NEW ENCYCLOPEDIA OF ZIONISM AND ISRAEL

NEW ENCYCLOPEDIA OF ZIONISM AND ISRAEL

GEOFFREY WIGODER,
Editor in Chief

2
K–Z

A Herzl Press Publication
•
Madison • Teaneck
Fairleigh Dickinson University Press
London and Toronto: Associated University Presses

The original edition of the *Encyclopedia of Zionism and Israel* was edited by Raphael Patai and published in 1971 by Herzl Press and McGraw-Hill, New York.

Associated University Presses
440 Forsgate Drive
Cranbury, NJ 08512

Associated University Presses
25 Sicilian Avenue
London WC1A 2QH, England

Associated University Presses
P.O. Box 338, Port Credit
Mississauga, Ontario
Canada L5G 4L8

Herzl Press
110 East 59th Street
New York, NY 10022

The paper used in this publication meets the requirements of the American National Standard for Permanence of Paper for Printed Library Materials Z39.48-1984.

Library of Congress Cataloging-in-Publication Data

New encyclopedia of Zionism and Israel / Geoffrey Wigoder, editor in chief.
p. cm.
ISBN 0-8386-3433-8 (alk. paper)
1. Zionism—Encyclopedias. 2. Israel—Encyclopedias.
I. Wigoder, Geoffrey, 1922–
DS149.N56 1994
320.5′4′095694—dc20 91-11828
CIP

PRINTED IN THE UNITED STATES OF AMERICA

NEW ENCYCLOPEDIA OF ZIONISM AND ISRAEL

K

KABRI. Kibbutz on the east rim of the Acre Plain. It was founded in 1949 by evacuated members of *Bet ha-Arava, later joined by others. The kibbutz engages in mixed farming and has industrial enterprises. Its site dates back at least to the Early Bronze period (third millennium BCE) and flourished in the Roman and Byzantine periods, when it was probably identical with "Kabrita" of the Talmud. The water from its four copious springs was directed ca. 7 miles (12 km.) south to Acre in an aqueduct built in 1800 on more ancient foundations. In the 1948 War of Independence, a Hagana unit was ambushed at Kabri and 46 men fell. Near Kabri are a government fruit tree nursery and a Jewish National Fund nursery for forest trees. Population: 726 in 1986.
E. ORNI

KACH (Kakh; "Thus"). Extreme right-wing political party. The Kach movement has its roots in the Jewish Defense League which was founded and headed by Rabbi Meir Kahane in 1968 in the United States. The Jewish Defense League took upon itself to physically defend Jews, synagogues, and Jewish property from anti-Semitic elements of the population. The League's activities often involved the use of violence.

After Kahane immigrated to Israel in 1971, he formed a Jewish Defense League in Israel and a youth movement also evolved. In 1973 the Jewish Defense League took part in the elections for the Knesset but failed to gain a seat. The name of the movement was changed to Kach; in the 1971 and 1981 elections, it again failed to gain a seat. In 1984, however, it got one seat (for Kahane) having received 205,907 votes.

Kahane's political platform was based on the premise that the State should be ruled in accordance with Jewish religious law. Thus it includes the idea that the State of Israel should be for Jews alone; any non-Jews wishing to live within the State would have to accept the status of a partial proselyte (accepting the seven Noahide commandments) and to accept the sovereignty of the Jews over the land. Any non-Jew not accepting these conditions would have to leave Israel. Kach also opposed mixed marriages between Jews and non-Jews. The bulk of Kach supporters come from the younger electorate. It was disqualified from the 1988 and 1992 elections because of its racist policies. In 1990, Kahane was assassinated in New York but his supporters continued their activities.

KADIMAH. *See* CONSERVATIVE JUDAISM AND ZIONISM.

KADIMAH. First Jewish nationalist students' society, formed in 1882 in Vienna by a small group of students, most of whom had come from eastern Europe. Its name means "Eastward" or "Forward." Kadimah's declared aims were to combat assimilation, strengthen Jewish national consciousness, and help Jewish settlement in Eretz Israel. The founders included Reuben Bierer, Nathan Birnbaum, Oser Kokesch, and Moritz Schnirer. They were assisted in their efforts by the Hebrew writer Peretz Smolenskin, who gave the society its name.

Kadimah rallied to Herzl soon after the publication of his *Jewish State*. Some of Kadimah's members became his close collaborators and played a prominent part in the work of the World Zionist Organization.

KADURI (Kadoorie). Farming school in Lower Galilee north of Mount Tavor. Its founding in 1933 was financed by a contribution of Sir Ellis Kadoorie to the Palestine Government. The pupils formed a unit of Hagana and later the nucleus of Palmah, whose training and organizational center was at Kaduri.
E. ORNI

KAHANEMAN, JOSEPH (the "Ponevezher Rebbe"). Rabbinical authority (b. Kuly, Lithuania, 1888; d. Benei Berak, 1969). Kahaneman studied in yeshivot in Telz and Radin. He was appointed head of the Grodno Yeshiva in 1916. As well as organizing and developing that yeshiva, he founded similar centers in other areas of Lithuania. In 1919 he was appointed rabbi of Ponevezh, where he had established a preparatory yeshiva; this grew to be the largest yeshiva in Lithuania. Kahaneman was a leader of Agudat Israel and was elected to the Lithuanian parliament as representative of Orthodox Jewry.

In 1940, he moved to Benei Berak, and after World War II devoted himself to developing a network of Torah institutions in Israel. He established 18 yeshivot around the country, to commemorate the 18 Lithuanian yeshivot destroyed in World War II. In 1944, the foundation was laid of the Ponevezh Yeshiva of Benei Berak which has a student body of over 1,000. The yeshiva complex includes a large library and a memorial to the Jews of Lithuania who perished in the Holocaust. In 1967, Kahaneman also established a branch of the yeshiva in Ashdod.

G. SHUSTER-BOUSKILA

KAHN, LEOPOLD. Lawyer and Zionist leader in Austria (b. Suceava, Bukovina, Austria, 1859; d. Vienna, 1909). After receiving a traditional education, Kahn studied law in Vienna, where he subsequently settled. He was an early adherent and close collaborator of Herzl and served on the Inner Actions Committee of the World Zionist Organization from 1898 to 1905.

Keenly interested in furthering Jewish culture, Kahn wrote the Zionist pamphlet *Warum? Die alte Lehre im Lichte neuer Katastrophen* (Why? The Old Doctrine in the Light of New Catastrophes, 1906) and *Durch Wahrheit zum Frieden: Ein Mahnwort an den VII Kongress* (Through Truth to Peace: A Word of Exhortation to the Seventh Congress, 1908).

KAHN, ZADOC. Chief Rabbi of France and early Zionist sympathizer (b. Mommenheim, France, 1839; d. Paris, 1905). Kahn studied at the Metz Rabbinical School and the Séminaire Israélite in Paris. In 1867 he became assistant to the Chief Rabbi of Paris, Lazare Isidor. A year later he became Chief Rabbi of Paris, and in 1889 Chief Rabbi of France. His religious opinions, tending to a moderate and almost skeptical attitude to daily observances, exerted a great influence on the French rabbinate. In 1892 he became honorary president of the Alliance Israélite Universelle, which he had joined in 1872. Kahn took a prominent part in the fight against anti-Semitism, particularly at the time of the Dreyfus affair and during the pogroms in eastern Europe in the early 1900s. He aided Baron Maurice de Hirsch in his colonization projects and in 1896 became a member of the Administrative Council of the Jewish Colonization Association (ICA).

An early adherent of the Hovevei Zion movement, Kahn helped persuade Baron Edmond de Rothschild to aid the Jewish settlers in Eretz Israel. He was among the first persons to be approached by Herzl and thereafter was in close contact with the Zionist leader, acting as his intermediary in his dealings with the Paris Rothschilds and the ICA. Zionism, in his eyes, was a means to alleviate the sufferings of persecuted Jews, but not a goal for Jews in emancipated lands.

Kahn helped found the Societé des Études Juives, of which he later became president, and participated in a number of French-Jewish philanthropic projects. In addition to numerous sermons and speeches, he wrote Talmudic and historical studies.

G. HIRSHLER—M. CATANE

KAKH. *See* KACH

KALISCHER, ZVI HIRSCH. Rabbi and pioneer Zionist (b. Leszno, Prussia, 1795; d. Thorn, Prussia, 1874). A student of Rabbi Akiba Eger and a strong opponent of Reform Judaism, Kalischer also acquired a knowledge of philosophy and other secular subjects. He spent most of his life as a rabbi in Thorn (now Torun, Poland), serving without salary. In 1832 he declared that the redemption of Zion would have to begin with action on the part of the Jewish people; the messianic miracle would then follow. He frequently had to defend these views against rabbinic opponents in both Europe and Eretz Israel who insisted that the Jewish people would have to wait for the Messiah without taking any action to hasten its deliverance. His volume *Derishat Tziyon ve-Hevrat Eretz Noshevet* (1862) was in effect the first Hebrew book to appear in eastern Europe on the subject of modern Jewish agricultural settlement in Eretz Israel

Zvi Hirsch Kalischer. [Zionist Archives]

Kalischer traveled through Germany asking wealthy and influential Jews to aid Jewish settlement projects. His influence inspired the founding of several settlement societies, and in 1864 he was responsible for the establishemnt of the Central Committee for Settlement in Eretz Israel in Berlin. Kalischer first interested the Alliance Israélite Universelle in aiding agriculture in Eretz Israel, an interest which led to the opening of the Mikve Yisrael Agricultural School in 1870. In reply to the argument from various quarters in Eretz Israel that conditions were not propitious for the establishment of agricultural settlements, he proposed that the settlers organize guard units whose members would combine farm work with defense against attack. Tirat Tzevi, a religious kibbutz in the Bet She'an Valley, is named for him.

An anthology of Kalischer's Zionist writings was edited by Israel Klausner in 1946.

I. KLAUSNER

KALKILIYA. Arab town in Samaria, on the eastern rim of the Sharon Plain, northeast of Kefar Sava. Kalkiliya was long considered a village and has preserved farming as an important element of its economy. In the 1936–1939 Arab riots, the 1948 War of Independence, and later, Kalkiliya inhabitants endangered nearby Jewish settlements. Under Israel administration after the 1967 Six-Day War, the town was peaceful and until the riots beginning in 1987 was much visited by Israeli shoppers. Kalkiliya's inhabitants are nearly all Moslems.

E. ORNI

KALLEN, HORACE MEYER. Philosopher, educator, "scientific humanist," creative American Jewish thinker (b. Bernstadt, Lower Galicia, Germany, 1882; d. West Palm Beach, USA, 1974). Brought from Germany to the United States in 1887, Kallen received his doctorate in philosophy in 1908 from Harvard University, where he served as assistant and intellectual heir to William James and George Santayana. He taught at the University of Wisconsin (1911–

1918) before joining the founding faculty of the New School for Social Research in New York City, an affiliation he maintained until his death.

Kallen's greatest contribution to American thought was his articulation of the concept of cultural pluralism, a formulation he first arrived at in 1905, when he began to search for a rationale which could justify his own intensifying commitment to the renationalization of the Jewish people even as he remained a loyal American citizen.

Kallen had adopted Zionism in 1903 as a secular alternative to a seemingly outmoded Jewish religious tradition. He had come to Zionism primarily through the influence of two Harvard professors, Barrett Wendell, who interpreted the Hebraic prophetic tradition of social justice as the inspiration for the American founding fathers, and William James, whose philosophy emphasized the validity inherent in the varieties of man's experience. Kallen extended Wendell's identification of Hebraic tradition with American idealism by defining Zionism as an opportunity to found in Eretz Israel a model democracy incorporating values of liberty and democracy similar to those in the United States. At the same time he applied James's concept of pluralism to America's ethnic communities, among them the Jews, arguing that preservation of cultural differences constituted the true measure of equality set forth in the American Declaration of Independence. In these terms Zionism became an ideology that fulfilled two important functions for Kallen: it helped him to retain his Jewish identity even as it affirmed him as a better American.

Kallen's Zionist formulation also met the needs of other American Jews who were wary of being accused of dual loyalties in a cultural climate that emphasized Americanization and a melting-pot ideology. The most important individual to have been influenced by Kallen was Louis D. Brandeis, who widely publicized Kallen's basic ideas after his own Zionist "conversion" and assumption of leadership of the American Zionist movement.

From 1914 until 1921, when disagreements with leading European Zionists caused Brandeis and Kallen to leave the Zionist movement, Kallen served as the behind-the-scenes philosopher of an Americanized Zionism, a "messianic-pragmatist" who attempted to reconstruct the American Zionist organization to reflect a "less ardent... more businesslike" attitude than that of the Europeans. During this period he used his own rationales for Zionism and expanded on his theory of cultural pluralism to try and influence a broad audience of non-Jews as well as Jews. For much of World War I he was the sole American link with Zionist activity in Great Britain. Kallen's most concrete expression of plans to create a state in Palestine reflecting ideals of economic and social justice was his "Constitutional Foundations for the New Zion," a series of proposals which forms the basis for the *Pittsburgh Program of 1918, the definitive statement of American Zionism as a reform movement influenced by early twentieth century American perspectives and values.

Kallen's books on Zionist themes include *Zionism and World Politics* (1921); *Judaism At Bay* (1932); *"Of Them Which Say They Are Jews" and Other Essays on the Jewish Struggle for Survival* (1954); and *Utopians at Bay* (1958), in which, after a visit to Israel, he wrote about the conflict between ideals and realities to be resolved by the new State. S. SCHMIDT

KALMAN, IMRE. Hungarian Zionist leader (b. Szabadka, now Subotica, Yugoslavia, 1883—d. Jerusalem, 1956). He studied law at Budapest University and served in the military during World War I, attaining the rank of captain and receiving many decorations for bravery. He obtained his doctorate in 1921 and practiced law in Budapest (1921–1951). Kalman was a Zionist from his student days: he joined the Zionist student organization Maccabea and belonged to it most of his life (1911–1951). He was a member of the executive of the Hungarian Zionist Federation from 1931 and one of the founders of the Zionist sporting club VAC. Kalman joined the New Zionist Organization (Revisionists) in 1935 and was chairman of its Hungarian branch and of Betar in Hungary. He was instrumental in organizing the first Betar group of "illegal immigrants" in 1937 and, after the Anschluss, another group of 150 Austrian and Hungarian Jews from the recently annexed territory of Eastern Slovakia. In all, Kalman organized the departure from Budapest of some 4,000 immigrants to Palestine and some 30,000 others who were refugees in transit; Kalman had obtained "stateless passports" for them from the Hungarian authorities. Having gained the confidence of the Slovak authorities, Kalman was particularly active in the rescue of Slovakian Jewry, collaborating with the Rescue Committee. Kalman and his family were among the Hungarian Jews who reached Switzerland in 1944 in the "Kasztner transport." He, himself, returned to Hungary in 1945, again participated in Zionist activities, and settled in Israel in 1951. E. EPPLER

KALWARISKI-MARGOLIS, HAYIM. Palestine pioneer, agronomist, and proponent of Jewish-Arab rapprochement (b. Suwalki District, Russian Poland, 1868; d. Jerusalem, 1947). As a youth Kalwariski joined the Hovevei Zion movement. He studied agronomy at the University of Montpellier, and after his graduation (1895) settled in Jaffa as secretary of the order Benei Moshe. In 1896 he became a teacher at the Mikve Yisrael Agricultural School and in 1900 chief administrator of the Galilean settlements of the Jewish Colonization Association (ICA), in which capacity he founded several new settlements and acquired land for others.

Under Kalwariski's influence, Baron Edmond de Rothschild agreed to establish a Hebrew-Arabic school for the children of the Arab village of Ja'uni, near Rosh Pina. While active in Galilee, Kalwariski-Margolis became closely associated with the members of Ha-Shomer (Jewish watchmen's organization). He helped found the settlements of Ayelet ha-Shahar, Mahanayim, Kefar Giladi, and Tel Hai, continuing to serve ICA until 1923.

Kalwariski devoted much attention to the problem of Jewish-Arab relations. In 1913 he arranged meetings between Nahum Sokolow and Arab nationalists in Damascus and Beirut. In 1922 he participated in Jewish-Arab negotiations in Cairo that were discontinued because of the opposition of the British government. He was one of three Jewish members of the Advisory Council established by Sir Herbert Samuel at the beginning of his service as High Commissioner for Palestine and served on the Executive of the Va'ad Leumi. From 1923 to 1927 he directed the Office of Arab Affairs of the Zionist Executive, and from 1929 to 1931 headed the combined office of the Jewish Agency and the Va'ad Leumi set up to deal with the Jewish-Arab problem after the 1929 Arab riots.

Kalwariski was among the leaders of all the groups that advocated Jewish-Arab cooperation including Berit Shalom (1926-early 1930s), Kedma Mizraha (late 1930s), the League of Jewish-Arab Rapprochement (from 1939), and Ihud (from 1942). A. COHEN

KAMERI (CHAMBER) THEATER. *See* THEATER IN ISRAEL.

KAMINKA, AARON. Pioneer Zionist, Hebrew scholar, author, poet, and educator (b. Berdichev, Ukraine, Russia, 1866; d. Tel Aviv, 1950). Kaminka studied at the Hildesheimer Rabbinical Seminary in Berlin, at the University of Berlin, and at the Sorbonne, in Paris. He occupied pulpits in Frankfurt on the Oder and Prague, and from 1897 to 1900 was Chief Rabbi of Osijek, Slavonia. He was active in the Hovevei Zion movement, joined the Zionist movement at its inception, and participated in the First Zionist Congress (1897), at which, at Herzl's request, he delivered an address on the settlement of Eretz Israel. He withdrew from active participation in the movement following differences with Herzl.

In 1900 he settled in Vienna, where he was secretary of the local office of the Alliance Israélite Universelle. He was also a lecturer at the Vienna Bet ha-Midrash and, from 1924 on, at the Maimonides Institute, which he founded.

Kaminka wrote Hebrew poetry and published several scholarly volumes on Judaica and rabbinical literature and became known as a translator of classical Greek and Latin authors into Hebrew. He first visited Eretz Israel in 1912.

In 1938 he was arrested by the Gestapo in Vienna. On his release, he moved to Tel Aviv, where he continued his literary and scholarly activities until his death.

A. ALPERIN

KAN, MARINUS L. Attorney and Zionist leader in the Netherlands (b. Amsterdam, 1891; d. Bergen-Belsen, 1945). After studying law in Amsterdam, Kan held various offices in the Dutch Zionist Federation, was named to the Dutch Zionist Executive, and became its vice-chairman (1936) and chairman (1939). He remained at the head of the Dutch Zionist movement until it was dissolved by the Nazis. Kan was deported first to Westerbork and then to Bergen-Belsen, where he died.

KANN, JACOBUS HENRICUS. Banker and Zionist leader in the Netherlands (b. The Hague, 1872; d. Theresienstadt, 1944). Kann attended the First Zionist Congress (1897) and offered the services of his own banking firm in The Hague in the establishment of the *Jewish Colonial Trust, of which he was vice-president from its foundation. He became a close friend of Herzl and David Wolffsohn and served on the Inner Actions Committee from 1905 to 1911. After his first visit to Eretz Israel in 1907 he published a book, *Eretz Israel, das jüdische Land* (Eretz Yisrael, The Land of the Jews, 1909), in which he set forth his travel impressions and his conviction that only the development of Eretz Israel as a Jewish State could save the Jews from the misery they suffered in other countries.

During World War I Kann arranged the transfer of *Jewish National Fund headquarters from Cologne to The Hague. He directed the new headquarters with Jean Fischer, Nehemia de Lieme, and Julius Simon. In 1924, however, he resigned from his directorship of the Jewish Colonial Trust and from active participation in the Zionist movement because of differences with the Zionist leadership on methods of settlement in Palestine. Eager to settle in Palestine, he sought and obtained the post of Netherlands Consul in Jerusalem in 1923 but had to return to the Netherlands in 1927 owing to his wife's illness. In 1930 he published his views on Zionism in *Some Observations on the Policy of the Mandatory Power in Palestine with Regard to the Arab Attacks on the Jewish Population in August, 1929, and the Jewish and Arab Sections of the Population*.

During World War II Kann and his wife were deported to Theresienstadt, where they died.

KAPLAN, ELIEZER. Labor leader and first Finance Minister of Israel (b. Minsk, Russia, 1891; d. Genoa, Italy, 1952). Born into a prominent Zionist family, Kaplan became active in Zionist affairs at an early age. In 1908 he was a founding member of Tze'irei Zion-Ha-Tehiya. Completing his engineering studies in Moscow in 1917, he continued to participate in Zionist affairs. He helped organize the founding convention of Hitahdut in Prague in 1920 and headed its Berlin central office from then until 1922. Beginning with the 11th Zionist Congress (1913), he served as a delegate to all Congresses.

Kaplan visited Palestine briefly in 1920 and settled there in 1923. He helped guide the activities of Solel Boneh and was active in other economic institutions associated with the Histadrut and in the municipality of Tel Aviv. In 1933 he became a member of the Executive of the Jewish Agency, heading its Finance and Administrative Department. He was a key planner and originator of economic and developmental projects in Palestine connected with the Agency, and he negotiated its first loan from Barclays Bank in London.

Moderate in his political views, Kaplan was a stanch follower of Chaim Weizmann and came into open conflict with David Ben-Gurion at the 22nd Zionist Congress (1946), where he headed the majority of the Mapai delegation that supported Weizmann against the minority headed by Ben-Gurion. After the establishment of the State of Israel he became Minister of Finance, retaining that post until shortly before his death, when he became Deputy Prime Minister. He died while on a journey abroad for medical treatment and was buried in Jerusalem. G. KRESSEL

KAPLAN, JACOB. Chief Rabbi of France (b. Paris, 1895). The son of an immigrant from Minsk, Kaplan served in the French Army during World Wars I and II. He received his licentiate in philosophy at the University of Paris in 1919 and was ordained at the Ecole Rabbinique de France two years later. In 1939, after having held pulpits in Mulhouse and Paris, he became assistant to the Chief Rabbi of France. He spent the war years in France, narrowly escaping deportation by the Nazis. In 1950 he was elected Chief Rabbi of Paris and two years later was named acting Chief Rabbi of France. In January, 1955, he was elected Chief Rabbi, a position he held until 1980, when he retired and received the honorary title "Chief Rabbi of the Central Consistory." He also served as honorary president of the Mizrachi of France and was active in the Religious Department of the Jewish National Fund.

Kaplan originated a new style in the Chief Rabbinate, in that he was more observant than his predecessors and ameliorated relations with the Christian hierarchy.

Kaplan published a number of books on Judaism. He holds the Croix de Guerre (1918, 1945) and is a commander of the Legion of Honor, and a member of the Institut de France (Académie des Sciences morales et politiques). M. CATANE

Eliezer Kaplan signs Declaration of Independence as David Ben-Gurion and Rabbi Yehuda Leb Maimon, at left, and Moshe Sharett, at right, look on. [Zionist Archives]

KAPLAN, MENDEL. South African businessman, Jewish leader and philanthropist (b. Parow, South Africa, 1936). A lawyer by training, he studied at Cape Town University where he later endowed a Center for Jewish Studies. He went into industry and headed his family business for manufacturing steel, wire, and wire products. Kaplan became deeply involved in Jewish communal activities, serving as National Chairman of the United Communal Fund (1974–78) and National Chairman of the United Israel Appeal (1978). On the international scene, he was Treasurer of the World Jewish Congress, a member of the World Board of Trustees of Keren ha-Yesod and, from 1987, Chairman of the Board of Governors of the Jewish Agency. He has been concerned with a variety of projects in Israel including the City of David Archeological Project, the Old Yishuv Court Museum, and the Jerusalem Tennis Center. He has written *From Stetl to Steelmaking* and *Jewish Roots in the South African Economy.*

KAPLAN, MORDECAI MENAHEM. Rabbi, religious philosopher and Zionist leader in the United States (b. Svencionys, Lithuania, 1881; d. New York City, 1983). Taken to New York in 1889, Kaplan graduated from City College of New York (B.A., 1900) and Columbia University (M.A., 1902). He was ordained in 1902 at the Jewish Theological Seminary of America, from which he obtained a doctorate in Hebrew letters in 1929. In 1922 he organized the Society for the Advancement of Judaism (SAJ), centered in a synagogue in New York which gave expression to Kaplan's religious philosophy and of which he remained the spiritual leader until 1944, when he became its rabbi emeritus.

Mordecai M. Kaplan. [Society for the Advancement of Judaism]

Kaplan was the founder of the Reconstructionist movement in Judaism (*see* RECONSTRUCTIONISM), the ideas of which were disseminated through the SAJ, *The Reconstructionist* (a bi-weekly founded in 1934), the Jewish Reconstructionist Foundation (founded in 1940), and, the Reconstructionist Rabbinical College (founded in Philadelphia in 1968).

Kaplan often designated Reconstructionism as "Zionist Judaism", in order to emphasize his view that Judaism is the evolving religious civilization of the Jewish people that attained its national consciousness in Eretz Israel. Inherent in that designation is the idea that the future of the Jewish people is primarily dependent on the remaking and revitalization of its national life and culture in its historical center. Kaplan argued that the ultimate task of Zionism "is to reconstitute our peoplehood, reclaim our ancient homeland, and revitalize our Jewish way of life." Thus, the basis of Judaism is the pulsating life of the Jewish group rather than a God-given set of doctrines and practices—traditionally categorized under the concepts of Torah or halakha. Judaism, in Kaplan's system, must undergo metamorphosis as the Jewish people responds to the challenges of its environment and of its own inner growth and maturation. Kaplan argued that in the modern world, the Jewish people will have to strive for a new type of unity, based on a full acceptance of diversity in spiritual outlook and observance among Jews. In order for that to happen, it will be necessary to reformulate the covenant that has bound Jewry together throughout the centuries. That covenant, which can be arrived at only through consensus among survivalist Jews, will have to reckon henceforth with the transnational character of the Jewish people. All this entails a mind-set that would make for a system of compromise decisions.

Although never wavering in his devotion to the Zionist cause, Kaplan affirmed the possibility and the desirability of Jewish life in the enlightened Diaspora, maintaining this position both before and after the establishment of the State of Israel. His philosophy of Jewish spiritual nationalism became particularly pertinent after 1948 when it became clear that the ingathering of the exiles would not and could not be accomplished in the foreseeable future. Kaplan believed that under conditions of freedom, men and women tend to live simultaneously in two civilizations, one which binds all citizens of a state together and another, which is that of their respective religious or ethnic groups. Even if many minority groups might, in the natural course of events, lose their will to survive, Kaplan felt that the Jewish experience would enable the Jewish people to continue a creative existence in freedom—even as a minority in the lands of the free Diaspora. The yishuv would stimulate the Diaspora communities to fashion their own forms of Judaism, while retaining a common sense of belonging to the Jewish people as a whole.

Kaplan was heavily involved in the practical affairs of the Jewish community. In his Zionist work, he served the Zionist Organization of America at various times as the chairman of its National Executive Committee and of its Commission on Basic Zionist Ideology and as a delegate to a number of Zionist Congresses. J. COHEN

KAPLANSKY, SHELOMO. Engineer, educator, and Labor Zionist leader (b. Bialystok, Russian Poland, 1884; d. Haifa, 1950). While still a student of mechanical engineering at the Vienna Institute of Technology, he helped organize the Po'ale Zion party and later became a secretary of the World Union of Po'ale Zion.

Settling in Eretz Israel in 1912, Kaplansky taught physics and mathematics at the Herzliya High School and was active on behalf of Po'ale Zion. He was associated with Franz Oppenheimer in the establishment of Merhavya, first of the Emek (Jezreel Valley) settlements. From 1913 to 1919 he was in charge of settlement affairs at the Jewish National Fund headquarters in The Hague. He was also a founder of Keren ha-Yesod. From 1921 to 1924 he was director of the Financial and Economic Council of the World Zionist Organization in London, then returned to Palestine to head the Settlement Department of the Palestine Zionist Executive, serving in this capacity until 1927. Between 1924 and 1929 he was also director of economics for the Histadrut. From 1929 to 1931 he was in London again, as a member of the Executive of the Jewish Agency.

In 1931 Kaplansky returned to Palestine and became head of the Haifa *Technion, a position he held until his death. He was a member of the National Council for Research and Development and of the Prime Minister's Council for Higher Education. In later years he was inclined toward left-wing socialism, leaving the Mapai party and supporting Mapam. He was the author of *Problems of Palestine Colonization* (1923), a collection of essays (1932), and other works dealing with Palestine and Israel.

KARAITE JEWS IN ISRAEL. The Karaites, a Jewish sect which emerged in the eighth century, accept the Pentateuch but not the rabbinical interpretations (the Oral Law) which have become basic to normative Judaism.

From the ninth and tenth centuries onwards, leading Karaite preachers called for mass immigration to Jerusalem and settlement there. They called on all Jews to give up the pleasures of this world and to mourn the destruction of Zion and Jerusalem by fasting and with sackloth and ashes. A prominent tenth century preacher was Sahl ben Matzliah ha-Kohen (for whom moshav Matzliah near Ramleh was named). He visited all the Jewish communities in the neighboring countries, preaching fervently for mass immigration to Eretz Israel. By virtue of this preaching, unique in Judaism, Jerusalem in that period became a world Karaite center, attracting many scholars and producing works of Bible commentary, grammar, and philosophy.

Karaite delegate greets Zalman Shazar on his appointment as President of Israel. [Karaite community in Israel]

Kindergarten at the immigration absorption center in Karmi'el [Israel Information Services]

The yearning for Zion characterized Karaism at all times. With the creation of the State of Israel, there was a mass immigration to Israel, particularly by the Egyptian Karaite community. Today there are about 25,000 Karaites in Israel, mostly in the Ramleh area, Ofakim, Moshav Ranen, Beersheba, Bat Yam, and Holon, as well as a sizeable number dispersed throughout Israel. Every place with a concentration of Karaites has a religious and organizational council, headed by a rabbi, cantors, ritual slaughterers, and circumcisers, providing all the religious services, and at the head of all the regions is the Supreme World Council uniting Karaites world-wide. They have their own religious institutions —synagogues and evening religious lessons; and a committee that has published a considerable portion of their literature on history and religious and legal exegesis; they have their own slaughterhouses, butchers, burial societies and cemeteries; and a law court that deals with matrimonial matters, although the Ministry for Religious Affairs supplies them with marriage certificates.

The oldest synagogue in the Jewish quarter in Jerusalem was built in the Middle Ages; it belonged to the Karaite community until the Old City fell into Jordanian hands in the 1948 War of Independence. After the Six-Day War, it was restored and returned to the Karaites.

The members of the Karaite community have been absorbed in the State, and may be found in all walks of life. Among them are lawyers, doctors, engineers, teachers, government servants, employees of the local authorities, agriculturalists, industrial and building workers; some are high-ranking officers in the police and in the regular army; and some have returned to the trades that were practiced in Egypt—goldsmithing and diamond polishing.

In 1955, Dr. Moshe Marzouk, an Egyptian physician who was a Karaite, was executed in Cairo on charges of spying for Israel. *See also* LAVON AFFAIR. C. HALEVI

KARELITZ, AVRAHAM YESHAYAHU. ("Hazon Ish"). Rabbinical authority (b. Kossow, Lithuania, 1878; d. Benei Berak, 1953). He studied with his father, Shemaryahu Yosef Karelitz, rabbi of Kozov. Karelitz never served as a rabbi in any official capacity but was a renowned religious leader by virtue of his intellect and personal charisma. In 1911, he published his first book on Jewish law, *Hazon Ish* which was the first of 22 volumes, four of which were published after he moved to Benei Berak in 1933. He became generally known thereafter as "the Hazon Ish." In Palestine, he quickly became a leader of the ultra-Orthodox camp which rejected the Chief Rabbinate. He was often in conflict with other ultra-Orthodox leaders, but nonetheless many of his decisions were adopted. He was influential in the creation of the *kolel* system, in which young men can pursue their religious studies after marriage and their families are housed within the *kolel* complex. He also encouraged the development of the Beis Ya'akov Girls' School system. He decided to allow Agudat Israel's Talmud Torah schools to conduct studies in Hebrew, not only in Yiddish.

He was extremely anti-Zionist and maintained that Zionism was the cause of the Holocaust. Although he was opposed to the modern State of Israel, he permitted ultra-Orthodox Jews to vote for the Knesset since it could benefit their interests. In 1952, he met with David Ben-Gurion to discuss the exemption of yeshiva students from military service. G. SHUSTER-BOUSKILA

KARESKI, GEORG (GEDALIAH). German communal leader (b. Posen, Germany, 1878; d. Ramat Gan, 1947). During World War I Kareski was employed in the management of industrial firms in Berlin and until Hitler's rise to power, was a member of the German Industrialists' Center.

Kareski was active in Jewish public life, helping to found the *Judische Volkspartei in 1919. As a member of this party, he was elected to the Berlin Community Council in 1920, serving as president of the community from 1928 to 1930. He was also a member of the Preussischer Landesverband der jüdischen Gemeinden (Prussian Association of Jewish Communities) institutions. Kareski served as chairman of the managing committee of the Jewish bank, Ivria. During the 1932 political crisis in Germany, Kareski advised Jewish voters to cast their ballots for the Catholic Zentrum party which, he held, defended the rights of the Jews better than the other parties. He himself was on the list of Zentrum candidates, but was not elected.

As a member of the Zionistische Vereinigung für Deutschland (German Zionist Union) Kareski belonged to the "political" conservative division, which worked to Zionize the communities. He was a member of the Revisionist faction which strongly opposed the political policy of the Zionist Union leadership among German Jewry and in the World Zionist Organization. In May, 1933, Kareski, at the head of a group of uniformed Beitar members, attempted to take control of the offices of the Berlin community. The community officials, however, refused to cooperate, and subsequently Kareski was dismissed from the Zionist Union. In 1934 Kareski founded and led the Revisionist Organization, Staatszionistische Organisation, which did not belong to the Zionist Union nor, for tactical reasons, to Jabotinsky's World Union of Zionist Revisionists.

With the support of the Gestapo, Kareski attempted in 1935 to take control of the Reichsverband jüdischer Kulturbünde (Reich Organization of Jewish Cultural Unions), and in 1937 of the representative institution of German Jewry, the Reichsvertretung der deutschen Juden. This attempt was thwarted by the strong opposition of the Reichsvertretung under Rabbi Leo Baeck. Following the bankruptcy of the Ivria bank in 1937, in which many small tradesmen lost their savings, Kareski resigned from the Berlin community council and immigrated in 1937 to Palestine.

There he was welcomed by rightist circles but was ostracized by the German Immigrants' Association. He was accused in their journal, *Mitteilungsblatt*, of trying to assume leadership of German Jewry with the aid of the Nazi party, of referring to the Zionist Union as a "breeding ground of the international Marxist spirit," of threatening to murder its chairman, and of responsibility for the collapse of the Ivria Bank. Kareski took the German Immigrants' Association to court on a charge of slander, but the Association was acquitted unanimously by the rabbinical court under Chief Rabbi Yitzhak Halevi Herzog.

In the last years of his life Kareski was active in the direction of Kupat Holim Le'umit (the National Sick Fund) of the Revisionist Movement. Y. ELONI

KARKUR. *See* PARDES HANA.

KARMI'EL. Town on the south side of the Bet ha-Kerem Valley which separates Lower from Upper Galilee. Founded as a development town in 1964, it absorbed Israelis and immigrants and achieved a reputation for its architectural planning, industrial base, administration, and the social amalgamation of its population. Its factories employ laborers from the neighboring Arab villages. Population: 8,800 in 1986. E. ORNI

Kindergarten at the immigration absorption center in Karmiel. [Israel Information Services]

KARNI, YEHUDA. Hebrew poet (b. Pinsk, Russia, 1884; d. Tel Aviv, 1949). Karni joined the Zionist movement at an early age, was active as an organizer and propagandist, and attended Zionist Congresses as a delegate of the labor confederation Po'ale Zion. In 1907–08 he was secretary of the Central Committee of Russian Zionists in Vilna.

Karni published articles and poems in Hebrew and Yiddish periodicals. He contributed to the weekly *Ha-Olam* and, after it moved to Odessa, became a member of its editorial staff. Settling in Palestine in 1921, he worked first as secretary of the local Shekel (Zionist membership fee) committee and later joined the editorial staff of *Ha-Aretz*.

Karni was deeply rooted in the cultural and Zionist traditions of Ahad Ha-Am and Hayim Nahman Bialik. In the beginning, his poetry had a lofty and detailed quality in which echoes of past grandeur and present aspirations were fused into lyrical and melodic poems. In Palestine his poetry underwent radical changes, reflecting more tangible aspects. The new landscape, and its spiritual aura especially of Jerusalem, captivated his poetic temperament.

Karni received the Bialik Prize in 1944. H. LEAF

KARTELL JUDISCHER VERBINDUNGEN (KJV). Association of Zionist student societies in Germany, formed in 1914 as a result of the fusion of the Bund Jüdischer Corporationen (Union of Jewish Student Societies) and the Kartell Zionistischer Verbindungen (KZV; Association of Zionist Student Societies). The Bund, founded in 1899, incorporated a number of Jewish student societies, the earliest of which had been organized in Berlin in 1895. The membership of these societies consisted of students imbued with a Jewish national consciousness, who in time became increasingly Zionist-oriented. The KZV had its origin in the Zionist student society Hasmonaea, which had been founded in Berlin in 1902. The Zionist activities of KJV included the promotion of the ideals of pioneering and the dissemination of the Hebrew language. In the early 1930s, KJV comprised student societies at 20 universities with an aggregate membership of about 2,000 (1,200 of whom were *alte Herren*, or alumni). Its official organ was *Der Jüdische Student* (The Jewish Student). KJV ceased its activities after Hitler's rise to power in 1933.

KARU (KRUPNIK), BARUKH. Hebrew author, journalist, critic, lexicographer, and translator (b. Czernevtsy, Podolia, Austria, 1899; d. Tel Aviv, 1972). Educated at the Yeshiva of Hayim Tchernovitz (Rav Tza'ir) in Odessa, at the Baron David Guenzburg Academy for Jewish Studies in St. Petersburg, and in Berlin, Karu edited Hebrew dictionaries in Warsaw in 1912–13. In 1922 he became associate editor of the Hebrew art periodical *Rimon* in Berlin; from 1925 to 1931 he was an editor and editorial secretary of the *Encylopedia Judaica* as well as of the *Eshkol Entziklopedia Yisre'elit* in that city.

Settling in Palestine in 1932, Karu was on the staff of *Ha-Aretz* from 1933 until 1942, when he joined the staff of *Ha-Boker*. He compiled several Hebrew and Aramaic dictionaries and encyclopedic works and translated English, French, Russian, German, and Yiddish masterpieces into Hebrew. Karu twice received the Tschernikowsky Award for classical translations. A member (1968) of the Advisory Committee of the Hebrew Language Academy, he was also a founder, and at one time vice-chairman, of the Israel Journalists Association and a member of the Council for Culture and Art of the Israeli Ministry of Education and Culture.

KASZTNER, REZSO RUDOLF (Israel). Journalist, lawyer, and Zionist leader in Romania and Hungary (b. Kolozsvar (Cluj), 1906; d. Tel Aviv, 1957). Kasztner worked on the Zionist daily *Uj Kelet* (New East) from 1925–1940 and was its political correspondent in Bucharest, 1929–1935. As a leader of the Zionist youth movement *Aviva—Barissia*, which eventually joined with Ha-Ihud ha-Olami, he edited its Hungarian-language paper *Noar* (Youth) 1926–1928. After the annexation of Transylvania to Hungary, Kasztner moved to Budapest in 1942 and joined the local Keren ha-Yesod office, was active in Ha-Ihud ha-Olami, and from 1943–1945 was vice-chairman of the Hungarian Zionist Federation. On his arrival in Budapest, Kasztner also joined the local *Vaad Ezra ve-Hatzala* (Relief and Rescue Committee) which organized rescue efforts on behalf of Jewish refugees from Poland and Slovakia. After the Nazi invasion of Hungary (19 March 1944), rescue operations were stepped up and Zionist contacts included the officers of the

RSHA (Reich Security Main Office) who, headed by Eichmann, came to Hungary to carry out the "Final Solution." Jointly with Joel Brand, Kasztner conducted negotiations with the Germans to exchange Jews for trucks and other material supplied from neutral countries. As a result of his negotiations, a transport of 1,786 Jews, including 500 members of youth movements, prominent Orthodox and Hasidic rabbis, Zionists and non-Zionists, left for Bergen-Belsen and were eventually transferred to Switzerland.

After the war, Kasztner settled in Palestine, received a government post and became active in the Mapai party, editing its Hungarian-language weekly *A Jovo* (The Future). He rejoined *Uj Kelet* in 1948. In a mimeographed leaflet written in 1953, Malkiel Gruenwald of Jerusalem accused Kasztner of collaboration with the Nazis, thereby hastening the destruction of Hungarian Jewry. As the person slandered was a government official, the Israeli Attorney General issued a writ against Gruenwald. On 22 June 1955 the judge found for Gruenwald. The Israeli Cabinet instructed the Attorney General to lodge an appeal. This caused a Cabinet crisis when the General Zionists refused to support the government on a no-confidence motion. Thus, the Kasztner case became a major issue in the 1955 elections. The appeal was heard, and on 17 January 1958 the Supreme Court quashed the lower court's decision and cleared Kasztner's name. Kasztner, however, was no longer alive. A Tel Aviv youth, Ze'ev Eckstein, influenced by the atmosphere created by the lower court's verdict, shot him in the street on 3 March 1957, and Kasztner died of his wounds nine days later. E. EPPLER

KATCHALSKI FAMILY. *See* KATZIR.

KATTOWITZ CONFERENCE. Conference of *Hovevei Zion (Lovers of Zion) societies held in Kattowitz, Prussia (now Katowice, Poland), in 1884. The various Hovevei Zion groups, which came into being in Russia in the early 1880s, had no central body to coordinate their activities. Appeals for the unification of all Russian Hovevei Zion groups and the establishment of a central committee were published in the Jewish press. A call to convene a congress and to elect a central body was also contained in Leo *Pinsker's *Autoemancipation* (1882).

In 1883 Rabbi Shemuel Mohilever attempted to form a central committee. A limited conference was held in Bialystok, Russian Poland, and a central board was elected. This board, however, was inactive. In September, 1883, a conference of Hovevei Zion groups convened by the Bene Berit Society of Kattowitz was held in that city. It was sparsely attended, with Russia represented by only two delegates from Warsaw and Romania by only one delegate. Bene Berit planned to convene a second conference in December. At that time, Pinsker took the first steps toward the organization of the movement in Russia, the convening of a congress, and the election of a central committee. He warned the Kattowitz society against premature and separatist action, urging it to wait until additional Hovevei Zion groups were organized in Russia. As a consequence, the second conference planned by Bene Berit was postponed. Also active in convening the congress was the Hovevei Zion group of Warsaw, which combined the proposal to elect a central committee with an Eretz Israel settlement project in honor of Sir Moses Montefiore. Various groups sent suggestions to the forthcoming conference, which was originally planned for Montefiore's 100th birthday (27 October 1884) but was not held until November 6 of that year. This conference was attended by 32 delegates (22 from Russia, 6 from Germany, 2 from England, and 1 each from France and Romania), Representatives from Russia included Pinsker, Mohilever, Israel Jasinovsky, Shaul Pinhas Rabinowicz, Rabbi David Friedmann of Pinsk, Kalonymus-Ze'ev Wissotzky, and Alexander Zederbaum, the editor of *Ha-Melitz*. Among the delegates from Germany was David Gordon, editor of *Ha-Maggid*. Charles (Kalman) Wohlrauch and Zerah Barnett came from England, Dr Karpel Lippe from Romania, and Yehiel Michel Rabbinowitz from France.

Pinsker, elected chairman of the conference, stressed in his opening speech the necessity for the Jews' return to agriculture in Eretz Israel but did not mention the aspirations for a national renaissance and political independence. This careful definition of aims was designed to gain the backing of the Jews of Western Europe. The conference resolved to establish the Montefiore Association (Agudat Montefiore, also known as Mazkeret Montefiore) for the support of Jewish settlements in Eretz Israel, chose a Central Committee, and decided to grant 10,000 francs to Petah Tikva and 2,000 rubles to the settlement of Yesud ha-Ma'ala. A delegate, to be chosen by the Central Committee, was to visit Eretz Israel to investigate the state of the settlements. No new settlements were to be established until after the existing ones had been consolidated. The Biluim, for whom support had been demanded at the conference by a group of 12 delegates organized in what might be called a "progressive" faction, were to receive the necessary aid after their situation had been thoroughly investigated. Funds collected by the Hovevei Zion groups, as soon as they amounted to 5,000 francs, were to be transferred by the Central Committee to Paris, to Michael Erlanger, who was to serve as secretary-general of the Montefiore Association.

Members of the 19-man Central Committee included Pinsker, Mohilever, Wissotzky, Sigmund Simmel (a Berlin banker), Moses Moses (Kattowitz), Dr. Max Mandelstamm (Kiev), Charles Wohlrauch (London), and the writer Samuel Joseph Fünn (Vilna). Odessa was named the temporary seat of the Central Committee, which was to be headed by Pinsker. A subcommittee was to function in Warsaw.

In his closing address, Pinsker expressed gratification that a union between religious and nonobservant elements had been achieved. The conference laid the foundation for an enlarged Hovevei Zion movement, concentrated mainly in Russia. I. KLAUSNER

KATZENELSOHN, NISSAN. Physicist, banker, Zionist leader, and statesman in Russia (b. Bobruisk, Russia, 1863; d. Libau, Latvia, 1923). He studied physics but, having inherited his father's banking business, left his profession and became prominent as a banker in Russia. He was one of the first prominent Russian Jews to join the Zionist movement. A cofounder of the Jewish Colonial Trust, he became one of its directors in 1899 and was elected chairman of its board in 1905. He was elected to the Actions Committee of the World Zionist Organization in the early years of the movement, acting as Herzl's personal representative in negotiations with the Russian government in 1903 and with Jacob H. Schiff, the American Jewish philanthropist, in 1904.

A leader in the struggle for the civil rights of Russian Jews, Katzenelsohn was elected (1906) to the Duma, the first Parliament of Tsarist Russia, as a representative of the province of Kurland. He was active in Zionist and Jewish political affairs until his death. A. ALPERIN

Aharon Katzir.
[Israel Govt. Press Office]

KATZIR (KATCHALSKI), AHARON. Chemist and educator (b. Lodz, Poland, 1913; d. Lydda (Lod) Airport, 1972). Taken to Palestine in 1925, Katzir studied at the Hebrew University of Jerusalem, obtaining a doctorate in 1946. In 1948 he became head of the polymer research department and chairman of the Science Committee at the Weizmann Institute of Science, a position he held until his death. He also served as visiting professor of physical chemistry at the Hebrew University. A member of the board of the Scientific Research Department of the Israel Ministry of Defense and of the Science Advisory Council of the Israel government, he held the rank of lieutenant-colonel in the Israel Defense Forces. He served as president of the Israel Academy of Sciences and Humanities and of the International Union of Pure and Applied Biophysics. His research and studies were on polyelectrolytes, and he conducted the initial investigation on the electrochemistry of biopolymers. He was also in the forefront or research on membrane phenomena from a biological and applied point of view. He received a number of science and academic awards, including the Israel Prize (1961). Katzir was the brother of Israel's fourth president, Ephraim *Katzir. He died in an attack by three Japanese terrorists, members of the extreme-left Japanese Red Star Organization, on passengers and visitors at Lydda Airport.

KATZIR (KATCHALSKI), EPHRAIM. Fourth President of Israel; scientist and educator (b. Kiev, Russia, 1916). Taken to Palestine in 1925, Katchalski studied at the Hebrew University of Jerusalem, receiving his doctorate in 1941. After serving as an assistant at the university's department of theoretical and macromolecular chemistry (1941–45), he was a research fellow at the Brooklyn Polytechnic Institute and at Columbia University (1947–48). Returning to Israel in 1948, he became acting head of the department

Ephraim Katzir.
[Israel Govt. Press Office]

of biophysics at the Weizmann Institute of Science. In 1951 he was appointed head of the department. He was also chief scientist of Israel's Ministry of Defense (holding the rank of lieutenant colonel in the Israel Defense Forces) and a member of the Israel Academy of Sciences and Humanities, the National Academy of Sciences of the United States, and numerous other scientific organizations.

In April 1973, Katzir was elected president of the State of Israel, in succession to Zalman Shazar. His term of office included the crucial period of the Yom Kippur War and, subsequently, President Sadat's historic visit to Jerusalem. In these developments, Katzir was deeply involved. On the domestic scene, he fulfilled the traditional functions of the Presidency, including a number of official visits abroad, while adding his own analytic approach. He gave increased emphasis to community service and volunteering as well as to the place of science in education and industry.

In May, 1978, upon completion of his term as President, he returned to his scientific research at the Weizmann Institute. At the same time, Professor Katzir initiated research in the field of practical application of biological knowledge at Tel Aviv University, where he established in 1980 a Center for Biotechnology. Katzir received many honors including Commander of the French Legion of Honor (the first Israeli so honored) and member of the Royal Institution of Great Britain and of the Academie des Sciences of the Institut de France.

While President, Katzir was a founder of the International Center of University Teaching of Jewish Civilization, a project to promote Jewish Studies on campuses throughout the world, with which he remained closely involved. He also was president of the international project of Academic Seminars for Zionist Thought, sponsored by the World Zionist Organization, which brought Jewish academics and intellectuals in many countries into a framework for discussing current Jewish, Zionist, and Israeli issues.

During his Presidency, an Ephraim Katzir Commission was appointed by the Ministry of Industry, Trade, and Tourism, in order to develop an area in Galilee, which came to be known as "Region 2000." This Commission was instrumental in laying the foundations for this region, now incorporating the towns of Karmiel and Ir ha-Veradim and the industrial center of Tefen, which has attracted high-tech industries that are successfully producing and exporting their products to markets the world over. In 1985 the World ORT Union established the ORT Braude International Institute of Technology in Karmiel, which was an integral part of the plans for this region. In 1986 Professor Katzir was elected president of the World ORT Union, and after making valuable contributions to the work of this organization, relinquished his post in 1990.

KATZNELSON, AVRAHAM. *See* NISSAN, AVRAHAM.

Berl Katznelson.
[Zionist Archives]

KATZNELSON, BERL. Labor Zionist leader and ideologist (b. Bobruisk, 1887; d. Jerusalem 1944). He became active at an early age in the Jewish Socialist groups of Russia, and belonged to several parties in turn, including Poale Zion and the Zionists-Socialists (S.S.). Katznelson's Zionism was Herzlian, being directed more towards the Jewish people than towards Eretz Israel. Believing that the Jewish people could not become a working people in the Diaspora, prior to his immigration to Eretz Israel he prepared himself for manual labor, by working at tinsmithing, blacksmithing, and turnery; he was deeply affected by his lack of skill in these occupations. Upon his arrival in Eretz Israel in 1909, he wandered about the country from one place of work to another: En Ganim, Hadera, Sejera, Ben Shemen, Kineret, Jerusalem. In the years preceding World War I, Katznelson participated in the strike organization at the Kineret Farm and helped foster labor unions in Galilee and Judea. He wished to unite the workers in a labor union and was opposed to the parties. During these years and through World War I, Katznelson continued to work in agriculture, acquiring some skill in the vegetable-growing sectors. His economic, cultural, and public activity during the war included the creation of *Ha-Mashbir*, the consumer cooperative, and the beginnings of Kupat Holim (Sick Fund). In 1917 Katznelson made an appeal for Labor unity in an address "Towards the Future"; the opportunity to work in this direction arose only after he joined the volunteers of the Jewish Legion. Katznelson feared that unification would not succeed, and indeed *Ha-Po'el ha-Tza'ir refused to join. *Ahdut ha-Avoda was consequently transformed from a general union into a party immediately upon its creation in 1919. In 1919 he began to edit his party's organ, *Kunteres*. In 1920 he participated in the struggles for the defense of Upper Galilee and vehemently opposed Vladimir Jabotinsky, who wished to abandon Upper Galilee. He supported Eliyahu Golomb in the latter's efforts to build the Hagana as a public organization not controlled by Ha-Shomer members. Thus Ha-Shomer and many leaders of the Third Aliya did not really accept Katznelson's leadership.

In 1921–22 Katznelson traveled to the U.S.A. to raise money for the creation of Bank Hapoalim and continued to distribute shares of this bank on every trip abroad in the following years. In 1925 he founded the Histadrut daily, *Davar*, becoming its first editor. In the 1920s Katznelson was one of the architects of the alliance between the Labor movement and Chaim Weizmann, an alliance that grew stronger as Jabotinsky's opposition to the policies of the Labor movement and the World Zionist Organization increased. Katznelson, like Weizmann, opposed Jabotinsky's declarations concerning the Arabs, but his own attitude hardened somewhat, especially after the events of 1929. He was suspicious regarding the British and had increasing reservations concerning the regime in the Soviet Union. Katznelson's views dominated *Davar*, and caused resentment among the left. Katznelson's doubts about the left increased when some of the leaders of the Gedud ha-Avoda left Palestine for the U.S.S.R. in 1927. Initially his doubts focused on the Ha-Shomer ha-Tza'ir movement, but in the thirties they broadened to include Ha-Kibbutz ha-Me'uhad, the movement of his relative and friend Y. Tabenkin. When Ha-Po'el ha-Tza'ir joined Ahdut ha-Avoda to form Mapai in 1930, this helped create a majority faction under the leadership of Katznelson, Ben-Gurion and others, against the radical minority faction led by Ha-Kibbutz ha-Me'uhad. Katznelson was close to Tabenkin in their joint opposition to the idea of partition in 1937 and in their ardent support of the Hagana and the "illegal" immigration movement. Katznelson, however, violently criticized the increasing radicalization of Ha-Kibbutz ha-Me'uhad's education programs, expressed in increasing leftist tendencies, an unwillingness to accept any compromise with the Revisionists, and even a growing sympathy with the Soviet Union. Between 1936 and 1939 Katznelson conducted a campaign to unite Ha-Kibbutz ha-Me'uhad with Hever ha-Kevutzot, in order to moderate this radicalization. With the White Paper of 1939, Katznelson's activism resembled the position ot the Ha-Kibbutz ha-Me'uhad, but after the outbreak of World War II he demanded, together with Ben-Gurion, Weizmann and others, the immediate creation of a Jewish State upon conclusion of the War. The support of the majority faction in Mapai for the Biltmore Program in 1942 constituted one of the bones of contention which caused Mapai to split in mid-1944. Already deeply affected by the Holocaust, katznelson suffered further from the split with Ha-Kibbutz ha-Me'uhad. He died a few months later. A complete edition of his works was published in 12 volumes (1946–50).

A. KAFKAFI

KAUFMAN, AVRAHAM IOSIFOVICH. Russian Zionist and communal leader (b. Mglin, Chernigov province, 1885; d. Tel Aviv, 1971). Born into a family of Habad Hasidim (he was a descendant of Rabbi Schneour Zalman of Lyady), he became an enthusiastic Zionist in his youth. He studied medicine at Berne, Switzerland, 1904–08, where he was vice-chairman of the Jewish Students' Association. On his return to Russia, he was sent by Jehiel Tschlenow on a mission to the Ural and Volga regions to propagate Zionism. He was a delegate to three Zionist Congresses. From 1912 he lived in Harbin, Manchuria, where he was involved in Zionist and communal affairs. He headed the Harbin community (1919–31 and 1933–45); was the representative in China of the World Zionist Organization, Jewish National Fund, and Keren ha-Yesod; and chaired the Zionist Organization of China. Professionally, he was chief physician of the Harbin Jewish hospital, of which he was a founder. When the Red Army occupied Harbin in 1945, Kaufman was arrested, sent to the Soviet Union and sentenced to 25 years' imprisonment of which he served eleven (three years in solitary confinement and eight years in prison camp). After his release in 1956 he was exiled to Kazakhstan. He succeeded in reaching Israel in 1961 and worked as a physician in Ramat Gan.

KAUFMAN, YEHEZKEL. Philosopher of Jewish history and Biblical scholar (b. Dunayevtsy, Ukraine, Russia, 1889; d. Jerusalem, 1963). He was educated at the modern yeshiva in Odessa, the Institute of Eastern Studies in St. Petersburg, and the University of Berne, where he obtained his doctorate in Kantian studies in 1918. Settling in Palestine in 1929, Kaufman taught at the Reali High School in Haifa (1929–49) and later served as professor of Bible at the Hebrew University of Jerusalem (1949–57). His two monumental works are *Gola ve-Nekhar* (Exile and Alienation, 1929–30), an exhaustive sociological study of the Diaspora in all its manifestations; and an eight-volume *History of the Jewish Religion* (1937–56). He also wrote commentaries on the Books of Joshua and Judges and essays on contemporary problems.

Kaufman differed from modern Biblical scholars in the chronological order he assigned to the various layers of the Pentateuch, seeking to prove that those portions which according to higher Biblical criticism were the latest, actually were the earliest. He also contended that the Pentateuch as a whole preceded the classical Prophecy. In addition, he claimed that monotheism did not result from a mythological faith by way of evolutionary process, but rather initiated the history of the Jewish people and was, in a sense, a revelation. He emphasized the religious factor in the history of the Jewish people and doubted that Zionism would assume a key role in modern times. He also questioned whether Zionism would manage to be the solution to the problem of the Diaspora. Nonetheless, he held that it was the test of Jewish nationalism to seek a solution to that problem and to the "eternal Jewish question." Kaufman felt a kinship with General Zionism, especially with the Ha-No'ar ha-Tziyoni movement. Shortly before his death a jubilee volume was published in his honor, and a posthumous volume of critical essays appeared in 1963.

G. KRESSEL—M. HARAN

KAUFMANN, RICHARD YITZHAK. Israeli architect (b. Frankfort on Main, 1887; d. Tel Aviv, 1954). He studied in Munich and worked in Germany before settling in Palestine in 1920. He was faced with the innovative challenge of planning both towns and villages of various ideological types (moshava, *moshav ovedim, kevutza*, kibbutz, and the cooperative farm). He grasped the need for zoning and for a social-cultural center in each settlement. His planning of moshavim differed completely from that of kibbutzim; whereas the former were closed concentricities, the latter were open, meant for expansion. This stemmed from their differing ideologies: the moshav sought to confine itself as a closed society, from which came the form of circle or ellipse (e.g., Nahalal, Kefar Yehoshu'a); the kibbutz was planned for growth and the adding of new members (e.g., Hulda, Ein Harod, Tel Yosef). Some of these evidenced classicism, and even a shade of baroque, although his first houses showed no sign of classicism. This was because he turned to house design some eight years after he had begun urban planning and in this period architecture had changed. His designs were always functional but he used shapes preferred by the first European modernists: horizontal lines with concrete embossments over the windows, and a preference for corner windows. He built interesting houses in the Rehavia neighborhood of Jerusalem; in the Jordan Valley for workers at the Dead Sea plant; and public buildings, such as the main structure at the 1939 Levant Fair in Tel Aviv, and Beit Ha'Am in Nahalal, which symmetry blends the influence of Erich Mendelsohn with elements of classicism.

A. ELHANANI

KEFAR BARUKH. Moshav in the Jezreel Valley. It was founded in 1927 by settlers from various countries, among them Mountain Jews from the Caucasus. The difficulties of the initial years were overcome when water for intensive farming became available. It was named for Barukh Kahana of Romania who gave his wealth to the Jewish National Fund. Population: 284 in 1986.

E. ORNI

KEFAR BLUM. Kibbutz in the Huleh Valley, founded in 1943 near malarial swamps, by the "Anglo-Baltic" group which included pioneers from the Habonim youth movement of England. It has highly-intensive farming, industry, a guest house, and the Bet Habonim cultural center. It was named for Léon Blum. Population (1987), 691.

E. ORNI

Kefar Blum. [Israel Government Tourist Office]

KEFAR DAROM. Site in the Gaza Strip south of Gaza, mentioned in the Talmud (*Sota* 20b). It was captured by the Moslems in 634, later became a Crusader fortress, was taken by Saladin in 1188, destroyed by Richard the Lionhearted in 1192, and later rebuilt by the Ayyubids. In 1946 it was one of the 11 Negev settlements founded on the same day. A religious kibbutz, it stubbornly resisted the Egyptian army onslaught in the 1948 War of Independence until ordered to evacuate the site. In 1949 the settlers founded their new kibbutz Benei Darom further north. Kefar Darom was rebuilt in 1970, becoming a transit camp for settlers in the Gaza Strip. E. ORNI

KEFAR ETZION. *See* ETZION BLOC.

Monument to the defenders of Tel Hai, in Galilee. [Israel Information Services]

KEFAR GILADI. Kibbutz on the northwestern rim of the Huleh Valley, founded in 1916 by members of Ha-Shomer as an outpost on land of the Jewish Colonization Association (ICA) to guard Jewish land holdings and increase the food supply to the country's starving Jews. In 1919, the adjoining outpost Tel Hai was established. The area was earmarked for inclusion in the French Mandate over Syria. The Arabs revolted and attacked Tel Hai, suspecting that French soldiers were hiding there. In the defense, Yosef *Trumpeldor and seven of his comrades fell. The settlers abandoned the site, but returned ten months later. In 1926, Kefar Giladi and Tel Hai merged. In World War II, the kibbutz participated in guarding the country's border against invasion by Vichy-French troops. Kefar Giladi has intensive farming, runs a large stone quarry, industry, and a guest house. Tel Hai is preserved as a national monument and serves as a youth hostel. The kibbutz, named for Ha-Shomer veteran Yisrael Giladi, has (1987) 731 inhabitants. E. ORNI

KEFAR HABAD. Rural center in the coastal plain southeast of Tel Aviv. Founded in 1949 on the initiative of the Lubavicher Rabbi Joseph Isaac Shneersohn, it was originally intended for Hasidic immigrants from Russia but soon became the Israel center of the Habad Hasidic movement. It comprises educational institutions including yeshivot (partly incorporating vocational training), and a teachers' seminary, a printing school, commemorating five children and their teacher murdered in 1955 by terrorist raiders, etc. Population (1987), 3,030. E. ORNI

KEFAR HA-MAKABI. Kibbutz in the Haifa Bay area, founded in 1936 by members of the Maccabi sports organization who remained in the country (without immigration permits) after participating in the Maccabia sports competition. The kibbutz runs intensive agriculture and industry. Population (1987), 369. E. ORNI

Kefar ha-Nasi. [Israel Government Tourist Office]

KEFAR HA-NASI. Kibbutz near the Jordan River south of the Huleh Valley. Founded in June, 1948, near the bridgehead established by the Syrians in the War of Independence, it was immediately engaged in fighting the Syrians. Its members, pioneers of the Habonim youth movement from English-speaking countries, developed intensive farming and industry. The name, "President's Village" commemorates Chaim Weizmann. Population (1987), 614. E. ORNI

KEFAR HA-RO'E. Moshav founded in 1934 in the Hefer Plain of the Sharon. It became a spiritual center of religious moshavim and set up a yeshiva of the Bnei Akiva youth movement, besides engaging in intensive farming. The name is composed of the initials of Rabbi Abraham ha-Kohen (Kook). Population (1987), 948. E. ORNI

KEFAR HASIDIM. Moshav and suburban settlement in the southeastern Haifa Bay area. Founded in 1924 by two groups of Hasidim, it was transferred to its permanent site

Synagogue of Kefar Hasidim, 1925. [Central Zionist Archives]

in 1927. The settlers, with much dedication, drained malarial swamps and developed intensive farming. In 1937 the agricultural school Kefar ha-No'ar ha-Dati was established nearby. In 1950 a second village, Kefar Hasidim B was established in the vicinity. Population (1987): Kefar Hasidim A, 400; Kefar Hasidim B, 216; Kefar ha-No'ar ha-Dati, 528. E. ORNI

KEFAR HITIM. Moshav shitufi in Lower Galilee, 3 miles (4 km.) northeast of Tiberias. It was established in 1936 by Bulgarian Jews near the site of a talmudic village not far from the Horns of Hittin volcanic hill, where Saladin decisively defeated the Crusaders in 1187 and the Druze erected their sanctuary Nebi Shueib. From 1839 onward Jews had planted citron groves there to supply *etrogim* for the Sukkot festival. In 1905, the Jewish National Fund acquired its land in one of its first purchases in the country. Settlement attempts in 1914, 1924, and 1932 failed. The moshav shitufi founded in 1936 was the first of its kind in the country and established the principles of this form of settlement. It has varied intensive farming. Population (1987), 277. E. ORNI

KEFAR MALAL. Moshav in the southern Sharon, near Kefar Sava. Founded in 1911 under the name En Hai. First experiments were made here towards establishing the moshav principles. Destroyed in World War I battles between Allied and Turco-German forces, it was rebuilt in 1921 but destroyed in 1921 by Arabs. Settlers from eastern Europe rebuilt it once again in 1922, taking the initials of M.L. Lilienblum for its name. The moshav's economy is based on intensive irrigated farming. Population (1987), 301. E. ORNI

KEFAR MENAHEM. Kibbutz in the southern coastal plain. The founding of a moshav here in 1936 heralded the drive to acquire land and set up settlements in the Negev. In 1937, the moshav was moved west becoming Kefar Warburg, and Kefar Menahem became a kibbutz developing intensive farming and industry. It is named after Menahem Ussishkin. Population (1987), 593. E. ORNI

KEFAR SAVA. City in the southern Sharon. Land was purchased here in 1892 by Hovevei Zion and taken over by Baron Edmond de Rothschild, who tried to convince settlers to raise plants for perfume production. In 1903 part of the land was bought by Petah Tikva farmers for their sons, and almond orchards were planted. Until 1912, the Turkish authorities sought to prevent the building of houses. In 1917, Kefar Sava set up a camp for 1,000 inhabitants of Tel Aviv, whom the Turks had expelled from their homes. In 1918, Kefar Sava was located in the no-man's land between the Allied and Turco-German forces, and the community was completely destroyed. Soon rebuilt, it again suffered destruction in the 1921 Arab riots. Shortly, however, the discovery of ample groundwater resources and the progress of the citrus industry brought prosperity. The struggle for the use of Jewish labor on the farms focused on Kefar Sava. A number of kibbutzim maintained temporary camps here before their permanent settlement elsewhere. From the period of World War II, industrial enterprises were established and immigrant housing quarters built. In the 1948 War of Independence, Kefar Sava repulsed Arab attacks and the neighboring Arab village Kafr Saba, abandoned by its inhabitants, was occupied. Kefar Sava grew quickly thereafter, numbering 30,000 inhabitants in 1962 when it received city status. The Bet Me'ir hospital and the Histadrut seminary and study center, Bet Berl, are located there. Population (1987), 52,800. E. ORNI

KEFAR SHEMARYAHU. Suburban settlement in the southern Sharon, near Herzliya, with municipal council status. Founded by immigrants from Germany in 1937 as a middle-class moshav, it was based on highly-intensive mixed farming. Its location transformed it into a middle-class garden city and a recreation and entertainment center, with relatively limited industrial enterprises. It bears the name of Shemaryahu Levin. Population (1987), 1,610. E. ORNI

KEFAR TAVOR. Moshava in Lower Galilee at the foot of Mount Tabor, founded in 1901 by the Jewish Colonization Association (ICA) with the aim of promoting grain cultivation by Jewish self-labor. Lack of water for many years impeded the progress of the village. Until World War I, it was a center of Ha-Shomer. Gradually, Kefar Tavor's situation improved and in the 1980s it made considerable progress. Population: 802 in 1986. E. ORNI

KEFAR URIYA. Moshav in the Judean foothills northwest of Bet Shemesh. In 1909 a farm was established here on land bought by individual Jews. Progress was slow and in the 1929 Arab riots the place was abandoned. The land became Jewish National Fund property and in 1943 Jewish stonecutters from Kurdistan settled there, but had to leave during the War of Independence. In 1949, the present moshav was set up by immigrants from Bulgaria, joined by others; and Kefar Uriya became an important link in the "Jerusalem Corridor." Ample ground-water was found, quantities of which are pumped up to Jerusalem. Population: 285 in 1986. E. ORNI

KEFAR VITKIN. Moshav in the Hefer Plain of the central Sharon. The founding group arrived in 1930, being the first in the area and pioneering in dune and swamp reclamation, but only in 1933 was it able to build its permanent settlement. It became one of the country's largest moshavim, basing its economy on citrus groves, dairy cattle, etc., later establishing small industry and resort homes as well. A youth hostel and certain offices of the moshav movement are located there. It is named after Joseph Vitkin. Population: 760 in 1986 E. ORNI

KEFAR YEHEZKEL. Moshav in the Harod Valley southeast of Afula. Founded in 1921, among the valley's first settlements, it developed intensive irrigated farming. It is named after Yehezkel Sassoon whose contributions aided the purchase of the Jezreel and Harod areas. Population: 556 in 1986. E. ORNI

KEFAR YEHOSHU'A. Moshav in the western Jezreel Valley, founded in 1927 by members of Gedud ha-Avoda and pioneers from Russia. Like its neighbor Nahalal, it was laid out in a circular pattern designed by the architect Richard

Kefar Yehezkel, 1923. [Jewish National and University Library]

Kauffmann. Named after Yehoshu'a Hankin, it has a regional museum of the history of settlement in the Jezreel Valley. Population (1987), 572. E. ORNI

KEFAR YONA. Village with municipal council status in the central Sharon, 4 mi. (7 km.) east of Netanya. Founded in 1932, it based its economy principally on citriculture. It expanded in the 1940s, and more so after 1948 when the transit camp Shevut Am was incorporated within its boundaries and industry was added to its economy. It was named after Jean Fischer of Belgium. Population (1987), 3,760. E. ORNI

KELLNER, LEON. Historian, scholar, Zionist leader, and author (b. Tarnow, Galicia, Austria, 1859; d. Vienna, 1928). From 1900 to 1918 he taught English at the Universities of Vienna and Czernowitz. A member of the Hovevei Zion movement and a close friend of Herzl, he was one of the first Jewish intellectuals in Vienna to join the Zionist movement and later participated in its leadership. He was one of the early editors of *Die Welt.* Herzl designated Kellner the executor of his literary estate and the editor of his Zionist writings. In 1920 Kellner published a biography of Herzl's early pre-Zionist years, *Theodor Herzls Lehrjahre* (Theodor Herzl's Apprentice Years). He also edited the original German edition of Herzl's *Diaries,* which appeared in Berlin in 1922–23. He also published many books on English literature and Shakespeare in particular. A. ALPERIN

KENESET YISRAEL ("Community of Israel"). Community organization of Palestine Jewry during the British Mandate for Palestine (1917–48). The Keneset Yisrael embraced the great majority of the entire Jewish population of Palestine. For its history and functions *see* YISHUV, SELF-GOVERNMENT IN THE.

KEREN HA-YESOD (Palestine Foundation Fund). One of the major fundraising arms of the *Jewish Agency and the *World Zionist Organization.

History. It was founded in July 1920 at the *London Zionist Conference, which was called to discuss the financing ot the creation of the Jewish national homeland in Palestine following the Balfour Declaration and the establishment of the British mandate. Two diametrically opposed views emerged at the conference. American Zionists, headed by Louis D. *Brandeis, favored financial institutions operating on a purely commercial and economic basis, arguing that private capital and free enterprise would build the country. The official Zionist leadership called for the creation of a central financial instrument to raise funds from the broad masses of world Jewry, based on voluntary contributions in the form of a Jewish tax. A third idea called for a national loan.

The conference resolved to create a central fund, called Keren ha-Yesod. A manifesto signed by Chaim Weizmann, Vladimir Jabotinsky, Berthold Feivel, Shemarya Levin, and other noted Zionist leaders proclaimed to world Jewry: "The key is in your hands." Funds would be raised to finance immigration, absorption, rural settlements, and the establishment of public economic enterprises together with private capital. Fundraising campaigns would be held among Zionists and non-Zionists alike. Keren ha-Yesod was registered as a company in Britain in March 1921 and set forth the following principles:

(*a*) To do all such acts and things as shall appear to be necessary or expedient for the purpose of carrying out the declaration of His Majesty's Government (commonly known as "the Balfour Declaration") incorporated in the Treaty of Sèvres, dated 2nd day of November, 1917, as to the establishment of a Jewish National Home in Palestine.

(*b*) To appeal for and to receive subscriptions, loans, gifts, legacies, bequests, and donations in money or any other form and to hold, realize, and invest the same or any part thereof....

In 1927 Keren ha-Yesod moved its headquarters from London to Jerusalem. When the 16th Zionist Congress (1929) created the Jewish Agency, with both Zionists and non-Zionists involved in the efforts to build the Jewish National Home, Keren ha-Yesod was made the principal financial instrument supplying the budget of the Jewish Agency. This provision remained in force thereafter in all countries except the United States, where the United Jewish Appeal (est. 1939) took over fundraising activities for the Jewish Agency. Keren ha-Yesod played a major role in funding the various activities of the Jewish community in Palestine during the Mandate era, among them immigration, absorption, settlement, education, housing, labor, Youth Aliya (from the early 1930s), and higher education. It helped rescue German Jews from Nazi Germany and Arab Jews from the Middle Eastern states. It helped purchase arms for the defense of the yishuv. Between 1920 and 1948 it raised £26,700,000. After World War II and the Holocaust, Keren ha-Yesod funds were used to rescue the survivors, prepare the yishuv for the coming war against the Arab states, and expand the industrial, agricultural, and educational infrastructure in Palestine. In 1948 it raised funds which helped pay for the costs of Israel's War of Independence.

Keren ha-Yesod became an Israeli company by a special act of the Knesset called the Keren ha-Yesod Law on 18 January 1956. After the establishment of Israel, its campaigns helped fund the massive immigration of some 1.8 million Jews to Israel and house, educate, and care for them in the initial absorption period. It helped fund immigration from the Soviet Union, starting in 1969, and from Ethiopia in 1985 (Operation Moses). In the first two decades of statehood (May 1948-April 1968) Keren ha-Yesod raised

Founding committee of Keren Ha-Yesod in London, 1920. Louis D. Brandeis is seated at the center of the dais. [United Israel Appeal]

some $400,000,000 in the 54 countries where it operated. Between 1968 and 1987 it raised an additional two billion dollars which included special emergency campaigns during the 1967 Six-Day War and the Yom Kippur War. These events unleashed an unprecedented and spontaneous expression of solidarity with Israel by world Jewry. In the Six-Day War Keren ha-Yesod raised $56,000,000 from 400,000 contributors, double its previous number of givers. Younger people, for whom the Holocaust and Israel's rebirth were past history, came forth to swell the ranks of volunteer workers who form the basis of Keren ha-Yesod operations, and their numbers grew dramatically.

Organization. Keren ha-Yesod's volunteers are organized in continental, territorial, and local committees. In each country it is an independent legal entity headed by local leadership assisted by local and Israeli-recruited professional staff. The Israeli staff is responsible to both the local leadership and the head office in Jerusalem, which directs operations and provides services for local campaigns in the form of speakers, emissaries, educational and publicity material, both written and electronic, and with specific projects.

The supreme body of Keren ha-Yesod is the 18-member World Board of Trustees (established 1978); half of its members are nominated by the World Zionist Organization, and the rest are major campaign leaders. The Board was headed initially by Phil Granovsky, who was followed by Mendel Kaplan. Keren ha-Yesod is headed by a World Chairman who is a member of the Zionist Executive. Among the chairmen were Arthur Hantke, Zvi Herman, Eliyahu Dobkin, Israel Goldstein, Ezra Shapira, Avraham Avi-Hai, and Shlomo Hillel. Day-to-day operations are directed by the Director-General (Moshe Ussishkin until 1968, S.J. Kreutner 1968–1980, and Ya'akov Gilead since 1980).

Projects. In 1977, Keren ha-Yesod heeded the call of Prime Minister Begin and adopted a number of Israeli neighborhoods under *Project Renewal. This work has since been expanded and in 1988 involved some 20 overseas communities which were "twinned" with Israeli neighborhoods, assisting them physically, financially, and through volunteer work. Leadership development abroad also became a major Keren ha-Yesod effort in the late 1970s, when it turned its attention to young Jews in business and the professions, recruiting and training them for both Keren ha-Yesod work and community involvement. Stress was laid on organizing study missions to Israel to provide a first-hand educational and emotional experience for participants. There has also been a growing demand for projects in the fields of education, child care, health, community centers, sports, and culture. Keren ha-Yesod helped set up more than 1,000 such projects from 1948 on. By

1988 Keren ha-Yesod was active in 47 countries, dealing with a population of some 2,000,000 Jews in the free world. M. MEDZINI

KEREN KAYEMET LE-YISRAEL. *See* JEWISH NATIONAL FUND.

KEREN TEL HAI. *See* TEL HAI FUND.

KERNER, MOSHE. Polish Zionist leader (b. Warsaw, 1876; d. Tel Aviv, 1966). Kerner was active in the 1906 *Helsingfors Conference and supported the **Gegenwartsarbeit* ("Work in the Present") program. He was elected to the special committee of the Polish region. During World War I he was exiled to Russia but returned at the first opportunity and began to represent the Zionist Organization on the Warsaw City Council. He was elected to the Polish Senate in 1922. One of the major figures in the Al ha-Mishmar faction (*see* POLAND, ZIONISM IN) he was a follower of Yitzhak Gruenbaum. Especially active in the cultural field, Kerner was the driving force for the establishment of the Central Library for Jewish Studies in Warsaw (1936) which served the Institute for Jewish Studies, founded in 1928. After the Nazi occupation he served for a short time on the Warsaw Jewish community council. He immigrated to Palestine in 1940, but ceased all public activity. M. MINTZ

KESSEL, JOSEPH. French journalist and writer (b. Clara, Argentina, 1898; d. Avernes near Paris, 1979). His parents were Jewish refugees from Russia who settled in a Jewish agricultural colony in Argentina, but emigrated to France in 1908. As a reporter for French papers, Kessel's taste for world-wide adventures, his curiosity for all beings, and his dramatic but simple style captured the public. He also wrote novels and film scenarios based on his recollections. Some of his works contain enthusiastic descriptions of Zionist realization: *Terre d'amour* (Land of Love, 1927), and *Terre de feu* (Land of Fire, 1948), and the expanded single-volume *Terre d'amour et de feu* (Land of Love and Fire, 1965). *Les Fils de l'impossible* (The Sons of the Impossible, 1970) praised the heroism of the soldiers who fought the Six-Day War. In his inauguration speech at the French Academy (1962) he spoke proudly of his Jewishness. M. CATANE

KESSLER, LEOPOLD. Zionist leader in South Africa and Great Britain (b. Tarnowskie Gory, Upper Silesia, Prussia, 1864; d. New York, 1944). After studying in Germany, he went to Rhodesia as a mining engineer and later to the Transvaal, where he worked as a general manager in mining operations. One of the earliest Zionist pioneers of South Africa, he was elected president of the Transvaal Zionist Association in 1899 and attended the Third Zionist Congress (1899). In 1903 Herzl appointed Kessler to lead the *El-Arish Expedition to investigate the possibilities of Jewish settlement in that location.

When David Wolffsohn became president of the World Zionist Organization (WZO), Kessler was one of his close collaborators. In 1906 Wolffsohn, Leopold Jacob Greenberg, Kessler, and others acquired the shares of the **Jewish Chronicle* and Kessler became a member and later chairman of its board of directors. From 1907 to 1921 he was on the Executive Committee of the Jewish National Fund. In 1909 he attended the Ninth Zionist Congress, and in 1912 he was elected president of the Zionist Federation of Great Britain and Ireland. He was also chairman of the Jewish National Fund in Great Britain and a member of the directorate of the Jewish Colonial Trust and other financial institutions of the WZO. After the 12th Zionist Congress (1921), he withdrew from official Zionist leadership. In 1918 he published a brochure entitled *History and Development of Jewish Colonisation in Palestine*. J. FRAENKEL

KEVUTZA. *See* KIBBUTZ.

KEVUTZAT YAVNE. Kibbutz in the coastal plain, 5 mi. (8 km.) south of the town of Yavne. Founded in 1941 by religious pioneers from Germany, who were later joined by immigrants from English-speaking and other countries, it became a center of the religious kibbutz movement, setting up the yeshiva Kerem be-Yavne and the teachers' seminary Givat Washington. Based on intensive, mostly irrigated, mixed farming and industry, it numbered 742 inhabitants in 1987. E. ORNI

KHAN YUNIS. Town southwest of Gaza. Until 1948 it was, apart from Gaza, the only population center of the southernmost coastal plain possessing at least a semi-urban character. At the beginning of the 14th century Yunis, a Mameluk governor, set up a wayfarers' inn ("khan"), laying the ground for a commercial center. The population of Khan Yunis increased from 11,220 in 1944 to 52,997 in the 1967 census, almost all Moslems, with 23,475 of them living in refugee camps. The town's economy is founded on farming, but hired labor in Israel became an important source of income after 1967. E. ORNI

KHOUSHI (HUSHI, SCHNELLER), ABBA. Israeli labor leader and public official (b. Turka, Galicia, Austria, 1898; d. Haifa, 1969). An early member of Ha-Shomer ha-Tza'ir and He-Halutz in Galicia, Khoushi settled in Palestine in 1920. A founder of Bet Alfa, he worked in road building, swamp drainage, and agriculture in the Jezreel Valley until 1927. That year he moved to Haifa, where he worked as a longshoreman and organized a union of port employees that comprised both Jews and Arabs. When the port of Haifa was built in the early 1930s, Khoushi made several trips to Salonika, where he recruited hundreds of young Jewish stevedores and other port employees for the Haifa project. In the course of his activities on behalf of labor, he acquired many Arab and Druze friends in Haifa and its environs.

Khoushi was a member of the Executive Committee of the Histadrut. From 1938 to 1951 he was secretary-general of the Haifa Labor Council, a position which he turned into a political office that soon made him one of the most important individuals in the city. He was also one of the organizers and leaders of Hagana in Haifa. In 1949 he was elected to the Knesset by the Mapai party but resigned in 1951 to become mayor of Haifa, a position he held until his death. During his administration he promoted Haifa's image as a working-class city and devoted particular attention to sanitation and landscaping, laying out parks, gardens, and playgrounds. He played a leading role in the building of Haifa's Carmelit subway, the Haifa Municipal Theater, and the Haifa University Institute.

KIBBUTZ ARTZI SHEL HA-SHOMER HA-TZA'IR. Kibbutz federation founded in 1927 with the aim of practising Zionism and Marxist socialism within the framework of kibbutz life. Its name means "Countrywide Kibbutz of *Ha-Shomer ha-Tza'ir."

In contrast to other kibbutz federations, which allowed freedom in political affiliation, the Kibbutz Artzi insisted on its members' accepting the official views of the Ha-Shomer ha-Tza'ir movement, considering such acceptance a prerequisite of the ideological collectivism it embraced. Politically, the Kibbutz Artzi is the mainstay of the *Mapam party. In addition to agriculture, several kibbutzim belonging to the federation engage in industry, often in partnership with private enterprises. The central bodies of the organization and its publishing house and press are located at Kibbutz Merhavya. In 1990 the Kibbutz Artzi comprised 83 kibbutzim with a total population of 41,515.

See also KIBBUTZ MOVEMENT

KIBBUTZ DATI. *See* HA-KIBBUTZ HA-DATI.

KIBBUTZ FESTIVALS. In the early days of the kibbutz agriculture and settlement of the land were among the main values. Appropriate ceremonies soon appeared to give expression to these purposes. By identifying with the biblical and post-biblical past when Jewish farmers tilled the soil, and by an emotional receptiveness to its contact with the soil, the kibbutz created a number of agricultural festivals. The *Haggada* (Passover ritual) and *Omer* (culling of the first barley sheaves) of Passover and *bikkurim* (the first fruits) of *Shavuot* are the most outstanding examples of the interaction between the kibbutz, the land, and Jewish heritage.

The Nature Festivals. A drift in community attitudes toward holidays shows up in the modifications and reinterpretations gradually introduced into the nature festivals which no longer command the central position they once held. This is especially noticeable on *Shavuot*. In the Diaspora this holiday was dedicated primarily to the commemoration of the revelation of the Torah at Sinai, while the aspect of the former Festival of the First Fruits was underplayed. The Diaspora aspect was completely absent from the festival as it emerged out of the secular kibbutz, with agriculture now acting as the holiday's foundation stone. The subsequent partial return to a historical focus has been attributed to the increased mechanization of agriculture. But what in fact occurred was a basic revision in the kibbutz community's relationship to agriculture. Shavuot no longer retains its former significance, as kibbutz industry moves forward to the position of major employer. The members who work in education or the domestic services also have minimal contact with the soil.

Children celebrating festival of Sukkot on Kibbutz Masada. [Kibbutz Masada]

Passover was a festival which came with a stock of pleasant, warm, and rich memories. Although there was a general revolt against traditional holidays among the old-timers, Passover was the holiday which suffered least from this rejection. Childhood and adolescent experiences of the Passover eve ceremony seem to have been sufficiently rewarding to protect Passover from the repudiation experienced by other holidays. This is evidenced by the creation of hundreds of kibbutz *haggadot* which, after a process of confrontation with the traditional *haggada* resulted in the fairly definitive versions in use today. At first these were artistically and graphically simple productions, compared to the esthetically attractive *haggadot* of today, but the message was the same: freedom achieved by natural means and not through supernatural redemption. There was no difficulty in reinterpreting Passover in this context since freedom is a major value of kibbutz life; neither was there a contradiction between this significant value of Passover and focal values of kibbutz culture.

Since Passover was the first holiday to undergo rejuvenation in the kibbutz, it became the repository of themes which had no echo in the traditional *haggada*. Whatever events seemed relevant in the Jewish world, whether in the kibbutz, in Israel or in the Diaspora, appeared in Kibbutz haggadot. The Arab riots of the 1930s, the sudden expansion of border kibbutzim prior to World War II, the first news of the Holocaust, the grim realization of the fate of European Jewry, the struggle for independence, the rise of the Jewish State—all these themes appeared in *haggadot* close to the time of their occurrence. Passover functioned as a ceremonial outlet by means of which kibbutz members identified themselves with the eternal struggle for freedom.

After the establishment of the State of Israel, many of the pre-State themes fell by the wayside, and Passover returned to itself. Israel's Independence Day was established in proximity to Holocaust Day and a Memorial Day for soldiers and civilians who fell in Israel's struggle for independence. These new holidays and days of memorial emptied the kibbutz Passover of its topical commentary and content, confronting the editors of *haggadot* with a new problem: how to restore the timelessness of Passover without returning to the rigid form of the traditional *haggada*. Because God's supernatural attributes are denied, entire sections of the traditional *haggada* offering praise to God, as well as the Grace after Meals, have been omitted. However, not all references to God were struck out. Psalms, and well loved songs from the traditional *haggada* such as "Who Knows One?" are read and sung at the table. Biblical sections, particularly from the Book of Exodus, are woven together to form a narrative outline of the Exodus from Egypt.

The kibbutz feels that its approach is an improvement on the traditional version, because it has made the retelling of the Exodus the focus of its *haggadot*. With God's role in the Exodus devalued, the figure of Moses becomes central. The puzzling omission of Moses from the traditional *haggada* has been rectified by the inclusion of narratively connected biblical verses portraying him as a shepherd, as the representative of his people confronting Pharaoh, and at the head of the "mixed multitude" leaving Egypt. Another major theme is the coming of spring. In the kibbutz *haggadot* spring serves as a short opening motif before giving way to the narrative. Portions from the *Song of Songs* interweave with selections from medieval Hebrew poetry on the cessation of the winter rains and the beginning of dew. The first *haggadot* to introduce this motif used the works of modern Hebrew writers, but as in the case with recounting of Exodus, classical and ancient texts outweighed modern writers.

A final theme in the kibbutz *haggada* is the ingathering of the exiles. The concluding cry of the *seder*—next year in Jerusalem—has been considerably enlarged by interposing poems by Judah Halevi and selections from Amos and Isaiah, all centering on the return of the Jewish people to their ancestral land.

The High Holidays. Unlike the pilgrimage festivals, Purim or Hanukka, the High Holidays cannot be connected to any event in the historical past or related to the cycles of nature. The Days of Awe are completely "religious" and resist adaptation to the national or agricultural themes prevalent in other holidays. Until recently, Rosh ha-Shana and Yom Kippur seemed consigned to spiritual exile, but they have now been restored to a more honorable position within the yearly kibbutz holiday cycle. With the depletion of the creative iconoclastic drive and the inclusion on the kibbutz agenda of questions of Jewish identity, Rosh ha-Shana and Yom Kippur can no longer be ignored. In addition, the Kibbutz movement has experienced a severe crisis of self-confidence, which has made the average member conscious of the failings of kibbutz life. Awareness of human limitations is a precondition to the reappearance of the days devoted in part to an evaluation of the human condition.

Rosh ha-Shana, like Passover, takes place around a festive meal in the dining room. There are no special foods, other than apples and honey, but the appearance is similar—a booklet with readings, a choir, community singing, and large quantities of food heaped on the tables. Clearly then, Rosh ha-Shana is not a "Day of Awe" on the kibbutz.

The themes within the ceremonial material remain broadly traditional—the return from exile, the New Year as a day of assessment of the relationship between man and man, man and society, man and his environment. A special kibbutz motif is the glorification of humanity, an outcome of the optimistic ideology that holds humans to be progressively developing in the direction of a fuller and more spiritual humanity. Faith and mutual trust in one's fellows are a pragmatic requirement of a cooperative society. Belief in the human being, for the kibbutz, becomes an ontological necessity.

Yom Kippur differs from the other holidays by reason of the absence of full community participation. Without the centrality of a communal meal and the active participation of children, the observance of the day can focus on its content alone. As a result, Yom Kippur "programs" attract few people. Young people in particular are accustomed to experiencing holidays as social events, generally ignoring content and message. Only a small minority mark Yom Kippur. The theme repeating itself in kibbutz literature on Yom Kippur is the recurrent necessity for a collective *heshbon nefesh*, a self-examination, evaluation, and joint stock-taking of the collective conscience of the community, as well as the personal conscience of the individual. In a kibbutz the interdependence of the collective and the individual requires periodic renewal.

The Extinct Holidays. The experimental mood of some of the cultural pace-setters led kibbutzim to attempt a "restoration" of certain minor holidays or traditions. A few kibbutzim sought to initiate holidays mentioned in Jewish sources and connected to special agricultural branches of their economy. One was called a "Vineyard Festival", another a "Shearing Festival". These efforts proved abortive, for an ancient practice fallen into disuse cannot be artificially resuscitated. Experience indicated that traditional holidays with a continuous history of practice can, however, be reconstituted. Another attempt to refurbish the past was the appearance of the Fifteenth of Av as a festival of love, but aside from a few sporadic celebrations, nothing has come of this. The new holidays failed to pass the test of experience. Antiquity was not enough.

The unique characteristics of kibbutz holiday as compared with a holiday in its customary setting are:

(1) The kibbutz holiday is a secular creation. No religious functionaries ensure its observance.
(2) The kibbutz makes no use of the synagogue for its ceremonies. Kibbutz ceremony is devoid of all prayer, praise or thanksgiving to a deity.
(3) Dance, song, decoration and communal spirit characterize the kibbutz festivals.

The future of kibbutz-style holidays is uncertain. The native-born generations have yet to reveal the creative urges that distinguished their parents and grandparents.

S. LILKER

KIBBUTZ ME'UHAD (Ha-Kibbutz ha-Me'uhad, or United Kibbutz). Organization of collective settlements in Israel, founded in 1927 on the initiative of En Harod (a Third Aliya kibbutz) and the remnants of *Gedud ha-Avoda (which had been formed in 1920). Its purpose was to utilize the collective form of settlement for large-scale absorption of workers in villages combining agriculture and industry. In the late 1930s, a left-wing opposition (Si'a Bet) crystallized in the Kibbutz Me'uhad against its Mapai-affiliated majority. In 1944 the Kibbutz Me'uhad founded the *Ahdut Avoda (United Zionist Labor party); in 1947 it rejected the Jewish State program and advocated placing Palestine under a UN mandate; and in 1948 it formed, with *Ha-Shomer ha-Tza'ir, the *Mapam party. In 1951 a split occurred; the former Mapai members (representing some 40 percent at the time) seceded from the organization and, with the *Hever ha-Kevutzot, formed the *Ihud ha-Kevutzot veha-Kibbutzim.

The Kibbutz Me'uhad was closely associated with the *Palmah (commando units); pioneered in new branches of primary economic production, such as quarrying, fishing, and seafaring; and had its own publishing house, press, and headquarters at En Harod. Affiliated with it were the youth movements *Dror and He-Halutz ha-Tza'ir in the

Diaspora. In 1954 it split from Mapam and reverted to Ahdut Avoda. In 1984 it united with Ihud ha-Kevutzot veha-Kibbutzim to form the Tenu'a Kibbutzit Me'uhedet (Takam).

See also KIBBUTZ MOVEMENT.

KIBBUTZ MOVEMENT. The kibbutz or kevutza (plural: kibbutzim, kevutzot) is a voluntary collective community unique to Israel based on the principles of communal ownership of the means of production, communal responsibility for all the needs of the community's members and their families, and equal distribution of wealth. The kibbutz movement in Israel had a population of 126,700 at the end of 1986, living in 269 communities and comprising 3.6 percent of the Jewish population. Its percentage of the Gross National Product was three times its percentage of the population, and it accounted for 57% of the total agricultural output of the country, in addition to its participation in an extraordinary variety of joint regional economic enterprises, partnerships with other groups in the Israeli economy, and extra-kibbutz activities. The kibbutz was described by the Israeli writer, Amos Oz, as one of the unique creations of the Zionist renascence.

History. The first kevutza (today the words kevutza and kibbutz are used interchangeably, but originally the term kevutza was used by those interested in a relatively small, intimate, organic community; those interested in a large, open, continuously expanding commune preferred the term kibbutz) was founded in 1909 on the banks of Lake Kineret. A group of pioneers working on a farm there operated by the Palestine Land Development Company undertook collective responsibility for its operation when it was in danger of closing down. They named the place Deganya.

These pioneers were among the first groups of young socialist-Zionist idealists who had begun to arrive in Eretz Israel in the early 1900s in what came to be known as the Second Aliya. They found a country which was largely barren; its wasted and eroded soil had to be reclaimed before even a meager living could be wrung from its arid, stony, or in other places swampy, soil. Their own ideological background, combined with the exigencies of the environment, made for the development of an ethic of continuous personal revolution based on the practical and ideological importance of physical labor as the basis of a Jewish democratic socialist communal society.

Various scattered attempts to establish such communities had been made previously. The idea of cooperative or collective settlement had been part of Zionist aspirations since the arrival of the First Aliya in the 1880s. It was, however, discouraged by the principal supporter of First Aliya settlement, Baron Edmond de Rothschild. It was later raised and suggested in the writings of Franz Oppenheimer, Nachman Syrkin and others. At the beginning of the Second Aliya a number of such experiments were attempted, led by such figures as Joseph Trumpeldor and Manya Wilbushewitz-Shohat (who, on a visit to the Canadian, Dukhobor communes, was impressed by them as a possible model for Jewish settlement in Eretz Israel). These experiments included a communal settlement at Sejera founded in 1907 by the Bar-Giora movement (the precursor of the Jewish self-defense movement), which lasted more than a year. David Ben-Gurion, Israel's future prime minister, was a member of this group. The kibbutz movement, as a movement, however, began with Deganya.

By 1914 there were eleven kevutzot established on Jewish National Fund land; the number grew to 29 by the end of 1918. These early kevutzot had transient memberships and were deliberately small, believing that the community should be intimate enough to constitute a kind of large extended family. Indeed, when Deganya felt that it was in danger of becoming "too large," it renamed itself Deganya Aleph (A) (its name to this day) and gave up part of its land for the establishment of another kevutza alongside it—Deganya (B) Bet.

The end of World War I brought larger numbers of pioneering youth who had experienced the ferment of the Russian revolution. Shelomo Lavi and others proposed to this group the establishment of large self-sufficient settlements with a mixed agricultural and industrial economy which would aim at absorbing large numbers. This approach naturally appealed to the members of the *Gedud ha-Avoda ("Labor Battalion"), who viewed themselves as mobilized for the establishment of a Jewish-socialist Palestine. They established Kibbutz En Harod and Kibbutz Tel Yosef which became prototypes for the "large, ever-expanding, kibbutz" as distinguished from the "small, intimate" kevutza.

Over the years the kibbutzim and kevutzot united to establish national federations according to their social, political, and communal outlook. *Hever ha-Kevutzot was founded in 1925; *Kibbutz Artzi of Ha-Shomer ha-Tza'ir and *Kibbutz Me'uhad were both founded in 1927, and *Ha-Kibbutz ha-Dati (founded by members of the religiously Orthodox Mizrachi movement) was established in 1935. After a number of shattering splits and reunifications (see below), Hever ha-Kevutzot united with some forty percent of the settlements of the Kibbutz Me'uhad—those leaning to *Mapai rather than to the *Ahdut ha-Avoda political party—to form in 1951, the *Ihud ha-Kevutzot ve-ha-Kibbutzim. This movement, in turn united with the Kibbutz Me'uhad in 1984 to form the Tenu'a Kibbutzit Me'uhedet (the Hebrew acronym is Takam) or—in English, the *United Kibbutz Movement. This is now the largest of the kibbutz federations—the others being Kibbutz Artzi, Ha-Kibbutz ha-Dati, and two kibbutzim of the ultra-Orthodox *Po'alei Agudat Israel. There is a great deal of cultural, educational, economic, and organizational cooperation both on the local and regional level and through a national coordinating body called the Berit ha-Tenu'a ha-Kibbutzit (Kibbutz Movement Association).

A major source of manpower for the kibbutz movement has been, historically, a network of Zionist pioneering *youth movements both in Israel and abroad. In many ways the history of these movements and the kibbutz movements is integrally intertwined. Kibbutz Artzi is actually the product of the Ha-Shomer ha-Tza'ir youth movement. The other federations, though founded independently, soon became associated with, or in some cases actually founded, their own youth movements. Among those relationships were Hever ha-Kevutzot with *Gordonia and later Maccabi ha-Tza'ir; Kibbutz Me'uhad with *Dror, *Ha-No'ar ha-Oved ve-ha-Lomed, *Mahanot ha-Olim, Ha-Tsofim and others; Ha-Kibbutz ha-Dati with Bnei Akiva; Ihud ha-Kevutzot veha-Kibbutzim with *Habonim, *Ha-Tenu'a ha-Me'uhedet, La-Merhav, Ha-Tsofim, *Young Judea, and the Takam, as the successor of these two, with all of them. Today there are also the youth movements of the Reform and Conservative religious groupings, among others. In pre-Hitler Europe these movements numbered hundreds of thousands of members. In Israel they numbered many thousands at the end of the 1980s, and the kibbutz movements invested in them heavily—financially, organizationally, and educationally.

The history of the kibbutz movement is, in a larger context, inseparable from that of the Israeli labor movement and its involvement in the Zionist movement and the establishment of the State. The founders and leaders of the kibbutz movement were in large measure among the founders and leaders of the labor movement, both in Israel and abroad, and were generally viewed, by themselves and by the larger movement, as a "vanguard"—a force to be mobilized in the forefront of every national endeavor, in the cities, in missions abroad, in "illegal" immigration, settlement, defense, education and culture, and in politics itself in both the narrower and broader sense.

The members of the smaller, intimate, organic kevutzot tended to be those adhering to the ethically (rather than Marxist) socialist philosophy, in a way Tolstoyan. This was closer to Jewish tradition, represented by A.D. Gordon, and consequently to the Ha-Po'el ha-Tza'ir sector of the labor movement in all its consequent metamorphoses. It was they who founded the Hever ha-Kevutzot. The members of what became Kibbutz Me'uhad were inclined to the more militant, stridently Marxist, aggressively socialist, militarily activist Ahdut ha-Avoda party, led by such figures as Yitzhak Tabenkin. Some of the left-wing elements of the Gedud ha-Avoda returned to the Soviet Union in the late 1920s in an illusory attempt to build Jewish communal socialism there. Some subsequently returned to Israel after years in the gulag; others perished there. The kibbutzim established by the graduates of the Ha-Shomer ha-Tza'ir youth movement were highly similar, as a result of their middle class intellectual youth movement background, to the kevutzot of Hever ha-Kevutzot. They, too, spoke of organic communities, based on "nuclei" of members who grew up and were educated as groups in the youth movement and of the kibbutz itself as a result of an all-embracing educational environmental process. In the course of time, however, Ha-Shomer ha-Tza'ir came to view itself not only as a youth movement or as a settlement movement but also as a political party—based on its position that economic, social, and political collectivism are inherently inseparable. In this they differed from Hever ha-Kevutzot and to a great extent from Ha-Kibbutz ha-Me'uhad. The latter also viewed themselves and the kibbutz as active instruments towards realizing political goals in society as a whole—a view which at times resulted in bitter internal struggle; nevertheless, they were much more open to a relatively large gamut of differing positions within the kibbutz. They did not believe in establishing independent political parties, aspiring rather to influence larger political organizations.

In the first years of the kibbutz movement the lines between individual settlements such as Kineret, Gan Shemuel, Kefar Giladi, Mahanayim, Heftzi-Ba, Bet Alfa, Geva, Yagur—which later became strongholds of the various federations—were not clearly drawn. People joined one, then left and joined another, and positions crystallized only with time.

The growth of the movement after World War I was hampered by a lack of funds both for land purchase and for minimal necessities. The existing kibbutzim were characterized by extremely difficult physical conditions and bitter poverty. During these years, however— between 1920 and 1930—the basic organizational framework of the kibbutz was established.

When Hever ha-Kevutzot was founded in 1925 at Bet Alfa, there were about 2,700 people in all the kibbutzim. The establishment of four kibbutzim by Ha-Shomer ha-Tza'ir and, consequently, of the Kibbutz ha-Artzi began the political evolution of what later became the *Mapam political party, dominated by Kibbutz ha-Artzi. Mapam gradually adopted an ultra-Marxist stance, focused on establishing close relations with the Soviet Union as a "second ideological homeland," and favored a bi-national Arab-Jewish state in Palestine. Meanwhile, Kibbutz Me'uhad, in keeping with its own ideological position, began to establish extra-kibbutz economic enterprises (a maritime company, work battalions in the cities, at the Dead Sea, in the building trades), developed central organizational structures, and played a decisive role in the Ahdut ha-Avoda party. Hever ha-Kevutzot, affiliated with the Mapai labor party, was deserted by many of its original member communities. Numbering some ten kevutzot, it maintained the original "Gordonist" Deganya approach, and was reinforced by receiving manpower from the Gordonia youth movement. It continued to establish smaller kibbutzim until after the establishment of the State; many of them were in the mountains (Kefar ha-Horesh, Hanita, Ma'ale ha-Hamisha) and became models of pioneering daring and inspiration.

If the 1920s were years of basic organization, the 1930s, though still characterized by difficult physical and economic circumstances, were years of growth and expansion, both internally and in influence beyond the movement itself. In 1931 the population of the kibbutzim was 4,291. By 1939 it had increased to 24,767 or 5.2% of the Jewish population. The General Zionist movement established kibbutzim through *Ha-No'ar ha-Tziyoni; the religious Mizrachi sector of the Zionist movement founded the Orthodox Ha-Kibbutz ha-Dati federation, and even the ultra-Orthodox Po'alei Agudat Israel established several kibbutz settlements. The movement was instrumental in expanding the map of Jewish settlement. In the late 1930s many were set up overnight as *"Tower and Stockade" settlements to forestall Arab attacks and British interference. By 1948 kibbutzim numbered 149 out of the 191 Jewish villages in the country.

In 1948 and 1949, the momentum of kibbutz expansion continued. Of the 175 new villages founded during these two years, 79 were kibbutzim. The newest immigrants, Jews from Moslem countries and survivors of the Holocaust, were less interested in kibbutzim than were the previous generation of pioneers, educated in the youth movements, and most of them preferred to settle in moshavim, in development towns, and in the cities. With the establishment of the State, some of the national activities of the kibbutz movement were taken over by the government e.g., security, settlement, and government departments, and some kibbutz members and prospective members chose government service as an idealistic challenge rather than kibbutz life. The kibbutz movement nevertheless continued to grow and expand in absolute numbers, although its percentage in the growing Jewish population of the country became somewhat smaller.

In the early 1950s support for pro-Soviet policies led to a split in Ha-Kibbutz ha-Me'uhad. This was a traumatic period which tore apart veteran kibbutzim. In a number of cases blocks of members moved en masse to other kibbutzim; sometimes they established new communities of the same name alongside the older ones, with those of one political persuasion living in one and of the other, in the second. The pro-Soviet section of Ha-Kibbutz ha-Me'uhad continued the federation and the political party to which it adhered, Ahdut ha-Avoda, united with Ha-Shomer ha-Tza'ir to form the Mapam party. The anti-Soviet grouping joined with Hever ha-Kevutzot to form Ihud ha-Kevutzot veha-Kibbutzim, identifying with the anti-Soviet, social democratic Mapai party.

It took a number of years for Ha-Kibbutz ha-Me'uhad and Ahdut Ha-Avoda to become disillusioned with their obsession with the Soviet Union and to realize that there was no hope for Communist-Zionist mutual understanding. Ahdut ha-Avoda left Mapam and ultimately merged again with Mapai to form the Israel Labor Party. Ha-Shomer ha-Tza'ir continued its pro-Soviet orientation for a longer time until the Khrushchev revelations and other developments resulted in a sobering reevaluation on its part as well.

The merger of Ahdut ha-Avoda and Mapai resulted in an increasing rapprochement between Ha-Kibbutz ha-Me'uhad and Ihud ha-Kevutzot veha-Kibbutzim. This was reflected on a local and regional level in the gradual unification of economic, cultural, and educational activities and institutions as well as on the national level. After a slow process of cooperative efforts and *de facto* merging, the two federations finally united formally in 1984 to create Ha-Tenu'a ha-Kibbutzit ha-Me'uhedet (Takam).

In 1987 the Takam federation numbered 167 kibbutzim, with a total population of 76,560; Ha-Kibbutz ha-Artzi of Ha-Shomer ha-Tza'ir 83 kibbutzim with a population of 41,515; Ha-Kibbutz ha-Dati 17 kibbutzim with a population of 7,307; and Po'alei Agudat Israel two, with a population of 1,367. The total population of the kibbutz movement was 126,745 comprising 3.6% of the Jewish population of Israel.

Structure. Organizationally the kibbutz is a direct democracy. A weekly general meeting of the members formulates policy, elects officers and full-time managerial personnel, and supervises the overall working of the community. Candidates for membership are usually accepted after a year's probation. Kibbutzim are incorporated enterprises, new members are generally expected to transfer all assets, other than personal effects, to the kibbutz. Should a member decide to leave, he is entitled to his personal effects and a cash grant proportional to the length of time he has been a member. Uniform national by-laws governing the rights of individuals vis-à-vis the kibbutz have been established by the federations.

Day-to-day management is conducted by elected committees and full-time managerial personnel. The principal committee is the kibbutz secretariat, which normally consists of an executive secretary, treasurer, coordinator of economic affairs, production manager, personnel coordinator, chairmen of certain committees, and others. There are additional committees in charge of education; cultural activities; budget and finance; basic issues related to the implementation of kibbutz principles in Israel's changing society; the personal needs of members; and in other areas. Elective positions are rotated. With time, many of the initial differences between one type of kibbutz and another disappeared. Most of those which believed in small, agriculturally-based communities have grown and established industry, leaving no difference between the small kevutza and the large kibbutz. Indeed, the income of the kibbutz movement in 1986 from non-agricultural sources was twice the income from agriculture (its 416 industrial plants sold products worth close to one and a quarter billion dollars).

From the early sixties on, new kibbutzim were established primarily through Nahal, a special corps of the Israel Defense Army, composed of youth movement graduates. Trained in "nuclear groups" for future kibbutz settlement as part of their army service, they spend some of it in established kibbutzim and the rest at points of future settlement. The Nahal is one of Israel's elite military formations; its soldiers maintain a fighting record in spite (or perhaps because) of spending almost half their service in settlement activity.

The kibbutz federations provide assistance to their member kibbutzim through national cooperative loan funds and negotiation with Zionist and Israel government agencies, banks, and other financial institutions, both in Israel and abroad. They offer technical advisory services ranging from economic consultancy to the planning of kitchens and centralized construction contracting, as well as central purchasing and marketing services and companies, and a national Kibbutz Industries Association.

Education and Culture. The movement operates a network of child and family guidance clinics (including central schools for children needing special education) and sponsors an extraordinarily wide gamut of economic, cultural, and educational activities.

At the Ruppin Agricultural Institute, near Netanya, a great variety of courses ranging from two weeks to two years is offered to kibbutz students in technical subjects such as mechanics, plumbing, and electricity; in farm subjects such as citriculture, banana growing, and water management; and managerial subjects for future kibbutz management. A Council for Higher Education-approved BA degree is offered in kibbutz management. The two largest Israeli teacher training colleges are operated by the kibbutz movement—Seminar ha-Kibbutzim in Tel Aviv with some 1,500 students and Oranim, the School of Education of the Kibbutz Movement, affiliated with the University of Haifa, situated in Kiryat Tivon with some 1,500 full-time students as well as another 1,500 part-time students. These schools train teachers for kindergartens, elementary schools, music, arts and crafts, and high school subjects ranging from Bible to history to physics. They maintain research and in-service training facilities. Together, they account for 25% of all the elementary school teachers in Israel. The movements maintain central seminar centers at Givat Haviva and Efal where thousands of people study for shorter or longer periods every year. Research centers exist at Yad Tabenkin in Efal, at Givat Haviva, at Oranim, and at the Center for the Study of the Kibbutz at Haifa University, and the movement maintains a joint ongoing project for the study of the kibbutz at the Center for Jewish Studies at Harvard University.

Recent years have seen the development of regional community colleges operated jointly by kibbutzim through the regional local councils; many thousands of people study at them part-time and in the evenings. Such colleges exist at Tel Hai in Upper Galilee, at Zemah in the Jordan Valley, at Ohel Sara in the Jezreel Valley, at Yad Natan in Western Galilee, and at the Sapir College in the Negev, and elsewhere.

The federations publish a number of literary magazines and journals of education and opinion such as *Mi-bifnim*, *Hedim*, and *Shedemot*. They own two of the major Israeli publishing houses—Sifriyat ha-Po'alim and Hotza'at ha-

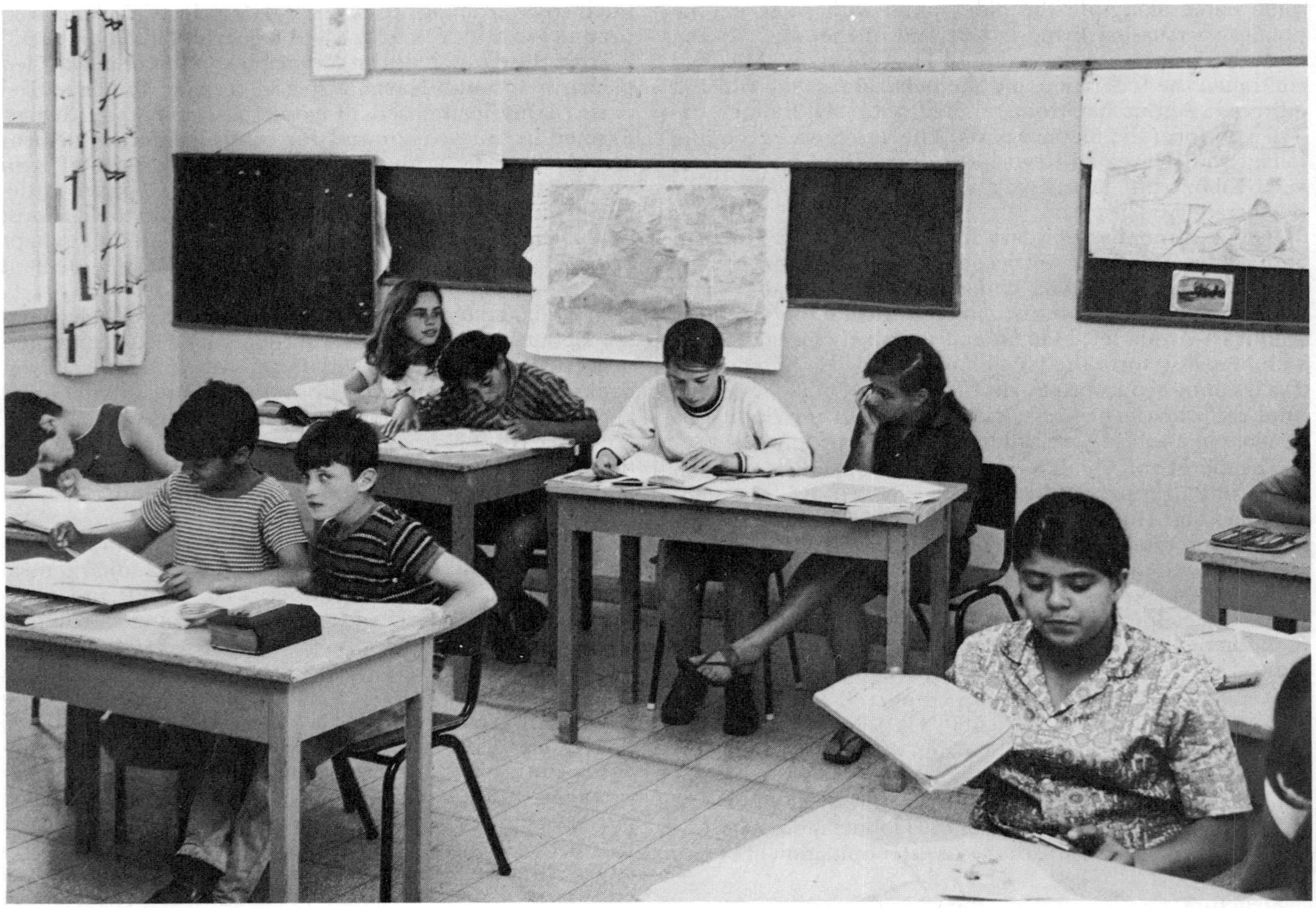

Classroom in the kibbutz Manara. [Keren Ha-Yesod]

Kibbutz ha-Me'uhad—which publish translated and original work in almost every cultural and academic field.

More than seventy museums are situated in kibbutzim, ranging from small archeological collections of artifacts found in the area to significant art museums, such as those in Ha-Zore'a and En Harod, and important museum centers on a national level such as the Ghetto Fighters' Museum at Kibbutz Lohamei ha-Geta'ot and the Settlement and Galilee Museum at Bet Allon at Ginosar.

There are countrywide kibbutz symphony and chamber music orchestras, choirs, and one of Israel's better-known dance companies is the Kibbutz Dance Ensemble, which performs both in Israel and abroad.

From its very beginnings the kibbutz movement viewed its educational system as a key factor in insuring its future and thus attempted to develop an all-encompassing system consonant with its aims and ideals. Until fifteen years ago this system was epitomized by children in children's houses (in all but a very small number of kibbutzim) which included sleeping quarters and play and study areas; it was hoped that the concepts of communal living could thus be inculcated from the very earliest age. The children were part of an organized children's community—living, eating and studying together—which constituted a miniature kibbutz. They conducted their own activities with the advice to teachers and group leaders and in many cases managed their own small farm economies. The kibbutz school differs from its city counterpart in its informal, egalitarian atmosphere, in its inclusion of physical work as an integral part of the curriculum, and its emphasis on the interaction between the school and the community.

From the 1960s on, the system was amended in an ever-increasing number of kibbutzim so that children now sleep in their parents' homes, in most cases until high-school age, when they move into a dormitory. This change is a function of changing kibbutz attitudes towards the place of the family in the kibbutz and is related to a whole series of changes in the same direction. The impact of the kibbutz and its educational system has been extensively researched and studied by observers both from Israel and abroad.

Recent Developments. By 1990, the fourth generation were operating many kibbutzim. Despite their communal upbringing, kibbutz children showed no evidence of "maternal deprivation." They served in elite units of Israel's armed forces, and their proportion among army officers was three or four times their percentage in the general population. They were in the upper percentiles of high-school matriculation examination results, and were represented favorably in every facet of Israeli life. Some fifty percent remained in the kibbutz despite the increasing attractions of city life in Israeli society. Research showed that the young kibbutz members were more direct and practical

Factory in Kibbutz Masada. [Kibbutz Masada]

than their parents and less given to ideological differences; they were the principal force pushing towards the ultimate unification of the movement.

One decade before the twenty-first century, the kibbutz movement faced major problems. In many ways, it was at an historic turning point. According to many of its own members, it was in fact undergoing a period of serious crisis. Kibbutz members pointed to the gaps between ideological aspiration and the often contrary direction of reality. One of the most serious problems was occasioned by the economic difficulties of the 1980s, exacerbated by the political victory of the Likud party and its allies, who were much less supportive of the movement than previous, Labor-based, governments. The period was characterized by galloping inflation and then a high-interest monetarist-favoring governmental policy which attempted to restrain the inflation. The kibbutzim at first joined the general stampede towards consumer-oriented spending and irresponsible over-investment. Due partly to mismanagement and partly to governmental policy, the stock market and bank-shares collapse which capped this inflationary period caused great damage to the kibbutz economy. The exorbitantly high interest policy which followed made things doubly difficult for both agriculture and industry. Dozens of kibbutzim reached the verge of bankruptcy. One large section of kibbutz industry was in the area of regional industrial enterprises, established by groups of kibbutzim (irrespective of federation affiliation) in various geographical sections of the country. These enterprises had grown into large conglomerates which owned and operated cotton gins, poultry packing plants, canning factories, silos and feed mixing plants, computer services, and transport cooperatives; and invested in research and development over and above the ability of any individual kibbutz to do so. Many of these regional conglomerates were dragged down with the nearly-bankrupt kibbutzim, becoming a major drain on the wealthier kibbutzim which were mobilized in their support. This resulted in despair in some kibbutzim, depressed morale in the movement as a whole, draconian belt-tightening, and many second thoughts about the very ideology and structure of the movement.

The gap between extremely poor kibbutzim and wealthy ones widened considerably, resulting in the more successful communities' insistence on greater accountability, professionalism, and managerial continuity as a condition of their continued support. Greater sensitivity surfaced regarding members who did not pull their weight, burdening the community's resources. An increased emphasis on individual responsibility and greater family-centeredness, typical of the moshav shitufi, was viewed not only as renewed social values but as a means of eliminating waste. It became clear that the kibbutz of the future must have a greater percentage of members with highly skilled trades and professions, many of which would be practised outside the kibbutz itself. On the other hand, it also seemed clear that this might imply changes in traditional negative attitudes towards hired labor within the kibbutz. The expensive kibbutz educational system also had to be revised: schools were enlarged and merged on an increasingly inter-movement basis, including partnerships with a variety of non-kibbutz populations in the surrounding areas. Consideration was given to the fact that science-based high-tech agriculture and industry might require a different approach to education, from the easy-going informal kibbutz children's society, to the philosophy of work and management, to regional and inter-kibbutz organization, production, and marketing.

As the concepts of classic socialist-Zionist ideology changed, defining the meaning of a tradition-based yet modern, imaginative and newly creative Jewish identity became more vital than ever, both for its own sake and to catch the imagination and allegiance of the young kibbutz member, who was continually comparing kibbutz life to the attractions of London and New York. It was no longer enough to recall nostalgically the days when the movement was the base of the Palmah, the prime factor in Youth Aliya, and a significant representative in every facet of political life. The question being asked was: What is the kibbutz's contribution to contemporary Israel?

In the late 1980s, all these questions and more were opened to an ongoing, often agonizing, reappraisal, with the general political and cultural dilemmas which faced Israel as a whole. The latter-day kibbutz would not be recognized by the founders of Deganya. The strength of the movement, however, has been its ability to change with the times while retaining its underlying idealism and principles.

M. KEREM

KIBUSH AVODA ("Conquest of Labor"). Doctrine developed by the Second Aliya (1904–14) and, in particular, by *Ha-Po'el ha-Tza'ir, stressing the importance of Jewish labor as the basis for a Jewish society in Eretz Israel. By the beginning of the 20th century, the development and consolidation of the Jewish agricultural settlements, especially those in Judea and Samaria, had reached a stage at which they were in need of hired labor. Most of the laborers employed were Arabs; some worked on a permanent basis, but by far the larger number were seasonal laborers drawn from neighboring Arab villages. Joseph Aronowicz, leader of the Ha-Po'el ha-Tza'ir party and editor of its weekly, preached the replacement of Arab labor by Jewish labor, not only because of the need to provide employment for Second Aliya immigrants but because without Jewish hired labor a Jewish majority in Eretz Israel would be unattainable. The country would not be made Jewish by the mere possession of title to properties or merely by Jewish management but only by Jews, performing their own manual labor, whether on the farm or in the factory; in other words, only the "Conquest of Labor" by Jews and not the mere "conquest" of the land by purchase would assure the realization of Zionism and the attainment of a Jewish majority. Aronowicz's appeal was directed both to the old settlers and to the new arrivals; to the settlers he pointed out the dangers inherent in Arab labor, and to the young workers he stressed the importance of becoming hired laborers themselves.

Kibush Avoda gave rise to considerable tension between the farmers of the First Aliya and the immigrants of the Second Aliya who were, on the whole, radical and permeated with the ideas of the Russian intelligentsia of the Revolution of 1904–05. The farmers were not always ready to pay the inexperienced new immigrants a higher wage than the one paid to the Arabs. In the course of time, however, wages were increased considerably, and the conflicts that arose were not due primarily to wage disputes. There was a feeling of estrangement between the farmers and the new immigrants. The latter, often better educated and politically oriented, felt superior to the rather conservative farmers, who resented the assertion of superiority and the radical slogans of the newcomers. In places such as Petah Tikva, acute conflicts developed because young workers, who generally were not observant, offended the sensibilities of the Orthodox elements, particularly by failing to observe the Sabbath. Since most of the new arrivals were unmarried, there was no compelling need for them to become attached to their places of employment, and their easy mobility from settlement to settlement and from Judea to Galilee earned them the reproof of Aronowicz.

Ha-Po'el ha-Tza'ir impressed the importance of Kibush Avoda both on the Hovevei Zion movement of Russia and on the Palestine Office of the World Zionist Organization headed by Arthur Ruppin. With their assistance the smallholders' settlement of En Ganim was founded near Petah Tikva in 1908, the intention being that the workers hold small tracts of land and cultivate them in their spare time, thus supplementing the income derived from their work in the orange groves of Petah Tikva. En Ganim was followed by Nahlat Yehuda, near Rishon le-Zion, and it was hoped that these developments would attach the new arrivals both to the land and to the status of hired laborers in the nearby settlement.

The total number of Jews employed in the settlements did not exceed 10 to 12 per cent of the labor force, and by 1914 it was estimated at 1,500. The doctrine of the "Conquest of Labor" was challenged by Joseph *Vitkin, who in 1908 appealed for the settlement of new arrivals on the land as self-employed farmers. Knowing the middle-class origins and the mentality of the Second Aliya, Vitkin realized that the status of hired farmhands would not appeal to them and that only the prospect of becoming independent farmers would attach them to the land. In this respect Vitkin was the precursor of the various kevutzot and smallholders' settlement which were established prior to World War I. Aronowicz, on the other hand, rejected Vitkin's policy: since the new immigrants had no financial means, they would be dependent on a settlement agency and dominated by it. Aronowicz preferred to have persons of means developing the economy of Palestine and employing Jews, thus avoiding the dangers of the *haluka* (philanthropic charity), from which not only the Old Yishuv was suffering. New settlements, he argued, would draw labor from the existing Jewish villages; their success, on the other hand, would create a demand for new labor, which would inevitably be Arab. Thus the establishment of Jewish workers as independent farmers would merely increase the demand for Arab labor and remove the prospect of a Jewish majority in the country.

The controversy over Kibush Avoda agitated the yishuv and the Zionist movement in the decade preceding World War I. Ahad Ha-Am, who devoted considerable attention to the problem, did not believe that it would be possible to create a Jewish working class to replace the Arabs employed in the settlements.

With the advent of the Third Aliya (1920–24), Kibush Avoda in agriculture was replaced by the principle of Avoda Ivrit (Jewish Labor) in all sectors of the rapidly developing economy of Palestine. During the period of the British Mandate for Palestine (1917–48), the application of this principle gave rise to a number of conflicts, nearly all in the citrus plantations of the old settlements. In Jewish-owned trades and industries, including the building trades, the principle was generally accepted. S. Z. ABRAMOV

KIBUTZ GALUYOT. *See* INGATHERING OF THE EXILES.

KINERET. Kibbutz, and moshava south-east of Lake Kineret. The land *Daleiqa-Umm Juni* was among the first holdings acquired by the Jewish National Fund. In 1908, Arthur Ruppin, director of the Zionist Organization's Palestine Office, decided to set up a training farm there for Jewish agricultural laborers. The farm administrator preferred cheaper Arab laborers to the Second Aliya pioneers. A strike broke out and the problem was not clearly solved, but Ruppin agreed to allocate the Umm Juni lands to seven workers for one year, thus laying the ground for the first kevutza, *Deganiya. In 1909, beginnings were made for the moshava Kineret. In 1912, a girls' agricultural training farm was added to Kineret. Pioneers from America, led by Eliezer Joffe, came to train there. The idea of the "large kibbutz" was formulated by leaders of the labor movement living at Kineret. In the 1920s, a date palm grove was planted to acclimatize this species in Israel, and the poet Rachel was buried there. During the same decade, Kineret served as a camp for members of Gedud ha-Avoda. The Kibbutz Me'uhad movement crystallized there, and it became a center of the Ha-Po'el ha-Tza'ir movement and of the Mapai party. Kevutzat Kineret has highly-intensive irrigated farming and industrial enterprises, and the moshava has besides irrigated farming a few tourist services. The convention buildings, the Oholo seminar center, and the Bet Yerah excavations lie within its boundaries. Population (1987) of Kevutzat Kineret 766, and of the moshava 273.

E. ORNI

KINERET (TIBERIAS), LAKE (Sea of Galilee). Part of the Jordan Rift Valley, bordering on Lower Galilee. With its water surface averaging 690 ft. (210 m.) below sea level, Lake Kineret is the lowest freshwater lake on earth. Its length is 13 miles (21 km.), its greatest width 7 miles (11 km.) and its area about 65 square miles. Its greatest depth, in its northeastern part, is about 147 ft. (45 m.). Lake Kineret is bounded by steep slopes in the south and by two valleys in the north: the valley of Ginosar in the northwest; and the valley of Bethsaida in the northeast.

Due to the low elevation, the summers are very hot, but the winters are mild, making the lakeshore an important winter resort area. The high temperatures also make the area suitable for the growing of subtropical fruits (dates, bananas) as well as early grapes and vegetables. The lake itself provides good fishing.

In ancient times Lake Kineret was a main center of population. In Roman times there were 15 large towns along its shores, where many of the early activities of Jesus of Nazareth and his disciples took place. Many sites along the

Old Turkish fortifications on the Lake Kineret shore of Tiberias. [Israel Government Tourist Office]

shore of the lake are now venerated by Christians as holy places and attract tourists and pilgrims. The only town of the area is *Tiberias. Y. KARMON

KING-CRANE REPORT. Report prepared by Henry C. King and Charles R. Crane of the American section of the Inter-Allied Commission on Mandates in Turkey, organized at the behest of the Council of Four of the Paris Peace Conference in 1919. At the time King was president of Oberlin College, while Crane was a Midwestern manufacturer interested in the Christian missions of the Middle East.

In March, 1919, Pres. Woodrow Wilson, confronted with the conflict of interests between France and Great Britain on the territories of the Middle East and subjected to pressures from anti-Zionist groups including Christian missionary interests, suggested that the Inter-Allied Commission be authorized to proceed to the Middle East to determine the wishes of the various peoples of the region on their political future and the needs of the area. Since Britain and France opposed such a mission, Wilson sent the two Americans, King and Crane, to undertake the task.

On 10 June 1919, the Commission arrived in Palestine. Its investigation consisted primarily in studying the petitions of various groupings and in holding interviews with representatives of political parties throughout Syria and Palestine.

In August, the Commission submitted its report to the American delegation for the use of the peace conference. Its conclusions were both anti-French and anti-Zionist. It advocated one mandate for a united Syria comprising both Lebanon and Palestine, to be assumed by the United States in conformity with the wishes of the large majority of the inhabitants of the region. If the United States declined to accept the mandate, it was to be given to Great Britain. With regard to Jewish aspirations for Palestine, the Commission recommended that "a greatly reduced Zionist program be attempted by the Peace Conference, and even that only very gradually initiated. This would have to mean that Jewish immigration should be definitely limited and that the project for making Palestine distinctly a Jewish commonwealth should be given up. There would then be no reason why Palestine could not be included in a united Syrian State...."

The report was not made public until 1922, by which time the political arrangements for the Middle East had been completed. Nonetheless, the Arabs subsequently used this document for political purposes and propaganda. H. PARZEN

KIRSHBLUM, MORDECAI (Max). Rabbi and communal and Zionist leader (b. Bialystok. Russian Poland, 1910). He received his rabbinical degree from the Rabbi Isaac Elchanan Theological Seminary (Yeshiva College) in 1931. In 1938 Kirshblum founded the Religious Department of the Jewish National Fund in the US. and served as its chairman for many years. From 1944 on he was rabbi of the Jewish Community Center of Bensonhurst, in Brooklyn.

From 1948 to 1963 he served as senior vice-chairman and member of the Committee on Administration of the American Zionist Council. From 1950 to 1953 he was co-treasurer, and after 1960 honorary chairman, of the Jewish National Fund in the US. From 1952 to 1957 he was president of the Mizrachi Organization of America.

In 1954 he was one of the founders of Bar-Ilan University. In 1956 he became a member of the Executive of the Jewish Agency for Israel-American Section and head of its Aliya Department and its Torah Culture Department. From 1961 to 1964 he was president of the religious Zionist movement of America, Mizrachi-Ha-Po'el ha-Mizrachi. In 1968 he moved to Israel, where he became a member of the Jewish Agency Executive in Jerusalem and associate head of the Agency's Aliya and Absorption Department.

I. HAMLIN

KIRYAT ANAVIM. Kibbutz in the Judean Hills, 8 mi. (12 km.) west of Jerusalem. It was founded in 1920 with the intention of working out methods for modern hill farming and afforestation. Despite severe hardships caused by insufficient aid from Zionist institutions, the settlers insisted on staying and declined the offer of a better site in the Jezreel Valley. With time, the kibbutz became an important supplier of foodstuffs to Jewish Jerusalem. In the 1948 War of Independence, it successfully defended a highly-endangered position and served as a base for military operations which opened the Jerusalem Corridor. In addition to fruit orchards and other farming, the kibbutz runs a resort hotel. Its name means "Town of Grapes". Population (1987), 399.

E. ORNI

KIRYAT ARBA. *See* HEBRON.

KIRYAT ATA. Town 9 mi. (14 km.) northeast of Haifa. Founded in 1925 as a rural settlement, it was abandoned in the 1929 Arab riots and resettled in 1934. Its economy was based largely on industry, notably the Ata textile factory. It developed as a satellite community of Haifa. Population (1987), 35,100.

E. ORNI

KIRYAT BIALIK, KIRYAT MOTZKIN. Two towns, founded in 1934 east and west of the Haifa-Acre highway, in the framework of the residential area north of the industrial zone of the Haifa Bay area. The local "Ahava" Youth Aliya center cares for children with educational problems. From the 1950s, both towns expanded, especially northward, now including industrial enterprises and gradually losing their suburban character. In 1987 Kiryat Bialik numbered 32,400, and Kiryat Motzkin 29,300 inhabitants. The first bears the name of Haim Nahman Bialik, and the second of Leo Motzkin.

E. ORNI

KIRYAT GAT. Town in the southern coastal plain, founded in 1955 to serve as the urban center of the Lachish development region, with industries initially based mainly on local agricultural products. Its largest factories those of the Polgat textile combine. Kiryat Gat is laid out with a centrally-placed business zone, cultural institutions, and a large public park. Its name was taken from the nearby ancient mound, which at the time was thought to be the site of Philistine Gath; later excavations, however, showed this identification to be mistaken. Population (1987), 27,400.

E. ORNI

KIRYAT MALAKHI. Town in the southern coastal plain 12 mi. (20 km.) northeast of Ashkelon. Built as a transit camp in 1950, it soon turned into a development town and became the secondary center of the Lachish Region, with abattoirs and other enterprises based on local farm products. The population is largely of Asian and African origin. Its name is the Hebrew translation of Los Angeles, whose Jews financed its first housing schemes. Population (1987), 13,800.

E. ORNI

KIRYAT MOTZKIN. *See* KIRYAT BIALIK.

KIRYAT SHEMONA. Israel's northernmost town, on the western rim of the Huleh Valley, founded in 1950 as the valley's urban center. An insufficient industrial base, dependence on neighboring kibbutzim for employment and, mainly since 1975, frequent shelling from across the Lebanese frontier nearby, caused a high turnover of settlers and very slow growth. The situation improved somewhat in the 1980s with stronger local initiative and increased government aid, but slowed again after the 1982 Lebanon War. Its name ("Town of Eight") commemorates Joseph Trumpeldor and seven of his comrades who fell in Tel Hai, a few miles away, when they were attacked by Arabs from the village of Khalisa, which stood on the site of present-day Kiryat Shemona. Population (1987), 15,500.

E. ORNI

KIRYAT TIVON. Town southeast of Haifa on the low Tivon Hills, which separate the Zebulun Valley from the Jezreel Valley. It was formed in 1957 by the merger of the workers' village Kiryat Amal (founded 1937) and the garden suburb Tivon (founded 1947). Recreation and tourist services form part of the town's economy, although many inhabitants commute to outside work. It stands near a large natural oak forest. The Bet She'arim antiquities lie within the town's municipal boundary. Basmat Tabun, a town housing formerly nomadic Bedouin, adjoins Kiryat Tivon in the northwest. Population (1987), 11,400.

E. ORNI

KIRYAT YE'ARIM. Institution for children with educational difficulties in the Judean Hills, 8 miles (13 km.) west of Jerusalem. In 1986 it had 223 inhabitants. The name Kiryat Ye'arim was given also to the nearby Telz-Stone suburban settlement of Orthodox Jews, mainly from English-speaking countries, which was founded in 1975 and in 1986 had a population of 1,060. The site is identified with Kiryat Jearim (Town of the Forests) on the border of the tribes of Judah and Benjamin (Josh. 15;9), where the Ark of the Covenant was placed after having been returned by the Philistines (I Samuel 6:21). The Crusaders considered Kiryat Ye'arim to be ancient Emmaus, but because of its springs also called it Fontenoid. *See also* ABU GHOSH.

E. ORNI

KISCH, FREDERICK HERMAN. Soldier and Zionist official (b. Darjeeling, India, 1888; d. Tunisia, 1943). In 1909 he entered the Royal Engineer Corps as an officer, and

Kiryat Shemona [Keren Ha-Yesod]

Frederick Kisch.
[Zionist Archives]

during World War I he saw active service in France and Mesopotamia.

In 1922, when he was attached to the staff of the British Embassy in Paris, he received an offer from Weizmann to join the Zionist Executive in Jerusalem. Kisch, Weizmann felt, would be able to negotiate with high British officials on equal terms. He arrived in Palestine in November 1922 together with Weizmann, and in January 1923 took up his duties as a member of the Executive and as chairman and director of its Political Department. From 1929 on he simultaneously served as head of the Palestine Executive of the Jewish Agency.

In his *Palestine Diary* (published in 1938 with a foreword by David Lloyd George), Kisch recorded his experiences in Palestine between 1923 and his retirement from official Zionist service in 1931. His task was to help the Palestine government get a better understanding of the yishuv and at the same time to foster goodwill between the Jews and the Arabs of Palestine. Convinced that agreement between Palestine's Jews and Arabs was vital if Zionist work was to be continued successfully, he pressed for direct high-level meetings between Jewish and Arab leaders without outside intermediaries. These efforts, however, were discouraged by the British authorities in Palestine.

Kisch vainly demanded that the British authorities support Arab moderates rather than the reactionaries led by Hajj Amin al-Husseini, the mufti of Jerusalem, pointing out that the Arab extremists would betray Britain in the event of a showdown with fascism. Kisch was on friendly terms with King Hussein of Hejaz and his son Abdullah, Emir of Transjordan, as well as with many Arab leaders in neighboring countries, who assured him of their support for Zionist endeavors in Palestine. He advocated the adoption of a program for closer Arab-Jewish cooperation, including mixed Arab-Jewish schools, and an Arab daily to counteract anti-Jewish propaganda in the Arab press.

When Weizmann failed to be re-elected to the presidency of the World Zionist Organization in 1931, Kisch retired from Zionist public service but decided to remain in Palestine, taking up residence in Haifa, where he went into business. He took an active interest in educational and cultural endeavors, serving as a member of the Board of Governors of the Haifa Technion, as chairman of the Ben-Yehuda Trust, formed to aid the completion of Eliezer Ben-Yehuda's dictionary of the modern Hebrew language, and as treasurer of the Palestine Orchestra (later Israel Philharmonic Orchestra). At the outbreak of World War II he rejoined the British Army as a lieutenant colonel. At the time of his death in action while clearing a minefield in Tunisia, he was chief engineer of the British Eighth Army, holding the rank of brigadier.

G. HIRSCHLER—N. ROSE

KISHINEV POGROM. Anti-Jewish riots in the Russian city of Kishinev, Bessarabia, in April, 1903, in which 47 Jews were killed and 92 severely injured. More than 500 suffered minor injuries, and hundreds of Jewish homes and shops were plundered.

The pogrom was the culmination of protracted anti-Jewish agitation by the Russian authorities, which gained added intensity in Kishinev early in 1903 as the result of a blood libel accusation. A violent anti-Jewish campaign, led by *Bessarabetz*, a government-subsidized newspaper, called for the death of the Jews. While the campaign was in full swing, secret societies were formed to massacre the Jews. On Easter Eve a rumor spread in the city to the effect that a Christian servant girl had been murdered by the Jews. Printed handbills were scattered, telling the people that the Russian authorities had given permission to inflict "bloody punishment" on the Jews during the three days of Easter. The police were in league with the pogrom plotters and made no attempt to suppress the circulars.

The pogrom began on Easter Sunday (6 April), 1903. Early in the afternoon a large mob attacked Jewish homes and stores. In the absence of police and military interference, the violence grew in intensity, and soon looting gave way to murder. When a group of Jews attempted to repulse the attackers, the police stepped in and disarmed the defenders. The looting and killing stopped at night, when the riot leaders met to plan further "operations." The massacre was resumed the next day and continued until the evening. Jews were brutally murdered and synagogues desecrated. A Jewish deputation requesting protection from Governor von Raaben of Bessarabia was told that he could do nothing without direct instructions from St. Petersburg. Only the following evening, when a telegram was received from Vyacheslav von Plehve, the Russian Minister of the Interior, were armed troops sent into the streets. At their sight the rioters disappeared without a single shot being fired. On the outskirts of Kishinev, which had not yet been reached by the military, the massacre and looting continued until late in the evening.

The Kishinev pogrom set off a wave of indignation and protest throughout the western world. Jewish organizations rushed aid to the victims of the slaughter. The pogrom had far-reaching effects on Russian Jewry. There was a sharp increase in emigration, not only to the United States but also to Eretz Israel and other countries. There was also a profound stirring of national sentiment among Jewish youth. Pinhas Dashevski, a Jewish student, made an attempt on the life of the editor of *Bessarabetz*, Pavolachi Krushevan. Ahad Ha-Am and others signed a proclamation for the organization of Jewish self-defense, and young Jews actually formed self-defense groups. The grief and shame they felt at what had happened in Kishinev were poignantly expressed in a stirring poem by Hayim Nahman Bialik, entitled "In the City of Slaughter."

The horrors of Kishinev had a profound impact also on the Zionist movement. Herzl intensified his efforts in two directions. He entered into negotiations with the Russian government, which was interested in the emigration of Jews, seeking its support for his endeavors to obtain a Charter from the Turkish government for Jewish settlement in Eretz Israel. He also intensified his search for a territory elsewhere that could serve as an immediate place of refuge for the Jews who had been driven from their homes. Thus when, a short time later, the British government offered the World Zionist Organization some territory in East Africa for a Jewish settlement (*see* EAST AFRICA SCHEME), Herzl and many other Zionist leaders were eager to consider it.

T. PRESCHEL

KISHON Seasonal river, 46 miles long (74 km.), watering the Jezreel Valley. Its headwaters irrigate the western slopes of Mount Gilboa, east of Jenin, and the hills of Umm el-Fahm. The Kishon crosses the Jezreel Valley in its center, breaks through the gap of Sha'ar ha-Amakim into the Zebulun Valley, and flows into the Mediterranean Sea at the southern edge of Haifa Bay. It flows intermittently after heavy rains and is subject to heavy floods and inundations that have turned most of the surrounding area into swamps. Its drainage, begun in 1925, facilitated the settlements of the Jezreel Valley. A dam, constructed in 1955 near Kefar Barukh, retains much of the floodwater and serves as a reservoir for the western Galilee water systems. The mouth of the river was turned into Kishon harbor, which serves as an auxiliary of the port of Haifa and as Israel's fishing harbor.

Y. KARMON

KISHON, EPHRAIM. Author and satirist (b. Budapest, Hungary, 1924). Kishon began to publish humorous essays and wrote for the theater while still in Hungary. In 1949 he emigrated to Israel where after two years he started a satirical column which appeared regularly in the easy-Hebrew daily *Omer* From 1952 he wrote for the daily *Ma'ariv*. His column was basically political and social satire although it included essays of pure humor.

Kishon directed and produced a number of feature films, including *Sallah Shabbati* and *Blaumilch Canal*, which also received international recognition. His play *Ha-Ketuba* (The Marriage Contract) had one of the longest runs in the Israel Theater. His sketches and plays have been translated and performed on the stage and television networks of several countries, being particularly popular in German-speaking countries. Collections of his humorous writings in English include *Look Back Mrs. Lot* (1960), *Noah's Ark, Tourist Class* (1962), and *The Sea-Sick Whale* (1963).

KITRON (KOSTRINSKY), MOSHE. Po'ale Zion leader and educator in Argentina (b. Pinsk, 1909; d. Tel Aviv, 1972). He belonged to the Freiheit movement which identified with the Borochov stream in Po'ale Zion. On his arrival

Harbor at the mouth of the Kishon River. [Israel Information Services]

in Argentina in 1927, he served as a teacher and later as Po'ale Zion party secretary. He was involved in all party activities, both in internal organization and in relations with other bodies. Kitron was one of the founders of the Committee against Anti-Semitic Persecutions in Germany (1933) and of the representative body of Argentinian Jewry, DAIA (1935). He supervised the party's relations with the Argentine Socialist Party and published many articles on problems of community organization, Zionist policy, and youth matters in the party organs, *Unzer Tzait*, and *Di Naye Tzait*, and the Dror youth movement organ, *Vanguardia Juvenil*. He was a delegate to the 22nd Zionist Congress. His principal activities centered on education of youth; he founded Dror in 1934, and was its spiritual and ideological leader, educating towards pioneering fulfillment in Eretz Israel. He organized seminars and summer camps and was among the founders of the Berl Katznelson Training Farm (1946). In 1949, his students and pupils founded Kibbutz Mefalsim, the first kibbutz to be founded by Latin American immigrants.

After the establishment of the State, Kitron immigrated to Israel (1949), serving as coordinator of the Ethnic Communities department at the Mapai Center and subsequently as secretary of Mapai in the Tel Aviv area. His last post was at the Histadrut Education and Culture Center.

S. SCHENKOLEWSKI

KJV. *See* KARTELL JUDISCHER VERBINDUNGEN.

KLATZKIN, JACOB. Hebrew writer and philosopher (b. Bereza, Kartuskaya, Russia, 1882; d. Vevey, Switzerland, 1948). A son of a renowned talmudic scholar, Rabbi Elijah ben Naphtali Herz Klatzkin (1852–1932), he received a traditional education. At 18 he went to Germany where he studied first at various universities including a period at the University of Marburg, where he pursued a degree in philosophy under the tutelage of Hermann Cohen. He earned his Ph.D. at the University of Berne in 1912. Concurrent to his studies, Klatzkin began a career as a Zionist publicist, writing principally in Hebrew. In 1909 he was appointed the editor of the prestigious organ of the World Zionist Organization, *Die Welt*, a position that he held for two years. Subsequently he was involved in publication projects, notably two which he undertook in collaboration with his friend Nahum Goldmann. In 1921–22, they founded and edited in Heidelberg the influential *Freie Zionistische Blätter* and they then established the Eschkol publishing company in Berlin which sponsored the monumental German-language *Encyclopaedia Judaica*, of which ten volumes—as well as two parallel Hebrew volumes—were published before Hitler's rise to power led to the suspension of the project. In 1933 Klatzkin left Germany and settled in Switzerland where he continued to write and lecture. During World War II he moved to the United States, but at the conclusion of the war he returned to Switzerland.

Decisively influenced by the psychologist and philosopher Ludwig Klages (1872–1956), Klatzkin's philosophy is best characterized as vitalistic. Following his mentor, he repudiated reason—and the life of the spirit—in the name of the biologically ground life-force called instinct. The advance of civilization and the enhancement of the rule of intellect, Klatzkin argues, have enfeebled human instinct and vitality. Modern man is increasingly estranged from the world and natural life. As a Zionist, he called upon Jews to reject both the spiritualized form of existence provided alternatively by traditional Judaism and the bourgeois civilization of the West. The return to Zion was an opportunity to return to a vital natural life. Grounded in the life of instinct and a wholesome relation to natural existence, Jewish life would be "normalized" and free of the life-estranging pursuit of the spiritual. Free of any pretensions to a spiritual vocation, the Jewish people would be content with the reacquisition of the normal parameters of peoplehood; a land and language of their own. These conditions, Klatzkin reasoned, would be sufficient to ensure the survival of the Jewish people. In the Diaspora, the Jews had no future; with the eclipse of religion, which had served to preserve the social distinctiveness of the Jews, and bereft of the land and language, modern Jews there were destined to disappear; moreover, "the *galut* can only drag out the disgrace of our people and sustain the existence of a people disfigured in both body and soul."

P. MENDES-FLOHR

KLAUSNER, JOSEPH GEDALIA. Historian, editor, and publicist (b. Olkieniki, Lithuania, 1874; d. Tel Aviv, 1958). Klausner studied at the modern yeshiva in Odessa and at Heidelberg University, receiving his doctorate in 1902. A Hovev Zion from his youth on, he was active in promoting the revival of the Hebrew language, participated in the First Zionist Congress (1897), was one of the founders of the Democratic Faction at the Fifth Congress (1901), and opposed the East Africa scheme. He was a delegate also to the Third (1899), Eighth (1907), and Tenth (1911) Congresses.

Klausner was the editor of the Hebrew monthly **Ha-Shiloah* from 1903 to 1926 (first in Odessa and from 1920 on in Jerusalem), adopting a completely negative attitude toward both the Jewish Diaspora and the Yiddish language and advancing his own concepts of "Jewishness and humanity."

Settling in Jerusalem in 1919, Klausner first taught history at the Jerusalem Teachers Seminary and then served as professor of modern Hebrew literature (from 1925) and of the history of the Second Temple (from 1943) at the Hebrew University of Jerusalem until his retirement in 1949. He was active in the Hebrew Language Academy and wrote numerous Hebrew works, including about 1,000 essays and articles. His first Hebrew essay was published in *Ha-Melitz* in 1893. Some of his books, among them *Jesus of Nazareth: His Life, Times and Teaching*, 1922 (published in English, 1927), *From Jesus to Paul* (1939–40), and *The Messianic Idea in Israel* (1909, 1927), were translated into several languages and widely circulated. His major works include *History of Modern Hebrew Literature* (first edition 1930; new edition in 6 vols., 1950);, *History of the Second Temple* (5 vols., 1948–57). He was the first editor-in-chief of the *Encyclopaedia Hebraica.*

From an ideological standpoint close to Revisionism and yet never officially a member of the Revisionist party, Klausner took an active part in the struggle for Jewish rights over the Western Wall in 1929, edited the monthly *Betar* (1933), and strongly opposed the plan for the partition of Palestine, proposed by the Peel Commission (1937). He was awarded the Israel Prize and other distinctions and in 1947 was elected an honorary foreign member of the American Academy of Arts and Sciences, in Boston. In 1949 he was the unsuccessful candidate of the Herut party for the Presidency of Israel.

J. NEDAVA

KLEE: Family of German Zionists.

Alfred Klee (b. Berlin, 1875; d. Westerbork, Netherlands, 1943) was an early Zionist and an eloquent orator who helped disseminate Zionism in Germany. He participated in the Third (1899) and subsequent Zionist Congresses and was a member of the Greater Actions Committee of the World Zionist Organization.

In 1920 Klee was elected to the Council of the Berlin Jewish Community as a representative of the Jüdische Volkspartei (Jewish People's party), which was formed by Zionists and other national Jewish groups, and in 1925 to the Council of the Preussischer Landesverband Jüdischer Gemeinden (Association of Jewish Communities of Prussia).

Klee founded the Binyan ha-Aretz faction, which sought to interest non-Zionist Jews in helping rebuild Palestine. In 1938 he emigrated to the Netherlands, where he died at the Westerbork concentration camp during World War II.

His son, **Hans Klee** (b. Berlin, 1906; d. Locarno, Switzerland, 1959) was a lawyer by profession. He was a member of the Central Committee of the Zionist Organization of Germany and served on the Presidium of the German Maccabi and of the Association of Zionist Academicians (whose organ, *Der Wille*, he edited). After emigrating to Switzerland, he continued to engage in communal activities. In 1947 he became president of the Association of General Zionists of Switzerland. He was also a vice-president of the Swiss Zionist Federation and a member of the Executive of the World Confederation of General Zionists. Klee was a delegate to Zionist Congresses and a member of the Actions Committee. A leading member of the World OSE Union and of the Swiss Federation of Jewish Communities, he was also editor (from 1954) of the *Israelitisches Wochenblatt* of Zurich.

S. HUBNER—ED.

KLEINBAUM, MOSHE. *See* SNEH, MOSHE.

KLEINMAN, MOSHE. Hebrew and Yiddish writer, editor, and Zionist leader (b. Podolia, Russia, 1870; d. Jerusalem, 1948). His first published work appeared in the *Berditchever Spiegel* in 1897. Joining the Zionist movement at its inception, Kleinman attended all Zionist Congresses from the Second (1898) to the 12th (1921) as a delegate and later Congresses as a journalist. He helped found the Ezra publishing house to disseminate Zionist ideas. Between 1904 and 1916 he edited Hebrew and Yiddish periodicals in Lvov and Odessa. In 1916 he was arrested by the Tsarist authorities for his Zionist activities. Released after the Russian Revolution of 1917, he settled in Moscow, where he became editor of the Hebrew weekly *Ha-Am* and took a leading part in the reorganization of Russia's Jewish communities.

In 1923 Kleinman took over the editorship, in Berlin, of *Ha-Olam*, the organ of the World Zionist Organization, a position he held until his death, moving with the paper first to London and then, in 1936, to Palestine. During his early years with *Ha-Olam*, Kleinman was editor also of the art journals *Rimon* (in Hebrew) and *Milgroim* (in Yiddish), and, in 1932, of *Tekufatenu*, a Hebrew quarterly. A collection of his Hebrew literary essays and articles, *Demuyot ve-Komot* (Figures and Statures), was published in Paris in 1928. Kleinman was the author also of monographs on Herzl and Chaim Weizmann. The first volume of his projected *Encyclopedia of Zionism* (in Hebrew) was published in Palestine in 1948.

KLEPFISZ, HESZEL. Rabbi, educator, author (b. Poland, 1912). He obtained rabbinical ordination in Warsaw in 1930, his Ph.D. at the University of Warsaw, and his D.Litt. in Zurich. He was active in pre-world Poland in Polish and Jewish intellectual life. During World War II he served as senior chaplain to the Polish forces on the western front, participating in the Normandy landings, the liberation of Europe, and was among the first to enter the concentration camps. After the war he taught in Glasgow, Scotland; Miami, USA; and founded the Hebrew School in San Jose, Costa Rica. From 1961–1978 he was rector of the Albert Einstein Institute in Panama and professor at the University of Panama. From 1961–1985 he was rabbi of Panama's Ashkenazi community. In 1985 he settled in Israel. He wrote books in various languages on Judaism, Jewish history, and education, including *The Mystery of the Land of Israel in Jewish History* (in Spanish).

KLUMEL, MEIR. Zionist leader, historian, and scientist (b. Vidzy, Kovno District, Lithuania, 1875; d. Tel Aviv, 1936). He studied philosophy and philology at the universities of Berlin and Strasbourg, where he organized Zionist student groups. His doctoral dissertation was a study of the Samaritans. After completing his studies, he settled in Warsaw, where he became prominent in the Zionist movement. For many years following World War I, he was president of the Polish Zionist Organization as well as of Tarbut, the Hebrew culture movement he helped create. A successful businessman, he made large contributions to Zionist and Hebrew educational work as well as to the Zionist national funds. With the outbreak of the dispute in the General Zionist Organization in Poland, at the Sixth Conference in 1923, Klumel supported Yitzhak Gruenbaum and the members of *Al ha-Mishmar* (*see* POLAND, ZIONISM IN). In 1933 he settled in Palestine, where he continued his Zionist and cultural work.

M. MINTZ

KNESSET. Parliament of the State of Israel. The name is derived from the Knesset ha-Gedola (Great Assembly), the legislative body of the Jewish people at the beginning of the Second Temple period in ancient Israel.

Early Beginnings. On 1 March 1948, in preparation for the establishment of an independent Jewish State, the *Va'ad Le'umi (National Council), the representative body of the Palestine Jewish community, adopted a resolution in consultation with the Executive of the Jewish Agency, calling for the establishment of a provisional government and of a Provisional Council of State on 15 May, the date fixed by the British government for the termination of the Mandate for Palestine. The Council was to consist of 37 members drawn from the Va'ad Le'umi and the Agency Executive as well as from other groups that had not been represented in either of these bodies. As the Mandate was still in force and the British authorities had not yet left the country, the newly constituted body assumed the temporary designation of Mo'etzet ha-Am (People's Council). Of the 37 members of this body, which was to act as a temporary legislative authority, 13 were chosen to act as an executive committee known as Minhelet ha-Am (People's Administration). The People's Council represented all the political parties in the proportions in which they had been represented in the Va'ad Le'umi and the Agency Executive, as well as Agudat Israel and the Communist party, which had not participated in those bodies. By virtue of the official proclamation of the State of Israel on 14 May 1948, the People's Council, by that time one month old, became the Provisional Council of State and the People's Administration became the provisional government of the new republic. Plans called for the election, by 1 October 1948, of a Constituent Assembly to draw up the Constitution of the State. Once a permanent legislative body and a Cabinet had been elected, the provisional government and the Provisional Council of State were to go out of office. The Provisional Council of State confined itself to the essentials of legislation required to administer the State. Its first act was to repeal the provisions of the British White Paper of 1939, thus abolishing all restrictions on Jewish immigration and land purchase in the Jewish State. Its main enactment, the Law and Administration Ordinance of 1948, laid down the procedure by which the authority formerly vested in the British Crown and exercised by the High Commissioner and his advisers was to be transferred to the government of the State of Israel. The main business of the Provisional Council of State was to prepare for the general elections which were to be held as soon as a proper register of voters could be prepared.

Constituent Assembly. Wartime conditions notwithstanding, the elections for the Constituent Assembly were held in January, 1949. Of 506,567 voters qualified according to the population census of November, 1948, 86.8 percent exercised their right to vote. The Constituent Assembly was officially opened in the Jewish Agency building in Jerusalem on 14 February 1949, by Chaim Weizmann, the President of the Provisional Council of State. Yosef Sprinzak was elected Speaker. On 16 February 1949, the Constituent Assembly passed the Transition Law, whereby Israel's legislative body was to be a single-chamber parliament known as the Knesset, with 120 members elected on a proportional representation basis. The Assembly then became the First Knesset. On the same day, the Assembly elected Weizmann first President of the State of Israel.

Constitutional Problem. On 24 February 1949, President Weizmann charged David Ben-Gurion, the head of the provisional government, with the task of forming a Cabinet. The new Cabinet with Ben-Gurion as Prime Minister, was approved by the Knesset on 8 March 1949. The Knesset held its sessions in Tel Aviv until 11 December 1949, when it decided to transfer its seat to Jerusalem, where it has met ever since. The Knesset sat in temporary quarters until the summer of 1966, when its permanent building was established with a grant from James de Rothschild. One of the most momentous debates in the Knesset took place in 1950 when the Knesset's Committee on Constitution, Law, and Justice, which had met to consider whether or not the State should have a written constitution, presented its report. The discussion went on for several weeks. It was not until

Knesset building in Jerusalem. [Israel Government Tourist Office]

June, 1950, that the following motion, a compromise between the views of the proponents and those of the opponents of the early drafting of a constitution, was adopted:

> The Knesset resolves to charge the Committee on Constitution, Law, and Justice with the task of preparing a draft Constitution for the State. The Constitution shall be constructed chapter by chapter in such a way that each chapter will constitute a Basic Law by itself. Each chapter shall be submitted to the Knesset. When the Committee has finished its work, all the chapters together shall be incorporated into the Constitution of the State.

In the years since this decision was taken, the Committee on Constitution, Law, and Justice has applied itself to the preparation of "constitutional" laws, but, as of 1987 only six of these had been submitted and ratified by the Knesset, on the President of the State; the Knesset: Lands in Israel (dealing with State-owned and publicly owned land); the Government (i.e., the executive branch); Economy of Israel; and the Armed Forces.

Powers and Duties. The Basic Law: the Knesset, enacted on 1 February 1958, sets forth the system of elections and the powers and duties of the Knesset. It provides for a unicameral parliament, consisting of 120 members, elected by secret ballot on the basis of proportional representation by all citizens of Israel who have attained the age of 18. Any citizen who has reached the age of 21, except persons who hold public office (that is, the President of the State, clergy who hold paid offices within their religious establishment, judges, army officers, and senior civil servants), may be elected to the Knesset. In later legislation candidates who had been convicted of treason, and party lists rejecting the democratic character of the State or its right to exist were banned. The Knesset is elected for a period of four years but may dissolve itself before the expiration of its term by enacting a special law to that effect, which law also fixes the election date. No quorum is required. All decisions are adopted by a majority of those present and voting; abstentions are not counted. All sessions are public unless a closed session is decided upon. The Knesset holds two sessions (winter and summer), the two together to last at least eight months. Any 20 members may call an extraordinary session of the Knesset during its recess. Members must draw a salary as provided by law and may not draw a salary from another source. The parliament building and its immediate

Knesset session marking 40th anniversary of defeat of Nazi Germany, 1985. [Israel Govt. Press Office]

Unveiling of Marc Chagall tapestry at the Knesset, 1969. [Israel Govt. Press Office]

vicinity enjoy immunity; order is maintained by the Knesset Guard, which is under the control of the Speaker. Members enjoy absolute immunity from criminal prosecution resulting from anything they may do or say in pursuance of their parliamentary function; in other areas they enjoy immunity from search, arrest, and prosecution unless such immunity is removed by a decision of the Knesset. The Knesset is the legislature of Israel, and the laws enacted by it are not subject to judicial review. The Knesset also performs functions in accordance with other laws. It is the Knesset that elects the President of the State and may, in certain circumstances, remove him from office. During the temporary absence of the President, the Speaker of the Knesset fulfills his function.

When a new government is formed, it presents itself to the Knesset and, through the Prime Minister designate, lays its program before the Knesset. Following a debate, the Knesset votes on a motion of confidence. After the Knesset votes favorably on the motion, the designated ministers take the oath of office. Thereupon the government is duly installed and remains in office as long as it enjoys the confidence of the Knesset. In this respect, the Knesset and its powers and functions are patterned on the model of the British Parliament, and it is in no way limited in the exercise of its legislative and other powers. Since the government is dependent on the Knesset, the latter has the duty of supervising and controlling the work of the former. This is achieved by debates in the plenary sessions, especially when the budgets of the individual ministries are debated, and in the committees, where ministers may be summoned to report on their activities and where, especially in the Finance Committee, approval is required for the exercise of delegated authority. Under the State Comptroller Law, enacted in March, 1958, provision is made for the appointment of a State Comptroller. His appointment is made by the President of the State upon the recommendation of the House Committee of the Knesset; he reports to the Knesset; a special committee discusses his report and presents its conclusions to the Plenary. In 1971 the State Comptroller was also charged with the function of Ombudsman.

Procedure. In accordance with the Basic Law: the Knesset, the procedure of the Knesset is governed by Rules of Procedure which have been devised and approved by the Knesset. These are supplemented by various precedents, rulings, and decisions handed down by the Speaker or by the Interpretations Committee of the Knesset.

Opening Session. The opening session of a newly elected Knesset is held on the second Monday after the week in which the election results are published. The Knesset is officially opened by the President of the State. After delivering his opening address, he yields the chair to the oldest member of the Knesset, who then administers the oath of office to the members: "I pledge allegiance to the State of Israel and promise faithfully to discharge my mandate in the Knesset."

Speaker. The first task of the new Knesset is to elect a Speaker, whose main duties, as prescribed by law, are to direct the affairs of the Knesset, to preserve its dignity, to maintain decorum, to enforce the Rules of Procedure, and to represent the Knesset at official functions. The Speaker has special powers of arrest and control within the Knesset buildings area. The Knesset Guard, under the command of a sergeant at arms, acts at the Speaker's direction to preserve order and discipline. Deputy Speakers numbering from two to eight are elected at the opening session or shortly thereafter.

Standing Committees. The Knesset works through standing committees much like those of other parliaments. As of 1988 there were ten such committees, each reflecting in proportion, as far as possible, the party composition of the Knesset Plenum: (1) Foreign Affairs and Defense; (2) Constitution, Law, and Justice; (3) Education and Culture; (4) Economic; (5) House; (6) Finance; (7) Labor and Welfare; (8) Internal Affairs and Ecology; (9) State Control; (10) Immigration and Absorption. Each Committee has 19 members and, from time to time, appoints subcommittees, permanent or temporary, to assist in its work.

The functions of the standing committees are (1) to examine, amend, and report on bills referred to them by the Knesset following the first reading, which are then submitted to the house for the second and third, or final, reading; and (2) to inquire into the workings of the executive branch and report their findings. The Knesset may also appoint committees of inquiry to study problems warranting more than a routine investigation by one of the regular standing committees and to inquire into the operations of the executive branch of the government. In addition, it may appoint ad hoc committees to consider particular bills.

Agenda and Day-to-Day Operations. Under the Rules of Procedure, the agenda of the Knesset sessions is set by the Speaker on the proposal of the government, apart from one session every week that is devoted to motions proposed by members on the floor or in response to private members' bills. At the beginning of each week the Speaker and his deputies confer with a representative of the government to draw up the agenda for the week to follow.

The Knesset meets three times a week, on Mondays, Tuesdays, and Wednesdays. The time allotted to each debate is decided in advance, thus eliminating such abuses as filibusters.

Legislative Process. The stages through which a bill must pass before it is enacted into law are as follows:

1. After preparing the draft bill, the government (most laws passed by the Knesset have been government-initiated) publishes it in the *Official Gazette* and places it on the Knesset table, where it must remain for at least 48 hours before the debate begins.

2. The first reading begins with an introductory speech by the Minister who would be responsible for the enforcement of the bill, if and when enacted, followed by a debate in which any member may take the floor, within a time limit decided *ad hoc* by the Speaker, from 10 to 20 minutes. The debate at the first reading deals primarily with principles of the proposed law; particulars of the bill are generally left for discussion in the committee stage. Upon the conclusion of the debate, the Minister in charge replies, thus winding up the debate. Thereafter, a vote is taken. This constitutes the conclusion of the first reading of the bill.

3. If the vote is favorable, the bill is referred to the appropriate Knesset committee for detailed discussion. The committee may revise or amend the bill as it sees fit. Each article of the bill is duscussed and voted upon. The meetings of the committees are not open to the public. Persons interested in presenting their views on a particular subject may appear before a committee, and a committee may invite persons whose views it wishes to ascertain to appear before it. A committee may also, with the consent of the Minister concerned, invite government officials to appear before it.

4. The bill is then returned to the Knesset plenum for its second reading. This phase begins with a report by the committee chairman, who informs the house of the principal points discussed in the committee and of the changes and modifications introduced. The debate at this point is not open to the entire house but only to those committee members who have submitted amendments during the committee stage or objected to any of its provisions. They are called upon to present their proposed amendments for adoption by the Knesset in short speeches before the house. After the committee chairman's reply, each amendment is voted on by the house. Once the voting on the amendments has been concluded, the second reading of the bill is completed. Such as have been adopted by the house are incorporated in the bill.

5. Once the second reading has been completed, the bill is given its third and final reading and is either passed or rejected in its entirety without any debate preceding the vote. After being signed by the Prime Minister, by the Minister responsible for its enforcement, and finally by the President of the State, it is published in the *Official Gazette* and becomes the law of the land.

State Budget. The most important item of Knesset business is the annual State budget, which is formulated as a bill including all the details of government revenue and disbursements. The first reading of the budget provides an opportunity for a comprehensive debate on the government's fiscal and economic policies, which follows a review given by the Minister of Finance. The budget is then referred to the Finance Committee for detailed consideration.

Question Time. The first half hour of every session is devoted to the institution known as question time, when members of the Knesset having submitted written questions to any Minister concerning matters that come within his jurisdiction hear the Minister's reply. This institution, like its counterpart in the British House of Commons, gives members an opportunity to question or obtain information on the day-to-day activities of the government. The Minister concerned or his deputy must answer the inquiry orally from the Knesset rostrum within 21 days (this deadline may be extended to a possible total of 49 days, subject to the Rules of Procedure). As opposed to the practice in the House of Commons in Great Britain, each questioner, and no one but the questioner, may put one supplementary question and no more to the Minister addressed. As many as 1,000 parliamentary questions may be asked and answered in one session of the Knesset. Recently all written questions have been answered in writing. Once a week an hour is devoted to urgent questions, selected by the Speaker, which have to be answered within 48 hours from presentation. In addition to the author of the question, two members— normally from opposite sides of the House— may be called upon to put a complementary question.

Motions to Add to the Agenda and Private Bills. According to the Rules of Procedure, the Knesset is proposed by the government and fixed in consultation with the Speaker, so that the bulk of Knesset business is actually controlled by the executive branch. However, at every second Wednesday session members may submit a motion to the agenda. This takes the form of a motion requesting a debate on a matter of public interest. The sponsor of the motion addresses the house, urging it to place the motion on its agenda. In his reply, the Minister having jurisdiction over the field to which the motion belongs may propose (1) that the Knesset debate the motion, placing it on the agenda; or (2) that the motion be referred to a Knesset committee for study; or (3) that the motion be rejected. The Knesset then votes on the Minister's proposal.

At the beginning of its session the House Committee assigns to each Party group a quota of motions and bills, in proportion to its numerical strength. This quota does not include urgent motions, recognized as such by the Speaker and his Deputies. A member wishing to sponsor a private bill submits the bill to the Speaker and Deputy Speakers. It is placed on the Knesset table and must be taken up no later than two months following its submission. The sponsor of the bill opens the debate by introducing the bill. If a representative of the government or another member of the Knesset moves that the bill be rejected, the sponsor returns to the rostrum and is given additional time in which to answer the objections. At the conclusion of the preliminary debate the house may vote either to reject the bill or to refer it to a committee. In the latter case, the committee having considered the bill may recommend (1) that the bill be placed on the Knesset agenda in the form submitted and given a first reading; or (2) that it be redrafted and given its first reading in the amended form; or (3) that it not be proceeded with.

Interparliamentary Relations. The Knesset maintains

contact with other legislative bodies the world over. From time to time delegations from other parliaments are received, and Knesset delegations visit the legislatures of other countries. The Knesset is affiliated with the Inter-parliamentary Union and sends delegations to its annual conferences. It has two representatives on the Council of the Union. The Knesset also sends two observers to the meetings of the Consultative Assembly of the Council of Europe in Strasbourg, and an advisory delegation of Knesset members sometimes joins the Israeli delegation at meetings of the General Assembly of the United Nations. Since 1978 it has exchanged delegations with the annual European Parliament. The Secretary General of the Knesset and his deputy are members of the Association of Secretaries General of Parliaments, affiliated to the Inter-parliamentary Union. Two of them—Moshe Rosetti and Netanel Lorch—were elected Presidents of that Association.

A. ZIDON—N. LORCH

SPEAKERS OF THE KNESSET

Yosef Sprinzak	1949–1959
Nahum Nir-Rafalkes	1959
Kadish Luz	1959–1969
Reuven Barkatt	1969–1972
Israel Yeshayahu	1972–1977
Yitzhak Shamir	1977–1979
Yitzhak Berman	1979–1981
Menahem Savidor	1981–1985
Shelomo Hillel	1985–1988
Dov Shilansky	1988–1992
Shevah Weiss	1992–

DATES OF OPENING AND CLOSING OF EACH KNESSET

1st Knesset	1949	1951
2nd Knesset	1951	1955
3rd Knesset	1955	1959
4th Knesset	1959	1961
5th Knesset	1961	1965
6th Knesset	1965	1969
7th Knesset	1969	1973
8th Knesset	1973	1977
9th Knesset	1977	1981
10th Knesset	1981	1984
11th Knesset	1984	1988
12th Knesset	1988	1992
13th Knesset	1992	

RESULTS OF KNESSET ELECTIONS.

Party	%	*Seats*
First—25 January 1949		
Mapai	35.7	46
Mapam[1]	14.7	19
Herut	11.5	14
General Zionists	5.2	7
Progressives	4.1	5
United Religious Front[3]	12.2	16
Communists	3.5	4
Arabs (associated with Mapai)	3.0	2
Others	10.1	7[4]
Second—30 July 1951		
Mapai	37.3	45
Mapam[1]	12.5	15
Herut	6.6	8
General Zionists	18.9	23
Progressives	3.2	4
National Religious Party	8.3	10
Agudat Israel and Po'alei A.I.[5]	3.7	5
Communists	4.0	5
Arabs (associated with Mapai)	4.7	5
Others	0.8	—
Third—26 July 1955		
Mapai	32.2	40
Ahdut ha-Avoda	8.2	10
Mapam	7.3	9
Herut	12.6	15
General Zionists	10.2	13
Progressives	4.4	5
National Religious Party	9.1	11
Agudat Israel and Po'alei A.I.	4.7	6
Communists	4.5	6
Arabs (associated with Mapai)	4.9	5
Others	1.9	—
Fourth—3 November 1959		
Mapai	38.2	47
Ahdut ha-Avoda	6.0	7
Mapam	7.2	9
Herut	13.5	17
General Zionists	6.2	8
Progressives	4.6	6
National Religious Party	9.9	12
Agudat Israel and Po'alei Agudat A.I.	4.7	6
Communists	2.8	3
Arabs (associated with Mapai)	3.5	5
Others	3.6	—
Fifth—15 August 1961		
Mapai	34.7	42
Ahdut ha-Avoda	6.6	8
Mapam	7.5	9
Herut	13.8	17
Liberals[2]	13.6	17
National Religious Party	9.8	12
Agudat Israel	3.7	4
Po'alei Agudat Israel	1.9	2
Communists	4.2	5
Arabs (associated with Mapai)	3.5	4
Others	0.7	—
Sixth—2 November 1965		
Alignment (Mapai and Ahdut ha-Avoda)	36.7[6]	45
Mapam	6.6	8
Rafi[7]	7.9	10
Gahal (Herut and Liberals)	21.3[8]	26[10]
Independent Liberals	3.8[9]	5
National Religious Party	9.9	11
Agudat Israel	3.3	4
Po'alei Agudat Israel	1.8	2
Communists	3.4	4[11]
Arabs (associated with Mapai)	3.3	4
Others	2.9	—
Seventh—28 October 1969		
Alignment (Mapai, Ahdut ha-Avoda, Mapam, Rafi)	46.22	56
Gahal	21.67	26
Independent Liberals	3.21	4
National Religious Party	9.74	12
Agudat Israel	3.22	4
Po'alei Agudat Israel	1.83	2
Communists	3.99	4
Arabs (associated with Mapai)	3.51	4
Others	6.61	8
Eighth—31 December 1973		
Alignment	39.6	51[14]
Likud (Gahal and smaller groups)	30.2	39

National Religious Party	8.3	10
Torah Religious Front[15]	3.8	5
Communists		
Democratic Front for Peace & Equality[16]	3.4	4
Sheli[17]	2.1	1[17]
United Arab List	2.5	3[18]
Independent Liberals	3.6	4
Citizens' Rights Movement (Ratz)	2.2	3
Kakh	0.8	—
Others	4.2	—
Ninth—17 May 1977		
Alignment	24.6	32[19]
Likud	33.4	43
National Religious Party	9.2	12
Agudat Israel	3.4	4
Po'alei Agudat Israel	1.4	1
Democratic Front for Peace & Equality	4.6	5
Sheli	1.6	2
Democratic Movement for Change (Shinui)	11.6	15
United Arab List	1.4	1
Independent Liberals	1.2	1
Citizens Rights Movement (Ratz)	1.2	1
Kakh	0.2	—
Others	5.8	3[20]
Tenth—30 June 1981		
Alignment	36.6	47
Likud	37.1	48
National Religious Party	4.9	6
Agudat Israel and Po'alei A.I.	3.7	4
Democratic Front for Peace & Equality	3.46	4
Democratic Movement for Change (Shinui)	1.1	2
Citizens' Rights Movement (Ratz)	1.4	1
Tehiya-Tzomet	2.3	3
Tami	2.3	3
Kakh	0.3	—
Others	2.75	—
Eleventh—23 July 1984		
Alignment	34.9	44
Likud	31.9	41
National Religious Party	3.5	4
Agudat Israel and Po'alei A.I.	1.7	2
Democratic Front for Peace & Equality	3.36	4
Democratic Movement for Change (Shinui)	2.6	3
Citizens' Rights Movement	2.4	3
Tehiya-Tzomet	4.0	5
Sephardi Torah Guardians (Shas)	3.06	4
Yahad	2.2	3
Progressive List for Peace	1.8	2
Morasha	1.6	2
Tami	1.5	1
Kakh	1.2	1
Ometz	1.15	1
Others	.85	—
Twelfth—1 December 1988		
Alignment	30.0	39
Mapam	2.5	3
Likud	31.1	40
National Religious Party	3.9	5
Agudat Israel and Po'alei A.I.	4.5	5
Democratic Front for Peace and Equality	3.7	4
Democratic Movement (Shinui)	1.7	2
United Arab List	1.2	1
Citizens' Rights Movement	4.3	5
Tehiya	3.1	3
Sephardi Torah Guardians (Shas)	4.7	6
Flag of the Torah	1.5	2
Moledet	1.9	2
Progressive List for Peace	1.5	1
Tzomet	2.0	2
Thirteenth—13 July 1992		
Labor	34.6	44
Likud	24.9	32
Meretz (Citizens' Rights, Shinui, Mapam)	9.5	12
Tsomet	6.3	8
National Religious Party	4.9	6
Shas	4.9	6
United Tora	3.2	4
Moledet	2.3	3
Democratic Front for Peace and Equality	2.3	3
Arab Democratic List	1.5	2

[1] In 1949 and 1951 Mapam included Ahdut ha-Avoda
[2] The General Zionists and Progressives merged in 1961 to form the Liberal Party. See also notes 8 and 9.
[3] In 1949 Mizrachi, Ha-Po'el ha-Mizrachi, Agudat Israel, and Po'alei Agudat Israel constituted the United Religious Front.
[4] Four Sephardim, one Yemenite, one WIZO, and one "Fighters."
[5] In 1951, 1955, and 1959, these two parties constituted the Torah Religious Front.
[6] Alignment (Mapai and Ahdut ha-Avoda); in Hebrew *Ma'arakh.*
[7] Rafi—Israel Labor List, formed in 1965 after a split in Mapai.
[8] Herut-Liberal Bloc (Gahal).
[9] Independent Liberals, formerly the Progressives.
[10] In 1967 three Herut Knesset members formed the independent Free Center faction.
[11] Three New Communist List (Rakah) and one Israel Communist Party (Maki).
[12] Ha-Olam ha-Ze—New Force.
[13] Including four National List, two Ha-Olam ha-Ze, two Free Center.
[14] Arie Eliav and Mordecai Ben-Porat withdrew from the party before the elections.
[15] In 1973 Agudat Israel and Po'alei Agudat Israel formed one list: The Torah Religious Front.
[16] In 1973 Rakah—New Communist List.
[17] In 1973 Moded (Focus) and Meri (Radicals)
[18] In 1973 Progress and Development (Arab) and Bedouin List.
[19] Moshe Dayan withdrew from the party after the elections.
[20] Flatto-Sharon 1 seat, Shelomzion 2 seats.

KOESTLER, ARTHUR. Newspaper correspondent, author of novels and other works (b. Budapest, 1905; d. London, 1983). Raised in an assimilated home, Koestler joined a Zionist fraternity while attending the Vienna Institute of Technology. He became a follower of Vladimir Jabotinsky and in 1926 left his studies to go to Palestine. He entered the kibbutz Heftziba, but left the same year to live briefly in Haifa and Tel Aviv. While in Palestine he became Middle East correspondent for the Ullstein newspaper chain of Berlin. Disillusioned by the economic depression and by what he called "the narrow chauvinism, the limited horizons of the Zionist settlers," he left Palestine in 1927, and in 1930, he joined the Ullstein editorial staff in Berlin. While in Berlin he briefly worked part time as executive secretary of the Revisionist party.

Joining the Communist party late in 1931, Koestler left Ullstein and traveled extensively through the Soviet Union in 1932–33. He then settled in Paris. In 1936 he went to Spain to cover the civil war for the London *News Chronicle.* Captured by General Franco's troops and condemned to death as a Communist spy, he was imprisoned for four months but released upon the intervention of the British government. Disillusioned with communism (he explained his change of heart in *The God That Failed,* edited by Richard Crossman, 1950), he left the Communist party early in 1938. After the outbreak of World War II he was briefly interned by the French authorities. He escaped to England, where he eventually took up permanent residence.

As the war continued, Koestler, who had never completely broken with Zionism, went to Palestine and covered the War of Independence for the foreign press. His novel *Thieves in the Night* (1946), a story of the growth of the "stockade and tower" settlements erected in the late 1930s by pioneers in Palestine, had a profound impact on Zionists and non-Zionists alike. In a non-fiction work, *Promise and Fulfillment* (1949), he assessed the State of Israel and its relationship to world Jewry.

KOFER HA-YISHUV. Fund for the defense of the Jewish community in Palestine, in existence from 1938 to 1948. The Arab riots of 1936–39 confronted the Jews of Palestine and the Hagana with the problem of strengthening their defense organization. Large sums of money were needed to maintain men on guard duty, to erect fortifications in the Jewish settlements, and to purchase arms. Previous fundraising efforts- contributions and allocations from national and municipal organizations—had proved inadequate. An institution was therefore needed whose sole purpose would be to supply the defense budget of the yishuv through voluntary self-taxation on the part of the Jewish community.

On 24 July 1938, the Va'ad Le'umi formed Kofer ha-Yishuv, representing all elements of the Jewish community in Palestine. Kofer ha-Yishuv imposed a levy on all Jewish breadwinners in Palestine in accordance with their income. Those who refused to cooperate were subject to social sanctions. A series of indirect taxes was imposed on goods and services such as travel, amusements, postage, cigarettes, matches, margarine, and liquor. A jewelry campaign, in which every Jew was requested to contribute personal jewelry to the defense fund, was initiated.

The Kofer ha-Yishuv fund enabled Hagana to expand its activities. Much of the fund's work was carried on by volunteers. During its first year of existence it raised about £150,000, covering 70 percent of Hagana's budget. Its success later led to the establishment of similar institutions based on the principle of voluntary taxation, such as the emergency tax to aid the unemployed, the Enlistment Fund to support volunteers in the Jewish units in the British Army, and the Rescue Fund to save Jews in Europe during and after World War II. Within this group of special funds, Kofer ha-Yishuv retained the revenues derived from levies on various goods and services for purposes of defense.

At the outset of the War of Independence, Kofer ha-Yishuv played a major role in the raising of funds for military needs. In September, 1948, after the establishment of the State of Israel, Kofer ha-Yishuv was dissolved and its activities were transferred to appropriate governmental agencies. Y. SLUTSKY

KOHAN-BERNSTEIN (BERNSTEIN-COHEN), JACOB. Zionist leader and communal worker in Russia (b. Kishinev, Bessarabia, Russia, 1859; d. Dnepropetrovsk, Russia, 1929). Kohan-Bernstein received the degree of doctor of medicine from Tartu University in 1889. He participated in the Kattowitz Conference, which founded the Hovevei Zion movement in 1884, and was a delegate to the movement's first convention in Odessa in 1890. With the advent of Herzl, he became a political Zionist and subsequently played a prominent role in Russian Zionism. Kohan-Bernstein was active also in Russian-Jewish communal affairs, organizing the first relief efforts for the victims of the Kishinev pogrom of 1903. He was a member of the Zionist Executive from 1905 until 1907, when he settled in Eretz Israel. There he served as physician to the new colonies in Galilee and in Petah Tikva and Jaffa. Returning to Russia in 1910, he settled again in Kishinev, where he soon took a leading part in Jewish and Zionist affairs.

After World War I, Kohan-Bernstein assisted Jewish refugees who went from Russia to Bessarabia, then part of Romania. A second attempt to settle in Palestine and to practice medicine there ended in failure, and in 1926 he went to Russia on behalf of the American Jewish Joint Distribution Committee to serve as physician to the Jewish settlements in the Crimea.

KOKESCH, OSER. Lawyer and early Zionist leader (b. Brody, Galicia, Austria, 1860; d. Vienna, 1905). He studied law at the University of Vienna and later settled in that city. While a student, he participated in the founding of Kadimah, the national Jewish students' fraternity. Kokesch was active in Admath Jeschurun, the Eretz Israel settlement society in Vienna, and in 1893 was one of the founders and leaders of Zion, the parent organization of Austrian Eretz Israel settlement societies of that name. He was also one of the early followers and collaborators of Herzl. At the First Zionist Congress (1897) he was elected to the Inner Actions Committee, serving in that capacity until shortly before his death.

KOL (KOLODNY), MOSHE. Israeli public figure (b. Pinsk, Russia, 1911; d. Jerusalem, 1989). Having engaged in Zionist work in his native city from his youth on, Kol settled in Palestine in 1932 and became a founder of Ha-No'ar ha-Tziyoni and of the Progressive party, which eventually developed into the Independent Liberal party. He was a delegate to every Zionist Congress from the 18th (Prague, 1933) on and a member of the Executive Committee of Histadrut from 1941 to 1946. In 1947 he became head of the Youth Aliya Department of the Jewish Agency, a position he held until 1966.

A signer of Israel's Declaration of Independence, Kol was a member of the Provisional Council of State (1948). Later he was a member of the Knesset, representing first the Progressive party and then the Independent Liberal party and serving as chairman of the latter's Executive Committee. In 1965 he became Minister of Development and Tourism, and from 1969–1977 he was Minister of Tourism.

Kol served as vice-president of the International Federation of Children's Communities (FICE) under the auspices of the UN Educational, Social, and Cultural Organization (UNESCO). He was the author of a history of Youth Aliya and books on education, Zionist personalities, etc.

KOL HA-AM ("Voice of the People"). Daily newspaper of the Israel Communist party. Founded in 1937, *Kol Ha-Am* became a daily in 1948. Its editor-in-chief for several years was Moshe Sneh (1954–1965). After becoming a weekly in 1970, the paper closed in 1974. M. NAOR

KOL ISRAEL. *See* BROADCASTING IN ISRAEL.

KOLLEK, THEODORE (TEDDY). Israeli civil servant and mayor of Jerusalem (b. Vienna, 1911). Kollek joined a Zionist youth movement and became active in Zionist work in Vienna. Settling in Palestine in 1934 he was one of the

Teddy Kollek, 1977.
[Hebrew University]

founders of Kibbutz Ein Gev on the eastern shores of the Sea of Galilee. In the late 1930s he carried out rescue missions in Austria and Germany and was engaged in Zionist political work in England. In 1942 he joined the Political Department of the Jewish Agency and served as liaison officer with the British military intelligence and with Jewish underground groups in Europe, operating out of Jerusalem, Cairo, and Istanbul. In 1947–48 he directed the illegal arms purchasing operations for the Hagana in the United States. Upon his return to Israel he was appointed director of the United States Division in the Foreign Ministry. Between 1950–52 he was the minister plenipotentiary at the Israel Embassy in Washington. Appointed Director-General of the Prime Minister's office in 1952, he displayed energy, vision, imagination, and capacity to mobilize people and funds. He laid the foundations for Israel's tourist industry as the person responsible for the Israel Government Tourist Corporation; he forged strong ties with Jewish art collectors and conceived the idea of a national museum in Jerusalem (the *Israel Museum opened in 1965); he led the effort to create a National Parks Authority in Israel and was active in promoting archeological digs and preservation of ancient sites. Considered one of the "doers," he was among the small group of younger civil servants and Labor Party officials who were cultivated by David Ben-Gurion.

In 1965, he joined Ben-Gurion's Rafi party and ran for Mayor of Jerusalem. In the elections of that year he was elected and was consistently reelected, whether under the banner of the Labor Party or later with his own One Jerusalem list.

He gained a national and international reputation for the orderly and peaceful manner in which he supervised the unification of Jerusalem after the Six-Day War. From a city of less than 200,000 inhabitants in 1967, Jerusalem became Israel's largest city with close to half a million inhabitants in 1988. He developed Jerusalem as an international center for the performing arts, instituted an annual music-dance-drama festival, and attracted to Jerusalem the best planners to help in the planning of the city. He led the effort to incorporate the Arab and Christian population in the life of the city. As the indefatigable head of the Jerusalem Foundation, he was responsible for raising over $60 million for various projects, among them theaters, parks, schools, community centers, playgrounds and facilities in both the Jewish and the Arab neighborhoods. He was awarded many prizes including the Israel Prize, awarded to him in 1988 for his life work for Israel and Jerusalem. He is the author of books on Jerusalem and an autobiography called *For Jerusalem.*

M. MEDZINI

KOLLENSCHER, MAX. Jewish and Zionist leader in Germany (b. Posen, 1875; d. Tel Aviv, 1937). He worked as a lawyer in Posen until 1920 and from 1920 to 1933 in Berlin. He joined the Zionist movement after the Sixth Zionist Congress (1903), following the Uganda crisis. The concrete settlement program proposed to the Zionist movement by the British government convinced Kollenscher that Zionism was not a utopian idea and brought him into the ranks of the political Zionists. He worked to change the nature of the Jewish community in Germany from a religious community (*Religionsgemeinde*) to a national community (*Volksgemeinde*), which would handle not only the religious needs but also the other special requirements of the Jewish community: education, culture, finance, and welfare. He hoped in this way to curb assimilation and to strengthen the Jewish community in its struggle for national survival. In a pamphlet, *Aufgaben jüdischer Gemeindepolitik* (1905) and in *Theses* on the *Gemeindepolitik* (1908), he outlined the policies which guided Zionist activity in Germany until the Nazi rise to power. Kollenscher specialized in the study of community law in Germany and in 1910 published *Rechtsverhältnisse der Juden in Preussen.*

He was one of the founders of the Jüdische Volkspartei (Jewish People's Party, 1919), which he represented in the Berlin community council and in the Prussian Jewish Community Organization, after moving to Berlin. In the Zionist Organization, Kollenscher belonged to the "conservative" section, which opposed the radical stream dominant in German Zionism. In 1920 he was one of the founders of the Binyan ha-Aretz opposition group, which was influenced by the views of Louis Brandeis, and in 1929 he founded the Independent Zionists Party, which opposed the Palestinian policies of the German Zionist leaders, considering them defeatist.

In 1933 he immigrated to Palestine, founding in 1934 Ihud, a religious German immigrant association with a rightist political orientation, which he headed until his death.

Y. ELONI

KOLODNY, MOSHE. *See* KOL, MOSHE.

KOL ZION LA-GOLA. *See* BROADCASTING IN ISRAEL.

KOMITEE FUR DEN OSTEN (Committee for the East). Committee initiated by German Zionist leaders during World War I for the protection of the rights of Eastern European Jewry and in hopes of furthering Zionist aims through support of the German cause. On 4 August 1914, Max Isidor Bodenheimer submitted to the German Ministry of Foreign Affairs a memorandum showing how the support of eastern European Jewry could be enlisted in furthering Germany's aim to destroy the Tsarist Russian Empire. The memorandum suggested that in the event of a final German victory a German-sponsored League of eastern European States, running approximately along the edge of the Tsarist Jewish Pale (from the Baltic to the Black Sea), should be set up, with the Jews cooperating with the Germans as a minority with national rights.

As a result of this memorandum and of subsequent discussions with German officials, it was decided to form a committee to be known as the Deutsches Komitee für die Befreiung der Russischen Juden (German Committee for the Liberation of the Russian Jews). Later the name was changed to the less provocative designation Komitee für den Osten. Franz Oppenheimer became its chairman, with Bodenheimer acting as his deputy in contacts with the German Foreign Ministry. Other members included Adolf Friedemann and the artist Hermann Struck. Later, representatives of non-Zionist groups, such as the B'nai B'rith and the Centralverein Deutscher Staatsbürger Jüdischen Glaubens (Central Union of German Citizens of the Jewish Faith), were admitted.

According to Friedemann, the official purpose of the committee was "to place at the service of the German government the founders' knowledge of and contacts with the Jews of eastern Europe and of the United States, thus contributing to the defeat of Tsarist Russia and to the securing of national autonomy for the Jews." The committee was to disseminate pro-German propaganda among the Jews in German-occupied eastern European territories and at the same time to act as an intermediary between eastern European Jewry and German and Austrian military occupation authorities. It was hoped that by fostering a sense of national identity among eastern European Jewry the cause of Jewish statehood in Palestine would also be furthered. Most of the active members of the committee were leaders in the Zionist Organization of Germany, but in order to give the committee a more nonpartisan character and to obviate the official involvement of the World Zionist Organization (which tried to maintain strict neutrality in the war), the leaders of the committee resigned from their Zionist posts. The committee briefly published an illustrated journal, *Kol Mevasser*, and (from 1916 to 1920) a monthly, *Neue Jüdische Monatshefte*.

After the retreat of German troops from southern Poland late in 1914, the committee began negotiations with Polish leaders about the integration of the Jews as a national group into the independent Polish state planned by the German empire and devoted much effort to securing national cultural autonomy for the Jews. To this end it commissioned a study of the community of language and culture among the Jews of Poland (by Vladimir Kaplan-Kogan) and published essays on the "Jewish language" by Hermann Struck and Heinrich Loewe. At the same time, the committee pursued its aim of gaining the sympathy of Jews in eastern Europe and in neutral countries for the German cause. It sent Dr. Isaac Straus to assist the German Ambassador in Washington as his adviser on Jewish affairs. In the intra-Jewish sphere, the committee became involved in a struggle with two opposing forces: the assimilationist and anti-Zionist tendencies of the leaders in the *Hilfsverein der Deutschen Juden (who subsequently founded their own organization, the Vereinigung für die Interessen der Osteuropäischen Juden, or Union for the Interests of the eastern European Jews), on the one hand, and the anti-Zionist Orthodox Jews from Germany (who also were active in German-occupied eastern Europe), on the other.

Much to the disappointment of Bodenheimer and his associates, who had believed that the interests of eastern European Jewry were in agreement with those of the Central Powers, the German government showed increasing coolness toward the work of the committee, and the attitude of the occupation authorities to the Jews in their territories worsened as the war wore on. By 1916 the committee had confined its work to philanthropic activities. It was dissolved after the war. Z. SHAIKOVSKI

KOMOLY, OTTO. Engineer and Hungarian Zionist leader (b. Budapest, 1892; d. there, 1945). He first became associated with the Zionist movement during his student years under the influence of his father, David Kohn, who had attended the First Zionist Congress. Less active in the 1920s and 1930s, Komoly played a decisive role during World War II as president of the Hungarian Zionist Federation. In January 1943, he became head of the Budapest Va'ad Ezra ve-Hatzala (Aid and Rescue Committee) which, under his leadership, carried out a vast rescue and relief operation to aid refugees from Nazi-occupied countries. After the Nazi invasion of Hungary in March 1944, the committee centered its efforts on the rescue of the Jewish community. He established contact with and was appointed a representative of the International Committee of the Red Cross and maintained close contact with the Hungarian underground lay and church leadership. He was murdered by the Hungarian Arrow Cross (Nazis) in January 1945. Parts of his diary relating to the period of Nazi occupation survived. A member of the General Zionist party, he was the author of *Cionista Eletszemlelet* (A Zionist View of Life) (1944).

R.L. BRAHAM—E. EPPLER

Abraham Isaac Kook. [Zionist Archives]

KOOK. Family of rabbinical authorities.

Abraham Isaac Kook. Chief Rabbi of Palestine (b. Griva, Latvia, 1865; d. Jerusalem, 1935). Kook studied at various eastern European yeshivot (talmudic academies) including the famed Yeshiva of Volozhin. In 1888 he became rabbi of Zimel, Lithuania, and in 1895 rabbi of Bauska, Latvia. In 1904 he settled in Eretz Israel, serving as rabbi of the Jewish community of Jaffa and of the newly established settlements. In 1914 he went to Germany to attend a conference of Agudat Israel. Stranded in Europe at the outbreak of World War I, he stayed in Switzerland until 1916, when he accepted a pulpit in London on condition that he be free to resign as soon as he could return to Eretz Israel. In 1919 he returned to Palestine as rabbi of the Ashkenazi community of Jerusalem. When the Chief Rabbinate of Palestine was established two years later, Rabbi Kook was chosen Ashkenazi Chief Rabbi of Palestine, an office he held until his death.

While still in Latvia, he wrote essays setting forth the ideals of a religious nationalism. While in Jaffa, he continued to develop his national-religious philosophy, aided the pioneers, and sought to influence them in favor of religious observance. In his treatise *Etz Hadar* (1907) Rabbi Kook sought to promote the sale of *etrogim* (citrons used at worship during Sukkot, the Feast of Tabernacles) from Eretz Israel. In 1909 he permitted the pioneers, under specific circumstances, to till their land during the sabbatical year and explained his stand in his treatise *Shabbat ha-Aretz*. He defended his views against sharp attacks by other Orthodox rabbinical authorities, pointing out that his ruling was in the interest of the upbuilding of the Jewish Homeland. When he accepted an invitation to attend a conference of Agudat Israel that was to be held in Frankfort on Main in 1914, he did so in order to win Orthodox Jews to the cause of rebuilding the Homeland. While in London during World War I, he publicly asserted the right of the Jewish people to Palestine and criticized the Anglo-Jewish assimilationists for their fight against Jewish nationalism. Following the issuance of the Balfour Declaration, he founded the Degel Yerushalayim (Banner of Jerusalem) organization, which aimed to introduce the ideals of Jewish law and religion into the Jewish renaissance in Palestine.

In Jerusalem he established his own yeshiva (later known as Merkaz ha-Rav), where he taught his disciples his ideals of a religious-national renaissance for the Jewish people: the renewal of the old and the sanctification of the new. Graduates of his yeshiva later played leading roles in the religious Halutz movement, in the educational system of the country, and in the struggle against the British mandatory authorities.

Although Rabbi Kook was closely associated with the Mizrachi movement, he was friendly to all the Zionist political parties, appreciating their role in the work of rebuilding the Homeland while at the same time seeking to imbue them with the ideals of Jewish tradition. His nationalist views and his kindly, tolerant attitude toward the irreligious Halutzim (who, he declared, were fulfilling a religious commandment by their pioneering work in Palestine) earned him the hatred of extreme Orthodox elements. Kook was fearless and outspoken in his criticism of the British administration. After the Arab riots of 1929, he charged the British with failure to take measures for the defense of Palestine's Jewish community. During the Arab-Jewish controversy regarding the Western Wall, he issued a proclamation to the effect that the Jews would never give up their right to this remnant of their holy Temple. During the last years of his life he was a central figure in the bitter controversy set off in the yishuv by the murder of Hayim Arlosoroff. Convinced that the Revisionists were innocent of the murder, Rabbi Kook took a leading role in the fight for the release and acquittal of the accused Jews.

A prolific writer, he published works in all fields of rabbinics, Jewish mysticism, and philosophy, as well as poetry. Several volumes of his letters have been published. Some of his treatises specifically expound his views on the religious, spiritual, and national renaissance of the Jewish people.

In his thought, the world is a harmonious whole and the search for truth starts with the quest for the unity behind the apparent multiplicity and chaos of the world. The world or reality does not exist apart from God and the cosmic evolutionary process directs the return of everything to its divine source. Man has a special place in creation and the Jewish people has a central role among mankind. In Eretz Israel, the Jew would regain his national creativity, lost in exile. In the Diaspora, the Jew is detached from the stream of holiness; only in Israel can he reach the pinnacle of piety. One danger is the lure of secular nationalism and he opposed any form of militant nationalism or advocating force for the acquisition of Eretz Israel. T. PRESCHEL

His son, **Zvi Yehuda Kook**. Israeli rabbi (b. Zimel, Lithuania, 1891; d. Jerusalem, 1984). He was taken to Eretz Israel in 1904 and studied at the Etz Hayim Yeshiva in Jerusalem. He helped his father administer Yeshivat Merkaz ha-Rav, and was an outstanding educator, calling for the Jewish people to return to the basic roots of Judaism, which included Zionism in its religious form.

After the death of his father, he headed the yeshiva together with his brother-in-law, Shalom Natan-Ra'anan. His positive attitude to the State of Israel greatly influenced the policies of the yeshiva. He became the spiritual leader of the National Religious Party.

A few weeks before the 1967 Six-Day War, Kook praised the State of Israel as a tangible sign of God's handiwork, while criticizing those who were satisfied to live in only a portion of the Land of Israel and taught that the redemption of the Land of Israel was as important as the redemption of the Jewish people. In 1967, after Israel's victory, his words were regarded by many of his followers as divinely inspired. He became the spiritual guide of *Gush Emunim and led his followers to Horon and Jericho. In 1979, he did not support those Gush Emunim settlers who had squatted on Arab lands in Jebel Kebir, ruling that this settlement violated the religious laws forbidding Jews from robbing non-Jewish residents of the Land of Israel.

His collected works *Li-Netivot Yisrael* (1967) deal with halakhic attitudes to current events. He also devoted himself to annotating, editing, and publishing the writings of his father. G. SHUSTER-BOUSKILA

Rabbi Kook Foundation (Mosad Ha-Rav Kook). Religious publishing house, research institute, and cultural center in Jerusalem, named for Chief Rabbi Abraham Isaac Kook. Founded in 1937 by the World Center of Mizrachi with the cooperation of the Jewish Agency, it publishes and subsidizes Jewish religious literature, books on religious Zionism, and works in all fields of traditional Jewish learning and scholarship. Over 1,500 volumes have been published, including new editions of Maimonides' writings (including his medical works); scholarly editions of Bible and Talmud commentaries; translations into Hebrew of classic Jewish scholarship; a hasidic encyclopedia; a history series concerning Jewish communities in Europe as well as Jews in Eretz Israel and modern Israel; and a biography series of outstanding rabbis and hasidic leaders. The foundation also publishes a bimonthly —*Sinai* —devoted to Jewish scholarship.

The Foundation's headquarters also house a large research library, the Archives for International Religious Zionism, and an auditorium. The annual conventions devoted to lectures on the Oral Law, inaugurated in 1958, have became major events in the country's religious-cultural life.

Rabbi Yehuda Leib Fishman (Maimon), initiator of the foundation, served for many years as its head and chief editor. He was succeeded by Yitzhak Raphael.

KOOK, HILLEL. *See* BERGSON, PETER.

KOOR. *See* LABOR ECONOMY.

KORAZIM. Area north of Lake Kineret, constituting a sill which separates the Huleh Valley to the north from the Kineret depression. Its basalt boulders make access difficult, although it has large pockets of fertile soil which were cultivated in antiquity. The ancient town of Korazim had an ornate synagogue, probably from the 3rd century CE. Until the end of the 1950s, the Syrians, in violation of the armistice agreement, held a military post there on Israel's territory. After they were driven off land reclamation could begin, and in 1961 the moshav Almagor was set up. Four more settlements were established in the 1980s, one of them named "Korazim". E. ORNI

KORKIS, ABRAHAM (Adolf). Zionist ideologist (b. Kamionka Strumilowa, Galicia, Austria, 1869; d. Lvov, Poland, 1922). Korkis studied law at the University of Lvov. A Zionist from his early youth, he became the spiritual guide of young Zionists in Galicia. In 1890 he founded and edited *Przyszlosc* (The Future), the first Polish-language Zionist periodical. Both before and after the advent of Herzl, he played a prominent role in outlining the cultural and spiritual aims of Zionism. N.M. GELBER

KORNGRUN, YERUHAM PHILLIP. Israeli jurist and Zionist leader (b. Ternopol, Galicia, Austria, 1883; d. Tel Aviv, 1960). Korngrün studied law at Lvov University, receiving his law degree in 1906 and his doctorate four years later. A Zionist from his high school days on, he was a founder of the Bar Kokhba Zionist academic organization in 1902 and attended the Seventh Zionist Congress (1905) as a correspondent for the Zionist press in Galicia. He was to attend the Eighth (1907) through the 14th (1925) Zionist Congresses as a delegate.

Korngrün practiced law in Vienna from 1908 until 1911, when he became a secretary of the Zionist Executive in Berlin, a position he held until 1913. A member of the Central Committee of the Zionist Organization of Galicia and Bukovina, he aided in the battle of Galician Jewry for national minority group rights. Following service in the Austro-Hungarian Army during World War I, he was a member of the Comité des Délégations Juives at the Paris Peace Conference (1919–20) and attended the London Zionist Conference of 1920. From 1920 to 1924 he was the director of the Palestine Office in Warsaw, serving also on the Jewish Community Council of that city.

Settling in Palestine in 1925, he engaged in private law practice in Tel Aviv until 1930, when he was appointed a judge in the Magistrates' Court of Tel Aviv. In 1937 he was named a judge of the Tel Aviv District Court, an office he held until his retirement in 1944 when he returned to private law practice.

In 1925 Korngrün was elected a member of the Asefat ha-Nivharim, the Va'ad Le'umi, and the Tel Aviv Municipal Council. He was also a member of the Executive Committee of the General Zionist party in Israel. His writings include *The Laws of the Ancient Orient* (1944) and *Jewish Military Colonization in Ancient Times* (1948), both in Hebrew.

KOTEL MA'ARAVI. *See* WESTERN WALL.

KOVNER, ABBA. Ghetto fighter and Hebrew poet (b. Sevastopol, Russia, 1918; d. Kibbutz En ha-Horesh, 1987). He studied at the Hebrew High School and the University

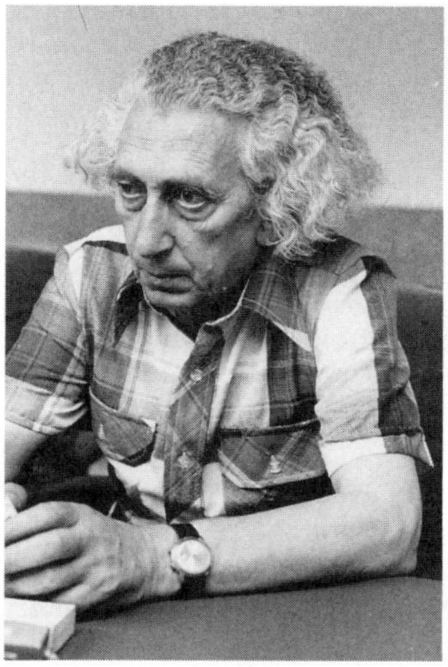

Abba Kovner.
[Israel Govt. Press Office]

of Vilna. After the Soviet occupation of Vilna in 1939, Kovner, who had been a member of Ha-Shomer ha-Tza'ir, helped organize "illegal" Zionist activities. With the capture of the city by the Germans in 1941, he assisted in the formation of the Jewish Fighting Organization there and later became its commander. In September, 1943, after the end of the fighting in the ghetto, he escaped with other surviving fighters and commanded a Jewish guerrilla force, Nekama (Vengeance), in the Rudniki Woods near Vilna.

After World War II, Kovner was active in the organization of "illegal" immigration to Palestine. He himself arrived there as an "illegal" and joined Kibbutz En ha-Horesh. Soon thereafter he was sent on a secret mission by the Zionist movement. Arrested by the British, he was held in a Cairo prison for some time. Eventually, he was freed by the Hagana and returned to Palestine. During the War of Independence he served as a staff officer with the Israel Defense Forces. Kovner was responsible for the basic plan of Beth Hatefutsoth, the Tel Aviv museum devoted to the history of the Jewish Diaspora.

Kovner began his literary career in prewar Vilna. In Israel he published two volumes of stories on the War of Independence, and several collections of poetry. Kovner is a symbolist poet who sets his recollections and experiences in the Holocaust against an eerie, dreamlike background. He lends mythical dimensions to the characters and images: the martyred mother and "little sister," the brave anti-Fascist partisan, the memory of the destroyed city. Kovner views Israel's wars as part of the historical Jewish struggle and often reinforces his synoptic vision by employing literary devices and allusions drawn from the Bible and the Hebrew prayer book.

His major works are *Admat ha-Hol*, 1961, *Ahoti Ketana* (1967), *Huppa ba-Midbar*, 1970, *Tatzpiyoth*, 1977, The Scrolls of Fire 1981. Translations of his poems include *A Canopy in the Desert* (selected poems) 1973, *Childhood under fire* (stories and poems) 1968, *Selected poems* (1971).
E. SPICEHANDLER

KOVNER, ABRAHAM URI. Hebrew author and literary critic (b. Vilna, Russian Poland, 1842; d. Lomza, Russian Poland 1909). After studying at several yeshivot (rabbinical academies), Kovner broke with Orthodox Judaism. He began publishing literary criticism in the Hebrew press, advocating a radical reevaluation of contemporary literature in the spirit of Russian positivist criticism. He dismissed Haskala (enlightenment) literature as trivial, romantic, and verbose. His essays are collected in *Heker Davar* (1866) and *Tseror Perahim* (1868).

Kovner was convicted for embezzlement of funds at the bank in which he was employed and was sentenced to Siberia. He married a non-Jewish woman and converted to Christianity. He spent his last years as a government clerk in Lomza, published memoirs in Russian and corresponded with leading Russian literati (Dostoievsky, Tolstoy, etc.) on the Jewish question. His selected works were published in 1947 (*Kol Kitvei Avraham Uri Kovner*).

E. SPICEHANDLER

KRAKAUER, LEOPOLD. Israeli artist and architect (b. Vienna, 1880; d. Jerusalem, 1954). He studied in Vienna and arrived in Israel in 1924 as an experienced architect and an expressionist artist. He first worked in the office of Alexander Baerwald in Haifa and was influenced by Baerwald's concepts of an Eretz Israel architecture, deriving from oriental sources. His first major architectural project was a large dwelling in Bet Alfa, with sharp and other arches, reflecting the cultural shock caused by his European background and the Eretz Israel landscape of the 1920, still dominated by the pastoral atmosphere of the sleepy Orient.

His buildings were few in number and most of them in kibbutzim (dining rooms, notably in Tel Yosef, children's homes) together with the Megiddo hotel on Mount Carmel, Haifa, and private homes in Rehavia, Jerusalem. His art was almost entirely devoted to the Jerusalem landscape, reflecting his absorption into his new surroundings. In many of his works he depicts Arab villages in the hills with their cube-like small houses clinging to the rock as if grown there. This morphology evidently inspired him when he came to design many of his cubistic houses.

A. ELHANANI

Lola Popper Kramarsky. [Hadassah]

KRAMARSKY, LOLA POPPER. Communal worker and leader in *Hadassah (b. Hamburg, Germany, 1896; d. New York, 1991). After completing her formal education, she taught at a religious school. In 1923 she and her husband, Siegfried Kramarsky, went to the Netherlands, where she subsequently organized committees for the rescue of children from Nazi persecution and helped send them on to Palestine. In 1940 she and her husband settled in New York, and she became involved with the work of Hadassah, serving as chairman of Hadassah's Youth Aliya Department, then as its national treasurer and vice-president, and, from 1960 to 1964, as its national president. She attended several World Zionist Congresses. Kramarsky was a member of Hadassah's National Executive and national chairman of the Hadassah Medical Organization. She served as a Fellow of the Morgan Library, member of the Art Committee of Columbia University, and a member of the Metropolitan Museum of Art.

M. LEVIN

KRAUSE, ELIYAHU. Agronomist (b. Berdyansk, Russia, 1878; d. Tel Aviv, 1962). After studying at the agricultural school of Mikve Yisrael and at an agricultural college in France, he entered the service of the Jewish Colonization Association (ICA). He helped establish an ICA agricultural school near Smyrna (Izmir), Turkey, and in 1901 was appointed director of the ICA farm at Sejera (Ilanya), where he was instrumental in establishing the first cooperative of Jewish agricultural laborers in Eretz Israel. In 1915 he became director of the Mikve Yisrael Agricultural School, a position he held until his retirement in 1954. During his administration he changed the school's language of instruction from French to Hebrew.

KRAUSZ, MOSHE (MIKLOS). Hungarian Zionist leader (b. Miskolc, Hungary 1908; d. Jerusalem, 1956). Under the impact of the 1929 Arab riots in Palestine, he established the Miskolc branch of He-Halutz and Ha-Po'el ha-Mizrachi with an agricultural training facility (*hakhshara*), expanding this activity to other localities in northern Hungary. In 1932 he moved to Budapest and was appointed general secretary of Mizrachi-Ha-Po'el ha-Mizrachi in Hungary; in 1934, he became Secretary of the Budapest Palestine Office. In these capacities Krausz strengthened the halutzic movement, established good relations with the British Consulate (representing the Mandatory Power) and the Hungarian authorities who issued passports to immigrants to Palestine. His contacts stood him in good stead when, after the *Anschluss* of Austria (1938) Jewish refugees began to arrive in Hungary. Krausz was able to arrange that every Palestine certificate holder could add a number of refugee children (mostly orphans) from Austria, Slovakia, Poland, and Croatia. Krausz continued his rescue and relief activities throughout the War. After the Nazi invasion of Hungary (19 March 1944), his contacts with Charles Lutz, the Swiss Vice-Consul in Budapest, resulted in Swiss Letters of Protection being issued and distributed, saving the lives of tens of thousands of Jews. After the war, Krausz settled in Jerusalem.

E. EPPLER

KREMENETZKY, JOHANN. Electrical engineer and Zionist leader in Austria (b. Odessa, Russia, 1850; d. Vienna, 1934). Kremenetzky studied engineering at the Berlin Technical Institute, helped build the Baku-Tiflis railroad, and then worked for a number of years in Paris with Paul Jablochov, inventor of the arc lamp. He himself was responsible for numerous inventions, including a method of railway signaling, and he built the first electric lamp factory in Austria.

A friend of Herzl before the formation of the World Zionist Organization, Kremenetzky was one of the first to respond to his call. He attended the First Zionist Congress

(1897) and was elected to the Inner Actions Committee, serving on that body until the Seventh Congress (1905). For many years thereafter he was a member of the Greater Actions Committee.

Kremenetzky's most important contribution to the Zionist movement was the organization of the *Jewish National Fund (JNF), with which Herzl had entrusted him. From its establishment in 1901 until 1907 he headed the Fund, which then had its main office in Vienna. He initiated many JNF projects, including the JNF boxes, the Golden Book, and JNF stamps.

Interested in bringing the electrical industry to Palestine, he built an electrical appliance factory in Tel Aviv after World War I, and in 1920 he and Boris Goldberg founded the Silicat brickworks in that city. Kremenetzky also played a major role in the acquisition of the Haifa Bay lands. Herzl's literary archives were housed in his Vienna home.

KRIEGEL, ANNIE BECKER. Historian and Zionist polemicist in France (b. Paris, 1926). After obtaining her doctorate in 1964 for a study of the beginnings of the French Communist Party, she was appointed (1969) professor at the Paris University in Nanterre. At first a Marxist, she became highly critical of Marxism and adopted a strong Zionist position. She headed the Paris Academic Seminary for Zionist Thought. Her writings include *Les Juifs et le monde moderne* (Jews and the Modern World, 1977); *Israël est-il coupable?* (Is Israel guilty?, 1982), and *Réflexions sur les questions juives* (Reflections on Jewish problems, 1984). From 1982, she coedited the biennial publication, *Communisme* and, from 1985, the periodical of Jewish studies *Pardès*.

M. CATANE

KRINITZI, ABRAHAM. Israeli industrialist and mayor of Ramat Gan (b. Grodno, Russia, 1886; d. near Haifa, 1969). An early adherent of Po'ale Zion, Krinitzi settled in Eretz Israel in 1905. In 1909, after having worked as a laborer, he established a furniture factory. He also founded the first sawmill in the country. In 1915 he worked for the Turkish authorities as supervisor of wood supply and sawing for the railroads of Palestine, Syria, and the Hejaz. Early in 1916 he left this position to become technical director of an armaments factory, and in 1917 he was in charge of barracks construction for the German Army in Damascus.

A member of Tel Aviv's first Municipal Council, Krinitzi was one of the founders and organizers of Hagana in the city. A co-founder of Ramat Gan, near Tel Aviv, he was elected chairman of that community's first local council, in May, 1926. In August, 1947, he was arrested with other Jewish leaders and interned in Latrun but was released a few weeks later. When Ramat Gan obtained municipal status, he became its first mayor, serving until his death. Krinitzi guided the development of Ramat Gan from a small semi-agricultural community to a thriving industrial and educational center. His autobiography, *Be-Khoah ha-Ma'ase*, was translated into English as *Reminiscences: Going My Own Way* (1963).

KROJANKER, GUSTAV. Editor and author (b. Berlin, 1891; d. Jerusalem, 1945). After studying economics in the universities of Berlin and Munich, he entered the family business. While at university, Krojanker joined the Students Zionist Association, *Kartell Zionistischer Verbindungen (KZV)*. holding that the modern Jew could retain his self-respect and his personal and cultural integrity only in the framework of Zionism. In 1922 he published his study of Jews in German literature, *Juden in der deutschen Literatur*. Krojanker was one of the few German Zionists who studied Hebrew and he published extensive essays on Agnon and Brenner. One of the leading Zionist authors in Germany, Krojanker joined the staff of the periodical, *Der Jude*, edited the *Jüdischer Wille*, the organ of the Kartell, *Kartell Jüdischer Verbindungen* and directed the *Weltverlag* and *Jüdischer Verlag* publishing houses. In 1932, with the rise of the Nazi movement, he published a work entitled *Zum Problem des deutschen Nationalismus*, in which he analyzed German nationalism from the Zionist point of view, stressing the positive aspects of Zionism as opposed to the danger of barbarity inherent in German nationalism.

Immigrating to Palestine in 1932, Krojanker contributed to *Ha-Aretz* and *Yedioth (Mitteilungsblatt)*, the organ of Central European immigrants. He edited the short-lived *Jüdische Weltrundschau*, which was intended as the main Zionist newspaper for German-speaking Jews throughout the world. On the capital transfer of immigrants from Nazi Germany to Palestine, he published *Der Transfer, eine Schicksaldsfrage der zionistischen Bewegung*, in which he supported the position of the Zionist Executive. In 1937 he edited a collection of speeches and articles by Chaim Weizmann. Krojanker also participated in public life, and was active in the Aliya Hadasha party. He wrote regularly for *Ammudim*, which he edited in the last months of his life.

Y. ELONI

KRONITZ, LEON ARYEH. Canadian educator and Zionist leader in Canada (b. Kletzk, Poland, 1917; d. Montreal, 1985). Kronitz received his early education in the Kletzker Yeshiva and the Tarbut Teachers' Seminary in Vilna. After emigrating in 1938, he earned degrees from McGill University, Montreal, and the Jewish Theological Seminary of America. A leading figure in Montreal educational circles from the time of his arrival, he was the founding principal of Herzliya High School and principal of the Solomon Schechter Academy, a founder and director of Camp Massad, director of the Keren ha-Tarbut, the Hebrew cultural organization, and one of the first Jewish members of the Protestant School Board of Greater Montreal. As executive vice-president of the Canadian Zionist Federation from 1972 until his death, he made education one of the priorities of that organization by instituting a biennial national education conference, scholarships in Israel for teacher training, and other programs.

A familiar figure at Zionist Congresses and at the World Jewish Congress, he served for nine years as president of the Labor Zionist Movement of Canada and for 15 years as an officer of the Canadian Jewish Congress.

M. BROWN

KRUPNIK, BARUKH. *See* KARU, BARUKH.

KUBOVY (KUBOWITZKI), ARYE LEON. Israeli diplomat and public servant (b. Kursenai, Lithuania, 1896; d. Jerusalem, 1966). Brought to Antwerp at the age of 10, Kubovy studied at the Universities of Brussels and Liège, receiving degrees in classical philology and jurisprudence. In 1916 he was a founder of Tze'irei Zion of Belgium and in 1920 was a delegate to the London Zionist Conference. Kubovy was also a delegate to several World Zionist Congresses. In 1920 he became the editor of the French-language Zionist fortnightly *HaTikva* and later also of the Yiddish fortnightly *Folk und Arbet*. From 1926 to 1940 he practiced law in Antwerp and Brussels. He was active in Belgium's Socialist movement and was elected a deputy member of the Antwerp Municipal Council in 1929.

After Hitler's advent to power, Kubovy was a co-founder of the world boycott movement against Nazi trade (1934). In 1936 he went to Poland to promote the idea of a World Jewish Congress, and later that year he was in charge of organizing its founding conference. After the outbreak of World War II he fled via France and Spain to the United States, where he joined the staff of the World Jewish Congress, heading its Rescue Department from 1943 to 1945. As secretary-general of the Congress (1945–48), he served on various postwar rescue and rehabilitation missions.

Settling in Israel in 1948, Kubovy became chairman of the board of the School of Law and Economics in Tel Aviv. He was Israel's Minister to Czechoslovakia and Poland from 1951 until 1952, when he was accused by the Czechs of complicity in a "Zionist conspiracy" (*see* SLANSKY TRIAL). He subsequently served as Minister (later, Ambassador) to Argentina and Chile (1953–58), Uruguay (1954–55), and Paraguay (1954–58). In 1959 he became chairman of *Yad va-Shem (Heroes' and Martyrs' Authority) in Jerusalem, a position he held until his death. He was the author of several books on Jewish issues.

KUGEL, HAYIM. Zionist leader in Czechoslovakia and mayor of Holon (b. Minsk, Russia, 1897; d. Holon, 1953). Kugel first went to Palestine as a young student, enrolling at the Herzliya High School in Tel Aviv. While he was on a visit to his parents in 1914, World War I broke out, forcing him to remain in Russia. After the war he became principal of the Hebrew High School in the Ruthenian city of Mukacevo. Active in the Zionist movement of Czechoslovakia, he represented the Zionist party in the Czechoslovak Parliament.

In 1939 Kugel returned to Palestine and became the first mayor of Holon, playing an active role in the economic and cultural development of the town. He was also active in the Association of Immigrants from Czechoslovakia.

G. KRESSEL

KUPAT HOLIM (Sick Fund). Comprehensive health insurance scheme of the Histadrut (General Federation of Labor) and the largest Histadrut mutual-aid institution in Israel.

Development. Founded in 1911 by the Federation of Judean Workers, the new organization soon had to rise to the challenges posed by problems beyond its original scope, such as post-World War I unemployment and a high incidence of illness and a high death rate among Yemenite immigrants. With the formation of the Histadrut in 1920, two health insurance funds (those of Ahdut Avoda and Ha-Po'el ha-Tza'ir) merged into one joint Sick Fund, which aimed to maintain its own medical staff rather than pay private physicians with organizational funds. During the early years of its existence, Kupat Holim physicians were pioneers in many fields of medicine and public health throughout Palestine.

By 1986 the enrollment in Kupat Holim, which had begun with 2.000 members, had reached a total of 3,300,000 (77 percent of the population). Throughout the years Kupat Holim played an important role in providing medical services for the masses of immigrants who, by arrangement with the Jewish Agency, were automatically given Kupat Holim coverage immediately after their arrival in Palestine/Israel. Many of these immigrants had never received medical care prior to their arrival. The remnants of European Jewry who came to the country after World War II also benefited from Kupat Holim membership. Indeed, almost every immigrant who arrived after the creation of the State of Israel joined Kupat Holim. A number of groups not affiliated with the Histadrut, including families of veterans, members of Po'alei Agudat Israel and of Ha-Po'el ha-Mizrachi, immigrant youth, and many welfare beneficiaries, also belong to Kupat Holim.

Organization. The basic units of Kupat Holim are clinics throughout Israel. These are aided by laboratories, specialized medical institutes, regional clinics with modern medical equipment, hospitals, medical centers, and convalescent and rest homes. Kupat Holim is also involved in an extensive program of preventive medicine. The organization is governed by the conference of Kupat Holim delegates, which appoints the National Supervisory Committee. The committee sets the annual budget, directs activities between conferences, and appoints the coordinator who supervises the day-to-day work of Kupat Holim. The country is divided into 15 regions for organizational purposes.

Kupat Holim is distinguished from similar institutions in other countries by the following specifications:

1. A uniform countrywide organization covering urban and rural workers, manual laborers and the free professions, salaried workers and the self-employed, old-timers and new immigrants. Thanks to this system of services based on the principle of mutual aid, efficient medical care is available even in the remotest regions of the country.
2. Medical care in its own clinics, auxiliary institutes, laboratories, and pharmacies. Hospitalization, the largest item in medical care, is given in Kupat Holim hospitals situated in rural and development areas and in hospitals maintained by the government and by municipalities.
3. Link between Kupat Holim and the Histadrut. Every Histadrut member is automatically a member of Kupat Holim and his insurance dues are included in the *mas ahid* (unified fee). Other workers' organizations such as Ha-Po'el ha-Mizrachi and Po'alei Agudat Israel, are also insured with Kupat Holim.

Benefits. Kupat Holim supplied its members with the following benefits: (1) medical care, (2) medical care for the families of the insured, (3) convalescent care, (4) mother and child care, (5) preventive medicine, (6) workmen's compensation treatment, (7) sick pay, and (8) treatment of chronic diseases.

Medical care includes the services of general practitioners, specialists, and nurses in clinics and at the patient's home, hospitalization in Kupat Holim and other hospitals, X-rays, physiotherapy and medical rehabilitation, laboratory tests, and drugs and medical appliances in Kupat Holim pharmacies. Preventive medicine includes mother and child care, industrial medicine, and health education.

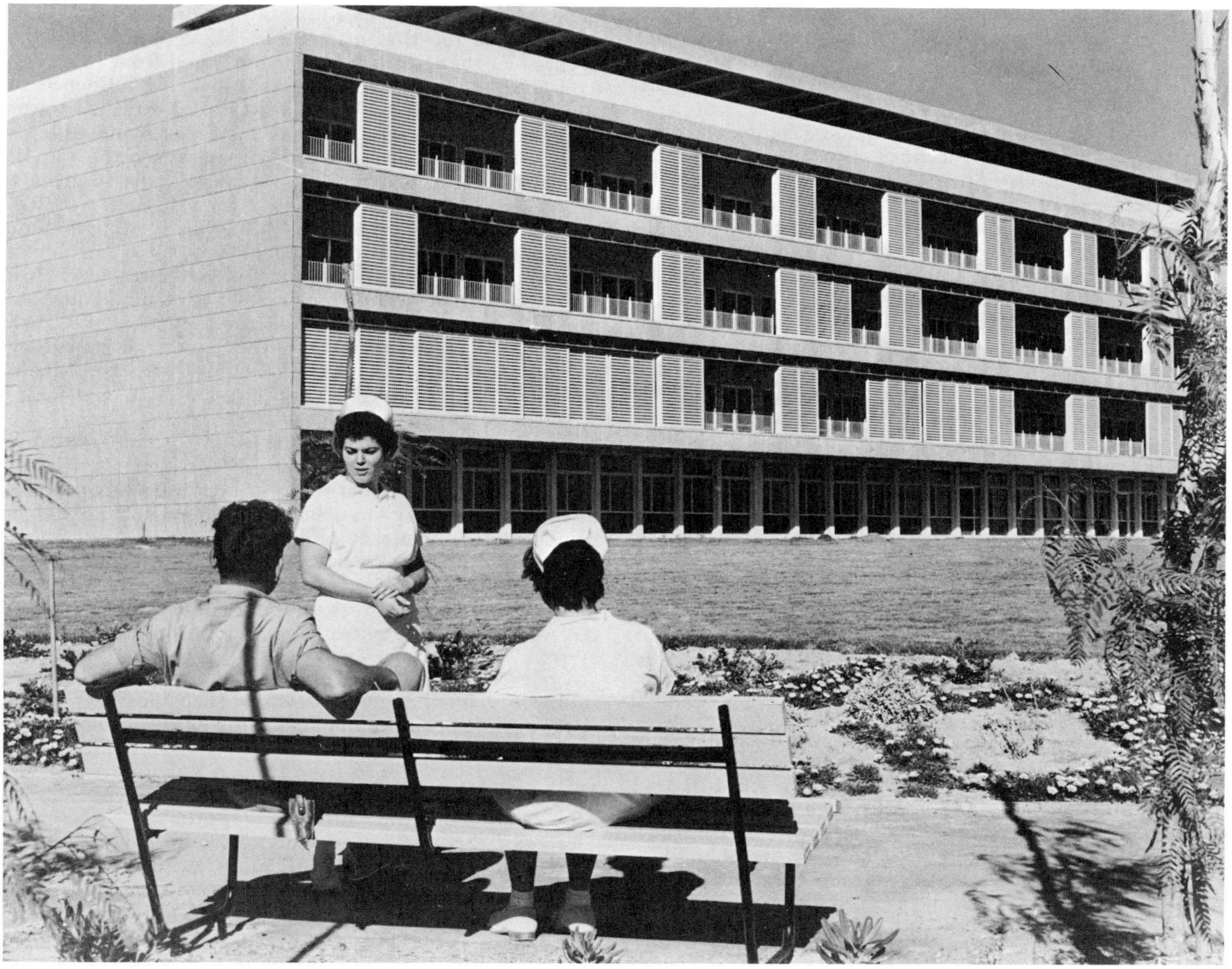

The Kupat Holim hospital in B'er Sheva' was opened in 1959. [Israel Information Services]

Choice of Doctors. Kupat Holim members who so wish may "choose" a self-employed doctor, practicing on his own premises, and receiving his fees directly from the insurance fund. Family doctors, pediatricians, and specialists may come into this category. Nearly 600 "self-employed" doctors work with Kupat Holim and members may make their choice from the list displayed in the Kupat Holim dispensaries.

Medical care to dependents is given in two forms: (1) family insurance (against payment of an additional 80 per cent of membership dues) entitling all dependents, including parents, to all types of medical treatment, including hospitalization, free of charge; (2) limited insurance, if no dues are paid for the family (in this case medical care is given to dependents against payment for certain treatments, to cover part of the cost).

Range of Kupat Holim Services in 1986: 14 general, psychiatric and physical rehabilitation hospitals, with a total of 5,400 beds. Agreements with government, municipal and private hospitals; 1,290 dispensaries and 550 laboratories and medical centers; 15 convalescent homes with 3,300 beds; 28,000 employees, including 5,000 doctors, 9,000 nurses, 2,600 pharmacists and laboratory assistants, 655 dentists and dental assistants, and 1,888 paramedics; 16 occupational therapy centers, 46 physiotherapy centers, 310 mother and child clinics, 34 X-ray centers, and 18 mobile units for treatment of patients in their homes.

A. BEN-YA'AKOV—ED.

KUPAT HOLIM LE-OVEDIM LE'UMIYIM (National Workers' Sick Fund). Israeli health insurance program, controlled and directed by the National Workers Federation (*Histadrut ha-Ovedim ha-Le'umit). In 1988, it had a membership of 300,000. Founded in 1933 to provide medical assistance for workers not affiliated with the Histadrut, it adopted from its inception an arrangement whereby each patient is free to select a physician of his choice from a panel.

The fund operates 200 clinics and dispensaries throughout Israel, in towns, settlements, and villages, including 50 in the Administered Areas as well as 30 in Druze and Arab villages, in addition to a network of health resorts and recreation centers; it employs physicians, nurses, and laboratory and pharmacy personnel. The health insurance offered its members covers full hospitalization and life insurance.

The fund conducts a broad educational campaign in the field of hygiene through lectures, brochures, and a periodical (*Beri'ut la-Kol*). Special efforts are devoted to the welfare of new immigrants, particularly those who have come to Israel from underdeveloped countries with substandard sanitary conditions. Within the framework of the State Health Service, the fund actively participates in the nationwide campaign of preventive medicine, is represented on the State Medical Council, on committees on public health and hygiene, and is affiliated with the International Social Security Association (ISSA) in Geneva.

I. BENARI—D. JUTAN

KUPER, SIMON MYER. Jurist and Zionist leader in South Africa (b. Johannesburg, 1906; d. there, 1963). A law graduate of Witwatersrand University, he practiced at the Johannesburg bar, becoming a queen's counsel in 1946. In 1933 he became a member of the Executive of the South African Zionist Federation and in 1950 was elected chairman. In 1945 he was appointed by the South African Jewish Board of Deputies to testify on behalf of South African Jewry before the Anglo-American Committee of Inquiry. He was named a judge of the Supreme Court of South Africa in 1955 and remained in office until his death.

KURDISH JEWS IN ISRAEL. Kurdistan is divided among three countries: the largest part is in Turkey, another part in Iran, and the smallest part in Iraq. Most Kurdish Jews lived in the Iraq region, some in the Iranian region, and only a few in the Turkish region. There were also Kurdish Jews in northern Syria and elsewhere. Their spoken language is Aramaic combined with Persian, Turkish, Kurdish, Arabic, and Hebrew words.

History: As early as the 16th century individual Jews came to Eretz Israel from Kurdistan, settling in Safed. They were among the first oriental Jewish immigrants in the country. Further Kurdish settlements dated from 1812. Initially a few families immigrated under the influence of emissaries from Eretz Israel, who visited Kurdish towns frequently and received generous donations from the Jews. Constant persecutions in Kurdistan increased the rate of immigration, and Kurdish Jews began to arrive in groups.

Two Kurdish immigrants who were flown to Israel by Operation Ezra and Nehemia. [Keren Ha-Yesod]

In 1916, 174 Kurdish Jews were recorded in Jerusalem and 222 in Galilee. Between 1920—1926, 1,900 Jews came to Palestine from Kurdistan, and 2,500 in 1935. The rate of legal and illegal immigration continued to accelerate. Most of the immigrants were from Iraqi Kurdistan and adapted rapidly to the conditions prevailing in the Holy Land. With the creation of the State of Israel, almost all remaining Kurdish Jews came to Israel in the "Ezra and Nehemiah" Operation, which brought Iraqi Jews 1950–51. Today they are dispersed in all the towns and settlements of Israel.

The first immigrants, from the town of Zakho, settled in Jerusalem. Joined by immigrants from other towns, they built housing, synagogues where they prayed according to their rites, and religious schools. They settled together in neighborhoods that they built themselves: Zikhron Yosef, Zikhron Ya'akov, Sha'arei Rahamim, etc. They were employed in various trades, as porters, donkey-drivers, stonemasons and stonecutters, builders, etc. Five of them received the municipality's "honored citizen of Jerusalem" award.

In Jerusalem several Kurdish committees were formed and were named after the towns of their members origin. They include: The Committee for the Kurdish Community (founded 1924) and The Committee for the Community of the Targum (immigrants from Iranian Kurdistan where the language of the Targum, i.e., Aramaic, is spoken; founded 1932; which at the time numbered approximately 300 families, with their own synagogue; and the Committee for Jews from Erbil (Arbil) (founded 1932, 200 families, two synagogues). In 1938 further committees were added representing Jews from Nisibis and Kamishli (50 families and a synagogue); Zakho (500 families, five synagogues); Dehok, (40 families); Barashe (60 families); Amadiya, (70 families with their own synagogue); and Sindur, (70 families, and a synagogue). In 1945 all these committees united under the general name Hitahdut Yehudei Kurdistan (Association of Kurdish Jews). In addition there are in Jerusalem an Association of Jews from Jezirah ibn Umar (in Turkish Kurdistan, numbering 500 and with two synagogues) and committees for immigrants from Jarmaq (1,500). Until 1953 the members of the Kurdish community in Jerusalem depended on the burial society of the Sephardi Community but in 1953 they created their own burial society. In 1971 the Igud Yotzei Kurdistan be-Yisrael (Union of Kurdish Jews in Israel) was created in Jerusalem. 1973 saw the founding of Ha-Irgun Ha-Artzi shel Yehudei Kurdistan be-Yisrael (The National Association of Kurdish Jews in Israel). Its mouthpiece is called *Hithadshut* and is edited by Habib Shimoni.

According to the 1948 Israel population census there were 1,520 Kurdish speakers (in addition to Hebrew) from age two upwards (681 males and 839 females). According to the 1961 population and housing census there were 8,560 Kurdish speakers (4,640 as a second language after Hebrew; 3,920 as a first language). They are dispersed in 14 regions: 4,090 live in urban settlements, 4,470 in rural settlements.

Kurdish immigrants celebrate Independence Day on their arrival at Lod Airport on May 10, 1951. [Keren Ha-Yesod]

At the time of the creation of the State of Israel the number of Kurdish Jews in Israel was estimated at 20,000; after the immigration from 1950–1952 their numbers increased greatly. According to a survey by the Hebrew University Folklore Studies Center, the overall number was estimated at between 80,000 to 100,000. They are dispersed in towns and settlements as follows: Holon (200–300 families, mostly from Iranian Kurdistan); Haifa (hundreds of families), Tiberias (700 families), Tirat Carmel (300–400 families); Yokne'am Illit (100–200 families), Jerusalem (30,000), in agricultural settlements and development towns (15,000), Kefar Yona (130–140 families), Mevasseret Tziyon—Maoz Tziyon Aleph and Bet (300 families), Nahariya (hundreds of families), Netanya (170–200 families), Pardes Hanna—Karkur (250–300 families), Petah Tikva (100–200 families), Safed (100-150 families), Kiryat Ata (hundreds of families), Kiryat Malakhi (147 families), Kiryat Shemona (100–150 families), Tel Aviv-Jaffa (hundreds of families). These figures include the total number of Jews from Iraqi Kurdistan, who all immigrated to Israel.

A. BEN-YAACOB

KURZWEIL, BARUCH. Literary historian, critic, and author (b. Pirnice, Moravia, 1907; d. Ramat Gan, 1971). Kurzweil received a traditional Jewish education but also studied in Czech and German schools. In 1921, he was sent to the Solomon Breuer yeshiva (rabbinical academy) in Frankfort on Main, a center of the neo-Orthodox movement. There he continued his secular studies as an extern. In 1928 he was admitted to the University of Frankfort, receiving his doctorate in German literature in 1933. During this period, he was also ordained as rabbi. From 1933–1939 he taught at the Hebrew high school at Brno (Moravia) and began publishing literary articles in German. In 1939, Martin Buber invited him to serve as his research fellow at the Hebrew University, Jerusalem. Kurzweil later moved to Haifa where he taught Hebrew literature at the Reali and then at the Hugim high schools until 1956, when he was appointed Professor of Hebrew literature at Bar-Ilan University.

His first book was *Masekhet ha-Roman* (Studies on the Novel, 1953). His other important works of criticism are *Sifruteinu ha-Hadasha— Hemshekh o Mahapehah* (Our Modern Literature, Continuum or Revolution, 1959), *Bialik ve-Tchernichowsky* (Bialik and Tchernichowsky, 1971), *Masot al Sipurei Shai Agnon* (Essays on S.Y. Agnon's Fiction, 1963), *Bein Hazon le-vein ha-Absurdi* (Between Vision and the Absurd, 1963), *Ba-Ma'avak al Erkhei ha-Yahadut* (On the Struggle for Jewish Values, 1969), *Be-Hipus ha-Sifrut ha-Yisraelit* (In Search of Israeli Literature, 1982).

A prolific writer, Kurzweil published almost 400 articles, at first in German but mainly in Hebrew. He also published a volume of short stories in 1972.

He is to be credited for the introduction of "Middle-European" critical analysis into the study of modern Hebrew literature. He insisted that the literary scholar must "attempt to discover the inner consistency" of the work of art. At the same time he stressed the cultural and sociological context in which a literary work was created. His central thesis was that modern Hebrew literature is a product of the secularization of Jewish life and therefore represents a revolutionary break with the Jewish past. The great modern Hebrew writers (Bialik or Agnon for example) attained their artistic stature because they gave expression to the *angst* which resulted from the crisis of loss of faith. Kurzweil dismissed as naive all attempts at synthesizing the tradition with modernity (Ahad Ha-Am for example). Most seminal are his close readings of the works of Bialik, Agnon, and Uri Tzevi Greenberg. E. SPICEHANDLER

L

LABOR ECONOMY IN ISRAEL (HEVRAT HA-OVEDIM)

Origins and Conception of Hevrat ha-Ovedim. Hevrat ha-Ovedim (Society of Workers) owes its creation to the "constructive socialist" ideology which crystallized during the Second Aliya, calling for an active, productive role of the Jewish worker in the upbuilding of the National Home. It assumed that Zionist and socialist fulfillment were interrelated. The idea that political power must precede the transformation of the economic order gave way to a growing realization that a new national economy must be created first, as a means to changing the social system.

In 1921 David Ben-Gurion launched the idea of Hevrat ha-Ovedim, based on the principles of central planning and management of a labor economy, *Histadrut ownership of the means of production and authority over the labor force, centralization of employment and control over wage rates by the Histadrut, central supply and equality in the living standard, "personal labor," and worker participation in management. This program thus was a social and economic platform aiming to create in Palestine a general workers' egalitarian society on cooperative foundations—a commune of all Histadrut members; i.e., to build from scratch a socialist society, without passing through the stages of capitalist construction and class struggle. Following searching debate, however, the program was modified. In 1923, at the second Histadrut Convention, Hevrat ha-Ovedim was established to organize the economic activities of all workers, and develop and expand these activities on the basis of mutual aid and responsibility. It was authorized to coordinate between relevant organizations, direct their activities for the common good of all workers, approve their programs, and supervise their managements. Its articles were approved by the Palestine government in March, 1924, as the constitution of Hevrat ha-Ovedim, the General Cooperative Association of Jewish Labor in Eretz Israel, Ltd.

The massive immigration and rapid urban development of the Fourth Aliya, in which private capital played a dominant role, led many urban workers to abandon pioneer aspirations in favor of current opportunities. From these processes Ben-Gurion concluded that socialist and Zionist fulfillment in the country did not coincide. Thus, rather than a socialist—i.e., planned national—economy, it was necessary to create a "labor economy" for which capitalist market relations existed between its enterprises, institutions, or settlements, and the surrounding economy, and between each other. According to this conception, which endures to this day, Hevrat ha-Ovedim has two main objectives: in the economic sphere to produce national assets and to fulfill a pioneering role in the "conquest of labor" (*see* KIBUSH AVODA), in the social sphere to serve as a strategic basis for the forging and strengthening of the working class.

In the first years of its existence, Hevrat ha-Ovedim was ruled by an expansionary approach which preferred rapid spurts of growth to careful, gradual development. Emphasis was on employment and immigrant absorption, "conquest of labor," and aid to labor settlements, rather than on economic efficiency. There was a feeling of urgency, with respect ot both Zionist fulfillment and reinforcement of the working class. This system of the 1920s was most evident in the overexpansion of the construction company, Solel Boneh, for purposes of expanding employment; but Ha-Mashbir, the wholesale supplier for consumers' cooperative, also expanded aggressively. At the same time, the establishment of new labor settlements, viewed as places for immigrant absorption and training, was given priority over the consolidation of existing ones. By contrast, the workers' bank, *Bank ha-Po'alim, applied from the outset a policy of prudence and economic efficiency. The "heroic" system led to the collapse of Solel Boneh in 1927 and years of crisis and deficits for Ha-Mashbir and the agricultural settlements. Therefore, the Third Histadrut Convention (1927) reexamined the expansionary conception and adopted an economic approach, which attached importance to considerations of economic effectiveness. Expansion was not abandoned, however, and in the following years Hevrat ha-Ovedim undertook national and social missions which often failed to conform to rational economic considerations.

After the establishment of the State of Israel, there was disagreement in the Labor movement concerning which functions should be transferred to the government, and the nationalization of the labor economy. It was resolved to maintain the economic autonomy of the working class by preserving Hevrat ha-Ovedim, since the Histadrut was to continue to combine the functions of trade unions with economic and social roles, and in particular play a "constructive" role in economic development and immigrant absorption. The labor economy would also strengthen the Histadrut on the organizational and trade union levels. The expansionary approach was thus continued, and all sectors and branches of Hevrat ha-Ovedim played an important role in absorption and geographic dispersal, development of agriculture and industry, and consolidation of border and development areas. In 1985, for example, the share of such areas in the activity of Koor, the Histadrut's industrial holding company, was 35% of investments, 29% of employment, and 32% of sales. The policy of maintaining employment caused Solel Boneh another severe crisis in 1985.

According to its social policy, Hevrat ha-Ovedim seeks to reduce wage differentials in its various enterprises and sections, to offer higher pay rates than in the private sector, and to provide better fringe benefits. It likewise endeavors to promote industrial democracy through development of worker participation in management and in profits. The coexistence of a labor economy and trade unions within the Histadrut is not, in general, a hindrance to union activities, but it creates problems for Hevrat ha-Ovedim managers. The realization of development and employment objectives and exemplary wage rates does not always coincide with economic efficiency and success within a competitive environment.

Structure of Hevrat ha-Ovedim. Hevrat ha-Ovedim has two basic components—public enterprises and cooperative societies, differing in their relations with the top management and in their legal form of association. The public concerns, for which Hevrat ha-Ovedim constitutes a roof organization, include those companies owned and controlled, or only controlled, by Hevrat ha-Ovedim, such as Koor Industries, Bank ha-Po'alim, Solel Boneh (construction); and companies in which Hevrat ha-Ovedim is only a partner jointly with the government or the World Zionist Organization (WZO), such as Yakhin-Hakal (agriculture) and Mekorot (water supply). In the cooperative societies, which are controlled by their members, Hevrat ha-Ovedim has direct or indirect rights of intervention on questions of principle. The cooperative economy has three different components: workers' agricultural settlements and their organizations—kibbutzim, moshavim, Ha-Mashbir ha-Merkazi, Tnuva (for marketing agricultural products), regional factories, etc.; the production and transport cooperatives; and the consumers' cooperatives.

Every member of the Histadrut is automatically a member of Hevrat ha-Ovedim. This membership does not constitute an investment in equity shares, but is a right to participate in electing the Convention. The supreme institutions of Hevrat ha-Ovedim are the convention, the council, and the management council, which are identical with the supreme institutions of the Histadrut (Hevrat ha-Ovedim's management council is identical with the Histadrut's executive committee). The executive bodies of the two organizations, however, are separate.

Development of the Main Enterprises. 1. *Ha-Mashbir* was founded in 1916, during World War I, against a background of unemployment, low wages, rising food prices, famine, and want, in order to supply the workers with reasonably priced goods. In 1919 it was also charged with marketing the produce of the labor settlements, a task taken over in 1926 by the newly created *Tnuva,* established on a regional cooperative basis for centralizing, processing, and marketing agricultural produce. In 1930 Ha-Mashbir Ha-Merkazi was founded to replace Ha-Mashbir as a cooperative wholesale supply center for settlements and consumers' societies, and to develop consumer cooperative stores in moshavot and towns. In 1947, in order to add retailing of clothing, footwear, and household items, Ha-Mashbir Ha-Merkazi and the consumers' societies created Ha-Mashbir La-Tzarkhan, which developed into a department store chain. In early 1952 Ha-Mashbir la-Oleh ("Ha-Mashbir for the immigrant") began to function as a common institution of Ha-Mashbir ha-Merkazi and of the consumers' societies, working in the *ma'abarot* and assisting in immigrant absorption. In the new moshav settlements, Ha-Mashbir la-Oleh established cooperative stores, supplied producer inputs, credit, etc. The infrastructure which it established served as a basis for the purchasing organizations of the moshavim in the following years. In the 1940s Ha-Mashbir ha-Merkazi began to establish and acquire industrial enterprises, including over the years the Shemen edible oil factory, the Selilim textile factory, flour mills etc., and in 1959 these enterprises were grouped in the framework of an industrial management. In 1985 the activity of labor economy marketing and supply agencies was as follows: Ha-Mashbir ha-Merkazi had six branches, including four in development areas. Total wholesale sales were $495 million, including 52% agricultural supply, 21% food and groceries, 8% technical and building equipment, 7% textiles, footwear and leather, and 12% other products. The consumers' societies had 217 branches throughout Israel, including 61 in development areas. Their sales totaled about $310 million in food products and groceries. Ha-Mashbir la-Tzarkhan had 21 branches, including 6 in development areas, with sales totaling $71 million— 62% clothing, textiles, footwear and leather goods and 38% others. Tnuva's wholesale sales totaled $730 million, while retail sales stood at $77 million, all of foodstuffs.

2. *Solel Boneh.* In early 1921, after the foundation of the Histadrut, two contracting offices became the Public Works and Building Office, which fulfilled a vital role in absorbing the pioneers of the Third Aliya. Initially the Office executed infrastructural works, such as roads and railroads; subsequently it undertook construction works in the towns and in labor settlements. The scope and variety of the Office's activities made it a central agency in the building sector of the yishuv until 1924, when Solel Boneh, the Jewish Workers Cooperative Association for Public Works, Building, and Manufacture Ltd. was founded. With its activity in these branches, Solel Boneh occupied a prominent role in the building sector in Palestine. In 1927 the company collapsed, principally due to a narrow capital base and over-expansion of its business activities. In place of Solel Boneh, contracting offices were established in 1927–1928 in several towns, and from 1929 the *Hanhalat ha-Avodot* operated in rural areas. In 1935 Solel Boneh was re-established in place of Hanhalat ha-Avodot and in the course of the following years it gradually united with the contracting offices, rapidly becoming the leading building contractor in Palestine, participating in all major settlement and defense projects of the yishuv. Solel Boneh also contributed to the Allied war effort in and beyond the bounds of Palestine, with construction works during World War II in neighboring countries—Syria, Lebanon, Iraq, etc. In the early 1940s Solel Boneh began industrial development, with the establishment and purchase, in the first half of the decade, of a series of factories: the Phoenicia glass works, the Vulcan foundries, and the Hamat metal works. In order to coordinate the activities of the Histadrut's industrial firms and to further their development, the Koor industrial holding company was created in 1944 as a subsidiary of Solel Boneh. After the creation of the State, Solel Boneh

filled an important role in public building for immigrant absorption and in developing infrastructure. From 1949 to 1957 it built 154,500 housing units. In addition to construction in Israel, Solel Boneh expanded its overseas activities, working extensively from 1957 in various countries of Africa; in different periods its projects extended over three continents—Asia, Africa and South America. Koor worked in the first decade of the State to bring industry to all areas of the country and to introduce new branches. Many of its plants were established in development and immigrant absorption areas, and despite the difficulties involved it endeavored to develop primary branches of industry— such as steel and chemical works.

With Solel Boneh's rapid development and growth after the creation of the State, difficulties in the functioning of its management and in the ability of Hevrat ha-Ovedim to impose its authority made reorganization of the company imperative. In 1958 it was split into three companies: Building and Public Works, Overseas and Harbor Works, and Industry. In 1963 the Building and Public Works Company and the Overseas Works Company reunited in the framework of Solel Boneh.

In 1985 Solel Boneh employed about 14,000 workers and carried out projects totaling $418 million in Israel, representing 12% of activity in the building sector in this country. Overseas the company's turnover in 1985 was about $200 million.

3. *Koor.* Since 1958 Koor has worked independently of Solel Boneh. Toward the end of the 1960s it was reorganized in order to adapt to the scope of activity and to diversify; factory groupings were consolidated in the branches of steel, chemicals, glass, ceramics, etc. In 1968 the company's name was changed from Koor Hevrat Haroshet u-Melakha to Koor Ta'asiyot (Koor Industries). Koor sales in 1985 totaled $1,847 million, with outstanding production in the branches: electronics and electricity, $721 million (39%); food and soft drinks, $223 million (12%); metal products, $207 million (11%); non-metal minerals, $202 million (11%); chemicals and medicine, $200 million (11%); base metals, $113 million (6%) and rubber and plastics, $103 million (6%). Koor exports in the same year, primarily electronic and electrical products, chemicals, and metal products, stood at $559 million. In 1985 Koor investments totaled $182 million and the number of employees stood at 33,540. The scope and diversity of Koor's activities has made it an important factor in the Israeli economy in general and in industry in particular. In 1985 it represented 13.5% of industrial sales in Israel, 13% of industrial exports, 17% of industrial investments, and 11% of employees in industry.

4. *Ti'us* was established by the government and Hevrat ha-Ovedim in 1958 in order to create sources of employment for residents of the development towns. In 1967 Hevrat ha-Ovedim purchased the government's share of the company. In 1985 Ti'us sales totaled $33 million, principally in the textile branch.

5. *Bank ha-Po'alim.* The need for a financial institution of the workers to assist production and settlement activity was recognized during the Second Aliya. Arthur Ruppin's motion calling for the creation of Bank ha-Po'alim was approved at the Zionist General Council in 1919, and the bank came into being (with WZO financing) in 1921 with the principal aim of assisting development and consolidation of cooperatives and labor enterprises; it was to be a major tool for the establishment of a labor economy. In the following years Bank ha-Po'alim served as a central credit institute for the various sectors of the labor economy—rural settlement, building, industry, marketing and consumers' societies. It did not, however, serve the individual worker, and to meet this need a network of credit cooperatives, loans and savings societies in towns and moshavot, was started in 1925 and rapidly expanded. In 1956, 25 such associations existed, with 32 branches and 132,000 members. In the 1950s Bank ha-Po'alim merged with these associations. In 1985 Bank ha-Po'alim had an extensive network of 259 branches throughout Israel, a total balance of $21,962 million, $17,550 million in loans to the public, deposits and loan deposits of $15,085 million and $639 million in equity capital. Its net profit was $54 million. In the Israeli banking system Bank ha-Po'alim ranked second after Bank Le'umi in 1985, while in the number of branches and in loans to the public and to the government it stood in first place. In addition to its activity in Israel, Bank ha-Po'alim is active on an international scale, maintaining a network of branches throughout the USA, Canada, Great Britain, Switzerland, France, and Latin America. Subsidiary companies include: *Bank Otzar ha-Hayal* (services to the defense forces); *Bank Yahav* (for civil servants); *Bank Masad* (for employees in education); *Mishkan—Bank ha-Po'alim* Mortgage Bank; the *Workers' Bank Investment Corporation*; and **Ampal*—American-Israel Corporation (fundraising in the US for investments).

6. *Ha-Sneh.* The Ha-Sneh ("The Bush") insurance company was founded in 1924 on the initiative of a group of public figures of the yishuv. Since it proved difficult to place the shares with the general public, most of them were sold to two private capitalists. In 1927 Ha-Sneh was purchased by Hevrat ha-Ovedim in partnership with the *Yidisher Natsionaler Arbeter Farband* (the US mutual aid society). In 1938 a reorganization of Ha-Sneh equity capital brought the company under Hevrat ha-Ovedim control. In the first years of Hevrat ha-Ovedim ownership, Ha-Sneh dealt with life insurance only, expanding in 1936 to coverage of other branches—fire, personal accidents, etc. Since its creation Ha-Sneh has augmented its turnover, absorbed and established a series of subsidiary companies, and become the largest insurance group in Israel. In 1985 the combined balance of the company totaled $555 million (25% of insurance sector activity in Israel); gross life insurance premiums stood at $71 million (21% of insurance sector activity in Israel); gross basic insurance premiums totaled $271 million (37% of insurance sector activity in Israel) and the combined equity capital was $31 million (26% of the insurance branch in Israel).

7. *Shikun Ovedim.* The idea of organized workers' housing engaged the Histadrut from the outset and in 1927 at the Third Histadrut Convention the need for institutionalized housing initiatives was acknowledged. In early 1928 the Workers' Housing Center was established in order to spread the idea of workers' housing, to organize the homesteaders and represent them before the municipalities, national institutions, and the government; to acquire land, deal with financial questions and neighborhood planning, etc. In 1935 the Housing Center was replaced by Shikun, Workmen's Housing Company Ltd., which was registered as a subsidiary company of Hevrat ha-Ovedim. Shikun, which worked mainly in the cities, constructed large workers' neighborhoods: Kiryat Hayim and Kiryat Amal on the outskirts of Haifa and Kiryat Avoda, the nucleus of the city of Holon, near Tel Aviv. In the course of its activity, from 1928

to 1954, the company built 24,850 apartments. As Shikun worked principally in the urban sector and lacked the means to expand into rural areas, the Neveh Oved company was founded in 1944 to provide housing for laborers in the moshavot, building 14,000 apartments up to the end ot 1954. After the creation of the State the two companies built for both new immigrants and veteran Israelis. In 1954 Shikun and Neveh Oved were merged to form Shikun Ovedim. Shikun Ovedim works in the following fields: purchase of lands for construction, promotion of construction, planning, registration, supervision, and sales of residential and commercial units. It undertakes low-income residential construction in development towns, in suburbs, and in cities. At the same time, construction of luxury residences is a source of finance for its socially orientated projects. In 1985 Shikun Ovedim commenced construction of 1,283 housing units, completed 1,213 units, and had 3,122 units under construction.

Hevrat ha-Ovedim and the World Zionist Organization. Extensive cooperation has always existed between Hevrat Ha-Ovedim and the WZO and its Funds, first of all in the promotion of cooperative and collective agricultural settlement. The WZO provided capital for the establishment of Bank ha-Po'alim, holding preferential powers on its Board of Directors until 1948. In the early 1920s the WZO helped the Office for Public Works to receive works, through provision of credit and guarantees. On the creation of Solel Boneh in 1924 the WZO provided part of the founding capital, and in 1926 organized a banking consortium to prevent the company's bankruptcy. The Zionist Executive also came to the assistance of Ha-Mashbir in the mid-1920s. This assistance to labor enterprises stemmed from recognition of their contribution to the realization of the Zionist endeavor.

In addition, joint enterprises were established by the WZO and Hevrat ha-Ovedim. In 1936 the Jewish Agency and Hevrat ha-Ovedim together founded *Bitzur* in order to create sources of employment. Following the creation of the State, Bitzur concentrated mainly on financing housing and public buildings in labor settlements. In 1959 the company's shares were purchased by Bank ha-Po'alim. 1936 also saw the founding of *Aviron* by the Jewish Agency and the Histadrut. This company, with its small fleet of planes which flew to the neighboring countries and even to Europe, played an important role in training pilots. After the creation of the State the Aviron company ceased to exist. In 1937 *Mekorot* was established by the Jewish Agency and the Jewish National Fund on the one hand, and by the Histadrut and the settlements on the other (*see* WATER AND THE UTILIZATION OF WATER IN ISRAEL) to develop water sources and supply. In 1957 the government became the chief partner of Mekorot. 1945 saw the founding of *Hakal*, Contracting Company for Agricultural Work in the Moshavot, by Yakhin, acting for the Histadrut and by PASA (Palestine Agricultural Settlement Association Ltd.), an organ of the WZO. In 1952 Yakhin and Hakal merged, becoming *Yakhin-Hakal*, under the joint ownership of Hevrat ha-Ovedim and the WZO. In 1945 the *Zim* Shipping Company was founded by the Histadrut in partnership with the Jewish Agency and *Hevel Yami le-Yisrael*. In the course of time, the company changed hands and it is now no longer owned by its founders.

Y. GREENBERG

LABOR FORCE IN ISRAEL, 1948–1984.

Definitions and Statistical Sources. The labor force is the stock of employed and unemployed in the economy during a specified period of time, generally a week. Young people under the legal working age (14 in Israel) and soldiers in the regular army (compulsory and standing) are not included in the labor force, but reserve duty soldiers, who occupy a regular place of employment, are. Also included in the labor force are persons temporarily absent from a regular job for other reasons.

Since 1954, Israel's Central Bureau of Statistics has prepared labor force estimates through surveys based on interviews with sample households. Since 1970, similar surveys have been conducted in the Administered Areas, both as regards those employed in the occupied areas and those working within Israel. Labor force estimates for the period prior to 1954 are based on information gathered from various sources.

Growth of the Labor Force (table 1): In 1984 the Israeli labor force numbered 1,444 million persons.

The most important event in its post-1948 history was its unprecedented growth between 1948 and 1951, at an annual average rate of 37 percent, so that by the end of 1951 the size of the labor force was 2.6 times what it had been at the end of 1948. This was a direct result of mass immigration, and of the release from the army of the 1948 veterans. This inordinate growth dictated a major part of the challenges to the labor market, and to the economy in general, for at least ten years. Firstly, employment had to be provided for the labor force; secondly, the occupational structure of the labor force, which included a high percentage of immigrants educated and trained abroad, had to be adapted to local market need and a vast training network was built. Thirdly, there was an effort to establish for the adult population a common language, and more broadly—a social and cultural common denominator through a network of adult schools.

These problems constituted a major cause for the steep decline in immigration between the years 1952–1954. Its renewal after 1955 was on a smaller scale, and up until 1973, the labor force annual growth rate remained at 3.7 percent. There were certain oscillations, caused by the economic recession of 1966–1967, and the entrance of workers from the Administered Areas into the Israeli labor market after the Six-Day War. After 1973 there was a further decline in the growth rate to 2.6 percent. Thus, the period 1955–1984 is characterized by a gradual decline in the labor force growth rate, together with the entrance of an increasingly large number of new members originating in the local population, so that the process of adapting labor market demands to the structure of the labor force became easier. Hence the developments in the labor market increasingly reflect internal changes in the economy, rather than immigrants' absorption. On the one hand, they mirror economic growth, developments connected with defense, the balance of payments and inflation, while on the other hand, they are influenced by changes in the educational and demographic structure of the local population.

Labor Force Participation Rates (tables 2 and 4): In 1984 the labor force constituted 50 percent of the working age population (14+). This percentage, which is considerably lower than the 57 percent characteristic of industrialized countries of Europe and North America is explained by the low participation level of both men and women, particularly in the age bracket 15 to 24. This, in turn, can be attributed mainly to the education system and army service. (Some of the difference, however, is compensated for by the fact that

TABLE 1
LOCAL LABOR FORCE,[a] DEGREE OF EMPLOYMENT, AND STANDING ARMY

			Israeli Civilian Labor Force Percentages			
Years	*Aver. Annual Growth Rate of Overall Labor Force* *(1)*	*Year*	*Unemployed* *(2)*	*Temporarily Absent*[c] *(3)*	*Part-Workers*[d] *(4)*	*Standing Army*[e] *(5)*
		1949(b)	18.7	. .	. .	. .
1948–1951	37.0					
		1951(b)	9.1	. .	. .	. .
1952–1954	2.3					
		1955	7.4	3.9	16.5	. .
1955–1965	3.7	1961	3.6	5.6	17.4	. .
		1965	3.6	5.5	15.8	4.4
1966–1967	0.8	1967	10.4	6.6	19.5	7.6
1968–1972	4.0	1972	2.8	5.7	16.1	6.8
1973–1984	2.6	1983	4.5	9.2	25.4	11.5

[a] Local labor force is the total Israeli civilian labor force plus the labor force from the administered areas employed in Israel—data on the latter from 1970 onwards. The percentage of employees in full-time employment is 100 minus the sum of columns (2) + (3) + (4).
[b] Includes estimate of potential labor force among residents of the immigrant camps.
[c] Generally employed, but absent from their work in the last week for reasons of illness, vacation, or army reserve duty.
[d] Employed 15–34 hours a week. Employees working 35 + hours a week are defined as full-time workers.
[e] The standing army is not included in the civilian labor force.

Sources: Columns (1)–(4): The Central Bureau of Statistics, *Statistical Yearbooks.* Column (5): The International Institute for Strategic Studies, *The Military Balance* (Various years).

TABLE 2
AGE-SEX-EDUCATION STRUCTURE OF THE POPULATION AGED 14+ AND OF THE ISRAELI CIVILIAN LABOR FORCE 1955–1983 (percentages)

		Age Group							
		All Ages (14+)	*14–17*	*18–24*	*25–34*	*35–44*	*45–54*	*55–65*	*65+*
A. Division of Population by Age									
1955		100.0		23.6	22.4	19.5	12.6	14.5	7.4
1973		100.0		29.7	18.0	15.2	14.1	12.9	10.1
1983		100.0		25.2	23.7	15.3	12.2	11.0	12.6
B. Division of Civilian Labor Force by Age									
1955		100.0	6.4	40.6		41.1		9.1	2.8
1973		100.0	4.5	18.0	24.0	18.9	17.7	14.8	2.9
1983		100.0	2.7	13.5	32.2	21.5	15.9	10.9	3.5
C. Proportion of Population's Participation in Labor Force[a]		all 14+							
1955	Women	26.5	31.7	32.2		26.2		17.0	5.1
	Men	80.1	42.2	80.9		96.4		82.3	38.3
1973	Women	31.4	15.8	45.5	38.7	34.8	35.7	25.0	5.7
	Men	68.3	23.8	45.5	89.5	93.6	93.9	86.5	33.1
1983	Women	36.6	8.7	37.2	55.1	53.5	45.4	26.4	5.9
	Men	63.5	14.5	42.2	84.0	91.1	89.9	78.3	24.1

D. Composition of Labor Force by Level of Education and by Sex[b]

	% Women in Labor Force	Years of Study of Labor Force		
		0–8	9–12	13+
1955	24.5	—	—	—
1961	27.5	51.7	35.3	13.0
1973	31.4	34.6	45.1	20.5
1983	37.2	23.5	47.8	28.7

[a] Labor force in age group as percentage of the population of that group.
[b] Labor force in age group as percentage of total labor force.
Source: Manpower surveys, and 1961 population census.

the participation rate of the 55+ group is higher in Israel.)

The proportion of the total population, including children, in the labor force in Israel is 34 percent as compared with 46 percent in industrialized countries. It reflects, in addition, the relatively higher percentage of the 0–15 age group in Israel. The overall low participation rate in the labor force means that a worker, on average, supports more people, resulting in a lower per capita standard of living.

Between 1955 and 1984 some changes occurred in the overall labor force participation rates, but these are secondary in importance to the far-reaching changes in the participation rates of specific population groups. In particular, female participation rose from 26.5 percent in 1955 to 37.6 percent in 1984. At the same time male participation fell from 80.1 to 63.2 percent. These trends are reflected in a change in the labor force compostion: the percentage of women rose from 24.5 to 37.2 in the aforesaid period.

Likewise the participation rates in the 14–17 and 18–24 age groups fell, parallel with the rise in the percentage of students in these groups; accordingly the percentage of young people in the labor force fell. All these changes are characteristic of the majority of developed countries and lead to an older labor force, with a higher percentage of women.

Unemployment: (tables 1 and 4). In the period of mass immigration and immediately thereafter, unemployment was very high, but already by the late 1950s it dropped to a rate considered low by any standard. This was a reflection of a very successful growth process within all sectors of the economy. A recession in the mid-1960s caused a social upheaval which resulted in a commitment to full employment by all subsequent governments until 1985. Thus, the slower pace of economic growth, from 1973 onwards, had no effect on unemployment until 1979, and between then and 1985—only a moderate one. Many other factors, besides explicit economic policies, helped to maintain near-full employment.

The percentage of the labor force (both male and female) temporarily absent from work rose from 5.6 percent in 1972 to 9.2 percent in 1983. Part of this increase stems from the greater number of women, particularly married with young children in the labor force: women tend to be absent from work slightly more often than men. Among men there has been an increase in absenteeism due to lengthening of the period of army reserve duty.

Another factor moderating unemployment was the rise in the number of part-time workers in the labor force (from 16.1 percent in 1972 to 25.4 percent in 1983), reflecting the growing percentage of women in the labor force and the increased percentage of workers in part-time employment, within each sex group.

Yet another factor contributing to low unemployment is the growth of the standing army. Its ratio to the civilian labor force rose from 4.4 percent in 1965 to 6.8 percent in 1972, and 11.5 percent in 1983. The expansion of the education system also tempered the growth of the labor force and unemployment. Last, there was a considerable expansion in public-sector employment, at times when almost no increase occurred in the private sector. All these factors created a situation, whereby economic stagnation was not accompanied by unemployment until the early 1980s. Only since 1985 has the government abandoned its full employment commitment.

Industrial Structure (tables 3 and 4): Some of the changes in this structure reflect the characteristic traits of economic growth in general: a fall in the proportion of the labor force employed in agriculture, and a rise in high-tech industry and service employment. But the Israeli experience differs from the general one in two respects: a major effort made in the 1950s to increase the proportion of labor employed in agriculture; and a high proportion employed in public services, exceeding that expected on the basis of economic development alone.

Agriculture: In contrast to most developing economies, in which the percentage employed in agriculture decreases over time, Israel in the 1950s expanded its agricultural employment. This was done for ideological reasons traditional in the Zionist movement. Moreover, agriculture was a convenient sector for absorbing immigrants: arable land was available due to Arab evacuation; there was a strong infrastructure of planning, training, and marketing, which could handle immigrants' absorption in employment on a large scale; and there was a shortage in food supply. However, already in the early 1960s, when the initial immigrant absorption had been accomplished, agricultural employment declined, and in 1983 it accounted for only 6% of total employment.

Public Services: An international comparison reveals that the percentage of total civilian employment in Israel's public services—30 percent in 1984—is one of the highest in the world. The military component should be added to this figure.

The civilian "surplus" of public services reflects the far-reaching influence of the country's balance of payments deficit: here the relevant distinction is between employment in tradables—exports and import substitutes, and non-tradables, such as public services. Israel's external deficit enables it to produce less tradables, part of which it receives gratis, and to concentrate on the production of non-tradables, particularly public services and residential construction.

The high proportion employed in public services further reflects the social priorities of the country: high standards of education, health, and housing. Last, since 1973 it also served as a preventive measure against potential unemployment. Today the effort to cut public services employment is part of the government's economic policy.

Manufacturing: The percentage of employed in this sector has remained stable throughout the period, but there has been a shift towards high-tech industries. While these have become a major export sector, their contribution to employment is not very large: they account for 8 percent of total employment.

Workers from the Administered Areas. Since 1968 Israel has been open to Arab workers living in the Administered Areas. While they account for a third to a half of total employment of the territories' labor force, their ratio to the Israeli labor force is small— only 7%. Their percentage in specific industries is, however, much higher; in particular, they constitute a large part of the labor force in construction, agriculture, and some services.

Quality of the Labor Force. It is difficult to construct appropriate indices to measure changes in the quality of the labor force. As an approximation, differences in salary between various kinds of workers are held to represent differences in quality. On this assumption, the principal factors which raise the quality of the labor force are the level of education and work experience. The latter is estimated indirectly through age, length of time in Israel (indicating local market experience), and sex (at any given age women accumulate, on average, less work experience than men). Table 2 shows the principal developments in these variables: there was a steep rise in the level of education, in the proportion of women in the labor force, and in the length of time in Israel.

The average level of education of the population dropped considerably in the early 1950s, due to the lower average of the arriving immigrants. A reversal was registered from the early 1960s, partly because the immigrants arriving in the 1960s and particularly in the 1970s, had a higher level of education than the local population; but principally because of the extremely rapid expansion in school attendance in all age groups. The education level of the labor force rose at a more rapid pace than that of the general population, since the tendency to join the labor force increases with education.

With regards to accumulation of work experience, several forces worked in diverging directions. The influence of the age element was not regular and cancels itself out. But the higher proportion of women in the labor force reduced the

TABLE 3
BRANCH STRUCTURE OF LOCAL WORKERS[a]

	1951	*1955*	*1961*	*1964*	*1967*	*1968*[b] *Old Classification*	*1968*[b] *New Classification*	*1972*	*1983*
Agriculture	13.8	17.5	17.1	12.9	12.6	11.4	10.4	8.7	6.0
Industry (A)[c]	23.5	15.8	16.4	17.5	18.1	16.8	18.1	16.6	14.3
Industry (B)[c]		5.5	7.3	7.9	8.0	9.2	5.9	6.8	8.2
Construction, electric., water	9.5	11.3	10.9	12.0	9.8	10.3	9.3	12.3	10.1
Transport	7.0	6.6	6.3	7.6	7.3	7.3	7.5	6.9	6.1
Business & Financial Services[d]		1.7	2.1	2.9	2.9	3.0	4.9	5.4	8.9
Commerce, entertainment & personal services	28.0	20.6	17.1	17.4	17.2	18.4	21.3	20.3	18.6
Public and Community Services[d]	18.2	21.0	22.8	21.8	24.1	23.6	22.6	23.0	27.8

[a] Includes, from 1972, residents from the administered areas working in Israel, with the industrial workers being attributed to industry (A); data on agricultural and construction workers exist separately. The other workers were attributed to commerce, entertainment, and personal services.
[b] The new branch classification drawn up in 1968 appears here from 1972. Details are given in notes c and d.
[c] Industry (B) is hi-tech, and includes printing and publishing, chemistry and oil, machinery, electricity and haulage equipment. Industry (A) covers all the rest. The detailed classification was changed in 1968, and this accounts for the drop in industry (B) between 1967 and 1972.
[d] Business services were included up to 1968 in public services, and thenceforth were combined with financial services. The trends from 1967 to 1972 are a result of the changes in classification.
Sources: Manpower surveys, and statistical yearbooks; and Klinov (1984).

level of experience. Lastly, experience in the Israeli market alone (as distinct from experience acquired abroad) increased, as the scope of immigration declined. These influences on the experience level offset each other and the main changes in the quality of the labor force are those originating from the increased level of education.

Conclusion. Generally speaking, two periods may be distinguished in the development of the labor force. During the first period, 1948–73, particularly in the 1950s, the labor force grew rapidly, and the absorption of the burgeoning labor force in employment, while at the same time increasing per capita production, was the major achievement of the Israeli economy. The labor market reached full employment as early as 1961, and this was maintained, with certain exceptions, up to the 1980s.

Since 1973, however, unemployment was prevented by mechanisms other than those at work previously: the proportion of the labor force serving in the army, working part-time, or temporarily absent from work increased, as did employment in civilian public services. The rise in the level of education of the labor force and the development of high-tech industry constituted the major achievements during this period.

Both the successes and the difficulties originated from the combined influence of three factors: education, foreign aid, and defense. The attendance rates in secondary and in post-secondary schools and universities are among the highest in the world, even when compared with developed countries; the result is an increase in the quality of the labor force and the development of high-tech industries, but another consequence is the excessive weight of public services in employment. Israel's heavy defense burden is an obstacle to growth and is responsible for much of Israel's external debt, though it did contribute to the reduction of unemployment and to the development of high-tech industry.

R. KLINOV

LABOR ZIONISM. Groups and parties in organized Zionism which are committed to the development of a Socialist form of society in Israel, socialism being interpreted in its broadest sense.

These parties and formations include *Ahdut Avoda, *Ha-Po'el ha-Tza'ir, *Ha-Shomer ha-Tza'ir, *Hitahdut, *Ihud Olami, *Israel Labor party, *Mapai, *Mapam, *Po'ale Zion, and *Tze'irei Zion.

Development of the Labor Zionist Movement. The second half of the 19th century was an epoch-making period in Jewish history. Migration, economic mobility, and social relocation, assuming proportions rarely experienced by Jews in the past, were revising the map of the Jewish world. The whole rhythm of Jewish living had undergone drastic alteration, and the traditional Jewish community structure was shaken to its foundations. The position of the Jew in the state of which he was an inhabitant shifted radically, and his relations with the non-Jewish world took on new forms. In the wake of these changes, there had arisen a number of movements which revolutionized Jewish life and produced a renaissance that was to culminate in the birth of the State of Israel. Among the movements were those which were

TABLE 4
INTERNATIONAL COMPARISONS (1979–1980)

	Labor force as % of pop.				*Employees in services*		
	Total	*Men*	*Women*	*Unemployment as % of labor force** *(aver. 1978–1982)*	*Public & personal*	*Business & financial*	*Employees in scientific, liberal and technical professions*
					(% of total employed)		
	(1)	*(2)*	*(3)*	*(4)*	*(5)*	*(6)*	*(7)*
Canada	47.7	58.5	37.0	8.3	34.5	5.0	14.7
USA	47.7	57.4	38.5	7.5	30.3	8.0	15.0
Japan	48.8	60.2	36.2	2.2	17.5	6.8	9.0
Belgium	42.1	54.1	30.7	(10.4)	27.8	6.1	. .
Denmark	51.3	58.5	44.3	(11.4)	33.2	7.0	17.0
France	43.3	54.4	32.7	6.9	23.7	6.8	
Germany	44.9	58.4	32.6	(4.2)	22.5	5.5	13.4
Italy	40.2	55.2	26.0	8.1	18.4	2.3	
Holland	37.7	52.9	22.8	(7.8)	28.2	6.8	16.2
Norway	46.9	55.9	38.0	2.1	29.5	5.7	18.6
Sweden	51.5	57.4	45.7	2.4	34.7	6.7	25.8
Gt. Britain	47.1	58.9	35.9	(8.8)	26.8	5.7	
Average	45.8	57.1	34.8	6.7	26.2	6.3	16.1
Israel: Labor Force							
Israel	34.0	43.1	24.8	4.2	35.8	8.2	22.6
Local	. .	. .	. .	. .	37.5	7.6	. .

*The figures not appearing in parentheses are estimates according to manpower surveys: those in parentheses correspond to employment service estimates. In countries where both systems of estimates exist, manpower surveys give a higher rate of unemployment.
Source: 1981, *ILO, Yearbook of Labor Statistics;* Unemployment—Bruno (1985).

based on faith in the redemptive power of the ordinary Jew and which relied on mass effort rather than divine intervention to cure social and national ills.

Although all these movements originated in a reawakening of Jewish initiative, from the beginning they divided into two main streams, one flowing in the direction of Zionism and the other in the direction of international socialism. The Zionists viewed the Jewish problem as a national problem, to be solved by the normalization of Jewish national life in a Jewish State in Eretz Israel. Socialists, on the other hand, saw the Jewish problem merely as a reflection of the evils of capitalism, which would automatically disappear once the prevailing economic system had been replaced by a classless society. The difference in approach and aims created a gulf between the two trends. It was this gulf that Labor Zionism set out to bridge.

The need for a movement to synthesize Zionism and socialism was proved by the spontaneous rise of Po'ale Zion groups in various parts of the world. The first group appeared in Minsk, Russia, in 1900. A few years later, groups were functioning in Galicia, Austria, Germany, England, and the United States. That they were making headway is indicated by the fact that the fifth convention of the *Bund (Jewish Socialist Workers party) found it necessary to pass a resolution opposing Zionism of all shades. There was at first no contact or coordination among the Labor Zionist groups, and their programs lacked clarity and sound theoretical grounding. While feeling their way toward the wider Jewish community, they were torn asunder internally by the struggle between those who could see Eretz Israel alone as the land of the future Jewish State and those who would have accepted the use of another territory as the Jewish National Homeland. Under the leadership of Ber *Borochov, this conflict was resolved in favor of Eretz Israel at a convention of the Russian Po'ale Zion in Poltava in 1906. A similar position was taken by the American Po'ale Zion and by Labor Zionist groups elsewhere.

In 1907, at a convention in The Hague, the various Po'ale Zion groups founded a world union which was solidly grounded in Eretz Israel and left no room for *Territorialism. The adherents of Territorialism organized the Socialist-Territorialist movements. The oldest Labor Zionist groups were augmented by groups which had never been associated with the parties of the Hague union (Ha-Po'el ha-Tza'ir, Tze'irei Zion, Ha-Shomer ha-Tza'ir; Ahdut Avoda joined the Hague union and was to lead the right wing in the 1920 split discussed below). What most of the groups shared was the conviction that Jewish national redemption could not be separated from the movements aiming at the liberation of the oppressed classes of all nations, that a Jewish State must give rise to a cooperative society, and that it could be built only by the labor of the Jews themselves. The question of how to achieve these basic objectives led to serious divisions and sharp conflicts which resulted in splits, regroupings, and protracted struggles. The differences of opinion crystallized into three main trends, identified with the three greatest names in Labor Zionist history: Ber Borochov, Nachman *Syrkin, and Aharon David *Gordon.

Influence of Borochov. Borochov interpreted Zionism in Marxian terms, but his was not a mechanical application of Marxian theories to Jewish reality. He filled a gap in these theories by showing the interrelationship of national conflicts and class struggles. Proceeding from this interrelationship, he showed how each class within the Jewish people was affected by the lack of a Jewish geographic center and pointed out the significance of the creation of a Jewish State for each. This fact determined the role of the classes in the realization of Zionism, which was historically inevitable because it responded to the specific socioeconomic needs of each stratum of the Jewish people while solving the problem of homelessness for the people as a whole. The class struggle was thus the instrument which created the Jewish State, and the role of the working class was not only to contribute its share to the building of the State but also to transform the State into a strategic base for the advance to socialism.

The Russian Po'ale Zion and their followers in other lands, who preferred to call themselves Social Democrats, accepted Borochov's program in full. This colored their relations with the World Zionist Organization (WZO), which they regarded as the instrument of the Jewish bourgeoisie in the process of creating the State. The Jewish working classes, it was contended, had no place in the WZO and had to retain freedom of action through their own organizations.

Influence of Syrkin and Gordon. Syrkin, too, accepted the basic tenets of Marxism, but with two far-reaching reservations. In the first place, he attributed greater significance to moral values as a motivating force in social processes. While Borochov based his prognosis on objective factors only, Syrkin laid greater stress on subjective forces and free will. He felt that Marxian methods of bringing about social revolution, while applicable to normal nations, could not be applied to a unique people like the Jews.

All Jewish classes, he maintained, shared a common vision of salvation of which Zionism was both symbol and practical expression. There was inherent in Zionism itself a universal promise which lifted it from the level of a mere nationalist movement to the lofty heights of a great social ideal. As against the Borochovist contention that Zionism would be realized through class struggle or not at all, Syrkin insisted that there could be no Zionism other than Socialist Zionism. The fight for socialism implied more than a direct combative confrontation between labor and capital. Since Jewish settlement in Palestine had neither the budgets of government nor the resources of private investment to back it, it could draw only on the so-called national capital, the funds raised by the Jewish people through Zionist institutions. The circumstance that these funds were contributed not for private gain but for national and social service offered Jewish labor the opportunity to build the Jewish Homeland as a cooperative commonwealth.

This approach was the common ground on which Syrkin and Gordon met in Zionism. Gordon was not a Socialist in the accepted meaning of the term. To him the complete and creative blending of man and nature was the highest social ideal. Only through labor—labor not merely as a means of deriving a livelihood but as an act of self-expression—could this unity be achieved. The closer a laborer was to the soil, the nearer he was to bringing his inner self into the sphere of social fulfillment. Where there were no individual involvement and commitment, there could be no community of interests. Gordon was opposed to organizational affiliation with international socialism, which both Borochov and Syrkin favored, because Jewish labor, facing tasks no other labor movement in the world had ever faced before, had to find its own way of combining social goals with national aspirations and of forging new human relationships. The *kibbutz was the concrete result of this combination, merging as it did practical functions with the opening of new social frontiers. It paved the way toward the ultimate in human striving: universal harmony.

Gordon was neither a writer nor a systematic thinker of the type of Syrkin and Borochov. His influence was direct and intimate, however. By his own emigration to Eretz Israel, where he turned farm worker at the age of nearly 50, he became a living example of the *hagshama atzmit* (self-fulfillment) he advocated. Labor Zionist parties such as Ha-Po'el ha-Tza'ir in Palestine and Tze'irei Zion in the Diaspora came closest to making his views the cornerstone of their ideologies. His influence extended also to the other parties in Labor Zionism, including those whose social orientation was directly opposed to his conceptions. Those parties frequently moved along Gordonian lines in their practical work even if they rejected the Gordonian philosophy. In general, it may be said that all three trends in Labor Zionism were interrelated and converged at one point or another.

Divisions in the Movement. The issues dividing the movement were exacerbated by the conflicts in international socialism, which separated it into two warring camps following the rise of the Soviet Union and the emergence of the Third (Communist) International. This division made a split in the Po'ale Zion ranks unavoidable, and one took place at a world conference held in Vienna in 1920. Two distinct federations of Po'ale Zion parties emerged from that conference. The Right Po'ale Zion, headed by the group in Palestine that assumed the name Ahdut Avoda, proceeded to translate into action the theories of Syrkin and Borochov, as broadened and synthesized by Berl *Katznelson, into a program that became known as Socialist constructionism. They intensified their building of kibbutzim and industrial and commercial cooperatives and established a network of cultural and political institutions that laid the foundation of the future State of Israel.

The Left Po'ale Zion evinced an ideological affinity for communism as the surest and shortest road to the realization of the aims of socialism. It also followed Borochov's early ideas about the division of labor among the various Jewish classes and their parties in the building of the Jewish State. According to these ideas, which Borochov was in the process of revising at the time of his death, the role of the working class was one of liberation rather than of upbuilding. Since upbuilding, he argued in his first works, required capital, political concessions, and international support, which only the bourgeoisie could provide in a capitalist world, it followed that the function of the working class was to supply the labor power, to safeguard and expand its economic interests, and to guide the building of the Jewish State into progressive channels.

In keeping with these theories, the Left Po'ale Zion concentrated most of their energies on political work. They did not participate in the Zionist Congresses and took very little part in creating kibbutzim or similar institutions in Palestine. On the other hand, they were a most active group within the Labor Zionist camp in the economic, political, and cultural life of Diaspora Jewry, as well as in the general social affairs of countries where Jews were living. They were also the greatest devotees of the Yiddish language and leaders in the fight for the place of Yiddish in Palestine and later in the State of Israel.

In 1930 Ahdut Avoda amalgamated with Ha-Po'el ha-Tza'ir in Palestine and together they formed the Mapai party, which emerged as the leading political force in the yishuv and, subsequently, in the State of Israel. In 1944 a group seceded from Mapai and organized itself into a new party under the old name Ahdut Avoda. It gained considerable influence by virtue of its leadership in the Kibbutz Me'uhad, the central body of some of the largest and most successful kibbutzim, and in Palmah, the commando formation of Hagana. In 1946 the Left Po'ale Zion, who had returned to the WZO in 1939 and had gradually changed their program in the direction of greater acceptance of the concepts of Socialist constructionism, merged with Ahdut Avoda, and the united party subsequently merged with Ha-Shomer ha-Tza'ir to constitute the Mapam party. That merger was short-lived; Ahdut Avoda and the Left Po'ale Zion withdrew. leaving Ha-Shomer ha-Tza'ir as the sole component of Mapam.

Labor Zionism since the Creation of the State. In the post-State era, Borochovist influence probably became strongest in Mapam (basically, the former Ha-Shomer ha-Tza'ir) and to a lesser extent in Ahdut Avoda, particularly in that segment which had come from the Left Po'ale Zion. In Mapai, by far the largest party in Labor Zionism, the Syrkin-Gordon influence remained more vital. Together, the Labor Zionist parties, headed by Mapai, were dynamic builders of Israel. In 1968 the Ahdut Avoda party merged with Mapai, and the reunited movement formed the Israel Labor Party. Mapam did not join in the merger. However, it later entered into a broad and programmatic front with the Israel Labor Party to fight subsequent elections to the Knesset and within the Histadrut. This front was known as the Ma'arakh (Alignment). After a Government of National Unity was constituted in 1985, Mapam withdrew from the Ma'arakh.

In the Diaspora, Labor Zionist groups, in addition to supporting their counterparts in Israel, continued to be active in the Jewish and general life of their countries. Po'ale Zion in England, for example, continued its participation in the British Labor Party, sponsored The Labor Friends of Israel and The Trade Union Friends of Israel organizations. Its sister organization *Pioneer Women, devoted its activities to support of Youth Aliya and kindergartens organized within the Histadrut framework in Israel. In the United States and Canada, Labor Zionism was subdivided in two main streams—the *Farband, whose followers were mostly of the older, Yiddish-speaking generation, and the Labor Zionist Organization, consisting mainly of the next and native-born generation of American Jews, many of whom had been members of the Habonim Youth Movement. These two organizations eventually united under the single banner of the Labor Zionist Organization of America. The large Pioneer Women organization of the US, has remained independent of the union and combines fundraising projects and education. In addition, in the US and Canada, the Histadrut Campaign, the fundraising arm of labor Zionism, initiates fundraising projects among American Trade Unions, in support of Kupat Holim and other Histadrut institutions in Israel, as well as acting as a bridge between the trade union movements of both countries. Po'ale Zion also has national branches in South Africa, Australia, and countries of western Europe, all identifying themselves ideologically and politically with the Israel Labor Party through affiliation to the World Union of Ihud Olami. C.B. SHERMAN—Y. MORRIS

LABOR ZIONIST FRATERNAL ORDER. *See* FARBAND.

LACHISH REGION. Development area in the Darom. Inaugurated in 1955, it comprises some 60 villages, half of which have been established since the beginning of the development project, and the city of Kiryat Gat, which is the regional center. The area covers 225,000 acres, of which 65,000 acres (in addition to natural pasturelands) are under cultivation. The villagers grow sugar beets, cotton, peanuts, vegetables, and other crops. They also engage in cattle raising and dairy farming. The region was named for the Biblical city of Lachish, which existed in the area. There is also a moshav of that name.

LAHAT, SHLOMO ("CHICH"). Army officer, mayor of Tel Aviv (b. Berlin, 1927). Lahat immigrated to Palestine with his family in 1933 and grew up in Rehovot. During the 1948 War of Independence he commanded a platoon and later a company in the Givati Brigade. Subsequently he studied law at the Hebrew University of Jerusalem, concurrently serving in the Israel Defense Forces (IDF). He was Governor of East Jerusalem and its environs during the Six-Day War, later becoming Commander of the Armored forces in Sinai. In 1970 he was appointed head of the Manpower Division of the IDF General Staff. Lahat left the army in 1972 and was elected mayor of Tel Aviv in 1974 as a candidate for the Liberal Party. He was reelected, in highly personalized campaigns, in 1978, 1983, and for a fourth term in 1989. (From 1988 he represented the Likud and Liberal parties following their amalgamation.)

As mayor, Lahat developed Tel Aviv's cultural institutions and its coastline, including the Herbert Samuel Promenade and adding various parks, notably the Darom Park. He reconstructed the center of Tel Aviv, attracting a younger population, and used culture as a means to urbanize the city.

He also reconstructed and developed Jaffa, especially in the fields of education and culture.

LAMDAN, YITZHAK. Hebrew poet and editor (b. Malinov, Volhynia, Russia, 1900; d. Tel Aviv, 1955). Born into a prosperous family, Lamdan received both a traditional Jewish and secular education. He witnessed the pogroms in the Ukraine following World War I and emigrated to Palestine in 1920 as a pioneer. In 1929, he joined the staff of *Moznayim*, the organ of the Hebrew Writers' Association. He founded *Gilyonot* in 1934 and served as its editor until his death.

Lamdan's long dramatic poem *Masada* became the anthem of the pioneers of the Third Aliya. It expressed their disillusionment with the Diaspora from which they had fled and with the Zionist experiment to which they were committed, but affirms that Eretz Israel, their last remaining fortress, must somehow be sustained. Despair of the possibility of survival serves as a source of faith that the struggle must go on.

Masada's style owes much to the expressionist movements of both Germany and revolutionary Russia. Its popularity overshadowed Lamdan's later works: *Ba-Ritma ha-Meshuleshet* (In Triple Harness, 1930), *Mi-Sefer ha-Yamim* (From the Diary, 1940), *Be-Ma'ale Akrabim* (On Scorpions' Path, 1945).

As editor of *Gilyonot*, Lamdan was fiercely independent, and he urged the depoliticization of the Zionist movement. Opposing those who advocated intensifying the class struggle, he believed that a new synthesis could be created between traditional Jewish values and the ideals of the labor movement. Many Hebrew writers of his generation were published in *Gilyonot*.

E. SPICEHANDLER

LAMEL SCHOOL. First modern Jewish school in Eretz Israel. Prior to its establishment, modern education was available to Jewish children only in the school of the British Mission. Almost all the Jewish children, both Ashkenazim and Sephardim, were educated in simple heders.

In 1855 Elisa Herz made a donation for the establishment of a modern Jewish school in Jerusalem in memory of her father, Simon von Lämel, an Austrian-Jewish industrialist who had died in 1845. Ludwig August Frankl (1810–94), secretary of the Jewish Community of Vienna and a noted German-Jewish writer and poet, was sent to Jerusalem to set up the school. The Ashkenazi Jews of the city strongly opposed his work, but the Sephardi majority supported it. Frankl rented an Arab house in the Old City, and soon the school was opened under the protection of the Austrian Consul. The first teachers were Sephardi Hakhamim (rabbis) who had some knowledge of European languages and taught the Bible. Of the first 40 pupils, 20 lived in the school dormitory and 20 came in daily. All of them were Sephardi children. At first the language of instruction was German, but eight years later the school adopted Hebrew. In 1888 the school was attached to Dr. Wilhelm Herzberg's orphanage, and Ephraim Cohn-Reiss, a native of Jerusalem who had been educated in Germany, became its principal. In 1903, with the help of the *Hilfsverein der Deutschen Juden, a new building was erected for the school in the new Zikhron Moshe quarter of Jerusalem.

The Lämel School's teachers included several pioneers of modern Hebrew education such as David Yellin, H. A. Zuta, Joseph J. Rivlin, and Yeshayahu Press. After World War I the school building came under the control of the Education Department of the World Zionist Organization, which opened in it a girls' school that is still called the Lämel School.

Y. SLUTSKY

LA-MERHAV. Israeli daily newspaper published in Tel Aviv. The founding of *La-Merhav* (Into the Open), which published its first issue on 6 December 1954, was a result of the split in Mapam when a considerable part of the membership seceded because of Mapam's pro-Soviet policy and formed a separate political party, Ahdut Avoda, with *La-Merhav* as its organ. The paper ceased publication in 1971; its staff was absorbed by the newspaper *Davar*.

La-Merhav incorporated the literary weekly *Masa*. Its literary supplement, edited by Aharon* Meged, succeeded in attracting many outstanding writers of the younger generation.

J. RUBIN

LANDAU, JACOB. Zionist journalist and publisher (b. Vienna, 1892; d. New York, 1952). Landau joined the Zionist movement while a student at the University of Vienna. A founder of the Austrian Blau-Weiss hiking club, he edited its publication, *Blau-Weiss*. In February, 1917, with the help of friends, he founded the Jewish Correspondence Bureau (Joodsche Correspondentie Bureau) in The Hague. The first international Jewish news service based on telegraphic reports from its own correspondents, the bureau presented the case of the Jewish people and of the Zionist movement to the world. In 1919 Landau, together with Meir Grossman re-established the bureau in London as a worldwide news service, the *Jewish Telegraphic Agency (JTA); Landau served as its president and managing director until his retirement in 1951.

Landau was a co-founder (1921) and director of the *Palestine Bulletin*, which in 1932 became the *Palestine Post* (subsequently the *Jerusalem Post*). In 1940, during World War II, Landau and a group of noted Americans including Jacob Blaustein, Herbert Bayard Swope, and William Allen White founded and directed the Overseas News Agency (ONA) which, based in New York, worked in close association with the JTA until 1949.

LANDAU, JUDAH LEO (Leib). Rabbi, Hebrew author, and Zionist leader in Europe and South Africa (b. Zalozhtsy, near Brody, Galicia, Austria, 1866; d. Johannesburg, 1942). While still in Galicia, Landau made a name for himself as a Talmudic scholar and writer of Hebrew belles lettres. After completing his studies in Vienna, he served briefly as a rabbi in Manchester, England. In 1903 he went to South Africa as rabbi of the Johannesburg Hebrew Congregation. For many years he served on the South African Zionist Executive, and from 1931 until his death he was honorary president of the South African Zionist Federation.

Landau's literary works include Hebrew poems, English essays on modern Hebrew literature, and plays. His wife, Annie Landau, became the first president of the Women's Zionist League of Johannesburg in 1914.

LANDAU, MOSHE. Israeli jurist (b. Danzig, 1912). After completing secondary school in Danzig, Landau attended the University of London. Settling in Palestine in 1933, he engaged in private law practice until 1940, when he was named a magistrate in Haifa. In 1948 he was appointed a judge of the Haifa District Court, an office he held until 1953, when he was appointed a justice of the Israeli Supreme Court, serving as its President from 1980–1982.

He was the presiding judge at the Eichmann trial in 1961–2. His public offices have included membership of the Board of Governors of the Haifa Technion, vice-chairman of the Council of Higher Education, membership of the Council of the Rubin Academy in Jerusalem, and President of the Zionist Court of the World Zionist Organization.

LANDAU, SAUL RAPHAEL. Lawyer, journalist, author, and early Zionist (b. Cracow, Poland, 1870; d. New York, 1943). Landau studied in Vienna, where he became active in pre-Herzlian Zionist circles, served as secretary of the Admath Jeschurun Palestine settlement society and of the Vienna branch of the Zion group, and engaged in varied journalistic activity. He also taught (1893–94) Polish literature and the history of the Jews of Poland at the Israelitische Theologische Lehranstalt (Rabbinical Seminary) of Vienna.

Landau was one of the earliest collaborators of Herzl and the first editor of *Die Welt*, but differences with Herzl led to his resignation from the paper after the First Zionist Congress (1897) and to his withdrawal from the World Zionist Organization in 1899. After the annexation of Austria by Germany (1938), he emigrated to the United States.

LANDAU, SHEMUEL HAYIM. Leader and ideologist of Ha-Po'el ha-Mizrachi (b. Matzivich, Poland, 1892; d. Jerusalem, 1928). Reared in Hasidic surroundings, Landau was ordained a rabbi at the age of 18. His secular education was self-acquired. At the end of World War I he became active in the Polish Mizrachi (Religious Zionist) movement. He contributed ideological articles to *Ha-Mizrachi*, the organ of the movement, speaking out against the negative attitude of Western Orthodoxy toward Zionism and discussing problems of religious Zionism. In 1921 he was chosen a member of the Executive of Tze'irei Mizrachi. At the Second Tze'irei Mizrachi Conference (Warsaw, 1922), he lectured on the ideology of religious *halutziyut* (pioneering). He became the recognized ideologist and leader of Tze'irei Mizrachi and He-Halutz ha-Mizrachi. Landau was active in organizing religious youth and instrumental in establishing training farms and craft workshops in Poland. At the 13th Zionist Congress (1923) he was elected to the Zionist Actions Committee. In 1925 he was chosen a member of the Executive of the Tora va-Avoda world movement and a member of the World Central Committee of Mizrachi. In 1926 he settled in Jerusalem, where he played a dominant role in Ha-Po'el ha-Mizrachi, in both the practical and ideological spheres.

G. BAT-YEHUDA

LANDAUER, GEORG. Zionist activist (b. Cologne, 1895; d. New York, 1954). He was a member of the Zionist student organization Kartell Jüdischer Verbindungen, from its foundation. Interrupting his studies, he served in the German army during World War I on the east European front. Impressed by east European Jewry, he wrote his doctoral thesis in 1923 on "Jewish Minority Rights" especially in eastern Europe. In 1918 he had founded the German branch of Ha-Po'el ha-Tza'ir, together with Haim Arlosoroff, Walter Preuss, and Rudolf Samuel (later professor of physics at the Haifa Technion). He was editor of the German Ha-Po'el ha-Tza'ir's *Die Arbeit.* When Arlosoroff moved to Palestine in 1924, Landauer became the leader of Ha-Po'el ha-Tza'ir. During 1924–5 he was head of the Palestine Office in Berlin. From 1926 to 1929 he served as secretary of the Labor Department of the Zionist Executive in Jerusalem. Returning for four years to Germany, he again served in Berlin as head of the Palestine Office and also headed the Zionist Organization in Germany. He was director of the Central Bureau for the Settlement of German Jews within the Jewish Agency in Jerusalem, from 1934 until 1954. He also played an important role in the development of Youth Aliya. His social and cultural projects on behalf of Jews from Germany, were of decisive importance for the integration of the 65,000 immigrants from Germany in Palestine. Having served from 1935 until 1946 as director of the PASA settlement company (for middle-class settlers from Germany), and of the water company Mekorot, he founded in 1942, together with Pinhas Rosen, the (liberal, middle-class) Aliya Hadasha-party. Historically it was the major political body founded by the immigrants from Germany. Until the breakup of the party in 1948, Landauer represented it in the Va'ad Le'umi. From 1948 until shortly before his death he was chairman of the Irgun Olej Merkas Europa (the central organization of immigrants from Germany and Austria). He supported the idea of a binational state as the only solution to the Jewish-Arab conflict.

E. ROTHSCHILD

LANDMAN, SAMUEL. Lawyer and Zionist leader in Great Britain (b. Zhvanets, Ukraine, Russia, 1884; d. London, 1967). Brought to England as a child, Landman graduated from the University of Leeds. From 1908 to 1911 he studied at the Sorbonne in Paris. On his return to England, he settled in London, where he became honorary secretary of the Joint Zionist Council of Great Britain (combining the English Zionist Federation and the Order of Ancient Maccabeans). Until 1914 he was one of the editors of the *Zionist* (formerly the *Zionist Banner*). During World War I he became associated with the political work which, under the leadership of Chaim Weizmann and Nahum Sokolow, led to the Balfour Declaration. From 1917 to 1922 he was general secretary of the London Office of the World Zionist Organization (WZO).

Landman was generally associated with the right wing of the Zionist movement. In 1935 he joined the New Zionist Organization, serving as its legal adviser and chairman of its Political Committee. In later years he became identified with the General Zionist movement and from 1955 until his death chaired the General Zionist Organization of Great Britain. He wrote a number of booklets and articles on Zionism and its history, including *Zionism: Its Organization and Institutions* (1915), *History of Zionism* (1915), and *Great Britain, Palestine and the Jews* (1936).

LAND OF ISRAEL. *See* ISRAEL.

LAND POLICY IN ISRAEL. Land policy in Israel is based on principles that antedate the establishment of the State.

The Land as Property of the People. The idea of land inalienably owned by the Jewish people as the basis for a morally just and economically healthy Jewish State was first proposed by Professor Hermann Schapira on the occasion of the establishment of the World Zionist Organization. As early as the Damascus blood libel in 1940, however, Colonel Charles Henry Churchill, voicing the need for a return of the Jews to Palestine, specifically urged that the "land should be the property of the nation." That same year, Rabbi Judah Solomon Hai Alkalai suggested the creation of a fund with aims similar to those adopted by the *Jewish National Fund (JNF) a half century later. Other thinkers, too, conceived this to be the surest way to create a desirable social and economic framework for the Return to Zion.

The idea achieved its practical and moral expression with the establishment of the JNF at the Fifth Zionist Congress (1901). Little could be done, however, to purchase land under the rule of the Turks, and it was only after the issuance of the Balfour Declaration under British administration that significant areas of land were purchased in the Jezreel Valley and elsewhere. In 1920 the London Zionist Conference adopted the following principles as the land policy of the Zionist Organization:

> 1. The fundamental principle of Zionist land policy is to make all land settled by Jews, whether in urban or rural areas, the property of the Jewish nation.
> 2. The organ for carrying out this land policy will be the Jewish National Fund, and its function will be to purchase land and make it the property of the nation. Funds for the purpose will be contributed by the people, and the acquired lands will be granted to groups and individuals for use only as hereditary leaseholds.

This land policy also specified that all lease contracts for national land were to be for a period of 49 years and that as long as the lessee continued to use the land for the purpose for which it had been leased, the lease could be renewed at the end of that term for an additional 49 years. The lessee was obligated to live on the leased land and, in the case of agricultural land, to work it himself. He had to pay an annual rent amounting to 2 percent of the value for agricultural land and to 4 percent for urban real estate. The amount of rent due was to be reassessed every seven years in accordance with changing land values. The size of the agricultural leasehold was to be that of a single family farm, cultivated by the lessee and providing him with a livelihood. This family "holding," therefore, could vary in size with the region, the quality of the soil, water resources, and the like. No lessee was permitted to hold more than one lease. In case of death, the holding could be transferred to only one heir in order to prevent parceling of the land. This provision applied to housing as well: one plot was leased to a family and could not be divided.

These principles stood the test of experience. However, they applied only to land owned by the JNF, which in 1947 consisted of no more than 3.5 percent of the land area of Mandatory Palestine. A similar amount of land was under private Jewish ownership and hence outside the scope of the Zionist land policy. Y. WEITZ

In the State of Israel. The ownership situation as regards the lands under the State of Israel's sovereignty is better organized than prior to Israeli independence. In 1928, new Land Settlement of Title ordinances were introduced through a law passed by the British mandatory authorities. This law was reformulated by the Knesset in 1969, as the Settlement Title of the Land Law, 1970, and by 1988 all lands had been reregistered in the land registers in an organized fashion, by a new, sophisticated method.

Land ownership in the State of Israel can be divided into four categories: 1) State lands, 2) Jewish national land, 3) private land, 4) Arab national land.

State lands constitute about 75 percent of all lands of the State; most of this land is registered in the name of the State of Israel, the titles having been passed from the Ottoman Empire to the British Mandate, and from the Mandate to the State of Israel. A small part is registered in the name of the Land Development Authority, a legally established body, under State control. Most of the State lands are rocky or arid desert lands, unsuited for agriculture, while the Land Development Authority for the most part controls agricultural land, or urban land suitable for construction. *Jewish national land* represents about 16.5 percent of all lands in the State; most of this land is registered in the name of the JNF, while a small part belongs to its subsidiary companies. This land was purchased over a period of almost 80 years with money contributed by the Jewish people for this purpose. Most of the Jewish national lands are agricultural lands; a small part is stony terrain.

Private land, totaling approximately 5.5 to 6.5 percent of all lands in Israel, is registered in the names of private owners, mostly Arabs, with a few Jews. The Jewish-owned lands were purchased and registered in the name of Jewish companies, whereas the private lands not under Jewish or Arab ownership, belong to various church bodies which purchased a foothold in Israel over the years out of religious, messianic, or missionary faith. The Arabs gained titles to private land in most cases by virtue of possession of the land over a long period, and in a few cases by virtue of a land grant by firman of the Turkish Sultan. The Jewish landowners purchased their lands from the Arabs or from churches, or from absentee effendi owners.

Arab national lands, representing about two to three percent of all the lands in the State, are registered in the land registry in the name of the Moslem *Waqf* (real estate endowments given to religious foundations) in the State of Israel. The Moslem *Waqf*, which owns most of these lands, received them from Moslem landowners, while the very small percentage belonging to the Christian *Waqf* was donated by private Christian landowners. In both cases, these donations were made mainly on the basis of religious faith, but also sometimes for other reasons, such as: the absence of heirs, tax evasion, or to ensure Moslem or Christian ownership of the land, which would become inalienable.

Use made of the various categories of lands.

State land is designed for public State objectives for the good of the population as a whole, according to the extent and type of land needs of each population sector. The uses made of these lands are varied; most extend over very large areas, while a minority extend over small areas. Uses include: parks and national parks, nature reserves, forestry reserves, sites of antiquities, water reservoirs, canals and water carriers, railroads, public roads, army camps and training areas, state and public industrial zones, allocation of lands to rural and urban settlements, allocation of lands for public needs in the framework of urban construction programs of the local authorities—for schools, sports facilities, housing projects, roads, drainage, and various public buildings. The State uses State lands, inter alia, for development of arid areas, construction of cities and towns for immigrant absorption and settlement of the land, and for the creation of community settlements to promote rural dwelling as opposed to town dwelling.

Most of the State-owned lands are in the southern part of the country, from the northern Negev to Eilat in the South, while a small part is scattered in relatively small blocs of land in Galilee, in Wadi Ara, and along the coastal plain. Effective use of State land for public objectives depends on the creation of uniform and unbroken land areas. Hence, when planning any area owned by the State or by the Land Development Authority, such as development of an industrial zone, expansion of an urban area for construction of public neighborhoods, or water or electricity projects, the Government must assure a continuous area under its ownership, if the planning is not to be a failure. The Government thus finds itself in conflict with the private landowners whose plots lie within the planned area, and is obliged to infinge on the rights of private ownership for the public good.

When private land lying within the planned State lands is liable to hold up or prevent the planning, the Government negotiates with the private owners. In the case of a refusal to sell, the Government is compelled to implement the 1943 Land (Acquisition for Public Purposes) Law, forcibly purchasing the land, but paying its full value. This kind of purchase is known as "expropriation."

Jewish national land. For the first period of the State, such land served for the establishment of 500 Jewish agricultural settlements, absorption centers, and Jewish education centers, while land was also allocated for industry. Land purchase and reclamation are the responsibility of the JNF. Jewish national land was not always available in places where settlements were necessary and initiatives to purchase land were not always successful. Consequently the place and scope of settlement were often determined according to the availability of national land.

The period from immediately after the establishment of the State until the early 1970s was marked by large-scale immigration and vast numbers of prospective settlers on the one hand, and tremendous areas of lands on the other, following the flight of many Arabs abandoning the lands which they occupied, but did not necessarily own. These lands were vested in the Custodian of Absentee Property, which sold them to the Development Authority, and the Authority in turn sold some of them to the JNF. The area of land purchased and placed at the disposal of Jewish settlement in this period by the JNF is estimated at about 10% of all State lands. This was the most fruitful and successful period of settlement.

The period from the early 1970s to 1990 was characterized by little land at the disposal of settlement, and a large demand by new immigrants and veteran citizens alike, wishing to be settlers. Unlike the initial settlement period, these potential settlers were not always guided by ideological motives.

Private land served its owners in the main for agriculture and to a small extent for construction and dwellings, principally within the cities, in the Arab villages, in the moshavot and various community settlements not included in the framework of cooperative settlement. Most private land is cultivable land, serving for plantations—olives, citrus fruits, and deciduous fruit trees, etc.—and irrigated or unirrigated land for crops. Agricultural land is concentrated in the rural area of Galilee, in the center of Israel, and in the northern Negev. The development and growth of the cities led to an increase in urban land designated for construction for homes and for industry, to the detriment of agricultural land.

Arab national land is held mainly by the Moslem *Waqf* of which there are various kinds. The main one, the "true *Waqf*," which holds most of the lands, is owned by the Moslem Higher Council in Palestine, which was declared absentee after the establishment of the State. Accordingly all the *Waqf* properties, both movable and immovable, were vested in the Custodian of Absentee Property of the State of Israel. The other *Waqf* lands are local family endowments and other kinds, over which the Moslem Higher Council was appointed as trustee. The trustees, who abandoned Israel after the establishment of the State were proclaimed absentee, and the property in their care was vested in the Custodian of Absentee Property of the State of Israel. Property serving ritual purposes, such as mosques, cemeteries, and other vital public purposes of the Moslems in the State of Israel, was handed over to a trustee appointed by the Custodian of Absentee Property to manage these lands and properties for the Moslem population in Israel and only for that population. The Moslem or Christian *Waqf* lands in Israel are destined for the use and benefit of the Moslems or Christians only. The Christian *Waqf* or endowment trust is made up mainly of churches, monasteries, and little land, belonging to the various Christian communities in Israel, which number about 15. Unlike the Moslem *Waqf* properties, almost no Christian trust properties were seized by the Custodian of Absentee Property, since the heads of the Christian communities in general remained in Israel following the establishment of the State of Israel.

Land acquisition and its influence on Jewish settlement policy. The growth of private Arab ownership influenced the scope of land acquisition by the JNF and by individual Jews, since the Arab owners received high prices for the semi-agricultural lands which they had obtained in the land regularization. From the 1960s until the Yom Kippur War, despite the rocketing land prices, land acquisition was at its peak, especially from Arab villages owning large tracts of land in Galilee. However, from the Yom Kippur War onwards, sales slowed and private buyers outside the JNF multiplied.

In the mid-1960s agricultural surveys carried out in Galilee showed that the agricultural land in this area was insufficient in quantity and quality for the creation of agricultural settlements according to the norms of the 1950s.

In the years following the Yom Kippur War, the need to accelerate Jewish settlement of Galilee intensified, and the settlement agencies joined the JNF in land acquisition activities. The heads of settlement in Israel, and above all in the Jewish Agency, were dissatisfied by the pace of settlement in that area. Hence, massive settlement, agricultural or otherwise, was universally seen as a vital need of the hour in order to ensure the full and effectve incorporation of Galilee in the State of Israel by virtue of a large Jewish population.

The urgent need for land to settle Galilee rapidly is one of the factors which led to the rise in land prices and the decline in land acquisition. Those responsible for settlement and their various emissaries in the field constantly wooed the owners of private land, transforming the low value land into very expensive land. The price eventually demanded was a political price beyond the real economic worth of the land.

Arab rural ownership had doubled through the Ottoman Land Law and the Land Holdings Law, which granted ownership of State land by virtue of possession. This land regulation continued to be the exclusive law for determining ownership of unregistered lands in the State of Israel, and continues to be the dominant law, but only as regards land not yet registered as owned by the State or by a private individual. The lot of the lands whose ownership had been determined conclusively by the land regularization as State land did not improve until the passing of the Israel Land Law in early 1970, which assembled all the land laws, excepting the regularization of land titles and clauses 20 and 78 of the Ottoman Land Law by which the individual could acquire the title to State lands and lands of another if the definitive ownership of this land had not yet been regularized. The Land Law introduced many essential and important changes; inter alia, it revoked the tenure by possession of regularized land which the state had not been able to include in the framework of the existing prescriptive law until that time. The revoking of tenure by possession applied both to state-owned and national lands. Notwithstanding, it was still feared that the Arabs would take control of state lands in the large outer circle of every single village, namely those lands distant from the village which were stony and uncultivable and had therefore been registered as State lands. Consequently, it was decided to create **Mitzpim*, where a small number of families would live, watching over the extensive areas owned by the State in order to warn of any attack on them by occupation of the land, even if this occupation does not grant the occupier ownership of the land.

After 1977, there was a decline in land sales. The main reason was the declaration made by the Begin government that there would be no more expropriation of Arab lands. This declaration was made to pacify the Arabs and dispel their suspicion of the Likud government. While achieving its political aim, the declaration also unintentionally dealt a hard blow to land purchases in the Arab sector.

The pacified Arab landowners no longer hastened to sell land located within the boundary of or near Jewish settlements. Not only was there no fear of expropriation, but the land value rose, since the Jewish Agency, which established the settlements, financed planning, infrastructure,and roads. Hence the land was improved without any investment by the landowner.

In fact nobody, Arabs or Jews, paid heed to one historic fact. No land expropriation was ever involved in the creation of Jewish agricultural settlements, which were established on Jewish national land, freely sold and fully paid for. Further, Jewish settlement in the State of Israel is established not by the State, but by the Jewish National Institutions, which are not empowered to expropriate land. Only the Government has the authority to expropriate land, and does so for the development and promotion of the interests of the general population, and not for national or private interests.

Land policy in Israel is determined in accordance with the type and extent of land ownership. For Jewish settlement, Jewish national land policy tends mainly to establish settlements on Jewish national land, without expropriation of lands by the state and without the use of State lands. Certainly, the Jews of Israel may receive a share of the State lands in accordance with their number and needs, as may the non-Jewish citizens of the State. The needs of the population which is to benefit from the state lands must be seen in relation to the amount of land privately owned by this population. Most of Israel's Arab population is concentrated in agricultural villages and owns large tracts of private land, while 95 percent of Israel's Jewish population lives in the cities and has almost no privately owned land. Hence the state allocates proportionally more lands to the landless Jewish population than to the Arab population which possess large stretches of private land, and is seen to be less in need of State land. A. HILLELI

LAND RECLAMATION IN ISRAEL. The aim of land reclamation is to convert into usable terrains areas which by virtue of their topographical, physical, or chemical characteristics are uncultivable, thus expanding the areas for agricultural utilization. Land reclamation also serves at times to prepare approaches to areas of difficult or impossible access, in order to allow the establishment of new settlements

Pioneers at Kineret reclaiming the land, 1930. [Central Zionist Archives]

or the erection of structures for housing, industry, and agriculture in existing settlements.

Land has been reclaimed in the Land of Israel since ancient times. The Bible mentions stone removal and digging for the planting of vineyards in hilly regions: "...My well-beloved had a vineyard in a very fruitful hill: And he fenced it, and gathered out the stones thereof, and planted it..." (Isaiah 5:1–2). Stone removal and preparation of hilly terrain are also mentioned in the Mishna and Talmud, and findings in the earth show that at various periods in the distant past terraces were built in sloping areas to prevent land erosion and to create surfaces for cultivation.

With the renewed settlement in Eretz Israel and the establishment of the first moshavot in the 1880s, land reclamation became a necessity. The wave of settlement in the present century, and in particular since the creation of the State of Israel, has called for land reclamation of all types in almost all areas where settlements were created.

The different types of land reclamation include:

Preparation of Hilly Terrain: In hilly regions, where the land in its natural state is strewn with boulders and stones, sliced by ravines, or steeply inclined, and does not therefore lend itself to uninterrupted and intensive cultivation. Land reclamation in these regions consists of stone clearing, removal of boulders—mainly by heavy machinery such as bulldozers and rooters—and terracing of sloping areas and gullies in order to prevent landslides and to allow the cultivation of contiguous areas.

Drainage: Of swampland, waterlogged for the whole or part of the year, or of areas where drainage is deficient and waterlogging prevents agricultural development. In the early period of Jewish settlement such swamps, infested by mosquitoes, also represented a health hazard for the settlers, many of whom succumbed to malaria.

Amelioration of Saline or Organically Poor Soils: Mainly in certain parts of the Negev and the Dead Sea-Jordan Valley region, where the soil is saline, or the sandy soils of the Negev which are poor in organic matter. The saline soils can be leached through the use of large quantities of salt-free water, while the sandy soils can be improved through organic fertilizers and improved cultivation methods.

Covering of Eroded Areas with Fresh Soil: Unique climatic conditions in certain areas of Israel, such as in several localities in the Arava, may contribute to the development of highly intensive agriculture; however, the land there cannot be reclaimed, however, either because of its composition or because of stony surface strata and substrata. In these special cases the terrain is covered with a 50 cm. layer, at least, of fertile soil.

Prevention of Erosion by Floodwaters and Winds: Land erosion in the loess and sandy regions of the Negev is attributable to the rains and to the movement of sand and loess by the winds. Several methods may be employed to prevent this destructive process. On sloping terrains, where erosion is common, wide terraces must be built. In the absence of stones and boulders in the area to reinforce the edges of the terraces, trees or perennial grasses and deep-rooted shrubs are planted to prevent the edges of the terraces from crumbling. Wind erosion may be effectively prevented by the planting of several parallel rows of trees to serve as windbreaks alongside the fields, thus reducing the force of the wind and preventing the removal of the loess.

Retention of Sand Dunes: The dune regions in several areas close to the Mediterranean shore and in the Negev are generally uncultivable; the dunes are swept by the wind and endanger the nearby agricultural areas and roads. To protect the neighboring agricultural lands and the roads, a variety of trees—including tamarisk, eucalyptus, and mimosa, which are resistant to sandy conditions and strike deep roots—are planted alongside the dunes and halt their advance.

Clearing of Scrub Soil: Certain areas in hill regions are choked with different kinds of flora, in particular the poterium thorn (*siziphys spina*), which impede plowing or agricultural cultivation. Clearance of these areas is required prior to agricultural exploitation.

In each region the reclamation methods must be suited to the local conditions. Indeed, all the methods mentioned above have been and still are employed by the farmers and by the institutions responsible for land development and reclamation. The initial reclamation works carried out in Eretz Israel in the 1880s, with the establishment of the first moshavot, consisted principally of drainage of swamps and swamplands. The settlers in Petah Tikva and in Hadera dug drainage canals for the swamps and planted eucalyptus trees to dry them out. The first settlers in the hilly or semihilly regions, Zikhron Ya'akov and Rosh Pina for instance, reclaimed the lands of the settlements by stone removal and construction of terraces prior to commencement of agricultural cultivation.

With the commencement of practical work by the World Zionist Organization (WZO) in the early 20th century and in particular under the British (1917–1948), land reclamation work expanded. The arm of the WZO entrusted with land purchase and reclamation, the *Jewish National Fund (JNF), in 1920 purchased the lands of the Valley of Jezreel. Most of this land was swampy, requiring drainage. The project, completed in 1927, was one of the great land reclamation activities of that period, calling for complex and comprehensive engineering work. Between 1920 and 1930 the JNF also purchased the Zebulun Valley in the Haifa Bay and the Hefer Valley in the central Sharon region. These two valleys were equally unsuited for immediate settlement, requiring drainage of swamps, in particular, and in some places the retention of sand dunes. A total of about 62,500 acres were drained in the Jezreel Valley, the Zebulun Valley, and the Hefer Valley, permitting dense settlement and intensive cultivation of the lands of the valleys.

Additional reclamation works carried out by the JNF in that decade were the reclamation of the hill lands in Kiryat Anavim near Jerusalem and in Atarot, north of the city. In the 1930s and 1940s settlement extended to additional areas, calling for further land reclamation. The settlements of Hanita, Eilon, and Matzuva were founded in the Galilee hills, and the Etzyon Bloc and Kibbutz Ma'ale ha-Hamisha were established in the Jerusalem hills. The extensive land reclamation required in all these localities was carried out by the JNF. In the Bet She'an Valley and the Dead Sea area where kibbutz Bet ha-Arava was established, leaching of saline soils was required.

Most of the land reclamation activities have been effected since the creation of the State of Israel in 1948, parallel to the extensive settlement in all parts of the country. By agreement between the Israeli government and the WZO, the JNF continued to be responsible for land reclamation work. In the period since the creation of the State up until 1987, the JNF reclaimed about 250,000 acres.

In the years of brisk settlement, between 1948 and 1958, about 7,500 acres were reclaimed yearly. From then until the Six-Day War in 1967, the rate of creation of new settlements slowed and the range of areas reclaimed fell to about 3,500 acres yearly. The renewal of large-scale settlement after the Six-Day War led to an increase in the scope of land reclamation, reaching the same proportions as in the 1950s.

In the hilly regions, principally Galilee and the Jerusalem hills, from the creation of the State until 1987 about 100,000 acres were reclaimed, while in the Golan about 25,000 acres were reclaimed.

One of the major swamp drainage land reclamation enterprises was the draining of the Huleh reservoir and the surrounding lands. This undertaking, which lasted from 1951 to 1957, brought into cultivation about 20,000 acres of fertile land.

Land reclamation in the Negev since the creation of the state up to 1987 encompassed about 40,000 acres, including 12,500 acres in the Arava area. In some of the Arava settlements, such as Yotvata, Ein Yahav, Hatzeva, and Gerofit, fertile soil had to be brought in to create new cultivable areas. The soil was brought from the Nahal ha-Arava, which in any case required widening and straightening, in order to prevent winter flooding.

Large areas were reclaimed after 1967 in the Etzyon Bloc, the Jordan Valley, and Judea and Samaria, to allow for the establishment of new settlements there. Likewise the project of establishing over 30 pre-settlements in Galilee between 1978 and 1984, required land reclamation, at times in difficult topographical conditions. A. ROKACH

LAND TRANSFER REGULATIONS OF 1940. Regulations issued by Sir Harold MacMichael, High Commissioner for Palestine, on Feb. 28, 1940, prohibiting or restricting the transfer of land in certain areas to persons "not being Palestinian Arabs." The enactment of the regulations was a sequel to the *White Paper of 1939, which envisaged restrictions on Jewish land purchases in the country and vested the High Commissioner with the authority to prohibit and regulate transfer of land.

The regulations delineated two zones, A and B, in which transfers of land were to be controlled. In Zone A, transfer was to be prohibited save in exceptional cases. In Zone B, too, transfer was forbidden, but under certain conditions permission for transfer could be requested and obtained from the High Commissioner. There were to be no restrictions on land purchases in areas not included in Zones A and B.

Zones A and B represented 64 per cent and 31 per cent, respectively, of the total area (6,717,250 acres) of Palestine west of the Jordan, leaving only about 5 per cent (335,750 acres) in which Jews were able to purchase land freely. The free area included all urban territories, the Haifa industrial zone, and the coastal plain between Tantura, 8 miles north of Caesarea, and the southern border of the Ramle Subdistrict. More than half of the land in the "free" area was in Jewish hands at the time.

The land regulations, which signified a further step in the implementation of the White Paper of 1939, aroused indignation throughout the Jewish world. Mass demonstrations took place in Palestine. In its protest, the Jewish Agency pointed out that it had asked the government on several occasions to provide the factual and statistical data on the displacement of Arabs which the government had cited to justify the regulations but that these requests had been consistently refused. The Agency drew attention to the fact that at the St. James's Conference in 1939 the Arabs

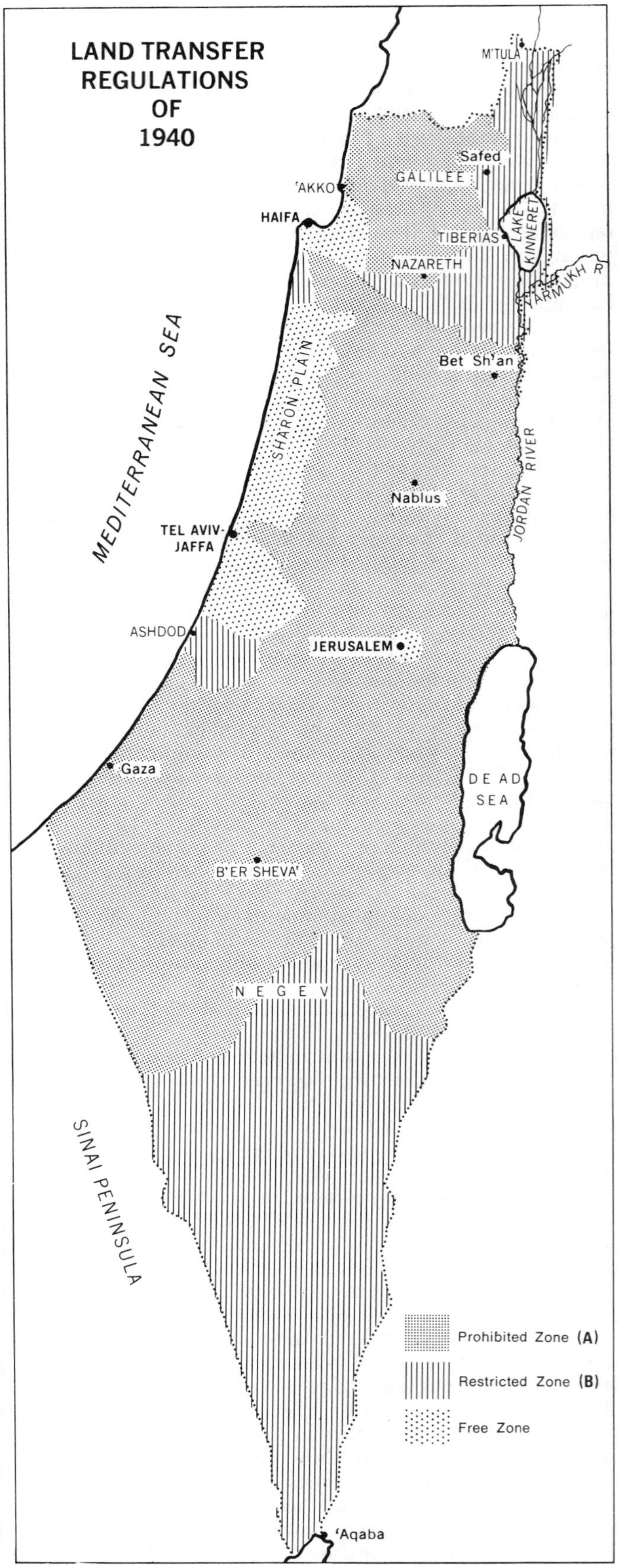

had admitted that there were about 19 million dunams (4,750,000 acres) of land in Palestine west of the Jordan, out of a total of less than 27 million dunams (6,717,250 acres), that had not been cultivated by the Arabs, who had found the land unarable.

On Mar. 6, 1940, British opponents of the regulations in the House of Commons made a motion of censure against the Government. The motion was rejected by a vote of 292 to 129. The Land Transfer Regulations remained in force until the departure of the British from Palestine in 1948.

T. PRESCHEL

LANGUAGE WAR (SPRACHENKAMPF). Campaign waged during the winter of 1913/14 by the Hebrew Teachers' Union in Eretz Israel against the *Hilfsverein der deutschen Juden over the issue of the language of instruction in Hilfsverein educational institutions.

The Hilfsverein had been founded in Berlin in 1901 by the cotton magnate, James Simon, and Dr. Paul Nathan; the first acting as president and the latter, director. One of the Hilfsverein's objectives was to raise the cultural standard of Jews in the Ottoman Empire.

Nathan laid the foundation of an extensive network of schools in Eretz Israel, from kindergartens to a Teachers' Training College which, unlike the Alliance Israélite schools, employed modern pedagogic methods. Instructors were competent and the Hilfsverein's educational director, Ephraim Cohn-Reiss, was an efficient administrator. Nathan was also responsible for introducing Hebrew as a language of instruction, believing that it would serve as a unifying factor for the polyglot composition of the yishuv. Scientific subjects, however, were taught in German.

Although the motives for introducing Hebrew in these schools were pedagogical rather than nationalistic, the Zionists fully appreciated the Hilfsverein's activities. Lacking sufficient financial resources to maintain their own school system, they willingly cooperated with the Hilfsverein. This relationship paved the way for partnership in a more ambitious project, Nathan's brainchild, the founding of a Technical College (Technikum or *Technion) in Haifa. Nathan and Shemarya Levin, a member of the Zionist Executive, managed to prevail upon Kalonymus-Ze'ev Wissotzky, a Russian tea magnate, to make a large financial contribution; Levin also interested Jacob Schiff, the celebrated Jewish financier and philanthropist in New York, in the project, receiving a sizable donation from him. Both Wissotzky and Schiff were represented on the board of the preparatory committee, chaired by James Simon; the Hilfsverein members were in a majority. Three Zionists, Ahad Ha-Am, Yehiel Tschlenow, and Shemarya Levin also joined the board, though in a private capacity. It was understood that the language of instruction for scientific subjects in the College would be German.

When the Hilfsverein-Zionist rapprochement took place in 1906, no serious difficulties were foreseen. Some German Zionist leaders, such as Arthur Hantke, Kurt Blumenfeld, and Richard Lichtheim, had grave misgivings about an association with anti-Zionist assimilationists, and even Ahad Ha-Am urged caution before entering into an agreement with the Hilfsverein; but expediency prevailed: the Zionists were in no position to renounce the partnership. Ironically, one of its first great enthusiasts was Shemarya Levin. The Hilfsverein's successful work enhanced Zionist confidence, but it was not long before a divergence of views appeared. Nathan feared that the partnership with the Zionists might prejudice the Hilfsverein's standing with both German Jewry and the Turks. He lost no opportunity to stress that his Association was completely detached from Zionism, its only purpose "the cultural and economic welfare of the Jews." Whereas the Zionists, as Chaim Weizmann put it, were struggling to weld the Jewish community in the country into "one creative unit", Nathan rejected Jewish exclusivism outright.

However disparate the two attitudes, the conflict which developed was not inevitable. Neither the Hilfsverein nor the Zionist Organization desired it. Otto Warburg, chairman of the Zionist Organization, continued to serve on the Hilfsverein Committee, and at the 11th Zionist Congress (1913), Chaim Weizmann publicly expressed his fear that the premature introduction of Hebrew into the Technical College might adversely affect the quality of teaching. Tschlenow, the Russian Zionist leader and a member of the College board, agreed: in an appreciative reference to the Hilfsverein's work, he went so far as to state that its educational program was compatible with "the national aim." Shemarya Levin thought differently: at the same Congress he declared that the Zionist Organization must fulfill its "unconditional obligation to concentrate in its hands the total cultural work in Eretz Israel," and to exclude those bodies "which lacked that banner." Nathan took offense, all the more since it was the Hilfsverein that had first grasped the importance of organizing the Jewish communities in the Middle East, and especially of educating the youth. It was unthinkable to him that this primacy, gained by heavy investment and pioneering work, should now be lost. He regarded the Teachers' Union, which the Zionist Executive in Berlin was "too weak" to restrain, as chiefly responsible for the now full-blown *Sprachenkampf*. But the teachers, too, had grievances; those in the Hilfsverein schools saw that since 1911 Hebrew had been repressed in favor of German and they placed the blame for this, during the Teachers' Union conference in August 1913, on Ephraim Cohn-Reiss, suspecting that he had submitted to "secret pressure exercised by the German Government."

Documentary evidence shows that this impression was mistaken: neither Berlin nor the German Consulate in the country was pushing German *Kultur* at the expense of Hebrew education. It was rather the Hilfsverein representatives themselves who repeatedly pointed to the Jews as a link between Germany and the Orient and praised the projected Technikum in Haifa as "a stronghold of *Deutschtum* in the Holy Land," arousing Zionist suspicions that Jewish settlement was to be subordinated to German political aspirations. Ephraim Cohn-Reiss, in particular, had incensed the teachers when, in 1913, he rejected their proposal to accelerate the Hebraization of his schools. The resignation of the Zionist representatives on the board of the Technikum heightened the tension. Before that meeting on 26 October 1913, Shmarya Levin appealed to Dr. Nathan, emphasizing that only Hebrew could provide the technical college with a semblance of neutrality. However, the Zionist members on the Technikum Board were in a minority and could not claim the exclusive right to draft its program. Moreover, the original agreement, to which all parties had committed themselves, stipulated that scientific subjects were to be taught in German. Ahad Ha-Am warned his fellow Zionists that, lacking Hebrew textbooks, adequate Hebrew terminology, and experienced staff to teach scientific subjects in that language, a speedy conversion of the

Technikum into a Hebrew institution was both impractical and unfair.

At the same time, he attempted to convince Dr. Nathan of the necessity of gradually introducing Hebrew into the Technikum. However, Nathan was unmoved. Ahad Ha-Am suspected that Nathan's inflexibility was determined by some secret agreement between the German government and the Hilfsverein. Though this was not the case, the episode served as the final fuse which sparked off the Teachers' Union struggle against "the complete suppression of Hebrew." Animated protest meetings were held throughout the country, and a strike was declared in the Hilfsverein schools. Dr. Nathan arrived in Eretz Israel in a militant mood and rejected all compromise solutions. Dismissal of certain teachers provoked a violent demonstration at the Lämel School in Jerusalem and elsewhere. These events took the Zionist Executive in Berlin entirely by surprise. The strike and particularly the teachers' exit *en masse* from the Hilfsverein schools, accompanied by their students, aroused general displeasure; the most outspoken critic was Ahad Ha-Am. Despite serious misgivings, however, the Executive could not desert the teachers. As soon as the struggle assumed a more positive character, a widespread campaign was launched in Europe and the United States to provide funds for the maintenance of independent Hebrew schools. Once involved, the Executive became a party to the conflict. It could not remain indifferent to the course pursued by the Hilfsverein and other segments of German Jewry, which tried to implicate the Zionist Organization in responsibility for the teachers' strike.

With Nathan's return to Berlin the campaign intensified. In January 1914 his pamphlet *Palästina und palästinensischer Zionismus* appeared, and the influential *Frankfurter Zeitung* opened its pages to him.

The Zionists replied in a pamphlet *Im Kampf um die hebraische Sprache*, and, judging from the generous response and the number of voluntary contributions for the Hebrew Schools Funds, it was clear that their arguments were gradually gaining ground. But it was not until the meeting of the Technikum's Board on 24 February 1914 that the Hilfsverein was decisively defeated. During that meeting the American and Russian members of the Board sided with the Zionists: by deciding to separate the affiliated Grammar School from the Technical College, they removed the principal bone of contention. In the Grammar School Hebrew would be used immediately as the exclusive language of instruction while in the College it would be introduced in the course of four years. Thus the Zionist Executive emerged triumphant.

Given the German Government's preference for the Hilfsverein, the Zionist victory on the political plane is the more surprising. (*See* GERMANY AND ZIONISM). Conrad von Wangenheim, the German Ambassador in Constantinople, expressed no objection to the superiority of Hebrew while Counsellor von Kühlman stated officially that "Germany would be sufficiently compensated if, besides Hebrew, German would also be cultivated." The primacy of Hebrew was thus fully conceded. After the War and throughout the period of the British Mandate, the sole language of instruction, from kindergartens to the Technion, was Hebrew.

I. FRIEDMAN

LASKI, HAROLD JOSEPH. Political economist and British Labor party leader (b. Manchester, England, 1893; d. London, 1950). The son of Nathan Laski, a Jewish communal leader in Manchester, he joined the Fabian Society while studying at New College, Oxford, from which he graduated in the School of Modern History in 1914. He taught history at McGill (1914–16) and Harvard (1916–20) Universities, and returning to England in 1920, joined the staff of the London School of Economics and devoted himself also to journalism and writing. In 1926 he became a professor of political science at the University of London.

Laski was a member of the Executive of Britain's Labor party from 1936 to 1949, serving as chairman of the party in 1945–46. Speaking at a meeting in Manchester in May, 1945, he declared that although at one time he had advocated Jewish assimilation, he now realized that the needs of the Jews could be fulfilled only in a territory of their own, which could only be Palestine.

Although Laski never officially joined the Zionist movement, he welcomed the decision of the Labor party to urge the right of the Jews to their Homeland. When the British Labor Government in 1945 repudiated its preelection promises, he denounced Ernest Bevin's Palestine policy as a "black stain on Britain's good name," and he later declared that Britain's attitude had been responsible for the invasion of Palestine by the Arab states. He long argued that anti-Semitism was a right-wing phenomenon, until he encountered the full force of Communist anti-Semitism which made him a Zionist rather late in life. He supported the concept of a bi-national state in Palestine long after it had been rejected by Arabs and Jews.

LASKOV, CHAIM. Israeli military leader (b. Borisov, Belorussia, Russia, 1919; d. Haifa, 1982). He was taken to Palestine in 1925 and joined the Hagana while in his teens. In 1938 he served with Wingate's Special Night Squad. In 1940 he joined the British Army, rising to the rank of major, and serving as a company commander in the Jewish Brigade. Between 1946–1948, he was on the permanent staff of the Hagana and during the War of Independence organized the first officers' course of the Israel Defense Forces. Later he served as battalion commander and saw action in Latrun. After the war he served as Commander of the Training Branch and Commander of the Air Force. In 1955 Laskov became Chief of Military Operations and Deputy Chief of Staff, and in June 1956 was appointed Commander of the Armoured Corps, fighting in Sinai during the 1956 Sinai War as Division Commander. He was subsequently appointed Officer Commanding the Southern Command and on 1 January 1958 succeeded Moshe Dayan as Chief of Staff. During his tenure he stressed the role of the armor and air force as well as meticulous training and discipline. He resigned in January 1961 following disagreements with Deputy Defense Minister Shimon Peres. Between 1962 and 1972 he was chairman of the Israel Port Authority, supervising the construction of the port of Ashdod. During his period of office the volume of tonnage in Israel's ports rose significantly. In November 1972 he became the Army's ombudsman. Following the Yom Kippur War he served on the Agranat Commission of Inquiry, which investigated the Army's state of readiness prior to the war and its conduct during the first three days. Laskov was known as a stern disciplinarian who demanded utmost dedication and devotion to duty and harshly criticized any lack of personal integrity or sloppy performance.

M. MEDZINI

LATIN AMERICAN JEWS IN ISRAEL. In the period between the issuance of the Balfour Declaration (1917) and the end of World War II only a few Latin American Jews settled in Palestine. Born in eastern Europe, most of these immigrants from Latin America felt strong ties with their native countries and hence on arrival in Palestine were absorbed into the communities of immigrants from Poland, Lithuania, Romania, and so on.

Immigration from Latin America until 1967. At the close of World War II a small group of young pioneers left for Palestine, and in early 1948 about 500 Latin American youths volunteered to fight in Israel's War of Independence. Many members of these two groups and their families remained in Israel.

Emigration from Latin America to Israel increased between 1956 and 1960 because of the growing prosperity of the State of Israel and the increasing pressure of economic and political crises in Latin America. While the younger immigrants joined existing kibbutzim or formed new ones, the older generation settled in towns and cities, finding employment in the crafts, the professions, business, and industry.

In July, 1961, violent riots instigated by neofascist and anti-Semitic groups broke out in Buenos Aires and Montevideo. This development came as a profound psychological shock to Argentinian and Uruguayan Jewry and particularly to the younger native-born generation, which had considered itself rooted in the culture and communal life of these countries. This shock aroused in certain segments of the Jewish population the desire to identify themselves completely with the State of Israel. The reaction in the Jewish communities not only of Argentina and Uruguay but throughout Latin America was expressed in a steep rise in the rate of immigration and in an increased emphasis on settlement in Israel. Between mid-1961 and mid-1965, over 13,000 Jews migrated from Latin American countries to Israel, more than in the preceeding 13 years.

The second half of 1965 saw a decline in this immigration. Conditions in Latin America had apparently improved, and political tensions diminished. On the other hand, some of the immigrants encountered difficulties in their adjustment in Israel, so that in many cases relatives who had remained in Latin America did not follow them. Nonetheless, the number of Latin American emigrants to Israel continued to be larger than that of the pre-1961 period, and emigration became a factor to reckon with in Latin American Jewish life. It was clear that the events of 1961 were an important impetus in this development, but the decisive factors lay far deeper and were more complicated. These factors included the Jewish national feelings of Latin American Jews; their Zionist affiliations and the cumulative influence of Zionist education over a score of years; the relative newness of their communities; the economic, social, and political crises, of which anti-Semitic outbreaks were only an external and secondary manifestation; the relatively great influence of the pioneer movement on fairly broad groups in these communities; the improved economic conditions in Israel and the rise in the standard of living there; and, finally, the possibility of active participation in the establishment of a new society and a new life, which was attractive to radical and progressive elements in the younger generation. All this resulted in the formation of a number of different aliya groups reflecting varying viewpoints and recruited from diverse social classes.

Adjustment to Life in Israel up to 1967. The immigration of Latin American Jews to Israel was the largest, both in absolute numbers and in relative percentage, of all countries of the free western world, and it reflected the special problems associated with Israel's immigration policy, which may be subsumed as follows:

1. The Absorption Departments of the Jewish Agency and the Israeli government had long been adapted to handle mass immigration from countries in which Jews had been persecuted. Only in the late 1950s were methods of individualized attention to immigrants and absorptive conditions of a higher standard developed. By 1966 this change was still in its early stages, and Latin American immigrants found themselves facing difficulties and misunderstandings which arose from insufficient preparation in their countries of origin or from shortcomings in the absorptive system in Israel.

2. The great majority of the immigrants became adjusted to the new environment in terms of housing and employment.

3. Aliya from Latin America was unusual in terms of the age of the immigrants: 30 percent were under 18; 30 percent, between 18 and 35; and 15 percent, between 35 and 50. The younger generation generally had had at least a secondary education and was accustomed to urban cultural life, but its roots in Jewish culture were weak and its knowledge of Hebrew was minimal. The older generation had been accustomed to a lively, effervescent communal life, in society in general and within the Jewish community in particular. On their arrival in Israel, many immigrants, owing to their lack of knowledge of Hebrew and the differences in both living conditions and general atmosphere, suddenly found themselves cut off from the mainstream of culture and the arts, from communal affairs, and from active participation in political life.

Despite these problems, the percentage of Latin Americans reemigrating from Israel was extremely low: between 1961 and 1965 only about 3 percent of the Argentinian immigrants, or close to 5 percent of all immigrants from Latin America, left Israel.

The Organization of Immigrants from Latin America filled an important function in serving as the intermediary between the new immigrants and Israel's immigrant absorption agencies and helped in accelerating the adjustment of the newcomers.

Immigration since 1967. By 1988, 75,000 Jews from South America had immigrated to Israel, about half of them since 1970. From 1967 various events and trends occurred which influenced the immigration and the immigrants absorbed in the country. These included, in Israel, the Six-Day War; the Yom Kippur War and the political upheaval in the aftermath; and the war in Lebanon. In the countries of origin there were continuing economic and social crises, internal wars and economic depressions in a number of countries, the war between Great Britain and Argentina, and the return to democratic government in Argentina, Brazil, and Uruguay; some of these events had a "push" effect on immigration, resulting in Jewish and non-Jewish emigration from South American countries. From Israel the "pull" effect was of varying effectiveness; at times so low that many Jews who left their countries of origin did not go to Israel, and among those who did arrive an increased percentage left, mostly to return to their countries of origin. Most of the immigrants came from four countries in South America: over half from Argentina; Brazil and Uruguay each contributed over 10%, and about 7% from Chile. From Mexico, Colombia, Venezuela, and Peru together nearly 10% arrived (over 3,000 from Mexico, about 1,500 from Colombia, and over 1,000 from Venezuela). Several hundred arrived from Bolivia, Ecuador, and Panama. About 1,000 additional immigrants came from the remaining Latin American countries. Generally, the number of immigrants is relative to the number of Jews in the countries of origin. However, from Uruguay the percentage of immigrants is markedly greater, relative to the size of the Jewish population, than is the case in Argentina, Chile, Peru, or Bolivia.

Basic characteristics of the immigrants from Latin America were:

a) A young aliya: in 1973, 36% of the immigrants from South America were between the ages of 18–29 at the time of their immigration, and among those who came in 1985 74% had not reached 34 years of age.

b) A large percentage of professionals and specialists: 54% of the immigrants who had worked in their country of origin were specialists in the sciences and other free professions or were academics; 22% had other professions, such as agents, teachers, para-medicine, technicians; 12.3% were clerks; and 7.8% were merchants.

c) Most of the immigrants were born in their country of origin. Recently only about 10% had themselves emigrated to South American countries before moving to Israel. This percentage was much greater in the past.

d) Only 8% of the immigrants defined themselves as religious. Their Zionist Jewish consciousness was very high, and was noted by them as being the main factor in their immigration.

e) In 1973, 50% stated that they had been active in Jewish and Zionist organizations before their immigration. Only 30% did not belong to such organizations.

f) In the 1950s and 1960s a large number of immigrants were absorbed in kibbutzim; also in 1985 out of a total of 836 immigrants from Argentina about 240 arrived in kibbutzim as the first stage of their absorption. However, internal migration from the kibbutz to the city has increased in recent years.

g) A recognizable portion of the immigrants had studied within the framework of Jewish education. In 1973, 15% of the immigrants spoke Hebrew fairly fluently at the time of their aliya. By the end of three years' residence about 90% spoke Hebrew freely.

Among the groups arriving after 1967 have been: students who came for studies at the universities and in other frameworks, many of whom were absorbed in Israel, and a group of political refugees resulting from the political oppressions in Argentina, Uruguay, and Chile during the 1970s. The latter group was relatively small, some having no Zionist motivation and many subsequently left. Quite a few of these had not been hurt personally but feared possible persecution, or chose not to live in the difficult atmosphere which prevailed. The political-social factor was accompanied by economic problems because the professionals and middle class were affected by the political and economic crises. In Israel, the drop in the standard of living experienced by the newcomers and economic difficulties made life hard for many immigrants from Latin America, who arrived without sufficient means or suffered from the undervaluation of their property. Immigrants with something to offer professionally found their absorption eased. But changes in social values and decreasing idealism of immigrants, together with the economic crisis, caused an increase in the number of emigrants from among the Latin American Jews. The return to democracy in the principal lands of origin, also had an influence in attracting them to return, although the economic difficulties which followed the political changes were a restraining factor. The fine balance between attraction and repulsion explains not only the arrival of Jews from South America in Israel but also the surge of emigration, which in the past had been very low. In 1973, of those immigrants from South America who had been in Israel for five years, the rate of emigration was 18%; in 1983 it reached 31%.

Organization of Latin American Jews in Israel. Many came to Israel to cease living a dual existence. Nevertheless the urge to preserve their distinctiveness and the wish to support new immigrants and work for immigration from their land of origin, brought them to organize various activities. Outstanding among these is the Association of Immigrants from Latin America with branches in 24 cities and towns, from the north to Eilat, with the main one in Tel Aviv. The Association is active in assisting the absorption of newcomers and in other areas. One of the problems of qualitative absorption characteristic of some of the Jews from Latin America results from their poisitive experience in the communities from which they came as active volunteers in Jewish organizations. With the structure of Israeli institutionalized public activity and the absence of a community framework, they missed this focus. The Association and other frameworks have offered a partial solution to this problem. The Association has a fund for mutual assistance and workers who advise and assist new immigrants in their contacts with institutions, in finding employment, etc. In addition there is a library, a theater, clubs, a monthly newspaper in Spanish, a Bible study circle, and so on. The main activity in the branches is in aiding absorption and in the cultural area—lectures, clubs, tours, and social activities.

The general tendency to integrate all the countries of Latin America, is countered by the tendency of each country to remain independent. Thus side-by-side with the Association of Latin American Immigrants, the immigrants from Brazil have a separate organization because of the language difference (Portuguese), and an informal organization of Mexican immigrants exists on a volunteer basis. For immigrants from other countries there are semi-formal groups which organize social meetings. Those from provincial towns in Argentina, especially from Jewish agricultural settlements, meet in active groups which organize a yearly meeting, sometimes attracting hundreds of participants. There are also Spanish-speaking working groups within the framework of Na'amat and WIZO.

The Association tries to function as an influential group and also as a pressure group in the interests of new immigrants and to further aliya, in the Ministry of Absorption and the Immigration Department of the Jewish Agency as well as active groups in such countries as Argentina. Immigrants from South America have not achieved significant weight in political institutions and parties in Israel. Due to the importance of youth movements of the Zionist Labor parties in their original communities, especially in Argentina, many of the immigrants were inclined over the years to support the Labor Movement. The Labor party and also other parties (Herut, Liberals, Mapam) have departments or committees which deal with the party organization of immigrants from Latin America—in information activities and in enlisting support, especially on the eve of elections. Three members of the Knesset have come from Latin American countries: Prof. Yitzhak Klinghofer of the Liberal Party (Brazil); Matityahu Drobles of Herut (Argentina); and Eliezer Ronan of Mapam (Mexico). Each of the parties mentioned publish political pamphlets in Spanish, generally twice a year. Immigrants from Latin America have taken a place in the leadership of the World Zionist Organization and the Jewish Agency (such as Arye Dulzin, Isaac Harkavi, Haim Finklestein) and in a number of its departments, in the kibbutz movement, in medical institutions, etc. The representation of Jews from Latin America is high in the diplomatic service, and in cooperative development programs with Latin American countries. By their service in Latin America and in Spain, they have been able to exploit the knowledge they acquired in their countries of origin and have contributed to the good relationships with these countries.

Employment. Latin American immigrants are to be found in all sectors and levels, but there are a number of professions and branches in which their presence is prominent. There was a period when most of the doctors in the Negev were from Latin America; they still take a large part in medicine in development areas and in border districts, and generally, in dentistry, architecture, sociology, and in developing analytical psychology and therapy; many professionals have taken graduate work in their countries of origin in their profession such as law, accounting, and teaching, and are now employed in these fields. Immigrants from Latin America are noteworthy in the economic area, in investment companies, and manufacturing (the Polgat, Rim, Clal Companies).

Cultural activities. Israel has two weeklies in Spanish; *Aurora* in Tel Aviv and *Semana* in Jerusalem. They fill various purposes, first in respect to Jews from Latin America, especially new immigrants and those who are not proficient in Hebrew; secondly in respect to diplomats, advanced students, visitors, and tourists who read Spanish; and thirdly for Spanish speakers outside the country, especially Jews who are interested in what is happening in Israel and who subscribe to the papers. In Israel they serve as a source of news on events in Latin America and the rest of the world. *Aurora* and *La Semana* also publish books in Spanish. Kol Israel broadcasts a daily program in Spanish directed toward immigrants.

The Association of Spanish-speaking writers in Israel unites tens of writers and organizes workshops, lectures, and literary competitions in cooperation with the Israel-Argentinian Friendship Society. The weekly *Aurora* publishes special art and literature supplements. The Institute for Cultural Ties with Countries of Latin America—Spain, and Portugal, contributes to the strengthening of cultural ties with those countries.

Trends in Absorption and Identification. A commonly designated phenomenon in the process of absorption is the "identification change" that happens to the immigrant. While they were in their native country they were "Jews", Argentinians, Mexicans, etc. of Jewish descent or people of the Jewish religion; upon their arrival in Israel they became Argentinians, Mexicans, etc.

In the countries of origin of most of the immigrants from Latin America, there is no formal separation of church and state; there exists a system of civil registration which makes possible intermarriage without any difficulty. Immigrants from South America who lived as Jews in a Catholic community and as citizens under an unstable government, at times oppressed, are sensitive to matters of human rights of the citizen and are inclined to resist what is called "religious coercion." The ban on conversion in Argentina and the hardship involved in other countries places an additional burden on instances of immigration of mixed couples. Most of the immigrants from Latin America are not religious according to the usual Israeli standards. With the development of Conservative and Reform congregations in Latin America, a flow has begun of immigrants who had been members of these congregations.

An additional paradox concerning the identification of these immigrants is reflected in the differences in the social framework between their life in the Diaspora and their life in Israel. The widespread affiliation in the Diaspora with Jewish organizations, in sports, economic, cultural, political, educational, and community affairs bestowed a feeling of belonging and a framework of identification. Upon their immigration to Israel they enter into an individualistic society whose formal and informal frameworks do not satisfy them. The system for their absorption is mainly bureaucratic and the immigrants do not find there an answer to their social needs, especially as in their countries of origin they did not need to apply personally for public services.

Jews from Latin America come from countries in which the lifestyle was middle class, generally pleasant, even in periods of political and social tension. In Israel, they miss this kind of ease. Those who go to kibbutzim find a social system which is inclusive and absorbing. The immigrants who identify themselves ideologically and come as pioneering groups are absorbed en bloc and overcome crises of adaptation by settling according to the ideals of their groups. Most of those who leave the kibbutzim settle in the city; a minority leaves Israel.

Two interesting experiments were tried by immigrants from Brazil. One group, identified with Mapam, tried cooperative living in Haifa. Another group, named after Dr. Michaelewitz of the Labor movement, immigrated in the late 1960s. Each family acquired an apartment in the Tel Aviv area where they were absorbed economically, but existed as a group for social and organizational needs.

For youngsters from Latin America, there are widespread long-term educational programs in Israel, conducted mainly by the World Zionist Organization, and in a large measure administered by veteran immigrants from these countries. The "Tapuz" program caters for thousands of young people who go to Israel for a two-month period, and there are also Jewish high school programs and study semesters in Israel. There are volunteer programs, and programs for absorbing students into the universities and other institutions of higher learning for a year or for regular studies. These programs, courses, and seminars for all ages, and the flow of tourists, serve as a bridge by means of which Jews from Latin America meet in Israel with those of

Latin American origin. Strong ties, with visits in both directions, characterize the Jews of Latin America in Israel, in spite of the great distances involved.

M. KITRON—D. SCHERS

LATIN AMERICA, RELATIONS WITH ISRAEL. In the UN Assembly debate of 1947 the attitude of the Latin American countries towards the creation of a Jewish State was not uniform. The liberal, democratic regimes were highly sympathetic, whereas the conservative, Catholic governments were influenced by the Vatican's anti-Zionist position at that time. Local Jewish communities played an important role promoting the creation of pro-Zionist committees, in which prominent public figures participated. In several countries, however, such as Chile and Honduras, the governments were influenced by the local Arab population.

Guatemala and Uruguay, together with Peru, participated in the *United Nations Special Committee on Palestine and were instrumental in getting the principle of the establishment of the Jewish State and the Partition Plan adopted. At the UN Assembly, in fall 1947, the Plan was opposed by two conservative Latin American countries, Columbia and El Salvador. In the last stage of the debates the USA exerted its influence in support of the Partition Plan, attempting to sway the undecided Latin American countries, such as Haiti and Paraguay. In the historic vote of 29 November 1947, 13 Latin American countries (Uruguay, Ecuador, Bolivia, Brazil, Guatemala, Haiti, Venezuela, Nicaragua, Panama, Paraguay, Peru, Costa Rica, and the Dominican Republic), voted in favor of the Partition Plan; one (Cuba) voted against; and six (El Salvador, Argentina, Honduras, Mexico, Chile, Colombia) abstained. Even the countries which had initially expressed reservations quickly accepted the existence of the Jewish State. Latin American support for Israel reached its peak on 11 May 1949, when 18 Latin American countries voted to accept Israel as a member of the UN and only two (El Salvador and Brazil) abstained. Almost all the first Latin American countries to recognize Israel belonged to the liberal camp: Guatemala, on 19 May 1948, followed during the next month by Uruguay, Nicaragua, Costa Rica, Venezuela, and Panama. The remaining countries officially recognized Israel between September, 1948, and April, 1949.

In January, 1949, Israel's first diplomatic representation in Latin America and her fourth in the world was established in Montevideo. In summer 1949 an Israeli legation was established in Buenos Aires, and an Argentinian legation in Tel Aviv. In 1952 Israel opened a legation in Brazil and in 1953 in Mexico. Between 1952 and 1955 Brazil, Uruguay, and Guatemala established diplomatic missions in Israel (the last in Jerusalem).

Bilateral ties between Israel and various Latin American countries developed particularly in the 1960s. Due to the reputation earned by Israel's rapid economic, technological, and social progress, Israeli technical assistance, especially in the agricultural field, was widely requested, especially after the advent of progressive democratic governments in several Latin American countries (including Argentina and Brazil) and of military regimes were geared towards accelerated economic development. Technical cooperation ties were established even with Cuba in the early stages of Castro's rule. The number of Israeli diplomatic missions in Latin America grew to 16, and the number of Latin American embassies in Israel to 15—ten of these in Jerusalem, constituting the bulk of the diplomatic corps in Israel's capital—while five Latin American representations remained in Tel Aviv (Argentina, Brazil, Mexico, Peru, and Cuba). Twenty-two technical cooperation agreements, 16 commercial agreements, and 16 cultural accords were signed in that period.

Latin American support of Israel was also expressed during this period at the UN and in international organizations (*see* UNITED NATIONS AND ISRAEL). Most of the Latin American countries voted against resolutions antagonistic to Israel's sovereignty (such as the appointment of a UN custodian of abandoned Arab property in Israel) and in favor of motions for Israeli-Arab negotiation (1951 and 1961–1964). Following the Sinai Campaign, in 1956–1957, the Latin American countries maintained their opposition to territorial conquests, supporting the resolutions calling for withdrawal of Israeli forces from Sinai. After the 1967 Six-Day War, however, 22 Latin American countries voted against a draft resolution by the non-aligned states which called for immediate and unconditional Israeli withdrawal from all the occupied territories. In the same debate 20 Latin American countries proposed an alternative resolution (which was not approved), positing a link between withdrawal and between cessation of hostilities and the establishment of peaceful coexistence. The Latin American bloc played a decisive role in the formulation of Security Council Resolution 242. The rate of support for Israel in the Latin American group (which had increased numerically through the independence of four new Caribbean States: Jamaica, Trinidad-Tobago, Barbados, and Guyana) was higher in 1960–67 than that of any other group, including the Western bloc.

In the late 1960s Latin America underwent fresh political changes. In 1968 a left-wing military regime was established in Peru. In 1969 a Communist-Socialist coalition headed by Salvador Allende came to power in Chile. In 1973 Juan Peron was reelected President in Argentina. These countries joined the non-aligned movement of which Cuba was already a member, and other Latin American countries followed. Furthermore the number of the Caribbean countries grew by the mid-1980s to 15. Many of them became increasingly radical also due to their ethnic attachment to Africa, and all joined the non-aligned states. These developments led to the formation of a broad Latin American radical group, following a sharply anti-American and anti-Israel line which was also active within the "G-77," the southern hemisphere organization (Latin America, Africa, and Asia) founded in 1964 in order to obtain preferential trade conditions from the rich industrialized countries of the north. Even though the G-77 had originally been established as an economic entity, it became active in the political sphere and began to adopt anti-Israel resolutions after the Conference held in Lima in 1971. In the 1980s the membership of the Non-Aligned grew to 95, and that of G-77 to 126—both organizations turning into factors of decisive weight in the international arena. Another development was the oil crisis which severely damaged the economies of most Latin American countries. The soaring oil prices in the years 1973–1974 and in 1979 created a dependence relationship with the oil-exporting countries, such as Saudi Arabia and Iraq, which controlled oil quotas and prices as well as the flow of petrodollar investments. Countries such as Brazil now adopted a pro-Arab foreign policy. Latin American oil-producing countries, such as Venezuela and

Ecuador which belonged to OPEC (Organization of Petroleum Exporting Countries), which benefit from the price increases, strengthened their relations with the Arab oil producers due to their joint economic interests. In several Latin American countries, policy was also influenced by an awakening of ethnical and political consciousness among the population of Arab origin now numbering over two and a half million (the Jewish population is estimated at only half a million). The seizing of power in such countries as Argentina and Chile by military juntas did not lead to a substantial change of attitudes. The military dictatorships which replaced the leftist governments continued to follow a pro-Arab policy, due to political and economic considerations.

These developments led to the rapid growth of diplomatic relations between the Latin American and the Arab countries and to the opening of PLO offices in Cuba, Peru, Mexico, Brazil, and Bolivia, and in Nicaragua following the 1979 Sandinista revolution. At the UN a radical change in the Latin American position on the Palestinian question was manifest. In 1974 seven Latin American countries voted in favor of Resolution 3236 recognizing the PLO as the representative of the Palestinian people and the right of the Palestinian people to national independence and sovereignty. In 1982 the number of Latin American countries supporting these claims rose to 20. Concurrently with this, Latin American support of resolutions condemning Israeli occupation of the territories and denial of the rights of the Arab population grew. In 1975 Brazil, Mexico, Cuba, Guyana, and Grenada voted in favor of the "Zionism is racism" resolution; Uruguay, El Salvador, the Dominican Republic, Haiti, Honduras, Nicaragua, Panama, Costa Rica, Bahamas, and Barbados voted against; and Ecuador, Argentina, Bolivia, Guatemala, Venezuela, Paraguay, Peru, Colombia, Jamaica, and Chile (the last having voted in favor in committee and the plenum) abstained. In the 1980s the voting patterns of the Latin American bloc resembled those of the African and Asian states. Several countries (Mexico and to a lesset extent, Argentina, Brazil, and Peru) began to support all anti-Israeli resolutions. The other Latin American countries supported most of the resolutions against Israel and abstained only on the harshest ones. Costa Rica, Haiti, El Salvador, Guatemala, the Dominican Republic, and Grenada (under the new regime established after the US intervention in 1983) have from time to time taken a more pro-Israel stand. Cuba, serving as chairman of the non-aligned from 1979 to 1983, was influential in determining the extremist policies of that group. The positions adopted by the Latin American countries in the UN affected their bilateral relations with Israel. After the adoption of the 1980 Knesset law proclaiming reunified Jerusalem the capital of Israel, 12 Latin American countries complied with Security Council demands and transferred their embassies to Tel Aviv. Notwithstanding, Costa Rica returned its embassy to Jerusalem in 1982 and El Salvador followed suit in 1984. Cuba severed ties with Israel in 1973, Guyana in 1974, and Nicaragua in 1982.

Israeli diplomatic representation in Latin America nevertheless continued to grow; embassies were opened in the Caribbean area and in Central America (Haiti, Jamaica, and El Salvador in the 1970s and Honduras in 1986). In 1986 there were 19 Israeli embassies in Latin America and 17 Latin American embassies in Israel. Israeli technical assistance in the 1980s included long-term programs in Costa Rica, the Dominican Republic, Colombia, and Honduras, and courses in agriculture, rural development, community development, and public health, both in Israel and in Latin America, with an annual participation of about 700 advanced students.

Commercial relations were always a subsidiary element in Israel-Latin American relations, totaling less than 50 million dollars in each direction in 1974. In 1980 Israeli exports were worth 150 million dollars and its imports from Latin America, 140 million dollars. Trade fell off in 1983–1984 due to the economic crisis in a number of Latin American countries, but exports again rose from 1985, reaching 185 million dollars in 1986 whereas imports went down to 82 million dollars. The main export items are in the field of chemicals, agriculture, machinery, and electronics. Israel imports meat, fish, cars, cocoa, coffee, sugar, and metals. Trade statistics do not cover defense exports and the import of strategic materials, such as oil and coal. Oil imports from Mexico in 1986 were estimated at 250 million dollars and coal imports from Colombia at 5 million dollars. An important economic role is also played by Israeli economic institutions in several Latin American countries —banks, building societies, and planning and agricultural development companies.

Cultural ties between Israel and Latin America were established in the 1950s. In 1956 the Central Institute for Cultural Relations between Israel and Iberoamerica, Spain, and Portugal was founded in Jerusalem. The Institute has promoted the creation of institutes in Latin America and fosters contacts with intellectuals, artists, and academic circles in countries in the area. There are now 30 subsidiary institutes in the capitals and important provincial towns of 17 countries. Writers' conventions, painters' and sculptors' workshops, and meetings with church dignitaries are held in Israel. Cultural agreements have been signed with 13 Latin American countries. On the academic plane, the Hebrew University in Jerusalem and Tel Aviv University, among others, have agreements with Latin American universities. Far-ranging scientific exchanges are effected between the Weizmann Institute and research institutes in Latin America.

The presence of Nazi war criminals in certain Latin American countries has sometimes clouded Israel's relations with them. Following Israel's capture of Adolf Eichmann in Buenos Aires in 1960, Argentina appealed to the UN Security Council, accusing Israel of a violation of the sovereign rights of the Argentine Republic resulting from Eichmann's illicit and clandestine transfer, and demanding appropriate reparation. A diplomatic settlement was eventually reached. Eichmann was tried in Jerusalem in 1961 and sentenced to death. J. BARROMI

LATRUN. Locality in the Judean Foothills, on the eastern rim of the Ayalon Valley; in antiquity it was situated on the crossroads of the Gaza-Gibeon and the Jerusalem-Jaffa connections. It has been one of the country's major battlefields throughout history; the Romans, Byzantine, and early Arab rulers fortified it, and Saladin destroyed the fortress in the 12th century. A Trappist monastery was built there about 1890. In 1946, leaders of the yishuv and Jewish underground fighters were held in a detention camp in Latrun. In the 1948 War of Independence, Latrun was a key position in the fight for Jerusalem. To open the road to the capital, Jewish forces repeatedly tried to take the Latrun police fortress held by the Arab Legion under the command of British officers; their failure necessitated the building of the "Burma Road" and, later, the "Road of Valor" to bypass the Arab position. According to the 1949 armistice agreement, Latrun remained a Jordanian enclave; it fell to the Israel army during the Six-Day War. The Jerusalem-Tel Aviv highway, opened in 1981, passes north of the monastery and the police fortress. On a hill facing the monastery is the interfaith settlement, Neveh Shalom.

E. ORNI

LATTES, DANTE. Writer, journalist, and teacher in Italy (b. Pitigliano, Italy, 1876; d. Venice, 1965). Trained as a rabbi, Lattes devoted himself to fostering Jewish culture and Zionist ideals among Italian Jewry. In 1896 he became a contributor, and later one of the editors, of *Il Corriere Israelitico*, a Trieste Jewish monthly. In 1916 he and Alfonso Pacifici founded a weekly, *Israel*, in Florence, and, about nine years later, a monthly supplement, *La Rassegna Mensile di Israel*. During World War II he lived in Palestine. Later he returned to Italy and resumed direction of the monthly, remaining its editor from 1945 until his death.

Lattes was active in disseminating Jewish knowledge among Italian Jews and gentiles. He taught modern Hebrew language and literature at the Institute for Slavonic and Oriental Languages in Rome and was on the faculty of the Collegio Rabbinico Italiano of Florence. Lattes helped create a network of Jewish centers and served as general secretary and president (later honorary president) of the Italian Zionist Federation. He was a delegate to Zionist Congresses prior to World War II.

His writings include *Bialik* (1926), *Storia del Sionismo* (The Story of Zionism, 1928), *Racconti palestinesi* (Palestinian Stories, 1949), *Letture del risorgimento ebraico* (Lectures on Jewish Rebirth, 1949), and *Aspetti e problemi dell'Ebraismo* (Aspects and Problems of Judaism, 1945). Lattes translated Hebrew classics and modern works into Italian. He also made literary translations from Italian into Hebrew and from French, German, and English into Italian.

G. ROMANO

LATVIA, ZIONISM IN. Under the long rule of the Tsars and later as part of an independent republic (1918–40), Latvian Jews, most of whom were of Lithuanian origin, always maintained their distinctive characteristics. They were intensely Jewish in spirit. When the ideas of national renaissance were first voiced in modern times, they found an immediate echo among Latvian Jews.

Early Years, 1880–1918. In the 1880s Hovevei Zion groups were formed in Riga, Libau (Liepaja), Dvinsk (Daugavpils), Krustpils (Kreuzburg), and Bauska. Two famous Latvian rabbis, Mordecai Eliasberg (1817–89) and Abraham Isaac Kook (1865–1935), played an outstanding part in spreading the idea of Jewish national revival. Both men were religious leaders of the small Jewish community of Bauska. Rabbi Kook subsequently settled in Eretz Israel, where he became Chief Rabbi of the Ashkenazim. At the first conference of the Hovevei Zion groups (1884), Riga was represented by two delegates, Wolf Lunz and Leib Shalit, both well-to-do merchants and communal workers. In 1891 a group of Jews from Latvia settled in Hadera.

Leib Shalit, of Riga, and S.J. Zaks, of Dvinsk, were delegates to the First Zionist Congress (1897). Soon afterward a group called Zion was established on the initiative of Abraham Meir Teiz, a shoemaker. Among its members were two men who played leading parts in the history of Latvian Zionism. One was Lazar Ettinger, who attended the First All-Russia Zionist Conference in Warsaw and the Second Zionist Congress (1898) and was a prominent figure in the Zionist movement for many years. The other pioneer was the lawyer Yeshayahu Thon (1864–1939). A gifted orator, Thon was a delegate to a number of Zionist Congresses and chairman of the Jewish National Fund in Riga. In 1935 he settled in Palestine.

Latvian Jewry was represented also at the Second All-Russia Zionist Conference in Minsk (1902). The delegate from Jelgava (Mitau) was Rabbi Mordekhai Nurock, who for a number of decades was a leading figure in the World Zionist movement and, later, in Israel's public life. Another outstanding Latvian Zionist was Nissan Katzenelsohn of Libau who was a close collaborator of Herzl and a member of the first Russian Duma. After the collapse of the Russian Revolution in 1905, Zionist activity was forbidden by law, but thanks to the ingenuity of a number of people the work was continued and younger persons joined the movement. A delegation of Latvian Zionists, which included Meir Berlin of Riga, took part in the Helsingfors Conference (1906).

The first Latvian Zionists were national-minded, religiously observant Jews, but gradually new social doctrines also made themselves felt in Latvian Zionism. In 1897 a Zionist Socialist students' circle was established in Riga. Dvinsk emerged as an important center of the Po'ale Zion party, which adopted a revolutionary program. In 1901 a group of Tze'irei Zion, whose program stressed *hagshama atzmit* (self-realization), was formed in Dvinsk. A number of its members subsequently settled in Palestine. In 1912 a Tze'irei Zion group was formed in Riga; this was the beginning of a movement that was to play an important part in the independent Latvian Republic. Among the leaders of the group were Ze'ev Levenberg, who was a delegate to the 11th Zionist Congress (1913), and Yerahmiel Vinnik, who participated in the Minsk Conference of Tze'irei Zion groups (1913) and became a well-known journalist and leader in the Labor Zionist movement. Vinnik died in a Siberian labor camp during World War II.

Despite the difficulties posed by the Russian authorities, and the hardships and deportations during World War I, Zionist work in Latvia was never interrupted. It was revitalized with the overthrow of Tsarism (March, 1917) and, especially, with the establishment of the Latvian Republic (November, 1918).

Zionism in Independent Latvia, 1918–34. The Jewish population in Latvia, about 100,000 strong, took full advantage of the new democratic regime, creating a center of Jewish life that became a model for many other Jewish communities. The Zionists, who had to cope with formidable opposition from the Bund and the religious movement Agudat Israel, became the leading force in Latvian Jewry. They formed a wide network of Hebrew schools, cultural institutions, and Yiddish-language papers and at the same time took an active part in parliamentary and municipal elections.

Outstanding among the Jewish members of the Latvian parliament were Prof. Max Laserson of Tze'irei Zion and Rabbi Nurock of Mizrachi. The former, who was well known as a scholar, lawyer, writer, and journalist, was a delegate to a number of Zionist Congresses. Both these Zionist parliamentarians conducted a campaign for Jewish national rights and for Latvian state aid to Jewish schools. Both were active in the Congresses of Minorities held after World War I.

Of special importance was the part played by Zionists in the development of the Yiddish press, including journals like *Dos Folk* (1920–27), *Der Weg* (1922–24), *Frimorgen* (1926–34), and *Ovent Post* (1932). An outstanding figure in Latvian-Jewish journalism was Jacob Hellman, a dynamic leader of the Labor wing of Zionism. He profoundly influenced the general development of Zionist life and was a well-known delegate at international Jewish gatherings.

The Hebrew school system in Latvia, which included both primary and secondary schools, was guided by the ideals of Zionism. There was close cooperation between Latvian Zionists in many fields, but there were also divisions along political and social lines. The large majority of the General Zionists supported Chaim Weizmann.

Latvia was the cradle of the Revisionist movement. A lecture in Russian by Vladimir Jabotinsky led to the formation of the first branch of the youth organization Betar in 1923. The student organization Hasmonea adopted the Revisionist program, and the foundation was laid for a strong party. For some time Dr. Joseph Schechtman, Jabotinsky's friend and close collaborator, was a member of the editorial board of *Dos Folk*.

The Mizrachi movement encountered strong opposition from Agudat Israel, led by Mordekhai Dubin, a member of the Latvian parliament. The guiding spirit of Mizrachi was Rabbi Nurock.

Tze'irei Zion was a popular movement in Latvia. It had deep roots both in general political life and among halutz (pioneer) youth and was active in many Jewish communal institutions. Between 1922 and 1931 there existed in Latvia a dynamic left-wing Zionist Socialist party which had a clear Socialist program and laid great stress on aliya (immigration). Composed of younger persons, it made a valuable contribution to the Jewish national revival movement. Many of its members subsequently went to Israel. In January, 1931, Tze'irei Zion and the Zionists-Socialists merged into one group. They were joined by some members of the Zionist Socialist student organization Ha-Shahar, led by Schneier Levenberg, who joined the Executive of the united party. Levenberg later became the chairman of the party and the editor of its organ, *Arbets-Volk*.

Latvia was a strong center of the Halutz movement. It had a number of active Zionist youth organizations including Ha-Shomer ha-Tza'ir, Gordonia, Borochov Youth, He-Halutz (with a Zionist Socialist outlook), Betar, Herzlia (General Zionist), and Tze'irei Mizrachi (Mizrachi Youth). These groups all trained their members for aliya. Jewish students had a number of Zionist organizations of their own: He-Haver (General Zionist), Ha-Shahar (Zionist Socialist), and Hasmonea (Revisionist).

The Jewish sports movement was also under Zionist influence. Its outstanding figure was Barukh Bag, who later became the head of the Wingate Institute in Israel. Zionist clubs included the Brenner Club and the Bialik Club (both Zionist Socialist) in Riga. Riga was an important center of Zionist life and was visited by numerous Zionist leaders.

From 1924 to 1935 about 6,000 Jews emigrated from Latvia. Of these, a large part went to Palestine. The total number of Latvian Jews settling in Palestine between 1919 and 1941 was 4,547 (503 went between 1920 and 1924, 2,253 between 1925 and 1934, 1,715 between 1935 and 1939, and 76 in 1940 and 1941). Immigrants from Latvia made a valuable contribution to the development of the kibbutz movement and set up a number of industrial enterprises in Palestine. For several years Latvia served as a transit center for aliya from the Soviet Union. In 1933, the last time Zionist Congress elections were held in Latvia, 22,536 shekels were sold and 19,474 voters elected 8 delegates.

Last Years. 1934–41. The initiation of an authoritarian regime in Latvia (May, 1934) came as a serious blow to the Zionist movement. All public activities were placed under strict government supervision. Zionist work, in a greatly restricted form, took on a semilegal or illegal character. Between 1934 and 1939 a number of leading Zionists left the country. The rest carried on under very difficult conditions. The occupation of Latvia by Soviet forces meant the end of the organized Zionist movement there. Thousands of Jews were deported as "bourgeois elements." The final blow came on 22 June 1941, when Nazi troops entered the country. According to eye-witnesses the Zionist spirit was kept alive even in the ghettos of Latvia until the start of mass-deportations.

See also RUSSIA, ZIONISM IN — S. LEVENBERG

LATZKY-BERTHOLDI, JACOB WOLF. Labor leader and publicist (b. Kiev, Ukraine, Russia, 1881; d. Tel Aviv, 1940). Latzky-Bertholdi studied at the Riga Polytechnic until 1901, when he was expelled because of revolutionary activities. He then went to Berlin where he was influenced by Zionism, met Nachman Syrkin, and helped him found Herut, a Zionist Socialist group. After his return to Russia in 1902, he was active in the Zionist Socialist movement and became one of its central figures. During the debate on the East Africa scheme he became a Territorialist. Again with Syrkin (whose ideas he basically shared), he was among the leaders of the Socialist Zionist Labor Party, founded in 1905, which adopted a platform combining Territorialism and revolutionary politics in Russia. In 1908 he visited New York on matters of Jewish migration.

After the Russian Revolution, Latzky-Bertholdi helped organize the Folkspartei (People's Party). In 1918 he was for a short time Minister of Jewish Affairs in the newly established Ukrainian Republic. Later he left Russia for Germany, where he devoted himself to cultural work and to the organization of Jewish migration. In the years 1923–25 he visited South American countries to study the possibilities of Jewish immigration and settlement there. Gradually he returned to Zionism. Settling in Riga, he became coeditor of the newly established Yiddish daily *Frimorgen* (1926). In 1935 he settled in Palestine, where he was active in the labor movement and served as deputy director of the Labor Archives of the Histadrut.

Latzky-Bertholdi contributed to numerous Yiddish periodicals on Jewish migration, culture, and art. In Palestine he was associated with various Hebrew publications.

LAUTERBACH, LEO. Attorney and executive secretary of the World Zionist Organization (b. Drogobych, Galicia, Austria, 1886; d. Jerusalem, 1968). Educated at the Universities of Vienna and Lvov, he received his law degree in 1913. In 1904 he was a founder of Agudat Herzl, a Zionist undergraduate student society in Przemysl, and in 1912–13 served as chairman of the Zionist Students' Association of Galicia. Moving to Vienna in 1914, he served in the Austro-

Hungarian Army from 1915 to 1918. In 1919 he joined the staff of the World Zionist Organization in London, becoming director of its Organization Department in 1921 and executive secretary in 1935. He moved to Palestine when his office was transferred there in 1936. Lauterbach retired in 1956.

LAVI. Religious kibbutz in eastern Lower Galilee, 8 mi. (12 km.) west of Tiberias, founded by pioneer immigrants from Britain. The kibbutz engages in farming, has a factory for synagogue furniture and a large guest house. It maintains a religious study center for immigrants. The name, resembling Lubiya, the former Arab village near the site, means "Lioness." Population (1987), 727. E. ORNI

LAVI (LOEWENSTEIN), THEODOR. Historian and writer (b. Turnu-Severin, 1905; d. Jerusalem, 1983). Lavi was a Zionist activist from his youth, and one of the first leaders of the Zionist Youth Association, ATS (1922–1927), the first youth movement in Romania. For several years he directed the Zionist Organization's organ *Stiri din Lummea Evreiasca* (News from the Jewish World). He received his Ph.D. at Bucharest University and was teacher and headmaster in Ploesti and in Bucharest until 1940. In 1940 he was elected to the Zionist Executive and was placed in charge of its Culture Department. In 1942 he organized the Jewish schools for the Jewish Center (the Romanian *Judenrat*), as an emissary of the Zionist Executive, but was dismissed by the Nazis.

After the Liberation, Lavi continued his Zionist activity until the disbanding of the Zionist movement; he was arrested in 1950 with Zionist leaders and sentenced to life imprisonment. Released in 1955, he immigrated to Israel the following year. From 1958 to 1975 Lavi was a researcher at Yad Vashem, coordinating the volumes on European Jewish communities; he edited *Toledot*, a periodical dealing with the history of Romanian Jewry, and directed the Center for Research of Romanian Jewry at the Hebrew University.

In addition to many articles on education and Zionist ideology, he wrote *Toledot Ha-Tziyonut, Antologia Ziyonit, Yahadut Romania be-Ma'avaka le-Hatzalata*, and finally *Ze Eino he-Hatul* in which he described his suffering in prison in Romania.

Lavi was influential in the shaping of Jewish and Zionist education in Romania during the war and contributed to the study of Romanian Jewry. He pioneered the study of the history of Romanian Jewry during the Holocaust period. E. OFIR

LAVON (LUBIANIKER), PINHAS. Israeli politician (b. Kopychintsy, Galicia, 1904; d. Gedera, 1976). He studied law in Lvov and was one of the founders of the pioneering Socialist youth movement, Gordonia. Immigrating to Palestine in 1929, he settled in Kibbutz Hulda, rose in the ranks of Mapai, and became a member of the Histadrut Central Committee. He was a promising leader and served as Secretary-General of the Histadrut between 1949–51. Elected to the Knesset in 1949, he served as Minister of Agriculture (1950–52), Minister without Portfolio (1952–54), and Minister of Defense (1954–55). A man of sharp intellect, quick wit, literary and oratorical skills, he was considered a possible successor to David Ben-Gurion. He was initially a moderate in foreign policy but became an ardent supporter of an activist policy against Arab terrorism and challenged the conciliatory policy of Prime Minister Moshe Sharett. During his brief tenure as Minister of Defense he attempted to reorganize that department and reduce the scope of its economic activities and defense industries, arousing the opposition of its Director-General, Shimon Peres, and the Chief of Staff, Moshe Dayan. Lavon's imperious manner and sharp tongue annoyed the Mapai leadership, who demanded that Ben-Gurion come out of retirement and resume his position as Defense Minister in view of the personality problems in the Defense Ministry and mounting security issues along the borders. The Lavon Affair (see below) focused on the question whether Lavon gave the order activating a covert Israeli network in Egypt. He was forced to resign in February 1955. The following year he resumed his post as Histadrut Secretary-General and instituted far-reaching organizational changes in the economic enterprises of that body. In 1960 he demanded to be rehabilitated, arguing that new evidence showed he had been framed in 1954. Ben-Gurion refused and Lavon turned to the press. Ben-Gurion was determined to oust him from the Histadrut and succeeded in doing so in 1961, threatening to resign if his demand was not accepted. Removed from office, embittered and ill, Lavon withdrew from public life. Even a 1964 letter to him from Prime Minister Eshkol, which was tantamount to his rehabilitation, failed to return him to public activity. In retrospect it was assumed that while he had not specifically ordered the operations in Egypt, he had known about them, failed to halt them, and gave what amounted to tacit approval.

Lavon Affair. In July, 1954, a series of bomb explosions at various American cultural institutes, cinemas, and libraries, rocked Cairo and Alexandria. They were carried out by young Egyptian Jews, part of an Israeli underground network recruited in the early 1950s, who were exposed and captured by the Egyptian police and brought to trial. The operation was authorized by Unit 139 of the Israel Army Intelligence, but serious doubt remains as to whether it was authorized formally by Lavon. He knew about the existence of the unit and discussed operations in Egypt with the Director of Military Intelligence, Colonel Benjamin Gibli, but claimed later that he never authorized the attacks. In January, 1955, an Egyptian military court sentenced to death two of the suspects; one committed suicide, and others were sentenced to long jail terms; they were released only in 1968.

A commission of inquiry, headed by Chief Justice Olshan, was appointed in Israel but failed to reach a decision as to "who gave the order?" Lavon resigned in February, 1955, after serious disagreements with the Chief-of-Staff, Moshe Dayan, and the Director-General of the Defense Ministry, Shimon Peres, and was replaced by David Ben-Gurion. At the time the entire matter remained top secret in Israel, which never admitted its involvement.

In 1960 the commander of the Jewish cell in Egypt was tried in camera by an Israeli court charged with being an Egyptian agent. In his trial he revealed that he was ordered to give false testimony before the Olshan Committee and that documents were forged on the instruction of Colonel Gibli. When Lavon heard of this he demanded of Ben-Gurion that the entire affair be reexamined. He also demanded public exoneration which Ben-Gurion refused to grant. Another commission was appointed, headed by Supreme Court Justice Haim Cohn, which confirmed that witnesses were suborned to give false testimony in the 1955 investigation, but this commission was equally unable to reach a decision as to "who gave the order?" Lavon now took his case before the Knesset Foreign Affairs and Security Committee and the affair became public when Lavon's revelations were leaked to the press. He claimed that he had been ousted from his post as Defense Minister by Dayan and Peres when he demanded accountability from them and wanted to reduce the scope of the ministry's authority. He accused them of working behind his back with Ben-Gurion and in the process, tarnishing the image of the army. They in turn accused him of mismanagement and irrational behavior. The affair now became part of the Ben-Gurion succession struggle between the younger elements in Mapai and the veteran leadership. The latter decided that Lavon would have to leave his post as secretary-general of the Histadrut in order to placate Ben-Gurion, but that Ben-Gurion would have to be curbed. They refused to heed Ben-Gurion's demand for another judiciary investigatory commission and were content when a ministerial committee found, in 1960, that Lavon did not give the order. Ben-Gurion refused to accept the findings, claiming they were political and not legal, and resigned, forcing the country into early elections in the summer of 1961, in which Mapai lost five seats. The veteran Mapai leadership came to the conclusion that in the wake of the Affair Ben-Gurion would have to give up the premiership and finally brought about his resignation in June, 1963. Even after he left office Ben-Gurion insisted that Lavon was guilty, but Prime Minister Eshkol refused to reopen the case. This led to a split in Mapai and the creation of the *Rafi party in the summer of 1965. Ben-Gurion continued to feel that justice and due process of law must be Israel's guidelines and not the political convenience of its leaders. Lavon proclaimed his innocence to his dying day. The affair contributed to the decline of Mapai's hegemony in Israeli politics. M. MEDZINI

LAVRY, MARC. Israeli composer and conductor (b. Riga, Latvia, 1903; d. Haifa, 1967). He was active as composer and conductor in Berlin during the years 1929–1934. With the rise of the Nazi regime he returned to Riga, where the growing anti-Semitism led him to compose a symphonic poem named *The Wandering Jew*. In 1935 he immigrated to Palestine, where he soon composed the song *Emek* which established his new style. Incorporating this song into a symphonic poem he made the syncopated pattern of the *hora* folk dance into a symbol of the new national style. In 1940 he composed an oratorio, *Song of Songs* and wrote an opera, Dan the Guard (*Dan ha-Shomer*), based on a libretto by Max Brod based on a play by Shin Shalom. Lavry soon became the chief spokesman for a popular style, deliberately appealing to a large audience, and dominated by tuneful melodies. Dan the Guard was the first original opera produced in the country and dealt with daily political and social problems of the Jewish people in general and the kibbutz in particular. Lavry was a conductor and program director at the Palestine radio station founded in 1936, and in 1950 became the director of the music department of broadcasts to the Diaspora (Kol Zion la-Gola). He was a prolific composer in all genres, including folk songs, arrangements, and chamber and orchestral works.

J. HIRSHBERG

LAW OF RETURN. *See* RETURN, LAW OF.

T. E. Lawrence. [Zionist Archives]

LAWRENCE, THOMAS EDWARD (Lawrence of Arabia). British soldier, statesman, adventurer, and author (b. Tremadoc, Wales, 1888; d. England 1935). In connection with his archeological and Arabic studies at Oxford University, Lawrence made a walking tour of Syria and Palestine. From 1910 on he participated in an excavation of the site of the ancient Hittite city of Carchemish on the Euphrates River. In 1913 he participated in the mapping of northern Sinai, the Negev, and southern Transjordan for the British High Command.

In 1915 Lawrence was named assistant to David Hogarth, head of the Arab Bureau in Cairo. The next year he was sent to Jidda, Arabia, where he aided the Arab uprising against the Turkish government in Hejaz (the rebellion of Sherif Hussein in June, 1916).

As an expert in Arab affairs, Lawrence was a member of the British delegation to the Paris Peace Conference. As political adviser to Winston Churchill, then Secretary of State for Colonies, he attended the Cairo Conference (March, 1921) that outlined British policy in the Middle East after World War I. In 1922 Lawrence considered his political career ended and joined the British Tank Corps. In 1925 he joined the Royal Air Force and served first in India and then in England, where he was killed in a road accident in May, 1935. His books, *The Seven Pillars of Wisdom* (1926) and *Revolt in the Desert* (1927), in which he described his exploits and the Arab rebellion, won wide acclaim.

Lawrence's contacts with Zionism occurred late in World War I and in the immediate postwar period. He met Chaim Weizmann briefly while serving with Gen. Sir Edmund Allenby in Egypt in the spring of 1918. When, on Allenby's advice, Weizmann visited Feisal, the leader of the Arab Army, in southern Transjordan (June, 1918), he again met Lawrence, who was Feisal's right-hand man and who participated in the discussion. In Lawrence's subsequent letter to Weizmann, he confirmed the understanding between Feisal and Weizmann concerning joint efforts of Arabs and Jews in Palestine and cooperation between Palestine and the expanded Arab kingdom that was then under discussion.

Similarly, Lawrence participated in negotiations between Weizmann and Feisal in Europe, at the opening of the peace conference, and drafted the document known as the Feisal-Weizmann Agreement (3 January 1919). The letter from

Feisal to Felix Frankfurter (1 March 1919), confirming Arab-Jewish cooperation in Palestine, was written in Lawrence's handwriting and signed by Feisal.

Weizmann testified that Lawrence's attitude toward the Zionist movement was "very positive, depite the fact that he was strongly pro-Arab, and was erroneously depicted as anti-Zionist; he was of the opinion—like Feisal—that the Jews would bring great benefits to the Arabs and that the Arab world would greatly profit from a Jewish National Home in Palestine" (*Trial and Error*). A. COHEN

LAWS OF ISRAEL. *See* LEGISLATION IN ISRAEL.

LAZARE, BERNARD (pseud. of Bernard, Lazare). Author, journalist, and defender of Alfred Dreyfus (b. Nîmes, France, 1870; d. Paris, 1903). Primarily a symbolist poet and an anarchistic publicist, Lazare was deeply shocked by the *Dreyfus affair and fought for the rehabilitation of the French army officer.

He was an ardent Zionist for a time, and was elected by the Second Zionist Congress (1898) to the Actions Committee. He later broke with the Zionist movement over the establishment of a bank to finance Jewish settlement in Eretz Israel. As an adherent of anarchist doctrines, he could not agree that the movement for the rebirth of the Jewish people should be turned into what he called a "capitalist enterprise."

Lazare published a number of literary, sociological, and historical works, including *Anti-Semitism: Its History and Its Causes* (1894), in which he praised assimilation and partially justified anti-Semitism. S. KLINGER—M. CATANE

Emma Lazarus. [Zionist Archives]

LAZARUS, EMMA. Poet and essayist in the United States (b. New York, 1849; d. there, 1887). Although her early literary work showed no affinity for Jewish history or thought, the Russian pogroms and the flight of Jews to the United States awakened her Jewish consciousness. Her outspoken reaction to the pogroms and her devoted work on behalf of the refugees established her as a leader among the Jewish intellectuals of her day.

Immersing herself in the study of her people, their language, history, and literature, Emma Lazarus became an early exponent of the rebirth of Jewish nationhood on its ancient soil. In "An Epistle to Hebrews," published in the *American Hebrew* in 1882–83, she declared that the only remedy for the suffering Jews of Europe would be "a home for the homeless, a goal for the wanderer, an asylum for the persecuted, a nation for the denationalized." She opposed the emigration of eastern European Jews to the United States, where society was "utterly at variance with their time-honored customs and most sacred beliefs," and suggested "repatriation and auto-emancipation in Palestine." In her opinion, any other suggested solutions to the Jewish problem were only of temporary value.

Emma Lazarus wrote ardent Zionist poems, such as "The Banner of the Jews," which were often recited at Zionist gatherings. Her sonnet "The New Colossus" is inscribed on the base of the Statue of Liberty in New York harbor.

J. DIENSTAG

LEAGUE OF BRITISH JEWS. Anglo-Jewish anti-Zionist organization formed to protect Jewish rights and interests. It was founded in 1917 as an outgrowth of the ideas put forward in the statement issued that year by the Conjoint Foreign Committee over the signatures of David Lindo Alexander, president of the Board of Deputies of British Jews, and Claude G. Montefiore, president of the Anglo-Jewish Association, opposing efforts to obtain the Balfour Declaration. Its declared objectives were to uphold the status of British subjects professing the Jewish religion, to resist the allegation that Jews constituted a separate political or national entity, and to facilitate the settlement in Palestine of such Jews as might desire to make their home there. The chairman of the league was Lionel de Rothschild, and the committee included Lords Bearsted and Swaythling, Leonard Montefiore, and Laurie Magnus. Magnus edited the *Jewish Guardian*, a weekly which expressed the views of the league but was open also to other opinions.

The League of British Jews ceased to exist in 1929. In 1944 a successor organization was founded under the name Jewish Fellowship. The leader of this group, Basil Henriques, appeared before the Anglo-American Committee of Inquiry in 1946, submitting that "there is not a Jewish nation to which all Jews belong, and it follows as a corollary that we reject the idea of a Jewish State." At the same time he said, "We look on Palestine as the Holy Land, as a Jewish religious and cultural center, and desire to help the Jews who need a place of refuge to settle there. That is fundamentally different from political Jewish nationalism." The Fellowship went out of existence on the establishment of the State of Israel. J. LEFTWICH

LEARSI, RUFUS (pen name of Israel Goldberg). Historian, educator, and Zionist publicist (b. Suraz, near Bialystok, Russian Poland, 1889; d. New York, 1964). Brought to the United States as a child of eight, Learsi (pen-name i.e., "Israel" read backward) was active in Zionist affairs in his student days. After his graduation he joined the staff of the *Maccabean*, which was then edited by Louis Lipsky. From 1918 on he worked for the Provisional Executive Committee for General Zionist Affairs in the United States and later became director of public relations of the Keren ha-Yesod. In 1920 he served as chairman of the first convention of the Tze'irei Zion in the United States. In 1925 he was a delegate to the 14th Zionist Congress in Vienna. In 1927 he was floor leader of the opposition at the Zionist Organization of America Convention, of which

Louis D. Brandeis was considered the mentor, and which attempted to unseat the Lipsky administration and replace it with a group headed by Judge Julian W. Mack. The effort failed, however, and Learsi resigned from his post with the Keren ha-Yesod.

Learsi subsequently entered the field of Jewish education, serving as director of organization and public relations of the Jewish Education Association of New York, and from 1939–44 as editor and director of public relations of the Jewish Education Committee of New York. He founded and edited *World Over*, the committee's magazine for children in Jewish schools.

His published works include *Israel: A History of the Jewish People* (1949), *Fulfillment: The Epic Story of Zionism* (1951), and *The Jews in America: A History* (1954).

D. GOLDBERG

LEBANESE JEWS IN ISRAEL. *See* SYRIAN AND LEBANESE JEWS IN ISRAEL.

LEBANON, ZIONISM IN. *See* SYRIA AND LEBANON, ZIONISM IN.

LEBANON WAR. Israel military operation, which began on 6 June 1982 as an operation to drive Palestine Liberation Organization (PLO) forces from South Lebanon, developed into a prolonged war and aftermath that brought the Israeli forces to Beirut and beyond, terminating only with the withdrawal of the Israel Defense Forces (IDF) in May, 1985. The proclaimed intention of the operation, codenamed "Peace for Galilee" was to put all the northern settlements in Israel out of range of the artillery of the Palestinian organizations which had been periodically bombarding them, and to create a 25—33 mi. (40—50 km.) security belt beyond the Israeli border; there was to be no clash with the Syrian army in Lebanon and no direct interference in the internal Lebanese struggle among the various sectarian groups. In the first few days of fighting, however, and, as it later became evident, also in prior planning, the objectives of the war were wider and included the demand for the evacuation of Syrian army formations and all PLO armed units from Lebanon, and the signing of a peace treaty between Israel and the new regime in Lebanon. This led to a head-on confrontation with the Syrian army on Lebanese soil; to the joining up with "the Lebanese forces: (the Christian militias under the control of the Phalangists (the militia of the Maronites) in east Beirut after taking control of the Beirut-Damascus highway; and to the besieging of PLO headquarters in western Beirut. The second stage, consisted of a two-year war of attrition in face of the guerrilla campaign of the Shi'ite population in the south. The events of summer 1982, the massacre in the camps of Sabra and Shatilla (see below), and the prolonged involvement in Lebanon stirred up a stormy public debate in Israel, and caused a sharp reverse in public opinion towards Israel in the western world, after an initial understanding of the campaign's defense motives.

The background. The roots of the war lay in the consolidation of PLO forces on Lebanese soil during the civil war waged in Lebanon, intermittently, from 1975, which led to the paralysis of the official government. Given the vulnerability of the Galilee settlement to shelling from over the border and the transformation of Beirut into an international center of terrorism, many in Israel began to think in terms of finding a far-reaching remedy against the danger. The PLO artillery bombardment reached its peak in the "Two-Week War" (10–17 July 1981), in the wake of which the town of Kiryat Shemona was virtually abandoned and thousands of Galilee families were forced to dwell in air raid shelters for days on end. To this was added the threat created when Syrian ground-to-air missiles were installed in the Bekaa Valley in Lebanon (April, 1981), contrary to the understanding reached through American mediation (June, 1976), by which the Syrian Forces in Lebanon would not act to reduce the Israel Air Force's freedom of operation. Beyond these considerations, at the root of the war was the hope of breaking the force of the PLO and of establishing a regime friendly to Israel in Lebanon, as well as the hope of dealing a heavy blow to the Syrian army and disrupting its preparations for future confrontation with the IDF. Israeli Defense Minister, Ariel Sharon, believed that the success of the war on Lebanese soil would improve Israel's geopolitical situation immeasurably and would create a new balance of power in the Middle East and these views were accepted by the Israeli government. The leaders of the Maronite community (the largest Christian Community in Lebanon, in union with the Vatican, but different from the Latin Catholics), and Bashir Jemayel in particular, worked to foster these hopes and to sustain Sharon and others with promises of an imminent treaty. In the series of contacts established in the year preceding the war, including a secret visit by Sharon to Beirut in January, 1982, a flimsy guideline was created for unwritten cooperation between Israel and the Phalangists, who had received generous aid from the IDF from 1976 onwards. Bashir Jemayel was to exploit the thrust of the Israeli campaign and to seize power; certain parties in the American government were aware of this plan and even gave their tacit agreement. Nevertheless, the full details of the "Oranim" plan with its far-reaching political implications, were not presented to the government plenary in Jerusalem. Consequently the joining up with Bashir Jemayel's troops in Beirut was not authorized a priori and the nature of the government authorizations for the attack on the Syrian army in the Bekaa Valley is also questionable.

The military campaign. Following the attempt on the life of the Israeli ambassador in London, Shlomo Argov, perpetrated by terrorists from the Abu Nidal group (3 June 1982), the IDF began a series of aerial bombardments on PLO facilities in Lebanon, and on 5 June towards midday, IDF forces began to move into Lebanon. Eight principal IDF formations were employed, supported by the absolute supremacy of the Israel Air Force; an effort was made to subdue the enemy rapidly. Because of the difficulties of mobility along the mountain tracks and the need to cross water courses and to fight in built-up areas, the plan called for the destruction of the PLO defense systems, the driving of wedges between the PLO and between the First Syrian Division to the east, and the controlling of the strategic positions. The clean-up operations were postponed to the second stage in order to allow the IDF to station along the Sidon-Jezzin target line within 48 hours. For the operation, forces were landed from the sea, north of Sidon. Control of an area of 30 mi. (45 km.) was completed in practice on the night of 7–8 June, when three formations joined up near Sidon: one that had landed from the sea, one that had passed through the Nabatiyah heights and the Zaharani river-bed, and one that had come up on the shore axis through Tyre. During this action, six squadrons of the PLO Kastel Brigade were wiped out, but fighting against the Palestinian refugee camps of Rashidiyeh near Tyre and Ein Hilwe near Sidon continued for over a week. At the same time another IDF formation went into action against the PLO Karameh Brigade and other units on the eastern sector, and additional large forces moved into the Shouf mountains. On the morning of 8 June the expansion of the war beyond the original government announcement became a fact, and the last-mentioned formation was ordered, following an Israeli government decision of October 6, to make all possible speed along the Shuf roads to the Beirut-Damascus axis on the mountain ridge. The formation was unsuccessful in its mission; it was stopped by Syrian armored and commando units about 4.5 mi. (seven km.) south of the high road. On 9 June in a lightning action, and without casualties, the Air Force destroyed 17 of the 19 Syrian ground-to-air missile batteries in Lebanon, and on 10 June the Syrian formation in the Lake Karaoun region was hit. At the same time the formations fighting to the west began to move towards Beirut. On 13 June the paratroopers joined the Phalangist militia men in the southern neighborhoods of the city, and west Beirut, which sheltered about 12,000 Palestinian terrorists and the 85th Syrian Army Brigade, was placed under siege. The siege was reinforced on 25 June when the IDF conquered the Aley-Bhamdoun region and stationed itself, albeit belatedly, on the Beirut-Damascus highway.

The Beirut Episode. During the following months the siege of west Beirut continued, accompanied by frequent air raids and massive artillery bombardments, disconnection of the electricity and water supplies, and capture of different areas on the edge of the besieged city. On 21 August an agreement was reached through the mediation of American envoy Philip Habib, and evacuation of the terrorists commenced, mainly by sea and partly in overland convoys under the protection of a multi-national force from the USA, France, and Italy. One of the central objectives of the war was thereby achieved and on 23 August another undeclared objective seemed to have been attained when Bashir Jemayel was elected President of Lebanon. Bashir Jemayel was not sworn into office however. He was murdered on 14 September by a Syrian agent, and with the threat of chaos and the collapse of the Phalangist militia pending, the IDF entered west Beirut, despite the previous agreement to stay out of this area. On 18 September the occupation of the city was complete. Opposition was weak, but Phalangist units were introduced in an attempt to take command of the Sabra and Shatilla refugee camps that were at that time in the IDF area of control. These units, without prior knowledge of the Israelis, slaughtered inhabitants of the camps (a minimum estimate gives about 360 dead, including women and children). The dimensions of the slaughter, when they became known, stunned Israeli and western public opinion and the internal crisis in Israel worsened, almost leading to the fall of Menahem Begin's government. Under heavy public pressure an inquiry committee was appointed under the chairmanship of Supreme Court President Yitzhak Kahan. At the request of the USA the IDF was withdrawn from west Beirut and the UN multinational force was returned to the city. The Kahan Commission's conclusions led to the resignation from office of Defense Minister Sharon, who was indicted of "personal responsibility" for the defects and shortcomings that were revealed. The Kahan Commission's conclusions, published on 9 February 1983, also led to the resignation of General Yehoshua Saguy from his position as head of Israel Army Intelligence, and included reprimands of other top officers, including Chief of General Staff Rafael Eitan and Minister of Foreign Affairs, Yitzhak Shamir.

Aftermath. The war led to an intensification of the debate in Israel concerning Israeli political trends; government functioning; and the performance of the IDF. At the center of the controversy was the accusation that Sharon misled the government and the Knesset, and partially even Begin, when he presented the "Peace for Galilee Operation" as a limited operation that gradually assumed broad dimensions because of the developments at the front, whereas from the beginning he strove for all-out objectives for which he had no authorization. Sharon and his supporters denied this, pointing to the fact that all decisions concerning the war had been taken by the government as a whole (which had not been the case in previous wars) and some of these decisions had even gone against Sharon's proposals. This debate did not terminate even after Begin resigned as Prime Minister, without giving any insight into his approach in this problem. In addition to the debate on questions of deceit, there were other basic questions such as: the projection of the IDF into a war for the achievement of conroversial political objectives, a war that could have been avoided; the employment of heavy fire against a noncombatant civilian population; the waste of human lives in face of the high loss rate; the extent to which Israel must rely on the use of force in the struggle against the Palestinians, etc. This prolonged debate created acute tensions within Israeli society, that subsided gradually only after the IDF withdrawal from Lebanon in May, 1985.

The withdrawal process was effected in stages. In August, 1983, the IDF was withdrawn from the outskirts of Beirut and the Shouf mountains to a new line along the Awali River. This withdrawal was aimed principally at preventing Israeli deaths in face of the guerrilla war and the continual escalation of terror by pro-PLO organizations, by pro-Syrian militia, and groups of Shi'ite zealots. In the wake of this withdrawal the *Druze defeated the Phalangist forces in the Shouf mountains and drove them back to the pre-war borders of the Christian enclave.

Israel still hoped at this stage for the implementation of the agreement that it had signed with President Amin Jemayel's government on 17 May 1983 on future defense arrangements in the south. Jemayel, however, was subjected to intense Syrian pressure and failed to ratify the treaty that had been worked out under the aegis of the Americans. The IDF was faced with the increasing insurrection of the Shi'ite inhabitants of the south, which progressed from demonstrations, strikes and stonethrowing to terror activities at the rate of 60–70 attacks monthly, including the dispatch of suicide drivers in booby-trapped cars. The IDF could not contain this new form of terror warfare. Only with the forming of a national unity government headed by Shimon Peres, was a resolution passed for an IDF withdrawal without an agreement, whilst a "security belt" was to be established under the control of the South Lebanese Army as a 6 mi. 8–10 km.) security barrier along the northern frontier.

With the end of the war it became clear that, despite the heavy price paid by Israel with more than 600 dead, the basic objectives had not been acheived: the PLO had indeed been apparently uprooted from its autonomous bases on Lebanese soil, initially by the IDF (in the south and in Beirut), and subsequently by the Syrians (in the Bekaa and in Tripoli) but already in late 1986 the Palestinian organizations had managed to renew their holds in Beirut, in Sidon and in Tyre, and had recommenced activities, although on a relatively smaller scale, against Israel. Moreover, the danger of pro-PLO terror was supplemented by the strong hostility against Israel that was borne among the Shi'ites and that was expressed in terror activities and shooting especially by organizations such as the pro-Iranian Hizballah. The dream of the establishment of a strong pro-Israel Christian government in Lebanon collapsed under Syrian pressure, and the Maronite militias, weakened and internally divided, were driven back from all the areas that they had seized under IDF protection. The Syrian army had suffered about a thousand dead, and the loss of 400 tanks and 100 fighter planes, but this blow led de facto to an accelerated pace of rearmament and to the increased danger of military confrontation. The Syrians regained their former strongholds in Lebanon and even prepared to take up positions closer to the Israeli border. In February, 1987, a Syrian division reentered Beirut and reestablished positions there. In practice, a wide consensus evolved in Israel, in the wake of the withdrawal, that the expansion of the war for the implementation of ambitious objectives had not yielded the anticipated fruits. This evaluation was reflected, among other things, in the policy of partial non-interference in the internal conflict in Lebanon and a return to the traditional approach that concentrates on efforts to secure the northern border against terrorist attacks. E. YA'ARI

LEGISLATION IN ISRAEL. The law of Israel consists of two distinct and chronologically separate parts, that is to say, the law in force in Palestine prior to 15 May 1948, and the law enacted by the Israeli legislature since that date.

The laws of mandatory Palestine, far from being homogeneous, were themselves of complex composition and origin. The basis of the law of Palestine was the Ottoman Law, as obtaining on 1 November 1914, Palestine having been a Turkish province on the date when the Ottoman Empire joined the Central Powers during World War I. The Ottoman Law, however, was in its turn far from being a uniform structure; its bottom layer was the Moslem Religious Law, on which were superimposed parts of the Napoleonic Code (the French Law that had been borrowed during the 19th century), and the family or personal laws of the Christian and Jewish communities. The Moslem Law, deriving its authority from the Koran, was concerned primarily with civil transactions, and was subsequently systematized into a civil code known as the Mejelleh; some parts of it still survive in present-day Israel. Matters of personal status of Moslems, that is to say, the laws regarding marriage, divorce, wills, and other family matters, were also dealt with in accordance with Moslem religious tradition. However, as the need to modernize the Empire grew acute, the Sultans borrowed the commercial, maritime, and civil procedure and the criminal code of the French. Indeed, French influence was so profound that the Ottoman jurists consulted French legal texts, and at times based their decisions on precedents set up by French courts of law, a practice that was followed by the courts of Palestine during the British Mandate.

This complicated body of law was overlaid by laws enacted or applied by the mandatory legislature of Palestine, and was generally patterned on English common law and the principles of equity. During the thirty years of British rule, substantial sections of the Turkish laws, primarily in the fields of public law, civil and criminal procedure, and criminal and commercial law were repealed and new laws were enacted, based on English law and interpreted in accordance with British judicial decisions. This law flowed into the legal system of Palestine both through specific legislative enactments and through Article 46 of the Palestine Order-in-Council of 1922, which provided that the substance of the English Common Law and the doctrines of equity in force in England would apply wherever there was a lacuna in the laws of Palestine. Through this aperture the English judges officiating in Palestine channeled more and more English law into what they regarded as lacunae in the local laws. The Supreme Court of Palestine, which also sat as a High Court of Justice with authority to issue original writs of habeas corpus, mandamus, and prohibition, became the protector of basic freedoms. The majority of the judges of the Supreme Court and all the presiding judges of the district courts were British, and they had brought with them their distinctive procedures and their flexible remedies and their individual opinions and dissents, which constituted a system that functioned through an independent judiciary. In a short time, the impact of English law and practice in Palestine under British rule became pervasive and far-reaching.

There was, however, one field of Ottoman law that the mandatory power scrupulously preserved: the personal law and the system of religious community courts. Originally the establishment of non-Moslem religious courts in the Ottoman Empire was regarded as an act of tolerance and goodwill toward the religious minorities, and was indeed welcomed by them. Both Jews and Christians enjoyed autonomy in matters of personal status, and favored the existence of their own religious courts. Thus there was no uniform Ottoman civil code dealing with domestic relations; there were, instead, the several codes of the religious communities, and one's personal status was determined by the law of his religion and his rights thereunder were adjudicated by the ecclesiastical court of the religious community to which he belonged.

The British confirmed this situation in the mandated territory and defined the scope of the jurisdiction of the communities already existing in Palestine, without enlarging their number. Consequently, some small communities such as the Maronites (an eastern offshoot of the Catholic Church) were confirmed in their status, while the Protestants whose membership was larger than that of the Maronites, were not accorded the status of a community with its own religious court, for the simple reason that within the Ottoman Empire their number had been significant.

Such was the maze of laws when the independence of Israel was proclaimed. War preceded and followed the Declaration of Independence; there was no alternative but to adopt the law as it existed in Palestine on the eve of independence. This was given effect in the first enactment by the Provisional Council of State, the Law and Administration Ordinance 5708–1948, which was passed with retroactive effect from 15 May 1948, the first day of Israel's independent existence. The circumstances in which the Jews of Palestine attained their sovereignty were such as to preclude any possibility of a serious consideration of what legal system to establish for the new state.

As a result of these provisions, the Law of Palestine became the law of the newly born state, with some exceptions bearing on matters of political import, such as the abolition of restrictions on Jewish immigration and land purchase, and on the abolition of the privileged status of English as an official language. Since that time a considerable part of the law has been changed by the Israeli legislature, but parts of the old law remain in force, most prominently the provisions dealing with the religious courts. Thus the link between religion and state that originated and developed in the peculiar circumstances of the Ottoman Empire, and was consolidated by the British rulers of Palestine, fell to the State of Israel as an inheritance. A.F. LANDAU

On 14 May 1948—the eve of the termination of the British Mandate—the Mo'etzet ha-Am (People's Council) consisting of 37 representatives of the yishuv and the Zionist movement issued the Declaration of Independence, proclaiming the establishment of the State of Israel. The Mo'etzet ha-Am declared that it would act as the Provisional Council of State until such time as elected and permanent authorities were set up in accordance with a constitution which was to be adopted by an elected Constituent Assembly not later than 1 October 1948. On the same day it issued a Proclamation constituting itself the legislative authority of the new State and repealing the restrictive provisions of the 1939 British White Paper, particularly those relating to Jewish immigration and land purchases. It also declared that all other laws, not inconsistent with this Proclamation, would remain in force until abolished or amended.

The first law enacted by the Provisional Council was the Law and Administration Ordinance, 5708/1948, laying down that the Provisional Council was the legislative authority and that every ordinance—as the laws were to be designated—duly signed by the Prime Minister, the Minister of Justice, and the responsible Minister would take effect from the date of its publication in the *Official Gazette*, unless another date was stipulated.

The Ordinance also gave legal effect to the regulations and directives published by the Jewish Agency, The Va'ad Le'umi and the Minhelet ha-Am (People's Administration) during the period between the date of the United Nations resolution on partition and the publication of the Ordinance (i.e., from 29 November 1947 to 21 May 1948). In repealing the restrictive White Paper provisions on immigration and land purchases, the Ordinance laid down that any Jew who had entered Palestine in contravention of the restrictions should be deemed to be a legal immigrant as from the date of his entry.

In terms of this Ordinance the Provisional Council was empowered to declare a state of emergency; in the event of such a declaration the Ministers of the provisional government were authorized to make emergency regulations deemed to be desirable for defense, public security, and the maintenance of essential supplies and services. They would be effective for three months unless renewed or revoked. The Provisional Council thereupon declared that such a state of emergency existed in Israel. (That declaration persisted throughout the first forty years of Israel's existence and has been the legal basis for innumerable Ministerial edicts.)

On 18 November 1948, 10 days after the population census, the Provisional Council adopted an ordinance providing for the holding of elections to a Constituent Assembly consisting of 120 members. The Assembly met for the first time on 14 February 1949. Two days later it passed its first law, the Transition Law 5709/1948, giving itself the name "*Knesset" (in this case the "First Knesset") and changing the mandatory and Provisional Council term "ordinance" to "law". It laid down the procedure for the adoption of such laws and their publication in the *Gazette* (to be known by the Hebrew term "Reshumot").

There were sustained debates in the Knesset as to whether the country should have a written constitution. In the end the Knesset, in 1950, charged its Committee on Constitution, Law, and Justice with the task of preparing a draft Constitution, adding that the Constitution would be built up, chapter by chapter, with each chapter, when passed, forming a Basic Law. The sum total of the chapters would eventually be incorporated into the State's Constitution. (It should be noted that, some 40 years later, the country was still without a comprehensive constitution, despite partial attempts at drafting individual chapters and the enactment of Basic Laws, dealing with the Knesset, Israel lands, the President of the State, the government, the army, State possessions and revenue, jurisdiction, and the State Controller). Meanwhile, there could be no restrictions limiting the legislative powers of the Knesset, nor could any law be invalidated by the Courts.

By and large the Knesset has been called upon to legislate on topics common to all democratic countries but several laws have been adopted arising out of the country's position as a Jewish state and as the fulfillment of the Zionist ideal, which do not have their counterpart elsewhere. Among them were those providing for the transfer of Herzl's remains, 1949, the Law of Return, 1950, guaranteeing the right of every Jew to settle in Israel, and the laws defining the relationships with the World Zionist Organization and the Jewish Agency. 1952, with the Keren Kayemet le-Israel (Jewish National Fund), 1953, and the Keren ha-Yesod, 1956.

Many laws were enacted relating to the Jewish religion, such as the Kasher Food for Soldiers Ordinance, 1948; Jewish Religious Services Budgets Law, 1949; the Chief Rabbinate Council Law, 1955; the Rabbinical Courts Jursdiction (Marriage and Divorce) Law, 1953; the Dayanim Law, 1955; the Prohibition of Pig Breeding Law, 1962; the Jewish Religious Services (Consolidated) Law, 1971; the protection of *tefillin* and *mezuzot*, 1974; and the prevention of fraud in *kashrut*, 1983.

A succession of laws deal with the Nazi Holocaust, such as the Punishment of Nazis and Their Collaborators Law, 1950; the Prevention and Punishment of the Crime of Genocide Law, 1950; the Remembrance of the Holocaust and the Valor Yad va-Shem Law, 1953; the Disabled in the War against the Nazis Law, 1954; the Payment of Compensation from Italy Law, 1955; the Disabled by Nazi Persecution Law, 1957; the Claims of Holocaust Victims (Regulation of Handling) Law, 1957 (amended in 1975); the Remembrance Day of the Holocaust and the Valor Law, 1959; the Abolition of Limitation in Crimes against Humanity Law, 1966; and a law in 1986 providing for a penalty of five years' imprisonment on anyone denying the existence of the Holocaust.

Two special legislative acts must be indicated here: the David Ben-Gurion Law, 1976, declaring his former Tel Aviv home to be a national monument and establishing a "Machon le-Moreshet Ben-Gurion" (an "Institute for Ben-Gurion's Heritage) at Sde Boker as part of the Ben-Gurion University of the Negev; and the 1980 Declaration of United Jerusalem as the capital of Israel and the seat of its President, the Knesset, the Government, and the Supreme Court. Under this law, the government was charged with responsibility for the development of the city and the protection of its holy places.

Apart from the Basic Laws cited above, enactments in the field of constitutional law include the State Controller Law 1949 (amended in 1972 and 1974); the Nationality Law 1952 (amended in 1980); the Passport Law, 1952 (amended in 1969); laws governing elections to the Knesşet and the remuneration rights, duties, and immunity of the members of the Knesset, 1952 (amended in 1964); the Entry into Israel Law 1952; and the Territorial Waters Law, 1958. Other fundamental issues were the laws on Identity Cards, 1969 (amended in 1971 and 1980); the protection of privacy, 1981, equal opportunities in employment, 1981, and the protection of consumers, 1982. In the same year the Prime Minister was given the right to dismiss one of his ministers without the government's resignation being necessitated. Also in 1981 the Knesset adopted a measure applying Israel law to the Golan Heights.

The civil judicial system is regulated by the Judges Law, 1953 (and amended in 1984) and the Courts Law, 1957. The Israel Criminal Procedure Law, 1965, and the Arbitration Law, 1968, replaced prevailing Mandatory Ordinances on these matters. Similarly the Chamber of Advocates Law, 1961, amended in 1975, superseded mandatory law. In 1976 came the Small Claims Court Law— and the entire system was amended and re-written in a consolidating law in 1984.

Questions of security have played a vital role. The Prevention of Terror Ordinance was promulgated in 1948, followed by the Civil Defense Law, 1951; the National Service Law, 1953 (revised and consolidated in 1986); the Prevention of Infiltration (Offenses and Jurisdiction) Law, 1954; and the Criminal Law (Security of the State, Foreign Relations, and Official Secrets) Law, 1957. Military matters are governed by the Security Service Law, 1949; the National Service Law, 1953; the Military Justice Law, 1955; and a comprehensive consolidating law of 1986. Compensation to soldiers is provided by the Rehabilitation of Disabled Soldiers Law, 1970, and by the War Injuries Law, 1971; rights of discharged soldiers were entrenched in a 1973 law, while the Army Pensions Law was passed in 1985.

Financial measures and taxes play a prominent part in Israel's legislation. They include the Absorption Tax Law, 1949; the Estate Tax Law, 1949; the Foreign Travel Tax Law, 1950—repealed in 1977 and reintroduced in 1983; the Purchase Tax Law, 1952; the Land Betterment Tax, 1963 (amended in 1974 and again in 1984); the Defense Levy Law, 1967; and measures to finance the country's war efforts by way of levy and loan in 1972, 1973, and 1982. The Property Tax and Compensation Fund Law, 1961 (amended in 1970) provides for a property tax in place of existing State and local taxes, and the Taxes on Services Law was adopted in 1973. There have been several comprehensive laws dealing with Income Tax (including those under conditions of inflation) such as those of 1974, 1975, 1977, 1978, and annually from 1981 to 1985 inclusive. The Inheritance Tax was adjusted for inflation in 1975 and abolished in 1981.

The unit of Israel's currency was changed from the *lira* to the *shekel* (the equivalent of 10 *lirot*) in 1980, and to the *New Shekel* (the equivalent of 1,000 old *Shekels*) in 1985.

The development of the economy is dealt with by the Capital Investment Encouragement Law, 1950, 1959, and 1971; the State Guarantees Law, 1950, 1954, and 1958; the Mortgages Guarantee Law, 1952; the Encouragement of Israel Films Law, 1954 (amended in 1972); the Savings Encouragement (Guarantee for Loans and Income Tax Relief) Law, 1969; the Foreign Trade Guarantees Law, 1959; the Tel Aviv Power Station Law, 1967; the Oil Pipeline Concession Law, 1968; the "Israel Company" Law, 1969 (sponsoring international capital for the country's development); the International Development Bank Law, 1976; the Tourist Services Law, 1976; the establishment of a National Energy Authority in 1977, and of a Development Authority in 1988. The Free Ports Law was adopted in 1969 and the town of Eilat was declared a Free Port in 1985.

In the field of communications a law establishing a public company called "Bezek" (The Israel Company for Communications Ltd.) was adopted, for the purpose of taking over State operations, in 1982 (amended in 1988). Laws setting up a Postal Authority and providing for cable television were both approved in 1986.

Control legislation applies to rents, insurance business, key money, commodities and services, hotel accommodation, hostels, sports betting, securities, electricity, licensing of businesses, safety in public places, and standards of manufacture.

Among a host of labor laws are those regulating hours of work and rest, annual leave, apprenticeship, youth labor, female labor, safety at work, organization of labor control, settlement of labor disputes and recourse to properly constituted Labor Courts; collective agreements, minimum wages, wage protection and guaranteed incomes, employment services, and severance pay.

There has been comprehensive legislation in the field of insurance. Basic allowances are entrenched—for retired and certain categories of needy persons—in the Bituah Le'umi (National Insurance) Law, 1953, which was amended in 1969 and thereafter annually from 1975 to 1986 inclusive. The original ordinance covering insurance in general was substantially rewritten in two laws passed in 1981. Other laws provide for benefits to disabled persons, military personnel, persons serving in the civil service, police and prisons services, volunteers for work in emergencies, and for the families of fallen soldiers, and for the right of disabled soldiers to return to their former employment. Motor vehicle insurance is the subject of a 1969 law, and compensation for accident victims is dealt with in a 1975 law (amended in 1985). In 1982 a law was passed providing compensation for persons evacuated from Sinai in consequence of the peace treaty with Egypt.

Laws relating to education, culture, and sport include the Compulsory Education Law, 1949, which was revised in 1953; the Broadcasting Authority Law, 1965 (amended in 1973); the Higher Learning Council Law, 1958; and the Israel National Academy of Sciences Law, 1961. A Memorial Institute in the name of Yitzhak Ben-Zvi, Israel's second President, was set up by law in 1969 for the purpose of promoting studies of the city of Jerusalem and of eastern Jewish communities. In terms of the Keren Wolf ("Wolf Fund") Law, 1975—a fund set up by a former Cuban ambassador to Israel—substantial cash prizes were to be awarded annually for outstanding work in physics, chemistry, medicine, agriculture, and mathematics, irrespective of country of domicile, race, color, religion, sex, or political outlook. Public Libraries were the subject of a law passed in 1975; a law on underwater diving was enacted in 1979; a law in 1988 provided facilities for children suffering from disabilities, and another in the same year dealt with qualifications of sports trainers.

Among laws dealing with health matters are the Magen David Law, 1950; the Anatomy and Pathology Law, 1953;

the Treatment of Mentally Sick Persons Law, 1955; the Prevention of Nuisances Law, 1961— broadened by the Pollution Law, 1970 and the Public Hygiene Laws of 1976 and 1984; and laws limiting tobacco smoking and tobacco advertising (both in 1983); and the use of hypnosis (1984).

Agriculture and water form the subject matter of a number of important laws, including the General Agricultural Council Ordinance, 1948; the Citrus Fruit (Control and Marketing) Ordinance, 1948; the Plant Protection (Goat Damage) Law, 1950; the Improvement of Agricultural Settlement Law, 1953; the Control of Export of Plants and Their Products Law, 1954; the Control of Water Drilling Law, 1955; the Protection of Wild Animals Law, 1955; the Plant Protection Law, 1956 (amended in 1970); the Control of Export of Animals and Animal Produce Law, 1957; the Drainage and Flood Protection Laws, 1957; the Groundnut (Peanuts) Production and Marketing Board Law, 1959; the Vegetables Production and Marketing Board Law, 1959; the comprehensive Water Law, 1959 (amended in 1971); the Petah Tikva Agricultural Authorities Law, 1959; the Poultry Branch (Production and Marketing) Board Law, 1963; the Streams and Springs Authority Law, 1965; and the Agricultural Settlement (Restrictions on Uses of Agricultural Land and Water) Law, 1967.

Topics relating to transport (mainly sea and air) are covered by the Ships (Nationality and Flag) Ordinance, 1948; the Ships Mortgages Ordinance, 1948; the Ships (Restriction on Transfer and Mortgage) Ordinance, 1948; the Shipping (Vessels) Law, 1960; the Ports Authority Law, 1961; the Air Services Licensing Law, 1963; and the Shipping (Restriction on Liability of Vessel Owners) Law, 1965. Aviation regulations were updated in 1971 and 1972, and again in 1980. An Airport Authority was created in 1977 and laws governing the use of seat-belts in motor-cars were passed in 1973. The Road Transport Ordinance of 1947 was amended in 1970 and 1979.

Laws affecting social welfare and youth are: the Social Welfare (Procedure in Matters of Minors, Mentally Sick Persons, and Absentees) Law, 1961, together with the Youth Law and the Juvenile Offenders Law, both of 1971; and the Rehabilitation of Disabled Soldiers Law, 1970.

Other matters dealing with the individual and the family include the Age of Marriage Law, 1950; the Equality of Women's Rights Law, 1951; the Names Law, 1956; the Personal Status (Consular Powers) Law, 1956; the Inheritance (Inheritance of Foreign Residents) Law, 1959; the Family (Maintenance) Law, 1959; the Adoption of Children Law, 1960, and its amendment in 1981; the Legal Competence and Guardianship Law, 1962; the Determination of Age Law, 1963; and the comprehensive Inheritance Law, 1965.

In the field of Civil Law, the Ottoman Civil Code (the "Mejelle") was gradually and systematically replaced by measures, including the Limitation Law, 1958; the Agency Law, 1965; the Pledge Law, 1967; the Guarantee Law, 1967; the Custodians Law, 1967; the Gift Law, 1967; and the Sale Law. The "Mejelle" as a whole was finally abolished in 1984. In addition to the laws amending the Civil Wrongs Ordinance, 1944, three laws deal with civil wrongs, namely, the Civil Wrongs (State Liability) Law, 1952; the Civil Wrongs (Reparation for Bodily Injury) Law, 1964; and the Prohibition of Defamation Law, 1965. Subsequently, the basic law of contracts was amended in 1969, in 1970 (breach of contracts), in 1971 (international sales), in 1973 and in 1981. In the realm of Company Law, the Mandatory Ordinance was amended in 1975 and 1980 and substantial changes were introduced in the Amendments to the Companies Law, 1981. The Amutot Law, 1980, provided an Israel substitute for the "Ottoman Society." Laws for the protection of tenants were enacted in 1971 and 1972, governing Letting and Borrowing, (1971); the Sales of Movables, (1971); Sales of Apartments, (1973); Building Contractors, (1974); and Foreign Judgments, (1974). A law providing for extensions of contractual liability due to military service was passed in 1975. The Execution Law, 1967, was amended in 1969 and 1970.

Land Legislation includes the Development Authority (Transfer of Property) Law, 1950; the Regulation of Seizure of Property during an Emergency Law, 1949; the Local Authorities (Land Transfer Fee) Law, 1949; the Petroleum Law, 1952; the Cooperative Houses Law, 1952; the Acquisition of Land (Confirmation of Acts and Compensation) Law, 1953; the Land (Conversion of Metrouke) Law, 1960; the National Gardens and Nature Reserves Law, 1963; the Acquisition for Public Purposes Law, 1964; the Registration of Public Housing Estates Law, 1964; the comprehensive Planning and Building Law, 1965; the Building and Evacuation of Rehabilitation Areas Law, 1965; and the Land Law, 1969. Pursuant to the Peace Treaty with Egypt, a law was adopted in 1980 enabling acquisition of lands in the Negev for public use— with appropriate compensation.

In dealing with the Criminal Law, the legislature began by systematically replacing the provisions of the Palestine Criminal Code Ordinance, 1936, with laws that will ultimately constitute an original Israel Criminal Code. Piecemeal measures in this context were: laws abolishing the death penalty for murder (except in military courts and in the case of Nazis and Nazi Collaborators) as well as the punishment of flogging and laws replacing the provisions of the ordinance with regard to bribery, assault of police officers, modes of punishment, offenses committed abroad, offenses by public officers, State security, foreign relations and official secrets, extradition, concealment of offences, bigamy, soliciting for prostitution, fraud, extortion and exploitation, use of a vehicle without permission, prohibited games, lotteries and betting, prohibition of defamation, and the prevention of nuisances. In addition the Palestine ordinances providing for collective punishment were repealed. The principal amendments to the Criminal Law were passed in 1969, 1973, 1977, 1980, 1981, 1982, and 1983.

The Amnesty Law was enacted in 1949, following the War of Independence, and the Pardon Law in 1967 after the Six-Day War of that year.

Thereafter concerted efforts were made at consolidation, such as the Criminal Penalties (Consolidated) Law, 1970 and more especially in the 1977 law finally abolishing the Palestine Ordinance of 1936 and comprehensively listing possible crimes and their penalties—the law contains no less than 505 sections! Similarly criminal proceedings were amended in 1965 and subsequently consolidated in a 1982 law (245 sections). Specific aspects dealt with were Traffic Offenses, 1971; Tightening Up Drug Control, 1971 and 1979; Control of Firearms, 1971; Wiretapping, 1979; and issuing checks without cover, 1981.

Laws relating to commerce and banking include: the Control of Insurance Business Law, 1951; the Standards Law, 1953 (amended in 1979); the Post Office Bank Law, 1951 (amended in 1975); the Bank of Israel Law, 1954; the Interest Law, 1957; the Restrictive Trade Practices Law, 1959; the Joint Investments in Trust Law, 1961; the Standard Contracts Law, 1954; the Protection of Designation of

Origin Law, 1965; the Patents Law, 1967; the Securities Law, 1967; and the Licensing of Businesses Law, 1968. Laws controlling and regulating professional practice include: the Notaries for Foreign Documents Law, 1950; the Auditors Law, 1955 (amended in 1974); the Engineers and Architects Law, 1958 (amended in 1972); the Chamber of Advocates Law, 1961; the Land Values Law, 1967; the Customs Agents Law, 1964; the Practice of Medicine Law, 1972, amending the Mandatory Ordinance (further amended in 1975); the Pharmacists Law, 1975, amending the Mandatory Ordinance; the Dentists Law, 1976; the Artisans Law, 1977; and the Anatomy and Pathology Law, 1980. The Credit Cards Law was passed in 1986 and the Restriction of Trade Law in 1988.

In the field of local government there have been numerous amendments to the Palestine Municipal Corporation Ordinance, 1934 and the Palestine Local Councils Ordinance, 1941; an original Israel law, the Union of Towns Law, 1955; and laws conferring new powers upon local authorities, such as the Local Authorities (Special Authorization) Law, 1956; the Local Authorities (Vesting of Public Property) Law, 1958; the Local Authorities (Social Welfare and Recreation Charge) Law, 1959; the Local Authorities (Regulation of Guarding) Law, 1961; and the Local Authorities (Sewage) Law, 1962.

A revolutionary measure was the 1975 law providing that the state would retain the Arnona tax and in its stead transfer 4.828% of its income to Local Authorities. Also in 1975 the Knesset changed election procedures by providing for direct elections of mayors and heads of Local Authorities. In 1976, a law changed the nature of meetings of Local Authorities, particularly by rendering them open to the public, subject to safeguards for security and certain other considerations. In 1978 the Knesset approved public funding of political parties' local electioneering expenses.

Other ordinances and laws relating to administrative matters include: the Abandoned Area Ordinance, 1948; the Absentees Property Law, 1950; the Germans' Property Law, 1950; the State Property Law, 1951; the Elections to Public Bodies Law, 1954; the Administrative Procedure (Reasons) Law, 1959; the State Service (Appointments) Law, 1959; the State Service (Restriction on Political Party Activity and Fund Raising) Law, 1959; the State Service (Discipline) Law, 1963; and the Population Register Law, 1965.

Generally speaking, Palestine legislation was based upon the corresponding British legislation, but the Israel legislature has not confined itself to such legislation in its search for suitable models for its own legislation, adapting European or American legislation, if found suitable. Whenever legislation is required upon any particular subject, the relevant principles of Jewish law on the subject, if any, are examined and, if found suitable, are incorporated in the legislation.

The same principle was applied to the Courts in a 1980 law which cancelled the priority given to British precedents in judicial decisions (enacted in the 1947 ordinance) and laying down that henceforth precedents were to be drawn from "Moreshet Israel" (the Jewish Heritage).

Despite the impressive number of ordinances and laws passed by the Israel legislature, much more remains to be done to replace the heterogeneous body of Israel law originally written (in part) in other languages by a homogeneous body of law written only in Hebrew and suited to the needs of the modern, progressive State of Israel.

H.E. BAKER—S. LEVIN

LEHI. *See* LOHAMEI HERUT ISRAEL.

LEHMAN, HERBERT H. Banker, political leader, and communal worker in the United States (b. New York, 1878; d. there, 1963). In 1908 he became a partner in Lehman Brothers, the family banking concern. During World War I he served first as aide to Assistant Secretary of the Navy Franklin D. Roosevelt, then as a colonel in the Quartermaster Corps, receiving the Distinguished Service Medal. Entering politics as a Democrat at the age of 50, he was elected lieutenant governor of New York in 1928. In 1932 he was elected Governor, serving until December, 1942, when President Roosevelt appointed him head of the Office of Foreign Relief and Rehabilitation Operations in the State Department. In 1945 he became Director General of the newly organized UN Relief and Rehabilitation Administration (UNRRA). From 1949 to 1956 he was United States Senator from New York, a leading figure in liberal politics.

Early in his career Lehman entered social work, and in 1914 he helped found the American Jewish Joint Distribution Committee (JDC). After World War I he became chairman of the JDC Reconstruction Committee and worked with its ancillary, the Agro-Joint.

Although he never joined a Zionist organization, Lehman's sympathies lay with the Zionist movement. He manifested his interest in Zionism especially in connection with the plans to expand the Jewish Agency that preoccupied many Zionist leaders in the 1920s. He helped organize the Palestine Loan Bank and the Palestine Economic Corporation. Lehman also took an active interest in the Hebrew University of Jerusalem, the Haifa Technion, and the Weizmann Institute of Science. He became convinced, particularly after World War II, of the need for a Jewish homeland in Palestine to receive victims of oppression.

In 1958 he was general chairman of the United States committee for the celebration of Israel's 10th anniversary. In his later years, Lehman stood for the unity of American Jewry in its support of Israel.

LEHMANN, SIEGFRIED, (b. Berlin, Germany 1892; d. Ben Shemen, Israel, 1958). Educator and philosopher, one of the key figures in village education in Palestine. The son of an affluent and assimilated Berlin family, he was influenced by Martin Buber and Gustav Landauer. As a young doctor, he came to know the Jewish proletariat in Berlin and the Jewish masses in eastern Europe. He was responsible for three main enterprises. The first was The Volksheim in East Berlin (1918–1922), a settlement house whose central activities were medical and social counseling, and vocational training and educational work with children and youth. The work was on a volunteer basis with the teachers and counselors living together with the young people. In 1922, on the invitation of Dr. Max Soloveitchik (Solieli), former Minister of Jewish Affairs in Lithuania, Lehmann went to Kovno to organize the work of assisting homeless Jewish children orphaned by war and pogroms. A derelict bath house on the edge of the city was converted into a modern educational and social institution called the Yidishe Kinderhoyz (Jewish children's home), where hundreds of youths were educated and thousands received educational, social, and medical aid.

Lehmann then went to Palestine where in 1927 he founded the Ben Shemen Youth Village on Lydda Plain. He overcame some of the financial and organizational difficulties with the aid of a circle of friends abroad, chief of whom was Wilfrid Israel. The first students immigrated with Lehmann from Kovno. They were joined by children born in Palestine who required boarding school education, primarily for social reasons. In 1932 the first group of *Youth Aliya children was brought to Ben Shemen. Up until the outbreak of World War II further groups of youth arrived from Germany, Austria, Czechoslovakia, and Poland. After the war Ben Shemen took in Holocaust survivors and, following the creation of the State of Israel, children of new immigrants from Islamic countries. In this way the village served as a workshop for the educational integration of immigrants from different cultural backgrounds among themselves, and between themselves and Israeli youth.

Lehmann based Ben Shemen's educational system on three principles: work, primarily agricultural; social life in integrated cells of an educating and learning community; and study. He defined the objectives of this education as the in-depth development of five attachments which together give meaning to human life: attachment to "the soil of the homeland" which a man should work with his own hands; to companions in work, with whom man lives cooperatively; to his people with its values of the past and hope for its future; to mankind as a whole; and to ethical law.

Lehmann was awarded the Israel Prize for Education in 1957. A. SIMON

Yeshayahu Leibowitz. [Hebrew University]

LEIBOWITZ, YESHAYAHU. Israeli scientist and intellectual (b. Riga, 1903). He studied chemistry and philosophy (Ph.D., Berlin 1924) and medicine (M.D., Basle, 1934). In 1935 he joined the Hebrew University of Jerusalem, where he was professor of organic and biological chemistry and neurophysiology. As emeritus professor, he continued teaching philosophy of science. Leibowitz was science editor and chief editor of many volumes of *Encyclopaedia Hebraica.* He was active in various Zionist organizations, including the Hagana.

Leibowitz proposed, defended, and applied a view of Jewishness, according to which it is characterized by its forms of life. Observance does not embody any distinct theology, world view, or mysticism. It manifests ideally total submission to the constitutive laws of worship.

From his views Leibowitz has drawn conclusions concerning various public affairs. Most important are his endorsement of strict separation between state and religion in Israel, and his forceful opposition to the continued occupation of the Administered Areas. Soon after the Six-Day War Leibowitz predicted many of the effects of occupation on the nature of Israeli society and the prospects of maintaining it as a Jewish state. A popular speaker, he found many Israelis agreeing with him on these points. After the Lebanon War he advocated a certain form of civil disobedience.

Leibowitz wrote numerous books and papers in Hebrew, including *Jewishness, Jewish People and State of Israel* (1975), *Faith, History and Values* (1982), *Conversations on the Eight Chapters of Maimonides* (1986), *Between Science and Philosophy* (1987) and *On Just About Everything* (conversations with M. Shashar, 1987). ASA KASHER

LESZCYNSKI, JACOB. Social scientist and pioneer ideologist of Labor Zionism (b. Gorodishche, Ukraine, Russia, 1876; d. Jerusalem, 1966). In his youth Leszcynski propagated Zionism and Hebraism. Later he joined the labor wing in Zionism, and subsequently embraced Territorialism, becoming (1904) a leader of the Zionist Socialist party. In 1917 he helped found the United Jewish Socialist party in Russia.

After publishing a number of studies on the economic situation of Russian Jewry in the years preceding World War I, Leszcynski left Soviet Russia in 1921 and settled in Berlin, where he headed the economic-statistical section of the Yiddish Scientific Institute (YIVO).

Leaving Nazi Germany in 1933, Leszcynski lived for a time in Riga, Warsaw, and Paris. In 1938 he settled in New York, where he worked with the Institute of Jewish Affairs of the World Jewish Congress and the American Jewish Congress. In 1959 he settled in Israel. He was the author of numerous pioneering studies on Jewish statistics and demography and social and economic history.

A. ALPERIN

LESZCZ, CHIEL. Revisionist activist in Uruguay and Israel (b. Poland, 1902; d. Tel Aviv, 1981). He initially identified with the Zionist center (General Zionists) but in 1928 joined the Revisionists. He worked for the party in an administrative capacity in Poland and in Austria, where he arrived in 1946, after escaping the catastrophe of World War II. Immigrating to Uruguay in 1947, he served as vice-president of the Ashkenazi Jewish community and of the Uruguayan Consejo Central Sionista at various periods, and was a member of its Education Committee. He was general secretary of the local Revisionist party, which he represented on the board of directors at the main office (in Jerusalem in 1949). Leszcz was coeditor of his party's organ in Uruguay, *Der Weg* (1957), and wrote for the community's local daily, *Folksblat.* Immigrating to Israel in 1962, he joined the Revisionist Party Executive, was a member of Misdar Jabotinsky, and participated in Zionist Congresses.

R.P. RAICHER

LEVEL OF LIVING IN ISRAEL. By the late 1980s the population of Israel attained the average income level of a medium developed country. According to the estimates of the National Accounts, Israel's Gross Domestic Product (GDP) per capita was equivalent in 1988 to about 10,000 US dollars. This income per capita was close to that of Italy, higher than that of Spain and Greece, somewhat lower than that of Great Britain, but only two-thirds and less the level of countries like the United States, Canada, Sweden, etc. The level of income was reflected in quite a high level of consumption expenditures (both personal consumption and collective expenditures for social services such as health, education, etc.). This was possible not only because of the high level of GDP but also because Israel benefited from a continuous flow of grants, donations, and other transfers which enabled it to finance the high level of consumption (about two-thirds of its GDP) in addition to its large expenditure on defense and investments. Consumption per capita in Israel was lower by some 45% than that of the US level, and 20–25% lower than that of Italy or Great Britain.

Changes in Income Level. In 1988 Israel's per capita Gross Domestic Product (at constant prices) was some 3.9 times higher than the 1950 level. This implies an average growth of 3.7% per year. Private consumption increased during this period at an average annual rate of 3.9%. By looking at sub-periods, however, a different picture emerges.

Between 1954 and 1965, GDP increased at a sustained high rate of 6.5 % per year, while private consumption grew at only 5.6 % per year. After the setback of the 1966–67 recession, the high rate of growth was resumed up to 1973: GDP increased by 7.4% per year and private consumption by 5.1%. Following the Yom Kippur War of 1973 and the world oil crisis the rate of growth decreased sharply to 1.2% per year, while private consumption grew by 3.1% per year.

Indicators of the level of living: A number of indicators demonstrate the level of living attained by the Israeli population:

1. The amount and type of consumption by the population.
2. The level of housing.
3. Ownership of durable goods.
4. Social and communal services.

LEVEL OF CONSUMPTION AND ITS COMPOSITION. The average Israeli household comprised of 3.5 persons in 1986/87. Among these households the majority (75%) were headed by a wage-earner (with 3.9 persons per household, 1.5 earners); 11% were self-employed (4.1 persons per houshold, 1.5 earners); and 32% were households whose head was not employed (2.6 persons per household).

Its consumption expenditure was distributed as follows:

Food	23.3%	
Housing	16.3%	(for the large part an imputed expenditure for owner-occupied housing).
Household Maintenance	8.9%	
Furniture & Household Equipment	6.7%	
Clothing & Footwear	7.3%	
Health	5.2%	(including health insurance)
Education, Culture, & Entertainment	12.6%	
Transport & Communication	14.0%	
Cigarettes, Cosmetics, Jewelry, etc.	5.7%	
Total	100.0%	

The increase in the general level of living from the 1950s brought about great changes in the structure of consumption:

(1) A continuous decrease in the percentage of the budget spent on food (in 1956/57, 39% of consumption expenditure was for food, declining to 23% in 1986/87).

(2) A decrease in the part of consumption devoted to clothing and footwear (from some 12% in 1956/57 to 7% thirty years later).

(3) An increase in the proportion of consumption devoted to transportation (especially for car ownership) and to cultural, leisure, and entertainment activities.

The differential between households of various income levels is also manifested in the percentage of total consumption which was devoted to food. In 1986/87 the 10% of households with the lowest income spent 39% of their consumption expenditure on food and beverages (these had on the average 4.9 persons per household), compared to only 16% spent on food by the 10% highest income households. On the other hand, expenditures on transport and communication was 7% in the lowest income households compared to 17% in the highest income group.

Food Consumption. A more quantitative physical measure of food consumption is provided by the statistics on all food consumed (as measured in the "Food Balance Sheets"). It was found that the average Israeli consumed 3,075 calories per day, 122 grams of fat, and 86 grams of protein. The number of calories consumed in 1986/87 was higher by 10% compared to 1959. Over 30 years fat intake per day increased by some 40% (animal fat by 54%; fat from vegetables etc., by 34%).

The average daily diet of the Israeli was composed of 280 grams of grains, 311 grams of vegetables, 370 grams of fruits, 190 grams of meat (mostly poultry), 33 grams of fish, 52 grams of eggs, and 280 grams of milk and dairy products.

OWNERSHIP OF DURABLE GOODS. Another indicator of the level of living is the extent of ownership of durable goods by households, and the changes which occurred in the type of durables owned. Thus the refrigerator was a rare item in the Israeli home in 1948, when the state was established. Even in 1958 only 34% of households owned a refrigerator (44% used iceboxes to keep their food). By 1961 refrigerators were found in half of all households, by 1970 in 90%, and in the 1980's in virtually every household. In 1986 some 10% of all homes also had deep freezers. A gas or electric stove can also be found in each apartment. In addition, new appliances began entering the Israeli kitchen, such as the electric mixer (found in 1986 in 73% of all households) and the dishwasher (in 10%). The washing machine, which was used in 9% of households in 1958, was to be found in 87% of all households in 1986, when half of all households also owned vacuum cleaners. Leisure goods took a prominent place in most homes. A television set, which was owned by only 2% of households in 1965 was to be found in 1986 in some 90% (80% having color TV). By 1986, 20% of all homes had added video sets to their leisure goods, and 41% had stereophonic sets. Personal computers had begun to appear also, and by 1986 could be found in more than 10% of all households.

There were telephones in only a minority of households in the 1950s. In 1970 they were owned by a third of households, while a large number waited for years for their phones to be installed. By 1986 they were operating in 85% of Israeli homes.

Private automobiles are highly taxed in Israel and are therefore very expensive. A new medium quality car costs some 2 years of the average worker's wage or salary. Nevertheless, a car was at the disposal of 43% of all households in 1986 (with some 5% of households owning two cars), compared to 5% of households in 1960 and less than 20% in 1970.

HOUSING CONDITIONS. The average housing unit in Israel was composed of 3.2 rooms in 1987 (as defined in Israel, kitchen and bathroom are not counted as rooms in measuring the size of the apartment). There were 3.6 people living in the average apartment, which means an average density of 1.5 per room. Average density for the Jewish population was 1.05 compared to 2 persons per room in the Arab population.

Impressive changes had occurred in this density (persons per room) and the housing standard: in 1957, after the "mass immigration" of 1948–51 was housed to a large extent, and a large investment made in housing by the government, a quarter of the Jewish population still lived in crowded conditions (density of 3 and more persons per room). A decade later this number had declined to 10%, concurrently with the general improvement of the level of living and following government investment, through the whole period, in special programs to help those in overcrowded conditions to move to better housing. By 1977 the percentage of persons living in apartments with 3 or more persons per room had declined to 2%; in 1987 it was only 0.8% (mostly very large families). The larger size of new apartments constructed and some decrease in the size of households contributed to the increase in the proportion of households living in density of less than 1 person per room: more than 60% in 1987 compared to less than 40% two decades earlier. Of the dwelling units constructed in 1987 or later, 71% were of 4 or more rooms (41% had 5 or more rooms) compared to 6% in 1960 and 28% in 1970. In addition, the area of the average room increased and the standard of housing and its amenities were of a much higher quality. The average area of a new dwelling started in 1987 was 135 square meters, compared to only 65 square meters in 1960 and 90 in 1970.

The 1983 Population and Housing Census found that 18% of dwellings had 2 or more lavatories per apartment; 85% had some permanent means of heating the apartment.

More than 70% of the dwelling units are owner-occupied, while 18% are rented under some rent control arrangement. Acquiring an apartment is the largest expenditure for the average family, and it is the major component of the family's wealth. The price of an average apartment could amount to some 7 years of the worker's average after-tax wage or salary, or some 4 years of the disposable income of the average household.

SOCIAL WELFARE. Israel has developed as a distinct welfare state, spending a large portion of its product on various social and welfare programs, including massive transfer payments. Israel developed most of the instruments for taking care of the general social and welfare problems of the various social groups with special attention given to the weak and disadvantaged parts of the population.

In 1987, social expenditures constituted 22% of total government expenditures (including expenditures by the National Insurance Institute). If debt and interest payments are excluded from total government expenditure, the percentage of social expenditure amounted to 40%. The second largest expenditure went to defense, which accounted for 34% of government expenditures.

Allotment of government's social expenditures.

a) Social services (health, education, culture, housing etc.), provided mostly in kind. These expenditures constituted 55% of government social expenditures. Some services were provided with the participation of non-profit organizations.

b) Transfer payments paid directly to households, through a very elaborate system of allowances and benefits, provided largely under universal criteria and administered by the National Insurance Institute, founded in 1954. (45% of all government social expenditures were spent on transfer payments.)

Social services. The largest expenditures on social services went to education and health. These services were financed mostly by government, but partly also by non-profit organizations and only to a small extent by private bodies.

Education. Israel spent some 8.5% of its GNP on education at different levels (from kindergarten and below, to university education). A third of the population (more than 1.4 million) was enrolled in an educational institution, practically all of them full-time students. Compulsory free education is provided to children between the ages of 5 and 16; it is free but not compulsory for ages 16–18. Among 3- to 4-year-olds 90–95% attended nursery school; practically all children aged 5–15 attended school, as did some 85% of those aged 17–18, some 10% aged 20–24, and 6% aged 25–29.

The percentage of total GNP spent on education increased from about 7% in 1962/63 to about 9% in the middle of the 1970s and remained at approximately the same level (with a small decline in the 1980s). In 1986, government financed two-thirds of the total expenditure on education, and local authorities some 10%. The remaining 22% was financed by tuition fees and by revenues of non-profit organizations, mostly from abroad. The portion financed by government declined in the 1980s (75% in the late 1970s).

Health. The population of Israel received most of its health services through the Health Insurance Plans managed by a few Sick Funds. 95% of the population are insured by one of these funds (the largest one, the General Kupat Holim of the Histadrut, covered some 85% of the insured population). This insurance provided for free clinic services (from a general practitioner to a variety of specialists), hospitalization, surgery, laboratory examinations, and tests, etc. Dental care was not covered by this insurance. Medical prescriptions were filled for a fixed nominal fee (for each medicine).

Israel spent 7.5% of its GNP on health services. 45% of these expenditures were allotted to hospitals and research, 33% to public clinics, and preventive medicine, and 12% to dental clinics; the remainder was spent on private physicians, medicine, and investments. Government financed 52% of health expenditures (this included the amount paid by employers to the National Insurance Institute). The portion financed by government decreased in the 1980s, from 60% to 52%; this was counterbalanced by an increase in the share paid by households particularly in premiums paid to the Sick Funds).

Housing. Subsidies to finance housing purchases and sometimes for rent were provided by government to specific disadvantaged groups. Financing was provided primarily through subsidized mortgages and by below-market rents, provided under special programs for those in overcrowded housing (defined as 3 or more persons per room), for young couples with limited economic means, and for new immigrants (especially in low-rent apartments).

An ambitious program was initiated in 1977 to improve the quality of housing, the environment, and the quality of life of distressed and slum areas. This program, in which large financial and organizational resources were invested, was named *Project Renewal.

Allowances and Benefits. A very elaborate system of income maintenance programs (massive transfer payments) was developed in Israel and administered largely by the National Insurance Institute. The Institute collected premiums from wages and salaries received by employees (at a fixed rate of 5.35% in 1987 up to an income ceiling), from employers (16% of wages paid, reduced in 1987 to some 11%), and from self-employed income. Government also contributed to these programs and in 1987 financed some 30% of the National Insurance Institute expenditures.

The NII's large number of benefits and allowances are shown in the following table. Other allowances and benefits were disbursed directly by the Ministry of Defense to survivors of those killed in military activities and to those disabled by army service injuries.

NUMBER OF RECIPIENTS OF BENEFITS AND ALLOWANCES (1987)

AND DISTRIBUTION OF EXPENDITURE BY TYPE OF BENEFITS

Type of Benefit	*Number of Recipients ('000)*	*Percent of total Expenditures*
Total	. .	100.0
Old age and survivors	410	39.1
General Disabilities	70	10.8
Employment injuries	71	5.2
Maternity grants	100	4.6
Maternity allowances	43	
Families receiving child allowances	533	22.0
Unemployment insurance	56	2.6
Payment for reservists	..	12.1
Income support & other	27	3.4

Eligibility for each of these allowances and their levels are determined by law. The laws and regulations include provisions for automatic indexing of the amount paid: some of these benefits are linked to the "average wage and salary," some to the consumer price index.

The old-age allowance was given to persons who were retired from their place of work (from age 60 for women, from 65 for men). The amount was not lower than 15% of the average wage and salary for a single elderly person. For those whose old-age allowance was the only source of income, an "income supplement" benefit was provided (a third of the group received this income supplement).

Women giving birth received a one-time maternity grant (covering hospitalization costs and a cash grant for other expenses for the child). Those women who were employed three months before giving birth were entitled to a maternity allowance of three months' salary. These constituted some 40% of all mothers giving birth in 1987. Child allowances were granted to more than half a million households, covering some 1.2 million children. For large families this allowance constituted an important contribution to the family income. For a family with 4 children it amounted to 23% of the average monthly wage, and for families with 5 children, to 33%.

Unemployment insurance benefits were paid from 1975 to the unemployed under some provisions of the law. The number of persons receiving unemployment benefits depended on the employment situation in the country. When the unemployment rate rose in the 1980s, the number claiming this type of benefit increased to 56,000 (in 1987).

The Disability Law (enacted in 1974) defined the type and degree of disabilities for which persons were entitled to various allowances.

In 1988 the Nursing Care Law was passed, providing that persons (generally the very elderly) who have some physical or other limitation which prevents them from taking care of themselves are entitled to receive some nursing help (for a certain number of hours a week, depending on their condition). By the end of 1988 some 15,000 persons were receiving this type of help.

Payment of benefits to soldiers doing reserve army duty for more than one day is also carried through the National Insurance Institute. A number of other, smaller benefits are paid by the National Insurance Institute; these include alimony for some divorced women, payments to those injured by enemy activities, etc.

In addition to all these allowances and benefits an "income support" program exists to give welfare needed support when it is not covered by any one of the programs mentioned.

DISPARITIES BETWEEN GROUPS IN THE LEVEL OF LIVING. The level of living of the various groups of the population increased during the four decades since the establishment of the state: for new immigrants and veterans, for those originating in Asia and Africa and those from Europe and America, those living in large cities, in development towns, in villages, etc. But the pace of increase was not the same in different periods for various groups and wide disparities continued to exist between groups. For some indicators it is found that gaps between groups did decrease, while for others they increased in some periods.

The income distribution of households shows that the lowest 20% of households (defined by the level of net income per "standard person") received about 8% of total income, while the highest 10% of the households received 40% of total income. The Gini Coefficient (which is a measure of income inequality ranging from 0 when all households have equal income to 1 when all income accrues to one household) was around 0.27 for disposable income of wage earner households. For all households (including households whose head was not employed) the coefficient was 0.33.

"The Luxemburg Study," a comparative study on income distribution and poverty in eight developed countries in the early eighties, carried out with the participation of the National Insurance Institute in Israel, showed the following results:

PERCENT OF EQUIVALENT NET INCOME, RECEIVED BY THE HIGHEST AND LOWEST HOUSEHOLDS.

	Percent of income received by		
	lowest 20%	highest 20%	Gini Coefficient
Sweden	10.6	31.1	0.21
England	9.0	36.1	0.27
Israel	7.5	40.3	0.33
USA	6.1	38.6	0.33
Norway	9.9	34.1	0.24
Canada	7.6	37.5	0.30
Germany (West)	7.5	43.0	0.35

Source: National Insurance Institute, *Annual Survey* 1984, Jerusalem 1985 p. 125

Studies on income distribution in Israel from the 1950s found signs that income inequality increased slightly from the beginning of the 1950s to the 1960s. From the 1960s fluctuations are found depending on the general economic conditions in the country (extent of unemployment, rate of growth of the economy, changes in transfer payments, etc.). Thus the Gini coefficients were as follows, for annual gross income of wage earners:

	1967	*1972*	*1975*	*1980*	*1984*
Per Household	0.36	0.30	0.28	0.32	0.35
Per Person	. .	0.22	0.20	0.24	0.27

Distribution of net income at the disposal of households was affected to a very large extent by government intervention: on the one hand by levying direct taxes (income tax and National Insurance payments), and on the other hand by transfer payments to various groups of the population.

Income tax and national insurance payments took in 1986/87 on the average 22% of gross income-but it ranged from 5% in the 10% lowest income households, 18% for middle income families, and 33% on the average on the 10% higher income households.

Income tax rates are very progressive. They ranged in 1988 from 20% of the income of lowest income households (receiving gross income of up to 1,100 shekels per month) to 30–35% marginal rates for middle income level households, and a maximum marginal rate of 48% for households with 4,000 shekels' income per month. The income on which income tax is levied is, with some exceptions, taken off gross income with deductions from the computed income tax based on number of children, working status of spouse, various payments for savings, health expenditures, etc. (*see* TAXATION IN ISRAEL)

Payments to the National Insurance Institute were proportional to gross income (in 1988 it was levied as 5.35% of gross income of a wage-earner up to a maximum income ceiling).

Income tax and national insurance payments reduced disparities in incomes of wage earners. The Gini coefficient was lower by 23% for net incomes compared to gross income (computed for 1984).

Transfer payments by the National Insurance Institute (as described in the section on Social Welfare) reduced inequality (as measured by the Gini coefficient) in the net income of households with transfer payments by 10% (compared to the coefficient of income before adding transfers). These payments accrue to a large extent to households from lower income levels.

Another measure of income disparity is provided by measuring the part of the population defined as "poor" by the National Insurance Institute. This definition of "poor" as having incomes below a "poverty line" is based on a relative concept of income distribution. The poverty line is defined as an income of 40% of the median income per standard person. According to this definition some 12% of households were defined in 1984 as being below the poverty line (based on net income per standard person, i.e., after deducting income tax and national insurance payments and after adding transfer payments). Transfer payments decreased the percent of households below the poverty line by some 60% compared to the distribution before adding transfer payments.

Disparities in level of living exist between households of various ethniç origins. Tha Arab population is at a much lower level of living than the Jewish population. Within the Jewish population disparities exist between households originating in various countries, those who immigrated from these countries and their descendants.

In 1987 the income of a wage-earner household born in Asia or Africa was 2,222 shekels per month while that of a household born in Europe or America was NIS 2,635 i.e., the Asia/Africa household had 0.84 of the gross income of the European-born households. As the number of persons in the Asia-Africa household was larger than the European household, disparity of income per person is larger (Asia/Africa households received 0.61 of the income per person of European-born households; this differential is decreased by direct tax to 0.64).

The gap between households in the income per person decreased to some extent in the period since the establishment of the state, but to a limited extent. Thus the income of a wage-earner per household whose head was born in Asia or Africa was, in 1971, 0.74 that of Europe and America; by 1975 it was 0.82 and remained at the same level through the 1980s. The income per person of households whose heads were born in Asia and Africa was 0.48 in 1971, 0.56 in 1980, and remained at the same level up to 1984.

M. SICRON

LEVENBERG, SCHNEIER. Zionist leader in Great Britain (b. Kursk, Russia, 1907). In his youth Levenberg was chairman of the student organization Ha-Shahar, then president of the Zionist Socialist party in Latvia and editor of its organ, *Arbets-Volk.* He was also a contributor to the Yiddish daily *Frimorgen* of Riga and the *Yidishe Shtime* of Kovno. Later, he was secretary of the editorial board of the Yiddish daily *Dos Vort* in Warsaw (1934–36).

Settling in London in 1936, Levenberg became chairman of Po'ale Zion in Great Britain. In 1941 he assumed the editorship of the *Zionist Review*, the official organ of British Zionism, and in 1949 became the representative of the Jewish Agency's office in the United Kingdom. He also served as London correspondent of the Histadrut daily *Davar* (1945–51) and as political representative of the Histadrut.

Dr. Levenberg was a member of the Zionist General Council and chairman of the European Executive of the Po'ale Zion. His publications include *British Labour's Policy on Palestine* (1938), *Zionism in British Politics* (1943), and *The Jews and Palestine* (1945).

LEVI, AUGUSTO. Lawyer, jurist, banker, and Zionist leader (b. Ancona, Italy, 1888; d. Ramat Gan, 1975). A member of the Italian Committee of Keren ha-Yesod from 1928 on and subsequently its president and reorganizer, Levi became president of the Italian Zionist Federation in 1933. In spite of the hostility of the Fascist regime, he was able to preserve the federation, keep the *hakhshara* agricultural training centers for Palestine open, organize Jewish National Fund work, and obtain government permission to forward the amounts collected. In 1938 he was the leading spirit of the resistance to the activities of pro-Fascist elements among Italian Jewry.

Levi was a delegate to the Zionist Congresses in 1935 and 1937. After his immigration to Palestine in 1938 (having barely escaped arrest by the Fascists), he took a leading part in cultural, industrial, and banking activities in Israel and directed numerous enterprises. In 1963 he was elected president of the Israeli Manufacturers' Association.

G. ROMANO

LEVI-BIANCHINI, ANGELO. Naval officer and Zionist diplomat in Italy (b. Venice, 1877; d. Transjordan, 1920). Descended from a distinguished Italian-Jewish family, he became an officer in the Italian navy at an early age. Levi-Bianchini taught at the Italian Naval Academy in Leghorn and the War College in Turin, and served as editor of *Rivista Marittima*, the organ of the Italian navy. He participated in naval actions in the Italo-Turkish War (1911) and was awarded several decorations. During World War I he commanded a warship and was sent by his government on diplomatic missions. At the end of the war he became an enthusiastic Zionist under the influence of Chaim Weizmann and was one of the two representatives of the Union of Italian-Jewish Communities appointed to the Zionist Commissions. From 1918 to 1920 he was active on diplomatic missions on behalf of both the Italian government and the Zionist Commission. Though this dual activity perplexed Weizmann, there is no doubt that Levi-Bianchini rendered great service to Zionism. At the San Remo Conference (April, 1920) he influenced the Italian Prime Minister, Francesco Nitti, to join in confirmation of the Balfour Declaration. After the conference he was appointed head of the Immigration Department of the Zionist Commission. In August, 1920, before assuming his new post, he went on a political mission to Damascus on behalf of the Italian government. On his return he was murdered by Bedouins near Dar'a. His body was discovered after searches by his brother in Khirbet Gazla.

E. LIVNEH

LEVIN, HANOKH. Israeli playwright (b. Tel Aviv, 1943). Levin studied Hebrew literature and philosophy at Tel Aviv University (1965–68). His first play, *Ani, Ata ve-ha-Milhama ha-Ba'a* (You, Me, and the Next War, 1968), was a satirical revue critical of the patriotic exuberance nurtured in the wake of the Six-Day War (1967). Levin's first full-length play, *Solomon Greep*, was staged that same year. Influenced by the theater of the absurd, its grotesque types and existentialist motifs would recur in most of his subsequent works.

Malkat ha-Ambatya (Queen of the Bathtub, 1970) stirred up violent public reaction. The opening performance was disrupted by demonstrators offended by Levin's jibes at Israeli patriotism, his use of obscenities, and his satirization of scriptures, and by those who supported his attacks on Israel's "triumphalism." The controversy ultimately forced the closing of the play.

Levin's first successful play, *Hefetz* (1982), won him a nomination for the Israel Prize, which he turned down. In *Jacobi ve-Lilienthal*, 1972, he contrasts the hidden yearnings of his characters' ids and the egotistical realities of their miserable lives. His other plays include *Schitz*, 1975), a musical drama, *Yisurei Iyov;e (Job's Torments, 1981), and Ha-Zona ha-Gedola mi-Bavel* (The Great Babylonian Whore, 1982).

Levin's plays are populated by gray, anonymous characters, living in the nameless, grim limbo of urban society. Devoid of any ideals or principles, incapable of real passion, they wallow in their psychological despair.

E. SPICEHANDLER

LEVIN, SHEMARYA. Zionist leader and author (b. Svisloch, Russia, 1867; d. Haifa, 1935). Levin studied at the Universities of Berlin and Königsberg. While a student in Berlin, he helped found a pre-Herzlian Zionist student society, the Russian-Jewish Academic Association. In 1896 he was appointed by the government to be rabbi in Grodno, later serving in the same capacity in Yekaterinoslav (Dnepropetrovsk) and Vilna. A brilliant orator, he attracted Jewish youth to his lectures on historical and cultural themes. In Vilna he also edited *Novaya Zarya* (New Dawn), a Russian-language Jewish daily. In 1906 he was elected to the Duma (Russian Parliament), where he championed Jewish rights. After the dissolution of the Duma by the government, he signed the Viborg Manifesto, a denunciation of Tsarist despotism. Forced to leave Russia, he settled in 1908 in Berlin, where he worked for the Hilfsverein der Deutschen Juden, winnng its support for the founding of the Haifa Technion. He was one of the leaders of the fight to

Sh'marya Levin.
[Zionist Archives]

make Hebrew the language of instruction at the institute (*see* LANGUAGE WAR).

A delegate to the Fourth (1900) and later Zionist Congresses, Levin was a proponent of practical Zionism. At the Sixth Congress (1903), he was a leading spokesman for the opponents of the East Africa scheme. Three years later he paid the first of numerous visits to the United States. In 1911 he was elected to the Zionist Executive. In 1913 he visited the United States on behalf of the Technion. Stranded in the United States by the outbreak of World War I, he plunged into the work of strengthening the Zionist movement in the country. One of the most brilliant propagandists and preachers of Zionism, he filled the American Jewish masses with enthusiasm for the movement and was instrumental in attracting influential Jews who had previously remained aloof from Zionism, among them Jacob H. Schiff.

As the sole member of the Zionist Executive in the United States when the war broke out, Levin, jointly with Louis Lipsky, issued the call for the extraordinary conference (1914) that created the Provisional Executive Committee for General Zionist Affairs, headed by Louis D. Brandeis. Levin worked closely with the committee and helped consolidate its status and authority on the Zionist scene. While in the United States, he also gave much of his time and energy to the propagation of Hebrew culture, helped found the Histadrut Ivrit of America, and co-edited the New York Hebrew weekly *Ha-Toren*. At the end of the war he returned to Berlin.

In 1920 Levin was put in charge of the Propaganda Department of the newly founded Keren ha-Yesod and in this capacity visited Jewish communities throughout the world. He became deeply involved in the controversy that developed between the pro-Weizmann and pro-Brandeis elements in the Zionist movement. In 1921 he was in the United States with Chaim Weizmann and played an active part in the internal development and growing rift that culminated in the Cleveland Convention of the Zionist Organization of America and the victory of the Weizmann forces that summer.

A close friend of Ahad Ha-Am and Hayim Nahman Bialik, Levin helped Bialik found the Devir publishing house. In 1924 he settled in Palestine.

Levin was the author of Zionist publications in Hebrew, Yiddish, Russian, and German. His memoirs (*Childhood in Exile*, 1929; *Youth in Revolt*, 1930; and *The Arena*, 1932) were reissued in an abridged edition by their translator, Maurice Samuel, as *Forward from Exile* (1967). H. LEAF

LEVIN, YITZHAK MEIR. Leader of the *Agudat Israel in Poland and Israel (b. Gora Kalwaria, Russian Poland, 1893; d, Jerusalem, 1971). Levin studied at the yeshiva of his uncle, Abraham M. Alter, the rabbi of Gora Kalwaria. During World War I he was entrusted by his uncle with work for Jewish war victims and with the organization of Agudat Israel in Poland. He devoted himself especially to the development of the Agudat Israel school system. Levin was an effective popular speaker; he contributed articles to the Aguda press, and maintained contact with the Polish government. Opposed to the Zionist political struggle for Jewish rights, he used traditional methods of obtaining the goodwill of government authorities. In 1929 he was elected to the Aguda Presidium. The next year he became president of the Polish Agudat Israel, and in 1939 president of the World Agudat Israel's Executive. After the Nazi occupation of Poland, Levin was appointed to the Judenrat (Jewish Council) in Warsaw, but some time later he fled Poland. Arriving in Palestine in 1940, he worked for the relief of Polish Jews.

Levin represented the Agudat Israel before the Anglo-American Committee of Inquiry (1946) and the United Nations Special Committee on Palestine (1947), after having reached an understanding with the Jewish Agency on the content of his testimony. Following the establishment of the State of Israel, he was elected Agudat Israel's representative to the Provisional Council of State. He was among the signatories of the Israel Declaration of Independence. Levin was subsequently elected to the Knesset, where he served until his death. From 1948 to 1952 he was Minister of Social Welfare. Y. SLUTSKY

LEVINSON, AVRAHAM. Tze'irei Zion activist in Russia and a leader of Hitahdut in Poland in the 1920s (b. Lodz, 1891; d. Tel Aviv, 1955). Levinson participated in the Tze'irei Zion Conference in May, 1917, and subsequently in the 7th All-Russian Zionist Conference. One of the founders of the Tze'irei Zion Popular Faction in the Zionist Organization in Russia, he edited its journal, *Erd Un Arbeit*. After World War I he moved to Poland where he was one of the heads of Hitahdut and one of its delegates to the first Polish Sejm (parliament). In 1936 Levinson immigrated to Palestine, where he directed the Histadrut Cultural Center. He was active in literary work and wrote history books. M. MINTZ

LEVINTHAL: U.S. family of Zionists.

Bernard Louis Levinthal. Rabbi and Zionist leader (b. Kovno, Lithuania, 1865; d. Atlantic City, N.J., 1952). Ordained to the rabbinate by Rabbi Isaac Elhanan Spektor and Rabbi Shemuel Mohilever, Levinthal went to the United States in 1891 to succeed his father-in-law as rabbi of Congregation B'nai Abraham in Philadelphia, a position he held for more than five decades. Considered the chief Orthodox rabbi of Philadelphia, he organized Orthodox Jewish communal institutions there and in 1902 helped found the Union of Orthodox Rabbis of the United States and Canada, becoming its first president and, later, honorary president. The same year Levinthal helped found the Mizrachi Organization of America, and for many years he was an honorary vice-president of the Federation of American Zionists. In 1917 he was one of the organizers of the American Jewish Congress and, two years later, one of the 10 delegates representing the organization at the Paris Peace Conference.

His son **Israel Herbert Levinthal.** Rabbi and Zionist leader (b. Vilna, Russia, 1888; d. New Rochelle, New York, 1982). He was brought to the United States in 1891. He graduated from Columbia University and was ordained at the Jewish Theological Seminary of America in 1910. After serving a number of synagogues in Brooklyn, he was called to the pulpit of the Brooklyn Jewish Center in 1919. He was president of the Rabbinical Assembly of America from 1930 to 1932 and of the Brooklyn Jewish Community Council from 1940 to 1944.

Levinthal was the first president of the Brooklyn region of the Zionist Organization of America (1932–35) and its honorary president from 1935 on. In the 1920s he was chairman of the fundraising campaign launched by the United Synagogue of America for the erection of a model synagogue center in Jerusalem. This center, which became the Jeshurun Synagogue, was intended to give the Jews in the new city of Jerusalem a synagogue that would be modern and architecturally appealing.

Levinthal's views on Judaism and Zionism appear in his writings, which include *Steering or Drifting—Which? Sermons and Discourses* (1928); *Judaism: An Analysis and an Interpretation* (1935); *A New World Is Born* (1943); and *Point of View: An Analysis of American Judaism* (1958).

Another son of Bernard Louis, **Louis Edward Levinthal** was a jurist, Zionist, and Jewish communal leader in the United States (b. Philadelphia, 1892; d. Jerusalem, Israel, 1976). He became interested in Zionism at an early age and headed the Zionist students' organization at the University of Pennsylvania, where he studied law. He combined a distinguished law career (he was judge of the Court of Common Pleas in Philadelphia from 1937 to 1959) with leadership in Jewish communal and Zionist endeavors. For many years he was chairman of the Publication Committee of the Jewish Publication Society of America, of which he was president from 1949 to 1954. In 1947–48 he served as special adviser on Jewish affairs to Gen. Lucius D. Clay and the European Command.

Levinthal's principal interest in Jewish life was the Zionist cause. From 1941 to 1943 he was president of the Zionist Organization of America, which made substantial progress

Louis E. Levinthal. [Zionist Archives]

during his administration. In the same years he also served as chairman of the Executive Committee of the Emergency Committee for Zionist Affairs. At the 22nd World Zionist Congress (1946) he was a member of the minority group that supported Chaim Weizmann. He was active on behalf of the United Jewish Appeal and the State of Israel bonds. In May, 1957, Levinthal was one of the founders of the American Jewish League for Israel. In 1962 he was elected chairman of the Board of Governors of the Hebrew University in Jerusalem, a position he held until 1968. He lived his last years in Jerusalem.

In addition to several books on legal subjects, Levinthal wrote *Credo of an American Zionist* (1942).

LEVITE, LEON. Zionist leader in Poland (b. Warsaw, 1878; d. Tel Aviv, 1944). Levite was one of the prominent leaders of Zionism in Poland before World War I. He attended early Zionist Congresses and the Helsingfors Conference of Russian Zionists (1906). During the war he was in Moscow, and after the Russian Revolution of 1917 he played a prominent role in the reorganization of the Russian-Jewish communities. After the Bolshevik takeover he returned to Warsaw, where he became a head of the *Palestine Office.

Levite was a representative of Polish Jewry in the Comité des Délégations Juives to the Paris Peace Conference. At the London Zionist Conference of 1920 he was elected to the Greater Actions Committee. Within the Polish Zionist Organization he led the Et Livnot faction, which supported Chaim Weizmann's plan for expanding the Jewish Agency and advocated building Palestine with private capital and enterprise. In 1925 he became head of the Central Committee of the Polish Zionist Organization, a position he held until 1929. He was the founder and president of the Polish-Palestine Chamber of Commerce in Warsaw and one of the founders of the anti-German boycott committee, which he headed until the invasion of Poland by Germany in 1939. He succeeded in escaping to Palestine, where he spent the last years of his life.

LEVONTIN, ZALMAN DAVID. Zionist pioneer (b. Orsha, Russia, 1856; d. Tel Aviv, 1940). Levontin was employed in commercial banks in southern Russia. He was active in the founding of Hovevei Zion groups until 1882, when he moved to Palestine. Levontin participated in the founding of the settlement Rishon le-Zion and headed the settlers' council, but economic difficulties compelled him to return to Russia. An early collaborator of Herzl, he became director of the *Jewish Colonial Trust in London in 1901. In 1903 he went to Palestine to open the Anglo-Palestine Company (later the Anglo-Palestine Bank; *see* BANK LEUMI LE-ISRAEL), whose establishment he had initiated, and served as its director until his retirement in 1924. In 1936 he was made an honorary citizen of Tel Aviv.

Levontin wrote *Le-Eretz Avotenu* (*To the Land of Our Fathers*, 1885; second ed., 1924) and several Zionist booklets, and also contributed to newspapers and magazines.

LEWIN-EPSTEIN, ELIYAHU ZE'EV. Zionist leader (b. Vilkaviskis, Lithuania, 1863; d. Bad Nauheim, Germany, 1932). Lewin-Epstein was the director of a Hebrew bookstore and publishing firm established in Warsaw by his father. One of the early followers of the Hovevei Zion movement, he together with Ze'ev Gluskin, re-established the Warsaw Hovevei Zion group in 1888. Accepted into the secret order *Bene Moshe in 1889, he founded its Warsaw chapter. He was also a founder of the Menuha ve-Nahala settlement society, visiting Palestine to purchase land on its behalf. On his way there, he represented the Warsaw Hovevei Zion at the first general meeting of the Odessa Committee in 1890. After purchasing the land on which Rehovot was founded, he returned to Palestine to administer the colony. He did much to further the progress of the settlement, which was to serve as a model for others.

Lewin-Epstein visited Europe on behalf of the Carmel Wine Company and settled in New York in 1900 as its representative in the United States. He was prominently associated with the activities of the Federation of American Zionists and served as its treasurer for some time. He was also prominently associated with the Provisional Executive Committee for General Zionist Affairs. In 1915 he visited Europe on a Jewish political mission, and in 1917 he served with Felix Frankfurter and others as a member of the United States political mission headed by Henry Morgenthau, whose purpose was to persuade Turkey to make a separate peace.

In 1918 Lewin-Epstein went to Palestine with the American Zionist Medical Unit, which he managed. He was also attached to the Zionist Commission. In 1921 he visited Europe and the United States to organize the sale of art and crafts of the Bezalel School, and from 1923 to 1925 he was active on behalf of the HIAS (Hebrew Immigrant Aid Society) in Europe and Palestine.

Lewin-Epstein published his memoirs in the periodical *Bustanai*. These later appeared in book form (*Zikhronotai*, 1932).

I. KLAUSNER

LEWINSKY, AKIVA. Zionist executive (b. Geneva, 1918). He immigrated to Palestine in 1934 and was a founding member of Kibbutz Ma'ayan Tzevi in 1936. In 1939, Lewinsky was sent on a special mission to the Palestine Office in Berlin to rescue children of Youth Aliya age. From 1940 to 1943 he was in charge of the Youth Aliya Department of the Hever ha-Kevutzot kibbutz movement. In 1943 he was chosen for a rescue mission to Turkey as Youth Aliya representative and remained there for two years. From 1945 to 1948 he was Youth Aliya representative for Europe. From 1952 to 1954 he represented Israel on the Inter-Governmental Committee for European Migration at its Geneva headquarters, and from 1957 to 1961, directed the economic affairs of the kibbutz federation Ihud ha-Kevutzot veha-Kibbutzim.

In 1961 he became managing director of Bank Hapoalim, which developed into one of the country's largest banks. During this period, from 1961 to 1978, Lewinsky was also adviser to the Organization of American States on the development of workers' banks in Latin America and the Caribbean, starting workers' cooperative banks in 12 countries.

From 1978 to 1987 Lewinsky was treasurer of the Jewish Agency and the World Zionist Organization.

Y. MORRIS

LEWINSKY, ELHANAN LOEB. Writer and communal worker (b. Paberze, Lithuania, 1857; d. Odessa, Russia, 1910). Lewinsky received a religious education and studied for a time at the University of Kharkov. After the 1881 pogroms in southern Russia, he joined a Bilu immigration group and went to Palestine, but an eye ailment forced him to return to Russia two months later. Subsequently he became well known as a feuilletonist and communal worker and was active as a publisher of Hebrew books. Among his best-known writings was the Utopian work *Masa le-Eretz Israel bi-Shenat Tat la-Elef ha-Shishi* (Journey to the Land of Israel in the Year 2040), which was first published in 1892.

A member of the secret order Bene Moshe, he helped organize Jewish emigration to Argentina, which was financed by Baron Maurice de Hirsch. In 1896 he became director of the Carmel Wine Company in Odessa. In 1907 the First World Conference of Ivriya (an organization for the development of Hebrew as a living language) at The Hague named Lewinsky head of its Russian Central Committee.

I. KLAUSNER

LEWIS, FRIEDA S. Zionist and Jewish affairs leader, educator, and guidance counsellor in the US (b. Great Neck, NY). Active in civic and educational affairs in her home community, she was a director of the Jewish National Fund, the Hadassah Zionist Youth Commission and the American Foundation for Jewish Culture. She served Hadassah, the Women's Zionist Organization of America, as national treasurer, vice-president in charge of Jewish Education and Youth Aliyah, and its 17th national president from 1980 to 1984. Subsequently she became chairman of the Hadassah Medical Organization. A delegate to six Zionist Congresses, she is a member of the Executive and National Board of the World Zionist Organization; a director of the Jewish National Fund; a director of the American Foundation for Jewish Culture; and a past chairman of the World Jewish Congress, American Section.

M. LEVIN

LIBERAL PARTY. Political party in Israel resulting from the merger of the General Zionist party (*see* GENERAL ZIONISM) and the *Progressive party in 1961. In the spring of 1961 negotiations were opened between the General Zionist Organization in Israel (then represented in the Knesset by eight members) and the Progressive party (six Knesset members) with a view to a merger. These negotiations were conducted under the impact of the Lavon affair, which seemed to have shaken the structure of the dominant political party. Although the Progressive party then formed part of the coalition Cabinet headed by David Ben-Gurion and the General Zionists were in the Opposition, it was felt by both groups that the time was ripe for the formation of a united liberal party which would derive its support from wide sections of the population.

On 25 April 1961, the merger of the General Zionist and Progressive parties and the formation of the Liberal party of Israel were announced. As an interim arrangement, pending a national convention of the new party, it was agreed that the numerical superiority of the General Zionists be ignored and that the governing organs of the party be constituted on the basis of parity (i.e., that equality of representation should be maintained regardless of the numerical strength of the constituent groups).

In its platform for the elections to the Fifth Knesset, which were held in the summer of 1961, the Liberal party endorsed the concept of a welfare state, in which social services would be maintained and administered by the State rather than by political or quasipolitical organizations. While acknowledging the importance of the cooperative sector as organized within the Histadrut and of a united trade union movement, the Liberal party called for equality of status for private initiative, greater consideration for the professional and middle classes, limitation of government intervention in economic affairs, and a more equitable distribution of the tax burden. Great stress was laid on the safeguarding of individual liberties, and the adoption of a written constitution was urged. In the election the new party gained almost 138,000 votes, or about 14 percent of the votes cast, and secured 17 seats in the Knesset. In the ensuing negotiations for the formation of a new Government conducted by Mapai, the Liberal party found itself forming the Opposition with the Herut party, which also had 17 representatives in the Knesset.

Pursuant to its election pledges, the Liberal party introduced a series of private bills designed to safeguard individual liberties; among these were a charter of human rights, abolition of military rule, and guarantees of the right of political asylum and the right of privacy; all were voted down. In matters of fiscal policy, the party urged the reduction of income tax rates in the middle-income brackets and, generally, a more moderate income tax. In the realm of economic policy, it advocated the abolition of monopolies and other forms of economic discrimination. To regulate labor-management relations, it introduced a bill calling for the compulsory mediation of labor disputes in public utilities and other essential services.

With the development of a rift within Mapai in 1964 and the negotiations opened by Levi Eshkol with a view to forming an alignment with the left-wing party Ahdut Avoda, widespread agitation developed in favor of a large non-Socialist bloc as a counterpart to the Ma'arakh (Labor Alignment). Herut officially approached the Liberal party with a view to forming a joint parliamentary bloc, that is, running a joint ticket in the forthcoming Knesset elections and acting as a single group in the incumbent Knesset. This was a scheme calling for a parliamentary partnership between two separate and independent political parties. The Central Committee of the Liberal party approved the scheme, but a minority withdrew from the party to form the Independent Liberal party.

Herut and the Liberal party signed an agreement in April, 1965, for a joint parliamentary bloc as well as for joint blocs in the municipal governing bodies. Shortly thereafter, a similar arrangement was effected within the Histadrut. The joint platform for the elections to the Sixth Knesset in November, 1965, was largely identical with the Liberal party platform in the 1961 elections. In September,

1965, elections were held within the Histadrut, and the joint list obtained more than 15 percent of the total vote, thus becoming the largest political grouping in it after the governing alignment. The joint list to the Knesset elections was known as *Gahal from the initials of the Hebrew words for "Herut-Liberal bloc."

See also INDEPENDENT LIBERAL PARTY

Haifa University Library. [Haifa University]

LIBRARIES IN ISRAEL. The first modern libraries in Israel were established at the end of the 19th century, when the Zionist movement saw them as an important factor in the return of the Jews to their homeland. In the following decades, the Israeli library system made great progress in serving the growing educational, scientific, and technological needs of a modern state.

Academic Libraries. Besides the *Jewish National and University Library in Jerusalem, which serves both a national and an academic function, there are eight universities, seven of which have large libraries. (Only the Open University has a small library.) The university libraries' collections, some of which operate on automated systems, total some 4,700,000 volumes. The Israel Standing Committee of National and University Libraries (SCONUL) serves as a forum for cooperation, planning, and communication among academic libraries.

Special Libraries and Information Centers. Israel has today some 400 special libraries and information centers connected with research institutes, industry, hospitals, government agencies (in particular the large Knesset library), and religious institutions. Many of them are computerized and offer online retrieval services. In 1961 the National Council for Research and Development established the Center for Scientific Information (COSTI) to sponsor and provide documentation and retrieval services and to publish directories and special guidebooks. By 1986 some 50 Israeli special data bases existed, 16 in the social sciences and humanities, and 34 in the natural and exact sciences, their number rapidly growing.

Public Libraries. Several bodies promote public libraries in Israel: The Ministry of Education and Culture, municipalities and local authorities, the Histadrut, and philanthropic organizations. The Library Law of 1975 provides for the further development and establishment of public libraries. In 1985 a total of 983 public libraries were functioning: 954 in Jewish settlements and 29 in non-Jewish settlements, serving some 973,000 readers. All inhabitants of urban Jewish localities, 79% of those in rural Jewish localities and 42% of the non-Jewish population, live in localities served by public libraries. Surveys show a high frequency of reading, although only some 26% are registered as library readers. The kibbutz population, with its 126,000 people, served by over two million volumes, is conspicuous for its high number of books per capita and high library use. The Center for Public Libraries, founded in 1965, provides services such as centralized acquisition and book processing; it also publishes special bibliographies, reference tools, and the professional journal, *Yad la-Kore* (in collaboration with the Israel Library Association and the Graduate School of Library and Archive Studies of the Hebrew University).

School Libraries. According to the Central Bureau of Statistics survey of 1982/83, 85% of the country's 1,277 primary schools and 91% of its 544 intermediate and secondary schools have library services provided to them. Sixty-four percent of all primary schools and 83% of all intermediate and secondary schools have reading rooms. The average number of volumes per school library was 3,060 for primary schools and 8,564 for intermediate and secondary schools.

Other Libraries. Several important libraries are maintained by foreign governments and non-governmental public bodies, such as the U.S. Information Service, the British Council, and the Alliance Française. A number of Jewish and Christian institutions, especially in Jerusalem, have important libraries, notably on theology, archeology, and Bible study. These include the Hebrew Union College, the Pontifical Biblical Institute, the schools of archeology, and the Ecumenical Institute at Tantur.

Professional Associations. The Israel Library Association, founded in 1952, numbers about 1,500 members from various types of libraries and archives. The Israel Society of Special Libraries and Information Centers was founded in 1966 and numbers some 600 members. It publishes the ISLIC bulletin. B.C. PERITZ

LIBRARY AND ARCHIVES, ZIONIST. The principal Zionist archives are the Central Zionist Archives in Jerusalem and the Zionist Archives and Library in New York.

Central Zionist Archives

Founded as *Archiv der Zionistischen Organisation* in Berlin in 1919, the earliest holdings of the Central Zionist Archives were the records of the Central Offices of the Zionist Organization in Vienna (1897–1905), Cologne (1905–1911), and Berlin (1911–1920). By 1933 when the Archives were moved to Jerusalem, additional groups of records had been acquired and the library, the collection of periodicals, as well as the collection of photographs had been started.

Reopened in the building of the National Institutions in 1935, the Central Zionist Archives (CZA)—this name was adopted at that time—also became *de facto* the historical archives of major Jewish institutions and organizations operating in mandatory Palestine. The acquisition of private papers of prominent persons was given a strong impetus with the transfer from Vienna of the archives of Theodor Herzl in 1937.

The 24th Zionist Congress (1956) accorded the Central Zionist Archives the status of "the historical archives of the Zionist movement, the World Zionist Organization (WZO), and the Jewish Agency (JA)." It was made mandatory for all

WZO and JA organizations and institutions: 1) to make over to the CZA their non-current records or to obtain their permission for the destruction of such records which do not merit preservation; 2) to furnish the CZA with one copy of all their publications.

The constant growth of the holdings of the CZA, led from the 1960s to the outhousing of large parts of their material. At the same time the use of these holdings by scholars and the general public steadily increased. To insure the proper functioning and full utilization of what had grown into the largest Jewish archival facility in the world—except for the State Archives of Israel—the Executive of the WZO and the JA decided in 1964 that a purpose-built structure be constructed for the CZA. This decision was implemented more than twenty years later, and in 1987 the Archives moved to their own building, located near the entrance to Jerusalem, which contains a comfortable reading-room and ample storage space.

By 1987, on the eve of the move to their new building, the CZA had assembled material which occupied c. 6,000 linear meters of shelves.

It comprised: a. the files of the Central Offices of the WZO since its foundation in 1897 and of the Jewish Agency since 1929: Vienna 1897–1905; Cologne 1905–1911; Berlin 1911–1920; London 1917–1955; Jerusalem from 1919/1921 onwards; New York from c. 1940 onwards. Among the files of the Jerusalem Office are, to name only the most voluminous record-groups, those of the Political Department, the Departments of Trade and Industry and of Labor (all of which terminated their activities upon the establishment of the State of Israel); of the Recruiting and Demobilization Offices (Jerusalem, Haifa, and Tel Aviv) 1940-1947, the "Rescue Committee" 1939–1948, and up to varying dates the files of the Treasury, the Immigration, Youth Aliya, and the Rural Settlement Departments and also those of the Education Department (the functions of which were transferred to the Va'ad Le'umi in 1932).

These files include the public papers (correspondence, memoranda, speeches) of leading personalities, among them Chaim Weizmann, David Ben-Gurion, Nahum Goldmann, Moshe Sharett, Eliezer Kaplan, and Berl Locker.

b. the files of the major branch offices of the WZO and the JA, among them those of the Palestine Office, Jaffa-Tel Aviv 1908-1920; the political Agency at Constantinople 1908–1917; the Copenhagen Office 1914–1920; the Geneva Office (representing the Jewish Agency at the League of Nations) 1925–1948; the Central Bureau for the Settlement of German Jews in Palestine (in London and Jerusalem 1933–1937 and 1933–1955 respectively) as well as the files of several Immigration Offices (including Istanbul, Tripoli, Marseilles, Rome) during and after World War II.

Central Zionist Archives, Jerusalem. [Central Zionist Archives]

c. the files of the Head Office of the Jewish National Fund [JNF/KKL]: Vienna-Cologne-The Hague 1902–1922 and Jerusalem 1922-1947, and of the Head Office of the Keren ha-Yesod: London 1920-1926 and Jerusalem 1926-c. 1965.

d. files of financial-economic institutions set up by the WZO, in particular those of the predecessors of Bank Le'umi (the Jewish Colonial Trust—Anglo-Palestine Company/Bank) 1899/1902-c. 1940 and of the Palestine (now Israel) Land Development Company 1908–1948.

e. files of organizations and institutions set up by or for the benefit of the Jewish Community in Palestine under Turkish and British rule, among them (to name again only the most voluminous) those of PICA (Palestine Jewish Colonization Association and its predecessors) 1882–1957, the Mikve Yisrael Agricultural School 1868–1948 and the Va'ad Le'umi 1918–1949.

f. remnants of the archives of Hovevei Zion Societies in Russia 1882–1917, Romania 1880–1900. and England 1890–1902; of some countrywide Zionist Federations, of youth movements and student organizations in various European countries.

g. files of some offices of the World Jewish Congress (WJC) (Stockholm, Buenos Aires, Jerusalem). According to an agreement with the WJC, the CZA serve as its historical archives and the files of the main offices of the WJC are expected to be transferred to Jerusalem.

h. the private papers of approximately 640 personalities, among them Theodor Herzl (who also retained most of his political papers in his private custody), Max Nordau, David Wolffsohn, Nahum Sokolow, Moses Hess, Menahem Ussishkin, Shemarya Levin, Leo Motzkin, Richard Gottheil, Israel Goldstein, Harry Friedenwald, Henrietta Szold, Rose Jacobs, Arthur Ruppin, Yitzhak Grünbaum, Pinhas Rosen (Felix Rosenblüth), Yitzhak Ben-Zvi, Israel Zangwill, Norman Bentwich, and Selig Brodetsky. The library of the Archives numbered in the summer of 1987 some 98,700 cataloged books; the periodicals collection comprised approximately 5,550 different newspapers, news sheets of kibbutzim and other periodicals. The collection of pictures contained over 300,000 photographs and negatives.

The Archives are associated with the publication of the writings of Theodor Herzl in Hebrew, English, and German, and they publish a bi-monthly bibliographical bulletin *Ha-Sifrut ha-Tziyonit*, which lists new publications on Zionism in Israel in modern times. M. HEYMANN

Zionist Archives and Library

The Zionist Archives and Library in New York is a research and information center for all aspects of life in Israel and other Middle Eastern countries and for Zionism and Judaism. It was established in 1939 under the aegis of the Zionist Organization of America (ZOA) and the Keren ha-Yesod. In 1942 the Keren ha-Yesod became its sole sponsor, continuing in this role until 1963, when the center was turned over to the Jewish Agency for Israel-American Section, Inc.

The initial collection consisted of 200 books and pamphlets, acquired from the ZOA, and about 1,000 letters and documents presented to it by Louis Lipsky. By 1988 the collection had grown to 45,000 books, pamphlets, documents, dissertations, and ephemera, mostly in English or Hebrew, some in German, Yiddish, and other languages;

4,000 periodicals (newspapers and magazines in English, Hebrew, Yiddish, German, French, and Swedish, including a set of *Die Welt*), of which 350 were currently received; and 35,000 photographs pertaining to Israel and to Israeli and Zionist history and leadership. Other holdings included a large microfilm collection, maps, nonmusical recordings, Israeli symphonic scores, and folk music, films and filmstrips.

The archival collection is rich in primary source material, such as correspondence, reports, and documents pertaining to the history of American and World Zionism. The archives contain original and microfilm copies from the files of Louis D. Brandeis, Benjamin V. Cohen, Jacob de Haas, Harry Friedenwald, Richard Gottheil, Louis Lipsky, Bernard G. Richards, Robert Szold, the National Archives in Washington, D.C., the Franklin Delano Roosevelt Collection in Hyde Park, N.Y., the American Jewish Conference, the ZOA, and the American Zionist Council as well as files of material from other Zionist and Jewish organizations.

From 1946 to 1956 the Zionist Archives and Library compiled and published *Palestine and Zionism*, a bibliography of books, pamphlets, and periodicals on Palestine, Israel, Zionism, the related fields of the Middle East, and Judaism. Special bibliographies have been compiled for individuals, groups, and specific events.

The collection and facilities of the library are available to all who desire authentic information in its field of competence. They have been utilized by governmental agencies, United Nations personnel, the press, radio, television, the motion-picture industry, students, researchers, authors, and educators. The library participates in an interlibrary loan program, thereby serving readers outside the New York area. Material for exhibits is also supplied. To acquaint the public with the library's services and collection, group visits are organized and orientation talks on the use of the library are initiated.

Sophie A. Udin was director of the Zionist Archives and Library from its inception until 1949. She was succeeded by Sylvia Landress, who served until 1982. Later, the director was Esther Togman. S. LANDRESS

LIBYA, ZIONISM IN. *See* NORTH AFRICA, ZIONISM IN.

LICHTHEIM, RICHARD. Zionist leader, editor, and diplomat (b. Berlin, 1885; d. Jerusalem, 1963). He was born into a German family whose members were either completely assimilated or converted to Christianity. From his early youth, Lichtheim felt their attitude to be one of insincerity, bordering on self-delusion. He found his way back to Judaism through Zionism, becoming active in the Zionist movement while a student at the Universities of Berlin and Freiburg (1905–10). In 1910 he visited Eretz Israel for the first time; the following year he became editor of *Die Welt* (until 1913) and published a brochure "Das Programm des Zionismus". In it he described the moral plight of the German Jews, who in their battle for civic rights had sacrificed their individuality. He regarded the formula "Germans of Jewish persuasion" as a deliberate distortion of Jewish identity to suit political convenience. Lichtheim rejected the notion that Jewish nationalism was incompatible with patriotism that it was a "return to the ghetto;" it was a bid for the emancipation of the Jews as a people as distinct from the emancipation of individuals, an endeavor towards their spiritual and cultural regeneration.

In 1913 Lichtheim was sent to Constantinople to assist Victor Jacobson in conducting Zionist political activity in Turkey, and soon afterwards assumed total responsibility for the job. Comparatively young—he was then thirty years old—he displayed maturity and balanced judgement, enjoying a unique talent to get on well with almost all successive German and American ambassadors in Constantinople. On 29 June 1914 the German Ambassador, Freiherr von Wangenheim, promised him that, should the Palestine Jews suffer from persecution, he would do his best to protect them.

Lichtheim's primary concern during World War I was to ensure the survival of the yishuv, and he was singularly successful. It was due to his endeavors that on 22 November 1915 the German Embassy in Constantinople, with Berlin's prior approval, issued far-reaching instructions to the German Consulate in Jerusalem (*see* GERMANY AND ZIONISM), which served as a cornerstone of their policy to protect the yishuv.

In June 1917 Lichtheim returned to Berlin and took charge of the Political and Propaganda Department of the Zionist Executive. He won over a section of the German press and a number of influential German personalities. On 28 August 1917, at the suggestion of the German foreign ministry, he and Arthur Hantke met *Jamal Pasha who was visiting Berlin; they prevailed upon him not to ill-treat Palestinian Jews. In two successive articles in the *Jüdische Rundschau* (16 and 23 November 1917), he found courage to praise the Balfour Declaration as "an event of world historical importance" and suggested that to fortify their position at the future peace conference, the Central Powers should follow suit.

In 1919 Lichtheim acted as adviser on Jewish affairs to the German delegation at the peace conference in Paris; the following year he moved to London to head the Organization Department of the Zionist Executive. In 1921 he was elected to the Executive but resigned two years later in protest against Weizmann's policy. A close friend of Jabotinsky, he joined the Revisionists. In 1933 he became a leading member of the Jewish State party. In 1934 he settled in Jerusalem. During World War II, as representative of the Jewish Agency in Geneva, he was one of the first to report the gruesome events of the Holocaust period.

In 1954 Lichtheim published two books: *Die Geschichte des deutschen Zionismus* (A History of Zionism in Germany) and *She'ar Yashuv: Zikhronot Tziyoni Mi-Germania* (The Remnant will Return: Memories of a Zionist from Germany); the latter appeared in German as *Rückkehr Lebenserinnerungem*, in 1970. I. FRIEDMAN

LIKUD ("Unity"). Israeli political party bloc, created in July, 1973, and consisting of *Gahal (the Herut-Liberal bloc, established in 1965), the Free Center party (an offshoot of Herut), and the La-Am party (consisting of former Rafi members who did not return to Labor). This electoral coalition was put together by Ariel Sharon who joined the Liberal party after his retirement from the Israel army a month earlier. It had become clear to Herut leader Menahem Begin and to Liberal leader Simha Erlich that, in order to defeat the dominant Labor party, they would have to combine forces with smaller nationalist parties under the ideological roof of preserving "Greater Israel" (i.e., the retention of those areas conquered in the 1967 Six-Day War) against the Labor Party doctrine of repartitioning the country for peace. Gahal had won 26 seats in the 1969 elections and felt it was likely to remain in opposition, unless it took drastic steps. The Free Center and La-Am sought the umbrella of a larger, better known political entity and found it in Gahal.

It was decided that each party would retain its structural and organizational independence. A committee would deal with the drawing-up of the Knesset list and allot seats according to each party's strength in the Knesset. The party platform called for retention of all the territories acquired in 1967, de-centralization of government control of the economy, greater focus on free enterprise, and closer cooperation with the national-religious elements in politics. The 1973 Yom Kippur War boosted the Likud and it won 39 seats in the 31 December 1973 elections, becoming the second largest party and major opposition group. It challenged the Labor governments' concept of withdrawal from the territories in return for security and US guarantees and arms, and opposed vehemently the 1974 Separation of Forces Agreements and the 1975 Israel-Egypt Interim agreement.

The Likud paid special attention to the underprivileged elements of Israeli society, mainly Jews from Arab and North African countries who had immigrated in the early years of statehood and often still lived in squalor in city slums and development towns, with a feeling of alienation from the mainstream of Israeli life for which they blamed the Labor Party. As Labor declined, the Likud intensified its efforts to appeal to the ethnic, traditional, less educated, younger and "hawkish" Israeli voter. Its platform for the May, 1977, elections called for settlement in all parts of Eretz Israel, application of Israeli law and administration and eventually sovereignty in the territories, peace through direct negotations with the Arab states, and full rights for all inhabitants of Eretz Israel. The campaign, run by Ezer Weizman, proved highly successful and the Likud won 43 seats, soon swollen to 45 by the addition of two seats won by Ariel Sharon who had run independently. Begin formed the first Likud cabinet in June, 1977, ending the long-standing domination of Israeli politics by the Labor party. He included in his coalition the National Religious Party, Agudat Israel, and Tami, later augmented by the 15-seat strong Democratic Movement for Change. The first cabinet was dominated by the Israel-Egypt negotiations leading to the Camp David Agreement and the Israel-Egypt Peace Treaty. A booming economy and an attack on the Iraqi nuclear facility near Baghdad, three weeks before the June, 1981, elections, combined with a divided Labor party under indecisive leadership, brought the Likud to 48 seats in the 1981 elections following which Begin formed his second cabinet. Begin was the acknowledged leader of Likud until his retirement from politics in September, 1983, when he was succeeded as Prime Minister by Yitzhak Shamir. While the Free Center and La-Am merged with Herut, opponents of the peace treaty with Egypt seceded from Herut and formed the Tehiya party. Ezer Weizman formed his own Yahad party and later united with the Labor Party.

By 1984, the Likud was seen as responsible for the 1982 war in Lebanon and its aftermath and for bringing the Israeli economy to the verge of collapse with an inflation rate of 448%. Likud's decline was also explained by the defection of many secular Israelis who resented what they saw as Likud's surrender to demands by the religious parties whose alliance the Likud needed to stay in power. In the July, 1984 elections the Likud received only 41 seats and was unable to form a government on its own. It joined the Labor party in establishing a Government of National Unity, with the office of Prime Minister and Foreign Minister rotating between Labor's Shimon Peres and Shamir.
Shamir.

In the first two years of the Government of National Unity the Likud supported Labor's efforts to end Israel's presence in Lebanon and to stabilize Israel's economy. The inflation rate declined to 28% in 1986 and to 18% in 1987. When Shamir resumed his premiership in October, 1986, he successfully blocked Shimon Peres' efforts to convene an international peace conference to promote an Israel-Jordan peace treaty. In the 1988 elections, Likud emerged as the largest party with 40 seats. Shamir reconstituted the National Unity Government, only this time it was agreed that he would serve as Prime Minister for the entire term. When the National Unity Government broke up in 1990, Likud—under Shamir—put together a coalition government of right-wing and religious parties but after the 1992 elections went into opposition. In 1993, Binyamin Netanyahu was elected leader of Likud. M. MEDZINI

LILIEN, EPHRAIM MOSES. *Jugendstijl* illustrator and early Bezalel teacher (b. Drohobitz, Galicia, Austria, 1874; d. Badenweiler, Germany, 1925). He studied art at academies in Cracow, Vienna, and Munich before becoming a noted illustrator for German periodicals in an *art nouveau* style. Settling in Berlin, he illustrated volumes on the Bible as well as Münchhausen's *Juda* and Morris Rosenfeld's *Songs of the Ghetto*. On his travels to Russia and Eretz Israel he made numerous source sketches of Jews. Lilien participated in the Fifth Zionist Congress (1901) and in 1906 joined Boris Schatz at the Bezalel School, but left after only a few months of teaching. He returned to Jerusalem on several occasions, the last time as an Austrian officer in World War I. His style left a lasting mark on early Bezalel teachers and students. M. RONNEN

Moshe Leib Lilienblum. [Zionist Archives]

LILIENBLUM, MOSHE LEIB. Hebrew writer and leader of the Hovevei Zion movement (b. Kaidan, Kovno District, Lithuania, 1843;d. Odessa, Russia, 1910). After receiving an Orthodox education, he became an adherent of the Haskala (Jewish Enlightment) and, together with the poet Yehuda Leib *Gordon, began in 1868 a campaign for reforms in the Jewish religion. His activities created a great stir among Russian Jews. Eventually despairing of the possibility of religious reform, he sought a solution to the

Jewish problem in the labor movement, particularly in agricultural work in Russia.

When his illusions were destroyed by the Russian pogroms in 1881, Lilienblum began to write a series of articles in Russian, "On the Rebirth of the Jews in the Land of Their Fathers," which presented a nationalist program. These were the first such articles to appear in Russian, predating even Leo *Pinsker's German writings. Thereafter Lilienblum was active in the Hibbat Zion movement, serving as Pinsker's deputy at the movement's Odessa headquarters until shortly before his death. He joined the Zionist movement but disagreed with Herzl on the role of practical work in Palestine, seeking a combination of both political and practical Zionism.

Lilienblum wrote several autobiographical books. A selection of his writings appeared in four posthumously published volumes. His works on Hibbat Zion and Zionism, in Hebrew, Russian, and Yiddish, were outstanding for their simplicity and logic, and they influenced an entire generation of Jewish intellectuals. G. KRESSEL

LINDHEIM, IRMA LEVY. Zionist leader in the United States and Israel (b. New York, 1886; d. Haifa, 1978). Raised in an assimilated family, she engaged in child study and social service work. Introduced to Zionism in 1918 through such Zionist leaders as Dr. Harry Friedenwald and Ben-Zion Mossinsohn, she served as chairman of the Seventh District (New York) of the Zionist Organization of America (ZOA) from 1919 to 1921. Interested in learning more about her Jewish heritage, she studied at the Jewish Institute of Religion in New York (1922–25) and also at Columbia University. From 1926 to 1928 she was a national vice-president of the ZOA and national president of Hadassah. She was a protégé and devoted disciple of Henrietta Szold.

Mrs Lindheim first visited Palestine in 1925. A gifted public speaker, she delivered lectures on Zionism throughout the United States. In 1933 she settled in Palestine, becoming a member of Kibbutz Mishmar ha-Emek, where she lived until her death. She returned to the United States on numerous occasions to lecture. She wrote *The Immortal Adventure* (1928), in which she described her impressions of Palestine, and an autobiography, *Parallel Quest: A Search of a Person and a People* (1962). M. LEVIN

LINTON, JOSEPH ISAAC. Zionist public figure and Israeli diplomat (b. Ozorkow, Poland, 1900; d. London 1982). Linton joined the staff of the London Central Office of the World Zionist Organization in 1919 and was appointed financial and administrative secretary in 1936 and political secretary in 1940. Linton worked closely with Chaim Weizmann as his political secretary. For many years he was honorary treasurer and vice chairman of the Anglo-Palestine Club in London. In 1948 he was a member of the Jewish Agency delegation to the United Nations.

Linton was the first diplomatic representative of the State of Israel in Great Britain (1948–49). Subsequently he served as adviser to the Israel Ministry of Foreign Affairs (1949–50), Minister to Australia and New Zealand (1950–52), Minister to Japan and Thailand (1952–57), and Ambassador to Switzerland (1958–61). From 1961 until 1971 he acted as consultant on international affairs to the World Jewish Congress in London. J. FRAENKEL

LIPPE, KARPEL. Physician, writer, and pioneer Zionist in Romania (b. Stanislav, Galicia, Austria, 1830; d. Vienna, 1915). After studying medicine in Galicia and Romania, Lippe practiced in Jassy, where he also engaged in extensive literary activity, particularly in the field of Jewish apologetics and anti-Christian polemics. He wrote in several languages and was a regular contributor to the Hebrew press. Lippe and Samuel Pineles were the guiding spirits of the Hibbat Zion movement in Romania, and Lippe lent considerable assistance in the founding of Zikhron Ya'akov and Rosh Pina by Romanian immigrants. He joined Herzl's Zionist movement and, as senior delegate, delivered the opening address at the First Zionist Congress (1897). He subsequently parted company with Herzl and devoted the last years of his life to literature and science.

G. KRESSEL

Louis Lipsky. [Zionist Archives]

LIPSKY, LOUIS. Journalist, author, and Zionist leader in the United States (b. Rochester, N.Y., 1876; d. New York, 1963). He went to work at the age of 15 in a cigar factory, then spent two years in a Rochester law office. At the age of 21 he entered journalism as the editor of the *Shofar*, a Rochester Anglo-Jewish weekly. In 1899 he moved to New York City, where he was an editor of the *American Hebrew* until 1914. Between 1910 and 1913 he wrote fiction and literary and drama reviews for the *New York Morning Telegraph*.

It was through his journalistic work that Lipsky first came to Jewish public life and to Zionism. In 1901 he was editor of the *Maccabean*, the official monthly of the Federation of American Zionists (FAZ), and guided its successor, the weekly *New Palestine*, until 1928. He was considered a foremost theoretician of the Zionist movement in the United States. In 1903 he became a member of the Executive Committee of the FAZ, serving as chairman of its Organization Committee (1904-06) and English Publication Committee (from 1906). From 1911, he was chairman of the FAZ Executive Committee. In 1914 he gave up other professional commitments to devote all his time to Zionist administrative work until 1930, when he became president of the Eastern Life Insurance Company.

In 1914 Lipsky, on behalf of the FAZ, joined with Shemarya Levin, on behalf of the World Zionist Organization, in issuing the call for the extraordinary conference that established the Provisional Executive Committee for General Zionist Affairs. He himself was a prominent member of the committee. In 1918 he became general secretary of the Zionist Organization of America (ZOA), then chairman of its Administrative Committee (1922) and its president (1925–30). The first Zionist Congress he attended was the 11th (Vienna, 1913); he attended all subsequent Congresses except for the 21st (Geneva, 1939). From 1921 on he also attended all meetings of the Zionist Actions Committee.

Lipsky was closely associated with Chaim Weizmann, whom he first met at the 11th Zionist Congress. In the controversy that developed in 1920–21 between the forces of Weizmann and Louis D. Brandeis in American Zionism, Lipsky emerged as the dynamic leader of the pro-Weizmann group before and during the ZOA's Cleveland Convention (1921). Following that convention and the withdrawal of the Brandeis supporters from the leadership, Lipsky, as head of the Administrative Committee, assumed responsibility with a group of like-minded men.

Lipsky actively worked for the establishment of Keren ha-Yesod, which he chaired in the United States for some time. He was an outspoken advocate of the democratization of Jewish organizational life, defining the concept in the spirit of American tradition and opposing those who held that it would invite charges of "dual loyalty." As early as 1913–15 he had represented the FAZ on a committee formed to set up an organization to support the Jewish National Home in Palestine and the democratization of American Jewish communal life and attainment of civil rights for Jews throughout the world. The organization became known as the *American Jewish Congress. Lipsky became its vice-president in 1934 and chairman of its Governing Council in 1942. He was also among the founders of the World Jewish Congress (1936). From 1939 to 1945 he was national co-chairman of the United Jewish Appeal, serving also as national co-chairman of the United Palestine Appeal.

During World War II Lipsky played a key role in mobilizing the American Jewish community to support the establishment of a Jewish State in Palestine. He was one of the founding members of the Emergency Committee for Zionist Affairs and an active participant in its leadership. A founder of the American Jewish Conference and co-chairman (1944–49) of its Interim Committee, he utilized the conference platform to create public support for the partition of Palestine and after the adoption of the UN General Assembly resolution (November, 1947), to prevent vitiation of the plan at the United Nations. From 1949 to 1954 he was chairman of the American Zionist Council. In 1957 Lipsky was one of the founders of the American Jewish League for Israel, which stressed solidarity with Israel as a whole rather than identification with any one political party there. He served as honorary president of the League until his death. At the time of his death he was also chairman of the American Zionist Committee for Public Affairs.

A prolific writer of articles, essays, and pamphlets on Zionism and Zionist thought, Lipsky was the author of *A Gallery of Zionist Profiles* (1956). An earlier three-volume collection of his writings (*Thirty Years of American Zionism, Stories of Jewish Life*, and *Shield of Honor*) was published in 1927. G. HIRSCHLER

LITERATURE, HEBREW. *See* HEBREW LITERATURE AND ZIONISM.

LITHUANIA, ZIONISM IN. The idea of a Jewish national revival had deep roots in Lithuania. In 1853 Abraham

Zionist pioneers in Lithuania, 1920s. [Central Zionist Archives]

Mapu, who was born in Slabode (Slobodka), a suburb of Kovno (Kaunas), published his famous novel *Ahavat Zion* (Love of Zion).

Early Years. Lithuanian Jews were among the first to propagate the idea of a return to the Land of Israel. A number of them played leading parts in furthering the Hovevei Zion movement: David Gordon (1831–86), Moshe Leib Lilienblum (1843-1910), Kalonymus-Ze'ev Wissotzky (1824–1904), Max Emanuel Mandelstamm (1839–1912), Prof. Hermann Schapira (1840–98), and Shaul Pinhas Rabinowicz (1845–1910).

Among the rabbis who were active in the Hovevei Zion movement were a number of Lithuanian Jews, including Mordecai Gimpel Jaffe (1820–91), Yitzhak Ze'ev Olswanger (1825–96), and Shemuel Mohilever (1824–98). Lithuanian-born writers and poets, too, made their mark in the work for the restoration of Zion; among them were Ben-Avigdor (1866–1921), Alter Druyanow (1870–1938), and Eliakum Zunser (1845–1913).

Among the members of the First Aliya (Bilu immigration movement, 1882) were Jews from the Kovno and Vilna Districts; several of them played major roles in the development of the new yishuv. Early in the 1880s Hovevei Zion societies sprang up in Lithuanian cities. The idea of land acquisition in Eretz Israel through small installment payments was popular among Hovevei Zion members in Kovno and its environs. Among the leaders of the Vilna society were the writer Arye Leib Levanda and the editor-biographer Samuel Joseph Fünn. The delegates to the Kattowitz Conference (1884) of the Hovevei Zion included Leib Klivansky and Moshe Bramson of Kovno. In 1889 a conference of the movement took place in Vilna.

The history of Zionism in Lithuania from the appearance of Herzl's *Jewish State* in 1896 until the establishment of an independent Lithuanian Republic in 1918 was closely linked with that of the movement in Russia. Jews from Kovno, Vilna, and the smaller townlets contributed to the development of Zionist ideas, the dissemination of Hebrew culture, and the emergence of the modern Zionist organization. A number of prominent Jews of Lithuanian origin played important parts in Russian Zionism. Among them were Abraham Tzevi Idelsohn (1865–1921), Dr. Julius Brutzkus (1870–1951), and Dr. Joseph Luria (1871–1937). Brutzkus and Luria subsequently settled in Palestine.

On 16 August 1903, Herzl visited Vilna, where he received a tremendous welcome. In 1905 Vilna became an important center of Russian Zionism. A special office was established under the direction of Itzhak Leib Goldberg. It existed until 1911, when a number of Zionist leaders were arrested and the main Zionist activities transferred to St. Petersburg. Vilna played an important part in the history of the Mizrachi movement; the first conferences of religious Zionists took place in that city.

Early in the 20th century, Po'ale Zion groups and, later, Tze'irei Zion societies sprang up in Kovno and Vilna. The Zionist Socialist newspapers *Der Proletarisher Gedank* (Proletarian Thought) and *Forverts* (Forward) were published in Vilna in 1907. Shneur Zalman Rubashow (Zalman Shazar) was connected with *Der Proletarisher Gedank*, which was closed by the Tsarist authorities after the appearance of the third issue, and its editor put in prison.

World War I was a time of great hardship for Lithuanian Jewry. In 1915 the Tsarist authorities embarked on large-scale deportations of the Jewish population. Jewish public life was destroyed. After the conquest of Vilna by the Germans, the city was cut off from Petrograd, the major center of Zionist activity. Moreover, economic conditions deteriorated. Nevertheless, the Zionist movement persevered in its educational and cultural work. In 1918, when it was again possible to communicate with Russia, Zionist activity increased in Vilna and the Zionist headquarters for Lithuania was set up there. It was decided to publish a daily newspaper, *Die Letzte Nayes*. The Zionists participated in communal elections.

Zionism in the Lithuanian Republic, 1918–39. The establishment of an independent Lithuanian Republic (1918) opened a new chapter in the history of Lithuanian Jewry in which the Zionist movement played the dominant part. The Balfour Declaration (1917) and the national-cultural autonomy granted the Jewish community led to a revival of the Zionist movement. There was a great upsurge of Jewish national sentiment, a rebuilding of Jewish life in towns and villages, a closer link with the yishuv in Palestine, and a remarkable development of Hebrew culture and the Yiddish press. The Lithuanian government established a Ministry for Jewish Affairs. Eighty Jewish communities were organized, a number of Jewish cooperatives were set up, Jewish economic life was reconstructed, and cultural life was developed on Jewish national lines. This work was directed mainly by Zionists, who at the same time managed to engage in intensive Zionist activity.

In 1918 three Zionists joined the first Cabinet of the Lithuanian Republic: Dr. Jacob Vigodsky, as Minister for Jewish Affairs; Dr. Shimshon Rosenbaum, as Deputy Minister for Foreign Affairs; and Dr. Nahman Rachmilevitz, as Deputy Minister for Trade and Industry. When the Lithuanian government moved its seat to Kovno, Dr. Max Soloveitchik (later Solieli) replaced (1919) Dr. Vigodsky as Minister for Jewish Affairs. Vigodsky remained in Vilna, which was incorporated into the new Polish Republic in 1920.

In January, 1920, the first conference of representatives of Jewish communities in Lithuania, held in Kovno, elected a National Council, with Rosenbaum as president. Among the members of its Executive were Leib Garfinkel, a Labor Zionist leader, and Dr. Jacob Robinson, a leader of the General Zionists. The Zionists, who were in the forefront of Jewish communal work in Lithuania, encountered strong opposition from the Folkists, who had a Diaspora orientation and favored cultural activity in the Yiddish language, and from extreme Orthodox elements. But the large majority of the Jews in Lithuania backed the Zionist leadership. In April, 1922, Dr. Soloveitchik resigned from the Cabinet in protest against the official policy of ignoring the rights of minorities. Brutzkus and, later, Rosenbaum took over the Ministry for Jewish Affairs. Thus, Zionists continued to represent the Jewish community in Lithuanian government circles.

On 20 November 1923, the Third Jewish National Assembly was convened in Kovno. All Jewish groups except the extreme Orthodox non-Zionist Ahdut participated in its election, which was held on the basis of democratic and proportional representation. A new National Council was elected; it consisted of 11 General Zionists, 11 Zionist-Socialists, 10 members of Mizrachi, 4 Artisans, 2 representatives of the Left Po'ale Zion, and 2 Folkists. In 1924 the reactionary forces triumphed. The Ministry for Jewish Affairs was liquidated and Rosenbaum left the country and settled in Palestine. The Zionists assisted the struggle for the social and economic rights of the Jewish population and trained Jewish youth for a pioneering life in Palestine. One of their achievements was the formation of Jewish people's banks; another was the establishment of the Jewish cooperative movement. This work was directed by such men as Isaac Brudni (Bareli) and Abraham Zabarski, who later became directors of the Bank ha-Po'alim (Workers' Bank) in Palestine. Azriel Walk played an important part in organizing the movement for people's banks in the provinces. The Jewish educational system in Lithuania was one of the greatest accomplishments of the Jewish national movement. In 1935 it controlled approximately 200 institutions with 18,000 pupils and 635 teachers. In no other country of the Diaspora was Hebrew so widely spoken and taught as in Lithuania; 70 percent of the Jewish children attended schools where Hebrew was taught, whereas only 17 percent were in Yiddish schools and 13 percent in general schools.

According to the *Lithuanian Statistical Yearbook* for 1937, 157,527 Jews, or 98 percent of the Jewish population of the country, indicated their adherence to the Jewish nationality group.

The Jewish press was a vital factor in upholding the Zionist spirit of the Jewish community. The oldest Jewish daily in Kovno was *Die Yidishe Shtime*, founded in 1920, which had a General Zionist orientation. Later the Zionists-Socialists published their own daily, *Das Vort*. The Revisionists, too, published a daily, *Moment*. Other Zionist groups had their own publications: Mizrachi, *Dos Yidish Vort*; the Jewish State party, *Yidenstat*; and Left Po'ale Zion, *Arbeter Zeitung*. In addition, a special feature of Zionist life in Lithuania was the publication, for longer or shorter periods, of a number of periodicals in Hebrew.

While the democratic regime prevailed in the country, the various Zionist groups devoted a great deal of time and energy to local matters, but beginning in 1926 the center of interest gradually shifted to Palestine affairs. For a large majority of Lithuanian Jews Zionism became both an ideal and a personal problem. This circumstance led to greater ideological divisions and to sharp controversies. At first, the General Zionists dominated the movement, but later the Zionists-Socialists became the majority.

Two factors influenced the development of the Zionist movement in Lithuania: the emergence of Revisionism and a right-wing group among the General Zionists. The mid-1930s saw the emergence of two General Zionist groups, each of which formed its own youth movement and issued its own literature. Group A, while critical of the

Labor Zionists, maintained its traditional liberal policy. Group B joined forces with the Revisionists and Mizrachi. As a result, Zionism in Lithuania was divided into right and left blocs, the latter being represented by the Labor Zionists. This development was due partly to objective reasons and partly to an artificial tendency toward polarization in the movement. The class struggle in Lithuanian Zionism led to a strengthening of the Labor wing and to the formation of Revisionist groups by former General Zionist supporters. The last Zionist Congress elections in Lithuania were held in 1935. On the basis of 50,830 Shekels sold, Lithuania obtained 17 mandates, divided as follows: Labor Zionists, 10; Mizrachi, 2; Jewish State party, 2; General Zionists B, 2; General Zionists A, 1.

At first, there were two distinct Zionist Socialist groups, the Zionists-Socialists, and Tze'irei Zion-Hitahdut, but in 1930 they merged to form one party. This party played an important part in Lithuanian-Jewish public life. It was the strongest force in the pioneer organization He-Halutz, the League for Labor Palestine, the Hebrew school system, Zionist fund-raising (including collections for the Palestine Workers' Fund), the Jewish press, the struggle for Jewish cultural autonomy, and the Jewish social-economic institutions. The Labor Zionists cooperated with the Lithuanian Social Democrats on general political issues.

The following Zionist youth organizations existed in 1935: Ha-Shomer ha-Tza'ir; He-Halutz; Kelal Tziyoni; Ha-Hakla'i; Maccabi; Betar; Berit ha-Hayal; and Menora. The Halutz (pioneer) movement played a significant part in educating Jewish youth for pioneering labor, Hebrew culture, and love of Zion. Many thousands of young persons passed through its ranks. Halutzim from Lithuania were among the builders of the kibbutzim Givat Brenner, Dafna (Galilee), and Bet Zera (Jordan Valley), of Kevutza Mishmarot, and of a number of other collective settlements. Lithuania was also an important transit center for aliya from Russia.

It is estimated that between 1923 and 1927 not fewer than 6,000 to 7,000 Jews left the country. Between 1928 and 1939, 13,898 Jews emigrated from Lithuania; of these 3,541 (25.5 percent) left for Palestine. According to Jewish Agency figures, 9,241 Jews from Lithuania, or 3 percent of the total number of immigrants, settled in Palestine between 1919 and 1941.

Final Years, 1939–41. The outbreak of World War II had a profound impact on the life of Lithuanian Jewry. In 1939, 15,000 Polish-Jewish refugees found temporary shelter in the country; of these, 5,000 managed to leave for foreign countries. Many of the refugees tried to leave for Palestine, but only a few were successful.

With the arrival of the Red Army on 15 June 1940, Jews were put on an equal basis with the other citizens, but the establishment of a Communist regime led to the gradual liquidation of Jewish public life and to the end of Zionist activities. In the middle of June, 1941, a week before the entry of German troops, the Soviet authorities began the deportation of "unreliable elements." During one week about 4,000 to 5,000 Jews (including many Zionists) were deported to the Soviet Union. At first they were kept in labor camps; later they were sent to the Asiatic regions of the USSR.

The occupation of Lithuania by the German troops led to the formation of ghettos for the Jewish population and to its ultimate extermination. Several illegal Zionist groups were active during the first stages of Nazi rule and helped keep up the morale of the Jewish population. A number of Zionists were active in the partisan movement. A few Lithuanian Jews managed to escape, but the large majority were murdered by the Germans with the assistance of local fascists. For the post-War period, *see* RUSSIA, ZIONISM IN. According to the Soviet census of 1970, there were 23,564 Jews in Lithuania. About 10,000 of these received Israeli visas between 1968 and 1977. S. LEVENBERG

LITVINOVSKY, PINHAS. Israeli portraitist (b. Odessa, Russia, 1894; d. Jerusalem, 1985). He went to Eretz Israel in 1910, studying briefly at the Bezalel School in 1912. In the 1930s and 1940s, he was in great demand as a portraitist, often working from photographs. He was famous for his virtuoso low-key oils of Zionist figures like Chaim Weizmann, David Ben-Gurion, Berl Katznelson and literary figures like Hayim Nahman Bialik, Saul Tchernichowsky, and Gershon Agron. In his later years, he abandoned portraiture for sketchy, modernist depictions of figure groups, notably of yeshiva students, all in high color. He was awarded the Israel Prize in 1980. M. RONNEN

LIVNEH (LIEBENSTEIN), ELIEZER. Israeli public figure and editor (b. Lodz, Russian Poland, 1902; d. Jerusalem, 1975). Livneh became active in Zionist youth groups and settled in Palestine in 1920. Until 1922 he was a farmhand and worked on road building, then served for a year as secretary of the Haifa Labor Council. In 1923 he joined the kibbutz En Harod and later became active in political work. He was in Germany as an emissary from 1928 to 1931 and again from 1933 to 1935, when he helped organize immigration to Palestine. From 1937 to 1939 Livneh studied in England. From 1939 to 1942 he was editor of the magazine *Maarakhot*, devoted to military affairs, and from 1940 to 1942 he headed the Political and Educational Department of Hagana. From 1942 to 1947 he was editor of *Eshnav*, Hagana's underground weekly. Meanwhile in 1942, he also became editor of *Be-Terem*, a political fortnightly.

Livneh was a Mapai member of the First and Second Knessets (1949–55). In 1957 he resigned from the Mapai party because of disagreement on basic party policies, devoted himself to independent journalism, and became a critic of the Israeli establishment. His main thesis was that reliance on outside financial assistance had an adverse effect on the morale of the yishuv and impeded progress toward economic independence.

A prolific writer, Livneh published numerous pamphlets, articles, and books on general and Israeli political, sociological, and philosophical questions. In *State and Diaspora* (1953) he stressed the need of American Jewry to identify itself more closely with the Land and the State of Israel through Aliya.

LLOYD GEORGE, DAVID (1st Earl Lloyd George of Dwyfor). British statesman and Prime Minister at the time of the *Balfour Declaration (b. Chorlton on Medlock, England, 1863; d. Llanystumdwy, Wales, 1945). A Liberal anti-imperialist member of the British Parliament for more than five decades, Lloyd George first entered the British Cabinet as President of the Board of Trade (1905). He was subsequently Chancellor of the Exchequer (1908–15), Minister of Munitions (1915–16), and Prime Minister (1916–22). He was raised to the peerage in 1945.

His first contact with the Zionist movement occurred in

July, 1903, when the law firm of which he was senior partner gave professional advice to Leopold J. Greenberg in the drafting of proposals to be submitted to the British government in connection with the East Africa scheme. In November, 1914, he expressed support for a proposal by Herbert Samuel, then also a member of the British government, that after the breakup of the Ottoman Empire, Palestine become the National Home of the Jewish people. In 1915 Charles Prestwich Scott, editor of the *Manchester Guardian*, first brought Chaim Weizmann to the attention of the then Minister of Munitions as an expert scientist. In his work *The Truth about the Peace Treaties*, Lloyd George described Weizmann as "one of the greatest Hebrews of all time."

Lloyd George brought Weizmann's Zionist work to the attention of Arthur James Balfour, the Foreign Secretary, who with Lloyd George's "zealous assent as Prime Minister" entered into the negotiations that culminated in the Balfour Declaration. The timing of the declaration, Lloyd George confirmed, had been determined by "propagandist strategy for mobilizing every opinion and force throughout the world which would weaken the enemy and improve the Allied chances". The Zionist leaders, Lloyd George went on, had promised that, in return for an Allied commitment to a Jewish National Home in Palestine, they would do their best to enlist Jewish support for the Allied cause throughout the world. "They kept their word in the letter and the spirit," Lloyd George stated, "and the only question that remains now is whether we mean to honour ours." As to the question whether the Jewish National Home involved the eventual establishment of a Jewish State in Palestine, Lloyd George declared that if the Jews became a definate majority of the inhabitants, then Palestine would become a Jewish commonwealth.

Lloyd George ensured the incorporation of the Balfour Declaration in the peace treaty with Turkey at the San Remo Conference (1920) and the assignment to Britain of the Mandate for Palestine. That same year he appointed Sir Herbert Samuel the first High Commissioner for Palestine.

For the rest of his life, Lloyd George remained consistent in his pro-Zionist views. In 1930 he denounced the Passfield White Paper in the House of Commons as a "breach of national faith," suggesting that if the mandate was too difficult for Britain to carry out, the only honorable alternative would be to ask the League of Nations to release it from its commitment and appoint another mandatory power to take its place. The following year, a kibbutz in the Jezreel Valley was named Ramat David in his honor.

He condemned the report of the Peel Commission (1937) as a violation of Britain's undertaking to the Jewish people. Two years later, in a broadcast to the British nation, he condemned the White Paper of 1939 as a breach of faith with the Jewish people, "who have honorably kept their part of the bargain." G. HIRSCHLER

LOCKER, BERL Zionist leader (b. Krzywiec, Galicia, Austria, 1887; d. Jerusalem, 1972). Active in Zionist youth and student societies, Locker joined the Jewish Socialist labor confederation Po'ale Zion in 1905. One of its early theorists and organizers, he became a member of its Central Committee in Austria and served as editor of *Der Yidisher Arbeter* from 1911 to 1914. During World War I, Locker was one of the four men who managed the Po'ale Zion office in The Hague and later in Stockholm, and he advocated Jewish minority rights in the Diaspora and unrestricted Jewish settlement in Palestine before the Socialist leaders.

Berl Locker.
[Keren HaYesod]

As secretary of the Central Office of the World Union of Po'ale Zion, Locker toured many countries to introduce his party's platform. In 1928 he became secretary of the Po'ale Zion in America. At the 17th Zionist Congress (1931), Locker was elected a member of the Zionist Executive, on which he served from 1931 to 1935. He was in charge of the Organization Department of the World Zionist Organization in London.

In 1936 Locker settled in Jerusalem, but before World War II he was appointed political adviser to the Zionist Executive in London. He was successful in British Labor circles, and the Labor party adopted a number of resolutions in favor of Zionism. In 1945 Locker was again elected a member of the Zionist Executive, and after the establishment of the State of Israel he served as its Jerusalem chairman (1948–56). He was also a Mapai member of the Knesset from 1955 to 1961.

Locker frequently addressed Zionist Congresses and conferences. He represented his party at various congresses of the International Federation of Trade Unions and was a member of the Executive of the Socialist International. Locker contributed to various journals and was the author of *A Stiff-necked People* (1946); its American edition is called *Covenant Everlasting* (1947). J. FRAENKEL

LOD. *See* LYDDA.

LOEWE, HEINRICH. Historian, folklorist, and early Zionist leader in Germany (b. Wanzleben, Saxony, 1869; d. Haifa, 1951). In 1891 he founded the Hovevei Sefat Ever (Lovers of the Hebrew Language) in Berlin, and the next year, with Willy Bambus, he organized Jung Israel, the first Zionist group in Germany. He also founded the Verein Jüdischer Studenten, precursor of the *Kartell Jüdischer Verbindungen. In 1893–94 he edited the Zionist periodical *Jüdische Volkszeitung*, and in 1895 he founded the monthly *Zion: Monatschrift für die Nationalen Interessen des Jüdischen Volkes*, which he edited until 1896.

In 1895 Loewe visited Eretz Israel; the following year he arranged the inclusion of a Palestine pavilion in the Berlin Exhibition of Trade and Industry and went to Jaffa with the intention of settling there. However, he returned to Europe as delegate of the settlers in Eretz Israel to the First Zionist Congress (1897) and remained in Germany to help strengthen the Zionist movement there. In 1897 he founded and became president of the Zionist Association of Berlin, where he settled and became librarian of the university. From 1902 to 1908 he was editor of the *Jüdische Rundschau*, which he turned into the central organ of German Zionism. Settling in Palestine in 1933, he was appointed director of the Municipal Library of Tel Aviv, a position he held until 1948.

A prolific author of books on Jewish history and folklore, including *Hibbat Zion* (Love of Zion, 1910) and *Wege zur jüdischen Kultur* (Roads to Jewish Culture, 1925), Loewe published Zionist writings under the pseudonym Heinrich Sachse. A biography of Loewe, *Aus der Frühzeit des Zionismus: Heinrich Loewe* (From the Early Days of Zionism: Heinrich Loewe) by Jehuda Louis Weinberg, was published in Jerusalem in 1946. G. HIRSCHLER

LOHAMEI HA-GETA'OT. Kibbutz in the coastal plain 3 mi. (5 km.) north of Acre, founded in 1949 by survivors of resistance movements and ghetto fighters against the Nazis in Poland and Lithuania including Yitzhak (Antek) Cukierman and Zivia Lubetkin, who were among the leaders of the Warsaw Ghetto revolt. It has a Holocaust Museum and an educational center. Besides intensive irrigated farming, the kibbutz runs an industrial enterprise. Its name means "Ghetto Fighters." Population (1987), 499. E. ORNI

Memorial meeting in Lohamei ha-Geta'ot. [Ghetto Fighters' House]

LOHAMEI HERUT YISRAEL ("Israel Freedom Fighters"). Underground Jewish organization in Palestine 1940–49, known by its acronym, LEHI. Its history can be divided into four phases: (a) Formation and establishment, 1940–1942; (b) interim and re-establishment, 1943–1945; (c) heyday, 1945–1947; (d) the decline, 29 November 1947 to March 1949.

(a) Its first manifestation came about after a split between Avraham *Stern and David *Raziel, the commander of *Irgun Tzeva'i Le'umi (Etzel) over the Irgun's suspension of anti-British hostilities on 11 September 1939 and the secret cooperation agreement signed in October with the British Inspector General of Police. Raziel accepted the authority of Vladimir Jabotinsky, who served as commander-in-chief of the Irgun and who supported Britain and its Allies in the war against Nazi Germany but Stern rejected the pro-British line.

"Wanted" poster for Lehi members. [Jabotinsky Institute]

Stern was influenced by Abba Achimeir, Yonatan Ratosh and Yehoshua Heschel Yeivin who called for a militant Zionist movement to seize power in Palestine immediately, without waiting until the Jews were a majority (which was Jabotinsky's policy). The turning points which convinced him that he must break with the Irgun and fight a war of independence were the hanging of Shelomo ben Yosef of Betar at the end of June, 1938, and the publication of the White Paper (17 May 1939).

Stern's contention that history is determined by force, as taught by Abba Ahimeir, reflected his opinion that an alternate ally to England should be found in order to realize the Zionist aim. However, his arrest in late August, 1939, prevented him from carrying out his plans until after his release on 18 June 1940. On 3 September of that year, learning that he could not take command of the Irgun, Stern formed his revolutionary underground movement which tried to conclude arrangements with the Axis powers, assuming they would win the war. He first tried to join up with Italy with the "Jerusalem Agreement" (15 September 1940), which never reached the Italians but became known and indicated clearly that Stern and his group wished to establish a Jewish State under Italian sponsorship. At the same time, the Stern group began a series of "expropriation" raids (bank robberies) for political financing since they had no public backing at all.

After Italy's defeats in Greece and in the Western Desert (in North Africa), Stern tried to approach Nazi Germany. His motives were based on his own belief that Nazi anti-

Oil installations in Haifa burning after Lehi bombing. [Jabotinsky Institute]

Semitism was not a new phenomenon but merely a new version of the traditional (primarily east European) anti-Semitism of the past, and just as he could negotiate with the anti-Semitic government of Poland, it should be possible to try to reach an agreement with the Germans.

Considering the wide publicity given to the Nazi's "Madagascar Plan", as a new home for Europe's expelled Jews, Stern assumed he could try and convince Hitler to agree to an evacuation of Jews from Europe to Palestine in return for establishing a Hebrew State to join the new German "political constellation." The failure of the mission to the Germans (a meeting between Naftali Lubenchik and Otto von Hentig in Beirut in early January 1941) led to a split in Stern's organization. His comrades, Hanokh Kalai and Binyamin Zeroni, left him and surrendered to the authorities. Stern was thus pushed by the extremists in his disintegrating band (Yoshke Lebstein-Eliav and Yehoshua Zetler) to acts of terrorism and further "expropriations." Failed attempts on 9 and 20 January led to the murder of the Tel Aviv Chief of Police and two of his officers and brought about Stern's own execution on 12 February 1942 at the hands of the British police, the arrest of his followers, and the collapse of his organization.

(b) The Lehi was re-formed in the summer of 1943 after the escape of Yitzhak *Shamir and Eliahu Giladi from prison (September, 1942) but only resumed its terrorist activities early in 1944, which coincided with the reactivation of the parent organization, the Irgun. Prior to that, Lehi was reinforced by 20 of its former members who escaped from the Latrun prison, led by one of Stern's former close assistants, Natan *Friedman-Yellin. The ensuing competition forced Lehi to seek new ideological and political paths and it turned to the socialist parties in the yishuv, meanwhile "freeing" itself from some of the Revisionist principles followed by Stern. Thus Lehi began to view their leftist pioneering settlements favorably but demanded that they too join the fighting underground for freedom from British rule.

At the same time, Lehi sought a new ally. Friedman-Yellin assumed that there was a historical rivalry between Britain and the Soviet Union and thus the Soviets would be the future allies of the Jewish people. Additionally, the Russians were showing signs of diminishing hostility to Zionism as well as developing a nationalist Communism which did not perceive Zionism as an ideological opponent and a vassal of British imperialism but rather as the struggle of a people for freedom as evidenced by the assassination of the British Minister Resident in the Middle East, Lord Moyne (6 November 1944).

The result of this murder was the decision of the Zionist leadership to cooperate with the British by handing over underground activists, although only Irgun members were kidnaped and surrendered. Lehi was forced to make an oral "deal" with the Hagana whereby they would cease all activity so as not to be a target for persecution.

(c) After the War, Lehi leaders were sure they now had a new opportunity when the "Hebrew Resistance Movement" was formed in October, 1945, incorporating members of all the underground movements, although they knew that the new body was an ad hoc arrangement made to strengthen the weak position of the Zionist leadership vis-à-vis the hostile British Labor government. Lehi, like the Irgun, felt free to call for a general revolt on the principle that even if it did not succeed, their own prestige would rise as the Hebrew Resistance Movement disintegrated. Indeed, the movement fell apart in the summer of 1946 and Lehi renewed its activities, despite the arrest of one of its central members, Yitzhak Shamir, in August of that year. Friedman-Yellin became the chief ideologist of the movement as well as its administrative head working to keep the third member of the central committee, Israel *Eldad (recently released from prison), from continuing his attempts to reunify the Irgun and Lehi, which he had been attempting since 1944.

At the same time, Friedman-Yellin continued his overtures to the Soviet Union. In September 1946 a "plan for the neutralization of the Middle East" was proposed, aimed at attracting the support of the USSR to Zionism by calling for the removal of western imperialism from the area. After the Soviet Foreign Minister, Andrei Gromyko's declaration of support in May, 1947, the ideology of Lehi became more socialist and pro-Soviet than ever before.

(d) After 29 November 1947, when the UN decided on the establishment of two states in Palestine, one Jewish and the other Arab, Friedman-Yellin announced the disbanding of Lehi in order to participate in the military struggle. The Lehi leader did not expect the outbreak of war for he felt such a war would only be caused by the active instigation of a "third party", Britain, fomenting discord between the Jews and Arabs. He also believed that the rise of progressive forces would prevent the war because only the reactionary Arabs were cooperating with the British.

As soon as he realized that the war was one of national survival, he reversed his opinion and pressed Lehi's force to the war effort. Nevertheless, he strongly decried the policies of Eldad and of Lehi's Jerusalem commander (Yehoshua Zetler) who endorsed the anti-Arab line of the Irgun leading to the attack on Deir Yasin, which Friedman-Yellin condemned.

In the summer of 1948 Lehi published its program combining elements adopted from both right and left, such as the maximalist Revisionist call for historical borders and the Revisionists' anti-socialist ideology together with socialist principles such as the need to fight imperialism and to prevent man from exploiting his fellow-man, nationalization, end state-planning.

At the end of August, 1948, Lehi officially requested recognition as a political party in Israel despite its opposition to the establishment of the State in only a small part of the Promised Land. It retained an "option" for independent action in Jerusalem and other "occupied territories" which were under the legal jurisdiction of Israel but not fully annexed by the State. The Lehi leaders decided to kill the UN mediator, Count *Bernadotte (17 September 1948) because of what they perceived as his anti-Israeli image which received expression in his plan to reduce the area of the State, as part of their cold war policies.

The government then outlawed Lehi and arrested many of its members, including Friedman-Yellin, who was tried and sentenced to eight years' imprisonment. The trial spoiled the chances of Lehi, who called itself the Fighters' List, in the first Knesset elections (25 January 1949) when it received 5,360 votes, and one seat.

In March of that year the Fighters' Party convened and found itself split between two factions, the supporters of Friedman-Yellin and Shamir who wanted the continuation of a party with a nationalist Bolshevik line and those of Eldad who preferred that the group leave politics and continue as an intellectual forum. The Fighters' Party existed until 1951 supporting a people's democracy and anticipating the collapse of the party system of the State following a large working-class immigration which, they assumed, would lead to an expansion of the borders and elevate their party to a central position in the country. J. HELLER

LONDON ZIONIST CONFERENCE OF 1920. First major international gathering of the World Zionist movement following the 11th Zionist Congress (1913). Held in London from 7–20 July 1920, it was attended by 280 delegates. Forty Zionist federations, operating in 40 different countries, were represented, as well as the "separate unions," including one from Russia. The conference devoted considerable attention to a review of the War years in their impact on the Zionist program.

The keynote speeches were delivered, in the following order, by Nahum Sokolow, Chaim Weizmann, Menahem Ussishkin (first vice-chairman of the conference), Justice Louis D. Brandeis (chairman of the conference), and Max Nordau (honorary chairman). In his speech Weizmann stated that the conference would have to deal with three basic tasks: to approve plans for work in Palestine, to find ways of defraying the cost of this work, and to reorganize Zionist administrative machinery to meet the new needs of the movement.

There were great divergences of opinion between the Palestinian and European groups, headed by Weizmann, on the one hand, and the American delegates, headed by Justice Brandeis, on the other. Moreover, there were differences of opinion even among the 42 delegates from the United States. Considering that the political aims of Zionism had been largely attained with Great Britain's acceptance of the Mandate for Palestine at the San Remo Conference, Brandeis saw the future tasks of the World Zionist Organization (WZO) to lie mainly in the economic field. He believed that non-Zionists, too, should aid in the upbuilding of Palestine through the Zionist movement. Weizmann and his associates, on the other hand, were convinced that the political work of Zionism was far from completed. They stressed the need for continued Zionist propaganda efforts and advocated contacts with important non-Zionist Jewish groups with a view to having them share in the rebuilding of Palestine through a Jewish Council (which later assumed the form of an expanded Jewish Agency). The proposals of the Brandeis group regarding the functions and character of the WZO were not accepted, a development that led to a cleavage between the followers of Brandeis and those of Weizmann.

Another controversial problem at the conference was the budget. It was decided to set up an "immigration and colonization fund" on a basis of £25,000,000, to be known as *Keren ha-Yesod (Palestine Foundation Fund). At least 20 percent of the funds collected by the Keren ha-Yesod were to be turned over to the Jewish National Fund. Of the remaining funds collected, not more than one-third was to be allocated to current expenditures for education, social welfare, immigration, and kindred purposes in Palestine, while at least two-thirds was to be invested in "permanent national institutions or economic undertakings." Brandeis, Julian W. Mack, and their associates were firmly opposed to such investments by the Keren ha-Yesod, insisting that the financing of commercial undertakings should be handled separately on a business basis. This view was not accepted.

Brandeis and his close associates were critical of the manner in which the financial affairs of the WZO were conducted, especially in Palestine, and were concerned to establish and maintain tighter supervision in the future.

The conference adopted a large number of resolutions, one of which stated that "at the moment when the Jewish people is preparing to concentrate its whole energies on the reconstruction of its historic Home, it solemnly declares its determination to live in peace and friendship with the non-Jewish population." The conference further declared the "fundamental principle of Zionist land policy" to be that "all land on which Jewish colonization takes place shall eventually become the common property of the Jewish people" and that the Jewish National Fund was to "combat speculation" and to "safeguard Jewish labor." Another resolution dealt with the setting up of Palestine Offices in all countries that could be expected to supply contingents of Jewish immigrants to Palestine.

The conference resolved to appoint a Board of Trustees, consisting of Sir Alfred Mond, Lord Rothschild, and Bernard Flexner, to superintend the disposal and employment of Zionist funds, and a Financial and Economic Council of persons well known in business and finance, and representatives of the WZO in order to advance Palestine's economic development. A new Zionist Executive was elected, with Brandeis as honorary president, Weizmann as president, and Sokolow as chairman.

The outstanding public event of the conference was a large rally held at the Albert Hall on July 12 with an audience of 10,000 gathered under the chairmanship of Lord Rothschild; one of the speakers was Lord Balfour.

Because of the clashes between Brandeis's supporters and Weizmann's, the conference ended on a somewhat pessimistic note. It disappointed the Jewish community of Palestine, which anxiously awaited practical results from the gathering. In retrospect, however, it appears that the London Conference laid the foundation for subsequent achievements in Palestine and for the further expansion of the Zionist movement. S. LEVENBERG

LOPEZ, SABATINO. Playwright, drama critic, and Zionist leader in Italy (b. Leghorn, 1867; d. Milan, 1951). President of the Italian Society of Authors from 1911 to 1919, he was also president of the Zionist Organization of Milan for many years, and served as counselor to the Italian Zionist Federation, the Jewish Community of Milan, and the Union of Italian-Jewish Communities. He was an outspoken advo-

cate of Jewish rights, and in view of his literary achievements he added prestige to the Italian Zionist movement.
G. ROMANO

LORJE, CHAIM. Forerunner of the Hibbat Zion movement (b. Frankfort on the Oder, Germany, 1821; d. Berlin, 1878). University-trained (graduating with the degree of doctor of philosophy), he was deeply religious, well-versed in Jewish lore, and inclined to mysticism. Kabbalistic speculation had led him to believe that the Messiah would arrive at the end of the 1840s and that all Jews would be gathered into the Land of Israel by 1860. When this hope was not fulfilled, Lorje concluded that the Messiah would come only if all Jews were pervaded by a fervent desire to return to Eretz Israel to reawaken its soil, not for the sake of their physical welfare but to cleanse themselves of the impurity of the Diaspora. Subsequently, he established the Colonisations-Verein für Palästina (Settlement Society for Palestine) in Frankfurt on the Oder, where he served as a teacher and directed a boarding home for children.

Lorje launched a widespread publicity campaign, elucidating the aims of his society and refuting those who doubted the feasibility of its plans. He succeeded in enlisting the aid of numerous prominent Jews. The society existed until 1864, when it disintegrated as a result of differences between Lorje and his chief supporters, who disliked some aspects of Lorje's propaganda activity. They also demanded that the seat of the society be transferred to a larger Jewish center, to which Lorje would not agree. With the cooperation of members of the Jewish community, they subsequently established a new settlement society in Berlin. As the Executive of the new society was inactive, Lorje's erstwhile supporters came to regret that they had removed the man who had worked with zeal and vigor for their cause. Though his society ceased to exist, Lorje remained faithful to the ideas he had preached and until his death continued to support those who furthered the settlement of Jews in Eretz Israel.

LOURIE, ARTHUR. Zionist leader and Israeli government official (b. Johannesburg, South Africa, 1903; d. Jerusalem, 1978). The son of Harry Lourie (d. 1960), one of South Africa's earliest Zionist leaders, he graduated from the University of Cape Town, received his master's degree from Cambridge University (1925), and studied at the Harvard Law School (1925–26). At Cambridge he was elected president of the University Zionist Society.

Lourie first visited Palestine in 1927. He practiced law in South Africa, lecturing on law at the University of Witwatersrand from 1927 to 1932, and was active in Zionist work in Johannesburg. In 1933 he gave up his law practice to become political secretary to the Jewish Agency in London, a position he held until 1940. That year he went to the United States, where he served as secretary of the Emergency Committee for Zionist Affairs until 1946. In January, 1947, he became director of the New York office of the Jewish Agency, which presented the Zionist case before the United Nations during its deliberations on the Palestine problem. Immediately after the establishment of the State of Israel, he was appointed Israel's Consul General in New York, a position he held until 1953. Between 1949 and 1953 he was also a member of the Israeli delegation to the UN General Assembly, serving again in 1956–57; in 1959 he was chairman of the delegation.

In 1953 Lourie moved to Israel to become Deputy Director General of the Ministry of Foreign Affairs, holding that office until 1957. He served as Ambassador to Canada from 1957 to 1959, Ambassador to Great Britain from 1960 to 1965, and Assistant Director General of the Foreign Ministry, 1965 to 1972.

LOVERS OF ZION. *See* HOVEVEI ZION.

Walter C. Lowdermilk.
[Zionist Archives]

LOWDERMILK, WALTER CLAY. American soil conservationist, Christian Zionist sympathizer, and originator of the *Jordan Valley Authority plan (b. Liberty, N.C., 1888; d. Berkeley, California, 1974). In 1938, as Assistant Chief of Soil Conservation in the U.S. Department of Agriculture, Lowdermilk was sent to Europe, Africa, and the Middle East to study the use of soil. Arriving in Palestine in 1939, he was impressed by Jewish efforts for the rehabilitation of the country through the demonstrated possibility of using irrigation to reclaim once-fertile lands that had become desert.

The initial result of Lowdermilk's Palestine survey was his widely noted book *Palestine: Land of Promise* (1944), in which he outlined his plan for the total utilization of Palestine's water resources for the irrigation of the country through full use of its rivers and subterranean water resources, including possible hydroelectric power development. For this purpose he suggested the creation of a Jordan Valley Authority, a project similar to the Tennessee Valley Authority in the United States. This program, he declared, might make it possible to settle in Palestine 4 million Jewish refugees in addition to the approximately 1.8 million Jews and Arabs who were then living there and in Transjordan.

Lowdermilk's proposals aroused great interest, especially among persons concerned with the future of Palestine. They were studied by the Commission on Palestine Surveys, which was headed by Emanuel Neumann. The detailed report of its engineering staff was eventually presented to the government of Israel and published in book form in 1948 under the title *TVA on the Jordan,* by James B. Hays.

The author of numerous articles setting forth his views on the Palestine problem, Lowdermilk criticized the separation of Transjordan from Palestine (letter to the *New York Times,* 16 August 1946) and the Palestine proposals of Count Folke Bernadotte (*New York Times,* 8 October 1948). Early in 1950 he revisited Israel on the invitation of the

Ministry of Agriculture, and that October he began a year's service as Special Adviser on Soil Conservation to the government of Israel, making a detailed survey of Israel's soil resources. He returned to Israel in 1954, and from then until 1957 he was professor of soil conservation at the Haifa Technion, where a special department was established to forward his ideas.

Tzivya Lubetkin-Zuckerman, 1949. [Lohamei ha-Geta'ot]

LUBETKIN-ZUCKERMAN (CUKIERMAN), TZIVYA. Heroine of the Polish underground and Zionist leader in Israel (b. Poland, 1914; d. Kibbutz Lohamei ha-Geta'ot, 1978). During her high school days in Poland she became active in the pioneering movement He-Halutz. After the outbreak of World War II and the disintegration of the He-Halutz movement in Poland, she maintained contact with He-Halutz members, traveling from town to town, to labor camps and ghettos, to teach them ways of defending themselves. She represented He-Halutz on the Central Committee of the Polish Resistance Organization. She became active in efforts to arrange for the escape of Jews from Poland to Palestine, crossing and recrossing borders on their behalf but refusing to leave Poland herself, insisting that she was needed by her fellow Jews there. She was a member of the command of the Jewish Fighting Organization of the Warsaw ghetto and participated in the battle in which the ghetto was crushed (spring, 1943). Until the end of the war she led guerrilla detachments in Nazi-occupied Poland.

In 1946 she settled in Palestine, and that year she attended the 22nd Zionist Congress in Basle, presiding at its 10th session as the representative of Ahdut Avoda. A member of the Zionist General Council from 1956 on, and a member of the Zionist Executive from 1948 to 1968, she lived in Kibbutz Lohamei ha-Geta'ot. Her husband Yitzhak (Antek) *Zuckerman, was a leader of the Warsaw Ghetto Revolt.

LUDVIPOL, ABRAHAM. Hebrew author, journalist, and delegate to the First Zionist Congres (b. Novograd Volynski, Russia, 1865; d. Tel Aviv, 1921). A member of the Hibbat Zion movement from his youth on, Ludvipol sailed for Eretz Israel in 1890 but was not permitted to land so he went to Paris where he studied and wrote for the French and Hebrew press. He covered the Dreyfus trial in 1894 and as a result of this he became known as a leading Hebrew journalist. As delegate to the First (1897) and subsequent Zionist Congresses, he was instrumental in obtaining general press coverage of Zionist affairs.

In 1903 Ludvipol became editor of the Warsaw daily *Ha-Tzofe*, modernized it, and made it one of the finest Hebrew papers of the time. He sought to establish a daily paper in Palestine, where he settled in 1907, but was unsuccessful. Turning to insurance sales for a living, Ludvipol played an active role in Jewish community affairs in Palestine. When the daily *Ha-Aretz* was founded in 1919, he joined its editorial board. He contributed to numerous Hebrew periodicals, and translated historical works from French into Hebrew. G. KRESSEL

LUNCZ, ABRAHAM MOSES. Scholar and Palestinographer (b. Kovno, Lithuania, 1854; d. Jerusalem, 1918). In 1869 he moved with his family to Eretz Israel, where he studied and worked with Israel Dov Frumkin, the early pioneer of printing and journalism. Luncz started to write for the Diaspora and Jerusalem Hebrew press but then turned to Palestinography. In 1876 he published the first Hebrew guidebook to Jerusalem, followed by essays on the history of the yishuv. Although he lost his eyesight, he continued to write and publish. Between 1882 and his death, he edited *Yerushalayim*, a 13-volume collection of essays on Eretz Israel and the history of the yishuv, and topographical studies contributed by leading local and European scholars. Between 1895 and 1916 he published *Luah Eretz Yisrael*, an annual (21 volumes) which included popular articles on the country as well as practical information. He published new editions of classic exploration studies (including those of Yehoseph Schwartz) and began work on a scholarly edition of the Jerusalem Talmud. Luncz was active in communal affairs in Jerusalem and on behalf of the Jerusalem School for the Blind. G. KRESSEL

LURIA, JOSEPH. Pioneer of Zionism, writer, and educator (b. Pampenai, Kovno District, Lithuania, 1871; d. Jerusalem, 1937). Luria studied at the University of Berlin and after his graduation served as principal of a modern Jewish school in Warsaw. While in Berlin, he helped found a pre-Herzlian Zionist student society. In 1897 he was a delegate to the First Zionist Congress.

As a contributor to Hebrew and Yiddish periodicals, he became (1899) editor of the Zionist Yiddish periodical *Der Yid* in Warsaw. He served in that capacity for four years. Subsequently he worked for the St. Petersburg Yiddish daily *Der Freind*, and in 1906 he assumed the editorship of the Zionist Yiddish weekly *Dos Yidishe Folk* in Vilna.

The following year he settled in Eretz Israel, where he continued his journalistic activities. His articles on contemporary life in the country, published in Yiddish and Hebrew periodicals in Russia, were very popular and were later issued in book form. After World War I, he became head of the Department of Education and Culture of the Zionist Executive (subsequently transferred to the Va'ad Le'umi), serving in this post until his death. He devoted himself to the problem of Arab-Jewish relations and worked in this field with Judah L. Magnes.

A. ALPERIN

LURIE, ZVI. Leader of Ha-Shomer ha-Tza'ir and a member of the Executive of the Jewish Agency (b. Lodz, Russian Poland, 1906; d. Jerusalem, 1968). Lurie immigrated to Palestine in 1925. After working as an agricultural laborer

in Petah Tikva, he joined in 1927 the Ha-Shomer ha-Tza'ir kibbutz group in En Ganim, which subsequently established Kibbutz En Shemer near Karkur. Devoted to the ideology of the movement, Lurie was active in establishing its kibbutz organization, the *Kibbutz Artzi shel Ha-Shomer ha-Tza'ir, in 1927. He became a member of the executive of the Kibbutz Artzi and editor of the movement's paper. From 1924 to 1931 and again from 1935 to 1937 he served on a mission to Poland, acted as secretary of the Executive of Ha-Shomer ha-Tza'ir (at the time seated in Warsaw), and edited the movement's weekly in Poland. From 1939 to 1943 he was secretary of the Jewish Agency's Land Settlement Department. In 1943 he was elected to the Asefat ha-Nivharim and became a member of the Va'ad Le'umi. He served as a member of the Provisional Council of State in 1948 and was among the signatories of the Declaration of Independence. From 1948 until his death he was a member of the Jewish Agency's Executive, in charge of the Organization Department.
Y. SLUTSKY

LUZ (LUZINSKY), KADDISH. Israeli legislator and labor leader (b. Bobruisk, Russia, 1895; d. Degania Bet, 1972). Luz served in the Russian Army during World War I and then pursued his education at the Odessa Institute of Agronomy (1917–19). A founder of the pioneer youth movement He-Halutz in Bobruisk, he settled in Palestine in 1920, joining kibbutz Deganya Bet in 1921. He was named a member of the Central Committee of Mapai in 1935 and was a member of the Central Comptroller's Commission of the Histadrut from 1935 to 1940 and of the Tel Aviv Labor Council in 1941–42.

Luz was a delegate to the 20th (1937) and 22nd (1946) Zionist Congresses. Serving in the Hagana, he saw fighting in the Jordan Valley during the War of Independence. From 1949 to 1951 he was secretary of the Hever ha-Kevutzot. A member of the Knesset from 1951 to 1969 and Minister of Agriculture from 1955 to 1959. From 1959 to 1969 he was Speaker of the Knesset. He was also a member of the Secretariat of the Ihud ha-Kevutzot veha-Kibbutzim. Luz published numerous booklets and articles on labor problems and on the kibbutz movement.

LYDDA (Lod). City in the coastal plain, 10 mi. (16 km.) southeast of Tel Aviv. Mentioned in the Bible (I Chron. 8;12), it became important in the Second Temple period. In 145 BCE it was annexed by Jonathan the Hasmonean and was a purely Jewish town, serving for a time as seat of the Sanhedrin, but it became impoverished and decimated by Roman oppression. The Romans called the town "Diospolis" but when the Christians predominated they named it "Georgiopolis" for St. George, who was reputedly buried there. After the Arab conquest in the seventh century,

Lod Airport. [Israel Information Services]

Lydda served as the country's capital until this designation was conferred on nearby Ramleh. The town expanded in the early 20th century and in 1919 became a railway junction. Before 1948, it numbered 44,000 Arab inhabitants, 80% of them Moslems and the rest Christians. After its capture by Israel forces, the great majority of its inhabitants abandoned it and soon Jewish immigrants settled there. In 1949 it received municipal council status. Modern housing estates were built around its oriental center and an industrial zone developed. Nearby is Israel's major airport (Ben-Gurion Airport), built by the mandatory government in 1946 and considerably expanded since 1948. Population (1987), 41,300, of whom 33,200 were Jews and 8,100 Arabs, the great majority of them Moslems. E. ORNI

M

MA'ABARA (immigrant transit camp). Temporary accommodation provided by the State of Israel for mass immigration between 1950 and 1954. During the first two years after the founding of the State of Israel (1948–50), the masses of penniless immigrants who poured into the Jewish Homeland were quartered in reception camps, where they were supported by the government and the Jewish Agency. This arrangement kept many of the immigrants in enforced idleness, retarded their integration, and placed a heavy economic strain on the infant State. In July 1950, the *ma'abara* system was inaugurated. It was designed to speed up the absorption process by encouraging the newcomers to become economically independent at the earliest possible moment. After passing through a clearance camp, all newcomers capable of working, and their families, were placed in *ma'abarot*, transit camps set up near existing towns or villages where employment was available, or in development regions where large-scale public works were in progress. There were two kinds of *ma'abarot*: those which were eventually to be converted into permanent settlements and those that were meant to be temporary, to be liquidated as the immigrants found employment. The newcomers were given tents or huts of wood, tin, or canvas, but each family had to get its own food, clothing, and furnishings. To help the newcomers in their adjustment, the government and the Jewish Agency provided labor exchanges, clinics,

Tent dwellings in a Ma'abara. [Zionist Archives]

Permanent housing erected near a Ma'abara. [Keren Ha-Yesod]

schools, and various social services in each *ma'abara*.

By 1952, there were in Israel 111 *ma'abarot* with a total population of 230,000. Thr primitive and crowded accommodations caused much hardship; the rainy season brought floods, and the tin huts made the summer heat unbearable. Dissatisfaction was rife. Adults protested and in some cases rioted. The young gave trouble, sometimes deteriorating into delinquency.

The State was compelled to move quickly to provide better and permanent housing for the immigrants. In many cases the permanent housing went up immediately adjoining the tents and huts. Or, the inhabitants of a *ma'abara* would be resettled elsewhere. By 1953 there were only 69 *ma'abarot* with a total population of 108,800. By the end of that year 47 *ma'abarot* had been converted into permanent agricultural settlements. To some extent the *ma'abara* was replaced by the Kefar Avoda (work village), where the immigrants were put to work on the soil. The newcomers in this type of village would be employed by the Jewish National Fund in land reclamation or afforestation projects. At the same time they built their own homes and were given agricultural training.

As the great wave of mass immigration subsided, a new plan for immigrant absorption, "From Ship to Village," was put into effect in September, 1954. This plan called for the immediate placement of every immigrant in specific agricultural settlements or development regions where housing or employment was available. By the late 1950s nearly all the *ma'abarot* had either been liquidated or turned into permanent settlements. G. HIRSCHLER

MA'AGAN MIKHA'EL. Kibbutz at the southern end of the Carmel Coast, founded in 1949 by graduates of the Israel scouting movement. It has variegated intensive farming, carp ponds, and industrial ventures and is one of the largest communal settlements, with 1,140 inhabitants in 1987. There is a nature reserve nearby at the split mouth of the Taninim (Crocodiles) River. The name, "Michael's Anchorage," commemorates PICA director Michael Pollak.

E. ORNI

MA'ALE HA-HAMISHA. Kibbutz in the Judean Hills, 8 mi. (13 km.) west of Jerusalem. It was founded by pioneers from Poland in 1938 at the spot where five of the group had been murdered by Arab terrorists, and hence named "Ascent of the Five." In the 1948 War of Independence it held out in an endangered position. In the 1967 Six-Day War, an attack from here on the nearby Jordanian "Radar Camp" opened the operation bringing Jerusalem and the West Bank under Israel's control. The kibbutz has fruit orchards and other branches of agriculture, an industrial enterprise, and a guest home. Large forests are planted around it. Population (1987), 453. E. ORNI

MA'ALOT-TARSHIHA. Town in western Upper Galilee, 12 mi. (20 km.) east of Nahariya. In 1957, two local *ma'abarot* (transit camps) were converted into the development town of Ma'alot. In 1963, the mainly Christian-Arab village of Tarshiha, lying 1 1/2 mi. (2 km.) further west was united with Ma'alot. Initial progress in Ma'alot was slow, due to the high percentage of welfare cases among the inhabitants, mostly of North African origin, and to the difficulties the local labor force had in adapting to modern industry. In 1974, a vicious attack on a school by Arab terrorists coming from beyond the Lebanese border left 27 dead, most of them children. Subsequently, increased government aid, vocational training, and, since 1973, regional development of the Tefen area brought conspicuous progress. The construction of new factories, some of them high-tech, and the adjacent neighborhood of Kefar Veradim, stimulated further growth. In 1987 the town numbered 8,660 inhabitants, comprising 5,760 Jews, and 2,900 Arabs, with a slight majority of Christians over Moslems.
E. ORNI

MA'APILIM ("illegal" immigrants). *See* "ILLEGAL" IMMIGRATION.

MA'ARAKH (Alignment). *See* AHDUT AVODA-PO'ALE ZION; ISRAEL LABOR PARTY; MAPAI.

MA'ARIV (literally "bringing in the evening"). Daily paper in Israel, founded by Azriel Carlebach who sought to publish a politically independent newspaper of superior quality. The first issue appeared on 15 February 1948, and until September of that year the paper bore the name *Yedi'ot Ma'ariv*. *Ma'ariv* achieved the largest circulation of any paper in Israel, and for many years bore the sub-title "the most widely circulated newspaper in Israel." Although nominally an afternoon paper, it appears in the early morning.

Maariv seeks to achieve a popular style without sensationalism. It maintains an independent network of reporters in Israel and abroad. An illustrated supplement appears with the newspaper almost daily (sport supplement, fashion supplement, men's supplement, financial supplement, Sabbath Eve supplement, etc.).

The newspaper's editors since its founding have been: Azriel Carlebach (1948–1956), Arye Dissentchik (1956–1972), Shalom Rosenfeld (1974–1980), Shmuel Schneider (1980–1985), and Iddo Dissentchik (1985-). M. NAOR

MACCABEANS. *See* ORDER OF ANCIENT MACCABEANS.

Parade of participants at fourth Maccabia, Tel Aviv, 1946. [Central Zionist Archives]

MACCABI WORLD UNION. Sports federation founded in 1921 at the time of the 12th Zionist Congress, replacing the Union of Jewish Gymnastics Clubs (*Jüdoscje Turnerschaft*) which had existed since 1903. The new framework was set up to unite the Jewish gymnastics associations and sports associations throughout the world in a single body. Another objective, in the wake of World War I, was to prevent Jews

Performance by Maccabi girls in Bessarabia, Romania, 1931. [Central Zionist Archives]

from joining organizations of a clearly German nature.

The Maccabi World Union, a non-party organization since its creation, aims to further physical, cultural, and social activity of Jewish youths throughout the world. Like the Union of Jewish Gymnastics Clubs, World Maccabi did not officially join the Zionist Organization, reasoning that official membership in the ranks of the Zionist Organization was likely to alienate many Jewish youngsters from its ranks. Its activity, however, was always of a clearly Zionist nature. Only after acceptance of the Jerusalem Program by the Zionist Organization in the early 1970s did the Maccabi Union join the Zionist Movement.

The main enterprise of the Maccabi World Union is the Maccabia, which was first held in 1932 in Palestine with the participation of 390 athletes from 14 countries. The second Maccabia was held in Tel Aviv in 1935 while the third Maccabia was held only after the creation of the State of Israel (1950). Since 1953 the Games have been held in the State of Israel every four years, one year after the Olympic Games. Some 4,000 athletes from 35 countries participated in the 12th Maccabia in 1985.

The Maccabi World Union has 35 regional branches in all continents. These branches hold national and continental meetings of Maccabi members. In order to guarantee greater participation in the Maccabia a special International Maccabia Committee was created in which organizations not belonging to the Maccabi World Union are also represented. The Maccabi World Union has its seat in the Maccabia village in Ramat Gan.

U. SIMRI

MCDONALD, JAMES GROVER. US diplomat (b. Coldwater, Ohio, 1886; d. Bronxville, N.Y., 1964). McDonald taught history and political science at Indiana University, served as chairman of the Foreign Policy Association, and was a member of the editorial board of the *New York Times*, president of the Brooklyn Institute of Arts and Sciences, and news analyst for the National Broadcasting Company. For many years he was associated with official and unofficial efforts on behalf of refugees, Christian as well as Jewish. It was in the course of these activities that he developed an interest in the Jewish problem and became an ardent champion of Zionism. From 1933 to 1936 McDonald was League of Nations High Commissioner for Refugees from Germany, and from 1938 to 1945 he was chairman of Pres. Franklin D. Roosevelt's Advisory Committee on Political Refugees. In 1938 he served as adviser to the United States representative at the International Conference on Refugees in Evian, France.

During and after World War II he sharply criticized Great Britain's policy in Palestine and called for the opening of the gates of Palestine to Jewish refugees. Serving on the *Anglo-American Committee of Inquiry on Palestine (1945–46), he was influential in framing its recommendation to admit 100,000 Jews to Palestine.

After the creation of the State of Israel, McDonald was named special representative of the United States to Israel. In 1949 he became the first Ambassador of the United States to Israel, serving in that capacity until 1951. Following his return to the United States, he was active as a speaker for the State of Israel bonds campaign. His writings include articles and pamphlets on the refugee problem and a book, *My Mission in Israel* (1951).

MACDONALD, JAMES RAMSAY. British Labor party leader and statesman (b. Lossiemouth, Scotland, 1866; d. aboard ship, Atlantic Ocean, 1937). The son of a laborer, Ramsay MacDonald became a journalist and early developed an interest in social reform. A Fabian Socialist, he joined (1894) the Independent Labor party, and his political career led him twice to the Prime-Ministership (January-November, 1924; 1929–35).

In January, 1922, MacDonald visited Palestine, where he met Jewish labor leaders, including David Ben-Gurion and Yitzhak Ben-Zvi, and visited a number of kibbutzim. In his articles, which were published in *New Palestine*, the organ of the Zionist Organization of America ("The Great Return: The Alluring Call of Palestine," 5 May 1922; "A Pilgrim's Impressions of Palestine," 23 June 1922; "The Great Jewish Return," 24 January 1924), he expressed his admiration for the work of Zionist pioneers in Palestine, praised Jewish labor for endeavoring to raise the living standards of Arab workers in the country, and declared that much of the trouble between the Jews and the Arabs had been caused by propaganda and fomented by the conservative Arab leaders. In one article (23 June 1922) he wrote:

> When our Mandate has been formally approved by the League of Nations, when Sir Herbert Samuel has a body of local officials heartily cooperating with him, and when some of the most objectionable and mischievous activities of the agents of disorder have been firmly dealt with, peace will come to Palestine.

Despite MacDonald's earlier sympathy with Zionist work in Palestine, during his term of office as Prime Minister the British government pursued an anti-Zionist policy. *See* PASSFIELD WHITE PAPER.

His son, **Malcolm John MacDonald** (1901–1981), was Secretary of State for the Colonies in 1935 and again from 1938 to 1940. His early favorable attitude to Zionism changed when he joined Neville Chamberlain's government. On 15 June 1939, he defended the *White Paper of 1939 before the League of Nations Permanent Mandates Commission in Geneva, denying that the policies envisioned by the document violated the British *Mandate for Palestine.

MACDONALD WHITE PAPER. *See* WHITE PAPER OF 1939.

MACHOVER, JOHN M. Zionist leader and attorney in the Mendel Beilis blood libel trial (b. Mogilev, Russia, 1880; d. London 1971). An early colleague of Vladimir Jabotinsky, Machover was a delegate to the Sixth Zionist Congress (1903) and to most subsequent Congresses until 1946. Settling in London in 1920, he served on the Zionist Actions Committee and as a member of the Zionist Congress Tribunal. He was a prominent member of the Revisionist movement, and after the split in the movement he joined the Jewish State party, serving as a member of the World Executive and chairman of the party in Great Britain.

Machover published a number of books and essays on Zionist problems, notably *Governing Palestine: The Case against a Parliament* (1939), an argument against the proposed Legislative Council in Palestine; and *Jewish State or Ghetto: Dangers of Palestine Partition* (1937).

J. LEFTWICH

Julian W. Mack. [Zionist Archives]

MACK, JULIAN WILLIAM. Jurist, communal worker, and Zionist leader in the United States (b. San Francisco, 1866; d. New York, 1943). After receiving an LL.B. degree from Harvard Law School in 1887, Mack opened a law practice in Chicago. He was a professor of law at Northwestern University (1895–1902) and the University of Chicago (1902–11). From 1903 to 1911 he was judge of the Circuit Court of Cook County, Ill., also presiding (1904-07) over the Juvenile Court of Chicago. In 1913, after two years on the US Commerce Court, he was appointed US Circuit Court judge, serving until his retirement in 1941.

Deeply interested in Jewish affairs and general social problems, Mack was (1906) one of the 50 charter members of the American Jewish Committee (AJC), of which he became vice-president and on whose Executive Committee he served until 1918. Largely owing to the efforts of Mack, Cyrus Adler, and Louis Marshall, the AJC adopted a resolution acclaiming the Balfour Declaration. In 1918 Mack resigned from the Executive Committee because of its objection to democratization of American Jewish communal life as advocated by the Zionists; but he retained his membership in the AJC, seeking to bring about harmony between the Committee and the Zionist Organization of America (ZOA), in which, by that time, he had also assumed a leading role.

Mack was drawn to Zionism by his growing conviction that democracy implied cultural pluralism rather than a melting pot, and through his friendship with Aaron Aaronsohn, the Palestine pioneer. His fellow jurists Louis D. Brandeis and Felix Frankfurter also helped convert him to the Zionist idea. From 1914 on he was closely identified with the Zionist movement. During World War I he was a member of the Advisory Council of the Provisional Executive Committee for General Zionist Affairs in the United States. From 1918 to 1921 he was president of the Zionist Organization of America, and at the same time was elected first president of the American Jewish Congress. Designated by the Congress as one of the seven spokesmen of American Jewry at the Paris Peace Conference in 1919, he was chosen chairman of the *Comité des Délégations Juives (this function was assumed by Louis Marshall when Mack had to return to the United States). That year, too, he led a delegation to President Woodrow Wilson endorsing the Balfour Declaration.

When Chaim Weizmann arrived in New York on his first visit to the United States, in the spring of 1921, he met with Mack, then president of the ZOA, who handed him a memorandum setting forth the conditions under which the Executive Committee of the ZOA would support Weizmann's primary mission: founding a United States branch of Keren ha-Yesod, which had been established by the World Zionist Organization the year before. Unlike Weizmann, the so-called Mack-Brandeis group believed in placing primary emphasis on the economic development of Palestine rather than on cultural and philanthropic activities there. The group believed that pro-Palestine investments (for economic purposes) and the donation of funds (for communal purposes in Palestine) should not be commingled and that Keren ha-Yesod in the United States should be strictly a donation fund largely under the control of the ZOA and not exclusively of the world movement. Weizmann refused to accept the conditions set forth in the memorandum, which he described as an "ultimatum." At the convention of the ZOA held in the summer of 1921, there was a showdown between the Mack-Brandeis forces and the supporters of Weizmann. The Mack-Brandeis group lost and resigned in a body from the ZOA's Executive Committee, having been defeated in its struggle to assert its point of view. However, it remained in the organization, and Mack was one of the ZOA's honorary vice-presidents at the time of his death.

He was particularly active in the Palestine Economic Corporation. He attended the 17th (1931) and 19th (1935) Zionist Congresses. He was also instrumental in the conception and founding of the Julian W. Mack School and Workshops in Jerusalem, a cooperative undertaking that sought to expose the children of the city to American progressive educational methods; and was an active supporter of the Hebrew University. In 1941 a kibbutz was named Ramat ha-Shofet (Height of the Judge) in Mack's honor.

MCMAHON CORRESPONDENCE. Exchange of letters (14 July 1915-10 March 1916) between Sir (Arthur) Henry McMahon, British High Commissioner for Egypt (representing the British government), and Hussein (Husayn) ibn Ali, Sherif of Mecca (later self-proclaimed ruler of the Kingdom of Hejaz), on the subject of independence for those Arab countries that gave active assistance to the Allied Powers against Turkey during World War I. The Arabs were later to cite this correspondence in support of their claim that Palestine had been promised to the Arabs before the issuance of the *Balfour Declaration and that the declaration as well as the *Mandate for Palestine was therefore illegal.

Of the 10 letters in the exchange, the ones of direct bearing on the Palestine question are the first letter, from the Sherif of Mecca to the High Commissioner on 14 July 1915, and that of McMahon to the Sherif on 24 October 1915.

In the 14 July letter, the Sherif requested the British government, in return for Arab aid to the Allied Powers, to acknowledge the independence of the Arab countries

> bounded on the north by Mersina and Adana up to the 37° of latitude, on which degree fall Birijik, Urfa, Mardin, Midiat, Jezirat (Ibn Umar), Amadia, up to the border of Persia; on the east by the borders of Persia up to the Gulf of Basra; on the south by the Indian Ocean, with the exception of the position of

Aden to remain as it is; on the west by the Red Sea, the Mediterranean Sea up to Mersina.

In his letter dated 24 October, McMahon accepted the limits specified by the Arab leader, with the following modification:

> The two districts of Mersina and Alexandretta and portions of Syria lying to the west of the districts of Damascus, Homs, Hama and Aleppo cannot be said to purely Arab, and should be excluded from the limits demanded.

Situated as it was to the southwest, or west-southwest, of Damascus, Palestine west of the Jordan River would come under this modification. However, there was no explicit mention of Palestine in the letter, and the loose wording of the pledge subsequently caused much controversy.

Initially, the Arabs made no attempt to invoke the McMahon letter as invalidating the Balfour Declaration or the British Mandate. In fact, Hussein's son, the Emir *Feisal, acting on behalf of the kingdom of Hejaz, met with Chaim Weizmann in London in 1919, a meeting that resulted in the Feisal-Weizmann Agreement (3 January 1919) concerning the rights of the Jews in Palestine. That same year, Feisal confirmed his goodwill toward the Zionist movement in a letter addressed to Felix Frankfurter (3 March 1919). In 1920 Hussein himself, in an interview with Col. Charles Vickery, who visited him on an official mission on behalf of the British government, "stated most emphatically that he did not concern himself at all with Palestine and had no desire to have suzerainty over it for himself or his successors" (letter from Vickery to the London *Times,* 21 February 1939).

Following the Arab riots of 1921, Winston Churchill, then Secretary of State for the Colonies, said in an official report in the House of Commons (11 July 1922) with regard to the McMahon letter that "His Majesty's Government have always regarded, and continue to regard Palestine as excluded by these provisos from the scope of their undertaking. This is clear from the fact...that in the following year they concluded an agreement with the French and Russian Governments under which Palestine was to receive special treatment."

During the years that followed, however, Arab nationalists used the McMahon letter of 14 October 1915, in support of their rejection of the Balfour Declaration. Thus, the Arab Executive declared to the League of Nations Permanent Mandates Commission in 1925 that, in view of McMahon's promise in the letter that "Great Britain is prepared to recognize and support the independence of the Arabs in all the regions within the limits demanded by the Sherif of Mecca," the declaration and the mandate were illegal. It was pointed out to the Arabs by the British government that they had cited the statement out of context, having failed to include the phrase directly preceding: "subject to the above modifications." However, it was admitted that although the British government's intent may have been clear, the wording of the letter to the Sherif was vague.

After the issuance of the *Peel Commission's report, McMahon himself, in a letter to the London *Times* (3 July 1937), went on record to clarify the text of his "pledge":

> Many references have been made in the Palestine Royal Commission Report and in the course of the recent debates in both Houses of Parliament to the "McMahon Pledge," especially to that portion of the pledge which concerns Palestine and of which one interpretation has been claimed by the Jews and another by the Arabs...
>
> I feel it my duty to state, and I do so definitely and emphatically, that it was not intended by me in giving this pledge to King Hussein to include Palestine in the area in which Arab independence was promised.
>
> I had also every reason to believe at the time that the fact that Palestine was not included in my pledge was well understood by King Hussein.

In March, 1939, the wording of the McMahon letter was examined by a joint commission of British and Arab representatives set up by the British government. At that time the British representatives concluded that "on a proper construction of the correspondence, Palestine was in fact excluded." They added, however, that they agreed that the language in which the exclusion was expressed was not so specific and unequivocal as it was thought to be at the time.

It is interesting to note that Thomas Edward *Lawrence (Lawrence of Arabia) was of the opinion that by giving the Arabs Transjordan, of which a large part was not "west of Damascus," the British government had completely fulfilled McMahon's promise to the Sherif." It is my deliberate opinion," he wrote to Prof. William Yale on 22 October 1929, "that the Winston Churchill settlement of 1921–22 (in which I shared) honorably fulfills the whole of the promises we made to the Arabs, in so far as the so-called British spheres are concerned."

J. LEFTWICH

MACMICHAEL, SIR HAROLD. British civil servant (b. Rowtor, Birchover in Derbyshire, England, 1882; d. Folkestone, England, 1969). He was educated at Magdalene College, Cambridge, where he obtained first class honors in Classics. He joined the Sudan Political Service in 1905 and served in the Sudan until 1934. He was Governor of Tanganyika (1934–7) and *High Commissioner for Palestine (1938–44).

MacMichael's first task as High Commissioner was to preside over the suppression of the final stage of the Arab Revolt. This was accomplished with considerable ruthlessness and by the spring of 1939 the force of the revolt was spent. For the remainder of MacMichael's period of office Palestinian Arab nationalism was a broken reed, with most of its leaders dead, imprisoned, or in exile.

The White Paper of May 1939 laid down the main lines of policy pursued by the British in Palestine during World War II. The land policy foreshadowed in the White Paper was given legal expression in the Land Transfer Regulations promulgated by MacMichael in February, 1940. Although these placed strict limitations on land transfers to Jews, they were not, in fact, effective in preventing large-scale 'under-the-table' purchases of land by Jews from Arabs during the war years.

MacMichael's implementation of the immigration provisions of the White Paper aroused fierce indignation among the yishuv and in the Jewish world in general. Every possible means, including the use of armed force and deportations, was used in order to counter the flow of "illegal" Jewish immigrants fleeing from Nazi Europe to Palestine. The incidents of the **Patria* and **Struma* evoked particularly emotional reactions directed against MacMichael personally, since he was seen (correctly) as an energetic advocate rather than a mere executant of the White Paper policy.

On general issues of policy MacMichael held and expressed strong views. He opposed the mandate. He called for the abolition of the Jewish Agency. He denounced what he termed the "almost Nazi control" of the Jewish leadership over the yishuv. He opposed the training of Jews for guerrilla activities in occupied Europe, arguing that this would be harmful to "the future internal security of this country [i.e. Palestine]."

Although MacMichael began as a strong opponent of partition, he changed his mind in the course of his term of office, and developed into a vigorous supporter of the idea. He set out his thinking on the subject in a major dispatch to the Colonial Secretary on 17 July 1944, shortly before relinquishing his office. On 8 August 1944, terrorists belonging to the *Lohamei Herut Israel organization made an attempt on his life: his chauffeur was killed and his wife slightly hurt but he himself survived unscathed. On 29 August, the eve of his departure, MacMichael broadcast to the people of Palestine, and declared his deeply-held conviction that: "The gravest threat [facing Palestine] ... is that political fanaticism which has been deliberately inculcated among the younger generation and regimented to ends which are the negation of all that is meant by democracy—that same impious will to power which reared its ugly head in Germany."

MacMichael lacked the outgoing charm of his predecessor, Wauchope, and of his successor, Gort. This defect compounded the unpopularity which he earned in the yishuv as a result of his responsibility for implementing the White Paper policy. Ben-Gurion called him "petty-minded, arrogant, bureaucratic", echoing the opinion of most Jews in Palestine. Nor was MacMichael notably successful in winning friends among the Palestinian Arabs. His departure from Palestine was little regretted. In retirement from 1946 to 1969 he devoted himself to collecting first editions, Sassanian seals, and Blue-John china. B. WASSERSTEIN

MAFDAL. *See* MIZRACHI.

Magen David on the wall around a portrait of Herzl at meeting of pioneers in Kishinev, Romania, [Central Zionist Archives]

MAGEN DAVID (Shield of David). Jewish symbol appearing on the flag of the Zionist movement and Israel (*see* FLAG, ZIONIST AND ISRAELI). In ancient times this symbol, which consists of two superimposed triangles forming a six-pointed star, or hexagram, was predominantly a non-Jewish decorative motif, sometimes with mystical significance. Only in recent centuries did it become a specifically Jewish symbol.

With the advent of Zionism the Magen David became the most prominent symbol of the Jewish national movement. Under the Flag and Emblem Law of 24 May 1949 enacted by the Knesset, the Magen David was incorporated in the flag of Israel.

Magen David Adom ambulance on the scene after parcel bomb explosion, Givatayim, 1980. [Magen David Adom]

MAGEN DAVID ADOM. ("Red Shield of David") Israeli organization, similar to the Red Cross organizations of other countries, that provides emergency medical services. The first Magen David Adom (MDA) group was founded in Tel Aviv in 1930; groups were formed in Haifa in 1931 and in Jerusalem in 1934. In December, 1935, a national organization was formed. The founding members were physicians, members of the Hagana, and private citizens. The groups provided medical services to the public and to the Hagana. During the 1936–39 Arab riots they gave first-aid training to the Hagana and the auxiliary police and provided medical aid to the wounded. During World War II, MDA worked within the general framework of the Civil Defense Organization.

When Israel was established, there were 16 MDA groups. Negotiations for MDA to become an affiliate of the International Red Cross came to naught because the latter refused to recognize the organization's emblem (red six-pointed star). The two organizations do maintain relations, however, and MDA representatives serve as observers at international conferences of the Red Cross.

In July, 1950, the Knesset ratified the Magen David Adom Law, which defined the tasks of the organization as (1) providing auxiliary services to the Army Medical Corps in wartime and preparing for such services in time of peace; (2) providing civilian first-aid services and temporary shelter in emergency situations; and (3) maintaining a blood bank for civilian use. MDA operates a network of first-aid stations, maintains ambulances, and supplies emergency blood services. Its Educational Department offers courses in first aid and mouth-to-mouth resuscitation for fire departments, bus drivers, teachers, students, and other groups. During Israel's wars since the foundation of the State MDA provided emergency care for the wounded and for war refugees. It also sends relief aid to other countries in such emergency situations as earthquakes, epidemics, and floods.

The organization's income is derived mainly from its members and supporters, from lotteries, and from national subsidies. "Friends of MDA" groups exist in the United States, South America, Western Europe, South Africa, and Australia. Y. SLUTSKY

Judah Leon Magnes. [Hebrew University]

MAGNES, JUDAH LEON. Rabbi, chancellor, and then president of the *Hebrew University of Jerusalem (b. San Francisco, 1877; d. New York, 1948). Having graduated from the University of Cincinnati in 1898, Magnes was ordained at the Hebrew Union College in 1900 and awarded his doctorate in Heidelberg in 1902. His early commitment to Zionism marked his life. He was English secretary (i.e., translator) to the Sixth Zionist Congress (1905), served as secretary of the Federation of American Zionists from 1905 to 1908, and visited Eretz Israel twice (1907 and 1912) before finally settling there in 1922.

Shocked by the Kishinev pogrom, Magnes became chairman of the Jewish Self-Defense Association in 1903, collecting funds for arms to send to Jewish self-defense groups in Russia. Later, this group also sent funds to Eretz Israel for the purchase of arms to protect Jewish settlements there.

Largely as a result of his Zionism and his increasing advocacy of more traditional Jewish observance, Magnes's career in the Reform rabbinate was short-lived. In 1910 he resigned from his position as rabbi of Temple Emanu-El, New York, in protest against assimilationist tendencies.

Feeling a need for an overall organization to speak for American Jewry and to act in its defense against anti-Semitism, he helped found the American Jewish Committee, serving as a member of its executive committee from 1906 to 1918. Meanwhile, in 1909, he helped found the Kehilla, which was intended to serve as the organized Jewish community of New York City, and remained its chairman until 1922. The Kehilla's outstanding accomplishment was in the field of Jewish education. A fervent advocate of the revival of the Hebrew language, Magnes induced Samson Benderley to establish the Bureau of Jewish Education under the Kehilla's aegis in 1910.

In the controversy over establishing an American Jewish congress which dominated Jewish communal politics from 1915, Magnes, who had been an early advocate of the idea, opposed the Zionists' support of a congress. He claimed that involvement in the controversy diverted the movement from its primary goal of mobilizing support for Zionist settlement in Eretz Israel. Following the 1915 Zionist convention which backed the congress, Magnes resigned from the Provisional Zionist Committee.

During the war years, Magnes was active in the work of the American Jewish Joint Distribution Committee, serving on its executive and also as one of its most successful fund-raising speakers. In 1916 he traveled to Germany and German-occupied Poland to investigate the condition of the Jews and the distribution of relief. During World War II he again served the JDC, this time as its adviser on Middle Eastern affairs.

In early 1917, as the United States edged towards war, Magnes adopted a militantly pacifist position. An outspoken critic of Wilson's policies after America's entry into the war, he himself became the center of controversy, alienating many of his supporters within the Jewish community. His pacifist beliefs were important in shaping his attitude towards the Arab question and Zionist politics in general.

Magnes was one of Chaim Weizmann's early co-workers in planning the Hebrew University. In 1925 he became chancellor, in which capacity he laid the foundations of a major university . He was particularly interested in building its institutes of Jewish Studies and Arabic Studies. Following severe criticism by Albert Einstein and an investigation by a committee headed by Sir Philip Hartog, the administration of the university was decentralized in 1935 and Magnes was named president, a mainly representative position he held until the end of his life.

Fearing that efforts to set up a Jewish State would lead to war, he advocated the establishment of a binational state in Palestine. In 1926 he helped found the *Berit Shalom and sought in vain to persuade the British authorities and the Zionist Executive to adopt his views. In a letter published in the *Manchester Guardian* (6 November 1935), he suggested that Palestine be made a permanently neutral state, exempt from war. At the meeting of the Jewish Agency in August, 1937, Magnes, representing the non-Zionists, introduced a resolution calling for the establishment of a committee of Zionists and non-Zionists to negotiate with the League of Nations, Great Britain, and the United States in order to study methods for the establishment of a binational state in Palestine. The motion was defeated, with Weizmann pointing out that the Arabs would never lend their cooperation. Magnes insisted that his contacts with Arabs—which angered Zionist leaders because they were unauthorized—proved the contrary. In response to the Biltmore Program, Magnes founded (1942) the *Ihud organization for better Jewish-Arab understanding but was unable to find Arab leaders who were willing to enter into negotiations with the Jews. Nevertheless, he continued his fight for a binational state, appearing on behalf of Ihud before the Anglo-American Committee of Inquiry. Appearing before the United Nations Special Committee on Palestine (UNSCOP) in 1947, he proposed a binational state in an unpartitioned Palestine that would be based on political parity between Jews and Arabs, and advocated a transitional period of trusteeship for Palestine under the United Nations, with Great Britain as the trustee, until the binational state could be set up.

The adoption of the partition resolution by the United Nations did not put an end to Magnes's efforts. The ensuing outbreak of hostilities, the escalation of fighting, and the Jewish reverses in the early months of 1948 led him to renew his efforts in support of an immediate truce and postponement of the UN partition decision. In March 1948, when the U.S. advocated a temporary trusteeship he drew the attention of Warren Austin, the United States representative at the United Nations, to the Ihud platform, and was invited to the United States to aid in efforts to obtain a truce in Palestine. On 26 April 1948, the Senate of the Hebrew University issued a statement dissociating the institution and its faculty from Magnes's political activities. After the establishment of the Jewish State, Magnes advocated the inclusion of Israel in a confederation of Middle Eastern States. In his Zionist outlook, Magnes gave equal weight to Eretz Israel and Diaspora, rejecting the notion of "the negation of the Diaspora." A flourishing yishuv, he believed, would enrich Diaspora Jewish life, not replace it. Where one wished to live a Jewish life was an individual decision.

H. PARZEN—G. HIRSCHLER—A. GOREN

MAHAL (Mitnadvei Hutz la-Aretz, or Volunteers from Abroad). Designation applied to volunteers from western Europe, North and South America, and South Africa who served with the Israel Defense Forces (IDF) during the War of Independence in 1948. All told, about 3,000 Mahal went to Israel, including large contingents from France, England, the United States, and South Africa. Most of them had been soldiers in the Allied armies during World War II. Some had held high rank and brought to the IDF a wealth of military skill and experience.

Mahal members served with all formations of the Israel Defense Forces. They played an important role primarily in the organization and operations of the Israel Air Force, which, at the beginning, used English for command communication. Most of the Israeli fighter, bomber, and transport planes were piloted by Mahal personnel, who also served as instructors. Mahal members also played an important part in artillery units and the Israel Navy, where they occupied some key positions, including that of chief of staff and the command of a number of ships. Their contribution was important in the medical services, particularly in certain types of orthopedic and plastic surgery. A Mahal officer Ben Dunkelman from Canada commanded one of the IDF's original 12 infantry brigades.

Jackie Cohen, Mahal volunteer pilot from South Africa, 1948. [South Africa Zionist Federation]

MAHANAYIM. Kibbutz south of the Huleh Valley. The land was bought by Jews in 1892 and settled by a few families in 1898 but soon abandoned. Three further settlement attempts failed between 1902 and 1918. In 1939, the kibbutz was established as a Zionist reply to the British White Paper. It developed intensive farming and an industrial enterprise. Near is the Mahanayim airfield servicing internal Israeli flights. Population (1987), 438. E. ORNI

MAHANOT OLIM. *See* HA-MAHANOT HA-OLIM.

MAHLER, RAPHAEL. Jewish historian (b. Nowy Sacz, eastern Galicia, 1899; d. Tel Aviv, 1977). After obtaining his doctorate from Vienna University, he taught Jewish history for many years in Jewish secondary schools in Warsaw. During the same period he continued to study Jewish history, worked with the historian Emanuel Ringelblum in further research, and was extremely active in the left-wing Po'ale Zion in Poland. In 1937 he emigrated to the USA, where he was engaged as a researcher at the YIVO Institute for Jewish Research, and wrote his works on the history of Polish Jewry (1946) and the Karaites (1949). Mahler immigrated to Israel in 1950, joined the staff of Tel Aviv University in 1959, and became a professor in 1963. In Israel he published books on Hasidism and on the Haskalah (1961) and parts of his multi-volumed, unfinished work on the history of the Jewish people in recent generations. His historiography was strongly Marxist in orientation.

M. MINTZ

MAIMON (FISHMAN): Family of Zionist leaders.

Yehuda Leib Hakohen Maimon (Fishman). Rabbi, religious Zionist leader, and author (b. Markuleshty, Bessarabia, Russia, 1876; d. Jerusalem, 1962). Educated at yeshivot in Lithuania, where he received rabbinical ordination, he was a member of the Hovevei Zion and of the Zionist movement. He served as a preacher in the town of his birth (1900–05) and as a rabbi in Ungeny, Bessarabia (1905–13). Rabbi Maimon was a founder of the Mizrachi in Vilna (1902), participating in the organization's first conference (Lida, 1903) and its first international conference (Bratislava, 1904). He was arrested more than once for his Zionist activities in southern Russia. In 1903 he settled in Tel Aviv, but two years later he and other Zionist leaders

Yehuda Leb Maimon. [Zionist Archives]

were arrested and then deported by the Turkish regime. During the remainder of World War I he was in the United States, where he became active in the Mizrachi movement. Returning to Palestine in 1919, he headed the movement there, editing its publication, *Ha-Tor* from 1921 to 1935 and helping develop its religious education system. In the summer of 1935 he was elected Mizrachi representative to the Executive of the Jewish Agency. In 1936 he founded the Rabbi Kook Foundation and began to publish the religious scholarly monthly *Sinai*.

Rabbi Maimon took an activist position in the political struggle against the British regime and for Jewish rights in Palestine. Although he remained within the framework of the organized community, he frequently expressed his esteem for dissident organizations such as the Irgun Tzeva'i Le'umi and Lohamei Herut Israel (Lehi). When the Hagana began to suppress the activities of the Irgun, Rabbi Maimon requested that Irgun members not be handed over to the British. When no agreement could be reached, he and Yitzhak Grünbaum left the Jewish Agency Executive for a short while. In October, 1945, he testified at the trial of a group of Irgun members and spoke out in harsh terms against the British, accusing them of closing the gates of Palestine to the survivors of the Holocaust; he proclaimed the right of every Jew to arm himself for self-defense and for the protection of his rights in Palestine. When the Jewish Agency Executive members were jailed on 29 June 1946 (a Sabbath day), Rabbi Maimon was forced into a car and taken to prison. He was released two weeks later because of ill-health.

In 1948 Rabbi Maimon was active in negotiations between the representatives of the Jewish Agency and the Irgun for the latter's cooperation with the Hagana and, later, with the Israel Defense Forces. He was a signatory to the Declaration of Independence and served as Minister of Religious Affairs and Minister of Welfare in the Provisional Government subsequently serving in the Cabinets of several Governments until 1961. He advocated the reestablishment of a Sanhedrin in Israel as the highest religious authority for Jews throughout the world. This suggestion was opposed by various religious groups.

In addition to political work Maimon was active in the literary field. He had a library of 40,000 volumes. A prolific author, he wrote voluminously on religious subjects, contributed to periodicals, and published a series of biographies of the sages of Israel. His memoirs record his meetings with men eminent in religion and Zionism. Among his books (all in Hebrew) are *Religious Zionism and Its Development* (1937), *For the Sake of Zion I Shall Not Keep Silent* (1954–55), and several other volumes of Zionist interest. He edited the series *Arim ve-Imahot be-Yisrael* (Great Jewish Communities), commemorating the Jewish communities destroyed in the Holocaust. Y. SLUTSKY

Ada Maimon (Fishman). Israeli pioneer and feminist leader, sister of Yehuda Leib Maimon (b. Markuleshty, Bessarabia, Russia, 1893; d. Tel Aviv, 1973). She settled in Eretz Israel in 1912, and two years later, after teaching in Petah Tikva and working as a farmhand, she founded a girls' school in Safed, where she taught for a time.

Ada Maimon was the earliest promoter of the working women's movement in Eretz Israel and occupied a prominent position in the Palestinian labor movement in general. She served as a member of the Central Committee of Ha-Po'el ha-Tza'ir (1914–20), of the Actions Committee of the World Zionist Organization, and of the Executive Committee of the Histadrut. From 1920 to 1948 she was a member of the Va'ad Le'umi and from 1921 to 1930 secretary of the Mo'etzet ha-Po'alot (Working Women's Council), which she had helped organize. In 1926 she was elected to the Central Committee of Mapai and to the Council of the World Union of Po'ale Zion-Hitahdut. She was a delegate to the 13th (1923) and subsequent Zionist Congresses.

In 1930 she became director of the Ayanot Agricultural High School near Nes Tziyona, which had been founded that year by WIZO and the Mo'etzet ha-Po'alot. From 1931 to 1939 she represented the women of Palestine at the International Labor Organization (ILO) of the League of Nations. In 1946–47 she was honorary director of the Histadrut's Immigration Department. She represented Mapai in the First and Second Knessets serving on the Economic and the Constitution, Law, and Justice Committees and actively championing women's rights.

Ada Maimon wrote several books and articles on the working women's movement in Palestine. Her book *Ha-Halutza be-Eretz Yisrael* was published in English as *Women Build a Land* (1962).

MAISEL-SHOHAT (MEISEL-SCHOCHET), HANNA. Educator and Zionist leader in Israel (b. Grodno, Belorussia, 1890; d. Tel Aviv, 1972). Hanna Maisel studied education at the University of Odessa and agriculture and natural sciences in Switzerland and France, receiving a doctorate in science. She early became active in the Po'ale Zion movement representing its Odessa branch at the Seventh Zionist Congress (1905). Settling in Eretz Israel in 1909, she founded (1911) a training farm for girls in Kineret, the first institution of its kind in the country. In 1912 she married Eliezer *Shohat. A year later she went to Vienna as a delegate to the 11th Zionist Congress.

In 1919 she founded a workers' kitchen in Tel Aviv that catered to pioneers of the Third Aliya, and she set up cooking courses for women pioneers, which later developed into the WIZO School of Domestic Science. In 1920 she became a member of the World Executive of WIZO. She was instrumental in the founding of the Girls' Agricultural School of Nahalal, of which she was principal from 1923 to 1960.

MAHLER-KALKSTEIN, MENAHEM. *See* AVIDOM, MENAHEM.

MAISLER, BENJAMIN. *See* MAZAR, BENJAMIN.

MAKHON BEN-ZVI. *See* BEN-ZVI, ITZHAK.

MAKHON JABOTINSKY. *See* JABOTINSKY, VLADIMIR.

MALAMUD, SAMUEL. Community and Zionist leader in Brazil (b. Mogilev Podolski, Ukraine, Russia, 1908). He arrived in Rio de Janeiro, Brazil, in 1923 and studied law. Active in Zionist organizations from his youth, he was a member of Po'ale Zion and was elected secretary-general of the Brazilian Unified Zionist Organization in 1945. In the period of the struggle for the State of Israel, he organized the Brazilian Christian Pro-Palestine Committee. He was president of the Federation of Jewish Institutions in Brazil (1969–72), secretary-general and vice-president of the Confederation of Brazilian Jewry, and president of ORT Brazil. From 1949 to 1952, he was honorary Israeli consul in Brazil, and attended various Zionist Congresses. His publications include *In ondenk of Praça Onze* on the history of the Ashkenazi community in Rio and *Do arquivo e da memoria*, memoirs of Brazilian Zionism. He has also contributed frequently to the journal *Idische Presse*.

MALBEN. *See* AMERICAN JEWISH JOINT DISTRIBUTION COMMITTEE.

MALCOLM, JAMES ARATOON. Engineer, financier, and Zionist sympathizer (b. Bushire, Persia, 1868; d. London, 1952). A British Armenian, Malcolm belonged to a family of merchants and shipowners that had represented British interests in the Persian Gulf countries.

Appointed liaison of the Armenian National Committee to the Foreign Office in London during World War I, Malcolm was in close touch with Sir Mark Sykes, the Undersecretary of State for Middle Eastern Questions. Malcolm later wrote that in 1916 he had suggested to Sykes that the Allied cause would get the support of American Jewry if Britain were to promise a Jewish homeland in Palestine after the war. He introduced Chaim Weizmann to Sykes and the subsequent contact between Sykes and Weizmann led to the events that culminated in the Balfour Declaration.

At one time during the war, Sykes entrusted Malcolm with the task of discussing the Palestine problem with Jaafar Pasha, an Arab nationalist leader then in London. On that occasion, Malcolm told the Arab leader that the all-important task at the moment was to help assure an Allied victory, because all small nations—not only the Jews but the Armenians and the Arabs as well—needed the help of the Allies to obtain self-determination. Malcolm subsequently went to Paris with Sykes and Nahum Sokolow when the latter two negotiated with the French. In the negotiations that followed, the French eventually yielded their claim to Palestine to Great Britain.

Malcolm remained a supporter of Zionism for the rest of his life, stressing that the Balfour Declaration was a contract binding on the British government. Soon after the creation of the New Zionist Organization in 1935 he became a Revisionist. In 1936 he published a pamphlet, *Partition of Palestine; Suggested Alterations in Proposed Frontiers*, in which he asserted that the boundaries contemplated by the Peel Commission were untenable from a strategic point of view and that, convinced of the benefits of Zionism to the world at large as well as to the Jews, he supported an "integral Jewish Palestine as comprised in the British Mandate."

G. HIRSCHLER

MANARA. Kibbutz on the Naftali Ridge of eastern Upper Galilee, at an altitude of 2,990 ft. (920 m.) on the Lebanese border. The occupation of the post by pioneers who climbed the precipitous slope from the Huleh Valley in 1943 was an outstanding feat. In the 1948 War of Independence, the "Arab Liberation Army" occupied the surrounding terrain, but Manara held out until the siege was lifted in "Operation Hiram" in October. The kibbutz tends fruit orchards on the border and fields in the Huleh Valley below. It runs an industrial enterprise and a guest house. Population (1987), 322.

E. ORNI

MANDATE FOR PALESTINE. The mandate system was created by article 22 of the Covenant of the League of Nations which formed part of the Treaty of Versailles of 1919. This declared that to territories inhabited "by peoples not yet able to stand by themselves under the strenuous conditions of the modern world there should be applied the principle that the well-being and development of such peoples form a sacred trust of civilization." The administration of such territories was to be "entrusted to advanced nations" to be exercised on behalf of the League. The mandate system was applied to non-European territories ceded by Germany and Turkey after World War I. The principal allied powers appointed the Mandatories subject to confirmation by the League of Nations. Mandated territories were assigned to one of three classes of mandate, "A", "B", or "C", depending on their degree of development. Palestine was assigned to Britain as an "A" mandate.

Political Background of the Mandate. The origins of the British mandate in Palestine lay in the confused wartime negotiations concerning the post-war division of the Ottoman Empire. France at first demanded Palestine as part of its claim to Syria, but in the Anglo-French treaty of 1916 (*see* SYKES-PICOT AGREEMENT), the Levant was divided into zones of direct and indirect British and French control. Central Palestine, comprising an area from north of Acre to a line from Gaza to Hebron in the south, and extending to the River Jordan in the east, was to be placed under a vaguely-defined "international" regime with the exceptions of British enclaves around Haifa and Acre.

Meanwhile, discussions had proceeded between British representatives and the Sherif Hussein of Mecca (*see* MCMAHON-HUSSEIN CORRESPONDENCE). The British object in these exchanges was to draw the Arabs of the Hejaz into the war against their Ottoman suzerains. To this end the British gave extensive but undefined undertakings concerning British support for the establishment at the end of the war of an independent Arab state headed by Hussein. Palestine was not specifically mentioned in the correspondence between Sir Henry McMahon and Hussein. Nor did the exchange of letters constitute a definitive agreement. Nevertheless, in later years Arab nationalists claimed that the correspondence committed Britain to the inclusion of Palestine in the putative Arab state. They further alleged that Britain had been guilty of double-dealing in its negotiations on the matter with the French, the Zionists, and the Arabs, to each of whom they had made conflicting promises. The failure of the British to publish the McMahon-Hussein correspondence officially until 1939 lent some color to these charges. The British government, on the other hand, argued that Palestine was not included in the area promised to the Arabs by Britain. This was also the view taken by British officials (including Sir Henry McMahon himself) who had participated in the negotiations.

The idea of British sponsorship of Jewish settlement in Palestine was first raised with fellow-members of the British Cabinet by Herbert Samuel in November, 1914, shortly after the entry of the Ottoman Empire into the war. In conversations with the Foreign Secretary, Sir Edward Grey, and others, he proposed the establishment, under British auspices, of a Jewish state in Palestine at the end of the war. In early 1915 he circulated a Cabinet memorandum in which he withdrew the suggestion of a Jewish state, but elaborated a scheme for Jewish autonomous development under British suzerainty. Although these proposals had no immediate effect, they raised Zionism to the status of a Cabinet-level issue, and helped ensure that the subject subsequently received serious attention.

The British decision to issue the *Balfour Declaration in November, 1917, however, flowed less from Zionist pressure than from strategic calculations. Foremost among these were the hope of drawing Russian and American Jews towards support for the Allied war effort and the desire to furnish a legitimate basis for British (rather than French) rule in post-war Palestine. In the following month the Egyptian Expeditionary Force, headed by General Allenby, occupied Jerusalem and inaugurated a British military administration in southern Palestine.

By the time of the Turkish armistice on 30 October 1918, Allenby's army had conquered the whole of northern Palestine as well as Transjordan, Syria, and Lebanon. An Arab regime, headed by the Emir Feisal, was set up at Damascus. Lebanon was placed under a French administration and the whole of Palestine west of the Jordan river was now incorporated into the British zone. Although these were interim administrative arrangements, supposedly without prejudice to the final territorial settlement, the fact that the British army was the only significant military force in the region gave the British a powerful lever for ensuring that the ultimate outcome reflected their wishes.

Negotiations for the partition of the Arab-inhabited parts of the former Ottoman Empire were complicated by the collapse of the Ottoman government and the rise of revolutionary forces headed by Mustafa Kemal (later known as Kemal Ataturk). The dying Ottoman government signed the Treaty of Sèvres with the allies in August, 1920, but the Kemalist revolt prevented the ratification of the treaty and it was subsequently abandoned. Meanwhile, French claims in Palestine had been withdrawn only gradually and grudgingly. In April, 1920, the allied powers, meeting at the *San Remo Conference, agreed to award the mandate for Palestine to Great Britain. The terms of the mandate were not yet decided and the legal basis of British rule in the country remained questionable pending the conclusion of a definitive peace treaty with Turkey. Nevertheless the British government proceeded immediately to establish a civil administration in Palestine, headed by a High Commissioner. Sir Herbert Samuel was selected for this position, and he arrived in Palestine on 30 June 1920.

Terms of the mandate. Negotiations concerning the terms of the mandate occupied more than two years after the institution of the civil administration. The Zionists pressed hard for terms which would guarantee the realization of the Balfour Declaration as they understood it. British officials, however, made it clear that Britain would not countenance a constitutional structure in which Jewish predominance was established in Palestine. The Zionists tried to obtain explicit recognition in the preamble to the mandate of "the historical connection of the Jewish people with Palestine and the claim this gives them to reconstitute Palestine as their National Home." These words were included in an early draft of the mandate prepared in June, 1920, but later deleted. The final version referred merely to the "historical connection of the Jewish people with Palestine and to the grounds for reconstituting their national home in that country."

The Zionists also sought the inclusion of a clause stating that the ultimate objective of the mandatory government was the establishment of a "Jewish Commonwealth," or, failing that, "a self-governing Commonwealth." The final text, however, referred only to "the development of self-governing institutions."

Crucial to the future status of the Zionist Organization was the clause in the mandate which detailed the status and functions of a recognized "Jewish Agency" for Palestine. An early draft of the mandate granted a "preferential right" to this *Jewish Agency "to construct or operate public works, services, and utilities, and to develop the natural resources of the country." This clause was watered down, and the reference to "preferential right" deleted in the final text. On the other hand, article four of the mandate declared that "an appropriate Jewish agency" would be "recognized as a public body for the purpose of advising and cooperating with the Administration of Palestine in such economic, social, and other matters as may affect the establishment of the Jewish national home and the interests of the Jewish population in Palestine, and subject always to the control of the Administration, to assist and take part in the development of the country." The Zionist Organization was recognized as such an agency, pending the establishment of a broader-based institution embracing all Jews "willing to assist in the establishment of the Jewish national home."

The mandate contained several other clauses favorable to Zionist interests. Thus article six required the government of Palestine to "facilitate Jewish immigration under suitable conditions" and to encourage "close settlement by Jews on the land." Article 22 recognized Hebrew as one of the three official languages of the country.

The mandate left open two constitutional questions of the utmost importance. The first was the question of the mode of termination of the mandatory system, since the mandate contained no provision for its own dissolution (except for a reference in article 28 to arrangements for the permanent safeguarding of rights with regard to the holy places), nor any indication of the process by which it might be terminated. Secondly, the mandate left unclear the question of who was the ultimate sovereign in Palestine. The form of government in Palestine between 1920 and 1948 was almost identical to that of a British crown colony and the High Commissioner exercised authority there under the authority of the King of England and by virtue of the provisions of the Foreign Jurisdiction Act passed by the British Parliament in 1890. But Palestine was not regarded as part of the British Empire, and under article 26 of the mandate the Mandatory agreed to an important limitation of its authority. This provided that in the event of a dispute relating to the mandate between the Mandatory and another member of the League of Nations such dispute should be submitted to the Permanent Court of International Justice. Until its demise at the beginning of World War II, the League of Nations exercised a nominal supervisory authority over the Government of Palestine through the Permanent Mandates Commission. But in no important instance was this ever an effective constraint on the actions of the government. The long-drawn-out negotiations for a Turkish peace treaty and simmering Anglo-French differences in the Near East delayed until 24 July 1922 the approval of the mandate by the Council of the League of Nations. The mandate could not, however, be said to have acquired full legal force until the conclusion of the Treaty of Lausanne between Turkey and the Allies on 24 July 1923. Since the USA was not a member of the League, a special Anglo-American convention was concluded and ratified in 1925, in which the United States agreed to the terms of the mandate, and the United Kingdom agreed that those terms would not be altered without the consent of the USA.

Boundaries of the Mandate. The mandate was granted to Britain, and the civil administration established in Palestine, without conclusive definition of its territorial boundaries and without prejudice to their final determination. The area governed at first by Samuel corresponded to that ruled by the preceding military administration. It included virtually all of Palestine west of the river Jordan. Shortly after assuming office Samuel asked the Foreign Office for permission to extend his authority east of the Jordan, but this was refused.

The south-western border of Palestine was identical to the pre-war Egyptian frontier. Since Egypt was under British occupation in 1920 this border seemed to require no further definition. The northern and eastern borders, however, were the subject of prolonged negotiations.

The Zionists sought to ensure that the eastern border of Palestine should be not the Jordan river but a line further to the east such as the Hejaz railway. As for the north, the Zionists wished to obtain the inclusion in Palestine of the northernmost Jewish settlements of Tel Hai and Metula and the headwaters of the Jordan and Litani rivers.

In the east, where a virtual state of anarchy existed for several months, a new situation arose in October, 1920, with the occupation of Transjordan by Abdullah ibn Hussein. He threatened to attack the French who in July, 1920, had captured Damascus and ejected his brother Feisal from the throne of Syria. In March, 1921, at a conference in Cairo of British officials, it was decided that Abdullah should be recognized as Emir of Transjordan. That region, which had hitherto been explicitly excluded by the British Government from the area administered by the Government of Palestine, was now attached to the Palestine mandate. Article 25 of the mandate, as approved in June, 1922, gave the mandatory government the right, subject to the consent of the League of Nations, "to postpone or withhold application" of any provisions of the mandate considered by the Mandatory to be "inapplicable to the existing local conditions." It was on this basis that the British government in 1922 excluded Transjordan from the area of the mandate to which the provisions regarding the establishment of the Jewish National Home were held to apply.

In the north the Zionists were partially successful in attaining their objectives. An Anglo-French Convention on the borders of Palestine, signed in December, 1920, failed to secure for Palestine the headwaters of the Litani. But the convention provided for a joint Anglo-French commission to delineate the frontier in consultation with "Zionist engineers" in such a way as to include the source of the Jordan in Palestine. The northern border, as finally agreed in 1923, included within Palestine all existing Jewish settlements in the north, and provided the necessary conditions for the establishment of Pinhas Rutenberg's hydro-electric plant on the bank of the Jordan.

Political History of the Mandate. During the period between the British occupation in 1917–18 and the arrival of the first High Commissioner on 30 June 1920, Palestine was ruled by a British military administration. Under the rules of international law governing the administration of occupied territory, no changes could be made to the legal status quo existing at the time of occupation. The effect was that, pending the establishment of the civil administration, the government delayed implementation of the Balfour Declaration. Although a *Zionist Commission was permitted to go to Palestine in the spring of 1918 in order to advise the government, Jewish immigration and land purchases, as well as other Zionist developments, were thus severely curtailed. Meanwhile, Arab nationalists, inspired by the ideal of a Greater Syria ruled by Feisal's government in Damascus, organized "Moslem-Christian Societies" which protested against Zionism with increasing vigor. In April, 1920, serious riots broke out in Jerusalem in which Arabs attacked and killed five Jews. With the installation of Samuel as first High Commissioner the position changed to the Zionists' benefit. Several officials of the military administration who had been hostile to Zionism were replaced. Steps were taken to facilitate Jewish immigration, land purchase, and the development of communal institutions such as the *Va'ad Le'umi. The outbreak of serious Arab anti-Jewish riots in May, 1921, however, led to the deaths of 47 Jews and 48 Arabs (most of the latter killed by British security forces). Following these disturbances the British government decided to redefine its policy in Palestine. A *White Paper was issued in June, 1922, in which the government announced that a constitution for Palestine would be established. The constitution, promulgated in August, 1922, provided for the election, on the basis of a restricted franchise, of a Legislative Council with limited powers. The proposal would have given the Jews only two seats on the 22-member Council, but the Zionist position was safeguarded by the presence of ten official members nominated by the High Commissioner and by the limitation of the council's powers. The Arab population, however, boycotted the elections to the Council in 1923. When Samuel sought to establish a nominated Advisory Council, the Arab nominees withdrew from participation. As a result the government was thereafter conducted by the High Commissioner without any elected institutions representative of the country as a whole.

Consequently article 2 of the mandate, providing for the development of self-governing institutions, was never implemented. In default of any all-Palestine representative body, the government consulted on a regular basis with the leaders of the major communities. In the case of the Jews, article four of the mandate provided for such consultation with the Jewish Agency. The mandate contained no provision for such consultation with the Arab majority of the population. A proposal by Samuel in 1923 for the establishment of an Arab Agency was rejected by leading Arab

Lord Plumer, High Commissioner for Palestine, inspecting veterans of the Jewish Legion in Jerusalem on Armistice Day, 1925. Walking behind him is Col. Frederick Herman Kisch. [Zionist Archives]

notables. In these circumstances the Supreme Moslem Council, which had been set up by the government in 1922, developed into the most important Arab institution in mandatory Palestine. The mufti of Jerusalem, Haj Amin al-Husseini, was appointed first head of the Council with the approval of the government. This gave him control of considerable patronage and of substantial funds. By the end of the 1920s he emerged as the foremost Arab politician in Palestine. A canny and ruthless intriguer, he gradually eliminated opponents within the Arab community, and put himself at the head of a popular anti-Zionist movement.

This period 1920 to 1936 was one of rapid development of the Jewish National Home. The Jewish population of Palestine, some 56,000 in 1918, grew to nearly 400,000 by early 1936 (nearly 30 percent of the population). During the first two decades of the mandate over £100,000,000 of capital was imported to Palestine by Jews. Jewish-owned land increased in area from 650,000 metric dunams (4 dunams¨ 1 acre) in 1920 to 1,533,400 in 1939. The Jewish trade union organization, the Histadrut, established in 1920, developed into a major economic power, and its political offspring, the Labor Zionist movement, became the dominant political force in the Jewish community.

Between 1921 and 1929 Palestine was comparatively peaceful. In 1925 Samuel was succeeded as High Commissioner by Field-Marshal Lord Plumer who remained in office until 1928. The main feature of his period in Palestine was the reduction of the British military garrison as part of a government economy drive. When renewed anti-Jewish violence erupted in August, 1929, British forces initially proved inadequate to the task of restoring order. The riots had grown out of a bitter Moslem-Jewish dispute over rights at the *Western Wall (Wailing Wall) in Jerusalem. The violence spread from Jerusalem to other cities, notably Hebron and Safed. A total of 133 Jews and 116 Arabs died in the course of the disturbances: most of the Jews were killed by Arab rioters, most of the Arabs by British security forces.

A British-appointed commission of inquiry into the causes of the riots (*see* SHAW COMMISSION) reported that excessive Jewish immigration in 1925 and 1926 had produced Arab unemployment. The commission proposed that an expert investigation be conducted into pressures on land resources in Palestine. Such a study was undertaken by Sir John Hope-Simpson, who reported that, given existing methods of cultivation, there was already insufficient land to support the Arab peasant population. Simultaneously with publication of Hope-Simpson's report in October, 1930, the British Government issued a policy statement (*see* PASSFIELD WHITE PAPER) in which it announced that Jewish immigration and land transfers would be subject to greater governmental control. The White Paper elicited a wave of Zionist protests. Following discussions between the Zionists and the British government, however, the Prime Minister,

J. Ramsay MacDonald, issued an explanatory public letter in which the Passfield White Paper was implicitly abrogated.

The period between 1933 and 1936 was one of large-scale Jewish immigration to Palestine, fuelled by the emergence of Nazism in Germany and of anti-Semitism in eastern Europe, notably Poland. Renewed Arab unrest in 1933 was followed three years later by the outbreak of a country-wide general strike which developed into a serious Arab rebellion against the mandatory government. The revolt took the form of attacks on the British and on Jews as well as internecine conflict between different Arab factions. All the major Arab political groups, however, joined in the Arab Higher Committee, whose dominant figure was the mufti of Jerusalem. A Royal Commission under Earl Peel (*see* PEEL COMMISSION) was appointed by the government to investigate the "underlying causes of the disturbances." The Peel Commission's report, issued in 1937, was strikingly radical both in its analysis of the issues and in its recommendations. It construed the mandate as having the "primary purpose ..., as expressed in its preamble and its articles,... to promote the establishment of the Jewish National Home." This objective, however, had been predicated on the political assumption that "Arab hostility to [the Balfour Declaration] would sooner or later be overcome." This assumption having proved mistaken, the Peel Commission declared the mandate "unworkable." The report argued that an equitable solution, which would give both parties what they chiefly wanted, "freedom and security," could best be obtained by a *partition of the country into an Arab and a Jewish state. If such a solution could not be achieved, and if the mandate were to continue, Jewish development should cease to be governed by the principle of economic absorptive capacity, which had reigned since 1922, and a "political high level" of Jewish immigration should henceforth be set by the mandatory government. The Peel Commission added that this level should be fixed for the next five years at a maximum of 12,000 per annum.

The partition proposal was rejected by the leaders of the Palestinian Arabs. The Arab revolt was renewed at a higher level of violence, evoking a determined response from the British army whose forces in Palestine were greatly reinforced. The scheme split the Zionist movement, but a majority supported the leadership of Weizmann in accepting the idea in principle while insisting that the borders of the proposed Jewish state should be the subject of negotiation with the British government. In the course of 1938, however, continuing Arab opposition to partition and the worsening international situation persuaded the British government to abandon its earlier support for the proposal. Meanwhile the Arab revolt in Palestine was crushed by the British army. A large number of Arab rebels were sentenced to death and hanged, others were jailed, and the political leaders of the Arab nationalist movement were sent into exile. Haj Amin al-Husseini, who had been deposed by the British from the presidency of the Supreme Moslem Council, succeeded in evading arrest and escaped to Lebanon. By early 1939 the revolt had been defeated. But the military and political cost to Britain had been considerable, and the government now reached the conclusion that the time had come to "crystallize" the Jewish National Home at roughly its existing size and level of development.

In February, 1939, the British government invited Arab and Jewish representatives to attend a conference on Palestine at St James's Palace in London. The government made it clear that in the absence of an agreed settlement it would find it necessary to impose its own solution. The Arab delegates refused to participate in official meetings with the Zionists although there were some unproductive private encounters. The British therefore held separate sessions with the Arabs and the Jews. By mid-March it was plain that the conference had failed. the government therefore set out its own policy in a White Paper which was published in May, 1939 (*see* [MACDONALD] WHITE PAPER OF 1939).

The MacDonald White Paper, which remained the most authoritative statement of British policy in Palestine until 1945, represented a reversal of the Balfour Declaration policy pursued during the previous two decades. The document declared "unequivocally" that it was not British policy that Palestine should become a Jewish state, but that, given "such relations between the Arabs and the Jews as would make good government possible," it was intended within ten years to establish "an independent Palestine state." The Jews would be a permanent minority in such a state, since the government declared that for the next five years a maximum of 75,000 immigrants would be permitted to enter Palestine (thus raising the Jewish proportion of the population to about one third). Thereafter, the White Paper announced, "no further Jewish immigration will be permitted unless the Arabs of Palestine are prepared to acquiesce in it." The High Commissioner was to be given "general powers to prohibit and regulate transfers of land" in order to protect Arab landholders. On this basis Land Transfer Regulations were promulgated in February, 1940. They restricted free acquisition of land by Jews to the five percent of the area of the country where Jews were already densely settled.

The White Paper was denounced by the Zionists and their supporters. Winston Churchill and Leopold Amery delivered powerful speeches in the British House of Commons denouncing it. The Palestinian Arabs, cowed by the repression of the revolt, evinced little reaction. The Permanent Mandates Commission of the League of Nations concluded that the White Paper represented a violation of the hitherto accepted interpretation of the mandate. But World War II broke out before the Council of the League could consider what action should be taken on the Mandates Commission's recommendations.

The restrictions imposed on Jewish immigration to Palestine came as pressure for Jewish emigration from Europe reached its height. With the Nazi occupation of Poland in September, 1939, and of the Low Countries and France in 1940, hundreds of thousands of Jewish refugees sought to escape from Nazi-held territory by any means. The British government, anxious lest Palestine be flooded with immigrants, used diplomatic, economic, and even military measures to seal the escape routes from Europe against Jewish refugees. Incidents such as the **Patria* and **Struma* tragedies, in which large numbers of would-be immigrants were drowned, aroused bitter Jewish resentment against the mandatory government. Having entered the war against Nazi Germany, however, Britain inevitably commanded the support of all Jews—except for the small fringe group, Lohamei Herut Israel (Lehi), founded by Avraham Stern, which entered into contact with German and Italian agents. The great majority of Jews in Palestine supported the war effort and large numbers volunteered to join the British army. Members of the Jewish underground army, the Hagana, undertook missions in occupied Europe in cooperation with British secret services. Many joined the Jewish

Brigade, formed within the British Army in 1944 after several years of Zionist pressure for the formation of a distinctive Jewish force.

During the early part of the war the British position in the Middle East appeared precarious. With the collapse of France Syria fell into the hands of Vichy French elements. In April, 1941, a pro-Nazi coup in Iraq, in which the mufti of Jerusalem played a major role, was overcome by British forces. In early 1942 the British position even in Egypt began to be threatened. Contingency plans were drawn up for a British withdrawal from Palestine, leaving the Jews to fend for themselves against Nazi attack. But the British victory in the Battle of El Alamein in November, 1942, preserved allied control of the Suez Canal and removed the threat of German occupation of Palestine.

The political situation in Palestine during the war remained relatively quiescent. In spite of their opposition to the White Paper policy, the Zionist leadership cooperated with the government in the war effort. The mufti of Jerusalem, who had fled to Berlin following the collapse of the coup in Iraq, broadcast anti-British propaganda to the Near East over Berlin radio. But the Palestinian Arabs showed no inclination to heed his message. After an economic recession at the beginning of the war, Palestine enjoyed an inflationary wartime boom. The Jewish community, however, became increasingly concerned about reports after 1942 of massacres of Jews in Europe. The continued resolve of the British government to restrict Jewish immigration evoked deep bitterness. Swelling hostility turned to violence in 1944 with attacks on government buildings and an attempt on the life of the High Commissioner, Sir Harold MacMichael. In November, 1944, the British Minister Resident in the Middle East, Lord Moyne, was assassinated in Cairo by two Palestinian Jews, members of Lehi. The Moyne assassination led the British Prime Minister, Churchill, to shelve indefinitely Cabinet discussion of a new Palestine partition plan.

All consideration of the future of Palestine was henceforth postponed until after the war. Meanwhile Britain had taken the initiative in sponsoring moves towards Arab unity (*see* *ARAB LEAGUE). As Axis defeat loomed larger on the horizon, Arab states successively joined the new *United Nations, which would inherit, together with other legacies from the League of Nations, responsibility for former mandated territories. At the founding conference of the United Nations at San Francisco in 1945 Arab representatives made a determined but unsuccessful effort to formulate Article 80 of the United Nations Charter in a way which would have denied to the Jews in Palestine rights previously recognized. The article was adopted in a form which would have preserved such rights intact in any transition from the mandate to a system of "trusteeship".

The Labor Party which won power in Britain in the general election of 1945 had taken up strongly pro-Zionist positions during the war. But the new government adhered to the essentials of the White Paper policy. The dominant force in policy-making on Palestine was no longer the High Commissioner, nor the Colonial Office, but the Foreign Office. The new Foreign Secretary, Ernest Bevin, took the problem in hand personally, and rashly declared that he would stake his political future on its resolution. Britain, strongly dependent at this time on American support, sought to associate the United States in responsibility for Palestine. In late 1945 the two countries agreed to set up an *Anglo-American Committee of Inquiry into the problem of Palestine and of Jewish refugees in Europe.

The Anglo-American Committee submitted its report in April, 1946. It recommended that the mandate continue, pending agreement on a new trusteeship arrangement leading ultimately to a binational state. The Committee's most controversial proposal, however, was for the immediate admission into Palestine of 100,000 Jewish victims of Nazi and fascist persecution. Most of the other recommendations were soon lost in a sharp disagreement on this point between the White House and the British government. The Americans urged Britain to admit the 100,000 to Palestine immediately, but the British insisted that such a step could be taken only if the Jewish underground military organizations in Palestine laid down their arms. (*see* "ILLEGAL" IMMIGRATION)

Meanwhile, the Zionist Mosad le-Aliya Bet organized the "illegal" immigration of Jewish refugees from liberated Europe to Palestine. The continued British blockade of Palestine against Jewish immigrants raised a storm of protest among Jews and their sympathizers, especially in the United States. Episodes such as the saga of the **Exodus* aroused fierce Jewish resentment against Bevin and the British government. Jewish resistance developed into terrorist warfare by the Irgun Tzeva'i Le'umi and the Lehi. For a while the Hagana made an effort to rein in these dissident groups under a joint command. However this had ended before the Irgun bomb attack in 1946 against the King David Hotel in Jerusalem, part of which was occupied by mandatory government offices. Ninety people, British, Arabs, and Jews, were killed in this incident.

Britain's decision in 1947 to give up the mandate and withdraw from Palestine was, however, less a reaction to such terrorist attacks than a logical consequence of the British withdrawal from India, the greatly reduced status of Britain in international diplomacy, and the heavy cost of maintaining large military and naval forces in and around Palestine to counter "illegal" immigration and the harassing tactics of the Hagana. Following the British announcement that it would submit the problem to the United Nations, a *United Nations Special Committee on Palestine (UNSCOP) was formed to investigate the problem and make recommendations to the General Assembly. A majority of this committee recommended the partition of Palestine into independent Arab and Jewish states. On 29 November 1947 the General Assembly of the United Nations voted by the necessary two-thirds majority to partition Palestine. The Zionists were fortunate at this time in enjoying the support of both the Soviet Union and the United States.

The partition plan was bitterly assailed by the Arabs, accepted with rejoicing by most Zionists, and greeted with hostility by the British government which announced that it would not cooperate in the implementation of any plan which did not have the approval of both Arabs and Jews. The British nevertheless held to their intention to withdraw from Palestine. The government made little effort to organize an orderly handover of authority; in places it actively sought to thwart any such transfer. The result was chaos and civil war. Before the formal end of the mandate Arab forces from outside Palestine had already entered the country. At midnight on 14/15 May 1948, Sir Alan Cunningham, the last British High Commissioner, took ship at Haifa. His departure marked the formal end of the British mandate, although a residual British presence was maintained at

Haifa for some weeks longer. A few hours before Cunningham's departure the Jewish state had been proclaimed at Tel Aviv, and a provisional government took office headed by David Ben-Gurion.

B. HALPERN—B. WASSERSTEIN

TEXT OF THE MANDATE FOR PALESTINE

The Council of the League of Nations:

Whereas the Principal Allied Powers have agreed, for the purpose of giving effect to the provisions of article 22 of the Covenant of the League of Nations, to entrust to a Mandatory selected by the said Powers the administration of the territory of Palestine, which formerly belonged to the Turkish Empire, within such boundaries as may be fixed by them; and

Whereas the Principal Allied Powers have also agreed that the Mandatory should be responsible for putting into effect the declaration originally made on the 2nd November 1917, by the government of his Britannic Majesty, and adopted by the said Powers, in favour of the establishment in Palestine of a national home for the Jewish people, it being clearly understood that nothing should be done which might prejudice the civil and religious rights of existing non-Jewish communities in Palestine, or the rights and political status enjoyed by Jews in any other country; and

Whereas recognition has thereby been given to the historical connection of the Jewish people with Palestine and to the grounds for reconstituting their national home in that country; and

Whereas the Principal Allied Powers have selected His Britannic Majesty as the Mandatory for Palestine; and

Whereas the Mandate in respect of Palestine has been formulated in the following terms and submitted to the Council of the League for approval; and

Whereas His Britannic Majesty has accepted the mandate in respect of Palestine and undertaken to exercise it on behalf of the League of Nations in conformity with the following provisions; and

Whereas by the aforementioned article 22 (paragraph 8), it is provided that the degree of authority, control or administration to be exercised by the Mandatory, not having been previously agreed upon by the members of the League, shall be explicitly defined by the Council of the League of Nations;

Confirming the said mandate, defines its terms as follows:

ARTICLE 1

The Mandatory shall have full powers of legislation and of administration, save as they may be limited by the terms of this mandate.

ARTICLE 2

The Mandatory shall be responsible for placing the country under such political, administrative and economic conditions as will secure the establishment of the Jewish national home, as laid down in the preamble, and the development of self-governing institutions, and also for safeguarding the civil and religious rights of all the inhabitants of Palestine, irrespective of race and religion.

ARTICLE 3

The Mandatory shall, so far as circumstances permit, encourage local autonomy.

ARTICLE 4

An appropriate Jewish agency shall be recognised as a public body for the purpose of advising and co-operating with the Administration of Palestine in such economic, social and other matters as may affect the establishment of the Jewish national home and the interests of the Jewish population in Palestine, and subject always to the control of the Administration, to assist and take part in the development of the country.

The Zionist organisation, so long as its organisation and constitution are in the opinion of the Mandatory appropriate, shall be recognised as such agency. It shall take steps in consultation with His Britannic Majesty's Government to secure the co-operation of all Jews who are willing to assist in the establishment of the Jewish national home.

ARTICLE 5

The Mandatory shall be responsible for seeing that no Palestine territory shall be ceded or leased to, or in any way placed under the control of, the Government of any foreign Power.

ARTICLE 6

The Administration of Palestine, while ensuring that the rights and position of other sections of the population are not prejudiced, shall facilitate Jewish immigration under suitable conditions and shall encourage, in co-operation with the Jewish agency referred to in Article 4, close settlement by Jews on the land, including State lands and waste lands not required for public purposes.

ARTICLE 7

The Administration of Palestine shall be responsible for enacting a nationality law. There shall be included in this law provisions framed so as to facilitate the acquisition of Palestinian citizenship by Jews who take up their permanent residence in Palestine.

ARTICLE 8

The privileges and immunities of foreigners, including the benefits of consular jurisdiction and protection as formerly enjoyed by Capitulation or usage in the Ottoman Empire, shall not be applicable in Palestine.

Unless the Powers whose nationals enjoyed the aforementioned privileges and immunities on the 1st August, 1914, shall have previously renounced the right to their re-establishment, or shall have agreed to their non-application for a specified period, these privileges and immunities shall, at the expiration of the mandate, be immediately re-established in their entirely or with such modifications as may have been agreed upon between the Powers concerned.

ARTICLE 9

The Mandatory shall be responsible for seeing that the judicial system established in Palestine shall assure to foreigners, as well as to natives, a complete guarantee of their rights.

Respect for the personal status of the various peoples and communities and for their religious interests shall be fully guaranteed. In particular, the control and administration of Wakfs shall be exercised in accordance with religious law and the dispositions of the founders.

ARTICLE 10

Pending the making of special extradition agreements relating to Palestine, the extradition treaties in force between the Mandatory and other foreign Powers shall apply to Palestine.

ARTICLE 11

The Administration of Palestine shall take all necessary measures to safeguard the interests of the community in connection with the development of the country, and, subject to any international obligations accepted by the Mandatory, shall have full power to provide for public ownership or control of any of the natural resources of the country or of the public works, services and utilities established or to be established therein. It shall introduce a land system appropriate to the needs of the country, having regard, among other things, to the desirability of promoting the close settlement and intensive cultivation of the land.

The Administration may arrange with the Jewish agency mentioned in article 4 to construct or operate, upon fair and equitable terms, any public works, services and utilities, and to develop any of the natural resources of the country, in so far as these matters are not directly undertaken by the Administration. Any such arrangements shall provide that no profits distributed by such agency, directly or indirectly, shall exceed a reasonable rate of interest on the capital, and any further profits shall be utilised by it for the benefit of the country in a manner approved by the Administration.

ARTICLE 12

The Mandatory shall be entrusted with the control of the foreign relations of Palestine and the right to issue exequaturs to consuls appointed by foreign Powers. He shall also be entitled to afford diplomatic and consular protection to citizens of Palestine when outside its territorial limits.

ARTICLE 13

All responsibility in connection with the Holy Places and religious buildings or sites in Palestine, including that of preserving existing rights and of securing free access to the Holy Places, religious buildings and sites and the free exercise of worship, while ensuring the requirements of public order and decorum, is assumed by the Mandatory, who shall be responsible solely to the League of Nations in all matters connected herewith, provided that nothing in this article shall prevent the Mandatory from entering into such arrangements as he may deem reasonable with the Administration for the purpose of carrying the provisions of this article into effect; and provided also that nothing in this mandate shall be construed as conferring upon the Mandatory authority to interfere with the fabric or the management of purely Moslem sacred shrines, the immunities of which are guaranteed.

ARTICLE 14

A special Commission shall be appointed by the Mandatory to study, define and determine the rights and claims in connection with the Holy Places and the rights and claims relating to the different religious communities in Palestine. The method of nomination, the composition and the functions of this Commission shall be submitted to the Council of the League for its approval, and the Commission shall not be appointed or enter upon its functions without the approval of the Council.

ARTICLE 15

The Mandatory shall see that complete freedom of conscience and the free exercise of all forms of worship, subject only to the maintenance of public order and morals, are ensured to all. No discrimination of any kind shall be made between the inhabitants of Palestine on the ground of race, religion or language. No person shall be excluded from Palestine on the sole ground of his religious belief.

The right of each community to maintain its own schools for the education of its own members in its own language, while conforming to such educational requirements of a general nature as the Administration may impose, shall not be denied or impaired.

ARTICLE 16

The Mandatory shall be responsible for exercising such supervision over religious or eleemosynary bodies of all faiths in Palestine as may be required for the maintenance of public order and good government. Subject to such supervision, no measure shall be taken in Palestine to obstruct or interfere with the enterprise of such bodies or to discriminate against any representative or member of them on the ground of his religion or nationality.

ARTICLE 17

The Administration of Palestine may organise on a voluntary basis the forces necessary for the preservation of peace and order, and also for the defence of the country, subject, however, to the supervision of the Mandatory, but shall not use them for purposes other than those above specified save with the consent of the Mandatory. Except for such purposes, no military, naval or air forces shall be raised or maintained by the Administration of Palestine.

Nothing in this article shall preclude the Administration of Palestine from contributing to the cost of the maintenance of the forces of the Mandatory in Palestine.

The Mandatory shall be entitled at all times to use the roads, railways and ports of Palestine for the movement of armed forces and the carriage of fuel and supplies.

ARTICLE 18

The Mandatory shall see that there is no discrimination in Palestine against the nationals of any State member of the League of Nations (including companies incorporated under its laws) as compared with those of the Mandatory or of any foreign State in matters concerning taxation, commerce or navigation, the exercise of industries or professions, or in the treatment of merchant vessels or civil aircraft. Similarly, there shall be no discrimination in Palestine against goods originating in or destined for any of the said States, and there shall be freedom of transit under equitable conditions across the mandated area.

Subject as aforesaid and to the other provisions of this mandate the Administration of Palestine may, on the advice of the Mandatory, impose such taxes and customs duties as it may consider necessary, and take such steps as it may think best to promote the development of the natural resources of the country and to safeguard the interests of the population. It may also, on the advice of the Mandatory, conclude a special customs agreement with any State the territory of which in 1914 was wholly included in Asiatic Turkey or Arabia.

ARTICLE 19

The Mandatory shall adhere on behalf of the Administration of Palestine to any general international conventions already existing, or which may be concluded hereafter with the approval of the League of Nations, respecting the slave traffic, the traffic in arms and ammunition, or the traffic in drugs, or relating to commercial equality, freedom of transit and navigation, aerial navigation and postal, telegraphic and wireless communication or literary, artistic or industrial property.

ARTICLE 20

The Mandatory shall co-operate on behalf of the Administration of Palestine, so far as religious, social and other conditions may permit, in the execution of any common policy adopted by the League of Nations for preventing and combating disease, including diseases of plants and animals.

ARTICLE 21

The Mandatory shall secure the enactment within twelve months from this date, and shall ensure the execution of a Law of Antiquities based on the following rules. This law shall ensure equality of treatment in the matter of excavations and archaeological research to the nationals of all States members of the League of Nations.

(1) "Antiquity" means any construction or any product of human activity earlier than the year A.D. 1700.

(2) The law for the protection of antiquities shall proceed by encouragement rather than by threat.

Any person who, having discovered an antiquity without being furnished with the authorisation referred to in paragraph 5, reports the same to an official of the competent Department, shall be rewarded according to the value of the discovery.

(3) No antiquity may be disposed of except to the competent Department, unless this Department renounces the acquisition of any such antiquity.

No antiquity may leave the country without an export licence from the said Department.

(4) Any person who maliciously or negligently destroys or damages an antiquity shall be liable to a penalty to be fixed.

(5) No clearing of ground or digging with the object of finding antiquities shall be permitted, under penalty of fine, except to persons authorised by the competent Department.

(6) Equitable terms shall be fixed for expropriation, temporary or permanent, of lands which might be of historical or archaeological interest.

(7) Authorisation to excavate shall only be granted to persons who show sufficient guarantees of archaeological experience. The Administration of Palestine shall not, in granting these authorisations, act in such a way as to exclude scholars of any nation without good grounds.

(8) The proceeds of excavations may be divided between the excavator and the competent Department in a proportion fixed by that Department. If division seems impossible for scientific reasons, the excavator shall receive a fair indemnity in lieu of a part of the find.

ARTICLE 22

English, Arabic and Hebrew shall be the official languages of Palestine. Any statement or inscription in Arabic on stamps or money in Palestine shall be repeated in Hebrew, and any statement or inscription in Hebrew shall be repeated in Arabic.

ARTICLE 23

The Administration of Palestine shall recognise the holy days of the respective communities in Palestine as legal days of rest for the members of such communities.

ARTICLE 24

The Mandatory shall make to the Council of the League of Nations an annual report to the satisfaction of the Council as to the measures taken during the year to carry out the provisions of the mandate. Copies of all laws and regulations promulgated or issued during the year shall be communicated with the report.

ARTICLE 25

In the territories lying between the Jordan and the eastern boundary of Palestine as ultimately determined, the Mandatory shall be entitled, with the consent of the Council of the League of Nations, to postpone or withhold application of such provisions of this mandate as he may consider inapplicable to the existing local conditions, and to make such provision for the administration of the territories as he may consider suitable to those conditions, provided that no action shall be taken which is inconsistent with the provisions of articles 15, 16, and 18.

ARTICLE 26

The Mandatory agrees that if any dispute whatever should arise between the Mandatory and another member of the League of Nations relating to the interpretation or the application of the provisions of the mandate, such dispute, if it cannot be settled by negotiation, shall be submitted to the Permanent Court of International Justice provided for by article 14 of the Covenant of the League of Nations.

ARTICLE 27

The consent of the Council of the League of Nations is required for any modification of the terms of this mandate.

ARTICLE 28

In the event of the termination of the mandate hereby conferred upon the Mandatory, the Council of the League of Nations shall make such arrangements as may be deemed necessary for safeguarding in perpetuity, under guarantee of the League, the rights secured by articles 13 and 14, and shall use its influence for securing, under the guarantee of the League, that the Government of Palestine will fully honour the financial obligations legitimately incurred by the Administration of Palestine during the period of the mandate, including the rights of public servants to pensions or gratuities.

The present instrument shall be deposited in original in the archives of the League of Nations, and certified copies shall be forwarded by the Secretary-General of the League of Nations to all members of the League.

Done at London, the 24th day of July, 1922.

MANDELSTAMM, MAX EMANUEL. Ophthalmologist and Zionist leader (b. Zagar, Kovno District, Lithuania, 1839; d. Kiev, Russia, 1912). He studied at the Universities of Tartu and Kharkov and, after working at various eye clinics in Germany, settled in Kiev, where he became one of Russia's leading ophthalmologists.

Although born of an assimilationist family, Mandelstamm identified completely with the Jewish nationalist movement and was active in Jewish communal affairs. His prominent position, coupled with his devotion to Jewish interests, made him a very influential figure in Russian Jewry. After the pogroms of 1881 he was one of the chief advocates of Jewish emigration from Russia. An early adherent of the Hovevei Zion movement, he joined political Zionism from its inception.

Mandelstamm participated in the First Zionist Congress (1897), was a member of the Zionist Actions Committee, and supported Herzl in the Uganda controversy. After the Seventh Congress (1905) had rejected the East Africa offer, Mandelstamm left the movement and helped Israel Zangwill found the Jewish Territorial Organization.

A close friend of Leo Pinsker and Herzl, Mandelstamm served as the model for Professor Eichenstamm in Herzl's **Old-New Land*.

MA'OZ HAYIM. Kibbutz in the Bet She'an Valley near the Jordan River. It was founded as a Tower-and-Stockade outpost during the 1937 Arab riots by four groups, three of which later founded their own kibbutzim in the Valley: Kefar Ruppin, Mesilot, and Neveh Eitan. During the War of Independence, Ma'oz Hayim held an advanced defense position. It was shelled in the 1967 Six-Day War. The kibbutz has highly intensive farming and industry. Its name commemorates Hayim Sturman, the Ha-Shomer veteran killed by Arabs on a land-purchasing mission in the Bet She'an Valley. Population (1987), 595. E. ORNI

MAPAI (Mifleget Po'alei Eretz Yisrael—Israel Workers' Party). Mapai is a Socialist Zionist party founded in 1930 by a merger of *Ahdut Avoda and *Ha-Po'el ha-Tza'ir. In 1968 it was joined by two smaller Socialist Zionist parties to form the *Israel Labor party.

Prior to the Establishment of the State of Israel, 1930–48. The formation of Mapai was the result of a lengthy process that began with the founding late in 1920 of the *Histadrut. Ahdut Avoda, which wanted to see all workers united in a single organization, had pressed for union with Ha-Po'el ha-Tza'ir since its formation in 1919. In the beginning Ha-Po'el ha-Tza'ir avoided identifying itself as a Socialist movement and remained aloof from the concept of class conflict, but in time some of its members raised the banner of what Hayim Victor *Arlosoroff called "populist Jewish socialism."

The strengthening of the right-wing Zionist groups during the Fourth Aliya and their demand for greater stress on the encouragement of middle-class and private initiative increased the pressure for a merger between the two labor parties. In the spring of 1929 a joint committee consisting of four members of Ahdut Avoda (David Ben-Gurion, Berl Katznelson, Zalman Shazar, and David Remez) and four of Ha-Po'el ha-Tza'ir (Joseph Aronowicz, Yitzhak Lufban, Eliezer Kaplan, and Yosef Sprinzak) met and drafted terms for unification, which were ratified by more than 80 per cent of the members of the two parties. The Arab riots of 1929 made unification even more urgent. On 5 January 1930, the founding convention of Mapai, representing 5,650 members, was held in Tel Aviv. This convention approved the party platform, which established the principle of unification and defined the aims of the united labor party as the "rebirth of the people of Israel in the land of Israel, as a free, working nation" and "the abolition of class slavery and social inequality in all their forms, the transfer of natural resources and means of productivity to the general working community, and the establishment of a society based on labor, equality, and freedom." It was decided that the weekly newspaper *Ha-Po'el ha-Tza'ir* would become the organ of the new party.

With this merger it appeared that the goal of complete identification of the labor movement (*see* LABOR ZIONISM) with the Histadrut was about to be realized. More than 80 per cent of the delegates attending the 4th Histadrut Conference (1933) were from Mapai. The merger in Palestine was followed by the merger of the parties close to Mapai in the Diaspora. Thus in August 1932, *Po'ale Zion merged with *Hitahdut (Zionist Labor party) to form the *Ihud Olami.

From its inception, Mapai had to fight for the status of the labor movement in the Zionist Executive in Palestine and in the World Zionist movement. The conflict, which was essentially between Mapai and the Revisionists, reached a climax when the latter openly declared their intention to "break" the Histadrut (November, 1932). In the 1931 elections to the Asefat ha-Nivharim, Mapai won 47 percent of the votes. At the 17th Zionist Congress (1931), 29 percent of the delegates were of the "labor group" (in which *Ha-Shomer ha-Tza'ir participated). That Congress was marked by a serious clash between the labor group and the Revisionists, who were then at the height of their influence and comprised 21 per cent of the delegates. Mapai carried the day, and two of its leaders, Arlosoroff and Berl Locker, were appointed to the Zionist Executive, with Arlosoroff becoming head of the Executive's Political Department in Palestine.

Following the Congress, the conflict between Mapai and the Revisionists intensified in Palestine and other countries. Within Mapai itself there was a debate between those who wanted to use force against the Revisionist group and another faction, headed by Berl Katznelson, that took a more moderate position. At the 18th Zionist Congress (1933) the labor party was the largest group, comprising 44 percent of the delegates. Four of its representatives, Ben-Gurion, Berl Locker, Eliezer Kaplan, and Moshe Shertok (Sharett), were elected to the Zionist Executive. In 1935, when the Revisionists seceded from the World Zionist Organization, Mapai's influence became even stronger, and its representatives occupied key positions in the leadership of the Zionist movement.

In the 1930s Mapai attained its greatest political and moral influence in the yishuv. It encompassed most of the Second Aliya and Third Aliya, the great majority of the moshav movement, the Kibbutz Me'uhad, Hever ha-Kevutzot, and most of the workers in the cities and moshavot. Its influence was decisive in the labor youth movements in Palestine and the Diaspora and in the pioneering movement. In May, 1941, on the eve of its 5th convention, Mapai had about 20,000 members: of these, 47 percent lived in kibbutzim and moshavim, 35 percent in cities, and 18 percent in moshavot. Many of Mapai's organizational and cultural activities were carried out within the framework of the Histadrut.

Mapai sought to expand its influence beyond the ranks of the working class. "The working class cannot liberate itself," said Berl Katznelson, "unless the entire nation is liberated with it." Ben-Gurion expressed the same theme in his slogan "From a class to a nation." Ideologically, the movement was far from united. Within it were groups (whose members included Shlomo Kaplansky and Yitzhak Tabenkin) that called themselves Marxists and others (including most of the moshav movement, Hever ha-Kevutzot, and members of Gordonia) that opposed Marxism. The general philosophy of the party could be defined as "constructivist socialism," and its leaders were agreed that the party's main function did not lie in any one ideological formulation but in joint action, that is, in efforts to recruit pioneers from the Diaspora, in the development of workers' settlements and cooperatives, in the creation of new employment opportunities in the cities, and in the support of Jewish labor in the moshavot. During those years most of the policies of the Histadrut, the Jewish community in Palestine, and the Zionist Organization were articulated by leaders of Mapai.

Soon, however, rifts appeared within the party. Even during the period of merger in the late 1920s, no agreement could be reached with Ha-Shomer ha-Tza'ir, then the largest pioneering youth movement in the Diaspora. Ha-Shomer ha-Tza'ir had begun as a movement with an undefined, nonpolitical ideology, but by the late 1920s it had adopted a Marxist ideology and a positive attitude toward the Soviet regime. Nevertheless, in view of the movement's significant educational influence on the Jewish youth of the Diaspora and its activities in the kibbutzim, Mapai was ready to absorb it into its ranks. However, Mapai refused to accept Marxism as the ideology of the entire party. Attempts at a merger continued throughout the 1930s, but without success. In the 1940s Ha-Shomer ha-Tza'ir became a left-wing Zionist Socialist party, competing with Mapai within the Labor Zionist movement.

A more dangerous split occurred when Mapai's leadership was unsuccessful in uniting its own affiliated cooperative settlement organizations, Kibbutz Me'uhad and Hever ha-Kevutzot. The kibbutz movement was far more influential within the party than the number of its members would indicate. It was responsible for the education and practical training of pioneering youth in Palestine as well as in the Diaspora. Attempts at unification met with resistance from a Kibbutz Me'uhad group headed by Tabenkin, whose opposition was based primarily on organizational principles. The division in the ranks of the kibbutz movement led to a rift also in the youth movements associated with Mapai in Palestine and the Diaspora and created an atmosphere of suspicion and mutual distrust.

The rift was most clearly reflected in the debate over the agreement made in 1934 between Ben-Gurion and the Revisionist leader Vladimir Jabotinsky for the purpose of ending the bitter clashes between Mapai and the Revisionists. The agreement included a special provision that workers belonging to the Revisionist party (who comprised a minority in their places of employment) had the right to seek to prevent strikes and to submit labor disputes to compulsory arbitration. The agreement aroused great opposition among many Mapai members. At the 3rd Mapai Convention (March, 1934) the delegates were divided on the issue, with 74 in favor of the agreement and 89 opposed. The agreement was brought to a referendum of Histadrut members. The Mapai elements that opposed it were joined by members of Ha-Shomer ha-Tza'ir and Left Po'ale Zion, and the agreement was defeated.

The dispute left a residue of bitterness. In 1937 a leftist opposition group, motivated mainly by local considerations, developed within Mapai in Tel Aviv. This group, known as Si'a Bet (Faction B), argued against the bureaucratization of the Mapai and Histadrut apparatus. Si'a Bet obtained a majority in the Mapai Council of Tel Aviv and joined with the opposition groups, which comprised a majority in the Kibbutz Me'uhad. A;though the 1937–39 debate over the partition of Palestine and the establishment of a Jewish State in part of the country did not follow faction lines (for instance, Berl Katznelson was a leader of the opposition to partition), it did help consolidate the various opposition groups, all of which were against the partition plan.

In the elections to the Mapai Convention of December, 1938, the opposition groups in the kibbutzim and cities united in Si'a Bet and obtained about one-third of the votes. Thereafter Si'a Bet fought for representation in proportion to its numbers within the party on local Mapai councils, on the electoral lists for various institutions, and in the collective movement.

During World War II the rift within the party widened, particularly with regard to relations with the Soviet Union. Si'a Bet joined the Soviet Union Friendship League, a Communist-influenced organization. The Mapai leadership did not join the league. Although Mapai won 70 percent of the delegates elected to the 5th Histadrut Conference late in 1941, one-third of its delegates were associated with Si'a Bet. Thus the Mapai majority was divided. Even though Si'a Bet did not now openly challenge party discipline, it occasionally demonstrated its opposition by abstaining from a vote.

This situation led to a paralysis of Mapai's organizational and propaganda activities. In October, 1942, the party held a conference at Kefar Vitkin to consider organizational problems. The majority of the delegates wanted to see party factions eliminated. The Si'a Bet delegates, who numbered about one-third of the total, boycotted the vote. When the party voted to dissolve its internal factions, Si'a Bet announced that it would ignore the resolution. The conference ended with the feeling that, instead of resolving the crisis, Mapai had now in effect, split in two.

In January, 1944, a Committee of Veteran Members was chosen to attempt to heal the schism, but the divisive forces grew stronger. The final split occurred at the February, 1944, meeting of the Histadrut Executive Committee at which delegates were to be elected to the London World Trade Union Conference, a body that, it was hoped, would form the basis for an international labor organization after the war. Ben-Gurion proposed that the Histadrut delegation seek the support of the conference for the Biltmore Program, the Zionist plan for an independent Jewish Commonwealth in Palestine. Si'a Bet did not agree that the Histadrut delegates be required to present the plan to the conference. Together with representatives of Ha-Shomer ha-Tza'ir and the Left Po'ale Zion, Si'a Bet therefore voted against the resolution, which, however, was passed by a majority of 24 to 21. It was clear that the fiction of a united party could no longer be maintained.

A decision to hold elections to the 6th Histadrut Conference was coupled with a demand that Mapai candidates pledge themselves to vote the party line. After Si'a Bet had refused to accept this demand, the split in the party became final. In the October, 1944, elections for the Histadrut Conference, Si'a Bet put up its own slate of candidates under the name Ha-Tenu'a le-Ahdut ha-Avoda and won 17.5 percent of the votes. Mapai polled 54 percent and retained its majority within the Histadrut. The vote indicated that three-fourths of Mapai's membership had remained loyal to the party leadership.

After World War II the task of leading the political and underground struggle against the British fell to Mapai. With the issuance of the White Paper of 1939, two trends took shape within the party concerning the struggle against the new British policy. The activists (including Ben-Gurion, Katznelson, and Eliyahu Golomb) urged a political and military struggle in the form of demonstrations and even an open show of strength that would prove to the British that Palestine's Jewish community would not resign itself to Britain's anti-Zionist policies. The more moderate group (including Yosef Sprinzak, Eliezer Kaplan, and Pinhas Lavon) sought to limit resistance to positive action such as accelerating "illegal" immigration and settlement, while seeking insofar as possible to avoid direct confrontation with the British regime. Following an acrimonious party debate in the middle 1940s, the moderates decided to leave the activists a free hand while reserving the right to criticize their activities. Even the secession of Si'a Bet (which favored active struggle against the British) from the party did not change the situation. Jointly with other civic groups, the Hagana, the Irgun Tzeva'i Le'umi, and the Lohamei Herut Israel, Mapai spearheaded the resistance movement to British rule. After the Black Sabbath (29 June 1946), when relations between the yishuv and the Zionist movement on one hand and the British on the other reached a low point, the moderates set forth their views in a pamphlet, *Examination of the Road*. The activists, led by Ben-Gurion, continued to lead the resistance to the British regime.

The survivors of the pioneering movement in Europe and many of the soldiers who had served in the Palestinian army units were eager for political and organizational unity. But as internal party disputes intensified in Palestine, this opportunity for the unification of the labor movement was lost. The great hopes which many people then placed in the Soviet Union, for both socialism and the Zionist cause (Soviet support of the proposed Jewish State in 1946–49), strengthened the parties and factions that leaned toward a Communist ideology. Early in 1948 these groups formed *Mapam, a left-wing party in which Ha-Shomer ha-Tza'ir, Ahdut Avoda, the Left Po'ale Zion, and the group led by Moshe Sneh, joined forces. The new party sought to challenge Mapai's leadership in the Histadrut, the pioneering youth movement, the Zionist Organization, and Palestine's Jewish community.

Mapai in the State of Israel. During the War of Independence and to an even greater extent in the early years of the new State, David Ben-Gurion became the outstanding figure and policy maker of Mapai. He also personified authority to many of the immigrants who poured into the country and who had no tradition of labor or pioneering and, in many cases, no concept of a democratic political party. Many of these immigrants identified Ben-Gurion's personal qualities with Mapai. The party's primary challenge during these early years of the State was to attract the masses who were grappling with problems of absorption, to help them become integrated in their new country, and in general to mold them into a constructive pioneering element.

After the establishment of the State, Mapai redefined its platform. It proclaimed the following aims: the gathering of a maximum number of Jews within the boundaries of the State of Israel; the settlement of undeveloped areas; the absorption of immigrants into the established community and their integration in the working class in Israel; the maintenance and development of a pluralistic economy with a public and governmental sector (including the workers' agricultural settlements and the economic institutions of the Histadrut) as well as a private-enterprise sector that would utilize private investments plus government aid; the promotion of the country's economic independence through agricultural and industrial expansion and increased exports; a guarantee of adequate wages for workers in accordance with their productive output and with the capacity of the economy; the promotion of friendly relationships between the secular and religious institutions in the State by avoidance of a *Kulturkampf* and provision for the special needs of religious citizens; the guarantee of peace on the borders by the strengthening of the Israel Defense Forces; a readiness to sign peace treaties with the neighboring Arab states; the development of a foreign policy based on friendly relations with nations willing to aid the

State of Israel; the breaking of Israel's political isolation and its siege by the Arab nations through the formation of alliances with the Afro-Asian bloc; and the unification of the Labor Zionist parties on a broad basis, as had been the goal of the party since its inception.

Mapai, as the largest political party in the State, occupied a central position between the extreme left and other political groups without which a coalition government could not be formed. Thus, every government in Israel from the establishment of the State until 1977 was formed by Mapai (as long as it was in existence) together with various partners on the left and the right. In every government the key Cabinet positions (Prime Minister, Minister of Finance, and Minister of Defense) were in Mapai hands. In municipal governments, Mapai candidates became mayors of the large towns and cities, and the party won most of the seats on the town and city councils. Mapai retained its hegemony in the Histadrut.

Mapai's publishing house, Ayanot, and the publishing houses Am Oved and Tarbut Hinukh, which are close to Mapai, printed works of party ideologists and spokesmen. Its cultural center for political studies was Bet Berl (established in 1947 and named for Berl Katznelson), with an extensive library which is the depository of the party archives. Mapai also sponsored a network of educational institutions.

As Mapai grew in membership, its ideological and organizational unity diminished, and various factions emerged. The two workers' settlement movements associated with Mapai, *Ihud ha-Kevutzot veha-Kibbutzim and Tenu'at ha-Moshavim, remained loyal to the party. In Tel Aviv and Haifa, however, blocs representing special interests of urban workers emerged. A group of younger men, headed by Moshe Dayan and Shimon Peres, took the position that Mapai must assume a powerful role in the guidance of the State and the realization of its aims and that government policies must be implemented through the State and its agencies rather than through the Histadrut. Pressure groups representing specific trade or professional interests arose within the party.

One of the serious problems facing Mapai was the transfer to the government of functions that had been controlled by the Histadrut prior to the founding of the State. This involved the disbanding of *Palmah, the elimination of labor-sponsored schools within the educational system, and the establishment of government labor exchanges. These transitions occasionally precipitated intraparty and interparty crises. Ben-Gurion's personal prestige played an important role.

In the early 1960s Mapai went through a difficult crisis. It began with the so-called *Lavon affair. Pinhas Lavon had resigned as Defense Minister in 1953 after a secret security operation had ended in failure. From 1956 on Lavon served as secretary-general of the Histadrut. After gathering documentary evidence in his support, he appealed for an examination of his responsibility for the failure of the operation. In 1960 a committee of seven ministers was set up by the government to investigate the matter. This committee arrived at the decision that Lavon had not been responsible for the operation that failed. Ben-Gurion refused to accept the conclusions of the ministerial committee, which he interpreted as a personal attack and an expression of lack of confidence in his leadership. In February, 1961, under pressure from Ben-Gurion, the Mapai center decided to remove Lavon from his position as secretary-general of the Histadrut. Some of the party members felt this decision was unethical and formed an opposition group called *Min ha-Yesod. This group, which included Yona Kesseh, Lavon, and Prof. Nathan Rotenstreich, demanded the democratization of Mapai, the right to form political-ideological groups within its framework, and adherence to the basic values of the labor movement. When its demand to overrule Lavon's dismissal was defeated, the group left Mapai (November, 1964). Although Min ha-Yesod was small in numbers and its influence limited to narrow intellectual circles and members of Ihud ha-Kevutzot veha-Kibbutzim of Gordonia background, its secession served as a protest against the ideological rigidity of the establishment, the control of the party hierarchy over Mapai, and the excessive authority granted the party's leader.

As Israel developed, sociological changes occurred in the population. There was a growing distance between the masses of new immigrants, mostly from Middle Eastern countries, and the older and generally more prosperous elements. As against the pioneering ideal, personal ambitions and the desire for individual professional and financial success came to the fore. The kibbutz movement and the pioneering role of the halutzim began to lose some of the aura of glory that had formerly attached to them.

On the other hand, the leftist parties and their youth movements became disenchanted with the Soviet Union and Communist ideology, so that the bitter debates between these groups and Mapai became a thing of the past. An article by Yitzhak Ben-Aharon (of Ahdut Avoda), "Daring to Change before Calamity Strikes" (January, 1963), called for an immediate union of all Socialist workers in Israel. Mapai and Ahdut Avoda began negotiations that lasted about two years and resulted in the formation of an alignment (Ma'arakh) in which the two parties were to present single electoral lists for the Histadrut and the Knesset. Within Mapai, David Ben-Gurion and the "younger generation" opposed the alignment. In February, 1965, a Mapai conference was called to consider the alignment proposal and the dismissal of Lavon. Levi Eshkol, Moshe Sharett, and Golda Meir opposed Ben-Gurion and his followers. The conference vote (59 percent for, 41 percent against) approved the alignment, and the agreement was signed in May, 1965.

The response of Ben-Gurion and six Mapai members of Knesset was to form a party of their own, *Rafi. Thus Mapai was split when Histadrut and Knesset elections were held in the fall of 1965. In the Histadrut elections (September, 1965) the alignment received 51 percent of the votes; Rafi got only 12 percent. In the Knesset elections (November, 1965) the alignment won 45 seats (by prior agreement 36 were allotted to Mapai and 9 to Ahdut Avoda), while Rafi won only 10 seats. Despite this upset, Mapai (with Ahdut Avoda) succeeded in maintaining its position as the principal party in the Histadrut and Knesset. Rafi's ambition to become a decisive political force in these institutions came to naught, and the elements that supported Ben-Gurion were unsuccessful in merging into a united party. Whereas one group was prepared to become a non-Socialist party, the majority, despite strong opposition from Ben-Gurion, wanted to rejoin Mapai. A further step toward merger was taken when, in October, 1966, the Mapai Secretariat decided to rescind Lavon's dismissal.

The tense period preceding and during the Six-Day War of 1967 increased the desire for a merger of Mapai, Ahdut Avoda, and Rafi. On 21 January 1968, the three parties met in Jerusalem and merged, the resulting party being called the *Israel Labor Party. Y. SLUTSKY

MAPAM (Mifleget ha-Po'alim ha-Me'uhedet; United Workers' Party). Left-wing Socialist Zionist political party of Israel.

History. Mapam was formed in January, 1948, when the struggle against the British mandatory power (*see* MANDATE FOR PALESTINE) was at its height, by the fusion of the *Ha-Shomer ha-Tza'ir Workers' party and the *Ahdut Avoda-Po'ale Zion party. The merger of these groups represented an amalgamation of the left wing of the Zionist movement, particularly its kibbutz-based sections. In 1930 the labor parties in mandatory Palestine, Ahdut Avoda and Ha-Po'el ha-Tza'ir, had formed *Mapai. Not satisfied with the program of this party, particularly in its socialist aspects, Ha-Shomer ha-Tza'ir declared itself an independent political trend within the Histadrut. By 1935 working people in the cities and villages who identified with its political and social views had founded the Socialist League. By 1946 Ha-Shomer ha-Tza'ir decided to change its traditional youth movement approach within Palestine, and its kibbutz movement, *Kibbutz Artzi, together with the Socialist League founded the Ha-Shomer ha-Tza'ir Workers' party.

The program of the Ha-Shomer ha-Tza'ir party continued to stress a platform of building the Jewish Homeland as well as advocating the class struggle. On the international scene it did not affiliate with the Second International, which it considered reformist and nonrevolutionary. Nor did it join the Third International, led by the Soviet Communist party, which it considered excessively centralist and which rejected Zionism as the national liberation movement of the Jewish people. Prior to the establishment of Israel, Ha-Shomer ha-Tza'ir proposed, as a solution to the Jewish-Arab conflict, a binational state with full civil and national rights for both Jews and Arabs, parity between Jews and Arabs, and guarantees for unrestricted Jewish immigration and agricultural settlement.

Meanwhile, a left-wing trend had emerged within the Mapai party. In 1944 this faction broke away from Mapai and formed the Tenu'a le-Ahdut ha-Avoda (Movement for the Unity of Labor). Opposed to Mapai's idea of a partitioned Palestine as well as to Ha-Shomer ha-Tza'ir's binational state, it sought a "Socialist Jewish state in the whole of Palestine."

There was also a smaller left-wing party, known as the Left *Po'ale Zion. Founded in 1920, this party had sought to join the Communist Third International on the basis of negotiations leading to Communist recognition of a Jewish Homeland in Palestine as the solution to the Jewish problem. The continued anti-Zionist stand of the Soviet Union led to the amalgamation of the Left Po'ale Zion with Ahdut Avoda in April, 1946.

At the end of World War II, when the struggle against the British Mandate in Palestine sharpened, the kibbutzim that formed the core of both left-wing Socialist parties had become the bases and training grounds for the underground defense forces of the Jewish community, for the Hagana and particularly its commando arm, the Palmah. Both parties played a prominent role in the organization of "illegal" immigration and in the establishment of kibbutzim in unpopulated areas in order to create security outposts as well as new economic and political realities. Both aimed at the establishment of a Socialist state in Palestine.

However, the two parties differed on two basic issues. Whereas Ha-Shomer ha-Tza'ir wanted a binational state, Ahdut Avoda-Po'ale Zion wanted a Jewish State in the whole of Palestine. Ha-Shomer ha-Tza'ir called for the unity of the two left-wing Socialist Zionist parties, while Ahdut Avoda-Po'ale Zion called for "total unity," a concept that included the Social Democratic Mapai. When the United Nations finally decided on the partition of Palestine into Jewish and Arab states and the concept of an unpartitioned Palestine, whether as a Jewish or as a binational state, became irrelevant, the two parties of the Socialist Zionist left united and formed Mapam in 1948. In the elections to the First Knesset (1949), Mapam received 19 seats and became the second largest party. But the fusion between the two groups failed and the fundamental differences persisted. A key question was the acceptance of Arabs as members of Mapam. The Ahdut Avoda leaders proposed a parallel but separate Arab party, while Ha-Shomer ha-Tza'ir held the view that in a sovereign state all political and economic entities must be organized on a territorial basis and not a nationality-group basis. Another crucial issue was the so-called "activism" or scope of military retaliation to Arab attacks and Israeli peace initiatives. Ahdut Avoda advocated sharp military responses to fedayeen (terrorist) incursions and were skeptical about Israel-sponsored peace initiatives. The majority in Mapam rejected this approach. Mapam's enthusiastic endorsement of Soviet Russia's policies changed with the Slansky trial in Prague (1952) and the 15-year imprisonment sentence passed on Mapam leader, Mordekhai Oren, who was visiting Czechoslovakia. A group led by Moshe Sneh which continued to support Soviet policies left Mapam in 1954 and joined the Israel Communist party (Maki).In September, 1954, Ahdut Avoda and a minority of Left Po'ale Zion left Mapam and after a period of independent existence rejoined Mapai to form the present-day *Israel Labor Party.

Mapam opposed the Sinai Campaign of 1956. It spearheaded the successful campaign to end the military administration in Arab areas of Israel and to secure equal membership rights for Arab workers in the Histadrut. It strengthened its role as a Jewish-Arab party, by obtaining the appointment of Abdul Aziz Zu'abi, one of its Knesset members, as Deputy Minister of Health, the highest position attained by an Israeli Arab in government. Mapam has been represented in every Knesset. From 1969 to 1984, it was part of the Labor Alignment (Ma'arakh) with the Israel Labor Party and when the latter formed the coalition with the Likud in 1984, Mapam left the Labor Alignment and went into opposition. In the 1988 elections, Mapam decided to run independently after an hiatus of 23 years. It had been part of coalition governments between 1948 and 1977 (with two exceptions, 1952–55 and 1962–65), with one or two ministers in each (Mordecai Ben-Tov, Israel Barzilai, Victor Shem-Tov, Natan Peled, Shelomo Rosen).

The decision to run independently followed a long and often sharp debate concerning the future of the Israeli Socialist-Zionist Left. Mapam received three seats in the 12th Knesset and became part of the opposition to the second National Unity (Likud-Labor) Government under Yitzhak Shamir. In 1992, it joined the Citizens' Rights and Shinvi parties to form Meretz which received 12 seats and became part of the government coalition.
sented on its Executive Committee. During its renewed independent existence in the Knesset after 1984, Mapam

had continued in an alignment with the Labor Party in the leadership of the Histadrut, together constituting 63 percent of the Histadrut electorate. In 1988, at the second session of its 10th Congress, the final severance of its organizational ties with the Labor Party was decided upon and an independent list to the 1989 Histadrut elections was nominated. Through the World Union of Mapam, with affiliates in 18 countries, it forms a constituent part of the World Zionist Organization and has been represented on the Zionist Executive and the Jewish Agency since 1949. It publishes a daily newspaper *Al ha-Mishmar*.

Ideology. As a working-class political movement, Mapam has followed a Marxist-oriented ideology whose broad outlines were set down by Ber *Borochov, the Socialist Zionist leader and theoretician. Borochov anticipated the crucial role of the national question in relation to the development of the class struggle and the attainment of socialism. He established the theoretical basis for a Socialist Zionist solution to the Jewish problem. Mapam holds that the right and duty of Jews to settle in Israel is universal. To achieve territorial concentration, it is necessary to build a National Home consisting of a productive citizenry that will bring about the social transformation of the Jewish people.

Political independence and Jewish statehood have preceded national and social liberation. In this context Mapam and, particularly, its ideological leader, Meir *Ya'ari, developed Borochov's analysis further in terms of the contemporary Israeli scene. Ya'ari's view conceived of two stages in the process of complete national and social liberation. The first stage took place in the process of the creation and development of the State of Israel. It involves the continuing cooperation of all elements within the Jewish people in encouraging and organizing the immigration of Jews from everywhere, in building and developing Israel as an economically and politically independent center of the Jewish people, and in increasing and strengthening a productive working class. The second stage is seen as a continuation of the first. It consists of the effort to establish the basis for a Socialist society in Israel. This endeavor seeks to preserve the foundations for a Socialist regime—public ownership of land, the cooperative and collective nature of 60 percent of Israeli agriculture, State and cooperative control of transportation in all its forms. The effort to maintain workers' wages and living standards must be intensified and the class struggle continued simultaneously with the constructive upbuilding of the country. The partnership between the kibbutz movement and wage workers in the cities and towns represented the symbol of this approach. This amalgam of theory and practice advocated by Mapam always took into account the fact that the Land of Israel also contained an indigenous Arab population. Mapam always sought Jewish-Arab cooperation in finding a solution to the Israel conflict. Yet, although Mapam has consistently opposed purely chauvinist attitudes and has advocated a foreign policy of neutralism and nonalignment, it stressed the fact that the roots of the Israel-Arab conflict lie in the refusal of most Arab leaders to recognize Israel's sovereignty and independence.

Six-Day War and Mapam Peace Plan. When the Six-Day War broke out in June, 1967, Mapam viewed it as a war of self-defense and survival and strongly supported Israel's right to territorial integrity and security. It proposed a peace plan (August, 1967) whose essential ingredients have been reiterated at subsequent party Congresses. Its main points include: a) no territorial annexation of the Administered Areas, with minor border rectification based on negotiations; b) a preference for a two-state solution, Israel and a Jordan-Palestinian state, but a readiness to accept any political set-up arrived at by the Jordanians and the Palestinians, including federation or confederation; c) Territory evacuated by Israel will be demilitarized and no military force will cross the Jordan River; d) United Jerusalem will remain the capital of Israel with extra-territorial status for holy sites of Islam and Christianity and a "borough" system with civic and cultural rights as well as choice of citizenship; e) rehabilitation and resettlement for Palestinian refugees within the borders of the Jordanian-Palestinian state with Israel contributing its share through reunion of families.

The continued Israeli presence in the Administered Areas after the Yom Kippur War and the historic visit of Sadat and the Camp David agreements leading to the peace treaty with Egypt brought the question of Palestinian self-determination to a new level. The Mapam approach was epitomized in 1974 by the Shemtov-Yariv formula (Victor Shemtov then Minister of Health and later Secretary-General of Mapam, and Maj. Gen. (Res.) Aaron Yariv, then Minister without Portfolio for the Israel Labor Party) which projected a readiness to enter negotiations with any Palestinian representation which accepted U.N. Resolutions 242 and 338, would forego terrorist acts, and adopted mutual recognition of Israel and the Palestinian entity as the basis for such negotiations.

The Tenth Mapam Congress (1988) took a further step in its political resolutions, by specifically including the Palestine Liberation Organization (PLO) as a possible partner in negotiations under the Shem-Tov-Yariv formula. This step evoked substantial response in international circles, particularly in the Socialist International (in which Mapam had been accepted as a full member in addition to the Israel Labor Party in 1983). It also resulted in invitations to its Secretary-General, Elazar Granot and other leaders by Egypt, China, Romania and other countries and their Socialist and Communist parties for political discussions and ongoing ties. It was the first time an avowedly Socialist-Zionist party had received such recognition.

A. SCHENKER

MAPU, ABRAHAM The first modern Hebrew novelist (b. Slobodka, Lithuania, 1807; d. Königsberg, Prussia, 1867). In his youth, he abandoned the kabbalistic tradition of his scholarly family and became a *maskil* (follower of the Haskala, Jewish Enlightenment movement). He quickly learned German, Latin, French, and Russian and read European literature eclectically. Throughout his life he earned his living as a Hebrew teacher, teaching privately in Georgenburg (1832–37), Russyeni (1837–1843), and Vilna (1844–1847). While in Russyeni, he was befriended by Senior Sachs, a leading *maskil* of the time. In Vilna, he joined the important circle of the city's *maskilim*. In 1848, he settled in Kovno where he taught at the modern Boys' School.

Mapu's first novel *Ahavat Tziyon* (Love of Zion, 1853) is a romantic novel, set in the Land of Israel during the reign of King Hezekiah. Written in a beautiful biblical Hebrew idiom, it depicts the idyllic life of Jews in a period when they were a free nation of farmers and shepherds living in their own homeland. The heroes of the novel became models for the new Jew which the *Haskala* movement strove to create: cultured, well-groomed, tolerant, and productive. *Ahavat Tziyon* was the first best-seller in modern Hebrew literature, reprinted in many editions. It was also translated into Yiddish, Russian, French, Ladino, Arabic, and Judeo-Persian.

Mapu's second novel, *Ayit Tzavu'a* (The Painted Hawk, or Hypocrite, 1857–1869) is the first Hebrew social novel. Set in mid-19th century Russia, its didactic tone is more strident. It condemns religious hypocrisy and intolerance on the one hand and assimilationism on the other. It applauds those *maskilim* who remain loyal to their people and urges Jews to engage in agriculture and other productive enterprises. In his introductions to various parts of the novel, Mapu argues that fiction rather than polemical articles affords a more effective medium for addressing the Jewish masses.

Mapu was influenced by the French romantic novelists. Like their works Mapu's were loosely constructed and full of hardly creditable heroic deeds and adventures. However, he had a masterful command of biblical Hebrew and in *Ayit Tzavu'a*, he incorporated later Hebrew elements in his style, leading to an increasing trend in that direction whenever contemporary life was portrayed in Hebrew fiction.

E. SPICEHANDLER

David Marcus.
[Zionist Archives]

MARCUS, DAVID. United States army officer, attorney, and military adviser to the Israel Army (b. New York, 1902; d. Jerusalem area, 1948). Born to an immigrant family on New York's lower East Side, Marcus received his secular schooling and traditional Jewish education in Brooklyn and studied at the City College of New York. Appointed to the US Military Academy at West Point in 1920, he received a law degree from Brooklyn Law School. He subsequently served as an assistant United States attorney for the Southern District of New York (1931–33) and with the New York City Department of Correction (first deputy commissioner, 1934–39; commissioner, 1940). Early in World War II Marcus reentered the US Army. He saw fighting in Normandy and in the Pacific theater of operations and served as legal aide at the conferences of Teheran, Dumbarton Oaks, Yalta, and Potsdam. In 1946 he was named chief of the US Army's war crimes branch.

Stationed as a colonel in the American-occupied zone of Germany, Marcus was deeply affected by the plight of the Jews in displaced-persons camps and became convinced that the only solution to their problems was resettlement in an independent Jewish State in Palestine. Returning to New York, he had just opened a law office when he was approached for help by a member of Hagana, who had come to the United States to recruit military experts who would survey the needs of the Jewish forces in Palestine and make appropriate recommendations. Late in January, 1948, Marcus left for Palestine. Here he accompanied Hagana guerrillas on raids, slipping in and out of the hands of British patrols. He dictated military manuals and made plans for Israel's defense.

Two weeks after the proclamation of Israel's independence, David Ben-Gurion appointed Marcus supreme commander of the Jerusalem front with the rank of brigadier general. He was killed on the road to Jerusalem on 10 June 1948. Buried in the cemetery of the US Military Academy, Marcus was posthumously (1951) awarded the Israeli Medal of Independence. A housing development for officer veterans of the Israel Army is named for him. His biography, *Cast a Giant Shadow*, by Ted Berkman, was published in 1962 and made into a film.

MARGOLIN, ELIEZER. Pioneer in Eretz Israel and Australian army officer (b. Belgorod, Russia, c. 1875 d. Perth, Australia, 1944). Margolin went to Eretz Israel with his parents in 1892 and took up farming in Rehovot. In 1902 after his parents' death, he left for Australia due to the difficult economic conditions prevailing at the time. He opened a small medical supplies factory in Sydney before moving to the mining town of Collie where he ran a cordial factory. He was naturalized in 1904, joining the local militia as a volunteer and was commissioned as a lieutenant in 1911 and promoted to captain in 1914. Margolin and his men joined the Australian Army during World War I and led his company which was among the first to fight at Gallipoli (1915–6) where he was cited for bravery. There he met volunteers of the Zion Mule Corps including Vladimir Jabotinsky. Later he served in France under General Sir John Monash, was wounded several times, and was promoted to Lt. Colonel. Margolin accepted Jabotinsky's proposal that he command the Second Battalion of the Jewish Regiment consisting mostly of Jewish volunteers from Canada and the U.S., and the 49th Royal Fusiliers (*see* *JEWISH LEGION).

He arrived in Palestine in 1918. Units of the Battalion broke through the Turkish lines on the Jordan River, capturing the town of Salt; Margolin was made its military governor. He cultivated friendly relations with the Eretz Israel volunteers, putting aside the normal customs of British military hierarchy.

In December 1919, when the Jewish Legion was officially named the First Judeans and given the *Menora* as its symbol, Margolin was named its commander. Though he encountered hostility from the British military command towards the Legion, he was able to implement his own ideas regarding the deployment of his command, as in the 1920 riots where his action averted further bloodshed.

During the 1921 Arab riots Margolin, without informing his superiors, mobilized both in-service and discharged legionnaires, providing them with arms from military stores and leading them in defense of Tel Aviv, which was under Arab attack. The British military authorities used this incident to disband the Legion, and Margolin chose to resign from the army rather than face a court martial.

He returned to Australia and went into farming and business without great success. A Zionist all his life, he served as vice-president of the West Australian Zionist Association. In 1950 Margolin's remains were reinterred in Rehovot.

E. HONIG

MARGOSHES, SAMUEL. Author, editor,and Zionist leader in the United States (b. Józefów, Galicia, Austria, 1887; d. New York, 1968). Margoshes became active in Zionism and general Jewish public life in early youth. He was associated with Dr. Judah L. Magnes in the founding of the Jewish Kehilla in New York. He also had a part in the founding of the Labor Zionist movement in the United States, the American Jewish Congress, the World Jewish Congress, and the Jewish Cultural Congress.

A veteran American Zionist, Margoshes was vice-president of the Zionist Organization of America and an associate member of the Actions Committee of the World Zionist Organization. A former editor of the *Day (Der Tog)* and dean of American Jewish journalists, Margoshes was the English columnist and an editorial writer of the *Day-Jewish Journal.* A. ALPERIN

MARGULIES, EMIL. Zionist leader, international lawyer, and leader in the struggle for Jewish rights (b. Sosnowiec, Russian Poland, 1877; d. Tel Aviv, 1943). Margulies settled in Austria in his early youth. In 1901 he graduated from the University of Vienna and joined the Zionist movement. He organized Zionist groups in various parts of Austria-Hungary and published articles in Austrian Zionist periodicals urging Jews to fight against assimilation. After World War I he became one of the organizers of Jewish communal and political life in the new republic of Czechoslovakia. He represented the Czechoslovak Jews in the Comité des Délégations Juives at the Paris Peace Conference. He attended Zionist Congresses and served as head of the Jewish party of Czechoslovakia.

After the rise of Hitler in 1933, Margulies and Leo Motzkin brought before the League of Nations the case of a Silesian Jew named Bernheim, who had lodged a complaint against the Nazi regime for breaking the German-Polish treaty, which guaranteed Jewish rights in Silesia. Margulies won the case, thus achieving international prominence. On the day of the German occupation of Czechoslovakia, he left for Palestine, where he continued his Zionist activities until his death. A. ALPERIN

MARGULIES, SAMUEL HIRSCH. Rabbi and communal leader in Italy (b. Berezhany, Galicia, Austria, 1858; d. Florence, 1922). After receiving a traditional education in Galicia, Margulies studied at the Jewish Theological Seminary and the University of Breslau, Germany. He held pulpits in Hamburg from 1885 to 1887 and in Weilburg, Hesse, from 1887 until 1890, when he became rabbi of Florence. In 1899 he was appointed dean of the Collegio Rabbinico Italiano, which was moved from Rome to Florence that year. A powerful personality, erudite scholar, and inspiring orator, Margulies had a profound influence on Italian Jewry and initiated its national and religious renaissance. He was active in the World Zionist Organization (WZO) and disseminated the message of Zionism in speeches and writings throughout Italy. In 1903 he arranged an interview between Herzl and King Victor Emmanuel III. In 1919 he attended a conference of religious Jewish organizations held in Zurich at the initiative of Agudat Israel, intending to mediate between that body and the WZO.

Margulies founded and edited the scholarly *Rivista Israelitica* (1904–15). In 1910 he founded *La Settimama Israelitica*, a weekly which served as the mouthpiece of the Pro Cultura movement, set up by his disciples to further the revival of Italian Jewry, and which Margulies directed until the end of 1913.

Lord Marks. [Zionist Archives]

MARKS, SIMON, LORD. English businessman and Zionist leader (b. Manchester, 1888; d. London, 1964). The son of an immigrant from Poland, Marks joined the department store chain founded by his father. At the time of his death he was chairman of the board of the establishment, which, as Marks and Spencer, Ltd., had become one of the best-known enterprises of its kind in England. Marks was introduced to Zionism by Chaim Weizmann, whom he met in 1913 while Weizmann was on the faculty of the University of Manchester. With his brothers-in-law Israel Moses Sieff (later Baron Sieff) and Harry Sacher, Marks was a member of the Manchester group of English Zionists who helped Weizmann reach wide circles in the British and Jewish public. During the period immediately preceding the issuance of the Balfour Declaration, he was in charge of the Zionist Office set up by Weizmann in London. After World War I, Marks was honorary secretary of the Zionist delegation to the Paris Peace Conference.

Marks and his family made munificent contributions to Zionist and Israeli causes. He was for some time chairman of the Keren ha-Yesod Committee in England and a vice-president of the Zionist Federation of Great Britain and Ireland. With Israel Sieff he set up the Sieff Research Institute, which became the nucleus of the Weizmann Institute of Science.

After Hitler's rise to power, Marks developed plans for the large-scale settlement of German Jews in Palestine in cooperation with the Jewish Agency.

He was knighted in 1944 and raised to the peerage as Baron Marks in 1961. At the time of his death he was president of the Joint Palestine Appeal in Great Britain.

MARMOREK. Family of Zionists.

Alexander Marmorek. Bacteriologist and Zionist leader in France (b. Mielnice, Galicia, Austria, 1865; d. Paris, 1923). He studied at the University of Vienna, obtaining his doctorate in medicine in 1887. An obstetrician at first, he later turned to bacteriology. When, in 1893, he was denied the post of assistant head of the department of medicine at the University of Vienna because of his religion, he accepted an invitation by Louis Pasteur to become head of laboratory research at the Pasteur Institute in Paris. There Marmorek developed an antistreptococcus serum and pioneered in the treatment of scarlet fever, tuberculosis, typhus, and diabetes. Several years before the outbreak of World War I he left the Pasteur Institute to pursue independent research in his own laboratory. During the war he served as a physician in prisoner-of-war camps in Transylvania. After the war he returned to Paris to work with the Nobel Prize winner Charles Richet.

Marmorek's association with Zionism began during his student days in Vienna, when he joined the Kadimah student Zionist organization. Together with his brothers the architect Oskar and Isidor (the latter, a lawyer in Austria, who attended the Third Zionist Congress in 1899), he became one of the closest friends and helpers of Herzl and Max Nordau. A founder of the French Zionist journal *L'Echo Sioniste*, Marmorek was for many years president of the Zionist Federation of France and a member of the Greater Actions Committee (1897–1913). He remained consistently faithful to Herzl's idea of political as against practical Zionism. Opposing the Zionist leadership, he criticized the Balfour Declaration and the British Mandate for Palestine as politically inadequate and incapable of promoting the realization of Zionist aims.

Prior to World War I Marmorek founded with others the Popular Jewish University, which became a center of Jewish intellectual life for new immigrants in Paris.

Oskar Marmorek, his brother, architect (b. Skala, Galicia, Austria, 1863; d. Vienna, 1909). He studied at the Institute of Technology in Vienna, where, together with his brother Alexander he joined the Kadimah student Zionist organization. Completing his studies in Paris, he returned in 1889 to Vienna, where he soon became a well-known architect, constructing synagogues and exhibition halls in Vienna and Budapest.

An early collaborator of Herzl, Marmorek was a founder of the World Zionist Organization (WZO) and a founder of and early co-worker on *Die Welt*, the WZO organ. He attended the First Zionist Congress (1897). The following year he was elected to the Inner Actions Committee, on which he served until 1905. In May, 1901, he accompanied Herzl to Constantinople. At the Fifth Zionist Congress (1901) he submitted plans for the construction of a permanent home for the Congress. In 1902 he took part in the *El-Arish Expedition acting as secretary of the party with the special task of investigating building and housing possibilities.

In 1904 he was elected to the Jewish Community Council of Vienna. Marmorek served as the model for the character of Steineck, the architect in Herzl's book **Old-New Land*. He was found dead from a bullet wound, presumably self-inflicted, at the grave of his father in Vienna.

MARSHALL, LOUIS. Cofounder of the expanded *Jewish Agency; constitutional lawyer and Jewish communal leader in the United States (b. Syracuse, N.Y., 1856; d. Zurich, 1929). After practicing law in Syracuse, he moved in 1894 to New York City, where he became known as an outstanding attorney and Jewish communal figure. In the sphere of Jewish interests, he responded to every call from Jewish communities in other countries and reacted promptly and vigorously to any infringement of the status of the American Jew or to any detraction of Jewish dignity, whether

Louis Marshall.
[Zionist Archives]

from government agencies or from private sources. He was the chief architect, leader, and organizer of the movement which led to the abrogation, in 1911, of a trade treaty with Tsarist Russia, in effect since 1832, because of Russia's refusal to honor American passports held by Jews. In the late 1920s he obtained a public apology from Henry Ford, retracting the slanderous series "The International Jew," which had been printed in Ford's *Dearborn Independent.*

In 1906 Marshall helped found the *American Jewish Committee, which soon emerged as a leading body of American Jewry. *De facto* leader of the committee from its inception, he was elected its president in 1912 and held that post until his death. While president of New York's Temple Emanu-El, the world's most influential Reform congregation, he was also chairman of the Board of Overseers of the Jewish Theological Seminary of America, the spiritual and academic center of Conservative Judaism.

At the outbreak of World war I, Marshall organized the American Jewish Relief Committee, which played a leading role in the formation of the American Jewish Joint Distribution Committee. Initially opposed to the convening of an American Jewish Congress, he later helped bring the congress into being and fully accepted its postwar program, including the demand for minority rights for the Jews in Eastern Europe, a demand about which he entertained serious doubts. He was a member, and subsequently chairman, of the *Comité des Délégations Juives at the Paris Peace Conference, where he played a major role in gaining the approval of many Jewish requests.

Initially inclined toward anti-Zionism, Marshall became the outstanding spokesman of the non-Zionists after the issuance of the Balfour Declaration in 1917. He endorsed the declaration, as did the American Jewish Committee, and worked for its implementation. In the 1920s he cooperated with Chaim Weizmann in organizing the expanded Jewish Agency for Palestine. He died a few days after the formal launching of the expanded Agency at a plenary assembly in Zurich, in 1929, where he had been elected chairman of the Jewish Agency Council.

C.B. SHERMAN

MARTON, ERNO. Lawyer, journalist, parliamentarian, and Zionist leader (b. Dicsoszenmarton, Transylvania, Hungary, 1896; d. Tel Aviv, 1960). In 1918 Marton founded and became publisher-editor of **Uj Kelet* (New East) in Kolozsvar (now Cluj, Romania), which emerged as the chief organ of Transylvanian Jewry until 1944. Active also in Romanian political life, he was named deputy mayor of Cluj in 1932 and was elected to Parliament as a candidate of the Jewish party.

Marton was a leading force in the Transylvanian Zionist movement. Shortly after the German occupation of Hungary (which after 1940 included northern Transylvania), he escaped to unoccupied Romania, where he engaged in rescue operations in behalf of Hungarian Jewry. In 1946 he testified in Vienna before the Anglo-American Committee of Inquiry on the status of Hungarian and Romanian Jewry and helped draft the Jewish proposals for the peace treaties with Romania and Hungary. After World War II he resumed publication of *Uj Kelet* in Tel Aviv, where it became the leading organ of the Jewish immigrants from Hungary. In addition, he published a number of historical, sociological, and statistical studies, including *A zsido nemzet Erdelyben* (The Jewish Nation in Transylvania, 1922) and *A Zsido nep vilaghelyzete 1941-ben* (The International Position of the Jews in 1941, 1942). R.L. BRAHAM

MASADA. Natural fortress in the Judean desert on the western shores of the Dead Sea. The rock rises almost perpendicularly above its surroundings. The fortified palace built by King Herod is on the upper plateau. In 42 BCE, Herod fortified Masada, the earlier site of a Hasmonean citadel, making it an impregnable stronghold. Soon after his death (4 BCE), the Romans set up a small garrison there. In the Jewish war against the Romans which began in 66 CE, a group of Zealots massacred the Romans and seized control. They lived there for six years and were the last outpost to hold out against the Romans. Eventually in 72 the 10th Roman Legion was moved up to besiege it and built an extensive rampart for heavy siege machines. After seven months, the 960 defenders led by Eleazar ben Yair took their own lives (except for 2 women and five children) rather than be enslaved by the Romans. Their heroic behavior became an inspiration for modern Israeli youth who come on pilgrimage and take the oath 'Masada shall not fall again'. Extensive excavations, led by Yigael Yadin, began in 1963 and uncovered Herod's palaces, storerooms, fortifications, a bathhouse and water supply system. A synagogue used by the Zealots was found, apparently on the site of an earlier one used in Herodian times, the earliest synagogue found in Israel. Many parchments, papyri and inscribed ostraca were also discovered. The site attracts many visitors and a cable car has been constructed to the top.

MASADA. Youth movement of the Zionist Organization of America (ZOA) which is active in 15 districts in various parts of the United States. Masada was organized in the 1940s under the auspices of the American Zionist Youth Commission, became independent in 1946, and played an active part in the struggle for Israel during the years 1947–48. Reorganized in 1952 under the name Young Zionists of the ZOA, it readopted its original name Masada in 1963. Internationally, Masada is affiliated with Israel ha-Tze'ira (of the *World Union of General Zionists) and with the Maccabi World Federation.

The movement is directed by its Executive Board, which is elected annually by the National Masada Convention. Masada is assisted by national, regional, and district ZOA youth committees as well as by the personnel of the ZOA Youth Department. The link with Israel is strengthened by emissaries sent from Israel by Israel ha-Tze'ira with the help of the *World Zionist Organization's Youth and he-Halutz Department. The summer activities of Masada consist of teenage, collegiate, and young adult tours and camps in Israel. In 1987 over 750 young people participated in these camps. Camp Yehuda in Michigan and Camp Kefar Masada are Masada-ZOA camps for youngsters aged 8 to 16; they include regional Masada leadership institutes.

Masada fosters aliya in its membership and keeps in close touch with its members who have settled in Israel. The Movement has hostels in Tel Aviv and Jerusalem where Masada members of settlement groups may live up to one year from the time of immigration. A. EVEN

MASLIANSKY, ZVI HIRSCH. Zionist orator (b Slutsk, Russia, 1856; d. New York, 1943). After his marriage in 1875 Masliansky settled in Pinsk, where he taught Hebrew. In 1881, when news of the pogroms in southern Russia reached him, he began to lecture from synagogue pulpits on the Return to Zion and became active in the Hovevei Zion movement in Pinsk. In 1888 he moved to Yekaterinoslav (now Dnepropetrovsk) and was among the founders of the Hovevei Zion center there. In 1892 he was sent on a tour through Russia to promote emigration to Eretz Israel. He traveled about for four years, helping found new Hovevei Zion groups and strengthening those already in existence. Masliansky was arrested many times during his travels and at one time was given a month to leave Russia. He subsequently wrote an account of his travel impressions.

In 1895 he went to the United States. On the way there, he stopped at Jewish centers in Germany, England, Belgium, the Netherlands, and France, where he addressed numerous gatherings. After extensive speaking tours in the United States, he settled in New York. From 1898 on he lectured regularly on behalf of the Jewish Educational Alliance in New York. He exercised great influence as a Zionist orator, championing the preservation of tradition and the cause of Zion in free America and drawing large audiences. From 1900 to 1910 he was vice-president of the Federation of American Zionists and in 1921 he took part in the 12th Zionist Congress, also visiting Palestine that year.

Masliansky was active also in various organizations supporting religious educational institutions in Brooklyn. From 1902 to 1905 he published the daily *Die Yidishe Welt*. Collections of his sermons, lectures, and memoirs, in both Hebrew and Yiddish, appeared in book form (1909–15, 1929). G. BAT-YEHUDA

MASSEL, JOSEPH EZEKIEL. Hebrew poet and Zionist leader (b. Vilna Province, Russia, 1850; d. Manchester, England, 1912). Arriving in England in the 1890s, Massel settled in Manchester, where he opened a printing and publishing office. A pioneer Zionist, he was active in the Dorshei Zion Society. At the First Zionist Congress (1897), he called for the amalgamation of the Hovevei Zion movement and the societies for settlement in Eretz Israel with the World Zionist Organization. He was a delegate also to the Second and Fourth Congresses (1898; 1900).

Massel translated English poetry into Hebrew, as well as poems of Jewish and general interest. Some of his original Hebrew poems were republished in Zionist papers and set to music. *Mi-Kenaf Ha-Aretz* (From the End of the Earth), an anthology of Massel's poems and translations from the English appeared in 1898. Massel edited *Ha-Makhela: Gallery of*

Hebrew Poets (1903), a unique collection of 94 biographies of Hebrew poets from 1725 to 1903. J. FRAENKEL

Foundation day of Kibbutz Masu'ot Yitzhak, 1945. [Central Zionist Archives]

MASU'OT YITZHAK. Religious moshav shitufi in the southern coastal plain, 8 mi. (13 km.) northeast of Ashkelon. It was founded in 1945 as a kibbutz in the Hebron Hills, as the Etzion Bloc's second settlement. When it fell to the Arab Legion in May 1948, its settlers became prisoners-of-war. After their release they established their kibbutz at the present site, a few years later changing the structure of their settlement. They engage in intensive farming and have a metal factory. The name Masu'ot Yitzhak honors Chief Rabbi Yitzhak Halevi Herzog. Population (1987), 492. E. ORNI

MATZKIN, ROSE ELLIS. Zionist community affairs leader, lecturer in the US (b. Ellis Island, N.Y.). Matzkin trained as a teacher. A dynamic speaker, she rose through the ranks of local community and Zionist affairs organizations to head most of Hadassah's national departments, and in 1972 began a four-year term as the Women's Zionist Organization's 15th president. She was a member of the Executive Board of the World Confederation of United Zionists and was vice-president of the American Zionist Youth Foundation. M. LEVIN

Immigrants arriving from Mauritius, 1945. [Central Zionist Archives]

MAURITIUS CAMPS. British detention camps on the island of Mauritius in the Indian Ocean, set up for "illegal" immigrants to Palestine (*see* "ILLEGAL" IMMIGRATION). From December, 1940 to August, 1945, about 1,500 "illegal" immigrants were held on Mauritius. Soon after arriving in Haifa in November, 1940, aboard the *S.S. Atlantic*, these refugees from Danzig, Austria, and Czechoslovakia, including 621 women and 116 children, had been forcibly transferred to British ships and taken to Mauritius. En route to Mauritius 22 of the deportees died of typhoid and a further nineteen of other causes. During their stay on the island, the immigrants suffered from the harsh camp regime and from tropical diseases. Some were released to join the Allied armed forces, but their dependants remained in detention. In 1945, the 1,310 surviving detainees were released; the majority returned to Palestine. B. WASSERSTEIN

MAY, MORTIMER. Businessman and Zionist leader in the United States (b. Laconia, N.H., 1892; d. Miami Beach, 1974). The son of immigrants from Germany, he was brought to Nashville, Tenn., as a child, then studied at Columbia University in New York, graduating in 1914. Returning to Nashville to enter the family business, he was first drawn to Zionism after World War I, partly through his admiration for Justice Louis D. Brandeis. He joined the Nashville Zionist District in 1926 and helped make Zionism fashionable among Jews in the South. Raised in German-style Reform Judaism and active in Reform congregational life (he was president of Nashville's Vine Street Temple from 1940 to 1943 and a member of the Board of Governors of the Union of American Hebrew Congregations from 1948 on), he urged the teaching of the Hebrew language in Reform religious schools.

Soon after joining the Zionist movement, May became interested in the American Jewish Congress and, in 1936, went to Geneva to attend the first meeting of the World Jewish Congress. Active in Jewish and general communal affairs, he attended the American Jewish Conference in 1943. He held leading positions in the Zionist Organization of America, serving as its president from 1954 to 1956. He attended the 21st to 24th and the 26th Zionist Congresses. In 1946 he became a member of the Zionist Actions Committee. He was a member of the Board of Directors of the American Committee for the Weizmann Institute of Science (from 1945 on), vice-president of the Council of Jewish Federations and Welfare Funds (1950–58), and a member of the boards of the United Israel Appeal and the America-Israel Cultural Foundation.

MAYER, ASTORRE. Manufacturer, philanthropist, and Zionist leader in Italy (b. Milan, 1906; d. there, 1977). Graduated as an industrial engineer in 1928, Mayer was president of the Italian Zionist Federation in 1947–48, honorary Consul General of Israel from 1950 to 1961, honorary president of the Italian Committee of the Jewish National Fund, and a member of the Council of the Union of Italian-Jewish Communities. While president of the Jewish Community of Milan, an office he held for many years, he built the school of the community, one of the finest Jewish educational institutions in Europe. In addition, he was president of the Standing Conference on European Community Services. He made generous donations to philanthropic, Jewish, and Zionist institutions and to various projects in Israel. G. ROMANO

MAZAR (MAISLER), BENJAMIN. Archeologist, historian, and president and rector of the *Hebrew University of Jerusalem (b. Ciechanowiec, Russian Poland, 1906). Mazar studied geography, history, and archeology at the Universities of Giessen and Berlin. Settling in Palestine in 1929, he engaged in archeological excavations in many parts of the country. In 1943 he was appointed instructor, in 1947 lecturer, and in 1951 professor of the history of the Jewish people in the Biblical period and of the archeology of Palestine, at the Hebrew University. Mazar was rector of the university from 1952 to 1961 and its president from 1953 to 1961, during which time he was largely responsible for the establishment of its Givat Ram campus. From 1967 Mazar was in charge of the excavations at the Western and Southern Walls of the Temple Mount.

Mazar was a member of the Israel Academy of Sciences and Humanities. In 1968 he was a recipient of the Israel Prize. His books include *History of Palestine* (1938), *Excavations at Beth She'arim* (1940), *Historical Atlas of Palestine: Biblical Period* (1942), *Ein Gedi* (1966), *The Excavations in the Old City of Jerusalem* (1971), and *The Mountain of the Lord* (1975).

MAZE, JACOB. Rabbi and communal worker in Russia (b. Mogilev, Russia, 1860; d. Moscow, 1924). Maze studied law at the University of Moscow. In 1882 he joined the Hovevei Zion movement, and two years later, as a student in Moscow, helped found the Benei Zion Society. An excellent orator, he visited various cities to establish Hovevei Zion groups. He also contributed articles to the Hebrew paper *Ha-Melitz,* advocating emphasis on the education of the young generation.

In 1890 Maze participated in the first general meeting of the Odessa Committee. With Dr. Nahum Zack, he founded a society for the establishment of a settlement in Eretz Israel by wealthy Moscow Jews. In 1891 he visited Eretz Israel on behalf of the society, opening negotiations for the purchase of land, but the project did not materialize.

In 1893 he was appointed government rabbi of the Jewish Community of Moscow, serving in that capacity until his death. In 1913 he testified for the defense in the Mendel Beilis blood libel trial. Maze was one of the founders of Tarbut (the Hebrew culture organization) in Moscow, and he interceded with the Soviet authorities to prevent the destruction of Hebrew cultural institutions.

MAZIA, AARON MEYER. Physician and pioneer in Eretz Israel (b. near Mogilev, Russia, 1858; d. Jerusalem, 1930). Mazia went to western Europe to pursue secular studies. After the Russian pogroms of the early 1880s, he became interested in settling in Eretz Israel and moved there after completing his medical studies in 1887. Mazia practiced medicine in settlements and was active in the field of public health. In 1902 he settled in Jerusalem, where he served as chief physician at the Bikur Holim Hospital.

Mazia devoted many years to research on Hebrew medical terminology, preparing a medical dictionary that was published posthumously by Saul Tschernichowsky in 1934. He was also an editor of *Ha-Refu'a*, the publication of the Hebrew Physicians Association in Palestine, and a founder of the Jewish Society for the Exploration of Palestine and its Antiquities, which published a collection of scientific essays in his memory in 1935. G. KRESSEL

MEDICINE IN ISRAEL. *See* HEALTH AND HEALTH SERVICES IN ISRAEL.

MEGED, AHARON. Writer of Hebrew prose (b. Wloczlavek, Poland, 1920). Meged was six years old when he was taken to Palestine. He was raised in Ra'anana and studied at the Herzliya Secondary School in Tel Aviv. Between 1939 and 1950 he was a member of Kibbutz Sedot Yam. He served as editor of the literary supplement, *Masa*, for many years.

Meged's first book of short stories, *Ru'ah Yamim* (Sea Wind, 1950) contains realistic short stories based on his experiences in his sea-faring kibbutz. Following the establishment of the State, Meged's fiction took on a satirical bent as it depicted the cynicism and loss of idealism following the War of Independence: *Hedvah va-Ani* (Hedvah and I, 1954), *Yisrael Haverim* (All Israel Are Friends, 1956), *Mikre ha-Kesil* (Fool's Fate, 1960). With the last work, Meged moved from realism to symbolism. *Ha-Beriha* (The Flight, 1962) employs motifs from the book of Jonah and *Nicaragua* deals with the alienation of a young Israeli from his Jewish roots. His other works include *Ha-Hai al-ha-Met*, 1965; (The Living on the Dead, 1970), *Asahel* (English translation, 1982), and, *Foigelman*, (1987). Meged also wrote for the stage. He dramatized *Hedvah and I*, and was the author of *Hannah Senesh, Genesis*, and *I Like Mike* which was made into a motion picture. E. SPICEHANDLER

MEGIDDO. Ancient fortress town which guarded the "Sea Road" connecting Egypt with Mesopotamia. Its mound is at the strategic point where the narrow thoroughfare of the Iron Valley issues into the broad Jezreel Valley. Excavations revealed over 20 strata of habitation beginning with the Chalcolithic era (4th millennium BCE). During the Early Bronze period (3rd millennium BCE), Canaanite temples stood there. In the Middle Bronze period (2nd millennium BCE), Megiddo was long ruled by the Egyptians. On the "fields of Megiddo," Deborah vanquished a big Canaanite confederation (Judges 4:5), but Megiddo was finally taken only by David and fortified by Solomon (I Kings 9:15). Excavations led by Yigael Yadin uncovered structures built by King Ahab, including large stables for chariot horses, water installations, fortification gates, etc. In 733/32 BCE the Assyrians took Megiddo and made it the capital of a province. Both Napoleon (in 1799) and Gen. Allenby (in 1918) defeated the Turks at Megiddo. The site ("Har Megiddo" or "Armageddon") symbolizes, principally in Christian tradition, the ultimate battlefield. The mound is open to visitors as an archeological site. In 1964, Pope Paul VI crossed the armistice line between Jordan and Israel near there and was welcomed at Megiddo by President Shazar.

In 1949, the kibbutz Megiddo was founded south of the mound. It engages in intensive farming and has industrial enterprises. Population (1987), 406. E. ORNI

MEI AMI. Moshav shitufi in the Iron Hills, founded in 1963 as a Nahal outpost on the pre-1967 Jordanian border near the Arab town Um al-Fahm. It engages in farming and has a factory. After 1967 it became a base for the founding of new settlements in northwestern Samaria. Its name "Water of My People" sounds similar to Miami (Florida), whose Jewish community helped finance the reclamation of the land. Population (1987), 170. E. ORNI

MEINERZHAGEN, RICHARD. Soldier-statesman, author, Zionist (b. London 1878; d. London 1967). He was educated at Harrow and joined the army in 1899, serving in India and East Africa and, during World War I, in Palestine and France.

Brought up in an upper-class family, Meinerzhagen might never have noticed the Jews and their problems had he not witnessed a pogrom in Odessa in March 1910 and resolved to help the Jews in the future. His chance came during 1917–1920 when serving as a Military Intelligence Officer in the East (1917) and later as Chief Political Officer in Syria and Palestine (1919–20). Aaron Aaronsohn, with whom he had collaborated, converted him to Zionism. Captivated by the Palestinian Jews, he believed that they would make good and that a Jewish State would eventually emerge.

In 1919 Meinerzhagen was a member of the British military delegation to the Peace Conference in Paris where he met Balfour, General Smuts, Weizmann, Emir Feisal and Lawrence of Arabia. He prepared a memorandum for Prime Minister Lloyd George advocating the British annexation of Sinai. The Peninsula was not legally owned by Egypt, and its possession, he claimed, could give Britain a useful base and a buffer between Egypt and the Jewish National Home.

In July 1919 he was appointed Chief Political Officer in Syria and Palestine where he had a constant battle with the pro-Arab British military administration. He tracked their involvement in the 1920 Easter riots in Jerusalem and was shocked to discover that British officers were actively implicated in this episode and plotting against their own government. His report incurred the wrath of General Allenby who demanded his summary dismissal. Although the Foreign Office insisted that Meinerzhagen had acted loyally and refused to accede to Allenby's demand, Meinerzhagen eventually had to go.

Both Lloyd George and Lord Curzon thought highly of him and when Winston Churchill was appointed Colonial Secretary in 1921, he invited him to join the Middle East Department as Military Adviser and Inspector-General of local troops in Palestine, Aden, and Mesopotamia. He stayed at the Colonial Office until 1924. Throughout this period he continued to argue boldly for increased Jewish immigration; for the exclusion of Haj-Amin el-Husseini, the Mufti; and for steps towards the creation of a Jewish State. His interest in Palestine and his connection with the region continued until the end of his life.

He published a number of books on ornithology, as well as *Kenya Diary* (1957) and *Middle East Diary, 1917–1956* (1959). I. FRIEDMAN

MEIR (MEYERSON), GOLDA (née Golda Mabovitch). Israeli stateswoman and labor leader (b. Kiev, Russia, 1898; d. Tel Aviv, 1978). In 1906 she was taken to the United States by her parents. The family settled in Milwaukee, where she was graduated from high school and enrolled in the Milwaukee Normal School. A Socialist as well as a Jewish nationalist, she joined Po'ale Zion in 1915. As a gifted propagandist in Yiddish and English, she attracted national attention.

Golda Meir. [Israel Govt. Press Office]

In 1921 she and her husband, Morris Meyerson, left the United States to settle in Palestine. They joined the kibbutz Merhavya in the Jezreel Valley, where Golda Meyerson soon became involved in political and social activities which took her away from the kibbutz. In 1928 she became executive secretary of the Mo'etzet ha-Po'alot (Working Women's Council), a task which required a two-year stay (1932–34) as an emissary in the United States to the American counterpart of the council, the Pioneer Women organization.

When she returned to Palestine in 1934, she was invited to join the Executive Committee of the Histadrut. She rapidly rose in the leadership of the Histadrut, becoming the head of its Political Department. In the 1940s, when Jewish Palestine was engaged in a struggle with the British mandatory power to bring in Jewish refugees, Meyerson was in the forefront of the conflict both as an exponent and as a practical organizer of its several facets. When the British, determined to crush the Hagana and Jewish resistance, arrested the male leaders of the yishuv, including Moshe Sharett (Shertok), head of the Political Department of the Jewish Agency, Golda Meyerson was chosen acting head, in which capacity she represented Jewish Palestine in the difficult negotiations with the British mandatory power. Since Sharett, upon his release from Latrun, left for the Zionist Congress and then the United States, Meyerson served as the de facto head of the Political Department in Jerusalem until the establishment of the State of Israel.

After the passage of the partition resolution in November, 1947, Meyerson became engaged in two major endeavors prior to the formal declaration of statehood. In January, 1948, she went to the United States to make the first of several appeals to enlist the aid of American Jewry. On 10 May 1948 (four days before the official establishment of the State), she had a secret meeting with King Abdullah in Transjordan, in the course of which she sought to persuade him not to join the Arab states in their attack on the Jewish State.

Following the establishment of the State of Israel, Meyerson was appointed Minister to Moscow, a post she held until April, 1949. After Israel's first elections in 1949, which resulted in a coalition headed by Mapai, Meyerson, as a leading Mapai figure, was invited to join the Cabinet. She returned to Israel to become Minister of Labor. Her tenure was marked by her vigorous pressure for a housing and road-building program.

In 1956 Golda Meyerson became Foreign Minister, a post she held until 1965. She Hebraized her name to Meir, and soon became a renowned figure on the international scene and at the United Nations. Among her achievements was the establishment of friendly relations with emergent African nations.

On her retirement from the Foreign Ministry, Meir became secretary of Mapai, a post she held until 1968. In March, 1969, following the death of Levi Eshkol, Golda Meir became Prime Minister of Israel. In view of her age, it was believed in some circles that she would hold the position only in a caretaker capacity until the elections called for later that year. As in the past, however, she proved herself a forceful leader. After the 1969 elections she formed a broad coalition government, including almost all parties, to guide Israel in its critical "no-war-no-peace" situation. That fall, too, she toured the United States (for the first time in her new position). She was received with full honors in Washington, where she conferred at length with Pres. Richard M. Nixon and other high American officials. She succeeded in maintaining a united home front in the face of serious external challenges and the opposition of Gahal, the parliamentary bloc of Herut and Likud led by Menahem Begin, who attacked her policies as being too conciliatory towards the Arabs.

Deeply concerned by the low economic status of immigrants from the Arab countries, she sought to close the gap between the underprivileged and more affluent sectors of the population. To promote social integration she introduced measures to provide better housing and special educational facilities. In her search for peace she held many secret meetings with international and Arab leaders, hoping that they might lead to negotiations with the Arab states. One of these meetings was with President Ceausescu of Romania in 1972. Although he informed her that President Sadat was willing to meet an Israeli leader, nothing came of this possibility at that time. In her Arab policy she favored direct negotiations and upheld the Labor Party program, whose chief features were those of the Allon Plan (*see* ALLON, YIGAL). In January, 1973, she was received at the Vatican by Pope Paul VI, the first time an Israeli prime minister was given an audience with the pope.

At the height of her international prestige, the surprise attack of the *Yom Kippur War in October, 1973, subjected her government to bitter criticism. Though the Agranat Commission of Inquiry absolved her of responsibility in Israel's initial setback and praised her actions during that period, she never recovered from the trauma of that war. Reelected as prime minister in December, 1973, accusations against her cabinet in the aftermath of the war and divisions within Mapai led her to resign her office in June, 1974.

After her retirement she wrote her autobiography, *My Life* (1975). At her death, after a long illness, she was generally viewed as one of the great political leaders of her time and one of its foremost women. M. SYRKIN

MEIR, YA'AKOV. Sephardi Chief Rabbi of Palestine (b. Jerusalem, 1856; d. there, 1939). A member of the Executive of the Sephardi community of Eretz Israel and its rabbinical court, he worked to establish harmony among the various communities. Active in Jerusalem communal affairs, he helped build several new neighborhoods and set up emergency medical and water supply units when the city was stricken with a cholera epidemic and drought.

Ya'akov Meir. [Zionist Archives]

In 1906 Meir was chosen chief rabbi of Jerusalem, but his appointment was vetoed by the chief rabbi of Constantinople because of his Zionist affiliations. He became chief rabbi of Salonika, founding many educational and philanthropic institutions. When Salonika was annexed by Greece, he gained the friendship of the Greek royal family and was able to secure a variety of services for his community. Toward the end of World War I he assisted the volunteer movement of Salonika Jews to form a corps to fight with the British in Palestine. He was also in constant touch with Zionist leaders.

He returned to Palestine after the war. After the Arab riots of 1920 he was a member of the delegation to the Colonial Office in London. In 1921 he was chosen one of the first two Chief Rabbis of Palestine, becoming Chief Rabbi of the Sephardi community, with the title Rishon le-Zion. He was a member of the First Asefat ha-Nivharim of the yishuv, a Mizrachi delegate to the 13th Zionist Congress (1923), and honorary president of the World Federation of Sephardi Communities. He received a number of decorations from foreign governments, including the French Legion of Honor. Y. RAPHAEL

MEIROVICZ, MENASHE. Pioneer in Eretz Israel (b. Nikolayev, Ukraine, Russia, 1860; d. Rishon le-Zion, 1949). The Warsaw pogroms of 1882, which he witnessed, convinced him that there was no future for the Jews in Russia. He joined a *Bilu group and emigrated to Eretz Israel. On his way there, he spent some time in Constantinople trying, with leading Bilu members, to obtain land in Eretz Israel from the Turkish authorities for the settlement of Jews. After his arrival, he went to Rishon le-Zion, where he worked as an agricultural laborer, and eventually settled there.

He conducted planting experiments and proposed the establishment of settlements with wine growing as the main industry. He also experimented with silkworms and wrote a booklet about raising them. Meirovicz wrote articles in the Hebrew and Russian-Jewish press on the development of the settlements and was one of the editors of the first Jewish agricultural periodical in the country (1893–95), which appeared first in Yiddish and later in Hebrew. He also edited a collection of Hebrew folk songs, *Shirei-Am Zion* (1897), and wrote a book about the settlements in Russian (1900).

In 1903–04 Meirovicz was the representative of the Odessa Committee in Eretz Israel. In 1903 he became the director of the Agudat ha-Koremim (Winegrowers' Association), serving in this capacity for 30 years. In 1913 he participated in the founding of the Union of the Settlements and, after World War I, when the union became the Hitahdut ha-Ikarim (Farmers' Federation), was elected its chairman. He was a member of the Va'ad Zemani (Provisional Council) of the Jews of Palestine and later a member of the Va'ad Le'umi. I. KLAUSNER

MEISEL-SCHOCHET, HANNA. *See* MAISEL-SHOHAT, HANNA.

MEKOROT WATER COMPANY LTD. (in brief *mekorot,* Hebrew for "sources"). Organization responsible for the construction and operation of Israel's national water supply system. Mekorot's shares are owned in equal parts by the government, the national institutions (Jewish Agency and Jewish National Fund) and the General Federation of Labor (Histadrut).

Mekorot was founded in 1937 for the purpose of constructing and operating the first regional water supply scheme, conducting water from wells in the neighborhood of Kefar Hasidim—Usha (Haifa Bay) to the city of Haifa and to the western Jezreel Valley, for irrigation. Levi Eshkol—who was later to become Prime Minister of Israel—instigated the foundation of the company and was its first director. A second regional water supply scheme was constructed in 1947, to bring drinking water to newly established settlements in the northern Negev.

After World War II, Mekorot was active in the preparation of a national plan for water resources development. After the War of Independence, a master plan for water resources development was finalized and the construction of regional water supply schemes, and later, of the National Water Carrier, was initiated. For this purpose, the technical department of Mekorot was enlarged and transformed into a national planning company called *Tahal, charged with the planning of the works, while Mekorot was entrusted with their construction and operation.

Mekorot is organized on a regional basis, comprising four regional offices, and one responsible for the operation of the National Water Carrier. The central offices as well as central workshops, stores, and laboratories are located in the Tel Aviv area. Mekorot has two subsidiary companies: one of them (Shaham, Hebrew acronym for electrical and mechanical services) supplies electrical and mechanical engineering services, and the other is in charge of construction of water works, and operates also as a building contractor in the private market, both in Israel and abroad.

In 1985, the company and its subsidiaries employed a staff of 3,500. It supplied 1.1 milliard cubic meters of water per year to 3,500 corporate consumers (towns, settlements, villages, industries, etc.). Peak daily supply amounted to 4.5 million cubic meters. The company's water supply network comprises 3,300 miles (5,000 km.) of pipelines, 375 operational reservoirs, 400 pumping stations, 25 storage reservoirs with a total capacity of 50 million cubic meters, and about 700 boreholes.

Annual energy consumption for the operation of the system amounted to 1,500 milliard kwh. Z. SHIFTAN

MELCHETT, 1ST BARON (Sir Alfred Moritz Mond). Industrialist, Cabinet Minister, and Zionist leader in England

Mekorot Water Company engineer (second from left) showing workers how pipes are to be transported. [Keren Ha-Yesod]

(b. Farnworth, England, 1868; d. London, 1930). The son of Ludwig Mond, who revolutionized the British chemical industry by his alkali manufacturing process, he entered his father's chemical firm, which he later headed, and expanded the business into the vast concern known today as Imperial Chemical Industries. He also organized the International Nickel Company of Canada.

A Liberal member of Parliament from 1906 to 1926, Mond was created a baronet in 1910, and served in the Cabinet of David Lloyd George as First Commissioner of Works (1916–21) and Minister of Health (1921–22). In 1926 he broke with the Liberals and joined the Conservative party. Brought up without any religious affiliation and married to a non-Jew, he first became interested in Zionism in 1917. In 1921 he contributed £25,000 to the Jewish National Fund. In 1921 he was named chairman of the new Economic Council for Palestine. That year he paid his first visit to Palestine with Chaim Weizmann. In 1927 he was president of the Joint Palestine Survey Commission that went to Palestine under the auspices of the Jewish Agency, and that same year he raised a fund of £25,000 for the relief of the unemployed in the yishuv. He became president of the English Keren ha-Yesod Committee and in 1928, the year he was raised to the peerage, president of the English Zionist Federation. When the Jewish Agency Council was expanded in 1929 he became its associate chairman and chairman of its Political Committee. He resigned from his Zionist and Jewish Agency offices in protest against the Passfield White Paper.

Melchett was an avowed and ardent Jewish nationalist. He built a villa for himself in Tiberias and founded the Tel Mond settlement, in the southern Sharon Plain, in 1929.

Melchett's son **Henry, the 2nd Baron Melchett** (1898–1949), an industrialist and economist, shared his father's Zionist interests. He was chairman of the Council of the Jewish Agency and honorary president of the British Maccabi and of the Maccabi World Federation. After the rise of Hitler, he formally adopted Judaism and took a leading part in the "Boycott Germany" movement. In his book *Thy Neighbor* (1936), he strongly advocated the cause of the Jewish National Home.

The 1st Baron Melchett's daughter, **Eva Violet, the Marchioness of Reading** (1895–1973), who along with her brother formally adopted Judaism, was active in the Zionist movement and served as president of the British section of the World Jewish Congress. Her husband, Gerald Rufus Isaacs (1889–1960), the 2nd Marquess of Reading, was counsel representing the Jewish Agency before the Shaw Commission, which investigated the causes of the 1929 Arab riots in Palestine. J. FRAENKEL

MENDELE MOKHER SEFARIM (pen name of Shalom Jacob Abromovich). Yiddish and Hebrew author (b. Kapuli, Belorussia, 1835 (?); d. Odessa, 1917). Mendele is considered to be the father of both modern Hebrew and Yiddish prose fiction. His life spanned several periods of Russian Jewish cultural life: the Haskala, Hibbat Zion, and modern Zionism. He is credited with forging the modern Hebrew and Yiddish idioms which served as a literary tool for several generations of realistic writers.

Orphaned at the age of 13, he wandered throughout Lithuania studying at various *yeshivot*. He thus experienced much of the world of the Jewish Pale of Settlement. He lived for six years in Kamenetz Podolsk (1853–1859), where he became the protege of the Hebrew poet and editor Abraham Dov Gottlober, who recommended Mendele's first article for publication (1856). From Kamenetz he moved to Berdichev (1858–1869) and then to Zhitomir (1869–1881), where he enrolled at a government Rabbinical Seminary and received his diploma as government rabbi in 1872. For political reasons, however, he was not permitted to serve in a congregation. In 1881, he became head teacher at the Odessa Talmud Torah, a position he held until his death.

While in Berdichev, Mendele began writing book reviews and articles for the Hebrew press. *Mishpat Shalom* (Peaceful Judgment, 1860) his first book, assumes the positivist approach then prevailing in Russian criticism without, however, denigrating the importance of classical Hebrew literature. During this early period, he published his first two fictional works, *Limdu Hetev* (Study Well, 1862), and *Avot u-Vanim* (Fathers and Sons, 1868), the former actually being a part of an earlier version of the latter. *Avot u-Vanim* is the first contemporary Hebrew prose work to appear after Mapu's *Ayit Tzavu'a*, and the first to deal with the conflict between generations.

Mendele's proclivity for realism was inhibited by the inadequacy of the Hebrew language of the 1870s. The world he described lived and spoke in Yiddish. Hebrew was a classical medium which lacked the suppleness of a spoken language. The Hebrew audience was restricted to a small elite, educated class; Yiddish appealed to a much larger audience. Mendele himself pointed out that Hebrew had no women readers at all. Later he insisted that he never "abandoned" Hebrew in his Yiddish period. However, his Hebrew writing in the 1870s was confined to non-fictional articles.

Mendele's first Yiddish work was *Das Kleine Mentschele* (The Little Man, 1865). There for the first time he introduces *Mendele Mokher Sefarim* (Mendele, the Seller of [Holy] Books), the name which he would later adopt as his pen name. This was followed by the *Vinshfingrel* (The Magic Ring, 1865) which he would later adapt and absorb in his later novel *Fishke der Krumer* (Fishke, the Lame, 1869). Mendele's arrival in Odessa coincided with the period of the Russian pogroms and the rise of the Hovevei Zion movement throughout Russia. Odessa itself became the capital of the new nationalist movement. A coterie of Hebrew writers assembled around Ahad Ha-Am with the aim of reviving the Hebrew language. Mendele shared the general disillusionment with the Haskala and its optimism about Jewish emancipation. His allegory *The Nag* was a condemnation of the Haskala's cultural and political program and is a bitter satire aimed at Russian liberalism. Mendele also translated Leo Pinsker's *Autoemancipation* into Yiddish (1904). He was, however, skeptical about the possibility of a return to Zion and about the capacity of unskilled and incompetent *shtetl* Jews to realize Zionism's lofty aims. His satirical work *Kitzur Masa'ot Binyamin Ha-Shelishi* (An Abridgment of the Third Travels of Benjamin, Yiddish 1878, and Hebrew 1896) is a hilarious picaresque novel about two quixotic *shlemiels* who undertake a frustrated voyage to the Holy Land. Nevertheless, the commitment of his Hovevei Zion friends to the revival of Hebrew had an impact upon him and the 1880s, with their enthusiastic encouragement, he returned to writing fiction in Hebrew. His major achievement was adapting and translating his Yiddish works to Hebrew. In doing so, he forged a new style which melded biblical Hebrew with mishnaic, midrashic, and talmudic Hebrew. The new idiom had the flexibility and vitality that his early Hebrew lacked. The so-called *nusah Mendele* (Mendele's style) became the prose vehicle used by more than a generation of Hebrew fiction writers.

The Hebrew University's Jewish Studies Institute prepared a definitive edition of Mendele's collected works.

E. SPICEHANDLER

MENDELEVICH, YOSEF. Aliya activist in USSR and Israel (b. Riga, 1947). In 1964 he joined the underground Zionist movement in his home city. The same year he enrolled at the Riga Polytechnical Institute where he studied electronics for four years. In 1969 he took an active part in organizing the "All-Union Coordinating Committee" of Zionist groups functioning in the USSR and was appointed editor of the Committee's underground publication. He also taught Hebrew and in the same year became an observant Jew. The Mendelevich family applied for an emigration visa in 1968 and was refused.

In 1970, Mendelevich, together with fifteen others, was arrested for participating in an attempt to hijack a plane in order to fly to Israel. He was sentenced to fifteen years imprisonment. In 1972, he participated in the organization of an underground Zionist movement in the labor camp and taught Hebrew. In 1975, he initiated a general strike of political prisoners at Camp 36 in Orel. In 1980, he held a 57-day hunger strike, demanding to be allowed Hebrew books.

As a result of his conduct and an international campaign for his release, the Supreme Soviet of the USSR issued, in 1981, a ruling ordering his deportation from the country. He was removed from the prison on the morning of 18 February 1981, and arrived in Israel the same night.

Between 1981 and 1984 he studied at the Merkaz ha-Rav Yeshiva in Jerusalem, and from 1984 was a student in the Beit ha-Midrash ha-Gavoha, in the rabbinical training program.

In 1983 Mendelevich became chairman of the newly-formed Soviet Jewry Education and Information Center, a grassroots organization of Jewish activists formerly from the USSR. In 1987, he founded Mahana'im, a Torah and Jewish Heritage Center which promotes religious Zionist education among Soviet Jews in Israel and in the USSR.

Mendelevich's memoirs, *Operation Wedding*, were published in Hebrew in 1985 and in Russian in 1987.

Y. STERN

MENDELSOHN, ERICH. Architect (b. Allenstein, East Prussia, 1887; d. San Francisco, 1953). He achieved international fame shortly after World War I when he built the Einstein Turm observatory in Potsdam. Later he abandoned his experiments with modernistic expressionism, and promoted the concept of the horizontal as the ideal form, notably in the Schocken department stores in Chemnitz and Stuggart. He first visited Palestine in the 1920s and, together with Richard Neutra, prepared a plan for a business center in Lower Haifa which, although never built, demonstrated his originality and regional approach with its arched colonnades and terraced structures leading to the sea. In 1934 he moved to Palestine. He designed the Weizmann house in Rehovot and the government hospital in Bat Galim but his main achievements are in Jerusalem. He drew inspiration from the massive buildings in the center of Hebron for his structure for the Anglo-Palestine Bank (later Bank Le'umi) in the center of Jerusalem. A modern building, it retains clear characteristics of Jerusalem style. He carefully preserved the skyline, and integrated the buildings into their surroundings. The Schocken House and Schocken Library in Talbieh were built along similar principles. In the Hadassah Hospital on Mount Scopus, Mendelsohn confronted specific problems, including the topographical lines of the mountain, on which he constructed retaining walls and terraces partly straight and partly rounded. The main entrance—a gate of stone pillars, supporting three concrete domes—was a clear gesture to the Old City of Jerusalem, clearly visible from the site. When World War II broke out, he moved to the United States and continued his work there.

A. ELHANANI

Seven-branched menora by British sculptor, Benno Elkan, in front of Knesset building, Jerusalem. [Israel Govt. Press Office]

MENORA. Seven-branched candelabrum of the Jerusalem Temple, adopted by the State of Israel as its emblem. The golden seven-branched candelabrum was one of the prominent vessels of the Sanctuary in the wilderness. Among the spoils carried off by Titus after the destruction of the Second Temple, the Menora is pictured on a bas-relief on the Arch of Titus in Rome in a scene showing the Roman triumphal procession. The Menora has also been a frequent ornamental feature in synagogues, recalling the Temple.

From early times the seven-branched candelabrum served as a symbol of Judaism. Drawings of it have been found among the decorations of synagogues, tombs, and sarcophagi dating back to the first centuries of the Common Era. In modern times a variety of Jewish organizations and associations, including the Jewish Legion of World War I, have used the Menora as their badge.

In February, 1949, the Provisional Council of the State of Israel proclaimed the Menora, flanked by two olive branches, as the emblem of the State. The design of the Menora on the emblem is based on the representation on the Arch of Titus.

MERCAZ. *See* CONSERVATIVE JUDAISM.

MERHAVYA. A kibbutz and a moshav in the Jezreel Valley east of Afula. In 1909, a first holding in the Jezreel Valley was acquired there on behalf of the Palestine Land Development Company and a Ha-Shomer group established a farm in 1911. Despite malaria, Arab attacks, and harassment by the Turkish authorities, they persevered and built the settlement as a cooperative following the ideas of Franz Oppenheimer. After World War I, the cooperative was replaced by another group which was not successful. In 1922 a group of pioneers from eastern Europe founded a moshav on land adjoining the original farm to the east. In 1929 a group of Ha-Shomer ha-Tza'ir from Poland revived the original Merhavya, making it an organizational center of its kibbutz movement, with a printing press and the Sifriyat Po'alim publishing house. The kibbutz and moshav both have intensive irrigated farming, and the former also engages in industry. In 1987 the kibbutz had 634 inhabitants, and the moshav 270. E. ORNI

Harvest in moshav Merhavya, 1924. [Central Zionist Archives]

MERIDOR, YAAKOV. *Betar leader and commander of *Irgun Tzeva'i Le'umi (b. Lipno, Russian Poland, 1913). In 1929 he joined Betar, the Revisionist youth movement, and in 1932, with 27 other Betar members, illegally crossed the Lebanese border into Palestine. In 1933 he joined the Irgun Tzeva'i Le'umi, which at the time was also known as the "national Hagana." During the Arab riots of 1936, Meridor assumed command of the Irgun units at Petah Tikva and three years later, with a group of selected Irgun leaders, entered the Irgun officers' school in Poland.

In 1941, at the outbreak of Rashid Ali's revolt in Iraq, which resulted in that country's joining the war on Germany's side, Meridor participated with the Irgun commander David Razi'el in a secret military mission on behalf of the British High Command in the Middle East. When Razi'el fell in action (May, 1941), Meridor assumed command of the Irgun. In 1943 he turned over the command to Menahem Begin and was appointed second in command. Arrested in February, 1945, by the British authorities, he was deported to Cairo and three months later was sent to detention camps in East Africa, where he spent more than three years. After eight unsuccessful attempts, he escaped from the camp in Gilgil, Kenya, with a group of internees and in April, 1948, reached Paris.

Returning to Israel on 15 May 1948, Meridor assumed responsibility for the integration of the Irgun units into the Israel Defense Forces. After the arrival from France of the Irgun's *S.S. Altalena*, carrying arms, ammunition, and volunteers, Meridor and other Irgun leaders were interned by the Israeli authorities in the fortress of Bet She'an. On his release, he joined the Herut movement, was elected to its Central Committee, and served in the First, Third, Fourth, Fifth, and Sixth Knessets, representing the Herut party on the Foreign Affairs and Defense Committee. In 1981 Meridor was appointed Minister for Economic Affairs in the Israel Cabinet, serving in that post up until the 1984 elections. He wrote *Long is the Road to Freedom* (1955).

I. BENARI—D. NIV

MERKAZ HAKLA'I. (Agricultural Center) Executive body of the Histadrut ha-Po'alim ha-Hakla'it (Agricultural Workers' Federation). An affiliate of the *Histadrut, the latter includes both agricultural laborers and members of kibbutzim and moshavim. The Merkaz Hakla'i maintains two departments: one that concerns itself with the needs of agricultural laborers and with the affairs of Yakhin, an agricultural contracting company operated by the Histadrut; and another that is in charge of settling members of the Histadrut on the land and generally handles the affairs of the labor movement's settlements. (The guiding spirit in the second department from its etablishment and for many years thereafter was Abraham Harzfeld.) The Merkaz Hakla'i is also engaged in training of youths and adults for agricultural work, and publishes professional literature including the agricultural periodical *Ha-Sadeh* (The Field). It represents the labor settlements vis-á-vis governmental and other public institutions active in land development and cultivation, such as the Jewish National Fund and the Palestine Jewish Colonization Association (PICA).

Y. SLUTSKY

MERON. Locality and moshav in eastern Upper Galilee, at the foot of Mount Meron. At a site not necessarily identical in all periods, a town of this name existed during the Second Temple period and Talmudic times. The front of a large synagogue of the 2nd-3rd century has been preserved. Traditionally, the sage Simeon bar Yohai and his son Eleazer lived at Meron and the putative site of their tombs are venerated there, especially on the minor festival of Lag ba-Omer, when thousands come from all over the country to light candles at the tombs and dance around bonfires; the same day, hasidic Jews give their three-year-old sons their first ceremonial haircut at the site.

In the 1948 War of Independence, Arab irregulars occupied Meron, which had long been Jewish property; later, the Israel army took it and in 1949 a religious moshav was founded. It developed fruit orchards and other hill farming branches, opened a yeshiva and built a conspicuous modern synagogue. Population (1987), 538. E. ORNI

METMAN-KOHEN, YEHUDA LEIB. Educator (b. Ostia, Russia, 1869; d. Tel Aviv, 1939). Metman-Kohen became a

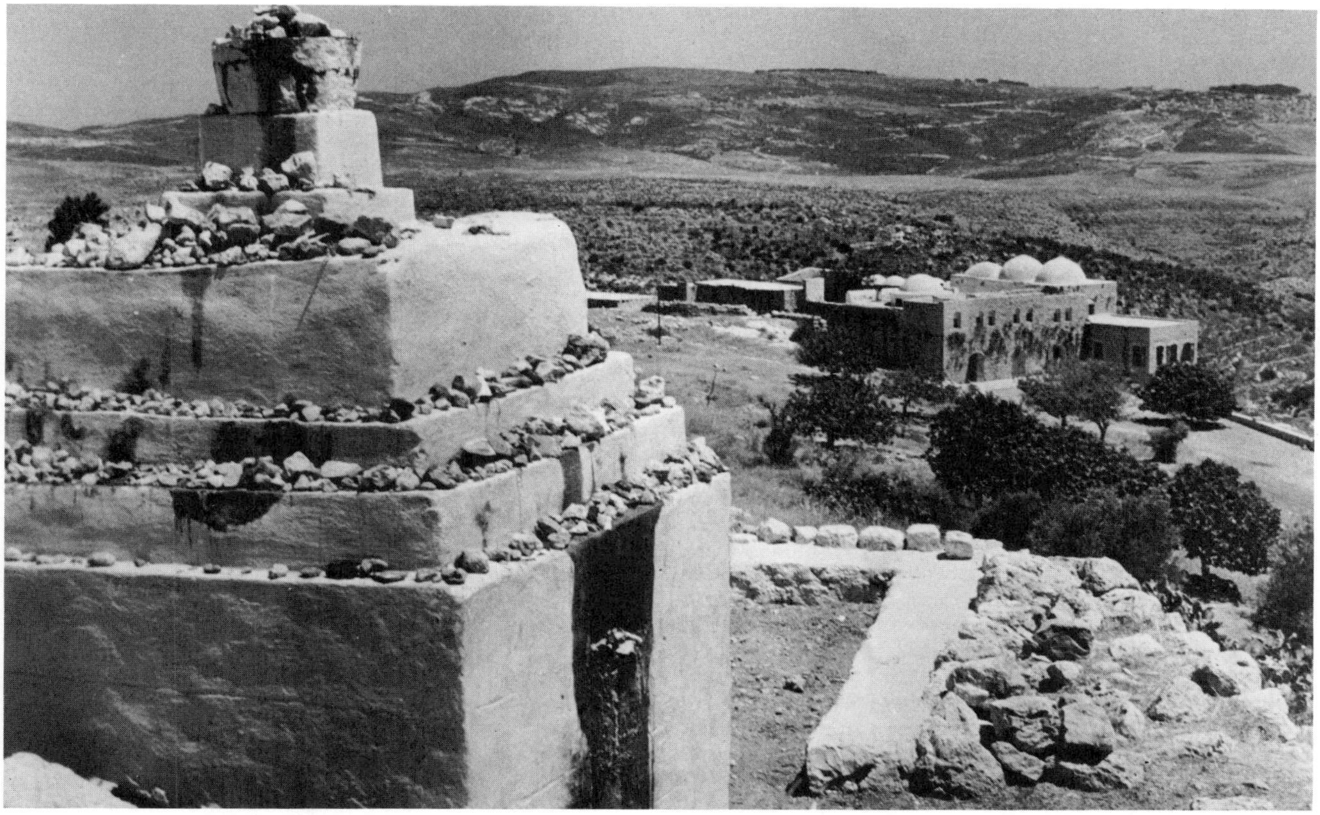

Tomb of Rabbi Shimon ben Yohai, pilgrimage site in Meron on Lag Ba-Omer. [Israel Government Tourist Office]

Hebrew teacher, and was active in the Hovevei Zion movement. In 1897 he moved to Odessa, where he studied at the university, headed a Hebrew school, founded a Hebrew kindergarten, and established the student organizations Sefat Zion and Tzeva ha-Tehiya, the latter intended to train a cadre of educators who would establish educational and cultural institutions in Eretz Israel. After graduating from the University of Berne (1904), he went to Eretz Israel to become principal of the school at Rishon le-Zion. In 1906 he founded the *Herzliya High School, where he taught until his retirement in 1936.

Metman-Kohen was one of the founders of Ramat Gan, where he established the first elementary school and the first high school. In the 1930s he edited *Ha-Ivri*, a vocalized Hebrew weekly for new immigrants. He was the author of Hebrew textbooks in botany and biology.

In Europe he had been a member of Po'ale Zion. After his arrival in Palestine he became active in Ahdut Avoda, which he represented in the First Asefat ha-Nivharim. In his last years he was identified with General Zionism.

His wife **Fania** (b. Bialystok, 1874; d. Tel Aviv, 1977) was one of the first teachers of the Hebrew high school in Jaffa. She was active in the Women's Federation for Equal Rights.

METULA. Northernmost Israeli village, on the Lebanese border ridge north of the Huleh Valley. Founded in 1896 on Baron Edmond de Rothschild's initiative, it was designed to defend itself on this isolated spot. Its progress was slow until the 1950s when water and electricity were supplied and a number of new immigrants enlarged the place. Besides hill farming Metula has a few resort hotels. Since the 1970s, it has served as a meeting place for contacts with South Lebanese Christians; a border crossing station is nearby. Population (1987), 694. E. ORNI

MEVASERET ZION. Urban community in the Judean Hills, 7 mi. (10 km.) west of Jerusalem; created by the amalgamation of Ma'oz Zion, which had been founded in 1951 to house and provide auxiliary farmsteads for immigrants from Kurdistan working in the nearby stone quarries, and Mevaseret Yerushalayim, developed since 1956 as a suburban settlement, mainly for immigrants. An immigrants' absorption center was opened in the 1970s. The site of Castel (the Roman Castellum) lies within the community's municipal borders. The name means "Herald of Zion." Population (1987), 10,900. E. ORNI

MEXICO, ZIONISM IN.

1. Origins and Organizational Development. The origins of Zionism in Mexico coincided with the arrival of the large-scale Jewish immigration to the country in the mid-1920s. Prior to this time, isolated manifestations of Zionist activity took place, such as the purchase of 28 *shekalim* in 1912—as stated in *Die Welt* in 28 November of the same year—and a celebration honoring the Balfour Declaration held in 1918.

An early attempt in the organizational direction occurred in July, 1922, with the establishment of the first Zionist Organization of Mexico, headed by Max Werner. This first attempt, however, was short lived due to the small number of Jews in Mexico. In that same year 500 *shekalim* were sent to Mexico, and on 23 April a benefit concert was organized for Keren ha-Yesod raising the sum of 18.43 (eighteen pounds, forty three shillings) which were sent to Keren ha-Yesod's headquarters in London.

With the foundation of the United Zionist Organization, Kadima, in 1925, Zionism in Mexico took a major step forward in stable organizational development. On 17 May 1925, Kadima's first General Assembly was held, with 83 members attending. The organization was headed by Jacob Rosenberg and Meier Berger. By 1925, the Ashkenazi Jewish community had risen to 5,000, becoming a propitious seedbed for Zionist activities. According to the newly-established organization, the 10,000 Sephardi and Arab-speaking Jews who inhabited Mexico then were oblivious to the Zionist idea. From the inception of Kadima, its leaders saw among its main objectives the organization of the new Mexican Jewish community with a Zionist orientation.

In 1926, Zionist activity in Mexico received an additional stimulus with the arrival of Dr. Ariel Bension, delegate of Keren ha-Yesod. He successfully reorganized the leadership of the Zionist Organization, appointing Wolf Sourasky as its new president and established the Zionist Sephardi Organization Benei Kedem, headed by Sol Shamah. He also organized a Keren ha-Yesod campaign and set up its permanent committee under the direction of Isaac Capon. Bension tried to establish first contacts with Mexican authorities at the ministerial level, meeting with the Ministries of Interior, Treasury, and Foreign Affairs. As early as 1927, with the gradual stabilization of Zionist organization, different conceptions developed leading to internal controversies. These centered around the question of the major focus of Zionist activity: should its work be ideological and educational in nature, or should it concentrate on the practical task of fundraising? The emphasis placed by the Zionist authorities in London on redoubling efforts to increase the amounts raised for the National Funds and to boost the sale of the *shekel* supported the latter attitude. While the leadership of Kadima, headed by Max Werner, considered fund-raising the major concern of Zionist activity, the younger activists led by Yosef Tjornitzky promoted a wider range of action within the movement. For them, education and the dissemination of Zionist ideology had preference. By the end of the 1920s, the two approaches became radically opposed, and when the leadership of Kadima suggested the total liquidation of the Zionist Organization, the youngsters took the initiative of reorganizing it, thus becoming the heads of the movement in the 1930s. Selling the *shekel* was an activity fraught with problems from the outset. The Zionist Organization of Mexico needed to sell 2,000 *shekalim* in 1927–28 in order to send a delegate to the Zionist Congress. This goal was not achieved at that time, nor in the 1930s when the United Zionist Organization of Mexico came into being. It was not until 1946 that Mexico was represented for the first time at a Zionist Congress.

Anti-Semitic demonstrations in Mexico at the beginning of the 1930s as well as the impact of Nazism on local nationalistic movements brought in its wake an expansion of Zionist work. By 1934, Jewish National Fund Committees existed in at least 10 Mexican cities and Zionist organizations had been established in the major Mexican cities.

The expansion of Zionist work and the organizational consolidation of the Zionist movement were characterized by the diversification of ideological currents and political parties. In 1930, the Socialist Labor Confederation Po'ale Zion was organized and it was active within the framework of the United Zionist Organization until December, 1934. In that year, it withdrew as a separate body—the Pro-Palestine League and founded the Keren Po'alei Eretz Israel (Kapai). In May, 1935, it became the Po'ale Zion-Tze'irei Zion party. A year later the Pioneer Women Organization was created. Throughout the decade the relations between this party and the United Zionist Organization were marked by strife and rivalry in fundraising and the sale of the *shekel*.

The Ashkenazi and Sephardi communities found it hard to collaborate in Zionist activities within the same organizational structure. Thus, the Zionist Sephardi Organization was founded in 1935, led by Victor Mitrani and Ricardo Levy.

During this period attempts were made to overcome the organizational division. In 1937, a committee was created to draw up the laws for a single Zionist organization. In 1938 all the groups—except Po'ale Zion—were united in a Central Committee in charge of the coordination and control of their work, while preserving the autonomy of the various factions in organizational matters. This attempt at unification was short-lived and was overshadowed by a constant trend towards a greater organizational diversification: the Revisionists formed the New Zionist Organization in 1936 headed by Dr. Jacob Kink; in 1938 the Women's International Zionist Organization (WIZO) was founded; and in the early forties Mizrachi was created under the leadership of Rabbi David Rafalin.

This trend towards structural diversity was also manifest during the 1940s in the Zionist youth movements. In 1940 Ha-Shomer ha-Tza'ir was founded, Ha-No'ar ha-Tziyoni in 1943, Betar and Bnei Akiva in 1946, and Habonim in 1948. Due to Natan Bistritsky's initiative while in Mexico, a Union of Zionist Youth Movements was established in 1943. It came as a response to the request of the Youth Department of the World Zionist Organization which sought to prevent the prevailing pattern of lack of coordination and unity within Zionism in Mexico. This Union, which lacked effectiveness at its onset, preceded the Youth Zionist Federation of Mexico which was established in turn in 1946. In December 1944, Moledet, the first *hakhshara*, was established and the first group of Ha-Shomer ha-Tza'ir, formed by 15 youngsters, received training.

The decade of the 1940s started with the institutionalization of the National Fund. In 1942 the local and national presidia of the Jewish National Fund were set up under the leadership of Teodoro Resnikoff, joined in 1943 by Mizrachi and Po'ale Zion.

The presence of emissaries such as Michael Graiver (1936 and 1940), Moises Senderey (1938), Leib Jaffe (1940), Dr. Yuris (1941), Abraham Mibashan (1942), Natan Bistrisky (Agmon, 1943) guaranteed the success of the Keren ha-Yesod campaigns, and stimulated general Zionist activity. This flux of external visitors continued during this period. Louis Lipsky and Emanuel Neumann (1943), and Dr. Israel Goldstein, Louis Segal and Maxa Nordau (1944) were among the most prominent.

During this period, the World Zionist Organization stressed the need to create a Zionist Territorial Federation in Mexico, in which all the political parties could participate and work together harmoniously. This appeal finally met with the positive response of the United Zionist Organization which decided to relinquish its organizational primacy, and after deleting the work "United" from its name, joined in October, 1947, the World Organization of General Zionists. This step was a consequence of the poor returns in the elections for the 22nd Zionist Congress. The United Zionist Organization received only 315 votes, while the Labor Front reached 746 and the National Front, formed by Mizrachi and the Revisionist party, 436 votes. Then, it called on all the parties to establish a federation. However, the latter was not formed for several years, due to disagreement among Zionist groups over the criteria to be used in setting up the Federation.

The educational and cultural work of the Zionist movement was intense during this first period. Prior to the early forties, all ideological and political currents coexisted in one educational institution, the Colegio Israelita de Mexico founded in 1924. The prevalent current viewing Yiddish as a national language was opposed by the Zionist faction that stressed the importance of Hebrew and of Zionist educational contents within the curricula. This opposition became an open conflict when Avner Alifaz, the Ha-Shomer ha-Tza'ir emissary arrived as a teacher to the school. Not being able to advance their position, in 1942, the Zionists broke away and founded the Tarbut Hebrew School, whose basic aim was to provide a Zionist education centered on the idea of national liberation and Eretz Israel. From the outset, the Hebrew language was seen as a decisive factor in the Jewish cultural renaissance and an instrument of national unification. On the practical level, this served as conduct of inter-communal unity. The oriental Jews' Mount Sinai Tarbut School and the Sephardi Tarbut School were founded in 1942 and 1944, respectively.

From the very beginning, one of the characteristics of the cultural work done by the different Zionist groups of Mexico has been the publication of newspapers and magazines to disseminate Zionist ideologies. Written in Spanish and Yiddish, these publications appeared intermittently, and many of them were short-lived: *Farn Folk* (1932–34), *Land und Arbet* (1935-36), *Oifboi* (1935–38), and *Ershter Mai* (1937) of the Po'ale Zion faction; *Unzer Shtime* (1936–39), *Zionistishe Tribune* (1939) of the Revisionists; *Idishe Tribune* (1939), *Unzer Tribune* (1942) which appeared with the supplement *Ha-Shomer ha-Tza'ir* and *Prensa Israelita* (1945) of the General Zionists; as well as various publications in Hebrew and Spanish of the Sephardi: *Mizraj* (1943), *Zion* (1945), and *Tikvatenu* (1947), to name just a few. Since 1943, WIZO has published its magazine without interruption.

From the early 1940s, an awareness of the increasing role that Latin America would be called on to play developed within the World Zionist Movement. As early as July, 1941, this was expressed in a letter written by Dr. Leo Lauterbach of the World Zionist Organization to I. Blumberg stating that in view of the destruction in Europe and the curtailment of Zionist activities within European Jewry, the communities of Latin America were called on to play a new and significant role. Thus, Dr. Leo Lauterbach submitted a proposal in 1942 for the establishment of an Advising Committee which in close cooperation with the Emergency Committee for Zionist Affairs of the United States would promote and coordinate Zionist activity in Latin America. Finally, in 1943, a Latin American Department of the New York Office of the Jewish Agency was established, headed by Rachel Sepharadi-Yardeni. At the Mexican community level, this awareness was evidenced in mounting concern for expanding the sphere of Zionist activity to domestic and national circles, which would later play a decisive role internationally in the establishment of the State of Israel. Thus, for example, the Zionist Convention that took place in October, 1943, in Mexico City, appealed to President Manuel Avila Camacho asking for Mexico's support for the Zionist idea. The Mexican Pro-Palestine Committee, headed by a member of the Mexican Supreme Court, Judge Alfonso Francisco Ramirez, successfully brought together non-Jewish Mexican intellectuals and politicians to support the Zionist cause. Intellectuals such as Antonio Castro Leal, rector of the National University, the prominent trade unions leader Vicente Lombardo Toledano, and former President Lazaro Cardenas were members of this Committee. Mexico participated as a sponsor in the World Conference on Palestine organized by the American Christian Palestine Committee, the American Palestine Committee, and the Christian Council on Palestine, held in Washington in November, 1945, to organize Pro-Palestine Committees throughout the world. At the same time, within the Jewish community in Mexico, the Jewish Emergency Committee for Palestine in Mexico was at work with the participation of Zionist leaders of different political convictions such as Arye Leon Dulzin, Elias Sourasky, Victor Mitrani, Jose Winiecky, Jose Silva, Rabbi David Rafalin, Arturo Woolfowich, Jose Kalach, and Lazaro Penhas among others. A prominent figure in the work of liaison between the Jewish community and leading Mexican figures was the Zionist leader Dr. Adolfo Fastlicht, who later became the first Honorary Consul of Israel in Mexico.

Subsequent to the establishment of the State of Israel the Pro-Palestine committee was dissolved, and the Institute of Mexico-Israel Cultural Relations was founded in December, 1949.

II. From the Establishment of the State of Israel to the Present. The foundation of the State of Israel gave further legitimacy to the Zionist idea and strengthened its activities within the Jewish community. This event, coupled with the annihilation of European Jewry, weakened the political importance of the traditional non-Zionist and anti-Zionist groups within Mexican Jewry, paving the road for Zionist hegemony within the community. A united Zionist Federation, however, was not created until 1950. During 1948 and 1949, conflicts over organizational criteria persisted and new struggles developed among the parties regarding the autonomy and coordination of fundraising campaigns for the National Funds. In December 1949, mediation was used to resolve these conflicts and a Territorial Shekel Committee was set up, with the participation of all political parties. This was the precedent for the establishment of the Zionist Federation created in June 1950.

By then, the following Zionist organizations existed in Mexico: Zionist Organization of Mexico, Po'ale Zion, Histadrut Mizrachi, Women's Mizrachi Organization, United Zionist Revisionist Organization, Mapam, Sephardi Zionist Organization, WIZO, Pioneer Women, Menorah-Hatikvah of the German Zionists, and United Zionist Organization of Monterrey.

The youth groups in the Youth Zionist Federation were: Ha-No'ar ha-Tziyoni, Youth Organization of General Zionists, Ha-Shomer ha-Tza'ir, Benei Zion, Ha-Po'el, Damascus Zionist Center, Sephardi Zionist Youth, Ahim Organization of Monterrey, and Habonim.

The elections of delegates to the 23rd and 24th Zionist

Congresses paved the way for the reorganization of the Zionist Movement in Mexico. It was not until 1953 that an effective operational method was worked out in the Zionist Federation and an agreement was reached on the creation of an Executive Committee in which all political parties would be represented. To preserve the ideological identity of the smaller groups, a veto was instituted enabling any member of the Federation to oppose decisions made by the majority and hold discussions of political and internal matters. This safeguard, however, was rarely enforced. Only Zionist political parties were represented in the federation. The Pioneer Women, WIZO, and the Sephardi Zionist Organization sent delegates, while the Youth Federation had an observer. All members of the Executive Committee and all political parties had equal voting power.

At the 23rd Zionist Congress, three Mexican delegates were elected for the first time to the Zionist General Council: Teodoro Resnikoff, Kalman Landau, and Arye Leon Dulzin, who later served as Chairman of the World Zionist Organization.

In the fifties, the Zionist movement expanded its cultural work. For more than two years the *Zionistishe Bleter*, a publication of the Zionist Federation, appeared in Yiddish and Spanish. Po'ale Zion published the magazine *Avantgard* (1949) and *Dos Vort* (1947–1960); the Revisionists, *Tribuna Sionista* and *El Heraldo de Israel* (1950–1959); and the General Zionists, *la Voz Sionista* from 1948 through the fifties.

Zionism was predominant in Jewish community life. Zionists led the main community institutions. In the November 1949 elections for the Comite Central Israelita de Mexico—the umbrella organization of Mexican Jewry—four of the six lists presented belonged to different Zionist groups, who won the majority of votes, with the General Zionists in the first place. In the 1962 elections in the Ashkenazi Kehila Nidhe Israel, the General Zionists again won over 50 percent of the votes.

Institutions promoting exchange and providing support for Israel's scientific and cultural activities, such as the Friends of the Hebrew University of Jerusalem—among the first organized Zionist associations, of the University of Tel Aviv, of Bar-Ilan, the Technion, and the Weizmann Institute became increasingly important. This reflects a general trend towards the development of multiple and direct relations between the Jewish community and the State of Israel. This trend affected the place and role played by the traditional organized Zionist bodies. Thus, the Zionist movement in Mexico had to reevaluate its role and its social bases of support. At the same time, the Zionist Federation launched a personal membership campaign in the late sixties, to expand its numbers. this campaign was opposed by traditional political parties which had been the only channel for joining the movement. During this process, youth organizations and new groups such as the Renewal Front demanded greater democratization of the Federation. They considered personal membership and elections as the only means by which the Zionist Federation could regain its place in the community. The fact that no elections had been held since the 24th Zionist Congress in 1956 was interpreted by these groups as one of the main reasons for its weakness. In 1972, elections were held for the 28th Zionist Congress. The continental awareness that developed within Latin American Zionism in the seventies was expressed in a proposal for a Convention of the continent's Zionist leaders during the 28th Zionist Congress. This Convention was held in May, 1972. (As early as 1946 on the eve of the 22nd Zionist Congress, Mexico had submitted a proposal to the World Zionist Organization to include delegates of Central American communities too small to be able to meet the *shekalim* required for representation.) By the mid-1970s, Ihud Habonim, Bnei Akiva, Ha-Halutz la-Merhav, Tze'irei Herut, and Ha-Agada le-ma'an ha-Hayal joined the Federation.

From 1947 to 1972 Mexico with 1,124 immigrants to Israel ranked fifth in Latin America aliya, after Argentina, Brazil, Uruguay, and Chile. Increased attention was payed to the Shenat Hakhshara (Year of Preparation) Program, in which over 120 youngsters participated in 1975. In educational and cultural activities, the Zionist Organization continued to support Jewish education, expanding its sphere of action to new areas, especially those aimed at the Dor Hemshekh (young leadership) and university students.

Mexican Zionism has achieved a prominent place among the fundraising campaigns of the National Funds, ranking first among Latin American communities—with the highest proportion of contributions per capita—and among the first six in world Jewry. World Zionist Congresses continue to provide a significant impetus for the activity of the organized movement. Prior to these Congresses intensive membership campaigns have been launched. Elections to the 31st Congress held in December 1987 were characterized by an upsurge of interest and political struggles. Eight lists were presented and six parties took part. As a result of the lack of consensus during the process, Mexico did not have an official delegation until the Congress was already underway.

In 1988, Mexico was the co-chairman of the Northern Area of the Latin American Zionist Council (Cosla), of the Latin American Federation of Zionist Students (FUSLA), and until the beginning of that year, was chairman of the Sephardi Latin American Federation (FESELA).

J.B. LIWERANT

MIBASHAN, ABRAHAM. Zionist leader in Romania and Argentina, journalist, and publisher (b Jassy, Romania, 1890; d. Buenos Aires, 1960). He was the son of the Hebrew author and Zionist leader Menachem Mendel Braunstein (Mibashan). After completing his studies at Berlin University, he taught in Palestine at the Herzliya Gymnasium in Tel Aviv. He also served as secretary of the Tel Aviv municipality. From 1924 he worked for the Romanian Jewish community and was active in Zionist information, editing Zionist periodicals. He was also a Romanian representative on the Jewish Agency Council. In 1936 he was sent to Argentina where his mission for the Keren ha-Yesod became permanent. He also served as the Jewish Agency representative. From 1944 to 1947 he helped to organize the Comité Pro-Palestina among non-Jewish personalities in Argentina. Mibashan regularly published articles on Jewish and Zionist subjects in the weekly *Mundo Israelita* and other Jewish periodicals. In 1943 he founded the Keren ha-Yesod illustrated journal *Eretz Israel* (in Spanish). In 1943 Mibashan organized and launched *Editorial Israel* and published books in Spanish on Judaica and, in particular, classic Zionist literature. Later he was one of the founders of the Candelabro publishing house. Mibashan was a General Zionist delegate at Zionist Congresses. Over the years he became increasingly involved in local community affairs and was appointed chairman of the Federacion Sionista (General Zionists). In 1955–1956 he served as chairman of the Buenos Aires community and subsequently, as chairman of the DAIA (the Argentinian Jewish community's representative body).

S. SCHENKOLEWSKI

MIFLEGET HA-AVODA HA-YISR'ELIT. *See* ISRAEL LABOR PARTY.

MIFLEGET HA-PO'ALIM HA-ME'UHEDET. *See* MAPAM.

MIFLEGET PO'ALEI ERETZ YISRAEL. *See* MAPAI.

MIGDAL. Moshava in the Ginosar Valley northwest of Lake Kineret, founded in 1912. Third Aliya pioneers who camped here in 1921 while building the Tiberias-Rosh Pina highway, founded Gedud ha-Avoda. Lord Melchett established a farm there near the lake shore in the 1920s. After 1948, Migdal was enlarged as new immigrants settled there. Irrigated subtropical farming constitutes the village's economic mainstay, together with a few resort hotels. In 1987, Migdal had 967 inhabitants. The name, "Tower," recalls its historical name "Magdala." E. ORNI

MIGDAL HA-EMEK. Town in Lower Galilee, 4 mi. (7 km.) southwest of Nazareth on the northern rim of the Jezreel Valley. It was founded as a development town in 1952, with most of its initial settlers originating from North Africa. After difficult beginnings, industry developed satisfactorily, including specialized branches such as leather clothing, cosmetics, and a few high-tech enterprises. Migdal ha-Emek is surrounded by the Balfour and other forests. Population (1987), 14,600. E. ORNI

MI'ILYA. Christian-Arab (Greek-Catholic) village in western Upper Galilee, 2.5 mi. (4 km.) from the Lebanese border. In the 13th century, German Crusader knights built a fortress there, "Chasteau du Roi," which is still partly intact and, in the Keziv river valley to the north, the castle Montfort (Burg Starkenberg). The ancestors of the village's present inhabitants came from the Lebanon in the 15th or 16th century. Population (1987), 1,980. E. ORNI

MIKHMORET. Moshav, village, and maritime training institute (Mevo'ot Yam) in the Hefer Plain of the central Sharon, founded in 1945 by World War II veterans. The original plan of developing a fishing harbor did not materialize and intensive farming became the economic mainstay. The village Mikhmoret B, later united with the moshav, also became a seaside resort. The name means "Fishing Net." Population (1987), 1,210. E. ORNI

MIKVE YISRAEL. Agricultural school southeast of Tel Aviv. Founded in 1870 by Charles Netter on behalf of the Alliance Israélite Française before there were any Jewish farming settlements in the country, it aimed to attract Jews to work on the land. First Aliya immigrants found their first employment there. Baron Edmond de Rothschild took over the main burden of the institution's upkeep. In the early years, French was the language of instruction, but from 1912 the "Language War" brought about its gradual replacement by Hebrew. Mikve Yisrael has a botanical garden, a soil research station, and an agricultural museum. In 1987 it had 919 inhabitants. The name, from Jeremiah 14:8 and 17:13, means "Israel's Hope." E. ORNI

MILBAUER, JOSEPH. Writer and public worker (b. Warsaw, 1897; d. Jerusalem, 1968). He grew up in Brussels and in 1921 went to Paris where he became a successful journalist and, editor of the *Univers Israélite*, but was compelled to resign because of his Zionist opinions. After fighting in World War II and in the French Jewish resistance, he settled (1944) in Jerusalem and became responsible for the French desk, and later member of the presidium, of Keren ha-Yesod.

He was an outstanding translator into French from Yiddish and wrote many books of stories and poems in French. He was one of the founders of a French literary circle in Jerusalem, which was the beginning of the *Amitiés Israël-France*" ("Israel-France Friendship League"). M. CATANE

MILEIKOWSKY, NATHAN. *See* NETANYAHU FAMILY.

MILLER, IRVING. Rabbi and Zionist leader in the United States (b. Kovno, Lithuania, 1903; d. Woodmere, N.Y., 1980). Miller was brought to the United States in 1912. A delegate to the founding session of the World Jewish Congress in 1936, he served as its secretary-general from 1942 to 1944, undertaking various missions on behalf of European Jewry. He subsequently became a member of the executive of the congress. Miller was elected chairman of the Executive Committee of the American Jewish Congress in 1942. In this capacity he testified before the Anglo-American Committee of Inquiry in Washington in January, 1946. He became president of the congress in 1949, serving until 1952.

A member of the National Executive Committee of the Zionist Organization of America (ZOA) from 1936 on, he was elected to the Zionist Actions Committee in 1939 and again in 1946, when he was also named chairman of the ZOA National Administrative Council. He was national president of the ZOA from 1952 to 1954 and chairman of the American Zionist Council from 1954 to 1963, years during which Zionism sought to redefine its role and objectives and was faced with numerous other challenges, including the Sinai Campaign and its effect on relations between Israel and the Eisenhower-Dulles administration in the United States.

Between 1961 and 1963 Rabbi Miller was the chairman of the Conference of Presidents of Major American Jewish Organizations. He wrote *Israel, the Eternal Ideal* (1955) and *The Zionist Movement Today: A Reappraisal* (1956).

MILLER, ISRAEL. Rabbi and Zionist leader in the United States (b. Baltimore, 1918). A graduate of Yeshiva College in 1938, Miller received an M.A. degree from Columbia University in 1949. He was ordained by the Rabbi Isaac Elchanan Theological Seminary of Yeshiva University in 1941. A year after his ordination, he became rabbi of the Kingsbridge Heights Jewish Center in the Bronx. In 1964 he was elected president of the Rabbinical Council of Amer-

Mikve Yisrael Agricultural School in 1945. [Keren Ha-Yesod]

ica. A chaplain in the US Army Air Corps during World War II, Miller served as chairman of the Commission on Jewish Chaplaincy of the National Jewish Welfare Board. He also served as a religious consultant to the US Department of Defense in Europe in June, 1954, and January, 1964, and in Japan in 1960 and 1965, conducting retreats for Jewish chaplains stationed overseas. In January, 1967, he was named chairman of the American Zionist Council. Other positions he held included chairman of the American Jewish Conference on Soviet Jewry, President of the Conference on Jewish Material Claims against Germany, and chairman of the Conference of Presidents of Major American Jewish Organizations. Rabbi Miller is Senior Vice-President of Yeshiva University.

MINERAL RESOURCES AND MINING IN ISRAEL. Mining and exploitation of mineral resources in Israel are as old as its history. Prehistoric men made tools from chert and flint occurring in many geological formations in all parts of the country. During various historic periods, copper was mined at Timna ("King Solomon's mines") and at other locations in the rift valley between the Dead Sea and Eilat. Glass was manufactured from sands in the coastal plain. There seems to be no certain evidence, however, that iron ores were utilized, despite indications in Deuteronomy (8;9) and other parts of the Bible. Asphalt from the Dead Sea was of great importance for a variety of purposes such as waterproofing vessels and mummifying the dead.

In modern times, interest in the country's mineral resources began in the mid-19th century, with the opening up of the country to scientific geological and geographical exploration. Interest focused mainly on the mineral wealth of the Dead Sea, on prospects for petroleum, on rock phosphates and bituminous rocks. Herzl, in his utopian novel *Altneuland* envisaged the industrial utilization of such resources. But in the period between the two world wars, the image of Palestine as a country poor in mineral resources took root, mainly because of its relative paucity of metallic mineral deposits and because systematic surveys in search of non-metallic minerals, especially phosphates, were still lacking.

Concentrated efforts for mineral exploration started after independence (1948) and laid the foundation for a mineral industry, which played an important part in the country's economic activity. Since the 1980s, Israel has had a significant share in world production of bromine (34%), potash (4%), and phosphates (2%). Most of Israel's mineral deposits are located in the Negev and in the Dead Sea-Judean Desert area.

Metallic Minerals *Copper.* Deposits of secondary copper minerals, mainly silicates and carbonates, are found 16 mi. (25 km.) north of Eilat, at Timna. These deposits are associated with a sandstone-shale sequence of Cambrian age. The minerals occur as vein fillings and also in disperse form

Extracting flint clay from Makhtesh Ramon, in the Negev. [Israel Government Tourist Office]

impregnating the rock. In ancient times, only small quantities of hand-picked highly concentrated ore were processed. The discovery after 1948 of notable quantities of an ore with 1–2 percent content of metallic copper made modern mining and processing possible. From 1960, the ore was mined open-cast, later also underground. After grinding, it was treated with sulphuric acid to convert it into copper sulphate, and subsequently with pig iron to produce copper cement, containing 75—80 percent of metallic copper. The copper cement was exported for further refining, mainly to Spain and Far Eastern countries. Production was discontinued in 1976 because of low prices on the world market.

Total production (1958–1976) amounted to 155,000 tons. Maximum annual production was 20,000 tons of copper cement. Reserves are estimated as 18 million tons of ore, most of it to be mined underground.

Manganese minerals are found in the same area and formation, but are so far not considered economically feasible.

Iron. Iron ores are found in a sandy shale-limestone sequence of Lower Cretaceous age in the Manara mountains, west of the Huleh depression and in some other locations in Galilee. Investigations showed that the iron content is about 28 percent of metallic iron and that the ore can be upgraded mechanically to a 40—50 per cent content. Proven reserves are estimated at 40 million tons. The deposits are regarded so far as not economic. Other iron ores are found in HaTira Crater (*Makhtesh Gadol*) in the Negev hills. Their high silica content makes utilization problematic. Hematite deposits with a 47–85 percent content of iron oxide occur in the Paran area, on the western border of the Arava depression. Reserves, however, are small and the deposit is not regarded as economic.

Non-Metallic Minerals *Phosphates.* The rock phosphate deposits of Israel are part of the Mediterranean phosphate belt extending from Morocco to Jordan. The phosphate occurs in limestones of Upper Cretaceous age containing the mineral calcium-fluorapatite. Economic deposits are confined to the Negev and the southern Judean Desert. In 1986, phosphates were mined (open cast) in the Arad (*Makhtesh Katan*), Oron (*Makhtesh Gadol*), and Tzin fields. The phosphoric acid content of the rock (23–27 percent P_2O_5) is enriched mechanically and/or by calcination. Numerous additional fields have been identified. Reserves are roughly estimated at 320 million tons, but are probably much greater.

Production of enriched phosphate for export amounted to 2.4 million tons in 1985/86, not including material used for the production of 180,000 tons of phosphoric acid and

200,000 tons of phosphate-based fertilizers. The mines and beneficiation plants were operated by Negev Phosphates Ltd., and the phosphoric acid and fertilizers plant by Rotem Fertilizers Ltd., both subsidiaries of the government-owned Israel Chemicals Ltd.

Dead Sea Minerals The average salinity of the Dead Sea water, of up to 32 percent, is higher than that of any other large lake on record. The high salinity is due to the Dead Sea being a terminal lake, draining a catchment area of over 40,000 sq.km. and losing water only by evaporation at a rate of about 2 m. per year. Bromine constitutes 1.5 percent of the dissolved matter, potassium about 2.3 percent, and magnesium about 1.5 percent. The salt content of the Dead Sea is estimated to be 43,850 million tons, constituting a practically unlimited reserve for the production of potash, bromine, and magnesia.

The utilization of the Dead Sea minerals was pioneered by Moshe Novomeysky, who started his investigation in 1911, but only in the 1920s did his ideas take the shape of a practical plan. After obtaining a concession from the British Mandatory Government, the Palestine Potash Co. Ltd. was founded and the first plant for potash and bromine production was erected in 1930, at the northern tip of the Dead Sea (Kalya). Because of the limited terrain available for evaporation pans in this area, additional pans and another plant were constructed at the southern end of the Dead Sea (Sedom) in 1934. During the 1948 War of Independence, the northern plant was destroyed. After the war (1952) a new company, Dead Sea Works Ltd., started efforts to renew production at Sedom. Among the difficulties that had to be overcome were transportation of the products to ports and lack of water supply for the washing of the evaporation pans. These problems were solved through the construction of a new road to Beersheba (and later, through the extension of rail transport to Arad) and the discovery of groundwater sources in the area. Production was made more efficient by the development of advanced production processes, the construction of a new plant with higher production capacity, and of a dam closing off the southern basin of the Dead Sea to convert it into a giant evaporation pan (1964-1968). Potash production is based on evaporation of the Dead Sea brines in pans, by solar energy, to effect precipitation of salt (sodium chloride), transfer of the remaining brines to other pans where carnallite (potassium-magnesium chloride) is precipitated, and processing of the harvested carnallite for the production of sylvinite (potassium chloride). Annual production of potash in 1985/86 was 1,992,000 tons. About 85 percent of the product was exported, and the remainder processed into potassium nitrate fertilizer by Haifa Chemicals Ltd.

Bromine is produced from the Dead Sea brines by the Dead Sea Bromine Group in two plants, one at Sedom and the other south of Beersheba (Ramat Hovav). Production in 1985/86 amounted to 165,000 tons representing about 34 percent of world production. Most of the bromine is exported to Europe.

Dead Sea Periclase Ltd. manufactures magnesium oxide from magnesium chloride contained in the brines, after the extraction of other salts, at a plant located between Sedom and Arad, using the locally developed Aman process. Production was about 20,000 tons in 1985/86, and expected to rise later to 55,000 tons. Hydrochloric acid (100,000 tons a year) was obtained as a by-product.

Ceramic Clays and Glass Sand *Flint clay* deposits found in the Ramon Crater ("*Makhtesh Ramon*") in the Central Negev occur as pockets and more or less continuous layers in beds near the Triassic-Jurassic transition. The clay is composed mainly of kaolinite, and contains additional minerals (boehmite, diaspore) which make it valuable for the manufacture of refractory materials. Production came to 20,000 to 30,000 tons a year. *Kaolinite clays*, are also found in the Ramon Crater. Production for use in the ceramics industry was about 25,000 tons. *Bentonite clays* occur in strata of Lower Cretaceous age along the cliffs of the Ramon Crater. Small amounts were mined (2,000 tons a year) mainly for use in the refining of oils and fats, as fillers and as binding material in chicken-feed.

Other clay deposits were mined for use in the ceramics industry, for cement manufacture and for various other uses, in the Negev and in other parts of the country.

Glass sand. The large amounts of sand found along the Mediterranean coastline cannot be used for the manufacture of glass because of a high iron content, except some sands in the Caesarea area which, however, would require magnetic removal of iron minerals. Good glass sand occurs in sandstone sequences of Lower Cretaceous age in the craters of the Central Negev. Glass sand mined from deposits in HaTira Crater (*Makhtesh Gadol*) were exploited at a rate of 70,000–85,000 tons per year. Deposits of good glass sand were also found near Eilat.

The exploitation of both ceramic clays and glass sand in the Negev was in the hands of Negev Ceramic Materials Ltd.

Miscellaneous Non-Metallic Deposits *Gypsum*, mainly used as plaster of Paris and in the manufacture of cement, is produced in Ramon Crater where it occurs in Upper Triassic strata and in the Gesher-Menahemiya area, in the Jordan Valley south of Tiberias, from Late Tertiary strata. Gypsum also occurs in various other formations, in the Negev mountains, and also in the Sedom salt mountain. Reserves suffice to supply the needs of Israel's cement factories for an indefinite period.

Common salt. Salt is mined for industrial use from the Sedom salt mountain and also produced in evaporation pans from sea water near Athlit and at Eilat. Part is refined into table salt by the Israel Salt Co. at their Athlit plant. Annual production amounts (1987) to about 125,000 tons.

Various non-metallic mineral occurrences associated with veins in the crystalline basement rocks of Eilat are sporadically exploited in small quantities, mainly *felspars, mica, baryte* and *quartz*. Small *baryte* deposits are worked sporadically in the Judean Desert.

Fossil Fuels (Petroleum, Natural Gas, Oil Shales, Asphalt, Coal) After the discovery of petroleum near Heletz in the southern coastal plain in 1955, and the development of this field for production, a few additional small fields were found in the same area (Kokhav, Beror Hayil, Ashdod). Production reached a peak of one to 1.5 million barrels per year between 1959 and 1968. After that, production declined to 220,000 barrels in 1977 and 66,000 barrels in 1985. Despite high hopes for further oil discoveries, only one other very limited oil field (Tzuk Tamrur, Rosh Zohar area) was found in 1982, and it went out of production by 1985. Exploration continued in various parts of the country.

A *natural gas* field was found in the early 1960s in the Rosh Zohar area west of the Dead Sea, which supplied energy to the phosphate and periclase industries operating in this area. This field produced up to 1985 about 16 million cu.ft. Production in 1985 was 1,650 million cu.ft. Some natural (methane) gas was found in the coastal plain

(Ashdod, Shikma) in Late Tertiary formations. Methane gas was found also in the Huleh basin in Upper Galilee. *Oil shales* occur in Upper Cretaceous strata in various parts of the country. Investigations defined several areas that could be considered for exploitation: the Tzefa-Ef'e area in the northern Negev, west of the Dead Sea (600 mill.t), Nahal Tzin in the north-eastern Negev south of the Dead Sea (500 mill.t) and the Beth Shemesh area in the Judean foothills belt, west of Jerusalem (1,000 mill.t). Average organic matter content of these deposits was found to be 14—15 percent. A smaller deposit near Ein Bokek, on the western shore of the Dead Sea (70 mill.t) contains an average of 18 percent of organic matter but would be difficult to exploit because of the need to protect a mine against flooding by Dead Sea water.

Asphalt blocks sporadically appear floating in the Dead Sea and are "fished" for use in the pharmaceutical industry. Asphalt is also found filling fissures in rocks along the western shores of the Dead Sea and west of Mount Sedom (Nahal Heimar, Nahal Admon).

Some *coal* seams were found in oil drillings in the subsurface of the Rosh Zohar area west of the Dead Sea. They are not considered for exploitation at the present time. Extensive peat deposits in the Huleh Valley (Upper Galilee) defy exploitation mainly because of environmental problems.

Building Materials *Cement.* The abundant limestone and clay deposits of central Israel are utilized for the manufacture of cement at three localities: near Haifa (Yagur) and between Tel Aviv and Jerusalem, at Ramleh and at Hartuv. The 1985 production amounted to about 1.9 million tons.

Building stones. A great variety of limestones and dolomites is available for use as building stones in most parts of the country. Stone buildings are indeed one of the characteristics of towns and villages in the hill areas. High-quality stones that can be utilized as ornamental "marble" are quarried mainly in Galilee and, to a lesser extent, in the Judean Hills and in the Negev. Production of building stones was estimated roughly as 10 million tons per year.

Sand, gravel and aggregates. Numerous limestone quarries produced crushed stone for road metal and for use as aggregates in the building industry. Gravel and a calcareous sandstone locally known as *kurkar* were quarried for the same purpose. Scoriaceous tuff from the Golan Heights was used for lightweight concrete mixtures and also as a substratum for growing of plants in nurseries.

Thermo-mineral springs arising along the shores of the Dead Sea and mud with therapeutical properties are used in spas for the treatment of skin (especially psoriasis), rheumatic and other diseases. Thermo-mineral springs are also used as spas around Lake Kineret (Tiberias, Hamat Gader).

Z. SHIFTAN

MINORITIES IN ISRAEL. *See* ARABS IN ISRAEL; CHRISTIAN COMMUNITIES AND CHURCHES IN ISRAEL; DRUZE COMMUNITY IN ISRAEL.

MINSK CONFERENCE. First official convention of Russian Zionists, held in 1902. An earlier conference of Russian Zionists had been held in Warsaw, prior to the Second Zionist Congress (1898), without the permission of the Russian authorities. However by 1902 the attitude of the Tsarist authorities, toward the Zionist movement was more tolerant, and permission was granted to hold a seven-day Zionist meeting for 300 persons.

Minsk Conference participants, 1902. [Jewish Labor Movement Archives, Tel Aviv]

More than 500 delegates and about 200 guests attended the Minsk Conference. Mizrachi, which had been organized that year by religious Zionists, and a group of political Zionists who opposed the pursuit of cultural activities by the World Zionist Organization, were represented by almost 160 delegates. There were also some 60 delegates from the Democratic Faction, which had been formed after the Fourth Zionist Congress (1900) and which demanded that the Zionist Organization engage in cultural activities. The majority of the delegates, who did not belong to any of the factions, organized themselves in a "neutral," or "independent," faction. Among the delegates were 50 Hebrew writers, about 200 persons of higher education, and 40 rabbis. Numerous correspondents representing the Jewish and Russian press were also present. The gathering was addressed by Yehoshu'a Eisenstadt (Barzilai), Israel Belkind, and Hemda Ben-Yehuda, wife of Eliezer Ben-Yehuda, who came as guests from Eretz Israel. Yehiel Tschlenow was elected president of the conference.

Problems of organization and culture were the main topics of the debate. Menahem M. Ussishkin's suggestion that Zionist work be conducted by appointed leaders was opposed by the Organizational Committee, which held that the basic unit of the Zionist movement was the Zionist group or society, whose elected leaders should represent it in the central institutions. Ussishkin also proposed the formation of a Zionist young guard to be composed of unmarried men, whose services as orators, organizers of schools, and the like would be available to the leadership over a period of two years. His call met with a warm response, and some delegates expressed their readiness to volunteer.

Ahad Ha-Am, though not a delegate, was invited to address the conference on cultural problems. He stressed that it was false and dangerous to think that Zionism could be concerned exclusively with diplomacy and financial transactions. He placed the emphasis on culture and education. He proposed the establishment of a separate organization for cultural activities and the election of two parallel committees to assure equal opportunities for conducting cultural activities among religious and non-observant elements. Nahum Sokolow wanted the conference to adopt a resolution declaring Hebrew the official language of the Zionist movement and urged the establishment of modern heders, training teachers, and the establishment by Zionist rabbis of a yeshiva conducted in the spirit of Jewish nationalism.

The debate on cultural problems was stormy. Ahad Ha-Am's proposal to establish a separate organization for cultural activities was rejected even by members of the Democratic Faction, who feared a splitting of Zionist forces. Rabbi Yitzchak Yaakov Reines, however, agreed to the naming of two parallel educational committees, religious and nonobservant, thereby restoring peace.

The conference resolved that the Jewish National Fund begin to purchase land as soon as possible instead of waiting until larger sums had been collected. It also recommended cooperation with the Odessa Committee of the Hovevei Zion in matters relating to settlement activities in Eretz Israel. The Conference fused the Russian Zionists together as one unit.

The fact that the Russian Zionists had been able to obtain a permit from the authorities to convene a conference of their own aroused hopes that the activities of the Zionist movement could be legalized. However, these hopes were soon shattered. The attitude of the Tsarist government toward the Zionist movement and toward Jews in general underwent a change for the worse, culminating in the Kishinev pogrom of the spring of 1903. In June of the same year, all Zionist activity was prohibited under the pretext that while in the beginning the main Zionist aim had been to promote Jewish emigration to Palestine, the Zionists were now concentrating on strengthening Jewish nationalism instead. I. KLAUSNER

MINTZ, BINYAMIN. Israeli legislator, and leader of *Po'alei Agudat Israel (b. Lodz, Russian Poland, 1903; d. Petah Tikva, 1961). Mintz worked briefly in journalism in Poland, where he helped found Po'alei Agudat Israel, of which he eventually became world leader. Settling in Palestine in 1925, he continued his political and journalistic activities and established a printing press. In Agudat Israel he advocated *halutziyut* (pioneering) and collaboration with Zionist institutions. Prior to the founding of the State, he served on the Jewish Agency's Rescue Committee for the Jews of Europe and on the yishuv's Security Committee. A member of the Provisional Council of State, he was elected in 1949 to the Knesset, where he represented his party until his death. He served on the Labor and the Education and Culture Committees and was chairman of the Internal Affairs Committee from 1949 to 1951. In 1951 he became Deputy Speaker, a position he held until 1960, when he was named Minister of Posts. His entry into the Government made him the target of sharp personal attacks from ultra-Orthodox circles. He wrote and edited several books.

MIRON, DAN. Hebrew literary scholar (b. Tel Aviv, 1931). He studied at the Hebrew University and received his Ph.D. in comparative literature at Columbia University, New York (1967). He was a founding editor of *Akhshav*, an avant garde literary magazine. Professor of modern Hebrew literature at the Hebrew University, he was also a visiting professor at Columbia University and at the Center of Yiddish Studies of the Yivo Institute, New York.

Although Miron does not overlook the esthetic and generic elements underlying a literary work, he studies it in the socio-historical context in which it was created. In *Bodedim be-Mo'adam* (When Lovers Come Together, A Portrait of Hebrew Literature at the Turn of the Century, 1987), he criticized the confining one-sidedness of formalist criticism and its failure to take into account that literature is a product of a literary community ("the republic of literature") whose authors and readers are subject to social, economic, and historical forces. Miron is a prolific writer whose works cover several periods of modern Yiddish and Hebrew literature and deal with many writers: Mapu, Oxenfeld, Mendele Mocher Seforim, Berdichevski, Bialik, Tchernichowsky, Shalom Aleichem, Berkowitz, Alterman, Hazaz, and others. In *A Traveler in Disguise*, 1973, he explores the role which Mendele played in the development of Hebrew and Yiddish fiction. He examines the achievement of Shalom Aleichem in *Shalom Aleichem Pirkei Masa* (second edition 1976) and his Yiddish essay "Der image fun shtetl". He wrote on Bialik's contribution to this literary period *Ha-Pereda min ha-Ani* (Taking Leave of the Impoverished Self, 1986), and *Bo'ah Laila* (Come Night, 1987), and edited a critical edition of Bialik's work, the first volume of which appeared in 1983. He was awarded an Israel Prize in 1993. E. SPICEHANDLER

MISGAV AM. Kibbutz on the Lebanese border on the Naphtali Ridge of northern Upper Galilee. In 1945, its founders had to climb steep footpaths to the site. During the 1948 War of Independence, Misgav Am was isolated for months. In 1982, artillery bombardment of the kibbutz from the Lebanon was one of the incidents precipitating the Lebanon War. The kibbutz tends hill orchards in the neighborhood and, in the Huleh Valley, crop fields and carp ponds. It also runs a factory. The name means "Stronghold of the People." Population (1987), 289. E. ORNI

MISHMAR HA-EMEK. Kibbutz on the southwest rim of the Jezreel Valley. The first settlement in its region, it was founded in 1926 and soon became a center of the Ha-Shomer ha-Tza'ir movement. In April 1948 the kibbutz resisted a strong attack of the "Arab Liberation Army" which was trying to break through to Haifa. The kibbutz has intensive mixed farming and factories. It maintains a regional school and a local museum. Adjoining it is the large Menashe Forest. The name means "Guard of the Valley." Population (1987), 799. E. ORNI

MISHMAR HA-YARDEN. Moshav near the upper Jordan course. In 1890, a Hovevei Zion group from Russia founded a moshava near the "Benot Ya'akov" Bridge over the Jordan. Baron Edmond de Rothschild supported the village, but its progress was slow because of its isolation and endemic malaria. In 1946 it was reinforced by a group of World War II veterans. In May 1948, the Syrian army crossed the Jordan here and established a bridgehead at Mishmar ha-Yarden. It evacuated the destroyed moshava only as a result of the 1949 armistice terms. In 1949, the moshav, as well as the kibbutz Gador (484 inhabitants in 1987), were set up somewhat further west. A monument to the defenders stands in the ruined moshava. The moshav settlers, mostly originating from Morocco, engage in intensive irrigated farming. The name means "Guard of the Jordan." Population (1987), 318. E. ORNI

MITRANI, VICTOR. Army officer and Zionist leader (b. Turkey, 1888; d. Mexico, 1952). In 1921, after serving in the Turkish Army in the Balkan Wars, he emigrated to Havana,

Cuba, where he organized Jewish institutions for the Sephardi community. Beginning in 1928 he held positions of leadership in many Jewish organizations, particularly Zionist institutions, in Mexico. E. WEINFELD

MITZPA. Smallest Jewish village in Israel. Founded in 1908 by pioneers from Russia on land of the Jewish Colonization Association in Lower Galilee west of Tiberias, it has preserved much of its original layout of closely-grouped farmsteads with a surrounding basalt stone wall. The name means "Lookout Point." Population (1987), 103. E. ORNI

Rafael metal plant in Mitzpe Ramon, 1976. [Israel Govt. Press Office]

MITZPE RAMON. Town in the central Negev Hills, on the north rim of the Ramon Crater 54 mi. (87 km.) south of Beersheba. In 1954, a camp of laborers employed in the construction of the first road to Eilat became permanent, initially as an "urban cooperative." This failed and the place was turned into a development town, absorbing immigrants from North Africa and elsewhere. Local industries and nearby mining sites were expected to provide employment. Progress halted from 1968 when the new Sedom-Eilat highway diverted most traffic from the town. Hopes that the peace treaty with Egypt and the transfer of large army camps from Sinai to the Negev would lead to development and prosperity were disappointed. In the mid-1980s plans were formulated to renew the town's growth. It has a museum of Negev geology and nature and a garden of abstract rock sculptures. To the north lies the Israel Astronomic Observatory. Population (1987), 2,350. E. ORNI

MITZPIM (outlook settlements). Small settlements, most of them in the hills of Galilee, founded with the purpose of holding state lands in reserve and preventing encroachment on them. The program was devised in 1978 by the Jewish Agency Settlement Department and endorsed by Israel's government. It was carried out mostly in 1979/80, and 28 such outposts were set up within a few months. About ten more were added in Galilee and others in the Iron hills. Their initial tasks included land reclamation, improvement of grazing land, afforestation, and, in a few cases, also tourist services. The settlers received temporary housing and were free to decide later on their definitive settlement form, whether kibbutz, moshav, community village, etc. Fifteen to twenty-five families per settlement were seen as a norm for the initial period, but some remained even smaller while others increased in size. *See also* LAND POLICY IN ISRAEL. E. ORNI

MITZPOT (outposts). Name given in 1943 to the first Negev settlements, Gevulot, Bet Eshel, and Revivim. Sometimes the name was applied also to the 11 settlements founded in the Negev in the night after the Day of Atonement, 1946. E. ORNI

MIXED ARMISTICE COMMISSIONS. *See* ARMISTICE AGREEMENTS.

MIZRACHI (Mizrachi-Ha-Po'el ha-Mizrachi World Movement). Religious Zionist movement based on the Basle Program, and dedicated to the establishment of the People of Israel in the Land of Israel in accordance with the precepts of the Torah.

The rabbis who joined the incipient Zionist movement gave political and organizational expression to the work of their precursors Rabbi Judah *Alkalai, Rabbi Zvi Hirsch *Kalischer, Rabbi Elijah *Guttmacher and other religious luminaries who had advocated a return to Zion in the mid-19th century.

They were prompted to urgent action through the deteriorating economic position of east European Jewry, which threatened their physical and spiritual extinction. They saw the common task of all Jews, irrespective of ideology and outlook, as the provision of a haven of refuge and the creation of a new, productive life. The object was, therefore, practical, not messianic; any thought that this was intended to expedite the Divine Redemption was discouraged. They maintained that the Land of Israel belonged to the people of Israel not only in the political sense, but that it had to be built on the religious tradition of the past. Hence their slogan: "Eretz Israel for the People of Israel according to the Torah of Israel." Total Judaism could flourish only in the Land of Israel.

Accordingly, religious Zionism assumed a double task: (1) To bring the message of Zionism to the masses of religious Jewry and to convince them that the practical work for the resuscitation of the Jewish people and the Homeland was not incompatible with the traditional Jewish belief in the ultimate coming of the Messiah; and (2) to mobilize religious Jewry for a joint effort with the non-religious in the rebuilding of the Homeland.

Early History. The question of the relationship between Zionism and Judaism was raised at the Second Zionist Congress (1898). The official attitude of the leaders of the *World Zionist Organization (WZO) was that religion was a personal matter, and that the Organization as such had no official stand on it. This did not satisfy the religious delegates, but as long as the Zionist program was limited to political and economic issues only, they were reluctant to disturb the unity of the WZO. When, however, the Fifth Zionist Congress (1901) resolved that education in the spirit of Jewish nationalism was an important aspect of Zionist activity and an obligation for every Zionist, the religious Zionists felt that there could be no compromise in spiritual matters, maintaining that "nationalist", i.e., secularist, education was liable to destroy Judaism.

This development provided the incentive for the foundation of a new organization to be called Mizrachi (a telescoping of the words *merkaz ruhani*—"spiritual center"). Thus, the Mizrachi Organization was established, in 1902, by Rabbi Yitzhak Ya'akov *Reines, as a religious-national party within the framework of the WZO, which was, in accordance with the resolution of the Fifth Zionist Congress, recognized as a separate federation.

The founding conference met in Vilna in the spring of 1902, with leading rabbis and religious laymen attending. At the conference two trends clashed. The political trend strove to maintain the political character of the Zionist movement and opposed the Congress decision to engage in cultural activity. The other trend did not oppose cultural activity per se. On the contrary, it appreciated its importance and demanded that Mizrachi intensify religious educational activities and bring its influence to bear on the Zionist movement and its work in Eretz Israel.

The task of composing the first Mizrachi manifesto was given to Ze'ev (Wolf) Jawitz, scholar, writer, historian, and philosopher. The gist of the manifesto was that Zionism had come not only to create a safe haven of refuge for the scattered and persecuted Jewish people, but also to rejuvenate the people spiritually, because in the Diaspora it was impossible for Judaism and its soul, the holy Torah, to flourish or for its commandments to be fulfilled in their entirety.

The Mizrachi program, adopted by the majority of delegates, stressed that all the organization's activities and projects must be directly related to Zionism. Likewise, the manifesto declared that the Mizrachi was to attempt to "mobilize those Zionists who wish to rid Zionism of all foreign influences which have no direct connection with its political and practical program." Whereas these resolutions reflected the political trend of the founders, the views of those advocating religious-cultural work found expression in the call for positive cultural activity "in accordance with local conditions and in the spirit of Orthodoxy." In his addenda to the proclamation, Reines urged the Mizrachi branches to consolidate their membership through Torah study and other spiritual activity. The leadership of the Mizrachi represented both trends. The central office was established in Lida, Russia, where Reines lived.

Three months after the founding conference, delegates from the various local Mizrachi groups met in Lida under the chairmanship of Reines, with Jawitz and Rabbi Zalman Gurland of Vilna among the members of the administration. By means of circular letters signed by Reines, a widespread propaganda campaign was launched on behalf of Mizrachi, and within half a year the organization had become a force to be reckoned with in the Zionist movement.

At the Minsk conference of Russian Zionists, which took place three months later, the "culture" question was prominent on the agenda. Mizrachi, represented by some fifty delegates, participated as an organized bloc. It insisted that national rebirth was impossible without a full educational program. Joined by the secular nationalists, headed by Ahad Ha-Am, the delegates reached the following agreement: "In order to fulfill the Zionist Congress resolution with regard to mandatory national-educational activity, and taking into consideration the fact that there are among us two equal trends—the traditional nationalist and the secular nationalist—the Congress is to name two committees on education, with each side appointing its own members." In this manner official recognition was given to complete autonomy of religious-national education, solely conducted by Mizrachi through a special education committee.

The first representative convention of Mizrachi was held in Lida in the spring of 1903. During the first year of its existence Mizrachi succeeded in organizing 210 branches in Russia alone (which then included part of Poland, Lithuania, Latvia, and other countries), and others in Galicia, Romania, Austria, Hungary, Germany, England, and Switzerland. Beginnings were made in organizing Mizrachi branches in Eretz Israel and the United States. Mizrachi's surprising organizational success stemmed largely from its decision to engage in educational work in both the Diaspora and Eretz Israel.

At the convention the opponents of cultural activity renewed their campaign and fought vociferously against Mizrachi's decision, taken at the Minsk Conference, to make educational activity mandatory in the program of political Zionism. After sharp debates a compromise was reached. It was resolved that the Mizrachi program should not include activities which had no direct relevance to political and practical Zionism. However, it was up to the local branches to engage in such activity. In addition, the convention decided "to publish a Zionist monthly with a religious outlook, whose purpose will be to demonstrate the justice and truth of Zionism." Jawitz was entrusted with the editorship of the new monthly, *Ha-Mizrachi*, which became the official organ of the organization.

Founding Program. In order to clarify the aims of the organization, adopt bylaws, and lay down guidelines for future Mizrachi activity, the first international convention was convened. It took place in Pozsony (Pressburg, Hungary, now Bratislava, Czechoslovakia) in the summer of 1904 with the participation of over 100 delegates. It was there that the foundation was laid for the Mizrachi World Organization, whose program was summarized as follows:

1. Mizrachi is a Zionist organization based on the Basle Program, striving for the national rebirth of the People of Israel. Mizrachi considers the existence of the Jewish people conditional on the observance of Torah and Jewish tradition, The fulfillment of the commandments, and the return to the Land of the Forefathers.

2. Mizrachi shall remain within the Zionist Organization and fight within it for its own views and outlook. However, it shall maintain its own organization for the purpose of conducting its religious and cultural activities.

3. The aim of Mizrachi shall be to spread its ideals in all religious circles, creating and disseminating religious-national literature and educating the young in its spirit.

Before adjourning, the convention elected an international committee consisting of Reines as president and including Rabbis Nahum Gruenhaus, Yehuda Leib Fishman (*Maimon), Jawitz, and Yehoshua Heshel Farbstein. A special committee was named for the western countries under the chairmanship of Rabbi Dr. Nehemia Anton Nobel, with its office in Frankfort-on-Main. The difficult situation of the Jews of Russia after the outbreak of the Russo-Japanese war and the subsequent pogroms (1905) made it impossible for the Mizrachi World Center, whose headquarters was in Russia, to function. It was therefore decided to move the world headquarters to Frankfort.

The Frankfort period brought systematic order into the work of Mizrachi. The organization was officially recognized as a Federation within the WZO (a status granted only to parties of at least 3,000 members), thus freeing it from the control of the local Zionist authority, and improving its position both materially and organizationally. It was during this period that the Mizrachi's educational program was launched.

Educational Program. The Russian Mizrachi leaders, called by Reines to a special conference in Lida in the winter of 1908, appreciated the vital importance of creating an educational network of their own, one that would train its students in Torah and *mitzvot* (commandments), while providing them with the secular skills and knowledge they needed for everyday life. In 1908, they sent Fishman to Eretz Israel to explore ways and means of launching an educational and cultural program. On his arrival, Fishman met with Chief Rabbi Samuel Salant, the writer Yehiel Mikhal Pines, Mizrachi leaders, and Abraham Isaac Kook, Chief Rabbi of Jaffa, by whom he was particularly encouraged. The religious-national Tahkemoni School in Jaffa was taken over by Mizrachi, becoming the organization's first educational institution in the country. In the following years similar institutions were established. During World War I these schools were placed under the supervision of a board and formed part of the WZO's educational system, at the same time retaining their own character and program. In 1920 the Zionist Executive, meeting in London, decided that these religious schools were to constitute a "religious trend" under a special Mizrachi School Supervision Committee, which was to be responsible for organizing religious schools, selecting appropriate teachers, and setting up proper curricula. (*See also* EDUCATION IN ISRAEL.)

Culture and Religion. At the 10th Zionist Congress (1911) the question of cultural activities was once again on the agenda. To determine its position, Mizrachi convened a pre-Congress meeting of its delegates, at which it was decided to oppose the introduction of cultural activity into the Zionist program. At the Zionist Congress itself Nahum Sokolow called for the establishment of a general program for cultural work in all countries. This proposal was opposed on behalf of Mizrachi by Reines, Hermann Struck, and Rabbi Meir Berlin (*Bar-Ilan). When the majority voted to introduce cultural work into the framework of Zionist activity, the Mizrachi delegation walked out in protest.

Immediately after the Congress, Mizrachi held its convention in Berlin, where the main problem was to determine its attitude toward the Congress decision. The Russian and Polish delegates favored fighting for their cause within the Zionist movement by any means short of secession, which they insisted could have disastrous consequences. Opposing them were the delegates from the Frankfort office and some of the Swiss and Hungarian delegates, who were in favor of seceding from the World Zionist Organization. Finally the majority decided that Mizrachi should not alter its basic concept of the unity of the WZO, but should remain in the WZO and fight for its views from within.

With the victory of the Zionist "loyalists", a split developed in the Mizrachi ranks. Leaders who headed the Frankfort office left the Zionist movement. As a result, Mizrachi headquarters was moved from Frankfort to Altona, near Hamburg, with Dr. Louis Frank as chairman. Following this move, a central office was established in Eretz Israel, headed by Fishman, to intensify the practical program of Mizrachi, particularly in the field of education, and to coordinate the work in Eretz Israel with that of the Diaspora.

The Hamburg office, recognizing the importance of engaging in settlement work, as well as education, announced the creation of a fund to establish religious garden suburbs, particularly for members of the Old Yishuv (hitherto dependent on Diaspora financial support), so that they might engage in agricultural work, enjoy the fruits of their own labors and become self-supporting.

During the Hamburg period Rabbi Berlin became the general secretary and chief organizer of Mizrachi. Thanks to his personality, energy, and abilities as orator and leader, the work of Mizrachi advanced rapidly. The center of Mizrachi activity shifted to the United States. Berlin first visited the United States in 1913 and again in 1914, touring the length and breadth of the country and laying the foundations for the American Mizrachi Organization, whose first convention was held in Cincinnati, Ohio, in the spring of 1914.

The outbreak of World War I brought Mizrachi activity in Europe to a standstill. Berlin revisited the United States during the war in an effort to strengthen Mizrachi in the US, where it began to play an increasingly important role in American Jewish life and in American Zionism. Berlin was joined in his work by Fishman, who went to the US after being expelled from Eretz Israel by the Turks.

Interwar Period. With the cessation of hostilities, the Mizrachi movement was revived. Spurred on by the Balfour Declaration (1917), Mizrachi set out to organize Orthodox Jews for the work of reconstruction in Palestine. New branches, youth movements, and pioneer groups were organized in many countries. In several countries Mizrachi set up a religious-national educational movement of its own (the Yavne school network in Poland and Lithuania, and Tahkemoni in Belgium). Mizrachi was strongest in Poland, where it was led by such prominent personalities as Rabbis Leib Kovalsky, Yitzhak Nissenbaum, Samuel Brot, and Yehoshua Farbstein. Mizrachi strength was reflected in the elections to the local community councils and it was represented in the parliaments of Poland and Latvia.

In Palestine Mizrachi played an active role in the organization of the Jewish community and of the legislative and executive bodies of the yishuv, the Asefat ha-Nivharim and the Va'ad Le'umi. As a result of Mizrachi's efforts, the Chief Rabbinate of Palestine and local rabbinic offices were organized within the framework of the Keneset Yisrael, as were the religious courts, which had jurisdiction over Jewish marriage, divorce, personal status, and inheritance. In addition, religious councils were set up to deal with religious problems on the local level. The party devoted its main efforts to the development and expansion of its network of schools.

HA-PO'EL HA-MIZRACHI.

The period between the two wars saw the formation of Ha-Po'el ha-Mizrachi. The Third Aliya of the immediate postwar years brought with it Orthodox pioneers, particularly from the Tze'irei Mizrachi (Mizrachi Youth) in Poland. These young settlers were loyal to the aims of the Mizrachi movement and sought self-fulfillment in a life dedicated to *Torah va-Avoda (Torah and Labor) in Palestine. This slogan became the basis of the religious labor movement, which soon developed into the Ha-Po'el ha-Mizrachi Organization. In 1921 Orthodox pioneers organized the first branches of Ha-Po'el ha-Mizrachi in Jaffa, Petah Tikva, Jerusalem, and Rishon le-Zion. In the spring of 1922 the Ha-Po'el ha-Mizrachi Organization of Palestine was founded with the following program: Ha-Poel ha-Mizrachi will endeavor to build the country in accordance with the teachings of Torah and tradition through labor. Its aim is to put its members on a firm material and spiritual footing, to develop and strengthen religious sentiment among the workers, and to make it possible for them to live as religious workers." The youth branch, *Bnei Akiva, was founded in 1922. In 1925 a worldwide movement was established embracing Ha-Po'el ha-Mizrachi in Palestine and Mizrachi youth, and pioneering movements in the Diaspora, adhering to the ideology of Ha-Po'el ha-Mizrachi, with headquarters in Jerusalem.

Ha-Po'el ha-Mizrachi in Palestine founded cooperatives, housing projects and credit institutions to help its members. In 1925 it established its first moshav, Sedeh Ya'akov, and in the 1930s it established its first kibbutzim. The Igud ha-Moshavim (the Ha-Po'el ha-Mizrachi Moshavim Union) has 97 moshavim and communal settlements, with many departments catering to every aspect of the life of its membership, with special attention to the younger generation.

Though Mizrachi and Ha-Po'el ha-Mizrachi were separate organizations, they collaborated within the Zionist movement, both advocating adherence to Jewish traditional concepts and values, and appearing on a joint list for elections to Zionist Congresses. Their halutzic movement *Bahad was founded in the 1930s and its kibbutz movement *Ha-Kibbutz ha-Dati in 1934.

World War II and the post-war period. During World War II Mizrachi and Ha-Po'el ha-Mizrachi in the free countries participated in efforts to aid Jews in Nazi-occupied Europe. In Palestine they cooperated in all efforts to consolidate and strengthen the yishuv. The movement grew in the free countries as a result of the arrival of refugees from the Nazi-dominated European continent. Many new branches were opened, and educational and cultural activities were conducted on a large scale.

During the years immediately following the war, Mizrachi and Ha-Po'el ha-Mizrachi participated in the struggle against Great Britain for Jewish immigration to Palestine. Their emissaries were active in the Displaced Persons camps, reestablishing the religious Zionist movement in continental Europe and preparing the survivors of the Holocaust for settlement in Palestine. They were also active in the *Beriha organization and in the organization of "illegal" transports to Palestine. Mizrachi and Ha-Po'el ha-Mizrachi took part in protests and special fundraising campaigns all over the world and in Hagana and settlement activities in Palestine.

At that time, Rabbis Fishman and Wolf Gold, representing Mizrachi, and Hayim Moshe Shapira and Shelomo Zalman Shragai, representing Ha-Po'el ha-Mizrachi were members of the Zionist Executive. Fishman was among the Jewish leaders arrested by the British in June, 1946. Gold was a member of the Jewish Agency delegation to the United Nations in 1947. In the period immediately preceding the establishment of the State of Israel, Shapira played a major role in getting the Hagana and the Irgun Tzeva'i Le'umi to agree to cooperate.

Development since the Establishment of Israel. After the proclamation of the State of Israel in May, 1948, Fishman and Shapira represented Mizrachi and Ha-Po'el ha-Mizrachi in the Provisional Government, the former as Minister of Religious Affairs and War Victims, and the latter as Minister of Immigration and Health. In the elections to the first Knesset Mizrachi and Ha-Po'el ha-Mizrachi joined with other religious parties to form the United Religious Front, which received 12.2 percent of the total vote and won 16 seats in the Knesset. In the next elections, in 1951, Mizrachi and Ha-Po'el ha-Mizrachi ran on a joint ticket without the other religious parties. They received 8.3 percent of the votes and 10 seats; and in 1955, 9.1 percent of the votes and 11 seats.

NATIONAL RELIGIOUS PARTY (MAFDAL).

In 1956 Mizrachi and Ha-Po'el ha-Mizrachi merged to form the National Religious Party (NRP—Miflaga Datit Le'umit). In 1959 the party received 9.9 percent of the vote and 12 seats in the Knesset; in 1961—9.8 percent and 12 seats; in 1965—8.9 percent and 12 seats; and in 1969—9.7 percent and 12 seats. It then held three portfolios: Interior (Shapira), Social Welfare (Yosef Burg), and Religious Affairs (Zerah Warhaftig).

The National Religious Party was a member of all coalition governments, with the exception of a short period in 1958–59, when the "Who is a Jew?" controversy caused its temporary withdrawal from the government. The party was headed by Moshe Shapira, who played a leading role in the establishment of the government of National Unity on the eve of the Six-Day War of 1967. Shapira held the party together, despite the various ideological trends within it. His death in 1970 left no unchallenged heir. Until 1967, the National Religious Party's main interest had been in advocating legislation of a religious nature and its role in external affairs had been passive. After 1967, however, it became dominated by those elements committed ideologically to the permanent settlement by Jews of the entire Land of Israel. This commitment to the retention by Israel of control over the Administered Areas meant a deeper involvement in aspects of Israel's foreign policy. The Party, led by Zevulun Hammer (who served as Minister of Education and later as Minister for Religions), joined the Likud-led coalitions of 1977 and 1981 and supported the policies of Menahem Begin. It was also a member of the 1984 and 1988 governments of national unity.

Although it maintained its strength of 11–12 members in the 1973 and 1977 elections, it dropped sharply to 6 members in 1981, 4 in 1984, and 5 in 1988. This was due to internal power struggle between the ideological factions, polarization, and defections to other religious and nationalist parties.

In 1988, its shift to the political right prompted the emergence of a new center religious party, called Meimad, which, however, failed to win any seats in that year's elections.

In the government, the Knesset, and the municipalities, the National Religious Party pressed for the public observance of the Sabbath and the Jewish holidays and the dietary laws. It constantly upheld the thesis that Jewish laws relating to personal status (marriage and divorce) are binding on all Jews living in Israel.

Structure of the World Movement. The World Mizrachi Executive is the supreme body of the movement, elected at the world convention. There are Mizrachi branches throughout the free world. Rabbi Meir Bar-Ilan (Berlin) served as president of the world movement from 1929 to 1949. The 18th world convention held in Jerusalem in 1949 elected a three-man presidium comprising Maimon, Gold and Leon Gellman, who was at the time president of the Mizrachi in the United States. From 1962 to 1967 Rabbi Bezalel Cohen served as chairman of the World Council. Subsequent chairmen were Rabbi Zemah Zambrowsky, Rabbi I. Dolgin, and Moshe Krone.

The World Mizrachi founded or sponsored a wide network of educational, financial, economic and cultural enterprises, ranging from kindergartens to the *Bar-Ilan University in Ramat Gan (founded in 1955); the United Mizrachi Bank, mortgage banks and building companies, the Mosad Rav Kook publishing house, the Talmudic Encyclopedia, the Institute for the Complete Israeli Talmud, synagogues, etc. The movement's main organ is the daily *Ha-Tzofeh*. It also publishes a number of periodicals in various languages, including Russian. It also sponsors the Mifal ha-Torah Medical Aid Fund for the yeshiva population. The Ha-Po'el ha-Mizrachi Trade Union has over 130,000 members, with its own (Gilad) Pension Fund, Tiferet Banim senior citizens' and economic cooperatives.

As an integral member of the WZO, the religious Zionist movement is represented on its Executive. In 1989, its two Executive members—Yitzhak Meir and Eliezer Sheffer were in charge of the Departments of Torah Education and Culture in the Diaspora, and the Youth Leadership and Volunteers projects, respectively.

The Center for Religious Education. In 1953 the Knesset disbanded the three separate trends of education, which had been in operation until then (the Labor, the Mizrachi, and the General Zionist trends) and set up one national framework comprising two streams—State and State Religious education.

With the passing of the State Education Act (*see* EDUCATION IN ISRAEL) it was no longer necessary to maintain independently the Mizrachi schools, which now became the responsibility of the Ministry of Education, with an autonomous section for religious education to oversee the teaching curriculum, the appointment of teachers, school supervisors and principals. Nevertheless, the struggle over education did not abate. Where religious schools already existed Mizrachi saw an obligation in promoting and enhancing them by additional hours of religious study; where no religious school existed, it sought to set one up and nurture it until it qualified for inclusion in the state system.

In 1963 the World Mizrachi and Ha-Po'el ha-Mizrachi decided at their world convention to revive the Center for Religious Education to handle all stages of religious education in Israel, to insure the equality and status of the religious department, and to safeguard the right of parents to choose the stream they preferred. In its public struggle the Center was backed by the religious section at the Ministry of Education, the Mizrachi representatives in the Knesset, the parents' associations, and activists and communal leaders. On the practical level the National Religious Women's movement, Emuna, established hundreds of kindergartens and day-care centers, which were the foundation stone for more religious schools in many locations all over Israel. The Center also promoted extra-curricular activities for pupils as well as parents, whose life style did not always match the education received by their children. This was done by way of evening clubs for parents, sponsored by Emuna, where lectures and discussions were conducted by rabbis, teachers, psychologists etc.

Hesder Yeshivot. Brought up on a national-religious ideology, graduates of Bnei Akiva and similarly motivated youth desired to continue their talmudical studies during their military service. Thus the idea of the hesder yeshiva was born,—the *hesder* (arrangement) with the Army being alternating periods of army training and studies.

The first to be so adapted was Kerem be-Yavne, established by Mizrachi in 1953. Following its success, other hesder yeshivot were established. In 1989 they numbered 14, with 3,250 soldier-students.

Mishmeret Tze'ira World Organization. World Mishmeret Tze'ira was established at the end of the 1950s to provide a framework for religious Zionist youth in the 20–40 age group, living in the Diaspora. Its aim is to foster aliya nuclei for young married couples; to prepare a young religious Zionist leadership and to encourage involvement in the local community. Several such nuclei have been set up in Israel.

Elitzur World Organization. Elitzur, Israel's religious sports association, the third largest in the country, established in 1939, combines sports activities with Jewish religious values. The association has over a hundred clubs with a membership of more than 25,000. They participate in all league games, except for football which is usually played on Saturday. In the wake of the first "Elitzuria" international sports festival, held in 1983, a World Association was founded, and there are now Elitzur branches in many major Jewish communities. The second Elitzuria, held in 1988, constituted a central part of Elitzur's 50th anniversary celebrations.

Yavneh Olami World Yavneh was established in 1984 as the world organization of religious students attending a university or yeshiva in various parts of the Jewish world. Its headquarters are in Jerusalem and it has branches in the USA, Canada, Argentina, Brazil, England, France, and Belgium, and representatives in 17 other countries. It provides a framework for religious students on campuses, enhancing their Jewish awareness and Israel orientation, providing material and speakers to counter anti-Zionist activities and propaganda. Yavneh Olami is recognized by the World Zionist Organization, with whose youth section it cooperates.

Emuna (formerly Mizrachi Women's Organization). Religious Zionist women's organization with a membership of over 130,000 women in 23 countries. It has a two-fold goal:

1) To support national religious education institutions in Israel.

2) To strengthen Judaism among Jewish women in the Diaspora through educational programs designed to deepen their Jewish roots and combat assimilation.

The organization was founded in 1977 with nine member countries. Its institutions in Israel included (1989) over 180 daycare centers and kindergartens, 4 children's homes, a children's village, 6 high schools for girls and a community college. Social welfare services offered by Emuna of Israel include family counselling services, literacy programs for women, parent-consciousness groups, community leadership development programs, golden-age daycare centers, and summer camps for mothers of large families.

In some countries where conditions require it, Emuna offers an intensive education program designed specifically for women of varying secular educational levels and different languages. Branches of Emuna in the Soviet Union were opened in 1988 with specially tailored educational material being sent to these groups in Leningrad and Moscow. It publishes the magazine *Kol Emuna*

World Emuna has member organizations in the following countries:

Israel, Argentina, Australia, Austria, Belgium, Brazil, Canada, Denmark, France, Gibraltar, Great Britain, Guatemala, Holland, Ireland, Mexico, Paraguay, South Africa, Spain, Sweden, Switzerland, United States, Uruguay, and the USSR.

Institute of Religious Zionism. The Institute in Jerusalem, established by Rabbi Judah L. Maimon, to preserve and promote the study of the contribution of Religious Zionist

Aerial view of Kefar Batya, the Bessie Gotsfeld Children's Village and Farm School, a Mizrahi Women's project in Ra'anana. [Mizrahi Women's Organization of America]

Jewry to the establishment and ongoing existence of the State of Israel. Among the goals of the Institute are 1) Publication of biographies and basic writings of the founders of religious Zionism.

2) The promotion of research, and publication of significant studies in the field of religious Zionist history.

3) The ongoing maintenance and expansion of the Archives of Religious Zionism.

4) Provision of financial incentives to students and scholars to encourage study and research of religious Zionism.

5) Providing libraries of books on religious Zionism to high schools to encourage their students to write school papers on religious Zionist subjects.

The Institute has sponsored the publication of some 25 volumes including the writings of Rabbis Kalischer, Alkalai, and Friedland; *Encyclopedia of Religious Zionism* (five volumes); and a biography of Rabbi Reines. The Institute is affiliated with Yad ha-Rav Maimon and the Rav Kook Institute.

Archives of Religious Zionism The Archives, established as part of the Institute of Religious Zionism, are housed in Mosad Ha-Rav Kook in Jerusalem. Their main purpose is the search for and accumulation of significant historic archival material concerning religious Zionism throughout the world. Such material includes documents, correspondence, minutes and records of meetings, conventions and gatherings; pamphlets, newspapers, books and photographs. The Archives contain some one and a half million items.

Amit Women (formerly American Mizrachi Women) Women's religious Zionist organization in the United States, founded in 1925 by Mrs. Bessie (Batya) Gotsfeld of New York. In 1988 Amit had over 80,000 members in 425 chapters in America and Israel. It is directed by a national board in the US and an Israeli executive board. Since its first educational project in Israel, the Beit Tzei'rot High School (today, Amit High School) opened in Jerusalem in 1933, Amit has grown to support and administer a network of 11 Technological Religious High Schools, 2 Youth Villages, 1 Junior College of Technology, 2 community centers, and 3 children's homes, serving over 8,000 children throughout Israel.

During World War II Amit was involved in US war-bond and blood-donor projects and afterwards in refugee relief and rehabilitation. Amit has been a non-governmental observer at the UN and a member of the National Women's Committee on Civil Rights. In 1948 it established the Annual America-Israel Friendship Award. In the 1960s, Amit was one of four authorized members of the United States Coordinating Committee for Youth Aliya.

The Israel Ministry of Education in 1981 designated the organization as its official network for religious secondary vocational and technological education, giving it a voice in educational policy-making and advisory status. This also gave Amit responsibility for additional religious high schools.

Amit has been caring for homeless and deprived children since its inception, but since 1983 has instituted a unique non-institutional childcare philosophy. In Jerusalem, at Bet ha-Yeled in Gilo, "Mishpahton" in Baka and Ma'on Amit in Talbieh, 216 children, aged 6–14, are living in "family units" composed of 12 children each, with a young married couple acting as surrogate parents and a "big sister", a girl doing national service. They live as a family in an apartment within the complex and all support services are provided by Amit. Y. GOLDSCHLAG—B. MINDEL

MIZRAHI. *See* MIZRACHI.

MIZRAHI, LEON (Arie), Romanian Zionist leader, lawyer, and publicist (b. Bucharest, 1899; d. Tel Aviv 1967). He studied law, literature, and philosophy at Bucharest University. From his early youth he was a Zionist activist, a founder of Ha-Talmid, a Zionist pupils' association and subsequently secretary of the Hasmonea Zionist students' association. In 1919 he was elected chairman of the Federation of Zionist Youth Organizations in Romania and was appointed editor and director of the Zionist literary journal, *Hasmonea*.

Mizrahi was one of the leaders of the radical Zionist association Renasterea (Revival) which was grouped around the Zionist leader Dr. Stern-Cochavi and which constituted the major stream of Romanian Zionism. In 1928 he was elected a member of the Zionist Executive and two years later chairman of the Zionist Organization. In this period he was one of the promoters and founders of the Jewish Party. In 1939–41 he was reelected chairman of the Zionist Organization and headed the Zionist movement during the persecutions of the Legionnaires (the Romanian fascists).

He represented the Romanian Zionist Movement at several Zionist Congresses and at the World Jewish Congress.

In 1941 Mizrahi immigrated to Palestine where he worked on behalf of the Jews of Romania; he was one of the founders of the Association of Romanian Immigrants and from 1948 was its chairman.

Mizrahi helped to influence the consolidation of Romanian Zionism through his public activity and his many articles which were collected and published in *Am Dori u-Ma'avakav*. E. OPHIR

MIZUG GALUYOT. Sociocultural concept forming one of the major basic tenets of Zionism and the reconstituted Jewish State of Israel. Mizug Galuyot (Heb., "Merging of the Exiles") is based on the historic fact of the Galut, or exile, which led to an increasing dispersion of the Jewish communities in many lands and ultimately resulted in the emergence of disparate Jewish Diasporas, each of which had absorbed definite social and cultural influences from its host country. Thus, especially in the wake of the emancipation and the ensuing Jewish assimilation, the Jewish people came to comprise, in actual fact, a large number of "exiles," each group with a distinct sociocultural physiognomy of its own. When these communities, or parts of them, began to gather in Eretz Israel, it soon became evident that certain sociocultural changes would have to take place within them in order to enable the yishuv to develop a distinct national identity. This process of mutual adjustment and fusion, which has become an ideological imperative for most of the yishuv leadership, is termed Mizug Galuyot. The related problems and challenges were particularly acute in the years following 1948. *See* ETHNIC GROUPS IN ISRAEL

Start of Hanukka torch relay race at Modi'in, 1978. [Israel Govt. Press Office]

MODI'IM (MODI'IN). Region and ancient town in the northern Judean foothills, 7.5 mi. (12 km.) east of Lydda (Lod); today the Arab village of Midya. Modi'in was the home town of Mattathias the Hasmonean, leader of the Maccabean revolt in the second century BCE. His son Simon built his family's mausoleum there. During the Hanukka festival, a torch is lit near the tombs, brought by runners to Jerusalem, and presented to the President of Israel. Since 1950, the Modi'im Forest has been planted further west, expanding the Herzl Forest. In 1965, the moshav shitufi Mevo Modi'im was founded as a Nahal outpost near the armistice border. The areas on the eastern side were developed with the founding of new settlements.

E. ORNI

MO'ETZA DATIT. *See* RELIGIOUS COUNCILS IN ISRAEL.

MO'ETZET HA-PO'ALOT (Working Women's Council of Israel). *See* NA'AMAT.

Shemuel Mohilever. [Zionist Archives]

MOHILEVER, SHEMUEL. Rabbi and early Zionist leader in Russia, founder of the *Hovevei Zion movement (b. Glubokoye, Vilna District, Russia, 1824; d. Bialystok, Russian Poland, 1898). Mohilever received his rabbinical ordination at the Yeshiva of Volozhin and was well versed not only in religious studies, kabbala, hasidism, and Jewish history but also in mathematics, engineering, Russian, German, and Polish. After five years in business, he entered the rabbinate, occupying pulpits in various communities and gaining a reputation as a public servant and spokesman of Russian Jewry.

Writing about Jewish affairs, Mohilever urged a positive attitude toward agriculture and manual labor and a strengthening of Jewish education by the addition of general cultural subjects to religious studies. After the pogroms in southern Russia in 1881–82 he helped organize Jewish emigration to Eretz Israel, and in 1882 he formed the first Hovevei Zion group in Warsaw. Meeting Baron Edmond de Rothschild in Paris, he persuaded him to support the settlement in Eretz Israel of several Jewish families from Russia, who founded Ekron, the first settlement project undertaken by Rothschild. Mohilever was a trusted mediator between the baron and the settlers in their disagreements. When the settlements faced economic disaster because of the *shemita* (sabbatical year) laws, he joined other rabbis (1899) in permitting the use of the land during the sabbatical year through a fictitious sale to a gentile. His Zionist activities in Bialystok led to his election as rabbi there.

As a member of the Executive Board of Hovevei Zion, Mohilever traveled to Eretz Israel with a group of settlers in 1890 and helped found Rehovot. He sought a basis in Jewish law for his Zionist outlook, citing the sages and commentators in support of his opinion that "God prefers to have His children live in their land even if they do not observe the Torah, rather than have them observe the Torah properly but live in the Diaspora." He called on Hovevei Zion to turn from philosophy to practical participation in, and monetary support for, the rebuilding of Eretz Israel.

In 1893 he became head of the Hovevei Zion in Bialystok. An early supporter of Herzl, Mohilever helped Herzl lay plans for the First Zionist Congress (1897) but was prevented by ill health from attending the assembly. In appreciation of his efforts the Congress elected him one of the four representatives from Russia to the Central Executive Committee, whose task was to carry out the resolutions of the Congress, transact Zionist business, and prepare for the next Congress. He exerted great influence on Jewish communities, and urged the observance of Jewish traditions within the ranks of the Zionist public.

Some of Mohilever's writings were published posthumously. Gan Shemuel, a kibbutz near Hadera, is named for him.

G. BAT-YEHUDA

MOKADY, MOSHE. Israeli painter (b. Tarnow, Galicia, Austria, 1902; d. Tel Aviv, 1974). Immigrating to Palestine in 1920, he made fine early paintings under the influence of Rubin, Lubin, Gutman, and others of the early Tel Aviv School. Between 1927–32 he studied in Paris, where the gloomy palette of the Jewish painters there influenced the work for which he is best known: anguished low-key portraits of waif-like boys set against somber backgrounds. Back in Palestine, Mokady also painted stage sets for the Habimah, Ohel, and Cameri (Chamber) theaters. Towards the end of the 1950s Mokady abandoned figurative painting for lively colorful abstraction.

M. RONNEN

MOKED, GABRIEL. Hebrew literary critic (b. Warsaw, 1933). He arrived in Palestine as a child (1946) and later studied at the Hebrew University, Tel Aviv University, and Oxford, receiving his Ph.D. in philosophy at Oxford. He taught Jewish philosophy at Tel Aviv University.

Moked published in two fields: literary criticism and philosophy. A founding editor of *Akhshav*, he was also an editor of *Ata*, a left-wing political journal. He published books on Kafka, Agnon, and works on Berkeley and esthetics. Among his works are *Iyunim be-Metamorfosis le-Franz Kafka* (Studies on Franz Kafka's 'Metamorphosis", 1956) and *Shivhei Adiel Amzeh* (In Praise of Adiel Amzeh [by Agnon], 1957). Moked published a series of literary-philosophical ruminations in various periodicals under the title of *Variatzyot* (Variations), some of which appeared in *Mivhar Variatzyot* (Selected Variations, 1979).

E. SPICEHANDLER

MONASH, SIR JOHN. Australian war hero, engineer, and lawyer who was commander-in-chief of the Australian forces in the Allied Armies on the western front during World War I (b. Melbourne, 1865; d. Melbourne, 1931). Monash was born into an immigrant family from Posen; his uncle was the historian Heinrich Graetz. An exceptional engineer and innovator, he introduced reinforced concrete to Australia and was involved in the design and construction of some of the main bridges in Victoria.

Monash was not a professional soldier. He volunteered for the local militia at the age of 19, was commissioned three years later, and at the outbreak of World War I was already a colonel. He commanded a brigade at Gallipoli, served in France, and in 1918 led the entire Australian and New Zealand Army Corps.

In 1920 he was appointed head of the Victorian Electricity Commission, directing a massive program to industrialize that State's natural resources for energy. He was elected Vice- Chancellor of Melbourne University in 1923. In that capacity he proposed the inclusion of Hebrew as a subject in the University curriculum.

Already as a young man, Monash expressed interest in the Jewish community and while not attracted by the ritual aspects of Judaism, he defined himself culturally as a Jew. In 1920 he presided over a Zionist public meeting addressed by Israel Cohen, making a donation, and indicating his readiness to help the Zionist movement. In 1927, when Alexander Goldstein visited Australia on behalf of Keren ha-Yesod, Monash accepted a position of official leadership, agreeing to become the honorary president of the newly-formed Zionist Federation of Australia. Although Monash's role was essentially passive, partly by choice, and perhaps due also to the lack of professional leadership which might have utilized his support of Zionist programs, his name lent great prestige to Zionism in Australia.

During the last five years of his life he endorsed the policies of the Zionist movement, including the stand taken by the Zionists on the Wailing Wall affair of 1929, a stand which precipitated strong anti-Zionist reaction on the part of Anglo-Jewish patrician leadership in Australia. Monash consistently denied any contradiction between being patriotic and loyal to the Empire, and being a good Jew and Zionist.

After his death the Zionist Organization in Australia organized a number of projects in his memory, and in 1945 the settlement of Kefar Monash was established in Palestine. E. HONIG

MOND, SIR ALFRED MORITZ. *See* MELCHETT, 1ST BARON. FORD, 1ST BARON.

MONSKY, HENRY. *B'nai B'rith leader, attorney, and convener of the *American Jewish Conference (b. Omaha, Nebr., 1890; d. New York, 1947). After receiving his degree from Creighton University in Omaha, he practiced law in his native city all his life. His election to the presidency of the local B'nai B'rith lodge marked the beginning of a career of volunteer social service which, in 1921, brought him to the presidency of District Six, the largest district of B'nai B'rith, and, in 1938, to the national presidency of the order—the first Zionist and Jew of Eastern European background to attain that office. He was reelected in 1941. Under his leadership, B'nai B'rith doubled its membership, becoming the largest Jewish service organization in the world. Monsky rapidly rose to national prominence. He threw himself into efforts to arouse American public opinion to the dangers of Hitlerism and participated in every project aiming to help the victims of Nazism. He was awarded many citations for patriotic work during World War II.

An ardent Zionist, Monsky was particularly active in promoting greater unity in Jewish community life. He was one of the organizers of the General Jewish Council in 1938 and of the National Community Relations Advisory Council (NCRAC) in 1944. His most significant achievement was the initiation of the American Jewish Conference. At the time of his death, Monsky was chairman of the Interim Committee, its administrative body. C.B. SHERMAN

MONTEFIORE, SIR FRANCIS ABRAHAM. Lawyer and Zionist leader in England (b. London, 1860; d. there, 1935). A grandnephew of Sir Moses Montefiore, whose baronetcy he inherited, he was one of Herzl's early followers. In 1900 Herzl, who regarded Sir Francis as his right-hand man in his efforts to win over the Rothschilds and other aristocratic and wealthy Jewish leaders, considered turning over to him the presidency of the World Zionist Organization (WZO) since Montefiore, unlike Herzl, was a man of independent means (Herzl's *Diaries*, entry for 25 April 1900). In 1899 Sir Francis presided at the inauguration of the Zionist Federation of Great Britain and Ireland, whose president he became.

He addressed the Fifth Zionist Congress (1901) on the subject of the Jewish Colonial Trust, expressing his confidence in the bank and calling for an objective evaluation of its situation and projects. It was in a letter to Sir Francis as president of the Zionist Federation that Herzl set forth his final declaration of policy with regard to the East Africa scheme. At the beginning of World War I, however, it seems that Sir Francis, like some other Englishmen, began to suspect the WZO of acting as a propaganda instrument for Germany and the Central Powers. Montefiore then resigned from the Zionist movement and had no further association with it. J. FRAENKEL

Sir Moses Montefiore.
[Zionist Archives]

MONTEFIORE, SIR MOSES. Philanthropist, Jewish communal leader, and supporter of projects in Eretz Israel (b. Leghorn, Italy, 1784; d. Ramsgate, England, 1885). A member of a well-to-do Sephardi family, he was brought to England in infancy and became one of London's most successful financiers. In 1824 he retired from business to devote all his time to Jewish communal and philanthropic work, in which he was aided by his wife, Judith Cohen Montefiore (1784–1862). From 1835 to 1874 Sir Moses (he was knighted in 1837 and created a baronet nine years later) was president of the Board of Deputies of British Jews. Throughout his life he not only gave large amounts of money to charity but also interceded with rulers and governments for the rights of Jews the world over and actively worked for the welfare of the Jews of Eretz Israel.

In England (where he became sheriff of London in 1837 and later a member of the city of London lieutenancy), Sir Moses and his brother-in-law Nathan Mayer Rothschild headed many deputations to Parliament, prime ministers, and peers to secure civic equality for Jews in Great Britain. Sir Moses and his wife were frequently invited to the court of Queen Victoria, who had visited his estate, East Cliff Lodge, in Ramsgate, two years before her accession to the throne.

In 1840 Montefiore interceded personally with Mohammed Ali, the ruler of Egypt, and with Sultan Abdul-Medjid I in the Damascus blood libel case. In 1846 and 1872 he visited Russia, where he called on Tsars Nicholas I and Alexander II to plead with them on behalf of their Jewish subjects. In 1859 he was in Rome to intercede in the Mortara forced-baptism case; five years later he visited Morocco, where he persuaded the sultan to enact a decree promising equality to his Jewish subjects. In 1867 he went to Romania, from where he had received reports of violent anti-Semitism. In each of these endeavors he had the support and cooperation of the British government.

In Eretz Israel, Sir Moses not only made generous financial donations but encouraged the Jews to engage in productive activities, particularly agriculture. He paid seven visits to the Holy Land, the first in 1827 and the last in 1875. On his first five visits he was accompanied by his wife, who recorded their travel impressions in a privately published volume, *Notes from a Private Journal of a Visit to Egypt and Palestine by Way of Italy and the Mediterranean* (1844). During his 1839 visit he sponsored the first census to be taken of the Jewish population in Eretz Israel since ancient times (*The Children of Israel Living in the Holy Land in the Year 5599–1839*). He then contemplated leasing land from Mohammed Ali and planned to form, following his return to England, a company for the cultivation of the land and to encourage Jews to return to Eretz Israel. "Many Jews now emigrate to New South Wales, Canada, etc., but in the Holy Land they would find a greater certainty of success," he noted in his diary. "By degrees I hope to induce the return of thousands of our brethren to the Land of Israel." On his return journey, he met with Mohammed Ali in Cairo and proposed the establishment of a joint bank with a capital of £1,000,000 and branches in Alexandria, Beirut, Damascus, Cairo, Jaffa, and Jerusalem. The project never materialized, but at the time the ruler gave Sir Moses assurances that he would favor a wide latitude for Jewish settlement in the Holy Land.

After his visit in 1849, Sir Moses founded a small textile plant in Jerusalem. In 1854 he initiated a fundraising drive for the relief of famine victims in Eretz Israel.

During his 1855 visit, Sir Moses provided funds to help Jewish families from Safed and Tiberias settle in rural areas, but the project did not materialize. However, he succeeded in founding in Jerusalem a girls' school in which the students were taught dressmaking, embroidery, and housekeeping in addition to other subjects. Probably influenced by Sir Moses' own strict adherence to Orthodox religious practice, some of the rabbis of the Old Yishuv, who then generally opposed modern education, gave their approval to the school. On that visit, Sir Moses bought land near Jaffa that was turned into the first Jewish orange plantation in the country. He also purchased land outside the walls of the Old City of Jerusalem in order to build a hospital with funds left by Judah Touro, the American Jewish philanthropist. Subsequently, however, he decided to build instead a housing project for the poor. This quarter, named Mishkenot Sha'ananim, was the first Jewish residential section outside the Old City of Jerusalem.

In 1874 Sir Moses again entertained the hope of establishing agricultural settlements, and he wrote to rabbis and Jewish communal leaders in Eretz Israel of his plans to ameliorate their situation by the employment of Jews in agriculture and in the trades. That year he retired as president of the Board of Deputies, which established a Testimonial Fund in his honor. Montefiore suggested that the money collected be used for settlement in Eretz Israel. In 1875, at the age of 90, he paid his last visit to Eretz Israel to report to the board on the situation. In his report he called for the establishment of garden suburbs and suggested that, if enough money was available, the board purchase land in various parts of the country for Jews to cultivate.

During the long years of its existence the Sir Moses Montefiore Testimonial Fund was instrumental in financing the construction of several new suburbs in Jerusalem, a number of which were named for Montefiore (Zikhron Moshe, Kiryat Moshe, etc.). In the last years of Montefiore's life the Hovevei Zion movement came into being, and the first agricultural settlements in the country were established. On his 99th birthday Sir Moses sent donations to six Jewish agricultural settlements: Rishon le-Zion and Yehud, near Jaffa; Gei Oni and Peki'in, near Safed; and Benei Bilu and Zikhron Ya'akov (then called Zamarin), near Haifa.

The Kattowitz Conference of the Hovevei Zion movement coincided with Sir Moses' 100th birthday, which was celebrated throughout England and by Jews the world over. At the suggestion of Leo Pinsker, the union of societies formed by the conference to promote the Hibbat Zion movement was named the Montefiore Association for the Promotion of Agriculture among Jews and Especially for the Support of the Jewish Colonies in Palestine.

G. HIRSCHLER—V.D. LIPMAN

MONTOR, HENRY. Zionist executive and communal worker in the United States (b. Nova Scotia, Canada, 1906; d. Jerusalem, 1982). Taken to the United States from his native Canada in 1908, he grew up in Pittsburgh, Pennsylvania and Steubenville, Ohio, and studied at the University of Cincinnati and the Hebrew Union College. Active in Zionist affairs from his early youth, he moved to New York in 1925 to become assistant editor of *The New Palestine*, subsequently becoming publicity director of the United Palestine Appeal (UPA). From 1930 to 1950 he was executive director of the UPA. A dynamic and sometimes controversial figure on the American Jewish scene, Montor was a key figure in the establishment of the United Jewish Appeal and of the Israel Bond Organization. During the period immediately preceding the establishment of the State of Israel, he stressed the primacy of Israel as a new home for survivors of the Holocaust and in the summer of 1945, at the personal request of David Ben-Gurion, organized some 40 top Jewish businessmen from all over the United States to channel supplies and equipment to the Hagana. This group, which met with Ben-Gurion at the home of the New York industrialist Rudolf Sonneborn, became known as the "Sonneborn Group" or "Sonneborn Institute." In 1948 Montor arranged for Golda Meir to address a meeting of Jewish communal leaders in Chicago, at which $50 million was raised for the defense of the fledgling Jewish nation fighting for its survival. He was chief executive officer of the

Israel Bond Organization from 1950 until 1955, when he resigned to form a consumer finance company, Finanziara Popolare, with branches in Milan and Turin, Italy. From that time on until his death he divided his time between Rome and Jerusalem. In 1960 Ben-Gurion referred to Montor as one of the top ten people "most responsible for the creation of the State of Israel." G. ḤIRSCHLER

MORAVIA, ZIONISM IN. *See* BOHEMIA AND MORAVIA, ZIONISM IN.

MORGENTHAU. US family.

Henry Morgenthau. Lawyer, businessman, philanthropist, Ambassador in Constantinople (b. Mannheim, Germany, 1856; d. New York, 1946). He arrived with his parents in the United States in 1876 and practiced law until 1899. Thereafter he became a businessman and an active member of the Democratic Party. In 1913 President Wilson appointed him US Ambassador to Turkey and told him: "Remember that anything you can do to improve the lot of your coreligionists is an act that will reflect credit upon America." Morgenthau faithfully followed this advice. He was not a Zionist and Zionism as a theory scarcely interested him, but he was deeply impressed by what he saw on a visit to Eretz Israel in April, 1914: the pioneers appeared to him to be the personification of a new type of Jew.

Morgenthau's good will did much for the Zionists during the war. In August, 1914, he alerted the Jewish relief organizations in the United States and on 6 October Maurice Wertheim, his son-in-law, arrived in Jaffa on the American warship *North Carolina* to hand over 250,000 francs in gold ($25,000) for emergency purposes. As the war went on and conditions worsened, more warships and additional funds were sent. Once an entire ship, the *S.S. Vulcan*, arrived loaded with provisions; it was thanks to this help that the Jewish population in the country remained alive. *Persona grata* with the Ottoman government, Morgenthau used his influence to prevent the destruction of the yishuv by Jamal Pasha.

In 1916 Morgenthau returned to the United States and assisted Woodrow Wilson in his presidential election campaign. In June, 1917, the President dispatched him on a secret mission to explore the possibilities of detaching Turkey from the Central Powers. The British government, for its part, learning about American objectives, dispatched Chaim Weizmann to counter the move. The latter met Morgenthau in Gibraltar (4–5 July) and managed to dissuade him from carrying out his mission. Outwitted, Morgenthau never forgave Weizmann for this maneuver and his attitude towards Zionism consequently soured.

He made his views known in a letter to the *New York Times* (12 December 1917) in which he paid tribute to the settlement work in Palestine but branded Zionism a dangerous ideology which could undermine the hard-won civil rights of Jews in countries of their adoption; it provided no solution to the Jewish problem. This was the classic doctrine of the Reform movement, of which he was an adherent. He wrote two books: *All in a Life-Time* (1922), an autobiography, and *Secrets of the Bosphorus, Constantinople, 1913–1916* (1928), an account of his diplomatic service.

I. FRIEDMAN

Henry Morgenthau Jr, his son. Statesman and Jewish communal leader (b. New York, 1891; d. Poughkeepsie, N.Y., 1967). He was prominent in New York State public affairs during the governorship of Franklin D. Roosevelt, a close friend, and served as Secretary of the Treasury during Roosevelt's presidency, from 1934 until 1945.

Morgenthau charged US State Department officials with taking no action when European Jews were being massacred and with holding up the transfer of funds that could have effected the rescue of 70,000 Jews in France and Romania in 1943. It was largely as a result of his report on this subject (January, 1944) that President Roosevelt set up the War Refugee Board, composed of the Secretaries of State, Treasury (Morgenthau), and War, which was charged with the preparation of plans and the inauguration of effective measures for the rescue and relief of victims of Nazi persecution.

Morgenthau attempted to influence the British to open Palestine to Jewish refugees, and gave political support to the Zionist movement and, later, to the State of Israel. Early in 1948 he spoke out in favor of lifting the United States arms embargo so that the yishuv would be able to resist Arab attacks.

He served as general chairman (1947–50) and honorary chairman (1951–53) of the United Jewish Appeal. An initiator of the State of Israel Bonds Organization, he was chairman of its Board of Governors from 1951 to 1955. He was also chairman of the Board of Governors of the Hebrew University of Jerusalem from 1950 to 1952. He paid several visits to Israel and at one time caused a stir in the country by calling for a regional pact embracing Israel and the Arab states to ward off Communism. The village of Tal Shahar (lit., "morning dew," or Morgenthau), near Hulda, is named for him.

MORIAH. Hebrew publishing house in Odessa, Russia. It was founded in 1901 by Hayim Nahman Bialik, Yeshoshu'a Hona Rawnitzky, and Simha Ben-Zion to produce textbooks and pedagogical literature designed to broaden Jewish education and to give it a traditional direction. Moriah's publications, which included selections from the Bible, the Midrash and the Talmud, medieval Hebrew poetry, and modern literature, in addition to its pedagogical literature were widely used.

In 1911 Moriah embarked on a program of literature for adults. Its publications in this field included anthologies of the writings of important modern Hebrew writers and the well known *Sefer Ha-Aggada* (Book of Aggada), legends from the Talmud and the Midrash systematically arranged and annotated by Bialik and Rawnitzky. Moriah ceased its activities after the outbreak of World War I, when the Tsarist government banned the printing of Hebrew books in Russia. Following the October Revolution of 1917 the Communist regime confiscated all of Moriah's assets. After his emigration from Russia, Bialik established in Berlin the Devir publishing house as the successor to Moriah. Devir was later moved to Palestine.

MOROCCAN JEWS IN ISRAEL. Jews lived along the North African coast from the time of the Phoenician expansion along the Mediterranean, and Spanish Jews settled there in the 15th century. All Jews were confined to the ghetto (*mellah*) as *dhimmis* (tolerated non-Moslems) under the protection of the ruler. Whether in the towns or the rural areas, they were mostly impoverished craftsmen or

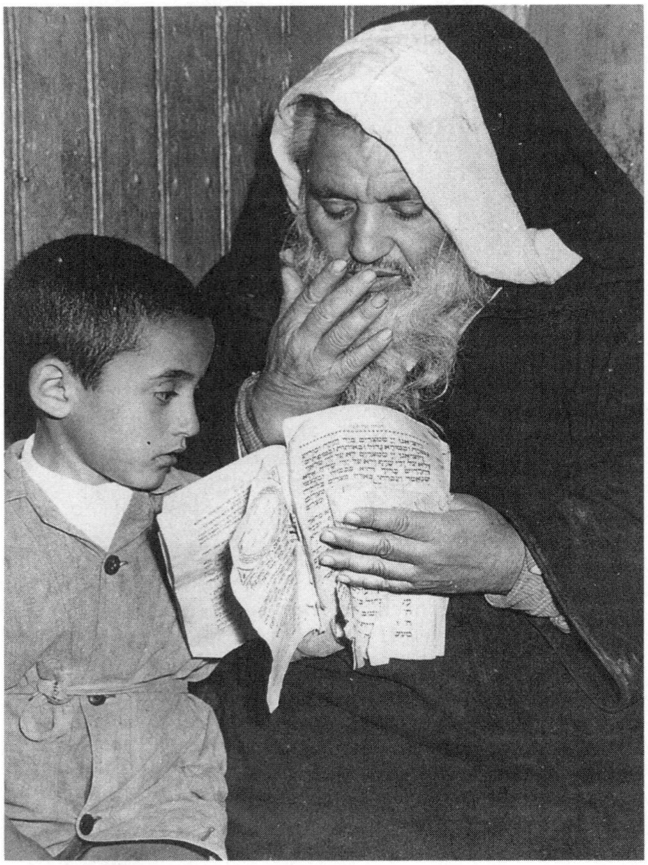

Moroccan Jews in Israel. [Yad Ben-Zvi]

Women of Moroccan origin celebrating the traditional Maimuna festival in Jerusalem, 1975. [Israel Govt. Press Office]

traders. The family was the axis of social organization; the synagogue with its elementary school, the center of the community; the yeshivot (rabbinic academies), the focus of spiritual life. Small groups of emigrants left the country regularly for the Holy Land.

Colonialism transformed Moroccan Jewry. From 1862, schools of the Alliance Israélite Universelle were set up; in addition to Jewish subjects, they taught the French language and secular courses. In 1953, 80 percent of all Moroccan Jews were city dwellers. While social problems accumulated in the overcrowded *mellah*, numerous Jewish professionals or businessmen now lived outside the *mellah* and were a part of French culture. These changes notwithstanding, and even though the Protectorate (1912) had abolished the special rules bound to the status of *dhimmi*, all Jews were still subjects of the sultan. The only way they could achieve their rights was through incessant lobbying with the authorities.

For most, the creation of Israel (1948) was seen as beginning the era of redemption. Nevertheless, while Jewish-Moslem relations were deteriorating, the relative advantages of the colonial situation held the majority in Morocco. In the aftermath of Morocco's declaration of independence, in 1956, however, the masses rallied behind the (now illegal) Zionist movement and emigrated, leaving minorities in Morocco and in France. The sinking of the *Pisces* carrying Jews bound for Israel, with 40 victims, near Morocco's shores was the dramatic peak of this period. (*see* OPERATION "YACHIN").

In total, about 230,000 Jews from Morocco immigrated between 1948 and 1964. They became the largest group of origin in Israel, representing 14 percent of the Jewish population, including the second generation (about 500,000 in the late 1980s).

Adjustments and community. The norms and patterns of the Moroccans soon created a cultural distance between them and the Israeli establishment. *Mizug galuyot* (the intermingling of the ingathered communities) was conceived by the absorbers in a largely secular context, tolerating the particular customs of each group only as part of the general Jewish culture. The Moroccans, who had arrived relatively late, had not participated in the formation of the dominant culture; their sense of Zionism was confused by its irreverence for longstanding values and patterns. In addition, their confrontation with an omnipresent bureaucracy was reminiscent of frustrating experiences with colonialism.

In reaction to this situation, as well as under the influence of the official policy of absorption, the Moroccans tended to concentrate among themselves. Only two or three percent joined kibbutzim, and ten percent went to moshavim; more than 50 percent settled (or were settled) in development towns and about one-third in metropolitan areas. In Galilee and the Negev, they constitute from 30 percent to 80 percent of numerous settlements. As for the big cities, Moroccans account for five percent of Tel Aviv, but 22 percent of one particular area; 14 percent of Jerusalem, and 30 percent of one neighborhood there; 10 percent of Haifa, but 33 percent of a single area. Marriages with non-Moroccan spouses are increasing in number, but at a moderate rate; in the 1980s almost 30 percent of Moroccan grooms and brides married spouses of their group (one-quarter married Ashkenazi spouses). Many other Jews from Moslem lands who marry Moroccans join their communities.

Parochialism is still strong. Circles of Moroccan rabbis study the *Zohar* (the classic of Jewish mysticism); their synagogues host festivals and celebrations; pilgrimages to holy tombs are massively attended. Traditional figures like the Baba Sali, the head of the revered Abuhatzeira dynasty, continue to be venerated. As for the young, ethnic music remains popular. Like all other groups, the Moroccans see themselves first as "Jews" or "Israelis." However, in contrast to the Ashkenazim but like other Oriental Jews originating in North Africa or the Middle East they also strongly identify with the token of their origin ("Moroccan") and with the more general ethnic label *Mizrahim* (i.e., originating in Moslem lands). On the other hand, the rabbis are losing much of their influence, as the younger generations experience the Israeli school, the army, and work settings outside the community. Family size has declined sharply, approaching the typical Ashkenazi four-person nucleus. New living standards diminish the Moroccans' cultural saliency.

Inequality and mobility: Social stratification. Groups like the Moroccans were *a priori* disadvantaged in the occupational sphere, in light of thieir weak educational and financial resources, as well as their initial dependency on an establishment in which the more veteran Ashkenazim were more numerous. Hence, in 1961, only 12 percent were professionals, clerks, or businessmen; 28 percent craftsmen, 25 percent peasants and agricultural workers, while 35 percent were (mostly unskilled) industrial workers or low-status employees.

The economic boom of the late 1960s and Israel's subsequent technological, industrial, and educational revolution changed this picture dramatically. In 1981, 29 percent were professionals, clerks, or businessmen; 47 percent were (now mostly skilled) workers in industry; 6 percent were agricultural workers, and 18 percent craftsmen, low-status, employees, or unskilled industrial workers. Similarly, whereas in 1961, 22 percent of all *Mizrahim*—including the Moroccans—born abroad, and 39 percent of those born in the country had a secondary education or more, in 1981 the figures were 46 percent and 82 percent respectively.

A wide stratum of middle- and upper-class *Mizrahim* (about 40 percent in the mid-1980s) has thus emerged. Among the Moroccans as well as among other Mizrahi cohorts, those who are socially mobile—principally in the professional track—are very close, both culturally and socially, to the well-to-do Ashkenazim; as a result, they are also less committed to their community of origin.

The political transformation. Underrepresentation in the political elite has been another aspect of inequality for the *Mizrahim*. Apparently because of their effervescent Diaspora experience, the Moroccans have exhibited the strongest reaction to deprivation. Among the Jews of Moroccan origin who have been prominent in political life are David Ben-Harosh, who led the riots which broke out in the Haifa slum of Wadi Salib in 1959; Charlie Biton, one of those who in the Katamon quarter of Jerusalem formed the Black Panther movement—a movement of protest and demonstration initiated by local youngsters that for a whole year (1970) was in the public eye for its activities in behalf of the poor and disadvantaged; Aharon Abu-hatzeira, who split from the National Religious Party to create the *Tami party; Rabbi Yitzhak Peretz, who created the ethnic orthodox *Shas Party.

While numerous Moroccan individuals take part in ethnic politics, many Moroccans prefer to express their animosity against the forces that absorbed them by giving their support to the nationalist Right. These allegiances are weaker among middle-class Moroccans who evolve in circles where social democracy is more popular. Yet, the floating of the Moroccan masses at the polls has generated meaningful changes. The Right now vies with the Left, and in the resulting competition floating votes gain an unprecedented weight. This accounts for new policies and impressive headway by politicians with origins from Morocco and other Moslem lands. Before the 1977 elections, there were 12 such members of the Knesset; in 1977, 18; in 1981, 24; in 1984, 31; in 1988, 38. About half of these non-Ashkenazi Knesset Members are Moroccan, which makes their rate of representation among Jewish Knesset members fairly proportionate to their group's ratio among the Jewish population. Two Jews from Moslem lands (non-Moroccans) were ministers before 1977; there were eight (five Moroccans) in 1988. Moroccans have been elected to mayorship in towns and cities like Ashdod, Ashkelon, and Yavneh.

Israel's *Project Renewal has been operating for the rehabilitation of poor neighborhoods (with relative success), and school programs have been developed to emphasize the contribution of Moroccan, as well as other legacies of the Oriental Jews, to Israeli culture. One expression among many others, the Jewish Moroccan "Feast of the Bread." the Maimuna, is now a national event at Passover time, celebrating Israel's cultural versatility. E. BEN-RAFAEL

MOROCCO, ZIONISM IN. *See* NORTH AFRICA, ZIONISM IN; OPERATION YACHIN.

MORRISON-GRADY PLAN (Cantonization Plan). British proposal for the solution of the Palestine problem. Presented by Deputy Prime Minister Herbert Morrison to the House of Commons on 31 July 1946, it proposed the "federalization" of Palestine under an overall British trusteeship to be implemented by a British "central government."

Background. The British government was not ready to accept the recommendations of the *Anglo-American Committee of Inquiry and indicated a desire to see the United States assume a share in the responsibility for implementing President Harry S Truman's recommendation to admit 100,000 Jewish displaced persons to Palestine. Truman's response was to appoint, in the summer of 1946, a special Cabinet committee, consisting of the Secretaries of State, War, and Treasury, to advise him on the policy to be pursued by the United States with regard to the Palestine problem and to negotiate with the British government on "various matters arising out of the recommendations of the Anglo-American Committee of Inquiry." These officials in turn appointed a working body of three representatives, headed by Henry F. Grady, who met in London with their opposite numbers in Britain, headed by Sir Norman Brook.

Provisions of the Plan. The committees headed by Brook and Grady proposed a solution for the Palestine problem which the British Foreign Office was willing to accept. Presenting the plan for debate in the House of Commons, Morrison observed that it was subject to approval by the United States government and to consultations with Arabs and Jews.

The plan provided for the division of Palestine into four areas: a Jewish province, an Arab province, a district of Jerusalem, and a district of the Negev. The Jerusalem district (which was to include the city of Bethlehem) and the Negev district (which was to extend from Beersheba to Akaba) were to be under the direct control of the central government. The Jewish province was to include about two-thirds of the coastal plain of Palestine (with the exception of an enclave around Jaffa), the Jezreel Valley, and eastern Galilee north of Bet She'an, or 1,500 square miles, as opposed to the 2,600 square miles originally allotted for a Jewish state in Palestine under the Peel Commission partition proposal.

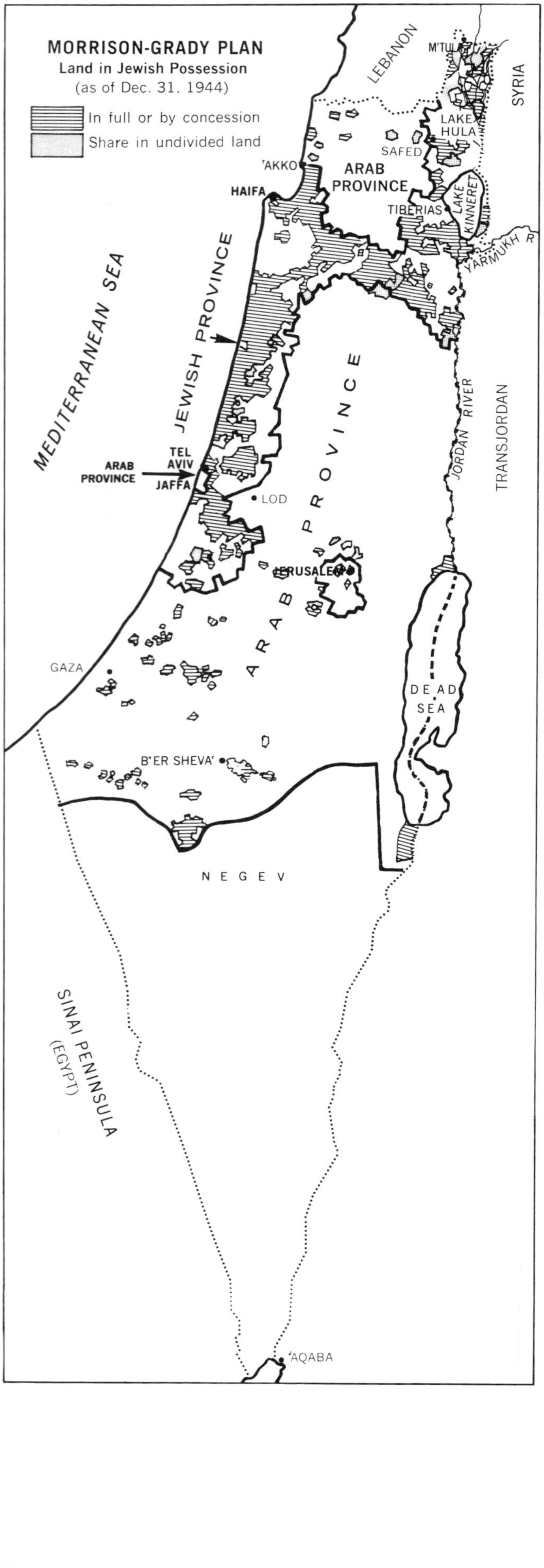

The Jewish and Arab provinces were each to have an elected legislative chamber. From the members of the two legislatures the High Commissioner was to choose two separate executive branches, consisting of a prime minister and a council of ministers. The legislative and administrative power of the provincial governments was to be confined mainly to subjects of provincial concern. The British central government was to retain exclusive jurisdiction over matters of defense, police, foreign relations, and customs and excise.

Final control of immigration was to rest with the central government. However, as long as immigration did not exceed the economic absorptive capacity of a province, the Palestine government would approve the volume of immigration desired by the provincial government. Thus, although the Arab province could exclude Jewish immigrants from its territory, the Jewish province was free to admit Jews to the extent warranted by its economic absorptive capicity. Both provincial governments would have the right to appeal to the UN Trusteeship Council. Immediately after inauguration of the plan, Palestine, in accordance with the recommendation of the Anglo-American Committee of Inquiry, was to admit 100,000 Jewish refugees, an operation which it was hoped could be completed within 12 months from its start.

The United States was to be requested to accept responsibility for the execution of the plan and to defray the cost of the transportation of the refugees to Palestine, as well as to supply food for them for two months. In addition, the United States was to be asked to make a substantial grant to the government of Palestine to be used primarily for financing Arab development projects and to help meet extraordinary expenditures during the transitional period. The United States also was to make available large-scale development loans to the Arab states in the Middle East.

Morrison announced that both the Jews and the Arabs would be invited to a conference in London to discuss the plan. Although the plan was presented in Parliament as the outcome of parleys of British and American teams of experts who had examined the recommendations of the Anglo-American Committee of Inquiry, it was in the main a British plan, prepared years earlier in the British Colonial Office, to which the American team had been persuaded to agree.

Reaction to the Plan. The Jews were unanimous in their rejection of the Morrison-Grady Plan, which would have made the admission of the 100,000 Jewish refugees contingent on Arab acceptance of the plan, closed the greater part of Palestine to Jewish immigration, and left the final determination of the country's economic absorptive capacity to the British government. Moreover, the Zionists argued that the creation of a Jerusalem district outside the Jewish province would tear out the very heart of the Jewish homeland and deprive the Jews of Jerusalem, who formed the majority of the city's population, of their political rights. As for the Negev, under the Morrison-Grady Plan it would be condemned to remain a wilderness forever. In effect, the plan would turn Palestine into a ghetto.

Immediately after Morrison's announcement, influential members of the US Congress of both parties voiced their outspoken opposition to United States endorsement of the plan. As a result of these protests, Truman had the State Department invite the six United States members of the Anglo-American Committee to meet in Washington with Grady and his two colleagues under the chairmanship of

Acting Secretary of State Dean Acheson. After two days of discussion (7–9 August 1946), this group unanimously recommended that the United States government reject the Morrison-Grady Plan in its entirety, with Judge Joseph C. Hutcheson, the chairman, terming the recommendations "a complete sell-out" which provided for a "ghetto in attenuated form," On 12 August 1946, Truman informed Prime Minister Clement R. Attlee that because of intense opposition to the plan in the United States it would not gain sufficient support from American public opinion to warrant United States endorsement.

The leaders of the Jewish Agency demanded the immediate admission of the 100,000 refugees and refused to participate in the Arab-Jewish conference planned by Bevin unless the British government were prepared to discuss the establishment of a viable Jewish state in an adequate area of Palestine. Meanwhile, the Arab Higher Committee rejected the plan because it opposed the idea of having any Jewish-owned land, much less a Jewish state, in what it considered Arab territory.

The conference, which met in London in September, 1946, ended in failure. It was attended by the British representatives, the representatives of the seven Arab states, and the Secretary-General of the Arab League. The Jews stayed away.

On 4 October 1946, Yom Kippur eve, Truman issued a public statement calculated to win Jewish support at the upcoming mid-term elections to the Congress. Though the statement was interpreted as offering support for the Jewish Agency's partition plan, what Truman in fact said was that he did not believe the gap between the British (i.e., the Morrison-Grady provincial autonomy plan) and the Jewish Agency (Partition) plan was "too great to be bridged by men of reason and goodwill." His statement endorsed the Jewish Agency demand for immediate, substantial immigration into Palestine. T. PRESCHEL—M.J. COHEN

MOSAD. (short for Ha-Mosad le-Modi'in ve-Tafkidim Meyuhadim, i.e., the institution for intelligence and special tasks). Israeli body responsible for intelligence activities outside the State. It was established in 1951 under Ha-Mosad ha-Merkazi le-Modi'in u-le-Vitahon (Central Institution for Intelligence and Security). Its head (whose identity is secret until he completes his term of office), who serves also as the chairman of the Committee of Intelligence Agencies, is directly responsible to the Prime Minister. It collects information on political, military, and security matters and executes special operations, including intelligence warfare. It cooperates with intelligence services of friendly countries, especially to counter terrorist activities. Its own operations have included the kidnaping of Adolf Eichmann in Argentina and his removal to Israel and activities against the Arab terrorists responsible for the 1972 massacre of Israeli sportsmen at the Olympic Games in Munich.

MOSAD BIALIK (BIALIK FOUNDATION). Publishing house in Jerusalem named for Hayim Nahman *Bialik. Its aim is to "encourage Hebrew writing, both literary and scientific, and to build a bridge between modern Hebrew literature and the literature of earlier generations, as well as between the literature of the Jewish people and world literature in general, and to encourage research in and advancement of the Hebrew language."

By 1986 the foundation had published about 800 books, including critical editions of Hebrew classics, source books, and studies in the religion, history, and literature of the Jews, Palestinography, belles lettres, and science, as well as translations of important works written by Jewish writers in foreign languages and Hebrew renderings of world literature. Larger projects of the foundation include the Hebrew *Biblical Encyclopedia*, the eight volumes of which were published between 1950 and 1982.

In 1984 the formal status of the foundation was changed from a department of the World Zionist Organization into an independent company wholly owned by the World Zionist Organization.

MOSAD HARAV KOOK. *See* KOOK, ABRAHAM ISAAC.

MOSCOVITZ, SHALOM. Israeli naîve painter; also known as *der zeigermacher* (the watchmaker) and later as Shalom of Safed, the name under which he became internationally famous. (b. Safed, 1887; d. Safed, 1980). He worked variously as a stonemason, scribe, silversmith, and watchmaker until 1948, when his watch repair shop was destroyed during the battle for Safed. After thw War of Independence, he began to make painted biblical toys based on traditional folk images of the Sacrifice of Isaac, and was first encouraged to paint in the early 1950s by painter Yosl Bergner. Self-taught and working at first solely in watercolors, he evolved a style related to that of early Safed and Jerusalem folk artists, concentrating almost exclusively on biblical subjects. In the 1960s, he also absorbed imagery from the biblical illustrations of Gustave Doré, without losing any of the enormous charm of his own vision and sense of color. From 1961, he was given one-man shows in museums throughout America and Europe. Some of his paintings were chosen for reproduction on UNICEF greeting cards. Many lithographs were made from his works at the Mourlot Studios in Paris.
M. RONNEN

MOSER, JACOB. Zionist leader in England (b. Kappeln, Schleswig, Denmark, 1839; d. Bradford, England, 1922). In 1909 Moser was elected freeman of his native town (by then part of Germany). Elected lord mayor of Bradford (1910–11), Alderman Moser held high positions in the Anglo-Jewish community.

A friend of Herzl and Devid Wolffsohn, Moser attended the Fifth Zionist Congress (1901) and subsequent Congresses. He was a member of the Zionist Actions Committee and one of the first to be inscribed in the Golden Book of the Jewish National Fund. He contributed generously to charitable institutions, especially to the Herzliya High School in Tel Aviv. J. FRAENKEL

MOSES, SIEGFRIED. Zionist leader and Israeli public servant (b. Lautenburg, Germany, 1887; d. Jerusalem, 1974). After receiving his doctorate in law from the University of Heidelberg in 1908, he practiced law in Germany between 1912 and 1937, with interruptions to serve as food controller in Danzig (1917–19), deputy director of the Union of German Municipalities (1919–20), and managing director of the Schocken department stores in Zwickau (1923–29). He was a delegate to several Zionist Congresses and between 1933 and 1937 (the first years of the Nazi regime) was president of the Zionist Organization of Germany. Settling in Palestine in 1937, he worked as managing director of Ha'avara (transfer of Jewish assets in Germany to Palestine) in Tel Aviv from 1939 to 1949, taking the initiative in pressing Jewish claims against Germany toward the end of World War II by setting forth individual and collective Jewish claims. In 1949 he was appointed Israel's first *State Comptroller, holding that position until his retirement in 1961.

A cofounder of the Progressive party in Israel, Moses was president of the Irgun Olei Merkaz Europa (Organization of Immigrants from Central Europe), of the Leo Baeck Institute, and, from 1957, of the Council of Jews from Germany (London, Jerusalem, and New York). He was the chairman of the Advisory Committee of the United Restitution Organization in Israel and a member of the board of Bank Le'umi. Moses wrote a number of books on legal and economic subjects, including *Jewish Postwar Claims* (1944), *The Income Tax Ordinance of Palestine* (1942, 1946), and reminiscences, *Bi-Shenei Olamot* (1962).

MOSHAV. (pl. moshavim). Cooperative farming village which became Israel's predominant type of rural settlement. Out of more than 800 rural agglomerations existing in 1986, 411 were moshavim. In 1948, when this form of settlement comprised only 80 out of 290 Jewish villages, the authorities responsible for settlement felt the moshav to be best suited to the needs and capabilities of newcomers arriving in mass immigration; all those who consented to try rural settlements were therefore directed towards moshavim.

The moshav is a cooperative farming village based on the following principles:

1) Settlement is on national land allocated to settlers for a period of 49 years, automatically renewable (*See* Jewish National Fund). According to law, a farm unit may be bequeathed to one son or daughter, but not split up among several heirs nor united with other farmsteads.

2) The family farmstead is based on the settler's own labor and that of his family members; in case of need, hired laborers may be employed but not permanently.

3) Marketing of produce and joint purchase of equipment and other necessities are organized through the moshav's cooperative agency.

4) Mutual aid and mutual responsibility guarantee the settler family's existence, by demanding aid from the other moshav members when a family's productive capacity is impaired by accident or sickness; the community's support continues until the crisis has passed.

5) Basic means of production, e.g., land and water, are equally distributed among the moshav members in such

The moshav K'far Hittim in 1948. [Zionist Archives]

amounts that enable them to earn their livelihood.

6) The moshav as a production unit is identical with the cooperative municipal unit which provides community services; the moshav's cooperative agency bears both tasks.

Though these basic principles form part of the articles of association of every moshav, numerous divergencies have resulted from technical and social developments.

The average moshav is comprised of about 80 farming families, plus 5–10 artisan families who do not own their own farms. The lowest number of family units of a moshav is 40, and the highest 140.

History. The moshav idea was conceived by settlers of the Second Aliya who reached the country in the first decade of the 20th century. More or less contemporarily with the first kevutza (*see* KIBBUTZ), a group settled close to Petah Tikva (*see* MOSHAVA) and established the village En Ganim, aiming to keep auxiliary farms while working in the moshav's citrus orchards. Nahlat Yehuda was founded in 1914, near Rishon le-Zion, with a similar purpose. These settlements or suburbs, at the time called *Moshevei Po'alim* (Workers Settlements), were seen as a transition stage toward settlement fully based on income from their own farmsteads. Among the proponents of the moshav was Berl Katznelson, who outlined the idea at the Conference of the Confederation of Judean Workers at Ben Shemen in 1912: the moshav was to be founded on the principles of self-labor, mutual aid, and settlement on national land. At the Fifth Galilee Laborers' Conference in 1914, Eliezer Shohat pointed out the necessity of gradually abandoning dependence on doing hired labor; the settlers' principal efforts should be directed toward the creation of independent agricultural farms. Similarly, Yitzhak Wilkansky (Elazari-Volcani) maintained that villages of hired laborers provided with auxiliary farms had no future; rather, there should be fully-fledged mixed farms, managed by the peasants and their families, producing their own food requirements and selling surpluses on the market. To ensure efficiency, Wilkansky suggested a cooperative format, with the cooperative supplying heavy machinery and taking responsibility for marketing surplus.

The most comprehensive and detailed proposal for a moshav ovedim (workers' moshav) for both its social, organizational, and agricultural structure, was made by Eliezer Lipa Joffe. His suggestions appeared in a booklet entitled "The Foundations of the Moshav Ovedim"; it was published in 1919 to serve the deliberations of the Agricultural Council of the Ha-Po'el ha-Tza'ir party. Joffe listed the basic principles of the moshav: full self-labor on the family farm, settlement on national land, mutual aid and cooperation in marketing of produce, with the farmer producing all his food and even his clothing requirements. He put the optimal number of farmer families in a moshav at 50-100. Each farmer family would be allocated seven hectares of land and base its production on diversified crops so as to assure a balanced work schedule throughout the year and prevent the need to employ hired laborers.

Accepting his suggestion, the Council resolved to take practical steps to implement the concept of the moshav. In September, 1921, members of Ha-Po'el ha-Tza'ir established the moshav *Nahalal in the western Jezreel Valley. Among the settlers were Eliezer Joffe and Eliezer Shohat. Some of the members had abandoned the first kevutza, Deganya, because they preferred the pattern of the family farm; among them was Shemuel Dayan, who later became one of the leaders of the moshav movement. At the end of that year, a second moshav, Kefar Yehezkel, was founded in the Harod Valley. The development of these moshavim and of others established later was made feasible by the financial and professional support of the Zionist Organization. Initially, the progress of the moshavim was relatively slow compared with that of the kibbutzim: between 1921 and 1930, 14 moshavim were founded, as against 30 kibbutzim. Toward the end of the 1920s moshav settlement increased when villages were established close to moshavot, where new settlers could work as hired laborers until their own farms were fully developed. This program was called *Hityashvut ha-Elef* (Settlement of the Thousand), for it hoped to absorb 1,000 families. Lack of land and money forced the program to be postponed until the early 1930s and reduced in scope to little more than 400 families, but it reinforced the movement with 16 moshavim founded in 1932/33. Moshavim were established where the Jewish National Fund had succeeded in acquiring suitable land, as in the Tel Mond bloc, in the Hefer Valley of the central Sharon, and in the Rehovot region. From the mid-1930s, immigrants from Germany, some with capital, established "middle class settlements" mostly on the moshav pattern. The settlers invested considerable sums of their own, thus reducing the need for national funds.

During the Arab riots from 1936–39, the number of moshavim increased more slowly than kibbutzim. With the end of World War II, establishment of moshavim was renewed, partly by soldiers demobilized from the Allied armies.

The big upsurge of the moshav sector followed the founding of the State, when mass immigration led to the creation of the immigrants' moshav (see below). The new moshavim were set up in most areas of the State, first in abandoned Arab villages primarily in the center and hill parts of the country, later in the South, the Negev, and along borders and armistice lines. The pace slowed down and nearly ceased from the end of the 1950s until the Six-Day War in 1967 due to a saturation of Israel-produced foodstuffs, and a lack of water, land, and suitable manpower.

After 1967, settlement which included moshavim was renewed mainly in the Arava Valley and in Galilee, within the pre-1967 boundaries, as well as in the administered areas. These new moshavim were populated principally by the second generation from existing settlements and by nuclei of urban youth; a minority were new immigrants, mostly from western countries. The total of 458 moshavim existing in 1990 had 150,000 members constituting 4% of Israel's Jewish population.

Structure. The "classical" moshav is a closed society, where the members owning farmsteads make most of the decisions regarding communal life. The settlers decide by mutual consent on their organizational structure. Their general assembly accepts new families by majority vote, after a trial period in which they demonstrate their ability to adapt to the community. All family members above the age of 18 hold voting rights in the general assembly and the right to membership in the moshav's institutions. An annual assembly session deals with the detailed budget, and its economic social-cultural, and municipal ramifications. For current administration, the moshav's cooperative association's council is elected by the assembly. Some moshavim also elect a larger board to advise the council and direct the moshav's economic and communal-municipal activities. Key positions in the council are held by the internal secretary (or farm manager), the external secretary, and the treasurer. In some instances, these individuals receive salaries which enable them to devote most of their time to their administrative tasks while employing outside labor on their own farms. Auxiliary committees deal with education, culture, mutual aid, control, social aid, etc.

The Association's current activity is financed from three sources: taxes raised directly from the moshav members; a certain percentage deducted from income from produce sold through centralized marketing; and payments from members for services provided to them. Many moshavim add to these the revenue from jointly operated branches, e.g., citrus groves, fruit orchards, grain farming, cotton, etc., which function more efficiently thus than they would within the separate family framework.

The degree of cooperation varies from moshav to moshav. Those keeping closely to the moshav ideology market produce and purchase farming implements and other necessities exclusively through the cooperative association. This enables the farmers to buy investment goods on credit. Every farmstead owner has his account in the communal book-keeping office, where the sums spent for his purchases are debited and the money due to him for produce sold is credited.

If the cooperative association lacks cash, it may take bank loans which are repaid when the income from produce sales comes in. This aids current financing but can cause difficulties, for example, when less efficient farmers accumulate debts which ultimately become the burden of their more successful colleagues. The cooperative association attempts to keep members solvent with bank loans when necessary; when a majority of members are in debt, however, this system can bring the entire moshav into crisis. Such a situation evolved in the 1979–1985 period, when Israel's galloping inflation and the linking of loans to the cost-of-living index loaded moshavim with overwhelming debts. Only government intervention in 1987, with the State suspending part of the debts and spreading out repayments of the remaining debts over a long period, enabled the moshavim to continue to function normally.

For the moshavim founded after 1948 without profound ideological motivation, thoroughgoing changes were found to be necessary when technological progress transformed their farming methods. Many farmers of these villages ceased to market produce through the cooperative association, preferring to market their produce personally. They also employed hired laborers in peak seasons, many even the year round. On the other hand, farmers engaged in salaried work outside the moshav in addition to maintaining their own farmsteads.

Since the associations of some moshavim no longer observed regulations, the Ministry of Labor's registrar of cooperative associations had to appoint councils (rather than letting them be elected by the moshav members) to supervise the functioning of these bodies.

Immigrants' moshavim. Between 1948 and 1967, about 280 immigrants' moshavim were founded, most in the first ten years of statehood. Of the moshavim established after 1967, most were populated by adult offspring of older settlements, and a few by new immigrants. The Jewish Agency's Settlement Department, which was responsible for rural settlement both before statehood and afterwards, planned the immigrants' moshavim and guided their settlers. Lack of time prevented preliminary training, so settlers were brought to the future villages even before permanent homesteads were built and were housed in temporary huts. Their lack of skills and of comprehension of the moshav's essence meant that the moshav had to be directed from above during a transition period.

Most settlers in the moshavim camp had come from Islamic countries. What little they knew of farming was of its most primitive form. They therefore had to be trained gradually, in the intensive and progressive farming methods and crops used in Israel and to be guided in moshav principles and in Israel's administrative practices.

Due to the pressures of mass immigration and the need to establish villages at utmost speed, the selection of the settlers was most superficial, taking into account only the prospective settlers' age and their health. Many of those directed to moshav settlements were eventually found unfit and had to be replaced.

In the initial period, most settlers were employed in building and infrastructure work. Simultaneously, they began work on their own farms under the supervision of agricultural guides with farmstead sizes at first limited. Towards the end of the transition period, their holdings were gradually enlarged to full size. The transition lasted relatively long, in some moshavim five to six, in others even ten years, until the agricultural guides could leave the settlers to work on their own.

The moshavim founded after 1955 differed from the earlier ones in their master plan and infrastructure. The earlier villages were not always located on suitable soil or topography. Later ones, such as those of the Lachish, Adullam, and Ta'anakh regions, were superior, partly because they were more ethnically and socially homogeneous, thus promising to become more stable communities. Settlement of large contiguous areas was based on the concept of regional structure, grouping moshavim in clusters around a rural center which provided various services. The system was first applied in the Lachish region and later copied elsewhere.

The second generation, born both in the 1948–1952 moshavim and in the later ones, received secondary education and professional training and was thus able to serve in responsible positions in its villages. As a result, the "immigrants' moshav" type ceased to exist from the end of the 1960s, and these villages subsequently functioned like veteran moshavim.

Moshav blueprints and farm types. Since the founding of the first moshavim in the 1920s, profound changes have occurred both in their physical and architectural planning and in their agricultural set-up. Before statehood, security considerations, the scarcity of available farming land, isolation of villages, and lack of irrigation water were major influences on the moshav. A basic planning principle at the time was to establish compact holdings where living quarters, farmyard, and crop fields were placed close to each other. This idea led the architect Richard Kaufmann to design Nahalal in concentric circles around the moshav's communal buildings, with the homes as an innermost circle, farm buildings constituting the second, and gardens and fields the outer circles. The proximity of fields to homes shortened the distance between the two, facilitated security arrangements, and fitted the mixed-farming concept which demanded from the farmer frequent visits to his installations and fields. As long as unirrigated crops remained the moshav mainstay, the individual holding had to measure 8–12 hectares (20–30 acres), until the mid-1930s the norm for villages in the plains. Moshavim on the hills, such as Atarot near Jerusalem, had to make do with a narrower unit of

1.5–2 hectares (3.5–5 acres), with their farms principally based on fruit orchards.

With the discovery of new water sources and the expansion of irrigated areas, concepts changed and the intensive family unit of about 2.5 hectares (6 acres) of irrigated land became the norm for the moshav, as programmed by Yitzhak Wilkansky (Elazari-Volcani) and named by him the "organic mixed farm." Like the previous extended farmstead, it was based on a variety of sectors. Such moshavim were established in the Jezreel Valley, the Hefer Valley of the central Sharon, the southern Sharon, and the southern coastal plain between Rehovot and Be'er Toviya. The cattle shed was to hold three to four milch cows, with fodder production adapted to its needs, and the poultry, vegetable, and fruit sectors kept at its side. Citrus groves were planted in the central region. In these cases the farm unit was set at 2–2.2 hectares (c. 5 acres), half for citrus and the rest for other intensive bran-sectors.

Settlement of the Lachish Region from the mid-1950s changed physical planning, the composition of the sectors, and the size of the farm units. Technological progress led to a gradual abandonment of the mixed-farming concept in favor of the specialized farm. The farming area now no longer had to be contiguous with the settler's living quarters. After 1955, each moshav settler's holding was distributed over several areas, generally three. One relatively small parcel remained as before near his home and was devoted to the most intensive crops; the two others at a distance, did not require his daily presence. This plan made it possible to place the living quarters relatively near the communal buildings and fostered closer links among the settlers. Concentration of certain crops on larger areas permitted joint cultivation, with heavy machinery, by only some of the moshav's settlers. The system also allowed more flexibility in the choice of village sites and cultivation areas, as there was no longer a need for continuous stretches of soil of uniform quality.

The transition from mixed to specialized farming entailed greater variations in the size of farmsteads according to farm type. So-called "field farms," principally based on vegetable and industrial field crops, required almost double the area needed by the "organic mixed farm."

Specialized farming also enabled the moshav family farm to make its production more efficient and increase its income. The part played by moshavim in Israel's total agricultural production grew steadily, especially in intensive branches like vegetable growing, flower cultivation in greenhouses, and milk and meat production, where cash income is high relative to area size.

The area farmed by moshavim in the late 1980s accounted for 28.6% of Israel's total agricultural surface, i.e., 120,000 out of 420,000 hectares (300,000 out of 1,050,000 acres). Because of the preference for intensive branches in the moshav sector, however, the moshavim provided about 40% of Israel's total agricultural production, and in certain branches even more—over 90% of Israel's flowers, 83% of the total number of eggs, 53% of poultry meat, 50% of vegetables, 44% of citrus fruit, and 40% of Israel's total milk yield.

These figures were attained despite the steady decrease in employment in agriculture, from 81% of the total labor force of the moshavim in 1951/52 to 75.2% in 1960, 66.2% in 1970 and only 44.7% in 1984. This was the result of mechanization and technological innovations which improved labor efficiency and enabled moshav settlers to take on outside employment and go over to part-time farming, while the remaining full farm units and their production expanded.

A. ROKACH

The moshava Rosh Pina about 1925. [Zionist Archives]

MOSHAVA (pl. Moshavot). Village based on private ownership of farmsteads and on settlers' personal initiative. In 1986, about 45 rural settlements functioned as moshavot although many of them were officially listed as "urban communities" because they numbered over 2,000 inhabitants. Three—Petah Tikva, Netanya, and Rishon le-Zion—had become large cities of over 100,000 inhabitants.

The moshava began in 1878 when Petah Tikva and Gei Oni (present-day Rosh Pina) were founded by Old Yishuv Jews from Jerusalem and Safed respectively. Both were abandoned after a short while and settled by First Aliya immigrants in 1882. Members of Hovevei Zion also founded Rishon le-Zion, Zikhron Ya'akov (1882), Nes Tziyona, Yesud ha-Ma'ala, Ekron (1883), and Gedera (1884). In 1889–1890 Bat Shelomo, Rehovot, Mishmar ha-Yarden, and Hadera were added, in 1894 Motza, and in 1896 Metulla. When the First Zionist Congress assembled in 1897, 18 moshavot already existed.

The founders of the early moshavot chose as their model the east European village, which basically subsisted on grain farming. After having spent most of their modest capital on land purchase, very little money remained for home construction and farming implements. Their lack of farming experience, the difficult environment and health conditions and the enmity of Arab neighbors would have soon led to complete failure had not Baron Edmond de Rothschild come to their rescue. He took almost all the moshavot under his patronage, providing the settlers with financial assistance, and sending expert French administrators. The settlers received monthly wages from Rothschild for managing their own farms. He advised them to replace grain with grapes and other fruits which were more suited to Mediterranean conditions and whose cultivation was familiar to his administrators from estates in southern France and North Africa.

In 1900, Rothschild transferred the moshavot administration to the *Jewish Colonization Association (ICA), which also started grain-farming villages in southeastern Lower Galilee. The moshava remained the sole Jewish village form until 1908, when the idea of cooperative settlement was first tried out by young Second Aliya immigrants. Even later, the moshava maintained its central role, showing that Jews were able to take root in the soil and modernizing local agriculture. In the first and second decade of the 20th century, the moshava also fulfilled the vital task of employing Second Aliya newcomers as farm laborers, thus enabling them to acquire basic agricultural skills before establishing their own villages. Citrus cultivation was, until statehood, mainly concentrated in moshavot. Even in 1985, 40% of this sector belonged to farms in moshavot or in former moshavot like Rishon le-Zion, Rehovot, Hadera, etc. The moshavot also owned about half of Israel's vineyards and fruit orchards.

Owing to the conditions, the moshavot grew at different rates: those in Galilee remained relatively small villages, while all those in the coastal plain became cities.

Only a few moshavot were established after the late 1920s. Under statehood, the sole new moshava within pre-1967 Israel was Karmei Yosef, founded in 1982 by children of moshavot farmers near Gezer in the Judean foothills, where moshavot veterans had maintained vineyards for several decades. In the Golan Heights, the moshava Kidmat Tzevi was founded in 1984.

The following are the social and economic characteristics of the moshava:

1) Membership in any party or organization strictly a matter of personal private choice;

2) Farmers market their produce as they choose and find most remunerative, although some of the moshavot have organized their marketing through Hitahdut ha-Ikarim (the Farmers' Federation) to which most of them are affiliated.

3) Owners determine who will work on the farm: themselves and their families, hired labor, or a combination of the two.

4) Moshava farmsteads are of different sizes; owners are free to choose which agricultural pursuits they prefer. In addition to farmstead owners, moshavot have always had landless inhabitants, some of whom worked as hired laborers on local farms, the rest otherwise employed in the moshava or outside.

5) The role of Zionist settlement authorities in planning and developing moshavot was always minimal because the farmsteads, as well as their land, were the settlers' private property. Only in rare instances did moshavot receive budgets from Zionist institutions, whose main contribution was professional guidance. From the 1930s onward, the coastal plain moshavot developed industry and local, regional and countrywide services. The ongoing importance of the citrus branch preserved the rural character of places such as Gedera, Herzliya, Ra'anana, Kefar Sava, and Pardes Hana.

A. ROKACH

MOSHAV MOVEMENTS. Israel's moshavim (*see* MOSHAV) belong to national associations called "Moshav movements," most of which are linked to political parties.

1. Tenu'at ha-Moshavim, the oldest movement, was founded in the fall of 1925 in a conference called at Nahalal by Eliezer Joffe, Berl Katznelson, and Yitzhak Wilkansky (Elazari-Volcani). Delegates of already existing moshavim and of groups preparing for settlement participated, deciding to outline the idea of the moshav and attract Jewish laborers to it. They elected a committee to prepare a basic moshav constitution and set up groups to safeguard their interests. At a second conference held in April, 1930, at Kefar Yehezkel, the Organization of Moshavim was formally founded. It elected both a Council and a narrower Executive. The former, later becoming the *Mazkirut* (Secretariat) of Tenu'at ha-Moshavim, guarded moshav interests in groups like Ha-Merkaz ha-Hakla'i (the Agricultural Center) of the Histadrut or in the World Zionist Organization. The Council convened the movement's General Conference, usually at four-year intervals, and took upon itself the following tasks: initiating and carrying out economic and financial measures promoting its settlements; activities related to vocational guidance, education and culture; youth work (inter alia establishing and aiding youth groups destined for future settlement); pursuing economic and organizational moshav interests in government and other public bodies; guarding moshav principles, and overseeing the creation of a moshav constitution.

When the movement grew with the establishment of numerous immigrant moshavim, after 1948, the veteran villages had to aid the newcomers. A department was established to provide instructions from the second generation of the veteran moshavim, some of them hired by the Jewish Agency Settlement Department, others volunteering without pay. The Secretariat opened a Tel Aviv office where veteran members held key positions but lower echelons included non-members from cities. The office had departments for farming, new settlers' absorption, education, youth, religious affairs, land matters, and communal affairs. The immigrant settlers' unfamiliarity with the moshav concept and structure made it necessary to fix the settlers obligations clearly through rules and eventually in a constitution, which was endorsed by the movement's Eighth Conference at Kefar Vitkin in 1951. The moshav was defined there as a cooperative taking over in leasehold the total of the village land and sub-leasing it to the farmer members. Relations between the settler, his moshav, and the entire movement were regulated. Since the movement lacked legal means to enforce such regulations, it strove from the beginning of the 1960s, to anchor them in state law. In 1971, a "moshav bill" was brought before the Knesset, but some leading moshav figures opposed it as a violation of the individual's liberties, and it was not passed.

As the movement's economic initiatives gradually increased, its financial arms were extended and new ones created. The most important are: Keren ha-Moshavim (the Moshav Fund), founded for mutual aid in 1930; En Hay Bank, a cooperative credit association which existed until 1986, when its activities were transferred to Bank Hapoalim; Keren Tagmulim, a savings fund for moshav members; and a mortgage bank for assistance in the construction and expansion of members' homes. The movement also established a number of regional purchasing organizations.

Throughout its existence, Tenu'at ha-Moshavim identified with labor parties, initially Ha-Po'el ha-Tza'ir, later Mapai, and finally the Israel Labor Party. In their policies regarding organization, immigrant absorption, and economics, the smaller moshav movements generally resembled Tenu'at ha-Moshavim.

2. Irgun ha-Moshavim shel ha-Po'el ha-Mizrachi was established in 1940 as a separate framework for religious moshavim. Most of them were linked to Ha-Po'el ha-Mizrachi or to the Mizrachi Movement.

3. Ha-Oved ha-Tziyoni Moshav Organization was founded at about the same time; its members were generally close to the General Zionist "A" Party (later the Independent Liberal Party).

4. Ha-Ihud ha-Hakla'i was created in 1944 by a merger of Irgun ha-Kefarim ha-Shitufiyim (Cooperative Villages' Organization), representing mainly middle-class villages founded in the 1930s by German immigrants, and Mo'etzet ha-Hakla'ut ha-Peratit (Private Farmers' Council, aslo representing middle-class settlements). Ha-Ihud ha-Hakla'i had cooperative farmers' groups and their marketing bodies, e.g., Tene (for sale of moshav products) and Haspaka (for purchasing farm implements, etc.) It defined itself as nonpolitical although many members belonged to the Liberal or the Independent Liberal Party. Its professional monthly publication was *Ha-Meshek ha-Hakla'i* (Agricultural Economy).

5. The Mishkei Herut-Betar organization was formed by a few villages founded by Betar; Nordiya near Netanya, and Ramat Razi'el, in the Jerusalem Hills were the veterans among them. More were founded in the administered areas after 1967.

6–7. The movements of **Po'alei Agudat Israel** and **Hitahdut ha-Ikarim** did not exclusively comprise moshavim, the first including also kibbutzim and the latter principally moshavot (*see* MOSHAVA), which were joined by a few moshavim in the 1980s.

A small number of moshavim do not belong to a regional framework. Most of these had initially not clearly defined their settlement form although it resembled that of the moshav. The national settlement authorities, however, demanded from all villages financed or aided by them to belong to a countrywide association which could to a degree take over guarantees for them. The organizational independence of such villages must therefore be regarded as transitional until each of them decides to join one of the movements.

The seven movements, with many problems and aspirations in common, set up an Inter-Moshav Committee to represent their interests to the Ministry of Agriculture and the Jewish Agency (Zionist Organization) Settlement Department. A. ROKACH

MOSHAV OVEDIM (workers' smallholders settlement). *See* MOSHAV MOVEMENTS.

MOSHAV SHITUFI ("Cooperative Moshav", plural: moshavim shitufiyim). Cooperative village, in its structure and principles midway between *kibbutz and *moshav. Its production is fully collective as in the kibbutz, but it resembles the moshav in that it permits individual consumption to the settler family. In 1988, Israel had 47 moshavim shitufiyim with a total population of 10,500.

The first settlement of this form was Kefar Hittin, founded by Bulgarian Jews in 1936 in eastern Lower Galilee. In 1938, it was followed by Shavei Zion in the Acre Plain and by Moledet in southeastern Lower Galilee, both established by Jews from Germany. The concept behind this settlement form, however, is much older. In 1912 a "work kevutza" took over Be'er Toviya in the southern coastal plain and in 1913 Arthur Ruppin suggested to the Jewish National Fund that the group works its land collectively while homesteads remain private. In 1933 Levi Eshkol advised a convention of the moshav movement to overcome the crisis of their villages by collective production with families retaining the right to "private" living and educational decision for their children. "Equality and cooperation in the obligation of work and in the moshav's income," he said, using for the first time the term "Moshav shitufi." The assembly did not accept his suggestion.

Only after World War II were three more moshavim shitufiyim founded, by soldiers demobilized from the British army. Further growth was slow, with certain villages exchanging this settlement form for the regular moshav, while others joined it. There was never a countrywide movement exclusively representing the moshav shitufi. In 1986, six moshavim shitufiyim belonged to Tenu'at ha-Moshavim, four to the Agudat Israel moshav association, others to smaller countrywide movements, while a few had joined the United Kibbutz Movement because they felt themselves close to the economic structure of the kibbutz. Twenty-five moshavim shitufiyim were founded after 1967.

Land, water, all farm branches and machinery as well as factories, resort hotels, etc. are operated cooperatively in the moshav shitufi as in the kibbutz, and they belong to the entire community, whose possessions cannot be divided or transferred. A member leaving the settlement cannot demand his share of the joint property, although he is entitled to compensation for the work place he abandons. Likewise, a moshav shitufi member cannot bequeath his home to his children because it is the community's property.

The labor force, as a production factor, is reckoned as part of the joint property, as in the kibbutz. Women do not give the community a full workday as they do in the kibbutz, since they have to devote part of their working hours to their home and children. The family members receive their household budgets as well as all health, social, and cultural services. The household budget covers the family needs in the way of food, clothing, furniture etc. Although the family is free to decide how to spend its budget, most villages impose certain reservations, some, for example, prohibiting private cars, employment of household help or enlarging the family home (if the latter is warranted by the growth of a family, the village's cooperative association takes the building costs upon itself). For members' use, the community often maintains a number of private cars which are available for each member's use for a fixed number of days.

Choice of services is more limited than in the regular moshav; for instance, determining which secondary school or sick fund members will join. On such matters the moshav shitufi leadership makes the decision for all its members. For their collective economy, all moshavim shitufiyim have accepted the kibbutz model.

The Members' Assembly is the supreme body of the community, while production and other daily matters are directed by the council of the local cooperative association, which also functions as the municipal authority. As on the kibbutz and the regular moshav, the council is aided by a number of specialized committees. Basic principles of the kibbutz and moshav also hold for the moshav shitufi, e.g., national ownership of the land, self-labor, and mutual aid.

Physical planning of the moshav shitufi resembles that of the kibbutz. A separate zone is devoted to community buildings. Farm installations are normally at a distance from living quarters.

Development tendencies are also similar to those of the kibbutz. Besides farming, the moshav shitufi is intent on engaging in other productive enterprises such as industry or resort hotels. In farming itself, branches are preferred which can be automatized and demand relatively little manpower. The moshav shitufi's ability to develop non-farming branches, mainly industry, brought about a preference for this settlement form over the regular moshav in areas where arable land is not widely available, like central Galilee. In the 1980s the scarcity of agricultural areas for new settlement opened up greater opportunities for the moshav shitufi than it had possessed in earlier periods.

A. ROKACH

MOSHEVEI OLIM. *See* MOSHAV MOVEMENTS.

MOSLEM COMMUNITY IN ISRAEL. *See* ARABS IN ISRAEL.

MOSSINSOHN, BEN-ZION. Educator, principal of the first Hebrew high school in Eretz Israel, and community leader (b. Andreyevka, Ukraine, Russia, 1878; d. Jerusalem, 1942). Mossinsohn joined the Zionist movement in his youth. In 1900–01 he served as teacher and principal in a Russian-Hebrew school in Berdyansk. From 1902 to 1906 he studied in Switzerland, where he was active in the student Zionist movement and received a Ph.D degree from the University of Berne. He first visited Eretz Israel in 1904, when he was sent by Menahem M. Ussishkin to fight the "Ugandist" tendencies spreading through the yishuv under the influence of Eliezer Ben-Yehuda (*see* EAST AFRICA SCHEME). Settling in Eretz Israel in 1907, he joined the staff of the *Herzliya High School in Jaffa, where he taught the Bible using a "modern" approach based on Biblical criticism and archeological findings.

From 1912–1915 and again from 1919–1941, Mossinsohn was principal of the Herzliya High School, which he helped establish as the country's outstanding Hebrew high school. During World War I he was deported by the Turkish regime. He spent the war years in the United States, where he was active on behalf of Zionism and the propagation of the Hebrew language. There he published his book on the prophets, *Ha-Neviim* (1919).

Active in communal affairs in Palestine, Mossinsohn belonged to the democratic wing of the General Zionist party, participated in many Zionist Congresses, and was a member of the Actions Committee. He was also a member of the Tel Aviv Municipal Council for many years, served as a delegate to the Asefat ha-Nivharim, and was a member of the Executive of the Va'ad Le'umi. Mossinsohn was active in the Hebrew Teachers Association and in 1941, was appointed to head the educational system of the Va'ad Le'umi. In this capacity he succeeded in eradicating the friction and distrust that had existed between the teachers and the Va'ad Le'umi's Education Department.

Y. SLUTSKY

MOTION PICTURES IN ISRAEL. Although regular cinematic activity by Jewish bodies in Palestine started in 1927, there were occasional cinematic "events" (film making, cinemas, importation, and screening of films, film reviews in the daily press) from 1896–7. The first cinematic "event" occurred with the arrival of Auguste and Louis Lumière's emissaries, at the same time that teams were sent to all parts of the Mediterranean, to film material for the Lumières' newsreels, screened from 25 December 1895 in Paris. The film shot in Eretz Israel, in the spirit of the travelogues characterizing the motion pictures made in Palestine until 1927, portray panoramas of Jerusalem, Jaffa, and Acre, the large centers of the yishuv of that period.

Other "pre-historic" events of great importance for the history of Israeli cinema are: a. The first motion picture screenings in the country in 1900 in the Goldmans' house in Rishon le-Zion, and by the Italian Colora Salvatore who went to Eretz Israel with a mobile projector and a selection of films that he screened at the Europa Hotel in Jerusalem. Among the first films screened was one on the Dreyfus Affair. The screening of the films was later transferred to the Abu Shakosh café in the Old City. b. Edison's team, that arrived in the framework of the competition between Edison and the Lumière brothers in 1902 with a dance team in order to film the first "feature" film, *A Dance in Jerusalem*. c. A group of German pilgrims and cineasts combed the country in 1903 and filmed its first "long" film (about 24 minutes). d. The opening of the first cinemas in Eretz Israel from 1908, and of the Eden cinema, the first Hebrew cinema in Tel Aviv, by Abarbanel and Weiser in 1914. e. The filming of the first Jewish oriented films by Murray Rosenberg and Akiva Aryeh Weiss. Rosenberg's film *The First Film of Palestine*, was shown in 1911 to the participants of the Tenth Zionist Congress in Basle. A film on Akiva Aryeh Weiss, one of the founders of Tel Aviv, was lost on its way back to the country. f. Filming of the first long feature film in Palestine, *From the Manger to the Cross*, by the American company K.A.L.M.N. Directed by Sidney Olcott, the film attempts to reconstruct the life of Jesus in the Land of Israel. g. The creation of the first film company in Palestine, *Menorah*, by Ya'akov Ben-Dov who made about ten films for the Jewish National Fund and the Keren ha-Yesod between 1917 and 1927. He established many of the production patterns of the Hebrew-Israeli film; many films would be produced for propaganda purposes out of public financing. h. The first Hebrew translations of films by Yerushalayim Segal, manager of the Eden cinema, in 1927.

Until 1926–7 it was impossible to speak of regular cinematographic activity. The conditions for this began to exist in the Jewish film industry in Palestine from the late 1920s: the Jewish population of Palestine increased considerably; the composition of this population changed with the introduction of many more urban-bourgeois bodies; the amount of money available for commerce and investment in cinema increased; there was a growing awareness of the entertainment value and the propaganda force of the cinema. Tel Aviv became the center of cinematographic life in the country. The center of gravity of Jewish cultural life moved from Jerusalem to Tel Aviv in the mid-1920s and a number of prominent personalities, such as Natan Axelrod and Baruch Agadati, arrived in Palestine and engaged in film-making. Vladimir Jabotinsky was also involved in the industry in the mid-twenties, writing profusely in praise of the cinema and was even the author of a screen play that was rejected by the Zionist institutions.

These changes led to the creation of several new cinemas in the Tel Aviv area and in other places throughout Palestine and the appearance of regular film reviews from 1927 (starting with Avigdor Hame'iri and the *Ha-Aretz* newspaper). An extensive range of creative cinematographic activity began with the founding of many production companies. For example Moledet (1927) was founded by Natan Axelrod and Yerushalayim Segal and the He-Halutz cooperative (1928) with the participation of Axelrod, Alexander Penn, Avigdor Hame'iri and others for the screening of a film with the same name as the company. (The film was never completed because of ideological and budgetary problems, since in its opening scene it presented a Petah Tikva pioneer collapsing from hunger on the streets of Tel Aviv).

Between 1927 and 1935 these companies' various cinematographic products were produced, including regular newsreels (about five-six a year) issued by the Moledet company between 1928 and 1934, and by Aga (owned by the Avigdor brothers) between 1931 and 1934. Many topical films and short documentaries were created for public bodies, such as the Jewish National Fund, the World Zionist Organization, the Keren ha-Yesod, the Histadrut, and private bodies, and cinemas which financed their production. Complete films were produced including *Va-Yehi bi-Yemei* ("And it came to pass," 1932) by Natan Axelrod, Hayim Ha-Lahmi and Zvi Goldman, the first long Palestinian feature film *Oded ha-Noded* ("Oded the Wanderer," 1932), *Tzabar* ("Sabra," 1932) by Polish director Alexander Ford; *Avoda* ("Labor," 1933) by the German stylistic cameraman Hermann Larsky; *Shirat Ami* ("My People's Dream," 1933) that portrayed the visit of the cantor Yossele Rosenblatt to Palestine, singing against a scenic background; Baruch Agadati's *Zot Hi Ha-Aretz* ("This is the Land"), which was a summary of 50 years of settlement in Eretz Israel using Ben-Dov's newsreel material; and *Le-Hayim Hadashim* ("Land of Promise," 1935) that was produced by the Keren ha-Yesod in conjunction with Margot Klausner and Yehoshua Branstatter.

During the same period (1927–1934) cinematographic activity was anchored in the framework of the law with the passing of legislation and the application of the British mandatory Palestine Cinema Law (1927), the Censorship Act (1929), and the Public Entertainment Act (1935).

Just when all the conditions for regular cinematographic activity in Palestine seemed right, however, the film industry suffered a crisis arising from internal reasons originating in the inability of Jewish society to finance and to consume such an extensive activity, and from external reasons—the Arab Revolt of 1936–1939 and World War II.

The only production company that withstood the crisis was that of Natan Axelrod, who in 1935 created a private company, Carmel Films. This became the main company on the Jewish cinematographic market in Palestine between 1935 and 1945; it produced a regular talking newsreel until 1941, a series of information films on agricultural topics in Arabic, and filmed a long series of short documentary films for the different Zionist institutions. It also attempted to film two full-length feature films, *Al ha-Horavot* ("On the Ruins," 1937) from a story by Zvi Liberman-Livneh on the exploits of children in the Second Temple period, and *Kol Mekarev* (1939), a love story between a singer who went to Palestine on a concert tour and a local girl.

The weakened Palestine film industry suffered a further crisis in 1942 when the importation of photographic raw material was interrupted almost completely. At the same time a British newsreel was supplied to the cinemas in addition to that of the French Pathé-Gaumont that was already provided free of charge.

Filming of the Carmel newsreel was interrupted; it reappeared in 1944 with the participation and partial funding of the Jewish National Fund. The newsreel thus lost the political independence that had characterized it and of which Axelrod was so proud.

The reappearance of the newsreel was accompanied by the revival of the film industry, expressed in the establishment of new cinemas throughout Palestine, and the production of many films, mostly financed and produced by American producers and the Zionist institutions. Among the most prominent producers of that period were Meyer Levin who wrote the scripts for two documentary films, *The Illegals* (1946), and the feature film *My Father's House* (1947). The latter was produced by Herbert Kline. Norman Lourie, a South African Jew, created and produced a series of documentary films between 1947 and 1949 for the Zionist institutions, the best known being *Bayit ba-Midbar* ("A House in the Desert") on the Bet ha-Arava settlement on the shores of the Dead Sea.

Joseph Leyts, a Polish Jewish producer who arrived in Palestine with the British Army in 1945, directed in 1947 *The Great Promise*, and Herman Larsky directed *Adama* ("Land").

Film production brought with it the importation of much equipment to the country, and the creation of another laboratory, Seret Le'umi, in addition to Axelrod's. However, even these two laboratories, with all the production equipment, were insufficient to cater to the needs of all the productions filmed in the country.

1948 was a turning point in the history of cinematographic activity in Israel; on the one hand it became organized and industrialized, and on the other, it changed its content.

Great efforts were invested in portraying the challenges facing the young State with the dual objectives of gathering money from abroad, and integrating the new immigrants. This effort was financed by public and state bodies (Jewish National Fund, Keren ha-Yesod, the Histadrut, and the Government Information Authority, etc.), and various production bodies were established including Geva (1951), owned by Yitzhak Agadati and Mordekhai Navon, and Herzlia (1953), owned by Margot Klausner and Yehoshua Branstatter. Geva was a studio and laboratory that concentrated on production of a newsreel to compete with Axelrod's Carmel newsreel, and on information films for state institutions, while the Herzlia studios dealt with production of films directed mainly at export markets.

The creation of the studios led to an imbalance between the equipment at the disposal of the film industry and the number of Israeli productions; balance was restored with the founding of the Israel Films Service headed by Yigal Efrati, and the Production Department of the Histadrut headed by Yosef Bernstein. The 1954 Encouragement of Israel Film Law settled the struggle between the Geva newsreel and the Carmel newsreel by determining alternate screening in Israeli cinemas, and made obligatory the screening of short Israeli films in the cinemas; it also assisted the Israel Films Service and the Histadrut Production Department in the creation of a large number of information films during the fifties. Patterns of work were developed along with a professional cadre that laid the infrastructure for the local film industry. In addition to the many scores of films created by these organizations between 1948 and 1960, local and foreign bodies also tried to produce feature films here. These were created at the rate of one or two yearly, and included Amar's *Hafuga* ("Cease-Fire"), and Sherman's *A Sword in the Desert* in 1949, *Faithful City* (Joseph Leyts, 1952), *Even al Kol Mil* ("Every Mile a Stone" Aryieh Lahola) and *Hill 24 Doesn't Answer* (Dickinson) in 1954, *Mafte'ah ha-Zahav* ("The Golden Key") (Sasha Alexander), *Ha-Etmol shel Mahar* ("Tomorrow's Yesterday" directed by Agadati) in 1955, *Dan ve-Sa'adya* ("Dan and Sa'adya" directed by Axelrod, 1956), *Be-En Moledet* ("Homeless" directed by Habib Nuri, 1957), *Amud Ha-Esh* ("Pillar of

Shooting reconstruction of Entebbe rescue at Ben-Gurion airport for film of Menachem Golan, 1976. [Israel Govt. Press Office]

Fire" directed by Frisch, 1959), and *Holot Lohatim* (Blazing Sands, 1959). In 1959 the Hollywood producer Otto Preminger produced *Exodus*, Israel's most widely viewed film. Encouraged by its success, local producer Baruch Dinar who had behind him a long line of short films including the international successes *Halutzim* (1950) and *Tent City* (1952), went on to produce *They Were Ten*, the first Israeli film to benefit from the aid proposed by the 1954 Law. Thus commenced a long tradition of full-length film production, which by 1987 encompassed over 300 long films, including five Oscar nominees and a prize winner at the Locarno Festival. Among the best known makers of these films initially were people with theater background, such as Menahem Golan, Ephraim Kishon, Peter Frye, Yoel Zilberg, and later, people who rose up in the film world such as Uri Zohar, Dan Wolman, Yitzhak Yeshurun, Judd Ne'eman, Avraham Hafner, Boaz Davidson, Assi Dayan, Dani Waxman, Uri Barbash, Shimon Dotan, and Eytan Garon.

In the 1960s the Committee for the Encouragement of the Israeli Short (Film) was created at the Ministry of Commerce and Industry. This Committee gave young directors the opportunity to produce their first films and to acquire the basic skills of the film industry.

In 1965 educational television was introduced in Israel and three years later, general television. Television greatly expanded the number of films created in Israel and the needs of the Israeli audience. It also led to a drop in the number of commercial cinemas from about 300 to 170.

The 1970s were characterized by the promotion of quality Israeli film productions, leading to the establishment of academic schools of cinema at Tel Aviv University and the the *Bet Tzevi* School of Stage Craft, the creation of cinematheques in Tel Aviv, Haifa, and Jerusalem from 1973 onwards, a Film Institute in 1974, and the appearance of quality film journals.

At this time the Histadrut's film department ceased production (1973); the Herzlia and Geva Studios merged to form the United Studios (1978); and the Foundation for the Encouragement of Quality Films was launched in 1978. The same period saw a decline in the popularity of ethnic fims in Israel, which had been popular in 1965, starting with *Sallah Shabbati*. Films on adolescence came into style following the production of *Eskimo Limon* (Lemon Popsicle), and encouraged the Israelis Menahem Golan and Yoram Globus to develop one of the largest private production companies in the world, Cannon.

The 1980s saw, along with a decline in the number of original television productions, a transition to feature film production along American story and production patterns as opposed to the European models that characterized many Israeli films in the sixties and seventies; and numerous attempts to break the monopoly of the single television network. M. ZIMERMAN

MOTZA. Two villages (Motza Ilit i.e., Upper Motza, and Motza Tahtit, Lower Motza), 3.5 mi. (5 km.) west of Jerusalem. A town of this name is mentioned in the Bible (Joshua 18:26) but its site is not necessarily identical with the present settlements. The Motza of the Mishna, where willow branches were cut for the Sukkot festival, is identical with the now abandoned adjoining Arab village Kalunya (Colonia). In 1859, Jerusalem Jews bought the land for farming and in 1894 the B'nai B'rith Order founded a small settlement there. In the 1929 Arab riots it was largely destroyed and seven of its settlers killed, but the Jewish settlement was restored soon after. In 1933 the moshav Motza Ilit was founded further west. Later, the Histadrut Sick Fund opened the Arza convalescent home on the hilltop, on the site where Herzl had planted a cypress in 1898. Since the 1960s, the moshav has gradually turned into a Jerusalem suburb, and luxury homes have been built at Ramat Motza near Motza Tahtit. In 1987, Motza Tahtit had 54 inhabitants, and Motza Ilit 720. E. ORNI

Leo Motzkin.
[United Israel Appeal]

MOTZKIN, LEO ARYE. Pioneer and cofounder of the World Zionist Organization, coauthor of the Basle Program, and co-founder and leader of the movement for Jewish minority-group rights in Europe (b. Brovary, near Kiev, Russia, 1867; d. Paris, 1933). The child of a wealthy, pious family, Leo Motzkin excelled in mathematics and, at the age of 15, was sent to Berlin to attend high school. Later, in 1885, he enrolled at the University of Berlin, where he studied mathematics and sociology. There, in 1899, he helped to found the Russisch-Jüdischer Wissenschaftlicher Verein (Russian-Jewish Academic Association), the first nationalist Jewish students' society in Berlin. Subsequently members of this group took an active part in the Jung Israel movement for German-Jewish students. Motzkin broke off his studies to devote his life to Jewish affairs.

Motzkin was one of the first to respond to the call of Herzl, helping the latter prepare the First Zionist Congress (1897). At that Congress he persistently fought for the adoption of a platform that would stress the political character of the new movement. The final version of the Basle Program was evolved by the Program Committee, of which he was a member. The First Congress commissioned Motzkin to make a survey of Jewish settlements in Eretz Israel, on which he made a report to the Second Congress (1898). A member of the Democratic Faction, he fought at subsequent Congresses for the democratization of Zionist leadership and for the introduction of educational activities within the framework of the Zionist program. After the outbreak of World War I, Motzkin, who sympathized with the Allied cause, left Berlin and was placed in charge of the *Copenhagen Bureau of the World Zionist Organization. After the war he settled in Paris. He presided over postwar Zionist Congresses (as vice-president of the 12th to 16th Congresses and as president of the 17th and 18th). In 1925 he was elected chairman of the Actions Committee, an office he held until his death.

Actively interested in the revival of the Hebrew language and culture, Motzkin was one of the organizers of the Berlin Conference for Hebrew Language and Culture (1909) and of the larger conference held in Vienna in 1913 under the chairmanship of David Yellin, Hillel Zlatopolsky, and himself. A strong advocate of *Gegenwartsarbeit* (political work on behalf of equal rights for Diaspora Jewry), Motzkin founded a news agency in Berlin in 1905 to publicize throughout the European press the pogroms then taking place in Tsarist Russia. He was commissioned by the Zionist Actions Committee to write a detailed report on these outrages. The result of his researches was *Die Judenpogrome in Russland* (2 vols., 1910), published under the pen name A. Linden. Later, he also published in western Europe factual information about the Beilis ritual murder case.

To Motzkin the struggle for Jewish rights in the Diaspora was a vital part of Zionism. His central ideal was the Jewish National Home in Palestine but, being a realist, he appreciated the value of *Gegenwartsarbeit*. In 1918 he published the *Copenhagen Manifesto, in which the postwar claims of the Jewish people were defined as national revival in Palestine and national minority-group rights for Jewish communities in other countries. The next year he became secretary-general of the *Comité des Délégations Juives at the Paris Peace Conference, a position in which he coordinated efforts to include guarantees of minority-group rights for Jews in the peace treaties with the newly established European republics. He initiated and helped form a central organization of all national minority groups in Europe, the European Minorities Congress, which sought to enforce the rights of minorities in countries where governments attempted to weaken or abolish these rights. He was a presidium member of the Congress until 1933, when he resigned over the refusal of the conference of that year to place on the agenda the situation of the Jews in Nazi Germany, and the Congress itself collapsed soon thereafter. A week before his death he traveled to London to confer with Weizmann and others on the German-Jewish refugee problem.

Motzkin aided Stephen S. Wise and Nahum Goldmann in their early efforts to organize a *World Jewish Congress. Early in the Nazi era, together with Emil Margulies, a prominent advocate of Jewish rights in Czechoslovakia, he brought before the League of Nations the Bernheim petition, which was based on a German-Polish treaty concerned with the rights of minorities in Upper Silesia. It was through this petition that the Nazi Nuremberg laws were later brought before the Council of the League of Nations, with the result that the rights of Upper Silesian Jews were fully respected until 1937, when the agreement expired.

Motzkin was reinterred on the Mount of Olives, Jerusalem, in 1934.

Mountain Jews delegates to Sixth Zionist Congress, 1903, standing next to portrait of Herzl (center). [Beth Hatefutsoth]

MOUNTAIN JEWS OF THE CAUCASUS IN ISRAEL. About half of the 65,000 Mountain Jews live in the autonomous, multi-national republic of Dagestan, on the western shore of the Caspian Sea in the east of the Caucasus. A third live in the Azerbaijan Republic, and the rest in areas neighboring on the aforesaid republics. Their language is Tat, an Iranian dialect mixed with Hebrew words and other words absorbed from the languages of the many different peoples of the Caucasus among whom the Jews have lived for generations. Little is known about immigration from this region to the Holy Land in the 19th century.

In 1893 Rabbi Sherbet Anisimov, one of the leaders of the community who visited Eretz Israel several times, counted in the cemetery on the Mount of Olives about one hundred tombstones engraved with names of Mountain Jews. He also noted most sorrowfully that about 200 immigrants from Dagestan had been compelled to return to their places of origin since they had not succeeded in finding sources of income in the Holy Land. After this emigration, only 60 Jews from Dagestan remained in Jerusalem.

In 1907, Yaakov Yitzhaki, rabbi of the Derbent Community, immigrated with his family and dozens more families of his community, who were among the founders of the moshava Be'er Ya'akov near Ramleh. The settlement was named after Yitzhaki, although he himself moved to Jerusalem. In 1902, a number of Caucasian families tried unsuccessfully to settle in the moshava Mahanayim in the Huleh Valley. Caucasian immigrants were also among the founders of kibbutz Hulata in 1936. From the time the first Caucasian immigrant arrived in Eretz Israel and up until World War I, many Caucasian Jews attempted to settle in the country; some were successful and some failed.

The Caucasian Jews accepted political Zionism from its outset. Two Caucasian delegates, Shlomo Mordikhaiev and Matityahu Bogatiraiov, participated in the Sixth Zionist Congress (1903) and made a great impression on the Congress participants with their imposing black beards and native costume. On their return from the Congress they founded the Zionist Movement of the Mountain Jews and commenced Zionist activity in all their communities. Scores of their families joined the Second Aliya. Their Zionism was nourished not only by the religious yearning for Eretz Israel but also, or principally, by the hostility and harsh persecutions of the Moslem peoples among whom they dwelt. In Eretz Israel, many of them identified with the labor movement. In view of their own tradition of self-defense, it was natural that several young Caucasian immigrants joined *Ha-Shomer*. One of them, Yehezkel Nisanov, was murdered in 1911 by Arabs while guarding the lands of Merhavya. Hundreds of young Mountain Jews responded to the call in 1917–18 to join the Jewish Legion and gave Jabotinsky a list of 800 volunteers. They were, however, unable to join because of the Civil War raging throughout Russia. Under the Soviet regime hundreds of Mountain Jews succeeded in immigrating to Palestine before the Jews of the entire Soviet Union were cut off and emigration was halted, except for a few exceptional cases, for almost fifty years.

When emigration was resumed in the 1970s, the Mountain Jews were the last of all the Jewish communities in the Soviet Union to be allowed to leave. The reason for this delay was the negative attitude of the local authorities. The regions settled by the Mountain Jews are also inhabited by a large Moslem population, and the Soviet media's acute agitation against Israel after the Six-Day War increased hostility to the Jews, especially among the Moslems. Only after Jewish representatives complained to the central authorities in Moscow were they permitted to leave and then only on a very small scale. The first 60 Mountain Jewish immigrants arrived in Israel in 1972; in 1973 there were 325. In 1974–1975 the numbers began to reach significant proportions: 1,570 and 2,270 respectively. From 1972 until 1985 a total of 10,857 members of the community arrived in Israel, almost none dropping out en route. The average family numbered 4.3. Children and youth up to age 18 constituted 50% of all the Mountain Jewish immigrants as against 28% among the total of Russian immigrants. The percentage of members of the academic, liberal, and technical professions (23%) was lower than among the other Russian immigrants; 55% were industrial workers. Yekutiel Adam, who served as deputy Chief-of-Staff of the Israel Defense Forces and who fell in the Lebanon War in 1982, was a member of the Caucasus community. Y. LITVAK

MOYNE, 1ST BARON (Walter Edward Guinness). British statesman (b. Dublin, 1880; d. Cairo, 1944). As Secretary of State for the Colonies (1941–42) and British Resident Minister in the Middle East (1942–44), Lord Moyne was responsible for the enforcement of British policy in Palestine. He made no secret of his outspoken opposition to Zionist aims. One of his most virulently anti-Zionist and anti-Jewish speeches was delivered on 9 June 1942, in a debate in the House of Lords on the motion of Lord Wedgwood for a Jewish fighting force to be recruited from Jewish refugees from Nazism and for permission to Palestine Jewry to raise an armed home guard.

"The Zionist claim," Lord Moyne asserted in his reply that day, "has raised two burning issues—first, the demand for large-scale immigration into an already overcrowded country, and secondly, racial domination by the newcomers over the original inhabitants....If a comparison with the Nazis is to be made it is surely those who wish to force an imported regime upon the Arab population who are guilty of the spirit of domination and aggression...." He went on to propose that Jewish refugees might be settled in Syria, Lebanon, and Transjordan, which were not as crowded as Palestine and which, if fear of Jewish domination could be removed, "might well be glad to welcome Jewish capital and industry."

Lord Moyne was shot and fatally wounded in Cairo on 6 November 1944, by Eliahu Hakim and Eliahu Bet Tzuri, two youthful members of Lohamei Herut Israel who had stolen across the Palestine border into Egypt. They were apprehended, tried, and executed by the Egyptian authorities.

MUFTI OF JERUSALEM. *See* AL-HUSSEINI, HAJJ AMIN.

MULLER-COHEN, ANITA. Communal worker and Zionist leader (b. Vienna, 1890; d. Tel Aviv, 1962). The daughter of a well-to-do family, who had been educated at a teachers' seminary and the University of Vienna, she early on became interested in Jewish and nonsectarian welfare work. Joining the Zionist movement at an early date, she paid her first visit to Eretz Israel in 1910. During World War I she organized relief work in Austria for thousands of Jewish refugees who arrived there from Galicia and Bukovina. In 1919 she was elected to the Vienna Municipal Council as a representative of the Jewish National party. The next year she initiated a movement in the United States, Canada, Argentina, and other countries in the western hemisphere for the adoption of children orphaned by the pogroms in Russia.

In 1925 Müller-Cohen visited Canada and the United States, where she addressed the opening session of the American Jewish Congress in Chicago. Early in 1936 she settled in Tel Aviv and immediately became active in social work in Palestine. During the Arab riots of 1936–39 she aided the refugees from endangered border areas. She was a founder of the Women's Social Service (now the Women's Social Service for Israel) and played a prominent role in the Mizrachi Women's Organization. When the Nazi annexation of Austria in March, 1938, led to the immigration of large numbers of Austrian Jews to Palestine, she helped revive and reorganize the Hitahdut Olei Austria (Association of Immigrants from Austria; *see* AUSTRIAN JEWS IN ISRAEL). She assumed an active role also in Youth Aliya, taking a particular interest in the resettlement of children from Orthodox families. After World War II she aided the Jewish underground and, following the independence of Israel, she joined the Herut movement. She attended several Zionist Congresses and at the 24th Congress (1956) was elected a delegate-at-large to the Greater Actions Committee.

MUSEUMS IN ISRAEL. Israel's national museum, the Israel Museum, was opened in Jerusalem in 1965. It comprises a number of institutions and collections that had been housed elsewhere in the city and many that have been added over the last two decades. The nearly-complete master plan brought together the Samuel Bronfman Biblical and Archeological Museum, an expanded version of the former archeological museum of the Israel Department of Antiquities; the Bezalel National Art Museum (founded by Prof. Boris *Schatz in 1905 and officially opened in 1927);

In the Israel Museum. [Israel Museum]

the Shrine of the Book, home to the Dead Sea Scrolls and the Bar Kokhba finds; and the Billy Rose Art Garden which contains a collection of neo-classical and modern sculpture.

Designed by Alfred Mansfeld and Dora Gad, it is located on a hill overlooking both the Knesset and the Givat Ram campus of the Hebrew University. The Bronfman Museum, places a unique emphasis on the Bible and contains outstanding examples of the cultures that flourished in Palestine and prehistoric Canaan, from Stone Age man through the conquests of Joshua and the Kings of Israel, to the conquests of the Greeks, Romans, Byzantines, and Arabs. Statues, altars, ceremonial objects, seals, coins, inscriptions, letters, glassware, pottery and weapons, most of them excavated in and around Israel, bring the biblical era to life.

The Bezalel section, which by now comprises a dozen pavilions, contains major collections of Jewish ceremonial folk art and ethnological costumes and objects from Jewish communities throughout the world; Far, Near and Middle Eastern art; a wing for the ethnology of distant cultures, African, pre-Columbian, and Oceanian. The Bezalel holdings include a huge collection of drawings and prints spanning the entire history of western art; a selection of Renaissance and Dutch painting and a wide range of modern art, from the French Impressionists to Picasso, the abstract and Pop New York School and a number of major international post-modernists.

The Bezalel's Israeli art pavilion houses a permanent overview of Israeli art and a huge gallery space for changing shows of contemporary Israeli works. The adjoining Billy Rose Pavilion is host to shows of international contemporary art, which will later be exhibited in a new wing for contemporary art. Permanently on view in the Bezalel section are Italian and German synagogues, an 18th-century French grand salon from the home of the Rothschilds, an English period dining room, an Italian Chinoiserie, and a Persian *mihrab* (prayer niche). The Youth Wing gives instruction in painting, sculpture, ceramics, graphics, puppetry, and drama to both Arab and Jewish schoolchildren and has its own exhibition galleries which feature didactic ethnological and other displays, both from Israel and elsewhere. Jerusalem's Arab children also attend art classes at the museum's Art Center in East Jerusalem.

The Israel Museum's Art Garden contains the work of sculptors from Rodin and Maillol to Chadwick, Moore, Picasso, and Tinguely; Israelis are also represented. A nearby pavilion houses outstanding collections of miniatures by Henry Moore and Honoré Daumier and the original plasters of heads by Jacob Epstein.

The Shrine of the Book, a dramatic, partly underground structure designed by Frederick Kiesler and Armand Bartos, is symbolic of an underground cave surmounted by a dome resembling the lid of an ancient storage jar. It features the splendidly preserved Isaiah scroll which was deposited in a jar in the Qumran caves nearly 2,000 years ago; other scrolls and fragments from the caves set out the ideology and rules of the Qumran sect and their belief in the account of the War of the Sons of Light against the Sons of Darkness, again symbolized by the juxtaposition of the Shrine's white dome with a black basalt wall backing onto the entrance. Also on display are relics of the Masada defenders; and Aramaic, Greek, and Hebrew letters from Bar Kokhba and his followers. In addition, the complex houses a scientific reference library. Also on the museum grounds is the Charlotte Bergman collection of paintings by Braque, Dufy, Moore, and others. In downtown Jerusalem, just off Jaffa Road, is an annexe of the Israel Museum at Bet Ticho, the former home of the late Jerusalem landscape artist Anna *Ticho and her husband, Dr. Avraham Ticho. The museum contains works by Anna Ticho and her art library, as well as Dr. Ticho's collection of Hanukka lamps.

Following the Six-Day War of 1967, the Palestine Archeological Museum in East Jerusalem again became accessible to Israelis. Opened in 1938 and endowed by a $1m. fund of the Rockefeller Foundation, the Rockefeller Museum, as it is popularly known, was placed in the administrative care of the Department of Antiquities and some of the staff of the Bronfman Museum. The collection has been augmented by exhibits from the Israel Museum and recent finds. The Rockefeller frequently hosts exhibitions of finds from new digs as well as changing didactic shows curated by Israel Museum staff. Otherwise, the exhibits in the main galleries remain exactly as presented in the 1930s and 1940s, since no changes were made by the Jordanians in 1948–67.

Jerusalem's first "site museum" of archeology is housed in the campus of Hebrew Union college, designed by Moshe Safdie. It is devoted chiefly to finds from excavations made under the aegis of the college's school of archeology, notably at Tel Dan and at Gezer. Its permanent didactic displays show all the finds from these sites.

Youth Wing, Israel Museum, Jerusalem. [Israel Museum]

Located in the heart of Jewish Jerusalem is the L.A. Mayer Institute —Islamic Museum which augments its permanent collection of Islamic ceramics, jewelry, textiles, rugs, and weapons with didactic loan exhibitions from international collections, which are well attended by classes of Israeli Arab schoolchildren.

Near Mount Herzl is the *Yad Vashem Holocaust Memorial complex. Below a Memorial Chamber, the floor of which is marked with the names of concentration camps in which most of the six million Jewish victims of Nazism perished, is a permanent exhibit of photographs and objects. An adjoining art museum contains another permanent display of drawings and paintings of eyewitness scenes and types in the camps and ghettoes, made by survivors either during or shortly after the war. The complex also features an avenue of trees planted for gentiles who saved Jewish lives; and a symbolic children's memorial with candles reflected in mirrors, designed by Moshe Safdie.

Smaller museums in the capital include the City Historical Museum at the Citadel; a collection of Jewish ceremonial objects at the Dor va-Dor Isaac Wolfson Museum in Hekhal Shlomo, seat of the Chief Rabbinate; a Museum of Natural History; musical instruments at the Rubin Academy of Music; the collection of the Pontifical Biblical Institute; the Armenian Treasures Museum in the Old City, chiefly church jewelry and vestments as well as sacramental objects and illuminations; a Museum of Taxes, from biblical times to the present, containing many Ottoman records; and a memorial museum to Lohamei Herut Israel (Lehi) and Irgun members preserved in the Mandatory prison.

Municipal Museums. Tel Aviv, Haifa, Holon, Herzliya, Ramat Gan, Petah Tikva, Bat Yam, Beersheba, Rehovot, Ein Hod, and Givatayim all have municipal art museums, chiefly for the presentation of Israeli painters and sculptors. Apart from Tel Aviv and Haifa, the most active municipal museums are those of Herzliya and the Museum of Israeli Art at Ramat Gan, which hosts both contemporary shows and didactic reviews of aspects and themes of Israeli art.

Tel Aviv Museums. The Tel Aviv Museum, housed in a huge modern building, is largely a museum of 20th-century art, though it also boasts a modest collection of post-Renaissance painting. It has a unique series of painted wooden reliefs by Osip Zadkine and a fine array of canvases by James Ensor. Its main permanent display is an overview of Israeli art from the days of Tel Aviv's inception until the present. International exhibits are also brought to the museum, which plays an active role in promoting shows of contemporary Israeli art and retrospectives of veteran Israeli artists. Visiting shows are often held at the museum's annex, the Helena Rubinstein Pavilion, first built to augment the Tel Aviv Museum's original modest home at Bet Dizengoff.

Tel Aviv also has a number of smaller, specialized museums. Biggest is the Land of Israel Museum at Ramat Aviv, comprising the former Ha-Aretz Museum with its pavilions devoted to ancient glass, ceramics, numismatics, ethnology, and folklore (with costumes displayed in dioramas of Yemen, Bukhara, Poland, and Kaifeng); science and technology; and an alphabet museum, the history of script with examples of Hebrew, Moabite, and Phoenician ostraca and manuscripts. Adjoining are the Tel Kasile excavations, where the visitor can see an Israelite city in 12 strata, from the Philistine period through that of the Kings of Israel and the Islamic conquest.

Nearby, on the campus of Tel Aviv University, is the

Beth Hatefutsoth, Museum of the Jewish Diaspora, Tel Aviv. [Beth Hatefutsoth]

Nahum Goldmann Museum of the Jewish Diaspora, Beth Hatefutsoth, a museum devoted to the 2,500-year history of Jewish communities in the Diaspora. This is an innovative museum of reconstruction in which there are no authentic objects but the exhibits have all been imaginatively created, relying heavily on audio-visual techniques. They include dioramas, models of famous synagogues down the ages, slide shows, documentary video films, and interactive computerized programs. The museum includes a Jewish Music and a Genealogy Center. Its changing exhibitions are often devoted to the history of Jewish communities, some of them exotic, some of them no longer in existence. In the course of its work, it has built up the world's largest Jewish photographic archive. The Museum of the Jewish Diaspora has also developed an extensive educational and outreach program, covering adult education, Israeli schoolchildren and soldiers, and seminars from abroad.

The Tel Aviv-Jaffa Museum of Antiquities, housed in the former Turkish prison in Jaffa, has finds from the surrounding area, chiefly pottery. The Tel Aviv Historical Museum, along with municipal memorabilia, shows old photographs of "Little Tel Aviv" and the early days when the town stood on sand dunes. At Bet Golomb, named for the Hagana leader Eliahu Golomb, is a defense forces and Hagana collection of weapons, uniforms, documents, and photos from the early days of the *shomerim* (watchmen) through the War of Independence to the present day. The Bet Bialik museum is the former home of Hebrew poet Hayim Nahman Bialik; it preserves his study and library and also contains a public reference library of Hebrew literature. David Ben-Gurion's home, containing an extensive library, is also open to the public. The Jabotinsky Institute is a memorial to Vladimir Jabotinsky and underground organizations that fought the mandatory authorities. Its Jabotinsky Archives relate to the history of the Revisionist movement and the Irgun Tzev'ai Le'umi. The Rubin Museum houses a collection of the paintings and drawings of the artist Reuven Rubin, but also holds occasional shows by other artists.

Haifa Museums. The Haifa Municipal Museum comprises the Haifa Museum of Modern Art and its ancillary pavilions of Israeli art, ethnology, musical instruments, porcelain and the separate Mané Katz Museum, the latter containing the paintings and sculptures of Mané Katz and his collection of Judaica. The ethnological collection is devoted to ceremonial objects brought to Israel by various communities and also to the preservation of the heritage of minority communities that have lived in the Holy Land for generations: Arabs, Druze, and Circassians.

The Tikotin Museum of Japanese Art has a large collection of ukiyo-e woodcut prints, painted screens, fans and the like; there are frequent didactic presentations. The Haifa Maritime Museum, devoted to the history of seafaring and local ports, displays antique finds, including hoards recovered from wrecks. There are ancient charts and navigational aids, old prints and engravings and records and pictures of Mediterranean sea battles, as well as a fine collection of models of naval craft from biblical times to the present day. A special section is devoted to the Israel Navy and blockade-running during the Mandate, when Jewish refugees landed "illegally". One of the small "illegal" immigration blockade-runners is permanently careened nearby.

South of Haifa is the Janco-Dada Museum at the artists' village of En Hod, named for and largely devoted to the artist, Marcel Janco, one of the signatories to the first Dada Manifesto and the founder and first mayor of the En Hod community. The museum mounts didactic shows on the history of Dada and related exhibitions by Israelis.

Settlement Museums. A number of kibbutzim boast professional art and archeological museums. The biggest, at En Harod, concentrates on a permanent collection of kibbutz painters, notably Menahem Shemi; it also displays major retrospectives of Israeli artists. At Kibbutz Lohamei ha-Geta'ot is a Holocaust Museum documenting Jewish resistance; it was founded by survivors of the last battle of the Warsaw Ghetto. In the Jordan Valley, at Ashdot Ya'akov, there is a display of paintings, photographs, and crafts by kibbutz artists at Uri and Rami House, named for two young brothers who lost their lives in the War of Independence. It was constructed with personal reparations payments from Germany donated by kibbutz members. Nearby, Kibbutz Sha'ar ha-Golan boasts an excellent collection of neolithic finds from its own fields, which were the crossroads of prehistoric Jordan Valley cultures, at the mouth of the Yarmuk River. Neighboring Bet Alfa has unearthed a sixth-century synagogue floor depicting Abraham's sacrifice of Isaac, and the zodiac. Bet Wilfred Israel, in Ha-Zore'a, has a fine small collection of early Chinese ceramics and temporary exhibits. A section of the former Acre Prison, where Jewish underground fighters were executed by the mandatory authorities and which was the scene of a famous "great escape," has been preserved, together with the gallows and trap.

Historic Sites. Israel is full of living museums in the form of historic sites, preserved and reconstructed. They include the great Roman theaters of Bet She'an and Caesarea, the sites of Megiddo and Hazor, the ancient fortresses and temples and churches of Caesarea, Shivta, Avdat, Montfort, Lachish, and Masada, and since June, 1967, Hisham's Ommayid palace at Jericho, Herodion, the "Essene village" at Qumran on the Dead Sea, and many sites in Samaria, such as the Judean-Hellenic-Roman fortress at Sebastia, near Nablus. Many of the Israeli sites have special local exhibit halls for finds that have not been turned over to the Israel Museum. M. RONNEN

MUSIC AND MUSICAL LIFE IN ISRAEL. Throughout the history of the yishuv and the State of Israel music has played an important symbolic and social role as part of the process of the formation of a national identity. Musical life on all levels—performance, composition, and musical organization —was dominated by strong ideological pressures and polemics, which underlined the importance of music as a cultural force. No ideological consensus as to the desired nature and components of the new national style has ever been reached, however, and the musical scene has been characterized by pluralism and coexistence of contrasting stylistic and ideological trends.

Most of the musicians who were influential in the shaping of musical activity in the pre-State years and even during the first decade of the State were immigrants, who received most or all of their education and professional training in their country of origin, while their absorption in their new home coincided with their ideologically motivated creativity. From the socio-cultural point of view, musical activity before the State consisted of two different divisions. Jewish immigrants from Europe between 1880–1948 brought along their predilection for formal institutions, public concert life, and curriculum-based music schools, whereas Jews from Arab countries, such as the large Yemenite immigration (arriving in the country already from the 1880s) and the local Sephardi community, made use of music for family- and community-oriented events, such as wedding ceremonies, holidays, and social gatherings, and this music as a rule was not easily accessible or understood by outsiders. Despite constant ideological pressure to turn to the east and to merge eastern and western traditions, it was only through an elaborate process of mediation that a certain limited encounter of eastern elements with western techniques was attained.

1880–1918. Western-oriented musical activity began in 1895 in the settlement of Rishon le-Zion where a community orchestra was formed, employing a professional salaried conductor and performing at local events, such as the historic visit of Theodor Herzl to the settlement (1898). Several pianos were brought to the settlement and symbolized European influence, opposed by some settlers as foreign to Zionist ideology. The influence of neighboring Arab villages was felt in the tendency of the Jewish farmers to learn folk songs in Arabic and provide them with Hebrew or Yiddish texts. In 1910 the German-born singer, Shulamit Ruppin, founded the first music conservatory in the country, which attracted students from Europe. Situated in Jaffa, its founding coincided with the opening of the

Rishon le-Zion Orchestra, 1897. [Jewish National and University Library]

Hebrew High School (later named Herzliya Gymnasium) where music was an obligatory and prestigious subject. After Shulamit Ruppin's death in 1912 the school was named after her. Under the directorship of the violinist Moshe Hopenko it maintained a purely European curriculum, with piano, violin, and theory classes, a choir, and a student orchestra. A branch opened in Jerusalem, soon becoming an independent institution. These first schools determined the western orientation of professional music education in the country for many years. The first expression of interest in the musical heritage of oriental Jews was effected by the monumental research project of Abraham Zvi *Idelsohn who worked in Jerusalem from 1907 (or late 1906) to 1921 with the declared intention of searching for the origins of ancient Jewish music through the methods of the emerging discipline of ethnomusicology. Idelsohn used the Edison phonograph to make thousands of field recordings of Yemenite, eastern Sephardi, and western Sephardi communities, the results of which were compiled in the ten-volume series of the *Thesaurus of Hebrew Oriental Melodies*, which soon became a major source for scholars and composers. The war years slowed the development of musical life but activity resumed soon after the establishment of British rule over Palestine.

Musical life and institutions 1919–1931. With the resumption of cultural activity following the World War, three ambitious projects emerged, intended to make Palestine into an international center for opera, oratorio, and Jewish music. A group of immigrants from Russia, who had been active members of the Society for Jewish Folk Music in St. Petersburg, among them the concert pianist and pedagogue Arieh Abileah (Nisvitzky) (1885–1984) and the singer Yehuda Har-Melah (Bergsalz), initiated an invitation to the opera conductor Mark (Mordekhai) Golinkin (1875–1963), then the conductor of the highly prestigious Mariansky Theater in St. Petersburg (Leningrad). Already in 1917 Golinkin had published in Russia a pamphlet circulated among Zionist activists there, in which he contemplated a Temple for the Arts in Palestine, an ambitious institution modeled after Wagnerian ideology, encompassing opera, ballet, orchestras, and a comprehensive art school. Golinkin's arrival in Jaffa in 1923 was hailed as a national event, but the grim economic situation in the small yishuv forced him immediately to forgo his ambitious plans and to concentrate on the establishment of a small opera company, which he considered the best vehicle to implement national ideas. The opera company commenced its performances in a festive atmosphere in July, 1923, with Verdi's *La Traviata*. This, as well as all subsequent performances, was produced in Hebrew, despite the severe difficulties of translating opera libretti into the still evolving modern Hebrew and the effort required by the Russian-born singers to relearn the repertory. The opera had good experienced singers, but the orchestra was the small student ensemble of the Shulamit school, the choir was a barely-paid amateur group, and production conditions were primitive. Alongside the classical opera repertory by Verdi, Mozart, and Puccini, Golinkin also produced operas by Jewish composers, such as Anton Rubenstein and Meyerbeer. The conflict between the great vision and the total lack of financial support pushed the opera into economic crisis, with a decrease in the number of productions until, after four seasons, it was forced to close. Golinkin's efforts to raise money abroad failed, and despite occasional revivals in the 1930s opera productions were sporadic and crisis-ridden for years to come.

More feasible economically was the project of the Hebrew Oratorio, mostly initiated by the conductor Fordhaus Ben-Zissi (1898–1979). A deeply religious youth, he considered the performance of oratorios on biblical themes as a great spiritual experience. Based on a dedicated amateur chorus, the Hebrew Oratorio began regular activity in 1927 with performances of works such as Mendelssohn's *Elijah* and Haydn's *The Creation*, with a somewhat free translation by the poet Aharon Ashman and a musical interpretation stressing slow and solemn tempi.

Another project was the endeavor to move the center for Jewish music research, performance, and publication from its older centers—St. Petersburg, Moscow, Vienna, and Berlin—to Palestine. With that object, the composer Yoel *Engel was urged to immigrate to Palestine. Engel settled in Tel Aviv in the end of 1924 and brought his publishing house, Yuval, from Berlin. The economic hardships forced him to work most of his time as teacher, composer, and arranger of children's songs, and his research and publication projects had to wait. His sudden death in 1927 put the whole project in jeopardy, but a group of his friends, including the pianist, pedagogue, and ideologist Prof. David Schorr (1867–1942) and the critic, conductor, and teacher Menashe Ravina (Rabinovitz) (1899–1968) reorganized the project as the Nigun Society, dedicated to the publication and performance of Jewish music, old and new. The society attracted a relatively large number of members, and despite its very limited budget organized regular series of concerts.

The ideology of all three projects—opera, oratorio, and Jewish music—was maximalistic and European-oriented. The purpose was to emphasize the significant role of Jews in world music and the wide range of music which could be defined as "Jewish." Consequently, it admitted as Jewish any music in which a single factor was related to Jewishness, such as performance in Hebrew translation, biblical or historical themes, Jewish descent of the composer, and even music with general humanistic values, such as Beethoven's music, described by David Schorr as not less Jewish than music written by Jews. It was linked to a socialist ideology of dissemination of music, whether through guided listening or through active participation in amateur choirs, among workers and farmers all over the country, many of whom were highly educated and responsive to musical activity. Schorr and Ravina inaugurated a large-scale project of organizing amateur choruses all over the country, gathering them occasionally for regional and national events. A contrasting ideology was represented by a small group of musicians and amateurs centered around Dr. Sandberg and the teacher and folk music composer Mordekhai Geshuri, who published a short-lived journal in 1930, proposing a total segregation of music in Palestine, abolishing all western influence, especially the commercial penetration of phonograph records and the newly developed movie soundtrack, and finding new inspiration in Arabic music. The actual influence of the segregationist group was minimal, but some of its ideas found their way into more moderately expressed reviews and essays.

The 1920s saw many attempts to organize symphonic orchestras. The conductor Max Lampel (1900–1987) organized a series of outdoor concerts in Tel Aviv in 1926–7, catering to large audiences numbering some 3,000 listeners. Yet, the paucity of professional players, the lack of funds for adequate salaries, and the musicians' need to earn their living at odd jobs, such as playing in movie houses, cafes, and hotels frustrated regular concert activity. In 1929 a small concert ensemble, directed by Tzevi Kompanetz, performed popular promenade-type programs for three seasons. Box office income alone could not guarantee a living for the musicians, and in 1932 the ensemble disbanded. Chamber music was much cherished in the yishuv, with concert societies organizing series of recitals performed by small groups of professional musicians and teachers, such as the cellist Thelma Yellin-Bentwich, her sister the violinist Marjorie Bentwich, and the violinist Shlomo Garter. The country also attracted many internationally renowned soloists, whether Jewish or not, among them the violinists Jan Kubelik and Jasha Heifetz, the pianists Leopold Godowsky and Artur Rubinstein, many of whom continued to visit the country frequently, performing with little or no pay and raising funds for cultural and educational purposes. Their activity helped to maintain a sensitivity to high artistic standards in the yishuv, but at the same time also limited the chance for local artists to build their own concert careers.

Composition of art music was very limited in the 1920s, mostly due to the lack of adequate performing ensembles for new music and the limited opportunities for professional composers to make a living in the small circle of educational institutions. The only active composer of the Engel group who immigrated to Palestine was Jacob Weinberg (1879–1958). His principal work composed in the country was a national folkloristic opera, *The Pioneers*, based on his own libretto and endorsing the Zionist ideology of abandoning the Diaspora way of life in favor of agricultural work on a kibbutz. Using sharply delineated musical symbols, such as quotations from traditional and new songs, cantorial modes, orientalistic motifs, and folk dances, it followed the trend of Russian folkloristic operas of the 19th century. Disenchanted by the lack of any opportunity for performing his large-scale works, Weinberg left for the United States in 1927.

Music and music institutions 1931–1948. The large immigration from central Europe in the 1930s effected a major change in the overall musical scene in Palestine. It brought to the country more than twenty professionally trained composers, some raised and educated in Germany (including Paul *Ben-Haim, Erich Walter *Sternberg, Josef *Tal, Stefan *Wolpe, Hanoch *Jacobi, Karel Salmon) and others born in Russia and Poland and professionally trained in other capitals, mostly Paris and Vienna (Alexander Uriah *Boscovich, Joachim *Stutschewsky, Verdina Shlonsky, Marc *Lavry, Joseph Kaminski, Oedoen *Partos). These were joined by younger composers who either arrived as advanced students (Haim *Alexander) or immigrated as children with their parents and later completed their studies abroad (Mordecai *Seter, Menahem *Avidom). They created an extensive repertory in all genres, which was judged by critics, journalists, and ideologists in the yishuv for its ideological stance no less than for professional quality. No group-school was formed, but three principal ideological attitudes dominated the creative activity of the small community of composers. They were located between the loose maximalistic attitude and the extreme segregationist approaches, neither of which was suitable for locally-based professional composing.

1. *The collective-nationalistic attitude.* As the best articulated of the five, this dominated the musical scene. Clearly stated by the composer Boscovich, it was based on the dialectics of time and place, viewing any musical culture as dependent, as far as its content and meaning were concerned, on the particular geographical or human environment where it originated, gaining international renown only at a later stage. Music suitable to a certain locality, such as Jewish folk and traditional music of eastern Europe, could be transferred to the new reality of life in Palestine. The special characteristics of landscape in the country, as well as the sound and rhetoric of Semitic languages (Arabic and modern Hebrew as spoken by those born in Palestine) had to be active factors in shaping the new national music. However, the technical achievements of western music should by no means be ignored but, conversely, adopted and used with discretion, accepting elements common to the Mediterranean basin as a whole, such as declamatory, recitative style, and rejecting typically European and especially German techniques such as fugue or chorale. The composer should act as the representative of a collective, expressing feelings and ideas common to the entire national group, and suppressing his personal emotions as irrelevant to his mission. The shaping of the new national music was to be a deliberate act rather than a natural process. Boscovich implemented his ideology in his early works written in the 1940s, especially in the second movement of the oboe concerto (1943) and in the *Semitic Suite* (1946). The term eastern-Mediterranean music was spelled out by Max *Brod in his monograph on the music of Israel (1951) and used by Avidom as the title of his *Mediterranean Sinfonietta*. Such music was dominated by dance rhythms, modal patterns, *taqsim*-like development; its harmony resulted from the superposition of the pitches of the melody, while the typical tonal directionality of western music was avoided in favor of static, repetitive patterns. Non-tempered intonations and micro-tones were feigned through coloristic minor seconds and frequent alternation of major and minor thirds. European instruments, mostly piano, as well as traditional chamber and orchestral ensembles, were utilized, and the compositions were intended for concert performance as well as for pedagogical purposes (Boscovich's *Pieces for Youth*, 1946).

2. *The popular-folk attitude.* While not contradicting the collective national attitude, this favored simple, light music, which would appeal to the public at large through easily grasped melodies and sensuous harmony. Its principal advocate was Lavry, who drew on simple, tuneful melodies, sharply delineated hora dance rhythms, as in his song *Emek* which was turned into a symphonic poem, and on realistic subjects, as in his national folk opera *Dan the Guard* (1945).

3. *The individualistic-national attitude.* Negating the collective-nationalistic attitude, it opposed any form of ideological pressure on any composer and maintained the traditional romantic attitude of the freedom of the composer to choose his personal form of expression. It considered that a national style would emerge as a natural outcome of regular and unforced compositional activity. The very fact that the composer would be active in Palestine as part of the community would itself render his contribution national. The supporters of this viewpoint also emphasized the need to maintain the cultural ties with the great achievements of western music and keep abreast of developments in new music, such as the Schoenberg school. The protagonists of this attitude, acting individually, were Stefan Wolpe who, however, left the country in 1938, Sternberg, and Tal. The ideology of this attitude was first articulated by Sternberg in an essay preparing the ground for the performance of his large-scale orchestral work, *The Twelve Tribes of Israel* (Musica Hebraica, 1938).

While certain composers strongly subscribed to one of

these ideological attitudes, others, such as Ben-Haim, avoided total identification with any definite attitude. While some of Ben-Haim's compositions reflect the eastern-Mediterranean attitude, such as his *Five Pieces for Piano* and his piano concerto, he never rejected western tonal organization or direction, and local coloristic sonorities of minor seconds and superposed fifths and fourths occur within a larger framework of tension-relaxation dialectics of western-based tonality and form. Such was also the case in direct quotes from traditional Jewish oriental tunes. Seter quoted traditional tunes of Iraqi Jews, derived from Idelsohn's *Thesaurus*, in his *Sabbath Cantata* (1944), but they were elaborated through western contrapuntal techniques based on Palestrina style, with twentieth-century dissonant harmony and the traditional four-part chorus and string orchestra. While quotations of tunes from a published document like Idelsohn's was an indirect approach to oriental music, it was only through the help of mediators that the western-minded composers established a more direct contact with the sonorities, intonation, and performance manner of Jews of "oriental" origins as well as of Arabs. Chief among these mediators was the singer Bracha Zefira who brought the traditional "oriental" songs into the concert hall context, and acquainted most of the composers active in the 1930s and 40s with the "oriental" Jewish repertory. Highly motivated by national ideology, she considered herself a "Hebrew" singer, free from any narrow ethnic commitment. Many of her songs were incorporated, either as full quotes or as motivic material, for further elaboration in large-scale symphonic and chamber works (as in Ben-Haim's symphonies, piano concerto, and clarinet quintet, Avidom's *Mediterranean Sinfonietta*, and many others). The oud player Ezra Aharon (b. 1903), one of the greatest Jewish musicians active at the Iraqi royal court, immigrated in 1935 and performed regularly in public concerts and in radio broadcasts from Jerusalem.

The founding of the Palestine Symphony Orchestra (later *Israel Philharmonic Orchestra) by the violinist Bronislow *Huberman and the initiation of Hebrew broadcasts from Jerusalem, both in 1936, were major events. Huberman's venture, begun as an idealistic quest for an international center for the arts to be situated in Palestine, soon became a rescue operation which brought to the country some of the best Jewish performers who lost their positions with major central European orchestras due to the rise to power of Nazism and anti-Semitic regimes. Adhering to high international standards from its first festive concert under Arturo Toscanini, the orchestra performed with the greatest conductors and soloists, and was a source of pride for Jews all over the world. The radio station focused on live classical music, established a small ensemble which soon developed into the radio orchestra, and promoted performances of locally composed works. Many immigrant musicians also filled important positions as professional teachers who shaped the locally-born younger generation of musicians and founded the music academies of Tel Aviv and Jerusalem. Musical activity was very intense during the years of World War II, when the very absence of visiting musicians encouraged local musicians to compose and perform.

Music and Music institutions since the establishment of the State of Israel. With the establishment of the State of Israel in 1948, individual musicians, such as the pianist Pnina Salzmann (who had studied in Paris under Cortot) and performing groups, notably the Israel Philharmonic, acted as cultural ambassadors for the young nation. The state encouraged composers and musical activity through limited financial funding and support for special events such as the sponsoring of festivals, but as a rule initiative remained mostly individual or institutional. The academies of music in Tel Aviv and Jerusalem, both founded in the 1940s, soon boasted graduates of professional ability, such as violinist Shmuel Ashkenazi and pianist Menahem Pressler. Internationally renowned teachers, among them Ilona Feher, Ilona Vinze, Thelma Yellin, Oedoen Partos (excelling as violin teacher no less than as composer), Lorand and Alice Fenyves, and many others developed generation after generation of fine violinists, including Pinhas Zuckerman, Yitzhak Perlman and Shlomo Mintz, cellist Uzi Wiesel, pianists Yahli Wagman, Varda Nishri, and Arie Vardi. The country also produced conductors of international standing: Gary Bertini, the founder of the Rinat National Choir and of the Israel Chamber Orchestra, who also made important contributions to the revival of opera and the performance of large-scale oratorios in the country, and Mendi Rodan, musical director of the Jerusalem Symphony Orchestra for nine years, following which he founded the Beersheba Sinfonietta. Later, younger conductors like Uri Segal and Yoav Talmi have continued the practice of dividing their time between regular positions in Israel and frequent performances in Europe and the US. The renewal of cultural ties with Europe and the US brought into the country influences of innovative trends, such as the post-war Darmstadt group, which stimulated changes of attitude and techniques among the composers. For example, Haim Alexander, whose early works for chorus (*Ve-Kibatzti ethem*) and for piano (*Five Israeli Dances*) reflected the collective-nationalistic attitude, turned in the 1950s and 1960s to dodecaphonic techniques, as in his song cycle *Ba Olam* to poems by Nathan Zach. However, no dogmatic dodecaphonic school ever emerged, and Alexander's *Patterns for Piano*, while sounding as though written in serial technique, is based on elaboration of a single pitch which remains a sonorous center of the work. More influential has been the search for new sonorities and esthetics of sound and form, as represented by Tal's pioneering activity in establishing the first studio for electronic music in Israel. In addition to production of electronic and computer music, Tal also applied innovative devices using sound and sonorities as a principal parameter, as in his Second Symphony, while still retaining the rigorous tradition of formal organization preserved by Schoenberg, as in his *Concertino for Flute* and his *Treatise for Solo Cello*. The direct influence of western avant-garde was frequently balanced by attempts to achieve syntheses of contemporary western techniques with related devices in oriental music such as Partos's serial treatment of maqam-like melodic figures (in his *Maqamat for flute and strings* and the *Psalm String Quartet*) and Boscovich's serialization of rhythmic elements of the Hebrew language in his orchestral work *Ornaments* (1964). The search for syntheses of advanced western compositional techniques and oriental elements has also characterized the work of the second and third generations of Israeli composers. These include Tzvi Avni (b. 1927), who, while making important contributions in the field of electronic music has also used traditional Jewish tunes (*By the Rivers of Babylon*), and Ben-Zion Orgad (b. 1926) who based many of his large-scale choral and orchestral works on prayer modes, sonorities, and rhythms, and on the inherent rhythm and accentuation of modern and old Hebrew texts (*mizmorim*). Ami Ma'ayani

Concert at sunset in the Roman amphitheater at Caesarea. [Israel Government Tourist Office]

(b. 1936) has maintained close ties with the musical idiom of the Mediterranean school, quoting and arranging traditional Jewish songs (*Sinfonietta on Jewish Folk Tunes*), and with the extended tonality and orientalism characteristic of that school (as in his *Ouverture Solennelle*). Haim Alexander has revived the Mediterranean idiom in his Piano Concerto.

The pluralism which characterized composition in Europe and the US during the 1970s and 1980s also prevails in the contemporary Israeli scene. Composers who were part of later waves of immigration have also tried to combine advanced techniques learnt in the West with eastern devices. Thus, Marc Kopytman (b. 1929, immigrated from Soviet Russia, 1972) has ventured into complex heterophonic writing and elaboration of traditional Jewish tunes, exemplified by his orchestral work *Memory* which combines the special voice quality of the Yemenite singer Gila Bashari with heterophonic elaboration of the melody through the large orchestra. The composer Tsippi Fleischer (b. 1946) combined Arabic and western elements in her song cycle, *A Girl is a Butterfly* (1977), set to poems by modern Lebanese and Syrian poets in two versions, the first in Arabic with Arab instruments, such as the oud, the other in Hebrew with flute, piano, and cello, combining maqam patterns with modern harmony and motivic work. The deliberate combination of languages and styles is used to make not only an ideological but also a political statement through music.

Since 1948 new performing institutions have been established, such as the Israel Opera. Founded by the singer Edis de Philippe, it performed regularly for over thirty years until her death, albeit with severe financial and artistic difficulties. A new opera company was formed in 1985. The Haifa, Beersheba, and the Israel Chamber Orchestras maintain regular subscription series. In 1971 the radio orchestra was expanded into a full symphonic orchestra (the Jerusalem Symphony Orchestra). In addition to the numerous amateur choirs active in the country several semi-professional and professional choirs have been formed. The Tel Aviv Chamber Chorus, founded by Eitan Lustig in 1940, evolved into a large oratorio chorus performing regularly with the Israel Philharmonic Orchestra. In 1956 the conductor Gary Bertini formed the chamber Rinat Choir, followed by Avner Itai with the professional Cameran Singers and the Chamber Choir of the Rubin Academy in Jerusalem. Professional music education leading to full academic degrees in performance, composition, and theory, is provided by the music academies in Tel Aviv and Jerusalem. The Israeli radio, Kol Israel, maintains an all-day classical music channel. The Israel Festival has sponsored major productions of operas, oratorios, and performances by leading soloists and chamber music ensembles from all over the world.

Music research and publication. Following the pioneer activity of Idelsohn, ethnomusicological research continued through Robert Lachmann (1892–1939) who was active in the country from 1935–39 and laid the foundations for the scientific collection, transcription, and analysis of the rich heterogeneous ethnic material which he found around him. Lachmann's project of a sound archive of traditional and folk recordings has been continued by Esther Gerson-Kiwi and Hanoch Avenary. In 1965 the first musicology department opened at the Hebrew University in Jerusalem, followed by departments at Tel Aviv and Bar-Ilan universities, where extensive research and teaching are done in the field of ethnomusicology (Amnon Shiloah's extensive study of Arabic writings on music and ethnic music, and the research laboratory developed by Dalia Cohen and Ruth Katz) and in the history of the music of the Jews (at the Center for Jewish Music Research headed by Israel Adler), as well as in traditional historical musicology (research of Renaissance music by Don Harran and of classical music by Bathia Churgin) and in music theory (Roger Kamien). The Israel Musicological Society sponsors a regular publication of studies by its members. During the 1980s, research and performance of far-eastern music, such as Javanese, Gamelan, and Indian, have been supported by the universities, with scholars like Dalia Cohen, Ben Brinner, and Uri Epstein expanding curriculum and practice accordingly. The Music Center in Jerusalem, founded by violinist Isaac Stern, sponsors regular master classes by internationally renowned teachers. Two important international performance competitions are regularly held in Israel: The Artur Rubinstein Competition for Pianists and the International Harp Competition.

(*See also* CANTORIAL MUSIC IN ISRAEL; FOLK MUSIC IN ISRAEL.)

J. HIRSCHBERG

N

NA'AMAT (abbreviation for Nashim Ovedot u-Mitnadevot, "Working and Volunteer Women"): Labor women's Zionist organization.

Israel: The Israel body, originally known as Mo'etzet ha-Po'alot ("Working Women's Council of Israel") is in effect the women's section of the *Histadrut, concerned with issues of special interest to women members of the Labor Federation and to working women in general. These have included the broadening of work opportunities for women, the integration of women immigrants, agricultural and vocational training for women, and family and child care. It seeks to increase the role of women in Israel public life and to assure them full representation in the institutions of the Histadrut and in Israel's public institutions.

Mo'etzet ha-Po'alot maintained "working women's farms", functioning as training and immigrant absorption centers; Batei Halutzot (working women's hostels); social and educational centers for single immigrants; and schools, children's homes, kindergartens, and nurseries. To meet the needs of wives of Histadrut members who are housewives with outside employment and to encourage their participation in public life, Mo'etzet ha-Po'alot established in 1930 the Irgun Imahot Ovedot ("Organization of Working Mothers"). Mo'etzet ha-Po'alot helped establish Pioneer Women, in the Diaspora (see below) and maintained relations with other Jewish women's organizations, such as WIZO. It also participated in social and educational work among Arab women.

In 1976, Mo'etzet ha-Po'alot and the Irgun Imahot Ovedot were restructured under the name of Na'amat. There has been continuity in the nature of the activities, which now includes professional and agricultural schools for girls, training of kindergarten teachers, youth clubs, facilities to assist working mothers, and cultural programs in the agricultural settlements.

Na'amat numbers (1989) some 750,000 members. It is active in 150 locations (including 25 Arab and 15 Druze villages) with more than 250 women's clubs in the towns and cities. It runs 45 community centers, 16 professional secondary schools, 30 professional training centers with 75 courses directed to Arab and Druze women; 475 child care centers for over 17,000 children; 30 kindergartens; three mixed agricultural schools; and 90 adult study circles. It publishes the monthly journal *Na'amat* (formerly *Devar ha-Po'elet*).

The organization is directed by a 900-member national council, which meets every four years; a 335-member national committee, meeting annually; a 114-member central committee meeting monthly; and a 28-member executive secretariat, meeting weekly. The secretary-general is assisted by a 23-member control commission. Overseas relations are maintained within a framework originally created under the name of Pioneer Women.

Diaspora: Under the name of Pioneer Women, the women's international labor Zionist movement was founded in the US in 1925 by seven women, with the endorsement of the American Po'ale Zion party. It held its first national convention in New York in 1926.

Ideologically a part of the Labor Zionist movement and affiliated with the *Ihud Olami, the World Union of Poale Zion groups, it retained full autonomy as an organization, formulating its own policies, pursuing its own activities in its fields of interest, and conducting its own educational and communal programs. Imbued with the national and social ideals of Labor Zionism, it dedicated itself to the following specific tasks: (1) "to give moral and material support to Mo'etzet ha-Po'alot;" and (2) "to strive...to educate the American Jewish woman to a more conscious role as coworker in the establishment of a better and more just society in America and throughout the world."

The central aim of its practical work was always support of and cooperation with Mo'etzet ha-Po'alot, now Na'amat. Through the Youth and He-Halutz Department of the *Jewish Agency, Pioneer Women took on the Child Rescue Fund, for which it raised considerable sums. In addition to collecting millions of dollars for Mo'etzet ha-Po'alot from its inception, it raised substantial amounts for the Jewish National Fund, the United Jewish Appeal, the Histadrut (independently of Mo'etzet ha-Po'alot), and other Israeli causes. NA'AMAT USA continues to support all these causes and remains faithful to its original goals. It raises several million dollars a year for its programs in Israel and in the USA.

Starting primarily as a Yiddish-speaking organization, Pioneer Women subsequently reached out to American-born Jewish women and drew them into Jewish community affairs. Active in Jewish education, and supporting Jewish youth work through *Habonim- Dror, it participates in all basic areas of the American Jewish scene. It also takes part in social action, cooperates with labor and progressive groups in behalf of liberal causes, and is active in the struggle for civil rights. It publishes *Na'amat Women*, a trilingual (English, Yiddish, Hebrew) magazine five times a year.

The activities of Pioneer Women in the United States stimulated the formation of similar bodies in the other countries. In July, 1964, at a conference in Tel Aviv, a world union of such organizations, comprising Pioneer Women groups from 14 countries, was formed. In 1966, the Canadian Pioneer Women, previously part of the US body, became a separate organization. C.B. SHERMAN—ED.

NA'AN. Kibbutz in the coastal plain southeast of Rehovot. It was founded in 1930 as the first settlement of Ha-No'ar ha-Oved youth movement. On "Black Saturday," 10 June 1946, it came under British army siege and 23 settlers were wounded. The kibbutz has highly intensive farming and industry. Population (1987), 1,200. E. ORNI

NABLUS (SHECHEM). Largest city of Samaria, situated in a narrow valley between Mount Ebal and Mount Gerizim. The biblical Shechem's excavated site, 1.5 miles (2 km.) east of modern Nablus, includes remains from the 19th century BCE, a strong fortress and Canaanite temple of the 18th-16th centuries BCE, the period when it is mentioned in stories of the Patriarchs. Under Joshua it was the site of a covenant of the Israelite tribes and Joseph was buried there (Joshua 24). After the split in the kingdom Jeroboam was crowned king there and made Shechem the first capital of the northern kingdom of Israel (I Kings 12). In 724 the Assyrians destroyed parts of Shechem, when they were bringing the kingdom to an end. Later Shechem was refounded and became the main center of the Samaritans. In 72 CE Vespasian rebuilt the then derelict city as Flavia Neapolis. In 636 the Moslem Arabs conquered the city, pronouncing its name "Nablus." Under them, it had a mixed population of Moslems, Persians, Samaritans, and Jews. In modern times Nablus became a center of Moslem fanaticism. In 1927, a severe earthquake destroyed large parts of the town. Under Jordanian rule, Nablus was the largest center of the Administered Areas. In addition to its traditional industry of soapmaking, the first modern factories made their appearance. On 7 June 1967, Nablus was taken by an Israel column coming from the east. Under Israel administration, the city's economic infrastructure broadened and it quickly grew from 44,000 inhabitants in 1967 (all Moslems, except for 370 Christians and 250 Samaritans)—or nearly double that number when adjacent villages and refugee camps were included. Near the traditional tomb of Joseph, venerated by Jews, Christians, and Moslems, a yeshiva (rabbinic academy) was installed by Gush Emunim supporters. The town has been a center of strong Palestinian Arab nationalism. E. ORNI

NAHAL. *See* ISRAEL DEFENSE FORCES.

NAHALAL. Moshav in the western Jezreel Valley. Founded in 1921 by pioneers of the Second Aliya, it became the prototype of the moshav settlement and initiated the Valley's development. During their first years, the settlers drained the malaria-infested swamps. The village layout in concentric circles, devised by architect Richard Kauffmann, was adopted as a pattern by other moshavim. In 1929, a girls' agricultural training school was founded by WIZO, later becoming a coeducational vocational school. Nahalal has mixed farming which has been intensive since sufficient water became available. The name is biblical. Population (1987), 1,080. E. ORNI

NAHALAT YEHUDA. Urban settlement in the coastal plain adjoining Rishon le-Zion. It was founded in 1914 to house Jewish farm laborers and provide them with auxiliary farms. Settlers made a living from their own small holdings, thus anticipating the moshav form. With the expansion of Rishon le-Zion, Nahalat Yehuda became contiguous with this city, though maintaining its status of an independent local council. It was named after Leo (Yehuda) Pinsker. Population (1987), 2,120. E. ORNI

NAHAL OZ. Kibbutz in the southern coastal plain on the border of the Gaza Strip, founded in 1951 as one of the first Nahal (Israel army unit preparing for cooperative agricultural settlement) outposts. Before both the Sinai Campaign (1956) and the Six-Day War (1967), the kibbutz suffered frequent terrorist attacks from the Gaza Strip. Later, it became an entrance gate to the Strip. The economy of Nahal Oz is based on intensive farming and it has an industrial enterprise. Population (1987), 501. E. ORNI

NAHARIYA. Coastal city six mi. (10 km.) north of Acre. Founded in 1934 by middle-class immigrants from Germany as an agricultural village, it soon developed also as a seaside resort and tourist center. The first Jewish settlement in the area, it was in a precarious position in the 1936/39 Arab riots and was isolated through long months during the 1948 War of Independence. After the establishment of the State, Nahariya grew rapidly, expanded to the east and north, developed an industrial zone, and increased its tourist services. Its name points to the Ga'aton River (*nahar*¨ river) which reaches the sea at this point. Near the shore, a Middle Bronze Age sanctuary has been excavated, probably dedicated to Asherat Yam (Astarte of the Sea). Population (1987), 29,400. E. ORNI

NAHON, SALOMONE UMBERTO. Journalist and Zionist leader in Italy and Israel (b. Leghorn, Italy, 1905; d. Jerusalem, 1974). After receiving a doctorate in economics, Nahon served first as secretary and later as vice-president of the Italian Zionist Federation (1927–39) and as secretary of the Italian Committee of the Keren ha-Yesod. From 1929 on he was an editor of the Italian-Jewish weekly *Israel*.

Nahon was a delegate to Zionist Congresses from 1931 to 1946. Settling in Palestine in 1939, he served as an emissary for Zionist funds in Egypt, Syria, Lebanon, and the Belgian Congo. In 1944 he joined the staff of the Jewish Agency and was its representative in Italy from 1945 to 1947. From 1947 on he was a senior official of the Organization Department of the Zionist Executive in Jerusalem. He directed the administrative office work of the 23rd to 26th Zionist Congresses (Jerusalem, 1951, 1956, 1960, 1964). He took a leading role in establishing Jerusalem's Italian synagogue

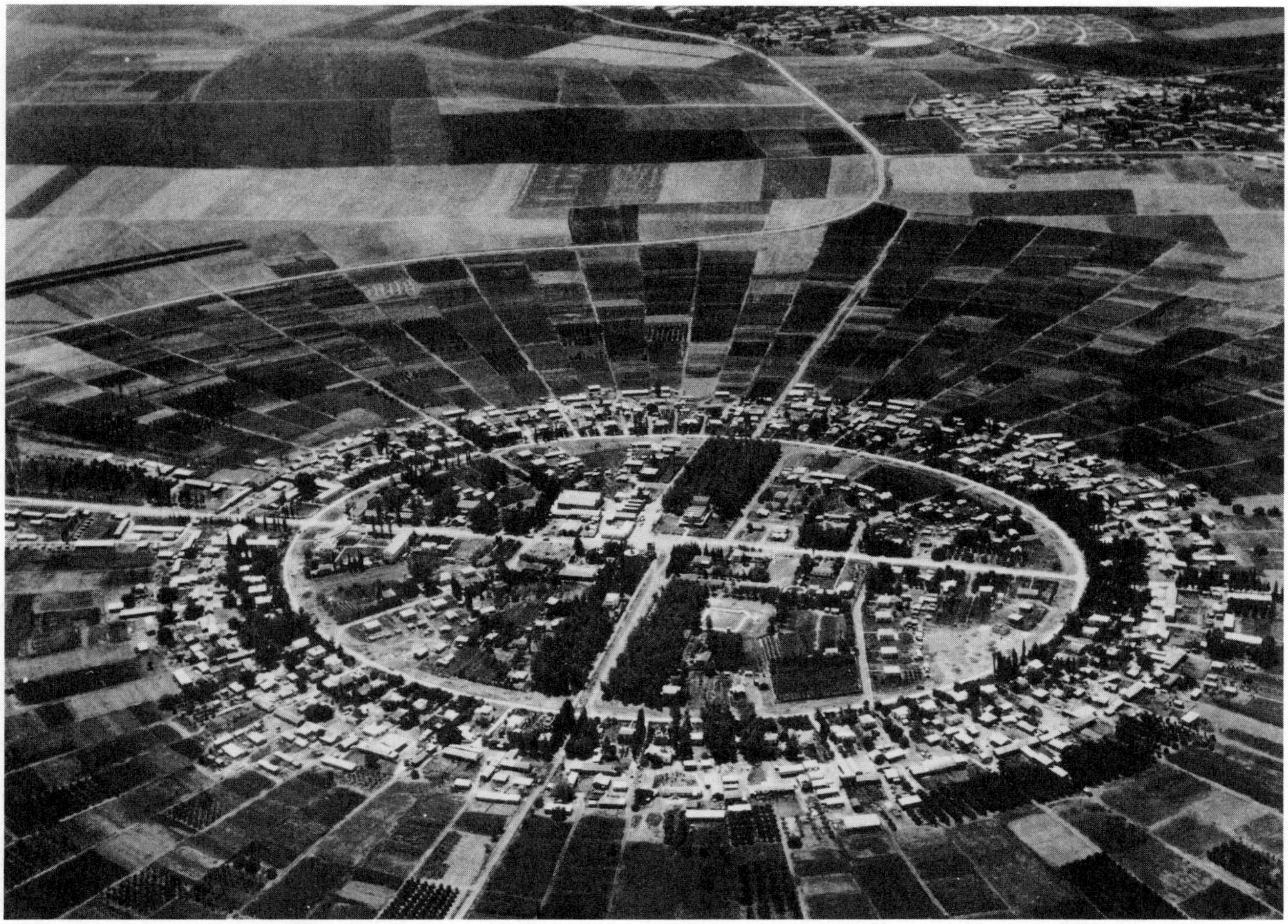

Aerial view of Nahalal, showing its circular layout. [Zionist Archives]

and its museum, which houses a collection of Jewish art from Italy. G. ROMANO

NAIDITSCH, ISAAC. Industrialist and Zionist leader (b. Pinsk, Russia, 1868; d. Paris, 1949). Naiditsch joined the Hovevei Zion movement in his youth. In 1889 he settled in Moscow and joined the Benei Zion Society. After the appearance of Herzl, he became one of the leaders of Russian Zionism. A rich industrialist (he owned large alcohol factories in Russia) with a deep interest in Hebrew culture and literature, he liberally supported Hebrew writers and Hebrew literary and educational enterprises.

He was also active in Russian-Jewish communal life. After the Bolshevik Revolution in November, 1917, he left Russia and settled in Paris, where he continued his industrial and Zionist activities until France's occupation by the Germans in 1940. During the rest of World War II he lived in the United States.

Naiditsch was a lifelong intimate friend of Chaim Weizmann. He was one of the initiators of the Keren ha-Yesod in 1920 and subsequently became one of its directors. From 1913 to 1927 and from 1939 until his death, he was a member of the Zionist Actions Committee. He contributed articles to Hebrew and Yiddish periodicals and was the author of a biography of Baron Edmond de Rothschild. A memorial volume containing some of his Hebrew poems and essays was published in 1956.

NAMIER, SIR LEWIS BERNSTEIN. Historian and Jewish Agency official (b. Wola Okrzyska, near Warsaw, 1888; d. London, 1960). Settling in England in 1907, Namier graduated from Oxford in 1915. He joined the British Army and served successively on the staff of the Propaganda (1915–17), Information (1917–18), and Political Intelligence (1918–20) Departments of the British Foreign Office. In 1920–21 he was a lecturer in modern history at Oxford. After two years in business, he pursued research work in history until 1929. That year he became political secretary of the Jewish Agency, a position he held until 1931, working closely with Chaim Weizmann. From 1931 to 1953 he was professor of modern history at Manchester University. Namier was a noted historian whose methods influenced an entire historical school. He took leave of absence from 1939 to 1945 to serve as political adviser to the Jewish Agency Executive in London. In this position Namier was an adviser to the Jewish delegation attending the St. James's Conference in London in the spring of 1939. He paid many visits to Palestine and Israel, the last in 1958.

Settlers of Nahal Oz on their way to work in the fields. [Israel Information Services]

Namier identified himself as a "national Jew." To him the Jewish people were a nation, religion being a private matter and having nothing to do with loyalty to the Jewish people. He himself had no Jewish religious affiliations, but was deeply devoted to the Zionist cause. He was knighted in 1952. He published a number of essays on the Jewish problem including "The Jews in the Modern World," in his book *In the Margin of History* (1939), and "The Jews," in *Conflicts* (1942, 1948). ED.—N. ROSE

NAMIR (NEMIROVSKY), MORDEKHAI. Israeli legislator, public servant, and mayor of Tel Aviv (b. Ukraine, Russia, 1897; d. Tel Aviv, 1975). In 1924, after graduating from the University of Odessa, he settled in Palestine. He worked for a year in a bakery, then became circulation manager of the daily *Davar* (1925–26). Namir was secretary of the Ahdut Avoda party from 1926 until 1929, when he was named director of the Statistical Department of the Histadrut, a position he held until 1936. In 1930 he joined the Central Committee of Mapai. In 1935 he was elected to the Tel Aviv Municipal Council, serving for one year. Continuing his career in the Labor movement, Namir was general secretary of the Tel Aviv Labor Council (1936–43) and a member of the Histadrut Executive Committee (1944–48). Active also in the self-defense effort of the yishuv, he served in the Hagana command of the district of Tel Aviv (1933–47) and in its national command (1947–48). A delegate to the Zionist Congresses of 1937 and 1946, he was also a member of the Actions Committee from 1946 to 1959.

In 1948 Namir was special envoy of the Israeli Ministry of Foreign Affairs to Bulgaria, Czechoslovakia, and Romania; in 1948–49, Counselor to the Israeli Legation in Moscow; and in 1949–50, Israeli Minister to the Soviet Union. He was elected to the Knesset in 1951 and served as general secretary of the Histadrut until 1956, when he was appointed Minister of Labor and Housing. In 1959 he was elected mayor of Tel Aviv, an office he held until 1969. Namir wrote numerous essays, articles, and statistical studies of economic and labor problems in Israel.

His wife **Ora** (b. Hadera, 1930), a member of the Knesset from 1974, was particularly involved with the social problems facing Israel and the issue of the status of women. From 1981-1984 she was chairman of the Knesset committee for Education and Culture and from 1984 chairman of the committee for Labor and Social Affairs. In 1992 she entered the cabinet as minister of the environment, later of labor and social affairs.

NAPHTALI, PERETZ (Fritz). Israeli economist and Cabinet member (b. Berlin, 1888; d. Tel Aviv, 1961). After attending the Institute of Commerce in Berlin, Naphtali worked for various banking and industrial firms. In 1919–20 he was editor of the trade column of the *Preussische Zeitung* and *Morgenpost*, and from 1921 to 1926 he edited the economic section of the *Frankfurter Zeitung*. As director of the Economic Research Bureau of the labor movement in Berlin (1926–33), he was an influential economic adviser to the Directorate of the German Trade Unions. A member of the German Socialist party, he was a lecturer in economics at the universities of Berlin and Frankfort and the author of two works that became basic economics texts of the Socialist movement in Germany.

Brought into the Zionist movement in the later 1920s through the influence of Kurt Blumenfeld and Zalman Shazar, Naphtali was chairman of the German League for Labor Palestine and served on the Board of Directors of the Zionist Organization of Germany. He was a delegate to the 17th (1931) and 22nd (1946) Zionist Congresses.

Settling in Palestine in 1933, Naphtali became a lecturer in political economy at the Haifa Technion (1933–36) and managing director of the Bank ha-Po'alim (1938–49). A member of the Tel Aviv Municipal Council (1937–49) and of the Asefat Ha-Nivharim, (1941–48), he represented the Mapai party in the first three Knessets. In 1948–49 he was chairman of the Economic Advisory Board to the Prime Minister. He joined the Cabinet in 1951 as Minister without Portfolio. From 1952 to 1955 he was Minister of Agriculture (and briefly, in 1955, Minister of Agriculture, Commerce, and Industry), and in November, 1955, he became Minister without Portfolio. In 1959 he was named Minister of Social Welfare but retired from both the Cabinet and Knesset that year because of ill health. G. HIRSCHLER

NARBONI, JOSEPH-GEORGES-ANDRE. Attorney and Zionist leader in Algeria and Israel (b. Algiers, 1912; d. Jerusalem, 1979). A graduate of the University of Algiers in 1934, Narboni became a judge of the Court of Appeals in that city. After serving in the French Army during World War II, he returned to Algiers, where he was a member of the North African Zionist Council and president of the Algerian Zionist Federation until 1961. At the 24th Zionist Congress (1956) he was elected to the Zionist Actions Committee, representing the World Confederation of General Zionists. In 1960–61 he represented the Progressive party in that body.

In 1961 Narboni settled in Israel and was appointed a deputy member of the Zionist Executive and later head of the Department for Zionism and social activity among the Sephardi and oriental communities. In 1964, together with André Chouraqui, deputy mayor of Jerusalem, he founded the Berit Am, an organization to facilitate the integration of French-speaking immigrants in Israel. He served as Hon. Pres. of the French and North African Jews' Association in Israel.

NARKISS, MORDECAI. Pioneer Israeli art curator (b. Skala, Poland, 1897; d. Jerusalem, 1957). He studied in Cracow and Vienna and went to Palestine in 1920, studying at the Bezalel School. In 1924 he was chief assistant to Boris Schatz at the Bezalel Museum. From 1925 until his death, Narkiss was the first director of the Bezalel National Museum, putting together the major part of the collections. He published many articles and books on Jewish art, archeology and art history, notably *Coins of Israel* (1936–38) and *Crafts of the Yemenite Jews* (1939).

His son, **Bezalel Narkiss** (b. Jerusalem, 1926) teaches the History of Art at the Hebrew University and is an authority on Jewish art. M. RONNEN

NASSER, JAMAL ABD EL-. President of Egypt, 1956–70 (b. Nile Delta, 1918; d. Cairo, 1970). In 1937, after completing his studies, he entered military academy. In 1948 he fought with the Egyptian troops in the Negev and was among those trapped in the "Faluja pocket." Like most officers of his generation, while fulfilling military tasks, he was deeply involved in political activity. In 1949 he established the organization known as the Free Officers—a small, clandestine group of intermediate-rank officers who were concerned with Egypt's condition resulting from the military defeat of 1948, the continued British presence in the Canal zone, endemic economic and social difficulties, and the rampant corruption in the political set-up.

In the hope of improving Egypt's situation the organization took control of the government in a military coup on 23 July 1952. A respected senior officer, Colonel Mohammed Najib, was made head of the government. A personal power struggle soon developed between him and Nasser; they also differed as to the direction Egypt should follow. In 1953 Nasser was appointed Minister of the Interior and Deputy Prime Minister and in 1954, Prime Minister. In a series of political maneuvers, with the support and loyalty of most of the Free Officers, Nasser managed to drain Najib's presidential role of all effectivity; he himself acquired uncontested control which he maintained until his death.

Nasser's regime totally changed the face of Egypt. He personally became a symbol and "Nasserism" evolved into a political and social concept. The revolution's successful entrenchment in the largest, most powerful, of the Arab countries, had a strong influence on the entire Middle East and Africa, and there were many attempts to imitate it.

Nasser's major achievements were far-reaching agrarian reform, construction of the Aswan High Dam on the Nile, economic and social reforms in the spirit of "Arab Socialism", securing the total evacuation of the British from Egypt (1954), institutionalizing the concept of holding Arab summit meetings (led by Nasser), and realizing the dream of unification of Arab states by unifying Egypt and Syria (establishment of the United Arab Republic—UAR—in 1958).

In the international arena, too, Nasser achieved prominence, sharing the status of a leader of the Third World with Marshal Tito and Pandit Nehru (1955). This position took on special importance during the "cold war" between the United States and the Soviet Union, when Nasser engineered the formation of a special relationship between Egypt and the USSR (1955).

Nasser's failures were almost as outstanding as his successes. Heading the list of disappointments and miscalculations were the disintegration of the UAR, the military entanglement in Yemen during the 1960s, and the defeats his forces suffered in their confrontations with Israel (1956; 1967).

Attitude to Israel. 1. *Ideology*: When Nasser and the revolutionary regime took over the government in 1952 they subscribed to no specific ideology, even in matters concerning the confrontation with Israel. They adhered to certain guidelines acquired in the course of their Islamic education and their military and political involvement in events in Palestine from 1936 on. But the Nasserist position did not crystallize until 1955, after which it quickly became the central conception motivating the entire Arab world (*see* ARAB STRATEGIES VIS-A-VIS ISRAEL).

Nasser's declared goal was the destruction of the State of Israel and the establishment in its stead of a state for the Arab majority that would return to live on those lands. To justify such action he developed a nationalist mythology that expounded a series of basic flaws in the Jewish State. One aspect of this mythology described the State of Israel as lacking inherent strength and viability, as an entity fostered by western imperialism and artificially injected into the Arab body to further the western world's imperialistic plans to divide and rule. The State of Israel was to be annihilated by means of an all-out, conventional war, so swift that the western countries would be unable to come to its defense. Arab unity was an obvious condition for realizing this objective. As a result of the disintegration of the UAR in 1961, Nasser postponed the war until after the construction of an Arab society that would be better able to shoulder the burden of unity. The postponement was opposed by Syria on the one hand and by the Fatah on the other (*see* PALESTINE LIBERATION ORGANIZATION).

In May-June, 1967, Egypt headed toward the *Six-Day War not because of any conceptual change, but because the country found itself in a shaky position in the pan-Arab world and hoped to retrieve its status by adopting a carefully controlled policy of brinkmanship. The war deprived Egypt of Sinai and the Gaza Strip which it had controlled since 1948, although it had never annexed the Strip or extended Egyptian citizenship to its population. At the postwar Arab summit conference in Khartoum (September, 1967) Nasser developed the concept of the three "noes:" no peace, no recognition, and no negotiation with Israel. Later (November, 1967), he accepted Resolution 242 of the *United Nations' Security Council, but he perceived it as part of his strategy of stages. The first stage was to be "eradication of the results of aggression," in other words: the return of Sinai, after which Egypt could put its original concept into practice. The intention was to retrieve Sinai by means of international arrangements, not through negotiation with Israel. Israel's refusal to agree to such a settlement brought Nasser in 1968 to develop the next stage on the way to destroying Israel: he declared that "what has been taken by force, will be returned by force." By this terminology he did not mean all-out war—this had to be avoided due to the relative strengths of the respective adversaries—but rather a controlled *war of attrition that would gradually wear down Israel's strength. Until the Six-Day War Nasser had considered armed conflict as almost the only means of eliminating Israel but, having been defeated, he was forced to turn to political means, thereby altering the nature of his struggle.

2. *War*: Under Nasser's leadership Egypt fought two total wars with Israel (the *Sinai Campaign in 1956; the Six-Day War of 1967), one limited war (of attrition, 1968–1970), and instigated dozens of border incidents and minor military confrontations (1952–1956, 1967–1970). Despite the severe setbacks he suffered, Nasser managed to extract political gain from his defeats. Thus in 1956 he gained ground in the sphere of external relations when the United States and the Soviet Union supported the full retreat of France, England, and Israel. In 1967 his gains were internal: On 9 June, Nasser resigned, but withdrew the resignation "under pressure of the masses." At the same time he refused to accept responsibility for the defeat and resign, as demanded by some of the senior officers led by his deputy, friend, and commander of the armed forces, Field-Marshal Amer. The officers were accused of conspiring to overthrow the regime.

3. *Contacts with Israelis*: These began in 1948–1949, when as a prisoner in the "Faluja Pocket" he met with Palmah commanders. After the revolution, when he rose to head the government (1952, 1954) Israel contacted the heads of the new regime and, in effect, between 1954–1956 negotiations were conducted between the two countries. The discussions covered a broad range of issues: past incidents and relationships, a draft proposal under which Israeli shipping would be permitted to use the Suez Canal; border incidents and the steps required to maintain the ceasefire agreements; even the question of the final settlement. In return for agreeing to make peace, Nasser demanded that Israel permit the 1948 refugees to return to their original homes in Israel, or at least be offered the choice of accepting compensation. He also demanded the creation of Arab territorial continuity in the Negev between Egypt and the Kingdom of Jordan. The first demand was rejected since from Israel's point of view it meant the demise of the State, while the second was rejected as infringing on the country's sovereignty.

The contacts were much influenced by military developments. Nasser was affected by the *Lavon Affair of 1954 and by a massive Israeli retaliatory act at Gaza (1955); the Israeli leadership was unfavorably impressed by Nasser's refusal to pardon the convicted spies involved with the Lavon Affair who were sentenced to death (1955), and by the big arms deal concluded between Egypt and Czechoslovakia (1955).

Communication channels between the hostile parties remained open during Levi Eshkol's premiership (1962–1968). However, generally, the Israeli leadership viewed Nasser as the consummate enemy who endangered the very existence of Israel. His radical concepts and his attempts to subvert the conservative, more moderate pro-western Arab regimes were a matter of concern to his Arab opponents as well. There were even some among them who appealed to Israel in the hope of making a common stand against him. As a result, cooperation developed between Israel and the Maronites in Lebanon, Morocco, Jordan, Tunis, and Saudi Arabia; Israel also made contact with non-Arab states in the Near East—Iran, Turkey, and Ethiopia—in order to evade what seemed to be the Egyptian threat against them.

M. KLEIN

NATANYA. *See* NETANYA.

NATIONAL CONFERENCE OF SYNAGOGUE YOUTH (NCSY). Jewish youth movement dedicated to the strengthening of Jewish values and Torah observance and attachment to Israel. Founded in 1954 by Rabbi Pinchas Stolper, its first national director, it is affiliated to the Orthodox

Union of Jewish Congregations of America. Its 400 chapters in eleven regions throughout America and Canada organize regular programs for pupils of both public and yeshiva day schools.

NCSY runs the LAVE (Leadership and Values Education) program in public schools, free Talmud Torah schools and educational programs, as well as consulting services. Cultural and social activities are provided around the country for pre-teens and alumni. NCSY produces a range of educational materials, books and publications as well as its national magazine "Keeping Posted."

NCSY sends three hundred youngsters to Israel annually on its Israel Summer Seminar and the Jerusalem Experience, an eight-day experimental seminar held three times a year for unaffiliated American high school students. NCSY graduates study in Israeli yeshivot and seminaries. The Orthodox Union of Jewish Congregations of America also maintains the Israel Center in Jerusalem, an educational and cultural center catering largely to Americans living in Israel. M. PERSOFF

NATIONAL COUNCIL. *See* VA'AD LE'UMI.

NATIONAL COUNCIL FOR RESEARCH AND DEVELOPMENT (NCRD). Department of the Israel Ministry of Science and Development responsible for the scientific and technological activities of the Ministry. Its specific functions include the formulation of a national science and technology policy for economic development and for improving the social welfare of the citizens of Israel; the fostering of international scientific relations and the implementation of existing agreements with foreign governments and international organizations and agencies; coordinating the research activities of the various ministries and initiating activities of central importance to Israel's research system not dealt with by other ministries; the management of research funds and scholarships for the advancement of basic and applied research in areas of national importance; and the continuous collection, analysis and dissemination of information on Research and Development (R&D) activities in Israel including the establishment of a data base on publicly-funded research and development projects.

The Council has a plenary composed of leading scientists, industrialists, and government officials. The plenary provides scientific advice to the government and guidance to

Solar turbine at the National Physical Laboratory. At the right is Tz'vi Tavor, director of the laboratory. [Israel Information Services]

NCRD staff in matters of policy and research priorities. The Director of the NCRD is appointed by the Cabinet and is responsible for its operations, assisted by a professional and administrative staff. Scientific fields covered by the NCRD encompass all areas of science and technology including the social sciences.

Research activities supported by the NCRD are implemented for the most part in the various academic and research institutions in Israel. This support is directed primarily to scientific and technological areas of high national priority. These include biotechnology, micro-electronics, electro-optics, computer sciences, environmental quality control, regional development, and space science.

Several organizations involved in R&D or science-related activities are administered by the NCRD or work in close coordination with it. These include:

1. The Weizmann Science Press of Israel a publishing company for scientific periodicals, including *Israel Journal of Botany, Israel Journal of Chemistry, Israel Journal of Earth Science, Israel Journal of Mathematics, Journal d'Analyse Mathématique,* and *Israel Journal of Zoology.* In most cases these journals are published and edited in close collaboration with the appropriate Israeli scientific societies. The press also publishes *Mada* (Science), a Hebrew quarterly devoted to the popularization of science for adults in Israel and *La-Da'at* for youngsters.

2. Several Regional Research Organizations for promoting R&D for the settlement and socio-economic development of certain regions in Israel, such as the Golan Heights, the Arava, the Jordan rift, and others.

3. Israel Institute of Applied Social Research, which collects and analyzes data on military and civilian problems. In 1955 the institute was chartered as an independent non-profit organization with its own Board of Trustees. To date, close to 1,000 projects have been carried out in research methodology, social psychology, sociology, psychology, and related disciplines. Its publications are *Yedion* (a quarterly bulletin in Hebrew) and a biennial research report (in English).

4. International Research Center on Contemporary Society—IRCSS, which addresses contemporary political, social, and economic problems and international affairs and strategic studies. Particular attention is devoted to the analysis of Soviet internal and foreign policy and military developments with special focus on aspects related to the Middle East and East-West relations.

Serial publications of IRCCS are: *Crossroads* —an international socio-political journal; *IRCCS Bulletin*—an analysis of major topics (different each issue) of current interest as treated by the Soviet press; *The Soviet Army*: Digest from the Soviet Press—a compilation with brief commentary of materials from specialized Soviet military publications, with bibliography of selected articles and books; *USSR Overview*, a monthly report of current Soviet developments and foreign policy; *The Middle East in the Soviet Press* (Hebrew)—brief annotations of current books and articles; and *Lexicon of Soviet Political Terms.*

The Center cooperates with a number of scholarly institutions and research centers in North America, Europe, Asia, and Australia.

The Israel Space Agency (ISA) was established by the Ministry of Science and Development in 1983 to develop an industrial, scientific, and human infrastructure to utilize space research for the benefit of the State and the wellbeing of its people. Relations have been established with similar organizations in France, West Germany, Japan, and the United States. In cooperation with NASA, a laser tracking station was inaugurated in Israel in 1985.

I. ATIYA—G. METZGER

NATIONAL FUNDS. *See* JEWISH NATIONAL FUND; KEREN HA-YESOD.

NATIONAL INSURANCE IN ISRAEL. *See* SOCIAL INSURANCE IN ISRAEL.

NATIONALISM, JEWISH. The concept that the Jews are not merely members of a religious "persuasion" but a nation like other nations in the modern sense of the term, with the right to develop a life and culture distinctly their own.

Early History. The concept of Jewish nationhood as such is rooted in the Bible and found its concrete expression in the Jewish Commonwealths that existed in Eretz Israel through more than 1,000 years. Deprived of political independence by the Roman conquest, the Jews continued to consider themselves a nation, but for centuries the idea of Jewish peoplehood of necessity found its expression primarily in terms of its spiritual and ethical aspects. Until the middle of the 19th century, the revival of political Jewish nationhood was closely linked with the belief in Messianic redemption, an act of miraculous divine intervention which would bring about not only the restoration of political independence for the Jews in their own country but also an era of peace and goodwill for all mankind.

Emancipation, with the breakdown of ghetto walls and the enactment of laws granting the Jews citizenship rights in the lands in which they lived, fostered assimilation and the belief that the age-old dream of a return to Jerusalem was no longer relevant to reality. Now that an enlightened world was ready to wipe out all religious barriers, it was felt, the Jews should regard themselves as part of the countries in which they lived and as Jews by religion only.

The rise of modern "racial" anti-Semitism in "enlightened" western Europe in the late 19th century and growing anti-Jewish excesses in eastern European countries made it clear that emancipation and assimilation did not hold the hoped-for answer to the "Jewish problem." Nor was it sufficient to adopt a passive attitude and wait for the advent of the Messiah, as some extreme Orthodox elements would have had the Jews do. Along with these disillusioning realities, Jewish thought on the future of Judaism and Jewry came to be influenced by the upsurge of nationalism that swept Europe during the 19th century.

The latter half of the 19th century and the early part of the 20th century saw the development of various types of Jewish nationalism:

**Galut Nationalism.* This doctrine, of which Simon *Dubnow was the most eminent advocate, asserted that Jewish nationhood was based not on territory or descent but on commonly held cultural ideals and common efforts to evolve spiritual values. Accordingly, the Jews would be able to develop their own distinctive culture even if they were living as minority groups in *Galut, or Diaspora, countries. To this end, provisions for national and cultural autonomy were proposed for Jews within countries having compact Jewish populations (*see* AUTONOMY, JEWISH).

**Zionism.* Modern political, or Herzlian, Zionism held that the healthy survival and development of the Jewish people necessitated a physical homeland to which those Jews who were unable or unwilling to live in other countries would be able to go, and which would serve as a cultural and spiritual center for Jews the world over. In the Zionist view, this homeland could only be Eretz Israel, the country in which the Jewish people had its roots and to which the Jews had remained attached through centuries of exile. At the same time the Zionists cooperated with other Jewish groups to secure civic, political, and nationality-group rights for Jews who would continue to live in the Diaspora.

**Territorialism*. This view, whose proponents included Israel *Zangwill and certain Jewish socialist elements, agreed with the Zionists that a homeland with a measure of political autonomy was needed, but considered Eretz Israel either unattainable or unsuitable for that purpose. The *Jewish Territorial Organization, formed after the Seventh Zionist Congress (1905), had rejected plans for Jewish settlement in an area in Kenya, East Africa, and investigated possibilities of establishing such a homeland in a variety of countries, among them Australia, Angola, Cyrenaica, and Iraq.

Jewish Nationalism since World War I. During and after World War I, a period that saw the emergence of many new nations, Zionists joined other Jewish nationalists in endeavors to secure nationality-group rights for Jews in countries of compact Jewish population where such rights were to be conferred on other nationality groups. Specifically, the rights demanded by the Jews included autonomous status in educational and cultural matters, with government assistance to Jewish schools, and the use of their mother tongue in conducting public affairs. Efforts to have guarantees of these rights incorporated in the various peace treaties and the constitutions of the newly independent countries were spearheaded by the *Comité des Délégations Juives to the Paris Peace Conference. Opposition came from organizations such as the American Jewish Committee and the Alliance Israélite Universelle, which feared that the fulfillment of Jewish demands for nationality-group status might jeopardize the achievements of emancipation. For the most part, the endeavors to secure the protection of Jewish minorities and the free development of their nationality-group rights ended in failure. In 1928 the government of the Soviet Union allotted *Birobidzhan, an autonomous region in eastern Siberia, for Jewish settlement, but before long this project to set up an autonomous Jewish region also was abandoned.

Since the destruction of European Jewry and the establishment of the State of Israel, most of Jewish nationalism has centered in Zionism and the upbuilding of the Jewish State.

G. HIRSCHLER

NATIONALITY, ISRAEL. *See* CITIZENSHIP IN ISRAEL.

NATIONAL LIBRARY. *See* JEWISH NATIONAL AND UNIVERSITY LIBRARY, JERUSALEM.

NATIONAL RELIGIOUS PARTY. *See* MIZRACHI.

NATIONAL WATER CARRIER. The waters of the Jordan River that are stored in Lake Kineret serve as the source for the National Water Carrier (NWC). which transports them over the main watershed of Israel to the coastal plain as far south as the northern Negev. The idea of transporting water from the Jordan Rift Valley to the coastal plain was originally conceived by Walter C. *Lowdermilk, but owing to political circumstances the plan had to undergo several changes before it found its final form in the NWC, which was completed in 1964.

The scheme starts at the northwestern edge of Lake Kineret, at Atar Kinrot, where powerful pumps lift the water to a canal, which lies about 500 feet (154 m.) above the level of the lake. A second pumping station at Tzalmon lifts the water to another canal which lies 615 feet (187 m.) farther up. Here the carrier crosses the first mountain range by a tunnel that leads it into the Bet Netofa Valley, at whose western end lies an operational reservoir.

From here the water is transported in a concrete pipe, 108 inches (270 cm.) in diameter, through three tunnels along the eastern edge of the coastal plain to the springs of Rosh ha-Ayin, near Petah Tikva. Here the NWC ends, but its waters are carried farther south in the pipe system of the Yarkon-Negev line, which was completed earlier. Its main conduits are two pipelines of 66-inch and 70-inch diameters, which provide water for Tel Aviv as well as for the southern coastal plain. Both lines meet at the reservoir of Tzohar and are distributed from there by smaller pipes to the Lachish region and the northern Negev.

Y. KARMON

NATIONAL WORKERS' SICK FUND. *See* KUPAT HOLIM LE-OVEDIM LE'UMIYIM.

NATONEK, JOSEPH. Rabbi and Zionist precursor (b. Komlo, Hungary, 1813; d. Bator, Hungary, 1892). Natonek studied at the yeshiva of Nikolsburg (Mikulov), Moravia. In 1850 he became principal of the Jewish school in Nagysurany, and in 1854 rabbi in Jaszbereny, Hungary. Under the impact of the Hungarian Revolution of 1848 he deplored the absence of Jewish national sentiment among his people. In a sermon (1860) he expressed the hope that the Jews would not be granted emancipation because their Homeland was not to be in Hungary but in Jerusalem. The sermon cost him his position but he was accepted as rabbi of Szekesfehervar.

In 1861 Natonek published his book *Messias* (in Hungarian), in which he declared that the Jews were not merely a religious group but also a national entity and called on them to work to regain their ancient Homeland. The book, which he had published under a pseudonym, was confiscated by the Hungarian authorities. After Moses Hess published *Rome and Jerusalem* (1862), Natonek kept in touch with Hess and with Rabbi Zvi Hirsch Kalischer. He conceived a plan to induce the Sultan of Turkey to turn over Eretz Israel to the Jews in return for payment. In 1866 he visited many cities in central and western Europe on behalf of Kalischer's Hevrat Yishuv Eretz Yisrael. In Paris he induced the Alliance Israélite Universelle to help further agriculture among the Jews of Eretz Israel. In order to devote himself completely to his work for Eretz Israel, Natonek gave up his rabbinical position. In 1867 he went to Constantinople on behalf of Kalischer and his supporters to negotiate with the Turkish authorities for permission to purchase land in Eretz Israel and for the protection of the future settlers against possible attacks by Arabs. Although he received a friendly reception, his talks yielded no concrete results.

Pipes of the National Water Carrier. [Israel Information Services]

After his return to Hungary, he settled in Budapest, where he edited (1872) a periodical, *Das Einige Israel* (United Israel), in which he propagated his ideas. Natonek was the author of theological and Hebrew philological studies and collaborated on *Pentaglotte*, a dictionary of the Hebrew, Latin, Hungarian, French, and German languages, of which only the letter A appeared.

T. PRESCHEL

NATZERAT ILIT (Upper *Nazareth). Town in Lower Galilee, east of Nazareth. Founded in 1957, its layout followed modern principles, with ample greenery echoing the beautiful mountain landscape and broad view of the Jezreel Valley. Its economy is based on relatively large industrial enterprises. Population (1987), 25,100 of whom 21,800 were Jews and 3,200 Arabs.

E. ORNI

NATZERET. *See* NAZARETH.

NAVON, YIZHAK. Fifth President of the State of Israel (b. Jerusalem, 1921). Navon was born into a Sephardi family which had settled in Jerusalem over three hundred years earlier. His father, Yosef Navon, was a member of the Asefat ha-Nivharim.

Yitzhak Navon. [Israel Govt. Press Office]

After completing his studies at the Hebrew University, Jerusalem, he taught high school pupils. From 1946, he directed the Arabic Department of the Hagana in Jerusalem.

From 1948–1951 Navon served as second secretary of the Israeli Consulate in Uruguay and Argentina. On his return, he was appointed political secretary to the Foreign Minister, Moshe Sharett and in 1952 became director of Prime Minister David Ben-Gurion's office, serving in this capacity until Ben-Gurion resigned from the premiership in 1963. From 1963 to 1965, Navon directed the Culture Department of the Ministry of Education and Culture. He initiated a literacy campaign mobilizing hundreds of women soldiers to teach Hebrew to illiterate adults in villages and development towns.

In 1965, he was elected to the Knesset as a member of Rafi—Ben-Gurion's newly formed party. In the following Knessets he was elected as a member of the Labor Party (Ma'arakh). Navon served in the Knesset as Deputy Speaker (1965–1974) and chairman of the Defense and Foreign Affairs Committtee (1974–1977). In 1978, Navon was elected President of the State of Israel. As President, he traveled extensively throughout the country and was a popular figure among all sectors of the population. He tried to bring together the various elements of the population and bridge the social and culture gap especially in the field of education. In October 1980, Navon made the first official state visit of an Israeli President to Egypt.

Upon completion of his term of office in 1983, he returned to politics. He was elected to the Knesset and appointed Deputy Prime Minister and Minister of Education and Culture in the National Unity Governments of 1984 and 1988–90.

Navon has served as chairman of the World Zionist Council and chairman of the America-Israel Cultural Fund.

Navon's literary works include *Romancero Sephardi* (1968), a musical presentation of sacred and secular songs of Sephardi Jewry; *Bustan Sephardi*, a dramatic presentation of culture and life among Jerusalem Sephardi families; and a book entitled *Six Days and Seven Gates*, a story of Jerusalem inspired by the Six-Day War. E. HOTER

NAVY OF ISRAEL. *See* ISRAEL DEFENSE FORCES.

View of Nazareth. [Israel Government Tourist Office]

Street scene in Nazareth. [Israel Government Tourist Office]

NAZARETH (NATZERET). City in lower Galilee. A Jewish hamlet in the Second Temple period, Nazareth kept its Jewish character for centuries after the destruction of the Temple. The Moslems who conquered the country in the seventh century found it in ruins. The Crusaders rebuilt the town in the 12th century and made it an ecclesiastical center. In 1263, the Mamluk ruler Baybars ordered the complete destruction of Nazareth. It remained in ruins until the 17th century, when the Druze emir Fakhr al-Din permitted Christians to return. The Bedouin ruler Dhahr a-Amr in the 18th century made Nazareth the administrative center of Lower Galilee. When British forces arrived in the town in 1918, they found 8,000 inhabitants, two-thirds of them Christian Arabs and the rest Moslems.

The home of Jesus as a boy and young man, Nazareth has long been a Christian pilgrimage site, and Christian institutions have been established there. Remains have been found of the first Church of the Annunciation, built in the fourth century. Remnants of the Crusader cathedral built on the site in the 12th century are preserved in the Franciscan museum, and a few have been incorporated in the new large cathedral completed in 1968.

Nazareth was taken by Israeli forces in July, 1948. It was the largest Arab center in Israel, increasing in size from 9,000 inhabitants in 1947 to 49,400 in 1987, with near to 30,000 Moslems and the rest Arab Christians. It has 25 churches and convents of different Christian denominations. Tourism and pilgrimage are important bases of its economy, besides small industries and administrative services. Many of its citizens are employed as laborers in neighboring *Natzerat Ilit.

E. ORNI

NE'EMAN, YUVAL. Israeli soldier, scientist, and politician (b. Tel Aviv, 1925). He studied at Herzlia High School, the Haifa Technion, and London University. He joined the Hagana in 1940, completed an officers' course in 1945, and fought as Brigade Operations Officer in the War of Independence. He later was Deputy Chief of Operations. Between 1952–1954 he served as director of the Israel army's Planning Branch and later as deputy director of Military Intelligence where he modernized the system. In 1958 he was appointed Defense Attaché to the United Kingdom and the Scandinavian countries. He left the Israel Army in 1961 to devote himself to science, serving as the scientific director of the Nahal Sorek Nuclear Center. Later he headed the Physics Department of Tel Aviv University and between 1971–1975 served as president of Tel Aviv University. In 1975 he became chief scientist of the Defense Ministry but resigned after the 1975 Israel-Egypt Interim Agreement which he opposed. In the late 1970s he served on various scientific committees of the Likud government. In 1979 he was one of the founders of the *Tehiya movement which bitterly opposed the Camp David Accords and the Israel-Egypt Peace Treaty. Elected to the Knesset in 1981 he was Minister for Science and Development between July, 1982 and October, 1984 and again from 1990–2. He resigned from the Knesset in 1989.

His political philosophy calls for the retention of all of Eretz Israel and a strong Israeli deterrent power. He won the Israel Prize in 1969. He is well known in the international scientific community for his "Eightfold Way" or SU(3) Invariance for the classification of the elementary particles of nature. M. MEDZINI

Monument to the defenders of Negba who lost their lives in the War of Independence. [Israel Information Services]

NEGBA. Kibbutz in the southern coastal plain, 6 mi. (10 km.) east of Ashkelon. It was founded as a "Stockade and Tower" settlement in July 1939, the first in a program to gain footholds toward the Negev (hence its name). In the 1948 War of Independence, the invading Egyptian army made special efforts to take Negba, completely destroying it above ground, but the kibbutz held out. The kibbutz's ruined water tower has been left as a monument. Later, the kibbutz economy was solidly based on intensive farming and industry. Population (1987), 693. E. ORNI

NEGEV. Southern, arid part of Israel, constituting almost two-thirds of the area of the State within its pre-1967 borders. The Negev has over 70 agricultural settlements and three development towns with a total of 44,000 inhabitants (1985). In spite of its generally barren and arid appearance, the Negev has diversified types of landscape, which appear in sections, running from southwest to northeast.

The northwestern section is the semi-arid Negev Plain, a

Kibbutz Lotan in the Negev, 1984. [Kibbutz Lotan]

rolling lowland covered with loess soil. This area, which until the creation of the State had been thought to be unarable and had been occupied only by Bedouins, was subsequently turned into fertile agricultural land with the aid of irrigation, mainly from the national water carrier. In the 1980s, it produced cotton, peanuts, almonds, citrus, and early vegetables. At its eastern edge lies the town of *Beersheba, the gateway to the arid Negev.

The next section is formed by the northern Negev Hills, which consist of a series of anticlines running from southwest to northeast. The anticlinal ridges rise in height from north to south, reaching altitudes of 2,460 feet (750 m.) in the center and more than 3,280 feet (940 m.) in the extreme southwest. Special features of this area are the huge erosion craters called makhteshim. The largest of these, Makhtesh Ramon, stretches for 24 miles (35 km.) and is bounded on the northwest by a sheer cliff 1,000 feet (300 m.) high. This area carries some exploitable minerals (fireclay, glass sand, gypsum) most important, phosphates (Oron, Tzefa-Ef'e and Tzin mines). In the northeast of the region lies the industrial and mining center of the Negev (potash, bromide, oil shales, phosphates) with nine—mainly urban-settlements, and 37,000 inhabitants(1985).

The central Negev Hills comprise a number of level plateaus and basins, divided by the two main riverbeds of the Negev, Nahal Paran and Nahal Iyon. It has no natural resources and is almost completely unpopulated.

The southern Negev is a complex mountain structure of granites, metamorphic rocks, and Nubian sandstone, capped in places by a thick layer of limestone. In its southern section it shows bizarre forms of landscape such as Solomon's Pillars. In its southernmost extremity it reaches the Red Sea in the Gulf of Eilat.

A separate section of the Negev is the *Arava; in its southern section, near Eilat, are situated the Timna Copper Mines, now abandoned. After water was found in great depth in the Arava, 18 new agricultural settlements were founded, with 7,000 inhabitants (1985). At its southern end lies the town of *Eilat, a major tourist resort and Israel's gateway to East Africa and the Far East. Y. KARMON

NEHER, ANDRE. Writer and thinker of religious Zionism (b. Obernai, Alsace, 1913; d. Jerusalem, 1988). Neher taught German in a Strasbourg high school. After being dismissed for being a Jew in 1940, he took shelter, together with his father, the popular storyteller Albert Abraham Neher (1879–1945), and his brother, the judge Richard Neher (1910–1981), in a village of central France, and there during the War they deepened their Jewish knowledge. After the War, André Neher became an intellectual leader of Jewish academic youth. He was appointed professor of the history of Alsatian Jews at the University of Strasbourg, but extended the scope of his chair to embrace Jewish studies as a whole. Under his influence, the youth chapel of the local synagogue became an activist Jewish center, particularly when he organized the reception for Algerian refugees in 1962. He was also on good terms with Christian leaders and obtained their public intervention on behalf of Jewish issues, including Zionism. In 1968 he settled in Jerusalem, continuing to publish works on Jewish philosophy and Bible studies, based principally on the notion of the covenant between God and His people Israel. His major writings are about Amos (1950), Ecclesiastes (1951), Moses (1956), and Jeremiah (1960); *Historie biblique du peuple d'Israeul* (Biblical History of the Israelites, 2 vol., 1962); studies about Rabbi Judah Loew of Prague; *Le Puits de l'Exil* (Exile's Well, 1966); *David Gans* (1974); and essays on the new Zionist life, e.g., *Dans tes portes, Jérusalem* (In Thy Gates, Jerusalem, 1972).

Renee-Rina Neher-Bernheim, his wife (b. Paris, 1922), has written several books on Jewish history.

M. CATANE

NE'OT MORDEKHAI. Kibbutz in the Huleh Valley, founded in 1946 by pioneers from Central Europe. After the split in Ha-Kibbutz ha-Me'uhad in 1951, the kibbutz remained unlinked to a countrywide kibbutz federation for many years. It has intensive, fully-irrigated farming and industry. It is named after the Argentinian Zionist Mordecai Rozovsky. Population (1987), 700. E. ORNI

NERIA, MOSHE TZEVI. Israeli rabbi and educator, (b. Lodz, 1913). Under the Soviet regime he studied in underground yeshivot. In 1930, Neriya moved to Jerusalem where he studied with Rabbi A.I. Kook. In 1940, he settled in Moshav Kefar ha-Ro'e where he founded the first Bnei Akiva yeshiva which had its basis in the pioneering, religious youth movement.

The Bnei Akiva yeshivot combine religious and secular education, and prepare their students for the Israeli matriculation certificate. Under his direction this movement also created study centers for girls, yeshiva-secondary schools, and yeshiva-technical high schools. After the 1967 Six-Day War, Neria helped to establish Yeshivat ha-Kotel, which pioneered the return of Jews to the Jewish Quarter of the Old City in Jerusalem.

Neria gave a weekly Talmud lesson on Israeli radio from 1948 until 1963. In 1969, he was elected to the Knesset on the National Religious Party (NRP) list. While in the Knesset he tried unsuccessfully to pass a private law to ban hunting for sport and another law to abolish military service for girls.

In 1978, he was awarded the Israel Prize for his contribution to the State of Israel.

In 1982 he was prominent in the movement to block the Israeli withdrawal from Sinai. Later that year he gave up active political involvement in the NRP.

G. SHUSTER-BOUSKILA

NES TZIYONA. Town in the coastal plain south of Rishon le-Zion. Founded in 1883 within the Arab hamlet, Wadi Hanin, it was one of the first moshavot. Its citrus groves attracted Arab laborers who settled within its precincts, and until 1948 it was the country's only rural settlement with a mixed Jewish-Arab population. After the Arabs left during the War of Independence, Nes Tziyona had 1,800 Jewish inhabitants. Until 1953 it absorbed many immigrants, but later its growth slowed although diverse industry was added to its intensive farming, with citriculture as the prominent branch. In the late 1970s expansion quickened again as the town became part of the outer ring of the Tel Aviv conurbation. Within its municipal borders are institutes of nuclear and biological research. The name "Standard towards Zion" was adopted at an anniversary celebration when the Jewish flag was unfurled. Population (1987), 17,800.

E. ORNI

NETANYA. City in central Israel on the Sharon coast. Founded in 1929 as a farming moshava by young members of the Benei Binyamin association, the village soon became the nucleus of settlement in its region. Netanya developed not only as a market and communication center, but also as a seaside resort and an industrial center with many branches, among them diamond polishing. The Laniado Hospital and the Wingate Sports Center are within its boundaries. Netanya is named after the US philanthropist Nathan Straus. Population (1987), 114,400. E. ORNI

NETANYAHU. Family of Zionist and Israeli public figures.

Nathan (Netanyahu) Mileikowsky. Rabbi and Zionist orator and campaigner (b. Krevo, Kovno District, Lithuania, 1879; d. Jerusalem, 1935). After studying at the Volozhin Yeshiva, he was sent in 1901 to campaign for Zionism throughout the towns of Siberia up to the Pacific Ocean. In 1903–5 he conducted vigorous Zionist agitation against both opponents of Zionism and supporters of the Uganda Scheme. He served as a delegate to the Seventh through the Tenth Zionist Congresses (1905–1911).

He was appointed head of Hebrew Studies at the Krinski Gymnasium (high school) in Warsaw in 1908 and, living alternately in Warsaw and Lodz, campaigned for Zionism in hundreds of Polish Jewish communities. In 1920 he settled in Palestine, working initially as headmaster of schools in Safed and Rosh Pina. In 1924 he was sent to England in behalf of the Jewish National Fund and from 1925 to 1929 he campaigned for the Keren ha-Yesod in the United States and Canada.

In 1930 he settled in Herzliya where he became a farmer. After the murder of Hayim *Arlosoroff, he was convinced of the innocence of those accused of the murder, and influenced Rabbi Abraham Isaac Kook to head a group of public figures dedicated to their defense.

Mileikowsky never joined a Zionist political party but worked for a unified Zionist front. His efforts led to negotiations between David Ben-Gurion and Vladimir Jabotinsky on the possibility of an agreement between Labor and the Revisionists. Some of Mileikowsky's speeches were published in *The Prophets and the People* (1913) and *Folk und Land* (1929, Yiddish).

Ben-Zion Netanyahu, his eldest son, Jewish historian Zionist campaigner (b. 1910, Warsaw, Poland). Settling in

Palestine with his family in 1920, Netanyahu studied at the Hebrew University, Jerusalem. Feeling a need for nationalistic Hebrew literature, Netanyahu joined forces with Yosef Ur in 1933 to publish a Hebrew monthly, *Betar*, edited by Joseph Klausner. He was a member of the central Revisionist Committee from 1933 until 1935. After the murder of Arlosoroff, Netanyahu launched a daily newspaper, *Ha-Yarden*, to give a voice to the Revisionist movement during the trial. He served as its editor until 1935. He devoted the following years to collecting and editing Herzl's Zionist writings and also edited the Zionist writings of Max Nordau and Israel Zangwill. In 1940 Netanyahu joined the Revisionist delegation in the US and began nationwide campaigning for a Jewish army. After Jabotinsky's death later in the year, he left the delegation. He joined the committee for a Jewish army but quit when it was unwilling to speak out against British rule in Palestine.

From 1942, he headed the activities of the Revisionist Party of America, editing the monthly *Zionews* from 1942–1944. From 1946–1948 he was a member of the Zionist Emergency Council led by Abba Hillel Silver.

In 1948 he returned to Israel after receiving a doctorate from Dropsie University. He became editor of the *Encyclopedia Hebraica* (overseeing volumes 2–15). From 1959–60 he coedited the *Jewish Quarterly Review*. In 1960 he moved to the US to become editor-in-chief of the *Encyclopedia Judaica* but left after six months and went to teach at Dropsie College, Philadelphia where he was appointed professor of Medieval Jewish History and Hebrew Literature in 1962. He taught at the Universities of Denver from 1968–71 and Cornell from 1971–1978. In 1979 he returned to Israel. His scholarly works deal with the Middle Ages, in particular the history of the Marranos and the Spanish Inquisition as well as the history of political Zionism. His publications include *Max Nordau to his People* (1941); *Road to Freedom* (Leon Pinsker's addresses and speeches, 1944); *Don Isaac Abravanel. Statesman and Philosopher* (1953) and *The Marranos of Spain* (1966).

His eldest son, **Jonathan Netanyahu** (b. New York, 1946; d. Entebbe, Uganda, 1976). After completing high school in the United States, he returned to Israel to serve in the army and was wounded during the Six-Day War, 1967. Following studies at Harvard and the Hebrew University he returned to the army where he participated in numerous secret military operations, in an elite military unit. He distinguished himself on the Syrian front during the Yom Kippur War, 1973. In 1976 he prepared and directed the ground operation to rescue the hostages from an Air France plane held by international terrorists in Entebbe, Uganda (*see* ENTEBBE OPERATION). He was killed while leading the raid to rescue the hostages. Following the rescue, the government of Israel renamed the mission Operation Jonathan. His letters, edited by his brothers, Benjamin and Iddo, are entitled *Self-Portrait of a Hero* (1980).

The Jonathan Institute, founded in his name, seeks to mobilize world opinion against international terrorism.

Benjamin Netanyahu, second son of Ben-Zion, Israeli diplomat (b. Tel Aviv, 1949), attended high school in the US and then studied at Harvard and MIT. In 1982, he was appointed as Israel's deputy chief of mission in the Israeli embassy in Washington and from 1984–1988 served as Ambassador and Israel's Permanent Representative to the United Nations. He was a member of the Israel delegation for talks on a strategic agreement with the US (1983). He was author of *Terrorism: How the West Can Win* (1986) and edited *International Terrorism, Challenge and Response* (1981). In 1988 he was elected Member of the Knesset for the Likud party and appointed deputy Foreign Minister. In 1992 he was elected leader of the Likud party.

Elisha Netanyahu. Third son of Nathan Mileikovsky, educator and mathematician (b. Warsaw, Poland, 1912; d. Jerusalem, 1986). After serving in World War II, he joined the staff of the Haifa Technion becoming head of its mathematics section and later, Dean. He helped to build the Technion into a center for research in function theory.

His wife **Shoshana Netanyahu,** Israeli jurist (b. Danzig, 1923) was educated at the Reali School, Haifa, and studied at the Jerusalem Law School of the Mandate authorities. In 1969 she was named a judge and from 1982–93 was a justice of the Israeli supreme court. E. HOTER

NETHERLANDS, RELATIONS WITH ISRAEL. The

President Ben-Zvi addresses congregation in Portuguese Synagogue, Amsterdam, 1958. [Israel Govt. Press Office]

Netherlands voted in favor of the partition of Palestine in 1947 and recognized the State of Israel soon after its establishment. It was the first country to establish its diplomatic representation in Jerusalem and maintained its ambassador there until the institution of the Jerusalem Law (1980) when it moved its diplomatic representation to Tel Aviv.

For many years the Netherlands was an outstanding supporter of Israel and on many occasions the Dutch people expressed their sympathy and identification. The Netherlands supported Israel in the UN and other international bodies; it helped Israel forge ties with the European Economic Community (EEC); and when the Soviet Union severed diplomatic ties with Israel in 1953 and again in 1967, the Netherlands represented Israeli interests in Moscow. The Dutch embassy there fought for the rights of Soviet Jews to leave Russia and assisted the Israeli consular delegation which arrived in Moscow in August 1988.

Political differences became increasingly marked after 1967 as a result of the situation created by the Six-Day War and by the Palestinian uprising which began in 1987. The Dutch media became much less sympathetic to Israel, and Holland supported the 1980 Venice Declaration which envisaged the participation of the PLO in Middle East peace negotiations. The Dutch government supported initiatives for an international peace conference as a framework for Arab-Israeli talks. It interpreted UN Security Council Resolutions 242 and 338 as advocating the exchange of "territories for peace" and the recognition of the rights of the Palestinian people, who in turn must recognize Israel's right to exist within secure, recognized borders. Following the EEC decision to accord to the agricultural produce of the Israeli administered areas the same export advantages as those accorded to Israeli agricultural produce, in the framework of the agreement between Israel and the EEC, the Dutch offered technical aid and advice to the Palestinian Arab farmers in order to enable them to benefit from these advantages. They saw this as a means of improving the quality of life in the Administered Areas and of helping to reduce tensions.

The disturbances in the Administered Areas from December, 1987, provoked at times violent reactions by Dutch personalities or institutions. Participation in certain events celebrating Israel's 40th anniversary in 1988 was at times cancelled or postponed. The Dutch Foreign Minister appeared twice before the Dutch parliament to state his government's position, condemning certain Israeli operations in the Administered Areas.

Trade relations between the two countries grew steadily. Despite the dimensions of Israel's agricultural exports to the Netherlands, especially flowers and citrus fruit, the balance was decidedly in the Netherlands' favor. Nevertheless, in the late 1980s the Netherlands replaced West Germany as Israel's third largest export market, after the US and Great Britain. In the first half of 1988, Israel's exports to the Netherlands rose to $256.7 million, an increase of 29 percent over the previous year. Over 600 Israeli exporters were active in the Netherlands. The Netherlands continued to be helpful to Israel in its negotiations with the EEC and helped to defend Israeli interests against agricultural competition by Spain and Portugal when they entered the Common Market.

Important cultural exchanges were effected by a cultural accord which also provided for scientific and technological cooperation. The two countries collaborated closely in an aid program for developing countries, partly financed by the Dutch and executed by Israelis. Over 1,500 Dutch citizens were awarded the title "Righteous of the Nations" by Yad Vashem for their assistance in rescuing Jews during the Holocaust. Israel participated in the popular Nijmegen march for many years and Dutch delegations took part in the annual march to Jerusalem. Thousands of Dutch tulips embellished Jerusalem each year, a gift of the Dutch people.

Leading figures, such as Holland's Princesses Beatrix and Juliana and their consorts and Israel's Presidents, Yitzhak Ben-Zvi and Chaim Herzog, made official visits to each others' countries. Prime ministers, foreign ministers and other members of the governments and of the parliaments of the two countries regularly paid mutual visits.

D. CATARIVAS

NETHERLANDS, ZIONISM IN. The Dutch Zionist Federation (Nederlands Zionisten Bond) was founded in 1899; one of its foremost members was Jacobus Henricus Kann, a banker and later member of the Zionist Executive. Zionism met with opposition from almost the entire rabbinical establishment with the exception of the Chief Rabbi of Amsterdam, Dr. J.H. Dünner, who strongly supported the young movement. Its first chairman was Abraham van Collem, a Dutch poet who left the movement after a year and joined the socialist organization. He was succeeded by Sigmund Seeligmann, a well-known bibliographer.

Group of Zionists in Rotterdam in 1915. [Zionist Archives]

Despite opposition from Jewish communal leaders and from Jewish liberals and socialists, the Zionist movement in the Netherlands made rapid headway. In 1905 the Dutch Zionist Federation began to publish a weekly, *De Joodse Wachter* which, interrupted only by the period of Nazi occupation, has served as the official organ of Dutch Zionism until the present. Also in 1905, the Zionist Federation opened the Zionist Book and Pamphlet Shop in Amsterdam. In 1906 the Dutch Zionist Students' Organization was founded. As a result of the founding of the Jewish Territorial Organization (ITO). the Federation lost many members but under the impact of the Eighth World Zionist Congress, held at the Hague (1907), its membership increased. At the same time a Zionist Youth movement, called Macbi, was founded by David Cohen, but after some years, only one branch, in Haarlem, remained in existence.

World War I. At the outbreak of World War I the Federation had 1,627 members and a strong chairman, Nehemia de Lieme. At the outbreak of the war the headquarters of the *Jewish National Fund was moved to the Hague and directed by Jean Fischer, a Belgian Zionist, Kann, and de Lieme. De Lieme, who was a dynamic director, formulated important principles for the policy of the Fund. The Federation was revitalized by the influx of a great number of Belgian (most of them East European) Jews, some of whom initiated the founding of Zionist youth groups, especially of the religious Mizrachi wing, and spread the knowledge of modern Hebrew. Zionists took an active part in aiding refugees and war sufferers. Following the official Dutch policy the Dutch Zionist Federation emphasized the necessity of complete neutrality on the part of Dutch Jews. In October, 1917, a delegation from the Dutch Po'ale Zion presented to the Dutch-Scandinavian Socialist Committee in Stockholm a memorandum favoring reforms in Palestine. In cooperation with the Dutch branches of the Alliance Israélite Universelle and the Jewish Territorial Organization an impressive demonstration was held in February, 1918, which adopted a resolution calling for minority rights for the Jews, emancipation, and the national concentration of the Jewish people in Palestine. The demonstration was followed by a petition supporting the resolution, which was signed by 46,578 Jews, 70% of the total adult Jewish population.

Between the Two World Wars. From the Hague Kann and de Lieme organized an opposition group in the World Zionist Organization, together with Julius Simon and Robert Szold. They attacked the economic and organizational policy of Chaim Weizmann and certain activities of the Jewish National Fund. Weizmann's conciliatory policy towards England was regarded by de Lieme as misguided. In addition he advocated an overhaul of the organizational structure of the World Zionist Organization; replacement of the shekel by an annual contribution; and the establishment of Zionist Federations in every country with membership on a personal basis, and not through political parties. As a result of the struggle against the WZO leadership, the Dutch Zionist Federations suffered in the years after the war from an internal strife between de Lieme and his adherents and their opponents. In 1925 a compromise was reached and Dr. A. Van Raalte was chosen as chairman of the Federation but de Lieme remained the dominating personality and from 1928 till 1940 all the chairmen were his followers (K.J. Edersheim: 1928–1931; Fritz Bernstein: 1931–1934; A.J. Herzberg: 1934–1939; M.L Kan: 1939-1941). The internal friction adversely influenced the membership which fell from 1,951 (1921) to 1,829 (1925) but rose from then on to 2,049 (1932).

From 1911, the Mizrachi (a Dutch branch was founded in 1909), led by Rabbi S. P. de Vries, was fully integrated in the Federation. In 1920 it hosted the international Mizrachi conference with delegates from Palestine, the United States, and seven European countries. Several attempts to found a branch of Po'ale Zion failed; efforts were renewed in 1933 by S. de Wolff and others and this time met with success. There was only a handful of Revisionists in the Netherlands; the small group split in 1938, when part of them founded a Dutch branch of the New Zionist Organization.

Keren ha-Yesod in Holland, founded in 1920, started its campaign with visits from Weizmann and Jabotinsky (1921); its board was composed of prominent personalities of the Jewish community, some of whom had not shown sympathy to Zionism in the past. Its most distinguished chairman was Dr. L.E. Visser, who later became President of the High Court of Justice at The Hague.

In 1920 the Joodse Jeugdfederatie (Jewish Youth Federation) was founded, and in the course of time had branches in almost all Jewish communities. It united all Zionist youth groups (General Zionists, Mizrachi, Ha-No'ar ha-Oved, Maccabi ha-Tza'ir). In the 1930s it grew to a powerful organization with a strong Zionist ideology and its membership rose to 2,009 (1938). It did not oblige its members to pioneering (*halutziut*) but many youngsters joined the ranks of the halutzim in the He-Halutz and the Bachad (Berit Halutzim Dati'im) or in the Hevrat Olim, an organization of pioneers who regarded themselves as "unconditional Zionists."

Hitler's advent to power in Germany in 1933, leading to a great influx of German Jewish refugees into the Netherlands, exerted a great influence on Dutch Jewry. Propaganda meetings of the Zionist Federation attracted thousands of Dutch Jews and many of them joined the Zionist Federation; in 1933 its membership rose to 3,249 and in 1939 to 4,246. Many Zionists were active in organizations in behalf of the refugees. Many of the young German Jews, housed in transitory centers, prepared themselves for aliya; a great working village was set up in the Wieringermeerpolder where about 50%, belonging to several youth movements, regarded themselves as halutzim. Many more centers for agricultural training were established with a mixed population of Dutch and non-Dutch halutzim.

The 1937 British proposal for the partition of Palestine was rejected by an overwhelming majority of Dutch Zionists. Nehemia de Lieme even left the Zionist organization in protest but was not followed by others. In 1938 a severe conflict broke out between the Zionist Federation and the Joodse Jeugdfederatie and the Zionist students. The leaders of the Zionist Federation condemned the stand taken by the youngsters on such topics as dissimilation from Dutch nationality, encouragement of cultural activities by the Zionist organization, and pioneering.

At the end of the 1930s the influence of Zionists in the Netherlands had been greatly enhanced. Not only were many of the Jewish communities and national organizations (like the Joodse Vrouwenraad, the Council of Jewish Women, which published the prestigious monthly *Ha-ischa*) led by Zionists but most of the Jewish journals were pro-Zionist and in 1938 the Jewish weekly with the highest circulation, the *Nieuw Israelietisch Weekblad*, got a mostly Zionist editorial board.

German Occupation 1940–1945. Immediately after the occupation of the Netherlands a Central Raad van de Zionistische Organisaties (Central Council of Zionist Organizations) was established, comprising representatives of the Federation, the Joodse Jeugdfederatie, and a pro-Zionist women's organization, which achieved harmonious cooperation among all the Zionist bodies. Efforts to broaden the Zionist influence were seriously hampered when the occupation authorities forbade all Jewish publication. Nevertheless all Zionist organizations intensified their activities and at the end of December, 1940, even held the annual convention of the Federation. A Central Council for Vocational Training was set up in order to finance the existing training centers and encourage *halutziut*; later, this body took over responsibility for all the Jewish vocational training in the Netherlands. The cultural department of the Central Council initiated Hebrew courses throughout the country. All these activities had to be stopped with the beginning of the deportation of the Jews to the death camps.

Altogether 110,000 Jews were sent to the death camps and only 5 percent survived. Some 10,000 Jews survived the occupation by hiding. Many Jews participated in underground activities but the only organized Jewish resistance group was the halutzim; by cooperation with a group of gentiles led by Joop Westerweel

46 percent of the halutzim survived the war and 80 of them went via Belgium and France to Spain and reached Palestine in wartime. The prominent Zionists who died in the Holocaust included J.H. Kann, M.L. Kan, Rudolf Cohen, Dr. B.A. Kahn, a director of Keren ha-Yesod, L. Nordheim; some committed suicide including Dr. E. Boekman, alderman of Amsterdam and a noted authority on Jewish demography. Thanks to an exchange plan with German nationals in Palestine against Jews of the Netherlands, several thousands of Jews were sent to the exchange camp of Bergen-Belsen and many of these survived, albeit in a very bad physical condition; 222 of them were released from Bergen-Belsen (June, 1994) and exchanged against Germans from Palestine.

Post-War Era, 1945–1948. Even before the liberation of the Netherlands, Zionist groups were organized, first in Brussels and afterwards in Eindhoven. In the Jewish Coordination Committee, which was established to handle Jewish affairs in the liberated parts of the Netherlands, the Zionists had the upper hand, most of them, former leaders of the Joodse Jeugdfederatie. In October 1945 the Zionist Federation held a convention and a board was chosen, headed by J. van Amerongen (Arnon), former chairman of the Joodse Jeugdfederatie and the Zionist student organization. Immediately after the war scores of young Jews participated in the "illegal" immigration into Palestine by soldiers of the *Jewish Brigade, stationed in Eindhoven and other places in the Netherlands. A new foundation for the encouragement of halutzic training (*hakhshara*), Hachsjarah en Alija, was formed; it set up 14 training centers, catering also to young people from other countries. Homes were established for orphaned children; some of them immigrated to Palestine together with the entire staff. Eventually the great majority of the postwar Zionist leadership immigrated to Palestine and Israel. Thanks to the presence of the Jewish Brigade it was possible to organize, together with the local teachers, courses and seminars for the study of Hebrew. The Dutch Zionist Federation took an active part in the struggle for the establishment of the Jewish State and tried to influence the government of the Netherlands and public opinion. However the government only reluctantly participated in the United Nations Special Committee on Palestine (UNSCOP) but supported the Palestine partition plan that resulted in the birth of the Jewish State.

Since 1948. While public opinion in the Netherlands favored the establishment of Israel (67% for, 10% against) the Dutch government delayed its *de facto* recognition until the end of 1948 and recognized Israel *de jure* only in January 1950. The main reason for this delay was the fear of unfavorable reaction from Indonesia, the former Dutch colony, with its mostly Moslem population. Nevertheless relations between Israel and the Netherlands were very sympathetic, and Dutch public opinion sided overwhelmingly with Israel, especially during the wars of 1967 and 1973. Eventually the Netherlands was the first country targeted by the oil embargo of the Arab states. The embargo had hardly any economic effect but politically the official policy became less pro-Israel and more in line with the policy of the other members of the European community. Public opinion also changed for the worse, especially in left-wing circles, and during the 1982 Lebanon War sympathy for Israel was at its lowest point.

Dutch Jews remained stanch supporters of Israel. After the establishment of the State K.J. Edersheim, who at that time was chairman of the Palestine Office, became Israel's first representative in the Netherlands, serving in that capacity until 1950, when a regular consular service was established in The Hague and Amsterdam (the latter was later abolished).

In 1948 the Zionist Federation increased its membership to 3,232 but in the following years it dropped steadily (1955:2,235; 1961:2,099; 1970:1,563; 1980:1,421) notwithstanding the affiliation of new groups: Herut and the organization of Liberal Zionists. This decline was not the result of lessened interest in the Zionist idea but of internal conflicts. The Zionist funds too enhanced their income greatly over the years. Financial aid to Israel was channeled from 1949 through the United Jewish Appeal, which raised its income from Hf1.400,000 in 1949 to 4 million in 1980 while the income of the Jewish National Fund rose from Hf1.200,000 (1948) to about two million in 1980. The JNF adopted the settlement Ashalim in the Negev as a special project of the Netherlands.

Cultural activities of the Zionist Federation included Hebrew language seminars, organized by the Jewish Agency's Department of Education and Culture and which were attended by many students (e.g., 1964:275; 1965:115). Modern Hebrew was also taught at some Universities (Leiden, Groningen) while the Juda Palache Institute of Amsterdam University (named after a Jewish professor who perished during the Holocaust) specialized in post-Biblical Hebrew but included also Yiddish and Jewish history in its curriculum.

Zionist youth organizations active in the Netherlands were Bene Akiva, Ihud Habonim-Dror, and the organization of Zionist students Iyar. J. MICHMAN

NETHERLANDS JEWS IN ISRAEL. Up to the 1930s aliya was not stimulated by the Zionist movement in the Netherlands, but was seen as a very personal decision. One of the first immigrants from Holland was Siegfried Hoofien, who went to Palestine in 1912 and became president of the Anglo-Palestine Bank. When the State of Israel was founded, Hoofien was still prominent in financial circles and became president of the board of directors of the Bank Le'umi.

It was the 1917 Balfour Declaration that led to a first small wave of immigrants from Holland. Among them was Siegfried van Vriesland, a successful Rotterdam lawyer, who was nominated treasurer of the Zionist Executive in Palestine. Most of the Dutch immigrants in the 1920s were well-to-do. In 1930 they numbered about 80. An enormous contribution was made by the Dutch *hakhshara* (pioneering) movement, the Deventer Vereeniging voor de opleiding van Palestina-pioniers, headed by Ru Cohen. It was founded in 1918 in order to give agricultural training mainly to Polish and Romanian Jews and to pioneers who came from Palestine (Degania) to Holland to learn dairy-farming. Dutch cows were shipped to Palestine and crossbred with a local strain to produce a strong climate-resistant cow with a high milk production. Up to 1933 about 300 pioneers received training in Holland, but few of them were Dutch. This changed from 1933 when the *hakhshara* movement grew quickly due to the influx of many young refugees from Germany. Dutch Jews started to join them from about the same year and made up about 30% of the total. Before the occupation of the Netherlands by Nazi Germany in 1940, more than 1,000 well-trained halutzim had gone to Palestine via Holland, 350 of them in the summer of 1939 arriving illegally on a ship called the *Dora* that had left Amsterdam with the silent approval of the Dutch government. One of the best-known immigrants from Holland Fritz (Peretz) Bernstein, who had exerted a strong influence on Dutch Zionism, went to Palestine in 1935; he was to become Israel's first minister of trade and commerce.

The total number of Dutch Jews in Palestine had grown to 1,000 in 1940. Many of those arriving in the 1930s were young and had less money than the immigrants of the 1920s. They were products of several Dutch youth movements, such as Zikhron Ya'acov and the Jewish Youth Federation, who had broken off their studies to move to Palestine. A nucleus for a Dutch kibbutz was founded in Amsterdam in 1934 and resulted in 1940 in the foundation of kibbutz Huli'ot or Sedeh Nehemia (called after the Dutch Zionist leader Nehemia de Lieme) in the Huleh district.

In May 1940, only days before the Germans occupied Holland, the Dutch in Palestine organized themselves in the "Advisory Bureau for Immigrants from the Netherlands." The organization was initiated by Miriam de Leeuw-Gerzon, who had come to Palestine in 1920 as a pioneer, and her husband Leib de Leeuw, an engineer working for potash industries. Because of the occupation, the Advisory Bureau was transformed into an organization representing the Dutch in Palestine and helped many Dutch Jews in Holland by sending them messages that they had been placed on exchange lists and would receive a certificate for immigration into Palestine. This prevented the immediate deportation of several thousands of Dutch Jews. In 1944 a group of German Templers in Palestine was exchanged against 222 Jews from Bergen-Belsen, half of whom were of Dutch nationality. In 1944 two groups of halutzim from Holland reached Palestine. They had escaped through Belgium and France and had crossed the Pyrenees into Spain. Among the kibbutim where Dutch pioneers settled were Yavneh, Metzuba, Bet ha-Shita, En Harod, and En ha-Natziv. In spite of strong ideological opposition in the Dutch group to forming a *landsmanshaft* the Bureau was changed into the "Irgun Olei Holland" (Dutch Immigrants Association) in April 1943 and as such continues to exist.

After the war only 25,000–30,000 Jews had survived the Holocaust in Holland. Thousands of them sought immigration certificates in 1945–46 and membership of the Nederlandse Zionistenbond rose to 3,232 in 1948, in spite of the decimation of the Jewish community. Several hundreds of young people went to Palestine on "illegal" ships leaving mainly from France. In 1946 about 400 Dutch Jews entered Palestine. Expectations of a large immigration from Holland did not materialize however. The British immigration policy was partly responsible; people who wanted to leave Holland immediately after the war, but did not receive a certificate, had by 1948 settled down again and found it difficult to make the move or had found a new home in the United States or Canada.

Between 1948 and 1953 a total of 1,500 Dutch Jews went to Palestine (600 in 1949). The total number of Jews leaving Holland in that period was 4,492, which means that most went to the United States, Canada, or other destinations.

Aliya from Holland slowed down during the 1950s and stabilized at around 50–100 a year. The 1967 Six-Day War brought a Zionist awakening among the young generation, born after World War II. Immigration numbers rose to about 300 a year for a period of several years after which it again stabilized around 100 a year. Compared to most Western European countries it is a high proportion.

Dutch Jews contributed considerably to the building of the State of Israel especially in the field of agriculture, the diamond industry, science, economy, and white collar professions. Two Dutch Jews became professors in Jewish subjects: Leo Seeligman was professor in Bible at the Hebrew University and Benjamin de Vries was professor in Talmud in Tel Aviv. Professor Jaap van der Hoeden, a bacteriologist, received the Israel Prize for his work and Ya'acov Arnon (van Amerongen) became director-general of the Ministry of Finance in 1956. Many Dutch Jews were in banking and accountancy. One of them, Eliezer Bawly, who had arrived in the 1920s, initiated the Israeli exams for accountants in 1948 to replace the British system. C. BRASZ

NETIVOT. Development town in the northwestern Negev, 9 miles (15 km) SE of Gaza. Founded in 1956 in the framework of Israel's regional settlement and population distribution policy, Netivot was planned to become a district town of an agricultural hinterland. Its progress, however, was handicapped by social problems among the settlers, almost all newcomers from Morocco and Tunisia, and by the proximity of two other development towns, Sederot and Ofakim. In spite of a high birth rate, growth was slow, from 1,231 inhabitants in 1957 to 4,830 in 1968 and 9,730 in 1988. Local industry originally included small to medium enterprises in textiles, wood, food processing, and diamond polishing. The oriental Orthodox-religious character of Netivot was increasingly emphasized. Israel Abu Hatzeira, the "Baba Salih", a holy leader revered by North African Jews lived there and gave religious advice. An annual remembrance and folklore day was instituted on the date of his death, that attracts multitudes from all over Israel.

E. ORNI

NETTER, CHARLES. Merchant and philanthropist (b. Strasbourg, France, 1826; d. Mikve Yisrael, 1882). Engaging in business in foreign countries and later in Paris, he was one of the founders of the *Alliance Israélite Universelle. In 1870 Netter, interested in the settlement in Eretz Israel of Jews from Islamic lands (especially Persia), who were then suffering from religious persecution, established, partly from his own fortune, the Mikve Yisrael Agricultural School on behalf of the Alliance.

He submitted a memorandum to the conferences of the European powers in Constantinople (1871), Berlin (1878), and Madrid (1880) on the status of the Jews in the Oriental and Balkan countries and in Morocco. In 1881, after the outbreak of the pogroms in Russia, he went to Brody, Galicia, where he organized the emigration of refugees to the United States. He sent a small group of children, accompanied by guides, to the agricultural school of Mikve Yisrael. In 1882 he became secretary of the Parisian Committee for Jewish Emigrants from Russia. At that time he opposed the movement for large-scale Jewish settlement in Eretz Israel because he saw the poor success of his enterprises and thought that the country would not be able to absorb the emigrants. However, when Baron Edmond de Rothschild became interested in the colonization of the country, Netter changed his views and went again to Eretz Israel to develop immigration, but, shortly afterwards, he fell sick and died. I. KLAUSNER—M. CATANE

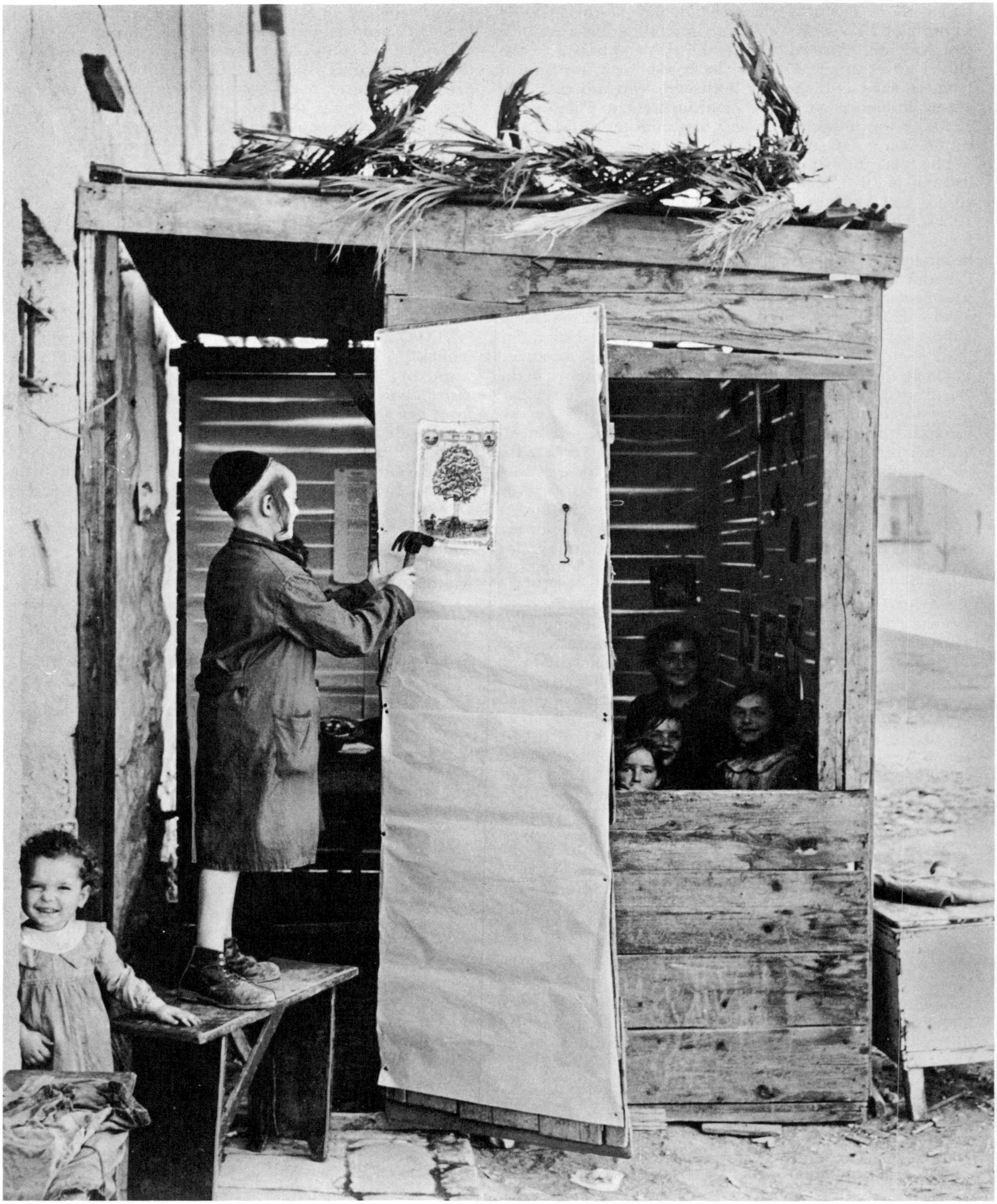

A young member of Neturei Karta lending a hand in decorating the Sukka. [Zionist Archives]

NETUREI KARTA (Aramaic, "Guardians of the City"). Group of Jewish religious extremists in Israel. Its members, estimated at 500 to 1,000, live in the Me'a She'arim section of Jerusalem. The group derives its name from a statement in the Talmud which refers to those who devote themselves to the study of Torah as the "guardians of the city." Neturei Karta adheres to the extremely Orthodox patterns of Jewish life imported from Hungary and Eastern Europe.

Members of Neturei Karta study in *hadarim* (religious elementary schools) and *yeshivot* (rabbinical academies), using the Ashkenazi pronunciation of Hebrew, like all other ultra-Orthodox groups. They speak and study in Yiddish. Yeshiva studies are limited to the Pentateuch (not the other parts of the Bible), Talmud and rabbinic codes. Their dress is indistinguishable from that of other ultra-Orthodox Jerusalemites, and, like them, the Neturei Karta were opposed to Zionism from the outset and to the creation of the State of Israel. In their eyes the very establishment of the State is an unpardonable sin, and the State must cease to exist.

Neturei Karta came into being when members of *Agudat Israel from Germany and Poland arrived in Palestine in the 1930s. A conflict developed between these newcomers and the leaders of the Agudat Israel party who were members of the Old Yishuv of Jerusalem. The German members of Agudat Israel and, to a lesser extent, its Polish members felt that, in addition to thorough religious training, the young had to be given a sound secular education. Furthermore, they realized that they could not hope to find a place in the economy of Palestine unless they cooperated with the Zionist institutions. Friction between the immigrants and the old leadership led to a reorganization of Agudat Israel in Palestine in which the latter lost its exclusive control of the movement. Some younger members of the Old Yishuv in Jerusalem, including Rabbis Amram Blau, Aharon Katzenelbogen, and Yeshaya Shoenberger, refused to accept the new arrangement and left Agudat Israel to form Hevrat Hayim, which later became Neturei Karta. The group took its first public stand in 1938, when it opposed the levying of a self-imposed tax for the support of the Hagana.

The break between the two groups became complete during World War II, when Agudat Israel, strengthened by the arrival from Poland of Agudat Israel leaders such as the rabbi of Gora Kalwaria (the Gerer Rebbe) and Rabbi Yitzhak Meir Levin, entered into increasingly close cooperation with the Zionist institutions. In 1944 Neturei Karta began to publish its own paper, *Ha-Homa* (now *Homatenu*), which attacked Agudat Israel. Demonstrations and clashes followed. In the 1945 elections to the committee representing the Ashkenazim of Jerusalem, Neturei Karta and sympathetic groups obtained a majority vote.

With the expansion of Ha-Eda ha-Haredit (the ultra-Orthodox community) and the tremendous growth of its *kashrut* (dietary laws) framework, the leadership of the community began to compromise in several areas of contact with the State institutions (principally in the field of medicine), a step which sent Neturei Karta back into the opposition. Both bodies forbid any direct contact with the State, but Neturei Karta calls for active militancy (identification with the PLO, burning of the national flag, declarations on the termination of the State, sackcloth and fasting on Independence Day).

During the struggle preceding the establishment of the State of Israel, Neturei Karta organized demonstrations, prayers, and fast days, and sent a memorandum to the United Nations protesting the creation of a Jewish State in Palestine. During the battle for Jerusalem it called for a truce, suggesting that the city be internationalized. Some members even declared themselves ready to live under Jordanian rule.

The hostility between Ha-Eda ha-Haredit led by the Rabbi of Satmer (Satu-Mare), Rabbi Moshe Teitelbaum, and Rabbi Yitzhak Yaakov Weiss, head of the Bet Din (Law Court) opposed to Neturei Karta, led to a wave of proclamations and mutual protests, until the Bet Din placed a *herem* (ban) on the more extreme side, the head of Neturei Karta.

Neturei Karta itself is divided into two groups. The extreme group was headed in the late 1980s by Rabbi Hayim Binyamin Katzenelbogen, son of Rabbi Yishaya Katzenelbogen and son-in-law of Rabbi Amram Blau, one of the founders of Neturei Karta. He was assisted by an extremist zealot from London, Yerahmiel Domb (also under a *herem*). The second group, headed by Amram Blau's son Uri Blau, accepted the legal authority of Ha-Eda ha-Haredit. The Neturei Karta yeshiva, Torah ve-Yira, belonged to the group headed by Rabbi Katzenelbogen (who was also known as Rabbi Levenstein).

In the decades after the establishment of the State of Israel, the activities of Neturei Karta contributed to increasing tension between the religious and secular groups of the country. Although small in size, Neturei Karta received support from time to time from many nonmembers who shared its views on specific issues without being in complete agreement with its philosophy or its methods. Its members often resorted to acts of violence which necessitated police intervention.

Before 1948 most Neturei Karta members were of Hungarian extraction; afterwards they were joined by the Hasidim of Satu-Mare, Romania, and designated the Satmarer Rabbi, living in Brooklyn, NY, as the rabbi of Jerusalem. A large proportion of the members, especially those belonging to the Old Yishuv, were supported by *yeshivot* and *kolelim* (*see* HALUKA), while others engaged in business or light industry.

M. FRIEDMAN—Y. ALFASI

NETZER OLAMI. International Reform Zionist Youth Movement, created in Jerusalem in 1980. The Netzer Olami platform includes the belief that the fates of Israel and Diaspora Jewry are inextricably linked; the establishment of Reform Zionist communities; Aliya as the highest expression of Reform Zionism, and the strengthening of Progressive Jewish communities in Israel.

Netzer Olami has branches in Israel (Tzofei Telem), South Africa (Netzer Maginim), Australia (Netzer), Britain (Netzer, Reform Synagogue Youth), Holland (Netzer-Kadima), and North America (Misgeret Netzer). They hold regular meetings, organize summer and winter camps, Israel tours, and counselor training. Settlement groups (*garinim*) have been formed in some of these countries. The main office of Netzer Olami is situated in Jerusalem.

NEUMANN, EMANUEL. Zionist leader in the United States (b. Libau, Latvia, 1893; d. Tel Aviv, 1980). Taken to the United States as an infant, Neumann received his traditional education in a private Hebrew school established by his father, Sundel Neumann, as the first Ivrit be-Ivrit school (in which only Hebrew was used in instruction) in the US.

Emanuel Neumann. [Zionist Archives]

The family spoke only Hebrew at home. Neumann received his secular education at Columbia and New York universities.

One of the founders of *Young Judaea (1910), Neumann was the editor of the *Young Judaean* magazine in 1914–15 and served as the educational director of the *Zionist Organization of America (ZOA) from 1918 to 1920. In 1920 he attended the London Zionist Conference and became involved in the controversy that developed between Louis D. Brandeis and Chaim Weizmann and their respective followers. At the Cleveland Convention of the ZOA in 1921, Neumann was among the foremost advocates of the pro-Weizmann policy and moved the resolution that resulted in the retirement of the leadership of Brandeis and Julian W. Mack. The same year he was a cofounder of the Keren ha-Yesod of the United States, serving as its national director until 1925. Later in 1925 he was instrumental in founding the United Palestine Appeal and served as chairman of its Executive Committee until 1927. From 1928 to 1930 he was president of the Jewish National Fund, serving at the same time as vice-president of the Century Bank in New York (1928–29) and of the Interstate Trust Company (1929–30).

Neumann was a delegate to Zionist Congresses from 1921. In the late 1920s he joined the Brandeis group and was closely associated with Brandeis. At the 17th Congress (1931) he was elected to the World Zionist Executive. Before going to Jerusalem to head the Jewish Agency's Economic Department, he organized the American Palestine Committee, composed of United States senators and representatives and of other persons prominent in American public life. During his stay in Palestine, Neumann conducted negotiations with Abdullah, then Emir of Transjordan, and obtained an option agreement that contemplated the beginning of Jewish settlement in Transjordan. Following his term of office, Neumann was active from 1934 to 1939 in various business enterprises in Palestine and served as director of the Industrial Financial Corporation of Palestine, Ltd., the Migdal Insurance Co., Ltd., Palroad, and the Tiberias Hot Springs Company.

After his return to the United States at the end of 1939, he took a leading part in the political affairs of the Zionist movement. From 1940 to 1942 he headed the Department of Public Relations and Political Action of the Emergency Committee for Zionist Affairs and in this capacity conducted negotiations with the State Department. Among his many activities was the revival of the American Palestine Committee, whose membership eventually grew to 15,000. In 1943 he organized and headed the Commission on Palestine Surveys, which, with the help of an Engineering Consulting Board, studied Walter C. Lowdermilk's proposals for the full utilization of Palestine's water resources and the setting up of a Jordan Valley Authority. In the summer of 1943 Neumann helped bring about the election of Abba Hillel Silver as chairman of the American Zionist Emergency Council, and he remained closely associated with Silver as a trusted friend. When Silver was forced to resign at the end of 1944 because of his militant policies, Neumann endeavored to have him reinstated. Silver resumed his office in the spring of 1945.

Neumann's Zionist work during this period included appearances before the Foreign Affairs Committee of the US House of Representatives in 1944. In December, 1945, the congressional hearings led to a resolution approved by both houses of Congress calling for free Jewish immigration to Palestine and for support of the upbuilding of the Jewish National Home. In 1946 Neumann undertook to organize the presentation of the Zionist case to the Anglo-American Committee of Inquiry and gave testimony himself. In December of that year he attended the 22nd Zionist Congress where he headed the Committee on Political Resolutions.

He was again elected a member of the World Zionist Executive and in January, 1947, participated in the Agency's last discussions with Britain's Foreign Secretary Ernest Bevin and his associates in London. Following the breakdown of these talks, Neumann returned to the United States and submitted a report to the extraordinary conference convened by Silver in Washington. The same year Neumann was elected president of the ZOA, an office he held until 1949. During his administration the organization was extremely active politically and reached its peak in the number of affiliated members. He served as president again from 1956 to 1958.

When Great Britain referred the Palestine problem to the United Nations in 1947, Neumann was a member of the Jewish Agency delegation that presented the Jewish case and negotiated with various other delegations to ensure the adoption of the partition proposal. In 1948 he visited Israel twice, to attend plenary meetings of the Jewish Agency Executive and sessions of the Zionist Actions Committee, where he successfully insisted on the principle of *hafrada*, the formal separation of the Executive from the government of Israel. Early in 1949 Neumann (together with Abba Hillel Silver) resigned from the Executive in protest against the choice of management of the United Jewish Appeal, but he returned to the Executive in 1951, serving first in Jerusalem and then in New York.

In 1954 he established the Theodor Herzl Institute as the adult education center for the Jewish Agency. He also established the Herzl Press and the Theodor Herzl Foundation, which published the monthly magazine *Midstream*, of which Neumann was editorial board chairman. Beginning in 1963 he served intermittently, and from 1968 to 1972, as chairman of the American Section of the Jewish Agency Executive. For many years he was actively associated with the leadership of the World Confederation of General Zionists; from 1963 on he served as president of the World Union of General Zionists.

An active proponent of the Hebrew language and culture throughout his life, Neumann in 1961 helped establish the Tarbuth Foundation for the Advancement of Hebrew Culture in America and was its president for several years. He contributed a large number of articles on Zionist subjects to the *American Zionist* and other Jewish periodicals. He also wrote a biography of Theodor Herzl that was published in several editions, and he was chairman of the editorial committee of the original edition of the *Encyclopedia of Zionism and Israel*.

NEUMANN, OSKAR (Yirmiyahu). Zionist leader in Czechoslovakia and Israel (b. Most, Bohemia, Austria, 1894; d. Be'er Tuvia, Israel, 1981). Neumann studied law at the universities of Prague and Vienna. A Zionist from his early youth, he founded the Blau-Weiss Zionist youth movement in Bratislava (Pressburg), where he settled in 1920.

After the Nazi annexation of Czechoslovakia in 1939, he helped found the Zentrale Jüdische Amtsstelle, an organization to aid victims of Nazi persecution. In 1940 he became chairman of the Zionist Organization of Slovakia. In 1943 he was appointed *Judenältester* (Head Jew) of Slovakia. As a member of the clandestine Working Group, he collaborated in underground rescue efforts. In 1944 he was arrested by the Gestapo on a charge of espionage. He was later held at the concentration camp of Sered, in Slovakia, and then sent to Theresienstadt, from which he escaped shortly before its liberation.

After World War II, Neumann helped reestablish the Czechoslovak Zionist Territorial Federation, serving as its first postwar chairman. In 1946 he settled in Palestine. From 1950 on he was honorary chairman of the Hitahdut Olei Tshekhoslovakia (Association of Immigrants from Czechoslovakia). Neumann was the editor of the *Jüdische Volkszeitung* in Bratislava and the author of several books, including *In the Shadow of Death* (in Hebrew and German), an account of the struggle of Slovakian Jewry during World War II.

NEVATIM. Moshav in the Negev, 5 mi. (9 km.) east of Beersheba. On 6 October 1946, it was the easternmost of the 11 settlements established in the Negev that night. Its original settlers were replaced later by immigrants from Cochin (southern India). Its farming in a region where annual rainfall amounts hardly reach 4 in. (100 mm.), is of the oasis type, largely concentrated on flower, early vegetable and fruit cultivation in hothouses. The name means "sprouts." Population (1987), 537. E. ORNI

NEW ISRAEL FUND (NIF; Ha-Keren he-Hadasha le-Yisrael). Organization whose aims include linking North American Jews and Israelis in an effort to promote equal social and political rights for all inhabitants of Israel; supporting citizens' action efforts by Israelis to achieve social justice and strengthen the democratic process in Israel; and encourage Israeli-Arab cooperation. To this end the NIF, from its formation in 1979 until 1988, provided support to almost 100 Israeli citizens' action organizations.

The projects sponsored by NIF, which has headquarters in New York City and an Israeli office in Jerusalem, include a Leadership Fellows Program; Shatil (founded in 1982), which seeks to provide technical assistance and training for Israeli citizens' action and self-help organizations; and a program sponsored jointly with the American University in Washington, DC, to bring Israeli lawyers to the United States for a special Master of Laws degree in civil liberties, followed by a one-year internship with an Israeli civil rights organization. G. HIRSCHLER

NEW PALESTINE, THE. *See* AMERICAN ZIONIST, THE.

NEW ZEALAND, ZIONISM IN. Jews first settled in New Zealand in the early 19th century. The first Jewish community was founded in Wellington in 1843. In 1990 New Zealand's Jewish population was about 4,500, most of whom lived in Auckland and Wellington.

Zionism in New Zealand dates to the beginning of the 20th century. In 1901 a few enthusiastic Zionists sold the first Shekels in the country. In 1903 a Zionist Social Club in Wellington and a Zionist Society in Auckland were formed. The movement relied for inspiration on periodic visits of Zionists from overseas. The first of these visitors was Samuel Goldreich, a South African Zionist leader. A speech he made inspired the formation of the Wellington Zionist League and led Frederick Ehrenfried Baume, a member of Parliament, to accept the presidency of the Auckland Zionist Society. Prof. Wolf Heinemann, a Hebrew scholar and linguist who had been active in the movement in England, founded the Dunedin Zionist Society. Another man prominent in local Zionism from the pre-World War I period was Rev. Samuel Aaron Goldstein, who assumed the presidency of the Auckland Zionist Society in 1912 and held this post, with only a year's interruption, for 20 years.

The most noteworthy Zionist in New Zealand was Louis Phillips, an Auckland attorney. He traveled through the country lecturing on Zionism, and his speeches paved the way for the enthusiastic reception accorded Israel Cohen, the first emissary of the Keren ha-Yesod, when he visited New Zealand in 1921. Cohen raised £21,000, a remarkable amount for the time. In subsequent years, emissaries of the Zionist funds and the World Zionist Organization greatly helped strengthen Zionist sentiment in the country.

In 1943 all the Zionist societies combined to form the Zionist Council of New Zealand, which was affiliated with the Zionist Federation of Australia and New Zealand. The first president of the council was Isaac Gotlieb. Other presidents included John Nathan, Gerhard Perl, Eugen Hirst, Dr. Herbert Ruben, Joseph Lewis, and Peter Wise. The Zionist Council, whose seat alternates between Auckland and Wellington then maintained a fortnightly newspaper, the *New Zealand Jewish Chronicle*. Its editor was Channa Durden. The first Zionist women's group in the country was the New Zealand Women's Zionist Society. Formed in 1921 under the leadership of Mrs. David L. Nathan, the society, which later became affiliated with the Women's International Zionist Organization (WIZO), was instrumental in introducing the Plunket nursing system to Palestine and opened three mothercraft centers in Jaffa and Tel Aviv. The only Zionist youth movement then was Habonim. Many young New Zealand Jews trained by Habonim settled in Israel.

The Jewish National Fund was always very active, and after the establishment of Israel it expanded its activities still further. United Israel Appeal campaigns were held with the participation of prominent visitors from other countries.

Work for Youth Aliya increased considerably over the years through the efforts of Gretel Lewis and, together with fund-raising for the Friends of the Hebrew University of Jerusalem, forms an integral part of Zionist activity in New Zealand.

In the late 1960s the Zionist societies of New Zealand decided to form their own federation together with WIZO, the Student Zionist Society, and the youth movements Habonim and Bnei Akiva. The decision to rotate the seat of the Executive every four years between Auckland and Wellington was maintained. The fortnightly *New Zealand Jewish Chronicle* became a monthly. Under the auspices of the Federation, the United Jewish Appeal and Jewish National Fund conducted their annual campaigns. The latter held annual bazaars in the Jewish community centers of Wellington and Auckland as a major source of income. On the initiative of the Zionist Federation, New Zealand-Israel Friendship Societies were started in Wellington, Auckland, and Hamilton following the establishment of the Jewish State.

To uphold Israel's position and to combat anti-Semitism in New Zealand the Jewish community established its Public Relations Council, with its seat in Wellington. Among its activities has been lobbying for Israel in parliament, support of the Russian Jewry Campaign, and fostering relations with the Maori community. Its first chairman was Wally Hirsch.

In 1979, an ecumenical "Prayer For Peace In the Middle East," held in the central Wellington Cathedral, was attended by the Ambassador of Egypt, the Prime Minister and Cabinet of New Zealand, and many other dignitaries.

Between 1977 and 1982, the former anti-Zionist and anti-Israel position of the New Zealand Student Organization changed. By 1982, the student bodies of four out of seven campuses had voted to adopt a neutral position towards the Middle East conflict and the left-wing national executive had been voted out of office.

New-Zealand—Israel Relations. It was not until 1975, that an Israel embassy was opened in Wellington as a result of an agreement between the labor governments of Israel and New Zealand. Notwithstanding the agreement, no New Zealand Ambassador was appointed to Israel and only in 1986 was the New Zealand Ambassador to the Hague appointed non-resident Ambassador to Israel. The new National Party Government headed by Robert Muldoon decided to maintain the status quo, namely that the Australian Embassy in Tel Aviv would continue to assume responsibility for New Zealand interests in Israel. The background to this decision was the emphasis New Zealand placed on its trade with the Arab countries and Iran and its policy of "even-handedness" towards the Arab-Israel conflict, in line with that of other Western countries. Trade and cultural ties between the two countries developed substantially. The main Israel exports to New Zealand consisted of computerized irrigation equipment, agricultural machinery, chemicals, clothing and foodstuffs. The Association of Friendship Societies expanded to 12 branches and a New Zealand-Israel Chamber of Commerce was established. Exchange visits between parliamentary delegations of both countries took place and a number of Israeli scientists and lecturers assumed appointments in New Zealand during their sabbaticals. H. RUBEN—Y. MORRIS

NEW ZIONIST ORGANIZATION (NZO). Independent worldwide Zionist body established when a plebiscite of the members of the Union of Zionist-Revisionists (*see* REVISIONISTS) resulted in secession from the World Zionist Organization (WZO). A considerable part of the Revisionist leadership felt that the prospects of gaining control of the WZO through an electoral victory were diminishing because elections to Zionist Congresses were based on the number of shekels acquired and majorities were obtained by parties possessing ample campaign funds. In March, 1935, the Actions Committee rejected the Revisionist appeal for a round table conference to create a united front in the Zionist movement, condemned the Revisionist mass petition to the British authorities for the opening of the gates of Palestine to free Jewish immigration, and decided to change the legend on the Shekel, obligating every voter to observe party discipline, thus precluding any independent Revisionist political action. These decisions prompted the long-maturing split. In September, 1935, at the Constituent Congress of the New Zionist Organization, which was elected by 713,000 voters and met in Vienna under the chairmanship of Jacob *de Haas, the aims of the Organization were outlined as follows: "First, the creation of a Jewish majority on both sides of the Jordan; secondly, the establishment of a Jewish State in Palestine on the basis of civil liberty and the principles of justice and in the spirit of the Torah; thirdly, the repatriation to Palestine of all Jews who wish to be repatriated there; fourthly, the liquidation of the Diaspora." The constitution further provided for the establishment of a parliamentary body to be known as the Zionist National Assembly, which was to meet every third year. The NZO called for the swift evacuation of Jewish masses from the danger zones of eastern and central Europe. A 10-year plan for the transfer to and absorption in Palestine of 1.5 million Jews was prepared in 1938. A major Revisionist activity was the "illegal" immigration. A considerable number of the "illegals" who landed in Palestine in 1937–40 were brought on ships chartered by the Revisionists.

In 1937 the NZO opposed the partition of Palestine as proposed by the Peel Commission. It gave full backing to the underground Irgun Tzeva'i Le'umi's operations during the 1937–1939 Arab riots, and to its armed struggle against British rule in Palestine in the wake of the White Paper issued by the British government in May, 1939.

At the outbreak of World War II the NZO leadership announced that the conflict between Zionist aspirations and British policy in Palestine would be shelved until the end of the war and that all efforts were to be concentrated on the destruction of the common enemy, Nazi Germany. Simultaneously, it advanced proposals for active Jewish participation in the struggle against the Third Reich: the formation of a Jewish army to take its rightful place as a cobelligerent alongside Allied armies; and the establishment of a pro tem Jewish World Council, which was to assume responsibility for mobilizing Jewish resources for the struggle against Germany and which, after victory, was to have a place at the peace conference.

With the arrival in New York (March, 1940) of an NZO delegation, headed by Vladimir Jabotinsky, demanding the creation of a Jewish army, the United States became the main field of NZO political activity. The NZO presented its demands at international meetings of the World War II Allies.

In May, 1943, when Prime Minister Winston Churchill arrived in the United States, the NZO voiced a public demand that Britain relinquish the Mandate for Palestine. Appeals to prevent civil war in Palestine and to undo the British White Paper of 1939 followed early in 1944. In July, 1945, on the eve of Pres. Harry S. Truman's departure for the Potsdam Conference, the NZO submitted to him a petition signed by 100 members of the U.S. Congress demanding that "Palestine in its historic boundaries be proclaimed as a Jewish State."

In August, 1945 the first postwar Zionist Conference, held in London, proclaimed the aim of Zionism to be the creation of a Jewish State. In the meantime, "illegal" immigration had become a major part of the Zionist effort. The Hagana began to cooperate with the active resistance groups, and Zionist opposition to the British regime in Palestine stiffened. Early in 1946 the NZO decided to rejoin the World Zionist Organization, because its leaders had come to the conclusion that WZO policies in regard to Jewish statehood, "illegal" immigration, and active resistance to the British regime in Palestine were coming closer to the Revisionist program and tactics.

J. SCHECHTMAN—D. NIV

NICARAGUA, ZIONISM IN. Although Jews probably settled in Nicaragua as early as the 16th century and there was some Jewish immigration in the 17th and 19th centuries, the present community originated with immigrants who arrived from central and eastern Europe between the two world wars. Nicaragua's Jewish community organization was founded in 1935.

The small Jewish community, of which the majority lived in Managua, the capital, took a lively interest in world Jewish affairs, Zionism, and Israel. The Jewish National Fund was active from 1935 on, and many members of the community were inscribed in its Golden Book. In 1941 Rahel Shiley, a Hadassah emissary from Canada, initiated the formation of a WIZO group, which eventually came to include all the women of the Jewish community. Beginning in 1947 annual campaigns for the United Jewish Appeal, to which all members of the community contributed, were organized. There were also drives for State of Israel bonds and regular Shekel (membership fee) campaigns.

Prominently associated with the work for the United Jewish Appeal were Morris Patzky, Laszlo Weis (who served as Israel's honorary Consul in Nicaragua from 1948 to 1955), Jose Retelny (honorary Israeli Consul from 1955 to 1960), Abraham Gorn, Saul Wolmer (honorary Israeli Consul from 1960 to 1965), Herman Biederman, and Desiderio Kellerman. Others active in Zionist and pro-Israel work included Max Najman (honorary Israeli Consul from 1965 on), Jacobo Schutzberg, and Freddy Luft. Olga Haring, Otilia de Kellermann, Raquel de Gesundheit, Marta de Lanczyner, Fanny de Czukerberg, Rosita de Hellemberg, Myriam de Biederman, Margarita Retelny, and Teresa Wiesner served as presidents of WIZO.

By the 1960s there was a decrease in Zionist activity because of emigration. Owing to the need to intensify the work of the Zionist movement and to discuss the internal organization problems of the community, Nicaragua sent a delegation to the Conference of Central American Communities and Zionist Organizations held in Panama in 1963 to deal with various problems common to all Central American countries.

Community work in general and Zionist activities in particular gained momentum in 1965, when a new Jewish Center was erected on a plot of land in downtown Managua donated by Desiderio Kellerman. The center, consisting of a synagogue, a library, and a club hall, became the gathering place for the whole community.

The Sandinista uprising, with the subsequent civil war and the installation of a quasi-Marxist government, led to the exodus of most members of the small community and the concomitant paralysis of Zionist activity. The new regime demonstrated from the outset pro-Arab leanings and the chairman of the PLO, Yasser Arafat, was one of the few foreign guests who attended the inauguration of President Ortega. Using the argument that the previous Somoza government had maintained close ties with Israel, Ortega broke off relations.

F. LUFT—N. LORCH

NIEMIROWER, JACOB ISAAC. Rabbi and communal and Zionist leader in Romania (b. Lvov, Galicia, Austria, 1871; d. Bucharest, 1939). Born of a family of Jewish scholars, Niemirower completed rabbinical studies in Berlin under Israel Hildesheimer and Abraham Biberfeld and received a doctorate from the University of Berlin in 1896. The following year he was called to a pulpit in Jassy, Romania, where he served until 1911 when he was appointed rabbi of the Sephardi community of Bucharest. In 1921 he became Chief Rabbi of Romania, a position he held until his death.

A friend of Max Nordau and Herzl, Niemirower attended several early Zionist Congresses and served as president of the Zionist Federation and the Jewish National Fund in Romania. An advocate of unity in Jewish life and culture, he founded a Society for the Science of Judaism (1927) in Romania and saw Palestine as the world center of Jewish learning. As Chief Rabbi of Romania, he was a member of the Romanian Senate, where he fought against anti-Jewish discrimination. In 1936 he escaped assassination at the hands of a fanatical Romanian nationalist. Niemirower was the author of a number of scholarly works in French and German.

NILI (Hebrew initials of Netzah Israel Lo Yeshaker). Jewish underground intelligence group organized during World War I, in the spring of 1915, to help the British forces conquer Eretz Israel from the Turks. Its name, which means "The glory of Israel will not fail," is taken from I Samuel 15;29. The initiator of Nili was Avshalom Feinberg, its leader, Aaron *Aaronsohn. Aaronsohn and Feinberg recruited members from among their families and the young people of the older settlements to gather military information for transmission to British headquarters in Cairo. By siding with Britain against the Turks, Nili hoped to secure Eretz Israel for the Jewish people after a British victory.

Nili's first attempts to get in touch with British headquarters in Egypt failed. Aaronsohn's brother Alexander, who managed to reach Cairo, was cold-shouldered by the British Intelligence staff, and the tentative contact Feinberg had established by sea was severed when Lieut. Leonard (later Sir Leonard) Woolley, British archeologist and discoverer of Ur of the Chaldees, was taken prisoner by the Turkish authorities in 1916. In July, 1916, Aaronsohn left for England via Germany and neutral Copenhagen. That October he succeeded in being "captured" in a sham arrest at a British port as a "Turkish spy." From England he was sent to Egypt, where he was attached to British Intelligence headquarters. Meanwhile, Feinberg tried to reestablish contact with the British through the Negev. Heading south, Feinberg and Joseph Lishansky were ambushed by Bedouin near El-Arish on 20 January 1917. Feinberg was killed. Lishansky was wounded and later brought to Egypt by a British patrol. Contact between Egypt and the agricultural experiment station at Athlit, which served as the center for Nili activities, was reestablished in February, 1917. A steamboat, the *Managem*, anchored offshore, collected the information gathered by Nili members in Eretz Israel. Levi Itzhak (Lyova) Schneurson acted as liaison officer between Egypt and Athlit.

Nili in Eretz Israel was headed by Lishansky and Sarah Aaronsohn, sister of Aaron and Alexander Aaronsohn. It numbered some 40 active members, who regularly gathered information on the military, political, and economic situation in the country. Aaron Aaronsohn submitted their reports, with additional vital background material, to the British authorities in Cairo. The leaders of the yishuv were at first strongly opposed to Nili, fearing Turkish reprisals if its activities were discovered. Attempts were made to suppress it, but following the expulsion of the Jewish population of Jaffa by the Turkish authorities in April, 1917, the yishuv's attitude changed. Aaronsohn made use of the arbitrary expulsion to arouse anti-Turkish sentiment throughout the world and arranged with the British authorities for the shipment of gold to the yishuv through Nili, thus to some extent relieving the hunger conditions prevalent in the country.

Negotiations between Meir Dizengoff, then the head of the yishuv, and leading members of Nili had ended in an agreement when the existence of the clandestine group came to the notice of the Turkish authorities. On 3 September 1917, a carrier pigeon was caught off Caesarea, and two weeks later Na'aman Belkind, a key Nili man, was caught while attempting to reach Egypt through the desert. The secrets of Nili were extorted from him. In October, 1917, Zikhron Ya'akov was besieged by Turkish troops. Sarah Aaronsohn was arrested and tortured for three days but refused to betray her friends. On 9 October 1917, she committed suicide. Lishansky, the second in command, fled from the settlement and, after surviving an attempt made on his life by members of Ha-Shomer, Nili's antagonists, was taken captive by a Bedouin shepherd and turned over to the Turks at Nebi Rubin. Reuven Schwartz, another member of Nili, died in a Nazareth prison; others were sentenced to imprisonment in Damascus or exiled to northern Turkey.

Following the suppression of Nili, several leading members of the yishuv were arrested and exiled. Belkind and Lishansky were sentenced to death and hanged on 16 December 1917. On 21 May 1919, Aaron Aaronsohn was killed in a plane crash. The British acknowledged Nili's contribution to the conquest of Palestine; the valuable contacts with British statesmen and military leaders established by Aaronsohn were an important factor in the events that led to the Balfour Declaration in 1917.

The activities of Nili were strongly opposed and denounced by the official leadership of the yishuv as adventurous, irresponsible, and dangerous to the security of the yishuv. It was not until November, 1967, that the rehabilitation of this group was made official by the military funeral accorded the remains of Avshalom Feinberg. Eulogizing Feinberg, Knesset Speaker Kadish Luz described the conflict with the yishuv as "one of the tragic misunderstandings with which Jewish history is so replete."

For many years a myth persisted to the effect that Avshalom Feinberg was murdered by his fellow-member of the organization, Lishansky, on account of their rivalry for the love of Sarah. However, following the Six-Day War in 1967, and the discovery of Feinberg's remains under a palm-tree, near the border of Sinai, the myth was dispelled as baseless, Lishansky's integrity was rehabilitated, and in 1979, following a government decision, his remains were transferred from the cemetery of Rishon le-Zion to Mount Herzl, Jerusalem. J. NEDAVA

NIRIM. Kibbutz in the western Negev. One of the 11 Negev settlements founded in the night of 6 October 1946, it was overwhelmed by Egyptian army forces in the 1948 War of Independence and destroyed by shelling above ground. A handful of armed settlers prevented the enemy from breaking into the settlement. After the war, the kibbutz was rebuilt a little north of the original site, facing the Gaza Strip. It has farming and industry. The name means "furrows."

Members of kibbutz Nirim going to work, 1947. [Israel Govt. Press Office]

A 6th century mosaic pavement of a synagogue discovered there is decorated with animals and symbols. It indicates that a Jewish community was living there at least until the Arab conquest in the 7th century. Population (1987), 464. E. ORNI

NIR-RAFALKES (RAFALKES), NAHUM YA'AKOV. Israeli lawyer, legislator, and Labor Zionist leader (b. Warsaw, 1884; d. Tel Aviv, 1968). Nir-Rafalkes studied at the universities of Warsaw, Zurich, St. Petersburg, and Tartu, from the last of which he received a doctorate in law. He then practiced law in Warsaw and, later, in St. Petersburg.

During his student days Nir-Rafalkes helped found Po'ale Zion in Poland. He was a delegate to several Zionist Congresses. After the Russian Revolution he became one of the leaders of Po'ale Zion in Russia and also held important positions in the revolutionary government. In 1918 he went to Poland, and in 1920 became secretary-general of the World Confederation of Left Po'ale Zion parties, continuing in that post after he settled in Palestine in 1925. In Palestine he practiced law and remained active in communal and political affairs.

As a member of Israel's Provisional Council of State, Nir-Rafalkes was a signatory of the Declaration of Independence (he adopted the Hebrew surname Nir, derived from his original initials). He was a member of the First, Third, Fourth, and Fifth Knessets, representing first Mapam and later Ahdut Avoda. He served as Deputy Speaker throughout, and briefly (March-November, 1959) as

Speaker. His writings include a number of works on economic and political issues and an autobiography, *Pirkei Hayim* (Chapters of Life, 1958). C.B. SHERMAN

NISSAN (KATZNELSON), AVRAHAM. Physician (b. Bobruisk, Russia, 1888; d. Petah Tikva, 1956). Nissan studied at the universities of St. Petersburg and Moscow. During World War I he served as a physician with the Russian Army. In 1919–20 he was director of the Istanbul office of the Zionist Executive, and from 1921 to 1923 he served in the head office of the Hitahdut in Vienna and Berlin. Settling in Palestine in 1924, he was director of the Health Department of the Zionist Executive, and later of the Va'ad Le'umi until the establishment of the State, when he became Director-General of the Ministry of Health.

He was a member of the Zionist Actions Committee for some time, a member of the Va'ad Le'umi from 1931 to 1948, and a member of the Provisional Council of State. In 1949–50 he was a member of the Israeli delegation to the United Nations. In 1950 he became Israeli Minister to the Scandinavian countries, serving in that capacity until his health failed several months before his death.

NISSENBAUM, YITZHAK. Rabbi and Zionist leader (b. Bobruisk, Russia, 1868; d. Warsaw ghetto, 1942 or 1943). Nissenbaum studied at talmudical academies and was active in the Hovevei Zion movement from 1887 on. In 1889 he settled in Minsk, where, in 1891, he founded a Safa Berura Society for the study of the Bible and the Hebrew language. That year he joined Netzah Yisrael, a secret Hovevei Zion society that had been founded at the yeshiva of Volozhin. When the yeshiva was closed in 1892, Nissenbaum was asked by Hayim Nahman Bialik to take over the leadership of Netzah Yisrael. In 1894 he was invited by Rabbi Shemuel Mohilever to serve as the secretary of the Hovevei Zion center that Mohilever headed in Bialystok.

Nissenbaum became an early adherent of political Zionism. After the death of Mohilever (1898), he worked for the Odessa Committee until 1910, traveling throughout Russia and addressing meetings. He did much to unite the Hovevei Zion with the political Zionists, remaining a stanch adherent of both political and practical Zionism. During the debate on the East Africa scheme, he helped Menahem Ussishkin organize the opposition to the plan.

In 1901 Nissenbaum settled in Warsaw, where he preached in the Zionist Moria Synagogue. Once a month he delivered his sermon in Hebrew. He attended the founding conference of the Mizrachi movement in Vilna (1902) and its first meeting in Lida (1903). However, it was not until 1919 that Nissenbaum officially became a member of the movement, in which he played an important role. In 1937 he was elected president of the Mizrachi of Poland.

Nissenbaum first began to contribute articles to the Hebrew press in 1889. From 1906 on he was a regular contributor to *Ha-Melitz*. In 1910 he joined the editorial board of **Ha-Tzefira*, of which he later became editor. He also served as editor of *Ha-Mizrach* the Warsaw Mizrachi weekly. In addition, he wrote for the Yiddish press.

He was considered one of the greatest Zionist preachers of his day. His sermons were immensely popular, drawing large crowds. He was killed in the Warsaw ghetto. Be'erot Yitzhak, a religious kibbutz in the Negev, was named for him.

Numerous Hebrew collections of Nissenbaum's sermons and other Zionist writings have been published including *Ha-Yahadut ha-Le'umit* (National Judaism, 1920), *Ha-Dat veha-Tehiya ha-Le'umit* (Religion and National Revival, 1920), and *Masoret ve-Herut* (Tradition and Freedom, 1939).
T. PRESCHEL

Rabbi Yitzhak Nissim.
[Jewish National Fund]

NISSIM, YITZHAK RAHAMIM. Sephardi Chief Rabbi of Israel (b. Baghdad, 1895; d. Jerusalem, 1981). Nissim received his rabbinical training in Baghdad. Although he refused to accept a pulpit, he took a prominent part in the religious leadership of Iraqi Jewry. In 1926 he settled in Jerusalem, where he served as adviser to Sephardi rabbis and communities. In 1955 he was elected Sephardi Chief Rabbi, holding office until 1972. Nissim contributed studies to rabbinic publications and edited responsa by famous Sephardi rabbinical authorities.

His son **Moshe Binyamin Nissim** (b. Jerusalem, 1935), a lawyer, became active in the Liberal Party in the 1960s. He held key Knesset and ministerial positions, including Minister of Justice (1980–1986), of Finance (1986–1988) and of Trade and Industry (1990–1992).

NITZANIM. Kibbutz and youth village in the southern coastal plain, founded in 1943. In the 1948 War of Independence, its resistance to the Egyptian army delayed the latter's advance but the settlers had to evacuate the site. After it was retaken by the Israel army, the kibbutz was rebuilt several miles south of the original site and in 1949 the youth village was established. The kibbutz is based on intensive farming. Its name means "buds." Population (1987), 385, the youth village 313. E. ORNI

NOAH, MORDECAI MANUEL. Author, diplomat, and Zionist visionary (b. Philadelphia, 1785; d. New York, 1851). Of Sephardi origin, Noah aroused attention by his early endeavors in journalism and was appointed American Consul in Tunis in 1813. After his return to New York in 1816, he continued his journalistic and literary career. His contributions to daily newspapers and the books and plays he published gained him great popularity.

Noah is remembered in Jewish history for the Jewish settlement he planned to establish in the United States. In

Raising the flag at the Nitzanim Youth Village. [Hadassah]

1820 he petitioned the New York State Legislature to permit him to purchase Grand Island in the Niagara River for the settlement of Jewish immigrants from Russia. In September, 1825, he issued an appeal to world Jewry for the support of the "city of refuge for the Jews," which he named Ararat, but since he met with no response, he was forced to abandon the project. In 1844 he broached the idea of a Jewish mass settlement once again, this time, however, stressing the necessity for the return of the Jewish people to Palestine as the only solution to the Jewish problem. He called upon America to help the Jews receive permission from the Turkish government to purchase land in Palestine and to hold it in security and peace.

A. ALPERIN

NOBEL, NEHEMIA ANTON (Zvi). Rabbi and religious Zionist leader in Germany (b. Nagymed, Hungary, 1871; d. Frankfurt on the Main, Germany, 1922). After his ordination at the Berlin (Hildesheimer) Rabbinical Seminary, he obtained a Ph.D. degree at the University of Bonn in 1895. He held pulpits in Cologne, Königsberg, Leipzig, Hamburg, and Frankfurt.

Nobel was a member of the governing body of the Zionist Organization of Germany, participated in the foundation of the Mizrachi World Movement at the Pressburg Conference of 1904, and was elected a member of the movement's Executive for Western Europe. In the last years of his life he was active on behalf of the Keren ha-Yesod. He was a delegate to the Sixth (1903) and 12th (1921) Zionist Congresses.

In 1921 Nobel was elected president of the Association of Rabbis in Germany, and in 1922 he was appointed professor of Jewish religious science and ethics at the University of Frankfurt.

At the turn of the century Nobel briefly studied in Marburg under Hermann Cohen, to whose anti-Zionist treatise *Deutschtum und Judentum* (Germanism and Judaism, 1915) he wrote a reply. His own philosophy was a synthesis of religious positivism and purely philosophical values, and of Orthodox Zionism and an acceptance of all shades of Judaism.

Max Nordau.
[United Israel Appeal]

NORDAU, MAX (Simon Maximilian Südfeld). Author, physician, and Zionist leader (b. Pest, Hungary, 1849; d. Paris, 1923). In his native city he received instruction in Hebrew and Ladino from his father, Gabriel Südfeld, an Orthodox rabbi and teacher of Sephardi origin. In later years Nordau drifted away from Jewish tradition. He started his journalistic career in Budapest in his early youth under the pseudonym Max Nordau, which he adopted as his legal name in 1873. Nordau studied medicine at the Universities of Budapest and Paris and in 1878 began to practice medicine in Budapest. In 1880 he moved to Paris, where he continued to practice medicine but devoted much of his time to writing. His thoughtful, incisive, and often provocative books were widely read and debated. By 1898 they had been translated into 18 languages, making Nordau one of the most influential and controversial writers of his time. *Die konventionellen Lügen der Kulturmenschheit*, 1883 (*Conventional Lies of Society*), in which he showed the essential falsity of some of the social, ethical, and religious standards of modern civilization, and *Entartung*, 1892 (*Degeneration*), in which he maintained that modern urban life resulted in a degeneration of man, attracted particular attention.

It was the growth of anti-Semitism in central and western Europe, particularly the Dreyfus affair, that first reawakened Nordau's Jewish consciousness. When, in July, 1895, Herzl broached to him the idea of a Jewish State, Nordau was psychologically ready for it. Herzl's purpose in coming to Nordau was to prove that his scheme was not a fantastic dream but the only practical solution for Jewish problems. He achieved his purpose, and Nordau became his first convert to Zionism. Before they parted, Nordau, grasping Herzl's hand, said to him: "You may be mad; but if you are, I am as mad as you." Later, on 9 August 1899, Herzl wrote to Nordau: "We met in a forest and recognized each other as brothers." Nordau himself felt that Zionism had given his life "purpose and a content."

At the First Zionist Congress (1897), Nordau delivered the first of his historic addresses on the situation of the Jews in the world. The delegates were fascinated by his depth of thought and masterly delivery. It was Nordau, too, who formulated the classic definition of Zionism's ultimate goal in the *Basle Program as "the creation for the Jewish people of a publicly recognized, legally secured Home in Eretz Israel" (only the term "publicly" was contributed by Herzl). Vladimir Jabotinsky called it the most classic of Nordau's writings: "In ten lines the aims and methods of the movement are exhaustively defined, with an architectonic beauty, grace and finesse which remind me of the temples on the Acropolis in Athens."

Nordau's addresses were the highlight of the ten Zionist Congresses in which he participated. Eloquent surveys of the situation of the Jews in Europe, they reflected Nordau's passion for justice and righteousness in every aspect of life. At the Sixth Congress, he vigorously defended the Uganda project submitted by Herzl, describing the East African site as a temporary expedient for which he coined the term *Nachtasyl* (overnight refuge). After Herzl's death, Nordau was offered the presidency of the World Zionist Organization, but he declined, remaining the political adviser to Herzl's successor, David Wolffsohn. A stanch and uncompromising "political" Zionist in Herzl's tradition, Nordau felt increasingly alienated by the ascendancy of the "practical" trend in the movement. The Tenth Congress (1911) elected an Executive composed solely of exponents of practical Zionism. It was the last Congress in which Nordau participated.

Nordau was strongly opposed to both the cultural Zionism of Ahad Ha-Am and the practical Zionism of Chaim Weizmann, to whom he referred as a "Hovev Zion at heart...the person least of all fitted to lead a political movement." Weizmann, in his *Trial and Error*, described Nordau as a mere "*Heldentenor*, a prima donna, a great speaker in the classical style; spade work was not his line."

During World War I, Nordau, an Austrian national, was expelled from France and took refuge in Spain, maintaining contact from there with the Zionist effort the world over. After the war, he was frequently urged to return to active leadership in the Zionist movement. He hesitated and, in reply to Weizmann's invitation to come to London, denounced the official Zionist policy as "sheer Hovevei Zionism, in direct conflict with that political Zionism for which I fight, and with the ideas of Herzl, my guide today as truly as he was twenty-two years ago..." Nordau did go to London in December, 1919, but he felt himself a stranger in the prevailing Zionist "establishment."

At the London Zionist Conference of 1920, he was named honorary president of that body. It was there that, in a lengthy discussion with the American delegation, he first broached his plan for the speedy transfer to Palestine of "at least half a million young men and women...to settle there at any cost, to toil there, to suffer there if need be...this is the only way of immediately establishing a [Jewish] majority in Palestine." Many of the listeners were shocked by the daring idea, which Nordau later fully developed in a series of ten articles published in *Le Peuple Juif* of Paris between 14 September and 20 November 1920. No one at that time was prepared to take the idea seriously, let alone endorse it. It was not until 1936 that Jabotinsky made the "Nordau Plan" the cornerstone of his own "evacuation" policy and of his Ten-Year Plan for Palestine.

Nordau returned to Paris in September, 1920, with the intention of moving to Palestine. However, he soon fell ill and, after a long illness, died on 23 January 1923. In 1926 his remains were transferred to Palestine and buried in Tel Aviv.

J. SCHECHTMAN

NORDHEIM, LION. Zionist leader in the Netherlands (b. Arnhem, Netherlands, 1910; d. near Amsterdam, 1945). Born of a conservative middle-class family, Nordheim became the principal ideologist of the Joodse Jeugd Federatie (Dutch Zionist Youth Federation), of which he was chairman from 1934 to 1936. Against the dominating trend in the Dutch Zionist organizations, he advocated cultural activities and support for halutzic activity. He spent the years of Nazi occupation in hiding, and was captured and executed by the Nazis a few weeks before the liberation of the Netherlands.

NORTH AFRICA, ZIONISM IN. The modern Zionist movement officially reached North Africa between 1897 and 1900, when the Zionist General Council appointed Dr. A. Valensin, a young doctor from Constantine, Algeria, to represent the movement in Algeria, Morocco, and Tunisia. Even before this date, a North African delegate had accompanied the French delegation to the First Zionist Congress (1897).

The development of the Zionist Movement in each of these North African countries was influenced by the situation of the local Jews, which differed from country to country.

ALGERIA

In this country, conquered by France in 1830, the Jews enjoyed full emancipation from 1870 when the Crémieux Decree granted them French citizenship. The consistorial leadership actively promoted this emancipation, bringing about a cultural assimilation which eroded broad sectors of the community. This integration of Algerian Jewry into French colonial society was widely opposed by the European population. Although the resultant virulent anti-Semitism came to the attention of the First Zionist Congress, few Algerian Jews were even aware of the holding of the Congress; indeed, with the exception of the traditional community of Constantine, which for many years was the only center of true Zionist activity, Zionism penetrated into Algeria only with great difficulty.

In the wake of the Balfour Declaration and the decisions of the San Remo Conference, various Zionist circles sprang up in a number of provincial towns, including Medeah and Mostaganem; in Algiers, an association known as the Union Sioniste Algérienne was founded and had 270 members in 1920, but according to its leader L. Smadja, these were simple people without influence. As in metropolitan France, Zionism was viewed with hostility by the consistorial leadership, which professed assimilation and related to Judaism only in the religious sense, leaving no room for national self-definition. This fundamentally negative attitude towards Zionism, however, did not prevent interest in what was happening in Palestine, so that for a very long period fundraising for the Keren ha-Yesod and the Jewish National Fund (JNF) remained the sole expression of Zionist activity in Algeria.

Only with World War II and the shock of the racist Vichy laws to which the Jews of Algeria were subjected, including the repeal of the Crémieux Decree, did a substantial change occur in the Algerian community's attitude towards Zionism. In late 1943, a local Zionist Federation was created under Benjamin Heller and Robert Brunschwig, which united over 20 Zionist associations operating throughout Algeria. The Federation was extremely active in the efforts to obtain the repeal of the racist laws which remained in force even after the American liberation (November, 1942). Following the establishment of the State of Israel, scores of Algerian Jewish ex-servicemen served as volunteers in the ranks of the Israel army. Hundreds of Algerian Jews immigrated to Israel in the following years, and Algerian Jewry was represented at all the Zionist Congresses of the 1950s. Notwithstanding, with the granting of Algerian independence (1962), almost all of the country's 130,000 Jews emigrated to France rather than to Israel. Algerian Jewry's passive attitude towards Zionism during all the years of its existence had a direct bearing on this exceptional, total migration of a Jewish community from one diaspora to another. (*See also* ALGERIAN JEWS IN ISRAEL).

TUNISIA

Tunisia became a French protectorate in 1881. In view of its non-colonial status and also in the light of the waves of anti-Semitism which had swept Algeria in the wake of the Crémieux Decree, French citizenship was not granted to Tunisian Jewry despite all the efforts of French Jewry in this respect. In consequence, the local community, while exposed to French culture, retained its traditional institutions.

Following the holding of the First Zionist Congress, Zionist associations were formed in the late 19th century in many localities in Tunisia, the most important of these being: Agudat Zion, under Alfred Valensi and Joseph Brami, and Yoshevet Zion, under Rabbi Boccara, in Tunis; Terahem Zion in Sousse; Ahavat Zion in Sfax; and Benei Zion in Beja. The participation of members of a high social standing and several rabbis in these organizations guaranteed their success among the Jewish population.

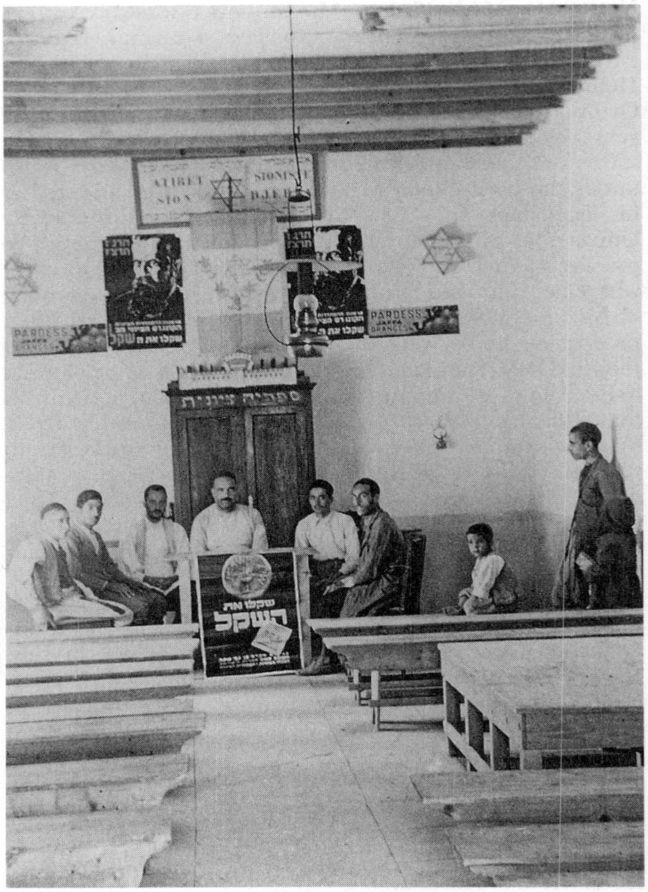

Meeting of committee of "Ateret Zion" Zionist movement, Djerba, Tunisia, 1930. [Beth Hatefutsoth]

As throughout the Jewish world, the Balfour Declaration gave a strong impetus to Zionist activity in Tunisia. New associations sprang up in all the large population centers, uniting in 1920 in the framework of the Zionist Federation of Tunisia. Granted immediate recognition by the authorities, the Federation enjoyed a wide freedom of activity and full freedom of expression through its two organs, *La Voix Juive* and *Le Réveil Juif*. Given the Federation's official status, and its successful direction by Alfred Valensi who represented Tunisian Zionists at the 12th Zionist Congress (1921), the Jewish elite did not distance itself from Zionist activity, although the great majority of the movement's members came from the popular strata. The public proclamation issued by the Zionist Federation in 1922 at the opening of the first Keren ha-Yesod Appeal was signed by all the community leaders, including the chief rabbi and the president of the community council.

From 1927 onward the Revisionists constituted the prime movers of Tunisian Zionism through the journal *Le Réveil*

Juif and its editor Félix Allouche, a follower of Vladimir Jabotinsky. On the eve of World War II the Revisionist Movement had almost 3,000 members. At a time when the Federation was paralyzed, the Revisionists strove to establish Betar youth clubs and to take an active part in community life, spreading the Hebrew language and intensifying Zionist information, while at the same time organizing large demonstrations against British policy in Palestine and boycotts of German-manufactured goods following Hitler's rise to power.

The Ha-Shomer ha-Tza'ir nucleus created in Tunisia in 1930 met with the open hostility of Betar and of the community leaders who shrank from the movement's revolutionary ideas: it existed for a bare four years.

In World War II, after two years under the Vichy regime, Tunisia was occupied for six months by the Germans, (November, 1942—May, 1943). Hundreds of Jews were placed in forced labor camps, while some were deported to the extermination camps in Europe.

The link with Palestine was renewed in June, 1943, when the first emissaries of the Tze'irei Zion pioneering movement arrived, forming branches throughout Tunisia. The members of the movement, almost all of whom came from the local Jewish bourgeoisie, were divided into several classes and groups, and shared the objective of forming a North African kibbutz. In addition to Zionist education, they engaged in defensive and agricultural training.

At the same time the Betar Movement enjoyed a broader public base, since the Revisionists continued to be the main stream in Tunisian Zionism. The Federation resumed activity in 1944, assuming direction of the Keren ha-Yesod and Jewish National Fund appeals, and of youth and information matters. However, continuous, regular work was impeded by the violent divergencies existing between the different streams. The main bone of contention was the allocation of certificates to potential immigrants to Palestine. Despite all these problems, the Zionist Movement remained a dominant force in community life in the years preceding the establishment of the State. Its two organs, *La Voix Juive* and *La Gazette d'Israël*, were likewise the two most important community publications.

After the establishment of the State of Israel, with the commencement of mass immigration, the number of agricultural training nuclei throughout Tunisia grew. Tze'irei Zion-Dror, Ha-Shomer ha-Tza'ir, Bnei Akiva, Habonim, and Betar united in order to organize Jewish youth for immigration to Israel, although a spirit of cooperation did not always rule between them or between them and the Zionist Federation, which itself split in 1950. In any event, with the declaration of Tunisian independence in 1954, the movement of emigration to Israel grew, reaching its peak in the early 1960s, when relations deteriorated between France and Tunisia which supported the Algerian liberation army. It is estimated that by the late 1960s almost half of Tunisian Jewry had immigrated to Israel. (*See also* TUNISIAN JEWS IN ISRAEL).

MOROCCO

While Morocco became a French Protectorate only in 1912, close ties already existed between Moroccan Jewry and the outside world through the European influence which had permeated the country and through the schools of the Alliance Israélite Universelle which had commenced activity in the early 1860s. Hence, the first Zionist associations in Morocco were established in the coastal towns which were exposed to European influence. In summer, 1900, Sha'arei Zion was founded in Mogador, while Shivat Zion was founded in Tetuan, on the initiative of a Russian-born Jewish doctor. Three years later Ahavat Zion came into being in Safi. Zionist activity in the interior of the country commenced only in 1908, with the establishment of the Hibbat Zion association in Fez, which included among its members all the city's rabbis. The fact that they had been led to see Zionism as a religious movement led to several misunderstandings between them and the movement's central institutions, which did not always demonstrate deep understanding of the mentality of the North African Jewish community.

The exaltation induced by the Balfour Declaration led to an intensification of Zionist activity in Morocco and a spontaneous organization of immigration to Palestine. Several families from the Sefrou region banded together and reached Jaffa harbor, but returned to Morocco after being refused entry to Palestine.

Toward the mid-1920s Zionist activity throughout Morocco declined for a variety of reasons, principally because of France's restrictive attitude towards the Zionist movement. Fearing the indignant reaction of the Arab populace, the French authorities placed many difficulties in the way of Zionist activity in Morocco, banning *inter alia* the distribution of the Zionist journal *Ha-Olam* and restricting fundraising for projects in Palestine. In view of this attitude, the community notables distanced themselves from the Zionist associations, thus detracting from their importance in the eyes of the Jewish population, which in any case had little sympathy with the secular aims of Zionism.

Recognizing the gravity of the situation, the central institutions in 1924 sent Yonatan Thurtz to Morocco, and he represented Morocco in all the Zionist Congresses up to the outbreak of World War II. The first problem facing Thurtz was the question of the legalization of Zionist activity in Morocco. While failing to obtain for the Moroccan movement the same status as that of the Tunisian Federation, with the aid of such eminent Parisian personalities as Léon Blum, he did persuade the French government to adopt a more tolerant attitude towards Zionist activity in Morocco and to recognize the Moroccan movement as a local section of the Zionist Federation of France. For information purposes, Thurtz founded in 1926 a periodical, *Avenir Illustré*, which gradually became the principal organ of Moroccan Jewry. He constructed a centralized, organizational infrastructure run by a small number of activists, almost all foreign nationals, apart from a few native Moroccans. In January, 1936, the first convention of Moroccan Zionists was held and the movement's regulations ratified. Two more conventions were held up to the outbreak of World War II.

After the war, Zionism in Morocco was completely transformed: in particular the effect of the Holocaust led to a national revival among educated youth while ties were strengthened with the yishuv in Palestine, which, because of the war, showed great interest in the Jewish communities in Islamic countries.

The Zionist movement resumed its activity in 1945, again as a regional branch of the French Federation, although in fact it maintained a direct, autonomous link with the central authorities. It was headed by its prewar directors—S. Kagan, P. Calamaro, S.D. Levy, J.R. Benazeraf -, except for Thurtz who had emigrated to the USA. The movement's efforts among youth were directed essentially at the associations of Alliance Israélite Universelle school graduates and especially at the members of the Karl Netter Club in Casablanca, which became a completely Zionist club, providing the members of the first settlement nuclei of Tze'irei Zion.

In Morocco, as in Tunisia, Zionism, with all its ideological shades, was directed at only a small sector of the population, in all several hundred young people—young French-educated town-dwellers, mainly from the middle classes. Their number would certainly have grown over the ensuing years as the education system grew, but the dramatic declaration of the establishment of the State of Israel was seen as the realization of the vision of the Prophets and the Jews of Morocco began to stream to Israel in their thousands. The process, which intensified with the granting of Moroccan independence in 1954, has continued without halt; according to estimates, two-thirds of Moroccan Jewry have immigrated to Israel, while the rest emigrated to France, Canada or Spain in the last thirty years. (*See also* Moroccans in Israel.)

LIBYA

Zionist organization commenced in Libya immediately after the Italian conquest of 1911, although informal contact with the movement's institutions existed even before then on an individual basis. From the inception of Zionist organization in Libya, Elijah Nehaisi, together with a group of local intellectuals, called for the revival of Jewish culture and the spread of the Hebrew language among Jewish youth. Unlike the other Zionist associations formed in the same period in North Africa, Nehaisi's Zion Society sought to take over the community institutions, and in 1917 he presented his candidates to the Tripoli community committee. While angering the traditional institutions, Nehaisi had the support of Italian Jewry, which supported his efforts to improve the cultural situation of Libyan Jewry while relying on the Zionist idea. Following Nehaisi's death in 1918, Zionist activity waned, although various associations continued to exist in Benghazi and in Tripoli, where a Zionist organ, *Degel Zion*, appeared in 1920. Real Zionist activity resumed only in World War II, when Jewish Palestinian soldiers arrived in the country with the British forces which drove Rommel and his Afrika Korps from the Egyptian desert and terminated Italian rule in Libya in early 1943.

With the authorization of the British authorities, the Palestinian soldiers began to organize educational activities for the Jewish communities and to assist in the difficult social problems. Some 60 orphans were taken to Palestine, and

Israel Independence Day celebration, Tripoli, Libya, 1949. [Yad Ben-Zvi]

Stamping first passport for Israel, Tripoli, Libya, 1949. [Beth Hatefutsoth]

teachers, nurses, and emissaries began to arrive from Palestine. At the same time the prewar Zionist associations were rehabilitated, and He-Halutz was founded to provide agricultural and ideological training for the young Jews intending to immigrate to Palestine.

The departure of the Jewish soldiers in 1944 was followed by a deterioration in the relations between the Jews and their Arab neighbors. One of the most shocking pogroms in the history of Libyan Jewry broke out in 1945, with the slaughter of scores of Jews in Tripoli and the burning and plundering of hundreds of homes and shops. These grievous events strengthened the Jews' desire to immigrate to Palestine, but until 1949 the British refused to grant them exit permits. From early 1949 until mid-1950 16,000 Jews immigrated to Israel from Libya, about fifty percent of Libyan Jewry. The process was accelerated with the granting of Libyan independence in 1952, and up to 1953, 31,000 Libyan Jews immigrated to Israel. The last Jews left Libya during the Six-Day War and after Colonel Muammer al-Qaddafi's rise to power in 1970. (*See also* LIBYAN JEWS IN ISRAEL; EGYPT, ZIONISM IN; EGYPTIAN JEWS IN ISRAEL.)

M. ABITBOL

NORWAY, RELATIONS WITH ISRAEL. Norway voted for the UN Partition Plan and a Jewish State in 1947. The former Norwegian Minister of Foreign Affairs and UN Secretary General, Trygve Lie, supported the establishment of the State of Israel. Norwegian de facto recognition was given on 5 February 1949. In 1954 diplomatic relations were established through an Israeli diplomat in Sweden, with a branch office in Oslo, and in 1960 an embassy was opened for Norway (and Iceland). The Norwegian office for Israel in Athens was later replaced by an embassy in Tel Aviv.

Norway supported Israel often in the United Nations, but did not fully approve of Israeli policy after the Six-Day War. In some instances Norway voted for resolutions criticizing or censuring Israel for not withdrawing from the Golan Heights and the Administered Areas or abstained from voting. Norway never recognized Jerusalem as Israel's capital, but always voted for Israel's sovereignty, for its right to secure borders, and against resolutions in the UN and its member organizations (ILO, WHO, UNESCO, UNO) which condemned Israel and Zionism as racist, and against efforts to exclude Israel from UN organizations. PLO diplomatic representation has not been admitted in Norway.

Israeli statesmen (among them David Ben-Gurion, Golda Meir, Abba Eban, and Moshe Dayan, who were very popular in Norway) have visited Norway, and prominent Norwegians have visited Israel. The Norwegian Labor Party and the non-socialist parties and their press have traditionally adopted pro-Israeli attitudes (not least those with a Christian orientation) as has the Trades Union Congress. But in the 1970s and 1980s certain union federations were influenced by anti-Israeli views, and left-wing groups and student groups demonstrated against Israeli guest lecturers, Norwegian-Israeli agreements, and visits by Israeli statesmen to Norway. The Lebanon war, in particular in its first phase, earned Israel hostile coverage in many newspapers, on television and radio. The demonstrations were mostly condemned by Norwegians. The authorities and most of the populace denounced terrorism against Jewish and Israeli institutions and individuals. On the other hand, the Lillehammer case (1973), where Israelis were involved in the murder in Norway of an Arab assumed to belong to a terrorist group, was criticized by many Norwegians for a time.

Norway has participated in United Nations Peace-Keeping Forces in the Sinai and, since 1978, in Lebanon. The Norwegian general, Odd Bull, headed the UN Truce Supervisory Organization from 1963-1970.

A number of Israeli writers have been translated into Norwegian. Norwegian authors have also visited Israel, as have numerous Norwegian tourists, many of them inspired by the land of the Bible, or interested in kibbutz life. Since the 1960s many Israelis have visited Norway.

Trade between Israel and Norway has developed. In the 1960s refrigerator boats for Israel were built in Norway. In the 1970s Arabs attempted to include in their contracts with Norwegian firms boycott provisos demanding that these firms give up contracts with Israel and with Israelis in their service, but the Norwegian authorities intervened to prevent this. In the 1980s trade between Norway and Israel expanded. Important exports from Norway are oil, fish, paper, pulp, aluminum, and metals, while Israel exports products such as vegetables and vegetable raw materials, fruit, nuts, chemical fertilizers, and equipment for telecommunications.

O. MENDELSOHN

NORWAY, ZIONISM IN. According to the census of 1910, 1,045 Jews lived in Norway, mainly in Oslo and Trondheim. In 1940, when Norway was invaded by the Germans, the number of Jews was more than 1,800, of whom 300–400 were refugees from Germany, Austria, and Czechoslovakia. During the German occupation 758 Jews were killed and 900–1,000 escaped to Sweden. In 1946, some 600 Jews lived in Norway; by 1990, their number had increased to 1,000.

Zionist Organizations before World War II. A Zionist organization was founded in Oslo in September, 1912, on the initiative of the leaders of the Oslo Jewish Youth Organization (J.U.F., founded in 1909). The same year a Zionist organization called Herzlia, was established in Trondheim. The years 1917–20 saw an upsurge of activity in the Oslo Zionist Organization, following the arrival of many Jews from abroad (most of them from eastern Europe). Among these were the architect Richard Kaufmann (later architect of the city of Tel Aviv), the journalist and author Pesach Ginsburg, and the artist Elieser (L.) Berson. These persons and others gave lectures for the Zionist groups. The Zionist leader Yehiel Tschlenow addressed a large meeting during his visit to Oslo in the fall of 1917, and after his death the following year a Palestine album was published by the Oslo group in his honor (reprinted 1984). The same year the Zionist Organization started its own publication *Jodisk Tidende* (The Jewish Times), which appeared five times. Osenselsky, the editor was the president of the Zionist Organization. The publication of the Oslo Jewish Youth Organization, *Israeliten*, also contained much Zionist material.

During the 1920s and the first half of the 1930s activities became more sporadic. The advent to power of the Nazis in Germany in 1933 spurred many young Jews to adopt Zionism. Nearly three hundred persons participated in the 25th anniversary of the Oslo Zionist Organization in 1937. The Jewish publication *Hatikwoh* published many Norwegian Zionist articles at that time.

The Trondheim Zionist organization, Herzliah, remained active through the 1920s. It too grew from 1933.

Jewish National Fund committees had been established during World War I, perhaps even earlier. The first Keren ha-Yesod drive was organized in 1921 with special committees in Oslo, as well as in Trondheim.

When the British White Paper of 1939 was issued, the Zionist Union of Norway (established 1935) together with the Jewish communities made representations to Norway's Foreign Minister.

Post-World War II developments. In Oslo the Zionist Organization was reestablished in December, 1945, and committees were elected for the Jewish National Fund and Keren ha-Yesod. The Jewish communities as well as Zionist and other groups protested to both the British and American embassies against England's negative attitude and policy towards Jewish immigration into Palestine. The Zionist organization also published a newsletter, *News from Israel*. Public meetings were organized when the Jewish State was proclaimed, and for the main anniversaries of the State of Israel (10, 20, 25, 30 years). Regular meetings of members of the Zionist Organization have not been frequent during the last 25 years. One of the most important activities has been the yearly drive of the United Jewish Appeal, organized by the local committees in Oslo and Trondheim. Trondheim had only 100–150 Jews in the 1950s. Zionist activities were conducted by a special committee of the Jewish Youth Club and then by the local appeal committee.

Women's Activities. A Jewish Women's Organization has existed in Oslo since 1913. In March, 1931, a WIZO group was established but it was not until 1937 that this group was organized as a Zionist organization and a member of International WIZO. This organization had its own committee for Jewish National Fund activities. Two years after its establishment, it had a membership of 75. In 1947, WIZO merged with the Jewish Women's Organization. In the years that followed the group sponsored meetings, fund-raising affairs, lectures, raffles, and collections of clothing. In 1957 WIZO embarked on a campaign to support youth institutions in Israel. WIZO holds an annual bazaar in aid of other WIZO activities in Israel. In 1976 a youth group, Aviv, was formed as part of the WIZO organization.

WIZO in Trondheim started in the late 1920s as the Kedimah club for young women. In 1934 they began actively to support Zionist activities, and took the name WIZO Kedimah. The following year they joined International

WIZO. After World War II this group merged with the local Jewish Women's Organization, founded in 1919. Its members did much in the post-war period to help Jewish refugees in central Europe and also to support Norwegian humanitarian institutions. First and foremost, however its efforts were directed in behalf of welfare in Israel, primarily support for the Amar home for tuberculosis patients. Trondheim WIZO has also been involved in information campaigns on Zionism and Israel, as well as on Judaism. In the early 1980s a non-Jewish Zionist group was founded.

Support of Youth Aliya. Money for Youth Aliya was collected in Trondheim in 1934–36 on a personal basis, while in Oslo an organization was established for this activity. In 1955 "Norwegian—Israeli Aid to Children" was formed. In 1964 it received a large legacy to be used in its work.

Between 1949–50, the Norwegian European Aid, in cooperation with Jewish organizations, established Camp Grefsrud near Holmestrand 60 mi. (100 km.) south of Oslo. Altogether about 400 children, most of them originally from Morocco, were sheltered for eight-month periods and trained for immigration to Israel by Norwegian and Israeli teachers. When in the fall of 1949 a plane bringing Jewish children to Norway crashed over Norwegian territory killing 27 of the 28 children aboard as well as the whole crew and the social workers, the Norwegian newspaper *Arbeiderbladet* launched a nationwide non-sectarian collection campaign to found a "Norwegian" village in Israel. The proceeds (about $100,000, including $29,000 from American Jews) were used to build moshav Norvegia, where the only survivor from the plane-crash settled. At the site of the accident, boy scouts raised a memorial in 1961.

Friends of the Hebrew University of Jerusalem. The Norwegian branch of the Friends of the Hebrew University was founded in the late 1930s. It was reestablished after the war in 1977. A Norwegian-Israeli Research Fund was also founded to provide scholarships for Norwegians to study and pursue research at the university in Jerusalem and for Israeli scholars to study in Norway and to support the work of the Hebrew University. There is also a committee supporting Tel Aviv University.

Israeli exhibitions of various types have been arranged in Norway. In addition there have been guest lectures, visits by Israeli artists, exchanges of artists and concerts as well as dance performances, much of this as part of the cultural agreement between Norway and Israel.

Other Norwegian-Israeli Organizations. The Norge-Israel (Norway-Israel) society was founded in November, 1948, to promote understanding, friendship, and cultural exchange between the two countries. In the mid-1970s a new organization was established, Med Israel For Fred, MIFF (With Israel for Peace) in order to disseminate information about Israel and counter anti-Zionist and anti-Israel propaganda in Norway. MIFF has some local subdivisions.

At the outbreak of the Six-Day War La Israel Leve (Let Israel live) was organized to bring material aid to Israel. Other organizations include the Norwegian branch of the friendship organization for the Jewish Institute for the Blind in Jerusalem and for the Sha'arei Zedek Hospital in Jerusalem.

Immigration. The first Jewish family from Norway settled in Palestine in spring 1937. Since World War II about 50 have settled in Israel in addition to two groups (comprising 150–200 people) of "displaced persons" who had moved to Norway from camps in Germany in 1947 and immigrated to Israel in 1948–49. O. MENDELSOHN

NORWEGIAN JEWS IN ISRAEL. *See* SCANDINAVIAN JEWS IN ISRAEL.

NOSSIG, ALFRED. Writer, publicist, sculptor, and active Zionist in Germany (b. Lvov, Galicia, Austria, 1865; d. Warsaw, 1943). Nossig's Jewish journalistic activities began in his teens when he was the editor of *Ojczyzna* (Homeland), the organ of the movement for Polish-Jewish assimilation. He gradually lost hope in the success of assimilation and turned to Zionism. In 1887 he published his *Essay on the Solution of the Jewish Problem,"* which advocated the establishment of a Jewish State. In 1902 he founded in Berlin the Society for Jewish Statistics. A delegate to the Sixth Zionist Congress (1903), at which the East Africa scheme was debated, Nossig opposed Herzl's policies. Later he left the Zionist Organization, and developed a new approach to Zionism—"integral Zionism"—which assumed responsibility for the Jewish people as a whole.

In 1909 he founded the General Jewish Colonization Organization in Berlin to promote the agricultural settlement of Jews in Eretz Israel, Syria, and the Sinai Peninsula on a humanitarian, nonpolitical basis. In 1919 he published a German pamphlet, *On the Solution of the Palestine Problem: Recommendations to the Peace Conference and to the League of Nations.* He subsequently engaged in world peace propaganda, and in 1928 he founded a Jewish branch of the Peace Federation of the Religions. He was killed in 1943 by Jewish partisans in the Warsaw ghetto for alleged collaboration with the Nazis.

Among Nossig's Zionist-oriented writings were *Das Jüdische Kolonisationsprogramm* (The Jewish Colonization Program, 1904), *Die Entwicklung des Zionismus* (The Development of Zionism, 1905), *Jüdische Realpolitik* (Practical Jewish Politics, 1907), and *Jüdische Landpolitik* (Jewish Land Policies, 1907). His other writings deal with politics, philosophy, and the social sciences. Most of his sculptures had biblical and Jewish themes.

Noterim guarding kibbutz En ha-Kore, 1945. [Central Zionist Archives]

NOTERIM (Guardsmen). Jewish Supernumerary Police recruited by the British in Palestine for defense duties during the Arab riots of 1936–39. They were also known by the

Arabic name Ghaffirim. At a later stage, the British organized the Noterim into the Jewish Settlement Police, which had its own mobile units. Other Noterim served as temporary policemen guarding the Iraq Petroleum Company pipelines, the lines of the Palestine Electric Corporation, railways, army supply depots, etc. In addition, the Jewish Supernumerary Police defended Jewish settlements, guarded lines of communication, and struck at Arab terrorists. By the end of the Arab terror in 1939 there were about 22,000 Jewish Supernumerary Police, including 14,000 part-time reservists who were liable to draft in case of need.

The Noterim, who were recruited through the offices of the Jewish Agency, were mostly members of Hagana. Though they were under British command, they also acted on secret orders of the undercover Jewish defense body.

NOTZERAT. *See* NAZARETH.

NOVOMEYSKY, MOSHE. Chemist, industrialist, engineer, and founder of the Dead Sea Works Company, Ltd. (b. Barguzin, Siberia, 1873; d. Paris, 1961). After graduating from the Technical High School in Irkutsk, Novomeysky went to Germany, where he attended the Royal Academy of Mines in Clausthal, the Technische Hochschule in Berlin, and Heidelberg University. Returning to his native Siberia, he pioneered in the exploitation of mineral resources. His contacts with political exiles in Siberia led him to join the Social Revolutionary party, but he soon became interested in Zionism. In 1906 he met in Berlin with Otto Warburg, the botanist and Zionist leader, to consult on professional matters. On that occasion Warburg showed him analyses made of the waters of the Dead Sea by a German geologist, Max Blanckenhorn, who had undertaken the research in Eretz Israel at the invitation of Herzl. These analyses interested Novomeysky in connection with his own efforts to extract minerals from the waters of Siberian lakes. In 1911 he first visited Eretz Israel, taking back with him to Russia samples from the Dead Sea waters for further analysis in his laboratory.

In 1920 he settled in Palestine. That year he got in touch with Sir Herbert Samuel, High Commissioner for Palestine, with a view to obtaining a franchise to operate a chemical plant near the Dead Sea. In 1921 he presented his plan to the British government. After eight years of struggle with the British Colonial Office and visits to England and the United States to raise funds, Novomeysky obtained (May, 1929) a 75-year franchise for Palestine Potash Ltd., which eventually became the Dead Sea Works Company. He served as managing director of this enterprise until it was taken over by the Israeli government. He then became honorary president. During the last years of his life he devoted much of his time to the building of a youth center for underprivileged children. He also published his autobiography in two volumes, *My Siberian Life* (1956) and *Given to Salt: The Struggle for the Dead Sea Concession* (1958). These two volumes were published in a Hebrew translation in 1958.

G. HIRSCHLER

NUDEL, IDA. Aliya activist in the USSR (b. Crimea, South Ukraine, 1931). She was trained in Moscow as an economist. Impressed by the Six-Day War, and the Leningrad trial of 1970, Ida along with her sister Elena and Elena's family, decided to immigrate to Israel and applied for exit visas in 1971. Elena, Ida's only relative, was permitted to go, while Ida was refused for "knowing state secrets". (She worked as an accountant in a non-secret planning institution). Nudel was dismissed from her job. Over the years she became highly active in the Jewish emigration movement and became known as the "guardian angel" of Jewish prisoners and their families. She corresponded regularly with the prisoners, visited camps, prisons, and transport points, sent them parcels of food, medicine, and books, and made representations on their behalf to camp administrations and to the authorities in Moscow. Through demonstrations, correspondence, and frequent meetings with foreigners visiting Moscow, she regularly exposed to the world public the violations of the prisoners' rights. Because of her activities, Nudel was frequently subjected to police harassment, being arrested and detained on numerous occasions. Several times she was physically abused. She was often placed under house arrest and her apartment searched and personal belongings confiscated, including a detailed file on all Jewish prisoners of conscience and their families which she had painstakingly compiled over the years.

On 1 June 1978 Nudel displayed a banner on the balcony of her apartment stating: KGB—GIVE ME MY EXIT VISA! She was put on trial on charges of "malicious hooliganism" and sentenced to four years of exile in Siberia. In Siberia she suffered immeasurable hardship, and after her release in 1982 had to drift from one refusenik home to another, as she was persistently refused the right of residence in the major cities. Eventually, she was allowed to settle in Bendery, Moldavia, which she was not permitted to leave. She said at the time: "I am fortunate because I add a page to the history of Jewish resistance, because my efforts have helped thousands of Jews to leave this barbarous country, because I have helped Prisoners of Zion to keep their spirit and survive in the hell which you cannot imagine. I know I must pay for this fortune in full. No matter how I am tormented, how weak I am, how lonely or senseless my present life, I do not regret or renounce any of my actions."

Ida Nudel was supported internationally by public figures, women's organizations, and personalities like actresses Jane Fonda (who visited Nudel in her Bendery exile), and Liv Ullmann (who starred in a film about her). On 2 October 1987 Ida Nudel was informed that she had been granted an exit permit. On 15 October, Nudel was welcomed by thousands of Israelis, including the country's leaders, at Ben-Gurion airport. She settled in Rehovot, near her sister.

Y. STERN

NUROCK, MORDEKHAI. Rabbi, religious Zionist leader, legislator, and Israeli statesman (b. Tukums, Latvia, 1884; d. Tel Aviv, 1962). Nurock was active from early youth in Jewish public affairs. He represented the Mizrachi movement at the Sixth Zionist Congress (1903) and participated in every Zionist Congress from 1921 on.

Before World War I Nurock was Chief Rabbi of Latvia. After the expulsion of the Jews from Latvia during the war he settled in Moscow, where he became active in Jewish political and social work. Returning to Latvia in 1921, he became a leader of Latvian Jewry and chairman of Latvian Mizrachi. From 1923, he was a member of the Zionist Actions Committee. In 1922 he was elected to the Latvian parliament, in which he served until its dissolution in 1934. After the annexation of Latvia by the USSR during World

War II, he was arrested (1941) by the Soviet authorities for his Zionist activities and imprisoned in Turkestan for 14 months. In the meantime the Nazis invaded Latvia, killing Nurock's entire family.

Settling in Palestine in 1947, he was elected to the Knesset in 1949, representing Mizrachi there until his death. Late in 1952 he was appointed Israel's first Minister of Posts, serving for one month. After the death of Chaim Weizmann that year, he was a leading contender fro the Presidency of Israel, receiving 40 votes to Itzhak Ben-Zvi's 62 on the final ballot.

NUSSBAUM, MAX. Rabbi and Zionist leader in the United States (b. Suceava, Bukovina, Austria, 1910; d. Hollywood, California, 1974). A graduate of the Jewish Theological Seminary of Breslau, he served as a rabbi in Berlin. After his arrival in the United States in 1940, he held a pulpit in Oklahoma and, in 1942, was appointed rabbi of Temple Israel in Hollywood, Calif. He became active in the American Zionist movement, attended several Zionist Congresses, and from 1962 to 1965 was president of the Zionist Organization of America. His associations with general and Jewish organizations included the vice-presidency of the American Jewish Congress, the chairmanship of the North American section of the World Jewish Congress, and membership on the Board of Governors of the State of Israel Bonds Organization and the Board of Directors of the United Jewish Appeal. In 1965 he became a member of the Zionist Actions Committee. His services as a Zionist speaker were in considerable demand.

NUSSENBLATT, TULO. Historian of Zionism (b. Stry, Galicia, Austria, 1895; d. Poland, 1941). Nussenblatt studied law at the University of Vienna and served as an officer in the Austro-Hungarian Army during World War I. In the 1920s he turned to writing and research on Herzl. His articles appeared in *Die Neue Welt, Die Stimme* (the official Zionist organ of Vienna), the Polish-Jewish dailies *Chwila* (Lvov), *Nowy Dziennik* (Cracow), and *Nasz Przeglad* (Warsaw), and other newspapers. When Moriz Reichenfeld (a relative of Herzl's wife) and Johann Kremenetzky, the executors of Herzl's will, founded the Herzl Archives in Vienna, Nussenblatt, with Adolf Böhm, Victor Kellner of the Chajes Gymnasium. Emil Krasny of the Zionist student union Ivria, and Oskar Grünbaum of the Zionist Federation of Austria, formed a committee to superintend the archives. Before the outbreak of World War II, the material of the Herzl Archives was transferred to the Central Archives in Jerusalem.

Nussenblatt published three books, *Zeitgenossen über Herzl* (Herzl through the Eyes of His Contemporaries, 1929), *Ein Volk unterwegs zum Frieden* (A People on the Way to Peace, 1933), and *Theodor Herzl Jahrbuch* (Theodor Herzl Yearbook, 1937), in which he included Herzl's literary testament and the unpublished material of several writers. He worked for the establishment of a Herzl institute and the production of a film on the life and work of Herzl, and he was preparing a second anthology of all Herzl's articles, comments, and speeches that had been published in *Die Welt* when the Nazis annexed Austria in March, 1938, and he was forced to go to Poland. In the Warsaw ghetto after the Nazi occupation, Nussenblatt participated actively in a cultural committee. He was murdered in a concentration camp.

J. FRAENKEL

O

ODESSA COMMITTEE. Executive body of the *Hovevei Zion (Lovers of Zion). The *Kattowitz Conference (1884) of the Hovevei Zion decided to establish a temporary Central Committee, headed by Leo *Pinsker, and resolved to ask the Tsarist Russian government to license the activities of the Montefiore Association for the support of Jewish settlement in Eretz Israel. For a number of years the Central Committee, which had its seat in Odessa, had to conduct its activities illegally, since the authorities refused to issue an official permit for its operation. In 1890, after endeavors in this direction had finally met with success, a Society for the Support of Jewish Agriculturalists and Artisans in Eretz Israel and Syria was founded. The statutes did not permit the establishment of branches outside Odessa. For this reason, representatives of the 26 Hovevei Zion societies then existing met prior to the first general meeting of the new society to plan its future activities. The first official general meeting of the society, held on 27 April 1890, elected an Executive Committee. As an indication that the new committee would continue the work of the former illegal body, Pinsker consented to serve as its chairman.

General Conference of the Society to support Farmers and Artisans in the Holy Land, held in Odessa, 1890. [Jewish National and University Library]

In the beginning the activities of the new committee proved successful. Membership and income were steadily increasing, as was emigration to Eretz Israel. Settlement societies were founded. The Jaffa Executive of the Odessa Committee, headed by Vladimir *Tiomkin, engaged in widespread activity. In the summer of 1891, however, immigration and settlement suffered a series of crises. The Jaffa Executive, having over-extended itself in the disbursement of funds, went bankrupt. Tiomkin was replaced by another representative of the Odessa Committee, who acted in accordance with instructions he received from the committee. The activities of the committee were directed toward the consolidation of economically weak settlements (Gedera, Mishmar ha-Yarden, etc.), the establishment of new settlements, and the setting up of auxiliary farms for workers. The committee also gave support to Hebrew education, encouraged handicrafts, and provided low-interest loans for settlers. After the death of Pinsker in 1891, Abraham Grünberg was chosen chairman of the Odessa Committee. He was succeeded in 1906 by Menahem M. *Ussishkin, who served in this capacity until the liquidation of the committee's activities following the Communist Revolution in November, 1917.

Since the Odessa Committee could not carry on all the activities of the Russian Hovevei Zion, the Merkaz Ruhani (Spiritual Center) was founded in 1893. This body, which was headed by Rabbi Shemuel *Mohilever, engaged in a variety of activities, including propaganda campaigns and the planting of a citrus grove in Eretz Israel for the export of etrogim (citrons), but did not assume an important place in the movement.

The Odessa Committee established a fund to assist Jewish workers in Eretz Israel. After 10 years of activity, it decided to change its approach and support only institutions and public needs, not private individuals. In 1903 the committee sent to Eretz Israel a delegation led by Ussishkin. This delegation convened a conference of representatives from all settlements at Zikhron Ya'akov, at which the formation of a central body for Jews in the country was approved. At the same time and place, a conference of Hebrew teachers was held which laid the foundations for the Hebrew Teachers' Association of Eretz Israel.

The widespread activities of the committee included the opening of information offices in Odessa, Constantinople,

Jaffa, Beirut, and elsewhere and the establishment, in cooperation with the Anglo-Palestine Bank (*see* BANK LE'UMI LE ISRAEL), of a credit institution which issued loans at low interest rates. The committee also participated in the development of Jerusalem and its environs (it acquired the land of Kefar Uriya), established workers' settlements near Jewish settlements (Be'er Ya'akov, near Rishon le-Zion), helped the Jewish watchmen's organization Ha-Shomer, sent propagandists all over Russia, and published books on the Hibbat Zion movement. In addition, it arranged the transfer of funds to Eretz Israel during World War I.

The average yearly membership of the Society for the Support of Jewish Agriculturalists and Artisans in Eretz Israel and Syria was about 5,200 (4,893 in 1890 and 2,724 in 1892, the year of the crisis; later, the number increased again). At its peak the society had a yearly income of 50,000 rubles. I. KLAUSNER

OFAKIM. Development town, with municipal status, in the northern Negev, 15 miles (25 km.) northwest of Beersheba. Ofakim was founded in 1955 as a regional center for the Merhavim region. The majority of the settlers came from North African countries. Industrial enterprises opened in the 1960s, only partly succeeded and were later replaced by others. The proximity of two other development towns, Sederot and Netivot, proved an impediment to progress. Unemployment, initially high, was temporarily overcome but again became a problem in the late 1980s. Population (1988), 13,400. E. ORNI

OHEL THEATER. *See* THEATER IN ISRAEL.

OIL PRODUCTION IN ISRAEL. *See* MINERAL RESOURCES AND MINING IN ISRAEL.

OLD-NEW LAND (Altneuland). Utopian novel interspersed with romantic interludes and graphic vignettes, written by Theodor *Herzl during the years 1899–1902. The author's objectives were to arouse the Jewish people and make them fully aware that Zionism was a practical movement, to inspire his followers with a prophetic vision of the future Jewish polity that would arise in Eretz Israel, and to leave for posterity a belletristic testament in which he could commemorate his friends as well as his opponents.

The characters appear wooden in spite of the fact that Herzl drew most of the dramatis personae from his own milieu. Thus the hero, Friedrich Loewenberg, is a composite figure of the author and his ill-starred friend Heinrich Kana. Similarly, Professor Eichenstamm, the first president of Old-New Land, is a prototype of Dr. Max E. *Mandelstamm, a noted oculist. Eichenstamm's successor, David Littwak, is modeled on David *Wolffsohn, who became the second president of the World Zionist Organization. The eccentric Steineck brothers, doyens of the technological revolution that transfigures Old-New Land, are identical with the Viennese architect Oskar *Marmorek and his brother, the eminent bacteriologist Alexander *Marmorek. Under other paraphrased names, Herzl also sketched Joseph *Cowen, a London businessman, Jozef Israels, the famous painter, his own sister Pauline, and many lesser-known persons.

The central theme of *Old-New Land* is systematically developed. Projecting 20 years in time to the spring of 1923, Herzl delineates the creation, by the Jews, of a model society in the Holy Land. Believing that the traditional political national state was moribund, he depicted a commonwealth directed by a giant cooperative association called the New Society. Through the utilization of modern technology and the application of the cooperative method to the production and distribution of goods, the New Society had successfully created a flourishing economy and reared a new civilization.

Herzl envisaged a settlement company dedicated to removing the Jews from Europe and elsewhere to a territory of their own. The company, a joint stock corporation, had successfully negotiated with the Turkish government for a political *Charter granting the Jews autonomous rights in Palestine. In exchange the Turks had received £2,000,000. In addition, they had retained ultimate sovereignty over the territory and were guaranteed annual payments of £50,000 for 30 years, plus one-fourth of the net annual profits of the settlement company or its successor. At the expiration of 30 years the net profits of the company were to be shared equally with the Turkish regime. If this arrangement proved unsatisfactory, the latter could select an alternative financial plan and receive instead a permanent annual tribute.

Immediately after gaining the Charter the company had launched an intensive propaganda campaign to prepare the Jewish masses for immigration. Simultaneously it negotiated with various governments for the safe exodus of their Jewish populations and for the liquidation of their assets. The company had then purchased property in Palestine, mobilized the necessary transport, and rapidly conveyed and settled Jewish immigrants in the newly acquired lands. When the settlements had become established, the company gradually relinquished its authority to a new structure, the New Society, formed by the settlers. The latter, a giant cooperative association, took over the capital, machinery, and responsibilities of the pioneer joint stock corporation.

The New Society considered itself a commonwealth. Its governmental apparatus included a Congress, a president, a board of directors, a managing director, and various departments. The 400 members of the Congress, or, to be more accurate, the delegates of the cooperative associations that composed the New Society, met for only a few weeks during each year and were chosen by periodic general elections. All constituents of the New Society were entitled to the franchise. Membership in the giant cooperative was open to any adult who had shown a sense of social responsibility by devoting two years of nonmilitary service to the commonwealth. Every seven years the Congress chose a president of the New Society. Candidates for this purely ceremonial office were nominated from among those individuals who had distinguished themselves in the service of the commonwealth.

Since the Congress was rarely in session, the day-by-day management of the New Society was entrusted to a board of directors. This board, created by each Congress before adjournment, carried out the mandates of the parent body. At the head of this executive group sat the director of the New Society, who was selected by the board, which then served as his cabinet. Each member of the board functioned as a minister heading one or more of the various departments that guided the economic and cultural life of the commonwealth.

The commonwealth was firmly founded upon modern technology. An elaborate watershed control system had been introduced to provide water for consumption and irrigation. A canal had been dug to join the Mediterranean to the Dead Sea. The 1,300-foot difference in levels between these two bodies of water had been harnessed to generate electric power. Industries had arisen along the banks of the canal, and the Dead Sea area had become a thriving industrial chemical center. Technological know-how, cooperative organization, and town planning had produced cities with distinctive characteristics. Haifa had become a bustling cosmopolitan seaport, and its residential area on Mount Carmel a thriving suburb. The Old City of Jerusalem had been preserved as a museum, and the new city had been developed into a prosperous modern metropolis. Tiberias had become a resort world-famous for its hot springs, and Jericho a popular winter vacation spot.

The second tenet guiding Old-New Land involved the application of the cooperative principle to every facet of economic life. Herzl's portrayal indicated a novel system, an intermediary form spanning capitalism and socialism which he called mutualism. Only mutualism, he believed, could allow private property to exist, and ensure that the individualist was "neither ground between the millstones of capitalism, nor decapitated by socialistic leveling...."

In its quest for the good life and social justice the New Society had introduced far-reaching land, welfare, labor, educational, and penal reforms, emancipated women, abolished military establishments, and repudiated religious and racial intolerance. Although the New Society was a Jewish entity, it did not bar other people from its organization or deny them the bounties of the land. Throughout the commonwealth's cities, towns, and countryside foreigners from every point on the globe and of every faith and creed—Christians, Moslems, Buddhists, and Hindus—rubbed shoulders with the Jewish majority and followed their respective pursuits and practiced their religious beliefs unmolested.

The humanitarian aspects of the New Society were best exemplified by many of its institutions. Outstanding in this respect were the Steineck Institute, the Jewish Academy, and the Peace Palace. Herzl fashioned the Steineck Institute after the Pasteur Institute of Paris. However, the Steineck Institute was more than a research center for the investigation of virulent contagious diseases. An integral part of the commonwealth's economy, it also used its resources to foster new industrial and agricultural techniques, and to devise products that would benefit all mankind. The Jewish Academy was patterned after the French Academy and its "40 immortals." Unlike the latter, however, Herzl's model was completely free of chauvinism, favoritism, and politics. The Peace Palace was, as its name suggested, primarily an institution consecrated to peace. What Herzl had in mind was a focal point for international cooperation on a permanent basis and not in terms of a special conference, so common in his day, called to resolve a particular knotty problem.

Although *Old-New Land* was Herzl's literary legacy to his faith in Zionism, it was not well received in many quarters. Some former Hovevei Zion, religious, and Socialist Zionists rejected his concept of a balanced industrial-agricultural economy. They were convinced that the Jews could only be redeemed by a return to the soil of Palestine and by the creation of a traditional type of peasantry. The severest criticism came from followers of Ahad Ha-Am. They saw nothing in the novel to encourage a renaissance of Jewish culture. It was, they believed, a work permeated with the spirit of western civilization and devoid of true Jewish content.

Nevertheless, despite the serious ideological, cultural, and literary flaws inherent in *Old-New Land*, its importance outlasted the censures of its detractors. Translated into many tongues and widely read, the book became a symbol of hope for succeeding Zionist generations. It provided them in dramatic and vivid form with the knowledge that the national redemption of Jewry in the Holy Land was not only possible but inevitable, for "... if you will it, it is no fable." J. ADLER

OLIPHANT, LAURENCE. British journalist, adventurer, and supporter of the return of the Jewish people to the Land of Israel (b. Cape Town, 1829; d. Twickenham, near London, 1888). After serving as a correspondent for the London *Times* in the Crimean and Franco-Prussian Wars and being involved for two years with the Brotherhood of the New Life in New York State (a group founded by the American mystic Thomas Lake Harris), Oliphant became an advocate of the return of the Jews to Eretz Israel. In 1878 he wrote to Prime Minister Lord Beaconsfield (Benjamin Disraeli) and other leading British public figures, urging the establishment of a Palestine development company under British auspices. In 1879 he left for Eretz Israel with official backing in search of a suitable site for his proposed settlement. Choosing the Gilead region in Transjordan, he started negotiations with the Turkish sultan but made no headway.

Oliphant visited eastern Europe, where he came in contact with Jewish leaders and the Jewish masses and propagated the idea of Jewish settlement in Eretz Israel. In 1882 he settled in Haifa with his secretary, Naftali Herz Imber, the author of "Ha-Tikva," assisting early Jewish settlers, writing articles on Jewish settlement, and maintaining correspondence with organizations and individuals in many countries. His writings included *Land of Gilead* (1880), and *Haifa, or Life in Modern Palestine* (1887), H. PINNER

OLSHAN, YITZHAK. Israeli jurist (b. Kovno, Lithuania, 1895; d. Jerusalem 1983). He settled in Eretz Israel in 1912 as a student at the Herzliya High School, and served in the Palestine Jewish Legion from 1918 to 1921. He was one of the founders of Hagana and from 1921 to 1923 was commander of the Tel Aviv-Jaffa district. After teaching school in Hadera for a time, he went to England to study at the University of London, where he received degrees in oriental studies (1924) and law (1927). While in London, he was liaison officer between the Histadrut and the British Labor party (1923–27) and secretary of the British Po'ale Zion (1924–27).

Returning to Palestine in 1927, he joined the law office of Mordecai Eliash in Jerusalem. He remained in private law practice until 1948, when he was appointed as one of the original five justices of Israel's Supreme Court. In 1953 he became Chief Justice, a position he held until his retirement in 1965.

OLSWANGER, EMANUEL (Immanuel Olsvanger). Folklorist, linguist, translator, and Zionist activist (b. Grajewo, Russian Poland, 1888; d. Jerusalem, 1961). Olswanger studied at the University of Königsberg, East Prussia, and received his doctorate from the University of Berne in 1916. In 1921 he joined the staff of Keren ha-Yesod, becoming a traveling lecturer for that organization and for the Zionist movement. His lecture tours took him to England, Romania, Hungary, South Africa, and remoter places such as India, Burma, and Singapore. In 1930 he settled in Palestine and joined the staff of Keren ha-Yesod in Jerusalem.

Olswanger won the 1946 Tschernichowsky Award for his translation of Dante's *Divine Comedy* into Hebrew. He also translated into Hebrew tales from Boccaccio's *Decameron*, the writings of the Chinese sage Fu Hsi, and a collection of Indian poetry. He wrote numerous anthologies in Yiddish, several volumes of Hebrew poetry, a Hebrew play, and a volume of poetry in Esperanto.

OMER. Suburban settlement in the northern Negev north of Beersheba. Founded in 1949 as an outpost confronting the armistice line of those days, it was at first a moshav, but later turned into a garden suburb with an academic and middle-class population, numbering 5,680 inhabitants in 1987. The name means "Sheaf of Grain." E. ORNI

Open University Headquarters, Tel Aviv. [Open University]

OPEN UNIVERSITY OF ISRAEL, THE (Everyman's University). Home study university established in 1974 by the Rothschild Foundation, in coordination with the government of Israel, in order to enable students to pursue a higher education without interfering with their professional or family obligations. The University, authorized by the Israel Council of Higher Education to confer B.A. degrees, offers a home study academic program, supplemented by tutorial sessions in its 35 regional study centers throughout the country, as well as by television and radio broadcasts, cassette tape recordings home laboratory kits, computers, and a broad spectrum of other educational aids.

The Open University, whose headquarters are in Tel Aviv, has a student enrollment of 12,000 students per semester, and offers about 200 courses in the fields of Natural Sciences, Life Sciences, Mathematics, Computer Studies, Social Sciences, Business Administration, Humanities, Education, Jewish History, and the Arts. The university prepares written textbooks expressly designed for self-study, and publishes 450,000 bound books annually, 200,000 of them purchased independently of course requirements.

The university's teaching method is designed to overcome the constraints of distance and time which constitute obstacles to many potentially capable students. It thus affords the opportunity of academic studies to people living in outlying and development towns far from conventional university centers. Kibbutz members constitute 10% of the university's student body, and soldiers on active duty while studying account for 12% of the enrollment. A further 16% are teachers, educators, and school principals seeking to attain a bachelor's degree and upgrade their own level of education.

Special study groups with additional and intensive tutorial guidance have been formed within the framework of Project Renewal communities and the Histadrut in order to assist these populations in their quest for self-improvement. They are also offered a pre-academic preparatory program as many of them lack a strong educational background and have been detached from a study framework for many years. Group programs are also organized in banks, in the Israeli military industries, and a variety of other frameworks, 350 tutors throughout the country supervise their studies and are available in tutorial sessions or by telephone contact.

In addition to its academic degree programs, the Open University offers varied professional programs, such as a technical engineering program in its School of Technology, continuing education in management in its Enrichment and Continuing Studies Program, and language studies in English, French, Spanish, Arabic, and Hebrew in its School of Languages. The University has also prepared Judaic Studies textbooks in English and Spanish which are used in Jewish communities all over the world.

OPERATION EZRA AND NEHEMIAH. Codename of the operation bringing Iraqi Jews to Israel beginning May, 1950. The operation was named for the Prophets Ezra and Nehemiah who headed the first return to Zion from Babylonia (i.e., Iraq) 2,500 years earlier.

The 130,000 strong Jewish community in Iraq had suffered greatly prior to this operation. Its recent history was paved with upheavals and vacillations which included anti-Jewish decrees, attacks, insults, restrictions, arrests, confiscation of property and pogroms which reached a climax in May-June, 1941, with the rise to power of Rashid Ali, who was allied with Nazi Germany. The slaughter in Baghdad on that occasion left 180 dead and several hundred wounded.

This pogrom and the continued harassment of the Jewish community, along with the struggle of the Zionist movement and the support of the Jewish community in Palestine, strengthened the determination of Iraqi Jewish youth to defend itself. A He-Halutz branch and youth organizations of various types were established, and in 1942 the Hagana organization was founded. The restrictions imposed on Jews wishing to leave Iraq for Israel forced thousands during 1949 and the beginning of 1950 to cross the border illegally into Iran and make their way from there to Israel.

In March, 1950, the Iraqi parliament passed a law granting permission to those Jews wishing to leave the country to do so within one year. The citizenship of those leaving was

Jews waiting at Baghdad registration point to waive Iraqi citizenship prior to immigration to Israel, 1950. [Beth Hatefutsoth].

canceled and their property confiscated. They were allowed to take out of Iraq 50 dinars ($140) for each adult and half of that amount for each child, as well as 66 lbs. (30 kgs), personal baggage per person, but no jewelry. The decree passed by the Iraqi parliament led to varying appraisals of the situation on the part of the emissaries operating in Iraq, as well as among the relevant institutions in Israel. The optimists claimed that 70,000 Iraqi Jews would want to emigrate to Israel. The pace of registration for passports and exit permits increased rapidly and even surpassed this estimate. Up to the end of the allotted period, 105,000 Jews had registered for immigration to Israel, and when the final date was extended by a few months, a further 20,000 Jews left.

The task of airlifting these immigrants was undertaken by the same Near East Air Transport Company which had carried out *Operation Magic Carpet from Aden. On 19 May 1950 the first airplane left Baghdad with emigrants. The Iraqi government insisted that they not be flown directly to Israel, but to a "neutral" country. Thus the planes were forced to extend their flights and touch down in Nicosia, Cyprus, and only then continue to Israel. About one-third of the Iraqi immigrants came by this route. Some time later the Iraqi officials waived this proviso of landing in Cyprus and the planes were permitted to fly directly to Lydda.

Up to the end of 1950, 26,757 Jews left Iraq and in 1951 another 89,205 emigrated. In early 1952 the Operation still continued, but during this period only a few isolated planeloads arrived.

In the "illegal" immigration from Iraq which came mainly through Iran, 1,700 Jews arrived in 1949, and in 1950 (up to May) a further 6,000. During this period, then, (1949–51) 123.000 Jews immigrated to Israel from Iraq and with the end of the Operation at the beginning of 1952 only 6,000 Jews remained behind. The majority of them later left. Only 300 stayed.

Y. DOMINITZ

OPERATION MAGIC CARPET (or "On Eagles' Wings"). Codename given to the airlift operation which brought the Jews of Yemen to Israel during 1949–50. The immigration of Yemenite Jews to the Holy Land in modern times began concurrently with or somewhat earlier than the immigration of the Biluim, in 1881. Subsequently, *Yemenite Jews continued to come in small or large groups, motivated by their yearning for redemption and the desire to return to Zion. By 1919 over 40,000 Yemenite Jews were living in Palestine, constituting 7.6% of the population and during the British Mandate a further 15,000 arrived. They traveled to the British Protectorate of Aden and from there through the Suez Canal to Egypt and on to Palestine.

The struggle of the Jewish community in Palestine against the British authorities, the UN decision on partition in 1947, and the Israel War of Independence all had repercussions on Yemenite Jewry. During 1946–47 there was a dire shortage of immigration certificates and very few were allocated to Yemenite Jews. In the Aden Protectorate Jews were persecuted and pogroms took a toll of several score victims; thousands of Yemenite Jews, who had come to Aden on their way to Palestine, were stranded there and unable to continue. The situation was tackled in various ways. Provisions were made for the thousands of Jews who had come to Aden, camps were set up, food, clothing and medical attention provided and arrangements made for them to leave Aden for Israel.

The Jewish Agency and the Joint Distribution Committee undertook this project and coordinated both assistance for the Jews in the camps and flights to Israel.

The first part of the Magic Carpet operation began in December, 1948, and within four months, 55 flights were carried out to alleviate the most urgent situation of the 7,000 Jews stranded in Aden. Their emigration to Israel brought in its wake a new wave of mass exodus from Yemen to Aden. This was preceded by negotiations which led to permission being granted by the Imam of Yemen for Jews to leave the country; arrangements were also made with the authorities through whose territories the Jews had to pass en route to Aden.

The main phase of the operation began in May, 1949. That year 35,000 Yemenite Jews reached Israel. In 1950 over 9,000 immigrants arrived and on 24 September 1950 Operation Magic Carpet officially came to an end with the arrival at Lydda of two planes from Aden with 177 Yemenite Jews on board.

Within the framework of this airlift operation a total of 430 flights were made, at first with American Alaska Airlines and during the main period with the Near East Air Transport Company, bringing 49,000 Jews, including some 1,800 residents of Aden and a further 400 from Djibouti and Asmara.

At the end of the operation some 3,000 Jews remained in Yemen. Over half of these immigrated to Israel in small groups by the early 1960s, and it is estimated that about 1,000 Jews are still living there. The political upheavals that have taken place in Yemen and in Aden have impeded further contacts with the remainder of the community.

Y. DOMINITZ

OPERATION MOSES. *See* ETHIOPIAN JEWS IN ISRAEL.

OPERATION SOLOMON. Airlift bringing the remaining Jews of Ethiopia to Israel in May 1991. Prior to this date some 20,000 Ethiopian Jews had been airlifted to Israel from 1984 onwards ("Operation Moses"). As civil war raged in that country, almost all the Jews still in Ethiopia moved to Addis Ababa in the hope of being taken to Israel but problems with the Ethiopian dictator, Mengistu Haile Mariam

Yemenite Jews in plane taking them to Israel in 1949. [Zionist Archives]

delayed the transport of all but small groups. As the rebels closed in on Addis Ababa, Mengistu fled his country and the mass operation, which had been planned for a long time, was swiftly carried out before Addis Ababa was taken over. Within 24 hours, 14,400 Ethiopians were flown to Israel in an operation conducted by the Israel Defense Forces in coordination with the Israel government offices, the Jewish Agency and other bodies, as well as the Ethiopian government. On arrival, the newcomers were immediately transported to absorption centers around Israel. The number remaining in Ethiopia (mostly caught behind the rebel lines) was uncertain but it was thought to be at least 2–3,000 in addition to an undetermined number who had converted to Christianity but wished to be taken to Israel.

OPERATION YAKHIN. Codename of the operation, beginning in November, 1961, which brought the Jews of Morocco to Israel. It was preceded by many months of secret negotiations through various channels. At the end of these negotiations the phase began of bringing tens of thousands of Jews to Israel in an orderly manner, without the publically announced official agreement of the Moroccan authorities, but also without persecution or anti-Jewish decrees. Public activities fostering immigration to Israel were not given official permission, but potential immigrants and those processing them were not harassed.

Operation Yakhin was initiated as a result of unceasing efforts following the pressure of Jewish and general public opinion throughout the world which was shocked in January, 1961, by the sinking of the ship *Egoz* in the Straits of Gibraltar with 43 "illegal" immigrants on board. Despite this disaster the Jews of Morocco themselves continued to press for immigration to Israel, insisting that they were prepared to take any risk if they were not allowed to emigrate in a regular manner. It was a combination of pressure by the Jews of Morocco, general and Jewish public opinion, the nature of the specific negotiations and the political situation at the time—Morocco's internal problems as well as its external relations—which led to a change in the attitude of the authorities to the question of immigration to Israel. From November, 1961, until 1988, over 127,000 Jews immigrated to Israel from Morocco.

Two periods of immigration by Moroccan Jews had preceded Operation Yakhin. One was under French rule, up to

Refugees in Aden wait to board Operation Magic Carpet plane. [Zionist Archives]

June, 1956, and the other came after Morocco gained its independence (in June, 1956). While the French ruled Morocco, Jews were free to leave the country in theory, but in practice the French authorities placed obstacles in the way of Jews (and Europeans) wishing to leave, believing that they constituted a group whose loyalty was reliable. To these difficulties had to be added internal problems within the Jewish community: it was during this period that the authorities in Israel imposed the principle of "selection", which was in force during part of this period (1948-1955) so that not all the possibilities of immigration from Morocco were exploited. Immigration increased during 1955 (25,000) when Moroccan independence was imminent, and the fear that a curtain would be rung down on this Jewish community caused the relaxation of the selective immigration regulations.

The year 1956, when Morocco gained its independence and joined the Arab League, was the turning point. One of the first acts of the newly independent Moroccan government was to close down the Kadima offices of the Jewish Agency Immigration Department and the Kadima transit camp. The camp had become overcrowded; originally designed to provide accommodation for 1,500 persons, it was soon holding 9,000. After negotiations between representatives of the World Jewish Congress and the Moroccan security services, permission was granted for 6,300 Jews to leave the camp. 36,301 Jews eventually emigrated that year (1956) and this was followed by five years of "illegal" emigration by devious methods and routes, clandestine activities carried out under dangerous conditions for both the immigrants and the activists processing them.

When the State of Israel was established in 1948 there were 270,000 Jews in Morocco; by the end of 1988, 262,000 had immigrated to Israel. Some tens of thousands of Moroccan Jews settled in France. and Canada and in other countries. At the end of 1988 it was estimated that only about 12,000 Jews still remained in Morocco.

Y. DOMINITZ

OPPENHEIMER, FRANZ. Economist, sociologist, and

Zionist (b. Berlin, 1864; d. Los Angeles, 1943). Oppenheimer practiced medicine in Germany from 1886 until 1896, when he turned to the social sciences. In 1909 he became a lecturer in economics at the University of Berlin, and from 1919 to 1929 he served as professor of sociology and economic theory at the University of Frankfurt. With the advent of Nazism he left Germany and, in 1938, accepted a post at the University of Kobe, Japan. In 1940 he settled in Los Angeles.

Oppenheimer sought to link classical economic theory with agrarian Socialist thought. He believed that the cause of all social evil was to be found in the monopolization of the earth's soil by the upper classes. To destroy this monopoly he suggested a vast cooperative effort on the part of the lower classes. Agricultural producer cooperatives, he felt, could lead to the highest form of human association, the cooperative settlement.

Captivated by Oppenheimer's concepts, Herzl invited him to address the Sixth Zionist Congress (1903) on his ideas of cooperative settlement as applied to Jewish settlement in Eretz Israel. At that Congress Oppenheimer was elected to the Eretz Israel Commission. After gaining the support of Po'ale Zion leaders, Oppenheimer urged the Ninth Congress (1909) to realize his ideas. This resulted in the establishment in 1911 of an experimental cooperative settlement in *Merhavya. Though the experiment was not entirely successful, Oppenheimer's proposals exerted great influence on the development of the cooperative settlement movement in Palestine.

During World War I and thereafter, Oppenheimer fought against anti-Semitism in Germany. In 1917 he championed national autonomy rights for minority groups, especially for the Jews of eastern Europe. In 1926 he was sent to Palestine by the Zionist Executive to report on the cooperative settlements there.

In addition to the important sociological studies which Oppenheimer published from 1895 on and which established his reputation as an outstanding socioeconomic theorist, he wrote the following Zionistically oriented studies (all in German): *Cooperative Settlement in Eretz Israel* (1910), *Cooperative Colonization in Eretz Israel* (1914), *Communal and Private Landed Property* (1914) and *Merhavya: Cooperative Settlement in Eretz Israel* (1914). In addition, several articles included in his volume *Sociological Excursions* (1927) deal with Zionism.

J. ADLER

ORDER OF ANCIENT MACCABEANS. Society linked with the Zionist movement, organized in London in 1891. Its founder, Ephraim *Ish-Kishor, was among the first to rally to Herzl when he addressed his first public meeting in Whitechapel in July, 1896. In 1970, the order became part of the Zionist Federation of Great Britain and Ireland.

In 1897 Herbert *Bentwich, grand commander of the order organized a Maccabean pilgrimage to Palestine (6 April-14 May) in which 21 persons participated, among them Israel Zangwill and other leading young Jews in England. Under Bentwich's leadership the order, intended originally as an auxiliary of the Zionist Federation of Great Britain and Ireland, developed into a rival of the federation. It grew to a size that enabled it to apply to the Executive of the World Zionist Organization for formal recognition as a separate union independent of the Zionist Federation. Although the federation refused to acknowledge these claims, the order was granted recognition, bringing to a head its differences with the federation. Protracted negotiations between the two groups led to the formation of a Joint Zionist Council in 1912. In 1913 a Maccabean Land Purchase Company was registered in England, and after World War I it purchased land in Palestine. Among the grand commanders of the order was Selig Brodetsky (1935–49).

J. FRAENKEL

OREN (Ohrenstein), MORDEKHAI. One of the leading members of Ha-Shomer ha-Tza'ir in Galicia and later of Kibbutz Artzi (b. Podhajce, 1905; d. Kibbutz Mizra, 1981). In a series of articles "On Drawing the Line" (1927), Oren formulated his radical leftist interpretation of the political platform of Kibbutz Artzi shel Ha-Shomer ha-Tza'ir. This leftist tendency characterized all his subsequent ideological and political activities in the movement. In 1929 he immigrated to Palestine, becoming one of the major Kibbutz Artzi activists, and representing the movement in the institutions of the Histadrut and the World Zionist Organization. For a time he represented Ha-Shomer ha-Tza'ir in the International Labor Movement. Oren was involved in arms deals in Czechoslovakia for the Hagana and later for the Israel army. In 1951 he was arrested in Czechoslovakia and used as a prosecution witness in the show trial against Rudolf Slansky. After his release in 1956, he returned to Israel but did not resume public or political activity. His book *Records of the Prisoner of Prague* was published in 1958. In 1962 the Czechs "rehabilitated" him.

M. MINTZ

ORGAD (BUSCHEL), BEN-ZION. Israeli composer and educator (b. Gelsenkirchen, Germany, 1926). He immigrated with his parents to Palestine in 1933. He studied composition with Paul Ben-Haim and Mordecai Seter and later with Aaron Copland in the USA. Orgad was in charge of music education in Israel's Ministry of Education and Culture, thus responsible for shaping curricula for public schools and conservatories throughout the country and in training music teachers. His own composition was motivated by national ideology, searching for a relationship between music and poetic texts, ancient and modern, as well as with religious and historical subjects, both in large-scale choral works, such as *Mizmorim*, as well as in short works like the Monologue for solo viola based on poetic rhythms of medieval Sephardi poetry.

J. HIRSHBERG

ORMSBY-GORE, WILLIAM GEORGE. *See* HARLECH, 4TH BARON.

ORNSTEIN, LEONARD SALOMON. Physicist and Zionist leader in the Netherlands (b. Nijmegen, 1880; d. Utrecht, 1941). After serving on the Dutch Zionist Executive for a number of years, he was its chairman from 1918 to 1922. During that period he was also a member of the Zionist Actions Committee. Ornstein was a member of the Board of Governors of the Hebrew University of Jerusalem from 1925 to 1940, and in 1933 he became the first chairman of Youth Aliya in the Netherlands. He was a professor of physics at the University of Utrecht from 1915 to 1940.

ORT (Organization for Rehabilitation through Training). Jewish vocational training agency, today the world's largest voluntary organization engaged in comprehensive education and technical training, encompassing hundreds of schools and educational training projects in 35 countries. Overall direction is provided by the World ORT Union, an international body whose 27 affiliate national membership organizations help to sustain and support the program.

ORT was founded in Russia in 1880, when Tsar Alexander II approved the petition of a group of Jewish philanthropists to establish a fund for the purpose of "ameliorating the position of the mass of our coreligionists ... (by) the thorough and systematic development of artisan and agricultural occupations among the mass."

ORT was legalized and established as a functioning organization after the 1905 Russian Revolution. During World War I, ORT launched programs of "relief through work" for thousands of homeless refugees and made its mark among large masses of Jews as an agency for economic rehabilitation. After the War, Dr. David Lvovitch and Dr. Aron Syngalowski emerged as the guiding spirits. During World War I ORT had continued its activities, concentrated on settling Jews on the land in southern Russia and on the organization of trade schools, workshops, cooperatives and training centers for artisans and small shopkeepers in Poland, Lithuania, Latvia, and Romania. After World War II, ORT played a significant role in teaching displaced persons new productive skills. It is now active throughout the Jewish world.

ORT Israel. In 1949, ORT began its program in Israel. The new country had three immediately pressing needs: economic development, integration of refugees, and defense. Many immigrants arrived with little or no education or vocational skills. ORT's beginning in Israel was in response to the overwhelming need for manpower for industry and services. Under the successive administrations of Jacob Oleiski and Joseph Harmatz, an ORT network began to expand in various directions. In cooperation with various municipalities and the ministries of Education and Labor, a network of vocational high schools was established, the largest such system in the country in terms of total enrollment, number of schools, and educational standards. The Syngalowski Center in Tel Aviv was considered an outstanding and well equipped vocational school. ORT pioneered in the introduction of training for new trades, including refrigeration, laboratory work, electroplating, textile technology, construction technology, and machine design, and in developing a number of centers for instruction in agro- and automobile-mechanics.

British Prime Minister Margaret Thatcher visiting Ort School of Engineering, Jerusalem, 1986. [Ort]

In view of the fact that large numbers of immigrant youth, especially those from pre-industrial cultures, could not readily absorb the regular vocational high school curriculum, centers for apprenticeship were established in the 1960s, in cooperation with the Ministry of Labor, at Tel Aviv, Jerusalem, Haifa (two), Ashkelon, Eilat, and Kiryat Gat. Women's American ORT helped to equip the centers. By the 1960s, ORT developed its own courses for the training of technical teachers in Israel.

There are 107 ORT schools in Israel, with an overall enrollment of 70,000. A teaching staff of 4,523 provides training and education in over 50 different fields. ORT Israel consists of junior technical colleges, technical and vocational high schools, comprehensive schools, apprenticeship centers, industrial schools, institutes for adult training, and the Moshinsky Pedagogical Center in Tel Aviv for the training of teachers and the development of educational resources. In 1976, ORT constructed a school of engineering on the campus of the Hebrew University in Jerusalem, extending the ORT educational system to the tertiary level. This school, as well as some other ORT schools, offers associate degrees in practical engineering. The ORT Braude International Institute of Technology is located in Karmiel, in the development area of Galilee slated to become the hi-tech center of the country. The school is named after Max Braude, the late Director General of World ORT Union (1956–1980).

ORT in Israel has pioneered in all fields of high technology including electronics, pneumatics, hydraulics, plastics, instrumentation and control, computers, CNC, CAD, avionics, robotics, automation, and biotechnology.

OSE (Obstchestvo Zdravochranienia Evrejev, or Society for the Protection of the Health of the Jews). International Jewish organization founded in St. Petersburg, Russia, in 1912. Its program was work in the fields of preventive medicine, medical education, public health and child care. OSE functioned especially in Europe until World War II after which it shifted its activities to North Africa and Latin America. Though already burdened with great responsibilities, OSE kept a watchful eye on developments in Palestine and strove to expand its activities there. The establishment of the State of Israel confronted OSE with new tasks.

During the mass migration of Jews from Moslem countries to Israel in 1948–49, when many European and North African ports were choked with masses of refugees who brought with them the threat of possible epidemics, it was OSE, particularly in France, which, with the support of the American Jewish Joint Distribution Committee and the Jewish Agency, set up a network of medical institutions for the screening and quarantine of thousands of immigrant applications. At the same time, work inside Israel was greatly intensified and expanded. OSE in Israel maintained five children's institutions, providing outpatient care for 1,060 children and 880 mothers in transit camps and small settlements. The entire program of OSE activities in Israel was carried out in cooperation with local governmental agencies and with the Kupat Holim of the Histadrut.

When OSE headquarters finally ceased activities, after more than 50 years of intense activity on behalf of Jewish populations in many parts of the world, their institutions in Israel were taken over by governmental or private organizations.

OSTERREICHER, BELA. Lawyer and Zionist leader in Hungary (b. Boldogasszony, 1862; d. Hungary, ca. 1936). After graduating from the Law School of the University of Budapest, he served as attorney general of Moson County. An ardent supporter of the Zionist cause from its inception, he was instrumental in launching the Zionist movement in Hungary and presided over the 1st Hungarian Zionist Conference, held in Pozsony (now Bratislava, Czechoslovakia) in 1902. He served for 10 years as president of the Hungarian Zionist Federation, in which capacity he frequently attended Zionist Congresses. R.L. BRAHAM

OSZTERN, LIPOT. Lawyer and Zionist leader in Hungary (b. Budapest, 1872; d. there, 1944). Osztern obtained a law degree at the University of Budapest and was appointed official Hebrew and Yiddish interpreter by the High Court of Hungary, 1916. In 1920 he was elected president of the Hungarian Zionist Federation. He served as an officer of various Jewish communal organizations, including the Jewish Community of Pest. He published articles in Jewish periodicals, including the *Zsidó Szemle* (Jewish Spectator) and *Mult és Jövö* (Past and Future). In the 1930s he served as president of the Palestine Office in Budapest. For two decades he was a member of the Board of Trustees of the Budapest Bar. R.L. BRAHAM—E. EPPLER

OTTOLENGHI, MARIO. Economist and Zionist leader in Italy (b. Florence, 1904; d. Ramat Gan, 1971). Ottolenghi was president of the Zionist Organization of Florence from 1929 to 1936 and secretary of the Italian Zionist Federation from 1933 to 1938. He served as editor-in-chief of the weekly *Israel* from 1936 until 1938, when the periodical was suppressed by the Fascist authorities. He also founded and directed the first *hakhshara* (agricultural training center), of Bachad, in Italy, at Ricavo di Castellina, near Florence, from 1934 to 1938. He settled in Palestine late in 1938.
G. ROMANO

OTTOMAN JEWRY AND ZIONISM. For generations, Ottoman Jews nourished deep feelings for the idea of the Return to Zion, which were manifested in Jewish tradition and religious beliefs. By contrast, their attitude towards political Zionism was conditioned by the policy of the Ottoman government. Ottoman Jewry was noted for its loyalty and was in no position to dissent. Thus throughout his negotiations with the Turkish government, Herzl could not expect the assistance of any Ottoman Jew. In fact Moses Halevi, the Chief Rabbi in Constantinople, warned the Chief Rabbi in Jerusalem, Jacob Saul Elyashar, not to become involved with a movement to which the Sultan objected. Elyashar, determined not to incur the government's displeasure, avoided meeting Herzl.

It was not until after the Young Turk Revolution of 24 July 1908 that the climate of opinion became more favorable. Early in September both Ahmed Riza, a prominent Young Turk leader (later President of the Chamber) and editor of *Mechveret*, and Tewfik Pasha, the Foreign Minister, made exceptionally friendly statements about Zionism and were willing to lift former restrictions on Jewish immigration to Palestine. Haim Nahoum, the Chief Rabbi of Turkey, confirmed to Victor Jacobson, head of the Zionist Agency in Constantinople, that the new régime viewed Jewish settlement in Palestine with favor although they would not allow Palestine to become politically autonomous. Jacobson, on his part, took great pains to dispel the notion that Zionism entertained separatist aspirations or ran counter to Ottoman interests. His efforts, as well as those of Jabotinsky who assisted him, bore fruit, since there was much latent sentiment for the idea of settlement in the Holy Land; the Jewish community of Salonica in particular proved a tower of strength.

The Salonica community. There were approximately 80,000 Jews in Salonica, out of a total population of 173,000. Jacob Meir, their chief rabbi (later Sephardi Chief Rabbi of Palestine), was very sympathetic to Zionism; so was Sa'adia Levi, the editor of *L'Epoca*, the local Jewish paper, and Joseph Na'or, the respected mayor of Salonica. But the greatest asset was Emmanuel Carasso, a prominent figure in the Young Turk movement and a deputy for Salonica in the Ottoman parliament. He thought that the leadership of the Committee of Union and Progress (C.U.P.) was not as hostile to Zionism as was generally assumed, although Zionist aims should be made more palatable to it. Of equal importance was the conversion to Zionism of Nissim Matzliah Effendi and Nissim Russo, both of whom were deputies to the Ottoman parliament. They were members of the small group that founded the C.U.P. and despite their youth, were very influential. Matzliah was secretary of the C.U.P. and later also of the parliament.

Like Carasso, Russo and Matzliah saw no incompatibility between patriotism and interest in Palestine. They were eager to convince Turkish politicians that opposition to Zionism was based on a misconception. In a meeting which took place on 31 December 1908 in the presence of Jacobson and Jabotinsky, they declared that they had decided to join the Zionist Organization and found an Ottoman branch, provided it would disclaim any separatist political aims. They suggested the C.U.P. should first be won over and, through it, the parliament and consequently also the government. Hilmi Pasha was singled out in particular. As the most influential statesman in the parliament and Minister of the Interior, he was the "man of the future". Russo was his former secretary and hoped to sway him. Jointly with Matzliah he considered submitting a memorandum to the C.U.P. and the Ministry of the Interior and, in order to keep the public in Constantinople better informed, they thought it absolutely essential that the Zionists establish a paper.

Turkish support for Zionism. Behor Effendi, who in 1908 was elected Senator (the only Jew to attain that eminence), became appreciably friendlier. This was also true of Faradji, who thought that the development of an intellectual center in Palestine was of crucial importance to world Jewry; the absence of anti-Semitism in Turkey made the idea realizable. This coincided with the proposal made by Carasso early in February, 1909 to found an Ottoman Immigration Company for Palestine and Turkey in general.

Russo and Matzliah soon approached a number of prominent C.U.P. leaders such as Ahmed Riza, Enver Bey, and Talaat Bey, and found them quite sympathetic; the most explicit statement was made by Niazim Bey, a leading member of the Unionist Central Committee. He would have liked to see six to eight million Jews in Turkey; they were the "most reliable element". He approved of Carasso's plan and was willing to join the board of the proposed Immigration Company, but with regard to Palestine he would allow no more than two to four million Jews to come; settlement in excess of this number would constitute "a danger".

Volte-face. Russo and Matzliah had hardly taken stock of the situation when the Young Turks staged their second coup in April, 1909, which brought in its wake a radical change in direction. Promises of equality for all Ottoman subjects without distinction of religion and race became invalid and slogans like Freedom and Liberty were discarded. Ottomanism gave way to Turkism and the dream of a free association of people in a multinational and multidenominational empire vanished for ever. Turkey became a centralized state and for the non-Turkish nationalities this was a crippling blow.

Attitudes towards Zionism also hardened. In consequence Ottoman-Jewish leaders became reserved and even Carasso, Matzliah, and Russo remained aloof. David Fresco, the editor of *El Tiempo*, the Judeo-Spanish periodical, with whom Jacobson had planned in 1908 to coedit a paper, turned against the Zionists and in a series of articles—from December 1910 to February 1911—accused them of disloyalty to Turkey.

In 1912–1914, Turkish policy towards Jewish settlement in Palestine changed markedly and *pari passu* Ottoman Jewry adopted a friendlier tone. But it was not until 1918 that they were able to come out openly in favor of Zionism.

Diplomatic overtures. Publication of the Balfour Declaration, coupled with the conquest of Jerusalem by the British, made restoration of Palestine to Turkey unlikely. To Talaat Pasha, the Grand Vizier, the only option that remained open was diplomacy. On 5 January 1918 he met German-Jewish leaders in Berlin and agreed to resuscitate the defunct Ottoman-Israelite Union for Immigration and Settlement in Palestine. Thereafter, he delegated to Emmanuel Carasso, his confidant, the task of negotiating with the German-Jewish leaders on the creation of the Jewish Center in Palestine under Ottoman sovereignty. Carasso considered the plan advantageous to Turkey. It also had a strong personal appeal for him; he had no difficulty in reconciling his duty as a Turkish patriot with that of a nationalist Jew.

Talaat invited the German-Jewish delegation (V.J.O.D.), which included the Zionists, to come to Constantinople, in order to bring the negotiations to a successful conclusion. Once again, Carasso had to work out the details. Accordingly, the Settlement Company was to be given the right to acquire land, administer concessions, regulate Jewish immigration and settlement, and grant local autonomy to individual settlements, so that in due course, the Jews would become a majority in the country. In Carasso's opinion—and so he had told the Grand Vizier—the fear that the Jews would ultimately go their own way had little substance. Should Turkey remain weak she would lose Palestine to the Arabs anyhow, whereas Jewish help in making Turkey a viable state was worthy of consideration. Once Turco-Jewish cooperation was established, a relationship of trust was likely to develop, and separatist tendencies would die out.

Nahoum also acted as one of the chief intermediaries between the Turkish government and a German-Jewish delegation. The negotiations proved abortive but indicative of the new spirit that prevailed among Ottoman Jews was Nahoum's statement, made a few years after the war, though under changed conditions:

> Jewish aspirations in Turkey center about the restoration of Palestine ... This back-to-the-land movement was the most important factor in the awakening of the desire for the repopulation of Palestine ... [and] it was proved that the regeneration of Palestine was possible. The Balfour Declaration became the basis for the settlement of the Jewish question and today the Jews of Turkey ... do not fail to cooperate with all their might with the rest of the Jews in the intellectual, economic, and commercial restoration of Palestine.

I. FRIEDMAN

OTTOMAN RULE IN PALESTINE. *See* ISRAEL, HISTORY OF.

OUZIEL, BENZION MEIR HAI. *See* UZIEL, BENZION MEIR HAI.

OVDAT. *See* AVEDAT.

OZ, AMOS. Israeli writer of fiction (b. Jerusalem, 1939). Oz, a member of Kibbutz Hulda, belongs to the group of authors who began publishing in the 1960s and marked the shift in Hebrew letters from themes of Zionist struggle and fulfillment to themes which stress the *angst* of the individual in the complex society of contemporary Israel where no unifying ideology obtains. Already in his first collection of short stories *Be-Artzot ha-Tan*, 1966 (Where Jackals Howl, 1981), Oz's major theme is the conflict between instinct (the jackal) and rationality (the kibbutz). His first novel *Be-Makom Aher* (Elsewhere, Perhaps, 1966) portrays the bleak emotional world of nonconformist kibbutz members. *My Michael* (1963) (1972 in English) depicts student life in Jerusalem in the aftermath of the War of Independence. It enjoyed great popularity and appeared as a motion picture. The protagonist, Hannah, is a sensitive, neurotic woman totally bored with the unpoetic routines of married life and escapes to a world of fantasy.

Oz sets most of his stories either in the kibbutz or in Jerusalem. In *Ad Mavet* (Unto Death, 1971) he deals with the problems of Jewish paranoia, His *Kufsa Shehora* (Black Box, 1986) depicts the tragic consequence of the break-up of a marriage.

Oz has deep Socialist Zionist commitments and has been politically active in various Zionist Progressive movements such as Peace Now. His collection of essays *In the Land of Israel*, 1983, contains brilliant reportage on the varieties of political views held by ordinary Israelis. In a literary essay, he insists that authors are not sociologists and tend to write about human folly and neuroses rather than present a balanced picture of the society in which they reside.

In 1993 he became professor of Hebrew literature at Ben-Gurion University of the Negev.

E. SPICEHANDLER

P

PACIFICI, ALFONSO. Lawyer, author, journalist, and philosopher (b. Florence, 1887; d. Jerusalem, 1981). Pacifici received a law degree in 1911 but turned to journalism, serving as comanager of the Italian-Jewish weekly *La Settimana Israelitica.* In 1916 he founded *Israel,* another Jewish weekly, and in 1924, the monthly *La Rassegna Mensile di Israel.* When a committee for the Keren ha-Yesod was founded in Italy, he advocated a revival of the *ma'aser* (Biblical tithe).

An orator and writer of extraordinary eloquence, Pacifici had a profound influence on a whole generation of Italian Jews, even those who disagreed with him when his religious views veered toward extreme Orthodoxy. Settling in Palestine in 1934, he continued to write articles for Italian-language Jewish periodicals. He also wrote a number of books in which he expounded his philosophy, among them *La nostra sintesi programma* (1957) and *Interludio I: Cinquant'anni intorno a un'idea* (1959). G. ROMANO

PAGIS, DAN. Hebrew poet and scholar of medieval Hebrew poetry (b. Radauz, Bukovina, 1930; d. Jerusalem, 1986). After spending his childhood in a concentration camp, Pagis arrived in Palestine in 1946. He studied medieval Hebrew poetry at the Hebrew University of Jerusalem and joined its faculty in 1962, receiving his professorship in 1972.

His first volume of verse, *She'on ha-Tzel* (Sun Dial, 1959) contains highly polished, but opaque verse. In his second volume *Shehut Me'uheret* (Late Leisure, 1964), objects and people still stalk ghost-like through the speaker's mind and he dissects them with scientific precision. At times the poet seems to make his peace with the fact that he cannot recover his lost identity.

In *Gilgul* (Transmigration, 1970) Pagis can now speak about the Holocaust and the volume contains a number of remarkable Holocaust poems. In *Mo'ah* (Brain, 1978) emotion gives way to a laboratory-like precision of diction. The same analytic cerebral poetry fills his last book *Milim Nirdafot* (Synonyms, 1982).

His studies of medieval poetry include: *Shirat ha-Hol ve-Torat ha-Shir le-Moshe ibn Ezra.* (The Secular Poetry and Poetics of Moses ibn Ezra, 1970); and *Hidush u-Masoret be-Shirat ha-Hol ha-Ivrit* (Innovation and Tradition in Secular Hebrew Poetry, 1976). He also edited editions of David Vogel's poetry (1966), the diwan of the medieval poet Levi al-Taban (1968), and completed Brody's edition of Moses ibn Ezra's secular poetry (1978). E. SPICEHANDLER

PALESTINE. Geographical area, known by a number of names in various periods of its history. Prior to its conquest by the Hebrews under Joshua, the Judges, Saul, and David, it was known as the Land of Canaan, the name being derived from the Canaanites, who inhabited certain parts of it. After its conquest by the Israelite tribes it became known as the Land of Israel (*see* ERETZ ISRAEL), a name still current among Jews. Following the death of King Solomon, the Land of Israel split into two kingdoms, Judah (Yehuda) in the south and Israel (Yisrael) in the north. The Greeks and the Romans referred to the country as Palaestina, after the Philistines who inhabited the southern coastal area. The Arabic form Falastin, or Filastin, was applied to the country throughout the period of Turkish rule. Because of the special sanctity attached to the country in the eyes of both Jews and Christians, the name Holy Land has become current among these two faiths.

As the official name of the territory mandated by the League of Nations to Great Britain (*see* MANDATE FOR PALESTINE), the term Palestine referred to an area which lay both to the west and to the east of the Jordan River and had clearly defined boundaries not only with Lebanon in the north and Egypt in the southwest but also with Syria, Iraq, and Saudi Arabia in the east. Subsequently, however, the term Palestine was applied to western Palestine only, while eastern Palestine was called *Transjordan. On 14 May 1948, with the establishment of the State of Israel, the name Palestine ceased to exist as a politicolegal term. It has received new currency with the claims of the Palestinian Arabs, especially since the 1960s. The Palestine Liberation Organization (of Palestinian Arabs) adopted in 1964 the first version of the "Palestinian National Covenant," stating its goal as the elimination of Israel and the establishment of an Arab-Palestinian state in "the whole of Palestine." However, it never formally defined its concept of Palestine and whether this included the area of Jordan.

R. PATAI—ED.

PALESTINE, HISTORY OF. *See* ISRAEL, HISTORY OF.

PALESTINE CONCILIATION COMMISSION. *See* ARMISTICE AGREEMENTS; UNITED NATIONS AND PALESTINE-ISRAEL.

PALESTINE CORPORATION LTD. Bank and investment company founded in 1922 by members of the Economic Board for Palestine in London. Both bodies were headed by Alfred Mond (later Lord Melchett) and Sir Robert Waley Cohen (an outstanding businesman and Jewish communal leader) and included Zionist as well as non-Zionist supporters of the Jewish National Home. The Palestine Corporation invested in various business enterprises, such as the Athlit Salt works and the Levant Bonded Warehouses, but mainly in commercial banking. Its banking business was merged in 1951 with the Central Bank for Cooperative Institutions (*see* PALESTINE ECONOMIC CORPORATION) into the Union Bank of Israel, later a member of the Bank Le'umi group. N. GROSS

PALESTINE ECONOMIC CORPORATION (PEC). *See* PEC ISRAEL ECONOMIC CORPORATION.

PALESTINE ELECTRIC CORPORATION, LTD. *See* ISRAEL ELECTRIC CORPORATION.

PALESTINE FOUNDATION FUND. *See* KEREN HA-YESOD.

PALESTINE JEWISH COLONIZATION ASSOCIATION (PICA). Society for Jewish settlement in Eretz Israel. Its beginnings go back to 1882, when Baron Edmond de *Rothschild first took an active interest in the establishment of Jewish settlements in the country. Until 1900 the settlements founded or aided by the Baron were under his personal administration. That year he transferred their administration to the *Jewish Colonization Association (ICA), which formed a Palestine Commission over which he presided. In 1924 the Baron established PICA as a separate organization; his eldest son James de Rothschild became its president and served in this capacity until his death in 1957. The death of James de Rothschild marked the termination of PICA activities. In a letter written shortly before his death and later given by his widow to David Ben-Gurion, James de Rothschild informed the Prime Minister that PICA had completed its settlement work and that he was transferring all remaining PICA land, leased and unleased, to the national institutions of the yishuv. In the same letter, which was read by Ben-Gurion to the Knesset on 22 July 1957, he also informed the Prime Minister of his gift of IL6,000,000 for the building of a new home for the Knesset.

History. When Rothschild came to the financial aid of the first settlements, he sought to consolidate their economic position chiefly by the introduction of viticulture. He had vineyards planted in the villages under his administration and established large wine cellars in Rishon le-Zion and Zikhron Ya'akov.

Although Rothschild's aid saved the settlements from ruin, his administrative methods had some adverse effects on the settlers. Many of his administrators were not in sympathy with the idealism of the settlers. They regarded the settlements not as a national enterprise but merely as objects of Rothschild's philanthropy. They took upon themselves the right to control the activities of the settlers, doling out support to them not in relation to the work they performed but according to the size of their families. This attitude dampened the idealism of the settlers and weakened their initiative, independence, and drive to achieve self-sufficiency. There were frequent clashes between the settlers and the baron's administrators.

The ICA administration opened a new chapter in the support of the settlements. Founded in 1891 by Baron Maurice de *Hirsch to assist Eastern European Jewry, the ICA by 1900 had established several Jewish villages in Argentina. As early as 1896 it had granted loans to settlers in Eretz Israel. Now it set out to improve the methods of the Rothschild administration. It did much to widen the market for wine from Eretz Israel (a lack of suitable markets was one of the reasons why viticulture had not been a financial success) and entrusted the settlers with the independent management and operation of the wine cellars. ICA gave priority also to wheat growing, thus helping reduce the settlers' living expenses and making them less dependent on the fluctuating world market. It introduced a credit system whereby the settlers could get loans on convenient terms. The administration concerned itself less and less with the internal affairs of the settlements and reduced its personnel accordingly.

In addition to devising means of putting the older settlements on a sound economic footing, ICA almost immediately began establishing villages whose principal product would be cereal crops. These new settlements were founded on land acquired partly by Baron de Rothschild and partly by ICA. During World War I, under the influence of Hayim Kalwariski-Margolis, who wanted the organization also to aid collective settlements, ICA provided land and financial assistance for the establishment of the kibbutzim Kefar Giladi, Tel Hai, Ayelet ha-Shahar, and Mahanayim in Upper Galilee.

PICA continued the work of ICA, aiding all types of settlements, conducting drainage and afforestation projects, and helping introduce and promote many industrial enterprises in the country, It helped Pinhas Rutenberg found the Palestine Electric Corporation, aided in the construction of the King David Hotel in Jerusalem, founded the Grands Moulin de Palestine (flour mills) in Haifa, had a major share in the foundation of the Palestine Salt Company at Athlit and the Palestine Brewery at Rishon le-Zion, and was one of the founding partners of Fertilizers and Chemicals, Ltd., in Haifa. PICA also encouraged village industry and crafts.

During the many years of its activity, PICA and its predecessors founded, helped establish, or aided about 50 settlements of all types. They included the oldest settlements, such as Petah Tikva, Rishon le-Zion, Rosh Pina, and Zikhron Ya'akov (some of which developed into cities), as well as some of the youngest, established after the creation of the State, such as Kefar Yeroham, Sedeh Boker, and Mashabe Sadeh.

Beneficiaries of PICA grants included the Hebrew University of Jerusalem, the Haifa Technion, yeshivot, hospitals, and other institutions. PICA also established a number of prizes for research. T. PRESCHEL

PALESTINE LABOR LEAGUE. Organization which originated in the Labor Palestine Committees which the Histadrut executive decided to establish in 1923, with the object of uniting the work of the different Socialist Zionist parties in the various countries of the Diaspora to further the work of the Histadrut in increasing Jewish settlement in Palestine. To this end a convention of all Diaspora parties and organizations supporting labor in Palestine met on 20 August 1923 immediately after the 13th Zionist Congress. The tasks allocated included: distribution of Bank ha-Poalim shares, and shares of other Histadrut companies, collection of equipment and material for the development of factories in Palestine, immigration, and pioneering. The committee, composed of representatives of Hitahdut, Right Po'ale Zion, Left Po'ale Zion (Barou and Revusky), Communist Po'ale Zion (Nir and Erem), the Tze'irei Zion Union, the Dror Federation (David Livshitz), and of He-Halutz (Meir Bugdanovski and Moshe Sharira), met in Berlin on 16 October 1923. The Histadrut in Israel, was represented by Eliezer Kaplan and Dov Hos. It was recommended: 1) to create territorial Labor Palestine Committees; 2) to raise funds for the Palestine Workers' Fund *(Kapai)*; and 3) to distribute Bank ha-Poalim shares.

The second convention meeting in Vienna in 1925 shortly after the 14th Zionist Congress, with the participation of Yosef Sprinzak and Berl Katznelson, resolved to convert the committees into Palestine Labor Leagues. In place of talks between the leaders of the existing parties for the promotion of labor in Palestine, the Leagues would become a direct organization of members paying minimal dues to *Kapai*. The Leagues were parallel organizations to the Histadrut in Palestine and served in time as a framework to unite the Socialist-Zionist force in various political systems in the different countries—in the elections to the Zionist Congresses, to municipal councils, and to community boards, for instance. The Socialist Zionist youth movements also maintained ties with the Leagues through their umbrella organization, He-Halutz. M. MINTZ

PALESTINE LAND DEVELOPMENT COMPANY (PLDC). *See* ISRAEL LAND DEVELOPMENT COMPANY.

PALESTINE LIBERATION ORGANIZATION (PLO). Umbrella body of Palestinian Arab organizations seeking to establish an independent Palestinian state. The foundation for the Palestine Liberation Organization (PLO) was laid by Ahmad Shukeiri and Arab heads of state at the first Arab Summit Conference held in 1964. The PLO was officially established, with Shukeiri as its leader, on 28 May 1964, during the "Conference on Palestinian Entity" in Jerusalem. The Organization was founded primarily for the purpose of recruiting the emerging younger generation of Palestinian Arabs—those growing up after the 1948 war—for political and propaganda activities. It also hoped to enable former Arab inhabitants of Palestine to regain their homeland. Although established under the aegis of all the Arab countries, the PLO had particularly strong support from Nasser's Egypt. Its objectives were meant to be realized with the assistance of the Arab countries and in accordance with a strategy approved by them.

At the time the Organization was founded it was challenged from within by the Fatah (see below) which maintained that the Palestinians constantly courted disaster because of their reliance on others. Only if they acted independently, by force of arms and by using guerrilla tactics, would the dream of liberation be realized. The Arab countries were defeated in the 1967 Six-Day War but terrorist actions were relatively successful. As a result, in 1968 the PLO was transformed into a roof-organization comprising a coalition of independent and semi-independent Palestinian organizations, as well as some supported by Syria and Iraq. It does not, however, include all groups that have been formed by the Palestinians (Abu Nidal, for example, is not a member of the PLO). Social and class distinctions also account for some of the organizational schisms: there are conflicting attitudes toward the Soviet Union on the one hand and the United States on the other; differences of opinion exist with regard to the scope of the "armed struggle" (a term encompassing terrorist activities, guerrilla warfare, and military operations). There are also many unsolved questions concerning the relation between the armed struggle and the political struggle.

Major Constituents of the Roof-Organization.

The "Fatah" (Conquest in Arabic; initials in reverse order of the words "Palestinian Liberation Movement") has a pragmatic orientation and, as the largest group within the PLO, sets the tone for the entire body. The Fatah was founded in Cairo in 1959 by a group of students of Palestinian origin, headed by Yassir *Arafat, Halil al-Wazir (Abu Jihad), Salah Khalaf (Abu-Iyad), Faruk al-Kadumi (Abu al-Lutf), Khaled al-Hassan (Abu Sa'id) and his brother Hani. As a pragmatic movement the Fatah has refrained from becoming involved in the internal affairs of the Arab countries and makes no effort to define its social doctrine. Its sights are focused on the "liberation" of Palestine, whether total, partial, or in stages. Once that will have been achieved, it will turn its attention to social issues, welfare, structure of the regime, and the role of religion. Due to its ideological flexibility and pragmatic approach the Fatah has succeeded in recruiting large numbers and has engulfed several smaller groups: a radical faction oriented toward Syria; an extremely pragmatic group that advocates even more moderate positions and wants to coordinate policies with those of Jordan, Egypt, and the moderate pro-western bloc in the Arab world. Then there is the middle-of-the-road faction led by Arafat; this is the principal group in the Fatah, both by virtue of its size and because it strives to rally the extreme elements around a more moderate internal consensus. Arafat's policy with respect to the Fatah coincides with his approach as the leader of the PLO. In the PLO, too, he has been faced with problems involving a coalition of different elements, but there it has been much more severe, even to the point of casting doubt on his personal status as leader. In the Fatah his leading position has not been brought into question.

Palestinians are not automatically granted membership in the Fatah; a candidate must first join a regional branch in one of the Arab countries. The important institutions of the Fatah are: the General Assembly which numbers some 120 people and meets at rare irregular intervals. The Revolutionary Council, which acts in the name of the General Assembly, is the legislative body of the organization and has a membership of some 35 people, and the Central Committee, which has 15 members headed by Arafat and is responsible for the organization's routine activities.

The Popular Front for the Liberation of Palestine is the second largest body in the PLO. It was established in December, 1967, by defectors from the "Arab Nationalists" (Kaumiyyun al-Arab) originally a secular, pro-Nasserist, pan-Arab Palestinian organization. During the 1960s, when ideological developments under Nasser brought about changes in Egyptian policy, and after the establishment of the Fatah, the Arab Nationalists began to adopt a Marxist-Leninist approach. The PFLP's ideology is rigid and formalized and it views the conflict with Israel as part of a world-wide struggle against imperialism. The movement identifies politically and operationally with movements throughout the world that subscribe to a similar ideology. Ideological criteria also determine its attitude to the Arab countries; consequently it did not join the PLO until 1972 when the roof organization tacitly accepted its demand to call for the destruction of the Hashemite regime in Jordan. In 1974 the Popular Front supported the PLO's "program of stages" (see below), but in 1983 it froze its participation in the PLO in view of what it considered Arafat's "reactionary deviation," claiming that the chairman was amenable to a political settlement that would forfeit Arab rights to areas of Palestine they had lost in 1948. It further objected that the projected settlement would be under the aegis of the United States, with Jordan, as part of the Palestinian representation, having a voice in the future Confederation. The Popular Front renewed its active participation in 1986 when Arafat canceled the agreement with King Hussein of Jordan that provided for political coordination between the PLO and Jordan (see below).

The most important body within the PFLP is the Executive Committee headed by Dr. George Habash. The organization publishes a weekly called *al Hadaf*.

The Democratic Front for the Liberation of Palestine was established in February, 1969, by a radical group that followed Nayef Hawatma when he broke away from the PFLP. At first its stands were very similar to those of the parent organization but after "Black September" (in September, 1970, fighting erupted between the Palestinian organizations and the Jordanian army following which the Palestinians were in effect evicted from Jordanian territory) the Democratic Front became so attached to the Soviet Union that it considers itself the Palestinian Communist Party.

Its most important body is the Central Committee and it publishes a weekly paper called *Al Huriyya*.

Al-Sa'ika (The Tempest in Arabic) was established in December, 1968, by the Syrian Ba'ath regime, its membership based on Palestinian members of the Ba'ath Party. It supports Syrian policy on the Palestinian question and has approved the steps taken by Syrian President Hafez al-*Assad after 1970 with respect to Arafat. It also advocates a close connection between the future Palestinian state and Syria. Since 1983, however, the organization has suspended activities in the PLO as a result of the sharp conflict between Assad and Arafat (see below).

The Palestinian National Covenant. This document expresses the collective credo of PLO members. It enjoys a status similar to that of a constitution or a holy document. The original version was written by Shukeiri and was approved by the first Palestinian Congress in June, 1964, together with the basic set of regulations of the PLO. Point 29 of the Covenant provides that it can be amended by no fewer than a two-thirds majority of all members of the National Council of the PLO, at a special assembly convened for this purpose. It was amended at the fourth assembly of the Council in July, 1968, when the Fatah and other guerrilla and terrorist organizations joined the PLO. In view of the sacrosanct nature of the Covenant on one hand and changing historical circumstances after 1968 on the other, the Palestinian National Council passed a number of binding decisions that in essence conflict with some of the Covenant's original provisions. These, together with the many divergent viewpoints upheld by the various Palestinian organizations, have given rise to a large corpus of commentary explicating the Covenant's provisions.

Point 2 of the Covenant declares that Palestine's borders are the frontiers that were recognized during the British Mandatory period. Point 5 declares that "the Palestinian personality" is a permanent, unchanging, fundamental characteristic that is transmitted from father to son. The land of Palestine belongs to the Palestinians, the "Arab citizens who lived permanently in Palestine until 1947, regardless of whether they were subsequently sent away or remained there." According to Point 6, "anyone born to a Palestinian father after this date (i.e., 1947), whether in or outside of Palestine, is a Palestinian." Point 17 "utterly repudiates" the "partition of Palestine in 1947 and the establishment of Israel" for the "claims of historical or spiritual ties of the Jews to Palestine are inconsistent with historical facts and with the components of the State in their real meaning." Judaism, according to Point 18, is a religion, not a nationality, and it has no substantive existence apart from the religion. Moreover, the Jews are not a single nation with a unique national personality, but are citizens of the countries in which they live. Point 19 of the Covenant maintains that Zionism is basically an imperialistic movement with aggressive, expansionist goals, essentially racist, fanatic, and fascistic in outlook and in the means it employs. Point 6 of an amended version of the Covenant states that only those Jews who resided permanently in Palestine until the beginning of the Zionist "invasion" are to be considered Palestinians, that is to say, only those who lived there before the Balfour Declaration of 1917 will be permitted to remain in the country. In 1968 Point 9 redefined the method by which the Palestinians' aims would be achieved: "Palestine will be liberated only by armed struggle."

Major Activities of the PLO. Particularly after 1967, the organization augmented its organizational, social, financial, educational, propagandist, and political activities with acts of terror and sabotage against Israel. At the height of its effectiveness, the PLO functioned inside the areas controlled by Israel, along Israel's borders, and against Israeli targets throughout the world. In June, 1985, it halted terrorist activities against targets outside of Israel. Most of the PLO's military operations of necessity have emanated from bases in the Administered Areas and South Lebanon: "Black September" in 1970 ended cooperation with Jordan, operating from Syria became difficult after Syria signed the Separation of Forces agreement with Israel in 1975, and President Sadat's peace initiative in 1978 made it impossible to operate from Egyptian territory.

Until 1974 the PLO's anti-Israeli activities were almost exclusively in the military sphere. However, after the 1974 Geneva Conference and the interim agreements that followed the Yom Kippur War, the Organization tried to become part of the political process. At the twelfth session of the Palestinian National Council in June, 1974, a political program for working in stages was approved. It centered around an agreement to initially establish a small Palestinian state in the Areas taken over by Israel in 1967. The PLO as a whole agreed on condition that implementation of this stage would not bar the way to a continued struggle for maximum realization of the Palestinians' objectives.

Acceptance of the "program of stages" was a very important landmark in the PLO's history because this was the first time that the Organization had made the slightest concession in its ideological and political concepts. Henceforth it would have to maneuver between the interim objective and the final goal, between "armed struggle" and political strategy, between the need for reconciliation with King Hussein of Jordan to facilitate entry into the Israeli-held territories and the demand of radical groups to "de-Hashemize" Jordan.

Most of the PLO's gains in fact have been achieved through political activity. Above all, to most Palestinians, it has acquired a secure position as their sole representative, a view supported by the Arabs inside the State of Israel as well as those in the Administered Areas. The PLO has been recognized politically by most of the countries of the world and since November, 1974, has enjoyed the status of an Observer-Member at the *United Nations. Nevertheless, this path has taken its toll: many of the political decisions made by the PLO's institutions have not been acceptable to the radical organizations. In 1983 there was an internal revolt against Arafat's leadership and, with the active encouragement of Syria, an attempt was made to form an alternative organization. The PLO's grudging attempts to seek a political settlement reached their peak in February, 1985, with the signing of an agreement providing for political cooperation with Jordan. The agreement made provisions for a confederation between Jordan and the Palestinian state that would be formed in the Administered Areas. The PLO and Jordan would participate in a joint delegation to negotiate the political settlement; negotiations, to be conducted under the aegis of the United States, would not deal with the question of the Golan Heights. The agreement indicated the change that had occurred in the relations between Jordan and the PLO. During the first decade of the PLO's existence (1964–1974) Jordan had persecuted the Organization, claiming that the Jordanian kingdom was the sole custodian of the Palestinian entity. But after the Arab Summit at Rabat in 1974 declared the PLO to be the only legitimate representative of the Palestinian people, Jordan accepted this position. Recognition of the PLO's representative nature did not however mean agreement with the Organization's political solution. A year later differences of opinion caused nullification of the agreement and a cooling of relations between Jordan and the PLO.

The PLO has failed in a number of important ways, most notably in that its major objective—the total or at least partial "liberation" of Palestine—has eluded it. Secondly, it has failed to establish a firm, long-lasting territorial foothold close to Israel, a situation that created even greater difficulties after the Lebanese war—in which the PLO was Israel's prime target. As a result of the war, the PLO's infrastructure on Lebanese soil was destroyed and most of its fighting force as well as its administrative bodies had to seek the hospitality of other Arab countries.

The important institutions of the PLO. These are the Palestinian National Council, a legislative body comprising some 400 members, convened at least once a year, working within the framework of the General Assembly and through sub-committees, and which is responsible for appointing the Executive Committee; the Executive Committee, responsible for implementing Council decisions and carrying out day-to-day activities. Its 15 members oversee the functioning of departments that have been established, among others, for political, military, welfare, higher education, administrative, and financial affairs; there are also centers for research and planning and a health organization ("The Palestinian Red Crescent"). Yassir Arafat is the chairman of the Executive Committee; organizational representation in it is based on parity.

Membership in the PLO is extended to all Palestinians by virtue of their origin. The various organizations belonging to the PLO appoint representatives to the body's institutions, while a certain number of people are chosen independently due to their public status. The PLO publishes the weekly *Falastin al-Thura* and the quarterly, *Shu'Un Falastiniyya.* M. KLEIN

PALESTINE OFFICES. Offices of the *World Zionist Organization (WZO), and later of the *Jewish Agency, that were set up in various countries to supervise the practical aspects of Jewish immigration to Palestine, including the registration and selection of candidates for immigration, the organization of immigrant groups, the granting of immigration certificates, the procurement of passports, visas, and transit permits, medical examinations, and the transportation of immigrants to Palestine. A precursor of this institution was the Palestine Office that had been set up in Jaffa in 1908 by a decision of the Actions Committee and charged with the duty of assisting in the settlement and absorption of immigrants.

At the 1917 Zionist Conference in Warsaw it was decided to prepare an organizational framework for the immigration to Palestine of He-Halutz members and to set up training farms for them. The Warsaw Palestine Office drew up a series of proposals and plans for action. Immediately after the cessation of hostilities on the Russian front, contact was resumed with key Zionist workers in Moscow, Kiev, and Petrograd (later Leningrad). After World War I the functions of the Palestine Offices were defined by the Zionist Executive in London. The offices in Warsaw, Vienna, and Constantinople were designated Central Palestine Offices. The Central Warsaw Office, established in October, 1918, supervised 54 branches throughout Poland, each headed by a Palestine Committee composed of representatives of the area's Zionist organizations. The Palestine Offices enjoyed official status in all countries, representing all Zionist groups in all matters relating to Jewish emigration to Palestine before the authorities of the countries in which they functioned.

With the rising interest in immigration, Palestine Offices

Pioneers about to immigrate outside Palestine Office in Warsaw, 1925. [Central Zionist Archives]

were opened also in Vienna (1918), Constantinople (later Istanbul), Trieste, Lvov, Cracow, Budapest, Prague, Bratislava, and New York (1919), as well as in such distant localities as Irkutsk, Siberia, and Harbin, in the Far East (1919). In April, 1919, an Immigration Department was established under the Zionist Executive in London to organize immigration in accordance with the absorptive capacity of Palestine and to facilitate the transportation of immigrants. In 1921 a Central Immigration Committee was established in Vienna.

In 1921 the British authorities in Palestine issued an Immigration Ordinance authorizing the Zionist Executive to allocate the immigration certificates made available to it by the British authorities every six months. The Executive, in turn, authorized the heads of the Palestine Offices to act as its representatives.

Following a resolution adopted by the London Zionist Conference of 1920, the Palestine Offices were reorganized and, with the participation of representatives of the Labor Zionist parties on the Palestine Committee, Labor Departments were set up to take charge of the immigration of pioneers and workers.

The composition of the committees of the Palestine Offices was a result of agreements reflecting conditions in the countries concerned. In the Palestine Office of Constantinople in 1921, there were four representatives from the labor factions and He-Halutz and one from the Zionist Federation; in Berlin, three representatives of the Zionist Organization, two of He-Halutz, and one each of Mizrachi, Po'ale Zion, and Ha-Po'el ha-Tza'ir, in addition to the director; and in Warsaw, three representatives of the Zionist Organization, two of Mizrachi, and one each of Tze'irei Zion, Hitahdut, He-Halutz, and the Labor Department, in addition to the director.

Upon their arrival in Palestine, the immigrants were received by the immigration offices of the WZO in Tel Aviv-Jaffa, Haifa, and Jerusalem. The main functions of these offices were to receive the immigrants at the port of debarkation; maintain immigrant hostels where the newcomers were given shelter and food during their initial period of adjustment; grant loans to immigrants to enable them to acquire permanent homes, household goods, and tools; find the immigrants suitable jobs; and assist Jewish residents of Palestine in obtaining immigration certificates for their relatives abroad. The immigration offices in Palestine functioned as branches of the Immigration Department of the WZO.

After the outbreak of World War II, the Jewish Agency bent every effort in behalf of the rescue of refugees temporarily residing in neutral countries. The Provisional Office of the Immigration Department, which was opened in Geneva in September, 1939, and the Department for Immigration of the Jewish Agency, which was opened in Istanbul in July, 1940, were in constant touch with the Palestine Offices, government institutions, and the Executive of the Jewish Agency in Jerusalem and in London. Frequently they were forced to use underground channels for immigration. During the period beginning at the end of 1935 and ending in June, 1943, a total of 5,851 immigrants were brought from Trieste to Palestine by the Palestine Office.

During the early days of the Nazi era, when the Nazi authorities still encouraged the emigration of Jews from Germany, Austria, and the other countries under their rule, the Palestine Offices in Berlin, Vienna, and Prague continued to function, even though the Zionist movement and its other institutions there had been closed down. In Nazi-occupied Poland, however, the Central Palestine Office and all its branches were closed down at once, and the emigration of Jews was prohibited. The Palestine Offices in Bucharest, Budapest, and Sofia functioned almost throughout the war despite the pressure brought to bear by the Nazi authorities on the satellite governments in Romania, Hungary, and Bulgaria. The Palestine Office in Trieste continued to function until June, 1940, when Italy entered the war on the side of the Nazis. Until the Nazi occupation of southern France, the Palestine Office in Paris routed the immigrants to Palestine via Marseilles. From 1940 to 1942 a total of about 3,000 immigrants were transported from Odessa to Istanbul by the Palestine Office in Kovno.

At the end of World War II, Palestine Offices were reestablished in France, Belgium, Italy, Hungary, the Netherlands, Czechoslovakia, Germany (Munich), Austria (Vienna), and elsewhere, and continued their work until the establishment of the State of Israel. H. BARLAS

PALLIERE, AIME. French pro-Zionist (b. Lyon, France, 1875; d. near Avignon, 1949). Brought up as a Catholic and intended for the priesthood, Pallière became attracted to Judaism in his adolescence on visiting a synagogue during Day of Atonement services. Although he never underwent formal conversion to Judaism (he died a Christian), he lived the life of a practicing Jew and was active in Jewish communal life, calling on Jews to return to the traditional values of Judaism. He wrote and lectured extensively on his own conception of the mission of Judaism.

An ardent supporter of Zionism, Pallière attempted to win Liberal Jews to Zionism. He was a member of the Zionist Federation of France and at one time was vice-chairman of the Jewish National Fund of France. During World War II he shared the plight of French Jewry under Nazi occupation.

Pallière's writings include an autobiographical work, *Le sanctuaire inconnu* (The Unknown Sanctuary, 1926), which was translated into English, German, and Hebrew and in which he describes his encounter with Judaism.

PALMAH (full name Pelugot Mahatz). Commando units of the *Hagana in Palestine and later shock battalions in the *Israel Defense Forces. The name means "shock companies." Recruited from members of active Hagana units and subject to complete Hagana control, the Palmah functioned as an independent entity under its own command.

The Palmah was formed during World War II by a decision of the Hagana command on 15–16 May 1941, as an "illegal" Jewish unit to provide the Hagana with a strategic reserve in the form of well-trained soldiers ready at any time to fulfill special functions. In the light of the Axis threats of 1941 and 1942 to Allied positions in the Middle East, it served in those years primarily in conjunction with British troops as an irregular force, while jealously guarding its independence from British control. Small groups of the Palmah participated in the conquest by the British Army of Syria and Lebanon in June, 1941. In 1942 the Palmah received intensive military training from expert British officers to form a guerilla group behind German lines if the Germans conquered Palestine. Members of the Palmah were called on to participate in groups of *parachutists to aid Jewish populations in Europe and to fulfill other tasks for the Allies. 32 parachutists were dropped behind German lines, over half of them being members of the Palmah.

From 1943 on the British, fearing that the Palmah might be used against them in the yishuv's attempt to resist the policy of the 1939 White Paper, were intent on destroying the Palmah, which numbered 2,000 effectives at the end of the war. By this time the Palmah was a permanently mobilized unit divided into 11 companies, one-third of whose members were young women. Stationed in kibbutzim, they worked 14 days a month and trained for 10; they thus paid very largely for their upkeep. Youth movement groups intending to settle on the land joined the Palmah as units. Other recruits came from kibbutzim and moshavim, while many were youths from the poor sections of Palestinian towns who received elementary schooling as part of their military training. A naval unit, Palyam, served as the nucleus of what was to become the Israel Navy. From 1946 a small group of pilots also was trained; they were among the first to man the future Israel Air Force. Discipline in the Palmah was strict, but relationships between officers and men were informal.

From the autumn of 1945 until the summer of 1946, the Palmah carried on the struggle against the British in spectacular actions such as the demolition of railway tracks in more than 200 localities on 31 October 1945, and the subsequent blowing up of bridges, radar stations, and other installations. These actions were carried out in conjunction with the *Irgun Tzeva'i Le'umi and the *Lohamei Herut Israel. On 29 June 1946, the British reacted against the Hagana and discovered some of the central arms caches. On the order of the Hagana command, Palmah now concentrated mainly on *"illegal" immigration. Palyam was largely responsible for the organization, communications, and command of the immigration ships. In addition, in daring frogmen's operations, British ships deporting immigrants to Cyprus were repeatedly sunk.

With the beginning of the Arab assault on the yishuv that followed the adoption of the UN General Assembly's partition resolution of November, 1947, the Palmah, now numbering some 5,000 effectives, was for several months almost the only mobile Hagana force. Organized in three brigades, it bore the brunt of the fighting. Its founder and first commander, Yitzhak Sadeh, left it to organize the first armored brigade of the Israeli forces, and it was under Yigal Allon, its commander in the *War of Independence, that the Palmah conquered Tiberias and Safed, held open the road to Jerusalem and took the Arab village of Kastel, and held the Negev front until the Israeli Army could be organized. With other forces of the army it participated in the conquest of Lydda, Ramle, and Beersheba and formed the spearhead of the great attacks on the Egyptians in October, 1948, and again in December, 1948-January, 1949. It suffered heavy casualties, losing more than one-sixth of its men. After a dramatic public discussion, during which Prime Minister David Ben-Gurion implied that the Palmah was too independent and was leaning too far to the left (with the Palmah vigorously protesting absolute and historically proven loyalty to the army command), the Palmah General Staff was dissolved.

Representing the flower of the youth of the yishuv, the Palmah was an elite corps both as a fighting force and as a closely knit community of dedicated men and women. Its heroism and special characteristics are reflected in contemporary Israeli literature. Y. BAUER

PALMERSTON, 3RD VISCOUNT, HENRY JOHN TEMPLE. British statesman, regarded as "champion of the oppressed" (b. Broadlands, Hants., 1784; d. Brocket Hall, Herts., 1865). During the years 1830–1841, 1846–1851 he served as Secretary of War, and Foreign Secretary, and during 1855–1858, 1859–1865 was Home Secretary and Prime Minister.

Lord Palmerston was a friend of the Jews. He saw no contradiction between his zealous support for their emancipation and their recognition as a people. Aware of their world-wide unity (like a "Free Mason fraternity") and of their ancient attachment to Palestine, he anticipated the Zionist movement.

On 31 January 1839, when establishing the British Consulate in Jerusalem, he gave instructions that the duties of the British Vice-Consul should include "to afford protection to the Jews generally ..."; the instruction was applied liberally, not only to British subjects and protégés but also to native Jews (*rayahs*) who were not eligible for consular protection. The move was motivated by a feeling of sympathy although, in the prevailing conditions of bitter rivalry among the Powers in the Near East, protection of the Jews brought Britain certain benefits, for, in contrast to the French who enjoyed a *locus standi* as the champion of the Catholics and to the Russians who supported the Greek-Orthodox, Britain had no comparable group to whom, by merit of common religion, she could extend her protection.

On 30 April 1840 Palmerston granted a sympathetic hearing to a Jewish committee, headed by Sir Moses Montefiore, and promised to use his influence both with the Egyptian ruler Mehemet Ali and the sultan of Turkey to put a stop to the atrocities against the Jews in Rhodes and Damascus. This he did most effectively.

The idea of Restoration of the Jews to the Holy Land was always vivid in evangelical England but Palmerston's motive was primarily political. On 11 August 1840 he wrote to Viscount Ponsonby, the British Ambassador in Constantinople:

> There exists at present among the Jews dispersed over Europe a strong notion that the time is approaching when their Nation is to return to Palestine; and consequently their wish to go thither has become more keen ... It is well known that the Jews of Europe possess great wealth; and it is manifest that any country in which a considerable number of them might choose to settle, would derive great benefit from Riches which they would bring into it.
>
> ... it would be of manifest importance to the Sultan to encourage the Jews to return to, and to settle in, Palestine; because the wealth which they would bring with them would increase the resources of the Sultan's Dominions; and the Jewish People, if returning under the Sanction and Protection and at the Invitation of the Sultan, would be a check upon any future evil designs of Mehemet Ali or his Successor ...

At the time Palmerston's mind was fully absorbed by various schemes of reforming Turkey and he hoped that Jewish capital and initiative would play a role in revitalizing the Ottoman economy. Palestine, inhabited by loyal and productive Jewish inhabitants could also serve as a bulwark against any possible incursions by Mehemet Ali or his successor. He instructed Ambassador Ponsonby to recommend this scheme strongly to the Turkish government. However, the Ambassador totally misrepresented Palmerston's case and the Turks rejected the scheme out of hand.

Palmerston's interest in the welfare of the Jews in the

orient did not diminish and British protection continued practically until the turn of the century when the usefulness of this policy was spent. I. FRIEDMAN

PANAMA, ZIONISM IN. About 6,000 Jews live in Panama—almost all in the capital, Panama City, but some in Colon, and a few in the provinces. The total population of Panama is over two million.

There are three congregations; Kol She'arith Israel, the oldest, founded in the second half of the 19th century (Reform), consisting mainly of descendents of the Sephardi exiles from Spain and Portugal during the period of the persecutions and Inquisition; Shevet Ahim, consisting of Jews of oriental origin, immigrants from the Near East and Arab countries; and Beth El, consisting of Ashkenazi Jews of central and eastern European origin. There are two Jewish day schools: Instituto Alberto Einstein, founded in 1955, and the Hebrew Academy, founded in 1978, both consisting of pre-primary, primary, and secondary schools. The directors are Israelis and the Jewish education is given by teachers from Israel, contracted through the Education Department of the World Zionist Organization. There is also a youth movement, Maccabi, with an Israeli instructor (madrikh).

Zionist activities are carried out by a Zionist Organization, Jewish National Fund and Keren ha-Yesod appeals and Israeli Bonds campaigns. A WIZO group is also active. The University of Panama has a chair for Hebrew and Hebrew Culture.

The Panamanian government has a tradition of friendly relations with Israel and there is also cultural, technical, agricultural, and scientific cooperation between the two countries. Panama was among the few nations that voted against the UN resolution equating Zionism with Racism. Leading Israeli personalities visit Panama, and leading Panamanians visit Israel. The former president of Panama Eric del Valle is a Jew, member of the Kol Shearith Israel, from a prominent Sephardi family, and on many occasions he has expressed his admiration for Israel's ideals and achievements. His uncle, Max Del Valle, was vice president of the country in the 1960s and a great supporter of Israel.

The membership of the Panama-Israel Cultural Institute includes prominent Panamanian statesmen and intellectuals and presidents of the country were among its founders. Its bulletin publishes studies and essays by university professors and other personalities. This Institute was among the first, decades ago, to demand human rights for the Jews of Russia. The Shalom organization consists of Christians who have undergone training in different fields in Israel. H. KLEPFISZ

PANN (Pfefferman), ABEL. Palestinian artist and illustrator (b. Kreslavka, Latvia, 1885; d. Jerusalem, 1963). He first studied with Yehuda Pen, teacher of Chagall and Lissitzky and worked as a lithographer in Vilna. After study at the art school in Odessa in 1898, he moved to Paris in 1903 and studied at the Grand Chaumière. In 1913 he went to Jerusalem to teach at the Bezalel School. He was caught by the war in 1914 on a visit to Paris. He made powerful drawings of pogroms in Russia for the *The Jug of Tears* series, 1916. He went to the US in 1917, and returned to teach at Bezalel in 1920, resigning in 1924 to publish his biblical illustrations made on his own imported lithographic press (still in service in Jerusalem). A brilliant illustrator, he was best known in the 1930s and 1940s for his romantic pastels of biblical heroes and heroines, the latter drawn from young Yemenite models. M. RONNEN

PARACHUTISTS, PALESTINIAN JEWISH A group of Jewish volunteers, who were dispatched in the years 1943–1945 behind the enemy lines into occupied Europe. The idea of penetration into occupied Europe emerged after the news of the extermination of European Jewry reached Palestine in late 1942. The objectives were to contact Jewish underground organizations, encourage them and organize their resistance, as well as to prepare the Jewish public in those countries for the likely Zionist struggle for Eretz Israel after the war. The delay was caused mainly by technical and operational obstacles.

The volunteers were recruited by the Jewish Agency from the German and Balkan sections of the *Palmah, as well as from the various kibbutz-movements which had sister-movements in the target countries; others came from the ranks of the Palestinian soldiers in the British army. About 250 men and women volunteered; 110 were trained, but only 37 were actually sent on missions. All but one were dispatched through cooperation with the British M.I.9 and Special Operations Executive, who needed their services for

Palestinian parachutists behind Nazi lines in Bari, Italy, 1944. Standing (right to left), Reuven Dafni, Zadok Burogoyer, Abba Berditchev; sitting (right to left) Shurika Brorman, Aryeh Fichman, Haviva Reik. [Israel Govt. Press Office]

the rescue of prisoners of war and liaison with resistance movements. One parachutist was sent to Italy through the American Office of Strategic Services.

The first parachutist, Peretz Rosenberg, was dropped in May, 1943, as a wireless operator of the British liaison mission to Tito's headquarters. The last of them, Hayim Waldner, was dropped in Austria in May, 1945, to rescue a prisoner of war camp. Nine parachutists were dispatched to Romania and played an important role in the evacuation of allied prisoners of war after the Romanian capitulation. They organized immigration and helped in the reconstruction of the Jewish community and youth movements.

Three parachutists, who jumped in Yugoslavia and penetrated into Hungary, were captured. Five were dropped in Slovakia in the summer of 1944 and participated in the Slovak revolt while helping the Jews who had found refuge with the rebels. Four of them were captured and executed. Two emissaries reached Bulgaria, but only after its occupation by the Russians. Three parachutists took part in the rescue operation of prisoners of war in northern Italy after the Italian surrender. Enzo *Sereni parachuted into occupied Italy in May, 1944, but was captured as he landed and executed. The rest of the parachutists were dropped in Yugoslavia, either on their way to the neighboring countries which they failed to penetrate, or as wireless operators of British liaison missions to the partisans. In all, 12 of the parachutists were captured, 7 of whom were killed in action. Their mission and sacrifice was the principal symbol of the yishuv's desire to assist the Jews of Europe during the Holocaust.

Y. GELBER

PARAGUAY, ZIONISM IN. Jews first went to Paraguay about 1900. By 1917 the country had approximately 600 Jews of Russian, Turkish, German, and French origin, and a Zionist society had been founded. Zionist work was carried on by the Consejo Representativo Israelita del Paraguay (Jewish Representative Council of Paraguay), which was Zionist-led and conducted pro-Israel fundraising. A branch of WIZO functioned in Asunción.

PARDES HANA-KARKUR. Predominantly rural township in the northern Sharon, 4 mi. (7 km.) northeast of Hadera, created in 1969 through the amalgamation of Pardes Hana and Karkur. The beginnings of Karkur go back to 1912, when the Palestine Land Development Company acquired 3,150 acres for English Jews. Members of Ha-Shomer guarded the site and tilled the land. Building of houses began in 1919, some of the English owners arrived in 1925/26, and citrus groves became the economic maintstay when abundant groundwater was discovered. After 1948, most of its settlers were from eastern Europe and from Yemen.

In 1929, Pardes Hana was founded on lands bought by Baron Edmond de Rothschild through the Jewish Colonization Association. Later, the moshava was merged with the neighboring village of Meged whcih had been founded in 1933. German Jews settled there in the 1930s, building the Tel Shalom quarter. After 1948, two large transit camps were opened in former British army camps. Some industrial enterprises were added to the farming, which was largely based on citriculture. In the town are the agricultural high school of the Farmers' Association, a yeshiva high school, and a dew research station. The name Karkur is derived from the Arabic; Pardes Hana commemorates a cousin of Baron de Rothschild. Population (1987) 16,200.

E. ORNI

PARTITION OF PALESTINE. The idea of the partition of Palestine, in order to attain as quickly as possible a Jewish majority and Jewish autonomy in part of the country, emerged at an early stage of Zionist thought. Herzl suggested in his negotiations with the Turkish sultan in 1902 that the Zionists be presented a *Charter to settle part of the country—the area from Haifa via the Jezreel Valley to Lake Kineret, including Galilee as far north as the Litani River. In 1907 Arthur Ruppin planned the concentration of Jewish settlement in Judea and around Lake Kineret so as to achieve dense Jewish settlement and the possibility of Jewish autonomy in these areas. During World War I he repeated this suggestion in the wake of discussions between German Jews and Zionists and the Turkish authorities. The idea of limiting Jewish settlement to several areas in the country was then rejected, for it would have prevented the spread of the Jews to other areas and their becoming a sovereign majority there.

The Zionist plan at the Paris Peace Conference of 1919 outlined the borders of a large Palestine, based on the assumption that, under a friendly international regime and with rapid immigration, the Jews would very quickly constitute the majority of the population. At this time Zionists were more deeply concerned with the absorptive capacity of Palestine for millions of Jews than they were with the problem of a Jewish majority, and they therefore requested as large a territory as possible. During the negotiations among the Allied Powers on awarding the Mandate for Palestine to Great Britain, the British desired maximal borders for the Jewish National Home in order to extend the area of their rule. Because of the strong stand taken by the French, areas of western Galilee to the Litani River and of the Golan Heights to the Yarmuk River were excluded from the Palestine mandated territory in 1920. Then, in 1922, the territory east of the Jordan River was excluded from the area of the Jewish National Home and placed under the rule of Emir Abdullah. The Zionists were forced to agree to this separation between the territories on either side of the Jordan.

In the wake of the new political situation resulting from the Arab riots of 1929 and the possibility of a retreat by the British from support of the Jewish National Home, the idea of partition was mentioned in a secret memorandum written in 1932 by Victor Jacobson, the World Zionist Organization representative at the League of Nations in Geneva. Jacobson suggested the partition of Palestine into a Jewish and an Arab area in order to allay Arab fears of the Jews becoming a majority. He proposed including in the Jewish area or State the coastal plain and the relatively sparsely populated valleys. Jacobson believed that under such an arrangement the Arabs would consent to the Zionist enterprise and the two states would collaborate with each other. From the Jewish point of view the plan presented serious difficulties such as the problem of land reserves for settlement, the future of Jerusalem, and the strategic position of the Jewish areas. Proposals for separation into Jewish and Arab administrative units as a solution to Palestine's constitutional problem were raised by both the British and the Jews in the 1930s. After the Arab Revolt of 1936, suggestions for the partition of Palestine were made in the press and in British diplomatic circles.

The *Peel Commission in its report proposed the partition of Palestine while rejecting the alternatives of common Palestinian citizenship and cantonization of the country. The partition of the country into a Jewish and an Arab State and a British-mandated area was designed to solve the rival claims of Jews and Arabs and, at the same time, to guard British interests by creating two states allied to Britain. The Jewish State proposed by the Commission embraced an area with a Jewish majority and included a land reserve for additional Jewish immigration and settlement. The Commission envisaged the necessity of financial aid by the Jewish to the Arab State. In defining the borders of the two states, strategic considerations were almost entirely disregarded, for the Commission assumed that partition would resolve the Arab-Jewish conflict.

The British government was inclined to accept the proposal of the Peel Commission and change its own status in Palestine from that of an internationally entrusted mandatory power to that of an ally of two independent countries tied to itself. There were differences of opinion among the Zionists. The majority was inclined to accept the partition proposal with certain emendations, in the hope that this would enable a large immigration of Europe's harassed Jews (1937–38).

The Arabs were absolutely opposed to the partition plan. (An exception was Emir Abdullah, who showed some inclination toward accepting it.) Arab opposition and the support given the Arabs by Nazi Germany and Fascist Italy induced the British government to reconsider its previous acceptance of partition. The British appointed the *Woodhead Commission, whose task was to investigate ways of implementing the partition proposal. However, the Commission concluded that the suggested plan was impracticable and put forward its own proposal, which was disadvantageous to the Jews.

The policy of the *White Paper of 1939 and, especially, the *Land Transfer Regulations of 1940 were based on certain aspects of the partition proposal that were detrimental to the Jews. The regulations limited the right of the Jews to purchase land to certain areas of the country. The Zionist *Biltmore Program of 1942 asked for Jewish rule over the entire area of Palestine, which was to absorb large-scale immigration from Europe.

The Churchill government appointed a ministerial committee to deal with the Palestine problem. Late in 1943 the Committee submitted to the Cabinet a proposal suggesting partition as the best solution to the problem. This plan, too, envisaged the partition of the country into Jewish and Arab states and a British-mandated area, which was to include Jerusalem. The Jewish and Arab states were to form a part of a federal organization of states in the area under the protection of Great Britain, France, and the United States.

The Labor government that came into power in 1945 did not favor partition and the granting of independence. Instead, it suggested a new plan of autonomous districts with ultimate authority remaining with the British, who would act as trustees (*see* MORRISON-GRADY PLAN). This plan was suggested in the wake of the report of the *Anglo-American Committee of Inquiry, which had rejected both partition and the granting of absolute authority to any one community over any part of the country. The Committee had envisaged the solution of the Palestine problem in preparing the country for binational rule.

Faced with the anti-Zionist policy of the British government and the necessity of obtaining United States support for Zionist demands, the Zionist leaders retreated in the summer of 1946 from their demand for a Jewish State in the whole of Palestine and informed Pres. Harry Truman of their readiness to accept a Jewish State in part of the country.

The *United Nations Special Committee on Palestine (UNSCOP), which was appointed after Britain had submitted the Palestine problem to the United Nations, was unanimous in its recommendation to grant independence to Palestine. The alternatives were the partition of the country into two sovereign entities or the establishment of one federated state with an Arab majority and a Jewish community enjoying autonomy. The Committee majority favored the first alternative. The partition plan proposed by UNSCOP included also an international area in Jerusalem. The Negev was to be included in the Jewish State as a land reserve for additional population, but during negotiations in the UN General Assembly part of the Negev was transferred from the Jewish to the Arab area.

The rejection of the partition proposal by the Arabs led to the War of Independence. In the summer of 1948, UN Mediator Count Folke Bernadotte proposed a new partition plan that would have further restricted the land area of the Jewish State.

The armistice agreements of 1949 left Israel in the possession of 20,700 of the 27,000 square kilometers of Mandatory Palestine. The rest of the country was occupied by the forces of King Abdullah and Egypt (the Gaza Strip). The cease-fire lines of 1967 left Israel in control of the entire area of Mandatory Palestine west of the Jordan River.

See also BOUNDARIES OF THE STATE OF ISRAEL. I. KOLATT

PARTOS, OEDOEN Israeli composer, violist, and pedagogue (b. Budapest, Hungary, 1907; d. Tel Aviv, 1977). At the age of twelve, he was accepted to the Liszt Music Academy as a pupil of Jenö Hubay (violin) and Zoltan Kodaly (composition). He graduated at the age of seventeen and was immediately appointed leader of an orchestra in Switzerland. In 1928 he settled in Berlin, where he composed popular and film music and played in chamber ensembles. The Nazi rise to power in 1933 forced him to return to Hungary; in 1934 he received a teaching position in Baku, Russia. In 1938 he accepted an invitation to join the newly founded Palestine Symphony Orchestra. He also became a member of the prestigious Israel String Quartet and one of the leading violin teachers at the Israel Music Academy (later part of Tel Aviv University), which he helped found, serving as its musical director from 1951. His early encounter with Hungarian methods of folklore research prepared him for his exposure to Arabic and Jewish traditional music, which he first learned from the singer Bracha Zephirah, for whom he did a series of arrangements. In the late 1940s he began concentrating on large-scale symphonic works and won the Israel Prize (1954) for his symphonic poem "Ein Gev." He composed two viola concerti and other works for viola which he himself performed frequently. In the 1960s he turned to writing in elaborate dodecaphonic technique. J. HIRSCHBERG

PASMANIK, DANIEL. Writer and Zionist leader (b. Gadyach, Poltava District, Russia, 1869; d. Paris, 1930). Pasmanik studied medicine in Switzerland and Bulgaria, and from 1899 he was an instructor in medicine at the University of Geneva. Joining the Zionist movement in 1900, he became one of its leading thinkers and publicists. He advocated the evolutionary concept of Zionism and practical work in Eretz Israel. Returning to Russia in 1905 to practice medicine, he joined the editorial boards of *Yevreiskaya Zhizn* and *Rassviet*. His articles appeared in Russian, Yiddish, German, Hebrew, Polish, and Croatian periodicals.

During the Russian Civil War (1917–21), Pasmanik sided with the anti-Bolshevist White volunteer army. In 1919 he emigrated to Paris, where he served as coeditor of the émigré paper *Obscheye Dyelo* from 1920 to 1922. His associations with White Russian circles alienated Pasmanik from the Zionist movement, and a partial reconciliation was achieved only shortly before his death.

Pasmanik's main writings include *The Economic Situation of the Jews in Russia* (1906); *Criticism of the Theories of the Bund* (1906); *The Theory of the Jewish Sejm* (1907); *The History of the Emancipation of Jews in Switzerland* (1907); *Die Seele Israels: Zur Psychologie des Diasporajudentums* (The Soul of Israel: On the Psychology of Diaspora Jewry, 1911), in German, Hebrew, and Russian; and *Qu'est-ce le judaïsme?* (What Is Judaism?, 1930). J. SCHECHTMAN

PASSFIELD WHITE PAPER. Statement of policy on Palestine issued by the British Government on 21 October 1930. Published under the authority of the Colonial Secretary, Lord Passfield (Sidney Webb), it appeared simultaneously with the *Hope-Simpson Report and was based on its findings.

The White Paper was inspired by the High Commissioner in Palestine, Sir John *Chancellor, and reflected his anti-Zionist views. Following the Arab riots of August 1929 the government had appointed a commission of inquiry under Sir Walter Shaw. The report of the Shaw commission published in March, 1930, recommended "a clear statement of policy...in such vital issues as land and immigration."

On the central constitutional issue, the Passfield White Paper announced that the government intended to make a renewed attempt to establish a legislative council. Recalling the earlier unsuccessful attempt to establish such a council in 1923, the White Paper warned that it would "circumvent" an attempt "on the part of any section of the population" to prevent the creation of such a body.

On the land question, the White Paper echoed the conclusions of the Hope-Simpson Report in asserting that "with the present methods of Arab cultivation there remains no margin of land available for agricultural settlement by new immigrants, with the exception of such undeveloped land as the various Jewish agencies hold in reserve." It alleged that "some of the attempts which have been made to prove that Zionist colonization has not had the effect of causing the previous tenants of land acquired to join the landless class have on examination proved to be unconvincing, if not fallacious." It declared that "consideration must also be given to the protection of tenants by some form of occupancy right, or by other means, to secure them against ejectment or the imposition of excessive rental."

Although the White Paper did not announce any specific change in immigration policy, it stated: "Any hasty decision in regard to more unrestricted Jewish immigration is to be strongly deprecated, not only from the point of view of the interests of the Palestine population as a whole, but even from the special point of view of the Jewish community."

The White Paper concluded with an appeal to the Arabs "for a recognition of the facts of the situation and for a sustained effort at cooperation," and to the Jews "for a recognition of the necessity for making some concessions on their side in regard to the independent and separatist ideals which have been developed in some quarters."

Overall it was the tone of the statement, rather than any particular shift in policy, which offended the Zionists, who reacted with a storm of indignation. Worldwide protests against the White Paper were orchestrated by the World Zionist Organization. Chaim Weizmann announced his resignation from the presidency of the Zionist Organization and the Jewish Agency as a gesture of protest. David Lloyd George denounced the White Paper as a breach of faith. Passfield complained of "the Jewish hurricane," and the minority Labor government felt compelled to draw back.

On 6 November 1930 the Cabinet decided to appoint a subcommittee to consider Palestine policy afresh. The committee held a series of meetings with Zionist leaders headed by Weizmann, who claimed to be acting merely as a private individual. The eventual result was the MacDonald Letter, made public on 13 February 1931, in which the Prime Minister sought to reassure the Zionists. In effect this amounted to the abrogation of the Passfield White Paper and the return of the British Government to the Balfour Declaration policy. B. WASSERSTEIN

PATAI. Zionist family of Hungarian origin.

Jozsef Patai (b. Gyongyospata, Hungary 1882; d. Tel Aviv, 1953). Hungarian and Hebrew poet, author, translator, and Zionist leader. Patai taught at the Budapest municipal high school. His first Hebrew verse collection appeared in 1902, followed by two anthologies of Hungarian poetry (1906, 1919). A selection of his poems also appeared in English (1920). He published five volumes of translations of Hebrew poetry throughout the ages (1921), and early recollections: *A Kozepso Kapu* (The Middle Gate, 1927); *A Feltamado Szentfold* (The Renascent Holy Land, 1926) on his first visit to Palestine; and *Star over Jordan*, his biography of Herzl.

Patai's ardent Zionism found its best expression in *Mult es Jovo* (Past and Future), the high-quality Zionist monthly he founded and edited from 1912 until 1938 when, as a result of the First Hungarian "Jewish Law," it closed down. The journal was the focal point of Jewish and Zionist interest, introducing Hungarian Jewry to Hebrew literature, art, and thought. In its pages Patai fought the anti-Zionists and around it, with some associates, he organized the League of Hungarian Jews for Palestine and arranged annual pilgrimages to Palestine.

In 1938 Patai emigrated to Palestine. At first he lived in Jerusalem, lecturing at the Hebrew University. A volume based on his lectures (*Mi-Sefurei ha-Shira*, 1939) and a three-volume selection of his writings (*Mivhar Kitvei Yosef Patai*, 1943) were published. He later settled in Givatayim.

E. EPPLER

Raphael Patai, Jozsef's son, anthropologist, Biblical scholar, and editor (b. Budapest, 1910). He settled in Palestine after receiving his Ph.D. in Semitic languages and literatures from the University of Budapest (1933). In 1936 he received the first Ph.D. degree awarded by the Hebrew University in Jerusalem, and his thesis, *Water: A Study in Palestinology and Palestinian Folklore in the Biblical and Mishnaic Periods* (1936), won the Bialik Prize. Returning to Budapest for a brief period, he was ordained at the city's Rabbinical Seminary. From 1938 to 1942 he was an instructor in Hebrew at the Hebrew University, where he subsequently (1943–47) held a research fellowship in Jewish ethnology. In 1944 he founded the Palestine Institute of Folklore and Ethnology, serving as its director of research until 1948 and (1945–48) as editor of its quarterly, *Edoth*.

After settling in the United States, he was professor of anthropology at Dropsie College from 1948 to 1957 and held a number of visiting lectureships and professorships, primarily in the New York area. From 1966 to 1976, he was professor of anthropology at Fairleigh Dickinson University. From 1956 to 1968 he was president of the American Friends of Tel Aviv University in New York.

From 1956 to 1971 Patai was professionally affiliated with Zionist cultural endeavors in the United States, serving as director of research of the Theodor Herzl Institute in New York and (from 1957) as editor of the Herzl Press; he was editor-in-chief of the first edition of the *Encyclopedia of Zionism and Israel*, published by the Herzl Press in 1971.

Patai's scholarly contributions mainly encompass the culture of the ancient Hebrews and Jews and the culture of the modern Middle East, including Israel. He is the author of several hundred articles and over two dozen books, including *Israel Between East and West* (1953, 1970); *Cultures in Conflict* (1958, 1961); *The Kingdom of Jordan* (1958); *Golden River to Golden Road: Society, Culture and Change in the Middle East* (1962, 1967, 1969); *Hebrew Myths: The Book of Genesis* (with Robert Graves; 1964, 1966, 1967); *The Hebrew Goddess* (1967); *Tents of Jacob: The Diaspora Yesterday and Today* (1971); *The Arab Mind* (1973, 1976); *The Myth of the Jewish Race* (with Jennifer Patai Wing; (1975); *The Jewish Mind* (1978); and *The Vanished Worlds of Jewry* (1981).

G. HIRSCHLER

"PATRIA." French ship to which 1,800 "illegal" immigrants were transferred in Haifa harbor for deportation to Mauritius. Early in November, 1940, two ships, the *Pacific*, which carried 1,100 "illegal" immigrants from Germany and Austria, and the *Milos*, carrying 700 "illegals" from Czechoslovakia, arrived in Haifa. After transferring the immigrants to the *Patria*, lying in the port, for the declared purpose of quarantine, the British mandatory government announced its decision not to admit the immigrants but to deport them to *Mauritius, a British colony where they were to be held for the duration of World War II. At the end of the war it was to be decided where the immigrants would be sent, since they would not be permitted to remain in the British colony or to enter Palestine.

On 24 November 1940, a third "illegal" ship, the *Atlantic*, carrying 1,700 immigrants, arrived in Haifa. The British authorities prepared to transfer the passengers to the *Patria*. On 25 November, after all protests against the deportations had gone unheeded, members of the Hagana blew up the *Patria*. The ship was sunk, and nearly 250 of the immigrants lost their lives.

British soldiers guarding the S.S. "Patria." [United Israel Appeal]

Following the tragedy, the British government by "special grace," permitted the survivors of the *Patria* to remain in Palestine. The number of permits granted to them was deducted from subsequent Jewish immigration quotas. Since the immigrants aboard the *Atlantic* had not yet been transferred to the *Patria*, they were not included in the "act of grace" but were deported to Mauritius on 9 December 1940. T. PRESCHEL

PATTERSON, JOHN HENRY. British soldier and Zionist sympathizer (b. Dublin, 1867; d. Bel Air, California, 1947). Patterson served as an officer in Africa and India and in the Boer War (1900–02), rising to the rank of lieutenant colonel. He made his first contact with Zionism when he was placed in command of the *Zion Mule Corps (1915) and became an ardent admirer of Joseph Trumpeldor and a lifelong friend of Vladimir Jabotinsky. An account of his service with the Mule Corps is given in his book *With the Zionists in Gallipoli* (1916).

In 1917, he was requested by the War Office to assume command of the 1st Judean Regiment (38th Royal Fusiliers; *see* JEWISH LEGION), which was officially formed in August, 1917. A devout Protestant and Bible student, Patterson saw to it that the soldiers under his command were able to observe the Sabbath and hold religious services whenever possible. Patterson's activities during this period, which he described in a book, *With the Judeans in the Palestine Campaign* (1922), earned him the admiration of Jews the world over but incurred the disfavor of the War Office.

Returning to England after World War I, Patterson continued to take an active interest in the Zionist cause, literally sacrificing his military career in so doing. He helped promote the work of Keren ha-Yesod in England and the United States, associating himself with the Revisionist movement.

During World War II, Patterson worked for the formation of a Jewish army, tirelessly pleading its cause before the British War Office and in the United States.

At the time of his death Patterson was serving as honorary chairman of the American League for a Free Palestine. G. HIRSCHLER

PATWA. *See* PROFESSIONAL AND TECHNICAL WORKERS ALIYA.

PEACE NOW (Shalom Akhshav). Extra-parliamentary movement in Israel. Founded in 1978, it has become the symbol for that political "camp" which advocates the return of the territories captured in the Six-Day War in exchange for a peace treaty which guarantees Israel's security. Its political supporters include people from the dovish wing of the Labor party, from the liberal center parties, and from the Left Zionist parties. The movement has established branches in Jewish communities throughout the world.

Peace Now was founded in order to press the Israeli government to respond positively to the challenge presented by President Sadat in his historic visit to Jerusalem. A letter sent to Prime Minister Begin in March, 1978, articulates the ideas which have remained the foundation of Peace Now:

> "We write to you out of the deepest concern. A government that will prefer the existence of Israel in the borders of the greater Israel to its existence in peace in the context of good neighborly relations will arouse in us grave misgivings. A government that will prefer the establishment of settlements over the "green line" (i.e., the pre-1967 borders) to the ending of the historic conflict and to the establishment of a system of normal relations will raise questions about the justice of our course. A government policy that will lead to the continued rule over one million Arabs is liable to damage the Jewish democratic character of the state, and would make it difficult for us to identify with the basic direction of the State of Israel."

This letter was signed by 350 reserve combat officers. Peace Now emerged out of the grassroots support which the "officers' letter" evoked. Its first activities were public demonstrations aimed to exert pressure upon the Likud government to reach peace with Egypt.

Following the signing of the peace treaty with Egypt, Peace Now focused its activity upon the Palestinian-Israeli conflict, seeking to support diplomatic initiatives and to oppose its perceived obstacles to the peace process, such as settlements in the Administered Areas.

Peace Now was prominent in the protest against the war in Lebanon, asserting that military action cannot solve the conflict with the Palestinians, that damaging the military arm of the PLO does not eliminate the PLO as a political force nor affect the likelihood of PLO terrorism in the future, and that the invasion of Lebanon was not necessary for Israel's defense. After the Sabra and Shatilla massacre, it organized a major demonstration condemning the massacre, denouncing the war generally, and calling for the dismissal of Minister of Defense, Ariel Sharon.

After the Lebanon War, Peace Now concentrated upon raising public opinion against settlements in the territories, against racist tendencies in Israel such as those manifested in Rabbi Meir Kahane's political party, and in favor of dialogue with the Palestinians towards the achievement of peace. After the outbreak of the Palestinian Arab uprising in December, 1987, Peace Now demonstrated against the policy of occupation, which in its view, necessarily corrupts the occupier, and leads to immoral acts committed by military authorities and settlers.

Peace Now maintains that continuation of the occupation of the Administered Areas, is destructive morally and socially for Israel. In its view, the occupation derails Israel from its original goal of creating a just society which would serve all its citizens, Jews and Arabs alike, and which would be a source of inspiration and attraction for Jews throughout the world. It claims that the principal obstacle to peace is the absence of mutual recognition between Israel and the Palestinians. Such recognition would have to include the right of the Palestinians to self-definition and the right of Israel to exist within secure borders.

Finally Peace Now holds that only a territorial compromise for the sake of peace with security would be able to restore Israel to its real self and preserve the democratic and Jewish character of the State. J. AVIAD

PEARLMAN, MOSHE (Maurice). Israeli writer and public servant (b. London, 1911; d. Jerusalem, 1986). In 1936 Pearlman went to Palestine to report on the Arab riots. In 1938 he worked as liaison officer with the Zionist Federation of Great Britain and Ireland.

During World War II Pearlman served with the British Army (1940-44), attaining the rank of major. In 1944–45 he was in the Intelligence Service of the British Foreign Office. After the war he took a prominent part in organizing "illegal" immigration to Palestine from Central Europe and the Balkan countries. At the outbreak of the War of Independence, he joined the Hagana with the rank of lieutenant colonel and settled in Israel. From 1948 to 1952 he was director of the Government Press Office. In 1952 he became Director of the Israel Broadcasting Service, holding this post until 1955, when he was named Director of Information Services and Adviser on Public Affairs to the Prime Minister. During the Six-Day War he served as Special Assistant to Defense Minister Moshe Dayan,

His books include *Collective Adventure* (1938) and *Adventure in the Sun* (1948), accounts of kibbutz life; *Mufti of Jerusalem* (1947), the story of Hajj Amin al-Husseini; *The Army of Israel* (1950); *The Capture and Trial of Adolf Eichmann* (1963); *Historical Sites in Israel* (1964); *Ben-Gurion Looks Back* (1965); *Pilgrims to the Holy Land* (1970), and *Jerusalem, History of 40 Centuries* (1968) (both with Teddy Kollek).

PEC ISRAEL ECONOMIC CORPORATION (formerly Palestine Economic Corporation). Oldest private Zionist investment corporation in Israel. In 1921 a group of American Zionists, led by Justice Louis D. Brandeis, established according to his principles (a) the Palestine Endowment Fund (now PEF Israel Endowment Funds Inc.) for philanthropic activities, and (b) the Palestine Cooperative Company for investments and encouragement of private enterprise in the yishuv. The latter, in cooperation with the American Jewish Joint Distribution Committee (the Joint), was reorganized in 1926 as the PEC. Among the leading figures and subscribers were Brandeis, Bernard Flexner, Herbert H. Lehman, Julian W. Mack, Louis Marshall, Julius Simon, Felix M. Warburg (the largest single subscriber), and Robert Szold. PEC's main investments in the 1920s and 1930s, some of them jointly with ICA (the Jewish Colonization Association), the Joint, and the Economic Board for Palestine, were the Central Bank for Cooperative Institutions (managed for many years by Harry Viteles), the Palestine Mortgage and Credit (later "and Savings") Bank, and the Loan Bank for small borrowers. It participated in the establishment of the Potash and Electric companies, the King David Hotel in Jerusalem, the Palestine Water Company, with the Jewish National Fund (JNF) in the development of the Haifa Bay region, and with JNF and PICA (Palestine Jewish Colonization Association) in the Thousand Families settlement project. In the activities of PEC and its subsidiaries, stress was laid on the encouragement of sound business practices and of small producers, whether independent or organized in cooperatives, both in agriculture (including citrus) and in urban industries. Profits were not an important objective of PEC, and the small ones made were mostly reinvested. After the establishment of the State of Israel, PEC's banks were gradually absorbed into larger firms, as part of the consolidation process in Israeli banking. Most important was the 1951 merger of the Central Bank and the banking business of the *Palestine Corporation into the Union Bank of Israel, which later became part of the Bank Le'umi group. PEC itself, run more on purely business lines, extended its investments in the development of manufacturing and also in the construction and service industries. In the 1960s it developed close ties with the Discount Bank group and eventually became part of it.

Total assets of PEC were evaluated (in current prices respectively) at $3.6 million in 1935 and $28 million in 1967.

N. GROSS

PEEL COMMISSION. Royal Commission appointed in August 1936 by the British Government to examine the Palestine problem. The chairman was Earl Peel, a former Conservative minister, but its most influential member was Reginald Coupland, Professor of Colonial History at Oxford University. The official terms of reference called on the Commission to "ascertain the underlying causes of the disturbances which broke out in Palestine in the middle of April; to enquire into the manner in which the Mandate for Palestine is being implemented...; to ascertain whether upon a proper construction of the terms of the Mandate either the Arabs or the Jews have any legitimate grievances;" and to make recommendations for the removal of any such grievances.

Although the decision to appoint the Commission was announced by the British Government in May 1936, its actual appointment was delayed pending the restoration of order in Palestine. It was not until November that, with the Arab general strike called off and much of the violence suppressed, the Commission set out for Palestine. During their stay in Palestine, from 11 November 1936 to 17 January 1937, the Commissioners heard evidence from 137 witnesses. At first, the Arab nationalist leaders boycotted the proceedings in protest against the continuation (albeit at a reduced level) of Jewish immigration, but towards the end of the Commission's stay they relented and agreed to give evidence. The leading Zionist spokesman before the Commission was Chaim Weizmann, whose public testimony created a powerful impression. The chief Arab spokesman, Haj Amin al-Husseini, mufti of Jerusalem, demanded a total cessation of Jewish immigration and alleged that the "Jews' ultimate aim" was the reconstruction of the temple on its ancient site. The Commission also held a number of closed sessions and paid a short visit to Transjordan to meet the Emir Abdullah.

The Commission's report, issued in July 1937, was one of the most perceptive and lucid analyses of the Palestine problem ever produced. The Commissioners went beyond their terms of reference in their central recommendation for the termination of the Mandate and the partition of Palestine into a small Jewish state (comprising Galilee, the Jezreel valley, and part of the coastal plain), an Arab state (including most of the rest of Palestine and also Transjordan), and a residual British-controlled area consisting of Jerusalem, a corridor to the coast, Acre, Haifa, and an enclave near Akaba. Justifying this solution, the Report (mainly drafted by Coupland) stated: "An irrepressible conflict has arisen between two national communities within the narrow bounds of one small country. About 1,000,000 Arabs are in strife, open or latent, with some 400,000 Jews. There is no common ground between them....In these circumstances to maintain that Palestinian citizenship has any moral meaning is a mischievous pretense....But while neither race can justly rule all Palestine, we see no reason why, if it were practicable, each race should not rule part of it....Partition seems to offer at least a chance of ultimate peace. We can see none in any other plan."

The report was roundly rejected by the Arabs (with the exception of the Emir Abdullah. The Zionists split over the issue of partition. Some, notably Weizmann, Moshe Shertok (Sharett), and David Ben-Gurion, accepted partition in principle, while reserving the right to negotiate the borders of the Jewish state. Others, among them Vladimir Jabotinsky, Menahem Ussishkin, Berl Katznelson, and Golda Meyerson (Meir), opposed the proposal. At the Zionist Con-

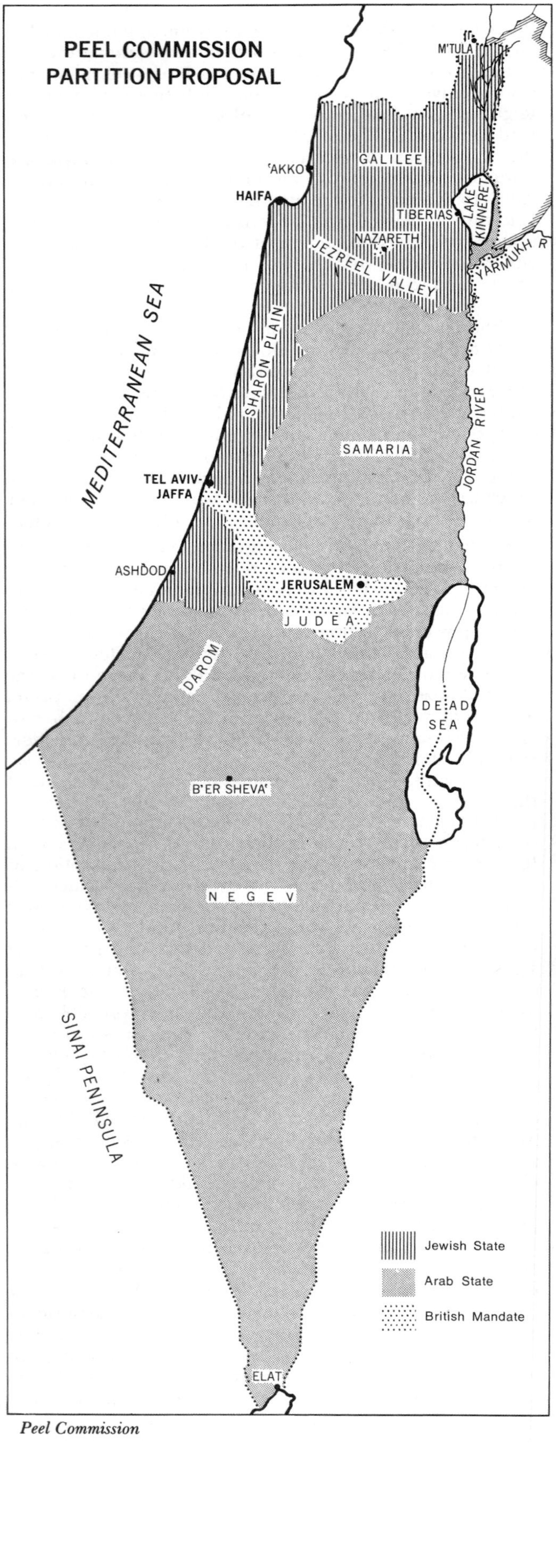

Peel Commission

gress in August, 1937, a compromise decision was taken which essentially represented a victory for the pro-partition faction.

The British Government initially accepted the Peel Report. In September, 1937, Foreign Secretary Anthony Eden declared that "partition is the only solution." But with the revival of the Arab revolt, the government's enthusiasm waned. A new commission under Sir John Woodhead was appointed to draw definitive frontiers for the proposed Jewish and Arab states. This commission received secret guidance from the British Government which led it to report that partition was impracticable. In November, 1938, the government announced its abandonment of partition.

The significance of the Peel Report lay, first, in its exceptionally clearheaded exposition of the Palestine problem; secondly, in the fact that, for the first time under the British mandate, the establishment of a sovereign Jewish state was placed on the political agenda; thirdly, in its revelation of severe internal differences among Zionists over the issue of partition; and finally, in its initiation of the process whereby, within little more than a decade, British rule in Palestine came to an end. B. WASSERSTEIN

PEKI'IN (Buqei'a). Village of Druze and Christian Arabs in central Upper Galilee. The place was inhabited by Jews at least from the Second Temple period and tradition venerates a local cave where Rabbi Simeon bar Yohai and his son Rabbi Eleazar are said to have hidden from Roman persecutions for 13 years in the 2nd century CE. Jewish peasant families lived in the village, alongside non-Jews, until the 20th century, claiming that their forefathers had never been

View of P'ki'in. [Israel Information Services]

in the Diaspora. Only one Jewish woman now remains. Its synagogue, built in 1873, contains in its walls fragments of a local synagogue of the Talmudic period. In 1955, the moshav Peki'in ha-Hadasha ("New Peki'in") was founded, north of Peki'in, with 231 inhabitants in 1987. Peki'in had 3,280 inhabitants, about two-thirds of them Druze, and the rest Christian Arabs. E. ORNI

PELUGOT MAHATZ. *See* PALMAH.

PERELMAN, CHAIM. Belgian philosopher (b. Warsaw, 1912; d. Brussels, 1984). Perelman settled in Antwerp in 1925. After brilliant studies at the University of Brussels, he became doctor of law in 1936 and doctor of philosophy in 1938; the same year he was appointed lecturer at the Faculty of Philosophy and Letters of the University of Brussels and professor in 1944. His main field of study was nonformal argument and justice in its legal and moral aspects. During the German occupation, Perelman participated in the resistance and was a member of the Comité de Défense des Juifs (C.D.J.), which he and his wife—Fela Liwer—had helped to establish and which rescued thousands of Jews. He also collaborated in the publication of illegal newspapers.

After the War, he directed, with the help of his wife, an "illegal" immigration movement which sent a boat from Antwerp in July, 1946. Perelman with some of his colleagues and friends founded the Belgian Friends of the Hebrew University which—with the help of a Ladies Committee headed by Fela Perelman—established at the University the Queen Elisabeth Institute of Archeology, the Collegium Fabiolanum, and the Faculty Club. Perelman was a member of the University's board of governors and received from it a doctorate *honoris causa.* In 1955, Perelman founded and presided over the Menorah Association which, through its conferences and a monthly newspaper, linked Jewish life in Belgium with cultural developments in Israel. From the inception of the Institut d'Etudes du Judaisme-Martin Buber, founded in 1971, he headed its scientific committee. He presided over several national committees including Monument National aux déportés (1965), Action Committee for Israel (1973), the Tribute Committee to Belgian Rescuers (1980), and the Information and Documentation Center on the Middle East (1976). A few weeks before his death, he was elevated by King Baudouin to the rank of baron. D. DRATWA

Shimon Peres.
[Israel Govt. Press Office]

PERES (PERSKY), SHIMON, Israeli labor leader and politician, Prime Minister of Israel 1984–1986 (b. Vishneva, Poland, 1923). He immigrated to Palestine in 1934. He graduated from Ben Shemen Agricultural High School and joined a pioneer training group that settled in Alumot. In 1943 he became secretary of the Labor youth movement, Ha-No'ar ha-Oved. In 1947 he was selected by David Ben-Gurion to serve in the Hagana headquarters. Between 1949 and 1952 he headed the Defense Ministry Mission to the United States. In 1952 Peres was appointed Deputy Director-General and a year later Director-General of the Defense Ministry, a position he held until 1959. In this position, under Ben-Gurion as Defense Minister, he was one of the architects of the 1956 Sinai war, helped to initiate defense ties with France and Germany, and encouraged the foundations of Israel's aviation and electronic industries and its nuclear energy programs. Active in Mapai politics as a leader of the younger generation of that party, he has sat in the Knesset since 1959. He was appointed Deputy Defense Minister holding that post until 1965 when he resigned to become Secretary General of the newly formed breakaway Rafi party headed by Ben-Gurion. The party was in opposition until 1969, when Peres was instrumental in bringing it back to Mapai and was one of the founders of the Israel Labor Party, serving as its Deputy Secretary General (under Golda Meir).

In 1969 he joined the cabinet and served until 1977 as Minister for Economic Development of the Administered Areas, Minister for Immigrant Absorption, Minister of Transport and Communications (1971–1974), Information (1974) and Defense Minister in the Rabin government (1974–1977). In the last capacity he worked to reorganize the Israel army following the Yom Kippur War, played a significant role in negotiating the second Interim Agreement with Egypt (September 1975), in planning the Entebbe Operation (1976) and the creation of the "Good Fence" policy with Lebanon. In two contests for the Labor Party leadership against Yitzhak Rabin he failed to win a majority, but after Labor lost the 1977 elections, he was elected Chairman of the Labor Party and led it through the seven years his party was in opposition to the Likud government. In 1978 he was elected Vice-President of the Socialist International. Following the 1984 general elections, which resulted in a stalemate between Labor and Likud, with neither being able to form even a narrow-based cabinet, Peres negotiated with Yitzhak Shamir the agreement that led to the establishment of the National Unity Government which Peres headed during its first two years (September 1984-October 1986).

As Prime Minister he brought about the termination of Israel's military involvement in Lebanon, in the initiation of an economic reform that reduced Israel's inflation rate from 448% in 1984/5 to 23% in 1985/6, and improved Israel's international standing. He held meetings with King Hassan of Morocco and President Mubarak of Egypt. Relations with African states progressed and those with the European Common Market were extended. Cooperation with the US attained new dimensions.

In October, 1986, he rotated offices with Yitzhak Shamir, according to the coalition agreement, and became Vice Prime Minister and Minister for Foreign Affairs. His efforts to reach an understanding with Jordan were unsuccessful in view of the opposition of the Palestine Liberation Organization, Syria, and his Likud coalition partners. Jordan's divesting of its claims and interests in the Administered

Areas in July, 1988, seemed to end Peres' policy which he called the "Jordan option." After the 1988 elections he was Vice Prime Minister and Minister of Finance in the renewed National Unity Government until 1990 when the Government broke up over Peres' advocacy of accepting US terms for advancing the peace process. In 1992 he was defeated by Yitzhak Rabin in elections to the leadership of the Labor party. After a Labor-led government was established later that year, Peres became foreign minister. M. MEDZINI

PERI, MENAHEM. Hebrew literary scholar (b. Binyamina, 1942). He studied at the Hebrew University and Tel Aviv University. Between 1963 and 1966 he was an instructor at the Hebrew University and since 1966 has taught literature at Tel Aviv University. He was secretary of the editorial board of *Ha-Sifrut* (1967–1970) and since 1970 the editor of *Siman Ker'ia*.

Peri belongs to the Tel Aviv school of semiologists and has written on Bialik's poetry and the technique of biblical narrative. E. SPICEHANDLER

PERLZWEIG, MAURICE LOUIS. Rabbi and Zionist leader (b. Poland, 1895; d. New York, 1985). Perlzweig studied at University College, London, Cambridge University, and the London School of Economics. He founded the Young Zionist Organization of the United Kingdom and was president of the London and Cambridge University Zionist Societies. On graduation he became a minister in the Liberal Synagogue of London. He served as honorary secretary of the Zionist Federation of Great Britain and Ireland, editor of the London *Zionist Review*, and deputy member of the Executive of the Jewish Agency (1935–1946). He was one of the founders of the World Jewish Congress (WJS) and first chairman of its British section.

In 1940 Stephen S. Wise invited Perlzweig to the USA as head of the WJC's International Affairs Department. The British Government used this opportunity of asking him to generate goodwill for Britain then facing the Nazi onslaught alone. His mission brough Perlzweig into contact with Jewish and non-Jewish leaders of public opinion including the highest echelons of the US Congress, State Department and administration. He was in the forefront of the struggle to rescue European Jewry from the Nazi murder machine and to secure relief for those in the ghettoes and concentration camps. As an ardent Zionist, he worked with Wise and Nahum Goldmann in their efforts to secure the establishment of an independent Jewish State. On the foundation of the United Nations Organization, Perlzweig became the WJC's permanent representative at the UN Economic and Social Council (ECOSOC), its Commission of Human Rights, and Sub-Committee on the Prevention of Discrimination. A great orator and superb draftsman of the innumerable WJC submissions to the UN, he had a paramount role in presenting the Jewish case and in securing the protection of Jewish rights by international legal instruments. With Alex L. Easterman (1890–1983), his counterpart in the WJC London Office, he fought for the rights of Jewish displaced persons not to be repatriated but to be allowed to go to Palestine and for the inclusion of Jewish demands in the Peace Treaties with Rumania, Hungary, and Italy. With Easterman and Dr. Gerhart M. Riegner, he went on several missions to North Africa, assuring the safety and right to emigrate for the Jews of Libya, Tunisia, and Morocco when those countries gained their independence. E. EPPLER

PERSIA, ZIONISM IN. *See* IRAN, ZIONISM IN.

PERSIAN JEWS IN ISRAEL. *See* IRANIAN JEWS IN ISRAEL.

PERSITZ, SHOSHANA. Publisher and political leader in Israel (b. Kiev, Russia, 1893; d. Tel Aviv, 1969). The daughter of Hillel *Zlatopolsky, Mrs Persitz became active at an early age in the promotion of the Hebrew language, serving as secretary of the Hovevei Sefat Ever and, later, of the Tarbut organization in Russia. After the Russian Revolution (March, 1917) she founded the Omanut Hebrew publishing house in Moscow, and that year she became a member of the Central Committee of the Russian Zionist Organization. After the Bolshevik Revolution (November, 1917), she moved to Kiev and then to Odessa, where she resumed her publishing activities. Later she left Russia and reestablished Omanut in Germany. In 1925 she settled in Palestine, transferring her publishing house to Tel Aviv.

From 1926 to 1935 Mrs Persitz was a member of the Tel Aviv Municipal Council, also heading the city's Department of Education. In addition, she was a member of the Department of Education of the Zionist Executive. Active in the General Zionist party, she represented the party from 1949 to 1959 in the Knesset, where she was chairman of the Committee of Education and Culture. She was a delegate to the London Zionist Conference of 1920 and the 16th Zionist Congress (1929).

Omanut, which became a major Hebrew publishing house, specialized in publishing books for the young. In 1968 Mrs. Persitz received the Israel Prize for her contributions to education.

PERU, ZIONISM IN. Zionism was introduced into Peru by Jews who settled there after World War I. In 1925 Bención Ariel, a professor at Madrid University, arrived in Peru as the first emissary of the Zionist movement. His visit evoked great enthusiasm, and after the first Zionist meeting a group of 40 young people founded the Zionist Organization of Peru. The first Zionist meeting was held in the building that had once housed the headquarters of the Inquisition. The organization chose as its leader Albert Miava; he was succeeded by Sason Sarfati. At that time the small Jewish community of Lima had no house of worship of its own, and religious services were held in the building of a Masonic temple. It was there that the first Zionist activities were concentrated. The group published a weekly, *Repertorio Hebreo*, which, though short-lived, had the distinction of being the first Jewish periodical in Peru. In 1926 the Ashkenazi Jews founded the Union Israelita del Peru, which became their main communal institution and was officially recognized in 1937.

The development of Zionist activities in Peru was greatly furthered by the arrival from Palestine of Dr. Haim Jacob Alcabes, a physician and the first Jewish professional to settle in the country. He eventually became the leader of the local Zionist Organization. The highlights in Peruvian Zionist life were visits of emissaries from abroad, Jewish National Fund and Keren ha-Yesod drives, and Balfour Day celebrations. In 1935 the *Peruaner Yidishe Tzeitung* was launched, and a short time later *La Voz Israelita* made its appearance. Both newspapers did much to spread Zionism. During the Hitler era, Nazi influence was strong in Peru, resulting in an anti-Semitic press campaign and in restrictions on Jewish immigration to the country.

During and after World War II, the Zionist Organization

of Peru grew into a strong body embracing all segments of the Jewish population, and it was therefore able to do its part in the struggle for the Jewish State. For some time after the establishment of the State of Israel, Zionist activities in Peru diminished; the generally-held assumption was that with the rise of the Jewish State, Zionism had achieved its purpose. In 1963, however, there was a revival in the local Zionist movement brought about primarily by the younger generation. In the late 1960s the Zionist Youth Federation played an important role in community affairs, and the Jewish community was linked closely to the Zionist movement.

Peruvian Jews contributed generously to the support of Israel. Annual drives on behalf of the United Israel Appeal were conducted jointly by all three communities (German, eastern European, and Sephardi Jews). There were also drives for State of Israel bonds, collections for the Jewish National Fund, and an active society of Friends of the Hebrew University of Jerusalem.

One of the outstanding achievements of the Zionist Organization of Peru was the Colegio León Pinelo (León Pinelo Jewish Day School). This school, established in 1946, educated hundreds of young Jews, many of whom subsequently went to Israel to continue their studies or to settle there permanently. At present about 700 pupils study at the Pinelo School and participate in its wide range of Zionist activities. For the last few years, a successful study program has been carried out at Alonei Yitzhak, an Israeli educational institution sponsored by Ha-No'ar ha-Tziyoni, where 11th grade pupils spend almost five months studying and learning about contemporary life in Israel. Peru was the pioneer of this program, which is now being followed in various Latin American and European countries.

Presidents of the Zionist Organization after World War II were Jaime Kirmayer, Dr. Marcos Roitman, Marcos Perelman, Dr. Isaac Wexelman, José Rosenbach, Bención Brodsky, Dr. Abraham Feldman, Benjamin Zusman, Eduardo Bigio, Jose Alalu, Jose Maiman, Fernando Gomberoff, Eric Topf, Sammy Loebl, Tobias Gabriel, and Marcos Kalikstein.

There were two Zionist women's groups, WIZO and Pioneer Women. Both had sections for younger women, *WIZO Aviv* and *Pioneras Shalva*. In addition, there were three youth organizations. Betar, founded in 1939, published much cultural material in Yiddish and Spanish and had considerable influence on youth but discontinued its activities in 1966 after 30 of its members went to Israel as pioneers. Ha-No'ar ha-Tziyoni was founded in 1946; it, too, provided pioneers and issued a periodical, *Zion*. A third youth group, Kineret, was organized in 1962.

The Jewish community today numbers 3,800 (among a total population of 20 million). Zionist life is conducted through the women's institutions such as WIZO and Na'amat. The WIZO Federation has taken on new life with the introduction of young leadership at the administrative level.

The sole youth movement today is Ha-No'ar ha-Tziyoni; it has 280 members and carries out typical youth movement activities. At a certain age, the older members tend to leave the movement, many to settle in the cities and kibbutzim of Israel or to study at Israeli universities.

The Jewish press has a daily bulletin (JTA) with a circulation of 600. In addition, abundant and rich Zionist material appears in *La Union* the Jewish Community of Peru's official monthly review, edited by Prof. Ya'acov Hasson. It has a circulation of 2,000.

In December, 1975, in reaction to the UN resolution equating Zionism with racism, the Jewish Community of Peru held a mass meeting, officially declaring itself the "first Zionist community of the entire Diaspora," a title which it assumed responsibly and proudly. The President of the Zionist Organization of Peru, Marcos Kalikstein, consolidated a large-scale Zionism membership drive.

A PLO Office has existed in Lima since 1979 despite the efforts of both Jews and non-Jews to prevent the presence of a terrorist entity on Peruvian soil. The PLO has intensified its activities in Marxist, university, and political circles, where it distributes Nazi, anti-Semitic, and anti-Zionist material. The PLO "chancellor" was received by President Garcia at the Government Palace in Lima. Likewise, at the Conference of the Non-Aligned States held in Zimbabwe, Africa, in 1986, President Garcia held meetings with Arafat and Libyan leader Mohammar Kaddafi, an action severely criticized in the press and in the local Jewish community.

While there is no official anti-Semitism in Peru, a number of small Nazi groups do exist, but without any great influence on national thought. The Israeli invasion of Lebanon (1982) met with considerable criticism in the press and on the part of political personalities, while the massacres of Sabra and Shatilla were even more severely condemned. The Jewish community countered these views in the print and broadcast media.

Y.I. HASSON

PETAH TIKVA ("Gateway of hope" cf. Hosea 2:17). City in the coastal plain 7 mi. (12 km.) east of Tel Aviv. In the 1870s a number of observant Jews from Jerusalem decided to earn their livelihood by working the soil and tried in 1872 to purchase land for the purpose near Jericho but the Turkish authorities did not consent to foreign subjects settling there. Continuing their search, an area of 850 acres near the Yarkon River was found in 1878. Attracted by its greenery, they disregarded warnings of the danger of malaria and laid the ground for the first modern Jewish village in the country. The founders, among them David Guttman, Yoel Moshe Salomon, Joshua Stampfer, Eliezer Raab, M.L. Katz, and others, succeeded in mobilizing more settlers, but malaria soon wrought havoc, the first harvest was a failure, and neighboring Arabs harassed them. They returned to Jerusalem and by 1881 Petah Tikva was abandoned.

A year later, the pioneers bought land in the nearby Arab village of Yahud, received some aid from the Hovevei Zion movement, and were joined by First Aliya newcomers. All the former difficulties repeated themselves, and in addition the Turkish authorities were hostile, but in 1887 Baron Edmond de Rothschild came to their aid, and initiated the plantation of vineyards, thus giving employment to the settlers. The direction of the village (moshava) passed into the hands of Rothschild's administrators. Tensions developed between them and the settlers, which lessened only slightly after the Jewish Colonization Association took over in 1900, at which time Petah Tikva numbered 818 inhabitants.

In the following decade, the situation improved, Petah Tikva was regarded as "the mother of the moshavot," became the center of the nascent Jewish labor movement, and in 1905 the parties Ha-Po'el ha-Tza'ir and Ahdut ha-Avoda were founded there. The settlers encouraged a watchmen's group headed by Abraham Shapira, which fought off Arab attacks and drove away Arab flocks grazing on Jewish fields. The moshava, which had suffered severe locust damage

Monument to Baron Edmond de Rothschild in Petah Tikva. [Israel Government Press Office]

and harassment by the Turkish authorities, faced a difficult period at the end of 1917 when it was between the lines of the German-Turkish and Allied armies.

After the war, the moshava absorbed many immigrants and in 1920 received local council status. In May, 1921, an Arab attack was repulsed by local youth, assisted by British troops, but four young men were killed. In subsequent years, Petah Tikva expanded quickly. The citrus branch became its economic mainstay, its first industrial enterprises opened, and by 1930 it numbered almost 9,000 inhabitants. In 1939 it attained city status with a population of over 20,000. The crisis of the citrus branch in World War II was compensated for by the progress of industry which supplied goods to the Allied forces stationed in the country. After World War II, Petah Tikva became the center of underground movements, especially the Irgun. It merged with adjoining workers' quarters and Jewish villages. In the 1948 War of Independence, the threat of Arab attacks was forestalled by the occupation of Arab villages in the area by the Israel Defense Forces. After 1948, Petah Tikva's expansion was rapid, bringing the population to 45,000 in 1953, 83,200 in 1970, and 132,100 in 1987. Its location in the Tel Aviv conurbation decisively influenced its development. Besides many large- and medium-sized enterprises of heavy and light industry in varied branches, citrus and other farming still played a role. Efforts to restrain expansion over the excellent farmland in the vicinity led, from the 1960s, to closer and higher building in the city. Petah Tikva has two big hospitals and the cultural institution Yad la-Banim, dedicated to the fallen in Israel's wars. E. ORNI

PEVSNER, SAMUEL JOSEPH. Engineer and pioneer in Palestine (b. Propoisk, Russia, 1878; d. Jerusalem, 1930). Pevsner studied at the Technische Hochschule in Berlin. An early follower of Herzl, he was the youngest delegate at the First Zionist Congress (1897). In 1905 he settled in Haifa, where he played a prominent role in the development of the local Jewish community and was one of the builders of the city's Hadar ha-Carmel section, where a street was named for him. Pevsner was a member of the Asefat ha-Nivharim and of the Haifa Community Council.

PICA. *See* PALESTINE JEWISH COLONIZATION ASSOCIATION.

PICARD, YEHUDA LEO. Israeli geologist (b. Wangen, Germany, 1900). He studied geology at the universities of Freiburg im Breisgau and Berlin, and was a member of the Blau-Weiss Zionist students' organization. After his immigration to Palestine in 1924, he established a geological department at the Hebrew University, becoming a lecturer in 1934, associate professor in 1939 and full professor in

1941. Most of Picard's work was related to basic geological investigation of the country, to the development of its groundwater and mineral deposits, and to prospecting for petroleum. He recognized the importance of the country's limestone formations as potential sources of groundwater and was responsible for many significant groundwater discoveries. Picard acted as consultant on groundwater resources to various international agencies and bilateral technical assistance projects. In 1967 he established the Hebrew University Groundwater Training and Research Center. Picard educated a generation of Israeli geologists and many of his pupils made important contributions to the development of the country's natural resources. In 1958 he was awarded the Israel Prize. His numerous publications include *Structure and Evolution of Palestine* (1943).

Z. SHIFTAN

PICK, HERMANN. Orientalist (b. Schildberg, Prussia, 1879; d. Jerusalem, 1952). After studying at the Hildesheimer Rabbinical Seminary and Berlin University, Pick served at various German scholarly institutions. Joining the Zionist movement in 1909, he was an early follower of Mizrachi. In 1920 he was elected to the Executive of the Mizrachi World Movement, and in 1921 he was appointed a member of the Zionist Executive and the director of its Immigration Department in Jerusalem. He served in that capacity until 1927, when he returned to Berlin, finally settling in Palestine in 1939. Pick was the author of several studies in Assyriology.

Louis Pincus. [Zionist Archives]

PINCUS, LOUIS (ARYE ABRAHAM) Israeli lawyer and chairman of the Executive of the Jewish Agency (b. Clocolan, Orange Free State, South Africa, 1912; d. Jerusalem, 1973). Pincus studied law and economics at Witwatersrand University. Admitted to the South African bar after his graduation (B.A. and LL.B., 1934), he opened a law practice in his native country. One of the founders of the Zionist Youth Movement Habonim in South Africa, he served as chairman of the Zionist Socialist Party (the major Labor Zionist group in South African Zionism) (1939–48) and as vice-chairman of the South African Zionist Federation (1940–48), and he represented the Labor Zionist party at the 22nd Zionist Congress (1946).

Settling in Israel in 1948, Pincus was Secretary-General and Legal Adviser of Israel's Ministry of Transport from the establishment of the State until 1949, when he was appointed managing director of El Al, Israel's national airline, a position he held until 1956. In 1957 he opened a private law practice in Tel Aviv.

Pincus's association with the Jewish Agency began in 1956, when he was appointed chairman of its Finance and Budget Committee. He was elected treasurer of the Agency Executive in 1965 and chairman of the Executive in 1966, a position he held until his sudden death in 1973. In 1968 he was also elected head of the Agency's Aliya Department. Pincus was a member of the Central Committee of Mapai and chairman of the party's Professional Bureau. He also served on the Executive of the World Union of Po'ale Zion. He traveled extensively in the United States, Canada, England, and South Africa on behalf of the Jewish Agency and Zionist fundraising. In 1969 he carried through an internal reorganization of the Jewish Agency, which involved the consolidation of departments and the reduction of the number of Executive members. At the same time, in collaboration with the American Jewish leader Max Fisher, he proceeded to put through a reconstitution of the Agency by including elements not necessarily represented by the World Zionist Organization (WZO) and its constituencies. Under this arrangement the Agency was to be responsible for work in and for Israel such as fundraising, immigration, absorption, social welfare, health, and Youth Aliya, while the WZO was to supervise information, youth activities, and educational and organizational activity in the Diaspora. An Assembly of the Jewish Agency was to be formed to act as the Agency's governing body. The Assembly, comprising up to 250 members, was to consist of representatives from Israel and the WZO (50 percent), the United States (30 percent), and other Diaspora countries (20 percent), including representatives of the major Jewish fundraising bodies in the United States and other countries (these mandates to be apportioned by a committee appointed for that purpose). The executive organ of the Assembly was to be a board of governors constituted in the same proportions. It was as a result of Pincus's untiring efforts that this reconstruction was approved, resulting in a significant broadening of the Jewish Agency for the first time since the expansion in 1929 carried out under the leadership of Chaim Weizmann.

PINE, MAX. Labor organizer and founder of the American Histadrut Campaign (b. Lyubavichi, Russia, 1866; d. Maywood, New Jersey, 1928). Arriving in New York in 1890, Pine spent his first years working in the needle trades. Before long, he started his organizing activities, and was elected general secretary of the United Hebrew Trades (Faraynikte Yidishe Geverkshaften) at a time when that body was the most powerful force in the American Jewish labor movement. He was a founder of the People's Relief Committee and had a part in forming the American Jewish Joint Distribution Committee.

Although sharing the anti-Zionist views that predominated among most of the official leaders in the Jewish labor movement until after World War I. Pine was the first prominent labor official to respond to the call of the Histadrut for support. In 1923, he organized the National Labor Committee for Organized Jewish Labor in Palestine, which launched the Histadrut Campaign on the North American continent. By the time of his death, he had succeeded in enlisting the cooperation of most of the Jewish trade unions.

C.B. SHERMAN

PINELES, SAMUEL. Zionist leader (b. Brody, Galicia, Austria, 1843; d. Galati, Romania, 1928). An early adherent of the Romanian Hovevei Zion movement, Pineles served as chairman of the Focsani Conference of Romanian Hovevei Zion societies (11–12 January 1882) and became secretary of the Central Committee of the movement. He assisted the Romanian emigrants who established the settlements of Rosh Pina and Zamarin (later renamed Zikhron Ya'akov). Shortly thereafter there was a decline in Hovevei Zion activity in Romania, and Pineles decided to withdraw from active work in the movement. He became active again in 1893, when the Hovevei Zion movement was revived in the country. Pineles headed the Galati committee, presided over the countrywide conference of Hovevei Zion societies which convened in January, 1895, and was chosen chairman of the newly elected Central Committee. The new committee bought land in the Golan (Gaulan) region from Baron de Rothschild for the purpose of settling Jews from Romania, but the Turkish authorities forced the settlers to leave the land.

Pineles was one of the first followers of Herzl, with whom he began to correspond early in 1897. Herzl entrusted him with the task of organizing Romanian Zionists for the First Zionist Congress and with establishing a countrywide Zionist committee. Pineles was a vice-president of the Congress, which he addressed on the situation of Romanian Jewry. He was elected to the Greater Actions Committee of the World Zionist Organization. Pineles was also prominently affiliated with Zionist institutions such as the Jewish Colonial Trust. Active in the promotion of aliya he was of assistance to the Russian halutzim who passed through Romania in 1920 on their way to Palestine. I. KLAUSNER

Yehiel Mikhel Pines.
[Jewish National Fund]

PINES, YEHIEL MIKHEL. Hebrew writer and Eretz Israel pioneer (b. Ruzhany, Grodno District, Russia, 1843; d. Jerusalem, 1913). He was one of the few eastern European Orthodox Jews to attempt to combine the best of Jewish tradition with western European education and culture during the haskala (Jewish Enlightenment) period. In his Hebrew articles he criticized the assimilationist and religious reformist tendencies of the haskala. He evolved a theory of Jewish nationalism with the Jewish religion as its main basis. A collection of his articles, *Yaldei Ruhi* (1872), made a great impression. Subsequently he advocated the settlement of Jews in Eretz Israel. He himself settled there in 1878, having been appointed director of the Sir Moses Montefiore Testimonial Fund, set up in England in honor of Sir Moses Montefiore for the establishment and organization of charitable institutions in Eretz Israel. Pines served in this position until 1901, when he was succeeded by his son-in-law, David Yellin.

Leo Pinsker.
[Zionist Archives]

PINSKER, LEO. Physician and *Hovevei Zion leader, author of *Autoemancipation* (b. Tomaszow, Russian Poland, 1821; d. Odessa, 1891). The son of a teacher and scholar, Pinsker first entered the teaching profession but later studied law and medicine. He established a medical practice in Odessa and contributed to *Rassviet*, the first Russian-Jewish weekly, which appeared in 1860. Later he helped edit the weekly *Zion*. As head of the Odessa branch of the Mefitzei Haskala (Society for the Promotion of Enlightenment among Russian Jews), he was active in the dissemination of secular culture among the Jews. He also contributed to the monthly *Diyen* (The Day), established by the society, which advocated assimilation.

The Odessa pogroms of 1871 and the subsequent change for the worse in the policies of the Russian authorities toward the Jews depressed Pinsker greatly. The 1881 pogroms that swept Russia caused him to revise his previous views on the position of the Jews in the Diaspora. Formerly a believer in the emancipation of the Jews in the countries where they lived, Pinsker came to the conclusion that the Jewish problem would be solved only by the concentrated settlement of Jews in a country where they would eventually form a majority and attain political independence. At a meeting of the committee of the Mefitzei Haskala in the summer of 1881, he called on the society to give up its activities, which he felt were pointless, and to concentrate on rendering practical aid to the resettlement of the Jews.

In 1882 Pinsker visited various European capitals in order to discuss his ideas with prominent Jews. In Vienna he conferred with Chief Rabbi Adolf Jellinek, to whom he explained the necessity of a Jewish exodus from Europe. Pinsker considered Eretz Israel a country suitable for settlement. Jellinek was not receptive to the ideas of Jewish nationhood and a Jewish State. The leaders of the Alliance Israélite Universelle in Paris also opposed him. The only one to agree with him was Arthur Cohen, chairman of the Board of Deputies of British Jews and nephew of Sir Moses Montefiore. Cohen encouraged him to put his ideas into writing, and in 1882 Pinsker published in Berlin a pamphlet in German entitled *Autoemancipation: A Warning of a Russian Jew to His Brethren,* in which he warned his fellow Jews to steer clear of the illusion that anti-Semitism was on the wane. He argued that the main source of the Jewish problem and of anti-Semitism was the fact that the Jews were a foreign element among the nations; even in countries where they had been granted equal rights under the law, they were not accepted as equals by the dominant society. As soon as the number of Jews in a particular country exceeded the "point of saturation," persecution would set in. Pinsker also pointed out that the bond of national solidarity among western Jews had weakened, whereas among the Jews of Russia and Romania there were stirrings of national consciousness, which found expression in the recognition of the need for a Homeland. Pinsker also expressed the hope that the peoples who oppressed the Jews would help them acquire a national and political center of their own. In his pamphlet Pinsker did not state where the Jews should establish their center—in America or in Eretz Israel—but merely called for a national congress to choose a country and organize emigration activities. Pinsker proposed the establishment of a national fund based on contributions for the settlement of immigrants without financial means.

Pinsker's pamphlet, which was eventually recognized as a Zionist classic, made a profound impression on the Hovevei Zion movement, whose basic manifesto it became. After its publication, Moshe Leib Lilienblum tried to induce him to commence activities for the settlement of the Jews in Eretz Israel, but Pinsker did not want to choose on his own the country to which Jews should emigrate. A year later, however, Lilienblum and Hermann Schapira prevailed on him to dedicate his energies to the settlement of Eretz Israel by joining the Hibbat Zion movement. Pinsker became the driving spirit of this movement and prepared the Hovevei Zion conference which was held in Kattowitz in November, 1884 (*see* KATTOWITZ CONFERENCE). It was presided over by Pinsker who was also elected chairman of the Central Committee. However, in his opening address at the Conference he did not mention the objective which he had defined as 'autoemancipation', namely the national revival of the Jewish people in their own land. He confined himself to the limited matter of assistance to the Jewish settlers in their land, since he wished to obtain the support of the German Jews who were afraid of a dual nationality, and since he feared that clearly nationalistic objectives would alarm the Turkish government which in any case was restricting the progress of Jewish settlement. He also felt that the Jewish people were not yet ready for independence. Thus Hovevei Zion activity was of a philanthropic nature, and Pinsker, given the great differences of opinion, had reservations about it from a doctrinal point of view.

The limited amounts contributed by individual societies to the central fund did not permit the granting of adequate support to the settlements in Eretz Israel or the broadening of settlement activities. This fact, coupled with differences of opinion within the movement and his poor state of health, caused Pinsker to become embittered and to tender his resignation at the Druskenik Conference in 1887. However, his resignation was not accepted. The more secularly inclined members in particular wanted him to continue to lead the movement for fear that its leadership might pass to the Orthodox element, led by Rabbi Shemuel Mohilever. Pinsker acceded to their request. He met with Baron de Rothschild, on the initiative of the latter, and obtained his support for the settlements in Eretz Israel, in collaboration with Hovevei Zion.

He continued to lead the Hovevei Zion until his resignation in 1889, when a conference in Vilna elected a new leadership.

After permission to organize the Odessa Committee had been obtained from the Russian government, Pinsker was again chosen head of the movement. The start of large-scale immigration to Eretz Israel in 1890 led him to hope once more that his aims were about to be realized. However, the cessation of immigration in 1891 by the Turkish authorities and the cancellation of land purchases by settlement societies brought new disappointment. Pinsker closely followed Baron Maurice de Hirsch's plans for the settlement of Russian Jews in Argentina, hoping that the project would solve the problem of concentrating masses of Jewish emigrants in one territory. Pinsker despaired of Eretz Israel, considering that the struggle for power over the Holy Places there would prevent the Jews from consolidating the land as a political reality. He felt that at the most it could serve as a spiritual center for the people.

I. KLAUSNER—S. LASKOV

PINSKI, DAVID. Playwright, pioneer in Yiddish literature, editor, and Labor Zionist leader (b. Mogilev, Russia, 1872; d. Haifa, 1959). Pinski's name first appeared in print in 1894, and he became an early co-worker of the great Yiddish author Isaac Leb Peretz, writing short stories, articles on current topics, and essays on popular science. As a pioneer of Jewish socialism, he reflected in his writings the struggles of Jewish workingmen for freedom and human dignity. After studying medicine for several years in Germany, Pinski settled in New York in 1899 and soon became known as a playwright, novelist, and editor.

Entertaining sympathies for the Bund in his youth, Pinski became an ardent Zionist during World War I and emerged as a leader of Po'ale Zion. He edited the *Yidisher Kemfer* for a number of years and was editor-in-chief of the Po'ale Zion daily *Die Zeit* throughout its existence. A member of the leading bodies of Po'ale Zion, he was elected president of the Farband (Labor Zionist fraternal order) in the 1920s, a position he held until he moved to Israel in 1950. He spent the last years of his life in Haifa and continued writing until the end, honored by the State and by his adopted city. The Haifa street where he lived has been named for him.

C.B. SHERMAN

PIONEERING. *See* HALUTZIYUT.

PIONEER WOMEN. *See* NA'AMAT.

PITTSBURGH PROGRAM. Program for the rebuilding of the Jewish National Home in Palestine, adopted by the 21st Convention of the Federation of American Zionists (*see* ZIONIST ORGANIZATION OF AMERICA), held in Pittsburgh, Pa., in June, 1918. Since the Pittsburgh Convention was the first assembly of American Zionists to be convened after the issuance of the (Balfour Declaration (2 November 1917), it was thought proper that the convention proclaim a code of social justice to guide the practical task of rebuilding the Homeland.

Justice Louis D. Brandeis had a decisive voice in framing the resolution as unanimously adopted by the convention on 25 June 1918. The main points were:

First
We declare for political and civil equality irrespective of race, sex, or faith of all the inhabitants of the land.

Second
To insure in the Jewish national home in Palestine equality of opportunity, we favor a policy which, with due regard to existing rights, shall tend to establish the ownership and control by the whole people of the land, of all natural resources and of all public utilities.

Third
All land, owned or controlled by the whole people, should be leased on such conditions as will insure the fullest opportunity for development and continuity of possession.

Fourth
The cooperative principle should be applied so far as feasible in the organization of agricultural, industrial, commercial, and financial undertakings.

Fifth
The system of free public instruction, which is to be established should embrace all grades and departments of education.

Sixth
Hebrew, the national language of the Jewish people, shall be the medium of public instruction.

Except for a few critics who attacked the resolution as a piece of thoughtless radicalism and irresponsible social experimentation, it was warmly welcomed by those who feared that the evils of monopoly and poverty might be transplanted to the new Jewish Homeland. The basic elements of the land policy set forth in the resolution were accepted by the *London Zionist Conference of 1920.

G. HIRSCHLER

PKP. *See* COMMUNISTS IN ISRAEL.

PLO. *See* PALESTINE LIBERATION ORGANIZATION.

PLUMER, HERBERT CHARLES ONSLOW. 1st Viscount Plumer of Messines and of Bilton, Yorkshire. British soldier (b. Torquay, 1857; d. London, 1932). Born to a middle-class family, Plumer was educated at Eton and entered the British army in 1876. He served in the Sudan, in the Boer War, and in World War I. He was British commander in 1917 at Passchendaele, one of the bloodiest battles of the war on the Western Front. From 1919 to 1924 he was Governor and Commander in Chief of Malta and from 1925 to 1928 he served as *High Commissioner for Palestine.

Plumer took a determinedly non-political approach to his task in Palestine: one of his first acts as High Commissioner was to discontinue the dispatch of regular monthly reports to the Colonial Office in London. He had no intellectual interest in Zionism but he endeared himself to the yishuv by his unwavering resistance to Arab nationalism. When an Arab delegation warned him that they could not be responsible for public tranquillity unless their demands were met, Plumer retorted that he did not expect them to take such responsibility—he would be responsible. Plumer resisted proposals in 1926 and 1928 for the establishment of an elected Legislative Council, arguing that it would be 'prejudicial to the interests of the people of Palestine as a whole.' He permitted, however, the enactment of a Municipal Franchise Ordinance in 1926 which provided for elected municipalities, albeit on a narrowly restricted franchise. The first such elections took place in 1927. Late in 1927 an autonomous Jewish organization based on religious affiliation was sanctioned under the Religious Communities Ordinance of 1926.

The most significant event during Plumer's term of office was the economic depression that struck Palestine in 1926–27. Although the mandatory government did not take active measures for economic rehabilitation, Plumer set up relief works for the unemployed, and the municipality of Tel Aviv was given a loan for this purpose. During the depression the number of immigration certificates was reduced, and a new category of immigrants, that of laborers, was established. 1927 was the first (and only) year in the history of the Palestine mandate in which Jewish emigration exceeded immigration.

Plumer was popular with his own officials in Palestine and with the yishuv. But his period of office was marked by a severe crisis in Zionism in which the movement came close to bankruptcy. His political immobilism was attractive to the Zionists in the short term but he bequeathed an unstable situation to his successors. In order to reduce public expenditures he scaled down the security forces. By 1928 the total contingent of British forces in western Palestine consisted of six armored cars and 5.8 (on average) serviceable aeroplanes, plus accompanying personnel. When severe anti-Jewish riots broke out in August, 1929, it was found that Plumer's economy measures had left a security apparatus so diminished as to be unable to restore order.

B. WASSERSTEIN

PO'ALEI AGUDAT ISRAEL. Religious labor movement dedicated to upbuilding the Land of Israel in the spirit of the Torah. Founded in 1922 in Poland as the workers' organization of *Agudat Israel, it was intended primarily to protect the rights of religious Jewish workers by implementing the Biblical ideals of social justice in Jewish life. The movement spread to other countries, particularly in Eastern Europe. With the deterioration of the Jewish position in Europe, the movement became increasingly oriented towards Palestine and began training its members as halutzim (pioneers). The first immigrants of Po'alei Agudat Israel arrived in Palestine in the late 1920s; a branch of the organization had been established in the country as early as 1923. In 1933 the pioneers founded the kibbutz Hafetz Hayim.

During the years preceding the establishment of the State of Israel, Po'alei Agudat Israel, collaborated with the World Zionist Organization in settlement endeavors. In the period immediately following World War II, it participated in the organization of "illegal" immigration to Palestine. After the establishment of the State, the movement was able to expand its organizational, educational, and settlement activities to a considerable degree. By 1988 it had established five settlements.

In the 1949 elections to the Knesset, Po'alei Agudat Israel formed part of the United Religious Front, which represented all religious parties. In the 1951 elections it campaigned independently. In the next two elections (1955, 1959) it formed a united list with Agudat Israel. In 1961, 1965, and 1969 Po'alei Agudat Israel again offered an independent list, obtaining two Knesset seats in each of these elections. The movement participated in various coalition governments. Binyamin Mintz, the world leader of the movement from 1944 on, was Minister of Posts from 1960 until his death in 1961. His successor in the world leadership, Rabbi Kalman Kahana, was Deputy Minister of Education in 1952 and again from 1961 to 1969.

Po'alei Agudat Israel maintained branches in Europe and in North and South America. The movement was greatly weakened by the death of its chairman, Yaakov Bruner, and branches remained active only in the USA and in two or three European countries. They provided financial support to the movement's institutions in Israel and new immigrants were recruited from their membership.

For many years Isaac Breuer was the principal ideologist of the movement. Rabbi Yeshayahu *Karelitz (known as the "Hazon Ish"), a revered figure in the rabbinic world, was closely related to the movement and advised the settlements on Halakhic problems, such as the observance of the Sabbath and the sabbatical year in agricultural work. Rabbi Meir Karelitz was for many years the rabbinical authority of the movement. After his death, Rabbi Asher Ze'ev Werner, rabbi of Tiberias, was appointed rabbi of Po'alei Agudat Israel, and he was succeeded by Rabbi Ṛefa'el Katznelbogen. After the latter's death in 1972, no rabbi was found to take his place.

The principal organ of the movement is *She'arim*, originally a daily but by the late 1980s a weekly, founded in 1951 and published in Tel Aviv. The youth affiliate of Po'alei Agudat Israel is the religious youth movement Ezra. Ezra was founded in Germany after World War I; its first branch in Eretz Israel was established in 1936. It educated its members in knowledge and strict adherence to the Jewish religious heritage (to be acquired through study in yeshivot) and toward creative participation in the building of the country, preferably by settling in a kibbutz of the Po'alei Agudat Israel. In 1988 Ezra had branches throughout Israel with a total membership of about 4,000. There were sister organizations in Great Britain, the Netherlands (where it was called Shalshelet), France (where its name was Yeshurun), and other countries. At the 1988 convention of Ezra it was decided to add to the name "Movement of Ultra-Orthodox Youth" the word "national," which has a serious implication in the Aguda dictionary. Po'alei Agudat Israel's central educational institution is Yad Binyamin, a Torah study and vocational training center, in the Nahal Sorek district.

In 1960 Po'alei Agudat Israel, originally part of Agudat Israel, became an independent organization.

The serious opposition of the Gerer hasidim to Binyamin Mintz' appointment as a government minister, and the influence of the heads of the "Lithuanian" yeshivot, who very violently opposed the nationalist character of Po'alei Agudat Israel, considerably weakened the movement. A small number, headed by the founders Yaakov Landau, Avraham Goldrat, Yehiel Grantstein, and others, even seceded to Ha-Po'el ha-Mizrahi. In the 1981 Knesset elections Po'alei Agudat Israel failed to win a single Knesset mandate. Despite the departure of the old leadership, their successors, under Avraham Werdiger, made little headway in reviving the movement.

In the 1985 Knesset elections, Po'alei Agudat Israel managed to unite with those who seceded from Ha-Po'el ha-Mizrachi, creating a new list, Morasha, and Werdiger obtained a seat in the Knesset. The bloc disbanded, however, before the next elections, when the heads of the Ha-Po'el ha-Mizrachi seceders returned to their party.

In 1988, when the heads of the "Lithuanian" yeshivot left Agudat Israel and created the Degel ha-Torah party, Po'alei Agudat Israel reintegrated with Agudat Israel, and the two movements stood together in the 1988 and 1992 Knesset elections and the 1989 municipal elections.

T. PRESCHEL—I. ALFASSI

PO'ALE ZION. Movement that sought to combine political Zionism with the class interests of the Jewish proletariat and the realization of socialism. Its earliest groups were formed in the late 19th century in Russia; most of the national European and American Po'ale Zion parties were established by 1907, when they formed the World Union (Berit Olamit) of Po'ale Zion. In 1920 the World Union was divided on the issues of the relationship to the Third International and the primacy of the upbuilding of Jewish Palestine. The Left Po'ale Zion was reorganized in 1924 after its extremist elements had broken away and abandoned Zionism. The right-wing group, which belonged to the World Zionist Organization (WZO), merged in 1925 with the Zionist Socialist party.

Russia. Po'ale Zion in Russia was founded about 1899 by groups that broke away from the general Zionist Organization and the Bund. Between 1901 and 1903 additional groups were established in the northwestern part of the Jewish Pale, southern Russia, and Poland. The ideological element uniting these groups was a concern for the economic fate of the Jewish laborer in particular, as distinct from the general working class. The groups claimed that the problem of the Jewish worker could be solved only by his territorial concentration in Palestine. They proposed a Zionist organization of the Jewish proletariat and joint activity within the WZO. The groups differed on the question of active participation in the revolutionary struggle within Russia. The Kishinev pogrom of 1903 radicalized their revolutionary stand.

Between 1903 and 1905 various schisms appeared in the party. One group became Territorialists; another (the so-called Sejmists) devoted themselves to fostering Jewish autonomy in the Diaspora. Early in 1906 the Social Democratic Jewish Labor party Po'ale Zion was formed under the leadership of Ber *Borochov, and it remained loyal to Eretz Israel. Borochov's philosophy, based on an analysis of Jewish economic processes, urged the development of a Jewish community in Eretz Israel and provided an objective impetus for aliya. Borochov held that, as a result of spontaneous economic processes and of the Jewish class struggle that would occur normally in Eretz Israel, the Socialist ideal would be realized within a concentration of Jewish population there.

Groups of Russian Po'ale Zion members settled in Eretz Israel during the period 1903–06, but the political paralysis that followed the 1906 reaction in Russia severely affected the party. Its leaders were jailed, and the organization was hounded. This situation fostered a more leftist trend in Po'ale Zion, and in 1909 it withdrew from the WZO.

Austria-Hungary. Following some early attempts, the year 1904 saw the formation of Po'ale Zion in the Hapsburg Monarchy by a group of Zionist laborers and intellectuals. Headed by Shelomo Kaplansky and Nathan Gross, they were opposed to Jewish Socialist antinationalist trends and joined the Austrian Zionist Organization. Later they left this organization but remained in the WZO and participated in the Zionist Congress. They viewed themselves as participating in the class struggle within the monarchy, but they

Founding convention of Po'ale Zion in the United States in 1905. [YIVO Institute for Jewish Research]

joined the WZO in order to help realize the latter's goals. At the Zionist Congresses the Austrian Po'ale Zion supported Franz Oppenheimer's program for the cooperative settlement of Eretz Israel, which it viewed as a manifestation of Zionist work for the Jewish proletariat.

The multinational character of the Austro-Hungarian Monarchy created many problems for the Po'ale Zion. The separate trade union groups of the Po'ale Zion opposed the internationalist line. In elections they supported Jewish nationalist candidates and, in second place, Social Democratic candidates. In the 1910 referendum they fought for the recognition of Yiddish as the Jewish national language. The Po'ale Zion also participated in elections to the Jewish communities and sought to secure wide authority for them.

United States. Po'ale Zion emerged in the United States in 1903 as an offshoot of the Russian groups. The Po'ale Zion groups differed from Jewish Socialist groups in their emphasis on Zionist activity and support of the Basle Program. The American group was influenced on the one hand by the increasing number of Russian-Jewish immigrants and the ideas they brought with them and, on the other, by the less doctrinaire social climate of America, which was free of political oppression and militant class consciousness.

In 1905 the group split into Territorialists and Palestinians, and late that year the Socialist Jewish Labor party Po'ale Zion in the United States and Canada was formed. In 1906 it began to publish *Der Yidisher Kemfer* (The Jewish Fighter). In 1909 the Territorialists, led by Nachman Sirkin and Baruch Zuckerman, rejoined the party after the program for the settlement of Jews had been amended to include the phrase "and in lands adjacent to Palestine."

Within the WZO the American Po'ale Zion groups, like the Austrian, stood for cooperation with nonlabor parties in active work for the upbuilding of Eretz Israel. They founded the Ahva cooperative for establishment of cooperative settlements and garden cities in Eretz Israel. The American group was active in raising money for the Jewish national funds and the Eretz Israel Workers' Fund and supported such workers' enterprises in Eretz Israel as the newspaper *Ha-Ahdut*, and the Ha-Shomer organization.

Eretz Israel. Po'ale Zion was founded there in 1906 by Russian immigrants of the Second Aliya. During the early stages of the party's existence there were different views concerning the value of Eretz Israel as the Jewish Homeland and the Hebrew language. In 1907, under the guidance of Itzhak Ben-Zvi, the party began to concentrate on the class struggle, formed trade union groups, and organized strikes. However, these trade union activities were not successful in the under-developed condition in the country. Po'ale Zion sponsored a Yiddish publication. It also demanded that the WZO carry out practical programs in Eretz Israel. From 1910 on, the party newspaper *Ha-Ahdut* was published.

The Young Turk Revolution of 1908 roused the party to political activity in the Ottoman Empire and awakened concern for the Jewish community in the empire. The party played down the call for a class struggle and favored a nonparty professional organization of agricultural workers and cooperative settlement under WZO auspices. In 1912 the World Union of Po'ale Zion began to function in Eretz Israel through the Eretz Israel Workers' Fund and the Labor Office, which opened an employment information center. These activities led to differences of opinion concerning the spheres of responsiblity of the party and its World Union, as well as between them and the other workers' organizations in the country. The Ha-Sho'mer defense organization functioned under the auspices of the party.

World Socialist Union of Jewish Laborers Po'ale Zion. This organization was founded in 1907 in The Hague by the Po'ale Zion parties of various countries in order to coordinate their activities. The World Union sought to carry out its own economic program on behalf of the Jewish workers in Eretz Israel. At its second convention (1909) it formed for this purpose the Eretz Israel Workers' Fund "in order to aid the aliya of Jewish laborers and their establishment in Eretz Israel." At its third convention (1911), it decided to open a workers' employment information center supported by funds from the Workers' Fund.

On the world scene the World Union opposed the dissolution of the Ottoman Empire and studied the problems of Jewish laborers in the Diaspora (e.g., migration, employment, and levels of productivity). It organized a public protest against the Jewish Colonization Association settlement projects in Argentina. Before World War I it attempted unsuccessfully to join the Socialist International.

The groups within the World Union participated in Zionist Congresses, but they refused to join the Actions Committee (Zionist Executive), which they considered bourgeois. At the Congresses the World Union favored practical programs in Eretz Israel, particularly cooperatives; it opposed utilization of the funds of the Jewish National Fund for the support of private settlement. It supported the farms established by the Palestine Office and was critical of proposals to establish a university in Eretz Israel.

At the fourth convention (1913), differences arose between the leftist group led by Borochov and the Austrian and American groups, toward which the Eretz Israel party was beginning to lean. The left demanded exclusive concentration on the organization of the proletariat and the class struggle and disassociated itself from the WZO; the other groups favored active participation in the WZO and support of cooperative programs in Eretz Israel.

In World War I the World Union was accepted in the Socialist International. It concerned itself with representing special Jewish interests during the war, particularly in conquered countries, and with preparing Jewish and Zionist demands for the forthcoming peace conference. Within the Socialist camp Po'ale Zion preached international responsibility for the Jewish question, demanded the right of the Jews to enjoy national autonomy within Russia, Austria, Romania, and Poland, and fought for the protection of Jewish settlement in Palestine. After the war the World Union of Po'ale Zion enjoyed full status in the conferences convened to renew the Second International. The 1919 meeting of the Standing Committee of the Socialist International in Amsterdam accepted Po'ale Zion's resolution concerning the right of the Jewish people to build a national life in Palestine under the protection of the League of Nations, while safeguarding the interests of the non-Jewish population.

During the war Po'ale Zion in the United States had initiated and activated the movement that resulted in the American Jewish Congress for the purpose of formulating demands for Jewish rights in the Diaspora. It also convened Jewish workers' meetings to adopt resolutions concerning Palestine. Po'ale Zion represented the extremist group in American Jewish life in its demands for Jewish national rights in the Diaspora and opposed the American Jewish Committee. The war years also led to sharp divisions of opinion between the members of Po'ale Zion who opposed participation in the war and those who favored mobilization for the Jewish Legion within the British army.

The Bolshevik Revolution in Russia and the formation of the Third International led to schisms within the World Union of Po'ale Zion. At the end of 1917 part of the Russian group broke away to form the Radical Po'ale Zion, with headquarters in Odessa; it sought cooperation with the WZO and the encouragement of Hebrew as a national language. The Russian Po'ale Zion was generally sympathetic to the Bolsheviks on local political issues. In the Zionist sphere, it urged the building of Palestine by the Jewish proletariat, without cooperation with bourgeois elements.

In 1919 a faction within the Russian Po'ale Zion urged complete identification with Bolshevism and postponement of Palestine projects until after the anticipated world Socialist revolution. The next year this group seceded and formed the Po'ale Zion JCP (Jewish Communist Party). In Austria, Poland, and Germany also, there were Po'ale Zion groups tending toward communism.

In Palestine, however, Po'ale Zion, under the leadership of Ben-Zvi and Ben-Gurion, joined with nonaffiliated workers to form the Zionist Socialist Union of the Workers of Palestine-*Ahdut Avoda, which was simultaneously an economic, trade union, ideological, and political organization. It eschewed Marxist definitions and class militancy in favor of the cooperative building of Palestine. A small group in Po'ale Zion opposed this united organization and the abandonment of the class struggle and of Yiddish, and formed a separate Socialist Labor party that became the nucleus of the Communist party in Palestine.

In 1919 the World Union of Po'ale Zion, under the leadership of Shelomo Kaplansky and Berl Locker, renewed its participation in the WZO and Zionist conferences, to which it even submitted political suggestions. It also was active in the conference held in 1919 to reorganize the Second International. Early in 1920 it sent a delegation to Palestine to investigate the possibility of building the country through cooperative projects, inspired by Nachman Syrkin.

Throughout this period Po'ale Zion was divided by the question of cooperation with "bourgeois" Zionism and participation in the Zionist Congresses. The final break in the World Union occurred at its fifth convention (Vienna, August, 1920), over the question of joining the Third International. The left demanded definite adherence to the Comintern, a proposal that divided the World Union. Most of the parties in Russia, Poland, Czechoslovakia, and Austria belonged to the left; the parties in Palestine, England, the United States, and Argentina, to the right. The British Po'ale Zion joined the British Labor party as a group. The attempt of the left to join the Third International was unsuccessful because of the Comintern's opposition to a world organization of Jewish workers and to Zionism, even proletarian Zionism. The leftists in Po'ale Zion disintegrated, but they regrouped in 1924 as the Left Po'ale Zion. They established a party in Palestine, which suffered further divisions because of the problems of Hebrew and pioneering immigration. In 1939 the Left Po'ale Zion again

Members of Po'ale Zion parade in Warsaw, 1927. [Yivo]

attended the Zionist Congress. In 1921 the right-wing Po'ale Zion joined the Second International (Vienna) and, in 1923, the renewed "Second-and-a-half" International. Its central party became the Palestinian Ahdut Avoda. In 1925 it united with the World Federation of Zionists-Socialists, which stressed Hebrew over Yiddish and pioneering immigration over the class struggle in the Diaspora.

At a conference held in Danzig in 1932, (two years after the creation of *Mapai, the World Federation (or Union) of Po'ale Zion and Zionists-Socialists united with the *Hitahdut (World Federation of *Ha-Po'el ha-Tza'ir and *Tze'irei Zion). Together they formed the *Ihud Olami (World Union of Zionists-Socialists), or Po'ale Zion-Hitahdut. The platform adopted in 1932 advocated "active Zionism" and "international socialism." From 1933 on the Ihud Olami became the major factor in the WZO.

I. KOLATT

In the United States in 1946 the members of the League for Labor Palestine, which had been organized in 1935 primarily in business and professional circles, joined with the Po'ale Zion-Tze'irei Zion to create a joint organization under the name Labor Zionist Organization of America-Po'ale Zion (LZOA). In 1968 LZOA merged with Ahdut Avoda to form a united organization known as Po'ale Zion-United Labor Organization of America.

An early institutional expression of Labor Zionism in the field of education in the US was the establishment of its own school system, a pioneering venture in the entire field of modern American Jewish education. A major aspect of Po'ale Zion activity remained the support of *Habonim, the Labor Zionist youth movement, and the promotion of American aliya. Two Labor Zionist publications, the *Yidisher Kemfer*, a Yiddish weekly, and the *Jewish Frontier*, an English monthly, were edited by Hayim Greenberg for some two decades, until his death in 1953.

In 1975, Po'ale Zion merged with Farband and American Habonim Associates to form the Labor Zionist Alliance.

PO'ALE ZION-HITAHDUT. *See* PO'ALE ZION.

PODLISHEVSKI, AVRAHAM. Polish Zionist leader (b. Lecwicz, 1862; d. Warsaw, 1930). Podlishevski supported Herzlian "political" Zionism and rejected Ahad Ha-Amist tendencies. He was an active proponent of the Helsingfors Program in 1906; subsequently he supported Yitzhak Gruenbaum's policies and belonged to the Al ha-Mishmar faction (*see* POLAND, ZIONISM IN). In the 1920s he enjoyed great influence in the Polish Zionist Organization; he sought to foster bridges to the radical Socialist elements in the Zionist camp, approving the idealistic foundations they brought to the movement.

M. MINTZ

POLAND, RELATIONS WITH ISRAEL. Poland was one of the first countries to recognize Israel, on 18 May 1948. Already in the period preceding the establishment of the State Poland unconditionally supported the yishuv in its struggle. This was expressed both by political and moral support of the Polish government and public, and also by practical aid. In 1948, even before the declaration of independence, a Hagana training camp was established in Poland, where 1,500 Jewish youth received military training before immigrating to Israel. During the War of Independence shipments of wheat reached Israel in Polish ships. In August, 1948, an Israeli legation was established in the Polish capital, one of the first diplomatic representations of the young state.

The cooling off of the eastern bloc's relations with Israel after 1950 affected the Polish attitude to Israel, which reached a low point in 1953 when the Polish government declared the Israeli envoy in Warsaw (and Prague), A.L.Kubovy, persona non grata, following a similar step taken by the Czech government after the Slansky trial. At the same time, two other Israeli diplomats were dismissed from Poland. With the rise of Wladyslaw Gomulka as general secretary of the Polish Communist Party in 1956, a certain amount of liberalization took place in the Polish internal policies, along with a more independent foreign policy, leading to a thaw in Polish-Israeli relations.

This was expressed first of all by a more generous emigration policy, and between the years 1956–60, 52,000 Polish Jews immigrated to Israel. In addition, the representations of both countries were raised to ambassadorial level. However, in the political arena, such as United Nations voting, little changed and Poland continued to follow the Soviet line. In those years Poland was in the forefront of the eastern bloc countries in cultivating ties with Israel in various areas, especially in scientific and cultural exchanges. The conference of the heads of Israeli diplomatic representations in eastern Europe which took place in Warsaw in 1966 with the participation of Foreign Secretary Abba Eban—who on this occasion held discussions with his Polish counterpart—epitomized the improved atmosphere between the two countries. This was the first time this type of gathering had taken place in an eastern European capital and the first visit of an Israeli foreign minister to an eastern European bloc country.

This period of improved relations came to an end with the outbreak of the Six-Day War. On 12 June 1967, following the USSR, Poland suspended diplomatic relations with Israel, adding that it would be prepared to renew them "when Israel removed the traces of her aggression." Even though public opinion in Poland obviously supported Israel, the Polish government organized a "spontaneous demonstration" at the Warsaw airport against the Israeli embassy officials leaving the country, which was characterized by vulgar anti-Semitism.

After the severing of relations and until around 1977, there was a total freeze in ties between the two countries in practically all areas: diplomatic, economic, cultural, tourist. The only surviving remnant from the period of ties was the Polish bank PKO (Polska Kasa Opieki) in Tel Aviv, which continued operating, with the agreement of the Israeli government. This bank had opened a branch in Tel Aviv during the British Mandate period in 1929, specializing mainly in business activities within the Polish immigrant community in Israel, and has continued to operate in recent years as a go-between in transactions between Israel and eastern European countries. More contacts in certain areas developed from 1977, starting with activities concerned with perpetuating the memory of victims of the Holocaust, especially within the framework of the Janusz Korczak Society, along with former partisan organizations.

The 1982 meeting of the former Polish foreign minister, Jozef Czyrek, and the Israeli foreign minister, Yitzhak Shamir, during their stay in New York for a United Nations assembly, represented the start of a new chapter in the relationship, when increased contacts on a non-governmental level were augmented by talks among official representatives of both governments. Foreign Minister Shamir again met with his Polish colleague in 1984 and 1985. At their meeting in October, 1985, the two foreign ministers agreed in principle that the two countries would exchange diplomatic representatives at adviser level, who would head interest offices. The Israel Interest Office would operate within the framework of the Dutch Embassy—which had been appointed to represent Israeli interests in Poland, while the Polish interests in Israel were handled by the PKO Bank. In May, 1986, representatives of the two foreign offices signed an agreement to carry out the basic agreement. In the fall of 1986 the Israeli representative returned to the Israel embassy building in Warsaw and the Polish representative arrived in Israel.

This agreement was the first breakthrough in Israel's relations with the Communist bloc (except for Romania which never ruptured its ties). Polish spokesmen stated that the renewal of the connection was not only a practical consideration, but also an expression of the historical tradition linking the Polish nation in a special relationship to the Jewish people. It may also have reflected the desire to improve Poland's image in the eyes of the west, especially the United States.

With the opening of the representation in Warsaw, contacts multiplied. In addition to the exchange of youth groups, which in recent years had almost become a tradition, Israeli tourism to Poland increased, and many Polish personalities—among them two former ministers of religious affairs and a minister of education visited Israel. Complementary visits of Israeli delegations also included Knesset members. Among the participants in the annual Jerusalem festival, Poland stood out in the number and level of its artistes and troupes. Polish journalists, writers, and composers also visited Israel and Polish scientists participated in every scientific congress which has taken place in Israel, while many Israeli scientists are invited to congresses in Poland. A phenomonon worthy of notice, undoubtedly a result of the increased contacts with Israel, is the widening interest in Poland in the long history of the Jewish presence there. An institute of Jewish Research was opened at the University of Cracow in 1987. An agreement was reached for the transfer of historic and documentary material to Israel from Polish state archives.

The self-imposed restrictions of the Poles in their relations with Israel are mainly felt in the political area, in which progress has been less impressive. With Poland continuing to try to maintain a low profile in its formal relationships with Israel, while placating Arab sensitivities, the matter of exchange of representatives with Israel was presented as a purely technical, consular matter.

The economic agreement signed between Poland and Israel in 1954 was renewed yearly until 1968. The major Israeli export products were citrus, cotton, and tires. Poland exported to Israel frozen meat, sugar, iron and steel products, and chemicals. The trade balance was mostly in Israel's favor, so that when the ties were suspended, Poland owed Israel $5,000,000. Contacts for the renewal of trade took place in 1985 when a Polish delegation visited Israel to investigate possibilities in this connection. With the setting up of interest offices efforts were increased to renew economic ties.

Diplomatic relations were resumed in February 1990 after an article appeared in the Polish government paper saying that the rupture in 1967 had been a mistake, for which it apologized to the Israeli people. In 1991 the Polish president, Lech Walesa, paid an official visit to Israel.

M. AVIDAN

POLAND, ZIONISM IN. From the rise of political Zionism to the extermination of Polish Jewry by the Nazis, Poland was one of the most important centers of the Zionist movement.

From the Rise of Modern Zionism to the End of World War I, 1897–1918. During the early period of political Zionism, Poland was not an independent nation but was divided among three neighboring powers: Russia, Germany, and the Austro-Hungarian Monarchy. Each area left its political, economic, and cultural imprint on Jewish life. The resultant lack of Jewish unity was also reflected in the field of Jewish nationalism. These differences necessitate a separate analysis of each geographical region.

The Jewish population of German Poland had always been small. By the beginning of the 20th century it had dwindled to 50,000 as a result of emigration to the German interior. The Jewish population was caught up in the process of assimilation to German culture and there was no interest in a Jewish renaissance movement or in Zionism, although some of the earliest Zionists—Rabbi Zvi Hirsch Kalischer and Rabbi Elijah Gutmacher—were active in this region and the first conference of the Hovevei Zion movement was held there, in Kattowitz (*see* KATTOWITZ CONFERENCE).

In the Russian Polish and Galician (Austrian) regions, however, the Jews responded wholeheartedly to the movement for a Jewish national revival. Political Zionism had been preceded by other manifestations of Jewish renaissance: the Haskala (Enlightenment), which had an emphatically Jewish national character in Russian Poland and Galicia, in contradistinction to its form in Germany; the development of a Hebrew and Yiddish press and literature; and the Hovevei Zion movement. The Jews in Russian Poland were part of the 6 million Jews of Russia, and the Jews of Galicia were part of the 2 million Jews of the Austro-Hungarian Monarchy. Nevertheless, in years preceding World War I, when domestic political activities (e.g., Jewish nationalism, the struggle for Jewish rights in the Diaspora) became part of the Zionist program, the Jews of

Members of "Ezra" a Hebrew-speaking Zionist society in Plonsk, Poland, 1905. [Central Zionist Archives]

these two areas found themselves in distinctive positions, different from those of both Russian Jewry and the Jewish communities in other parts of the Austro-Hungarian monarchy.

Russian Poland. The Jewish population in the area of Tsarist Russian rule was almost three times greater than that of Galicia. The Zionist movement grew mainly as a result of the activities of Jews who had migrated from Lithuania and other Russian districts to the so-called Congress Poland (central provinces of Poland) in search of better economic conditions. At first the local Jews were skeptical. Many of them, particularly the hasidim, the assimilationists, and the Bundists (*see* BUND), were opposed to Zionism. Eventually, however, they came to join the Zionist ranks, particularly after Herzl had gained the support of such leaders as Nahum Sokolow. The advent of Ahad Ha-Am and his Benei Moshe (Sons of Moses) movement, which found many supporters in Poland, also strengthened the Zionist movement. Zionist societies were established in cities, towns, and villages. In the beginning their activities were only propagandistic and educational, but they soon expanded into practical endeavors, especially the solicitation of funds for settlement efforts in Eretz Israel.

The initial reaction of the gentile Polish population to Zionism was positive, for it viewed the settlement of Eretz Israel as hastening the exodus of the Jews from Poland. The authorities saw in Zionism a useful means of keeping the Jews out of revolutionary movements, and although all communal activities were suspect in their eyes, they placed no special difficulties in the way of the Zionist movement. When, however, it became apparent that Zionism also aimed at strengthening Jewish national identity and encouraged the fight for Jewish civil and political rights, the Poles initiated anti-Zionist propaganda and the authorities tended to proscribe Zionist activities, particularly among young people and the lower economic classes.

In addition, the Zionist movement in Poland had to cope with internal challenges. It was split as a result of the controversy over the East Africa scheme. At first the local Zionist Organization took no clear stand on the issue, but later it joined the Eretz Israel-centered Tziyonei Zion. Some, including a number of leaders, left the Zionist movement and joined the Jewish Territorial Organization. Zionists from the ranks of labor who sided with Territorialism formed their own organization, that of the Zionists-Socialists, and for a time were able to attract sizable numbers. Another crisis arose when Zionism developed a program of progressivism, which attracted radical intellectuals and the Socialist workers, who were strongly opposed to Herzl's negotiations with the Russian government and especially with Vyacheslav K. von Plehve, the Russian statesman who was considered responsible for the pogroms at the beginning of the century. Nonetheless, the Zionist movement continued to expand its ideological framework to encompass all matters affecting the Jewish public and particularly the defense of its civil and national-group rights in the Diaspora.

In 1906 Russian Zionists, with the vigorous participation of Polish Zionists, adopted the Helsingfors Program. Similar to the earlier Cracow Program of the Austrian Zionists, it marked the beginning of the fierce struggle of the Polish Zionists against assimilation, for the strengthening of Zionist influence in the Jewish communities, and for Jewish civil and nationality-group rights. At first the Zionists boycotted elections to the Russian Duma (Parliament), but later they decided to participate in elections to the Fourth Duma. They succeeded in electing their own representative in Lodz and in preventing the election of an anti-Semitic representative in Warsaw. Their efforts resulted in the election of a Polish Socialist, but they also led to strained relationships with the Polish nationalist movement and to an unsuccessful boycott of Jewish goods (which continued to be sold in the interior districts of Russia). These developments made Zionism an ever-greater factor in Polish-Jewish life, without, however, diminishing regular Zionist activities and the role of Polish Zionists in the World Zionist Organization (WZO). Nahum Sokolow, who headed the movement in Poland, became a member of the World Zionist Executive. Funds were raised for the settlement effort in Eretz Israel. Zionist influence was apparent in the cultural life of Polish Jewry—in the Jewish newspapers, in the publication of books (particularly Hebrew books), and in the establishment of schools with Hebrew or Yiddish as the language of instruction. However Polish Zionist participation in aliya (immigration to Eretz Israel) was relatively small during this period, as compared with that of the Russian Zionists, from whose ranks came the early Bilu settlers and the pioneers of the Second Aliya.

Throughout this period the Zionist movement in Poland maintained a united front. Although both the religious Zionists and the Labor Zionists sought new adherents, they remained within the organizational framework of the movement. This loyalty was particularly true of the Mizrachi movement, whose spiritual fathers were Rabbi Shemuel Mohilever of Bialystok (during the Hibbat Zion period) and Rabbi Yitzhak Ya'akov Reines of Lida, the ideological and organizational creator of the movement. Mizrachi gained ground among observant Jews despite the boycott of Zionism by the hasidim and by organized Orthodox Jewry.

In the course of time the identification of the Labor Zionists with the Zionist Organization grew weaker; the fact that they had come to view Zionism primarily as the solution to the problem of the Jewish working class kept them apart from the other segments of the Zionist movement. Large groups within Labor Zionist ranks broke away from the Zionist Organization to form the Territorialist Socialist Zionists, or Sejmists, who sought national autonomy as a solution to the Jewish problem. Even those who remained within the movement were identified more closely with the Po'ale Zion in Russia, who stressed their class character and did not cooperate with other Zionist organizations. Their independent position was more distinct in domestic politics and in Socialist and trade union activities, where they competed with the Bund. Whereas the general Zionist Organization enjoyed a semilegal status, Po'ale Zion, like other Socialist movements in Russia, was illegal and was often harassed by the police.

With the outbreak of World War I, Zionist activity in Poland ceased. After the occupation of Congress Poland by German and Austrian forces and the resulting cancellation of some of the repressive Tsarist decrees, however, the Po'ale Zion began to function openly. In time, the Central Powers came to favor the idea of a Jewish National Home in Palestine as a means of blocking the political ambitions of Great Britain and the other Western Powers. Nonetheless, they were very cautious in local political affairs. Thus, for example, it was only with difficulty that permission was obtained to open Jewish schools with Hebrew or Yiddish as the language of instruction. The local Polish population continued to display animosity despite Zionist proclamations supporting the establishment of an independent Polish state.

Galicia. The development of the Zionist movement in Austrian Galicia was quite different. The Austrian government was more liberal in its attitude toward communal activity than were the Tsarist authorities. Nonetheless, there were many similarities between the Zionist movements in Galicia and Congress Poland. In Galicia, as in Congress Poland, Zionist grew out of the Haskala movement, developed with Hibbat Zion, and found strong adherents among intellectuals and university students. With the birth of political Zionism the movement spread throughout Galicia; it was affiliated with the Austrian Zionist Organization (*see* AUSTRIA, ZIONISM IN) and coordinated its activities through district committees. The scope of activities in Galicia was even broader than in Congress Poland and included organizations of Labor Zionists, religious Zionists, and university and secondary school student Zionists, as well as an active women's Zionist organization.

The Galician Zionists also took a position on domestic political affairs concerning Jewish national-group rights and representation in the legislative bodies, particularly the Austrian Parliament, the special Galician Parliament (Sejm), and the local municipalities. As for civil rights, these had been largely accorded to Austrian Jews by this time. A further goal was Zionist control of the Jewish communities, most of which were headed by assimilationists.

In the Austro-Hungarian monarchy the Jews were considered not a national group but a religious group. In eastern Galicia this circumstance led to attempts by the Poles to outvote the Ukrainians by including the Jews within Polish ranks. The Zionists challenged this step. They also sought to improve the depressed economic condition of Galician Jewry and urged Jews to engage in local political activity. However, some Zionists saw a danger in such activity and sought to limit Zionist work to education and fundraising. Thus, when the Cracow Conference of 1906 voted in favor of domestic political activities, a compromise resolution was passed to the effect that activity in this area was not to be undertaken by the Zionist Organization itself but by a newly created Jewish National party.

In theory, the Cracow Conference was all-Austrian in composition—Markus (Mordekhai Z.) Braude of Galicia and Adolf Böhm of Vienna drew up the platform. In fact, however, the Galician Zionists were the most active in it. It soon became apparent that the resolution to establish a separate Jewish National party was merely theoretical, for other Jewish groups did not seek to join the party and in practice domestic policies remained an important part of the Zionist program. In 1907 four Jewish National party representatives, one from Bukovina and three from Galicia, were elected to the Austrian Parliament. Adolf Stand headed the "Jewish faction," the first of its kind in the history of Diaspora Jewry.

Other areas of Zionist domestic political activity included the battle for the right to list Yiddish and Hebrew as national languages in the census, the attempt to improve the economic status of Galician Jews (the formation of a national Jewish bank, as against various "family" banks, and of the ICA Credit Cooperatives), the battle against anti-Jewish discrimination, the effort to strengthen Zionist influence within the leadership of the *kehillot* (religious communities), and the demand for Jewish representation in the Galician Sejm and in the municipalities. These activities attracted large groups to the Zionist movement, which continued to expand its activities. The Zionist idea was propagated through Yiddish- and Polish-language newspapers. *Voskhod,* the weekly of the Galician Zionists, was for many years also the organ of the Zionists in Congress Poland, who had no official permit from the authorities to publish their own newspaper. Galician Zionists formed their own settlement, Mahanayim, in Eretz Israel, actively supported settlement in the country in general, and raised sizable sums for the building of the Hebrew High School in Jerusalem.

Deeply concerned about education, Galician Zionists developed a network of modern *heders* and Hebrew-language schools and introduced a more positive Jewish content into the Baron de Hirsch schools, whose original philosophy had been assimilationist. This effort was guided by Solomon Schiller. The Hebrew language, Jewish studies, and Zionist philosophy were disseminated among secondary-school and university students.

Zionist academic associations were an important part of Galician Zionism. Some of them had been in existence even before the advent of modern political Zionism. Some followed in the footsteps of the gentile academic societies; they stressed social activities and emphasized their willingness to fight for the honor of their comrades and of the Jewish people, thus emulating the *schlagende Verbindungen* (dueling fraternities) of German and Austrian universities. Gradually, however, more and more emphasis came to be placed on Zionist content. The illegal Zionist youth organizations on the secondary school level worked secretly but managed to form a nationwide young Zionist organization, Tze'irei Zion, whose purpose was purely educational. A scouting movement with Jewish educational content was formed; it later changed its name to Ha-Shomer. During World War I these two Jewish youth groups merged.

In Galicia as in Congress Poland, the Mizrachi and Po'ale Zion groups were consolidated within the framework of the Zionist Organization. Po'ale Zion attracted thousands of workers, particularly among white-collar employees. They took an independent position in domestic politics and generally cooperated with the Jewish National party. Their newspaper, *Der Yidisher Arbeter,* published first in Vienna, then in Cracow, and finally in Lemberg (Lvov), became the most important organ of Labor Zionism.

In Galicia, too, Zionist activity was paralyzed by the outbreak of World War I. The area was conquered and occupied by Russian forces for almost a year, during which time almost half of the Jewish population fled to the interior of Austria (particularly to Vienna). Those who remained suffered greatly. The center of Galician Zionism was moved to Vienna. With the liberation of the country, Zionist activity was revived but on a limited scale because of uncertainty regarding the political future of the region. At first there was talk of a Polish state, including Galicia, within the Austro-Hungarian monarchy. With the growing disintegration of the Hapsburg Monarchy by the end of the war, however, it became apparent that it would be necessary to find a new political solution. These developments were fraught with grave dangers for the Jews of Galicia, caught as they were between the mutually inimical Polish and Ukrainian populations.

Independent Poland, 1919–39. The development of Polish Zionism between the two world wars was characterized and determined by four basic phenomena:

1. The tremendous increase in membership and in Zionist influence on Jewish communal life. Zionism became the most decisive force in Jewish life in Poland. Its closest competitor was the ultra-Orthodox Agudat Israel, but that organization exerted much less influence in the political sphere than did the Zionists. In the second half of the 1930s the Bund's influence grew again, but Zionism remained the central pillar of Jewish life.

2. The merger of the Zionist movements of the various regions of Poland. This merger was limited and was successful mainly among the religious Zionists and the left-wing Zionist camps (later in the ranks of the Revisionists as well). The General Zionists remained divided both geographically and, especially in Congress Poland, ideologically.

3. The development within the movement of a number of parties whose ties to one another were minimal. The various trends with their individual ideological characteristics crystallized into independent parties; even the General Zionists became a party with its own point of view. Only a few groups—the Radical wing in what was formerly Congress Poland and, to a much smaller extent, the Zionist Organization in western Galicia—tried to maintain the tradition of a movement that could accommodate Zionists of all shades of opinion. Occasionally the interparty differences gave rise to bitter struggles.

4. The intensity of Jewish life in Poland, which led to an extension of Zionist activity into every field. The Halutz (pioneer) movement came into being, educational activities were expanded, and Zionism became a decisive influence in the press, in literature, and, to some extent, in economic life as well. This period was the zenith of Polish Zionism. No other country, with the exception of Palestine and, to a degree, Lithuania, experienced so encompassing a Zionist impact on Jewish life. *Zionist Organization and Activities.* The unification of the formerly foreign-held areas through the establishment of an independent Polish state paved the way for a merger of the Zionist movements in Poland, but such a merger did not materialize. At first, unity was hampered by uncertainty as to whether the united provinces would actually remain part of an independent Poland. Internally, the Zionist movement in the various regions had developed differences in ideology and approach. The groups with specific social philosophies were the first to separate from general Zionism. Greatly influenced by the developments in Russia, they lost factions to the Communist camp.

In the 1920s the Labor Zionist movement itself was split into two or three trends. The Polish Po'ale Zion was inclined largely to the radical trend and was not prepared to cooperate with "bourgeois" Zionism. The popular element in the Zionist movement, which before and during World War I had formed Tze'irei Zion (not to be confused with the Galician group of secondary school students bearing the same name), also sought an independent existence and was divided into two trends. One trend, the left-wing Tze'irei Zion (also known as Berit ha-Mizrah), formed a party of its own. The other trend remained for a time but eventually became the Hitahdut Labor Zionist party. The left-wing group later merged with the right-wing Po'ale Zion to form the Po'ale Zion (united with the Zionists-Socialists).

Following the lead of the left-wing groups, the religious Zionists affiliated with Mizrachi also presented themselves as an independent party. Only the General Zionists remained within the old framework and they, too, were unsuccessful in their attempts to create a united Zionist framework for the three territorial regions of Poland (Congress Poland with the eastern border provinces, eastern Galicia, and western Galicia). Within Congress Poland, the party was split into two factions, Et li-Venot (Time to Build) and Al ha-Mishmar (On Guard). This division originally arose over the plan of an expanded Jewish Agency: Et li-Venot supported it, while Al ha-Mishmar joined the extremists who opposed the idea. After the expanded Jewish Agency had been formed in 1929, the rift was continued along social-ideological lines. Al ha-Mishmar viewed Zionism as common to all elements in Jewry but stressed social progress, whereas Et li-Venot became more and more a middle-class movement that looked with disfavor on the growing status of the labor movement in Palestine and stressed free enterprise. This was also the position of the General Zionists in eastern Galicia; those of western Galicia sought to retain the all-inclusive character of the organization, but in time they too became more middle-class in ideology. Upon the consolidation of the Revisionists with their own fundraising and aliya program in the 1930s, the Polish Zionist movement was split once more. The Mizrachi party was generally more stable, but some of its younger members broke away to form their own party, which stressed pioneer activities and was spiritually akin to the labor movement in Palestine. The Revisionist movement in Poland, as elsewhere, split; a minority remained in the WZO, while the large majority established the New Zionist Organization.

Almost all the Zionist parties in Poland formed youth groups which, while following the ideological line of the parent organizations, stressed *hakhshara* (agricultural training) and aliya. Some of them were active in disseminating the Hebrew language and culture among the Jewish population. One independent youth movement, Ha-Shomer ha-Tza'ir, was born on Polish soil and spread from there to other countries. It was sympathetic to left-wing Zionism but retained its independent posture and maintained contact with the Kibbutz Artzi shel Ha-Shomer ha-Tza'ir in Palestine. The pioneering movement He-Helutz developed well and then split into ideological factions. Gordonia, also born in Poland, was ideologically close to Hitahdut.

Paradoxically, this fragmentation of the Zionist movement and the struggle among the factions did not have a negative effect on the influence and strength of Zionism in Poland. Polish Zionism grew in strength and retained its decisive role in Jewish community life. Only the ranks of the General Zionists in Congress Poland suffered from internal dissension. Eventually the influence of the General Zionists declined in local politics as well as within the movement.

It is significant that with two exceptions all Zionist parties and youth movements remained within the WZO and were represented in its institutions. The exceptions were the extreme left-wing Po'ale Zion and the Revisionists. The influence of the former was to be found primarily among Jewish workers; the latter appealed mostly to the younger generation. In the mid-1930s the Revisionists created a stir in the Jewish community with their plan to "evacuate" a large proportion of the Jewish population of Poland to Palestine. The plan, which did not materialize, was received favorably by the Polish government but aroused great opposition among the Jews, who viewed it as supporting the anti-Semitic Polish position and as endangering their civil status.

The number of Jews sympathetic to Zionism was far greater than that of those formally affiliated with its parties and undoubtedly constituted the majority of Poland's Jewish population. Nonetheless, there were groups of anti-Zionist Jews. Aside from the assimilationists, whose numbers decreased greatly after World War I and who had no influence on Jewish life in Poland during the interwar period, the opponents of Zionism were concentrated within the extreme Orthodox camp, whose spokesmen were the Agudat Israel and the various hasidic rabbis (although some of the latter were neutral or even pro-Zionist); among the Bundists and Communists; and among the Folkists, who had a following among middle-class artisans in the early 1920s. Orthodox opposition sprang from the secular nature of Zionism (the Mizrachi movement was not religious enough for the Agudat Israel) and from the belief entertained by many of the Orthodox that the redemption of Israel was in the hands of the Lord and should not be hastened by human means. Later, Orthodoxy also tended toward cooperation with the Polish government. Zionism, on the other hand, stressed an independent Jewish policy and, as anti-Semitic tendencies grew in the Polish population and government, became more and more of an opposition party. The Bundists and Folkists were united in their hatred of Zionism, holding that the only solution to the Jewish problem was through the improvement of the position of the Jews in the countries where they resided. They also opposed Zionism in that they stressed Yiddish, which they viewed as "progressive," in contrast to the "reactionary" policy of nurturing the Hebrew language and culture. Outside these groups, the Jewish population looked with favor on Zionism and was willing to accept its leadership, particularly in questions relating to Palestine and national Jewish politics.

The relationship between Zionism and the Polish people and government was quite different. Anti-Jewish feeling had been a widespread phenomenon in Poland for generations, and it was intensified during the 1930s until it became one of the major elements in Polish life. It did not distinguish between Zionists and other groups in the Jewish population. Nonetheless, the Polish government generally did not place obstacles in the way of the movement and even aided it, particularly in the international arena, on the assumption that this would increase the flow of Jewish emigration from Poland to Palestine. On the domestic political scene, however, relations continued to be strained, since the Zionist movement headed the battle against anti-Jewish prejudice. This relationship deteriorated in the 1930s, with the progressive disintegration of democracy in Poland and the growth of anti-Semitism, particularly during election periods when the government attempted to strengthen its position and weaken the opposition. Nonetheless, the legality of the Zionist movement was not placed in question, nor were its pro-Palestine educational and fundraising activities curtailed. The anti-Semitic propaganda that permeated almost the entire Polish population was rarely aimed specifically against Zionism as such.

Domestic Politics. As it had before World War I, the Zionist movement devoted an important part of its activities to local political affairs, and it now set the tone for the Jewish community in this area. The emphasis was on safeguarding the civil and national rights of the Jews, who were legally recognized as a national minority group and enjoyed civil rights, although in practice the government tended to disregard this fact and often violated Jewish rights.

It was thus an important task of Zionist domestic policy to defend the Jewish population against the growing anti-Semitism of the authorities and the population and against the policy of discrimination, which was felt in all spheres of life. In the 1930s discrimination was directed particularly against the economic position of the Jews, with the clear intention of impoverishing them and forcing them from the country. Anti-Semitism also took the form of pogroms. The main battlegrounds in the Zionist fight against the attacks on Jewish rights were the Polish Parliament (the Sejm and the Senate) and, particularly in the 1930s, the municipalities, which retained a degree of freedom while democracy foundered on the national level and the parliament became a tool in the hands of a semifascist government.

The Jewish community was the scene of a battle between the Zionist movement and anti-Zionist Orthodoxy (Agudat Israel) for community control. Immediately after World War I the Zionist movement initiated the formation of a Jewish National Council, whose main purpose was to provide Jewish representation in the national parliament and to safeguard Jewish rights in the laws passed by the parliament. Of the 13 Jewish representatives in the First Polish Parliament, six were Zionists and one was sympathetic to the movement. The Zionists were thus the decisive element in the parliamentary representation, especially in view of the fact that the non-Zionist parliamentarians included two assimilationists who had been appointed by the government as representatives of the Jews of eastern Galicia and had no influence in parliament. In the Second Parliament, as a result of the national minorities' bloc organized by the Zionists during the elections and of the boycott of the elections by the Ukrainians in eastern Galicia, the number of Jewish representatives increased almost fourfold. Of the 47 Jewish representatives, 32 were Zionists, so that it was the Zionists who decided the policy of the Jewish parliamentary bloc.

A crisis arose in the Zionist camp when two of its leaders, Leon Reich and Osias Thon, both of Galicia, entered into negotiations with government representatives for the guarantee of certain benefits to the Jewish community in exchange for the latter's support of government policies. Representatives from the former Russian-held areas, headed by Itzhak Grünbaum, opposed these negotiations, and the storm that was aroused in the Jewish community left its mark long after its cause had been eliminated by the formation in 1926 of a new Polish regime headed by Marshal Jozef Pilsudski. The two political tendencies within

Zionism then crystallized to a great extent. The Galician representatives concentrated on the practical needs of the moment (a principle generally supported by the Mizrachi and Agudat Israel camps), whereas the Zionist representatives from the former Russian area sought open confrontation, fighting for Jewish rights without retreating from their antigovernment position. These internal disputes led to the decline of Zionist influence as the decisive factor in domestic political affairs. The situation worsened when Agudat Israel and the merchant element among the Jews became inclined to cooperation with the new regime, to the extent of relinquishing the principle of independent Jewish politics.

In subsequent parliamentary elections the government exerted increasingly heavy pressure on opposition parties in order to ensure its own success in the elections, and there was a sharp decrease in the number of Jewish representatives. In the Third Parliament there were 22 Jewish representatives, of whom 16 were Zionists; in the Fourth the number of Jewish representatives again was halved (to 11, of whom six were Zionists; four of the remainder were elected on the government party list). The Fifth Parliament had six Jewish representatives (including three Zionists), and the Sixth and last had seven (with four Zionists). The Zionist representatives, despite their numerical majority in the Jewish group, were no longer able to set the policies for the other Jewish representatives, most of whom belonged to the government bloc despite the latter's increasingly anti-Semitic policies. Moreover, as democracy disintegrated in Poland, the parliament lost its effectiveness. The main role of the Jewish representatives now was the protection of the Jewish population from growing anti-Semitic onslaughts, which were carried out with the active participation of the authorities. What was left of the democratic parliamentary regime in the country was now to be found in the municipalities. There the Zionists continued to exert influence until the early 1930s, after which they were superseded by the Bund, which the Jewish masses were used to regarding as the main fighter against the rampant anti-Semitism.

Within the *kehillot*, whose authority under Polish law was limited to religious affairs, considerable influence was wielded by the Orthodox groups, especially Agudat Israel. In the 1930s the government, exploiting the differences of opinion within the Jewish community, frequently transferred the direction of the *kehillot* to appointees of its own.

All in all, Zionist achievements in the area of domestic policies during this period were far from encouraging. The lack of success was due to internal disputes in the movement, spiritual disintegration within the Jewish population, rising Polish nationalism, diminishing democracy, and growing anti-Semitism, particularly in the 1930s.

Zionism and Palestine. Between the two world wars Polish Jewry played an outstanding role in Zionist activity as a result partly of its past tradition, partly of religious influence, and, particularly, of the effectiveness of Zionist propaganda, which reached every Jewish home. Identification with Zionism was expressed in fundraising, in demonstrations attended by hundreds of thousands of persons (e.g., after the Arab riots of 1929 and 1936), and, especially, in emigration to Palestine. With the isolation of Russian Jewry under the Communist regime, Poland became the primary source of aliya from eastern Europe. Most of the emigrants were young and labor-oriented (although the Fourth Aliya was made up of largely middle-class persons with capital to invest).

In order to set up *hakhshara* programs, the young Zionist groups in Poland formed He-Halutz, and eventually similar organizations were established by the various Zionist parties. Some *hakhshara* units were agricultural; others specialized in other skills needed in Palestine (e.g., quarrying) or worked in vocations that would provide the members with employment there. Life within the *hakhshara* groups was almost always organized along cooperative lines, much as in a kibbutz. Hebrew was taught; the national and social problems of Palestine were studied, as were the particular ideological issues of the various parties. The *hakhshara* members were not always able to emigrate immediately after they had completed their training, for the British Mandatory power limited entry permits for Palestine. The permits that were made available were distributed by a Palestine Office maintained jointly by all the Zionist parties. They were allotted in proportion to the strength of the parties and the number of their members in *hakhshara*. During the 1930s, 20,000 young people were in *hakhshara* and at least three times as many were members of Halutz groups. Most of these eventually reached Palestine, either "legally" or "illegally". Those who remained in Poland under Nazi rule were among the underground and ghetto leaders.

Zionism and Jewish Culture. Jewish literature, journalism, and art were influenced definitively by Zionism. Almost all the daily papers of Polish Jewry expressed a Zionist position, in varying degrees, the only exceptions being the organs of the Bund and Agudat Israel. Most of the Jewish clubs for literature, music, sports, and other interests, which existed in almost every town, had a Zionist character.

During the 1930s the network of schools established by the Jewish community catered to more than 250,000 Jewish children. Most of these were Orthodox institutions (*heders*, yeshivot, supplementary courses); the majority of the non-Orthodox schools were of Zionist orientation. The Tarbut schools, in which Hebrew was the language of instruction, stressed Zionism and *halutziyut*. The Mizrachi schools and the bilingual (Polish-Hebrew and Yiddish-Hebrew) educational institutions were also Zionist. A large proportion of Jewish students emigrated to Palestine after having completed their studies.

End of Zionism in Poland. During the early years of Nazi control the Zionist movement in Nazi-held Poland was active in the cultural and educational life of the ghettos. The youth groups in particular played an important role in the Jewish underground and the ghetto revolt. In the end the last manifestations of Jewish life were silenced, and Polish Jewry, numbering over 3 million in 1939, was almost totally annihilated in the Nazi Holocaust.

Following the war, with the return of refugees from the Soviet Union, the Jewish population of Poland grew to almost 200.000 and the Zionist political parties were revived. Before long the larger part of the Jewish population emigrated, mainly to Israel. The Communist take-over in Poland put an end to Zionist activity.

Summary. From a historical perspective, one must conclude that of the three philosophies that molded Polish Jewry after the disappearance of assimilation as a practical factor—Zionism, Orthodoxy, and the non-Zionist left—Zionism exerted by far the greatest influence. The Orthodox members of Agudat Israel and the hasidic leaders were more numerous than the Zionists, and during the later years of the period between the two world wars the influence of the Bundists undoubtedly grew. Nonetheless, it is

Reception at the New Zionist Club, Warsaw, in 1938. Seated third from the left is Vladimir Jabotinsky. [Zionist Archives]

clear that all the influence of Orthodoxy was limited to matters of religion; in other matters its adherents tended to follow the Zionist line. This was most apparent in matters pertaining to Palestine; the Agudat Israel even had a Halutz movement of its own. Nor did the Bund, despite its strength within the working class, exert any influence even approaching that of the Zionist movement. During the years of democracy in Poland the Bund did not succeed in electing a single representative to the Polish Parliament; the Yiddish-language schools it sponsored together with the Left Po'ale Zion ranked far behind the Zionist schools. Even at the height of Bundist influence, in the late 1930s, the sphere of Bundist political activity was limited to domestic politics in municipal elections.

Polish Zionism played an outstanding role in World Zionist affairs. Various Zionist parties (particularly those of the Zionist left, the Halutz movement, and Revisionism) were born or assumed their mature form on Polish soil. Hebrew and Yiddish culture, which achieved the heights of expression in Poland, were clearly of Zionist content and helped mold the character of Polish Jewry. This character still influences the Jewish world wherever Polish Jews are now scattered. It is reflected in a rich literature of personal reminiscences and memoirs and is particularly apparent in Israel, where a large percentage of immigrants are of Polish origin.

A. TARTAKOWER

POLICE IN ISRAEL. The Israel Police Force is national in character and was founded with the establishment of the State of Israel on 15 May 1948. The Force is commanded by the Commissioner of Police who is appointed by the government upon the recommendation of the Minister of Police. The duties and powers of the Force are laid down in the Police Ordinance (New Version) 1971.

Historical Background. Towards the end of the 19th century, when Jewish settlements began to flourish in Eretz Israel, and with them a growing hostility on the part of the Arab neighbors, the need for defending life and property became vital. In 1909, the *Ha-Shomer (Watchman) Organization was secretly established. Ha-Shomer members declared themselves to be the "nucleus of Hebrew police and Hebrew gendarmerie in the Land of Israel." Ha-Shomer was highly selective in recruiting new members, insisting on high standards of personal integrity, Zionist patriotism, shrewdness, and professional skills. Ha-Shomer members were encouraged to build friendly relationships with the Arab neighbors (for crime prevention purposes) and to professionalize themselves for the sole purpose of ensuring security and protection for the Jewish inhabitants and their property. The Ha-Shomer Organization (although illegal because of Ottoman prohibitions) founded and manned a police station in Tiberias. In 1920, Ha-Shomer was merged into the *Hagana, which was composed of legally super-

Police speedboat patrolling Lake Kineret. [Israel Information Services]

numary Jewish police (paid or volunteer) officers. In 1921, the Palestine Police Force and Gendarmerie were founded and served under British supervision. The Chief Inspector of Police and Prisons commanded a national force. He was responsible for all those functions and duties delegated by the Police Ordinance.

When the Mandate came to an end the mandatory authorities refused to arrange for an orderly transfer of the functions of government and administration and police organization was gravely affected. The withdrawing forces took with them most of the equipment such as transport, armament, laboratory equipment, and police dogs. Most of the records and archives of the police were also removed, including large numbers of outstanding case files and exhibits. Convicts and detainees were released adding to the confusion and disorder. The withdrawal of the British and Arab personnel left the manpower of most police formations in a sorely depleted state.

Early in 1948, the leaders of the yishuv prepared for the police needs of the future Jewish state. The future Israeli Force was planned by a small team led by Yechezkel Sahar (Sacharov) who later became the first Inspector-General of the newly established Israel Police Force. With the departure of the British, the new State was faced with the problem of ensuring law and order. All the police roles and posts had to be filled overnight with Jewish personnel. Veterans who had formerly served as officers in the British Army were drafted to replace the British supervisory personnel, along with senior members of the Hagana. However, these men had no experience in the civilian policing of the country. In addition, recruits had to be found who had been in Israel long enough to have acquired a thorough knowledge of Hebrew and the basic values of the country. It had to be impressed on every policeman, that he, too, was subject to the laws he was duty bound to enforce.

Organization and Structure. The Israel Police Force is commanded by a Commissioner, whose headquarters in 1969 moved from Tel Aviv to Jerusalem. The Commissioner is assisted by a staff of senior officers that forms the National Headquarters. The staff consists of the heads of five departments; Policing & Security Department, Investigations Department, Quartermaster's Department, Personnel Department, and Planning & Organization, each with the rank of Major General. The country is divided into four police districts, which in turn are divided into subdistricts and stations. The districts are:- the Southern district, the Central district, the Tel Aviv district, and the Northern district.

Two separate bodies within the police force are the Border Police, founded in 1953, which is in fact a Gendarmerie force, and the Civil Guard, founded in 1974, both of which report directly to Headquarters. After the Six-Day

War of 1967, the Israel Police was required to provide law enforcement services in the Golan Heights, and the Administered Areas. East Jerusalem became part of the subdistrict of Jerusalem. Several hundred Arabs who had been policemen under Syrian, Jordanian, and United Arab Republic authorities were retained to serve in areas under Israeli control.

In 1987, the total number of members in the police force in Israel came to 16,227, including 4,150 in the Border Police and about 500 sworn officers (not including volunteers) in the Civil Guard. There are 3,020 policewomen serving in all the branches.

Training. The National Police Training Academy, located at Shefaram in Galilee, offers many types of courses: basic, advanced, and specialized. The basic course is for the training of patrolmen and CID staff. The advanced courses are for sergeants and inspectors. Specialized courses are held periodically for detectives, laboratory experts, dog handlers, instructors, youth investigators, traffic accident investigators, and so on. An Officers' College is located in Ne'urim, Netanya, for senior officers.

The training base for the Border Police is located at Bet Horon; members of the Border Police are also trained as bomb-demolition experts and sappers, and learn to handle suspicius objects.

J.L. PRAG

POLISH JEWS IN ISRAEL. Immigration of Jews from Poland to Eretz Israel began during the First Aliya (1882–1903). The immigrants became agricultural settlers, city builders, industrial developers, craftsmen, and construction workers and in general contributed greatly to urban development. The number of immigrants was small, for no particular pressures then forced Jewish emigration from Poland in general or migration to Eretz Israel in particular. Polish Jews had not been affected by the harsh edicts issued against Jews in Russia proper by the Tsarist regime, which had spared them, intending to use them as tools for the Russification of Poland.

In 1883 a group of 11 families left Bialystok to settle in Petah Tikva. That same year 25 immigrants from Suwalki and Miedzyrzec founded the settlement of Yesud ha-Ma'ala. In 1884, five farmers from the Grodno District settled in Ekron, and in 1890 a Warsaw settlement organization, Menuha ve-Nahala, founded Rehovot.

Polish immigrants played an important role in the Second Aliya. Immigrants from Plonsk included David Ben-Gurion, Shelomo Lavi, and Shelomo Zemach. Others who came to the country at that time included groups from Bedzin and Brody. Among the immigrants from Brody were Joseph Aronowicz and Asher Barash. Shemuel Yoseph Agnon came from Buchach, and Dr. Ya'akov Thon from Lvov.

The immigrants of the Old Yishuv, especially those in Jerusalem, were associated with *kolelim* (religious charity organizations) based on their places of origin. The Kolel census of 1916 conducted by the Palestine Office listed the following Polish *kolelim* in Jerusalem: Kolel Galicia, 1,000 members; Kolel Warsaw, 1,400; Kolel Grodno, 1,100; Kolel Volhynia, 1,000; and Kolel Vilna, 1,400. Other Polish immigrants lived in Safed, Tiberias, and Hebron. The number of Polish Jews in the Old Yishuv in 1916 was estimated at 6,000 or more; the total number throughout the country, at 10,000.

Toward the end of World War I many Jews in Poland, particularly members of the younger generation, were beginning to contemplate emigration to Palestine. The Third Convention of Polish Zionists, held in 1917, called for the establishment of centers to prepare pioneers for settlement on the land. As a result, *hakhshara* training farms were formed in Grochow and Czestochowa. Immediately after the war, about 500 Polish Jews left for Palestine. Not all were able to overcome the obstacles in their way, but some succeeded in arriving after months of wandering.

During the Third Aliya (1919–23), 9,158 immigrants arrived in Palestine from Poland, or about 30 percent of the total immigration of 35,000 in this period. From 1924 to 1931, during the Fourth Aliya, 38,605 of the 80,000 immigrants were from Poland. The Polish immigrants of this period were generally assumed to be members of the middle class who had fled the Grabski decrees. This assumption is not valid, for the majority of these immigrants were laborers. Nor did all those who allegedly came with funds of their own really possess the capital registered in their names. Sometimes such a financial registration had been "arranged" so that the immigrants could obtain immigration certificates (legal permits authorizing entry into Palestine). Between 1924 and 1926, 9,751 immigrants allegedly possessing capital arrived; 13,434 came as laborers. The 1926 census of Jewish laborers in Palestine indicated that 37.6 percent of the total were from Poland.

At that time, too, the followers of the hasidic rabbis of Yablonov and Kozienice decided to settle in Palestine and become farmers. They founded Nahlat Ya'akov and Avodat Yisrael, neighboring settlements in the vicinity of Haifa. Although the attempt was not entirely successful (some of the hasidic pioneers eventually left the settlements and the country), a nucleus remained which, with additional settlers, founded Kefar Hasidim. Religious Jews from Poland also founded Beei Berak.

Although Polish immigration during this period was not mainly of the middle class, it did play an important role in the development of industries and crafts in Palestine. Polish immigrants pioneered in the textile industry. The Lodzia company was founded by immigrants from Lodz, an energetic but unsuccessful attempt was made to establish a Jedeh-Manor textile mill near Haifa, and the Yerushalmi brothers opened a rope factory. Polish immigrants also built many small factories, some of which eventually developed into important industrial enterprises, and contributed greatly to the building of Tel Aviv and the development of other areas.

In 1927 the British mandatory government halted immigration for all practical purposes. However, in Poland there was increased pressure among pioneer youth and Jewish workers for emigration to Palestine. Certificates were obtained by circuitous means. The first Maccabia in 1932, for example, sparked a wave of "tourism" that continued almost until the end of 1933. Although a Jew could not get an immigration permit to Palestine, he could obtain a tourist visa for a deposit of 60 Palestine pounds as a guarantee that he would leave the country on the expiration of his visa. Thousands of Jews took advantage of this arrangement, with the prior intention of settling permanently in Palestine. By the end of 1933, according to the estimate of the mandatory government, about 15,000 such "tourists" had remained in Palestine beyond the expiration dates of their visas. At least two-thirds of these tourists were estimated to be Polish Jews.

Between 1932 and the end of World War II, 325,000 immigrants reached Palestine; of these 105,235, or about 30

Polish-Jewish refugee children arriving in Palestine during World War II. [United Jewish Appeal]

percent, were from Poland. They were mainly pioneer youths, laborers, and middle-class people. Between 1946 and 1948 about 17,129 Polish Jews came to Palestine, many of them as "illegal" immigrants. Many "illegal" ships sailed before, during, and after World War II, and a large number of their passengers (often the majority) were from Poland.

Since the establishment of the State of Israel there have been various waves of Polish immigrants: concentration camp survivors, inmates of the Cyprus camps, and so on. Of the 151,185 Polish Jews who arrived after the creation of the State, two-thirds came before 1950. Many more Polish Jews arrived in Israel via Germany, France, Austria, and almost all the countries of North, Central, and South America and were thus registered as immigrants from these countries. Statistics showed that in 1965 there were 331,312 Polish immigrants in Israel, to which figure must be added the children born to these immigrants after their arrival. The number of Jews of Polish origin living in Israel in 1990 may therefore be estimated at well over 400,000.

Hundreds of associations of Polish Jews from various towns are to be found in Israel. About 200 of these are actively involved in providing social services for their members. Some 150 were organized in the Association of Immigrants from Poland, which was founded in the early 1920s. In 1925 the association presented its own list of candidates for election to the Tel Aviv Municipal Council, winning four seats. It maintained a broad program of social services, including finding work for unemployed immigrants and serving the aged and the sick.

Polish immigrants to Israel played an important and responsible role in civic, political, and Zionist affairs. A high proportion of prime ministers and cabinet ministers have been of Polish extraction and Jews of Polish origin have played a dominant role in all aspects of Israeli life, setting a stamp on the country's ethos that has only changed in recent years with the rise of the Jews from Moslem Lands.

A. REISS

POLITICAL PARTIES IN ISRAEL. Most features of Israel's political parties have changed considerably over the years and the party system has been totally reshaped since the 1970s. Some features, however, have remained the same since the days of the yishuv prior to the establishment of the State. One such feature is the multiplicity of parties. In the 1984 national elections a new record was reached, with 31 lists, not all of them real parties, in the running. This multiplicity in the past has been variously attributed to historical factors, such as the role of parties and party-linked organizations in the development of the yishuv; psychological factors, such as loyalties to causes and leaders; ideological factors relating to long-range adherence to basic ideas and issues; and legal factors, predominantly the extreme form of proportional representation in Israel's parliamentary system, which makes the entire country one multi-member constituency and thus encourages fractionalization. More recently, with a growing voters' volatility, the proportional representation election system seems to have become the single most important factor accounting for the extreme multiplicity of parties.

Multiparty system. Numerically the extreme multi-party system has been fairly stable, despite the growing tendency of fusions and fissions of parties and the emergence of party blocs and alliances. But the relative strength of parties which had been comparatively steady until the 1960s has since fluctuated greatly. No party has ever had a majority in the Knesset, the closest being the 56 seats (out of 120) which the Israel Labor Party (ILP)-Mapam Alignment achieved in the 1969 elections. But until the 1970s the ILP (and its predecessor, Mapai) was the dominant party, having a substantial plurality of between 32 and 38 percent of the vote. Throughout that earlier period Mapai/ILP was the governing party, providing the candidates for the offices of Prime Minister and all other major ministries. In the public image Mapai/ILP was widely identified with the State and the established political regime. Other parties were sometimes part ot the coalition and at other times were identified with the opposition. Some of these parties, such as the Independent Liberals (previously the Progressive party), the National Religious party (NRP, previously Mizrachi and Ha-Po'el ha-Mizrachi), and Ahdut ha-Avoda (after its split from

Election posters. [Israel Information Services]

Mapam and prior to its merger with Mapai to form the ILP), have been almost constant coalition members. Others vacillated between coalition and opposition, among them Mapam and the General Zionists (later the Liberals). Finally there were the parties in opposition on principle. Among these Herut was by far the largest and most important, having been the second largest party in the Knesset since 1955. Herut was, however, a member of the Government of National Unity during 1967–1970. Other parties in this group were the Communists (split into two parties in 1965) and Agudat Israel (in opposition to the Labor majority from 1951).

The 1977 electoral upheaval changed all of this, and since then the Israeli party system can best be described as a two-party system. The Likud bloc, composed primarily of Herut and the Liberals, emerged as the largest faction in the Knesset with 43 seats. Together with the one-time electoral success of Dash (Democratic Movement of Change), which became briefly the third largest party (15 seats), the old Labor-dominated system came to an end. Instead, and with the rapid disappearance of Dash, a new two-party bloc system emerged in 1981, with a balance between the two main blocs (1981: Likud—48 seats, Alignment—47 seats; 1984: Alignment—44 seats, Likud—41 seats; 1988: Likud—40 seats, Alignment—39 seats).

Around these two new blocs a number of realignments of parties have taken place. The most important of these concerns the so-called religious camp, the parties of which have attached themselves in varying degrees to the Likud and which by 1988 as a camp had regained previous losses. Within this camp the NRP has lost heavily (1977: 12 seats; 1988: 5 seats), and new ethnic-religious parties have been founded, first Tami, a breakaway from NRP and now defunct, and in 1984 Shas, an Oriental Aguda-style party (gaining 4 seats). Tehiya is a new radical nationalist party on the right of the political spectrum, with 5 seats in 1984 and 3 in 1988, when two more such parties appeared: Tzomet and Moledet, each with 2 seats. On the other side of the spectrum are new parties such as the Civil Rights Movement with 5 seats in 1988 and Shinui with 2 seats. The left-wing socialist Mapam also reappeared as an independent party after splitting off the Labor Alignment and gained 3 seats. The Communists (labeled Democratic Front for Peace) and the Progressive List for Peace, new in 1984, and the Arab Democratic Party, new in 1988, got 1 seat each in 1988. Together they received the bulk of the Arab vote, while the former so-called Arab electoral lists built around notables disappeared from the scene. The majority of the combined seats of the Likud-centered camp in the 1977 elections made possible the first ever change of the party in power, and in 1981 a bare majority extended the tenure of this coalition. But the balanced results between the two camps in the 1984 and 1988 elections made Governments of National Unity with full equality between the two major parties in 1984 and of almost full equality a necessity, leaving an opposition of only 20 Knesset Members in 1984 and of 23 in 1988.

No single sociological or ideological factor can account for the electoral support and party affiliations of the various sectors of the population. Nor is there any one explanation for the notable overall decline of party membership of Israelis from about 20% of adults in the early 1960s to below 10% in the mid-1980s, other than a disenchantment in general with parties and politicians as such. This might explain also the ever-growing phenomenon of voter volatility and change of party support. Even the nationality-based cleavage—in the first two decades of the State accounting for a majority of Arabs voting for so-called Arab party-lists but no longer attracting much support—declined in importance in recent elections, with a growing percentage of Arabs voting for the Communists or "mixed" or Jewish parties. Beyond this, complex combinations of factors of geographical proximity, city or village place of residence, and religious and *hamula* (clan) affiliation, as well as age, continue to play a role in the Arab voting decision.

ISRAELI PARTY SYSTEM:
SHARING BY TWO LARGEST PARTIES OF 120 KNESSET
SEATS AND COMPETITIVENESS RATIO, 1949–1984

	Largest Party	*Second Largest Party*	*2 Largest Parties Combined*	*Percentage of 2 Largest Parties*	*Competitiveness ratio*
1949	Mapai:46	Mapam:19	65	54%	.41
1951	Mapai:45	Liberals:20	65	54	.41
1955	Mapai:40	Herut:15	55	46	.38
1959	Mapai:47	Herut:17	64	53	.36
1961	Mapai:42	Herut:17 Liberals:17	59	49	.40
1965	Alignment b:45	Gahal c:26	71	59	.58
1969	Alignment d:56	Gahal c:26	82	68	.46
1973	Alignment d:51	Likud e:39	90	75	.76
1977	Likud e:43	Alignment d:32	75	62	.74
1981	Likud e:47	Alignment d:47	95	79	.98
1984	Alignment d:44	Likud e:41	85	71	.93

a Competitiveness ratio = second largest party/largest party
b Mapai and Ahdut ha-Avoda
c Herut and Liberals
d Labor Party and Mapam
e Gahal and others

Among Jewish voters the propensity of two sociologically identifiable sectors to vote for specific parties is eminently apparent: the politically significant cleavage between religious Jews and others finds its expression in the vote of a plurality of religious Jews for so-called religious parties, but it is hard to explain sociologically either the temporary decline of the overall vote for these parties in the early 1980s or the growth of the ultra-Orthodox parties at the expense of the moderate ones. The main Jewish ethnic divide, of little electoral significance during two earlier decades, became preponderant in the 1970s and early 1980s when up to 70% of Likud support came from the Sephardi/Oriental sector and a similar percentage of the votes for the Labor Alignment were provided by Ashkenazis. This ethnic dichotomization seems since to have abated only slightly.

Class stratification and class consciousness, inasmuch as they exist, find little clear expression in voting behavior, and to the extent that they do are strongly correlated with the ethnic factor. Working-class and low-income citizens constitute the mass of supporters of almost all parties in nearly equal proportions. Nor does class structure explain the division of votes between the various parties of the labor movement when they ran separately in elections. Even the continuously solid labor vote in the kibbutz and moshav movements recently has at least slightly dissipated. In any event, support for the ILP is derived in large measure from non-working-class voters. On the other hand, the Likud gains more support from low-income groups than from middle-class and other non-working-class strata, and a substantial part of its vote comes from the most underprivileged among the Jewish population. Again, this more recent tendency is strongly correlated with the ethnic or country-of-origin criterion. Nevertheless, in addition to social status, this increasing tendency can be explained by political culture, a reputed affirmative approach to traditional religious values, and a hawkish foreign policy orientation. This has been amply proved by the support of some of these groups for newer parties, such as Tehiya and Rabbi Meir Kahane's Kach party.

Until the 1970s younger voters did not evince a voting behavior different from that of older voters. Since then, however, the younger the age of the voters the more pronounced are the leanings towards the Likud and the other nationalistic parties, for ethnic-demographic and ideological reasons. Women do not vote in a manner significantly different from men.

Party ideologies. During the first two decades or so of the State, ideological and policy specificity of all parties was perhaps their major characteristic. Parties took exact positions on a number of intersecting axes, such as the socioeconomic structure of society, foreign and security policy, and religious issues. Later, and especially after 1967, other issues came to the fore in the national agenda, chiefly the future of the Administered Areas, but also Israel-Diaspora relations. Some of the older issues have been sidetracked, while still others have been exacerbated. At the same time the ideological stands of most parties—certainly of the two major "catch-all" party agglomerates, the Labor Alignment and the Likud— had become blurred, so that within each of them a wide range of ideological and policy positions is to be found, and views on many issues cut across these and other parties. Most parties also have found it possible to collaborate in a national unity government. Only some of the smaller parties on the political map have been mindful of a need to preserve their ideological uniqueness. Nevertheless, and in spite of the continuing Government of National Unity, starting roughly in the mid-1980s, the ideological split over the national-territorial issue and Israel-Palestinian relations has reemerged as the dominant divisive element in Israeli politics.

Thus in the 1980s, of the three broad, major policy areas which are at the heart of public controversy, the one which has to do with the Palestinian question, has become the least consensual. There still is wide agreement, but by no means unanimity, to disallow the establishment of a Palestinian state, but beyond that there is a wide range of views, and an ever-widening gap between those advocating the full annexation of the whole of western Palestine and maximal Jewish settlement of all of that area, and those supporting a repartitioning of Palestine, creation of a Jordanian-Palestinian state, and total or virtual stoppage of further settlement on the West Bank. The second policy area concerns the economic and social system. Although there is widespread agreement on the necessity for a comprehensive welfare state, opinions range from Marxists on the one extreme to private-initiative proponents on the other. Here again the middle ground is dominant, which favors the continuation of a tripartite economy of private, State and labor-owned and -run sectors, with substantial governmental control and activity in investments, fiscal and monetary measures, and particularly heavy involvement by government in the social services. However, deregulation, lifting of controls, and some elements of privatization have become acceptable to most, excepting only the emphatic left. Third, in matters of state and religion, the range of positions runs from demands for a theocracy, i.e., a "Torah" State, to complete separation of state and the religious establishment, with a majority accepting a wide variety of potential middle-of-the-road solutions. Coercion is rising on the one side, and on the other its imposition meets increasing resentment, as a result of which tension between the so-called religious and secular camps is on the increase.

Structure and Functions. Conforming with the general political and administrative tendency in the country, almost all parties are extremely centralized. In spite of formally far-reaching democratic internal structures and processes, parties are run on rather oligarchic lines, although in recent years substantial democratizing measures have variously been introduced. Some parties are little more than tenuous coalitions of loosely connected notables or religious leaders. At the same time, most parties are highly bureaucratized organizations; they have comparatively large party headquarters with salaried personnel and branch offices throughout the country. Most parties hold party conferences, nowadays as a rule elected by party members and meeting rather infrequently; party councils, usually elected by the conferences; and "secretariats" or "executive committees," where internal power is really located, which are responsible for the operations of the party.

Israeli parties function as more than electoral and governmental-supporting apparatuses which participate in the public policy-making process. Many of them, directly or by way of subsidiary organizations, are active in cultural and educational activities, operate commercial enterprises such as banking, housing, and construction, and function as labor unions and the like. None of this is really peculiar to Israeli parties; what is outstanding is the cumulative propensity of many parties to engage in these multiple functions. In recent years there has been a slight tendency of at least some parties to forego some of these activities, but so far the parties have rejected the enactment of a party law which would regulate certain, and perhaps even prohibit a number of, these functions.

Politics come dear in Israel; day-to-day operations and large staffs cost a good deal of money, and electoral expenses are extremely high. Since the 1970s these expenses are covered by allocations from the public purse to parties represented in the Knesset according to the proportionate number of their Knesset members. In addition, parties are allowed to raise funds through membership dues and other contributions. All these financial transactions are subject to the surveillance of the State Comptroller.

Since the 1960s political movements of a quasi-party character have become part of the political scene. The more prominent ones, such as Gush Emunim and Peace Now, have been very influential, more so even than some regular parties. Some of these have transformed themselves into parties, either fully and openly or under other labels and more hesitantly. E. GUTMANN

POOL, DE SOLA: U.S. Zionist family.

David De Sola Pool, rabbi, and author (b. London, 1885; d. New York City 1970) studied at Jews' College, London, the University of London, the Berlin Rabbinical Seminary, and the universities of Berlin and Heidelberg. In 1907 he was invited to become rabbi of Congregation Shearith Israel (the Spanish-Portuguese Synagogue) in New York, the oldest congregation in the United States. He served there until 1956, when he became rabbi emeritus.

Sola Pool early took an interest in the Young Judaea movement, serving first as an adviser and then as its president from 1915 to 1919 and again from 1924 to 1927. From 1919 to 1921 he was a member of the Zionist Commission to Palestine, and he also represented the American Jewish Joint Distribution Committee, which did relief work among the yishuv. Returning to his congregation in 1922, he occupied a leading position in various rabbinical and communal organizations and wrote extensively on the history of American Jewry and on Jewish and Zionist issues. He also published a number of prayer books for the Sephardi Jews, with his own English translation and commentaries.

His wife **Tamar De Sola Pool** (b. Constantinople, 1893; d. New York City 1981) was an educator and Zionist leader. She was taken to the United States by her parents in 1904 and studied at Hunter College and Columbia University in New York and at the Sorbonne and the Collège de France in Paris. A Zionist from her youth, she became active in Hadassah, of which she was national president from 1939 to 1943. She was the editor of the *Hadassah Newsletter* from 1936 to 1951. Thereafter she headed several of Hadassah's major committees, represented the organization on the Actions Committee of the World Zionist Organization, and was a cofounder of the Hebrew University-Hadassah Medical School. She and her husband were coauthors of a number of books on Jewish life in America. A. ALPERIN

POPKIN, RUTH WILLION. Zionist and Jewish leader in the US (b. Queens, New York). She rose from the ranks in Hadassah work to become the 18th national president, 1984–88. She was an innovative chairman of Purchasing and Supplies for Israel and of the National Youth Activities department of the organization, co-Treasurer of the World Jewish Congress, and vice-president of the National Jewish Community Relations Advisory Council. A member of the Presidium of the Jewish Agency General Council, she has been a delegate to five Zionist Congresses and served as Chairman of the Presidium and as President of the World Zionist Congress in December, 1987, in Jerusalem, the first woman to be elected to this position. In 1990 she was elected US president of the Jewish National Fund.

M. LEVIN

POPULATION OF ISRAEL.

Size and growth of the population. Since the establishment of the State, its population has increased as shown by Table 1.

The Jews living in the Administered Areas are included in the Jewish population in Table 1. This population increased from about 1,500 in 1972 to 53,300 at the end of 1986 (of which: 51,100 in Judea and Samaria and 2,100 in Gaza.

The Arab population of these territories has evolved as shown by Table 2.

The growth of the Jewish population of Israel was very strong in the first fifteen years or so after the establishment of the State, and was due largely to immigration. With the slackening of immigration and reduction of the rate of natural increase, the yearly rates of growth of the Jewish population and of the total population of Israel have strongly decreased. The average rate of growth of the non-Jewish population (which is practically the result only of natural increase) has remained comparatively high, despite recent reduction in fertility. The Arab population of the Administered Areas has had a strong rise in its natural increase. With progressive reduction in the volume of emigration from those territories, the yearly rate of growth has strongly increased in the course of time.

Determinants and consequences of these basic trends are described below.

At the end of 1988, Israel's population reached 4,476,800 of whom 3,659,000 (81.7%) were Jews, 634,600 (14.0%) Moslems, 105,000 (2.4%) Christians, and 78,000 (1.7%) Druze and other religious communities. In 1988, the Jewish population grew by 1.6% (1.7% in 1987) and the Moslem by 3.3%.

2. Immigration. Table 3 shows the size of Jewish immigration to Israel (*see* ALIYA) during 1948–86. The table indicates: 1) the absolute number of immigrants (including "potential immigrants" viz. persons entering Israel for more than three months and entitled to obtain the status of immigrants); 2) the yearly average rate of immigrants per 1,000 of the Jewish Diaspora population, from which immigration originates; and 3) per 1,000 of the Jewish population of Israel by which immigration is absorbed; 4) the percentage of immigrants born in Europe and America (including Oceania). The difference between 100 and this percentage indicates the percentage born in Asia and Africa.

The analysis of these data, of comparable rates for the period of British Mandate, and of detailed data on Jewish immigration by countries of origin, leads to the following general conclusions:

1) Since 1919 immigration has been a continuous feature and still remains so. It has originated and continues to originate from almost all Diaspora Jewish communities. The continuity and cosmopolitan character of the immigration suggest continuous action of immigration determinants felt throughout the Jewish Diaspora.

TABLE 1. POPULATION INCREASE AND ITS MAIN SOURCES.

Dates	Size of population (thousands)	Yearly rate of growth per 1000 in the period between two dates	Percentage of growth due to	
			migratory balance	natural increase
		Total Population		
15 May 1948	805.6			
		78	64.6	35.4
End of year 1960	2,150.4			
		32	37.7	62.3
End of year 1971	3,115.6			
		24	19.6	80.4
End of year 1982	4,033.7			
		18	5.1	94.9
End of year 1986	4,331.3			
1948–1986		44	40.5	59.5
		Jews		
15 May 1948	649.6			
		86	68.9	31.1
End of year 1960	1,911.2			
		30	45.0	55.0
End of year 1971	2,662.0			
		21	25.1	74.9
End of year 1982	3,349.6			
		15	6.3	93.7
End of year 1986	3,561			
1948–1986		44	47.7	52.3
		Non-Jews		
15 May 1948	156.0			
		36	0.1	99.9
End of year 1960	239.2			
		41	0.3	99.7
End of year 1971	453.8			
		37	2.1	97.9
End of year 1982	684.1			
		30	2.3	97.7
End of year 1986	769.9			
1948–1986		42	1.6	98.4

TABLE 2. ARAB POPULATION OF JUDEA, SAMARIA, AND GAZA.

Dates	Size of population (thousands)	Yearly rate of growth in the period between two dates	Average yearly	
			Balance of population (thousands)	Natural increase (thousands)
September 1967	966.7			
		9	−20.5	+24.2
End of year 1971	1,001.4			
		19	−13.6	+37.3
End of year 1982	1,226.6			
		30	−9.4	+46.0
End of year 1986	1,381.0			
of which:				
Judea & Samaria	836.0	1967–86: 19	1967–85: −8.8	1967–85: +20.7
Gaza	545.0	1967–86: 19	1967–85: −5.4	1967–85: +14.9

2) However, propensity to immigrate (measured in terms of yearly rates of immigration to Israel per 1,000 Jewish population in each Diaspora community) changes enormously from place to place and from time to time. Generally speaking, this propensity has been strong among the Jewish population of eastern Europe, the Balkans, and Asia and, in certain periods, in central Europe and North Africa. Progressive disappearance of the Jewish communities in these areas has probably constituted a major determinant of the downward trend of immigration.

3) Today the Jewish Diaspora is mainly constituted by the communities in the Americas, Eastern and Central Europe, South Africa and Oceania, where propensity to immigrate to Israel has been generally low, and by the Jewish population of the USSR, from where the Jewish emigration is largely dependent upon Soviet Government policies.

4) Economic, political, and social difficulties in Israel have presumably contributed to the shrinkage of immigration from Western countries, which started after the 1973 Yom Kippur War and still continues.

TABLE 3. DIMENSIONS OF JEWISH IMMIGRATION IN ISRAEL (1948–1985)

Years	*Absolute number of immigrants*		*Percentage immigrants born in Europe and America*	*Average annual number of immigrants per 1000*	
	Whole period	*Annual average*		*Jews in the Diaspora*	*Jewish population of Israel*
1948–51 (1)	686,739	189,184	50.1	16.57	184.2
1952–54	54,065	18,022	23.6	1.54	12.3
1955–57	164,936	54,979	31.7	4.60	33.4
1958–60	75,487	25,162	64.0	2.04	18.7
1961–64	228,046	57,012	40.6	4.41	27.5
1965–68	81,337	20,334	50.3	1.51	8.7
1969–73	227,258	45,452	81.3	3.25	17.2
1974–78	119,586	23,917	90.1	2.39	8.0
1979–83	100,878	20,176	78.6	2.01	6.2
1984–86	40,128	13,376	52.7	1.02	3.8

(1) Starting 15 May 1948

5) Immigration from the Diaspora was the dominant factor of the Jewish demography of Israel in 1948–51, and played a very important part at the time of the waves of 1955–57, 1961–64, and 1969–73. Since then, it has had low levels. In 1984–86, the yearly rate of immigration has been only about 1 per 1,000 Diaspora Jews and less than 4 per 100 Israeli Jews.

3. Emigration. As in previous period, in recent years also, part of the immigration is offset by *emigration (*"Yerida"*). The statistical measurement of size, composition, and directions of emigration is fraught with many technical difficulties. To indicate a few points:

1) According to a rough estimate, the total volume of the emigration of Jews from Israel to abroad between 1948 and 1985 has been 300,000—330,000.

2) The yearly rate of emigration per 1,000 of the Jewish population of Israel has been 7–8 during 1948–1959, 5 during 1960–67, 2 during 1968–72, and 4 during 1973–1985,

3) In consequence of the emigration and other factors, the migratory balance of the Jewish population of Israel has during 1948–1986 been 1,407,800 as compared to a total of 1,783,400 immigrants.

Part of the emigration was caused by re-emigration of recent immigrants who did not succeed in settling satisfactorily in Israel. However, since the 1960s emigration also developed of people other than new immigrants, largely connected with the desire to improve individual economic conditions. Broadly speaking, it may be estimated that emigration is more frequent at young labor ages and is lower for children and old people; that men emigrate more than women, single more than married, people of European-American origin more than people of African-Asian origin. Emigration is largely directed toward the USA, Canada, etc.

Under the circumstances described above, the natural increase became the dominant factor in the growth of the population.

4. Marriage, divorce, and the family. New families are generally established in Israel by spouses belonging to the same religion. Unlike in the Diaspora, the number of mixed Jewish-non-Jewish couples is thought to be small (despite lack of statistics on this topic).

Among the Jews, preference in marriage between people originating from the same country, which in the past was very strong, is decreasing.

During the first decades of statehood, tendency to marry has continued to be very high among Jews, Moslems, and Druze (while being rather weak among the Christians). In the past, the proportion of Jews, Moslems, and Druze remaining single throughout their entire lifetime was very small.

The marriage patterns of Moslems, Jews of Asian-African origin, and certain extremely Orthodox Jewish religious groups have been largely influenced in the past by traditional nuptial customs, and in particular by the custom of marrying girls at very young ages. Jews immigrating from Europe brought very different nuptial customs. In the course of time, evolution has brought a standardization of nuptial habits to most Jewish groups and a decrease in differential marriage patterns.

Among Moslems, the general tendency until recently has been that an overwhelming majority of those reaching adulthood marry and do so at rather young ages. However, very young marriages have almost disappeared in consequence of the introduction of a legal marriage age of 17.

New immigrants tend to have strong nuptiality and this has created high peaks of nuptiality in periods of mass immigration. With declining rates of immigration, however, nuptiality has tended to return to more normal rates.

All these traits together led to the consequence that the proportion of the fertile period spent by Jewish, Moslem, and Druze women in married life was comparatively very high in Israel.

However, in the last decade or so, the marriage scenario of Israeli Jewish society has been changing rapidly, under the impact of the weakening of family, analogous to that occurring among all advanced populations and Diaspora Jews.

The decline in familistic orientation was presumably later and possibily weaker in Israeli society than in many Western countries. However, signs of changes are evident. A few examples are given below with regard to Jewish population. similar evolution is taking place among other population groups:

1) Marriage rates per 1,000 Jews aged 15 and over have declined as follows:

	1969–73	1974–78	1979–83	1984–86
Males	27.3	25.9	21.8	19.6
Females	27.1	25.3	21.4	18.8

Considering in a more specific way people aged 20–29, the following rates are found:

MARRIAGES PER THOUSAND NEVER MARRIED

	Grooms		Brides	
	1975	1985	1975	1985
20–24	135	72	226	164
25–29	243	226	178	171

2) The proportion single per 100 in each age group has increased as follows:

AMONG JEWISH MALES AGED

	20–24	25–29	30–34
Census of 1972	76.8	27.5	9.3
Estimate for 1985	83.9	37.8	12.6

AMONG JEWISH FEMALES AGED

	20–24	25–29	30–34
Census of 1972	47.1	15.8	6.2
Estimate for 1985	54.4	18.5	9.7

3) The age at first marriage of Jewish brides is increasing. For example: the median age of these brides moved from 21.5 in 1975 to 22.7 in 1985; the proportion married at age 19 or below decreased from 29.6 in 1975 to 19.0 in 1985.

4) The frequency of divorce is increasing (divorces per 1,000 ever-married males aged 15–49: 1973–74: 6.6; 1984–86: 9.0; females: 1973–74: 5.4; 1984–86: 7.7).

According to data up to 1985, for the cohort of couples married in 1964–65 (exposed to the risk of divorce for 20 years), the proportion of marriages ending with divorce was about 12%. In more recent cohorts, this proportion is expected to be large, but it will still be much lower than those found in some Western countries. The proportion of divorcing couples with children is increasing (1975: 46.6%; 1982–94: 61.6%).

5) No statistics are available on unmarried cohabitations; but it is known that this phenomenon is spreading considerably.

6) The proportion of births out of wedlock tends to increase (1970: 0.7% births; 1983–85: 1.1%). However, this level is much lower than that found in many other comparable populations.

7) There has been a considerable increase in the proportion of one-person households (from 13% in 1970 to 17% in 1985). This is due to the joint action of changes in marriage habits indicated above, increased tendency of young people to live outside the parents' home, and the enlarged proportion of elderly people living alone.

The proportion of one-parent households has somewhat increased in the past decade, and has reached a level of 4% of all households.

5. Fertility and Abortions.

1) *Among the Jews*: Table 4 shows total fertility rates for the population of Israel between 1950 and 1985. These rates indicate the average number of children which would be born to a woman, under the conditions indicated by the specific birth rates for women of each age in the year under survey.

TABLE 4. AVERAGE NUMBER OF CHILDREN PER WOMAN

Years	*Jewish women born in*				*Moslem*	*Christian*
	Israel	*Asia-Africa*	*Europe America*	*Total*	*women*	
1950–53	3.52	6.09	3.10	3.94		
1961–64	2.73	4.68	2.42	3.37	9.4	4.7
1972–75	3.01	3.81	2.81	3.20	8.24	3.36
1976–78	2.93	3.40	2.84	3.00	7.29	3.14
1979–81	2.76	3.03	2.68	2.75	6.09	2.62
1982–83	2.83	3.10	2.82	2.81	5.40	2.30
1984–85	2.88	3.25	2.72	2.84	4.74	2.33

It can be seen from the table that in the 1950s and 1960s, total fertility had very different levels among the various population groups in Israel. The lowest fertility was found among Jewish families born in Europe; fertility of women born in Asia and North Africa was almost double. These women were primarily immigrants of the 1948–1951 period, coming from communities still largely oriented toward traditional high nuptiality and fertility habits. From those differentials in fertility, it ensued that a considerable proportion of Jewish children were born in families with poorer socio-economic conditions. This led, together with other factors, to political and social tensions.

Later, there was a rapid transition of Asian-African women toward lower levels of fertility. This can be explained by rising educational standards, growing urbanization, the impact of modern (particularly more secular) views on the part of the young generation, and growing familiarity with birth control ideas and methods. Among Jews of Asian-African origin in Israel, the fertility of first-generation immigrants in Israel is generally lower than that which prevailed among the Jews in their countries of origin; fertility of those born in Israel (second generation) is lower than that of the first generation.

Transition of Jews of European origin to lower fertility levels had occurred already in the British mandatory period and was followed by a "baby boom" in the 1940s and 1950s. In the 1960s, it fell again. However, in the course of the last decade or so, it has risen to a plateau of around 2.7–2.8 children per woman. This level is much higher than that of comparable Diaspora Jews.

Due to those opposite trends, differentiation between people born in the different continents tends almost to disappear. In an analogous way, fertility of women born in Israel to families of Asian-African origin or European origin tends to converge.

In the past few years, average fertility rates for the entire Jewish population have oscillated around a level of some 2.85. This is a level much higher than the average level of Diaspora Jews and of advanced world populations. However, a recent feature is the considerable decline of fertility rates to women aged less than 25. This results probably from decrease of nuptiality at young ages.

The comparatively remarkable level of Jewish fertility in Israel is largely due to the fact that the majority of Jewish families in Israel desire to have a number of children larger than that generally desired by contemporary advanced populations. In this regard, the following provisional findings can be quoted, for 741 Jewish married women aged 19–39 (out of some 1,800), included in a current inquiry conducted by the School of Public Health of the Hebrew University, under the sponsorship of the UN Fund for Population Assistance: the average number of children actually had by these women until the time of the inquiry was 2.52; the total number desired was 3,50; the total number considered as desirable, if there were not economic or health difficulties, was 4.08.

While origin has lost its place as an important factor of differentiation of fertility in Israel, other factors of differentiation persist, such as the following:

a) Jewish women belonging to families or groups with religious outlook and allegiance tend to have higher fertility than those secularly oriented. The ultra-Orthodox have very high fertility.

b) Average fertility differs among different types of localities: it is comparatively higher a) in Jerusalem (due in considerable part to the influence of comparatively large religious groups), and b) at least until recently, in the kibbutzim (where the economic burden of child raising falls on the community, which is interested in keeping a large number of children), and c) in some small towns and rural settlements. It is comparatively lower in Tel Aviv and Haifa.

c) Fertility tends generally to decline with increasing levels of education of mothers and fathers.

d) The number of children of working mothers is somewhat lower than that of non-working mothers of the same age.

Studies carried out in the past two decades have shown an increase among all population groups in their tendency to plan the number and spacing of the children and to use modern birth control. However, there is still considerable resort to abortion. After legalization of abortion (for specific reasons), the number of interruptions of pregnancy at authorized hospitals was as follows:

	1979–80	*1981–83*	*1984–85*
Absolute number	15,316	15,645	18,677
Per 100 Jewish births	21.7	21.5	25.0

It may be noted that while in 1979–80 interruption of pregnancies was legal for family or social circumstances, since then abortion has been permitted only in cases of danger to the woman's life, or physical or mental defects in the fetus, the woman's age, and non-marital relations. Besides legal abortions, an unknown but not negligible number of illegal abortions is known to be performed.

Referring all legal abortions (including those undergone by an unspecified but presumably small number of non-Jewish women) to Jewish births, it is found that there are today about 25 abortions per 100 live births. This proportion is very similar to the average number of abortions per 100 live births (24.7%) in 14 countries of western Europe and North America for which data for 1984 are available. However, it is much smaller than the proportions found in eastern European countries. Differences between countries are also due to different degrees of liberalization of abortion by law. b) *Fertility among the Non-Jewish population.* Until the 1960s the Moslem population of Israel had an exceptionally high fertility (over 9 children per woman), exceeding that of other Middle Eastern Moslem populations. This was due largely to the permanence of traditional orientation, typical of a predominantly rural society in which high fertility was greatly esteemed and in which the nuclear families were integrated in clans. The enormous progress in health conditions and improvement in socio-economic conditions presumably acted also in a first stage to maintain fertility levels. However, later trends have been mainly directed toward a "modern" evolution. Education levels have risen considerably; many large villages have turned into small towns; and the urban proportion among the Moslems has increased very rapidly. The influence of modern ways of life is making its impact through extensive schooling, increasing contacts with the Jews at work, increasing influence of mass media of communication. As shown by Table 4, the decrease of Moslem fertility during the 1970s and early 1980s has been very rapid. However, its level remains considerably higher than that of the Jews.

2) *Among the Christians:* Fertility has constantly been much lower than among the Moslems, due to various factors, such as (a) the lower propensity to marry among the Christians; (b) the much higher educational and urbanization level. In recent years the fertility of the Christians has become lower than that of the Jews. (See Table 4).

6. Health and Mortality. The population of Israel, in all its sectors, has reached health levels comparable to those of the most advanced world countries.

In the following some indicators are given on levels of mortality in Israel:

TABLE 5. AVERAGE LENGTH OF LIFE AT BIRTH

Years	*Jews*		*Non-Jews*	
	Males	*Females*	*Males*	*Females*
1965–69	70.2	73.4	69.3	71.7
1970–74	70.5	73.6	68.9	72.4
1975–78	71.6	75.2	68.9	71.8
1979–82	72.7	76.1	70.4	73.5
1983–85	73.5	77.0	71.6	74.7

1) The average length of life (expectation of life at birth) has continued to improve both among Jews and non-Jews, as shown by Table 5 and it is only slightly shorter for the latter than for the former. The average length of life of 75.3 for males and 77.0 for females in the entire population of Israel in 1985 can be compared to an estimate of 73.0 in developed world countries (1984).

2) Infant mortality rates have further decreased among

all population groups, as shown by Table 6; however they are still higher among Moslems than among Jews and Christians. The average rate for the entire population of Israel (1984–86: 12.0 per 1,000 live births) can be compared to an estimate of 16.9 for all developed world countries (1984).

TABLE 6. INFANT DEATHS PER 1,000 LIVE BIRTHS

Years	*Jews*	*Moslems*	*Christians*	*Total population*
1955–59	32.1	60.6	46.1	36.5
1965–69	20.8	43.8	32.7	25.5
1970–74	18.7	40.1	29.6	23.5
1975–79	15.0	32.6	20.9	18.9
1980–83	12.2	23.5	19.0	14.8
1984–86	9.9	19.6	13.6(*)	12.0

(*) 1984–85

Detailed data for mortality by cause among the Jews show that heart diseases, malignant neoplasms, and cerebro-vascular diseases are the leading groups. Mortality from malignant neoplasms has been on the rise, while mortality related to acute myocardial infarction and cerebrovascular diseases has recently declined considerably. Mortality due to perinatal causes has decreased too. Mortality due to infections and parasitic diseases is much smaller than in the 1950s. However, certain infectious diseases such as hepatitis and gastro-intestinal disorders still constitute public health problems.

7. Natural increase. Table 7 shows the current annual rate of births, deaths and natural increases per 1,000 population. Birth rates are affected by fertility (discussed above) and age structure (see below); death rates are affected by age-specific mortality and age structure; rates of natural increase are obtained by subtracting death rates from birth rates.

TABLE 7. RATES PER 1,000 POPULATION

	Jews			*Moslems*		
Years	*Births*	*Deaths*	*Natural increase*	*Births*	*Deaths*	*Natural increase*
1955–59	25.6	5.9	19.7	46.3	8.0	38.3
1965–69	22.5	6.7	15.8	51.0	6.1	44.9
1970–74	24.3	7.3	17.0	49.5	5.8	43.7
1975–79	23.6	7.2	16.4	44.5	5.0	39.5
1980–83	21.8	7.2	14.7	37.4	3.9	33.5
1984–86	21.5	7.3	14.1	34.9	3.5	31.3

	Christians			*Total population*		
Years	*Births*	*Deaths*	*Natural increase*	*Births*	*Deaths*	*Natural increase*
1955–59	34.4	7.3	27.1	27.7	6.2	21.5
1965–69	30.4	5.9	24.5	25.4	6.6	18.8
1970–74	26.9	7.0	19.9	27.4	7.1	20.3
1975–79	24.5	6.3	18.2	26.4	6.9	19.5
1980–83	20.7	5.8	14.9	24.0	6.8	17.2
1984–86	19.8	5.7(*)	13.1(*)	23.4	6.7	16.7

(*)1984–85

It is seen from Table 7 that the birth rate has declined in the course of the period considered, much more among the Moslems and Christians than among the Jews, in consequence of the strong decrease of fertility of the non-Jews. However, the rate of births of Moslems still considerably exceeds that of the Jews. Paradoxically, the death rate of non-Jews is lower than that of the Jews, despite the fact that the age specific mortality rates are generally somewhat higher for the former than for the latter. The reason for that is that mortality is today largely concentrated at old ages and that the proportion of old people in the population is much higher among the Jews than among non-Jews. Despite the decline in the natural increase of the Jewish population of Israel, this increase is today considerably larger than that found on an average in the developed world countries (1984: 5.9 per 1,000 population), but it is smaller than that found in developing world countries (20.2). It stands in sharp contrast with the situation prevailing among most Diaspora Jewish populations in which death rates exceed birth rates.

8. The structure of the population.

a) *Sex balance.* The sexes have been in the past and are still rather well-balanced in Israel's population, despite the influence of migratory increase on its development (Table 8). This is because immigration has also been, in general, well-balanced by sex.

TABLE 8. MALES IN THE POPULATION (PERCENTAGES)

Years	*Total population (incl. Druze)*	*Jews*	*Moslems*	*Christians*
1948		51.67		
1955	50.82	50.78	51.52	50.12
1972	50.29	50.17	51.26	49.12
1982	49.93	49.81	50.64	49.04
1986	49.89	49.73	50.86	48.70

The age distribution of Israel's population (Table 9) subsumes the distribution of many different groups with dissimilar types of determinants and courses of evolution.

The age distribution of the Jews of European origin has been affected by their lower fertility; that of Jews of Asian-African origin has been affected over the course of time by a fall in their formerly high fertility. Besides this, the age distribution of both sectors of the Jewish population has been affected by the size and age composition of their immigrant components. This has depended, in turn, on the age distribution of the Jewish community of origin and of selectivity by age of the immigration: these factors have varied greatly from community to community and from period to period; consequently, the age distribution of immigrants has differed considerably from wave to wave.

The age distribution of the Moslem population has generally been rather regular and very young, with a high and rapidly increasing proportion of children. This is in line with the regime of high fertility and declining child mortality in this population.

The age distribution of the Druze is similar to that of the Moslems, while, due to lower fertility, that of the Christians shows a lower proportion of children. On the whole, the age distribution of the entire population is rather similar to that of the majority group (the Jews).

However, under the impact of the very young structure of the non-Jewish population groups, Israel's total population has a somewhat larger proportion of children than the Jewish population; children under age 15 constitute about a third of the total population. No significant change in this age group has occurred in the course of time. On the other hand, during the past thirty years the proportion of the elderly has grown considerably, from 4.8% in 1955 to 8.8% in 1986. In the Jewish population alone, their proportion has increased from 4% in 1948 to 10.1 in 1986.

TABLE 9. PROPORTION OF AGE GROUPS, 1955–1986
(Percentages)

Years	*Total*	*0–4*	*5–14*	*15–24*	*25–34*	*35–44*	*45–64*	*65+*
1955	100.0	14.2	21.1	15.3	14.5	12.6	17.5	4.8
1965	100.0	11.8	22.6	17.6	12.1	11.5	18.3	6.1
1970	100.0	12.0	20.9	20.0	12.0	10.3	18.0	6.8
1975	100.0	12.7	20.2	18.8	16.9	9.7	16.7	8.0
1982	100.0	11.6	21.8	16.8	15.9	10.1	15.5	8.4
1986	100.0	11.3	21.0	17.7	14.9	11.8	15.0	8.8
1986: Jews	100.0	10.5	19.4	16.1	15.1	12.5	16.3	10.1
Moslems	100.0	16.1	29.5	22.3	13.5	8.0	8.1	2.6
Christians	100.0	9.8	21.2	18.9	16.6	11.9	15.9	5.8

c) *Ethnic-religious structure of the population.* The Jews have constituted the large majority of the population since the establishment of the State of Israel; at that time they formed 80.6% of the population. Following the mass migratory influx of 1948–51 their percentage reached 89% in 1951. Between 1951 and 1964 their proportion was subject only to minor fluctuations. Since 1964 it has tended to decline, descending to 82.0% at the end of 1987. This has come about inasmuch as the natural increase of the Jews is much lower than that of non-Jews and because of the drop in their net migratory increase.

The proportion of Moslems rose from 7.5% in 1951 to 13.7% at the end of 1986 due both to their strong natural increase and to the incorporation of East Jerusalem into Israel after the 1967 war. The proportion of Christians fluctuated slightly during 1948-1986, hovering around the level of 2.3%. The proportion of Druze and others increased from 1% in 1948 to 1.7% at the end of 1986.

d) *Population structure by origins.* At the end of the first post-State migratory wave in 1951, 75.5% of the Jewish population had been born abroad and more than half of this group had been in the country five years or less. With the slowing of immigration, the proportion of foreign-born in the population declined steadily, falling to a proportion of 39.1% by the end of 1986. Among the Israeli-born, who constituted in 1986 a majority of 60.9% in the Jewish population, 31.2% belonged to a third or greater generation born in the country.

Among those born abroad, 79.5% immigrated up to 1971, 13.7% during 1972–79, and 6.8% after 1980.

At the establishment of the State the great majority of the foreign-born population was of European origin. In the course of time the proportion of those of Asian origin, and later of those of African (mainly North African), background, has grown significantly (Table 10).

The classification of the foreign-born and their children according to their country of origin (1986) shows that the groups with over 100,000 persons are those originating from Morocco and Tangier (483 thousand); Poland (302.1); USSR (293.2); Romania (278.5); Iraq (266.9); Yemen (165.0); Iran (126.2); Algeria and Tunisia (124.9).

e) *Linguistic and educational structure.* The new immigrants

TABLE 10. JEWISH POPULATION OF ISRAEL BY CONTINENT OF ORIGIN
(Percentages)

Continent of origin	*Foreign-born*		*Foreign-born and their children**	
	1948	*1986*	*1961*	*1986*
Europe (incl.) America	84.9	55.6	55.9	46.8
Asia	12.5	20.7	26.6	26.0
Africa	2.6	23.8	17.5	27.2

*Children of foreign-born fathers are classified according to the continent of birth of their father.

brought with them a great variety of linguistic, cultural, educational, and socio-economic characteristics, creating an extremely heterogenous population in the first years after the establishment of the State.

Since then, Israel society has speedily homogenized under the impact of mutual cultural influences, prolonged residence in the country by the foreign-born, a larger proportion of second and succeeding generations in Israel, the development of the educational system (including adult education), and policies pursued by the government and other institutions.

In the domain of language, an enormous change has taken place in the population's Jewish sector: Hebrew has become the main language in cultural, educational, social, and political endeavors, in business and daily life. In 1954 the percentage of Jews using Hebrew only or first language had fallen from 75% to 61%, due to mass immigration. The proportion of Hebrew speakers among people aged 15 and more later increased from 81% in 1972 to 84% in 1983.

Education is today compulsory until age 16, being given in Hebrew in the Jewish sector and in Arabic in the Arab sector. Due to this and to the rapid development of secondary, vocational, and agricultural schools, universities and other post-secondary educational institutions, an enormous change has occurred in the educational level of all population sectors (Table 11). Illiteracy has practically disappeared among younger age groups, while it still exists in considerable proportion among Jewish women and non-Jewish women aged 45 and over.

Civilian labor force participation of males aged 14 and over has declined rather drastically, from about 80% in 1955 to about 70% in the early 1970s. It continued to

TABLE 11. EDUCATIONAL ATTAINMENT OF THE POPULATION AGED 14 AND OVER

a) Percentage of illiterates or persons who did not attend school

	Jews			*Non-Jews*		
	Males	*Females*	*Total*	*Males*	*Females*	*Total*
1954	8.2	21.7	15.0	35.9	79.0	57.2
1972	4.6	12.9	6.8	17.9	49.5	33.6
1986	2.8	6.8	4.9	8.1	23.7	15.8

b) Of those who attended school, number of years of schooling (total population).

	1–4	*5–8*	*9–12*	*13–15*	*16+*	*Total*
1961	9.7	41.3	38.3	6.8	3.9	100.0
1986	4.1	19.9	51.3	14.2	10.5	100.0

recede slowly (to 63%-64%) in the early 1980s. This decline has been due largely to population aging and to the decline in participation between ages 14–24 due to an extended tendency to attend school. On the other hand, female participation continuously increased: from 27% in 1955 to 39% in 1986.

For both sexes together, participation declined from about 54% in 1955 to about 50% in the late 1960s; since then it has not changed considerably.

9. Geographical distribution of the population. At the establishment of the State, the Jewish population was largely concentrated in very limited areas: 64% lived in the two larger municipalities of Tel Aviv-Jaffa and Haifa and their surroundings. A large number of rural settlements and a few small towns were found in a belt extending from just north of Haifa to somewhat south of Tel Aviv; over 80% thus lived in the coastal plain and about 12% in the town of Jerusalem.

With the large influx of immigrants, mainly in the early 1950s, large changes took place in the population distribution under the impact of population dispersal policies. The number of rural settlements more than doubled between 1943 and 1955, the new settlements being largely spread over new or almost-new development areas in the northern and southern peripheral regions and in the region between Jerusalem and the Mediterranean Sea. Between 1952 and 1955, and to a lesser extent until the middle of the 1960s, many new towns were established. Systematic policies fostered the growth of small and medium-sized towns, mainly in peripheral regions.

Whereas the proportion of Jewish population residing in the Southern district stood at 0.9% in 1948, it grew to 12.9% by 1986. No large changes occurred in the geographical distribution of the non-Jewish population, found mainly in northern areas and in Jerusalem. On the whole, the proportion of population defined as urban increased between 1955 (70.1%) and 1986 (89.5%).

The comparison between the censuses of 1972 and 1983 shows that in this period, the main changes in geographical distribution of the population were a) a slow but significant decline in the importance of the Tel Aviv-Jaffa and Haifa metropolitan areas and surrounding regions; and b) a parallel increase in the population share of the Jerusalem area, as well as peripheral Southern regions.

These changes in the geographical distribution of the population are the result of various determinants. First, while in the period after the establishment of the State new immigrants were largely directed toward more peripheral zones, those immigrants who arrived after the first decade have largely preferred other localities, with Jerusalem heading the list. Second, the forces of internal immigration have played a part, as detailed below. Finally, there are regional differentials in natural increase. The birth rate is considerably higher in the peripheral Northern and Southern districts, where the population is comparatively younger.

Among the complex patterns of internal migration the following are of special importance:

a) *Periphery to core migration*: This spontaneous movement has been going on since the early 1950s, following the settling down of new immigrants in the periphery. Due to differential migration rates, the result has been a gradual regional segregation on the basis of origin: Jews of Asian-African origins constituted a larger share of peripheral zones, while those of European origin tended to concentrate in the central part of the country.

b) *Suburbanization processes*: This largely spontaneous movement toward new, low-density communities situated around major cities was partly checked by a strong agricultural land preservation policy.

c) *Migration from the core to the periphery*: This trend is encouraged by the government by means of various incentives. One form of incentive has been to build new towns for veteran inhabitants, another has been to build new neighborhoods of owner-occupied low-density dwellings in existing development towns.

10. The Arab population of the Administered Areas. The estimates given in Table 2 for the Arab population of those territories are based on the only population census carried out there (in 1967), updated on the basis of current registration of vital events and migratory movements. Despite some incompleteness of those registrations and methodological difficulties in their interpretation, the following conclusions seem to be warranted:

1) The population of the Administered Areas is undergoing a very rapid demographic transition, the first expressions of which is a rapid decrease in mortality rates per 1,000 population (according to rough estimates, from 22 in 1968 to 7.6 in 1983–86 in Judea and Samaria, and from 20 to 7.1 in Gaza). This decline has presumably been fostered by development of health services and educational network in these areas. It can be guessed that while expectation of life at birth was in 1967 still around 48, in the mid-1970s, it was around 55 and in the early 1980s 62. This level was, however, considerably below that of the non-Jewish population of Israel (see Section 6).

2) Fertility was and still is traditionally high in both areas, although it did not reach there the record levels attained by Israel Moslems (9.9 children per woman in 1964–65). At the census of 1967 the average number of children per non-single woman aged 45–49 was 8.6 in Samaria and Judea, 8.3 in the Gaza Strip. Estimates of birth rates per 1,000 population (in 1983–86—41.6 in Judea and Samaria; 46.8 in Gaza) also suggest a persisting high level of fertility; however, the rates for more recent years for Judea and Samaria may suggest that there are some first signs of transition of fertility to slightly lower levels.

3) In consequence of high birth rates and rapidly falling death rates, the average rate of natural increase has become very strong both in the Gaza area (yearly average for 1983–86: 39.7 per 1,000) and Judea and Samaria (33.9).

4) Emigration, directed largely to Arab countries, was a typical feature of both territories already long before the 1967 war. Immediately after the war, large emigration movements took place. Current estimates available as given by Table 2 indicate that net outmigration has considerably decreased in recent years (net migratory balance per 1,000 population in 1985–86:—6.6 in Judea and Samaria; -7.3 in Gaza.

5) Due to the combination of large and growing rates of natural increase and high levels of emigration, the yearly rates of population growth were moderate in Judea and Samaria during 1975-81 (12.7 per 1,000); however, with the decrease of emigration they reached in 1983–86 a level of 28 per 1,000. In the Gaza area—due mainly to lower emigration level—the yearly rates of population growth have been comparatively very high and reached in 1983–86 33 per 1,000.

6) The Arab population of Judea and Samaria grew from 583,100 at the end of 1968 to 838,000 at the end of 1986;

the population of the Gaza area in the same period grew from 356,800 to 545,000.

11. Population Projections, Evaluation of Future Trends. Future population developments cannot be predicted with certainty, but important information can be obtained from population projections. These are calculations based on the knowledge of size, age, and sex structure of the present population and on alternative hypotheses on future levels of fertility, mortality, and migrations. Here projections wil be quoted: a) for the population of the State of Israel; b) for the Arab population of the Administered Areas; c) for the world Jewish population. Among the many alternative projections available those quoted will be labeled "medium" which are based on hypotheses—which at the moment seem reasonable—of only mild future changes in the present demographic trends. Projections a) and b) have been prepared by the Central Bureau of Statistics of Israel, projection c) has been prepared by the Division for Jewish Demography and Statistics of the Institute of Contemporary Jewry of the Hebrew University of Jerusalem.

a) Projections for the population of Israel (thousands).

	End 1987	*1990*	*2000*	*2010*	*Average yearly increase per 1,000 (1987–2010)*
Jews	3,612	3,740	4,212	4,703	+11.5
Non-Jews	792	868	1,158	1,458	+22.8
Total	4,404	4,608	5,370	6,161	+14.7
Percentage of non-Jews in the population	18.0	18.8	21.6	23.7	

b) Projections for the Arab population of the Administered Areas (thousands)

	End 1985	*1992*	*2002*	*Average yearly increase per 1,000 1986–2002*
Judea and Samaria	838	959	1,211	+23.3
Gaza	545	655	866	+29.4
Total	1,383	1,614	2,077	+25.7

c) Projections for the World Jewish Population (millions)

	1985	*2000*	*2010*	*Average yearly change per 1,000 1985–2010*
Diaspora	9.5	8.2	7.3	−10.5
Israel	3.5	4.2	4.7	+11.8
Total	13.0	12.4	12.0	−3.2

If further developments will not be strongly different from the projections, it can be expected that: 1) the Jewish population of Israel will continue to increase but at a moderate rate; 2) the non-Jewish population of Israel will grow at a rate double than that of the Jews; 3) the Arab population of the Administered Areas will grow at an even more rapid pace than the non-Jews of Israel; 4) the proportion of non-Jews in Israel will grow accordingly from 18% in 1987 to about 23.7% in 2010. Including in the calculation the Administered Areas, the proportion of the non-Jews which was in 1986 37.7% will grow to about 41% by 2,000. The Diaspora population has not recovered from a demographic viewpoint after the Holocaust. Since about 1970, it has declined, due to low fertility, aging of population, losses due to mixed marriages and assimilation, etc. In the future, if there will be no changes in trends, it is expected that the Diaspora population will decrease strongly. The natural increase of the Jews of Israel will not be sufficient to compensate for such losses and the entire world Jewish population will decrease. Thr proportion of old people within this population will further increase.

These statements are not forecasts, but indications of events which may happen, should present trends continue unabated, and if unpredictable political or other events will not induce unforeseeable changes.

Aging and shrinking of the population are regarded today as unfavorable trends in many developed countries, due to their implications for the structure of the labor force, social security services, and general security.

For the Diaspora, the possibility of a continuation of present trends appears to be even more worrying. It implies (a) a prospect of a decline of some 30% between 1970 and 2010 to a population which already lost about one-third of its size in the Holocaust, and (b) a proportion of old people much higher than in any other population.

With regard to Israel, there appears to be a rather general consensus in world Jewry on the desirability of further strengthening its Jewish population for political, social, economic, security, and other reasons. Current and projected rates of growth do not appear to be in line with this aim.

12. Population policies.

a) *Policies in Israel having a bearing on demographic problems, until 1986.*

In Israel, population policy has been (and still is) very largely focused on fostering immigration. In 1968 the Government (under Prime Minister Levi Eshkol) endorsed the recommendations of a Committee for the problems of natality (which had been appointed by the former Prime Minister David Ben-Gurion). This committee indicated the dangers implied in the decrease of Jewish natality in Israel and in the Diaspora, the social and economic problems of many of the families with large numbers of children, and problems due to lack of any public control on induced abortions. The Government established a small unit, the Demographic Center (formerly in the Prime Minister's Office, and later in the Ministry for Labor and Welfare), which has been active since then in various fields such as: giving advice to Government offices in fields related to the conditions of mothers and children, increasing further awareness for demographic problems, sex and family education, research in demographic fields, etc. On the subject of abortions, awareness of the contrast between the very severe legislation inherited by the British Mandate and actual lack of any control generated the regulations adopted by the Knesset in the late 1970s. According to them, interruption of pregnancy is legal, only if carried out in public hospitals for special reasons (see above Section 5).

In the 1970s much public attention was given to the social problems of children growing in unfavorable conditions and there was a continuous expansion of welfare policies, such as: grants to every mother giving birth in hospital (a measure that was designed and has actually worked to foster hospitalization of practically all births); maternity allowances to working mothers during maternity leave of up to 12 weeks; child allowance for every child under 18 years of age; activities directed to improve the educational and social conditions of underprivileged children (born mainly to large-sized families); expansion of the network of day nurseries; help to the newly-wed in solving housing problems; improving housing conditions of underprivileged large-sized families, etc.

This expansion of policies for the welfare of mothers (and especially working mothers), children, and families was dictated largely by general political, social, and economic reasons, and not by demographic considerations. However, it is possible that some of these measures and the general climate that they have created may have had some positive influence in strengthening familistic attitudes and keeping the fertility rate of the Jewish population of Israel at a level much higher than that of Diaspora Jewry and most advanced countries.

During the 1980s, the rapid deterioration of the country's financial situation, the enormous inflation, and the resulting severe budgetary restraints have determined a reversal of many of these policies. Welfare measures have been reduced or even revoked for lack of funds; allowances for first children have been cancelled, allowances for second and third children have been reduced, by eliminating their tax-free status, etc.

Research undertaken recently has put in new light the problems resulting from the demographic trends both in Israel and in the Diaspora, as discussed in Section 11.

b) *Developments since 1986.*

On 11 May 1986 the Government of Israel devoted a special session to the demographic problems of the Jewish people. The Government accepted the principle that demographic trends prevailing both in Israel and the Diaspora are to be given much more attention than in the past, taking into consideration the influence that these trends may have in the long run in political, security, economic, social, and ecological matters. The Government made clear that it does not have a magic formula which can quickly and easily change demographic habits deeply rooted in society, but is opposed to indifference in the field of demography and considers that attempts should be made along many coordinated paths in order to mitigate adverse trends.

In its decision, the Government indicated that, as in many other countries, Israel must plan and then implement comprehensive, long-term coordinated policies. Taking into consideration the strong ties binding Israel and the Diaspora, it is desirable to cooperate with institutions representing world Jewry or Diaspora Jewries in specific fields regarding Jewish population.

According to this decision of principle, demographic policies should be designed, among other goals, to attempt to insure the rate of population increase considered to be desirable in each period, and also to try to insure qualitative characteristics which are considered desirable. Demographic policies should be based on an understanding of the determinants of the trends and on an evaluation of the possible alternative methods which may influence them and limitations of those methods.

Demographic policies should be based on orientation and coordination of means which may have influence on population increase, such as: fostering the establishment of new families and their desire for children; strengthening families and elimination of obstacles in their paths; avoiding unnecessary abortions by means of proper advice; helping families having difficulties in child raising; fostering immigration and immigrant absorption; taking steps to restrain emigration and to encourage the return of emigrants to Israel.

Demographic policy should insure coordination of the activities of government ministries and other institutions in fields such as health, education, labor, and welfare, housing, economic development, etc., which may have influence on population trends.

Following the general decision on goals and methods for demographic policies taken in May, 1986, the Government established a working group formed by representatives of the relevant ministries and the Jewish Agency, coordinated by the Demographic Center, to prepare a program for such policies.

In October 1987 a Conference on the Demography of the Jewish People was convened in Jerusalem at the initiative of the Government of Israel, the World Jewish Congress, the World Zionist Organization, the Jewish Agency, and the Institute of Contemporary Jewry of the Hebrew University. The Conference consisted of two parallel and integrated symposia. A symposium of researchers in the demography and sociology of the Jewish people drew a provisional general picture of the demography of the Jewish people in the world. In order to open the way for insuring proper information, it suggested the initiation of a coordinated series of national sample surveys in the main Diaspora countries to be integrated in a survey of World Jewish population around 1990.

A second symposium of leaders of Jewish communities and institutions all over the world, discussed ways to arouse and deepen awareness of the importance of socio-demographic trends for the future existence of the Jewish people, and to identify objectives, directions, and means for demographic policies.

The 31st Zionist Congress (1987) discussed the demographic problems of the Jewish people and endorsed the proposals of the Demographic Conference.

R. BACHI

PORTUGAL, RELATIONS WITH ISRAEL. At the time of Israel's establishment Portugal was ruled by the pro-Fascist dictatorial regime of Antonio de Oliveira Salazar. Portugal was one of the few European countries which refrained from extending recognition to the newly-born Jewish State. Only in 1958 was an Israeli Consulate-General opened in Lisbon. Portugal was admitted to the UN in 1955. At the UN General Assembly, Portugal maintained a cautious attitude vis-à-vis the Arab-Israeli conflict, usually abstaining on critical issues. Israel, on the other hand, supported the resolutions against Portuguese colonialism in Africa, adopted in the Assembly from 1961 onwards.

In 1973, during the Yom Kippur War, Portugal—then under the government of Marcelo Caetano who succeeded Salazar in 1968—enabled the airlift of military supplies to Israel by allowing the American planes engaged in the operation to refuel in the Azores Islands.

In 1974 the Caetano regime was overthrown by a left-wing military revolution. The new government quickly granted independence to the Portuguese colonies in Africa. In the UN Portugal followed the lead of the Non-Aligned Countries and consequently moved to an outright pro-Arab line. In 1975 Portugal was the only western European country to vote in favor of General Assembly Resolution 3379, which equated Zionism with racism (*see* UN AND ISRAEL).

Portugal's international line and its attitude towards Israel changed again following the defeat of the extreme-left coup in 1975, and the ensuing 1976 elections, which brought to power the Socialist Party under the premiership of Mario Soares. The Israeli Labor Party had maintained friendly ties with the Portuguese Socialist Party when it still operated underground in the pre-1974 period. Contacts between Portugal and Israel were soon established both at party and at official level. In April 1977 the Prime Minister of Portugal, Soares, and the Foreign Minister of Israel, Yigal Allon, met in Amsterdam on the occasion of a conference of the Socialist International and decided upon the establishment of diplomatic relations between the two countries. The Israeli Consulate-General in Lisbon was immediately raised to the rank of Embassy. Portugal announced that it would establish in due course an embassy in Israel. In May, 1977, an Agreement of Agricultural Cooperation between Israel and Portugal was signed in Lisbon. A regular El-Al service to Lisbon was inaugurated in September, 1977.

The element of party solidarity in the relations between the Portuguese and Israeli governments disappeared after the Likud government came to power in Israel in 1977. However the main factor which hampered the further development of Israeli-Portuguese relations was Portugal's sensitivity to adverse reactions by the Arab States. Accordingly, the embassy in Israel was not opened. In 1979 Portugal again shifted briefly to leftist and pro-Arab positions under the government of Maria de Lurdes Pintasilgo. In that year a pro-PLO international conference was held in Lisbon, with the participation of Yasser Arafat. Arafat was received by the Portuguese President Antonio Ramalho Eanes with the honors reserved for a head of state. Subsequent Portuguese governments reverted to a more neutral policy. In 1985 Portugal was admitted to the European Economic Community and since then it has adjusted its stand on Middle Eastern questions to the relatively balanced common policy of the European Community. In 1991 it announced it was opening an embassy in Israel.

J. BARROMI

PRACTICAL ZIONISM. Trend within the World Zionist Organization (WZO) prior to the issuance of the Balfour Declaration (1917). It grew out of the dissatisfaction of some Zionist leaders with "political" Zionism, represented by the disciples of Herzl, which considered the central aim of Zionism to be the establishment of an autonomous Jewish settlement with international legal and political guarantees or under a "Charter" to be obtained from the Turkish government (which then held Eretz Israel). The "political" Zionists asserted that large-scale Jewish settlement endeavors in the country would be realistic and successful only if they were preceded by legal and political guarantees. The "practical" Zionists argued that it would be unrealistic to demand political rights without having any practical settlement work on which to base their request. Practical activity to promote the extension of Jewish interests in Eretz Israel, the practical Zionists pointed out, would also strengthen the political potential of the Zionist movement. The practical Zionists drew support from the Hovevei Zion movement and the opponents of the East Africa scheme. Among their leaders were Otto Warburg, Jacob Kohan-Bernstein, Julius Simon, and Menahem Ussishkin.

The differences between the two trends, which emerged as early as the First Zionist Congress (1897), took up a major part of the agenda of the Seventh Congress (1905), at which the East Africa scheme was rejected. The Eighth Congress (1907) resolved that the WZO begin practical work in Eretz Israel. It was at the Eighth Congress, too, that Chaim Weizmann declared the need for a synthesis between political and practical Zionism (*see* SYNTHETIC ZIONISM). The practical Zionists won the day within the movement at the 10th Congress (1911), when Otto Warburg became head of the WZO and an Inner Actions Committee composed entirely of practical Zionists was elected. G. HIRSCHLER

PRATO, DAVID. Rabbi and Zionist leader in Italy (b. Leghorn, Italy, 1882; d. Rome, 1951). He served for many years as director of the Collegio Rabbinico Italiano of Florence and in 1927 was chosen chief rabbi of Alexandria, Egypt. Becoming chief rabbi of Rome in 1937, he served there until 1939, when, as a result of mounting anti-Semitic persecution, he left Italy for Palestine. Settling in Tel Aviv, he became director of the city's rabbinate office and was prominent in local religious affairs. In 1945 he returned to Rome, serving as spiritual leader of the community there until his death.

An ardent Zionist, Prato was an aide to Chaim Weizmann during the San Remo Conference (1920). In 1922 he was secretary of the Jewish National Fund and the Keren ha-Yesod in Italy. He was also a delegate to Zionist Congresses, representing Italian, and later Egyptian, Zionists. During his service in the rabbinates of Alexandria and Rome he fought assimilation and championed the ideals of the Jewish national renaissance in his communities. After World War II, while chief rabbi of Rome, he greatly aided Jewish "illegal" immigration to Palestine through Italy.

G. ROMANO

PRESIDENCY OF ISRAEL. Israel is a parliamentary democracy, and its executive branch, the government, is responsible to the legislative branch, the Knesset. This being the constitutional setup, the position of the President of the State is largely analogous to that of the sovereign in Great Britain, where the head of state, devoid of executive powers, symbolizes the unity of the nation. The laws regulating the position of the President of the State of Israel were incorporated in the Basic Law: the President of the State, passed by the Knesset on 16 June 1964. This law provides that the State is headed by a President, the seat of the Presidency is Jerusalem, and any Israeli citizen who is a resident of Israel is qualified to be a candidate for election as President.

The President is elected by the Knesset in secret ballot, by a simple majority of the entire membership, at a meeting convened solely for that purpose. If no candidate obtains the required majority, the balloting continues until one candidate does obtain a majority. Any 10 members of the Knesset are entitled to nominate a candidate for the office, by submitting a proposal in writing to the Speaker together with the consent in writing of the candidate.

The law provides that the election of the President must take place not earlier than 90 days and not later than 30 days before the expiration of the term of office of the officiating President. If the office of President becomes vacant before the expiration of the term of office, the election must be held within 45 days from the date when the vacancy occurs. If the date of the election does not fall during a session of the Knesset, the Speaker must convene the Knesset in order to hold the election of the President.

The President's term of office is five years; he can be elected for another term but (since 1969) not for a third term. If the office of President becomes vacant prior to the expiration of his term and another election is held by the Knesset, the Speaker of the Knesset functions as Acting President of the State in the interim period.

The most important function of the President is to charge a member of the Knesset with the task of forming a new government. This is done after consulting representatives of political parties. He also accredits the diplomatic representatives of the State, receives the accreditation of diplomatic representatives of foreign states, signs treaties with foreign states that have been approved by the Knesset, signs all laws except laws concerning his own powers, receives from the government a report of its meetings, and performs any other functions assigned to him by law. The

Chaim Weizmann taking the oath of office as Israel's first President. [Israel Government Press Office]

Student from Gabon being greeted by Pres. and Mrs. Itzhak Ben Zvi. [Histadrut Foto-News]

Ezer Weizman being sworn in as seventh President. To his left are Shevah Weiss (Knesset speaker) and outgoing President Haim Herzog.

President has the power to pardon criminal offenders and to lighten penalties by reduction or commutation of sentence.

The other functions of the President as prescribed by law are as follows. Under the State Comptroller Law of 5709 (1949), the President appoints the State Comptroller on the recommendation of the House Committee of the Knesset. Under the Magen David Adom Law of 5710 (1950), he

Pres. Zalman Shazar (seated, in center) listening to an address by Sheikh Amin Tarif at a Druze festival in Kefar Hittim. [Israel Information Services]

appoints the president of the Magen David Adom (Red Shield of David) society established by that law. Under the Bank of Israel Law of 5714 (1954), he appoints the Governor of the Bank of Israel on the recommendation of the government. Under the Basic Law: Judicature (1984), the Dayanim Law of 5715 (1955), the Kadis Law of 5721 (1961), and the Druze Religious Courts Law of 5723 (1962), he appoints the members of the civil judiciary and the judges of the religious courts, respectively, on the recommendation of competent Nominations Committees. Under the Military Justice Law of 5715 (1955), on the recommendation of the chief of the General Staff submitted by the Minister of Defense, he appoints an officer as President of the Military Court of Appeal. Under the Defense Levy Law of 5716 (1957), on the recommendation of the government, he appoints a Defense Levy Council. Under the Council for Higher Education Law of 5718 (1958), on the recommendation of the government, he appoints the members of the Council for Higher Education.

If the President has charged a Member of the Knesset with the task of forming a new government but that member does not succeed in forming a Cabinet, the President chooses another Knesset Member for the purpose.

With regard to the immunities of the President, the Basic Law provides that he shall not be tried by any court or tribunal for any matter connected with his functions or powers and that he enjoys immunity from any legal act for any such matter. He is not obliged to state in evidence anything that has become known to him in the performance of his function as President of the State. These immunities are also available to him after he has ceased to be President of the State. The President may not be brought before a criminal court.

A President cannot be impeached except by a vote of three-fourths of the entire Knesset membership acting on a recommendation submitted to it by the Knesset Rules Committee, which considers the complaint and adopts the recommendation by a three-fourths vote of its membership. Provision was made for the President to defend himself against any complaint or accusation, both before the Knesset Rules Committee and before the plenary session of the Knesset. Provision was also made for the President's temporary or permanent suspension from office in the event of his inability to perform his duties on grounds of health. During a period when the President has temporarily ceased to perform his functions, or when he is abroad, the Speaker of the Knesset officiates in his stead.

S.Z. ABRAMOV

	dates of birth (death)	*dates of office*
Chaim Weizmann	1874–1952	1949–1952
Yitzhak Ben-Zvi	1884–1963	1952–1963
Zalman Shazar	1889–1974	1963–1973
Ephraim Katzir	1916–	1973–1978
Yitzhak Navon	1921–	1978–1983
Chaim Herzog	1918–	1983–1993
Ezer Weizman	1924–	1993–

PRESIDENTS' CONFERENCE. *See* CONFERENCE OF PRESIDENTS OF MAJOR AMERICAN JEWISH ORGANIZATIONS.

PRESS, YESHAYAHU. Teacher and historian (b. Jerusalem, 1874; d. there, 1955). Press studied at the Lämel School in Jerusalem and at a Jewish teachers seminary in Hanover, Germany. After his return to Eretz Israel he taught at educational institutions operated by the Hilfsverein der Deutschen Juden. In 1908 he became principal of the Lämel School.

Press was a founder of the Hebrew Teachers' Association of Eretz Israel and of the Jewish Society for the Exploration of the Land of Israel and its Antiquities, and he served as president of B'nai B'rith in the country. He helped found the first Hebrew kindergartens and the Zikhron Moshe quarter in Jerusalem.

A well-known Palestinographer, Press contributed articles on topographical research to a variety of publications and wrote several books on Palestine. His most important work is *Eretz Yisrael: Entziklopedia Topografit-Historit* (A Topographical-Historical Encyclopedia of Palestine, 4 vols., 1946–55).

PROFESSIONAL AND TECHNICAL WORKERS' ALIYA (PATWA). Non-political, voluntary organization founded in London in 1944 and dedicated to promoting the immigration to Palestine-Israel of young Zionists (mostly serving then in H.M. Forces), whose professional and technical training and experience equipped them for service in the Jewish National Home or in the projected Jewish State.

PATWA members were organized in 10 professional groupings (medical, medical auxiliaries, nurses, engineers, legal, economic and administrative staff, scientists, teachers social workers, office personnel, and general). They were encouraged to study Hebrew, keep abreast of Eretz Israel affairs and start savings to finance their contemplated aliya after the war. Seven of the nine original founders immigrated, including the first two national chairmen, Prof. Eli Davis (later director-general of Hadassah Medical Organization) and Walter (Ettinghausen) Eytan (later director-general of Israel's Foreign Ministry). After the war, Palestinian employers visiting the United Kingdom began interviewing PATWA candidates for job vacancies. To develop this "market research," PATWA arranged a two-way representation, sending Tamar Woolf, a London economist, to open a liaison office in Jerusalem and bringing Alfred Ranan (later director of Israel's Postal Services) as the first PATWA emissary to the UK. In 1948, PATWA Jerusalem became part ot the Jewish Agency's Youth and He-Halutz Department. Branch offices were opened and membership bodies were promoted in the US, Africa, Canada, France, Australia, and other countries.

PATWA organized summer programs in Israel for visiting students and young graduates, as well as pilot tours for professionals investigating their own immigration prospects. In the first years of the State, hundreds of PATWA families from the UK arrived in Israel. Many found employment in the civil service, commerce, and industry as well as the universities. In turn, they helped to absorb hundreds of British Mahal volunteers in the country and to found the British Settlers' Association in 1950. By 1969 British PATWA, it is estimated, had assisted thousands of professionals to settle in Israel. PATWA's emphasis on careful vocational guidance later served as a pattern for activities developed by the Jewish Agency's Aliya Department.

L. HARRIS

PROGRESSIVE PARTY. Political party established in October, 1948, through the unification of three groups: *Ha-Oved ha-Tziyoni, consisting of graduates of the General Zionist youth movements of Europe who subscribed to Zionist national principles and rejected Socialism; the *Aliya Hadasha, the organization of immigrants from central Europe and of those close to them in their non-partisan approach to current problems; and the Union of General Zionists (group A), which supported the policies of Chaim Weizmann. These groups united chiefly on the basis of their common approach to social problems. They announced that the realization of Zionist aims and the strengthening of the State of Israel required class cooperation and national discipline with regard to private interests, a guarantee of the place of private enterprise in Israel's economy, public economic activities, the strengthening of individual rights and freedoms, and depolitization of the civil service.

The new party was called upon to participate in the government coalition and did so for 11 years through Pinhas *Rosen, who served as Minister of Justice. It supported the removal of education from the control of the political parties and the establishment of state-controlled education (1953), the removal of employment service from partisan control and the establishment of government employment bureaus (1959), and the enactment of a law to restrict political activities of civil servants (1959). The Progressives also demanded, but did not secure, government-operated health services.

The Progressive party opposed all forms of coercion of religion or conscience. While affirming Jewish religious and traditional values, the party opposed the broadening of the judicial authority of the Rabbinate.

The party supported economic planning but demanded that the needs of all economic sectors, including private enterprise, be considered in planning. It demanded the abolition of unnecessary governmental controls in favor of economic liberalization. On this basis the Progressives refused to join the government at the end of 1951 and remained in the opposition for about a year and a half.

The party supported the academicians in their struggle to better their position and favored a salary policy that would guarantee suitable compensation for executive or professional personnel. It opposed the egalitarian salary policies of the leftist parties. It was over these issues that Rosen resigned from the government in 1956 and did not return until Progressive demands had been essentially fulfilled.

The Progressives generally supported the foreign and security policies of those governments in which they participated. In regard to the Arab minority, they demanded the cancellation of most of the military government restrictions. Rosen, as chairman of the Ministerial Committee, obtained such a recommendation in the Committee.

The Progressives kept an average of five members in the Knesset, but they lacked mass appeal. Accordingly, a proposal was made to establish a parliamentary bloc with the General Zionists. This proposal was rejected at the party's 1954 convention.

In the Executive of the Jewish Agency the party held the portfolio of Youth Aliya, which was headed by Moshe Kol, the chairman of the party's Executive. In the Histadrut, Ha-Oved ha-Tziyoni had about 5 per cent of the votes and participated in the activities of the labor unions. Here, too, the Progressives demanded national discipline, arbitration in labor disputes, and the transfer to the government of governmental functions which the Histadrut had fulfilled before the establishment of the State. Ha-Oved ha-Tziyoni demanded the limitation of the Histadrut's economic activities to the development regions and fields which private enterprise did not enter. Ha-Oved ha-Tziyoni established a network of kibbutzim and moshavim as well as a number of agricultural schools. For some time the party issued a daily paper, *Zemanim* (Times).

The Progressives were a branch of the Liberal International. In April, 1961, the Progressive party united with the General Zionist party to form the *Liberal party. This union succeeded in securing 17 seats in the Fifth Knesset, but it did not endure. In 1965 the former General Zionists decided to form a parliamentary bloc with the Herut party (*see* GAHAL). This move was opposed by the former Progressives, and the result was a split in the Liberal party.

See also INDEPENDENT LIBERAL PARTY

G. HAUSNER

PROJECT RENEWAL. Joint program of the Jewish Agency (JA) and the government of Israel for the redevelopment of distressed neighborhoods. 87 neighborhoods and towns throughout Israel with a combined population of about 600,000 residents have participated in the project which was initiated in 1977 by the government of Israel. In each neighborhood service levels are raised through comprehensive neighborhood programming which integrates physical renovation, enlargement and construction of housing and public facilities, and social programming.

In late 1977, the Prime Minister of Israel, Menahem Begin, invited Jewish leadership from abroad to participate as partners in the program and the Jewish Agency, the implementing agency for Diaspora communities, became a partner in the discussions with government agencies. Diaspora Jewish leadership concluded that the most promising basis for support by world Jewry would be a direct community-neighborhood relationship. Thus the idea of twinning specific Jewish communities with particular Israeli neighborhoods was born.

A resolution of the 7th annual Assembly of the Jewish Agency in 1978 ratified the decision taken by world Jewish leadership to join the government of Israel as partners in Renewal. In addition to assigning the name "Project Renewal" to the program, the Assembly established that the project was to be a joint effort of the government of Israel, local municipalities, residents, the Jewish Agency, and communities from abroad. Renewal activities were to be undertaken according to a comprehensive plan dealing with both the physical and social needs of the locality, with local residents taking an active part in the planning, Funding for each neighborhood was to be done through the Jewish Agency by each community directly to each neighborhood. Commitments of communities from abroad were to be on the basis of a multi-year budget of limited time duration.

Initially, 11 neighborhoods were included in the project, but by 1979 there were 30. Twinnings were established between some of the neighborhoods, and the first tentative activity began. It was not until 1981, however, that the director general of the JA Project Renewal Department could report that there was full activity in 69 neighborhoods, twinned with over 200 Jewish communities all over the world. In 1982, 13 neighborhoods were added to make a total of 82, and in 1986, a decision was taken by the Board of Governors of the Jewish Agency and the government of Israel to include five-six new neighborhoods each year until the task of rehabilitating all of the distressed neighborhoods in Israel should be completed. By March 1987, there were 87 neighborhoods in the project. Total Project Renewal expenditures as of 31 March 1987, were $202.5 million, while the combined ministries of the government of Israel have expended more than $400 million.

The Renewal Process. The organizational structure of Project Renewal consists of a partnership between the government of Israel, local municipal governments, Diaspora communities, and neighborhood residents. It places emphasis on coordinated policy-making, planning, and implementation. Authority in the project is derived from the joint government/Jewish Agency Project Renewal Committee, cochaired by the deputy prime minister and by the chairman of the Executive of the Jewish Agency. Policy and coordination of activity on a national level is within the authority of the interministerial team. The team which approves all neighborhood programs consists of representatives of both the government ministries participating in the project and those of the Jewish Agency, and is chaired by the director general of the JA Project Renewal Department and the head of the Social Planning Team of the Ministry of Housing. Government ministries taking part in the program are: Construction and Housing, Labor and Welfare, Education and Culture, Health, Interior, and Finance.

A central element in the organizational structure is the Local Steering Committee established in each neighborhood. It consists of local residents who comprise 50% of the membership, professionals, representatives of the municipal authority, representatives of the government agencies at the regional and local levels, and of the Jewish Agency. The committee's tasks are: to weigh program and project recommendations, to set priorities in view of available funds and financial framework, to approve the annual proposed program and budget, and to approve the comprehensive plan.

The project is administered in each neighborhood by a Project Manager.

All projects and programs designated for Jewish Agency implementation are funded on the basis of a predetermined multi-year budget framework by twinned communities from abroad. In the United States, the UJA (United Jewish Appeal) acts as the liaison with the Renewal Department in Israel and through them to the neighborhoods. In the rest of the world, Keren ha-Yesod—UIA fulfills this function. The community, acting in cooperation with the UJA or Keren ha-Yesod, encourages mission groups and individuals to visit the neighborhoods creating an ongoing linkage between the residents of the neighborhood and members of the community. At least once a year, community representatives are invited to visit their twinned neighborhood to review its budget proposals, projects, and programs.

Impact of Project Renewal. In 1987, in over half of the first 69 neighborhoods, multi-year budgets are being phased down and essential programming transferred to regular government funding, local municipalities, voluntary organizations, and resident participation. More than 600,000 people throughout Israel have been directly or indirectly affected by Project Renewal and before the project is completed 20% of Israel's population will have been affected by it.

Over 35,000 housing units have been renovated and expanded. More than 200 community and neighborhood centers have been built, improved, or enlarged as part of the total of more than 500 public service facilities which the project has made available to neighborhood residents. These facilities have included Early Childhood Development Centers, Family Health and Dental Clinics, Day Centers for the elderly, playgrounds, etc. The physical infrastructures, roads, sewage and drainage systems, street lighting, etc., have been upgraded in all neighborhoods through government and municipal funding, greatly improving the general appearance of the neighborhood. With the improvement in the quality of life in the neighborhoods, the steady outmigration of stronger population groups has been all but halted. Apartment prices, which had been much lower than market prices, have risen steadily as demand has increased.

"Second Chance" programs designed to raise educational levels and improve or provide educational skills, currently include 16,000 neighborhood residents, with more than 5,000 adults learning basic Hebrew language skills in adult education classes each year. Technological and scientific vocational education projects, initiated by Project Renewal, have made it possible for residents of development areas to enroll in pre-technological preparatory courses and graduates of the first courses have already begun studies in practical engineering courses. Technological and scientific equipment has been installed in development town high schools to upgrade educational opportunities for local youth and adults. A number of other courses provide in-house technological training, management training, and educational upgrading for Renewal area residents.

Improving parenting skills and school preparation levels are the target of a number of programs including the Etgar pre-school development program involving 6,000 parents each year. In addition more than 15,000 pre-school and school children participate regularly in Project Renewal-sponsored enrichment and educational reinforcement programs. Courses for local lay leaders have been offered in almost all neighborhoods, and in 1987 200 residents completed a leadership program leading to a BA through the "Everyman's (Open) University".

The twinning relationship has had an impact on Israel-Diaspora relations. More than 20,000 Jews from all over the world have visited their Renewal neighborhoods since the inception of the project. Young people from all over the world have performed voluntary service in their twinned neighborhoods and many neighborhood youth have given service abroad in their twinned communities. Budget consultations with twinned communities were held in 45 neighborhoods in Israel in preparation for the 1987/88 fiscal year.

The Project Renewal twinning relationship has provided an opportunity for Israeli citizens to meet with Diaspora Jews in Israel, in their homes, at community gatherings, and in committee meetings. At least 4,000 Israeli families have hosted visitors from their twinned communities in their homes in Israel. Research and evaluation has accompanied the work of Project Renewal from the earliest days and the Project's success has been confirmed by international experts in urban renewal.

AFFILIATIONS WITH CITIES IN ISRAEL—AUGUST 1987

AFULA	FRESNO, California, USA
	SELERICO DE BEIRA, Portugal
	ALLAUCH, France
	ENGELHEIM, West Germany
	STAMFORD, Connecticut. USA
ACRE	LA ROCHELLE, France
	RECKLINGHAUSEN, West Germany
	PISA, Italy
	CORPUS CHRISTI, Texas, USA
ARAD	WILMINGTON, Delaware, USA
	DINSLAKEN, West Germany
ASHDOD	MOBILE, Alabama, USA
BERLIN	SPANDAU, West Germany
	BORDEAUX, France
	OPORTO, Portugal
ASHKELON	COTE ST. LUC, Quebec, Canada
	PORT ELIZABETH, South Africa
	SEINE-SUR-MER, France
	CARDIFF, Wales
	PORTLAND, Oregon, USA
AZUR	KARMOY, Norway
	BOUJON, Belgium
BAKA EL-GARBIEH	SENNORI, Italy
BAT-YAM	LEGHORN, Italy
	BERLIN NEU KOELN, West Germany
	VILLE URBAINE, France
	VALPARAISO, Chile
BE'ER YA'AKOV	BAD OLDESLOE, West Germany
	COTIGNOLA, Italy
BEERSHEBA	SEATTLE, Washington, USA
	MIAMI, Florida, USA
	WINNIPEG, Manitoba, Canada
	WUPPERTAL, West Germany
	LYONS, France
	SAN SEBASTIAN, Spain
	PARAMATRA, Australia
BINYAMINA	ATTENDORN, West Germany
BENEI BERAK	BROOKLYN, New York, USA
BET SHE'AN	TARASCON, France
BET SHEMESH	LANCASTER, California, USA
	HOLSTEBRO, Denmark
DIMONA	ST. AMANDE LES EAUX, France
	ANDERNACH AM RHEIN, West Germany
	OGDEN CITY, Utah, USA
	SEPT ILES, Canada
EILAT	LOS ANGELES, California, USA
	DURBAN, South Africa
	KAMEN, West Germany
	ANTIBES, France
	GORIZIA, Italy
EVEN YEHUDA	SPARTA, Greece

GAN YAVNE	PUTEAUX, France
GIVATAYIM	ESSLINGEN, West Germany
	CHATTANOOGA, Tennessee, USA
	BENEVENTO, Italy
GIVAT SHEMUEL	STADE, West Germany
HADERA	BESANCON, France
	TOMAR, Portugal
	GATINEAU, Quebec, Canada
	MINNEAPOLIS, Minnesota, USA
	ST. PAUL, Minnesota, USA
	STAVENGER, Norway
	HAREN, Holland
	RAVENNA, Italy
HAIFA	HACKNEY, LONDON, Great Britain
	PORTSMOUTH, Great Britain
	CAPE TOWN, South Africa
	DUSSELDORF, West Germany
	MAINZ, West Germany
	BREMEN, West Germany
	MARSEILLES, France
	ANTWERP, Belgium
	ROTTERDAM, Holland
	SAN FRANCISCO, California, USA
	LIMASSOL, Cyprus
	SYDNEY, Australia
	AALBORG, Denmark
HERZLIYA	MARLE, West Germany
	TOULON, France
	SAN BERNARDINO, California, USA
HOLON	SURESNES, France
	BERLIN WEDDING, West Germany
	JACKSONVILLE, Florida, USA
	CLEVELAND, Ohio, USA
	LACHINE, Quebec, Canada
	MUNDEN SAARLAND, West Germany
HATZOR HA-GELILIT	BRIEY, France
JATT	BERNALDA, Italy
KADIMA	LA FRANCAISE, France
KARMIEL	DENVER, Colorado, USA
	BERLIN WILMERSDORF, West Germany
	METZ, France
KEFAR SABA	DELFT, Holland
	WIESBADEN, West Germany
	BINGHAMTON, New York, USA
KEFAR TABOR	WINFIELD, Kansas, USA
	BJERKREIM, Norway
	EPPELBORN, West Germany
	ATRI, Italy
KIRYAT ATA	BERLIN REINICKENDORF, West Germany
KIRYAT BIALIK	BERLIN STEGLITZ, West Germany
KIRYAT EKRON	AKRON, Ohio, USA
KIRYAT GAT	BUFFALO, New York, USA
	MONCRIBO, Portugal
	CHERASCO, Italy
KIRYAT MALAKHI	RUEIL-MALMAISON, France
KIRYAT MOTZKIN	BAD KREUZNACH, West Germany
	TACOMA, Washington, USA
	BAD SEGEBERG, West Germany
KIRYAT ONO	DRACHTEN, Holland
KIRYAT SHEMONA	HAMPSTEAD, Canada
	COLUMBUS, Ohio, USA
	NANCY, France
KIRYAT TIVON	TAMARAC, Florida, USA
	BRAUNSCHWEIG, West Germany
	PUTTEN, Holland
KIRYAT YAM	BERLIN KREUZBERG, West Germany
	CRETEUIL, France
LOD (LYDDA)	ULZEN, West Germany
	STAFFELSTEIN, West Germany
	TIVOLI, Italy
MA'ALOT TARSHIHA	HAMM, West Germany
	HARRISBURG, Pennsylvania, USA
MAZKERET BATYA	MEUDON, France
METULLA	ROUGEMONT, Quebec, Canada
	POCKING, West Germany
	NEUDORFEL, Austria
	RONCIGLIONE, Italy
MITZPE RAMON	GREEN RIVER, Wyoming, USA
	WEST HOLLYWOOD, California, USA
MIGDAL HA-EMEK	ANAGNI, Italy
NAHARIYA	BERLIN TEMPELHOF, West Germany
	OFFENBACH, West Germany
	BIELEFELD, West Germany
	PADERBORN, West Germany
	SORRENTO, Italy
	DELRAY BEACH, Florida, USA
NAZARETH (NOTZERAT) ILIT	ST ETIENNE, France
	LEVERKUSEN, West Germany
	ROODEPOORT, South Africa
	CANTU, Italy
	ASHEVILLE, N.C., USA
NETANYA	NICE, France
	LEEDS, Great Britain
	AARHUS COUNTY, Denmark
	GIESSEN, West Germany
	DORTMUND, West Germany
	GOLD COAST, Australia
MENAHEMIYA	SALBRIS, France
NES ZIONA	GRAND-QUEVILLY, France
	SOLINGEN, West Germany
	ALATRI, Italy
	LEVIN, Quebec, Canada
NESHER	FONTENAY-SOUS-BOIS, France
	DOREN, West Germany
OFAKIM	SOIGNIES, Belgium
	SUCY-EN-BRIE, France
	ST. HYACINTHE, Canada
OMER	PAGE, Arizona, USA
OR YEHUDA	BERLIN CHARLOTTENBURG, West Germany
PARDES HANA-KARKUR	GRASSE, France
PETAH TIKVA	ODENSE, Denmark
	NORRKOEPING, Sweden
	TRONDHEIM, Norway
	MEERBUSCH, West Germany
	LAVAL, Quebec, Canada
	KOBLENZ, West Germany
RA'ANANA	OPSTERLAND, Holland
	BRAMSCHE, West Germany
	MARGATE, Florida, USA
RAMAT GAN	CHERRY HILL, New Jersey, USA
	NEW HAVEN, Connecticut, USA
	MIAMI BEACH, Florida, USA

	BARNET, LONDON, Great Britain
	DIJON, France
	MANNHEIM, West Germany
RAMAT HA-SHARON	GEORGSMARIENHUETTE, West Germany
	TRIESTE, Italy
RAMAT YISHAI	LIESTAL, Switzerland
REHOVOT	GRENOBLE, France
	ROCHESTER, New York, USA
	MANCHESTER, Great Britain
	HEIDELBERG, West Germany
	VITERBO, Italy
RAMLE	GIRONA, Spain
	UPPER MARLBORO, Maryland, USA
	MORS, West Germany
RISHON LE-ZION	HEERENSVEEN, Holland
	MUNSTER, West Germany
	NIMES, France
	ARVADA, Colorado, USA
	BALTIMORE, Maryland, USA
	TERAMO, Italy
ROSH HA-AYIN	BIRMINGHAM, Alabama, USA
SAFED	OAK PARK, Michigan, USA
	TOLEDO, Spain
	GUARDA, Portugal
	LILLE, France
SEDEROT	BERLIN ZEHLENDORF, West Germany
	ANTONY, France
SHAVEI ZION	BAD SALZGITTER, West Germany
SHELOMI	ROESER, Luxembourg
	AUREC, France
TEL AVIV	PHILADELPHIA, Pennsylvania, USA
	COLOGNE, West Germany
	BONN, West Germany
	FRANKFURT, West Germany
	TOULOUSE, France
	BUENOS AIRES, Argentina
TIBERIAS	TUDELA, Spain
	ALLENTOWN, Pennsylvania, USA
	MONTPELLIER, France
	MONTECATINI, Italy
	WORMS, West Germany
TIRAT HA-CARMEL	CASTELET, France
YAVNE	SUNRISE, Florida, USA
	FREJUS, France
	PROVO, Utah, USA
	LUBBIO, Italy
YEHUD	ATLANTA, Georgia, USA
	PERIGNEUX, France
YEROHAM	DESERT HOT SPRINGS, California, USA
YOKNE'AM	WIEHL, West Germany
ZIKHRON YA'AKOV	CHARENTON-LE-PONT, France

PRO PALASTINA KOMITEE. Associations of public, mainly non-Jewish, figures in different countries who supported the Zionist aspirations for the creation of a national home in Palestine. Associations with this or similar names were created in the 1920s in France (1924) under the patronage of the President of the Republic, and in England (1926) with the participation of representatives of the House of Commons, and in Austria, Italy, Belgium, Romania, and Bulgaria (1927–1930). Nowhere was the influence of these associations felt in the Jewish and non-Jewish public of their countries as strongly as in Germany.

The first German committee was founded on 25 April 1918. It was the brainchild of Victor Jacobson and the culmination of efforts begun in August, 1917, when the Zionist Executive (at its meeting in Copenhagen) decided that a body comparable to the British Palestine Committee should be formed in Germany. The board included such worthies as Professor Carl Ballod, who was elected chairman, Professor Hans Delbrück, Konstantin Fehrenbach, President of the Reichstag, Georg Gotheim (Liberal), Johannes Junck (National Liberal), Gustav Noske (Social Democrat), Ludwig Raschdau, former Ambassador and member of the Reichstag, and Major Endres. The council covered the political spectrum: Count Kuno Westarp, leader of the Conservative party, Matthias Erzberger, leader of the Center party, Philipp Scheidemann, Ludwig Quessel, and Oskar Cohen-Reiss, leading members of the Social Democratic party; also included were distinguished academicians and writers like Professors Max Weber, Werner Sombart, Karl Meinhoff, Otto Auhagen, Gottfried Zoepfl, and Otto Hoetzsch, and Dr. Adolf Grabowsky and Dr. Ernst Jäckh. Such a broad coalition was an unusual phenomenon in German politics.

The aims of the Committee were formulated as follows:

> to support the aspirations of Zionism for the free development of a Jewish culture in the ancient home of the Jewish people....The regeneration of Palestine will be a great help to our ally Turkey, and thereby further German culture and influence in the Near East.

Moreover, as Ludwig Raschdau pointed out, Palestine offered "the soundest solution for millions of Jews living in miserable conditions in eastern Europe".

The committee reached the conclusion that, given adequate political, economic, and legal conditions, Palestine could absorb millions of Jews whose talent, emotional attachment, and command of financial resources would make the country flourish in a relatively short period. Turkey would derive enormous benefit and Germany would gain the sympathy of the Jewish people and expand her influence in the Orient.

This committee ceased its activity after the Allied victory, without officially disbanding, "in the hope of change in the political situation". On the initiative of Kurt Blumenfeld, secretary of the Zionist Organization in Germany, the Pro-Palästina Komitee was re-founded in 1926. The Presidium of this Committee was headed by Baron Bernstorff, former German Ambassador in Constantinople, and was composed of members of all the parties, from the German Nationalists to the Social Democrats, excepting the Communists and the Nazis. The Jewish members of the Committee consisted of representatives of the Zionist parties and non-Zionists such as Leo Baeck and Albert Einstein, and their numbers this time equaled those of the non-Jews. This composition was designed among other things to forestall the Liberal Jews' accusation that the Zionists' aspirations contradicted the loyalty of German Jews to their homeland and would endanger their citizen status. Similar considerations guided the Committee in the wording of its objectives:

"The Committee, convinced that the development of the Jewish National Home according to the Palestine Mandate —as an achievement of human progress and welfare—is entitled to German sympathies and the active participation of German Jewry, will endeavor to inform the German public about the Jewish settlement work in Palestine, will foster its relations with Germany and, generally, spread the knowledge that the Jewish work of upbuilding Palestine is an excellent instrument for the economic and cultural relations and the reconciliation of peoples".

During the years of the Committee's existence its prominent members participated in public meetings on behalf of the Zionist endeavor in Palestine and in Keren ha-Yesod appeals. When the Nazis seized power, the Committee was dissolved, but its non-Jewish members remained faithful to its program. J. WALK—I. FRIEDMAN

PROTESTRABBINER (Protest Rabbis). Expression coined by Herzl in an article in *Die Welt* (16 July 1897), in which he ridiculed a statement issued by the anti-Zionist Association of Rabbis in Germany in the wake of the convening of the First Zionist Congress. The rabbis had asserted that the aim of the "so-called Zionists" to establish a national state in Eretz Israel was incompatible with the Messianic ideal, while it also went against the concept that Judaism obligates all believers to be faithful to their native land. However the German Rabbinical Association claimed that philanthropic support for agricultural settlements was permissible because it was not connected with the establishment of a Jewish national State. It was mainly due to this letter that the First Zionist Congress was not held at Munich, as originally planned, but at Basle.

A survey was carried out 70 years after the publication of the protest letter which showed that almost all the children, grandchildren and great grand-children of the "protest rabbis" had settled in Israel.

PUBLIC HEALTH IN ISRAEL. *See* HEALTH AND HEALTH SERVICES IN ISRAEL.

PUBLISHING IN ISRAEL. A printing industry in Eretz Israel has existed since Eliezer and Abraham ben Isaac Ashkenazi opened the first print shop in Safed in 1577. Nevertheless, the main world centers for printing and publishing Jewish religious texts remained among the great concentrations of European Jewry, such as Vienna, Vilna, Leipzig, Warsaw, Berlin, and Amsterdam. In 1831, Israel Bak set up a printing house first in Safed, and then in Jerusalem. However, publishing as such began in Eretz Israel only in the early 20th century, with emphasis still on the production of books and tracts of a religious and devotional nature. After the establishment of the British Mandate, and following the immigration of Jews from Europe during the 1920s and 1930s, a new—general and secular—publishing industry began to take shape. At the same time, modern printing machinery, and especially the linotype system which replaced hand setting, began to be imported, and with the development of a variety of Hebrew typefaces, the foundations for a modern publishing and printing industry began to be laid. Some major Hebrew publishing houses that had been established in Europe were transferred, together with their owners, to Palestine. These included Moriah, which had been founded by the poet Chaim Nahman Bialik and others in Odessa in 1911. Moriah merged with Dvir (established in Berlin in 1922) in Tel Aviv in 1923. Sreberk came from Vilna in 1933; Rubin Mass from Berlin in 1927; and Schocken from Berlin in 1938.

Following the destruction of European Jewry during World War II, the world center of Hebrew publishing was firmly established in Israel, although some Hebrew publishing and printing continued elsewhere, especially in New York. After the War of Independence and the influx of hundreds and thousands of new immigrants, there was suddenly a need for a great deal of new educational and reading material; textbooks at all levels and especially for Hebrew teaching; translations of world literature; increasing quantities of technical and scientific material; and a growing demand for leisure reading of all sorts. Today, Israel has a large and thriving printing industry with almost 1,000 printers of various sizes, from one man, desktop publishing shops, to sophisticated enterprises offering a full range of electronic phototypesetting, high-speed one-to four-color presses, rotary presses, and the latest in fully automated paperback and casemaking machinery, all under one roof.

Israel's publishing industry is one of the world's largest on a per capita basis, with some 180 publishers publishing between five and 150 new books per year. In the year 1986–7, a total of nearly 13.5 million copies of 4,822 books were published. Of these, 2,003 (43.5%) were new books or new editions, and the remainder reprints. Of the new books, 56% were published by 18 "large publishers" (more than 51 books per annum), 36% by 81 "medium-sized publishers" 10–50 books per annum), and less than 8% by 84 "small publishers" (less than ten books per annum). The average print run in 1987 reached 2,900 copies per title, a substantial improvement over 1985 when the figure dropped to 1,900 as a result of the country's economic difficulties. In 1986–7, 12% of all books were printed in more than 5,000 copies each: an increase from only 7% in 1985.

Languages. 88% of the books published in 1986–7 in Israel were in Hebrew. There is a small output of books in English, Arabic, and other languages. A large proportion of foreign language books is destined for export, and some 20 million dollars of books and printing work are exported every year, the main clients being the USA, Britain, France, and Germany. With a high literacy rate and growing familiarity with foreign languages (especially English) and despite the inevitable decline in the relative size of the immigrant population vis-à-vis local-born, there remains a substantial local demand for imported books in languages other than Hebrew. This has, in turn, led to a more sophisticated approach to translations, so that the Hebrew edition of an important or best-selling book is now likely to be available virtually simultaneously with the original. Where this is not the case, a meaningful part of the potential market would be able to cope with the book in its original language. At the same time, the market has been steadily dwindling for books in once important languages such as Yiddish, Hungarian, Polish, Romanian, German, etc., where there is no new generation of readers. An upsurge in Russian language publishing resulted from the arrival of new immigrants from the Soviet Union in the 1970s, and with the advent of *perestroika*, this may well increase enormously.

Subjects. Local publishers cover every topic and sphere of interest, and there is intense competition among publishers, both for local authors and for the works of leading foreign writers. At the same time, in some fields, Israel is unique. In the first place, it has become, inevitably, the world's main source for books of a Jewish nature. This includes prayer books, the Bible and Talmud, exegesis and biblical scholarship, and also includes books of a more secular character, such as works of archeology, Jewish history, flora and fauna of Israel, travel and guide books, and Judaica and Jewish art.

At the same time, there is a substantial output of books having a clear but non-Jewish connection with the land. Many publishers specialize in books for the Christian world, a large number of them written by Christian scholars resident in Israel, and dealing with the Holy Sites, comparative religions, early Christianity, and the life of Jesus. Another field in which Israel leads relates to the Middle-East conflict and Arab-Jewish relations.

With seven major universities active in a wide variety of scientific pursuits, there is a growing output of academic books in the natural and exact sciences and the humanities. Some of these are co-published with leading university publishers abroad. Israel has a surprisingly large output of poetry. Several publishers specialize in the publication of poetry and the country's literary magazines and Friday supplements of the major daily newspapers print a great deal of new poetry: perhaps as many as 10,000 new poems appear in print in Israel every year. Unlike most other countries, these books enjoy an encouragingly large sale—3,000–5,000 copies of a volume of poetry is not unusual—a remarkably high quantity considering the size of the market.

Translations. As the Hebrew language has undergone a rapid and dynamic change in this century, many of the world's great classics, translated 40 or 50 years ago, sound very stilted to the average Israeli today. Consequently, many are already being retranslated and reissued. The quality of translation has greatly improved, not only from other languages into Hebrew, but also from Hebrew into other languages. Increasingly, publishers abroad are commissioning Israeli translators to do such work in Israel, providing the additional benefit for the translator of being able to work closely with the author. In 1986–7, some 68% of all new books were written in Hebrew, 19% in English, and 3% in Arabic.

One of the most interesting publishing phenomena in Israel was the creation in 1958 of the Israel Program for Scientific Translations. Originally established as part of the Prime Minister's Office, it was financed by the American National Science Foundation as a means of using up surplus American funds in Israel. Within a few years, IPST became one of the world's largest institutes of scientific translation, with tens of thousands of pages of Soviet literature in a wide variety of subjects being translated into English. Created because of American concerns over the perceived gap in knowledge as to scientific developments in the Soviet Union, within a decade the publication gap for a vast amount of Soviet literature had been virtually eliminated. IPST was then eventually phased out, becoming part of the Keter Publishing Company which was also publisher of one of the most important English-language Jewish publishing events of modern times, the 16-volume "Encyclopaedia Judaica," and its annual yearbooks.

The Institute for the Translation of Hebrew Literature is a publicly-funded institution providing technical and financial help to publishers throughout the world who wish to publish Hebrew work in translation, particularly in the less common languages. It also publishes a quarterly journal, *Modern Hebrew Literature*.

The Publishers. Broadly speaking, Israel's publishers can be divided into three main categories: institutionally-owned, newspaper-owned, and privately-owned. The first of these categories include some of the country's most distinguished houses, such as Am Oved (owned by the Histadrut—the General Federation of Labor); the two publishers owned by the kibbutz movements, Sifri'at Po'alim (Kibbutz Artzi) and Ha-Kibbutz ha-Me'uhad; the Bialik Institute, owned by the World Zionist Organization; the Magnes Press, owned by the Hebrew University of Jerusalem; and the publishing house of the Ministry of Defense, which specializes in military history and strategy.

The publishers owned by newspapers include Edanim (*Yedi'ot Aharonot*), Schocken (*Ha-Aretz*), and the Ma'ariv Book Guild (*Ma'ariv*). The English-language daily, *The Jerusalem Post*, publishes some books in English and distributes an increasingly large number of books for other publishers in Israel and abroad. The privately-owned publishers tend by nature to be the most volatile of the groups. Some of them are among the largest and most important publishers in the country, while others come and go. Among the leaders in this group are Keter, Yavne, Zmora-Bitan, and Massada. Smaller, but important, publishers include the long-established Achiasaf, Amichai, Eked (for poetry), Kiriat Sefer, Sinai, Sreberk, Tcherikover, and Yezre'el. Newer publishers who are making an impact include Modan, Kinneret, and Domino. A few companies specialize in productions for overseas co-publishers; notable among them are the Jerusalem Publishing House, Carta (which specializes in maps and mapmaking), Sadan, Ariel, and Makor (facsimile reprints of Judaica).

Costs. Up to the early 1970s, books in Israel were very inexpensive in comparison to other countries— a major consequence being that publishing profits were low and tended to discourage major investments. Combined with the usually low print runs in a country with such a small potential market, the whole publishing business was, financially, extremely marginal. However, in recent years the attitude has changed and books have become very much more expensive. Prices today are more economically viable for a thriving industry and, in the final analysis, healthier for both publisher and reader, as they allow investments to be plowed back into more projects as well as into non-profitable but important publishing ventures. Moreover, Israeli book prices are rarely higher than overseas, despite the low print runs. One beneficiary of this is, of course, the author. Royalties vary from an average of 10% to 15% for original Hebrew work, and from about 8% to 15% for translations. Nevertheless, very few Israeli writers are able to support themselves solely from their work (except for a handful of well-known literary figures such as Amos Oz, A.B. Yehoshua, Aharon Appelfeld, Yehuda Amichai, Ephraim Kishon, and David Grossman whose local sales are substantial or who have been widely translated into other languages).

While there is no long tradition of paperback publishing, there is an increasing use of this medium. Am Oved's *Sifriya le-Am* ("Popular Library") and *Ofakim* are two important paperback series. The idea of simultaneous hardback and paperback publication has not proved viable in Israel, partly because of the low print runs.

Trade Organizations. Eighty-five publishers are currently (1987) members of the Book Publishers' Association of Israel, established in 1939, which serves as the trade association of the industry and is affiliated to the International Publishers' Association. In addition to the normal representation and lobbying activities, the BPAI also serves as a central paper-buying authority for its members, who thus obtain a reduced price from the country's monopolist paper mill, the American-Israel Paper Mills in Hadera. The Association also maintains two jointly-owned publishing imprints, Ma'alot for school textbooks, and Yahdav for university textbooks. In addition, the Association runs a literary agency and organizes Hebrew Book Week (see below).

Approximately 100 publishers and printers belong to the Book and Printing Center of the Israel Export Institute. This institute works through a series of specialized centers in order to encourage exports of Israeli goods. The Book and Printing Center publishes a quarterly, *Books from Israel*, with news about Israeli books, and the biennial *Israel Book Trade Directory*. It arranges and administers Israel's participation on collective stands at international book fairs, especially the Frankfort and Moscow Book Fairs; organizes the Exhibitors' Club at the Jerusalem International Book Fair, and generally serves as a clearing house and information center for publishers and printers from abroad wishing to become acquainted with the market.

Literary Agencies. Until the mid-1970s, the concept of a literary agency was barely known in Israel. The agency Jaap Bar-David (no longer extant) did a certain amount of representation of foreign publishers (but not Israelis abroad), but overwhelmingly, rights were bought and sold by direct negotiation between publishers. This situation changed radically with the creation in 1976 of the Barbara Rogan Literary Agency, now called the Rogan-Pikarski Agency. Today, a large number of Hebrew rights are bought through this agency or through others that have been established in the meantime. These include the agency run as part of the Book Publishers' Association of Israel (which serves mainly but not exclusively the interests of its members), the Pecker Literary Agency, the Jonathan Silverman Agency, Norma Schneider Agency, and Domino. All these agencies serve in a two-way capacity, i.e., also attempting to sell the works of Israeli writers to publishers overseas.

Jerusalem International Book Fair, 1965. [Israel Govt. Press Office]

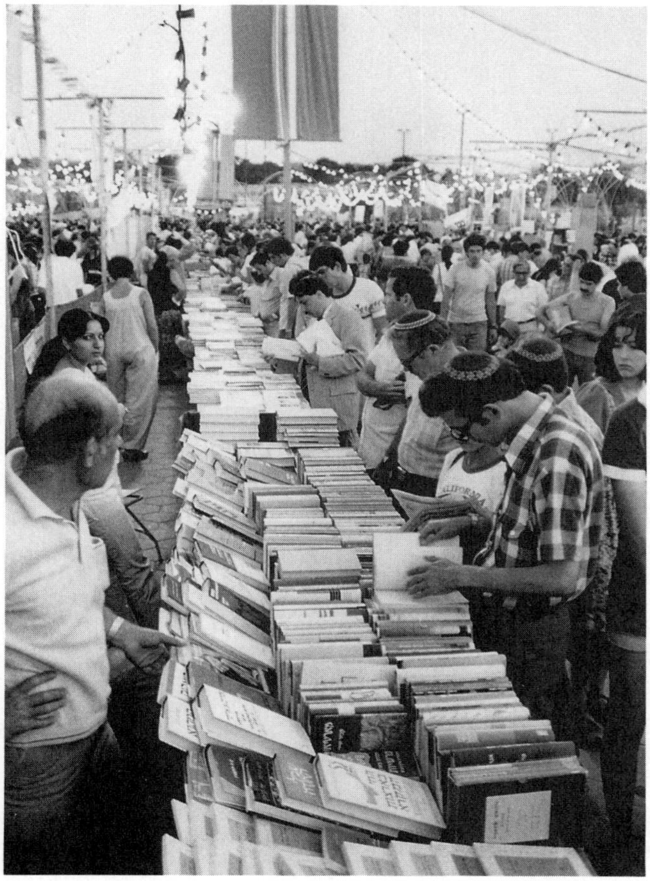

Annual Hebrew book fair, Jerusalem, 1980. [Israel Govt. Press Office]

Sales and Distribution. There are over 300 points-of-sale of books in Israel, although probably no more than 100 of them are "legitimate" book shops, and that number has been steadily declining over recent years. More and more, the trade has become concentrated in the hands of a few major chains. By far the largest of these is Steimatzky, with shops of its own and franchises in its name in all the main towns as well as the hotels and airports. Steimatzky's main strength is in foreign book sales, which may account for as much as 70% of retail foreign book sales in Israel, bearing in mind that they are also wholesalers to all the other shops. The stores of Shekem, the chain belonging to the Ministry of Defense and serving the armed forces and their families, have book departments, as does the Ha-Mashbir department store chain. Another chain belongs to Keter Publishing House; and Massada also franchises bookshops in its name.

While most of the larger publishers have their own distribution departments, most smaller ones prefer to use one of the distribution companies such as Steimatzky, Sifri, Chemed (with a branch in New York), Alim, Ofer, etc. In 1986–7, book sales in Israel were divided as follows:The annual Hebrew Book Week, organized by the Publishers' Association, is enormously successful. Held throughout the country in all the major towns, and through bookmobiles to villages and settlements, the event has taken on the nature of a popular festival with open-air booths, author appearances, autographing sessions, and everything at special discounted prices. Some Israeli publishers maintain that the "Week" accounts for as much as a third of their annual turnover.

Another major event is the biennial Jerusalem International Book Fair. First held in 1963, the JIBF has become perhaps the third most important international book event in the world (after the annual Frankfort Book Fair and the ABA, the annual meeting of the American Booksellers Association). Among the many events that take place congruent with the Fair is the awarding of the Jerusalem Prize for the "Freedom of the Individual in Society." Recipients have included Bertrand Russell, Simone de Beauvoir, Jorge Luis Borges, Eugene Ionesco, Graham Greene, and Milan Kundera.

Several attempts have been made in the past to establish Israeli book clubs, with no great success or impact, although some of them, such as the Hebrew Book Club and the *Mo'adon ha-Sefer ha-Tov* ("The Good Book Club"), continue to exist.

Foreign Sales. World interest in books emanating from Israel fluctuates enormously—to some extent in accordance with political events. In the euphoric days following the Six-Day War of 1967, the world was flooded with commemorative albums, war stories, books on all aspects of Jewish history, the Holy Land and the Holy Sites, many of them of dubious value. There has been a steady falling off of interest since then, and the world market has become far more discerning. At the same time, a market always exists for well-written and well-illustrated books, as well as memoirs by leading personalities. Some of the best-selling Israeli authors abroad are not writers at all, but political figures such as Abba Eban, Chaim Herzog, and the late Golda Meir, Yigael Yadin, and Moshe Dayan. With very few exceptions, most "big name" Israeli writers, whether literary or political in nature, are not represented by Israeli agents or publishers, but by agents in New York or London. This sometimes leads to the surprising result of Israeli publishers having to acquire Hebrew rights to Israeli authors from agents abroad.

Literary Magazines. All the major daily newspapers publish a special literary supplement in their Friday (weekend) issue. This is often the first opportunity for promising new writers to be exposed to the reading public. In addition, there are several literary magazines, including *Moznayim* (published by the Israel Authors' Association), *Iton 77*, *Ahshav*, and *Siman Keri'a*. *The Jerusalem Post*, *Israel Scene* and *Jerusalem Quarterly* are respectively, daily, monthly, and quarterly English-language publications each of which devotes substantial coverage to books and publishing. Israel's leading non-Hebrew cultural and arts magazine is the quarterly *Ariel* which is regularly published in English, French, Spanish, German and Russian editions, with the occasional issue in other languages.

A. WEILL

R

RAAB, JUDAH. Eretz Israel pioneer and farmer (b. Szenstisvan, Hungary, 1858; d. Petah Tikva, 1948). After engaging in agricultural work in Hungary, he went to Eretz Israel in 1875. He spent some time in Jerusalem, then joined the group of pioneers who founded Petah Tikva, the first Jewish agricultural settlement in the country. Raab gave the benefit of his farming experience to the settlers there and elsewhere. He published a number of articles on farming, and was one of the two first Jewish guardsmen of Petah Tikva. During the last years of his life, he wrote his memoirs, which appeared posthumously under the title *Ha-Telem ha-Rishon* (The First Furrow, 1956)

Esther Raab, Judah's daughter (b. Petah Tikva, 1899; d. Tivon, 1981) was a poet. She joined kibbutz Degania in her youth. After her marriage she lived in Egypt for 5 years, then returned to Petah Tikva. Her poetry is characterized by its descriptions of the Israeli landscape. These are collected in *Kimshonim* (1935) and *Shirei Esther Raab* (1963). *Poems of Esther Raab* (an English translation) appeared in 1986. G. KRESSEL

RA'ANANA. City in the southern Sharon northeast of Herzliya, founded in 1922 by American Jews. Their initial plan to raise cattle met with little success, but following the discovery of rich groundwater citriculture was developed. Middle-class immigrants of the Fourth and Fifth Aliya were absorbed in the 1920s and 1930s. In World War II, the settlers went over to mixed farming and industry. After 1948, Ra'anana grew quickly, with inhabitants from the adjacent transit camp receiving permanent housing. The city gradually became included in the outer ring of the Tel Aviv conurbation, with industries and services superseding agriculture. The name means "Fresh Green." Population (1987), 48,000. E. ORNI

RABAN (Rawicki), ZE'EV. Early Palestinian decorative artist and teacher (b. Lodz, Poland, 1890; d. Jerusalem, 1970). He studied in Munich and Paris, absorbing *jugendstil-art nouveau* styles, and went to Jerusalem to teach at the Bezalel School in 1912. He taught *repoussé*, anatomy, modeling, and composition, designed major Bezalel artifacts, and helped set the style of "Bezalel Ware." In 1923, he opened Jerusalem's first industrial design studio together with another Bezalel teacher, Meir Gur-Arie; their first commission was to help decorate the new YMCA building in Jerusalem, working chiefly on sculptural reliefs. M. RONNEN

RABBI BINYAMIN. *See* RADLER-FELDMAN, YEHOSHU'A.

RABBINATE OF ISRAEL. The institution of the Chief Rabbinate has its origin in the period when Eretz Israel was a province of the Ottoman Empire. It was the policy of the Sultan to exempt the religious minorities in the Empire from the application of some of the laws of the land, i.e., the Moslem religious law, and bestow upon these minorities a measure of cultural and religious autonomy, primarily through their own religious courts for the adjudication of matters of personal status. Such autonomy was enjoyed by the Jewish community as well. According to Ottoman regulations, the sultan would appoint an eminent Turkish rabbi as Chief Rabbi of the Jews of the Ottoman Empire, which included Eretz Israel. Residing in Constantinople and bearing the title hakham bashi (literally, "chief sage"), he was the official spokesman of the Jewish community to the authorities, and by *firman* (the sultan's decree) he exercised broad authority over all the religious activities and spiritual concerns of members of the Jewish community throughout the Ottoman Empire. He appointed representatives, who also bore the title hakham bashi, to the important communities of the Ottoman Empire, of which Jerusalem was one. Each hakham bashi was assisted by two commissions, one for religious matters and the other for public affairs, and was attended by two uniformed guards (*kavasses*) who served as his "guard of honor".

Rishon le-Zion. The hakham bashi of Jerusalem bore the title Rishon le-Zion (first in Zion), which, it seems, was introduced in the 17th century. Although he was merely the personal representative of the hakham bashi in Constantinople, the Rishon le-Zion in Jerusalem, by virtue of his residence in Jerusalem and his erudition, often wielded a powerful influence among the communities of the Near East. Thus the Rishon le-Zion gradually came to assume authority over all the religious affairs of the Jews of Eretz Israel.

The post of hakham bashi was always held by a rabbi of the Sephardi community in Jerusalem, which originally constituted the majority of the yishuv. Until the British conquest of Palestine in 1917, there was no hakham bashi who did not affix to his signature S.T., the Hebrew initials for *sephardi tahor* (pure Sephardi). As the Ashkenazi population in Jerusalem and throughout the country (as well as other "non-pure Sephardi" communities, such as that of the Yemenite Jews) grew, along with its institutions, the Ashkenazim came to occupy important and respected positions in the yishuv. Nevertheless, the post of hakham bashi remained in the hands of the Sephardim. The Rishon le-Zion retained, as before, jurisdiction over every project, every organization and appointment, every decision and law within the Jewish community; in practice, however, the hakham bashi did not exercise in full his jurisdiction and legal authority but delegated to each Jewish group and large *kolel* the right to establish and maintain its own autonomous institutions, such as courts of law and yeshivot.

As the Ashkenazi community in Eretz Israel grew, serious confrontations developed between the Ashkenazi religious leadership under Rabbi Shemuel Salant and the leadership of the Sephardi community under the hakham bashi. Ashkenazi demands for independence included a request to conduct their own supervision of *shehita* (ritual slaughter) separately from the Sephardim.

With the British conquest it was found necessary to establish a united rabbinate comprising the entire Jewish community. Several elements cooperated in establishing a supreme rabbinic authority—the Chief Rabbinate: the British mandatory government, the World Zionist Organization, and the Mizrachi movement.

Mandatory Government. The British government, acting in accordance with the Mandate of the League of Nations, which stipulated (Article 9 of the Mandate) that the rights of the several religious communities be respected, retained the Ottoman system.When the British conquered Jerusalem, they found the Jewish community splintered into many factions. The position of hakham bashi after World War I had become vague and somewhat discredited as a result of Palestine's isolation from the Ottoman Empire and because of a sharp dispute over the nature of the office that had arisen within the Sephardi community even before the war. While the British government wished to preserve the *status quo* so as not to deprive the Sephardi community of this post, it could not ignore the need for a supreme religious authority that would represent the entire Jewish community of Palestine and not only the Sephardim.

World Zionist Organization. The Zionist Commission, headed by Chaim Weizmann, arrived in Palestine in 1918 after the British had occupied the southern part of the country. It encouraged the leaders of the yishuv to organize unified communities in the cities as well as to set up a central organization of Palestinian Jewry, with the local and central organizations making provision for religious institutions. Because the British government intended to retain the *status quo* regarding religious communities as it had existed under Ottoman rule, which provided for separate ecclesiastical courts for Moslems, Christians, and Jews with jurisdiction over matters of personal status and family law, it was necessary to solve the question of the legal position of the rabbinate. This led to the concept of a united rabbinate, composed of representatives of all the Jewish ethnic groups in Palestine and serving all the Jewish communities there. The Zionist Commission at first assumed responsibility for the budget needed to support this institution.

The powers of the local rabbinical courts were set out in article 53 of the Palestine Order-in-Council, which gave these courts exclusive jurisdiction in matters of marriage and divorce, alimony, and confirmation of wills, as well as jurisdiction in any other matter of personal status when all parties concerned consented to the jurisdiction. The Chief Rabbinical Council was the Court of Appeals for the local rabbinical courts.

Mizrachi Organization. Through most of the history of the Diaspora the rabbinate derived no authority from outside sources (governments or law courts), nor was it common for Diaspora rabbis to be officially recognized as government rabbis. The authority of the Diaspora rabbis was derived solely from Jewish law, and from their scholarly attainments and moral standing in the community. At times, the rabbi was more than merely a religious leader, a teacher, guide, and judge but was also the leader and spokesman of the community, and the arbitrator in matters of philanthropy and charity. This was the position that Mizrachi leaders wished to secure for members of the Rabbinical Council. They hoped that once the rabbinate was established in Palestine on a firm legal basis, it would become a spiritual religious authority.

In efforts to achieve this goal a dominant role was assumed by Rabbi Avraham Yitzhak *Kook, the first Ashkenazi Chief Rabbi, who viewed the establishment of the Palestinian Rabbinate as the fulfillment of the prophetic promise, "I shall restore your judges as of old" (Isaiah 1:26). He envisioned the establishment of a great Rabbinical Court in Jerusalem as the first step toward the reestablishment of the ancient Sanhedrin and sincerely believed that, through its participation in the projects of national rebirth, the rabbinate would help fulfill the prophecy "For out of Zion shall go forth the law, and the word of the Lord from Jerusalem" (Isaiah 2:3) to all corners of the Diaspora.

Chief Rabbinate of Palestine. Sir Herbert Samuel, the first High Commissioner of Palestine, appointed a commission headed by Norman Bentwich, then legal adviser to the mandatory government, which recommended the establishment of an electoral college of 100 members (two-thirds officiating rabbis and one-third lay representatives of city and village communities) to choose two chief rabbis and a Council of the Chief Rabbinate.

Following the presentation of Bentwich's request, a controversy arose concerning the insistence of the government of Palestine that there be established a rabbinical appeals court to hear appeals from the rabbinical courts of the first instance. The rabbis contended that, in accordance with Jewish religious law, a judgment of a rabbinical court (Bet Din) is final, and is not subject to appeal. The government, however, refused to give way, insisting that a court of appeal was essential in any civilized judicial system. The ultra-Orthodox rabbis would not yield and did not participate in the Assembly that was to become the Rabbinical Council. The other rabbis, however, agreed to the setting up of the appellate court.

In 1921 the electoral college met in Jerusalem, and at its sixth meeting, chaired by Rabbi Yehuda Leib Fishman (later Maimon), it elected Rabbis Kook and Ya'akov *Meir as Ashkenazi and Sephardi Chief Rabbis and presidents of the Council of the Chief Rabbinate of Palestine. Three Sephardi and three Ashkenazi rabbis were named to the Council; in addition, two chief secretaries (one Ashkenazi and one Sephardi) and three lay advisers were elected.

The election was not accepted by the ultra-Orthodox community in Jerusalem, which created its own council, Ha-Eda ha-Haredit. This council elected to its head Rabbi

Yosef Hayim Sonnenfeld, who was succeeded by Rabbi Yosef Tzevi Duschinsky. The Eda Haredit did not recognize the election of Rabbi Kook, violently opposing both him and the Rabbinical Council in word and deed.

The Sephardi Chief Rabbi retained the title of Rishon le-Zion in addition to that of Chief Rabbi.

Initially the supreme institution of the Rabbinate was to be a judicial institution (a court of appeal for judgments of lower courts); Rabbi Kook, however, wished to see in the Rabbinate a spiritual leadership for the Jewish people in the Holy Land. Despite his demand that the electoral college be composed of rabbis only, it comprises lay representatives too.

The mandatory government accepted the newly composed Chief Rabbinate of Palestine as exercising sole jurisdiction in matters of personal status. The office of hakham bashi was abolished, and the judgments of the Rabbinate were enforced by the civil courts.

Under the terms of its constitution, the Chief Rabbinate was elected for a period of five years only, but in actual fact no elections were held during Rabbi Kook's lifetime (he died in 1935), the government periodically extending the Council's life. In 1936 the High Commissioner issued statutes governing the Va'ad Le'umi of the Jewish community, which included provisions for the election of the Chief Rabbinate.

On 12 January 1936, new elections were held, and Rabbi Yitzhak Halevi *Herzog was chosen Ashkenazi Chief Rabbi and Rabbi Meir reelected Sephardi Chief Rabbi. As Rabbi Meir was ill (he died two years later), Rabbi Ben-Zion Meir Hai *Uziel was elected his acting representative. New members were elected to the Rabbinical Council to replace those who had died. Owing to World War II, elections were not held again until 1945, when Chief Rabbis Herzog and Uziel were reelected.

The election of Rabbi Herzog met with serious opposition, since he held a university doctorate which to many was incompatible with the office of Chief Rabbi of Palestine, despite Rabbi Herzog's piety. This was a serious dispute on principles. The opposition candidate was Rabbi Ya'akov Moshe Harlap, a close disciple of Rabbi Kook.

Chief Rabbinate in Israel. The chief rabbis preside over the bet din gadol (Rabbinical Supreme Court) which hears appeals, while their associates are permanent *dayanim* (rabbinical judges). The first elections for the Council of the Chief Rabbinate were held in March, 1955. Chief Rabbi Herzog was reelected and Rabbi Yitzhak Rahamim *Nissim was chosen to replace Rabbi Uziel, who had died in 1953. The old statutes of 1936 governing the elections were found unsuitable, but owing to differences of opinion within the government no permanent rules for the election of the Chief Rabbinate were enacted. Elections to the Chief Rabbinate were held in 1964 in accordance with provisional rules. Rabbi Nissim was reelected Sephardi Chief Rabbi, and Rabbi Issar Yehuda *Unterman, the Chief Rabbi of Tel Aviv, was elected Ashkenazi Chief Rabbi to succeed Chief Rabbi Herzog, who had died in 1959. Ten members (five Ashkenazi and five Sephardi) were elected to the Rabbinical Council. In 1969 the term of the Chief Rabbinate expired, but as no agreement could be reached, the Knesset extended the term of office for another five years. The main bone of contention was the composition of the electoral college and the provision of adequate representation for lay representatives on it. In 1972 Rabbi Shelomo *Goren, who had served as chief chaplain of the Israel army and as Chief Rabbi of Tel Aviv, was elected as Ashkenazi Chief Rabbi, and Rabbi Ovadia Yosef—also Chief Rabbi of Tel Aviv—was elected as Sephardi Chief Rabbi and Rishon le-Zion.

The relations between the two Chief Rabbis were not always harmonious. Even in the time of Rabbi Kook there were confrontations between the two chief rabbis, although the public rarely heard of them. The situation under Rabbis Unterman and Nissim was more serious, while the differences of opinion between Rabbis Goren and Yosef, both great Torah scholars, were widely publicized and harmed the workings of the Rabbinate, affecting the halakhic rulings and the day-to-day verdicts passed by the Rabbinical Council. One of Rabbi Goren's prominent rulings, which Rabbi Yosef opposed, was the approval of the recitation of the complete *hallel* prayer with its benedictions on Israel's Independence Day. Only in 1980 was the breach between the two chief rabbis healed.

The period of office, dominated by Rabbi Goren, was marked by many extremely controversial halakhic rulings. In one such ruling, a brother and sister who had been declared *mamzerim* (offspring of a forbidden union) by the rabbinical courts, were freed of the taint. The ultra-Orthodox community responded with a manifesto proclaiming Rabbi Goren's rulings invalid. Other controversial decisions were: the ruling against the archeological excavations in the City of David; the decision permitting access to certain places and in certain conditions on the Temple Mount (a personal decision by Rabbi Goren); the interdiction on the National Religious Party to enter a government coalition until the passing of the "Who is a Jew?" Law; the ban on withdrawing from territories. Important rulings included: the implementation of a divorce to prevent the taint of *mamzerut*; the recognition of the Ethiopian Jews as Jews; a new halakhic way of solving the problem of the Sabbatical Year; the authorization of organ transplants; the establishment of a study institute for converts to Judaism; the indexing of the sums mentioned in the *ketuba* (marriage contract) to the cost of living.

Both Chief Rabbis were Torah scholars; at the same time they were very dominant personalities and acquired both followers and opponents. These were both decisive factors in frustrating their reelection. In 1983, after a difficult struggle, two new chief rabbis were elected, Rabbi Avraham Elkana Kahana-Shapira, who served as a member of the Rabbinical Supreme Court and as head of the Merkaz ha-Rav Yeshiva, and Rabbi Mordecai Eliyahu, who also served as a dayan. The new Council of the Chief Rabbinate was made up of younger rabbis.

Rabbi Avraham Shapira, former Ashkenazi Chief Rabbi of Israel. [Israel Govt. Press Office]

Rabbi Mordecai Eliyahu, former Sephardi Chief Rabbi of Israel. [Israel Govt. Press Office]

In recent years the standing of the Chief Rabbinate has declined. Non-official rabbinic institutions, such as those of Agudat Israel and the ultra-Orthodox Eda Haredit, as well as the major Hasidic centers, competed for the allegiance of the Orthodox. Some of the decisions of the Supreme Court of Israel invalidating decisions of the Chief Rabbinate, on the grounds that the latter exceeded its jurisdiction, also adversely affected the standing of the Rabbinate.

The Chief Rabbinate has expressed definitive opinions on political issues such as "Eretz Yisrael ha-Shelema" (The Undivided Land of Israel) and on "no return of territories for peace".

The Council of the Chief Rabbinate, with the aid of various departments and committees, decides matters of religious law and supervises kashrut and the activities of *mohalim* (ritual circumcisers) and Torah scribes in Israel. It supervises the appointment of local rabbis and religious teachers, conducts examinations of candidates foe *semikha* (rabbinical ordination), reviews the eligibility requirements for judgeships in the rabbinical courts, and establishes the procedure for these courts. The Rabbinical Courts Jurisdiction (Marriage and Divorce) Law of 1953 defines the powers of the rabbinical courts (i.e., that they have exclusive jurisdiction in matters of marriage and divorce of Jews residing in Israel), while the Dayanim Law of 1955 sets forth the procedures for the appointment of dayanim. The Council of the Chief Rabbinate publishes guidelines in matters of religious law, maintains contact with practicing rabbis in Israel, and guides them in various aspects of Torah knowledge. It also maintains contact with Orthodox rabbis in the Diaspora, helps in the solution of problems of religious law, and endeavors to supply Jewish communities throughout the world with spiritual leaders. It maintains, however, no contact with the Conservative or Reform movements and has prevented the granting of any recognition to Conservative and Reform rabbis in Israel.

The official number of rabbis in Israel, namely, rabbis of cities, moshavot and moshavim, kibbutzim and yeshivot (not including rabbis of synagogues) is 520.

See also RELIGIOUS COUNCILS IN ISRAEL.

M. HACOHEN—Y. ALFASSI

CHIEF RABBIS

	Ashkenazi	*Sephardi*
1921	Avraham Yitzhak Kook	Ya'akov Meir
1936	Yitzhak Halevi Herzog	Ben-Zion Meir Hai Uziel (acting Chief Rabbi from 1936)
1945	Yitzhak Halevi Herzog	Ben-Zion Meir Hai Uziel (acting Chief Rabbi from 1936)
1955	Yitzhak Halevi Herzog	Yitzhak Rahamim Nissim
1964	Issar Yehuda Unterman	Yitzhak Rahamim Nissim
1972	Shelomo Goren	Ovadia Yosef
1983	Avraham Elkana Kahana-Shapiro	Mordecai Eliyahu
1993	Yisrael Lau	Eliyahu Bakshi-Doron

RABBINICAL COURTS IN ISRAEL. The rabbinical courts, alongside the courts of the Moslem and Christian religious courts, are part of the general judicial system of Israel. The scope of their authority is confined to the adjudication of matters of family law affecting members of the respective religious communities. These courts were firmly established by the British mandatory power in the years 1918–1948, but their origin dates to the period of the Ottoman Empire, of which Palestine was a province.

The law prevailing in the Ottoman Empire was that of Islam, the Sharia. In one domain only, in matters of personal status, the Sharia law was not made applicable to non-Moslems, the religious minorities, the Christian and Jewish communities. The Ottoman rulers afforded a measure of autonomy to the religious minorities and recognized their right to set up their own religious courts to deal with matters of personal status. Thus personal status was determined by the law of a person's religion and his rights were adjudicated by the ecclesiastical court of the religious community to which he belonged. These courts were regarded as an act of tolerance and good will toward the religious minorities within the Ottoman Empire. It was welcomed by those religious minorities as well as by the European powers which had assumed the role of protectors of the Christian communities in the Empire in general and in the Holy Land in particular. Such protection was also extended to those Jews in Eretz Israel who were nationals of the European powers.

After the conquest of Palestine by the British and the setting up of a civil administration in 1920, the new rulers retained the Ottoman system of ecclesiastical courts. They were enjoined to follow in the footsteps of the Ottomans by the terms of the Palestine Mandate approved by the League of Nations, under which the British assumed the administration of Palestine. Article 9 of the Mandate provided that "respect for the personal status of the various peoples and communities and for their religious interests shall be guaranteed."

While there were no problems in the setting up of Moslem and Christian ecclesiastical courts for the adjudication of matters of personal status, the Jewish community presented a complex situation. Under Ottoman rule, the official head of the Jewish community was the Hakham Bashi (Chief Sephardi rabbi) who was appointed by the Sultan in Constantinople. His authority, however, was recognized only by the Sephardi Jews. The Ashkenazi Jews, who comprised a majority of the Jewish community and were predominantly nationals of European powers, refused to recognize the authority of the Hakham Bashi and maintained a number of religious courts (*Batei Din*). The latter had no official status. Chaim Weizmann, who arrived in Palestine in 1918 as head of the Zionist Commission, tried repeatedly to persuade the rabbis to establish a central rabbinic authority but failed in his efforts.

In the fall of 1921, the British High Commissioner, Sir Herbert Samuel, appointed a committee of rabbis and laymen, headed by Attorney-General Norman Bentwich, to study the problem of creating a central rabbinical authority. The committee recommended the convening of an assembly (two-thirds rabbis and one-third laymen) to elect two Chief Rabbis, one Ashkenazi and one Sephardi, and a Rabbinical Council. A thorny problem arose when the Palestine government insisted that there be established a rabbinical appellate court, in addition to district courts, as courts of the first instance. The rabbis contended that, in accordance with Jewish religious law, the judgment of a Bet Din is final, and is not subject to appeal. The government, however, refused to give way, insisting that a court of appeal was essential in order to remedy possible mistakes in judgments and thereby give litigants additional confidence, knowing that their cases might receive further consideration. The rabbis of the Old Yishuv also refused to yield on this point, and did not participate in the Assembly. Realizing that the government would not otherwise give recognition to any rabbinical court, the other rabbis agreed to the setting up of a court of appellate jurisdiction. A Rabbinical Council of eight rabbis was subsequently established; four of them were Sephardim and four Ashkenazim; two Chief Rabbis were selected. Those elected were Yaakov Meir for the Sephardim and Abraham Isaac Kook for the Ashkenazim.

After the rabbinate was set up, the government of Palestine announced that "the appointment of Hakham Bashi no longer exists in Palestine," and that "no person is recognized by the government as a Chief Rabbi in Palestine except the Rabbis elected by the Assembly." Official recognition was accorded to the Rabbinical Council elected at the Assembly: "The Government of Palestine will recognize the Council and any Bet Din (religious court of law) sanctioned by it, as the sole authorities in matters of Jewish law." It would execute through the civil courts judgments given by the Bet Din as a court of first instance and judgments given on appeal.

Thus, by dint of law, the Jewish religion became an established religion for the Jews of Palestine. In an important legal sphere, the religious law became binding on Jews and the Rabbinical Council was made its sole authority. By implication, the Jewish religion was equated with Orthodoxy, and Jewish religious law was to be interpreted by Orthodox rabbis.

The scope of this jurisdiction was set out in Article 5 of the Palestine Order-in-Council, 1922, as follows:

"The Rabbinical Courts of the Jewish Community shall have:

(a) Exclusive jurisdiction in matters of marriage and divorce, alimony, and confirmation of wills of members of this community, other than foreigners as defined in Article 59.

(b) Jurisdiction in any other matters of personal status of such persons, where all the parties to the action consent to their jurisdiction.

(c) Exclusive jurisdiction over any case as to the constitution or internal administration of a Wakf or a religious endowment constituted before the Rabbinical Courts according to Jewish law.

The exclusive jurisdiction conferred on the rabbinical courts in matters of family law and confirmation of wills was limited to Jews who were not nationals of a foreign state. The British government apparently felt that it would not be fair to impose a religious law on residents of Palestine who were not citizens of Palestine. Thousands of Jews living in Palestine had retained foreign nationality, and could thus contract civil marriages before consular officers. Marriages contracted abroad and decrees of divorce issued abroad were recognized as valid by the civil courts of Palestine, which unhesitatingly applied the principles of private international law.

The rabbinical courts and the Chief Rabbinate were thus the creation of the British authorities in Palestine. The Mizrachi and the New Yishuv in general, as well as the leadership of the Zionist organization, promoted the rabbinical establishment, hoping that it would lead the Old Yishuv to become an integral part of a unified community. This hope failed to materialize. The leaders of the Old Yishuv in Jerusalem, who from the early 1920s had regarded themselves as the Palestinian branch of the ultra-Orthodox World Agudat Israel, rejected the Assembly and the Rabbinical Council, refused to accept their authority, and set up their own Bet Din. The Sephardi Jews, on the other hand, did acknowledge the authority of the Rabbinical Council, and in spite of occasional controversies made themselves part of the organs of Jewish self-government.

As subsequently transpired, the Rabbinical Council, headed by the two Chief Rabbis, played a rather minor role in the development of religious life in Palestine during the thirty years of British rule. The growing secularization of the yishuv was not conducive to the development of Orthodoxy, nor did the dissension that occasionally developed between the Ashkenazi and Sephardi rabbis enhance the standing of the rabbinate. The first Rabbinical Council was elected for three years, but when it became impossible to reach agreement on procedures for the election of a new Rabbinical Council, the same rabbis stayed in office for over twelve years. The Old Yishuv leadership, now identified as Agudat Israel, disowned the official rabbinate as a creation of the Mizrachi, and accused it of association with the secularists; at one time some of their extremists assaulted the widely revered Rabbi Kook.

On 21 May 1948, six days after the Proclamation of Independence, the Provisional Council of State enacted its first law: "Law and Administration Ordinance 5708 (1948)." Article 11 of the Ordinance provided: "The law which existed in Palestine on 14 May 1948 shall remain in force, insofar as there is nothing therein repugnant to this Ordinance or to the other laws which may be enacted by or on behalf of the Provisional Council of State, and subject to such modification as may result from the establishment of the State and its authorities." By virtue of this enactment the system of ecclesiastical courts was carried over into the newly-born state.

The most important legislative enactment relating to the Rabbinical Courts was passed in 1953, defining the scope of its jurisdiction as follows:

1. Matters of marriage and divorce of Jews in Israel, being nationals or residents of the state, shall be under the exclusive jurisdiction of rabbinical courts.

2. Marriages and divorces of Jews shall be performed in Israel in accordance with Jewish religious law.

3. Where a suit for divorce between Jews has been filed in a rabbinical court, whether by the wife or by the husband, a

rabbinical court shall have exclusive jurisdiction in any matter connected with such suit, including maintenance for the wife and for the children of the couple.

4. Where a Jewish wife sues her Jewish husband or his estate for maintenance in a rabbinical court, otherwise than in connection with divorce, the plea of the defendant that a rabbinical court has no jurisdiction in the matter shall not be heard.

5. Where a woman sues her deceased husband's brother for Halitza (ceremony rejecting levirate marriage) in a rabbinical court, the rabbinical court shall have exclusive jurisdiction in the matter, also as regards maintenance for the woman until the day on which Halitza is given.

6. Where a rabbinical court, by final judgment, has ordered that a husband be compelled to grant his wife a letter of divorce or that a wife be compelled to accept a letter of divorce from her husband, a district court may, upon expiration of six months from the day of the making of the order, on the application of the Attorney General, compel compliance with the order by imprisonment.

7. Where a rabbinical court, by final judgment, has ordered that a man be compelled to give his brother's widow Halitza, a district court may, upon expiration of three months from the day of the making of the order, on application of the Attorney General, compel compliance with the order by imprisonment.

While Article 2 did not specify what "Jewish religious law" was to be, it was obvious that it meant the *halakha* (Jewish law) as traditionally interpreted. This understanding was never challenged, especially since the official rabbinate consisted of Orthodox rabbis only. Thus the civil law left the interpretation and application of *halakha* to the rabbinical courts, headed by the Rabbinical Court of Appeal as the chief of halakhic authority. In this way the Israeli legislature not only divested itself of its sovereign right to provide the substantive law in matters of family relations, and to amend and alter such law, but by delegating this right to the Orthodox rabbinate, created a situation where the law applicable to these matters could only be interpreted, and neither amended not altered, for the *halakha*, understood as divinely ordained, cannot admit of legislative change. This immutability of the ancient law is at the root of a good deal of the tension between a large segment of the Jewish population of Israel and the civil as well as religious authorities.

Only a narrow field of family relations is not within the exclusive jurisdiction of the rabbinical courts. When a suit for maintenance is brought other than in connection with divorce proceedings, the civil and religious courts have concurrent jurisdiction. But even civil courts, when dealing with a matter of family law, or where personal status is incidental to a litigation, are bound to apply the religious law of the person concerned. This means for a Jewish person that *halakha* is to be applied. In such cases the civil courts deviate from the *halakha* in only two instances: when principles of private international law are involved, in which case these principles take precedence over *halakha* and in matters of procedure and of the rules of evidence, when the courts have ignored the principles of *halakha*. On several occasions the rabbinic courts attempted to invalidate marriages contracted abroad on the ground that they were not in accordance with the *halakha*. The Supreme Court, however, ruled that a marriage that was valid in accordance with the law of the country in which it was celebrated, would be valid also in Israel, this being in conformity with principles well established in private international law. It also stressed that this ruling was supported by Rabbinical Courts' Jurisdiction (Marriage and Divorce) Law that "marriages and divorces of Jews shall be performed in Israel in accordance with *halakha*", i.e., that the *halakha* applied only to marriages and divorces performed in Israel and not abroad.

In the exercise of their authority under the law bestowing upon them jurisdiction in matters of marriage and divorce as well as matters relating to the observance of *kashrut* (the dietary laws), the rabbinic courts gave rise to considerable controversy and tension. The prohibition of a Cohen—a presumed descendant of the priestly caste which ministered in the Temple of Jerusalem—marrying a divorcée or a woman converted to Judaism was a frequent bone of contention, and direct or indirect attempts to invalidate such marriages were frustrated by decisions of the Supreme Court. The imprisonment of a husband who refused to give his wife a bill of divorce in contravention to a rabbinical court order was not always effective, especially in cases where the recalcitrant husband was sentenced by a civil court to a long term or life imprisonment. The wife in such cases shared the same fate awaiting a childless widow whose brother-in-law refused to perform the rite of *halitza*: both were deprived of the possibility of remarriage.

Controversies between the Chief Rabbinate—the supreme judicial authority of the rabbinic courts—and the government were frequent occurrences, and the case of the Bene Israel Jews of India led to a major controversy. Bene Israel, an old Jewish community, arrived in the thousands in Israel in the 1960s, and the Rabbinate refused to marry them until each case was investigated "whether the mother and grandmother of a Bene Israel applicant, as far back as possible, was a Jewess" or whether "the parents of the applicant and their parents as far back as possible had married after divorce..." Under pressure of public opinion, the government passed a resolution later approved by the Knesset that, "it regards the Bene Israel of India as Jews in all respects without exception, who are equal to all other Jews in respect of all matters, including matters of personal status." In the debate in the Knesset Prime Minister Levi Eshkol stated, "Out of consideration of Kelal Israel (the total Jewish community), our law has entrusted matters of personal status to the hands of the rabbis: but the deed of trust carries with it an obligation: the rabbinate is duty bound to observe the greatest *mitzva* (precept) of the age and to promote *kibbutz galuyot*—the ingathering of exiles." The Chief Rabbinate yielded. A similar conflict developed on the arrival of Ethiopian Jews in the mid-1980s.

From time to time tension developed between the Chief Rabbinate and the Supreme Court of Israel, primarily where the Rabbinate exceeded the scope of its jurisdiction. Thus the Supreme Court overruled the rabbinate when it attempted to impose norms of *kashrut* unrelated to food. When, under the pressure of the Rabbinate, the Ministry of the Interior refused to register as a Jew one who had been converted in the Diaspora under Reform or Conservative auspices, the Supreme Court ordered that such a person be registered, on the ground that the *Law of Return treats all conversions performed abroad as valid, whether Orthodox or of other Jewish religious groups. In 1988 a woman was appointed to the town of Yeruham's Religious Council, a local administrative body concerned with the maintenance of religious institutions and services. She was, however, excluded by the rabbinate from this council on grounds of being a woman. The matter reached the Supreme Court, the Chief Rabbinate contending that it had inherent jurisdiction in all matters relating to religion. The Supreme Court rejected this claim and stressed that the rabbinate is a creation of a Knesset legislative act and can exercise only that jurisdiction that the Knesset had accorded it. It concluded that, while a local religious council deals with matters related to religious affairs, its composition is regulated by law, which does not discriminate against women, and a woman, therefore, can be a member of this council.

From its very inception, the Chief Rabbinate was confronted with considerable difficulties. The ultra-Orthodox (*Eda Haredit*) refused to accept its authority and set up their own Bet Din; though deprived of official authority, it was accepted by the ultra-Orthodox as a spiritual guide. This situation did not change following the establishment of the State of Israel. The ultra-Orthodox of the Neturei Karta type refused to recognize the very legitimacy of the State. Agudat Israel accorded a measure of *de facto* recognition but attached no religious significance to the State. Both treat the Chief Rabbinate as an institution set up by the State and maintained by it. The Chief Rabbinate cannot ignore the ultra-Orthodox and therefore leans towards a strict interpretation of the *halakha*. S.Z. ABRAMOV

RABIKOVITZ, DALIA. Israeli writer (b. Ramat Gan, Palestine, 1936). She was educated at Kibbutz Geva and the Hebrew University. Rabikovitz's poetry has a surrealistic childlike quality and is full of mythological figures, fairy tales, and magic. Her major works are *Ahavat Tapuah ha-Zahav* (The Love of the Orange, 1958–9); *Ha-Sefer ha-Shelishi* (The Third Book 1969); *Tehom Kore* (The Abyss Calls, 1976). She has also published a volume of short stories. Rabikovitz has translated works by Yeats, Poe, and Eliot.

Her work in the 1980s represents a shift away from formal verse towards a more conversational tone. Rabikovitz was dismayed by the victory of the political right in Israel. After the Lebanese War, she wrote an increasing number of protest poems supporting the peace movement. E. SPICEHANDLER

RABIN, YITZHAK. Israeli military and political leader, Chief of Staff 1964–1967, Prime Minister of Israel 1974–1977, 1992– (b. Jerusalem, 1922). He studied in Labor Movement schools in Tel Aviv and Givat ha-Shelosha and was graduated from the Kadoorie Agricultural High School. As a member of the Palmah, he participated in military operations in Lebanon and Syria in June 1941. Later he attended various military courses and rose in the ranks of the Palmah. Arrested by the British on 29 June 1946, he was interned in Rafiah for five months. During the War of Independence he was Palmah Operations Officer and later commanded the Harel Brigade, which fought in the Jerusalem corridor and tried to lift the siege of the city. Later he served as Deputy Commander of the Southern Front (under Yigal Allon) and participated in the final campaigns against the Egyptian army. He also took part in the Rhodes negotiations but returned home expressing disapproval of the armistice agreement. After commanding the Battalion Leaders' School he served in the Operations Branch, then studied in a British Command and Staff College. Upon his return he became head of the Training Branch and was promoted to Brigadier-General. In 1956 he was appointed Commanding Officer of the Northern Command, followed

Prime Minister Yitzhak Rabin appearing at the National Press Club in Washington, 1976. [Israel Govt. Press Office]

by stints as Chief of Military Operations and Deputy Chief-of-Staff. On 1 January 1964 he became Chief-of-Staff and served in that capacity during the *Six-Day War; he had been instrumental in preparing the Israel Army for its victory. At the end of 1967 he retired from the army and was appointed Israel's Ambassador to the United States. During his five-and-a-half years in Washington, he forged close links with President Nixon and National Security Adviser Henry Kissinger and became a respected figure on Capitol Hill. He negotiated many financial and military arrangements with the US.

Returning to Israel in 1973 he became a Knesset member representing the Labor Party and in March 1974 was appointed Minister of Labor. After the resignation of Premier Golda Meir on 10 April 1974, he contested the party leadership against Shimon Peres and won by a comfortable majority, becoming Prime Minister on 3 June 1974.

His foreign policy focused on the continuation of "Step by Step" diplomacy leading to a better understanding with Egypt under American sponsorship. He presided over the negotiations that led to the signing of the Israel-Egypt Interim Agreement of 1 September 1975 and the corollary Memorandum of Understanding with the US, which committed the latter to supply Israel with arms, oil, and political information regarding future diplomatic moves. Relations with the US, strained during the negotiations, improved considerably. He pursued an active anti-terrorist policy and authorized the *Entebbe operation.

On the home front he set out to rehabilitate the Israel army after the Yom Kippur War trauma, restock its arsenals, and elevate its morale. He sought to stabilize the shattered economy and reduced the inflation rate. As a party leader, however, he displayed little interest in the daily functioning of the Labor Party and was plagued by a series of setbacks. The Labor Party showed signs of decline and was badly hurt by disclosures of scandals involving high level party and government officials. The Rabin Cabinet finally fell over a clash with the National Religious Party, which abstained in a no-confidence motion brought about by the tardy arrival of newly-acquired jet fighters, almost causing the desecration of the Sabbath. The revelation that Rabin and his wife had kept a personal bank account in Washington, illegal at the time, forced him to resign from his position as party leader. After the Labor Party was defeated in the May 1977 elections, he worked for its rehabilitation, traveled extensively, and wrote his memoirs. In October, 1984, he was appointed Minister of Defense in the Government of National Unity. In this capacity, he was responsible for the tough army policy towards the Arab disturbances in the Administered Areas which broke out in December, 1987. He retained the Defense Ministry following the creation of the Government of National Unity in December 1988 until the break up of that government in 1990. In 1992, Rabin was elected chairman of the Labor Party which he led to victory in elections later that year. He established a coalition government in which he was prime minister and minister of defense. M. MEDZINI

RABINOWICZ, OSKAR KWASNIK. Banker, Zionist leader, and historian (b. Aspern, Austria, 1902; d. White Plains, N.Y., 1969). Rabinowicz attended the Universities of Brno and Prague (1921–23), where he received a Ph.D. degree. From 1925 to 1939 he was, with short interruptions, president of the Revisionist organization and, later, the New Zionist Organization (NZO) in Czechoslovakia (*see* CZECHOSLOVAKIA, ZIONISM IN). He was also a member of the Zionist Actions Committee (1931–35) and the World Executive of the NZO (1935–38), a delegate to the Zionist Congresses of 1931 and 1933, and the editor of *Medina Ivrit (Judenstaat)*, a weekly published in Prague (1934–39). After the Nazi invasion of Czechoslovakia (1939) he settled in England, where he was managing director of the Anglo-Federal Banking Corporation of London (1946–56).

In 1956 Rabinowicz moved to the United States, where he was active in many Jewish organizations. He wrote numerous scholarly books of which the following deal with Zionist issues: *Vladimir Jabotinsky's Conception of a Nation* (1946); *Fifty Years of Zionism* (1950, 1952), a historical analysis of Chaim Weizmann's *Trial and Error*; Winston Churchill on Jewish Problems (1956, 1960); and *Herzl, Architect of the Balfour Declaration* (1958).

RABINOWICZ, SHAUL PINHAS (known as Shepher). Hebrew writer and leader of Hovevei Zion (b. Tauragé, Kovno District, Lithuania, 1845; d. Frankfurt on Main, Germany, 1910). Settling in Warsaw in 1875, he worked on the newspapers *Ha-Tzefira* and *Ha-Melitz*. Joining the Hovevei Zion movement in the early 1880s he was the moving spirit behind the *Kattowitz Conference and afterward served as secretary of the Warsaw branch of the Hovevei Zion movement until 1886. With the advent of Herzl, Rabinowicz joined the political Zionist movement attending the First (1897) and subsequent Zionist Congresses. He published a number of books and edited three volumes of the annual *Keneset Yisrael* (1886–88). His major literary work was his Hebrew translation of Heinrich Graetz's *History of the Jews* (1888-98), to which he added his own and others' supplementary material. G. KRESSEL

RABINOWITZ, ALEXANDER SISKIND. Hebrew author and Labor Zionist leader (b. Lyady, Russia, 1854; d. Tel Aviv, 1945). Rabinowitz received a traditional Jewish education in Lyady and from the age of 15 supported himself by teaching Hebrew in various towns and villages. From 1888 to 1905 he taught at a Hebrew school in Poltava. One of the first members of the Hovevei Zion movement, he was a delegate to the First Zionist Congress (1897) and helped his disciples Ber Borochov and Itzhak Ben-Zvi found the Po'ale Zion party in Russia. Notwithstanding his Socialist views, he was sympathetic to Orthodoxy, particularly to the Hasidim.

Rabinowitz's literary career began in 1882, when his first article (in Russian), "In Defense of the Melamedim," appeared in the *Russki Evrei*. His first Hebrew feuilletons were printed in *Ha-Melitz* in 1899. He also published some works in Yiddish but discarded that language after settling in Eretz Israel in 1905. Because of the Socialist character of his stories, novels, and articles, he was regarded as a leader of the Jewish workers in the country. A leader in Ahdut Avoda, he became a founder of the Histadrut. He was greatly respected in later years as the dean of Hebrew writers, and the village Kefar Azar was named for him (from his initials). In addition to works of fiction, Rabinowitz wrote *Toledot ha-Yehudim be-Eretz Yisrael* (History of the Jews in Eretz Israel 1921, 1936).

RABINOWITZ, LOUIS ISAAC. Rabbi and Zionist leader (b. Edinburgh, 1906; d. Jerusalem, 1984) Educated at Yeshivat Etz Hayim, Jews' College, and the University of London (M.A., 1928; Ph.D., 1934), he held various pulpits in London from 1926 to 1929. During World War II he served in the British Army as senior Jewish chaplain in the Middle East and Europe. In 1945 Rabinowitz was called to the chief rabbinate of the United Hebrew Congregations of Johannesburg and appointed professor of Hebrew at Witwatersrand University in that city. In 1948 he became chief rabbi of the Federation of Synagogues of the Transvaal and the Orange Free State. He assumed an active role in all phases of Zionist work as honorary president of the South African Zionist Federation and honorary vice-president of the United Israel Appeal. During the Zionists' struggle with Great Britain in the post-World War II period, Rabinowitz was an ardent supporter of the Irgun Tzeva'i Le'umi and in the months prior to the establishment of the State he participated in the negotiations in Palestine between the Hagana and the Irgun for cooperation.

In 1961 he settled in Israel, where he became an associate editor of the *Encyclopedia Judaica*. He was prominently associated with the Herut movement. In 1969 he headed the Gahal list to the Jerusalem municipal elections and served for a time as a deputy mayor of Jerusalem.

Rabinowitz was a columnist for several newspapers and his books included *Soldiers from Judea* (1944), *Far East Mission* (1952), as well as volumes of sermons.

Pilgrims at the tomb of Rachel. [Israel Government Tourist Office]

RACHEL (RACHEL BLUVSTEIN). Hebrew lyric poet (b. Vyatka, Russia, 1890; d. Tel Aviv, 1931). Rachel endeared herself to Hebrew readers by her warm and melodic poems of the Palestinian countryside. Arriving in the country at the age of 19, she mastered the Hebrew language.

Rachel worked as a laborer first in Rehovot and later at the agricultural training farm of Kinneret in the Jordan Valley. In 1913 she went to France to study agriculture and from there to Russia, where she spent the years of World War I teaching refugee children. While in Russia she contracted tuberculosis. After the war she returned to Palestine. She lived for some time at Deganya, but ill health forced her to leave the kibbutz. Her illness lent a sad and nostalgic mood to her poetry. Love of country and of her fellow beings are the dominant themes of her poems, many of which have been set to music. She was buried at Kineret.

H. LEAF

RACAH, GINO. Lawyer, journalist, writer, sportsman, and Zionist leader in Italy (b. Milan, 1865; d. there, 1911). One of the first Italian Zionists and founder (1901) of the Zionist Organization of Milan, of which he was secretary, Ricah was a friend of Max Nordau and one of Herzl's close aides during the Zionist leader's visit to Milan in 1902. After 1907 he was president of the Milan group. He was active also in many areas of Italian public life.

G. ROMANO

RACHEL, TOMB OF. Tomb at entrance to Bethlehem. The Bible (Gen. 35:19) relates that Rachel "was buried on the way to Efrat which is Bethlehem." The identification of the tomb near Bethlehem with Rachel's last resting place stems from early Christian sources. In the Middle Ages, the tomb was marked by 11 stones, symbolizing Jacob's 11 sons born before Rachel died. There was a cupola over the tomb, resting on four pillars. Later, walls were built so that the grave was enclosed in a small room. Sir Moses Montefiore received permission from the sultan to repair the cupola and enclosure. He also added another room to the structure. The tomb was a place of pilgrimage, especially for women praying for sons to be born. Between the 1948 War of Independence and the 1967 Six-Day War, the tomb was under Jordanian control and inaccessible to Jews. Throughout recent centuries a picture of the Tomb was

Rachel (seated left) with friends of the Second Aliya. [Central Zionist Archives]

commonly found in Jewish homes in the Diaspora, providing a visual symbol of their links with the Land of Israel.

E. ORNI

RACHMILEWITZ, MOSHE. Hematologist (b. Mskislavi, Russia, 1899; d. Jerusalem, 1985). Rachmilewitz came from a Zionist family. He studied medicine in Königsberg and Berlin and in 1926 emigrated to Palestine where he worked at the Bikur Holim hospital in Jerusalem. After four years working and studying abroad, he returned to Palestine, joining the Hadassah Rothschild hospital in Jerusalem where he worked in the department for internal medicine.

From the opening of the Medical Center of Hadassah Mount Scopus in 1939 until 1969 Rachmilewitz was head of its department of internal medicine. In this capacity he started weekly training sessions at the hospital to update doctors working in the clinics with developments in the field of medicine.

Rachmilewitz was one of the architects of the Hebrew University Hadassah Medical School, where he taught internal medicine from its opening in 1949, serving as Dean in 1957–61.

In 1969–85 he also served as a visiting professor in the Beersheba and Tel Aviv medical schools. His research work was centered around the metabolism of vitamin B.12 and folic acid, Mediterranean fever, liver diseases, the mechanisms regulating blood creation, and nutritional anemia. He served as vice-chairman of the National Health Council and was a member of the World Health Organization's expert committee on nutritional anemia. In 1964 he received the Israel Prize for Medicine.

E. HOTER

RACKMAN, EMANUEL. Rabbi and scholar (b. Albany, New, 1910). Born into a rabbinical family, Rackman studied at Yitzhak Elhanan Yeshiva in New York and then at Columbia University. He served as a chaplain in the US army during World War II and after the Allied occupation of Europe worked as advisor in Jewish affairs, aiding the escape of Holocaust survivors to the American zone and establishing Jewish schools in the transit camps.

He was president of the New York Board of Rabbis, 1955–57, and vice-president of the Religious Zionist Council of America. He served as rabbi of the Fifth Ave. Synagogue, New York, and Shaarey Tefila, Far Rockaway Congregation, New York. A specialist in the area of Jewish family law, he tried to improve the position of women within the Jewish legal framework. He was professor of Jewish studies at City University of New York, professor at Yeshiva University, and professor of Jewish Law at New York Law School. In 1977 he became president of *Bar-Ilan University, in which capacity he worked for mutual respect between religious and secular elements. In 1986 he was appointed Chancellor of Bar-Ilan University.

He has published essays and reviews and the books, *Israel's Emerging Constitution* and *One Man's Judaism.*

E. HOTER

RADICAL ZIONISTS. Zionist party formation founded at the 13th Zionist Congress (1923), at which several delegates from Poland formed a faction called Al ha-Mishmar (On the Watch) in opposition to the methods of the Zionist leadership and to the Zionist policies represented by Chaim Weizmann. The original group, influenced by the ideas of the Democratic Faction in the Fifth Zionist Congress (1901), was joined by small Zionist circles in Austria, Czechoslovakia, Romania, Germany, and Palestine. The Radical Zionists were headed by Itzhak Grünbaum, Max Soloveitchik (Solieli), Nahum Goldmann, Robert Stricker, Moshe Glickson, and others. The party had 21 delegates at the 13th Congress, 15 at the 14th (1925), 11 at the 15th (1927), 12 at the 16th (1929), 8 at the 17th (1931), and 15 at the 18th (1933).

The burden of the criticism leveled by the Radical Zionists against Weizmann's policies was expressed in their opposition to his attitude toward the British government, which they considered too conciliatory and compromise-seeking, and in which they saw a willingness to forgo Jewish rights in Palestine. They were even more strongly opposed to Weizmann's plan to set up an expanded Jewish Agency by including, along with the Zionist leadership, prominent Jewish philanthropists who were willing to support Jewish settlement in Palestine without subscribing to national Zionist ideology and to Zionist political aims. Grünbaum and his followers considered this plan a vitiation of the character of Zionism as a popular, democratic movement and its transformation into an exclusive group of Jewish notables.

In essence this view of the Radical Zionists was close to the position of Vladimir Jabotinsky, who during the same period organized the Zionist Revisionist Organization. At first both parties sent out feelers with a view to joining forces. However, it soon became evident that their views on the social aspects of Zionism and the methods of work and settlement to be followed in Palestine were in sharp contrast. Whereas the Revisionists were critical of the Zionist labor movement and of the methods of labor settlement, and their relationship with the Zionist "left" deteriorated from year to year, the Radical Zionists held that labor was the basis of Jewish settlement in Palestine and that the Halutz youth movement must pioneer in the rebuilding of the Homeland and must therefore be given priority in immigration and settlement. The Radicals regarded the Labor Zionist movement and the Histadrut as primary instruments for Zionist settlement work, even though they disapproved of their Socialist character. On this basis the Radical Zionists struggled within the World Zionist movement in Poland with the rightist Et li-Venot party, which proposed precedence to middle-class settlement in Palestine.

In June, 1925, the Radical Zionist groups, headed by the Al ha-Mishmar faction in Poland, resolved to set up a Union of Radical Zionists. At the Union's founding conference in Berlin, it was resolved that the ultimate aim of Zionism was "the redemption of the Jewish people as expressed in changing the structure of Jewish life" and that a national settlement must be developed in Palestine, based insofar as possible, on nationally owned land (i.e., land owned by the Jewish National Fund) and on Jewish self-labor. The Union also upheld "aid to healthy private initiative" (the word "healthy" was used in order to exclude such phenomena as land speculation and the exploitation of unorganized, cheap labor). Although the Union supported work for Jewish rights in the Diaspora in the political, cultural, and economic fields, it emphasized the national character of this acitivity and demanded "the revival of Jewish culture on the basis of the Hebrew language." The Union also fought for the secularization of Jewish life in both Palestine and the Diaspora.

When the resolution to establish the expanded Jewish Agency was adopted by the 16th Zionist Congress (1929), the Radical Zionists accepted it but continued to fight for the retention of the democratic and Zionist character of the new framework. At the 18th Congress (1933) Itzhak Grünbaum became a member of the Jewish Agency's Executive.

From its foundation until its merger with the World Union of General Zionists, the Radical Zionist faction was the party of Itzhak Grünbaum, whose speeches and writings expressed the essence of its views. While he personally was reticent toward General Zionism as a party, his followers in Poland, as in the sections of the Radical Union in other countries, nourished a close affinity to the progressive wing of General Zionism. In June, 1935, after Grünbaum had settled in Palestine and a split occurred in the ranks of the General Zionists, the Radical Zionists united with the progressive wing of General Zionism, forming the World Union of General Zionists (General Zionists A).

Y. SLUTSKY—D. SCHA'ARY

RADIO IN ISRAEL. *See* BROADCASTING IN ISRAEL.

RADLER-FELDMAN, YEHOSHU'A (pseudonym, Rabbi Binyamin). Author and journalist (b. Zborov, Galicia, Austria, 1880; d. Jerusalem, 1957). He received a traditional and a secular education and studied for some time at an agricultural institute in Berlin. In 1906 he moved to London, where he founded, with Yoseph Hayim Brenner, the periodical *Ha-Me'orer*. In 1908 he settled in Palestine, where he served as secretary of the Jaffa office of the World Zionist Organization and was especially active in the promotion of Jewish immigration from Yemen. During World War I he interceded with the German and Austrian military authorities in Palestine on behalf of the local Jewish population. For several years after the war he was director of Mizrahi headquarters in Palestine and was editor of its publications. He also helped found several urban residential developments. In 1926 he became the editor of *Ha-Hed*, the religious monthly published by the Jewish National Fund, remaining in charge of it throughout its existence of more than a quarter of a century.

A lifelong advocate of Arab-Jewish understanding and friendship, Radler-Feldman was one of the founders of *Berit Shalom (1927) and similar organizations and served as editor of thier mouthpieces *She'ifotenu* and *Ner*. He contributed to a variety of periodicals and wrote a number of books, including biographies of Herzl and David Wolffsohn. He also translated Herzl's *Diaries* into Hebrew.

RAFALKES, NAHUM YA'AKOV. *See* NIR-RAFALKES, NAHUM YA'AKOV.

RAFI (*Reshimat Po'alei Yisrael*, Israel Workers' List). Political party founded in July, 1965, by David *Ben-Gurion and seven other Knesset members. The founders of Rafi seceded from *Mapai in consequence of the dissension created by the controversy over the *Lavon affair. Subsequently Moshe Dayan joined the new party, which advocated self-reliance in matters of national security, peace with the neighboring countries from a position of strength, electoral reform aiming at a constituency system, general secondary education, rapid modernization of the economy, a state health service, and a democratic society with division of powers and social justice.

Rafi participated with its own slate in Histadrut, Knesset, and municipal elections held in 1965. In the Histadrut elections it received 12.1 per cent of the votes. In the Knesset elections it obtained 95,328 votes (7.9 per cent) and 10 seats. In the municipal elections in Jerusalem, its candidate, Teddy Kollek, received the largest number of votes and was subsequently elected mayor of the city. Rafi remained in opposition to the government until the eve of the Six-Day War of 1967, when it entered the Government of National Unity, Moshe Dayan becoming Minister of Defense. In January, 1968, Rafi joined Mapai and Ahdut ha-Avoda to form the *Israel Labor party. Ben-Gurion and a group of his followers, who opposed this move, established a new party. Appearing under the name Reshima Mamlakhtit (State List), it received 3.8 per cent of the votes in the Histadrut elections in 1969. In the elections to the Seventh Knesset of the same year, four of its candidates obtained seats. In the elections to the 8th Knesset (1973), the State List appeared as part of Likud.

RAFIAH (RAFA). Southernmost urban settlement in the southern coastal plain, on the Egyptian border. First mentioned in Egyptian documents of the 2nd millennium BCE,

Egyptian and Mesopotamian armies battled for Rafiah in the period of the First Temple, as did forces of the Ptolemies and Seleucids in Second Temple times. Its prosperity as a Hellenistic city dates mainly from the 1st century BCE when it was rebuilt by the Romans. Jewish and Samaritan communities lived there under Byzantine and Arab rule. Rafiah ceased to exist at the time of the Crusades. The British mandatory authorities built large army camps on the site, thereby attracting a considerable number of people. Most settled on the Palestinian side of the frontier and a minority on the Egyptian side. After Israel's 1948 War of Independence, refugees were housed in the abandoned army camps, swelling the population from 2,500 in 1945 to 49,812 in the 1967 census (of whom 39,000 were refugees), all of them Moslems. In the 1979 peace agreement with Israel, the border divided the town again. E. ORNI

RAKAH. *See* COMMUNISTS IN ISRAEL.

RAMALLAH AND AL-BIRA. Twin towns 9 miles (15 km.) north of Jerusalem. Ramallah may be identical with biblical Rama, or with Ramathaim-Zophim, or with both and al-Bira is supposed to be the site of the biblical Beeroth. Under the British Mandate, Ramallah's population was more than 85 percent Christian-Arab and the rest Moslem, while al-Bira had over 90 percent Moslems. Because of Ramallah's elevation, 2610 feet (870 m.) above sea level, it was chosen in the 1930s as the site of the country's broadcasting transmitters. Its brisk climate promoted the town as a summer resort, which, after 1948, gained impetus under Jordanian rule. As a result of the 1967 Six-Day War, both towns came under Israel administration. The census of the fall of 1967 revealed that the population had more than tripled since 1948, largely through the installation of refugee camps, to 12,134 inhabitants in Ramallah and 13,037 in al-Bira. The percentage of Ramallah Christians had fallen to 57 percent, while al-Bira had become almost exclusively Moslem. In the following two decades, the Christian percentage further weakened. E. ORNI

Diamond Center building, Ramat Gan. [Israel Govt. Press Office]

RAMAT GAN. City in the coastal plain, bordering on Tel Aviv. In 1914 a group was formed called Ir Ganim ("garden city") to create a garden suburb; the plan was realized only from 1921 onward. Avraham Krinitzi became its first mayor and held the post for decades. Because land prices were cheaper than in Tel Aviv, relatively large industrial enterprises chose Ramat Gan for their locations and the town grew rapidly. Care was taken to ensure green areas and numerous public gardens and playgrounds were laid out. After 1948, Ramat Gan's expansion quickened even more, and it was the country's fourth largest city. From the 1970s, however, its population remained stable, partly as a result of a tendency of its residents to move further out. Industry, however, continued to gain in size. Ramat Gan has Israel's largest sports stadium and is the site of the Bar-Ilan University, the Maccabia (sports) Village, the 500 acre National Park which includes a zoo and the Safari Park. The name means "Garden Height." Population (1987), 115,600. E. ORNI

RAMAT HADAR. *See* HOD HA-SHARON.

RAMAT HA-KOVESH. Kibbutz in the southern Sharon, northeast of Kefar Sava, founded in 1932. The settlement suffered heavily during the 1936–39 Arab riots. In 1943, the British police and army conducted an arms search there, the settlers resisted, and in the ensuing fight one of them was killed and several wounded. In protest, the yishuv proclaimed a general strike. During the 1948 War of Independence, it was the scene of much fighting between Jewish and Arab forces. The kibbutz has intensive farming, especially citriculture, and industrial enterprises. Population (1987), 638. E. ORNI

RAMAT HA-SHARON. City in the southern Sharon, adjoining Tel Aviv from the north. Founded as a moshava in 1923, it was in its first period primarily based on citriculture, and during World War II went over to other farm branches. After 1948, its population increased quickly when the inhabitants of a local transit camp were gradually transferred to permanent housing. Large and medium-sized industrial enterprises opened. Population (1987), 35,800. E. ORNI

RAMAT RAHEL. Kibbutz south of Jerusalem. It was founded in 1926 by Gedud ha-Avoda members who were employed in construction work in Jerusalem. Destroyed in the 1929 Arab riots, it was rebuilt in 1930. In the 1948 War of Independence, it was a forward position in the defense of Jerusalem and was heavily attacked by Arab Legion, Egyptian, and other Arab forces, occupied by them and changed hands several times. Eventually it remained in Israel's hands. It had been completely destroyed but was soon rebuilt. The kibbutz has some farming and industry, and runs a guesthouse and seminary. Its name ("Rachel's Height") was chosen for the view of Rachel's Tomb from the kibbutz site. Within the kibbutz perimeter are ancient remains, including a Judean royal fortress, and from Byzantine time, remnants of a monastery and a church. Population (1987), 306. E. ORNI

RAMLEH (Hebrew: Ramla). Town in the coastal plain, 28 mi. (42 km.) southeast of Tel Aviv. It was founded in 717 CE by the Caliph Suleiman, to replace nearby Lydda as the

Highway passing through a residential section of Ramle. [Israel Information Services]

country's capital, which it remained until the Crusader period (11th century). Moslem, Jewish, Karaite, and Samaritan communities flourished there. The earliest archeological remains are the 8th-century Uneiziya cisterns (Pool of St. Helena). The Great Mosque in the town center was originally the St. John's cathedral of the Crusaders (12th century). The square White Tower which dominates the town dates from 1318; it was the minaret of a mosque otherwise preserved only below ground.

The Jewish community ended with the Crusader occupation and was renewed in the 14th-17th centuries. Late in the 19th century, small numbers of Jews again settled in Ramleh but under the British Mandate, few Jews remained there. The town was captured by Israel forces in July, 1948 and the great majority of its 17,000 Arab inhabitants left. It was soon repopulated with Jewish immigrants, growing quickly in the 1950s, but slower subsequently. Population (1987), 43,900 of whom 36,700 were Jews, and 7,200 non-Jews. Ramleh has two industrial zones with enterprises comprising various branches, most important among these being Israel's largest cement factory. The name means "sands" in Arabic. E. ORNI

RAMOT HA-SHAVIM. Moshav in the southern Sharon near Hod ha-Sharon, founded in 1933 by middle-class immigrants from Germany who made painstaking efforts to become farmers and made their village a showplace of successful mixed intensive farming, with poultry breeding prominent. Population (1987), 692. E. ORNI

RAPHAEL, YITZHAK. Israeli religious leader (b. Sasov, Galicia, Austria, 1914). Raphael studied first at the University of Lvov. Settling in Palestine in 1935, he completed his studies at the Hebrew University of Jerusalem and continued research in history at the University of London. He taught at the Ma'ale High School in Jerusalem. With the establishment of the Rabbi Kook Foundation, he was named its director.

Raphael was a member of the Va'ad Le'umi and, from 1948 to 1954, of the Executive of the Jewish Agency for Israel, heading its Aliya Department. He was also a member of the Second and subsequent Knessets. In the Third Knesset he served as chairman of the Constitution, Law, and Justice Committee. From 1961 to 1965 he was Deputy Minister of Health. Raphael was also a member of the Executive of the National Religious party, and of the Central Committee of World Mizrachi, and chairman of the board of the Rabbi Kook Foundation and of the Yad ha-Rav Maimon.

From 1940 to 1947 he edited the weekly *Ba-Mishor*. and from 1963 of *Sinai* a monthly on Judaica. He also edited some of the basic literature of religious Zionism and the *Encyclopedia of Religious Zionism* (1958–1965) and was the author of a number of books on Hasidism, folklore, literary history, and other subjects.

RASSVIET. Name of three Jewish Russian-language weeklies, published (1) in Odessa (1860–61) by Ossip Rabinowitsch and advocating equal rights and assimilation for Russian Jews; (2) in St. Petersburg (1879–83), under the editorship of Alexander Zederbaum, with a similar program; and (3) in St. Petersburg (1907–18) and Moscow (1918–19) by the Russian Zionist Organization and edited by Abraham Idelsohn. The name means "Dawn."

The third *Rassviet* advocated practical settlement work in Eretz Israel and active Zionist participation in the defense of the rights and interests of the Russian-Jewish community, thus laying the foundation for the concept of Synthetic Zionism, which combined Herzl's political Zionism with immediate settlement activities in Eretz Israel and the struggle for Jewish survival and national organization in the Diaspora countries.

Rassviet became the leading and most widely read Russian-language Jewish periodical in the country. It was suppressed by the Soviet authorities in October, 1919 and from that time on no Zionist organ was permitted to appear in the Soviet Union. In 1922 it resumed publication in Berlin, where it was put out by the émigré Federation of Russian-Ukrainian Zionists, with Shelomo Gepstein as editor. Until February, 1923, it took no stand on internal Zionist controversies, but soon after the resignation of Vladimir Jabotinsky from the Zionist Executive the journal became the mouthpiece of activist Zionism as preached by Jabotinsky, endorsing his appraisal of the political situation in Palestine and his criticism of the official Zionist political line.

In December, 1924, *Rassviet* moved to Paris, where it appeared under the editorship of Jabotinsky, Michael Berchin, and Joseph Schechtman. The ideology, program, and tactical line of the World Union of Zionists-Revisionists, founded in April, 1925, was largely molded by the *Rassviet* group. The paper's readership consisted of Jewish émigrés from Russia in Western European countries and elements of the yishuv and the Jewish communities in eastern and southeastern Europe that had a Russian-language background. As its Russian-reading public shrank, however, the journal's financial position became precarious. It had to be converted from a weekly to a biweekly, and even in this form it appeared irregularly. It was finally discontinued in 1935. J. SCHECHTMAN

RATNER, YOHANAN. Israeli soldier and architect (b. Odessa, Russia, 1891; d. Haifa, 1965). After studying in Germany, he served in the Russian Red army in World War I. In 1923 he immigrated to Palestine and became a professor at the Haifa Technion, where he established the faculty of architecture. In 1928, he was chosen to design the National Institutions building in Jerusalem. By nature a man of understatement, his architectural work is characterized by thought and analysis combined with complex composition and attention to detail. Ratner achieved distinctiveness, avoiding inflated monumentalism, by creating a dignified rounded courtway entrance, with three separate entrances to the institutions: the Jewish Agency, the Jewish National Fund, and the Keren ha-Yesod, arranged according to hierarchy. His other buildings (including the small school in Nahalal, the Eden Hotel in Jerusalem, the Faculty of Aeronautics at the Technion, the Kefar ha-Yarok agricultural school, and the Bet Berl Seminar) sought a synthesis between the tones of the local past and the new directions of architecture in the world.

As a soldier, he played a leading role in the Hagana from his arrival in the country. He headed its territorial command in 1938–39, and in 1947 became a member of its high command. After the establishment of the Israel Defense Forces, he directed the general headquarters' department, with the rank of general. He served as Israel's military attaché in Moscow, 1948–51. A. ELHANANI

RATOSH, YONATAN. Hebrew poet and political activist (b. Warsaw, 1909; d. Tel Aviv, 1981). Ratosh was the son of Yehiel Halperin, a well-known Hebrew educator. He migrated to Palestine in his childhood (1921) and graduated from Tel Aviv's Herzliya High School (1926). He was one of the militant nationalist intellectuals who joined the Revisionist party. He was a staff member of *Ha-Yarden*, the movement's daily newspaper, but was forced to resign in 1937 because of his ultra-radical views, especially his call for the immediate establishment of a Jewish state. He formulated a new ideology which ultimately led to the founding of the *Canaanite movement. He argued that Israelis constitute a new Semitic nation which must sever its connection with Jews and Judaism and integrate into the "Semitic area." He believed that the new nation would lead in developing the Middle East. He became editor of *Aleph*, the organ of the movement.

Ratosh's early poetry was highly nationalistic. Many of these poems were published in *Hupah Shehora* (Black Canopy, 1941) and other collections. Ratosh developed an idiosyncratic "primitive" Hebrew style based on what he considered to be an ancient Hebrew poetic vocabulary drawn from early strata of the Bible and from Ugaritic epic poetry. His collected poetical works appeared in 1975–1977.

Ratosh is considered one of the key poets of his generation. Contemporary critics are fascinated by his use of primitive Hebrew-Canaanite myth. Of special interest are his critical studies of Bialik's poetry. He was also a prolific translator. In the course of his career, he coined hundreds of neologisms, many of which have been incorporated into standard Hebrew. E. SPICEHANDLER

RATZ. *See* CITIZENS' RIGHTS MOVEMENT.

RAVENNA, FELICE. Lawyer, Zionist, and communal leader in Italy (b. Ferrara, 1869; d. there, 1937). With Angelo Donati and Carlo Conigliani, Ravenna was one of the early Zionists in Italy. A member of the Council of the Italian Zionist Federation and its president for more than 20 years, he participated in many Zionist Congresses as a delegate from Italy, beginning with the Second (1898). He was a confidant and friend of Herzl, with whom he corresponded regularly. In January, 1904, he accompanied Herzl to Rome when the latter was received in audience by King Victor Emmanuel III and Pope Pius X.

Ravenna was a prolific writer on Zionist problems and an effective debater. He served as president of the Jewish Community of Ferrara from 1920 to 1931, when he was named Government Commissar of the newly created Union of Italian-Jewish Communities (Unione delle Comunità Israelitiche Italiane). He was elected president of the union in 1933, holding this office until his death. G. ROMANO

RAWNITZKY, YEHOSHUA HANA. Hebrew writer and literary critic (b. Odessa, Russia, 1859; d. Tel Aviv, 1944). Starting his literary career in 1879, Rawnitzky advocated in Hebrew and Yiddish articles the ideas of the Hovevei Zion movement and of the Jewish national renaissance. An early follower of Ahad Ha-Am, he helped found the Benei Moshe order.

He founded the literary miscellany *Pardes* (1892) and edited the Yiddish periodical *Der Yid.* In 1901 Rawnitzky, with Hayim Nahman Bialik and Simha Ben-Zion, established the Moriah Hebrew publishing house. With Bialik he edited textbooks, the *Sefer ha-Aggada*, and books of medieval Hebrew poetry. He also contributed to numerous periodicals, wrote on Yiddish philology, and was a founder and editor of *Reshumot*, a Hebrew periodical for Jewish folklore and ethnography.

In 1921 he settled in Palestine, where he helped found the Devir publishing house, of which he served as director and editor until his death. He was also prominent in Jewish life in Palestine and held leading positions in a number of cultural institutions there.

RAZI'EL, DAVID Commander of the *Irgun Tzeva'i Le'umi (b. Smorgon, Vilna District, Russia, 1910; d. Iraq, 1941). He was brought to Eretz Israel as a small child in 1914, but during World War I the family was expelled by the Turkish authorities and returned to Palestine only in 1923. After graduating from the Tahkemoni High School in Tel Aviv, Razi'el studied at the yeshiva of Rabbi Abraham Isaac Kook and at the Hebrew University of Jerusalem.

With the formation of the Irgun Tzeva'i Le'umi following a split in the Hagana after the Arab riots of 1929, Razi'el became one of its early members. He soon rose in rank, broadening his knowledge of military affairs by a thorough study of the literature on the subject, and eventually authoring a military training manual for the use of his organization. He played a leading role in the reorganization of the Irgun in 1937 (following a split in the Irgun's ranks) and in its transformation into an activist fighting force. That year he was commander of the Irgun in Jerusalem and a member of the countrywide high command. In November, he led the first reprisal action against Arabs in Jerusalem. Chosen commander of the Irgun in 1938, he became military leader of the organization. Under his command the Irgun intensified its activities in Palestine as well as in Europe.

In 1939, after having left Palestine clandestinely, Razi'el joined Vladimir Jabotinsky in a conference in Paris at which relations between the Irgun and the Revisionist movement were clarified. He was arrested by the British soon after his return to Palestine. With the outbreak of World War II, the Irgun ceased its anti-British activities and Razi'el was released a short time later. In 1941, during the pro-Axis revolt of Rashid Ali in Iraq, Razi'el, with a small group of his followers, volunteered to go to Baghdad on an important British sabotage and intelligence mission, in which he was killed.

He was buried in Iraq. His remains could not be transferred to Israel immediately upon the establishment of the Jewish State because of political obstacles. In 1955 they were transferred from Iraq to Cyprus, where they were interred in the Jewish Cemetery of Margo. In 1961 they were brought from there to Israel and reinterred on Mount Herzl in Jerusalem. T. PRESCHEL—D. NIV

READING, MARCHIONESS OF. *See* MELCHETT.

READING, 2ND MARQUESS OF. *See* MELCHETT.

RECANATI FAMILY.

Avraham Recanati. Greek Zionist and author (b. Salonika, 1888; d. Tel Aviv, 1980) was an active Zionist leader in Salonika. He tried to merge the Revisionist and Mizrachi political streams in Greece and in the Jewish world in general and was a delegate to the 12th, 13th, 14th, 15th, and 17th Zionist Congresses. In 1929 he was appointed vice mayor of Salonika. He moved to Palestine in 1934 and was a member of the first Knesset, representing the Herut party.

As a journalist, he contributed to the Salonikan Judeo-Spanish newspaper *El Avenir*, was a correspondent for the *Jewish Chronicle* and *Die Welt*, and published the newspapers *Le Courrier* and *El Progreso*. In 1917, he was one of the founders of the French weekly newspaper *Pro-Israel* and served as its editor for ten years. When in 1924 the Greek government passed legislation forbidding work on Sundays, endangering Jewish Sabbath observance, Avraham Recanati used *Pro-Israel* as a mouthpiece to fight this discriminatory law.

He wrote *La Poriza dela Familia Judia, Ke es el Tsionismo*, and *Los Judios de Rusia Sofrin Eyos Como Judios*. He also translated Herzl's *The Jewish State* into French.

His brother **Leon Recanati**, community leader and banker (b. Salonika, 1890; d. Tel Aviv, 1945), was the owner of the Fumero tobacco factory in Salonika and was elected president of the Jewish community of Salonika in 1933. After immigrating to Palestine in 1935 he founded the Palestine Discount Bank, later the *Israel Discount Bank. He played an active role in encouraging and financially backing the "illegal" immigration of Greek Jewish refugees fleeing Greece by sea to escape the Holocaust and reach Palestine via Turkey. In public life in Palestine, he was a leader of the Organization of Greek Immigrants and president of the settlement company Banim li-Gevulam which founded and strengthened the Sephardi settlements Kefar Hitim and the moshavim Beit Hanan, Tzur Moshe, and Bet ha-Levi.

His son, **Raphael Recanati** (b. Salonika, 1924) was the head of the "illegal" immigration in activities in Egypt in 1945–46. After the death of Leon he and his brothers **Harry** and **Daniel** managed and expanded the bank.

The sons of Avraham Recanati have been active in restoring the tradition and memory of Salonikan Jewry. **Shemuel Recanati** (b. Salonika, 1920) was the main force in raising the funds and constructing the Heikhal Yehuda synagogue in north Tel Aviv, named in memory of Leon Yehuda Recanati. **David Recanati** (b. Salonika, 1923) compiled and edited two major works on Salonikan Jewry, *Zikhron Saloniki, volumes I and II.* Y. KEREM

RECONSTRUCTIONISM AND ZIONISM. The Jewish Reconstructionist movement, founded by Rabbi Mordecai M. *Kaplan, has from its inception placed Zion in the center of its philosophical view of Jewish peoplehood. The centrality of the Land of Israel in the Reconstructionist scheme is the inevitable consequence of the view that Judaism must be understood as constituting an "evolving religious civilization." Kaplan, in his first major work, *Judaism as a Civilization* (1934), made Jewish nationhood or peoplehood, rather than religion, the central ingredient of Judaism, which encompasses land, language, mores, traditions, literature, art —in short, all the elements of a total culture.

Because in modern times Jews in the free nations have been permitted to participate fully in the cultures of the people among which they reside, they participate of necessity in two civilizations, with the Jewish civilization reduced to an ancillary role.

In light of these developments, Judaismnow requires one place in the world where it is the majority culture. No civilization can be creative unless it has the soil in which to grow. Thus from the Reconstructionist viewpoint, Zionism was the inevitable outgrowth of the Jewish will to live as a modern people. Witn the establishment of the State of Israel, however, a "new Zionism" is required, one that grows more from the philosophy of Ahad Ha-Am than from that of Herzl. This new Zionism calls for the reconstitution of the Jewish people as a worldwide entity, united by its common spiritual Homeland in Zion and dedicated anew to the age-old ideal of Judaism: ethical nationhood or peoplehood.

With the aid of Israel's Jewish community, Diaspora Jewry, despite the distractions of majority cultures, should be able to motivate Jews to develop a Zionist Judaism. This requires the establishment of organic Jewish communities wherever Jews live; an active and intelligent concern on the part of Israel for the future of these communities; the intensification of education, especially a knowledge of Hebrew; ever-growing reciprocity between Israel and the Diaspora; and finally, widening appreciation of the fact that only with the naturalistic approach to religion, Torah, and the Jewish people can the Jewish people hope to win the active participation and support of its secularly educated men and women of the coming generations.

I. EISENSTEIN

REFORM JUDAISM AND ZIONISM. Reform Judaism in Germany was a derivative of the late 18th century Emancipation, which Reform leaders hailed as a spiritually and politically liberating movement. They perceived it as reopening the way for the renewed and authentic expression of Judaism as uniquely religious, committed to the universalistic teachings of Israel's prophets, and endowed with a mission to lead humanity toward a Messianic era of peace and justice. They also were convinced that both the new age which helped induce Reform, and their own reformulation of Judaism, would bring Jews into a safe harbor of freedom and security.

Meeting in Braunschweig in 1844, the first German Rabbinic Conference appointed a committee to report on whether the Hebrew language was necessary in religious services, and how the messianic idea was to be considered in worship. The Frankfort Convention met in 1845 to deal with the questions raised in Braunschweig.

One of its decisions was that "the idea of Messiah deserves a high recognition in the prayers; yet all political-national conceptions must be excluded from it."

At the Leipzig Synod (1869), the following resolutions were presented by Abraham Geiger: "The national side of Israel has to be pushed into the background. The separation of Israel from other nations ought no longer to find expression in our prayers. The hope of the unification of the whole human family in truth, justice, and peace should be emphasized. The hope that...all Israelites be gathered from every corner of the globe and return to the promised land has vanished entirely from our consciousness."

A head-on collision between Reform and Zionism came when the new World Zionist Organization's Basle Program of 1897 was proclaimed. The five-member Executive Committee of the German Rabbinical Assembly protested: "The efforts of so-called Zionists to erect in Palestine a Jewish national state run counter to Judaism's messianic hopes, as expressed in Scripture and later religious sources."

With the development of the Reform movement in America, its attitudes towards Zionism went through several phases: (1) Anti-Zionism (1885–1917); (2) Moderating anti-Zionism and growing non-Zionism (1917–1935); (3) Progression toward Zionism (1935–1943); (4) Support of Zionism (1943 to the present).

In their first statement of principles, a group of American rabbis, meeting in Philadelphia in 1869, had defined universalism as the "union of all the children of God in the confession of the unity of God." This was considered to be in conflict with "restoration of the old Jewish State under a descendant of David, involving a second separation from the nations of the earth."

The Pittsburgh Platform (1885), which preceded the founding of the Central Conference of American Rabbis, stated: "...We recognize, in the modern era of universal culture of heart and intellect, the approaching of the realization of Israel's great Messianic hope for the establishment of the kingdom of truth, justice, and peace among all men. We consider ourselves no longer a nation, but a religious community, and therefore expect neither a return to Palestine, nor a sacrificial worship under the sons of Aaron, nor the restoration of any of the laws concerning the Jewish State."

In 1890, at its first Convention, the Central Conference affirmed as its basis the decision of previous Conferences starting in Braunschweig in 1844.

At the 1898 Convention, the Committee on the President's Message issued the following resolution, which was unanimously adopted: "Resolved, that we totally disapprove of any attempt for the establishment of a Jewish State. Such attempts show a misunderstanding of Israel's mission, and do not benefit, but infinitely harm our Jewish brethren where they are still persecuted, by confirming the assertion of their enemies that the Jews are foreigners in the countries in which they are at home, and of which they are everywhere the most loyal and patriotic citizens."

Nevertheless some of American Jewry's leading Zionist leaders, spokesmen, and thinkers emerged from the ranks of the Reform movement. In 1898, Richard Gottheil wrote "The Aims of Zionism" and became the first president of the newly-founded Federation of American Zionists. His father, who was Rabbi of Temple Emanuel in New York, was also a Zionist, a fact which provoked dismay in his congregation. "The Justification of Zionism", by Professor Casper Levias of the Hebrew Union College, appeared in the Central Conference Yearbook of 1899. After declaring that even the most universalist of prophets believed in the national existence of the Jews, Levias continued, "Nationalism is a genuinely Jewish idea, running like a thread through all our history, from its very beginning to our days."

Bernhard Felsenthal became actively identified with Zionism toward the end of his career. In 1907, he submitted a series of resolutions to the Central Conference, affirming the compatibility of Zionism and Reform Judaism, denying the need for dispersion as a requisite for promoting the mission of Israel, and maintaining that a Jewish state would be best qualified to advance the mission. Maximilian Heller was an unequivocal Zionist, seeking to achieve ideological unity between Jewish religion and Jewish nationalism. He was honorary Vice-President of the Zionist Organization of America from 1911–1929, and became President of the Central Conference of American Rabbis.

With the Balfour Declaration (1917) and following the end of the First World War, Reform Judaism entered its second period of confrontation with Zionism. Under the leadership of Stephen Wise and Abba Hillel Silver, a growing number of Zionist Rabbis pressed their positions with increasing intensity. In 1917 Heller presented the following resolution: "There is nothing in the effort to secure a publicly and legally safe-guarded home for Jews in Palestine which is not in accord with the principles and aims of Reform Judaism."

A motion offered by Rabbi Stoltz and passed by 68–20 stated: "At a time of universal conflict and suffering, such as the present, it is of prime importance that the Conference emphasize not the differences that divide us, but those sacred principles which all Jews hold in common, and those great tasks which it is our paramount duty at the present moment to promote and perform together for the alleviation of human suffering and the healing of the Jewish people." This resolution established the presence and legitimacy of the Zionist rabbis. In principle the Conference remained anti-Zionist, but less virulently so.

In 1920, the Central Conference declared, "We rejoice...at the decision of the San Remo Conference to give to Great Britain a mandate over Palestine in line with the Balfour Declaration." At the 1920 Convention, Professor Gotthard Deutsch submitted two controversial proposals. The first, approved without dissent, stated that "the sentence of a long term of imprisonment against Lieut. Vladimir Jabotinsky, of Jerusalem, and a number of his associates, whose only crime was to defend their co-religionists against an attack by a mob when the constituted authorities failed to act, has aroused just indignation all over the world", and sought their liberation. The second recommendation by Deutsch read: "While this Conference expressed first in 1897 and on subsequent occasions its disapproval of political Zionism your Committee deems it timely to revise this attitude. The Jewish homeland in Palestine is now an internationally acknowledged fact...Your Committee proposes that this Conference express its sympathy with all activities which shall develop the resources of Palestine and raise the economic and intellectual state of its Jewish population..."

The Conference also stated: "It is the duty of all Jews to contribute to the reconstruction of Palestine, insofar as Jews may place themselves there and to make it a good place for them to live in. But the cooperation of Jews who reject Jewish nationalism is made difficult, nay impossible, as long as the Zionist Organization is committed to such nationalism. For such cooperation would mean the tacit acceptance of the program and ideals of Zionism. We, therefore, hold that it is the duty of all Jews to make clear the character of the practical world now demanded for Palestine, leaving to the Jews there, and not to any partisan organization, to determine their own destiny. We hope that for the sake of unity in Israel, and, above all, for the sake of the practical help to Palestinian Jews, some plan for the union of Jewish forces may be devised..." There may have been an opportunity in 1920 for a closer relationship with the Zionist Organization of America, but it was lost because the Zionist Organization failed to respond to overtures of cooperation. At the 1922 Convention, the Central Conference announced an agreement with the Palestine Development Council for joint efforts developing Palestine, predicated upon the understanding that neither party, as an organization, would be committed to any political-national program. Another resolution welcomed the proposed Jewish Agency.

In 1935 the Central Conference officially passed from anti-Zionism into its third (and more positive) phase. The anti-Zionist chapter was officially concluded with the passage of its resolution "...that in keeping with its oft-announced intentions, the Central Conference of American Rabbis will continue to cooperate in the upbuilding of Palestine, and in the economic, cultural, and particularly spiritual tasks confronting the growing and evolving Jewish community there."

By the 1930s, the Hebrew Union College, while not necessarily congenial to Zionism, did not officially combat it. Though most of the Faculty was anti- or non-Zionist, some scholars were Zionistically engaged and could teach in freedom. Zionist sermons by students could be heard from the College pulpit. Student societies for propagating modern Hebrew and studying Zionist thought flourished. A chapter of the student Zionist Organization, Avukah, met regularly on the premises of the College. During the transition toward Zionism, the following Reform Rabbis provided Zionist leadership within the Central Conference and within the Zionist movement, nationally and internationally: Stephen S. Wise, Abba Hillel Silver, James C. Heller, Barnett Brickner, Max Nussbaum, Arthur Lelyveld, Morton M. Berman, Jacob Weinstein, Samuel Blumenfield, Leon Feuer, Moses Cyrus Weiler, Joachim Prinz, Louis I. Newman, Leon Kronish, Joshua Trachtenberg, Samuel Wohl, Felix Levy, and others.

In 1937, at Columbus, Ohio, the Central Conference adopted a document called "Guiding Principles of Reform Judaism." It stated in part: "...We affirm the obligation of all Jewry to aid in Palestine's upbuilding as a Jewish homeland by endeavoring to make it not only a haven of refuge for the oppressed but also a center of Jewish culture and spiritual life." The Union of American Hebrew Congregations adopted a similar course soon afterwards.

In 1942, the Central Conference passed a resolution, after an intense debate, expressing its complete sympathy with the demand of the Jews of Palestine "that they be given the opportunity to fight in defense of their homeland on the side of the democracies under allied command to the end that the victory of democracy may be hastened everywhere." As a consequence of "the Jewish Army" debate, opponents of Zionism within the Central Conference organized the American Council for Judaism. The Conference was threatened with a split which was averted by a confrontation in June, 1943, in which the Zionist position predominated. After a formidable debate by Rabbis Fineshriber, Schachter, Levy, and David Polish, and after long general discussion, the following resolution was adopted: "...Without impugning the right of members of the Conference to be opposed to Zionism, for whatever reason they may choose, the Conference declares that it discerns no essential incompatibility between Reform Judaism and Zionism, no reason why those of its members who give allegiance to Zionism should not have the right to regard themselves as fully within the spirit and purpose of Reform Judaism." Rabbinic members of the Council for Judaism were asked to withdraw, and most did.

The turn toward Jewish nationalism affected all aspects of life within the Reform community, particularly transforming its religious life. In recent decades, the Reform community experienced an explosion of Israel-related observance. Much of the music in the services is Israeli. Some congregations observe the second day of Rosh ha-Shana out of spiritual identification with Israel. Israeli art and artifacts are found within many synagogues. The new Reform Haggada contains the prayer, "Next year in Jerusalem," and the new prayer book, *Gates of Prayer* includes special services for Israel Independence Day, as well as prayers for the State of Israel in the regular liturgy.

Working in the fields of Kibbutz Yahel, founded by the Reform movement, 1984. [World Union for Progressive Judaism]

Reform Judaism in Israel. When the Hebrew University was dedicated in 1925, its first Chancellor and then President (from 1935) was Judah Leon Magnes, ordained at the Hebrew Union College in 1900. With Magnes, the presence in Israel of the Reform Rabbinate began.

In 1951, the Central Conference undertook to support the construction of a new high school building for the Leo Baeck School in Haifa. During the 1950s, Jay Kaufman, whose organizational gifts advanced Zionist action within the Reform movement, served as chairman of the Israel Committee of the World Union for Progressive Judaism.

The institutionalization of the Progressive Movement in Israel gained authority with the building of the Hebrew Union College School in Jerusalem in 1952. Under the leadership of its President, Nelson Glueck, it soon became the intellectual and spiritual center of the Progressive Movement in Israel. In 1970, the College became the first Jewish seminary to require all students to spend their first year in Jerusalem, and in 1986 its expanded campus was dedicated. Concurrently, through the World Union for Progressive Judaism, progressive congregations began to take root in Israel. Among the early pioneers were Shalom Ben-Chorin, the founder of the Har-El Synagogue in Jerusalem, Rabbi Moshe Zemer of Tel Aviv, and Rabbi Reuven Samuels, principal of the Leo Baeck School in Haifa. By 1989 there were congregations in Jerusalem, Tel Aviv, Haifa, Ramat Aviv, Upper Nazareth, Nahariya, Netanya, Ramat Gan, and Beersheba.

In 1970, the Central Conference held its first convention in Israel and it was decided that the Conference would meet in Israel at least every seven years. During the 1970 convention, representatives of the Central Conference undertook to enter into a series of spiritual dialogues with the kibbutz movement. Several years later, a decision was made to sponsor a Progressive kibbutz under the auspices of the World Union for Progressive Judaism; the decision led to the founding of Kibbutz Yahel in 1976. In 1983 Kibbutz Lotan was organized, and Moshav Har Halutz was founded in 1985.

From 1972–74, the Central Conference, the Union of American Hebrew Congregations and the World Union each joined the World Jewish Congress. The Union for Progressive Judaism joined the World Zionist Organization in 1975.

The World Union formally transferred its international headquarters to Jerusalem in 1974. Under the guidance of its director, Rabbi Richard Hirsch, the World Union intensified its Israel program. Hirsch represented the Reform position to the Israeli community and conducted a campaign on behalf of the religious rights of the Progressive community, especially in the "Who is a Jew" issue. From 1988–92 he was chairman of the Zionist General Council.

In 1978, under the sponsorship of the Union of American Hebrew Congregations, the Association of Reform Zionists of America (ARZA) came into being, under the leadership of Roland Gittelsohn, its first president, and David Polish. It fostered the creation of a world body, *Artzenu. In 1987, the Reform Zionist bodies achieved a significant representation at the Zionist Congress and for the first time received a portfolio in the Zionist Executive (Rabbi Henry Skirball as head of the Department of Education and Culture in the Diaspora, 1988–92). D. POLISH

REFUSENIKS. Jews in the USSR who applied for permission to emigrate to Israel from 1970 onward and were refused.

INITIAL PERIOD (1967–1971). During the 1960s nationalist oriented Jewish groups spread throughout the USSR, and Zionist motivation became increasingly pronounced, but it was the Six-Day War that marked the rebirth of the mass Zionist movement (*see* RUSSIA, ZIONISM IN).

The Soviets expressed their anger and frustration at the results of the Six-Day War by cutting off diplomatic relations with the State of Israel and by waging an enormous anti-Israel/Zionist/Jewish propaganda campaign (*see* RUSSIA, RELATIONS WITH ISRAEL). The latter acquired additional political meaning in light of the official anti-liberal mood following the events in Czechoslovakia and Poland in 1968. The Jewish reaction to the increasingly antagonistic attitude of the authorities was further alienation from the regime, growing protest against official anti-Semitism and defamation of the Jewish State, and a search for ideological and practical alternatives. At the same time, the disappearance of the Israeli diplomatic presence in the Soviet Union made it possible for aliya-oriented Zionist activism to develop without being dependent on good relations between the USSR and Israel. Emigration to Israel became an open demand. From that time until the Gorbachev "Glasnost" experiment, the dynamics of the situation were such that governmental pressure, discrimination, and defamation of the Jews produced more protest and desire to emigrate, while Jewish protests and emigration increased governmental paranoia and harassment. In the post Six-Day War years the major reservoir of activists was drawn from that part of the Jewish population which had inherited or developed its Zionist dream years ago: the remnants of partially destroyed communities in Baltic states, Western Belorussia, Ukraine, and Bessarabia (now Moldavia); traditional oriental communities of mountain Georgian and Bukharan Jews; and survivors of underground Zionist groups, old (1920–30s) and new (1950-early 60s). These activists were joined by a growing number of youngsters with no Jewish upbringing—but also without the fear resulting from previous repressions. The first cases of public protest which became known to the outside world occurred in the late 1960s. On 13 June 1967, Yakov Kazakov, a 22-year-old Moscow Jew who had discussed his desire to immigrate to Israel with the Israeli embassy before its expulsion from Moscow, sent a letter to the Supreme Soviet renouncing his Soviet citizenship, declaring himself a citizen of Israel, and demanding the right to go there. In September, 1968, Boris Kochubievsky took part in an unofficial memorial meeting in Babi Yar, site of the Nazi massacres of Kiev Jews, and then protested to the authorities against anti-Semitism, declaring, "I am a Jew. I want to live in the Jewish State. That is my right." He was arrested in December, and five months later sentenced to three years in labor camp for slandering the Soviet regime. In August, 1969, eighteen Jewish families from Georgia sent a letter to the UN Human Rights Commission which ended with an appeal, "Let us go to the land of our forefathers!" After some hesitation the Israeli government made the letter public. In most cases the authorities yielded to the pressure. In 1969 more than 3,000 Jews were allowed to leave for Israel— the largest number since the establishment of the Jewish State. Meanwhile, emigration fever spread. Unofficial Hebrew study groups (*ulpanim*) were created to serve the future immigrants. In Moscow alone more that ten *ulpanim* operated simultaneously. Hebrew textbooks and dictionaries, as well as translated Zionist and Jewish materials, were copied by the hundreds and even thousands. In August, 1969, representatives of groups from Moscow, Leningrad, Riga, Kharkov, Kiev, Orel, and Georgia met in Moscow to discuss the establishment of a national coordinating committee; the publication of a joint periodical (called *Iton*, this periodical was subsequently started in Riga, with 22-year-old Zionist activist Yosef Mendelevich responsible for its production); different legal and illegal activities; and ways of expanding *ulpanim*.

The Soviets responded to this spreading activism by reducing the number of emigration visas (1,044 in 1970), thus creating the "refuseniks." By this time the Jewish movement had gathered such momentum that the frustration of the activists resulted in a dramatic step which became a turning point for the whole movement. On 15 June 1970, a group of Jews, mostly from Riga, and two non-Jewish dissidents were arrested. They planned to hijack a small aircraft in order to fly to Sweden; from there they hoped to go to Israel. They were tried for "betrayal of the Motherland" the severest charge in the USSR. Two of them (Eduard Kuznetsov and Mark Dymshits) were sentenced to death while the others received prison terms ranging from four years to 15 (Yosef Mendelevich, Yuri Fedorov). 24 December, the day the sentences were handed down, was afterwards commemorated by Jewish activists in the USSR as "Prisoner of Zion Day." The great public outcry in the West was only slightly relieved when Soviet authorities changed the death sentences to the maximum of 15 years' imprisonment. In Israel the Leningrad trial caused the first massive public movement on behalf of Soviet Jewry, led by recently arrived Soviet Jewish activists. The authorities attempted to crush the movement by new mass arrests of activists in different cities throughout the USSR. In May-June 1971, three groups of Jewish activists were put on trial for defaming the Soviet regime: nine in Leningrad (Hillel Butman was sentenced to ten years in prison, Mikhail Korenblit to seven; others got between one and five years in labor camp), nine in Riga (including a woman, Ruth Alexandrovich, who was sentenced to one year in labor camp with a strict regime, while the maximum three-year sentence was given to Arkady Shpilberg), and nine in Kishinev (with sentences ranging from one to five—in the case of David Chernoglaz—years in prison). In addition, in 1971–72 twelve individual trials were held in Moscow, Leningrad, Kharkov, Sverdlovsk, and Odessa.

Solidarity rally with Russian Jewry at Western Wall, Jerusalem, 1970. [Israel Govt. Press Office]

Nevertheless, the authorities were forced to recognize that emigration demands had become widespread and could not be suppressed without offering the "carrot" along with the "stick." In March, 1971, the number of exit visas was sharply increased, reaching 13,033 by the end of the year.

YEARS OF EXODUS (1971–1980). From the time of the Leningrad Trial until the end of the decade, the Soviet Jewry movement grew within a context of: 1) international pressure, especially effective as long as the Soviets were interested in preserving the atmosphere of "detente"; 2) a relatively easy—though always restricted—emigration of the majority of those who were applying for exit visas; 3) constant harassment of a relatively small number of activists and refuseniks.

Emigration policies. The Leningrad Trial and the unprecedented reaction to it around the world turned the plight of Soviet Jewry into an international issue. The Israeli government which had previously pursued so-called "quiet diplomacy," finally approved the public campaign that had been constantly demanded by Soviet Jewish activists themselves. This policy shift was earmarked by the first World Conference on Soviet Jewry, held in Brussels in February, 1971.

Under the combined internal and external pressures, the Soviet regime allowed large-scale Jewish emigration, although never agreeing to recognize officially either the principle of freedom of emigration or the specific right of the Jews to repatriate to their historic homeland, Israel. The process of applying for emigration permission has never been an easy one. The only legitimate reason for making such an application was family reunification. An affidavit from a relative in Israel had to be produced, or the notorious OVIR (Department of Visas and Registration of the Ministry of Interior) offices would not even supply the needed application form and questionnaires. These affidavits had to be received via regular mail, in a special, immediately identifiable envelope. Thus people who asked for an affidavit to be sent to them were aware that the KGB would definitely register them as potential emigrants even if they did not actually apply. The applicants also had to produce numerous reference letters, e.g., from their place of work or study, neighborhood administration, and family members remaining in the USSR. Every step was accompanied by embarrassment, emotional stress, and hostility on the part of officials, neighbors, and co-workers. Nevertheless, a growing number of Jews applied for emigration visas and most were permitted to leave. From 1971-1979, an average of 2,000 Jews left the USSR monthly, and there were two or three new requests for affidavits from Israel for every Jew permitted to leave.

Emergence of the refusenik movement. However, there was always a percentage of applications which was turned away, i.e., these applicants became refuseniks. In many cases, the refuseniks lost their jobs, professionals among them could not find employment in their fields, and they faced social isolation and even harassment. The frightening possibility of becoming a refusenik was a successful deterrent to many potential applicants. The by-product of this Soviet policy was the creation of a certain social stratum of people who were both committed and able to conduct a systematic pro-emigration campaign as well as independent Jewish cultural activities. Unemployment also meant free time and freedom from reprisal from employers; disruption of normal social contacts encouraged communication and cooperation with other Jews seeking to emigrate; while the human drama generated sympathy in the free world and led to the creation of direct links between the refuseniks and Jews around the world. The leading role in the movement at this time was played by assimilated Jewish intellectuals, particularly scientists, whose percentage among the refuseniks was disproportionately high. In 1972 the unemployed refusenik scientists organized a seminar as a means of continuing their academic life and sustaining professional levels. The following seminars, led primarily by Professor Alexander Lerner and by Dr. Victor Brailovsky, became for years not only one of the major institutions and intellectual forces in the refuseniks' life, but also an important channel of their international communications. Ideological influence, political leadership, and spokesmanship of the refusenik scientists shaped in many ways the behavior of the whole movement, especially vis-à-vis the outside world.

The major preoccupation of this movement was the campaign for aliya (immigration to Israel) and/or emigration rights. At the same time, when it became clear that many of the refuseniks would be denied exit visas for indefinite periods of time, an increasing amount of their energy began to be invested in developing a community life of their own and cultural activities aimed at reaching out to a larger Jewish population.

The Aliya campaign. The major forms taken by the activists' campaign were: individual and collective petitions addressed to the Soviet authorities and/or Western politicians and public; demonstrations, sit-ins, and hunger strikes; defense and support of persecuted activists, especially those imprisoned for Jewish and Zionist activities (Prisoners of Zion); and the monitoring of Soviet practices in Jewish and emigration issues, with subsequent communication of the results abroad. An integral part of the aliya activities was the pro-Israel and Zionist educational effort. Public demonstrations became a constant feature of the Jewish movement starting in February, 1971, when groups of Jews demonstrated in Moscow near the Supreme Soviet of the USSR and in Riga near the local OVIR office. On 28 February, thirty Moscow Jews, protesting their refusals, staged a sit-in in the building of the Supreme Soviet. Demonstrations in Moscow (where the Jews were actually received by shocked KGB and OVIR officials) and Riga took place again in March, and on 10 March 146 Jews from Latvia, Lithuania, and Moscow sat for an entire day in the Supreme Soviet. The next day 50 Jews arrived without warning at the Ministry of the Interior of the USSR, demanding and finally receiving an interview with the minister, Nikolai Schelokov. In July, Georgian Jews demonstrated in Tbilisi and then in Moscow. A major petition campaign culminated in a letter signed by 1,185 Jewish families, altogether 4,056 people, from throughout the USSR. The letter was sent to the UN and governments of the free world, appealing to them for help because "life in the Soviet Union has become absolutely unbearable." Over the years, while large-scale emigration continued, the Jewish demonstrations and petitions became less massive and less shocking to the authorities though the participants were in many cases harassed, detained, and even imprisoned. The primary addressee of Jewish actions and appeals was the free world. The Soviet Jewish activists saw public and political pressure from Israel, world Jewry, and the international community in general as the major vehicle for changing Soviet emigration policies as well as for protection against repression.

The principal stage in the process of internationalization of the issue was reached in 1972–73. President Nixon's visit to Moscow in May, 1972, was preceded by mass petitions of the Jews appealing for his help in obtaining emigration visas. During the visit almost every active refusenik was detained, including Vladimir *Slepak, a *de facto* leader of the Moscow refusenik community. On the eve of Nixon's visit on 17 April, the US House of Representatives resolved that the Presidency should request that the Soviet government permit its citizens to emigrate. In the fall of that year Senator Henry Jackson introduced an amendment (sponsored in the House by Congressman Charles Vanik) that linked Soviet attainment of "Most Favored Nation" status in trade to the easing of emigration restrictions. The vocal support of Jewish activists in the USSR played a critical role in the Jackson-Vanik Amendment's being adopted against the desire of the US Administration, and despite the hesitation of the American Jewish establishment. The issue of Soviet Jewry became a constant feature of Soviet-American relations. The idea of linkage between East-West exchanges and emigration was now a major strategic concept of the activist movement. Meanwhile, an important battle was won when the Soviet authorities introduced, in August, 1972, an "education tax" on professionals emigrating to Israel, and then abolished it in March, 1973, after the outrage and pressure from the West which were initiated by the refuseniks' protests. The worldwide campaign on behalf of Soviet Jewry became both an example of and a factor in the emergence of the human rights issue as a vital part of the general East-West agenda. The culmination of this process was the signing of the Helsinki Accords on cooperation and security in Europe on 1 August 1975. The human rights obligations of the signatories, among them the USSR, included specific provisions for family reunification as well as guarantees of the rights of minorities. Monitoring Soviet fulfillment of those obligations was the reason for several aliya activists (Dr. Vitaly Rubin, Vladimir Slepak and Natan *Sharansky in Moscow, Dr. Eitan Finkelstein in Vilnius, and Dr. Grigory Goldstein in Tbilisi) to join Helsinki Watch Groups, established by human rights activists in the USSR. This step was disputed by some circles in the Jewish movement. Their position, as well as that of the Israeli officials dealing with the Soviet Jewry issue, was to show a clear distinction between the Jewish and any other human rights campaign in the USSR. The relationship between the Jewish movement and other democratic human right forces continued to be one of the major topics of dispute among Soviet Jewish activists and among their supporters abroad, even after the dissident movement was practically crushed by Soviet authorities at the end of the 1970s.

Cultural activities. Paradoxically, the very people whose main determination was to leave the Soviet Union and go to Israel, were the ones who contributed the most to the revival of Jewish culture and religion inside the USSR. Cultural and educational activities were the cornerstones of underground Zionism until the Six-Day War, but were overshadowed by the aliya campaign. Most aliya activists believed that all efforts should be invested in securing immediate exit from the Soviet Union, while Hebrew classes, massive Jewish gatherings around the synagogues and sites of Holocaust atrocities etc. were seen merely as preparation for emigration. However, in 1974, emigration dropped and the first signs of the *neshira* (drop-out) phenomenon appeared when about 20% of those Jews leaving decided to go to places other than Israel. Many activists consequently decided to give higher priority to cultural and educational work, though others feared, not groundlessly, that this would weaken the political campaign against Soviet anti-emigration measures. The argument between "Kulturniks" and those promoting political protest actions continued through the decade. Meanwhile, a whole network of cultural activities was created, including :*ulpanim*, seminars on Jewish topics, publications, commemorations of Holocaust victims, celebrations of Jewish holidays, Jewish education of children, performances and art exhibitions. Towards the end of the 1970s religious observance and studies became an important part of this newly emerged, unofficial Jewish life.

1. Hebrew teaching was, at first, provided by old-time Zionists or religious Jews, by remnants of pre-Soviet Hebrew education in Western parts of the USSR, and even by some Hebrew speakers. Soon, as students and self-educated enthusiasts themselves became teachers, the number of *ulpanim* grew and the study of Hebrew spread throughout the USSR. By the end of the decade an estimated 2,000 people were learning the language in various places. Several attempts were made over the years to register Hebrew instruction as an official, private form of employment, like other kinds of private tutoring. In June, 1977, the authorities gave a clear message to the activists. Dr. Yosef Begun, Moscow refusenik and one of the principal fighters for the legalization of Hebrew instruction, was sentenced to two years' internal exile on charges of "parasitism," since his teaching practice was not a recognized form of employment.

Moscow gradually became the center of Hebrew activities, which were aimed also at provincial cities. The veteran refusenik Yuli Kosharovsky, an electronics engineer by profession, was an unofficial leader of the network, which included: copying and distributing teaching materials; special "Hebrew only" weekly seminars for teachers; short, intensive courses for future teachers who either traveled to Moscow or studied in their home towns with teachers who came from Moscow. Dozens of study groups, generally consisting of three to ten people, existed simultaneously. In 1979 a month-long summer retreat for Hebrew teachers from all over the USSR was organized in the Crimea. It was repeated the following year, but this time the authorities reacted by arresting Yuli Kosharovsky and detaining him for thirteen days on charges of "hooliganism."

2. While Hebrew classes became the major network of revived unofficial Jewish cultural life, the most popular attraction, drawing thousands, was the Jewish gatherings outside synagogues in major cities on Jewish holidays, especially Simhat Torah, attended by thousands. The activists played a crucial role, both in publicizing the gatherings and in organizing the entertainment. The authorities were fully aware of the importance of this mass, albeit superficial, Jewish involvement. Starting in 1973, dozens and sometimes hundreds of Jews showed up at picnics in the woods outside Moscow, organized by activists on spring and fall Jewish holidays: Israel Independence Day, Lag ba-Omer, Sukkot, etc. The picnics' programs included lectures on the meaning and customs of the particular holiday, performances of Jewish music, Jewish song competitions, and sports events. The KGB and police were always visible, usually keeping their distance but sometimes trying to disturb the celebrations. Other kinds of outdoor Jewish gatherings, such as Holocaust memorial services, received harsher treatment, and throughout the decade, dozens of activists were detained or prevented from leaving their places of residence while attempting to set up a memorial rally at Babi Yar in Kiev.

3. Jewish artistic activities, both official and unofficial, had been well developed in the Baltic republics, but already in the first years of massive emigration, most members of local performing groups left for Israel, where some of them (for example, the singer Nechama Lifshitz and the "Anahnu Kan" folklore ensemble) continued to perform. By the end of the 1970s in Moscow, a Hebrew singing group, regular "Purimshpiels", and occasional theater performances created entertainment, not only for the refusenik community but also for a larger Jewish audience. A unique Leningrad contribution to this cultural process was the establishment in 1975 of the artists' group "Aleph," some of whose members later became well-known Israeli painters (E. Abezgaus, T. Korenfeld, A. Okun).

4. Jewish history, tradition, philosophy, Israeli society and politics were among the subjects of numerous home seminars for audiences of 10–100 people throughout the USSR, Among the best known were seminars in Kishinev, Leningrad, Minsk, Riga, and Vilnius. There were several seminars or study groups in Moscow. Arkady Mai, who had been educated as an historian, but due to Stalin's anti-Semitic campaign was forced to choose a technological occupation, organized a seminar devoted exclusively to social sciences and culture. The Moscow seminars, and to a lesser extent those in other cities, were frequently addressed by visiting Western and Israeli lecturers. This international connection was important, not only in terms of the content and level of the presentations but also for creating international publicity of the Soviet Jewry issue and protection for the Jewish activities. The most powerful illustration of this was an abortive international symposium on "Jewish Culture in the Soviet Union— Present and Future." In March, 1976, a committee of thirty Jews from all over the USSR, chaired by Professor Benyamin Fain, was set up to organize the seminar. Invitations were sent to hundreds of Jewish scholars and intellectuals abroad and to official Soviet institutions. Ultimately the Soviets did not permit the seminar to take place; instead there were home searches and house arrests. This entire drama symbolized the new interest in developing cultural life that the Jewish movement was to take, and the continuing prohibition of Jewish cultural expression on the part of the Soviet government.

5. A new dimension that became increasingly pronounced in the movement towards the end of the decade, was a revival of religious Judaism within the predominantly assimilated refusenik and activist community. Along with different seminars and Hebrew classes, Torah study groups appeared, centered around two newly observant Moscow refuseniks, both educated as mathematicians: Iliya Essas (associated with Lithuanian "mitnagdim") and Vladimir Shakhnovsky (affiliated with Habad).

6. In 1978 two refusenik families in Moscow, the Tzirlins and the Chernobilskys, decided that since they were unable to leave Russia, they must create a preschool educational system of their own for their small children. Together with a few friends they set up an unofficial Jewish kindergarten, which soon became too small to accommodate all who wished to participate. The more religious parents set up a separate kindergarten, and eventually there were three or four kindergartens functioning. In the kindergartens, Hebrew, Jewish songs, tradition and festivals were taught along with the usual preschool subjects.

7. Different trends, groups, and opinions found expression in various *Samizdat* publications which appeared in Moscow (most influential were "Jews in the USSR," founded by Professor A. Voronel and Yakhot in 1974, and "Tarbut," edited by I. Essas); Riga ("Jewish Thought," *Din u-Metzi'ut* [Law and Reality]); and occasionally in other cities. Original creations by Soviet Jews, reproductions of works by past Russian Jewish Zionists, such as Jabotinsky, documents and announcements concerning the movement, and regular reviews of the situation could be found in these publications.

Official harassment. Neither aliya nor cultural activities of the Jewish movement were fully tolerated by the authorities. There was continuous harassment and a wide range of punishments, such as expulsion from jobs and university studies; searches of homes; house arrests; defamation in the media; beatings; short-term detentions; arrests that led either to internal exile or imprisonment. From 1971–1980, over 80 Jews were tried and sentenced for their Jewish activities or desire to emigrate. In many cases they were accused of anti-Soviet activities. Many demonstrators were accused of "hooliganism." Young people who asked not to be drafted into the Soviet Army since they planned to emigrate were charged with draft evasion. Unemployed refuseniks were sometimes imprisoned for "parasitism" while some would-be emigrés who had been employed in construction or commercial trades were accused of "economic crimes." The most serious trumped-up charges employed against Jewish activists were "treason" and "espionage." These could have resulted in capital punishment, though in fact they ended in long prison sentences. After the Leningrad trial of 1970, the harshest sentence meted out was Anatoly Sharansky's. Sharansky, who served as spokesman for the refusenik community and had established especially good relations with Western correspondents working in Moscow, was arrested in March, 1977, accused of espionage, and sentenced in 1978 to 13 years' imprisonment.

Rather than breaking the movement, the repressions and arrests became a focal point of new protest actions, support activities, and international campaigns. Inside the USSR, the Prisoners of Zion were supported not only by petitions and appeals in their defense, but also through provision of food, medicine, and clothes to the prisoners themselves, and financial support to their families. A Moscow refusenik, Ida *Nudel, was called "the angel of the Prisoners of Zion" because of her devotion to that kind of vital care. As for the western world, the release of the Prisoners of Zion became not only one of the central demands of the movement, but also the strongest single appeal in terms of rank-and-file involvement and media attention.

Summary of the Decade's Achievements and Crises. From 1971 through 1980, about a quarter of a million Jews, close to one-tenth of the entire Jewish population, left the USSR, two-thirds of them arriving in Israel. Simultaneously, against all odds and on a very limited scale, a sort of Jewish community had formed in the USSR. After decades of isolation, communication was restored with Israel and the rest of the Jewish world.

The Zionist idea and the national movement it inspired created this turning point. At the height of the movement's achievements, however, its ideological integrity was shaken. From the beginning of the mass exodus, the activists' appeal for Jews' right to live in the Jewish State was in complete accord with the mood of their followers. Until 1973 practically every Jews leaving the USSR made his way to Israel; in 1975, the number dropped to 50%, and in 1979 only 33%, with the rest going mostly to the USA and Canada. Objective difficulties and mistakes in the immigrants' resettlement in Israel were only partially responsible for the new "drop-out" trend. Clearly, the wider the circles of those joining the growing emigration, the more the lack of Jewish identity, created by decades of state-organized cultural genocide, determined the emigré's choice of destination. At a later stage the snowball effect, typical of any human migration, became a factor in itself: the first Soviet Jewish arrivals in North America created an infrastructure of personal and family relations, attracting and accommodating additional immigrants. The emergence and growth of "drop-outs" constituted a major challenge to the movement in the USSR and its supporters abroad. Two polar positions developed: the denial of legitimacy and condemnation of any support of Jewish emigration to places other than Israel; and, on the other hand, the proclamation of the freedom of choice and of the obligation to help unequivocably every Jew wishing to leave the totalitarian and anti-Semitic Soviet state. Disputes revolved around periodic appeals by the Israeli government to the American Jewish community to stop financial assistance to drop-outs, to deny political refugee status to those arriving with Israeli visas, and different suggestions for making "dropping out" technically impossible via selective sending of affidavits or the introduction of direct flights from the USSR to Israel. Russian Jewish intellectuals who led the political campaign for emigration rights in the seventies, were generally opposed to any coercive solutions. On the other hand, cultural and religious activists tended to support a rigorous anti-drop-out position. Discussions notwithstanding, the massive drop-out seriously weakened the movement internally and contributed to its isolation from the Jewish rank and file, including the majority of those interested in leaving the USSR. This accumulation of internal weakness coincided with a new negative turn in official policy, earmarked by the arrests in 1977–78 of some of the leading refusenik activists, including Natan Sharansky, Yosef Begun (second term), Vladimir Slepak, and Ida Nudel in Moscow, and Grigory Goldstein in Tbilisi, and the parallel release of some others, including Dina and Iosif Beilin, Dr. Alexander Luntz and Professor Vitaly Rubin. In 1978–79, while emigration figures were increasing and reached an all-time high of over 4,000 per month, a new policy was worked out and implemented to bring emigration almost to an end.

SUPPRESSION OF EMIGRATION. In the fall of 1979 in Kharkov and several other cities in the Ukraine, the OVIR offices began turning down emigration applications on the grounds of "lack of sufficient kinship" with the supposed relative in Israel. The following year Moscow authorities dramatically reduced the number of exit permits, while the majority of those who had applied were simply left with no answer. Rumors connected this with OVIR's supposed preoccupation with processing visas for foreign tourists coming for the Summer Olympics of 1980. The games came and went and the situation did not improve. Towards the end of the year the "Ukrainian experiment" of 1979 became the general rule in most parts of the USSR; Moscow was among the few places where emigration applications based on an invitation from a non-first degree relative in Israel would even be considered.

This sharp reversal of emigration policy was never officially announced or elaborated by the Soviet Union and was explained in different ways in the free world. The official Israeli and Zionist position was that the main reason for this change was the growing drop-out, which supposedly eroded the unique excuse that the Soviet authorities had in permitting emigration of Jews and not Soviet citizens in general. Some of the semi-official declarations and hints of the Soviets seemed to support this theory, as did statistics showing that the initial crackdown on emigration was mostly in cities with the highest rate of drop-outs.

On the other hand, almost all the Sovietologists, as well as many campaigners and uninvolved observers, emphasized that the slow-down of Jewish emigration was part of a larger reversal of Soviet internal and international policies unconnected with the Jewish drop-outs. In 1979, when the US Congress failed to ratify the SALT II agreement, USSR-USA relations began to deteriorate. This was aggravated by the Soviet invasion of Afghanistan in December of that year, and detente collapsed. The Soviet aggressiveness in foreign relations was related to an anti-liberal drive inside the country: in the late 1970s the human rights movement was nearly completely suppressed, culminating in Andrei Sakharov's exile to Gorky without a trial in January, 1980.

Not only Jewish emigration was cut down from the 51,000 mark of 1979 to 2,700 in 1982, 1,300 the next year and only 900 in 1984, but all other emigration suffered a similar blow: while 9,000 ethnic Germans were permitted to emigrate annually in 1976–78, only 900 left in 1984; the number of Armenians permitted to emigrate to the USA reached a peak of 6,100 in 1980 and went down to only 88 persons in 1984.

Several attempts by refuseniks and activists to protest the emigration restrictions were suppressed. A group of Jews from Kiev that came in 1980 to petition the highest authorities in Moscow were sent back home, where they were harassed by officials. In May, 1981, a group of about 30 refuseniks in Kishinev, who had notified the authorities of their intention to demonstrate against the denial of exit visas, were arrested outside the synagogue and two of them, Osip Lokshin and Vladimir Zukerman, sentenced to three years in labor camp. On 11 November 1980, the opening day of the Helsinki Agreement follow-up conference in Madrid, about a hundred Jews demonstrated and presented a petition to the Supreme Soviet of the USSR. There was no police intervention, but two days later Dr. Victor Brailovsky was arrested and later sentenced to five years of internal exile. Many thousands of Moscow Jews, most of whom had been denied any answer, were so desperate that a newly emerging group of young activists succeeded in organizing a chain of demonstrations, petitions, visits to officials, etc., all of this escalating toward the Communist Party Congress at the end of February, 1981. The officials' concern over possible disorder during this event was probably among the main reasons for a temporary policy change. A month before the Congress was opened, hundreds of Jews started receiving invitations to the city OVIR with a positive answer to their applications. This continued for three to four months, in Moscow only, and among those released were most of the young leaders who had set up the campaign. With this exception, the period from 1981–86 saw a nearly complete standstill in the emigration process.

THE JEWISH MOVEMENT IN THE EARLY 1980S. Leonid Brezhnev died in 1982 and two of his successors, Yuri Andropov and then Konstantin Chernenko, reached the top position for a few months only before dying. In March, 1985, Mikhail Gorbachev was elected Secretary-General of the Communist Party. His policy at first largely followed the previous course, although a few changes did slowly occur, developing toward 1987 into a profound reshaping of the human rights, economic, foreign, and other policies of the USSR. Until then, the Jewish movement passed through a most difficult period.

The mass exodus of the previous decade and its subsequent suppression left the remaining activists and those who joined their ranks very isolated from the surrounding—even Jewish—population. The authorities attempted a systematic destruction of all the networks and frameworks of the Jewish movement throughout the country. Dr. Brailovsky's arrest was a hard blow to the refusenik scientists' seminar that he had led for years. Heavy pressure was put on the Jewish cultural seminar in Leningrad, and in 1981 one of its participants, Dr. Evgeny Lein, was arrested and sentenced to one year in exile. The same year an unofficial Jewish university in Kharkov was crushed and its leader, Dr. Alexander Paritsky, was sentenced to three years' imprisonment. Outdoor celebration of Jewish festivals in the Moscow countryside had been halted for years. Of the few Jews still active in Kiev, Kim Fridman, Dr. Vladimir Kislik and Dr. Stanislav Zubko were arrested and sentenced to terms in labor camp. One of them was accused of possessing a gun and drugs, which police had planted in his flat during the search; this trick was then repeated with several other activists. In 1982 Dr. Felix Kochubievsky, the best-known Novosibirsk refusenik, was arrested and sentenced to two and a half years in labor camp after founding a friendship association between the USSR and Israel. In the city of Sverdlovsk two Hebrew teachers, Lev Sheffer and Vladimir Elchin (a non-Jew) were sentenced to five years' strict regime in labor camps for "anti-Soviet agitation and propaganda."

Hebrew and religious studies were subjected to increasing pressure until the major wave of arrests began in August, 1984, first in Moscow (Kholmiansky and Edelstein, who had taken over from Yuli Kosharovsky responsibility for the network of Hebrew teaching across the USSR), then in Odessa, Kiev, Kharkov, etc. This wave of imprisonments continued until June, 1985, when two veteran refuseniks and teachers, Dr. Leonid Volvovsky and Dr. Roald Zelichenok, were arrested in Gorky and Leningrad respectively. Besides Hebrew teachers, other refuseniks and activists were tried in Moscow, Leningrad, Chernovtsy, and other places. This was the most massive and consistent attack on Jewish activism since 1970–71, and even Gorbachev's appointment did not bring immediate relief. Three refuseniks, Dr. Vladimir Lifshitz (Leningrad), Alexei Magarik (Moscow), and Bezalel Shalolashvili (Tbilisi) were arrested in 1986 before this kind of anti-Jewish repression was stopped. Altogether, not less than fifty activists and refuseniks were put on trial in 1981–86, two of whom had already been Prisoners of Zion in the 1970s (Shimon Shnirman of Kerch and then Kishinev was imprisoned for the second time for "draft evasion," while Yosef Begun was imprisoned for the third time, accused of "anti-Soviet propaganda," and sentenced to seven years of imprisonment with an additional five years of internal exile). Despite these conditions, the Jewish movement succeeded in preserving and even expanding all those activities and community structures that had been developed. An important development in the cultural field was the significant growth of religious observance and education, which attracted dozens of young people not only in major cities but also in relatively small towns. This new *baal teshuva* (return to religion) movement encompassed a variety of trends, from religious Zionists (Piotr Polonsky's group) to anti-Zionist Satmar Hasidim. Another interesting, though less pronounced, phenomenon was a revival of Yiddish. These and other cultural developments included a large number of Jews who were not planning emigration and became an important factor in a kind of open Jewish revival under Gorbachev's *Glasnost*.

As for the aliya campaign, the official suppression of emigration by massive denial of exit visas to those who had no close family in Israel caused a new movement of Soviet Jews requesting Israeli citizenship and demanding repatriation to Israel as a national right, as opposed to the personal issue of "family reunification." This movement gained momentum at the end of 1984-beginning of 1985, when several hundred Jews throughout the USSR signed a "Letter on Repatriation" and/or claimed citizenship of Israel (quite a few of them denouncing their Soviet citizenship).

GLASNOST—THE NEW PAGE. The process of profound change in Soviet policies on Jewish issues started in 1986 along with changes in some other areas of human rights. The Jewish struggle in the USSR and supporting international pressure were definitely among the major factors that caused the Soviet recognition of the fundamental link between their growing economic backwardness and their denial of elementary freedoms to their citizens. As a result, Prisoners of Zion were released, Jewish emigration jumped from nine hundred in 1986 to 19,000 in 1988 to 185,000 in 1990, the persecution of Jewish culture as well as suppression of contacts between Soviet and Western Jews was mostly stopped, and governmental anti-Semitism was reduced dramatically. Most of the long-term refuseniks and known aliya activists were permitted to emigrate, while large numbers of new people joined the remaining activists in setting up Jewish clubs, societies and performing groups in all parts of the Soviet Union. On the other hand, unofficial grassroots anti-Semitism became the ideology of popular nationalistic groups (like Pamyat [Memory] Society) patronized by part of the governing bureaucracy.

At the end of the 1980s the Jewish national movement faced new challenges and new opportunities. An important dimension was added by the former leadership that arrived in Israel in the late 1980s and which organized itself into a natural force for supporting cutural revival in the USSR and promoting aliya to Israel. Y. STERN

REGALSKY, MARCOS (MORDECHAI), (pseudonym of Itzhak Berlin). Po'ale Zion leader and journalist (b. Moscow, 1885; d. Buenos Aires, 1959). He finished his secondary studies in Warsaw, studied literature and philosophy at the New University of Berlin, and commenced his public activity in 1903 in Warsaw as a supporter of Herzlian Zionism. He was subsequently drawn to Labor Zionism and in 1904–1905 was a member of the S.S. Party Committee, working also in Zhitomir and in Kovno. He was arrested twice by the authorities for his political activity. After his release from jail (1909) he moved to Berlin, where he published articles on Jewish life in Germany in the eastern European Jewish press.

In late 1914 Regalsky moved to the USA, where he was one of the founders of the People's Relief Committee. After the Balfour Declaration he worked for the unification of the Territorial Socialists and Po'ale Zion. Sent to Argentina in 1918 as a Po'ale Zion emissary, he reorganized the local movement. From 1918 his articles were published in the party organ *Di Naye Tzait* and from 1933 in the party periodical *Unzer Tzait*. From 1923 he was the permanent correspondent of the large circulation daily *Di Yidishe Tsaytung*. The bulk of his articles were political commentaries on world events and, the Jewish and Zionist scene in particular. He also covered the local Jewish community and supported democratization of its institutions. In the 1930s and 1940s he was a member of the DAIA (Argentinian Jewry's Representative Organization) governing board. He participated in the 19th and 22nd Zionist Congresses (1935, 1946). A selection of his writings were published in *Zwishen Zvay Veltmilkhomes* (Between Two World Wars, 1946).

S. SCHENKOLEWSKI

REGELSON, ABRAHAM. Hebrew poet (b. near Minsk, Russia, 1896; d. Tel Aviv, 1981). He was taken to the US in 1905 and his early poems were published from 1920 onward. He lived in Eretz Israel from 1933 to 1936 and again from 1949, working for various newspapers. His collected poems appeared in *Hakukot Otiyotayikh* (1964) which includes both his original verse and his translations from English and Yiddish. Among his prose works are critical essays, philosophical reflections, and works for children.

REGEV, YOSEF. *See* GRAVITSKY, YOSEF.

REHOVOT. City in the coastal plain, 13 mi. (20 km.) south of Tel Aviv. It was founded as a moshava in 1890 by a group of Hovevei Zion from Warsaw together with immigrant Jews already in the country. The settlers attempted to make themselves self-supporting from the start and employed Jewish labor and, later, also Jewish watchmen. Rehovot became a social and cultural center for Second Aliya immigrants. At first, the main crops were grapes and almonds but before World War I, Rehovot developed into a center of citriculture. By 1913 it had 600 inhabitants. In the 1921 Arab riots, 6,000 Arabs attacked the moshava but were beaten back. In the 1930s, the first industrial enterprises were established, notably citrus packing plants and other enterprises based on farm crops. Later, industry became increasingly sophisticated. In 1948 Rehovot had a population of 12,522 and in 1950 it was granted municipal status. The city's growth, which had slowed down somewhat in the 1960s, quickened again when Rehovot became part of the Tel Aviv conurbation's outermost ring and many chose to live there while commuting to work elsewhere in the coastal plain. Rehovot is the seat of the Weizmann Institute of Science, the Faculty of Agriculture of the Hebrew University of Jerusalem, and the Volcani Institute of Agricultural Research of the Ministry of Agriculture. The Kaplan Hospital is situated in the city. Chaim Weizmann lived and died there and a memorial, Yad Chaim Weizmann, was established near his home. The name is biblical although the biblical Rehoboth was elsewhere. Population (1987), 71,900.

E. ORNI

REICH, LEON. Zionist leader in Galicia and member of the Polish Parliament (b. Drohobych, Galicia, Austria, 1879; d. Lvov, Poland, 1929). He began to participate in Zionist activities at an early age and soon became one of Galicia's most prominent Zionist leaders. In 1907 and 1911 he was a candidate in the elections to the Austrian Parliament. From 1908 on he participated in all Zionist Congresses, and from 1913 until his death he was a member of the Greater Actions Committee.

In 1918 Reich was elected chairman of the Jewish National Council of Eastern Galicia, and in 1919–20 he was a member of the Jewish delegation to the Paris Peace Conference (*see* COMITE DES DELEGATIONS JUIVES). From 1922 to 1929 he was a member of the Polish Parliament, where he served as chairman of the Jewish Club. In this capacity he negotiated and, in 1924, signed an agreement for Polish-Jewish cooperation with Premier Wladyslaw Grabski. When the agreement brought no positive results, Reich was removed from the presidency of the club, which by then was torn by strife.

From 1920 to 1929 Reich headed the Zionist Organization of Eastern Galicia. He contributed numerous articles to the Jewish press.

N.M. GELBER

REINES, YITZHAK YA'AKOV. Rabbi and founder of the *Mizrachi movement (b. Karlin, near Pinsk, Russia, 1839; d. Lida, Russia, 1915). In 1869 he became rabbi of Svencionys, where, in 1882, he founded a yeshiva (rabbinical school) whose curriculum included secular as well as Jewish subjects of instruction. This innovation incurred the disapproval of ultra-Orthodox elements, and after four years he was forced to close the institution owing to lack of funds and to the pressure brought to bear on him. In 1884 he was made rabbi of Lida, a position he held until his death. In 1905 he revived his project of a modern yeshiva in Lida, which then attracted a large number of students from throughout Russia.

Reines was the author of many books on halakha (Jewish Law) and Aggada. In *Hotam Tokhnit* (2 vols., 1880–81) he advocated a new method of Talmud study based on the analysis of comprehensive halakhic concepts.

Reines was an early adherent of the Hovevei Zion movement. In 1887 he proposed to Rabbi Shemuel Mohilever the establishment in Eretz Israel of a network of settlements and educational institutions to restore the country as a spiritual center of the Jewish people. After the advent of Herzl, he became an adherent of political Zionism, participated in Zionist Congresses, and spread the ideas of Zionism by speech and writing. Although he was attacked by some Orthodox rabbinical and lay groups for joining the Zionist movement and collaborating with nonreligious elements, he continued to work untiringly for the Zionist cause, insisting that Zionism signified the beginning of the redemption of the Jewish people and expressing the hope that nonobservant Zionists would ultimately return to religious practices. He put forward these views in *Or Hadash Al Tziyon* (1901) and other writings. In 1902, seeking to win the religious masses to Zionism and to strengthen the influence of religious Jews in the World Zionist Organization (WZO), he called a conference of rabbis and laymen in Vilna at which the Mizrachi movement was founded. A year later Mizrachi's second conference was held in Reines's hometown, Lida. In 1903, at the Sixth Zionist Congress, Reines and most of the delegates of his party voted for the acceptance of the East Africa scheme with its prospect of immediate relief for the suffering Jewish masses of eastern Europe. In the same year he founded *Ha-Mizrah*, Mizrachi's first organ. In 1904 he convened the First World Conference of the Mizrachi in Bratislava.

At the early Zionist Congresses Reines and other religious delegates had objected to the inclusion of cultural work in the Zionist program for fear that such activity would have an antireligious character. It was this objection, among other considerations, that had moved Reines and like-minded men to establish the Mizrachi movement. At the 10th Congress (1911) Reines and the Mizrachi fought fiercely against the decision that the WZO engage in cultural work. Despite his defeat and disappointment, however, Reines did not share the view of some Mizrachi leaders that the party should leave the WZO but continued untiringly in his Zionist work. The 11th Zionist Congress (1913) was the last he attended.

T. PRESCHEL

REISS, ANSHEL (Anzelm). Civil engineer, Labor Zionist leader, and publicist (b. Jaroslaw, Galicia, Austria, 1886; d. Kefar Sava, Israel, 1984). Reiss was one of the founders and leaders of the Po'ale Zion party in Galicia. He served as a lieutenant engineer in the Austro-Hungarian Army during World War I. After the war he was one of the organizers of Jewish self-defense in Lvov.

Reiss settled in Palestine in 1925 and became director of the Technical Department of the Zionist Executive in Jerusalem. In 1928 he became general secretary of the Po'ale Zion World Movement and went to Warsaw. With the outbreak of World War II he returned to Palestine, where he served with Histadrut institutions. He attended all Zionist Congresses from 1913 on and was a member of the Actions Committee from 1929 and of its presidium from 1951.

Reiss was one of the founders of the World Jewish Congress, representing Labor Zionism in its leadership. During World War II he organized the "Representation of Polish Jewry" and helped establish the Rescue Committee (Va'ad Hatzala) in Palestine. He published many articles in labor and Zionist periodicals in Poland, Israel, and other countries.

RELIGIOUS COUNCILS IN ISRAEL. Jewish religious councils were established in cities and in a large number of villages throughout Israel to meet the Jewish religious needs of the Israeli public. Working in cooperation with the Chief *Rabbinate and the local rabbinates, the councils undertook kashrut supervision, the supervision of Sabbath observance, religious guidance, the registration of marriages, and the building and maintenance of synagogues, ritual baths, and other religious institutions. Their budget was supplied by the local civic authorities, the Ministry of Religious Affairs, and revenue from some of the services they rendered.

The institution goes back to the mandatory period when religious councils were set up under the Jewish Community Regulations (*see* YISHUV, SELF-GOVERNMENT IN THE). Since the establishment of the State, the composition of the councils and the scope of their activities have been governed by Knesset legislation. In 1988 there were 185 religious councils in the country.

The provision of Jewish religious services is regulated by the Jewish Religious Services (Consolidated Version) Law 5731 (1971), as amended. Under that law such services are to be provided by the Jewish religious councils established thereunder, which are empowered to provide such services in accordance with the approved budget, and for those purposes such councils are empowered to enter into contracts, to hold property on lease, and to acquire movable property.

A draft budget must be prepared by such a council (*mo'etza datit*) at such time and in such manner as are prescribed by the Minister of Religious Affairs and must be submitted by the council for approval to the local authority within the area of jurisdiction whereof the persons to whom the services are supplied reside or, if there is no such local suthority, to the Minister of Religious Affairs. In the event of a difference of opinion between the council and the local authority with regard to the draft budget submitted for approval, the government will approve the budget with or without modifications. When the draft budget has been so approved, it will come into effect and the council may not expend any money save in accordance therewith.

Under the Jewish Religious Services Budgets Regulations, 5728 (1968) as amended, made by the Minister of Religious Affairs, the services for which provision may be made in the budget of a Jewish religious council are (1) rabbinate and marriages, (2) kashrut and shehita (ritual slaughter), (3) family purity, (4) burial services, (5) the Sabbath and the *eruv* (ritual fence), (6) Tora culture, and (7) supported institutions (synagogues and others). The law provides that the government shall meet one-third, and the local authority two-thirds, of a budget approved by a local authority or by the government in the case of a difference between the council and the local authority, but it empowers the Minister of Finance and the Minister of Religious Affairs jointly to increase the government share of the budget for the council of any particular place if, in their opinion, the special conditions in the place justify such increase. The expenditure of a budget approved by the Minister of Religious Affairs will be borne periodically by the government within the Budget Law in force.

The number of members of a Jewish religious council will be fixed by the Minister of Religious Affairs, but it may not exceed the number of members of the local authority. Of that number 45 percent must be proposed by the Minister, 45 percent by the local authority, and 10 percent by the local rabbinate; and all three, the Minister, the local authority, and the local rabbinate, must together give their opinion regarding the candidates to be appointed as members of the council from the point of view of their personal suitability to serve as such and from the point of view of their being suitably representative, within the council, of the bodies and communities interested in the maintenance of the religious services in the place concerned. If the local authority or the local rabbinate does not propose its quota of candidates within the prescribed time, it will be proposed by the Minister of Religious Affairs. If there are differences of opinion between the Minister, the local authority, and the local rabbinate, the matter will be decided by a committee composed of the Minister, the Minister of Justice, and the Minister of the Interior or their representatives, and if the Minister appeals against the decision of the committee, the government will decide. Every Jewish religious council must be reconstituted every four years.

The Minister of Religious Affairs is charged with the implementation of the law and empowered to make regulations for that purpose, including regulations for the appointment of members of a council in place of members whose place has become vacant, elections of rabbis in areas having a municipal corporation or local council (known as "town rabbis"), the licensing of Jewish burial societies, and the establishment of Jewish cemetery boards. Jewish religious councils, Jewish burial societies, and Jewish cemetery boards may, with the approval of the Minister of Religious Affairs and in accordance with regulations made by him, levy fees for their services.

Under a 1973 amendment to the above Law, the Minister for Religious Affairs is empowered to demand of a Religious Council which, in his opinion, has not fulfilled a particular duty or function imposed on it under the Law, to take the necessary action within a specified time. If the Council fails to comply with the Minister's demand, the Minister, after consultation with the head of the Local Authority, may appoint a person whom he regards as suitable to fulfill the duty or function, provided that person's remuneration and expenses are paid from the budget of the Council. Under a 1980 amendment to the Law, provision is made for the establishment of a disciplinary tribunal to deal with a complaint of the Minister for Religious Affairs that a Town Rabbi has acted wrongly in the performance of his duties, has acted in a manner inconsistent with his standing as rabbi in Israel, or has been convicted of an offense involving moral turpitude. If the tribunal finds that the rabbi is unworthy of continuing to fill his position, the minister shall bring the tribunal's conclusions before the president of the Chief Rabbinate Council, which shall remove the rabbi from office.

H.E. BAKER—A.F. LANDAU

David Remez.
[Israel Information Services]

REMEMBRANCE DAY. *See* INDEPENDENCE DAY OF ISRAEL.

REMEZ, DAVID. Israeli statesman (b. Kopust, Russia, 1886; d. Jerusalem, 1951). As a young man, Remez taught in White Russian villages and in Warsaw and had verses published in *Ha-Shilo'ah.* In 1911 he went to Constantinople to study law. In 1913 he immigrated to Eretz Israel, where he engaged in agricultural work in Kastina, Karkur, and Zikhron Ya'akov and was active in war refugee relief work. Moving to Tel Aviv, he helped found Ahdut Avoda in 1919 and the Histadrut in 1920 and, until 1927, headed the Bureau for Public Works (later Solel Boneh). For 13 years he was secretary-general of Histadrut and later directed various economic and settlement agencies.

From 1944 to 1949 Remez was chairman of the Va'ad Le'umi. In 1946 he was imprisoned in Latrun by the British Mandatory authorities with other yishuv leaders. On 1 March 1948, at a plenary session of the Va'ad Le'umi, he proposed the establishment of the Provisional Council of State, which was to be the legislative body of Israel until the First Knesset was convened. On 13 February 1949, the eve of the Knesset's first meeting, it was Remez who adjourned the final session of the Va'ad Le'umi. He was a Mapai member of the first two Knessets, serving as Minister of Communications from 1948 to 1950 and as Minister of Education and Culture in 1950–51.

His poetry and articles on contemporary events, linguistics, and archeology appeared in a posthumously published volume *Turim.*

G. KRESSEL

REPARATIONS, GERMANY-ISRAEL. *See* GERMAN-ISRAEL AGREEMENT.

RESHIMA MAMLAKHTIT. *See* RAFI.

RESHIMAT PO'ALEI YISRAEL. *See* RAFI.

RETAIL TRADES IN ISRAEL. *See* DISTRIBUTIVE TRADES IN ISRAEL.

RETURN, LAW OF. Law adopted on 5 July 1950 formally establishing the principle that the State of Israel is open to every Jew wishing to settle there. The declared aim of the Zionist movement was the reestablishment of Jewish sovereignty in the Land of Israel, the ultimate objective being the *"ingathering of exiles." From the early 19th century, Jews wishing to settle in what was then Ottoman-ruled Eretz Israel encountered difficulties in gaining admission to the country. During the period of British rule, large numbers of Jews were allowed to immigrate to Palestine, the number of arrivals varying in accordance with changing political circumstances. The right of Jews to settle in their homeland was the crucial element in the relationship between the Zionist movement and the British mandatory power, and the last few years of British administration were characterized by mounting tension within the yishuv caused by the drastic curtailment of immigration, promulgated in the White Paper of 1939. Israel's Declaration of Independence of 14 May 1948, proclaimed: "The State will be open to Jewish immigration, and for the ingathering of exiles." To give legal effect to this principle, the Knesset, on 5 July 1950, enacted the Law of Return (see inset).

This law was amended on 23 August 1954, to authorize the Minister of the Interior to deny an immigrant's visa to "a person with a criminal past, likely to endanger public welfare." It was further amended on 10 March 1970 by the addition of a definition of a Jew. Section 4B provides that "for the purposes of this Law, "Jew" means a person who was born of a Jewish mother or has become converted to Judaism, and who is not a member of another religion."

The underlying theory of this law is that a Jew in the Diaspora is a potential citizen of the Jewish State and is entitled by right to settle in Israel. He may exercise this right at any time, either when applying for an immigrant visa or after establishing residence. In pursuance of this principle, a person arriving in Israel on an immigrant visa acquires Israeli nationality as from the date of his arrival (Nationality Law of 1 April 1952).

The Law of Return does not apply to Jews or other persons wishing to enter the country as tourists or as temporary residents. These cases, as well as those of persons wishing to enter the country as immigrants, are regulated by the "Entry into Israel Law" of 26 August 1952. Persons entering Israel otherwise than under the Law of Return may acquire Israeli nationality through naturalization.

It was inevitable that the Law of Return would call for a definition of the term "Jew." The controversy over "Who is a Jew?" has raged since the early days of the State and continues unabated, leading at times to political crises. In general, the religious rather than the ethnic element was the determining criterion, the exception being the Brother Daniel (Rufeisen) case: a Jew who had converted in Poland to Catholicism, and subsequently been admitted to the priesthood, claimed the status of a Jew under the Law of Return. The Supreme Court ruled (H.C. 72/62) by a majority vote that the term "Jew" is to be interpreted in accordance with its popular meaning, and therefore rejected Rufeisen's claim. He later acquired Israeli nationality by naturalization.

The definition of the term "Jew" in the 1970 Amendment to the Law of Return did not terminate the controversy over this issue. This amendment, which provided that a Jew is an individual born of a Jewish mother or converted to Judaism, was in all respects a *halakhic* definition, i.e., in accordance with Jewish religious law. It was introduced in the Knesset as a joint initiative of the then-dominant Labor Party and the National Religious Party and was passed by an overwhelming majority of the Knesset, against the opposition of the small Agudat Israel party. The demand of the latter to add the words "in accordance with the *halakha*" (i.e., Jewish religious law) after the words "converted to Judaism" was rejected. Since then Agudat Israel, supported by the National Religious Party, has agitated unremittingly in favor of adding to the definition of "conversion to Judaism" the words "in accordance with the *halakha*." The immediate result of such a change, if adopted, would be to deny an immigrant visa to a person converted to Judaism by rabbis affiliated with non-Orthodox congregations.

S.Z. ABRAMOV

The Law of Return states:

1. Every Jew has the right to immigrate to the country.

2. (a) Immigration shall be on the basis of immigration visas.

(b) Immigrant visas shall be issued to any Jew expressing a desire to settle in Israel, except if the Minister of Interior is satisfied that the applicant:

(i) acts against the Jewish nation; or

(ii) may threaten the public health or State security, or

(iii) is a person with a criminal past, likely to endanger public welfare.

3. (a) A Jew who comes to Israel and after his arrival expresses a desire to settle there may, while in Israel, obtain an immigrant certificate.

(b) The exceptions listed in Article 2 (b) shall apply also with respect to the issue of an immigrant certificate, but a person shall not be regarded as a threat to public health as a result of an illness that he contracts after his arrival in Israel.

4. Every Jew who migrated to the country before this law goes into effect, and every Jew who was born in the country either before or after the coming into force of the law shall be deemed to be a person who has come to this country as an immigrant under this law.

Rights of members of 4A. (a) The rights of a Jew under this Law and the rights of an immigrant under the Nationality family Law, 5712–1952 (2), as well as the rights of an immigrant under any other enactment, are also vested in a child and grandchild of a Jew, the spouse of a Jew, the spouse of a child of a Jew and the spouse of a grandchild of a Jew, except for a person who has been a Jew and has voluntarily changed his religion.

(b) It shall be immaterial whether or not a Jew by whose right a right under subsection (a) is claimed is still alive and whether or not he has immigrated to Israel.

(c) The restrictions and conditions prescribed in respect of a Jew or an immigrant by or under this Law or by the enactments referred to in subsection (a) shall also apply to a person who claims a right under subsection (a).

Definition 4B. For the purposes of this Law, "Jew" means a person who was born of a Jewish mother or has become converted to Judaism and who is not a member of another religion.

5. The Minister of the Interior is delegated to enforce this law and he may enact regulations in connection with its implementation and for the issue of immigrant visas and immigrant certificates. Regulations for the purposes of section 4A and 4B shall require the approval of the Constitution, Legislation and Judicial Committee of the Knesset.

REVADIM. Kibbutz in the southern coastal plain, 5 mi. (8 km.) south of Gedera. The original kibbutz of this name was established in the Etzion Bloc in 1947. Its settlers fell into Jordanian captivity on 13 May 1948 and on their release in November, 1948, founded the present kibbutz. They were later joined by pioneer immigrants from Bulgaria and elsewhere. The kibbutz has intensive farming and an industrial enterprise. The name, "terraces," records their first work in the mountainous Etzion Bloc. East of the present kibbutz is the large site of the ancient Philistine city of Ekron, where excavations began in the 1980s. Population (1987), 372.

E. ORNI

REVISIONISTS (Union of Zionists-Revisionists-Ha-Tzohar). Zionist political party, founded in 1925 by Vladimir *Jabotinsky. It reflected the demand in Zionist ranks for a revision of the Zionist Executive's conciliatory policy toward the British mandatory government and of the system and tempo of the Zionist settlement activity in Palestine.

Based on Herzl's concept of Zionism as an essentially political movement, Revisionist ideology considered Chaim Weizmann's policy of unconditional priority for the advancement of Jewish economic positions in Palestine within the steadily deteriorating political situation as self-defeating. The Revisionist stand, formulated by Jabotinsky, was to "buy acres, build houses, but never to forget politics; ninety percent of Zionism may consist of tangible settlement, and only ten percent of politics, but that ten percent is the precondition of success and the ultimate guarantee of survival." In the Revisionist conception, the Zionist aim was to provide an integral solution to the worldwide Jewish problem in all its aspects—political, economic, and spiritual. To attain this objective, the Revisionists demanded that the entire mandated territory of Palestine, on both sides of the Jordan River, be turned into a Jewish state with a Jewish majority. In 1928 the Revisionists were instrumental in forming the Seventh (Palestine) Dominion League, which consisted of a group of British and Jewish political leaders who advocated the implementation of Colonel Josiah Wedgwood's plan for the establishment in Palestine of a Jewish Dominion within the British Commonwealth.

The contention of the Revisionists was that deliberate worldwide political pressure must be exerted in order to induce Britain to abide by the letter and spirit of the Palestine Mandate. They stressed the imperative necessity of bringing to Palestine the largest number of Jews within the shortest possible time, even at the risk of postponing the attainment of highly desirable social, economic, and educational goals. Since agricultural settlement was a slow process, the Revisionists focused attention on industrial development, middle-class settlement, individual initiative, and private capital. Major Revisionist demands also included the reestablishment of the *Jewish Legion, the formation of Jewish units within the Palestine security forces, and systematic training of Jewish youths for defense as an essential feature of their education.

Before World War II, Eastern and Central Europe, the Jewish distress areas, constituted the stronghold of Revisionism. The impoverished Jewish masses, anxious to emigrate, rallied to the Revisionist banner of fast, large-scale aliya. In addition to the regular Revisionist organization (Ha-Tzohar), a wide network of subsidiary groups sprang up. The Revisionist union of Jewish veterans (*Berit ha-Hayal), founded in 1932, had 23,000 registered members by 1937. By 1938 Berit Trumpeldor (*Betar), the Revisionist youth organization, had more than 100,000 members in 26 countries. Orthodox adherents were represented by Ahdut Israel, women by Berit Nashim Le'umiyot, high school students by Masada, collegiate youth by Yavne ve-Yodefeth, and sports by Nordia. The financial instrument of the movement was the *Tel Hai Fund.

Within the World Zionist Organization (WZO), Revisionism met with increasingly strong resistance, particularly from the labor groups. Tension reached its peak after the assassination of Hayim *Arlosoroff, the outstanding labor leader and member of the Zionist Executive. The murder was ascribed to two young Revisionists, Abraham Stavsky and Zvi Rosenblatt, who later were acquitted.

The World Union of Zionists-Revisionists was founded in 1925 as an integral part of the WZO. The seat of the Union's Executive alternated between Paris and London, with Jabotinsky as president and Meir Grossman and Richard Lichtheim as vice-presidents. The Russian-language weekly **Rassviet*, published in Paris and edited by Jabotinsky, Michael Berchin, and Joseph Schechtman, served as the movement's central organ. The Yiddish weekly *Der Naier Weg* (edited by Yeshayahu Klinov and Joseph Schechtman) appeared in Paris and, later, in London.

The Revisionists strongly opposed expansion of the Jewish Agency by including prominent non-Zionists, which, they felt, would dilute the Zionist content, undermine the democratic character, and hamstring the freedom of political action of the Zionist movement. From 1929, when the expanded Jewish Agency took over the political prerogatives of the WZO, Jabotinsky consistently urged increasing independence for the Revisionist Union. In 1933 he assumed personal responsibility for the conduct of Revisionist affairs, a move endorsed by 93.8 percent of the membership. His opponents, headed by Meir Grossman and Robert Stricker, seceded and founded the *Jewish State party, which remained a small splinter group until it merged with the Revisionist Union in 1946.

A major Revisionist political activity was the 1934 worldwide petition signed by 600,000 Jews and addressed to Great Britain's King and Parliament and to the governments of 24 countries of which the petitioners were citizens, urging the opening of the gates of Palestine to Jewish immigration. Late in the fall of 1934, Jabotinsky and David Ben-Gurion met in London and negotiated three important agreements. The first enjoined all Zionist parties to refrain from employing means of party warfare other than political ideological discussion and specifically outlawed libel, slander, and insult of individuals and groups. The second offered a comrpomise between the Histadrut and the *Histadrut ha-Ovedim ha-Le'umit (National Workers Federation), including the highly controversial issues of strikes and compulsory arbitration. The third provided for the suspension of the two-year-old Revisionist boycott of the national funds and the restoration of the right of members of Betar to receive immigration certificates. Ratified by the Revisionist World Conference, the agreements were overwhelmingly rejected by a referendum among the membership of Histadrut.

In 1935 a referendum held among Revisionists resulted in their secession from the WZO and the establishment of an independent *New Zionist Organization (NZO). Eleven years later, when ideological and tactical differences between the NZO and the WZO had diminished, the NZO decided to give up its separate existence. The United Zionists-Revisionists (the merger of the Revisionist Union and the Jewish State party) participated in the elections to the 22nd Zionist Congress (1946), to which it sent 42 delegates.

On 14 May 1948, two Revisionist representatives were signers of Israel's Declaration of Independence. In the elections to the First Knesset, the *Herut (Freedom) Party, founded by the *Irgun Tzeva'i Leumi, and the Revisionists put forward separate lists of candidates. After a year of negotiations, unity was restored in the form of the worldwide Berit Herut ha-Tzohar (World Union of Herut-Zionists-Revisionists), with Herut as its only territorial organization in Israel and Ha-Tzohar as the sole standard-bearer of the Union in the Diaspora countries.

At the August, 1948, session of the Zionist Actions Committee, two Revisionist representatives, Meir Grossman and Joseph Schechtman, were elected to the executive of the Jewish Agency and the WZO, which for the first time in its history included all Zionist parties. At the 23rd Zionist Congress (1951), at which the Revisionists were represented by 33 delegates, the labor parties prevented the election of Revisionist representatives to the Executive. The exclusion of Revisionists from participation in the Executive was continued at the 24th Congress (1956), in which the Herut-Revisionist delegation numbered 52, and at the 25th Congress (1960–61). In March, 1963, when the Zionist General Council elected Joseph Schechtman to the Executive, the exclusion came to an end.

The seat of the World Executive of Berit Herut-ha-Tzohar is in Tel Aviv. There are branches in the Diaspora countries. J. SCHECHTMAN—S. KATZ

REVIVIM. Kibbutz in the Negev, 21 mi. (34 km.) south of Beersheba. It was founded in 1943 as the southernmost of three early outposts set up to explore Negev conditions. The 15 young settlers experimented with diverting flash floodwaters for irrigation and other uses and with farming various crops. In 1947, with the outbreak of the hostilities which culminated in the War of Independence, Revivim repulsed Bedouin attacks and after May 1948, held out against the invading Egyptian army until Israel forces broke through to relieve it in December, 1948. The kibbutz had to be built up again from scratch. It developed farming, including tropical and subtropical crops, as well as industry. The original patio-fortress was reconstructed as a local museum. The name, "Dew Drops" is from Psalm 65:11. Population (1987), 650. E. ORNI

RHODESIA AND ZAMBIA, ZIONISM IN. *See* ZIMBABWE AND ZAMBIA, ZIONISM IN.

RIBALOW, MENAHEM. Literary critic and editor (b. Chudnov, Ukraine, Russia, 1896; d. New York, 1953). Ribalow began his literary career in Russia. At the time of the Communist Revolution in November, 1917, he was living in Moscow, where he worked for the Hebrew daily *Ha-Am* (The People). In 1921 he settled in the United States, where he became an outstanding standard-bearer of the Hebraist movement. For more than 30 years he was the editor of the American Hebrew weekly **Ha-Do'ar*. He also edited *Sefer Ha-Shana*, an annual literary omnibus (11 vols.). Shortly before his death he initiated a Hebrew literary journal, *Mabu'a*, and published an anthology of Hebrew poetry in the United States. His own works were published in five volumes. Ribalow participated in Zionist conferences and lectured extensively on Hebrew literature and culture.

H. LEAF

RIFTIN, YAKOV. A leader of Kibbutz Artzi shel Ha-Shomer ha-Tza'ir (b. Kolo, 1907; d. Kibbutz Ein Shemer, 1977). In the 1920s Riftin was one of the first leaders of Ha-Shomer ha-Tza'ir in Poland and worked to consolidate and run the League for Labor Eretz Israel. Immigrating to Palestine in 1929, he joined Kibbutz Ein Shemer, and was a prominent leader of his movement on the executive of the Histadrut. He was a civilian leader of the Hagana and represented it in the political domain. A member of the Zionist political delegation to the United Nations in 1947, Riftin subsequently served as political secretary of Mapam and was a Mapam member of the Knesset. Riftin was close to Moshe Sneh when the latter was about to secede but he did not follow him. In 1969 he stood at the head of the opposition to the founding of the Alignment between the Labor Party and Mapam. He left Mapam and founded the Independent Left Zionist Socialist Alliance. Its failure ended his career in politics and in public life.

M. MINTZ

RIMALT, ELIMELEKH S. Israeli politician and educator (b. Bochnia, Galicia, Austria, 1907). Rimalt received a doctorate from the University of Vienna in 1931, and the following year was ordained to the rabbinate at the Vienna Rabbinical Seminary. From 1933 until 1938 he was rabbi of Jewish communities in the Tirol and Vorarlberg. Thereafter he served as director of the Emigration Department of the Jewish Religious Community of Vienna. Settling in Ramat Gan in 1939, he was the principal of elementary and secondary schools. From 1947 to 1953 he directed the Ramat Gan Department of Education. In 1948 he was a member of the Committee on Education and Security of the provisional government of Israel.

Rimalt was first elected to the Knesset in 1951, and was a member until 1977, representing the Liberal party. From 1952-1955 he served as chairman of the Liberal Labor movement in the Histadrut. He was a member of the Knesset Foreign Affairs and Defense Committee and, from 1965, served as chairman of the Committee on Education and Culture. He was chairman of a special Knesset committee for reforms in the educational system (1966–68) and of the Executive Committee of the Liberal party (1971–73). Rimalt was a delegate to the 11th (1956) and 13th (1958) sessions of the UN General Assembly.

E. HOTER

RINGEL, MICHAEL. Zionist leader in Poland (b. Borislav, Galicia, Austria, 1880; d. USSR, during World War II). Ringel studied law at the University of Vienna and opened a law practice in Galicia. While still a high school student, he had been active in the Zionist movement of Galicia and eventually became one of its leaders. In 1907 he was elected to the Central Committee of the Austrian Zionist Federation and to the Central Committee of the Zionist Organization of Galicia. A General Zionist, he attended the Seventh Zionist Congress (1905) and many subsequent Congresses. In 1918 he was chairman of the Jewish National Council of Eastern Galicia, and in 1919 a member of the Comité des Délégations Juives at the Paris Peace Conference.

A contributor to numerous Zionist publications in Polish, German, and Yiddish and the author of several pamphlets, Ringel helped found (1918) in Cracow the *Nowy Dziennik*, the first Polish-language Zionist daily. In 1926 he helped found in Lvov the Yiddish Zionist daily *Der Morgen*. He was a member of the Polish Senate from 1922 to 1928. After the occupation of eastern Poland by Soviet forces in 1939, he was arrested in Lvov, where he then resided, and deported to the Soviet Union, where he died.

RINGELBLUM, EMANUEL. Educator, historian, Po'ale Zion leader, and an organizer of the Warsaw ghetto revolt (b. Buchach, Galicia, Austria, 1900; d. Warsaw, 1944). From 1920 to 1927 Ringelblum served on the Central Committee of the Labor Zionist Young Workers' Federation of Poland and wrote for its journal. He taught history at a high school in Warsaw until 1939 and also was active in the Left Po'ale Zion movement. In the last few years before World War II he was on the staff of the American Jewish Joint Distribution Committee (JDC) and wrote studies on the history of the Jews in Poland.

In the late summer of 1939 he was in Geneva, attending the 21st Zionist Congress. When news of Nazi mobilization reached the Congress, Ringelblum and the other representatives of his party returned to Poland. Ringelblum set up JDC soup kitchens and organized resistance in the Warsaw ghetto. At the same time he gathered a staff to help him record the story of the ghetto. He was killed in March, 1944, after the Gestapo discovered the underground shelter in Warsaw where he, his family, and other Jews were hiding. His journal was found after the war and published in 1958 under the title *Notes from the Warsaw Ghetto*.

RISHON LE-ZION. City in the coastal plain, 7 mi. (12 km.) southeast of Tel Aviv. It was founded as a moshava in 1882 by 10 immigrants headed by Z.D. *Levontin; they were joined by Bilu pioneers who had gone through some farm training at Mikve Yisrael. The payment of the land price, search for water, building of homes, and purchase of farming implements soon totally exhausted the settlers' resources, and they were enabled to continue through the help extended by Baron Edmond de Rothschild. The Baron switched Rishon le-Zion's farming program from grain cultivation to viticulture, and later almond groves. In 1889 he set up there the large Carmel Oriental wine cellars. His administrators, however, stifled the settlers' initiative. The situation improved when the Jewish Colonization Association took over in 1900. The world's first Hebrew kindergarten and elementary school were opened here in the 1880s. The original settlers were joined by laborers who immigrated from eastern Europe, and later from Yemen. Herzl's visit to the moshava in 1898 was a landmark in its history. In World War I, the Turkish governor allocated to Rishon le-Zion 5,000 acres of sand dunes in the west as far

The wine press in Rishon le-Zion. [Central Zionist Archives]

as the sea shore. The moshava had meanwhile made citriculture its principal farming branch. In 1920, it numbered 2,200 inhabitants. In the 1930s, industry began to take root, besides agriculture. In 1948 it was a town with a population of 12,000 and grew rapidly in the first years of Israel's statehood. Its major growth rates were registered from the 1970s onward, when it had become part of the Tel Aviv conurbation's outer ring. The name, "First in Zion," derives from Isaiah 41:27. Population (1987), 120,100.

E. ORNI

RISHON LE-ZION. *See* RABBINATE OF ISRAEL.

Israel Rokach [Zionist Archives]

ROKACH: Family of early Zionist settlers in Eretz Israel.

Shimon Rokach. Communal leader in Eretz Israel (b. Jerusalem, 1863; d. Vienna, 1922). Born to a family that had immigrated to Eretz Israel from Galicia, he moved (1884) from Jerusalem to Jaffa, then the country's main port of entry, to supervise road tax collections, an office he and his father had leased from the Turkish government. He formed the Ezrat Israel organization, which founded a Jewish hospital and purchased land for a new cemetery, and in 1887 he helped found Neveh Tzedek, the first Jewish neighborhood in Jaffa.

In 1890 he was one of the founders of the United Ashkenazi-Sephardi Jewish Community of Jaffa, serving as its president for many years. In 1900 he was instrumental in founding Pardes, the cooperative citrus-marketing organization, and was its general manager. Rokach's contacts with Arab leaders benefited the Jewish community of Jaffa as well as other Jewish settlements in Eretz Israel. During World War I Rokach supplied lumber to the Turkish Army for locomotive fuel.

Israel Rokach, Shimon's son, Israeli public servant, General Zionist party leader, and Cabinet minister (b. Jaffa, 1896; d. Tel Aviv, 1959). He studied in Switzerland, first in Lausanne and then at the Federal Polytechnic School in Zurich, graduating as an electrical engineer in 1920. After working in England for two years, he returned in 1922 to Palestine, where he combined business activities with a career of municipal leadership in the rapidly growing city of Tel Aviv.

Rokach was a member of the Tel Aviv Municipal Council (1922–53) and in 1936, after having served as deputy mayor on several occasions, was appointed mayor by the British High Commissioner to succeed Meir Dizengoff. A member of the Council of the Federation of General Zionists in Palestine, he was one of the founders of the newspaper *Ha-Boker*, and a member of its board of directors, and served on the Executive Committee on Education of the Keneset Yisrael. He was also president of the Maccabi athletic association.

Suspected of helping the Jewish resistance to British rule and to the 1939 White Paper policy, he was arrested by the British Mandatory authorities in 1947 and detained at Latrun with several other mayors of Jewish municipalities. In 1949 he was elected to the Knesset, serving as a representative of the General Zionist party there until his death. He continued to serve as mayor of Tel Aviv until December, 1952, when he was appointed Minister of the Interior. Resigning from his Cabinet post when the General Zionist party left the Government coalition in 1955, he again sought the mayoralty of Tel Aviv, but his party named Hayim Levanon instead. He served as Deputy Speaker during the Third Knesset. During his 16 years of service as mayor of Tel Aviv, Rokach led the largest city in Israel through an important phase of growth and development.

ROKEAH, ELEAZAR. Early pioneer in Eretz Israel and member of Hovevei Zion (b. Jerusalem, 1854; d. Drogobych, Galicia, Austria, 1914). After receiving a traditional Jewish education in Jerusalem, Rokeah was married at the age of 13 and moved to Safed. Drawn in early youth to the Haskala (Jewish Enlightenment) movement, he wrote articles, most of them anonymously, for Hebrew newspapers outside Eretz Israel on the state of the Jewish community of Safed. He criticized the communal leaders and the Haluka (religious charity) system and advocated the establishment of Jewish agricultural settlements. His activities earned him the wrath of communal leaders. In 1878 a group of Safed Jews, including some followers of Rokeah, founded a settlement at Ge-Oni (where Rosh Pina was later established), and Rokeah attempted to raise funds to aid them.

In the early 1880s he was active in Romania. He helped found the Hovevei Zion movement there and disseminated its ideas in the Hebrew *Yezre'el* and the Yiddish *Die Hoffnung* and *Der Imigrant*, newspapers he had founded. From Romania he went to Galicia and Russia. In 1888 he returned to Eretz Israel as secretary to Kalonymus-Ze'ev Wissotzky, who made him secretary of the Jaffa office of the Hovevei Zion. Rokeah was a sharp critic of Baron Edmond de Rothschild's administration of settlements in Eretz Israel. After the advent of Herzl he vigorously fought political Zionism until the end of his life.

In 1897 he left Eretz Israel again, living in Romania and Galicia and never remaining long in one place. The author of hundreds of newspaper articles, he founded and edited the Hebrew papers *Talpiot* (Jassy, 1898–99) and *Ha-Yarden* (Buchach, 1906). He died in poverty.

ROMANIA, RELATIONS WITH ISRAEL. Israel's first representative to Romania, the artist Reuven Rubin, arrived in Bucharest in September, 1948, but for many years relations were cool, with Romania following the lead set by the USSR. Trade was modest and cultural ties sparse. Improvement followed as Romania grew more independent of the USSR. The first high-level Romanian economic delegation visited Israel in March, 1967, followed shortly afterward by a reciprocal Israel trade delegation to Bucharest, headed by the Minister of Finance. Comprehensive trade agreements were signed. The trade balance reached $20,000,000 in 1968. Cultural relations also expanded and tourism grew. After the 1967 Six-Day War, Romania was the only eastern bloc country to retain its diplomatic relations with Israel and declined to participate in the Soviet anti-Israel campaign. In 1969, diplomatic representation in both Bucharest and Tel Aviv was raised to embassy level. Romania continued to maintain a delicate fabric of political and economic relations, and generally permitted the emigration of Romanian Jews to Israel. The two countries maintained a friendly dialogue, despite disagreements on a number of basic issues connected with the Israel-Arab conflict, including the Jerusalem Law, the Golan Heights Law, and attitudes to the Palestine Liberation Organization.

In the framework of this dialogue, Romanian President Nicolae Ceaucescu played an important, if not decisive, role in Egyptian President Anwar al-Sadat's visit to Jerusalem in November, 1977. Ceausescu was also active in different stages of the Lebanon War and was instrumental in the exchange of prisoners-of-war between Israel and Syria and the PLO.

The two countries maintain cultural and scientific ties in the framework of a cultural agreement signed between them in 1979, and the regular economic relations include commercial exchanges and cooperation in the fields of agriculture, marine transport, aviation, and tourism.

Israeli exports to Romania are composed principally of phosphates, pest controls, citrus fruits, and electrodes. Imports from Romania mainly consist of metals, wood and its by-products, chemicals, and food products. For Israel, the best year of trade exchange was 1980: $35,000,000—export and $48,000,000—import.

Until the end of 1989 the regular framework of relations between Romania and Israel stemmed from two principal factors. The first was related to the personality and qualities of Nicolae Ceaucescu, a political maneuverer in domestic and foreign policy. The second formed part of the basic principles of his general foreign policy, which included recognition of the independence of all countries of the world and respect for their sovereignty, the desire to develop relations with all countries of the world, and support of the solution of all conflicts by peaceful means through negotiation. Hence the decision to maintain diplomatic ties with Israel and the support of the Camp David Accords and the Israel-Egyptian peace treaty, in opposition to the position of the other countries of the Soviet bloc. After the major changes in eastern Europe at the end of 1989, other countries reestablished diplomatic relations with Israel and the Romanian position instead of being exceptional was now part of a general pattern. A. GEFEN

ROMANIA, ZIONISM IN.

From the Pre-Herzlian Period up to World War I. The Jews of Romania were the forerunners not only of the Zionist idea but also of its implementation in the modern period. Yishuv Eretz Israel societies were organized in the towns of Nicoresti and of Tecuci in southern Moldavia in 1873, and in 1874 Moshe David Schub organized another group in Moinesti, traveling to Eretz Israel in the same year to buy land for settlement. As Romanian Jewry's hopes of improving its situation were disappointed, Yishuv Eretz Israel societies multiplied, under a variety of names and groups such as Hevrat Yishuv Eretz Israel al Yedei Avodat Adama (Society to Settle Eretz Israel by Working the Land) and Hevrat Ovedei ha-Adama be-Eretz ha-Kodesh appeared. In 1880 Eleazar Rokeah founded an Eretz Israel settlement society in Bucharest, and the prominent Jewish leader of the town of Galati, Samuel Pineles, founded another in 1881. In November 1881 over 20 societies existed, and the necessity of coordinating the activities for settlement of Eretz Israel became apparent. On 18 November 1881 a preparatory meeting of representatives of the various societies was held in Focsani, and on 11–12 January 1882 they convened a meeting with the participation of 56 representatives of 33 societies, representing about 70,000 people who wished to immigrate to Eretz Israel —the first representative gathering of the Jewish public in modern times. The conference's principal resolution determined that "the aim of the Movement is the solution of the problem of Romanian Jewry by immediate immigration to Eretz Israel, agricultural settlement there, and work of the settlers with their own hands." The conference elected a central committee, and Samuel Pineles was appointed secretary to centralize the movement's activity.

In March 1882 an exploratory delegation was sent out, and Schub subsequently purchased the lands of Gei Oni for the Moinesti society. In August, 1882, 228 settlers, mostly from Moinesti, sailed for Eretz Israel on the S.S. *Thetis*. In October, Emil Franck purchased the lands of Zamarin (Zikhron Ya'akov) and Tantura.

In late 1882 about 10,000 Romanian Jews registered for emigration to Eretz Israel, but the financial crisis in the settlements and the Galati committee's inability to assist them nearly destroyed the movement. The Hovevei Zion Kattowitz Conference in September, 1883, and the subsequent convention in Galati in 1894 resurrected it under the name *Hovevei Zion*, with Pineles serving as its president until the First Zionist Congress. Herzl's *Der Judenstaat*, translated in 1896 into Romanian by Martin Spiner of Botosani, made a strong impression not only on the *Hovevei Zion*, but on the majority of Romanian Jewry. The Romanian *Hovevei Zion* societies were the first to offer organized support to Herzl and his activities. The Third conference of *Hovevei Zion*, held on 14–15 April 1897, with representatives of most of the Romanian Jewish community participating, expressed massive support for Herzl. In addition to three of the movement's representatives (Pineles, Dr. Karpel Lippe, and Heinrich Rosenbaum) to the First Zionist Congress, representatives of *B'nai B'rith*, which also wished to participate in the Congress, were elected. The Romanian delegation was received with great honor, and the Congress was opened by a speech of the oldest delegate, Lippe. Pineles was elected vice-president of the Congress.

During the fourth conference of Hovevei Zion in 1898, in Galati, the Basle Program was accepted. The Zionist idea quickly spread and by 1899 there were about 136 Zionist associations in Romania. Initially the Movement's main supporters came from the middle classes and the poor. From the early 20th century, however, the Zionist movement grew stronger and as Romanian anti-Semitism increased, effectively barring the large-scale assimilationist attempts of the Jewish intelligentsia, the movement's ranks were swelled by a number of intellectuals including Rabbi Dr. Jacob Niemirower, and the historian Moshe Schwarzfeld.

Pineles was chairman of the Zionist Federation until 1905 and was succeeded by Heinrich Rosenbaum who occupied an important post in the Zionist Organization's Colonial Bank; Heinrich Schein was chairman of the Zionist Federation from 1908 until the end of World War I. The Zionist Organization had its center in Galati until World War I, but a Zionist spiritual center existed in Jassy, where in 1909 the poet and writer Adolf Steuerman-Rodion brought out *Rassaritul*, the first Zionist publication in Romanian. (Most previous Zionist publications had been in Yiddish.) On the eve of World War I, A.L. Zissu published a periodical in Hebrew, *Ha-Mekitz*, in Piatra Neamtz, conducting a publicity campaign for the study of the Hebrew language. In 1913 Ha-Sharon, a cultural association, was created by a group of Zionist intellectuals in Bucharest, headed by Dr. Niemirower. Zionist ideas also penetrated to schools; in 1909 pupils' clubs were created in Focsani and Galati. In 1914 a Zionist students' society, Hasmonaea, was organized in Bucharest University; it published a journal of the same name in the inter-war period. With the entry of Romania into the war in the summer of 1916 and the occupation of part of the country by the Germans, Zionist activity ceased. The Zionist movement received a new impetus with the Balfour Declaration, although the German occupation prevented any public display of enthusiasm.

Between the Two World Wars. Following World War I Romania enlarged her territory with the provinces of Bukovina, Bessarabia, and Transylvania. Jews living in these areas, who differed from the Jews of "Old" Romania both in their historical past and their cultural background, maintained autonomous Zionist Organizations, working with the Zionist Organization of Old Romania only in certain cases such as the fight for Jewish civil rights in Romania and the creation of the "Jewish Party." The youth organizations had joint frameworks in Old Romania, Bessarabia, and Bukovina.

The Zionist Convention which met in fall 1919 transferred the center of the Romanian Zionist Organization (the new name of the Romanian Zionist Federation) from Galati to Bucharest. Adolf Bernard served as the chairman of the new organization's executive from its inception until 1931. This Zionist leadership, which held office for a record length of time, laid the organizational foundations for Zionist work in the Old Kingdom. The movement engaged principally in raising capital for the National Funds, endeavoring to attract affluent Jewish circles to Zionist ideas. Wishing to keep the Zionist Organization intact, and influenced by political considerations of the World Zionist Movement, the Romanian Zionist Organization adopted a neutral position in the country's internal politics. Most of the young generation of Zionists thought that the Jews should demand national autonomy together with involvement in Romanian political life. In the years following the war all the Jewish

Zionist center in Bessarabia, 1922. [Jabotinsky Institute]

Demonstration to welcome Zionist delegation, Belzy, Bessarabia, 1921. [Central Zionist Archives]

organizations (Dr. W. Filderman's Union of Romanian Jews—UER—and the Zionist Movement) fought to obtain civil rights in the spirit of the Paris minorities treaty. They formed a list of Jewish delegates under the name Menora for the elections to the Romanian parliament, but the elections were rigged, and not one candidate succeeded in entering parliament. A.L. Zissu's journal *Mantuirea* ("The Deliverance") campaigned strongly for the creation of a Jewish political party. This journal ceased to appear in 1922 after its editorial offices were damaged in anti-Semitic riots by Bucharest university students.

The Zionist Organization's organ *Stiri Din Lumea Evreiasca* (News from the Jewish World) first came out in the same year and continued to appear until 1940. In 1920 a group of Zionists from Bessarabia and radical Zionists founded Tze'irei Zion in Romania. In 1924 Samuel Stern (Cochavi) brought out the weekly *Renasterea Noastra* (Our Revival), attracting a large group of Zionist intellectuals who became the radical faction militating for Zionist involvement in Jewish politics in Romania. Following Vladimir

Jabotinsky's visit to Romania in 1925, his supporters organized into a Revisionist Party and began publishing the journal *Drumuri Noua* (New Directions).

Religious Zionism was expressed in the Mizrachi movement, headed by Rabbi Zvi Guttman and by, Ha-Po'el ha-Mizrachi and Women's Mizrachi.

The emergence of the various parties aggravated the disagreements in the Zionist movement and led to a change of leadership in the Zionist Organization at the 19th Conference, when the coalition of radicals (the *Renasterea* group) and the Tze'irei Zion headed by S. Stern-Cochavi replaced the long-standing executive of the General Zionists with A. Bernard.

In 1932 a new coalition was formed with the two aforesaid factions, together with Meir Grossman's Revisionist faction (Jewish State Party) and the General Zionists, led by Mishu Weissman-Amir (later to be the first Israeli ambassador to the Benelux countries).

1933 saw the formation of a small coalition with members of *Renasteraea* and the Jewish State Party led by Philip Rosenstein, as chairman of the Executive.

At the same time there was a split in the Revisionist Movement; the majority formed the New Zionist Organization under Edgar Kanner, while the minority remained in the Zionist Organization as the Jewish State Party led by Philip Rosenstein.

In 1934 Leon Mizrahi was chairman of the executive. In 1935 Rabbi Dr. Jacob Niemerower formed a coalition among all the Zionist factions (except for the Jewish Party), which he led until his death in 1939, guiding the Zionist Organization through the difficult period of rising anti-Semitism, the Goga-Cuza government, and the state dictatorship, up until the outbreak of World War II.

A section of Romania's Zionists, the General Zionists, were active in the Union of Romanian Jews (UER) led by Dr. Wilhelm Filderman who opposed independent political activity by the Jews of Romania and limited his activity to the defense of Jewish civil rights through pacts with the Romanian ruling parties; Filderman was a member of the Union of the Jewish Communities direction and in 1929 was elected UER member of the enlarged Jewish Agency. Other Zionist factions, such as the Radicals, the Jewish Party, etc., supported the approach of the Zionist organizations of Bukovina, Bessarabia, and Transylvania, which favored an independent Jewish party to fight for the interests of the Jewish national minority. After many efforts they succeeded in 1931 in creating the Jewish Party, which intermittently managed to send five to six delegates to the Romanian parliament. The Party ceased activity in early 1938. The above situation imposed neutrality on the Zionist Organization in Romania and also explains the philanthropic nature of Zionist activity between the two world wars (activity for the Funds, the Shekel, emigration to Palestine, and assistance to the training farms).

Youth Movements. Most of the Zionist youth organizations commenced their activity after the war in Bukovina and in Bessarabia. Ha-Shomer ha-Tza'ir was created in Czernowitz by young people who returned from Vienna at the end of the war, and by 1924 it had spread to the other regions of Romania. At first the youth movements were devoid of pioneering or Jewish ideology.

In Bessarabia refugees from the USSR created He-Halutz which directed the young Zionists towards fulfillment as pioneers and immigrants to Palestine; they also acted as a catalyst for the creation of other youth movements. In Old Romania the various youth circles which came into being after the war united in the framework of the Asociatia Tineretului Sionist (Association of Zionist Youth—ATS).

In 1927 most of the ATS merged with Ha-Shomer ha-Tza'ir; later Ha-Noar ha-Tziyoni, Dror, Gordonia, Bnei Akiva, Betar, Habonim, Berit ha-Kana'im (the Jewish Party youth) came into being. In the various regions of Romania other youth movements existed which were connected to these movements: Busselia, Ha-Shomer, Barisia, Aviva, Benei Avoda, Ha-Oved, etc. Most of the groups were part of a single framework in Bukovina. Bessarabia, and the Old Kingdom, while maintaining separate organizations in Transylvania. The majority received agricultural or vocational training in the framework of He-Halutz in preparation for immigration to Palestine; in 1936 there were six permanent training farms and about 40 seasonal groups, including a fishing group. The number of halutzic (pioneering) immigrants was dependent upon the number of permits received and consequently subject to variation. The "boom" period seems to have been between 1920 and 1926 when 1,340 halutzim (pioneers) moved to Palestine. Immigration was subsequently restricted during certain periods by the Mandatory Government; between the end of 1937 and early 1938 about 180 halutzim immigrated. On 15 March 1938 He-Halutz was dismantled by the state dictatorship; after many efforts a semi-legal framework, Hakhsharat Olim, was set up and received authorization to create four training farms, which served as centers for the halutzim until 1941. Youth movement activity and pioneering aliya constituted the principal Zionist activities in Romania between the two wars.

Women's Organizations. The Asociatia Culturala a Femeilor Evreice (Cultural Association of Jewish Women—ACFE) was created after World War I and for a time was affiliated with WIZO. In 1937 it had about 5,000 members in 33 branches. The organization was active in the appeals of the Zionist funds, in welfare and assistance activities, and in support of the halutzic groups. In addition to the young women organized in the youth movements, there was an organization of young Avoda women affiliated to Young WIZO. The ACFE established the Ayanot agricultural school in Palestine.

World War II. In 1938 the Zionist movement in Romania passed through a difficult period, with the institution of King Carol II's dictatorship and the dismantling of the Jewish Party. The Zionist Organization continued its activity mainly towards increasing aliya, and with the occupation of Poland in 1939 endeavored to assist Jewish refugees arriving in Romania. As the only large Zionist movement still functioning in Europe, it also helped to organize legal and "illegal" immigration from Romania. With the occupation of Bessarabia and north Bukovina by the USSR (in accordance with the Ribbentrop-Molotov agreement), Zionism in Romania, and in particular the halutzic movement, suffered heavy losses; many of the halutzim were from these regions, and despairing of any chance of immigrating to Palestine, they left the Zionist movement.

In January 1940 the new executive formed under L. Mizrahi was faced with extreme anti-Semitic terrorism; power had been seized by the Iron Guard, the Romanian fascist party, and a dictatorship established by General Ion Antonescu. The Zionist leadership requested authorization to continue Zionist activity and immigration, and this was viewed positively by the Romanian regime, which wished to rid itself of the Jews in a "humanitarian" way. The anti-Jewish terror paralyzed Zionist activity and *inter alia* harmed the training groups of the halutzic movements; in January, 1941, at the time of their revolt members of the Iron Guard carried out a pogrom, arresting and torturing many members of the youth movements, and murdering Moshe Orikhovsky, director of the Palestine Office.

In spring 1941, following the aliya of some of the Zionist leaders, an executive was elected, composed of most of the Zionist parties, and headed by Moshe Benvenisti. He obtained official permission to continue Zionist activity, namely to continue organizing emigration to Palestine and to create frameworks for "training of immigrants" which made possible the continued existence and activities of the groups of halutzim and youth movements, albeit in a semi-clandestine way. With the outbreak of the war against the USSR and the increased Nazi influence-which led to the annihilation of the Jews of Bessarabia and Bukovina and serious harm to the Jews of Old Romania-the Zionist Movement became increasingly involved in Jewish community affairs, closely cooperating with the other Jewish organizations and in particular with the Union of Jewish Communities leadership and its president, Dr. Filderman.

In February 1942 the Centrala Evreilor (Jewish Center) was created, under the influence of the Nazis, as an alternative leadership to the legitimate Romanian Jewish leadership (the UER, which was dissolved in December 1941). After considerable hesitation the Zionist leadership decided to participate in the Center's activities in order to guide them in the desired direction. Theodor Loewenstein (Lavi), who was responsible for Jewish schools, intensified national Jewish education, but his activity ran counter to the designs of the Germans, and he was dismissed shortly after the banning of the Zionist movement in July, 1942. The dissolution of the Jewish organizations was followed by the formation of a clandestine leadership, Sfatul Evreiesc (The Jewish Council) under Chief Rabbi Dr. Alexander Safran, with the participation of M. Benvenisti and Dr. Filderman.

In March, 1943, the Zionist Organization, despite the opposition of the Nazis, managed to transfer a group of about 75 children via Bulgaria to Palestine; subsequent German pressure on Bulgaria, however, prevented the transfer of a second group of children.

In late 1943 there was serious disagreement in the Zionist Movement over Aliya Bet ("illegal" immigration) by sea, as demanded by the Jewish Agency delegation in Constantinople. Some of the Zionist and halutzic leaders were arrested in January, 1944. New leadership, comprised of a group of Zionist activists led by A.L. Zissu, immediately took over. With the aid of Romanian political personalities, members of the Red Cross, and foreign diplomats, Zissu obtained the release of the imprisoned Zionists in the summer of 1944. As the fortunes of the war changed and the climate in the Romanian regime improved, Zissu obtained official recognition for the Palestine Office and for himself as representative of the Jewish Agency and organizer of emigration; this status enabled him to issue official documents to Jewish refugees who had escaped from Poland and Hungary, thereby ensuring that they were not sent back into Nazi hands.

Zissu helped organize "illegal" immigration to Palestine, which was renewed in March, 1944. Most of the pioneer Zionist youth organizations continued to work underground, and their members and ex-members were largely responsible for the implementation of this emigration. A liaison network was created among the various regions to assist the flight of the refugees from Poland through Czernowitz (which was close to the Nazi-occupied territory) to the center of Romania. The halutzim also sent help to the deportation zones and to their comrades in the forced labor squads. Benvenisti managed to create training farms in order to maintain nuclei of pioneers. With the German occupation of Hungary, the halutzic movement established a number of rescue stations along the border (Turda and Arad), thus saving several thousand Hungarian refugees. Nine parachutists from the yishuv dropped into Romania between October 1943 and the Liberation (23 August 1944); four were captured and five reached the Zionist underground, guiding and encouraging the Zionist movement and the youth organizations in particular. Their activities ambraced aliya, rescue from Hungary, and self-defense. As the Soviet front drew near, paratrooper Yitzhak Ben-Ephraim helped the youth movements organize self-defense groups in case the Germans attempted to exterminate the Jews of Bucharest (the largest Romanian community).

Throughout the war the Zionist organizations maintained links with the Palestinian delegations in Constantinople and Geneva and with other Jewish organizations abroad which afforded them material and moral aid and guidance, while they themselves provided information on the situation of the Jews in the occupied zone.

Throughout the war the Romanian authorities allowed "illegal" immigrant ships to leave the country; from 1938 to 1941 about 20 ships sailed from Romanian ports carrying approximately 17,000 immigrants, mainly refugees from Central Europe; this aliya was organized by the Revisionist Aliya Committee and the Zionist Organization's Mosad le-Aliyah Bet with the assistance of the Romanian Zionist organizations. Despite the risks involved in such voyages during the war and their high price in human lives, there were constant departures of Romanian Jews for Palestine. In February, 1942, the S.S. *Struma,* with 769 immigrants aboard, was sunk by a Soviet submarine, but even this did not halt immigration to Palestine in 1942–43. In 1944 "illegal" immigration was again organized by members of the Mosad Le-Aliyah Bet; refugees from Transnistria, Poland, and Hungary were the first to leave. Seven ships transported 2,700 "illegal" immigrants up to 23 August 1944, when the fascist regime was overthrown. During this period the S.S. *Mefkure,* with 320 on board, was sunk by a German submarine.

In May 1944 Transylvanian Zionist leaders who had been smuggled into Romania organized a committee, headed by Erno Marton, to assist the Jewish refugees (in 1940 northern Transylvania, with over 150,000 Jews, was annexed to Hungary) who had managed to escape extermination at Auschwitz. Following Romania's liberation the committee, together with Romanian Jewish leaders A.L Zissu and Dr. W. Filderman, persuaded the Romanian government to intercede with the Hungarian and German governments in an attempt to save the Jews of Transylvania who were yet alive.

From the End of World War II until the Dissolution of the Zionist Movement. Upon Romania's liberation from the Nazi yoke, all the organizations of the Zionist Movement resumed activity; the Jewish Party reappeared and the Romanian branch of the World Jewish Congress was established.

The Zionist Movement emerged from the war greatly respected for its activities under the fascist regime and for its nuclei of activists, particularly in the youth movements, who could take credit for most of the clandestine achievements. Despite the uncertain conditions of the Soviet occupation, the Romanian Zionist Movement not only firmly reestablished itself but became a central body in Jewish life; by April 1946 it had about 40 branches and over 110,000 members. This period was marked by the growing strength of the organizations and movements connected with the League for Labor Palestine (the union of Mapai, Mishmar, Ha-Shomer ha-Tza'ir, and their related youth movements). At the first Zionist Conference after the war, held on 29 April 1946, the League for Labor Palestine had 165 delegates (45%), the General Zionist Union (Renasterea, General Zionist Center, Democratic Zionists, Ha-Oved ha-Tziyoni and their related youth movements had 122 delegates (33%), Mizrachi (including Torah va-Avoda and Bnei Akiva) had 60 delegates and the Revisionists 14.

The first president of the Zionist Organization after the liberation was A.L. Zissu; in the national conference in 1946 Adv. Rohrlich was elected; he was followed by M. Benvenisti.

Romanian Jewry identified strongly with Zionism and any appeal of the Zionist Executive met with an enthusiastic mass response. The petition prior to the arrival of the Anglo-American Committee of Inquiry was signed by 90,000 Jews aged 18 and over from the Old Kingdom and from southern Bukovina. Prior to the Zionist Congress in 1946, 92,500 shekels were purchased.

The youth movements organized more rapidly than the adult Zionists. The emissaries guided the youth movements in joint activities in several fields, despite differences of opinion. All the movements which had functioned before the war renewed their activity. He-Halutz was recreated after the Liberation as a joint training framework for most of the movements, and in November, 1944, each movement had at least two training groups, with a total of about 400 members in training. Within a year the youth movements had reached every vicinity where Jews lived; they also created orphanages for refugee children. In October, 1947, 22 training farms, 68 training groups and 10 orphanages stood at the disposal of the halutzim with 2,600 halutzim and about 1,000 children; the number of members of the youth movements was estimated at 20,000.

The Zionist press was reestablished and for four years three widely-distributed weeklies were circulated: the Renasterea Group's *Renasterea Noastra*, the Union's *Viata Evreeasca*, and Zissu's *Mantuirea*; journals and publications of other Zionist movements and organizations also appeared. A publishing house, Bikkurim, was created, which in conjunction with the Zionist Organization printed and translated basic books of Zionist ideology.

While the Romanian Jewish community was strongly attracted to Zionism, seeing immigration to Palestine as the sole solution to their situation after the suffering endured during the war, there was also a counter tendency in the initial period to embrace Communism as a means of assimilating in the new regime being created in Romania.

During a four-year period, the Communist Party gradually took control of the Romanian political system. The Jewish community was one of its targets, and the Zionist Movement the principal obstacle in its way. The Party initially supported Zionist activity and the right of Jewish emigration. It promoted the creation in June, 1945, of a front organization for the anti-fascist struggle, Comitetul Democratic Evreesc (CDE—the Jewish Democratic Committee), with the participation of the Jewish Communists and of the League for Labor Palestine parties; the youth movements organized in He-Halutz participated in a youth framework paralled to the CDE, the Union of Socialist and Communist Working Youth. It was hoped that adherence to the Communist framework would make continued legal Zionist activity possible under the new political conditions. Hence, while the yishuv and the Zionist Movement were fighting British policy in Palestine, the Romanian pro-Communist government supported the activities of the Zionist Movement and aliya. A League for Labor Palestine delegate, Asher Dascalu, was elected to the first parliament after the liberation, and Petru Groza, Prime Minister and subsequently President of the Romanian People's Republic, affirmed the government's political support for the Jews' emigration to Palestine. With the creation of the State of Israel and the growing desire of many Jews to leave for that country, the USSR changed its stand and the Romanian Communist party followed suit. A press campaign was conducted in *Unirea* and the other CDE publications against the "illegal" emigration and Zionism, which, by promoting aliya, was "sabotaging the construction of the new regime." The Jewish Communists replaced the representatives of the Zionist bodies on the committees, and in fall 1947 they took control of the communities and their central organizations. In late 1948 strongmen of the CDE occupied the branches and centers of the Zionist organizations in Bucharest. The heads of the National Funds were arrested on fictitious charges of "tax transgressions" and the Zionist press eliminated.

Under pressure by Jewish Communist leaders, the Zionist organizations and youth movements decided to halt their activities "voluntarily;" all the Zionist movements and organizations were disbanded and the World Jewish Congress ceased to operate in Romania. Romanian Jews continued hoping that they could leave for Israel, despite the anti-Zionist propaganda conducted by members of the CDE, even in the synagogues; from 1948 until 1951 more than 140,000 Jews left Romania.

In summer 1950, the leaders of the Zionist movement and of the youth movements (about 120 people) were arrested; after four years of interrogations, show trials were held in which the prisoners were accused of "spying for imperialism," "endangering state security," and "sabotage of the regime;" they were sentenced to various terms of imprisonment. Some of the prisoners died in jail (A. Yampolski, A. Orenstein, and A. Shein) and others died later as a result of the conditions of imprisonment (A.L. Zissu and M. Abir). Between 1955 and 1956 the "Prisoners of Zion" benefited from an amnesty, and after a certain period they were allowed to leave for Israel. At the same time the Communist Party disbanded the Democratic Jewish Committee, apparently because of its failure to curb the nationalistic longings of Romanian Jewry. By the 1990s only 15,000 of the approximately 430,000 Jews remaining after the Holocaust were still in Romania; the others were in Israel.

E. OFIR

ROMANIAN JEWS IN ISRAEL.

Immigration from Romania: The first Jews arriving in Eretz Israel from Romania, in the 17th century, settled in Safed and Jerusalem. Immigration of Romanian Jews who wished to live productively in the Holy Land commenced with the arrival of members of the Hevrat Yishuv Eretz Yisrael al yedei Avodat Adama (Society for the Settlement of Eretz Israel by Working the Land) in 1882 (*see* romania, zionism in). Under the banner of Hovevei Zion, Jews continued to arrive from Romania throughout the period of the First Aliya. Few data are available on the number of Romanian immigrants in the Second Aliya.

During the Third Aliya (1920–1924), 1,404 immigrants arrived in Palestine, mainly Ha-Shomer ha-Tza'ir and Tze'irei Zion pioneers from the annexed territories of Bessarabia and Bukovina.

During the Fourth Aliya (1924–1926), with the economic growth of the yishuv the number of immigrants doubled, reaching about 2,825, while during the slump of 1927–1928 only 150 immigrants arrived. The riots of 1929 spurred aliya, with immigration figures of around 1,141 in the years 1930–1932.

Hitler's rise to power in Germany and increased anti-Semitic activities in Romania, combined with an increase in the possibilities of aliya, resulted in a large growth in the number of immigrants, who numbered 1,374 in 1933; 1,705 in 1934; 3,596 in 1935; and 1,348 in 1936.

Various factors, principally the limitations placed on immigration by the British mandatory authorities, restricted the number of immigrants despite the increase in anti-Semitic persecutions in Romania under the Goga-Cuza government, and subsequently during the state dictatorship. Between 1937 and 1940 2,078 Romanian Jews arrived in Palestine legally. Following the reduction in the quota of immigrants imposed by the British 1939 White Paper, the Zionist Organization, the Revisionists, and private individuals began to organize "illegal" immigration from 1938 onward; at the same time refugees from Nazi-occupied countries began to arrive in Romania. The "illegal" immigrant boats sailing from Romania carried refugees from Germany, Austria, Czechoslovakia, Poland, etc., together with the Romanian Jews. From 1938 until the outbreak of the war in 1939 about 13,797 Jews left Romania in 22 "illegal" immigrant ships. From the end of 1939 until late 1941 about 9,628 "illegal" immigrants left Romania for Palestine in eight ships. In 1941 around 600 Jews immigrated from Romania legally.

While Romania was a member of the Axis and adopted the anti-Jewish policy of Nazi Germany, with persecutions, deportations, and massacres, the Romanian dictatorship preferred to rid the country of its Jews "humanely" and allowed Jewish aliya throughout the war; the drop in aliya during this period stemmed from other difficulties—the danger of sailing in the Black Sea, the dearth of sailing vessels, and need for permits to pass through various countries. Notwithstanding the difficulties, Romania's Jews did not cease their aliya attempts; despite disasters, such as the sinking of the S.S. **Struma* with 769 "illegal" immigrants on board in February, 1942, several hundred young people set sail for Palestine in all kinds of seagoing crafts. In 1944 "illegal" sailings to Constantinople resumed; 2,652 "illegal" immigrants were taken to Palestine up to the liberation, although the price in human lives was high: during this period the S.S. *Mefkure* went down with 320 immigrants aboard. With the Soviet occupation of Romania, immigration to Palestine continued; about 1,500 immigrants left the country in 1944, including Hungarian, Polish, and Transnistrian refugees. After the war, from 1945 until the founding of the State of Israel, "illegal" immigration continued from Romanian ports by permits accorded at irregular intervals by the Communist authorities. In 1946, the S.S. *Max Nordau* brought 1,666 immigrants, in 1947 about 4,000 arrived on the S.S. *Ge'ula* and the S.S. *Jewish State*, and in June, 1948, about 15,000 arrived on the S.S. *Pan York* and the S.S. Pan Crescent; exact numbers of Romanian immigrants are not known, since a large number arrived through the *Beriha organization.

Following Israel's Declaration of Independence (May, 1948) the Romanian government allowed practically no aliya until November of that year when it began to grant exit permits to the elderly, to "elements which had not been absorbed in the new regime," and to special cases; the aliya was in tri-weekly sailings on the S.S. *Transylvania*. In this way about 108,940 immigrants arrived in Israel from Romania up to 1951. Most went to the transit camps (*ma'abarot*), yet despite the difficult conditions the large majority eventually integrated successfully by their own efforts; some built farm holdings in the "From Transit Camp to Farm" and "From Ship to Settlement" operations.

During this period the Jewish Democratic Committee in Romania (an institution similar to the Soviet *Evsektsiia*, the Jewish Section of the Communist Party) conducted sometimes violent propaganda among Jews against Jewish aspirations to immigrate to Israel. Realizing that the ban on the Zionist organizations in no way subdued these desires, the Romanian authorities arrested the leaders of the Zionist organizations; after years of imprisonment and interrogations they were charged in 1954 with "sabotage of the building of socialism by encouraging the emigration of the Jews: and sentenced to varying periods of imprisonment. The Jews persisted in their wish to leave, and thanks to the efforts of the Israeli government and various international organizations, aliya was renewed, initially to permit unification of families, and subsequently for other applicants; between 1952 and 1960 32,004 immigrants arrived in Israel; from 1961 to 1971 98,919; from 1972 until 1982, 22,116; and from 1983 until late 1986, a further 5,901. (Given the abnormal circumstances and conditions of immigration in this period, many of these figures are estimates).

Settlement in Israel: In 1863 the rabbi of Moinesti and his family immigrated, settling temporarily in Haifa. Later he returned to Moinesti where he convinced 30 more young people to join him in Haifa. A year later he returned once more to Romania to advocate agricultural settlement in Eretz Israel. His nephew David Yankovitz (David Schub) was subsequently similarly active. In 1882 David Schub and David Buchstater purchased the lands of Gei Oni (later Rosh Pina), which were settled by immigrants from Moinesti in October, 1882. In the same month the lands of Zamarin and Tantura were purchased and December, 1882, saw the establishment of Zikhron Ya'akov, the second moshava of Romanian immigrants. In 1883 they participated in the founding of Ekron. Romanian immigrants from the First Aliya were among the founders of Mishmar ha-Yarden, Kefar Tavor, Menahemiya, and Shefeya. In 1894 an attempt was made to build a moshava on land purchased by Baron Rothschild in the Golan, but the settlers eventually abandoned the site, which was difficult to defend. Israel Marcus from Bucharest founded in Romania the Carmel La Mare company which purchased 50 acres near Neveh Sha'anan for construction of a neighborhood. In 1922 Marcus founded the Ahuzat Sir Herbert Samuel cooperative with over 1,000 members, for whom he purchased 850 acres of land on the Carmel. Immigrating to Palestine in 1923, he commenced construction, and in 1925 the first houses were already standing.

Between the two world wars Romanian immigrants came mainly from the pioneer movements which constituted the principal strength of the Zionist Movement in Romania. Ha-Shomer ha-Tza'ir pioneers began to arrive in the Third Aliya, and in the framework of Ha-Kibbutz ha-Artzi, founded the kibbutzim of Ma'abarot, Sha'ar ha-Amakim, Sarid, Daliya, Shamir, Ruhama, Dan, and Reshafim, and after 1948, Evron, Barka'i, Zikim, and Magen. Members of this movement also joined kibbutzim Gazit, Shomrat, Gat, Shuval, Nir Yitzhak, etc.

Gordonia pioneers joined Ihud ha-Kevutzot veha-Kibbutzim and created the kibbutzim of Masada, Hulda, Nir Am, Hanita, and Ramat David; groups of pioneers also joined other kibbutzim.

Members of Dror (from Bessarabia, Bukovina, and Old Romania) and of Habonim from Transylvania created Bet Oren, Heftziba, Givat Hayim (Ha-Kibbutz ha-Me'uhad), Gesher, Kefar Glickson, and Ma'agan, participated in the creation of Eyal, Nahsholim, Malkiya, Bet Guvrin, Misgav Am, Hukok, Menahemia, and Gadot-Guvrin, and joined another ten or so settlements. Ha-No'ar ha-Tziyoni pioneers were among the founders of Usha, Kefar Glickson, Nitzanim, Alonei Abba, and also joined Shoresh, Mavki'im, Kefar Shemu'el, Kefar Bin Nun, and Talmei Yafeh.

Bnei Akiva religious pioneer youth settled in Alumim, Kefar Jawetz, Kefar Etzion, and Kefar Hasidim. Members of the religious Agudat Israel movement settled on moshavim: Komemiyut, Kefar Gidon, Benei Re'em, and Yesodot. Betar settlers participated in the founding of Ramat Tiomkin, Tel-Tzur (Nahalat Jabotinsky), Yad 14, Kefar Avi'el, Misgav Dov, Amikam, Nili, and Ramat Raziel.

Romanian Jews also settled in other agricultural settlements including the moshavim Olesh and Adanim.

Many Romanian immigrants were absorbed in the towns, notably, Haifa, Tel Aviv and its suburbs, and Beersheba; in 1944 they founded the Givat Shemu'el quarter (near Benei Berak), named after Samuel Pineles, one of the first Romanian Zionists.

The war effort: Romanian immigrants took part in all the yishuv's underground activities. In addition, they participated in all fields of the Palestinian war efforts. Ten native Romanians, members of the kibbutz movement, were parachuted behind enemy lines during the war; of the nine who were dropped into Romania, four were captured. The others organized rescue, aliya, self-defense, and the encouragement of Romanian Jewry. Abba Berdichev, who jumped into Slovakia, was killed. Romanian immigrants were well represented in the defense forces prior to the creation of the State and 384 fell while fighting in the ranks of the Israel Defense Forces during the War of Independence.

Romanian Jews in Israel: An estimated 370,000 Romanian Jews live in Israel. Their contribution is expressed in most fields of life and artistic creativity. They include:

In public life: Yitzhak Ben-Aharon (Nussenbaum), member of Kibbutz Givat Hayim, former government minister, former secretary-general of the Histadrut; Natan Peled (Friedel), member of Kibbutz Sarid, former Minister of Absorption and Knesset Member; Yitzhak Korn, former deputy Minister of Finance and former Chairman of the Israel branch of the World Jewish Congress; Yitzhak Artzi (Herzig), former Knesset Member and deputy mayor of Tel Aviv; Idov Cohen and Gustav Badian, former Knesset Members. Former and present members of the diplomatic corps include Misu Weissman-Amir, Shemu'el Ben-Tzur (Patarpi), and Meir Rosenne, former ambassador to the US.

A large number of Romanian-born scientists are active in all fields in universities in Israel. Romanian Jews are also prominent in the Israeli art world: among Israel's most important painters are Reuven Rubin, who studied at the Bezalel School of Art prior to World War I and was Israel minister to Romania; and Marcel Janco, a founder of the Dada school in European painting and head of the Ein Hod Artists' Village; Avigdor Arikha studied at Bezalel and the Paris Ecole des Beaux Arts. In musical life in Israel: composers Alexander Uriah Boscovich, Sergiu Natra, conductors Mendi Rodan, and Sergiu Commissiona, songwriter Dubi Zeltzer, the pianist Mindru Katz.

Prominent in the country's intellectual life and literary creativity are Yisrael Zmora, Chaim Robinson, B.Y. Michali, K.A. Bertini, J. Rabi, A.B. Jaffe, Aharon Appelfeld, and Ezra Fleischer; Appelfeld and Fleischer are both Israel Prize laureates.

Prominent in Israeli theater are actors: Batya Lancet, Lea Koenig, Ya'akov Bodo, Shimon Bar, and Mosco Alkalai.

Romanian periodicals include the daily *Viata Noastra* and the weekly *Adevarul* in Romanian and *Uj Kelet* in Hungarian, which appeared in Romania and continue to appear in Israel. Other publications are *Minimum, Facla*, and *Revista Mea*, while several political parties have periodicals in Romanian. General organizations of Romanian immigrants are: The Organization of Zionist Communal Workers from Romania, the Rabbi Dr. Niemerower Lodge of B'nai B'rith in Tel Aviv with a branch in Jerusalem, an organization of former Hasmonaea members (Zionist student organization at the universities of Bucharest and Jassy), and ACMEOR (International Cultural Organization of Romanian Jews).

The Romanian Immigrants' Association, created prior to World War II to assist the absorption of immigrants from that country, continues its activities. In the 1960s immigrants from Bessarabia and Bukovina created their own organizations; the former publishes a journal in Yiddish and the latter in German.

Romanian immigrants are members of all Israeli political parties and occupy important positions both in the national political sphere and in the municipal sphere. Prior to elections each party brings out publications in Romanian.

Romanian Jews have proved adept at integrating into Israel with a minimum of fuss. Today Romanian immigrants constitute one of the largest ethnic groups in Israel.

E. OFIR

ROME AND JERUSALEM. *See* HESS, MOSES.

RONAI, JANOS. Jurist and Zionist leader in Hungary (b. Gyulafehervar (now Alba Julia, Romania), 1849; d. 1919). In 1897 he attended the First Zionist Congress and became the first president of the Hungarian Zionist Federation. Ronai was a prolific writer, whose books include *Nationalism and Cosmopolitanism, with Special Emphasis on the Contemporary Situation of Jewry* (in Hungarian, 1875) and *Zionism in Hungary* (in German, 1897).

ROOSEVELT, FRANKLIN DELANO. Thiry-second President (1933-45) of the United States (b. Hyde Park, NY, 1882; d. Warm Springs, Ga., 1945). Roosevelt's connection with the Palestine issue goes back to the administration of

Woodrow Wilson, in which he served as Assistant Secretary of the Navy. For almost a decade after he came to the White House he went along with Secretary of State Cordell Hull in assuming that the Mandate for Palestine was a British responsibility and that the Middle East was a British sphere of influence. This assumption, a carry-over from his post-World War I Republican predecessors, gave the 1924 United States-British Palestine Convention a very narrow interpretation, insisting that Washington could intervene only if changes in the Mandate jeopardized the rights of American citizens in the Holy Land. From the first, Roosevelt automatically forwarded all correspondence, petitions, and the like arriving at the White House to Hull, who, knowing little of the Middle East, in turn sent all White House material pertaining to the region to the Division of Near Eastern Affairs of the State Department. The Chief of the Division was Wallace Murray, whose basic anti-Zionism stemmed in large measure from a fear that a Jewish Palestine would be radically oriented. Murray always maintained that he wanted a fair settlement in Palestine, but he pressed plans stemming from non-Zionist or anti-Zionist sources including the American Council for Judaism and the Ihud platform of Judah L. Magnes. As Chief of the Division of Near Eastern Affairs and later as Political Adviser in the State Department hierarchy, Murray made many of the crucial decisions touching on Palestine and the entire Middle East. After the outbreak of World War II in 1939, the President had little time to devote to secondary war issues; he therefore continued to relegate them to Hull, who usually turned Palestinian problems over to Murray.

From time to time, Roosevelt bypassed the State Department by issuing statements on Palestine or else by considering independent solutions for the Jewish plight during the nightmare Axis years. Roosevelt displayed a keen interest in Zionist endeavors and undoubtedly would have liked to solve the problem of Jewish homelessness, preferably, because of political conditions, in some underdeveloped region outside Palestine. However, prior to American entrance into the war he was bound by the isolationist shackles of the time and thereafter he could not see how a Jewish Commonwealth could be established in Palestine in the face of great Arab opposition. So, acting entirely in character, the President moved from one idea to another: the transfer of Arabs to Iraq in order to clear western Palestine for the Jews; a deal with King Ibn Saud of Saudi Arabia, an idea he never entirely abandoned until his interview with the King in 1945; and numerous extraterritorial schemes, all of which proved abortive. Most of these ideas were not the President's own. The Iraqi scheme was urged on him by Edward A. Norman of New York, and the proposed deal with Ibn Saud came from a British Arabist, H. St. John Philby.

Roosevelt never exerted sufficient pressure on London to modify the White Paper of 1939, which practically put an end to Jewish immigration to, and land purchases in, Palestine. He refrained from intervening when the White Paper was issued, possibly for fear that isolationist Anglophobes in the United States would capitalize on a Washington-London rift.

World War II. During World War II, the President was under considerable pressure not to force Britain's hand. This pressure came from the State Department, oil lobbyists, and special emissaries whom Roosevelt dispatched to the Middle East (Halford Hoskins and Patrick J. Hurley). United States archival material reveals similar pressure from American consular officials in Jerusalem, Cairo, and other Middle Eastern centers. Oil specialists persuaded Roosevelt that the domestic reserves of the United States would be exhausted by 1958, necessitating for future defense purposes Saudi Arabian oil, which would not be forthcoming if the White House allowed Congress to pass a pro-Zionist resolution. This point of view was pressed on Roosevelt by James V. Forrestal, who was promoted to the position of Secretary of the Navy after the death of his chief, Frank Knox, in 1944. Most important in Roosevelt's thinking, however, was the insistence of Allied military authorities that a pro-Zionist stand would jeopardize the shipment of war matérial to the Soviet Union, the bulk of which had to pass through Arab or other Moslem countries.

Although these reasons help explain Roosevelt's stand in the earlier war years, they do not explain why the President hesitated to act in behalf of the Zionist cause after the entire Middle East had been cleared of Axis forces. At this juncture, British Prime Minister Winston Churchill assured the President of his ardent support of Zionism and promised that the two leaders would jointly recompense the Jewish people after victory. However, pleading political as well as military reasons, the Rooosevelt administration obstructed the passage in Congress of resolutions supporting a Jewish Homeland in Palestine.

In an interview on 9 March 1944, Roosevelt authorized Rabbis Abba Hillel Silver and Stephen S. Wise to issue the following statement:

> The President authorized us to say that the American government has never given its approval to the White Paper of 1939. The President is happy the doors of Palestine are open today to Jewish refugees and that when future decisions are made, full justice will be done to those who seek a Jewish National Home for which our Government and the American people have always had the deepest sympathy and today more than ever, in view of the tragic plight of hundreds of thousands of homeless Jewish refugees.

A few days later (13 and 17 March 1944), however, Roosevelt informed Ibn Saud and Emir Abdullah of Transjordan that "no decision altering the basic situation of Palestine should be reached without full consultation with both Arabs and Jews." He sent similar messages to Egypt and Yemen. These communications had been sent in response to protests from the Arab world against deliberations in Congress on a pro-Palestine resolution.

Meanwhile, on 13 March, Silver and Wise, encouraged by the reception they had had four days earlier at the White House, drafted a statement for issuance by the President explicitly committing the United States to the support of Zionism. The statement would have urged the opening of Palestine to further immigration, development, and settlement and declared that the American people favored a Jewish Commonwealth. No reply was ever sent by the White House to this communication.

During the 1944 electoral campaign, on 15 October, Roosevelt said in a message to the National Convention of the Zionist Organization of America: "I know how long and ardently the Jewish people have worked and prayed for the establishment of Palestine as a free and democratic Jewish commonwealth. I am convinced that the American people give their support to this aim; and if reelected, I shall help to bring about its realization." However, after the election (15 November 1944), Roosevelt agreed with Secretary of State Edward R. Stettinius that it would be "unwise" to push pro-Palestine resolutions in Congress. They agreed that Wise should be informed to this effect; Stettinius gave the news to Wise two days later. On 21 November, Roosevelt sent Wise and Silver protests from Arab and pro-Arab groups that had been transmitted by the Cairo Legation.

On 14 February 1945, Roosevelt met with Ibn Saud on the Mediterranean. Two weeks later, in his last speech to Congress (1 March), Roosevelt remarked on how much he had learned about the Palestine question from his recent interview with Ibn Saud. On 5 April, Roosevelt wrote him that "no decision [would] be taken with respect to the basic situation in that country without full consultation with both Arabs and Jews." He assured the King that he would take no action "in my capacity as Chief of the Executive Branch which may prove hostile to the Arab people." Despite these assurances made to the Arabs on the eve of Roosevelt's sudden death, there is evidence that in his very last days the President was turning over in his mind a plan to have the newly formed United Nations create a Jewish State and defend it. It is impossible to say how seriously Roosevelt meant these statements, made to Rabbi Stephen S. Wise and Undersecretary of State Sumner Welles, for he had been repeatedly warned by his Ambassador in Moscow that the Soviet Union would use such a stand to gain influence among the 50 million Arabs. All that one can say for certain is that Roosevelt had thought, as early as 1943, that the United States must share in the final disposal of the Palestine question. Furthermore, public opinion polls taken in the mid-1940s clearly indicated the existence of strong public sentiment favoring a pro-Zionist solution for the Palestine problem.

Refugee Problem. The Palestine issue aside, Roosevelt evinced his concern for the tragedy of the millions of Jews crushed by the Nazi juggernaut. He protested German anti-Jewish atrocities and sent representatives to various unsuccessful international conferences on refugees, including the Evian (1938) and Bermuda (1943) Conferences. In 1943 he appealed, without avail, to Pope Pius XII to condemn Nazi excesses. On 16 January 1944, in response to detailed reports of genocide and a stern admonition from Secretary of the Treasury Henry Morgenthau Jr. that the administration had failed to extend tangible help to the Jews, he established the War Refugee Board. Thousands of Jews were rescued late in the war, but there was still no place for them to go. In July, 1944, a total of 982 refugees (Jews and non-Jews) were shipped from Italy to Fort Ontario, Oswego, NY, where they were detained until the end of 1945, when President Harry S Truman gave them the option of permanent asylum in the United States. Resting on the researches of Arthur D. Morse and David S. Wyman, historians feel that Roosevelt failed to cut State Department red tape and overcome congressional obstacles in dealing with the refugee problem. Had he done so, far fewer Jews would have perished in the Nazi Holocaust. A similar conclusion in regard to Palestine was reached by the Zionist leadership in the United States toward the end of the war, with the faction controlled by Rabbi Wise dissenting. Rabbi Silver, voicing the majority American Zionist opinion, told the 22nd Zionist Congress (1946):

> Throughout the Roosevelt administration the United States Government was determined to take no action whatsoever and to make no representations whatsoever to the British Government either to open the doors of Palestine to Jewish immigration or to live up to other obligations it had assumed under the Mandate.

S. ADLER

Pinhas Rosen.
[Israel Information Services]

ROSEN (ROSENBLUTH), PINHAS FELIX. Zionist leader and Israeli statesman (b. Berlin, 1887; d. Kefar Saba, 1978). He studied at the universities of Freiburg and Berlin, subsequently serving as a judge and engaging in private law practice. A Zionist from his youth on, he became a leader in the Zionist students' organization Kartell Jüdischer Verbindungen. In 1911 he helped found the Blau-Weiss (Blue-White) youth organization. He served as an officer in the German Army in World War I, in the course of which he came in contact with eastern European Jews. In 1918 he was named honorary secretary of the Pro Palästina Komitee. He was first secretary, then chairman (1920), of the Zionist Organization of Germany.

From 1926 to 1931 Rosen was a member of the Zionist Executive in London and head of its Organization Department. He settled in Palestine in 1931 and, while engaging in private law practice, continued to be active in public life. He was one of the founders and leaders of the Association of Immigrants from Germany (later Organization of Immigrants from Central Europe) and president (1941–48) of the Aliya Hadasha party, the political successor of the association. He was also a member of the Tel Aviv Municipal Council for many years.

In 1948 Rosen was one of the founders of the Progressive party, which he led until 1961, when it merged with the General Zionist party to form the Liberal party. He was one of the leaders of the united party until it split again in 1965, with the bulk of the former Progressives forming the Independent Liberal party. Elected to the Knesset at its inception in 1949, he continued to be a member thereafter. Rosen was Minister of Justice in the provisional government (1948–49) and held the same post in subsequent coalition governments, with one short interruption, until 1961. During his tenure he laid the foundation for the legal system of Israel and for the establishment of a judiciary independent of Knesset and Cabinet alike. In 1968 he resigned his seat in the Knesset. He published articles on Zionist themes in Hebrew, English, and German.

ROSENBERG, ADAM. Early Zionist leader in the United States (b. Philadelphia, 1858; d. 1928). The son of a rabbi who had gone to the United States from Germany, Rosenberg studied rabbinics and law in New York. In 1886 he became active in the city's Hovevei Zion movement, and in 1891 he was one of the founders of the Shavei Zion settlement society, serving as its chairman. He proposed that the Hovevei Zion in Vienna call a conference of all Hovevei

Zion groups, to be held in Paris in August, 1891, in order to establish a unified movement. That year he went to Eretz Israel on behalf of the Shavei Zion society to purchase land in the Gaulan Heights. When the transfer of these lands encountered difficulties, Baron Edmond de Rothschild undertook to acquire and register them in the name of the settlers. However, obstruction by the authorities continued, and at a Paris meeting of the land purchasers in 1893, Rosenberg announced the withdrawal of his society from the purchase.

Rosenberg drafted a constitution for a centralized Hovevei Zion movement and participated in the Paris Conference, held in January, 1894, that decided to establish a Central Committee. In 1895, when it seemed that the Turkish authorities were willing to facilitate the settlement of Jews in the Gaulan area, he reorganized the Shavei Zion society. He went to Eretz Israel and started to set up a farm as the basis for a settlement, but the Turks obstructed his activities, members of his society ceased to send him funds, and he was forced to leave the place and abandon the project.

In 1897 Rosenberg attended the First Zionist Congress, which he addressed on the situation in Eretz Israel and on the position of Jews in the United States. After his return to the United States, he was active in the American Zionist movement.

I. KLAUSNER

ROSENBLATT, BERNARD ABRAHAM. Judge and Zionist leader in the United States (b. Grodek, Bialystok District, Russian Poland, 1886; d. New York, 1969). Brought to the United States at the age of six, Rosenblatt graduated from Columbia University in 1909. He was appointed a judge in the Magistrates Court of the city of New York in 1916 and subsequently held several other civic posts. He joined the Zionist movement and in 1914 organized the *American Zion Commonwealth, a land-purchasing agency. From 1921 to 1923 he served as American representative on the Zionist Executive in Jerusalem. During this time he was instrumental in launching the Tel Aviv bond issue that was floated in the United States. After his return to the United States he served as president of the Jewish National Fund, from 1925 to 1927. During World War II he was chairman of the Keren ha-Yesod in the United States. He was active in various Israeli enterprises, as a director of the Israel Land Development Company and the Migdal Insurance Co. Ltd., and as board chairman of the Tiberias Hot Springs.

Rosenblatt wrote extensively on economic and Zionist subjects, including *Social Zionism: Selected Essays* (1919), *Federal Palestine and the Jewish Commonwealth* (1941), and *The American Bridge to the Israel Commonwealth* (1959). His autobiography, *Two Generations of Zionism: Historical Recollections of an American Zionist*, appeared in 1967.

ROSENBLUTH, MARTIN MICHAEL. Zionist official (b. Messingwerk, near Berlin, 1886; d. Tel Aviv, 1963). A brother of Pinhas *Rosen, he attended the Universities of Berlin and Kiel (Ph.D., 1909). In 1910 at the suggestion of David Wolffsohn, president of the World Zionist Organization, he joined the Central Zionist Office in Cologne as secretary to Wolffsohn and the Inner Actions Committee. As secretary of the World Zionist Executive (1915–20), he directed the activities of the Copenhagen Bureau. In 1921 he was appointed director of the Palestine Office in Vienna; he then served as Keren ha-Yesod representative in Central Europe (1922–24), executive vice-president of the Zionist Organization of Germany in Berlin (1925–29), and director of Keren ha-Yesod in Germany (1929–33).

In March, 1933, Rosenblüth led a small delegation of Jewish leaders sent to London by German Minister of the Interior Hermann Goering to negotiate the immediate cessation of alleged atrocity propaganda against Nazi Germany. After conveying the true state of affairs in Germany to his friends in London, Rosenblüth returned to Germany to report to the German Foreign Office, then left Germany for London, where he established an office as representative of the Zionist Organization of Germany. When the 18th Zionist Congress (1933) decided to set up in London a central office for the settlement of German Jews in Palestine, Rosenblüth was put in charge of it (1933–40). Moving to New York, he served the United Palestine Appeal as director of information (1941–48). In 1949 he was appointed representative of the Israeli Ministry of Finance for the Western Hemisphere and held this position until his retirement in 1961.

ROSENBLUTH, PINHAS FELIX. *See* ROSEN, PINHAS FELIX.

ROSENFELD, MAX. Galician Po'ale Zion leader (b. Drohobycz, 1884; d. Vienna, 1919). After receiving his doctorate in law from the University of Lvov, he studied the Jewish national problem and questions of national autonomy. In 1904 Rosenfeld was one of the first Po'ale Zion members in Galicia. Ideologically, he supported Social-Democrat revisionism and was in agreement with Shelomo Kaplansky concerning the practical objectives of Zionism in Eretz Israel (creation of a national economy by the furthering of cooperative settlements and enterprises), considering the main emphasis in the Diaspora to be the struggle for civil rights and national autonomy. Rosenfeld participated in the founding convention of the World Union of Po'ale Zion parties in 1907. After World War I he worked to further Jewish national organization, and was involved in self-defense efforts. In 1919 he was elected to the Polish Sejm as a representative of the Chelm region in Congress Poland but died a few days after his election.

M. MINTZ

ROSENSOHN, ETTA LASKER. Communal worker and Zionist leader in the United States (b. Galveston, Tex., 1885; d. New York, 1966). She studied at the University of Texas (1901–03) and the New York School of Social Work (1914–16). She became acquainted with Zionism while visiting Eretz Israel in 1914 and was subsequently drawn into Zionist activity by her husband, Samuel Julian Rosensohn, whom she married in 1918. From 1928 until her death she was a member of the National Board of *Hadassah, serving as national treasurer from 1932 to 1937 and again in the early 1940s and as national president in 1952–53. Together with Ira Hirschmann she headed the first joint campaign of Hadassah and the Hebrew University of Jerusalem for the university's Medical School.

A sister of the philanthropist Albert D. Lasker, she interested other members of her family in Zionism; one sister, Loula D. Lasker, was chairman of the editorial board of the *Hadassah Newsletter* for some years. Mrs. Rosensohn was a member of the Board of Governors of the Hebrew University, the Board of Directors of the American Friends of the Hebrew University, and the Zionist General Council. She was active also in the National Council of Jewish Women, serving on its board as immigration chairman for a number of years.

ROSH HA-AYIN. Town in the coastal plain, 3 mi. (5 km.) east of Petah Tikva. Its population consists almost exclusively of Jews hailing from Yemen. In 1950, immigrants found shelter here in a former British army camp and in 1955, the place received municipal council status. Most breadwinners commute to work in the Tel Aviv conurbation. The name, "Head of the Spring," refers to the nearby springs feeding the Yarkon River. Population (1987), 11,600. E. ORNI

ROSH HA-NIKRA. The cape on the northern extremity of Israel's coast protruding slightly into the Mediterranean Sea, and marking the western end of the border between Israel and the Lebanon. The waves have carved picturesque grottoes in the limestone cliffs. On top of the ridge lies a border station. A railway tunnel beneath has been out of use since 1947. On the southern slope of the ridge lies Kibbutz Kefar Rosh ha-Nikra, population (1987), 594. Together with other small capes to the north, it was called in antiquity "Sulam Tzor" ("Ladder of Tyre"). E. ORNI

ROSH PINA. Moshava in eastern Upper Galilee, on the slope of Mount Canaan, south of the Huleh Valley. It was first founded in 1878 under the name "Gai Oni" ("Valley of My Strength" adapted from the name of the nearby Arab village Ja'uni) by Jews from Safed who wished to live by their own labor instead of on the charity of the haluka. Lacking both funds and farming experience and harassed by Arabs, they had to give up after two years, but in 1882 the village was renewed by First Aliya pioneers from Romania and Russia, and was given its present name, "Corner Stone" (derived from Psalms 118:21). Although Baron Edmond de Rothschild extended his aid to the moshava, it made little headway, mainly owing to its isolation. Attempts to grow tobacco and mulberry trees for silkworm-raising failed. In the 1936–39 Arab riots, Rosh Pina suffered repeated attacks. A Betar group based itself in the village; in 1938 three of its members attacked an Arab bus, were caught, and one, Shelomo Ben-Yosef, was hanged in Acre prison and buried in Rosh Pina. After 1948, immigrants from a nearby transit camp were absorbed, but most of them later transferred to the nearby development town of Hatzor ha-Galil. Its farming includes grain crops, cattle, and fruit orchards. There is a sizable writers' quarter. Population (1987), 1,540. E. ORNI

ROSMARIN, HENRYK. Zionist leader in Poland (b. Peratyn, Russian Poland, 1882; d. Tel Aviv, 1955). Rosmarin studied at the Universities of Lvov, Vienna, and Berlin. An active Zionist from his youth on, he eventually became a member of the Central Committee of the Polish Zionist Organization. In 1918 he was one of the founders and the editor of the Polish Zionist daily *Chwila*.

Rosmarin was a deputy to the Polish Sejm (Parliament) from 1932 to 1938 and Consul General of Poland in Pal-

View of Rosh Pina, with old section in the foreground and new settlement in the background. [Israel Information Services]

estine from 1938 to 1945. He was a member of the Greater Zionist Actions Committee and president of the Polish branch of the Maccabi World Federation.

N.M. GELBER

ROSOV, ISRAEL BINYAMIN. Industrialist, financier, and Zionist leader (b. Dokshitsy, Russia, 1869; d. Jerusalem 1948). Rosov enrolled at the University of Moscow but because of the expulsion of the Jews from Moscow could not graduate. In 1895 he was appointed managing director of the Caucasus Oil Company, and in 1913, director of the Russian Oil Company in St. Petersburg. Rosov joined the Hovevei Zion movement in his youth and took an active part in Jewish and Zionist political and communal affairs. He represented the Russian Zionist Organization and, later, the Zionists of Palestine at the Fifth to the 19th Zionist Congresses (1901–35), and was a member of the Zionist Actions Committee from 1907 to 1931.

In 1904 Rosov participated in the underground conference of Jewish self-defense units in Odessa. He represented the Russian Zionist Organization in the Political Advisory Committee formed to assist Jewish deputies in the Russian Duma (Parliament). In 1909 he was elected a director of the Jewish Colonial Trust in London. In 1915 he took part in the consultations of Zionist leaders in Copenhagen, and in 1917 he served on the committee that formulated the Jewish political demands to the provisional revolutionary government of Russia. Two years later, Rosov settled in Palestine, where he served on the board of directors of the Mortgage Bank. From 1925 to 1931 he was director of the Society for Geological Research in Palestine.

Rosov joined the Revisionist movement in 1925. From 1930 to 1932 he served as chairman of the Revisionist Central Committee in Palestine, and he represented the movement in the Second and Third Asefat ha-Nivharim. After the split in the Revisionist ranks in 1933, Rosov backed the *Jewish State party headed by Meir Grossman, but in 1936 he joined Vladimir Jabotinsky's *New Zionist Organization and served on its governing bodies in Palestine.

I. BENARI

ROTENSTREICH. Zionist-Israeli family.

Efrayim Fischel Rotenstreich (Rottenstreich). Zionist leader in Poland (b. Kolomya, Galicia, Austria, 1882; d. Jerusalem, 1938). He graduated from the University of Vienna with a degree in German languages and literature, but later became a prominent economist. From his youth he was active in the Zionist movement, eventually becoming the chairman of the Jewish National Council in the short-lived West Ukrainian State (1918–19). When the district reverted to Polish rule, he was arrested for his Zionist activities by the Poles and imprisoned for nearly a year. From 1922 to 1927 he was a member of the Polish senate, and from 1927 to 1930 a member of the Polish Sejm (parliament), elected in both instances as a representative of the Jewish community. As a legislator he devoted himself largely to economic affairs, gaining vital experience for his later role as head of the Jewish Agency's Department of Trade and Industry in Jerusalem. He served in this capacity from 1935 until his death. In these few years he did much to strengthen the industrial basis of the yishuv's economy, and vigorously promoted foreign Jewish investment. Throughout his life he contributed to the Jewish press on ideological and economic matters, writing in Hebrew, Polish, and Yiddish.

Nathan Rotenstreich, son of Efrayim Fischel Rotenstreich, Israeli educator and philosopher (b. Sambor, Galicia, Austria, 1914), was active in his youth in the Gordonia movement. Settling in Palestine in 1932 he studied at the Hebrew University where he earned a Ph.D. in 1938. For nearly a decade he served as principal of the Youth Aliya Teachers College in Jerusalem. After two years of post-graduate studies at the University of Chicago, he returned in 1951 to the Hebrew University as a lecturer in philosophy, attaining the rank of full professor in 1955; he served this institution as the dean of humanities from 1957 to 1961 and as rector from 1965 to 1969. He is a founding member and vice-president of the Israel Academy of Science and Humanities. He was the first chairman of the Committee for Higher Education (1973–1979). For his varied contribution to Zionist thought and Israeli culture he received many awards, among them the Tschernichowsky Award (for his translation with S.H. Bergman of Kant) in 1954, and the Israel Prize for humanities in 1963.

His scholarship moves along two parallel vectors: the first a critical examination of modern continental philosophy; the second an analysis of modern Jewish thought. To both these fields he has contributed historical and original works. Among his writings on Jewish thought are his study, *Jewish Thought in Modern Times* (Hebrew, 2 vols., 1945, 1950, and second, revised ed. 1987); an abridged English version, *Jewish Philosophy in Modern Times: From Mendelssohn to Rosenzweig* (1968); *Tradition and Reality* (1972), *Jews and German Philosophy: The Polemics of Emancipation* (1984). Among his works in Zionist thought and current Israeli affairs are *The Jewish Situation and the State of Israel* (1963) and *Essays on Zionism and the Contemporary Jewish Condition* (1980). Reflecting his conception of Zionism as the renewal of Jewish culture in conjunction with the participation of Jews as Jews in the highest expressions of the universal human spirit are his translations into Hebrew (with Shemuel Hugo Bergman) of Immanuel Kant's three *Critiques* and *On Eternal Peace*.

As a Zionist thinker he endeavored to introduce a rigorous mode of philosophical analysis of the movement's ideological principles, particularly in the light of the new historical realities that have emerged with the establishment and existence of the State of Israel and the fact that the center of the Diaspora has shifted from the East, where the salient issue was emancipation, to the West, particularly the USA, where Jews have unambiguously achieved full civil rights. This achievement, however, has intensified the decline of Jewish culture and identity. A national culture can exist only when there is a correspondence between the individual's axiological and spiritual universe and the majority culture. With respect to Jewry, such a situation can exist only in the State of Israel. In the past, Zionism benefited from the "negative energizing force" of anti-Semitism; today, in the general absence of persecution, the movement must depend on a "positive energizing force," which Rotenstreich believes can and, indeed, must be generated by the unfolding national culture of the State of Israel.

Yehoshua Rotenstreich, son of Efrayim Fischel Rotenstreich, Israeli jurist (b. Kolomya, Galicia, Austria, 1910; d. Tel Aviv, 1988). He immigrated to Palestine in 1933, after qualifying in law at the University of Lvov. A distinguished lawyer, he was head of the Israel Bar Association from 1963 to 1974 and for almost 40 years headed the Censorship

Appeals Tribunal (Press Council). Rotenstreich served on a number of official inquiry commissions, including the one to establish operational norms for the General Security Services (Shin Bet). P. MENDES-FLOHR

ROTH. Family of scholars.

Leon Roth (Hayim Yehuda). Philosopher, faculty member of the Hebrew University of Jerusalem (b. London, 1896; d. Wellington, New Zealand, 1963). After serving in the British Army in France (1916–18), Roth received MA and PhD degrees from Oxford University. He was a lecturer in philosophy at the University of Manchester (1923–28) and then went to Palestine to become a professor of philosophy at the Hebrew University, a chair he held until 1953. He also served as rector of the Hebrew University (1940–43) and as dean of the Faculty of Humanities (1949–51).

In 1926 Roth was named an *officier de l'Académie* and in 1948 a fellow of the British Academy. A prolific writer, he published numerous studies in philosophy and comparative religion and contributed articles to specialized periodicals in English, French, and Hebrew. He also edited a series of translations of philosophy classics into Hebrew. His works include *The Hebrew University and Its Place in the Modern Jewish World* (1944), *Jewish Thought as a Factor in Civilization* (1954), *God and Man in the Old Testament* (1955), and *Judaism: A Portrait* (1960).

Cecil Roth, Leon's brother, Jewish historian (b. London, 1899; d. Jerusalem, 1970), taught at Oxford until 1964 when he settled in Jerusalem. He was editor-in-chief of the *Encyclopedia Judaica* and wrote extensively on Jewish history and art.

ROTH, STEPHEN (SIEGFRIED) J. Zionist leader in Hungary and Britain (b. Gyoengyoes, Hungary, 1915). He received his doctorate in law from the University of Budapest and was an active leader of the Zionist youth movement in Hungary. In 1940 he joined the Executive of the Hungarian Zionist Federation. During World War II he was one of the founders of the Clandestine Zionist rescue committee (Va'ad Ezra ve-Hatzala). During Hungary's occupation by Nazi Germany (1944–1945), he was a leading member of the Zionist underground, organizing the illegal escape to Romania, and was arrested by the Gestapo and imprisoned for 3 1/2 months. After the war, he was elected to the Executive of the reconstituted Jewish community of Budapest and also founded the Hungarian Section of the World Jewish Congress, becoming its first Director. In 1946 he was invited to join the World Jewish Congress (WJC) European head office in London. He was Executive Director of the WJC European Branch (1947–1980) and General Secretary of its British Section (1947–1966). In 1966 he was appointed Director of the Institute of Jewish Affairs (of the WJC), serving until 1988. Roth was delegate to several Zionist Congresses and, in 1985, was elected Chairman of the Zionist Federation of Great Britain and Ireland. An international lawyer, specializing in problems of human rights, he has frequently contributed to books and learned journals. E. EPPLER

ROTHEMBERG, NEHEMIE. Religious Zionist leader in France (b. Safed, 1892; d. Paris, 1970). Rothemberg became active in the Zionist movement at an early age. After serving as secretary of the Jewish National Fund (JNF) in France, in 1935 he was elected vice-president, and in 1939 president, of the Mizrachi Organization of France. In 1948 he was again elected to the presidency of the Mizrachi, and in 1955 he became treasurer of the JNF campaign in France. In 1962 he was elected president of the Zionist Federation of France, the first religious Zionist to hold that office.

Rothemberg was active also in general Jewish communal life. In 1945 he became a member of the Jewish Consistory and treasurer of the Comité de Bienfaisance, the central philanthropic institution of Paris. Between 1951 and 1961 he was president of the Yavne Grammar School. In 1964 he was elected president of the Traditional religious congregation Rue de Montevideo, Paris.

S. KLINGER—M. CATANE

ROTHENBERG, MORRIS. Judge and Zionist leader in the United States (b. Tartu, Estonia, 1885; d. New York, 1950). Taken to the United States at the age of eight, Rothenberg received a law degree from the New York University Law School in 1905 and opened a law practice in New York. He lectured widely on labor law and was frequently asked to arbitrate industrial disputes. In 1937 he was appointed a judge of the Magistrates Court of the city of New York.

Rothenberg early became interested in Zionism, and from 1916 to 1918 he served as chairman of the Zionist Council of Greater New York. He was a delegate to the international conference of the Comité des Délégations Juives and to the International Relief Conference, both of which met in Carlsbad, Czechoslovakia, in 1923. He was a delegate to several Zionist Congresses and became a close associate of Chaim Weizmann. Along with Weizmann, Louis C. Marshall, Felix M. Warburg, and others he collaborated in creating the expanded Jewish Agency in 1929, and he was elected cochairman of the Jewish Agency Council. Rothenberg was a member of the Zionist Actions Committee and, from 1932 to 1936, president of the Zionist Organization of America (ZOA).

Rothenberg was an incorporator of the American Jewish Joint Distribution Committee in 1914 and helped organize the People's Relief Committee during World War I. He was president of the Jewish National Fund (1943–49) and a member of the international Board of Directors of Keren ha-Yesod. In 1949–50 he served as cochairman of the United Jewish Appeal and chairman of the United Palestine Appeal. A founder and executive board member of the National Jewish Welfare Board, he took an active interest in the rescue and resettlement of refugees from Nazi Germany and became a board member of the National Refugee Service. For some time he served as chairman of the Executive Committee of the American Jewish Congress.

ROTHSCHILD FAMILY. Prominent family of bankers and philanthropists, many of whom were active supporters of Zionism and Israel.

FRENCH BRANCH: The youngest of the five sons of the founder of the family, **Meyer Amschel Rothschild** of Frankfort, **James Rothschild** (1792–1868) settled in Paris. One of his sons was **Baron Edmond de Rothschild** (see separate entry).

James' granddaughter, **Bathsabée** (b. 1914), established

the Batsheva Dance Company in Israel, and was awarded the Israel Prize in 1989 for her contributions to dance in Israel. Her brother, **Guy** (b. 1909) was also deeply involved with Israel and was president of the Comité de Solidarité avec Israel (1956). **Edmond de Rothschild** (b. 1926), grandson of Baron Edmond, became one of the largest foreign investors in Israel. Particularly concerned with the economic development of the State of Israel, he made generous contributions to the national funds. President of the company that built an oil pipeline from Haifa to Eilat, and of a corporation founded to develop Caesarea, he also served as president of the European Committee for State of Israel Bonds and of the board of governors of the Israel Museum. M. CATANE

BRITISH BRANCH: Nathaniel Meyer Rothschild (1840–1915) was the first Jew to be elevated to the British peerage, as Baron Rothschild. Herzl at first placed great hopes in the British branch of the Rothschild family and, in 1895, composed a lengthy "Address to the Rothschilds," in which he set forth his plans for a Jewish State. In 1902 he addressed a letter to Baron Rothschild asking for an interview, which took place at the Rothschild office in London in the presence of Lord Rothschild's younger brother, Leopold (1845–1917). Lord Rothschild's friendship was useful to Herzl in his political work. Later, however, Rothschild joined Israel Zangwill in the International Council of the Jewish Territorial Organization. As a philanthropist, Nathaniel Meyer Rothschild supported various projects in Palestine and, among others, helped maintain the Evelina de Rothschild School in Jerusalem, named in memory of his sister.

James-Armand de Rothschild (1878–1957), the son of Baron Edmond de Rothschild, who became a naturalized British subject and a member of Parliament, was an active Zionist. During World War I he served with the Jewish Legion in Palestine, where his cousins Evelyn de Rothschild and Neil Primrose were killed in action. He was attached to the Zionist Commission that went to Palestine in 1918 with Chaim Weizmann and became president of the Palestine Jewish Colonization Association (PICA), which administered the settlements established by his father. In his will he left IL 6,000,000 for the construction of the new Knesset building in Jerusalem.

Nathaniel Meyer's son, **Lionel Walter, 2nd Baron Rothschild** (1869–1937), was honorary president of the Zionist Federation of Great Britain and Ireland at the time of the Balfour Declaration. It was to him that the declaration was addressed. Lord Rothschild was also a vice-president of the Board of Deputies of British Jews. In December, 1917, he presided over a meeting held at Covent Garden to celebrate the issuance of the Balfour Declaration. As vice-president of the London Zionist Conference of 1920, he took the chair at many of its sessions. During World War I he was a supporter of the Jewish Legion and head of its Comforts Committee. J. FRAENKEL

ROTHSCHILD, BARON EDMOND DE. Banker, philanthropist, patron of scientific and cultural projects, and developer and supporter of Palestine projects (b. Boulogne-sur-Seine, France, 1845; d. there, 1934). Rothschild was concerned with Jewish problems from his earliest youth. In 1882, following the pogroms in Russia, he first became interested in the settlement work done in Eretz Israel by the Hovevei Zion movement, his attention having been drawn to the movement by Rabbi Zadoc Kahn, chief rabbi of Paris and Rothschild's adviser on philanthropic matters. It was at Kahn's suggestion that Rothschild received Rabbi Shemuel Mohilever and Joseph Feinberg, a leader of the new settlement Rishon le-Zion, who had come to Paris to seek funds for the relief of the needy settlers. At about the same time Charles Netter drew his attention to the financial difficulties of Rishon le-Zion. Rothschild donated 30,000 francs to save the settlement from collapse. Late in 1883 he purchased land for the founding of a model agricultural settlement, Ekron, which he set up at his own expense and which was later renamed Mazkeret Batya in memory of his mother. He continued to support Rishon le-Zion and Ekron and subsequently took under his wing Rosh Pina and Zamarin, which was later renamed Zikhron Ya'akov in memory of Rothschild's father.

Baron Edmond de Rothschild. [Zionist Archives]

After his first visit to Eretz Israel in 1887 (he was to visit there four more times, in 1893, 1899, 1914, and 1925), Rothschild met Leo Pinsker in Paris to discuss various aspects of Jewish settlement in the country and to offer help and cooperation to the Hovevei Zion. The *Bilu pioneers in the settlements under his patronage resented what they considered the paternalistic attitude of Rothschild and of the experts he employed to supervise agricultural work. Only much later, after the settlements had begun to prosper, did this attitude of distrust and resentment give way to one of respect and appreciation. In time Rothschild became known as Ha-Nadiv ha-Yadu'a (the Well-known Benefactor) and the Father of the Yishuv.

By the time Herzl published *The Jewish State*, Rothschild had invested millions of francs in various enterprises in Eretz Israel, including the wine industry, which he had started by building the wine cellars of Rishon le-Zion and Zikhron Ya'akov. Anxious to win Rothschild's support for his projected Jewish State, Herzl met Rothschild in Paris in July 1896, but was received coolly. Rothschild considered Herzl's plan impractical. He thought that Eretz Israel would not be able to support mass immigration and that the Turks would never countenance such a project. In general, he believed that any such plans would have to be preceded by quiet, practical settlement work. Besides, he feared that the notion of a Jewish State might lead anti-Semites the world over to suggest that all the Jews be expelled from the countries where they lived and sent to Eretz Israel.

In 1899, when he was seriously ill, he turned over the administration of his Palestine enterprises to the Jewish Colonization Association (ICA), giving ICA 14,000,000 francs to put it on a self-sustaining basis. A quarter of a century later, in 1924, he founded the *Palestine Jewish Colonization Association (PICA), making his son James-Armand de Rothschild its president. During his lifetime, Edmond de Rothschild and his settlement association founded more than 30 settlements in all parts of Eretz Israel.

In addition to developing the wine industry in the country, he founded a glass factory (1892), an olive oil processing plant (1894), a salt refinery in Athlit, and the Grands Moulins de Palestine in Haifa. In 1921 he was a cosponsor of the Palestine Electric Corporation, Ltd., and two years later he set up Palestine's first modern dairy plant in Binyamina. In addition, he sponsored swamp drainage near Hadera, Athlit, and other communities to fight malaria.

An observant Jew throughout his life, Rothschild established synagogues wherever the settlers requested them. During a crisis in 1923 he made a large donation to keep the Zionist schools of the yishuv from closing down but insisted that his views on Jewish education be respected. He demanded that the schools show respect for religious tradition by refraining from criticizing religious observances and from teaching biblical criticism. In general, he believed that any Jewish commonwealth in Palestine could draw the world's attention only by disseminating culture. Accordingly, he aided Chaim Weizmann with funds to establish the Hebrew University of Jerusalem.

During World War I Rothschild used his influence to secure France's endorsement of the Balfour Declaration and, later, of the award of the Mandate for Palestine to Great Britain. Nevertheless, he admitted that he had influenced the anti-Zionist speech of Sylvain Lévi, the representative of the Alliance Israélite Universelle, at the Paris Peace Conference. He explained that he had done so to keep the idea of a Jewish state from being brought up at the conference in such a blatant manner as to incur Arab ill will while the Jews in Palestine had no means of defending such a state. He was, as he put it, "opposed to raising slogans and to building Eiffel towers without foundations." Yet he stressed that he had always thought in terms of establishing a Jewish commonwealth at some future date. In 1929 he was made honorary president of the newly founded Jewish Agency. It was in this capacity that he wrote a letter to the London *Times* registering his protest against the Passfield White Paper.

Edmond de Rothschild and his wife were reinterred near Zikhron Ya'akov in 1954. G. HIRSCHLER

ROUND TABLE CONFERENCE OF 1939. *See* ST. JAMES'S CONFERENCE.

ROVINA, HANNA. Actress (b. Berezino, Minsk Province, 1889; d. Tel Aviv, 1980). She studied Hebrew in a modern *heder* and prepared to be a teacher in the Froebel Institute in Warsaw. The director Nahum Zemach took her into a Hebrew-speaking troupe in Warsaw. During World War I she returned to kindergarten teaching but when Zemach established the Habimah company in Moscow, he invited Rovina to join and she created many of the female lead roles in the classical Habimah repertoire, notably as Lea in Anski's *The Dybbuk*, Portia in *The Merchant of Venice*, and Medea. When the company moved to Tel Aviv, she became regarded as the leading actress in the country and eventually as the "first lady of the Israel stage." Later in her career, she played a series of mother roles (mother of the Messiah in *The Eternal Jew*, Capek's *Mother*, etc.).

Hanna Rovina in the original production of the "Dybbuk" in Moscow, 1922. [Habima Theater]

ROYAL COMMISSION. *See* PEEL COMMISSION; SHAW COMMISSION.

ROZENTAL, SALVADOR (JOSHUA). Zionist leader in Colombia (b. Edineti, Bessarabia, 1908). After studying medicine in Spain, he went to Peru in 1925 but returned to Spain during the Spanish Civil War and served on the Madrid front as school doctor for refugee children. In 1938, he settled in Colombia where he worked first on behalf of Spanish Republican refugees and then for refugees from Nazi Germany, as secretary of the Centro Israelita. In 1939 Rozental was elected president of the Centro Israelita and devoted himself to communal and Zionist activities. In 1945 he founded the Christian Committee for a Jewish Palestine and established the Zionist Federation of Colombia. He edited the review *Atid* and was cofounder of the Jewish school in Bogota. Rozental also established Cultural Institutes between Israel and Colombia, Ecuador, and Venezuela. He founded Committees for Soviet Jewry in Latin America, acting as General Secretary until 1974.

RUBASHOW, SHNEUR ZALMAN. *See* SHAZAR, SHNEUR ZALMAN.

RUBIN, REUVEN. Israeli painter and diplomat (b. Galale, Romania 1893; d. Caesarea, 1974). He studied for one year (1912) at the Bezalel School in Jerusalem and continued in Paris, Italy, and Romania. His first solo show was sponsored by Alfred Stieglitz in New York, 1920. Rubin settled in Tel Aviv in 1922, painted family portraits, did woodcuts, stage sets, and was the first artist to have a one-man show at the Tower of David in Jerusalem, 1924. He developed a widely influential Palestine naïve style, in both portraits and landscapes, which he abandoned in the 1930s for sweeter and more romantic versions of Palestinian genre, as well as landscapes of Jerusalem surrounded by silvery olive trees. His one-man show inaugurated the Tel Aviv Museum in 1932 and he was given a retrospective there in 1947. From

Reuven Rubin.
[Israel Information Services]

1948–50, he was Israel's minister-plenipotentiary to Romania. Rubin represented Israel at the Venice Biennale in 1948, 1950, and 1952. His *Glory of Galilee*, commissioned for the Knesset, hangs in the Cabinet Room. In 1969 he designed a stained glass window for the President's Residence in Jerusalem. In 1966 he was accorded a retrospective at the Israel Museum. In his later years, Rubin lived in Caesarea and completed numerous albums of lithographs for leading US publishers. He was awarded the Israel Prize for Art in 1973. A Rubin Museum was established in Tel Aviv by his widow, Esther Davis Rubin. M. RONNEN

RUFEISEN, JOSEPH. Economist, jurist, and pioneer Zionist (b. Moravska Ostrava, Moravia, Austria, 1887; d. Tel Aviv, 1949). While a law student at the University of Vienna, he was active in Zionist youth groups and for a time was the head of Ha-Ko'ah, the Austrian Zionist sports association. After World War I he participated in the establishment of the Jewish National Council in Czechoslovakia. In 1920 he became chairman of the Czechoslovak Zionist Territorial Federation, in which capacity he served for almost two decades.

A delegate to Zionist Congresses, beginning with the 12th in 1921, Rufeisen was elected to the Actions Committee in 1925. In 1939 he settled in Palestine, where he became active in the General Zionist party and in several economic institutions. He lectured at the School of Law and Economics in Tel Aviv on economic management and marketing. These lectures were published in two volumes in 1946. A. ALPERIN

RUHAMA. Kibbutz in the southern coastal plain, 7 mi. (12 km.) east of Sederot. Since 1911 there had been Jewish settlement attempts on the site and the place had for a time been the southernmost Jewish outpost. In 1917, the Turks ordered its evacuation in face of the advance of the Allied forces. Resettled in 1920, it was abandoned in the 1929 Arab riots, again occupied in 1932, but given up in the 1936–39 Arab riots. It was finally established in 1944 as part of the project extending the settlement network southward. Its first task was reclamation of the local loess badlands. The kibbutz held out under irregular and Egyptian army attacks in the 1948 War of Independence. It has variegated farming as well as industrial enterprises. Population (1987), 632. E. ORNI

RULF, ISAAC. Rabbi, Jewish communal worker, and early Zionist in Germany (b. Rauisch-Holzhausen, near Marburg, Germany, 1831; d. Bonn, 1902). Ordained a rabbi in 1857, Rülf received his secular education at the universities of Marburg and Rostock. In 1865 he obtained a Ph.D. degree and became district rabbi of Memel. In this post he engaged in relief work for Russian Jewry and for immigrants from eastern Europe. In 1883 he wrote his famous treatise *Arukhat Bat Ami* (The Healing of the Daughter of My People), which anticipated the ideas of political Zionism.

With the rise of Herzl, Rülf joined the Zionist movement, attending the first five Zionist Congresses (1897–1901). At a conference held in Frankfurt on the Main on 31 October 1897, which later gave rise to the Zionist Organization of Germany, Rülf was elected to the Central Committee, which transacted the business of the new organization. A fierce opponent of the *Protestrabbiner (German anti-Zionist rabbis), he spent the last years of his life in Bonn, actively aiding in the dissemination of Zionism throughout Germany.

Rülf was the author of a number of books and treatises on philosophy and social problems, including *Das Erbrecht als Erbübel* (The Law of Inheritance as Inherited Evil, 1893). From 1872 until his departure from Memel, he was editor-in-chief of the *Memeler Dampfboot*, a political daily.

Arthur Ruppin.
[Zionist Archives]

RUPPIN, ARTHUR. Zionist leader and organizer of agricultural settlement in Palestine (b. Rawicz, Posen Province, Prussia, 1876; d. Jerusalem, 1943). Because of his family's poverty, Ruppin had to leave school at the age of 14 and was apprenticed to a firm of wholesale grain merchants in Magdeburg. He soon advanced to a position of responsibility, meanwhile continuing his studies to prepare himself for admission to a university. After passing the secondary school examination in 1898, he attended the universities of Berlin and Halle, receiving a doctorate in law in 1902. In 1904 he accepted the invitation of Alfred Nossig to become secretary-general of the Verein für Statistik der Juden (Society for Jewish Statistics), which Nossig had founded, and published his sociological study *Die Juden der Gegenwart (The Jews of Today*, 1913). The following year Ruppin became editor of the *Zeitschrift für Demographie und Statistik der Juden* (Journal of Jewish Demography and Statistics).

Ruppin joined the World Zionist Organization in 1905. In 1907 David Wolffsohn asked him to go to Palestine to make a study of Jewish settlements on behalf of the Inner Actions Committee. In the report he submitted to the Actions Committee after his return from an 11-week tour, Ruppin recommended that the settlements in Judea and Galilee be developed into a nucleus with a Jewish majority and that the greater part of the soil be owned by Jews. His recommendations included detailed proposals regarding land purchases and the industrial and cultural development of Jewish Palestine. This journey was the turning point in Ruppin's life. From then on he devoted all his energies to the upbuilding of the yishuv. In 1908 he settled in Palestine to become director of the *Palestine Office set up in Jaffa by the Zionist Executive. On Ruppin's initiative, six workers from the Kineret farm signed a contract with the Palestine Land Development Company, undertaking to work the land allotted them as employees of the company in return for a monthly salary and half of the net profits. This was the start of the Kevutza Deganya (1909). Ruppin also helped found the all-Jewish garden suburb near Jaffa, which later became Tel Aviv, and he was active in civic and communal affairs.

When the yishuv was cut off from the Diaspora by the outbreak of World War I, Ruppin turned his energies to obtaining aid for Palestine Jewry. Before long his activities became suspect to Ahmed Jamal Pasha, commander of the Turkish Army in Syria, and in 1916 Ruppin was expelled from the country. He went to Constantinople, where, with the aid of the German Embassy, he served as the sole link between the Palestine Office in Jaffa and the Zionist Executive in Berlin. He helped transfer funds from abroad to the Palestinian settlers and aided Palestinian Jews in Constantinople.

After his return to Palestine in 1920, Ruppin was named to the Zionist Commission, and in 1921 he was elected to the Palestine Zionist Executive. Until 1925 he was in charge of the Land Settlement Department. On his initiative a number of banks, among them the Bank ha-Po'alim and the Palestine Loan Bank, were founded to provide loans on easy terms for workers who sought to set up cooperatives of their own. He bought and developed land in various parts of the country, including the Rehavia quarter in Jerusalem. In 1925 he was appointed lecturer in Jewish sociology at the Hebrew University of Jerusalem.

When Hitler came to power in Germany, Ruppin was appointed head of a new department set up by the Executive to deal with the resettlement of Jewish refugees from Nazi persecution. Seeking to consolidate and increase Jewish settlement in Palestine, he advocated the introduction of mixed farming so that the settlers need not depend on a single crop. Deeply concerned about the yishuv's relations with the Arabs, he emphasized the necessity to avoid offending Arab sensibilities when buying land and made a point of stressing the fact that the Jews bought only barren soil that had been of no use ot the Arab peasants. In the early 1920s he had helped found the Berit Shalom movement, which advocated the establishment of a binational Arab-Jewish state in Palestine, but after the Arab riots of 1929 and the massacre of the Jews in Hebron he resigned from the group and from then on refused to consider any concessions regarding Jewish immigration or land purchases.

In addition to the books mentioned above, Ruppin was the author of *Jüdische Zukunftsarbeit in Palästina* (1918); *Der Aufbau des Landes Israel* (1919); *Die Landwirtschaftliche Kolonisation der Zionistischen Organization in Palästina*, 1925; (*The Agricultural Settlement of the Zionist Organization in Palestine*, 1926); *Soziologie der Juden* (1930); *Bauern und Pflanzer: Landwirtschaftsprobleme im Aufbau von Palästina* (1932); *The Jews in the Modern World* (1934, reprinted 1973); *Three Decades of Palestine: Speeches and Papers on the Upbuilding of the Jewish National Home* (1936); *The Jewish Fate and Future* (1940); and *Agricultural Achievements in Palestine* (1943). Ruppin's three-volume autobiography, *My Life and Work*, edited by Alex Bein, was published in Hebrew in Jerusalem in 1968. His *Memoirs, Diaries and Letters* appeared in English in 1971, edited by A. Bein. I. PHILIPP

RURAL SETTLEMENT. The idea of bringing Jews to farming and other productive work in Eretz Israel emerged in the 1830s. Following the Safed earthquake (1837) Rabbi Nissan Bak built Kefar Jermak on Mount Meron lands which he had received from the governor, Ibrahim Pasha, but the village was soon abandoned. In 1855 Jews purchased land at Koloniya west of Jerusalem, but only in 1894 did the moshava Motza come into being there. In 1870, Alliance Israélite Universelle opened the agricultural school Mikve Yisrael under the management of Charles Netter near Jaffa, to train Jews in farming.

In 1878, Jews from Safed attempted to settle and farm at Gei Oni on the eastern slope of Mount Canaan in Upper Galilee, and Jews from Jerusalem purchased a relatively large area northeast of Jaffa. Both enterprises failed after some time but, in 1882 and 1883 respectively, the *moshavot of Rosh Pina and Petah Tikva were renewed on the two sites.

Hovevei Zion of the First Aliya settled in 1882–1884 in these two moshavot and founded Rishon le-Zion and Nes Ziona south of Jaffa, Zikhron Ya'akov on the southern spur of Mount Carmel, and Yesud ha-Ma'ala on the bank of Lake Huleh. The Benei *Bilu association set up Gedera, its only village, in the southern coastal plain. All settlers encountered enormous obstacles—hostility of Arab neighbors and Turkish authorities, lack of water, absence of working capital, illnesses caused by malaria, the unfamiliar climate and bad sanitary conditions, and their own inexperience in farming. They would have failed, had not Baron Edmond de Rothschild intervened from 1883, taking most of the moshavot under his protection, aiding them financially, and sending French experts as administrators and farming guides. He let grain cultivation be largely replaced by vineyards and other fruit plantations and bought land for a few more moshavot for the second generation of settlers e.g., Shefeya and Bat Shelomo near Zikhron Ya'akov, and Mazkeret Batya near Rishon le-Zion. However, farms were mostly run with hired Arab labor and the moshavot assumed a patriarchic-philanthropical character which affected the settlers' pioneering spirit.

When in 1890–1891 immigration took a new upturn, Rehovot south of Rishon le-Zion and Hadera in the northern Sharon came into being. Metula and Mishmar ha-Yarden widened the settlement network to the north and Be'er Toviya to the south. The moshavot, in spite of all their shortcomings, demonstrated the ability of Jews to work the soil.

Sharp criticism of the moshavot regime moved Rothschild, in 1899, to transfer the villages' administration to ICA the (*Jewish Colonization Association). Striving to gradually transform settlers into self-working independent farmers and therefore preferring grain-farming ("grande culture") to vineyards, ICA bought land between 1901 and 1909, mostly in eastern Lower Galilee where it established the Sejera (Ilaniya) farm and moshavot like Kefar Tavor, Menahemia and Yavne'el-Bet Gan, with generous land units of 60–75 acres for each settler. Lack of water, however, did

Early view of Binyamina. [Zionist Archives]

not permit the diversifications of farming and, without machinery, hired Arab labor was again needed for grain farming. Jewish laborers who demanded higher wages were little welcomed by the ICA administration.

From 1904, young Second Aliya immigrants sought to insist on Jewish labor in the veteran moshavot. Arthur Ruppin, who in 1908 opened in Jaffa the Palestine Office of the Zionist Organization, took on Yehoshua Hankin as a land acquisition expert. On the land purchased, training farms for Jewish laborers were installed, especially Kineret near the southwest corner of the Sea of Galilee. When quarrels developed between the Kineret director and the laborers, Ruppin was inclined to support the latter and permitted some of them to work part of the land on their own responsibility (1909). They then created Degania, the first kevutza, with principles of collective direction by the village members, full self-labor, equality of men and women, and education of the children by the collective. A farm cooperative on lines suggested by Franz Oppenheimer was founded in 1911 in the center of the Jezreel Valley at Merhavia; it did not succeed as hoped, but nevertheless became the cornerstone of settlement in the valley, and from 1921 a *moshav and a *kibbutz developed on its land. Other Zionist farms at Hulda and Ben Shemen, the latter directed by Yitzhak Elazari-Volcani, tried out new branches and laid the ground for "mixed farming" which Ruppin enthusiastically advocated.

In World War I the Jewish villages persevered in spite of Turkish hostility. In Upper Galilee, new settlements, Kefar Giladi, Tel Hai and Ayelet ha-Shahar, were even established, originally intended by ICA as temporary expedients in order to provide food for urban Jews threatened by famine. Their continuing existence and later resistance to Arab attacks resulted in the inclusion of their region within the borders of the British Mandate.

The 1920 London Zionist Conference endorsed the principles of national land and self-labor. It resolved that the *Jewish National Fund concentrate its efforts on the acquisition, reclamation, and afforestation of land which was to be allocated in hereditary leasehold to settlers. Keren ha-Yesod was founded to finance settlement building and other Zionist purposes. In the same year, the Histadrut was founded, comprising the older Agricultural Workers Union. It formed the Merkaz Hakla'i as its instrument for rural settlement planning and execution and for agricultural production. The moshavot set up Histadrut ha-Ikarim.

Young socialist pioneers of the Third Aliya, some having received basic farm training in the Diaspora, united in 1921 in the He-Halutz movement. In Palestine, their groups took on road building, swamp draining, and other infrastructural tasks. In their new settlements, they clearly defined the form of the Kevutza, with the accent on human relations and no rigid insistence on growing beyond a defined limit; also of the "large and growing kibbutz", striving to maximize its economic potential, and of the moshav, based on family holdings but cooperative in the principles of national land, self-labor, mutual aid, and the common sale of produce and common purchase of production means. The period's outstanding settlement achievements were in the Jezreel and Harod Valley where by 1923 the kibbutzim En Harod, Tel Yosef, Bet Alfa, Heftziba, Geva, Ginegar, and Mizra, and the moshavim Nahalal, Kefar Yehezkel and Tel Adashim came into being. Kibbutz Kiryat Anavim was founded in the Judean Hills and, on ICA land in the northern Sharon, Moshava Binyamina. Countrywide associations started to group villages according to settlement forms and political views. In 1925, Tenu'at ha-Moshavim was established at a congress at Nahalal; it identified with what was to become the Mapai party. The kevutzot close to Ha-Po'el ha-Tza'ir formed the Hever ha-Kevutzot organization. In 1927, the larger kibbutzim set up the *Kibbutz Me'uhad, and those of the Ha-Shomer ha-Tza'ir movement organized in the *Kibbutz Artzi. All associations supported their member settlements economically with credit bodies and other institutions and aided them in education, culture, and recreation.

In the Fourth Aliya, starting in 1924, the lower middle-class element was prominent. It preferred urban life, but also strengthened the rural sector. In the central coastal plain, it reinforced veteran moshavot and settled in new ones, like Ra'anana, Herzliya, Ramatayim (Hod ha-Sharon), Pardes Hana, and Netanya, all based principally on a citrus economy.

In the 1929 Arab riots, Be'er Toviya and Hulda were temporarily destroyed and the progress of other settlements slowed. Simultaneously, the world economic crisis caused severe difficulties. To overcome the stalemate the Hityashvut ha-Elef ("settlement of the thousand") scheme of 1932 planned the creation of intensive farms with family holdings of only 4 acres near coastal plain moshavot, where in the initial stage farmer-settlers could earn their upkeep by doing hired labor. The scheme financed only 437 farmsteads, but the moshavim of Kefar Bilu and Gibeton near Rehovot, Neta'im and Bet Oved near Nes Ziona, Gat Rimon near Petah Tikva, Kefar Hess near Tel Mond, Givat Hen near Ra'anana and Ganei Am near Magdiel, and the kibbutzim Gan Shelomo (Kevutzat Schiller) and Givat ha-Shelosha enriched the settlement map. Acquisition by the JNF, from 1928, of the Haifa Bay (*Zevulun Valley) and Hefer Valley lands resulted, after 1932, in the creation of the first villages in those regions.

Many newcomers of the Fifth Aliya in the 1930s, which brought 240,000 Jews to the country, turned to rural settlement. Pioneers joined existing kibbutzim and founded new ones whose growth was reinforced by Youth Aliya.

The majority of its groups were absorbed in kibbutzim and the rest in youth villages and moshavim, subsequently constituting nuclei for future villages. Settlement progressed in the Jezreel Valley and the Hefer Valley where farming became intensive, with 4–6 acres allocated to the moshav or kibbutz family unit.

The 1936–1939 Arab riots and their political aftermath spurred an intensified effort in land acquisition and settlement which reinforced several regions and encompassed new ones, e.g., the Bet She'an and Huleh valleys, the northwest corner of mountainous Upper Galilee, and the southern coastal plain. The *Stockade and Tower method was devised, creating new outposts capable of repulsing Arab attacks already on their founding day. In 1936, 10 such settlements were founded; 16 in 1937; 15 in 1938; 17 in 1939. The moshav shitufi, an additional settlement form, intermediate between kibbutz and moshav, was founded at that time; its first villages were Kefar Hitin (1936) and Moledet (1937) in eastern Lower Galilee and Shavei Zion (1938) on the coast near Nahariya. Immigrants from central Europe who had brought some capital, set up "middle-class-settlements," in which the financial participation of the national institutions was limited; some of these had small family holdings (1–2 acres); in their social order most of them resembled the moshav. Further countrywide associations were formed, namely Ha-Kibbutz ha-Dati (religious kibbutzim, set up 1938), Irgun Moshevei ha-Po'el ha-Mizrachi (religious Moshavim, 1940), Ha-Oved ha-Tziyoni (liberal Moshavim, 1936), the Ihud Hakla'i (middle-class villages, 1944).

Even during World War II settlement activity did not cease. On the promulgation of the 1939 White Paper and the 1940 Land Laws, the JNF reacted by further stepping up its work, particularly in regions where the laws forbade Jewish land purchase. From 1938 until 1947, the JNF purchased 110,00 acres, on which 47 new villages were founded, among them, in 1943, the first three Negev outposts—Gevulot, Bet Eshel, and Revivim—and in one night of 1946, 11 more settlements in the south and the Negev. Another effort was directed to the Hebron Hills where the four settlements of the Etzyon Bloc were formed in 1943–1946. Soldiers demobilized after World War II founded a number of moshavim and kibbutzim.

On the eve of the establishment of the State of Israel (May 1948), 25% of the country's 645,000 Jews lived on the land: in 44 moshavot (86,000 inhabitants), 39 middle-class settlements (14,000), 68 moshavim (19,000), 146 kibbutzim (44,000), and a number of training farms and schools (2,000).

In the War of Independence, the four kibbutzim of the Etzyon Bloc were abandoned, as well as the moshavim of Atarot and Neve Ya'akov north of Jerusalem, Kibbutz Bet ha-Arava north of the Dead Sea, and Kibbutz Kefar Darom south of Gaza. East of Gaza, Kibbutz Be'erot Yitzhak was destroyed. All these settler groups soon established new villages elsewhere in Israel. Kibbutzim Yad Mordekhai and Nitzanim in the southern coastal plain, evacuated in the fighting, were rebuilt soon after their sites were recaptured by the Israel army. Mishmar ha-Yarden, temporarily occupied by the Syrians, was later rebuilt not far from its former site.

About 80 outpost settlements were in 1947/48 set up by pioneer youth, some under enemy fire, prominent among them being Kibbutzim Beror Hayil on the northern Negev limit and Kefar ha-Nasi near the Upper Jordan. Soon after the end of hostilities, security settlements, mostly kibbutzim of Israel-born and immigrant pioneer youth, were built to secure defense positions close to former front lines. Their dual military and development assignment was institutionalized in 1949 by Nahal, the army's pioneer youth units.

Large scale immigration, which by the end of 1951 had nearly doubled the number of Israel's Jews, necessitated a new approach in rural planning. In November-December 1948, the settlement authorities prepared the immediate founding of 96 villages, but only one-third of the needed candidate groups were available. Masses of immigrants, on the other hand, were in transit camps without work. This generated the idea of the Moshav olim (immigrants' moshav) which in the course of time would become a normal moshav (*see* MOSHAV).

A total of 299 pioneer settlements and moshevei olim were established between 1948 and 1952, as against 277 rural settlements founded in the preceding 65 years. Of the 299, 57 were populated by immigrants from eastern and central Europe, 18 from Balkan countries and Turkey, 46 from Yemen, 28 from Iraq and Iran, 38 from North Africa, 8 from English-speaking countries, 6 from South America, and 1 from India. Settlers, agriculturally untrained and not ideologically motivated, tended to leave new villages at the first opportunity. This explains the large turnover of inhabitants in moshevei olim in their initial years. None, however, was abandoned.

From 1952, the Jewish Agency and Ministry of Agriculture authorities started planning according to a comprehensive regional concept. The number of farm units of each future moshav was decreased from 100–120 to 60–80. Clusters of four-five moshavim were grouped around a "rural center" providing economic, administrative, educational, and cultural services. These settlement groups were in turn linked to a center or directly to a regional town or city where more sophisticated services were available. The idea first guided the planning of middle-class villages in the Gedera region, around the rural center of Aseret. In the northwestern Negev, seven moshavim were set up near the town of Ofakim, and in the Jezreel Valley south of Afula the Ta'anakh Region was planned around rural centers. The scheme was perfected, from 1955, in the Lakhish Region, an area comprising parts of the southern coastal plain and the southern Judean foothills. The scheme was devised by Ra'anan Weitz. Arye Eliav headed the team which implemented the scheme on the spot. In addition to 12 settlements founded earlier, mainly in the region's northern and western part, 22 villages were set up over 18 months, of which 13 were immigrant moshavim, three moshavim shitufiyim, and two kibbutzim, as well as the two regional centers of Nehora and Even Shemu'el, the regional center Deganim (Merkaz Shapira), and the town of Kiryat Gat. Renewed immigration, mainly from North Africa, aided in populating the region. The Lakhish method was applied also to the planning of the Ta'anakh Region and, from 1957, to the Adullam Region in the Judean foothills and hills.

All the immigrant moshavim had been based on mixed farming, but from the mid-1950s it became clear that villages had to specialize in a limited number of branches in order to make their farming efficient and rewarding and to improve and cheapen ancillary services. This entailed a change in village layouts: instead of the former "towel shape", with homesteads spread along the sides of a single long road and the fields behind their yards, the new ones were built more compactly, thereby strengthening their economic and social coherence.

The pace of new settlement largely depended on the rate of immigration. In 1954 eight villages were founded, 21 in 1955 and again 21 in 1956, five in 1957, 13 in 1958, but only 28 during the period 1959–1966. In the 1960s settlement commenced in the Arava Valley which, apart from Kibbutz Yotvata, had previously been totally desolate; beginning as Nahal outposts, there were 3 moshavim in the northern and two kibbutzim in the southern Arava. Attention turned also to mountainous Galilee, where in 1965–1967 four moshavim and one kibbutz were added.

In the years preceding 1967, agriculture was constantly intensified, aided by supplies from the National Water Carrier which started to function in 1964. Farming was rationalized and mechanized, with progressive branch specialization of moshav farmers. Consequently, fewer farm workers were needed. Kibbutzim, some of whom had installed factories even before statehood, now opened one or more plants to employ surplus labor and broaden and balance their income sources. Regional factories belonging to several kibbutzim were often built at sites not registered as having permanent population (e.g., Tzemah south of Lake Kineret). Their use of hired non-member laborers led to ideological discussions, because as a matter of principle the kibbutz movements negated hired labor.

After the Six-Day War, existing villages were strengthened and new ones added within the pre-1967 borders. The principal change, however, consisted in efforts to extend settlement into the Administered Areas. Pioneer settlement in new regions was often begun with Nahal outposts. The first initiative came from children of the Etzyon Bloc which had been lost in 1948: in September 1967 Kibbutz Kefar Etzyon was restored in the Hebron hills. In 1987, the Bloc numbered 10 villages (three kibbutzim, one moshav shitufi and six "community settlements"), as well as the semi-rural center of Alon Shevut and the town of Efrata.

Settlement also began in the Golan Heights, where the first branch developed was beef cattle. Later, emphasis shifted to vegetables and fruit. In 1987, 28 rural settlements, two rural centers (Hispin and Benei Yehuda) and the town of Katzrin existed on the Golan Heights.

In 1968 it was decided to secure the Lower Jordan Valley border by establishing new villages. The scheme also extended along the western shore of the Dead Sea. Moshav Mehola opened the program, Yigal Allon drew up a plan, reserving for development those parts of the Administered Areas which had only a minute Arab population and were deemed vital for Israel's defense. Settlement proceeded there until 1977. In 1987, the Lower Jordan Valley, together with the waste eastern slopes of Samaria and Judea and the Dead Sea shore, was the site of 23 rural settlements and the urban center of Ma'ale Efrayim. Highly intensive farming, largely out-of-season crops, was introduced there.

In Sinai, settlement spread along the Eilat Gulf coast down to the Tiran Straits, and near the Mediterranean shore as a barrier between Egypt and the Gaza Strip. In the Eilat Gulf strip, four settlements were created, based mainly on tourism. In the north-east, the town of Yamit and 19 settlements were built, but in accordance with the peace treaty with Egypt, all were evacuated, and most of them flattened, in April 1982. In the Gaza Strip, efforts were directed mainly at emptying sand dunes where 10 villages existed in 1987, besides four further north.

The Likud and its political allies, opposed to the Allon Plan, strove to spread settlement all over Judea and Samaria and in 1974 succeeded in establishing Kedumim and Ofra in the mountainous area. When they took over the government in 1977, large-scale founding of villages began there. As hardly any but waste public land was available for the purpose and the chances for agriculture were minimal, a new form of the "community village" was devised which enabled settlers to commute to outside employment. Community villages were then set up elsewhere in the country, particularly in mountainous Galilee. Each such village hoped to attract 150–350 families, but by 1987 most of them had only 20–30 families. *Gush Emunim was particularly active in populating Judea and Samaria and the Gaza Strip and in 1977 established its settlement movement, Amana. In 1987, some 80 Jewish rural settlements existed in Judea and Samaria (besides those of the Etzyon Bloc), as well as the urban centers of Ariel, Immanu'el, Ma'ale Adumim, Givat Ze'ev, and Kiryat Arba.

Inside pre-1967 Israel, Negev settlement was energetically furthered after the evacuation of Sinai. On dune land east of the restored Egyptian border and south of the Gaza Strip, the "Peace Salient" was developed after 1982, with six moshavim and two kibbutzim, to grow vegetables and flowers, partly in greenhouses. In the Arava Valley, the number of settlements reached 21 by 1987. This was aided by the discovery of water sources and by research into the exploitation of brackish soil and water. In the 1980s, the settlement network was augmented also in the northern Negev close to the southern reaches of the Hebron hills.

In mountainous Galilee, outposts were created in areas empty of Jews to prevent public lands from being illegally appropriated by the local population. To expedite settlement, the *mitzpim system was devised, consisting of minute outposts initially averaging only 5–10 families, often without a chance to commence farming. Even larger new settlements were planned as *kafatim*, i.e., deriving their livelihood exclusively from industry. *Mitzpim* which became permanent in the course of time adopted one of the regular settlemnt forms, i.e., kibbutz, moshav, moshav shitufi, or community village. At the base of planning was the regional concept, aiming at four new regions—Segev, Tefen, Tzalmon, and Nahal Tzipori. Between 1980 and 1987, 58 new villages were established, 38 of them in the new regions and 20 in other parts of Galilee. Similarly, *mitzpim* were set up in the Iron Hills of northwestern Samaria.

In the 1980s, new settlement was matched by endeavors to reinforce existing villages, enlarge their productive capacity, redeem land for farming, factories and housing estates, carry out housing programs, build roads, render supply and marketing services more efficient, improve the educational and cultural network in the rural sector, find employment for the young generation of moshav farmers by establishing factories in such villages and in industrial zones belonging to groups of moshavim, etc.

Of the 3.5 million Jews in Israel in 1987, 10.2% lived in rural areas. Of the 936 Jewish villages, 248 had been founded before statehood. Of 370,100 Jewish rural inhabitants, 145,600 lived in 409 moshavim, 10,900 in 47 moshavim shitufiyim, 126,000 in 268 kibbutzim, 13,300 in 32 rural institutions (farming schools etc.) and 68,400 in 180 other rural places (of which 18,600 were in 95 community villages and 8,700 in 24 rural centers) (*see also* AGRICULTURE IN ISRAEL).

R. PERLMAN

RUSSIA, ZIONISM IN. Political Zionism in Russia, as in many other countries, was preceded by a *Hovevei Zion movement.

Initial Period (1897–1900): The first reports of Theodor Herzl's political activity reached Russia in late 1895. When he arrived in Russia a year later, he was greeted stormily by the members of the *Odessa Committee, who led the Hovevei Zion movement. Herzl's activities were initially viewed in a positive light, but opposition began to emerge as it became evident that his aims were not identical with those of the Hovevei Zion movement. The Odessa Committee did not, however, interfere with Herzl's activities and even encouraged him to convene a Zionist Congress. Herzl, for his part, urged the heads of Hibbat Zion (members of Hovevei Zion) to join his movement, promising both through emissaries and in writing that his activity would in no way harm the movement in Russia.

The First Zionist Congress in 1897 was attended by 44 delegates from Russia, and another twenty or so students from eastern Europe, who were studying in universities outside Russia, and who served in the Congress as representatives of the Russian Zionist societies. The total Russian delegation accounted for over a third of the Congress delegates. Despite their original disagreement with Herzl's ideologies and their initial demand for a fundamental change in his programs, the Russian delegates came away from the Congress fired with the same enthusiasm for Herzl's grandiose project as the other delegates. This enthusiasm quickly spread: within a year 379 Zionist societies had been created in the Pale of Settlement, as opposed to a total of only forty Hibbat Zion associations in the seven previous years (1890-1897).

Four Russian delegates, Jacob Bernstein-Cohen, Max Mandelstamm, Isidore Jasinowski, and Rabbi Shemuel Mohilever, were elected as members of the Zionist General Council and each accepted a function in the organization of the Zionist movement in Russia, undertaking to promote the movement and to disseminate its doctrine among Russian Jewry. The refusal of the Odessa Committee to join either the Zionist movement or the Zionist leadership in Russia stemmed not only from the official government ban on "political" activities in Russia, but more from their ideological opposition to Herzl and his movement which became increasingly acute.

Within a few years the Zionist movement had become a major public body in Russia. The violent opposition campaign mounted in 1899, in the main by hasidic circles, did not initially affect the spread of the movement. In 1900 1,147 societies existed with over sixty thousand shekel-holding members. The movement's success continued until late 1902 and can be credited not only to Herzl, who succeeded in infusing great hope into the masses, but to the Zionist organization created in Russia. The Russian delegates who headed the movement there increased after a year from four to ten, and built up a cadre which maintained thousands of activists. Jacob Bernstein-Cohen for several years directed the movement from the "Postal Bureau" in Kishinev, working alongside a number of community workers from southern Russia, including Menahem Ussishkin, Vladimir Tiomkin, and Victor Jacobson (nicknamed the "Southerners"). In order to make the existence of the movement more widely known they conducted propaganda campaigns, sending scores of speakers to tour through the cities and towns to win membership for the movement.

The "southern" leadership gradually took over the movement's administration, and imposed its ideologies and directions of activity on Russian Zionism, often in opposition to the "political" ideology of Herzl. The idea of Hibbat Zion prevailed, emphasizing traditional "practical" Zionism, and the principle that "cultural" activity as propounded by Ahad Ha-Am constituted an indivisible part of Zionism. The "cultural" work, holding that the Jewish masses must be educated to their nationality through spiritual preparation, eventually came to characterize the Zionist movement in southern Russia. The delegates added further nuances which differed from Herzl's political doctrine.

The Zionist movement in 1897–1900, in content and in spirit, superficially constituted a continuation of the previous activity of the Odessa Committee, but differed both quantitatively and in the additional "Herzlian" elements. Its presence was felt throughout the Pale of Settlement and its communal workers began to constitute an important influence in Jewish public life. Opposition by ultra-Orthodox circles stemmed less from ideological reasons than from the fact that Zionism supplanted them in Jewish public life, and this opposition escalated as Zionism spread, reaching a climax in 1899–1900 when the movement won support in localities which had never been favorable to the Odessa Committee.

Transformation of the Movement's Activity, 1900–1905. From 1899 and in particular in 1900, the heads of the Zionist movement in Russia began to change the direction of their activity. As the success of Herzl's diplomatic efforts became increasingly less probable and his political goal appeared unattainable, even utopian, the activists found other objectives which would enable the continued growth of the movement. The movement's objectives were now directed

Zionist youth group in Bobruisk in 1902. [YIVO Institute for Jewish Research]

towards the solution of existential problems, leaving the global Zionist solution to await the end of days! For several years, Zionism was almost entirely a political and social movement, working in the field of education, and in almost all fields related to the Jewish community. In time even the state officials began to see its representatives as the authentic heads of Russian Jewry, and in the summer of 1903 the Russian Minister of the Interior, Viacheslav von Plehve, issued a directive banning all Zionist activity. The movement's leaders were required to return to the traditional Hibbat Zion-type activity. The directive did not become a statutory law, but it intimidated the activists and affected the expansion of the movement.

In 1901 Bernstein-Cohen was replaced by Victor Jacobson, and the office of information took the place of the "Postal Bureau", which had centralized Zionist activity from Kishinev. These modifications were symptomatic of the changes in the entire movement's administration. While Bernstein-Cohen had centralized, shaped, and directed the activity, achieving coordinated, uniform processes, Jacobson acted more as a liaison officer among the delegates. He would not and perhaps could not direct and unify the overall Zionist activity in Russia as had his predecessor. Consequently, with the creation of the bureau of information, the delegates began to do as they saw fit within their "districts". Within two years (1901–1903) the movement's organizational infrastructure became chaotic, resulting in a severe crisis.

The organizational struggle in the Russian Zionist movement led to a split. In addition to the separate and uncoordinated functioning of the delegates in their districts, several Zionist parties, such as the Mizrachi, the Democratic Faction, and the Po'ale Zion emerged, considering themselves different from the rest of the movement and demanding organizational privileges. This reflected not only the organizational divisions in the movement, but also the new **Gegenwartsarbeit* (work in the Diaspora) activity. Zionism may be perceived from 1902 not as one body representing a monolithic ideology, but as an organization with a common, distant, and unrealistic objective, made up of a multitude of societies each wishing to move in a separate ideological direction. The creation of the office of information was accompanied by the decentralization of activities, suspension of the belief in a rapid Herzl-type Zionist solution, and the beginnings of *Gegenwartsarbeit*, activities. The outcome in the long term was unavoidably a crisis in the movement. Paradoxically, the *Minsk Conference, the second all-Russian Conference of the movement in Russia, which also marked the zenith of the Russian Zionist movement's growth, did not reflect the true situation at that time, offering rather a picture of the state of affairs under Bernstein-Cohen. The functional and organizational crisis inside the movement gradually led to paralysis.

In late 1900 the Zionist Organization also underwent a crisis, which had its source with the movement in Russia. While the Zionists in Russia had adopted several "Herzlian" ideological elements, principally those related to the need for open political activity, they also disagreed with many of his principles. Most were in favor of practical Hibbat Zion work and cultural activity as proposed by Ahad Ha-Am, and were basically opposed to any territorial solution outside Eretz Israel. These differences of opinion were openly stated from the first conference of the heads of the Zionist movement held in Bialystok (November, 1897) and reached their peak at the Minsk Conference. Herzl saw the Russian Zionists as the principal beneficiaries of his program and they in turn recognized that there was no alternative to Herzl or to the movement which he had built up.

Y. GOLDSTEIN

After Uganda. Herzl's journey to Russia in the summer of 1903, when he sought an audience with Viacheslav K. von Plehve, the Tsarist Minister of the Interior, in an abortive attempt to obtain a more favorable attitude toward the Zionist cause, provoked violent criticism on the part of the Russian delegates to the Sixth Zionist Congress (1903). The Russian delegation also constituted the bulk of the 177 who opposed Herzl's proposal to appoint a commission to investigate the *East Africa scheme and walked out after the proposal had been accepted. At that time Russian Zionism, with its 1,572 local groups, was the major force in the World Zionist Organization. In October, 1903, a conference of Russian Zionist leaders met in Kharkov and presented Herzl with an ultimatum either to give a written pledge to abandon the East Africa scheme and to concentrate on Eretz Israel or face an organized secession at an early date. An open conflict was averted, but after Herzl's death the Seventh Congress (1905) was split when the majority categorically rejected the British offer. In the minority group, which seceded and created the *Jewish Territorial Organization, Russian Zionists were represented by Mandelstamm and Nachman Syrkin.

While Territorialism as an idea and as a movement never gained much ground in General Zionist circles in Russia, it crystallized into a considerable force in Labor Zionist circles. The Zionist Socialist party, founded in 1904–05, repudiated the Eretz Israel solution of the Jewish problem as utopian and devoted its main attention to problems of Jewish migration, which, it believed, would automatically develop into a movement of settlement and thereby solve the Jewish problem.

Another Socialist group, whose general philosophy was close to that of the Russian Social Revolutionaries, emerged in 1905–06; it opposed Eretz Israel and any other Territorialist solution of the Jewish problem and advocated Jewish national autonomy in Russia, based on an elected Jewish national assembly; its members were called Sejmists, from the Polish word *sejm* (parliament). Both groups later merged into a United Socialist party, known as the Fareinigte. Even by early 1917, their combined membership did not exceed 13,000.

The Eretz Israel orientation was represented among Jewish labor and intelligentsia by Po'ale Zion, whose leading theorist was Ber Borochov. His concept of Zionism was strictly materialistic, expressed in Marxist terms: the Jewish problem could be solved only if a Socialist state were created in an economically viable country to which the Jews would emigrate. Eretz Israel was both geographically and economically best suited for this purpose. The first Po'ale Zion cells emerged in 1900 and for a time worked within the general framework of the Zionist Organization; later, increasing emphasis was put on proletarian class-consciousness, preventing continued cooperation with the middle-class Zionist movement. An intermediate position was taken by numerous groups of Tze'irei Zion, which began to gain ground from 1903 on. Their orientation was Socialist and non-Marxist, with no stress on the class struggle. The majority gravitated toward Ha-Po'el ha-Tza'ir. Tze'irei Zion constituted the backbone of the Halutz movement in Russia and was prominently represented in the Second Aliya (1904–14).

Prior to the 1905 Revolution, the Russian Zionists deliberately abstained from active participation in Russia's political life. Adhering strictly to the concept of the "negation of the Diaspora," they had little faith in the possibilities of collective Jewish national existence in Russia. From 1905 on this position underwent a radical change as a result of political developments in Russia and the need for an answer to the immediate problems of the Jewish masses. The Zionist press, including the Russian weeklies **Rassviet* of St. Petersburg, *Yevreiskaya Mysl* (Jewish Thought) of Odessa, and the Vilna Yiddish weekly *Dos Yidishe Folk* (The Jewish People), played a leading role in molding the Zionist short-term program. An All-Russia Zionist Conference at Helsingfors (Helsinki), Finland (21-27 November 1906), with 72 delegates representing 56 localities (*see* HELSINGFORS CONFERENCE), saw the emergence of the concept of Synthetic Zionism, which organically combined the traditional Zionist negation of the Diaspora with the struggle for Jewish survival and national organization in the Diaspora countries. The Helsingfors Program demanded not only complete civic equality for the Jewish population of Russia but also the recognition of the Jews as a national group with the right of self-determination in all Jewish national affairs and the acceptance of Hebrew and Yiddish as official languages in the schools, in the courts, and in public life. It was decided that the Zionists could not join any faction in the political struggle then going on in Russia but were to act as an independent party; cooperation with other groups was recommended for specific purposes only. The Zionists nominated their own candidates in the election to the First Duma (parliament); five of the 12 elected Jewish deputies

B'nei Zion (Sons of Zion) in Moscow celebrate 25th anniversary, 1910. [Jewish National and University Library]

were Zionists. In the Second Duma only six deputies were Jews, of whom one was a Zionist. After 1907 the Tsarist Russian government clamped down on the country's political life with an iron hand. Together with all other parties and groups, Russian Zionism was largely paralyzed.

The debate between the Russian Zionists and the World Zionist Executive over practical work in Eretz Israel continued after Herzl's death. This was apparent in the resolutions adopted at the Fifth All-Russia Zionist Conference, which opened prior to the Ninth Zionist Congress (1909) and concluded simultaneously with the latter. Despite these differences of opinion, the 1910 meeting of the Zionist Executive in Berlin decided to discontinue the discussion for the sake of the movement, and the Tenth Zionist Congress (1911) no longer reflected the conflict over this issue, which had been so noticeable at previous Congresses. The Polish and Russian Zionists were given representation on the World Zionist bodies. A similar situation existed prior and immediately subsequent to the 11th Zionist Congress (1913). J. SCHECHTMAN

1917: Between February and October. The Zionist movement in Russia had become largely inactive during World War I because of lingering government repression and the prohibition of printing in Hebrew and Yiddish. The fall of the Tsarist regime in February, 1917, followed by the abolition of all restrictions on the Jews and other minorities, had an especially exhilarating effect on the Zionists. They now saw the field clear for assuming the leadership of the Jewish community in Russia.

The Seventh Congress of Russian Zionists took place in May in the capital (then still Petrograd) with the participation of 552 delegates representing 140,000 shekel-holders. Menahem Ussishkin and Yehiel Tschlenow were elected to the presidency of the Congress, which reaffirmed the Helsingfors Program, and called for national autonomy for the Jewish minority in Russia in addition to support of the struggle for a homeland in Palestine. Party activists immediately went to work in order to secure maximum Zionist representation in the forthcoming elections for the Constituent Assembly, the planned Russian Jewish Congress, and the *kehillot* (local Jewish communities). Zionist cultural activity grew apace, and numerous newspapers made their appearance in Hebrew, Yiddish, and Russian. An educational center, "Tarbut", was also founded, which was later suppressed by the Soviets but took the lead in Hebrew education in those former parts of the Tsarist empire which did not come under Soviet rule.

First meeting of committee of Zionist Jewish Youth in Siberia, 1917. [Central Zionist Archives]

After October. The Bolshevik revolution in October (according to the western calendar: 7 November 1917) had no immediate effect on the Zionist renaissance, which at that very time was greatly encouraged by news of the Balfour Declaration. Zionism did not, as some expected, decline with the disappearance of oppression. In the elections for the Constituent Assembly the Zionists did very well, and in some cases formed election blocs with the Orthodox. In election after election they gained a majority of delegates, with all the parties of the left together (Bund, Po'ale Zion, United Jewish Socialists) generally managing to get only a quarter of the votes. Unfortunately, these election successes soon lost any meaning since the Russian Jewish Congress never convened, the Bolsheviks dispersed the Constituent Assembly, and the *kehillot* were soon liquidated by them in their efforts to bring Communism to the "Jewish street".

In their first year of rule the Communists closed the central Zionist Hebrew newspaper *Ha-Am*, together with the rest of the Hebrew press. This represented a victory for the Yiddishists, many of whom left the disintegrating Jewish Socialist parties to join the newly formed Jewish sections of the Communist party (Evsektsiia). The first big victory for the Evsektsiia and its government partner, the Evkom (Jewish Commissariat), came in July, 1919, with a decree declaring Yiddish and not Hebrew the language of the Jewish masses. This put an end to the Zionist-sponsored Tarbut schools, which had Hebrew as their language of instruction. Later that year the central Zionist organ in Russian, *Khronika evreiskoi zhizni*, was closed. It would, however, be an exaggeration to attribute all persecutions of Zionism to the "Evsektsiia". The Jewish Communists were willing tools in the hands of a government which had reasons of its own for not tolerating the Zionist movement. One of these was the decision to put an end to all political parties except the Communist party and Po'ale Zion (see below). Another was opposition to emigration. After the *SS Roslan* was allowed to sail for Palestine in 1919 with many Hebrew writers and cultural activists aboard, emigration became a matter of individual initiative, connections, and luck.

Serious harassment of Zionists had begun in the Ukraine in 1919 under the Communist regime then in the region, On 12 July, at the instigation of the leftist Jewish Komfarband, all Zionist organizations except Po'ale Zion were banned. The civil war in the area rendered the ban temporary, but when Communist rule was firmly established in what was to become the Soviet Union, there was, beginning in 1920, continuing and increasingly severe harassment of Zionist activity. Without imposing a formal ban the authorities, as time went on, made it impossible for the Zionist movement to function in the country.

The first serious blow came on 23 April 1920, the third day of an all-Russian Zionist conference convened in Moscow. Of 109 delegates and guests 75 were arrested, and while most were freed a few months later, some were sentenced on trumped-up charges to prison terms of up to five years. They were, however, freed after intervention by the American Jewish Joint Distribution Committee and after promising to cease further Zionist activity. An appeal by the visiting British Zionist leader, David Eder, to the Soviet Foreign Commissar, Chicherin, early in 1921 brought only evasive answers; Chicherin denied that Zionism was persecuted and pointed to Po'ale Zion as an example. The

Russian Zionist organization now went underground, with clandestine headquarters organized by Eliezer Tcherikover. For most of the decade there were arrests, prison sentences, and exile to Siberia. In some cases these sentences were commuted to expulsion to Palestine. In the mid-1920s 30,000 adherents of the movement were still claimed, but by 1930 the Zionist Organization of Russia had ceased to exist.

Tze'irei Zion. This labor-oriented but non-Marxist party convened in Kharkov in May, 1920, shortly after the last Moscow Zionist conference. On the basis of the conference decisions, which led to a split, the left wing formed a new party: ZS (Zionist-Socialists), with a pro-Soviet platform. The initials of this party were chosen to distinguish it clearly from the pre-war Zionist-Socialists, known by their Russian initials SS, who had actually been territorialists. ZS's hopes to enter the workers' councils (soviets) and to participate in Soviet life remained unfulfilled. ZS maintained an underground center in Leningrad until 1926 and for a few years following in Moscow.

The Tze'irei Zion faction, which remained loyal to democracy, later took the name Zionist Labor Party, or STP: Sionistskaia Trudovaia Partiia. It rejected the Kharkov conference decision, and went underground. Fifty-one delegates were arrested during its founding conference in Kiev on 4 May 1922. Thirty-seven were put on trial and the authorities, capitalizing on the agreement between the Zionist leader, Vladimir Jabotinsky, and the Ukrainian nationalist leader, Simon Petliura, attempted to put Zionism itself on trial at the time (August 1922). A number of those arrested were sentenced to prison, but Tze'irei Zion—STP maintained its organization for some time. In May, 1923, at an illegal Moscow conference, it was decided to join the World Union of Ha-Po'el ha-Tza'ir-Tze'irei Zion established in 1920 in Prague. Decimated by arrests, STP disbanded by the end of the decade.

Both wings of Tze'irei Zion had youth movements: From May, 1923 ZS had its "Zionist-Socialist Youth League" (Tsionistish-Sotsialistishe-Yugend Farband) while STP sponsored the competing United All-Russian Organization of Zionist Youth (Edinaia Vserossiiskaia Organizatsiia Sionistskoi Molodezhi, abbreviated EVOSM), founded in 1924. In 1926, when it formally joined STP, EVOSM, became EVTOSM by adding Trudovaia (Labor) to its name.

Ha-Shomer Ha-Tza'ir. In Russia Ha-Shomer ha-Tza'ir grew out of the Hebrew scout movement and the "Maccabi" sports organization during the Soviet period. As a separate group with the new name, it dates from a meeting which took place in Moscow (May, 1922) in the home of the "Maccabi" leader Yitzhak Rabinovich. Its first convention took place in Kharkov in May, 1923, and a second one in Kiev in July, 1924. From that year on Ha-Shomer ha-Tza'ir was split along the lines of the Tze'irei Zion youth organizations, with whom it maintained contact, into a right, or National Labor wing, and a left, or National-Class, i.e. proletarian, wing. Both existed under conditions of illegality. The left wing, after a period of rapid expansion, claimed 12,000 members and ca. 170 branches at the end of 1925. After that year increased repressions and arrests decimated the movement, the illegal conventions ceased, and by the end of the decade little was left. Sporadic attempts to pursue small-scale activity continued until 1935.

Po'ale Zion. The Bolshevik revolution led to a schism at the international convention of Po'ale Zion parties in Vienna (1920). The left wing, which included most Russian delegates, applied for admission to the Comintern but was refused. In Soviet Russia, however, the left, which renamed itself The Jewish Communist Workers' Party Po'ale Zion, was not banned but, alone among all non-Communist political parties, allowed to exist legally for ten years, while the old Social-Democratic Po'ale Zion was suppressed. Various explanations have been offered for this tolerance, including the need for a token remnant of Zionism, and such services to the new regime as spying in Poland. The party was weak, with membership in the hundreds rather than in the thousands, and found itself under constant attack by the "Evsektsiia", to which a number of members defected over the years. The Communist Po'ale Zion stressed their loyalty to the Soviet system without giving up hope for a Socialist Jewish home in Palestine. In 1921 they formed a youth movement called Yugnt-Po'ale-Zion. The increasing political harshness of the late twenties brought formal liquidation to the party and its youth movement at the end of June, 1928. Some activity took place illegally even afterwards, and a number of members and former members were arrested during the purges of the 1930s.

He-Halutz. He-Halutz grew out of a pioneer sub-organization of Tze'irei Zion in 1918. Its main principle was productive work, preferably in agriculture or workshops, in preparation for emigration to Palestine. Its members also obligated themselves to study Hebrew.

He-Halutz spread from the Ukraine to the Russian Republic, where it had its founding convention in Petrograd (today Leningrad) in January, 1919. It was influenced by the idealism of Joseph Trumpeldor into emphasizing self-fulfillment, and decided to be politically unaffiliated ("above-party"), although some of its leaders also were active in party structures. Many members were employed in artisan cooperatives, but the pride of the movement were its farm settlements, supported by the Joint Distribution Committee. The largest and best-known of these was Tel-Hai in the Crimea.

He-Halutz suffered from the usual harassment of its activities until its leadership, after much effort and tedious negotiations, obtained a legalization statute from the government in September, 1923. However, many members objected to the exposure to government inspection, and to a resolution adopted in April of that year, which accepted the "class struggle" as a principle of the organization. A split followed, and henceforth there existed two He-Halutz organizations: the Class He-Halutz, which was legal, on the left, and the illegal Labor He-Halutz on the right, which soon had thousands of members. Efforts by David Ben-Gurion and the World He-Halutz Federation to heal the split proved unavailing. The legalization of part of He-Halutz did not stop harassment, which was felt more in the cities than on the farms. In the course of time many members of He-Halutz branches were able to get to Palestine, in a number of cases after spending time in prison. The legal He-Halutz and its newspaper were liquidated on 1 March 1928 and its farms disbanded. Two farms of the illegal He-Halutz, Mishmar in the Crimea and Bilu in Belorussia, continued to exist until May, 1929. The last arrest of He-Halutz leaders was in September, 1934, in Moscow.

World War II. The Soviet expansion into western Poland, the Baltic States, Bessarabia, and northern Bukovina in 1939–1940 brought about the liquidation of local Zionist activity and the deportation of many of the leaders to Siberia, the far north, and Central Asia. The hundreds of thousands of Polish Jews who fled east after Hitler's attack on the Soviet Union in June, 1941, also included Zionists who in some cases carried on clandestine activity in Soviet Central Asia. These two groupings—the Jews from Poland and the western territories—had a "nationalizing" effect on the new generation of Soviet Jews as well.

A. GREENBAUM

Post-World War II. Although no Zionist movement as such existed in the Soviet Union at the end of World War II, the termination of the War found the surviving Soviet Jewish population with a markedly stronger Jewish nationalist orientation and identification than had characterized that population in the mid- and late 1930s. In the first place, the very fact of the Holocaust, including the extermination on Soviet territory of between 1.5 and two million Jews (no precise statistics have yet been published), inevitably had a traumatic impact. Hardly a Jew who had not lost one or more close relatives. Secondly, there had been numerous instances of collaboration by the non-Jewish population (especially Ukrainians and Lithuanians) with the Nazis in the extermination of Jews. Thirdly, the Soviet establishment itself was manifesting a new, official anti-Semitism that complemented and encouraged the popular, social anti-Semitism. Both manifestations naturally led to a widespread disillusionment with the Soviet Communist experiment with which so many Jews had actively been associated in the pre-war period as a result of the removal of the restrictions that had limited Jewish existence in Tsarist Russia. Finally, the Soviet Jewish population now included a not insignificant number of Jews from the western territories and Poland who had conducted a very Jewish existence prior to their annexation by the USSR, and contact with whom reawakened Jewish and often specifically Zionist feelings among Jews who had been severed from the Jewish world outside for an entire generation.

These sentiments were not merely the lot of the older generation, Jews in their fifties and sixties, who had been Zionists in their younger days before Zionism had become illegal. Many youngsters in their twenties and even in their teens, who had survived the ghettos, fought with the partisans, or been evacuated with their mothers and grandmothers as their fathers fought at the front, had been exposed to personal experiences that led them to similar conclusions. When a Jewish state was voted into existence at the United Nations in 1947 and proclaimed in May, 1948, large numbers of Soviet Jews demonstrated their enthusiasm and even identification with it. Younger Jews, including some still in uniform in the Soviet armed forces, filed applications to be allowed to volunteer for action in Israel's War of Independence, and when Israel's first diplomatic envoy, Golda Meyerson (later Meir), arrived in Moscow in September the Jews were unable to restrain themselves. At the fall 1948 High Holy Day services at Moscow's central Choral Synagogue in which the Israeli diplomatic mission participated, tens of thousands of Jews openly demonstrated their excitement in the synagogue and the street outside on a scale that Moscow had not seen since the October Revolution.

The Black Years. The reaction of the authorities was not long in coming. The Jews had felt encouraged to display their support of Israel as a result of the Soviet government's own sympathetic attitude to the new Jewish state which its UN delegation had helped to come into being. The Soviet authorities' assumption had apparently been that their Jewish citizens had become integrated and assimilated and were therefore not directly affected by developments in Palestine. They now lost little time in clarifying the situation. In the months that followed the High Holy Days many of those who had participated in the demonstrations, not to speak of those who actually applied to go to fight in Israel, were arrested and charged with betrayal of the motherland. So too were the members of Zionist groupings, mostly students and young people, which had come into being in many Soviet cities and smaller towns in the postwar years and particularly in 1947–8.

Repression mounted throughout what have come to be known as the "black years" of Soviet Jewry, reaching its climax with the "Doctors' Plot" in early 1953—when a group of doctors was accused, among other things, of espionage activity on behalf of foreign (including the Israeli) intelligence services—and the subsequent severance of diplomatic relations with Israel in February, just a month before Stalin died. Yet even in this period there was considerable, albeit clandestine, Zionist activity throughout the length and breadth of the Soviet Union. Mostly, this took the form of small groupings (usually five to 10 people) who would discuss Israeli news broadcasts and other topics of Jewish interest. The majority of these groupings were either students, young people who were probing for the meaning of their Jewishness at a time when there was no Jewish cultural expression in the USSR and discrimination against individual Jews was high, or older people who were already pensioners and therefore had nothing to risk with regard to their professional careers. Neither age group was immune from arrest, however, and large numbers of Jews, many of them with unequivocal national inclinations but many also whose Jewish activity and identity were negligible, were sent to the camps on charges of Jewish bourgeois nationalism.

Paradoxically, the prisons and camps both in this and in the subsequent post-Stalin period played an important role in promoting Zionism in the Soviet Union. Here—having lost their personal "freedom" and jeopardized their family ties and professional careers—Jews felt freer to conduct genuinely Zionist activity than they had dared when still at liberty. Here older Jews taught their younger colleagues Jewish and Zionist history and even the Hebrew language. The ties formed as a result of shared camp experience became the nucleus of connections between different groupings and different cities, which were normally extremely difficult to maintain, given the fear and lack of mutual trust that the regime so systematically instilled into its citizens. De-Stalinization brought little respite to Soviet Jewry. While the excesses of the "black years" were not repeated, Jewish culture was not rehabilitated and the Jews continued to feel discriminated against both as a national grouping and as individuals. Indeed, the fact that discrimination and anti-Semitism persisted served to convince many Jews that these were not the concomitants of the distortions of Communism, attributable to the aging, paranoid mind of the deceased ruler, but an integral component of Soviet life. This conclusion enhanced the tendency to Jewish consciousness.

Jewish nationalism in the 1950s. The strength of the Jewish national awakening became manifest in the second half of the 1950s. In the first place, the authorities permitted the holding of Yiddish recitals or "concerts" which attracted huge crowds wherever they took place not so much on account of the artistic level of the performances, usually low, but because they gave Jews a precious opportunity to glimpse their folklore and to meet with fellow-Jews. Secondly, the major Jewish festivals, especially Simhat Torah, brought large numbers of Jews, especially young people, to the synagogues, first of all in Moscow and Leningrad and by the turn of the decade in a number of other cities where synagogues still remained. Thirdly, a number of international tournaments, exhibitions, and the like, brought Israelis to the Soviet Union. The participation of an Israeli team in a sports championship, especially when it won and *Ha-Tikva* was played and the Israeli flag flown in the stadium, was invariably a source of excitement for Soviet Jews who came in the thousands, often from afar, for the occasion.

The most important of these events, in that it both brought to the Soviet Union a large Israeli delegation and enabled the local populace to mingle with relative freedom with the foreign guests, was the World Federation of Democratic Youth Festival held in Moscow in the summer of 1957. The Israeli artistic performances drew enormous crowds and the constant maneuvering of the authorities to minimize their effect was to no avail. Not a few of the Jewish national movement's later activists were to trace their interest in and association with Israel to the Youth Festival.

Toward the end of the 1950s and increasingly in the 1960s, Jews, again particularly youngsters, began learning Hebrew. While the *ulpanim* (intensive Hebrew courses) as a widespread phenomenon date only from the late 1960s-early 1970s, considerable numbers were able to study privately or in small groups. Dictionaries and primers were always in demand, wherever Israeli diplomats, sportsmen or other representatives appeared. By the early-mid 1960s, the Israeli broadcasts to Russia, Kol Zion la-Gola, were including Hebrew lessons. Even records and cassettes of Israeli songs were circulating in the decade between 1957 and the Six-Day War.

All this activity exacted a price. Throughout these years central figures of the Jewish "national movement" wer arrested on charges of Jewish bourgeois nationalism, "hooliganism", anti-Soviet propaganda and activity, contact with hostile foreign representatives, and espionage. The media, towards the end of the 1950s launched a major campaign against Israel, Zionism, and even the Jewish religion. Often synagogues were closed down on the pretext that they were being used for anti-Soviet activity and propaganda. The Israeli diplomatic mission was under constant open surveillance and its members were periodically declared *persona non grata* in the USSR. Finally, the slight Jewish emigration of the years 1954–56, mostly of elderly relatives of Israeli citizens—some 750 left the Soviet Union in the first ten months of 1956—ceased after the 1956 Sinai War. The Soviet authorities seem to have hoped that this emigration would give them political leverage with Israel, which they could use to enhance their influence as potential arbitrators of the Arab-Israeli conflict. True, there was a considerable Polish Jewish repatriation to Poland as of late 1956 and through 1959 and it was common knowledge that many of the repatriates sought to reach Israel, yet this was a necessarily limited operation and could hardly affect the most Soviet Jews.

The Six-Day War. Neither administrative measures nor implied threats had any marked effect. Right up to the Six-Day War, Soviet Jews continued to attend synagogues in large numbers on festivals (by the mid-1960s thirty to thirty-five thousand thronged Moscow's Choral Synagogue and the street outside on Simhat Torah), to flock to concerts, where the most popular Jewish singer, Nehama Lifshitz, was including Hebrew songs in her repertoire and where the audience would dance the *hora* in the foyer in the interval, and to attend Israeli events. The pre-Six-Day War period came to a finale with the performances of the Israeli singer Geula Gil in a number of cities in summer, 1966, which were the occasion for wild enthusiasm, and three agricultural exhibitions (two in Moscow and one in Kiev), which again drew vast crowds to the Israeli pavilion. And many tens, if not hundreds, of thousands were listening regularly to Israeli broadcasts.

The Six-Day War was a further turning-point. First, in the period of anticipation that preceded the War, the Arab threat to the very existence of Israel brought home to large numbers of Jews, even many who had not previously identified with Israel, how important Israel was to them, how much it was a part of them. The Israeli victory filled them with pride, relief, and joy. Paradoxically, the anti-Israeli attitude of the Soviet authorities in 1967 had the same result as had their pro-Israeli stand in 1948. Then, the knowledge of Moscow's support for Israel gave the Jews encouragement to express their own sympathy for the Jewish state. Now, awareness of the Kremlin's active support of the Arabs, especially the supply of weaponry for Israel's destruction, stressed the polarization of the two positions and made any attempt at concealing the difference or reaching a compromise a lost cause. The Jews' feeling of alienation increased. Moreover, the virulence of anti-Israeli propaganda was exacerbated and it became virtually impossible to distinguish between anti-Zionism and anti-Semitism. Finally, the growing nationalism of other ethnic groupings not only strengthened their anti-Jewish sentiments (notably among the Great Russians) but provided a legitimization for the Jews to give vent to their own.

The lack of any direct relations between the USSR and Israel may also have had a salutary effect on the Jewish national movement. If until May, 1967, Zionist inclinations were given their most open expression in the context of Israeli events, and the Israel Embassy in Moscow was their focus and fulcrum, the departure of the latter left the initiative and leadership in the hands of the local Jews.

Immigration to Israel. The end of the decade thus saw a new catharsis that was further highlighted by the Soviet regime's somewhat severer policy toward dissident movements in the context of a certain reaction to Khrushchev's liberalization in the early Brezhnev period. Jews had played a considerable part in dissident activity, both cultural and political. Yet the virtual helplessness of the Democratic movement was brought to the fore by a series of trials against writers and intellectuals and by its ineffectiveness in face of the Warsaw Pact invasion of Czechoslovakia in 1968. The resultant frustration led many Jews to abandon efforts to change the regime. Instead they joined those who were seeking to replace existence in the Soviet Union by life in a country of their own.

The Soviet authorities, within the framework of their general policy of terminating dissident activity (Zionist activity was seen by them essentially as such, since the desire to leave the Soviet mother country can only be interpreted as anti-Soviet), seem to have decided to permit the emigration of the leading activists of the Jewish movement in the hope that without leadership it would die out. (Once again emigration had grown prior to an Arab-Israeli war and ceased on its outbreak). In fact, the opposite occurred. The emigration of some 3,000 Jews in 1969 fed new hopes and when it was followed by renewed restrictions on emigration—in 1970 the number was only about 1,000—the Jews resolved to take decisive action. Petitions to foreign governments and public figures, notably, but not solely, that of the 18 Georgian Jews to Israeli Prime Minister Golda Meir, and constant contact with western correspondents in Moscow, had helped bring the Jewish movement to the public eye. Now, a series of hunger and sit-in strikes and finally the major trial of a group of Jews (and two non-Jews) who had planned to hijack a plane to get to Israel brought the outcry in the West to new heights.

There was at this point unquestionably a Jewish national movement in the Soviet Union. The audacity of its central figures, their inventiveness as they sought ways to embarrass the authorities, their unified actions and solidarity, inevitably made their mark and the movement swelled. The Jews were greatly helped at this time by the struggle on their behalf in the West. Deprived of the active backing of a permanent Israeli presence, the Soviet Jews established contact with other westerners: correspondents, tourists, delegations. This passing-on of information was of vital importance as a constraint vis-à-vis the Soviet authorities; the knowledge that any action they took against the Jews would become known at once in the West, and would arouse a storm of protest, restricted their inclination to take such action. During the course of the 1970s extensive use was made of telephone calls to Israel and the West for the express purpose of exchanging information: Soviet Jews would tell their news and learn what was being done on their behalf. All this activity in the West had become politically meaningful as a result of the détente that characterized the Soviet-American relationship in the 1970s. The USSR's need for western technology and desire for major agreements on arms limitations provided new opportunities to bargain on behalf of Soviet Jewry's struggle for emigration to Israel. The consolidation of the struggle in the West, however, which reached its peak in the Jackson-Vanik amendment that prevented the Soviet Union from receiving most favored nation status in trade with the US so long as it limited emigration, brought about a major change in the nature, and perhaps in the long-term fortunes, of the Soviet Jewish national movement. In the first years of the decade as the emigration figures jumped—from 1,000 in 1970 to 14,000 in 1971 to over 30,000 in 1972 and 1973—over 95 percent of the Jews went to Israel. Many of the emigrants had long been Zionists, who had been dreaming for years of going to Israel. A considerable number came from the western territories where Jewish feeling and identity had remained strongest and where middle-aged people had still gone to Jewish, often even Hebrew-speaking, schools. Others came from Georgia where the Jewish religion had remained a living force and where the Jews traditionally looked to Zion as the object of their aspirations. By the mid-1970s, a large proportion of these Zionists had left and although there remained a basic nucleus of activists who taught and studied Hebrew and continued to see Israel as their ultimate destination, a new group of Jews began to seize the possibility to leave the USSR as a fundamental human right. These thousands of Jews had no particularly Jewish motivation and wished solely to escape anti-Semitism and discrimination. They opted to leave for the West, particularly the US, rather than for Israel; and by 1979, the last year of large-scale emigration—when, after dropping to approximately 15,000 per year in the middle of the decade, emigration figures soared to 51,000 as the Soviet Union sought ratification by Congress of SALT II—only one-third of the emigrants were reaching Israel.

In the 1980s the Jewish movement in the USSR has looked very different. Deprived of its positive motivation, the desire to live a Jewish life in a Jewish state, it dwindled to a minor phenomenon, centering on the small nucleus of activists who aspired to go to Israel. The Soviet authorities, as part of their renewed hardline policy in the domestic arena as a whole, in an effort to put an end to the weakness, inefficiency, and corruption that seemed to have characterized the last Brezhnev years, virtually closed the gates of emigration once again. Still at 20,000 p.a. in 1980, emigration had shrunk to less than 1,000 by the middle of the decade. Even the renewal of détente, or at least the search for a working relationship with the US by Secretary Gorbachev as of 1985, did not lead to a renewal of large-scale emigration. It appeared that the Soviet authorities were concentrating on de-Zionizing the Jewish movement. They allowed the emigration of veteran refuseniks and young Hebrew teachers, clearly hoping to clip the movement's wings.

When the chances of leaving are slight and there is a likelihood of considerable inconvenience for those who apply to leave, not many wish to burn their bridges by filing an emigration application, even on the basis of family reunification in countries outside Israel. Many seemed to believe that they would benefit from the new slogans of Gorbachev's regime: openness (*glasnost*) and restructuring (*perestroika*). Students of Soviet and pre-revolutionary Russian Jewish history have expressed doubts concerning the long-term success of any such orientation.

The entire situation underwent a complete change from 1989 when the gates were opened to large-scale emigration. Under evidence of open, popular anti-Semitism, Jews decided to leave in large numbers and large numbers of these went to Israel. In 1990 alone, 185,000 Russian Jews went to Israel. The rate diminished in 1991 to 148,000 in view of the Gulf War and the reports of economic difficulties experienced by Russian immigrants in Israel and further dropped in 1992 to 64,000, but the gates were still open and many Russian Jews continued to arrive.

See also REFUSENIKS; RUSSIAN JEWS IN ISRAEL Y. RO'I

The Drop-Out Controversy. 81.4 percent of Soviet Jewish emigrants were abandoning plans to go to Israel from Vienna, in favor of other destinations, mainly the US. Deliberations were held in Israel and in the Diaspora countries over the way to deal with this "drop-out" phenomenon. Jewish organizations in the US considered it correct to provide physical assistance to the Jews emigrating from the Soviet Union and desiring to go to the US. The American government granted them refugee status thereby enabling these Jews to enter the US without having to wait for long periods until their turn came, as was the general practice for immigrants. In addition, financial assistance was provided by the Federal government for settling in through the Jewish agencies that dealt with their absorption.

The Israel Government and the Jewish Agency claimed that Jews leaving the Soviet Union on an Israeli visa should immigrate to Israel, and argued that the continued processing of the Soviet Jews by the American Jewish organizations encouraged Soviet Jews to drop out, and the phenomenon itself negated the Zionist basis of the struggle for the freedom of immigration to Israel from the USSR.

Among American Jews there were those who supported the Israeli-Zionist stand; in Israel there were those who disapproved of the "drop-out" phenomenon, but did not believe that Jews should be brought to Israel under coercion. The approach of the American Jewish organizations was based on the principle of "freedom of choice", that every Jew, even those leaving the Soviet Union on an Israeli visa, should have the right to settle wherever he chose, and was entitled to communal aid in implementing his choice.

The controversy continued when Jewish emigration almost came to a standstill, or when hope rose once more for its renewal. In 1988, it was announced that emigrating Soviet Jews would henceforth be flown directly to Israel via Bucharest. With the large-scale emigration starting in 1989, the situation changed. The US placed a limit on the numbers of Russians it would receive each year (initially 40,000) and the remainder made their way to Israel by various routes, eventually directly from the Russian republics (including in 1993 flights from *Birobidjan). Below is a table showing the numbers leaving the Soviet Union, immigration to Israel and "drop-outs," during 1956–1992.

EMIGRATION OF SOVIET JEWS—IMMIGRATION TO ISRAEL AND DROP-OUTS

Date	*Total emigration*	*Immigration to Israel*	*Drop-outs*
1956	454	454	
1957	149	149	
1958	12	12	
1959	3	3	
1960	66	66	
1961	202	202	
1962	184	184	
1963	305	305	
1964	537	537	
1965	891	891	
1966	2,047	2,047	
1967	1,390	1,390	
Total 1956–1967	6,240	6,240	
1968	223	223	
1969	2,979	2,979	
1970	1,027	1,027	
1971	13,022	12,966	56
1972	31,681	31,432	249
1973	34,733	33,283	1,450
1974	20,944	17,065	3,879
1975	13,221	8,293	4,982
1976	14,261	7,258	7,003
1977	16,736	8,253	8,483
1978	28,865	11,998	16,876
1979	51,333	17,277	34,056
1980	21,471	7,393	14,078
1981	9,448	1,757	7,691
1982	2,692	731	1,961
1983	1,314	378	936
1984	895	335	560
1985	1,140	348	792
1986	914	206	708
1987	8,080	2,083	5,997
1988	19,251	2,231	17,020
1989	71,238	12,277	58,961
1990	204,742	185,242	19,500
1991	189,839	147,839	42,000
1992	117,457	64,057	53,400
Total 1968–1992	610,587	413,729	196,878
Total 1956–1992	616,809	419,969	196,878

Y. DOMINITZ

RUSSIA AND THE SOVIET UNION, RELATIONS WITH ZIONISM AND ISRAEL.

UNDER THE TSARS. Under the Tsarist regime the Zionism movement, though not legalized, was on the whole tolerated rather than persecuted. A change for the worse occurred in midsummer of 1930: a secret circular of the Ministry of the Interior, dated 24 June 1903, instructed the local authorities to take strict measures for the suppression of the national and Zionist movement among Russian Jews. They were to forbid meetings, grant no permission for the organization of congresses, prevent the *magidim* (traditional religious preachers: this Hebrew word was used in the circular) from conducting Zionist propaganda campaigns in the synagogues, close all Zionist organizations in Russia, and make it impossible for Zionist leaders to travel abroad to attend Zionist Congresses and conventions. The distribution and sale of shares of the Jewish Colonial Trust was to be banned, and if such shares were found anywhere, they were to be confiscated. The circular particularly instructed the local authorities to watch Jewish schools and *heders* (traditional Tora schools) and to withhold official confirmation from persons in the posts of chairmen of Jewish communities or communal rabbis if they were found to be connected with the Zionist movement.

The purpose of the circular was clearly the destruction of the Zionist movement in Russia. Yet Russian Zionist leaders were not excessively disturbed by it. Russian Jews had long been accustomed to repressive measures on the part of governmental authorities and had learned to circumvent them. Herzl felt differently, and it was largely in the hope of securing a change for the better that he sought and obtained an interview with Viacheslav K. von Plehve, the all-powerful Minister of the Interior in Russia. After their first meeting, on 8 August 1903, Von Plehve sent Herzl an official letter whose text, according to him, was approved by the Tsar. This letter was made public during the Sixth Zionist Congress (1903). It stated that insofar as Zionism aimed at establishing an independent state in Palestine, which would lead to the emigration of a "certain number of Jewish subjects from Russia," the Russian government might have considered the movement favorably. However, Zionism had begun to diverge from its direct goal and to engage in propaganda of Jewish national unity within Russia proper; such a trend could not be countenanced by the government, because it might lead to the emergence in Russia of groups of people who were alien and hostile to the patriotic sentiments on which every state is based. Nonetheless, if Zionism returned to its original program, it could expect to enlist the moral and material support of the Russian government, particularly after its practical measures had reduced the size of the Jewish population in Russia. In such an event, the Russian government was prepared to support the Zionist appeals to Turkey, to facilitate Zionist activities, and even to issue subsidies to emigration societies, if not from the state Treasury, then from special Jewish levies.

The practical outcome of Herzl's negotiations with Von Plehve was, however, very limited. Zionism remained illegal; from time to time Zionist gatherings were invaded by the police, and many Zionists were arrested and deported to Siberia.

IN SOVIET RUSSIA. Soviet rule was established in Russia in November, 1917. In January, 1918, the Evkom (Jewish Commissariat) was set up. It was manned largely by men with little or no specifically Jewish background who had no strong motivation for anti-Zionist action. They concentrated their efforts on winning the Jewish masses for the Communist cause through appeals in Yiddish and on liquidating the existing Jewish community councils. The Evkom had neither time nor inclination to indulge in an anti-Zionist crusade. For such an attitude it was strongly criticized by the so-called Jewish section (Evsektsiia) of the Communist party, which was largely composed of converts from traditionally anti-Zionist parties (Bund and Fareinigte): they were eager to settle old scores with the Zionists, whose political hegemony in Russian Jewry they had been unable to shake by the democratic process. The second conference of Evsektsiia and Evkom groups, held in Moscow in June, 1919, demanded the dissolution of the "counterrevolutionary...clerical and nationalistic Zionist Organization," which was branded the "instrument in the hands of the Entente imperialism in its war against the proletarian revolution.

Developments in the Ukraine. In the Ukraine, however, a full-scale anti-Zionist campaign was unleashed in the summer of 1919. Large sections of the Fareinigte and the Bund embraced the Communist cause and, in May, 1919, formed the Komfarband (Communist Union). On 4 July, this body addressed a memorandum to the Ukrainian Commissariat of Internal Affairs, insisting that it was "absolutely necessary to liquidate the activities of the Zionist Party and all its factions." Two days later, the homes of many prominent Zionists in Kiev were searched by the Cheka (secret police), accompanied by Komfarbandists, and on 12 July the Commissariat ordered 15 Zionist organizations (Po'ale Zion was exempted), as well as Tarbut and the organized Jewish community, to cease functioning at once. The only reason why repression did not assume a permanent countrywide character was that by mid-1919 most of the Ukraine had been occupied by Anton Denikin's Volunteer Army. It was resumed early in 1920, after the final defeat of Denikin's forces, whose rule had been marked by bloody pogroms. Scattered contemporary reports indicate that the ruined and terrorized Ukrainian Jews were yearning for speedy emigration to Palestine: in Cherkassy, in central Ukraine, 1,823 of the 2,118 families polled stated that they were preparing for immediate emigration; in Novoarkhangels, Kherson Province, "the entire Jewish population was ready, at the first opportunity, to abandon its town and leave for Palestine"; in several towns, Zionist groups established special Palestine Offices that enlisted prospective emigrants in resettlement cooperatives, prepared statutes, and collected funds. In October, 1920, a Zionist conference took place in Simferopol to discuss emigration possibilities for Jews of the Crimea. But the country's frontiers were almost hermetically sealed, with one notable exception: in the fall of 1919, shortly before the consolidation of the Soviet regime in the Ukraine, the S.S. *Roslan* sailed from Odessa, bound for Palestine, with some 600 emigrants aboard.

Developments in the early 1920s. Handicapped for some time by general political developments in the Ukraine, the anti-Zionist drive was activated in Soviet Russia itself, and on 1 September 1919, the Cheka closed Zionist headquarters in Petrograd, imprisoned its director, confiscated its documents and 120,000 rubles in cash, and closed the central Zionist publication *Khronika Yevreisko Zhiny* (Chronicle of Jewish Life). Arrests in Moscow followed the next day; and the Russian-language weekly *Rassviet* was suppressed as an "organ of the bourgeoisie." Although arrested Zionists were released after a brief internment, harassment of local Zionist groups continued intermittently in several towns. The heaviest blow came in April, 1920, when an All-Russia Zionist Conference met in Moscow, attended by 109 delegates and guests. On the third day of its deliberations, Cheka agents arrested 75 of the participants on charges of possessing compromising documents, of having made pro-British utterances, of collaborating with American Zionists in giving aid to Admiral Aleksandr Kolchak, a counter-revolutionary, and of supporting anti-Soviet forces elsewhere. In mid-July, 68 of the detainees were released, following intervention by representatives of the American Jewish Joint Distribution Committee. Others were sentenced to forced labor for periods of six months to five years; they were later released on condition that they refrain from all further Zionist activities. The Zionist Central Committee then decided to go underground. A clandestine headquarters, headed by Eliezer Tcherikover, continued to coordinate the work of the still-existine local Zionist groups until the end of the 1920s.

During the first months of the New Economic Policy (NEP), inaugurated by Lenin in 1921, the general relaxation of governmental pressure made life somewhat easier for the Zionist groups as well. But the breathing spell was short-lived. Suppression was resumed by mid-1922. The main object of suppression was the *Tze'irei Zion party. This dynamic Zionist formation split at its May, 1920, conference in Kharkov. The left wing, outspokenly pro-Marxist and pro-Soviet, seceded and organized a Zionist Socialist party; the right wing maintained its non-Marxist program, refused to extend overt support to the Bolshevik regime, remained within the World Zionist Organization, moved underground with other Zionist groupings, and assumed the name Zionist Labor party. It constituted the mainstay of the underground Zionist movement and was particularly strong in the Ukraine. In May, 1922, its Third All-Ukraine Conference, which met in Kiev, was apprehended by the Cheka; 37 of the 51 arrested delegates appeared on 20 August before a Soviet court in a three-day show trial. The indictment charged that the Tze'irei Zion, under the guise of democracy, had sought to "corrupt Jewish youth and throw them into the arms of the counterrevolutionary bourgeoisie in the interests of Anglo-French capitalism"; 12 of the accused were sentenced to two years at hard labor, 15 to one year, and 10 were released. After 13 months, those sentenced to two years were permitted to apply for emigration to Palestine. Arrests continued. In September, 1922, more than 1,000 Zionists were arrested in Odessa, Kiev, Berdichev, and other urban centers in the Ukraine. Undaunted, the right-wing Tze'irei Zion persevered in its underground work, maintaining contact, no matter how tenuous, between the local cells and issuing circulars and information bulletins. In the summer of 1924, the Zionist Labor party circulated a memorandum among delegates to the session of the Soviet of Nationalities in Moscow protesting the willful destruction of all existing Jewish cultural institutions and the general suppression of Zionist work: "In spite of the terror," the memorandum claimed defiantly, "the Zionist Labor party lives on and continues its revolutionary struggle." The Soviet regime retaliated with mass arrests. During the night of 2 September 1924, more than 3,000 Zionists in some 150 localities were seized.

The arrests continued through October. This time there were no public show trials at which, in the past, audiences had frequently evinced open sympathy with the accused; interrogations were conducted and verdicts pronounced behind closed doors. The usual sentence was 3 to 10 years at hard labor in isolation camps in central Russia, the Solovetski Islands, Siberia, the Ural Mountains, Kirgizia, or Soviet Central Asia. This new wave of government terror had an adverse effect on the Zionist underground but failed to break its spirit. In October, 1924, Zionist youths in Odessa marched in the streets singing the "Ha-Tikva" Zionist anthem; they were dispersed by mounted police, and 32 were arrested. By the end of 1924, thousands of Zionists were languishing in Soviet prisons and detention camps. Julius Margolin, himself one of the detainees, related that as late as 1941 he met Russian Zionist leaders in the deportation camps in the Soviet far north; some of them had spent 16 or 17 years there.

The pro-Soviet left-wing Tze'irei Zion, though drastically depleted by defections, managed to maintain headquarters in Leningrad until 1926 and in Moscow until 1928–29, when it disbanded. By that time, the miniscule, outspoken Communist, left-wing Po'ale Zion, too, had ceased to exist.

The only sector of the Zionist movement tolerated by the authorities during the first decade of the Soviet regime was *He-Halutz. At its second conference in January, 1919, the organization enjoined all its members to train at collective farms for pioneer work in Palestine. This step strongly appealed to the Soviet regime's ideology. In the spring of 1922 He-Halutz had some 75 local groups, and by the end of 1923 its cadres comprised 100 groups with some 3,000 members. In August, 1923, He-Halutz cells in the agricultural settlements, but not in the urban areas, obtained formal legalization. Yet about one-third of the members were opposed to accepting this legal status, which, they insisted, would be exploited by the Soviet regime for infiltration and destruction of their Zionist content. The dissidents formed an independent Halutz Le'umi-Amlani (National Pioneer Labor Organization).

Both wings of the He-Halutz movement had their troubles with the Soviet authorities, particularly in the Ukraine and the Crimea. Arrests started in 1924 and were intensified in 1926. The 10 existing He-Halutz farms were successively liquidated; the last, Al Mishmar, was disbanded in May, 1928. Minute remnants of the "illegal" He-Halutz carried on until 1934. Unlike the other Zionists, the arrested halutzim (pioneers) were permitted to opt for emigration to Palestine as an alternative to imprisonment or internment in deportation camps.

Zionist activites were effectively crippled. The last citadel of organized underground Zionism, the Moscow Central Executive Committee of Tze'irei Zion and the Union of Zionist Youth, was liquidated in September, 1934; its members received long prison sentences.

Crimea Project. The Soviet government did not rely solely on administrative suppression. On two occasions it attempted to offer its Jewish citizens what it considered a constructive alternative to the Zionist solution of the Jewish problem.

In 1926 Mikhail Kalinin, the Chairman of the Supreme Soviet Presidium, advanced the scheme of territorial concentration of "a compactly settled [Jewish agricultural peasantry" on the Crimean Peninsula, between the Black Sea and the Sea of Azov. Kalinin believed that such mass resettlement would provide the framework for the "preservation of the Jewish nationality"; other Communist leaders expected that the Crimea project would divert Jewish loyalties from Zionist efforts in Palestine. A string of relatively prosperous Jewish agricultural settlements started to emerge in the Crimea. But when, in 1929–30, in the process of "collectivization", the government launched a relentless campaign against the kulaks (well-to-do Russian peasants), the Crimean Jewish colonists were among its first victims. Within a few years the Crimean scheme had petered out, to be revived in 1944 when a number of leading Jewish public figures suggested—in the wake of the deportation of the Crimean Tatars—that the Crimea be allotted for Jewish settlement. The proponents of this suggestion, most of them members of the presidium of the Jewish Anti-Fascist Committee, were arrested in Stalin's last years, charged with being nationalists, bourgeois Zionists, and agents of American imperialism who had plotted to separate the Crimea from the Soviet Union and establish there a "Jewish National Bourgeois Zionist Republic," which would serve as an American military base against the USSR.

***Birobidzhan.** Another, much more ambitious "substitute for Zionism" was announced in March, 1928: an area of some 10 million acres in the Birobidzhan Region, close to the Manchurian border, was set aside for compact Jewish settlement. On 7 May 1934, Kalinin signed a decree establishing a Jewish Autonomous Oblast (region) as part of the Russian Soviet Federated Socialist Republic. On 29 August 1936, the Central Committee of the USSR declared that "for the first time in the history of the Jewish people, its burning desire for the creation of a homeland of its own, for the achievement of its national statehood, has found fulfillment." Birobidzhan, however, at no time succeeded in attracting significant numbers of Jews. The climate and living conditions were extremely difficult and the region was remote and difficult of access, with none of the cultural and other facilities that the Jews, who were largely urban, felt they needed. While it had its ups and downs (in the immediate post-World War II years the project was again boosted as a solution for the surviving Jews of the Ukrainian townships), Birobidzhan at no stage boasted more than a tiny percentage of Soviet Jewry. Remaining officially until this day a Jewish Autonomous Oblast, it had less than 10,000 Jewish inhabitants in 1993 when some of its Jews began to be flown to Israel.

World War II. By the end of the 1930s, the last visible vestiges of Zionism as idea and movement had been ruthlessly and efficiently eradicated in the Soviet Union. Whatever Zionist beliefs and feelings had survived the pressure and persecution of the mighty, all-pervading authoritarian apparatus were deeply hidden in the minds and souls of the then 3 million-strong Soviet Jewish community. The regime considered "the Zionist chapter" fully and irretrievably closed.

It was dramatically reopened on the eve and in the early stages of World War II. On the basis of the Hitler-Stalin pact of August, 1939, Soviet troops began to occupy eastern Poland on 17 September 1939. The German-Soviet Boundary and Friendship Treaty, concluded on 28 September, provided for the annexation by the Soviet Union of Poland's eastern and southeastern provinces, with a Jewish population of about 1,200,000 to 1,250,000; some 300,000 Jews later came in as refugees from the German-occupied area. In June, 1940, the USSR annexed the Romanian provinces of Bessarabia and northern Bukovina, with a Jewish population of 277,949 according to the Romanian census of 1930. The almost simultaneous annexation of Latvia, Estonia, and Lithuania added 265,000 Jews. Within nine months the Jewish community of the USSR had increased by more than 2 million.

Zionists constituted a high percentage of the newly incorporated Jewish population. Polish Jewry was the backbone of the World Zionist Organization. Forty-three per cent of the Jewish councilmen elected by a total of 274,398 Jewish voters in the 1934 Polish municipal elections belonged to various Zionist groups. The two Zionist-sponsored Hebrew school systems, Yavne and Tarbut, comprised 403 institutions with 59,241 pupils. In the 1931 census 243,339 Jews listed Hebrew as their mother tongue; 4 weeklies and 24 other periodicals appeared in Hebrew. A similar pattern, in varying degrees, prevailed in the other annexed areas. The Soviet Union saw itself saddled with a largely Zionist "new" Jewish minority of more than 2 million.

The Soviet machinery of repression went into action to remedy this state of affairs. What had been done to "indigenous" Soviet Zionists for more than two decades was now inflicted on those from the newly acquired areas in a far shorter period. It is estimated that nearly 400,000 of the newcomers along with many more non-Jews from the same areas were sent to concentration and forced-labor camps in the forests of Arkhangelsk, the Komi ASSR, the Siberian tundra, or the mines of the Don basin in southeastern European Russia. In June, 1941, the Soviet-German idyll came to an abrupt end. Hitler's armies invaded Soviet territory and hundreds of thousands of Jews were massacred. However, persecution of Zionists by the Soviet authorities continued throughout the war years. At the same time, the Soviet government was assiduously courting Jewish public opinion in the western democracies, intermittently indulging in conciliatory gestures toward Zionism and the Zionist work of upbuilding Palestine. In May, 1943, Solomon Mikhoels, director of the Jewish State Theater in Moscow, said in London that "Zionism is a great idea," though it was inapplicable to Soviet Jewry, which had "deep roots in our country"; and in November, 1944, Shakhno Epstein, secretary of the Jewish Anti-Fascist Committee, wrote in the committee's organ, *Ainigkeit*, that "the Jewish people has a right to political independence in Palestine" and that "no sensible and freedom-loving person can have any objection to the Jews there continuing to develop in freedom the Home that they had set up through hard, constructive work, on the basis of self-government." In January, 1944, permission was granted for a display in Moscow of farm produce from the Jewish agricultural settlements in Palestine.

The increasingly militant struggle of the World Zionist movement, and primarily of its Palestinian vanguard, against British policy in Palestine apparently somewhat mitigated the traditional Communist notion of Zionism as an inveterate and conscious "tool of British imperialism." When, in 1946, Bartley Crum, member of the Anglo-American Committee of Inquiry on Palestine, asked Ukrainian Foreign Minister Dmitri Manuilsky in London whether Moscow still believed in the validity of that slogan, Manuilsky smilingly retorted: "They [the Zionists] are not active tools of British imperialism, but Dr. [Chaim] Weizmann and his group have such confidence in the integrity of the British that Russia feels sometimes they are the unconscious tools of British imperialism." It was, rather prematurely, considered a major departure from traditional Communist hostility when at the Founding Conference of the World Federation of Trade Unions held in London in February, 1945, the Soviet delegation endorsed a resolution stating that "the Jewish people must be enabled to continue the rebuilding of Palestine as their National Home.

Attitude toward the Formation of Israel. The Soviet government welcomed Great Britain's submission, in the spring of 1947, of the Palestine issue to the United Nations as signifying the end of British rule in Palestine and converting the country's future into an international problem. While stressing that the Soviet Union had "no concern in the Palestine problem" since the "Jewish population in the Soviet Union does not have much interest in immigration to Palestine," Soviet Deputy Foreign Minister Andrei A. Gromyko clearly stated that Moscow's interest was of an "exclusively political" character. It was in this connection that Gromyko unexpectedly volunteered a significant statement on the substance of the Jewish claim to Palestine. He told the UN General Assembly on 14 May 1947:

> During the last war [in Europe], the Jewish people underwent exceptional sorrow and suffering. Without any exaggeration, this sorrow and suffering are indescribable. It is difficult to express them in dry statistics of the Jewish victims of the Fascist aggressors. The Jews in territories where the Hitlerites held sway were subjected to almost complete annihilation. The total number of members of the Jewish population who perished at the hands of Nazi executioners is estimated at approximately 6 million. Only about a million and a half Jews in western Europe survived the war.... The aspirations of an important part of the Jewish people are bound up with the question of Palestine and with the future structure of that country....It is impossible to justify a denial...of the aspiration of the Jews for a creation of a state of their own... particularly if one takes into account the experiences of this people in the Second World War.

Gromyko's statement that "the population of Palestine consists of two peoples, Arabs and Jews" and that "each of these has its historical roots in Palestine" was certainly a long way from accepting the Zionist concept of the historical connection of the Jewish people with Palestine, but it could be interpreted as a step in that direction. When told by a Jewish Telegraphic Agency reporter that his statement was interpreted as "indicating a significant departure from the [Soviet] official opposition to Zionism," Gromyko seemed to be not at all embarrassed; he simply withheld comment. Prior to Gromyko's speech, the Soviet United Nations delegation voted for granting a hearing to the Jewish Agency, which, it well knew, was identical with the Executive of the World Zionist Organization.

For a time, the Soviet delegation still hesitated between the two solutions offered by the United Nations Special Committee on Palestine (UNSCOP): the majority's proposal of the country's partition into a Jewish and an Arab state, and the proposal by the minority calling for the establishment of a binational Arab-Jewish state. The Zionists endorsed and advocated partition. On 13 October 1947, Semeon K. Tsarapkin, Counselor of the Soviet Embassy in Washington, officially announced the Soviet Union's support for the partition plan. On 29 November, the entire Soviet bloc (except Yugoslavia, which abstained) voted for partition.

The very next day Arab bands, organized by the Arab Higher Committee and reinforced by contingents from neighboring Arab countries, launched attacks against the yishuv. When the American United Nations delegation introduced in the Security Council a resolution calling "upon Arab and Jewish armed groups in Palestine to cease acts of violence immediately," Gromyko, on behalf of the Soviet delegation, denounced the United States proposal as "inequitable and unjust" and submitted an amendment insisting on the "immediate withdrawal of all armed groups which have invaded Palestine from the outside" and calling for the "prevention of the invasion of such groups into Palestine in the future." In March, 1948, when the United States delegation withdrew its support from the United Nations partition decision and tried to substitute for it a "temporary trusteeship," Gromyko (on 30 March) told the Security Council that the United States was "burying" the partition of Palestine and demanded the full implementation of the 29 November 1947 decision.

Developments under Stalin. Soviet support in the United Nations for the creation of a Jewish State was undoubtedly motivated primarily by the desire to eliminate Great Britain from Palestine and to weaken western domination of the Middle East. During 1948, in particular, the USSR rendered political and military aid to the Jewish State. It was the first great power to afford formal *de jure* recognition and its support was crucial to Israel's acceptance into the UN. Military aid was given in the form of arms—through Czechoslovakia—and emigration of Jews from the Soviet-bloc countries (between 15 May 1948, and 15 May 1952, 296,813 immigrants from Poland, Romania, Hungary, Czechoslovakia, and Bulgaria landed in Israel) although the Soviet authorities persisted in their traditional policy of preventing their Jewish citizens from leaving for Palestine. In 1925–26, a total of 8,157 Jews had still been able to reach the shores of Palestine. In the following four years (1927–30) the number had dropped to 1,297, and in the period between 1931 and 1936 a mere 1,848 immigrants arrived from the Soviet Union. Immigration to Israel was practically barred. From 15 May 1948, to the end of 1951, only four elderly women and one disabled ex-serviceman were permitted to leave for Israel.

In the early stages, hostility to Zionism rather than to the State of Israel appears to have been the dominant feature of the Kremlin's policies. The Jewish minority in the USSR, with its deep-seated sentiment for Israel and its strong sympathies for the Jewish communities of the western world, was viewed by the Stalin regime as inherently "unreliable," and Israel was regarded as a major "diversionary" source of this alleged unreliability. Anti-Jewish, anti-Zionist, and anti-Israel tendencies of the Soviet regime were organically interconnected. When, on 13 January 1953, *Pravda* announced the infamous "doctors' plot," the six Jews among the nine indicted physicians were charged with being in league not only with American and British agents but also with "Zionist spies." The same day, *Izvestia* berated "the dirty face of Zionist espionage." When on 9 February 1953, a bomb exploded on the premises of the Soviet Legation in Israel, the USSR, disregarding apologies by the Israeli government, immediately broke off diplomatic relations with the Jewish State.

Malenkov and Khrushchev Regimes. During the short-lived post-Stalin regime of Georgi Malenkov, the anti-Zionist drive subsided somewhat. The charges against the doctors were withdrawn, and open anti-Jewish propaganda disappeared from the Soviet press. Although the accusation of Zionism as a world conspiracy was never retracted, the USSR resumed diplomatic relations with Israel in the summer of 1953. There also was a more cooperative response to individual Jewish applications for emigration permits: between July, 1953, and October, 1956, over 800 immigrants from the USSR, chiefly old people, reached Israel and were reunited with their families.

Nikita S. Krushchev, who had become first secretary of the Central Committee of the Communist party in September, 1953, increased his power during 1954. In February, 1955, he nominated Nikolai Bulganin to succeed Malenkov as premier. In 1958 Krushchev replaced Bulganin as premier while continuing as party leader.) During the 10 years of Krushchev's leadership, Soviet policy became more aggressively anti-Zionist, though the *Great Soviet Encyclopaedia* had dismissed the Zionist movement as "moribund" as early as 1944. The intensified crusade against Judaism and Israel was combined with an anti-Zionist barrage.

Great Britain's agreement (1954) with Gamal Abdel Nasser of Egypt, abrogating the Anglo-Egyptian treaty of 1936 and providing for the withdrawal of British forces from the Suez Canal Zone by 1956, gave the USSR a new wedge to enter the Middle East, which it was quick to use. By 1955 the Soviet government was diligently courting the Arabs. High Soviet officials, including Foreign Minister Viacheslav M. Molotov, assured the Arabs of Soviet support in defending themselves against "imperialist oppressors" and praised the "great Socialist experiment" Nasser was carrying out in Egypt. On 27 September 1955, Nasser announced that an agreement for arms deliveries to Egypt had been concluded with Czechoslovakia. This transaction, which had been arranged under the auspices of the Soviet Union, was the beginning of massive Soviet shipments of modern weapons to the Arab nations. From then on Soviet relations with Israel deteriorated. In July, 1956, the USSR vigorously supported Nasser's seizure of the Suez Canal. Following the concerted action by Britain, France, and Israel against Egypt (*see* SINAI CAMPAIGN) that fall, Moscow was prompt to condemn Israel as an aggressor and went so far as to offer the services of "volunteers" to "help Egypt repel the invaders." (The offer was made after the conclusion of hostilities.) On 5 November 1956, Premier Bulganin sent a personal letter to Prime Minister David Ben-Gurion, declaring that "acting on instructions from abroad, the Israeli government is criminally and irresponsibly playing with the fate of peace, with the fate of its own people." He also informed Ben-Gurion that he was recalling the Soviet Ambassador from Tel Aviv. Meanwhile, it was reported that Soviet arms and technicians had arrived in Syria, which was to come increasingly under Soviet domination. On 6 November, the Soviet Union canceled contracts for the delivery of crude petroleum to Israel. The USSR demanded strong sanctions against Israel at the United Nations. Faced with the danger of Soviet armed intervention on behalf of the Arabs (and veiled hints of nuclear attack against Britain and France) and the implicit threat of a third world war, the United States joined the USSR in forcing Britain and France to withdraw from Egypt and in coercing Israel to quit unconditionally the Egyptian territory it had occupied.

On 7 September 1957, Eliahu Hazan, an attaché of the Israeli Embassy in Moscow, was accused of having given anti-Soviet literature to a Soviet citizen. Hazan was abducted and threatened with death unless he agreed to spy for the USSR. After 26 hours of questioning he was released and soon thereafter returned to Israel.

During 1956 and 1957 only a few individuals, mostly old people with relatives in Israel, were permitted to go on aliya from the Soviet Union. In an interview with Mrs. Franklin D. Roosevelt in the fall of 1957, Krushchev said it was difficult for a Jew who wanted to settle in Israel, or even to visit there, to leave the Soviet Union. He also told Mrs.

Roosevelt that "if Israel continues her present policy she will be destroyed."

In 1958 the first group of Jewish tourists from the Soviet Union, mostly writers and members of the professions, visited Israel. On their return to the USSR, they wrote disparaging reports of Israel and its institutions. Clearly the tour had been intended by the Soviet government as part of its program to discredit Israel in the Soviet Union.

Anti-Zionist propaganda in the Soviet press continued unabated. An article on the petroleum industry, appearing in *Pravda* (15 August 1958), stated that Chaim Weizmann had "shown a great capacity to write about or even to register patents in his own name in fields well known and well described in Soviet literature." The article alleged: "Apparently the appetite for things which do not belong to them is great among certain men in Israel, and this hunger is not confined to Arab lands, but extends also to scientific discoveries."

A Ukrainian-language radio broadcast from Kirovograd (9 December 1959) said: "Judaic sermons are the sermons of bourgeois Zionists." In December, 1959, the Soviet radio in Moscow linked Israel with international bankers, Wall Street, and imperialism. Attacking the Histadrut and Mapai, Israel's major labor party, the broadcast described Israel's technical assistance to the new African nations as evidence that "Mapai's so-called Socialists are anxious to try their hand at exploiting the Negroes." When Prime Minister Ben-Gurion that month requested a meeting with Khrushchev, he received no answer until April, 1960, when he was told that a visit by him to the Soviet Union would be "premature." It is estimated that the USSR shipped more than $500,000,000 worth of armaments to the Arab states, as well as lavish economic assistance between 1955 and 1959.

Still, Israel did not give up hope that its relations with the Soviet Union would improve. In December, 1961, the Knesset Committee on Foreign Affairs and Defense agreed unanimously that Israel wished "to establish friendly relations with the Soviet Union, as it wishes such relations with all the nations of the world." The Knesset requested the Soviet government to "give the Jewish community of the USSR the opportunity to live its own national, cultural and religious life without discrimination and in accordance with the guarantees of the Soviet constitution."

However, the Soviet anti-Zionist campaign was intensified and augmented to a growing extent by frankly anti-Semitic propaganda. The Kuibyshev daily *Volzhkaia Communa* wrote on 30 September 1961: "The character of the Jewish religion serves the political aims of the Zionists—the awakening of a nationalistic frame of mind." A pamphlet by A. Edelman, *In the Name of the God Yahve*, published in 1963, was devoted to the "debunking of Jewish bourgeois nationalism, Zionism, the spiritual source of which is Judaism.... Zionism and Judaism concluded an alliance... to isolate the Jewish working masses and distract them from the class struggle."

Sentiment for Israel and latent interest in emigration to the Jewish State, both highly unpalatable to the regime, were invariably ascribed to "Zionist propaganda" —propaganda of a movement decreed defunct long ago. On 10 January 1960, *Radianska Ukraina* reported that "believing the Zionist lies," one Nekhama Fogel had decided to go to Israel. The trade union daily *Trud* (17 July 1960) published a letter by a "group of Jews" who, "deceived by Zionist propaganda, had left the Soviet Union for Israel." The popular magazine *Ogonek* (August, 1960) sadly told the story of two members of the Gershuni family who, "succumbing to Zionist propaganda, emigrated to Israel." *Sovetskaia Belorussia* (26 February 1961) assailed "deceitful propaganda of the bourgeois Zionists." *Sovetskaia Moldavia* (27 May 1961) upbraided the Zionists for "kindling nationalist feelings."

Under Khrushchev's regime the attitude and practical approach to allowing Soviet Jews to be reunited with their families in Israel hardened. Requests for exit visas were left unanswered, rejected, or granted only after considerable delay, unpredictably, in small numbers, and mostly to older people. Those who obtained permission to leave originated overwhelmingly from the "incorporated" former Baltic states (Latvia, Lithuania, Estonia) or former Romanian territories (Bessarabia, Bukovina); very few came from the Ukraine and almost none from the Russian Socialist Republic (RSFSR).

Developments after 1964. In mid-October, 1964, Khrushchev was replaced by Aleksei N. Kosygin as Prime Minister of the Soviet Union. A rabidly anti-Zionist policy continued unabated, climaxing in October, 1965, when the Soviet representatives on the Third (Social, Humanitarian, and Cultural) Committee of the UN General Assembly, dealing with the draft Convention on the Elimination of All Forms of Racial Discrimination, attempted to inveigle the United Nations into equating Zionism with Nazism. The Soviet move was triggered by an amendment to the draft, introduced jointly by the United States and Brazil, specifically condemning anti-Semitism as one of the prime "isms" conducive to racism. Partly because of their own increasing sensitivity to any mention of anti-Semitism, of which they themselves were being accused, and partly to curry additional favor with the Arabs, but also because of their deeply ingrained animosity to Zionism, the Soviet delegates offered an amendment of their own, equating Nazism with Zionism. In the ensuing customary give-and-take, they agreed to withdraw this motion in exchange for the retraction of the United States-Brazilian amendment, thus achieving their objective. In the compromise resolution finally adopted, all references to particular "isms," including anti-Semitism, were dropped. The result was a bland, safely general statement of opposition to racial discrimination, which everyone could interpret to his liking.

An unobtrusively favorable change in the Soviet authorities' treatment of Jews wishing to be reunited with their families in Israel came in 1965–66. There were months when as many as 300 immigrants came from Russia, and the total for 1966 reached 2,700. The new arrivals were, on the whole, younger; some came with wives and children; liberal professions and technical skills were represented; and geographic distribution was wider even than in earlier years.

High hopes were attached to a statement made by Kosygin in Paris on 3 December 1966. In reply to a question by the correspondent of United Press International, the Soviet Premier said: "We shall do all possible for us if some families want to meet or even if some among them would like to leave us, to open the road for them, and this naturally does not raise here any problem of principles and will not raise any."

Kosygin's statement was reproduced in both *Izvestia* and *Komsomolskaia Pravda* on 5 December 1966; it also appeared in various provincial newspapers. This suggested that the Soviet Premier's remarks were not made merely for external consumption and were not a spontaneous, impromptu reaction to a correspondent's query but were based on prior consultation with his government. Soviet Jews were greatly encouraged, and there was a considerable increase in the volume of applications by those who had previously been deterred from applying by official hostility. It was known that in previous years applicants had often risked intimidation by security officials, demotion in their jobs (applications must be accompanied by character references from the management of places of employment, exposing people to the possibility of reprisal), or expulsion from universities of students whose parents included their names in family requests for reunions. Cases were also known of young children who had been made to stand before their classmates and promise that they would refuse to accompany their parents if the latter were to leave the Soviet Union. It was hoped that these harassments would now cease. On 2 January 1967, the *New York Times* reported from Moscow that Jews were arriving at passport offices in the various Soviet republics carrying copies of *Pravda* and *Izvestiia* in which Kosygin's remarks in Paris were reported. These applicants were said to have included Jews who had already been refused permission to join relatives as well as others who were applying for the first time.

But it soon became evident that there was strong resistance in Soviet official circles to the idea of easing conditions for Jews wishing to join relatives abroad. A series of articles in the Soviet press, strongly discouraging applications for exit visas, suggested that the initial interpretation of Kosygin's remarks in Paris had been overoptimistic. The campaign began in *Sovetskaia Moldavia* on 18 January 1967, with the article "The Promised Land" without Embellishment—the 'Free World' as It Is." The article contained a long description of allegedly appalling conditions in Israel and disclosed that Soviet Jews seeking to go there were being sent to hear the "truth" from Jewish emigrants who had returned to the USSR; the article warned those who persisted in applying to leave that they would have to suffer the consequences. Even more ominous was a bitter attack in *Sovetskaia Latvia* on 1 February 1967, in which Jews were told that to seek reunion with relatives in Israel was unpatriotic, anti-Communist, and an insult to the feelings of the Soviet people. Prospective applicants were urged to subordinate their family feelings to their sacred responsibilities to the Soviet fatherland. The meaning of such articles was unmistakable and served as a strong deterrent to further applications.

In the wake of the Six-Day War of 1967, in which the Arab states, armed and encouraged by the USSR, were decisively defeated by the Israel Defense Forces, the Soviet government together with the other Bloc states except Romania, broke off diplomatic relations with Israel and withdrew permission to leave for Israel from a number of Soviet Jews who had already obtained exit visas, purchased tickets for the trip to Israel, given up their homes, and sold their belongings. Speaking in the Israeli Knesset on 28 November 1967, Prime Minister Levi Eshkol said that blocking the trickle of immigration to Israel was "an inhuman step, bereft of all moral, political or practical justification."

Simultaneously, a violent radio and press campaign was launched in which, characteristically, Zionism and Zionists were pictured as the real villain: a pointed distinction was made between "criminal Zionism" and the ordinary Israeli citizen. A broadcast by Moscow Radio in Hungarian on 6 July 1967, insisted that the propagators of Zionism were not to be confused with the people of Israel. The theme that Zionism was evil and the Israeli people merely one of its victims was picked up on 15 July by *Komsomolskaia Pravda*, which reaches an estimated 15 million readers, and *Za Rubezhom* (4 August). In an article, "What Is Zionism?," *Sovetskaia Latvia* (5 August) described Zionism as a kind of international "*Cosa Nostra*" (Mafia organization) which was active behind the international scene through the "wide network of Zionist organizations, with a common center, a common program and funds." This new version of *The Protocols of the Elders of Zion* claimed that "the latest aggression of Israeli militarism against the Arab states" was "a classic example of the practices of the Zionist corporation," so powerful that Israel's ruling circles were only its junior partners. In a broadcast in Czech and Slovak on 7 September, Moscow Radio argued that Zionism had no justification for identifying itself with the State of Israel, where there were exploited and exploiters, working people and racialists and reactionaries: Zionism, "the enemy of all working people," was, in the first place the enemy of the Jews.

In January, 1969, there was an unexpected increase in exit permits. Until early April about 200 Soviet Jews reached Israel each month; after April the number of monthly arrivals decreased to a handful. However, a small but steadily growing number of Jews in the USSR defiantly demonstrated their firm determination to break through the barrier of official Soviet anti-emigration policies and secure permission to leave for Israel. A number of individuals, couples and families in Riga, Moscow, and Kiev wrote letters to the highest Soviet authorities, stating their wish as Jews to live in their "motherland Israel," renouncing their Soviet citizenship, and requesting exit visas. In many cases the petitioners saw to it that their actions received worldwide publicity. The response of the Soviet authorities did not follow a set pattern. Some of the requests were simply left unanswered. Some petitioners were arrested, while others were given permission to leave for Israel.

On 10 November 1969, the Israel Ambassador to the UN, Yosef Tekoa submitted an appeal, sent to him by 18 Jews from Soviet Georgia, to UN Secretary-General U Thant, asking him to use his good offices on their behalf; Tekoa was told that the Secretary-General would do whatever he could and that the appeal would be accredited as a General Assembly document. Tekoa noted that this was the first time Israel had formally brought the question of Soviet Jews before the United Nations. In a major change in Israeli policy on the question of Soviet Jewry, the Knesset on 19 November 1969, called on parliaments the world over to "employ the full weight of their influence" in enabling Soviet Jews to emigrate to Israel. Prime Minister Golda Meir declared that the days of "quiet talks and quiet diplomacy" were over. Soviet Jews, she said, had become more courageous and were now openly declaring that "their homeland is the State of Israel."

J. SCHECHTMAN

From the 1970s. In the 1970s, the emigration movement from the USSR reached unprecedented heights despite Moscow's uncompromisingly negative attitude toward Israel and the absence of official relations between the two states. The reasons seem to have been domestic and foreign, a congruence of factors with the same general purport. Within the USSR the Jewish national movement was becoming a major source of disturbance and unrest, notably in Moscow but also in a series of provincial capitals (Riga, Vilnius [Vilna], Kiev, Kishinev) and other cities (*see* RUSSIA: ZIONISM IN). The Soviet authorities seem to have believed that by allowing the emigration of a few thousand Jews they would deprive the movement of its leadership, of its ability to unsettle other sectors of the Jewish, and perhaps also of the non-Jewish, population, and to attract the attention of the outside world as a whole and foreign correspondents in the Soviet capital in particular. In the international arena, the détente, which the Soviet Union badly needed in order to remove the military threat, inherent in western strategic superiority, to enable it to divert its attention and resources from military to civilian development and to open it up to western capital investment and technological know-how, made the Kremlin more susceptible to foreign pressures. At a time when the Soviet Jewry movement was gaining momentum in the US and other western countries and acquiring political clout. The question of Soviet Jewish rights and above all of the right of emigration, which were the focus of the struggle both inside and outside the Soviet Union, became a central issue on the Soviet-US agenda. The US traditionally saw in human rights a yardstick for measuring Soviet intentions in the international arena. Desirous of ridding itself of Jewish trouble-makers for its own domestic reasons, the Soviet leadership found itself in a situation in which it could exact a price for them in its negotiations with the US. As a result, Jewish emigration figures catapulted from a mere 1,000 in 1970 to over 14,000 in 1971 and over 30,000 in each of the years 1972 and 1973. In the middle years of the decade the numbers dropped—thirteen, fourteen, and seventeen thousand respectively for the years 1975, 1976, and 1977—only to rise again towards its end: 30,000 in 1978 and a new peak of 51,000 in 1979. These fluctuations seemed to reflect first the fortunes of détente, which went through some difficult times in the wake of Secretary of State Henry Kissinger's Middle East diplomacy following the Yom Kippur War and Soviet intervention in the Horn of Africa and Angola, and secondly Soviet sensitivities in the face of the congressional debate that culminated in the Jackson-Vanik amendment, that limited US-Soviet trade as long as the USSR limited emigration. In 1978–9, on the other hand, the Soviets were pressing for the ratification by Congress of the SALT II Agreement and in this context Jewish emigration was a meaningful bait.

In the 1980s emigration dwindled to a mere trickle (less than 1,000 per year in the middle of the decade) although it was to grow to mass proportions under Gorbachev at the end of the 1980s. As of the invasion of Afghanistan (December, 1979) and until the appointment of Mikhail Gorbachev as The Communist Party General Secretary in early 1985 détente was replaced by a new period of tension between the two superpowers. At home, too, the relative liberalism and laxity of the early 1970s gave way to an atmosphere of severity and repression *vis-à-vis* the Soviet citizenry in general with the purpose of improving work morale and motivation and boosting the economy. The new trend has been attributed to the KGB chief who succeeded Brezhnev in November, 1982: Iuri Andropov (whose star had begun to shine well before Brezhnev's death and who, among others was mentor to Mikhail Gorbachev). Inevitably its repercussions were felt by the Jews—policy toward whom must always be seen in the broader framework of domestic trends and developments. This was especially true since their large-scale emigration had been depicted throughout by the media basically as defection from the Soviet fatherland and was broadly seen as socially demoralizing and economically harmful.

Indeed, Israel and Zionism continued throughout the 1970s to receive an inordinate amount of attention in the Soviet media in the general vein that had prevailed in the previous period. The intention of this campaign was clearly to alienate from Israel any potential Jewish emigrants, to give vent to feelings of frustration and discontent for which Jews were a traditional outlet, to highlight the insiduousness of US imperialism that relied on such adventurist, amoral, and aggressive tools, and perhaps also to provide apologia for Soviet support of the Arabs.

In the Middle East, the USSR continued its support of the Arabs. The measures it employed to come to Egypt's help when that country's air defenses were demolished by the Israel Defense Forces in the War of Attrition included the dispatch of Soviet pilots to fly combat missions above Egyptian territory—the first time since World War II that Soviet pilots or military personnel participated actively in ongoing hostilities—and the supply of SAM-2s and -3s manned by Soviet crews. Although Nasser's death and Sadat's succession to the Egyptian leadership led to difficulties in the Soviet-Egyptian relationship that were brought to light by the dismissal of the USSR's 20,000 strong military mission in Egypt (July, 1972) and although the Soviets refrained from providing the Egyptians with the offensive weaponry for which they asked, Moscow supplied Sadat with the weaponry that enabled him to initiate the Yom Kippur War in October, 1973.

Egypt's subsequent defection from the Soviet partnership brought about no change in the negative Soviet position toward Israel. While continuing throughout to proclaim its recognition of Israel's right to exist within recognized frontiers and giving the impression that it accepted the borders of the 1949 Armistice Agreements (those of 4 June 1967)—although Soviet maps always gave Israel's borders as those of the 29 November 1947 partition resolution—the USSR joined hands with the Arab radicals against Israel. It supplied weapons to Syria and the PLO in quantities, and of a quality, that might enable the former to attain on its own military parity with Israel.

The main Soviet purpose was not apparently to encourage a further round of hostilities but rather to guarantee Syrian, and PLO, dependence on Moscow so as to make certain that in all discussions and negotiations toward a Middle East, Arab-Israeli settlement, the USSR would necessarily be included as a foreign power of equal status with the US. As of the mid-1970s it began periodically proposing outlines for a settlement which would, moreover, secure for it not only its place and role in reaching and concluding a settlement but also in its implementation through great power guarantees.

Throughout the period subsequent to the Yom Kippur War, the Soviet Union conducted sporadic talks with Israeli representatives. Foreign Minister Gromyko met with his Israeli counterpart at the opening session of the Geneva Conference in December, 1973 and other meetings took place at the UN and various western capitals; lower-level Soviet representatives even visited Israel. These contacts were upgraded simultaneously with Gorbachev's endeavors to renew détente and the US demand that Moscow resume diplomatic relations with Israel as an earnest of its desire to normalize international relations and demonstrate its responsibility. In the early 1990s there were signs that the

Soviet Union was contemplating a full renewal of relations with Israel. This was signaled by the reopening of diplomatic representations and in May 1991 the Soviet Foreign Minister, Alexander Bessmertnykh, paid a historic first visit to Israel in the framework of Soviet attempts to enter the Middle East peace process and in 1992, full diplomatic relations were restored.

Despite endeavors to prove the contrary, Soviet relations with Israel have been not so much the outcome of the usual foreign policy considerations that determine relations between states and particularly between superpowers and small states: specific issues of a purely bilateral level (such as trade); the great power's interests in the region in which the smaller country is situated; and the customary jostling between the powers. The issue is complicated by the presence within the USSR of a sizeable Jewish minority for whose plight Israel takes a certain responsibility by virtue of its own understanding of its essence and historical role and for some of whom at least Israel's existence is a precious boon and even an object of identification. It was also complicated by the traditional Soviet attitude toward Zionism as a tool of imperialism and a valuable propaganda instrument, which in turn entails many aspects of a deep-seated anti-Semitism inherited in part from pre-revolutionary Russian culture. Only in the framework of the new viewpoints of the Gorbachev and Yeltsin regimes as well as the Russian interest in being involved in the peace process (which began at the end of 1991) did a new more positive relationship emerge. This was also carried forward to almost all the separate Republics who established relations and economic ties.

See also ANTI-ZIONISM. Y. RO'I

RUSSIAN JEWS IN ISRAEL. Geographically and politically, this article deals with Jews from Russia both under the Czars (except for Congress Poland) and as the USSR within the borders determined at the end of World War II (except eastern Galicia and northern Bukovina).

Old Yishuv. In 1777 more than 300 Jews, mostly Hasidim from Russia, went to Eretz Israel and settled in Tiberias and Safed. In 1809 a large group of disciples of the Vilna Gaon settled in Safed. Some of these immigrants succeeded in supporting themselves; others were forced to rely on public support and live on the funds of religious charity organizations (*see* HALUKA). One of the leading personalities of the Old Yishuv was Rabbi Shemuel Salant (1816–1909), who went to Eretz Israel and settled in Jerusalem in 1840. He was accepted by the Old Yishuv, and later by the New Yishuv, who appreciated his moderate attitude towards the Haskala movement and Zionism. Through his intervention, the Turkish authorities accorded to the Ashkenazi community a legal status equal to that enjoyed by the Sephardim. He promoted the unification of the small communities (*kolelim*) in Jerusalem under a single umbrella organization and management—the "Keneset Israel General Committee." For 31 years, from 1878 until his death, he served as Ashkenazi chief rabbi.

Another prominent personality, accepted by the Old and the New Yishuv alike, was Rabbi Yehiel Mikhel Pines (1843–1913), thinker and writer, whose religious and nationalistic views subsequently became ideological foundation stones of the Mizrachi movement. He migrated to Jerusalem in 1878 and coordinated the affairs of the Hovevei Zion executive in Eretz Israel for many years. He secured the lands of Gedera for the *Bilu and was one of the founders of the moshava Motza. Unable to agree with Ahad Ha-Am on religious and educational matters, he was dismissed from his office in the Hovevei Zion executive and worked for the rest of his life as one of the main spokesmen of the Old Yishuv.

First Aliya, 1882–1903. The wave of Bilu immigration, while modest in numbers, was strong in vision and ideology. The Bilu organization had about 500 members; the first group to reach Eretz Israel in 1882 numbered only 14 but its impact extended far beyond the narrow confines of the movement proper.

Immigrants, mainly from Russia, had been coming to the country even before the Bilu movement. Five of the first settlements established in the early 1880s were the fruit of the labor and vision of Russian Jewry: Rishon le-Zion, Yesud ha-Ma'ala, Ekron, Nes Tziyona, and Gedera. In the course of time Russian Jews also founded Rehovot, Hadera, Be'er Tovya, Kefar Saba, and Mishmar ha-Yarden. Among the outstanding figures of this period were the Levontins, Eisenbergs, Lewin-Epsteins, Yoseph Feinberg, Israel Belkind, and Mikhael Halpern, a romantic and heroic figure in Russia, who was part Zionist, part collectivist, and part revolutionary and a blend of austerity and fierce courage. Eliezer Ben-Yehuda, who settled in Jerusalem in 1881, was the first to advocate and practice the use of the Hebrew language in everyday conversation. 25,000 Jews from Russia were in the First Aliya.

Second Aliya, 1904–14. In 1905, at a low point in the settlement of Eretz Israel and the history of the Zionist movement (due to the crisis over the East Africa scheme and the death of Herzl), Joseph Witkin who settled in Eretz Israel, (1897) issued an appeal to Jewish youth in Russia outlining the basic principles of the Zionist labor movement. By that time some of the movement's founders—Aharon David Gordon and others, all of Russian origin—had settled in the country, but it was Witkin's appeal that laid the foundation for the Second Aliya, whose members established the first cells of collective and cooperative agricultural settlements (Deganya, Merhavya, Kineret). Some 40,000 Jews immigrated from Russia during this period.

Among the distinguished Russian Jews of the Second Aliya were men such as Gordon, Yoseph Hayim Brenner, David Shimoni, Itzhak Ben-Zvi, Shemuel Yavne'eli, Berl Katznelson, Yosef Sprinzak, and Joseph Trumpeldor (who was expelled during World War I). The Russian Jews who came to Eretz Israel with the Second Aliya initiated and headed many major projects. A group of educated young men established a secondary school for Jewish children. The Herzliya High School was founded by Yehuda Metman-Kohen, Hayim Bograshov, and Ben-Zion Mossinsohn. Pioneer teachers included Itzhak Epstein, Simha Vilkomitz, Joseph Azaryahu, and Joseph Luria. The founder and first manager of the Anglo-Palestine Company (the first Jewish bank in Eretz Israel), Zalman David Levontin, was of Russian origin. One of the founders of Tel Aviv was the Russian-born Meir Dizengoff, who except for a two-year period served as its mayor until his death in 1936. The first Jewish school for arts and crafts, the Bezalel School, was established in Jerusalem and administered by Boris Schatz, a Russian Jew. Russian Jews were active in the experimental ventures of the country's industry also at the turn of the 20th century. On the eve of World War I there were about 50,000 Jews from Russia in Eretz Israel, in a total Jewish population of about 85,000.

Interwar Years. The Third Aliya (1919–23) emerged from the ruins of Russian and Eastern European Jewry at the end of World War I. At the risk of their lives young pioneers and Jews of various social strata sought to reach Palestine. The obstacles were tremendous: emigration from Russia was forbidden by the Soviet authorities, and immigration to Palestine was obstructed by the British mandatory government. In 1918 a small group left Siberia and, traveling via Japan, reached Palestine a year later. Joseph Trumpeldor and his friends arrived in Jaffa at the end of 1919. The SS *Roslan* sailed from Odessa and arrived in Jaffa at the end of 1919 with 630 immigrants aboard. Thereafter, Zionism was outlawed in Russia; emigration to Palestine was considered desertion. Nevertheless, in the early years of the Soviet regime (1919–23), 15,800 Russian Jews found their way to Palestine; about the same number (15,500) emigrated during the period 1924–31. For a short time Zionist prisoners were occasionally offered a choice between imprisonment, exile in Siberia, and "exile" to Palestine. Thereafter only a trickle of Jewish political prisoners, Zionist-motivated Jews and victims of persecution and want, managed to reach Palestine and later Israel from the USSR.

State of Israel. The establishment of the State of Israel awakened enthusiasm and hope in the hearts of Russian Jews. With the arrival of Golda Meyerson (Meir), the first Israeli Minister in Moscow, large numbers of Jews applied for immigration visas. Many of them paid for this spontaneous move with prison or concentration camp sentences and with economic and social hardships. Except for a few cases, emigration from Russia was not allowed. Nevertheless, from the creation of the State of Israel in 1948 until the Six-Day War in June 1967, thousands more Russian Jews reached Israel disguised as Polish citizens, and on one occasion as Turkish immigrants. Many of them were former residents of the areas of east Poland (western Ukraine and Belorussia and the Vilna region annexed by the USSR). During World War II these Jews had lived in the USSR as refugees. Mostly genuine, but sometimes fictitious, marriages with Polish refugees were used to enable those who were not former Polish citizens to leave Russia. Some employed ruses in order to obtain certificates attesting to their Polish citizenship prior to the War. Immigration from Poland was made possible through accords between the USSR and Poland on repatriation from the USSR to Poland of former Polish citizens. These accords were signed in 1944, 1945, and 1957. In addition to these immigrants, the Soviets permitted the emigration of 5,837 Soviet Jews between 1960 and May 1967. Most of these immigrants were also residents of the border areas annexed to Russia in World War II, not only from former areas of Poland, but also from the Baltic countries, Bessarabia, and Bukovina. They were mostly elderly, disabled, and chronic invalids. In the forty years ending 1988, 185,499 Jews immigrated from the USSR. Altogether, 205,246 Jews who immigrated said they were of Russian birth, the difference being accounted for by those Soviet Jews who lived outside the USSR before coming to Israel. To these should be added 52,350 Jews who immigrated from the USSR in the period 1919–48.

Contributions of Russian Jews. Numbers and percentages do not reflect the weight and influence of Jews from Russia in every aspect of Israel's life. To mention a few of the outstanding figures involved in the development of the country: The first three Presidents of Israel—Chaim Weizmann, Itzhak Ben-Zvi, and Zalman Shazar—were of Russian origin, as were two of the first three Prime Ministers, Moshe Sharett and Levi Eshkol. In the hands of Menahem Ussishkin, who served as its chairman from 1923 to 1941, the Jewish National Fund became the principal land redemption instrument, and contributed to the expansion of the borders of the State that rose afterwards.

Russian-Jewish farmer in K'far Hasidim in 1937. [United Israel Appeal]

Some of the outstanding intellectual and artistic figures of Russian Jewry settled in Palestine. They included the philosopher Ahad Ha-Am, the historians Joseph Klausner, Benzion Dinur, Binyamin Mazar, Avigdor Tscherikover, and Shmuel Ettinger; the poets Hayim Nahman Bialik, Saul Tschernichowsky, Abraham Shlonsky, Rachel, Yitzhak Lamdan, and Nathan Alterman; the writers Yosef Hayim Brenner, Sh. Benzion, Alexander Suskind Rabinovitz, Ya'akov Fichman, Mordecai Ben-Hillel Ha-Cohen, Moshe Smilansky, and Hayim Hazaz, the linguist Avraham Even-Shoshan, the orator and political leader Shemarya Levin, and members of the Habimah Theater such as Yehoshua Bertonoff, Aharon Meskin, and Hanna Rovina.

Berl Katznelson, David Remez, Yosef Sprinzak, and Yitzhak Tabenkin, all Russian Jews, played a leading part in the foundation of the Histadrut in 1920. Jews from Russia also founded (1920) the pioneer kevutzot, moshavim, and kibbutzim. During the 1920s many settlements, both collective and cooperative, were established in the Jezreel and Jordan Valleys through the initiative and driving force of Jews from Russia. The Palestine Electric Corporation, Ltd. was founded by Pinhas Rutenberg. In 1929 Palestine Potash, Ltd., predecessor of the Dead Sea Works Company, Ltd., was formed and headed by Moshe Novomeysky, who had come to Palestine from Siberia.

The influence of the members of the Second and Third Aliya on the social, spiritual, and cultural life of the yishuv far exceeded their comparative numerical importance. They were responsible for the founding of the Zionist-

Socialist Labor Movement with its various parties and ideological streams.

The first leaders of the two Zionist right-wing parties were also of Russian origin: Menahem Ussishkin led the General Zionists and Vladimir Jabotinsky founded and led the Revisionist Party.

After 1967. Israel's victory in the Six-Day War led to a reinforced national awakening among very wide circles of Soviet Jews. It strengthened the desire to immigrate to Israel in circles fired by Zionism, and also inspired completely assimilated Jews who had been totally estranged from their religious origin and identity. Among the former were Holocaust survivors, inhabitants of the annexed regions, and also members of the non-Ashkenazi communities: Georgians, Bukharans, and Caucasians.

From 1969 there were strong fluctuations in the numbers of Jews leaving the USSR, probably reflecting the internal hesitations and reversals in the Soviets' consideration of this matter. (*For statistics see* ALIYA). Between 1969 and 1988 168,950 Russian Jews immigrated to Israel. The number of Russian immigrants leaving Israel has been low in comparison to the groups of other immigrants. In the three years following their aliya 8% of Russian immigrants left Israel. Bearing in mind that some leave Israel after three years or more, it may be assumed that about 10% of Soviet immigrants reaching Israel from the Six-Day War up to 1988 have left. Since 1989, with the large-scale Jewish emigration from Russia, great numbers of Russian Jews have been arriving in Israel.

About 107,000, i.e., some 65% of the Russian immigrants who went to Israel between 1968 and 1986, emanated from the European regions of the Soviet Union. Although a high percentage of these immigrants were of working age, many were of retirement age (19%). About 56% of working age immigrants benefited from higher education; nearly half of these were engineers. There was also a very high percentage of doctors (17%). Many hundreds of scientists and top specialists were successfully absorbed in institutes of higher education, scientific and research establishments, and high tech industries, and their contributions to these areas are of major importance. Conversely, thousands of academics had to be retrained, due to the lack of demand in Israel for their areas of specialization (mining, forestry and railway engineers, Russian language and literature specialists, Marxist philosophers, etc.).

The immigrants also included many artists, particularly musicians (among them famous virtuosos), who reinforced Israel's orchestras and the teaching staff in the music academies, and who made it possible to create new institutions of this kind in the provincial towns. Hundreds of music teachers have raised the level of music teaching in Israel and introduced music education into many schools, community centers, and youth clubs throughout Israel.

Due to the high percentage of members of the labor force, to the fact that both men and women work, to the high levels of education, and to the professional training, the economic absorption of the European Russian immigrants was generally successful. Most of them enjoyed a higher income level and higher living standards than they had known in the USSR and higher than the average in the Israeli population. They mastered the Hebrew language; after five years in the country 87% of European Russian immigrants and 65% from the southern regions, aged 18 to 54, spoke Hebrew fluently or almost fluently.

Despite the satisfactory command of Hebrew, there was relatively little social intercourse between the Russian immigrants and the veteran population in Israel, and the immigrants' social and cultural life was centered principally in groups of people of the same origin. The spiritual and cultural world of the intellectuals among the immigrants—the writers, poets, journalists, artists, and specialists in the humanities—was, with some exceptions, immersed entirely in Russian culture, and they did not succeed, or if so only partially, in joining the intellectual and cultural life in Hebrew in Israel. This, however, is a common phenomenon among all first generation immigrants, who have been uprooted from their natural surroundings; it disappears from the second generation in Israel onwards since the children learn in schools and serve in the Israel army together with all other Israelis.

The situation was revolutionized with the mass emigration of Jews from the USSR starting in 1989, following the opening of the gates of Russia and the threat of widespread anti-Semitism. As the US limited its intake of Russian Jews, large numbers moved to Israel, which was faced with a massive challenge in housing and absorbing the newcomers.

Y. LITVAK

Pinhas Rutenberg. [Zionist Archives]

RUTENBERG, PINHAS. Engineer, industrialist, founder of the Palestine Electric Corporation, and leader of the *yishuv (b. Romny, Russia, 1879; d. Jerusalem, 1942). Rutenberg joined the Russian revolutionary movement as a student in St. Petersburg and played a prominent part in it. Forced to flee from Russia, he went to Italy, where he worked as an engineer, later specializing in irrigation works. He went to the United States in 1915 to organize the movement for the *Jewish Legion and joined in efforts to convene the first *American Jewish Congress. At the same time he worked on a comprehensive irrigation plan for Palestine.

After the overthrow of the Tsarist regime in 1917, Rutenberg returned to Russia, where he served as a military commander of Petrograd in the Kerenski government. He was among the last defenders of the Winter Palace, the seat of the provisional government, and upon its surrender was imprisoned by the Bolsheviks. Released in the spring of 1918, he went to Moscow. Later he fled to Kiev and Odessa, where he joined the anti-Bolshevist forces. When Odessa was about to fall, he escaped to Paris and, after a while, decided to give up Russian politics. He settled in Palestine late in 1919.

In Palestine Rutenberg worked out the details of his plan for the Jordan River Valley. As a first step, he decided to exploit the waters of the Jordan and Yarmukh Rivers for hydroelectric purposes. During the *Arab riots of 1920 he cooperated with Vladimir *Jabotinsky in organizing Jewish self-defense in Jerusalem. Despite the opposition of various British circles, the mandatory government granted Rutenberg a concession in 1921, and in 1923 he established the Palestine Electric Corporation, Ltd. The electrification project proved a success, revealing his skill as an engineer, financier, and manager.

After the 1929 Arab riots, Rutenberg became chairman of the *Va'ad Le'umi (National Council). In 1930 he became a member of the Executive of the *Jewish Agency. He resigned from both posts the next year. Rutenberg helped establish the port of Tel Aviv and founded a Palestine aviation company. After the outbreak of World War II he invested great effort in the unification of the Yishuv and was again chosen chairman of the Va'ad Le'umi. Illness forced him to resign this office in 1941.

In his will Rutenberg made an impassioned plea for the unity of the yishuv, directed that all his property be utilized to establish a Rutenberg Endowment Fund, the proceeds of which were to be devoted to the education of Jewish youth, and asked that no streets or villages be named for him.

S

SA'AD. Religious kibbutz in the northwest corner of the Negev, 4 mi. (6 km.) southeast of Gaza, founded in 1947 by Youth Aliya graduates from Germany. In the 1948 War of Independence, the village was completely leveled in long and bitter battles with the invading Egyptian army, but the settlers held out and later rebuilt the kibbutz further east. They developed industrial enterprises and model intensive farming based on many branches, and they conduct religious and cultural programs for immigrants. Population (1987), 722.

E. ORNI

SABBATH AND HOLIDAYS IN ISRAEL. Already in 1948, with the founding of the State, the Jewish sabbath (Friday sundown to Saturday sundown) was determined as the official day of rest for the Jewish population. Allowance was made for a day of rest on Friday for Moslems and Sunday for Christians. The Work and Rest Hours Law of 1951 legislated that Jewish employees were to be given their weekly day of rest on the sabbath and their festival vacations on Jewish holidays. Certain sectors were regulated by municipal ordinances, in accordance with local coalition agree-

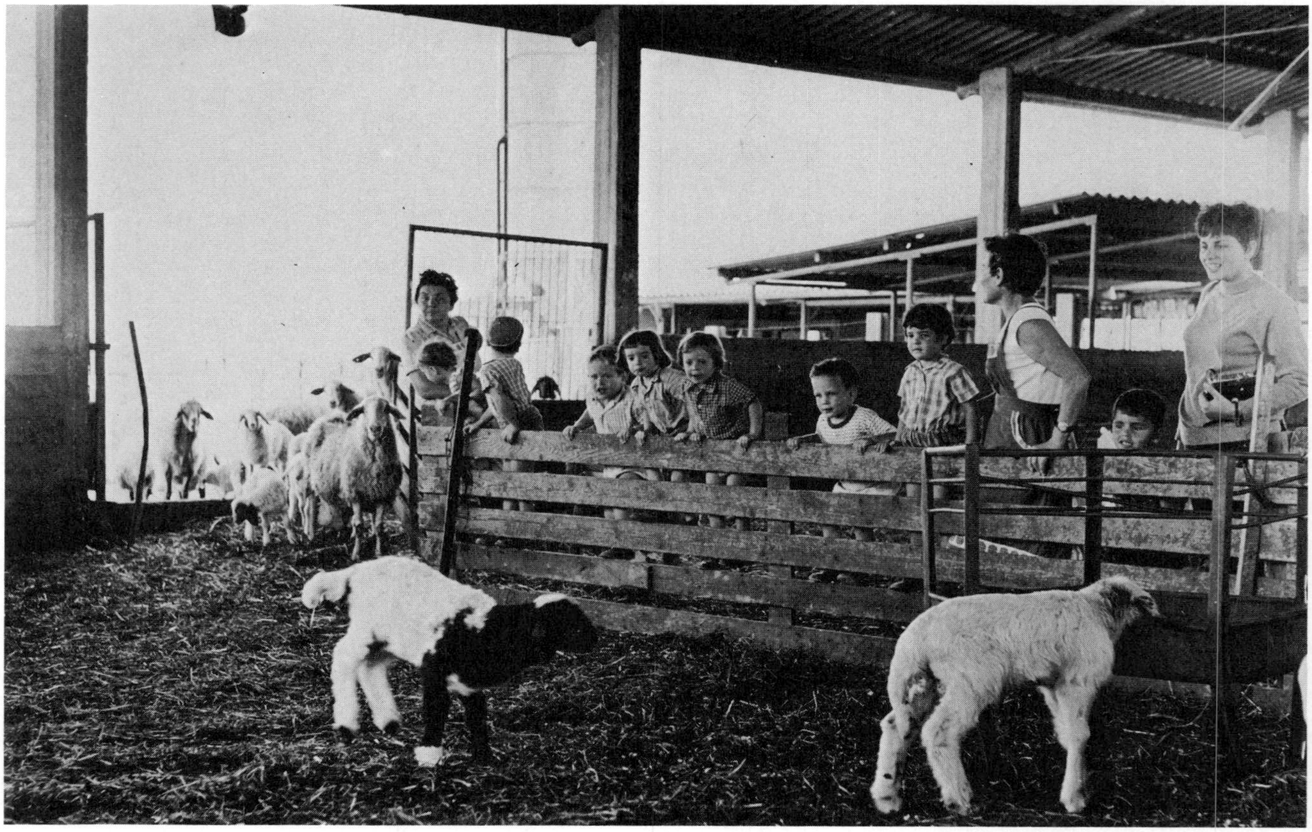

Watching sheep feed at the kibbutz Sa'ad. [United Israel Appeal]

Purchasing lulav *and* etrog *for the festival of Sukkot.* [Israel Government Press Office]

ments in each city. However, permits to work on sabbaths and holidays could be issued for essential services and for security operations where the traditional principle of *piku'ah nefesh* (danger to life) was deemed at stake. Such licences were granted by the Ministry of Labor. Under the *status quo* principle, arrangements in force under the Mandate were extended under Israel rule. As a result, public bus service continued to function in Haifa on the sabbath while there was no public transportation on the sabbath in other cities. The political power of the religious parties within municipal or local council also affected local legislation: cafés were allowed to be open during certain hours on the sabbath in Tel Aviv, but not Jerusalem; all streets were closed to traffic in Benei Berak; cinemas and other forms of entertainment were open in some towns, not in others.

Inevitably the sabbath was kept in different ways by the Orthodox and non-Orthodox. The Orthodox observed the sabbath according to traditional practice, and each municipality had a religious council which constructed and maintained an *eruv* (a symbolic fence) around the city, making it religiously permissible to carry articles on the sabbath. For the non-Orthodox, the sabbath was a day of leisure, with high attendance at football matches in the winter and at the beaches in the summer. Orthodox political parties and groups campaigned to reduce what they regarded as sabbath violation, achieving some success through coalition agreements at the national and municipal levels which resulted in appropriate legislation or ordinances. Informally, the ultra-Orthodox in particular conducted protracted demonstrations to protest sabbath traffic in roads close to

Planting trees on Tu bi-Shevat [Israel Information Services]

Orthodox quarters, the opening of cinemas, cafés, etc. In 1976, the coalition government headed by Yitzhak Rabin fell when it was deserted by its religious coalition partners: the ceremonies marking the arrival of the Israel Air Force's first F15 planes, involved the desecration of the sabbath. Following the principle of the Mandatory *status quo*, sabbath radio broadcasts were continued under the State. When television was introduced in the late 1960s, the Orthodox endeavored to veto sabbath programs on the grounds that this was an innovation, but the Supreme Court ruled that TV should be regarded as an extension of radio broadcasting and that they should be permitted.

The Festivals. The traditional festivals (New Year, Day of Atonement, Sukkot, Simhat Torah, Passover (first and last days) and Shavuot) are days of rest, as is Independence Day (5 Iyar). The last is not observed among certain extreme Orthodox circles. In accordance with ancient tradition, festivals (except the New Year) that are observed for two days in the Diaspora are kept for only one day in Israel. The Day of Atonement is respected by all segments of the Jewish population. Broadcasting is suspended and everyone refrains from driving cars, leaving the streets open to pedestrians, many dressed in white on their way to and from the *synagogues. Many Israeli characteristics have been imparted to festivals, with the *Western Wall serving as a focus on many of these occasions. On the evening after Simhat Torah, the custom has developed of dancing with the Scrolls of the Law in public places, according to traditions of different communities. *Tu bi-Shevat* (the New Year for Trees) is the occasion of mass tree planting by children. On Purim, fancy dress parades, known as *Adloyada*, are held, and for a few days costumed children fill the streets. Before Shavu'ot, children of younger school age attend school wearing wreaths of flowers on their heads. Lag ba-Omer is a day for bonfires, and many of the Orthodox make their way to the reputed grave of Rabbi Shimon bar Yohai at Meron, where boys who have reached the age of three are given their first haircuts. For the many special observances that have been developed in the kibbutzim, *see* KIBBUTZ FESTIVALS. Non-Jews including Moslems and Christians are also legally allowed to observe their holidays. Christmas and Easter are the main Christians holidays, the former being observed on different days by the Latin Christians (25 December), the Greek Orthodox (6 January), and the Armenian Orthodox (19 January).

Sounding the ram's horn on Mount Zion, Jerusalem, 1958. [Israel Govt. Press Office]

SABRA. Popular appellation for native-born Israelis. It is derived from the Arabic name of the cactus plant (Heb., *tzabar*) which grows freely in the country and whose sweet, refreshing, and juicy fruit is enclosed in a tough skin that is studded with long thorns. The name refers to the character of the Sabras, who are supposedly tough on the surface but gentle within.

Cactus from which the name of the native-born Israeli is derived. [Israel Information Services]

SACERDOTI, ANGELO. Chief rabbi of Rome and Zionist leader (b. Florence, 1886; d. Rome, 1935). As chief rabbi of Rome from 1912 until his death, Sacerdoti exerted a profound influence on Italian Jewry. During World War I he was senior chaplain on the Italian front. He was the initiator of a revision of the Law of Jewish Communities of Italy and a member of the Consulta Rabbinica from 1932 until his death.

Active in the Zionist movement, he represented Italian Jewry as well as the Italian government at the opening of the Hebrew University of Jerusalem in 1925. Sacerdoti, then a member of the Executive of the Comité des Délégations Juives, participated in the World Jewish Conference held in Geneva (5–8 September 1933; 20–23 August 1934) preparatory to the organization of the World Jewish Congress. A selection of his writings was collected in a memorial book entitled *In memoria di Angelo Sacerdoti*, published by the Jewish Community of Rome in 1936. G. ROMANO

Harry Sacher. [United Israel Appeal]

SACHER: Family of British Zionists.

Harry Sacher, Editor, lawyer, and Zionist leader (b. London, 1881; d. London, 1971). Born in London's East End, Sacher studied at the Universities of London (1900–01), Oxford (1901–04), Berlin (1904–05), and Paris (1905) and was called to the bar in 1909. He first became acquainted with Zionism during a vacation trip in 1903, when he stopped off at Basle to visit the Sixth Zionist Congress. After his return to England he founded the first student Zionist society there. In 1905 he joined the staff of the *Manchester Guardian* as an editorial writer, serving on that paper until 1909 and again from 1915 to 1919, after a period with the London *Daily News*. He met Chaim Weizmann soon after the latter's arrival in Manchester, and it was he who introduced Weizmann to Charles Prestwich Scott, the editor of the *Manchester Guardian*, and to the political journalist Herbert Sidebotham, who later rendered historic services to the Zionist cause. He also won over to Zionism Simon Marks and Israel Sieff, who were to become his brothers-in-law and with whom he formed the small group of Weizmann disciples known as the Manchester group.

In 1920 Sacher went to Palestine to open a law practice in Jerusalem, where he remained for 10 years, representing various business firms and providing legal services to the Zionist movement, including the defense of Jews arrested during the Arab riots of 1921. From 1927 to 1929 he was a member of the Zionist Executive in Palestine and from 1929 to 1931 of the Jewish Agency Executive in Jerusalem and London. In 1930 he returned to England to become a director of the Marks and Spencer chain stores.

The author of numerous pamphlets and essays on Zionism, Sacher edited (with Sir Leon Simon) the Manchester monthly the *Zionist Banner* (1909) and (with Sidebotham) a fortnightly journal, *Palestine*, dedicated to the education of public opinion in favor of Zionism, and the *Jewish Review* (1932–34). In 1916 he edited *Zionism and the Jewish Future*, a volume of Zionist essays by many authors, which became an important propaganda instrument in the period preceding the issuance of the Balfour Declaration. He also wrote *Israel: The Establishment of a State* (1952) and *Zionist Portraits and Other Essays* (1959).

Miriam Sacher, Harry's wife, WIZO leader (b. Manchester, 1892; d. London, 1973). She was one of the early founders of WIZO and while in Palestine in 1924 helped to found WIZO's Jerusalem Baby Home. After her return to England, she played a leading role in the Federation of Women Zionists of Great Britain and Ireland and was the benefactor of many projects in Israel, including Jerusalem's Sacher Park.

Michael Moses Sacher, son of Harry and Miriam, industrialist and Zionist leader in England (b. Manchester, 1918; d. London, 1986). He entered the family business, Marks and Spencer, and served as vice-chairman from 1972–84. During World War II he served in the Royal Army Service Corps in the Western Desert. His public Zionist work began in 1950 when he was appointed treasurer of the Jewish National Fund in England, later becoming its President. He also served, among other things, as Joint President of the Joint Israel Appeal (United Kingdom), member of the Jewish Agency Executive, and Vice-President of the Jewish Colonization Association.

SADAN, DOV. Author and literary scholar (b. Brody, Poland, 1902; d. Jerusalem, 1989). Sadan received a traditional Jewish education, then attended a Jewish secular school and later a government secondary school, where he acquired his interest in literature and general history. In Lvov, where his family moved during World War I, he became active in He-Halutz, and later served as the editor of *He-Atid*, the movement's periodical. In 1925, he migrated to Palestine and worked as a halutz in the coastal plain. His writing drew him to the attention of Berl Katznelson, who invited him in 1927 to join the editorial staff of *Davar*, the newspaper published by the Labor movement.

In 1928, he was sent to Germany to represent the He-Halutz movement. There he enrolled in Berlin's *Hochschule* for Politics, Geopolitics, and Education; there he discovered the then-prevailing critical literary and aesthetic trends, particularly the application of psychoanalytic theories in literary analysis. Returning to Palestine, he spent several years teaching in Galilee but in 1933 rejoined *Davar*, serving intermittently as the editor of its weekly literary supplement. He became the first professor of Yiddish Literature at the Hebrew University in 1952, enjoying immense popularity as teacher and literary mentor until he retired in 1963. In 1965 he was appointed professor of Hebrew Literature at Tel Aviv University, retiring in 1970. He was elected a member of Israel's Academy of Sciences in 1965. Sadan served in the Knesset as a Labor member from 1965–67. He resigned his seat in protest against the decision to send a Knesset delegation to Germany. In 1968, he was awarded the Israel Prize in Jewish Studies.

Sadan was a brilliant and prolific author, having published more than sixty volumes. The range of his interests was extremely wide: prose fiction, poetry, philology, and folklore.

He was one of the earliest Hebrew literary scholars to employ Freudian techniques in his literary studies and demonstrated uncanny skill in dissecting the symbolic language of major Hebrew writers such as Bialik and Agnon.

Sadan dates the beginning of modern Hebrew literature from the period of the Chmielnicki pogroms (1648) in the Ukraine. His major thesis is that Hebrew literature cannot be viewed in isolation but rather as an important segment of modern Jewish literature, which includes not only Hebrew but also Yiddish and Jewish literature written in European languages. This literature must be viewed as a single, if multi-faceted, corpus. A major task of the historian and critic is to uncover the linguistic and contextual links as well as the dialectic clash between these three segments. In his Bialik studies, he engages in meticulous symbol analysis. He also suggests that Bialik's genius was thwarted by the negative influences of Ahad Ha-Am's positivism, Mendele Mokher Seforim's realism, and the anti-mystical and rational prejudices which he encountered at the Volozhin yeshiva.

Sadan's belle-lettres include several volumes of short stories, a number of autobiographical reminiscences: *Mi-Mehoz ha-Yaldut* (From Childhood's World), *Shenot Hayim* (Life's Years), and others. His collection of Jewish humor, *Ke'arat Tsimukim* (A Bowl of Raisins) and *Ke'arat Egozim* (A Bowl of Nuts), were highly popular. He also published translations of literary works and essays.

His major critical-historical works are *Avnei Bohan* (Touchstones, 1951), *Al Shai Agnon* (On S.Y. Agnon, 1959), *Avnei Bedek* (Stones of Repair [or Scrutiny], 1962), *Bein Din ve-Heshbon* (Between Judgment and Reckoning, 1963), *Bein She'ilah ve-Kinyan* (Between Borrowing and Acquisition, 1969) and *Avnei Geder* (Definitions, 1970). Much of his Yiddish criticism appears in *Avnei Miftan* (Threshold Stones, 1962–70). E. SPICEHANDLER

SADAT (EL-SAADAT), ANWAR. President of Egypt, 1970–1981 (b. a village in the Egyptian delta (Mitoatbul-Kum), 1918; d. Cairo, 1981). He graduated from military academy in 1938 and during his subsequent military service was active in political life. As a result of his traditional background and ideological leanings he was close to the Moslem Brotherhood. During World War II he organized a group of anti-British officers who contacted the Nazi forces in North Africa; Sadat was imprisoned from 1942 to 1945. In 1949 he became a member of the "Free Officers" whose military coup led by Gamal Abdel *Nasser, overthrew the monarchy in July, 1952.

Because of Sadat's association with the Moslem Brotherhood, he was excluded from high governmental circles during the years in which the Nasser regime was in conflict with the Brotherhood—from 1954 to to 1957. In 1957 he was appointed chairman of the "National Unity" (the only authorized political body) and between 1959 and 1969 presided over the Parliament. In 1969 he was chosen as Nasser's sole deputy and upon the latter's sudden death in 1970, Sadat became president.

At that time he was still considered a rather colorless personality lacking executive experience and seen as a compromise between the left and right wings of Nasserism. This assessment, however, soon changed radically, with the sweeping de-Nasserization that began in mid-1971. Egypt's international orientation was deflected from the Soviet Union to the United States and the West, which meant an influx of economic and military aid to help replenish the country's empty treasury and supply depots. Parliamentary life and political party activities were renewed (including legitimization of the Moslem Brotherhood), and the attitude to Israel changed. Sadat was murdered by members of one of the many extreme religious fundamentalist organizations that flourished in Egypt at the end of the 1970s. Their objective was to destroy his regime which they believed promulgated an heretical approach by failing to implement all aspects of traditional Islamic law, by failing to prevent social and cultural westernization, and by encouraging the idea of a national state that conflicts with the principle of the absolute sovereignty of God. The peace with Israel was seen as one of Sadat's major transgressions.

Attitude to Israel: Sadat followed a circuitous path that led him all the way from war to peace. In all his moves he showed himslef to be pragmatic and cautious, a man with a comprehensive strategic conception and political outlook. These traits helped him jettison the concept that a political settlement could be reached with Israel through repeated military actions and convinced him that the differences had to be solved by means of direct and open negotiations. This change in his approach was the result of internal social and economic pressures exacerbated by Egypt's conflict with Israel. Egypt's economic, political, and military situation would benefit from changing the nature of the confrontation, and Sadat incorporated his new policy toward Israel into his overall position. In addition, while Israel exhibited a new flexibility in view of the outcome of the *Yom Kippur War, there was a growing feeling in Egypt that the country had achieved as much as possible by means of war, and that it was now likely to be more advantageous to look toward peace.

Essentially, this process had been set in motion as early as 1971 when Sadat expressed readiness in principle, although still in rudimentary form, to make peace with Israel in return for an overall settlement that would include Israel's total withdrawal from the areas conquered in 1967; he even indicated readiness to negotiate a partial settlement in the Sinai. When his call elicited no response and the situation continued unchanged, Sadat decided to provoke a reaction by means of a limited military engagement—the Yom Kippur War of 1973. Thereafter, with the mediation of the United States, a Separation of Forces and two Interim Agreements were signed. The first (January, 1974) provided for a minor pull-back of Israeli forces in return for Egypt's undertaking to seek ways of making peace. The second (September, 1975) had a three-year limitation and included a deeper Israeli pull-back in Sinai as well as the return of the Abū Rodeis oil field to Egypt, while providing for the demilitarization of those areas and their surveillance by United Nations' forces. Egypt guaranteed not to resort to armed conflict with Israel, and to permit passage through the reopened Suez Canal of non-military cargoes to and from Israel.

In the late summer and early fall of 1977 Sadat's peace initiative included indirect contact and then direct—but still secret—communication with the Israeli government leadership. Then, when it became clear to the Egyptian President that the end of the second Separation of Forces agreement with Israel was imminent with nothing satisfactory to replace it, he became convinced that a dramatic breakthrough was needed to confront Israel with the choice of peace for territory. The ground having been prepared with the help of the good offices of the President of Romania, Nicolai Ceausescu, and at a secret meeting in Morocco between Sadat's adviser and Gen. Moshe Dayan, Sadat had reason to believe that a daring public initiative would not be rejected by Menahem Begin, head of the new Israeli government. And indeed, in November, 1977, Egypt's President was officially and publicly received in Jerusalem. Sadat's coming to Jerusalem and his declaration in the Knesset that "...we welcome you among us... we agree to live in permanent and just peace with you..." opened new avenues to direct public negotiations which eventually led to the signing of the *Camp David accords in 1978. In 1979 Israel signed a peace treaty with Egypt, the largest and strongest of all the Arab states (*see* CAMP DAVID FRAMEWORK ACCORDS; EGYPT, RELATIONS WITH ISRAEL). M. KLEIN

SADEH (LANDSBERG), YITZHAK. Israeli soldier, labor leader, and writer (b. Lublin, Russian Poland, 1890; d. Petah Tikva, 1952). He served in the Russian Army during World War I, was decorated, and after the Russian Revolution was a company commander in the Red Army at Petrograd. In 1919 he joined Joseph Trumpeldor in organizing the He-Halutz pioneering movement in the Crimea. Settling in Palestine in 1920, he became a leader in Gedud ha-Avoda and later worked as a foreman at the Rutenberg works and at the Athlit quarry. A proficient athlete, he was a founder of Ha-Po'el, the sports organization of the Histadrut.

Soon after his arrival in Palestine, Sadeh became active in the Hagana, the self-defense organization of the yishuv, in which he held leading posts. He was largely responsible for the organization of the Pelugot Sadeh (Field Units), a Hagana mobile force, and in 1941 founded Palmah, the striking arm of Hagana, serving as its commander until 1945. In the beginning of the War of Independence, serving as a Hagana commander, he led battles against Arab forces at Mishmar ha-Emek and in Jerusalem. Soon after the establishment of the Israel Defense Forces he became commander of the Eighth Armored Brigade. His popular, enthusiastic style of leadership gained him widespread affection and respect. Many of the commanders of the Hagana and the Palmah, and—subsequently—the Israel army were his disciples, including Yigal Allon.

After the war, in 1949, Sadeh resigned from the Israel Defense Forces. He assumed a leading role in the Mapam party, which he represented on the Tel Aviv Municipal Council. He devoted the last years of his life to literary pursuits and served as mentor to a new generation of young authors. He wrote a regular column for the newspaper *Al ha-Mishmar*, in which he recalled the early days of Palmah and criticized the spit-and-polish discipline of modern army life. He was also the author of a number of stories and plays.

SAFED (TZEFAT). Town in Upper Galilee, 25 mi. (40 km.) north of Tiberias, 2,780 ft. (850 m.) above sea level. It is mentioned in the Jerusalem Talmud. The Crusaders built a strong fortress at the site in the 12th century. A Jewish community existed there from the 11th century onward

View of Safed. [Israel Information Services]

and it was greatly strengthened by an influx of Jews from Spain after 1492. In the 16th century, the town attained its highest spiritual and material level. It was the center of Kabbala (Jewish mysticism) and home of Rabbi Isaac Luria (The "Ari") and of Joseph Karo, author of the standard legal code, the *Shulhan Arukh*. Jews established famous textile and printing workshops and traded in farm produce, silk, spices, etc. Together with Jerusalem, Hebron, and Tiberias, Safed was counted as one of the four "holy towns" in the Land of Israel. With the deterioration of Turkish rule in the 17th century a decline set in, and became more severe in the following century, with epidemics and earthquakes causing the death and the departure of many Jews. An earthquake in 1837 killed 5,000 inhabitants, 4,000 of them Jews. Toward the end of the 19th century, Jewish settlers returned to Safed. The community numbered 6,620 in 1895 and 11,000 (out of a total population of 25,000) in 1913, existing mostly on charity (*haluka*). Cut off from its sources of support in World War I, the community was decimated by hunger and disease and dwindled to 2,986 (out of a population of 8,760) in 1922. When part of the Safed hinterland was included within the borders of Lebanon, the Jewish community shrank further, numbering less than 2,000 (out of 12,000 inhabitants) by 1948. Living in its narrow northern quarter, it came under siege when the evacuating British permitted Arab forces (among them Iraqi and Lebanese army detachments) to occupy key positions. A Palmah force entered the Jewish quarter through hidden paths and on 11–12 May, against all odds, captured the Arab positions. The Arab troops and the entire Arab population fled. Jewish immigrants from different countries thereafter settled in Safed. Its economy was based on some industry and on summer tourism. Painters and sculptors made the picturesque artists' quarter a tourist attraction, alongside the municipal Glicenstein Museum and six famous ancient synagogues. There are also several Moslem monuments, and parts of the Crusader fortress on the hilltop were excavated by Israel archeologists. Despite plans in the 1970s and 1980s to enlarge Safed's population to 100,000 in the framework of Galilee development, the town stagnated, numbering 16,400 inhabitants in 1987.

E. ORNI

ST. JAMES'S CONFERENCE (Round Table Conference of 1939). Conference of Arabs and Jews called by the British

Leaders of the Jewish Agency at the St. James's Conference, London, in 1939. [Zionist Archives]

government to discuss the future of Palestine. It was held in St. James's Palace, London, from 7 February—17 March 1939. In November, 1938, the British government announced that after studying the report of the Palestine Partition Commission (*Woodhead Commission) it had reached the conclusion that the proposal to create an Arab and a Jewish State in Palestine was impractical, so that an alternative solution to the Palestine problem would have to be found. "The surest foundation for progress and peace in Palestine would be an understanding between the Arabs and the Jews," the government declared, and to this end it proposed to invite representatives of the Palestinian Arabs and of the neighboring states and representatives of the Jewish Agency to a conference in London.

To make its delegation as representative as possible, the Agency established a conference committee of leading Jews, both Zionist and non-Zionist, from Great Britain and other countries. The function of the committee, which was to remain in session in London throughout the conference, was to advise and assist the Jewish negotiating body in the conduct of the talks. The Jewish delegation was led by Chaim Weizmann. The Palestine Arabs were represented by followers of Hajj Amin al-Huseini, the mufti of Jerusalem, and of the rival and more moderate Arab National Defense party of the Nashashibis. Among the mufti's delegates were men who had been deported by the British from Palestine to the Seychelles Islands. These individuals were accepted by the British as delegates although the government had previously announced that it reserved the right to exclude from the conference "those leaders whom they regard as responsible for the campaign of assassination and violence." Egypt, Iraq, Saudi Arabia, Yemen, and Transjordan sent leading representatives of their governments. The British government was represented by Colonial Secretary Malcolm Macdonald, Foreign Secretary Viscount Halifax, and Under-secretary for Foreign Affairs R.A. Butler, who were aided by a staff of high-ranking officials of the Foreign and Colonial Offices.

The Arab delegates at the St. James's Conference. [Central Zionist Archives]

Although one informal meeting was held between some representatives of the Arab countries and the Jewish delegates the Arabs refused to meet officially with the Jewish delegates on the grounds that the Arabs did not recognize the Jewish Agency. The British government therefore had to conduct negotiations with each side separately. The Arabs even used different entrances to the palace so as to avoid meeting the Jews. Since the Arab delegations were dominated by the defiant and uncompromising attitude of the mufti's followers, the negotiations led nowhere. On 15 March 1939, after having proposed suggestions as a basis for discussion, which had been rejected by the Jews, the British government presented the Jewish and Arab delegates with detailed proposals in the same vein as the previous suggestions, providing for the eventual establishment of an independent Palestinian state. In the interim, a total of 75,000 Jews were to be admitted during the subsequent five years, provided the absorptive capacity of the country warranted it, and the High Commissioner was to be authorized to regulate Jewish land purchases in Palestine. The proposals were open to discussion, but the basic points were not subject to change. The Jews rejected the proposals as a breach of the Balfour Declaration, and the Jewish delegation disbanded. The Arabs, too, rejected the government's terms as a basis for discussion.

In calling the conference, the British government had stated that if the discussions did not produce an agreement it would make its own decision and announce its policy. On 17 May 1939, the government issued a *White Paper on its policy in Palestine, which in the main embodied the proposals submitted to the St. James's Conference.

T. PRESCHEL

SALAMON, MIHALY. Publicist and religious Zionist leader (b. Transylvania, Hungary, 1897). Salamon attended the Jewish Teachers Seminary of Budapest and later studied at the University of Budapest. Attracted to Zionism at an early age, he became a member and leader of the Mizrachi. Between 1934 and 1944 he was the head of the Palestine Office in Budapest. Following the Nazi invasion of Hungary in March, 1944, he led Zionist rescue and relief work. He was among the leaders of the Zionist underground operation in the "Glass House" under the protection of the Swiss Legation, where 70,000 letters of protection and false papers were prepared. Several thousand Jews were saved in the Glass House itself, the adjacent headquarters of the Hungarian Football Federation, and Swiss protected houses. From 1946 to 1948, Salamon was president of the Hungarian Zionist Federation. In 1949 he settled in Israel, where for more than three years he edited and published *Népunk* (Our People), a Hungarian-language religious Zionist organ, and served on the staff of the Hungarian-language journal *Uj Kelet*.

R.L. BRAHAM—E. EPPLER

SALANT, SHEMUEL. Ashkenazi Chief Rabbi of Jerusalem and a leader of the Old Yishuv (b. Bialystok, 1816; d. Jerusalem, 1909). He studied at the rabbinical academies of Vilna, Salant, and Volozhin. He was ordained as a rabbi by the time of his barmitzvah. His second wife was the daughter of Rabbi Joseph Salant, who inspired the Musar movement (the Orthodox moralistic movement).

Salant was considered the head of the moderate wing of the ultra-Orthodox community in Jerusalem because he generally opposed the use of bans and excommunications. Upon settling in Eretz Israel in 1841, he created and headed the Ashkenazi *Beth Din* (rabbinical court). He encouraged members of his community to live in settlements outside the wall of the Old City of Jerusalem. Among his followers were Yosef Rivlin and Yoel Moshe Salomon, who founded Petah Tikva. Many of his supporters founded the Jerusalem neighborhood called Nahalat ha-Shiva. He was instrumental in founding Bikur Holim Hospital, as well as the Etz Hayim Talmud Torah and Yeshiva (religious school and academy). In 1878, he became Chief Rabbi of the Ashkenazi community, although this position never gained official recognition under Ottoman rule.

Although a moderate, he joined Rabbi Y.L. Diskin in banning I.D. Frumkin and his paper *Ha-Havatzelet*. He was also one of Eliezer Ben-Yehuda's main opponents; his opposition contributed to the arrest of Ben-Yehuda and the closing of his paper, *Ha-Tzevi*. Salant was a significant factor on the Jerusalem religious scene for more than 60 years.

G. SHUSTER-BOUSKILA

SALOMON, YOEL MOSHE. Printer, publisher, and early advocate of Jewish agricultural settlement in Eretz Israel (b. Jerusalem, 1838; d. there, 1912). Salomon engaged in talmudic studies under the guidance of noted rabbinical authorities. In 1859 he left Eretz Israel and studied printing and lithography in Königsberg, East Prussia. Returning to Jerusalem, he opened in 1862 the second Hebrew print shop in the city and in the spring of 1863 began printing *Ha-Levanon*, the first Hebrew-language newspaper in the country, which he helped edit. However, the paper was forced to cease publication after religious zealots had denounced it to the Turkish authorities.

Salomon was active in the communal life of Jerusalem and helped establish the new Jewish residential quarters Nahlat Shiva (1869) and Mea She'arim (1874). He also helped organize a settlement society called Hevrat Yishuv Eretz Yisrael for the purpose of purchasing and settling farmland in Eretz Israel.

In 1877–78 Salomon published *Yehuda vi-Yrushalayim*, a journal in which he developed his ideas on the development of a productive Jewish community and Jewish agricultural settlements in Eretz Israel. In the fall of 1878 he joined the group of pioneers who founded Petah Tikva. Eventually he returned to Jerusalem and continued his communal activities there until his death.

A history of the family, *Three Generations in the Yishuv* was published in Hebrew in 1942 by Salomon's son Mordekhai, a farmer in Petah Tikva.

SALZ, ABRAHAM. Zionist leader in Galicia (b. Tarnow, Galicia, Austria, 1864; d. there, 1941). Salz helped found the Zionist youth group Ha-Tehiya in his native city and, later the Ahavat Zion society, which worked for the establishment of Jewish settlements in Eretz Israel. While studying law at the University of Vienna, he was a member of Kadimah, the pre-Herzlian student Zionist organization. During that period, too, he assisted Nathan Birnbaum in the editing of his paper, *Selbst-Emanzipation*.

Returning to Tarnow in 1887, Salz opened a law practice and became active in Zionist affairs in western Galicia. He contributed articles to the Lvov Polish young Zionist weekly *Przyszlosc* (The Future). In October, 1893, Salz, who was then chairman of the Executive Committee of the Jewish National party of Galicia, together with Birnbaum issued invitations to a special conference to be held in Cracow on 1 November 1893, in order to establish a Zionist organization in Austria.

Salz played an active part in the preparations for the First Zionist Congress (1897), of which he was a vice-president. In 1899 he helped found the settlement Mahanayim in Galilee, but the project was short-lived. As opposed to Herzl, who emphasized political work, Salz devoted his efforts to practical, piecemeal settlement work.

From 1918 to 1939 he concentrated on Zionist activity in Tarnow.

SAMARIA. Northern section of the central highlands of Eretz Israel, bounded in the north by the Jezreel Valley and separated from the Judean Mountains to the south by steep river valleys. Samaria is 31 miles (50 km.) long and 23 miles (37 km.) wide.

The mountains of Samaria are composed of alternating soft and hard limestone, dissected by steep riverbeds and interspersed with small interior basins, especially in their northern half. These basins, around which most of the settlements are concentrated, are filled with fertile alluvial soil. Altogether, the landscape is much more open than the compact Judean Mountains and is crossed by many roads (ancient as well as modern).

The main transverse valley follows the Nahal Shechem, a tributary of the Alexander River. In its center lies the historic capital of the region, the town of Shechem (Arab., Nablus), situated in a narrow valley and flanked by the two highest mountains of the region. Mount Ebal (3,084 feet) (950 km.), to the north, and Mount Gerizim (2,887 feet) (887 km.), to the south. The latter, according to tradition, is the "mountain of blessing" (Joshua 8:33). The *Samaritans still go there to pray and perform the annual Passover sacrifice. Near the exit of the valley into the coastal plain lies the town of Tulkarm. Another important transverse valley crosses the mountains near their northern edge: the Dotan Valley, which connects the northern Sharon Plain on the coast with the Jezreel Valley. At its narrow exit into the Jezreel Valley is Jenin.

Samaria is the most densely settled part of the Central Mountains. A chain of Arab villages along the northwestern and western edge of the mountains was ceded to Israel by the 1949 armistice agreement with Jordan. Between 1948 and 1967, only its extreme northern and western fringes were within Israel territory, the rest was in Jordan. The entire area was occupied by Israeli forces during the Six-Day War of 1967,

Under Israeli rule, the biblical name "Samaria" gradually came to denote the area, which lacks exact geographical definition. In international usage it continued to be regarded as part of the "West Bank of Jordan." For administrative purposes, it remained divided, with minor changes, according to the Jordanian subdistricts (*Kadha*) Jenin, Tulkarm, Nablus, and Ramallah. The area of the region is approximately 1,000 square miles.

Few exact data exist for the changes in population, as only one census was conducted in almost fifty years: the census of 1967 made by the (Israeli) Central Bureau of Statistics, which showed a total population of 390,000. For the 1980s there does not exist even an estimate, but the natural increase is very high.

The economy, and especially the agriculture, showed tremendous progress, as agricultural exports made their way to Israel as well as to Jordan and the Arab states, and unemployment disappeared as tens of thousands found jobs in the surrounding areas of Israel. The area became a center of disturbances from December 1987.

Shortly after Israeli rule began, a movement of Jewish settlement started. Unlike previous Jewish settlements in Palestine/Israel, these were not based on agriculture; the majority of the settlers were employed within Israel proper or in services in the settlements. This movement grew especially in the 1980s and by 1988 there were about 70 settlements, including 15 or so of the Nahal type (funded and populated by soldiers preparing for agricultural settlement) and about 20 in their initial stages. About 27,000 people live in the other settlements, almost half of them children.

Y. KARMON

SAMARITANS. Descendants of the Samaritans mentioned in the Bible. They take their name from their geographical origin, the area of Samaria, but, based on historical and archeological sources and tradition, they are identified as Israelites descended from the tribes of Ephraim and Manasseh and led by priests directly descended from Ithamar son of Aaron. At the beginning of the Second Temple period, the people were split between the Jews, faithful to the Jerusalem center, and the Samaritans, whose ritual center was and still is, on Mount Gerizim near Shechem. While the Second Temple stood, there were periods of enmity and hostility between the Jews and the Samaritans, but common opposition to foreign rule in the country led to their cooperation at other periods. It has been estimated that at their peak, in the fourth—fifth centuries C.E., there were about one million two hundred thousand Samaritans, living in many cities and villages from southern Syria to northern Egypt. In the late fifth and sixth centuries, Byzantine authorities' decrees against the Samaritans provoked great revolts which led to the annihilation of over two-thirds of the Samaritan people. Persecutions, pogroms, and forced apostasy under Islamic, Crusader, Mameluke, and Ottoman rule further depleted the number of Samaritans, until at the beginning of the 20th century they numbered less than 150. At that time many prophesied the imminent end of the Samaritan community.

In the 1920s the situation of the Samaritans improved and Samaritan settlement was strengthened with the beginning of the British Mandate over Palestine and the renewed Jewish settlement. Some of the Samaritan survivors in Shechem settled in the coastal cities of Jaffa and Tel Aviv and found many friends among the Jews, who were prepared to assist the revival of the Samaritan community. At their head stood Yitzhak Ben-Zvi, who later became the second President of the State of Israel. With his aid and inspiration, the Zionist Executive in the 1920s and 1930s founded a school for the Samaritans in Shechem and sent teachers there to teach the modern Hebrew language alongside Samaritan teachers who taught the ancient script and language. Ben-Zvi mobilized economic aid for the Samaritans from institutions in Palestine and abroad and helped to find employment for many Samaritans. Their revival was further aided by the renewal of marriage, after an interval of two thousand years, between Samaritans and Jewish women.

With the creation of the State of Israel the community was split into two centers. Most of the community remained in Shechem, which was under Jordanian rule, but a minority lived within the borders of the State of Israel. Ben-Zvi supported a number of steps to have them recognized as citizens with equal rights and obligations in the State of Israel. The Law of Return was applied to them, so that any Samaritan who moved from Shechem to the State of Israel was recognized as a new immigrant. From 1928 to 1982, Yefet ben Abraham Tsedaka headed the Samaritan community outside Shechem and a Samaritan center was established in Holon near Tel Aviv. In Shechem the community continued to live in a separate neighborhood in the western part of town, where they had settled in 1927 after an earthquake destroyed almost all the ancient Samaritan neighborhood. Thanks to the intervention of Ben-Zvi, the American Joint Distribution Committee gave them monthly financial aid through the Red Cross. In the years 1951-1967, in the framework of the cease-fire agreement between Israel and Jordan, the Samaritans in the State of Israel were allowed to cross the border to celebrate Passover in a closed camp on Mount Gerizim together with their brethren from Shechem. The Six-Day War ended the separation. Since then the community has grown, its economic situation has improved, and there are signs of a renewed cultural blossoming with the publication of Samaritan works and a fortnightly paper, *A.B.- The Samaritan News* (established in 1969) which appears in ancient Hebrew, modern Hebrew, English, and Arabic.

In January 1989 the community had 531 members, 239 women and 292 men, 220 of whom were married, 284 single, and 27 divorced or widowed. Fifty-seven per cent of the community were aged 25 and under. About half the community lives in Shechem and the rest in Holon. In 1988 a third Samaritan settlement was founded in Kiryat Lusa, the Samaritan neighborhood on Mount Gerizim, composed mainly of young couples. Their cemeteries are on Mount Gerizim and in the Samaritan plot at Kiryat Shaul in Tel Aviv. Samaritan doctrine has remained unchanged for thousands of years. The tradition is guided by four principles of faith: 1.) Belief in the God of Israel; 2.) Belief in one prophet—Moses, son of Amram; 3.) Belief in one holy scripture—the Pentateuch alone; 4.) Belief in one holy place—Mount Gerizim. The Samaritans celebrate only festivals mentioned in the Pentateuch. The community is led by a high priest, traditionally descended from Aaron. The oldest priest in the family of priests is elected the High Priest.

Samaritans at prayer in their synagogue in Holon. [Israel Information Services]

To be identified as an Israel Samaritan, a member of the community must observe four principles: 1. Permanent settlement in Eretz Israel by virtue of which they fulfill the true meaning of Zionism; 2. Participation in the Passover sacrifice on Mount Gerizim; 3. Strict Sabbath observance in accordance with the word of Scripture; 4. Strict observance of the laws of purity and impurity, according to the Pentateuch.

In 1981 an Institute of Samaritan Studies was founded in Holon; it affords academic aid to scholars and students researching topics related to the Samaritans. Not only in Holon, but in Shechem too, there are clear signs of social integration in Israeli society, such as the community's extensive sports activity. The Samaritans in Holon have two basketball teams in the official Israeli league -Elitzur Hai Hashomrom Holon and Betar Hashomron Holon; in Shechem they have a basketball team which competes against Arab teams and those from the Israeli settlements in Samaria.

B. TSEDAKA

SAMPTER, JESSIE ETHEL. Poet, educator, and Zionist (b. New York, 1883; d. Givat Brenner, 1938). Born into a wealthy, assimilated Jewish family (her father was one of the founders of the Ethical Culture movement), she was raised in a cultured and intellectual atmosphere and was graduated from Columbia University. She was attracted in her youth to the Unitarian Church but subsequently came under the influence of Henrietta Szold and Mordecai M. Kaplan and recognized the importance of the revival of the Jewish people in its own land. Sampter became an ardent Zionist. She served as the director of the School of Zionism, a lecture course organized by Hadassah in 1914, and became increasingly active in Jewish communal and Zionist affairs. In 1919 she settled in Palestine, making her home first in Jerusalem and then in Rehovot. She spent the final years of her life in a vegetarian convalescent home which she had founded at the kibbutz Givat Brenner.

Miss Sampter's published volumes of prose and poetry (in English) include *A Guide to Zionism* (1920), *The Emek*

(1927), *Modern Palestine* (1933), and *Brand Plucked from the Fire* (poems, 1937). Toward the end of her life she began to write poetry in Hebrew also. A collection of her poems was translated into Hebrew and published in 1945.
G. HIRSCHLER

SAMUEL, MAURICE. Author and lecturer (b. Macin, Romania, 1895; d. New York, 1972). Brought to Manchester, England in 1900, Samuel attended the university there from 1911 to 1914, when he settled in the United States. He served in the United States Army from 1917 to 1919, spending some time in Poland as an interpreter with the Pogrom Investigation Commission headed by Henry Morgenthau and later, with the reparations commissions in Berlin and Vienna. Returning to the United States in 1921, he soon gained a reputation as an author, essayist, translator from Hebrew and Yiddish and as a lecturer in the Jewish field. He was one of Zionism's most brilliant exponents.

In his youthful days a Socialist and pacifist, Samuel became closely identified with Zionism and with Yiddish and Hebrew culture during his first years in the United States. He was deeply influenced by Shemarya Levin and became close to Louis Lipsky and Meyer Weisgal.

In 1919 he paid the first of many visits to Palestine and Israel. For several years during the 1920s he was employed by the Zionist Organization of America (ZOA) as a writer and lecturer, and from 1927 to 1929 he served on the Zionist Actions Committee. He enjoyed a close association with Chaim Weizmann, whom he described as "the central figure in my dominating life interest" and with whom he worked on the latter's memoirs, *Trial and Error*.

Samuel was in great demand as a lecturer. The main themes of his writings and lectures, in addition to Zionism and the challenges which the State of Israel presented to world Jewry, were the position of the Jew in the western world and the nature and effects of anti-Semitism.

Samuel's Zionist writings include *What Happened in Palestine* (1929); *On the Rim of the Wilderness: The Conflict in Palestine* (1931); *Harvest in the Desert* (a description and history of the Zionist movement, 1944, 1945); *Level Sunlight* (observations on the story and growth of the Jewish State, (1953); and *Light on Israel* (the story of Israel seen in the light of the *Six-Day War of 1967 and its aftermath, 1968). Among his other books are translations of the works of Hayim Nahman Bialik, Shemarya Levin, and Sholem Asch; *You Gentiles* (1924), *The Great Hatred* (causes and effects of anti-Semitism, 1940); *The World of Shalom Aleichem* (1943); *Prince of the Ghetto* (tales of Isaac Leib Peretz, 1948); *The Gentleman and the Jew* (1950); *Certain People of the Book* (1955); *The Professor and the Fossil: Some Observations on Arnold J. Toynbee's "A Study of History"* (1956); *Little Did I Know* (an autobiography, 1963); and *Blood Accusation: The Strange Story of the Beiliss Case* (1966). His novel of Renaissance Italy, *The Web of Lucifer* (1947) was widely praised, while his last novel, *The Second Crucifixion* (1960), dealt with the Ebionites. One of his most brilliant books, *In Praise of Yiddish*, appeared in 1971. After his death his translations of Bialik were reissued, and his radio dialogues with Mark van Doren on the Bible, edited by his wife Edith, were published: *In the Beginning, Love* (1973) and *Dialogues on the Psalms* (1975).
J. DIENSTAG—S. NARDI

Sir Herbert Samuel. [Zionist Archives]

SAMUEL, VISCOUNT (SIR HERBERT LOUIS SAMUEL). British statesman and first British *High Commissioner for Palestine (b. Liverpool, 1870; d. London, 1963).

Early Years. Born into a distinguished Anglo-Jewish banking family, Samuel was educated at University College School, London, and at Balliol College, Oxford. While a student at Oxford he became involved in Liberal politics and in 1902 was elected to the House of Commons as Liberal M.P. for Cleveland. In 1905 he was appointed Under-Secretary at the Home Office and in 1909 he became the first non-baptized Jew to attain Cabinet office in Britain (as Chancellor of the Duchy of Lancaster). Later he served as Postmaster General (1910–14 and 1915–16), President of the Local Government Board (1914–15), and Home Secretary (1916 and 1931–2). He was leader of the Liberal Party from 1931 to 1935.

Samuel was brought up in a traditional Jewish home. Although he ceased to practice Orthodox Judaism when a young man, he remained a member of the Jewish community and retained a lifelong interest in Jewish problems. He took an interest in Zionism at an early stage but was not initially drawn to support it because he saw no prospect of its realization.

The entry of Turkey into World War I on the side of the Central Powers prompted Samuel to take action. In a conversation with Sir Edward Grey, the Foreign Secretary, in November, 1914, Samuel outlined a scheme for setting up a Jewish state in Palestine that "might become the center for a new culture" and would also secure British interests in the Middle East. In January, 1915, he submitted a draft Cabinet memorandum on the future of Palestine to Prime Minister Asquith, and in March he circulated a revised version to the Cabinet, in which he referred to the possibility of establishing an autonomous Jewish State in Palestine but went on to advocate turning Palestine into a British protectorate, under which "facilities would be given to Jewish organizations to purchase land, to found colonies, to establish educational and religious institutions, and to cooperate in the economic development of the country." He went on to propose that "Jewish immigration, carefully regulated, would be given preference, so that in the course of time the Jewish inhabitants, grown into a majority and settled in the land, may be conceded such degree of self-government as the conditions of that day might justify."

Although Grey, David Lloyd George, and other members

of the Cabinet sympathized with the proposal, no immediate decision was taken. Samuel, however, worked quietly behind the scenes to promote the Zionist cause, collaborating closely with Weizmann, who was surprised to find in him an enthusiastic ally. With the fall of the Asquith Government in December, 1916, Samuel refused Lloyd George's invitation to join his Government. Although out of office, he nevertheless took an active part in the developments leading to the Balfour Declaration in 1917, personally participating in the first official contacts between British representatives and Zionist leaders. In 1918 and 1919, although not a member of the World Zionist Organization, he was active as chairman of a committee that drew up a statement of political proposals for submission to the government and of another on the economic planning of the proposed Jewish National Home. Late in 1919 he was asked by the Foreign Office to go to Palestine to report on "financial and administrative conditions there, and to advise concerning the line of policy to be followed in future in these respects, should the Mandate fall to Great Britain." On his return journey in April, 1920, he attended the San Remo Conference. While there Lloyd George offered him the post of High Commissioner for Palestine, which he accepted despite the opposition of Gen. Allenby, High Commissioner for Egypt, and Lord Curzon, British Foreign Secretary, to the appointment of a Jew to this office.

First High Commissioner for Palestine. Samuel served as first British High Commissioner for Palestine from 1920 until 1925. He was instrumental in the formulation of British policy in Palestine and laid the foundations of the mandatory system of government. His term of office can be divided roughly into two parts: (1) From his arrival on 30 June 1920 to 1922, when British policy in Palestine was crystallized in the White Paper of June, 1922, and the mandate was approved by the League of Nations; and (2) the period of stabilization from 1922 to 1925.

The immediate task that confronted Samuel was the establishment of a civil government to replace the British military administration in Palestine. During his first year of office he was preoccupied mainly with the administrative and judicial organization of the country. An Advisory Council consisting of 11 British officials, 4 Moslems, 3 Christians, and 3 Jews, was set up; it functioned for two years. In addition, an Executive Council of officials and a system of courts were established. In August, 1920, the first Immigration Ordinance was enacted, and a quota of 16,500 Jewish immigration certificates was fixed for the first year. An ordinance enacted in 1921 authorized the organization of local councils. The Chief Rabbinate was established and given authority in matters of personal status. Hajj Amin al-Husayni, an ultranationalistic Arab leader, was appointed mufti of Jerusalem and later made President of the Supreme Moslem Council. The Arab riots of May, 1921, led to a reformulation of policy in the White Paper of June, 1922. The Arabs were assured that the mandatory government was not intended to promote Jewish dominance in the country. The criterion of "economic absorptive capacity" of the country was introduced as the basis for decision-making on immigration quotas. Jewish immigration, which had been halted during the May riots, was resumed two months later and rose in 1924 and 1925 to unprecedented levels.

Following the 1921 riots Samuel made repeated attempts to conciliate Arab nationalist opposition to Zionism. He proposed the establishment of an elected Legislative Council (with limited powers), but the elections were boycotted successfully by the Arab nationalists and the scheme was abandoned. Efforts to establish an appointive Advisory Council and an Arab Agency (akin to the Jewish Agency) were abortive. Henceforth, and for the entire mandatory period until 1948, Palestine was ruled by British officials without the aid of any elected body representative of the country as a whole.

Although from the early days of his administration Samuel had urged the British Government to extend his authority over Transjordan, the proposal was rejected at first. In 1921, however, the inclusion of Transjordan in the area of the Palestine was approved by the British Government, and subsequently also by the League of Nations. This expansion was subject to the proviso that the Jewish National Home provisions of the mandate should not apply to Transjordan.

The relative political tranquillity between 1922 and 1925 enabled the British mandatory administration headed by Samuel to focus on the peaceful development of the country. Jewish land purchase and settlement proceeded apace despite some Zionist dissatisfaction with the government's efforts (not wholly successful) to protect Arab peasants from eviction. Communications were improved, and sanitation and education were carried forward. Between 1918 and 1925 the Jewish population grew from 55,000 to 108,000. Jerusalem, Haifa, and Tel Aviv made rapid strides; and modern industrial development began. The opening of the Hebrew University of Jerusalem on Mount Scopus in April 1925 was the culminating event of Samuel's administration.

Later Years. Samuel's interest in the National Home continued unabated after his departure from Palestine in July 1925. In 1936 he became chairman of the board of directors of Palestine Electric Corporation. In the controversy over partition in the wake of the Peel Commission Report of 1937, Samuel strongly opposed the division of the country into separate Arab and Jewish states. In 1939 he pressed the British government not to proceed with the anti-Zionist policy adopted in the White Paper of that year. Following Hitler's rise to power, he had assumed the chairmanship of the Council for German Jewry and during World War II he pleaded with the British government to adopt a more generous policy towards Jewish refugees from Nazism.

Samuel was regarded as the leading Anglo-Jewish statesman of his generation. For almost half a century his interest in the development of Zionism was unflagging. He was the first British statesman to raise the Zionist project to the level of serious political discourse and he played a major role in the discussions which led to the Balfour Declaration. Although many Zionists expressed dissatisfaction with his record as High Commissioner, regarding him as too ready to give in to Arab pressure, Weizmann later hailed his "great services to [the] consummation of this ideal."

I. KOLATT—B. WASSERSTEIN

Edwin Herbert Samuel (2nd Viscount Samuel), Herbert's son, civil servant, lecturer, and writer (b. London 1898; d. Jerusalem, 1978). Educated at Balliol College, Oxford, he went to Palestine in 1917 as a junior officer in the British army. From 1920 to 1948 he served as an official in the British mandatory administration in Palestine, finally as Director of Broadcasting (1945–8). From 1954 to 1969 he lectured in the political science department of the Hebrew University of Jerusalem. Upon his father's death, he succeeded to the viscountcy. He sat on the Labor party benches in the House of Lords. During his later years he divided his time between London and Jerusalem. He wrote a number of books and articles, including several collections of short stories and *A Handbook of the Jewish Communal Villages of Palestine* (1938, 1945). His memoirs, *A Lifetime in Jerusalem* (1970), give an evocative picture of mandatory Palestine and a human portrait of his father.

David Herbert Samuel, 3rd Viscount Samuel, Edwin's son, Israeli scientist (b. Jerusalem, 1922). Professor of Physical Chemistry at the Weizmann Institute in Rehovot, he succeeded his father to the viscountcy.

B. WASSERSTEIN

SAN REMO CONFERENCE. Meeting of the Supreme Council of the Paris Peace Conference, held 18–26 April 1920 in San Remo, Italy, to consider problems arising from the peace conference. Among those participating were the British Prime Minister, David Lloyd George; the Foreign Secretary, Lord Curzon; and the French statesmen Alexandre Millerand and Philippe Berthelot. Chaim Weizmann and other Zionist leaders also traveled to San Remo to seek a pro-Zionist outcome of the deliberations. Although France had already effectively conceded British primacy in Palestine, the French representatives waged a formidable rearguard action against the British claim. But the anti-Jewish riots in Jerusalem a fortnight earlier had persuaded the British government that further uncertainty about the future of Palestine was undesirable. The British therefore urged immediate recognition of their mandate over Palestine. On 25 April the Supreme Council assigned the mandate to Britain although the terms of the document were to await the decision of the League of Nations following ratification of the peace treaty with Turkey. The conference also reaffirmed the Balfour Declaration. With the British mandate thus assured, Lloyd George decided to move speedily to replace the military administration in Palestine with a civil government. Herbert Samuel, who was also present at San Remo, accepted the British government's invitation to take office as head of the new civil administration.

B. WASSERSTEIN

SAPIR, JOSEPH. Israeli politician (b. Jaffa, 1902; d. Petah Tikva, 1972). Sapir studied at the Hebrew Teachers Seminary but was forced to interrupt his studies in order to take over the management of his family's farm in Petah Tikva. He put great effort into the development of citriculture and went abroad to study citrus-growing methods. In 1928 he became a member of the Executive Board of the Hitahdut ha-Ikarim (Farmers' Federation) and subsequently was active in organizing the middle class in the settlements and cities for the defense of free enterprise. In 1939 he became manager of the Pardes syndicate of Palestine. From 1940 to 1951 he served as mayor of Petah Tikva, which expanded greatly under his leadership. Throughout his public career he remained a stanch advocate of the free enterprise system.

A prominent leader of Israel's General Zionist party, Sapir was a member of the Knesset from 1949. From 1952 to 1955 he was Minister of Transport and Communications. In 1967 he became a Minister without Portfolio, representing the Gahal alignment, and in December, 1969, he was appointed Minister of Commerce and Industry. With other Gahal leaders he resigned in 1970 over the American peace proposals.

Pinhas Sapir.
[Israel Information Services]

SAPIR (KOSLOWSKY), PINHAS. Israeli Labor leader (b. Suwalki, Russian Poland, 1909; d. Nevatim, Negev, 1975). He joined He-Halutz while a student at a Jewish religious secondary school in Warsaw and immigrated to Palestine in 1929, settling in Kefar Sava. He worked in the orange groves in the Plains of Sharon and as a part-time bookkeeper. In the early 1930s he was prominent in the struggle for the employment of Jewish labor in the citrus groves and was instrumental in organizing several strikes.

A member of Mapai, he was its representative on the local council of Kefar Sava, where he also founded a workers' housing project and loan fund. In 1937 he became Levi Eshkol's assistant in the newly founded Mekorot Water Company and remained there until 1947. In February 1948 he was placed in charge of the Quartermaster General's Branch of the Hagana. The following August he was sent to Geneva as head of the Defense Ministry's arms purchasing mission in Europe. From 1949 to 1953 he served as Director-General of the Defense Ministry, followed by two years as Director-General of the Finance Ministry, (1953–1955). In 1955 he joined the cabinet as Minister for Commerce and Industry and became the key figure in Israel's economic growth, concentrating on building new industrial plants to provide work for new immigrants, chiefly in the development towns. When Levi Eshkol became Prime Minister (1963), Sapir took over the Finance Ministry and held this office until 1968 and again, after a brief tenure as Secretary-General of Mapai, from 1969 to 1974. He was first elected to the Knesset in 1955, and, as one of its veteran leaders, became a major figure in Mapai. He opposed Israel's continued presence in the territories after the Six-Day War and was critical of policies pursued by Golda Meir. After the Yom Kippur War he refused to succeed Golda Meir as Prime Minister, initially backing Abba Eban for that post and then Yitzhak Rabin. He resigned from the cabinet in June, 1974, and was elected Chairman of the Executive of the Jewish Agency, a position he held until his death.

M. MEDZINI

SASA. Kibbutz in central Upper Galilee, near the Lebanese border. A Jewish village stood there in Roman times. In the 1948 War of Independence, Israeli columns advancing from west and east met at the abandoned Arab village of Sa'sa. In 1949, the kibbutz was established by pioneers from North America. They developed hill farming on rocky ground they reclaimed, basing it principally on fruit orchards, and establishing industrial enterprises. Sasa runs a regional high school of the Ha-Shomer ha-Tza'ir movement. Population (1987), 496. E. ORNI

SASSON, ELIYAHU HAI. Israeli public servant and diplomat (b. Damascus, 1902; d. Jerusalem, 1978). Educated at St. Joseph's College in Beirut, Sasson in 1920 became editor of *el-Hayat,* a Damascus Arabic-Jewish newspaper that sought to promote better relations between Arabs and Jews. Settling in Palestine in 1927, he briefly engaged in business and then was active as a journalist and lecturer on Middle Eastern problems. In 1933 he was appointed head of the Arab Department of the Jewish Agency, a position he held until 1948, serving also as member of the Zionist delegation to the United Nations in 1947 and 1948, in the capacity of specialist on Arab affairs.

From 1948 to 1950 Sasson was director of the Middle East Department of the Israel Ministry of Foreign Affairs; in 1949 he was a signatory of the armistice agreement with Egypt at Rhodes and went to Lausanne as a member of the Israel delegation to discuss peace between Israel and the Arab states. He served as Israel's Minister to Turkey (1950–52), as Minister (1953–57) and Ambassador (1957–60) to Italy, and briefly, in 1961, as Ambassador to Switzerland; in 1961 he was also a member of the Israel delegation to the United Nations. Sasson was appointed Minister of Posts that November, serving until 1967, when he was appointed Minister of Police, which post he held until 1969. He was elected to the Knesset in 1965 representing the Alignment.

His son, **Moshe Sasson** (b. Damascus, 1925), Israeli diplomat. He was head of the Israeli delegation in Turkey, 1960-66, Israeli ambassador to Rome, 1973–77, and to Egypt, 1981–88.

SAVYON. Garden city with local council status in the coastal plain, in the outer ring of the Tel Aviv conurbation south of Petah Tikva. Founded in 1954 on the initiative of South African immigrants, it became the prototype of an upper middle class center. Population (1987), 2,480. E. ORNI

SCANDINAVIAN JEWS IN ISRAEL. A small but steady wave of immigrants has gone to Israel from the Scandinavian countries since the 1950s. Some 3,000 such immigrants now live in the country, concentrated in the urban centers and on kibbutzim.

The majority of the immigrants are young, from strongly pro-Israel communities, and many are graduates of Zionist youth and student organizations such as Bnei Akiva, the Scandinavian Jewish Youth Organization (SJUF), and Habonim.

There are difficulties in defining immigration "from Scandinavia," because of the large-scale waves of refugees who reached Sweden and Denmark before, during, and after World War II. Over 4,500 refugees from Germany, Austria, and Czechoslovakia passed through Denmark in the years 1933–1940; some stayed there, but at least 1,100 are known to have been *halutzim.* Most of the latter found their way to Israel, where they organized a group called *Dengang i Danmark* (That Time in Denmark), arranging periodic gatherings for the former refugees.

Some 3,000 Jews fled to Sweden before the war broke

Hanukka party of Swedish Jews in Israel, 1987. [Swedish Immigrants' Association]

out, and more than 10,000 survivors of the Holocaust found refuge there after the war. Many of these refugees later moved to Israel. The statistics concerning immigrants to Israel from Scandinavia fail to distinguish clearly between immigrants who were born and raised in Scandinavia and those who only "passed through."

Among the first Scandinavian immigrants was the Danish Dr. Frankel, who settled in Modi'in in 1898. The majority of those who came in the first half of the 20th century were inspired by the Zionism advocated by the Russian Jews reaching Scandinavia and later by the *halutzim* being trained on Danish/Swedish farms. Motivated by a desire to build the land, many of these early Scandinavian immigrants joined kibbutzim. Under the influence of Swedish Chief Rabbi Dr. Marcus Ehrenpreis, Prof. Hugo Valentin of Sweden, Rabbi Aronsson of Norway, Rabbi Marcus Melchior of Copenhagen, and others the attitude of Scandinavian Jewry gradually changed into an appreciation of the importance of settling in Palestine, later Israel.

When the War of Independence broke out in 1948, Mahal groups were formed in Scandinavia. The small Jewish community of Finland sent more than 25 volunteers, most of whom had spent four to five years fighting against the Russians in the two Finno-Russian wars.

SJUF, together with Patwa and Shenat Sherut (a year's volunteer service in Israel), introduced several programs for Scandinavian Jewish youth in Israel in 1958 and reported that 32 participants had left for Israel and a similar number attended Summer Institutes that year. This marked the beginning of an annual tradition; from then on, Scandinavian Jewish youth have attended the Institute for Youth Leaders from Abroad and the Bnei Akiva Scholarship Institute.

Since the late 1970s, groups of schoolchildren from all the Jewish day schools in Scandinavia have made organized visits to Israel.

The gradual increase in the rate of immigration since the 1970s can be attributed largely to the Zionist awareness generated by closer contact with Israel.

According to Israel's 1983 population census there were 1,187 immigrants who had arrived from Sweden, 869 from Denmark, 524 from Finland, and 336 from Norway. In relative terms this means that some 40% of the Finnish Jewish community has settled in Israel. Most of the immigrants are in business or the social professions (doctors, dentists, social workers, technicians, etc.). A majority of the students attending universities can be found in the faculties of humanities and social sciences.

Among others who have made contributions to Israeli life, mention should be made of Professor Ozer Schild, born in Denmark, who immigrated in 1957 and has been Rector of Haifa University; Herbert Pundik, senior reporter at *Davar* until 1969, and since then chief editor of *Politiken*, an important daily in his native country, Denmark; Rabbi Moshe Edelman, director of the Bureau for Cultural Services to Communities of the World Zionist Organization. who represented the Scandinavian Zionist Federation in Israel in the 1970s; and ethnographer Avi Nilsson Ben-Zvi (1949–1985), originally from Sweden, who was instrumental in documenting the material culture of Swedish Jewry and in acquiring the bulk of the Ashkenazi ethnological collection of the Israel Museum, where a room is named in his memory. The Association of Scandinavians in Israel (*Hitahdut Olei Scandinavia*) was founded in 1975 to help new immigrants adjust to Israeli society. S. SCHUBAK

SCHACH, ELIEZER. Rabbinical authority (b. Lithuania, 1897). Schach was a brilliant student in yeshivot in Russia and Lithuania. Before the outbreak of World War II, he headed a yeshiva in Luninec, now part of Soviet Belorussia. When the Soviets invaded eastern Poland, he escaped to Vilna in independent Lithuania. In 1940, after Lithuania was annexed to the Soviet Union, Schach and his family escaped to Benei Berak in Palestine.

The head of the Ponevezh Yeshiva in Benei Berak, a stronghold of the anti-hasidic wing of ultra-Orthodox Judaism, he was for many years cochairman of the Council of Torah Sages (Mo'etzet Gedolei ha-Torah), the ruling body of Agudat Israel. He shared the post with Rabbi Simha Bunim-Alter, the head of the Ger hasidic movement and their cochairmanship represented an uneasy coalition between two conflicting ultra-Orthodox factions.

Schach has been involved in political affairs in Israel, but insists that Israel is still in exile. He pressed his supporters in the Knesset and in the government to exert themselves to protect the observance of the Sabbath, to exempt women from military service, and to pass legislation to prohibit abortions. He also declared that Ethiopian Jews must undergo a complete conversion, including circumcision and ritual immersion, like any non-Jew who decides to become part of the Jewish people.

In 1984, he was one of the mentors of Shas, a new party of Sephardi ultra-Orthodox Jews.

Schach has published nine volumes of *Avi Ezer*, a commentary on the teachings of Maimonides.

G. SHUSTER-BOUSKILA

SCHAFFER, SCHEPSEL (Shabbetai). Rabbi and early Zionist leader in the United States (b. Bauska, Latvia, 1862; d. Baltimore, 1933). After attending high school in Libau, Latvia, Schaffer went to Germany for advanced study, receiving a Ph.D degree from the University of Leipzig in 1888 and ordination from the Hildesheimer Rabbinical Seminary in Berlin in 1889. Unable to obtain a pulpit in Germany because of his Russian citizenship and unwilling to return to Russia, he went to the United States in 1893 to become rabbi of Congregation She'arith Israel in Baltimore, a position he held until his death.

Strictly Orthodox in his religious beliefs, Schaffer stated that he could not separate Zionism from Judaism, and in 1895 became president of the Baltimore Zion Association. In 1897 he attended the First Zionist Congress in Basle as the only official delegate from the United States representing an existing Zionist organization. He was a delegate also to the Fifth Congress (1901). At the First Annual Conference of American Zionists (July, 1898), he was elected a vice-president of the Federation of American Zionists and later served on its Executive Council.

SCHALIT, ISIDOR. Early Zionist and secretary to Herzl (b. Ukraine, Russia, 1871; d. Tel Aviv, 1954). Schalit grew up in Vienna, where he studied medicine and lived until he left for Palestine after the annexation of Austria by Germany in 1938. He joined Kadimah, the Zionist student group, in 1888 and eventually became its leader. On the publication of Herzl's *Jewish State*, he cast his lot with Herzl, serving as his secretary and assisting him in the publication of *Die Welt*. Schalit, who took a leading part in the preparations for the First Zionist Congress (1897), participated in almost all the Zionist Congresses that followed and opened the first Zionist Congress to be held in Jerusalem, in 1951.

During the Greco-Turkish War (1897), he sought to organize a Zionist students' battalion to aid Turkey in order to gain Turkish support for Zionism. When the Austrian authorities prohibited the recruitment of Jews for that purpose, he organized a Zionist medical mission to aid the Turks. The mission was well received but did not bring the expected political gains.

Schalit formed the Viennese Zionist societies Ahva and Jordania to win the support of Jewish workers and was secretary of the Zionist Executive from 1897 to 1905. He later became president of the Zionist Federation of Austria. He fought for minority-group rights for the Jews of Galicia and Bukovina and for that purpose organized a political committee consisting of all the national minority groups of the Austro-Hungarian Monarchy. In 1918 he helped form a Jewish self-defense corps in Vienna.

Hermann Schapira. [Zionist Archives]

SCHAPIRA, HERMANN (Zvi). Mathematician and Zionist leader (b. Taurage, Kovno District, Lithuania, 1840; d. Cologne, 1898). Schapira received a traditional education and while still young served as rabbi and head of a yeshiva. At the age of 22, he decided to leave his rabbinical position and turn to secular studies. He spent some time in Kovno, where he was befriended by the Hebrew novelist Abraham Mapu, and in Vilna; he then enrolled at the Berlin Technical Institute. Lack of funds forced him to interrupt his studies and return to Russia. He lived in Odessa, earning his livelihood as a Hebrew teacher and then as a bookkeeper. Later he engaged in business, and after saving enough money, he returned to Germany to complete his studies and received his doctorate at the age of 40. He then settled in Western Europe.

Schapira regarded the pogroms in southern Russia (1881) not as a passing phenomenon but as an outbreak of hatred against a people which had no country of its own. In 1882 he published in *Ha-Melitz* a letter in which he appealed for the unity of observant and nonobservant Jews and suggested the establishment of an institution of higher learning in Palestine to serve as an educational center for the entire people. He also believed in developing a strong Jewish settlement in the country but maintained that it should be built only by Jews who would go there of their own volition rather than because of persecution elsewhere.

In 1883 Schapira was appointed a lecturer at the University of Heidelberg. That summer he attended a scientific conference in Odessa and, while there, visited Leo Pinsker in the company of Moshe Leib Lilienblum. He persuaded Pinsker to help put into practice the ideas he had advocated in his *Autoemancipation*. At a subsequent conference, attended also by Prof. Max Emanuel Mandelstamm, it was decided to set up a central committee of all emigration societies for the purpose of creating a center for Jewish settlement, preferably in Eretz Israel. The central committee was to be chosen at a conference to be convened the ensuing year (*see* ODESSA COMMITTEE). This decision laid the foundation for the establishment of the Central Committee of *Hovevei Zion.

In 1844, in Heidelberg, Schapira founded a society, Zion, to spread knowledge of the Hebrew language and of Jewish history and literature, to help in the settlement of Jews in Palestine, and to advance the idea of establishing an institution of higher learning there. He could not attend the Kattowitz Conference of the Hovevei Zion but sent a telegram in which he called attention to the need for a *Jewish National Fund for the purchase of land in Palestine. In the years that followed, Schapira dedicated himself completely to his scientific work.

Although, like many Hovevei Zion, Schapira originally opposed political Zionism, he responded to Herzl's call and attended the First Zionist Congress (1897). He was a member of the committee that drafted the *Basle Program, and in a stirring speech called on all the delegates to submerge their differences and prejudices in order to work together for Zionism, the cause they all held dear. He presented to the Congress a written resolution containing the principles on which the Jewish National Fund was later formed. At the same Congress he introduced a resolution concerning the establishment of a seat of higher learning in Jerusalem and proposed that a special committee be chosen to draw up a program toward this end and to find competent individuals to prepare textbooks. I. KLAUSNER

SCHAPIRO, ABRAHAM. Pioneer in Eretz Israel (b. Novy Mikhailovka, Ukraine, Russia, 1870; d. Petah Tikva, 1965). The son of a pious merchant, Schapiro was taken to Eretz Israel by his family when he was ten years old. The family later moved to Yahud with the rebuilders of Petah Tikva. While still young, Schapiro participated in the defense of Petah Tikva against Arab marauders and was made head of the settlement's watchmen. By the time he was 30, he had become a legendary figure and enjoyed the respect even of the Bedouin tribesmen whom he had fought.

During World War I he was arrested by the Turks on suspicion of underground activity in Nili and taken to Damascus, where he was tried at a court-martial. He was acquitted and drafted into the Turkish Army. In 1921 he led the counterattack of the people of Petah Tikva against marauding Bedouin tribesmen and was arrested by the British Mandatory authorities. Accused of killing some of the attacking Arabs, he was acquitted of the charges. He subsequently insisted that Sheikh Abu Kishek, the leader of the Bedouin attack, not be released from prison until he arranged a formal *sulha* (peace) ceremony with the Jews. The chieftain eventually complied with Schapiro's request, and the two men became good friends.

Schapiro was for many years a familiar figure at public functions such as the Tel Aviv Purim Adloyada (carnival procession) which he led on horseback.

Boris Schatz, 1909.
[Central Zionist Archives]

SCHATZ, BORIS. Sculptor and founder of *Bezalel Arts and Crafts School (b. Varno, Lithuania, 1866; d. Denver, Co., USA, 1932.). In 1882 he went to Vilna, studied art and attended yeshiva classes and at the same time joined Smolenskin's Hovevei Zion group. In 1888, he studied in Warsaw and made the first of his famous copper reliefs. The following year he began studies in Paris, first under the sculptor, Mark Antokolski. Schatz concentrated on themes of Jewish suffering and also heroism, of which his bronze of Mattathias the Hasmonean (1894) is a famous example. In 1895, he left Paris for Sofia, where he became one of the founders of the Academy of Fine Arts and court sculptor, representing Bulgaria at the St. Louis World Fair, 1904. He first met Herzl in 1903 and in 1905 presented a proposal to the Seventh Zionist Congress to establish the Bezalel School in Jerusalem. The School was opened the following year with the aim of promoting Jewish art as well as Jewish craftsmanship. Schatz brought many noted artists to teach in Jerusalem and organized Bezalel exhibitions and friendship societies in the Diaspora. Despite the initial success of arts and crafts at the school, it closed for lack of funds and support in 1929. Schatz died in the US three years later

while trying to raise money to reopen the school. Schatz's children, Bezalel and Zohara, both became well-known Israeli artists.
M. RONNEN

SCHECHTER, SOLOMON. Scholar, theologian, and Zionist ideologist (b. Focsani, Romania, 1847; d. New York, 1915). After receiving his basic rabbinical education in his native land, Schechter moved to Vienna in 1871 to broaden his knowledge of Jewish literature and to acquire a scientific approach to Jewish learning. In 1879 he transferred to the Hochschule für die Wissenschaft des Judentums (Academy of Jewish Studies) in Berlin, enrolling also at the University of Berlin. In 1882 he moved to England as tutor to Claude G. Montefiore. There he joined the faculty of Cambridge University as reader in rabbinics. In 1896 he was responsible for the recovery of the Geniza (cache of antique manuscripts) stored in a synagogue in Cairo. This material proved to be an inexhaustible source for the enrichment of Jewish literature and history and brought Schechter international renown.

In 1902 he moved to New York, where he assumed the presidency of the Jewish Theological Seminary of America and laid the foundations for Conservative Judaism, whose philosophy he set forth in a number of books and speeches. In Schechter's concept of Conservative Judaism, Jewish nationalism and Zionism played an integral part. He emphasized that Judaism is a unique entity, an indivisible whole wherein religion and nationalism are inextricably linked. *See also* CONSERVATIVE JUDAISM AND ZIONISM.

Schechter did not join Herzl's political Zionist movement at once, because of the lack of religious loyalty in many leaders of the movement, who seemed to him to be out of touch with the faith and the soul of the Jewish people. He felt that Eretz Israel must become the center of Judaism and not merely a "National Home." In this respect he shared, to some degree, the opinions of Ahad Ha-Am.

However, in December, 1905, he joined the Federation of American Zionists, having become convinced that Zionism was "a genuine manifestation of the deeper Jewish consciousness; deeper, perhaps, than several of its leaders realized." In 1906 he wrote "Zionism: A Statement," which the Federation published in English and in a Yiddish translation. It served as a "declaration of Jewish independence from all kinds of slavery, whether material or spiritual." Basically, though he respected every aspect of Zionism, Schechter was a religious Zionist.

He violently opposed the East Africa scheme and the idea of Territorialism. "Zionism, with Palestine," he wrote, "is an ideal worth living and dying for; without it, Zionism means nothing....Any autonomous State of Jews outside Palestine means the destruction of Judaism and an utter break with all our traditions."

After joining the Federation of American Zionists, Schechter took an active part in its gatherings, He was present at the 11th Zionist Congress (1913). He wrote that although he did not divide Jews according to their political convictions, he felt closest to the views of the representatives of Mizrachi at the Congress for he still feared what he called "exaggerated secular nationalism" in Zionist leadership.
H. PARZEN

SCHECHTMAN, JOSEPH B. Author and Zionist leader (b. Odessa, 1891; d. New York, 1970). Educated in Germany (University of Berlin) and Russia (University of

Joseph B. Schechtman. [Zionist Archives]

Novorossiysk), Schechtman was active in Zionist work from his early youth. In 1917 he was elected to the All-Russia Jewish Congress (Petrograd) and to the Ukrainian National Assembly (Kiev), and a year later to the Ukrainian National Secretariat, the highest executive body of Jewish national autonomy in the Ukraine. He left Soviet Russia in 1920 and became coeditor of the Russian Zionist weekly *Rassviet* in Berlin (1922–24) and Paris (1925–34) and of the Yiddish weekly *Der Naier Weg* (Paris, 1929–31). A close associate of Vladimir Jabotinsky for three decades, he was a founder of the Zionist Revisionist movement and of the New Zionist Organization. Schechtman served on the Revisionist Executive in Paris, London, and Warsaw and was a member of the Actions Committee of the World Zionist Organization (1931–35, 1946–70). He was a deputy member (1948–51) and member (1963–65, 1966–68) of the Executive of the Jewish Agency for Israel, chairman of the United Zionists-Revisionists of America, and a member of the Executive of the World Jewish Congress.

Schechtman wrote several studies on Jewish, Zionist, and population problems. *The Pogroms in the Ukraine under the Ukrainian Governments* (in French, 1927) and *The Pogroms of the Volunteer Army* (in Russian, 1932) are standard works on the subject. *Transjordan within the Framework of the Palestine Mandate* (in German, 1937) was the first extensive study on Transjordan. His two-volume biography of Jabotinsky, *Rebel and Statesman* (1956) and *Fighter and Prophet* (1961), was translated into Hebrew and Spanish.

In 1941 Schechtman settled in the United States, where he served as a fellow in the Institute of Jewish Affairs (1941–43), as director of the Research Bureau on Population Movements, which he helped establish (1943–44), and as consultant for the U.S. Office of Strategic Services in Washington as a specialist on population movements (1944–45) on which he wrote a number of books. *The Refugee in the World: Displacement and Integration* appeared in 1963. Among his other publications are *The Arab Refugee Problem* (1952), *On Wings of Eagles: The Flight, Exodus and Homecoming of Oriental Jewry* (1961), *Star in Eclipse: Russian Jewry Revisited* (1961), *The Mufti and the Fuehrer* (1965), *The United States and the Jewish State Movement* (1966), *Jordan: A State That Never Was* (1969), and (with I. Benari) *History of the Revisionist Movement* (vol. 1, 1970).
I. HAMLIN

SCHEIB, ISRAEL. *See* ELDAD, ISRAEL.

SCHENK, FAYE ZEICHIK. Communal worker and leader in *Hadassah, the Women's Zionist Organization of America (b. Des Moines, Iowa, 1909; d. Jerusalem, 1981). She received B.A. and M.A. degrees from Drake University, where she also taught science for a time. From 1939 to 1949 she and her husband, Rabbi Max Schenk, lived in Sydney, Australia, where she was active in WIZO. Returning to the United States in 1949, Mrs. Schenk became active in Hadassah, serving as its national president (1968–1972), and in the American Zionist Federation. She was a delegate to five Zionist Congresses from 1956 on. In 1978 Schenk settled in Jerusalem, where she headed the Organization Department of the World Zionist Organization until her death. She also served on the Board of Governors of the Hebrew University, the Presidium of the Zionist General Council, and the Board of Directors of the United Israel Appeal and of the Jewish National Fund. M. LEVIN

SCHENKER, AVRAHAM. Zionist executive (b. Brooklyn, N.Y., 1918). From 1937 to 1941 he taught school in Chicago and New York. In 1938–39 he was secretary of Ha-Shomer ha-Tza'ir Zionist Youth, and from 1942 to 1944 served as executive secretary of the He-Halutz Organization of America. From 1944 to 1946 he was in the United States Army.

Schenker was administrative secretary of the National Committee for Labor Israel from 1947 to 1951, executive director of Progressive Israel Projects from 1951 to 1954, and a member of the World Executive of the World Union of Mapam from 1955, a deputy member of the Executive of the Jewish Agency and head of its Youth and He-Halutz Department in the U.S. from 1956 on, and national secretary (1961–64) and national vice-chairman (from 1964) of the American Zionist Council. In 1963 he became a founder, trustee, and secretary of the American Zionist Youth Foundation. In 1968 he moved to Israel when he was elected a member of the Jewish Agency Executive, in charge of the Department for Organization and Information. From 1978–86, he headed the World Zionist Organization's Department of Development and Community Services.

SCHIFF, JACOB HENRY. Banker, philanthropist, and Jewish communal worker in the United States (b. Frankfurt-on-the-Main, Germany, 1847; d. New York, 1920). Schiff went to the United States at the age of 18, and in 1875 he joined the banking house of Kuhn, Loeb and Company. By 1885 he was the head of the firm and soon became one of the most prominent financiers in the United States. His outstanding achievement in international finance was the floating of a $200,000,000 bond issue for the Japanese government during the Russo-Japanese War (1904–05). Schiff had welcomed this opportunity of aiding Japan because of the Tsarist government's anti-Jewish excesses. He was also active in raising funds for victims of the Kishinev pogrom and, convinced of the need for an organization to fight for the rights of Jews the world over, helped found the American Jewish Committee.

For many years Schiff was an outspoken opponent of Jewish nationalism. Nonetheless, in April, 1904, Herzl sought an interview with Schiff, who was then in Frankfurt. Because of Herzl's failing health, this meeting did not take place, but on 2 May 1904, Schiff met in London with Nissan Katzelnelsohn, the Russian-Jewish banker and physicist, to discuss Herzl's plans, which Schiff considered impractical and utopian. When Solomon Schechter joined the Zionist movement, Schiff engaged in a public discussion with him in the *New York Times* (August, 1907), asserting that Zionism was incompatible with citizenship in the United States. Nevertheless, he visited Palestine in 1908 and gave generous assistance to educational projects there, particularly the Haifa Technion, toward whose founding he donated $100,000. He also supported the agricultural experiment station planned at the time by Aaron Aaronsohn.

When World War I made it obvious that many Jews would not be able to maintain themselves in Eastern Europe, Schiff took a more positive view of Jewish settlement in Palestine and, in an address before the League of Jewish Youth (April, 1917), admitted the necessity for a religious and cultural center for the Jewish people there. He welcomed the issuance of the Balfour Declaration although he did not approve Zionist efforts to obtain an independent Jewish State. Neverthless, at one point he offered to join the Zionist Organization of America (ZOA) on condition that the organization publish his views opposing Jewish nationalism. The ZOA refused, and Schiff remained outside the Zionist movement.

SCHILLER (BLANKENSTEIN), SOLOMON. Zionist ideologist and educator (b. Michalowo, near Bialystok, Russian Poland, 1863; d. Jerusalem, 1925). He was active among the pre-Herzlian Zionist students of Galicia and contributed articles to the Polish Zionist periodical *Przyszlosc* (The Future). He attended the First Zionist Congress (1897) and after his return toured Galicia in behalf of the Zionist movement. In speeches and articles he stressed the political and spiritual aspects of the Jewish national renaissance. He devoted his efforts to the dissemination of Hebrew culture and the Hebrew language and organized Hebrew schools and courses in Galicia and Bukovina.

Settling in Eretz Israel in 1910, Schiller became a teacher and later principal at the Hebrew High School of Jerusalem. During World War I he was exiled by the Turks to Damascus, where he continued to be active in the field of Jewish education. After the war he resumed his pedagogical work in Jerusalem and participated in the creation of the new communal institutions of Palestinian Jewry. A prominent leader in the Ha-Po'el ha-Tza'ir Zionist labor party, he was its delegate to the Asefat ha-Nivharim and a member of the Va'ad Le'umi. An anthology of his writings was published in 1927. N.M. GELBER

SCHIPPER, IGNAZ (Isaac). Polish-Jewish historian, public figure, and Zionist leader (b. Tarnow, Galicia, Austria, 1884; d. Maidanek, 1943). Schipper studied jurisprudence, philosophy, and economics in Cracow and Vienna but devoted most of his time to Jewish history. He contributed to numerous publications, and some of his studies appeared in book form. His major works deal with the history of the Jews of Poland during the Middle Ages, and the history of Jewish theatrical art and drama.

A Zionist from his high school days, when he helped found a Zionist students' group, Schipper joined the Austrian Po'ale Zion in 1903 and became one of its prominent leaders. In 1910–11 he edited its organ, *Der Jüdische Arbeiter*. In 1922 he joined the General Zionists. From 1919 to

1927 he was a deputy in the Polish Sejm (Parliament). Schipper was prominently associated with Jewish cultural, communal, and Zionist institutions. He lectured at the Institute for Jewish Studies in Warsaw, was active on behalf of ORT, OSE, and HIAS, and from 1935 to 1939 was director of the Keren ha-Yesod of Poland.

During World War II he was interned in the Warsaw ghetto, where he engaged in cultural activities. From there he was deported to the death camp of Maidanek.
N.M. GELBER

SCHLESINGER, AKIBA JOSEPH. Rabbi and pioneer in Eretz Israel (b. Bratislava, Slovakia, Hungary, 1837; d. Jerusalem, 1922). An early advocate of settlement in Palestine, he settled in 1870 in Jerusalem, where he organized an association called Mahzirei ha-Atara le-Yoshna (Restorers of Ancient Glory), which stood for agricultural settlement, the use of Hebrew as a spoken language, and self defense. Despite the extreme Orthodoxy of his religious views, he incurred the opposition of the ultra-Orthodox in Jerusalem.

Schlesinger was among the first settlers of Petah Tikva, where he owned some land, regarding settlement there as a sacred act. He spent the last years of his life in Jerusalem.
G. KRESSEL

SCHLOSSBERG, JOSEPH. Labor pioneer in the United States and president of the Histadrut Campaign (b. Kaidanovo, Russia, 1875; d. N.Y.C., 1971). Arriving in the United States in 1888, Schlossberg was almost immediately drawn into efforts to abolish the sweat-shops. His trade union and Socialist activities span the entire history of the American Jewish labor movement. He was the editor of the Yiddish daily *Ovenblat* (1899–1902) and of the Yiddish weekly *Der Arbeter* (1904–11). Both periodicals were identified with the Socialist Labor party. In 1914 he played a decisive part in organizing the Amalgamated Clothing Workers of America, serving as its general secretary and editor of its publications from the beginning until his retirement in 1940.

Schlossberg was one of the very few Jewish trade union pioneers to bring Jewish national consciousness and a deep appreciation of Jewish values into general labor activities. He manifested Zionist sympathies at a time when Zionism was rejected by virtually all the leaders of the Jewish labor movement. In 1918 he was one of the conveners of the first American Jewish Labor Congress for Palestine, and he was a founder of the Histadrut Campaign, serving as its chairman and president from 1934 on.
C.B. SHERMAN

SCHMORAK, EMIL. Zionist leader (b. Shchirets, Lvov District, Galicia, Austria, 1886; d. Jerusalem, 1953). After graduating from the School of Law of the University of Vienna, he settled in Lvov. Active in Zionism from his youth on, he held leading positions in Jewish communal life and in the Zionist movement of Galicia. He was the chairman of the Zionist Organization of Eastern Galicia and the first chairman of the pioneering organization He-Halutz in eastern Galicia.

From 1910 on he was a delegate to all Zionist Congresses and from 1925 a member of the Greater Actions Committee. In 1938 he was appointed a member of the Jewish Agency Executive in charge of the Department of Trade and Industry and settled in Jerusalem. He held this position until 1947. From 1947 until 1951 he was the comptroller of the Jewish Agency and the World Zionist Organization and his critical report of the Organization's bureaucracy caused a storm at the 1951 Zionist Congress. During the last years of his life, Schmorak, who was a leading figure in the General Zionist movement, served on the advisory board of Bank Le'umi le-Israel.
N.M. GELBER

SCHNEIDER, JACOB. Brazilian communal leader (b. Barlidon, Bessarabia, Russia, 1887; d. Rio de Janeiro, Brazil, 1978). He emigrated to Brazil in 1903 and after a few years in Franca, in the state of Sao Paulo, moved to Rio de Janeiro where he went into business. In 1913, he founded the first Zionist group in Brazil, Tifereth Zion. Three years later he organized a welfare committee called Achiezer to assist new Jewish immigrants to the country. Active in many communal organizations, he was especially involved in Zionism. When the Zionist Federation in Brazil was established in 1922, he was elected its president and remained in the position until Zionism was declared illegal during World War II. With the resumption of Zionist activities in 1945, he was again elected president of the United Zionist Organization. In 1951, he was a delegate to the first Zionist Congress to be held in Jerusalem.

Scyla Schneider, Jacob's wife, was the founder of WIZO in Brazil and its first president.
S. MALAMUD

SCHNIRER, MORITZ TOBIAS. Physician and early Zionist leader in Austria (b. Bucharest, 1861; d. Vienna, 1941). Schnirer was one of the group of young men in Vienna who in 1882 founded Kadimah, the first nationalist Jewish students' union, and later he was instrumental also in founding the Zion society, forerunner of the Zionist Federation of Austria. In 1896 he was a member of the delegation that delivered a resolution of confidence from both these groups to Herzl. The young physician soon became one of Herzl's close friends and disciples, and he played an important role in the organization of the First Zionist Congress (1897). For some years thereafter he was a member and vice-president of the Zionist Inner Actions Committee. In 1898 he went with Herzl to Eretz Israel, where he was a member of the Zionist delegation that was received in Jerusalem, on November 2, by the German emperor Wilhelm II. Soon after Herzl's death in 1904, Schnirer withdrew from public participation in Zionist activity, but he retained a keen interest in Zionist affairs.

SCHOCKEN. Family of publishers.

Shelomo Salman Schocken, Zionist leader, publisher and philanthropist (b. Margonin, Germany, 1877; d. Pontresina, Switzerland, 1959). With his brother Simon, Schocken pioneered in developing modern scientific retailing, by 1933 owning a chain of 20 department stores in central and southern Germany. He joined the Zionist movement in 1910, made several long study trips to Palestine, and became a member of the Financial and Economic Council of the World Zionist Organization and a director of the Jewish National Fund. In the latter capacity he was instrumental in acquiring the Haifa Bay region for the Fund in 1928; it subsequently became one of the major industrial areas of Israel.

Schocken settled in Jerusalem in 1934 and soon became chairman of the Executive Council of the Hebrew University of Jerusalem. During World War II he went to the United States. An ardent collector of rare books, Schocken assembled the world's largest private library of Judaica now housed in the Schocken Institute for Jewish Research in Jerusalem, and its research institutes, the Research Institute for Medieval Poetry and the Institute for Jewish Mysticism. In 1961 the library and its research institutes were taken over by the Jewish Theological Seminary of America. His lifelong friendship with men like S.Y. Agnon and Martin Buber led to the establishment of the Schocken publishing houses (Berlin, 1931; Jerusalem-Tel Aviv, 1934; New York, 1945). The Schocken Verlag, Berlin, was closed by the Nazis in 1939.

Gershom Gustav Schocken, Shelomo Salman's son, Israeli publisher (b. Zwickau, Germany, 1912; d. Tel Aviv, 1990). He settled in Palestine in 1933 and in 1936 took over the editorship and eventually the ownership of the Hebrew daily **Ha-Aretz*, which his father had bought. In 1939 he became the manager of the Schocken Publishing Company, Ltd., which had transferred its operations from Germany to Palestine. Schocken was a member of the Third Knesset (1955–59), in which he represented the Progressive party.

Gershom Scholem. [Hebrew University]

SCHOLEM, GERSHOM GERHARD. Scholar who founded the modern study of Jewish mysticism (b. Berlin, 1897; d. Jerusalem, 1982). Scholem was born to an assimilated Jewish family, and grew up with no knowledge of Judaism or Hebrew. In his youth he began to be interested in Zionism, and started to study Hebrew and Jewish sources. He joined the circle of young Zionists led by Martin Buber, and was influenced by Franz Rosenzweig. While studying mathematics and Semitic languages in the universities of Berlin and Munich, Scholem became interested in the kabbalah and decided to write his Ph.D. thesis on the subject. Published in Leipzig in 1923, his thesis included a translation of the first work of the kabbalah, the Book of Bahir, into German, with detailed commentary and notes. In 1923 Scholem settled in Jerusalem, where his first job was at the Jewish National Library (later the Jewish National and University Library). Here he developed his system of cataloguing Judaica books. In 1924 the Institute of Jewish Studies was established (it was incorporated the next year in the Hebrew University of Jerusalem); Scholem delivered its inaugural lecture and was then nominated to teach Jewish mysticism at the Hebrew University, a position he held until his retirement in 1965. Scholem was active in the university's affairs, and to a large extent set the standards of scholarship and research which the university demanded from its teachers.

Scholem collected an unparalleled 24,000 volume library, exhaustive in its collection on kabbalah and related subjects; after his death it was bequeathed to the National and University Library, where it is housed in a special hall. He published over 40 books and 600 articles, most of them dealing with the history of Jewish mysticism. His main books are: *Major Trends in Jewish Mysticism* (1941); *Ursprung und Anfange der Kabbala* (1962; English, 1987); *Jewish Gnosticism, Merkabah Mysticism and Talmudic Tradition* (1960); *Sabbatai Sevi- The Mystical Messiah* (1957; English 1973); *On the Kabbalah and Its Symbolism* (1965); and *The Messianic Idea In Judaism* (1971).

Scholem's main contribution to Jewish studies was the detailed study of the history of Jewish mysticism from the Talmudic period up to modern Hasidism, describing the inter-relationship between mystical ideas and Jewish religious culture as a whole. He emphasized the place of the early kabbalists of the 13th century in the ideological struggles of that period, and the special role that mystical messianism played in Judaism after the expulsion of the Jews from Spain in 1492 and the establishment of the Jewish center in Safed in the 16th century. He identified Rabbi Moses de Leon of Castile (died 1305) as the author of the Zohar, and described the impact of the kabbalistic system of Rabbi Isaac Luria (died 1572) on Jewish thought in the 17th-18th centuries. His history of the Sabbatian movement identified the heretical elements in Judaism and their role in shaping modern trends in Jewish culture.

Scholem saw the Zionist movement as the active expression of the Jewish decision to take an active role in history. He refused to attribute messianic elements to Zionism and insisted on its political-secular function. The attempts of some critics to reveal a connection between Scholem's views of Sabbatianism and Zionism (Kurzweil, Biale) have no factual basis: according to Scholem Sabbatianism was a mystical movement, whereas Zionism is a modern national movement based on rational political thought.

His main contribution to Zionism and to contemporary Israeli culture was the definition of the role of Jewish studies as a strict scholarly-historical discipline within national Jewish culture. His insistence on a philological approach to texts, without apolegetics, is exemplified in his books and papers, and his views concerning the nature of Jewish history and culture as a dynamic expression of Judaism had a shaping influence on modern Jewish thought.

J. DAN

SCHONFELD, JOZSEF. Lawyer, publicist and Zionist leader in Hungary (b. Tiszapéterfalva, 1884; d. Budapest, 1935). He studied at the Budapest Rabbinical Seminary and the University of Budapest, obtaining a law degree. A cofounder and president of the Makkabea (Maccabi) Zionist student organization, he played a leading role in the Hungarian Zionist Federation, editing its official weekly organ *Zsidó Szemle* (Jewish Spectator), with brief interruptions, for over 20 years. He wrote a large number of articles propagating the Zionist idea, which were also published in two anthologies (in Hungarian), *Back into the Ghetto!* (1919), and *In Battle for Jewry* (1928), and translated Herzl's *The Jewish State* into Hungarian. R.L. BRAHAM

SCHORR, MOSES. Rabbi, orientalist, and communal and Zionist leader in Poland (b. Przemysl, Galicia, Austria, 1874; d. Uzbekistan, 1941). Schorr studied at the Universities of Vienna and Berlin and at the Vienna Rabbinical Seminary. He became known for his oriental studies and works on Polish-Jewish history. He served as a professor at the University of Lvov and in 1923 became a rabbi in Warsaw, where he also taught at the university and helped found and headed the Institute for Jewish Studies. Active in Jewish communal affairs and Zionist work, he did much to advance Jewish education. From 1936 to 1938 he was a member of the Polish Senate, where he vigorously fought for Jewish rights. His Zionist activities included the chairmanship of the Polish Friends of the Hebrew University of Jerusalem and of the Jewish National Fund in Poland. Shortly before the outbreak of World War II he headed a relief committee for Jewish victims of Nazi persecution. During the war he was arrested by Russian troops and died in a Soviet prison camp.

SCHREIBER, DAVID. Zionist leader and member of the Polish Parliament (b. Lvov, Galicia, Austria, 1874; d. 1942). Schreiber studied at the University of Vienna, the Vienna Rabbinical Seminary, and the University of Lvov. One of the first organizers of the student Zionist movement, he rose to be a prominent leader in Galician Zionism. He was a member of the Zionist Central Committee of Galicia and a founder of the Organization of Galician Hebrew Schools. In 1918 he was president of the Jewish National Council of Galicia, and a year later he helped found *Chwila*, the Polish-language Zionist daily in Lvov.

From 1922 to 1927 Schreiber was a member of the Polish Sejm (Parliament) and, from 1928 to 1931, of the Polish Senate. From 1928 on he was also a member of the Lvov Jewish Community Council. He was killed by the Nazis. N.M. GELBER

SCHWADRON (SHARON), ABRAHAM. *See* SHARON, ABRAHAM.

SCHWARTZ, JOSEPH J. Jewish communal leader in the United States (b. Novaya Odessa, Russia, 1899; d. New York City, 1975). Brought to the United States in 1907, Schwartz was ordained to the rabbinate by the Rabbi Isaac Elchanan Theological Seminary (now part of Yeshiva University) in 1923 and received a doctorate from Yale University in 1927. He taught at the American University in Cairo (1928) and at Long Island University (1930-33). Schwartz began his career in Jewish social work with the Federation of Jewish Charities of Brooklyn (1929) and became secretary of the *American Jewish Joint Distribution Committee (JDC) in 1939. He was executive vice-chairman of the *United Jewish Appeal from 1951 to 1955, when he became vice-president of the State of Israel Bonds Organization, a position held until 1970. In 1966 he was named to the Executive of the World Zionist Organization and the Jewish Agency, a position he held until 1968.

In his work as chairman of the European Executive and director general of the JDC (1940–51), Schwartz supervised relief and welfare programs in 30 countries involving more than one million people, conferring with leading statesmen throughout Europe, the Middle East, and North Africa. During World War II, with the approval of the U.S. War Refugee Board, he successfully negotiated through neutral emissaries the rescue of tens of thousands of Jews from Nazi Germany and Nazi-occupied Europe. During the years that followed Schwartz directed the transfer to Israel of more than 500,000 Jews from Europe, North Africa, and the Middle East, and helped more than 100,000 Jewish displaced persons to emigrate to the United States, Canada, and South America. He organized JDC Malben institutions in Israel to care for Holocaust survivors.

SCHWARZ, KOPPEL. Labor Zionist leader (b. Bolekhov, Galicia, Austria, 1889; d. Tel Aviv, 1954). Schwarz studied at the Universities of Lvov and Vienna and was active in the Zionist movement from his youth on, spreading the Zionist idea in speeches and articles. After World War I he was active in the pioneering youth organization He-Halutz, was one of the founders and leaders of the Hitahdut, and was elected to the Polish Sejm (Parliament) as a representative of this party. Schwarz was a member of the Presidium of the Keren ha-Yesod in Galicia and of the Executive of the Lvov Palestine Office. In 1940 he settled in Palestine, where he served on the Central Committee of Mapai and on the Council of the Histadrut. N.M. GELBER

SCHWARZ, YEHOSEPH. Rabbi and Palestinographer (b. Floss, Bavaria, Germany, 1804; d. Jerusalem, 1865). Schwarz went to Eretz Israel in 1933 and immediately became interested in exploration of the country, which was then conducted exclusively by non-Jews. His work was summarized in a series of books, the most important being *Tevuot ha-Aretz* (1845), the first modern Hebrew volume to be devoted to the biblical and talmudic topography of the country. He was active also in communal affairs in Jerusalem, particularly among immigrants from western Europe. In 1849 he went to the United States, where his book was translated into English by Isaac Leeser under the title *A Descriptive Geography of Palestine* (1850). G. KRESSEL

SCHWARZBART, ISAAC (IZAK) IGNACY. Zionist leader in Poland (b. Chrzanow, Galicia, Austria, 1888; d. New York, 1961). He was originally interested in socialism but soon was drawn to Zionism, becoming president of Ha-Shahar, the association of Zionist academic youth, in 1911. At the end of World War I he became general secretary of the newly formed Zionist Organization of Western Galicia and Silesia, serving as its president from 1923 to 1939. Between 1921 and 1924 he edited *Nowy Dziennik*, a Polish-language Zionist daily published in Cracow. He struggled for coordination within the Zionist movement in the Jewish community of Poland, and became a member of the coordinating committee for all Zionist groups in western Galicia and Silesia.

On the international Zionist scene, Schwarzbart founded the World Union of General Zionists, serving as its first president, from 1931 to 1935. From 1935 to 1946 he was president of the General Zionists, group B. From 1933 until his death he was a member of the Zionist Actions Committee.

In 1938 Schwarzbart was elected to Poland's last prewar Sejm (Parliament). After the outbreak of World War II he fled to Romania, where he stayed until 1940. That year he was appointed to the National Council of the Polish government in exile, serving first in France and then in England. He fought anti-Semitic attitudes in the Council and brought out information about the Nazi massacres of Jews. In 1946 he settled in the United States, where he was appointed director of the Organization Department of the World Jewish Congress, a position he held until 1960.

SCHWARZMANN, MOSES. Physician and Zionist leader (b. Balta, Russia, 1880; d. London, 1946). Schwarzmann served as a radiologist at the Imperial Medical Academy in St. Petersburg. After the Bolshevik Revolution he left Russia, lived for some years in Berlin, and then settled in London, where he was senior radiologist at the London Jewish Hospital.

While still a student in Odessa, he was an active Zionist and played a leading role in the Odessa Jewish Community, which he headed from 1918 to 1920. He was a cofounder of Keren ha-Yesod (1920) and a member of the Zionist Actions Committee from 1920 to 1924. An early follower of Vladimir Jabotinsky, he was elected to the Executive of the World Union of Zionists-Revisionists at its founding conference in 1925. From 1935 to 1938 he was a member of the Presidium of the *New Zionist Organization and later was active for a time in the Jewish State party.

Schwartzmann attended several Zionist Congresses and contributed to Zionist periodicals in Russian, Yiddish, German, and English. He was prominently associated with Jewish relief organizations and was one of the leaders of OSE (Society for the Protection of the Health of the Jews).

SCHWEID, ELIEZER. Israeli philosopher, educator, and literary critic (b. Jerusalem, 1929). After the War of Independence he became a founding member of Kibbutz Tzora. In 1953 he enrolled at the Hebrew University where he studied, and since 1965, has taught medieval and modern Jewish thought. Among his many scholarly books in Hebrew are *Studies in Maimonides* (1965), a critical edition of Joseph Albo's *Sefer Ha-Ikarim* (1967), *A History of Jewish Thought in Modern Times: The Nineteenth Century* (1977), and *Homeland or Land of Destiny* (English, 1985). He has also devoted many books to contemporary issues of Jewish existence and Zionist thought, among them: *Judaism at the Crossroads* (English, 1973), *Judaism and the Solitary Jew* (Hebrew, 1974), *Orthodoxy and Religious Humanism* (Hebrew, 1977), *Jewish Nationalism* (Hebrew, 1982), *Democracy and Halakhah* (Hebrew, 1978), *Judaism and Secular Culture* (Hebrew, 1981), *The Cycle of Appointed Times. The Meaning of Jewish Holidays* (Hebrew, 1984).

As a Zionist thinker his main preoccupation has been with what he regards as the ambiguous cultural legacy of Labor Zionism. On the one hand, he proudly acknowledges the single contribution of Labor Zionism to the revival of Hebrew as a spoken language, to the renewal of a vibrant Hebrew folklore of song and dance, and to the promotion of a modern, diversified Hebrew literature; Labor Zionism is also to be credited for fostering Jewry's spiritual attachment to the Land of Israel. On the other hand, the secular Hebrew culture sponsored by Labor Zionism was often so radically secular and detached from the spiritual heritage of traditional Judaism that it failed, in Schweid's judgment, to provide the matrix for a meaningful Jewish culture and identity. Jewish culture, he contends, must be grounded in Judaism, which in the first instance consists of the entire corpus of Jewish writings, "Scripture, Mishna, Talmud, Midrash, medieval and rabbinic exegesis, the responsa literature, kabbala," and even modern literature in all its genres, at least to the extent that this literature draws upon the classical sources. Together with the traditional liturgical calendar, this literature provides the genuine basis for the unity of Jewish people sought by Zionism as well as the wellsprings of a creative, existentially engaging Jewish culture.

Schweid acknowledges that the spiritual heritage of Judaism posits certain theological principles that require the affirmation of religious faith. The Zionist commitment to the revival of Judaism, however, obliges one to accept the challenge to consider various strategies to reappropriate faith and the sacred texts, liturgy, and even ritual practices of the tradition as the ground of Jewish culture and creativity. But in consonance with the modern appreciation of personal integrity, endorsed by Zionism, the act of reclaiming the heritage and religious faith of traditional Judaism must allow for individual inclinations and judgment. Thus Schweid envisions the emergence of a pluralistic, democratic Judaism.

P. MENDES-FLOHR

SCOTT, CHARLES PRESTWICH. British editor and Christian Zionist (b. Bath, England, 1846; d. Manchester, 1932). In 1871 Scott joined the *Manchester Guardian*, becoming editor in 1872 and proprietor in 1905. A Liberal member of Parliament from 1895 to 1906, he was a close friend and confidant of David Lloyd George.

Meeting Chaim Weizmann by chance at a party in September, 1914, Scott was impressed by the Zionist leader and soon became a warm supporter of Zionism. After Turkey entered World War I, Scott began to link the future of Palestine with British interests, asserting that a friendly Palestine was essential to Great Britain for the defense of the Suez Canal and that, in any partition of the Ottoman Empire after an Allied victory, Palestine should come under British rather than French control. When Lloyd George became Prime Minister in December, 1916, Scott's close association with him placed him in an advantageous position for advocating the Zionist cause in high government circles. A constant and devoted friend and adviser of Weizmann in the Zionist negotiations that led to the issuance of the Balfour Declaration, Scott was a member of the British Palestine Committee, which was founded late in 1916 to argue the case for British sponsorship of Zionist aspirations.

SCOUTING IN ISRAEL. *See* HATZOFIM.

SEA OF GALILEE. *See* KINERET, LAKE.

SECOND ALIYA. *See* ALIYA.

Members of the kibbutz Sedeh Boker. In the center is former Prime Minister David Ben-Gurion. [Israel Information Services]

SEDEH BOKER. Kibbutz in the central Negev Hills, 11 mi. (19 km.) south of Yeroham. Founded as a pioneer outpost in 1952, it long remained Israel's most isolated rural development and was not affiliated to any countrywide settlement association. It experimented with methods of desert farming and water preservation. Later, it added small handicraft and industrial enterprises. From 1953, David Ben-Gurion made his home there. After his death his home was preserved as a museum in his memory. A study center was founded at Ben-Gurion's initiative in 1965, 3 mi. (5 km.) south of the kibbutz, later named Midreshet Ben-Gurion. In addition to a branch of the Beersheba Ben-Gurion University dedicated to desert research, it comprises an agricultural boarding high school, a school of field studies, and courses for immigrants and students from abroad, with a large library and exhibits of Negev nature and history. David and Paula Ben-Gurion's tombs are nearby on the north rim of the wild Zin Canyon. In 1987 the kibbutz numbered 307 inhabitants, and Midreshet Ben-Gurion 676.

E. ORNI

SEDEH YA'AKOV. Moshav in the northwestern Jezreel Valley. Founded in 1927 as the pioneering venture of religious Zionists, it struggled hard in its initial years to overcome difficulties. It included the Youth Aliya village of Neveh Amiel. Its economy is based on intensive mixed farming. Its name commemorates Rabbi Yaakov Reines, founder of Mizrachi. Population (1987), 677.

E. ORNI

SEDEROT. Development town in the southern coastal plain, 11 mi. (18 km.) south of Ashkelon opposite the northern end of the Gaza Strip. Originally a camp for new immigrants, then a transit camp, it was declared a town in 1956. There was a large turnover of inhabitants, but Jews from North Africa continued to constitute the bulk of the population. Difficulties remained in providing full employment, even after packing factories for agricultural crops were established along with textile and metal plants. Sederot failed to attract more sophisticated branches. Population (1987), 9,380.

E. ORNI

SEDOM (SODOM.) Site at the southwestern corner of the Dead Sea, where the Dead Sea Works are located. The biblical story of the destruction of Sodom and Gomorrah appears to have its origin in the region's seismic lability,

Sederot residents of Moroccan origin in town center, 1972. [Israel Govt. Press Office]

which produced earthquakes and abrupt topographical changes. Mount Sedom, 6.8 mi. (11 km.) long and 1–1.8 mi. (1.5–3 km.) wide, is regarded as the remnant of an older Dead Sea. It rises to 760 ft. (250 m.) above the Dead Sea level. Construction of the Dead Sea Works began at Sedom in 1937. The United Nations included the area within the borders of the future Jewish State, and it was held in the 1948 War of Independence by factory laborers and Hagana forces. The *Dead Sea Works were reactivated after the Beersheba-Sedom road was built in 1952. E. ORNI

SEDOT YAM. Kibbutz on the coast of the northern Sharon, near Caesarea. Founded by graduates of Ha-No'ar ha-Oved youth movement and of Youth Aliya in 1940, the kibbutz initially saw its principal branch of economy as sea fishing, but soon abandoned this and turned to intensive mixed farming and industrial enterprises. It also operated the seaside resort "Kayit ve-Shayit." A cultural center with an archeological museum is named for Hannah Szenes, who was a member of the kibbutz. Population (1987), 705.
E. ORNI

SEGAL, LOUIS. American Labor Zionist leader (b. Lowicz, Russian Poland, 1894; d. New York, 1964). Arriving in the United States in 1911, he worked as a hatmaker in St. Paul and soon became prominent in trade union activities. Before long he was elected organizer of the United Hatters Cap and Millinery Workers Union in St. Paul. He held this post until he was called to New York in 1924 to serve as assistant secretary-general of the Jewish National Workers Alliance, which later became the *Farband (Labor Zionist fraternal order). In 1926 he was elected general secretary of the organization holding that position until his death.

Under his leadership, Farband developed into a significant factor in American Jewish life generally and in the Zionist movement in particular. Especially noteworthy was Segal's vigorous role in Jewish cultural and communal affairs. He was a member of the Central Committee of the Po'ale Zion party, of the Actions Committee of the World

British soldiers guarding kibbutz members at Sedot Yam during a search. [Central Zionist Archives]

Zionist Organization, of the Executive of Ihud Olami (World Union of Zionists-Socialists), and, from 1954 until his death, of the Executive of the Jewish Agency.
C.B. SHERMAN

SEJERA. *See* ILANIYA.

SELF-GOVERNMENT IN THE YISHUV. *See* YISHUV, SELF-GOVERNMENT IN THE.

SELF-LABOR. Principle of the *Labor Zionist movement according to which every individual must earn a living by his own work, to the exclusion of income or profit derived from the employment of hired labor. A distinction must be made between the concept of self-labor and that of Jewish labor, although there is a close relationship between the two. The attitude toward labor as a central value in Zionist ideology in general and in Labor Zionism in particular stems from the Haskala (Jewish Enlightenment) movement that began late in the 18th century. One of the aims of the Haskala was the introduction of a change in the Jewish attitude toward labor. The impetus for such a change came from the non-Jewish world. All those who sought to reform Jewish life beginning with the late 18th century (Christian

Wilhelm von Dohm in Prussia, Abbé Henri Grégoire in France, and others) argued that the Jews must be encouraged to engage in physical labor, particularly in agriculture. Before long the idea had been taken up by the Jews who sought to leave the ghetto and become integrated in the world around them.

From Haskala the concept of self-labor passed into modern Hebrew literature finding forceful expression in the writings of Mikha Yosef Berdyczewsky (Mikha Yosef Bin-Gorion) and Yoseph Hayim Brenner and in the poetry of Hayim Nahman Bialik and Saul Tschernichowsky. Self-labor occupied a central place also in the writings of Herzl.

The concept guided the founders of the first moshavot in Eretz Israel. The bylaws of the Bilu pioneering movement (1884) emphasized that it was Bilu's purpose to create a situation in which every Jew in Eretz Israel would "make a living for himself and the members of his household without utilizing the help of others."

In time, however, many of the moshavot deviated from the principle of self-labor; the farmers not only ceased doing their own work but drew upon Arab fellahin and Bedouin for cheap labor. This practice came under strong criticism not only from the leaders of the Hovevei Zion but also from the settlers themselves. In 1891 a group of young men, headed by Meir Dizengoff, founded the Ha-Aretz veha-Avoda Society, which called for "the rearing of a new generation which will work its soil literally with its own hands."

The young pioneers who came with the Second Aliya (1904–14) linked self-labor to the problem of Jewish labor (*see* KIBBUSH AVODA). Their basic assumption was that each nation acquired the right to its land by working its soil and that the future of the Jewish people in Eretz Israel depended on whether a Jewish working class would develop there. These assumptions were given either moral-national or Socialist Marxist underpinnings) Ha-Po'el ha-Tza'ir and Po'ale Zion respectively).

The pioneers drew their inspiration from the personality and teachings of Aharon David *Gordon, who conceived of physical toil as a central value in the life of the individual, representing his link with nature. When the Jewish people were exiled, Gordon taught, they had suffered a great loss by having been denied the opportunity to engage in physical labor. Now the Jewish people had to return to labor. "We must place labor into the center of all our endeavors," he declared, "and base our entire structure upon it."

During the first years after their arrival, the pioneers conceived their destiny to be Kibbush Avoda ("Conquest of Labor") in the Jewish moshavot. Before long, however, they discovered that the prospect of remaining an agricultural laborer all one's life, without property of one's own, completely dependent on one's employers and in constant competition with cheap Arab labor, could not draw young people to Eretz Israel in large numbers. On the other hand, it was feared that if the pioneers were given land to cultivate they would eventually become employers themselves and succumb to the temptation of hiring non-Jewish workers. This dilemma gave rise to the concept of "free labor," or the creation of new forms of labor and settlement based on self-labor.

The forms of collectivist (kevutza and later the kibbutz) and cooperative (moshav ovedim) settlements that were included in the concept "labor settlements" had been advocated toward the end of the Second Aliya by the founders of Degania (Joseph Bussel and his friends). They were supported also by Eliezer Lipa Joffe, Isaac Wilkansky (Yitzhak Avigdor Elazari-Volcani), the leaders of the Agricultural Workers' Federation (Berl Katznelson, Yitzhak Tabenkin), and such writers as Yoseph Hayim Brenner.

At the time of its founding in 1920, the Histadrut stated its goals to be the transformation of the Jewish people, as it returned to its Homeland, into "a working people without classes, deprivation, discrimination, exploitation or subjection [of one class by another]" (David Ben-Gurion) and "to bring the entire [Jewish] people to labor" (Tabenkin). The principle of self-labor was placed at the basis of the ideologies of the World Federation of He-Halutz and of Halutz (pioneer) youth movements in Palestine and the Diaspora (Ha-Shomer ha-Tza'ir, Gordonia, Dror, Habonim, Ha-No'ar ha-Tziyoni, Maccabi ha-Tza'ir). The rebuilding of the Homeland by Jewish self-labor was recognized as the central principle also outside the strictly Socialist Zionist movement; it was supported by the Radical Zionists and by the Torah va-Avoda movement of Ha-Po'el ha-Mizrachi.

Y. SLUTSKY

SELIGSBERG, ALICE LILLIE. Social worker and *Hadassah leader in the United States (b. New York, 1873; d. there, 1940). Reared in the intellectual atmosphere of the Ethical Culture Society, Seligsberg was graduated from Barnard College and later did graduate work at Columbia University and the University of Berlin. Soon thereafter she embarked on a career of social work, taking special interest in orphans and underprivileged children.

Realizing that the philosophy of Ethical Culture did not meet her religious needs, Miss Seligsberg began to study Jewish history, Biblical literature, and Hebrew, eventually joining Mordecai M. Kaplan's Society for the Advancement of Judaism at its inception. Her studies in Judaism and her association with Henrietta Szold, who was to become her lifelong friend, led her to Zionism, and she was a member of the original group that met to organize Hadassah in 1912.

Seligsberg was appointed by Hadassah to its activities for the *American Zionist Medical Unit, which went to Palestine in 1918. The next year the American Jewish Joint Distribution Committee appointed her executive director of its Palestine Orphans Committee. In this position she introduced modern methods of work with orphans and dependent children, with emphasis on the importance of play and recreation. Returning to the United States in 1920, she continued her activities in Hadassah, serving as national president in 1921–22 and as an honorary associate of the National Board of Directors for many years. From 1924 until her death she was intermittently active as senior adviser to Junior Hadassah, the Hadassah affiliate she helped organize on a national scale in 1920.

From 1922 to 1936 Seligsberg was executive director of the Jewish Children's Clearing Bureau, in New York, a pioneer agency for the study of the situation and placement of dependent children. The Alice L. Seligsberg Vocational High School for Girls in Jerusalem, and later the Seligsberg-Brandeis Community College resulted from Hadassah's resolution, at the time of Seligsberg's death, to allocate $25,000 for the establishment in Palestine of the Alice L. Seligsberg Fellowship Center to serve Jewish and Arab children and adolescents.

SEMITIC ACTION. *See* CANAANITES AND SEMITIC ACTION.

Opening of a new building of the Alice L. Seligsberg Vocational High School for Girls, Jerusalem, in 1958. [Hadassah]

SENATOR, DAVID WERNER. Social scientist, welfare worker, and administrator (b. Berlin, 1896; d. Atlanta, Ga., 1953). Senator became interested in Palestine problems while still a student in Germany and wrote his doctoral thesis on Jewish settlement in Palestine. He worked for Jewish welfare organizations in Germany, became acquainted with the problems of the Eastern European Jewish immigrants, and later joined the European branch of the American Jewish Joint Distribution Committee, rising to the position of general secretary of its European Headquarters. He settled in Palestine in 1924 but was sent on a mission abroad, returning in 1930. Senator was a leading member of the Berit Shalom and Ihud movements and a supporter of Judah L. Magnes's political work advocating a binational Jewish-Arab state in Palestine.

At the plenary session of the Council of the *Jewish Agency held in Basle, Switzerland, in 1931, Senator was elected a non-Zionist member of the Executive in Jerusalem serving until 1935. He played an active role in the work of the Agency for several years. He became administrator of the Hebrew University of Jerusalem, in effect running the University during crucial periods in World War II and the Israel War of Independence. In 1949 he was appointed executive vice-president of the university. A. ALPERIN

SEPARATE UNIONS. Whereas *Zionist territorial organizations (ZTOs) have existed under various names and in various forms from the very beginning of the *World Zionist Organization (WZO) to the present day, separate unions (SUs) emerged at a later stage and were dissolved with the promulgation of the new constitution of the WZO in 1960. The ZTOs originally were meant to embrace all Zionists, regardless of their views, in given countries, but the SUs were intended to be worldwide organizations of Zionists who within the broad context of their Zionist convictions, subscribed to a specific ideology and were subject not only to Zionist discipline in general but to the discipline of a particular SU as well.

It may be said that, apart from the "horizontal" division into ZTOs, there was a "vertical" division into SUs (*Sonderverbände).* The latter were defined by the 1921 constitution of the WZO (which with numerous amendments remained in force until 1960) as associations of Shekel payers who represented a specific point of view within the WZO (article 11). An SU had to fulfill two initial requirements: it had to include at least 20,000 Shekel payers, and it had to be approved by the Zionist General Council. If such approval was denied, the applicants had the right to appeal to the Zionist Congress. According to the 1921 constitution, members of an SU could simultaneously belong to a ZTO (federation); this was the case in countries such as the Netherlands that had an all-embracing Zionist framework. The SUs maintained territorial branches in the various countries.

The English version of the constitution of 1921 defined

an SU as a "party association." This definition was not entirely accurate, for one SU, the Order of Ancient Maccabeans in England, was not a party and not every Zionist party was recognized as an SU. The first SU, the Mizrachi, was founded in 1902; Po'ale Zion followed in 1907. However, it was only at the 10th Zionist Congress (1911) that the institution of the SU was formally incorporated in the constitution of the WZO, as an exception to the rule of the "horizontal," geographical pattern of organization.

In the first years of the Zionist movement, SUs were exceptional. They grew apace, however, and eventually comprised a majority, if not of the permanently organized Zionists, then at least of Shekel payers and the electorate as well as of the Congress delegates. At the 12th Congress (1921) the two then-existing SUs, Mizrachi and Po'ale Zion, together accounted for 27 percent of the representation (19 and 8 percent, respectively). Six years later, at the 15th Congress (1927), Mizrachi's representation had declined to 16 percent, but that of Po'ale Zion-Hitahdut had risen to 22 percent, thus increasing the total SU representation to 38 percent. At the 19th Congress (1935) the SUs had 60 percent of the delegates. At the 21st Congress (1939), Mizrachi had 12.3 percent of the representation, Po'ale Zion-Hitahdut 41 percent, and the Jewish State party 1.5 percent.

By 1939 there were five SUs within the framework of the WZO. Mizrachi had 16 territorial branches; Po'ale Zion-Hitahdut, 18; and Ha-Shomer ha-Tza'ir and the Jewish State party, 12 each. The fifth SU, the Order of Ancient Maccabeans, had become affiliated with the Zionist Federation of Great Britain and Ireland. Each of the other four SUs represented a specific ideology, respectively Orthodox Zionism, Labor Zionism, a blending of Zionism with Marxist Socialism, and radical anti-Socialist nationalism. The Jewish State party, the smallest and youngest of the SUs, included those Revisionists who had seceded from the Revisionist party in 1933 but continued to subscribe to the basic tenets of Revisionism. As for Labor Zionism, both components of Po'ale Zion-Hitahdut had been recognized as SUs before their merger into one group.

In time the distinction between the SUs and other Zionist parties became blurred. In the early years an SU enjoyed special prerogatives such as assured representation on the Zionist Actions Committee and authority to conduct Shekel drives among its members without outside interference. After World War II, however, these prerogatives were reduced to mere formalities such as the privilege to submit a worldwide election list regardless of the number of lists the SU had presented in the various countries. For all practical purposes, the differences between SUs and other Zionist parties ceased to exist.

At the same time, the status and nature of the General Zionist party was changing and approaching that of the SUs. Originally, "General Zionists" were the members of Zionist federations (ZTOs) who, in contradistinction to the members of the SUs, did not subscribe to a specific ideology. Later the tendency arose to adopt a liberal ideology of their own and become a party, and in some places this trend prevailed within General Zionist groups. Furthermore, in 1931 the General Zionists split into A and B wings. This breach was healed, but at the 24th Congress (1956) the General Zionists were divided into the "World Union" and the "World Confederation" of General Zionists, which for practical purposes (though not legally) were SUs like the others.

The 1960 constitution of the WZO no longer provided for SUs but referred merely to "Congress groupings" and "parties". However, the institution of the SU was reintroduced in 1973 in another form and under another name but with nearly the same content when, by an amendment of the Constitution, the *Zionist World Unions were established. A. ZWERGBAUM

SEPHARDIM. *See* WORLD SEPHARDI FEDERATION.

Enzo Sereni (right) and Mordechai Nahumson in Iraq with local Jews when they were organizing Iraqi Jewish illegal immigration to Palestine, Baghdad, 1942. [Beth Hatefutsoth]

SERENI, ENZO HAYIM. Zionist pioneer and emissary (b. Rome, 1905; d. Dachau, 1944). Educated in Italy, he received his Ph.D. in Rome in 1924. Attracted by Zionist socialism, he engaged in Zionist work in Italy and immigrated to Palestine in 1926. He was among the founders of Kibbutz Givat Brenner in 1928, but as a prominent member of the Zionist labor movement and Mapai party he was soon chosen for political and educational missions abroad. In 1931–1932, and again in 1933–1934 he was in Germany, where he organized the local halutz movement, as well as youth immigration and transfer of Jewish property after the Nazi seizure of power. In the following years he wrote numerous articles on Zionist and socialist issues, displaying an outstanding intellect among the leaders of the Zionist labor movement.

In 1940 Sereni volunteered for the British army as a candidate for a subsersive mission to Italy. The operation was put off, and he remained in Egypt where he edited on behalf of the British a propaganda newspaper for the Italian community and prisoners of war. In 1941 he was discharged after being accused of disseminating 'Communist' propaganda through his paper. In 1942 he went on a clandestine mission to Iraq, to organize a halutz movement and "illegal" immigration. In May, 1943, his activities were uncovered, and he had to return to Palestine. For a while he was in charge of the Iraqi desk of the Mossad for "illegal" immigration, until he was appointed liaison officer with the British secret services which sent parachutists into occupied Europe.

In February, 1944, Sereni accompanied a group of parachutists to Bari, in the liberated part of Italy, on their way to Yugoslavia. In spite of his age and Mapai leaders' objections, he decided to relinquish the role of staff officer and volunteered for an operational mission, utilizing his personal connections with British officers in charge of subversive operations in occupied Italy. He parachuted in May, 1944, was captured upon his landing, transferred to Dachau concentration camp, and executed there in November, 1944. Y. GELBER

His wife **Ada Sereni** (b. Rome, Italy, 1905) took part in many of his missions. She was a leading figure in the organization of "illegal" immigration to Palestine via Italy at the end of World War II. In the 1960s she organized and led the Associazione Italie-Israele in Rome and from 1959–68 she worked as public relations liaison for Soviet Jewry from Rome.

She published a book about the "illegal" immigration to Palestine entitled *Sephimot Lelo Degel* (1973). E. HOTER

SERLIN, YOSEPH. Lawyer and leader of General Zionism (b. Bialystok, Russian Poland, 1906; d. Tel Aviv, 1974). Serlin studied law at the University of Warsaw, receiving his degree in 1929. He early became active in Zionist work, first in his native Bialystok, then in Warsaw, where he headed a group of Zionist academicians and served as private secretary to Nahum Sokolow, and later in Pinsk.

Settling in Palestine in 1933, Serlin established a law practice and was active in the General Zionist party. He attended the 21st (1939) and 22nd (1946) Zionist Congresses. A member of the Knesset from 1949–1969, he first represented the General Zionist party and later Gahal. He was Minister of Health from 1952 to 1955 and served as Deputy Speaker of the Knesset from 1961 to 1969. He was also chairman of the World Union of General Zionists Israeli office and a member of the Executive of the Liberal Party.

SEROUSSI, ELIAS. Jewish leader in Uruguay (b. Alexandria, 1896; d. Tel Aviv, 1983). Active in the organization of Sephardi community life and at the general community level, his criteria of association between the different ethnic communities and of global Zionism transcended party considerations. He immigrated to Uruguay in 1926, participating in the founding of the Circulo Social Sefaradi (1930), and of the Sephardi Jewish Community of Uruguay (1932) of which he was the first president. He helped to organize B'nai B'rith (1935–36), and was cofounder of the Comité Central Israelita del Uruguay (1940), a Jewish community roof institution which represented the community before the Uruguayan authorities, serving as its president for ten years. Seroussi participated in the Comité's diplomatic activities during the period of struggle for the creation of the Jewish State. He immigrated to Israel in 1974.

R.P. RAICHER

SETER (STAROMINSKY), MORDECAI. Israeli composer (b. Novorossisk, Russia, 1916). His parents took him to Palestine in 1926. From 1932–37 he studied composition in Paris. In 1944, he composed his *Sabbath Cantata*, which established his austere, contrapuntal style, based on a synthesis of Palestrina-type counterpoint, with modern, dissonant harmonies, combined with quotes of traditional Jewish tunes. During the 1940s and early 1950s he concentrated on composing intense meditative chamber pieces, culminating with the sonata for solo violin. He also composed works for a capella choir. He later composed orchestral works, among them the powerful cantata *Tikun Hatzot* (Midnight Vigil), echoing the soundscape of prayer at a Yemenite synagogue. His later works, such as the Ricercar for string trio, stress his introvert nature and his predilection for abstract, concentrated contrapuntal style. Seter was a professor of composition at the Academy of Music in Tel Aviv (later part of Tel Aviv University). J. HIRSHBERG

SHA'ALVIM. Religious kibbutz in the northern Judean foothills, on the northern side of the Ayalon Valley. It was founded in 1951 by members of the Ezra youth movement, later joined by immigrants from English-speaking and other countries. It developed mixed farming and workshops and became a spiritual center of Po'alei Agudat Israel, building a large synagogue and opening a yeshiva (rabbinical academy). In 1987, Sha'alvim numbered 902 inhabitants. The biblical town of Sha'albim stood on the site. The mosaic floor of a Samaritan synagogue was discovered there. E. ORNI

SHA'AR HA-GOLAN. Kibbutz south of Lake Kineret, near the Yarmuk-Jordan confluence, established as a Tower and Stockade outpost in 1937. The kibbutz came under heavy Syrian, Iraqi, and Jordanian attacks in the 1948 War of Independence and had to be abandoned, but was recaptured two days later. Until the Six-Day War, it still suffered harassment from time to time from nearby Syrian and Jordanian positions. However, it developed intensive farming and an industrial enterprise. Remains of a Neolithic culture were discovered in the vicinity and are housed in a museum on the kibbutz. Population (1987), 670. E. ORNI

SHABTAI, YAAKOV. Israel novelist (b. Tel Aviv, 1934; d. there, 1981). Shabtai was raised in Tel Aviv. In 1957, he joined Kibbutz Merhavya where he lived for ten years, returning to Tel Aviv in 1967. He wrote several plays and short stories while still in Merhavya but gained prominence as a novelist.

Shabtai portrays the world of contemporary Israeli society, in which the Socialist-Zionist ideology which nurtured the first generation of Jewish settlers no longer sustains their sons, who now find their lives utterly devoid of purpose. Shabtai's major novel *Past Continuous* (1977) is set in

Swimming pool in the kibbutz Sha'ar Ha-Golan. [Israel Government Press Office]

modern Tel Aviv and depicts the urban malaise of several members of its intelligentsia. He employs contemporary literary techniques, particularly flashbacks and stream of consciousness. Both *Past Continuous* and his posthumous novel *Sof Davar* (1984, Past Perfect, 1987) have been translated into English. E. SPICEHANDLER

SHAKED, GERSHON. Hebrew literary scholar (b. Vienna, 1929). Shaked's family migrated in 1939 to Tel Aviv. He studied at the Hebrew University and at the University of Zurich, joining the faculty of the Hebrew University in 1964. He was awarded an Israel Prize in 1993.

Shaked was a seminal and prolific scholar whose major works are: *Bein Tzehok va-Dima* (Between Laughter and Tears, 1967), a study of Mendele Mokher Sefarim; *Gal Hadash ba-Sifrut ha-Ivrit* (A New Wave in Hebrew Literature, 1971); *Ha-Mahaze ha-Ivri ha-Histori* (The Hebrew Historical Drama, 1970); *Omanut ha-Sipur shel Agnon* (Agnon's Narrative Art, 1973); *Le-lo Motza* (Dead End, 1973); essays on Brenner, Bin-Gorion, and others. His history of modern Hebrew fiction (*Ha-Siporet ha-Ivrit*), of which the first three volumes appeared by 1989, was of great significance. Shaked dealt with contemporary Zionist problems in *Ein Makom Aher* (There Is No Other Place). His study on American Jewish authors was translated to English (The Shadow Within, 1987). E. SPICEHANDLER

SHALI'AH (pl. *shelihim*). Emissary from the Land of Israel to Diaspora communities. The institution has been known for centuries when the emissary (formerly known as *meshulah* or *shadar*) from the Holy Land (and especially from the "holy communities" of Jerusalem, Hebron, Tiberias, and Safed) was a familiar figure throughout the Jewish world as he came to raise funds for institutions in Eretz Israel.

With the beginning of the rebuilding of Eretz Israel by the Zionist Movement, *shelihut* (the "mission" of the emissaries) took on new forms. First of all, the *shaliah* went to Diaspora countries to describe the new way of life being built by the young pioneers. He personified the principles of Zionism, having settled on the land, and helped prepare young Jews abroad who had committed themselves to immigration, besides encouraging others to do so.

In the aftermath of World War II, *shelihim* from Palestine followed in the wake of the troops in a desperate effort to rescue survivors of the Holocaust and bring them "illegally" to the shores of Palestine, despite the attempts of the British mandatory authorities to stop them.

After the establishment of the State of Israel *shelihim* were sent to Jewish communities in North Africa and Asia to help organize mass immigration to Israel. In the years since, young Israelis have also been sent by their youth movements with funds allocated by the World Zionist Organization (WZO), to serve two-to-three-year periods in the Diaspora communities, mainly in the countries of the West, to strengthen the activities of the movements, and encourage immigration.

Over the years the functions of the emissary expanded to included *shelihut* to entire communities. As new generations grew up with less and less Jewish knowledge, the *shaliah* not only had to serve personally as a role model, but also had to educate young Jews in the basics of Jewish life. This resulted in more professional selection and training; the selection process included personal interviews by qualified professionals; a battery of tests examining general, Jewish, and Zionist knowledge; and behavioral workshops in simulated situations, where the candidates were observed by trained personnel. The *shaliah* was required to be proficient in the language of the country to which he was destined, and all candidates had to attend an intensive two-month training course at the WZO's Emissaries' Training Institute.

In 1981 the Central Emissaries' Authority was created by the WZO Executive as a roof body for the recruiting, selection, and training of *shelihim* sent on behalf of all WZO Departments. The Emissaries Authority determines the conditions of service, collates information on the work of *shelihim* throughout the world, monitors their activities, and supplies them with updated information on events in Israel.

In 1988 over seven hundred emissaries were active in 31 countries on the continents of North America, Europe, Central and South America, Oceania, and Africa. The majority (over 400) were Israeli teachers sent to Jewish schools by the WZO Departments for Education in the Diaspora; about two hundre were sent under the auspices of the Youth and he-Halutz Department to Zionist youth movements, to Jewish youth organizations, and to serve at Jewish community centers, as well as entire Jewish communities. The Aliya Department had some 60 emissaries active in main Jewish communities; the remainder represented or worked on behalf of other Departments of the WZO and the Jewish Agency.

The majority of *shelihim* are qualified teachers whose function in the Jewish schools is to teach Hebrew and participate in Jewish study programs. The *shelihim* to youth movements are required to help in the organization and administration of their movements; design and implement educational programs for the various age groups; plan and run summer and winter camps; organize programs related to the Jewish festivals, teach about life in Israel, and encourage senior members to emigrate to Israel. They are assisted in this task by local youth movement leaders, usually not much older than the children they are in charge of, and the emissary trains them to fill this role. The community emissary carries out many of these functions, but in addition he plans programs for adults, works closely with local Jewish organizations, runs Hebrew classes, lectures on aspects of life in Israel to Jewish and non-Jewish audiences, organizes Israel programs, and carries out interviews with potential immigrants. The aliya emissary interviews potential immigrants, advises them regarding their prospects in Israel, and deals with the process of the immigration.

In 1985 the Chairman of the WZO-Jewish Agency appointed a public committee, headed by former Supreme Court President Moshe Landau, to examine the institution of *shelihut*. The committee heard reports from former *shelihim*, reviewed the situation in a number of Diaspora countries and examined the system of recruitment, selection, and training. As a result of the public committee's recommendations, a WZO Executive Committee for *shelihim* was appointed which redefined the roles of the different categories of *shelihut*; resolved to establish and operate unified territorial missions; appointed heads of missions; and defined their powers. It set criteria for modes of operation and gathering feedback, and for streamlining the system. It also fixed new criteria for short-term *shelihut*.

S. KETKO

SHALIAH. *See* EMISSARIES.

Yitzhak Shamir.
[Israel Govt. Press Office]

SHAMIR, MOSHE. Hebrew novelist (b. Safed, 1921). Shamir was raised in Tel Aviv and attended the Herzliya secondary school. He became a member of Ha-Shomer ha-Tza'ir and joined Kibbutz Mishmar ha-Emek (1941–47). Between 1944–48, he served in the Palmah and edited several of its literary publications. Following the Six-Day War, he quit the Zionist left and went over to the nationalist right. He became a founder of the Greater Israel movement and a leader of the La-Am wing of the Likud, serving in the ninth Knesset as a Likud member. After the Camp David Agreement, he resigned from the Likud and was a founding member of the Tehiya party (1979).

Shamir's first novel, *Hu Halakh ba-Sadot* (He Walked in the Fields, 1947), caught the public's imagination during Israel's War of Independence. Uri, the hero of the novel, is a rough and ready Sabra native to a kibbutz. In contrast to his intellectual father, his commitment to the national cause is instinctive and has more to do with his sense of comradeship and adventure than with ideological convictions. The novel enjoyed an enormous success and its dramatized version drew enthusiastic audiences. *Be-Mo Yadav*, (1951; With His Own Hands, 1970) is a sensitive, somewhat fictionalized portrayal of his brother, Elik, who fell in the war. *Tahat ha-Shemesh* (Under the Sun, 1950) and *Ki Erom Ata* (You Are Naked, 1959) are social novels. The first deals with the struggle of Jewish farm workers against Jewish farmers during the Second Aliya and the latter with the world of the Labor-Zionist youth movements.

Shamir's realistic historical novels are set in ancient Israel. *Melekh Basar va-Dam* (1954; A King of Flesh and Blood, 1958), is a literary *tour de force*. Written in Mishnaic Hebrew, it depicts the reign of Alexander Yannai, the great Hasmonean king. Shamir's Alexander is a complex machiavellian empire-builder who ruled with few moral constraints. The novel draws a panoramic portrait of the Jewish world of the second century BCE and often implies that there are parallels between the relationship of the ancient commonwealth and its diaspora and that of modern Israel and contemporary world Jewry. *Kivsat ha-Rash* (David's Stranger, 1965) takes up the conflict between King David, the powerful and crafty monarch, and Uriah the Hittite, an idealistic soldier who falls prey to the wiles of the king he faithfully serves.

Shamir's later novels have been part of a trilogy of epic proportions which seeks to portray the saga of a pioneering Israeli family from its European origins until modern times *Rahok mi-Peninim* (More Precious than Pearls). Two parts have appeared; *Yona mi-Hatzer Zara* (Pigeon From a Different Yard, 1973) and *Hinomet ha-Kala* (Bridal Veil, 1984).

Hayai im Yishma'el, (1968; My Life with Ishmael, 1970) is an autobiographical essay with distinct political overtones. He asserts that Arab intransigence has led him to advocate maximalist territorial demands. He has also written plays, some of which are based on his novels, children's books, war reportage, and literary criticism. E. SPICEHANDLER

SHAMIR (YEZERNITSKY), YITZHAK (b. Rozinai, Poland, 1915). Lehi (*Lohamei Herut Israel) underground leader and Prime Minister of Israel (1983–1984, 1986-). He graduated from a Hebrew Secondary School in Bialystok and studied law in Warsaw, where he was active in Betar. He immigrated to Palestine in 1935 and studied at the Hebrew University. In 1937 he joined the Irgun Tzeva'i Le'umi and in 1940 followed Yair Stern into Lohamei Herut Israel (Lehi). Arrested by the British he escaped and between 1942 and 1946 was one of the three heads of Lehi, responsible for organization and operations. Arrested again in 1948 he was deported to Eritrea, from where he escaped, returning to Israel by way of Ethiopia and France the same year. He went into business but in 1955 joined the Mosad, where he served for a decade, reaching senior positions. In 1965 he returned to business. In 1969 he joined the Herut party, becoming head of its immigration and organization department.

President Reagan and Yitzhak Shamir in front of White House, 1983. [Israel Govt. Press Office]

Elected to the Knesset in 1973, he served on its Defense and Foreign Affairs Committee. Reelected in 1977, he became the Speaker of the Knesset. In 1978 he abstained in the vote on the Camp David Accords. Upon the resignation of Moshe Dayan, Shamir became Foreign Minister in March, 1980, and held that post until October, 1986, even while serving as Prime Minister for a year after the resignation of Menahem Begin (October 1983-October 1984). During his year as Prime Minister he sought to deal with Israel's growing economic difficulties, mounting inflation, and deep military involvement in Lebanon.

Shamir supported Israel's retention of all the territories held since 1967, opposing any concessions to the Egyptians in 1978 and 1979 and to Jordan. As Foreign Minister during Israel's war in Lebanon, he defended Israel's position and sought to restore its international standing and image. During his tenure as Foreign Minister Israel reopened a dialogue with eastern Europe, culminating in the reopening of an Israeli office in Warsaw (October, 1986), Budapest (1988) and in increased contacts with other Communist bloc nations. Diplomatic relations between Israel and a growing number of African nations were restored in the mid-1980s. A "Free Trade Zone" agreement with the United States was successfully negotiated.

Following the 1984 General Elections, he negotiated with Shimon Peres a "rotation" agreement that led to the creation of the National Unity Government and served during its first twenty-five months as Vice Prime Minister and Minister for Foreign Affairs. He opposed various diplomatic initiatives undertaken by Prime Minister Peres regarding possible talks with Jordan and a Palestinian delegation; he opposed the idea of an international conference to resolve the Arab-Israel conflict, or making concessions to Egypt on the Taba dispute in return for normalization of relations with Israel. He supported the ending of Israel's military presence in Lebanon. In October, 1986, he reassumed the position of Prime Minister. For the next two years, while supporting in general a process leading to peace between Israel and its neighbors, he opposed moves initiated by his Foreign Minister, Shimon Peres, towards an agreement with Jordan over the future of Judea and Samaria. In October, 1988, he led the Likud to a narrow victory in the general elections for the 12th Knesset and reestablished a Government of National Unity with himself as Prime Minister. In May 1989 he launched an Israeli peace plan calling for elections in the Administered Territories and a transitional period of autonomy. The plan stalled over an American request that the Palestinian delegation should include Palestinian Arabs known to be supporters of the Palestine Liberation Organization as well as Palestinians from Jerusalem (which Israel did not accept as part of the Territories). When the Ma'arakh, feeling that Shamir's policy on these matters was too rigid, introduced a vote of no-confidence, the Government was voted out of office in March 1990. Shamir subsequently established a new narrower-based government based on a coalition with right-wing and religious parties. In 1992 he was defeated in the general election and resigned the leadership of his party.

M. MEDZINI

SHAPIRA, (HAYIM) MOSHE. Israel politician and religious leader (b. Grodno, Russia, 1902;d. near Tel Aviv, 1970). He studied at the Grodno Yeshiva and the Hildesheimer Rabbinical Seminary in Berlin. Active in the Mizrachi Youth organization in Poland and Lithuania, he was one of the founders of He-Halutz ha-Mizrachi (Mizrachi Pioneer). In 1925 he was a delegate to a Zionist Congress for the first time, was elected a member of the world leadership of *Torah va-Avoda, and in this capacity settled in Palestine. Subsequently he held important positions in the Mizrachi and Ha-Po'el ha-Mizrachi, eventually becoming chairman of the united Mizrachi-Ha-Po'el ha-Mizrachi movement.

For many years Shapira was a member of the Executive

of the Jewish Agency and director of its Department for Immigration. In the period preceding the establishment of the State of Israel, he was instrumental in securing cooperation between the Hagana and the Irgun Tzeva'i Le'umi. After the establishment of the State he was the initiator of the *United Religious Front at the elections to the First Knesset. Shapira was Minister of Immigration and Health in the provisional government (1948–49). He was elected to the Knesset in 1949 and, with one short interruption, served in the Cabinet continuously thereafter. He held the portfolios of the Interior (1949–53, 1955) and of Social Welfare and Religious Affairs (1953–58). In 1959 he again became Minister of the Interior, an office he held until his death. He was also a member of the Ministerial Committee on Defense and Foreign Affairs. J. STAVI

Moshe Shapira. [Zionist Archives]

SHARABI, ISRAEL YESHAYAHU. *See* YESHAYAHU, ISRAEL SHARABI.

Anatol and Avital Sharansky on the latter's arrival in Israel, 1986. [Israel Govt. Press Office]

SHARANSKY, ANATOLY (NATAN). Aliya activist in USSR and Israel (b. Donetsk, Ukraine, 1948) He graduated from the Physical Technical Institute in Moscow as a computer scientist. In 1973 he first applied for an emigration visa and was refused on "security" grounds. In July, 1974, he married Natalya (Avital), whom the Soviet authorities forced to leave the USSR a few hours after their wedding. Sharansky, with his command of English and analytic ability, became a liaison between the refusenik community and foreign journalists in Moscow, virtually the spokesman for the aliya movement. He also represented the Jewish movement in the unofficial Helsinki Monitoring Group, which he joined in 1976. In March, 1977, *Izvestia* published an article in which he was accused of collaborating with the CIA.

Within 10 days he was arrested on the charge of treason and espionage and imprisoned in Moscow Lefortovo Prison, in complete isolation for one and a half years. During the period of his solitary confinement, before he was brought to trial, hundreds of Jews all over the USSR were interrogated in connection with his case. The false accusation leveled against Sharansky was intended as the forerunner of threats and intimidation against Jews applying to emigrate to Israel. Sharansky defended himself throughout the trial. In his last words to the Court, he spoke of two thousand years of exile of the Jewish people among the nations and of the persecution of Jews in the USSR. He ended his words with the declaration of faith: "Next Year in Jerusalem." Though the USA denied any connection between Sharansky and the CIA in the most official manner, including President Jimmy Carter's personal statement, he was pronounced guilty and sentenced to 13 years' imprisonment: three years in isolation and ten in a labor camp. Of the nine years he actually spent in confinement, not more than one and a half years were spent in the labor camp, where he was in punishment cells and the internal camp prison for two-thirds of the time. In 1981 he was accused of "being a bad influence" on other prisoners, tried again, and sentenced to another term in prison. He himself felt that the brutal pressure applied to him was aimed at coercing him to sign a document admitting cooperation with the CIA—a document whose implications could have been disastrous for the whole Jewish movement.

In 1982, all basic prisoner rights were denied him. He was not allowed to meet with relatives or even to send letters to his family. As a protest, Sharansky refused to eat for 110 days starting from Yom Kippur, 1982, and was forcefed by the prison authorities. After the authorities acquiesced in his demand (the right to communicate), he ceased the hunger strike. He then weighed 35 kilos, was hospitalized, and began to suffer from heart problems.

The international campaign waged by his wife made Sharansky the best known Soviet Jewry activist and led, finally, to his release on 11 February 1986. He arrived in Israel the same night and was welcomed by thousands of people who gathered spontaneously at Ben-Gurion airport. Since his release Sharansky has been a tireless promoter of the cause of Soviet Jewry, his international standing enabling him to present this issue to world leaders. He played a central role in mobilizing the American Jewish community for the biggest ever solidarity rally in Washington, on 6 December 1987, the eve of the second Gorbachev-Reagan summit.

In May, 1988, he was elected chairman of the newly formed Soviet Jewry Zionist Forum, an umbrella organization of Soviet Jewish activists in Israel. Sharansky's memoirs, *Fear No Evil,* were published in Israel and in the USA in 1988. Y. STERN

SHAREF, ZE'EV. Zionist and Israeli public official (b. Izvor-Szeletin, Romania, 1906; d. Jerusalem, 1984). Sharef early became active in the Po'ale Zion youth movement in his native country. Settling in Palestine in 1925, he was an official of the Palestine Workers' Fund (Kupat Po'alei Eretz Yisrael) from 1925 to 1928. From 1929 to 1931 he was a member of kibbutz Shefayim. During the next four years he traveled on Zionist missions to Poland, Latvia, Austria, and Finland. From 1935 to 1940 he was secretary of Ha-Po'el, the athletic association of the Histadrut. From 1940 to 1943 Sharef was engaged in administrative work for the Hagana. He then became secretary of the Political Department of the Jewish Agency, serving until 1947, when he was charged by the Provisional Council of State with the task of preparing the essential administrative machinery that was to begin operations as soon as the British left Palestine.

From 1948 to 1957 Sharef was Secretary of the Cabinet, and from 1957 to 1959 Director-General of the Prime Minister's Office. He also served as Civil Service Commissioner (1951–52), Director of the Revenue Department of the Ministry of Finance (1954–61), and Chairman of the Port Authority (1962–66). Elected to the Knesset in 1965 as a representative of the Ma'arakh, or Labor Alignment he was named Minister of Commerce and Industry in 1966 and assumed the portfolio of finance as well in 1968. In 1969–73, he was Minister of Housing.

Sharef is the author of *Three Days* (1962), a description of the crucial events immediately preceding the Proclamation of the State of Israel in May, 1948.

SHARETT (SHERTOK), MOSHE. Labor movement leader, Zionist statesman, Israel's first Foreign Minister and second Prime Minister, (b. Kherson, Russia, 1894; d. Jerusalem, 1965). His father, Ya'acov Yehudi Shertok, was a member of the original Bilu group which emigrated to Eretz Israel in 1882 but he returned to Russia in 1886 due to severe economic problems and poor health. Moshe was strongly influenced by his father's liberal, social, and political views. He was educated in a modern religious school and a Russian high school. In 1906, the Shertok family emigrated again to Eretz Israel. They leased a farm and a mill in Ein-Sinya, an Arab village on the Jerusalem—Nablus road, where young Shertok gained firsthand knowledge of the Arabic language and Palestinian customs. The attempt to settle in Samaria failed economically, and the family moved to Jaffa in 1908. The following year, Ya'acov Shertok was among the founders of Ahuzat Bayit, the Jaffa suburb that later became the nucleus of Tel Aviv. Moshe Shertok attended the Herzliya High School, and subsequently went to study law at the University of Constantinople. After a year, the university closed down on the eve of World War I, and Shertok returned to Eretz Israel and began to teach at the Herzliya High School. Maintaining that the Jews of Eretz Israel should become Ottoman citizens and enlist in the Turkish army, he and a few hundred of his fellow high school graduates enlisted in that army in 1915 and served in various places in the Middle East, Shertok being commissioned as an officer.

After the collapse of the Turkish Empire and its army, Shertok returned to Palestine and was appointed secretary of the Department for Land and Arab Affairs of the Zionist Commission, under Yehoshua Hankin. In this capacity, Shertok traveled throughout Palestine, the Golan Heights, and Transjordan, establishing contacts, and often friendly relations, with Arab notables. Under the influence of his old friend and schoolmate, Eliyahu Golomb, Shertok joined the new Ahdut ha-Avoda party and served on its Executive. However, from 1920 he studied economics at the London School of Economics. While in London, Shertok worked for the Hagana, and as the London representative of Ahdut ha-

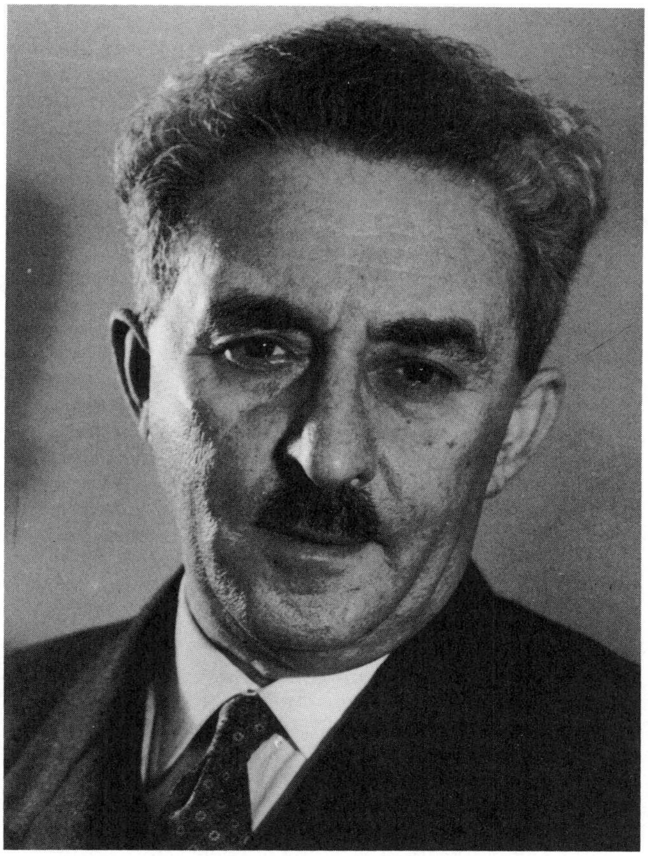

Moshe Sharett. [Zionist Archives]

Avoda, he became involved in the British Po'ale Zion Party. In these capacities he served as a liaison with the British Labor Party.

In 1923, Shertok's political mentor Berl Katznelson had suggested that he should return to Palestine to work with a new Hebrew daily newspaper that Katznelson was planning. In 1925, when this plan materialized, Shertok joined the editorial board of *Davar*, the daily launched under the sponsorship of the Histadrut, continuing in this post until 1931; from 1929 he also edited *Davar*'s English supplement.

Shertok played an important role in planning organizational reforms of the Histadrut and of his party. He also played a role in the unification of Ha-Po'el ha-Tza'ir and Ahdut ha-Avoda, which led to the establishment of Mapai in 1930. Shertok served on most of the united party's governing bodies, and was also a Labor delegate to Zionist Congresses, devoting considerable time to the development of the Labor Bloc youth movements.

When Mapai joined the ruling coalition of the Zionist movement Haim Arlosoroff, head of the Political Department of the Jewish Agency, demanded that Shertok be appointed as the political secretary of that Department. In this capacity, Shertok conducted negotiations with Emir Abdullah of Transjordan and with Palestinian Arab leaders, designed to reduce tension between the Jewish and Arab communities in the country. Arlosoroff and Shertok worked harmoniously until the former's assassination in 1933. At the Zionist Congress held later the same year,

Shertok was elected Arlosoroff's successor as head of the Political Department and as a member of the Zionist Executive.

Shertok was now the yishuv's senior representative in negotiations with the British, Arabs, and the League of Nations. In view of the 1936 Arab Revolt he initiated and helped organize the Noterim (Jewish Supernumerary Police.) Later in 1936, he directed the planning and preparation of the Jewish Agency's case before the Peel Commission. When the Commission proposed the partition of Palestine and the establishment of a Jewish State, Shertok joined Weizmann and Ben-Gurion as a stanch supporter of the proposal. At this time, Shertok chaired a secret Security Committee of the Jewish Agency which, among other things, dealt with the organization and financing of the Hagana. Early in 1939, Shertok directed the planning and presentation of the Jewish Agency's position at the St. James's Conference, in which the Zionist leaders unsuccessfully fought British plans to temporarily freeze the development of the yishuv.

During World War II, Shertok was particularly active regarding the yishuv's defense, recruiting Jewish soldiers for the British Army, and aiding Jews in Nazi-occupied Europe. He participated in the planning of the yishuv's defense in the event of a German invasion into Palestine; he persuaded the British authorities to train Palestinian Jewish units within the British army for underground resistance in such an eventuality; he convinced British authorities in Egypt and London to train Palestinians and Jewish commandos for operations behind German lines in eastern Europe, and he organized Jewish resistance to the Nazis. At the same time, he was a leading figure in the yishuv's struggle against the restrictions of the 1939 British White Paper.

After 1941, Shertok was deeply involved in the efforts to rescue Jews from the Holocaust and helped organize and conduct the "illegal" Jewish immigration.

In 1946, he prepared the Agency's case and was a principal witness before the Anglo-American Committee of Inquiry. In June, 1946 (on "Black Saturday"), he and other senior members of the yishuv political elite were arrested by the British and interned at Latrun for four months.

The following year Shertok focused his activities on the United Nations. He was the leading yishuv and Zionist figure in the campaign to secure a positive resolution from the United Nations Special Committee on Palestine (UNSCOP). Together with Abba Hillel Silver, he led the diplomatic and political effort on behalf of the Zionist movement and the yishuv, which culminated in the establishment of the State of Israel.

One of the signatories to Israel's Declaration of Independence, he became Israel's first Foreign Minister. In 1949, he Hebraized his last name to Sharett. He negotiated the *de jure* recognition of Israel by the US, and established intimate diplomatic relations with this superpower. In his direction of the Armistice negotiations following Israel's War of Independence, he considered the possibility of establishing an independent Palestinian state rather than the annexation of the West Bank to Jordan. He advocated respect fot the United Nations and its peacekeeping efforts, and cooperation with other international bodies. Sharett created the Israeli Foreign Ministry and Foreign Service, shaping their structure and major procedures.

In 1949, Sharett was elected to the Knesset on the Mapai list. During his years as Foreign Minister, he developed a moderate foreign and defense strategy (known as the "Sharett line"), and Israel's policy vis-à-vis the Palestinians and Arab states was based on a liberal political stance, and a moderate approach to the protracted Arab-Israeli conflict. He held that since the conflict was virtually insoluble, it should be managed carefully and moderately. To this end, he initiated secret negotiations with Presidents Naguib and Nasser of Egypt, meant further to reduce regional tensions, and advocated only closely controlled and limited retaliations against Palestinian infiltrators and their sponsors. These attitudes and policies led to many clashes with Ben-Gurion.

Nevertheless, upon the latter's resignation in December, 1953, Sharett, the next senior leader of Mapai, became the second Prime Minister of Israel, retaining control over the foreign affairs portfolio. During his tenure, he continued his moderate policies in Arab affairs despite the bitter disagreements they caused with his Defense Ministers, Pinhas Lavon, and later Ben-Gurion over the retaliation policy, political attitudes toward the Arab states, and policies vis-à-vis the superpowers. During the same period, the Lavon Affair had occurred without Sharett's knowledge or consent, leading Sharett and Mapai to oust Lavon and recall Ben-Gurion as Defense Minister.

Sharett served as Prime Minister until the November, 1955, elections when upon the decision of Mapai, Ben-Gurion returned to the position. Sharett served under Ben-Gurion as Foreign Minister until his resignation in June, 1956, following his unflagging opposition to launching a war against Egypt, as was being planned by Ben-Gurion and Moshe Dayan.

After leaving the government, Sharett headed the Am Oved publishing company and was ambassador at large. At the 1960 Zionist Congress, he was elected Chairman of the Jewish Agency Executive. When the Lavon Affair surfaced again in the early 1960s, Sharett was instrumental in pushing Ben-Gurion into deciding to leave Mapai and establish his own separate party.

His published works include a number of books: *Mishut be-Asia* (Roaming through Asia, 1957), describing his journeys in the Far East on political missions; *Be'Sha'ar ha-Umot* (At the Gates of the Nations, 1958), *Orot she-Kavu* (Burned-Out Lights), a collection of poems translated from the Russian; *Yoman Medini* (Political Diary, 1975, 5 volumes), his political diaries of the years 1936–1941; and *Yoman Ishi* (Personal Diary, 1978, 8 volumes), covering the period 1953–1957, which described the inner struggles among Israel's senior political elite. G. SHEFFER

SHARON (SHEINERMAN), ARIEL. Israeli soldier and politician (b. Kefar Mahalal, 1928). Upon graduating from high school he joined the Hagana, fought in the War of Independence, and was wounded in the battle of Latrun. He remained in the Israel army until 1973 serving in many capacities, among them Commander of the Special Operationa 101 Unit and of the paratroopers. He commanded many retaliatory raids in the 1950s and led the parachutists in their jump into the Mitla Pass during the 1956 Sinai War. He was appointed Chief of Staff of the Northern Command in 1962, and head of the Training Branch in 1966 and promoted to Brigadier General. In the 1967 Six-Day War he commanded a division which fought valiantly in Sinai. Between 1970 and 1973 he served as Officer Commanding the Southern Command and restored law and order in the Gaza Strip by unconventional means. He left the army in 1973, when it became clear that he would not be appointed Chief of Staff, and joined the Liberal Party. He was instrumental in putting together the *Likud bloc in the summer of 1973 and ran for the Knesset. In the Yom Kippur War he commanded a division which established a bridgehead over the Suez Canal and changed the fortunes of war in the Southern front by crossing into Egypt. He subsequently left the army, sat briefly in the Knesset, and resigned to become security adviser to Prime Minister Yitzhak Rabin. He left this post in 1976 and in 1977 formed the Shlomzion party, which won two seats in the May 1977 general elections. Sharon joined the first Begin cabinet as Minister of Agriculture (1977–1981). He was the key figure pushing for Jewish settlements in the Administered Areas and in Galilee. Though he supported the Camp David Accords and the Israel-Egypt Peace Treaty, his proclamations on defense and foreign affairs sometimes caused serious rifts between himself and his colleagues in the cabinet. In July 1981 he was appointed Defense Minister and immediately planned the war in Lebanon, which he led in the summer of 1982 (*see* LEBANON WAR). The War lasted far longer than the two-three days he anticipated and took on wider dimensions, causing far more casualties than expected. He led the army to the gates of Beirut and saw the PLO leave that city. The massacre committed by Lebanese Christian forces in the Sabra and Shatilla Palestinian refugee camps in Beirut (September, 1982) led an Israeli commission of inquiry to demand his resignation as Defense Minister. He left this post in March, 1983, retaining his cabinet seat as Minister without Portfolio. He helped put together the Government of National Unity after the deadlocked 1984 Knesset elections and was appointed Minister of Commerce and Industry. Sharon opposed the return of any part of Eretz Israel to the Arab nations and advocated Israel's annexation of at least parts of the Administered Areas. In 1990–92, he was Minister of Housing.

M. MEDZINI

SHARON (SCHWADRON), AVRAHAM. Zionist journalist and founder of the collection of Jewish autographs and portraits now in the Jewish National and University Library in Jerusalem (b. Bienuv, Eastern Galicia, 1878; d. Jerusalem, 1957). He started his collection of Jewish autographs and portraits in his early youth and invested in it almost all of his own modest resources. Schwadron graduated from the University of Vienna where he studied philosophy, law, and chemistry. He was a founding member of a Zionist association, "Ha-Tehia", in Vienna. Moving to Palestine in 1927, he settled in Jerusalem. He was a prolific publicist, who wrote extensively on Jewish and Zionist issues, his style was very polemic and satiric and sometimes quite aggressive. In his articles he preached the need to compel, if necessary, all Jews in the Diaspora to immigrate to Eretz Israel in order to put an end to the *galut* (exile) which in his mind was an abnormal and undignified situation. Making Eretz Israel a "spiritual center" for the Jewish people without eliminating the Diaspora was insufficient and would not solve the "problem of the Jews" abroad.

After the massacres of Jews by Arabs in 1929 in various places in Palestine, he advocated a systematic effort to convince Palestinian Arabs to emigrate of their own free will, with every possible incentive offered them, to neighboring Arab countries. He believed there to be no chance of Jews and Arabs coexisting peacefully together in the same country and that for the good of both peoples there had to be a physical separation between them. He called for modesty in public life in Israel and opposed the preservation of ethnic differences among the various Jewish communities gathered there.

He published more than 150 booklets, tracts, and articles, in German and Hebrew. Some of his writings were published in his book *Mi-Shenei Evrei ha-Sha'a* (1946).

M. YEGAR

SHAS (abbreviation of Shomerei-Torah, Torah Guardians). Israeli religious political party, established in 1984. Its members and supporters, many of Moroccan origin, were drawn from the ranks of *Agudat Israel and *Tami. Led by Rabbi Yitzhak Peretz and supported by former Sephardi Chief Rabbi Ovadia Yosef, the party was established as the result of the growing disenchantment of its Sephardi members and followers with the Aguda's traditional Ashkenazi leadership and activists, and with the performance of Tami. It demanded greater representation in the party's bodies including the Knesset list. Its founders claimed to represent large, low-income families from North Africa and Middle Eastern countries. Its platform insisted on the supremacy of the Torah and its later authoritative rabbinic interpretations as the exclusive law of the land; religious legislation insuring the sanctity of the Sabbath and Jewish holidays and kashrut; opposition to military service for women and religious students, and special allocations for yeshivot. The stand of the party resembled that of Aguda but stressed the special problems of the religious-Sephardi Jews. It espoused dovish views on foreign policy and took a liberal position in economic matters, both considered secondary to religious issues. In its first appearance on the political arena, the elections in 1984 to the 11th Knesset, the party received 63,605 votes (or 3.06% of the total votes) gaining four seats in the Knesset. It was invited to join the Government of National Unity and agreed to do so on condition that Rabbi Peretz become Minister of the Interior. After joining the Cabinet, Shas concentrated on pursuing religious legislation. In the 1988 elections Shas gained six seats and retained the Ministry of the Interior. In the 1990 government it also received the Ministry of Communications. In 1992 it received 6 seats and joined the Rabin coalition in which Arye Deri was a minister.

M. MEDZINI

SHAVEI ZION. One of the country's first villages of the moshav shitufi type, founded on the coast of the Acre Plain in 1938 by immigrants from Germany descended from generations of farmers and cattle merchants in the Wuerttemberg village of Rexingen. Besides intensive farming, Shavei Zion developed as a seaside resort. Although not strictly Orthodox, the settlers preserved traditional Judaism as part of their social organization. The name means "Returners to Zion." Population (1987), 698.

E. ORNI

SHAW COMMISSION. Commission of inquiry appointed in September, 1929, by Lord Passfield, British Colonial Secretary, to investigate the Arab riots in Palestine. Sir Walter Shaw, a veteran staff official of the Colonial Office, was chairman, and the members represented the three British political parties, Conservative (Sir Henry Betterton), Liberal (Hopkin Morris), and Labor (Harry Snell; afterward Lord Snell). The Commission sat in Jerusalem as a public court of inquiry. The Jewish Agency was represented by Sir Frank (later Lord) Boyd Merriman and Lord Erleigh (later 2nd Marquess of Reading).

The Commission's report was published in March, 1930, with a minority report by Lord Snell. The latter had dissociated himself from the majority opinion, which held that the Arabs were alarmed by Jewish immigration and land purchases which allegedly created a landless Arab proletariat. Specifically, the report blamed the Arab "outbreak" on "racial animosity on the part of the Arabs, consequent upon the disappointment of their political and national aspirations and fear for their economic future." The conflict between the Jews and the Arabs was due mainly to the opposing interpretations placed by Arab and Jewish nationalists on Britain's wartime pledges to each side. "A National Home for the Jews," the report admitted, "in the sense in which it was widely understood, was inconsistent with the demands of Arab nationalists, while the claims of Arab nationalism, if admitted, would have rendered impossible the fulfillment of the pledge to the Jews." While the Arabs appeared to have had no objection to the "unobtrusive minority" that the Jews had formed in prewar Palestine, the report stated that they feared the postwar pioneers, who had greater energy and initiative than the veteran Jewish residents of the country and who represented an "international organization" enjoying what seemed to the Arabs to be unlimited financial support. When Jewish immigration in the 1920s was followed by a depression, the Arabs came to regard the Zionist movement as the cause of the country's economic troubles.

The main recommendations of the report were (1) the issuance by the government of a clear statement of the policy it intended to pursue in Palestine, including a definition of the passages in the Mandate for Palestine concerning the safeguarding of the interests of non-Jewish communities in the country; (2) a revision of the methods of regulating immigration to prevent "a repetition of the excessive immigration of 1925 and 1926" and to provide for consultation with non-Jewish representatives in this respect; (3) the initiation of a scientific expert inquiry into "the prospects of introducing improved methods of cultivation in Palestine" and the regulation of land policy in accordance with the results; and (4) a reaffirmation of the statement made in 1922 that "the special position assigned to the Zionist Organization by the Mandate does not entitle it to share in any degree in the government of Palestine."

The report pleased the Arabs, particularly so since the issuance of immigration certificates was suspended until Sir John Hope-Simpson, who arrived in Palestine in May, 1930, to conduct the inquiry recommended by the Commission, should have completed his work. In contrast, the report caused great indignation among the Jews. Chaim Weizmann said it implied an exoneration of the Arab mobs and their inciters.

See also HOPE-SIMPSON REPORT; PASSFIELD WHITE PAPER.

J. FRAENKEL

SHAZAR (RUBASHOW), SHNEUR ZALMAN. Third President of the State of Israel (b. Mir, Russia, 1889; d. Jerusalem, 1974). His surname is composed of the initials of his original name, Shneur Zalman Rubashow. He spent his childhood in the town of Stolbtsy, near Mir, where he had been brought by his parents, Yehuda Leib and Sarah Ginzburg Rubashow. Shazar was reared in an atmosphere

Zalman Shazar. [Israel Information Services]

of Habad hasidism, combined with Talmudic erudition and early Zionism, In 1905 he joined the Zionist labor movement *Po'ale Zion and subsequently organized Jewish self-defense in Stolbtsy and the vicinity. As a delegate to the clandestine conference of Po'ale Zion held in Minsk in 1906, he met Yitzhak Ben-Zvi, who was by then a leader in the Labor Zionist movement and an authority on practical conditions in Palestine. In 1907, while working in Vilna on the Po'ale Zion paper *Der Proletarisher Gedank* (Proletarian Thought), Shazar was arrested by the Tsarist police and imprisoned with the rest of the editorial staff. After his release that autumn, he entered the Academy for Jewish Studies founded by Baron David Guenzburg in St. Petersburg. There he studied for four years under the guidance of such distinguished teachers as Guenzburg himself, the historian Simon *Dubnow, and the talmudist and writer Judah Loeb Katznelson (pseudonym, Buki ben Yogli). At the same time he was employed on the editorial staff of *Der Yidisher Immigrant,* published by the Jewish Colonization Association (ICA).

In the summer of 1911 Shazar made his first journey to Eretz Israel and worked for a time at Kibbutz Merhavia. After a pilgrimage to the Western Wall, he wrote his first Hebrew article, "On the Eternity of the Past," for *Ahdut,* the Po'ale Zion paper in Jerusalem. Returning to Russia, he reported for military service but was exempted and went to Germany to study history and philosophy at the universities of Freiburg and Strasbourg.

World War I found him in Germany; as an enemy alien he was confined to Berlin, where he devoted his time to study and to Zionist and cultural work among German Jews. He helped edit the **Judische Rundschau* and played a leading role in organizing the Labor Zionist movement and He-Halutz in Germany. In 1919 he completed his studies in history and philosophy at the University of Berlin. That year the World Conference of Po'ale Zion in Stockholm named him to the study commission that it sent to Palestine; he edited the commission's report. In 1921 he wqs a delegate to the 12th Zionist Congress. At the 13th Congress (1923), he was elected to the Zionist Actions Committee. In 1920 he married Rachel Katznelson (see below).

From 1922 Shazar lectured in Jewish history at the Hebrew Pedagogium, the Jewish teachers' training seminary in Vienna. In 1924, he settled in Palestine. In Tel Aviv he was appointed to the Executive Committee of the Histadrut, and in June, 1925, he joined the editorial board of *Davar*, the newly established labor daily, of which he was to become editor-in-chief, serving until 1949.

In 1929 Shazar was elected to the Executive of the Va'ad Le'umi, and in 1930, with Hayim Arlosoroff, he edited the monthly *Ahdut Ha'Avoda*. He also took part in the founding conference of Mapai, the Palestine Jewish labor party. In 1933 he went to Warsaw, where he founded, and for a time edited, the Yiddish daily *Dos Vort*. He was sent on a number of missions to Jewish communities in other countries and represented the Histadrut and Mapai at international conferences of the Socialist and cooperative movements. In 1938 he attended the International Conference on Refugees at Évian, France. In 1943 he wrote the manifesto in which the Va'ad Le'umi drew the attention of the world to the Nazi Holocaust in Europe.

During the pre-State struggle with the mandatory power, Shazar participated in the 1946 hunger strike of the leaders of Palestine's Jewish community, and in 1947 he was named by the Zionist General Council to the Political Committee collaborating with the Zionist Executive in its negotiations at the United Nations. He appeared on behalf of the Histadrut at the hearing of the United Nations Special Committee on Palestine (UNSCOP) in Jerusalem and was a member of the Political Committee of the Jewish Agency at Lake Success when the UN Assembly decided on the establishment of the Jewish State. During his meetings in the United States with the rebbe (rabbi) of Lubavich, the world spiritual leader of Habad hasidism, it was decided to found Kefar Habad in Israel for refugees from Russia belonging to the Habad movement. Early in April, 1948, Shazar drafted the resolution passed by the Zionist General Council on April 12, announcing that Jewish independence would be established after the end of the Mandate. In 1949 he was elected to the First Knesset, serving also in the Second and Third Knessets (1951–59). He was appointed Minister of Education and Culture in the first regular Cabinet of Israel, a position he held until 1951. During his term he put the Free and Compulsory Education Law (1949) through the Knesset and supervised its implementation.

In 1951 Shazar resigned from the Cabinet to become Ambassador to Moscow. When the appointment did not materialize because of the opposition of the Soviet Government, he was elected to the Jewish Agency Executive (1952), taking charge of the Information Department. In 1954 he became head of the World Zionist Organization's Department of Education and Culture in the Diaspora. He was elected acting chairman of the Jewish Agency in Jerusalen in 1956. The next year he convened a world ideological conference on the basic problems facing the Zionist movement after the Holocaust and the emergence of the State.

On 21 May 1963, Shazar was elected President of the State of Israel to succeed Yitzhak Ben-Zvi. During his first term, he represented Israel at the funerals of President John F. Kennedy and Sir Winston Churchill and made official visits to Nepal, Uruguay, Brazil, Chile, the United States, and Canada. In 1964 he welcomed Pope Paul VI to Israel. On 26 March 1968, he was elected to a second five-year term of office. Little more than a year after its completion he died on 6 October 1974.

Shazar's writings include *Al Tilei Bet Frank* (On the Ruins of the House of Frank, 1923), a study of the Frankist movement; *Toledot Bikoret ha-Mikra* (A History of Biblical Criticism, 1925), in collaboration with Max Soloveitchik (Solieli); *Kokheve Boker*, 1950 (*Morning Stars*, 1967), a volume of autobiographical sketches; *Or Ishim* (The Light of Personalities, 2 vols., 1955), reminiscences of outstanding personalities, for which he received the Ussishkin Prize. His newspaper and magazine articles, from 1911 to 1948, were collected in *Be-Hazar ha-Mattara* (1974). In 1971 the Histadrut, Israel's General Federation of Labor, issued two volumes of Shazar's writing on the Labor Movement *Tziyon ve-Tzedek*. Under the title of *Orei Dorot* Shazar's studies in Jewish history were published in 1971: prominent among them are his seminal essays on the Shabbatean movement. The poet in Shazar was reflected in two small collections of his verse published shortly before his death: the Yiddish *Farsich* (1972) and the Hebrew *Liviat Mir* (1974).

As a memorial to Zalman Shazar, the Israel Historical Society established the Shazar Center which aims to strengthen knowledge and understanding of Jewish history among Israeli youth. S. NARDI

Rachel Katznelson Shazar his wife, Israeli editor and Zionist leader (b. Bobruisk, Russia, 1888; d. Jerusalem, 1975). After graduating from high school in Russia, Rahel Katznelson studied German language and literature in Berlin, where she also attended the Academy of Jewish Studies. Later she enrolled at the Women's College in St. Petersburg. Settling in Eretz Israel in 1912, she taught Hebrew at a training farm for girls in Kinneret and worked kibbutzim in Galilee and in Jerusalem. She was active in the women workers' movement and in 1919 became a member of the Cultural Committee of the newly established Ahdut Avoda party. She was a member of the Executive Committee of Mo'etzet ha-Po'alot (Working Women's Council) from 1930 on, a member of the Presidium of the Zionist Actions Committee, and a delegate to numerous Zionist Congresses. From 1934 to 1959 she was editor of *Devar ha-Po'elet*, a working women's monthly.

Mrs. Shazar frequently went abroad in connection with her Zionist work. She visited the Pioneer Women organization in the United States and Canada in 1933, conducted a He-Halutz seminar in Poland in 1938, worked with young Jewish men and women in the displaced-persons camps in Germany under the UN Relief and Rehabilitation Administration (UNRRA) in 1947, and attended international congresses of Socialist women in Stockholm and London. In 1946 she received the Yoseph H. Brenner Prize for a volume of essays and literary criticism, *Masot U-Reshimot* (Essays and Notes). In 1958 she was awarded the Israel Prize for her cultural and literary work.

SHECHEM. *See* NABLUS.

SHEFARAM (Shafa Amr). Town on the eastern outskirts of the Haifa Bay area. It is mentioned in talmudic sources as the seat of the Sanhedrin in the 2nd century CE, and was known as Safran in the Crusader period. From the 17th century, Jews, mostly farmers, lived in the town; in the 19th century, however, their numbers dwindled gradually and in 1920 the last Jews left, leaving behind a synagogue and cemetery. In the 1948 War of Independence, many Moslem, Christian-Arab, and Druze inhabitants left but others were absorbed and the proportion of Druze increased. Later, gaining importance as a market town, it attracted Arabs from Galilean villages, as well as Bedouin, and small industries were opened. Population (1987), 19,400, with the Moslems constituting the largest community.
E. ORNI

SHEFELA (literally, lowland). Hilly region in the southern part of Israel, at the foot of the Judean Mountains, extending from the vicinity of Lydda almost to Beersheba. The Shefala is 46 miles long and about 6 miles wide. It is covered with soft limestones and chalk and gradually ascends from the coastal plain toward the east. Dissection by rivers is strong only at its eastern flank, while in the west, dry rivers form wide valleys that are covered with fertile alluvial soil and bordered by soft hills. The climate become semi-arid toward the south.

The Shefela is an area of historic trade routes and dense settlement. Its largest part is now included in the planning area of the Lachish region, whose central town is Kiryat Gat.
Y. KARMON

SHEINKIN, MENAHEM. Zionist (b. Ula, Vitebsk District, Russia, 1871; d. Chicago, 1924). Sheinkin received a traditional education and, after his marriage, attended high school and later the University of Odessa while earning his livelihood as a teacher. In 1898 he founded in Odessa Benei Zion, the first local political Zionist group, which he represented at the Second Zionist Congress in Basle that year. He engaged in widespread Zionist and Hebrew cultural activities. In 1900 he visited Eretz Israel to study the conditions of the country, and from there he went to London to attend the Fourth Congress. The next year he was chosen government rabbi of Balta, in Bessarabia. While serving in this position, he continued his Zionist activities as the representative for the Zionist district of Podolia, Volhynia, and Bessarabia. In 1905 he was reelected to his rabbinical position, but the local Russian authorities refused to confirm his election because of his Zionist activities. He then went to Eretz Israel, where he helped found the Herzliya High School in Jaffa. In 1906 he settled permanently in the country and worked at the information and immigration offices of the Hovevei Zion in Jaffa. He helped found Tel Aviv and often visited Russia to disseminate the Zionist idea, raise funds, and persuade people to buy land or make investments in Eretz Israel.

At the beginning of World War I, Sheinkin was expelled from Eretz Israel as an enemy alien and went to the United States, where he helped found the American Zion Commonwealth and publicize the Jewish Legion. In 1919 he returned to Palestine to direct the Immigration Department of the Zionist Executive. Later he revisited the United States on behalf of the American Zion Commonwealth. He was killed in a traffic accident in Chicago and was buried in Tel Aviv.

Sheinkin favored the development of Palestine through private initiative, and in his writings he carried on a running debate concerning public ownership of land and self-labor. A collection of his Zionist writings appeared in 1935.

SHEKEL (plural, Shekalim). Designation of membership dues in the World Zionist Organization (WZO). The Shekel was introduced at the First Zionist Congress (1897) and existed, in various forms and with various functions, until the 26th Congress (1968). Its name was taken from the biblical coin and tax (Exodus 30:13).

Payment of the Shekel entitled the contributor to vote in elections to Zionist Congresses. Until 1960, when individual membership was abolished, it also entitled the contributor to a membership card in the WZO. In addition, the Shekel served as a basis for apportioning delegates to the Zionist Congresses. The number of Shekalim required to elect one delegate varied. During the early years of the movement it was set at 100 to 400; during the 1920s it was 2,000; later, it was set at 1,500 for the first five seats and several thousands for additional seats. Beginning with the 25th Congress (1960–61), the Congress representation for each country was no longer computed on the basis of the yield of the Shekel drive but was determined by a special commission according to the size of the Jewish population and the extent of Zionist activity in the country in question. Until the formation of the Keren ha-Yesod in 1920, the Shekel was the main source of income of the WZO.

The mode of Shekel distribution evolved as follows:

1898–1921. Shekalim were issued not by world headquarters but by each of the countries concerned, and were turned over to the local Zionist associations and societies for distribution among their members.

1921–25. Shekalim were printed by the Zionist executive in London, which then sent them to the *Zionist territorial organizations (ZTOs; federations) and to the *separate unions (SUs), which in turn distributed the Shekalim among their members.

1925–64 (the "Unified Shekel"). The Shekalim were printed and distributed by the Zionist Executive, which sent them to the various countries, where they were distributed by national Shekel boards, composed of representatives of all local Zionist groups and parties. In some countries and within some large Zionist organizations, a system of "automatic distribution" developed; that is, each individual belonging to an organization (e.g. Hadassah in the United States and the Histadrut in Palestine-Israel) automatically received the Shekel by virtue of his membership in the organizations, unless he had expressly opted out, so that part of his membership dues was allocated to payment of the Shekel.

Not only "organized" Zionists (members of ZTOs and SUs) but all individuals subscribing to the Zionist program printed on the Shekel receipt and to the "discipline clause" introduced after 1933 were eligible to purchase the Shekel. As a result, the total of Shekel payers (WZO members at large) was much greater than the total membership of the above-mentioned Zionist bodies, which in fact, carried on most of the ongoing Zionist activities.

During the first two decades of the Zionist movement the annual Shekel figures did not exceed 100,000. Following the issuance of the Balfour Declaration (1917), there was a sharp upswing: 778,000 Shekalim were sold in 1921. After a decline for some years, the 1921 record was surpassed in 1935, with 978,000 Shekalim. In 1939 the million mark was exceeded: 1,042,000 Shekalim were sold that year. The largest Shekel figure ever achieved was 2,148,000, in 1946. The latest-recorded figure (1964) was 2,148,000 of which 737,000 were from Israel and 1,044,000 from the United States.

At the beginning of the movement the amount to be paid for the Shekel was set at 1 Austrian crown, 1 German mark, 1 French franc, 2 shillings (Great Britain), half a ruble (Russia), and half a dollar (United States). The intent was to keep the price low in order to enable as many individuals as possible to acquire a Shekel. Neverthless, some elements within the movement opposed what they called a "paid franchise." The regulations for the implementation of the constitution of 1960 specified that the price of the Shekel be set independently by each country but that it should not be less than the equivalent of U.S.$0.15 or more than U.S.$0.50.

Since only Shekalim purchased during Congress years entitled the purchaser to a vote, the number of Shekalim sold during the years when no Congress was held was 50 and even 70 per cent below the Shekel purchases of Congress years. To achieve more constant Shekel proceeds, the 21st Congress (1939) made the right to vote dependent on the acquisition of a Shekel for each year between Zionist Congresses ("annual Shekel"). Under the constitution of 1960 only one Shekel drive was to be conducted before each Congress.

Beginning in the 1950s there was an increasing demand for the abolition of the Shekel. The system had been working quite well in most countries, particularly in the smaller and middle-sized countries, such as Switzerland and, especially, South Africa, where more than 50 per cent of the total Jewish population purchased Shekalim and Shekel Day was tantamount to a Jewish census of sorts. However, some abuses occurred: the Shekel drive, which formerly had entailed individual canvassing, became an impersonal transaction. Zionist parties purchased Shekalim en bloc to increase the number of seats allotted to the parties; the parties then distributed these Shekalim gratis or completed the Shekel forms with the help of a directory and never distributed the Shekalim at all. Moreover, the "membership Shekel" was frequently acquired automatically by individuals who had no conception of the aims of Zionism.

As a result, the proposal to abolish the Shekel met with little opposition and was carried out by the 27th Congress (1968). In Resolution 51 (incorporated in the constitution as article 19) it was specified that Congress delegates "should be elected according to a method consistent with generally accepted democratic principles." Thus, the Shekel as an obligatory and worldwide institution was, in effect, abolished because each country became free to choose Congress representation on a basis other than the Shekel. If a country wishes, it may introduce a Shekel of its own, but such a Shekel is optional and valid only within that country. However, very few countries have availed themselves of this option. A. ZWERGBAUM

SHELOMI. Development town in the Plain of Acre, close to the Lebanese border. Founded in 1950, Shelomi made little headway and remained one of the smallest of the development towns, partly because it could not compete with nearby Nahariya. Most inhabitants hailed from North Africa and Middle East countries. The number of social welfare cases was high and there were few industrial or other enterprises. Population (1987), 2,260. E. ORNI

SHERMAN, CHARLES BEZALEL. Labor Zionist theorist and sociologist (b. Kiev, Russia, 1896; d. New York City, 1971). He left for the United States in 1911 settling in Chicago. He moved to New York in 1936.

He was a member of Ha-Tehiya, a branch of the Knights of Zion, from 1912 to 1915 and then joined the Po'ale Zion party. After the party split in 1920, he joined the Left Po'ale Zion in 1923 and became its secretary-general, editor, and pamphleteer. With some interruptions, he was engaged in these activities until 1949, when he resigned and rejoined the Labor Zionist Organization of America-Po'ale Zion a year later. He was particularly involved in theoretical attempts to give Zionism generally, and Labor Zionism in particular, a grounding in the processes shaping American Jewish life.

The author of books, pamphlets, and numerous articles in Yiddish and English on Zionist issues, Sherman also wrote extensively on the sociology of the American Jew.

SHERTOK, MOSHE. *See* SHARETT, MOSHE.

SHIELD OF DAVID. *See* MAGEN DAVID.

SHIMONI (SHIMONOVITZ), DAVID. Hebrew poet (b. Bobruisk, Russia, 1886; d. Tel Aviv, 1956). Settling in Eretz Israel in 1909, Shimoni worked for a year as a farmhand and watchman in Jewish settlements. Later he studied at universities in Germany. With the outbreak of World War I, he returned to Russia where, after the Kerensky Revolution, he was secretary of the Hebrew newspaper *Ha-Am*. Returning to Palestine in 1920, he served as instructor in literature at the Herzliya High School in Tel Aviv.

Shimoni was a prolific poet. Although his first writings were individualistic and lyrical in style, his creative talents found their fullest expression in idylls portraying the life and experience of the pioneer and the many odds he faced on his return and adjustment to the land. Despite the difficulties they depict, Shimoni's earlier idylls ("In the Woods of Hadera," "The Jubilee of the Drivers," "Yardenit") are filled with optimism, cheerfulness, and humor. His later idylls ("The Movement," "Drops of the Night") portray the tragic results of the Arab riots, World War II, and the extermination of European Jewry.

He also wrote satirical verses, some political, directed against the administration of the British Mandate for Palestine. He translated into Hebrew works by Lermontov, Pushkin, Tolstoy, and Heine and was the recipient of the Israel Prize for 1954. Shimoni was chairman of the Israeli Authors Association, a member of the Academy of the Hebrew Language, and chairman of the Israeli Organization of Friends of the Hebrew University and a member of its Board of Trustees. H. LEAF

SHIN BET. (abbreviation for Sherut Bitahon Kelali, i.e., General Security Service). Institution responsible for the prevention of activities against the security of the State of Israel, planned or executed within its borders. This takes the form of intelligence gathering and of practical measures to forestall or prevent actions by hostile elements. The Shin Bet organizationally is responsible to the Prime Minister. In the wake of the Six-Day War which brought Judea, Samaria, and Gaza under Israel military government, its mission has been considerably broadened. The identity of the Head of the Shin Bet and of its functionaries is secret.

SHIPPING IN ISRAEL. *See* TRANSPORTATION IN ISRAEL.

Bekhor Shitrit.
[Israel Information Services]

SHITRIT, BEKHOR SHALOM. Israeli statesman (b. Tiberias, 1895; d. Jerusalem, 1967). Member of a Jewish family whose ancestors had come from Morocco to Eretz Israel in the 18th century, Shitrit was educated at the Alliance Israélite Universelle school in Tiberias and at a yeshiva. After teaching in the Alliance school system, he joined in 1919 the police force set up by the British Mandatory government and in 1927 became head of the Tel Aviv police. In 1930 he qualified as a lawyer, in 1935 was appointed a magistrate, and in 1945 became chief magistrate of Tel Aviv.

When the State of Israel was established, Shitrit was appointed Minister of Police and of Minorities, and from 1948 to 1966 he served as Minister of Police. In 1949 he was elected to the Knesset, where he remained a member until his death, representing the Mapai and (in 1966) Labor Alignment lists. He played an important role in establishing and organizing the police of Israel.

SHKOLNIK, LEVI. *See* ESHKOL, LEVI.

SHLONSKY, ABRAHAM DAVID. Hebrew author and translator (b. Krayukov, near Kremenchug, Ukraine, Russia, 1900; d. Tel Aviv, 1973). In 1921 Shlonsky settled in Palestine, where he worked as a laborer for several years. After a short stay in Paris, he returned to Palestine and joined (1925) the editorial board of *Davar*. Later he worked for *Ha-Aretz*.

Shlonsky began to write poetry at an early age. Some of his early verses reflected the experiences of the pioneers of the Third Aliya. He also wrote extensively on the evils of city life. A leading exponent of Hebrew modernism, he helped Eliezer Steinmann edit the Hebrew weekly *Ketuvim*, the modernists' main platform. In 1933 he established the literary periodical *Turim*. In 1939 he became attracted to Ha-Shomer ha-Tza'ir and from then on was closely identified with the left wing of the Labor Zionist movement. He served as editor of many of its literary publications and of Sifriyat Po'alim, the publishing house of Ha-Shomer ha-Tza'ir. He was also active in the international peace movement.

A prolific writer, Shlonsky published articles, essays, and poetry, including children's literature, much of which appeared in book form. He was a brilliant translator and rendered numerous books into Hebrew, including classic plays and novels, among them *Hamlet* by William Shakespeare and *Eugene Onegin* by Alexander Pushkin. His collected works *Kitvei Avraham Shlonsky* (5 vols) appeared in 1971.
E. SPICEHANDLER

SHOHAT. Family of pioneers in Eretz Israel.

Eliezer Shohat. Labor leader (b. Liskova, Grodno District, Russia, 1874; d. Nahalal, 1971). In the early 1900s Shohat was among the first members of Po'ale Zion in Grodno. In 1904, with his brother Israel, he settled in Eretz Israel, where he worked as an agricultural laborer in Petah Tikva and helped to found *Ha-Po'el ha-Tza'ir. Later he went to Lower Galilee to organize the Jewish workers in the Jewish settlements there and was a founder of Ha-Horesh (1907), a society of Jewish agricultural workers in Galilee.

Shohat was a delegate of Ha-Po'el ha-Tza'ir to the Eighth (1907) and 11th (1913) Zionist Congresses. He was among the first settlers of Merhavya. After the Arab attack on the settlement in May, 1911, he was one of those arrested by the Turkish authorities. For about a year, he was imprisoned in Nazareth and Acre.

His article "National Creation and Stock-Taking" (1910) was one of the classic essays of the Jewish labor movement in Eretz Israel. He was among the first to conceive the idea of Moshevei Ovedim (workers' smallholders settlements; *see* MOSHAV), and he helped found Nahalal. From the beginning of his communal activity he fought those who advocated the use of coercion in the internal political disputes of the yishuv. Though he was one of the founders of the Histadrut he did not agree to the union of Ha-Po'el ha-Tza'ir and Ahdut Avoda and joined Mapai only because he did not want to part from his friends. Thereafter he devoted himself to collecting and publishing the literature of the Palestine Jewish labor movement. He edited *Pirkei ha-Po'el ha-Tza'ir* (with Hayim Shurer, 13 vols., 1935–39) and *Sefer ha-Aliya ha-Sheniya* (with Berakha Habas, 1947), and he helped edit the writings of Eliezer Joffe (1947), Aharon David Gordon (1951-54), and Joseph Witkin (1961). *Bi-Netivei Avoda*, a collection of his important essays, appeared in 1967.

His brother, **Israel Shohat.** Lawyer, pioneer, and founder of Ha-Shomer (b. Liskova, Grodno District, Russia, 1886; d. Tel Aviv, 1961). Joining the Po'ale Zion movement in Russia soon after its founding, Shohat studied at a business college in Warsaw and at the Halle Agricultural Institute. In 1904 he settled in Eretz Israel, where he found employment as a day laborer in Petah Tikva. In 1907 he was one of the initiators of Bar Giora, a small group of recent arrivals from Russia who advocated that the protection of Jewish settlements be entrusted to Jewish watchmen. Two years later he organized and became the first leader of the Ha-Shomer defense organization. In 1910 he was one of the leaders of the newly founded Legion ha-Avoda (Legion of Labor), which organized laborers for contractual work in agriculture.

In 1911 he moved to Haifa, where he organized the construction of the Technion and a number of other buildings and settlement projects. A year later, with Itzhak Ben-Zvi and David Ben-Gurion, he went to Constantinople to study law. Upon the outbreak of World War I he proposed to the Turkish military authorities the formation of a Jewish-Arab civilian militia. The Turks, who suspected him of Jewish nationalist motives, exiled him and his wife, Manya Wilbuschewitz Shohat, to Anatolia. In 1917 Shohat was allowed to go to Stockholm, to attend a Socialist conference. After the war he returned to Palestine and worked in Kibbutz Kefar Giladi.

Shohat attended several Zionist Congresses and participated in the founding convention of the Po'ale Zion World Movement in the Hague and in the London Zionist Conference of 1920. The same year he opened a law practice but continued to be active in the Histadrut and in community affairs. From 1921 until 1926 Shohat served on the Va'ad Le'umi. Y. SLUTSKY

Manya Wilbuschewitz Shohat. Pioneer of the Second Aliya and leader in the Eretz Israel labor and self-defense movements, wife of Israel Shohat (b. near Grodno, Russia, 1880; d. Tel Aviv, 1961). Reared in a well-to-do family that was among the earliest adherents of the Hovevei Zion movement, she became active in the Russian revolutionary movement. Later she organized a legal, nonrevolutionary workers' party. She settled in Eretz Israel in 1904, joining her three brothers, who had gone there before her. During a visit to Paris, she obtained funds from Baron Edmond de Rothschild for Jewish self-defense in Russia, and participated in smuggling arms there. Returning to Eretz Israel she began to promote the settlement of Jewish pioneers in the Golan region. To raise funds for this purpose and for Jewish self-defense she went abroad again in 1907, this time to the United States, but succeeded in obtaining money only for the self-defense efforts of the Jews in Russia, who were under the constant threat of pogroms.

After marrying Israel Shohat, she settled in Sejera, in Lower Galilee. She participated with her husband in founding Ha-Shomer. During World War I the couple was deported by the Turks, first to Damascus and then to Anatolia. After their return they settled in Kefar Giladi. In 1921, with Yosef Baratz and Berl Katznelson, she went to the United States on behalf of the newly founded Histadrut and in the 1920s and 1930s was prominently active in the Hagana. After the 1929 Arab riots she helped found the League of Jewish-Arab Rapprochement. After the issuance of the White Paper of 1939, she conceived a plan for bringing "illegal" immigrants to Palestine, traveling abroad several times for that purpose. Manya Shohat spent the last years of her life in encouraging and assisting new immigrants in ma'abarot (transit camps).

SHOLEM ALEICHEM (Sholom Rabinowitz). Yiddish novelist and humorist (b. Ukraine, Russia, 1859; d. New York, 1916). His first stories describing Jewish life in the small towns of eastern Europe appeared in 1883. Later he also wrote of the life of Jewish immigrants in the United States, which he visited several times and where he spent his last years.

Although he did not believe that the Jewish masses would take practical action in behalf of building the Jewish Homeland, Sholem Aleichem supported the Hibbat Zion movement and its projects in Russia, and in 1888 he formally joined the movement. The following year he helped found an Eretz Israel settlement society in Kiev, and in 1890 he participated in the foundation of the Odessa Committee, the Society for the Support of Jewish Agriculturists and Artisans in Eretz Israel and Syria. That same year his Zionist story *Zelig Mekhanik* appeared.

Sholem Aleichem
[Zionist Archives]

Deeply impressed by Herzl, Sholem Aleichem wrote two Zionist pamphlets in Yiddish (1898), *Auf was Bedarfen Yidn a Land?* (Why Do the Jews Need a Homeland?) and *Zu Unzere Shvester in Zion* (To Our Sisters in Zion), as well as a Zionist novel, *Meshiah's Zeiten* (The Days of the Messiah). In 1904 Sholem Aleichem wrote a biography of Herzl in Yiddish. His Zionist play *David Ben-David* was published in 1959 by his son-in-law, I.D. Berkowitz. G. KRESSEL

SHOMER. *See* HA-SHOMER.

SHOMER DATI. *See* BNEI AKIVA.

SHOMER TZA'IR. *See* HA-SHOMER HA-TZA'IR.

SHOVAL. Kibbutz in the northern Negev, 16 mi. (25 km.) northwest of Beersheba. It was founded by youth from South Africa and Palestine on 6 October 1946, as one of the 11 outposts set up in the same night. The kibbutz pioneered in Negev-type land reclamation and established friendly relations with Bedouin of the vicinity, later developing farming and an industrial enterprise. Population (1987), 569. E. ORNI

SHRAGAI, SHELOMO ZALMAN. Religious Zionist leader and Israeli public official (b. Gorzkowice, Russian Poland, 1899). The son of a hasidic family that early embraced the Zionist cause, Shragai was a founder of the Tze'irei Mizrachi (Mizrachi Youth) movement in Poland, which later gave rise to Ha-Po'el ha-Mizrachi. He also founded the first hakhshara (agricultural training camp) for religious pioneers in Czestochowa. A member of the Central Committee of the Mizrachi World Organization and of the Executive of Ha-Po'el ha-Mizrachi, he represented the latter at every Zionist Congress beginning with the 15th (1927) and on the Zionist Actions Committee.

In 1924 he settled in Palestine. In 1929 he was elected to the Va'ad Le'umi and later served as head of its Department of Press and Information. In 1946 he was elected to the London Executive of the Jewish Agency. In this position, which he held until 1948, he was entrusted with the task of making contact with non-Jewish religious organizations in England to win them to the Zionist cause.

After the adoption of the United Nations partition resolution (November, 1947), he was sent to Poland to obtain the support of the Polish government for the establishment of the Jewish State.

In 1951 Shragai was elected mayor of Jerusalem, but resigned in 1952. In 1954 he became a member of the World Zionist Executive and head of the Aliya Department of the Jewish Agency, a position he held until early in 1967.

An outstanding exponent of the ideology of *Torah va-Avoda (Torah and Labor), Shragai wrote several books, among them *Tehumim* (1951), *Hazon ve-Hagshama* (1956), and *Pa'amei Ge'ula* (1962–63). D. TELSNER

SHULMAN, MAX. Attorney and Zionist leader (b. Libau, Latvia, 1885; d. Chicago, 1937). Brought to the United States in 1897, Shulman received a thorough Jewish education, remaining strictly Orthodox in his religious beliefs throughout his life. At the turn of the century he was one of the three young men who organized in Chicago the Herzl Literary Club, which aimed to spread Zionism among American Jewish youth. Graduating from the John Marshall Law School in Chicago in 1905, he established a law practice and devoted himself to Zionist activities. At various times over a period of 30 years he was president of the Chicago Zionist Organization, representing it at the 11th Zionist Congress (1913). In 1921 he resigned from the presidency to devote himself to the Jewish National Fund and the Keren ha-Yesod. In the late 1920s he served a term as vice-president of the Zionist Organization of America.

Active also in Jewish religious and communal work, Shulman helped found the Hebrew Theological College in Chicago and for many years was secretary of the city's United Jewish Charities.

SHULMAN, REBECCA BILDNER. Communal worker and leader in *Hadassah (b. Snyatyn, Galicia, Austria, 1896). Taken to the United States in 1899, she attended Hunter College in New York City. After holding almost every chairmanship in Hadassah, she served as national president of the organization from 1953 to 1956. She attended nearly every Zionist Congress from the 16th (1929) on. Mrs Shulman represented Hadassah in Israel during two wars: the War of Independence, when she remained in Israel for nine months, and during the Six-Day War of 1967. She was among the first to visit Mount Scopus, within 24 hours after its liberation in 1967. M. LEVIN

SICK FUND. *See* KUPAT HOLIM.

SIDEBOTHAM, HERBERT. British journalist and Christian Zionist (b. Manchester, England, 1872; d. Roehampton, England, 1940). Sidebotham, a member of the editorial staff of the *Manchester Guardian*, and Charles P. *Scott, the editor, who first met Chaim Weizmann in September, 1914, were devoted friends of Zionism. Sidebotham considered Palestine a matter of mutual interest to the Jewish people and Great Britain. An editorial, his first important article, on Palestine, appeared in November, 1915. He was a cofounder of the British Palestine Committee and the editor of its magazine *Palestine*, which sought to acquaint British readers with Zionist affairs. "The first object of any political settlement of Palestine must be the establishment of a State whose civilization shall be predominantly Jewish, and its ultimate goal self-government," Sidebotham stated (*England and Palestine*, London, 1918). In his article "The Future of Palestine," published in 1922, he wrote: "The Jewish interest in Palestine is not merely that of the Jews who are at the moment actually present there; it is the interest of the entire body of Jews throughout the world." Years later, especially in his *Britain and Palestine* (1937), he sharply criticized the British government for its failure to implement the Balfour Declaration.

Sidebotham wrote editorials for the London *Times* and published articles under the name Scrutator in the *Sunday Times* and under the name Candidus in the *Daily Sketch*. J. LEFTWICH

SIEFF. Family of industrialists, philanthropists, and Zionists in Great Britain.

Israel Moses Sieff: Baron Sieff of Brimpton (b. Manchester England, 1889; d. London, 1970), was the son of an immigrant from Lithuania. He took a degree in commerce and economics at the University of Manchester and entered business, eventually becoming chairman of the board of Marks and Spencer, Ltd., one of the largest chain stores in Great Britain. He and his wife, Rebecca, were introduced to Zionism shortly before World War I by Chaim Weizmann, who was then a lecturer in chemistry at the University of Manchester. During the war Sieff was a member of the political committee set up in London to conduct Zionist work. After the war he went to Palestine as honorary secretary of the Zionist Commission. As a member of the Board of Directors of Keren ha-Yesod, he was largely responsible for a series of loans given to the Fund by Lloyds Bank of London between the two world wars.

The Sieff family made impressive contributions to the Joint Palestine Appeal and to numerous Zionist causes. In 1934 Sieff and his wife established the Sieff Research Institute in Rehovot (*see* WEIZMANN INSTITUTE OF SCIENCE) in memory of their son Daniel, who had died the year before. In 1966 Sieff was created a baron (life peer). He served as honorary president of the British Zionist Federation and of the Joint Palestine Appeal, president of the Anglo-Israel Chamber of Commerce, and chairman of the European Executive of the World Jewish Congress. His memoirs appeared in 1970.

Rebecca Doro Marks Sieff: his wife, founder of *WIZO (Women's International Zionist Organization) (b. Leeds, England, 1890; d. Tel Aviv, 1966). A sister of Simon *Marks, she was educated at the University of Manchester. Together with Israel Moses Sieff, whom she married in 1910, she joined the Zionist movement shortly before World War I. She was a founder (1918) and the first president of the Federation of Women Zionists of Great Britain and Ireland. In 1920 she founded the Women's International Zionist Organization (WIZO), on whose behalf she traveled extensively in Europe, South Africa, Australia, and North Amer-

Israel Sieff (right) and his brother-in-law, Simon Marks. [Beth Hatefutsoth]

ica and of which she was honorary president at the time of her death.

As chairperson of the Women's Appeal Committee of the Central British Fund for German Jewry, she helped in the work of rescue and rehabilitation of victims of Nazism and, in 1938, was instrumental in bringing 1,000 Jewish children from Germany to England. After World War II she visited displaced-persons camps to assist survivors of the Holocaust. She made her home in Tel Mond, Palestine (Israel).

E.S. FRANKEL

Joseph Edward Sieff: younger brother of Israel Moses Sieff (b. Salford, England, 1905; d. London, 1982). He joined the family business, Marks and Spencer in 1933, becoming vice-chairman and joint managing director in 1963, chairman 1967–72, president 1972–79, and thereafter honorary president.

He was an active Zionist, preferring to work behind the scenes. He was connected with the Joint Palestine Appeal (later the Joint Israel Appeal) from its inception and served as chairman of its administration committee from 1951–65 when he was elected president. In December, 1973, he narrowly escaped death when a terrorist forced his way into his London home and shot him in the jaw. Subsequently he became president of the Zionist Federation of Great Britain and Ireland, having served since 1965 as vice-president.

Marcus Joseph Sieff: son of Israel Moses Sieff (b. Salford, England, 1913) Second Baron Sieff. He joined the family business in 1935. During World War II he served in the Royal Artillery. He became vice-chairman of Marks and Spencer in 1965, chairman 1972–1984, president 1984–1985, and honorary president in 1985.

Deeply involved in Zionist activities, he was chairman of the Export Committee for Israel (1965–1968), President of the Anglo-Israel Chamber of Commerce from 1975, Honorary President of the Joint Israel Appeal from 1984, and was chairman of the First International Bank of Israel Financial Trust Ltd. from 1983. His memoirs—*Don't Ask the Price*—appeared in 1986.

E. HOTER

SILBERG, MOSHE. Israeli jurist (b. Skaudvile, Lithuania, 1900; d. Jerusalem, 1975). After studying at yeshivot in eastern Europe, Silberg studied law at German universities. He was active in the Zionist movement in Germany and directed the Hebrew-language evening school established by the Zionists in Frankfurt on Main. In 1929 he settled in Palestine, where he taught Talmud at the Tahkemoni High School in Tel Aviv and later practiced law. In 1948 he was appointed district court judge in Tel Aviv and some time later became a justice in Israel's Supreme Court. In 1965 he was appointed Deputy President of the Supreme Court, from which he retired in 1975.

Silberg, who was a visiting professor of the law of personal status at the Hebrew University of Jerusalem, wrote numerous articles on legal, philosophical, and general subjects and was the author of the Hebrew books *Personal Status in Israel* (1957; awarded the Bialik Prize) and *Principia Talmudica* (1961). In 1969 he received the Israel Prize.

Abba Hillel Silver. [Zionist Archives]

SILVER, ABBA HILLEL. American rabbi and Zionist leader (b. Neustadt, now Kudirkos-Naumiestis, Lithuania, 1893; d. Cleveland, 1963). Silver was taken to the USA in 1902. His father, Moses, a Hebrew teacher and an ordained rabbi, instilled a love of Jewish learning and Zionism in his children.

The Herzl Zion Club, a Hebrew-speaking Zionist boy's club which was the first of its kind in the US, was created under Moses Silver's tutelage and held its first meetings in 1904 in the Silver home on the lower east side of New York. Moses' eldest son, Maxwell, was the group's first president and Abba Hillel succeeded his brother a year later. Silver began his involvement in the American Zionist movement as a youth, when he outspokenly represented the Herzl Zion Club at a convention of the Federation of American Zionists.

Though himself a product of Orthodox education and upbringing, Silver enrolled in the rabbinical program of the Hebrew Union College in Cincinnati. Apart from his spiritual identification with Reform Judaism, Silver considered it a challenge to try to change the Reform movement's fervent anti-Zionist position. He was ordained in 1915 and graduated the same year from the University of Cincinnati. He later received doctoral degrees from the Hebrew Union College (1925) and Western Reserve University (1928).

Silver's first pulpit was in Wheeling, West Virginia, in 1915. In 1917, he was appointed rabbi of the prominent and influential Congregation Tifereth Israel in Cleveland, known as The Temple, where he served until his death. Throughout his career, he vociferously advocated liberal and social causes, emphasized the necessity of an intensive Jewish and Hebrew education, and continuously stressed the importance of Zionism in Judaism and in American Jewish life. Silver attended the 1920 London Zionist Conference where, like most of the American delegates, he supported Justice Louis D. Brandeis in his controversy with Chaim Weizmann. Later Silver accepted Weizmann's leadership while sometimes strongly differing with him on policy. In 1937, when Weizmann favored consideration of the Peel Commission's plan to partition Palestine, Silver expressed strong opposition. Between the two world wars Silver represented the American Zionist Movement at numerous Zionist Congresses. He was a founder and cochairman (1938–1944) of the United Jewish Appeal and president (1938–1943) of the United Palestine Appeal.

Silver exerted strong leadership in the American Zionist movement during the crucial years of World War II and its aftermath. Unlike other American Zionist leaders, he advocated the energetic pursuit of public opinion and the firm utilization of political pressure to achieve Zionist aims. A dynamic personality as well as a brilliant orator, Silver helped mobilize American and Jewish public opinion for the creation of a Jewish state. In an address before the National Conference of the United Palestine Appeal (2 May 1943), he became the first responsible Zionist leader to attack publicly the position of President Franklin D. Roosevelt and the State Department on the issue of Palestine. Silver was named chairman of the American Zionist Emergency Council in 1943. That year his speech before the American Jewish Conference contributed to the latter's adoption of a resolution endorsing the Zionist demand for a Jewish Commonwealth. Even after Roosevelt's reelection in 1944, Silver persisted in his attempt to obtain passage of the Palestine resolution in the US Congress against the continued opposition of the Roosevelt administration. As a result of his unyielding position, he was forced to resign from the Emergency Council by the faction headed by Stephen S. Wise, who felt that it was not proper for the Jews to press for special measures during wartime. After the revelation of Roosevelt's correspondence with King Ibn Saud, Silver's activist views were vindicated and he was recalled to the chairmanship, serving until 1948. He played an important role in the reorganization of the council, placing it on an entirely new footing, with adequate budget and staff.

Silver's leadership ushered in a new era in American Zionism, the era of political activism. He vigorously opposed those Zionists whom he considered overly cautious in the use of political action to influence the United States Government and public opinion on behalf of Zionist aims. Under Silver the American Zionist Emergency Council won overwhelming public support for the Zionist cause and the endorsement of Jewish statehood by both the Democratic and the Republican parties. Unlike most American Jewish leaders, Silver was a Republican and he gained the friendship of powerful Republican figures such as US Senator Robert A. Taft, Governor Thomas E. Dewey, and later of President Dwight D. Eisenhower, as well as that of Democratic figures.

Silver was president of the Zionist Organization of America (ZOA) from 1945 to 1947 and honorary president until his death. As a chairman of the American Section of the Jewish Agency (1946-1948), he was responsible for planning the strategy to be followed by the Zionist movement in its relations with the government of the United States and with the United Nations. During the final struggle for Jewish statehood he opposed cooperation with the Anglo-American Committee of Inquiry, which he considered a stalling device on the part of the British and US governments. During the summer of 1946 he opposed the idea that the Jewish Agency take the initiative in discussions with the British by advancing proposals for the partition of Palestine. The Agency, he felt, should not deal with the question unless or until it were proposed by a government. In protest against such a move, which he considered a political and tactical blunder, he resigned from the Jewish Agency Executive, but his policy was upheld by the 22nd Zionist Congress (1946), and he remained in office. Silver's subsequent conversation with British Foreign Secretary Ernest Bevin convinced him that the latter had no intention of consenting to the creation of a Jewish state in any part of Palestine, and that the British proposal for a Round Table Conference was merely another stalling tactic.

When the Palestine problem was finally brought before the United Nations, Silver was the Agency's representative and leading spokesman in the debates that led to the UN resolution on 29 November 1947 approving the partition of Palestine and the establishment of a Jewish state. When in March, 1948, the US State Department withdrew its support for the partition resolution and called for a temporary UN trusteeship, Silver announced before the UN Security Council that the establishment of the Jewish state would take place as scheduled on 15 May. Knowing that a Security Council session scheduled for 11 a.m., Friday, 14 May, was designed to postpone implementation of the partition resolution, Silver and his colleagues asked the Jewish leaders in Palestine to announce the declaration of the Jewish state one hour earlier, that is, at 10 a.m. New York time (or 4 p.m. Israel time). At the opening of the session, Silver announced to the Security Council that the State of Israel had already been declared.

After the establishment of Israel, Silver's leadership of the Zionist movement in the United States was successfully challenged by a combination of non-Zionists and backers of Ben-Gurion's Mapai Party. The United Palestine Appeal (UPA), of which Silver was the most powerful figure, had now assumed new importance as a source of foreign currency for the State of Israel. Silver's attempt to retain the Zionist Organization of America's traditional dominance of the UPA was thwarted by UPA executive director Henry Montor, who sought to expand the appeal's financial base by including non-Zionist leaders in policy decisions. Montor's position was backed by Mapai supporters, who wished to diminish the UPA's dependence on the ZOA, which supported Israel's oppositionist General Zionist Party. In an action made possible by a special meeting of the Jewish Agency Executive, Montor was ultimately established by United Jewish Appeal (UJA) Chairman Henry Morgenthau, Jr., as chief executive officer of the UJA on behalf of the UPA. Montor's victory was unacceptable to Silver, and he resigned his chairmanship of the American Section of the Jewish Agency Executive in early 1949. Silver's resignation was regarded as a victory for the supporters of Ben-Gurion, who had regarded Silver as a strong political contender and as a symbol of unwelcome Diaspora influence on the State of Israel. Many of Silver's followers, for their part, regarded his defeat as a cynical political maneuver which deprived Silver of his rightful leadership, as soon as he was no longer needed.

Subsequently, Silver was chairman of the Board of Governors of the State of Israel Bonds Organization. He was also a director of the American Society for the Technion-Israel Institute of Technology, Inc., and a member of Technion's Board of Governors. In addition, he was on the Board of Directors of the American Friends of the Hebrew University, served as a governor of the university, and at one point was offered the presidency of the university. In 1951 he was honored by the General Zionists with the establishment of Kefar Silver, an agricultural training institute near Ashkelon.

A leading figure in the American Jewish Reform Movement, Silver served as president of the Central Conference of American Rabbis from 1945 to 1947. He was the author of a number of scholarly works dealing with the philosophy of Judaism and its relation to the modern world.

G. HIRSCHLER—B. MARINBACH

SIMON, ERNST AKIVA. Educator (b. Berlin, 1899; d. Jerusalem, 1988). Educated at the Universities of Berlin, Frankfurt, and Heidelberg (Ph.D., 1923), Simon early came under the influence of Nehemia Anton Nobel, Martin Buber, and Franz Rosenzweig, became active in the Jüdisches Lehraus in Frankfurt (founded by Rosenzweig), and with Buber edited the monthly *Der Jude* (1923–28). In 1928 he settled in Palestine, where he taught at the Mizrachi Teachers' Seminary in Jerusalem (1928) and the Reali High School in Haifa (from 1930). Shortly after Hitler's rise to power he returned to Germany as an instructor for Jewish teachers and youth leaders preparing for immigration to Palestine. Upon his return to Palestine, he joined the staff of the Hebrew Teachers' Seminary in Jerusalem (1936) and acted as educational adviser to Youth Aliya. From 1939 until his retirement in 1968 he was on the faculty of the Hebrew University of Jerusalem, becoming professor of education in 1955 and codirector of the School of Education in 1965.

An advocate of close Jewish-Arab cooperation and of a binational state in Palestine, Simon was honorary secretary of *Berit Shalom (1928–32) and a member of the Board of Directors of *Ihud, editing *Be'ayot*, the Ihud monthly (1945–47). In 1967 he received the Israel Prize for education. His major publications include *Ranke und Hegel* (1928); *The Teaching of Pestalozzi* (1953; Hebrew); *The Demarcation Line—Nationalism, Zionism and the Jewish-Arab Conflict in Buber's Thought & Practice* (Hebrew, 1973); *Are We Still Jews?*—Essays (Heb. 1982); *The Right to Educate, The Obligation to Educate* (Heb. 1983); and *Chapters in My Life; Building Up in the Time of Destruction* (Heb.; 1986).

SIMON, JULIUS. Economist and Zionist (b. Mannheim, Germany, 1875; d. New York, 1969). Drawn to Zionism through contact with Herzl and his associates, Simon was active in the World Zionist Organization, the Jewish National Fund, and the Jewish Colonial Trust before World War I. In 1913 he was a member of a Zionist mission that studied the situation of the Jewish settlements in Eretz Israel. During the war he lived in the Netherlands, but in 1920 he moved to England where, until 1921, he was a member of the World Zionist Executive.

Simon belonged to the group that rallied around Justice Louis D. Brandeis. In 1920 he visited Palestine again as a member of a special three-man commission (the other members were Nehemia de Lieme and Robert Szold) and prepared a report recommending reorganization of the work of the Zionist Organization in Palestine. In 1922 he took up residence in New York, where he became a partner in a brokerage firm and served as director of the Palestine Cooperative Company until 1926, when he became one of the founders of the Palestine Economic Corporation (PEC). In 1928–29 he was vice-president of PEC, and in 1930 he became president, holding that office until 1955. He was president emeritus and a member of the PEC administrative board until his death.

In 1934 Simon went to Palestine to take charge of PEC operations there, remaining through World War II. He played a prominent part in the development of the Dead Sea Works Company, serving on the board of directors of Palestine Potash, Ltd. He also served on the boards of the Central Bank of Cooperative Institutions in Palestine, Ltd., the Palestine Mortgage and Credit Bank, Ltd., and Palestine Hotels, Ltd.

SIMON, SIR LEON. British civil servant and Zionist (b. Southampton, England, 1881; d. London, 1965). Simon served as Director of Telegraphs and Telephones of the General Post Office (1931) and of National Savings (1935). He was a disciple of Ahad Ha'Am, whose biography he wrote (*Ahad Ha'Am*, 1960) and whose works he translated into English.

One of the early British Zionists, Simon was responsible for much early Zionist propaganda and was the first honorary secretary of the London Zionist League. In 1909, with Harry Sacher, he edited the *Zionist Banner*; with Sacher and Albert Hyamson, he was one of the editors of *Zionism and the Jewish Future* (1916). He went to Palestine in 1918 as a member of the Zionist Commission.

A leading exponent of cultural Zionism and of the Hebrew language and culture, Simon took an active interest in the Hebrew University of Jerusalem. He was knighted in 1944. After his retirement from the British civil service (1946), he settled in Jerusalem, where he served as chairman of the Executive Council (1946–49) and chairman of the Board of Governors of the Hebrew University (1949–50). In 1951 he received the Tschernichowsky Award for his Hebrew translation of Plato's *Dialogues*.

J. FRAENKEL

SINAI. Peninsula and land bridge between Asia and Africa, with a surface area of 23,000 square miles. No part of Sinai receives rainfall in amounts sufficient for agriculture, and the southern portion is extremely arid. Sinai consists of two entirely different regions, the peninsula and the continental bridge.

Sinai Peninsula. The peninsula part of Sinai is a triangle, bounded by the Gulf of Suez in the west and the Gulf of Eilat (Akaba) in the east. Its core is a steeply dissected granitic massif which reaches its peak in Gebel Musa (7,496 feet). Because of the identification of this peak with Biblical Mount Sinai, one of the earliest Christian monasteries was erected at the foot of the mountain. Near it lies Feiran, the only oasis of the area. The generally impassable massif is bounded in the north by a narrow sandstone plateau, on whose western edge are found the manganese mines of Umm Bugma. Rising from its northern margin is the almost perpendicular wall of the limestone plateaus of Egma and Tih (5,341 feet); the upper edge of the scarp encloses in the form of a half circle the drainage basin of Wadi el-Arish, which collects the runoff from more than half of Sinai. Both plateaus slope toward the center of Sinai, which resembles the inside of a bowl. All the mountainous parts of the peninsula form a maze of cliffs and scarps, dissected by canyons and steep valleys; they are completely roadless. Except for a few monks in the monastery and the few inhabitants of Feiran, the area is uninhabited.

The mountains reach the east coast of the peninsula along its total length, leaving no coastal plain or even room for a coastal road. Only near the southern extremity does the coast widen at the promontory of Ras Nazrani, which forms the small cove of Sharm el-Sheikh, opposite the island of Tiran. This place was fortified by Egypt until 1956 to blockade the entrance to the Gulf of Eilat. The blockade brought about the *Sinai Campaign of 1956 and the *Six-day War of 1967.

The west coast consists of a wider plain, which carries the road from Suez to Sharm el-Sheikh. Here lies the small town of Et-Tur, which was an important harbor in medieval times and since the 19th century served as a quarantine station for Muslim pilgrims returning from Mecca. Farther north there are oilfields.

Continental Bridge. This region is mainly a low plateau, bounded by the Mediterranean on the north and by the foot of the Tih plateau on the south, along which runs the historic route from Suez to Eilat. It consists of wide expanses of gravel, through which the tributaries of Wadi el-Arish have created wide, sandy riverbeds. The low northern margin is covered by a belt of sand dunes, which in some places attains a width of 30 miles. The center is crossed by two rows of folded limestone ridges, which form a direct continuation of the folded mountains of the Negev. Along the gaps between the ridges and along the coast run important historic routes (now turned into surfaced roads), which facilitated easy communication between Asia and Africa throughout the centuries and formed the main lines of advance during the wars of the 20th century.

The low coast is separated from the Mediterranean by a sand spit which encloses the saline lagoon of Bardawil. It runs from the lagoon of Port Said almost to El-Arish and prevents any use of the coast for harbors. This spit is regarded by many archeologists as the road of the Biblical

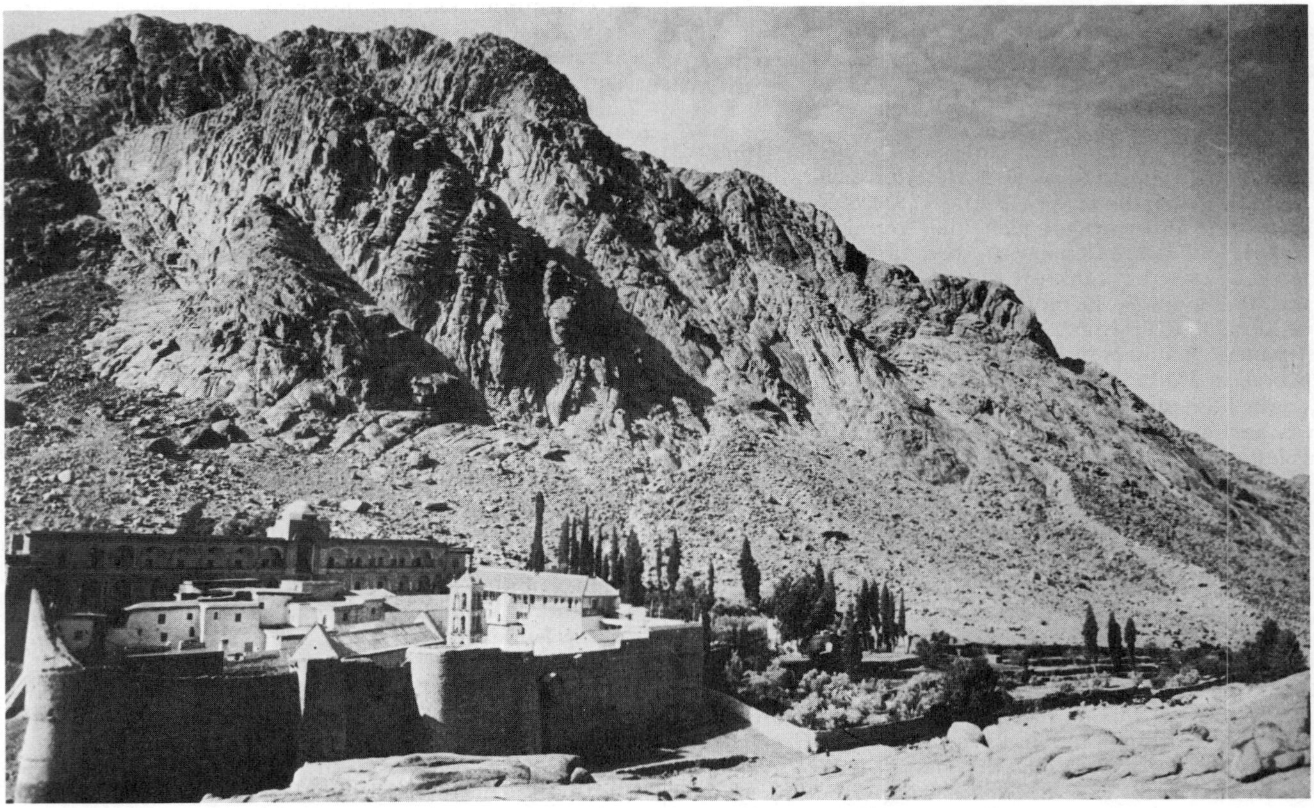

St. Catherine's Monastery, Mount Sinai. [Israel Information Services]

Exodus. The only settlement in the whole region was El-Arish, which utilizes the floodwaters of Wadi el-Arish, reaching the sea near the town, and underground water for extensive palm groves. El-Arish serves also as the Egyptian administrative center; it has about 25,000 inhabitants.

History. In the 19th century, Sinai was regarded as a borderland between Egypt and Turkey, but no boundary was fixed. The town of El-Arish was administered by Turkey, which also claimed half of Sinai, either its northern part or the area bounded by a line from El-Arish to the southern edge of that peninsula. In 1906 Britain forced Turkey to retreat to the line, which later was to form the boundary of the Mandate for Palestine and which, for most of its length, became the armistice boundary of Israel in 1948. In 1903 a delegation dispatched by the Zionist Congress visited El-Arish to study the possibility of Jewish settlement in northern Sinai (*see* EL-ARISH SCHEME).

Sinai was occupied by Israel in 1956–57. After its return to Egypt it served as a major concentration area of Egyptian forces. It was again occupied by Israel after the Six-day War of 1967 and returned in the framework of the peace agreement with Egypt. Y. KARMON

SINAI CAMPAIGN. Israeli military operation against Egypt from 29 October to 5 November 1956, undertaken to eliminate the marauder bases in the Gaza Strip and to thwart Egyptian plans for an all-out attack in Israel.

Background to Conflict. The armistice agreements signed by Israel and its immediate Arab neighbors in 1949 did not result in a transition to peace, as had been hoped and, indeed, intended by the authors of the United Nations resolution calling for their negotiation. On the contrary, secured by these agreements against the prospect of further military defeats, the Arabs gradually stiffened in their attitude toward Israel. A blockade of Israeli ships and of trade to and from Israel through the Suez Canal and the Gulf of Eilat (Akaba) was maintained on the ground that the Arab nations were still in a state of war with Israel. An economic boycott was initiated, and companies trading with Israel were named on blacklists prepared by the Central Boycott Office.

Tension increased following the Eygptian-Czechoslovakian arms deal of October, 1955, which resulted in a continuous flow of cheap and modern armaments into Egypt, in addition to the considerable amounts supplied to Arab countries by western powers. Meanwhile, there was active warfare on Israel's frontiers. Fedayeen, irregular commando troops, engaged in raids across the border directed exclusively against civilians, and although only a few men, women, and children were killed or wounded in any one incident, morale was ominously undermined in

Israeli warship in the Strait of Tiran. [Israel Information Services]

Israeli motor column advancing toward Nakhl. [Israel Information Services]

certain frontier settlements of recent immigrants. The fedayeen were organized, trained, and paid by the Egyptian Army. Their main headquarters were at Khan Yunis in the Gaza Strip, but beginning in 1955 they were operating also from bases in Syria and Jordan.

Until the summer of 1955 Egypt denied responsibility for the fedayeen raids, but on 26 August it acknowledged them officially, acclaiming the fedayeen as national heroes. Reprisal raids undertaken by Israel from time to time against military targets across its frontiers failed to put a stop to these raids. On 24 October 1956, a unified command of Arab states under an Egyptian general was established. The aim stated in a training directive issued by the commander of an Egyptian division in February, 1956, was: "Every officer must prepare himself and his subordinates for the inevitable struggle with Israel with the object of realizing our noble aim namely, the annihilation of Israel and her destruction in the shortest possible time and in the most brutal and cruel of battles."

At the same time Egypt was involved in a major crisis resulting from the nationalization of the Suez Canal in July, 1956. France and Great Britain, having failed to achieve their purpose of international control of that waterway by diplomatic means, had made preparations to seize it by force. Secret negotiations, culminating in a conference at Sèvres, near Paris, on 22 October 1956—with the participation of David Ben-Gurion, Guy Mollet, the French Premier, and Selwyn Lloyd, the British Foreign Secretary, resulted in an agreement under which an Israel operation would be followed by an ultimatum by Great Britain and France to both Egypt and Israel to withdraw 10 miles (15 km.) from the Canal. Once—as expected—Egypt would reject that ultimatum, British and French land, air, and naval forces would initiate a military operation against Egypt (Operation Musketeer). During the first crucial days, when Israel would be fighting alone, certain elements of the French air forces were to be stationed in Israel, to assist in defense against Egyptian bombing attacks, and naval units were to be ready to assist in naval defense. In the event, these forces were not called upon to act.

Operation. The Sinai operation, also known by its code name Kadesh, achieved its objectives within 100 hours. Most of Egypt's ground forces, consisting of about 10 brigades numbering 45,000 men, were located east of the Suez Canal, with the main concentration in the Gaza Strip and the triangle area of Rafa, Abu Ageila, El-Arish, lying astride the two major approaches from the north into Egypt, the desert, and the coastal road. In its plan of operation, Israel's General Staff had to take into consideration the possibility of simultaneous fighting on the Jordanian, Syrian, and

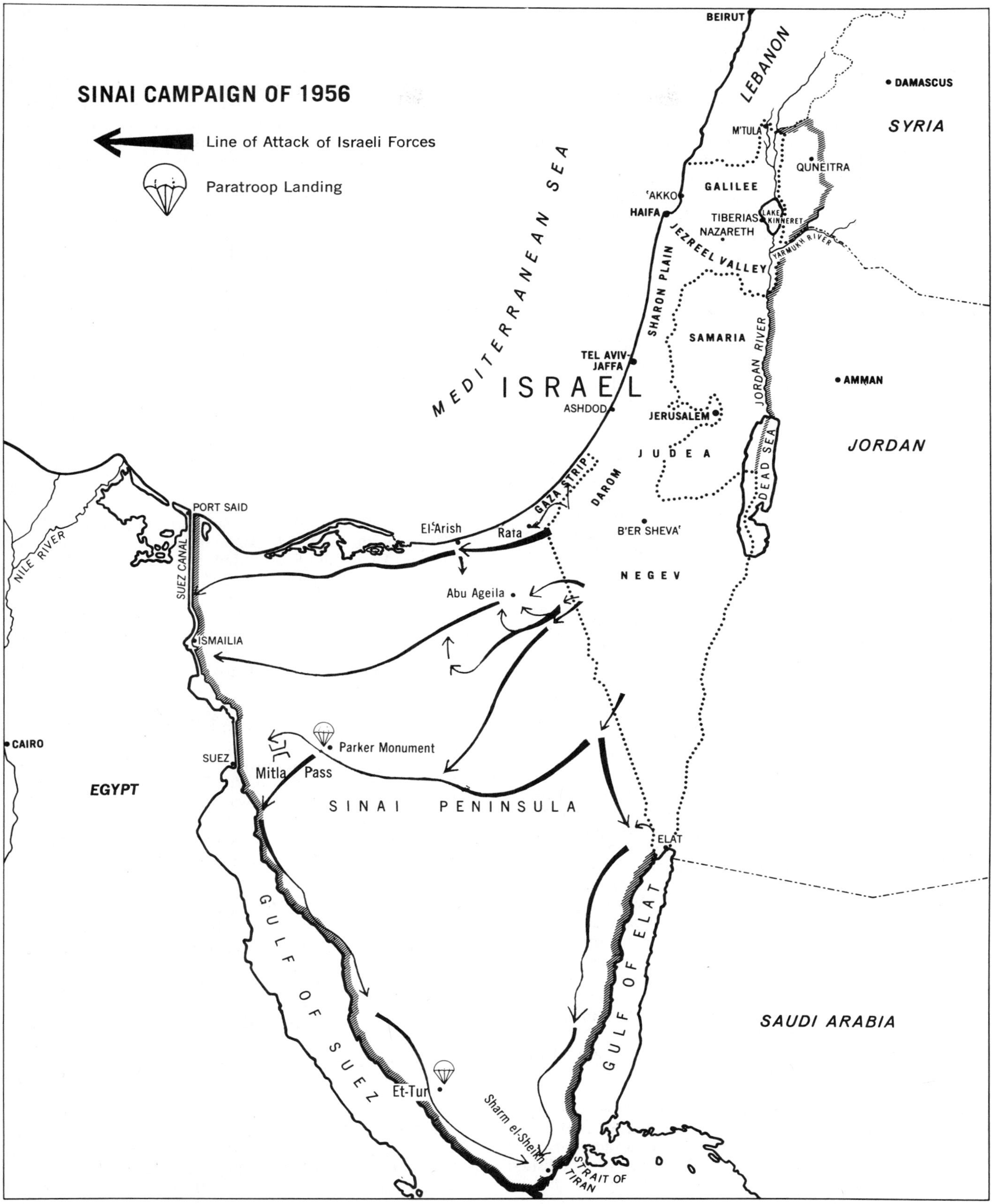
SINAI CAMPAIGN OF 1956
Line of Attack of Israeli Forces
Paratroop Landing
BEIRUT
LEBANON
DAMASCUS
SYRIA
M'TULA
QUNEITRA
MEDITERRANEAN SEA
'AKKO
GALILEE
HAIFA
TIBERIAS
LAKE KINNERET
NAZARETH
JEZREEL VALLEY
YARMUKH RIVER
SHARON PLAIN
SAMARIA
JORDAN RIVER
TEL AVIV-JAFFA
ISRAEL
AMMAN
ASHDOD
JERUSALEM
JUDEA
DEAD SEA
JORDAN
GAZA STRIP
DAROM
PORT SAID
El-'Arish
Rafa
B'ER SHEVA'
NILE RIVER
SUEZ CANAL
NEGEV
Abu Ageila
ISMAILIA
CAIRO
Parker Monument
SUEZ
Mitla Pass
EGYPT
SINAI PENINSULA
ELAT
GULF OF SUEZ
GULF OF ELAT
SAUDI ARABIA
Et-Tur
Sharm el-Sheikh
STRAIT OF TIRAN

Lebanese fronts. The forces assigned to the Egyptian front were therefore smaller than those of their opponents and consisted largely of reserves mobilized within hours immediately preceding the operation. Moreover, because of political considerations, the Israel Air Force was ordered not to participate in the operation unless the Egyptian Air Force went into battle first.

The opening move consisted in dropping a parachute battalion near the Mitla Pass, about 40 miles (60 km.) east of Suez and 100 miles (150 km.) beyond the Israel border, or well to the rear of Egypt's main fortifications and concentrations. During the 24 hours that followed, this battalion was to be reinforced overland by the two remaining battalions of the Airborne Brigade, while no initiative was to be taken in other sectors so as to leave the Israeli government free to decide on the next steps to be taken in accordance with political and military developments and, if necessary, to limit the operation to what might be termed a major retaliatory raid. Nevertheless, the Mitla battalion, which, as expected, attracted fierce Egyptian counterattack owing to its proximity to the Suez Canal and the threat it posed to Egyptian supply lines and to Suez itself, was able to hold out until the arrival of reinforcements.

After 24 hours, operations began in the south and in the north. In the south a reserve brigade, equipped mainly with civilian transports, made its way along the west shore of the Gulf of Eilat, following a track previously considered unusable. Aided by light motorboats, which had been rushed overland to Eilat and assembled there, the brigade, with a minimum of resistance, was able to overrun the strongly fortified positions of Sharm el-Sheikh, whose mission had been to blockade the Gulf of Eilat to all shipping to and from Eilat.

The heaviest and bloodiest fighting took place in the north, the area of major Egyptian fortification and troop concentration. Although Abu Ageila was taken from the rear, its principal fortified position, farther east, was able to repulse the initial Israeli attack. The crossing of the minefields covering the southern approaches to Rafa and the barbed wire defenses surrounding its strongly fortified position was achieved only after considerable effort, involving outstanding acts of individual heroism. Close coordination between infantry and armor brought about the capture of Rafa and the consequent sealing off of the Gaza Strip, which subsequently fell without major opposition.

Once it was permitted to operate, the Israel Air Force played an essential role in the outcome, emerging victorious from all encounters, even when heavily outnumbered by Russian MIGs. The Israel Navy was able to capture an Egyptian destroyer, which had been attacking its Haifa base. At a cost of fewer than 180 dead and 4 prisoners of war, the Israel Defense Forces were able to rout the entire Egyptian force east of the Suez Canal, inflicting casualties of about 1,000 dead and 6,000 prisoners of war and capturing considerable quantities of armaments and equipment. The rest of the Egyptian forces fled.

Although the road to Suez was now open, Israel's advance was brought to a halt as agreed 10 miles east of the Canal. Subsequently, under the combined pressure of the United Nations, the United States, and the USSR, the Israeli government was compelled to order the withdrawal of its forces from Sinai, once appropriate arrangements had been made for the introduction of the newly established United Nations Emergency Force. However, despite mounting pressure culminating in threats of sanctions, Israel refused to evacuate the Gaza Strip and the western shores of the Gulf of Eilat. Only in March, 1957, after an understanding had been reached with the United Nations and the United States that Israel's rights of free shipping to and from Eilat would be respected and that the UN Emergency Force, which was to be deployed in the Gaza Strip and in the Sharm el-Sheikh area, would prevent raids from the Gaza Strip and further interference with Israeli shipping, were Israeli forces withdrawn behind the armistice lines.

Results. Israel's place as a regional military power in the Middle East was enhanced as a result of the Campaign. The "collusion" with two former colonial powers, suspected already at the time, undermined its relations with certain Third World countries. Relations with the US—which had not been informed beforehand—became strained, for a while. The cessation of border raids and the initiation of shipping to and from Eilat with its potential for trade with East Africa, South Asia, and the Far East were viewed as considerable gains. However, the defeat inflicted on the Egyptian Army failed to result in peace negotiations or in the abandonment of the belligerent Arab attitude toward Israel. N. LORCH

SINAI SCHEME. *See* EL-ARISH SCHEME.

SINGER, BERNAT. Rabbi and Zionist thinker in Hungary (b. Sátoraljaújhely, 1868; d. Szabadka [now Subotica, Yugoslavia] 1916). Singer attended the Budapest Rabbinical Seminary (1887-93) and earned his Ph.D degree at the University of Budapest in 1894. He served as rabbi in Tapolca (1894—1902) and Szabadka. He wrote extensively on subjects of theological and Zionist interest in *Mult és Jövö* (Past and Future), *Zsidó Szemle* (Jewish Spectator) and other Jewish and non-Jewish periodicals. R.L. BRAHAM

SINGER, LUDWIG. Attorney and Zionist leader in Czechoslovakia (b. Kolin, Bohemia, Austria, 1876; d. Prague, 1931). Joining the Zionist movement in 1907, Singer served as chairman of the Zionist District Committee for Bohemia (1910–15). Much of his life was devoted to a struggle to improve the position of the Jews in Czechoslovakia as a national minority. Shortly before his death, in 1930, he was elected president of the Jewish Community of Prague.

SINIGAGLIA, GIUSEPPE. Businessman and Zionist leader (b. Ferrara, Italy, 1899; d. Italy, 1973). Sinigaglia was president of the Italian Committee of the Jewish National Fund from 1926 to 1938 and the founder, in 1929, of Perachia, Ltd., which promoted investments in Palestine among Italian Jewry. Settling in Palestine with his family in 1935, he was the founder and first president of the Israel-Italian Chamber of Commerce and cofounder of an Israeli company for deep-sea fishing in the Atlantic.

G. ROMANO

SIRAT, RENE SAMUEL. French rabbi (b. Bône [Annaba], 1930,). He settled in France in 1948 and studied at the Aix-les-Bains yeshiva and Paris Rabbinical Seminary, where he was ordained in 1952. He was a youth chaplain and director of religious education in Paris, 1955–1963. From 1966 he taught Hebrew at the Inalco (National Institute for Oriental Languages and Civilizations) and from 1969 at the Sorbonne. After two years in Israel (1970–1972), when he directed Hebrew courses for French-speaking students at the Hebrew University, Sirat became French general inspector for Hebrew teaching and significantly developed its organizational basis. The number of pupils in Hebrew courses grew from 440 in 1973 to 2,740 in 1980 in 46 state high schools. Several research centers in Hebrew and Jewish studies were established, and Franco-Israeli educational cooperation expanded. From 1981–1988 he was Chief Rabbi of France. As Chief Rabbi he fostered Jewish education and ties between the French Community and Israel.

M. CATANE

SIX-DAY WAR OF 1967 (Arab-Israeli War of 1967). The 10 years following the Sinai Campaign of the fall of 1956 proved another period of uneasy peace, intermittent border warfare, and reprisals. Whereas Israel's southern border, patrolled by the UN Emergency Force (UNEF), was relatively quiet, and shipping through the Straits of Tiran to the Gulf of Eilat (Akaba) went on unhindered, sabotage and infiltration across the Syrian and Jordanian frontiers continued.

Background to Conflict. Habib Bourguiba, President of Tunisia, was the first Arab leader to come out openly in favor of a basic change in the Arab attitude toward Israel, advocating recognition of and coexistence with the Jewish State. Other Arab governments, however, particularly those having common frontiers with Israel, did not change their political aim of ultimately destroying the State of Israel. The threat of war increased when the Arab governments decided to divert the headwaters of the Jordan River to deprive Israel of its main water resources. The Arab diversion scheme was frustrated, and the first stage of Israel's Jordan-Negev project, the vital artery of its economy and agriculture, went into operation in 1964.

In the mid-1960s Syria came to the forefront of Arab extremism. The leftist Ba'ath government installed in Damascus, energetically supported by the Soviet Union and eager to gain a position of leadership among the Arab countries, was foremost in organizing, financing, directing, and executing raids across the border, directed primarily against the Jewish settlements at the foot of the controlling range of hills held by the Syrians. An attempt initiated by the United Nations, early in 1967, to reactivate the Syrian-Israeli Mixed Armistice Commission (*see* ARMISTICE AGREEMENTS) failed dismally because of Syrian intransigence. The Syrian government did not conceal its support for the popular "war of liberation," as the guerilla warfare originating from its territory was called. When reminded of its obligations under the armistice agreement to prevent hostile acts emanating from its territory, Syria argued that it was not obliged to serve as the guardian of Israel's frontiers. After lengthy forbearance, Israel decided to strike back on 6 April 1967. When, on that day, Syrian fortified positions on the hills overlooking Lake Kineret opened fire once more on Israeli tractor drivers in the plain below, Israeli planes went into action, wiping out the artillery positions, bringing down six Syrian MIGs and going on to fly over Damascus, all without encountering serious resistance. The Syrian government, which, evidently under Soviet influence, had entered into a mutual defense agreement with the United Arab Republic (UAR, or Egypt) a short time before, sent an angry complaint to President Nasser for not having come to the aid of his allies in their hour of need.

Shortly afterward, the Soviet Ambassador in Israel presented a stern note to the Israeli government in which he protested against an alleged concentration of Israeli forces near the Syrian border and a presumed Israeli plan to attack Syria in order to overthrow its government. The Soviet Ambassador refused an invitation by Prime Minister Levi Eshkol to accompany him to the border to see with his own eyes that there was no basis of truth to the allegation.

Following Israel's Independence Day, which fell on May 15 that year, events moved swiftly. Egypt, nettled by the criticism of other Arab countries and encouraged by the Soviets, was put on a war footing and huge concentrations of tanks and infantry units were built up in Sinai close to the Israeli border.

On 18 May 1967, the government of the United Arab Republic requested the immediate withdrawal of the UN Emergency Force from its positions along the Israeli-UAR border. UN Secretary-General U Thant agreed. While the Secretary-General was on his way to Cairo, President Nasser blockaded the Gulf of Eilat by closing the Straits of Tiran to all shipping to and from the port of Eilat.

The United States and a number of other maritime nations reiterated their view that the Straits of Tiran were to be considered an international waterway through which free and innocent passage for ships of all nations must be secured. It soon became evident, however, that diplomatic action would not induce President Nasser to alter his decision.

Nasser openly proclaimed that he would consider an attempt to break the blockade an act of war, taunted Israel to do so, and predicted a war which would result in Israel's annihilation. His confidence was no doubt based on the huge amount of Soviet equipment which he had received during the preceeding years, ranging from supersonic MIG-21 planes, through modern T-55 tanks with infrared equipment and ultramodern artillery, up to and including the most up-to-date type of ground-to-air missiles, which had been designed for the aerial defense of the Soviet Union itself. In addition, he had signed a mutual defense agreement with Syria, and on 30 May, despite the deep rift which had been in evidence between Egypt and Jordan, he signed a similar pact with Jordan under which the Jordanian armed forces were to be put under Egyptian command. This pact was followed within hours by an agreement with Iraq. Thus, in contrast to the situation in 1956, the principal Arab countries seemed to be politically and militarily united, mainly supported by the Soviet Union, while Israel stood alone.

Observers throughout the world agreed that the Arab armies enjoyed an advantage in numbers, quantity, and quality of equipment, and that if the Israelis stood a chance, it was due to their superior organization, motivation, skill, and morale. However, Moshe Dayan, who was appointed Israel's Minister of Defense on 3 June, made it clear in his first news conference that if war should come, there was no doubt about Israel's ability to win it.

Course of the War. In the early hours of 5 June 1967, the Israel Air Force bombed practically all the UAR's military airfields and destroyed most of the combat planes of the Egyptian Air Force on the ground.

Simultaneously, Israel sent a warning to King Hussein of Jordan, cautioning him to stay out of the war. When that warning went unheeded and Jordanian forces shelled the

Israeli children in an air-raid shelter. [Histadrut Foto-News]

Israeli sector of Jerusalem, subsequently attacking and capturing United Nations headquarters, the Jordanian Air Force came in for similar treatment. Later in the day, Syria's airfields were similarly attacked and its air force decimated. The sum total of Arab losses during the first 16 hours of the war was well over 400 planes, as against 19 Israeli planes lost in the air. Most Israeli civilians had spent 5 June in air-raid shelters. The world outside was tense, listening to Arab "news" broadcasts about bombings in Tel Aviv and the destruction of oil refineries in Haifa. Israel, on the other hand, maintained an almost complete blackout on news. By the end of the first day of fighting, Israel had won complete air superiority over its neighbors.

Simultaneously, Israeli columns advanced into Sinai, in

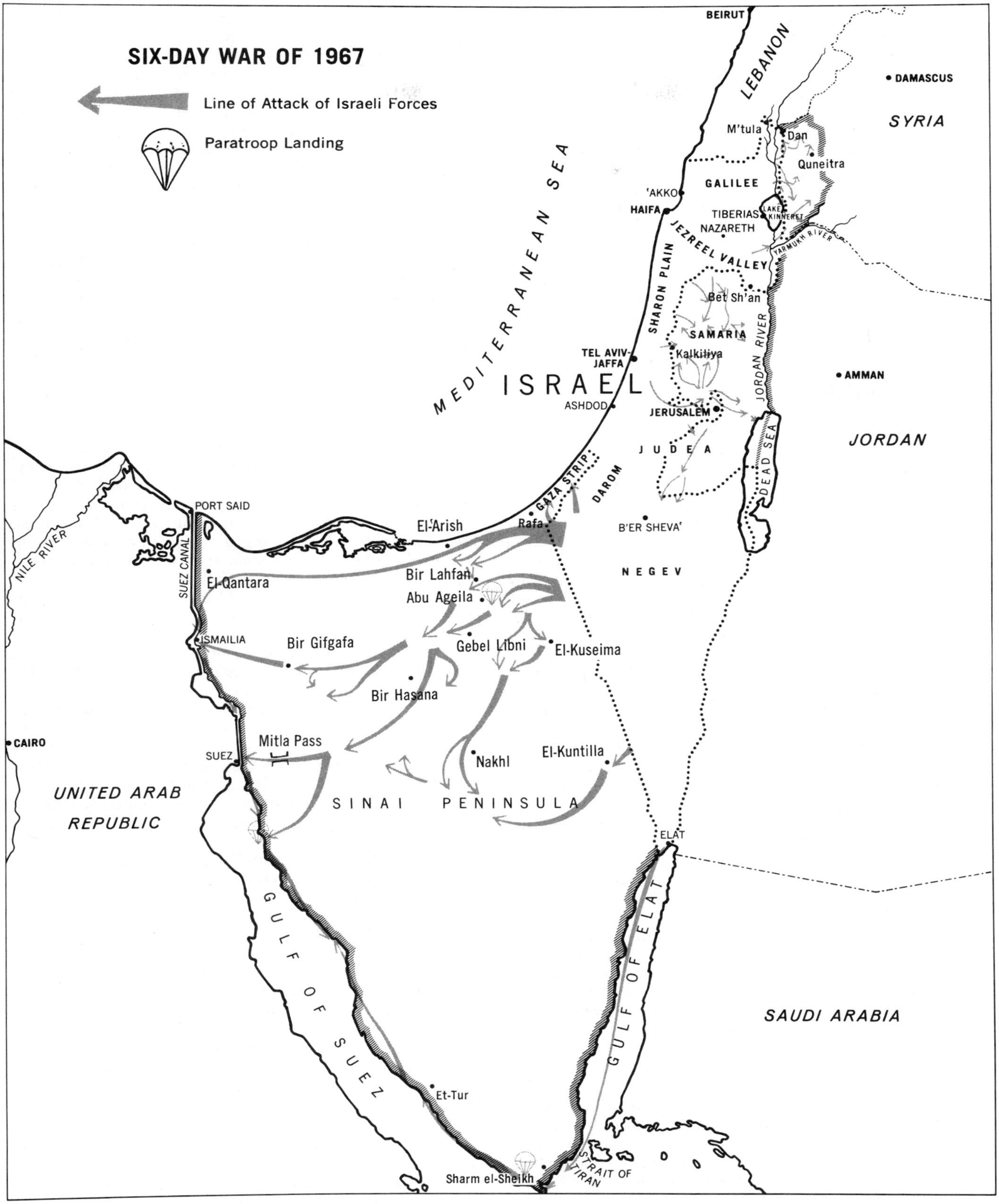
SIX-DAY WAR OF 1967
Line of Attack of Israeli Forces
Paratroop Landing
BEIRUT
LEBANON
DAMASCUS
SYRIA
M'tula
Dan
Quneitra
'AKKO
GALILEE
HAIFA
TIBERIAS
LAKE KINNERET
NAZARETH
YARMUKH RIVER
JEZREEL VALLEY
Bet Sh'an
SHARON PLAIN
SAMARIA
JORDAN RIVER
TEL AVIV-JAFFA
Kalkiliya
MEDITERRANEAN SEA
ISRAEL
AMMAN
ASHDOD
JERUSALEM
JUDEA
JORDAN
DEAD SEA
GAZA STRIP
DAROM
PORT SAID
El-Arish
Rafa
B'ER SHEVA'
NILE RIVER
SUEZ CANAL
El-Qantara
Bir Lahfan
Abu Ageila
NEGEV
ISMAILIA
Bir Gifgafa
Gebel Libni
El-Kuseima
Bir Hasana
CAIRO
Mitla Pass
SUEZ
Nakhl
El-Kuntilla
UNITED ARAB REPUBLIC
SINAI PENINSULA
ELAT
GULF OF SUEZ
GULF OF ELAT
SAUDI ARABIA
Et-Tur
Sharm el-Sheikh
STRAIT OF TIRAN

the direction of Rafa and El-Arish in the north, Abu Ageila and Bir Gifgafa in the center, and El Kuseima in the south. A major battle took place on and around the strong fortifications of Abu Ageila. A combined Israeli force of parachutists, which came down in the rear of the Egyptian outposts to put artillery out of action, infantry, sappers, and armored troops supported from the air captured the fortified position of Abu Ageila during the night of 5–6 June. The outskirts of Gaza witnessed another bitter encounter. While Israeli armor pushed relentlessly forward, close air support helped wipe out Egyptian resistance and supplies were parachuted to the advancing units. By the end of the second day of fighting and despite Egyptian assertions to the contrary, the Egyptian retreat had turned into a rout.

Sharm el-Sheikh, the Egyptian position overlooking the Straits of Tiran from which the blockade was to be enforced, was captured on Tuesday, 6 June. Parachutists about to be dropped were informed that the position had already been taken from the sea, and they were able to land without opposition.

Jordan's entry into the war triggered a swift reaction. Additional Israeli forces which quickly poured into the city of Jerusalem were able to take the High Commissioner's Palace, which served as the United Nations headquarters and which had been captured by Jordanian forces, and to break through to the isolated outpost on Mount Scopus, which had constituted an Israeli enclave behind Jordan lines since 1949. Out of respect for the holy places, strict orders were given to avoid damage to the Old City insofar as possible. After 36 hours of fierce fighting, the Old City of Jerusalem was isolated, with all roads leading to it from the east, north, and south cut. On Wednesday, 7 June, Israeli forces entered the Old City itself, and Israeli soldiers, headed by the chief army chaplain sounding the shofar, prayed at the Western Wall for the first time in 19 years.

Heavy fighting took place in and around Jenin, the site of an unsuccessful battle in 1948, and in and around Kalkiliya, an Arab town from which long-range guns had shelled Tel Aviv. By the end of the third day of fighting, Israel forces were in control of the Sinai Peninsula, taking up positions on the east bank of the Suez Canal, and had captured most of the west bank of the Jordan River, from Bet She'an down to the Dead Sea.

When the UN Security Council, after days of wrangling, finally adopted a cease-fire resolution, Israel was the first to accept it. Jordan followed soon after. Egypt rejected the call at first but acceded 24 hours later, on Thursday, 8 June.

While Lebanon, although it had joined in the clamor for war, had taken no action during the Six-Day War, Syria, the noisiest advocate of war, had been shelling Israeli border villages. An attempt to capture one of them, Dan, had failed. Nevertheless, Syria held out and refused to accept the cease-fire. The time had come for the concentration of Israeli forces against Syrian positions. The tremendous tactical advantages the Syrians enjoyed all along the border, combined with the strong fortifications constructed during the preceeding years, were bound to make an uphill assault difficult and costly. However, in the course of 20 hours of intensive fighting a breakthrough was achieved at the northern tip of the Syrian line, near Dan, and a broad strip of Syrian territory, up to and including Quneitra, was captured by Israeli forces before the cease-fire came into effect also on the Syrian border on Sunday, 11 June 1967.

Results. In less than six days, at the cost of over 700 dead and well over 2,500 wounded, many of them officers (as against enemy losses of thousands killed, wounded, captured, and missing), Israel alone had routed three neighboring nations supported by a number of other countries. More than 400 Arab planes had been destroyed (about 60 in the air), and over 500 tanks had been destroyed or captured. During the Six-Day War the three Arab armies had lost 70 per cent of their heavy equipment, representing well over $1,000,000,000 worth of armaments. The unity, discipline, and determination of the people of Israel were matched by an unprecedented outburst of solidarity and sympathy from Jews the world over as well as the support of non-Jews in many countries.

The UN Security Council rejected a Soviet sponsored draft calling for unconditional Israel withdrawal and an Emergency Session of the General Assembly was unable to agree on any resolution. It was only in November 1967 that the Security Council adopted resolution 242 (*see* UNITED NATIONS). Two months earlier, at their summit meeting in Khartoum, the heads of Arab States had reiterated their three "No's": no recognition of Israel, no negotiations, and no peace with her.

N. LORCH

SLANSKY TRIAL. Communist purge trial held in November, 1952, in Prague. Rudolf Slansky, a former secretary-general of the Communist party and Vice-Premier of Czechoslovakia, and 13 other high party and state officials were charged with "Trotskyite-Titoist-Zionist" activities. They were accused of having participated in a worldwide Zionist plot and of having been agents of imperialist sabotage and espionage services. All the defendants "confessed." Two Israeli citizens, Mordecai Oren (a Mapam leader) and Shimon Ohrenstein, who were arrested in Prague, "admitted" Zionist espionage activities. Slansky, the chief defendant, and ten of the others were Jews. All these men had been violently opposed to Zionism and Jewish nationalism all their adult lives. Eleven of the accused, including Slansky, were condemned to death and subsequently executed. Three were sentenced to life imprisonment.

The trial was part of the wave of great anti-Jewish purges, accompanied by anti-Semitic and anti-Israel campaigns, which swept the Soviet Union and the satellite countries in the years preceding the death of Stalin in 1953. In addition to state and party officials of Jewish origin, those arrested in Czechoslovakia included both Zionists and non-Zionists. In Czechoslovakia the purge continued even after the death of Stalin, into 1954.

Ohrenstein and Oren were secretly tried in 1953 and sentenced to life and 15 years' imprisonment, respectively. Protests by the Israeli government against their arrest and against the charges were of no avail.

In the years that followed, the victims of the purge trials were gradually released. Ohrenstein was freed in 1954 and Oren in 1956, but it was not until 1963 that the authorities officially exonerated those indicted in the Slansky and other purge trials. The exoneration made no mention of the Zionist plot charge or of the anti-Jewish character of the purge.

During the "Prague Spring" of 1968, further details of the trial came to light, including the false accusations against Zionism and the State of Israel. In reaction, many Czech and Slovak liberals developed an appreciation for the Jewish state. Several of the surviving victims of the trial and some close relatives of those executed left Czechoslovakia following the Warsaw-Pact invasion of their country. Their published memoirs became best-sellers and a source of theater and movie scripts, and the inspiration of the spiritual resistance in Czechoslovakia. ED.—Y. JELINEK

SLEPAK, VLADIMIR. Aliya activist in USSR (b. Moscow, 1927). His father, Simon was a devoted communist from the early days of the Soviet state and worked for many years as one of the editors at the Soviet news agency Tass. He named his son "Vladimir" in honor of Vladimir Lenin. (When Slepak informed his father about his plans to emigrate to Israel, Simon Slepak disowned him and refused to see him until his dying day in 1978.) Slepak received a Ph.D in radio engineering and had a successful scientific career becoming head of a laboratory in the Scientific Institute of Television Research in Moscow.

He and his wife, Maria, a medical doctor (b. 1926), became active in the campaign for Jewish emigration in 1969. The same year, he resigned from his post to facilitate his departure from the USSR. Nevertheless, when the Slepaks applied for an exit visa in April, 1970, they were refused on the grounds that his work was classified. Slepak became tha vanguard of the emigration movement, as well as a central source of moral support and practical advice for *refuseniks and for other Jews interested in leaving the USSR for Israel. His apartment, located in the center of Moscow, was always an "open house" for Jews from all over the USSR and for a growing number of foreign tourists, politicians, and journalists seeking contacts with refuseniks. In 1976 Vladimir, together with Anatoly Sharansky, joined the Moscow Helsinki Monitoring Committee, headed by Yuri Orlov and Andrei Sakharov.

During the 1970s the Slepaks' apartment was repeatedly raided and searched; their telephone was disconnected; they were often detained or kept under house arrest and Vladimir was vilified in the Soviet media, which described him as a "soldier of Zionism inside the Soviet Union" and accused him of espionage and treason.

In 1978, Maria and Vladimir Slepak were arrested for displaying a banner from their window saying, "Let Us Go To Our Son In Israel." He was sentenced to five years of internal exile in Siberia on charges of "malicious hooliganism." Maria Slepak was given a three-year suspended sentence, but voluntarily shared the fate with her husband when she learned of his sentence. Maria made the long trip to Moscow periodically in an effort to retain her residency permit in the capital. Vladimir, despite ill health, worked at odd jobs, often outdoors in sub-zero temperatures.

In December, 1982, the Slepaks returned to Moscow. They reapplied for exit visas but were refused again with the explanation that it was still considered a "security risk." It was only in October, 1987, on the eve of the second Gorbachev-Reagan summit meeting, that they were granted permission to emigrate. They arrived in Israel on 29 October 1987, and settled in Tel Aviv. Y. STERN

SLOUSCHZ. Family of Zionists.

David Solomon Slouschz. Rabbi and early Zionist (b. Odessa, Russia, 1852; d. there, 1906). Occupying the pulpits of various synagogues in Odessa from 1879 and in Odessa's Moldavanka suburb from 1881, Slouschz was one of the first Russian rabbis to join the Zionist movement. He wrote newspaper articles attacking the anti-Zionist rabbis, as well as a number of books, including *Tzidkat Moshe O Tuv ha-Aretz* (The Piety of Moses or the Best of the Land, 1885) and *Mikhtav le-David* (A Letter to David, 1905), a defense of Zionism against charges of un-Jewishness. A stanch supporter of Herzl, he was an enthusiastic proponent of the East Africa scheme. He wrote a second volume entitled *Mikhtav le-David* (which appeared only after the scheme had been shelved), in which he presented arguments in favor of East Africa and Territorialism. Slouschz was killed in a pogrom in Odessa.

Nahum Slouschz, his son, writer, scholar, and Zionist leader (b. Smorgon, Vilna District, Russia, 1872; d. Gedera, 1966). He went to Eretz Israel in 1891 but fell ill and went to Odessa, where he was active in Zionist and Hebraist circles. In 1896 he returned to Eretz Israel. Beginning with the Second Zionist Congress (1898), he was a close associate of Herzl. Slouschz completed his studies at the Sorbonne in 1903. His dissertation on the history of Hebrew literature, the first of its kind, was published in French, Hebrew, and English. He became a lecturer in modern Hebrew at the Sorbonne and was sent by the French Academy to explore antiquities in North Africa. During this expedition he took a special interest in Jewish antiquities and in the situation of the Jews in the regions he visited, which he described in several volumes. Continuing to be active in Zionism, he worked to enlist the support of French leaders for the Balfour Declaration (1917).

Returning to Palestine in 1919, Slouschz became the first Jewish archeologist to dig in and around Tiberias. He wrote extensively, in Hebrew and in French, on historical subjects and translated French literature (works by such authors as Gustave Flaubert and Émile Zola) into Hebrew. Slouschz was the editor of the first volumes published by the Society for the Exploration of the Land of Israel and Its Antiquities. G. KRESSEL

SMILANSKY, MOSHE. Hebrew writer and leader of agricultural settlements (b. Talpino, Kiev Province, Russia, 1874; d. Rehovot, 1953). Smilansky emigrated to Eretz Israel in 1890. At first he worked as a laborer in Rishon le-Zion. Later he settled with a sister and two brothers on land his father had bought in Hadera, but epidemics forced them to abandon their homestead. In 1893 he built a farm in Rehovot. Devoting his spare time to communal affairs, he soon became one of the leaders of the young settlements. In 1900 he helped form the Ahdut ha-Moshavot (Union of Settlements) and in 1901 was a member of its delegation to the Odessa Committee of the Hovevei Zion movement and to Baron Edmond de Rothschild. In 1905 he participated in the Seventh Zionist Congress.

During World War I Smilansky joined the Jewish Legion. Later he took a prominent part in the organization of Jewish communal life in the country, in developing Jewish economic activities, and in the purchase of land. He helped establish the Hitahdut ha-Ikarim (Farmers' Federation of Israel) and led it for many years. In the 1930s he became attracted to the ideology of Berit Shalom.

Smilansky began his literary activities in 1898 with journalistic articles, and from then on he contributed to numerous Hebrew periodicals. For a long time he was political editor of *Bustanai*, the weekly organ of the Hitahdut ha-Ikkarim, and he also served as editor of the daily **Do'ar ha-Yom*. Best known among his belletristic writings were his stories of Arab life. He also wrote historical studies of the modern settlements, biographies of pioneers, and personal memoirs. S. SKULSKY

SMOLENSKIN, PERETZ. Hebrew writer of the haskala (Jewish Enlightenment) period, forerunner of modern Jewish nationalism (b. Monastyrshchina, Russia, 1842; d. Meran, Tyrol, Austria, 1885). After receiving a traditional Jewish education, Smolenskin spent some time wandering in the Russian Pale of Settlement and became attracted to Jewish Enlightenment. In 1862 he settled in Odessa and began to write articles and short stories for *Ha-Melitz*. In 1868 he went to Vienna. There he edited (1868–85) the Hebrew monthly *Ha-Shahar*, which was devoted to belles lettres and Jewish studies and engaged in haskala-inspired criticism of old-fashioned Jewish life. At the same time the monthly sharply opposed assimilation and the denial of Jewish nationalism. In Vienna Smolenskin also helped found Kadimah, the first Jewish national student association.

Smolenskin himself contributed numerous articles to *Ha-Shahar*, in which most of his writings were published. These included his autobiographical novel, *Ha-To'e be-Darkhei ha-Hayim* (The Wanderer on the Paths of Life). His novel *Kevurat Hamor* (A Donkey's Burial) criticizes the Jewish community organizations, while *Gemul Yesharim* (The Reward of the Honest) describes the tragic situation of the Jews caught between the Russians and the Poles at the time of the 1863 Polish uprising. In various articles Smolenskin sharply attacked the "enlightenment" of Moses Mendelssohn, which he accused of paving the way for the assimilation of the Jewish people. He developed a theory of the Jewish people as a people based not on a territory but on the spirit—the Torah.

With the outbreak of the Russian pogroms in 1881 he espoused the idea of the Return to Zion, and in his story "Nekam Berit" (The Vengeance of the Covenant) he described the change that took place among the young Jews of Russia. He felt that the time was ripe to establish a center in Eretz Israel in anticipation of a Jewish state. He foresaw a spiritual center in Zion but practically emphasized that the economy of the country would have to include industry and not rely solely on agriculture. He may be seen as a precursor of modern Zionism. Smolenskin exerted considerable influence on the Jewish youth of his day and on the Hebrew literature of the second half of the 19th century.

Y. SLUTSKY

SMUTS, JAN CHRISTIAAN. South African military leader and statesman, Prime Minister of the Union of South Africa (1919–24, 1939–48), and ardent friend of Zionism (b. near Riebeck West, Cape Colony, 1870; d. Irene, near Pretoria, 1950). A deeply religious Christian, Smuts found inspiration in the Bible for his advocacy of both the Jewish claim to Palestine and the League of Nations.

Invited by Prime Minister David Lloyd George in 1917 to join the British Imperial War Cabinet, Smuts actively participated in the framing of the Balfour Declaration and in the efforts to establish the Jewish Legion. Smuts saw in the Balfour Declaration "an act of national reparation which will rank as one of the highest achievements in the world...the foundation of a great policy of international justice."

After the publication of the Passfield White Paper of 1929, he sent an angry cable to the British government, charging that "our present Palestine policy marks retreat from the Balfour Declaration...[which] represents a debt of honor that must be discharged in full at all costs; I would most solemnly urge that a government statement should be issued that the terms of the Balfour Declaration will be carried out in good faith, and that the government's Palestine policy be recast accordingly."

During World War II Smuts said in an address, broadcast on 1 November 1941, that in the face of the tragedy that had befallen the Jewish people, "the case of the Balfour Declaration has become overwhelmingly strong," and urged: "Instead of the horror of new ghettos in the twentieth century, let us carry out our promise and open up the National Home; the case has become one not merely of promises and international law, but for the conscience of mankind; we dare not fold our hands without insulting the human spirit itself."

During Smuts's lifetime a settlement was established in his honor in Palestine, in the Zebulun Valley; it bears the name Ramat Yohanan. J. SCHECHTMAN

SNEH (KLEINBAUM), MOSHE, Israeli statesman, physician, and editor (b. Radzyn, Russian Poland, 1909; d. Jerusalem, 1972). Sneh received a doctorate in medicine from the University of Warsaw (1935), where he was active in Zionist student groups. Subsequently he joined the General Zionist party where he adhered to the radical wing led by Yitzhak Gruenbaum. He was a member (1931–1935) and chairman (1935–1939) of the Central Committee of the Polish Zionist Organization and chairman of the Palestine Office in Poland (1935–37). While in Poland, he was editor of the daily *Ster* and subsequently the weekly *Opinia*, the organs of Jewish academicians in Poland, and political editor of *Hajnt*, the Warsaw Yiddish-language daily, from 1933 to 1939.

Arriving in Palestine in 1940, Sneh joined the Hagana, eventually becoming its chief, a post he held until 1946. In this capacity he organized "illegal" immigration operations and conducted the Hagana's armed resistance against Britain's anti-Zionist policy; in 1945–46 he headed the Jewish Resistance Movement which coordinated the activities of the Hagana, Irgun Tzeva'i Le'umi, and Lohamei Herut Israel in the armed struggle against British rule. In 1945 he became a member of the Executive of the Jewish Agency, serving as director of the Political Department of the Agency's European office in Paris in 1946–47.

In 1947 he resigned from the Jewish Agency Executive. He joined the Mapam party, on whose Executive Committee he served until 1953. From 1950 until 1953 he was coeditor of its newspaper, *Al ha-Mishmar*. In 1953, after the Prague trials, he left Mapam and formed Mifleget ha-Smol ha-Sotzialisti, an independent left-wing group that merged with the Communist party of Israel (*see* COMMUNISTS IN ISRAEL) a year later. He was a member of the Knesset from 1949 to 1965, representing Mapam until 1953 and the Communist party thereafter. A split occurred in the Communist party in 1965, when the followers of the strict Moscow line, most of them Arabs, withdrew and formed the New Communist party (Rakah). Under the leadership of Sneh and Shemuel Mikunis, the Israel Communist party (Maki) adopted a policy independent of Moscow, criticized the actions of the Soviet government toward Israel, and considered the Six-Day War of 1967 an act of legitimate self-defense. Immediately following that war, Sneh prepared an Israeli peace plan and demanded that the government take the initiative in negotiating with representatives of Palestinian Arabs in the administered territories. In 1969 Sneh was reelected to the Knesset.

For several years Sneh was editor of *Kol ha-Am*, the daily newspaper of his party. In the last years of his life he published hundreds of articles and interviews in the Israeli and international press, in which he expressed his ideological and political thought. He preached a rebirth of Marxist thought and wrote commentaries on Communism, crystallizing a new concept which recognized Zionism as the national movement of the Jewish people, and distinguished between its progressive and reactionary streams.

Y. TSABAN

SOCIAL INSURANCE IN ISRAEL. Social insurance, in the modern sense of a state-administered national insurance plan covering various benefits, was introduced in Israel soon after the establishment of the State. However, this development had important precedents in the yishuv. One example is *Kupat Holim Kelalit* (General Sick Fund), the outgrowth of a mutual health insurance scheme established in 1911 by the Federation of Judean Workers.

Over the years the Histadrut established voluntary institutions in various fields of social insurance: contributory provident and pension funds administered by the trade unions for their members, to provide them with old-age pensions. These funds also covered survivors, and other benefits. A number of mutual-aid provident funds, established for employees of voluntary social insurance institutions, covered the greater part of the population and paved the way for compulsory insurance legislation.

National Insurance Law. The Government of Israel appointed an inter-ministerial committee in 1949 to draft a social insurance plan. The committee proposals were presented to the government in 1950, and the National Insurance Law was enacted by the Knesset in November, 1953. The Law, which became effective in April, 1954, established an independent government agency, the National Insurance Institute (N.I.I.), which administers the program. There is a compulsory contribution, about 4% of income of all wage earners, with employers transferring about 9% of the income earned. The self-employed are required to make payments of about 11% (percentages are modified slightly as programs are added or because of changes in fiscal policy). The original law provided for old age and survivors insurance, maternity benefits, and work-injury insurance.

Israel adopted the fixed-rate pension system, that is, a basic equivalent pension for all, unrelated to previous earnings. There are small increments based on years of coverage beyond the minimum of ten years the law requires and, in cases of deferred retirement, for women from age 60 to age 65 and for men from age 65 to age 70. At age 60 or 65 respectively, retirees may receive their grants if they have no income or if it is below a level set by the N.I.I. All insured males 70 years or more and all insured females above age 65 are eligible for the pension, regardless of other income. The percentage of aged has been rising steadily; it reached 9% in 1986 and is expected to account for 10% of the population at the end of the decade. Approximately 310,000 persons received old age pensions in 1986, and more than 90,000 persons received survivors' benefits. All burials are covered by the N.I.I.

The N.I.I. administers a non-statutory, non-contributory old age pension program which serves all aged individuals not covered by the statutory program. This includes immigrants who did not work at all or whose period of employment was less than required for N.I.I. rights. The program is budgeted from regular tax funds and payments similar to those under the regular program. However, while about 40% of statutory payment recipients require supplementary income over 90% in the non-statutory category receive this.

The maternity insurance program provides two forms of benefits: maternity grants and maternity allowances. Maternity grants cover hospitalization costs and a layette allowance, given to the mother in cash. Virtually 100% of the annual 100,000 births occur in hospitals. Maternity allowances are paid to all employed or self-employed women for up to twelve weeks of leave. The allowance amounts to 75% of the average wage or salary of the women during the three months preceding the maternity leave. The law permits the women to take nine additional months of unpaid leave with job security guaranteed. In recent years about 42% of the women who received maternity grants were also recipients of the maternity allowance.

Work-injury insurance covers both employed and self-employed workers. Benefits include financial compensation, survivors' pensions in cases of work-related death, medical care and rehabilitation, as well as vocational retraining when needed. In 1985, 56,000 individuals received financial payments.

The large family allowance program was the first of many additions to the original National Insurance Law. Introduced in 1959, it initially made payments to all families with four or more children. In the mid-sixties, the third child became eligible. A 1975 revision of the Law guaranteed allowances for all children in the family, beginning with the first, but an emergency regulation enacted in 1985 restricted payment for the first child to specific low income families (those living on income maintenance grants or whose income from work was less than 80% of the average salary). There is a fixed basic payment for each child, with additional amounts given to the children in "four-plus" families. Additional sums are also granted for children in families where at least one parent has served in the armed forces. Allowances to families with five children (under age 18) who are eligible for the military service supplement was 36% of the average wage and for a family with seven children, close to 60% (1986).

A national Unemployment Insurance Law was enacted in 1972. Unemployed persons who have completed the qualifying period are eligible for payments, which are calculated on the basis of average earnings during the three months prior to unemployment.

The Alimony-Guarantee of Payment Law became effective in October, 1972. This is a non-contributory program administered by the N.I.I. Women eligible for alimony payments on the basis of court order, and not receiving them from those ordered to make payment, are granted payments as determined by the court and within certain regulations. The Law releases the women from the task of having the court order executed and puts the responsibility on the N.I.I. to collect what is due from the debtor. At any one time about 9,000 women are receiving alimony payments.

General Disability Law—1974. Disability benefits are

paid to persons who, as a result of physical, mental, or psychological limitations existing from birth or caused by illness or accidents, meet certain criteria such as restricted earning capacity or total inability to support themselves. A housewife with a medical disability of 50% or more is eligible for payments. In cases of limited physical mobility, a special mobility allowance is granted for car purchase.

Income Support Benefits Law—1980. Effective January, 1982, public assistance for the needy was transferred from local public welfare offices to the N.I.I. This is a means-tested program for those with no sources of income or with income below the minimum level as defined in regulations. Approximately 30,000 persons were receiving these benefits in mid-1986. The payment to a two-parent family with two children is approximately 50% of the average salary.

Reserve military service insurance provides compensation to all reservists called for more than one day of military service at a time; it is related to regular income.

N.I.I. includes a number of smaller programs, most of them unique to Israel, such as insurance for persons injured while performing volunteer activities, and insurance for workers whose employers have gone into bankruptcy. The workers are guaranteed unpaid salaries, severance pay, and premium payments to pension funds. Victims of terrorist attacks and persons imprisoned in their original countries for Zionist activities are eligible for payments, budgeted by the government and administered by the N.I.I.

J. NEIPRIS

SOCIALIST-TERRITORIALISTS. *See* JEWISH TERRITORIAL ORGANIZATION.

SOCIAL SERVICES IN ISRAEL. Social Welfare, defined broadly, includes health, education, the personal social services, and income maintenance. Until 1982 most personal social services, and some income maintenance programs were the responsibility of the Ministry of Labor and Social Affairs, and carried out by the local social welfare bureaus. These social services remain within the domain of the Ministry while public assistance, often denoted relief, has been transferred to the National Insurance Institute (N.I.I.). The social welfare system of Israel accounts for 22% of the national budget, with about 45% of this allocated to income maintenance, i.e., old-age pensions, family allowances, income support, 30% for education, 20% for health, and 5% for the personal social services (1986).

The Ministry of Social Welfare, established in 1948, existed until 1977 when it was amalgamated with the Ministry of Labor and renamed the Ministry of Labor and Social Affairs. The Ministry carries both direct and indirect responsibility for the bulk of the personal social services although some statutory programs and various voluntary ones are carried out by other Ministries, as well as public or non-profit organizations. The N.I.I., for example, offers social services to those handicapped as a result of birth defects, illness, or injury. The Ministry of Defense, through the Department of Rehabilitation, cares for citizens with disabilities that resulted from their military service and grants them disability pensions. It also grants maintenance pensions to the widows and orphans of persons killed in military service. The Ministry of Health has a range of social services in medical and psychiatric settings, both institutional and ambulatory. The programs of the central government employ over 1,000 social workers.

Personal social services in non-governmental agencies include the social services of the Department of Immigration and Absorption of the Jewish Agency, the Health Fund (Kupat Holim) of the Histadrut, the Israel Federation of Labor, the public hospitals such as Hadassah in Jerusalem, and the specialized non-profit organizations such as *Akim* for the mentally handicapped and *Alyn* for the physically handicapped.

The responsibilities of the Ministry of Labor and Social Affairs are carried out in part by Ministry-employed personnel in the centralized services and in part by personnel employed by the local authorities. Under the comprehensive Social Welfare Services Law (1958), all local authorities are required to maintain a welfare office. Originally called welfare bureaus, these are now known as the Department of Family and Community Services. Staffed by professionally trained, licensed social workers, they offer individual and family treatment and services as well as institutional or foster home care, school social services, and services to populations at risk, such as the blind, the deaf, and the aged. The social workers offer referral or brokerage services to other agencies, and supervise children in and out of home placements. There are about 10,000 children, exclusive of delinquents, mentally handicapped or mentally ill, who are placed annually with foster families or in institutions. The personal services include day-care programs, summer day camps, and homemaker services for the indigent aged or chronically ill. The Ministry supervises the professional activities of the local services through its area offices and covers 75% of the budget of most activities.

Statutory Ministry Activities. The basic law, as noted, is the Social Welfare Services Law of 1958. Activities not covered by specific legislation are carried out within the framework of this law and the social service regulations promulgated by the Ministry within this law.

An early specific law was the Youth Law—Treatment and Supervision, 1960, which authorized the Minister to appoint special personnel with authority to intervene on behalf of children whenever or wherever they are deemed to be in physical or psychological danger. The law permits the immediate removal of the child from his environment, with later judicial review.

Adoption of children and youths under age 18 was codified in the Adoption Law of 1960, revised in 1981. The Ministry, through its Department of Children's Services, is responsible for screening all potential adoptive parents, represents the child before the court and supervises the placement until the final adoption order has been made by the court. The unit offers supportive services and housing where necessary for the pregnant woman offering her child for adoption.

All settings housing 3 or more children, the aged or handicapped, are licensed and supervised by the Ministry as stipulated in the Law of Supervision of Homes, 1965. Services for the mentally retarded have been a function of the Ministry since the early years of the State. In 1969, with the passage of the Welfare Services Law—Care for the Retarded, the Ministry was authorized to establish diagnostic centers and professionally staffed diagnostic boards. The same law made it compulsory for all persons, who in the course of their professional work suspect a child to be retarded, to report such cases to specially appointed social workers. The law requires the parents of such children to have the child studied in a diagnostic clinic. The objective of the legislation is to allow for early treatment and educational planning, as well as supportive services to the family.

Services for delinquent youth have been recognized as a social service. Treatment and supervision of adjudicated delinquents is the responsibility of the Ministry, under the Youth Law—Treatment of Delinquents, as is the case of those sentenced by the juvenile court to institutions. In 1985, there were about 10,000 youths between the ages of 12 through 17 referred to the probation service for pre-trial social histories. Approximately 3,300 were convicted of juvenile crimes and 2,100 were in care under probation orders. The delinquency rate in Israel is about 5.6 per 1,000 in the relevant age group. The adult probation service of the Ministry supervises about 2,000 persons per year, including those sentenced to do community service in lieu of prison terms.

Ministry services not based on specific laws include programs for the blind, the aged, and youths at risk (pre-delinquent), as well as community-oriented programs, especially those in the framework of Project Renewal, the program to upgrade both the physical and social conditions in selected low-income communities.

Social Work Education. Training of personnel for the social services began in 1934 with the establishment of a course in Jerusalem within the social department of the Va'ad Le'umi. The school was transferred to the Ministry of Welfare in 1948 and continued to train personnel until 1958. A comparable two-year school was established by the Municipality of Tel Aviv in 1951. The two schools were phased out with the opening of the first three-year academic program at the Paul Baerwald School of the Hebrew University in 1958. In the mid-1960s schools of social work were opened at Bar-Ilan University and Haifa University, and at that time the Tel Aviv branch of the Paul Baerwald School was transferred to Tel Aviv University. A fifth training program was instituted at Ben-Gurion University in 1981. Approximately 400 Bachelor of Social Work graduates enter the field each year. Masters' degree programs are also offered in most of the schools. The Ministry continued its Institute for Training of Social Workers to prepare staff for the local public welfare offices from 1958 until the early 1980s when direct training ceased. The focus of the Institute has become in-service training and programs for the continuing education of social workers.

The Social Welfare Services Law created a legal status for social workers. While the law does not require this certification for general social work practice, it is requisite for certain functions such as representing the Ministry in adoption cases before the court. During recent years certification has become a condition for employment in services sponsored or supported by the Ministry of Labor and Social Affairs, the local family and community service departments, and by the other Ministries offering social services. It is estimated that there are about 6,500 certified social workers in the country, of whom about 5,000 are employed in some form of social service. J. NEIPRIS

SOCIETY FOR THE PROTECTION OF THE HEALTH OF THE JEWS. *See* OSE.

SODOM. *See* SEDOM.

SOILS OF ISRAEL. Israel's small area encompasses a wide variety of environmental conditions differing in geology, climate, topography, vegetation, etc., which all play a role in soil-forming processes. Therefore, the country has a great variety of soil types, both on a regional scale, in accordance with changing environmental conditions or soil-forming factors, and locally along a slope, as the mass and moisture movement intensities vary downslope. The development of characteristic soil features may last from a few hundred years, in clayey floodplains or recent debris screes, to several million years on stable desert surfaces and plateaus.

Both coarse and fine-grain textured soils are common. The latter are usually dominated by the swelling type of clay minerals, where permeability is reduced when they are wetted. On moderately or insufficiently wetted porous surfaces, calcium carbonate (lime) is relocated to the depth of wetting, where it forms irregularly shaped nodules, characteristic of most of the loess-derived soils. In the desert, insufficient leaching has led to an accumulation of airborne salts, and of gypsum at greater depth on stable desert pavement surfaces.

In the better watered Mediterranean regions, the calcium carbonate is apt to be leached out, but only the soil associations of the sandy Coastal Plain are non-calcareous. In soils associated with limestone, the amount of remaining carbonates depends mainly on the hardness of the rock; there is little in Terra Ressa soils on impermeable hard rock, but a much greater amount on soft porous limestone, resulting in a highly calcareous Rendzina soil. The weathering products of basalt in Israel are mainly heavy, clayey soils which swell when wetted and shrink again when dry. Over the millennia both the limestone and basalt hills and their associated soils have been subject to erosion, frequently as a result of exceptional climatic conditions and later also due to deforestation. The eroded material accumulated partly on the footslopes and in inland valleys, forming plains with thick deposits of fertile, though frequently poorly drained, heavy clay soils.

Israel lies within the region where cultivation and irrigation began some 9,000 years ago. Though in historical times arable soil has not exceeded one-fifth of the country's total area, man's influence on the landscape and its soils has been considerable, both destructive and constructive. Cultivation has reduced the original organic matter content by more than half. Yet the soils are inherently fertile, especially where they are sufficiently deep and have a high capacity to hold water. Most require irrigation to replenish water deficits of the dry summers. Replenishment of exhausted nutrients, particularly nitrogen, by fertilization increases yields. Irrigation with brackish water, without the simultaneous addition of gypsum, may be harmful by increasing the soil's sodium saturation and thus reducing its permeability.

In respect to geology, topography, and climate, Israel's soils can be grouped into a number of major soil landscapes, each with one or several characteristic soil types and a distinct pattern of local soil variations. In recent decades, a detailed, well-defined soil classification system has been devised by the Israel Ministry of Agriculture's Committee on Soil Classification, using some established traditional names, like Hamra and Nazaz on the coastal plain, and Terra Rossa and Rendzina for soils associated with the limestone hills, as well as other names which conform to newer definitions of diagnostic horizons, such as Grumusol for the clayey shrink-swell soils with deep cracks during the dry season, or Arid Brown soils for the loess soils with calcium carbonate nodules at some depth.

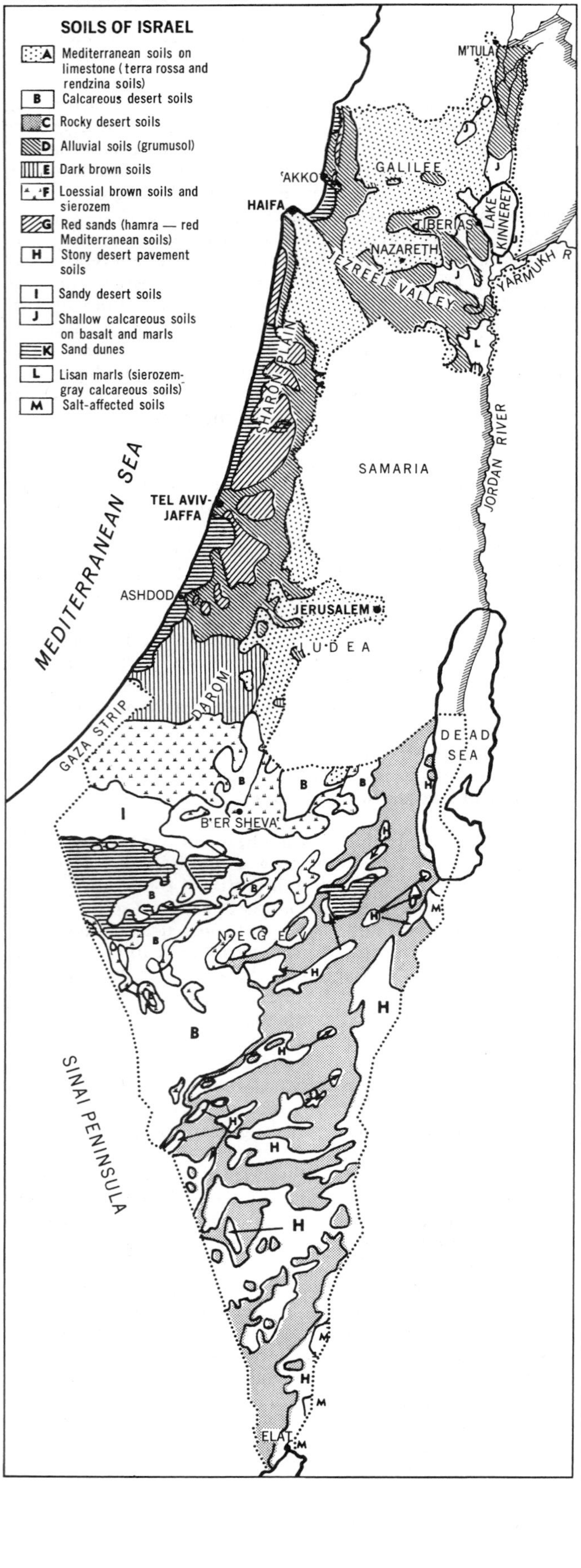

For determining general soil maps, the best unit is the soil association, frequently named after the dominant or characteristic soil or soils of the region. On a small-scale map the effect of climate and parent material on the nature of soils are well expressed when comparing soils associated with the same parent rock, for example limestone, in both the Mediterranean regions (where it is associated with Terra Rossa or Rendzina soils) and in desert regions (where it is associated with stony brown Serozems [dry-type soils] or rocky slopes without much soil cover). Basalts weather to shallow Protogrumusol or deep Grumusol soils. The effect of the time (age) factor can be seen by comparing the coastal plain soils of recent yellow sand dunes with the red Hamra soils, which originate from the same kind of sand dunes but are much older and have been enriched by imbedded clay from airborne dust and also reddened by iron oxides due to weathering.

In Israel the contribution to soils by dust blown in from the Sinai and Sahara deserts is of utmost importance. There is hardly any soil in Israel which does not include significant contributions of airborne dust material. The rate of deposition was in the past, and is still today, highest in the semiarid desert fringe region. The Serozems and Arid Brown soils have been formed from the thick blanket of airborne loess. This is a silt-dominated calcareous sediment serving as parent material for a whole sequence of different soils, generally of high fertility. Some of the airborne dust has been deposited in transit in the Negev Hills and has eventually accumulated in wadis. Large amounts of dust have been transported beyond the desert fringe region and contributed to the soil cover in the subhumid and Mediterranean regions. In the fertile Hamra and Nazaz soils the clay is of airborne origin, just like a large part of the fine clay and silt in soils associated with basalt and limestone.

Within each climatic region the local topography affects the rate of runoff and erosion, resulting in a chain-like sequence of soils going downslope. A good example is the association of Hamra-Nazaz-Grumusol soils in the coastal plain which results from the increasingly greater imbedding of airborne clay down the sandy slope.

Vegetation depends on and interacts closely with the soil. There are thus many similarities between Israel's vegetation and soil maps although only remnants of the original natural vegetation can be identified, due to man's interference with and destruction of it during the last few millennia. Modern study of Israel's soils commenced with the founding, by the Palestine Zionist Executive, of the Agricultural Experiment Station in Tel Aviv soon after the establishment of British mandatory rule. Later, soil laboratories were established both at the Hebrew University in Jerusalem and at the Jewish Agency Agricultural Experiment Station at Rehovot.

Following the establishment of the State of Israel in 1948, intensive surveys and mapping, including the Negev, were carried out by the Soil Conservation Service and by the Agricultural Research Station of the Ministry of Agriculture. Detailed and reconnaissance soil surveys, soil association maps and general soil maps on various scales were prepared. Studies on the genesis and nature of the soils are carried out at the Hebrew University, and those on the management of soils by the Volcani Agricultural Research Center of the Ministry of Agriculture and at the Lowdermilk Faculty of Agricultural Engineering at the Haifa Technion. While only a few specialists are engaged in soil survey and soil genesis research, close to 100 soil scientists study various applied aspects of soil use and management.

Soils are essentially a non-renewable natural resource and must be treated as such. They are the only resource for sustained agriculture and forestry. In Israel about 20% of the total area is cultivated, not very different from the proportion in the past. This is not likely to change much in the future due to water constraints. Improved management and efficient irrigation were the main reasons for continuously increasing yields. About 2% of Israel's area is covered by ancient forest remnants, and a larger area by planted forests. About 5% is built-up areas and roads, increasing by some 30,000 dunams (7,500 acres or 300 sq. km.) per year. Care must be taken that the most fertile soils are not built on. The remainder, about 60% is open area, mostly rocky slopes and stone-covered desert pavements, mountain slopes in non-desert areas, and sand dunes. The coastal sand dune areas are important as sources of groundwater recharge and need to be preserved. About one third of the open areas were designated national parks and nature reserves. A large proportion of the rest are military training areas.

D.H. YAALON

SOKOLOW, NAHUM. Hebrew journalist, author, and Zionist leader (b. Wyszogrod, Russian Poland, 1859; d. London, 1936). Sokolow received an intensive traditional education in Jewish classics and was early recognized as a prodigy in Talmudic studies. He taught himself secular subjects and was completely at home in the arts and sciences and in world literature. An accomplished linguist, he spoke and wrote in German, French, English, Italian, and Spanish as well as in Hebrew, Yiddish, Polish, and Russian. While still a young man he acquired a reputation as an outstanding Hebrew journalist. In the late 1870s, he moved to Warsaw, where he soon joined the staff of **Ha-Tzefira.* By 1885 he had become a partner and, shortly thereafter, sole owner and editor of the Hebrew periodical. Sokolow transformed *Ha-Tzefira* from an informative but dull weekly into an interesting and popular daily. His columns acquainted the reader with the general European scene as well as with Jewish life, presenting information and personalities hitherto alien to Eastern European Jewry. His style was unique, utilizing the rich treasures of Hebrew literature. Moreover, he knew how to appeal to traditionalist and modernist alike without offending either.

Despite the fact that Sokolow wrote most of *Ha-Tzefira*'s material, he had the time and energy to engage in other projects. He wrote for periodicals in various languages; for a time, he edited a Polish-language paper for the Jewish community of Warsaw and, at another period, a Yiddish journal. In addition to scholarly studies, he wrote poems, stories, and essays. Seeking to introduce a novel element into Hebrew literature, he decided to publish a literary annual, *He-Asif,* of which six volumes appeared between 1885 and 1894 and which had a tremendous impact on the revival of the Hebrew language. In 1907, when he became an officer in the World Zionist Organization (WZO), he made a further contribution to Hebrew journalism by founding and personally editing for a time the Hebrew Zionist organ, **Ha-Olam.*

Sokolow's literary talents also found expression in a number of books. Even before he moved to Warsaw, he had written a Hebrew geography, *Metzukei Aretz.* In 1882 he published *Sinat Olam le-Am Olam* (Eternal Hatred for an Eternal People), an anthology of articles analyzing anti-Semitism. In 1901 he wrote *Le-Maranan ve-Rabanan* (To Our Masters and Teachers). This book, in which he undertook to demonstrate to religious Jews why they should be Zionists, persuaded many who had had qualms about the nonreligious character of Zionism to identify themselves with the movement. When Herzl's **Old-New Land* appeared, Sokolow translated it into Hebrew under the title *Tel Aviv,* whence the name of the city in Israel.

In 1918 Sokolow published his *History of Zionism,* a massive two-volume study in English of the Western roots of the Zionist idea. Always attracted to history, he wrote in 1929 an impressive study of Amsterdam Jewry and its most famous son, Spinoza. The following year he published a sociological study of the Jewish people, *Ha-Ani Ha-Kibutzi* (The Collective Ego). In 1934 came *Hibbat Zion,* a history in English of the pre-Herzlian movement that had worked to settle the Holy Land. This was followed in 1935 by what many consider his finest work, *Ishim* (Personalities), a three-volume series of brilliant biographical essays.

Sokolow's eminence in Hebrew letters was matched by his distinction as a Zionist leader. Prior to the 1st Zionist Congress (Basle, 1897) he had taken a neutral position on Palestine. The activities of the Hibbat Zion movement were too petty and unorganized to elicit his involvement, but Zionism thrilled him with its breadth of vision, its international scope, and its systematic manner of pursuing its goal. Without underestimating its cultural aspects, Sokolow espoused the political aims of Zionism. He became one of the principal spokesmen of the movement in Eastern Europe, and *Ha-Tzefira* came to be an important medium of Zionist expression.

Financial difficulties forced Sokolow in 1906 to suspend temporarily the publication of *Ha-Tzefira.* Shortly afterward, Herzl's successor, David Wolffsohn, invited Sokolow to move to Cologne to become secretary-general of the WZO. Sokolow accepted the offer and from 1907 to 1909 conducted the affairs of the movement, taking charge also of the German-language Zionist organ, *Die Welt,* and *Ha-Olam.* However, he did not agree with many of Wolffsohn's policies. In particular, he did not believe that Zionism should be confined exclusively to diplomatic negotiations and sided with those who insisted that it must include pratical work, and settlement. The rift grew to the point where Sokolow could not continue working with Wolffsohn, and he resigned in 1909.

When the 10th Zionist Congress (1911) elected a new administration, Sokolow became a member of the Zionist Executive, and he moved to Berlin when Zionist headquarters was transferred there. He was given the political portfolio and spent the next three years trying to win sympathizers for the Zionist cause, particularly in England and the United States. In 1913 he also traveled to the Middle East and met Arab leaders in Syria and Lebanon. When World War I broke out in 1914, each member of the Executive was assigned to a different country. Sokolow moved to England, where he and Chaim Weizmann shared the task of convincing the Allies of the justice of the Zionist cause and of securing Allied support. In addition to meeting with influential non-Jews, Sokolow and Weizmann sought to gain the cooperation of prominent British Jews. They also made efforts to obtain pledges of support from other governments.

Sokolow's task was to win support from the governments of Italy and France and the Vatican. Despite the difficulty of wartime travel, he went back and forth from London to

Nahum Sokolow and his wife. [Jewish National Fund]

Paris and Rome. Displaying remarkable diplomatic skill, he succeeded in eliciting sympathy and promises of support. Thus in May, 1917, he obtained an official pro-Zionist statement from the French government. He then returned to England to join Weizmann in laying the groundwork for the Balfour Declaration. After the war Sokolow headed the Zionist delegation to the Paris Peace Conference of 1919, where he eloquently and effectively pleaded the Zionist cause but at the same time argued for Jewish civil rights in the Diaspora.

At the London Conference of February, 1919, Sokolow and Weizmann were elected to head the interim administration that had been chosen to represent the Zionist movement until the first postwar Zionist Congress could be called. The next London Conference (*see* LONDON ZIONIST CONFERENCE OF 1920) confirmed the choice of Weizmann and Sokolow, entrusting both men specifically with the Political Department of the WZO. In the conflict between Weizmann and the Brandeis faction in American Zionism, Sokolow supported Weizmann's aim to establish the Keren ha-Yesod (Palestine Foundation Fund) on a worldwide basis, and in the following years he spent much of his time traveling throughout the world on its behalf.

At the 12th Zionist Congress (1921), which reelected Weizmann president of the WZO, Sokolow was elected chairman of the Zionist Executive. During the years immediately following, he traveled constantly on behalf of Zionism, visiting a large number of countries the world over. In Italy, in 1927, he was received by Pope Pius XI and Benito Mussolini; the latter then authorized the establishment of an Italian pro-Palestine committee. Sokolow was to be received by Mussolini again in 1933.

At the 16th Zionist Congress (1929), Sokolow supported Weizmann's demand for an expanded Jewish Agency. At the 17th Congress (1931), he succeeded Weizmann as president of the WZO. His program did not differ greatly from that of Weizmann; he favored economic, social, and political measures with a view to furthering good Arab-Jewish relations in Palestine. He was sure that in time Britain would be impressed by the devotion and tenacity of the Zionists and give its full support to Zionist aims. During his presidency Sokolow visited Palestine several times and traveled to the United States and various European countries.

When Weizmann was returned to office in 1935, Sokolow was elected honorary president of the WZO. He was also named head of a newly formed Cultural Department but was not given the funds needed to execute a program. He returned to writing and campaigning in behalf of Keren ha-Yesod.

Sokolow did not belong to any one Zionist party. His vast erudition and universal outlook placed him above partisan politics. He was respected by all who believed in the cause of the Jewish Homeland and the renaissance of Hebrew culture. In 1956 the State of Israel had the remains of Sokolow and his wife brought from London to Israel for reinterment on Mount Herzl. The Tel Aviv municipality presents an annual journalism award in his name, and the Israel Journalists Association has named its Tel Aviv headquarters Sokolow House. S. KLING

SOLIELI (SOLOVEITCHIK), MAX (Menahem). Biblical scholar and Zionist leader (b. Kovno, Lithuania, 1883; d. Jerusalem, 1957). Active in the Zionist movement in Russia, he was a founder of and contributor to the important Russian Zionist periodical *Yevreiskaya Zhizn* (later *Rassviet*). After World War I Solieli was elected to the newly formed Lithuanian Sejm (Parliament), and in 1919 he was appointed Minister for Jewish Affairs in the Lithuanian Cabinet. Following his election in 1921 to the Zionist Executive in London, he resigned from the Cabinet. In 1923 he withdrew from his London post because of disagreement with the policies of Chaim Weizmann and settled in Berlin, where he helped found the *Radical Zionist faction. In 1929 he was elected to the Administrative Committee of the enlarged Jewish Agency. In 1933 he settled in Palestine. He was head of the Education Department of the Va'ad Le'umi from 1944 to 1948, and after the establishment of the State of Israel he served as the first director of the Israel Broadcasting Service. Solieli published several books on the Bible including a geographical-historical atlas. He was also editor of the Bible section of the German-language *Encyclopedia Judaica*. S. HUBNER

SOMMERSTEIN, EMIL. Member of the Polish Parliament and Zionist leader (b. Hleszczawa, Poland, 1883; d. Middletown, N.Y., 1957). Sommerstein studied law at the University of Lvov and subsequently practiced in that city. He joined the Zionist movement as a student and in 1909 founded the Jewish students' center at the University of Lvov, the first of its kind in Europe. From 1918 to 1939 he was vice-president of the Zionist Organization of Galicia. He played a prominent part in numerous Jewish communal endeavors in Poland and served as vice-president and board member of the Jewish cooperative movement of the country from 1925 to 1939. From 1922 to 1939 he was a member of the Polish Parliament.

After the outbreak of World War II, Sommerstein fled to the USSR and was imprisoned by the Soviet authorities. Following his release he became a member of the first postwar Polish government and served as chairman of the Central Jewish Committee of Poland from 1944 to 1946. In this capacity he negotiated for and organized the repatriation of some 140,000 Jews from the USSR to Poland. Most of the repatriates subsequently went on to Israel, with Sommerstein's assistance. He settled in the United States in 1946. That year he helped found the Economic Department of the World Jewish Congress, of which he became chairman. N.M. GELBER

SONGS OF THE LAND OF ISRAEL. From the beginning of the First Aliya and until the end of the War of Independence, several thousands of songs in the Hebrew language were circulated and sung. Of these, 3,854 were put into print. Printed publication and distribution took many and varied forms, including songbooks, collected lyrics, songsheets, song postcards, schoolbooks, periodicals, concert and recital programs, calendars, and almanacs.

1882–1903. Before 1882, the musical life of the yishuv found expression in liturgical and para-liturgical song. Profane songs—with Hebrew lyrics, but of non-canonical origin—were, with few exceptions, almost never sung.

Beginning in 1882, the first immigrants arrived from eastern Europe and the same year witnessed the beginning of immigration from Yemen. Yemenite influence, however, on Hebrew song in the Holy Land was not felt as long as the Yemenite newcomers lived in insulated community frameworks, separating themselves from their surroundings.

A variegated musical life emerged during the First Aliya. In addition to liturgical and para-liturgical song, musical life included community singing in Hebrew about various events in their lives; group dances to the tunes of the songs—often until dawn; choirs performing Hebrew songs; orchestras founded in Rishon le-Zion, Zikhron Ya'akov, and elsewhere.

This period saw the rise of two central, interlinked processes, which exerted a significant influence on the composition, distribution and performance of songs with Hebrew lyrics: the establishment of educational institutions—kindergartens and schools; and the beginning of the process of turning the Hebrew tongue into an everyday language. With the setting-up of the educational institutions, the problem arose of the complete lack of songs with Hebrew words, suitable for infants and children of school age.

A number of solutions were found, the main ones being: a. The use of "imported" songs, composed especially for the various European educational frameworks; b. The school and kindergarten teachers themselves composing Hebrew lyrics, and adapting them to well-known and recognized melodies; c. The translation of well-known songs from European languages and Yiddish into Hebrew.

The immigrants brought with them to their new homeland songs with Hebrew lyrics (either sung from memory by those who knew them well, or contained in songbooks). The main theme of all of these was Love of Zion. Others described the suffering in the Diaspora, redemption of The Land of Israel and its people, and so on. These are known as *Songs of Zion.*

The first Hebrew songbook published in Eretz Israel was entitled *Songs of the People of Zion*, printed and distributed by Menashe Meirovitz in 1895, in Rishon le-Zion. It contained the words to nine songs with well-known melodies, but since the notation was lacking, a note was inserted at the head of each peace, saying, "to be sung to the well-known melody..." or "to be sung to the tune of...". This book included *Ha-Tikva, Shir ha-Shofar* (song of the Shofar), and *Rishon le-Zion*, the words all written by Naphtali Hertz Imber; *Rishon le-Zion*, words by a member of the settlement, Yom Tov Lipman Shalit, music by Y. Igli; and *Song of Thanks to Baron de Rothschild.*

The first commercial collection of songs to be published and distributed was *Kinor Zion* (Lyre of Zion), issued in 1903, by the publishing house of Abraham Moshe Luncz in Jerusalem.

The number of Hebrew songs circulated in print had reached more than a hundred by the end of this period. They can be divided into 1. Liturgical songs, also performed outside the synagogues; 2. Para-liturgical songs, also performed at non-religious or non-traditional functions; 3. "Songs of Zion"; 4. Songs for pupils of the various educational institutions. Many others did not appear in print and became forgotten. The musical activities of the song-writers were carried out in addition to their regular everyday work. For example, Dr. Aaron Meir Maze (*Quarry the Mountains*) was a doctor; Y. Igli (*Rishon le-Zion*) was an instructor in horticulture; and Noah Shapira (*Ya Halili*) was a laborer.

1904–1914. A number of interdependent factors influenced the quantity of songs produced in Palestine during the period of the Second Aliya, including: The general development of Jewish settlement in the country; the development and expansion of the educational system (the founding conference of the teachers' organization was held in Zikhron Ya'akov in 1903); acceleration of the process of turning the Hebrew language into an everyday spoken language; the personal activism and initiative of the teachers, and the "singing teachers" in particular, both within and outside of the framework of the educational institutions, in composing song, lyrics, and melodies.

The inclusion of singing in the school curricula, and the existence of both amateur and professional musicians on the teaching staffs, made these institutions foci for musical activity, with the singing teacher initiating and establishing musical bodies (usually choirs or orchestras) according to their individual capabilities and directing them. Lacking suitable musical material for the singing lessons, or for local and school events (mostly musical settings for the Hebrew lyrics), the teacher would him/herself compose the necessary material. Performances by school choirs and orchestras at every local and school function, celebration or festival, became permanent features. Among the singing teachers who wrote music during this period, two names stand out: Hanina Karchevsky, at the Herzliya High School in Tel Aviv, and Abraham Zvi Idelsohn, who taught at the Laemel School and the Jerusalem Teachers' Seminary. The latter also edited *The Book of Songs*, Vol. I, published by Ha-Ezra, in 1911, containing 100 songs with Hebrew words. In this book the editor tried to match the various Hebrew texts with melodies originating in the various ethnic Jewish communities.

Many printed publications of songs with Hebrew words were distributed in the country, most of them having been printed in Europe; other songs were published and distributed in Eretz Israel. Among these were: *Alei Yom Tov* (O Holiday), by K.Y. Silman, the *Had Gadya Page* (The Only Kid), put out by Y. Dushman, the *Song Notebooks, A and B*, published by A. Idelsohn. These comprise the first publications in the country of individual composers.

A large part of the *Songs of the Second Aliya* grew out of the circumstances of the life of the pioneers together with their experiences as a social group, and characterized, among other things, by their communal singing and wild *hora dances. Community singing was a very common form of amusement, being a sign of recognition and identity. The pioneers celebrated and entertained through song. They went to work in song, sang at their work, and returned the same way. The excursions they made through the land were always accompanied by song. For many, community singing replaced community prayer.

The dances too, which accompanied the songs—especially the hora and the rondo—fulfilled similar social functions, and the intercombination of song and dance together was very common. Descriptions of songs and dances, found in the memoirs of the members of the Second Aliya, contain no mention of names of any particular people who initiated or organized them. They appear to have been completely spontaneous.

The main body of songs from the Second Aliya can be found in the collection, *From the Songs of the Second Aliya* (1948), *Collected, Recorded, and Edited by Samuel Shapira*. Most of the music of these songs originates in Russian, Polish, or Yiddish songs (one comes from Sweden), and all the songs without words come from the eastern European hasidic tradition. Three songs are specifically indicated as "Arab Melody" and "Arab Tune."

Several hundred songs have been added from this period to the general store of songs, especially from the following groups: Songs of Zion, similar to those coming from the first period, and to which were added songs written in memory of Herzl; songs for the various educational institutions, most of which were similar to those of the same type published during the first period. The exceptions were the result of Idelsohn's efforts to adapt words to the ethnic music of Jewish communities from Islamic countries. The repertoire of songs expanded considerably in this period, and it is possible to discern the beginnings of a process of "repertoire turnover," with "new" songs of one kind, taking the place of "old-timers" of another. Except for a few oriental and Arabic melodies, the sources of the remaining song music were western and eastern European.

1915–1923. The musical life of the yishuv was greatly enhanced and enriched during the period of the Third Aliya. Various mass events, among them concerts and "celebrations," were held throughout the country, often featuring "Songs of the Land of Israel," both new and old.

Alongside the veteran composers, new names, like David Ma'aravi, Joseph Milet, Nachum Nardi, Shalom Postolski, Joel Walbe, Moshe Bik, Matityahu Weiner (Shalem), and others, were beginning their musical activity.

Four groups of songs were added to the repertoire in this period: 1. Songs for which both words and music had been composed in the country; 2. Songs for which the words, but not the music, had been composed locally; 3. Songs for which the music had been taken from ethnic Jewish communities and adapted to new Hebrew lyrics; 4. Songs for which neither words nor music had been composed locally.

Most of the European song publications designated for Hebrew educational institutions were also published in Palestine. Only a small portion of those printed, however, were suitable in content for use by local pupils, because most were completely divorced from the Holy Land milieu. Descriptions of snows in winter and forests stretching from horizon to horizon; the squirrel, bear, cuckoo and nightingale; chimney-sweeps, *muzhiks* and nobility—all these, together with descriptions of the *heder*, the *rebbe*, and life in the *shtetl*, were utterly strange to children born and brought up in the new Land of Israel. The Ashkenazi pronunciation of the eastern European songs, stressing the penultimate syllable, no longer suited the Sephardi style now being spoken in the schools.

The teachers at kindergartens and primary schools continued to fill the need for children's songs, translating and writing their own words and adapting them to well-known and familiar melodies. One of the most active was the poet, Levin Kipnis. In all the works he wrote for the very young in their early school years, Kipnis included dozens of songs, most of them his own works, with the music mainly original melodies composed by musicians then living in Palestine—Idelsohn, Karchevsky, and Shapira, who had immigrated during the second period, and Milet, Ma'aravi, Vered, and Greenshpon, who arrived in the third. Another composer of this period was Yedidia Gorochov (Admon), who had been raised and educated in the country from the age of twelve. To his remaining poems, Kipnis himself fitted the "folk" tunes which he recalled. Because there was a lack of songs suited to certain holidays or seasons, many of these songs were dedicated to them.

Pioneers of the Third Aliya adopted the ideology of their predecessors in the Second Aliya, including their customs of community singing and dancing the hora, as well as a large number of the songs which they used to sing at every opportunity. Nevertheless, the way of life taken up by the Third Aliya immigrants, and their special type of society, brought forth many new songs reflecting the events of the time: Tel Hai; the difficult economic situation, the special life-style of the workers' camps. Now, however, what had once been spontaneous and fortuitous, became organized and institutionalized, so that communal singing turned into an integral part of every event, "party," gathering, demonstration, etc.

In the repertoire of songs by the end of this period, it is possible to see a clear acceleration of the "turnover process," in which the older songs were gradually yielding place to new ones often with words and/or music composed locally. The *Songs of Zion* group gradually diminished while *Songs for the Schools* increased, with a significant growth in number of those composed (both words and music) in Palestine. Particularly prominent within this group, in a class by itself, was a group called *Shirei ha-Hagim* (Festival Songs).

1924–1933. Many hundreds of new songs were now being written and performed on different and varied stages at public gatherings and events, both large and small. Concerts featuring Hebrew songs, with the participation of soloists, choirs, and orchestras, were arranged with considerable frequency at various places in the country. Hebrew songs were often performed at concerts of artistic music, and even cantors in concert devoted part of their programs to songs of the Land of Israel.

One of the most important institutions encouraging the writing of Hebrew songs, but engaged mainly in their distribution, was the Jewish National Fund (JNF), which saw in the songs of the Land of Israel, a unique and valuable instrument for education and dissemination of the Zionist ideal, both inside the country and abroad. In 1929, the JNF published a songbook entitled *From the Songs of Our Country*, containing more than 90 songs. In addition, production was initiated on nine different series of song cards, suitable for mailing as postcards. On each card were printed the complete words and music of a song of the Land of Israel, with the Hebrew words printed at the side, and their transliteration embodied in the usual way in the music. The JNF also put out guidelines and suggestions for celebrating holidays, festivals, and memorial days, with songs claiming an important place. Other public bodies and institutions were also active together with the various publishing houses, printing and distributing new and old songs of Israel.

It was during this period that books of the songs of individual composers also began to see publication. These included: *Shirat ha-Dor* (Songs of This Generation), by composer Puah Greenshpon (1929), *Lehu Neranena* (Let us Go and Sing), by poet K.Y. Silman (1928), *Be-Keren Zavit, A and B* (On a Corner), songs by composer Yoel Engel and poet Y. Heilperin (1927),

Among the composers whose first published works were to be found during this period, were Yitzhak Edel, Gabriel Gard, Joel Walbe, David Zahavi, Mordechai Zeira, Sara Levi-Tanai, Emanuel Amiran, Shalom Postolski, and Matityahu Shalem.

1934–1941. This was a period of greatness for the songs of the Land of Israel; they continued their rapid development, begun in the previous period. Hundreds of new songs were composed by dozens of composers and poets—veterans and newcomers, amateur and professional. There was hardly an event, large or small, where songs of the country did not appear as an official—or even unofficial—part of the program: mass celebrations and intimate ones, cultural events of all sorts, sports meets, political rallies, demonstrations, memorial services, festival celebrations, and so forth.

Various organizations took part in distributing the songs, either directly or indirectly: the national institutions—The Jewish Agency, the JNF, Keren ha-Yesod with its Department of Education, and educational institutions, school teachers' and kindergarten teachers' associations, the Histadrut, labor councils, municipalities, cultural committees, kibbutz movements, youth movements, various publishing companies etc. The Palestine Broadcasting Service too, which commenced its broadcasts in 1936, devoted a number of special programs to Hebrew songs, initially during the Hebrew hour and later in school broadcasts.

The composers themselves also circulated their songs, at special concerts and performances before many different audiences. Often, singers and choirs would participate in performing the songs. Many new songs were written for every special event, festival and holiday, some of them quickly circulated among the various audiences, even before they were published. Various music word-books were put into print and immediately set to music, sometimes by more than one composer.

A modest contribution was made by the theater arts, mainly the light stage, which presented songs and tunes. It was at this time that records of songs from Palestine appeared, and films containing Hebrew songs began to be shown in the cinemas. At this time, too, a new concept appeared on the scene of the country's musical life—the community-song leader. The Histadrut and the Music Institute gave courses in the new occupation. Throughout the country, in the cities, cooperative settlements and kibbutzim, cultural activities were taking place, devoted entirely to community singing.

In the Diaspora various publications of Hebrew songs were circulated, but most of the material in them, apparently, had been copied from works printed earlier in Palestine, especially those put out by the national and public institutions.

Among the most important composers whose songs were being sung and even published, mention should be made of Nahum Nardi, Daniel Sambursky, Nissan Nissimov, B. Omer, Menashe Ravina, Moshe Wilensky, and Yehuda Sharett.

1942–1949. This period also regarded the song as a tool for promoting community singing, with a massive addition of Israeli songs composed throughout the period (about 40 percent of the general repertoire). It is nevertheless different from the previous period in a number of aspects: the institutional aspect, where significant changes were taking place, both during and near the end of the period; the increase in the number of subjects not seen in songs of the preceding period; greater use of the radio as a means of dissemination of the Israeli song; the attempts to define the musical substance and characteristics of the Israeli song.

Significant changes were taking place in the institutional realm. Intensive activity by the Histadrut organization in putting out song-publications led the national institutions—the Jewish Agency and the JNF—to change the direction of their own work in this field, especially for American Jewry (for instance, the *Classified Palestine Songs* series, published during 1943-1945). This was in addition to material which they were bringing out in Palestine itself.

The educational network continued to grow and expand in all sectors. A number of bodies were added to the framework, engaging in circulation of songs of the Land of Israel. The most important of these was the Center for Worker Education and Organization, which distributed to its members various publications containing Israeli songs. The National Organization of Music Teachers (founded in 1942) distributed to its members the *Ron Dafron* series (four issues), as well as special song-sheets for holidays, festivals, and memorial days.

When Jewish Palestinians joined the British army in World War II, it was important to keep contact with them, and this was done through the efforts of various committees and societies set up for this purpose. One of the most active bodies was the Committee for Jewish Soldiers which, among its other activities, distributed a collection of songs, *Mizmorim la-Hayal ha-Yehudi* (Songs for the Jewish Soldier) which appeared in three different editions (1942, 1943, 1945). The last edition, *Shir u-Mizmor la-Hayal* (Songs and Melodies for the Soldier), contained 105 songs.

Upon its establishment in 1948, the Israel Defense Forces began to distribute song collections. All those printed appeared together with music. New, meaningful themes in this period began to change the make-up of the repertoire of songs, with many songs devoted to each subject appearing in the various publications published by public, private, and State bodies and institutions. One of the most important of these themes was *Songs of the Jewish Town in the Diaspora*, which arose in the wake of the Holocaust and the desire to preserve European Jewish culture, even if only through songs. In the various publications of songs of the period, special sections and booklets were devoted to *Songs of the Diaspora*.

The period of the struggle for independence—especially in the framework of the Palmah, the period of the War of Independence (which saw the beginning of the army troupes such as the *Chizbatron* and the *Chishtaron*) and the establishment of the State of Israel yielded an impressive crop of songs which appeared in a wide range of publications from private or State-run publishing houses. Much of the sheet-music was arranged for "popular" instruments, especially the recorder, accordion, mandolin, and guitar.

1950–1967. The waves of mass immigration, problems of absorption, security, economic stability, social integration, and politics—all found expression in the content and style of songs being written throughout the period. A number of different, important processes changed the character of the Songs of Israel.

The main processes included the rapid increase in size of the Jewish population in Israel and the change in ethnic composition, as well as the radical change which took place during this period in the dissemination of songs, mainly by means of the radio and through records.

The folk-dance movement now began to expand significantly. Dozens of new dances were composed every year, some to the tunes of existing songs and others with new ones written for them (words and music). Many of the dances were composed under the influence of the folk-dances of various ethnic communities (mainly Yemenite) and the Israeli-Arab minority. In addition to the composers who had begun writing in the preceding period, and to whose music "folk-dances" were adapted including Nira Chen, Emanuel Zamir, Emanuel Amiran, Sasha Argov, Moshe Wilensky and others, new names appear, such as Amitai Ne'eman, Gil Aldema, Effie Netzer, Joseph Hadar, and Yossi Spivak.

Visits to Israel of singers and groups from abroad, the advent of easily available home record-players and radios at affordable prices (especially when it became possible to purchase transistorized, battery-operated radios and portable tape-recorder/players), circulation of imported European and American song-records and their acquisition by wide segments of the Israeli population, circulation of magazines devoted especially to popular song hits etc.—all these encouraged the penetration of waves of foreign-language songs, changing the face of the Israeli song. One example is the influence of French songs of the 1950s, most prominently represented by Yohanan Zarai; other influences exerted during this period were those of Greek, Spanish, and Italian songs, as well as English and American.

The conclusion of the War of Independence, and the organization of the Israel Defense Forces into corps and commands, led those in charge of the army's cultural activities to set up army entertainment troupes, resembling those functioning at the end of the war. The programs were oriented mainly toward light entertainment (songs, tunes, and amusing sketches), with each troupe attempting to reflect the uniqueness of its own particular command or corps.

The contributions of the army troupes to Israeli song were expressed on a number of planes: 1. A large number of new songs; 2. Singers received training in these troupes and, on release from military service, they were already experienced in appearing onstage before an audience; 3. A new vocal style and mode of instrumental accompaniment was introduced (originally based mainly upon accordion and guitar), which later grew into a full-fledged background sound including brass, electric and electronic instruments, and sets of drums. 4. The training of musical arrangers and managers who, on their release from the army, continued their musical activities which also included original compositions. Composers such as Doubie Zeltzer, Arie Levanon, Nissan Cohen ha-Baron, Ya'ir Rosenbloom, and many others began their musical writing careers within these frameworks.

The various ensembles included Ran and Na'ama, the Duda'im, the Theater Club Quartet, Green Onion, The Tarnegolim (Roosters), and The Yarkon Bridge Trio.

Inclusion of the stage as an additional dimension in performance of a song, including stage props, lighting and positioning, together with the vocal and instrumental arrangement turned a large number of such songs into "Songs for the Ear", no longer suitable for singing in a crowd, but preferably only for listening to. In the content of the songs too, a revolution was taking place, with the "lyric" songs, which accorded greater chance for individual expression, claiming greater prominence.

An increase in the numbers of performers, both soloists and ensembles, stimulated a great demand for new Israeli songs, and throughout this period, composers like Naomi Shemer, Nahum Heyman, Nurit Hirsch, and others became well-known. One of the most important State activities to encourage composition of original Israeli songs was undertaken by the Israel Broadcasting Authority and the Committee for Independence Day Celebrations, who, in 1960, announced the establishment of a competition for the writing of an "original Hebrew song." These competitions, which almost every year concluded with a festival, usually as Independence Day drew to a close, led to the contribution of many songs and the fame of many composers.

1968–1985. Only after the wave of songs which came in the wake of the Six-Day War had abated did new musical and lyrical trends and directions begin to appear in Israeli song.

Composers who had begun to write in previous periods but wrote much in this period, and whose songs mark a continuation of the style of the songs from the previous period include Sasha Argoc, Naomi Shemer, Shayke Paikov, Nahum Heiman, Efi Netzer, Moni Amarilio, and Yaakov Hollander. Sasha Argov and Naomi Shemer received the Israel Prize for their unique contribution to Israeli song.

The end of the previous period had seen the burgeoning of "rock" songs, influenced mainly by various foreign groups. The opening of a national television channel at the end of the 1960s and the broadcasting of foreign song programs on the various broadcasting networks greatly speeded up the introduction of "rock" music into Israeli songs. The youth enthusiastically welcomed the new styles of western music, while the young songwriters, performers and orchestrators, mostly native Israelis, began to incorporate various elements of western rock styles in their songs and programs. Of note in this respect are Arik Einstein, Shmulik Kraus, Zohar Levi, Shalom Hanokh, Danny Sanderson, Yitzhak Klefter, Mikki Gabrielov, Yoni Rechter, and Shlomo Grunich. The army groups, which reached the reak of their growth at the beginning of this period, increasingly began to introduce elements of rock music into their programs. Orchestrators who set the musical orientation of these groups included Yair Rosenblum, Kobi Ashrat, and Eldad Sharim.

In addition to the army groups (which were suspended in the mid-1970s, new song groups were founded based mainly on rock music. Among the groups formed in the period were Kaveret, Aharit ha-Yamin, Berosh, Ha-Klik, and Machina. Many of the "protest songs" penned in Israel during this period were in this style.

Since 1970 a Hasidic Song Festival has been held regularly in Israel. The songs sung here are distinctive in that all their lyrics are taken from biblical sources, while the new melodies have modern musical scores embracing most musical styles, including rock. They won a following in various population sectors which had not previously found a song style to suit them.

Already in the previous period, songs based on elements of eastern Jewish ethnic music had begun to appear, although not in the institutionalized frameworks. These musical elements were expressed rpincipally in the Magamat programs, with typical oriental instruments, such as the canon, the oud, the hand drum, etc., and in the ways the songs are performed. The large circulation of these songs among an ever-growing public in the course of this period, led to the institution of an "Oriental Song Festival" by the Israel Broadcasting Authority. The Ha-Bereira ha-Tivit group succeeded in creating a synthesis of several eastern styles, including Indian music. The expansion of the framework of eastern styles and the increased demand for such songs led many song writers, not necessarily of eastern origin, to write songs which in some way amalgamated musical styles of east and west.

Several singers who became stars at the end of the previous period and during this period also chose to write their own songs. Sometimes the actual composers chose to perform the songs that they had penned. In this category are Matti Caspi, Shalom Hanokh, Yehudit Ravitz, Tzvika Pik, Corinne Elal, Shlomo Artzi, Avi Toledano, and Shlomo Grunick.

A social manifestation which became very common in this period is that of the song circles. In these circles, various groups, ranging from a few dozen to a few hundred, meet in order to sing Hebrew songs together, led by a moderator and using slides and/or printed songbooks. These song circles, sometimes called "song clubs", exist in various localities throughout Israel and are estimated to comprehend hundreds of thousands of members.

Song clubs at times constitute a meeting place for various song companies which were formed in Israel in the course of this period. The song company, as an amateur performing group, numbers about 14–40 participants and its repertoire is made up mainly of Hebrew songs from the various periods, with scores written for several voices and with a small instrumental accompaniment. At the end of the period there were almost 400 active song companies in Israel, including Ha-Gevatron, Pina-ba-Emek, Mateh Asher, Ha-Irusim, Shir Li, and Ha-Tel Avivim. Since 1983, "Hebrew Song Festivals" have been held in Arad, in which scores of song companies appear with new and old Hebrew songs.

N. SHAHAR

SONNE, AVRAHAM. Poet and educator (b. Przemysl, Galicia, Austria, 1883; d. Ramatayim, 1950). Sonne received a traditional and a secular education and later studied at the universities of Vienna and Berlin. Before World War I he taught for a short period at the Hebrew Teachers Seminary in Jerusalem. During the war he was in Vienna and Galicia. At the end of the hostilities Sonne went to London, where he worked for the World Zionist Organization, and in 1920 became secretary of the Zionist Executive. He later resigned from this post and returned to Vienna, where he was first a teacher and later principal of the Hebrew Pedagogium, founded by Chief Rabbi Zvi Peretz Chajes. In 1938 he settled in Palestine.

Sonne was a harbinger of modernist Hebrew poetry. Though his published poems were few (he used the pseudonym Avraham Ben-Yitzhak), they were a significant contribution to Hebrew poetry on nature. A collection of his poems was published in 1952, and an edition with an English translation appeared in 1957.

N.M. GELBER

SONNENFELD, JOSEPH HAYIM BEN ABRAHAM SOLOMON. Rabbinic authority (b. Verbo, Slovakia, 1849; d. Jerusalem, 1932). He studied with Abraham Samuel Benjamin Sofer in Pressburg (Bratislava). In 1873, he settled in Jerusalem, where, together with Rabbi M.J.L. Diskin he founded schools, an orphanage, and opposed secular education. He founded Batei Ungarin, the Hungarian religious neighborhood in Me'a She'arim, as well as a number of other quarters in Jerusalem, and headed Shomerei ha-Homot (Guardians of the Walls), the Hungarian Orthodox community.

Rabbi Sonnenfeld (center) accompanying President Thomas Masaryk of Czechoslovakia on a tour of Jerusalem, 1927. [Central Zionist Archives]

Strongly opposed to Zionism and secularism, he was a founder of Agudat Israel in Eretz Israel. He lobbied to keep institutions of the Old Yishuv from coming under Zionist control and objected to Orthodox Jewish participation in Keneset Yisrael, the general community. Although personally on good terms with Rabbi A.I. Kook, he opposed Kook's appointment as Chief Rabbi of Palestine. In 1920, he was elected the first rabbi of the separatist Orthodox community. Representing this body in official meetings and before the King-Crane Commission, he expressed a positive attitude to Zionism and Jewish settlement and worked to build bridges with the Arab community.

His publications included *Salmat Hayim*, responsa on sections of the Shulhan Arukh code (1938–1942).

G. SHUSTER-BOUSKILA

SONNINO, GIUSEPPE. Rabbi and Zionist leader in Italy (b. Ancona, Italy, 1861; d. Genoa, 1930). Chief rabbi of various Italian-Jewish communities, including those of Naples and Genoa, Sonnino was one of the first Italian Zionists. He was the first Italian delegate to a Zionist Congress, the Second, held in Basle in 1898. G. ROMANO

SOSKIN, SELIG EUGEN. Agricultural expert (b. Crimea, Russia, 1873; d. Tel Aviv, 1959). A Zionist from his student days in Germany, Soskin settled in Eretz Israel in 1896 and served as an agronomist for the Palestine Executive of the Odessa Committee of the Hovevei Zion movement. In 1903 he took part in the *El-Arish Expedition and was elected by the Sixth Zionist Congress to the Palestine Commission of the World Zionist Organization. Subsequently, he was one of the editors of the commission's monthly, *Altneuland*.

From 1906 to 1915 Soskin was employed by the economic services of the German colonies in West Africa. In 1918 he became director of the Land Settlement Department at Jewish National Fund headquarters in The Hague. At that time he first advocated the employment of intensive agricultural methods in Palestine. He stressed especially the importance of hydroponics in view of the limited agricultural potential of the country. He traveled in many countries, primarily to investigate the conditions necessary for the settlement of large masses of people in limited areas. Returning to Palestine, he was instrumental in founding *Nahariya, and introduced chemical farming into the country.

Soskin was prominently affiliated with the Revisionists and, later, with the Jewish State party. His published writings include *Small Holding and Irrigation* (1920) and *Intensive Cultivation and Close Settlement* (1926).

SOURASKY: Family of philanthropists in Mexico.

Elias Sourasky. Banker, philanthropist, and active Zionist (b. Bialystok, Russian Poland, 1899; d. Mexico City, 1986). In 1917 he settled in Mexico City, where he and his brother Leon set up a textile plant. In 1936 he founded a group of major banking enterprises in Mexico City, and in 1959 he established the Jaysour Mortgage Bank Ltd. in Israel. Active in Jewish communal and Zionist affairs, he founded in Mexico City the Colegio Hebreo Tarbut. He was a leading member of the General Zionist Society of Mexico. He received decorations from the State of Israel in 1948 and 1969 for services rendered to the State during the War of Independence and the Six-Day War of 1967 particularly in procurement of vital airplane fuel. In 1968 he was awarded the Aguila Azteca, Mexico's highest decoration.

His brother **Leon Sourasky.** Business executive and Zionist philanthropist in Mexico (b. Bialystok, Russian Poland, 1889; d. Mexico City, 1966). Settling in Mexico in 1917, he established and developed various financial institutions and industrial enterprises there. In 1935 he founded and became chairman of the Near East Bonded Warehouses Co. Ltd. in Haifa. His philanthropic work began in 1930, when he became honorary president of the Beneficencia Israelita in Mexico. In 1953 he became president of the Michael Weitz-Sourasky Foundation. His book *The History of the Jewish Community in Mexico, 1917–42* was published in 1959.

SOUTH AFRICA, RELATIONS WITH ISRAEL. Israel's complex and vacillating relationship with South Africa may be divided into four distinct phases. The first stage commenced with the establishment of the State of Israel in 1948 and extended until 1961. During this period, which coincided with the consolidation of Afrikaner power in South Africa, Israel maintained conventional diplomatic relations with Pretoria. An Israeli legation was established in South Africa, while Britain represented South African interests in Israel. Israeli Foreign Minister Moshe Sharett visited South Africa in 1951 at the behest of the leaders of the Jewish community, and in 1953 South Africa Premier D.F. Malan was the first foreign prime minister in office to visit Israel, albeit on an unofficial visit. Economic and commercial ties at this juncture were, however, negligible.

The second stage in Israeli-South African relations, one of perceptible coolness, commenced in 1961 and continued until 1967. During this period Israel revised its policy towards South Africa at the initiative of the Foreign Minister Golda Meir, who was the architect of Israeli efforts to cement ties with the new states of sub-Saharan Africa. In 1961 Israel supported an anti-apartheid censure in the United Nations, and repeated this vote in 1962. In 1963 Israel's diplomatic representative in Pretoria was recalled as Israel reduced its formal ties with South Africa to the consular level. Israeli officials avoided any unnecessary association with the South African regime and contacts, except with the Jewish community of South Africa, dwindled to a trickle. The new Israeli policy reached its culmination in 1966, when Israel voted with the UN majority to relieve South Africa of its mandate over Namibia.

Following the Six-Day War (1967) Israeli-South African relations began to thaw. The South African government praised Israel's performance in the war, made efforts to establish commercial contacts, and set up a South African consulate in Tel Aviv. Although Israel resisted South African requests to upgrade its representation in South Africa and continued to back anti-apartheid resolutions (including offering a donation in 1971 to the Liberation Committee of the Organization of African Unity), ties with South Africa gradually improved in the transitional period between 1967 and 1973.

The events of 1973 constituted a turning point in Israeli relations with South Africa. The Yom Kippur War, the Arab oil embargo, and the massive rupture of diplomatic relations by all but four African states laid the groundwork for the launching of a third phase in Israel's South African connection (1973–1987).

In January, 1974, partly in response to its setback in Africa, Israel reinstated its diplomatic representation in Pretoria, appointing Yitzhak Unna as its first ambassador to South Africa. In that year senior Israeli officials visited South Africa, and the South African Minister of Information, Dr. Connie Mulder, visited Israel. Following the United Nations condemnation of Zionism as racism in 1975, South Africa appointed its first ambassador to Israel, Dr. Charles Fincham. These series of exchanges culminated in April, 1976, with the official visit of South African Prime Minister B.J. Vorster to Israel. A comprehensive agreement that covered a range of commercial, trade, fiscal, and scientific spheres was signed on this occasion. A joint ministerial committee was created to oversee the implementation of these agreements. A decade of increasingly ramified relations between Israel and South Africa ensued.

Economic relations between Israel and South Africa expanded rapidly during the latter part of the 1970s and the first half of the 1980s. The total volume of trade increased tenfold during this period (from $20.9 million in 1970 to $285 million in 1984), 0.5% of Israeli exports and 0.75% of Israeli imports, not including the diamond and military-related trades. A series of joint economic ventures were launched, including the creation of Iskoor (a company owned by the South African Iron and Steel Corporation and Koor Industries). South African investors funded a variety of hydro-electric, construction, regional development, and industrial projects in Israel. Some Israeli firms, such as Tadiran, established plants in South Africa, and private Israeli entrepreneurs invested in the South African homelands of Transkei, Ciskei, and Bophuthatswana. South Africa, for much of this period, was Israel's sole supplier of coal. Relations in the cultural sphere also expanded during this period. The Israel Philharmonic Orchestra, the Bat Dor and Batsheva dance troupes, and the Jerusalem Song and Dance Ensemble toured South Africa. Various South African musical groups visited Israel at this time. Several Israeli cities (Haifa, Acre, Ariel) forged twin-city agreements with South African towns. Some Israeli sportspeople defied international sanctions against South Africa, participating in tennis and boxing matches in the country. Tourism between Israel and South Africa increased rapidly during this period as the South African Tourist Corporation established an office in Tel Aviv and the government-owned South African Airlines (SAA) was granted landing rights in Israel. Israel's improved relationship with South Africa was also expressed on the multilateral level. In 1976 Israel absented itself for the first time from an anti-apartheid vote in the UN, a practice it continued until 1987. The close association with the government of South Africa hampered Israel's efforts to restore diplomatic relations with sub-Saharan African states. Criticism was repeatedly voiced against Israel at the United Nations, and the South African connection became an issue in relations between blacks and Jews in the United States.

A military tie between Israel and South Africa began to develop in 1967 when South Africa supplied Israel with spare parts for its Mirage planes after France had imposed an arms embargo on Israel. Arms-related trade between the two countries expanded in the following decade, including items such as missile-carrying boats, electronic equipment and a license to manufacture certain Israeli-developed light arms. In the early 1980s substantial joint military research and production developed. During the public debate which accompanied the Israeli government's reassessment of relations with South Africa in early 1987, the existence of this trade was officially acknowledged. However, persistent media reports to the effect that there was collaboration in the nuclear sphere between Israel and South Africa have been consistently denied by both countries.

Israel's ties with South Africa were justified by Israeli government leaders on the grounds of its legitimate, pragmatic national interest as well as of concern for the wellbeing of the South African Jewish community. Explanations for Israel's policy also underlined the fact that it was being singled out for activities conducted on a much more comprehensive scale by other states.

The declaration of a state of emergency in South Africa in 1985 and the subsequent global denunciation of apartheid, coupled with increasing Israeli concern over the political costs of the South Africa relationship, led to a systematic reassessment of official policy. Israeli condemnation of racial discrimination in South Africa became more vocal. In late 1986 and early 1987, under pressure from the United States, a range of options for policy change was tabled. On 18 March 1987 the Israeli cabinet announced a change in policy towards South Africa, placing a ban on all new military sales to South Africa, reiterating Israel's abhorrence of apartheid, calling for a reduction of cultural and sports links with South Africa, and appointing a committee to work on a detailed list of additional Israeli measures against South Africa. The new policy signaled the beginning of the fourth phase in Israeli-South African relations.

Israel's ties with South Africa were gradually circumscribed in 1987 and 1988. Cultural and sports contacts virtually ceased. A reduction in formal trade was registered. While delivery on old military contracts continued apace, there was no evidence of new military agreements. Special efforts were made to establish contacts with leaders of the anti-apartheid struggle in South Africa. Black trade unionists participated in specially designed courses sponsored by the Afro-Asian Institute for Labor Cooperation of the Histadrut. Several activists visited Israel in the course of 1987 and 1988.

In September, 1987, the inner cabinet decided to adopt more stringent measures against South Africa, in accordance with the proposals put forth by the interministerial committee established for this purpose. The ten provisions limit economic, cultural, scientific, and sports ties, and include a pledge not to allow Israel to serve as a midway station for bypassing sanctions imposed by other countries. In addition, an embargo was placed on steel imports from South Africa. These measures put Israeli policy in line with that adopted by the European Economic Community. South Africa issued a statement deploring these moves, while the UN Committee on Apartheid praised Israel's policy change, which was followed in November, 1987, by the first Israeli vote against South Africa in the United Nations General Assembly in over a decade. N. CHAZAN

SOUTH AFRICA, ZIONISM IN. South African Jewry began as an incidental offshoot of British Jewry in the 19th century, was consolidated between 1880 and 1930 by a broad wave of immigration mainly from Lithuania, and augmented by a small influx of German Jewry in the 1930s. Between 1880 and 1911, the Jewish population rose from an estimated 4,000 to 46,926. According to the census of 1946 there were 104,156 Jews constituting 4.39% of the white population. When the country became the Republic of South Africa in 1960, there were 114,762 Jews and the census of 1980 showed 117,963, constituting 2.6% of the whites and 0.5% of the total population.

Distinctive Character of Zionism in South Africa. In the comparative perspective of Diaspora Jewish communities, especially in English-speaking countries, the distinctive features of Zionism in South Africa were its preeminence in the institutional structure of the Jewish community as well as its major role in shaping the normative mode of identity of South African Jews. Three major factors may explain this: 1) The peculiarities of South Africa's societal and political systems which not only segmented the entire population into racially defined groups, but even divided the absolutely dominant white group into Afrikaners and English-speakers. The consequently inchoate nature of South African national identity was conducive to the expression of Jewish identity in the national mode provided by Zionism. (2) The very considerable previous exposure to Zionism of the predominantly Lithuanian Jewish immigration to South Africa. (3) The fact that this formative immigration wave was not confronted by a well-established communal leadership generally opposed to Zionism, as was the case in Britain and the United States.

The Zionist Federation and its Components. A Hovevei Zion society was founded in South Africa as early as 1896 in the Transvaal while a society called Bene Zion was formed in Cape Town in late 1897. The first association affiliated with the Zionist Organization founded by Theodor Herzl was the Transvaal Zionist Association, formed in April, 1898. When the South African Zionist Federation was established in December, 1898, it was the first countrywide organization of South African Jewry. In the circumstances resulting from the Boer War at the turn of the century it became, *de facto*, the first representative body of the community vis-à-vis the British governmental authorities. The Zionist leadership established the view that Zionist were obliged "to take part in all Jewish work and to care for all Jewish interests in order to accustom Governments to regard them as representatives of the Jewish people." Therefore it at first resisted attempts to establish a South African Jewish Board of Deputies on the Anglo-Jewish model. Even after such a Board was founded in 1903 and extended countrywide in 1912, the Zionist Federation consistently maintained, through the present, its preeminent position in the communal structure, according to criteria such as membership, fundraising capacity, scope of activities, press resources, political vitality, and youth affiliates.

The South African Zionist Federation has been held as a model of an all-embracing territorial Zionist organization. Membership has always been by societies rather than individuals. It has encompassed and coordinated all Zionist societies and parties and initiated a wide scope of activities. Only between 1937 and 1946, and for a few years in the late 1950s, was this unity disrupted when the Revisionist Zionists left the Federation. Its headquarters in Johannesburg and offices in Cape Town and other provincial cities were supplemented in 1948 by an office in Tel Aviv controlled by a council of South African Zionists settled in Israel. The latter has played a major role in assisting the integration of immigrants from South Africa into Israeli life. In contrast to the situation in many other countries, the Jewish Agency (both as constituted in 1929 and reconstituted in 1969) had and still has no independent presence in South Africa. The South African Zionist Federation has represented its interests, and emissaries performing specialized tasks have always done so under direct contract to the Federation itself.

Committee of Zionist Federation, Cape Town, 1902. [South African Zionist Federation]

Since 1908 the Zionist Federation has maintained its own press organ, the *Zionist Record* (originally monthly and later weekly, incorporating the *South African Jewish Chronicle*). The Zionist Revisionist organization was served by its own weekly, the *Jewish Herald*, while the Mizrachi Organization and the Po'ale Zion produced monthlies, the *South African Jewish Observer* and the *South African Jewish Frontier*, respectively. Women's Zionist societies, founded as early as 1899 and unified in the Women's Zionist Council in 1932, were incorporated as a department of the Federation although also affiliated to WIZO. Always the major generator of grassroots Zionist activities, the Women's Zionist Organization of South Africa had some 15,000 members in more than 100 branches in the 1980s. It has extensively promoted educational programs, raised funds for the Keren ha-Yesod, Youth Aliya, and the Jewish National Fund, and supported a number of its own projects in Israel. Another major department of the Zionist Federation has been the Maccabi organization (with some 6,000 members in the 1980s). Although essentially a sports organization, Maccabi has also served as a medium through which Jews were initiated into fundraising projects and identification with Zionist aims.

Significant above all, however, have been the Zionist youth movements, all affiliated to the Zionist Federation through its Zionist Youth Council. In South Africa virtually all organized youth activity has been of a Zionist character. By 1920 there were 33 "Young Israel Societies" affiliated to the Zionist Federation. In 1931 the first uniformed junior youth movement, Habonim, was founded on scouting lines, and by 1948 the number of youth movements, which had multiplied on the basis of Zionist political ideologies, included Noar ha-Po'el ha-Mizrachi (later Ha-Shomer ha-Dati and Bnei Akiva), Ha-Shomer ha-Tza'ir, the United Zionist Party Youth (later Bene Zion), the Zionist Socialist Youth (later Dror), and the Revisionist Youth Front and Betar. By 1948 the total membership of the various Zionist youth organizations was about 10,000. From the late 1930s onwards probably as much as two-thirds of the youth were exposed to the influence of those Zionist youth movements. In 1966 a census revealed that 6,800 youths were in the youth movements, distributed as follows: Habonim (which had incorporated Dror in 1959 and Bene Zion in 1961) 3,618; Betar 1,483; Bnei Akiva 1,478; Ha-Shomer ha-Tza'ir 221. In the 1980s the Zionist youth movements, Habonim-Dror, Betar, Bnei Akiva, and Maginim (of Progressive Judaism), continued to be a vibrant and major component of South African Zionism. Similarly, the South African Union of Jewish Students (SAUJS), an affiliate of the Zionist Youth Council, provided a significant Zionist presence among Jewish university students.

Although the Zionist Federation never created a school system of its own, it was instrumental in creating the Board of Jewish Education in 1928; the ideological premises of Jewish education were essentially Zionist: "Jewish education based on broadly national-traditional lines." After 1948, the main emphasis in Jewish education shifted from supplementary afternoon schools to day schools. By the mid-1980s

65% of the Jewish school-going population attended the Jewish schools. By agreement with the Jewish Agency, considerable financial assistance has been provided to these schools from Zionist funds.

The *per capita* record of South African Jewry in Zionist fundraising since the early 1920s was unequaled in the world. Between 1922 and 1939 its contribution to the Keren ha-Yesod, even in absolute figures, was second only to United States Jewry. In 1950 the Keren ha-Yesod merged with the South African Jewish Appeal to form the Israel United Appeal (IUA), which took on the form of a voluntary tax encompassing nearly 90% of the community. One of the characteristic strengths of South African Zionism lay in the subordination of the IUA to the Zionist Federation, and in the IUA's primacy over all other fundraising campaigns for local or overseas causes. During the 1970s, however, the IUA became increasingly independent, and in 1983 it ceased to be a department of the Zionist Federation. In 1986 it merged with the United Communal Fund to form a fundraising body which combines local needs with those of the Jewish Agency.

Settling in Israel (*see* SOUTH AFRICANS IN ISRAEL) was always part of the program of South African Zionism. In comparison with other English-speaking countries, aliya from South Africa has represented a higher percentage relative to the size of the home community. However, it was not until 1933 that the first *hakhshara* (agricultural training farm) was set up and prepared the first group of halutzim (pioneers), 12 in number, for their immigration in the mid-1930s. In the late 1940s the training of halutzim reached its peak when Ha-Shomer ha-Tza'ir, Habonim and the United Zionist Party Youth each maintained its own training farm, and candidates for aliya reached a few hundred.

Political Groupings. Political parties developed late in South African Zionism. Before World War I the Zionist Federation, particularly under the leadership of Samuel Goldreich, followed a political Zionist line loyal to Theodor Herzl and his successor David Wolffsohn. The General Zionists originally comprised the great bulk of South African Zionism. Small groups of Po'ale Zion and Mizrachi emerged in 1918 and 1919 respectively, but proved ephemeral. It was only out of the wave of post-World War I immigrants, some of whom had first gone to Palestine and later left for South Africa, that more durable political groupings of Tze'irei Zion (later the Zionist Socialist Party) and Revisionist Zionists emerged in the 1920s. Nine delegates were sent to the 1929 Zionist Congress; six General Zionists, two Zionist-Socialists (Tze'irei Zion), and one Revisionist. (Out of a Jewish population of 80,000, 13,500 were shekel (membership fee) holders and 2,761 votes were cast.) The visits to South Africa of Vladimir Jabotinsky in 1931, 1937, and 1938 strengthened his following there considerably. South Africa became an important outpost of Zionist Revisionism, and its New Zionist Organization acted independently of the Zionist Federation from 1937 until 1946.

At the 19th Zionist Conference in July 1943 the parties succeeded in politicizing the Zionist Federation's constitution. Its executive was to be elected on the basis of party lists rather than on an individual "best-man" basis as in the past. Much of the internal politics of South African Zionism thereafter consisted of forming a non-party "Association of South African Zionists" (merged in 1952 with the United General Zionists to form the United Zionists Association) who struggled to reverse this development and re-organize the structure of the Federation on a non-party basis. They did not succeed, although from the 1960s onwards various modifications were introduced to provide for executive co-option of individuals not associated with parties. Out of a total of 39,945 shekel holders (in a Jewish population of 104,156) no less than 28,876 cast their votes in the elections to the World Zionist Congress of 1946. The vote was divided (in percentages) thus: United Zionist Party 36, United Zionist Revisionist Party 32, Zionist Socialist Party and Ha-Shomer ha-Tza'ir 27, Mizrachi and Ha-Po'el Ha-Mizrachi 5. In the elections of 1952 29,011 shekel holders voted. The percentage return was: United General Zionists 28.3, Association of South African Zionists 17.8, Zionist Socialists 22.8, United Zionists-Revisionists 20.8, Mizrachi 10.

The decline of South African Jews' interest in the Zionist parties was evident during the nineteen years until the next elections were held in 1971. Although 30,000 purchased shekels, only 16,763 voted. The Revisionist Zionist Organization emerged, for the first time, with the greatest percentage vote (35.99), followed by the United Zionist Association (25.18), Habonim Zionist Youth (15.68), Labor Zionists (10.99) and Mizrachi-Bnei Akiva (12.16). No further elections were held in the following years but at the 1986 Conference of the Zionist Federation a new grouping, Magshimim, composed of all Zionists who committed themselves to personal aliya, won independent representation on the Federation's executive, as did the numerically powerful Women's Zionist Organization. This portends a further weakening of the role of the already effete political groups.

Attitude of South African Governments. Throughout its history the South African Zionist Federation enjoyed the sympathy of South African governments and of many major political leaders, both English and Afrikaner. General Jan Christiaan *Smuts was one of the foremost gentile supporters of Zionism in the world. His ardent, Christian-rooted belief in the historic justice of the Zionist cause was shared by others in his political camp, most notably by Jan Hofmeyr. Afrikaner nationalists also evinced sympathy for Zionism. In 1926 the first Afrikaner nationalist government, under the premiership of General J.B.M. Hertzog, issued a formal statement in support of the objectives of the Zionist Organization. However, from 1933 to 1948, the extreme Afrikaner nationalists, headed by Dr. Daniel

Zionist demonstration in Durban, 1975. [South African Zionist Federation]

Malan, succumbed to anti-Semitic influences and fervently opposed Jewish immigration to South Africa. It was only in the first decade after 1948 (the year which marked the contemporaneous emergence of the State of Israel and the final ascendance of Afrikaner nationalists to power) that a rapprochement with Jews gradually took place, facilitated by growing sympathy for Israel and accompanied by renewed understanding of the Zionist Federation's activities.

South African Jewry's unique situation as part of the privileged white minority dominating the other population groups under the racist apartheid system has plagued the conscience of many Jews. Some Jews—proportionately more than other segments of the whites—have actively opposed the system, while the community's leadership has faced a perpetual dilemma. The Zionist Federation has consistently left representative functions in relation to internal South African issues to the Jewish Board of Deputies, although there is much overlap of leadership personnel between the two bodies. As a matter of policy, it has therefore not concerned itself with the morally disturbing and increasingly volatile problems of South African society.

Impact of South African-Israel Relations. Relations between South Africa and Israel (*see* SOUTH AFRICA, RELATIONS WITH ISRAEL), however, have concerned the Zionist Federation, and fluctuations in these relations have had a deep impact on South African Zionism. In the 1950s the Zionist Federation was instrumental in fostering trade and diplomatic relations between the two countries. These suffered a serious setback in the 1960s when Israel's foreign policy in Africa placed it in the forefront of those condemning apartheid. Between 1961 and 1967 the South African government reacted by withdrawing facilities for transfer of IUA funds to the Jewish Agency in Jerusalem. After 1973, in the wake of the unilateral break in relations with Israel by most African states, full diplomatic relations were instituted between Israel and South Africa. On the surface, these have been low profile and conventional, but there has been increasing behind-the-scenes cooperation and the South African government has been sympathetic to the extensive Zionist activities of South Africa's Jewish citizens.

In the mid-1980s South African Zionism (together with South African Jews in general and the entire society) entered a highly critical stage marked by the resurgence of widespread, radical resistance to apartheid and white supremacy, and growing world pressure for trade sanctions against South Africa. Concern was aroused by hostile attitudes towards Jews—largely in the guise of "anti-Zionism"—which became evident among black political groups, especially of Moslems. At the same time anti-Semitism is prevalent, as in the past, among extreme right-wing whites who oppose any modifications of the apartheid system. Although nearly 2,000 South African Jews settled in Israel between 1985 and 1988, it was estimated that this number was exceeded by those choosing to move to other countries. Attendant upon the aggravation of moral dilemmas and of doubts about the future of South African society, aliya became, more than ever before, a critical concern of Zionists. G. SHIMONI

SOUTH AFRICAN JEWS IN ISRAEL. Most of the Jews in South Africa, numbering 118,000 in 1980, stem from Lithuania. The fact that the Jewish community was so homogeneous, with most communal leaders being pro-Zionist, resulted in one of the most united and ardent Zionist communities in any of the free countries of the Diaspora, with strong leadership centralized in the South African Zionist Federation (*see* SOUTH AFRICA, ZIONISM IN).

From the beginning, there was a belief in ultimate Zionist fulfillment through immigration to Israel. The record of *aliya* by South African Zionists is considerably higher than that of other English-speaking communities. By 1906, 35 had left the Transvaal for Jerusalem. When Israel celebrated its 40th anniversary in 1988, the Tel Aviv office of the South African Zionist Federation estimated that 17,000 South Africans (including first-generation children) were settled in Israel, i.e., nearly 15% of South African Jewry itself. A noteworthy feature of this immigration is the high percentage of Zionist leaders who participated, such as Lazar Braudo, Joseph Janower, Katie Gluckman, Louis Pincus, Sam Levin, Felix Landau, Nicolai Kirschner, Israel Dunsky, Zvi Infeld, Sydney Berg, Inez Bernstein, Joseph Herbstein, Sol Liebgott, Harry Hurwitz, and Isaac Kalmanovitz.

Pioneering Capital. In the 1920s and 1930s several prominent South African businessmen settled in Israel and invested "pioneering capital" in enterprises important to the development of the country. Among these were the Binyan Mortgage Company, which lent money at low interest rates to home-builders at a time when interest rates were generally oppressive; Palestine Cold Storage, the country's first cold storage plant, which made a great contribution to agriculture; Peltours, which pioneered in travel and tourism; Binyan Insurance Company, which later merged with Migdal to form one of the largest insurance groups in the country. Another company, the Palestine Land Development Corporation, acquired land in strategic sites for Jewish settlement, and, in particular, developed the Tiberias foreshore, where a renowned hotel, the Galei Kineret, was built. The overall South African holding company was the African Palestine Investments Corporation (the API).

In the early 1950s, Prime Minister David Ben-Gurion made Ya'akov Geri, of the Africa Palestine Investments, Minister of Commerce, although he was a non-party man. A large number of other South African enterprises were launched after the State was established, but their comparative importance diminished due to the vast sums being invested by American and other western Zionists, and by restrictions on getting capital out of South Africa.

Among later successful large-scale South African commercial enterprises was API's development of Savyon, a commuters' suburb outside Tel Aviv.

A particularly interesting industrial contribution was a result of medical research by a South African plastic surgeon, Professor Isaac Kaplan of Beilinson hospital, whose contribution to laser beam surgery led to the creation of a muti-million-dollar enterprise exporting lasers all over the world.

Pioneering. In 1933 a Halutz (pioneer) farm was established in the Transvaal, and many young Zionists trained there to become settlers in moshavim and kibbutzim in Palestine, later Israel. This drive towards pioneering settlements on the land was strongly reinforced from the late 1940s onwards when Habonim, which became a powerful influence among Jewish youth in South Africa, adopted immigration and pioneering as major objectives.

As a result, South Africans played important roles in setting up several kibbutzim and moshavim. Settlements that South Africans helped to launch or where they are now settled include Shuval, Tzora, Tuval, Moshav Ha-Bonim, Ma'ayan Barukh, Yizre'el, Timorim, Amatzya, Barka'i, Galed, Kefar Blum, Ha-Solelim, Sedeh Nitzan, Kefar Giladi, Sheluhot, Nirim, Zikim, Moledet, Ramat Yohanan, Manof, Nahshon, Talmei Yosef, Neveh Ilan, Kokhav Ya'ir, and Orot.

***Mahal** (*Mitnadvei Hutz la-Aretz*; Overseas Volunteers). When it became manifest in 1947 that war between Israel and the surrounding Arab states was imminent, emissaries went to South Africa to recruit personnel to help set up what were to become the Israel Defense Forces (IDF). South African Jewry was in a position to supply such recruits, because many thousands of Jews had served in the South African forces during World War II.

Although Israel had a nucleus of trained fighting men from the Jewish Brigade, the Palmah and Hagana, and others who had served in various armies in World War II, the need for the South African veterans was acute.

Of the many who volunteered, about 700 were selected and went to Israel. They were by far the largest contingent relative to the size of the home communities of the volunteers. While members of Mahal served in all branches of the service, their influence was most marked in the nascent Israel Air Force and in the Medical Corps. In both these branches, experienced officers were given key positions and helped to shape the character of the air force and medical corps throughout the years to come. Many of the Mahal volunteers remained or returned as settlers.

Ashkelon. During World War II, a South African Organization, the South African Jewish War Appeal, collected a considerable sum of money for the aid of victims of the Holocaust. Most of the survivors were brought to Israel.

The strategic planners of Israel decided that the defense and economy of the country required that a new town be built on the sand dunes next to the Mediterranean, some eight miles north of the Gaza Strip. The Government of Israel suggested to the SA Zionist Federation and the War Appeal that the funds of the Appeal be allocated to launching such a town.

The idea was accepted, and the South Africans undertook the financing, planning, and building of Ashkelon, at a site where once a thriving Philistine city had existed. The South Africans built several hundred housing units, a civic and commercial center, a hotel, a nursery school, a watertower, gardens and parks, piazzas, roads, a family and community health center, along with the requisite infrastructure. Later South Africa contributed to the financing, planning, and building of the Ashkelon hospital and of a football stadium. Help was given to launch several enterprises, including Miromit, founded by moshav Timorim, the first firm to manufacture solar heaters in Israel.

This South African-built town was later absorbed, along with the former community of Migdal, and became one of the five residential units of greater Ashkelon. The unit is now known as Afridar.

The first two mayors of Ashkelon were former South Africans, Henry Sonnabend and Leo Tager.

Medicine. South African doctors made a meaningful contribution to medicine in Israel. Even before they arrived with Mahal to serve in the IDF, Dr. Mary Gordon had gone to work among the refugees in the detention camps in Cyprus; later she served Yemenite immigrants in the Rosh ha-Ayin *ma'abara* (transit camp).

When the Mahal contingent arrived, Dr. Lionel Meltzer, who had been awarded the Military Cross during World War II, was appointed second-in-command to Dr. Chaim Sheba in the Medical Corps. Meltzer mobilized several South African specialists in the treatment of war trauma. Among them was the psychiatrist, Dr. Louis Miller, who set up psychiatric services in the IDF for the Air Force and later for the Ministry of Health.

After the War of Independence ended, South African doctors and lawyers financed the establishment of the Leopold Greenberg Forensic Medical Institute in Tel Aviv, which was established by Dr. Okkie Gordon, a South African pathologist.

Professor Sidney L. Kark was responsible for setting up, with an initial staff consisting almost entirely of South Africans, the Hadassah Family and Community Health Service, serving a community of 20,000 in Kiryat ha-Yovel, a Jerusalem suburb. Moving the initial staff to Israel was planned and financed by the SA Zionist Federation.

In the field of administration, Dr. Jack Karpas became the associate director-general of the Hadassah-Hebrew University Medical Center in Jerusalem, and held the post for many years.

The SA Zionist Federation established a special committee to encourage and help the aliya of doctors and to serve as a liaison between Israel and South Africa, finding the specialists most needed in Israel. By the 40th anniversary of the State, over 300 former South African physicians were settled in Israel, many of them holding key positions in hospitals. Professor Joseph T. Borman, of Hadassah, performed the first successful heart transplants in Israel.

Sport. Sport is an important aspect of the quality of life in South Africa, and South Africans have done a great deal to encourage the sports they enjoyed before immigrating.

Among the best-known is Dr. Ian Froman, a one-time Davis Cup player for South Africa. He promoted the Israel Tennis Centers, which have established over 100 courts in Israel and have revolutionized the game in the country.

Many sports were virtually non-existent in Israel in 1948, and were set up by South Africans. Among these are lawn bowls, to which Max Spitz made a particularly important contribution, cricket, squash, rugby, hockey, and archery. Most of the players in the first years of the Caesarea Golf Club were South Africans.

Former South Africans represented Israel in the Maccabia Games and other major events in many of these sports.

Personalia. A number of South Africans achieved prominence in the Jewish Agency and in government service. Arye (Louis) Pincus was chairman of the World Zionist Organization and of the Jewish Agency. In 1987 Mendel Kaplan was elected Chairman of the Board of Governors of the Jewish Agency. Raphael Kotlowitz was a member of the Jewish Agency executive in the 1970s and Harry Hurwitz was adviser on Diaspora Affairs to Israel Prime Ministers.

Felix Asher Landau and Leonard Rabinowitz became district judges; Colin Gillon was state attorney for several years; and Israel Dunsky was mayor of Kefar Shmaryahu. Arthur Lourie and Michael Comay were leading Israeli diplomats and South-African born Abba Eban served in various governments. Norman Lourie was a pioneer in Israel film production. Joan Comay wrote many popular books on Israel.

The Zionist Federation Office in Tel Aviv. South African aliya and absorption in Israel have been greatly facilitated by the financial and imaginative support given by the Israel office of the SA Zionist Federation, whose offices are in Tel

Aviv. This has included housing and other loans, aid to members of various professions to get their qualifications recognized, setting up hostels providing temporary accommodation, running Israel's first hotel course in English. An experimental project, initiated in 1987, was bringing immigrants directly to their own apartments in Rishon le-Zion rather than sending them to absorption centers. Another new project is the Protea home for retirees. P. GILLON

SOUTHERN RHODESIA, ZIONISM IN. *See* ZIMBABWE AND ZAMBIA, ZIONISM IN.

SPIRE, ANDRE. Poet and spokesman for Zionism in France (b. Nancy, France, 1868; d. Paris, 1966). Together with a career in the French civil service and enthusiastic activity for the improvement of the social conditions of the working class, Spire became one of the finest modern French poets. His Jewish background and his passion for justice influenced his reaction to the Dreyfus affair, and Jewish destiny, Jewish hopes, and the redemption of the Jewish people became an important theme of his poetry and of his political action. This led him to Zionism. During World War I he helped mobilize public opinion in favor of Zionism. He founded (1918) the Ligue des Amis du Sionisme (League of the Friends of Zionism) and edited its bulletin, *La Palestine Nouvelle* (The New Palestine). Spire was invited by the World Zionist Organization to be one of the spokesmen to present the Zionist case before the Paris Peace Conference in 1919. His speech to the leaders of the conference was an event of considerable moral and political significance for Zionism. Spire was active in defending and assisting refugees from Nazism. From 1941 to 1946 he taught university courses in the USA in poetry and French literature.

Spire's published works include poems directed against anti-Semitism, and favoring a Jewish homeland. He wrote short stories and essays. A. ALPERIN—M. CATANE

SPIRITUAL ZIONISM. *See* CULTURAL ZIONISM.

SPORTS AND PHYSICAL EDUCATION IN ISRAEL. Physical education was introduced into Eretz Israel in the last decade of the 19th century by classroom teachers who had been trained in Germany. Yeshayahu Press introduced physical education at a boys' school in Jerusalem in 1894, and Heinrich Loewe at a girls' school in Jaffa a year later.

In 1898 Max Nordau made his famous speech on *Muskeljudentum* ("Muscular Jewry") at the second Zionist Congress, and as a result Jewish gymnastics and later sports clubs came into being all over Europe. As early as 1899 Theodore Weiss attempted to create a gymnastics club in Jaffa and asked the Executive of the Zionist movement for assistance. The Executive agreed in principle but shied away from the project, probably for lack of funds.

The first teacher to make physical education his profession was Abraham Zvi Goldsmit, who started working in Jerusalem in 1904 after having been fascinated with the subject as a rabbinical student in the Netherlands. Goldsmit was instrumental in creating one of the first two gymnastics clubs in the country, the Bar-Giora club in Jerusalem, which was founded by the students' association of the local teachers seminary in 1906. The same year a public club, the Rishon le-Tzion club, was founded in Jaffa.

The second teacher to enter the physical education field was Zvi Nishri, in 1907. Nishri's major contributions to the field were the creation of a Hebrew terminology for physical education and sports (Goldsmit before him had taught in German); the introduction of Scandinavian gymnastics, in 1911; the publication of several books in Hebrew, starting with two books on gymnastics and football, in 1913; and the foundation of the *scouting movement after World War I and of the Physical Education Teachers' Association in 1927.

Competitive Sports. The first organized sports competitions in the country took place in Rehovot in 1908. That year the youth of the village organized an annual spring festival during Passover, in which sports played a dominant part. The Rehovot Festival was an immediate success and was held six times before World War I, which brought it to an end. The festival included track and field events, wrestling, shooting, and horseback riding.

The creation of the first clubs in 1906 was followed by attempts to form clubs in various settlements, but many of these proved unsuccessful. However, the *Maccabi club, formed in Jerusalem in the winter of 1911 by Aviezer Yellin, met with immediate success and soon had 300 active members. This club, together with the clubs of Jaffa and Petah Tikva, called a meeting in Jaffa in September, 1912, from which the national organization of the Maccabi developed. Within two years the Maccabi organization comprised about 20 clubs with an aggregate membership of 1,000.

World War I brought great hardships to the yishuv, whose precarious position made it impossible to engage in any sports activity. Following the British occupation of the country in 1917–18, sports began to flourish, soon replacing gymnastics as the major physical activity. The Football Association became the first national sports federation to be established, in 1928.

Earlier, a split had occurred in the sports movement. In 1926 the Histadrut founded *Ha-Po'el, a workers' sports organization, which in 1927 became associated with the Socialist Workers' Sports International (SASI). Maccabi and Ha-Po'el did not cooperate, except in soccer, until after the establishment of the State of Israel in 1948. Other sports organizations created in that era were *Betar, of the Revisionists, and Elitzur, of Ha-Po'el ha-Mizrachi.

While Ha-Po'el catered primarily to the masses and by 1935 had already become the largest sports organization in the country with more than 10,000 active members, Maccabi continued to emphasize competitive sports. It was due to Maccabi's initiative that the Sports Federation was founded in 1931 and the Palestinian Olympic Committee in 1933.

The climax of the activities of the Maccabi was the international *Maccabia Games, which were first held in 1932 and which replaced the national meetings of that organization that were started already in 1919. The Maccabia Games, held under the auspices of the Maccabi World Union (founded in 1921), have subsequently been organized 12 times and have since 1953 been held in the year following the Olympic Games. In recent games as many as 4,000 Jewish athletes from close to 40 countries have participated.

Ha-Po'el started its own national meetings back in 1928 and after the establishment of the State turned the Ha-Po'el Games into international events. These games too are held

Israeli contingent at opening ceremonies of the Maccabia. [Israel Information Services]

on a quadrennial basis, in the year before the Olympic Games, and were held for the 13th time in 1987. Whereas the Maccabia Games are undoubtedly the most important national sports event, the Ha-Po'el Games are the most important international sports event in the State of Israel.

The yishuv tried to establish its place in Asian sports by attempting to create relations with the neighboring countries and by sending, as early as 1934, six athletes to the Western Asian Games in New Delhi. After the establishment of the State, Israel made great efforts to integrate into Asian sports, an effort which came to an abrupt end in 1974, when the Asian sport bodies for all practical purposes expelled Israel under political pressure from all Arab countries. By then Israel's athletes had participated in four Asian Games, in which they had gained 53 medals.

Israel's flag was raised for the first time at the Olympic Games at Helsinki in 1952. An invitation to the Olympic Games held in Nazi Germany in 1936 had been declined for obvious reasons by the Palestinian Olympic Committee, while during the London Olympics of 1948, Palestine, as a mandated territory, no longer existed, and hence its Olympic Committee was no longer recognized. The new Israel Olympic Committee was to be accredited only in 1951. Since 1952 Israel has participated in all Olympic Games, with the exception of the 1980 Moscow Olympics, at which time Israel joined the boycott organized by President Carter.

Israel's participation in the 1972 Olympic Games in Munich was terminated by a tragedy, when Arab terrorists brutally killed 11 members of Israel's Olympic delegation—athletes, coaches, and referees. Nevertheless, Israel has not forsaken the international sports arena and following the political developments on the Asian continent, Israel has tried to integrate into European sports. These efforts were only partially successful, mainly due to the opposition of the Eastern European Socialist countries. The best achievements by athletes from Israel in the European arena have been the second place gained in the continental basket-ball championship in 1977 and the victories of Maccabi Tel Aviv in the European Basketball Champions' Cup in 1978 and 1981. In 1970, the Israel soccer team reached the last 16 of the World Cup in Mexico City.

Physical Education. Until World War II the yishuv had only 80 physical education teachers, 40 of whom had been

Aerobic dancing in Hebrew University Sports Center. [Hebrew University]

trained in Scandinavia. The war cut Palestine off from Europe, and to meet the growing need for physical educators local teacher training was started in 1944. What started out as a one-year course has since become (in one of the five institutions now training physical educators) a fully accredited four-year academic program, and so far over 5,000 teachers have been trained in Israel, 3,000 of whom belong to the Physical Education Teachers' Association.

On the eve of World War II the Va'ad Le'umi created a Physical Training Department, which was taken over by the Ministry for Education and Culture at the establishment of the State. In 1960 the department was replaced by the Sport and Physical Education Authority within the same ministry. The Council also decided, in 1944, to establish a national center for physical education and sports, but only in 1957 did the Wingate Institute open its doors. U. SIMRI

Yosef Sprinzak. [Israel Information Services]

SPRINZAK, YOSEF. Israeli labor leader and statesman (b. Moscow, 1885; d. Jerusalem, 1959). Born of a prominent family of manufacturers who were permitted to live outside the Jewish Pale. Sprinzak was brought to Kishinev and later to Warsaw. Early active in Zionism, he helped found the Tze'irei Zion of southern Russia in Kishinev in 1905. He represented Tze'irei Zion at the Helsingfors Conference of 1906 and was a delegate to Zionist Congresses, beginning with the Eighth (1907). In 1908 he went to Beirut to study medicine at the American University, but that year he was called to Eretz Israel to serve as secretary of Ha-Po'el ha-Tza'ir. During World War I he was the workers' representative on the committee for the relief of the yishuv.

A cofounder of Hitahdut, Sprinzak helped organize its inaugural conference in Prague (1920). In 1921 he was appointed to the Zionist Executive, heading its Labor Department until 1927 and its Aliya Department from 1929 to 1931. He served on the Board of Directors of Keren Ha-Yesod and on the World Executive of Po'ale Zion. Sprinzak was instrumental in organizing the Va'ad Le'umi (National Council) and Asefat ha-Nivharim (Elected Assembly), the two representative bodies of the yishuv under the British Mandate for Palestine.

In 1946 he became chairman of the Zionist General Council, a position he held until his death. By the time the State of Israel was established in 1948, he had been secretary-general of the Histadrut (1945–48) and a member of the Tel Aviv Municipal Council. He was made chairman of the Provisional Council of State, and when the First Knesset met in 1949, he was unanimously elected Speaker, holding the office for the rest of his life. In this capacity he served several times as Acting President of Israel during the absence or illness of Chaim Weizmann and as Interim President from Weizmann's death until the election of Yitzhak Ben-Zvi (November–December, 1952).

Sprinzak was universally respected for his dignified and impartial conduct of Knesset affairs. He frequently deplored the tendency in some Israeli circles to disparage Zionist activity in the Diaspora, asserting that it was a mistake to expect all Zionist leaders to move to Israel. His letters were published in 1965 under the title *Igrot Yosef Sprinzak.*

STAMPFER, JOSHUA. Early pioneer in Eretz Israel (b. Szombathely, Hungary, 1852; d. Petah Tikva, 1908). The son of a rabbi, Stampfer was reared in strictest Orthodoxy, but also received a secular education. He became a tutor at the home of his uncle Eliezer Raab, who later, along with Stampfer, was to become one of the founders of *Petah Tikva. He supported the Hibbat Zion idea and devised a plan to establish in Eretz Israel yeshiva settlements whose inhabitants would devote their time to farming and Talmudic studies. Inspired by the successful bid of the Hungarian revolutionaries for national freedom, he became imbued with the ideal of Jewish national independence and at the age of 17, against the wishes of his parents, left Hungary for Jerusalem which he reached after a journey of five months, having traveled largely on foot.

In Jerusalem he studied at a yeshiva and later joined a group that sought to buy land and establish an agricultural settlement. In 1872 this group bought land near Jericho, but the sale was invalidated by the Turkish authorities. In 1878 Stampfer participated in the purchase of land for Petah Tikva and was among the first settlers to establish themselves there. He toiled on the land and defended it against Arab marauders. When the pioneers were forced to abandon the settlement, Stampfer returned to Jerusalem. In 1882 he visited the United States on behalf of the Hungarian Kolel (charity organization). During all his travels in America and Europe he spoke on behalf of the settlement of Eretz Israel. When settlement efforts were resumed in Petah Tikva, he returned there. In 1885 he visited Russia and western Europe and influenced the Hovevei Zion and Baron Edmond de Rothschild to give material aid to the settlement.

STAMPS OF ISRAEL. The first post offices in the Holy Land were established by the European great powers. In 1852 France inaugurated a new shipping line to the Orient, with post offices at ports of call, among them Jaffa. In addition, the French Consulate in Jerusalem acted as a letter-collecting agency for the Jaffa office. At about the same time Austria established post offices in Jerusalem and Jaffa, and later, Russia, Germany, and Italy followed suit. The postal services of the great powers were extended also to Haifa, but attempts to establish offices elsewhere met with strenuous opposition from the Turkish authorities, who had begun to operate their own state postal services after 1865.

The Austrian (Jaffa) post office was able to maintain agencies in the Jewish settlements of Rishon le-Zion and Petah Tikva for relatively short periods with permission of the local governors.

Despite the very doubtful legal basis of the foreign post offices (the so-called capitulations), the Ottoman Empire succeeded in suppressing them only after Turkey's entry into World War I, in 1914. Philatelic material from this period showing postmarks of places in Eretz Israel is highly coveted by collectors today.

The Turkish post offices in their turn came to an end with the conquest of Palestine by the forces of Gen. Edmund H. Allenby (1917–18). During the war both British and Turkish fighting forces operated army post offices. With the end of hostilities the British military post offices were made accessible to the civilian population and became the basis for the civilian post offices of the mandatory era.

During World War II army post offices of the Allied forces (British, Australian, Polish, Greek, Belgian, etc.) again operated in the country. When the mandatory post offices were closed (April-May, 1948), an interim stamp issue was hastily prepared by overprinting Jewish National Fund seals with the Hebrew word *do'ar* (post) to enable the post offices of the yishuv to carry on. These stamps were in circulation from 1 May 1948 on.

Stamps of the State of Israel. In April, 1948, it became clear that after the termination of the British Mandate (15 May), no postage stamps of any kind would be available, and plans were made to prepare stamps for the emerging State of Israel. A series of nine stamps, ranging in value from 3 to 1,000 prutot and depicting ancient Hebrew coins, was decided upon. The actual printing began on the night of 2 May 1948, which left only 12 working days before the opening day of the post offices of the new State (16 May). The stamps appeared according to plan, though their preparation encountered great difficulties. The stamps had to be printed in absolute secrecy, under war conditions: the first printing plate was destroyed by enemy shells. Neither gummed paper nor special machinery for printing and perforating the stamps was available. The stamp sheets had to be checked at night by candlelight. Since the name of the new State was not known when the printing started, the stamps were given the imprint "Do'ar Ivri" (Hebrew post).

After the Proclamation of the State a new postal department, the Philatelic Services, was entrusted with the design and production of new stamps, their distribution to post offices, and their sale to collectors. Great care was taken to improve the printing and the artistic quality of new issues. Israel postage stamps reflected every aspect of Jewish history and religion, Israel's struggle for independence and security, the development of agriculture and industry and of the arts and sciences, and the position of Israel in the comity of nations. Within a relatively short time, Israeli stamps won an important place in international philately. Some of the country's earlier stamps, especially the Do'ar Ivri set of 1948, have become coveted rarities and command high prices.

The Philatelic Services, since their establishment in 1948, have issued more than 900 stamps, some of which have received international awards for their attractive design. They have included definitive series of ancient coins, the twelve tribes, signs of the zodiac, emblems of Israel's towns and cities, the country's flora and fauna, annual commemorative issues for the Jewish New Year and Israel Independence Day, and many other subjects. Philatelic clubs, both in Israel and abroad, devote themselves to the stamps of Israel.

M.G. HESKY—ED.

STAND, ADOLF. Zionist leader and public figure in Austria (b. Lvov, Galicia, Austria, 1870; d. Vienna, 1919). Stand studied law at the University of Lvov. A Jewish nationalist from his youth on, he was an active participant in the work of the Zion society of Lvov. One of the founders and leaders of the pre-Herzlian Zionist Organization of Galicia, he became a zealous follower of Herzl.

An eloquent orator, Stand disseminated Zionism among the Jewish masses of Galicia and led the battle against the assimilationists and for Jewish national rights. From 1907 to 1911 he was a member of the Austrian Parliament, representing the district of Brody, and was a leading member of the Jewish Club of that body. He was a member of the Greater Actions Committee of the World Zionist Organization and a leading proponent of Synthetic Zionism. While an émigré in Vienna during World War I, he took an active part in the relief of Jewish refugees from Galicia. In 1919 he headed the Viennese delegation of the Jewish National Council of Eastern Galicia.

Stand was also active as a writer, editing the Galician Zionist periodicals *Przyszlosc* (The Future) and *Voskhod* (East) and the *Rocnik Zydowski* (Jewish Yearbook).

STANDARD OF LIVING. *See* LEVEL OF LIVING.

STATE COMPTROLLER OF ISRAEL. Like most democratic countries, Israel instituted a state control institution very soon after its independence under the State Comptroller's Law enacted by the Knesset in 1949. The State Control Institution has developed substantially in Israel and today plays an important role alongside the country's executive, legislative, and judicial authorities. The Basic Law: The State Comptroller, which the Knesset enacted in 1988, is one of the Basic Laws forming in effect the Constitution of the State of Israel, and is thus an expression of the prominent status accorded to this institution.

The State Comptroller submits to the Knesset a comprehensive annual report (over 900 pages), with findings on faults in the administration of state finances and the management of state-controlled institutions, together with sug-

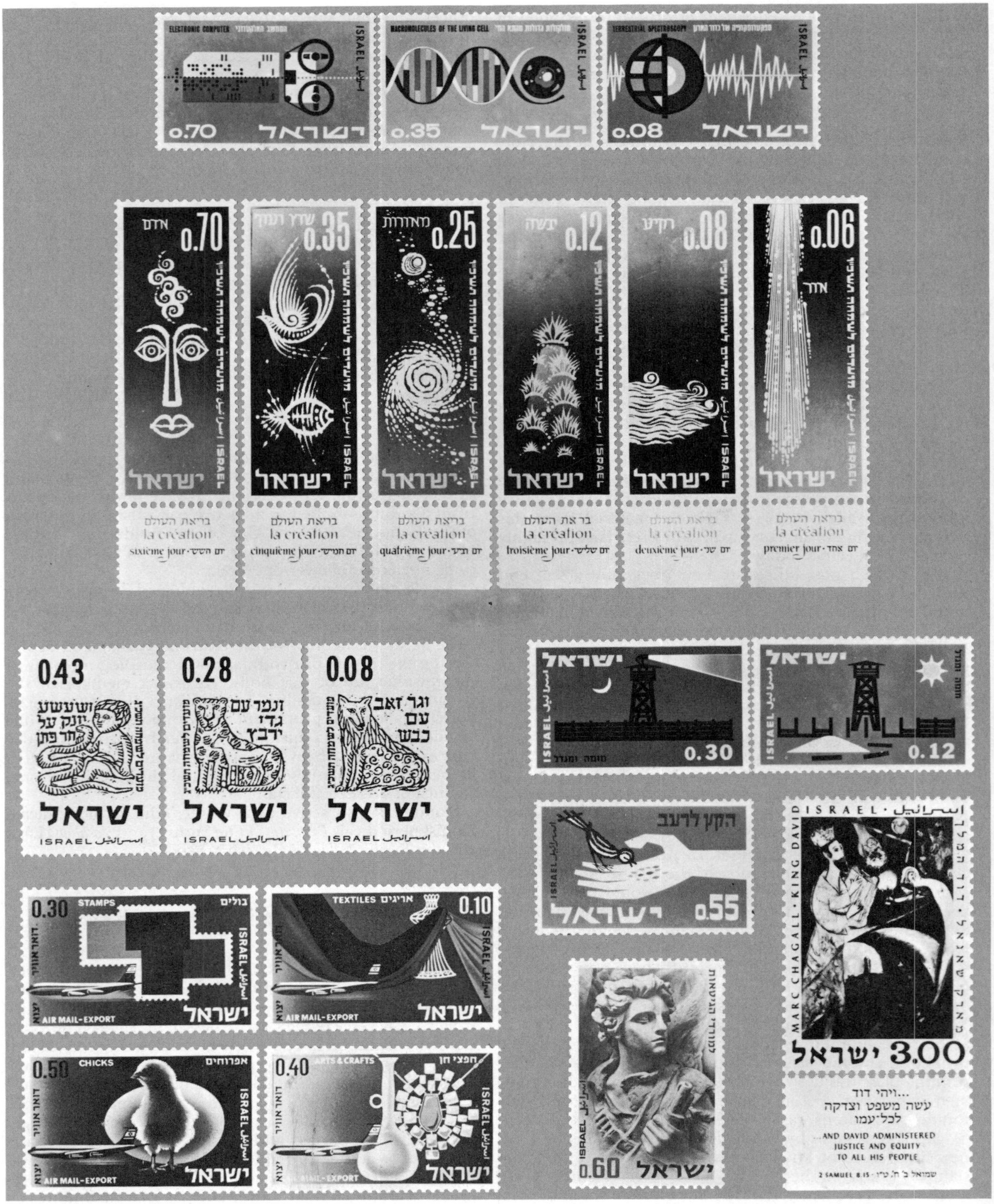

Israeli postage stamps. [Israel Philatelic Agency in America]

gestions for their rectification. In addition to these reports, hundreds of reports on local authorities, statutory corporations, and government companies have been presented.

The task of the State Comptroller is to review the State economy, the property, finances, commitments and administration of the State, of government offices, of every enterprise, institution or corporation of the State, of local authorities and of other bodies or institutions subject by law to the State Comptroller's inspection.

In accordance with the new Basic Law the Comptroller is elected by the Knesset by secret ballot. The election procedures are similar to those prescribed for the election of the President of the State of Israel (previously the Comptroller was appointed by the President, on the recommendation of the Knesset committee). The new Basic Law sets a five-year term of office for the Comptroller, with the possibility of serving no more than two consecutive terms.

By virtue of the Basic Law, the Comptroller is independent of the Government, and is responsible to the Knesset alone. The Law obliges everybody subject to the State Comptroller's inspection to transmit to him, on request and without delay, information, documents, explanations, and any other material which the Comptroller considers necessary for fulfilling his duties.

The State Comptroller maintains contact with the Knesset through the State Control Committee of the Knesset. The budget of the Comptroller's Office is determined, at the suggestion of the Comptroller, by the Knesset Finance Committee.

The bodies subject to the State Comptroller's inspection include not only government ministries and State enterprises and institutions, but also all local authorities, any corporation subject to control by law, any body in whose management the Government participates, and any body supported directly or indirectly by the Government or by an inspected body. The scope of the inspection includes legality of activities, integrity, proper management of the inspected bodies and whether they have operated economically and efficiently.

Any defects found in the course of inspection are brought to the notice of the inspected body and of the minister concerned, together with the Comptroller's demands for rectification; serious defects may be brought to the notice of the State Control Committee of the Knesset even before the submission of the formal report or, where there is reason to suspect the commission of a criminal offense, to the notice of the Attorney General.

In special cases the State Control Committee of the Knesset is entitled, on its own initiative or at the suggestion of the Comptroller, to decide on the appointment of a commission of inquiry in accordance with the 1968 Inquiry Commissions Law.

The fact that the State Comptroller has no authority to impose direct sanctions on those responsible for the mistakes and defects he uncovers is seen by some as a weakness, and there has been some demand for the direct mention, in the Control Reports, of those responsible for the defects revealed by the Comptroller. On the other hand, it has also been argued that that could be interpreted as an assumption of duties imposed on other State authorities and would lead to an unclear delimitation of powers. Furthermore, such a procedure could affect the right of every individual to a fair trial by due process.

From the beginning of his activity the State Comptroller dealt with complaints lodged by citizens concerning inspected bodies. In 1971 an amendment to the Law prescribed that the Comptroller would also serve as Public Ombudsman, and would be authorized to inquire into complaints concerning inspected bodies and employees or office-holders in those bodies. According to that amendment, a complaint reviewed by the Ombudsman could be an act or an oversight which affects the complainant directly or deprives him directly of a benefit, where the act contravenes the law or has been effected without legal authority or contrary to proper management, is excessively inflexible or blatantly unjust.

A special unit in the Comptroller's Office—the Ombudsman—deals with complaints lodged by the public, and is empowered to demand the agency concerned to answer the charges and to furnish all the documents and explanations required. On completion of the investigation the Ombudsman decides whether the complaint is justified, and is also entitled to indicate the need for rectification of the defect and the method and time limit for such rectification. If the matter is not rectified, the Ombudsman may inform the relevant minister or the State Control Committee of the Knesset accordingly. The Ombudsman receives about 5,000 complaints annually, over 40% of which are found to be justified.

Israel's State Comptroller cooperates closely with the state comptrollers of other countries and is an active member of the international organization of supreme control institutions. He also cooperates with Ombudsmen of other countries.

The first State Comptroller was Siegfried Moses (1949–1961); he was followed by Yitzhak Nebenzahl (1961–1982); Yitzhak Tunik (1982–1986); Ya'akov Maltz (1986–1988); and Miriam Ben-Porat (1988–). S. GUBERMAN

STATE LIST. *See* RAFI.

STATE OF ISRAEL BONDS. Israel government stock issued in a number of countries to raise capital for economic development. The great wave of immigration following the establishment of the State of Israel confronted the new government with serious financial burdens. Early in September, 1950, Prime Minister David Ben-Gurion convened a conference in Jerusalem of some 50 outstanding Jewish leaders from the United States and other countries to discuss Israel's difficult economic situation.

After placing the facts before them, the Prime Minister proposed that an Israel Bond issue be floated in the United States as a means of opening up a new source of urgently needed funds. The conference delegates approved the proposal in a four-point program, which also called for increased support of the United Jewish Appeal and the stimulation of private investment and aid from foreign governments.

Six weeks later, in October, a national conference of the representatives of major American Jewish organizations and communities, meeting in Washington, endorsed the plan for an Israel Bond campaign in the United States. Ben-Gurion visited the United States in May, 1951, to launch the Israel Bond drive. His visit was the occasion for enthusiastic public demonstrations of sympathy for Israel, which gave dramatic impetus to the sale of the first Israel Bond issue in the United States.

The launching of the Israel Bond Organization was beset with many problems and difficulties. When the financial world showed no interest in the Bonds, the Israel program was established as a volunteer community enterprise based on American Jewish concern for the welfare of Israel. An army of volunteers in communities throughout the country was marshaled for the task of selling Israel Bonds. Volunteers were recruited from synagogues, women's groups, and from the general Jewish community.

This concept of volunteer community effort remained the backbone of the Israel Bond drive. With very rare exceptions, every organized element in American Jewish life, religious, communal, cultural, and social, cooperated actively with this far-flung enterprise, which became a decisive factor in the economic development of Israel.

In time, other countries joined in the Israel Bond drive. Sales in Latin America began late in 1951, in Canada in 1953, and in western Europe in 1954. By 1986, Israel Bonds were sold in more than 30 countries of the free world.

From its inception in 1951 through 1986, the State of Israel Bond Organization sold $8 billion in Israel Bonds. Approximately 80 per cent of this amount was realized in the United States. The balance came from Canada, Europe, and Latin America. More than $4.5 billion had been repaid on time.

After the Yom Kippur War, which stimulated a record $515 million in Bond sales, the Bond Organization began to develop new financial instruments in its effort to help Israel recover from the economic after-effects of the war. By 1988 the new securities also included two variable rate Bonds.

The 1970s and 1980s saw an expansion of the campaign into the corporate world, financial institutions, labor unions, pension plans and other employee benefit funds.

By 1986, the Bond Organization was on its way towards an annual sale of $600 million.

STAVSKY TRIAL. *See* ARLOSOROFF, HAYIM.

STEED, HENRY WICKHAM. British journalist and Christian Zionist (b. Long Melford, Suffolk, England, 1871; d. Wootton-by-Woodstock, Oxfordshire, 1956). Steed joined the staff of the London *Times* in 1896, serving as a correspondent in Berlin, Rome, Vienna, and London. In 1914 he was named foreign editor of *The Times*, a position which he held until 1917 and in which he was responsible for the foreign policy views of the paper. He met Herzl first in 1896 and again, in Vienna, in 1902. Impressed by Herzl's analysis of anti-Semitism and its causes, Steed became convinced that Zionism would offer a cure for the social, political, and economic aspects of the "Jewish problem" in the Hapsburg Monarchy. In addition, he came to feel that Zionism would present a counterpoise to those Jewish elements that embraced revolutionary movements. In his book *The Hapsburg Monarchy* (1913), in which he discussed the situation within Austro-Hungary, he referred to the growth of Zionism as "the most hopeful sign noticeable in Jewry for centuries" and added that "Zionism in its territorial aspects is now an integral, if not indeed the most significant, part of the Near Eastern question, at least as regards the future of the Ottoman Empire." Early in World War I he supported the efforts of Vladimir Jabotinsky and Col. John Henry Patterson to recruit a Jewish regiment from London's East End (*see* JEWISH LEGION). During the negotiations culminating in the issuance of the Balfour Declaration, he was in constant touch with British and Zionist leaders and came to feel great admiration for Nahum Sokolow and Chaim Weizmann. On numerous occasions during 1917 he threw the weight of *The Times* into the scales on the Zionist side, using the paper's editorial columns to refute the arguments of anti-Zionists, including the Anglo-Jewish assimilationists. During the 1930s he took an outspoken stand against Nazi anti-Jewish excesses.

STEIN, LEONARD JACQUES. Lawyer, Zionist leader, writer, and lecturer in England (b. London, 1887; d. London, 1973). Stein studied at Oxford University and was president of the Oxford Union in 1910. Interested in Zionism from early youth, he became active on behalf of the Jewish National Fund. He opened a law practice in 1912 but left it at the outbreak of World War I to serve as an officer in the British Expeditionary Force (1914–15, 1917–18) and as a member of the War Trade Intelligence Department (1915–17). From 1918 to 1920 he served as a staff captain in the Palestine military administration, acting as a military governor of Safed, and later joined the political staff of the Egyptian Expeditionary Force in Jerusalem and at general headquarters in Cairo.

A close friend of Chaim Weizmann, Stein was political secretary of the World Zionist Organization from 1920 to 1929. In 1921 he accompanied Weizmann on the latter's first visit to the United States, where he endeavored to arrange a compromise between the views of the Weizmann and Brandeis factions in the Zionist Organization of America. He took an active part in negotiations for the expanded Jewish Agency and served as honorary legal adviser to the Agency from 1929 to 1939. After the issuance of the Passfield White Paper in 1930, he was one of the Zionist negotiators responsible for the letter written the following year by Prime Minister Ramsay MacDonald to Weizmann, which explained away the anti-Zionist statements in the Passfield document. He was a member of the Jewish delegation to the St. James's Conference.

From 1939 to 1949 Stein was president of the Anglo-Jewish Association, which opposed restrictions on Jewish immigration and land purchases in Palestine. He was cochairman with Selig Brodetsky of the Joint Foreign Committee set up by the Association and the Board of Deputies of British Jews. In 1943 the Board of Deputies, under Zionist influence, formed its own Foreign Affairs Committee and the following year advocated the establishment of a Jewish State in Palestine as part of the British Commonwealth of Nations. This policy was opposed by the Anglo-Jewish Association under Stein's leadership. In later years, Stein devoted most of his time to research activities and pro-Israel causes.

His published writings include *Zionism* (1925; new ed., 1932); *Syria* (1926); and *The Balfour Declaration* (1961). He co-edited the first volume of *The Letters and Papers of Chaim Weizmann* (covering 1889–1902). He was awarded the Order of the British Empire in 1953. S. LEVENBERG

STEINHARDT, JACOB. Israeli woodcut master and painter (b. Posen, Germany, 1887; d. Nahariya, 1968). He studied at the Berlin Academy under Lovis Corinth and Hermann Struck and was a member of the Pathetiker Group, 1912. In World War I, he served in the German

Army on the eastern fronts. In the early 1920s, Steinhardt made woodcuts based on German mythology in an expressionist mode. Settling in Jerusalem in 1933 he gave private art classes. In the 1940s he taught woodcut at the Bezalel School and became head of the prints department in 1950 and director of the Bezalel School, 1953–57. Steinhardt established himself as a master of the woodcut medium, also with color woodcuts made in the 1950s and 1960s. Both his paintings and graphic work deal chiefly with biblical subjects, Jerusalem genre, and the Israeli landscape, but he also had a lifelong preoccupation with grotesques in the Gothic tradition. M. RONNEN

STEINSALTZ, ADIN. Rabbinical scholar (b. Jerusalem, 1937). Although he grew up in a home that was secular and socialist in nature, he was tutored in the Talmud and sent to a religious high school. He studied chemistry and mathematics at university. At age 22, he was principal of a high school.

The first volume of his edition of the Babylonian Talmud, *Talmud ha-Mevu'ar*, appeared in 1967. It included vowels and punctuation, as well as translations of the Aramaic passages into modern Hebrew. His own commentary appears alongside the traditional ones. The Institute for Talmudic Publications, which he heads, published the 20th volume of this work in 1988.

The first edition of Steinsaltz's Jerusalem Talmud was published at the end of 1987. This text is full of linguistic and contextual problems, which Steinsaltz helps to make intelligible to the modern Hebrew reader. Steinsaltz is also undertaking an annotated English translation of the Babylonian Talmud.

Steinsaltz heads several religious institutions, including Yeshivat Shefa in Jerusalem. He was awarded the Israel Prize in 1988, in recognition of his achievements.

His works in English include the mystical *Thirteen-Petaled Rose; The Essential Talmud*; a commentary on the stories of Rabbi Nahman of Bratslav, *Beggars and Prayers*; and his Passover Haggada has also been published in English.
G. SHUSTER-BOUSKILA

STERN, AVRAHAM ("Yair"). Leader of the underground movement *Lohamei Herut Israel, Lehi (b. Suwalki, Poland, 1907; d. Tel Aviv, 1942). In 1915, his family was exiled to the Bashkir region in the Urals where he attended a Russian school and became a member of the Communist Party youth group. Returning to Suwalki in 1921, he studied at the Hebrew high school. Stern emigrated to Palestine in 1926 where he spent a year at the Hebrew high school (Gymnasium) in Jerusalem and then enrolled at Hebrew University, majoring in literature and history.

During the 1929 riots he joined the Hagana and served in Galilee and Jerusalem; in 1932 he joined the *Irgun Tzeva'i Le'umi underground where he completed an officers' command course. In 1933 he left for Florence to work on his doctoral dissertation in classical Greek literature but before its completion returned to Palestine to participate in underground activities. He was appointed as aide-de-camp to Avraham Tehomi, commander of the Irgun. Following the split in the Irgun in 1937 Stern was appointed secretary of the command. Already beforehand he accepted the authority of Vladimir Jabotinsky.

The ideological split, however, reached its peak during the third World Convention of Betar in Warsaw when arguments raged between the advocates of militant Zionism (M. Begin and Y. Scheib-Eldad) and Jabotinsky who favored political Zionism. Stern supported Jabotinsky's opponents behind the scenes and rejected Jabotinsky's dominance imposed in the Paris agreement of January 1939. In March, 1939, Stern and his supporters denounced Jabotinsky but did not feel the time to be ripe for a breakaway. That point was reached on 17 May 1939 with the publication of the White Paper and the detention of David Raziel, the Irgun commander. Stern and his colleagues, following Ratosh, advocated an immediate seizure of power by the Jewish minority in Palestine without waiting for a majority.

Just before the outbreak of the War, Stern, pursuing his belief in social Darwinism, called for the imitation of the use of force on the model of other liberated nations. The day before World War II broke out, he and all the Irgun high command were arrested by the British authorities. The final break in the Irgun followed Jabotinsky's call to suspend resistance to opposition to Britain and actively support it against Hitler. Stern opposed unconditional support of Britain without first receiving at least a promise of a Jewish State.

From this point, while under arrest, his strong opposition to military service in the British army or even in any of the Allied Forces, developed into hatred of Britain and concurrently support for the Axis victories. Upon his release in June, 1940, the schism occurred. Since Stern failed to convince Vladimir Jabotinsky to replace Raziel with himself as chief of the Irgun, he made every effort to take over the Irgun and the Revisionist Party. His goal was to turn them into an armed force to fight for independence from Britain on a model drawn from mixed sources, namely the Irish 1916 Easter Rebellion, Pilsudski's activities in Poland in World War I, NILI and Jewish messianic movements such as those of Eleazar ben Jair and Bar-Kokhba.

On 15 September 1940, Stern's organization "Irgun in Israel" (formed two weeks previously) signed the "Jerusalem Agreement", a blueprint for an agreement with Fascist Italy but he was never able to make direct contact with the Italians. Stern conceived that Mussolini might conquer the Middle East and that then it would be possible to establish a Jewish State under his sponsorship. With the defeat of the Italians in Greece and the Western Desert, Stern conceived the idea of signing a pact with Nazi Germany on the understanding that Hitler was winning the war. He felt it important to go in with him before it was too late, in order to participate in the new order. Stern did not assess the true extent of Nazi anti-Semitism and perceived World War II purely as an imperialistic struggle to take over the world, with no ideological basis. He felt Hitler need only be persuaded to move the Jews to Palestine, instead of Madagascar, and establish a Jewish State in return for opposing Britain.

In the late summer of 1941 when the failure of the mission to the Germans became known, "Irgun in Israel" began to disintegrate. Extremist factions from within then took over the group, intensifying their terrorist activities. Their efforts to cooperate with the Axis powers became known to the British, to the Jewish leadership, and to the Irgun movement, which strongly denounced this policy. Still, the Hagana and the Irgun were willing to hide him from the authorities. After members of the group had killed the Tel Aviv police chief and two of his officers, the British stepped up their search and Stern was caught and killed on 12 February 1942. Y. HELLER

STERNBERG, ERICH WALTER. Israeli composer (b. Berlin, 1891; d. Tel Aviv, 1974). After studying law at Kiel, he moved in 1918 to Berlin where he devoted himself to composition under Hugo Leichtentritt. He was influenced by the innovative trends which prevailed in German music in the 1920s. His early works, such as the First String Quartet, reflect the influence of Alexander von Zemlinsky and of Arnold Schönberg in their dense contrapuntal and highly chromatic texture. He endeavored to reach a synthesis of the purely German technique with national Jewish spirit by quoting and elaborating Yiddish songs of eastern Europe and traditional cantillation in the Quartet as well as in his piano suite, *Visions from the East*. From 1924 Sternberg made yearly visits to Palestine, and in 1931 he settled there. Sternberg was strongly opposed to the ideological pressures for a collective, national style, and in the periodical *Musica Hebraica* (1938) he defended the rights of the composer to "walk his own path and speak his personal language, emanating from himself." In the large-scale orchestral works composed in Palestine, *The Twelve Tribes of Israel* (1938) and *Joseph and his Brethren* (1939), he made extensive use of historically related tonal techniques. His chamber works tended to a more dodecaphonic, austere, and abstract style. Sternberg was the President of the Israel Composers' League. He was also very active in organizing concerts of new music in Israel. J. HIRSCHBERG

"STOCKADE AND TOWER" SETTLEMENTS (Homa u-Migdal). Fortified settlements of the period of the Mandate for Palestine that could be set up within a single day. The Arab riots in the spring of 1936 brought Jewish settlement work in Palestine to a halt. When it became apparent that the riots were going to continue, new means were sought to extend Jewish rural settlement in the face of Arab attacks, and a method of erecting fortified settlements within a day was devised. The basic blueprint for such a settlement included a courtyard surrounded by a hollow wooden wall or stockade filled with gravel. In the center of the court stood a watchtower, topped by a searchlight. The cabins of the settlers were located in the corners of the yard. The entire compound was surrounded by barbed-wire fences. the tower and stockade would be prefabricated in sections at nearby settlements, and on the day that the new settlement was to be founded hundreds of people would set out in a convoy of cars and trucks, accompanied by Hagana men and guards, to erect the fortifications. Their job done, the builders would return to their homes, leaving behind a nucleus of 20 to 40 armed settlers who would begin to cultivate the land while remaining on a 24-hour alert against attackers. In the course of time, the neighboring Arabs would come to accept the existence of the new settlement. The settlers would then begin to construct homes and farm buildings outside the stockade, and the temporary camp would be turned into a permanent settlement.

The first settlement erected in this manner was Kibbutz Nir David in the Bet She'an Valley, which was founded in 1936. Prior to World War II, a total of 52 "stockade and tower" settlements were established despite the continuing attacks of marauding Arab bands. The heaviest attacks were against Tirat Tzevi and Ma'oz Hayim in the Bet She'an Valley.

The 1937 proposal of the British Peel Commission for the partition of Palestine between the Arabs and the Jews

Gravel chain on foundation day of Stockade and Tower settlement of En Gev. [Jewish National Fund]

added political importance to the "stockade and tower" settlements which had expanded the areas of Jewish settlement in the Bet She'an Valley, the northern Huleh region, Mount Carmel, and elsewhere. The high point of this settlement was reached with the founding of Hanita on the Lebanese border in March, 1938, which brought western Galilee within the area of Jewish settlement in Palestine.

Y. SLUTSKY

STOCK EXCHANGE IN ISRAEL. *See* BANKING AND FINANCE IN ISRAEL.

STONE, DEWEY DAVID. United States businessman and Zionist leader (b. Brockton, Mass., 1900; d. there 1977). Stone served in the United States Army during World War I and graduated from the Boston University College of Business in 1920. An ardent Zionist from his youth on, he met Chaim Weizmann during the latter's visit to the United States in 1940. He headed the U.S. operation to acquire boats to bring Holocaust survivors into Palestine. Stone had early taken an interest in the Sieff Research Institute, the nucleus of what later became the Weizmann Institute of Science, and he served as chairman of the Institute's Board of Governors from its founding in 1944. In 1960 he was elected an honorary fellow of the Institute, and from 1970 he was chairman of the Board of Directors of the American Committee for the Weizmann Institute of Science.

A former vice-president of the Zionist Organization of

America, Stone was elected to the World Zionist Executive in 1966. That year he became chairman of the United Israel Appeal. He was national chairman of the United Jewish Appeal from 1955 to 1963, thereafter becoming honorary chairman. From 1970 he was also a director of the PEC Israel Economic Corporation, the Israel Foreign Trade Credits Corporation, the State of Israel Bonds Organization, the America-Israel Cultural Foundation, the American Friends of the Hebrew University, the American Society for Technion-Israel Institute of Technology, Inc., and many other Zionist and pro-Israel organizations and institutions in the United States.

STRABOLGI, 10TH BARON (Joseph Montague Kenworthy). British Labor party leader and Zionist supporter (b. 1886; d. London, 1953). Kenworthy was, like his colleague and friend Josiah Clement *Wedgwood, drawn to Vladimir Jabotinsky's activist brand of Zionism. In 1926 he published a much-discussed article, "Transjordan—the Future Jewish Irredenta," in which he condemned the exclusion of Transjordan from the territory of the Jewish National Home as being "wrong not only politically but also economically." In 1927, together with Wedgwood and (James) Ramsay MacDonald, he organized the Palestine Mandate Society for the purpose of disseminating pro-Zionist information in England. He was one of the first to endorse Wedgwood's idea of converting a predominantly Jewish Palestine into a self-governing Dominion within the British Commonwealth of Nations. In the House of Commons, Kenworthy strongly attacked the Passfield White Paper of 21 October 1930.

In 1934 he succeeded his father as Baron Strabolgi. In a debate in the House of Lords (July, 1937), Strabolgi criticized the Peel Commission's partition scheme. During World War II he was president of the Committee for a Jewish Fighting Force, whose purpose was the creation of a Jewish army that would fight alongside the Allied forces on all fronts of the struggle against Nazi Germany.

J. SCHECHTMAN

STRAUS: U.S. family of Zionist sympathizers.

Nathan Straus. Merchant, philanthropist, and supporter of health and social service institutions in Palestine (b. Otterberg, Germany, 1848; d. New York, 1931). Brought to the United States in 1852, Straus had a distinguished career in business. He devoted the last decades of his life to social and philanthropic work in Palestine, which he first visited in 1904. His second visit, in 1912, with Judah L. Magnes, resulted in the establishment in Jerusalem of a domestic science school for girls. During that visit he also opened a soup kitchen for the poor in the Old City of Jerusalem and set up a Health Institute with headquarters in Jerusalem to cope with malaria, trachoma, and other illnesses resulting from lack of sanitation.

In June, 1913, Straus and his wife, Lina Gutherz Straus (1854-1930), returned to the country. They brought with them the first two nurses, Rachel Landy and Rose Kaplan, who started *Hadassah's pioneer work in the Health Institute. During that visit, too, Straus established a Pasteur Institute which, with the Health Institute, played an important role in the control of rabies and epidemics during World War I. In 1915 he supplied half the cargo of $100,000 worth of provisions sent from the United States to war-ravaged Palestine on the collier *Vulcan*.

On his next visit (1923–24), he established the Nathan and Lina Straus Health Center in Jerusalem and, later a similar Health Center in Tel Aviv. In 1927 he returned to lay the cornerstone of the Health Center building in Jerusalem. The two centers were intended to serve all residents irrespective of creed. Straus also made donations to a Moslem orphanage in Jerusalem and to poor Arabs in Jaffa. His known gifts to Palestine totaled $2,000,000, and Mrs Straus donated her jewels to Hadassah.

The Israeli town Netanya, on the Mediterranean coast, was named for him.

Oscar Solomon Straus, brother of Nathan, diplomat, jurist, and philanthropist (b. Otterberg, Germany, 1850; d. New York, 1926). He was also brought to the United States in 1852. After practicing law for a time, he became active in his family's extensive business enterprises. Straus served as U.S. Minister (1887–90, 1898–1900) and Ambassador (1909–10) to Turkey. He was appointed American member of the Permanent Court of Arbitration at the Hague (1902, 1908, 1912, 1920), and from 1906 to 1909, during the administration of Pres. Theodore Roosevelt, he served as Secretary of Commerce and Labor, the first Jew to be named to the U.S. Cabinet.

Straus first visited Eretz Israel in 1888, at the time of his first mission to Turkey, and used his influence to help defend the rights of the Jews there. While in Vienna in 1899, he met Herzl and advised him to go to Constantinople to conduct personal negotiations with Sultan Abdul Hamid II. He urged him, however, to consider Mesopotamia as an alternative to Eretz Israel, which he felt Herzl would never be able to obtain. A few years after Herzl's death, Straus was instrumental in arranging a meeting between the leaders of Zionism and the Jewish Territorial Organization in London to arrive at a common basis for action. After World War I he again visited Palestine, this time at the suggestion of Sir Herbert Samuel.

STRICKER, ROBERT. Zionist leader (b. Brno, Moravia, Austria, 1879; d. Auschwitz, 1944). Stricker was cofounder and president of the Zionist student association Veritas. Settling in Vienna, he advocated participation by Zionists in the political life of the countries where they lived (this policy was referred to as *Landespolitik*) and edited the official Zionist organ, *Die Jüdische Zeitung*.

During World War I he founded the Jewish War Archives, which he directed with Nathan Birnbaum. After the war the Jewish National Council, later called Jewish National party, was established in Austria with Stricker as president. In 1919–20 he was a member of the Austrian Parliament. He founded the Jewish daily *Wiener Morgenzeitung* (1919–28) and the weekly *Die Neue Welt* (1928-38).

At the 12th (1921) and 13th (1923) Zionist Congresses Stricker proposed the election of Chaim Weizmann to the presidency of the World Zionist Organization, but he soon became an opponent of Weizmann's policies, disapproving the enlargement of the Jewish Agency and insisting on defining the aim of Zionism as the establishment of a Jewish State. He resigned as vice-president of the Zionist Actions Committee, became cofounder of the *Radical Zionist party, and, in 1926, joined the *Revisionists. In 1933, following a split in the Revisionist movement, Stricker, together with Meir Grossman and others, formed the *Jewish State party.

Stricker was vice-president of the Zionist-oriented Jewish Religious Community of Vienna. He was also a founder of the World Jewish Congress in 1936, becoming president of its Austrian section.

Immediately after the Nazi occupation of Austria, Stricker was arrested but was subsequently released and given an opportunity to leave the country. He refused, however, insisting that he owed it to his "constituents" to remain with them. The Nazis deported him to Dachau and Buchenwald and later interned him and his wife, Paula, in Theresienstadt. In October 1944 both were moved from Theresienstadt to Auschwitz, where they were killed in the gas chambers. J. FRAENKEL

STRUCK, HERMANN. Graphic artist and Zionist leader (b. Berlin, 1876; d. Haifa, 1944). Struck early demonstrated a talent for sketching and painting and enrolled at the Berlin Academy of Art. He attained international fame as an etcher; his book *Die Kunst des Radierens* (The Art of Etching, 1909) became a standard work on the subject. In 1912 he was named a member of the Royal Society of Painter-Etchers and Engravers in London. He is best known for his portrayals of famous Jewish and gentile contemporaries such as Hermann Cohen, Albert Einstein, Sigmund Freud, Ignacz Goldziher, and Henrik Ibsen. In 1903 he made a well-known etching of Herzl.

A strictly Orthodox Jew throughout his life, he made it a practice to sign his work "Hayim Aharon ben David" or with a Magen David along with his initials. He traveled extensively throughout Europe and the Middle East in search of Jewish types. During World War I he served as a noncommissioned officer in the German Army and was a liaison officer between the German Army and the Jewish population of Poland and Lithuania.

Struck first visited Eretz Israel in 1903 and on his return illustrated Adolf Friedmann's *Reisebilder aus Palästina* (Pictures from Travels in Palestine, 1904). He early became active in the Zionist movement. A close friend of Herzl, he attended a number of Zionist Congresses and later became a director of the Jewish National Fund. He was a founder of the Mizrahi movement in Germany and served on the Central Committee of the Mizrahi World Organization and on the Zionist Actions Committee. In 1922 he carried out his long-cherished plan to settle in Palestine and made his home in Haifa. He helped found the Tel Aviv Museum, and he served on the Board of Directors of the Bezalel School in Jerusalem.

"STRUMA." "Illegal" immigrant ship (*see* "ILLEGAL" IMMIGRATION) that sailed for Palestine from Romania late in 1941. The venture was organized by a Greek shipowner and a member of the Revisionist party, who chartered an old Bulgarian coal barge flying the Panamanian flag to transport 600 immigrants to Palestine. The barge was totally unseaworthy, but the plight of the refugees was such that 769 of them nonetheless boarded the vessel in Romania.

The *Struma* reached Istanbul on 14 December 1941. It was in no condition to proceed, but the Turkish authorities refused it permission to land unless British approval for immigration to Palestine was forthcoming. Only five disembarked and eventually reached Palestine. On 19 January 1942, and on several subsequent dates, the Jewish Agency requested British permission for the refugees to land under the immigration schedules of the *White Paper of 1939. This permission was refused, on the grounds of alleged lack of food supplies in Palestine and the danger of there being Nazi spies among the refugees. A request to admit children, submitted on 30 January 1942 was not answered until February 15; the British then stipulated that children between the ages of 11 and 16 (the limits were later extended to include those of 4 to 11) be allowed to land.

On February 13 the chief rabbis of the yishuv saw the High Commissioner for Palestine, Sir Harold MacMichael, and on February 18 the Jewish Agency urgently requested the British authorities to reconsider their decision regarding the adults. This was ignored. The British assured the Agency, however, that the Turks would be informed of their decision to permit the children to land, but the Turks later denied any knowledge of this. On 24 February 1942, the Turks drove the barge out into the Black Sea, where it was sunk by an unidentified attacker (most probably a Soviet submarine) with the loss of all but one of the passengers aboard. The tragedy was a turning point in British-Zionist relationships. Y. BAUER

STUTSCHEWSKY, JOACHIM. Israeli composer and cellist (b. Romny, Ukraine, 1891; d. Tel Aviv, 1981) He graduated from the Leipzig conservatory. In 1914–1924 he was active as a cellist in Switzerland. He then moved to Vienna where he founded the Austrian String Quartet, which made important contributions in performing new works of the Viennese school. He was also active in the field of Jewish music, contributing regularly to the Jewish periodical *Die Stimme* and maintaining close contacts with Jewish musicians in Russia and in Palestine (*see* MUSIC AND MUSICAL LIFE IN ISRAEL). After the Nazi *Anschluss* in 1938 he immigrated to Palestine. In Tel Aviv he organized a series of concerts of Jewish music, for which he commissioned new works, covering the concert expenses mostly from his own pocket. He made research into hasidic music and published a monograph on the *kleizmerim* (Jewish folk musicians). As a great cello teacher he published an innovative methodics, *Das Violoncellspiel*, and a monograph on the lives of the great cellists. Stutschewsky was a prolific composer of music for the cello, arrangements of folk songs, chamber and vocal works, and numerous pedagogical works for children. He published an autobiography, *Life without Compromise* (1977). J. HIRSCHBERG

SUDFELD, SIMON MAXIMILIAN. *See* NORDAU, MAX.

SUKENIK, ELEAZAR LIPA. Israeli archeologist (b. Bialystok, Russian Poland, 1889; d. Jerusalem, 1953). Sukenik studied at talmudical academies in Poland. He was active in the Po'ale Zion and in 1912 settled in Eretz Israel, where he became a schoolteacher. During World War I he joined the Jewish Legion.

From 1919 to 1921 Sukenik was secretary of the Education Department of the Palestine Zionist Executive. Becoming interested in archeology, he did research at the École Biblique in Jerusalem, attended the University of Berlin (1923), became a fellow of the American School of Oriental Research in Jerusalem (1925), and obtained a Ph.D. degree from Dropsie College in Philadelphia (1926).

In 1925 he joined the faculty of the newly opened

Hebrew University of Jerusalem and until his death remained associated with that institution, as a lecturer (1935–38), professor (1938-43), and head of the department of Palestine archeology (from 1943). From 1937 until his death he was also director of the university's Museum of Jewish Antiquities.

Between 1925 and 1927 he worked on the excavation of the Third Wall of the ancient city of Jerusalem. He subsequently conducted excavations on the sites of the ancient synagogues on the Greek island of Aegina, in Bet Alfa, and elsewhere. In 1947 he was the first scholar to recognize the antiquity of the Dead Sea Scrolls, and was able to acquire some of them on behalf of the Hebrew University. Sukenik was the only Jewish member of the Board of Directors of the Palestine (Rockefeller) Archeological Museum.

His writings include *The Third Wall of Jerusalem* (1930), *The Ancient Synagogue of Beth Alpha* (1932), *Ancient Synagogues in Palestine and Greece* (1934), *The Ancient Synagogues of El Hammeh* (1935), and *The Dead Sea Scrolls of the Hebrew University* (published posthumously, 1955).

One of Sukenik's sons was Yigael *Yadin.

SULLAM, ANGELO. Lawyer, university lecturer, and Zionist leader in Italy (b. Venice, 1881; d. there, 1970). Interested in Jewish affairs and Zionism from his early youth on, Sullam earned his law degree (1902) with a thesis entitled "Zionism and International Law." In 1903 he founded the Zionist group in Venice. A delegate to the Sixth Zionist Congress (1903), he was elected to the East Africa Commission (*see* EAST AFRICA SCHEME). He worked with the pioneer Italian Zionists Felice Ravenna, Carlo Conigliani, and Giuseppe Levi, maintaining contact also with Herzl and Max Nordau and, later, with other leaders such as Chaim Weizmann and Vladimir Jabotinsky.

Active in communal and Zionist life, Sullam was president of the Jewish Community of Venice from 1919 to 1929, a member of the Union of Italian-Jewish Communities, and president of the Italian Committee of Assistance for Jewish Immigrants from 1921 to 1964. During World War I he was consultant on Palestine to the Italian Ministry of Foreign Affairs and worked for the welfare of the Jews of the Balkans and the Mediterranean basin. He recommended that Angelo Levi-Bianchini be appointed to the Zionist Commission. During World War II he volunteered to work (1944–45) for the Allied armies and for the British Admiralty in the Mediterranean.

A writer on juridical problems and economic questions, Sullam collected and arranged documents and material pertinent to the history of the Jews of Italy.

G. ROMANO

SULTANIK, KALMAN. Zionist organization executive (b. Miechow, Poland, 1917). He became active in Jewish communal and Zionist activities in his early youth. During World War II, he was transported to a concentration camp in Plaszow, Poland, and was later liberated from the death march in 1945. In 1946 Sultanik organized the General Zionist movement in Germany. The same year, he was elected Zionist delegate to the 22nd Zionist Congress held in Basle in 1946 representing the D.P. camps in Germany. In 1947 he was elected to serve on the Central Committee of Liberated Jews in Munich. In 1956 he was elected a member of the Zionist General Council.

Kalman Sultanik (left) presenting an award to Isaac Bashevis Singer.

Since 1972, Sultanik has been a member of the Executive of the World Zionist Organization and is chairman of the Theodor Herzl Foundation in New York (elected in 1975), which sponsors the monthly literary publication *Midstream*. In 1977 Sultanik was elected vice-president of the World Jewish Congress, and in 1980 was elected president of the Federation of Polish Jews in the United States. In 1981 he was appointed member of the United States Holocaust Memorial Council by President Carter, on which he served until 1991. He has been a member of the International Council of the Auschwitz Museum by the Polish government since 1988, was elected its vice-chairman, and has been serving until the present. Sultanik frequently writes articles for various publications on Zionism, World Jewry, anti-Semitism, the Holocaust, and Israel. He currently serves as the chairman of the WZO American Section and is vice-chairman of the United Israel Appeal.

SULZBERGER, CYRUS L. Merchant, communal and civic worker, philanthropist, and early Zionist leader in the United States (b. Philadelphia, 1858; d. New York, 1932). In 1877 Sulzberger settled in New York and entered business there. He became prominent in municipal and state politics, served on various city and state commissions, and was a candidate (1903) for the office of borough president of Manhattan. At the same time he was deeply concerned with Jewish social, cultural, and educational endeavors.

Aroused to Zionism as a result of the Kishinev pogrom of 1903, Sulzberger served as vice-president of the Federation of American Zionists in 1904–05. Subsequently he became interested in the Territorialist movement, formed a branch of the Jewish Territorial Organization, and sponsored the visit of Israel Zangwill to the United States for the Territorialist cause (1905-06).

After World War I Sulzberger became disillusioned with the emphasis on nationalism and renounced all Jewish aspirations. Nevertheless, he continued to identify himself with the cultural efforts supported by Zionism. After a visit to Palestine, he became a devoted supporter of the Hebrew University of Jerusalem.

SUPERNUMERARY POLICE. *See* HAGANA; NOTERIM.

SUPRASKY, YEHOSHUA. Zionist leader (b. Goniadz, Bialystok Province, Russian Poland, 1879; d. Tel Aviv, 1948). A Zionist from his youth on, he engaged in many Zionist and Jewish communal activities in southern Russia, where he was occupied as a manufacturer and grain merchant. Suprasky participated in the Minsk Conference of Russian Zionists (1902) and was a member of the Central Committee of Russian Zionists. He devoted great effort to persuading Jews to make investments in Eretz Israel and to settle there themselves. After the Revolution of March, 1917, he was a member of the All-Russia Council of the Kerensky government and of the Central Board of the Russian-Jewish Communities. Following the Bolshevik takeover, he settled (1920) in Palestine.

Suprasky was active in land-purchasing societies and other economic enterprises. A leading figure in the General Zionist movement, he headed the General Zionists in Palestine, was a member of the Va'ad Le'umi (National Council) and the Municipal Council of Tel Aviv (1925–32), and served as a vice-president of the Jewish Community of Tel Aviv-Jaffa.

He attended every Zionist Congress from the Sixth (1903), where he voted against the East Africa scheme, to the 20th (1937), and was a member of the Greater Actions Committee from 1921 until his death.

SURINAM, ZIONISM IN. Surinam (formerly Dutch Guiana) has one of the oldest Jewish communities in the Americas. In the 17th century, a Jewish region called Joden Savanne (the Jewish Savanna) was established and its capital named Jerusalem-on-the-Riverside. This was surrounded by some 40 agricultural settlements with Hebrew names, e.g., Mahanaim, Goshen, Mitzpeh, Beersheba, Succoth, and Sharon. In 1987 the number of Jews in Surinam was 180.

Zionist activity began in Surinam in 1938, when J.D. Oppenheim, a native of the Netherlands who had lived in Palestine from 1923 to 1938, settled there as a citrus agronomist working for the government. He became one of the three editors of the Dutch-Jewish monthly *Teroenca (Teru'a*; founded by Michael Levi) and organized a small nucleus of active Zionists at whose meetings he lectured regularly. When Oppenheim left for Palestine (1945), the leadership of the Zionists fell to Ph. A. Samson, a lawyer and magistrate, who served as president of the group from 1945 to 1954, when his brother Jules A. Samson became acting president. During that period the Jewish community was rapidly declining. From 1966 on Mrs. A. Azijnman was in charge of Zionist activities, expressed mainly in work for the Jewish National Fund. Following the Six-Day War of 1967, a pro-Israel campaign conducted in Surinam raised $30,000, earmarked for the Magen David Adom of Israel.

The Israeli ambassador in Colombia is also accredited to Surinam. S.J. MASLIN—M. ARBELL

SWEDEN, ZIONISM IN. A Swedish Jew, Josef Seligmann, attended the first Zionist Congress in Basle (1897), but upon his return did not attempt to spread Zionism among the Jews of Stockholm. The first Zionist club was founded after the turn of the century in Malmö in southern Sweden by Cantor A. Hurwitz and Salomon Blumenthau and was, like its successors, established by immigrants to Sweden and not by native Jews. Another club was organized in 1903 in Lund, not far from Malmö. The inspiration for these initiatives came from Copenhagen, Denmark, where a Danish Zionist group had already been formed. These clubs in southern Sweden were unable to sustain themselves and when the Stockholm Zionist Organization (Zionistföreningen) was finally organized in 1910 by Mauritz Tarschis, with the help of Josef Nachemson of Copenhagen (who also owned a store in Stockholm), it was the only one in Sweden.

In 1910 there were 6,122 Jews in Sweden, about half of whom lived in Stockholm. Since non-Swedish citizens could not be members of the local Jewish communities, most Zionists were excluded and therefore unable to directly influence the policies of the small but wealthy and prestigious "Mosaic Communities." It is, indeed, remarkable that they were indirectly able to work so successfully. The election of Marcus *Ehrenpreis, Chief Rabbi of Bulgaria, to the post of Chief Rabbi of Stockholm was due to the intervention of the local Zionists. A protest petition circulated in 1912 resulted in reopening of the candidature after it had officially been closed, and one of several non-Orthodox, anti-Zionist German rabbis appeared certain of election. Ehrenpreis was permitted to apply and was chosen to follow Gottlieb Klein, a rabid anti-Zionist for whom the Jewish national idea was treachery, an act of abandoning Judaism's essential mission to the nations.

The new Chief Rabbi was an internationally famous personality and could therefore assist in numerous relief actions organized by Zionist and non-Zionist organizations during and after the war. He had an active Zionist past but was in the process of redirecting his energies. Consequently he influenced the Stockholm community towards cultural Zionism but never actively involved himself in Zionist groups such as the Jewish National Fund Committee, the Zionist Club, or ad hoc committees for various projects.

Kurt Blumenfeld, the General Secretary and Chief of Information for the World Zionist Organization, visited Stockholm and Gothenburg on 9–17 April, 1912. He received extensive coverage in the national press, gaining extra prominence from Rabbi Gottlieb Klein's opposition. Klein's newspaper attack on Zionism was met by Pastor Lindhagen, the executive secretary of the Lutheran Churches' Conversionalist "Mission to the Jews," who accused him of not caring for his people.

Blumenfeld inspired the Stockholm Zionist Club to initiate a Zionist Conference, called for 5–6 January 1913. Dr. Gerson Bloede was sent by the World Zionist Organization, then in Cologne, to address the membership, the major purpose of the meeting being to unite Scandinavian Zionists for political and educational purposes. The meeting tightened the bonds between the Zionist clubs in Denmark, Norway, and Sweden, and led to the publication of a Swedish-language magazine, *Zionisten*, in Stockholm. Despite the capable editing of Leopold Turitz, a native-born Swedish Jew and a college graduate, *Zionisten* survived only from July to November 1913. World War I divided the Zionists into two camps, and until the *Copenhagen Bureau was established in neutral Denmark, the Zionists on the opposing sides kept in touch via telegrams often re-forwarded by Josef Nachemsohn in Copenhagen and Mauritz Tarschis in Stockholm. World War I was a period of heightened activity. Numerous Russian Jewish immigrants passed through Scandinavia although relatively few remained in Sweden after the peace. An afternoon Hebrew School, Iwriah, was set up in Stockholm but failed. The most important and lasting achievement during the war years was the founding of the Stockholm Blau-Weiss Club in 1916 by Lea Tarschis, who had attended the Second Scandinavian Zionist Conference, held in Copenhagen on 28–29 May 1916. She returned and organized the Blau-Weiss Hiking Club, which four years later changed its name to Youth Club Blau-Weiss. In 1925 the organization again changed its name and its goals, now emphasizing social activities and calling itself Jewish Youth (Judisk Ungdom).

In 1918 the non-Zionist Mosaic Community of Stockholm reacted to the formation of Blau-Weiss by helping Jewish university students establish a club of their own (Judiska Akademiska Klubben). This organization is still functioning today. In a remarkable development, Blau-Weiss' choral group, founded in February 1923 as Hasomir under the leadership of Cantor Felix Saul, became the choir of the non-Orthodox Great Synagogue in 1924. It is a significant comment on the lack of dogmatic doctrinairism within Stockholm's Jewish community that the children of Zionist immigrants were now singing at the non-Orthodox religious services held at the bastion of assimilated Swedish Jewry. Three other events of importance occurred in Sweden during the years of World War I. Vladimir Jabotinsky's visit in 1916 was the occasion of his first lecture about the need for a Jewish legion. Jabotinsky also convinced several Zionist leaders of Stockholm to sign a secret resolution attacking the work and the venue of the Central Zionist Organization, which he believed should be moved from Germany.

More significant was the establishment of the Po'ale Zion office in Stockholm in 1917. Berl Locker and Leon Chasanowitsch were permanently posted in Stockholm to direct a political office and publish a bulletin of Jewish news in several languages. They and several other leading Zionist Socialists—Ya'akov Zerubavel (Witkin), Shlomo Kaplansky, and Ber Borochov—had been invited by the Holland-Scandinavian Committee headed by Camille Huysmanns and Karl Hjalmar Branting to represent the Jewish Zionist Workers' Party—Po'ale Zion—at the International Socialist Conference held in Stockholm during the summer of 1917. This meeting led to the publication of a statement, "Program for the Peace" published in the fall of 1917, the first time that autonomous Jewish rights in the Diaspora and Jewish rights to settle in Palestine ever appeared in an International Socialist document.

The Po'ale Zion political and news centers in Stockholm worked closely with the Socialist parties and published significant news releases. But the internal bickering between Locker and Chasanowitsch led to much wasted energy. In 1919 Leon Motzkin and Chasanowitsch published in Stockholm a collection of political documents concerning Jewish rights, and Chasanowitsch reported in the same year on the pogroms in eastern Europe. The Stockholm office closed in late summer 1919 after a long and disorganized series of meetings and disagreements by renowned opponents representing the various branches of the Po'ale Zion movement.

The local Zionist clubs in Sweden were devoted to fulfilling Herzl's goal of "Capturing the Communities," but knew that as immigrants, they were unequipped for the task. They lacked wealth and status. Whenever major projects were initiated in Sweden, they were directed by world centers of the Zionist movement and involved international leaders. The outstanding example of this process is the complicated series of behind-the-scene contacts which eventually resulted in the transfer of American relief funds to the yishuv in Palestine. The money was sent on several occasions to the Copenhagen Bureau, then forwarded to Isaac Feuerring, a German industrialist temporarily living in Stockholm, who arranged for the Swedish National Bank to send it in gold coin to Germany. From Berlin it was transferred to the Zionist Office in Constantinople where Arthur Ruppin supervised its distribution. In 1917 the money was sent from Denmark, and in early 1918 from Stockholm. Though the local Zionist clubs knew about the relief transactions, the actual contacts and arrangements were made by Feuerring, Ehrenpreis, the wealthy Jewish philanthropist Oskar Hirsch, and other well-connected individuals. This and other rescue activities led to close cooperation between Zionists and non-Zionists which was to be repeated in World War II and even during the post-war periods. Sweden's proximity to Poland, the Baltic States, and the Soviet Union made it a center for organizing relief.

Swedish Social Democracy evinced a historical sympathy for Zionism and evolved a working relationship with Israel's Labor Party. The leader of the Swedish Social Democratic Workers' Party, Carl Hjalmar Branting, participated in Zionist gatherings, sending a message to the public meeting after the Balfour Declaration and attending the celebration following the San Remo agreement in 1920. Mayor Carl Lindhagen of Stockholm, a leading Social Democrat, was also a stanch supporter of Zionism and participated in public demonstrations. This warm relationship continued throughout the years of Social Democratic government, except for a relatively brief period in the late 1970s and early 1980s when, on several occasions, the prime minister Olof Palme consulted with and even invited Yassir Arafat, the leader of the PLO, to Stockholm (May 1983) and when Palme condemned Israel's war in Lebanon. His successor, Ingvar Carlsson, himself worked on a kibbutz and retains close personal contacts with leading Israelis in the Labor Party.

Most of the Russian Jewish immigrants left Sweden in the last year of World War I and the years following. Some of those previously active in Zionist work ceased their activities. Turitz left the club. Mauritz Tarschis moved to Germany but returned later to Sweden, where he resumed the chairmanship. Though the club lost most of its dynamism a young native-born generation was growing up: Daniel and Simon Brick and later Emil Glück began to assume responsibility for various activities. The magazine of the Scandinavian Youth Federation (Sjuf), *Israeliten*, founded in Oslo in 1919, was taken over in 1932 by Daniel Brick, who made it into Sweden's Zionist voice. His brother Simon was the managing editor and a great supporter of Jewish athletics, attending the First International Maccabia in 1932. By this time Simon Brick was already involved in Jewish National Fund work and remained its president until 1949; he was succeeded by Max Kornblom, who was active until the presidency was assumed by Harry Rock in 1965.

In general, the end of World War I resulted in a decline in Zionist activities. Ernst Blumenthal, a German Zionist employed by Feuerring (who had also left Sweden to return to Germany) was transferred to Stockholm and found a Zionist desert there in the early 1920s. Except for a few fund-raising activities the Zionist Club and indeed the entire Scandinavian Union was dormant. There were a few bright rays: Dr. Abraham Brody, with the assistance and participation of Rabbi Ehrenpreis, organized a Hebrew-Speaking Club in 1925. Ehrenpreis was already engaged in translating major Jewish works into Swedish and in supporting new cultural efforts. For this purpose he received financial support from wealthy community leaders, several of whom were themselves publishers. They helped him to form the Jewish Literature Society and to prepare a series of books. *New Hebrew Lyrical Poetry* appeared in 1920, translated by the Chief Rabbi and Ragnar Josephson, who would later become a famous literary critic, theater director, and a member of the prestigious Swedish Academy. This work is one of the earliest translations into a modern European language of Bialik, Tschernichowsky, Ahad Ha-Am, and other authors writing in Hebrew. *Israel's Present and Future* a collection of essays by Buber, Brod, Dubnow, and others followed the next year. In 1924 Ehrenpreis published an original work by the young native Swedish Zionist, Hugo Valentin, *Jews in Sweden* (Judarna i Sverige). S.J. Agnon's *The Crooked Shall Be Made Straight* was the next translation.

In the 1920s, the Jewish population in Palestine was growing and new trends were developing. The assimilated Jews of Sweden were anti-Zionist in principle but almost always prepared to assist needy co-religionists. Collections were made on behalf of the victims of anti-Semitic violence in Eastern Europe, and an effort to purchase Swedish-made farm machinery for shipment to Palestine in 1926 was extremely successful. The famous author and adventurer, Sven Hedin, participated in these efforts and Fredrik Böök, a literary critic for the newspaper, *Svenska Dagbladet*, wrote positively about Zionism as the solution of the Jewish problem in eastern Europe. Böök had recently returned from Jerusalem, where he had been the Stockholm Zionists' official delegate to the opening of the Hebrew University in Jerusalem. Rabbi Ehrenpreis was added as a second representative, and he and Böök wrote later about their experiences in *Journey to Jerusalem* (Resa till Jerusalem), a collection of their articles that appeared weekly in *Svenska Dagbladet*. In 1927 Ehrenpreis founded and later, together with Hugo Valentin, published *Judisk Tidskrift* (Jewish Magazine) which appeared eight times a year. It was a cultural magazine of national repute; its monthly review of Jewish events analyzed developments in Palestine and elsewhere. Translations of Yiddish and Hebrew classics were also made available to the Swedish public. This magazine survived until the 1950s. In the early 1930s efforts were made to provide Zionist activities for Swedish youth. Willy Gordon, later a world-renowned sculptor, was instrumental in founding Herzelia in Malmö, the first committed Zionist youth movement; Zerej Mizrachi, was formed in Stockholm in 1934 by the then Chief Rabbi of Finland, Dr. Simon Federbusch. This youth group was very active and many of its members later assumed positions of leadership in the Swedish Zionist Federation (founded 1933). This Federation made its mark on Swedish society through the personality and position of its leading spokesman, Hugo Valentin. A well-known historian and expert on both the general history of anti-Semitism and the history of the Jews in Sweden, Valentin was a scion of an old-established Jewish family. As the president of the Zionist Organization, he challenged the Jewish establishment's anti-Zionism and its assimilationist policies and gave the new Jewish nationalism access to broad press and radio coverage.

Another native-born Swedish Jew, Emil Glück, a doctor of veterinary medicine, organized a He-Halutz branch in Sweden. Working in close cooperation with German and Danish He-Halutz, Glück helped in placing young Zionists on Swedish farms to learn agriculture while waiting for certificates of entry to Palestine. His book, *Pa vag till Israel* (On the way to Israel) was published in 1985 by the Society for Nordic Jewish Studies and relates how Glück successfully involved even the Jewish establishment in the support of individuals and of small *hakhshara* groups and how these pioneers participated in rescue actions during the war. The *hakhshara* farms were jointly operated by He-Halutz and the religious Berit Halutzim Datiyim (Bachad).

About 1,000 Jews arrived in Sweden during the 1930s mostly central European refugees from Germany, Austria, and Czechoslovakia. Some of these were Zionists and joined the small Zionist Organization, providing the numbers and the inspiration for new initiatives. One important Zionist project was support for the establishment of the Self-Help Organization (Immigranternas Självhjälp) in November 1938. Youth Aliya took its first group to Palestine the same year.

Fritz Hollander, who after the war played a major role in the "Conquest of the Community for Zionism," was personally involved in the various wartime rescue efforts directed from Sweden. The first leader of this work was Dr. Shalom Adler-Rudel, who was sent by the Jewish Agency from England to Sweden. Adler-Rudel succeeded in uniting all the various factions of Swedish Jewry to finance a transfer of young Danish pioneers from Denmark to Sweden, an action that saved the lives of every member. A national committee was soon organized for rescue work; the Zionist Organization was represented and active. During the last years of the war, the Swedish section of the World Jewish Congress was responsible for saving thousands of Jews. Those directly involved were Hillel Storsch, who worked behind the scenes, and Norbert Mazur, a former German Jew and a devoted Zionist, who met with Heinrich Himmler in April, 1945. His book, *A Jew speaks with Himmler* (En jude talar med Himmler) gives the background and describes the conversation. During these years Raoul Wallenberg was dispatched to Budapest to attempt to save Hungarian Jews and packages were sent to Bergen-Belsen and Theresienstadt. The October 1943 rescue action which transported the Danish Jews to Sweden was initiated by the Jewish community, but all segments of Swedish Jewry and even Swedish governmental authorities participated. Not to be forgotten is Rabbi Eliezer Berlinger of Malmö, who on Yom Kippur, 1943, sent his Orthodox congregation from the synagogue to the beaches with food and clothing; and Karl Berman, then a young, dynamic Social Democratic politician and active Zionist, who acted as contact man between the parties. Ivar Philipsson, an assimilated Jewish lawyer from Stockholm and stanch anti-Zionist, contributed great amounts of time and money. Cooperation between all branches of Swedish Jewry transcended all ideological and political differences.

Almost 15,000 Jewish survivors were brought to Sweden from the liberated camps in the last stages of the war. Most of these left for Israel or America upon recovering their health, and almost the entire Danish and Norwegian Jewish refugee population in Sweden returned to their homes after the War. Nevertheless, those remaining doubled the pre-war Jewish population. In 1950, there were about 14,000 Jews in Sweden. Most of the newcomers were traditional Jews and Zionists and were concerned with the Jewish education of their children. Under the leadership of Fritz Hollander, Anna Rock, Kantor Idy Bornstein, Joseph Ettlinger, and numerous others, a new political party was founded inside the Jewish community with the goal of intensifying the Jewish and Hebraic content of Jewish education in Sweden. Small but important changes had already occurred. Swedish volunteers—Jewish and non-Jewish—

Meeting between David Ben-Gurion and representatives of Swedish Zionist Organization, Helsingborg, Sweden, 1946. [Beth Hatefutsoth]

Prof. Hugo Valentin (left) and Simon Brick (right) presenting King Gustaf V of Sweden with a certificate of a forest planted in his name in Palestine, in 1945. [Swedish Zionist Federation]

had fought in the Israel War of Independence. The Jewish community leadership and the Zionist Organization had formed a defense committee, which later became the Keren ha-Yesod (Förenade Israelinsamlingen). An Israel Passport Office had opened in 1948 with Daniel Brick authorized as Israeli Consul to Sweden to issue visas; it functioned until Israel's Legation was established in Stockholm in 1949. The first Israeli emissary arrived in 1953. A branch of Bnei Akiva was established in the 1950s.

Taking advantage of the new climate, the Zionists in Stockholm established Chinuch (education), an organization which founded a Jewish kindergarten and day school. Technically, Chinuch and the Zionist Federation (established in the late 1940s) were two separate organizations, but the same people sat on both boards. Chinuch received the moral support of Chief Rabbi Kurt Wilhelm, who was severely criticized by the leadership of the Jewish community in Stockholm on the grounds that segregation for educational purposes was a step towards ghettoization. For the same reason the community initially opposed the establishment of Jewish Sports Clubs and worked against a Jewish Community Center. These political battles, fought in the 1950s and 60s, resulted in Zionist victories. The Jewish community now supports the day school and the Center and works closely with all Zionist organs in Sweden and Israel.

In 1967, shortly before the outbreak of the Six-Day War, the Zionist Federation took the initiative in forming a Solidarity Committee for Israel, with the support of almost every Jewish organization in Sweden. Under Leon Gerson it has presented Israel's case to the Swedish public by means of exhibitions, lectures, press coverage, and it has published several pamphlets and books. In 1966, S.J. Agnon and Nelly Sachs received the Nobel Prize in literature; at a gala celebration held in their honor at the Jewish Center in Stockholm, the Jewish Youth Federation (Stiftelsen Judiska Ungdomsfonden) was established by Chinuch and the Zionist Federation. This foundation funded activities for immigrant Jewish university students who fled to Sweden during the period of Polish anti-Semitism, and has supported the Hillel School, the Jewish Center and other youth institutions and activities throughout the country. In the early 1980s the Jewish community of Stockholm rewrote its by-laws and became one of the first European communities to declare as one of its goals the strengthening of "closer connection with the Jewish people and with the State of Israel." Of the almost 20,000 Jews in Sweden today, about 25–30% are directly or indirectly affiliated with the Zionist Federation through membership in one or several Jewish organizations. The various athletic clubs in Stockholm, Malmö and Gothenburg are all affiliated with the Maccabi World Union and participate in the European Games and the Maccabia in Israel. The most active Zionist organization in Sweden is WIZO, which, under the leadership of Charlotte Ettlinger, has gained a national reputation. Zionist organizations are active in Malmö and Gothenburg, where the communities work very closely with them.

Figures are uncertain but immigration to Israel from Sweden since 1948 is roughly estimated at 2–3,000. This is a relatively large number for a country with a total Jewish population of less than 20,000.

M. NARROWE

SWEDISH JEWS IN ISRAEL. *See* SCANDINAVIAN JEWS IN ISRAEL.

SWITZERLAND, RELATIONS WITH ISRAEL. Switzerland had an early connection with Zionism, as the scene of the First and many subsequent Congresses. Diplomatic relations between Switzerland and Israel were established in 1949. Switzerland has carefully maintained a policy of neutrality and has refrained from pronouncing opinions on international conflicts or from taking positions or initiatives. This neutrality and the defense of its extensive economic interests—in the Arab world, *inter alia*—formed the basis for its behavior in the international arena.

At the same time, Switzerland placed itself at the disposal of other countries, offering its services to host conferences, meetings, negotiations, etc. It was in Lausanne, for instance, that the Palestine Conciliation Commission met in May, 1949, with the participation of representatives from Israel, Egypt, Syria, and Jordan, in an effort to reach an agreement on the problems of the refugees, the internationalization of Jerusalem, and the determination of frontiers. Neither this meeting, nor its sequel in Geneva, bore fruit.

Geneva was also the site of a conference on 21–22 December 1973 following the Yom Kippur War; this meeting led to the signing of separation of forces agreements between Israel, Egypt, and Syria.

Swiss neutrality was aided by its not being a member of the United Nations: it therefore did not have to vote in the General Assembly or at the Security Council on the problems of the Middle East. Geneva is the seat of the International Red Cross Committee, through which many, often successful, prisoner exchange negotiations were conducted.

Notwithstanding this tradition of neutrality, in the 1980s leaders of Swiss foreign policy tended to some extent to express themselves on certain aspects of the Middle East situation.

On basic issues, no areas of disagreement have emerged between Switzerland and Israel. An Israeli security agent who killed an Arab terrorist attacking an El Al plane in Zurich in 1969, was judged under the best possible conditions by the authorities, who were obviously displeased at the use made by Arab terrorists—and the Arab states employing them—of Swiss territory. An attack on a Swissair plane which exploded in flight in 1970, heightened the angry Swiss response to Palestinian terrorism. In the 1980s, Switzerland recognized the rights of the Palestinian people to self-determination, as well as Israel's rights to secure recognized borders.

Since the Swiss federal government, on principle, recognizes only states, it does not recognize the PLO. This did not, however, prevent Swiss Foreign Minister Pierre Aubert from receiving his opposite number in the PLO, Farouk Kadoumi, in 1981. A former president of the Swiss-Israel Friendship League, and a declared friend of Israel, Pierre Aubert hoped to act as mediator or intermediary between Israel and its enemies. Unlike Swiss Foreign Ministers in general, who are reluctant to leave their country, Aubert has visited both Tunisia and Israel.

The PLO took advantage of its UN Observer status in order to maintain an office in Geneva—seat of the UN European Bureau—where its primary function is to produce PLO propaganda. In this work, it is aided by leftist groups and certain social democrat groupings, the main Swiss political parties being more traditionally pro-Israel.

Another result of Swiss neutrality is the absence, in the Swiss Foreign Office, of a class of Arabists such as exists in many other countries; even Swiss officials who have served in Arab countries are generally little influenced by their years of service.

One problem that arose in relations between the two countries related to the signing of a Social Benefits Agreement. Drawn up in 1980, this agreement was to have been signed in Israel, but after the passing of the Jerusalem Law the Swiss refused to sign it in Israel's capital, and through the late 1980s, no formula had been found which would allow the final signing of the agreement.

The action of the Swiss-Israel Friendship Leagues, with branches in the main cities, the effective activities of the Swiss Jewish community in its support of Israel, and the traditional friendship of the military establishments (Israel modeled its system of army reserves on Switzerland's, and important military transactions are negotiated between Israel and Switzerland) are all factors which contribute to maintaining an atmosphere generally favorable towards Israel, even if this is not always reflected in the press.

Switzerland's economic relations with Israel are on a smaller scale than with the Arab countries. Some 150,000 Israeli tourists visit Switzerland annually and Swiss tourists in Israel number around 30,000 a year. Israeli exports to Switzerland total almost $200 million annually in diamonds, electronic items, food and chemical products, textiles, citrus fruits, and even some watches: Swiss exports to Israel amount to nearly $700 million a year (490 million without the raw diamonds), in electronics, machine tools, medicines, watches, and jewelry; these figures do not include Israeli military arms sales to Switzerland. In its commercial relations with Switzerland, Israel enjoys the status of a developing country, benefiting from preferential customs tariffs.

In addition to its embassy in Berne, Israel has a general consulate in Zurich and a permanent delegation at the UN European Bureau in Geneva.

Switzerland represented Israel in certain countries after their diplomatic relations with Israel were ruptured in 1967 or in 1973.

D. CATARIVAS

SWITZERLAND, ZIONISM IN. The history of Zionism in Switzerland does not show a unified process of development. Zionism evolved along different paths among Switzerland's various Jewish elements such as the official Jewish communities, the groups of Jews from Eastern Europe, and the intellectuals. Frequently there was little contact between these circles. Switzerland was the headquarters of a number of international Jewish organizations, many of which held conventions in Geneva, Berne, and Zurich. Accordingly, no history of Zionism in Switzerland is complete without at least passing mention of the Bund, which had its headquarters in Geneva for a long time, the Jewish Territorial Organization, the Yiddishist organizations which had Chaim Zhitlowsky as their chief spokesman in Berne, and the various Jewish Socialist groups, all of which were engaged in a running debate with the Zionists. In addition, a considerable part of Switzerland's Orthodox Jews joined the Agudat Israel in 1912. The conflicts within the ranks of the Zionist movement in Switzerland concerned problems of political and practical Zionism, Territorialism, cultural Zionism, and, later, the attitude to be taken by the movement toward the Triple Entente and the Central Powers. Many of the participants in these debates emigrated to Israel or the United States, where they became leaders in Jewish life.

One of the Swiss guests at the First Zionist Congress (Basle, 1897) was Jean-Henri Dunant, who brought about the founding of the international Red Cross. As early as 1873 this philanthropist, who shared the Nobel Peace Prize of 1901 with Frédéric Passy, had founded several organizations for the establishment of a neutral Jewish State. Among the conveners of the First Zionist Congress was Dr. David Zvi Farbstein, who delivered a paper entitled "The Economic Basis of Zionism." The author of the draft constitution of the Jewish National Fund (JNF), Farbstein became the first president of the Keren ha-Yesod of Switzerland in 1920.

The first few Zionist Congresses did not make much impression on the Jewish population of Switzerland, which in 1900 numbered only 12,264. Zurich, the largest Jewish community in the country, then had only 2,713 Jews. The delegates to the Congresses were elected at local conferences. The first such conference was held in Zurich at the Mueller Shul, a small synagogue attended by Jews from Eastern Europe who either were in the city temporarily or had been stranded there on the way to North or South America.

The First Zionist Congress had 15 delegates from Switzerland. In October, 1897, the Judaea-Kolonisationsverein (Judea Colonization Society) was founded under the chairmanship of Farbstein, but the organization did not survive long. Soon thereafter the first local branch of the World Zionist Organization was founded under the chairmanship of Isidor Horn, and the first student Zionist group, named Hessiana, for Moses Hess, was established. The first meeting of the Zionist branch, with a membership of 45, was held in Basle on 19 November 1897. In addition, Basle had a Jung-Zion (Young Zion) movement for young people between the ages of 15 and 20. Other branches of the Zionist Organization were founded in Geneva, Lausanne, Berne, Endingen, and Biel. By the time the Second Zionist Congress met in Basle in 1898, with Nachman Syrkin as one of the Geneva delegates, Switzerland had six local branches. Among the delegates from Geneva at the Third Congress (1899) was Dr. Chaim Weizmann, and at the Fourth Congress (1900) one of Geneva's delegates was Dr. Daniel Pasmanik.

The first preliminary meeting for the founding of the Swiss Zionist Federation was held on 11 December 1898. The founding conference itself took place on 12 October 1901. The first annual Conference of Delegates was held on 21 December 1902, in Biel, where, according to the Congress report, the entire Jewish population belonged to the local Zionist branch. The chairman at that conference was Dr. Pasmanik; Weizmann was vice-chairman, and Moritz Levy secretary. Among the delegates from Zurich was Dr. Berthold Feiwel. The JNF began work in Switzerland in 1902, and the name of Jean-Henri Dunant was the first entry in its Golden Book.

In the years that followed, the delegations to the Zionist Congresses were composed of representatives from all the cities of Switzerland. Among the Swiss delegates to the Ninth Congress (1909) were Hayim Israel Eis (who later became a leader in the Agudat Israel), Dr. David Farbstein, Dr. Pasmanik, Dr. Camille Lévy, and Dr. David Strauss. At the Seventh Zionist Congress (1905) the Swiss delegates were among those who rejected the East Africa (Uganda) scheme; and in 1929 they voted for the expansion of the Jewish Agency.

Parties and factions did not appear in the Swiss Zionist movement until after World War I. The delegations to the Zionist Congresses consisted of General Zionists and members of Mizrachi. Only after Switzerland had been allotted additional delegates on the basis of the shekel levy did delegations include one representative each of the General Zionists, the Mizrachi, and the Po'ale Zion, as well as a nonpartisan delegate representing the national funds. At recent Congresses, shekel sales amounted to 5,000 for each Congress, in a total Jewish population of 20,000.

Berne and Geneva were the major centers of debates between Zionist and Socialist students' groups. At these debates, some of which lasted through entire nights, the Socialists were represented by men such as Georgi Plekhanov, Vladimir Medem, the Axelrod brothers, Salomon An-Ski, Lev Davydovich Bronstein (who later assumed the surname Trotsky), Vladimir Ilyich Lenin, Alexander Helphand-Parvus, and Chaim Zhitlowsky, while the Zionists had among their spokesmen Weizmann, Daniel Pasmanik, Zvi Aberson, Mordecai Robinson, Ber Borochov, Hayim Bograshov, Israel Auerbach, Bertha Ratnowsky, Yitzhak Avigdor Wilkansky (Elazari-Volcani), Baruch Kahane, Abraham Burstein, Jacob Klatzkin, Julius Becker, Jakob Meir Salkind, and Felix Lazar Pinkus. Debate within the Zionist movement revolved chiefly around practical and political Zionism, cultural Zionism, and the East Africa problem.

During World War I, Swiss Zionist sympathies were divided between the Allies and the Central Powers, with the Allied cause soon gaining ascendancy under the leadership of Felix Pinkus, who published a pamphlet entitled *Vor der Errichtung des Judenstaates* (Before the Founding of the Jewish State) after the issuance of the Balfour Declaration. As the result of conferences with the Swiss Federal Council in 1918, Pres. Félix Calonder, on behalf of the Council, promised to accord full recognition and support to the declaration. At the time of the Paris Peace Conference the Eastern European delegates to the Comité des Délégations Juives conferred under the chairmanship of Dr. George Steinmarder, then chairman of the Zionist delegates of Zurich, before going to Paris.

The years immediately following World War I saw a rapid exodus of the Jewish refugees who had taken up temporary residence in Switzerland, but in the period immediately preceding and during World War II the refugee problem gained prominence once more. After a heated election campaign Dr. Hans Klee, a General Zionist and member of the Zionist Central Committee and later a delegate to various Zionist Congresses and a member of Zionist Actions Committee, was chosen chairman of the Refugee Council.

The establishment of the State of Israel in 1948 brought a decline in the importance of the Swiss Zionist Federation. Many Jews left Switzerland, a considerable number of them settling in Israel. However, those who remained in Switzerland showed increasing interest in the new State, as indicated by the fact that the revenue raised in Switzerland for the JNF and the Keren ha-Yesod was among the highest per capita in the world and that many Swiss Jews visited Israel or settled there. Swiss Zionists also took an active interest in the Hebrew University of Jerusalem, the Weizmann Institute of Science in Rehovot, Youth Aliya, Berit Ivrit Olamit, and other institutions active in or on behalf of Israel. The Swiss Women's International Zionist Organization (WIZO) had almost 3,000 members, with almost every Jewish family in Switzerland represented on its rolls.

The Swiss Zionist Federation holds annual congresses (called Delegates' Day) to which the parties elect or nominate representatives. Recent chairpersons have included Dr. Moritz Bernstein, Mrs Bluette Nordmann, and Max Bessermann. Party activity as such has dwindled and plays little role in the community.

Emissaries of the World Zionist Organization's Aliya Department have played an active role in promoting aliya and helping Jews from Switzerland to immigrate to Israel. Many organizations are active in developing solidarity with Israel or aiding specific projects. These include the Swiss-Israel Friendship Association, WIZO, Youth Aliya (which has a special interest in the Swiss children's village of Kiryat Ye'arim), Keren ha-Yesod, the Jewish National Fund, and the Friends of the institutes of higher learning in Israel.

L. WOHLMANN—V. WYLER

SYKES, SIR MARK. British traveler and diplomat (b. London, 1879; d. Paris, 1919). Educated in Monaco, Brussels, and Cambridge, Sykes served as a soldier in the South African War (1902) and traveled for some time in Syria, Mesopotamia, and Kurdistan. Several years later he was appointed honorary attaché to the British Embassy in Constantinople. In 1915 his special knowledge and qualifications, particularly with regard to the Middle East, won him an appointment as one of the two assistant secretaries to the British War Cabinet, a position in which he prepared regular intelligence summaries on the Middle East for the Cabinet's information. Thus, too, he came to participate in the Anglo-French talks in London on the "Syrian" question, talks that culminated in the *Sykes-Picot Agreement of 1916.

It was some time between the provisional signing of the agreement in January, 1916, and its official ratification in May of that year that Sykes first read the memorandum sent by Sir Herbert Samuel to all members of the Cabinet the year before, suggesting British sponsorship of the Zionist cause. With the encouragement of Samuel, Moses Gaster began an exchange of views on Zionism with Sykes. Eager to see Britain gain a firm foothold in Palestine, Sykes felt that if Britain were to show active sympathy for the Zionist cause, it might be able to extricate itself from the Palestine provisions of the Sykes-Picot Agreement by pointing out that the Jews were overwhelmingly in favor of British trusteeship in the Holy Land.

In 1917 he first met Chaim Weizmann and Nahum Sokolow. By that time he had become attracted to Zionism per se, because he viewed it as a movement to lead the Jews away from urban commercialism and back to what he considered the healthier life and attitude of the tiller of the soil. He envisioned an eventual partnership between the Zionists and the Arabs and Armenians (whom he considered friendly toward the Entente) to preserve the stability of the Middle East after the collapse of the Ottoman Empire. At his first important meeting with nine Jewish and Zionist leaders in London on 7 February 1917, Sykes stated his conviction that the Arabs would come to terms with Zionism, particularly if they received support from the Jews in other matters. While in Rome in 1917, Sykes used his influence as a distinguished Catholic layman to explain to the Vatican authorities that Zionism would not clash with Christian or Catholic wishes concerning the holy places in Palestine. He participated in the drafting of the *Balfour Declaration; the final Zionist draft, submitted on 18 July 1917, had his approval, and Leopold S. Amery, a secretary of the War Cabinet, was to stress in future speeches and writings that the issuance of the declaration was due in large measure to Sykes's faith and energy.

Sykes addressed many Zionist meetings and, in a speech on 2 December 1917, said: "It might be the destiny of the Jewish race to be the bridge between Asia and Europe, and to bring the spirituality of Asia to Europe and the vitality of Europe to Asia." At the same time, he was on friendly terms with the Arabs. As a staff member of the Foreign Office he went on several missions to Egypt. In 1918 he went to Aleppo in the hope of reconciling French and Arab aims. His death, from influenza, at the Paris Peace Conference was greatly mourned by Zionists the world over.

SYKES-PICOT AGREEMENT (in official terminology, the 1916 Asia Minor Agreement), secret agreement reached during World War I between the British and French governments pertaining to the partition of the Ottoman Empire among the Allied Powers. The terms were specified in a letter dated 9 May 1916, which Paul Cambon, the French Ambassador in London addressed to Sir Edward Grey, the British Foreign Secretary. It was ratified in a letter from Grey to Cambon on 16 May. Russia was also privy to the discussions and consented to the terms. The Agreement became official in an exchange of notes among the three Allied Powers on 26 April and 23 May 1916. In a subsequent stage Italy too gave her agreement and the notes, which had been exchanged between 10 April and 27 September 1917, were confirmed in the Treaty of St. Jean de Maurienne.

Background. When Sir Henry McMahon, the British High Commissioner in Egypt, had reached a crucial stage in his negotiations with Sharif Hussein of Mecca (*see* MCMAHON-HUSSEIN CORRESPONDENCE), Grey expressed concern that the advocated support of Arab demands on Syria would cause the impression in France that the British merely intended to establish their own interests at the expense of the French. "Our primary and vital object," he emphasized, "is not to secure a new sphere of British influence, but to get the Arabs on our side."

An agreement with France was indispensable to avoid the impression that Britain had acted in bad faith. France regarded Syria as a dependency and a separate arrangement with the Sharif without France's participation could have had a chilling effect on the cordiality of the *entente*. Grey therefore suggested that Paris send a competent representative to discuss the matter.

The first round of discussions took place in London on 23 November 1915. The French Government was represented by François-Georges Picot, a professional diplomat with extensive experience in the Levant, who before the war was Consul-General in Beirut. The British delegation was led by Sir Arthur Nicolson. Picot was uncompromising; he insisted that Syria was a purely French possession, and by Syria he meant the region bounded by the Taurus ridges in the north and the Egyptian frontier on the south.

The second round of discussions took place on 21 December. The British were represented by Sir Mark Sykes, a leading expert on the East. This time Picot was in a more accommodating mood. Having juxtaposed the desiderata of all the parties concerned, he British, the French, and the Arabs, the two statesmen worked out a compromise solution.

Terms of the Agreement. It was agreed that France was to exercise direct control over Cilicia, the coastal strip of Syria, the Lebanon, and the greater part of Galilee, up to the line stretching from north of Acre to the north-west corner of Lake Kineret (Sea of Galilee) referred to as the "blue zone." East of that zone, in the Syrian hinterland, an Arab state was to be created under French protection (Area "A"). Britain was to exercise control over southern Mesopotamia (the "red zone"), the territory round Acre-Haifa bay in the Mediterranean, with rights to build a railway from there to

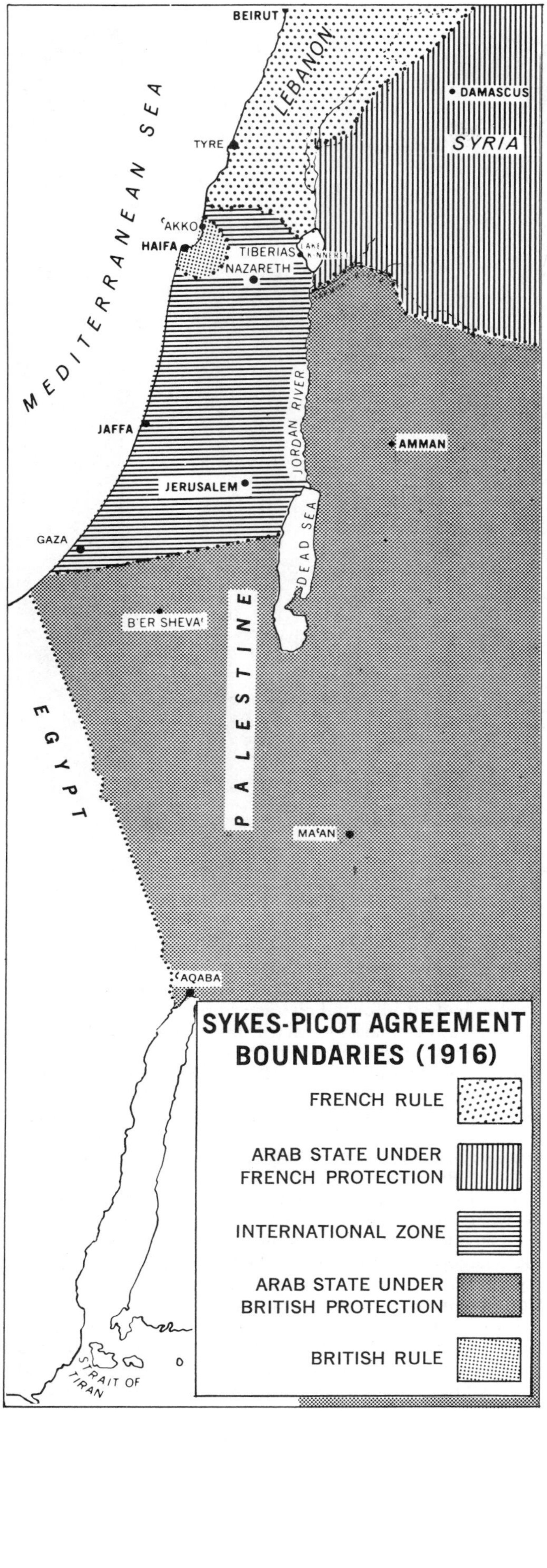

Baghdad. The territory east of the Jordan river and the Negev, south of the line stretching from Gaza to the Dead Sea, was allocated to an Arab State under British protection (Area "B"). South of France's "blue zone," in the area covering the Sanjak of Jerusalem, and extending southwards towards the line running approximately from Gaza to the Dead Sea. was to be a "brown zone" under international administration.

Assessment. In the years that followed, the Sykes-Picot Agreement became the target of bitter criticism, both in France and in England. Lloyd George referred to it as an "egregious" and a "foolish" document. He was particularly indignant that Palestine was inconsiderately mutilated. As seen through the glasses of 1917 this was, perhaps, true but in the winter of 1915–16, when negotiations were in full swing, the strategic importance of Palestine had not yet been fully appreciated in British official circles. The overriding aim was to make an Arab uprising possible, and this hinged on French concessions to Arab demands in the Syrian hinterland. Nor could military operations on the eastern front take place without French concurrence. Without a British offensive, there could have been no Arab revolt, and without the Sykes-Picot Agreement there would have been no British offensive. The compromise solution with the French was the price that the British had to pay. The true progenitor of the Sykes-Picot Agreement was the McMahon-Hussein Correspondence.

From this point of view Arab criticism is even less justified. The two negotiations showed meticulous consderation for Arab interests and blended it with healthy realism. The power vacuum created by the destruction of the Ottoman Empire had to be filled by a new authority; the alternative was chaos. Absolute independence for the Arabs would have invited anarchy or an outside invasion. There was no material incompatibility between the Agreement and the pledges made to Sharif Hussein.

The Agreement and Zionism. During the discussions Sykes and Picot took note that Jews throughout the world have "a conscientious and sentimental interest" in the future of the country. Zionist aspirations were passed over. This lapse was severely criticized by William R. Hall, head of the Intelligence Department of the British Admiralty. He pointed out that the Jews have "a strong material, and a very strong political interest in the future of the country and that...in the Brown area the question of Zionism...[ought] to be considered."

It took Sykes several months to appreciate the fact that he had committed a blunder. The growing awareness of Germany's ambition to dominate the Middle East was the decisive factor that prompted him to embrace the concept of a British-controlled Palestine. A condominium with France in Palestine was fraught with danger, since the very principle of an international regime left the door open to Germany. Hence, as the historian Sir Charles Webster put it, "a situation had to be created in which the worst features of the Sykes-Picot Agreement could be got rid of without breaking faith...In these circumstances Dr. Weizmann's offer was an attractive one." Herein lay the *raison d'être* of the alliance with British Zionism. It provides a way to outmaneuver the French without a breach of faith, and a useful card at the future peace conference to play against any move by Germany.

The Agreement was officially abrogated by the Allies at the San Remo Conference in April 1920, when the Mandate for Palestine was conferred upon Britain.

I. FRIEDMAN

Stained-glass windows by Marc Chagall adorn the synagogue of the Hebrew University–Hadassah Medical Center, 'En Kerem. [Hadassah]

SYNAGOGUES IN ISRAEL. The role played by the synagogue in Israel is, in many ways, more restricted than in the Diaspora where it often tends to be the focal point of Jewish identity not only in the religious but also in the social and educational spheres. Functions assumed by the synagogue elsewhere are not in its purview in Israel: births, marriages, and deaths are solemnized and registered through the ministries of Religious Affairs and the Interior; education, including religious education, is the concern of the Ministry of Education; the role of community center is met by other institutions. Consequently, the synagogue is almost exclusively a *bet tefilla* (house of prayer) rather than a *bet ha-keneset* (assembly house).

The life of the Old Yishuv was synagogue-centered but the pioneers arriving from the late 19th century on were primarily secular and socialist-oriented, rebelling against their east European religious background. Synagogues were attended by committed worshipers, usually without a rabbi but adequately conducted by laymen whose Jewish scholarship enabled them to provide sermons and study-group leaders. This tradition was further strengthened by the mass immigration after 1948 from Moslem lands, whose Jewish communities were strongly traditional and who founded many small congregations united by their origin from a common country, region, or town. The typical synagogue had an informal character and the only examples that bore any similarity to their Diaspora counterparts were a few central urban ones and those placed by Baron Edmond de Rothschild in the early moshavot under his sponsorship, such as Pardes Hanna and Zikhron Ya'akov. Synagogues were also uniformly Orthodox, since the religious establishment was Orthodox and, until the German immigration of the 1930s, only a handful of settlers identified with Progressive Judaism.

The mass immigration led to an explosion in the number of synagogues and by the late 1980s, their number was estimated at some 7,000, ranging from historically fascinating synagogues of the Samaritans and Karaites to the growing number—if still a small proportion of the total—of Conservative and Reform congregations.

Four main patterns of worship, not mutually exclusive, can be distinguished. There is the total synagogue that is a direct continuation of the combined religious study and social center of east European and oriental Jewry, still re-

Israel Goldstein Synagogue on Hebrew University's Givat Ram campus. [Hebrew University]

taining many of the characteristics of the pre-Emancipation era, including the Diaspora Ashkenazi pronunciation of Hebrew, and meticulously adhering to the liturgical rites of the Diaspora locality from which its founders hailed. Synagogues of this type can be found in the ultra-Orthodox centers of Benei Berak and Me'a She'arim in Jerusalem and their offshoots in all parts of the country, attended by graduates of the traditional yeshivot, followers of the various hasidic rabbis, and older immigrants who feel more comfortable with the prayer-style of the "old country".

The second pattern might be termed the west European cathedral, central, or "representative" synagogue. In these "Great" synagogues in the larger cities—in Jerusalem, Tel Aviv, Haifa and Ramat Gan—services are more formal with a part-time cantor and sometimes a choir. The buildings are usually imposing and are used for official services on state occasions. Services are conducted according to the Orthodox rite as current in the Diaspora save for the Israeli pronunciation of Hebrew and the east-European "Lithuanian" cantillation of the Bible readings.

A third pattern is the small "ethnic" congregation, ranging from the ultra-Orthodox *stiebel,* transferred from eastern Europe, to the many variants of synagogues of Jews originating from Moslem lands. These have no official rabbi but are conducted informally by the members, according to the customs and melodies of their places of origin.

The fourth pattern is the native Israeli one, that has emerged from the melting-pot of the State religious school system with its daily services, the army which provides religious amenities including synagogues at every base, and the religious kibbutz and pioneer youth movements. Its keynote is informality, community singing, regular Torah study circles, and the conducting of services by the members in rotation. Often the traditional status symbols of the different honors accorded in the service, the sale of offerings, and the bench of honor along the eastern wall have disappeared. The prayer for the State of Israel, the Armed Forces, the full liturgical recognition of Israel's Independence Day as a festival, and the Israeli pronunciation of Hebrew are essential features. The egalitarian influence of the kibbutz and the impact of the religious nationalism and fervor of the Merkaz ha-Rav and Bnei Akiva yeshivot are unmistakable. Oriental, hasidic, and even "pop" nuances surface in the synagogue tunes, in the popularization of which television, radio, and the cassette industry play a considerable role. The basic components of the prayer book are the same for all, and the army chaplaincy developed a uniform service for soldiers from all origins. The one family ceremony which has remained synagogue-centered in the barmitzvah and this has contributed, along with the pull of such festivals as the High Holidays and Simhat Torah, to the revival of the synagogue in certain secular communities such as a number of kibbutzim.

Israeli synagogues are independent in that the order of service, seating arrangements and the like depend entirely on the initiative of the worshippers themselves. There exists a loose roof organization known as the United Synagogue of Israel, sponsored by Hekhal Shelomo, the religious center and seat of the Chief Rabbinate in Jerusalem. Its activities consist mainly of issuing an annual calendar and yearbook, the holding of an annual conference, and an occasional world conference of Orthodox rabbis. All recognized synagogues (as well as churches and mosques) receive financial help from the Ministry of Religious Affairs, the local authority, and government development funds. Synagogue facilities are included in the planning of new suburbs and neighborhoods but the main burden falls on the worshipers themselves and whatever endowments they can obtain from Diaspora and Israeli philanthropists. They also lobby for public funds. In their architecture and design, Israel's major new synagogues have been influenced by styles prevailing in the West. Sometimes the architect has drawn his model from the past: the Belz synagogue in Jerusalem is directly modeled on the original building in Belz, whilst the four Ben-Zakkai synagogues in the Old City of Jerusalem (where all synagogues had been destroyed by the Jordanian between 1948 and 1967) are not precise reconstructions but modern halls evoking the atmosphere of the originals. In sharp contrast to recent developments in the Diaspora, there is seldom a creative partnership with sculptors and artists and only the exceptional synagogue shows originality. Occasionally, stained glass windows are incorporated, the most notable being Marc Chagall's twelve windows portraying the Twelve Tribes in Jerusalem's Hadassah synagogue. Some synagogues incorporate furnishings rescued from European synagogues including 28 arks brought from Italy. One of the finest of these is to be found in the grand synagogue hall of the Ponivezh yeshiva in Benei Berak. Some of the most attractive and original synagogues are found in the religious kibbutzim.

*Reform and *Conservative synagogues are not recognized by the religious establishment but their numbers have grown, especially since the 1960s. Many have been specially built for their congregations. A distinguishing feature is the joint seating for men and women. A. NEWMAN

SYNTHETIC ZIONISM. Fusion of two schools of early Zionism, the political Zionists, who regarded political efforts for the purpose of achieving a *Charter for Eretz Israel from Turkey as the immediate task of the Zionist movement, and the *practical Zionists, who insisted that the movement embark immediately on settlement activities. The term was probably coined at the Helsingfors Zionist Conference of 1906 and became associated with Chaim Weizmann, who at the Eighth Zionist Congress (1907) made an ardent plea for a synthesis between the two Zionist conceptions.

SYRIA AND LEBANON, ZIONISM IN. The Zionist movement in Syria and Lebanon, which developed in the first decade of the 20th century and ceased to exist with the establishment of the State of Israel, differed from its sister movements in Europe and the Americas in that, because of the political situation, it never had legal status and could not function openly. Arab nationalism, which was extremely strong in Syria and somewhat less so in Lebanon, regarded Zionism with suspicion, viewing it as a movement seeking to steal Palestine from the Arabs. Whereas in Syria the authorities forbade all Zionist activity, the movement in Lebanon enjoyed a certain amount of freedom owing to the support of the Maronites, although official, organized Zionism was forbidden there as well.

As a consequence, Zionist activity in both Syria and Lebanon had to be conducted under the guise of religious activity and was expressed through cultural work, Hebrew education, Zionist lectures before semi-secret groups, and emigration to Eretz Israel. He-Halutz and Ha-Halutz ha-Tza'ir groups were formed, as well as Maccabi and Ha-Po'el sports organizations. A Revisionist youth group , Betar, was formed in Aleppo, Syria. The Hebrew language, which served as a means of expressing Zionism, was studied in the Alliance Israélite Universelle schools in Syria and Lebanon, whose Hebrew curriculum was patterned on that of the Hebrew schools in Eretz Israel.

In 1910, when Abraham Elmaleh arrived from Eretz Israel and established in Damascus the first Hebrew kindergarten completely staffed by teachers from Eretz Israel, the Zionist movement in Syria embarked on a broad program of activities. Two community schools, teaching mainly in Hebrew, were established as a continuation of this kindergarten. The children began by singing Zionist songs in Hebrew, and as their command of the language increased, lectures and other cultural events were held in Hebrew, until that language was heard throughout the Jewish ghetto in Damascus and became the foundation for subsequent Zionist activities. After Elmaleh's return to Jerusalem, Yehuda Burla, the writer, administered the Hebrew schools for boys, while the future professor Joseph Joel Rivlin headed the girls' school.

During World War I, owing to the arrival in Damascus of many Jews who had been expelled from Eretz Israel by the Turks, Zionist educational activity in Syria expanded. Among the exiles were David Yellin and his son Aviezer, Abraham Elmaleh, and the writer and poet Ovadia Kimhi. These men helped propagate the Hebrew language and Hebrew culture and set up courses in the history and geography of Eretz Israel. Under the guise of cultural activities, the Zionist spirit permeated the Jewish community of Damascus and, on a smaller scale, that of Aleppo as well.

After the war, the network of Hebrew schools expanded and the teaching staff, headed by Burla, Rivlin, and Bezalel Basrawi, provided a Hebrew and Zionist education for thousands of students. Basrawi devoted his energies to the formation of the Maccabi and Young Maccabi sports organizations, which embraced all the upper-grade students of the Hebrew schools. This golden period did not last long; in 1923 most of the Hebrew schools had to close for lack of financial support from the Damascus Jewish community.

However, the seeds sown began to bear fruit. Groups of young people who had received a Zionist education set up their own organizations and established the Lev Ehad and Ha-Tzevi movements. But these were short-lived, and the young people became restless as they sought methods and ways of expressing their Zionism. In 1928 Yehuda Kopeliovitz (later Almog), a member of a kibbutz, visited Damascus and helped form a Halutz (pioneer) organization there. One of its early members was Eliahu Luzya, a leader of the Jewish community in Damascus. This pioneering movement, which was started in Lebanon as well, helped spread Zionism through the Jewish communities. Its main purpose was to encourage settlement in Palestine. Both Syria and Lebanon forbade migration to Palestine, but although the local and French authorities knew that illegal migration of Syrian and Lebanese Jews to Palestine existed, they disregarded it.

Zionist activity in Lebanon enjoyed relative freedom. The Lebanese Maronites viewed Zionism with favor, and the Maronite Patriarch and Bishop Mubarak were supporters of Zionism. The Maccabi organization paraded openly in Lebanon with the blue-and-white Zionist flag. Hebrew was taught in the Jewish schools and even in the French secondary school. Eliahu Elmaleh taught in the latter school and also directed the Alliance Israélite Universelle school in Beirut. Jewish students could choose Hebrew as their second language in the official baccalaureate examinations.

Following World War II, when Joseph David Farhi, an active Zionist and president of B'nai B'rith, headed the Beirut *kehilla*, Rahel Yanait Ben-Zvi came from Palestine to recruit Jewish girls in Syria and Lebanon for the agricultural school she directed in Jerusalem. Jewish students from Palestine at the American University of Beirut helped Hebrew and Zionist activities in Lebanon. Among them was Eliahu Epstein (Elath), later president of the Hebrew University of Jerusalem. The students' organization Kadima won many people to Zionism and was a center of lively Zionist activity both within the university and in Beirut generally.

A Jewish Arabic-language paper, notable for its articles on Zionism and Palestine, was published in Beirut. Lebanon was also a source of immigrants to Palestine, with Eliahu Elmaleh representing the Jewish Agency in Beirut.

Syrian and Lebanese Jews appeared before the Crane Commission (*see* KING-CRANE REPORT). Abraham Elmaleh urged the heads of the Jewish communities in those countries to declare themselves in favor of Britain as the Mandatory for Palestine. At the same time, Arab nationalist leaders exerted pressure on the Jews of Syria and Lebanon to support their demand for an independent, united Syria, including Palestine as its southern sector and with Palestine enjoying a certain degree of internal autonomy but not separated from Syria. The Jewish representatives in those countries did not yield to this pressure, and when they appeared before the Crane Commission, they emphasized that they, as Jews, sought free Jewish migration to Palestine, where they wished to settle, to establish settlements, and to develop the country's economy. "It is clear," they declared in their testimony, "that Palestine has always been, in a geographic and administrative sense, separate from Syria, and it is our intense desire that it once again become the national home for our people." A. MASHIAH

SYRIAN AND LEBANESE JEWS IN ISRAEL. Late in the 19th century several prominent rabbis from Aleppo (Halab) immigrated to Jerusalem. An Aleppan (Halabi) community was registered with the Ottoman authorities in Jerusalem in 1880. The motivation of the migration was primarily religious.

World War I interrupted this migration. In fact, many

families returned to Syria, while some emigrated to the Americas. During the period of the Mandate for Palestine immigration of Syrian and Lebanese Jews to Palestine was resumed, both legally and illegally. The new immigration was stimulated in part by a small Zionist movement that had been formed in Damascus as a result of contact with Palestinian Jewish exiles during World War I. Of great significance were the continuing economic difficulties of Jews in Damascus and Aleppo, the two main centers, the increasingly anti-Jewish and anti-Zionist tone of Syrian Arab nationalism, and the closure of the United States to large-scale Syrian immigration after 1924. The Syrian Jews from Aleppo and Damascus were primarily small-scale merchants, peddlers, and craftsmen. One of the major crafts engaged in by Damascus Jews was copper engraving, which was particularly hard hit by foreign competition in the 1920s and 1930s.

It is estimated that about 9,000 Jews immigrated to Palestine from Syria, mainly illegally, during the mandatory period. While Jerusalem continued to attract them, more and more went to Haifa and Tel Aviv. A small number, especially from Damascus, went to kibbutzim in Galilee. Much of this immigration took place in the 1930s and 1940s, when Arab nationalism was at its height. This period was marked by new manifestations of Arab nationalism and, briefly, by a Nazi threat in the form of Vichy France's occupation of Syria.

In the first decade of the State of Israel (1948–58), 5,600 immigrants came from Syria and Lebanon. The demographic picture of Syrian Jews in Israel is complicated by a number of factors: (1) Persons whose origin group is Aleppan or Damascan or who stem from other Syrian and Lebanese areas may have been born in Palestine, Egypt, or elsewhere (e.g., the Americas) and are thus not counted by the census as Syrian or Lebanese. (2) There has been a high birthrate among Middle Eastern Jews in general, and Syrian Jews are no exception. (3) While it is difficult to make an exact estimate, many Israelis of Syrian and Lebanese origin are temporarily away from Israel or permanent residents of the United States or South American countries, where there are substantial Syrian-Jewish communities. (4) According to data supplied by the Central Bureau of Statistics of Israel, intermarriage with other groups is increasing among Syrian Jews.

Synagogues identified as Syro-Lebanese, Damascan, and Aleppan can be found in Jerusalem, Tel Aviv, and Haifa. In some cases, these synagogues draw their congregations solely from Syro-Lebanese Jews, while other synagogues have become general Middle Eastern houses of worship. Syro-Lebanese synagogues follow the ritual common to most Sephardi and Middle Eastern Jews in Israel.

A noteworthy feature of the Syro-Lebanese synagogues is the midnight and early morning singing of certain sacred Hebrew songs, called *bakashot*. The *bakashot* are sung in accord with *maqamat*, the Arab musical modes. They are sung on Sabbaths from Sukkot to Passover. While this custom appears to have originated in Aleppo and Damascus, it has been adopted by other Middle Eastern Jews in Jerusalem. The singing is a living tradition in which new *bakashot* continue to be composed and stylistic changes appear.

Few occupations can be considered typically Syrian, and there are no specifically Syrian handicrafts. Aleppan Jews have been particularly prominent in religious and communal activities in Jerusalem. Many rabbis of Aleppan origin are graduates of the Porat Yosef Yeshiva in Jerusalem, and Aleppan Jews in the Diaspora have contributed funds to maintain this institution of Torah learning as well as other Sephardi institutions in Israel. During the mandate period an individual of Aleppan origin, E. Shama, was active in promoting commerce in Jewish Jerusalem. Although the number of Syrian Jews in kibbutzim has always been small, both immigrants and Israel-born Jews of Syrian origin have been members of collective settlements. Like their fellows of other origins, Syrian Jews served in various underground organizations that fought for Israel's independence.

Syrian Jews are found in all strata from the Cabinet level down. Prominent Syrian Jews in recent years have been Eliyahu Hai Sasson, a Damascan Jew who served as a diplomat and as Minister of Posts and of Police; Menahem Yedid and Abraham Abbas, members of the Knesset; Rabbi Ovadia Hadaya, a halakhist and kabbalist who received the Israel Prize in 1968; Yitzhak Shammush, a scholar in Arabic literature and editor of the Arabic-language newspaper *al-Yom*; and Amnon Shammosh, novelist, many of whose works deal with the life of Syrian Jews. W.P. ZENNER

Nachman Syrkin.
[Zionist Archives]

SYRKIN. Zionist family.

Nachman Syrkin. Ideological founder of Socialist Zionism (b. Mogilev, Russia, 1868; d. New York, 1924). The son of a prosperous middle-class family, Syrkin received a traditional Jewish education and also studied at a Russian high school. While still in his teens, he became active in the Hovevei Zion movement and in anti-Tsarist revolutionary circles. In 1888 he left home to study in Germany. He received his doctorate in Berlin and soon began to advance his theories, which subsequently were crystallized in the platform of Socialist Zionism.

In 1898 Syrkin published (in German) *The Jewish Problem and the Socialist Jewish State*, in which he broke theoretical ground for the program of Socialist constructivism, a program adhered to by the majority of the Jewish labor parties in Eretz Israel from the second decade of the 20th century on. Syrkin recognized that the Jews, like all other peoples, were divided into classes, but to him the class struggle was not the only road to socialism. All Jewish classes, he maintained, shared a common vision of redemption, of which Zionism was both symbol and practical expression. Zionism held a universal promise that elevated it above the level of a mere nationalist movement to the height of a great social ideal. Throughout his active life Syrkin insisted that "there can by no Zionism except Socialist Zionism." The Jews had not prayed and died for a Return to Zion, he said, merely to see another state come into being with all the evils and injustices of existing states.

Jewish socialism, Syrkin argued, derived its spiritual sustenance from the visions of the Hebrew prophets no less than from the needs, interests, and aspirations of the exploited classes. People were moved not only by material compulsions but also by the yearning of the soul. This was true particularly of oppressed peoples, and all the more so of the Jewish people. This, Syrkin contended, explained why voluntarism had played so decisive a role in the development of nations in general and in the history of the Jewish people in particular.

According to Syrkin, the fight for socialism implied more than a direct confrontation between capital and labor. Since Jewish settlement work in Eretz Israel had neither the budgets of government nor the resources of private investment to back it, it could draw only upon the so-called Jewish national capital—the funds raised by the Jewish people through Zionist institutions. These funds were not given for private gain but for national and social service, and this circumstance offered Jewish labor the opportunity to build the Jewish Homeland on a foundation of free cooperative enterprise. Practical statebuilding needs and the forging of new social relations were joined in this program of cooperative effort, which found its concrete expression in the kibbutz movement and in the other collective institutions established by Jewish labor in Eretz Israel on a foundation of voluntary cooperation.

Syrkin was no ivory tower theoretician. He was a man of action who found himself in the thick of every fight for the honor of the Jewish people and the dignity of the working classes. No sooner was he seized by an idea than he set out to implement it. It was this social impatience that made him at the same time an inspiring popular leader and the lonely figure he could be when, ahead of his time, he championed causes that did not gain immediate acceptance. His strong desire to see social programs put into immediate effect impelled him, on the defeat of the East Africa scheme, to join the Territorialist movement for a brief period.

Active in a number of European countries, Syrkin spent his most productive years in the United States, where he arrived in 1907. Upon rejoining the Labor Zionist movement in 1909, he became its most eloquent spokesman and its most effective organizer. He soon emerged as a highly influential leader in world Labor Zionism, which was largely shaped by his ideas and pursued policies he formulated. He was also one of the proponents of the Jewish Legion.

Syrkin's remains were transferred to the State of Israel in 1951. A street in Tel Aviv and a village (Kefar Syrkin) are named for him. C.B. SHERMAN

Marie Syrkin, his daughter. Educator, author, and Zionist publicist; (b. Berne, Switzerland, 1899; d. Los Angeles, 1989) Taken to the United States in 1907, she graduated from Cornell University (B.A., 1920). From 1925 to 1948 she taught at high schools in New York City and from 1950 to 1966 was an associate professor of English at Brandeis University. She first became known as a translator of Yiddish poetry into English and later was widely known as a critic of Jewish life on the American scene. In 1948 she became editor of the *Jewish Frontier*, a position she held till 1969. She was a member of the Jewish Agency Executive in New York from 1965 to 1968. Her books include *Your School, Your Children*, a study of the American public schools (1944), *Blessed Is the Match* (the story of Jewish resistance in Nazi-occupied Europe, based on her interviews in Palestine in 1945 with survivors of the Jewish underground; 1947), *Nachman Syrkin, Socialist Zionist* (1960), a biography of Golda Meir (*Golda Meir: Woman with a Cause*, 1963; rev. ed., *Golda Meir: Israel's Leader*, 1969), and *The State of the Jews* a volume of selected essays, (1980). She wrote many articles and pamphlets on Zionist problems and literary and general themes. Her translations of Yiddish verse appeared in numerous anthologies. *Gleanings, a Diary in Verse*, was a selection of her original verse (1979). She edited a *Hayim Greenberg Anthology*, (1968); and *A Land of Our Own*, an oral autobiography, by Golda Meir, (1973). She was on the editorial board of and a frequent contributor to the journal, *Midstream*.

SZEKELY, BELA. Journalist, writer, and Zionist leader (b. Betlen, Hungary, 1892; d. Chascomus, Argentina, 1955). Szekely began his career in Nagyvarad (Oradea). He was a founder, with Erno Marton, of the newspaper *Uj Kelet* in Kolozsvar and editor of *Keleti Ujsag* (Eastern Journal) and *5 Crai Ujsak* (Five O'Clock Journal) of the same city. An active Zionist, he was a leading figure of the Transylvanian Jewish National Association and of the Pro-Palestine Association of Hungarian Jews. He was the founder and president of the Aviva Girls' movement which, by the late 1920s, had branches in 16 countries. A prolific writer and poet, Szekely was also active as a translator and as the Hungarian representative of the Jewish Telegraphic Agency. In 1938 he emigrated to Argentina, where he engaged in teaching and wrote a number of books, including one on anti-Semitism.

R.L. BRAHAM

Hanna Szenes at kibbutz Sedot Yam, 1939. [Israel Govt. Press Office]

SZENES (SENESH), HANNA. Poet and Palestinian Jewish resistance heroine in World War II (b. Budapest, 1921; d. there, 1944). The daughter of a Hungarian author and playwright, she was raised in an assimilated home but was drawn to Zionism in the late 1930s, probably under the influence of increasing anti-Semitism in Hungary and of the growing menace of Nazism. Against the wishes of her widowed mother, she began to study Hebrew and to prepare for aliya. Arriving in Palestine in 1939, she studied for two years at the agricultural training school for girls at Nahalal, where she first began to write poetry. On completion of her training, she joined Kibbutz Sedot Yam, near Caesarea.

In 1943 she conceived the idea that she must go back to Hungary to help organize an aliya of young people from there and to rescue her mother. Subsequently she enlisted in the British Army, volunteering for the group of Palestinian Jewish *parachutists who were being trained in Egypt to operate behind enemy lines as organizers of anti-Nazi resistance. She was dropped over Italy and made her way to Yugoslavia, from where she tried to continue into Hungary. In June, 1944, she was captured near the Hungarian border and interrogated in prison in Szombathely. From there she was taken to Budapest. Hanna's mother was taken to counterintelligence headquarters, where she was brought face to face with her daughter in an effort to make the girl reveal what she knew of underground activities. Hanna was brought to trial late in October and shot in November. Her remains were taken to Israel in 1950 and reinterred on Mount Herzl.

Her biography (in Hebrew), *Hanna Szenes: Her Life, Her Mission, and Her Death* (1954), includes excerpts from her diary, her poems, a one-act play, *The Violin* (dealing with a girl who gives up a career in music to help build a kibbutz), and reminiscences by her mother, who settled in Israel after the war. Her best-known poem, "Blessed Is the Match," was written in May, 1944, while she was in Yugoslavia.

Henrietta Szold. [Hadassah]

SZOLD, HENRIETTA. Educator, author, social worker, and founder of *Hadassah (b. Baltimore, 1860; d. Jerusalem, 1945). Influenced by her father, Dr. Benjamin Szold (1829–1902), a prominent rabbi, Hebrew scholar, and pioneer member of the Hovevei Zion movement in Baltimore, Henrietta Szold received an intensive Jewish education at home and was graduated from the Western Female High School in her native city. Before she was 19, she was writing articles for various Anglo-Jewish periodicals under the pen name Shulamith.

While teaching school in Baltimore, she became interested in the Americanization problems of the immigrants who came to Baltimore from Eastern Europe. In 1889, she established formal night classes to train immigrants for U.S. citizenship, thus initiating America's first night school. It was later incorporated into the Baltimore public school system.

Her interest in the Jewish homeland antedated the advent of Herzl. She gave her first Zionist address in 1895 at a meeting of the Baltimore section of the National Council of Jewish Women. In 1893 she became literary secretary of the Jewish Publication Society of America, a position she held until 1916. Her work included proofreading, the rewriting and revising of books and articles, and the translation into English of a number of important works published by the society, including Louis Ginzberg's *Legends of the Jews*, Moritz Lazarus' *Ethics of Judaism*, and Nahum Slouschz's *Hebrew Renaissance*. She also participated in and edited the English translation of Heinrich Graetz's monumental *History of the Jews*.

In 1903 Szold moved to New York, where she enrolled as a special student at the Jewish Theological Seminary of America, and from 1904 to 1908 edited the Jewish Publication Society's American Jewish Yearbook. Her apartment became a gathering place for early Zionist leaders and Jewish scholars of renown. In 1909 she visited Eretz Israel. Returning to New York, she reported on the pressing health problems which then beset the country. In 1907 she had been invited by Emma Gottheil to join the Hadassah Study Circle. In 1912 this group became the first chapter of a National Women's Zionist Organization founded by Szold, who served as its president (1912–1921; 1923–1926) and honorary president (1926–1945). In 1917 Justice Louis D. Brandeis, then chairman of the Provisional Executive Committee for General Zionist Affairs in the United States, charged Szold with organizing the *American Zionist Medical Unit, which went to Palestine in the summer of 1918. Szold settled in Palestine in 1920 and directed the Hadassah Medical Organization from 1920 to 1923. In 1927 the Zionist Congress elected her a member of the Zionist Executive, the first woman to hold such a position, assigning her the portfolio of health and education. In 1930 she was elected to the Va'ad Le'umi, in conjunction with the opening of a Department of Social Welfare, of which she took charge.

Following Hitler's rise to power in Germany, Szold in 1934 became involved with *Youth Aliya, which rescued Jewish children from Nazi persecution in Europe. She became its noted leader. Beginning in 1934, at the age of 73, she was on hand to welcome each ship as it docked and supervised the placement of the children in institutions and schools in accordance with their religious background. In 1941 she made a survey of the needs of vocational education for girls, on the basis of which Hadassah subsequently founded the Alice L. Seligsberg Vocational High School for Girls in Jerusalem.

Kefar Szold, a settlement established in 1935 near the Syrian border, as well as many streets in towns and numerous institutions throughout the country were named for her. G. HIRSCHLER—M. LEVIN

SZOLD, ROBERT. Attorney and Zionist leader in the United States (b. Streator, Ill., 1889; d. New York City, 1979). A graduate of Knox College (1909) and Harvard Law School (LL.B, 1912), he briefly served as assistant attorney general for Puerto Rico in 1915. Later that year he was named assistant to U.S. Solicitor-General John W. Davis, a position he held until 1919. Brought to Zionism through his friendship with Justice Louis D. Brandeis, to whom he remained attached and loyal throughout his long Zionist career, Szold was president of a Zionist circle in Washington from 1915 to 1917. In 1919 he served on the Zionist Commission in Palestine. The next year he was a member of the Zionist Reorganization Commission. In 1921 he established a law practice in New York. After the Cleveland Convention of the Zionist Organization of America (ZOA), together with Brandeis, Julian W. Mack, and their disciples, he temporarily left active Zionist leadership and turned his attention to work for the economic development of Palestine.

Szold was president (1922–26) of the Palestine Cooperative Company; treasurer, president, and chairman of Palestine Endowment Funds, Inc.; director, vice-president, president, and finally, chairman (1925–57) of the Palestine Economic Corporation; life member of the Council of the Jewish Colonial Trust; life member of the Jewish National Fund; director of the Palestine Mortgage and Savings Bank (1930–59); director and chairman of the Central Bank of Cooperative Institutions in Palestine (1930–56); director of Palestine Potash Ltd; and a founder-member and cochairman of the American Economic Committee for Palestine, Inc. (1939–54).

In 1930 Szold returned to Zionist leadership as president of the ZOA, serving through the following year, when he was vice-chairman of the Council of the Jewish Agency. In 1939 he was the ZOA delegate to the St. James's Conference in London, and later that year he helped found the Emergency Committee for Zionist Affairs, serving on its Presidium from 1940 on and as chairman of its Budget Committee from 1942 to 1944. In 1943 he was a member of the Executive Committee of the American Jewish Conference.

Zip Falk Szold, Robert's wife, communal worker, and Zionist leader in the United States (b. Savannah, Ga., 1888; d. New York City, 1979). A graduate of Bryn Mawr College (B.A., 1910), she was employed as a social worker in Bloomfield, N.J., organizing a district nursing service and getting the local public schools to open evenings for group recreation for young people. She subsequently served as secretary of the National Consumers League in Washington, where she also acted as its legislative representative.

Zip Szold was active in Hadassah for almost five decades, serving as National Board member of that organization from 1921 on and as Hadassah's president from 1929 to 1931. In 1920 she sponsored the young women's Zionist group that later became known as Junior Hadassah, and subsequently took an active part in the building of the Hadassah-University Hospital on Mount Scopus in Jerusalem. She was at various times editor of the *Hadassah Newsletter* and chairman of Hadassah's national UN committee. She was an effective spokesman for Zionism and Hadassah in the 1930s and 1940s among influential political circles in Washington, DC. Through her activity, Hadassah first entered political activity in the US in an organized fashion.

G. HIRSCHLER—M. LEVIN

T

TAANACH REGION. Farming area in the southern Jezreel Valley, developed since 1955 on the planning principles devised at the time for the Lachish and other regions, viz., moshavim grouped around rural centers. Nine villages were established, with three centers; the proximity of Afula, 3–6 mi. (5–10 km.) to the north, later made these centers redundant. The moshavim, on good soil and with an adequate water supply, based themselves on intensive mixed farming. The name Taanach is taken from the biblical site, principally known from Deborah's victory over the Canaanites (Judges 5;6). Most names of the region's settlement were taken from the Song of Deborah. E. ORNI

TABENKIN, YITZHAK. A leader of the Israel kibbutz movements (b. Bobruisk, 1887; d. Tel Aviv, 1971). He studied in Bobruisk and Warsaw, and later at the universities of Vienna and Berne, becoming deeply versed in Jewish, Russian, and European culture. Tabenkin was one of the founders of Po'ale Zion. He immigrated to Eretz Israel in 1912, worked as a watchman in Rehovot, and then at Kineret. After World War I he was one of the founders of Ahdut ha-Avoda, the Hagana, and the Histadrut in 1920. In 1921, as a member of a Gedud ha-Avoda group, he settled in En Harod. Together with Shelomo Lavi he took the En Harod farm out of Gedud ha-Avoda in 1923 in order to implement the idea of the large collective. In 1925–26 he was a He-Halutz emissary in Poland. In 1927 he founded Ha-Kibbutz ha-Me'uhad in En Harod, together with other farms and groups; in 1930 he unenthusiastically supported its union with Ha-Po'el ha-Tza'ir in order to form Mapai. The 1930s saw continuing quarrels between Tabenkin and his friends in the Mapai leadership, over such subjects as the nature of He-Halutz education and the orientation of its workforce; the Peel Committee Partition Plan; Berl Katznelson's program to unite Ha-Kibbutz ha-Me'uhad and Hever ha-Kevutzot; and relations with the Soviet Union. Between 1938 and 1942 the disagreements worsened and led to the creation of Faction B in Mapai, an alliance between the opposition to the party's leadership in the cities and the Ha-Kibbutz ha-Me'uhad leadership. From 1942 the internal party opposition took on a political aspect: in 1942 Faction B opposed the Biltmore Program and also opposed the priority accorded to recruitment into the British army rather than fostering the Palmah.

The social, ideological, and political power struggle in Mapai terminated in a split in 1944. Tabenkin's faction was called Ahdut ha-Avoda, and after its unification with Po'ale Zion in April 1946 the party was called Ahdut ha-Avoda-Po'ale Zion. He contributed greatly to the Palmah, putting Ha-Kibbutz ha-Me'uhad farms at its disposal as work and training bases, and many members of his movement served as soldiers and officers in the ranks of the Palmah. On the eve of the War of Independence the Zionist left-wing, which rejected the partition proposal, united with the United Workers' Party, Mapam, which included Tabenkin's party. Tabenkin was a Mapam member of the Knesset 1949–51. When Mapam left the government, Tabenkin found himself in a left-wing opposition party to which most of Ha-Kibbutz ha-Me'uhad belonged. In 1954, Ahdut Avoda split off from Mapam to resume an independent policy and from 1954 to 1959 Tabenkin served as an Ahdut Avoda member of the Knesset but, as before, his leadership did not stem from any formal position. His opposition to the creation of an Alignment in the mid-sixties and to the union between his party and Mapai, delayed the creation of the Labor Alignment until after the Six-Day War. Tabenkin joined the Greater Israel Movement founded after that War, and worked to prevent support by Ha-Kibbutz ha-Me'uhad for Yigal Allon's plan which called for only limited settlement in the Administered Areas, which was delayed until after his death. A. KAFKAFI

TABOR (TAVOR), MOUNT. Mountain in Lower Galilee northeast of the Jezreel Valley, 1,930 ft. (588 m.) high, conspicuous for its isolated position and domed shape. Marking the boundary between the tribes of Manasseh, Issachar, and Zebulun, it is mentioned in Judges 4 in the description of Deborah's and Barak's victory over the Canaanites. Christian tradition locates there Jesus's transfiguration, and monasteries were built on the top. The moshava of Kefar Tavor lies southeast of the mountain, and the Kadourie farming school to the northeast. E. ORNI

TAGER, ARYE LEO. Businessman, Zionist leader, and Israeli public official (b. Rezekne, Latvia, 1900; d. Ashkelon, 1967). Tager studied law at the universities of Petrograd and Moscow. He early became active in Labor Zionist circles

Mount Tabor. [Israel Information Services]

in his native country, serving on the Central Committee of Tze'irei Zion in Latvia. He was a cofounder and editor (1921–25) of the Riga Yiddish-language daily *Unzer Weg.*

In 1925 he first went to Palestine, settling in Rishon le-Zion, where he became a member of the town council. In 1929, he moved to Johannesburg as an emissary to build a strong Labor Zionist movement in South Africa and remained there until 1952. Tager was a member of the Executive Committee of the South African Zionist Socialist party (1929–52) and its chairman (1930–32, 1948–52), vice-chairman of the South African Zionist Federation, and national chairman of the federation's Israeli United Appeal (IUA, 1948–52). A delegate to many Zionist Congresses, he was a member of the Zionist General Council from 1951 to 1956 and for many years served on the Board of Directors of Keren ha-Yesod.

In 1952 he returned to Israel, where he played a leading role in the Afridar Housing Corporation, whose housing development became part of the city of Ashkelon. In 1956 Tager was appointed mayor of Ashkelon by the Minister of the Interior, a position in which he was confirmed in subsequent elections and which he held until 1965.

TAHAL (Hebrew acronym for "Water Planning for Israel Ltd."). Company offering consulting services in almost the entire range of engineering and associated disciplines. It was founded in 1952, for the purpose of planning Israel's National Water Carrier and the national water sector in general. The government is the major shareholder. Part of the shares are held by the Jewish National Fund. The company is the official consultant to the National Water Commission (acting under the Ministry of Agriculture) on all matters concerning the planning of water works and use of water on the national scale. In addition, it provides consulting services also to public agencies, such as municipalities, and to private clients.

During its first decade, most of Tahal's activities were related to the planning of the National Water Carrier and the peripheral water works related to it, such as regional water schemes based on boreholes, for exploitation of groundwater, storage reservoirs, and waste-water disposal schemes. Since its completion in the early 1960s, activities have related mainly to the planning of the optimal exploitation of Israel's water resources, covering a wide range of subjects such as the economic use of water in agriculture, conservation of water resources and optimization of their use, development of marginal resources (e.g., use of brackish water, desalination, artifical rain), and re-use of urban effluents.

In 1961, a subsidiary company named Tahal Consulting Engineers Ltd. (TCE) was established for offering the accumulated experience and know-how to developing, and later also to industrialized, countries. Tahal's services to private clients in Israel are also provided through TCE.

Realizing the need for an integrated approach to the planning of resources development, especially in connection with work in developing countries, Tahal diversified its fields of activity to include agriculture, irrigation, and agro-industries. Later, the company turned to additional fields of engineering, and particularly public works and infrastructure, sanitation and environmental protection, energy, oil and gas conveyance and storage, integrated development and systems engineering.

Up to 1988, Tahal had performed hundreds of projects, mainly in water resources, irrigation, and agricultural development, but also in other fields such as planning of road networks, bridges, hospitals, and tourist resorts, in more than 40 countries of Africa, Asia, Latin America, Europe, and the Middle East. Many of these projects were funded by international agencies such as the World Bank Group, the Inter-American Development Bank, and United Nations agencies.

The company employed in 1988 about 450 professionals and about 200 technicians and administrative staff.

Z. SHIFTAN

TAKAM. *See* UNITED KIBBUTZ MOVEMENT.

TAL (GRUNTHAL), JOSEPH. Israeli composer, pianist, and pedagogue (b. Pinne (Pniewy), Poznania, 1910). Tal studied at the Staatlichen Akademischen Hochschule in Berlin. He immigrated to Palestine in 1934, eventually settling in Jerusalem. During the 1940s he was active mostly as a solo pianist. He also taught theory at the Jerusalem Music Academy, and from 1960, taught at the Hebrew University, where, in 1965 he was among the founders of the country's first musicology department in which he was a professor. His early works, written in the 1940s, were chamber pieces. Tal opposed any ideological or group pressure to compose in any specific "national" style, supported the freedom of personal choice of techniques and styles, and advocated the maintenance of ties to the great historical heritage of Europe, into which he injected eastern elements, such as portions of traditional tunes of Jews from Arab lands, and local folk songs. In 1960 he founded the first studio for electro-acoustic music in the country and produced purely electro-acoustic works, as well as a series of piano concerti with magnetic tape, and a full scale opera, *Masada* for voices and tape. In 1971 his opera *Ashmedai*, to a libretto by the poet Israel Eliraz, was staged in Hamburg, opening the way for a series of operas by Tal and Eliraz produced in Hamburg and at the New York City Opera. He also conducted a research project into the development of notation for electro-acoustic music. Tal was awarded the Israel Prize in 1970.

J. HIRSCHBERG

TANNENBAUM, BERNICE. Zionist and community leader in the US (b. Brooklyn, NY). A graduate of Brooklyn College, Tannenbaum has been a member of Hadassah since 1940, founding the Kew Gardens Chapter in 1944, and in 1948 was an organizer of Hadassah's Long Island Region. She later was a founder of the Queens and Nassau-Suffolk regions of Hadassah. In 1953, she was sent to Israel by National Hadassah as its Speakers' Bureau Fellow-of-the-Year and in 1957 became National Chairman of Junior Hadassah. In 1968, she was chairman of Hadassah's tribute to Israel's 20th Anniversary and also headed the first mid-winter conference to be held in Israel. She became Hadassah's 16th national president in 1976, serving for four years, and then headed Hadassah's medical work for four years. In 1982–83, she was chairman of Hadassah's 70th Anniversary Committee. In 1984, Tannenbaum established the Hadassah Medical Relief Organization (HMRO), which had its first international conference in Paris in March, 1986, and became its chairman. HMRO, an organization of friends of Hadassah, has members in 20 countries and a membership of more than 5,000. Tannenbaum was elected chairman of the American Section of the World Zionist Organization in 1982 and reelected in 1987; she is a member of the Executive of the WZO and of the Jewish Agency Executive. She is co-president of the World Confederation of United Zionists, and chairman of the Status of Women Commission of the World Jewish Congress.

M. LEVIN

TARBUT. Hebrew term, meaning "culture," used between the two world wars to designate Hebrew-language movements, mainly in eastern European countries. The Tarbut movement was the fruit of many earlier attempts to unite the supporters of the Hebrew renaissance, such as the Hovevei Sefat Ever in Russia, the Safa Berura Societies in the Austro-Hungarian Monarchy, and the Doreshei Sefat Ever in the United States. During World War I and especially after the Russian Revolution of 1917, the Hebrew-

Greetings to the Hebrew University on its opening in 1925 from the Central Board of Tarbut in Poland. [Hebrew University]

language movement showed a pronounced upsurge in Russia. On the establishment of the Communist regime, however, the movement, together with Zionism and the practice of the Jewish religion in general, was declared counterrevolutionary and suppressed. The main center of the movement then shifted to Poland, where the Tarbut organization was established in 1922 and, strongly supported by the Zionist movement, played a substantial role in Jewish life. Of special significance was the Tarbut network of educational institutions, such as kindergartens, elementary and high schools, teachers' seminaries, and evening classes, whose overall attendance, despite financial difficulties and a hostile government, reached 45,000 in the 1930s. There were also many other Hebrew-language activities, including newspapers, libraries, and theaters.

No less intensive, though much smaller in numbers, was the Hebrew-language movement in the other eastern European countries, especially Lithuania, Romania, and Bulgaria. In the 1930s, the number of pupils in Hebrew schools in Lithuania reached 14,000, or 90 percent of the Jewish schoolchildren in the country. Equally impressive were the achievements in Bulgaria, where Hebrew served as the language of instruction in all Jewish schools, and in Bessarabia, where, after the cession of the province from Russia to Romania, the Jewish population established a network of Hebrew schools that it managed to maintain despite persecution by the anti-Semitic Romanian authorities. All the Tarbut schools in eastern Europe remained in close contact with the Jewish community of Palestine and had a distinct Zionist orientation.

During World War II the Tarbut movement in eastern Europe disappeared. It was liquidated in eastern Poland, the Baltic countries, and Bessarabia after the Soviet occupation of these territories, and subsequently by the Nazis in the course of their destruction of Jewish life in the occupied countries. The only country in eastern Europe where an attempt was made after the war to reestablish the Hebrew-language movement, and especially the Hebrew schools, was Poland. There, in the immediate postwar years, 12 Hebrew schools were functioning with a combined enrollment of more than 1,000. With the consolidation of the Communist regime and the domination of Jewish life by Communists, however, the Hebrew schools in Poland were gradually broken up.

A. TARTAKOWER

TARTAKOWER, ARYE. Sociologist (b. Brody, Galicia, Austria, 1897; d. Jerusalem 1982). After completing his law studies at the University of Vienna in 1920, Tartakower left for Palestine, where he worked on farms and on road construction. Returning to Europe for medical treatment, he studied sociology at the University of Vienna. From 1922 to 1939 he was general secretary of the Association of Hebrew High Schools in Lodz, Poland, and from 1931 to 1939 lectured at the Institute for Jewish Studies in Warsaw. He was also secretary of the Hitahdut party from 1927 to 1932.

Tartakower spent the years of World War II in the United States, where he worked for the World Jewish Congress (WJC). In 1946 he became a lecturer in sociology at the Hebrew University of Jerusalem, and from 1948 to 1971 he was chairman of the Israel Executive of the WJC. For the last few years of his life Tartakower also served as chairman of the Brit Ivrit Olamit, the World Association for Hebrew Language and Culture. His extensive research in sociology is reflected in articles, books, and monographs in Hebrew, German, and English on such topics as the history of the Jewish labor movement, the essence and history of Jewish nationalism, and the Jewish and Israeli communities.

G. KRESSEL

TAXATION IN ISRAEL. The basic tax system in use during the mandatory period continued with the establishment of the State of Israel. It consisted of two main categories: income and property tax (direct taxation) and taxes on expenditure and business (indirect taxation). Government fees, namely payments collected for specific services offered by the government, were generally included in the category of indirect taxes, while compulsory loans on revenue, which played an important role in part of the period under survey, usually came under the heading of direct taxes.

The tax system's role in the economy greatly increased after the establishment of the State. The share of taxes and of compulsory payments in the gross national product (GNP). which was about 10% towards the end of the British Mandate and in the early years of the State, increased gradually over the years, reaching approximately 20% in 1960, 30% in 1970, 42% in 1975, and a little over 50% from the late 1970s up to the late 1980s (about 54% in 1986). During the early years of the State, taxes on manufactured goods were increased as the tax system became the principal instrument of fiscal policy for financing the State budget, reducing inequalities in the distribution of revenues, and contributing to the achievement of various economic goals: economic growth, immigrant absorption, and encouragement of geographical population dispersion. The increased use of the taxation system was made possible both by the real growth in the sources at the disposal of the economy (manufactured goods and fuel imports), and by the constant development of the tax collection apparatus and the legal and administrative instruments at its disposal, together with the population's acceptance of the growing tax burden. By the mid-1980s, however, the negative economic influences of an elevated tax burden were increasingly apparent. As in other countries, there was a growing trend in Israel towards the reduction of the direct tax burden, for fear of the influence of elevated marginal tax rates on the will to invest and to work, and on the growth of economic activity outside recognized frameworks (the "black" economy). Many amendments were introduced in the tax system. Initially these focused on constructing the tax authority and tax laws, and on educating the populace to a large number of taxes at sufficiently high rates while adapting the system to economic fluctuations, namely: changes in the economy's rate of growth; periods of rapid inflation; and intensified efforts in times of war and during the rehabilitation of post-war periods. Subsequently, the stress was again placed on the use of taxes as an instrument for renewed growth and to ameliorate the balance of payments.

The development of the tax system can be divided into two basic periods: the first, up to 1970, saw a gradual increase in the tax burden, with rapid adjustments of the system to the changes in the economy. The second, from 1970, was marked by a sharply accelerated increase in the tax burden with the aim of solving, through budgetary means, several problems, which included: the deficit in the balance of payments (the 1970s "package deal"); the heavy defense burden of the Yom Kippur War (1973); and the

Israel Ministry of Finance. [Israel Information Services]

negative economic developments after 1973 (the world energy crisis and the accelerated rate of inflation). During this period, important reforms were introduced in the direct and indirect taxation system. 1987 may have initiated a third period, characterized by stability and a possible lessening of the tax burden, with a simplification of the Tax Law and, in particular, a lowering of the marginal income tax rates.

The number of taxes making up the Israeli tax system gradually decreased for reasons of economic and administrative efficiency. The basic direct taxes included income tax (on individuals and on companies), property tax (essentially abolished by 1985), and estate tax (abolished). Until the 1970s, compulsory loans were also an important part of state revenues. Indirect taxes included customs duties, purchase tax, excise duty on various products such as fuel, tobacco, and liquors, foreign travel tax, stamp duty, and entertainment tax. Following the introduction of a value-added tax (VAT) in 1976, some indirect taxes were abolished, and the others diminished in importance. Today the most important tax is income tax, both in scope and in its economic and social influence. The most significant indirect tax, by virtue of its universality and scope, is VAT.

Income tax was first introduced in Palestine in the framework of the 1941 Income Tax Ordinance. Tax rates were very high in 1948-50, due to the urgent financing needs of the state budget. In addition to a direct increase in the tax rates, a Defense Levy and an Absorption Tax were also imposed. In 1951 these additions were combined in a uniform, egalitarian system of rates, which were lower than the previous overall rates for low and medium incomes, but higher for upper income brackets. The new scale included a regular system of rates, a surtax, and a tax supplement which was to go to the local authorities. The maximum marginal tax bracket in the year reached 86% and company tax stood at 53.75%. At the same time, all "personal deductions" for tax purposes became "credits". Several important new principles were introduced: a working wife became entitled to a separate tax assessment; wage earners were granted a 10% tax reduction as compensation for tax deduction at source; and special tax rates were determined for overtime and for productivity bonuses. Moreover, the Minister of Finance was empowered to impose a capital gains tax. In 1952 it was determined that the total income tax would not exceed 50% of income, thus reducing the marginal rate from 80% to 53%. A tax exemption was also introduced for the first time on the cost-of-living allowance. Until 1957, no other substantial amendments were introduced in the Income Tax Law, apart from changes in the tax rates in 1953 and 1955, which further increased the tax burden. 1957 saw the introduction of important amendments in the tax assessment system: the successive taxation formula was replaced by successive taxation rates on defined income groups and personal credits again gave way to personal deductions. The special supplement for local authorities was abolished, the maximal marginal tax rate was reduced from 70% to 60%, and the ceiling tax was abolished. In 1958, deduction of company tax was allowed for purposes of calculating income tax on companies. This important modification in the tax assessment system reduced the tax burden on companies from 53% to 46%. Tax rates on individuals were also greatly reduced in 1960.

As a result of the partial amendments introduced periodically in the Income Tax Law in the first 15 years of the State's existence, an overall reexamination of the direct taxation system became necessary. In May, 1963, the Minister of Finance appointed a public committee (the Zadok Committee) to examine the existing income tax system. The committee's recommendations led to change in the Law at the beginning of the 1964 fiscal year. The principal amendments were: the abolition of the existing exemption on the cost-of-living allowance and its inclusion in the regular system through changes in the personal deductions and in the tax rates (without abolishing the principle of cost-of-living allowance exemption for the future); introduction of a capital gains tax (with several important exemptions); and changes in exemptions and discounts stemming from social payments, etc. In 1964 two laws were passed which exempted various linkages from tax, in the wake of the 1962 devaluation of the currency.

The yearly rate of changes in the Income Tax Ordinance accelerated from 1966 onwards (from 1966–77 the ordinance was amended 21 times). In 1966 tax rates were again increased, whereas in 1967, the year of the Six-Day War, tax evaders were given the possibility of declaring revenues which they had not admitted in the past, with the tax on the difference in income being limited to 25%. Only 1,500 tax payers responded. Tax rates were again increased in this year, through a Defense Levy at a rate of 8.3% of tax. The levy was raised to 10% in 1968, but tax discounts to families with children were increased simultaneously. In 1970, the levy rose to 15%, and the capital gains tax was increased from 25% to 32.5%. In 1971 many concessions for social aims were introduced, along with several concessions meant to provide work incentives.

With the cumulative increase in the tax burden from 1967–70, another public committee was appointed to examine the tax system. The Asher Committee submitted its recommendations in stages from 1970–73, covering broad aspects of income tax (rates, deductions and credits, business expenses, social insurance, and tax collection). The recommendations adopted were implemented from 1972–74. The main ones were: replacement of the different levies and loans by regular income tax rates; reduction of the maximum marginal income tax rate from 80% to 65%; a marked limitation of deductions; assimilation of the exemption from cost-of-living allowances in the system of rates and deductions; limitation of exemptable business expenses; and various modifications in the system of deductions for social costs.

The accelerated annual rate of inflation, in particular from 1973, led to a sizable increase in the effective income tax burden, despite implementation of the Asher Committee recommendations. In December, 1974, the Finance Minister appointed the Ben-Shahar Committee to reexamine the income tax system. The main problem facing this committee was the high marginal tax imposed on the middle-income bracket, which resulted in tax evasions and blatant inequality in distribution of the tax burden. The committee adopted a number of principles, according to which it recommended a system of income tax rates: (1) Direct taxation was to be universal, without preference to any group. Hence all special rates for income from various sources were to be abolished; (2) The taxation structure should be simple to understand and to implement, with a tax scale comprising only five categories; (3) Direct taxation was to fill a major role in redistribution of revenues, hence there would be a system of progressive rates, going from 25% to 60%, and a system of credits; (4) The tax should contribute to economic efficiency, and therefore the marginal rates should be reduced; (5) Tax scales were to be adjusted to inflation through linkage to the consumer price index. The committee's recommendations were approved almost in their entirety in 1975. The subsequent rate of inflation in the country made it necessary to adapt the tax rates and the tax structure accordingly. Such amendments were introduced partially up to 1982, through full linkage of parts of the system to the consumer price index, and, more fully, through the Taxation in Inflationary Conditions Law—1982, which is one of the most advanced and complex laws on the collection of income tax in periods of inflation. In 1985 the Law was again amended, in the wake of the lessons drawn from implementation of the Inflation Law. With the lower rate of inflation achieved from 1986, marginal tax was lowered in 1987; the maximal tax rate on individuals was reduced from 60% to 48%, the maximum tax rate being imposed on incomes of over 41,000 shekels a year (about US $25,000).

The tax levied on corporations (including cooperative societies), in the framework of the Income Tax Law, amounted in 1975, to 61% (40% in the framework of company tax, and 21% as income tax on the company's profits). In 1987, income tax on companies was reduced from an effective rate of 21% to a rate of 5%, and the overall tax rate on undistributed dividends of a company stood at 45%. Industrial companies and companies with revenue from "improved investments" were entitled to a further deduction in tax rates. The Law for the Encouragement of Industry—1969, designed to promote growth of industrial plants, investment in new equipment and modernization, and to facilitate company mergers beneficial to the economy, provided for deductions in tax rates on undistributed profits, depreciation allowances, and tax concessions on profits from mergers. The tax concession remained at 10 percentage points from the inception of the law until 1987, when the overall tax rate on an industrial company was 52% (as against 63% on a regular company). In the same year the special concession was abolished and the tax rate was fixed at 45%, as for all companies. A company with revenues deriving from an "approved investment" (i.e., approved by a specific government agency, in consideration of the contribution of the investment to exports, to employment, and to the economy's infrastructure), also benefited from special concessions, in accordance with the Law for the Encouragement of Capital Investments— 1959, which underwent many amendments over the years. The law provided for concessions and exemptions in the tax rate and in depreciation, through indirect taxes and in financing and grants. The other major taxes, apart from income tax, were property tax and estate tax. Property tax, one of the oldest taxes in the country, was adopted by the Israeli government on the establishment of the State, in the same form as at the end of the British Mandate. It actually included two taxes: the urban property tax and the rural property tax; in 1961 the two taxes were merged in one law. The basis for calculating the tax, which was levied on immovable property, buildings, equipment and stock, was the net worth of the property. The revenues from this tax were small, and in 1981 most of its sections were abolished. Property tax is levied today only on vacant lots.

Estate Tax was introduced in Israel in 1949, and was imposed on the heirs, at progressive rates, in accordance with the degree of closeness to the deceased. Never an important element in the tax system, and unaccompanied by a legacies tax, it could be evaded very simply. Following a tax revision in 1979, fewer than 2% of all estates were taxed, and in 1981 the tax was abolished.

The second main group of taxes is comprised of indirect taxes, or taxes on expenditure. Revenues from this group were about 70% of all revenues from taxes in the early years of the State, but gradually decreased and stabilized by the 1980s at about 50% of all revenues. Until the introduction of VAT in 1976, there were two main indirect taxes—customs duties and purchase tax—and a number of lesser ones. Customs duties, inherited from the mandatory government, always constituted an important element in the system, both in the scope of revenues, and in order to attain various economic goals, such as financing the budget, improving the balance of payments, and protecting Israeli produce. During the period when a fixed exchange rate was in force, customs duties and import duties helped prevent lower prices of imports at times of local price rises. Potentially viable industries received considerable protection through customs duties. From 1962, this protective policy was replaced by one which gradually exposed Israeli produce to imports, and in 1975, a cooperation agreement was signed with the European Common Market (EEC). By the late 1980s the protective element on Israeli produce constituted a relatively minute component in customs duties, to be further reduced with the full implementation of the free trade agreement signed with the USA.

Purchase tax, imposed on manufactured goods and services (imported or manufactured in Israel), was generally paid at the wholesale commercial stage or at the production stage. Instituted in 1949 as a luxury tax on a relatively small number of products, the tax was extended in 1952 to a larger number of products, becoming known as purchase tax. From 1965 purchase tax was also imposed on several services and, with rates varying from 10% to over 100%, constituted a very important part of the tax system. Following the introduction of VAT, the importance of purchase tax decreased, and by the late 1980s only a small number of durable consumer goods remained subject to purchase tax, as a supplement to VAT.

The main indirect tax became the value-added tax (VAT), first introduced in July, 1976, after a long preparatory period and after study of the use of this tax in EEC countries. Within a short time it became the principal element in fiscal policy, competing in scope with income tax. VAT was levied in Israel on all products and services (except for a minute number of exemptions) at a uniform rate. In the financial sector, VAT was not levied on total turnover, but on salaries and profits. The taxation system was both simple and efficient, and prevented double taxation on the various production stages. Further, it effectively exempted imports and investments from tax without preventing refund of the taxes paid to the producers and investors. In this way the tax also helped to achieve the goals of improving the balance of payments and of promoting growth. Initially fixed at 8%, VAT was raised to 12% in 1977, and stood at 15% in 1988. The automatic control system incorporated in the tax (anyone paying this tax was entitled to deduct from tax on his sales the tax paid on his purchases, provided he had the relevant receipts) made it possible to collect large sums with a relatively small bureaucratic establishment and with relatively limited possibilities of tax evasion.

Other indirect taxes in Israel are stamp duty, imposed on legal documents stamped in Israel; foreign travel tax, levied on tickets for overseas travel purchased in Israel; and various duties levied by government ministries to cover specific services, including vehicle licence fees, driving licences, fees on issue of passports and other certificates, and legal fees.

One of the major goals of the taxation system in Israel, and particularly income tax, is to reduce unequal distribution of wealth. In every modern state the reduction of inequalities through progressive taxation on the one hand, and subsidies and social services on the other, is considered to be one of the roles of budgetary policy. It is, however, extremely difficult to evaluate to what extent this goal is achieved, due to conceptual problems (definition of income, reference to income by wage earner or by family, etc.) and to problems in obtaining data. The studies carried out in Israel in the 1980s show a greater inequality among the families of nonsalaried wage earners than among families of wage earners, and among families of individuals (including many elderly) and large families than among couples without children. It is generally accepted that inequality of income in Israel is not greatly different from that existing in other developed countries.

B-A. ZUKERMAN

TECHNION (Israel Institute of Technology). Leading university of the engineering sciences in Israel. Located in Haifa, it is the oldest institution of higher learning in the country. At the opening of the academic term in October, 1985, the Undergraduate School had an enrollment of 6,325, the Graduate School had 1,919 students, and the affiliated Junior Technical College had 1,564 students. The academic staff numbered 1,100 teachers. The National School for Senior Technicians, operated by the Technion in cooperation with tye Ministry of Labor, offered refresher courses that were attended by 2,060 adults in 1985/1986. In addition, the Technion Extension Division conducted numerous courses and symposia attended by both adults and youths.

The idea of a technical college in Eretz Israel was first broached before World War I and received immediate support, including generous financial help from individual Jewish philanthropists in Russia, Germany, and the United States. Although construction began in 1912, when the country was still part of the Ottoman Empire, a controversy erupted over the language of instruction, foreigners insisting on German while local citizens demanded Hebrew (*see* *LANGUAGE WAR). This dispute continued until the outbreak of World War I and subsequent dislocations delayed the formal opening of the Technion until 1924, when the first classes were held. Until the establishment of the State the

Original building of Haifa Technion. [Central Zionist Archives]

Campus of the Technion, in Haifa. [Israel Information Services]

growth of the Technion was slow. In 1948 it had an enrollment of some 600 students, jammed into old, overcrowded buildings in central Haifa. It became clear that the future progress and security of the country depended largely on the development of science and technology and that a full-fledged technological university had to be built to provide the new nation with a supply of trained engineers, architects, technicians, and research specialists. The American Society for Technion-Israel Institute of Technology, Inc., together with sister organizations in England, Canada, South Africa, France, Mexico, Argentina, Australia, and elsewhere, pledged wholehearted support for the plan to erect on Mount Carmel a modern, fully equipped campus for a technological university and continued to give financial, technical, and moral support to the institute. The government of Israel deeded to the Technion 300 acres of land on a slope of Mount Carmel near Neve Sha'anan. Construction of Technion City began in 1952 and the establishment of new laboratories, libraries, dormitories, classrooms, and other facilities proceeded apace. In the 1985/86 academic year, the last two faculties remaining on the old campus moved to the new Technion City, completing the process begun 34 years before.

Since its inception, the Technion has trained more than 25,000 engineers, scientists, architects, and physicists to fill vital positions in all areas of Israel's economy. These included more than 70% of Israel's engineers, and one quarter of its scientists. The Technion pioneered in such areas as aeronautical engineering and created the infrastructure for original design and development of aircraft in Israel. Its Faculty of Agricultural Engineering played a paramount role in the implementation of revolutionary water management techniques and in the design of sophisticated, computerized farm machinery. The only university in the country authorized to licence architects and town planners, the Technion helped in the establishment of modern new cities such as Carmiel in the north and Arad in the south.

The new campus overlooks the Zebulun Valley. By 1986 more than 100 buildings, including student dormitories, had been completed. In addition to the construction of campus facilities, funds from Technion Societies organized in numerous countries were used for the acquisition of special equipment and technical literature, the training of faculty members and graduates in specialized institutions in various parts of the world, research projects, and other programs, including scholarships, student loan funds, lectureships, and permanently endowed chairs.

In 1987, the principal departments of the Technion included: civil engineering (including mining and metallurgy), architecture and town planning, mechanical engineering, mathematics, physics, chemistry, nuclear engineering, chemical engineering, agricultural engineering, aeronautical engineering, industrial and management engineering, computer sciences, materials engineering, biology, food engineering and biotechnology, biomedical engineering, medicine, general studies, and education in science and technology.

The Technion is administered by a Board of Governors, consisting of civic leaders from both Israel and various communities in other countries, alumni, faculty, and representatives of the Israel government and quasi-governmental agencies. The Council of the Technion, elected by the Board of Governors, governs the institute between the annual meetings of the board. Executive authority is vested in the president of the institute. The supreme authority in academic matters is the Senate, composed of the president of the Technion, the vice-presidents, all full-time professors, the deans, the director of the library, and elected representatives of the senior academic staff.

The particular significance that Israel attaches to research, especially applied research, is reflected in the Technion Research and Development Foundation, an institute affiliated with the Technion, which serves as Israel's principal center for research keyed to the country's industrial, agricultural, housing, defense, and general development programs. Among the units on the Technion campus that bear the burden of Israel's day-to-day applied research programs are those dealing with construction research, the construction materials testing laboratory, food industry instruction, farm equipment testing and development station, hydraulics testing laboratory, chemical testing laboratory, the Israel Institute of Industrial Design, and the Israel Institute of Metals, the Solid State Institute, the Transportation Research Institute, the Biomedical Engineering Institute and the Institute for Advanced Studies in Science and Technology. The 22 Technion libraries contain more than 800,000 engineering, scientific and technical works in Hebrew, English, and the principal European languages, including more than 250,000 technical and scientific periodicals in many languages.

Today, the overriding majority of Technion students are Israeli-born. Many technical students are from South America and return there to aid in the development of science and industry. Women comprise approximately 20 per cent of the total enrollment, an unusually high percentage for a technological university. The average age of students at the time of enrollment is 21 or 22 years, since many have had to complete their military service before coming to the Technion.

In 1987, the Technion, fully accredited by the Council for Higher Education in Israel, offered the following degrees: bachelor of science in specific disciplines of science and engineering, bachelor of architecture in architecture and town planning, engineer, bachelor of arts, master of science, medical doctor, doctor of science, and doctor of science in technology.

D.C. GROSS—A. SHERMAN

TEHIYA (Renaissance). Israeli political party founded in 1979 by members of the Likud, National Religious Party, Land of Israel Movement, and Gush Emunim. Tehiya's founders opposed the Camp David Agreements and the Israel-Egypt Peace Treaty, fearing the creation of a Palestinian Arab state in the Administered Areas, and arguing that these pacts would herald the return to the pre-June 1967 borders thereby endangering Israel's security and survival. Its platform called for the immediate annexation of Judea, Samaria, and Gaza and for a massive Jewish settlement in these regions.

Its leaders were Yuval *Ne'eman, Ge'ula Cohen, and Hanan Porat. These three were elected on its behalf to the Tenth Knesset in the 1981 elections; the party obtained some 45,000 votes, including 12% of the soldiers' vote. Between 1981 and April, 1982, Tehiya organized the Movement to Stop the Withdrawal from Sinai. It supported the Lebanon War and on 26 July 1982 joined the Likud-led coalition, receiving a promise from Prime Minister Begin to accelerate Jewish settlement in the territories. Ne'eman became Minister for Science as well as deputy chairman of the Cabinet Settlement Committee, which initiated some forty new settlements in the territories between 1982 and 1984. The party voted against the 17 May 1983 Israel-Lebanon Treaty, expressing disapproval of the security arrangements envisioned for South Lebanon.

Meanwhile, the party consolidated its organizational infrastructure and appealed to nationalist-religious elements dissatisfied with the policies of the National Religious Party. In the 1984 elections to the 11th Knesset, Tehiya doubled its votes when six members were elected, among them former Chief of Staff Rafael Eytan. Their votes again derived mainly from Likud and National Religious Party followers who were unhappy with their party's vague stand on the future of "Eretz Israel." When the Government of National Unity was formed in September, 1984, Tehiya decided to remain in the opposition, voting against the Israeli withdrawal from Lebanon, and other government moves designed to bring about negotiations between Israel and a Jordanian-Palestinian delegation. In 1987, Rafael Eytan broke away to establish his own faction. In the 1988 elections, it received three mandates. In 1990, after the breakup of the National Unity Government, Tehiya joined the coalition government under Yitzhak Shamir. However, in the 1992 elections it received no mandates in the general elections. Eylan's Party, called Tzomet, obtained eight seats.

M. MEDZINI

TEKHELET LAVAN. *See* BLAUWEISS.

TEL ADASHIM. Moshav in the Jezreel Valley, 3 mi. (5 km.) north of Afula. In 1913, members of Ha-Shomer set up a camp there. In 1923, pioneers from eastern Europe founded the moshav, which was based on mixed farming. Population (1987), 406.

E. ORNI

TEL AVIV-JAFFA. City on Israel's Mediterranean coast. Jaffa served for many centuries as Eretz Israel's principal port. Its easily defensible hill, jutting slightly into the sea, forms small bays to its north and south where ancient ships anchored. Another sheltered anchorage lay 4 mi. (6 km.) to the north in the Yarkon river estuary.

Existing at least since the Neolithic era, Jaffa was con-

Members of the Second Aliya laying the cornerstone of Tel Aviv in 1909. [Israel Information Services]

began functioning there under Arthur Ruppin. Wholly Jewish quarters, like Neveh Tzedek and Neveh Shalom, were built. In 1914 Jaffa had close to 40,000 inhabitants, of whom about 15,000 were Jews.

The beginnings of Tel Aviv. Seeking a healthier environment than crowded, noisy Jaffa, Zionists founded the Ahuzat Bayit company, and purchased twelve and a half acres of dune land northeast of Jaffa. On 11 April 1909 they assembled there to portion out building plots. A Jewish National Fund loan of 300,000 francs enabled them to construct the first 60 houses. In 1910, the garden suburb's name became "Tel Aviv", based on the name of a Babylonian city mentioned in Ezekiel 3:15, and chosen by Nahum Sokolow as the title of his Hebrew translation of Theodor Herzl's novel *Altneuland*.

By 1914, the area of Tel Aviv grew to 250 acres and its population reached 2,026. The Herzliya High School building became its outstanding building. In World War I, the Turkish authorities harassed the Jaffa and Tel Aviv Jews and expelled them all in March, 1917. After the British conquest (November, 1917), they returned and were joined, from 1919 on, by Third Aliya immigrants. Arab riots in May, 1921, drove many Jaffa Jews to Tel Aviv which was accorded "town council" status and set up municipal enterprises. In 1922, the Jewish quarters of Jaffa were quered by Pharaoh Thutmose III in 1469 BCE when it was a Canaanite town. It was allocated to the Dan tribe (Josh. 19:46) but the Sea Peoples (Philistines) ruled there from the 12th century BCE. The fortress on Tell Qasila near the Yarkon, however, seems to have been Israelite, at least in King Solomon's time. In the 8th century BCE, the Assyrians conquered Jaffa and gave it to seafaring Sidon. After the death of Alexander the Great, the partly Hellenized city fell in 301 BCE to the Egyptian Ptolemies but was wrested from them at the beginning of the second century by the Seleucids of Syria. The Maccabean Simon annexed it, making it "a window to the sea" for the Hasmonean state (140 BCE). In the Roman-Jewish War (66 CE), Jaffa Jews harassed

Tel Aviv, with the Shalom Tower in the background, as seen from Jaffa in the 1960s. [Israel Government Tourist Office]

Roman shipping; the Roman commander, Vespasian, launched an attack from the land side; the Jews took refuge in ships, but a storm threw them onto the shore where the Romans massacred the survivors. From the end of the first century, a strong Jewish community formed again, but was repeatedly persecuted by the Christians under Byzantine rule. In 636, Jaffa fell to the Moslems. Jaffa was the first port of the Crusaders (1099) and vantage point for the conquest of Jerusalem. In 1268, the city finally fell to the Mamluks who largely destroyed it, like other shore towns, so as to prevent further Christian invasions. After the Ottoman takeover, Jaffa's status hardly improved. Only later did its sea-trade gradually increase.

Early Jewish Settlement. Between 1810 and 1820, the Turkish city governor Abu Nabut furthered its rebuilding, and the rule of Ibrahim Pasha on behalf of Muhammad Ali (1831–1839) brought more improvement. North African Jews settled in Jaffa and in 1856 the Jewish community numbered about 400. The German Templer sect founded in 1866 a German quarter which contributed to progress. In the 1880s, Jaffa harbor was improved, new quarters began to be built outside the city walls, which were soon razed, and orange groves were planted in Jaffa's vicinity. First and Second Aliya immigrants made Jaffa the center of the "New Yishuv", founding health and educational institutions. The Anglo-Palestine Bank opened its office in Jaffa, and in 1908 the Palestine Office of the Zionist Organization annexed to Tel Aviv. Tel Aviv's population reached 34,000 in 1925. New quarters, mainly in the southeast, came into being and Tel Aviv was now home to the Habimah and Kumkum theaters, the Opera, Histadrut offices, and all Hebrew daily papers. The Fifth Aliya brought a big expanse in building, commercial, and industrial activity, and population grew to 120,000 in 1931 (36% of all Palestine Jews), and 160,000 in 1939. In May, 1934, Tel Aviv was recognized as a city. When Jaffa port was paralyzed by the 1936 Arab riots and general strike, Tel Aviv port was opened, although its business never attained significant proportions and it ceased to function in World War II.

World War II paralyzed building, but industrialization intensified. In 1943, Tel Aviv's area was doubled to 3,150 acres, incorporating the rest of Jaffa's Jewish quarters. By 1948, Tel Aviv was the country's largest city, with 210,000 inhabitants. Jaffa then numbered about 100,000 inhabi-

Dizengoff Street, Tel Aviv. [Trans World Airlines]

tants, of whom about 70,000 were non-Jews. Its industry had developed, but not to the same extent as Tel Aviv's. Jaffa port, closed in the war for security reasons, hardly recovered in the following years.

The War of Independence. Jaffa Arabs, reinforced by Arab military units from abroad, severely shelled Tel Aviv from December, 1947. Until April, 1948, the British prevented an all-out Jewish attack, but on 13 May 1948, Jaffa fell to Jewish forces and most of its Arabs abandoned it. A day later the State of Israel was proclaimed in the Tel Aviv Museum building. The German Templer quarter, Sarona, empty since the expulsion of Germans in World War II and now acquired by Jews, became the Government center (the "Kirya"). On 24 April 1949, both cities were amalgamated into Tel Aviv-Jaffa. The city boundaries were widened to 10,000 acres, to include abandoned Arab villages to the east and northeast. Jaffa's apartments, deserted in the Arab mass flight, soon absorbed many thousands of new Jewish immigrants. In Tel Aviv proper, the focus of social and commercial life shifted to the northeast, to Dizengoff and Ibn Gabirol Streets and the new municipal building on Malkhei Yisrael Circle.

The modern city. From the 1950s, new quarters were built north of the Yarkon River. Jaffa Hill was transformed into a tourist, art, and entertainment center. Tel Aviv's sea shore was replanned and, with Israel's largest concentration of high-class hotels, became a major entertainment and recreation center. From 1956, *Tel Aviv University began to function as one of Israel's prime academic institutions.

The city had become the nucleus of Israel's largest conurbation, which in the 1980s stretched from Rishon le-Zion, Holon, and Bat Yam in the south to Herzliya in the north and from the sea to Petah Tikva in the east. Together with its outer ring, it contained in the 1980s over one third of Israel's total population and a considerable part of the country's industry and commerce. While the conurbation's outer cities, especially those in the south, continued to expand vigorously, Tel Aviv-Jaffa itself lost population, and numbered 319,500 inhabitants at the end of 1987.

Meir Dizengoff, one of Tel Aviv's founders, served as Tel Aviv's mayor from 1911 until his death in 1936. He was followed by Israel Rokah (1936–1953), Haim Levanon (1953–1959), Mordekhai Namir (1959–1969), Yehoshua Rabinowitz (1969–1973), and Shlomo Lahat (from 1974).

E. ORNI

TEL AVIV UNIVERSITY. Institution of higher education. In 1953–54, the municipality of Tel Aviv-Jaffa set up two university institutes: the Institute of Sciences and the Institute of Jewish Studies. Their development led to the establishment of the University in 1956. Authorization to grant

Students in the Central Square of Tel Aviv University. [Tel Aviv University]

degrees was received in 1960 and the University became fully autonomous in 1963.

In 1986 Tel Aviv University comprised nine faculties (Engineering, Exact Sciences, Humanities, Law, Life Sciences, Management, Medicine, Social Sciences, and Visual and Performing Arts), and 11 schools (Education, History, Jewish Studies, Language and Literature, Mathematics, Physics and Astronomy, Chemistry, Continuing Medical Education, Communication Disorders, Dental Medicine, and Social Work) and the Rubin Academy of Music. The Faculties comprised 92 departments and programs.

In the 1985/86 academic year the University, with the largest enrollment in Israel, had 19,500 degree-seeking students and an additional 8,600 students in in-service training and extension courses and other non-degree programs. The faculty numbered 2,295 members with at least the rank of Lecturer.

The University maintained or was affiliated with 65 research institutions and centers and had 84 endowed academic chairs which also served as research units. The research units include the Zionist Research Institute of Hebrew Literature, the Diaspora Research Institute, and the Institute for Research, as well as the Stellar Observatory, the only one in the region, an Electron Microscope Laboratory, a Center of Biotechnology, the Institute for Computer Sciences, the Institute of Advanced Studies, the Institute for Electronic Research, the Interdisciplinary Center for Technological Analysis and Forecasting, and a whole string of medical research units ranging from cancer to cardiological research, and from epidemiology to human reproduction and fetal development, and also includes research in both environmental and occupational health.

Notable among the research facilities were the Dayan Center for Middle Eastern and African Studies, and the Jaffee Center for Strategic Studies, both of which concentrate largely, but in different fields, on the unique and critical problems facing Israel in its geopolitical and strategic relations. The Faculty of Humanities was the largest faculty at the University. It comprised four schools (History, Jewish Studies, Language and Literature, and Education) and 22 departments. It offered a program in general BA studies, the only such program in Israel, and its popularity indicated that it answered a real need. Judaic Studies offered by the Faculty of Humanities included Bible, Talmud, Hebrew Language and Literature, Jewish History and Philosophy and Semitic Linguistics.

The School of Education was actively involved in furthering Jewish and Zionist education beyond the borders of Israel. It had academic responsibility for the Herzlia Day School system in Cape Town, South Africa, for which it formulated a comprehensive model and provided curriculum material. For several years, the School of Education provided the Hebrew Teachers Training College in Buenos Aires with its director and several staff members, and conducted in-service training at the University for third-year students of the College and members of its faculty.

The Faculty of Engineering was established in 1971 to meet the need for engineers that the existing facilities in the country were unable to supply. The Faculty provided training and research in mechanical, electrical, and industrial engineering, and planned to focus on electronics, computers and robotics in the 1990s. The Faculty developed biomechanical instrumentation to measure gait and postures (standing, sitting, etc.), for diagnosing and evaluating treatment in orthopedics and rehabilitation processes; this instrumentation won international recognition and prizes.

A shortage of electronics engineers led the Faculty to introduce in 1985 a six-semester, two-year intensive course, including summer studies, to upgrade electronics technicians to engineers with a B.Sc. degree in Electrical Engineering and Electronics. This course was able to inject highly qualified electronics engineers into industry more quickly than would otherwise be the case.

The Faculty of Natural Sciences, the oldest unit in the University, grew so rapidly that in 1972 it was divided into Faculties of Life Sciences and Exact Sciences. The Faculty of Life Sciences had departments of Biochemistry, Botany, Microbiology, and Zoology and offered graduate studies in Biotechnology. The Faculty maintained a botanical gardens and the Canadian Center for Ecological Zoology, with the only wildlife research zoo in the region, the Cereal Crops Improvement Institute, and the Nature Conservation Research Institute.

The Faculty of Exact Sciences comprised three major schools (Physics and Astronomy, including an observatory in the Negev, Mathematics and Chemistry), and a department of Geophysics and Planetary Sciences. The Faculty of Social Sciences included departments of Economics, Sociology and Anthropology, Political Science, and the School of Social Work.

Medical studies at the University began with a Faculty of Continuing Medical Studies which expanded into a School within the Faculty of Medicine. It offered graduate and post-graduate specialization courses in some 25 disciplines to more than 1,000 physicians every year. The Faculty of Medicine, inaugurated in 1965, became the largest Medical School in Israel by the late 1980s, enrolling some 80–85 students every year in a six-year curriculum leading to the MD degree. In addition, it enrolled 40 students from New York State and 20 from other American states in a four-year American-style program of clinical studies towards a degree that enabled them to practice in their home states. The Medical School was affiliated with seven major general hospitals, six psychiatric hospitals and a 270-bed rehabilitation center covering the entire spectrum of rehabilitative medicine.

In the late 1980s the School of Dental Medicine had some 70 students working towards a D.M.D. Degree. Academic studies were also offered in Communication Disorders, Nursing, and Physical and Occupational Therapy.

An innovation in the scene of medical education was the introduction of a Master's degree program in Health Systems Management, a joint venture with the Faculty of Management to support an urgent need for trained personnel in this vital field.

The Faculty of Management—Graduate School of Business Management was the largest business school in Israel. The Faculty conducted a number of highly popular and widely attended non-degree programs for business and industrial executives, and conducted research over a wide field including business policy, international trade, international banking, financial markets, etc.

Law Faculty graduates occupied leading positions in the legal profession as well as in public life. The Faculty is the oldest and largest law school in Israel. In order to broaden the horizons of prospective legal students, the Faculty initiated a one-year pre-law program a few years ago, together with the Faculty of Humanities, and about half the freshman LL.B. classes were graduates of the pre-law program.

The Faculty of Visual and Performing Arts (originally named the Faculty of Fine Arts) offered studies in the History of Art, Film and Television, Musicology and Theater Arts, as well as education and training for instrumentalists and singers at its Rubin Academy of Music.

The University's library contained 620,000 volumes and 85,000 microfilm publications. Other large libraries were the Library of Exact Sciences and Engineering (125,000 volumes), the Library of Law (70,000 volumes), the Library of Social Sciences and Management (150,000 volumes), the Library of Medicine and Life Sciences (120,000 volumes), and the Wiener Library (80,000 books and journals). Units such as the School of Education and the School of Social Work also had specialized libraries.

The University is governed by an international board of governors which generally meets once a year. An executive council meeting at least once monthly runs day-to-day affairs. The principal academic body is the University senate, chaired by the rector. The senate supervises all academic affairs, elects the rector and vice-rector, and approves the appointment of deans of faculties and the senior academic staff. The senate steering committee is the senate's main standing committee. Faculty councils elect the deans, are responsible for syllabi, and appoint study and other advisory committees.

In addition to the rector who heads the academic establishment, the principal officers of the University are the president, elected for four years, the Board of Governors' chairman also elected for four years, the chairman of the executive council, elected for two years, and a director-general appointed by the Executive Council.

The Ramat Aviv campus has some 45 buildings. The Stellar Observatory is located at Mitzpe Ramon in the Negev, and a number of units, such as the Department of Geography, the Office of the Registrar, and the Meyerhoff Technical College, are situated outside but adjoining the campus.

Tel Aviv University enjoys support from active Associations of Friends in North and Latin America, in most countries of Western Europe, and in Australia and South Africa.

George S. Wise was president of the university 1963–1972 (chancellor 1972–1988). He was succeeded by Yuval Neeman (1971–1977), Haim Ben-Shahar (1977–1983), Moshe Many (1983–91) and Yoram Dinstein (1991–).

TELEVISION IN ISRAEL. *See* BROADCASTING IN ISRAEL.

TEL HAI FUND (Keren Tel Hai). Financial instrument of the World Union of Zionists -*Revisionists, registered in London in 1929. Originally, its main object was to promote the physical training of Jewish youths, with special emphasis on defense sports and paramilitary discipline, in order to prepare trained cadres for the self-defense of the yishuv and for prospective Jewish military units. The name of the fund was derived from the settlement Tel Hai, in Upper Galilee, where Joseph Trumpeldor and some of his comrades fell in 1920 while defending the settlement against bands of Arab marauders. The program also included training for self-defense in countries where the Jewish population was exposed to anti-Semitic attacks. The first Governing Council was composed of Vladimir Jabotinsky, Lieut. Col. John Henry Patterson, Meir Grossman, and representatives of the Revisionist World Union and of Betar, the fund's main beneficiary. Other youth groups engaged in similar activities were also eligible for its support, which consisted mainly in providing competent instructors for all forms of physical self-defense. The fund's budget was covered by members' fees, Blue Box collections, and registration in the Iron Memorial Book. More recently the fund has undertaken to help Betar pioneers in Israel obtain work and settle on the land. The headquarters of the fund is located in Tel Aviv. J. SCHECHTMAN

TEL MOND. Moshava in the southern Sharon, 6 mi. (10 km.) north of Kefar Sava. It was founded in 1929 upon the initiative of Sir Alfred Mond (Lord Melchett) who planted large citrus groves in the area. The moshava became the center for a group of moshavim (Tel Mond bloc). After 1948 immigrants were absorbed in the village which in 1987 numbered 3,250 inhabitants. E. ORNI

TEL YOSEF. Kibbutz in the Harod Valley, 8 mi. (13 km.) southeast of Afula. Founded in 1921 at the foot of Mount Gilboa as a work camp of Gedud ha-Avoda, together with En Harod, its members participated in draining the malaria-infested swamps. After En Harod seceded from Gedud ha-Avoda, Tel Yosef remained with it and only in 1928 joined Ha-Kibbutz ha-Me'uhad. In 1929 it moved to its present site on the northern slope of the Harod Valley. In the 1951/52 split of Ha-Kibbutz ha-Me'uhad, it joined Ihud ha-Kibbutzim. Tel Yosef has highly-intensive irrigated farming and various industrial enterprises, and is also a partner in regional factories. Bet Trumpeldor, containing the archives of Gedud ha-Avoda, is at Tel Yosef, while the regional museum, Bet Sturman—maintained together with En Harod—and a regional open-air stage, are located in the space between the two kibbutzim. It is named after Joseph Trumpeldor. Population (1987), 491. E. ORNI

TEMPLERS. Members of a pietist Protestant community, the "Temple Society" (*Tempelgesellschaft*), founded in 1861 in the kingdom of Württemberg by Christoph Hoffmann and Georg David Hardegg. Their struggle against the contemporary church which, in their opinion, had degenerated, eventually led (1859) to their expulsion from the established church. Their belief that the Kingdom of Heaven

The kibbutz Tel Yosef. In the background are the hills of Galilee. [Israel Information Services]

would shortly return and that the Ottoman Empire was on the verge of collapse, combined with political and economic motives, led them to emigrate to the Holy Land as the pioneers of "God's People" to whom the prophets had promised the Holy Land.

During the years 1868–1875 about 750 Templers—approximately a quarter of the society's members—settled in the Land of Israel. After this period their immigration almost ceased. The Templers did not manage to expand their numbers sufficiently to fulfill their initial aim of dominating the Holy Land. In the early days of settlement their security, economic, social, climatic, and sanitary problems were so grave that spiritual matters were not given priority. This tendency was strengthened in the second generation among those who had not taken part in their parents' struggle against the Evangelical Church in Württemberg. Instead of the concept of "the assembling of God's people in Jerusalem" which could not be implemented, it was now decided to place the emphasis on improving the situation in the Holy Land and providing a good example for its inhabitants. During the fifty years of Templer residence under the Turkish regime, seven settlements were established: in Haifa, Jaffa (both in 1869), Sarona (1871), Jerusalem (officially in 1878), Wilhelma (1902), Galilean Bethlehem (1906), and Waldheim (1907) whose settlers belonged to those Templers who in the meantime had returned to the Evangelical Church. The three last named, as well as Sarona, were agricultural settlements, while those in Jaffa and Jerusalem (the "German Colony") were urban, and that near Haifa was agricultural at first and later became mainly an urban colony. With the exception of Bethlehem and Waldheim, which did not have time to develop properly before the outbreak of World War I, the German settlements reached a level of development unparalleled at that time in Palestine. The Haifa colony, with its pretty suburb "Carmelheim", the first residential quarter on Mount Carmel, was the largest and most impressive and successful of the urban settlements. Sarona (now in the Kirya district of Tel Aviv) was the most prosperous of the agricultural colonies, particularly successful in viticulture and the export of wines. The members of the Jaffa community, like their colleagues in Haifa and Jerusalem, engaged mainly in commerce, trade and industry, tourist promotion, and various free professions.

The most prominent German settler was perhaps Gottlieb Schumacher of the Haifa colony. He not only erected numerous buildings of importance (e.g., the first winecellar in Rishon le-Zion) but made an outstanding contribution to the cartography and the archeological research of late Ottoman Palestine and its adjacent regions. The Templers played a particularly important role in transport. The Haifa settlers were the first to introduce the wheel-cart into the north of the country, adapted the roads from Haifa to the district capital of Acre and to Nazareth and Tiberias to carriage traffic, and organized a regular passenger service. They were also the first to organize (in 1874) a regular carriage service from Jaffa to Jerusalem, then the most-traveled route in the country. The German settlers pioneered in establishing hotels at European standards, developing modern industry, utilizing motors for irrigation purposes, and setting up steam-operated flour mills.

The number of German settlers (about 2,200 in 1914)

dwindled after World War I. With the conquest of the country by the British, the Germans were expelled, but in 1920–22 were allowed to return to their colonies. As German subjects, many of whom, mainly among the younger generation, joined the Nazi party in the 1930s, the Templers were again expelled from Palestine at the outbreak of World War II or were interned. Most of the remainder were finally evacuated by the British Mandate authorities in April, 1948. A part (54 mi.DM) of the very considerable value of the Templer properties in Palestine was in 1956–1963 paid by Israel to the Federal Republic of Germany and delivered to the Temple Society for distribution among its members. A. CARMEL

TENU'AT HA-MOSHAVIM. *See* MOSHAV MOVEMENTS.

TERRITORIAL FEDERATIONS. *See* ZIONIST TERRITORIAL ORGANIZATIONS.

TERRITORIALISM. The name of Jewish movements whose aim was to settle Jews in a territory of their own, with cultural, religious, and, as far as possible, political autonomy. The most important was the *Jewish Territorial Organization.

Territorial conceptions appeared as early as the first half of the 19th century, in the perspective of compact Jewish settlement in one territory in the USA (Mordecai Manuel Noah) and supported theoretically by the Verein für Wissenschaft des Judentums, a clear focus of Jewish nationalist thought in Germany in the 1820s. The idea was echoed subsequently by the ideological thinking of members of Am Olam in Russia (1881) who hoped by their personal example to steer Jewish emigration to the USA and to effect large-scale agricultural settlement in a territory designated for a Jewish state. Leon Pinsker's *Auto-Emancipation* and subsequently Theodor Herzl's *Judenstaat* essentially advocated the creation of a Jewish state in any territory whatever, without emphasis on the exclusivity of Eretz Israel. In addition to getting away from the economic plight and political discrimination experienced by Jews in European countries, the primary aim of the territorial ideologies was to create a "formal balance" between the passive status of the Jews seeking protection and civil rights in the countries of their dispersion and an active status in an independent state of their own, as with all nations enjoying sovereignty. In other words, auto-emancipation was a prerequisite for emancipation.

Po'ale Zion Territorialists in Minsk. [YIVO Institute for Jewish Research]

The ideologists of this approach saw no formal difference between Territorialism in general and Eretz Israelism in particular, except that the latter had its roots in the Jewish historical ethos.

The confrontation between Territorialism and Eretz Israelism came to a head with the Uganda controversy (1903–1905) and ended with the secession of the Uganda Scheme supporters from the Zionist Organization at the Seventh Congress in 1905, and the creation of the Jewish Territorial Organization (ITO) under Israel Zangwill. At the same time a split occurred in the Po'ale Zion camp, and numerous circles in Russia and Poland united early in 1905 in the framework of the Zionist Socialist Workers' Party (SS), led *inter alia* by Nahman Syrkin, Jacob Ze'ev Wolf Latzky-Bertholdi, Shmuel Niger, and Moshe Litvakov. The SS established a connection with the ITO.

In 1931 a Jewish group in Berlin revived the ITO plan to colonize the Portuguese territory of Angola, in southwestern Africa, by initiating a project to take over almost a million acres of land belonging to the Societa Pecoaria d' Angola. Three years later, however, agitation in the press persuaded the Portuguese government to forbid Jewish mass settlement in Angola.

With the issuance of one British White Paper after another restricting Jewish immigration to Palestine, and with the increasing need for places of refuge because of Hitler's rise to power, efforts were made to revive the ITO. In July, 1935, a group of prominent English Jews, headed by Moses Gaster, met in London to constitute the Freeland Movement for Jewish Territorial Colonization. Among its leading members were Leopold Kessler, Myer S. Nathan (formerly treasurer of ITO), Zangwill's widow, and her sister, Barbara Ayrton-Gould, who later was to support Zionism in the British parliament. The group explored settlement possiblities in South America, Africa, and elsewhere.

Similar groups were organized independently in Germany, Poland, France, and the United States. In January, 1941, the Freeland League for Territorial Settlement was founded in New York under the presidency of Jacob Levin. Its leaders included Ben-Adir (Abraham Rosen), Isaac Nachman Steinberg, and Mordkhe Schaechter. The establishment of the State of Israel did not put an end to the Freeland League. At its conference in New York in October, 1948, it stated that while it welcomed the founding of the Jewish State, it felt that because of the limited area and hostile neighbors, it "dare not allow the whole Jewish future to depend solely on Israel." M. MINTZ

THEATER IN ISRAEL. Hebrew drama is mainly a product of the 20th century. In the absence of a theatrical tradition or an established current practice, it first emerged as an occasional offshoot of literature, written almost exclusively by novelists or poets who hardly had in mind theatrical production. Some sporadic attempts by amateurs to stage Jewish plays (such as Lilienblum's *Zerubavel* in Jerusalem, 1890, or Goldfaden's *Shulamit* in 1894) led to the establishment, in 1904, of an amateur theater group, "The Lovers of Dramatic Art," later known as "The Lovers of the Hebrew Language," when they switched from performing in Yiddish to playing in Hebrew. During World War I all theatrical activity in the country practically stopped.

The attempts at mounting stage productions or forming Jewish amateur groups in the Diaspora culminated with the triumph of the Habimah ("The Stage") troupe, which was

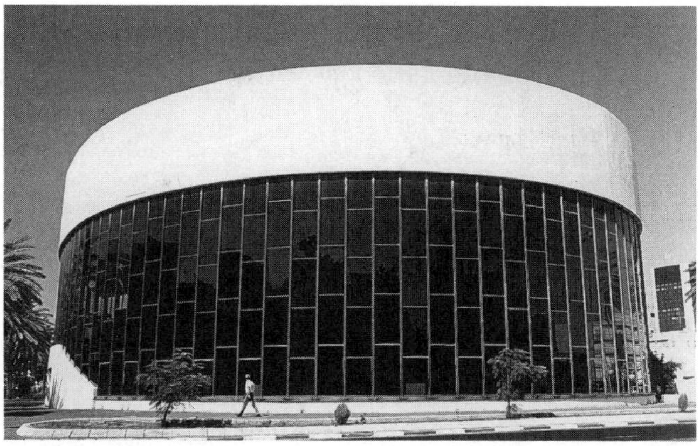

Habimah Theater, Tel Aviv. [Habimah]

founded in 1917, during the turbulent days of the Bolshevik Revolution, with strong attachment to the Moscow Art Theater. Under Nahum Zemach's dynamic leadership, Habimah made its name especially with Yevgeni Vakhtangov's highly expressionistic production of Anski's *The Dybbuk* (after the 1922 Vakhtangov version had been kept in repertory for almost half a century, two celebrated directors came to the Habimah to restage the play: the American J. Chaikin and the Polish A. Wajda). Habimah left Moscow in 1926. In the course of a tour in Europe and the United States during the following years, a split occurred among the Habimah players: Zemach, with some actors of the company, decided to settle in the United States, while the remaining group headed for Palestine. The latter group visited Palestine first in 1928, went on to Berlin (then a capital of the European theater), to return to Tel Aviv in February, 1931). Since then Tel Aviv has been the permanent home of Habimah. In 1945 the theater moved into its present building in the center of town. Its traditional structure as a collective organization having been disbanded, the Habimah was in 1958 proclaimed the National Theater of Israel. It now operates in its three auditoria: the 1,150-seat Rovina auditorium, the 300-seat Meskin auditorium, and the 200-seat Bertonov auditorium (all named after the star actors of the company, who remained with the Habimah from its inception in Moscow until after it became the National Theater of Israel).

The Habimah success inspired the formation of several other permanent companies in Palestine. In 1920 the first professional group ("The Hebrew Theater") was established, operating until 1927, when it closed for lack of funds. The TEI ("The Theater of the Land of Israel"), established 1925, gave way two years later to "The Art Theater". The Ohel ("Tent") Theater was formed in 1926 by Moshe Halevi (who left Habimah in Moscow) under the auspices of the Histadrut, which subsidized it until 1954. Owing to this affiliation, it was initially considered socialist-orientated, but before long its artistic policies could hardly be distinguished from the other major repertory companies of the country until it closed in 1968 for lack of funds. Two satirical theaters were formed during the twenties: the short-lived Kumkum ("Kettle"), founded by Avigdor Hame'iri in 1927, to be replaced about a year later by the Matateh ("Broom"). The latter flourished under the British mandatory rule, satirizing the British, but ironically disbanded soon after the establishment of the State of Israel,

From a performance of Kafka's "The Trial" at the Habimah Theater. [Habimah]

which was too young as yet to satirize its own shortcomings.

The prestigious stand of Habimah in Palestine from 1931 was later challenged by companies constituting the present theatrical scene in Israel: first the Cameri ("Chamber") Theater, founded in 1944 by Yosef Millo as a youthful, West-oriented company reacting against the stagnation of Habimah in its classical and East European traditions. Now operating from its main auditorium in the center of Tel Aviv (inaugurated 1961) and several other rented venues of various seating capacity, it presents a mixture of popular musicals, classical, modern and Israeli plays. In 1969 the Cameri became the established Municipal Theater of Tel Aviv. Next came the Haifa Municipal Theater, opened in 1961 under Millo, which later, especially during the seventies and the eighties, became the focus of some political scandals owing to its daring repertory. Completing the peripheral theatrical scene (as opposed to the Tel Aviv hegemony as the capital of theater in Israel), the Be'er Sheva Theater (under Gershon Bilu) and the Jerusalem Khan Theater were formed in the early seventies. Owing to the relatively small distances within Israel, all theaters regularly tour the country all year round. The Omanut la-Am ("Art for the People"), a semi-governmental organization, brings mobile theaters into remote places within the country. Fairly short-lived, were the Zira ("Circle") Theater which functioned in Tel Aviv between 1949 -1958, providing the Hebrew stage with some of the more fashionable and avant-garde plays of the period, like those by Sartre, Beckett, and Ionesco; and Zavit ("Corner"), an off-Broadway-like theatrical enterprise which operated between the late fifties and the early seventies. The two major Arabic-speaking companies are the Bet ha-Gefen ("Vine House") Theater in Haifa, and the more radical Palestinian company "El-Hakawatti" (founded by François Abu-Salem) in East Jerusalem.

From the early 1980s, the annual Acre Fringe Festival served as a proving-ground for new playwrights, directors, actors, and designers. The 1980s also saw the most established companies traveling frequently to various international festivals. Several plays, especially by Yehoshua Sobol and Hanoch Levin, were translated and produced in Europe.

In 1989, the budget of the major theaters ranged from about IS 16 million ($8 million) for Habimah to IS 9 million ($4.5 million) for the Haifa Theater. Habimah, the Cameri, Haifa, Khan, Be'er Sheva, and the Children and Youth Theater (founded 1969 by Orna Porat) are partly subsidized by the Arts' Council of the Ministry of Education and Culture—a subsidy which has decreased over the years. While the Ohel and Cameri, founded before the establishment of the state, followed the Habimah example in starting as cooperatives, this system was later abandoned. However, most companies still have a nucleus of permanent actors, and this often creates the problem of members of the company being under-employed, but fully paid. The general tendency in the Israeli theaters, however, is currently limited-period or even per-production contracts, and thus most Israeli actors are regularly on the move from one company to another according to the rules of the free market. Actors are trained mainly in the three major drama schools in the country: the state-subsidized Advanced School of Stage Arts ("Bet Tzevi"), "The Studio," directed by Nissan Nativ, and the "Seminar ha-Kibbutzim" drama school.

See also HEBREW DRAMA. A. OZ

THIRD ALIYA. *See* ALIYA.

THON: Family of Zionists.

Osias (Yehoshua) Thon, Rabbi in Poland (b. Lvov, Galicia, Austria, 1870; d. Cracow, Poland, 1936). Thon studied at the University of Berlin and the Hochschule für die Wissenschaft des Judentums (Academy of Jewish Studies), receiving his Ph.D. degree in 1895. While still a high school student in Lvov, he had helped found a pre-Herzlian Zionist youth group, and while in Berlin he was active in Jung Israel. He early became a follower of Herzl. In 1897 he assumed a pulpit in Cracow, which he held until his death.

Thon helped build the Zionist Organization in Poland and was a delegate to numerous Zionist Congresses. He was a member of the Zionist Actions Committee and of the Administrative Committee of the Jewish Agency and president of the Tarbut organization of Poland. A leader of Polish Jewry, he was a member of the Jewish delegation to the Paris Peace Conference in 1919 (*see* COMITÉ DES DÉLÉGATIONS JUIVES). From 1919 to 1935 he was a deputy in the Polish Sejm (Parliament), where for several years he was president of the Jewish Club.

He wrote books on Zionism and philosophy and contributed journalistic and scholarly articles to a variety of Jewish periodicals.

Yaakov Yohanan Thon his brother (b. Lvov, Galicia, Austria, 1880; d. Jerusalem, 1950). While a law student at the University of Lvov he helped found the Emunah Zionist students' fellowship (1899). He founded and served as the first editor (1903–04) of *Moriah*, the first Polish-language Zionist youth monthly. In 1904 he moved to Berlin, where he assisted his close friend Arthur Ruppin in managing the Society for Jewish Statistics.

Settling in Eretz Israel in 1907, Thon served as assistant director (1908–16) and director (1916–20) of the Palestine Office. In 1921 he became managing director of the Palestine Land Development Company, a position he held untl his death. He was one of the founders of Tel Aviv and was instrumental in the purchase of the Jezreel Valley, the Rehavia section of Jerusalem, and other urban areas. During World War I he was taken as a hostage by the Turkish authorities. After the British occupation of Palestine he became chairman of the Va'ad Zemani (Provisional Council) and a founder of the Asefat ha-Nivharim, in which he represented Ha-Po'el ha-Tza'ir. A vice-president and president of the Va'ad Le'umi until 1930, he represented that body at the founding conference (1929) of the Jewish Agency, becoming a member of the Agency's Council. He was also a Presidium member of the Council of the Jewish Community of Jerusalem and a delegate to numerous Zionist Congresses.

Thon contributed articles to many periodicals and was the author of several books, including *Sefer Warburg* (1948), the life, letters, and speeches of Otto Warburg.

N.M. GELBER

TIBERIAS (TEVERYA). Town on the west shore of Lake Kineret. Its municipal area ascends westward from 690 ft. (210 m.) below sea level on the lake shore to 817 ft. (249 m.) above sea level on the Poriya Ridge. This results in noticeable differences in temperature, rainfall, and vegetation cover within the town. The town was first built by Herod Antipas in the early 1st century CE, and named after Em-

Old section of Tiberias. The buildings are constructed of the local black basalt. [Israel Government Tourist Office]

peror Tiberius. Pious Jews initially shunned Tiberias because it was said to stand on tombs. In the 2nd century, Rabbi Shimon bar Yohai declared Tiberias clean of tombs and chose it as his residence. It became the seat of the Sanhedrin and a center of Judaism, where most of the Jerusalem Talmud was composed and many famous sages resided. In the 6th century, it had a Jewish academy. Later, under Moslem domination, the Masoretic spelling and vocalization of the Bible were devised at Tiberias. Its Jewish community continued to exist until the Crusades. The body of the great medieval scholar, Moses Maimonides, was brought there from Egypt for burial in 1206.

The ruined town was allocated in 1562 by the Turkish sultan to Joseph Nasi, Duke of Naxos, who unsuccessfully tried to rebuild it as a Jewish center. In the 18th century, the governor Dhahir al-Amr invited Jews to participate in Tiberias' reconstruction. From then on, it was considered as one of the four holy cities of the Land of Israel. A severe earthquake in 1837 destroyed much of the town and its walls, and 1,000 Jews lost their lives. In 1912–14, the first Jewish quarter was built outside the Old City confines. From 1919, Tiberias served Gedud ha-Avoda as a base and in 1920 the construction of the Kiryat Shemuel quarter, named after Sir Herbert Samuel, began high above the Old City. It was a winter health resort, based on its hot springs. Until 1948, Jews constituted ca. 60% of Tiberias' population.

In the 1948 War of Independence, it was attacked by local Arabs. Following the Hagana counterattack, all Arab inhabitants fled and Tiberias was the first of the country's mixed towns to become all-Jewish, with about 4,000 inhabitants. Many of the Old City's dilapidated buildings were razed and comprehensive building started. In 1949, a large transit camp for new immigrants was opened above Kiryat Shemuel. Later, this was partly replaced by permanent buildings and in the 1950s the construction of Upper Tiberias (Poriya Quarter) began. Lake fishing continued to occupy some citizens, but tourism and recreation remained its principal economic base. New hotels were built, largely near the lake shore, the hot springs facilities for healing rheumatic and other ailments were doubled in capacity, and the tourist season extended to function all the year round. Tiberias has a number of archeological and historical sites, among them beautiful mosaic floors of synagogues of the Byzantine period near the Hot Springs, sections of the Crusader and 18th-century walls, as well as venerated traditional tombs of sages, among them Rabbi Meir Ba'al ha-Nes. Population (1987), 30,800. E. ORNI

TIBERIAS, LAKE. *See* KINERET, LAKE.

TICHO. Jerusalem family.

Abraham Albert Ticho. Ophthalmologist (b. Boskovice, Moravia, Austria, 1883; d. Jerusalem, 1960). After receiving a doctorate in medicine from the University of Vienna in 1908, Ticho served on the staff of a hospital in that city until 1912. That year he accepted a call of the Lema'an Zion Society of Frankfurt on Main to head its eye clinic and hospital in Jerusalem, a position he held until 1917. During World War I he served as ophthalmic surgeon with various Austrian, German, and Turkish army units and also became associated with Hadassah's health program, notably the campaign against trachoma in Palestine. From 1920 to 1922 he was head of the ophthalmic department of the Hadassah health clinic in Jerusalem.

Ticho also built up an extensive private practice and had his own eye clinic in Jerusalem, in which he remained active until his death and where he treated many patients, both Jewish and Arab, free of charge. A skilled surgeon (he performed 40,000 eye operations during his lifetime), he soon became famous throughout the Middle East.

Anna Ticho.
[Israel Museum]

Anna Ticho, his wife, Israeli artist (b. Brunn, Austria, 1894; d. Jerusalem, 1980). She began her art studies in Vienna in 1909 and moved to Jerusalem in 1912, assisting her husband as a nurse. Between 1917–19, she fled to Damascus with her husband. Anna Ticho at first drew from nature, concentrating on Jerusalem sites and olive trees and figures of Arab women but in the 1960s began her great series of imaginary but archetypal Judean hill landscapes, all chalk-charcoal drawings. She was awarded the Israel Prize in 1980. The Ticho home in Jerusalem after her death became an annex of the Israel Museum, displaying a collection of her work and Avraham Ticho's collection of Judaica. M. RONNEN

TIOMKIN. Zionist family.

Vladimir Tiomkin. Russian-Jewish leader (b. Yelizavetgrad, Russia, 1861; d. Paris, 1927). Tiomkin studied at the St. Petersburg Technological Institute, graduating as an engineer. Originally an assimilationist, he was made aware of his Jewish identity by the Russian pogroms of the 1880s and joined the Hovevei Zion movement. He founded the Ahavat Zion society in St. Petersburg and was a delegate to the Druskenik Conference (1887) of the Hovevei Zion. With the establishment (1891) of the Jaffa office of the Odessa Committee he served as its first director. On his return to Russia he was appointed government rabbi of Yelizavetgrad (now Kirovograd). An early follower of Herzl, he helped prepare for the First Zionist Congress (1897), and at the Second Congress (1898) he was elected to the

Greater Actions Committee. A leader of the Democratic Faction, he took a leading part in the Second Conference of Russian Zionists (1902; *see* MINSK CONFERENCE). During the controversy over the East Africa scheme he was a leader of the opposition and the chairman of the Kharkov Conference (1903).

Tiomkin was one of the principal speakers of the Seventh Conference of Russian Zionists, held in Petrograd in May, 1917, shortly after the overthrow of the Tsarist regime, and was a member of the Presidium of the Jewish National Council of the Ukraine (1918). With the consolidation of the Bolshevik regime, he left Russia. He lived for some time in Berlin, where he was a member of the Central Committee of Russian Zionist émigrés and participated in the reconstituted journal *Rassviet.* Later he settled in Paris, where he joined the Revisionist movement at its inception.

Zinovi Tiomkin, Zionist Revisionist leader, his brother (b. Kherson, Russia, ca. 1865; d. Saint-Raphaël, France, 1942). He studied medicine in Russia, then in Berlin, and practiced as a physician in Berlin and later in Russia. During World War I he was in charge of a Russian hospital train. After the war he lived successively in Constantinople, Berlin, and Paris. In Constantinople he was representative both of the Joint Distribution Committee and of the Palestine Office. In London (1921) he was chosen as general director of Emigdirect, an agency for fostering and financing Jewish emigration from eastern Europe and in 1926 he was among the founders of the Bank Ivriyya for this purpose. He was also active in the direction of ORT and OSE.

From 1924 to 1933 Tiomkin was a member of the editorial office of *Rassviet.* In 1925 the First Revisionist Conference elected him to the Revisionist World Executive, and from 1925 to 1931 he was the chairman of the French Revisionist organization in Paris. In 1932, he resigned from the Revisionist World Executive in protest against its policies, which at the time were influenced by Meir Grossman. In 1935 Tiomkin was elected to the Executive of the New Zionist Organization, serving until 1938.

ED.—M. CATANE

TIRAT CARMEL. Urban settlement on the west slope of Mount Carmel, south of Haifa. Founded in 1949, it became part of the outer ring of this city's conurbation. It has a number of industrial enterprises, but many citizens commute to work in Haifa. Population (1987), 15,000.

E. ORNI

TIRAT TZEVI. Religious kibbutz in the Bet She'an Valley, founded in 1937 by pioneers from Germany as the valley's southernmost tower-and-stockade outpost. During the Arab riots in that period, it had to repulse frequent attacks. There was a heavy assault early in the 1948 War of Independence, the repulsing of which constituted a turning point in the war. Tirat Tzevi has from its beginnings occupied a central role in the religious settlement movement. It has intensive mixed farming and some industry, including a sausage and meat processing factory. It was named for Rabbi Tzevi Hirsch Kalischer. Population (1987), 700.

E. ORNI

TNUVA. *See* LABOR ECONOMY.

TOLKOWSKY, SAMUEL. Israeli agronomist and diplomat (b. Antwerp, 1886; d. Ramat Gan, 1965). Tolkowsky studied at the Gembloux Institute of Agronomy. In 1911 he settled in Eretz Israel, where he introduced many new methods for the growing and sale of citrus fruit. During World War I he served with the Belgian forces. Afterward he was in England as a member of the London Political Committee of the World Zionist Organization (1916–18) which negotiated the Balfour Declaration. He served as honorary secretary of the Zionist delegation at the Paris Peace Conference (1919).

Tolkowsky was a member of the Tel Aviv Municipal Council (1920-24), chairman of the Jaffa Citrus Exchange (1934–40), and secretary of the Palestine Citrus Marketing Board (1940–47). He helped found (1937) the Palestine Maritime League and served as its chairman, and in 1945 assisted in the formation of the Zim Shipping Company, of which he was also a director. In 1949 he was appointed Israel Consul General in Switzerland, and from 1951 to 1956 he served as Israel Minister to that country.

He wrote on the citrus trade, economics, maritime affairs, and archeology.

His son **Dan Tolkowsky** (b. Tel Aviv, 1921) served in the R.A.F. during World War II. He joined the Israel Air Force from 1948 and from 1953–58 was its commander.

TOMB OF RACHEL. *See* RACHEL, TOMB OF.

TOPIOL, MEILICH (MICHEL). Zionist leader in France (b. Staszow, Russian Poland, 1910). Topiol settled in France in 1931 and was one of the founders of the Zionist youth organization Bleu-blanc (Blue-white, 1932). He became a leader of the General Zionist Organization (leftist group A) in France and attended the 19th Zionist Congress (1935) and all subsequent Congresses. Having taken refuge in Nice after France's defeat in 1940, he was the head (1942) of the Committee for Jewish Assistance there and represented the Federation of Jewish Societies in the political commission gathered by J. Fisher-Ariel (1943) to prepare a united direction of French Jewry (today the CRIF). After the liberation of France, Topiol served the Zionist movement as vice-president of the Zionist Federation and the Keren ha-Yesod of France. From 1951 he was a delegate to Zionist Congresses and a member of the Zionist General Council. He was a member of the Zionist Executive in 1981–1982 and of the Board of Governors of the Jewish Agency. In 1967 he was cofounder of the United Jewish Appeal of France and was elected its cochairman (with David de Rothschild). He also devoted much attention to the development of Jewish education and participated in the construction of dozens of Zionist day-schools in France.

M. CATANE

TORAH VA-AVODA (Torah and Labor). Philosophy of the *Ha-Po'el ha-Mizrachi movement (*see also* MIZRACHI) which combines adherence to the Jewish religious-national tradition and observance of the precepts of the Torah with active participation in the upbuilding of the Land of Israel. It maintains that the revival of the nation in its historic land is organically bound up with the betterment of the individual and of society.

Torah va-Avoda grew out of opposition to Labor Zionist ideology, which was largely secular, and out of dissatisfaction with the Mizrachi movement, which, while it represented religious Zionism, limited its activities to exerting political influence and setting up educational institutions. Its basic philosophy was developed by Shemuel Hayim Landau, Rabbi Yeshayahu Shapira, Yeshayahu Bernstein, and Shelomo Zalman Shragai. In 1925, when the Mizrachi pioneer and youth groups in different countries that subscribed to the ideology of Torah va-Avoda established at a convention in Vienna the World Confederation of the Tze'irei he-Halutz and Ha-Po'el ha-Mizrachi, it was resolved to call the new federation by the name World Confederation of the Torah va-Avoda Movement.

The Torah va-Avoda ideology was determined mainly by the conviction that the success of Zionism as a movement of Jewish renaissance depended on whether its proponents acknowledged the link of Zionism with the Jewish ideal of redemption. Israel's redemption from its long exile, it was felt, must find its expression primarily in spiritual revival. Under no circumstances could Zionism be considered simply a movement aimed at delivering the Jewish people from material persecution.

There can be no renewal of the life of the individual Jew or of the Jewish people if religion and religious tradition are neglected. True Jewish revival implies, and depends upon, religion brought to its full expression. The Torah as the Law of Life, must be the guide in all spheres of existence: in the life of the spirit and in the sphere of action, in the social order as well as in politics.

According to Torah va-Avoda, the idea of unity is a basic concept in Judaism: "Israel, the Torah and God are one." Related to this concept is the idea of the unity of the Torah, the People of Israel, and the Promised Land. Only through this union can the Jewish people attain perfection. The aspirations to return to Zion and to lead a productive life are the two sides of the coin of revival. Similarly, the concepts of Torah and labor are two manifestations of revival. Torah va-Avoda aims at creating a feeling for this synthesis as the expression of Jewish completeness. Only when a man lives by the labor of his hands can he be certain that his bread has not been won at the expense of his neighbor and is not tainted with exploitation and abuse.

An especially strong emphasis is placed on the demand for social justice. It was this concept that led the adherents of Torah va-Avoda toward productivity and, particularly, toward the cooperative agricultural way of life, in which the movement saw the best possibility of realizing its ideals. For a concept is of no value if it does not lead to practical action.

The demand for the creation of a better society led to a confrontation with the general Socialist labor movement in the yishuv and in Israel. Discussions of the relationship between the Torah va-Avoda adherents and the general labor movement became a constant feature in both the practical and theoretical fields. One group held that the very fact of a common ideal of the creation of a better society was conducive to rapprochement between the adherents of the ideals of Torah va-Avoda and all those, whatever their general outlook, who aspired to the abolition of the wrongs and injustice existing in the social order. Others argued that religious sentiment and observances were integral elements of Torah va-Avoda and that opposition to them, or even a fight against them, actually characterized the general labor movement in the yishuv and in Israel. There could therefore be no rapprochement beyond the day-to-day contacts necessitated by practical concerns, all the more so since the attitude of Torah va-Avoda on questions of class struggle and compulsory arbitration revealed differences that transcended the ideological sphere.

Parallel to this controversy was a disagreement with the Mizrachi, with which the Torah va-Avoda movement was organizationally connected. The members of Mizrachi, who were essentially bourgeois, disagreed with the Socialist tendencies that found acceptance in the ideology of Torah va-Avoda. M. UNNA

TORCZYNER: Family of Zionists.

Numa Torczyner, diamond merchant and Zionist leader (b. Brody, Galicia, Austria, 1885; d. Amsterdam, 1948). After spending his youth in Vienna, Torczyner moved to Antwerp in 1910. Following the outbreak of World War I, he returned to Austria to serve in the army, was captured by the Russians, and remained a prisoner of war in Siberia until 1920. After his return to Belgium he was elected president of the Zionist Federation of Belgium in 1923 and again in 1929. From 1933 to 1940 he also headed a committee to help German refugees and was a member of the Central Consistory of Belgian Jewry.

During World War II Torczyner moved to the United States, where he founded the Diamond Trade Association and served as its president until his death. He was active in the World Jewish Congress and in the Zionist Organization of America (ZOA), and in 1946 was elected to the Zionist Actions Committee.

Jacques Torczyner, his son, member of the World Zionist Executive (b. Antwerp, 1914). He studied at the Solvay Institute of the University of Brussels and settled in the US in 1940. He was one of Abba Hillel Silver's followers who assumed the leadership of the ZOA in 1945. Torczyner was among the founders of the Friends of Hagana in the United States. From 1956 on he served as a member of the Presidium of the Zionist Actions Committee, and in 1965–70 was president of the ZOA, a position he held until 1970. In 1983 he was elected honorary president of the ZOA. Since 1972, he has been a member of the World Zionist Executive, and of its American Section. He is the chairman of the Theodor Herzl Institute, the only adult education center of World Zionist Organization, and chairman of the Publications Committee of the World Jewish Congress and a member of its Executive. From 1978 he was president of the World Union of General Zionists. He attended every Zionist Congress from 1946. In 1982 he was appointed a member of the United States National Commission for UNESCO and in 1984 was appointed to the special monitoring panel that made the decision that the United States should leave UNESCO. He was a founder and vice-president of the American-Israel Chamber of Commerce. He is a founding member of the Board of Governors of the State of Israel Bonds.

TOURISM IN ISRAEL. Tourism to Israel has grown steadily from 1949, when there were 23,000 visitors, to 1985 when the figure reached 1,436,000. In the latter year, tourism yielded an income of $1,109m. and was rated as one of Israel's main export items. The natural increase, however, is often offset by negative factors especially Middle East tension and security incidents within Israel. Currency fluctuations can also affect tourism, both negatively and positively.

The increase in non-Jewish tourism has been significant; in 1950 72% of all visitors were Jewish whereas in 1983 only 39% of visitors were Jewish. The others included a constantly growing nymber of Christian pilgrims and, after the

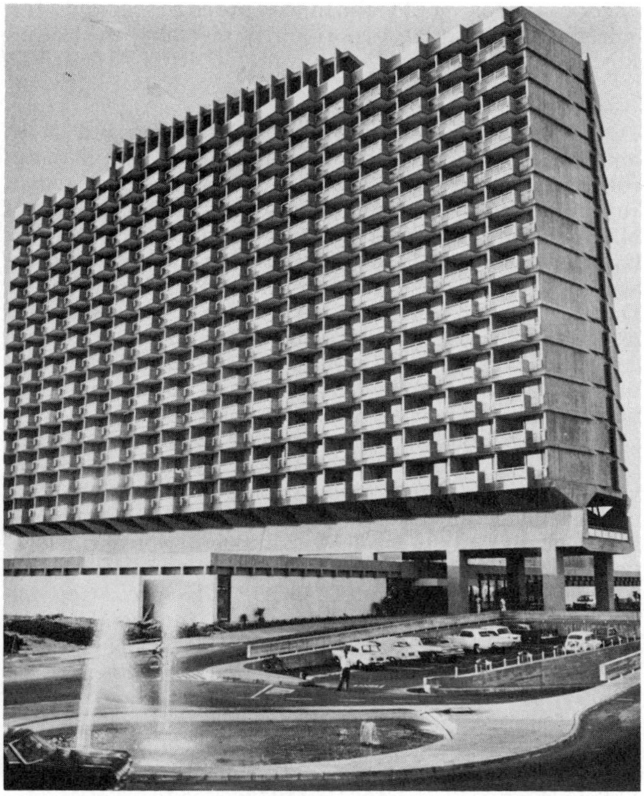

Hilton Hotel, Tel Aviv. [Israel Government Tourist Office]

Tourist park on shore of Lake Kineret near Kibbutz En Gev [Israel Govt. Press Office]

Six-Day War, many visitors from Arab lands, coming via the Jordan bridges, often to visit their families in Israel.

The Prime Minister's Office was at first responsible for the development of tourism to Israel. The Government Tourism Corporation was established in 1960 and a separate Ministry of Tourism in 1964. In 1988 the Ministry operated 21 official tourist bureaus and 23 overseas information offices (in New York, Chicago, Los Angeles, Atlanta, Montreal, Buenos Aires, London, Paris, Amsterdam, Stockholm, Zurich, Frankfort, and Rome). The task of the overseas offices was to promote tourism to Israel: they dispensed information and distributed publicity material and also fostered and maintained contact with local travel agents, international institutions, and organizers of international conferences. In addition, they were responsible for publicity campaigns in newspapers, on the radio, and on television.

The Israel offices functioned as information centers, organized special events such as folklore evenings and tourist forums at the larger hotels in the main cities, operated a program known as "Meet the Israeli", which enabled tourists to visit Israeli families. They also supervised all tourist services within their respective areas, including tour managers, travel agencies, hotels, guides, and car rental offices. The Ministry of Tourism provided professional training courses in hotel management for guides, travel clerks, receptionists, waiters, and members of other associated branches of the tourist industry.

Travel to Israel. In the 1960s, in addition to the El Al Israel Airlines and the Zim-Israel Shipping Company, Ltd., more than a dozen international airlines offered direct jet services linking Israel with Europe, the United States, South Africa, the Middle and Far East, and Australia, and steamship companies operated regularly scheduled sailings to and from the United States, Central and South America, Europe, and parts of Asia. In addition, many Mediterranean and round-the-world cruise ships made Haifa a regular port of call. One of the steamship companies also offered a fast and reasonably priced car-ferry service, bringing Israel within "driving" distance of European Mediterranean ports.

Health and Visa Regulations. International travelers arriving in Israel no longer require vaccination certificates. Citizens of Austria, Bahamas, Barbados, Belgium, Bolivia, Colombia, Costa Rica, Denmark, Dominican Republic, Ecuador, El Salvador, Fiji, Finland, France, Greece, Guatemala, Haiti, Hong Kong, Iceland, Jamaica, Japan, Liechtenstein, Luxembourg, Maldives, Mauritius, Mexico, Netherlands, Netherlands Antilles, Norway, Paraguay, Surinam, Swaziland, Sweden, Switzerland, Trinidad and Tobago, and the United Kingdom can enter Israel with a valid passport without a transit or visitors' visas. Nationals from other countries require a valid passport and visa. Citizens of Argentina, Australia, Brazil, Canada, Central African Republic, Chile, Germany (Federal Republic of, born after 1 January 1928), Italy, New Zealand, San Marino, South Africa, Uruguay, and the United States of America are issued with visas free of charge on arrival in Israel. Nationals of Cyprus, Yugoslavia, and Germany (Federal Republic of, born before 1 January 1928) must apply for a visa prior to their departure, nationals of other countries are issued a visa on application to an Israeli diplomatic or consular representation and pay the applicable visa fee. A visitor's visa is valid for 3 months from the date of entry. A transit visa, issued to persons en route to other destinations is initially issued for a period of 5 days and may be extended after arrival for an additional period of 10 days on application to the Ministry of the Interior. Cruise and airplane passengers who wish to stay in the country during a short period and provided they leave by the same boat or airplane may be issued a landing-for-the-day card by the frontier control authorities and do not require any other documents to land.

Climate. Israel's Mediterranean coastline has a climate similar to that of southern Italy, Greece, Florida, and southern California. Seaside resorts in this region enjoy an unbroken eight months of summer, from mid-April to mid-

December when the temperature along the coastal strip ranges from 60°F in May to 85°F in July and August. The hill regions, including the areas around Jerusalem and Safed, enjoy a slightly cooler and considerably drier climate.

As a result of its unusual geography, with two regions lying below sea level and a third in the subtropical south, Israel also has a winter tourist season lasting from November until the end of March. Winter is the time to visit Tiberias on Lake Kineret (Sea of Galilee), which lies 780 feet below sea level; Sedom on the Dead Sea, at 1,290 feet below sea level (the lowest spot on earth); and Eilat on the Red Sea, with a dry, year-round-resort climate. Even in January mean temperatures in these areas range from 55°F to 68°F. *See also* CLIMATE OF ISRAEL.

Accommodations. In 1985 there were some 300 hotels in Israel that were recommended for tourists, ranging from simple, moderately priced pensions (one star) to first class establishments (5 star) of the Hilton and Sheraton type. In accordance with the decentralization policy of the Ministry of Tourism, these accommodations were not concentrated only in the larger tourist centers such as Tel Aviv, Jerusalem, and Haifa but spread over all parts of the country, offering overnight facilities to visitors even in small, out-of-the-way places.

Unique to Israel were the kibbutz guesthouses where one might not only find excellent and reasonably priced accomodations but also gain an insight into the way of life of a communal settlement. Most guesthouses were situated at sites of particular scenic beauty such as Ayelet ha-Shahar in Upper Galilee, Nof Ginosar on Lake Kineret, and Kiryat Anavim and Ma'ale ha-Hamisha, overlooking the main Tel Aviv-Jerusalem highway.

Also available were various Christian hospices in Jerusalem, Nazareth, and Tiberias. Israel, which was affiliated with the International Youth Hostels Association, operated 16 youth hostels in various parts of the country.

A popular form of vacationing is represented by small self-contained holiday villages, with simple accommodations, sports and on-the-spot entertainment facilities. In 1985, 14 holiday villages were dotted throughout the country. A number of well-equipped camping sites were set up at Horshat Tal, in the Huleh Valley; En Gev, on the shore of Lake Kineret; and Akhziv and Sedot Yam, on the Mediterranean. Accommodations in all recommended hotels, pensions, and kibbutz guesthouses are graded according to the official list published by the Ministry of Tourism.

Organized guided tours, by either sightseeing bus or limousine, are run by the principal tour operators and cover all parts of the country, These include tours to Galilee, Negev tours, and desert tours by jeep or command car operated out of Eilat and Neot ha-Kikar, at the southern end of the Dead Sea.

International Conventions. Israel has become a popular venue for international conventions. The interest shown in the country's scientific, technological, and agricultural achievements has brought many experts in these fields to see and discuss past and future projects. In addition, numerous religious, political, economic, and cultural world organizations, as well as Jewish organizations of all types have found in Israel a congenial international meeting place.

Shopping. In 1984 384 shops and stores were recommended and graded for tourists. These displayed a special tourist emblem in their windows. Most knitwear stores gave a 15 per cent discount on purchases paid for in travelers' checks. Tourists could also make purchases in duty-free stores at Lod (Lydda) Airport and at several of the leading hotels.

M. GIDRON—H. KLEIN

TOV, MOSHE. Zionist leader in Latin America and Israeli diplomat (b. Buenos Aires, 1910; d. Tel Aviv, 1989). Involved from his youth in Zionist activity, he was chairman of Juventud Cultural Sionista (Zionist Cultural Youth) and of Macabi. From 1938, as a member of the DAIA governing board, he conducted negotiations with the Committee against Racism and Anti-Semitism working in Argentina. On the invitation of Nahum Goldmann, he moved in 1946 to Washington where he headed the Jewish Agency's Latin American Department. In this post he toured all the countries of Latin America in 1946–1947 and directed information activities in favor of the creation of the State of Israel at governmental and parliamentary levels and in intellectual circles. He organized Pro-Palestine Committees and activated the Jewish communities on the continent to the same end. He kept in close contact with the Latin American representatives at the UN and with their diplomatic delegations in Washington. In 1947 he was one of three Jewish Agency liaison officers with UNSCOP (UN Special Committee on Palestine). After Israel declared its independence, he was appointed to the Israeli delegation at the UN and until 1959 was director of the Latin American Department of the Ministry of Foreign Affairs.

Tov founded the Israel-Latin America, Spain and Portugal Cultural Exchange Institute. In 1968 he was appointed resident ambassador in Guatemala, Honduras and El Salvador, and from 1971 to 1975 served as ambassador in Chile.

S. SHENKOLEWSKY

"TOWER AND STOCKADE" SETTLEMENTS. *See* "STOCKADE AND TOWER" SETTLEMENTS.

TOWN PLANNING IN ISRAEL. *See* ARCHITECTURE IN ISRAEL.

TRADE UNIONS IN ISRAEL. The trade unions in Israel are part of the *Histadrut (General Federation of Labor), forming its largest division. Each worker or employee applies individually for membership in the Histadrut and, upon being admitted, also becomes a member of a specific union according to his trade, profession, or occupation. In addition to being the supreme authority of the unions, the Histadrut owns numerous large industrial enterprises, which contribute about 25 percent of the gross national product to the national economy and form the Hevrat ha-Ovedim (Society of Workers), which pursues ideological, social, and economic laborite goals.

The Trade Union Council, which is elected by the Histadrut Executive Committee, is in charge of implementing policies on wages, social security payments, cost-of-living and family allowances, working hours, and employment problems, in accordance with directives laid down by the Histadrut General Conference and the governing bodies elected by it. The Trade Union Council supervises the activities of unions and, in general, has authority to call a strike in a major labor-management conflict. It acts as an arbitrator in disputes between management and workers in Histadrut-owned enterprises and in grievances submitted by the workers' committees in private and public establishments.

Most salaried workers in Israel, as well as members of the liberal professions and artisans, are organized in professional trade unions affiliated to the Histadrut. These trade unions are: actors and producers; agricultural workers; civilian army employees; artistes; biochemists and microbiologists; building and building material workers; chemists; civil aviation; diamond workers; El Al; electricians and electronics specialists; engineers and technicians; film and TV workers; food workers; fuel workers; glass and ceramics workers; government employees; guides; hairdressers and cosmeticians; workers in Histadrut enterprises; journalists; knitwear workers; lawyers; leather and clothing workers; lifeguards; medical practitioners; metal workers; workers in the military industries; musicians; nurses; occupational therapists; paramedics; pharmacists; physiotherapists; airline pilots; plastic and rubber workers; printing workers; road transport workers; seamen; service workers; social workers; teachers; university lecturers; woodworkers; and X-ray technicians. Each union operates autonomously in executing wage policies, within the framework approved by the Histadrut. It decides on its wage scale and differentials according to working conditions and industrial disputes. The constitution (which is not strictly observed) calls for new elections every four years in each union.

Most of the unions are organized by trade or craft, but in most places of employment there is an all-inclusive workers' committee, usually associated with the union, to which the majority of employees belong. The committee is the basic unit of workers' representation. In some cases there are two committees, one for employees who receive wages on a daily basis, and the other for those on monthly salaries. In enterprises with two committees, joint representation for all unspecific questions is the rule. Each worker is represented before management by the committee, but he remains in contact with his particular union and in many cases is paid according to the wage scale of his trade. Another practice, found in larger firms, is to put all workers on a local, all-inclusive wage scale. Work committees function permanently in factories, offices, building sites, and plantations. Their members are chosen by direct election and serve on the committees without pay.

Both national legislation and Histadrut decisions guarantee equal pay and rights to all workers. Arab workers are full members in the Histadrut and the trade unions. Women receive equal pay for equal work. This rule is observed strictly in the professions, but in manufacturing, women are concentrated mostly at the lower-paid levels.

The Tenth Histadrut Conference, held in January, 1966, adopted a resolution calling for direct participation by workers in the management of Histadrut-operated economic enterprises and the institution of profit-sharing plans in these establishments. The Histadrut Executive Committee then elected a new Department for Workers' Participation, charged with the implementation of this reform, but the resolution was only partially implemented.

In order to increase labor productivity, save materials, and improve quality, the Histadrut has created joint productivity committees in private, public, and Histadrut enterprises.

Through their unceasing activities, the trade unions prepared the ground for progressive labor legislation. Legislation guarantees a minimum of 14 days' paid vacation, severance pay of two weeks' to a month's salary for each year of work, equal pay for women, and a ban on night work for women (unless they desire it) and youths. Of special importance is the Collective Agreements Law, which gives the Minister of Labor the right to extend the applicability of collective agreements to non-union enterprises. The unions oppose compulsory arbitration, even in public services, accepting arbitration only if both sides to a dispute agree on that course. The Ministry of Labor has a Supervisor of Labor Relations who acts as mediator in industrial disputes but has no right to force his authority on disputing parties. There is a law for settling labor disputes.

The Histadrut is affiliated with the International Confederation of Free Trade Unions (ICFTU), and the individual unions are very active in their international counterparts. The Histadrut and its affiliated unions maintain close relations with international labor organizations, and there is a constant flow of delegations and visitors to Israel from all parts of the international labor movement. On many important occasions the ICFTU and national trade union organizations have expressed support and sympathy for the cause of labor in Israel.

See also SOCIAL INSURANCE IN ISRAEL; LEVEL OF LIVING IN ISRAEL.

Y. YUDIN—ED.

TRAINING, AGRICULTURAL. *See* HAKHSHARA.

TRANSFER AGREEMENT WITH GERMANY. *See* HAAVARA.

TRANSJORDAN. Name applied to the area of the Land of Israel east of the Jordan River. Historically, Transjordan (Heb., Ever ha-Yarden) or parts of it have often been united with western Eretz Israel. In biblical times the tribes of Gad, Reuben, and half of Manasseh settled in the mountainous plateau of Gilead, and King David conquered the whole of Transjordan. In the reign of King Solomon the conquests of David were consolidated, but under his weak successors most of Transjordan was lost or held only temporarily. It was intermittently conquered and lost by the Maccabees and the Herodian dynasty. From the fifth to the seventh centuries of the Common Era, Transjordan was under Byzantine authority. In CE 635 it was overrun by Moslems. After a brief interlude (1115–81) of Crusader rule, Transjordan reverted to Moslem domination, first of the Egyptian Mamelukes and later (16th century) of the Turks, who administered it as part of the Ottoman Empire.

Development to 1928. Throughout the area's eventful history, it always had larger or smaller Jewish settlements. In 1884 the Jews of Safed established on the Transjordanian side of Lake Kineret a settlement, Benei Yehuda, that by 1900 had 31 settlers on 800 acres of land. In 1896 there were in the Golan (biblical Bashan) area four Jewish settlements in addition to Benei Yehuda. In 1894 Baron Edmond de Rothschild acquired 17,500 acres in the Golan. Tracts were also bought by various Hovevei Zion groups, among them the Shavei Zion of New York, Agudat Ahim of Yekaterinoslav, Ezra Mi-Tza'ar of Jassy and the Hovevei Zion of England. Turkish restrictions on Jewish immigration prevented large-scale settlement. According to official Turkish sources, Transjordan's sparse population, almost exclusively Arab, was 141,982 (not including the nomadic tribes) at the beginning of World War I.

Meeting between Transjordanian sheikhs and Zionist leaders, Jerusalem, 1933. Fourth from the left in the front row is Chaim Weizmann. [Zionist Archives]

At the time of the Balfour Declaration (1917) and for at least three years thereafter, no distinction was made between the two banks of the Jordan River. On 26 June, and again on 11 August 1919, Arthur James Balfour, head of the British delegation to the Paris Peace Conference, wrote to Prime Minister David Lloyd George: "In determining the Palestine frontiers the main thing to keep in mind is to make a Zionist policy possible by giving the fullest scope to economic development in Palestine....Palestine should extend into the lands lying east of the Jordan." The first draft of the *Mandate for Palestine, submitted to the Council of the League of Nations on 6 December 1920, contained no provision exempting Transjordan from the scope of the Jewish National Home. T.E. Lawrence (Lawrence of Arabia), who had played a leading role in shaping British Middle East policy, later told Professor Lewis Bernstein Namier that as late as February, 1921, the intention had been "to include Transjordan in Palestine, to make it indistinguishable from Palestine, and to open it to Jewish immigration." The British Royal Commission of 1937 authoritatively stated, on the basis of official documentation and testimony heard, that "the field in which the Jewish National Home was to be established was understood, at the time of the Balfour Declaration, to be the whole of historic Palestine," that is, including Transjordan.

The first tentative indication that Transjordan would be treated in a different manner from Cis-Jordan was made by Sir Herbert Samuel, the first British High Commissioner for Palestine. On 20 August 1920, he told an assembly of sheikhs and notables at Es-Salt that Transjordan was under British control but that Great Britain favored a system of local self-government. Within the next six months a completely extraneous set of events, in no way connected with the Jewish National Home policy, created a new situation.

In July, 1920, the French occupation forces in Syria had ousted Feisal, son of Sherif Hussein of Mecca, from his Damascus throne. Eager to avenge this event and to recapture the Syrian domain from the French, Emir Abdullah, Feisal's older brother, appeared in February, 1921, with a force of 2,000 Bedouins from the Hejaz. French troops advanced to meet his forces. The British did not relish the prospect of seeing the French on the eastern bank of the Jordan but were unwilling themselves to assume the task of expelling *Abdullah and his Bedouins. Winston *Churchill, British Secretary of State for the Colonies, who was touring the Middle East at the time, chose to come to some understanding with the Arab chieftain. On 27 March 1921, he invited Abdullah to Jerusalem for a conference, which was attended also by Herbert Samuel and Lawrence. It was agreed that Abdullah would abstain from action against the French, administer Transjordan in the name of the mandatory, and receive a monthly subsidy of £5,000 for a period of six months.

Like many other similar "temporary arrangements," this one came to achieve permanence: expediency became policy. On 24 July 1922, a revised draft of the Palestine Mandate was published, including Article 25, which entitled the mandatory "to postpone or withhold application of such provisions of the Mandate as he may consider inapplicable to the existing local conditions...in the territories lying between Jordan and the Eastern boundary of Palestine." On the basis of this proviso, Great Britain informed the League of Nations on 16 September 1922, that all the provisions of the Palestine Mandate concerning the Jewish National Home were inapplicable to Transjordan. On 23 April 1923, Samuel declared in Amman that "His Majesty's Government would recognize the existence of an independent government in Transjordan by means of an agreement to be concluded between the two governments." An agreement to this effect was signed on 20 February 1928. Two months later an Organic Law of Transjordan was promulgated. It covered an area of 34,740 square miles with an estimated population of 300,000. Of this total, some 50,000 were nomads and 120,000 seminomads; the settled population numbered about 130,000.

Emirate and Kingdom, 1928–48. The Zionist Executive reluctantly acquiesced to the agreement. The Revisionist opposition had since 1925 refused to recognize the separation of Transjordan and made the demand for an "undivided Palestine" a major part of its program. Underpopulated though it was, Transjordan was consistently barred to settlement by Jews. This policy was imposed by the British authorities, apparently against the wishes of the local Arab population and of Emir Abdullah. In 1933 two members of the Executive of the Jewish Agency, Yehoshua Heshel Farbstein and Emanuel Neumann, were approached by Abdullah's emissary with a view to enlisting Jewish participation in the development of 17,000 acres of land. They later met Abdullah himself. According to the report given by Neumann to the Political Committee of the 18th Zionist Congress (1933), Abdullah at that time not only was interested in the financial aspect of the transaction but also saw in it a beginning of a new era in Jewish-Arab relations which he wished to inaugurate. On 18 July 1933, the *New York Times* reported that an agreement had been reached providing an option on a lease of 33 years, renewable for two similar periods, with an annual payment of 2,200 Palestine pounds. When the Palestine Arab leaders learned of the agreement, a violent campaign against Abdullah started in the papers controlled by the mufti of Jerusalem, Hajj Amin al-Husseini. Even more vigorous pressure was exerted by the British authorities, and Abdullah was compelled to recant publicly. Yet several Arab sheikhs were eager to enlist Jewish cooperation and offered plans for leasing some of their lands. To prevent such an eventuality, the British submitted to the Transjordan Legislative Council a draft law prohibiting land sales to foreigners; the draft was rejected 13 to 3. The 23rd session of the Permanent Mandates Commission of the League of Nations also argued that no obstacles be put in the way of leasing land to Jews. But the British insisted on barring Jews from Transjordan while traffic from the east to the west bank of the Jordan was free, permitting large-scale smuggling of arms to the Arab terrorist gangs and a steady influx of cheap Arab labor, both from Transjordan proper and from the adjacent Syrian province of Hauran. The *Hope-Simpson Report put the number of such infiltrators at 110,000 during the decade 1921–31; additional tens of thousands infiltrated between 1932 and 1935.

On 22 March 1946, a 25-year treaty of alliance terminated the British Mandate. Transjordan was recognized as an independent state, the Hashemite kingdom of Transjordan (later, Jordan), with Abdullah as sovereign. For subsequent history, *see* ABDULLAH; HUSSEIN.

J. SCHECHTMAN

TRANSPORTATION IN ISRAEL.

The Ottoman Legacy. The first Zionist settlers found a primitive transportation system in Eretz Israel. A carriage ride from Jaffa to Jerusalem took at least 11 hours in 1876. Most roads, however, were not suitable for carriages and very few could be traveled in any weather.

Following the opening of the Suez Canal in 1869 and the increase in pilgrims and tourists visiting the country, the number of steamships frequenting its ports increased considerably by the end of the 19th century. However, no port had proper piers. Jaffa was the main port for both passenger and cargo traffic, most notably citrus exports. In 1910, 870,000 crates of citrus were shipped from Jaffa. As a result of the bad state of land transportation, most of the commerce of the north of the country was conducted through Acre, and later Haifa.

In 1892 the first railroad line in the Middle East was opened between Jaffa and Jerusalem. To avoid tunneling, the narrow-gauge (100 cm.) track followed the winding course of the Sorek Valley, making it 40 percent longer than the road. A second line, opened in 1904, connected Haifa to the Hejaz line in Syria. It later served the settlement areas in the Jezreel Valley through which it passed.

The main impetus to rail development in Palestine was the outbreak of World War I. Both the Turks and British built networks to facilitate their troop movements. The Turks and Germans built a narrow-gauge (105 cm.) line from north to south along the foothills so as to avoid naval bombardment. This line was continued to Beersheba and Sinai. The British built a line from the south across the Sinai to Gaza and later through Lydda to Haifa.

During the war both sides also built roads suitable for motor vehicles. The road network, however, was concentrated predominantly in areas which were inaccessible to rail such as the mountains of Judea and Galilee. The all-weather network in 1918 totaled 300 miles (450 km.) in length.

Transportation during the British Mandate. The British mandatory authorities developed the transportation system in Palestine mainly to serve the interests of the British Empire. The existing railroads were purchased and formed into a government unit, to serve as part of the imperial transportation system in the Middle East. Until the mid-thirties rail development was given precedence over roads. The rail system, however, suffered from a number of handicaps. The British and Turkish rails were of different widths. The system was thus in effect two different systems. The lines built during the war were of inferior quality and required high maintenance expenditures, as did the old equipment. They were located according to military needs and did not serve well the main economic centers, mainly Tel Aviv. The financing costs of the initial purchase limited the possibilities of the railroad management to invest resources in modernizing the system. As a result of these factors the level of service of the railroads was low, and the number of passengers did not grow as fast as the population. Still, the railroad played a central part in cargo traffic throughout the mandatory period.

Until the mid-thirties roads were built primarily on routes not served by rail. Despite growing motorization the total length of all-weather roads reached only 630 miles

(950 km.) in 1932. The road from Tel Aviv to Petah Tikva was completed only in 1928, and the road from Tel Aviv to Haifa through Hadera was delayed until 1937.

After 1938 military needs took precedence over economic considerations. First, roads were built in Galilee to thwart infiltrations from Lebanon, as part of the British effort to put down the Arab revolt of 1936–9. Later, during World War II, additional roads were built to facilitate troop movements, as Palestine became an important base for the British Army in the Middle East. In total 1,770 miles (2,660 km.) of new roads were built during this period.

The first deep-water port in Palestine was built by the British in Haifa. Its construction was completed in 1933. It was intended also to serve parts of Transjordan and Iraq. An oil pipeline from Iraq to Haifa was completed in 1934, and plans were made for a railway line from Haifa to Baghdad. With its deep-water port, Haifa became the main port for Palestine for both passengers and cargo.

Jaffa port was also expanded. Between 1934 and 1936 a breakwater, wharfs, and piers were built. In 1936, however, the access of Jews to the port was impeded as a result of the Arab general strike. Consequently the port of Tel Aviv was inaugurated in 1937 to serve the needs of the Jewish population.

Most of the ships calling at Palestinian ports were tramps, without fixed routes or schedules. Most of the sea trade was with western Europe. Shipping ceased almost completely during World War II. In the years immediately after the war shipping was hampered by the world-wide shortage of merchant ships.

The first airfields in Palestine were built during World War I. Commercial aviation, however, dates to 1924, when Imperial Airways began to use the field at Gaza as a staging point for their Cairo to London flights. Seaplanes landed in Haifa Bay and on Lake Kineret near Tiberias. Gaza continued to serve as the main land airport until the thirties when Haifa (1934) and Lydda (1937) airports were opened. Following Arab attacks on Jewish traffic to Lydda a single-runway airport was opened north of Tel Aviv (the present day Sedeh Dov airport) in 1938. It was used by Palestine Airways, founded in 1937 by Pinhas Rutenberg. This company closed down after the outbreak of World War II. During the war several military airfields were built by the British.

With cruising ranges of about four hours, long distance flights in the thirties and forties were made in stages of not more than 530 miles (800 km.). The Palestinian airfields thus served as staging points for flights between Europe and the Far East; they also served as departure points for local flights to Beirut, Cairo, Nicosia, and Baghdad.

After 1948. The transportation system has undergone a dramatic transformation since the establishment of the State of Israel in 1948. Until the early 1960s it was typical of that of a developing country. During this period many resources were invested in infrastructure as a prerequisite to economic growth. Such growth was rapid during the late fifties and early sixties, and the deregulation of the vehicle market in 1961 created a growing demand for transportation services. This demand was met during the 1960s and early 1970s by parallel increases in both public and private transportation expenditure. During this period transportation planning was institutionalized at both the national and metropolitan levels: the first metropolitan transportation studies were undertaken and the first comprehensive masterplans prepared.

The economic recession following the Yom Kippur War in 1973 slowed the development of the transportation sector. This slowdown manifested itself differently in the various subsectors. In the air and sea subsectors demand for both freight and passenger transport declined, and consequently the implementation of development plans was deferred. In contrast, in the land transportation subsector car ownership levels rose while public expenditure declined. A growing gap resulted between demand and supply in this subsector, lowering the level of road service. One attempt to overcome this problem was the construction of limited-access highways.

As a result of the growing concern for both road safety and the environment, and the continuing scarcity of land, especially in built-up areas, the cost of supplying the demand by new infrastructure escalated, while the resources available to the transportation system diminished. Consequently, emphasis in the 1980s was placed on managing the existing system rather than on development.

Land Transportation. The armistice lines at the end of the War of Independence severed several major roads and railroad lines. Many of the new immigrants in the early 1950s were settled in the periphery, in the north, south, and the Jerusalem corridor. Consequently, major investments were required to restore and provide basic access to all parts of the country. Major roads built in this period included the central road to Beersheba, the roads to Sedom on the Dead Sea, to Eilat on the Red Sea, and the new road to Jerusalem bypassing the section of the road controlled by Jordan at Latrun.

Most of the roads built in the 1950s were narrow, as traffic demand was low. The import of vehicles was regulated until 1961. In 1951 only 28 percent of vehicles were private cars. Deregulation of car imports and rapid economic growth led to a rapid increase in the rate of motorization after 1961. The number of private cars rose dramatically. By 1970 55 percent of vehicles were private cars, and by 1983 78 percent.

The growth in the rate of motorization, the change in modal split from public transportation to private cars, and growing suburbanization led to the deterioration of the level of service of roads, especially in metropolitan areas. For this reason the emphasis in road development changed in the late 1960s from the provision of access to peripheral areas to relieving congested arteries in metropolitan areas. The first limited-access highways were planned and built during the 1970s. In the early 1970s metropolitan and national transportation planning units were formed to plan and implement such projects. As a result of the economic recession following the Yom Kippur War of 1973, the resources at the disposal of transportation projects were reduced. With the exceptions of 1978 and 1979 budgets were cut annually from 1973. At the same time road standards were improved for safety reasons, increasing road construction costs.

An additional factor limiting road development was the fragmentation of resources. The interurban system is the responsibility of the Public Works Department, originally part of the Ministry of Labor and currently part of the Ministry of Housing and Construction. Another important budget source for the interurban system is the Ministry of Defense. The Ministry of Transportation allocates most of its resources to metropolitan projects in conjunction with local municipalities. The main recipient of these funds for more than a decade was the Netivei Ayalon project in Tel

Aviv, the major highway through the city along the Ayalon stream. Each of these bodies allocates its funding independently according to its own priorities. No overall transportation development policy had been set up to the end of the 1980s.

The growth differential in the rate of motorization on the one hand, and in the budget structure on the other, resulted in a sudden decline in service to metropolitan areas. Traffic congestion became a major problem in all metropolitan areas. However, Netivei Ayalon was the only major metropolitan project carried out between 1975 and 1985. Bypasses to congested areas and rapid rail systems are planned but their implementation has been stalled due to budget constraints. Traffic management schemes were implemented as an interim measure to alleviate some of the congestion by more efficient use of existing infrastructure.

In the interurban system, national projects such as the settlement of Galilee or the redeployment of the army in the Negev, following the withdrawal from Sinai in 1982, led to construction of a few major roads, mostly in the late 1970s and early 1980s, thus limiting the deterioration of service.

The public transportation system in Israel is dominated by buses. There are two main bus companies: Egged with some 4,000 buses operating throughout the country, and Dan with approximately 1,500 buses serving the Tel Aviv metropolitan area. Both companies are cooperatives which grew through mergers of smaller local and regional cooperatives formed during the British Mandate period. Bus fares and lines are regulated by the government. Tariff and subsidy policies are determined mainly by macro-economic and welfare considerations, and not as part of an overall transportation policy.

Taxis operate both on fixed routes and individual hire basis. The taxi sector is not subsidized by government, although the Ministry of Transport controls entry into this sector and supervises tariffs. The taxi and para-transit industries are especially important among the Arab population.

The number of passengers traveling by rail peaked in 1964. Since then the number has declined continuously as a result of the improvements in roads, the growing rate of motorization, and suburbanization. With the establishment of the State in 1948, the main north-south railway was cut at Tulkarm. Furthermore, as the Palestine government had developed the railroad according to British interests, the existing rail network was ill-suited to serve the needs of the Jewish sector, and consequently of the new State. In the early 1950s an effort was made to develop the rail system to suit the State's growing needs. A new, direct line was built between Haifa and Tel Aviv and a line to Beersheba was opened in 1953. New locomotives and cars were financed by the reparation funds received from Germany. Since the early 1960s, however, only few additional improvements have been made, comprising mainly the extension of the line in the Negev to Dimona (1965) and later to Oron (1970) and Zin (1977). The speed of major passenger lines was not improved significantly. Since the mid-sixties the main emphasis for rail development was directed towards freight, especially bulk freight. Grain, phosphates, and potash accounted for 75% of the freight hauled by rail. In the future coal is expected to become one of the main commodities transported by rail, as more power stations will use coal.

With the establishment of the State of Israel railroads became a government unit, under the Ministry of Transport. In 1988 the government decided to merge the railroads with the Ports Authority. At that time the main development plans for the railroad included the extension of the Negev line to Eilat, the construction of a line through Tel Aviv on the Netivei Ayalon axis, and the development of a commuter service in the Tel Aviv and Haifa metropolitan areas.

Traffic jam at entrance to Tel Aviv. [Israel Govt. Press Office]

A subway system was proposed for the Tel Aviv metropolitan area in the early 1970s. However, due to the high cost involved, the plan was dropped. Currently the only subway line operating in Israel is the Carmelit, opened in 1959, connecting Mount Carmel and downtown Haifa.

The dominant mode of freight transportation in Israel is trucks. In 1977 84.8 million tons, 95 percent of all commodity transport in Israel, were carried by truck. However, the total number of mileage traveled by these trucks was only 85 percent of the total distance over which commodities were conveyed, since the average distance of truck haulage was 27 miles (40 km.) whereas for trains it was 85 miles (128 km.). The dominance of trucks in commodity transportation in Israel is explained by the country's small size and its physical structure, both unconducive to rail transport.

The trucking industry is very sensitive to changes in the economy. Periods of economic growth, such as the early 1970s, are characterized by high profits that bring new entries into the field. Conversely trucks are less in demand during economic recessions. In contrast to railroads, trucking is a very competitive industry, with hardly any government involvement and many small operators. In 1977 26 percent of the total 13,600 trucks in Israel were privately owned in cooperatives, and a further 30 percent were independently owned. This resulted in many empty trips.

Shipping. With the establishment of the State all the land borders were closed, severing all business and trade relations with neighboring countries. Since then almost 99 percent of Israel's imports and exports have been transported by ship. This makes the shipping sector vital for the Israeli economy.

The foundation for a Jewish merchant marine was laid already at the end of the British Mandate period with the establishment of Zim in 1945 by the Jewish Agency, the Histadrut, and the Israel Maritime League. In 1947 Zim purchased its first passenger ship. Two additional ships were bought in 1948. These ships helped transport the large number of refugees and immigrants streaming to the country. With the establishment of the State the vessels which were confiscated by the British for transporting "illegal" immigrants were added to the company. In 1949 Zim purchased a few old freighters and opened its first line to northern and western Europe. From 1952 while immigration slowed, Israel's economy developed and freight traffic from, and particularly to, Israel increased. Consequently, Zim purchased additional freighters, and new companies were formed, the most notable being El Yam founded in 1953 and the Maritime Fruit Carriers founded in 1964.

The strategic importance of the shipping sector for the economy, and the reluctance of many foreign companies to enter Israeli ports due to the Arab boycott led the government to make a special effort in the first 20 years to build an Israeli commercial fleet. The German-Israeli reparations agreement enabled the government to finance the modernization and expansion of the Israeli merchant marine in the 1950s and 1960s. From a fleet of 31 vessels in 1952, most of which had seen 20 years or more of service, the fleet grew to 113 vessels in 1968, mostly modern. The most important technological trend was the growing specialization of ships and loading facilities. After the specialization of tankers and bulk carriers during the 1960s, container ships were introduced during the 1970s to carry general cargo. In 1985 Israeli companies owned 20 container ships of 379,000 ton deadweight. Half of this tonnage was employed in international traffic, as Zim operates a shipping line from Israel through North Mediterranean ports to the USA and Far East.

Following the closing of the Suez Canal in 1967, tankers carrying oil from the Persian Gulf to Europe and America were forced to use the route around the Cape of Good Hope. Israel reached an agreement with Iran to build a pipeline from Eilat to Ashkelon, thus shortening the distance and lowering transportation costs for Iranian oil exports. Between 20 and 30 million tons of oil were transported through the pipeline annually. This transit traffic enabled Israel to build a large tanker fleet. However, with the fall of the Shah, Iran canceled the agreement, and by the end of 1985 only 918,000 tons deadweight of tankers remained in Israeli ownership.

Today Israel owns no passenger ships. Passenger shipping became unprofitable after the introduction of jet aircraft. The last two passenger ships were sold in 1974. The only such ships now reaching Israel are cruise liners plying the ports of the Mediterranean.

Demand for shipping is influenced by two factors: the Israeli economy and the conditions of the world shipping market. Since 1973 the world shipping market has been characterized by a surplus of shipping capacity, causing a collapse of freight rates. At the same time the Israeli economy's rate of growth declined. This situation led to the liquidation of the Maritime Fruit Carriers Company and to considerable losses for Zim as from 1983. Despite reorganization Zim remained in a precarious position.

Ports. Three ports existed in 1948: Haifa, Jaffa, and Tel Aviv. Haifa was the only deep-water port. In 1949 1,410 ships visited the port, 78 percent of the total number of ships reaching Israel. 70 percent of the cargo and most passengers went through Haifa port. As a result congestion developed in peak periods. Already in 1951 a small complementary harbor was being built nearby, at the mouth of the Kishon, and it was opened in 1955. As Haifa was far from the developing southern half of the country, the government decided in 1956 to build a new port at Ashdod. Work started in April of 1961 and was completed on 21 November 1965. Following the opening of Ashdod the ports of Jaffa and Tel Aviv were closed in 1966.

After the Sinai Campaign of 1956, the Tiran Straits at the southern tip of the Sinai Peninsula were opened for Israeli shipping from Eilat. Consequently an open-water port was built in Eilat in 1957.

The three ports of Haifa, Ashdod, and Eilat are operated by the Port Authority, established in 1961. The Port Authority Law required that these ports sustain themselves. Tariffs are set so that revenues will cover both operation and development costs.

In the 1970s two additional specialized ports were opened: the oil terminal at Ashkelon and a coal terminal at the Hadera power station. These open-sea off-shore ports are operated by special port administrations independent of the Israel Ports Authority.

Growing ship specialization has also led to specialized wharfs, increasing productivity at the water line by reducing handling time. This productivity increase reduced ship turnover time and increased the demand for storage space. Such space grew from 65 square meters per meter of wharf in 1967/8 to 120 square meters in 1982/3.

Table 3 shows the changes in the relative standing of the ports. After overcoming labor problems in its early years Ashdod became the largest port, handling 50.6 percent of the total freight passing through the Port Authority ports in 1983/4, compared with 42.2 percent passing through Haifa and 7.2 percent through Eilat. The decline in the movement through Eilat is linked to the reopening of the Suez Canal. Most of the bulk exports originate in the Negev and are thus exported through Ashdod, while most grain imports pass through the Dagon granary at Haifa. Consequently, Table 3 shows that exports in Ashdod are double the imports while in Haifa the situation is the reverse.

Air Transportation. Four factors affect international aviation to Israel. The first is aircraft technology. Until the early 1960s most planes were propeller and turbo-props. With the advent of jet aircraft in the early 1960s, the range, speed, and capacity of planes increased, allowing more nonstop service. Since 1973 the trend has been to develop quiet, low-cost, fuel-efficient aircraft, rather than faster ones. The increase in capacity allowed the number of arriving passengers to increase at a faster rate than the number of landings, delaying the need for major investments.

The second factor is the world aviation's institutional structure. Until the mid-sixties aviation operated as a cartel. After 1966 charter flights were allowed for specific destinations, mainly Scandinavia. In 1978 the skies were opened to charters without limitations on destinations, leading to a dramatic increase in such flights. In August, 1984, new regulations came into effect, limiting charter flights from destinations within 100 miles (150 km.) from destinations served by *El Al and preventing the mingling of Israelis and foreign tourists on flights traveling regular airline routes. This led to a decline in charter flights.

The third factor is geopolitics. With the establishment of the State all regional routes were closed, except to Nicosia and Istanbul. Most links are to western Europe and North America. As a result of the accession to power of the Khomeini regime in Iran, the line to the Far East was disconnected in 1979. Following the peace treaty with Egypt the line to Cairo was reopened.

Conditions in the world aviation market are the fourth factor. The market entered a stagnation period in 1979/80 due to concurrent increases in fuel prices and an economic recession in many developed countries. The deregulation of the airlines in the USA led to a general decrease in tariffs. The increase in expenditure and decrease in revenues brought heavy losses to many regular companies. El Al lost approximately $300 million. This, together with labor unrest, forced the company to cease operations temporarily. After major structural changes, including a 20 percent decrease in the workforce, the company resumed operations in January 1983.

The domestic aviation sector has three parts: regular, agricultural, and general. Arkia, founded in 1950, is the sole regular-aviation operator. With the short distances in Israel limiting development potential, 70–90 percent of all regular flights are between Tel Aviv and Eilat. The period between 1967 and 1982 was characterized by high levels of demand for flights to Sinai. The number of passengers using the internal aviation's services rose from 166,000 in 1966 to 295,000 in 1969 and 715,000 in 1975. With the return of Sinai to Egyptian control the number of passengers dropped to 300,000 in 1982/3.

Agricultural aviation is highly developed in Israel. The two companies in this sector fly some 90 planes. The general aviation sector, including air taxis, is relatively small with some 180 planes. Four flying schools operate from Herzliya, Jerusalem, and Haifa.

The major civilian airport in Israel is Ben-Gurion Airport in Lod (Lydda). Located in the center of the country near major highways, Ben-Gurion is easily accessible from all major urban centers. The airport is situated at the center of an industrial complex which is one of Israel's main employment centers.

Ben-Gurion Airport is the hub of a complex airport system which is the base for all Israeli civilian aviation. The two complementary fields are Sedeh Dov in northern Tel Aviv, which specializes in internal aviation, and Herzliya, which is the major base for agricultural and general aviation. Other noteworthy airports are Eilat which handles both internal and charter flights, and Atarot near Jerusalem. This latter field was developed by the Jordanians from a British dirt strip. Since 1967 the Israeli government has tried to divert traffic to it. However, due to its proximity to Ben-Gurion, its short runway and the refusal of most countries to allow flights originating in them to land there, these efforts have been largely unsuccessful.

Most of the civilian airports are operated by the Airports Authority, established in 1977. The Authority is an economically independent body, funded by government-supervised landing fees, and by concessionaire sales. (*See also* AVIATION IN ISRAEL).

E. FEITELSON

TREIDEL, JOSEPH. Engineer and pioneer in Eretz Israel (b. Mayen, Germany, 1876; d. Haifa, 1927). Treidel completed his studies as a land surveyor and development engineer and in 1898 settled in Eretz Israel, where he worked for several years with the Jewish Colonization Association (ICA) in Haifa. In 1905 he and Aaron Aaronsohn set up a land office that was the forerunner of the Palestine Office founded by Arthur Ruppin.

In 1908 Treidel participated in the geological expedition to Transjordan headed by Aaronsohn and the German geologist Max Blanckenhorn. In 1910 he went to East Africa for a year to study methods of water conservation for agricultural purposes. After his return to Eretz Israel, he helped survey the land for the settlements of Migdal and Merhavia, of which he was a founder.

TRIETSCH, DAVIS. Zionist writer and statistician (b. Dresden, 1870; d. Ramatayim, 1935). From 1893 to 1899 Trietsch lived in New York, where he made a study of the problem of Jewish immigration and proposed, as a solution, the Jewish colonization of Cyprus. Joining the Zionist movement, he attended the First Zionist Congress (1897). However, he opposed Herzl's political platform and advocated immediate Jewish settlement in a Greater Palestine that would include Cyprus and El-Arish. He also maintained that rapid Jewish resettlement would be possible only on an industrial basis in connection with the establishment of garden cities. Although the World Zionist Organization did not accept his plans for colonization in Cyprus, some of his suggestions for settlement work in Eretz Israel were eventually adopted by Zionist Congresses. In 1907 Trietsch became a member of the Zionist Actions Committee.

After World War I he was one of the chief advocates of Zionist maximalism, which strove for the immediate emigration of hundreds of thousands of Jews to Eretz Israel and their settlement there. He published his views in 1919 in *Volk und Land*, a Berlin weekly founded and edited by him. He settled in Palestine in 1932.

Trietsch helped found (1902) the publishing house Jüdischer Verlag in Berlin and (1902–03) the monthlies *Ost und West* and *Palästina*. A prolific writer, he published many books, including *Palästina-Handbuch* (1907; 5th ed., 1922), *Bilder aus Palästina* (1912), *Levante-Handbuch* (3rd ed., 1914), *Jüdische Emigration und Kolonisation* (1917, 1923), *Palästina und die Juden: Tatsachen und Ziffern* (1919), *Atlas der jüdischen Welt* (1926), *Palästina-Wirtschaftsatlas* (2nd ed., 1926), *Der Wiedereintritt der Juden in die Weltgeschichte* (1926), and *Die Fassungskraft Palästinas* (1930).

TRIVUS, ISRAEL. Lawyer, writer, and Zionist leader (b. Crimea, Russia, 1882; d. Tel Aviv, 1955). A graduate of the Odessa University Law School, Trivus became a Zionist in his early youth and in 1901 was a cofounder of Yerusholayim, the first Zionist student organization in Odessa. In 1903 he headed the committee responsible for the formation of the first Jewish student self-defense unit in Russia.

In 1906 Trivus, Vladimir Jabotinsky, and others founded in Odessa the Zionist weekly *Yevreiskaya Mysl*; the same year Trivus participated in the Helsingfors Conference. In 1908 he was secretary-general of the Central Committee of the Russian Zionist Organization and from 1914 to 1918 served as chairman of the Zionist Organization of Odessa. In 1917 he was elected to the Municipal Council of Odessa and served as chairman of the Jewish faction; in 1918 he headed the Zionist faction of the Odessa Jewish Community (kehilla). In 1919, with Zinovi Tiomkin, he organized the first Jewish immigrant group to arrive in Palestine from Soviet Russia on the S.S. *Roslan*.

In 1920 Trivus was a delegate to the London Zionist Conference. From 1921 to 1923 he served in Berlin as the representative of the Keren ha-Yesod; in 1923 he joined the editorial board of *Rassviet* and the activist group, headed by Jabotinsky. In 1924 he settled in Paris, where he became a founder of the Revisionist movement and served on the Revisionist World Executive.

In 1926 Trivus founded in Paris the Crédit Mutuel Ivriya, the first Jewish credit institution in France, which was supported by the Cooperative Bank of France and served Jewish emigrants and political refugees. In 1939 he settled in Palestine where he was a regular contributor to the Hebrew dailies *Ha-Mashkif, Ha-Boker,* and *Herut* and edited a history of the British Mandate for Palestine.

I. BENARI

TRUMAN, HARRY S. Thirty-third President (1945–53) of the United States (b. Lamar, Mo., 1884; d. Kansas City, 1972). In 1939, as United States Senator from Missouri, Truman strongly condemned in the Senate the British White Paper of 1939, which severely limited Jewish immigration to, and land purchase in, Palestine. In May, 1944, he wrote to the Washington bureau of the Zionist Organization of America, stating that "when the right time comes I am willing to help make the fight for a Jewish homeland in Palestine." As soon as Truman became President, he was subjected to pressure from anti-Zionist State Department officials to handle "the question of Palestine...with the greatest care." Secretary of State Edward R. Stettinius warned Truman against endangering world peace by any hasty action. On the other hand, Sen. Robert F. Wagner of New York pointed out to Truman (in a letter of 18 April 1945) that on several occasions Pres. Franklin D. *Roosevelt had supported Jewish immigration to Palestine and the founding of a Jewish Commonwealth there, and he urged Truman to follow this policy. Nevertheless, at the urging of Acting Secretary of State Joseph C. Grew, Truman, in answer to a letter from Emir Abdullah of Transjordan, reaffirmed Roosevelt's assurances that the United States would not act on the Palestine issue without "prior consultation with Arabs and Jews" (17 May 1945).

Refugee Problem. Truman commissioned Earl G. Harrison, the United States member of the International Committee on Refugees, to investigate the condition of the displaced persons in the camps and ascertain their needs and wishes. On 24 August 1945, Harrison reported that the

Chaim Weizmann, first President of Israel, presents a Tora scroll to Pres. Harry S Truman on a visit to the White House in 1949. [United Jewish Appeal]

International symposium on Harry S Truman at the Hebrew University. [Hebrew University]

Jewish displaced persons "want to be evacuated to Palestine now" and that "the only real solution" was "the quick admission of one hundred thousand Jews into Palestine." Thereupon, on 31 August, Truman wrote to British Prime Minister Clement Attlee, stressing the need for immediate action to permit 100,000 Jewish refugees to enter Palestine.

Instead of granting this request, the British government, on 19 October 1945, formally proposed an Anglo-American inquiry into the Palestine problem. The proposal was accepted by Truman, was made public on 13 November, and drew strong protests from the Zionists and others who considered it one more dilatory move. Truman appointed six American members to the *Anglo-American Committee of Inquiry, which was set up soon thereafter and which submitted its report on 22 April 1946. Truman endorsed the Committee's recommendation for the admission of 100,000 refugees and offered ships and funds for the transfer. However, he refused to become involved in a possible settlement of the Palestine question by force.

***Morrison-Grady Plan.** In order to find a political solution to the Palestine question acceptable to both Arabs and Jews, Truman appointed a Cabinet committee which, under the chairmanship of Henry F. Grady, acting for the Secretary of State, left for London in July, 1946, to meet with a British Cabinet committee headed by Herbert S. Morrison. The resulting Morrison-Grady Plan (envisaging a federated Jewish-Arab state in Palestine under British rule), which was opposed by Jews and Arabs alike, at first seemed acceptable to Truman, but energetic Jewish and general political protests moved him to instruct the United States delegation to continue negotiations instead of going ahead with the federation plan.

On Yom Kippur Eve (4 October 1946), Truman issued a statement which, in effect, expressed his hope that a way could be found to bridge the gap between the Morrison-Grady Plan and the Zionist bid for the partition of Palestine as presented to the State Department in August, 1946, and endorsed by Department officials. During the nine months that followed, Truman moved to a position of supporting the establishment of a Jewish State in Palestine. He did this primarily because he hoped that the problem of the displaced Jews of Europe would thus be settled, and that a democratic Jewish State would contribute to stability in the Middle East. On 28 October 1946, in reply to a letter from King Ibn Saud, Truman wrote: "The United States...took the position...that a national home for the Jewish people should be established in Palestine." At the same time, he still did not commit himself to any specific manner in which the Jewish National Home in Palestine should be set up. Throughout this period Truman was, to a considerable extent, caught between pressures from the State Department, on the one hand, and from public opinion—including the Congress of the United States, which had been aroused by Zionist efforts led by Abba Hillel Silver—on the other.

United Nations. Following the submission of the Palestine problem by Great Britain to the United Nations (February, 1947), Truman was determined that the young international body should be successful in solving this, its first major international issue. In the ensuing months Zionists and their sympathizers in the United States importuned the President to throw the weight of the United States behind the Palestine *partition proposal, while the State Department was untiring in reminding him of the need for Arab friendship and oil concessions. However, by the time the final vote took place in the United Nations on the Palestine partition proposal (29 November 1947), the United States delegation took the lead in voting for it, with the majority. The question whether or not Truman instructed the United States delegation to bring pressure to bear on other delegations in the United Nations to vote for the partition resolution remains a matter of argument. *See also* UNITED NATIONS AND PALESTINE-ISRAEL.

Trusteeship Issue. Following the passage of the resolution, Truman expressed the hope that it would be possible to carry it out by peaceful means. When this hope proved vain and Arab attacks on the yishuv threw Palestine into chaos, Truman made a last unsuccessful appeal to the Arabs for pacification. He was privy to most of the State Department moves to substitute partition with trusteeship in March, 1948, but was surprised at the timing and by the determination of the State Department officials. On 18 March 1948, persuaded by his friend Edward Jacobson, Truman received Chaim Weizmann, who obtained from him assurance that he would continue to support the partition plan. However, before Truman could take action, on the very next day, Warren R. Austin, United States Ambassador to the United Nations, told the Security Council of the American trusteeship proposal, calling for a suspension of all efforts aimed at partition. Truman apparently had not given his formal approval to the proposal, and he now felt that it had been released on 19 March in order to force his hand. The Zionists and many political leaders in the United States were dismayed by what seemed to be a reversal in the American attitude. The President thereupon pointed out, in a statement on 25 March, that the trusteeship proposal had merely been "an effort to fill the vacuum soon to be created by the termination of the Mandate on 15 May".

At the 2nd Special Session of the UN General Assembly (16 April—14 May 1948), it became clear that the trusteeship proposal, like partition, could not be implemented without the commitment of armed forces. On 22 April, in an attempt to prevent further violence between Jews and Arabs, Truman stated that he was prepared to send troops to Palestine to enforce a temporary trusteeship if an international police force were set up for that purpose.

Recognition of Israel. On 14 May 1948, the US State Department advised Eliahu Epstein, (later Elath), then the representative of the Jewish Agency in Washington, that the new State would be granted recognition if he, Epstein, were to submit a formal request to this effect. The same day, Epstein drafted a letter to the President and the Secretary of State requesting immediate recognition.

On 15 May, within minutes after the expiration of the Mandate (shortly after 6 P.M. Washington time on 14 May), Truman announced that "the United States recognizes the provisional government as the *de facto* authority of the new State of Israel." On 31 January 1949, Truman was to extend *de jure* recognition to Israel.

During the United States presidential election campaign of 1948, Truman's policy and action indicated that he did not wish to use the Israel problem as a political maneuver. Although the Bernadotte Plan, drastically reducing the area allotted to Israel, was put forward in September and accepted within a week by Secretary of State Marshall in the name of the United States, aroused a storm of Zionist protests, Truman refused to take a stand against the plan. Only after the Republican candidate, Gov. Thomas E. Dewey, had accused Truman of betraying United States pledges to Israel, did the latter, on 24 October, reiterate his support for the Democratic platform plank accepting Israel's boundaries as set up by the partition resolution.

Early in 1949 he supported a loan from the Export-Import Bank to Israel of $100 million (later increased to $135 million).

On 25 August 1949 Truman pledged the full support of the United States to the UN Economic Survey of the Middle East, headed by Gordon R. Clapp, chairman of the Board of Directors of the Tennessee Valley Authority. United States government circles felt that assistance to the underdeveloped areas of the Middle East would strengthen the position of the Western powers there and might provide an economic solution to the Arab refugee problem.

On 31 October 1951, Truman signed a bill under which, as part of the program of the newly established Mutual Security Agency, Israel was to receive $64,950,000 for economic aid, of which $50,000,000 was earmarked for the relief and resettlement of Jewish refugees. On 15 July 1952, he signed the appropriation bill of the Mutual Security Program for military, technical, and economic aid to members of the North Atlantic Treaty Organization (NATO) and most other non-Communist countries; under this bill Israel received $70,228,000 for aid for the resettlement of Jewish refugees and $2,772,000 for technical assistance.

After his tenure in the White House, Truman continued to be active in support of Israel. On 28 January 1956, he joined Mrs. Franklin D. Roosevelt and the labor leader Walter P. Reuther in a statement that, in order to counteract Soviet attempts to gain power in the Middle East, "the United States should now provide the defensive arms needed by Israel to protect itself against any aggression made possible or incited by the introduction of Communist arms." On 24 April 1958, he was among the dignitaries attending ceremonies at Philadelphia's Independence Hall, marking the opening event in the celebration of the 10th anniversary of Israel's statehood.

Ian J. Bickerton's detailed analysis of Truman's position on the Jewish State reveals that, despite the overwhelming consensus of Zionists, congressmen, the Democratic National Committee, and the press that he should support the foundation of a Jewish State, he was at first reluctant to do so. When he finally did act, he did so because he believed in the justice of the Jewish cause, wished to support the United Nations in endorsing its partition resolution, hoped that peace in the Middle East would be the outcome of the partition of Palestine and the establishment of a Jewish State, and was convinced that this was in the national interest of the United States.

In Israel the village of Kefar Truman and the Hebrew University's Truman Peace Center were named in his honor.

See also UNITED STATES, ATTITUDE TO ZIONISM AND ISRAEL

R. PATAI—Y. FREUNDLICH

Trumpeldor with the medals awarded him in the Russo-Japanese War, 1905. [Central Zionist Archives]

TRUMPELDOR, JOSEPH. Soldier, pioneer of the Second and Third Aliya, and the molder of the *He-Halutz movement in Russia (b. Pyatigorsk, 1880; d. Tel Hai, 1920). His father had been a "cantonist" (Jewish child conscript to the Tsarist Army) who, despite the 25 years that he had to spend in the service of the army, had not forgotten that he was Jewish; but he was cut off from the traditional Jewish way of life and Trumpeldor grew up in an atmosphere that was remote from Judaism. Trumpeldor took up the study of dentistry after he was barred by the *numerus clausus* from attending high school in Rostov-on-Don, where the family lived. This was his first encounter with anti-Semitism, and it was to have a profound effect on his life. In his early years, Trumpeldor was attracted by Tolstoy's teachings, especially the Tolstoyan idea of a commune. Under the impact of the First Zionist Congress (1897), Trumpeldor became a Zionist and organized a Zionist society in Pyatigorsk, where one of his brothers lived. As a disciple of Tolstoy, he opposed militarism but made no effort to escape military service (as many Jews did) in order to prove that Jews were no cowards. He was drafted in 1902.

In the Russo-Japanese War (1904—1905) Trumpeldor distinguished himself in the fighting at Port Arthur and lost his left arm in battle. Recovering from his injury, he asked to be sent back to the front; his request was granted. He was promoted to non-commissioned rank (rare for a Jew in the Tsarist Army) and was cited for bravery. For his distinguished service he was awarded all four degrees of the St. George Cross and the George Medal—an array of decorations matched by no more than four persons in the entire country. When Port Arthur fell, on 2 January 1905, Trumpeldor was one of the great number of Russian troops whom the Japanese took prisoner. In Japanese captivity he organized schools and workshops in which Russian soldiers—Jews and non-Jews—learned a trade as well as how to read and write. He also founded a Zionist Society in the P.O.W. camp and edited "*Yevreskaya Zhizn* (Jewish Life), of the sons of Israel in Japanese Captivity". He also organized a group of Jewish soldiers with whom he planned to go to Eretz Israel and form a cooperative (a plan which was not put into effect).

On his return to Russia, Trumpeldor was made a reservist Second Lieutenant, becoming one of the few Jews ever to be appointed to commissioned rank in the Tsarist Army. He took up residence in St. Petersburg, and graduated in law from St. Petersburg University in 1912. The political outlook that he acquired was a combination of anarcho-socialism and Zionism, calling for Eretz Israel to be settled by agricultural cooperative groups. For Trumpeldor the concept of cooperative living was an ideal to be pursued for itself within the framework of the realization of Zionism, an exclusive view in those times. His search for partners who would join him in the implementation of his ideas was successful and in 1911 he met with a group of like-minded Zionists in Romny (Ukraine) to elaborate their views and make practical decisions. The meeting decided to establish in Eretz Israel a cooperative—and shortly thereafter five of the participants left to make a start on their project. They found agriculture work at the Migdal farm, functioning as a cooperative. Trumpeldor and others joined this advance party in 1912. At its peak, the group numbered 16 members. In 1913, the group disbanded; it did not have the financial means to acquire its own land, there was not enough work available, and the deprivations from which its members suffered led to serious quarrels among them. That same year Trumpeldor attended the 11th Zionist Congress and spent some time in Russia, in order to promote the Jewish National Fund and make propaganda for Aliya. He then returned to Eretz Israel where he worked as an agricultural laborer in Deganya.

After Turkey entered World War I in 1914 Trumpeldor—a Russian national who refused to become an Ottoman citizen—was expelled to Alexandria, Egypt. There he met Vladimir Jabotinsky who, together with Pinhas Rutenberg, was proposing the formation of a *Jewish Legion which would fight with the British in the struggle for Eretz Israel. Jabotinsky and Trumpeldor joined forces, planning to recruit the regiment from among the refugees from Eretz Israel. Jabotinsky withdrew from the project when the British refused to give their consent to a fighting unit which would in time be posted to the front in Eretz Israel; but Trumpeldor thought otherwise and accepted the British offer to establish an auxiliary unit, a mule corps. Trumpeldor was appointed deputy commanding officer of the unit (which came to be known as the *Zion Mule Corps) with the rank of captain. He served with the unit in Gallipoli and towards the end of the campaign became its commanding officer, remaining until the evacuation of the British forces from the peninsula.

When the Mule Corps was disbanded, Trumpeldor again joined with Jabotinsky, then in London, who was continuing his efforts in behalf of a Jewish fighting unit. In March, 1917, following the February Revolution in Russia, Trumpeldor left for his native country, his purpose being to form a Jewish Legion there which would fight its way to Eretz Israel, by way of the Caucasus or Iran. The plan, calling for a force of 100,000, was submitted to the Provisional Government, which was inclined to give its approval. The Bolshevik regime, when it took over, confirmed the creation of the Legion (in December, 1917), but changed its mind and at the end of January, 1918, ordered the Legion to be disbanded.

The growing unrest in the country and the concern that pogroms might break out induced Trumpeldor to form Jewish self-defense organizations, first in Petrograd and then in other parts of the country. He envisioned employing the Legion for this task, but the Bolshevik government soon prohibited the existence of any self-defense organizations.

Trumpeldor was also involved in the He-Halutz movement and launched the unification into a single organization of all the various He-Halutz groups that had sprung up in Russian towns. At the He-Halutz Convention in Petrograd (6 January 1919) he was instrumental in consolidating the movement's ideas. In his view, He-Halutz was to be an advance "army" of toilers who would prepare the ground in Eretz Israel for the creation of a Jewish entity made up of workers' cooperatives ready to serve any national purpose. In due course, governmental power in Eretz Israel would be in the hands of communes. He-Halutz would prepare its members for the tasks awaiting them before they left for Eretz Israel, teach them the required civilian skills, and train them as soldiers. The Convention decided to send Trumpeldor to Southern Russia, to organize He-Halutz branches in that part of the country and then to Eretz Israel for an inspection of conditions there. According to plan he was to return to Russia for another He-Halutz conference. Before leaving Petrograd, Trumpeldor established a training farm ("Hakhshara") in the outskirts of the city. He then proceeded on his trip south, setting up He-Halutz branches in the cities along his route, mainly in the Crimea. From there he continued to Constantinople where many Jewish refugees gathered on their way to Eretz Israel and he established there an information office for laborers' groups.

Trumpeldor arrived in Palestine in October, 1919. His offer to Allenby to form a legion of 10,000 Jews from Russia was rejected. However, his main effort at this stage was to bring about the unification of the two workers' parties within the framework of a single, non-partisan trade union, believing that such an organization was indispensable for the absorption of the masses of Jews who were fleeing the pogroms in Russia and were trying to enter Palestine. In an appeal that he published in the workers' press, he stressed the urgency of his proposal and outlined its basic features. Trumpeldor thus became one of the principal advocates for the establishment of the General Federation of Labor (*Histadrut), which eventually was founded, after his death, in December, 1920.

At this time the Jewish settlements in Upper Galilee were

being subjected to frequent attacks by the Beduin in the area, and Trumpeldor was asked to inspect the situation there and make recommendations for countermeasures to be taken. Arriving on the scene at the end of December, 1919, he intended to stay there for a short while only and then go back to Russia as originally planned. The precarious conditions that he found persuaded him, however, to accede to the request that he take over the command of the defense of the three settlements in the Galilee panhandle—Metula, Kefar Giladi, and Tel Hai. This was where he spent the last two months of his life. On 1 March 1920 five of the men under his command were killed in a Beduin attack, and Trumpeldor himself also suffered fatal wounds. His last words were: "Never mind, it is worthwhile to die for the country" (better known in the form to which it was changed by J.H. Brenner "it is good to die for our country"). The bodies of the fallen defenders were taken to Kefar Giladi and buried there. In 1924, the bodies were reinterred in a new cemetery nearby, between Kefar Giladi and Tel Hai. Since 1934 the site has been marked by the statue of a roaring lion, the work of sculptor Abraham Melnikov.

Trumpeldor had been a living legend and ever since his heroic death his memory has been cherished by the whole Zionist movement. Both the labor movement and the Revisionist party adopted him as their symbol and source of inspiration; Labor took over his socialist ideas, while the Revisionist party hailed his fighter's image and the military program that he had formulated.

A collection of his letters was published under the title *"Mi-Hayei Yoseph Trumpeldor"*—(Tel Aviv, 1953, third ed.). Zionist youth groups make annual pilgrimages to his tomb on the anniversary of his death. On 25 August 1920, a group of members of the Russian He-Halutz, who had reached Palestine illegally via Constantinople, established a labor battalion in Trumpeldor's name (*see* GEDUD AVODAH), a force dedicated to serving the country in the spirit of Trumpeldor's vision. The communal settlement Tel Yosef and the Revisionist youth organization Berit Trumpeldor (*Betar) were named for Trumpeldor. S. LASKOV

Saul Tschernichowsky. [Zionist Archives]

TSCHERNICHOWSKY, SAUL. Hebrew poet (b. Mikhailovka, South Russia, 1875; d. Jerusalem, 1943). Tschernichowsky's parents, although traditional, provided him with a modern education in Jewish and Russian schools. At the age of 15, he was sent to Odessa to a Jewish commercial secondary school and later to a state school, but he preferred a more academic education. On his own, he prepared himself for admission to a university, concentrating on learning foreign languages: Latin, Greek, French, German, and English. This enabled him to read extensively in classical and European literature. While studying in Odessa, he became active in the Zionist movement. He published his first poem in 1892 and his first volume of verse in 1898, *Hezyonot u-Manginot* (Visions and Melodies).

In this early period, Tschernichowsky already employed various poetic *genres* prevailing in European literature to a degree hitherto unequaled by any modern Hebrew poet. Like *Bialik, he adopted the accented line which had recently been introduced into Hebrew poetry. His vocabulary, though mainly biblical, was free of the *pastiche* style (*melitza*) of the preceding generation. In content, these early poems reflect his eye for his native landscape, his zest for life, and his experiences of romantic love. While he advocated a militant Zionism and expressed a deep disdain for life in the Exile, his work is animated by humanistic and even socialist optimism.

In 1899, after failing to gain admission to a Russian university because of anti-Jewish quotas, he enrolled at the University of Heidelberg as a medical student. He completed his medical degree at Lausanne University in 1906. His poems of this period are evidence of the broadening of his range. His encounter with South Germany produced an array of lyrical verse portraying its beautiful landscape and his uninhibited flirtations. At the same time, he began writing ballads and epic poems. *Barukh mi-Magenza* (Baruch of Mainz), set in medieval Mainz during the Crusade period, describes the massacre of the Jews of that city and the avenging heroism of the protagonist. Away from Russia, his "idylls" depict with nostalgic charm the simple life of the Jews of his native province. Yet his contact with Nietzschean ideas then prevailing in Heidelberg and Lausanne led him to criticize the puritanical morality of traditional Judaism and to advocate the Hellenistic ideals of natural and physical beauty. He sings paeans to the pre-Judaic Hebrews and writes sympathetically of ancient Canaanite paganism in poems such as *Ashtarte li* (My Astarte). In "Nocturno" he expresses a romantic, pantheistic view of nature.

When Tschernichowsky returned to Russia in 1906, his lack of a Russian degree made it difficult for him to obtain a proper medical post except in remote areas of South Russia. Finally, in 1910, after receiving a Russian degree, he settled in St. Petersburg. He served as a medical officer during World War I and returned to St. Petersburg following the Russian Revolution. In 1919 he moved to Odessa, where he barely subsisted on a meager medical practice. He was able to leave Russia for Berlin in 1922.

Despite the war, the revolution, and his economic difficulties, Tschernichowsky produced not only a great body of poetry but of prose as well; short stories, scholarly articles, and translations (Anacreon's Poems, 1920; Plato's *Symposium*, the *Iliad*, selections from the *Greek Anthology* as well as Longfellow's *Hiawatha.* Poems written in this turbulent period record his experiences as a military doctor. In the sonnet sequence *La-Shemesh* (To the Sun), Tschernichowsky describes the terror and agony of war but at the same time reasserts his faith in human civilization. Several of his short stories also depict life in the Russian army. A number of additional Idylls were again set in his native Crimea, drawing on memories of the landscape of his childhood and the simple folk who inhabited it.

Tschernichowsky appears to have tried to move to Palestine, after he left Odessa via Istanbul but was unable to find suitable medical employment there. He therefore settled in Berlin, where he struggled to earn a living as a writer. For a time, he served as the literary editor of *Ha-Tekufa*, a prestigious Hebrew periodical, and as editor of the medical and natural science sections of the Hebrew encyclopedia, *Eshkol*.

During the German period, he wrote a great number of short-stories, including and feuilletons. He also published numerous translations: *Renke, the Fox*, by Goethe, *Twelfth Night* and *Macbeth* by Shakespeare, Sophocles' *Oedipus Rex*, and Homer's *Odyssey, The Gilgamesh Epic*, and the *Kalevala*. He also wrote *Bar Kochba*, an historical play and a literary essay on the Italian Hebrew poet Immanuel of Rome (1925). In 1934, toward the end of his sojourn in Germany, a ten-volume edition of his collected works appeared.

The epic poems *Mayim shelanu* (Our Waters) and *Al ha-Dam* (On the Blood) describe the deprivations he experienced in Odessa during the revolution. Gone is the optimism which permeated his earlier works. Love seems to be replaced by faith, and the light-hearted devil-may-care attitude of the younger poet toward women gives way to a mystical yearning. The poet's belief in the redemptive power of art and beauty now is modified by his awareness that full aesthetic attainment is beyond his reach. His failure to settle in Palestine filled him with anguish. During this period, he wrote some of his more moving "Zionist" lyrics, e.g., *Omerim yesh sham Aretz* (They say there is a Land). He finally found the opportunity to migrate to Palestine when he was invited to edit a trilingual lexicon of medical and natural science terminology. When the lexicon was completed, he was appointed as physician to the Tel Aviv school system. In 1936, Schocken Publishing House put him on an annual retainer, enabling him to devote his efforts exclusively to writing, and shortly thereafter he moved to Jerusalem.

After several years of acclimatization to his new environment, Tschernichowsky resumed his habitual literary output. He adopted the Sephardi pronunciation of Hebrew with its shift of accent. Thematically, he now dealt with the struggles of the yishuv under the Palestine Mandate, taking a strong nationalist position. As World War II engulfed European Jewry, he returned to the tragedy of Jewish fate, depicting the persecution of Jews in medieval Europe in. These events became metaphors for the Holocaust which was decimating contemporary European Jewry. The tragedy of the Holocaust softened his anti-traditional bias. The *Idylls* written in this period tend to idealize the world of his childhood. As his years in Palestine lengthened, his poems became somewhat less enthusiastic about life there, often revealing slight feelings of alienation. The long poem *Ama di-Dehava* is probably the most important long poem written by any Hebrew poet in the 1930s. It is an attempt to reconcile the conflict between the poet's sense of alienation and his longing for his native land with his love for his historic homeland. He accepts the fact that he will never succeed in "feeling at home" either in his place of birth or in his newly acquired homeland: he is a citizen of the world who embraces the culture of all mankind. The passages depicting the landscapes of Palestine, the rich and graphic description of the world of bee-raising, and the mature humor of the speaker of the poem are poetry on its highest level.

While Tschernichowsky's worldview was not startlingly original, his zest for life, his powers of observation, the versatility of his craft, and his keen ear earned him great esteem. As a Hebrew poet, he was considered second only to Bialik. E. SPICEHANDLER

TSCHLENOW, YEHIEL. Physician and early Zionist leader (b. Kremenchug, Russia, 1863; d. London, 1918). Tschlenow was reared and educated in Moscow, where he practiced medicine. As a youth he was active in Hovevei Zion work with Menahem Ussishkin, and even after his acceptance of Herzlian Zionism and posts in the World Zionist Organization (WZO), he continued to emphasize the ideology of Hovevei Zion: gradual settlement in Eretz Israel and dedicated efforts to revive Hebrew literature and culture. He was elected to the Greater Actions Committee at the Second Zionist Congress (1898), became head of the Moscow Zionist District and director of the Jewish National Fund, and worked as a Zionist organizer, propagandist, and fundraiser. Calm and deliberate, he prevented many clashes and held together dissenting groups of extremists.

When Herzl presented the Uganda proposal to the Sixth Congress (1903), Tschlenow led the walkout of those who insisted in Eretz Israel as the only possible Jewish Homeland. He continued to oppose Uganda but avoided a break with Herzl because he was concerned with the unity and preservation of the WZO.

Tschlenow was offered the presidency of the WZO after Herzl's death but declined it, preferring to continue as head of the Russian Zionists. He took part in the Language War resulting from the dispute over the language of instruction to be used at the Haifa Technion. When the supporters of the German language on the Technion Board of Governors gained the majority, Tschlenow resigned, along with Ahad Ha-Am and Shemarya Levin, and proceeded to raise funds and win supporters for the cause of Hebrew as the language of instruction in all Jewish schools in Eretz Israel.

In 1913 he was elected vice-chairman of the World Zionist Executive. He moved temporarily to Berlin, seat of the new Zionist headquarters, to perform administrative tasks. After the outbreak of World War I, Tschlenow was forced to return to Moscow but continued to carry on his work. Despite his poor health and the personal risks involved, he traveled to Executive meetings held in Copenhagen and supported neutralism on the part of the WZO rather than alliance with any of the belligerent powers. He helped formulate the postwar demands of the Zionists, namely, Jewish autonomy in Palestine and equal rights for Jews elsewhere.

Late in 1914 he went to London with Nahum Sokolow as emissary of the Zionist Executive and met Chaim Weizmann and other Zionist leaders. He was invited by the Provisional Executive Committee for General Zionist Affairs to go to New York but felt that his duty lay in Moscow. He returned and headed Jewish relief work there, aiding refugees fleeing or driven back from the eastern front.

After the downfall of the Tsarist government, Tschlenow was chairman of the All-Russia Zionist Conference in Petrograd at which the Russian Zionist position was formulated. Even after the Anglo-Zionist negotiations for a pro-Zionist declaration on Palestine were under way, he clung to the policy of neutrality. He considered that any departure from neutrality would expose the yishuv to repression by the Turkish military authorities.

Urged by Weizmann and Sokolow to come to London to participate in the final stages of the negotiations with the British as the representative of Russian Zionism, he heeded their call despite his poor health. He welcomed the Balfour Declaration as a sign of recognition of the Jews as full-fledged members of the family of nations.

Tschlenow was not a colorful, controversial figure. He

represented middle-of-the-road leadership and kept the Zionist movement unified even in times of stress without ever surrendering his principles. He was loved and respected by all factions. S. KLING

TSUR (TCHERNOWITZ), JACOB. Israeli diplomat and administrator (b. Vilna, Russia, 1906; d. Jerusalem 1990). Tsur went to Palestine with his family in 1921. He studied in Florence and at the Sorbonne in Paris, and upon his return to Palestine in 1929 entered the service of the Zionist movement. During World War II he headed the Jewish Agency's office in Egypt; after the liberation of Greece (1944) he headed the rescue mission to that country sponsored by the UN Relief and Rehabilitation Administration (UNRRA). In 1948 he became Israel's first diplomatic representative in South America, serving until 1953 as Minister Plenipotentiary to Argentina, Chile, Paraguay, and Uruguay. From 1953 to 1956 he was Ambassador to France. In 1956 he was elected chairman of the Jewish National Fund, a position he held until 1977. He also served as chairman of the Executive Board of the Bialik Foundation and president of the Central Institute for Cultural Relations Israel-South America, Spain, and Portugal.

Tsur wrote numerous articles and several books including *Sunrise in Zion* (English ed., 1968), *Paris Diary* (in Hebrew, 1968; in French, *Prélude à Suez*, 1968, and edited *Portrait of the Diaspora* (Hebrew, 1975).

TUL KARM. Arab district town in Samaria, on the rim of the Sharon Plain 9 miles (15 km.) east of Netanya. According to archeological evidence, it was inhabited at least from the Roman period. Its Arabic name is derived from the Aramaic "Tur Karma" ("Vineyard Hill"), given by its Samaritan inhabitants of the Middle Ages. Farming citrus and other partly-irrigated crops, it expanded in the 20th century, as the Haifa—Lydda railroad and a highway passed nearby. A farm school for Arab youth was built with the contribution of the Jewish financier Y. Kadourie to the mandatory government. In the 1949 armistice agreement, Tul Karm was left under Jordanian rule but Israel's border included some of its land and the railroad line. In the Six-Day War, Tul Karm was taken by Israel forces on 7 June 1967. Under Israel administration, the town grew rapidly from 10,157 inhabitants, in 1967, nearly all Moslems. Several thousand live in a refugee camp which in effect is part of the town. E. ORNI

TUNISIA, ZIONISM IN. *See* NORTH AFRICA, ZIONISM IN.

TUNISIAN JEWS IN ISRAEL. Tunisian Jewry always had a strong link with Eretz Israel. Famous rabbis and talmudists (Zemah Sarfati, Nathan Borgel, and Yehuda Sfez) spent the last years of their lives in the Holy Land. The awakening of political Zionism in the early 20th century gave a strong impetus to the Zionist movement, expressed in political activity, the multiplication of newspapers and youth movements, and the teaching of Hebrew.

After the departure of the Nazis (1943), emissaries of the *Mosad created a Hagana network which took root in many towns. In 1947, two ships, the *Yehuda Halevi* and the *Shivat Zion*, left the port of Algiers with over 400 "illegal" immigrants on board. The creation of the State of Israel was greeted with joy and between 1948 and 1953, pushed by Zionist and religious ideas, over 15,000 Tunisian Jews realized the age-old promise: "Next year in Jerusalem."

Immigrants from Tunisia preparing red peppers for processing. [Keren HaYesod]

The immigration of young people was organized by Youth Aliya, and departures did not cease, even after a plane from Tunisia carrying young people destined for Israel crashed in Norway in November 1949, leaving 29 children dead. Youth Aliya continued its work, absorbing several thousand young people in its network of institutions in Israel.

The struggle for Tunisian independence accelerated the general aliya of Tunisian Jewry, and between the declaration of internal autonomy (1954) and the declaration of the Republic (1957), nearly 18,000 Jews immigrated to Israel. Arriving during the period of consolidation of the moshavim and the development towns, they were settled throughout Israel in the framework of Operation "Ship to Village."

The disbanding of Jewish institutions in Tunisia, the expulsion of all Israeli emissaries and the rupture of postal ties with Israel (1958) gave a further impetus to the process, and in this period alone nearly two thousand Tunisian Jews arrived in Israel. The Bizerta crisis between Tunisia and France (1961) further precipitated Jewish emigration, but at this time most of the community had left the country.

Over half the Jewish population of Tunisia (55,000 out of the 1948 population of 105,000) arrived in Israel up to 1988 (600 before 1948; 15,000 in 1948–1953; 18,000 in 1954–1957; 4,500 in 1958–1961; 6,000 in 1962–1966; 5,500 in 1968–1970; and 5,400 in 1971–1988). Not only the poor masses but also the elite were attracted to the Zionist idea, which was seldom the case elsewhere in North Africa. This is perhaps one reason for their successful absorption in Israeli society and their positive reputation in the country. Tunisian Jewry also integrated well into the political scene, with a representation completely disproportionate to their numbers (including Aharon Uzan, the first Minister of Immigration in an Israeli government, Knesset members, mayors and senior officials).

Tunisian immigrants settled throughout Israel. The first arrivals in the 1940s lived in the alleys of old Jaffa, or settled at the edge of the desert in Beersheba. Kiryat Gat and the moshavim of the Lachish region and elsewhere became home to the immigrants of the 1950s. There are 16 exclusively or mainly Tunisian moshavim: Gilat, Sharsheret, Yanuv, Berekhiya, Azrikam, Kelahim, Petahya, Kefar Avdon, Nir Yafeh, Eitan, Bet ha-Gadi, Zimrat, Zohar, Telamim, Sedeh Tzevi, and Tzerufa.

Jews from the vibrant communities of southern Tunisia can be found in Safed and Tiberias, while many from La Goulette (Halq al-Wadi) settled in Netanya. Other immigrants live in Ashkelon, Netivot, Ofakim, Lydda, Ramleh, Dimona and the large cities, permanent home to the middle calsses and the immigrants recently arrived via France. The members of the kibbutzim (Regavim and Karmiya) include intellectuals who once trained the militants and leaders of the Zionist movement in Tunisia.

Official organizations, both academic and in the arts, have manifested an increasing interest in the past and the cultural and spiritual patrimony of Tunisian Jewry. The Jews of Djerba reconstructed the Ghariba synagogue in Ofakim. On 7 May 1984, Israel Independence Day and the 41st anniversary of the Allied liberation of Tunis, Tunisian immigrants planted a forest in commemoration of the Tunisian vicitms of the Nazis and of the heroes of the Resistance; and Beth Hatefutzoth (the Museum of the Jewish Diaspora) in Tel Aviv organized a successful exhibition in 1986 on Tunisian Jewry, entitled "From Carthage to Jerusalem: The Jewish Community of Tunis." C. SITBON

TURKEY. *See* OTTOMAN JEWRY AND ZIONISM.

TURKEY, RELATIONS WITH ISRAEL. Israel's first Prime Minister, David Ben-Gurion, from the establishment of the State attempted to promote a rapprochement with Moslem, non-Arab countries which formed part of or bordered the Middle East, in an attempt to offset Israel's encirclement by hostile Arab nations. As part of this strategy ties were developed, *inter alia* with Iran, Ethiopia, and Turkey.

Because of Moslem solidarity and its own interest in continuing British influence in the Middle East in case of a Soviet attack, Turkey voted against the partition of Palestine in 1947. However, it extended to Israel *de jure* recognition in 1949 and established diplomatic relations. The first Israeli Ambassador to France, Maurice Fisher, considered relations with Turkey of such importance that he had no hesitation in ceding his ambassadorship in order to head a legation in Ankara. Initial relations between Israel and Turkey were marked by a desire for cooperation. A trade agreement was signed in 1950, followed by an air transport agreement in 1951, inaugurating regular Israeli and Turkish flights between both countries.

During this period Turkey viewed Israel as a pro-western, secular, democratic, "European"-style country, constituting to some extent an island in a Moslem and Arab sea of dictatorships. Fearing Syrian aggression (after its conflict over the *sanjak* of Alexandretta) and the cooperation between Armenian and Palestinian terrorists, Turkey felt it had certain common interests with Israel.

From 1955, however, following the signing of the Baghdad Pact, Turkey began to move closer to the Arab countries and to diminish its relations with Israel. In the wake of the 1956 Sinai Campaign, it reduced the level of diplomatic representation, leaving its legation under a chargé d'affaires. Nevertheless, Arab pressure for complete

Israel's first consul in Turkey celebrating Israel Independence Day, 1949. [Beth Hatefutsoth]

severance of diplomatic ties was resisted.

The Cyprus troubles in 1963–64 and the aggravation of the conflict with Greece led Turkey increasingly to seek the support of the Arab world in the UN, and after 1967 it joined the bloc of countries condemning the "acquisition of territories by force." In 1971, the Israel consul in Istanbul, Ephraim Elrom, was kidnaped and murdered by terrorists. The Turkish government ascribed the crime to left-wing circles whose action was directed not only against Israel but against the Turkish regime.

Rapprochement with the Arab and Moslem world was further strengthened following the 1980 coup and in the wake of economic and energy problems. Relations with Israel were reduced to a minimum, and after the passing of the Jerusalem Law (1980), Turkey placed its diplomatic representation under a second secretary. Up until 1985, political relations remained at the lowest possible level.

From 1983, with the amelioration in the economic situation, and the decline in the importance of the Arab market, Turkey manifested a desire to improve relations. Oil became a less effective weapon and Turkey's interests lay in the direction of the European Economic Community and the USA.

The first new agreements between Turkey and Israel were in the field of trade relations, development of which has since been constant but cautious, since the Turks wish to keep a low profile in their relations with Israel.

Turkey's behavior can be attributed to its need to improve its image as much as possible in the USA in light of attacks by the Greeks and the Armenians, and because of the military regime which held power for several years. Turkey's longstanding resistance to the pressures of Israel's enemies and its failure to adopt a more hostile policy to Israel lie in its wish not to alienate American sympathies. In 1986 Turkey agreed to restore the level of diplomatic representation to that of Minister Plenipotentiary.

The Lebanon War and the disturbances in the Israeli Administered Areas from December 1987—and above all their presentation in the media—had repercussions in Turkish public opinion and in its media. Criticisms of Israeli policies, both by left-wing and right-wing elements, were accompanied at times by an anti-Semitism quickly denounced by the authorities when it involved attacks on Jews, as in the terrorist attack on Istanbul's main synagogue in 1987.

Official reactions were less direct. Turkey, like other western countries, condemned certain aspects of Israeli policy in the Administered Areas, and supported the principle of an international conference to resolve the Arab-Israeli conflict. Unlike Greece, however, it offered little effective support to the Palestinian cause. It participated in the work of the Islamic Conference, but did not play a major role, wary of spreading Moslem fundamentalism. Trade relations are a good index of the relations between the two countries, since these can only develop with the permission of the authorities. Commercial exchanges between Israel and Turkey totaled 50 million dollars in 1987; Israel's 33 million dollars of exports were comprised mainly of agricultural produce, phosphates, textiles, plastics, chemical products, metallurgy, and light manufactured goods. Israel imported mostly dried fruit and vegetables.

Turkey remained subject to strong Arab and Soviet pressures for a more active support of the Arab positions, but also had to take into account American reactions. The search for a balance in its relations with the two superpowers determined, to some degree, its policy towards Israel. Israel, for its part, endeavored to make allowances for a certain Turkish "sensitivity" caused by its inevitable feelings of Moslem solidarity. D. CATARIVAS

TURKISH JEWS IN ISRAEL. The main immigration from Turkey to Israel occurred immediately after the establishment of the State (1948–50), when almost half of the Jews of Turkey moved to Israel. 4,362 Turkish Jews immigrated in 1948 but then there was a hiatus of several months as the result of Arab pressure. However, the movement was renewed in 1949 and Turkey allowed its merchant ships to transport the migrants. 26,295 went to Israel in 1949–50. Afterwards the numbers dropped, although there was no prohibition. Between 1948 and 1970, 37,000 Turkish Jews immigrated to Israel, of whom about a tenth returned to Turkey. There has been a constant record of aliya with increases particularly noticeable during times of crisis in Turkey and special periods in Israel, such as in the wake of the Six-Day War.

The large immigration of 1948–50 included many of the poorer elements, as well as numerous idealists and affluent and educated Jews who were attracted by the challenge of a Jewish State.

By 1988, it was estimated that over 60,000 Turkish Jews were living in Israel. There were several geographical concentrations. Many of the poorer Jews who arrived in 1948–50 settled in Yahud, where they have moved up the socioeconomic ladder. Those from the middle classes who arrived in the 1960s and 1970s live largely in Bat Yam, where there are also many Turkish clubs and restaurants. The wealthy and professional immigrants have settled in the north Tel Aviv area. Turkish Jews are also to be found in Ramleh, Lydda, and Tel Hanan. Turkish Jews are also scattered in many towns and villages. Turkish Jews founded the moshavim of Burgeta, Geva Carmel, and Tal Shahar, and the kibbutzim of Ha-Gosherim and Ruhama. Among places where Turkish pioneering groups were to be found from the 1940s were Kefar Giladi, Ashdot Ya'akov, Nir Eliahu, Tel Yosef, Ayelet ha-Shahar, Afikim, and Givat Brenner.

In their occupations, they are workers, businessmen, and professionals. Few are to be found in public positions and offices; since the foundation of the State there has only been one Knesset member of Turkish origin.

Three organizations aim at bringing Turkish-Jewish culture to public attention and to work with the Turkish Jews. The Association of Immigrants from Turkey, after a period of inactivity, has been revived and developed an extensive program; Morit is a foundation for the establishment of a center for Turkish-Jewish culture in Israel; and there is an active Turkish lodge of B'nai B'rith. The Turkish Jews around the country usually retain close connections with others from Turkey and with the Turkish organizations. Altogether, they have proved a well-adjusted and successful element who have made many positive contributions to Israeli society.

TUR-SINAI, NAPHTALI HERZ (Harry Torczyner). Hebrew philologist (b. Lvov, Galicia, Austria, 1886; d. Jerusalem, 1973). He studied at the universities of Vienna and Berlin and at the Vienna Rabbinical Seminary. From 1910 to 1912 he taught at the Hebrew High School of Jerusalem and from 1913 to 1919 at Vienna University. He was a founder and principal of the Hebrew Pedagogium in Vienna (1918–19) and taught at the Hochschule für die Wissenschaft des Judentums in Berlin (1919–33). In 1933 he became professor of Hebrew philology at the Hebrew University of Jerusalem, a position he held until his retirement in 1955.

Tur-Sinai wrote numerous scholarly works on the Bible and on Hebrew philology and edited a German translation of the Bible and the final volumes of Eliezer *Ben-Yehuda's thesaurus of the Hebrew language. He was cochairman of the Va'ad ha-Lashon ha-Ivrit (*see* HEBREW LANGUAGE ACADEMY) from 1943 to 1953, when he became its president. From 1934 to 1954 he was the editor of its periodical *Leshonenu* (Our Language). In 1956 he was awarded the Israel Prize for Jewish studies. Prominently associated with movements to propagate the knowledge of Hebrew and Hebrew literature, he served as chairman of the preparatory committee for the convocation of the Congress of Hebrew Culture, which was held in conjunction with the 11th Zionist Congress in Vienna in 1913.

An active Zionist from his youth on, Tur-Sinai was a delegate to the 12th Zionist Congress (1921).

TZE'IREI ZION. Zionist movement of eastern European origin. Its name means "Youth of Zion." Zionist youth

Group of Tze'irei Zion in Kishinev, 1905. [Central Zionist Archives]

groups known as Tze'irei Zion or Ha-Tehiya sprang up in Russia and Galicia at the beginning of the 20th century. Here and there (e.g., Ha-Tehiya in Warsaw, 1903; Tze'irei Zion in Kishinev, 1906) attempts at separate program formulations were made. But in contrast to the Po'ale Zion movement, Tze'irei Zion considered itself an integral part of the World Zionist Organization (WZO), stressing allegiance to the Zionist Congress and to the revival of Hebrew. Tze'irei Zion derived its inspiration from *Ha-Po'el ha-Tza'ir in Eretz Israel. The First World Conference of Tze'irei Zion was held in Vienna in 1913 simultaneously with the 11th Zionist Congress. this conference was attended by delegates from Ha-Po'el ha-Tza'ir.

World Tze'irei Zion headquarters was set up in Warsaw. By 1914 the movement embraced 165 groups throughout Russia with a combined membership of more than 8,000. Its organ was *Shaharit*, a bimonthly edited by Samuel Eisenstat. With impetus of the Russian Revolution of 1917, Tze'irei Zion became a mass movement; its following numbered in the tens of thousands. At a Tze'irei Zion conference held in May, 1917, in Petrograd, several differing ideological trends emerged. The "Socialist-popular" trend stressed the vital necessity of changing the economic structure of the Jewish people if any improvement was to be effected in the situation of the Jews in Palestine as well as in the Diaspora. The "laborite" trend, on the other hand, held that although the movement should be based on working people and youth, it should dissociate itself from Socialist slogans. The conference decided to organize Tze'irei Zion as a "popular faction" within the WZO. During the Russian Revolution, Tze'irei Zion played a significant role in the founding of the pioneering organization He-Halutz in Russia and in the formation of Jewish self-defense groups.

After the Bolshevik takeover, Tze'irei Zion was forced underground in Russia. Tze'irei Zion groups were formed in Poland, Lithuania, Latvia, and Bessarabia. At a conference held in Prague in March, 1920, the delegates from Tze'irei Zion and those from Ha-Po'el ha-Tza'ir (including such leaders as Hayim Arlosoroff, Samuel Hugo Bergmann, Martin Buber, and Eliezer Kaplan, representing the Tze'irei Zion groups of Europe, and Joseph Aronowics, Aharon David Gordon, and Yosef Sprinzak, representing Ha-Po'el ha-Tza'ir of Palestine) decided to merge in a movement to be called the World *Hitahdut. The left wing of Tze'irei Zion thereupon seceded and constituted itself the Tze'irei Zion-Tzioyonim Sozialistim (Zionist Socialist) party.

Following systematic suppression by the Soviet regime, both wings of T1ze'irei Zion ceased to exist in Russia. Outside Russia Tze'irei Zion-Tziyonom Sozialistim united with the Right Po'ale Zion in 1925 under the name Po'ale Zion-Tziyonim Sozialistim. In 1932, under the impact of the unification of the workers' parties in Palestine (*see* MAPAI), the Hitahdut and Po'ale Zion-Tziyonim Sozialistim merged into the *Ihud Olami (World Union of Zionists-Socialists).

Members of Tze'irei Zion of all trends played leading roles in the workers' movement of Palestine.

Y. SLUTSKY

TZE'IREI ZION HITAHDUT OF AMERICA. Zionist faction in the United States established in 1920 by a group of radical Zionists who were critical of the policies of the leadership of the Zionist Organization of America (ZOA). Its founding convention, which met in Rochester, N.Y., in November, 1920, adopted resolutions to the effect that Tze'irei Zion would consider itself a part of the World Zionist Organization and a faction within the ZOA with certain autonomous rights; that it would advocate the nationalization of the land and industry of Eretz Israel (which was to be built on the principle of social justice by Jewish labor without exploiters or exploited), and the establishment of cooperative banks and institutions for aliya; that it would organize He-Halutz groups in the United States for the training of craftsmen who would settle in Palestine; that it would help organize the Jewish masses of the United States in a socioeconomic and Jewish cultural sense; and that it would be active in Jewish educational institutions, participate in activities on behalf of world Jewry, and support Hebrew as the national language of the Jewish people.

A resolution was also introduced that the organization join the World *Hitahdut (the union of the *Tze'irei Zion in Europe and Ha-Po'el ha-Tza'ir of Palestine), which had been formed in March, 1920. Action on this resolution was deferred until the next convention. The second convention, which met in Philadelphia in 1921, adopted the resolution, adding that Tze'irei Zion would also cooperate with the ZOA. This decision was the cause of frequent friction among the leaders, and it was decided at the third convention (Rochester, 1922) that Tze'irei Zion function as a separate, independent Zionist organization. Some of the members who disagreed with this decision left the party.

In 1923 Tze'irei Zion began to publish a Yiddish biweekly, *Farn Folk*. It developed a diversified cultural program that was intensified with the arrival in 1924 of the Hitahdut leaders Hayim *Greenberg and Dr. David Rebelsky. A party seminar and an open forum headed by Greenberg were established in New York. These soon attracted hundreds of regular participants.

Tze'irei Zion members were active in raising money for the Jewish National Fund. In 1921 the organization established the Keren he-Halutz, the proceeds of which were to support the Halutz (pioneer) movement in Europe, particularly in Russia. It sold shares for the Bank ha-Po'alim in Palestine and aided the Geverkshaften Campaign to raise money for the Histadrut and its institutions. The members taxed themselves a day's earnings for the various funds and for Jewish labor in Palestine.

By 1924–25 there were 40 Tze'irei Zion branches in the United States and Canada, with a total membership of well over 3,000. Tze'irei Zion made educational work among American Jewish youth a prime objective, establishing English-speaking branches for this purpose. In 1925 youth groups were organized under the name Gordonia, modeled on the *Gordonia youth movement in Europe. A group of Tze'irei Zion members organized a Bet he-Halutz in Philadelphia to train prospective pioneers for Palestine. In 1927 this group went to Petaluma, Calif., to train in various phases of agriculture before going to Palestine to live on a kibbutz. The Tze'irei Zion was also instrumental in the establishment in 1929 of the *hakhshara* training farm in Hightstown, N.J.

Hayim Arlosoroff, who visited the United States and Canada in 1926 and 1927, engaged in propaganda work for the Tze'irei Zion. Under his leadership the party embarked on an elaborate program of English-language Zionist educational publications under the title *The Young Jew Series.*

The biweekly *Farn Folk* became a weekly in November 1926. Between February, 1927, and February, 1929, it was edited by Hayim Greenberg. It gained prestige from its serious articles and editorials on Zionist and general Jewish affairs as well as on educational, cultural, and literary matters.

Following the merger in Palestine of Ha-Po'el ha-Tza'ir and Ahdut Avoda in 1930, Tze'irei Zion and Po'ale Zion in America decided to merge in October, 1932, at a joint convention held in Philadelphia. L. RUBINSTEIN

TZEMAH, SHELOMO. *See* ZEMACH, SHELOMO.

TZEFAT. *See* SAFED.

TZIYONEI ZION. Trend within the World Zionist Organization in 1903–05 that opposed the consideration of East Africa or of any territory other than Eretz Israel as a Jewish Homeland (*see* EAST AFRICA SCHEME). The Tziyonei Zion group was formed in opposition to the resolution taken by the Sixth Zionist Congress (1903) to send a commission of inquiry to East Africa to evaluate the feasibility of Jewish settlement there. The opponents of that resolution were mainly the Russian Zionists, who remained loyal to their primary attachment to Eretz Israel and active settlement work even though they had accepted Herzl's political Zionism.

At the time of the Congress Menahem Ussishkin was in Eretz Israel, endeavoring to establish an organization of the Jews of the country. An outspoken opponent of the East Africa scheme, he set about organizing the Russian Zionists against Herzl. In October, 1903, he convened the Kharkov Conference, which rebelled against Herzl's leadership, demanded a limitation to his authority, and called for effective control of his political activities and expenses. It also clamored for abandonment of the East Africa proposal and of any future proposal for Zionist settlement outside Eretz Israel. The conference warned Herzl that if this were not done, all Zionist work would be stopped and a separate organization established.

This extreme opposition brought a reaction of support for Herzl, expressed in a conference held in Warsaw. Herzl himself refused to receive a delegation sent to him by the Kharkov Conference, but he was impressed by its stubborn adherence to the Land of Israel. At the last session of the Zionist General Council in which Herzl participated (April, 1904), he demanded obedience to the resolution of the Congress but declared his basic allegiance to Eretz Israel.

After Herzl's death, the Tziyonei Zion strove to assume leadership; the East Africa plan seemed impractical because of a negative report submitted by the commission of inquiry. But the problem turned out to be a problem of principle: could any territorial solution outside Eretz Israel be considered by the Zionist Organization? The election campaign for the Seventh Zionist Congress (1905) concentrated on this crucial problem. The debate cut across national organization and party lines. Those who emphasized the urgency of a solution and the economic need of the Jewish masses were opposed by those whose deep-rooted loyalty to Eretz Israel precluded any other consideration.

Tziyonei Zion carried the day at the Seventh Congress. Territorialism was rejected, and steps were taken for more active work in Eretz Israel according to Ussishkin's policy as formulated in what he called "our program."

I. KOLATT

TZIPORI. Moshav in Lower Galilee, 3 mi. (5 km.) northwest of Nazareth, founded by immigrants from Bulgaria in 1949 near the abandoned Arab village of Saffuriyye. There was a turnover of settlers, leaving immigrants from North Africa in the majority. The economy is based on mixed farming. There is a Jewish National Fund forest and tree nursery and large afforestation projects have been carried out in the vicinity. This is the site of the ancient city of Sepphoris (Tzipori), capital of Galilee in Second Temple times and seat of the Patriarchate in the late 2nd -early 3rd centuries CE. In 1987, Tzipori numbered 309 inhabitants.

E. ORNI

TZIYON. *See* ZION.

TZOHAR. *See* REVISIONISTS.

U

UGANDA SCHEME. *See* EAST AFRICA SCHEME.

UJA. *See* UNITED JEWISH APPEAL.

ULPAN (Heb. "place of study," plural: ulpanim). Intensive Hebrew courses. After the establishment of the State of Israel, Ulpanim were set up to meet the needs of thousands of new immigrants who arrived in Israel without knowing how to communicate in modern Hebrew. The first Ulpan, Ulpan Etzion, was established in Jerusalem in 1949. Many of the students lived on the premises and were freed from the responsibility of earning a living for the duration of the intensive-study course.

Ulpanim teaching Hebrew to adults subsequently opened all over the country under the auspices of the Ministry of Education and Culture in conjunction with the Jewish Agency. The Israel army, faced with the immediate need to teach basic Hebrew to the many soldiers originating from all over the world, also opened Ulpanim at Camp Marcus.

The Ulpan network's general aim is to facilitate the absorption of new immigrants from different social and economic backgrounds. The Ulpan stresses the imparting of a language and a culture as opposed to teaching a second language. It also tries to give the students an understanding of fundamental Jewish and Israeli values to help acclimatize and integrate the student into Israel's economic and social life.

Several types of Ulpanim are available in Israel today. The most popular is the Absorption Center Ulpan which is a 5-month program for the families living at the center. In 1988 there were 360 Ulpan classes with 5,280 students in these centers under the auspices of the Jewish Agency and Ministry of Absorption. There are also a number of immigrant hostel Ulpanim where the immigrants maintain themselves. Another alternative is the Kibbutz Ulpan which caters for 17–35 year-olds. In these 5-month Ulpanim the students study for half the day and work the other half. In 1988 there were 59 classes at various kibbutzim containing 1,201 students. There are also a number of non-residential Ulpanim, usually run by local authorities, where students can study mornings or evenings. Another option is the "Ulpaniot" where students study 2–3 times a week for a year. In 1988 there were 235 classes run by local authorities and various public institutions, with 4,066 students. Other Ulpan programs include vocational retraining Ulpanim, a study month program, university Ulpanim for overseas students, and a special program given at Ulpan Akiva, Netanya to teach Hebrew to Arabs, Druze, and Samaritans.

In the mid-1980s a new type of Ulpan was required to meet the needs of a new wave of immigration from Ethiopia. These new immigrants had previously lived in isolated circumstances; many were illiterate even in their mother-tongue and so the Ulpan had to expand its aims in order to teach basic learning skills and help the immigrants overcome the cultural shock of a modern society. The Ministry of Education developed a new integral program to teach the basics of the Hebrew language as well as other subjects including arithmetic, religious practices and tradition, to bridge the gap between the two diverse cultures while paying particular care to respect the Ethiopian culture. The Department of Adult Education at the Ministry of Education and Culture is responsible for preparing and publishing all Ulpan curricula and for establishing the teaching methods to be employed. Hebrew is taught in Hebrew to small classes of 15–20 students. Teaching material emphasizes the development of the students' communicative ability. Lessons are built around linguistic situations constituting a topic with vocabulary and paradigm incorporated according to linguistic and didactic considerations. The Ulpan system calls on the active involvement of the student in the classroom.

On the basis of the success of the Ulpan method in Israel, Ulpanim for the intensive study of Hebrew have been established in other countries. Furthermore the system has been adapted to teach other languages abroad. E. HOTER

UM AL-FAHM. Moslem-Arab town on the "Iron Hills" east of the "Iron Valley." It incorporates a number of villages in the valley and on the hills. It received town status in 1985, but still found it hard to finance the necessary municipal services for its citizens. Its name, "Mother of Coal", points to the region's woodland vegetation which through centuries served as a raw material for local charcoal burning. Population (1987), 23,100. E. ORNI

UNGAR, BELA. Lawyer, editor, and Zionist leader (b. Nagyteteny, Hungary, 1899; d. Jerusalem, 1974). Ungar completed his studies at the Universities of Budapest and Pozsony (now Bratislava), where he earned the degree of doctor of laws in 1922. He was a founder of Hasmonea, a high school students' Zionist organization, and served as president of Makkabea (Maccabi), the Hungarian Zionist students' organization, from 1917 to 1919. He played a leading role in the Hungarian Zionist Federation, first as its national secretary (1923—24) and then as editor of the Zionist weekly *Zsido Szemle* (Jewish Spectator) (1924–27), as a member of its National Executive Committee (1927–39), and finally as its vice-president (1922–44). He also served as first secretary of Hungarian Mizrahi in 1939-40.

Following the Nazi invasion of Hungary in 1944, Ungar was active in rescue and relief work. After the war, he was among the organizers and leaders of the Hungarian section of the World Jewish Congress and, as its delegate, attended conferences of Prague, London (1947), and the Second Plenary Assembly, Montreux (1948). He also served as a Hungarian director of the American Jewish Joint Distribution Committee, in charge of the Department for the Provinces (1946–48), and as Legal Counselor of the Israeli Consulate in Budapest. In 1950, he settled in Israel, where he worked as an editor of the weekly *Nepunk* (Our People), and served as president of the Hitahdut Olei Hungaria (Association of Immigrants from Hungary), (1957—1959).

R.L. BRAHAM

UNION OF KEVUTZOT AND KIBBUTZIM. *See* IHUD HA-KEVUTZOT VE-HAKIBBUTZIM.

UNION OF ZIONISTS-REVISIONISTS-HATZOHAR. *See* REVISIONISTS.

UNITED ISRAEL APPEAL. *See* UNITED JEWISH APPEAL; UNITED PALESTINE APPEAL.

UNITED JEWISH APPEAL (UJA). Joint annual fundraising campaign in the USA for the development of the Jewish National Home in Palestine and, from 1948 on, of Israel, and for the relief and reconstruction of stricken Jewish communities all over the world. Over the years, the United Jewish Appeal has steadily grown in importance as a concrete, material expression of the American Jewish community's support for fellow Jews in other lands and for the State of Israel. The UJA began to function as a continuous operation in 1939. Previous intermittent attempts at unified fund drives had failed because of meager financial results and ideological differences over the building of the National Home. Despite these differences on the national level, in 1938, the last year prior to the establishment of the UJA, no fewer than 299 localities in the United States conducted local combined drives for the *United Palestine Appeal (UPA) and the *American Jewish Joint Distribution Committee (JDC), and 156 Jewish Welfare Fund communities allotted funds to the national organizations. When the Nazis perpetrated the infamous *Kristallnacht* (Crystal Night pogrom, during which there was wholesale destruction of synagogues) on 10 November 1938 throughout Germany, the JDC Executive acceded to the suggestion of Rabbi Jonah B. Wise, who had visited Germany and returned with the idea of establishing a UJA. It was decided in December to launch the United Jewish Appeal for 1939.

Participants in the UJA were the UPA, the JDC, and the National Refugee Service, an American organization for aiding Jewish refugees from Nazi-controlled countries in Europe which joined as a beneficiary and not as a principal partner. The main advocates of UJA were leaders of the local communities, who recognized the advantages of one combined drive for overseas Jewish needs and local communal requirements.

During the initial period of UJA activities, some budgetary controversies arose. After settling them, the UJA continued to operate without interruption, despite recurrent differences of opinion among its participants, and it still functions as the largest annual fundraising campaign on the American scene.

After the establishment of the State of Israel, the UJA underwent certain technical changes. The UPA was transformed into the United Israel Appeal (UIA). After the *Jewish National Fund ceased being a beneficiary in 1953, the UIA represented only the *Keren ha-Yesod (Palestine Foundation Fund). The funds raised by the UJA were divided between the JDC and the UIA, the latter turning over its share to the Jewish Agency. In addition, the United HIAS Service, which provided for transportation of oppressed Jews and for their resettlement in nations other than Israel, and the New York Association of New Americans, which assisted Jewish refugees in the United States, were beneficiaries of one-time grants from the UJA.

Between 1960 and 1966 annual UJA income averaged more than $60,000,000. After the *Six-Day War of 1967, the UJA for some years conducted two campaigns, the regular campaign and an Israel Emergency Fund campaign. Income from the regular campaign was divided between the UIA and the JDC according to a formula arrived at 10 years before. Proceeds from the Israel Emergency Fund were allocated to the UIA only. In 1967 the regular campaign brought in $63,000,000, and the Israel Emergency Fund Campaign $173,000,000; in 1968 the two campaigns yielded $71,000,000 and $83,000,000 respectively. Following the 1973 Yom Kippur War, income reached a new high, with $480 million in pledges for both regular and emergency campaigns in 1974. It subsequently leveled off at around $400,000,000 annually, of which (net after expenses and allocation to HIAS) 87.5% is allocated to UIA and 12.5% to JDC. The figures constitute UJA share of local community campaigns, the aggregate of which amounted to some $750,000,000 in 1987. On the local scene, the UJA maintains a separate relationship with each of the community federations and negotiates with each of them individually over allocations in light of local conditions. It cultivates local leadership, including the major donors, and is especially active at the community level through its Young Leadership division. The local campaign thus has some characteristics of a business partnership, a cooperative endeavor between the federations and the UJA.

In addition to its regular and emergency campaigns, the UJA also conducts special fundraising drives for *Project Renewal in Israel (administered jointly by the Jewish Agency and the Israel government) and (since 1964) for the Israel Education Fund.

Signers of the agreement creating the United Jewish Appeal in 1939, left to right: William Rosenwald, for the National Coordinating Committee for Aid to Refugees and Emigrants Coming from Germany; Rabbi Abba Hillel Silver, for the United Palestine Appeal; and Rabbi Jonah B. Wise, for the American Jewish Joint Distribution Committee. [United Jewish Appeal]

The UJA maintains an office in Jerusalem whose main function is organizing study missions for leadership and community groups from the United States; in the 1980s those missions took on growing significance as a means of increasing participants' awareness of and commitment to Israel's needs. H. PARZEN—E. STOCK

UNITED KIBBUTZ. *See* KIBBUTZ ME'UHAD.

UNITED KIBBUTZ MOVEMENT (Hebrew Takam, acrostic abbreviation Ha-Tenu'a ha-Kibbutzit ha-Me'uhedet). Largest of the three major federations of kibbutzim, established with the merger of *Ihud ha-Kevutzot veha-Kibbutzim and the *Kibbutz Me'uhad. The merger was decided upon in 1979, undertaken in 1981, and finalized at the first convention of the united movement in 1985.

The history of the *kibbutz movement has been marked over the years by a series of mergers, divisions, and reunifications. Ha-Kibbutz ha-Me'uhad was founded originally in the 1920s by members allied with the Ahdut ha-Avoda wing of the Israel Labor Party. This was a grouping which adopted a left-wing militant socialist, often Marxist, stance, believing in establishing large variegated communities, based on a mixed economy and committed to a centralized direction. Ihud ha-Kevutzot veha-Kibbutzim was established in 1951 as a merger of *Hever ha-Kevutzot and Ihud ha-Kibbutzim. Hever ha-Kevutzot was the federation of the smaller, more agriculturally-minded, kevutzot aligned with the non-Marxist socialist wing of the Israel Labor Party, whereas Ihud ha-Kibbutzim was made up of larger kibbutzim which had split from Ha-Kibbutz ha-Me'uhad primarily on the issue of its pro-Soviet political stance at that time.

By 1979, and indeed much before this date, the political differences between these groupings had all but disappeared. The pro-Soviet stance and the militant socialism that marked Ha-Kibbutz ha-Me'uhad of the early 1950s had evaporated. The Ahdut ha-Avoda party had been reintegrated into the Israel Labor Party. All kibbutzim were interested in industry as well as in agriculture. Size had ceased to be a matter for ideological contention. In many areas a *de facto* merger had already taken place. Joint schools, economic enterprises, and seminar centers were operating successfully. Both federations felt that there was no point in separation and that a merger would enhance the social, economic, and political influence of the movement.

In 1989, the federation numbered 167 settlements with a population of some 75,000. It is the most heterogeneous of the kibbutz federations. Most of its kibbutzim define themselves as secular but there are two Reform and two Masorti (Conservative) communities. It includes a number of moshavim shitufiyim as well as kibbutzim which are affiliated with *Ha-No'ar ha-Tziyoni which at the end of the 1980s was politically part of the Progressive wing of Shinui. Most of the membership votes Labor and Takam is a major force in the Labor Party. There are, however, significant groups which vote for other parties.

The economic crisis which hit the kibbutz movement in the 1980s resulted in a social crisis as well and in a movement for change in which basic concepts were being reexamined, such as the degree of individual responsibility to the commune and vice versa. This reexamination was conducted in the Takam more so than in the other federations because of its very size and relative heterogeneity.

In June, 1989, the merger was completed and Muki Tzur was elected secretary-general for the entire movement. Previously the merger agreement had called for two secretaries—one from each of the original uniting federations.

M. KEREM

UNITED MIZRAHI BANK (Bank ha-Mizrahi ha-Me'uhad B.M. [Ltd.]). One of the oldest banks in Israel and in 1988 the fourth largest. It was established in Tel Aviv by the World Mizrachi Organization on 6 June 1923, with the object of assisting the promotion and development of the *Mizrachi party's program of religious Zionism. The bank's original name was the Mizrahi Bank Ltd., but in 1969, following the acquisition of the Ha-Po'el ha-Mizrahi Bank Ltd., its name was changed to the present one. The first foreign representative office was opened in New York in 1975, becoming a subsidiary called UMB Bank and Trust Company in 1978. This was followed by European subsidiaries in Zurich in 1981 and in London in 1983. In 1984, Mizrahi's overseas operations were concentrated in the United Mizrahi International Holding Company, registered in Amsterdam and in which Mizrahi holds a majority 54 percent stake. At the end of 1986, Mizrahi had 80 branches in Israel and 4 abroad (New York, Los Angeles, London, and Zurich).

In 1980, Mizrahi bought control of Bank Tefahot, Israel's biggest mortgage bank, from the Israeli government, and in 1984 it transferred control of its small Finance and Trade Bank subsidiary to Tefahot. Following the crisis in the banking industry that began in October 1983, Mizrahi undertook a program of selling non-banking assets, including real estate and investment companies under its control.

Assets: As of 31 December 1986, the bank's assets totaled NIS 8,876 million ($5,917 m.) and shareholder's equity stood at NIS 289 m. ($193 m.), with a further NIS 16 m. ($10.7 m.) in deferred capital notes and convertible bonds. Total deposits from the public amounted to NIS 3,870 m. ($7,111 m.) and loans to the public to NIS 5,209 m. ($3,473 m.).

Control and Direction: Control of the bank is vested in the World Mizrachi Organization, which holds special shares giving it dominant voting rights. The share capital is widely held, but became part of the "bank share arrangement" under which the Israel Treasury undertook to buy the bank's shares from their holders in October 1988 at their value prior to the crash of 6 October 1983.

P. LANDAU

UNITED NATIONS AND PALESTINE-ISRAEL.

Palestine Debate: 1947–48. On 18 February 1947, British Foreign Secretary Ernest Bevin announced in the House of Commons that His Majesty's government saw no prospect for a settlement of the problem of Palestine and had no choice but to submit "the whole problem of Palestine" to the United Nations. On 2 April, the British delegation to the United Nations requested the UN Secretary-General to "summon as soon as possible a special session of the Assembly for the purpose of constituting and instructing a special Committee" that would report to the regular fall session.

The special session of the General Assembly met on 27 April 1947. The first stage was taken up by what later became known as the "battle of the agenda," a major effort by the delegations of the five Arab member states—Egypt, Iraq, Lebanon, Saudi Arabia, and Syria—to prejudge the United Nations decision at the outset. The Arab states demanded that an additional item, "The termination of the *Mandate over Palestine and the declaration of its independence," be appended to the session's agenda. This proposal was overwhelmingly defeated.

Whereas the Arab case was fully stated during the discussion of the agenda, no hearing was given to Jewish spokesmen. On 22 April, the American Section of the Jewish Agency had submitted a formal request for permission, as a matter of "simple justice," to be heard on behalf of the Jewish people. The Agency's application met with nearly general acceptance among the non-Arab and non-Moslem delegations, but considerabls controversy developed with regard to the forum before which the Agency was to be allowed to state its case.

The Agency's application asked for a "seating" in the General Assembly. The representative of the United States, Ambassador Warren R. Austin, objected to the request, arguing that there was no provision in the UN Charter that permitted a non-governmental agency to appear before the General Assembly; he therefore held that the proper forum would be a special subcommittee to be appointed by the Assembly. The Jewish Agency strongly opposed the relegation of the presentation of the Jewish case to an ad hoc body. The United States delegation later dropped its original proposal, replacing it with a motion "to refer all the requests for a hearing" to the prestigious First (Political and Security) Committee. The Assembly decided, by a vote of 44 to 7 with 3 abstentions, to instruct the First Committee to grant a hearing to the Jewish Agency.

A number of other nongovernmental organizations asked to be heard on the Palestine problem, but their requests were denied, leaving the Jewish Agency as the sole spokesman for the Jewish cause. On 8 May 1947, Abba Hillel Silver took his seat between Cuba and Czechoslovakia to make the first presentation of the Jewish case. He was followed on 10 May by Moshe Shertok (Sharett), the head of the Agency's Political Department, and on 22 May by David Ben-Gurion, the chairman of the Agency's Executive. Later, Shertok and Emanuel Neumann were to participate on a regular basis in the work of the UN Ad Hoc Committee on Palestine and of Subcommittee 1, which was appointed to prepare a detailed plan for the *partition of Palestine into two states, one Jewish and one Arab.

The main item on the agenda of the special session of the General Assembly was the formation of a committee of inquiry on Palestine. Two proposals were submitted on the composition of the planned committee. The American delegation, supported by the representatives of Great Britain and several Latin American countries, proposed that the committee be made up exclusively of smaller, "neutral" powers which had no direct interest in Palestine; this proposal would have eliminated the Big Five (United States, USSR, France, Great Britain, and China). The representative of Argentina, stressing the international importance of the Palestine issue, proposed an 11-member committee consisting of the Big Five, one representative of the Arab states, and five members to be selected on an equitable geographical basis. The Jewish Agency opposed the proposal that would place on the inquiry committee a representative of Great Britain, thus permitting the mandatory power, the object of the international investigation, to act as a full-fledged partner in the conclusions and recommendations of the investigating committee. Even less acceptable was the prospect of having an Arab state both as a member of the inquiry committee and as a claimant before it. The 11-member *United Nations Special Committee on Palestine (UNSCOP) that was eventually appointed by the General Assembly included no representatives of either the great powers or the Arab states.

There was a sharp debate on the question of whether the

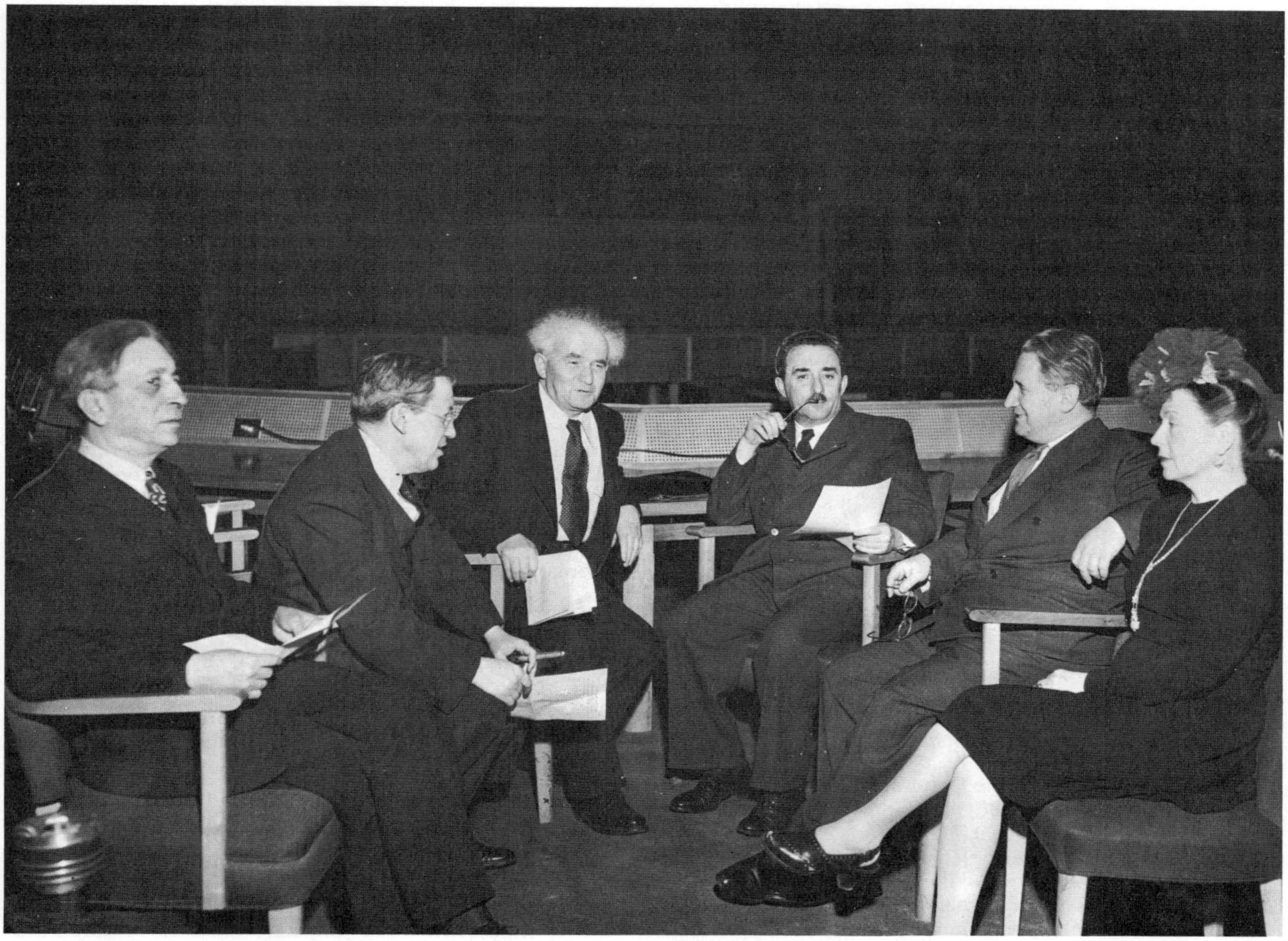

Representatives of the Jewish Agency at United Nations headquarters on May 9, 1947. Left to right: Hayim Greenberg, Emanuel Neumann, David Ben-Gurion, Moshe Sharett, Nahum Goldmann, and Mrs. Rose Halprin. [Alexander Archer]

inquiry committee should visit the displaced-persons camps in Europe and the detention camps for Jewish "illegal immigrants" in Cyprus. Although the Arab delegates claimed that the plight of the Jewish displaced persons had nothing to do with the Palestine problem, Silver and Shertok said that it was "the crux of the matter" and that the rights and interests of Jews outside Palestine were inextricably linked with the status of Palestine and its inhabitants. The final decision was that the UNSCOP should "have the widest powers to ascertain all questions and issues relative to the problem of Palestine."

During the ensuing three months, the center of United Nations activity and attention with regard to the Palestine issue shifted to Europe and the Middle East. In Palestine the UNSCOP gathered factual information from the mandatory government and the Jewish Agency, toured the country, and heard 34 witnesses at 13 public meetings and 18 closed sessions. Since the Arab Higher Committee boycotted the hearings, most of the testimony was presented by Zionist leaders and Palestine government officials.

From Palestine the UNSCOP went to Beirut, Lebanon, where it met with representatives of the governments of Egypt, Iraq, Lebanon, Saudi Arabia, and Yemen and heard their views on the Palestine problem. It then proceeded to Geneva, from where a subcommittee visited a number of Jewish displaced-persons camps in Germany and Austria and reported that "practically all the persons in the Jewish assembly centers wish, more or less determinedly, to go to Palestine....A main reason given for this wish to go to Palestine was that Palestine was a Jewish country, 'our country.'" The subcommittee concluded that "if only because of the extraordinary intensity of the feeling displayed in this direction, such a situation must be regarded as at least a component in the problem of Palestine."

The UNSCOP was unable to arrive at unanimous conclusions. Its final report, signed in Geneva on 31 August 1947, consisted of a minority plan and a majority plan. The minority plan, signed by the representatives of India, Iran, and Yugoslavia, proposed the creation, after a brief period of transition, of an independent federal state of Palestine. The federation was to comprise two subordinate states, one Arab and one Jewish, and to have two federal legislative bodies, one elected on the basis of proportional representation by all the inhabitants of Palestine and the other giving equal representation to Arabs and Jews. The majority plan, signed by seven committee members (the delegate from Australia refused to sign either plan), proposed the establishment of two states in Palestine, one Jewish and one Arab, to be joined in an economic union. After a period of two years, each state would become fully independent, provided it adopted a constitution and agreed to guarantee religious and minority rights and to establish adequate safeguards for the holy places. The city of Jerusalem was to be placed under a United Nations trusteeship.

On 23 September 1947, the regular fall session of the General Assembly referred the UNSCOP report to a Special (Ad Hoc) Committee on the question of Palestine, composed of representatives of all the member nations. It was before this Committee that Silver, on 2 October, stated the position of the Jewish Agency on the UNSCOP majority proposal to partition Palestine into an Arab and a Jewish State. While Silver made it clear that partition was not the Jewish Agency's proposal and that it would entail "a very heavy sacrifice on the part of the Jewish people," he said that the Agency would be prepared, albeit reluctantly, "to assume the responsibility of recommending acquiescence to the supreme organs of our [Zionist] Movement... because the proposal makes possible the immediate establishment of a Jewish State." Silver rejected the UNSCOP minority report, because

> under the constitutional provisions envisaged in this recommendation, Palestine would become an Arab State with two Jewish enclaves, in which the Jews would be in the frozen position of a permanent minority of the population.

In the early stages of the General Assembly session both the Soviet and the United States delegations hesitated to reveal their stand on the UNSCOP majority report. As a result, most of the other delegations were also reluctant to commit themselves; they awaited a sign from the two great powers before taking sides themselves. Meanwhile, the proceedings of the Ad Hoc Committee on Palestine dragged on. On 11 October, the United States delegate, Ambassador Herschel V. Johnson, had told the General Assembly that his country "supports the [UNSCOP] majority plan for partition and immigration." Two days later, Semyon K. Tsarapkin announced the support of the Soviet delegation for the partition plan. By virtue of their stand on the Palestine issue, the two superpowers found themselves in unaccustomed agreement on a major international issue.

Nevertheless, debate on the UNSCOP partition plan continued for weeks in the Ad Hoc Committee. The committee named two subcommittees: Subcommittee 1, to deal with the majority report; and Subcommittee 2 (consisting almost exclusively of Arab and Moslem states), to work on the minority proposal. The representatives of the Jewish Agency were allowed to attend all meetings of Subcommittee 1 and to offer comments, opinions, and suggestions on every point under discussion.

One of the major problems facing Subcommittee 1 in its deliberations was the confused territorial arrangement envisioned by the partition plan. The map attached to the report divided Palestine into six segments, three Jewish and three Arab (with additional enclaves), by splitting the country in half vertically and into three sections horizontally. Thus, the Jewish and Arab areas were interlocked in a checkerboard design. The Jewish Agency considered the proposed boundaries unsatisfactory and pressed for an increase of the territory of the planned Jewish State by about 200,000 acres, with stress on areas best suited for mass Jewish settlement and on easily defensible boundaries. On the other side, there were suggestions, mostly from the United States delegation, aimed at reducing the area to be allocated to the Jewish State. It was largely through the influence of the United States that the city and port of Jaffa, which the UNSCOP majority report had assigned to the Jewish State, was allocated to the proposed Arab State. Most of western Galilee, too, was assigned to the Arab State. The decision to internationalize Jerusalem dealt a severe blow to Jewish hopes. As against these losses, the Jewish Agency representatives succeeded in salvaging the Bet Netofa Valley and Lydda Airport, and in obtaining important border rectifications in Lower Galilee, the Bet She'an Valley, and the Gilboa region of the Jezreel Valley. Most important, as a result of a visit paid by Chaim Weizmann to Pres. Harry S Truman, the latter issued last-minute instructions to the United States delegation to change its stand on the Negev, whereupon that area, too, was included in the proposed Jewish State. Thus, of the 10,000 square miles of Cis-Jordanian Palestine that had been under the British Mandate, 5,579 square miles (an area that at the time had an Arab population of 397,000, or 46.46 per cent of the total population there) was allotted to the Jewish State.

On 25 November 1947, the Ad Hoc Committee voted on the reports of both subcommittees. The plan worked out by Subcommittee 2 was defeated by 29 votes to 12, with 16 abstentions. The partition plan presented by Subcommittee 1 was approved by the substantial majority of 25 to 13, with 17 abstentions and 2 members absent, or by just one vote short of the two-thirds majority of those present and voting that would be needed for acceptance in the final vote to be taken by the General Assembly.

The vote of the General Assembly on the partition plan was held on 29 November 1947. There were 33 votes in favor of the partition plan, 13 opposed, 10 abstentions (including the United Kingdom), and 1 nation (Siam) absent. The outcome was a little better than the required two-thirds majority. The voting was as follows:

For partition: Australia, Belgium, Bolivia, Brazil, Belorussia, Canada, Costa Rica, Czechoslovakia, Denmark, Dominican Republic, Ecuador, France, Guatemala, Haiti, Iceland, Liberia, Luxembourg, the Netherlands, New Zealand, Nicaragua, Norway, Panama, Paraguay, Peru, the Philippines, Poland, Sweden, Ukraine, Union of South Africa, USSR, United States, Uruguay, and Venezuela.

Against partition: Afghanistan, Cuba, Egypt, Greece, India, Iran, Iraq, Lebanon, Pakistan, Saudi Arabia, Syria, Turkey, and Yemen.

Abstentions: Argentina, Chile, China, Colombia, El Salvador, Ethiopia, Honduras, Mexico, United Kingdom, and Yugoslavia.

Immediately after the Assembly vote for partition, the Arab delegations denounced the decision, declared that they would refuse to honor it, and left the chamber pledging to use force to oppose its implementation. The Arabs lost no time in carrying out their threat. The very next day violence broke out in Palestine. By 18 January 1948, the number of Jews, Arabs, and members of the British security forces killed in armed clashes had risen to 720, and 1,532 had been wounded.

When the Assembly passed the resolution on the partition of Palestine into Jewish and Arab states, it called on the Security Council to assist in the implementation of this

The Israeli flag is raised at United Nations headquarters in Lake Success on May 12, 1949, after Israel's admission to the world body. Just left and right of the flag are Amb. Abba Eban and Foreign Minister Moshe Sharett. [Israel Information Services]

decision and to take all necessary measures to preserve peace in Palestine. By the time it adjourned, however, no provisions had been made for maintaining the authority of the United Nations in Palestine or for safeguarding life and property during the transition period from British Mandate to independence. A leading role among the Arab attackers was assumed by "volunteers" from neighboring Arab countries (openly recruited by the Egyptian, Transjordanian, and Syrian governments), who infiltrated the frontiers of Palestine by land and sea.

The Security Council made several ineffectual attempts to stop the fighting. On 30 March, the United States delegate introduced a draft resolution calling "upon Arab and Jewish armed groups in Palestine to cease acts of violence immediately." The Jewish Agency objected to this motion which, it insisted, distorted the true state of affairs in Palestine: the motion conveyed the impression that the armed conflict was a local affair, involving only the two segments of the country's population, when in fact the root of the violence was "the presence of Arab aggression from outside, sponsored and organized by Arab States, members of the United Nations, in an effort to alter by force the settlement envisaged by the General Assembly's resolution of 29 November 1947." As a precondition for accepting the truce, the Jewish Agency demanded "the withdrawal of foreign invaders," but the Security Council disregarded these objections and adopted the United States motion. The resolution had no effect. On 15 April, the Council again called for the cessation of "all activities of a military or para-military nature." This time, apparently taking notice of the Jewish Agency objections, the resolution contained a specific reference to "the entry into Palestine of armed bands and fighting personnel groups and individuals, and weapons or war material." The Arab countries paid no heed to this implicit admonition.

The General Assembly had appointed a five-member Palestine Commission, consisting of Bolivia, Czechoslovakia, Denmark, Panama, and the Philippines, to supervise the implementation of the partition plan. But the British mandatory government declared that it "would not regard favorably any proposal by the Commission to proceed to Palestine," and the Commission had to remain at the United Nations headquarters in Lake Success, N.Y.

Meanwhile, the U.S. State Department withdrew its support for the United Nations partition resolution. On 19

March 1948, Ambassador Austin told the Security Council that the Assembly's vote of 29 November 1947 had been only a "recommendation" and not a binding decision. On the grounds that partition "cannot be implemented by peaceful means" and that "the maintenance of international peace is at stake," the United States delegation proposed that "a temporary trusteeship for Palestine be established under the UN Trusteeship Council." Great Britain, it was proposed, should be induced to retain the Palestine Mandate, at least for the time being, and the proclamation of the Jewish State, originally scheduled for 15 May 1948, be postponed. On 24 March Silver, speaking on behalf of the Jewish Agency and the Va'ad Le'umi, announced before the Security Council that the two Jewish bodies would oppose any proposal designed to prevent or postpone the establishment of the Jewish State, that they would reject any plan to set up a trusteeship regime, even for a short period, and that on 15 May 1948, a "provisional Jewish government would commence to function in Palestine."

In April, the General Assembly reconvened for a special session to consider the trusteeship proposal. A desultory debate on a succession of compromise formulas continued as 15 May drew closer.

War of Independence and Armistice: 1948–56. The State of Israel was proclaimed on 14 May 1948. On the same day, the United States extended de facto recognition to the new State, followed three days later by the USSR's de jure recognition. On 15 May, the armies of five Arab states—Egypt, Syria, Lebanon, Transjordan, and Iraq—invaded the new Jewish State. In response to the complaint of the provisional government of the State of Israel, the Security Council met several times, but each time it adjourned without reaching a decision or taking action. While the Arab armies were swiftly advancing, the British and Syrian representatives on the Council employed delaying tactics to enable the Arabs to strengthen their positions. Fighting stopped only on 11 June 1948, in response to a UN Security Council resolution. Four weeks later the fighting broke out again, and a second cease-fire came into effect after 10 days of intensive fighting (8–18 July), in which the Israeli Army occupied considerable areas of the country. The advance of the Israeli Army was thus halted. The truce was repeatedly broken.

In September, Count Folke *Bernadotte, who on 20 May had been appointed UN Mediator for Palestine by the five permanent members of the Security Council, submitted a set of proposals that amounted to a major revision of the territorial dispositions made in the 1947 partition plan: while all Galilee was to go to the Jewish State, all the Negev, as well as Ramle and Lydda, was to become part of the Arab State, which was to be united with Transjordan. The area of the State of Israel was to be reduced from 5,579 to 2,124 square miles. The day after he signed his report, Bernadotte was assassinated in Jerusalem (17 September 1948). After a protracted debate at the UN Political Committee in Paris, the Bernadotte Plan, which had the strong support of Great Britain, was defeated (4 December) by an ill-assorted combination of various pro-Israel, pro-Arab, and pro-Soviet delegates.

On 6 January 1949, Egypt agreed to enter into armistice negotiations with Israel at the headquarters of Acting UN Mediator Ralph J. *Bunche on the island of Rhodes. Under the aegis of the United Nations an Israel-Egyptian armistice was concluded on 24 February 1949; agreements were signed with Lebanon of 23 March, with Transjordan on 3 April, and with Syria on 20 July.

In the hope of converting the armistice agreements into a permanent peace settlement, the General Assembly decided to establish a Palestine Conciliation Commission consisting of France, Turkey, and the United States, each to be represented by delegates nominated by and responsible to their respective governments, not the United Nations. Since the delegates on the Commission were acting as agents of their governments, serving their national interests rather than those of the United Nations as such, the Commission could not be objective in its attitude, nor was it capable of recording any constructive achievements.

The UN Truce Supervision Organization (UNTSO), which was set up by the United Nations to supervise the observance of the four armistice agreements, was hardly more successful. Admittedly, UNTSO was understaffed, overworked, and usually lacked the support of the Arab states, Israel, and United Nations headquarters, with both sides in the conflict questioning the impartiality of the leading staff members.

In general, the frontiers between Israel and the Arab neighbor states, as worked out by the United Nations-sponsored armistice agreements, were neither natural nor reasonable. They had been determined solely by the positions held by the forward troops of the opposing armies at the time of the cease-fire. The frontiers with Jordan (329 miles) and Egypt (164 miles) were particularly haphazard, long, and vague. They were to become the most sensitive, explosive, and bloody borders and to figure recurrently and prominently on the United Nations agenda for years to come.

Much of the early trouble came from the Hashemite kingdom of Jordan (comprising Transjordan and the part of Palestine which the United Nations had assigned for an Arab State but which had been conquered and annexed by Transjordan). Between 1949 and 1953, 176 Jews were killed and 282 wounded in a total of 1,182 incursions from Jordan; there were 147 cases of mining, 1,427 armed clashes, and 3,487 cases of robbery. Attacks by Jordanian military and paramilitary forces reached a climax in the first half of October, 1953. On 14 October, Israel retaliated by sending a paramilitary force into Jordanian territory, attacking the village of Kibya.

When the UN Security Council took up the Kibya incident, Ambassador Eban stated that the government of Israel "regards the loss of life in Kibya with profound and unreserved regret," but pointed out that "the mood and background of the Kibya incident can only be understood in the light of the atmosphere in which our struggle for security and peace is conducted...." The Security Council, Eban insisted, was "not a police court of lower instance which convenes only to analyze and record single turbulent incidents." It should not "isolate single events from their context" but should "criticize all acts of violence." However, the Council refused to distinguish between the immediate deed and its background and motivation. A resolution adopted on 24 November vaguely took note of the fact that there was "substantial evidence of crossing of the demarcation line by unauthorized persons often resulting in acts of violence" and "requested the Government of Jordan to continue and strengthen the measures which they were already taking to prevent such crossings." On the other hand, the

Israel emerged from the *armistice agreements with a territorial accretion of 2,268 square miles. On 11 May 1949, the General Assembly approved Israel's application for membership in the United Nations by a roll-call vote of 33 to 11, with 13 abstentions.

Golda Meir as Foreign Minister with Amb. Michael S. Comay at the United Nations. [Israel Information Services]

On 29 March 1954, eight of the nine members of the Security Council voted for a resolution that censured Egypt for continuing to maintain discriminatory blockade practices in the Suez Canal. The resolution was defeated by a veto of the Soviet representative, and the issue remained deadlocked. Six months later, on 28 September, Israel lodged a complaint with the Council against Egypt's seizure of the unarmed Israeli vessel *Bat Galim*, which was passing the Suez Canal en route to Haifa with a cargo of meat, plywood, and hides. To forestall a vote of censure, Egypt released the 10-man crew. However, Egypt refused to release the ship and its cargo. Nevertheless, the Security Council, on 13 January 1955, closed its deliberations on the issue without any formal resolution and recommendation; nor was any reference made to Israel's right of free passage through the Suez Canal. As early as March, 1954, Ambassador Eban stated that in fact "no resolution recognizing Israel's fundamental rights under the General Armistice Agreement appears capable of adoption by the Security Council; resolutions opposed strongly by Israel, on the other hand, have been allowed free passage." In each case, he said, the alternative had actually been between a resolution acceptable to Arab interests or no resolution at all. Under the circumstances, Eban stated, the question arose "whether there exists the basic condition of judicial equity in which Israel should have recourse to the Security Council."

On 14 March 1956, Israel lodged a strongly worded complaint with the Security Council on breaches of peace along the border of the Egyptian-held Gaza Strip, listing 180 cases of minelaying, shooting, and killing in the period from December, 1955, to March 1956. Another complaint was lodged on 4 April. Two weeks later, the Council President declared that "there was no need for any new action by the Council at present." Nevertheless, UN Secretary-General Dag Hammarskjöld went to the Middle East in an attempt to establish a United Nations presence in the area. While the Secretary-General was still in the Middle East, fedayeen incursions were carried out with full vigor, from both the Gaza Strip and Jordan. Reviewing the situation on the country's borders, Prime Minister Ben-Gurion told the Knesset on 15 October 1956: "The apparatus of the United Nations has demonstrated its incapacity—I do not say its unwillingness—to prevent the continued and systematic murder of citizens of Israel."

United Nations and the Sinai Campaign: 1956–57. Two weeks later on 29 October 1956, Israel launched the Sinai

Campaign, the aim of which was, as Ambassador Eban told the Security Council, the elimination of fedayeen bases in Egyptian territory. A few days later, Britain and France attacked the Suez Canal area. Within a week, Israeli forces had occupied the Gaza Strip and the entire Sinai Peninsula, including the strategically crucial position of Sharm el-Sheikh at the mouth of the Gulf of Eilat.

On 30 October, the Security Council met to consider a draft resolution submitted by the United States, which accused Israel of "violating the armistice agreement between Egypt and Israel" and called on Israel "immediately to withdraw its armed forces behind the established [1949] armistice line." Arkady Sobolev, the Soviet delegate, "warmly welcomed" the United States motion, which was approved by 7 of the 11 Council members; Australia and Belgium abstained. The negative votes of France and Britain, both permanent members of the Council, killed the resolution. Deadlocked in the Security Council, the issue went to an emergency session of the General Assembly, which, on 2 November, adopted the United States motion by a vote of 64 to 5 (Australia, Britain, France, Israel, and New Zealand), with 6 abstentions. The basic aim of the Assembly, like that of the Council, was a prompt return to the territorial status quo established by the 1949 armistice agreement. The Assembly directed Secretary-General Hammarskjöld to form a UN Emergency Force (UNEF) to maintain the peace in the territory to be vacated by the Israeli forces.

Yielding to unrelenting international pressure, led by the United States, the Israeli government on 14 January 1957, pledged itself to evacuate the Sinai Peninsula except for the Sharm el-Sheikh area by 22 January; no mention was made of the Gaza Strip. Israel honored its promise on the indicated date. Then, on 2 February the General Assembly, by a vote of 74 to 2, called on Israel to withdraw from both Gaza and Sharm el-Sheikh, with the proviso that the UNEF would be stationed in these two areas. On 1 March, Israeli Foreign Minister Golda Meir announced in the Assembly that her country would abide by the United Nations decision. The UNEF entered the Gaza Strip on 7 March. Four days later, the Egyptian government appointed a civilian administration for the area, and Egyptian troops and officials returned to the area in greater strength than before. Israel's withdrawal, enforced by the threat of international sanctions, left her confined to the same borders that had been the source of trouble since the signing of the armistice agreements. The only positive after- effect was that, in the 10 years that followed, the UNEF, stationed in the Gaza Strip, on the Sinai border, and at Sharm el-Sheikh, effectively sealed the Israeli border from Egypt-based terrorist incursions and enabled ships bound for Israel to pass through the Strait of Tiran.

"Status Quo": 1957–67. Between 1947 and 1967 the General Assembly and the Security Council passed 253 resolutions on matters pertaining to Israel. During the years immediately following the Sinai Campaign, however, the number of cases the United Nations dealt with diminished considerably. Perennial items on the agenda were the annual reports of the UN Relief and Works Agency for Palestine Refugees in the Near East (UNRWA) and the routine debate on the *Arab refugee problem.

In December, 1961, 16 delegations (nine African nations, five Latin American nations, the Netherlands, and Haiti) submitted a draft resolution on the Middle East, calling on the General Assembly to appeal to "all governments concerned" to undertake "direct negotiations with a view to finding a solution acceptable to all the parties concerned, for all the questions in dispute between them." Israel strongly supported this initiative; the Arab delegations rejected and opposed it. The motion was defeated in the Assembly's Special Political Committee by a vote of 44 to 34, with 20 abstentions and six members absent. In April 1962, the Security Council, by a vote of 10 to 0 (with France abstaining) condemned Israel's raid on a Syrian military post on the eastern shore of Lake Kineret, undertaken in the wake of repeated harassment of Israeli fishing and police boats.

The Council was particularly occupied with the "Palestine question" in 1966, when this item was listed as the main order of business in 28 of its 70 meetings. In October of that year, following a series of outrages by Syrian-based terrorist groups, the Israel government lodged a complaint with the Security Council, charging that Syria's military junta was responsible for the terrorist attacks. The Council discussed the matter for three weeks. Six Council members (Argentina, Japan, the Netherlands, New Zealand, Nigeria, and Uganda) submitted a draft resolution that contained no censure of Syria but merely "invited" the Syrian government "to strengthen its security measures for preventing incidents that constitute a violation of the General Armistice Agreement" between Israel and Syria. Israel was asked "to cooperate fully with the Israel-Syria Mixed Armistice Commission." On 14 November, 10 of the 15 Council members voted for this resolution, with the United States, Britain, France, and New Zealand joining the six sponsors, Nationalist China abstaining, and four Council members (Bulgaria, Jordan, Mali, and the Soviet Union) casting negative votes. The Soviet vote amounted to a veto—the first cast by the USSR against a motion sponsored by African countries. Ambassador Nikolai T. Fedorenko of the USSR declared that the majority resolution was one-sided, since it implied that the Syrian government might have been able to prevent terrorist incursions into Israel. Three weeks later, on 25 November, the Security Council, by a vote of 14 to 0, with New Zealand abstaining, censured Israel for a retaliatory raid against the Jordanian village of Es-Samu. The resolution warned that "military reprisal cannot be tolerated and...if...repeated, the Security Council will have to consider further and more effective steps... to ensure against...repetitions"; this was an implied threat to invoke sanctions.

Israel's chief delegate, Michael Comay, thereupon charged that although the Security Council took prompt and resolute action on complaints against Israel's reactions to Arab terrorism, it had proved unable in 15 years to adopt a single resolution in response to Israel's complaints about attacks on its territory.

J. SCHECHTMAN

United Nations and the Six Day War The starting point of the 1967 crisis was the sudden decision of the Government of the United Arab Republic (UAR, Egypt's official name in the years 1961–1971) to demand the immediate withdrawal of UNEF from Sinai and the Gaza Strip. The request was first transmitted by the UAR military authorities on 16 May 1967 to the UNEF Commander and was formally conveyed to the Secretary-General of the UN, U Thant, by the UAR Permanent Representative on 18 May. By that time the Egyptian army had already forcibly ousted the UNEF forces from their positions along the Egyptian-Israeli demarcation lines and at Sharm el-Sheikh. The Secretary-

General replied on the same day that he acceded to the Egyptian demand. On 22 May, while the Secretary-General was en route to Cairo, President Nasser announced the establishment of a blockade against Israeli shipping in the Straits of Tiran and the Gulf of Akaba.

The Security Council met on 24 May. A report submitted to the Council on 26 May by the Secretary-General stressed the gravity of the situation and urged all the parties concerned "to exercise special restraint, to forgo belligerence and to avoid all other actions which could increase tensions". During the debates the Arab delegations took a militant stand. The UAR representative declared that the Gulf of Akaba was " a national inland waterway subject to absolute Arab sovereignty". The Soviet delegate took exception to the "hasty" convening of the Council and asserted that "the real culprit...once more is Israel". The western and the Latin American delegations urged restraint. Only the U.S. representative stressed the need to maintain free passage in the Straits of Tiran.

Three draft resolutions were tabled. One sponsored by Canada and Denmark supported the efforts of the Secretary-General to calm the situation. Another draft submitted by the USA encouraged "international diplomacy to seek reasonable, peaceful, and just solutions". A text, orally proposed by the UAR, called on Israel to respect the Egyptian-Israeli Armistice Agreement. None of these three motions was put to a vote.

The war broke out on 5 June. Israel, facing three Arab States, the UAR, Syria, and Jordan, quickly attained the military advantage. The Security Council met on the same day, but could agree only on the request for a cease-fire. On 7 June, after the Israeli forces had swept the Sinai Peninsula and the West Bank, Israel, the UAR, and Jordan indicated their compliance with the cease-fire. Hostilities between Israel and Syria continued in spite of a further Security Council resolution demanding an immediate halt to the fighting and ended only on 11 June after Israel had taken the Golan Heights.

During the Security Council debates the Arab States and the USSR urged the immediate withdrawal of the Israeli forces and demanded that Israel be condemned as an aggressor and ordered to pay reparations. The majority of the Council, however, did not follow suit. On 14 June a Soviet draft resolution on the aggressive activities of Israel, which embodied these concepts, was defeated with 11 votes against and only four in favor (the Soviet Union, Bulgaria, India, and Mali). The USSR then moved for the convening of an emergency session of the General Assembly on the situation in the Middle East. The Soviet government apparently expected to rally a majority in the 122-member Assembly, where the Afro-Asian bloc and the non-aligned countries had a decisive weight. The Fifth Emergency Session met between 17 June and 21 July. The Soviet delegation, led by Premier Aleksei Kosygin, presented a proposal of its own, on the lines of the one which had been rejected in the Security Council. The Soviet bloc also backed a comparatively milder draft resolution, sponsored by Yugoslavia and other non-aligned countries, whose essential provision was the immediate and unconditional withdrawal of the Israeli forces to the positions they held prior to 5 June 1967. The western countries supported a draft submitted by 20 Latin American states, based on the link between the Israeli withdrawal from all the occupied territories and the termination of belligerence. The voting took place on 4 July. The Soviet draft was squarely defeated in a paragraph by paragraph vote. The Yugoslav draft obtained a plurality (with 53 votes in favor, 46 against, and 20 abstentions), but was rejected for lack of the required two-thirds majority. The Latin American draft, with a tally of 57 in favor 45 against, and 18 abstentions, drew the largest plurality but also fell short of the two-thirds majority. The voting pattern reflected to a considerable extent the lines of the east-west contest. While the western and Latin American countries solidly voted against the Soviet and non-aligned proposals the African bloc split into three roughly equal voting groups: the pro-western and pro-Israeli, the pro-Soviet and pro-Arab, and the abstainers. On 4 July the Assembly also voted on a draft resolution on the status of Jerusalem introduced by Pakistan and adopted it by 99 votes to 0, with 20 abstentions. The resolution declared invalid the measures taken by Israel to change the status of the city and called on Israel to rescind them. Israel did not participate in the voting. A second resolution on the status of Jerusalem which reiterated the earlier call was adopted on 14 July.

On 21 July the Emergency Session temporarily adjourned. It resumed for one day on 18 September when it decided to place the item on the situation in the Middle East on the agenda of the next regular session of the General Assembly. Nevertheless the question of the Middle East was not discussed during the 1967, 1968, or 1969 sessions of the Assembly.

Security Council Resolution 242. Following the impasse arrived at in the General Assembly the focus of diplomatic activity shifted again to the Security Council. India, Mali, and Nigeria made an attempt to persuade the two Latin American members of the Council, Argentina and Brazil, to support a draft resolution aimed at securing a prompt Israeli withdrawal from all the occupied territories. To this purpose they tabled a proposal couched in terms largely similar to those of the draft submitted by 20 Latin American countries during the Emergency Session. This move, however, was firmly opposed by the United States and the other western countries. Eventually a general agreement was reached on a compromise text prepared by the United Kingdom based on two principles: a) "withdrawal of Israeli armed forces from territories occupied in the recent conflict" and b) the right of every state in the area "to live in peace within secure and recognized borders". The text also included the following elements: the concept of "inadmissibility of the acquisition of territory by war"; the necessity of "guaranteeing freedom of navigation through international waterways in the area", and of "achieving a just settlement of the refugee problem"; and the request made to the Secretary-General to designate a Special Representative "to maintain contacts with the states concerned in order to promote agreement".

The draft was unanimously adopted on 22 November 1967 and became Security Council Resolution 242. Israel and the Arab States directly concerned later signified their acceptance. Their respective interpretations, however, differed. While Israel affirmed that Resolution 242 recognized the need to establish by mutual agreement new and secure borders, the Arab States maintained that it provided for a return to the pre-war borders. A bone of contention was the discrepancy between the original English text which spoke of withdrawal "from territories" and its translation into French which read "from the territories".

The Secretary-General appointed as Special Representative Dr. Gunnar Jarring of Sweden.

1967–1973; Deterioration of Israel's position in the UN.

The alignment which withstood the Arab-Soviet requests in June-November 1967 proved to be short-lived. The western countries, mindful of their interests in the Arab countries, soon adopted an attitude of neutrality. The political and social conflicts and changes which shook Latin America caused a number of Latin American states to relinquish their previous pro-US and pro-Israel positions. In Africa and Asia the influence of the Non-Aligned Movement grew and in consequence nearly all the states of those regions gradually joined the pro-Arab camp. Moreover the western and pro-western forces lost over the years much of their political clout as a result of the admission to the UN of new African and Asian states. The overall UN membership rose from 122 in the 1967 Emergency Session to 127 in 1970, and 159 in 1985, with the western and Latin American States becoming a shrinking minority.

The first indication of the new state of affairs was the adoption by the General Assembly in 1968 of a resolution on the establishment of a "Special Committee to Investigate Israeli Practices Affecting the Human Rights of the Population of the Occupied Territories". The voting tally was 60 in favor, 22 against and 37 abstentions. Israel asserted that the Special Committee would be unable to take an impartial stand because of the biased terms and the unilateral nature of its mandate which ignored the human rights deprivation affecting the Jewish communities in Arab countries. Israel also pointed out that the Special Committee was composed of countries with which it had no diplomatic relations and consequently denied it all cooperation and facilities, including access to the Israeli-held territories. The Special Committee, whose members were Ceylon (presently called Sri Lanka), Yugoslavia, and Somalia (later replaced by Senegal), submitted, from 1970 onwards, annual reports highly critical of the Israeli administration. The resolutions based on these reports were adopted each year by increasing majorities. The resolution submitted in 1972, which accused Israel among other things of looting the resources of the occupied territories, of pillaging their archeological and cultural heritage, of deporting population and of interference in the freedom of worship in the Holy Places was adopted by 63 votes to 10 with 49 abstentions. Only two western countries (US and Canada) voted against, together with Israel and seven Latin American and African states.

Another weighty development, which took place during the General Assembly debate on the UNRWA Report in 1969, was the introduction of a draft affirming "the inalienable rights of the people of Palestine". The text, which became part B of the resolution on the UNRWA Report, was adopted by 48 votes to 22 with 47 abstentions. Subsequently, resolutions on the Palestinian people's rights, which comprised express references to the right of self-determination, were adopted each year. In 1972 the vote was 67 to 21 (mainly western and Latin American countries), with 37 abstentions.

The consideration of the item on the situation in the Middle East was resumed by the General Assembly in 1970. A draft resolution introduced by Yugoslavia and 21 Afro-Asian countries reaffirmed the principles of Security Council Resolution 242, urged its speedy implementation, and added to it the new element of Palestinian rights. The vote was 57 to 16 with 39 abstentions.

The War of Attrition between Egypt and Israel. In the meantime the mission of the Special Representative of the Secretary-General continued, against a background of heightening tension in the region. In October, 1968, Egypt initiated the war of attrition in the Suez Canal area and from then Egypt and Israel became involved in continuous and increasingly severe hostilities. However, in July, 1970, both countries agreed to a temporary cease-fire. In February, 1971, Dr. Jarring conveyed to Egypt and Israel identical proposals based on mutual prior commitments which included the readiness to enter into a peace agreement and the withdrawal of the Israeli forces to the previous international border. Egypt gave a positive reply, while Israel announced its willingness to withdraw "to the secure, recognized, and agreed boundaries to be established in the peace agreement". The Israeli note stressed that Israel would not return to the pre-5 June 1967 lines. In a resolution adopted in 1972 the General Assembly deplored Israel's attitude and invited Israel to declare publicly its adherence to the principle of non-annexation of territories through the use of force. The vote was 87 to 7 (Israel and six Latin American states) with 31 abstentions, including the US.

During the years 1968–1973 the Security Council repeatedly dealt with Israeli reprisals for incursions and terrorist attacks originating from Jordan and Lebanon and passed several resolutions condemning Israel or its military actions. Some of these texts, such as the resolutions unanimously adopted in December, 1968, after the Israeli retaliatory action against Beirut airport, and in August, 1973, following the temporary seizure of a Lebanese airliner by Israel, also carried the warning that the Council would consider taking adequate measures if such acts were repeated.

The Security Council also passed a number of resolutions against measures taken by Israel in Jerusalem which changed or affected the status of the city. In September, 1969, after an arson attack in the El Aksa Mosque, the Council adopted a particularly strongly worded resolution stating that "any encouragement of, or connivance at, any such act may seriously endanger international peace and security". Israel stressed that the arson was committed by a deranged person of Australian nationality, who was subsequently tried and convicted.

In September, 1972, after the slaughter perpetrated by PLO terrorists on the members of the Israeli athletic team at the Munich Olympic games, the United States interposed for the first time a veto in the Arab-Israeli context. Following the Munich massacre and the Israeli bombing of PLO targets in the vicinity of Damascus and in Southern Lebanon, three non-aligned states submitted a draft resolution which called on all parties to cease immediately all military operations. The United States cast the decisive negative vote (veto), objecting to the omission of any reference to the Munich outrage. One country abstained (Panama) and the remaining 13 members of the Council voted in favor. In July, 1973, the US vetoed a draft submitted on Egypt's initiative which, after reaffirming resolution 242, stated that a peaceful solution could be achieved only on the basis of respect for "the rights of all States in the area and for the rights and legitimate aspirations of the Palestinians". The vote was 13 to 1 (with China not participating). The US representative emphasized that the draft was highly partisan and unbalanced and would have fundamentally changed resolution 242, the one agreed basis on which a settlement could be constructed.

The Yom Kippur War. On 6 October 1973 Egypt and Syria unleashed a sudden and concerted attack on Israel. At the beginning of the war the Egyptian army swept the eastern bank of the Suez Canal and the Syrian army overran the Golan Heights. No action was taken by the Security Council at this stage. On 18 October Israeli forces established a bridgehead across the Suez Canal, posing a serious threat to the Egyptian Third Army still deployed on the eastern bank of the Canal. The possibility of a Soviet military intervention to rescue the entrapped Egyptian units loomed. On 20 October US Secretary of State Kissinger flew to Moscow and held urgent consultations with the Soviet leaders. The terms of a cease-fire were agreed upon by the two superpowers and were accepted by Egypt and Israel and subsequently by Syria. On 22 October the Security Council met at the request of both the US and the Soviet Union and unanimously adopted Resolution 338.

Like Resolution 242 the wording of the new resolution was carefully balanced and gave partial satisfaction to both the Arab and the Israeli viewpoints. Its main elements were: 1) a cease-fire within 12 hours; 2) the "immediate implementation of Resolution 242 in all its parts"; 3) the opening of "negotiations between the parties under appropriate auspices aimed at establishing a just and durable peace in the Middle East". In spite of the resolution, heavy fighting continued in the Suez Canal area and the cordon around the Egyptian Third Army was further tightened. On 24 October the American forces were put in a state of overall alert to forestall a threatened Soviet intervention on behalf of the entrapped Egyptian forces. Military operations along the Suez Canal ended on 26 October and on the same day the Security Council adopted Resolution 340 on the establishment of a new UN peace-keeping force (UNEF) between the Egyptian and the Israeli lines.

The pattern of stiffly-bargained agreement between the US and the Soviet Union and subsequent legitimization or acceptance by the UN emerged again in the question of the Geneva Peace Conference. The convening of the Conference was the result of the original agreement between the superpowers, embodied in Resolution 338. One of the fine points of the resolution was the wording "under appropriate auspices", which meant in practice American-Soviet auspices. The non-aligned countries however wanted the Conference to be under UN control and at their request the Security Council adopted on 15 December 1973 resolution 344, which referred to "the auspices of the United Nations" and expressed confidence that the Secretary-General would play a full and effective role at the Conference. The voting was 10 in favor and none against. Both the US and the USSR abstained, together with the UK and France. In practice the Conference was held under the cochairmanship of the United States and the Soviet Union while the role of UN Secretary-General was confined to a ceremonial one. The Conference met on 21 December and adjourned the next day.

At this point the United States took up the task of mediating between the parties. The "shuttle diplomacy" of the US Secretary of State, Henry Kissinger, led to the first disengagement agreements which brought about the withdrawal of Israeli forces from the western sector of the Sinai Peninsula and from parts of the Golan Heights. The Security Council confined itself to taking note of these agreements and providing the required peace-keeping forces: UNEF along the Egyptian-Israeli lines (which served until the Egyptian-Israeli Peace Treaty in 1979) and UNDOF (United Nations Disengagement Observers Force), set up by Resolution 350 of 31 May 1974, along the Israeli-Syrian lines.

The Anti-Israel campaign in the General Assembly. While in the Security Council the Arab states and their allies were forced, in the aftermath of the Yom Kippur war, to come to terms with the hard facts of military realities and Great Power interests, in the General Assembly an atmosphere of passion and aggressiveness prevailed. To a large extent the two phenomena were related. The Arab States, being unable to achieve by military or diplomatic means a quick change in the question of the territories, moved to strike at Israel in the Assembly in order to isolate it and weaken its international position. They knew that the balance of power in the Assembly and on the world scene had markedly evolved in their favor. The Non-Aligned Movement—in which the Arab states had played a central role since its inception in 1961—had grown in numbers and had drawn new strength by upholding the claims of the poverty-stricken countries of the southern hemisphere against the industrialized north. The new policy of economic confrontation was first introduced at the Fourth Summit Meeting of the Non-Aligned, held in Algiers in September, 1973.

The successes of the non-aligned strategy in the UN were largely due to the emergence of an external factor: the huge increase in oil prices during the years 1973–1974 and the consequent meteoric rise in political power of the OPEC oil cartel. The fact that the Arab states formed the core of OPEC gave to this state of affairs an anti-Israeli twist. The European countries, bowing to undisguised blackmail (e.g., the oil sanctions proclaimed by OPEC against Holland for its support of Israel during the Yom Kippur war) agreed to revise in a pro-Arab sense their policies vis-à-vis the Middle East conflict. Most Latin American countries changed their stand likewise. A parallel development was the collapse of the Israeli diplomatic network in Africa. Over the years 1972–1973 29 African countries severed their diplomatic ties with Israel.

By the end of 1973 Israel appeared in the UN scene considerably weakened. The Arab States, on the other hand, had become a central factor in a wide range of interconnected, southern-oriented, regional and international groups and organizations: the Islamic Conference (founded in 1969 after the fire in the El Aksa Mosque), the African and Asian groups of the UN, G-77 (the organization set up by the developing countries from Africa, Asia, and Latin America for the purpose of obtaining better trade and financial terms from the industrialized states of the Northern Hemisphere) and the Non-Aligned. On Arab-Israeli issues the Arab-led and Soviet-supported coalition in the General Assembly wielded an overwhelming majority. In 1974, in the Nineteenth Session of the General Assembly, this shift in the balance of power was acutely felt and the outcome was the passing of unprecedented anti-Israeli resolutions. Resolution 3210 inviting the PLO "to participate in the deliberations of the General Assembly on the question of Palestine in plenary meetings" was adopted on 14 October 1974 with 105 votes in favor, 4 against (US, Bolivia, Dominican Republic, Israel), and 20 abstentions. The invitation constituted a break with previous UN practice and rules which limited appearance in the Assembly's plenary meetings only to representatives of states. The PLO leader, Yasser Arafat, was received by the president of the General Assembly with the honors normally reserved for a head of state. Resolution 3237, which issued a general invitation to the PLO to take part as an observer in all the sessions of the General Assembly and in all the conferences convened by the Assembly—thus granting it a status similar to that of a state—was approved on 22 November 1974 with 95 votes in favor, 17 against, and 19 abstentions. The Assembly also adopted Resolution 3236, which affirmed the right of the Palestinian people to national independence and sovereignty (89 votes to 8 with 37 abstentions).

One of the decisions taken by the Nineteenth Session was the rejection of the credentials of the Soutn African delegation and the consequent exclusion of South Africa from the General Assembly's deliberations. In the summer of 1975 the Arab States made known the plan to bring about by the same technique, in the forthcoming Twentieth Session, the exclusion of Israel. The reaction of western public opinion and of a number of governments to this threat was emphatically negative. Henry Kissinger declared that in case of Israel's expulsion the UN would become "an empty shell". Eventually the Arab group refrained from a confrontation on the question of Israel's credentials and decided instead to introduce a draft resolution against Zionism. In effect the Arab drive against Zionism had begun earlier. The resolution passed in 1973 on the "Policies of Apartheid of the Government of South Africa" referred to "the collusion between Portuguese colonialism, the apartheid regime, and zionism". The Declaration of Mexico on the Equality of Women adopted in July, 1975 by the International Women's Conference demanded the elimination of "colonialism and neo-colonialism, foreign occupation, zionism, apartheid, and racial discrimination". The Arab draft in the General Assembly went further by bluntly determining that "zionism is a form of racism and racial discrimination". After a long and highly emotional debate the draft was adopted on 10 November 1975 with 72 votes in favor, 35 against, and 32 abstentions and became Resolution 3379. A number of African states which had severed diplomatic relations with Israel two years earlier voted against or abstained. On the other hand two major Latin American countries considered as friendly to Israel, Brazil and Mexico, voted in favor. (Chile voted in favor in committee and switched to abstention in the plenary). After the vote the Israeli delegate, Chaim Herzog, at the end of his statement tore up the text of the resolution, in a gesture of defiance and protest. Resolution 3379 represented in a sense the nadir of Israel's fortunes in the UN.

Concurrently, the Arab pressure to further upgrade the PLO's status in the UN continued. On 4 December 1975 the PLO was invited for the first time to take part in a Security Council debate, the item being Israeli air raids in Lebanon. The invitation was made, moreover, under article 37 of the Council's Provisional Rules of Procedure, which deals with the invitation of states. The decision was adopted by 9 votes to 3 (Costa Rica, UK, US) and 3 abstentions (France, Italy, Japan). The question was considered a procedural matter on which the veto does not apply. This became a precedent for the invitation of the PLO on the same terms in subsequent Security Council meetings on Middle East matters. In July, 1977, the PLO was admitted to the Economic Commission for Western Asia on the same footing as a Member State of the UN. In addition PLO influence was bolstered by the creation of special UN bodies set up to deal with Palestinian matters. In 1975 the General Assembly established a permanent Committee of 20 states (raised to 23 states in 1976) on the exercise of the inalienable rights of the Palestinian people. In 1977 the Assembly authorized the setting up of a Division for Palestinian rights within the UN Secretariat.

The Security Council held debates on Israeli air attacks in Lebanon in 1975 and on the Middle East problem, the status of Jerusalem, and Palestinian rights in 1976. However, all the draft resolutions on these items, submitted by the non-aligned, were rejected because of the US negative vote. In July, 1976, the Security Council met in the wake of the hijacking by Palestinian terrorists of a French airliner to Entebbe, Uganda, and the liberation of the hostages by Israel. A Non-Aligned draft resolution which would have condemned "Israel's flagrant violation of Uganda's sovereignty and territorial integrity" and would have demanded from Israel to pay full compensation met with the opposition of all the Western powers. The UK and the US submitted a draft resolution which condemned all hijacking and called upon all states to take every necessary measure to prevent and punish all such terrorist acts. The Non-Aligned draft was not put to a vote. The UK-US draft received only 6 votes in favor (while Panama and Romania abstained and the USSR, China, and the Non-Aligned did not participate in the voting) and thus failed to obtain the required majority.

The anti-Israel campaign also encompassed the other organs of the United Nations System. In 1974 UNESCO virtually excluded Israel from its regional activities. Such a situation aroused a wave of protests and provoked the temporary suspension of U.S. contributions to the organization. In 1976 this problem was solved with the admission of Israel to the European Regional Group. On the other hand, UNESCO General Conferences periodically adopted resolutions condemning Israel for violating UNESCO decisions on the preservation of the cultural heritage of Jerusalem and on the respect of the educational rights of the population of the occupied territories. The World Health Organization, for its part, passed each year resolutions on the deterioration of the health situation of the population of the territories. In 1979 the Arab States tried without success to obtain the suspension of Israel's membership rights in the Organization. Resolutions concerning the rights of Arab workers in the territories were adopted by the International Labor Organization. Similar decisions referring to various aspects of the situation in the territories were taken by other UN bodies and agencies. Moreover, on the basis of the above-mentioned resolution 3237 of the UN General Assembly, the PLO was admitted as an observer by all the UN Specialized Agencies.

The Peace with Egypt followed by new crises. The rapprochement between Egypt and Israel which began with President Sadat's historic visit to Jerusalem (November, 1977) and led to the Camp David Agreements (September, 1978) and to the Peace Treaty between Israel and Egypt (March, 1979) encountered in the UN General Assembly the antagonism of the pro-Arab majority. In 1979, 1980, and 1981 the General Assembly passed special resolutions on this subject. Resolution 36/220, adopted in 1981, expressed "strong opposition to all partial agreements and separate treaties which constitute a flagrant violation of the rights of the Palestinian people". The vote was 88 to 21 with 36 abstentions. From 1982 a special paragraph rejecting "all agreements and arrangements in so far as they violate the recognized rights of the Palestinian people" was included in the main resolution submitted each year on the situation in the Middle East.

A noteworthy point is that no role was played by the Security Council in the implementation and supervision of the 1979 Peace Treaty, due to the negative attitude of the Arab-Soviet-Non-Aligned coalition. In view of the fact that no Security Council approval could possibly be attained for the establishment of a UN peace-keeping force linked to the Treaty, a Multinational Force and Observers (MFO) was constituted outside the UN framework.

The issues which claimed most attention in the UN were the Palestinian question and the armed clashes along the Israeli-Lebanese border, caused by the concentration of large PLO forces in that area. In July, 1980, the Seventh Emergency Session of the General Assembly was convened to deal with the Middle East problem. Resolution Es-7/2, which affirmed for the first time the right of the Palestinian people to establish its own independent state, was adopted by 112 to 7 (US, Norway, Australia, Canada, Dominican Republic, Guatemala, Israel) with 24 abstentions.

Israel's increasing isolation and vulnerability in the UN was aggravated by a change in United States policies in the Security Council. The US, from 1973 onwards, had blocked all significant anti-Israel moves in the Council through the use of its veto. Under the Carter administration, however, the tendency prevailed to promote compromise decisions or to abstain, leaving the veto only as a last resort. Consequently, in the years 1978–1980, a considerable number of Security Council resolutions adverse to Israel were approved. In March, 1978, following a large-scale Israeli military action in Southern Lebanon in response to PLO attacks against Israeli towns and villages (the Litani River operation), the Security Council adopted Resolution 425 which called upon Israel to withdraw forthwith and established a new UN Force, UNIFIL. Resolutions critical of Israel's activities in Southern Lebanon were passed in May, 1978, in January, 1979, in April, 1980, in June, 1980, and in December, 1981. In March, 1979, the Council approved by 12 to none with 3 abstentions (US, UK, Norway) a resolution on the establishment of a three-member Commission to examine the situation created by Israeli settlements in the occupied territories, including Jerusalem. On 1 March 1980 the Council unanimously adopted Resolution 465, which strongly deplored the establishment of Israeli settlements and called "upon the government and people of Israel" to dismantle them. Two resolutions on the expulsions of the mayors of Hebron and Halhul and a resolution condemning the assassination attempts on the lives of the mayors of Nablus, Ramallah, and Al Bireh were passed in May—June 1980 by 14 to none with the abstention of the US. In June, 1980, after the submission to the Knesset of a bill affirming the indivisibility of Jerusalem and proclaiming the city as the capital of Israel, the Security Council adopted a resolution urgently calling on Israel to desist forthwith from persisting in such policy. The vote was again 14 to none with the US abstaining. On 20 August 1980, following the approval of the law by the Knesset, the Security Council unanimously passed Resolution 478 which censured in the strongest terms the enactment of the law and called upon the states that had established diplomatic missions in Jerusalem to withdraw them. In compliance with this decision, the 13 foreign embassies located in Jerusalem left the city and were transferred to the Tel Aviv area.

In June, 1981, after the bombing by Israeli aircraft of a nuclear installation in Baghdad, Iraq, the Security Council unanimously adopted Resolution 487 which strongly condemned the Israeli military attack "in clear violation of the charter of the United Nations and the norms of international conduct" and stated that Iraq was entitled to appropriate redress. The question of the Israeli attack was also dealt with by the General Assembly. In November, 1981, the Assembly passed by 109 votes to 2 (Israel, US) with 34 abstentions a resolution which: a) strongly condemned Israel: b) requested the Security Council to take effective enforcement action to prevent Israel from further endangering international peace; c) demanded that Israel pay prompt and adequate compensation. In September, 1982, the General Conference of the International Atomic Energy Authority rejected by 41 votes to 39 with 5 abstentions the credentials of the Israeli delegation, thus barring Israel's participation in that session.

In the meantime a new major crisis had erupted, due to a law approved by the Knesset on 14 December 1981, on the enforcement of Israeli jurisdiction in the Golan region. On 17 December 1981 the Security Council unanimously adopted Resolution 497, which decided that the Israeli enactment was null and void and demanded that Israel rescind it forthwith. However, on 19 January 1982, the US vetoed a draft resolution defining the annexation of the Golan as an act of aggression and requesting all member states to take concrete and effective measures to nullify it. Five countries abstained. The pro-Arab coalition reacted by convening the Ninth Emergency Session of the General Assembly. On 8 February 1982 the Assembly adopted an extremely harsh resolution (Es/9/1) whose more salient features were: a) Israel's decision constituted an act of aggression and a threat to international peace and security; b) Israel's record and actions confirmed that it was not a peace-loving state (a requirement which according to the Charter is indispensable for admission to the UN; c) all member states were requested to sever diplomatic, trade, and cultural relations with Israel. The vote was 86 to 21 with 34 abstentions.

The Lebanon War. The close ties that the United States, under the Reagan Administration, maintained with Israel were evidenced by a return to the policy of stalling anti-Israel action in the Security Council by making frequent use of the veto power. In April, 1982, the US vetoed two draft resolutions: one on the removal of the mayors of Nablus and Ramallah and another on incidents which had occurred in Jerusalem in the area of the El Aksa Mosque.

On 6 June 1982 Israeli forces entered Southern Lebanon, destroyed the PLO military positions in that region, clashed with Syrian units and by mid-June encircled Beirut. The war created the risk of a confrontation between the two superpowers and the consequence was, once again, a partial paralysis of the Security Council. Yet the situation was not identical with that of 1973. The United States gave Israel only guarded support and at times disagreed openly with specific Israeli moves. The Soviet Union maintained an unusually low profile. It took no initiatives of its own in the Council or in other UN bodies and it refrained from voicing threats of military intervention. The non-aligned adopted a wait-and-see attitude. On the other hand, France and other western countries developed an independent diplomatic effort which at times clashed with that of the United States.

On 5 June the Security Council unanimously approved a call for a cease-fire. On 8 June the US vetoed a Spanish draft, which demanded the immediate and unconditional withdrawal of the Israeli forces. The other Council members voted in favor. A draft resolution submitted by France asking for an immediate 10-kilometer withdrawal of Israeli forces engaged around Beirut, and a simultaneous withdrawal of Palestinian forces from Beirut to their camps, was likewise defeated on 25 June by the US veto. During this period the Council unanimously adopted two resolutions of a humanitarian nature—one, on 19 June, calling on the parties to facilitate the distribution of aid provided by UN agencies and the International Red Cross, and the second on 4 July, calling for the restoration to the civilian population, particularly in Beirut, of vital facilities such as water, electricity, food, and medical provisions.

By the end of July, the aggravation of the situation in Beirut, caused by the continuing siege and the bombardment of the city by Israel, elicited a flurry of activity by the Security Council. A resolution on the lifting of the blockade and on the dispatch of supplies to the civilian population of Beirut was passed on 29 July by 14 votes to none (with the US not participating). On 1 August the US joined the other Council members in supporting a resolution which demanded the immediate cessation of all military activity within Lebanon. On 4 August the Council adopted by 14 votes to none, with the US abstaining, a resolution which expressed shock at the advance of Israeli forces in Beirut, demanded their withdrawal, and took note of the PLO's decision to evacuate the city. On the other hand the US vetoed on 6 August a Soviet draft condemning Israel for non-compliance with the Council's decisions and requesting all member states to refrain from providing Israel with weapons and military aid. On 12 August an additional resolution on the immediate lifting of the blockade of Beirut and the free entry of supplies to meet the needs of the civilian population was passed, this time unanimously.

The tension in Beirut subsided with the deployment of an international peace-keeping force and the evacuation of the PLO and Syrian military personnel on 21 August. Later fighting between Israeli troops and local militias flared up and on 15 September Israeli forces entered West Beirut.

On 17 September the Security Council unanimously adopted a resolution condemning the Israeli incursions into Beirut and demanding the immediate return of the Israeli forces to previous positions. On 19 September, after the slaughter in the Sabra and Shatila camps, another unanimous resolution was passed which condemned the "criminal massacre" of Palestinian civilians in Beirut.

On the whole, throughout the Lebanon war the Security Council remained on the sidelines and avoided taking a stand on the central issues. The American-French-Italian peace-keeping force, which acted in the Beirut area in August, 1982, and again between September, 1982, and January, 1983, was a non-UN body. On the other hand UNIFIL stayed in its positions in Southern Lebanon and was unable to play any significant role. The evacuation of PLO troops was negotiated outside the UN, while the Security Council had no bearing on later developments, such as the evacuation of the PLO troops, the Israel-Lebanese agreement of 17 May 1983 (abrogated by Lebanon on 5 May 1984), and the Israeli withdrawals of August 1983 and May-June 1985. The General Assembly dealt with the Lebanon war when the Seventh Emergency Session resumed. A resolution adopted on 28 June 1982 reiterated the demand for an Israeli withdrawal. The vote was 120 to 2 (Israel, US) with 20 abstentions. At the beginning of the 37th Regular Session of the General Assembly in October, 1982, Iran proposed an amendment to the Report of the Credentials Committee which would have had the effect of excluding Israel from the deliberations of the 37th session and the possibility of a de facto permanent exclusion. In order to avoid the risk of a straight vote on Israel's membership in the unfavorable political climate created by the Lebanon war, the western bloc preferred to act on purely procedural grounds. The four Nordic countries (Denmark, Iceland, Norway, and Sweden) moved that the Iranian amendment not be put to a vote. From a political viewpoint the key factor was the threat of the United States to quit the Assembly in the event of Israel's exclusion. The results of the voting on the Nordic motion were 74 in favor, 9 against, and 32 abstentions. Egypt supported the motion, Algeria and Libya voted against. The other Arab states did not participate. In December, 1982, the General Assembly passed a resolution which condemned "in the strongest terms the large-scale massacre of Palestinian civilians in the Sabra and Shatila refugee camps" and resolved that the massacre was "an act of genocide". The vote was 123 to none with 22 abstentions (Israel abstained). Another resolution, unanimously adopted, called for the restoration of the exclusive authority of the Lebanese government throughout its territory up to the internationally recognized boundaries.

The UN and the Arab-Israeli conflict in the eighties A major factor on the UN scene, since the beginning of the eighties, has been the new assertiveness of the United States. The US openly declared that it would apply its leverage, on the international and bilateral levels, to affect the course of UN events.

A combination of political and economic pressure on individual states and budgetary pressure on the UN as a whole proved effective up to a point on a number of critical issues, although South-Soviet control of the General Assembly was not substantially impaired. An illustration of this situation was the dispute over a United Nations Declaration scheduled to be solemnly signed at the Fortieth Session of the General Assembly. The US objected to the inclusion of a section on the Middle East because of its anti-Israel connotations and refused to subscribe to the document. The outcome was that the whole declaration project was abandoned.

A development which directly affected the Middle East was the war between Iran and Iraq, which broke out in 1980 and caused a split in the Arab camp. On the other hand Israel's political stand was strengthened by the relative tranquillity which prevailed along its borders after 1982. In these circumstances the position of Israel at the UN was to a certain extent eased. An example was the challenge to Israel's credentials initiated by Iran in 1982. From 1983 the Arab States solidly supported the move and from 1984 sponsored it. Yet the proposal was rejected each year—through the technique of the "Nordic motion"—by a larger majority.

The proportion of Israel-related items debated in each General Assembly remained unusually high. They included the Question of Palestine, the Situation in the Middle East, Human Rights of the Population of the Occupied Territories, Palestine Refugees in the Middle East, Living Conditions of the Palestine People in the Occupied Palestinian Territories, Israeli Economic Practices in the Occupied Palestinian and Other Arab Territories, Armed Israeli Aggression against Iraqi Nuclear Installations, and Relations between Israel and South Africa. In 1985 the Assembly passed 49 resolutions either dealing directly with Israel or comprising critical references to it. The voting trend pointed to a decrease in support for the Arab States and to a growing unwillingness to back extreme anti-Israeli proposals.

During the years 1983–1986 the Security Council acted only when the United States showed its willingness not to interpose the veto. On 4 October 1985, after the bombing by Israeli aircraft of the PLO headquarters in Tunis, the

Council unanimously adopted Resolution 573 which vigorously condemned "the act of armed aggression perpetrated by Israel against Tunisian territory" and considered Tunisia entitled to appropriate reparations. In September, 1986, the Council passed by 14 votes to none, with the US abstaining, a resolution condemning attacks committed against UNIFIL. In December, 1986, the Council adopted, by the same majority, a resolution deploring the opening of fire by the Israel Army, which resulted in the death and wounding of students of Bir Zeit University. Otherwise the Council confined itself to the periodic renewal of the mandate of UNDOF and UNIFIL.

The campaign against Israel in the UN Specialized Agencies continued. In 1982 the Conference of the International Telecommunications Union (ITU) rejected a move of the Arab States to exclude Israel from the Organization. In 1984 the Arab States introduced in the Congress of the Universal Postal Union a motion to expel Israel. The Congress decided not to take action on the proposal.

In 1992, the UN General Assembly voted to repeal the Zionism-racism resolution of 1975.

J. BARROMI

Security Council Resolution on the Middle East, November 22, 1967

THE SECURITY COUNCIL,

Expressing its continuing concern with the grave situation in the Middle East,

Emphasizing the inadmissibility of the acquisition of territory by war and the need to work for a just and lasting peace in which every state in the area can live in security,

Emphasizing further that all member states in their acceptance of the Charter of the United Nations have undertaken a commitment to act in accordance with Article 2 of the Charter,

1. *Affirms* that the fulfillment of Charter principles requires the establishment of a just and lasting peace in the Middle East which should include the application of both the following principles:

(i) Withdrawal of Israeli armed forces from territories of recent conflict;

(ii) Termination of all claims or states of belligerency and respect for and acknowledgment of the sovereignty, territorial integrity and political independence of every state in the area and their right to live in peace within secure and recognized boundaries free from threats or acts of force;

2. *Affirms further* the necessity

(a) For guaranteeing freedom of navigation through international waterways in the area;

(b) For achieving a just settlement of the refugee problem;

(c) For guaranteeing the territorial inviolability and political independence of every state in the area, through measures including the establishment of demilitarized zones;

3. *Requests* the Secretary General to designate a special representative to proceed to the Middle East to establish and maintain contacts with the states concerned in order to promote agreement and assist efforts to achieve a peaceful and accepted settlement in accordance with the provisions and principles in this resolution.

4. *Requests* the Secretary General to report to the Security Council on the progress of the efforts of the special representative as soon as possible.

UNITED NATIONS SPECIAL COMMITTEE ON PALESTINE (UNSCOP). Special committee appointed by a special assembly of the UN summoned in April-May, 1947. Its majority report served as a basis for the United Nations resolution of November, 1947, on the *partition of Palestine and the establishment of a Jewish State.

When the British government submitted the Palestine problem to the United Nations, it insisted that it was not relinquishing the mandate for Palestine but merely requesting advice on ways to administer or amend the mandate. It requested a special session of the General Assembly for the purpose of "constituting and instructing a special committee to prepare for the consideration" of the problem of Palestine and its future government for the next regular session of the Assembly.

The debate in the Assembly was confined mainly to the composition and terms of reference of the proposed Committee. In the end the Assembly approved an Anglo-American motion that excluded the Big Five (the United States, the United Kingdom, France, China, and the Soviet Union) and the Arab states from the investigating body. The Committee appointed included representatives of Australia. Canada, Czechoslovakia, Guatemala, India, Iran, the Netherlands, Peru, Sweden, Uruguay, and Yugoslavia. Of great significance, was the address by the Soviet delegate Andrei Gromyko, to the special session. He stated that a single, bi-national state, with equal rights for both communities was the solution "most deserving attention," but if that was found to be impracticable, owing to the nature of their relations, the alternative of partition would have to be considered. Potential Soviet support for partition upset the calculations of all those who had been certain that partition would never secure a majority vote at the UN.

UNSCOP's terms of reference gave it "the widest power to ascertain and record facts, and to investigate all questions and issues relevant to the problem of Palestine," thus rejecting an Arab request to exclude the problem of the displaced Jews as irrelevant. From 16 June to 24 July 1947, it pursued its inquiries in Palestine. The Palestine mandatory administration presented a memorandum that blamed the pro-Zionist provisions of the mandate for upsetting the balance between Jews and Arabs. The testimony of the Jewish Agency sought to eliminate any suggested solution other than a Jewish State (e.g. continuation of the mandate, joint trusteeship, cantonization, an Arab state, or binational parity) as unworkable and inequitable. Although all the Arab League states except Transjordan testified at the UNSCOP hearings, the Palestinian Arabs did not cooperate with the Committee. [King Abdullah met with the Committee in secret.]

The UNSCOP report was published on 31 August 1947. The committee recommended unanimously that the British Mandate over Palestine be terminated and that the British withdraw from the country. In solution of the Palestine problem, the Committee insisted on independence, democratic institutions, obedience to the basic principles of the United Nations, the economic unity of Palestine, strict observance of the sanctity of the holy places, and respect for the rights of the various parties there. The report also urged the United Nations to take steps to alleviate the plight of 200,000 Jews in displaced-persons camps in Europe.

In the application of these principles, UNSCOP was divided into a majority, recommending partition, and a minority (consisting of the delegates of India, Iran, and Yugoslavia), recommending a federated Jewish-Arab State. The delegate from Australia abstained.

The majority scheme suggested two independent states,

Members of the UN Special Committee on Palestine, left to right: Roberto Fontaina (Uruguay), Nasrollah Entezan (Iran), N. S. Blom (Netherlands), Alberto Ulloa (Peru), Emil Sandström (chairman, Sweden), Sir Abdur Rahman (India), Kavel Lišický (Czechoslovakia), Ivan C. Rand (Canada), John D. L. Hood (Australia), Jorge Garcia Granados (Guatemala), and Josha Brilej (Yugoslavia). [Zionist Archives]

one Jewish and the other Arab, and an economic union of the two. The Jewish territory was to consist of eastern Galilee, the coastal plain from a point south of Acre to a point north of Ashdod, and the Negev. Jerusalem, Bethlehem, and their suburbs were to form the Jerusalem enclave, to be administered by the United Nations under permanent trusteeship.

The Jewish Agency announced its acceptance of the majority report, but the Arabs rejected both proposals, and declared that they would resort to armed resistance.

I. KOLATT—M.J. COHEN

UNITED PALESTINE APPEAL (UPA). American fundraising organization established in 1925 for the purpose of coordinating and unifying the several Zionist fund drives, which had been campaigning independently. The Zionist leadership, aware of the desirability of setting up such an organization, was prompted to take action when the *American Jewish Joint Distribution Committee (JDC) launched its United Jewish Campaign in order to raise $15,000,000 in three years for the relief and reconstruction of eastern European Jewries, with emphasis on the Crimea settlement scheme. Although a conference of Jewish leaders convened by the JDC (Philadelphia, September, 1925) passed a resolution to establish rapport between the JDC and the Zionist organizations, no such rapport developed. Thereupon Emanuel Neumann, the national director of *Keren Ha-Yesod from its inception in 1921, initiated among Zionist leaders the discussion of a plan to unify Zionist fundraising activities into one appeal with a goal of $5,000,000 for the year 1925–26. This program was adopted, and Neumann was entrusted with its implementation. As a result of his negotiations, Keren ha-Yesod, the *Jewish National Fund (JNF), *Hadassah, the *Hebrew University Fund, and the Mizrachi combined their resources and efforts to raise the designated amount. Neumann persuaded Stephen S. Wise to assume the chairmanship of the campaign.

The first extraordinary UPA Conference (such conferences were to become annual events) met in Baltimore in November, 1925, and officially launched the first UPA campaign with Wise as chairman, Neumann as chairman of the Executive Committee, and Morris Rothenberg as chairman of the board. The first drive achieved its $5,000,000 quota.

The annual UPA campaigns continued until the end of 1929 despite internal disagreements and external struggles with non-Zionists. In 1930 the *Jewish Agency assumed direction of fundraising for Palestine, and the UPA became a wraith but was revived late in 1935.

The Zionist Organization of America (ZOA) proceeded to organize a united Zionist front to restore the UPA under Zionist leadership. To this end a preliminary conference was held in New York on 1 December 1935 in order to mobilize the Zionist organizations, including the Keren ha-Yesod and the JNF, as well as national organizations in sympathy with the building of the Jewish National Home in Palestine. The conference approved the inclusion of the

Keren ha-Yesod and the JNF on a parity basis into one agency, the United Palestine Appeal, and aimed at raising $2,500,000 in 1936, to be divided equally between the two. This plan was approved by a conference that met in Washington on 1 February 1936; it increased the goal to $3,500,000 and elected a permanent administration in which the ZOA was dominant.

The UPA—renamed the United Israel Appeal (UIA) in 1950—has functioned continuously ever since, despite initial difficulties with the JDC over the allocation of funds after it combined with the JDC in 1939 to form the *United Jewish Appeal (UJA). Where the JDC had at first been the major beneficiary of the combined drive, after the establishment of the State of Israel the UIA became predominant. For many years the ratio was fixed contractually at two-thirds of the UJA proceeds for the UIA and one-third for the JDC; in more recent years it was set at 87.5% UIA to 12.5% JDC for the regular campaigns.

In 1952 the JNF, by mutual consent, became independent of the UIA. The Keren ha-Yesod was eventually also eliminated as intermediary between the UIA and the Jewish Agency, the latter being the ultimate beneficiary.

The UIA itself became part of a process of reorganization in 1960, brought on by a ruling by the US Internal Revenue Service that tax-exempt philanthropic funds sent abroad must be controlled by an American organization recognized as tax-exempt by the IRS. Consequently a new agency was created called Jewish Agency for Israel, Inc. (JAFI) in which was vested control of UIA funds destined for the Jerusalem Jewish Agency.

Of JAFI, Inc.'s Board of Directors of twenty-one (initially), fourteen were appointed by the UIA and seven by the American Zionist organizations. The next logical step was the merger of the JAFI, Inc. and the UIA in 1966, with the UIA label being retained for the merged body. Thus the UIA, once the agent of the Jewish Agency for fundraising purposes now became the principal, and the Jewish Agency its operating, agent. At the same time, this continued the process of disengagement of the UIA from the World Zionist Organization.

Since the reconstitution of the Jewish Agency in 1971, the UIA has played a major role in that body, appointing 30 percent of the Agency's Board of Governors and Assembly. On the American scene, the UIA has been active in obtaining loans from banks for emergency needs in Israel; in securing government grants for programs in Israel on behalf of east European immigrants; and more recently also on behalf of Jews from Ethiopia.

The UIA maintains an office in Jerusalem whose main function is oversight of the programs operated on its behalf by the Jewish Agency (*See also* ZIONIST MOVEMENT, FINANCES.). H. PARZEN—E. STOCK

UNITED STATES JEWS IN ISRAEL. In the 18th century the interest of American Jewry in Eretz Israel was stimulated by the messengers sent by the various communities in the country to collect funds for their needy Jews. In 1825, Mordecai Manuel Noah dedicated the project of Ararat, a city of refuge for the Jews on Grand Island in the Niagara River in upstate New York and his *Discourse on the Restoration of the Jews*, written in 1844, called for the return of the people of Israel to its ancestral homeland.

In 1844 Warder Cresson, the United States Consul in Jerusalem, embraced Judaism and changed his name to Michael Boaz Israel. In 1852 he announced his intention of establishing a farm near Jerusalem to serve as a beginning of Israel's return to its ancestral soil. However, although he had the support of Jewish individuals in various countries, as well as a group in Jerusalem, his plan did not materialize.

The face of Jerusalem was changed in the middle of the 19th century due to the estate of Judah Touro, a native of New Orleans, Louisiana. When Touro died in 1854, he left $60,000 to build housing for the needy of Jerusalem, designating Sir Moses Montefiore to execute the project. That structure, the first outside the walls of the Old City of Jerusalem, was named Mishkenot Sha'ananim and the adjacent neighborhood came to be known as Yemin Moshe, in honor of Montefiore. Touro's generosity was marked by a plaque erected when the building was completed in 1860.

In 1870 Simon Berman, a Galician Jew who had lived in the US for many years, arrived in Eretz Israel. Advocating the establishment of Jewish agricultural settlements, he organized the Holy Land Settlement Society in Tiberias, which had a membership of 150, but the Society's plan to found a settlement was never realized.

Hundreds of American travelers descended on the Holy Land in the second half of the 19th century. Although the number of Jews among these tourists is not known, perhaps the outstanding individual in this category was David Lubin. In 1882, as a successful merchant in California, he fulfilled a vow by bringing his mother to Eretz Israel. From his letters during his six-month stay, it appears that he had decided to remain. However, he found the local agriculture such a source of inspiration that he decided to devote himself to this vocation on a world-wide basis and early in the 20th century, he founded the International Institute For Agriculture which he headed until his death.

The initial land purchase for American Jewish colonization occurred in 1891. Adam Rosenberg of New York, a representative of the Shavei Zion Society of that city, went to Eretz Israel and bought over 6,000 acres in Golan for members of the group. A dispute subsequently arose over the title to the land, so that only a few of the purchasers were ever able to settle there, but Rosenberg's mission was indicative of the desire on the part of a segment of American Jewry to settle in Eretz Israel even before the founding of the Zionist movement.

The first organized group of American Jews in the country, established in 1896 and still in existence, was known as Kolel America Tiferet Yerushalayim. By the end of the 19th century, the number of American Jews living in Jerusalem, most of whom were naturalized American citizens, had grown to 1,000. This made it possible for them to challenge the recognized practice of distributions of funds from abroad (*halukka*). That process was controlled by an organization, the Va'ad ha-Kelali of Jerusalem, which acted in an undemocratic fashion in its decision-making. To demonstrate the Va'ad's intractability, Americans in Jerusalem organized Kolel America to enable them to receive their funds directly from contributors in the USA. Their action led to the elimination of the Va'ad and ultimately to the downfall of the entire system.

When the American School of Oriental Studies opened in Jerusalem in 1901, Rabbi Martin Meyer was the first student. A graduate of the Hebrew Union College, he won his place at the Jerusalem School in a nationwide competition among colleges throughout the USA. During his stay, his articles from Jerusalem appeared in Anglo-Jewish newspapers and provided an American perspective of the land.

He later published his letters to his parents in the *Reform Jewish Advocate* of Chicago and also wrote children's stories about Eretz Israel. When he returned to the United States, he was commissioned to prepare the article on "Modern Jerusalem" for the *Jewish Encyclopedia*.

In 1904 He-Halutz, whose aim was to train members for immigration to Eretz Israel, was founded in the USA preceding the eastern European He-Halutz by many years. Five of its members emigrated to Eretz Israel in 1911 and worked initially on the Kinneret Farm. One of the group, Berl Klai, was a noted horseman, and a member of Ha-Shomer. He was killed in an Arab attack in 1915. Eliezer Lipa Yoffe, the best known of this pioneering circle, became a leading figure in the Labor Movement and was instrumental in defining the organization and structure of the moshav ovedim, which soon became a widespread form of settlement.

In 1913 *Hadassah, which had been founded a year earlier by Henrietta Szold, sent two American Jewish nurses, Rose Kaplan and Eva Levin, to Jerusalem where they treated thousands of children for trachoma and gave instruction in maternal care. During World War I, Hadassah organized the American Zionist Medical Unit. In June, 1918, 44 men and women of the Unit, including physicians, nurses, social workers and administrators, arrived in Palestine. They were later joined by additional Americans and local personnel. Many of the Unit's members remained in Palestine where they continued to be active in the medical institutions and health services established by the Unit and played a prominent role in the country's public health activities.

Also in 1918, 1,600 American volunteers, along with 400 Canadian volunteers, came as a part of the *Jewish Legion to Palestine. After the disbandment of the Jewish battalions, about 500 of the American volunteers remained in the country to assist in its rebuilding. Two of them, Jacob Tucker and Zev Scharf, died at the side of Joseph Trumpeldor in the defense of Tel Hai in March, 1920.

When the capture of Jerusalem by General Allenby was imminent in December, 1917, the Turkish authorities expelled all foreign nationals from the city. Among the population were 151 Americans, most of whom had derivative citizenship via naturalized American relatives. For almost a year they lived with the other exiles in Damascus, supported by the American Jewish Relief Committee. Among this group was Eliezer Rivlin, a scholar and an authority on Jerusalem history.

In 1919 Dr. Harry Friedenwald of Baltimore, a former president of the Federation of American Zionists, came to Palestine as the chairman of the Zionist Commission, the quasi-legal body which acted as the agent for the Jewish people until the mandate was established. Friedenwald was accompanied by Dr. David de Sola Pool, the rabbi of the Spanish and Portuguese Synagogue in New York, and Rudolph Sonneborn of Baltimore, who served as the secretary of the Commission. Sonneborn, who had just completed his tour of duty in the US Army and who came over in uniform, was to be the chairman in the 1940s of the Committee in the USA which purchased secret arms for the Hagana.

Between the end of World War I and 1927, some 4,300 settlers went to Palestine from North America, most of them setting up private enterprises in the growing towns and villages. The first members of the American Po'ale Zion, Gordonia, and other Labor Zionist groups began to arrive in Palestine during the Fourth Aliya (1923–28). Some joined established villages in ones and twos; others came in larger groups: for example, 12 members of the Detroit Kevutza settled at Ramat Yohanan.

The 1920s also witnessed the land purchasing activities of the *American Zion Commonwealth. Founded in 1914 as Zion Commonwealth Inc., its name was changed in 1919 to American Zion Commonwealth Inc. The purpose was to raise money for the purchase of land in Palestine through the sale of shares with the shareholders taking possession of their property when they settled on the land. Another goal was to ensure that "social justice, in harmony with the ideals of the prophets of Israel, may be the cornerstone of the Jewish Commonwealth." Relatively few shareholders moved to Palestine but the land purchases themselves were significant. Major areas of Herzliya, Ra'anana, Afula, and Balfouria were bought by the American Zion Commonwealth. Sections of Haifa, Tel Aviv, and Jerusalem were also among the purchases. A 1925 settlers' list of Herzliya included the names of 26 Americans.

During the 1920s, American Jews went to Palestine to organize specific projects in the economic, health, or educational fields. One was William Topkis of Wilmington, Delaware, a Zionist activist who previously had been a partner in Goldwyn Pictures with the DuPont family. In 1923 he opened the American Information Bureau in downtown Jerusalem and promoted the use of Jewish guides by American and other tourists. Topkis also wrote and directed a film produced in Palestine in which an American businessman, after seeing the country, decided to settle there. An American settlers' organization was established in 1923 in Tel Aviv under the name of The Organization of American Jews in Palestine. Active in aiding members in financial straits, the group organized a boycott of a Tel Aviv store which they claimed was charging unfair prices. In 1927 in Jerusalem another organization for American Jews was founded, known as Agudath Ahim Anshe America. In the early 1930s it merged with a Tel Aviv group of Americans but by the mid-decade, it had disappeared.

In 1931 Ha-Shomer ha-Tza'ir, the pioneer youth movement, sent its first group to Palestine and eventually founded Ein Ha-Shofet (named for Justice [*shofet*] Louis Brandeis), the first kibbutz established by Americans. Similar pioneer Zionist youth organizations were subsequently formed in the United States and Canada, and they systematically began to train young people for life on a kibbutz.

Between 1933 and the establishment of the State of Israel in 1948, around 6,000 Americans, including about 850 who had originally gone there as tourists, settled in Palestine, many of them after doing volunteer work in the European underground and manning ships carrying "illegal" immigrants to Palestine. On 5 April 1939 an organization, the American Jewish Association of Palestine, was founded at a meeting held in the Young Israel Hall in Tel Aviv. In 1940 the Association, working with Dr. Judah L. Magnes, Dr. Jacob Kligler, Deborah Kallen and the American consulate in Jerusalem, arranged for several hundred beds in Jerusalem to accommodate, if the need arose, "American Jewish evacuees from Haifa and Tel Aviv." The major success of this group came in 1942 when it persuaded the US Congress, through delicate lobbying, to pass an amendment extending until after World War II the date when naturalized American citizens had to set foot on American soil to maintain their citizenship. At the time of this Congressional action, 3,500 American Jews in this category were resident in Palestine.

All in all, during the 30-year period between 1918 and

the founding of the State of Israel, no more than 9,000 Americans settled in Palestine. Of these, 8,600 were registered immigrants from the United States. The rest entered under a variety of categories, both official and "illegal." By 1948 American and Canadian pioneers had established, in partnership with youth groups from other countries, the villages of Avihayil (founded by former members of the Jewish Legion), Ein ha-Shofet, Kefar Menahem, Kefar Blum, Beit Herut, Hatzor, Ma'ayan Barukh and Ein Dor.

This period saw significant contributions by individual Americans. Among them were Dr. Magnes, first head of the Hebrew University of Jerusalem; Henrietta Szold, an outstanding leader in social work; Deborah Kallen, who started the first progressive school in the country; Judge Shimon Agranat, later Chief Justice of the Supreme Court of Israel; Gershon Agronsky (later Agron), mayor of Jerusalem and founder and editor of the English language daily *Palestine Post* (later *Jerusalem Post*); Jessie Sampter, the poet; Irma Lindheim, former Hadassah president; and Dr. Israel Jacob Kligler and Louis Cantor, who were instrumental in introducing and developing public health services. Other Americans who conrtibuted to the development of the yishuv were Israel Goldstein, treasurer of the Jewish Agency and head of the Keren Hayesod; Robert Kesselman, an executive of the Federation of American Zionists and chief auditor of the Zionist Commission; and Elias Passman, representative of the American Zion Commonwealth and later of the American Jewish Joint Distribution Committee.

The proclamation of the State on 14 May 1948 was highlighted in Jerusalem by the flying of a handmade Israeli flag, fashioned from a bedsheet by Rebecca Affachiner, an American resident of the city since 1934. During the War of Independence 1,770 Americans and Canadians enlisted in Mahal, the organization of volunteers from overseas who joined the fighting forces in Israel. Of these, approximately 500 eventually settled in Israel, mostly in urban areas, engaging in white-collar jobs, professions and academic life, with a few on kibbutzim or cooperative settlements. Between 1948—1967, 7,500 Jews from the US settled in Israel. Among the villages they founded or helped to start were Sassa, Barka'i, Ha-Soleiim, Yiftah, Gesher ha-Ziv, Kisufim, Urim, Galon, Orot, Nahshon and Kefar Darom as well as the agricultural suburb of Bet Hatzor. Two entire communities of hasidic Jews also moved from the US to Israel.

A statistical survey of American and Canadian immigration was compiled from the close of 1961 through 1966 by the Association of Americans and Canadians in Israel (AACI). Of the immigrants who settled during that period, 34 percent were 30 years of age or below, 17 percent were aged 31—45, 10.5 percent were 46—60, and 22.5 percent were over 60. The ages of 16 percent were not listed.

A survey dating from March, 1963, showed 789 Americans and Canadians in a total of 94 kibbutzim and 239 in a total of 34 moshavim. It is estimated that another 200—250 had joined kibbutzim and moshavim by the end of 1966; an additional 400 were in private agricultural settlements. By 1968, it was estimated that of 23,000 settlers of all types from the North American continent some 10 percent were pioneers, somewhat less than the national average. More than 17,000 were settled in towns and cities, engaged in trade, in the professions, in studies or academic life, in technical and social work.

Many immigrants from the United States held key positions in Israel in the 1960s. Heading the list of officials was Golda Meir, Prime Minister. At the Hebrew University, the Technion in Haifa, the Negev Institute for Arid Zone Research, and the Weizmann Institute of Science, heads of departments and prominent research scientists and instructors were of American origin.

The educated, physically healthy, and technologically oriented manpower emigrating from the United States was essential to Israel's developing agriculture, industry, science and art and left its mark on numerous aspects of the new State's life and culture. Efforts were made to understand and solve some of the problems specific to members of this particular immigrant group. In the 1960s the largest number of immigrants arriving from the western hemisphere were young professionals. These individuals required conditions that would enable them to follow their professions and to maintain a standard of living for their families not too far below that to which they had been accustomed in their former homes. Relatively lower salaries and higher expenses for housing inferior to their previous housing created difficulties. The profusion of rules, laws and customs inherited from the Turks and the British, added to attempts at reorganization and modernization on the part of Israeli legislative bodies, made the initial formalities of immigration confusing and inefficient.

Early in 1968 a new aliya group, the Association of Americans and Canadians for Aliya (AACA), was established in affiliation with the American Zionist Council and the AACI. In the wake of the Six-Day War and the desire on the part of American Jews to immigrate, the AACA's purpose was to facilitate the absorption of North Americans in Israel. By May, 1968, membership exceeding 600 was reported and a considerable portion of the members prepared for immigration to Israel in the summer of that same year. The AACA subsequently became the North American Aliya Movement. From 1969–1974, 32,000 American Jews immigrated. A similar number came between 1975–1986. A recent study on the return of Americans to the United States places the percentage at 27 percent; however, other estimates suggest that the number is higher.

The period between 1969–1986 was one of major growth for American Jews integrating into Israeli society and contributing to it. Immigrants from the United States who held significant positions included Moshe Arens, Minister of Defense and Foreign Affairs; Yehuda Ben-Meir, Deputy Minister of Foreign Affairs; and Judge Stephen Adler, a member of the National Labor Court.

The key voice of the North American segment of Israel's population has become the AACI. Organized in 1951, the AACI, in its first quarter of a century of existence, was a resource body to which immigrants could turn. However, it did not have a high profile within general Israeli society because of its limited numbers and because it sought to act in a subdued fashion.

With the change of professional leadership in 1978, a new direction was sought by redefining the relationship of the AACI with the Jewish Agency to parallel the new understanding of aliya in American Jewish life. Community aliya projects were established in the USA and hometown groups were created for American immigrants in Israel with ties to the local federations in the communities of origin. The American Israeli came to be considered as an extension of the former community rather than being divorced from it. This linkage was further concretized by the loan funds established by 15 USA communities, administered through the AACI, by which former hometowners could be given direct assistance if needed. However, only three communities, Florida, Los Angeles, and Baltimore, have created mortgage funds for former residents now living in Israel.

The AACI, as of the fall of 1988, had 52,000 individuals affiliated with it. Educated estimates suggest that an additional 10,000 American Israelis may be resident in the country. As an activist organization, the AACI, in conjunction with the Israel Cancer Society, spearheaded the lobbying effort which produced a bill in 1984 banning smoking in public places. In the elections of the 1970s and the 1980s, the AACI published a non-partisan voters' guide on the parties and their platforms. Copies of the 1984 edition were used by the Israel army in courses for officers on democratic values. To aid new immigrants, the AACI published a guide in English listing every elementary and high school in the country, including principal's name, school's address and phone number. The most copied work of the AACI was the *Jerusalem Consumers' Guide*, published in 1983 with a second expanded edition in 1988. Similar guides for Tel Aviv, Netanya, Haifa and Beersheba followed. In 1987 a serving in the Israeli army. This contrasts with the typical eral consumer-oriented organizations and was sold widely.

While the number of American Jews who immigrate each year is relatively small, their significance may well be far greater than the actual numbers suggest. American immigration to Israel is one of the few examples, presently, of "free migration." Secondly, American immigrants, for the most part are college-trained. No other immigrant group has such a high concentration of professionals.

Even though American immigration appears to be monolithic, there is still a sub-group which moves to Israel specifically to join pioneering settlements. Three percent of immigrants in 1986 settled in kibbutzim and moshavim; 35 percent in Jerusalem; 35 percent in the central area around Tel Aviv; 10 percent in Netanya and another 15 percent in various cities and towns in the north and south. Two percent of the new immigrants settled in the Administered Areas. During the period 1969–1986, kibbutzim were started by American Orthodox immigrants at Ma'alei Gilboa and Bet Rimonim. The Reform Movement established two kibbutzim, Yahel and Lotan in the Arava; and the Conservative Movement founded Kibbutz Hanaton in Galilee. Young Judaea alumni started Kibbutz Ketura in the Arabah. Numerous moshavim and *mitzpim* (hilltop small communities) were founded by American immigrants in this period. A new phenomenon, beginning in 1969, were Americans settling in a *moshav kehillati* (community village) in the Administered Areas. While no official statistics have been compiled, it has been estimated that between 7,500 and 10,000 settlers in that area are of American origin; certainly, the percentage of American settlers there is higher than their number in the general population of the country.

A study of the religious preference of American immigrants arriving in 1986 showed the following: Orthodox, 37 percent, Conservative, 24 percent, and Reform, 10 percent. Whereas the Orthodox group has a natural power base in the country with representation in the Knesset, the Conservative and the Reform Movements have, on their own, begun to develop a network of institutions (*see* CONSERVATIVE JUDAISM AND ZIONISM: REFORM JUDAISM AND ZIONISM).

While American immigrants had been elected to the Knesset previously, the election in 1984 of Rabbi Meir Kahane (of the *Kakh Party) pointed to a small percentage of American immigrants with an ultra-nationalist orientation. In 1988 his Kakh party was ruled to be illegal so Rabbi Kahane could not run for reelection.

Certain areas of Israeli society have benefitted directly from the participation of American settlers. One is volunteerism. A key facet of American society, American Jews helped to develop the spirit of volunteerism in Israel, and succeeded in infusing it into the running of schools, hospitals, museums, and even government agencies. Another such area is sports. The arrival in the late 1960s of Tal Brodie, a noted American Jewish basketball player, gave a fillip to sports as leisure activity and spectator entertainment for all Israeli society. In order to speed up the development of teams at championship levels, foreign players—especially from the US—were imported, notably in basketball. Brodie, spent his entire Israeli career with the Tel Aviv Maccabi team and in 1977 led them to their first European championship. When Brodie retired in the 1980s, he set up basketball schools for youth throughout the country in which he emphasized sportsmanship as well as athletic expertise. For his efforts he was awarded the Israel Prize, the first athlete to be so honored. He is one of 14 American immigrants to receive the Israel Prize in their fields of distinction.

In 1984–1985 the percentage of senior citizens among US immigrants reached 16 percent. Since 1969, there has been a steady flow of senior citizens to Israel, most settling in Jerusalem or Netanya. The first American senior sheltered housing project, Nofim, was built in Jerusalem by the AACI and similar projects are being planned for other cities. Programming and networking for seniors have increased with activities for this age group in English being held almost daily in ten different cities in Israel. Camping programs, trips, cooperative buying, health care and exercise programs are all part of the American senior life-style in Israel.

The religious category of the "newly repentant" (*ba'al teshuva*) has added to the ranks of Americans in Israel. the first designated *ba'al teshuva* yeshiva (academy) in Israel was opened by an American rabbi in the early 1970s. A number of others have been developed which specifically cater to Americans. Men and women, seeking Jewish spiritual fulfillment, have come to Israel and enrolled in these yeshivot. The instruction is primarily in English and the life-style is strictly Orthodox. Spouses are found for the students and assistance is provided for newly-married couples and couples with children. Some of these yeshivot tend to be anti-Zionist and they discourage their adherents from serving in the Israeli army. This contrasts with the typical American immigrant who joins the army and fulfills the responsibility of Israeli citizenship. Over 100 American immigrants, men and women, who have been killed in battle or in terrorist attacks, are memorialized in a forest overlooking the Jerusalem-Tel Aviv highway. D. GEFFEN

UNITED STATES OF AMERICA, RELATIONS WITH ZIONISM AND ISRAEL. Long before the emergence of modern political Zionism, large segments of public opinion in the United States were favorably disposed toward the idea of Jewish national restoration in Eretz Israel. This was in keeping with the tolerant, liberal climate prevailing in the United States and was probably also due to the impact of the Restoration movement in England. In October, 1818, Pres. John Adams wrote in retirement to Mordecai Manuel Noah: "I really wish the Jews again in Judaea, an independent Nation, for, as I believe, the most enlightened men of it have participated in the amelioration of the philosophy of the age...." At the same time, the President expressed the wish that "your nation may be admitted to all the privileges of citizens in every part of the world...."

On 5 March 1891, William Blackstone of Chicago, a deeply religious Protestant who had visited Eretz Israel in 1888, submitted to Pres. Benjamin Harrison a "memorial" proposing the restoration of the persecuted Jews of Russia to the Holy Land ("What Shall Be Done for the Russian Jews?"). Among the 413 signers of the document were such men as Chief Justice Melville W. Fuller, Speaker Thomas B. Reed of the House of Representatives, and Congressman William McKinley (who later became President of the United States). The President received the memorial kindly and promised to give it his consideration. The publication of this document initiated much discussion in the American Jewish and non-Jewish press.

Twenty-five years later, in May, 1916, Blackstone revived his memorial and persuaded the Presbyterian General Assembly to adopt a resolution in favor of a Jewish Homeland in Palestine. In a speech before the National Geographic Society, former Pres. William H. Taft stated that a definitive solution of the Jewish problem should be put on the agenda of the postwar peace conference.

However, prior to World War I the attitude of the government of the United States was indifferent and even unfriendly to Zionism as a political movement and to the planned increase of the Jewish population in Eretz Israel. As late as 10 February 1912, Secretary of State Philander C. Knox was of the opinion that "problems of Zionism involve certain matters primarily related to the interest of countries other than our own...and might lead to misconstruction."

The election of Woodrow *Wilson as President in November, 1912, introduced a powerful new factor in the attitude of the executive branch toward Zionism. Wilson's interest in the Zionist cause was cultivated by Louis D. Brandeis, who was to become the key figure in the American involvement in Palestine. During the first year and a half of Wilson's tenure, however, there was no marked change in the attitude of the State Department. It was not until Turkey's entry into World War I in the fall of 1914, when the yishuv faced persecution and destruction, that Wilson's pro-Zionist stand made itself felt, resulting in the assumption by the United States of diplomatic protection of the Jews in Palestine.

World War and the Interwar Years. As a nation with no stake of its own in the Middle East, the United States occupied a unique position of influence with both the Allies and the Central Powers. It was largely due to American intercession in Constantinople and to American philanthropy that the depleted yishuv survived. The U.S.S. *Tennessee*, then in the eastern Mediterranean, was made available for the transportation to Port Said of Jews expelled from Eretz Israel by the Turkish administration. Owing to the intervention of Henry Morgenthau, United States Ambassador in Constantinople, the expulsions were discontinued by March, 1915; and in April and May, relief funds for the starving remnant of the Jewish community and for the support of Zionist settlements began to arrive. The transfer of funds was permitted even after the United States broke diplomatic relations with Turkey in April, 1917.

When the Turks resumed their anti-Jewish persecution and the Jews of Jaffa were forcibly evacuated, Secretary of State Robert Lansing officially requested the Washington envoys of the major neutral powers to join the United States in a protest to the Turkish government. Although the United States did not declare war on Turkey, no obstacles were put in the way of the call for enlistment of American Jewish youths in the Jewish Legion (1917-18). The American public evinced considerable interest in and sympathy for the Zionist cause.

In private talks with Rabbi Stephen S. wise and Justice Brandeis in May and June, 1917, President Wilson expressed approval of Zionist aspirations. These assurances were given without the concurrence or knowledge of Secretary Lansing, nor was a written commitment obtained from the President. There is no evidence that the forthcoming Balfour Declaration was discussed with the President during British Foreign Secretary Arthur James Balfour's visit to the United States in May, or that Wilson in any way committed the United States to the acceptance of British Palestine policy. It was only in mid-October that, on Wilson's instructions, Col. Edward M. House, the President's special representative, informed the British government that "the formula they suggest as to the Zionist Movement" met with the President's approval. Official Washington received the Balfour Declaration without comment. In December, 1917, at Lansing's insistence, Wilson acquiesced in withholding any announcement of the American stand, and this attitude became the State Department's official position during the 10 months of war that followed.

The first interruption of Washington's studied silence came on 31 August 1918, when, after an interview with Rabbi Wise, the President wrote a letter expressing his "satisfaction with the progress of the Zionist Movement...since the declaration by Mr. Balfour on behalf of the British government." He also hailed the founding of the Hebrew University of Jerusalem. This was the first of a long series of statements of sympathy for the Zionist cause issued by American Presidents.

Apparently issued without consultation with Lansing, the letter was neither then nor in the years that followed considered by the State Department an official United States endorsement of the Balfour Declaration. On many crucial occasions during the peace negotiations, the Department had ample opportunity to put forward its own line of thinking. The four American Commissioners Plenipotentiary at the Paris Peace Conference did not favor the Zionist approach to Palestine; indeed, they repeatedly expressed skepticism and even antagonism to Zionism. Lansing's memorandum of September, 1918, which was intended as a general guide for the Commissioners though not as a set of explicit instructions, included a provision for the creation of an autonomous state of Palestine under a protectorate, but it made no reference to any special status for the Jews in the country. On the other hand, the "Outline of Tentative Report and Recommendations," submitted in January, 1919, by the Intelligence Section of the American peace delegation (Dr. Sidney E. Mezes, Dr. Isaiah Bowman, and W.J. Westerman), was outspokenly pro-Zionist. It contained a broad statement of policy on Palestine, which recommended that "the Jews be invited to return to Palestine, being assured by the [Peace] Conference that it will be the policy of the League of Nations to recognize Palestine as a Jewish State as soon as it is a Jewish state in fact." There was, however, no lack of anti-Zionist influence, issuing mainly from Christian missionary groups, Jewish assimilationists, and pro-Arab circles.

Wilson himself seemed to be consistently pro-Zionist. In a statement issued from Washington on 2 March 1919, he reiterated his "personal approval of the declaration of the British government regarding the aspirations and historic claims of the Jewish people in regard to Palestine." As a firm believer in the principle of "self-determination of peoples," which he made the cornerstone of the American position at the Paris Peace Conference, Wilson could do nothing but endorse the proposal of an inter-Allied commission to investigate the desires of the population of Syria, of which Palestine was then considered a subdivision. Because Britain and France were withholding the nomination of their delegates, Wilson appointed a purely American team, consisting of Henry C. King and Charles Crane.

The *King-Crane Report, submitted after a hasty survey of public opinion throughout Syria (60 communities were visited in 40 days), stated that both Christian and Moslems were strongly opposed to the ultimate creation of a Jewish State in Palestine; it advocated Palestine's inclusion in a "United Syrian State" under a United States or British Mandate and strict limitation of Jewish immigration. This report, which was filed with the United States delegation in Paris, was not made public and in no way influenced the American stand and the deliberations of the peace conference.

After the signing of the peace treaty with Germany in June, 1919, the conference itself lost both authority and initiative. Simultaneously, President Wilson was losing his battle against isolationist forces in the United States, where the Senate and the electorate successively repudiated the Treaty of Versailles. The United States thus eliminated itself as an effective force in the framing of the terms of the Palestine Mandate. When, in February, 1920, the question of Palestine's boundaries became acute, Wilson, in response to Brandeis's plea, instructed the American representatives in Paris to support the Zionist demand for inclusion of the economically vital Litani River Valley and the western and southern slopes of Mount Hermon. But by that time Wilson was already desperately ill and largely dependent on his Secretary of State, who was unsympathetic to the Zionist cause.

The United States had become no more than an onlooker at international conferences. At the San Remo Conference of the Supreme Council of the Allied Powers in April, 1920, at which Britain was awarded the mandate over Palestine, the United States was represented by a mere observer. The isolationist administration of Pres. Warren G. Harding, which took over in March, 1921, had neither interest in nor sympathy for Zionism and Palestine. Harding himself addressed a friendly letter to the Zionist Palestine Restoration Fund, but Charles Evans Hughes, his Secretary of State, was firmly opposed to any pro-Zionist gesture. Reports received by the State Department from American consular representatives in Palestine were anything but fair, let alone friendly to Zionism, describing the Zionist leaders in the country as dangerous radicals, thus strengthening the determination of official Washington to eschew any Zionist involvement.

In contrast to the negativism of the administration, both houses of Congress were outspoken in their support of the Zionist cause. Despite the covert hostility of the State Department, they passed on 11 September 1922, a joint resolution (*Lodge-Fish Resolution) embodying the terms of the Balfour Declaration. Signed by President Harding, the resolution was of great moral significance for the Zionists, but it was not an indication of the Palestine policy the United States government was following in the early 1920s. Negotiations between Washington and London on a treaty defining American rights in Palestine lasted several years. The Palestine Convention, signed by Britain and the United States on 3 December 1924, and ratified exactly a year later, provided for United States acceptance of the terms of the Palestine Mandate and for American participation in all rights and benefits extended to members of the League of Nations.

For almost a quarter of a century the 1924 convention served as the basis for the official American attitude toward Palestine and Zionism—an attitude of aloofness, not shaken even by the bloody Arab riots of August, 1929, during which 8 (according to some sources, 12) American Jews were murdered. American Consul General Paul Knabenshue cabled the State Department from Jerusalem that the "Moslem attacks were precipitated by provocative acts of the Jews." The forceful indictment of Britain's "great betrayal" by Stephen S. Wise and Jacob de Haas left official Washington unmoved.

World War II and the Immediate Postwar Years. Throughout the interwar period and in the early days of World War II, it was a basic concept of United States foreign policy that the entire Mediterranean Basin was an area of British interest and responsibility, in which the United States had no immediate concern. There was in this respect little if any difference between the Republican administration and that of Pres. Franklin D. *Roosevelt (1933–45). Article 7 of the 1924 Palestine Convention provided that "any modification" in the terms of the Palestine Mandate had to be "assented to by the United States." The British White Paper of 7 May 1939, which drastically reduced Jewish immigration and, after a five-year period, made it fully dependent on Arab consent, undoubtedly was a major modification of the mandate. Nevertheless, the State Department, in October, 1939, declared that article 7 did not "empower the Government of the United States to prevent the modification of the terms of any mandate."

When the five-year period of grace during which limited immigration was still permitted was about to expire, President Roosevelt authorized Rabbis Wise and Abba Hillel Silver to publish in his name a statement that "the American Government has never given its approval to the White Paper of 1939." Yet, almost immediately following this seemingly definitive pronouncement, secret diplomatic dispatches to Arab capitals explained that although the United States had never approved of the 1939 White Paper, it had never disapproved of it, and that no decision would be reached on Palestine without full consultation with both Arabs and Jews. Despite the developing Nazi drive against the Jews no positive American action was taken to induce Britain to abolish or relax the White Paper restrictions on Jewish immigration to Palestine and thus to open an avenue of escape for Jewish refugees from Nazi-dominated countries. Official Washington endorsed the British view that the problem of Jewish escapees from Nazism must be handled as "part of the overall refugee problem" without special consideration for Palestine as a haven of refuge.

At the Anglo-American conference held in Bermuda in April, 1943, a dozen countries were mentioned as possible "clearinghouses" for refugees, but Palestine's name was omitted. Moreover, as revealed in official documents published by the Department of State (*Foreign Relations of the United States*, vols. III and IV), when the military situation in the Middle East was deteriorating and Palestine appeared in immediate danger of falling into German hands, highly placed State Department officials tried in 1941 to induce Zionist leaders to reach "some sort of understanding with the Arabs" in order "to avert a possible massacre" of Jews, who would be left "face to face with the Arabs, without any screen of protective force." The attempt to frighten the American Zionists into a downward revision of their political claims failed. Instead, an all-Zionist conference held at the Biltmore Hotel in New York in May, 1942, vigorously advanced the demand that "Palestine be established as a Jewish Commonwealth integrated in the structure of the new democratic world" (*see* BILTMORE PROGRAM). American public opinion, appalled by reports of what had happened to the Jews in the Nazi death camps, overshelmingly endorsed this demand. In the summer of 1944, both the Democratic and Republican party conventions incorporated strong pro-Zionist planks into their platforms. In the fall of 1944, 411 of the 535 members of the 78th Congress went on record as approving the Zionist call for immediate American action in favor of a Jewish Commonwealth in Palestine; there was virtually no distinction between the percentages of Democratic and Republican supporters. Resolutions urging the United States to "use its good offices and take appropriate measures to the end that the doors of Palestine shall be opened for free entry of Jews into that country, and that there shall be full opportunity for colonization so that the Jewish people may ultimately reconstitute Palestine as a free and democratic Jewish commonwealth" were introduced early in 1944 in the House and Senate. A clear majority of representatives and senators were pledged to vote for the resolution, but action was blocked on 17 March by the intervention of Secretary of War Henry L. Stimson, who notified the House Committee on Foreign Affairs that it was "the considered judgment of the War Department" that such a resolution "at this time would be prejudicial to the successful prosecution of the war." The objection was withdrawn in October, 1944. That same month President Roosevelt sent a strongly pro-Zionist message to the National Convention of the Zionist Organization of America (ZOA). The House Committee resumed hearings and reported favorably on the resolution, but concurrent action in the Senate Foreign Relations Committee was blocked when the State Department, with the approval of President Roosevelt, declared that "the passage of the resolution at the present time would be unwise from the standpoint of the general international situation."

A third and final attempt to secure the passage of pro-Zionist resolutions was made 10 months later in the 79th Congress, with the approval of the new President, Harry S *Truman. The resolutions were passed by an overwhelming majority of both houses in December, 1945.

The moral significance and impact of the congressional vote were substantial. Yet the clue to United States action on Zionist aspirations in Palestine lay in the executive branch as personified by the President and his administration. The attitude and policies of President Roosevelt and, later, of President Truman were of decisive importance. During Roosevelt's 12-year tenure numerous statements of sympathy and support for the Zionist cause appeared, but they were not followed by action. Former Under-secretary of State Sumner Welles explained this discrepancy by Roosevelt's firm belief that a just and practical settlement of the Palestine problem could be found through direct negotiations between Jewish and Arab leaders and by his consequent reluctance to jeopardize the prospects of such a settlement and antagonize the Arabs by urging a Zionist solution.

Roosevelt had therefore temporized, making public promises to the Jews and afterward explaining them away to the Arabs in secret diplomatic messages. The result of this strategy was that both Jews and Arabs became increasingly distrustful. In the process, however, Arab influence increased. After an encounter with King Ibn Saud in Alexandria in February, 1945, Roosevelt told Congress that by talking to the King "for five minutes" he had "learned more about that whole problem" tha he "could have learned in an exchange of two or three dozen letters." On 2 April the President, in a message to Ibn Saud, gave his personal assurance that he "would take no action...which might prove hostile to the Arab people." Since any action leading to increased Jewish immigration to Palestine and the establishment there of a Jewish Commonwealth was considered by Arab leaders to be "hostile to the Arab people," such an assurance practically precluded constructive American efforts on behalf of the Jewish cause.

Harry S Truman, who became President on 12 April 1945, was under pressure from anti-Zionist State Department officials to continue handling "the question of Palestine...with the greatest care." Undaunted by this advice and moved by the plight of the Jewish refugees in postwar Europe, he commissioned Earl G. Harrison, the United States member of the Intergovernmental Committee on Refugees, to investigate the situation of the refugees and their needs and wishes. On 24 August 1945, Harrison reported that the Jewish displaced persons "want to be evacuated to Palestine now" and that "the only real solution" was "the quick admission of one hundred thousand Jews into Palestine."

Forwarding Harrison's report to the British Labor Government, Turman urged the granting of 100,000 certificates but accepted instead the British proposal for a joint *Anglo-American Committee of Inquiry. The Committee's unanimous report, submitted on 20 April 1946, endorsed the immediate issuance of 100,000 certificates and denounced the policy of the 1939 White Paper which forbade the sale of landed property to Jews and which held that "there should be no further Jewish immigration into Palestine without Arab acquiescence." The British government refused to act on the report without ascertaining "to what extent the United States would be prepared to share the resulting additional military and financial responsibilities." In response to the President's inquiry, the Joint Chiefs of Staff advised against "United States armed forces involvement in carrying out the Committee's findings"; otherwise "the USSR might replace the United States and Britain in influence and power in the Middle East."

Instead of action, a new British-American team of negotiators, headed by Henry F. Grady of the State Department and Herbert Morrison of the British Labor Cabinet, met on 21 July 1946. While endorsing the 13-month-old United States plea for 100,000 certificates, it advocated the division of Palestine into three parts under an overall British trusteeship with the Jewish area covering 1,500 square miles. Originally approved by Secretary of State James G. Byrnes, the *Morrison-Grady Plan was rejected on 4 October by President Truman following strong criticism by leading members of Congress and by all Jewish organizations. The President, however, indicated the possibility of eventual United States support for a suggested Jewish Agency proposal for a viable Jewish State in control of its own immigration and economic policies in an adequate area of Palestine instead of the whole of Palestine.

When, in the spring of 1947, the British government submitted the Palestine problem to the *United Nations, Ambassador Herschel V. Johnson, the chief American delegate, stressed its importance "not only to the parties involved but to the whole world." He also expressed the certainty that "every member of the United Nations looks forward to the day when Palestine will be a free and independent state." Yet the American delegation remained consistently noncommittal concerning the envisaged character, scope, and timing of Jewish statehood which had been endorsed by the *United Nations Special Committee on Palestine (UNSCOP). The majority report of UNSCOP (31 August 1947) favored the partition of western Palestine into a Jewish and an Arab State, bound by an economic union, with Jerusalem under United Nations trusteeship. United States hesitation was motivated largely by uncertainty regarding the Soviet position; it was dispelled early in October, when the Soviet United Nations delegation endorsed the partition scheme; the American delegation followed suit on 11 October. At a later stage, the United States representatives solicited propartition votes among the United Nations member states and were thus largely instrumental in securing the required two-thirds majority on 29 November 1947.

The implementation of the United Nations partition decision met with armed resistance from the Arabs, while the British Mandatory authorities refused to cooperate with the UN Commission of Five, comprising representatives of Bolivia, Czechoslovakia, Denmark, Panama, and the Philippines, which had been set up by the General Assembly to facilitate the implementation of the partition plan and serve as a liaison between the outgoing mandatory government and the two prospective provisional governments in Palestine. Faced with these obstacles and unwilling to commit the United States to the enforcement of partition, the American delegation submitted on 19 March 1948, a proposal to the UN Security Council for a "temporary Trusteeship for Palestine" under the Trusteeship Council; in the meantime, the Commission was to suspend its efforts to implement the partition plan. This reversal of the declared American position pleased the British but aroused indignation among the American public.

The American working paper, submitted on 16 April to the UN General Assembly's First (Political and Security) Committee met with a cool and inconclusive reception. With the 15 May expiration date of the British Mandate approaching, United States officials urged the Zionist leaders to postpone the Declaration of Independence set for the same day and implied that economic and other sanctions might be imposed in case of noncompliance. Nevertheless, the State of Israel was formally proclaimed on the scheduled date. J. SCHECHTMAN

From the Establishment of the State of Israel. Eleven minutes after the State of Israel was proclaimed on 14 May 1948, the White House announced that President Harry Truman had extended diplomatic recognition to the new state. This act has come to symbolize the close and warm relationship which, in the main, has characterized contacts between the United States and Israel. This does not mean that there have never been differences, even serious differences, between Washington and Jerusalem. Still less does it mean that the United States established the State of Israel. However, a special affinity has existed between the two countries from the very beginning.

In the summer of 1948, Secretary of State George Marshall's endorsement of the plan of UN Mediator Count Bernadotte to detach the Negev from Israel and award it to Jordan severely upset President Truman who was charged with reneging on his support for the partition program. In both instances President Truman succeeded in overcoming State Department machinations and reasserted America's firm commitment to the principles of partition. Likewise in June, 1948, the President overrode State Department objections and appointed James G. McDonald as his Special Representative to the State of Israel (and subsequently as the first US Ambassador to Israel).

Only in one vital area did the President stay his hand and refrain from overturning State Department policy, and that was in the matter of the arms embargo on the sale of weapons to the Middle East imposed on 5 December 1947. This prohibition critically affected the fledgling Jewish State's prospects for survival. Considerable domestic pressure was brought to bear on Truman to lift the embargo, on the ground that diplomatic recognition warranted such a step. However, Truman was dissuaded from lifting the embargo, largely because both the British Foreign Office and the State Department warned that such a move would jeopardize Anglo-American relations by pitting the two powers against one another in a burgeoning Middle East arms race.

When Israel completed its first Knesset elections, President Truman, in February, 1949, moved to accord *de jure*, and not only *de facto*, recognition of the government of Israel. The US administration also acted to gain Israel's admission to the United Nations, which took place in May, 1949. Truman also aranged for the US Export-Import Bank to extend a loan of $100 million to allow Israel to promote the integration of the hundreds of thousands of newly arrived immigrants.

Moreover, these manifestations of warmth to the new Jewish state were not affected even when differences arose between Washington and Jerusalem over such matters as the fate of Arab refugees and the future of Jerusalem. According to the Israeli government the issue of the refugees could not be resolved except as part of an overall peace settlement. According to the United States, the readmission of the refugees would represent the first step toward a comprehensive settlement.

On the issue of Jerusalem, Israel maintained that the events of 1948 had aborted the entire scheme for the internationalization of the city. It rejected as a fiction the American assertion that the UN resolutions on Jerusalem still had a bearing on the status of the city. Although the United States persisted in treating Jerusalem as a separate and single entity, with the American consul reporting directly to Washington and not via the embassy in either Amman or Tel Aviv, this did not affect relations in any serious manner.

Arab refusal to sign a peace treaty with Israel coupled with an Arab search for arms and calls for a "second round" against Israel prompted Israel to turn to the United States to redress the arms balance. Instead, Washington prevailed upon its western allies, Great Britain and France, to join it in a common announcement that the three powers would act to forestall the development of any serious arms race in the Middle East. The 1950 Tripartite Declaration which they issued also proclaimed that they would treat as aggression any attempt to modify Middle Eastern boundaries by force.

The 1950 Declaration was widely regarded as the next best thing to a formal peace treaty in the effort to stabilize the region. The Soviet Union was not a party to the 1950 Declaration; in fact the Declaration was essentially directed against Soviet encroachment in the area.

US Attempts to Build a Mid-East Security Network. The entry of the Eisenhower administration into office in January, 1952, marked a turning point in efforts to "shore up" the Middle East against Soviet influence. John F. Dulles, the new Secretary of State, after a quick tour of Middle Eastern capitals, proclaimed the creation of a Middle East security network as a matter of the highest priority. There was a strong suggestion that Israel was hindering the formation of a regional security network. Dulles implied that Israel's concern over such a network would not be permitted to stand in the way. The Eisenhower administration's relentless pursuit of Arab support for a Middle East security pact foreshadowed a radical departure from the Truman administration's partiality toward Israel. It reflected a line of thinking according to which the emergence of Israel had created a stumbling block to consolidating western defense of the Middle East. If the stumbling block could not be removed, at least it should be humbled (in size). It is not surprising that relations between Washington and Jerusalem plummeted since they were marked by a considerable air of crisis throughout this entire period. At no other time in the course of the forty years that have elapsed since Israel emerged as a State did relations reach the nadir that they attained during these critical years.

American efforts to enhance Arab military strength before the Middle East dispute was settled caused consternation in Israel. Remarkably enough these demarches also antagonized Egypt, which viewed the projected security network as a euphemism for imperial domination. Nasser rejected American overtures to join the proposed Middle East network on the ground that Egypt was not fully sovereign so long as Britain continued to occupy part of its territory, and until Egypt recovered its full sovereignty it could not contemplate joining any security grouping. For Dulles the implications were clear: the British presence in Suez must be terminated. It was to this goal that he set his sights in 1953-54. His efforts were crowned with success in August 1954 when Britain agreed to evacuate Suez while reserving a "right of return" in the event of a great power threat to the Middle East. Dulles assumed that removal of the Suez stumbling block would clear the way for creation of the Middle East security network. Suez was to serve as a fulcrum around which the whole scheme would revolve. Since Nasser remained vehemently opposed to Egyptian participation in any regional defense pact, US efforts in this field remained frustrated.

Dulles now focused his attention on creating a northern defense network in the Middle East, that would initially embrace only those states immediately bordering on the Soviet Union such as Turkey, Iran, and Iraq. The move to include Iraq, an Arab state and moreover Egypt's rival, incensed Nasser. Given the opposition of both Egypt and Israel, it was decided that the United States would not, for the moment, become a full-fledged party to the Baghdad Pact, signed on 30 March 1955. Washington would furnish weapons and supplies but would not assume formal membership. This would also help spare the administration a tough battle from the pro-Israel Senate whose advice and consent would be required for the approval of a treaty.

Israel's concern over America's resolve to arm Iraq, a state which, alone among Arab belligerents, had refused to even conclude an armistice agreement with Israel, was compounded by the news of the Egyptian-Czech arms deal announced in September, 1955. In a very real sense, the policies of Dulles had brought about the very development—Russian penetration of the Middle East—which American policy had, since World War II, sought to preclude at all costs. But if the new situation emerging in the Middle East was fraught with dangers for western interests, it was positively ominous for the security of Israel. Notwithstanding the force of international conventions and the terms of the armistice agreement, Egypt had steadfastly refused passage to Israeli ships or cargoes through the Suez Canal. Likewise, Egypt had blockaded the entrance to the Gulf of Eilat (Akaba) by denying passage through the Straits of Tiran. The Security Council had in 1951 condemned the Egyptian blockade of the Canal, but its resolution effected no change in Egyptian policy.

Egypt's embroilment in 1956 in a dispute with Britain and France over ownership and control of the Suez Canal opened the way for concerted international action against Nasser. The outcome was the Suez Campaign of October-November, 1956, in which Israel captured all Sinai, approaching the Canal, including the Egyptian fortifications at Sharm el-Sheikh which had been employed to impose the blockade through the Straits of Tiran.

However, the Eisenhower administration, still wedded to the policies which had so contributed to the Suez explosion and still bent on courting Nasser, insisted that Israel forego the fruits of conflict and expose itself once again to the varied manifestations of Nasserite belligerency. The United States demanded an immediate and unconditional Israeli withdrawal from Sinai. The confrontation which ensued between Washington and Jerusalem was a reflection of the obtuseness which had characterized America's Middle East policy since the Eisenhower-Dulles team had entered office. Nowhere was this better revealed than in the American stand on the Straits of Tiran as an international waterway. Israel demanded that, besides the stationing of a UN force at Sharm el-Sheikh to guard the straits, it was essential that the United States, in conjunction with other seafaring states, confirm the international character of the waterway. The Eisenhower administration was not inclined to accede to the Israeli demand or offer any assurances in return for an Israeli withdrawal. By early 1957 an impasse had been reached and the US resolved to support the call for Security Council sanctions against Israel for its failure to withdraw from Sinai. It was at this point that Israel's support in the US Senate induced a change of policy. The then Senate Majority Leader, Lyndon Johnson, made it clear to the White House that Congress would balk at the imposition of sanctions against Israel. The crisis was finally resolved when Israel agreed to accept a letter from President Eisenhower which confirmed freedom of passage through the Straits of Tiran. Israeli evacuation of Sinai followed in short order.

Whereas the first five years of the Eisenhower administration's terms of office were marked by a placatory attitude toward Nasser's aggressive policies and persistent efforts to woo the Egyptian leader in the western-sponsored Middle East Defense Organization, the final three years of office reflected a deep disillusionment with Nasser and his policies. In the earlier period an attempt was made to forestall Russian penetration and domination of the Middle East by enlisting Nasser's aid, while in the later period this goal was to be achieved despite Nasser's opposition. The

Eisenhower administration's disillusionment with Nasser was given expression in the proclamation of the Eisenhower Doctrine on 5 January 1957, whose purpose "to deal with the possibility of Communist aggression, direct and indirect." The United States gave notice that it would even employ its own armed forces, if need be. Belatedly, the Eisenhower-Dulles team was awakening to the realities of Middle East politics. Soviet penetration of the region was now a fact, confirmed not only by the arms deal but even more, by the contest of arms reflected in the Suez war whose main purpose had been to restore western influence in the Middle East. Henceforth, East and West would share influence in the area.

Israel was an indirect beneficiary of the reorientation in America's Middle East policy. Recognition by Washington that Nasser was committed to promoting Russian influence in the Middle East at the expense of western influence cast Israel in a new light in relation to American policy interests in the region. By the time the Eisenhower administration ended its second term of office, relations between Washington and Jerusalem, although not overly warm, were at least cordial and marked with a new spirit of cooperation. The departure of Secretary of State John Foster Dulles from the scene with his death in 1958 and his replacement by Christian Herter heralded a new era in US-Israeli relations.

US Guarantees Israel's Security. The improvement in ties took a major leap forward with the entry into the White House of President John F. Kennedy in January, 1961. Kennedy was the first US president to guarantee Israeli security. At a meeting with Foreign Minister Golda Meir in December, 1962, the President assured her that "in case of an invasion the United States would come to the support of Israel." This presidential commitment placed relations between the two countries on a new level of association, for it was tantamount to a *de facto* alliance. While subsequent US-Israeli relations have been marked by an ebb and a flow, the bedrock of the relationship has remained the firm American pledge to ensure Israel's security. The ties had been given a practical boost when the Kennedy administration in September, 1962, announced that Washington would furnish Israel with Hawk anti-aircraft missiles. This was the first occasion that the United States undertook to furnish Israel with a major weapons system—albeit a defensive one.

However, it should not be assumed that Kennedy spurned opportunities to build bridges to the Arab world. On the contrary, in the opening stages of his administration he adopted a pragmatic approach to the questions involved and while assuring Israel of support, sought to explore possibilities with Nasser. The Kennedy administration increased aid to Egypt and was particularly generous in grants of wheat. But these efforts were torpedoed by Egypt's involvement in the civil war which broke out in Yemen in 1962: Nasser backed the revolutionaries while Saudi Arabia (in which the United States had vital interests) supported the new imam.

In contrast to Kennedy, Pres. Lyndon Johnson did not go out of his way to try and court Nasser. There was the feeling that the United States had gone as far as it could to accommodate Nasser's whims and there was nothing much that Washington could, or should, do to further appease him. In any case, the United States had become embroiled in Vietnam and the problems of the Middle East were placed on the "back burner." So long as no immediate crisis enveloped the region, Washington felt it could safely ignore a dispute which had now dragged on for more than a decade and a half.

The Six-Day War. Any expectation that the Middle East would oblige and remain quiescent was dashed by Nasser's bold aggressive moves in May, 1967. Moscow, it appears, had spread a rumor that Israel was preparing to attack Syria. Nasser decided to capitalize on this and on 16 May 1967 ordered the withdrawal of the UN Emergency Force from the Egyptian-Israeli border, as well as from Sharm el-Sheikh. On 23 May after massing troops in Sinai, Nasser proclaimed a blockade on Israel through the Straits of Tiran. (In 1957, when Israel had withdrawn from Sinai, it had made clear that any attempt to impede freedom of passage to Israeli ships in the Gulf of Eilat (Akaba) would constitute a *casus belli.*) In an effort to avert war, Israel turned to the US to restore the *status quo ante* and enforce freedom of passage through the straits. The Johnson administration did not now relish the prospect of becoming engaged militarily in the Middle East. Washington called upon other western states to join it in creating an international flotilla of warships to secure passage. For Israel, time was of the essence and in the absence of an adequate response from Washington, a decision was taken to act unilaterally. The Israeli move came on the morning of 5 June 1967. Six days later all of Sinai as far as the Suez Canal, east Jerusalem and the entire West Bank of the Jordan River, as well as the Golan Heights, were in Israel's hands.

Prime Minister David Ben-Gurion with Pres. John F. Kennedy. [Israel Information Services]

Visit of Prime Minister Levi Eshkol to the United States. Shown (left to right) are Mrs. Eshkol, Prime Minister Eshkol, Amb. Avraham Harman, Pres. Lyndon B. Johnson, and Mrs. Johnson. [Hadassah]

Israel's lightning campaign spared the United States any involvement in the conflict. Only when the Russians hinted that they were contemplating intervention was the United States compelled to react—by strategically placing the US Sixth Fleet athwart any possible line of attack from the sea. The war was over before outside intervention could materialize and as a result no East-West confrontation transpired.

However, Washington was active in defense of Israeli interests on the diplomatic front. In contrast to 1956, the Johnson administration was resolved that restoration of the *status quo ante* not be effected until the causes of war in the Middle East were eliminated. It therefore rejected both during and after the conflict, every call at the United Nations for an unconditional return to the lines of 5 June. Return of territories, Johnson stressed, must be accompanied by peace. The United States joined repeatedly with a majority of UN members to reject Arab and Soviet demands for an immediate and unqualified withdrawal from territories. American diplomatic support for Israel was unequivocal. Only on one point was there a divergence of views, namely, on the issue of Jerusalem. Israel, in the aftermath of the conflict, had reunited the city as an administrative step. Washington expressed its reservations. In the UN General Assembly a resolution on Jerusalem was adopted calling upon Israel to restore the city to its former status. The United States abstained in the vote while Israel voted against.

Aftermath of the Six-Day War: the Rogers Plan. President Johnson's stand on a negotiated settlement was essentially incorporated into Security Council resolution 242, adopted on 22 November 1967, which henceforth became the touchstone of American policy in the Middle East. (*see* UNITED NATIONS AND PALESTINE-ISRAEL). With the entrance into the White House of Pres. Richard Nixon in January, 1969, US policy underwent a subtle but significant change. The United States continued to pay lip service to direct negotiations. However, in practice, US policymakers began to outline the "contours" of the proposed settlement. In an attempt to bridge the gulf between the parties, Secretary of State William Rogers outlined a plan which called for a near-total Israeli withdrawal from all Arab territories in return for peace. Only "insubstantial" adjustments in the borders would be permitted. Israel, however, now viewed the matter quite differently. It insisted on direct negotiations between the parties as a sign of mutual acceptance and as the only real guarantee for a settlement.

By the end of 1969, US—Israeli relations had seriously deteriorated as a result of divergent approaches to the substance and procedure of peace negotiations. In December, 1969, Prime Minister Golda Meir formally rejected the Rogers Plan. A major crisis between Jerusalem and Washington was only averted by Egyptian intransigence and, even more significantly, by the dramatic entry of the Russians onto the scene.

Russian entrenchment. The Rogers Plan had been submitted to the Soviet Union as a proposed basis for negotiations. Egypt, however, adamantly refused to entertain the Plan even as a starting point, and so the Russians dismissed it out of hand. Washington felt it could not fairly attempt to wring more concessions from Israel than envisaged under the Rogers Plan and so the talks were stalled. Meanwhile the stationing of over 20,000 Russian troops in Egypt in early 1970, followed by SAM ground-to-air missiles and MIG fighters to counter Israel's air supremacy, altered the regional power balance. The entrance of Soviet troops into a combat role represented a new and dangerous escalation in the Arab-Israeli dispute. It portended the possibility of a major American-Soviet clash—even a nuclear one —over the Suez Canal. American policymakers were determined to forestall any such development. Two moves resulted. The first was to bolster Israel's defenses by replenishing Israel's losses in war planes. In effect, Israel was now serving as America's first line of defense in the Middle East against Russian penetration and domination. The second step was to secure a ceasefire along the canal which would make the Russian presence in Egypt unnecessary. Secretary of State Rogers succeeded in doing this, and on 7–8 August 1970 the ceasefire entered into effect.

However, no sooner had the hostilities ceased than the Egyptians, with the active connivance of the Russians, rushed to deploy ground-to-air missiles along the entire length of the Canal—notwithstanding the commitment they had made to maintain a military standstill within 50 kilometers of the waterway. This brazen violation of the terms of the ceasefire agreement dashed any hope for meaningful peace talks between the parties. American policymakers reacted strongly to the Egyptian-Soviet duplicity. There was the feeling that the Russians, rather than promoting peace, were bent on entrenching themselves more deeply in Egypt. The Suez Canal was now fully within their grasp with all that this implied for global power politics.

In September, 1970, Palestinian Arabs hijacked three airliners to a Jordanian desert airstrip and Syrian tanks were poised to intervene on behalf of the hijackers. The US interpreted the incident as Russian-orchestrated and as part of Russia's plan to gain control of the Middle East. The United States responded vigorously to the Russian challenge. The US Sixth Fleet was moved into the eastern Mediterranean, the 82nd Airborne Division in Germany and the United States was put on alert, and giant transport planes in Turkey were readied for instant action. These measures, however, did not halt the Syrian advance. Urgent consultations were held between Washington and Jerusalem whereupon Israel made it known that its air force stood ready to smash the Syrian advance. This warning had the desired effect and the Syrian forces were withdrawn. The crisis receded.

In effect, Israel added substance to America's Middle East deterrent and helped contain what, in President Nixon's words, was "the gravest threat to world peace since this administration came into office—Vietnam not excluded." American aid to Israel in 1971 and 1972 increased. For the first time it also included Phantom jets. As long as the Russians remained in Egypt, the United States was determined to bolster Israel's strength.

President Sadat's Initiative. The resultant stalemate which gripped the Middle East after 1970 was anathema to President Sadat who had succeeded President Nasser as Egypt's head of state. The Soviet presence in Egypt, while essential for Egypt's air defense, operated as a brake against military action, since the Soviet Union did not want to underwrite anything which might lead to a confrontation with the United States. Yet, so long as the Russians remained, the avenue to negotiations via Washington was blocked. On 18 July 1972, Sadat cut the Gordian knot and expelled the Russians from Egypt. This act restored Egypt's freedom of action and allowed Egypt to prepare for an all-out cross-canal attack, timed to coincide with a Syrian attack from the north and set for the day of Yom Kippur, 6 October 1973.

The Yom Kippur War provided American decision-makers with an opportunity to attain manifold policy goals. As explained by the new Secretary of State, Henry Kissinger, these were a) ensuring Israel's survival; b) producing a ceasefire which would facilitate negotiations between the parties; c) preventing unilateral Soviet gains; and d) avoiding a nuclear confrontation with the Soviet Union. The United States, in fact, succeeded in achieving all of its policy objectives. Thus, even though Washington rallied to Israel's aid with an enormous military airlift, the door to Cairo was kept open for the period following hostilities. Nuclear confrontation with the Soviet Union was avoided, although a crisis did arise in the final hours of the conflict, and the Soviet Union was unable to exploit developments so as to reestablish itself in Egypt. The natural outcome of a war in which neither side gained a knockout victory and in which Russia was prevented from exploiting the situation, was an American-Egyptian rapprochement. This paved the way for the US to pursue an active diplomatic role. Initially, it helped produce disengagement agreements aimed at stabilizing and extending the ceasefire and, ultimately, it acted as a midwife of the Egyptian-Israeli peace treaty. In a real sense, the United States was positioned to institute a form of Pax Americana in the Middle East to the exclusion of a Soviet role in the peace-making process.

The key figure in this diplomatic initiative was Secretary of State Henry Kissinger who in the course of the two years after November 1973 made eleven trips to the Middle East. He won the confidence of both the Egyptian and Israeli leaders and gradually succeeded in extracting concessions from both sides in a series of step-by-step negotiations. There was one interlude in this process during which the parties met at Geneva under the joint auspices of the United States and the Soviet Union as was provided for in Security Council Resolution 338. However the Geneva Conference turned out to be mere window dressing since the parties themselves preferred to dispense with the international forum and rely rather on the direct services of the United States in reaching an accommodation. By the time Kissinger left office in January 1977, substantial progress had been made in reducing tension in the Middle East and in moving the area from belligerence to actual peace—at least along the Egyptian-Israeli boundary.

President Nixon with Golda Meir, 1973. [Israel Govt. Press Office]

A measure of the crucial role which the United States had come to play in the peace process is indicated by the special supervisory function it assumed in Sinai and by the secret supplementary agreements with which it furnished Israel. Thus, the United States set up the Sinai Field Mission composed of 200 technicians to man three early warning stations, and provided Israel with the necessary participatory assurances for its security.

The Egyptian-Israeli peace process was consummated during the next stage of negotiations, after Kissinger had already left the scene. In the interval two further significant changes in personnel had taken place. First, President Carter had entered the White House in January 1977. Moreover in May 1977, Menachem Begin, head of the Herut party, had, for the first time in Israeli politics, succeeded to the reins of government.

The real breakthrough came after Pres. Sadat announced, in a speech before the Egyptian parliament on 9 November 1977, that he would be prepared to address the Knesset in Jerusalem if that would bring peace. This dramatic announcement undermined, and made purposeless, Pres. Carter's earlier efforts to reconvene the Geneva Conference under joint Soviet-American auspices. It confirmed that neither Egypt nor Israel cared to grant the Soviet Union an effective role in the peacemaking process. President Carter had obviously misread the situation and had failed to appreciate that progress along the road to peace had emerged only because of Russia's absence from the negotiating table.

The Camp David Accords. Sadat's historic appearance before the Knesset on 19 November 1977 launched a new era in the peacemaking process, in which the United States was assigned a pivotal role. This role was highlighted by the shuttle mediation undertaken by Secretary of State Cyrus Vance and other State Department officials and, most importantly, by the convening of the Camp David conference (*see* CAMP DAVID AGREEMENT) on 5 September 1978. The conference, which lasted for two weeks, was attended by Pres. Carter, Prime Minister Begin, Pres. Sadat, and senior officials from all three governments. Carter and his staff prodded, cajoled, pressured, and browbeat the parties until an agreement was hammered out. The "Framework for Peace in the Middle East" included an agreement for the conclusion of an Egyptian-Israeli peace treaty to be completed within three months of the accords and an agreement for instituting a five-year transition period for the West Bank (Judea and Samaria) and the Gaza Strip during which the local population would be accorded "full autonomy." During this period the parties, including Israel, Egypt, Jordan, and the representatives of the inhabitants of the West Bank and Gaza, would meet "to determine the final status of the West Bank and Gaza and its relationship with its neighbors and to conclude a peace treaty between Israel and Jordan by the end of the transitional period."

America's role as mediator was also highlighted in the subsequent stage of the negotiations during which the terms of the Egyptian-Israeli peace treaty were concluded. Again, after much pressuring and prodding by the US government, and extensive shuttle diplomacy, the agreement was signed on the White House lawn on 26 March 1979. America's role had been crucial throughout, and in two respects. First, the United States extracted concessions from both sides and devised compromise terms of agreement which proved acceptable to both sides. Second, the US administration supplemented the agreements with guarantees indispensable to both sides. The guarantees extended to security matters, such as the creation of a multinational force to guard the Sinai but also to economic matters, such as the promise to ensure Israel's oil supply for fifteen years in return for Israel's surrender of the Sinai oil wells to Egypt.

The US Contribution to Autonomy Discussions. By the time Pres. Carter was replaced in the White House by Pres. Reagan on 20 January 1981, no recognizable progress had been made in the autonomy talks for the West Bank and Gaza. Furthermore, two major points of dispute had arisen between Washington and Jerusalem. The first was the decision of the Carter administration in March 1978 to sell 60 FI5 planes to Saudi Arabia. (It was presented as part of an arms package deal which also entailed the sale of arms and planes to Israel and Egypt.) The Israel lobby in Washington strenuously fought the move and ultimately the sale to Saudi Arabia was made subject to restrictions which would prevent use of the planes in an offensive capacity. The second bone of contention was that of Jewish settlements. The Carter administration was sharply critical of the Begin government's policy of promoting Jewish settlement in the West Bank and Gaza while the talks were stalled. In contrast, the Reagan administration adopted a more tolerant attitude toward the issue of the settlements which it refused to condemn as illegal. Nonetheless, matters relating to the autonomy discussions had not been appreciably advanced in the interim. In fact, the Reagan Plan, announced by the President on 1 September 1982, only tended to congeal positions.

According to the President, the United States envisaged some sort of permanent tie-in between the West Bank, Gaza, and Jordan. This somewhat preempted the purpose of the negotiations between the parties toward the end of the five year autonomy period, since the Camp David accords had envisaged that the parties would themselves resolve the issue of the future of the territories. Israel objected to the Reagan Plan, *inter alia*, on this ground. (On one point, however, the Reagan Plan seemed distinctly to favor Israel namely, with reference to near-exclusive Israeli control over Jerusalem.)

The Lebanon Conflict. The years 1982–85 were marked by heavy Israeli involvement in Lebanon. The US had given its implicit blessing to the initial Israel incursion in June, 1982, but as the campaign dragged on the American attitude became one of disillusionment and ultimately, of sharp criticism. The US at one point assumed a peacekeeping role in Beirut which enabled the PLO and its leader, Yasir Arafat, to safely leave the city. Subsequently, after the headquarters of the US Marines in Beirut attacked by a terrorist car-bomb, with the loss of 241 American lives, Pres. Reagan ordered an end to the US peacekeeping role and the American forces were withdrawn. The differences between Washington and Israel over Lebanon were resolved when Israel announced its withdrawal in May, 1985. The question of the status of the West Bank and Gaza (not excluding the issue of Jerusalem) was postponed. Until the population of these territories resolved just who was to represent them—King Hussein or Yasir Arafat—the US was unable to promote the convening of a forum for resolving the issue.

US-Israel Relations: Conclusions. In general, the period of the Reagan administration was one of unprecedented cordiality between Israel and the United States. When the United Nations, as a result of Russian opposition, was unable to enlist the necessary international personnel to compose the Mutinational Force and Observer team to supervise the peace between Israel and Egypt in the Sinai, the United States, in 1981–82, undertook to supply the bulk of the forces. This step saved the Egyptian-Israeli peace treaty from foundering. Furthermore, Washington and Jerusalem concluded numerous binational agreements such as a Memorandum of Strategic Understanding and later a Free Trade Agreement between the two countries.

American-Israeli relations have been affected by various influences at each stage of the way. In the first phase, during the Truman administration, pro-Zionist commitments made by earlier US administrations together with strong humanitarian sentiments in the wake of the Holocaust competed with considerations of *realpolitik* based on the strategic value of Arab countries and their possession of vast oil reserves. The Truman administration was torn within itself—the White House versus the State Department—and found it difficult to adopt and adhere consistently to one firm line of policy. Ultimately, the President prevailed and the United States gave valuable diplomatic, although not military, support to the nascent Jewish state. No doubt domestic political considerations also influenced the decisions of the Truman administration, as they have influenced the decisions of almost every administration since then.

However, these considerations were not as crucial as is ordinarily assumed.

With the entry into office of the Eisenhower administration, considerations of global policy in the burgeoning Cold War with the Soviet Union prompted a far more critical stance on American-Israeli relations. Convinced that the Arab states, and especially Nasser, could be enlisted in the cause of the West only with payment in Israeli coinage, Eisenhower and especially his Secretary of State John Foster Dulles, repeatedly called on Israel to make the necessary sacrifices for the greater good. In their futile endeavor to forestall Russian entry into the Middle East, Eisenhower and Dulles unwittingly contributed more than anyone else to that very outcome. Their failure to perceive and appreciate the real nature of Nasser's imperial drive, and the proxy role it was assuming on behalf of Russia. led them fatally to refrain from reacting vigorously and adequately to the challenge Nasser posed. Worse still, they even prevented others from reacting appropriately. With the undermining of British and French authority in the Middle East there followed the further penetration and bolstering of Russian influence in the area. Belatedly, the Eisenhower Doctrine was designed to fill the void resulting from the dismissal of the British and French from the region, but its effect was minimal. The Cold War had not only penetrated the Middle East; it had divided it territorially—with western interests under siege. Only now did the Eisenhower administration come to appreciate Israel's value as a potential ally in the contested area which the Middle East had become. The Kennedy administration, from the very beginning, took due account of the new facts of global competition which had superimposed themselves on the Middle East. Kennedy's efforts to dissuade Nasser from pursuing an imperialist goal were aimed at uncoupling the local, from the global, competition; but these efforts were unsuccessful. Nasser could not be diverted. This fact was forcefully revealed during the tenure of Lyndon Johnson. Nasser threatened Israel with economic strangulation and military force. When Israel moved to remove the threat, the United States "held the ring" by defeating Russian diplomatic moves in the United Nations and by neutralizing Russian threats to intervene in the fighting directly. In the aftermath of the Six-Day War the US refused to allow the immediate reinstatement of the *status quo ante* without resolution of the deeper causes of the Arab-Israeli dispute. In effect, Washington was allowing Israel to use the territories as bargaining chips to secure peace. The next stage in the Arab-Israeli dispute highlighted the extent to which US-Israeli relations had become a coefficient of the Cold War.

The Nixon administration's first moves were directed to extracting concessions from Israel in the hope that this would inject new life into the stalled peace process. However, the encampment of 20,000 Russian troops in Egypt undermined these efforts and reminded Washington of Israel's role as a barrier against Russian encroachment in the Middle East. The ensuing deadlock which settled on the Middle East was broken by Sadat's expulsion of the Russians from Egypt followed by a military offensive across the Canal. In the aftermath of the 1973 Yom Kippur War the United States had become the ally of the two leading protagonists—Israel and Egypt—and was in an unrivaled position to effect a Pax Americana for the region which would facilitate an Israeli-Egyptian reconciliation. This effort culminated in the Carter-inspired Camp David agreement of 1978 and the Egyptian-Israeli peace treaty of 1979, both of which signified a new form of American primacy in the area. American policy had not yet resolved the entire gamut of the Arab-Israeli dispute; it had, however, succeeded in resolving the most salient front in that dispute by means of the first treaty of peace to be concluded between Israel and a neighboring Arab state. S. SLONIM

UNITED STATES OF AMERICA, ZIONISM IN. Jewish immigrants who came to the United States from eastern Europe in the early 1880s brought with them the ideas of the Hibbat Zion, and by 1890 *Hovevei Zion organizations existed in the large Jewish communities of New York, Chicago, Baltimore, Boston, Philadelphia, and elsewhere. At the same time, newspapers propagating Hibbat Zion ideas appeared, among them *Shulamit,* edited by J.I. Bluestone in Yiddish, and *Ha-Pisgah* (The Summit), 1888–1889, a Hebrew paper edited by W. Schur. Following a mass meeting in New York on 4 May 1898, supporters of Zionism established an organization which *Die Welt* called the Zentralverein der amerikanischen Zionisten (Central Union of American Zionists). Other Zionist organizations appeared in the months before the First Zionist Congress at Basle (1897). Opposition was expressed by upper-class Jews and Reform rabbis (*see* REFORM JUDAISM AND ZIONISM). The Central Conference of American Rabbis passed a resolution in July, 1897, denouncing Zionism in sharp terms:

> Resolved that we totally disapprove of any attempt for the establishment of a Jewish state. Such attempts show a misunderstanding of Israel's mission which, from the narrow political and national field, has been expanded to the promotion among the whole human race of the broad and universalistic religion first proclaimed by the Jewish prophets.

By 1898 two major Zionist organizations developed in New York City: the Federation of Zionist Societies of Greater New York, under the leadership of Richard Gottheil, and the League of Zionist Societies of the United States of North America, under Rabbi Philip Klein and Michael Singer. They united in February, 1898, into the Federation of Zionists of Greater New York and Vicinity. Consolidation at the national level in July, 1898, resulted in the establishment of the Federation of American Zionists (FAZ), under the presidency of Gottheil, with Stephen S. Wise as first secretary.

Despite initial progress, the FAZ encountered organizational difficulties. Many Zionist organizations did not recognize its authority. The most recalcitrant were independent Zionist organizations in New York based on *Landsmanschaften* and in Chicago on the Knights of Zion, who organized in October, 1898, under the leadership of Leon Zolotkoff. Only in 1913 did the Knights accept the authority of the FAZ. Another obstacle to the growth of the FAZ was the opposition to Zionism from the left, namely from east European immigrants who adhered to socialist organizations and regarded socialism as the solution to Jewish problems as well. Difficulties were increased by the reluctance of the membership, which was primarily from eastern Europe, to accept the leadership of "Germans," who differed from them in their life style as well as social class. In 1902 Jacob de Haas moved to the US as editor of the FAZ's official paper, *The Maccabean*, and secretary of the organization. He tried to cope with the various organizational and administrative problems and to include more organizations under Richard Gottheil's leadership. De Haas instituted the "Shekel Day" and developed elaborate Zionist propaganda. In 1904 Gottheil resigned and Harry Friedenwald became president. In early 1905 de Haas also resigned and was replaced by Judah Magnes as secretary. With the two new leaders, the Zionist orientation of the FAZ changed. Gottheil and de Haas were "political Zionists" who supported Herzl, whereas Friedenwald and Magnes were "cultural Zionists," who tried to adapt Zionism to the American scene. Other important cultural Zionists were Solomon Schechter, president of the Jewish Theological Seminary, and Israel Friedländer, also of the Seminary, a Semitic scholar and communal leader. These "cultural Zionists" saw Zionism as a renaissance of traditional Jewish values and a check on assimilation. Although Eretz Israel was for them a cultural center, they did not negate the American Diaspora, which they viewed as equal in importance. The American cultural Zionists created a new Zionist position which, over the next decades, became accepted by growing segments of American Jewry.

The first Labor Zionist (*Poale Zion) organization was founded in New York City in March, 1903. Its ancillary Jewish National Workers Alliance (*Farband) was established as a benevolent organization in 1910, in part to attract members who might otherwise join the Socialist, anti-Zionist *Workmen's Circle. In its initial stages, Po'ale Zion was rejected by the Socialists and regarded with suspicion by the Zionists. Labor Zionism combined Jewish national aspirations with a social philosophy dedicated to the establishment of a new political and economic order in Eretz Israel. During its first decade, the platform included as priorities: the furthering of Jewish settlement in Palestine, and also the struggle against assimilation, aid to Jewish workers, and the building of Yiddish folk schools. Its organs, *Der Yidisher Kemfer* (1905, with interruptions) and *The *Jewish Frontier* (1934, under the editorship of Hayim Greenberg) exerted influence in liberal and progressive circles as well as within Zionist ranks. In 1911 a new FAZ administration, whose members were mostly east European, was elected. Friedenwald remained honorary president, but the affairs of the organization were handed over to the chairman of the executive, Louis Lipsky, who was becoming one of the important figures in American Zionism. He shared the responsibility with Abraham Goldberg, Bernard Rosenblatt, and Senior Abel, who founded the Yiddish organ of the movement, *Dos Yidishe Folk* (1909). Until World War I attempts were made to improve administration. Newly founded organizations gradually established ties with the FAZ: Po'ale Zion, *Hadassah Women's Organization, founded by Henrietta Szold (1912), and the *Mizrachi Organization of America (1914). The latter was established in 1911 by Meir Berlin (Bar-Ilan). In time it became a central component of the World Mizrachi Organization by virtue of its numbers and resources.

World War I and After. Early in 1914 the Federation of American Zionists, and American Zionism in general, were small and weak; membership was static and organizationally it suffered from financial stress. It did enjoy the support of the *Day* and *Morning Journal*, two leading Yiddish dailies. The *Forward*, however, was sharply anti-Zionist out of socialist conviction until the 1920s, when it became more sympathetic. With the outbreak of World War I, an international coordinating Zionist body was established in the US, where the Provisional Committee for General Zionist Affairs was established. Louis D. Brandeis, who had his first contact with Zionism through Jacob de Haas, Nahum Sokolow, and Bernard Richards, accepted its chairmanship. He took up his role with great energy and drew to the Zionist movement Felix Frankfurter, Julian W. Mack, and Bernard Flexner, who were also attracted by its democratic and progressive ideas. Under Brandeis' leadership, the financial situation of the FAZ improved, and membership and political influence increased. Brandeis and his associates were influenced through Horace Kallen and others by the idea of cultural pluralism, the essence of which is that America is a nation of nations in which different cultures are blended. This theory served to reconcile "Americanism" with Zionism. After Brandeis' elevation to the Supreme Court in June, 1916, he resigned as active chairman but continued to lead the movement through his associates, notably de Haas. In 1916 the Po'ale Zion and Mizrachi organizations withdrew from the Provisional Zionist Committee, and in 1918 American Zionism was reorganized in the *Zionist Organization of America (ZOA), which was based on territorial districts. Brandeis became honorary president, Judge Julian W. Mack president, Jacob de Haas and Louis Lipsky heads of departments. After the war Brandeis visited Palestine (July, 1919) and formed plans to build its future on the basis of large-scale investment and centrally-controlled public corporations. He wanted the ZOA to collect funds for specific economic projects. At the London Conference of 1920 his views clashed with Chaim Weizmann's who wanted to found the Keren ha-Yesod as a general fund to support the economy and settlements in Palestine, as well as to establish educational institutions. The Brandeis group refused to accept the decisions of the World Zionist Organization, represented by Weizmann. During Weizmann's visit to the United States, in the spring of 1921, both men, and the sectors of the Zionist movement behind each of them, clashed in what came to be known as the "Brandeis-Weizmann struggle." The main issue became the standing of the American movement in the World Zionist Organization: Brandeis and his associates proposed a reorganization of the world movement along federative lines, which would allow each national organization (in their case, the Zionist Organization of America) greater liberty of action. At the Cleveland convention of the ZOA in June, 1921, which debated the issues, a majority rejected Brandeis's views, and he and his close associates consequently seceded from the mainstream of Zionist activity in the US and concentrated their efforts on fostering the economic development of Palestine as, for instance, through the *Palestine Economic Corporation. Louis Lipsky, who led the opposition to Brandeis, became president, with Abraham Goldberg, Emanuel Neumann, Morris Rothenberg, and others as his collaborators. The Keren ha-Yesod was established in the United States. The Weizmann-Brandeis struggle was one of the major crises that shook American Zionism and its consequences undermined Zionist efforts in the United States during the 1920s. The Lipsky administration remained in office until 1930. During this period the ZOA concentrated on fundraising but without much success. Article 4 of the League of Nations Mandate had made specific provision for the recognition of a "Jewish agency" to advise and cooperate with the administration of Palestine as representative of the Jewish people. US Jewry, by reason of its numbers and resources, was a decisive factor in "enlarging" the *Jewish Agency. Louis Marshall, the leading American "non-Zionist," convened two nonpartisan conferences in 1924 and 1925 to consider Palestine problems. These meetings resulted in proposals to include non-Zionist

Group of Halutzim (pioneers) in 1921. Golda Meyerson (later, Golda Meir) is first from the left in the second row. [YIVO Institute for Jewish Research]

representation in an enlarged Jewish Agency. The proposal to enlarge the Agency by the cooption of non-Zionists was also approved in principle by the Zionist Congress in 1927, and in that year, following publication of a preliminary agreement between Weizmann and Marshall, a Joint Palestine Survey Commission was appointed. It made recommendations for practical work in Palestine upon which both Zionists and non-Zionists could agree. In August, 1929, the constitution of the enlarged Agency was approved and the Americans received the largest number of the 112 seats allotted to non-Zionists (44). However, due to the death of Marshall in 1929, the onset of the economic depression, the subseqnent political events, and the disorganization of the American section of the Jewish Agency, the Zionists continued to control most activities and policies of the Agency.

The riots in Palestine in 1929, coupled with the US economic crisis, further lowered the morale of the ZOA, whose membership declined to 8,000. There was a general clamor for the return of Brandeis and his associates, who were seen as necessary for a revitalization of the movement. At the convention in 1930, an executive committee of 18, composed mainly of Brandeis's circle, was elected, with Robert Szold as its chairman from 1930 to 1932. From 1932 to 1936 Morris Rothenberg functioned as president; Stephen S. Wise succeeded him from 1936 to 1938, followed by Solomon Goldman in 1938, Edmund Kaufmann in 1940, and Judge Louis E. Levinthal in 1941.

World War II. With the outbreak of World War II, the ZOA formed the American *Emergency Committee for Zionist Affairs, which later became the American Zionist Emergency Council (AZEC), presided over by Stephen Wise and Abba Hillel Silver. On 9–11 May 1942, at New York's Biltmore Hotel, a Zionist Convention consisting of delegates of the ZOA, Hadassah, Mizrachi, Po'ale Zion and with the participation of European and Palestinian leaders like Weizmann, Ben-Gurion, and Nahum Goldmann, adopted the *Biltmore Program, which defined the postwar Zionist aim as the establishment of Palestine as a Jewish commonwealth. Misunderstandings between Wise and Silver hampered the activity of the AZEC at the beginning. Wise had been a leading figure in American Zionism since its beginnings, and he considered Silver a brash newcomer. There were also political differences. Wise was a Democrat, close to Roosevelt and unwilling to apply pressure tactics against the Administration. Silver, a Republican, was convinced that a much more activist attitude should be taken by the Zionists in their dealings with the American government. Gradually Silver's position was accepted, and he became the leading figure in the AZEC. From 1945 the Zionist Emergency Council directed the energies and resources of the movement which grew enormously in those years, to influence the entire Jewish community, the US government, and public opinion, to support its demands in Palestine. Through these efforts American Zionists contributed decisively to the political prerequisites for the establishment of the State of Israel on 14 May 1948. During and after World War II, a dissident group, called at first the Committee for a Jewish Army and later the Hebrew Committee for National Liberation, agitated in the US mainly through newspaper advertisements, expounding and supporting the ideas and acts of the Irgun Tzeva'i Le'umi (Etzel) in Palestine. The group was headed by an Etzel leader, Hillel Kook (who appeared in America under the name of Peter Bergson), and enlisted the support of several prominent Jews and non-Jews. The style and tactics of the *Bergson Group were the subject of sharp controversies in Zionist circles.

In addition to their efforts in the political field, American

Chaim Weizmann addressing the Biltmore Conference, New York, 1942. [YIVO Institute for Jewish Research]

Zionists were among the most active participants in practical aid to the yishuv in its struggle after 1945; they helped with "illegal" immigration, the Beriha, secret shipment of arms to the Hagana, and large sums of money. The greatest number of volunteers to the yishuv's fighting forces, which were called *mitnadevei hutz la-aretz* (Mahal), came from the United States. After World War II, under the impact of the Holocaust in Europe and, later, the establishment of the State of Israel, Zionism became much more popular among the bulk of the Jewish community in America.

Opposition to Zionism. From the beginning Zionism had encountered strong opposition from Jewish socialist circles (under the Bund's influence) and especially from *Reform Judaism. Among the staunchest, most influential, opponents were Rabbis Emil G. Hirsch and Kaufmann Kohler. Other prominent Reform rabbis, however, such as Gustav Gottheil, Jacob Raisin, Bernard Felsenthal, and Maximilian Heller, supported the movement. In 1907 Professors Max Margolis, Henry Malter, and Max Schloessinger, all strong Zionist sympathizers, resigned from the Hebrew Union College faculty, while the Zionists charged that they were forced to resign by the college's anti-Zionist president, Kohler. Among the younger generation, Stephen S. Wise, Judah L. Magnes, and Abba Hillel Silver were notable exceptions to the anti-Zionism of the Reform rabbinate. The main body of the Central Conference of American Rabbis was anti-Zionist and railed against Zionism until 1920. After the Balfour Declaration (1917) and the San Remo decision on Palestine (1920), the Reform movement gradually adopted, although unofficially, a non-Zionist position which allowed cooperation with Zionists in philanthropic enterprises. In 1935 they revised their collective negative stand on Zionism in favor of individual choice, and further conciliation occurred after the *"Columbus Platform" of 1937. A small minority group, however, persisted in its opposition to Zionism.

In November, 1942, the *American Council for Judaism was formed, composed of Reform rabbis and influential lay leaders, such as Lessing Rosenwald, with Rabbi Elmer Berger as its head. Whereas the Reform movement as a whole tended to pro-Zionism, the Council continued its anti-Zionist activities and upon the establishment of the State of Israel it stated:

The State of Israel is not the state or homeland of the Jewish people: to Americans of Jewish faith it is a foreign state. Our single exclusive national identity is in the United States.

Jewish Orthodox circles were divided nearly from the beginning on the Zionist issue. While the Zionist Mizrachi and the Ha-Po'el ha-Mizrachi found many adherents among the east European Jews, Agudat Israel, a smaller but articulate group, was anti-Zionist out of conviction that Zionism was secularist and incompatible with Orthodox Judaism. Only during World War II did these groups abate their anti-Zionism, and in 1945, with some internal opposition, Agudat Israel declared its willingness to cooperate with the Zionists. On the extreme fringe of Orthodoxy, opposition to Zionism was perpetuated by the Satmar Rebbe Joel Teitelbaum, who condemned the Zionists for trying to hasten the redemption by establishing a "heretical" state. Within the lay leadership of American Jewry, Zionism at first found an opponent in the *American Jewish Committee, whose leadership and supporters included at various times, among others, Mayer Sulzberger, Cyrus Adler, Irving Lehmann, Louis Marshall, Jacob Schiff, Felix Warburg, Oscar Straus, Cyrus Sulzberger, and Julius Rosenwald, all wealthy, of German background, and non- or anti-Zionists. During World War I the American Jewish Committee (AJC), an oligarchic group, opposed the "Congress Movement," which was advanced by the Zionists and based on mass support. In 1916, however, a compromise was worked out. After the Balfour Declaration, the Committee tacitly recognized the ZOA as the main representative of those concerned with the welfare and development of Palestine. A gradual change in the attitude of the German-Jewish leadership became evident. During the 1920s the leaders of the AJC were approached by Weizmann in order to establish the enlarged Jewish Agency. Louis Marshall and some of his associates were ready, despite the opposition of extreme anti-Zionists, to reach accord with the WZO. In 1923 Weizmann, with the approval of the Zionist Executive, initiated negotiations with influential American non-Zionists. He found sympathetic co-workers in Marshall and Felix M. Warburg and their friends. Zionist "Diaspora nationalism," however, which the AJC saw as a threat to its position and patriotism, remained an issue of contention. Thus, opposition to the Zionists continued in various forms until January, 1948, when Judge Joseph M. Proskauer, under the pressure of the pro-Zionist Jewish consensus in the US, declared the Committee's acceptance of the Jewish State as recommended by the United Nations Special Committee on Palestine (UNSCOP). However, the AJC remained apprehensive about the status of American Jews in the light of a Jewish state. It was willing to support Israel while remaining wary of direct interference by Israel in its affairs. In 1950 David Ben-Gurion, as prime minister, exchanged letters on the subject with Jacob Blaustein, president of the AJC. Ben-Gurion stated that Israel represented only its own citizens and made no claim to speak in the name of the Jews in the Diaspora. The Jews of the United States, as a community and as individuals, owed political loyalty only to the United States, and the Jews in Israel had no intention of interfering in the affairs of Jewish communities abroad. The result of these letters was the cooperation of the AJC with Israel within defined areas of agreement.

Mass Support and Fundraising. Dedicated supporters of the Zionist movement had come from the ranks of *Conservative Judaism since the establishment of that movement in the US. Solomon Schechter and his faculty at the Jewish Theological Seminary supported Zionism despite the objection of the Reform-oriented board of directors of the Seminary. The meetings of the Rabbinical Assembly of America were consistently characterized by expressions of sympathy for Zionism. The *Reconstructionist movement, under the leadership of Rabbi Mordecai M. Kaplan, also was always pro-Zionist. It viewed the endeavor in Palestine as a means to achieve a renaissance in Jewish life in America as well, guided by Rabbi Kaplan's concept of "Jewish peoplehood." Reconstructionist leaders worked within the Zionist movement to achieve their twofold aim.

From the 1920s on the ZOA devoted more and more attention to fundraising, mainly in the United Palestine Appeal (UPA). There was considerable rivalry with local and non-Zionist overseas agencies, especially the *American Jewish Joint Distribution Committee (JDC), for the allocation of funds raised in local communities. In 1939–40 the UPA and JDC combined into the *United Jewish Appeal (UJA). The frequent consequence of such cooperation was a lack of emphasis on Zionist ideology in Zionist circles. The situation changed from the 1940s, when fundraising and political ideology became indistinguishable. Zionist fundraising became a major expression of Jewish identification and communal participation. In April, 1960, following criticism from a US Senate committee and other sources of the practice of returning a small proportion of funds raised for Israel for educational activities in the US, an agreement was reached between the Jewish Agency and the leadership of the UJA to establish an entirely American body, the Jewish Agency for Israel, Inc., to budget and allocate funds raised in the United States for social needs in Israel. This body was charged with authorizing the expenditure in Israel of funds contributed in America, thus giving American Jewry a direct say and responsibility in administering its funds in Israel. Aid to Israel by Jews in the US was channeled through the UJA and other overseas agencies, and through the Israel Bond Organization. From 1948 through 1968, the UJA provided over $1.16b. In times of crisis for Israel, the sums collected reached unprecedented proportions, as evidenced at the time of the Six-Day War: in 1966 the sale of Israel Bonds totaled $11m.; in 1967, $175m. In 1970-71, facing threats to Israel's security, the target was the largest ever: $1b. In addition to fundraising, private investment was fostered by bodies such as the Palestine Economic Corporation (PEC). Many American contributors and investors were not only declared Zionists, but Jews who felt a sense of identification with the Jewish people. American Jewish philanthropy found a balance between its support of American Jewish causes and its support of Israel.

Aliya and Youth Movements. Aside from the increase in funds, there was also evidence of swelling American immigration to Israel (aliya), the ultimate expression of commitment to Zionism. In the first three and a half years of the State's existence (May, 1948-December, 1951), out of a total of 684,201 immigrants to Israel, only 1,909 were Americans. Until 1961 immigration from the United States was less than 1.1% of the total number of immigrants. Between 1960 and 1967 immigration to Israel from the US was 2,000 per year; immediately after the Six-Day War this figure rose to 5,000 per year. After 1967 a grassroots immigration movement developed independently of the Jewish Agency, and in 1968 formed the Association of Americans and Canadians for Aliya. The resolutions of the 27th Zionist Congress (1968) stated that all necessary help be extended to this and all other organizations seriously contemplating

American delegation to the World Zionist Conference in London in 1945. From left to right: Louis E. Levinthal, Daniel Frisch, Emanuel Neumann, Juliette Benjamin, Naomi Chertoff, Abba Hillel Silver, Judith G. Epstein, Stephen S. Wise, Rose Halprin, Meyer Weisgal, Israel Goldstein, James G. Heller, Louis Lipsky, and Samuel Margoshes. [Zionist Archives]

immigration. Immigration in 1970 and 1971 was approximately 7,000 annually. The 1970s and 1980s saw a strong increase in immigration by Orthodox Jews from the US. The Zionist movement in America financially assisted established educational institutions and youth movements (Ihud Habonim, Young Judea, Bnei Akiva, etc.), summer camps, and also organized tours to Israel. In the 1950s and 1960s membership in these movements declined, mostly as a result of the growing Jewish affiliation to the various religious movements and their youth groups; in most cases these were developing strong programs of Israeli consciousness including group visits to Israel.

Mass rally in New York to celebrate first anniversary of Israel's independence, 1949. [Central Zionist Archives]

Organizational and Cultural Impact. After World War II, as a continuation of the framework created by the American Zionist Emergency Council, an American section of the Jewish Agency Executive was established in New York, consisting of leading members of the ZOA, Hadassah, the Labor Zionists, and Mizrachi. They participated regularly in plenary sessions of the Executive, whose center remained in Jerusalem.

In 1957 Mizrachi and Ha-Po'el ha-Mizrachi (founded in 1925) united into the Religious Zionists of America. The women's organizations of both groups, as well as their respective youth groups, Mizrachi ha-Tza'ir and Bnei Akiva, remained separate organizations. In 1923 Labor Zionism formed the Histadrut Campaign, which raised funds for the various institutions of the Histadrut in Israel. Pioneer Women, founded in 1926, made its main function raising funds for the women's division of the Histadrut (Mo'etzet ha-Po'alot). The youth affiliated to Labor Zionism, Habonim, administered summer camps and year-round social and cultural programs in North America. In the late 1960s Zionists became concerned with increasing their propaganda activities through new tactics and approaches, especially on the American campuses where the New Left and black nationalists developed an explicit anti-Zionist ideology which denied Israel's right to exist and supported Arab aims against Israel—an ideology which attracted a number of Jewish students as well. Independent radical campus groups (e.g., the Radical Zionist Alliance) emerged throughout the US to counter this ideology from a Jewish point of view.

Partly under the impact of this Zionist revival in the new generation, an important reform took place in the structure of American Zionism. Instead of the relatively weak coordinating body called the American Zionist Council, in which the main parties and organizations were represented, the Zionist Federation of America was established in 1970. Zionist affiliation of individuals became possible henceforth without the intermediary of a particular party or organization. The voluminous literature and extensive ideological debates on the relationship between American Jewry and Israel indicated the impact made on the Diaspora by the State of Israel. American Jews showed themselves more willing and ready to be identified as Jews, to affiliate with Jewish organizations and institutions, and to send their children to Jewish schools. Israel occupied an important place in synagogue activities, sermons, and various religious celebrations, and Israel's Independence Day assumed an important place in the American Jewish calendar. The Israeli flag was frequently displayed in synagogues and community centers. In many synagogues prayers for the welfare of the State of Israel and world Jewry were recited on Sabbaths and holidays following that for the welfare of the United States. Both the Conservative and Reform branches also established themselves in Israel through rabbinical schools and various educational programs and kibbutzim.

Another impact of Israel was the use of the Hebrew language in contrast to the decline of Yiddish. Hebrew songs and Israeli folk dances became part of American Jewish popular culture at weddings, bar mitzvot, and on many college campuses. Jewish art, which traditionally concentrated on east European themes, expanded to include Israeli symbols; Israel's crafts found a wide market among American Jews. Fiction on Israeli life increased rapidly and an extensive periodical literature was directed from Israeli institutions toward American Jewry. Israel had a profound impact on the ideologies of American Jews. The anti-Zionist American Council for Judaism was the only American Jewish organization which claimed that any suggestions of an ethnic bond among Jews, especially the ideas of Zionism and the creation of the State of Israel, harmed the position of the Jews in America because it placed in question their loyalty to the United States. With the progress of the State of Israel and particularly after the Six-Day War, many of its members and supporters shifted to a more pro-Israel stance, and the Council's influence dwindled considerably. Agudat Israel, on the other hand, which before the establishment of the State held that any Jewish state not governed by halakha (Jewish Law) would be illegitimate, accepted the State of Israel, as did almost all other Orthodox Jewish groups in America.

Jewish religious and welfare institutions in America, such as the National Council of Jewish Women, B'nai B'rith, and the Jewish War Veterans, as well as civic organizations such as the Anti-Defamation League and the National Communal Relations Advisory Council, all adopted an official stand of "non-Zionism." In practice, however, they supported the State of Israel and demands for an American policy of friendship toward Israel. As a consequence, they rejected the suggestion that Jewish ethnic traditions involving Zionism and the existence of the State of Israel create conflicts of dual loyalty.

New Religious and Ideological Issues. There remained, however, issues of concern to some of these organizations. Orthodox Jewry in America felt itself intimately involved in the course of religious affairs in Israel, pressing the State to pursue official religious policies in accord with its own religious beliefs. Israeli rabbis commanded influence and respect among similar circles in the United States. The Conservative and Reform movements, on the other hand, were concerned that the legal establishment of religious Orthodoxy in Israel involved discrimination against non-Orthodox Jews there. Some demanded the separation of state and religion or the adoption of forms of religious practice closer to their own points of view. The concern of the American religious groups implied that the religious forms practiced in Israel were of direct relevance to American Jews.

After the establishment of the State of Israel controversies also arose between Israelis and American Zionists over their relationships in the future. The Americans demanded a separation of the activities of the State from those of the Jewish Agency and the World Zionist Organization, whereas the Israelis wanted Jerusalem to be the center of all Zionist activities. American Zionists wanted to be recognized as the liaison for all activities between American Jews and Israel. They demanded that, through legislation, Israel recognize their leading position in fundraising and practical work, a demand practically achieved in 1952 through the passage of the Zionist Organization and Jewish Agency Law in the Knesset and the covenant signed subsequently between the Israeli government and the Jewish Agency. In addition, there was a great controversy about the meaning of the Diaspora and the obligation to immigrate to Israel. The Americans claimed that America was not *galut* (exile) because Jews were secure and not oppressed there (Rose Halprin) and that the Zionist Organization should not submit to the authority of Israel (Abba Hillel Silver).

The definition of the relations between American Zionism and Israel was discussed from the 1950s on. A commission on Zionist ideology submitted to the ZOA convention in 1958 a report which balanced the interests of Israel with those in the Diaspora, an approach that had been one of the characteristics of American Zionism from its early years: "Zionism should pursue the following aims: 1. It should promulgate and translate into action the supreme importance of the centrality of the State of Israel to the survival and spiritual enhancement of the Jewish People throughout the world... 2. It should develop in the Diaspora, to the maximum degree, the creative potentialities of Jewish life, culture and religion..."

American Zionists maintained that the most crucial issue for the Jews was their survival as a people. Since Jews would continue to live in the Diaspora, only a Zionism that recognized the essential ethnic elements of the Jewish people could keep them from cultural disintegration. For this reason a strong emphasis on cultural continuity, Hebrew, and a strong bond with Israel are the tasks of American Zionism (Ben Halpern), although since 1967, encouraging aliya from the US also became a legitimate part of Zionist activity in America. In essence this was a new-Ahad Ha-Am position which perceived Israel as the cultural center of the Jewish people but simultaneously dependent on the moral, political, and financial assistance of the Diaspora.

In the 1970s and 1980s, American Zionism underwent further ideological developments. The process of "Zionization" of American Jewry, that had already begun in previous decades, adopted new expressions in this period. There was greater identification betwen the American religious movements and an American brand of Zionism. That process was evident both in the Orthodox and the Conservative movements, but especially visible in the American

Reform movement which, during the 20th century, had undergone an interesting evolution from anti-Zionism to non-Zionism and finally to pro-Zionism. The 1976 San Francisco Conference of the Central Conference of American Rabbis, the prestigious organization of Reform rabbis, gave a resounding expression to the movement's identification with Israel and its support for it.

There were clear indications that the American religious movements which had undergone a process of "Zionization," especially the Conservative and Reform, were searching for a more influential role in Israel, and were increasingly ready to confront the opposition of the Orthodox establishment. The presence of both movements in Israel grew, represented by immigrants, kibbutzim, Israelis who adopted their religious positions, various synagogues, and rabbinical institutions. In 1973, the World Union for Progressive Judaism WUPJ (Reform) established its central office in Jerusalem and in 1976 the WUPJ affiliated officially with the World Zionist Organization. The Conservative movement also affiliated in 1976. (For organizational developments since 1970 *see* AMERICAN ZIONIST FEDERATION.) *See also* UNITED STATES JEWS IN ISRAEL.

J. REINHARZ

UNITED SYNAGOGUE YOUTH. *See* CONSERVATIVE JUDAISM AND ZIONISM.

UNITED WORKERS' PARTY. *See* MAPAM.

UNITED ZIONIST LABOR PARTY. *See* AHDUT AVODA.

UNITED ZIONISTS-REVISIONISTS. *See* REVISIONISTS.

UNIVERSITY LIBRARY. *See* JEWISH NATIONAL AND UNIVERSITY LIBRARY, JERUSALEM.

UNIVERSITY OF HAIFA. Institute of higher learning, founded in 1963 as Haifa University College, under the academic supervision of the Hebrew University. In 1970 it was granted independent status and the name was changed to "University of Haifa." In 1972 it received full academic accreditation from the Council for Higher Education.

The university stands on the crest of Mount Carmel in a campus (designed by the architect Oscar Niemeyer) which blends modern architecture with the natural beauty of the Carmel Forest. The 30-story Tower adjoins a cluster of buildings which house research and teaching facilities, a computer center, a sports complex, dormitories, and a library which operates on a computerized system enabling it to service the entire north of Israel. The university maintains two branch campuses—Tel Hai in Upper Galilee and Ohel Sara in the Jezreel Valley—to serve outlying areas of Galilee. The Hecht Museum, two art galleries, and numerous displays throughout the main buildings enhance the environment.

The university offers courses of study leading to bachelor's, master's, and doctoral degrees in the faculties of Humanities, Social Science, and Mathematics, the School of Education, the School of Social Work, and Oranim—the School of Education of the Kibbutz Movement. In addition, the university offers pre-academic studies, continuing education in the School of Social Work, in-service education in the School of Education, and a full range of extension studies in Management, Business, and the Professions. The Unit for Bridging the Gap, prepares students from disadvantaged backgrounds to qualify for and adjust to university studies. The university also houses research centers and institutes among which are its Institute of Holocaust Studies,its Institute for Zionist and Israel Studies, the Jewish-Arab center and Institute for Middle Eastern Studies, the Institute for Archaeology and Maritime Studies, and the Center for the Study of Psychological Stress.

The faculty comprises some 500 teachers and researchers, many of whom are internationally recognized experts in their fields. Students at the University of Haifa come from diverse backgrounds. The 6,500 undergraduate, graduate, and diploma students include men and women from all sectors of society—native "sabras" together with new immigrants, students from developing areas and those from established cities, and the highest percentage of Arab and Druze students at any university in Israel. Exchange students spend a semester or year at the university within the framework of the Overseas Program. The majority of the university's graduates remain in the north after completing their studies.

A. SHERMAN

UNNA, MOSHE. Leader in Israeli religious community (b. Mannheim, Germany, 1902; d. Sedeh Eliyahu, 1989). Before moving to Palestine in 1927, Unna had a varied education. He studied at the Humanistic High School in Mannheim, at the Berlin Rabbinical Seminary, and the Agricultural College of Berlin. For many years he was active in the development of the Kibbutz ha-Dati movement. In the early 1930s he was sent to Germany and eastern Europe to prepare Jews for pioneer life in Palestine. He returned to Palestine in 1934 and was one of the founding members of Kibbutz Tirat Tzevi where he lived until 1941. He helped to found the Religious Youth Village at Kefar Hasidim and was active in its administration. In 1944, he joined Kibbutz Sedeh Eliyahu.

Unna's political career led to a variety of posts. In 1940, he was elected to the Va'ad Le'umi. As treasurer of the Ha-Po'el ha-Mizrachi he served on the movement's executive committee from 1942 to 1949. He was often a delegate to World Zionist Congresses and was sent on foreign missions. He was a representative of the National Religious Party in the first to the sixth Knessets. He served two terms as chairman of the Council for State Religious Education (1955–1966 and 1967–1978), and was Deputy Minister of Education, 1956–1958. A member of the Board of Directors of the Jewish National Fund, 1970–83, Unna was also co-founder of Oz ve-Shalom, a dovish ideological and political movement of religious Zionism in Israel in the 1980s.

He wrote books and many articles on Judaism, education, and the religious kibbutz.

G. SHUSTER-BOUSKILA

UNSCOP. *See* UNITED NATIONS SPECIAL COMMITTEE ON PALESTINE.

UNTERMAN, ISSAR YEHUDA. Ashkenazi Chief Rabbi of Israel (b. Brest Litovsk, Russia, 1886; d. Jerusalem, 1976). Unterman served as rabbi in various localities in Russia. In 1923 he received a call to Liverpool, England, where he officiated until 1946, when he became chief rabbi of Tel Aviv. In 1964 he was elected Ashkenazi Chief Rabbi of Israel to succeed Chief Rabbi Isaac H. Herzog.

An early adherent of the Mizrachi movement, Unterman was a delegate to the 12th Zionist Congress (1921) and to several subsequent Congresses. During his service in England, he was active on behalf of Zionism as vice-president of the national councils of the Jewish National Fund and the Keren ha-Yesod and as president of the Mizrachi Organization of Great Britain. In 1946 he pleaded the Jewish case before the Anglo-American Committee of Inquiry on Palestine.

An eloquent speaker, Unterman wielded great influence in the communities he served. He contributed articles to rabbinic journals and was the author of a halakhic treatise, *Shevet mi-Yehuda* (1955).

Rabbi Unterman addressing Israel's Christian and Moslem leaders, 1967. Next to him, Prime Minister Levi Eshkol. [Israel Govt. Press Office]

URBACH, EPHRAIM ELIMELECH. Israeli educator and rabbinic scholar (b. Wloclawek, Poland, 1912; d. Jerusalem, 1991). Urbach studied at the Rabbinical Seminary of Breslau (today Wroclaw), as well as the universities of Breslau and Rome. He taught at the Breslau Rabbinical Seminary from 1935 until 1938 when he immigrated to Palestine.

During World War II, he served as an army chaplain. After the war he became principal of the Ma'ale Religious High School in Jerusalem. He taught at high schools in Jerusalem and was a high school inspector. From 1953, he taught aggada and rabbinic literature at the Hebrew University of Jerusalem. He was awarded the Israel Prize in 1956. Urbach was president of the Israel Academy of Sciences and Humanities, 1980–1986, and edited the Hebrew journal *Tarbiz* from 1970.

His major works on the Talmud and rabbinic literature are *Ba'alei ha-Tosefot* (1956), a history of the Tosafists and their work, and *Hazal* (1969; English edition *The Sages, Their concepts and beliefs*), a comprehensive presentation and analysis of rabbinic theology. G. SHUSTER-BOUSKILA

URIM. Kibbutz in the western Negev, established by pioneers from Bulgaria as one of the 11 Negev outposts set up in the night of 6 October 1946. It is based on partly-intensive farming and an industrial enterprise. Population (1987), 628.

E. ORNI

URUGUAY, ZIONISM IN. The founding Zionist associations came into being during the first decade of this century, at the same time as the initial community organizations. Their members were central European Ashkenazim and Sephardim from Mediterranean lands and the Middle East, and immigrants of the same extraction from Argentina and Brazil. In addition to their Zionist objectives, they, like other groups, were concerned with the local conduct of Jewish life.

Dorshei Zion, founded in Montevideo in 1911, was attached to the Zionist Federation of Argentina. In 1917, the Dr. Yehiel Tschlenow Society was founded by Zionists of the centrist and traditionalist streams, while left-wing Zionists founded Po'ale Zion. Uruguayan volunteers enlisted in the Jewish Legion, and the Balfour Declaration was celebrated by the Jews in the streets of Montevideo. In 1918 the Dr. Teodor Herzl Society was organized, with a Sephardi majority. The youth organization, Shahar, was active in the early 1920s. On these organizational bases, the Keren ha-Yesod was founded in Montevideo in 1921.

The Jewish population of Uruguay was swollen by the waves of immigration of the 1920s and 1930s, and these immigrants stimulated the development of the ideologies predominating in the Jewish world from where they had come. Zionism and the Jewish left (Communists, Bundists) polarized the Jewish population. The community was largely pro-Zionist, but the organization of the Zionist movement as such remained limited.

In those years a wide range of Zionist affiliations was established in Uruguay: General Zionists, Po'ale Zion-Tze'irei Zion, Liga Pro Palestina Qbrera (founded 1933), Mizrachi (founded 1933), Revisionists (from 1932), WIZO (from 1933), Warburg group (founded 1937, German-speaking), Keren ha-Yesod, and Jewish National Fund. The Jewish Agency Representation in Uruguay (founded 1937), attached to the head office in Buenos Aires, was made up of Zionists (General, Liga, Mizrachi) and community leaders. From 1933, the following youth movements were active (with ups and downs): Ha-No'ar ha-Tziyoni, Ha-Shomer ha-Tza'ir, Bnei Akiva, Betar.

The Zionists, together with the community, defended Zionism in time of crisis, protesting the 1929 riots in Palestine and the 1939 White Paper. Together with non-Zionist sectors, they organized actions against anti-Semitism in Europe, and for the reception of Jewish refugees in Uruguay.

During World War II, the movement expanded its political and community activities. The youth reorganized their pioneer movements and the Sephardim founded the Dr. Herzl Society (1941); Zionist students formed Kadima (1940). The centralizing and representative institutions, *Consejo Central Sionista* (C.C.S. 1942) and the *Federació;ni* Juvenil Sionista (F.J.S. 1944), were organized. The community umbrella institution, the *Comité Central Israelita del Uruguay* (C.C.I.U. founded 1940), defended the Zionist cause. The C.C.S. and the C.C.I.U. acted together with the *Comité Uruguayo Pro Palestina* (founded 1944) in mobilizing support in non-Jewish political and intellectual circles in favor of the creation of the Jewish State. Officials in the Uruguayan government supported Zionist stands.

The local Zionist organization and its influence were strengthened after World War II. The struggle for the creation of the Jewish State was backed in Uruguay by massive campaigns, and contacts with the government were promoted by the Uruguayan Zionists, pro-Zionists, and communities. Recognition of the Jewish State by the U.N. was celebrated on the main street of Montevideo, with the

Group of Zionists in Montevideo. [Zionist Archives]

participation of Jewish non-Zionist left-wingers. The local Jewish Agency representation was established in 1947. Agricultural training centers were organized (by Ha-No'ar ha-Tziyoni, 1946; Ha-Shomer ha-Tza'ir, 1948; Ihud Habonim, c. 1955). The first immigrants left for Israel in 1948, and in the same year the United Appeal was established. Continental Zionist Congresses have had their seat in Montevideo since the First Latin American Zionist Congress (May, 1945).

The Zionist Organization of Uruguay (O.S.U.) established its primacy during the 1950s and 1960s, with the affiliation of all the parties and a non-party organization (founded 1955), the F.J.S., community organizations, WIZO, and Pioneras (founded early 1950s). Together with the Jewish Agency, it has acted to promote Jewish primary, secondary education and a teachers' training school. During the Six-Day War, together with the C.C.I.U., it promoted the political and financial mobilization of the community.

In 1973 military rule was instituted in Uruguay. This change of regime, and the situation of Israel following the Yom Kippur War, had an impact on local Jewish and Zionist life. The strict governmental controls instituted in the country did not lead to organizational changes in the community, but activities were limited. There was no change of leadership—instead of elections, the O.S.U. prolonged its mandate in 1976. However, groups which had been estranged began to participate in Zionist and community affairs, and the Zionist Organization grew in strength. The emigration to Israel increased. Most of the immigrants emanated from elements unconnected with the community institutions, except for students with a background of activism in youth movements. The terrorist attacks on Israel in the 1970s gave rise to protest campaigns conducted by the O.S.U. and the C.C.I.U., directed at the Uruguayan non-Jewish public.

Civil rule was restored in Uruguay in March 1985. This democratic development made itself felt at all levels including the opening up of the Zionist movement. All groups and ideological tendencies are now represented in the O.S.U. The F.J.S. also embraces all parties and trends. The O.S.U. has 11,000 members, and the F.J.S. 2,000, approximately.

Between 1948 and 1985, 8,139 Jews from Uruguay including 6,076 native-born, emigrated to Israel.

R.P. RAICHER

USHA. Kibbutz on the eastern outskirts of the Haifa Bay area, founded in 1937 as a Tower-and-Stockade outpost by pioneer immigrants from Galicia (Poland). It is based on intensive, largely irrigated farming and also has industry. It was the site of the Sanhedrin after the Bar-Kokhba revolt (about 140 CE). Population (1987), 400.

E. ORNI

USSISHKIN, MENAHEM MENDEL. Zionist leader (b. Dubrovno, Mogilev District, Russia, 1863; d. Jerusalem, 1941). Born into a hasidic family, Ussishkin received a traditional Jewish upbringing. He also attended high school and

Menahem Mendel Ussishkin. [Zionist Archives]

the Moscow Technical Institute. After the pogroms of 1881, he helped found a youth group whose aim was to settle in Eretz Israel and some of whose members went there with the Bilu. In 1884 he helped found in Moscow the Benei Zion Society, a student association that engaged in cultural activities in the spirit of Jewish nationalism and Zionism. In 1885 Ussishkin was chosen secretary of the Moscow *Hovevei Zion movement and put in charge of spreading its ideas in Russia. In 1887 he served as secretary of the Druskenik Conference of the Hovevei Zion. He contributed articles to the Hebrew periodical *Ha-Melitz* on problems facing the movement and participated in the first meeting of the Odessa Committee, which was established with the permission of the Russian authorities in 1890. He also joined the secret order Benei Moshe, which was guided by Ahad Ha-Am. In 1891 he visited Eretz Israel. When Ahad Ha-Am, who visited the country at the same time, published a series of articles in *Ha-Melitz* that were critical of the settlement work supported by the Hovevei Zion, Ussishkin entered into a controversy with him.

In Yekaterinoslav, where he settled, Ussishkin established a committee for the publication of Jewish nationalist and Zionist literature and organized an Eretz Israel settlement society. In the summer of 1896 he met Herzl in Vienna, and in 1897 he participated in the First Zionist Congress as its Hebrew secretary. At the Second Zionist Congress (1898) he was elected to the Actions Committee. From the Third Zionist Congress (1899) on he served as the representative of the World Zionist Organization (WZO) in the district of Yekaterinoslav (which included the Caucasus), developed widespread educational and propaganda activities, engaged in the distribution of Shekalim (membership fees) and of shares of the Jewish Colonial Trust, and raised funds for the Odessa Committee. He was a member of the delegation which in 1901 requested Baron Edmond de Rothschild and representatives of the Jewish Colonization Association to change administrative procedures in their settlements in Eretz Israel. At the All-Russia Zionist conference held in Minsk in 1902, he suggested the formation of Zionist youth cadres whose members would put themselves at the disposal of the movement for one to two years of service. Ussishkin visited Kishinev soon after the pogrom of 1903 and arranged for the transfer of pogrom orphans to Eretz Israel and their placement in the Kiryat Sefer Agricultural School. That summer he again went to Eretz Israel, where he attempted to establish a central representative body of the Jewish population. For this purpose he convened a conference in Zikhron Ya'akov that passed a resolution to establish an organization of the Jews of the country. The organization did not develop as had been hoped, but the Hebrew Teachers Association, which he founded at the same time, grew into a well-organized body.

Ussishkin vehemently opposed the East Africa scheme, regarding it as a "betrayal of historic Zionism," and became the leader of the opposition to Herzl. At the Kharkov Conference (October, 1903), which was attended by the majority of the representatives of the WZO in Russia, it was decided to send a delegation to Herzl with an ultimatum that he give up the East Africa project. Ussishkin and his friends organized a strong faction called *Tziyonei Zion, which demanded that the WZO devote all its efforts to Eretz Israel. At the time of his struggle against the East Africa project, Ussishkin published a booklet, *Our Program* (1904), in which he called for practical work in Eretz Israel, land purchase and settlement, and educational-cultural activities, without, however, neglecting political action, and recommended the establishment of agricultural training farms for youths. Graduates of the farms would receive plots of land which they would be required to cultivate without the help of hired labor. He also suggested the formation of workers' groups, each member of which would be obliged to go to Eretz Israel and work on farms there for three years. Ussishkin's booklet exerted a great influence on the young Jews then leaving on aliya.

In 1906 Ussishkin was chosen chairman of the Odessa Committee. Under his leadership the committee ceased to assist individuals and rendered support only to communal bodies. It supported the establishment of workers' settlements near existing "settlements" and aided schools, the publication of periodicals, and the like. After the Young Turk Revolution of 1908, Ussishkin visited Constantinople to study the new political climate, met with the leaders of the local Jewish community, and helped set up a Zionist Office in the Turkish capital.

In 1913 he visited Eretz Israel for the third time. He published his impressions in a Russian booklet in which he suggested that aid be given not only to the Jewish villages but also to the communities in the cities, especially to the Jews of Jerusalem. From then on he devoted particular attention to the development of Jerusalem.

During World War I Ussishkin opposed the establishment of a Jewish Legion to fight against the Turks and did his utmost to render aid to the Jews of Eretz Israel. He advocated strict neutrality for Zionism, believing, however, that a German victory would ensure Jewish progress in the country. But when the Balfour Declaration was issued in 1917, he organized mass demonstrations in honor of the occasion. That same year he participated in a conference of representatives of national minority groups in Russia and addressed the gathering in Hebrew. In 1918 he was elected chairman of a conference of representatives of Ukrainian Jewry and, despite objections from the Yiddishists, opened the conference with a Hebrew speech.

Ussishkin was a member of the Jewish delegation at the Paris Peace Conference in 1919 and later settled in Palestine, where he headed the *Zionist Commission (later the Palestine Zionist Executive) for more than three years. During this period he effected the purchase of a substantial part of the Jezreel Valley. In 1921 he visited the United States with Albert Einstein, Shemarya Levin, and Ben-Zion Mossinsohn in behalf of the Keren ha-Yesod. The drive was successful despite the opposition of the Brandeis group. In

Ben-Zion Uziel.
[Zionist Archives]

1923, after differences had developed between himself and Chaim Weizmann, he was not reelected to the Zionist Executive. The same year he was elected chairman of the Executive Committee of the Jewish National Fund, in which capacity he was instrumental in the purchase of large stretches of land. In 1927 he visited Canada in behalf of the fund and raised $1,000,000 for the purchase of the Hefer Valley.

Ussishkin was a vehement opponent of the British proposal for the partition of Palestine (1937). He participated in the 1939 St. James's Conference in London and, despite the great political obstacles which Zionism encountered, remained steadfast in his belief in the establishment of a Jewish State. I. KLAUSNER

UZIEL (Ouziel), BEN-ZION MEIR HAY. Chief Rabbi of Israel (b. Jerusalem, 1880; d. there, 1953). Uziel studied at yeshivot in Jerusalem and later taught at various educational institutions in the city. In 1914 he became Hakham Bashi, or the officially recognized chief rabbi, of Jaffa and its environs. During World War I he frequently intervened on behalf of the Jewish population against the oppresive measures of the Turkish authorities. After the war Uziel served in Salonika for two years. Returning to Palestine in 1923, he became Sephardi chief rabbi of Tel Aviv-Jaffa, a position he held until 1939, when he was chosen Rishon le-Zion, or Sephardi Chief Rabbi of Palestine, an office he held until his death.

Uziel was greatly esteemed by all sections of the yishuv. He played a leading role in the Mizrachi World Movement. He was a founder of the Mizrachi Organization of Palestine and one of its representatives in the Asefat ha-Nivharim. He was a delegate to the 14th and 15th Zionist Congresses (1925, 1927) and a member of the Zionist Actions Committee and of the Council of the Jewish Agency.

On a number of occasions Uziel represented the yishuv before British and international authorities. He was a member of the yishuv's delegation to the Permanent Mandates Commission of the League of Nations (1926) and to the St. James's Conference (1939), and he testified before the Anglo-American Committee of Inquiry (1946) and the United Nations Special Committee on Palestine (UNSCOP; 1947).

Uziel's published writings include rabbinical responsa, Talmudic novellae, sermons, essays, and articles.

V

VA'AD HA-LASHON HA-IVRIT (Hebrew Language Council). *See* ACADEMY OF HEBREW LANGUAGE.

VA'AD LE'UMI (National Council). Executive of the *Keneset Yisrael, the statutory Jewish community (*see* YISHUV, SELF-GOVERNMENT IN THE), OPERATING UNDER MANDATORY LAW (*see* MANDATE FOR PALESTINE) and chosen by the annual sessions of the *Asefat ha-Nivharim (Elected Assembly) to administer the affairs of Palestine Jewry under the mandate. It was recognized by the British Mandatory government as the official spokesman of the organized Jewish community in Palestine. The number of its members was not fixed, but its composition reflected the various parties and factions represented in the Asefat ha-Nivharim.

The Va'ad Le'umi drafted the constitution of the Asefat ha-Nivharim, which was recognized by the High Commissioner for Palestine and was officially gazetted on 1 January 1928. In cooperation with the Chief Rabbinate, it drew up the regulations on the system of election or appointment of the Rabbinical Council and the rabbinical offices of local communities. These were subsequently approved by the Asefat ha-Nivharim, confirmed by the High Commissioner, and officially published on 9 April 1936. In 1931 the Va'ad Le'umi prepared the regulations for the elections of committees of local communities. These regulations were

Session of the Va'ad Le'umi. At the head of the table are David Remez (left) and Itzhak Ben Zvi (right). [Central Zionist Archives, Jerusalem]

basically identical with those drafted for the elections to the Asefat ha-Nivharim.

A very important task of the Va'ad Le'umi was the publication of the Register of Adult Jews in the country. The register was compiled every four years before the elections to the Asefat ha-Nivharim and included all Jews age 18 and over who had been residents of Palestine for at least three months. Relevant parts of the register were published in various parts of the country, and during a period of one month every adult Jew had the right to ask that his name be added to the register if it had been omitted or to demand that his name be struck from the register if he did not want to belong the Keneset Yisrael. Only adults who were included in the register were members of Keneset Yisrael, with duties and privileges belonging thereto, and were subject to the jurisdiction of the Rabbinate. The register served as a basis for the compilation of the voters' lists for the elections to the Asefat ha-Nivharim and to committees of local communities.

The fact that membership in the Keneset Yisrael was optional constituted one of the weaknesses of the community organization, because those who did not want to pay taxes or to subject themselves to the jurisdiction of the Rabbinate could evade these obligations simply by leaving the Keneset Yisrael. According to reliable estimates, about 5 percent of Palestine Jewry were not members of the community organization. In order to strengthen its cooperation with the communities, the Va'ad Le'umi arranged periodical joint meetings with the representatives of the communities.

The Va'ad Le'umi did not confine its activities to the narrow sphere allotted to it by the law. Palestine Jewry, serving at the frontline of the Zionist struggle, was most sensitive to all developments in the realms of politics, security, and economy, and consequently the sessions of the Va'ad Le'umi became its most important platform for the discussion of the political situation.

During the 28 years of its existence (it functioned until the convening of the Provisional Council of the State of Israel on 14 May 1948), the Va'ad Le'umi was headed consecutively by David Yellin, Ya'akov Thon, Yitzhak Ben-Zvi, Pinhas Rutenberg, and David Remez. M. ATTIAS

VA'AD ZEMANI (Provisional Council). *See* ASEFAT HA-NIVHARIM.

VALENSI, ALFRED. Tunisian Zionist (b. Tunis, 1878; d. Auschwitz, 1944). Valensi studied law in Montpellier from 1897, obtaining his doctorate in 1905, and being called to the bar in Tunis. Inspired with Zionist militancy, Valensi created in 1910, together with Chief Rabbi Jacob Boccara and Joseph Brami, the first Zionist organization in Tunisia, Agudat Zion. From 1920, he was active in developing the Keren ha-Yesod in Tunisia. In 1920, he became President of the Zionist Federation of Tunisia which was legally recognized by the French Protectorate authorities. In 1921 Valensi represented Tunisia at the 12th Zionist Congress.

From 1922 to 1926 he traveled frequently to France, participating in the creation of the French Betar movement in 1923.

Valensi was the author of incisive articles, such as *le Sionisme*, which was translated into Judeo-Arabic in 1906, published as a brochure, and sold for the benefit of the victims of pogroms in Russia. In 1919 a collection of his articles was published under the title: *Sion et Liberté* (1919).

He moved to France, where he continued intensive Zionist activity until his deportation to Buchenwald during World War II. He died in Auschwitz. C. SITBON

VAMBERY, ARMINIUS (HERMAN WAMBERGER), Orientalist and traveler (b. Dunaszerdahely, Hungary (now Dunajska Streda, Czechoslovakia), 1832; d. Budapest, 1913). Born to extremely poor Orthodox Jewish parents, Vámbéry, lame from birth, applied himself to study, and at a very early age showed a remarkable aptitude for languages. After studies at the universities of Pozsony (now Bratislava), Vienna, and Pest, where he graduated in Oriental languages, he traveled to Constantinople in 1854.

Nominally becoming a Moslem, he entered Turkish service and was for a time secretary to Mehmet Fuad Pasha. During his stay in Constantinople he mastered numerous oriental languages and dialects and published various linguistic works, including a Turkish-German dictionary (1858).

After receiving a grant from the Hungarian Academy of Sciences (1861), Vámbéry, disguised as a dervish, explored Armenia, Persia, and Turkestan, traveling as far as Bukhara and Afghanistan. Returning to Europe in 1864, he embraced Protestantism and wrote a book describing his adventures. In 1865 he was made professor of oriental languages at the University of Budapest.

A stanch advocate of British imperialism, Vámbéry frequently carried out diplomatic missions for Great Britain. He was also frequently consulted on foreign problems by the Sultan of Turkey. Herzl solicited Vámbéry's aid in arranging an interview with the Sultan, which took place on 7 May 1901. After Herzl's death, his successor, David Wolffsohn, continued to consult Vámbéry on Zionist political problems. In addition to several hundred scholarly works, Vámbéry wrote an autobiography, *The Story of My Struggles : The Memoirs of Arminius Vambery* (2 vols. 1904).

J. ADLER—E. EPPLER

VAN PAASSEN, PIERRE. Writer and journalist (b. Gorinchem, Holland, 1895; d. New York, 1968). Born to a strict Calvinist family he became one of the most fervent non-Jewish Zionists. In 1911 he moved to Toronto where he studied for the ministry. After serving with the Canadian Expeditionary Force in World War I and studying theology in Paris, he turned to journalism. He traveled throughout the world and was outspoken in his anti-fascist views and advocacy of democracy. His books and articles reflected his enthusiastic attitude to Zionism.

In 1942 he was one of the heads of the committee for a Jewish army active in the United States. His book, *The Forgotten Army* (1943), was a sharp indictment of British anti-Zionist policy. His other pro-Zionist publications include *Days of our Years* (1939), *To Number Our Days* (1964), *Jerusalem Calling* (1956), and *Nazism, an Assault on Civilization* (1934, edited with J.W. Wise). E. HOTER

VAN RAALTE, ALBERT. Chemist and Zionist leader in the Netherlands (b. Dordrecht, Netherlands, 1871; d. Amsterdam, 1938). Van Raalte served for many years as a spokesman for the Zionist movement and wrote several Zionist pamphlets. A long-time honorary editor of *De Joodse*

Wachter, the Dutch Zionist weekly, he was chairman of the Dutch Zionist Executive from 1925 to 1927. He was active in organizations on behalf of Jewish refugees and chief editor of the weekly *De Joodse Middenstander* (Journal for the Jewish middle-class) 1933–1935. On his retirement from his post as head of the Food Control Department of the city of Amsterdam (1921–1937) he became director of the Jewish National Fund in the Netherlands. J. MICHMAN

VAN VRIESLAND, SIEGFRIED A. Attorney and Zionist leader in the Netherlands and Palestine (b. Amsterdam, 1886; d. Jerusalem, 1939). A founder of the Dutch Zionist Students' Organization during his student days at the University of Leiden, Van Vriesland served as honorary secretary of the Dutch Zionist Executive from 1913 to 1918, when he settled in Palestine. He was a member of the Zionist Commission from 1919 on, treasurer of the Zionist Executive from 1923 to 1925 and manager of Palestine Potash, Ltd. (*see* DEAD SEA WORKS COMPANY, LTD.) from 1929 to 1938. In 1938 he became director of the port of Tel Aviv. For a time he also served as Dutch consul and, later, consul general in Jerusalem.

His wife, Jeanette, a sister of Eliezer Siegfried *Hoofien, was an honorary editor of *De Joodse Wachter* from 1913 to 1918 and a correspondent for several Dutch newspapers in Jerusalem. She was killed in an Arab attack on a United Nations convoy near Latrun in October, 1948.

VATICAN, RELATIONS WITH ZIONISM AND ISRAEL. In view of the concern of the Catholic Church for the Holy Land and for its *holy places there, it is only natural that modern political Zionism, and later the State of Israel, should have been matters of interest to the papacy and the Vatican. The following factors with direct or indirect bearing on this basic concern have variously influenced the attitude of the Vatican toward Zionism and Israel: the strong desire to safeguard the Catholics' rights in the holy places through internationalization and other means; the Church doctrine concerning the Jews according to which their exile was a punishment for their having killed Jesus, a doctrine which has been modified only recently; the notion that the Jews are condemned to exile until and unless they recognize Christ; a fear of the spread of atheist communism; and, since the creation of the State of Israel, a fear of Arab reprisals against Catholic communities. Positive influences in more recent years have been the political realism of the Vatican, which has obliged it to take into account the existence of the State of Israel, the world-wide sense of guilt and outrage at the murder of 6 million Jews, and liberal and reformist trends within the Catholic Church.

Basically, the pattern followed to date by the Vatican in its approach to the Zionist program has been one of resistance to changes in the status quo with regard to the holy places, followed by slow accommodation to the realities created by developments over the years. Most official papal pronouncements since the War of Independence have sought to stress neutrality in the Middle East conflict, emphasizing that "our apostolic mission" has imposed an attitude of "perfect impartiality" on the Pope, placing him "above the conflicts that are rending human society."

From Herzl to the San Remo Conference: 1896–1920. Within months of the appearance of *The Jewish State*, Herzl had an interview (19 May 1896) with Msgr. Antonio Agliardi, the Papal Nuncio in Vienna, with the aim of enlisting the support of the Catholic Church for the Zionist movement. Although Herzl explained to Agliardi that he did not want a Jewish "kingdom" in the Holy Land and that he would be prepared to accord extraterritorial status to the holy places, the Nuncio gave him a cold reception. Nonetheless, Herzl persisted in his efforts. On 22 January 1904, he was received by Rafael Cardinal Merry del Val, the Papal Secretary of State. The Cardinal made it clear to Herzl that the Church could not allow the Jews to take possession of the Holy Land as long as they denied the divinity of Jesus Christ. In answer to Herzl's assurances that the holy places would have extraterritorial status, Merry del Val said that the holy places could not be regarded as entities separate from the Holy Land. Three days later, on 25 January, Herzl was accorded a lengthy audience with Pope Pius X, who had assumed the papacy the year before. Although Pius X had good personal relations with the Jews, he too told Herzl that the Church could not favor Israel's return to Zion as long as the Jews did not accept Jesus as the Savior. Herzl quotes the Pope in his *Diaries* as having said:

> We cannot prevent the Jews from going to Jerusalem but we could never sanction it...The Jews have not recognized our Lord; therefore we cannot recognize the Jewish people.

Regarding the fact that the Ottoman overlords of Palestine also were not Christians, the Pope said:

> I know, it is not pleasant to see the Turks in possession of our Holy Places. We simply have to put up with that. But to support the Jews in the acquisition of the Holy Places that we cannot do.

"If you come to Palestine and settle your people there," the Pope finally said to Herzl, "we will have churches and priests ready to baptize all of you." Several weeks later, however, perhaps to soften the effect of Vatican rejection, Cardinal Merry del Val promised Herzl's close associate Heinrich York-Steiner that if all the Jews wanted was to be "admitted" to the land of their ancestors, he would regard that as a "humanitarian" endeavor and would not impede their efforts to found settlements in the Holy Land.

Insofar as the Vatican was concerned, the matter rested there until World War I, when the anticipated collapse of the Ottoman Empire made Palestine an object of interest and rivalry for Britain, France, and Italy and the Zionist dream stood a good chance of becoming a reality under the protectorate of the victorious allied powers. Sir Mark Sykes, the British diplomat who was negotiating in 1917 with the Zionists in England and was himself a Catholic, went to Rome to sound out the Vatican on its attitude toward having Protestant Britain rather than France, which was officially entrusted by the Vatican with the role of protector of Catholic interests in the Levant, assume the protectorate over the Holy Land. On 11 April 1917, Sykes saw Msgr. Eugenio Pacelli (later Pope Pius XII), who was then Under-Secretary for Extraordinary Affairs at the Papal Secretariat of State. A few days later, he had an audience with Pope Benedict XV. From these talks Sykes assumed that the Vatican was ready to accept Britain as the mandatory power in Palestine.

At Sykes's suggestion, Pacelli received Nahum Sokolow on 29 April 1917, when Sokolow came to Rome on behalf of the Zionist Executive to seek Vatican support for the planned Jewish National Home in Palestine. Pacelli was interested but insisted that the Zionists stay clear of an area extending well beyond the holy places. On 1 May, Sokolow was received by the Papal Secretary of State, Pietro Cardinal Gasparri. Gasparri, too, discussed the holy places and claimed for the Church a "reserved Zone" (similar to the one provided for in the Sykes-Picot Agreement), including not only Jerusalem but also Bethlehem, Nazareth and its environs, Tiberias, and Jericho. As long as the Vatican's requirements concerning the holy places were met, Gasparri said to Sokolow, the Holy See wished the Zionists well in their attempt to set up a state in Palestine. When Sokolow said that the Zionists wanted only an "autonomous home," Gasparri assured him that he might count on the sympathy of the Church.

On 4 May 1917, Sokolow was received in private audience by Benedict XV. Aware of Britain's interest in Zionism, the Pope listened attentively to Sokolow and declared that the return of the Jews to Palestine was a providential event and in keeping with God's will.

> The problem of the holy places is for us of extraordinary importance. The sacred rights must be protected. We will settle this between the Church and the Great Powers. You must respect those rights to their full extent.

Sokolow gave assurance that the Zionists would respect the holy places, and the audience ended with the words of the Pope: "Yes, yes," he told Sokolow, "I think we shall be good neighbors."

On the strength of Sokolow's report, Chaim Weizmann felt justified in telling a Zionist conference in London that the Church would not oppose Zionist aims in Palestine. On the eve of his departure from Rome, on 6 May, Sokolow received a cable from Weizmann about the deportation of Jews from Jaffa and Jerusalem. De Salis, the British Representative to the Holy See, was informed by Sokolow and, in turn, brought the matter to the attention of Cardinal Gasparri. Several days later Gasparri replied that, according to his inquiry, there had been no killing of Jews by the Turks. De Salis stressed the fact that Weizmann's cable concerned the deportation of 8,000 Jews from Jaffa and not the killing of Jews.

It seems, however, that the issuance of the Balfour Declaration in November, 1917, and Gen. Edmund H.H. Allenby's conquest of Jerusalem stirred misgivings in the Vatican concerning the safety of the holy places under the new regime in Palestine and its apprehension that Palestine would not be placed under international rule, as envisioned in the Sykes-Picot Agreement. At any rate, by December, 1917, Pope Benedict XV had expressed his concern to De Salis lest the Jews gain direct control over Palestine's affairs to the detriment of Christian interests.

When Sykes revisited Rome in the winter of 1918, he noted a marked change in the Vatican's attitude toward Zionism. He now found Cardinal Gasparri thoroughly unsympathetic. On 1 March 1919, the *Tablet* published a denial of reports that the Pope had ever supported Zionism. On 10 March, while the peace conference was meeting in Paris, Pope Benedict told a secret consistory in Rome that "it would be for us and all Christians a bitter grief if infidels [in Palestine] were placed in a privileged and prominent position." Although the Pope did not specify who the "infidels" were, he was evidently seeking to influence the peace conference. Cardinal Gasparri told the Belgian representative that the danger he feared most was the creation of a Jewish State in Palestine. The Vatican was probably ready to accept a British Mandate, but with no privileges for the Zionists and, preferably, with international status for the holy places. The Pope had probably been influenced by the reports sent to him from England by Francis Cardinal Bourne, who had visited Palestine in that period and wrote anti-Zionist letters also to Foreign Secretary Arthur James Balfour and Prime Minister David Lloyd George. The British government gave assurances to the Vatican on the safeguarding of Catholic interests in the holy places, in case Britain were to receive the mandate, but it seems that the Vatican still preferred the internationalization of Palestine.

In June, 1919, some Catholic papers urged that the protectorate over Palestine be awarded to Italy, which, incidentally, had its own political ambitions in the Middle East and was not eager to have the British establish themselves there. By November, 1919, Col. Richard Meinertzhagen, then Chief British Political Officer in Palestine, reported to the Foreign Office that the Vatican was "violently opposed to Zionism"

From San Remo to Lake Success: 1920–47. On 26 April 1920, only days after the San Remo Conference had awarded the Palestine Mandate to Great Britain (subject to the approval of the League of Nations), the Vatican made known its fears that Jewish elements might become predominant in Palestine under British rule. These fears were discussed in Catholic circles even in England, where Cardinal Bourne told a nationwide Catholic conference in Liverpool that "a new non-Christian influence was being deliberately set up in the land whence countless generations of Christendom had longed and striven to oust a non-Christian power."

By this time the Vatican appeared to have been influenced also by the fear of Communism. In 1921 representatives of the Zionist movement visiting Rome were informed by a Vatican spokesman that the Holy See did not wish to "assist the Jewish race, which is permeated with a revolutionary and rebellious spirit," to gain control over the Holy Land. Obviously, the Pope had been impressed by anti-Semitic reports that the Jewish pioneers were Bolshevists who were seeking to establish a Communist regime in Palestine. In June, 1921, Benedict XV protested that the Christians in Palestine were now worse off than under Turkish rule "through the new civil ordinances put in force which tend to turn Christianity out of the positions it has occupied up to now and to put Jews in its place," and called on the governments of all Christian states, Catholic and non-Catholic, "to bring vigilant pressure to bear on the League of Nations" in order to protect the "just rights of the Christians"—all this despite repeated assurances from the British that they would afford ample protection to the holy places and that, as Sir Ronald Storrs put it to the Pope, the Jews in the administration were in proportion to their numbers, known to be a minority.

Popes Benedict XV and Pius XI (who succeeded Benedict in January, 1922) were further influenced against the British and the Jews by lurid reports from Msgr. Luigi Barlassina, Latin Patriarch of Jerusalem. Barlassina, who overlooked no opportunity to side with the Arabs, told Roman and Vatican audiences that the Balfour Declaration had enabled the Jews to come out openly with their plan to set up "the Zionist kingdom," that some kibbutzim in Palestine were run according to extreme Communist principles, and that Jerusalem alone now had 500 prostitutes.

In the spring of 1922 Weizmann arrived in Rome to try to convince the Holy See to accept the approval of the Mandate. He had two interviews with Cardinal Gasparri, who was still Papal Secretary of State. Gasparri wrote in those days that the Vatican was opposing the Zionist plan to establish a Jewish state. Gasparri assured Weizmann that he was fully satisfied by his declaration that all peoples would have the place they deserve in Palestine with no privileges for anyone. According to Weizmann's memoirs, *Trial and Error*, it seemed to him that Gasparri somehow considered the World Zionist Organization (WZO) a branch of Britain's Palestine government. After Weizmann had reported to Gasparri on Jewish settlement and reconstruction work in Palestine, Gasparri remarked that he was not worried about Jewish settlement in the Holy Land. "It is your university that I fear," the Cardinal said, referring to the Hebrew University of Jerusalem. In a note to the British Embassy, Gasparri stressed again that "the Holy See is not opposed to Jews in Palestine having civil rights equal to those possessed by other nationals and needs. But it cannot agree that the Jews will obtain a privileged position." The Vatican was opposed to the Zionist plan to establish a Jewish State.

On 15 May, 1922, Gasparri submitted a memorandum to the League of Nations Council, which was then about to ratify the British Mandate for Palestine, on the same line of his note. This theme was repeated on 1 June by *L'Osservatore Romano*, the semiofficial Vatican paper, which agreed to the British Mandate in principle but demanded modifications in the declaration because Zionism would be detrimental to peace in Palestine and would rob the native population of its rights.

On 11 December 1922, Pope Pius XI, in an allocution at a secret consistory, made a special reference to the question of the holy places and the rights of the Holy See, which should be assured not only in front of Jews and infidels but also before all other non-Catholic religions. At a secret consistory on 23 May 1923, he declared that the Church would defend the "undeniable, obvious and overwhelming rights of Catholicism to the Holy Places in Palestine." In a papal bull of May, 1924, he again called for the solution of the problem of the holy places in accordance with Catholic interests.

When Benito Mussolini's Fascist party first assumed power in Italy (October, 1922), its attitude toward Zionism was cool. On various occasions the Vatican exerted pressure on the Mussolini government to take an anti-Zionist stand. Later, Marchese Alberto Theodoli, the Italian Representative to the League of Nations Permanent Mandates Commission, assumed an anti-Zionist position, claiming to protect the rights of the Catholics in Palestine. In 1927 Mussolini told Victor Jacobson that he had to take into account the feelings of his "neighbor" (i.e., the Vatican), which was implacably opposed to Zionist aspirations.

Meanwhile, Vatican officials and highly placed Church circles continued their campaign against Zionism. Barlassina, now a cardinal and Latin Patriarch in Jerusalem, alleged that the Zionists were driving Arab workers out and replacing them with thousands of their "coreligionists from Russia."

Late in November, 1929, *L'Osservatore Romano* carried an editorial headlined "The Jewish Danger Threatening the Entire World." The 3 October 1936 issue of the Jesuit paper *Civiltà Cattolica*, which was close to the Holy See, said that "the Jews constitute a serious and permanent danger to society...." "Zionism," said another issue of that year, "might offer a way out, but the creation of a Jewish state would increase the Jewish menace." The publication of the Peel Report on the partition of Palestine in 1937 worried the Holy See because it created a distinction between Jerusalem and Nazareth and the Holy See "could not believe that a Christian nation would tolerate that Nazareth and the Lake of Tiberias should be withdrawn from Christian influence and subjected to a non-Christian authority." In an editorial (2 April 1938), the same paper suggested that the best thing for the Jews to do was to relinquish their claims on Palestine and, if possible, leave the country altogether. *Civiltà Cattolica* was to be singularly consistent in its opposition to Zionism and later to Israel. (It had a record of anti-Semitism going back to the 1880s, when it published outright accusations of ritual murder against the Jews.) Msgr. Tardini of the Secretariat of State said to a British diplomat that "the Jews with their messianic notion were still a peculiar people, a world influence, and there was no real reason why they should be back in Palestine; why should not a nice place be found for them in South America?"

In May, 1939, after the British White Paper on Palestine was issued, the Vatican paper *Osservatore Romano* wrote that the Paper denied "the historical rights of Zionist claims."

During World War II the throne of St. Peter was held by Pius XII. Some high Church dignitaries, such as Msgr. Andrea Cassulo, the Nuncio to Romania, and Msgr. Angelo Roncalli (later Pope John XXIII), who spent most of the war years as Apostolic Delegate in Istanbul, quietly intervened to save Jewish lives. However, the moral issue of the silence of Pius XII on Nazi atrocities against Jews still remains open.

In May 1943, in the middle of World War II, while Jews were desperately seeking a refuge from Nazi persecutions, Secretary of State Cardinal Luigi Maglione, wrote to the Apostolic Delegate in the United States, Cicognani, that it would not be difficult

> "if one wants to establish a 'Jewish home', to find other territories [than Palestine] which could better fulfill this aim, while Palestine, under Jewish predominance, would bring new and grave international problems, would not satisfy the Catholics of the world, would provoke the just complaint of the Holy See, and would not be in harmony with the charitable assistance that the Holy See had and will continue to have in favor of non-Aryans."

In 1944 Msgr. Thomas J. McMahon, national secretary of the American Catholic Near East Welfare Association (CNEWA) expressed the fear that while Islam could not "expel Jesus from Palestine", a Jewish state would do just that. He therefore proposed the internationalization of Palestine with predominant Christian control.

On 10 April 1945, Moshe Shertok (Sharett), then head of the Political Department of the Jewish Agency, had an audience with Pius XII. Shertok told the Pope that the murder of 6 million Jews by the Nazis had been possible only because the Jews had no state of their own, that a radical change must take place in the life of the Jewish people after the war, that he knew of no conflict of interest between Zionist aspirations in Palestine and the interests of Christianity and Catholicism there, that the Jewish State to be set up in Palestine would undertake to protect the Christian holy places, and that the Jews hoped for the "moral support" of the Catholic Church for "our renewed existence in Palestine." The Pope's questions and answers were courteous but noncommittal.

Meanwhile, Arab countries were beginning to exert heavy pressure on the Pope to mobilize the Catholic Church against the establishment of a Jewish State in Palestine. On

3 August 1946, Pius XII was visited by a delegation from the Palestine Arab Higher Committee, which requested his intervention against the Zionists. The Pope's reply was as follows:

> We deplore all resorts to force and violence from whatever quarter they come. Thus we also deplored repeatedly in the past the persecutions that fanatic anti-Semitism unleashed against the Hebrew people.
>
> We always observed [an] attitude of perfect impartiality...and we are determined to conform to it in the future.
>
> But it is clear that this impartiality, which our apostolic mission imposes on us and which places us above the conflicts that are rending human society, cannot signify indifference especially at this difficult moment. [We will] endeavor that justice and peace in Palestine may become a beneficial reality, that an order springing from the efficient cooperation of all interested parties may be created and may guarantee to each of the parties now in conflict security of existence as well as physical and moral living conditions on which may be established a normal situation of material and cultural welfare.

The representative of the Franciscan Custodia Terrae Sanctae, appearing before the United Nations Special Committee on Palestine in 1947, expressed the fear that the establishment of a non-Christian government would modify the status quo in the Holy Places.

When the partition of Palestine came to a vote at the United Nations on 29 November 1947, most of the Catholic countries in the world body approved the action that cleared the way for the creation of the Jewish State, particularly since the plan provided also for the internationalization of Jerusalem.

The Vatican and the State of Israel: 1948—. To many conservative and traditional interpreters of the Gospels and the writings of the Church Fathers, the establishment of the State of Israel came as something of a shock. According to the views held in these circles, the Jews had been condemned to homelessness because of the crime of deicide they had committed. To them, the reestablishment of a Jewish State in the Holy Land and the revitalization of the Jewish people which this development implied seemed contradictory to the will of God as they understood it. They found it difficult to accept the possibility that such a State should be permitted to survive and to prosper.

Pius XII himself viewed the War of Independence with apprehension for the Holy Places. Vatican spokesmen at the time said that although the Pope scrupulously avoided taking sides in the conflict, he would have welcomed and supported any move for conciliation. But he himself did not initiate steps toward that end. Basically, Pius XII is said to have felt that peace and quiet in the Holy Land and the safety of the holy places would best be served by the continuation of a mandatory regime. In view of the fact that both Jews and Arabs lived in Palestine in large numbers, he feared that whichever side won the war would have to set up a police state, with disastrous consequences to Christian communities and the holy places.

The Pope's official reaction to the war was contained in three papal encyclicals. The first, *Auspicia quaedam* (1 May 1948), expressed concern for the holy places and offered a prayer that the "situation in Palestine be at long last settled justly." The second, *In multiplicibus* (24 October 1948), was promulgated when it was clear that the Israelis were winning. In the encyclical the Pope said that for "it would be opportune to give Jerusalem and its surroundings an international character which seems to offer a better guarantee for the protection of the sanctuaries." Pleading for the internationalization of Jerusalem and the holy places, the Pope mentioned that, speaking before a "delegation of Arab dignitaries" who "came to render us homage," he had

> manifested our lifelong solicitude for peace in Palestine, condemning every recourse to violence [and that] peace could only be realized in truth and in justice, that is, in the respect of the rights of the acquired traditions, especially in the religious field and also in the strict fulfillment of the duties and obligations of each group of inhabitants.
>
> When war was declared, without abandoning the attitude of impartiality imposed on us by our apostolic mission, which places us above the conflicts which agitate human society, we did not fail to do our utmost...for the triumph of justice and peace in Palestine and for the respect and protection of the holy places.

In his third encyclical, *In Redemptoris nostri* (15 April 1949), which appeared two days after the signing of the armistice agreement between Israel and Jordan the Pope, recalling his previous appeal for an international regime, said that for the protection of the Holy Places also in other cities a "juridical statute, guaranteed by some form of international agreement" was necessary. He sought to persuade the governments, and all those who possess a power of decision on such an important question, "that the Holy City and its surroundings must be given an adequate juridical status, the stability of which...can be guaranteed only through common ground between the peace-loving countries." Again, he pleaded the necessity of guarantees for

> all those rights in the holy places which were acquired [by Catholics] many centuries ago and time and again defended valiantly, and which our predecessors have solemnly and effectively reaffirmed....

As for the *Civiltà Cattolica*, it made its sympathies clear. In reporting on the war, it referred to Israeli setbacks as "Arab victories" and to Israeli victories as "advances," Only Egyptian and Jordanian communiqués were quoted in full. In its issue of 19 June 1948, the paper reported that "two Zionist emissaries" had been caught trying to poison the wells in Gaza.

When, in the spring of 1949, the State of Israel sought admission to the United Nations, several Catholic states under the pressure of the Pope opposed its application on the ground that Israel had "failed to carry out the full internationalization scheme" proposed by the United Nations for Jerusalem. No such accusation was made against Jordan, which had most of the holy places in its territory and had refused even to consider relinquishing its rule over these places and over the Old City of Jerusalem.

The Holy See refused to recognize any part of Jerusalem as the capital of Israel, or the State of Israel itself, for that matter. The Apolostic Delegate to Jerusalem and Palestine resided in the Arab sector of Jerusalem, and the Vatican exerted pressure on Catholic states to establish their embassies and legations in or near Tel Aviv rather than in Jerusalem.

Only after it became obvious that the Jewish State was viable and vigorous, and that the United Nations was incapable of enforcing its resolutions regarding the internationalization of Jerusalem and the holy places, did the Vatican make its first tentative attempts at a rapprochement with the Israelis, if not with the State of Israel. On 27 March 1952, Pope Pius XII received Moshe Sharett, now Israel's

Foreign Minister, in a private unofficial audience. Sharett assured the Pope that Israel would respect Christian rights. The Pope did not take any stand on the subjects raised by Sharett. In the years that followed, Israel was visited by a number of eminent Catholics including some Latin American prelates, who subsequently spoke in highly complimentary terms of what they had seen in the country. A growing number of Catholic priests began the serious study of modern Hebrew. In 1955 a group of Jesuits, Dominicans, and Franciscans spent six months in an intensive Hebrew-language course, studying side by side with new Jewish immigrants.

Some Vatican authorities were impressed by Israel's attitude toward the holy places. In November, 1955, Israel's Ministry of Religious Affairs presented a check to Msgr. Antonio Vergani, the Latin Patriarchial Representative in Israel, in final compensation for war damage to Catholic institutions. In a formal letter (16 November 1955) to the Israeli government, Vergani thanked the government for the "constant assistance I was given in the settlement of the various questions outstanding between the Roman Catholic Church and the State of Israel within the latter's territory."

The official Vatican, however, still seemed reluctant to mention the State of Israel by name. In May, 1955, several months prior to Vergani's letter, the Israel Philharmonic Orchestra had been granted an audience by the Pope and had given him a private concert as a gesture of gratitude for the help the Church had given to Jewish victims of Nazism. In its review of the concert, *L'Osservatore Romano* simply said that the Pope had addressed "Jewish musicians of fourteen different nationalities." Not a word was mentioned about the actual nationality of the players.

The accession of Pope John XXIII in 1958 inaugurated an era of liberalization in the attitudes of the Catholic Church. The new Pope, formerly Angelo Cardinal Roncalli, had maintained cordial relations with Jews and, on his election, exchanged messages of goodwill with the President and Chief Rabbi of Israel. His coronation was attended by Eliyahu Sasson, then Israel's Ambassador to Italy, who attended the ceremonies as a "special delegate of the government of Israel." In 1962 Saul Colbi, Director of the Department for Christian Communities of the Israeli Ministry of Religious Affairs, attended the opening ceremonies of the Vatican Council.

Still, the Vatican did not establish official diplomatic ties with the State of Israel. In this it was motivated to no small extent by fear of Arab reprisals against Catholic communities or institutions in Arab lands. The extent of the pressure the Arab states were capable of exerting can best be seen from what transpired during the Vatican Council, which, begun by John XXIII and continued by his successor, Paul VI, met in four separate sessions from 1962 to 1965.

When the 1963 session discussed a "statement on the Jews" absolving them from guilt in the Crucifixion, the Coptic Patriarch of Alexandria, United Arab Republic, warned that if such a statement were approved, "we shall have to face the music from the Arab nations." To admit that the Jews had not been guilty in the death of Christ would mean that they had a right to their Homeland after all, and this the Arabs could not tolerate. Such warnings, combined with religious opposition from conservative clerics, prevented that session from taking up the statement.

During the 1964 session, when the statement was discussed again, the Arab League countries instructed their diplomatic representatives in Rome (October, 1964) to get in touch with the cardinals and bishops and make plain to them the political implications of a pro-Jewish statement on the part of the Council. Arab newspapers warned that the matter of the Jewish declaration would be raised at the conference of leaders of nonaligned nations that was meeting in Cairo at the time. When the Council gave preliminary approval to a strongly worded statement condemning anti-Jewish discrimination and declaring that it was wrong to consider the Jews a "deicide" people, Foreign Minister Kadri Toukan of Jordan said that the act would encourage Israel to "continue its aggressive policy." Ten Christian members of the Jordanian parliament sent a message to Pope Paul calling the statement a "stab in the heart of Christianity."

Two days after the passage of the pro-Jewish statement, the Pope, in an effort to pacify the Arabs, arranged to meet with Charles Helou, the Christian President of Lebanon. Augustin Cardinal Bea, in a front-page editorial in *L'Osservatore Romano*, stressed the purely religious significance of the declaration, denying that it had any political aims or intentions. The statement finally ratified when the Ecumenical Council closed in October, 1965, was a considerably watered-down version of the draft declaration passed the year before.

In January, 1964, Pope Paul made a pilgrimage to the Holy Land. After arriving in Jordan on 4 January, he spent 5 January visiting Megiddo, Nazareth, Tiberias, and Capernaum, repeatedly announcing that he had come strictly as a pilgrim to worship at the holy places there. The Arab world exploited the occasion for propaganda purposes. Reporters arriving in Jordan from all over the world to cover the Pope's visit were given kits from the Jordanian Office of Information containing violently anti-Jewish material. The Arabic version of the Jordan radio's response to the Pope's greeting declared that "two thousand years ago the Jews crucified Christ and fifteen years ago they attacked the people of Palestine...the Jews are the enemies of God and of all religions in the world."

In his response to an address of welcome from President Zalman Shazar, who met the Pope as he entered Israel, Pope Paul referred to the President as "Your Excellency" and expressed his thanks to the "authorities" who had been kind to him, but he never referred to "Israel" or to a "Jewish State." On the other hand, he instructed Eugène Cardinal Tisserant, who had accompanied him on the journey, to kindle memorial lights and to recite a prayer in the Memorial Chamber on Mount Zion. And when he left, Paul VI told the Israeli Chief of Protocol that "we saw today a living people at work, a calm and serene people." He also accepted a medallion with the words "State of Israel engraved upon it in Hebrew, and said "Shalom, shalom" in Hebrew. Following Israel's victory in the Six-Day War, the Pope at a secret consistory held on 26 June 1967, recalled that he had wanted to spare Jerusalem the suffering and the damages of the war, that he was very saddened by the conditions of Palestinian refugees, and that the Holy City of Jerusalem should have its own internationally guaranteed statute. According to the Vatican spokesman who released the report of the consistory to the *New York Times*, Israel's assurance that it would afford all faiths free access to the holy places was not enough to satisfy the Vatican.

However, the Vatican apparently was willing to come to terms with the new situation created by Israel's victory. In July, 1967, a series of meetings was held in Jerusalem be-

Pope Paul VI receiving Foreign Minister Abba Eban in October, 1969. [Pontificia Fotografia Felici]

tween Prime Minister Levi Eshkol and Msgr. Angelo Felici, the Vatican Under-secretary for Extraordinary Affairs. A joint communiqué issued by Felici and Ya'akov Herzog, Director General of the Prime Minister's Office, described the talks as having been marked by "cordiality and mutual understanding." The meetings had come about in response to a special message Eshkol had sent the Pope through Herzog, who had made a trip to Rome for that purpose. A week before the Jerusalem talks, Ehud Avriel, Israel's Ambassador to Italy, had been received by the Pope. In September, 1968, Herzog met in Rome with Msgr. Agostino Casaroli of the Papal Secretariat of State, and Avriel had another audience with the Pope when he left his post in Rome in 1968.

The attitude of the Vatican on the internationalization of Jerusalem had changed. Whereas in 1948 the Vatican advocated the internationalization of the entire city and its environs, the Pope, in his allocution of 23 December 1968, spoke of his desire to see "an internationally guaranteed agreement on the question of Jerusalem and the Holy Places."

The Vatican, which maintains diplomatic relations with nearly all the Arab countries, has not established such ties with Israel. In December, 1968, following Israel's attack on Beirut International Airport, the Pope dismayed Israel by sending a cable to President Helou of Lebanon in which he confined himself to deploring violent acts whatever their origin. The Pope had had nothing to say about the act that had precipitated the attack, the Arab terrorist raid on an El Al plane in Athens, which unlike the Beirut raid, had involved loss of life.

In a message of September, 1969, to the Islamic Summit Conference held in Rabat, Morocco, the Pope proposed that the three monotheistic religions should reach an agreement in order to safeguard the unique and sacred character of the Holy Places and of Jerusalem in particular. The following month, on 6 October, the Pope received Israeli Foreign Minister Abba Eban in an official audience. The meeting consisted of an exchange of ideas between the Pope and Eban concerning the status of the holy places. Reporting on the interview, Eban said: "I found an atmosphere of esteem and profound respect for our sovereignty and for our historical evolution." He also noted that he had seen an Israeli flag on display in a corridor in the Vatican. According to the communiqué published after the meeting, the Pope and Eban discussed "the question of peace and understanding between the peoples of the region," as well as "the refugees, the holy places, and the unique and sacred character of Jerusalem."

In December, 1969, the Vatican Secretariat for the Promotion of Christian Unity released a document concerning Catholic-Jewish relations in which it stated that "Jews have indicated in a thousand ways their attachment to the land promised to their ancestors" and that "the existence of the

State of Israel should not be separated from this perspective."

On 22 December 1969 the traditional Christmas wishes for the (Arab) refugees and the special mention of the Christian communities in Palestine were supplemented by a new preoccupation. "They have diminished and they are diminishing, the faithful of Jesus in that blessed earth," said the Pope. This was the first time that the Pope expressed publicly his worries about the diminishing number of Catholics in the Holy Land, a preoccupation which featured time and again in his later speeches.

In August, 1970, Pope Paul VI said: "The destiny of the Holy Land is always very important to us, not because of territorial or political interests, but because of the religious values linked to it." He then expressed the hope that since the conflict involved three peoples recognizing the same monotheism, reference to the same God could lead to the discovery that we were all brothers.

In March, 1971, the Pope called for the "recognition of the peculiar needs of the holy places in Palestine, of the continuing residence of the Christians in the blessed country, and of an appropriate statute for Jerusalem."

The idea of a special statute, internationally guaranteed for Jerusalem, in order that the city could become a center of peace, was reiterated by the Pope in June and December, 1971.

In January, 1972, Deputy Secretary of State Msgr. Giovanni Benelli visited Israel and held several talks with Minister of Finance Pinhas Sapir, and Minister of Justice Ya'akov Shimshon Shapiro, on the question of the sale of the Notre Dame de France convent to the Hebrew University. The Assumptionist Order had sold the convent and according to the Vatican the sale had to be considered null and void because Canon Law imposed the requirement of authorization by the Vatican. A case which began before an Israeli Court in Jerusalem was interrupted by the Israeli government decision to cancel the sale but no conditions were imposed. The Vatican transformed the convent into a modern hotel and for years refused to pay municipal taxes until 1987 when the Vatican agreed to pay a symbolic sum to the Municipality.

In February, 1972, Chaim Herzog, later to become President of the State, was received in a special audience by the Pope and presented him with the *Encyclopaedia Judaica*, published in Israel.

On 22 December 1972 in his allocution to the Holy College, the Pope criticized "situations without a clear juridical basis, internationally recognized and guaranteed", in a reference to Jerusalem in which the followers of Christ "must feel themselves fully 'citizens'." He spoke also of the sons of the Palestinian people waiting for years "for an equitable recognition of their aspirations, not in contrast but in the necessary harmony with the rights of other peoples".

On 15 January 1973, Israeli Prime Minister Golda Meir was received in a private audience by the Pope. It was the first official visit of this kind. The final communiqué recalled the suffering of the Jewish people; the Pope in his humanitarian mission was interested in the (Arab) refugee problem and that of the (Christian) communities living in the Holy Land, while in his religious mission he dealt with the holy places and the universal and holy character of Jerusalem. The importance of this event was greatly diminished by the communiqué issued by Prof. Alessandrini, the spokesman of the Holy See. Immediately after the event he stressed to the media that the audience was not a sign of preference, since the Pope had also received King Hussein and other important personalities of the Arab world. He also emphasized that the audience had been requested by Mrs. Meir, and that the stand of the Holy See towards the State of Israel remained unchanged. He also explained that the Pope accepted the request of Mrs. Meir to help the weakest people and in the first place the Palestinian refugees. The Pope wanted to defend the rights of the three monotheistic religions linked to the universal and pluralistic character of Jerusalem. This constituted an unprecedented lack of diplomatic courtesy and the Israeli press was highly critical.

Some days later in an interview with an Israeli paper, Mrs. Meir said that the Pope had thanked her for the care that was being taken of the holy places in Jerusalem; he never mentioned the internationalization of Jerusalem but stressed the need to pursue the dialogue between the Catholic Church and Israel.

At the end of the same year, after the Yom Kippur War, the Pope devoted most of his yearly message to the Cardinals (21 December 1973) to the Middle East. He expressed his appreciation of the Peace Conference convening that day in Geneva, "although, at least for the moment, incomplete in its participants," hinting probably at the non-participation of the Palestinian Arabs. The Holy See was ready "to offer willing cooperation (...) (towards) agreements that may guarantee to all parties concerned a calm and secure existence and the recognition of respective rights." The Pope spoke about the hundreds of thousands of (Arab) refugees "living in desperate conditions"; even if their cause "has been endangered by actions that are repugnant to the civil conscience of the peoples and are in no way justified, it is a cause that demands human consideration and calls with the voice of abandoned and innocent masses for a just and generous response." Again the Pope spoke about rights and "legitimate aspirations" of members of the three monotheistic religions in Jerusalem and in the Holy Land. He also said that "the deference shown by the Israeli authorities assures us of the possibility of having our voice heard when those questions are submitted to a concrete discussion."

Some months later the Pope, inviting contributions to help the Church in the Holy Land, said about the Christians there:

> "If their presence would cease, the glow of a living witness near the shrines would vanish, and the Christian Holy Places of Jerusalem and the Holy Land would become similar to museums."

On 16 July 1974, in a message to the President of the Pontifical Mission for Palestine, the Pope repeated his support for the legitimate aspirations of the Palestinians; the situation had wrought in them "a sense of frustration and in some of them such a mortification and despair that pushed them to actions of violent protest, which we, in pain, cannot but deplore." According to the Pope, the "adequate solution" for the holy places should be found also for the Jewish and Moslem ones, not only the Christian.

On 9 December 1974 Archbishop Hilarion Capucci, the Greek Catholic (Melkite) Archbishop of Jerusalem and vicar of the Patriarch Maximos, was sentenced by an Israeli court to 12 years' imprisonment. He had been found guilty of smuggling arms and explosives from Lebanon into Israel in his car on behalf of el-Fatah, exploiting the diplomatic immunity granted by Israeli authorities. Next day the Vatican declared that the sentence conflicted with the Holy Land tradition of respect for religious leaders, while an Israeli spokesman was "surprised" that the Vatican statement contained no mention of Msgr. Capucci's crimes. Some years later, on 6 November 1977, President Ephraim Katzir, in response to a personal letter from the Pope, commuted the sentence and Archbishop Capucci was immediately released. In January, 1978, he was relieved of his pastoral responsibility in Jerusalem and became a Papal Legate to Latin America, but the written promise of the Pope that Msgr. Capuccini would not "bring any harm to the State of Israel," i.e., would no more indulge in political activity, was not respected and the prelate participated in many propaganda activities organized by the PLO.

At a Seminar on Islamic-Catholic Dialogue, held in Tripoli (Libya) on 1–5 February 1976 a declaration was approved stating that the two parties consider "Zionism an aggressive racist movement extraneous to Palestine" (Par. 20),, "affirm the national rights of the Palestinian people and their right to return to their lands" and "affirm the Arab character of the city of Jerusalem" (Par. 21). The Holy See later declared that it could not accept paragraphs 20 or 21.

On 20 November 1977, the Pope referred to the visit of President Sadat to Jerusalem that day: "it is a great event, hope rises again." Israel's Foreign Minister, Moshe Dayan, was received in private audience by the Pope on 12 January 1978. The Pope again stressed his concern for the question of Jerusalem and the holy places, and "the preeminently religious nature of the Holy City"; in the words of Paul VI, negotiations for a just peace must take place "with the participation of all interested parties" and should combine "the basic demands of both security and justice for all the peoples of the area". But the Israeli Minister did not receive the same appreciation for the efforts of his government in favor of peace as had been received by the Ambassador of Tunisia in December, 1976, or the same praise for the contribution of his country to the cause of peace as had been expressed to the Ambassador of Iraq in December, 1977. President Sadat was received in February, 1978, by the Pope who was "following with active interest the initiative that he had promoted" for peace. The Pope hoped that a solution could be found to all the outstanding problems: Lebanon; the "legitimate aspirations of the Palestinian people"; and the assurance of the juridical conditions for Jerusalem in which the local communities of the three religions should "coexist in a peaceful equality of rights." In 1978 Paul VI died and was succeeded by Pope John Paul I, who had been Patriarch of Venice and as such had had good relations with the Jews. At the beginning of the Camp David meeting between Presidents Carter and Sadat and Prime Minister Begin, the new Pope in his first general audience, on 6 September 1978, said: "I would like to pray together for the success of the Camp David meeting, that those conversations would open the way to a just and complete peace.(..) Complete, without leaving unsolved any problem: the problem of the Palestinians, the security of Israel, the holy city of Jerusalem". It was the first time in history that a Pope had spoken of the necessity of guaranteeing the security of Israel. A few days later, on 10 September, he again prayed for the success of the three leaders at Camp David. Concerning the Jewish people who had known difficult times in the past, he said "never will God forget His people." As the Catholic Church has considered itself the "verus Israel" and "the people of God," it was a novelty to hear a Pope speaking about the Jews as the people of God. But a few days later John Paul I died.

The new Pope, John Paul II, was born in Poland and was the first Pope in centuries who was not an Italian. When he met for the first time with Jewish leaders on 12 March 1979, he evoked "the dedicated and effective work of my predecessor Pius XII on behalf of the Jewish people." He also hoped that "the city of Jerusalem will be effectively guaranteed as a center of harmony for the followers of the three great monotheistic religions." In his address to the General Assembly of the United Nations, the Pope stated:

> "I also hope for a special statute that, under international guarantees, would respect the particular nature of Jerusalem, a heritage sacred to the veneration of millions of believers of the three great monotheistic religions: Judaism, Christianity, and Islam."

The observer of the Holy See to the United Nations made a declaration on Jerusalem on 3 December 1979 in which he explained the meaning of a "special statute internationally guaranteed" for Jerusalem. The content of this statute would include two orders of guarantees: parity for the three religious communities of freedom of worship and of access to the holy places; equal rights for the three religious communities, with guarantees for the promotion of their spiritual, cultural, civil, and social life including adequate opportunities for economic progress, education, and employment.

On 5 October 1980 the Pope spoke in Otranto commemorating the death of Antonio Primoldo and his 800 companions at the hands of the Moslems 500 years before and said:

> "The Jewish people, after tragic experiences connected with the extermination of so many sons and daughters, driven by the desire for security, set up the State of Israel. At the same time the painful condition of the Palestinian people was created, a large part of whom were excluded from their land."

Yitzhak Shamir, Israeli Minister for Foreign Affairs, was received on 7 January 1982 by the Pope who stressed the importance of the Palestinian question, which should find a solution "taking into account also the problem of security of the State of Israel." The Pope also spoke about "a just and agreed upon solution for the question of Jerusalem." Shamir emphasized the concessions made by Israel in order to reach the peace agreement with Egypt, his preoccupation with the arms race in the area, and the serious problem of terrorism.

Later in the same year, on 15 September, the Pope received Yasir Arafat, who had just been forced to leave Beirut, thus according him a political victory after a military defeat. Prime Minister Menahem Begin said on this occasion:

> "The Church, which did not say a word about the massacre of the Jews for six years in Europe and has not much to say about the killing of Christians for seven years in Lebanon, is now ready to meet a man who committed the killings in Lebanon and who wants the destruction of Israel in order to complete the work carried out by the Nazis in Germany."

After the meeting the Holy See issued a press communiqué stressing the three principles of the Vatican: 1)- opposition to acts of terrorism and the use of reprisals; 2)- The

Palestinians were entitled to a homeland of their own; 3)- The Holy See recognized the *de facto* existence of the Jewish State and its right to secure and defined borders.

The Pope dedicated a whole Apostolic Letter, "Redemptionis Anno", on 20 April 1984 to the question of Jerusalem and the Holy Land. After explaining why Jerusalem is holy to the Christians, the Jews and the Moslems, he recalled the Holy See's appeals for an adequate solution. He said: "Not only the monuments or the sacred places, but the whole historical situation and future cannot but affect everyone and interest everyone." Therefore solutions like extraterritoriality, as proposed by Herzl, could not be accepted by the Vatican since it was not a matter of single sanctuaries but the whole "historical Jerusalem", nor could one forget the people (as Paul VI had stressed). A just solution, the Pope said, could "be safeguarded in an adequate and efficacious manner by a special Statute internationally guaranteed," a formula already used by his predecessors. He then went on:

> "For the Jewish people who live in the State of Israel and who preserve in that land such precious testimonies to their history and their faith, we must ask for the desired security and the due tranquillity that is the prerogative of every nation and condition of life and of progress for every society.
>
> The Palestinian people who find their historical roots in that land and who for decades have been dispersed, have the natural right in justice to find once more a homeland and to be able to live in peace and tranquillity with the other people of the area."

Shimon Peres, then Prime Minister, was received by the Pope on 19 February 1985 and discussed the peace process.

No mention of Israel was made by the Pope during his historic visit to the Great Synagogue of Rome in 1986, nor at other meetings with Jewish delegations in Rome and elsewhere. In Miami in 1987, the Pope repeated his previous statements concerning Israel and the Palestinians.

The outstanding issue between Israel and the Vatican remains the absence of normal diplomatic relations. Among the reasons given by the Holy See for refusing to exchange ambassadors are: the unresolved nature of the boundaries between Israel and some of its neighbors; the disposition of the city of Jerusalem; and the security of Christian communities in Arab countries. Theological reasons are not quoted, and in September, 1987, when Jewish leaders were received by the Pope at Castel Gandolfo, near Rome, the official communiqué stated that no theological reasons prevented full relations but that the problems were solely political.

The 1985 "Notes" on the teaching of Jews and Judaism was the first official Vatican document to refer to the State of Israel. While inviting Christians to understand the religious attachment of Jews to the State of Israel it continues that for Christians, "the existence of the State of Israel and its political options should be envisaged not in a perspective which is itself religious but in their reference to the common principles of international law". While averting theological obstacles this denies the spiritual basis of Zionism.

In 1992, the Vatican announced that it was opening negotiations with Israel with a view to "normalization" of relations. The Vatican spokesman expressed the hope that this would lead to diplomatic ties.

S.I. MINERBI

VENEZUELA, ZIONISM IN. The first Jews to settle in Venezuela were Sephardim from the West Indies, who arrived about 1850; by 1873 there were 30 Jewish inhabitants in the country. By World War II, the community consisted overwhelmingly of immigrants from eastern Europe who had come to Venezuela after World War I and of Jews who had fled Nazi oppression in the 1930s. As of 1988 the Jewish population of Venezuela numbered 30,000 (60 percent Ashkenazim) in a total population of 18,000,000. 95 percent of the Jews lived in Caracas, the capital, 400 families in Maracaibo, the second largest city, and 50 in Valencia and Maracay, and 45 families on the island of Margarita.

There are two communities in Venezuela: Union Israelita de Caracas, embracing approximately 2,500 families (mostly Ashkenazi) and Asociacion Israelita de Venezuela with approximately 2,200 families (mostly Sephardi). These two communities together with the Zionist Federation and the B'nai B'rith, constitute the Confederation of Israeli Associations in Venezuela (CAIV), which officially represents the entire community and identified with Zionism.

Zionist activity in Venezuela is centered for the most part in Caracas and Maracaibo. Originally supported by immigrants who came from eastern Europe in large numbers in the 1920s, Zionism eventually won over the Sephardi Jews and received enthusiastic support from the refugees from Nazi persecution and the survivors of the Holocaust who reached Venezuela after World War II.

Activity on behalf of the Jewish National Fund (JNF) began as early as the 1920s. The early 1940s also saw the founding of the first children's Zionist groups by young people who had recently arrived from Europe. These groups met on Saturdays to discuss various aspects of Judaism and Zionism, sing Palestinian Jewish songs, and learn folk dances. They also arranged celebrations for the Jewish holidays and excursions. An older youth group organized public meetings and rallies on behalf of Palestine. It was only in 1949 that an official Zionist Organization, with a building of its own, was set up. Eventually the Zionist movement and local communal life were closely linked, especially in fundraising and education.

The Zionist Federation was founded in 1956 and today has its own community center. It embraces all Zionist groups, each organization being represented on its board by one delegate; it also accepts individuals.

B'nai B'rith: Activities in Venezuela started in 1953. In 1967, after a district division of the Latin America area, Venezuela was assigned to District 23, which extended from Mexico to Colombia. In 1988, Caracas became the headquarters of this district. B'nai B'rith has approximately 1,000 members in eight lodges for men, women, and youth. Although they conduct cultural and social programs, their most important activity is related to human rights. The Human Rights Commission has campaigned for the right of Russian Jews to emigrate to Israel.

Keren ha-Yesod began operations in Venezuela in 1941. In the 1960s approximately 900 Jews from Caracas, Maracaibo, Valencia, Maracay, and Barquisimeto participated in the annual fundraising campaign. Today there are 2,000 members and 120 activists working for the regular campaign, Women's Division and Dor Hemshekh (Young leadership). The last is considered of special importance not only for the institution, but for leadership within the community. The "Ben-Gurion Book" was instituted for the main donors.

The Jewish National Fund began in Venezuela as early as the 1920s, but it was not until the early 1940s that fundraising was organized, with the help of emissaries from Pal-

Zionist group in Venezuela, 1943. [Margot de Labunsky]

estine. Collections are made by the usual means: blue-and-white boxes, the Golden Book, the Bar Mitzva Book, and the Sefer ha-Yeled (Book of the Child). It is common to plant trees to honor people and events.

Women are organized under the Jewish Women of Venezuela (Unión de Damas Hebreas). WIZO, the largest organization, was founded in 1942 with branches in Caracas, Maracaibo, Maracay, and Valencia, pursuing social and cultural activities and helping in fundraising campaigns. In 1958 it founded an orphanage in Holon, which in 1988 cared for 200 children from six months to five years of age. WIZO has eight branches. WIZO Aviv is the organization of the younger generation. The Hatikvah group, another women's organization, was founded in 1953. It works for Magen David Adom and Youth Aliya in Israel, besides aiding local causes in Venezuela such as the Institute for the Blind, Children's Hospital, etc. Other women's organizations are Friends of ICA of Venezuela, supporting the Israel Cancer Association and Shaare Zedek Women's Committee, which works for its hospital in Jerusalem. *Schools*: The community supports two schools with 2,800 students. Two to three hours a day are dedicated to learning Hebrew and Jewish subjects. Study trips to Israel are organized either directly or through the Jewish Agency.

Hebraica is a social club founded in 1978 by both communities. It was the venue of the 1987 Latin American Maccabi Games with the participation of 1,600 athletes from North, Central, and South America. Its ethnic dance group is very well known.

The Venezuelan-Israeli Cultural Institute handles cultural and scientific matters.

Nuevo Mundo Israelita, the local pro-Zionist community newspaper, was founded in 1973 and is distributed free of charge to all Jewish homes and offices.

Israeli academic institutions that have offices in Caracas are the Hebrew University of Jerusalem, the Technion, Tel Aviv University, Bar-Ilan University, and the Weizmann Institute of Science. These raise funds and foster cultural interchange.

Youth Groups: Ha-Shomer ha-Tza'ir of Venezuela, which was founded in 1955 and later renamed Ken Nahshon, caters for children and teenagers. Several of its members have settled in Israel.

Israel Independence Day and the anniversary of the Warsaw Ghetto Uprising are commemorated by the whole community, some 80 percent of whom have visited Israel at least once.

R. PERLI

VIGEE, CLAUDE (originally Claude Strauss). Poet and literary critic (b. Bischwiller, Alsace, 1921). During World War II he was active in Zionist resistance in Toulouse, and in

1943 fled with his parents to the USA, where he became professor of French at Brandeis University. Appointed to a similar position at the Hebrew University (1963), he moved to Jerusalem. Vigée published various books of poems, combining sensitive poetry, philosophical thoughts, and subtle criticism. M. CATANE

VITERBO, CARLO ALBERTO. Lawyer, journalist, and Zionist leader in Italy (b. Florence, 1889; d. Rome, 1974). Coeditor of the weekly *La Settimana Israelitica* in Florence with Alfonso Pacifici, Quinto Sinigaglia, and David Prato, Viterbo was active in Zionist affairs in the 1920s and served as vice-president of the Italian Zionist Federation. He was an Italian delegate to the 12th Zionist Congress (1921) and an organizer of the Italian Zionist Conference (1925). Beginning in 1931 he was president of the Italian Zionist Federation, succeeding Dante Lattes. In 1933 he was a member of the Central Committee for German-Jewish Refugees. From July, 1936, to March, 1937, he carried out a mission among the Falashas of Ethiopia for the Union of Italian-Jewish Communities. Arrested at the outbreak of World War II, he was first imprisoned in Rome and then sent to the concentration camp of Sforzacosta, in Macerata Province, where he remained for more than a year.

Viterbo was a delegate to various conferences of the World Jewish Congress and to Zionist Congresses from the 22nd to the 26th. In 1945 he revived the Italian weekly *Israel*, which had been forced to suspend publication in 1938, and from that time on was its editor and main contributor. In 1951 he was a lecturer in the Hebrew language at the University of Rome. From 1945 to 1947 and again from 1951 to 1961, he was president of the Italian Zionist Federation and was honorary president thereafter.

G. ROMANO

Yoseph Vitkin

VITKIN, JOSEPH. One of the founders of modern education in Eretz Israel and a precursor of the Second Aliya (b. Mogilev on the Dnieper, 1876; d. Tel Aviv, 1912). Vitkin, who came from a religious Zionist family, immigrated to Eretz Israel in 1897, spent his first few months in the country as a laborer in Rishon le-Zion, and in the summer of 1898 turned to teaching which remained his vocation for the rest of his life. He served as teacher and headmaster in Gedera, Rishon le-Zion, and Kefar Tavor. He was one of the first educators to introduce natural sciences, agriculture, and physical training into the curriculum, and he emphasized the need for thorough instruction in the Bible which he regarded as the major source for the study of Hebrew and for the inculcation of moral and national values. Vitkin introduced Hebrew as the main language in his schools in the face of a strong opposition from the settlers, who, owing to the French influence of Baron Edmond de Rothschild's appointees in the settlements, aimed at worldly careers for their children. Late in 1904, while at Kefar Tavor, Vitkin wrote a pamphlet entitled "A call to young Jews whose hearts are with their people and with Zion," which was a passionate appeal to Jewish youth in the Diaspora to come to Eretz Israel and infuse new life into the yishuv whose continued existence was threatened by the decadence that had set in under the regime of patronage practiced by Rothschild's representatives and later by ICA. The pamphlet was distributed in Russia in 1905 by Hovevei Zion, and at first did not cause much of a stir. After a while, however, the pamphlet came to be regarded as one of the elements that inspired the Second Aliya; indeed, the leaders of that wave of immigration felt that it was a cornerstone of their movement, and it was this pamphlet to which Vitkin owed his subsequent renown.

For Vitkin, the workers who had come to Eretz Israel with the Second Aliya were the embodiment of the yishuv's hopes and he decided to join the founders of Ha-Po'el ha-Tza'ir, the first political party to be established by that aliya. He called on the party and its adherents not to restrict themselves to "the conquest of labor" (*see* KIBBUSH AVODA) but to dedicate themselves also to "the conquest of land" to be used for the settlement of immigrant workers in agricultural units. At the time, this idea was not popular among the labor parties, whose aim was to create a proletariat made up of wage-earning workers, and one of the leaders of Ha-Po'el ha-Tza'ir, Joseph Aharonowitz, attacked Vitkin on this score. Vitkin was the first to argue that the Jewish National Fund should be the agency to settle immigrants on the land and he worked out a detailed proposal on this issue (in 1907) which in its contents was almost identical with the plan that Arthur Ruppin drew up the following year for the Palestine Land Development Co. (Hakhsharat ha-Yishuv). In 1907 and 1908 Vitkin spent about half a year in southern Russia as an emissary for Hovevei Zion and Ha-Po'el ha-Tza'ir.

In 1911 he went to Vienna, where he underwent surgery for the removal of a cancerous growth from his throat. The operation was not successful and he returned to Eretz Israel to die there. In accordance with his request, he was buried in Rishon le-Zion. A village in the coastal plain, Kefar Vitkin, was named after him. A collection of Vitkin's writings was published a few months after his death and was republished, in an expanded edition, in 1961.

S. LASKOV

VOGEL, DAVID. Hebrew poet and novelist (b. Satanov, Russia, 1891; d. in a German concentration camp, 1944?). He received a traditional education, studied at a yeshiva (rabbinical academy) in Vilna and, after a period of wandering in Galicia and Podolia, moved to Vienna in 1912. Vogel settled in Paris in 1925 or 1926. In 1929, he went to Palestine but, unable to find gainful employment, returned to Europe in 1930. From 1931 until the outbreak of World War II he lived in Paris. The war found him at Hautville, near Lyons. When the Nazis invaded the Vichy area, he was deported to Germany. It is presumed that he died in a concentration camp.

Vogel is one of the early post-Bialik modernist poets. Although he published in all the leading Hebrew journals, he enjoyed only moderate critical acclaim. Literary tastes at the time favored a more traditional poetic idiom. Even those writers who rebelled against the Bialik tradition favored Russian modernist trends rather that the kind of poetry written by German and Yiddish poets which appealed to Vogel. Only one volume of his poetry, *Lifnei ha-Sha'ar ha-Afel* (Before the Dark Gate, 1921), appeared in his lifetime. His novel, *Hayai Nesu'im* (Married Life, 1929–30), received only grudging recognition.

Interest in Vogel was revived in the 1960s when a new generation of poets led by Natan Zach rediscovered him and hailed him as a forerunner of the new Hebrew modernism. Zach and others admired Vogel's spare style, his elliptic "line which is drawn from the not-yet-molded void of the authentic experience which lay at the base of a poem."

Dan Pagis gathered and published his *Collected Poems* in 1966 and issued an expanded edition in 1972. Aharon Komem rediscovered and published Vogel's literary remains, including a complete manuscript of a proposed volume of verse, which he published in 1983 (*Le-ever ha-Demama*, Toward Stillness). E. SPICEHANDLER

VOLCANI, YITZHAK AVIGDOR. *See* ELAZARI-VOLCANI, YITZHAK AVIGDOR.

VOLCANI INSTITUTE OF AGRICULTURAL RESEARCH. *See* AGRICULTURAL RESEARCH ORGANIZATION.

VON WEISL, ZE'EV (Wolfgang). Physician, author, and Zionist leader (b. Vienna, 1896; d. Gedera, 1974). During World War I he served as a lieutenant in the Austro-Hungarian Army and, after the collapse of the monarchy, with the Jewish defense unit in Vienna. After graduating from the Medical Faculty of the University of Vienna in 1921, Von Weisl went to Palestine, where he worked as a laborer and, later, as a physician while directing the first Hagana officers' school in Tel Aviv. In 1923 he returned to Vienna, where he practiced medicine, took an active part in Zionist work, and contributed articles to the *Neue Freie Presse* and the *Wiener Morgenzeitung*. In 1924 he was appointed political correspondent for Palestine and the Near East of the *Vossische Zeitung* (Berlin) and the *Chicago Tribune*. He became one of the founders of the Revisionist movement in Palestine, and in 1928 he joined the editorial board of *Do'ar ha-Yom*. During the Arab riots of 1929 he was seriously wounded. In 1930 he was elected chairman of the Revisionist Central Committee in Palestine, and the next year he became editor of the movement's daily, *Ha-Am*.

In 1932 Von Weisl returned to Vienna. In 1936 he was elected to the World Executive of the New Zionist Organization. In 1940 he was in Palestine once again, and in 1942 he assumed the chairmanship of the Palestine branch of the New Zionist Organization. In June, 1946, he was interned in Latrun but was released after a hunger strike of 19 days. In 1947 he was again interned at Latrun together with leaders of the yishuv. He was wounded during the War of Independence. In 1955 he joined the General Zionist party.

He wrote *Der Kampf um das Heilige Land* (The Struggle for the Holy Land, 1925), *Allah ist gross* (Great is Allah, 1937), *Ein Volk im Streit* (A Nation at War, 1934), *Ninety-two Days of Detention and Fasting* (1946), and other works.

I. BENARI

VRIES, SIMON PHILIP. Rabbi and Mizrachi leader in the Netherlands (b. Neede, Netherlands, 1870;d. Bergen-Belsen, 1943). Vries attended the Netherlands Rabbinical Seminary in Amsterdam and from 1892 to 1940 served as rabbi in Haarlem. He became a Zionist early in life, published a pamphlet entitled *Ma'ane le-Tziyon* (Response to Zion, 1905), and founded the Dutch Mizrachi Organization, of which he remained the most prominent leader throughout his life, and for many years was editor of its monthly journal. He influenced several generations of the Dutch Mizrachi. Among his published works is *Joods Palestina* (1935).

H. BOAS

VYGODSKI, YAKOV. Zionist leader in districts of Lithuania and Vilna (b. Vilna, 1857; d. 1942 under the Nazi occupation). After completing his medical studies, Vygodski practiced as a physician in Vilna up until World War I. In 1905 he became active in the struggle for civil rights for Jews in Russia and was involved in the Committee for National Minorities talks in Vilna. At the same time he also worked within the Constitutional Democrat (Kadet) Party, which he represented at the 1905 conference. He contributed to the renewal of public Jewish life through the organization and running of community boards, in line with the resolutions of the Helsingfors Conference, and participated in the Kovno conference in November, 1909, which convened in order to draw up a program. He took a prominent part in the aid and rehabilitation activities of the Vilna community during the German occupation in World War I. In his vigorous defense of Jewish rights he came into acute confrontation with the German authorities and in March, 1917, he was arrested and deported to a prisoner-of-war camp in western Prussia, where he remained until 1918. Subsequently Vygodski joined the Lithuanian Zionist Organization, participating in its conference in December, 1918. One of the seven Jewish representatives elected to the Lithuanian *Taryiba* (National Council), Vygodski served as Minister for Jewish Affairs. After the Polish capture of Vilna, he fought against the Polish army's brutalization of the town's Jewish population. Following the community's reorganization in 1919 he became one of its leaders, and was elected as its head in 1920, embodying the desire of the Vilna Jews for a community which would realize national autonomy, and fighting for the recognition of Yiddish as an official language. In 1922 he was one of the National Minorities Bloc delegates elected to the Polish Sejm. Vygodski continued his communal and municipal council activities throughout this period (even in his eighties) up until the dispersal of the Jewish community with the annexation of Lithuania to the USSR in 1940. During the Nazi occupation he was not initially elected to the Jewish Council where his active participation in anti-Nazi committees before the war would have placed him in immediate danger. In July, 1941, however Vygodski was included in the expanded *Judenrat* (Jewish Council) was arrested for the first time on 6 August, and again on 24 August. He died in prison.

M. MINTZ

W

WACHSBERGER, MOSHE. Hebrew scholar (b. Galicia, 1879; d. Adelaide, Australia, 1965). He went to Hungary at age 13, and attended a yeshiva which he was asked to leave at 16 because he was discovered reading Hebrew *haskala* and German literature. Reaching the capital, he entered the teachers' seminary, obtaining qualifications to teach Hungarian and German language and literature. He was employed as a teacher in the schools of the Jewish Community of Pest which enabled him to travel in Europe and in 1909, Egypt and Eretz Israel. He joined the Zionist movement, attended the 11th Zionist Congress (1913) and several other Congresses. During World War I he served in Silesia as an auxiliary. After the war, he taught in secondary schools, achieving his dream of teaching the Hebrew language in the Jewish High School (Gymnasium) only towards the end of his career. A pioneer in the diffusion of Hebrew, Wachsberger organized courses and Hebrew-speaking clubs, translated and published a volume of modern Hebrew short stories, edited a Hebrew grammar, and was chairman of Brit Ivrit Olamit in Hungary. After the death of his wife in 1950, Wachsberger tried to settle in Israel but old, alone, and with badly-impaired vision, in 1952 he joined his daughter in Australia where he continued to teach Hebrew until his death. E. EPPLER

WAHRHAFTIG, ZERAH. Religious Zionist leader, scholar, and politician (b. Volkovysk, Russia, 1906). After studying at yeshivot in Poland and at the University of Warsaw, he practiced law in Warsaw. Active from his youth in the Tora va-Avoda and Mizrachi movements, he held leading positions in both. He was vice-president of the Mizrachi Organization of Poland and served on the Executive of the World Jewish Congress.

From 1939–1941 he was a refugee in Lithuania and Japan. During these years he was active in attempts to rescue Jews and take them to Palestine. In 1941 he arrived in New York where he served as deputy director of the Institute of Jewish Affairs of the World Jewish Congress and as vice-president of Ha-Po'el ha-Mizrachi of America. Wahrhaftig settled in Palestine in 1947, and became a member of Israel's Provisional Council of State. He was one of the signatories to the Declaration of Independence.

A member of the Knesset from 1949–1981, he was Deputy Minister of Religious Affairs from 1949 and from 1961–1974 served as Minister of Religious Affairs. He taught in the Law Department of the Hebrew University from 1949–1963 and was one of the founders of Bar-Ilan University, serving as chairman of its executive. He was also among the founders of Yad Vashem and of Heikhal Shelomo.

He published books on Jewish Law and articles on the problems of religion and state. His autobiography, *Remnant and a Survivor*, appeared in 1988. In 1983, he was awarded an Israel Prize for his contribution to Law and Society.

J. STAVI—E. HOTER

WAILING WALL. *See* WESTERN WALL.

"WALL AND TOWER" SETTLEMENTS. *See* "STOCKADE AND TOWER" SETTLEMENTS.

WARBURG, FELIX MORITZ. Banker, philanthropist, and communal worker in the United States (b. Hamburg, Germany, 1871; d. New York, 1937). Warburg married the daughter of Jacob H. Schiff, moved to New York, and joined the banking firm of Kuhn, Loeb and Co., of which he was a senior partner at the time of his death. Throughout his life he took an active interest in Jewish philanthropy and communal life, playing a leading role in the American Jewish Joint Distribution Committee and the United Jewish Appeal.

When Chaim Weizmann visited New York in 1923, Warburg invited him to his office and questioned him about Zionist work in Palestine. Warburg and his wife visited Palestine at Weizmann's suggestion and returned deeply impressed. From that time on, although he never became a Zionist, Warburg devoted much of his energy to aiding the cultural and economic development of the yishuv.

In 1926 he helped found the *PEC Israel Economic Corporation, of which he became honorary president. In 1929 he was elected a director of Keren ha-Yesod and, together with Louis Marshall, represented the non-Zionists in negotiations with the World Zionist Organization for an expanded *Jewish Agency. After Marshall's death (1929), he became chairman of the Agency's Administrative Committee. In 1930 he resigned the chairmanship in protest against the Passfield White Paper, which he called "a cruel betrayal of trusteeship," but remained a member of the Agency's Council. In 1937 he opposed the plan for the partition of Palestine proposed by the Peel Commission; he was convinced that a Jewish State set up along the lines of the Peel proposal would not be able to survive and that a peace arrangement should be made with the Arabs before the Agency began negotiations with the British. At the August 1937 sessions of the Jewish Agency Council Warburg was instrumental in formulating the Council's resolution regarding negotiations with the British for the establishment of a Jewish State in Palestine and efforts to reach a peaceful accommodation with the Arabs.

Frieda Schiff Warburg (1876–1958), his wife, took an active role in Hadassah, serving as chairman of the building fund campaign for the Hadassah University Hospital in Jerusalem. In 1949 she established a $100,000 fund for medical scholarships at the hospital, and in 1951 she contributed $650,000 to the United Jewish Appeal for the housing and education of new immigrants in Israel. At the time of her death she was honorary president of the American Friends of the Hebrew University and honorary vice-president of the International Youth Aliya Commission.

Otto Warburg. [Zionist Archives]

WARBURG, OTTO. Botanist and Chairman of the Executive of the World Zionist Organization (b. Hamburg, Germany, 1859; d. Berlin, 1938). A graduate of the universities of Bonn, Berlin, and Strasbourg in philosophy, mathematics, and natural sciences; he specialized in botany at the University of Tübingen. His book *Beiträge zur Kenntniss der papuasischen Flora* (1889–91), the first in a series, established his name as an authority in this field. He was cofounder of numerous companies, notably of the Kolonial-Wirtschaftliches Kommittee (1896), edited its periodical *Der Tropenwirt*, and was greatly respected in German academic and official circles.

It was rare for a man of his standing in Germany to turn to Zionism. His father-in-law, Gustav Gabriel Cohen, a pre-Herzlian Zionist, was influential in this respect. In 1896 he joined the Esra Society, a philanthropic body which aimed to promote the settlement of east European Jews in Turkey, and he soon became a member of its Central Committee. In the following year he joined the newly-established Zionist movement, being particularly attracted by the socio-economic experiment in Eretz Israel and the pressing need to ameliorate the position of the Jews in eastern Europe. His enthusiasm for settlement projects was tempered by his trained scientific thinking.

In 1903 Herzl appointed him chairman of the newly-founded Palestine Commission, of which Franz Oppenheimer and Selig Eugen Soskin were also members. He contributed a number of articles to the periodical *Palästina* and served on the editorial board of *Altneuland* (1904–1906), the Commission's monthly. In 1904 he conceived the idea of the Olive Tree Fund (subsequently appropriated by the Jewish National Fund), which was to serve a dual purpose: (a) to provide employment and serve as a training ground for the newly arrived pioneers, and (b) to assist financing (when the olive trees reached maturity) cultural enterprises in Eretz Israel. From 1905 he served as chairman of the Jewish National Fund. He helped to found the Bezalel School in Jerusalem (1905), the Jaffa Office of the Zionist Organization, and of the Hevrat Hakhsharat ha-Yishuv (1908). He also furthered private enterprise.

From 1905 he was a member of the Inner Actions Committee and succeeded David Wolffsohn as head of the World Zionist Organization, following Wolffsohn's resignation at the Tenth Zionist Congress (9–15 August 1911). However, Warburg refused to become president and confined himself to the role of chairman of the executive. In this capacity he served until 1920. He stood firmly by his convictions but his innate modesty and understanding made him an ideal chairman. It was largely due to his personal qualities that relations within the movement were harmonious.

A leading exponent of the "practical" school of thought, he took politics seriously. At the Eleventh Zionist Congress (1913) he stated: "Our work in Eretz Israel is not merely a factor of equal work with our political work but is the necessary forerunner of our political efforts".

Following the outbreak of World War I he outlined the Zionist policy of neutrality between the warring camps: Zionism was an international movement and the future of Eretz Israel would be decided only during the peace negotiations. He urged that the traditional policy of loyalty to the Ottoman Empire be followed. His prime concern was the preservation of the yishuv during the war. Jamal Pasha, the Commander of the IV Ottoman Army in Syria and Palestine, was inimical and his intent to institute a policy of massive deportations could have brought utter destruction to the Zionist enterprise in Eretz Israel. Warburg's high standing in official German circles stood him in good stead and it was largely owing to his persuasiveness, as well as that of his colleagues, that the German government emerged as the chief protector of the yishuv.

In 1920 he stepped down gracefully in favor of Weizmann. In 1922 he went to Palestine to lay the foundation of the Agricultural Station in Rehovot. He became its head jointly with Isaac Wilkansky (*see* ELAZAR VOLCANI). When the Hebrew University in Jerusalem was founded he was invited to head its Department of Botany. However, he continued to reside in Germany, visiting Palestine each year for several months.

I. FRIEDMAN

WAR EFFORT OF THE YISHUV. Palestinian Jewry made a substantial contribution to the Allied war effort against the Axis powers in World War II. The participation of the

Jews in Jewish Brigade in recruiting parade in Tel Aviv. [Jewish National Fund]

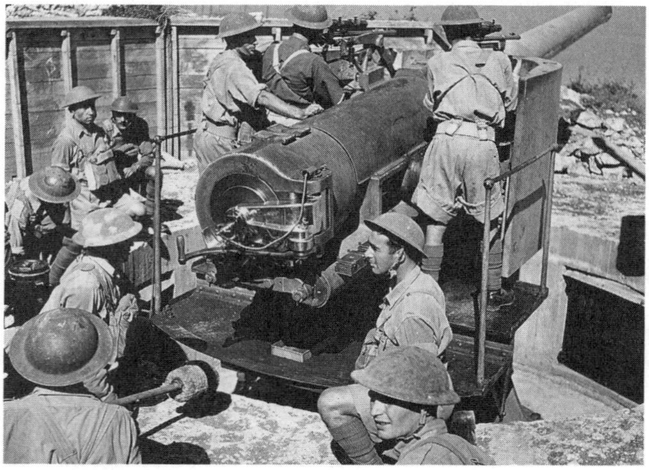

Jewish Palestinians in British Royal Artillery man a coastal gun near Haifa, 1941. [Israel Govt. Press Office]

yishuv in the war was twofold: large numbers of its young people served as volunteers in various formations of the British armed forces, and its industry and agriculture filled many of the needs of the Allied troops stationed in the Middle East.

Immediately after the outbreak of war in 1939, the yishuv declared its readiness to give all the aid it could to the Allies in their struggle against Nazi Germany. A growing number of young men and women enlisted in the British army, navy, air force, ATS (Auxiliary Territorial Service), and WAAF (Women's Auxiliary Air Force). Units of Palestinian Jewish soldiers served in various theaters of the war. Their contribution was especially noteworthy in the desert war in Libya, where they participated in the defense of Tobruk. A special camouflage unit created the fake 10th Corps in the Libyan Desert, which was designed as a ruse to trick the enemy.

A Palestinian Jewish volunteer unit paved the way for the Allied advance into Syria and Lebanon in 1940. In 1941, when the Axis forces advancing in the Soviet Union and Libya threatened the whole Middle East, the British military authorities assigned the Jewish Settlement Police and units of *Hagana vital defense tasks and trained them for this purpose. In the spring of 1941 a Jewish intelligence and sabotage unit penetrated pro-Axis Iraq. Between 1943 and 1945 Palestinian Jewish *parachutists were dropped behind the enemy lines in central and southern Europe. In 1944 the British authorities at last acceded to the yishuv's request for a separate Jewish fighting unit, and the *Jewish Brigade Group was established.

While about 30,000 young Palestinian Jews were serving in the regular forces, agriculture and industry, the technical skill of the yishuv as well as the inventiveness of its scientists played an important role in filling the needs of the large contingents of Allied troops stationed in the Middle East. In the early 1940s, when the Mediterranean became a major theater of war and shipments from Great Britain became extremely difficult because of a scarcity of shipping and a shortage of labor in Britain, the British relied heavily on Palestinian Jewry's agricultural, industrial, and technical potential. Palestinian Jewish agriculture supplied the forces stationed in the country with large quantities of potatoes, other vegetables, and dairy products. Canned foods and preserves were furnished to Allied troops in Palestine and neighboring countries. Jewish factories in Palestine produced tools and machinery needed for the war effort, including precision instruments for the Royal Air Force. Jewish textile mills supplied large quantities of tents, tarpaulins, rope, twine, camouflage netting, and socks and sweaters for the soldiers. Palestinian factories also produced armaments and large quantities of land mines. Pharmaceutical plants produced essential medical supplies, including drugs and vaccines discovered or prepared by the country's scientists. These provided the needs of large segments of the civilian population and the Allied forces in the Middle East. Some medical supplies were shipped also to the troops in the Far East.

The potash works of the Dead Sea were the principal source of potash throughout the British Empire. Palestinian research laboratories contributed greatly to the production of scarce but essential materials and devised improvements in precision instruments. Jewish technicians carried out major repair work.

The small Palestinian Jewish merchant marine was at the disposal of the British Admiralty. It undertook dangerous missions in the eastern Mediterranean, including bringing vital aid and supplies to British forces locked in battle in Libya.

T. PRESCHEL

WAR OF ATTRITION. A war fought, fundamentally on static lines.

Egyptian Front, 1968–70. Soon after the termination of the *Six-Day War, in June, 1967, Egyptian President Nasser outlined a three-stage program: phase one, to stand firm and steadfast, to be followed by a second phase of active deterrence, and ultimately, once the Egyptian armed forces were fully reconstituted and close coordination instituted with other Arab armies, by final liberation of Sinai. Consequently, the armistice lines with Egypt were at first kept relatively quiet, in order to deprive the Israel Defense Forces (IDF) of any possible pretext for renewing the fighting. Clashes that took place towards the end of 1967 bore a local character and were related to the delineation of the armistice lines, along the Suez Canal itself (important for the eventual use of the water way which had been closed since the Six-Day War) and in the northern sector, where Egyptian troops occupied positions to the east of the Canal. On 21 October 1967 an Israel destroyer, the *Eilat*, was sunk by an Egyptian torpedo using Soviet-made missiles. To warn against a repetition of similar actions, a massive Israel attack paralyzed Egyptian refineries, petrochemical industries, and oil tanks near the city of Suez. In February, 1968, the Israel submarine *Dakar* was lost without trace, en route from Portsmouth to Haifa.

The second phase, that of active deterrence, began in September, 1968, with a series of massive Egyptian artillery barrages along a 66 mile (100 km.) front, clearly designed to cause a maximum amount of casualties, affecting Israeli morale in view of its extreme sensitivity to casualties, and at the same time boosting Egyptian morale both at the front and in the rear. It was this phase which became known as the War of Attrition. The IDF replied in kind with artillery fire directed against targets on the west bank of the Suez Canal while at the same time reinforcing the fortifications established along the east bank, *inter alia*, using the rails of the abandoned Sinai railroad line to provide bomb-proof roofs.

When these tactics proved insufficient, the IDF, from 31 October 1968 onward, provided a diversion with raids deep into Egypt. In the course of the first of these—to Naj Hammadi— some 235 miles (350 km.) from the nearest point in Israel hands, a bridge, a dam, and a transmission station on the Aswan-Cairo high powerline were blown up. President Nasser established a popular militia to guard strategic objectives in the rear, while maintaining steady pressure of varying intensity along the front, both in the form of artillery fire and armored and infantry patrols east of the Canal designed to capture at least one fortification, and to improve the training and self-confidence of the Egyptian troops. No fortification fell to the Egyptians. Israeli raids continued in the course of 1969— with coastal stations along the west side of the Gulf of Suez as the main targets— attacked by either airborne or naval units; one spectacular raid was directed against the heavily fortified Green Island, just west of Port Tewfik, in July, 1969.

In the same month, air attacks were added to artillery shellings, directed against anti-aircraft installations, headquarters, and petrol and ammunition dumps. In September, 1969, IDF landing craft with tanks landed on the western, Egyptian side of the Gulf of Suez; the armored column ranged freely along dozens of miles, destroying Egyptian outposts, raiding Egyptian army camps and radar installations before returning home safely. The most spectacular raid consisted in the capture and transfer, intact, to Israel of a 7-ton Russian-made radar installation. Egyptian Soviet-made and -installed anti-aircraft emplacements, artillery, radar, and missiles, had by now been severely damaged, and the interior of Egypt was no longer sealed against Israeli air penetration. Israel planes ranged freely near Cairo and beyond. On a desperate gamble, Nasser visited Moscow and demanded direct Soviet intervention in the protection of Egyptian skies with pilots and missile crews, until Egypt could handle its own defense. Failing a favorable Soviet response, he threatened to resign and publicly to accuse the Soviet Union of having failed its ally. Soviet crews were dispatched to Egypt in the early months of 1970; they soon moved missiles forward, closer to the Suez Canal. Five Israeli planes were brought down in an attempt to neutralize the new system. July witnessed the only encounter in the air between Russian and Israeli pilots, in which four Russian planes were downed without Israeli losses. Major power direct involvement with its concomitant risks of further escalations prompted the US administration to undertake an initiative, named after Secretary of State William Rogers, calling for a ceasefire— standstill, and a simultaneous effort to bring about a peace agreement, under Ambassador Jarring of Finland. Both Israel and Egypt accepted the initiative, with Egypt limiting its agreement to an initial period of 90 days. Immediately after the ceasefire came into effect, on 8 August 1970, and before any supervisory machinery had been introduced, the Soviets and Egyptians once more erected an anti-aircraft missile system extending to the Suez Canal, something they had been unable to do while fighting was in progress. In retaliation the government of Israel suspended its participation in the Jarring talks, which were about to be renewed. The system thus installed was to play a major role in the first phase of the Yom Kippur War in 1973.

Israel's consent to the Jarring talks had included an express commitment to "withdraw" from territories occupied in 1967. This caused Gahal, under the leadership of Menahem Begin, to leave the government, thus bringing to an end the National Unity Government which, in one form or another, had been in power since the eve of the Six-Day War.

In the course of the War of Attrition about 400 Israeli soldiers lost their lives in battle. N. LORCH

Jordanian Front, 1967–70. After the Six-Day War with the consequent loss of bases for the terrorists in Judea and Samaria, Jordan became the principal base for activities of Palestinian terrorists against Israel, and they in fact took over parts of the eastern Jordan Valley. From Jordanian territory, they shelled the border districts in the Bet She'an Valley and the Kinarot Valley, while terrorist bands infiltrated the long, winding border in order to attack Israeli settlements. Jordanian army units helped the terrorists to cross the Jordan, covered them during retreat, and even fired on Israeli settlements on their own initiative.

The IDF retaliated by establishing a defense system designed to close off the Jordan Valley completely. The frontier was fenced and mined, and electronic warning systems and sophisticated detection means were installed. Observation posts and Nahal settlements were created at strategic points. Ambuscades were set nightly close to the river, and from mid-November 1967 tanks were also stationed in the Valley.

The IDF also carried out preventive actions, launched by the infantry, armored forces, artillery, and air force, which severely damaged the terrorist bases and led the terrorists to withdraw in April, 1968, to the western districts of Gilead, and in the course of time to the mountain heights on the eastern bank. The inhabitants of the region fled to refugee camps in the Amman area.

With the Valley closed off, the terrorists attempted to infiltrate via the Dead Sea. A blocking system was likewise installed in this sector.

The activities of the terrorists and of the Jordanian army continued for three years, coming to an end only when the Jordanians expelled the PLO in "Black September" (September, 1970). During this period, 5,840 enemy actions were carried out on this front (mostly shelling and shooting from over the border), including 660 against civilian settlements; 141 Israelis were killed and about 800 injured. Some 1,000 terrorists were killed and approximately 400 captured. The Jordanian army suffered about 300 dead. Several score soldiers of the Iraqi division were also killed.

The Golan Heights, 1969–70. With Israel's relatively deep front after the Six-Day War and the stationing of its forward troops at only 40 miles (60 km.) from Damascus, the Syrian leadership was extremely cautious about carrying out hostile actions. From February, 1969, however, the number of terrorist infiltrations increased, for the most part for mine-laying operations, but there were also penetrations by large 15–25 man units. The IDF retaliated by air attacks on Fatah bases. The conference of Arab chiefs-of-staff, held in Damascus on 8 July 1969, decided to activate the eastern front, and the Syrian army came into action. The IDF retaliated by attacking a convoy of Syrian gunners in northern Jordan and a terrorist base on the slopes of the Hermon. The Syrians in turn shelled the Hermon outpost and bombarded the entire frontier line.

In March, 1970, the Syrians began to operate commando units and set many ambushes for patrols and vehicles in the Golan Heights. In retaliation, the IDF attacked objectives deep in Syria. When the Syrians stepped up shelling of villages and outposts in June of that year, the situation degenerated into open warfare. IDF attacks were designed to prevent further escalation on the eastern front, and in a "three-day war" Israeli forces inflicted a serious blow on the Syrian army. After that, the front was calm. Only the terrorist units continued to act on the Syrian border, and this activity was now on a reduced scale.

Lebanon, 1968–70. In 1968, with the deterioration of their situation in the Jordan Valley, Palestinian terrorists began to establish bases on the south-west slopes of Mount Hermon, which served as a departure point for large-scale actions. In 1969, 97 actions against objectives in Israel were carried out by terrorists from this area.

From their bases the terrorists infiltrated Israeli territory, blew up buildings, set ambushes, fired on settlements, and attacked IDF border patrols. They bombarded targets in Israel mainly civilian settlements, with mortar shells and "katyushas." The terrorists also attempted to settle in bases west of the Hatzbani river, but were opposed by the Lebanese army and violent encounters ensued between the Lebanese and the terrorists, leading to a government crisis in Lebanon and clashes between Moslems and Christians. With the mediation of Nasser, an agreement was signed between the Lebanese government and the terrorists giving the PLO the right to settle in the south-east sector of Lebanon ("Fatahland") and to maintain regular contacts with their rearguard bases in Syria. The terrorists undertook not to shell Israeli settlements from Lebanese territory, but violated the agreement.

In 1969, the IDF went over to the offensive and attacked terrorist bases and traffic axes with planes and artillery. Terrorist activity increased, in particular the shelling of Kiryat Shemona and the settlements in the Galilee panhandle. In order to eradicate the terrorists, large forces deployed in May and September, 1970, deep in Fatahland, with artillery and air force cover, which succeeded in reducing the terrorist activity. B. MICHELSOHN

WAR OF INDEPENDENCE (Arab-Israeli War of 1948). War fought from November, 1947, to July, 1949, by the Jewish population of Palestine, and subsequently by the people of the newly created State of Israel, in order to gain and defend their political independence, and assure their very survival.

The war can be divided into two main periods. The first, beginning on 30 November 1947, on the morrow of the partition resolution of the General Assembly of the United Nations, ended with the termination of the British Mandate for Palestine and the establishment of the State of Israel on 14 May 1948. The second began with the official invasion from neighboring Arab countries on 15 May 1948, and continued until the signing of the last of the general *armistice agreements, that with Syria, on 20 July 1949. In the first phase of the war, the yishuv was faced with violence from armed elements of the local Arab population, assisted by irregular volunteers from neighboring Arab countries. In the second, the defense forces of Israel, which from 30 May 1948 on were known as the *Israel Defense Forces (IDF), fought principally against the regular armies of Egypt, Iraq, Jordan, Syria, and Lebanon, which had invaded Palestine on the morrow of the British evacuation, assisted by volunteers from Saudi Arabia, Libya, and Yemen. The declared objective of the Arabs in the first phase was to frustrate the implementation of the partition resolution and prevent the establishment of the State of Israel; in the second—to liquidate the newly born state and, when that was frustrated, to limit its territory and undermine its viability.

Hostilities during the first phase were conducted by loosely organized bands, commanded and directed by the emissaries of political bodies of Palestinian Arabs. Early in October, 1947, the Arab League urged its member states to train volunteers and mobilize financial means and armaments in order to assist the Arabs of Palestine. The Jewish force, whose task was to counter any Arab aggression, consisted primarily of the *Hagana, with its small full-time component and its larger militia element. The fully mobilized force prior to the war included four battalions of the *Palmah (commando units), with 2,100 fighters in October, 1947, and about 1,000 reservists who had completed their tour of duty but could be recalled at short notice; and the HISH (Hel Sadeh, or field army), with about 1,800 full-time members of the Jewish Settlement Police and about 10,000 reservists. In addition to headquarters units, service formations, and a military industry component, the High Command of the Hagana could dispose of about 32,000 members of HIM (Hel Mishmar, or garrison army), most of whom were elderly persons tied down to the defense of their places of residence in villages and cities; and the Gadna (Youth Battalions), consisting of youngsters who were being trained for auxiliary tasks, with the idea that when they grew older they would join the HISH or the Palmah. In the arsenals of the Hagana there were, on the eve of the War of Independence, somewhat over 15,000 rifles of various types, light machine guns, and a few dozen medium machine guns and 3-inch mortars. Hand grenades, dynamite, and sub-machine guns of the Sten gun type were being produced in the Hagana's secret workshops. In addition to the Hagana, there were two other underground organizations in the yishuv, the *Irgun Tzeva'i Le'umi (Etzel) and the *Lohamei Herut Israel (Lehi), which operated on their own at the beginning of the war (in fact, before the war clashes had occurred between them and the Hagana). In the course of the war, however, they disbanded, and their members joined the Israel Defense Forces. It is estimated that at the beginning of the war the Irgun consisted of 5,000 men and the Lehi of 1,000.

The command structure and organization of the Jewish military force underwent significant changes in the course of the war and reached a certain stage of stability only toward the end. The Hagana, as the illegal military arm of the legal and recognized Jewish Agency, was controlled by a High Command consisting of a chief appointed by the chairman of the Jewish Agency Executive and of delegates of various political parties. The highest ranking officer was the chief of the small General Staff. At the beginning of the war David Ben-Gurion, chairman of the Jewish Agency Executive, had overall responsibility for all military and defense affairs; Israel Galili was chief of the High Command, and Ya'akov Dori was chief of the General Staff. With the establishment of the State and Hagana's emergence from underground status, the function of chief of the High Command was abolished and control of the newly formed Israel Defense Forces was vested directly in the provisional government, through the Minister of Defense, who was simultaneously Prime Minister.

Partition Resolution to Operation Nahshon, 29 November 1947–3 April 1948. The existence of a considerable number of Jewish settlements interspersed in areas populated primarily by Arabs, the presence of mixed cities with both Jewish and Arab inhabitants, and Arab control of the greater part of the mountainous areas and of the major communication arteries—these were the factors that determined the character of Arab aggression from its first manifestation, the attack on a Jewish bus near Lydda Airport. Soon after a general strike had been declared by the Arab Higher Committee, an Arab mob broke into the old commercial center of Jerusalem and destroyed it. At the same time fire was opened on Jewish residences and shops in Haifa and on the boundary between Jaffa and Tel Aviv. On 10 December 1947, mobs attacked Jewish vehicles in the Negev and on the road from Jerusalem to the Etzion Bloc. It soon became evident that static defense would not be a sufficient deterrent, and both the Hagana and the Irgun undertook retaliatory operations against the hotbeds of Arab gangs, each in its own way. The month of December also saw a process of segregation of Jewish and Arab areas throughout the country. Marginal quarters in the mixed cities changed hands in several cases; mixed houses and mixed quarters were evacuated by their Jewish or Arab inhabitants. The battle for lines of communications became fiercer. The Arabs soon gained the upper hand, particularly because of the position of the British Army, still ubiquitous in the country, neutral in theory, but often pro-Arab in fact. The possibility of evacuating 33 Jewish settlements, which in accordance with the partition resolution should have been included in the Arab state, was discussed but was rejected, and the decision was taken by the Jewish High Command to defend each and every one of the settlements and the communications with them, wherever they might be.

On 10 January 1948, 900 Arabs of the so-called Palestine Liberation Army, which had been trained and organized across the borders, attacked Kefar Szold in Upper Galilee but were defeated by its defenders, assisted by a British unit. The following day, Arab attacks were launched against isolated Jewish settlements in the Judean Mountains and the Hebron Hills, in Upper Galilee, and in the Negev. The target of a major attack was Kefar Etzion, the main settlement in the Etzion Bloc, lying isolated near the road leading from Bethlehem to Hebron. Though the attack was repulsed by the defenders, the Etzion Bloc begged for reinforcements and the replenishment of its stocks of arms and ammunition. Since the main road was still controlled by

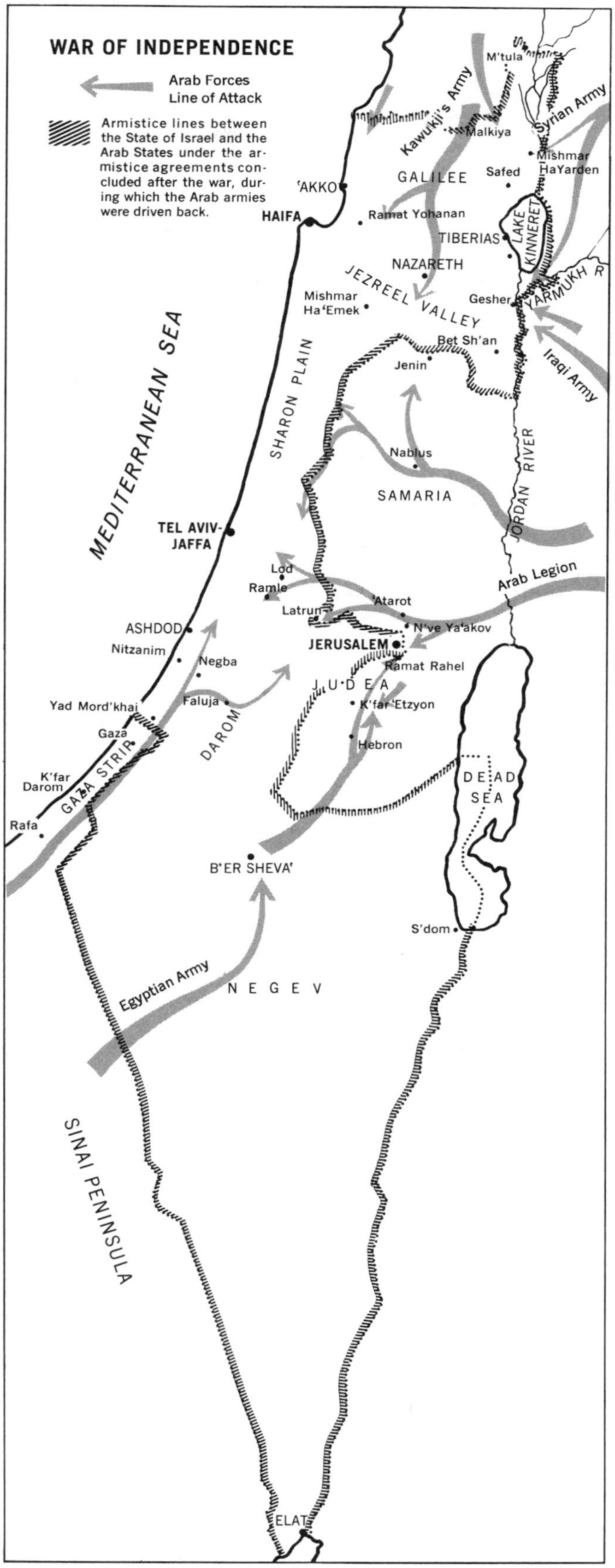

British forces, a platoon of 35 soldiers, half Palmah and half HISH, was sent out on foot to reinforce the bloc. It was spotted by an Arab shepherd, surrounded by villagers from the neighboring villages, and annihilated. The soldiers had fought to the last bullet—some of them were found in death clutching rocks in their hands. Simultaneously, terrorist activities were continued against the centers of Jewish population and against Jewish workers in mixed enterprises. Vehicles filled with dynamite were smuggled into Jewish sections of Haifa and Jerusalem. In Jerusalem the editorial offices of the *Palestine Post*, a large part of Ben-Yehuda Street, and the Jewish Agency headquarters were either blown up or damaged by such vehicles. Outlying quarters southeast of Jerusalem were being isolated from the center of the city. By now most Jewish traffic moved in armored cars and in convoys, which whenever possible set out at irregular times and along varying routes, at night or by roundabout ways. Nonetheless, traffic to a number of Jewish quarters in Jerusalem and along some of the major arteries in the country was soon to grind to a halt.

On 16 February 1948, the Liberation Army attacked Tirat Tzevi, in the Bet She'an Valley, but was obliged to ratreat after suffering heavy casualties. In view of the failure of attempts to attack and capture at least one Jewish settlement, in March the Arabs directed their main efforts against Jewish road traffic. Simultaneously, however, they continued their attacks on outlying Jewish settlements and quarters. There were some remarkable Jewish successes: an armored convoy that had set out from Negba succeeded in reaching isolated Gat, farther east; an Arab convoy carrying arms from Lebanon was intercepted and annihilated by an ambush in Kiryat Motzkin, near Haifa. All the same, the Arabs gained their major successes in this war of communications. Attacks on the convoys on the road to Jerusalem became heavier and more costly. From 26 March on, following the introduction of electric mines by the Arabs, Jewish traffic along the coastal road to the Negev was completely interrupted. A convoy that, against tremendous odds, had managed to reach the Etziyon Bloc was ambushed by Arabs on its return to Jerusalem, near Nebi Daniel. The men were obliged to abandon the armored cars and take shelter in a ruin not far from the road. Following the intervention of the Red Cross, they were permitted to return to Jerusalem, but without their arms and vehicles. Thus, most of the homemade armor that had provided the means of transportation to Jerusalem was lost. Far to the north, another convoy, which had gone from Haifa to the isolated settlement of Yehi'am, was ambushed and destroyed.

Thus, at the end of March the Negev was isolated from the center of the country, Jerusalem was isolated from the coast and the outlying settlements from Jerusaldm, and the settlements of western Galilee were similarly cut off. On the other hand, during the months since the partition resolution the armed forces of the yishuv had been built up; by the end of March about 21,000 men between the ages of 17 and 25 were fully mobilized. Simultaneously, there had been considerable progress in the manufacture of antitank weapons, submachine guns, and dynamite. Substantial quantities of light arms, which had been acquired in Czechoslovakia, were en route to Palestine. The "aerial service" of the yishuv consisted of about 30 light planes, which could perform missions of reconnaissance and transport small quantities of arms and ammunition and key personnel to isolated areas. But the local Arab force, organized within the framework of the "national guard" and other organizations, was also increasing, and the number and military proficiency of volunteers from neighboring countries were rising steadily.

Operation Nahshon to the Invasion, March-15 May 1948. The military reverses of the month of March coincided with the tendency of the United Nations and, particularly, of the United States government to weaken in their resolution to implement partition and to seek alternatives whose practical implications would have meant indefinite postponement of the establishment of a Jewish State. A reversal of military fortunes thus became a political necessity; at the same time, it had become a military possibility in view of the steady strengthening of the Jewish forces and the progress of British evacuation, which permitted the Hagana greater freedom of maneuver. Thus, the Hagana decided to take the initiative in order to gain control of all the areas assigned to the Jewish State according to the partition resolution and to create conditions that would enable it to face a possible invasion from neighboring Arab countries; it also called for the establishment of secure communications with outlying settlements, including those outside the area allotted to the Jewish State. The plan in which these operations were included was implemented gradually, coordinated with the progress of British evacuation and the development of the fighting in the various sectors.

First priority was given to the opening of a secure road to Jerusalem. For this purpose Operation Nahshon was mounted, bringing together for the first time 1,500 fighters, or about three battalions, armed to a large extent with Czech weapons, which had arrived in the country secretly on 1 April. In preparation for the operation, the headquarters of Hassan Salame, commander of Arab troops in the Shefela (coastal plain area), was captured and destroyed, and the village of Kastel, controlling the road about 6 mi. (9 kilometers) east of Jerusalem, was taken by Hagana troops. The operation itself began on 6 April. Its purpose was to capture and secure a corridor on both sides of the main road to Jerusalem, which would make it possible to move along the road without armored cars or convoys. In the course of the operation a number of Arab villages lying within the corridor both in the Shefela and in the mountain area, among them Hulda, the camp of Wadi Sarar, and Der-Mukheizin, were captured. Arab resistance was particularly violent in Kastel, which changed hands a number of times before it was finally evacuated by the Arabs on 10 April, after Abd el-Kadr al-Husseini, commander of Arab forces in the Jerusalem district, had been killed in battle the previous day. Before Operation Nahshon was terminated on 15 April, three convoys laden with supplies, food, and armaments had reached Jerusalem.

While Nahshon was under way in the Jerusalem area, the Arab Liberation Army, presumably to divert forces from Jerusalem and thus reduce the pressure on Arab forces there, once more attempted to capture a Jewish settlement, and attacked Mishmar ha-Emek. Forces under Fawzi al-Kawukji, commander of the Liberation Army, shelled Mishmar ha-Emek with artillery on 4 April, but the subsequent infantry assault was repulsed. The attack was renewed the following day but was interrupted by British forces. In the course of the ensuing cease-fire, women and children were evacuated from the village. Subsequently, the Hagana forces developed a counterattack, and on 12 April, they occupied a number of strongholds southeast of Mishmar ha-Emek and destroyed an Arab force that was en route to attack the settlement through the wooded area to its south. Once Kawukji realized that it now was his turn to face the danger of isolation, he retreated toward Jenin, and his artillery was transferred to the Jerusalem front, where it began to shell the Jewish areas of the city early in May.

Facing defeat in Mishmar ha-Emek, al-Kawukji turned to the commander of the Druze mercenary battalion, which was located in Shefaram and asked him to come to the rescue. Between 12 and 14 April, the battalion attacked the Jewish settlement of Ramat Yohanan but was repulsed with heavy casualties. From then on the Druze battalion did not participate actively in the war against the yishuv.

The success of Operation Nahshon in the Jerusalem corridor and the failure of the Arab attack on Mishmar ha-Emek and Ramat Yohanan encouraged the forces of the Hagana to continue, with redoubled vigor, to implement the various phases of the plan, to the extent that the British evacuation made this possible. On 18 April, the forces of the Golani Brigade cut the Arab part of Tiberias in two, and in the days that followed the Arabs evacuated the city. On 21 April, when the British army began to concentrate its forces in the port area of Haifa prior to final departure, the battle for Haifa began; it was terminated within 24 hours by the complete capture of the city by Jewish forces. Haifa was abandoned by most of its Arab inhabitants. They left by sea or land, having been encouraged to do so by their leaders in Beirut, who had promised the inhabitants a speedy return in the wake of the "victorious Arab armies."

The liberation of Tiberias and the opening of routes to eastern Galilee made it possible to reinforce the small Jewish forces in the finger of Upper Galilee. As early as 14 April, a platoon of the Palmah had infiltrated the besieged Jewish quarter of Safed, strengthening its desperate defenders. Within the framework of Operation Yiftah, whose objective was the capture of Upper Galilee and control of its major lines of communications, Hagana forces had seized the police fortress of Rosh Pina and the adjoining army camps, which had been evacuated by the British a few days earlier. Through the capture of the Arab villages Birya and En Zeytun, a corridor was opened from the rear to the Jewish quarter of Safed. On 1 May, Arab forces launched a concentrated attack on the neighboring Jewish settlement of Ramot Naftali, which had long been besieged. The artillery and armor of the Lebanese Army took an active part in this attack. However, the defenders of the besieged settlement stood fast, with help (more moral than material) from the "Galilee flight," consisting of a number of Piper Cub planes.

Meanwhile, preparations for Operation Yiftah continued unabated. On 3 May, another Palmah battalion reached the Safed area, having swept up the area of the Betekha, near the mouth of the Jordan River, en route. The attack on the Arab parts of Safed began on 6 May with an unsuccessful assault, and soon Arab reinforcements were streaming into the city and concentrated shelling of the Jewish quarter began. On the night of 9–10 May, the Jewish assault was renewed, and the following day witnessed the flight of the Arab inhabitants of Safed and their allies, who had infiltrated from neighboring countries. The citadel atop the mountain and the police fortress were captured by the Palmah. The flight of the Arabs of Safed, who had gained a reputation for being stubborn fighters, became the signal for the flight of many thousands of villagers from the Huleh area, so that by the eve of the invasion all the Jewish areas in Upper Galilee were connected with each other.

On 29 April, a unit of the Golani Brigade seized Tzemah and the large police fortress adjoining the city, which had been evacuated by British forces some time earlier; another police fortress, near Gesher, was occupied at the same time. The forces of the Arab Legion, which attacked Gesher, supported by artillery and armor, were repulsed. Bet She'an fell into Jewish hands on 12 May, and at the same time Arab villages were captured in the area of Mount Tabor: the Arab village of Sejera, Bet Lehem ha-Gelilit, the former German colony of Waldheim, and others. In the short and brilliant Operation Ben Ami, the Carmeli Brigade captured the outposts of the city of Acre and a series of villages north of Acre as far as the Lebanese border; the isolated and besieged settlements of Yehi'am and Hanita were now relieved. The capture of Acre itself was completed on 17 May.

Farther south, in the course of Operation Hametz (Leaven, so called because it started on the eve of Passover), units from three brigades captured a number of villages on the outskirts of Jaffa-Tel Aviv, which had formerly formed a ring around the Jewish city. At the same time the Irgun penetrated the northern quarters of Jaffa, including Manshiye; the Irgun attack encountered heavy Arab resistance; moreover, British reinforcements were rushed into the city, which was to be included in the future Arab state. The attack began on 26 April, and within a few days the Manshiye quarter had been isolated. On 29 April, following the containment and encirclement of Jaffa, many of its 70,000 Arab inhabitants fled. The city surrendered only on 13 May, following the British evacuation.

Information was now received concerning British intentions to advance the date of the final evacuation of Jerusalem; as a result, the Harel Brigade of Palmah was transferred from the corridor of Jerusalem to the city itself. Its removal from the Jerusalem corridor was soon exploited by the Arab Liberation Army, which once more seized the hills on either side of the Jerusalem-Tel Aviv road, so that Jerusalem was isolated. In spite of the fact that the information concerning an early British evacuation of Jerusalem was not confirmed, it was now decided to undertake Operation Jebusi in order to restore communications with the outlying Jewish settlements Neve Ya'akov and Atarot to the north of Jerusalem, Mount Scopus and the Hebrew University to the east, and the isolated quarters south of the city. An attack launched against the imposing and dominating observation post of Nebi Samuel on 22 April failed; Harel forces, which had captured the Sheikh Jarrah quarter on the road to Mount Scopus on 26 April, were forced to evacuate if by a British ultimatum backed by British artillery. An attempt to capture the Augusta Victoria Hospital on the Mount of Olives and thus gain control of the Jericho road, which was undertaken two days later, similarly failed. On the night of 28–29 April, the battle for the Monastery of St. Simon in Katamon began. The monastery was captured, but obstinate counterattacks by Iraqi soldiers of the Liberation Army, lasting throughout the day, exhausted both sides; the battle was decided by reinforcements, which arrived toward evening, from the Jerusalem Brigade. The capture of the Katamon quarter made it possible to move reinforcements to the isolated quarter of Mekor Hayim. Some days later, on 11 May, another attempt was made to reopen the road to Jerusalem, through Operation Maccabee. A number of villages and strongholds were captured, including the detention camp near Latrun, but only a convoy of a few dozen cars moved to Jerusalem on 17

May, before the road was blocked once more.

As soon as the last British soldiers had abandoned Jerusalem, on 14 May, the Jerusalem (Etziyoni) Brigade undertook Operation Kilshon (Pitchfork), whose objective was to seize the abandoned security zones which had previously been occupied by British forces, and to prepare Jewish Jerusalem for defense against a possible attack by the Arab Legion. Once the Allenby Barracks, Der Abu Tor, and the police school in Sheikh Jarrah, as well as the Russian compound, the Central Post Office, and their vicinity, had been captured, Jewish Jerusalem became a singly continuous area for the first time. Had it not been for these achievements immediately following the British evacuation and before the Egyptians in the south and the Arab Legion in the north and east were fully prepared for their attack on the city, the outcome of the war in Jerusalem might have been different. However, not all the objectives of Kilshon were achieved: Arab enclaves were left to the north of the city, and no corridor was cut to the Jewish quarter of the Old City.

Just before the Arab invasion, the isolated Jewish settlements to the south and north of Jerusalem either fell or were evacuated. The Etzion Bloc, which had been subjected to almost continuous harassment since the all-out attack in January, was the objective of a concentrated assault on 4 May, in which Arab Legion armored units, still nominally under British command, and four British tanks participated. This attack was repulsed; the defenders suffered heavy casualties and losses in arms and ammunition, which, in the prevailing condition of almost complete isolation, could not be replenished. On the eve of 12 May, Arab attackers succeeded in cutting the bloc in two; the following day, the rocky outpost between Kefar Etzion and Masu'ot Yitzhak was captured and armored forces broke into Kefar Etzion itself. The village surrendered, having fought practically to the last bullet; the survivors, except for four who escaped to tell the story, were massacred by villagers from the Hebron area under the eyes of the Arab Legion officers. On 14 May, the villagers of the three remaining settlements in the bloc were taken prisoner by the Arab Legion and transferred to Transjordan. North of Jerusalem the defenders of Atarot managed to gain control of the military airfield nearby, which had been evacuated by the British, but when they found that the plan to fly reinforcements to them had been abandoned, they evacuated the village and retreated to Neve Ya'akov on 15 May. That settlement in its turn was attacked by armored units of the Arab Legion, which had not been evacuated with the British forces, and the commander of Neveh Ya'akov decided to evacuate soldiers and civilians alike on foot to Mount Scopus. The evacuation took place on the night of 16–17 May. Thus, no obstacles were left on the road to Jewish Jerusalem from the north and south, while from the east defenders from the potash works at the northern end of the Dead Sea and of Bet ha-Arava were unable to stop the progress of the Arab Legion along the Jericho-Jerusalem road.

In the six weeks preceding the establishment of the State of Israel and the invasion of regular Arab armies, Haifa, Jaffa, Safed, Tiberias, and about 100 Arab villages had been captured, and Acre had been surrounded. Most of the main arteries in the country, excluding the Latrun portion of the Jerusalem road, were open to Jewish traffic. The military forces of Palestinian Arabs had practically been defeated, and the Arab Liberation Army had suffered heavy setbacks in the battles of Mishmar ha-Emek and the Jerusalem corridor. But the yishuv too had suffered considerable casualties. However, its fully mobilized defense force had now been increased to more than 30,000 young men and its state of armament had been considerably improved, particularly following the arrival of the first Czechoslovak arms shipment and the acquisition of light artillery and antitank and antiaircraft guns. On the other hand, the yishuv still did not possess field artillery, fighter planes, or tanks.

Invasion to the First Truce, 15 May-10 June 1948. The invasion by the regular Arab armies began on 15 May. The plan of attack, as envisaged by the Arab chiefs of staff when they met in April, called for a rapid operation with its main thrust in the north, where components of four Arab armies—the Syrian, Lebanese, Iraqi, and Jordanian—were to thrust toward Haifa, capturing its port and its refineries and clearing the area north of the Jezreel Valley. The Egyptians were to attack along the coastal route toward Tel Aviv, while the Arab Liberation Army was to maintain control of the rest of Palestine and exert pressure on Jerusalem. For political and military reasons this plan was not put into operation; indeed, John Bagot Glubb Pasha, the British commander of the Arab Legion, in his memoirs denies the very existence of the plan, although it is quite possible that since he was a foreigner, it had not been communicated to him. In any case, the Arab Legion was instructed by King Abdullah to gain control of as much of Arab Palestine as was feasible without major battles, concentrating its efforts on Jerusalem and its vicinity. In order to avoid a vacuum farther north, the Iraqis, operating in close conjunction with the Arab Legion of Transjordan, moved into the breach and occupied the general area of the triangle Nablus-Jenin-Tulkarm. No effective, unified Arab command ever came into being.

In the north the Syrian Army opened its attack on the eve of 16 May with an artillery barrage on the outlying settlements En Gev, Massada, and Sha'ar ha-Golan, east and south of Lake Kinneret, and Syrian planes shelled the Jordan Valley settlements at dawn. The main Syrian infantry column moved toward Tzemah, attacking Masada and Sha'ar ha-Golan en route, but was repulsed. On 18 May, Syrian armor outflanked Tzemah, which had been abandoned by Israeli forces following the battle of the previous day; Massada and Sha'ar ha-Golan also were abandoned by their defenders. Thus, on 20 May, the Syrians found themselves outside the two Deganyas, the oldest kibbutzim in Israel. Infantry, supported by light tanks, was deployed for an all-out assault. The defenders of Deganya A and of the neighboring Jordan Bridge were able to repulse the attacking column, which retreated as far as Tzemah. A Syrian attack on Deganya B was also stopped. Light field artillery from France, the first artillery to arrive in Israel, which had been received a few days before, was rushed to the Jordan Valley to the great surprise of the Syrians, and the shelling of Syrian Army concentrations near Tzemah caused the withdrawal of the Syrian forces from that city and from neighboring locations.

In the northernmost finger of Upper Galilee the Palmah captured the police fortress of Nebi Yusha, dominating the ridge high above the valley, in a bloody battle, and the village of Malkiya. Detachments crossed the border into Lebanon and blew up the Litani Bridge, as well as the Baniasn Bridge in Syrian territory. A particularly successful raid against the Syrian customhouse opposite the Benot Ya'akov Bridge not only caused the destruction of a large

Medical convoy bound for Jerusalem. [Israel Information Services]

reservoir of equipment and arms, which the Syrians had built up preparatory to their invasion, but also convinced a small Beduin tribe in the area that the Jews were the winners in this war, and they sided with the Jewish forces thereafter.

The Iraqi expeditionary force penetrated Palestine in the area of Gesher and Kaukab el-Hawa, the ancient Crusader castle of Belvoir; simultaneously, the Arab Legion, on 14 May, captured the installations of the Palestine Electric Corporation, which were located in the area of Transjordan. Subsequently, the Iraqis, having failed to capture Gesher and Kaukab el-Hawa, concentrated their main efforts in the Triangle area.

The transfer of the Yiftah Brigade from the northern to the central front, undertaken without any attempted concealment, and its replacement by a relatively new and inexperienced brigade facilitated the second Syrian attampt at invasion, which was carried out farther north, across the Benot Ya'akov Bridge. Following six days of fierce fighting, the Syrians captured Mishmar ha-Yarden on the day the first truce came into force. A Syrian attempt to capture En Gev just a few hours before the truce failed. Farther north the Lebanese recaptured Malkiya on 5 June, making it possible for Kawukji to penetrate central Galilee once more; however, his forces did not achieve their major objective, the capture of Jewish Sejera (Ilaniya). On 24 May, after the arrival of the Iraqi vanguard in Nablus, the Triangle front came to life. An Israeli attack was launched against Jenin, primarily as a diversion, to pin down the considerable Iraqi forces then in the Triangle area. The Carmeli Brigade was able to capture a number of villages lying on either side of the main road to Jenin, but under pressure of an Iraqi counterattack it was obliged to abandon the city itself and its surrounding heights soon after their capture. On 6 June, the Alexandroni Brigade captured the village of Kakun, on the western outskirts of the Triangle. *Jerusalem Front.* The Arab Legion devoted its main effort to an attempt to capture the city and its environs while sustaining a minimum of casualties; the legion had to remain intact as the main support of Abdullah's regime. One column crossed the Jordan over the Damiya Bridge and moved south and west. On 18 May, it took possession of the Latrun police station. Another column crossed the Allenby Bridge westward; on 19 May, the first legionnaires were observed in the Old City of Jerusalem. On the same day, Arab Legion forces took possession of the police school in Sheikh Jarrah, once more isolating Mount Scopus and endangering the Jewish quarters in the northern part of the new city. Some 2,500 Jews, mostly elderly persons with only a handful of defenders, had now been trapped in the Jewish quarter of the Old City. Their clamor for immediate reinforcement or rescue became more and more urgent. Although it was not said aloud, the massacre at Kefar Etzion, which had occurred a few days previously, was clearly in their minds. Desperate attempts were made by the Etziyoni Brigade in conjunction with a detachment from the Irgun Tzeva'i Le'umi to capture the Citadel and penetrate the Jewish quarter by the Jaffa Gate. The attempts failed; however, a simultaneous attempt by the Harel Brigade to capture Mount Zion and penetrate the Jewish quarter by the Zion Gate was crowned with success on the night of 18–19 May. There was an emotional reunion with the defenders of the Jewish quarter after weeks of complete isolation. Reinforcements and ammunition, taken from the meager reserves of Jewish Jerusalem, which in its turn had been besieged, were now rushed to the Jewish quarter of the Old City. The newly established link did not last long; as day broke, the Arab Legion counterattacked and recaptured the Zion Gate. Further attempts to reestablish communications with the Jewish quarter of the Old City did not succeed. On 28 May, the Jewish quarter surrendered, and all able-bodied men were taken into captivity in Transjordan. This was the Arab Legion's major success in Jerusalem. Its attempts to penetrate the heart of the Jewish city in the Mandelbaum and Notre Dame sectors were repulsed. The Arab Legion's armored vehicles, although not yet matched by anything on the Jewish side, did not prove effective in built-up areas. Meanwhile, semiregular Egyptian forces, made up primarily of members of the Moslem Brotherhood, attacked Ramat Rahel to the south of the city. Between 22 and 25 May, the settlement changed hands several times, the Jews attacking by night and the Arabs counterattacking during the day. Finally, it remained in Jewish hands. From then until the beginning of the first truce, both the Arab Legion and the Egyptians concentrated primarily on merciless shelling of the Jewish city. The victims were primarily civilians, of whom some 1,200 were wounded or died in less than four weeks. The Hagana, in its turn, was engaged primarily in static defense, localized skirmishes, and straightening the line of defense; it tried unsuccessfully to recapture the police school in Sheikh Jarrah.

Once more it became evident that the key to the future of Jerusalem was the road leading to the city. Supplies of food and ammunition had run dangerously low in the besieged city; if fighting were to last much longer, the Arab Legion could be justified in anticipating the city's early surrender. And the key to the reopening of the road to Jerusalem was the Latrun area. On 25 May, the newly formed 7th Brigade, composed to a large extent of immigrants who had arrived in the country only a week before, attempted to capture Latrun. The attack was late in starting; the force was discovered and fired upon long before it reached the target area, and was forced to retreat with heavy casualties. After a few days of regrouping, some armored cars of the 7th Brigade tried once more and succeeded in penetrating the police fortress; however, they were forced to retreat forthwith, since no infantry was there to exploit their success and their flanks were exposed. Harel attacks to the east, in the mountainous area, which were intended to capture a number of villages on the flanks and in the rear of Latrun, were similarly unsuccessful. Latrun was to remain in Arab hands for 20 years. Just as the battle for Latrun seemed completely hopeless, however, a route that would open communications with Jerusalem and avoid the Latrun junction was discovered farther south. At first barely negotiable with pack animals, this route was rapidly improved so that jeeps, trucks, and ultimately, normal passenger vehicles could use it. It was by way of this "Burma Road" that Jerusalem obtained eagerly awaited medium machine guns, light artillery, and vital foodstuffs just a few days before the first truce.

South and the Negev. The defense of the south and the Negev against an Egyptian invasion was entrusted to the Negev and Givati Brigades. The former was based on 27 Jewish settlements in the Negev south of the Faluja-Ashkelon road; the latter, north of that line. During the last days before 15 May, Givati had been engaged in a mopping-up operation, capturing a series of Arab villages in its area and creating a continuous area under Jewish control. The Egyptian forces invaded Palestine along two routes, the coastal road and the interior road, leading from El-Auja to Beersheba. The light forces of the Egyptian Army, including volunteers from the Moslem Brotherhood, reached Bet Guvrin and from there continued to Hebron, Bethlehem, and Hartuv.

The invasion of the regular forces was preceded, on 11 May, by an Egyptian attack on Kefar Darom, an isolated Jewish village south of Gaza, lying about 800 meters off the coastal road, which was considered potentially dangerous to free movement along that road. The attack was led by members of the Moslem Brotherhood. It was repulsed, but the village remained isolated from then on. On 15 May, the regular Egyptian Army attacked Kefar Darom and Nirim, another kibbutz not far from the main artery. Once more the attacks were repulsed, but both settlements were neutralized and unable, for the time being, to interfere with Egyptian traffic along the coastal road. Next came Yad Mordekhai, farther north next to the road. It was attacked furiously, day after day, between 23 and 29 May, by Egyptian infantry supported by armor and fighter planes, and ultimately fell to the invader. Now the road was clear, and the Egyptians moved swiftly northward, linking their forces with Egyptian battalions that had landed from the sea at Majdal (Ashkelon).

On 29 May, an Egyptian column pushed north toward Ashdod, a mere 24 mi. (35 kilometers) from Tel Aviv. On that day, only a handful of soldiers stood between the Egyptians and the heart of the yishuv. They were ordered to halt the Egyptians at any cost. The first fighter planes, Messerschmitts which had just arrived from Czechoslovakia, were sent to the aid of Givati; these planes helped stop the Egyptians and force them to abandon their vehicles and dig in. However, an attack designed to destroy the Egyptian force was called off on 2 June, when news of an impending truce was received. On the same day, the Egyptians opened a resolute attack on Negba, close to the lateral road connecting the coastal and interior roads. Tanks and artillery were used by the Egyptians, who were able to penetrate the outer defenses but were then stopped and repulsed. A combined counterattack, carried out by the Negev and Givati Brigades against the Egyptian dispositions near Ashdod, took place on the night of 2–3 June, although they were unable to capture the Egyptian positions, they forced them to forgo a further advance toward Tel Aviv and the settlements in the south. The Egyptians now turned their attention to mopping up foci of resistance in the rear; thus they attacked and captured the settlement of Nitzanim, whose residents went into Egyptian captivity. Mopping-up operations, and the capture of various isolated Arab villages in the rear of the Jewish force, took place at the same time; the Negev Brigade also captured Bir Asluj, south of Beersheba, and the neighboring police station. An attempt to capture the police fortress of Iraq Suweidan, dominating Negba and the neighboring junction, failed.

Naval and Air Force Operations. The initial clear superiority of the Egyptians, Iraqis, and Syrians in terms of fighter planes and bombers made it possible for them to support their ground forces and attack centers of civilian popula-

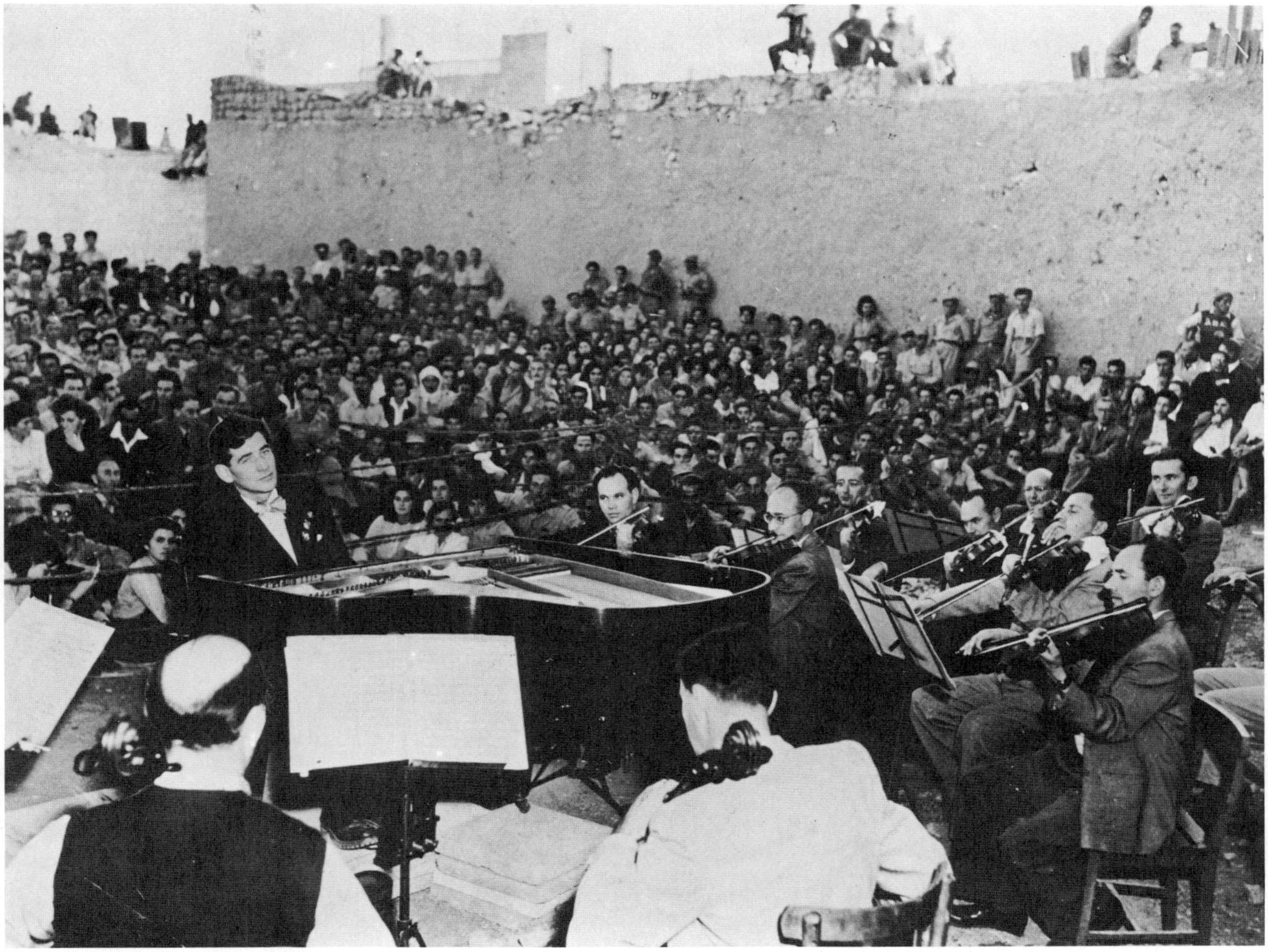

Leonard Bernstein, pianist and conductor, playing with the Israel Philharmonic Orchestra in Beersheba in a concert for the armed forces during the War of Independence. [Zionist Archives]

tion. At dawn on 15 May, the Egyptians bombed the central bus station in Tel Aviv and various targets in Ramat Gan, Rishon le-Zion, and settlements in the Negev. The Iraqi Air Force bombarded Gesher and supported its ground forces in the Triangle. The Syrian Air Force chose as its targets the settlements of the Jordan Valley and Upper Galilee. At that time Israel did not possess a single fighter plane. The situation began to change when Israel received the first Messerschmitts. The first aerial encounter took place on 3 June, when an Israeli fighter plane brought down two Egyptian Dakota bombers, which were en route to Tel Aviv and to settlements in the south. About the same time Israeli planes undertook their first offensive action, attacking Amman. Some days later, on the eve of the first truce, they attacked Damascus. The effect of both attacks was primarily psychological, but they did demonstrate that Israel had acquired some sort of aerial capacity. Most Israeli planes were still not military planes; they operated primarily at night and thus could not support the ground troops in attack or in defense.

The Egyptian Navy, which at the time consisted of some 45 units, was engaged primarily in supplying and supporting Egyptian ground forces, which were moved north along the coastal route. On 2 June, Egyptian warships shelled the settlement of Sedot Yam. Troop carriers were sighted off the coast of Tel Aviv on 4 June, but whether or not they had planned a landing, they were driven away by Israeli naval and air forces.

First Truce, 11 June-8 July, 1948. In accordance with a resolution of the UN Security Council, fighting stopped on most fronts on 11 June 1948, at 6 A.M., when the first truce came into effect. The Council had decreed that the truce should last 28 days. The fighting before the truce had not produced a military decision. Although some Jewish settlements had fallen into enemy hands and heavy casualties in dead and wounded had been inflicted on Israeli forces, the Arab invasion had not attained its main objective, the capture of Palestine and the prevention of the establishment of a Jewish State. The first truce was advantageous in a way to both sides. It made it possible for the Arab Legion to renew its reserves of ammunition and fuel, which were fast diminishing, and for all Arab forces to rest and reorganize. In spite of the embargo that had been imposed officially on the supply of arms and ammunition to all the states participating in the war, men and supplies continued to stream

Foreign Minister Moshe Shertok conferring with Count Folke Bernadotte before the first truce. [Zionist Archives]

to Arab countries and from there to the Palestinian front. The Jewish forces spent the 28 days of the truce in training, reorganizing, preparing plans for the future, and setting up fortifications, and managed to get some rest. It was during this first truce that the *Altalena* incident took place (*see* IRGUN TZEVA'I LE'UMI).

Ten Days' Fighting, 9–18 July 1948. On 9 July, fighting was renewed on all fronts. Now the initiative in some sectors was taken by Israel. In the north, the Carmeli Brigade undertook Operation Berosh with the aim of dislodging the Syrians from the bridgehead they had established near Mishmar ha-Yarden. The operation failed in its main objective, but it prevented the Syrians from breaking out from the bridgehead to cut the road to Upper Galilee. Farther south, in Operation Dekel, the 7th Brigade, with units from Golani and Carmeli, captured Nazareth and a series of villages in Lower Galilee. The Liberation Army, under the command of Kawukji, was forced to forgo its attack on the Jewish settlement of Sejera, and it was only with great difficulty that Kawukji and part of his forces were able to extricate themselves and escape to neighboring territory. South of the Jezreel Valley, the Iraqis were able to consolidate their positions in the Gilboa area, forcing Golani to give up the Dotan Valley.

The major effort of the Israel Defense Forces during the 10 days' fighting was directed against the Arab Legion forces in the area of Lydda and Ramle. Operation Dani, named for the commander of the 35 men who had died en route to Kefar Etzion, aimed at the capture of these two cities and the opening of the Latrun-Jerusalem road. For the first time, large elements of three brigades, including one armored brigade, participated in a single operation. The plan envisaged a pincer movement, from the south and the north, against the rear of both cities, followed by a frontal attack once they would have been cut off from Arab Legion bases farther east. The Yiftah Brigade, jumping off from the south, captured a number of villages, while the 8th Brigade captures Lydda Airport from the north; both forces converged on the Jewish village of Ben Shemen, which had been isolated for many weeks. Once the encirclement of Lydda and Ramle was completed, a commando battalion broke into Lydda from the east and in a swift thrust passed through that city into Ramle. Having encountered heavy opposition from the police fortress between the two cities, it turned back, reaching Ben Shemen after less than an hour. The battalion had not captured any Arab Legion positions but had surprised and dismayed the Arabs in both cities, who hitherto had considered themselves immune from attack. Lydda was captured the following night; the next day Ramle surrendered without fighting. During the following days Israeli forces advanced farther east, toward the Latrun-Ramallah road, but encountered increasingly heavy opposition from the Arab Legion, which was determined to prevent the complete isolation of Latrun. Egyptian pressure in the south prevailed on the Israeli High Command to transfer the commando battalion to the southern front and thus contributed to the abandonment of the second phase of Operation Dani, the capture of Latrun. Just north of the Dani area of operation, the Alexandroni Brigade captured from the Iraqis the headwaters of the Yarkon, the major source of water for Tel Aviv and, prior to the war also for Jerusalem.

In the Jerusalem corridor, the settlement of Hartuv was recaptured from Egyptian hands, and the neighboring village of Tzora was taken, thus widening the narrow corridor lifeline of the city. Farther east, near Jerusalem itself, the corridor was widened through the capture of Malkha, En Kerem, and Tzova. On the eve of the second truce, an attempt was made to break into the Old City. The attampt failed, while the Arab Legion attacked the Mandelbaum sector. The fighting there continued for some time after the second truce came into effect.

In the south, during the first truce, the Egyptians had broken the commitment they had given to the United Nations to permit the passage of supply convoys to the isolated Negev settlements. On 8 July, before the truce came officially to a close, the Egyptians renewed their attacks, capturing a series of strongholds near the junction of Iraq Suweidan in order to ensure their freedom of passage from east to west and simultaneously cutting Israeli communications from north to south. The Egyptians still enjoyed a considerable advantage, particularly during the day, when their superiority in the air and in artillery and armor was brought into play. Their strongholds, after being captured by Jewish forces during the night, were frequently abandoned again during the day under enemy pressure. On 12 July, having failed in another attempt to capture Negba and the neighboring outposts, the Egyptians moved their attacks farther south. On 15 July, they attacked Be'erot Yitzhak and captured part of it, but were compelled to withdraw. The arrival of a commando battalion enabled the Israelis to take a local initiative and capture a number of villages, thus relieving the siege of Ruhama. However, this was not enough to cut the lateral road connecting Egyptian forces along the coast with those in the Judean Mountains nor to restore communications between the isolated settlements in the Negev and the rest of Israel.

Naval and Air Operations. In the course of the 10 days'

Houses in Negba destroyed by enemy shelling in August, 1948. [Zionist Archives]

fighting, the Egyptian Air Force continued to shell settlements in the Negev and Tel Aviv; a number of bombs also fell on Jerusalem. At the same time, three Flying Fortresses acquired by Israel arrived in the country, bombing Cairo while en route to Israel. The Israeli Air Force was now in a better position to support the infantry, operating, *inter alia*, against Quneitra in support of Operation Berosh. The Syrian and Iraqi Air Forces limited their operations during this time, evidently because of reluctance to risk encounters with Israeli planes.

Second Truce. After the renewed fighting had been going on for several days, the UN Security Council decided, under insistent pressure from Great Britain, on a second truce, this time one of unlimited duration. The intensive efforts by Israel to mobilize its forces and acquire arms and military equipment, unhampered by the presence of the mandatory government and its forces, had by now borne fruit. The fate of the Negev was still in the balance. Arrangements made by United Nations observers, according to which Egyptian east-west traffic would alternate with Jewish north-south traffic, proved unworkable. Although the Negev had been allotted to the Jewish State under the partition resolution, the plan of UN Mediator Count Folke *Bernadotte envisaged its assignment to the Arabs. No doubt, the military situation was a factor in drawing up that plan. Thus, it was imperative for Israel to bring about a military decision, relieving the isolated settlements and consolidating Jewish control.

During the second truce, the Negev Brigade had been sent north for a long-overdue rest and was replaced by the Yiftah Brigade. The movement of troops was carried out partly by planes but primarily on foot, by means of infiltration through Egyptian lines. Transport planes of the Israel Air Force, having completed their airlift from abroad, were engaged in the transportation of considerable quantities of arms and supplies to the Negev. The Egyptians, aware of increased air activity, attacked the Khirbet Mahaz area, close to the Ruhama landing strip, in order to interfere with the airlift to the Negev, but they failed despite heavy fighting. A supply column, which left for the Negev on 14 October, was attacked by Egyptian troops; this was the signal for the Israeli Army to undertake Operation Yo'av (Ten Plagues). The operation was preceded by a surprise attack by the Israel Air Force on Egypt's forward airfields in Sinai and its manor troop concentrations in Gaza, Bet Hanun, Majdal, and Faluja. During the following night Yiftah drove a wedge in the Egyptian lines near Bet Hanun, threatening to cut off Majdal. This operation was intended primarily as a diversion, compelling the Egyptians to concentrate troops in the west. Soon afterward, Givati, operating from the north of the isolation belt, cut the Majdal-Bet Guvrin road, but an attempt to capture the tel of Itaq el-Manshiye, which dominates a good part of the road, failed. The element of surprise had by now been lost; it was evident that any attack on an Egyptian stronghold on either side of the isolation belt would be risky. Thus, it was decided to go straight for the heart of the Egyptian defenses along the lateral road, near the junction of Iraq Suweidan. On the night of 16–17 October, in heavy fighting that culminated in hand-to-hand struggles, these strongholds fell to Givati.

Simultaneously, and farther to the east, the Harel Brigade attacked the light Egyptian forces which were still in position in the area of Hartuv and the Hebron Hills. They cleared the western slopes of the hills and reached the outskirts of Bet Jala.

The last outpost near the junction was captured by Givati on the eve of 20 October; finally, after many months, a secure road to the Negev was opened. Quickly exploiting success, the Negev Brigade was rushed south and captured Beersheba, in a surprise move, on 21 October. The Egyptian brigade in the Faluja and Iraq el-Manshiye area now found itself encircled and completely isolated in a pocket, while the Egyptian forces in the Majdal sector, in view of the threat of isolation, retreated along an improvised road along the beach. The Faluja pocket was further reduced with the capture of the Iraq Suweidan police fortress early in November.

The capture of Beersheba by Israel's forces had isolated the Egyptian detachment in the Hebron Hills from the main Egyptian body. As a result, the Egyptians were evacuated from the area and replaced by the Arab Legion of Transjordan. No major operation had taken place on the Arab Legion front since the beginning of the second truce. An almost nightly exchange of fire, particularly in the urban areas where opposing positions were very close to each other, caused many casualties but did not change the overall situation. In August, Israel's forces attempted to gain control of the slopes of the High Commissioner's Palace, seat of the United Nations command in Palestine. On the last night of Operation Yo'av an attack was launched against the heights above Bet Jala and places farther to the west, south of the railway line, whose possession by Israel would have enabled it to use that vital link with Jerusalem. The nature of the terrain and the short time available were among the reasons why the attack failed. A few weeks later a "sincere cease-fire" was signed by the Transjordan and Israel commanders on the Jerusalem front, effectively terminating fighting in that sector.

Naval and Air Operations. During the period of Operation Yo'av the Israel Air Force carried out 150 sorties against enemy bases, primarily in close support of ground forces. The Israel Navy operated against coastal targets and transported commando units, which operated against the railway line in the Sinai area. Close to the end of Operation Yo'av the navy achieved its major success of the war when a small, highly trained detachment of saboteurs attacked and sank the flagship of the Egyptian Navy, the *Emir Farouk*, off the coast of Gaza.

Final Operations. The second truce did not end the war, and a number of operations were undertaken before armistice agreements were finally negotiated and signed. Kawukji's Liberation Army was still active in Upper Galilee, to the north of the Bet Netofa Valley. Moreover, using an argument that was to be heard many times in years to come, Kawukji did not consider himself bound by the cease-fire resolution of the Security Council, on the ground that he did not represent a member nation of the United Nations. When on 22 October, Kawukji's forces captured Sheikh Abed, thus isolating Manara in Upper Galilee, the Israel High Command decided to strike. In an operation lasting less than 60 hours, the Israeli forces, jumping off from the coast in the west and from Safed in the east, contained Kawukji's forces in Upper Galilee; although he and a part of his forces were able to escape into Lebanon, the whole of Upper Galilee was now in Israeli hands. In pursuit, Israeli forces crossed into Lebanon, capturing 14 villages (Operation Hiram).

In the south, it became evident early in December that the Egyptians were reorganizing their forces, possibly with the aim of recapturing Beersheba. In view of this and of the fact that despite the call of the Security Council no negotiations for an armistice were in sight, the government of Israel decided on a final operation in that area: Operation Ayin, whose aim was to force the Egyptians to withdraw completely from the southern Negev and from the Gaza-Rafa sector. The operation began on the eve of 22 December with air strikes against Egyptian troop concentrations in the west, in Rafa, Khan Yunis, and Gaza, and with an artillery bombardment of the Egyptian strongholds in the area. This was intended to be a diversion as much as a softening-up operation. To strengthen the diversionary effect, the Golani Brigade attacked a number of Egyptian positions in the sector, astride the Gaza-Rafa road. Simultaneously, the Negev and Harel Brigades, which were to make the main effort of the operation, were moved across country along unpaved routes that had not been previously considered passable, particularly for tanks, to the rear of the Egyptian dispositions along the Beersheba-Asluj-El-Auja road. Before the Egyptians were aware of that movement, the Negev Brigade had captured the Temile stronghold from the rear and the 8th Brigade had taken up its positions astride the Rafa-El-Auja road and was ready to strike at El-Auja itself. Once all approaches to El-Auja from the north-east, south, and west had been blocked, the outpost itself fell after brief fighting on 27 December. A few hours later, the mopping up along the El-Auja-Beersheba road was completed; the Egyptians had not yet recovered from the surprise that the Jewish forces should be moving from the west to the northeast, toward Beersheba rather than away from it. Many Egyptians abandoned their vehicles and fled into the desert, where they were subsequently rounded up and taken prisoner.

In the second phase of the operation, which began on the eve of 29 December, an armored column moved for the first time into Egyptian territory and captured Abu Ageila; the following day, the airfield of El-Arish was captured, and the isolation of the Egyptian forces in the Gaza Strip was effectively completed. However, under heavy political pressure from the United States and Great Britain, Israeli forces were ordered to retreat to what was formerly Palestinian territory. A last effort was made to attack and destroy the Egyptian forces in the Gaza-Rafa area through a direct attack; Golani captured the cemetery hill, and Harel approached Rafa itself, along the El-Auja-Rafa road. By this time, however, the Egyptians had indicated their willingness to negotiate an armistice, and thus on 7 January 1949, a cease-fire order was given. A few days later, on 12 January, armistice negotiations with Egypt began on the island of Rhodes, with the achievements of Operation Ayin constituting an important factor in the deliberations.

Parallel with the first phase of Operation Ayin, the Alexandroni Brigade attempted the liquidation of the Faluja pocket but was repulsed. However, during those days En Husub was captured, and the area of Sedom, at the southern tip of the Dead Sea, was linked with Israel after an isolation of more than six months, during which its only contact with the outside world had been by Piper planes.

After lengthy negotiations the armistice agreement with Egypt was signed on 24 February. The armistice lines drawn up on the maps attached to the agreement were based on the positions held by both sides when negotiations began. It was emphasized that they did not constitute political boundaries and had been agreed upon without prejudice to the position of either side. The soldiers surrounded in the Faluja pocket were now permitted to return to Egypt, prisoners were exchanged, and a Mixed Armistice Commission was constituted under the chairmanship of a United Nations observer.

As a result of the armistice agreement, Egypt renounced all claims to possession of the southern Negev, the triangle reaching down to Eilat on the Red Sea. The Negev had been allotted to the Jewish State under the partition resolution, but Israeli forces had not taken effective possession of its southern part. Arab Legion units patroled some parts of the area, particularly Umm Rashrash, the primitive police station that stood where the city of Eilat is today. In Operation Uvda (Fact), Israeli forces, moving south along the Arava and through the Negev desert, took effective possession of that territory, and on 10 March, the Israel Defense Forces hoisted a primitive handmade flag over the Umm Rashrash-Eilat police station.

The armistice agreement with Egypt served as a reference base for later armistice agreements. Even before Operation Uvda, on 1 March 1949, parallel negotiations were initiated with Lebanon and Jordan. The main stumbling block in the negotiations with Lebanon was the matter of the evacuation of the 14 villages captured in the course of Operation Hiram. Israel at first insisted that they would be evacuated only after the Syrians removed their forces from the Mishmar ha-Yarden bridgehead, on the ground that the Lebanese and Syrian front had to be considered as one, since Syrian forces had operated from Lebanese territory, particularly in the last stages of the war. However, largely on account of French pressure, which was brought into play to assist Lebanon, Israel gave up this claim and agreed to evacuate the villages without any reciprocal advantage.

Negotiations with Transjordan were far more complicated; however, when a deadlock was reached in the overt part of the negotiations, which took place in Rhodes under the chairmanship of UN Mediator Ralph J. *Bunche, secret negotiations were conducted with Emir Abdullah in Transjordan. Finally, an agreement was reached. It included a number of territorial adjustments, aimed at giving the slender waist of Israel in the maritime plain further depth, thus enabling it to reactivate the railway line to Jerusalem. The Old City of Jerusalem remained in the hands of Emir Abdullah. A number of questions were left open for further discussion: the opening of the Latrun road, access to the Western Wall, and reactivation of the water pipeline. The agreement was signed in Rhodes on 3 April 1949.

The negotiations with Syria were the most difficult and the most prolonged. Syria had been the only country to capture territory allotted to the Jewish State under the partition plan; moreover, it endangered Israeli communications in eastern Upper Galilee. After tortuous negotiations, a formula was found that entailed the withdrawal of Syrian forces from the Mishmar ha-Yarden bridgehead. This formula was open to conflicting interpretations, giving rise to many bloody incidents in later years.

The armistice agreement with Syria was signed on 20 July 1949, which date is generally considered the termination of the War of Independence. The war had lasted 20 months and had cost the new State more than 6,000 killed, or almost one per cent of its population at the time of its inception.

See also BOUNDARIES OF THE STATE OF ISRAEL.

N. LORCH

WASCHITZ, EPHRAIM. Lawyer and Zionist (b. eastern Galicia, Austria, 1879; d. Jerusalem, 1945). Waschitz studied law at the University of Vienna and subsequently practiced law in Lvov. He was active in the Zionist movement, serving from 1904 to 1910 as secretary of the Zionist Council of eastern Galicia. He edited the weekly *Der Yud*, participated in the founding and editing of the Lvov daily *Togblat*, and was a founder of Ha-Shomer, the Zionist scout movement. In 1918 he was a leader of the Jewish self-defense movement in Lvov.

In 1920 Waschitz settled in Palestine, and shortly after his arrival participated in the defense of Jerusalem Jewry during the Arab riots. He continued to practice law and was prominent in communal affairs. In 1930 he joined the Revisionist movement and became a member of the party's Central Committee in Palestine. He represented the party on the Zionist Actions Committee, on the Va'ad Le'umi, and on the Council of the Jewish Community of Jerusalem. He was a delegate to several Zionist Congresses.

N.M. GELBER

WASSERMANN, OSKAR. Banker and Jewish communal worker (b. Bamberg, Germany, 1869; d. Garmisch, Germany, 1934). A member of an old-established banking family, Wassermann received a thorough Jewish education and was active in his family's banking house until 1912, when he became a board member of the Deutsche Bank, later serving as a member of the General Council of Germany's Reichsbank until Hitler's rise to power in 1933. He also held directorships in many other German commercial and industrial enterprises.

Although Wassermann never joined the Zionist movement, he wanted to see the Jewish National Home in Palestine develop into a "Jewish power station, a center of Jewish energy." Palestine, he once said, had to be more than a refuge for oppressed Jews: "It must be a center which will react also on our position in Germany. Only in Palestine can there grow up a free Jewish life; only there can religion and life intimately coalesce." Soon after the establishment of the Keren ha-Yesod, he became its chairman in Germany, and in 1929 he was elected to the Board of Directors of the World Keren ha-Yesod, later becoming chairman of that body. In 1927–28 he participated in the preparations that paved the way for the expansion of the Jewish Agency to include non-Zionists. A signatory to the charter of the expanded Jewish Agency he served as chairman of the Agency's Finance and Budget Committee and until his death was a member of its Administrative Committee, which for a time he also chaired.

WATCHMEN. *See* HA-SHOMER; NOTERIM.

WATER AND THE UTILIZATION OF WATER RESOURCES IN ISRAEL. The northern parts of Israel are situated in the semi-humid to semi-arid region of the eastern Mediterranean. The southern part, the Negev, is semi-arid to arid. Practically all of the annual rains fall during the winter months (November-March). The amount of annual rainfall varies considerably from year to year and drought years are common. These climatic conditions are the reason for the country's historic water problem. Already during early historic times, the inhabitants applied ingenious methods to ensure the supply of water for human and animal subsistence, such as the construction of canals, reservoirs, and cisterns for the collection and storage of rain water and surface run-off, digging of wells in the Negev, and excavation of underground galleries (e.g., Megiddo, Hazor, Shiloah Canal) to supply water to towns. During later periods (Hellenistic-Roman, Turkish) aqueducts were constructed to supply important towns, such as Jerusalem, Caesarea, and Acre. Irrigation, however, remained confined to areas adjoining springs and spring-fed rivers.

The emergence of Zionism, accompanied by the ideal of land settlement, comprised the vision of the development of water resources for large-scale irrigation, as already expressed by Herzl. During the period between the two World Wars, the introduction of modern well construction methods and the discovery of previously unknown groundwater sources, together with the construction of some small-scale schemes for the utilization of natural springs and rivers (Bet-She'an, Jordan Valley, Yarkon), transformed many parts of the coastal plain, the Jezreel Valley and some Galilean valleys into irrigated areas. Large-scale development of water resources, however, was not possible because of the dispersed nature of Jewish land holdings and of existing legislation.

Specific plans for full-scale utilization of available water resources emerged during, and shortly after, World War II. The discovery and intensive development of important groundwater aquifers provided the quantities required for a rapid expansion of irrigated agriculture during the years of the massive ingathering of the exiles. Simultaneously, a national master plan for water resources utilization was prepared, based on the concept of transfer of water surplus from the relatively humid northern parts of the country to the wide irrigable plains of the drier southern coastal plain and northern Negev (*See also* NATIONAL WATER CARRIER). With the completion of this scheme Israel attained a rate of utilization of its available water resources unparalleled in any other country.

Supplies available from natural, conventional sources within the 1948 armistice lines are (in million cu.m./year):

To these quantities, some marginal sources such as brackish groundwater and non-renewable ground-water resources of the Negev, amounting to another 100 million cu.m./year, may be added.

Water consumption on the eve of Independence (1948) amounted to 230 MCM/year (million cubic meters per year), has increased steadily since to 1,400 MCM in 1962, 1,750 MCM in 1971, and reached a maximum of around 2,000 MCM in the mid-1980s. The imbalance between the long-term average replenishment of fresh water sources and the high consumption during this period was covered by increasing re-use of treated effluent wastes, of brackish water, and by drawing upon reserves stored in the groundwater reservoirs.

It was expected that the imbalance between consumption and available average long-term replenishment of sources would be restored through a variety of measures. These are more extensive use of brackish water and treated waste water in irrigation, together with more efficient irrigation methods (drip irrigation, automatic computer-controlled operation of irrigation systems), selective allocation of water for different crops, and other water policy measures. Another non-conventional method of increasing available supplies is artificial enhancement of rainfall by country-wide cloud seeding, despite doubts concerning the effectiveness of this method. Desalination of sea water for irrigation water supplies is not considered feasible under existing

Water desalinization plant in Elat. [Israel Information Services]

technological and fuel cost conditions. The water supply of the town of Eilat, however, is based in part on desalination of sea water by the multi-stage flash evaporation process and in part by desalination of brackish groundwater water by the reverse osmosis process. This process is also applied to upgrade brackish groundwater for use in some other areas of acute water shortage.

Of the total annually available water, the agricultural sector used to consume (1960–1975) approximately 75%, the urban-domestic sector approximately 19% and the industrial sector 6%. In ensuing years, agricultural consumption declined to about 70%, urban-domestic consumption increased to about 20%, while industrial consumption, in relative terms remained static. This tendency was due, on the one hand, to greater efficiency of irrigation and of industrial water use and on the other hand to an increase in urban population and a rise in the standard of living.

Future water resources policy was expected to concentrate on the conservation of water quality to stave off salinization and contamination hazards and on re-allocation of the available water in accordance with trends of economic developments. In view of an expected increase in demand for urban-domestic supplies and, possibly, also industrial supplies, a reduced allocation of fresh water from conventional sources for irrigation was considered inevitable, but was expected to be replaced, at least in part, by water of marginal quality such as treated waste water and brackish water, as well as by continued improvement of irrigation techniques. (*See also* AGRICULTURE IN ISRAEL; MEKOROT; TAHAL). Z. SHIFTAN

WAUCHOPE, SIR ARTHUR GRENFELL, (b. Edinburgh, 1874; d. London, 1947). British soldier and *High Commissioner for Palestine. He had a distinguished military career, serving in South Africa, in Europe during World War I, and as a military member of the Overseas Settlement Delegation to Australia and New Zealand. From 1924–1927 he was chief of the British section of the Military Inter-Allied Commission of Control in Berlin where he encountered the problem of refugees in Europe.

Succeeding the unsuccessful Sir John Chancellor, Wauchope was sppointed High Commissioner in 1931, after the stormy period of 1929—1930. He served a full term (1931–1935) and part of a second term (1935–1938). When he arrived in Palestine, the country was, on the surface, politically calm, and economically prospering. But underneath there were mounting tensions, since Jews and Arabs were reorganizing their forces and their autonomous organizations. In full agreement with the British Colonial Secretary, Sir Philip Cunliffe-Lister, and in accordance with their shared imperial conceptions, Wauchope introduced a new set of policies in Palestine. He pursued a liberal, moderate, and evenhanded course vis-à-vis the two communities in Palestine, which were already locked in a protracted conflict. This new approach was based on the notion that a well-controlled economic development should reduce British government costs of ruling Palestine; create prosperity and hence stability; increase the chances for three-sided cooperation among Jews, Arabs, and British; and, ultimately, allow Jewish numerical equality with the Arabs. The overall aim was to maintain British rule over a binational mandated area. This liberal approach was supplemented by a policy of minimal intervention in the internal affairs of the two communities, and by control through the communities' respective notables. Thus Wauchope established friendly working relations with Jewish and Arab leaders.

Between 1931 and 1935, Wauchope relaxed the existing immigration regulations. Consequently, the Jewish population grew in an unprecedented manner. During that period, more than 100,000 German and Polish Jews, who had found themselves in distress in their native countries, immigrated and settled in Palestine. An important component of Wauchope's new policy was the gradual and controlled encouragement of self-government for the two communities. He revived an old plan for a legislative council. The British pre-condition for the implementation of this plan was, however, its symmetrical acceptance by both communities. As a first step in this direction local government was expanded according to a new Municipal Corporation Ordinance of 1934. Municipal elections were then held in the country. However, emanating from diametrically opposed considerations, the two communities respectively showed marked ambivalence and lack of enthusiasm for the plan, which lingered on until 1936 and was then shelved.

Toward the end of 1935, tensions mounted in the region and in Palestine. The adverse ramifications of the Italian-Ethiopian War, which had been felt in various parts of the Middle East, the upsurge in the Arab quest for independence in all parts of the region, the rapid processes of political modernization and radicalization within the Palestinian—Arab community, the vehement reactions to the high rate of Jewish immigration, all culminated in the violent eruption in 1936.

Wauchope was confident of his ability to control the Arab community, but after establishing the Arab Higher Committee, the Arabs started, in April 1936, a general strike which soon deteriorated into the Arab Revolt. At first Wauchope tried to pull strings and manipulate the Arab leaders, opposing the use of military force to quell the Revolt. As part of his efforts to maintain normal life in the territory, the Jews were allowed to open a port in Tel Aviv to insure the flow of imports into the country, and, despite Arab demands, Jewish immigration continued unhampered. For a few months Wauchope prevented the application of harsh measures by the military against the Arab leadership, in the hope of restoring stability and calm. Only when the situation further deteriorated did he agree to the use of force, and encouraged the mediation of Arab rulers (especially Nuri Said of Iraq) in order to bring about an end to the Revolt. As a result a temporary truce was achieved in the winter of 1936. This truce enabled the British government to dispatch the prestigious Peel Commission to explore solutions. Although it contradicted Wauchope's previous policy, he wholeheartedly supported the Peel Commission's final recommendation to partition Palestine, and to establish two separate states under British auspices.

The degree of Wauchope's own failure became evident when the Revolt was resumed in the summer of 1937. Despite Wauchope's pleas the British government decided to dispatch additional military forces, and to employ severe tactics against the Arab leadership. Following the assassination of Acting District Commissioner Lewis Andrews of Galilee, the Arab Higher Committee and other Revolt committees were outlawed. Arab leaders were arrested, some deported, and Haj Amin al-Husseini was relieved of his office as mufti of Jerusalem (and, disguised as a woman, fled from Palestine to Lebanon). In November, 1937, military courts were established under emergency regulations, and firm measures were taken to fight terrorism. Eventually, British efforts restored order to the country. Then the British government appointed the Woodhead Commission which recommended a withdrawal from the Peel Commission partition plan.

Realizing his failure, Wauchope left Palestine in March 1938, after stability had been restored. Wauchope maintained an active interest in Palestine, as well as his contacts with Arab and Jewish leaders, even after his retirement.

G. SHEFFER

WEDGWOOD, JOSIAH CLEMENT (Baron Wedgwood). British statesman and supporter of Zionism (b. Barlaston, Staffordshire, England, 1872; d. London, 1943). He was a descendant of Josiah Wedgwood, the 18th-century founder of the Wedgwood pottery firm. A British Radical politician and a member of the Labor Government in 1924, he was a stanch supporter of Zionism and an outspoken critic of the British government's policy of whittling down the promises of the Balfour Declaration. Like his colleague Lord Strabolgi, Wedgwood was drawn to the more militant Zionist spirit of Vladimir Jabotinsky.

In 1926 Wedgwood toured the United States for the Keren ha-Yesod, which afterward published his speeches in a pamphlet entitled *Palestine: The Fight for Jewish Freedom and Honor*. In 1928 Wedgwood published his book *Palestine: The Seventh Dominion*, advocating the establishment of a self-governing Jewish Dominion in Palestine as part of the British Empire. In 1929 he formed the Seventh Dominion League; Lord Strabolgi, Sir Martin Conway, Lord Hartington, Dr. Drummond Shields, and several other parliamentarians were associated in it along with him.

A vigorous spokesman for Zionist demands in the House of Commons and in the House of Lords, to which he was elevated in 1942, Wedgwood strongly criticized British Palestine policy and defended "illegal" Jewish immigration into the country.

J. FRAENKEL

WEINSHALL. Family of Zionists.

Abraham Weinshall. Lawyer (b. Kyurdamir, Baku District, Russia, 1893; d. Haifa, 1968). He studied law at German and Swiss universities. An active Zionist from his youth on he helped found in 1911 the Zionist student organization He-Haver and in 1913–14 was a member of its

Central Committee. In 1916 he edited a Jewish national periodical, *Das Erwachen*, in Zurich. After his return to Russia, he was active on behalf of Zionism and headed a Jewish people's university in the Caucasus. In 1920 he settled in Haifa, where he worked as a lawyer. As an expert in land law, he helped arrange large Jewish land purchases. He edited *Ha-Tzafon*, a Haifa newspaper (1926–27), and contributed articles to numerous other newspapers.

Weinshall joined the Zionist-Revisionist movement at its inception and for many years was chairman of its Palestinian branch. He also served on the Haifa Jewish Community Council from 1925 to 1931, and from 1927 to 1933 he was a member of Asefat ha-Nivharim and the Va'ad Le'umi. In 1947 he was arrested by the British with other Palestinian Jewish leaders and was detained for 40 days. From 1951 to 1959 he served as president of the Israel Bar Association.

Jacob Weinshall, his brother, physician, novelist, one of the founders of the Revisionist Movement (b. Tiflis, Caucasus, 1891; d. Tel Aviv, 1981). An active Zionist from his youth, he studied medicine at the universities of Munich, Geneva, and Dorpat (Estonia). He served as a medical officer in the Russian army joining Joseph Trumpeldor in 1917, after the February Russian revolution, in an unsuccessful attempt to organize Jewish soldiers of the Russian army to invade Turkey, conquer Palestine, and establish a Jewish State. In 1922, Weinshall settled in Palestine.

He was employed by the Hadassah Medical Center , Jerusalem, and Kupat Holim Sick Fund in Tel Aviv. He was a founder of the Kupat Holim le-Ovedim Le'umi (The National Workers' Sick Fund) and joined their medical staff in 1933.

He was among the founders of the Union of Zionist Revisionists (1925) and chaired its Central Committee in Palestine until 1928. He was also a member of the municipal council of Tel Aviv (1925-1928), a delegate to the First and Second Asefat ha-Nivharim, and a member of the Va'ad Le'umi.

In 1939 he published a bi-weekly called *Ha-Hevra*, with an English version entitled *Commonwealth*. In addition to his political and historical articles, Weinshall wrote biographic and historic novels.

Meyer W. Weisgal.
[Weizmann Institute of Science]

WEISGAL, MEYER WOLF. Journalist, Zionist leader, and president of the *Weizmann Institute of Science (b. Kikl, Russian Poland, 1894; d. Rehovot, 1977). Brought to the United States at the age of 11, Weisgal was educated in the public schools of New York City and at Columbia University, where he studied journalism. A Zionist from his earliest youth (he was one of the first members of the Bronx Zionist society Ha-Shahar), he became a disciple of Louis Lipsky and Chaim Weizmann and served as editor of the *Maccabean* (later the *New Palestine*) from 1917 to 1930. From 1921 to 1930 he was national secretary of the Zionist Organization of America.

In 1931–32 Weisgal was publisher and editor of the *Jewish Standard* of Toronto. He produced two pageants that focused national attention on the sufferings of the Jewish people: "The Romance of a People." (1933) at the Chicago World's Fair and "The Eternal Road" (1937). Weisgal conceived the idea of a Palestine Pavilion for the 1939 New York World's Fair and supervised its construction, securing for it the status of a national pavilion.

In 1940 Weisgal became Weizmann's personal political representative in the United States. Shortly thereafter he organized the American office of the Jewish Agency, serving as its executive secretary until 1946. In that post, he helped organize the Biltmore Conference in 1942 and was one of the five organizing secretaries of the American Jewish Conference in 1943.

In 1944 Weisgal was one of the group that conceived the idea of the Weizmann Institute of Science. He became chairman of the Executive Council of the institute in 1947 and president and chief executive officer in 1966 (retaining the Executive Council chairmanship as well), in which capacity he served until 1969. In 1970 he was named chancellor. Under his presidency the institute expanded greatly and developed into one of the foremost scientific institutions of Israel. In 1957, at the request of Prime Minister David Ben-Gurion, he assumed the chairmanship of the World Committee for the Observance of Israel's Tenth Anniversary.

Weisgal edited *Chaim Weizmann, Statesman, Scientist, Builder of the Jewish Commonwealth* (1944); *Chaim Weizmann: A Biography by Several Hands* (1963), and was general editor of *The Letters and Papers of Chaim Weizmann* (1968 ff.).

WEISL, ZE'EV (WOLFGANG) VON. *See* VON WEISL, ZE'EV.

WEISSBURG, HAYIM. Zionist leader (b. Diosfalva, Hungary, 1892; d. Israel, 1959). Weissburg studied law at the University of Budapest, where he became a member, and subsequently secretary, of the Makkabea (Maccabi) Zionist student organization. He visited Eretz Israel in 1913–14, and upon his return lectured widely and wrote extensively about his impressions of the Jewish Homeland. He served in World War I, and as a prisoner of war in 1915 continued his Zionist campaign in Siberia. On repatriation in 1918, he became active in Transylvania, organizing Zionist groups, launching Zionist papers, and establishing Jewish cultural and educational institutions. He attended several Zionist Congresses. In 1923 he helped found Kefar Gidon and was responsible for the settlement of 40 Transylvanian families there and for the purchase and development of land in the Zevulun Valley. He settled in Palestine in 1925.

R.L. BRAHAM

WEITZ, YOSEF. Settlement and afforestation planner (b. Burmel, Volhynia, 1889; d. Jerusalem, 1972). Upon immigrating to Eretz Israel in 1908, Weitz found employment as an agricultural laborer in Rehovot. He helped establish the Union of Agricultural Laborers in Eretz Israel (Histadrut ha-Po'alim ha-Hakla'im be-Eretz Israel) and was one of the first members of Ha-Po'el ha-Tza'ir. During World War I he was manager of the Sejera farm and in 1919 began working in the Jewish National Fund (JNF) as inspector of planting and afforestation and as assistant to Akiva Ettinger.

Appointed director of the JNF's Land Development and Afforestation Divisions in 1932, he played a central role in the 1930s and 1940s in land acquisition and in the planning and execution of agricultural settlement enterprises. He was involved in the acquisition of the Emek Hefer lands in the early 1930s; the bypassing of the British restrictions on land acquisition in the wake of the 1939 White Paper and the 1940 Land Law; the Tower and Stockade settlements; the establishment of Hanita and Beria; and the creation of eleven lookout settlements in the Negev (1943). He was an ardent supporter of settlement of the border regions—Galilee, the Negev, and the mountain areas.

He initiated and headed the "Negev Committee," which dealt with all the affairs of this region during the War of Independence. In 1950 he was elected to the JNF Board of Directors and in 1960 worked for the transferral of lands from the JNF to the State of Israel and the creation of the Israel Lands Authority, which he directed from its inception until 1964. He wrote many books, principally on the subject of the settlement and afforestation of Israel, and children's stories. His diary, published in six volumes, is a valuable historical source.

His son **Ra'anan Weitz** (b. Rehovot, 1913), was one of the architects of agricultural settlement in Israel. He entered the Jewish Agency Settlement Department in 1938, working in key positions, including head of the Department, from 1963–1984. He helped plan and implement the major settlement projects from the establishment of the state, and was involved in important developments in settlement strategy and concept, such as: the transition from a mixed economy to a specialized economy; the system of regional planning, first tried in Lachish; the development of areas—particularly the Arava and Besor—with agricultural production geared principally toward the export market; industrialization of the settlement sector and the creation of industrial villages; and the "lookout" settlements in Galilee. He was Development Planning Professor at the universities of Haifa and of Bar Ilan and in 1963 founded the Settlement Study Center in Rehovot. He was awarded an Israel Prize in 1990.

WEIZMAN, EZER. Israeli soldier and politican; seventh President of Israel. (b. Tel Aviv, 1924). A newphew of Chaim Weizmann, Israel's first President, he graduated from high school in Haifa, and in 1939 joined the Hagana. During World War II he served in the Royal Air Force, seeing service in India. In December, 1946 he appeared in Basle before the 22nd Zionist Congress in order to convince the delegates of the necessity for developing military and civil aviation in Palestine. In the summer of 1947 he took charge of the squad of nine pilots who brought supplies to besieged settlements.

After the establishment of the State of Israel (May, 1948), Weizman was assigned the task of bringing to Israel the German Messerschmitt planes that the fledgling Israel Air Force had bought from Czechoslovakia and of training the first pilots to handle them. He participated in Israel's first air attack on Egyptian forces. In 1949 he was named commander of the First Wing of the Israel Air Force and set up the first staff command course of the IAF. As lieutenant colonel, chief of operations (1950–53), commander of a group of Israel's first jet fighter planes (1953–56), chief of the Air Force General Staff (1956–58), and brigadier general and commander of the Israel Air Force (1958–66), he developed and supervised the training program of the IAF. As chief of operations of the General Staff of the Israel Defense Forces (from 1966 on) Weizman played a crucial role in Israel's victory in the Six-Day War of 1967. In 1969–70 he was Minister of Transport, representing the Herut party of which he was elected chairman in 1971. In 1977 he organized the Likud's successful election campaign, following which he became Minister of Defense. In this capacity he played a leading role in advancing the peace process with Egypt. In 1980 he resigned from the cabinet following a disagreement with Prime Minister Begin on the continuation of the peace process.

He was reelected to the Knesset in 1984 as head of a new faction, Yahad, which eventually joined the Alignment. From 1984 he was Minister in the Prime Minister's office with special reference to Arab affairs and in 1986 he became Minister without portfolio in the Ministry of Foreign Affairs. In 1988–90, he was Minister of Science. In 1993 he was elected President of Israel.

His books include *The Battle for Peace* (1981) and an autobiography, *On Eagles' Wings* (1976).

WEIZMANN, CHAIM. Scientist, president of the *World Zionist Organization (WZO), and first President of the State of Israel (b. Motol, near Pinsk, Russia, 1874; d. Rehovot, 1952). Son of a timber merchant who was an early adherent of haskala (Jewish Enlightenment), Weizmann attended a traditional heder in Motol and, at the age of 11, entered high school in Pinsk. After graduation he studied chemistry at the polytechnic institutes of Darmstadt and Berlin and at the University of Freiburg, where he received a doctorate with honors in 1899. In 1901 he was appointed lecturer in chemistry at the University of Geneva, and in 1904 moved to the University of Manchester. He began his academic career at Manchester as an unpaid research assistant with the prospect of a paid fellowship and taking on students. He gradually rose to lecturer and, in 1913, was appointed reader in biochemistry.

Weizmann began to engage in Hovevei Zion activities at an early age. Although he aided preparations in Russia for the First Zionist Congress (1897) and was chosen a delegate from Pinsk, he could not travel to Switzerland because he was in Moscow trying to sell a patent. However, he attended the Second Congress (Basle, 1898), met Herzl, and soon became a member of the early Zionist opposition. He believed that the Jewish State could not be obtained through political shortcuts or solely through high-level negotiations with important statesmen. To attain its aims Zionism had to founded on the moral and practical support of the Jewish people as a whole. In 1901 Weizmann helped found the *Democratic Faction within the Zionist movement, a group that emphasized cultural, educational, and practical settlement activity in Eretz Israel. At the Sixth Congress (1903) Weizmann voted, after initial doubts, against the *East Africa scheme. At the Eighth Congress (1907), he preached the idea of *Synthetic Zionism: political activity to obtain a *Charter for a Jewish National Home, supported by constructive pioneering and cultural work in Eretz Israel.

In the early period the dominant aspect of Weizmann's

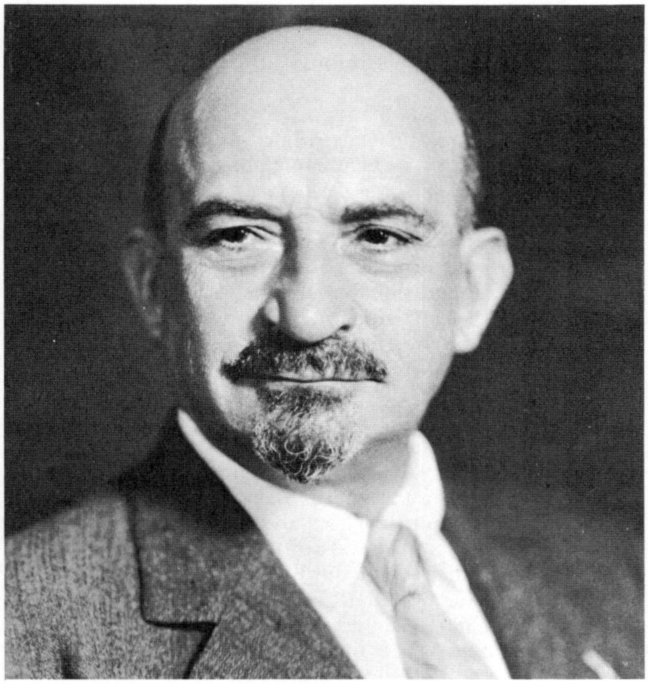

Chaim Weizmann [Weizmann Institute of Science]

own cultural work for Zionism and Eretz Israel was his interest in the founding of a *Hebrew University. As early as the Fifth Congress (1901) he had supported a motion to investigate the possibilities for such an institution. At the Eleventh Congress (1913), he was to submit detailed plans for what he felt would be a "home for homeless Jewish intellectuals," whom the *numerus clausus* (Jewish quota) had barred from studies in other countries.

Weizmann first went to England in 1900 to attend the Fourth Zionist Congress. He had early conceived an admiration for England, whose tradition of freedom, moderation, and practical common sense appealed to him. During his years of world Zionist leadership, Weizmann was convinced that, despite the difficulties and setbacks, the interests of Britain and Zionism coincided.

Although he admired England and believed it might play a role in the fulfillment of Zionism, he moved to Manchester in 1904 mainly to further his scientific work and career which had reached a deadlock in Geneva. In addition to his work at Manchester University, he conducted chemical research for a private concern. In Manchester, Weizmann gathered around him a small group of Jewish friends, including Simon Marks, Israel Sieff, and Harry Sacher, who were destined to play an important role both in Zionist political work in England and in the development of Palestine and Israel. In 1906 one of his friends, Charles Dreyfus, a local Zionist leader and Conservative party member, introduced Weizmann to Arthur James Balfour, who was to remember the meeting when he and the Zionist leader met again in 1915.

In 1907 Weizmann made his first journey to Eretz Israel. One of the purposes of the trip was to explore possibilities for setting up a chemical industry in the country.

Weizmann's active political work for Zionism began at the outbreak of World War I. He was firmly convinced that Britain and its allies would be victorious, that Turkey would lose its empire, including Eretz Israel, and that the destiny of Zionism and the Jewish Homeland lay with the western democracies, primarily Great Britain. Accordingly, he loosened his contacts with the central office of the WZO in Berlin and the office it had set up in Copenhagen and began to get in touch with British politicians and journalists, explaining to them the Zionist program for a revival of the Jewish people in its ancient Homeland. He was greatly aided in these efforts by Charles Prestwich Scott of the *Manchester Guardian*, who introduced him to such leading British political figures as David Lloyd George.

Having offered his services to the British government soon after the outbreak of the war, Weizmann was asked by the Admiralty (of which Winston Churchill was then First Lord) to produce large quantities of acetone, a vital constituent in the manufacture of cordite. In 1916 he moved to London to become the director of the Admiralty laboratory. While in London, he widened his political contacts on behalf of Zionism. A significant breakthrough was the meeting between Weizmann, and other Zionist leaders, and Sir Mark Sykes, assistant secretary to the War Cabinet, at the home of Moses Gaster in February, 1917. This turned out to be the beginning of the official negotiations that led to the issuance of the *Balfour Declaration. Except for membership in the Zionist Actions Committee, Weizmann held no leading position in the WZO at this time. In order to facilitate his political work, the British Zionists gave him official status by electing him (1917) president of the English Zionist Federation.

The months that followed were a time of intense political effort for Weizmann. In the endeavors to secure Britain's official support for the Zionist cause, not only hesitation and reluctance in some official British circles but also strong opposition from influential Anglo-Jewish organizations and individual British Jews had to be overcome. In 1917, at the suggestion of the Foreign Office, Weizmann went to Gibraltar to meet Henry Morgenthau, who was on his way to implement a plan he had conceived for detaching Turkey from the Central Powers. Weizmann's task, in which he succeeded. was to convince the American diplomat of the futility of his aim to neutralize the Ottoman Empire. After the issuance of the Balfour Declaration (2 November 1917), Weizmann and his associates were faced with the task of obtaining the endorsement of the document by the Allies and ensuring that the Mandate for Palestine would be entrusted to Britain. They were to achieve both these aims at the Paris Peace Conference (1919) and at the San Remo Conference (1920).

In 1918 Weizmann went to Palestine as head of the *Zionist Commission to study conditions and make recommendations to the British authorities, who by that time were in control of part of the country. During his stay in Palestine he participated (24 July 1918) in the cornerstone laying of the Hebrew University on Mount Scopus. Seven years later (April, 1925), he was to take part in the official opening of the institution. Deeply concerned with the importance of Arab-Jewish cooperation, Weizmann traveled to Aqaba in

June, 1918, to enlist the support of Emir Feisal for Jewish development work in Palestine. On 3 January 1919, in the presence of Col. Thomas Edward Lawrence (Lawrence of Arabia), he signed a formal agreement with the Arab ruler.

At the London Zionist Conference of 1920, Weizmann was elected president of the WZO; he was reelected at the 12th Zionist Congress (1921). He held that office (as well as the presidency of the *Jewish Agency from 1929 on) until 1931, and again from 1935 until 1946. As the Zionist leader, Weizmann had the task of representing Zionism in talks with each British High Commissioner in Palestine, the British government in London, and many leading world statesmen. He cautioned his fellow Zionists against the illusion that, with the Balfour Declaration, a Jewish state in Palestine was automatically assured. He warned that only by unremitting practical work in Palestine, which would require the moral and financial support of the masses of the Jewish people, could Jewish aspirations to statehood be fulfilled.

Although Weizmann avoided identifying himself with any one party in the Zionist movement (he considered himself as representing the movement as a whole), he felt close to the halutzim, who were laying the foundations of the National Home on a solid agricultural basis. Political formulas, he stressed over and over again, would be meaningless if they were not the outgrowth of hard work on the soil of the Homeland. Throughout his years of Zionist leadership he was to occupy a central position in Zionist ranks, rejecting the extremes of radical socialism on the left and Revisionism on the right.

In April, 1921, he made the first of a series of frequent visits to the United States. This visit, on which he was accompanied by Albert Einstein and Menahem Ussishkin, was to settle organizational differences that had arisen over the Keren ha-Yesod, and to raise funds for the Hebrew University. These questions sparked a heated controversy with American Zionists, particularly those led by Brandeis and Mack. The controversy ended in the defeat of the Brandeis group, since Weizmann's point of view was supported by the majority of the American Zionist leadership. At the same time, Weizmann was eager to mobilize as many Jewish organizations and influential individuals as possible to assist the practical work of reconstruction. To this end, he was able to enlist the help of non-Zionists such as Louis Marshall and Felix M. Warburg, and after years of negotiations with Jewish leaders and organizations in the United States and Europe, the expanded Jewish Agency, which included non-Zionists, was constituted in Zurich in August, 1929.

In his efforts to fulfill Zionist aims Weizmann was inspired by the belief that a Jewish Commonwealth or State would ultimately materialize if there were sufficient Jewish immigration and if enough funds could be raised to promote Jewish agricultural settlement and industrial development in Palestine. His hope, as he had expressed it at the Paris Peace Conference in 1919, was that the Zionists, by diligent, patient effort, would be able to create such political, economic, and administrative conditions that in a given time Palestine would become as Jewish as England was English. His "foreign policy" approach was marked by a concern to obtain as wide an international constituency as possible for Zionism while effecting a visible working partnership with the mandatory power, Britain, although these sentiments were sometimes strained as the result of the disappointments he suffered at the hands of successive British governments.

Convinced that in the final analysis Great Britain would not betray the trust vested in it by virtue of the League of Nations mandate, Weizmann reluctantly accepted, as did the Zionist Executive, the severance of Transjordan from Palestine (1921) and the White Paper of June, 1922 which stipulated that future Jewish immigration to Palestine should be based on the economic absorptive capacity of the country.

The Passfield White Paper of 1930 came as a shock to Weizmann, and he and Lord Melchett resigned in protest from the presidency and chairmanship, respectively, of the Jewish Agency. The negotiations with Prime Minister (James, Ramsay MacDonald which followed under Weizmann's leadership resulted in a modification of the White Paper. This, however, did not satisfy those Zionists who had become disillusioned with Great Britain. As a result of general dissatisfaction, heightened by a newspaper interview in which Weizmann was quoted as saying that he did not consider a Jewish majority in Palestine essential to the fulfillment of Zionist aims, the 17th Zionist Congress (1931) did not reelect him president of the WZO.

During the next four years, Weizmann devoted his energies to his scientific work while continuing his endeavors on behalf of Zionism. He made fund-raising trips to the United States and South Africa and sought to induce European scientists to join the staff of the Hebrew University, of which he was chairman of the Board of Governors (1932–49) and honorary president (1949–52). At his suggestion the Marks and Sieff families provided funds for a research institute in Rehovot. This institute, which bears the name of Daniel Sieff, who had died as a young man, was opened in 1934 and later became part of the larger complex of the *Weizmann Institute of Science. It was in his Rehovot laboratories that Weizmann spent as much time as he could spare from his Zionist work. It was in Rehovot, too, that he and Mrs. Weizmann became active in the resettlement in Palestine of German-Jewish refugees, among them scientists.

In 1936–37 Weizmann, who had been returned to the presidency of the WZO in 1935, presented the Zionist cause before the Peel Commission, which proposed the partition of Palestine. He bitterly attacked the White Paper of 1939 and fought British efforts to restrict Jewish immigration and land purchases. But when World War II broke out in September, 1939, he offered Britain the full cooperation of the Jewish people in the defense of freedom and democracy. He engaged in scientific work for the British war effort mainly in the fields of synthetic rubber, high octane aviation fuel, and synthetic foodstuffs, and spent much time in the U.S.

Just as he had supported Jabotinsky's efforts to form the Jewish Legion during World War I, Weizmann now pressed the British government to organize a Jewish fighting force to fight alongside the Allied armies in the struggle against Nazism. Eventually, in 1944, with the support of Churchill, who by then was Britain's Prime Minister, the British government agreed to the formation of the Jewish Brigade. During the darkest years of the war, Weizmann was sustained by his talks with Churchill and his hopes that an Allied victory would bring a solution to the Palestine problem that would provide for the needs of the Jewish people and favor Zionist aspirations. In 1942, in an article in the

American magazine *Foreign Affairs*, he resumed his public advocacy of the creation of a Jewish State as a solution to the plight of the Jewish people.

Weizmann's disappointment with British policy reached its climax when the Labor party assumed power in 1945 and failed to keep its preelection promise to adopt a pro-Zionist policy. He felt that in the light of Britain's attitude, as shown by the new Prime Minister, Clement R. Attlee, and his Foreign Secretary, Ernest Bevin, only the Jews themselves could deal with the problem of receiving and resettling in Palestine the hundreds of thousands of refugees from the Holocaust. Accordingly, he demanded sovereign powers for Palestine's Jewish community, although he still had hopes that the Jewish State would be able to retain some link with Great Britain or the British Commonwealth of Nations. Early in 1946 he testified before the Anglo-American Committee of Inquiry on Palestine. This was one of Weizmann's last official acts as president of the WZO, for the 22nd Zionist Congress, which met in December, 1946, did not reelect him to the presidency. This Congress, the first to meet after the war, felt that Weizmann, now aged and unwell, had lost touch with the realities of the Palestine problem and postwar relationships between the great powers. While Weizmann had been ready to accept Britain's invitation to a new conference in London to discuss the future of Palestine, the new Zionist leadership, notably David Ben-Gurion and Abba Hillel Silver, favored a more active policy seeking to arouse broad segments of public opinion to put pressure on the British (though in February 1947 they led the Zionist movement in unofficial talks with the British government).

In 1947, though Weizmann no longer held an official position in the WZO, he appeared, at the request of the Va'ad Le'umi and the Jewish Agency, before a hearing held in Jerusalem by the United Nations Special Committee on Palestine. At the request of the Jewish Agency, he also testified before the UN Ad Hoc Committee on Palestine at Lake Success, N.Y. Through his contacts with Pres. Harry S Truman he was largely instrumental in obtaining the inclusion of the whole of the Negev within the boundaries of the Jewish State under the United Nations partition plan as well as an American loan of $100 million for the new state. At the instance of a close friend, Eddie Jacobson, President Truman met with Weizmann on 18 March 1948. When, on the next day, the U.S. ambassador to the UN, Warren Austin, announced the reversal of American support for the partition plan, Weizmann wrote a personal letter to Truman. Truman then told Judge Samuel I. Rosenman, adviser to the late President Roosevelt, that Austin's announcement, which reflected the views of the State Department, did not meet with his approval.

On 17 May 1948, Weizmann was elected President of the Provisional Council of State of the newly established State of Israel. On 23 May he and Mrs. Weizmann went to Washington as official guests of President Truman. On 16 February 1949, Weizmann was inaugurated as the first President of the State of Israel. Weizmann differed with Ben-Gurion on the concept of the presidency. He wished to put his vast experience, in some way, at the service of Israel; Ben-Gurion, on the other hand, saw the presidency strictly as a figurehead office, a role Weizmann detested.

As President, Weizmann again visited Truman in Washington in April, 1949. He had hoped to see Israel a Middle Eastern Switzerland, making its contribution as a mediator in the cold war. During the last year of his life Weizmann, whose health had been poor since the World War II years, was a virtual invalid, but he remained in office until his death.

Weizmann occupied a unique position in Jewish history. He was regarded as the uncrowned head of the Jewish people and his name was universally identified with Zionism and with Palestine whether he was in or out of office. Like Herzl, he was driven to his Zionist labors by a compelling inner force to which he had to give way, sometimes to the detriment of both his private life and his scientific work, and at times even to his health. He was no orator in the generally accepted sense, for he shunned the outward mannerisms of the acclaimed popular speaker. Weizmann held his audiences by his sincerity, the clarity of his exposition, apt quotations from the sacred books, and the wistful telling of a story or the use of a saying gleaned from Jewish life in the Russian ghettos. He was at his best in private conversation when he could give full play to his persuasive powers and to his gift of winning support for his ideas. His personality seems to have appealed most to Englishmen and Americans who saw in him a dedicated leader, a blend of the Hebrew prophet steeped in Jewish history and in the moral and ethical traditions of his people, the wise scientist, and the cultured statesman.

His writings include an autobiography, *Trial and Error* (1949), which was translated into several languages.

Vera Chatzman Weizmann, his wife (b. Rostov-on-Don, Russia, 1882; d. London, 1966) was the daughter of a relatively well-to-do Jewish family. Vera Chatzman studied medicine at the University of Geneva, where she met her future husband. She graduated in 1906, and they married soon thereafter in Zoppot. Weizmann had taken an academic post at Manchester University, but as Mrs. Weizmann's Swiss degree did not allow her to practice medicine in England, she resumed her medical studies in Manchester in 1911, graduating in 1913. Until she left Manchester for London in 1917, she was a medical officer at Manchester schools for mothers and at children's clinics.

In 1913 she dissuaded her husband from leaving Manchester for Berlin to take up a position at Zionist headquarters—a decision which vitally affected the course of Zionist history. Her interest in Zionism and Palestine grew steadily as a result of her active participation in her husband's work and her increasing contacts with Zionist leaders and Jewish personalities in England and on the Continent. In their home in London she created a political *salon* where Zionist leaders, scholars, and British and other statesmen found a congenial meeting place.

Mrs Weizmann was a cofounder of the Women's International Zionist Organization (WIZO), for many years chairman of its Executive, and, later, honorary president. During World War II she became active in Youth Aliya, of which she was chairman from 1940 to 1948. She was a member of the British tribunals for German refugees and gave assistance in air-raid shelters during the air bombardment of London. In 1937 she set up a home in Rehovot, where the Weizmanns lived intermittently; after the establishment of the State of Israel in 1948 they settled there permanently.

In Israel she devoted much time and effort to the Israel Disabled Veterans Organization, the War Veterans Fund, World Jewish Child Day, and the Magen David Adom. After her husband's death (1952), she helped in the collection and preservation of the Weizmann Archives and took an active interest in the affairs of the Weizmann Institute of Science.

A volume of Mrs. Weizmann's memoirs, *The Impossible Takes Longer*, was published posthumously, in 1967.

J.I. LINTON—N. ROSE

WEIZMANN INSTITUTE OF SCIENCE. Center of scientific research and graduate study in Rehovot. Its scientific staff numbers some 1,800—researchers, engineers, and technicians—among them 500 scientists-in-training pursuing M.Sc. and Ph.D. programs at its Graduate School.

The campus of some 40 buildings— including research, administration, and auxiliary facilities—grew out of the Daniel Sieff Research Institute founded in 1934 by Chaim Weizmann.

Weizmann organized his fledgling Institute as an experiment in scientific pioneering: it would subject itself to the disciplines of practical problems arising from the Land of Israel and its economy while not neglecting pure science. Its standards of performance would be measured by international standards.

With a staff of ten accomplished scientists, Weizmann—who by then had already made significant contributions to organic chemistry and industrial fermentation—started work on projects related to the citrus industry, dairy farming, silk and tobacco, and to the production of chemical products of medical value.

To honor Weizmann on his 70th birthday in 1944, a group of his friends, led by his close associate Meyer W. Weisgal, later President and Chancellor of the Weizmann Institute, set up a committee to plan a radical expansion of the Sieff Institute into a wide-ranging research facility bearing Weizmann's name. On 2 November 1949, when the Weizmann Institute of Science was formally dedicated, it comprised eight main buildings and some 60 laboratories.

By the end of the 1980s the Institute carried out some 640 basic and applied research projects in its 21 units each year, grouped administratively into five faculties, each headed by a Dean. The Faculty of Biology was actively tackling the problem of cancer, the functioning of the immune system, the basis of Hormone operation and aging, as well as research into plant genetics and metabolism. Scientists in the Faculty of Biophysics-Biochemistry examined the details of how cells manufacture the substances they need to live, function, and develop. Nerve tissue, muscles, cell membranes, algae and bacteria were among the materials under study. Aspects of inorganic, organic, physical and polymer chemistry were all being investigated in the Faculty of Chemistry. Various materials of commercial value and processes bearing on water resource expansion and solar energy exploitation resulted from this research. The Faculty of Mathematics was engaged in both theoretical and applied mathematics. Computer technology and methodology, as well as theoretical geophysics, were among the interests of Institute mathematicians. In the Faculty of Physics, research ranged from probing the secrets of the nucleus, elementary particles and astrophysics to applied physics where magnetism, laser, and holography projects were under way and the design of electronic devices, for medicine and industry, was in progress.

Cutting across departmental lines were a number of intellectual centers in such fields as aging, agriculture and plant science, energy research, industrial research, molecular biology of tropical diseases, molecular genetics, neurosciences and behavioral research, nutrition, photosynthesis, structural biology, theoretical physics, and wheat science.

In addition, a Department of Science Teaching was responsible for the development of new science curricula, textbooks, TV programs and teaching methods. It also

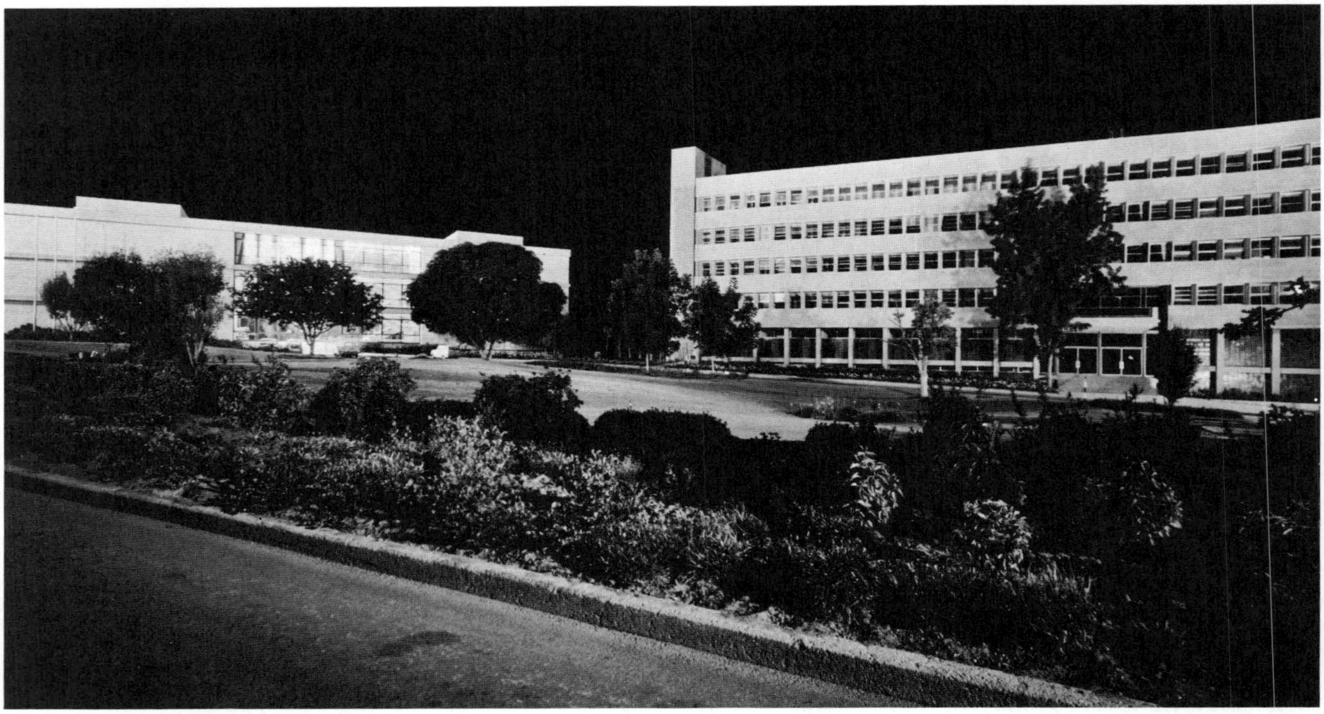

Section of campus of Weizmann Institute of Science. [Weizmann Institute of Science]

The Koffler accelerator in the Weizmann Institute of Science. In background, town of Rehovot. [Weizmann Institute of Science]

sponsored science summer camps for young people from Israeland abroad, a Science Fair, a Mathematics Olympiad, science clubs, and special courses for scientifically talented children from all over the country, including development towns and disadvantaged neighborhoods.

Among the auxiliary facilities available at the Institute was the Wix Central Library which, together with departmental libraries, held a total of 185,000 books and bound periodicals.

Virtually all the scientific and administrative computing at the Institute was carried out in its Computer Center, which operated an IBM 3081-D computer system, and terminals for remote access to the central computer in most of the Institute's buildings.

Institute scientists participated in major international scientific conferences (a dozen of which are held on campus each year), and Rehovot researchers held key positions in various international scientific organizations. Also significant in this regard is the fact that some 100 visiting scientists and their families annually spend extended periods in Rehovot. Foreign students constituted 20% of the enrollment at the Institute's Graudate School, where almost all lectures were given in English.

Responsibility for broad policy and for fundraising is borne by an international Board of Governors and its Executive Council, while the administration of the Institute is the responsibility of the President, aided by three Vice-Presidents.

Much of the Institute's budget is allocated by the Planning and Grants Committee of Israel's Council for Higher Education. Research grants and contracts, mostly from abroad, are an additional source of funds as are private donations.

The main purpose of the Yeda Research and Development Company at the Weizmann Institute is to develop the results of research at the Institute for commercial application and to promote research contracts with commercial enterprises. Through a separate corporation (SIDCO—Science-Based Industries Development Co.), efforts are made to facilitate the establishment of science-based industries in a nearby industrial park, Kiryat Weizmann. Thirty companies were already at work there in 1988 in fields ranging from electro-optics to genetic engineering.

The area of Yad Chaim Weizmann, established in memory of Chaim Weizmann, includes the Weizmann House, which is open to the public, the Weizmann Archives, containing Dr. Weizmann's letters and papers, and the Weizmann Institute.

WELT, DIE. Zionist weekly founded by Herzl and published in Vienna from 1897 to 1905, in Cologne from 1906 to 1911, and in Berlin from 1911 to 1914. The original German edition of *Die Welt* (The World) was followed by a shortlived Yiddish publication of the same name and, in 1907, by a Hebrew weekly under the title **Ha-Olam.* Herzl devoted much of his energies and a great part of his private assets to the creation of *Die Welt.* He attended to the minutest details connected with its operation during its first years, but refused to act as its official editor or publisher for fear that this would jeopardize his position on the *Neue Freie Presse.* This concern, however, did not prevent him from contributing numerous articles and a weekly review of all Zionist activities.

The first editor of *Die Welt* was Saul Raphael Landau. He was soon followed by Dr. Siegmund Werner. Other editors at various times included Erwin Rosenberger, Isidor Marmorek, Julius Uprimny, and Berthold Feiwel. Paul Naschauer, Herzl's brother-in-law, figured for a time as the paper's publisher.

Die Welt was a new force in Jewish life. Its columns carried accounts of developments in Jewish affairs as related to the political, economic, and social events of the day. In addition, the paper stressed Zionist activities, Hebrew culture (particularly literature), and Jewish history and art.

The last issue of *Die Welt* appeared on 31 July 1914.

J. ADLER

WELTSCH. Czech Zionist family.

Felix Weltsch. Philosopher, author, and Zionist editor (b. Prague, 1884; d. Jerusalem, 1964). After completing his studies in Prague, Weltsch became an official, and eventually the vice-director, of the Prague University library. On 15 March 1939, the day the Nazis occupied the city, he left Prague for Palestine. In Jerusalem he was appointed to the Jewish National and University Library, where he continued to work, even after his official retirement, until a month before his death.

Weltsch's first philosophical book, *Anschauung und Begriff* (Perception and Concept), which he wrote in collaboration with his close friend Max Brod, was published in 1913. This was followed by a number of other works, most of them dealing with the nature of politics and the philosophy of religion. A work entitled *Nature, Ethics, Politics* was published in Jerusalem in 1950 in a Hebrew translation. From 1920 to 1939 Weltsch was the editor of *Selbstwehr* (Self-defense), a German-language Zionist weekly published in Czechoslovakia, and was considered one of the intellectual leaders of German-speaking Zionists in that country. His countless articles and essays on Zionism and Jewish nationalism are outstanding for their clear logic and awareness of moral values.

Robert Weltsch, his brother, writer and journalist (b. Prague, 1891; d. Jerusalem 1982). He studied at the University of Prague, where he became a member of the Bar Kokhba Zionist student organization. From 1919 until his emigration to Palestine in 1938 he was editor of the **Jüdische Rundschau* in Berlin. Between 1933 and 1938 he

Die Welt.

Nr. 1. I. Jahrgang.

Erscheint jeden Freitag.

Wien, 4. Juni 1897.

Redaction und Administration: Wien II., Rembrandtstraße 11.

Preise der Anzeigen: Die viermal gespaltene Petitzeile 10 kr.

Zuschriften sind nicht an einzelne Personen, sondern an die Redaction oder Administration Wien, II., Rembrandtstraße 11, zu richten.

Unfrankirte Briefe werden nicht angenommen und Manuscripte nicht zurückgesendet.

Bezugspreise.
Für Oesterreich:
Halbjährig 3 fl. = 6 Kr.
Ganzjährig 6 fl. = 12 Kr.
Für das Ausland:
Halbjährig 4 fl. = 8 Kr.
Ganzjährig 8 fl. = 16 Kr.
Einzelne Nummern 15 kr.

Programm.

Unsere Wochenschrift ist ein „Judenblatt".

Wir nehmen dieses Wort, das ein Schimpf sein soll, und wollen daraus ein Wort der Ehre machen.

„Die Welt" ist ein Blatt der Juden. Welcher Juden? Etwa der Starken, denen man ohnehin hilft? Nein, nein, die brauchen keine Unterstützung.

„Die Welt" ist das Blatt der Armen, der Schwachen, der Jungen, aber auch aller derjenigen, die sich, ohne selbst in bedrängter Lage zu sein, zu ihrem Stamme heimgefunden haben. Wage es Niemand, zu sagen, daß wir den Klassenhaß in das Judenthum hineintragen, wenn wir uns der Schwachen unter unseren Brüdern annehmen. In unseren Reihen stehen Männer genug, die weder „Proletarier", noch Umstürzler, noch Tollköpfe sind. Die Sache, der wir dienen, ist groß und schön, ein Werk des Friedens, die versöhnende Lösung der Judenfrage. Ein Gedanke, wohl geeignet, edlere Menschen — sie seien Christen, Mohammedaner oder Israeliten — zu begeistern.

Wir möchten, um es mit den unseren Freunden schon vertrauten Worten zu sagen:

Eine völkerrechtlich gesicherte Heimstätte schaffen für diejenigen Juden, die sich an ihren jetzigen Wohnorten nicht assimiliren können oder wollen.

First issue of Die Welt, *published in Vienna on June 4, 1897.* [Zionist Archives]

showed great courage in calling on German Jewry to become aware of its Jewish heritage and to bear Nazi persecution with dignity. In Palestine he edited the short-lived *Jüdische Weltrundschau* (1939-40) and later became a member of the editorial staff of *Ha-Aretz,* serving for many years as its London correspondent. During the British Mandate for Palestine, when the country had a large Arab majority, Weltsch was among those who advocated the establishment of a binational Jewish-Arab state (*see* IHUD). He wrote *Zionistische Politik* (Zionist Policies, 1928), *Ja-Sagen zum Judentum* (Saying Yea to Judaism, 1933), and *Martin Buber, 1930–1960* (1961) and contributed to numerous German, Hebrew, and English publications. From 1955 on he served as editor of the yearbook of the Leo Baeck Institute in London.

S. HUBNER

WERKLEUTE (Men of Action). Jewish youth movement in Germany, officially founded in 1932. It existed, however, prior to this date as a branch of the Kameraden youth movement (founded 1916) which together with the *Blau-Weiss movement (founded 1912) constituted a Jewish response to the exclusion of Jews from the popular German youth movement, Wandervogel, whose unique spirit and life style were adopted by both Jewish movements. Some of the members of these movements also found support for their feelings of Jewish independence in the Zionist idea.

Against the background of the serious economic crisis and the social, political, spiritual, and ideological ferment prevailing in the wake of Germany's World War I debacle, anti-Semitism became acute in Germany, to the perplexity of many sensitive young Jews who saw in this the undermining of 150 years of social and cultural integration of German Jewry. The large number of Jewish youth movements and their frequent splits reflected the range of reactions among young Jews to the growth of anti-Semitism, and the profound change which this anti-Semitism brought about in their conscious identity as Jews and as Germans. The constant wave of emigration from eastern Europe in this period also contributed to this change.

In 1932 the Kameraden movement split into three different movements: Das schwarze Fähnlein (a romantic name reminiscent of a small military unit in the 16th-17th century wars in Germany), with assimilationist Jewish-liberal leanings; Freie deutsch-jüdische Jugend (Free Jewish-German Youth), which professed extreme left, assimilationist leanings; and Der Kreis (The Circle), the largest faction which, under Hermann (Menahem) Gerson, called itself Werkleute. The first two factions disbanded after the Nazi rise to power and only Werkleute continued its activities under the new conditions.

At the time of the movement's founding, most of its members were young intellectuals whose ideological platform was based on three principles: a religious leaning with emphasis on humanitarianism and social ethics; commitment to the Jewish people and the wish to make a cultural and social contribution to the Jewish community in the Diaspora; and a revolutionary socialism which was to lead to a human existence based on justice. The common denominator was the emphasis on ethical humanitarianism, but the religious yearning did not lead to established religion, just as the revolutionary socialism did not lead to the Communist party nor did the Jewish awareness yet lead to pioneering Zionism.

In the attachment to Judaism and to Jewish education, Martin Buber had a pronounced philosophical and personal influence on the Werkleute leadership. Together with the impact of the German youth-culture styled after the youth movements, this influence determined the form of Werkleute, its spiritual climate, its general and Jewish intellectual activity, and its educational methods. The members were attracted to the social ethos of the Prophets and to the social and political left of the period;—although disillusionment with the German Social-Democrat party led them to conclude that only by revolutionary activity could socialism be attained (despite their rejection of Communist ideology).

The Nazi rise to power constituted a turning-point in the development of Werkleute. The survival of the Jewish people became a question of personal and collective survival. The halutzic kibbutz movement in Palestine now seemed the natural continuation of the trend of the movement. Immigration to Palestine and agricultural training were declared as obligatory for all members of the movement, and in 1934 the first Werkleute immigrants, temporarily assembled in Hadera, prepared to establish their own kibbutz. In 1936 Kibbutz Ha-Zore'a was founded on the western outskirts of Jezreel Valley. In 1938 it joined the Kibbutz Artzi-Ha-Shomer ha-Tza'ir movement, which professed similar ideological and political beliefs concerning the essence and structure of the kibbutz, its educational methods, and its position on the Jewish-Arab problem.

In the year of its founding, the Werkleute movement numbered about 1,000 members in approximately 25 branches throughout Germany. It organized intensive and comprehensive educational activity (excursions, camps, ideological debates, study of Hebrew and the Bible, etc.) and its membership increased to about 1,200. Most of the movement's members immigrated to Palestine legally, "illegally", or with Youth Aliya. Some 150 Werkleute members settled on Kibbutz Ha-Zore'a. Z. RA'ANAN

WERSES, SHMUEL. Critic and literary scholar (b. Vilna, 1915). After graduating from the Tarbut Gymnasium (high school) in Vilna, Werses went in 1935 to Palestine, where he studied at the Hebrew University. He was appointed to its faculty of Hebrew literature, eventually serving as professor. A prolific scholar, Werses published many articles and major books: *Ha-Sipur ve-Shoresho* (The Story and its Origins, 1971), dealing with the development of Hebrew fiction; *Bikoret ha-Bikoret* (Critique of Criticism, 1981–82), on the criticism of major Hebrew and Yiddish writers; *Mi-Mendele ad Hazaz* (From Mendele to Hazaz, 1988), essays on Mendele, Feierberg, Bin-Gorion, and Hazaz; and *Haskalah ve-Shabeta'ut* (Haskala and Shabbataism, 1988), which examines the early attitudes of Haskala towards Shabetai Tzevi. Werses also published hitherto unpublished works of Josef Perl (1970) and a selection of Bin-Gorion's Yiddish writings. He was awarded the Israel Prize in 1989.

E. SPICEHANDLER

Western Wall. [Israel Govt. Press Office]

WESTERN WALL (Kotel Ma'aravi; also called Wailing Wall). Part of the retaining wall that surrounded the Temple Mount in *Jerusalem after the extension of the outer courtyard of the Temple area by Herod, King of Judea. As the last remnant of the Second Temple precinct, the Western Wall is Judaism's most sacred site and has served for centuries as a place of pilgrimage and prayer. (*See also* HOLY PLACES IN ISRAEL.)

Since the destruction of Jerusalem in C.E. 70, Jews have made the pilgrimage to the ruins of the Temple to bewail its destruction and to offer prayers. Talmudic sages expressed the opinion that the *shekhina*, the Divine Presence, would never depart from the Western Wall and that it would never be destroyed. References to the Western Wall as a place of worship are frequently found from the 11th century on. Special prayers were composed to be recited at the Wall. It was a long-established custom for Jews to take off their shoes on approaching it. Since the prayers took the form of lamentations on the destruction of the Temple, the Wall also came to be called the Wailing Wall. According to Jewish legend, the Wall itself sheds tears on Tisha be-Av, the anniversary of the destruction of the Temple.

Access to the Temple area was not always granted to the Jews. During Roman and Byzantine rule over Eretz Israel the Jews were for long periods banished from Jerusalem, and only on Tisha be-Av were they permitted, for a fee, to come to the site of the Temple and bewail its destruction. Under Arab rule they were again permitted to settle in Jerusalem, and held regular services at the Temple site. The Turkish rulers of the country recognized the right of the Jews to pray at the Wall, although the Jews had to pay a special tax to the Porte for its exercise. From time to time, the authorities or local rulers would place restrictions on the worshipers, such as the prohibition against bringing tables and chairs to the Wall. In the second half of the 19th and the early 20th century, the Jews attempted without success to acquire the narrow area in front of the Wall in order to secure free and undisturbed worship.

With the growth of Arab anti-Jewish sentiment in Palestine, the Arabs attempted to exploit the status of the Western Wall by interfering with Jewish worship and urged the British authorities to limit it. The declared policy of the British was to maintain the status quo, as it had evolved during the centuries of Ottoman rule in Palestine.

On the Day of Atonement in 1925 the British police, acting in accordance with Moslem demands, removed seats and benches placed at the Wall for the use of aged and infirm worshipers. Three years later, again on the Day of Atonement, the police forcibly removed a screen dividing men and women, alleging that its installation constituted an infraction of the status quo. In the wake of this incident, which aroused worldwide Jewish indignation and protests, the British Colonial Secretary published (November, 1928) a memorandum in which he justified the action and also set forth the government's view of the status quo: the Wall itself as well as the strip of pavement in front of it was Arab property, but the Jews had the right of access for devotional purposes. However, they might bring to the Wall only those appurtenances of worship permitted them under the Turkish regime.

Meanwhile, the Arab leaders, who had received the memorandum with gratification, intensified their campaign against Jewish worship at the Wall, inciting the Arab masses with the allegation that the Zionists coveted the Moslem holy places of the Temple Mount. The Moslems also claimed that the Wall itself was sacred to them, being the place where Mohammed's steed Buraq was tethered when he visited the Temple Mount, from which he rose to heaven. They harassed Jewish worshipers at the Wall in a variety of ways, such as stationing in the vicinity a muezzin whose loud calls to prayer were calculated to disturb the Jews. The British did not interfere with this innovation. The Arabs also instituted ritual dances by dervishes (*zikr*) near the Wall to annoy the worshipers, and they began building operations that caused the worshipers inconvenience. Arab agitation culminated in the bloody riots of August, 1929, which began in the Old City of Jerusalem and spread to other parts of the country.

In September, 1929, the Palestine administration issued temporary instructions for the use of the Wall. These instructions set forth in detail the appurtenances of worship that could be brought to the Wall, prohibiting the use of benches, chairs, and stools and the installation of a screen or curtain for the separation of men and women or for any other purpose. They also contained regulations to prevent Moslem passersby from disturbing the worshipers.

In 1930 the British government, with the approval of the League of Nations, appointed a commission to determine the rights and claims of Moslems and Jews in connection with the Wall. The Commission consisted of Eliel Löfgren, a former Swedish Minister of Foreign Affairs, who acted as chairman, Charles Barde, a Swiss, and I. van Kemper, a Dutchman. It held hearings in Jerusalem in June-July, 1930, during which it heard 52 witnesses, 21 called by the Jews, 30 called by the Moslems, and 1 British official. Both sides submitted documents in support of their claims.

The Moslems, who claimed to represent coreligionists from all over the world, demanded that the Jews be prohibited from approaching the Wall. They argued that the Wall was sacred Moslem property and that the area before it, as part of the adjacent Maghribi quarter inhabited by Moslem pilgrims from Morocco, was also sacred Moslem property. The Jews, whose counsel were Mordecai Eliash, David Yellin, and Rabbi Moshe Blau, demanded that recognition be given to the immemorial claim that the Western Wall was a Jewish holy place and that the Jews had the right to pray there without interference or interruption. They denied the Moslem contention that the Wall and the Maghribi quarter facing it were Moslem holy places.

In its conclusions the Commission declared that the Moslems were sole owners of the Wall as well as of the area in front of and adjacent to it. The Jews should have free access to the Wall for devotional purposes, subject to the limitations regarding appurtenances of worship set forth in the temporary instructions of September, 1929 (which with one modification were to be made permanent). The Jews also were not permitted to blow the shofar (ram's horn) at the Wall. Moslems were under obligation not to engage in any building activity on their property that was liable to impair access to the Wall or to inconvenience the worshipers. The restrictions in the temporary instructions designed to prevent disturbance of the worshipers by passersby were to be made permanent.

The report of the Commission was published in June, 1931. The Jewish representative bodies expressed dissatisfaction with the limitations on the Jewish rights of worship, but no recourse to appeal was open to them. However, Jewish protests against the ruling found expression in the defiant blowing of the shofar at the Wall at the end of the Day of Atonement. Despite arrests by the British, the shofar was blown each year at the Wall by a member of Betar, and later of the Irgun Tzeva'i Le'umi, until 1947, the last time High Holiday services were held before the War of Independence, during which the Old City was occupied by the Arabs.

In the negotiations between Israel and Jordan that led to the armistice agreement of April, 1949, free access to the holy places was agreed upon in principle. The Jordanian authorities, however, did nothing to translate this agreement into reality, and during the almost 20 years of Jordan's occupation of the Old City, the Western Wall was inaccessible to Jews from Israel.

The Old City was taken by Israeli forces on 7 June 1967, the third day of the Six-Day War. The shofar was blown, and festive thanksgiving services were held at the Wall by Chief Chaplain Rabbi Shelomo Goren soon after Israeli soldiers reached the place. Within hours, the President of the State, the Prime Minister, and other high dignitaries made the pilgrimage to the Wall.

To accommodate the large numbers of persons who were expected to come to the Wall, the praying area in front of it was greatly enlarged by the removal of old, dilapidated houses. On the feast of Shavu'ot (14 June), the first day when the area was open to the public, 200,000 Jews made the pilgrimage to the Wall. In subsequent weeks, Jews came from all over Israel and the Diaspora.

The area has since been considerably improved. The pavement in front of the Wall has been lowered, exposing tiers of stone blocks that had been covered and increasing the height of the Wall. Arks to house Torah scrolls and tables have been installed for the convenience of worshipers, who gather there from early morning until late into the night. The area in front of the Wall has been partitioned to separate men from women. Tens of thousands of worshipers gather at the Wall on Jewish holidays and fast days, especially Tisha be-Av. Many special religious and national ceremonies are held in front of the Wall, including the swearing-in of soldiers and barmitzvahs for Jewish boys from Israel and the Diaspora.

From 1969 the continuation of the Wall to the east was uncovered when old houses that had been leaning against it were removed. Archeological excavations were undertaken near these parts of the Western Wall as well as near the remains of the Southern Wall of the Temple Mount.

T. PRESCHEL

WHITE PAPER OF JUNE, 1922 (Churchill White Paper). Official British government policy statement (Cmd. 1700 of June, 1922), consisting of correspondence among the British government, the Palestine Arab delegation, and the Zionist Organization concerning the future of Palestine. The statement was issued following fruitless talks in London between the British government and the Palestine Arab delegation headed by Musa Kazem Pasha al-Husseini. It was issued by the British Colonial Secretary, Winston Churchill, but its terms were mainly formulated by the High Commissioner for Palestine, Sir Herbert Samuel, following lengthy consultations with the Colonial Office and with Arab and Zionist representatives.

The White Paper was carefully designed to mollify the Arab nationalists while reassuring the Zionists. In a key passage, intended for Arab eyes, the British government stressed that it had never

> at any time contemplated, as appears to be feared by the Arab delegation the disappearance or the subordination of the Arab population, language or culture in Palestine. They would draw attention to the fact that the terms of the [Balfour] Declaration ...do not contemplate that Palestine as a whole should be converted into a Jewish National Home, but that such a Home should be founded in Palestine....It is also necessary to point out that the Zionist Commission in Palestine ... has not desired to possess, and does not possess, any share in the general administration of the country.

The statement sought to furnish a definitive interpretation of the Balfour Declaration:

> When it is asked what is meant by the development of the Jewish National Home in Palestine, it may be answered that it is not the imposition of a Jewish nationality upon the inhabitants of Palestine as a whole, but the further development of the existing Jewish community, with the assistance of Jews in other parts of the world, in order that it may become a centre in which the Jewish people as a whole may take, on grounds of religion and race, an interest and a pride. But in order that this community should have the best prospect of free development and provide a free opportunity for the Jewish people to display its capacities, it is essential that it should know that it is in Palestine as of right and not on sufferance. That is the reason why it is necessary that the existence of a Jewish National Home in Palestine should be internationally guaranteed, and that it should be formally recognized to rest upon ancient historic connection.... This, then, is the interpretation which His Majesty's Government place upon the Declaration of 1917; and, so understood, the Secretary of State is of the opinion that it does not contain or imply anything which need cause either alarm to the Arab population of Palestine or disappointment to the Jews.

The White Paper confirmed the right of Jews to immigrate to Palestine but stipulated that this immigration must not exceed the economic absorptive capacity of the country. The statement neither prescribed nor precluded the eventual establishment of a Jewish State in Palestine. (A proposal, some months earlier, that the Zionists should acquiesce in an explicit exclusion of such a possibility was vehemently rejected by Weizmann.) The Arab nationalist contention that the British government was committed by the *McMahon Correspondence to the placing of Palestine under Arab rule was rejected by the White Paper. But the British Government announced its intention to foster "a full measure of self-government... by gradual stages". Both Arab and Zionist leaders were invited to commit themselves to accept the White Paper policy.

The Zionists had some reservations about the White Paper, but felt compelled to register their acceptance because the British government had made it clear that the special position of the Zionist Organization foreseen in article 4 of the *Mandate for Palestine could be granted only if the policies of the British and the Zionists were seen to be consistent. The Zionist Executive accepted the policy in a letter to the Colonial Office on 18 June 1922. The fifth Palestine Arab Congress which met at Nablus in August, 1922, rejected the White Paper outright. The British government nevertheless pressed forward to secure League of Nations approval of the Mandate and to put into effect the constitutional arrangements for Palestine (including a plan for an elected Legislative Council) envisaged in the White Paper. These, however, proved abortive. In spite of this failure of its central constitutional provisions, the White Paper remained the most authoritative statement of British policy in Palestine for nearly a decade.

B. WASSERSTEIN

WHITE PAPER OF 1931. *See* SHAW COMMISSION.

WHITE PAPER OF 1939 (MacDonald White Paper). Statement on policy on Palestine issued by the British government on 17 May 1939. The MacDonald White Paper (so called after Malcolm MacDonald, the Colonial Secretary) embodied in the main the proposals for the future of Palestine submitted by the British government to the abortive *St James's Conference of February-March, 1939. It declared that since the proposal for partition recommended by the *Peel Commission had been found to be impracticable, the government deemed it necessary to devise an alternative policy that would be consistent with Britain's obligations to both Jews and Arabs and would also solve the Palestine problem. The Balfour Declaration, the document stated, had not envisaged the conversion of all Palestine into a Jewish State but merely the establishment in that country of a "Jewish National Home," which meant the development of Palestine's existing Jewish community into a center for the Jewish people. Since the Jewish population in the country had increased to about 450,000, approaching one-third of the total population, the government considered that it had carried out its obligation in this respect. On the other hand, the government adhered to the view that all Palestine west of the Jordan River had been excluded from Sir Henry McMahon's pledge (1915) to the Sherif of Mecca to support and recognize Arab independence (*see* MCMAHON CORRESPONDENCE).

Under the *Mandate for Palestine, Britain was charged to "secure the development of self-governing institutions" in Palestine. It was contrary to the spirit of the mandate for the country's population to remain forever under the tutelage of a mandatory power. The government therefore desired the ultimate establishment of a Palestine state in which the two peoples of Palestine, the Arabs and the Jews, would share governmental authority in such a way that the essential interests of each were safeguarded. It was the government's objective to establish such an independent Palestine state within 10 years. The new state would provide satisfactorily for the commercial and strategic requirements of both countries. The constitution of the independent state would include adequate provision for the security of and freedom of access to the holy places. The proposal for the establishment of the independent state involved consultations with the Council of the League of Nations with a view to terminating the mandate.

The establishment of the state was to be preceded by a transitional period during which the British government would retain responsibility for the country and would give the people of Palestine an increasing share in the administration of the country. Britain would do all it could to create conditions that would enable the independent state to come into being within 10 years. However, if at the end of this period circumstances required the postponement of independence, the government would then consult with the people of Palestine, the Council of the League of Nations, and the neighboring Arab states.

On the subject of future Jewish immigration to Palestine the White Paper declared that the Arabs fears of continued immigration leading to a Jewish majority in the country, had to be taken into account. In the subsequent five years, only 75,000 Jews would be admitted, subject to the criterion of economic capacity, which would bring the Jewish population to about one-third of Palestine's total population. After that period no Jewish immigration would be permitted without the agreement of the Arabs. The number of illegal Jewish immigrants would be deducted from the 75,000 quota.

In order to prevent Arabs from becoming landless and to help Arab farmers maintain their standard of living, restrictions were to be imposed on land transfers to Jews. The High Commissioner for Palestine was therefore empowered to prohibit and regulate transfers of land throughout the transitional period (*see* LAND TRANSFER REGULATIONS OF 1940).

Immediately after its publication, the White Paper was denounced by the Jews as a "breach of faith" with the Jewish people, because it left Palestine Jewry at the mercy of the Arab majority and closed the country to Jews fleeing Nazi persecution. Arab extremists also rejected the White Paper, which still did not meet their demands, but some Arab moderates accepted it.

In Britain itself, the Labor and Liberal parties condemned the White Paper, as did many members of the ruling Conservative party. The House of Commons (268 votes to 179) approved the new Palestine policy of the government.

In June, 1939, the Permanent Mandates Commission of the Council of the League of Nations unanimously declared that the policy set forth in the White Paper "was not in accordance with the interpretation which, in agreement with the Mandatory Power and the Council, the Commission had always placed upon the Palestine Mandate." However, the Commission also considered "whether the Palestine Mandate might not perhaps be open to a new interpretation which, while still respecting its main principles, would be sufficiently flexible for the policy of the White Paper not to appear at variance with it." A majority held that it could not state that the White Paper was in conformity with the mandate. A minority expressed the view that existing circumstances could justify the policy of the White Paper, provided the Council of the League of Nations did not oppose it. In its comments on the report of the Commission, the British government sought to defend the White Paper, insisting that the new policy was faithful to the fundamental aims of the mandate.

In August, 1939, the 21st Zionist Congress, meeting in Geneva, rejected the White Paper as "violating the rights of the Jewish people and repudiating the obligation towards them entered into by Great Britain in the Balfour Declaration and the Mandate, and endorsed by the civilized nations of the world." and declared that "the sacred bond between the Jewish people and their historic homeland cannot be severed, and nothing will prevent the Jews from returning to their country and rebuilding their National Home."

Because of the outbreak of World War II in September, 1939, the Council of the League of Nations did not meet again to discuss the report of the Permanent Mandates Commission. Although the British government did not receive legal sanction for its new policy, it took steps to implement the White Paper. Jewish immigration to Palestine was greatly curtailed, and, twice, all legal immigration was stopped for a period of six months. On 28 February 1940, the High Commissioner, in accordance with the authority conferred upon him by the White Paper, issued the Land Transfer Regulations, which permitted unrestricted purchases of land by Jews only in a small zone, constituting about 5 per cent of the area of the country.

The White Paper remained the basis of British policy in Palestine until, forced by mounting Jewish resistance and world opinion, in February, 1947, the British referred the Palestine problem to the United Nations and, in the wake of the partition resolution of 29 November 1947, evacuated the country in May, 1948. T. PRESCHEL

WIESELTIER, MEIR. Hebrew poet (b. Moscow, 1941). He arrived in Israel in 1949 and studied at the Hebrew University. His major works are: *Tiyul be-Iyon* (Travels in Ionia, 1963); *Kah* (Take, 1974); *Davar Optimi Asiyat Shirim* (Making Poems Is an Optimistic Thing, 1976); *Penim ve-Hutz* (Inside and Outside, 1977); *Motza el ha-Yam* (Outlet to the Sea, 1981); and *Mikhtavim ve-Shirim Ahadim* (Letters and Some Poems, 1986). He translated Virginia Woolf's *To the Lighthouse*, Shakespeare's *Macbeth* and selected poems, *Pegimot* (Defects, 1979).

Wieseltier's poetry represents a break with the dominant Hebrew poets of the 1950s (Natan Zach, for example), rejecting their low-keyed tone for a more expressionist mood. His verse is passionate, biographical, and expansive rather than intellectual and controlled. Unlike the verse of older poets, he has often expressed political views which were pacifist and socially radical. E. SPICEHANDLER

WILBUSCHEWITZ MANYA. *See* SHOHAT, MANYA.

WILKANSKY, ISAAC. *See* ELAZARI-VOLCANI, YITZHAK AVIGDOR.

WILSON, (THOMAS) WOODROW. Twenty-eighth President (1913–21) of the United States (b. Staunton, Va., 1856; d. Washington, 1924). Although an idealist and generally an advocate of peace he led the United States into World War I in 1917 when Germany unleashed unrestricted submarine warfare. He was the author of the Fourteen Points, a program of war aims that included open diplomacy, self-determination for all peoples, and the establishment of a League of Nations.

Wilson early became interested in the situation of the Jews in Eretz Israel under Turkish rule and in 1913 told Henry (Morgenthau, his Ambassador to Constantinople, that "anything you can do to improve the lot of your coreligionists is an act that will reflect credit upon America." He was predisposed in favor of Zionism by his religious background (he stemmed from a long line of Presbyterian ministers) and by his friendship with such prominent Zionist leaders as Justice Louis D. Brandeis, Felix Frankfurter, and Stephen S. Wise. On the other hand, he was subjected to anti-Zionist pressures from the Department of State, certain American business interests, missionary groups working in the Middle East, and prominent Jewish friends who were indifferent or hostile to political Zionism during the war years.

Early in September, 1917, Col. Edward Mandell House, Wilson's confidant and adviser, transmitted to the President a message from Lord Cecil, British Under-secretary of Foreign Affairs, inquiring whether Wilson would favor a British "declaration of sympathy" for the Zionist cause. Although, in a letter to Wise (7 February 1917), House had expressed the hope that "the dream which we have may soon become a reality," he now urged Wilson to proceed with caution before taking a definite stand on the issue. Relying on House's advice and preoccupied with momentous international developments, including the Russian Revolution, Wilson sent a discouraging reply to London. However, in response to Britain's warning that Germany was seeking to capture Zionist support, Wilson, probably influenced by Brandeis, wrote that he favored such a declaration.

In these talks and contacts, Wilson had bypassed the Department of State, headed by Secretary Robert Lansing. As a result, the Department subsequently was to insist (until 1948) that the United States government had never committed itself officially to support of the Jewish National Home in Palestine. In December, 1917, after the issuance of the declaration, Lansing wrote a memorandum to the President, arguing against official United States support of the Zionist cause. He pointed out that the United States could not support any plan that gave the appearance of seeking to take territory from a nation (i.e., Turkey) with which it was not at war, that the Jews themselves could not agree on whether they wanted the National Home, that it was unwise to favor any one sector or faction, and finally, that "many Christian sects and individuals would undoubtedly resent turning the Holy Land over to the absolute control of the race credited with the death of Christ." For practical purposes, Lansing suggested that only the first argument be cited for the refusal of the United States to commit itself.

On 27 August 1918, Wise visited the President and urged him, in keeping with a previous promise, to speak out in favor of it. As a result, Wilson, in a letter (31 August 1918) addressed to Wise, made known his official endorsement of the Balfour Declaration.

This official communication by the President produced protests from American business interests (notably the Standard Oil Company of New Jersey), the State Department, anti-Zionist Jews, Christian missionaries active in the Middle East, and United States consular officials stationed there. Meanwhile the newly founded American Jewish Congress prepared a "Memorial on Palestine" for submission to the President, asking the Paris Peace Conference to recognize Zionist aspirations in Palestine. The signatories to the memorandum—Judge Julian W. Mack, Louis Marshall, Bernard G. Richards, and Wise—called on Wilson at the White House on 2 March 1919. They were assured by the President that he approved the Balfour Declaration and was "persuaded that the Allied nations with the fullest encouragement of our Government and people are agreed that in Palestine there shall be laid the foundations of a Jewish Commonwealth."

In Paris later that month, however, Wilson, surrendering to pressure from Howard J. Bliss, president of the Syrian Protestant College in Beirut, persuaded the Supreme Council of the Allied Powers to send a commission to the Middle East (*see* KING-CRANE REPORT) to reascertain the wishes of the inhabitants of former Turkish possessions (including Palestine) with regard to their destiny. This development caused consternation in Zionist ranks, but it seems that Wilson was unaware of the potential threat it held for Zionism. In response to a plea from Frankfurter, Wilson registered surprise that Frankfurter thought it "necessary [for me] to give you any renewed assurance of my adherence to the Balfour Declaration and so far I have found no one who is seriously opposing the purpose which it embodies...." The report was pigeonholed and not given consideration by the Allied Powers.

In February, 1920, Wilson, by then a semi-invalid after a stroke, came to the aid of the Zionist cause when France sought to deprive Palestine, in favor of Syria, of a large stretch of arable land. In response to a plea from Brandeis, Wilson instructed Lansing to transmit to the United States Ambassador in Paris Wilson's disapproval of the French plan. Lansing, just before his forced resignation as Secretary of State, sent the message but made it clear that the order from the White House had been motivated by Brandeis.

G. HIRSCHLER

WINGATE, ORDE CHARLES. British officer and Christian Zionist (b. Naini Tal, India, 1903; d. Naga Hills, on the border between Assam and Burma, 1944). Wingate received a military education and in 1927 was sent to the Sudan, where he was stationed until 1933. In 1936 he was ordered to Palestine as an intelligence officer to study the political and security situation there. He traveled through Palestine and met many Jewish and Arab leaders. Noting that the regular British Army would be unable to deal effectively with the guerrilla warfare conducted by the Arab terrorists, he organized and trained the Special Night Squads, composed of Jewish volunteers, which helped beat back the Arab marauders. In these operations, for which he received his first Distinguished Service Order, he had assistance from regular British troops and valuable intelligence information not only from Jews but also from friendly Arabs who were anxious to see the terrorists stopped.

Within weeks after his arrival in Palestine, Wingate had zealously espoused the Zionist cause, to the extent that at times he became impatient with the Zionist "establishment," which he did not consider sufficiently militant. Ar first the leaders of the yishuv were suspicious of the eccentric, high-strung British officer, but before long they grew to trust and respect him, and he was accorded the cognomen of Ha-Yedid (the Friend).

In the spring of 1938 Wingate testified before the Woodhead Commission in Jerusalem, declaring that whatever progress the Arabs had made in Palestine was due to the Jews and that a modern industrial Jewish State under British protection would make the British Mediterranean impregnable and should also represent "the best hope of the Arab world." While on leave in London early in 1939, he met with many high British officials, to whom he voiced his conviction that the only way for Britain to restore peace in Palestine was to adopt a pro-Zionist policy. In May, 1939, he received orders to leave Palestine at once. There is no doubt that this was the result of official British disapproval of Wingate's enthusiastic espousal of the Jewish cause.

After the outbreak of World War II, Wingate hoped to be put in command of a Jewish army to fight alongside the Allied forces and offered to raise an army of 60,000 Palestinian Jews to drive the Italians from North Africa. The British did not act upon his offer. In 1940–41 Wingate served in Ethiopia at the head of guerrilla forces fighting for the liberation of that country. Subsequently he was sent to India, where he organized the Chindits, who fought in Burma behind the Japanese lines.

He was killed late in March, 1944, when his plane, flown by an American crew serving the Chindit forces, crashed. He was later reinterred in Arlington Cemetery in the United States. Wingate memorials in Israel include the Wingate Institute (a center for physical education) and a forest planted by the Jewish National Fund on the slopes of Mount Gilboa.

WISE, GEORGE SCHNEIWEIS. Businessman, sociologist, and educator (b. Pinsk, Russia, 1906; d. Miami, 1987). Two years after his arrival in the United States, he graduated from Furman University (B.S., 1928), and in 1950 received a Ph.D. degree from Columbia University. Active as a director or head of many business concerns in the United States, Mexico, and Israel, he also taught at institutions of higher education, serving as a lecturer in sociology at Columbia University in 1951–52 and as a visiting professor at the National University of Mexico in 1956–57. Interested in the Hebrew University of Jerusalem for many years, he was national president of the American Friends of the Hebrew University from 1951 to 1955 and chairman of the university's Board of Governors from 1953 to 1962. In 1963 he was elected president of Tel Aviv University, in which capacity he developed that institution into a major university, serving as its chancellor from 1971 until his death.

WISE, STEPHEN SAMUEL. Rabbi, Zionist leader, communal leader, educator, and social activist (b. Budapest, 1874; d. New York, 1949). The son and grandson of rabbis, Wise went to New York as a child, attended public schools and earned a B.A. and Ph.D. from Colombia University. He pursued Jewish studies with his father and informally with teachers at the new Jewish Theological Seminary, then went to study in Vienna with Adolf Jellinek, one of the chief exponents of *Wissenschaft des Judentums*. After receiving ordination from Jellinek, Wise returned to New York and served briefly as rabbi of Congregation B'nai Jeshurun.

Stephen S. Wise.
[American Jewish Congress]

In 1900 Wise accepted the pulpit of Congregation Beth Israel in Portland, Oregon, then still a semifrontier society. In the six years he lived there, Wise set the pattern which he would follow the rest of his life. A dynamic speaker, he attracted large audiences to his sermons, and pioneered in the practice of pulpit exchanges; he was a welcome guest speaker at many churches. With reform sentiment sweeping the country, Wise, unlike most rabbis at the time, spoke out about public issues, condemning corruption, and even endorsing political candidates. Within the congregation, he established one of the first social reform programs in the country.

In 1907, he founded the Free Synagogue in New York, which he headed until his death, on the basis of Reform Judaism, Zionism, a free pulpit, and social involvement in the larger community.

For the next forty years, Wise epitomized the socially involved rabbi he believed essential not only in terms of traditional prophetic Judaism but of American democratic idealism as well. Wise led the Jewish equivalent of the Social Gospel movement, in which his close friend and frequent collaborator, John Haynes Holmes, was active. He founded a downtown branch of the Free Synagogue where he preached to the immigrant East Side Jews, and from which the congregation ran an outreach program to them.

Wise was a longtime critic of Tammany Hall, the New York City Democratic organization, which was then one of the most corrupt political machines in the country. He early and enthusiastically backed Woodrow Wilson for President, and was on speaking terms with many of the Democratic party's leaders.

Although Wise was nominally a Reform Jew, and belonged to the Central Conference of American Rabbis, he seriously differed from the classic Reform doctrine then expounded at Hebrew Union College, especially regarding Zionism. Wise had been a founder of the Federation of American Zionists in 1897, and participated in the Second Zionist Congress (1898), the first of many he would attend. There he met Theodor Herzl and was elected to the Greater Actions Committee. Although he never abandoned Zionism, the internal bickering and especially the European dismissal of the American movement as inconsequential led him to retire from an active role when he moved to Portland.

He returned, however, with the advent of Louis D. Brandeis to the movement's leadership in 1914, and became one of Brandeis's key lieutenants. When Brandeis went on to the

Supreme Court, Wise succeeded him as chairman of the Provisional Executive Committee for General Zionist Affairs in the United States. Wise spearheaded the drive to create an American Jewish Congress, a pro-Zionist and democratically constituted body which vied for community leadership with the aristocratic and anti-Zionist American Jewish Committee. Wise's friendship with Woodrow Wilson played a key part in securing American endorsement of the Balfour Declaration. In 1918 the Congress elected him one of the delegates to the Paris Peace Conference.

In 1921 he joined with others in the Brandeis entourage in resigning from positions of leadership in the Zionist Organization of America following the dispute with Chaim Weizmann and the European Zionist leadership over the establishment of the Keren ha-Yesod. Unlike many of Brandeis' other followers, however, Wise remained on good terms with both Weizmann and Louis Lipsky, a close associate since the early days of American Zionism.

During the 1920s Wise devoted himself to building up the American Jewish Congress. Although nominally only vice-president from 1922 to 1925, he was the driving force in efforts to create a role for the Congress in Jewish communal life, and in 1925 became president in name as well as fact, a position he held with only one interruption until his death.

Wise also established the Jewish Institute of Religion in 1922 as an alternative seminary for the training of Reform rabbis. The Institute, which Wise headed from its inception until its merger with Hebrew Union College in 1948, differed from the Cincinnati school primarily in its emphasis on social activism, pro-Zionist attitude, and its requirement that students have a baccalaureate degree before matriculating for rabbinic studies.

In 1925 Wise re-entered Zionist life with his acceptance of the Chairmanship of the United Palestine Appeal campaign. Although he welcomed the involvement of non-Zionist Jews in building up Palestine, he opposed Weizmann's plan for an enlarged Jewish Agency, claiming it would give control of Zionist affairs to wealthy Jews who had little sympathy with the broader Zionist vision.

Two crises precipitated Wise's full return to Zionist activities: the British withdrawal from the Balfour promise and Hitler's rise to power in Germany. Together with Jacob de Haas, Wise penned a powerful indictment of British policy in *The Great Betrayal* (1930) and remained a persistent critic of British policy thereafter, although during the war he insisted that Palestine should not be an issue thwarting full American support of its ally.

Wise was one of the first American Jews to recognize the danger Hitler and Nazism posed not only to the Jewish people but to democracy as well. Throughout the decade Wise spoke out against anti-Semitic measures in Germany, much to the discomfort of the German-American Jewish elite in the American Jewish Committee, who believed that private negotiations would be more effective than public criticism. The American Jewish Congress was the driving force in anti-Fascist public protests, and in 1936 Wise founded the World Jewish Congress to bolster the fight against the Nazis.

During this period Wise did not neglect his duties at the Free Synagogue nor abandon his role as a leading civic reformer. He and John Haynes Holmes led a campaign that culminated in the resignation of New York's corrupt mayor James J. Walker, and the eclipse of Tammany's power during the administration of Wise's friend, Fiorello H. LaGuardia.

He used his influence with President Franklin D. Roosevelt to block the British from closing immigration to Palestine in 1936, although the British Government finally adopted a restrictive policy in the 1939 White Paper. Wise's efforts to fight fascism have been criticized by some scholars as ineffective, and they charge that his friendship with Roosevelt, and his unwillingness to embarrass the administration, prevented him from taking a more strident and, they allege, therefore a more effective position. They point particularly to Wise's initial knowledge of the Holocaust, transmitted by the World Jewish Congress Geneva office in 1942, which he held secret for several weeks at the request of the State Department while the government attempted to verify the information. Wise's reluctance to criticize Roosevelt resulted in a split between him and his cochairman of the American Zionist Emergency Council (founded in 1939 after the outbreak of the war to coordinate Zionist activities), Abba Hillel Silver, who had no faith in the President. Though still committed to the ideals of Zionism and democracy in his old age, Wise was uncomfortable with the new Jewish militancy epitomized by Silver and by David Ben-Gurion. When power shifted to the militants, Wise was forced out of the leadership of the Emergency Council. Nevertheless, in 1945 he attended the United Nations Conference in San Francisco as one of the special representatives of the Jewish Agency. The following year he testified before the Anglo-American Committee of Inquiry in Washington, and his eloquence still stirred listeners. At the 22nd Zionist Congress (1946), the last he attended, he backed his old antagonist, Chaim Weizmann, in a losing battle against Silver and Ben-Gurion.

Despite his ouster from Zionist leadership and ill health, Wise's last few years proved rewarding. The American Jewish Congress began to exert the influence Wise had hoped it would. especially in matters concerning social justice. The merger of the Jewish Institute of Religion with Hebrew Union College marked the acceptance by the Reform establishment of the ideals of Zionism and social justice Wise had long preached, and ensured the survival of the Institute. Most satisfying was the establishment of the State of Israel, for which Wise had devoted much of his life.

Wise's autobiography, *Challenging Years* (1949), appeared shortly after his death. There are two published collections of his letters: *The Personal Letters of Stephen S. Wise* (1956), edited by his children, James Waterman Wise and Justice Wise Polier, and *Stephen S. Wise, Servant of the People* (1969), edited by Carl Hermann Voss. M.I. UROFSKY

WISSOTZKY, KALONYMUS-Z'EV. Merchant and philanthropist (b. Zagare, Kovno District, Lithuania, 1824; d. Moscow, 1904). Wissotzky engaged in business and settled, together with a group of other Jews, as a farmer in Dubonivo, a village near Dvinsk. Crop failures forced him to leave the village and return to study and business. In 1858, after having studied for some time under Rabbi Israel Salanter in Kovno, he settled in Moscow, where he established a tea trading company that developed into one of the most important companies of its kind in Russia.

A great philanthropist, Wissotzky was also an ardent supporter of movements for the settlement of Jews in Eretz Israel. He supported Rabbi Zvi Hirsch Kalisher, the Sir Moses Montefiore Testimonial Fund, and the Hovevei Zion. He wanted his large contributions to be turned into permanent endowment funds, the income from which would be used to benefit national institutions. In 1884 he participated in the Kattowitz Conference of the Hovevei Zion and sought to establish a fund for the development of industry in Eretz Israel. The next year he visited Eretz Israel on behalf of the Hovevei Zion and formed an actions committee in Jaffa. He contributed generously to a variety of Jewish institutions in Eretz Israel and supported Hebrew writers and literary enterprises, including the periodical *Ha-Shilo'ah*.

I. KLAUSNER

WITKIN, YA'AKOV. *See* ZERUBAVEL, YA'AKOV.

WIZO (Women's International Zionist Organization). An apolitical, voluntary movement, founded in London on 11 July 1920, at an international conference of women Zionists convened by the Federation of Women Zionists of Great Britain and Ireland, which had been established two years earlier. The leaders of the new movement were Rebecca Sieff, Vera Weizmann (wife of Chaim Weizmann), Romana Goodman, Edith Eder, and Henrietta Irwell. Rebecca Sieff, elected as first president, held this office until her death in 1966.

World WIZO's establishment coincided with the beginning of the British civil administration in Palestine under the British Mandate. At the same time, there was considerable Jewish emigration from Russia to Palestine resulting from the Communist revolution in Russia. These two events motivated the women Zionist leaders to devote themselves to fostering the welfare of women immigrants in the belief that these women, perhaps even more than men, would have to adjust to a new way of life, and that women Zionists would be more sensitive to this than the Zionist movement in general. WIZO's original program was divided into three categories: professional and vocational training for women, with special emphasis on preparation for agricultural pioneering; education of women to relate to their society as informed and civic-minded citizens; and the care and education of children and youth.

In the first 20 years of its existence, WIZO's headquarters were in London while a network of federations was established throughout Europe (with the exception of the USSR) and in most other countries of the world except the United States (where *Hadassah served as the women's Zionist Organization). With the rise of Nazism in the 1930s and throughout World War II, WIZO federations were engaged in the rescue and relief of Jews wherever possible and cooperated with the activities of various Jewish appeals, particularly Youth Aliya.

After World War II the number of federations was considerably reduced since those in the Communist bloc and most Moslem countries were disbanded. In 1949 the seat of the Executive was transferred from London to Tel Aviv. WIZO today has 50 federations with a membership of approximately 250,000. The largest federation is in Israel itself, with a membership of 90,000. Its overall governing body is the WIZO World Conference, which meets every four years.

WIZO is the only Zionist organization recognized by the

WIZO conference held in Jerusalem in 1951. [Zionist Archives]

United Nations as a Non-Governmental Organization and has consultative status with the UN Economic and Social Council (ECOSOC) and the UN Children's Emergency Fund (UNICEF). WIZO is a member of the World Zionist Organization and the World Jewish Congress.

World WIZO's activities are administered by an Executive residing in Israel, composed of a chairperson and 20 department heads, all voluntary members. WIZO conducts and maintains over 670 institutions and services throughout Israel, caring for and educating more than 36,000 children and youth and providing activities for hundreds of thousands of women, including those of the minority communities (Arab, Druze, Bedouin, and Circassian). All its projects are supported through the fundraising activities of its federations, with the participation of government and local authorities, and parents' fees. WIZO's projects include 201 institutions for child care: daycare centers, kindergartens, toddlers' homes, play centers, student clubs, therapeutic child centers, etc., 11 agricultural, vocational, and general academic schools; 81 youth clubs and 190 women's clubs and branches.

WIZO works to advance the rights and status of women, initiating and lobbying for legislation on this subject. Its 26 Legal Advice Bureaus on Family Matters offer counseling to disputing couples and represent women in the rabbinical courts.

WIZO's work for the community and for family welfare includes assistance for families of war casualties and for the absorption and integration of new immigrants, most recently those from Ethiopia. WIZO conducts a variety of vocational, cultural, educational, and social activities; it maintains two shelters for battered wives in cooperation with the Ministry of Labor and Social Welfare and the National Insurance Institute and conducts activities for young women in distress. WIZO also conducts summer camps for disadvantaged mothers of large families and offers week-long holiday programs throughout the year to these and other needy groups.

In recent years WIZO has added the "Third Age" to its sphere of activities, running clubs for senior citizens in various branches throughout the country and recently establishing a WIZO Parents' Home in Tel Aviv which accommodates 120 elderly residents.

WIZO's basic aims are to promote Jewish and Zionist education to its worldwide membership, and thus to strengthen the bond between World Jewry and the State of Israel; foster the physical and emotional welfare and cultural development of women, children, youth and the aged, regardless of race, creed, or color; and to advance the status of women.

COUNTRIES WITH A WIZO ORGANIZATION

Argentina
Australia
Austria
Barbados
Belgium and Luxembourg
Bolivia
Brazil
Canada
Chile
Colombia
Costa Rica
Curaçao
Denmark
Hong Kong
Israel
Italy
Japan
Jamaica
Kenya
Mexico
New Zealand
Norway
Panama
Paraguay
Peru
Portugal
The Dominican Republic
Ecuador
Finland
France
Germany
Gibraltar
Great Britain and Ireland
Greece
Guatemala
Holland
Honduras
Singapore
South Africa
Spain
Sweden
Switzerland
Trinidad
USA
Uruguay
Venezuela
Zaire
Zimbabwe

WOHLMANN, LEON. Attorney, public official, and Zionist leader in Switzerland (b. Sanok, Galicia, Austria, 1900; d. Zurich, 1968). Wohlmann moved to Switzerland as a young man, receiving his law degree from the University of Zurich in 1929 and studying at the University of London in 1930. In 1931 he became secretary of the municipality of Zurich. A member of the World Council of General Zionists, he became vice-president (1945) and president (1958) of the Federation of General Zionists in Switzerland. He was a delegate to the 25th Zionist Congress (1960–61). From 1929 until his death he was on the staff of the *Israelitisches Wochenblatt*, writing extensively on Zionist topics.

David Wolffsohn. [Zionist Archives]

WOLFFSOHN, DAVID. Second president of the World Zionist Organization (b. Darbenai, Lithuania, 1856; d. Homburg, Germany, 1914). Wolffsohn received a traditional Jewish education and in 1872 moved to Memel, East Prussia, where he came under the influence of the Zionist precursor Rabbi Isaac Rülf. He later lived in Lyck, East Prussia, at the home of David Gordon, editor of *Ha-Maggid*. Eventually he became a partner in a large lumber concern and in 1888 settled in Cologne, where he made his home for the rest of his life. Wolffsohn took great pride in his Eastern European background; although he was no longer strictly Orthodox, he retained a deep attachment to the customs and traditions in which he had been raised. In the early 1890s he was active in the Jewish Literary Society of Cologne, lecturing there on subjects such as the Talmud, Russian Jewry, and the ideas that later became known as Zionism. It was at a literary society meeting that he first met Max Isidor Bodenheimer, with whom he founded (1893) the Cologne Association for the Furtherance of Agriculture and Handicrafts in Eretz Israel, an organization along the lines of the Hovevei Zion.

Wolffsohn began to correspond with other Hovevei Zion groups and with such Hovevei Zionists as Naftali Zvi Hirsh Hildesheimer and Willy Bambus. It was Bambus who informed him of the imminent publication of Herzl's *Jewish State* (1896). Wolffsohn immediately went to Vienna, sought out Herzl, and became the latter's devoted lieutenant and close friend. With his Eastern European background, intelligence, levelheadedness, and business experience, Wolffsohn became an ideal complement to Herzl, who had no experience in business dealings and no knowledge of Jewish life in Eastern Europe. To his surprise, Wolffsohn found that Herzl had not known of the work of his Zionist forerunners. Herzl, in turn, was surprised when Wolffsohn told him at their first meeting that the success of his idea of political Zionism would depend on how it was received by the Jewish masses in Eastern Europe. It was Wolffsohn who is said to have chosen the colors for the Zionist flag: blue and white, from the traditional *tallit* (prayer shawl).

From 1897 until 1904 Wolffsohn was a member of the Inner Actions Committee. In the fall of 1898 he accompanied Herzl to Constantinople and Eretz Israel, where he was a member of the deputation which, led by Herzl, was received by Wilhelm II outside Jerusalem. Earlier that year, he had been sent by Herzl to London to rally the British Hovevei Zionists to the idea of political Zionism and to meet with Jewish financiers for the purpose of setting up the Jewish Colonial Trust. This, the financial instrument of the World Zionist Organization (WZO), was officially founded in London in 1899 and began operating in 1901. Wolffsohn became its first president and remained its chairman until his death. In his work with this Zionist "bank," aided by Jacobus Kann, Wolffsohn frequently came into conflict with Herzl. Herzl saw the bank as a political asset, which was needed before a Charter could be requested from the Turkish government. Wolffsohn, on the other hand, looked upon the bank as a business enterprise that had to be managed in a businesslike manner, and he pleaded with Herzl to leave its management to experienced businessmen. But before long, Herzl was giving orders to James H. Loewe, the bank's secretary in London, over Wolffsohn's head; in response to complaints, most of them anonymous he also had the books of the bank examined. At one point, both Wolffsohn and Kann were ready to resign from their positions with the bank.

His frank disagreements with Herzl notwithstanding, Wolffsohn remained absolutely loyal to his chief. Herzl referred to him as "Daade" and named for him David Litwak, the character in *Old-New Land* who was made President of the new Jewish Commonwealth because "he did not want to." Wolffsohn never aspired to positions of official leadership and was content to act as an intermediary between Herzl and his opponents within and outside the Zionist movement. Thus, when the East Africa scheme virtually split the Zionist movement, Wolffsohn, who opposed the plan, did not participate in the discussion but kept himself in reserve as a possible mediator if the need for one arose.

After Herzl's death, Wolffsohn (with Leon Kellner and Johann Kremenetzky) took charge of Herzl's literary estate and, in accordance with Herzl's instructions, assumed the guardianship of the Herzl children, raising a fund to provide for their support and education.

Despite opposition from the practical Zionists and his own unwillingness to accept the office, Wolffsohn was elected in 1905 as Herzl's successor in the presidency of the WZO. During his term of office he concentrated on consolidating the ranks of the movement and preserving its "political" character. Between 1906 and 1908 he traveled widely, visiting South Africa, Eretz Israel, Russia, Hungary, and Turkey. In Russia he conferred with Prime Minister Pyotr Stolypin and Foreign Minister Aleksandr Izvolski to induce them to ease Tsarist restrictions on Zionist activity. He obtained promises that Zionist efforts, particularly work for the Jewish Colonial Trust, would be facilitated. In Hungary he discussed with Minister of the Interior Count Gyula Andrássy the question of legalizing Zionist activity in that country. In Constantinople he negotiated indirectly with Sultan Abdul Hamid II. After the take-over by the Young Turks in 1908, Wolffsohn called for adherence to the Basle Program but abandoned the idea of a Charter and of great power guarantees for the National Home in Eretz Israel.

In 1911 due to opposition from the practical Zionists and the Democratic Faction, Wolffsohn was not reelected president of the WZO. Although he suffered from a heart ailment brought on by exhaustion, he remained chairman of the Jewish Colonial Trust. He presided at the 11th Zionist Congress (1913), where there was much debate about the Zionist banking enterprises, and succeeded in keeping them from being turned over to the cultural Zionists, whom he considered unbusinesslike. At that Congress, Wolffsohn made the first substantial donation toward the Hebrew University project presented to the assembly by Chaim Weizmann.

Wolffsohn wanted to settle in Eretz Israel, but his illness and the outbreak of World War I prevented him from carrying out his plan. In his will, he earmarked the major part of his estate for the erection of a meeting hall for Zionist Congresses or a building for the Hebrew University. Bet David Wolffsohn (today the Hebrew University Law Faculty Building), on the Mount Scopus campus of the university, was dedicated in 1930. G. HIRSCHLER

WOLFSBERG, YESHAYAHU. *See* AVIAD-WOLFSBERG, YESHAYAHU.

WOLFSON, SIR ISAAC. Merchant and philanthropist (b. Glasgow, 1897; d. Rehovot, 1991). The head of Great Universal Stores, one of Britain's largest merchandising enterprises, he was the founder of the Wolfson Foundation for the advancement of health, education, and youth activities, appeal chairman of the Joint Palestine Appeal, honorary president of the Weizmann Institute of Science Foundation, treasurer of Hekhal Shelomo, and president of Britain's United Synagogue. He received a baronetcy in 1962 for his philanthropic activities.

Although Sir Isaac's association with Zionist activities came late, he headed Zionist fundraising activities in Great Britain for Israel, which found expression particularly in Hekhal Shelomo, the religious center in Jerusalem, which he established in memory of his father. He helped to build synagogues and youth clubs throughout Israel, and with his wife Edith dedicated the Great Synagogue in Jerusalem in 1982. He was much concerned with business developments in Israel and participated in a number of Israeli commercial, industrial, and investment enterprises. He made his home in Rehovot.

J. FRAENKEL

WOMEN IN ISRAEL. Jewish resettlement of Eretz Israel during the final decades of the 19th century was undertaken primarily by families— whether of Sephardi or east European origin— who essentially subscribed to traditional notions regarding the gender-based division of social and familial functions. Although women as well as men populated the early settlements (moshavot), such as Petah Tikva and Rosh Pina, land was registered exclusively as belonging to men and the only women employed in agriculture were Arab.

By contrast, the women pioneers of the Second Aliya (1905–1914) who came from eastern Europe were, like their male colleagues, motivated both by the horrors of pogroms and by revolutionary socialist ideals. They differed from the men in that they were on average slightly less educated and in that only 30% (compared to 60% of men) already spoke Hebrew upon arrival in the country. Furthermore, they came not as wives accompanying their husbands, but as single individuals spurred by the dream of participating in the rebuilding of a Jewish homeland. The question of women's emancipation had not been raised in the European Labor Zionist movement, though powerful feminist movements existed in most of the countries from which the pioneers came. Possibly this was because it was presumed that the socialist elimination of exploitive relationships would automatically eliminate sexual discrimination. Alternatively, the overriding need to insure the very existence of the Jewish people may have relegated female emancipation to secondary importance. On the other hand, the explanation might lie in the male pioneers' traditional beliefs regarding women's subservient role and status. Whatever the reason, the halutzot (women pioneers) found themselves engaged in a twofold struggle: like the men, they encountered hostility to Socialist Zionism, but in addition they encountered hostility, or, at best, indifference to their expectations of an egalitarian partnership between men and women. The farmers of the First Aliya, who objected to hiring the halutzim, objected even more strenuously to hiring women laborers and many of the halutzot were obliged to undertake non-agricultural employment, and work as seamstresses or domestics.

The pioneers' first response to the farmers' hostility was to organize themselves into collectives. Though women were accepted into these groups, they were at first merely employed by the men, rather than being equal partners. Furthermore, criteria for women's membership were significantly different from those applied to men; women had to be intelligent, of good character and well-intentioned, not merely efficient workers. Even then, their wages were usually lower than those of the men. Next, the pioneers established their own cooperative settlements, the first of which was founded at Sejera in Galilee in 1907, with six women among its 18 members. Though the women's primary responsibility was providing meals and other domestic services, they also shared the agricultural work and nightly guard duty with the men. Finding that farming the fields was not the most suitable work for women, they experimented with other types of work, notably vegetable gardening and poultry-keeping.

As a result of the Sejera experience, one of the women members, Hanna Maisel (Shohat), who had studied agriculture abroad before coming to Sejera in 1909, founded the Agriculture School for Women at Kineret in 1911, encouraged by Arthur Ruppin of the Palestine Office and financially assisted by a group of Women Zionists in Germany. The expertise thus gained by some women, as well as an increased demand for more members from the Workers' Groups, enabled them to determine the terms under which they returned to these groups. Some preferred to join separate, self-supporting women's groups. In such groups of six—ten, they were able to act as significant mentors for younger women, sometimes moving together from place to place in search of new employment.

The women's experience in cooperative aid proved to be useful training for their political struggle for equal representation in decision-making forums. In 1914, in protest at the failure of the Galilee Agricultural Union to invite a woman representative to its fifth conference, the Women's Workers Movement (Tenu'at ha-Po'alot) was established, led by Ada Maimon. The women convened their own conference, with 30 delegates representing 209 workers from Judea and Galilee. At the four further conferences held before the end of World War I, various issues constantly reemerged as demanding response: the need for adequate training and sources of employment, the need to expand women's role beyond the kitchen and laundry, the men's failure to comprehend or support women's endeavors and yearning for equality, and the problem of combining child-care with gainful employment. The solution found for the last of these was the collectivization of child-care, but it is significant that, while the entire community was held responsible for covering expenses incurred in building child-care facilities, the care itself was relegated exclusively to women. Even the revolutionary women's movement stopped short of challenging the gender-specific nature of parenting.

Concurrently with the efforts of the Women Workers' Movement, the women members of Ha-Shomer were conducting their own struggle. Twenty-three of the 105-member group were women, but only six enjoyed full membership rights. Despite their yearning for full partnership in all the movement's activities, these women too were relegated to domestic roles, the single women working in the kitchens of the single men. The nomadic nature of Ha-Shomer life prevented the development of an agricultural base which might have provided women with an alternative pioneering role and, consequently, an independent source of status accumulation. Lack of communal child-care and similar services further intensified the women's dissatisfaction, but their anger was particularly directed against their exclusion from decision-making. Following a statement issued in 1917, which indicated that further exclusion would result in women leaving the group, Ha-Shomer's annual meeting decided that women with serviceable qualification would henceforth be eligible for membership, but the organization was disbanded before that decision could be fully implemented.

In 1920, when the Histadrut was founded, the Women Workers' Movement demanded that it recognize the legitimacy of a separate women's council, Mo'etzet ha-Po'alot. This was established in 1921, and conducted a determined struggle to break down occupational barriers and develop non-traditional employment opportunities for women. The ensuing decade was characterized by great innovativeness and an emphasis on women's acquisition of the personal, social, and professional skills necessary for full participation in the creation of a new society, but the 1930s saw a marked weakening of the transformative and creative orientation of the Working Women's Movement and a shift toward the provision of child-care and other services for working mothers, which subsequently remained its major concern.

The issue of women's suffrage was first discussed in 1903, when delegates of the yishuv assembled in Zikhron Ya'akov to decide on the establishment of their first elected body of representatives. On this occasion an overwhelming majority, led by Orthodox Jews of east European origin, decided against granting women voting rights. In June, 1918, another meeting called to compose the constitution for a "Founding Assembly" reached a similar decision, bringing about the foundation of a Women's League (Agudat Nashim) that worked on a local basis to further women's political representation. These local groups joined forces in 1919 to found the Jewish Women's Federation for Equal Rights in Eretz Israel. The majority of members were middle-class urban women who had benefited from a higher degree of education than their rural sisters. In December, 1918, the Founding Assembly passed a resolution granting women the vote, but without referring to their right to be elected. This attempt at a compromise angered both the women and their opponents, leading to frequent postponements in the date of the elections. When these were finally held in April, 1920, separate polling booths were established for the ultra-Orthodox men, who were allowed two votes, one for themselves and one on behalf of their wives. Of the Women's Federation, which ran with its own independent list, seven members were elected who, together with a further seven women elected by the various workers' parties, constituted 4.5% of the total number of representatives.

Only in 1925 were the principles of equal voting and election rights finally accepted, with 103 representatives voting in favor and 53 against. Nevertheless, on a local level women remained discriminated against until 1941 and even at the end of the 1980s over 25% of moshavim and villages still denied women the right to vote.

The modern State of Israel has from its inception assured political equality to women, expressing this assumption in the 1948 Declaration of Independence. However, this equality is in fact confined primarily to enfranchisement. Israeli women vote equally with men, but they are elected well below their proportion in the general population. In none of the eleven Knessets elected between 1949 and 1988 did women constitute more than 10% of members. In the Seventh—Ninth Knessets, only 6.7% of members were women; in the 10th and 11th, 7.4% and in the 12th, 5.6%. In the late 1980s a woman mayor was still a rarity; less than 8% of elected members of local government were women.

This striking disproportion was further evidence of the discrepancy between principle and practice obtaining in virtually all issues of equality between the sexes. For example, though Israel was the first state to institute compulsory military service for women, conscription was in fact far from universal since women could request exemption on a variety of grounds and were, in any case, legally exempt or discharged from service if they were married or pregnant. Consequently, only approximately 65% of 18-year-old women were conscripted for their two years' compulsory service (as against men's three years). Women were eligible for reserve duty only to the age of 24 (compared with 55 for men), many of them receiving exemption immediately upon completing their compulsory service. No women served in the front line after the War of Independence, the dominant conception of the Women's Corps being that inherited from the British Auxiliary Territorial Service, in which a considerable number of women from Palestine served during World War II. In the 1980s, and particularly during the 1983–1988 period when Amira Dotan (the first woman to attain the rank of Brigadier-General, which is the norm for heads of all army corps) headed the Women's Corps, an increasing number of women were integrated into the various units of the Israel Defense Forces (IDF), acting as training officers of future combat forces, among other new positions. By 1985, almost 60% of the occupations existing in the IDF were, in principle, open to women, compared to only 29.6% in 1976. Nevertheless, the general taboo on women's service in active combat continued to restrict them to non-combat functions, while they still constituted the overwhelming majority of clerical and service forces. In addition, few women were able to attain senior rank and comparatively few selected a professional career in the defense forces.

Similar anomalies characterized the role and status of women in the Israeli economy. Between 1954 and 1988, the proportion of women in the civilian labor force grew from 21% to 40% and among Jewish women to 45%. Of all non-singles, i.e. married, widowed, or divorced, Jewish women, 46.6% were in the civilian labor force in 1988. The more educated the woman, the more likely she was to be employed, so that participation rates for women with 16 or more years of education was the same as for men (77%). Since a continually increasing number of women attended university, more women were likely to enter the work force with the passage of time. (In the academic year of 1987–88, women constituted 50.3% of students for the first degree, 48.4% of students for a second degree, and 40.7% of doctoral candidates.)

However, women are heavily concentrated in only three of the nine aggregated occupational categories—semi-professional and technical workers, clerical, and service workers, in each of which they constituted approximately 60% of the total employed. Moreover, despite the Equal Pay for Equal Work Law introduced in 1965 and amended in 1973 to apply to work that is essentially equal, women's real earnings were only approximately 71% of men's, a drop from 78% a decade earlier. This was partly because the law applied only to the basic wage, while real earnings include the many fringe benefits such as car allowances which accrue primarily to men. It was also partly the result of the sex segregation which has ghettoized women into lower-paying service occupations.

As for the theoretically egalitarian kibbutzim, work there became increasingly segregated according to sex: by 1988 75% of the women members were employed in services and education, while 65% of men work in the production occupations, which were more highly regarded. Similarly, in elected positions relating to kibbutz government and administration, women were to be found, if at all, primarily as heads of the education and culture committees or, at best, in the secretariat or work committees; no woman headed a kibbutz industry.

In general a large proportion of married women elected to work only part-time, in order to fulfill their family roles as wives and mothers, thus effectively denying themselves the opportunities for promotion and/or managerial authority associated with full-time employment. In 1987, 44.8% of employed women worked part-time (compared with 17.6% of men).

Israeli labor legislation traditionally protected and favored working mothers. The Women's Employment Act (1954) granted women 12 weeks' maternity leave with pay.

No woman could be dismissed on grounds of pregnancy or maternity, and in certain professional areas working mothers' salaries were calculated on a more liberal scale than that of their male colleagues, so that the woman's full-time job involved fewer hours of work than the man's.

Ongoing debate regarding the advantages and disadvantages of protective legislation led to considerable legislative revisions during the 1980s. Restrictions on nightwork were rescinded in 1987. 1988 saw not only legislation mandating equal retirement age for both sexes but also a major revision of the Equal Opportunities in Employment Law of 1981, providing for parental leave. Certain collective agreements now permitted both parents to utilize their sick leave for care of other family members—a privilege previously restricted to women. However, changes in legislation did not necessarily change behavior patterns, and considerable educational efforts remained to be made in order to induce the average Israeli man to do more than "lend a hand."

Undoubtedly, the schism between traditional beliefs, dictating women's primary roles as being the home-based familial ones of wife and mother, and modern egalitarianism, which typified the early years of renewed Jewish settlement in Eretz Israel, lay at the root of the paradoxes and anomalies that characterized the status of women in late 20th-century Israel. All issues of personal status (e.g., marriage and divorce) fell under the sole jurisdiction of the religious courts, in which all the judges were Orthodox men. In officially sanctioned religious rituals, women were segregated from men and banned from any public role. Thus Jewish women in Israel, as elsewhere, found themselves "second-class citizens" not only in the important realm of spirituality, but also in that cycle of ritual which constituted a universal element of the life of a Jewish male, whether or not religiously observant. While Diaspora Jewry developed alternative denominations, such as Conservative, Reform, or Liberal Judaism, as well as a distinctly new liberal "Modern Orthodoxy," no such frameworks attained legal recognition as a religious authority in Israel, where traditional Orthodox practice was the law.

In a resolutely secular state, absence of ritual alternatives was less distressing to the majority of women (and men) than the discriminations and apparent injustices frequently found in the workings of the religious courts; thus, while only a few Israeli women attempted to develop alternative types of feminist ritual, an increasing number of grassroot and mainstream women's groups and organizations actively advocated reform of the religious courts and alleviation of the distress of deserted wives and those denied a *get* (bill of divorce) by their recalcitrant husbands.

An increasingly active women's movement, a greater readiness to identify as feminists (to be found even in the traditional and very established women's organizations, which for several decades devoted themselves primarily to education and welfare), as well as a marked increase in media attention to women and women-related issues are evidence of changing attitudes. Nonetheless, a 1987 survey by the Israel Women's Network indicated that of the 241 recommendations made by the Prime Minister's Commission on the Status of Women in Israel (an *ad hoc* body appointed in 1975 and chaired by Ora Namir, which submitted a comprehensive report in February, 1978), only 71 had so far been implemented. Public policy lags behind public sentiments.

Women's status continued to be considered (even by many women) a secondary issue, overshadowed by political party considerations. Since the eradication of gender discrimination and the creation of equal opportunity for women and men were not yet perceived as central to the essence of a modern state, much less as the basis of public policy, education, and social norms, there appeared to be little hope for any radical changes towards the utopian realization of full and equal partnership, egalitarian ideals which inspired the 19th-century women pioneers of the Second Aliya. A. SHALVI—D.N. IZRAELI

WOMEN'S INTERNATIONAL ZIONIST ORGANIZATION. *See* WIZO.

WOODHEAD COMMISSION. Commission under Sir John Woodhead, appointed in 1938 by the British government to explore possible ways of dividing Palestine into two self-sufficient states, Jewish and Arab, as suggested by the *Peel Commission. The statement made by the Peel Commission that the British Mandate for Palestine was unworkable brought many new factors into play pending the change in the political status of Palestine. Some Arab elements nearly agreed to the British proposals, but, faced with adamant opposition on the part of the Palestinian Arabs, they demurred. After some debate, the Zionist movement finally agreed to consider the British proposals. The League of Nations asserted its right to approve or reject any plan concerning the political status of a country under the League's auspices. On the other hand, local Arab opposition and terror were growing, and British prestige was diminishing owing to the German-Italian rapprochement and the advance of the Nazis.

In this situation, the Woodhead Commission was appointed either to stall for time or to examine the practicability of the Peel recommendations. It was a technical commission. Under its terms of reference, it used the Peel recommendations as the basis for its agenda but could suggest modifications. The Woodhead Commission had to suggest boundaries to make the existence of two self-sufficient states feasible; this meant the smallest possible number of Arabs and the smallest possible areas of Arab lands and enterprises in the Jewish area, and vice versa.

The Commission, whose report was published in October, 1938, considered three alternative plans of *partition. The first (Plan A) was that of the Peel proposal, which the Commission unanimously advised against, since under it the Jewish State would have included a large Arab minority and much Arab-owned land. The second (Plan B) reduced the area of the suggested Jewish State by making Galilee a Mandatory area, while a portion south of the Jerusalem enclave that had been destined for the Jewish State was to be given to the Arab State. This plan was recommended by only one of the four members of the Commission. The third (Plan C), which had the backing of the chairman and one other member, reduced the projected Jewish State to a coastal strip between Zikhron Ya'akov and Rehovot and proposed the inclusion of two additional areas in the British Mandatory territory: (*a*) Haifa and the Haifa Bay area, the Jezreel and Bet She'an (Beisan) Valleys, the Huleh Basin, and all of Galilee; and (*b*) the Negev. The fourth member, while agreeing that Plan C was the best that could be designed under the Commission's terms of reference, regarded both Plans B and C as impracticable.

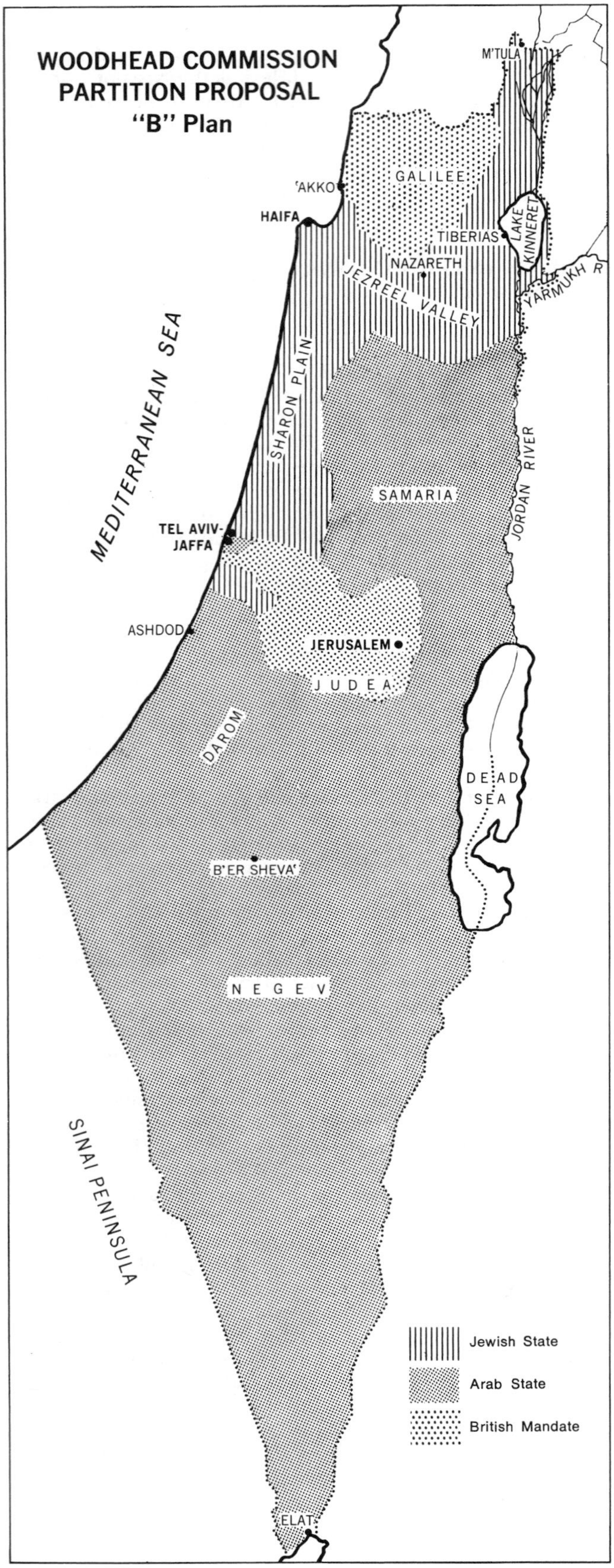
WOODHEAD COMMISSION
PARTITION PROPOSAL
"B" Plan
M'TULA
'AKKO
HAIFA
GALILEE
TIBERIAS
LAKE KINNERET
NAZARETH
JEZREEL VALLEY
YARMUKH R
MEDITERRANEAN SEA
SHARON PLAIN
JORDAN RIVER
SAMARIA
TEL AVIV-JAFFA
ASHDOD
JERUSALEM
JUDEA
DAROM
DEAD SEA
B'ER SHEVA'
NEGEV
SINAI PENINSULA
ELAT
Jewish State
Arab State
British Mandate

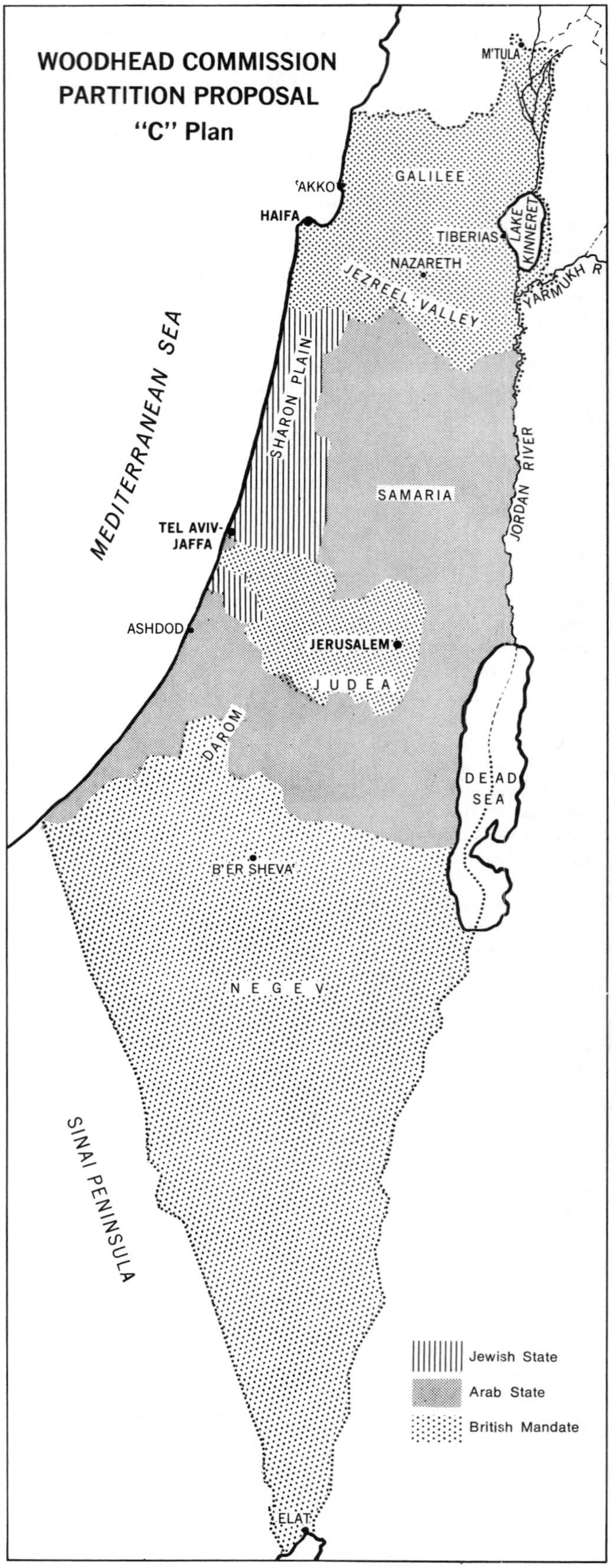
WOODHEAD COMMISSION
PARTITION PROPOSAL
"C" Plan
M'TULA
'AKKO
HAIFA
GALILEE
TIBERIAS
LAKE KINNERET
NAZARETH
JEZREEL VALLEY
YARMUKH R
MEDITERRANEAN SEA
SHARON PLAIN
JORDAN RIVER
SAMARIA
TEL AVIV-JAFFA
ASHDOD
JERUSALEM
JUDEA
DAROM
DEAD SEA
B'ER SHEVA'
NEGEV
SINAI PENINSULA
ELAT
Jewish State
Arab State
British Mandate

The Commission pointed out that under either plan, while the budget of the Jewish State was likely to show a substantial surplus, the budgets of the Arab State (including Transjordan) and of the mandated territories were likely to show substantial deficits. On economic grounds, a customs union between the two states and the mandated territories was essential, but any such scheme would be inconsistent with the grant of fiscal independence to the Arab and Jewish states. The Commission therefore concluded that "on a strict interpretation of their terms of reference, they have no alternative but to report that they are unable to recommend boundaries for the proposed areas which will afford a reasonable prospect of the eventual establishment of self-supporting Arab and Jewish States."

On the basis of the report of the Woodhead Commission (officially called the Palestine Partition Commission) the British government declared in November, 1938, that it was faced with the necessity of finding an alternative solution for the Palestine problem. With this end in view, the government proposed to invite representatives of the Palestinian Arabs and of the neighboring Arab states, on the one hand, and of the Jewish Agency, on the other, to a conference in London (*see* ST. JAMES'S CONFERENCE). I. KOLATT

WORKMEN'S CIRCLE. US Jewish labor-oriented fraternal order conducting a program of social, cultural, and educational activities. Organized in 1900, it had 210 branches with a combined membership of 55,000 in the United States and Canada in 1987. It had $75 million of insurance in force, and its assets totaled $13,500,000. During its early years it largely shared the assimilationist views prevailing among most Jewish labor leaders of the time, but it embarked on a more positive Jewish program during World War I.

In addition to supporting the American labor movement and the labor movement in Israel, the Workmen's Circle participated in efforts to improve the condition of the Jewish people. It worked with the People's Relief Committee during World War I. In 1934 it founded the Jewish Labor Committee, remaining the mainstay of the committee throughout the latter's existence. It also sponsored a network of Jewish secular schools and was a leading source of Yiddish educational and cultural materials.

An anti-Zionist spirit pervaded the national bodies of the Workmen's Circle until the 1940s, although Zionist-oriented branches had always existed without interference. In the post-World War II years and with the establishment of the State of Israel, the Workmen's Circle gave increasing attention to the support of Israel and its institutions. In 1987 it had fundraising divisions for the Histadrut, ORT, United Jewish Appeal, and State of Israel Bonds. In the 1980s it raised millions of dollars for an absorption center in Ashkelon and dormitories for Kibbutz Lohamei ha-Geta'ot. In 1987 it sold $300,000 worth of Israel Bonds.

Its current publications include *Kultur un Lebn* (Culture and Life) in Yiddish and the *Workmen's Circle Call* in English.

WORLD COMMITTEE FOR PALESTINE. International organization of Christian groups supporting the establishment of a Jewish State in Palestine. The initiative for the formation of this worldwide body came from the American Christian Palestine Committee (*see* AMERICAN PALESTINE COMMITTEE), which, in 1945 convened an International Christian Conference for Palestine. The nearly 50 delegates who attended were prominent in politics, government, education, and journalism. They included Sir Ellsworth Flavelle, of Canada; Judge K.J. van Erpecum, president of the Supreme Court of Dutch Guiana; the widow of Gen. Orde Charles Wingate, from England; J.A.C. Allum, mayor of Auckland, New Zealand; Dr. Henry A. Atkinson, Congresswomen Helen Gahagan Douglas, Dr. Walter C. Lowdermilk, Dr. Carl Hermann Voss, and Sen. Robert F. Wagner, from the United States; and Dr. Pedro Zuloaga, Venezuelan representative on the Displaced Persons Committee of the UN Relief and Rehabilitation Administration (UNRRA).

The International Christian Conference for Palestine formed the World Committee for Palestine, including coordination of the activities of the various national pro-Palestine committees; planning for a more effective expression of "the aroused conscience of Christendom to its responsibility for the establishment of Jewish security"; drawing attention to the plight of the European Jewish survivors of World War II; and fostering the concern of the nations of the world that Palestine should become "legally and in fact" the Jewish National Homeland.

More specifically, the Committee urged the free immigration of Jews into Palestine under the administration of the Jewish Agency; the unhampered right of the Jewish people to purchase and settle on land throughout Palestine; and the ultimate establishment of Palestine as a free and democratic Jewish Commonwealth with international rights guaranteed through the United Nations, equal civil, religious, and cultural rights of all groups, separation of church and state, and the protection of the holy places under international law. The headquarters of the Committee was located at first in Washington and later in New York.

By June, 1947, the Committee included 30 non-Jewish national organizations in the United States, Canada, Latin America, Scandinavia, the United Kingdom, and the Union of South Africa, their chairmen forming the Executive Council of the World Committee. G. HIRSCHLER

WORLD CONFEDERATION OF UNITED ZIONISTS. The World Confederation is an heir to the central stream in the Zionist movement, the stream to which Herzl and Weizmann belonged, which has been characterized by unswerving devotion to the ideals of the movement throughout its history. This body outspokenly supported the demand for Jewish statehood, which received ratification at the 22nd Zionist Congress. Here the cornerstone was laid for the State of Israel, resting on the foundation of the Balfour Declaration. One of the far-reaching resolutions adopted at the founding conference of the confederation in 1946 provided for the creation of a constructive enterprise fund (Keren L'Mifalim Konstructivim—known as KMK) to serve as a financial arm of the movement for the purpose of directing the General Zionists' work in the land of Israel and helping in absorption of newcomers. Even though during this period the confederation can register achievements, it became increasingly evident that it was a house divided. In an atmosphere of tension and unease, the 3rd World Conference of World Confederation convened in Jerusalem in 1956 on the occasion of the 24th Zionist Congress. It was a clash between the two irreconcilable camps: those who favored identification with parties in Israel and those who remained faithful to traditional principles of general Zionism not to interfere in Israel's politics.

In March 1958 the reconstituted Confederation of General Zionists met in London, headed by representatives from Hadassah, the Zionist Federation of Great Britain, and the continents of Europe and Latin America. The conference adopted a platform outlining the aims and purposes of the confederation, without identification with any political parties in Israel. Dr. Israel Goldstein and Mrs. Rose Halpern were unanimously elected co-chairmen, and Kalman Sultanik was elected executive vice-chairman of the reconstituted World Confederation.

In 1971 the World Confederation of General Zionists changed its name to the World Confederation of United Zionists in order to emphasize its non-party character. The confederation advocated a change in the structure of the WZO, considering its actual party structure obsolete and demanding its depolitization. The World Confederation of United Zionists is the largest Diaspora grouping in the WZO. It is unaffiliated with any political parties in the Israeli Knesset and derives its inspiration and strength from the whole spectrum of Israeli life. At the last Zionist Congress in July 1992 in Jerusalem, the World Confederation of United Zionists held its conference with 140 delegates and 80 delegates to the Congress, the largest Zionist union from the Diaspora.

K. SULTANIK

WORLD FEDERATION OF SEPHARDI COMMUNITIES. In the 1920s, the Sephardim attempted to form a world organization which would also operate within the framework of the Zionist movement. On the eve of the 13th Zionist Congress (1923), the Sephardi delegates from Palestine and from the Diaspora met to discuss the intensification of Zionist propaganda among Sephardi Jewry, increased Sephardi participation in Zionist activities, and the building up of Eretz Israel. Recognizing that Zionism had not sufficiently penetrated the Sephardi community, they resolved on the establishment of a bureau in Jerusalem to prepare a world convention of the representatives of Sephardi Jewry. This convention would consolidate the world unity of Sephardi Jews, who would then seek formal representation in the institutions of the Zionist movement, with their members taking part in determining policies and in decision-making processes. Particular stress was laid on the point that the new framework was not being created to lead to a scission within the Jewish people, but rather to contribute to its unification.

Dr. Yitzhak Levi was elected president of the newly-formed bureau; Yitzhak Eliachar and Abraham Elmalech served as vice presidents. The bureau's seat was in Jerusalem and it had branches in Hebron, Haifa, and Jaffa, and also in the Diaspora.

After prolonged preparations, 62 delegates met in Vienna in 1925 on the eve of the 14th Congress, representing 15 countries, including Palestine, Bulgaria, Greece, Yugoslavia, and Austria, which sent most of the delegates. The convention approved as its objective the cultural, national, and religious development of the Sephardi community, and an increased Sephardi participation in the work in Palestine. The means for achieving these objectives included: the publication of a journal, the circulation of relevant printed material, the utilization of emissaries, the training of teachers and religious functionaries, the establishment of institutions for promotion of immigration to Palestine, and rural settlement, and the exploitation of the influence of the Sephardi delegates at Zionist Congresses. It was expressly laid down that the association would not intervene in the internal affairs of the local communities. Moses Peixotto of Manchester was chosen as president of the association. A Palestine executive based in Jerusalem, and a Diaspora executive based in Paris, were also elected. In mid-1926 the association was formally registered in Jerusalem. In its initial years the association established several branches in Palestine—Tel Aviv, Jaffa, Haifa, and Safed -, and throughout the world—Beirut, Damascus, Aleppo, Cairo, Alexandria, Belgrade, Sarajevo, Munster, Nice, Skopje, Polipopoli, Vienna, Paris, Manchester, New York, Rochester, N.Y., and in Latin America in Argentina, Uruguay, Brazil, Peru, Chile, and Cuba.

The establishment of a world framework for Sephardi Jewry as a part of the World Zionist Organization received the support of major personalities in the Sephardi communities and in the World Zionist Organization, including Chaim Weizmann, and Menahem Ussishkin and the Zionist Executive in Palestine.

The principal opponents of the idea among the Sephardi communities were the Jews of Bulgaria, who maintained that even in Herzl's time they had participated in the Zionist Congresses and in all Zionist work, and did not consider themselves anything but full partners with the Ashkenazim both in rights and in obligations. They negated Sephardi isolationism, maintaining that the Sephardim should join the rest of the community and fulfill their obligations. In their opinion, most of the bureau's objectives were identical with the objectives of the Zionist Organization and could be realized without the Sephardi Association.

While the representatives from Palestine had played a decisive role in the organization of the Vienna Convention, their role in the interterritorial conventions held in 1930 (Belgrade), 1935 (London), and 1938 (Amsterdam) was more marginal. At the 1930 Convention, the delegates, reacting to Peixotto's proposed course of action, stressed that all activities for the building of the yishuv would be coordinated with the national institutions. Sephardi Jewry throughout the world should be asked to make very generous contributions to the national funds, but on express condition that their money would be used only for Sephardi Jewry in Palestine. The demand was to be aggressive enough to pressure the Zionist Executive into recognizing its mistakes in this regard.

At the 1935 convention the association's name was changed to the World Federation of Sephardi Communities; new regulations were determined and a program of action was drawn up, which did not include activity in Palestine. The fundamental objective of the program was an amelioration in the educational and cultural condition of the Sephardi communities in the world, while the political issues were to be left to the official institutions. In this way joint activity of the members of the various parties was made possible alongside the nonparty members, together with Sephardi communities which did not identify with the political line of the Sephardim in Palestine (such as the Bulgarians). The 1938 convention in Amsterdam resolved on the creation of a rabbinical college in Jerusalem. The establishment of a Jewish Agency Section for Sephardi Affairs was greeted positively, and it was decided to insist on appropriate representation for the Sephardim in all the national institutions in Palestine and on the safeguarding of their rights. Nonetheless, in comparison with the Vienna Convention, this was a significant retreat with regard to Zionism and to settlement in Palestine.

During World War II the World Federation ceased activity. Shortly after the war a new central committee, organized in New York, laid down new regulations and invited community councils in Palestine to join it; the Sephardi community council in Jerusalem responded to the invitation. This committee, like its predecessors, wished to convene a world Sephardi convention with the primary objectives of unifying the Sephardi forces and fostering education and agriculture. Because of the extensive activity and the events surrounding the establishment of the State of Israel and the War of Independence, the convention was postponed, and was held eventually in Paris in 1951. The World Sephardi Federation was revived, with the aim of strengthening the link between the Sephardi communities and the State of Israel.

Other congresses were held in May, 1954, and in November, 1987, both in Jerusalem. Over the last twenty years, and principally since the election of Nissim Gaon as its president (1973) and during the presidency of Eliahu Eliachar in Israel, the World Sephardi Federation has initiated a Department for Sephardi communities in the World Zionist Organization. It has worked for the development of a training program for community activists at Israel's universities and has participated in the scholarship funds for Sephardi research students, and in activities for fostering of the Sephardi heritage and the dissemination of this heritage among the general public. A. HAIM

WORLD HEBREW FEDERATION. *See* BRIT IVRIT OLAMIT.

WORLD JEWISH CONGRESS. Organization established in 1936 as "a voluntary association of representative Jewish bodies, communities, and organizations throughout the world," whose purposes are:

"a) To foster the unity of the Jewish people, to strive for the fulfillment of its aspirations, and to ensure the continuity and development of its religious, spiritual, cultural, and social heritage." It seeks: "(1) To intensify the bonds of world Jewry with Israel as the central creative force in Jewish life and to strengthen the ties of solidarity among Jewish communities everywhere; (2) To secure the rights, status, and interests of Jews and Jewish communities, and to defend them wherever they are denied, violated, or imperiled; (3) To encourage and assist the creative development of Jewish social, religious, and cultural life throughout the world; (4) To coordinate the efforts of Jewish communities and organizations with respect to the political, economic, social, religious, and cultural problems of the Jewish people; (5) To represent and act on behalf of its participating communities and organizations before governmental, intergovernmental, and other international authorities with respect to matters which concern the Jewish people as a whole.

b) "to cooperate with all peoples on the basis of universal ideals of peace, freedom, and justice."

Its constitution states that "Participation in the World Jewish Congress shall in no way affect the autonomy of Jewish communities and organizations with regard to their respective internal and religious affairs nor imply any authoriztion of the World Jewish Congress to intervene in the domestic political affairs of their countries." Leaders in the forefront of the Zionist movement initiated the establishment of an international Jewish organization with the object of securing and defending the civic, religious, and political rights of the Jews in the Diaspora.

Just as the shock of the Dreyfus affair and the tragedies of persecution, pogroms, and discrimination in Tsarist Russia and Romania represented a major impulse for the creation of the World Zionist Organization (WZO), so the insecurity of the large Jewish minorities of eastern Europe, arising out of World War I, drove home the necessity of concerted international Jewish action to deal with the grave problems of the future rights and freedoms of Jews and Jewish communities.

In the United States, the *American Jewish Congress was established in 1916 but, owing to the war situation, its first meeting could not take place until mid-December, 1918. The Congress resolved that as soon as peace was declared, it would "instruct its European delegation to take necessary and effective steps in cooperation with representative Jewish bodies in other countries for the convening of the World Jewish Congress". It elected a delegation which was to proceed to the Paris Peace Conference and which included Julian W. Mack, Stephen S. Wise, Louis D. Marshall, Jacob de Haas, and Nahman Syrkin.

By the time the Peace Conference assembled, a large number of Jewish delegations from many lands had found their way to Paris. It became clear to responsible Jewish statesmen that their first task was to coordinate the activities of these delegations. On 25 March 1919, a **Comité des Délégations Juives auprès de la Conférence de Paix* (Committee of Jewish Delegations to the Peace Conference) was formed, composed of delegations from Palestine, the United States, Canada, Russia, the Ukraine, Poland, eastern Galicia, Romania, Transylvania, Bukovina, Czechoslovakia, Italy, Yugoslavia, and Greece, speaking in the name of democratically elected Jewish congresses, national Jewish councils, or federated Jewish communities. The WZO and the B'nai B'rith were also represented on the *Comité*. The *Comité* claimed to be the spokesman of more than 10 million Jews. Its Secretary-General was Leo Motzkin.

Only the *Alliance Israélite Universelle* and the Joint Foreign Committee (of the Board of Deputies of British Jews and the Anglo-Jewish Association) separated themselves from the others. The *Alliance* would not even hear of national rights advocating only the recognition of Jews as a religious community, and the Joint Foreign Committee decided to stand by the *Alliance*, although it was in favor of the minorities being granted "the autonomous management of their religious, educational, charitable, and other cultural institutions".

The *Comité* was intended to be an *ad hoc* organization for the duration of the Peace Conference. However, it soon appeared that the insertion of the basic Jewish demands in the peace treaties was not an end but a beginning, and that unremitting vigilance would be essential to ensure their implementation. Accordingly the *Comité* decided, at the end of the Paris Peace Conference, to drop the words *auprès de la Conférence de Paix* and to remain a permanent body. At the same time that it was taking action on every threat to, or restriction of, Jewish rights, the *Comité* engaged in the task of bringing into existence a world-wide Jewish organization which would be recognized by Jews and non-Jews alike as the Jewish representative body to deal with the problems of the Diaspora.

Under the impact of the rising tide of Nazism, efforts to establish such a body assumed an even greater urgency. Preparatory conferences of Jewish, chiefly Zionist, leaders from 20 countries were held in 1932, 1933, and 1934 in Geneva. A resolution of the 19th Zionist Congress (1935) called upon " Zionists and Zionist groups to take part in the World Jewish Congress and in the preparations for it". In August, 1936, again in Geneva, the participating organizations, through 280 delegates from 33 countries, formally established and adopted the principles for a constitution of the World Jewish Congress (WJC). Stephen S. Wise was elected chairman of the Executive, Nahum Goldmann chairman of the Administrative Committee, and Louis Lipsky chairman of the General Council. Julian W. Mack was elected president.

Having established a political office in Geneva at the League of Nations, with Nahum Goldmann in charge (the WJC head office was in Paris), the WJC engaged in intensive political and diplomatic activity at the League and elsewhere to combat Nazi anti-Jewish attacks, to deal with the many grave Jewish problems arising from them, and by extensive propaganda to induce world opinion to realize that Hitler's terrorist acts against German, Austrian, and Czechoslovak Jews were only a prelude to his real and ultimate objective—a Nazi "New Order" for all the world. A major activity initiated by the newly-created WJC was an appeal for a world-wide Jewish economic and financial boycott of Nazi Germany. However, Jewish response was inadequate and the campaign failed.

After the outbreak of World War II in 1939, and the Nazi occupation of the major part of Europe, the headquarters of the WJC moved to New York. A parallel center was developed simultaneously in London, while the WJC maintained its Geneva office whose head, Dr. Gerhart M. Riegner, in August 1942 informed leaders of the WJC and, through them, the Allies, of the "Final Solution" decided upon by the Nazis in January that year. At first incredulous, the Allies obtained confirmation of the news from "independent sources" and on 17 December 1942, issued a joint declaration promising retribution for the perpetrators. The major tasks of the WJC during the war were (1) to inform governments, politicians, and the world press of the persecution and murder of Jews throughout Nazi-occupied Europe; (2) to prevail upon the Allies to assist in the rescue and relief of Jews living under Nazi terror; (3) to make plans for the rehabilitation of surviving Jewish victims of Nazism; and (4) to formulate internationally recognized political and legal measures to punish the Nazis found guilty of crimes against the Jews, to obtain indemnities from Germany for surviving Jewish victims, restitution for Jewish private and communal properties expropriated and destroyed by the Nazis, and global reparations for the human and material losses suffered by the Jewish people through Nazi crimes. These aims were set forth in detail by the WJC War Emergency Conference in Atlantic City, N.J. (November 1944). With the exception of the rescue of European Jews, this program was, in large measure, successfully carried out, in stages, between 1945 and 1965. Perhaps the greatest single achievement in which the leaders of the WJC played a decisive role was the signing by Germany of the Luxembourg Agreements in 1952 (*see* GERMAN-ISRAEL AGREEMENT), which eventually resulted in billions of marks being paid to the government of Israel and to the large numbers of victims who had settled in Israel. Both directly and through the Conference on Jewish Material Claims against Germany, which it helped to establish, the WJC played a notable role in the reconstruction of the Jewish communities of Europe. Restitution and compensation legislation was also enacted by the Federal German Republic for individual victims of Nazism and additional legislation was enacted and funds provided to compensate Jewish refugees, victims of Nazism who left their native east European countries after the Federal Compensation Law (1953) came into effect.

Since World War II the international character of the WJC has underlined its many political and diplomatic actions to assure and defend the rights and freedoms of the Jews in many countries. Negotiations with the leaders of independence movements of Morocco and Tunisia resulted in complete civic equality and religious and political liberties for the Jewish citizens of these countries and assured the survival of their institutions and freedom of Jewish emigration when the two countries became sovereign states in 1955. Similar formal assurances were obtained by a resolution of the United Nations when Libya attained independent status. However, the new kingdom of Libya failed to honor its undertaking. In cooperation with its affiliated Jewish communities of Latin America, the WJC has taken energetic political action to combat and suppress widespread and dangerous anti-Semitic movements in South American countries. In 1941, the WJC and the American Jewish Congress set up the Institute of Jewish Affairs in New York to study problems facing Jewry after World War II. The IJA moved to London in 1966 and has become an internationally recognized research body. Since the 1950s, the grave problem of the religious, cultural, and communal discrimination and frustration suffered by Soviet Jewry has been a major preoccupation of the WJC as has the emergence of neo-Nazi and anti-Semitic organizations since the war.

The WJC was the first international Jewish non-governmental organization (NGO) to be granted consultative status with the UN Economic and Social Council (ECOSOC) (1947) and the UN Educational, Scientific, and Cultural Organization (UNESCO, 1945). It is also represented at the International Labor Office (ILO). In June 1961 "relations of general cooperation" were established between the Organization of American States (OAS) and the WJC. The WJC has consultative status, category 1, at the Council of Europe. It has been closely and actively associated with the UN Human Rights Commission and played a prominent role in the framing of the Universal Declaration of Human Rights. The WJC has also been in the forefront of the movement for improvement of Christian-Jewish Relations.

Presidents of the WJC have been: Rabbi Dr. Stephen S. Wise (1936–1949); Dr. Nahum Goldmann (1949–1977); Philip N. Klutznick (1977–1979); Edgar M. Bronfman (1979 Acting—and from 1981, President).

Its four Branches, (Israel, North America, Latin American Jewish Congress, European Jewish Congress) embrace Jewish communities in 66 countries and 26 regional and international organizations. The WJC's organs are the Plenary Assembly, the General Council, the Governing Board, and the Executive. Headquarters are in New York, with offices in Jerusalem, London, Paris, Geneva, Rome, and Buenos Aires.

The WJC is in a unique position to be of service to the State of Israel. It has done so effectively on a number of occasions since 1948, particularly in asserting the legal right and freedom of Jews to emigrate to Israel. In certain countries, where official restrictions on this freedom had been imposed, it negotiated successfully for their removal. The WJC maintains close relations with appropriate departments of the government of Israel on matters of common interest in relation to Jews in other lands and is in special

World Jewish Congress leaders at a meeting of the Conference on Jewish Material Claims against Germany, New York, 1959. Left to right: Alex Easterman, Monroe Abbey, Nahum Goldmann, Saul Hayes, Hendrik van Dam, Gerhart Riegner, Shad Polier, Maurice L. Perlzweig, José Ventura, and Isaac Schwarzbart. [Zionist Archives]

relationship with the World Zionist Organization.

A.L. EASTERMAN—A.M. MELAMET—E. EPPLER

WORLD LABOR ZIONIST MOVEMENT. The product of a number of mergers in the Labor Zionist ranks throughout the years (*see* LABOR ZIONISM). The movement serves in 20 countries on five continents as the roof organization of political bodies, all of which have a common belief in the principles of Zionist Socialism and support the platform of the Israel Labor Party. Its goals are: fostering immigration to Israel, to which end it supports pioneering activities; active participation in local, national, and world Zionist institutions; rejuvenation of the Zionist organization as an ideological movement with the purpose of bringing about a revolution within the Jewish people and in the situation of the individual Jew; expansion of Jewish education in the Diaspora, which is Israel-centered, and based on the national identity of the Jewish people; and teaching the younger generation the principles of Zionism.

The World Labor Zionist Movement's governing body is a World Convention held every four years, which formulates policy and delineates the elections to the World Zionist Congress, insuring that every affiliate is represented by at least one delegate. The Convention elects the Chairman, Secretary-General, the World Bureau (consisting of 101 members and responsible for the running of the Movement during the inter-Convention period), and a five-person Control Committee. The decision-making body consists of the Movement's representatives on the World Zionist Organization Executive and the Zionist Council Presidium, as well as, *ex officio*, the Minister of Absorption, the Israel Labor Party Secretary-General, the Secretary-General of Na'amat, and the Secretary of the United Kibbutz Movement.

Among the activities of the World Labor Zionist Movement are the support of the pioneering youth movement *Habonim-Dror, and assistance in immigration and absorption in Israel of groups of young people; the publication and distribution of materials in various languages, including monthly newssheets (*Background* and *From the Rostrum*), as well as periodicals published in New York, Paris, and Buenos Aires; training activists from Israel and the Diaspora at the Sharett Institute in Jerusalem (established in 1964); working closely with the World Conservative and World Progressive Movements to promote Jewish religious pluralism; and running ideological seminars and conventions for an exchange of views on a national, continental, and international basis.

The World Labor Zionist Movement has associate status in the Socialist International.

Yigal Allon was chairman from 1978 until his death in 1980; Yehiel Leket from 1978 to 1990; and from 1990 Judi Widetsky (formerly secretary-general) was acting chairman.

WORLD UNION OF GENERAL ZIONISTS. Designation assumed in July, 1963, by the General Zionist faction led by Emanuel Neumann. (For the original faction of that name, which was founded in 1931 and split up after 1935, and for the developments leading to the formation of the present organization of that name, *see* GENERAL ZIONISM.) The World Union of General Zionists considers itself a middle-of-the-road faction that wants to see Israel develop as a western-style democracy based on free economic initiative.

In 1970 the World Union of General Zionists included

the Zionist Organization of America (ZOA), the General Zionist organizations of Central and South American countries, Europe, Canada, Australia, and New Zealand, and the Liberal party of the State of Israel. The World Union was governed by two bodies, a World Executive and a World Council. The World Executive, which had headquarters in New York and branch offices in Israel, Argentina, and Europe, included representatives from the United States, Israel, South America, Australia, and New Zealand. Also affiliated with the World Union was an Israeli youth movement, Israel ha-Tze'ira, which had a representative on the Union's World Executive.

In contrast to the World Confederation of United Zionists, the World Union of General Zionists advocates a linkage with the Israeli Liberal Party. The two organizational pillars of the World Union of General Zionists are: the ZOA and the Liberal Party in Israel. Since 1978, the World Union has formed, together with Herut, the Likud alignment in the World Zionist Organization.

B. WEINSTEIN—D. SHA'ARI

WORLD UNION OF JEWISH STUDENTS (WUJS). Organization established at a conference in Antwerp in 1924. Its founder and first chairman was Zvi (Hersch) Lauterpacht, then a doctoral student at the London School of Economics and later a distinguished international lawyer. Its first president, elected in 1925, was Albert Einstein.

WUJS was created largely in response to growing pressure on Jewish students in eastern Europe, particularly as a result of the *numerus clausus* (restriction on numbers of Jews admitted to universities) in Hungary, Poland, and Romania. The *numerus clausus* caused a flood of Jewish students to emigrate to western Europe in hope of gaining admission to university there. Many became destitute, while others flourished. Lauterpacht and Einstein hoped that uniting Jewish students across Europe would create more favorable conditions for Jews seeking higher education. Einstein, who had witnessed student anti-Semitism at first hand as a lecturer in Berlin, was a keen supporter both of the Hebrew University and of plans in the 1920s to establish a Jewish university in Europe under the auspices of the League of Nations.

The early program of WUJS concentrated on three major areas: first, to lobby international bodies such as the League of Nations and International Labor Organization to insure better conditions for Jewish students in eastern Europe; second, to provide assistance to emigré students forced to travel westward; third, to unite all the national Jewish student groupings under one banner in order to campaign for Jewish rights and the development of Zionism.

One of WUJS' first projects was an attempt to establish a student hostel at the Hebrew University in Jerusalem. Land for this purpose was donated by Herbert Bentwich, but the students were unable to raise the necessary funds. After initial enthusiasm, the support for the Union declined in the later 1920s but was revived in 1933 in response to Hitler's rise to power in Germany. Maurice Perlzweig was elected chairman, while Einstein continued as president. Joining the list of vice-presidents were Chaim Weizmann, Sigmund Freud, and Stephen S. Wise. In 1939 the Union's offices were transferred to Switzerland.

After the end of World War II, the Union cooperated closely with the World Jewish Congress in post-war reconstruction in Europe. A WUJS Congress held in Prague in 1948 saluted the establishment of the State of Israel, and in 1949 the Union extended its activities to the United States with the affiliation of the B'nai B'rith Hillel Foundations. At the 1950 Congress Brian Sandelson of Britain was elected chairman, but shortage of funds led the Union once more into decline. In 1962 the Union was revived once more, with Dan Bitan appointed as Secretary-General. A successful Congress (the 13th) held in Jerusalem in 1963 was dominated by the issue of whether to recognize the Jewish student union in Germany. Manfred Gerstenfeld of Switzerland was elected chairman. In 1964 the young Israeli author A.B. Yehoshua became Secretary-General, based in Paris. The 1960s saw the rapid development of WUJS both in Israel and the Diaspora, largely as a coordinating body for national member unions. Prior to 1967, its major campaign was for Soviet Jewry, whose position was deteriorating due to renewed anti-Semitism in the Soviet Union.

In June, 1967, the Union led Jewish student support for Israel, both politically and by organizing groups of volunteers to go to Israel and help the war effort. At the 14th Congress held in Jerusalem in 1967, soon after the end of the Six-Day War, Michael Hunter of Britain was elected chairman. In protest at French policy towards Israel, the headquarters of the Union were transferred from Paris to

World Union of Jewish Students activists protesting Pope's meeting with President Kurt Waldheim, 1987. [World Union of Jewish Students]

London (where they remained until 1979). In 1968 the WUJS Institute in Arad was established to serve as a seminar center for students in Israel and as an absorption center for those wishing to immigrate.

In 1968, WUJS officially joined the World Zionist Organization, and the following year its North American union, Network, was founded. The Jewish Student Press Service, organized by the national Network office in New York, encouraged and assisted the development of well over 100 student publications, primarily in the US and Canada. WUJS sponsored a number of important international conferences in North America and Europe, geared primarily towards Jewish creativity and education. WUJS leaders and members were caught up not only in the renewed Jewish cultural consciousness, but also the heightened political activities of the late 1960s and early 1970s, which created tensions between the generations in the Zionist movement. Many young Jews felt that they should be publicly involved in general student protest movements concerned with apartheid, Biafra, and Vietnam. Objecting, the majority of adult Jewish leaders felt that the students could not afford to dissipate their energies. The adult movement was further antagonized when the 15th WUJS Congress, held in Arad in 1970, adopted the Arad Program, which called for a two-state solution to the Israel-Palestinian conflict. From then on the students and adults were at loggerheads. In 1972, though WUJS narrowly avoided being expelled from the WZO, its budget was cut. Throughout the 1970s the Union was in conflict with the mainstream WZO leadership, until in 1979 the Union was in effect taken over by a specially-created Student Division of the WZO.

Despite these problems, WUJS managed to initiate a number of major educational projects around the world. Among them was Areivim, which trained students and sent them out as volunteers to help develop small Jewish communities around the world.

From 1979 to 1983 WUJS was based in Jerusalem but was hardly active. At the 1983 Congress a number of member unions attempted to wrest control back from the WZO. Danny Katz from Australia was elected chairperson, and when he resigned in 1984 David Makovsky of the US took over. From 1984 to 1986 the Union attempted to reestablish its activities and independence. Links were renewed with the World Jewish Congress and campaigns launched in the traditional areas of education, politics, and aliya. WUJS was particularly active in the resettlement of Ethiopian Jews in Israel and the campaign for Soviet Jewry. In 1987 the 20th Congress was held in Jerusalem, preceded by a gathering of more than 2,000 students from around the world, and Yosef Abramowitz of the US was elected chairperson.

M. KALMAN

WORLD UNION OF ZIONISTS-REVISIONISTS. *See* REVISIONISTS.

WORLD UNION OF ZIONISTS-SOCIALISTS. *See* IHUD OLAMI.

WORLD ZIONIST ORGANIZATION (WZO). Worldwide official organization of the Zionist movement, founded on the initiative of Herzl at the First Zionist Congress (Basle, 1897). Originally known as the Zionist Organization, it came to be called the World Zionist Organization, which name was officially adopted in 1960.

HISTORY

Herzl first suggested the establishment of a body to represent the interests of the Jewish people wishing to establish a National Home for itself in *The Jewish State*, which he published in 1896. The organization he set up a year later in Basle actually represented the realization of the "Society of Jews" described in his treatise. The Zionist Organization was defined as the body "comprising all Jews who accept the Zionist program (*see* BASLE PROGRAM) and pay the *Shekel."

During Herzl's presidency (1897–1904), two of the main financial instruments of the WZO were created: the Jewish Colonial Trust (1899) and the *Jewish National Fund (Keren Kayemet le-Israel) (1901). The same period saw the emergence of the first separate union (*Sonderverband*), the Mizrachi, (1902), which was not a part of the Zionist territorial union, the Zionist roof organizations uniting all Zionist groupings within each country (*see* SEPARATE UNIONS).

Under the presidency of Herzl's successor, David Wolffsohn (1904–11), the seat of the Zionist Organization was transferred from Vienna to Cologne, where Wolffsohn lived. In that period, as well as under the presidency of Otto Warburg (1911–20), emphasis was placed on practical work in Eretz Israel. In 1907 another separate union, the Po'ale Zion, was founded.

The outbreak of World War I not only halted the work in Eretz Israel but also brought organizational activities to a virtual standstill because the battlefronts separated the Zionists in the countries of the Entente from those living in the territories of the Central Powers. The Zionist head office, which from 1911 on was in Berlin, was unable to maintain contact with Zionists in the western countries and Russia. Therefore in 1915 a Zionist liaison office was opened in neutral Copenhagen (*see* COPENHAGEN BUREAU). With the issuance of the Balfour Declaration (1917), the political center of gravity was transferred to London, where a World Zionist Conference, the first Zionist gathering after the war, met in 1920 (*see* LONDON ZIONIST CONFERENCE of 1920). At this conference large-scale settlement activities were initiated through the establishment of the *Keren ha-Yesod (Palestine Foundation Fund), and Chaim Weizmann was elected president of the WZO, which position he retained until 1931.

At the 16th Zionist Congress (1929) the expanded *Jewish Agency was set up. After the 18th Congress (1933) had decided that allegiance to the WZO took precedence over allegiance to any other Zionist body, the majority of the Revisionist party, founded in 1925 and headed by Vladimir Jabotinsky, seceded from the WZO and established the *New Zionist Organization (NZO). A minority, led by Meir Grossman, remained in the fold of the WZO, as the Jewish State party. From 1931 to 1935 Nahum Sokolow was president of the WZO. From 1935 to 1946 Chaim Weizmann was president again. In 1946 the Revisionists returned to the parent body and resumed their participation in Zionist Congresses, beginning with the 22nd in Basle in 1946.

The 23rd Zionist Congress (1951), the first to meet after the establishment of the State of Israel and to take place in Jerusalem, accepted the so-called *Jerusalem Program, supplementing the Basle Program. From 1956 to 1968 Nahum Goldmann was president of the WZO.

In 1960 a new constitution that put the WZO on a federative basis was promulgated. The 27th Congress (1968) adopted the new Jerusalem Program. It elected no new president to succeed Nahum Goldmann—nor did any of the subsequent Zionist Congresses. The legal standing of the WZO in Israel and its relations with the government of the State of Israel were defined in the "Law of the Status of the WZO", first promulgated in 1952 and amended in view of the Reconstitution of the Jewish Agency in 1975.

In 1986 the Jerusalem Program was supplemented by the following statement of principle adopted by the Zionist General Council: "Zionism is a movement which adheres to the basic principles of Justice, Equality, and Democracy and which rejects discrimination based on origin, nationality, or race".

See also ZIONISM, HISTORY OF.

STRUCTURE

The work of the WZO is carried on through a number of major organs.

Shekel. Until the adoption of the new constitution of 1960, the Shekel served not only as a certificate of membership but also as a voting card and, until 1956, as a basis for Congress representation as well, seats being apportioned among the various countries on the basis of the total number of Shekalim (plural of Shekel) sold. In 1907, when the number of Shekalim was first recorded exactly, it was 164,333. In 1964 it was 2,147,997.

The constitution of 1960 replaced the individual membership of Shekel payers by the collective one of *Zionist territorial organizations and other Zionist bodies but retained the Shekel as a token of Zionist allegiance and as a voting card. The 27th Congress (1968) abolished the Shekel as a universal and world-wide institution, not expressly but by implication: it stipulated that each country determine for itself the system of Congress elections, which need not necessarily be based on the Shekel. On the other hand, each country was entitled to keep the Shekel as a legitimation of membership in the Zionist territorial federations and as a basis of voting for Zionist conventions.

Zionist Congress. The Congress is the legislative body and the supreme forum of the WZO. It determines the general and financial policy of the WZO and elects the representative and governing bodies of the Zionist movements. Until 1964 the Congress was elected by the Shekel payers either in elections with balloting or in "uncontested elections" with a "united slate." No elections of any kind took place for the 27th Congress (1968), which, as an exceptional case, was composed on the pattern of the previous one, apart from one important innovation, the inclusion of nonparty delegations of youth, student and Aliya movements. Characteristic of the subsequent Congresses is the participation of appointed representatives with limited voting rights of international Jewish bodies, apart from the elected delegates of Zionist World Unions. At the 30th Zionist Congress (1982), there were five such non-political bodies.

Until 1960 the number of seats due to each country was computed on the basis of Shekel figures. From 1960 on proportions were stipulated in the constitution for Israel (38 percent) and the United States (29 percent), while the numbers of delegates for other Diaspora countries were determined by a special committee "having regard to the size of the Jewish population and the totality of the conditions and activities of the Zionist Movement in the country concerned."

General Council. The *Zionist General Council, known also as the (Greater) *Actions Committee, is the supreme organ of the WZO in the inter-Congress period, having legislative functions, deciding general policy, and controlling the *Executive. It is (1986) composed of 144 members with voting rights, apart from a number of members who serve in an advisory capacity. The Council meets at least once a year and *inter alia*, decides on the WZO budget in non-Congress years, either by itself or through its Permanent Budget and Finance Committee. Its composition reflects that of the Congress with, in general, one Council member for each five Congress delegates of Zionist World Unions and parties, while the proportion is one to three as far as international Jewish bodies are concerned. Elections—with or without balloting—were again held at the 28th (1972), 29th (1978), 30th (1982), and 31st (1987) Zionist Congresses.

Executive. The Executive of the WZO, formerly known as the Inner Actions Committee, and of the Zionist General Council is charged with implementing the resolutions of the Congress and the current business of the WZO. Its seat is in Jerusalem, but for many years an American section of the Executive has existed. Several times a year, plenary sessions are held in Jerusalem, where questions of special importance are decided, while day-to-day matters are handled in the twice monthly meetings of the Jerusalem Executive.

The Executive has been headed by a chairman; at times, by two chairmen, one responsible for the American section and the other for the Israeli section of the Executive. The number of members of the Executive has grown from 5 in Herzl's time to 15 after World War I and to 36 in 1985.

Comptroller. The task of the comptroller and of his office is to "inspect the financial and economic activities of the WZO and its institutions and offices of every kind."

Judicial Organs. (*see* ZIONIST SUPREME COURT) The judicial branch of the WZO comprises the *Congress Tribunal (combining since 1960 the functions of the former Congress Court and Court of Honor) and the attorney of the WZO. The Court consists of a maximum of 30 members including the president and up to five deputy presidents. The Court has always enjoyed the highest esteem in the movement, largely owing to the eminence of the men who have headed it, among them, in the last decade, justices of the Supreme Court of Israel. The attorney of the WZO (formerly the Congress attorney) represents the WZO before the Court and advises central Zionist bodies on legal matters.

PATTERN OF ORGANIZATION

The WZO was originally organized on a territorial basis: the Shekel payers were grouped into local societies that formed territorial committees or federations (*Landesverbände*). Even in Herzl's lifetime, however, with the foundation of the first separate union, the Mizrachi, in 1902, this horizontal organization was supplemented by a vertical one. Whereas the separate unions represented special points of view, Zionists who did not subscribe to a particular ideology, primarily the adherents of General Zionism, were organized in territorial federations.

According to the constitution of 1960, Zionist territorial federations constitute the most important category of members. Other categories are Zionist territorial and inter-territorial associations, Jewish national and international bodies that as a whole accept the Zionist program without obliging each of their members to be a Zionist, and Zionist World Unions which have replaced the former Zionist Separate Unions with tasks and functions similar to those of their predecessors.

Zionist Federations. The WZO Constitution of 1960 recognized three different types of Zionist territorial organizations as members of the WZO: those based on the collective membership of Zionist bodies (parties and non-political organizations) called Zionist federation; those based on the personal membership of Zionist individuals, called Zionist union; and a third called Mixed Zionist Federation because it includes both individual and corporate members. In 1973 the Constitution was amended and the pattern of organization changed. It was laid down that all Zionist territorial organizations should be based on personal membership of individuals. Collective membership of Zionist bodies was no longer recognized. However, the name of Zionist Federation, which had become generally used for Zionist territorial organizations, was transferred to what had become the sole recognized form of a Zionist territorial organization.

Just as *International Jewish Bodies are members of the WZO alongside Zionist Federations, a national branch of such body or a national Jewish (in contradistinction to Zionist) body, which accepts the Jerusalem Program as such without obliging each of its members to be personally an organized and committed Zionist, may affiliate with a

Zionist Federation on a collective basis. Zionist Territorial and Interterritorial Associations, mentioned in the Constitution, namely Zionist bodies operating in countries in which there is no Zionist Federation, no longer exist. Before the establishment of the American Zionist Federation, the USA offered examples of Zionist Territorial Associations directly affiliated with the WZO rather than with a territorial framework e.g., Hadassah.

There has never been a Zionist Federation in Israel. In former times the Central Shekel and Election Board constituted a common Zionist framework mostly for the purposes of Congress representation. Now the Zionist Council for Israel, a loose roof association of parties, professional organizations, Settlers' Associations, etc., is partly filling the void and exercising functions elsewhere incumbent on the Zionist Federation.

Until World War II Zionist activities could be pursued nearly everywhere—with the exceptions of Russia and Turkey—and Zionist organizations operated in all countries with a Jewish population. Later on a "shrinking process" set in and the Zionist map became smaller and smaller. A few years after World War II, Zionist Federations still existed and were active in countries like Poland, Hungary, Czechoslovakia, Romania, and China. By 1950 all Zionist bodies were dissolved by the Communist regimes in these countries and very often key Zionist workers were persecuted and jailed. Legal Zionist activities in Moslem countries came to an end in the mid-fifties, with the termination of French rule in North Africa. The downfall of the Shah in Iran also meant the end of the semi-clandestine Zionist work in that country which had been carried on until then.

In 1986, 33 Zionist Federations were in existence: 2 in North America, 3 in Central America, 9 in South America, 14 in Europe, 1 in the Near East, 2 in Africa, and 2 in Australia-New Zealand. In a few countries, the Jewish community (congregation) or one of its departments performs the activities and tasks of a Zionist Federation. In others, the Committees of the United Israel Appeal (*Magbit*) conduct Zionist work beyond fundraising, and elsewhere dedicated individuals without a permanent organizational framework are active in some field of Zionist endeavor. Thus the total number of countries within the orbit of the WZO may be put at about 50.

THE DEPARTMENTS OF THE WZO *see also* JEWISH AGENCY: DEPARTMENTS)

As a result of the reconstruction of the JA and the separation of the WZO from the JA in 1971, the various departments which had hitherto been common to the joint body, had to be divided between either the JA or the WZO. The largest departments as far as size, budget, and scope of activities were concerned—namely *Immigration and Absorption, Settlement and Youth Aliya*—were assigned to the JA. However, in view of certain legal requirements and the requirements of fundraising, sections for Immigration and Absorption and for Settlement were also set up within the WZO. The latter were in charge of immigration from free countries—in contradistinction to emergency and rescue immigration—as well as of settlement in the Administered Areas with which the JA, for the reasons mentioned, could not deal. In 1986/87 the Section for Immigration and Absorption received the greatest share of the total WZO budget, namely $16,200,000 out of approximately $61,000,000.

The next largest allocation went to the *Department for Youth and He-Halutz* with $11,650,000. Established in the mid-1940s, it was charged with the guidance and support of Zionist pioneering youth movements and youth organizations. It carries out various projects in Israel and also in the Diaspora with the object of strengthening the Jewish identity of youth, promoting their knowledge of, and attachment to, Israel and in this way to prepare the ground for immigration. It holds annual Summer Institutes of several weeks' duration offering short seminars and camps. Thus, every year some 1,000 youngsters are brought to Israel from South America in the framework of the *Tapuz* program. The Institute for Youth Leaders in Jerusalem has been operating since 1946. Kiryat Moriah in Jerusalem is an education center for Diaspora youth and a venue for many of the Department's programs. Much of its work abroad is carried out by *emissaries, (shelihim) sent to youth movements, community centers and other bodies, either solely by the Department or shared with other organizations. Jewish students abroad are used as counsellors and instructors in youth camps. The Department's activities in Israel aim at bringing together the youth of the country with their counterparts from the Diaspora in order to promote mutual understanding and make Israeli youth conscious of the unity of the Jewish people and aware of their responsibilities towards the Diaspora.

The dichotomy in the Israel educational system—the state schools being divided into general and religious (Orthodox) schools—is reflected in the existence of two separate education departments in the JA, namely, the *Department for Education in the Diaspora* and the *Department for Torah Education in the Diaspora*. They were set up in 1940 and 1951 respectively. Both departments are concerned with the promotion and intensification of formal and informal Jewish education and the enhancement of Jewish cultural values in the Diaspora. They train teachers—both in Israel and abroad—(and the Torah Department also trains religious officials) and send teachers from Israel to Jewish communities all over the world, in particular to small and remote ones, supplying textbooks and other educational material, promoting the study of Hebrew, etc. Both the Hayim Greenberg and the Rabbi Gold Institutes for the training of teachers—called after former heads of the Departments—have been operating for several decades in Jerusalem. The Jerusalem College for Torah and Judaism provides facilities for intensive Jewish studies for boys. The "General" Department co-operates closely with the Reform and Conservative movements while the Torah Department has a natural affinity to the Orthodox trend. In 1987 emissaries of the General Department were active in 70 schools in 20 countries while emissaries from the Torah Department were to be found in 85 schools in 20 countries. Each Department operated on an annual budget of $4,300,000.

The *Organization Department* is the oldest of all the departments of the WZO, having been set up in Berlin prior to World War I. It has also the widest jurisdiction because in principle everything not assigned to any other department falls into its province. The Organization Department is responsible for the convening and organization of the governing bodies of the WZO, such as the Zionist Congress and Zionist General Council. It is also in charge of the WZO's membership drive and the preparation and supervision of Congress elections. It maintains contact with the member-organizations of the WZO—Zionist Federations, Zionist World Unions, and Jewish International Bodies. It assists the work of the Zionist Federations by financial allocations and by sending emissaries who usually serve as their general secretaries or undertake other responsible tasks. The

Department convenes continental and regional conferences of Zionist bodies and arranges seminars in Israel and abroad for voluntary Zionist key-workers and professionals. One of the Department's more recent ventures is the Academy of Zionist Studies, set up after the 30th Zionist Congress (1983) in cooperation with Israeli universities, for studying at an academic level the history and processes of the WZO. The Zionist Library, founded by the Department in the 1950s, publishes Zionist classics and standard works. The Organization Department is in charge of the maintenance and operation of Mount Herzl with the tomb of the founder of the WZO and the Herzl Museum. Attached to the Department are the *Central Zionist Archives. The Department's budget in 1987 amounted to $3,800,000.

The *Information Department* has been an independent unit since the 28th Zionist Congress in 1972 prior to which it had usually formed part of the Organization Department. It conducts Zionist information work within the Jewish public, its main target groups being Zionist and Jewish leadership, and Jewish opinion-makers. It has been involved in a struggle against anti-Zionist trends and phenomena, such as the resolution passed in 1975 by the UN General Assembly equating Zionism with racism. Its publications include a press service for Jewish newspapers abroad, the monthly *Israel Scene*, the quarterly *Forum*, and the Yiddish journal *Folk un Zion*. It has organized two international conferences of the Jewish media, "information caravans" to tour Jewish communities of the Diaspora and produces or coproduces films, slideshows, and other audio-visual programs. It maintains Zionist Information Centers in various countries. Its budget in 1987 was $1,750,000.

The *Department for External Relations*, with a budget of $990,000 in 1987, maintains contact with non-Jewish pro-Israeli groups, including friendship leagues for Israel, pro-Israel parliamentary groups, and societies for Christian-Jewish cooperation. It arranges in Israel suitable programs for visitors from such groups.

Other units of the WZO include: *The Young Leadership and Volunteers Department*, established in 1973, whose budget in 1987 was $450,000. It is in charge of the 25–40 age group and endeavors to ensure the continuity of the movement by recruiting and training new key workers.

The *Department for Sephardi and Oriental Communities*, established in 1972, with a budget of $650,000 in 1987, strengthens the links between the WZO and Sephardi and Oriental Jewry, in particular its roof organization, the Sephardi World Federation which had branches in many countries. In Israel its activities aim primarily at promoting Zionist ideas among the non-Ashkenazi sector of the Jewish population and dealing with the so-called "cultural gap" between some of the newcomers and the rest of the country.

The *Department for Development and Community Services*, one of the newest units, has the following functions: cooperation with organizations not yet formally affiliated with the WZO, such as B'nai B'rith; activities among academics, intellectuals, and professionals; assistance to the *Brit Ivrit Olamit (World Hebrew Union); and liaison with the Bialik Institute. Its Jewish Family Heritage project fosters interest in Jewish genealogy and the preservation of family tradition. Its budget in 1987 amounted to $650,000.

The *Bureau for Spiritual Services*, in operation since 1974, had a budget of $450,000 in 1987. It seeks to combat assimilation by strengthening and preserving the values of Jewish religion and tradition in Diaspora communities, especially in small ones which are not self-sufficient in this respect. It trains rabbis and other religious leaders for these communities and supplies them with books and religious objects.

The function of the *Finance Department* (Treasury) and the *Manpower Division* are indicated by their names. The *Office of the Comptroller of the WZO*, who so far has always been identical with the Comptroller of the JA, is independent of the Executive of the WZO. The Comptroller's task is to inspect and supervise the financial, economic, and administrative activities of the offices, institutions, and companies of the WZO, periodically reporting his findings to the Congress and Zionist General Council.

The number and jurisdiction of the various Departments of the WZO has not been laid down in the Constitution nor is it determined by the Congress or General Council; this remaining the prerogative of the Executive. The proliferation of the Departments is to a large degree due to political considerations.

AMERICAN SECTION

In the 1970s and 1980s the American Section's activities were expanded. Some of its members head the American branches of major departments of the WZO like Education and Culture and Torah Education and Culture. Special emphasis was placed on political work and information activities on the American scene in general and within the Jewish public. Thus a *Department for Interreligious Affairs and Community Relations* was established in order to promote better understanding of the Zionist Movement among Christian organizations, and the black and Hispanic communities, by means of special missions by their leaders to Israel, participation in seminars, etc.

Through its participation in the *Conference of Presidents of Major Jewish Organizations, the American Section endeavored to strengthen support for Israel within the American Jewish community, striving to maintain a united stand on the part of American Jewry in its relationship to the Jewish State.

The American Section conducted an information campaign to back the position of the Government of Israel and the JA regarding the *nosherim* (emigrants from the Soviet Union who decided to settle in the USA). On the other hand, it advised and aided Israeli residents of the USA who planned to return to Israel, in particular through its Aliya Center.

The establishment and functioning of the American Section is based on article 42 of the WZO Constitution which states, after laying down that the Executive's seat is in Jerusalem, that the Congress or General Council "may establish one or more divisions of the Executive abroad."

A. ZWERGBAUM

WORLD ZIONIST ORGANIZATION
MEMBERS OF THE ZIONIST EXECUTIVE BEFORE THE STATE OF ISRAEL

1st Congress 1897	*2nd Congress 1898*	*3rd Congress 1899*
T. Herzl (Pres)	T. Herzl (Pres)	T. Herzl (Pres)
O. Kokesch	L. Kahn	L. Kahn
J. Kremenetsky	O. Kokesch	O. Kokesch
A. Minz	O. Marmorek	O. Marmorek
M. Shnirer	M. Shnirer	M. Shnirer
4th Congress 1900	*5th Congress 1901*	*6th Congress 1903*
as before	T. Herzl	as before
	L. Kahn	

O. Kokesch
O. Marmorek

7th Congress 1905
L. J. Greenberg
J. Kann
J. Kohan-Bernstein
A. Marmorek
M. Ussishkin
O. Warburg
D. Wolffsohn
(Chairman)

8th Congress 1907
as before

9th Congress 1909
as before

10th Congress 1911
A. Hantke
S. Levin
N. Sokolow
O. Warburg
(Chairman)

11th Congress 1913
A. Hantke
S. Levin
N. Sokolow
Y. Tschlenow
O. Warburg
(Chairman)

12th Congress 1921
C. Weizmann
(Pres of Z.O.)
N. Sokolow (Pres
the Executive
J. Cowen
M.D. Eder
B. Feiwel
G. Halpern
V. Jabotinsky
R. Lichtheim
L. Motzkin
I. Naiditsch
H. Pick
B. Rosenblatt
A. Ruppin
M. Soloveitchik
(Solieli)
Y. Sprinzak
M. Ussishkin

13th Congress 1923
C. Weizmann (Pres
of Z.O.)
N. Sokolow (Pres of
Exec)
J. Cowen
B. Feiwel
G. Halpern
F. Kisch
L. Lipsky
I. Naiditsch
H. Pick
A. Ruppin
M. Soloveitchik
(Solieli)
S. Van Vriesland

14th Congress 1925
C. Weizmann (Pres
of Z.O.)
N. Sokolow (Pres of
Exec)
J. Cowen
B. Feiwel
G. Halpern
F. Kisch
L. Lipsky
I. Naiditsch
H. Pick
A. Ruppin
Y. Sprinzak
S. Van Vriesland

15th Congress 1927
C. Weizmann (Pres
of Z.O.)
N. Sokolow (Pres of
Exec)
M. D. Eder
F. Kisch
L. Lipsky
P. Rosenbluth
(Rosen)
H. Sacher
H. Szold

16th Congress 1929
C. Weizmann (Pres
of Z.O.)
N. Sokolow (Pres of
Exec)
L. Barth
M. Berlin
(Bar-Ilan)
S. Kaplansky
F. Kisch
L. Lipsky
P. Rosenbluth
(Rosen)
A. Ruppin
H. Sacher
Y. Sprinzak
H. Szold

17th Congress 1931
N. Sokolow (Pres)
H. Arlosoroff
S. Brodetsky
Y. Farbstein
B. Locker
E. Neumann

18th Congress 1933
N. Sokolow (Pres)
D. Ben-Gurion
S. Brodetsky
I. Gruenbaum
V. Jacobson
E. Kaplan
L. Lipsky
B. Locker
A. Ruppin
M. Shertok
(Sharett)

19th Congress 1935
N. Sokolow (Hon.
Pres)
C. Weizmann (Pres)
D. Ben-Gurion
S. Brodetsky
Y. Fishman
(Maimon)
I. Gruenbaum
E. Kaplan
E. Rottenstreich
M. Shertok
(Sharett)

20th Congress 1937
N. Sokolow (Hon.
Pres)
C. Weizmann (Pres)
D. Ben-Gurion
S. Brodetsky
Y. Fishman
(Maimon)
I. Gruenbaum
E. Kaplan
E. Rottenstreich
M. Shertok
(Sharett)

21st Congress 1939
C. Weizmann (Pres)
D. Ben-Gurion
S. Brodetsky
Y. Fishman
(Maimon)
I. Gruenbaum
E. Kaplan
E. Schmorak
M. Shertok
(Sharett)
N. Goldmann*
L. Lipsky*
A. Ruppin*
M. Ussishkin*

22nd Congress 1946
no president
D. Ben-Gurion
P. Bernstein
S. Brodetsky
E. Dobkin
Y. Fishman (Maimon)
Z. Gold
N. Goldmann
H. Greenberg
Y. Gruenbaum
R. Halprin
E. Kaplan
M. Kleinbaum (Sneh)
B. Locker
G. Meyerson (Meir)
E. Neumann
M. Shapira
M. Shertok (Sharett)
S. Z. Shragai
A. H. Silver
M. Kol (from 1948)

*members of the Executive with restricted rights

MEMBERS OF THE ZIONIST EXECUTIVE AFTER 1948

23rd Congress 1951
B. Locker
(Chairman of Ex.
in Jer.)
Y. Braginsky
E. Dobkin
L. Eshkol
Z. Gold
Z. Hermann
G. Josephthal
M. Kol
E. Neumann
Y. Raphael
Z. Shazar

N. Goldmann
(Chairman of Ex.
in New York)
D. Beth Aryeh
B. Browdy
I. Goldstein
H. Greenberg
R. Halprin

24th Congress 1956
Jerusalem Executive
N. Goldmann
(Chairman of
WZO, Zionist Ex.)
D. Beth Aryeh
Y. Braginsky
E. Dobkin
A. L. Dulzin
L. Eshkol
M. Grossman
A. Harman
D. Joseph
M. Kol
Z. Lurie
Z. Shazar
S. Z. Shragai

New York Executive
I. Goldstein
R. Halprin
(Chairman of Ex.
in New York)
M. Kirshblum
E. Neumann
L. Segal

25th Congress 1960
N. Goldmann (Pres
of WZO & Chair of
Ex.)
D. Beth Aryeh
E. Dobkin
A. L. Dulzin
L. Eshkol
I. Goldstein
D. Joseph
M. Kol
C. Levanon
Z. Lurie
M. Sharett
Z. Shazar
S. Z. Shragai
A. Zisling

R. Halprin
M. Kirshblum
E. Neumann
L. Segal
A. Schenker
(deputy member)

Z. Lurie
B. Zuckerman

26th Congress 1965
N. Goldmann (Pres of WZO)
M. Sharett (Ch. of Z.O. d. 9.7.65)
D. Beth Aryeh
M. Erem
I. Goldstein
E. Dobkin
A. L. Dulzin
I. Harkavy
R. Weitz
C. Levanon
Z. Lurie
A. Narboni
L. Pincus (acting chairman from 1965)
M. Kol
S. Z. Shragai
N.Y.
E. Neumann
R. Halprin
M. Kirshblum
M. Syrkin

27th Congress 1968
L. Pincus (Chairman of Executive)
E. Avriel
M. Bar On
A. L. Dulzin
C. Finkelsteyn
I. Goldstein
R. Jaglom
M. Kirshblum
J. Klarman
M. Krone
A. Narboni
M. Rivlin (from 1971)
A. Schenker
E. Shapiro (from 1971)

The Diaspora
R. Feuer
S. Greenberg (r. 1969)
B. Halpern
A. Hertzberg (from 1969)
A. Mayer
E. Neumann
C. Jacobson (chair)
E. Rackman
S. Rothberg (from 1970)
J. Schwartz
Lord Sieff

28th Congress 1972
L. Pincus (Chairman of Executive)
M. Bar On
A. L. Dulzin
C. Finkelsteyn
R. Hirsch
R. Jaglom
M. Kirshblum
J. Klarman
M. Krone
M. Rivlin (assoc.)
A. Narboni (assoc.)
E. Shapiro
A. Schenker
J. Tsur
R. Weitz

America
C. Jacobson (chair)
A. Hertzberg
I. Miller
A. Pollack
E. Rackman
K. Sultanik
J. Torczyner

America
E. Bernstein
H. Jacobs
C. Jacobson (Chair)
A. Levine
A. Pollack
A. Schindler
K. Sultanik
J. Torczyner
I. Yudovin (r. 1979)
R. Gittelson (from 1979)

31st Congress 1987
S. Dinitz (Chairman of Executive)
A. Avi-Hai
M. Drobless
U. Gordon
S. Grawitz
R. Jaglom
Y. Meir
U. Narkis
A. Ohayon
I. Peled
D. Puder
E. Sheffer
M. Shitrit
H. Skirball
C. Weinberg
J. Wernick
N. Zvili

America
A. Schindler
K. Sultanik
B. Tannenbaum
J. Torczyner

America
B. Tannenbaum (chair)
J. Berman
R. Gittelson
A. Levine
A. Schindler
S. Shalom
K. Sultanik
P. Sutker
H. Taubenfeld (assoc)
J. Torczyner

29th Congress 1978
A. L. Dulzin (Chairman of Ex.)
Y. Aridor
A. Avi-Hai
E. Eyal
T. Friedman (r. 1981)
R. Hirsch
M. Jaffe
R. Jaglom
A. Katz
R. Kotlowitz
M. Krone
A. Lewinsky
A. Narboni d. 1979
F. Schenk d. 1981
A. Schenker
Y. Shapira
E. Tavin
M. Topol (from 1981)

30th Congress 1982
A. L. Dulzin (Chairman of Ex.)
D. Avayou
A. Avi-Hai
M. Borsuk (assoc. member)
A. Ohayon
E. Artzi
M. Drobless
U. Gordon
R. Hirsch
A. Lewinsky
N. Zvili
Y. Warszawski
R. Jaglom
M. Jaffe
A. Katz
U. Narkiss
H. Fishman
I. Peled
C. Aron
E. Sheffer
E. Even
M. Rivlin
M. Dayan
Y. Ellinson
A. Schenker/
D. Puder
E. Tavin

32nd Congress (1992)
S. Dinitz (Chairman of Ex.)
I. Ben-Nun
H. Ben-Yehuda
C. Chessler
A. Duvdevani
P. Edelstein
E. Eyal
U. Gordon
S. Gravetz
D. Hagoel
A. Handler
Z. Hasson
R. Hirsch
R. Jaglom
D. Kaplan
C. Klein
Y. Leket
D. Puder
E. Sheffer
J. Wernik

America
Z. Heller
A. Schindler
K. Sultanik
B. Tannenbaum
J. Torczyner
M. Wolke
S. Meridor
Y. Michaeli
A. Ohayon

WZO. *See* WORLD ZIONIST ORGANIZATION.

Y

YA'ARI (WALD), MEIR. Israel labor leader and ideologist (b. Rzeszow, Galicia, 1897; d. Kibbutz Merhavya, 1987). Ya'ari studied at the Vienna Agricultural Academy and at Vienna University. He served in the Austrian army in World War I and until his immigration to Palestine in 1919 was the leader of *Ha-Shomer ha-Tza'ir in Vienna. Under Ya'ari's direction this organization, initially a romantic scouting movement, rapidly became one of the most important and widespread Zionist pioneering movements in eastern Europe. Zealously insisting on the use of the Hebrew language, the movement provided a satisfying identity for Jewish youth from the intelligentsia in a crumbling Jewish world; it emphasized the collective and the self-consolidation of Zionist youth independent of adults' party affiliations. From the outset ties were established with Martin Buber; the inspiration of the German educator and philosopher Gustav Wyneken and his "Youth Culture" was also significant. The Russian revolution and the mass movement which brought it about had very little impact. The image of Ha-Shomer ha-Tza'ir was determined by the small collective and not by masses, and Ya'ari was one of the formulators of this image.

Ha-Shomer ha-Tza'ir's ideological platform was far closer to Ha-Po'el ha-Tza'ir than to Marxism when Ya'ari and his friends arrived in Palestine. Ya'ari led his friends in difficult physical labor in Upper Bitania and was the first secretary of Ha-Shomer ha-Tza'ir in Palestine. He was a founder of Kibbutz Merhavya and became the first secretary of *Kibbutz Artzi (the kibbutz movement of Ha-Shomer ha-Tza'ir) in 1927. From this influential position he worked for the adoption of Marxism as the accepted ideology of the movement. Combining Marxism and some of Ber Borochov's central ideas, Ya'ari crystallized the doctrine of Ha-Shomer ha-Tza'ir in the country—a synthesis between Zionism and Socialism.

In the framework of Ha-Shomer ha-Tza'ir, Ya'ari was one of the founders of the Histadrut in 1920; and Ha-Shomer ha-Tza'ir participated in the general framework of the Gedud ha-Avoda. Ha-Shomer ha-Tza'ir also created its own party, headed by Ya'ari, whose efforts to expand were crowned with success in January, 1948, when Ha-Shomer ha-Tza'ir and Ahdut ha-Avoda—Left Po'ale Zion merged to form *Mapam (The United Workers' Party), which was intended to provide a left-wing, Marxist-Leninist alternative to Mapai.

Although initially Ya'ari had no official role in Mapam, he was, as the leader of Ha-Shomer ha-Tza'ir, one of its undisputed leaders. Throughout this period Ya'ari represented his movement and party in the Zionist and the Histadrut institutions, and, after the creation of the State, in the Knesset. When Mapam participated in the government, at the time of the founding of the State and from 1955, Ya'ari did not accept an executive role as a government minister, but concentrated rather on educational and ideological leadership of his movement and party, of which he became secretary.

During the Cold War, and particularly in the wake of the Prague trial, Ya'ari contributed to the successful struggle to maintain the Zionism of Ha-Shomer ha-Tza'ir youth against Moshe Sneh and his followers, who went over to the Communist Party. After the 1954 Mapam split, Ya'ari consolidated and led the majority in the party, returning to the framework of a small left-wing party based on Ha-Kibbutz ha-Artzi of Ha-Shomer ha-Tza'ir. This party participated in Israel's governments from 1955, even though it was at times violently opposed to political decisions, such as the 1956 Sinai Campaign. Together with Ahdut ha-Avoda and Mapai it founded the Alignment (Ma'arakh) in 1968. Ya'ari served as a Knesset member until 1973, when he resigned from the Knesset and from his office of party secretary.

Meir Ya'ari was the leading ideologist of Ha-Shomer ha-Tza'ir. His writings include: *Be-Fetah Tekufa* (Dawn of an Age, 1942), *Be-Derekh Aruka* (The Long Road, 1947), *Kibbutz Galuyot ba-Aspaklarya shel Yamenu* (Ingathering of the Exiles in our Time, 1954), *Be-Mivhan Dorenu* (Trials of our Generation, 1957), *Ben Hazon le-Metzi'ut* (From Vision to Reality, 1963), *Be-Siman Ahdut ve-Atzma'ut* (For Unity and Independence, 1968), *Be-Ma'avak le-Amal Meshuhrar* (selection of writings and speeches, 1972). A. KAFKAFI

YAD BEN-ZVI. *See* BEN-ZVI, ITZHAK.

YAD HARAV HERZOG. *See* HERZOG FAMILY.

YADIN, YIGAEL. Archeologist and military commander (b. Jerusalem, 1917; d. Michmoret, 1984). The son of the archeologist Eleazar Lipa *Sukenik, Yadin was educated at

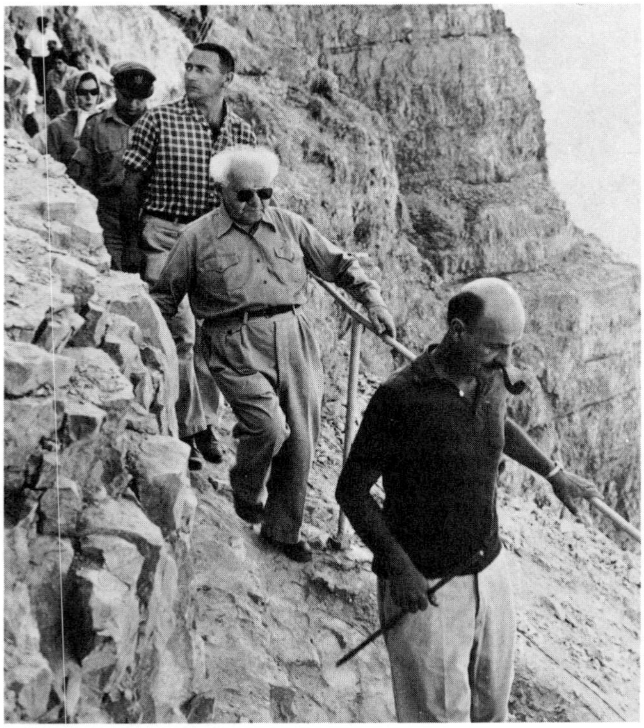

Yigael Yadin leading David Ben-Gurion to Herod's palace in M'tzada. [Israel Information Services]

the Hebrew University of Jerusalem. He became a lecturer at the university in 1953, an associate professor in 1959, a professor and chairman of its department of archeology in 1963.

Yadin was active in the Hagana, the Palestinian Jewish self-defense organization, from his early youth. During Israel's War of Independence he headed the Hagana's operational branch, and after the creation of the Israel Defense Forces (IDF) he was their chief operational officer. In 1949 he was a delegate to the Israel-Arab armistice negotiations at Rhodes, and from 1949 to 1952 he served as chief of the General Staff of the IDF. During his three year term of office he reorganized the IDF, establishing compulsory military service and the system of long-term reserve duty.

After concluding his army career Yadin returned to archeology, devoting himself particularly to the study of the Dead Sea Scrolls and to excavations in Hazor, Megiddo, and other places. He explored the caves of the Judean Desert, discovering documents and articles from the Bar Kokhba era (2nd cent. C.E.), and headed the excavations at Masada.

In 1977 Yadin entered party politics, founding the *Democratic Movement for Change which hoped to reform the Israeli electoral system by introducing constituent representation. His party joined Begin's first government and Yadin became deputy prime minister. The Democratic Movement officially dissolved in 1981 and Yadin retired from politics to return to his academic career.

A brilliant popularizer as well as a distinguished archeologist, his books include *The Message of the Scrolls* (1956); *Hazor* (with N. Avigad; 3 vols., 1957–62); *A Genesis Apocryphon* (1957); *The Art of Warfare in Biblical Lands* (1963); *The Finds from the Cave of Bar Kochba* (1963); and *Masada* (1966). G. KRESSEL

YAD MORDEKHAI. Kibbutz in the southern coastal plain, near the northern side of the Gaza Strip. It was founded by a pioneer group from Poland in 1943, when Jews were trying to enlarge their settlement network in the south and the Negev. In May, 1948, a small number of settlers held back for six days a concentrated attack by the invading Egyptian army which employed artillery, tanks, aircraft, and infantry. The settlers then slipped through the ring of the siege to reach Jewish positions some miles away, carrying their wounded. In October, 1948, the site was retaken and the kibbutz was built up anew. Yad Mordekhai has intensive farming and industrial enterprises. It maintains a reconstruction of the 1948 battlefield and a museum of the Holocaust and ghetto resistance. A large bronze statue below the ruin of the water tower, destroyed in 1948, commemorates the ghetto fighters of World War II. The kibbutz is named for Mordekhai Anilewicz, leader of the Warsaw Ghetto revolt. Population (1987), 728. E. ORNI

Statue of Mordekhai Anilewicz in Yad Mordekhai. [Central Zionist Archives]

YAD VASHEM. Israel's official authority (The Holocaust Martyrs' and Heroes' Remembrance Authority) for the commemoration of Jewish heroes and martyrs who were murdered during the Holocaust. The name, meaning "Monument and Memorial" is derived from Isaiah 56:5—"Even unto them shall I give in My house and within My walls a monument and a memorial .... I will give them an everlasting memorial, which shall never be cut off." The authority was established by law of the Knesset (19 August 1953) for "the commemoration in the Homeland of all those members of the Jewish people who gave their lives, or rose and fought against the Nazi enemy and its collaborators" and for the purpose of setting up "a memorial to them and to the communities, organizations and institutions which were destroyed because they belonged to the Jewish people."

Yad Vashem has established the world's largest archives on the Holocaust period, numbering some 50 million documents, and has collected a vast number of eyewitness reports and testimonies. It has a library of 100,000 volumes and publishes works of historical research pertaining to the Holocaust in Hebrew, Yiddish, English, French, and Spanish. It publishes a bulletin at regular intervals, conducts seminars for students and educators from Israel and

Yad VaShem, Jerusalem. [Israel Government Press Office]

abroad, organizes bienniel international historical conferences, gatherings of survivor organizations, as well as the official state ceremonies for Holocaust Martyrs' and Heroes' Remembrance Day. The authority suppled much of the evidence used at the trial of Adolf Eichmann, and assists in the provision of documentary evidence to legal authorities throughout the world dealing with the prosecution of suspected Nazi war criminals.

Located on the Mount of Remembrance beyond Mount Herzl in Jerusalem, the Yad Vashem complex consists of a library, archives and administration building, the historical museum containing Yad Vashem's permanent exhibit "From Holocaust to Rebirth," a museum of art from the Holocaust, the Hall of Names, a synagogue commemorating the synagogues destroyed by the Nazis, the Hall of Remembrance, the Avenue of the Righteous commemorating gentiles who heroically saved Jewish lives in the Holocaust, and a children's memorial. Dedicated in 1961, the Hall of Remembrance contains the ashes of unknown Jewish martyrs and an Eternal Flame; on its floor are inscribed the 22 most notorious death sites in Nazi occupied Europe. Adjacent to the complex is the Valley of Remembrance, memorializing the destroyed communities of Europe.

The directorate of Yad Vashem includes representatives of the Israeli government, the Jewish Agency, the Jewish National Fund, and other public bodies. M. FOGEL

YAFFE, BEZALEL. *See* JAFFE, BEZALEL.

YAFO. *See* JAFFA.

YAGUR. Kibbutz in the Haifa Bay area, at the foot of Mt. Carmel, 7 mi. (11 km.) southeast of Haifa. Founded in 1922 by a Gedud ha-Avoda group, it soon became the country's largest kibbutz, developed intensive irrigated farming and industrial enterprises and sent members to hired work in Haifa port and in industry. In 1946 the kibbutz was subjected to a severe search by the British army and an essential arms cache of the Hagana was discovered. It runs a vocational school of metal work, electronics etc. Population (1987), 1,340. E. ORNI

YAHIL (HOFFMAN), HAYIM. Israeli government official (b. Velke Mezirici, Moravia, Austria, 1905; d. Jerusalem, 1974). He first went to Palestine in 1929. There he joined Kibbutz Givat Hayim, but remained only a short time before returning to Europe. He studied at the universities of Prague and Vienna and from 1933 to 1939 served as director of the Jewish Social Service Center of Prague. Returning to Palestine in 1939, he joined the staff of the Histadrut, serving first (1939–42) as director of its Education Department in Haifa and then (1942–45) as a member of the Executive Committee. From 1945 to 1949 he was in Munich, where he served as representative of the Jewish Agency (1945–48) and Israel Consul (1948–49).

From 1949 to 1951 Yahil was director of the Jewish Agency's Department of Immigrant Absorption in Jerusalem and from 1951 to 1953 head of the Information Department of the Ministry of Foreign Affairs. Between 1956 and 1959 he first was Minister to the Scandinavian countries and later served as Ambassador to Sweden and Minister to Norway and Iceland. In 1960 he was appointed Director General of the Ministry of Foreign Affairs, a position he held until 1964. In 1965 he became chairman of the Israel Broadcasting Authority. For several years he served as head of the Center for the Diaspora (Merkaz la-Tefutzot) of the Jewish Agency in Jerusalem.

A delegate to numerous Zionist Congresses, Yahil published essays on Zionism, sociology, and politics. His books include *A History of the Israel Labor Movement* (1939) and *Scandinavian Socialism and its Implementation* (1961). Y. JELINEK

YAHUDA, ABRAHAM SHALOM EZEKIEL. Biblical scholar, Orientalist, and Zionist (b. Jerusalem, 1877; d. Saratoga Springs, N.Y., 1951). Scion of an old Sephardi family, Yahuda studied at German universities and taught at academic institutions in Germany, Spain, England, and the United States. At the age of 20 he attended the First Zionist Congress (1897). During World War I, when he was teaching Hebrew at Madrid University, he intervened (together with Max Nordau who was then an exile from France in Spain) with King Alfonso XIII and Spanish governmental authorities in behalf of the yishuv. Yahuda was largely responsible for bringing the plight of the yishuv to the attention of Oscar Straus and other leaders of American Jewry. He also endeavored to obtain the support of Spain for the ratification of the Mandate for Palestine.

After the war Yahuda went to England with Nordau and lived in London until he moved to the United States during World War II. He was an early supporter of the concept of a Hebrew University and helped interest Albert Einstein in it. In Zionist politics he was a close follower of Nordau, a consistent critic of Chaim Weizmann, and a supporter of Vladimir Jabotinsky. J. FRAENKEL

YA'IR, ABRAHAM. *See* STERN, ABRAHAM.

YARKON. Largest of Israel's coastal rivers, entering the Mediterranean Sea in the northern section of Tel Aviv. It drains a large part of the Judean Mountains as well as the southern Samaria Mountains. All its tributaries are dry wadis, carrying water only after heavy rains and subject to sudden floods. The Yarkon is perennial only for its last

Yarkon River at Tel Aviv. [Israel Government Tourist Office]

winding stretch of about 20 miles. The source of its perennial waters consists of large springs of Rosh ha-Ayin, east of Petah Tikva. Most of these waters are now caught and transported in a large pipeline for irrigation in the Lachish area and the northern Negev (Yarkon-Negev system).

Y. KARMON

YASSKY, HAYIM. Physician and director of the *Hadassah Medical Organization (b. Odessa, Russia, 1896; d. Jerusalem, 1948). Yassky studied medicine at the University of Odessa. Late in 1919, several weeks before he was due to take his final examinations, he left Russia for Palestine. He went to Switzerland in 1920, completed his medical studies at the University of Geneva, and returned to Palestine in 1921. He volunteered his services as an ophthalmologist to the Hadassah eye clinic in Haifa. In 1924, as acting director of the ophthalmology department of the Hadassah Hospital in Tel Aviv, he was assigned the task of organizing a campaign against trachoma in Judea. He also engaged in other public health work, including the reduction of infant mortality. Yassky's plans for combating trachoma were adopted by French authorities for use in French colonies.

In 1928 he became assistant to Dr. Ephraim Michael Bluestone, medical director of Hadassah, who was about to leave Palestine. In 1931 he became director of the Hadassah Medical Organization, a position he held until his death. During his tenure he helped secure the consent of the Rothschild family to transfer the ownership of the Rothschild Hospital in Jerusalem to Hadassah, and he served as chairman of the building committee for the Hebrew University-Hadassah Medical Center. After the outbreak of World War II he offered the services of the medical center to the British Middle East Command. On 13 April 1948, he was shot and killed when Arabs attacked the medical convoy in which he was traveling to Mount Scopus, bringing food and medical supplies to the Hadassah-University Hospital. The Hayim Yassky Hadassah Negev Hospital in Beersheba is named for him.

YAVNE. Town in the coastal plain, 5 mi. (8 km.) southwest of Rehovot. Mentioned in Josh. 15:11 (Jabneh) as a town of the tribe of Judah, it remained a Philistine center. In the Hellenistic period known as Iamnia, it was an important trade and strategic center. Its Jewish population increased gradually and during the Roman siege of Jerusalem in 66–70 C.E., Rabbi Yohanan ben Zakai obtained permission to open there his school, which remained the seat of the Sanhedrin until this was transferred to Galilee after the Bar Kokhba revolt (2nd century C.E.). The Moslem Arabs took the town in 634. The Crusaders called it Ybellin, making it a rallying point for their attacks against Ashkelon. Later, it remained the Arab village Yibna which grew quickly in the early 20th century, thanks to the nearby Jewish markets of Gedera, Rehovot, etc. In May, 1948, Hagana forces occupied Yibna, thereby halting the march of the invading Egyptian army towards Tel Aviv. From the end of 1948, Jewish immigrants were housed in the now abandoned Arab village, which was later classed as a development town. Initially suffering from too narrow an economic base, Yavne made quick progress from the 1960s, thanks to its position halfway between Tel Aviv and Ashdod and a flourishing farming hinterland. Important industrial enterprises were transferred there and new ones opened. Population (1987), 20,100.

See also KEVUTZAT YAVNE. E. ORNI

YAVNE. *See* KEVUTZAT YAVNE.

YAVNE'EL. Moshava in the Yavne'el Valley of eastern Lower Galilee, southwest of Tiberias. It is mentioned as a town (Jabneel) of the tribe of Naphtali (Josh. 15:11). The modern settlement was founded in 1901 by the Jewish Colonization Association on land bought by Baron Edmond de Rothschild. Pioneers from Russia settled there to develop grain farming but because of the lack of water the village made little progress until a groundwater horizon was tapped in the 1940s. After 1948, an immigrants' transit camp was set up near the village, some of whose inhabitants, hailing from Yemen, North Africa, etc., were absorbed in Yavne'el. The veteran moshava Bet Gan and the moshavim Mishmar ha-Shelosha and Semadar were also united with Yavne'el. Its farming is composed of grain crops, fruit orchards, cattle etc. Population (1987), 1,580.

E. ORNI

YEDI'OT AHARANOT ("Latest News"). Israeli daily. The newspaper with the largest circulation in Israel (approaching 400,000 copies of the Friday edition), it was founded in 1939 by Yehuda Moses and edited by Dr. Azriel Carlebach until May 1948, when Carlebach and several of the paper's leading journalists left in order to found *Ma'ariv*, plunging *Yedi'ot Aharonot* into a severe crisis which took several years to surmount. For many years the paper was directed by No'ah Moses (son of the founder) as responsible editor and Dov Judkovski as coordinator of the editorial board. Dr. Herzl Rosenblum, a signatory of the Declaration of Independence, served as editor-in-chief. After the death of Moses (1986) and the retirement of Rosenblum shortly afterwards. Judkovski became the paper's editor-in-chief.

Yedi'ot Aharonot appeals to a broad strata of the population with strong political and security writers and columnists and a high level of social, financial, literary, sport, and cultural coverage. Although nominally an afternoon paper, it appears in the early morning. *Yedi'ot Aharonot* publishes *La'Isha*, Israel's most popular women's magazine, and is part owner of *Koteret Rashit*, a weekly news magazine, and of the Edanim book publishing house. M. NAOR

YEHOSHUA, (AVRAHAM) A.B., Israeli novelist (b. Jerusalem, 1936). Since 1972, he has served on the faculty of Haifa University. Yehoshua began as a writer of highly symbolistic short stories, in which the main characters are alienated individuals forever struggling against allegorical figures representing social or metaphysical authority, such as *Mot ha-Zaken* (Death of the Old Man), 1963. His second volume of short stories, *Mul Ye'arot* (Facing the Forests), 1968, moves towards realism. Since the 1970s, he has turned novelist and his writing is increasingly realistic. Both *Ha-Me'ahev* (The Lover) 1977, and *Gerushim Me'uharim* (A Late Divorce) 1982, as well as *Molkho* (1986) and *Mr. Mani* (1993) are set in contemporary Israel. In these novels Yehoshua skillfully manipulates the "point of view" of the narrative from one character to the other. Behind his realism, abstract social ideas still hover: the nature of Israeli society, the Arab problem, the pull of emigration, the religious problem, etc.

Yehoshua deals openly with Zionist themes in a penetrating collection of essays *Bi-Zekhut ha-Normaliyut* (in Favor of Normalcy) 1980. Here he argues against the Jewish historic proclivity toward wandering and exile and against the thesis that suffering and persecution are the cauldron which refined the Jewish genius. E. SPICEHANDLER

YEHUD. Town in the coastal plain, 8 mi. (12 km.) east of Tel Aviv. It is mentioned in Josh. 19;45 as a town of the tribe of Dan. Settlers from Petah Tikva, who evacuated their village temporarily because of the danger of malaria, stayed at Yehud for a number of years after 1882. The local Arab village of Yahudiyya was taken by Israeli forces, together with the nearby Lydda Airport in July, 1948, and its inhabitants left. At the end of 1948, the first Jewish settlers were housed there. Yehud soon became urbanized, received municipal status in 1951, and industry began to develop. It grew in size thanks to its position in the outskirts of the Tel Aviv conurbation and numbered 14,500 inhabitants in 1987. E. ORNI

YEIVIN, YEHOSHU'A HESCHEL. Hebrew writer and editor (b. Yinnitsa, Ukraine, 1891; d. Jerusalem, 1970). After completing his studies in medicine at Moscow University Yeivin served as a doctor in the Russian army during World War II. Subsequently he left the medical profession in order to work in journalism and literature. He published his articles and stories in the Hebrew periodicals *Ha-Olam*, *Ha-Shiloah*, and *Ha-Tekufa*.

In 1924 he moved to Palestine where in 1928 he was one of the founders of the Revisionist movement, becoming an editor of its press for which he also wrote extensively. From 1928–1933 he was one of the editors of *Do'ar ha-Yom*. He established and edited the Revisionist newspaper *Hazit ha-Am* (with Abba Ahimeir, 1931–4) and from 1935–47 he worked on the newspaper *Ha-Boker* while regularly publishing articles in the monthly periodical *Sulam*. His articles and novels were on historical subjects. In 1959 he won first place in the Israel Bible Contest.

His books include *Sipurim* (1928), *Be-Sod ha-Talim* (1936), *Uri Tzevi Greenberg-Meshorer Mehokek* (1938), and *Mi-Me'orat Arayot* (Stories of the underground movement, 1954).

E. HOTER

YELLIN: Prominent family in Eretz Israel.

Yehoshua Yellin. Communal leader (b. Jerusalem, 1843; d. there, 1924). He sought to direct the old yishuv toward work in agriculture and crafts. In the 1860s he bought land outside Jerusalem to accomodate a wayfarers' inn and plan-

David Yellin.
[Zionist Archives]

tations. He also helped found the first Jewish residential quarters outside the walls of the Old City (Nahlat Shiva, Me'a She'arim, etc.) He tried his hand at agriculture for a while. Despite the opposition of Jerusalem's religious zealots he sent his son to a "modern" school. From 1897 to 1901 Yellin was a member of the Jerusalem municipality.

Yellin remained active in public affairs throughout his life. His *Memoirs of a Jerusalemite,* covering the history of Jerusalem and the yishuv during the years 1834–1918, appeared in 1924.

His son, **David Yellin**, author, educator, and public figure (b. Jerusalem, 1864; d. there, 1941), was educated at yeshivot in Jerusalem and at the Alliance Israélite Universelle school, where he later taught Hebrew and Arabic. He taught at the Lämel School as well. He supported Eliezer Ben-Yehuda in efforts to teach Hebrew as a living language.

Yellin was active in communal life in Jerusalem and helped found several new residential quarters in the city. He also helped found the Va'ad ha-Lashon ha-Ivrit (Hebrew Language Council) and the Midrash Abarbanel, which became the nucleus of the Jewish National and University Library. In addition, he was active in B'nai B'rith and was one of the founders of the first Hebrew kindergarten in the city (1903). He helped organize the first convention of Hebrew teachers, in Zikhron Ya'akov, and became the first president of the Histadrut ha-Morim (Hebrew Teachers Association).

From 1904 Yellin taught at the teachers' seminary of the Hilfsverein der Deutschen Juden in Jerusalem, becoming its assistant principal in 1910 and serving until the outbreak of the *Language War of 1913, in which he was one of the leading champions of Hebrew. He became one of the founders of the network of Hebrew schools and established the Hebrew Teachers' Seminary in Jerusalem, which he headed until 1926 when he joined the faculty of the Hebrew University of Jerusalem. He lectured on medieval Hebrew poetry at the university and in 1937 was named chairman of its Institute of Jewish Studies.

For many years Yellin was a member of the municipal government of Jerusalem. During World War I he was exiled to Damascus by the Turkish authorities. On his return, he served as chairman of the Jewish Municipal Committee of Jerusalem (1919–21), deputy mayor of Jerusalem (1920–26), and chairman of the Va'ad Le'umi (1920–29). He was a leading witness before various commissions of investigation sent to Palestine during the British Mandatory regime.

A prolific writer, Yellin was the author of journalistic articles, research studies on the Bible, the Hebrew language, and medieval poetry, and Hebrew translations from Arabic and English. He was coauthor with Eliezer Ben-Yehuda of the first modern Hebrew textbooks to be published in Eretz Israel. G. KRESSEL

YELLIN-MOR (Friedmann-Yellin), NATHAN. Leader of *Lohamei Herut Israel (b. Grodno, Poland, 1913; d. Tel Aviv, 1980). In Poland he was a member of Merkaz ha-Tzohar (Union of Zionists-Revisionists) and of Betar. He supported the maximalist faction in Ha-Tzohar, and the *Irgun Tzeva'i Le'umi, under the influence of Avraham Stern. From 1934 to 1938 he edited the Irgun organ *Di Tat,* disseminating the ideas of the maximalists, and demonstrating mounting hostility towards the ideas of Vladimir Jabotinsky. With the outbreak of World War II he fled from Warsaw to Soviet-occupied Vilna, and from there to Palestine (early 1941), where he joined Stern and his underground group, opposing the pro-British policy of Ha-Tzohar. In late 1941 he was sent by the Irgun to meet German representatives in the Balkans, to attempt to persuade them to send their Jews to Palestine in exchange for an Irgun undertaking to fight against Great Britain. Before he could complete his mission, he was apprehended near Aleppo, Syria (February, 1942). In the same year Stern was murdered and the Irgun disbanded.

After escaping from Latrun prison on 1 November 1943, together with 20 colleagues, Yellin-Mor joined Yitzhak Shamir and Yisrael Eldad in establishing Lohamei Herut Israel (Lehi). The new group adopted the ideology of the Revisionist maximalists, but had to modify this ideology slightly in order to justify the movement's existence in light of the competition of the Irgun when it resumed operations under Menahem Begin (early 1944). In late 1943, while seeking formulas which would be acceptable to the organized yishuv and the Labor movement, Yellin-Mor put out feelers to the USSR, hoping to find a new ally to assist in the fight for national liberation.

In early 1944 there was a rapprochement with the yishuv through meetings held with Hagana leader Eliyahu Golomb. In May, 1944, Yellin-Mor promised to cease terror activities and to coordinate his activities with the Hagana and the Irgun. In late 1945 Yellin-Mor mediated the alliance of the three underground movements into the Hebrew Resistance Movement (Tenu'at ha-Meri ha-Ivri), hoping to bring about a change in yishuv policies and to initiate a general revolt against Britain. With the collapse of this movement, Yellin-Mor began to crystallize a new policy in the field of foreign affairs: "Neutrality of the Middle East" (September, 1946). After the Gromyko Declaration (May, 1947), with the partial realization of Yellin-Mor's hopes of an alliance with the Soviet powers, there was a more far-reaching change in the approach to the USSR, with a willingness to adopt the model of "popular democracy." At the same time Yellin-Mor attempted to combine this with his Arab policy. He nurtured the belief in the rise of "progressive" Arab bodies who would prevent the outbreak of a Jewish-Arab war.

Hoping that such a war would not break out, he decided on the dismantling of Lehi after the UN resolution of 29 November 1947. When this hope proved false, he reversed the decision and Lehi joined the war. On 17 September 1948 Lehi was disbanded following the leadership's planning of the assassination of the UN mediator, Count Bernadotte. Yellin-Mor was arrested at the end of that month on the eve of an attempt to escape to Czechoslovakia and tried at the end of the year. Despite denials of his involvement in the assassination, he was sentenced to eight years' imprisonment. He was released, however, and elected to the First Knesset on the Lehi ticket. When the Lohamim party (successors of Lehi) split, he headed a majority which professed a national-Bolshevik platform (a combination of a rightist outlook and leftist elements such as nationalization and planning). Unsuccessful in the new Israeli arena, his party was disbanded in 1951. In the 1950s Yellin-Mor renounced political activity, but joined Ha-Pe'ula ha-Shemit (Semitic Action) towards the end of that decade. In the late 1960s he joined the Shalom u-Bitahon movement, and advocated granting self-determination to the Palestinians, in contradiction to his pre-1951 position. He stood for the Knesset on the Nes (socialist left) list in 1969, but the list failed to gain a seat in the elections. Y. HELLER

YEMENITE JEWS IN ISRAEL. Stimulated by reports of the development of the yishuv in Eretz Israel, and spurred by the political retributions suffered in Yemen, the number of immigrants to Eretz Israel from this diaspora increased in the 19th century. These were only individual immigrants, however, who left practically no impression on the yishuv. Only in 1881 did Yemenite immigrants begin to create their own distinct community in the country. That year saw the beginning of an uninterrupted flow of immigrants from Yemen. Such an emigration, estimated at about fifty to sixty thousand, was considered large-scale by the standards of those times and in relation to the size of the mother community. The process continued for about seventy years (1891–1951). By 1948, nearly half the Jews of Yemen already dwelt in Israel, and the other half, about 55,000, immigrated between 1949 and 1951 (*Operation Magic Carpet), but the process is not quite complete. Of the Jews who remained in Yemen, hundreds of individuals went to Israel until 1962, the eve of the republican revolution in Yemen. An estimated few thousand Jews still live in Yemen today.

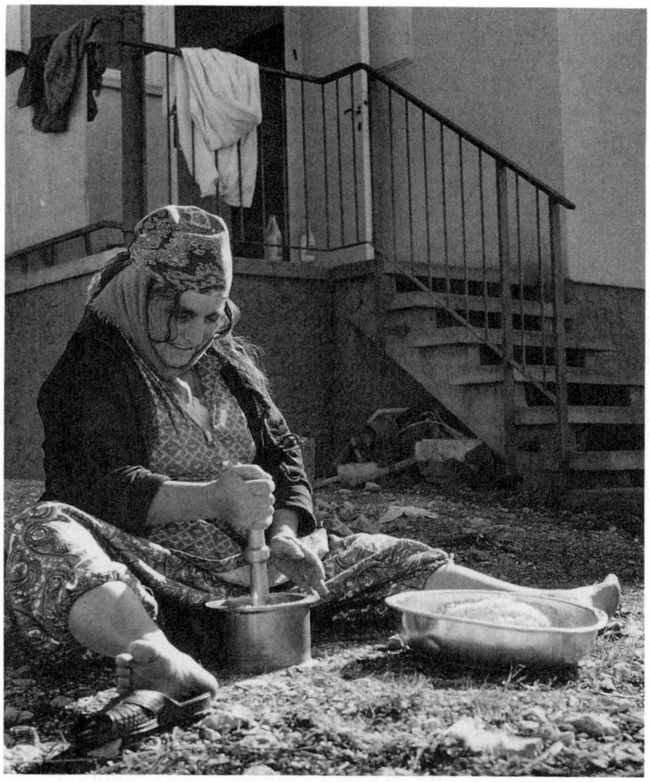

Yemenite woman pounding food in front of her home in Moshav Shetulim, 1969. [Israel Govt. Press Office]

Pre-nuptial ceremony at Yemenite bride's home. [Israel Govt. Press Office]

The modern phenomenon of secularity was completely unknown in Yemen, and no modern Zionist movement whatsoever was created there. Immigration from Yemen to Eretz Israel was the direct result of the political activity of Jewish personalities and institutions, from the 1870s, for the return of the Jewish people to their land; the climax was the aliya organized by the State of Israel in the first years of its independence. Two powerful factors were of prime importance: the traditional belief in the coming of the Messiah and the ingathering of the exiles; and the difficult situation of the Yemenite Jews under the rule of Zaydi Islam in that country. Yemenite Jews in Eretz Israel therefore identified totally with the Zionist undertaking, even in its early stages, although, with the exception of some individuals, they knew almost nothing of modern Zionist ideology. However, they saw in the activity of the Zionist Movement the clear materialization of the vision of the Prophets concerning the return of the Jewish people to their land. Indeed, quite a few even saw the Jewish representatives of government in the country, firstly British High Commissioner Herbert Samuel and subsequently the first Prime Minister of the State of Israel, David Ben-Gurion, as a kind of embodiment of the longed-for-Messiah; this is even expressed in Yemenite Jewish poetry and correspondence.

The first community of Yemenite Jews in Palestine was founded in Jerusalem, and between 1881 and 1906 most Yemenite immigrants settled there (a lesser number went to Jaffa). In this period they were under the protection of the flourishing Sephardi community in Jerusalem, although they began to develop their independent community institutions, principally in the educational and spiritual spheres. Despite their settlement in an urban community, they had always wished to work the land but all attempts to found agricultural settlements of Yemenite immigrants failed completely, for different reasons. The Yemenite immigrants in Jerusalem became part of the old yishuv.

Living conditions in Jerusalem were extremely difficult. Despite the assistance of various institutions and personalities in the construction of housing and the provision of food for the Yemenite immigrants, a feeling of failure and powerlessness prevailed in the poverty-stricken community, especially when the anticipated moral and financial support from the mother community in San'a the capital of Yemen, was not forthcoming, and when it became clear that in practice nothing was to be gained from a merger with the Sephardi community. After a disagreement broke out between the two communities on payment of exemption tax from army service, an independent community of Yemenite immigrants was established in Jerusalem with the authorization of the Turkish authorities.

From 1907 onwards most of the Yemenite immigrants settled in the new neighborhoods that they constructed on the outskirts of the new moshavot: Sha'arayim in Rehovot, Shivat Zion in Rishon le-Zion, Mahane Yehuda in Petah Tikva, and the Yemenite quarter in Zikhron Ya'akov, etc. In the wake of their great success in the difficult competition with the Arab worker, the heads of the Palestine Office sent Shemuel Yavne'eli to Yemen in 1910 in order to stimulate more immigration. Following his mission, many immigrants arrived from the Yemen and the Zionist institutions took it upon themselves to settle them on the land. These institutions, however, discriminated against the Yemenites in favor of settlers from Europe, and even the European settlers did not see them as full participants in the Zionist enterprise, but only as auxiliary workers. The Yemenite immigrants were helped to a certain extent by the young pioneers from the Second Aliya, but the departure of the Yemenites from the Kineret moshava on the charge that they were not a suitable "element" for secular socialist ideas, caused troubled relations not only between the Yemenites and the people of these settlements, but also between the Yemenites and members of the Labor party.

The bitter deterioration of relations finally led to the creation in 1922 of the Hitahdut ha-Teimanim (Yemenites' Association), an institution encompassing the Yemenite immigrants in Jerusalem, Jaffa, and moshavot, and designed to represent the problems of the Yemenites in Palestine and of their brethren in Yemen, in the representative institutions of the yishuv and the Zionist Movement in general.

The Yemenite representatives constituted a significant and active part of the yishuv (about 7% on average). Until 1940 most of the Yemenites belonged to the religious-conservative faction and to the civic faction of the yishuv, with almost no attachment to the Labor Movement. However, the new immigrants from Yemen all settled in urban neighborhoods, principally in Tel Aviv and its surroundings, and in Jerusalem, rather than in the agricultural settlements. Thus, it is not surprising that with the growth of the movement of revolt against the British Mandatory government, young Yemenite immigrants were drawn towards the Irgun rather than the Hagana. In this period, those who shaped the new culture of the Jewish people in their land were searching among the Yemenite immigrants for the roots of Israeli culture, as expressed in the spheres of artistic creativity (silver work, music, and dance). The intensive activity of the different Yemenite organizations, principally in religious and educational spheres, was sufficient to ensure strict preservation of the community's tradition alongside participation in the life of the yishuv.

Labor Party involvement. A very significant change began in the early 1940s, following the agreement between the Histadrut and the Hitahdut ha-Teimanim. The leadership of the Yemenite immigrants in Palestine passed to Yemenite members of the Labor Party, which controlled most of the institutions of the incipient state. The Yemenite immigrants, particularly the young, were more exposed to secular socialist ideas which were inevitably conducive to a negative attitude towards the tradition of the past. The influence of the Labor Movement was expressed in the organization of immigration from Yemen from the early forties, when young Yemenite Labor Party emissaries worked in the Aden "Geula" transit camp as educators and representatives of the new culture in Palestine. The Labor Party continued this activity indefatigably among tens of thousands of Yemenite immigrants in the early years following the creation of the State, in a perennial struggle with the religious parties over the votes of unsophisticated immigrants. The Israeli government, under the leadership of the Labor Party, also sent many thousands of Yemenite immigrants to the scores of new agricultural settlements located in the Jerusalem hills, in the northern Negev, in Galilee, and in the Sharon plain.

In practice, with the creation of the State of Israel, the Yemenite organizations collapsed, although the Hitahdut ha-Teimanim did manage to send one member to the first and second Knessets. It was no longer possible, however, to maintain a separate education system or law courts. Consequently, second and third generation Israelis of Yemenite origin struck deeper roots in the social life of the State on the one hand, and distanced themselves from Yemenite tradition on the other.

However, in recent years, with the financial, social, and cultural consolidation of a sizable proportion of the Yemenite immigrants, a movement of rediscovery of the sources has developed, which finds expression not only in strengthened religious attachment, but also, and perhaps more so, in a revival of interest in the history of the community and its traditions, together with an active desire to reinforce the community's influence on spiritual life in Israel.

Y. TOBI

YERIDA. *See* EMIGRATION.

YEROHAM. Development town in the central Negev Hills, 9 mi. (14 km.) south of Dimona. Founded in 1951, it was initially intended to be based on farming, but when this failed it became largely dependent on mining in the nearby Great and Ramon craters. Industries brought to Yeroham were only partly successful and its importance diminished after it was bypassed by the Sedom-Eilat highway. Hopes for an improvement to result from the transfer of army camps from Sinai to the Negev after 1978, were only partly realized. Population (1987), 5,890. E. ORNI

YERUSHALAYIM. *See* JERUSALEM.

YESHAYAHU (SHARABI), ISRAEL. Israeli politician and labor leader (b. San'a, Yemen, 1910; d. Tel Aviv, 1979). Settling in Palestine in 1929, he worked initially as a laborer in vineyards and as a road builder. He served as Head of the Department for Yemenite and Eastern communities in the Histadrut from 1934–1938. He was also a member of the Va'ad Le'umi.

In 1948–1949 he helped organize *Operation Magic Carpet, which airlifted virtually all the Yemenite Jews from Aden to Israel. He helped to found cooperative settlements of Yemenite Jews throughout Israel. In 1951 he became a member of the Knesset on the Mapai list. For 12 years from 1955–1967 he was Deputy Speaker of the Knesset, Minister of Posts, 1967–1969; Secretary-General of the Labor Party, 1970–1971; and Speaker of the Knesset, 1972–1977.

He edited two periodicals, *Mi-Teman le-Tziyon* (From Yemen to Zion), *Shevut Teman* (Return of Yemen) and other books. E. HOTER

YESHIVOT (RABBINICAL ACADEMIES) IN ISRAEL. Yeshivot flourished in Eretz Israel from late Second Temple times until after the Palestinian Talmud was completed in the fifth century.

A yeshiva existed in Jerusalem in the 10th century, and Rabbi Yehiel of Paris founded a famous yeshiva in Acre in the 13th century which existed for almost forty years.

Active yeshiva life resumed in the 16th century when Jews expelled from Spain after 1492 began contributing to the flourishing of yeshivot in the Holy Land. The yeshivot in Jerusalem and Safed were renowned. A further revival commenced in the 18th century.

In modern times, the first Ashkenazi yeshiva was Etz Hayim, founded in 1840, which until recently was the main Ashkenazi yeshiva in Jerusalem. The first Hasidic yeshiva in Jerusalem, Hayei Olam, was founded in 1876. Torat Hayim, established in 1887, enjoyed great influence and was characterized by a relatively "liberal" attitude toward the developing yishuv. All these institutions were ultra-Orthodox. Renowned also was the Ridbaz Yeshiva in Safed.

The first "European" yeshiva was the Slobodka Yeshiva which arrived in 1924. It settled in Hebron until 1929, when many of its pupils were slaughtered in the Arab pogrom, and then moved to Jerusalem. It was followed by the Lomza yeshiva, which established itself in Petah Tikva. The Gur Hasidim founded their yeshiva, Sefat Emet, in Jerusalem in 1925.

The great wave of immigration to Palestine after the Balfour Declaration led to the creation of other yeshivot. In the wake of the Holocaust, scores of yeshiva heads arrived in the country and refounded the yeshivot which had ceased to exist in Europe. These included the yeshivot of Mir (in Jerusalem), Ponievecz (in Benei Berak), Telz (in Telz-Stone near Jerusalem), and Grodno (in Ashdod).

After the establishment of the State of Israel and the exemption of yeshiva students from military service, pupils streamed into the yeshivot, turning Israel into the most extensive yeshiva center in Jewish history. Although most of the yeshivot are situated in Jerusalem and in Benei Berak, yeshivot also exist in other religious centers and in all Israel's major cities.

The categories of yeshivot are:

YESHIVOT GEDOLOT (rabbinical colleges)

a. *The Lithuanian Yeshivot*

These continue the tradition of the Volozhin Yeshiva in Lithuania. There is no differenc today between the methods of study at these yeshivot. The emphasis is on Talmudic erudition, and only Talmudic tractates are taught in the curricula. The yeshiva head gives regular lessons. These yeshivot tend towards extremism.

The most prominent of these yeshivot are: Hebron, Mir, Itri, and Ateret Yisrael in Jerusalem, Ponievecz and Slobodka in Benei Berak, and the yeshiva of Kefar Hasidim. In some of these yeshivot, studies are conducted in Hebrew; elsewhere, the language of instruction is Yiddish.

b. *The Hasidic Yeshivot*

Every important Hasidic rabbi has his own yeshiva. Of the scores of such yeshivot, the major ones are Gur, Belz, Vizhnitz, Satmer, Siret-Vizhnitz in Haifa, Slonim, Kozienice, Nadworna, and Kefar Habad. In all, except at Kefar Habad, tuition is in Yiddish.

c. *Zionist Yeshivot*

The most prominent Zionist yeshiva is the Merkaz ha-Rav in Jerusalem. Ha-Kibbutz ha-Dati yeshiva, founded in 1986, was an innovation in this movement's system of thought.

In 1988 there were about 10,800 students studying in the Yeshivot Gevohot (advanced Talmudic institutions for adults), not including the Neturei Karta yeshivot, which are not registered with the Ministry of Religious Affairs and which account for a further 600 students.

YESHIVOT KETANOT (Talmudic schools)

These are intermediate yeshivot between the Talmud Torah schools and the Yeshivot Gedolot. Tiferet Tzevi at one time enjoyed great prestige. However, as each Hasidic leader founded his own yeshiva, the value of these yeshivot declined. The most famous and important of the Yeshivot Ketanot is the Kol Torah yeshiva in Jerusalem. Very few of these yeshivot offer secular studies. 4,700 students were studying in the Yeshivot Ketanot in 1988.

Yeshivot Tikhoniyot (high school yeshivot)

These combine Jewish studies and secular studies leading to the school matriculation examination. The first yeshivot of this kind were the yeshiva of Ha-Yishuv He-Hadash (established by Rabbi M.A. Amiel) in Tel Aviv and Aluma in Jerusalem. Subsequently Midreshet No'am was founded in Pardes Hana. The first Bnei Akiva yeshiva was founded in Kefar ha-Ro'eh; it introduced secular studies.

In 1988 about 20 high school yeshivot existed, mostly in the framework of the Bnei Akiva yeshivot. On graduation, the students enter the Yeshivot Hesder (*see below*), the Yeshivot Gevohot, or the Israel army. From the 1980s some graduates received the army's authorization to go on to the Jerusalem Technological Institute, which combines Talmudic and technological studies.

About 10,000 pupils were enrolled in the high school yeshivot in 1988.

Yeshivot Hesder

These yeshivot combine advanced Jewish studies with active military service. During the four and a half year course of study, a year and a half is devoted to army service. The best known of these yeshivot are Kerem be-Yavneh, Yeshivat ha-Kotel (Jerusalem), Yeshivat ha-Golan (Golan Heights), Nir Kiryat Arba (Kiryat Arba, Hebron).

3,300 students studied in these Yeshivot in 1988.

Yeshivot for Newly Orthodox

Yeshivot for the newly religious multiplied in the 1980s. 3,295 students studied in these yeshivot in 1988. (See BA'ALEI TESHUVA MOVEMENT)

Kolelim

The great number of yeshivot has led to an extraordinary growth of *Kolelim*—study institutions for married yeshiva students. The *Kolelim* pay a small stipend to students, and their income is usually supplemented by their wives, generally graduates of the ultra-Orthodox girl's schools. All the yeshivot mentioned above have *Kolelim*. Several *Kolelim*, and in particular the Harry Fischel Institute in Jerusalem, have begun to specialize in training rabbis and *dayanim* (religious judges). Other *Kolelim* specialize in the training of Torah scribes or in Torah-related occupations. Of note is the extensive development of *Ulpanot* (study centers) for religious women, with an external framework similar to that of the yeshivot. Many students from other countries attend the Yeshivot.

17,400 students attended *Kolelim* in 1988

Sephardi Yeshivot

These was also an unprecedented growth in Sephardi yeshivot, more than 50 new ones being opened in the 1980s. The oldest Sephardi yeshiva is Porat Yoseph in Jerusalem but the Kol Ya'akov Yeshiva counted more students. Also important are the She'erit Yoseph Yeshiva in Beersheba, Ohel Moshe in Benei Berak, and Or Barukh and Or ha-Hayim (for the newly religious) in Jerusalem. Sephardi yeshivot are to be found throughout the country.

Y. ALFASSI

Group in Yesud ha-Ma'ala, 1911. [Jewish Labor Movement Archives]

YESUD HA-MA'ALA. Moshava in the Huleh Valley, established by First Aliya immigrants from Poland in 1883 on the banks of Lake Huleh. The settlers endured great hardships, due to malaria and lack of both capital and farming experience. The aid by Baron Edmond de Rothschild did little to improve the situation. Attempts to cultivate perfume herbs and mulberry trees for the tending of silkworms failed. In the 1940s, the situation improved somewhat when PICA (Palestine Jewish Colonization Association) transferred the land to the settlers. Further small steps forward came with the absorption of immigrants after 1948 and the drainage of Lake Huleh in 1958. Farming is fully irrigated and includes field crops, fruit orchards, carp ponds, etc. In 1987 Yesud ha-Ma'ala numbered 778 inhabitants. Adjoining the moshava is the Huleh Nature Reserve, preserving a sample of the former lake and swamps and their unique vegetation and wildlife.

E. ORNI

YIDISHER KEMFER. Weekly publication of the Labor Zionist Organization of America-Po'ale Zion. Founded in 1906 in New York and Philadelphia, the *Yidisher Kemfer* (Jewish Fighter) gave way to the daily *Zeit*, published by Po'ale Zion from 1920 to 1922. It resumed publication as the *Yidisher Arbeter* (Jewish Worker) in 1923 and in May, 1932, reverted to its original name under which it appeared regularly thereafter in New York. Although the organ of a party, it was never narrowly partisan and served as a forum for free expression on all issues of concern to the Jewish people and the rebuilding of Israel. It also devoted much space to problems pertaining to Yiddish and Hebrew literature and culture, counting among its contributors outstanding creative writers in both languages. In time, it established itself as a leading Yiddish weekly. Its editors included Kalman Marmor, Itzhak Zahr, Ber Borochov, Barukh Zuckerman, David Pinski, Hayim Greenberg, Jacob Glatstein, and Mordecai Strigler.

C.B. SHERMAN

YISHUV. Hebrew term, meaning "settlement," denoting the Jewish community of Eretz Israel prior to the founding of the State of Israel.

YISHUV, SELF-GOVERNMENT IN THE. Efforts on the part of the yishuv to set up publicly recognized institutions of self-government in pre-Israel Palestine began with the First Aliya (from 1882), were expanded during the mandatory era (1918–48), and culminated in the establishment of the State of Israel, when the officially recognized institutions of the yishuv were replaced by the various branches and departments of the Israeli government. Under Turkish rule Jewish self-government was on a local level; under the British Mandate it was placed on a countrywide basis.

Old Yishuv: Palestine's Jewish Communities before 1882. The Old Yishuv, which was maintained predominantly by Jewish charity funds raised in the Diaspora (*see* HALUKA) and was committed to a strictly religious way of life, showed no interest in developing institutions of self-government. It was divided into Sephardi and Ashkenazi communities, which had little contact with each other; each community maintained its own religious and charitable institutions. The Sephardim accepted the authority of the Hakham Bashi, their chief religious dignitary, who was recognized also by the Turkish government. The Ashkenazim were split among a score of Kolelim (small congregations) and *Landsmannschaften* (groups of persons coming from the same town in eastern or central Europe) who were supported and usually housed in special quarters by Haluka funds raised in their hometowns. Regarding themselves, as they did, as a purely religious group devoted entirely to the study and strict observance of the Torah, the Jews of the Old Yishuv had no political ambitions and saw no need to set up their own self-governing institutions.

New Yishuv: 1882–1918. Unlike the Old Yishuv, the pioneers of the New Yishuv regarded themselves primarily not as members of a religious community but as part of a national entity. They sought to develop a Jewish community in Eretz Israel that would not depend on charity but be self-supporting and productive. This attitude, along with the problems and challenges they faced as modern pioneers, led them to develop institutions of self-government.

As early as 1880 the founders of Petah Tikva, the first Jewish village to be established, decided to draw up Regulations of the Founders of the Yishuv Petah Tikva, which were to be binding on all the residents of the village. This was a true constitution, regulating the economic, religious, and educational life of the settlers and providing for village administration. These regulations were the first attempt made by the yishuv in modern Eretz Israel to draw up a constitutional instrument for a territory, however small, inhabited exclusively by Jews. The regulations provided, *inter alia*, that "the Rabbi will be vested with authority, with full power to see that the holy Torah is observed ... and that members who disobey him be punished." It was the duty of every person to assist the rabbi in the enforcement of his rulings. The rabbi was the sole authority in adjudicating "matters, minor and major, be they damage to property or damage to person. At appointed periods, the rabbi shall personally inspect the gardens, fields, and vineyards to see whether everything is being done in accordance with the law ... including tithes to the priesthood." The rabbi, whose salary was to be paid by the community, was also authorized to perform marriages and grant divorces. Detailed provisions were made for compulsory synagogue attendance, a ritual bath (mikve), and burial services. This first modern attempt at Jewish self-government in Eretz Israel was basically theocratic; it reflected the spirit of the Old Yishuv, from which the founders of Petah Tikva originated. However, this constitution was short-lived. In 1881 a new instrument was drawn up with a view to attracting new settlers. Although provision was made for religious observance and some of the theocratic features of the earlier document were retained, the new constitution introduced the principle of democracy in self-government: "Everything in the community shall be decided by a majority of those who have a house therein, and each homeowner, be he rich or poor, shall have one vote." The administration of the village was to be entrusted to an elected committee headed by "the most respected person among them," who was also to "act as trustee for the treasury."

In 1883 a group of Russian Jews, who founded the village Yesud ha-Ma'ala in Upper Galilee, drew up a Book of Regulations providing for a democratically elected management committee. To prevent members from appealing the decisions of the committee to an outside body (presumably the rabbis of Jerusalem), it was stipulated that "none of the decisions of the committee shall be subject to appeal." Although the Book of Regulations made provision for the upkeep of a synagogue, it contained no reference to a rabbi or to rabbinical authority.

In 1891 the inhabitants of Rehovot evolved a constitution under which a democratically elected committee was given control of all village affairs, including religious matters. The Rehovot constitution served as a model for village governments set up elsewhere in the country.

Thus the early years of the 20th century saw the evolution in the country of a pattern of Jewish self-government based on the village as a territorial unit. It was a democratic form of government from which all vestiges of rabbinic authority had been eliminated. Although the committees that administered the villages lacked statutory power to enforce their decisions, including the collection of taxes for the maintenance of local communal services, they experienced no serious difficulties in asserting their authority because the pioneers of the New Yishuv had a highly developed sense of communal solidarity. The committees administered local schools, hired watchmen to guard the villages, and maintained offices for the issuance of title deeds. The Turkish authorities showed little inclination to interfere with these committees as long as they received their taxes on time.

These units of democratic government operated on a strictly local basis. There was no organized Jewish self-government on a national scale. In 1903 a delegation representing the Hovevei Zion of Russia, headed by Menahem M. Ussishkin, arrived in the country with the object of establishing a nationwide representative body of Jewry and of uniting "all the material and spiritual forces of the Jewish population, in order to promote and accelerate the development of the Jewish element in the country, both in quantity and in quality." In consultation with local Jewish leaders, the delegation decided to convene a Kenesiya (Assembly) to develop a plan for a nationwide organization of the yishuv. It was agreed that all males who had resided in Eretz Israel for one year, and who did not live on Haluka funds, would be eligible to vote. This plan would have excluded the Old Yishuv, which at the time constituted about three-fourths of the Jewish population. Elections were duly held, and the Kenesiya met in Zikhron Ya'akov on 23 August 1903. Much of the debate was devoted to the problem of female suffrage, which was vehemently opposed by the Orthodox.

The first attempt to organize the New Yishuv was unsuccessful. A total Jewish population of 12,000 was hardly an adequate basis for the countrywide organization of self-government. Thus, the Old Yishuv and the New Yishuv each went its own way, with each repudiating the views and ways of the other and each mindful only of its own ideals and ambitions.

Mandatory Era: 1918–48. The expulsion of the Turks from Palestine, the issuance of the Balfour Declaration (November, 1917), and the establishment of the mandate, which committed the British to place Palestine "under such political, administrative and economic conditions as will secure the establishment of the Jewish National Home," opened a new chapter in the history of yishuv self-government. It was generally realized, both in Palestine and by the leaders of the Zionist movement abroad, that the building of a Jewish National Home would require the utmost efforts of a united Palestine Jewry. The rigid barriers separating the Old from the New Yishuv and Sephardim from Ashkenazim had to be overcome, and only a representative body of the entire Jewish community would be able to deal with internal issues as well as with the relationship between the yishuv and the British administration. Moreover, under the terms of the mandate provision was made for local autonomy to be enjoyed by each community in Palestine, Jewish and Arab, in the fields of education, social welfare, and religion. All this called for the merger of Palestine's numerous Jewish groups into a closely knit national entity.

Immediately after the British occupation of southern Palestine, a conference of representatives of Jewish settlements and other Jewish communal leaders met in Petah Tikva in order to convene a fully representative assembly. After the conquest of Jerusalem by the British, a gathering of an even more representative character met in Jaffa (2 January 1918) and elected a provisional committee charged with the task of arranging for the election of delegates to a Constituent Assembly. The question of female suffrage was raised again, but no decision was made.

Because the progress of the British forces was slow and northern Palestine was still held by the Turks, a second Preparatory Assembly was held in Jaffa in the summer of 1918. This meeting was addressed by Chaim Weizmann as chairman of the Zionist Commission; he stressed the importance of unity in Palestine Jewry's response to the opportunities opened up by the Balfour Declaration. In the debate on the qualification of voters for the Constituent Assembly, the question of female suffrage threatened to cause a serious rift. To appease the Orthodox, it was agreed to use the name Elected Assembly (*Asefat ha-Nivharim) instead of Constituent Assembly. This change allowed the Orthodox in Jerusalem to hold their own polls, from which women would be excluded; for the sake of fairness, it was agreed that each vote from these all-male polling places should count as two. Everywhere else women were allowed to vote, and elections were duly held on 19 April 1920.

The opening of the Elected Assembly in Jerusalem on 7 October 1920, was a solemn occasion. It was the first time that the Old and New Yishuv, the Orthodox and the secular, Ashkenazim and Sephardim, had met in a democratically elected gathering. It was decided to elect a National Council (*Va'ad Le'umi) as the executive organ of the Elected Assembly, with the duty of administering the affairs of the yishuv between the sessions of the Assembly and of preparing a draft constitution for the autonomous Jewish community, including the qualification of voters. At its first session, the Assembly proclaimed itself the "Supreme Authority in dealing with the public and national interests of the Jewish people in Palestine" and its "sole representation" for internal and external affairs. It further "charged the Va'ad Le'umi with the task of obtaining recognition from the Palestine Government." These resolutions were submitted to Sir Herbert Samuel, the first High Commissioner for Palestine, who replied that the Palestine government would be prepared to recognize the Assembly, provided that the Assembly retained its representative character and that it was clearly understood that "it is not within the scope of the authority to deal with matters affecting the whole of Palestine, but merely to deal with the internal matters of the Jewish community." Samuel added the significant proviso that "such recognition would not prevent any sect, group, or individual of any faith from applying to the Government in any matter, nor from laying any complaint."

The difficulties involved in securing a legal framework for the yishuv sprang from two sources: (1) lack of unity within the Jewish community because of differences between the Orthodox and the majority of the yishuv, and (2) the insistence of the British government on treating the Jewish population of Palestine as a religious rather than a national entity. It took nearly eight years for the British government to enact a law that was to serve as a basis for Jewish autonomy; and when the law finally materialized, it fell short of Jewish expectations. Taking advantage of the disunity within the yishuv, the British were able to place substantial restrictions on the scope and powers of Palestine's Jewish community.

The framers of the constitution for the yishuv had to overcome difficulties from various quarters. The ultra-Orthodox Agudat Israel opposed the constitution; it refused to accept female suffrage and insisted that the supremacy of Jewish religious law be recognized. The Rabbinical Council, as the officially recognized authority in matters of Jewish marriage and divorce, insisted that it be granted preferred status in the organs of self-government. The British government took exception to the provisions making membership in the community compulsory for all Jews in Palestine and granting the organs of the community the authority to levy taxes. After protracted negotiations, the High Commissioner promulgated (1 January 1928) the Jewish Community Regulations, which within the framework of the Religious Communities Ordinances (1926) served as the official and legal basis of Palestine's Jewish community organization until the establishment of the State of Israel.

Of the several organs of the Jewish Community of Palestine (known in Hebrew as *Keneset Yisrael), the first to be dealt with were the Rabbinical Council, as the central ecclesiastical authority, and the local ecclesiastical offices. The regulations provided for the establishment of these central and local rabbinical authorities. The budget for the Rabbinical Council was to be drawn up jointly by the Council and the Va'ad Le'umi, and the Va'ad Le'umi would then supply the funds for the maintenance of the Rabbinical Council. Rather than leave it to the democratically elected organs of Keneset Yisrael to decide whether and in what fashion they would maintain an ecclesiastical establishment, the regulations imposed on the organized yishuv a rabbinical establishment, delineated its authority, and made its maintenance the financial responsibility of the yishuv.

The regulations next provided for an Elected Assembly as the democratically elected body of Keneset Yisrael. It was to hold office for three years; its function was to determine policy, approve a budget, and provide for taxation to cover the budget. The budget and taxes were both subject to the approval of the Palestine government. The regulations promulgated in March, 1930, provided for direct elections by secret ballot, universal suffrage (every member of the Jewish community 20 years of age and over), and proportional representation (the whole of Palestine was declared one electoral area, with voters electing party lists rather than individual candidates). The Assembly was to have 71 seats (the number of seats was increased to 171 in 1944).

The executive organ of Keneset Yisrael was the Va'ad Le'umi, elected annually and allocated an annual budget by the Asefat ha-Nivharim. The Assembly was also empowered to authorize a local community "to levy a tax upon its members" for the purpose of providing for the budget of the Va'ad Le'umi. It was the Va'ad Le'umi that drew up a budget for submission to the Asefat ha-Nivharim; after approval by the Assembly, the Va'ad Le'umi submitted the budget to the High Commissioner for his approval, without which the budget could not come into operation.

Although in accordance with the regulations the community was constituted the Community of the Jews in Palestine, membership was not obligatory. It was provided that as soon as the regulations came into force, the Va'ad Le'umi "shall forthwith draw up a register of adult Jews who have been resident in Palestine not less than 3 months, and the relevent portions of the register shall be published in every town and village in which one or more registered persons reside." Any person whose name was omitted might request the addition of his name to the register. On the other hand, "any person who desires his name to be struck off the register shall, within one month of the publication of the relevant portion thereof, give notice, either personally or by an agent duly authorized in writing, to the Va'ad Le'umi, which shall acknowledge the receipt of the notice, and strike off his name accordingly." It was further provided that in the month of Iyar of each year persons wishing their names to be added to or struck off the register could do so. A person whose name was struck off the list was exempted from paying communal taxes.

Finally, the regulations dealt with local communities. "There shall be not more than one local community in each town or village, but any section of such community comprising not less than 30 adults may claim the satisfaction of its religious and cultural needs according to its own principles." In towns or villages or in quarters where the population was Jewish, the mayor and councillors of such locality also constituted the governing body of the community. In those places there was complete identity between the local municipal authority and the Jewish community, and because the bulk of the yishuv resided in areas where it constituted a majority of the population, the municipal authority simultaneously discharged the functions of the local community, except with regard to such persons as opted out of the community. As a result of this provision, the local governments in parts of Palestine where the population was Jewish maintained the local rabbinate and religious services, such as ritual slaughterhouses, ritual baths, and kashrut certification.

The constitution of the Community of the Jews in Palestine reflected a compromise between the conflicting interests of three parties: the British administration, the great majority of the yishuv, and the Agudat Israel. The British government wished to soft-pedal the nationalist aspect of the yishuv and stress its religious character; hence the prominence given to the rabbinate, and the duty imposed on the democratically elected organs of the community of maintaining the rabbinical establishment. This amounted to the imposition by an outside party of an established religion, since the regulations that served as the constitution of the community could not be altered or modified by that community but only by the British High Commissioner. As a further limitation on the scope of Jewish autonomy, the budgets voted by the Elected Assembly were subject to the approval of the High Commissioner, as were any taxes that the community wished to levy. The extent to which the British administration was determined to go in its treatment of the yishuv as a religious rather than a national entity was apparent in its insistence on using the words "General Council" as its official version of the Hebrew "Va'ad Le'umi," which literally means "National Committee." It was only by way of compromise that the British agreed to have the Hebrew "Va'ad Le'umi" follow the English "General Council" in brackets in the English version of the regulations.

Agudat Israel succeeded in obtaining a provision that enabled any Jew who so desired to opt out of the community and thus be exempted for the payment of communal taxes. The arrangement pleased both the Aguda and the British administration, for it weakened the position of the Keneset Yisrael. It was thought that this provision would suit not only the ultra-Orthodox but also all persons who would simply rather not pay communal taxes.

Although in many ways a disappointment, the Jewish Community Regulations nevertheless afforded a framework for the development of Jewish self-government in Palestine. First, the regulations recognized only one community on the national and local level, so that only the Va'ad Le'umi could act as the officially recognized spokesman for Palestine Jewry. Second, the Asefat ha-Nivharim, by virtue of its authority to levy taxes, was able to develop countrywide activities in several fields. The fact that on the local level municipal authorities also discharged communal functions tended to strengthen the national-secular aspect of Jewish self-government in Palestine under British rule.

Whereas the publication of the regulations merely failed to elicit enthusiasm in the yishuv, it evoked an immediate adverse reaction from Agudat Israel and other ultra-Orthodox circles. The date of the promulgation of the regulations, 1 January 1928, was proclaimed a fast day by Agudat Israel, and the group gathered at the Western Wall to mark the event. The ultra-Orthodox elements outside Agudat Israel organized themselves into a separate community, the Adat Israel. Together the two groups formed a committee of dissidents from the Jewish community; they urged their followers to opt out of the community and applied to the High Commissioner for recognition as a separate community with powers to tax its members, basing themselves on the provisions of the Religious Communities Ordinances. They also made representations to the Permanent Mandates Commission of the League of Nations. However, the Palestine government rejected their request and denied them recognition.

The rather narrow legal framework fixed by the mandatory power for Jewish self-government in Palestine, the limitations imposed on its powere of taxation, and, finally, the right of any Jew to opt out of the community hindered the development of Jewish self-government in Palestine. Yet despite all these handicaps the self-discipline of the yishuv brought a steady growth and a strong consolidation. The withdrawal of Agudat Israel and the other anti-Zionist ultra-Orthodox elements put an end to the interminable quarrels over female suffrage; even more important, it made harmonious cooperation possible between the Va'ad Le'umi and the Executive of the World Zionist Organization (WZO). After 1929 this applied equally to relations between the Va'ad Le'umi and the newly established *Jewish Agency, which was the all-inclusive organization of world Jewry, Zionist and non-Zionist, working on behalf of the Jewish National Home. The Executive of the Jewish Agency was in charge of relations with the British government in London and Jerusalem; it was responsible for fundraising activities for the building of Palestine and, through its offices in Jerusalem, was concerned with agricultural settlement, urban development, and a variety of economic activities. The political parties represented in the Asefat ha-Nivharim were also represented on the WZO and, through it, on the Executive of the Jewish Agency. The Mizrachi participated actively in both the WZO and the governing organs of the Community of Jews in Palestine; relations between this Orthodox party and the secular majority were generally harmonious. Mizrachi participated in the elections to the Asefat ha-Nivharim, in which it consistently obtained between 7 and 10 per cent of the votes.

It was in the fields of education and health services that Jewish self-government in Palestine scored its greatest success. From 1919 until 1933 the WZO, through its Department of Education (in cooperation with the Jewish Agency Executive after 1929), administered and was largely responsible for financing the network of Jewish schools in Palestine. Thus the country had two separate and officially organized public school systems, one for Arab children, maintained and administered by the Education Department of the British Palestine government, and the other for Jewish children, administered and maintained by the WZO with some financial aid from the mandatory power. In 1933 the administration of the Jewish schools was transferred from the Jewish Agency to the Community of Jews in Palestine, and the Va'ad Le'umi set up a Department of Education for that purpose. Whereas in 1919 the WZO had provided nearly 89 per cent of the education budget, in 1947 its share in the budget was about 9 per cent, the balance being furnished by the Va'ad Le'umi and the local communities, with the Palestine government providing an annual grant-in-aid. Thus it came about that, in effect, Keneset Yisrael assumed total responsibility for the education of Jewish children in Palestine.

The Va'ad Le'umi had a Political Department, headed by Yitzhak Ben-Zvi, which was concerned with the relations of the yishuv and the Palestine administration. Another department was in charge of health services. The Department of Social Welfare was headed for many years by Henrietta Szold. There was also a department in charge of the local communities, their budgets, and other problems. With the Department of Education these comprised the network of activities of Jewish self-government; thus the Va'ad Le'umi, as the executive branch of Keneset Yisrael, was able to exercise a considerable measure of real autonomy.

After the establishment of the State of Israel, the Va'ad Le'umi and Asefat ha-Nivharim were dissolved. The departments of which the Va'ad Le'umi had been in charge were transferred to the provisional government of the new State.

Despite the limitations imposed by the British authorities, self-government afforded the yishuv invaluable training in democratic practice and procedure. Since the organs of Jewish self-government in Palestine during the mandate era enjoyed only limited coercive power, their effectiveness depended largely on voluntary cooperation between the various Jewish groups. Thus, the experience of self-government endowed the Jewish State with a democratic tradition of harmonious coöperation between widely differing groups and a modus vivendi between the nonobservant majority and the moderate Orthodox elements. As for religious life, the State inherited from the Keneset Yisrael a "religious status quo": an established religion and a tax-supported rabbinic establishment exercising judicial powers, a "religious trend" in the public school system, and the existence of religious parties as an integral part of the political party system. S.Z. ABRAMOV

YISRAEL. *See* ISRAEL.

YIZHAR, S. (Yizhar Smilansky). Hebrew author and educator (b. Rehovot, 1916). Yizhar is the first and most prominent prose writer of the "native school" of modern Hebrew literature. He was raised in Rehovot, studied at the Hebrew Teachers Seminary and at the Hebrew University in Jerusalem, and served in the Palmah during Israel's War of Independence. He was a Labor member of the Knesset from 1941–1967.

His first story "Efrayim Hozer la-Aspeset" (Ephraim Goes Back to Alfalfa, 1938) is a landmark in the development of Hebrew literature. Both in content and form it reflects the world of the first generation of Hebrew writers born in Eretz Israel. It is set in a kibbutz and, although conforming to its Zionist-socialist ideals, depicts the clash between the individual and the collectivist society in which he chose to live. Yizhar's prose style while still "literary" attains the flexibility of a native speaker of the language. Most of his other stories are set in the rural areas of Israel. Their characters are drawn from the world of the kibbutz and the moshav, and their plots involve the tensions which beset them when their personal wishes clash with the collective will. The intimate and introspective voice of writers like Brenner and Gnessin influenced Yizhar's style. It is to Gnessin in particular that he is indebted although he further develops the use of interior monologue. Like other "nativist" authors, Yizhar has a penchant for lyrical descriptions of his native landscape.

Yizhar's mammoth novel *Yemei Ziklag* (Ziklag Days, 1958) has been called the great epic novel of Israel's War of Independence. It portrays the psychological world of a platoon of soldiers. Its outward plot, seven days of fighting in the arid mountain country of the Negev, is subsidiary to the probing of the emotional world of its characters. Besides their gnawing personal concerns, in the terror of battle, they often question the basic premises of the Zionist endeavor and, at times, reject the sacrifices it exacts. Yizhar skillfully employs the *Akedah* (the sacrifice of Isaac) motif as the underlying metaphor of his novel. All of Yizhar's works are animated by a strong moral sense. He was the first to write sympathetically of the plight of the Arab refugees and the moral conflicts engendered whenever the realities of the Arab-Jewish conflict clashed with the ideals of Labor Zionist humanism. When his two stories on these themes, *Ha-Shavuy* (The Prisoner) and *Sipur Hirbet Hizah* (The Story of Hirbet Hizah) appeared, nationalist elements vehemently rejected his "moralizing." He continues to deplore the moral damage which he believes is inflicted on the Israeli society as a result of the persistent Palestinian problem.

In later years, Yizhar confined his writings to the fields of education and literary criticism. He dealt with the problem of teaching ethical values in the school system (*Al Hinukh ve-Arakhim*—On Education and Ethical Values, 1974) and has written critical works on the art of the short story.

E. SPICEHANDLER

YIZRE'EL. Kibbutz in the Jezreel Valley, on the northwest slope of Mt. Gilboa. The site is assumedly that of biblical Jezreel (I Kings 21) where King Ahab had his summer residence and took from Naboth his vineyard. In the 1948 War of Independence, the strategically situated Arab village of Zar'in on the site served the Arab Legion for harassing the Harod Valley Jewish settlements. On 30 May, 1948, a Palmah group stormed the village and a few weeks later set up the kibbutz which was joined by pioneers from English-speaking and other countries. Yizre'el has highly-intensive farming and an industrial enterprise. Population (1987), 542. E. ORNI

YIZRE'EL VALLEY. *See* JEZREEL VALLEY.

YODEFAT. Moshav shitufi in central Lower Galilee, 9 mi. (15 km.) southwest of Carmi'el. Founded in 1962, initially as a kibbutz, where shortly before a Jewish National Fund forest center and watchtower had been built. Fruit orchards and vegetables, partly in greenhouses, are the principal farming branches. There are also handicraft workshops. In 1987 Yodefat numbered 212 inhabitants. According to archeological evidence, Yodefat was the last Galilean fortress resisting the Romans, where Josephus Flavius surrendered to Vespasian (The Jewish Wars, III:7). E. ORNI

YOKNE'AM. Moshav on the northwestern rim of the Jezreel Valley, below the southeast corner of Mt. Carmel. Founded in 1935 as a moshava by Jews from Holland and other countries, it developed intensive mixed farming. In 1987, it was a moshav affiliated to Ha-Ihud ha-Hakla'i. Population (1987), 683. Nearby is the mound of biblical Jokneam (Josh. 21:34) of the tribe of Zebulun. E. ORNI

YOKNE'AM ILIT. Development town near the Yokne'am (Jokneam) mound in the Jezreel Valley, founded in 1950. A metal factory of the defense industry forms its main economic base. Population (1987), 5,640. E. ORNI

YOM HA'ATZMA'UT. *See* INDEPENDENCE DAY OF ISRAEL.

YOM HA-ZIKARON. *See* INDEPENDENCE DAY OF ISRAEL.

YOM KIPPUR WAR. Arab-Israel war, 6–24 October 1973, fought by Israel against Egypt and Syria, who received military assistance directly from Jordan and Iraq and indirectly from other Arab states.

Background. The *Six-Day War of 1967 left Israel in possession of all of the territory captured in the course of that war. Security Council Resolution 242, adopted in November 1967, while being pursued with varying degrees of rigor over the years, had not led to fruitful negotiations. The Arab doctrine of "three no's" adopted at Khartoum (September 1967), i.e., no recognition of Israel, no negotiation with Israel, no peace with Israel, still governed at least the public conduct of the Arab governments. The *War of Attrition, designed by President Nasser of Egypt to unfreeze the status quo, had failed in that purpose. His successor, Anwar *Sadat, adopted his predecessor's motto: what had been taken by force would be returned by force. The obliteration of the humiliation suffered by the Egyptian armed forces in 1967 became a major policy objective. Sadat proclaimed the year 1971 "the year of decision;" when nothing happened in the course of that year he was held up to ridicule in Egypt and beyond.

On the Israel side, when a major mobilization ordered in the spring of 1973 had turned out to be a costly reaction to a false alarm, both political and military authorities were lulled into the belief that a major Arab offensive designed to retake the "territories" was highly improbable. This belief was sustained by the conception that Arab governments would not risk a major war as long as Israel's Air Force enjoyed clear superiority and controlled the skies. The months of September-October, just before the winter, were known to be the usual season for both Egyptian and Syrian maneuvers. These factors enabled both of these countries to proceed, in the summer and fall of 1973, with massive preparations for a major offensive operation. While the relevant troop movements, by their very nature, were well known to the Israel Defense Forces (IDF), their purpose—an offensive rather than a maneuver—remained secret until less than 12 hours before zero hour.

Following talks between Egyptian and Syrian political and military leaders during May-June, 1973, Sadat had visited Damascus on 12 June. It was then agreed to prepare for simultaneous joint attack against Israel, with the objective, in the first phase, of recapturing territories taken by Israel in the course of the Six-Day War. The method was to be a "meatgrinder" attack along as wide a front as possible, forcing Israel to disperse its counterattack. The tentative date for Operation Badr (lightning)—6 October—was fixed primarily for military reasons: a moonlit night, with currents in the Canal suitable for crossing operations; a night during which an attack would not be expected—during the month of Ramadan, for Moslems, and on Yom Kippur, a day of fasting for Jews. Zero hour—2 p.m.—was a compromise between Egypt and Syria, each of whom wished to fight with the sun at its back. In the fall of 1973 attempts were made—with Saudi support—to include Jordan in the alliance; however, in view of the latter's military weakness and its losses in 1967, its task was primarily limited to tying up Israel forces along the Jordan River, and preventing a flank attack through Jordan into southern Syria. The entire plan was kept in strict secrecy—even senior Egyptian officers were informed only at the very last moment.

The War. On the morning of 5 October, IDF intelligence began to reassess its assumptions concerning the "low probability" of war; it was only at 1.30 a.m. on 6 October that they finally determined that an attack was to be expected in the course of that very day. Even then there was a mistake concerning the exact hour of attack. There was not enough warning time for a large-scale mobilization and movement of troops to the front which required 48 hours under the best circumstances. Some of that time was wasted in discussing the extent of the mobilization, until the Prime Minister, Golda Meir, decided at 9 a.m. on an all-out mobilization, following the advice of the chief of general staff, David Elazar. At the same time she decided against a preemptive air strike, to avoid Israel being branded as the aggressor.

On the northern front the attack began at 1.50 p.m. with a strafing attack by Syrian Mig 17 fighter planes and simultaneous artillery bombardment against IDF positions on the Golan Heights, followed immediately by three Syrian infantry divisions with hundreds of tanks, backed up by two tank divisions, sweeping across the ceasefire line. The IDF position on Mount Hermon—"the eyes and ears of the State," vitally important for purposes of intelligence gathering—was captured by helicopter-borne infantry; three other positions were evacuated under orders. An Israeli force of 180 tanks held the line against a Syrian force which rapidly increased to 1,400 tanks. The main threat was directed towards the Nafah junction where Syrian forces came to within 7 miles (10 kms.) of the Jordan; a secondary thrust further south came within sight of the Sea of Galilee. At this stage the northern command, under General Rafael Eitan, was augmented by another division even though reinforcements at first arrived piecemeal and were sent into battle before they were able to group in their organic units. Northern command at that stage, with heavy support from the air force, launched a counterattack on 8 October. By Wednesday, 10 October, at 10 a.m., Israeli forces had driven the Syrians back to the 1967 ceasefire lines. Some 300 Syrian tanks and armored personnel carriers were abandoned or destroyed in the northern sector, at the foothills of the Hermon, by the 7th Brigade, in what came to be known as the Vale of Tears.

On Thursday, 11 October Israel counterattacks continued into Syria, in the general direction of Damascus, coming on the following day within 26 miles (40 kms.) of the Syrian capital, whose outskirts were now within Israel artillery range. Two Iraqi armored divisions arriving in the theater of operations at that time inadvertently found themselves in the jaws of an IDF pincer and were forced to withdraw with heavy casualties. A similar fate awaited Jordanian forces in their attempt to strengthen the Syrian left flank. On 21–22 October, just before the ceasefire (see below) came into effect, the IDF finally succeeded in recapturing Mount Hermon. In 16 days of fighting the Syrians had lost 1,100 tanks, including many Soviet-manufactured T-62's, the latest model not yet supplied even to Russia's Warsaw Pact allies. The Russian-provided land-to-air SAM missile system had been totally destroyed by Israel as were the main components of the Syrian air force, enabling Israel's air force to concentrate on deep penetration operations against strategic targets in Damascus and other centers, including the refinery in Tripoli. 370 Syrians and 65 Israelis had been taken prisoner on the opposing sides.

Simultaneously with the Syrian attack in the north, at 2 p.m. on Yom Kippur (6 October) five Egyptian divisions crossed the Suez Canal under cover of an unprecedented air and artillery barrage. Unlike the north—where IDF troops were at least tactically on the alert—the 500 Israel troops, mainly reservists from Jerusalem manning the strongholds of the Bar-Lev line, were taken by complete surprise by the assault of 70,000 Egyptians, who bypassed the strongholds taking up positions to the east, at their rear. Israeli armored forces rushing to previously prepared positions found them occupied by Egyptian infantry provided with large quantities of Sagger antitank missiles, causing heavy casualties. The Israel air force's main effort, at that time, was directed at the northern front, in view of its proximity to major population centers. When the air force was able to turn to the south it met massive opposition, not only from the missile sites which had been moved right up to the canal immediately following the adoption of the ceasefire standstill ("Rogers") initiative in 1970, but also from infantry-operated SAM 7 land-to-air missiles and conventional anti-aircraft guns, which combined to cause heavy casualties to the Israel air force.

The Egyptians established three major bridgeheads east of the canal: in the north, based on Kantara; in the center, on Ismailia; and in the South, north of Suez. The first two operated by the second, the last by the third, Egyptian army. Most of the Bar-Lev line was captured and abandoned by the third day. Only one stronghold, at the northern extreme of the canal at Baluza, held out throughout the war; the most southerly, at Port Tewfik facing Suez, surrendered after a week, having run out of ammunition and supplies.

It had been the IDF's plan to undertake a major counterattack as soon as mobilization had been achieved. The chief of general staff, on the night of 8–9 October, indeed confidently announced that such an attack was imminent, in the course of which the Egyptian forces would be smashed. The attack on that day was stillborn, adding considerably to the despondency, in certain quarters bordering on despair, which had widely prevailed ever since the outbreak of hostilities.

On 14 October, the Egyptians, under pressure from the Syrians, moved their last remaining armored division east of the canal, attempting to break out from the bridgeheads at four points. These attempts failed, with the Egyptians losing some 250 tanks on that day. It was only then that General Haim Bar-Lev, newly appointed commander of the southern front, authorized a major counterattack. During the night of 15–16 October, elements of General Ariel Sharon's division crossed the Suez Canal to the north of the Great Bitter Lake, establishing a bridgehead in Egypt proper. When the Knesset convened at 4 p.m. on 16 October for its first session since the beginning of the war, the Prime Minister was able to announce that Israeli troops were operating west of the canal. The Egyptian high command was taken by surprise, and when apprised of the facts did not give them due weight. It was only after about 24 hours that they moved, on the east bank of Suez, to close the Israel corridor leading up to the canal, threatening Sharon's lifeline to the rear. General Avraham (Bren) Adan's division bore the brunt of the fighting to keep that corridor open, with some of the heaviest fighting—possibly the most intensive concentrated armored battle in military history—taking place in the "Chinese farm," in the northern part of the corridor. By 17 October two bridges across the canal had been established—under fire—by Israel army engineers. The northern division now crossed the canal, its first mission being to destroy anti-aircraft missiles so as to open an air corridor for the air force, and to advance southwards in the direction of the Genifa hills, and beyond, towards the city of Suez. Egyptian commando counterattacks, against the paratroop brigade which had been the first to cross, failed. With most of the SAM missiles out of the way, the Israel air force had achieved superiority and freedom of action. On 19 October a third Israel division, commanded by General Magen (the original commander, General Mandler, had been killed at the end of the first week) crossed the Canal, its mission being to undertake a broad sweep in the sparsely defended area west of the Genifa hills towards the port of Adabya on the Gulf of Suez, far to the south of the canal.

Once the IDF had crossed the Suez canal on 16 October, the Soviets, previously unwilling to take any action to stop the fighting, hastily invited the US Secretary of State, Henry Kissinger, to Moscow, and—in agreement with him—asked the UN Secretary General to convene the Security Council to an urgent meeting on 21 October. The Council adopted Resolution 338 for an immediate ceasefire, effective at 5.59 p.m. on 22 October. Immediately after the ceasefire, negotiations were to start between the parties concerned on the "implementation of Security Council Resolution 242 in all its parts," aimed at establishing "a just and durable peace in the Middle East." Fighting continued, however, with the Third Egyptian Army now completely surrounded, struggling desperately to break out and reestablish a link with Egyptian forces west of the canal. The southern Israel division consolidated its gains and closed the ring by the capture of Adabya. An Israel force penetrating the town of Suez encountered heavy opposition. The continuation of fighting, despite the ceasefire order, with consequent risks of further losses for its Egyptian protégé, caused the Soviet

Union to insinuate the possibility of unilateral military intervention, which in turn motivated a highly visible worldwide defensive "condition 3" alert, for all US forces. On 24 October the Security Council convened once more, to adopt Resolution 339 reiterating the call for an immediate ceasefire and return to the lines of 22 October; this time the call was combined with arrangements for the immediate despatch of UN observers. Fighting finally stopped on that day, with Egyptian forces holding two main bridgeheads along the east bank of the canal, to a depth of some 7 miles (10 kms.)—and Israel occupying some 640 square miles (1,600 sq. kms.) inside Egypt, with the most westerly point some 46 miles (70 kms) east of Cairo. The Third Army, with about 20,000 soldiers and 300 tanks, was isolated. Egypt had lost about 1,000 tanks; 8,000 Egyptian prisoners were in Israeli hands, as against 240 Israeli prisoners of war in Egypt.

In several naval engagements the Israel navy, which had played a secondary role in previous wars, destroyed most of the Syrian and part of the Egyptian navies, gaining complete control in the theater of operations, i.e., the eastern Mediterranean and the northern part of the Red Sea.

Air and sea lifts of unprecedented dimensions—by the Russians with equipment and arms for the Syrians and the Egyptians, and subsequently by the US for Israel—played a vital role in the supply efforts of the opposing sides. On 11 November, a six-point ceasefire agreement between Egypt and Israel was signed under UN auspices at kilometer 101 on the Suez-Cairo Road. On 18 December 1973 the General Peace Conference opened, with the US and the USSR as cochairmen, and Egypt, Jordan, and Israel as participants. On 18 January 1974—with Henry Kissinger as the main mediator—a disengagement agreement was signed between Israel and Egypt; several months later a similar agreement was signed between Israel and Syria. In the course of negotiations with Syria, fighting flared up once more. While the agreement with Egypt was followed by another, and ultimately crowned by the Peace Treaty of 1979, predicated on the vindication of the honor of the Egyptian forces coupled with the realization that Sinai could not be recovered by force, the agreement with Syria was not followed up.

Casualties were high, on both sides, with 2,700 Israelis and an estimated 3,500 Syrians, and 15,000 Egyptians killed. Exchange of prisoners with Egypt was effected with relative ease and speed; Syria utilized information about Israeli prisoners, and subsequently their return, in order to gain maximum advantage in the course of the negotiations.

N. LORCH

YORK-STEINER, HEINRICH. Author, editor, and Zionist (b. Senica, Slovakia, Hungary, 1859; d. Tel Aviv, 1934). A prominent journalist and editor in Vienna, York-Steiner was one of the first to join Herzl in launching the Zionist movement. Early in 1897 he participated in a small conference at which, under Herzl's leadership and initiative, the decision was made to convene the First Zionist Congress. From then on, York-Steiner worked closely with Herzl and helped him publish *Die Welt*, the first official periodical of the World Zionist Organization. He later assisted Herzl in his political endeavors. York-Steiner settled in Palestine in 1933. During the last years of his life he was a member of the Revisionist movement.

York-Steiner wrote several books including *Die Kunst als Jude zu leben* (The Art of Living as a Jew, 1928).

A. ALPERIN

Rabbi Ovadia Yosef (right) watches Rabbi Shelomo Goren bless Menahem Begin on his return from Egypt, 1977. [Israel Govt. Press Office]

YOSEF, OVADYA. Rabbinical scholar and Sephardi Chief Rabbi of Israel (b. Baghdad, 1921). Brought to Palestine at the age of three, he displayed outstanding academic aptitudes from an early age. He studied at the Porat Yosef Yeshiva in the Old City of Jerusalem. In 1945, he was appointed as a dayan (judge) of the *beth din* (rabbinical court) of the Sephardi community. In 1947–50, he served as head of the Cairo *beth din*. Although the Egyptian Secret Service, convinced that he was preaching Zionism in his Hebrew sermons, followed his actions and raided his home, he managed to complete his full term there.

Upon his return to Israel, he was appointed to the Petah Tikva *beth din* where he remained until 1958, and was then transferred to the Jerusalem District Rabbinical Court. In 1965, he was appointed to the Rabbinical Supreme Court. Yosef was elected chief rabbi of Tel Aviv in 1969 and in 1972, became the Rishon le-Zion, the Sephardi Chief Rabbi of Israel, serving until 1983.

An influential leader of the Sephardi communities, Yosef has been the religious leader and leader of the Sephardi *teshuva* (religious penitence) movement, which stresses Jewish education dedicated to Torah learning and the observance of the *mitzvot* (commandments). He is the patron of many institutions that help the newly observant renew their contact with their roots as well as fill the spiritual void they have encountered in their secular life. He is also one of the spiritual guides of the political wing of this movement, the *Shas party.

A noted halakhic authority, he has written several volumes of responsa and published *Hazon Yosef*.

G. SHUSTER-BOUSKILA

YOTVATA (Yotveta). Kibbutz in the southern Arava Valley, 26 mi. (41 km.) north of Eilat. Founded as a Nahal (army pioneering agricultural unit) outpost in 1951. it became a permanent village in 1958, pioneering in desert oasis farming, based on a relatively strong, although slightly brackish, spring. It emphasized the reintroduction of date palm

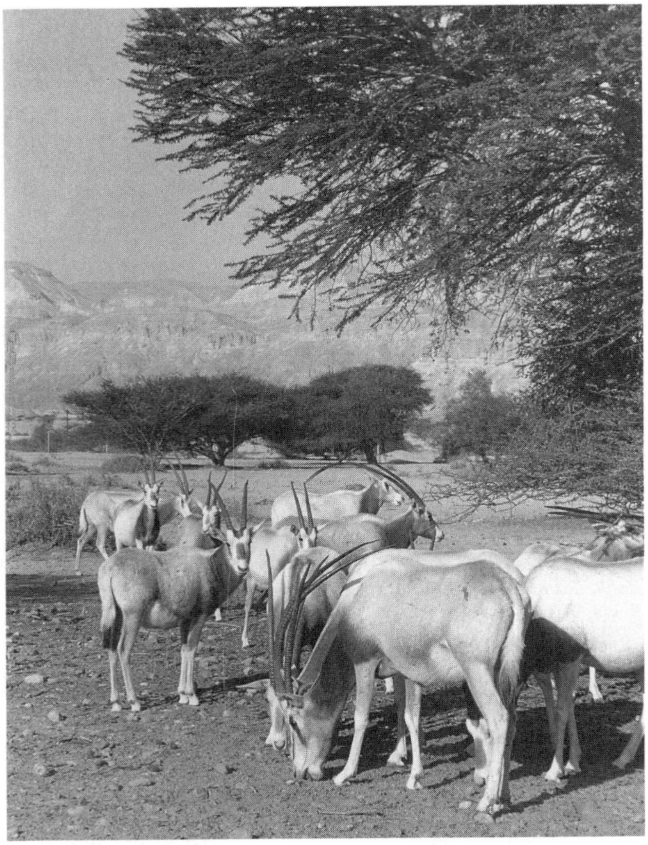

Reindeer in Yotvata Wildlife Reserve. [Nature Reserve Authorities]

groves and the breeding of pedigree cattle. Yotvata started to supply most of the milk products needed in Eilat and to market special products in all of Israel, also operating some industry. Nearby is the Hai-Bar wildlife reserve. Population (1987), 534. E. ORNI

A Young Judea volunteer in Tiberias absorption center with children from Ethiopia. [Hadassah—Young Judea]

YOUNG JUDAEA. Oldest Zionist youth organization in the United States, officially founded in 1909. It emerged from Zionist study clubs, of which one of the first, and the nucleus for Young Judaea, was the Herzl Zion Club, established in 1904 by Abba Hillel Silver, Max Silver, and Israel Chipkin. They defined their objective as "the dissemination of the Zionist ideal and self-cultivation in Hebrew among the Jewish youth of this city."

At the instigation of Henrietta Szold and Judah Magnes, a special conference was held in New York in 1909 and the Young Judaea organization was founded. Fifty delegates from independent youth groups attended and Professor Israel Friedlander was elected president. The aim was "to advance the cause of Zionism, to promote Jewish culture and ideals..." and the Basle Program was adopted. Later Rabbi David de Sola Pool served as president for an extended period. For several years the officers of the movement were adults although the members themselves were not more than 21. In 1910 the *Young Judaean* magazine began to appear; and in 1916 a Training School for Teachers was set up with Jessie Sampter as director of leadership training. Throughout, Hebrew played an important role in the organization's programs.

From 1919 Young Judaea was affiliated with the Zionist Organization of America (ZOA). In 1924, it established a relationship with the Jewish scout movement in Palestine. By 1935, there were ten regional organizations. In that year Hadassah began to grant an annual subvention of $2,500 to help "effect the educational program of Young Judaea."

In 1940, the American Zionist Youth Commission (AZYC) was set up, under the sponsorship of Hadassah and the ZOA, to service the youth movements Young Judaea, Junior Hadassah, Masada, and Avukah "and to coordinate and develop general Zionist youth activities in the US" and from 1941–67, Young Judaea received its funds from the AZYC. It was able to expand its activities: a senior (high school) movement was formed in 1948 and in the same year Tel Yehuda, the first national senior camp, was held and in the following years five junior camps were established. In 1950 the Leaders' Association was organized and in that year Young Judaea was the first Zionist youth organization to send teenagers to Israel for a summer. In 1956 it organized the first one-year program in the Israel workshop program.

In 1967, the partnership between Hadassah and the ZOA was dissolved and Hadassah established Hashahar (Dawn) an overall movement under its sole sponsorship. Its activities include a year-round club program with its own publications. There are two distinct levels: Young Judaea, for boys and girls from 9 years of age through the final year of high school, and Hamagshimim (The Fulfillers or Realizers) whose members are college age through age 30, based on campus and providing Zionist activities and Israel program opportunities to its members. In 1973 a group of Hamagshimim members founded Kibbutz Ketura, 30 miles north of Eilat. Israeli emissaries from the scout movement in Israel work with Young Judaea through the national office in different regions and at camps.

Young Judaea members participate in the Hashahar Year Course in Israel (The Jerusalem Institute) based at the Hadassah Youth Center in Jerusalem which accommodates 120 young people; the Mahon Leadership Training Institute based at Kiryat Moriah Educational Center in Jerusalem; and the Hashahar Israel Experience, Israel Hadrakha Seminar and summer programs, all in cooperation with the

American Zionist Youth Foundation and the Youth and he-Halutz Department of the World Zionist Organization.
M. FREUND-ROSENTHAL

YOUTH ALIYA. Movement for the transfer of children and young people to Israel and their settlement there.

In 1932 the first six boys of Youth Aliya, recruited by Recha *Freier in Berlin, arrived at the Ben Shemen youth village and in 1934 the first group of youngsters from Germany arrived at Kibbutz En Harod. Mrs. Freier, the wife of a Berlin rabbi, was in contact with the kibbutzim and with leaders and institutions in Palestine in an effort to facilitate the transfer of young people from Nazi Germany. She thus laid the foundations of the Youth Aliya movement. The idea was implemented under the leadership of Henrietta *Szold, who dedicated the last 12 years of her life to the movement. During this period more than 15,000 children and youth from Germany and the Nazi-occupied countries were absorbed in Youth Aliya, which acted *in loco parentis*, replacing absent or lost parents. The election of Henrietta Szold as head of Youth Aliya largely determined its character as an educational movement and as a national organization maintaining close cooperation with many voluntary organizations, first and foremost with *Hadassah. Among Miss Szold's main assistants were Dr. Georg Landauer and Hans Beyth (who acted as her successor until he was murdered by Arabs in 1947). Dr. Landauer was director of the Jewish Agency's Department for the Settlement of German Jews, of which the Youth Aliya Office, as it was called in the early days, was part. It was Landauer who, in 1935, signed the agreement between Youth Aliya and the Hadassah organization which made the latter the official agency of Youth Aliya in the United States and provided an enormous incentive for the rescue, immigration, and integration of children and youth from all countries of Europe.

In Great Britain and in continental Europe, committees were organized for Youth Aliya whose active membership was composed of Zionist women, Women's International Zionist Organization (WIZO) members, and interested non-Jews. In the course of time, the Pioneer Women and the Mizrachi Women's Organization of America in the United States, the Hadassah-WIZO Organization of Canada, and the South African Women's Zionist Council rallied to the cause of Youth Aliya. In most countries, Jews and Christians worked together in a Friends' Committee for Youth Aliya, notably in Great Britain and Switzerland. From the beginning of 1947, Moshe *Kol, a member of the Jewish Agency Executive, headed the Youth Aliya Department; he served as chairman of the Board of Directors of the movement until 1966. Kol was succeeded by Yitzhak Artzi, who served until 1968 when he was in turn followed by Joseph Klarman, Yoseph Shapiro, and Uri Gordon.

The success of Youth Aliya in rehabilitating children res-

Eleanor Roosevelt with Moshe Kol, head of Youth Aliya [Hadassah]

Youth Aliya children arriving in Palestine, 1936. [Beth Hatefutsoth]

cued from the Holocaust and immigrant youth from 80 countries was due to the thousands of educators, housemothers, home attendants, teachers, field-workers in cooperative settlements, youth villages, educational establishments, and youth day-centers, and foster families. The central team of the department's Executive, educational supervisors, social workers, and professional personnel in the psychological clinics and in every section of Youth Aliya's work—many of them idealists who regarded these tasks as their mission in life. During its more than 55 years of existence, Youth Aliya has gathered, absorbed, educated, and rehabilitated more than 35,000 children and adolescents from a great variety of cultural and educational levels, many from remote and isolated Jewish communities. Youth Aliya turned them into constructive, independent adults, and in the course of time many of the integrated trainees became educators themselves and helped integrate other children.

In the 1980s Youth Aliya continued to meet the needs of Jewish children from various parts of the world. More than 2,000 youngsters from Iran were educated by Youth Aliya during the period which immediately preceded the ascent to power of Ayatollah Khomeini. In the mid-1980s more than 3,000 children and youth from Ethiopia, many of them orphans, were absorbed and educated in the religious villages affiliated with Youth Aliya.

In the late seventies, Youth Aliya initiated a new program: a year-long educational experience aiming to strengthen the Jewish roots and attachment of young people from the Diaspora. But the bulk of Youth Aliya's student population since the early seventies has been socially, economically, and scholastically disadvantaged children and youth, mostly the offspring of first and second generation immigrants. In 1987 they represented 80% of Youth Aliya's 18,000 students. Special foster programs were introduced to cope with the scholastic and social lag of these children (some of these programs were subsequently adopted by the Ministry of Education and Culture, the Ministry of Social Welfare, and by the Israel Army).

The movement has aroused interest and attention among the older, developed nations as well as in the newly developing countries, all of which had to cope with the difficult problems of youth and were seeking ways to prevent young people from going astray and becoming delinquents. The educational experience of Youth Aliya in theory and in practice attained wide recognition iin the International Union for Child Welfare and the International Federation of Children's Communities.

Youth Aliya is a part of the Jewish Agency and the World Zionist Organization, but it raises a substantial part of its budget from friends and supporters the world over. The implementation of its work is carried out in full partnership with the agricultural settlements and particularly with the kibbutz movement and Zionist women's organizations, which support both its youth villages and its educational establishments.

From the inception of Youth Aliya until the establishment of the State, nearly 30,000 trainees were absorbed; another 205.000 were integrated during the period from the establishment of the State to 1987. In the late 1980s Youth Aliya was responsible for the care of more than 18,000 trainees. Youth Aliya education is based on formal schooling, work, training, and social education. Youth Aliya is concerned with the individual within the group and considers him no less important than the group as a whole. In the day centers, set up especially in the development towns, care is provided for drop-outs and educationally underprivileged adolescents and children.

A study of the absorption and education of the first 50,000 graduates of Youth Aliya showed that 95 per cent of them remained in Israel and 2 per cent fell in World War II and in Israel's War of Independence. Only 3 per cent left the country. In no other category of immigrants was the percentage of those striking permanent roots in the country so high.

Since the 1960s, the agricultural training and kibbutz-oriented education have been one aspect of education in Youth Aliya; nowadays, the majority of its youth population receives vocational and academic training. Thanks to scholarships awarded by Youth Aliya, many of its graduates have gone on to universities, or schools of art. Among the graduates of the movement are painters, musicians, sculptors, scientists, senior army officers, teachers, politicians, and writers who have held important positions in Israel. They set up more than 50 kibbutzim and cooperative smallholders' settlements, either independently or with youth from the Zionist youth movements, and continued to regard themselves as members of the Youth Aliya family. Always aware of the security problems of the country, Youth Aliya graduates form a considerable proportion of Nahal, the special military educational and social formation within the Israel Defense Forces.

International seminars were held under the auspices of Youth Aliya (and Hadassah) in 1968, 1978, and 1984, as well as two international conferences (in 1958 and 1981) of the FICE (International Federation of Children-Communities, a UNESCO-affiliated organization) of which Youth Aliya is a founding member.

M. KOL—M. GOTTESMAN

YOUTH MOVEMENTS IN ISRAEL. Israel's youth movements were modeled on Jewish youth organizations established in central Europe before World War I. They followed the pattern of the Baden-Powell scouting movement in England, with its group organization, age-level structure, camping and fieldcraft, tracking, first-aid, signaling, etc.

From the European Jewish youth organizations they derived the spirit of revolt against traditions and certain modes of behavior through the cultivation of specific mannerisms, simplicity of dress, the ideals of equality, and a desire to alter the social structure. The implementation of these ideals brought Jewish youth to Eretz Israel and they played a significant role in the birth of the cooperative settlement movement and in particular the kibbutz. The new settlers drew upon the youth movement framework for their forms of organization and for this reason many of the Israeli movements are affiliated to settlement groupings.

In 1988 the following youth movements were affiliated to the Council of Zionist Youth Movements in Israel: (*Betar, *Bnei Akiva, *Ezra, *Ha-Mahanot Ha-Olim, *Ha-No'ar ha-Dati ha-Oved veha-Lomed, *Ha-No'ar ha-Le'umi ha-Oved veha-Lomed, *Ha-No'ar ha-Oved veha-Lomed, *Ha-No'ar ha-Tziyoni, *Ha-Tzofim, *Ha-Shomer ha-Tza'ir, Maccabi ha-Tza'ir (*see* MACCABI WORLD UNION). They counted some 250,000 members in all, active in 820 branches throughout the country run by 11,000 youth leaders (including 355 branches in development towns and under-privileged areas). In addition to the formation of groups which train together in the Israel Defense Forces within the framework of Nahal prior to settlement on the land, senior members of these movements give a year's voluntary service in development towns. S. KETKO

YUGOSLAVIA, RELATIONS WITH ISRAEL.

Before 1948: Shortly after the Balfour Declaration, the head of the Serbian Mission in the United States, Vesnitch, wrote a letter of support to Dr. David Albala, the Zionist leader of Belgrade. After the creation of the Yugoslav state, Zionist and other communal Jewish activities continued unhindered and anti-Semitism was practically unknown during the inter-war period. During World War II, friendly ties were established between the Yugoslav partisans and representatives of the yishuv. Palestinian parachutists were dropped into liberated areas of Yugoslavia and helped mostly in communications with the Allied Command in Italy.

The attitude of Socialist Yugoslavia, which came into being in the wake of World War II, towards the Zionist struggle for independence was one of comprehension and active aid, by letting transports of "illegal" immigrants, as well as some shipments of arms, pass through its territory. This assistance was mainly motivated by anti-imperialist considerations (on the ideological level), but stemmed also from a genuine will to assist the Jewish struggle for statehood, particularly as it comprised Socialist elements.

Yugoslavia participated in the 1947 United Nations Special Commission on Palestine (UNSCOP). The Yugoslav delegation showed understanding for the Jewish aspirations, but eventually aligned itself with the minority opposing partition.

After May, 1948: Yugoslavia recognized the new State and diplomatic missions were exchanged. Reciprocal visits by trade union delegations, members of parliament, etc. took place and relations were correct, even cordial. Commercial ties developed to mutually satisfactory levels. That state of affairs continued until the Bandung Conference of non-aligned nations in 1955. From then on, there was a gradual cooling-off on Yugoslavia's part, as it strengthened its ties with the Arab World, especially with Nasser's Egypt. The personal friendship between Tito and Nasser, both ambitious to become leaders of the third-world countries, may have played a part in this process. Another turning-point causing a deterioration was the Sinai campaign of 1956, depicted by Yugoslav officials and press, as "unprovoked aggression" on Israel's part, and thereafter Yugoslav friendship to Israel declined steadily. Yugoslavia openly abandoned any semblance of neutrality in regard to the Arab-Israeli conflict, unequivocally siding with the Arabs. Following the Six-Day War Yugoslavia broke off relations unilaterally following a visit by Tito to the Soviet Union.

Since the breaking of diplomatic ties: The critical stance of the Yugoslav leadership vis-à-vis Israel gained momentum as Yugoslavia invested in and forged new economic links with the Arab countries. In the international field, this policy led to anti-Israel votes, including the sponsoring of anti-Israel moves at the United Nations and in other international bodies. Yugoslavia also voted for the UN resolution calling Zionism racist. This wholly one-sided pro-Arab policy was pursued until the death of Marshal Tito. In the post-Tito period, Yugoslavia suffered a certain number of setbacks, and some disenchantment set in with its relations with Arab nations, although its policy was not officially reappraised. Nevertheless, and despite the continual flow of information from Palestine Liberation Organization and other Arab sources, the local press, in particular the popular and widely circulated Belgrade weekly *Nin*, has advocated the view that the breaking of relations with Israel may have been a mistake. This idea was first voiced by a political scientist, Vekaritch, repeated by the former foreign minister, Kocha Popovitch, and also by a prominent journalist, Gustincic. In late 1987 this trend accelerated and spread in the Yugoslav media generally, more particularly in Ljubljana, capital of the Slovene Republic.

The first direct political move, apart from the meeting of Foreign Ministers Peres and Dizdarevic in New York, was a visit in 1987 by a two-member *Mapam* delegation to Belgrade, invited by the League of Communists, the first encounter of this nature for 20 years.

The tourist trade between the two countries has been one-sided: namely, with a few Yugoslav exceptions, such as participants in international conferences held in Israel and a few Jewish groups on commemorative and family visits, it has been Israeli citizens who have traveled to spend vacations in Yugoslavia. In 1987, some 28,000 Israelis visited Yugoslavia, despite the complicated process of obtaining entry permits. The Slovene-owned Adria airline, in December 1987, started regular and direct weekly flights to Israel. Cultural relations also began to develop in the latter part of 1987 with a visit of the Habima theater to Belgrade and performances by Yugoslav music and dance groups in Israel.

During 1988 the question of renewing full diplomatic relations with Israel was repeatedly raised in Yugoslav public forums. A deputy from the Republic of Slovenia put the question to the Government in a session of the Federal Parliament. The same query was addressed to Raif Dizdarevic, the Foreign Minister. In both cases the official response was negative. The media seemed on the whole unconvinced and continued to deal with the problem, pleading for a more balanced approach to the Arab-Israeli conflict. Some newspapers and television stations featured Israeli viewpoints.

The rather one-sided tourist trade, as the number of Israelis visiting Yugoslavia reached 30,000, was on the increase but ceased with the breakup of Yugoslavia and the ensuing fighting there.

Commercial ties have been steady, without great advances. In March 1989 a bilateral Chamber of Commerce was inaugurated in Tel Aviv, but after the dissolution of the country relations with the successor states were in a state of flux.

Z. LOKER

YUGOSLAVIA, ZIONISM IN. In 1918 Yugoslavia had about 60,000 Jews. Owing to the influx of refugees from Central Europe, their number had grown to 75,000 by the eve of Nazi occupation in April, 1941. One-third were Sephardim, concentrated south of the Sava and Danube Rivers; the rest were Ashkenazim. About 5 per cent of the Jewish community belonged to Orthodox congregations which opposed political Zionism; the rest were members of congregations affiliated with the general Jewish community. Down to the 20th century almost all the Sephardim were faithful to the religious-nationalist tradition, and most of them still spoke Ladino. By contrast the Ashkenazim, by and large, were assimilationist.

Zionist Precursors. Two rabbis active in the 19th century were the forerunners of Zionism in Croatia. Rabbi Yekuthiel Hirschenstein, a former student of Rabbi Moses Sofer of Pressburg (Bratislava), was interested in the settlement of Eretz Israel as early as 1807 and remained active in this endeavor even after becoming the rabbi of Varazdin, in northern Croatia, in 1812. Whereas Rabbi Hirschenstein's activity made little impression on Croatian Jewry, Rabbi Judah ben Solomon Hai *Alkalai exerted considerable influence on the Jewish community of Serbia. Following anti-Jewish manifestations in the town of Sabac (Shabatz) in 1865, all its Jewish residents were ready to emigrate to the Holy Land.

Impact of Political Zionism. David Alkalai (1862–1933), a member of the family of Rabbi Judah ben Solomon Hai Alkalai, and his wife Rachel were among the few from the South Slavic countries to participate in the First Zionist Congress in 1897. Immediately after the Congress, Alkalai established the first Zionist organization in Serbia. From 1924 until his death he served as president of the Zionist Organization of Yugoslavia. Young men returning from their studies in Vienna, capital of the Austro-Hungarian monarchy, influenced their contemporaries in Zagreb. In 1898 the Literary Society of Secondary School Youth was established; it soon became the focus of the Zionist movement in Croatia and later in Yugoslavia as a whole. Alexander Licht (1884–1948), first the leader of his own circle, soon became the undisputed head of Yugoslav Zionists. A champion of integrated Zionism, he knew how to smooth over party disputes and to preserve the unity of the Zionist Organization of Yugoslavia.

Yugoslav Zionism in the early 20th century had to contend with the indifference of the Jews of Croatia and Slavonia in general, and with opposition from communal leaders and heads of the philanthropic organizations in particular. Fortunately, the Jewish community included not only the Sephardim, whose numbers had grown, but also Jews who had come from Galicia to Bosnia-Herzegovina when the latter had been conquered by the Hapsburgs in 1878, and who had been adherents of the Hovevei Zion movement. They responded enthusiastically to Herzl, joining the World Zionist Organization as soon as it was formed. The influence of such men as Gustav Seideman, a bookdealer, Nathan Landau, a teacher (who organized a Zionist group in 1897), and Yohanan Thau, a government employee, spread from Bosnia over all the Serbian-Croatian-speaking Jewish communities. These men were active in propaganda, organization, and fundraising for the Jewish National Fund from its inception and also worked on the first South Slavic Zionist periodical, *Zhidovska Smotra* (1906–14), edited by Alexander Licht and others.

At the same time a number of rabbis from eastern Europe and other strongholds of traditional Judaism were active in Zionism. They were Dr. Hosea Jacobi, in Zagreb; Dr. Simon Bernfeld in Belgrade; Dr. Mordechai (Marcus) Ehrenpreis, in Djakovo, who was one of Herzl's chief assistants in preparations for the First Zionist Congress; and Dr. Moses Margel, author of a German-Hebrew dictionary. These men were joined by Dr. Moritz Levi, in Sarajevo, and by Dr. Isaac Alkalai, in Belgrade.

A group of university students from the South Slavic countries founded the Bar Giora society in Vienna (1902), while Sephardi students organized their own association, called Esperanza. The two societies became the prime movers in the student conferences that convened biennially between 1904 and 1910. The Judea Jewish student society, organized in Zagreb in 1909, played an important role in strengthening Zionism in Yugoslavia.

A prominent figure in the student Zionist movement was Hugo Spitzer, who attended the First Zionist Congress. He later became president of the Zionist Organization of the South Slavic countries within the Austro-Hungarian monarchy (founded in 1909) and then co-chairman of the Zionist Organization of Yugoslavia, from its founding in 1919 to 1924.

Before World War I, David Albala (1887–1942) organized a youth group called Gideon in Belgrade; a nationalist group was active in Sarajevo; and an association of Jewish officials was established in Zagreb by Herman Licht who, like his brother Alexander, was a pillar of Croatian Zionism. There were a Maccabi sports club and a Benot Zion club for girls.

World War I, with the mobilization of the younger people for military service and the passing of the older generation of leaders, temporarily disrupted Zionist activity. In 1917, however, work was resumed under the leadership of Lav Stern (1888–1959) and in September, 1917, the first issue of *Zhidov* (The Jew), a Zionist weekly, appeared. It was published until just before the German invasion of Yugoslavia in 1941, when it was forced by the government to suspend publication. Russian prisoners of war and Austrian soldiers from eastern Europe brought new views to the peripheral Jewry of Croatia, which was the prime mover in Yugoslav Zionism between the two world wars.

The Serbian government-in-exile was the first Allied power to endorse the Balfour Declaration, in a letter from the Serbian representative in the United States, Milenko Vesnic, to Capt. David Albala (dated 27 December 1917). On 6 January 1919, one month after the Serbo-Croatian-Slovenian monarchy, the modern state of Yugoslavia, had been proclaimed, the founding conference of the Zionist Organization of Yugoslavia was held in Zagreb. The authorities were friendly, because they considered that a union of Jews from different language areas (Hungarian, German, Italian, and Spanish) would make for greater unity within the monarchy and act as a counterpoise to the separatist and irridentist movements in Yugoslavia. It was only with the growth of reactionary forces in the country and the development of Socialist trends in the Zionist ranks, that the movement as a whole became suspect. The Yugoslav Secret Service then established close surveillance over all Zionist activities and built up dossiers that served as the basis for the persecution of Zionist leaders during the Nazi occupation.

The Zionists in Yugoslavia soon had groups paralleling all the trends that existed in the World Zionist movement. Pioneers of the Third Aliya who passed through Zagreb in 1919 exerted considerable influence on the young. Because of the Jewish quota enforced at Polish universities, scores of Jewish students from Poland came to Zagreb after World War I. They organized a Borochov Society, providing the Jews of Yugoslavia with their first opportunity to become familiar with Yiddish literature and folk songs. Politically, this development also affected the youth movements, which joined the Po'ale Zion in Sarajevo. From this, Mattathia, an organization of working youth developed. Influenced by the Prague Conference, the Ha-Po'el ha-Tza'ir movement arose, with headquarters in Zagreb. However, the spiritual and political leadership of the Zionist movement in Yugoslavia remained in the hands of Alexander Licht, the supporter of integrated Zionism. Leftist tendencies found expression in the youth movements, but the ideological and practical struggle was, in the main, between personal fulfillment through pioneer work in Palestine, and the comforts of bourgeois life in Yugoslavia.

The first hakhshara training farm was organized in 1920, and a Palestine Office was set up under the leadership of Dr. Abraham Werber, who had come from eastern Europe. There was a pause in hakhshara activity after the first hakhshara groups left for Palestine, but work was soon resumed on an expanded scale and continued up to the Nazi invasion in 1941. Bet She'arim, the first agricultural settlement of pioneers from Yugoslavia, was established in 1926. Immigration to Palestine from Yugoslavia remained very small, and it was only the Ha-Shomer ha-Tza'ir movement and, to some extent, the Netzah—Tekhelet-Lavan, that managed to start a program of intensified agricultural training and to send members to Palestine. Before the Nazi invasion, Akiva, a General Zionist youth group, was active as well and organized an agricultural training program. The Revisionists in Yugoslavia organized themselves under the leadership of Dr. Julius Dohany and formed a Betar youth group.

Because of the small number of Jews in Yugoslavia and their lack of cohesion, their Zionism was in constant need of inspiration from the centers and leaders of Jewish and Zionist life, such as the visit of David Wolffsohn to the Zionists of Croatia and Slavonia. Between the two world wars, the visits of Nahum Sokolow, Menahem Ussishkin, Vladimir Jabotinsky, Nahum Goldmann, and other Zionist leaders had an impact, as did fund representatives, Women's International Zionist Organization (WIZO) and youth movement spokesmen, and Hebrew teachers. These contacts with the Zionist world outside led to an active Zionist movement with a spiritual and cultural content that would otherwise have been inconceivable in such a barren ground. In addition to *Zhidov*, weeklies that appeared (in Sarajevo) were *Zhidovska Sviyest* (from 1918) and *Yevreyski Zhivot*, both of which later merged into the *Yevreyski Glass*. Jüdische Zeitung/Georgiske Norine was started at Nori Sad in the 1930s. There were youth monthlies and *Ha-Aviv*, a monthly for children, which was stopped only by the Nazi invasion. *Omanut*, a monthly edited by the writer Hinco Gottlieb, began to appear in 1937; it fought Nazism down to April, 1941.

Emigrants to Israel at Belgrade railroad station, 1948. [Federation of Jewish Communities of Yugoslavia]

World War II and the Postwar Era. The Nazi onslaught brought destruction to the Jews of Yugoslavia and to the Zionist movement there. Less than one-fifth of the Jewish population escaped the Holocaust. Some survived as prisoners of war, and others fled to areas occupied by the Italians; some were rescued in Hungary, while others joined in the guerilla warfare of the Yugoslav partisans. The liberation of Yugoslavia and its reconstitution as a Socialist state did not bring a revival of the Zionist movement there. Some of those who had fled to Italy went on to Palestine; others crossed the Atlantic. The new government of Yugoslavia maintained a friendly attitude toward the Jews and Zionist aspirations. Yugoslavia served as an important base and transit area for "illegal" immigration during the period of the British Mandate in Palestine and the struggle over Israel. With the establishment of the State of Israel, Yugoslavia permitted Jewish citizens to emigrate to Israel, and most of them did so in several waves starting in December, 1948, and continuing up to 1951. There were c. 6,000 Jews in Yugoslavia at the time of its break-up, as against the 9,000 to 10,000 who had emigrated to Israel and about 1,000 who were scattered in other countries.

Z.I. ROTEM—Z. LOKER

YUGOSLAV JEWS IN ISRAEL. The first scheme for pioneering immigration from Yugoslavia started in the early 1920s, when a moshav was planned in Bet She'arim. A score of youngsters came from Yugoslavia, but the conditions were unfavorable and the plan failed. The immigrants dispersed, some of them even returning to Yugoslavia. Others became prominent in their fields, such as the agronomist Hugo Zaloscer, who came in 1922 and was an active, innovative director of the Pardes Hanna Agricultural School, and Dr. Avraham Werber/Avishur, a well-known hydrologist, employed both by the government of Palestine and the Jewish Agency. Some succeeded in private farming, like Yehuda Altmann in Hadera (who became a town councillor). However, the aliya was no more than a trickle until the early 1930s, when the first Ha-Shomer ha-Tza'ir group arrived at Magdi'el. They, together with a Romanian contingent, were among the founders of Kibbutz Sha'ar ha-Amakim. By the mid-decade, another kibbutz, Gat, was established in the south (an amalgamation of Yugoslav and Galician pioneers from the same movement). Some forty families from the Yugoslav branch of Blau-Weiss, affiliated with Kibbutz ha-Me'uhad and Mapai, were successfully absorbed in Kibbutz Afikim. At about that time a certain number of holders of "A" certificates, i.e., so-called capitalists, arrived from Yugoslavia, including several intellectuals including Dr. Zvi Rotem, member of the editorial staff and secretary of *Davar*, and editor of *Omer* (a daily in easy Hebrew for newcomers), Yakir Eventov (former editor of the Zionist weekly *Zhidor* in Zagreb), and Dr. Otto Mandl, a trade expert. Sarolta (Shari) Berger (née Kohn) was an early Zionist activist who became one of the leading figures of Hadassah. One group of holders of immigration certificates from the town of Bitolj (Monastir) in Macedonia, near the Greek border, consisted mainly of laborers, artisans, and peddlers. They settled in Jerusalem, where they founded their own synagogue called Yagel Ya'akov, and formed a quiet and hardworking community.

In 1934, the Association of Yugoslav Immigrants was founded. It endeavored to encourage and assist newcomers while also assuming more ambitious tasks, such as the furthering of cultural ties with the old homeland and fostering friendly relations between the yishuv, later the State of Israel, and Yugoslavia. At the same time, a Historical Commission was established and collected documents, on the initiative of Yakir Eventov, resulting, in 1970, in the first book ever to be published on the history of Yugoslav Jews (in Hebrew), written by Eventov and edited by Rotem. The archives have been deposited in Jerusalem, in the Central Archive for the History of the Jewish People.

The Immigrants' Association also published several translations into Hebrew of works of Yugoslav Jewish authors (Isaac Samokovlija and Dr. H. Gottlieb) and a memorial brochure on Dr. Alexander Licht, the president of the Zionist Federation in the inter-war years. (In 1955, his remains were brought to Israel from Switzerland, where he died, for reburial in Jerusalem.)

During the summer of 1944 a few hundred Holocaust survivors arrived from Italy. After the establishment of the State, in 1948/49, several thousands of immigrants came from Yugoslavia and most of them found a niche in the socio-economic pattern of the country. Yugoslav immigrants founded the moshavim of Kidron and Rishpon. Jews of Yugoslav origin have also entered the professions as engineers, pharmacists, lawyers, physicians, chemists, biologists, and other paramedical personnel, including hospital matrons. They have made a notable contribution in the military field participating actively in all Israel's wars and suffering proportionately high casualties. This group has also provided several members of the officer corps, including two commanders-in chief (Haim Bar-Lev, although born in Vienna, was raised in Zagreb, Yugoslavia and went to Israel as part of a Youth Aliya contingent from Yugoslavia, and David Elazar, born in Sarajevo, capital of Bosnia). Another general was Dr. Reuven Eldar, who headed the Army Medical Services.

Among journalists prominent positions have been achieved by Dr. Zvi (Cvi) Rotem (see above); Yosef Lapid of *Ma'ariv* and for a time head of the Israel Broadcasting Authority; and R. Teitelbaum of *Yedi'ot Aharonot*.

Z. LOKER

Z

ZACH, NATAN. Hebrew poet and literary critic (b. Berlin 1930). He was taken to Palestine in 1935. While studying at the Hebrew University, he became the leader of a group of young writers who revolted against the Shlonsky-Alterman school of literature. Together with Benjamin Hrushovsky (Harshav) he edited their iconoclastic literary journal *Li-Kerat* which advocated the freeing of Hebrew poetry from traditional rhythmic and rhyme patterns. Formal devices were to be used only if they stressed a poetic image or idea. The old ideologies were to be shunned. The individual world of the writer lost in a tragic, faithless age must be the central theme of modern writing: Zach's criticism marked the shift of Hebrew literature away from its eastern European influences and in the direction of the new poetry written in America (Eliot, Pound, e.e. cummings, and others) and Germany (Rilke, Else Lasker-Schüler).

His poems manifest a decided shift from metaphor to synecdoche, from the romantically lyrical to the ironic. In the 1980s, compelled by the political and military crises which troubled Israel's intellectuals, Zach, in violation of his previous "neutrality" in matters political, penned several "political" poems critical of the Lebanese War.

His major works are: *Shirim Shonim* (Various Poems, 1964), *Tzefonit Mizrahit* (North East, 1979), *Anti-Mehikon* (Against Erasure, 1984). E. SPICEHANDLER

ZACKS, SAMUEL JACOB. Industrialist, art collector, and a communal and Zionist leader in Canada (b. Kingston, Ontario, 1904; d. Toronto, Canada, 1970). He studied at Queen's (Canada), and Harvard universities and in his later years lectured widely on art and was chairman of the art gallery of Ontario. He was active in the National War Finance Committee, the Central Committee for Interned Refugees, the Boy Scouts Association of Canada, the Community Chest, tha Canadian Opera Company, the Jewish Theological Seminary of America, the United Jewish Welfare Fund of Toronto, and other institutions.

For many years Zacks was one of the leading Zionist personalities in Canada. In 1943 he helped found the Canadian Palestine Committee. During the struggle for Israeli independence he assisted in the procurement of shipping for "illegal" immigrants and of weapons, and was the chief architect of a wide-ranging program designed to win Canadian government support for the establishment of a Jewish state in Palestine. He served as president of the United Zionist Council, which coordinated the various Zionist groups in Canada in the 1940s and 1950s; as one of three members of the presidium of the Zionist Organization of Canada (ZOC) from 1944 to 1946; and as president of the ZOC from 1946 to 1950. Over the years he held the posts of vice-president of the World Confederation of General Zionists and of the Canadian Friends of the Hebrew University, vice-president and member of the board of governors of the Weizmann Institute, a founder (1938) and president (1942) of the United Welfare Fund of Toronto, member of the administrative committee of the World Zionist Organization, trustee of the America-Israel Cultural Foundation, and director of the Palestine Economic Corporation. M. BROWN

ZAMBIA, ZIONISM IN. *See* ZIMBABWE AND ZAMBIA, ZIONISM IN.

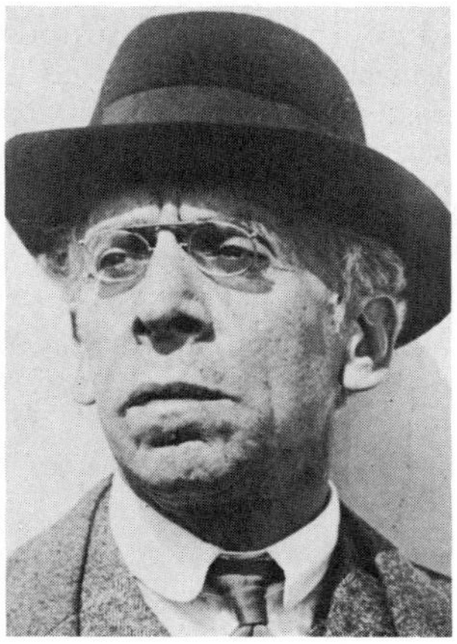

Israel Zangwill.
[Zionist Archives]

ZANGWILL, ISRAEL. Anglo-Jewish author (b. London. 1864; d. East Preston, England, 1926). Zangwill became well known as a novelist after the publication of his *Children of the Ghetto* (1892), *Ghetto Tragedies* (1893), and *The King of Schnorrers* (1894). When Herzl arrived in London on 21 November 1895, his first call was on Zangwill, to ask him to arrange a meeting with the leaders of Anglo-Jewry. The conference, which took place under Zangwill's chairmanship at a gathering of the Order of Ancient Maccabeans on 24 November, was Herzl's first Zionist meeting. Herzl again addressed the Maccabeans under Zangwill's chairmanship in July, 1896. In April, 1897, Zangwill joined the first Maccabean pilgrimage to Eretz Israel, and after his return to London published his impressions of the trip. He attended the First Zionist Congress, which he described in his *Dreamers of the Ghetto* (1898), and subsequent Congresses. The British press often quoted him as a spokesman for Zionism.

Zangwill was one of the most fervent supporters of the *East Africa scheme, and after the Seventh Zionist Congress (1905), which rejected all plans for Jewish settlement outside Eretz Israel, he left the World Zionist Organization and founded the *Jewish Territorial Organization (ITO), whose object was to acquire land in East Africa or elsewhere for a Jewish settlement. During World War I he supported the efforts of Vladimir Jabotinsky to create a Jewish Legion. In 1917 a reconciliation took place between Zangwill and Chaim Weizmann, and Zangwill was one of the speakers at the grand celebration of the Balfour Declaration held on 2 December 1917, at Covent Garden. Gradually, the activities of the ITO came to an end, and it was officially dissolved in 1925. Zangwill called for a radical Zionist policy, and advocated the transfer of Palestinian Arabs to other Arab countries. He criticized the British government for failing to fulfill its obligation under the Balfour Declaration and the Zionist leadership for not pressing for the establishment of a Jewish State.

J. FRAENKEL

ZARITSKY, JOSEF. Israel artist and founding father of the New Horizons movement (b. Borispol, Ukraine, 1891; d. Kibbutz Tzova, 1985). He graduated from the Kiev Academy in 1914 and settled in Jerusalem in 1923. After studying in Paris 1927–29, he returned to settle in Tel Aviv where he began his greatest watercolor landscapes, painted between 1929–45, all freely brushed over the basic composition of pencil lines. In 1947/8 he helped to establish the New Horizons modernist movement, of which he soon became the leader, supported by his former students, Yeheskel Streichman and Avigdor Stematsky. In the 1950s, Zaritsky moved to total abstraction of the landscape, leading what were called the lyrical abstractionists. He worked on a large scale in oils, while continuing to make small watercolors like the *Yehiam* and *Tzova* series, maintaining a home and studio at Kibbutz Tzova. He was awarded an Israel Prize in 1960. In 1954–56 Zaritsky worked in Paris and Amsterdam and was accorded a one-man show at the Stedelijk Museum, Amsterdam, 1955. His first retrospective was at the Bezalel National Museum in 1952, and a major retrospective was held at the Tel Aviv Museum, 1985.

M. RONNEN

ZEBULUN VALLEY (Emek Zevulun). Section of the coastal plain of Israel, 12 miles (19 km.) long and 6 miles (10 km.) wide. Bounded by Mount Carmel on the south, Haifa Bay on the west, and the hills of Lower Galilee on the east, it is drained by the Kishon and Na'aman Rivers. Since the drainage of these rivers was impeded by the sand dunes that fringe the coast, the valley through most of history, was a swampy area occupied chiefly by Bedouins. After its acquisition by the Jewish National Fund in 1928, it became the first region of Palestine to benefit from regional planning. Its southern section developed into the industrial zone of Haifa, bordered on the north and west by residential areas known as the Kerayot. Its northern and eastern sections became prosperous agricultural settlements, and the former swamps were utilized in part as fishponds. From the 1920s, the northwestern section also became increasingly urbanized.

Y. KARMON

ZEDERBAUM, ALEXANDER. Hebrew and Yiddish writer and editor (b. Zamosc, Russian Poland, 1816; d. St. Petersburg, 1893). Zederbaum lived in Odessa from 1840 to 1871, when he moved to St. Petersburg. In 1860, after receiving permission to publish a periodical, he founded and edited *Ha-Melitz*, the first Hebrew weekly in Russia. Later he founded *Kol Mevaser* (1862), the *Yidishes Folksblatt* (1881), and the *Vyestnik Russkich Yevreyev*. In 1886, *Ha-Melitz* began to appear as a daily.

At first Zederbaum fought for Haskala (Jewish Enlightenment); later he became an ardent advocate of the Hovevei Zion movement. He attended the Kattowitz Conference of the Hovevei Zion in 1884 and tried to obtain legal permission from the authorities for the founding of Hovevei Zion groups in Russia. As a result of his efforts, permission was granted in 1890 for the establishment of a Society for the Support of Jewish Agriculturalists and Artisans in Eretz Israel and Syria, whose seat was in Odessa. After the first general meeting of the society, Zederbaum visited western Europe to raise funds for a settlement in Eretz Israel.

I. KLAUSNER

ZEID, ALEXANDER. Leader of the *Ha-Shomer watchmen's organization (b. Balagansk, Siberia, 1886; d. Jezreel Valley, 1938). Arriving in Eretz Israel in 1904, he worked as an agricultural laborer in Rishon le-Zion, Petah Tikva, Zikhron Ya'akov, and other agricultural settlements.

In 1907 he was one of the founders of a secret defense organization, called Bar Giora, set up in Jaffa. Its aim was to guard and defend the country's Jewish population; it developed into Ha-Shomer where Zeid was also influential in decisions on policy and development.

He was one of the founders of Tel Adashim, Tel Hai, and, in 1916, Kefar Giladi. He left Kefar Giladi in 1926 over an ideological dispute concerning the level of independence to be achieved by the kevutza. He settled on the land of Sheikh Abrek (near Kiryat Tivon of today) and worked guarding Jewish National Fund land in the Jezreel Valley.

Zeid was murdered on guard duty during the 1938 riots by local Arabs. He left a diary and notes about his work as one of the *shomerim* (guards) of the yishuv.

In 1943 Kibbutz Givat Zeid in the Jezreel Valley was founded in his name, near the site of his death. On a hill opposite the kibbutz is a statue of Zeid on his horse.

E. HOTER

ZEITLIN, HILLEL. Author, philosopher, and publicist (b. Korma, Mogilev District, Russia, 1871; d. Treblinka, 1942). Educated in a hasidic environment, Zeitlin acquired a general education and in the early 1890s moved to Gomel. There he met Yoseph Hayim Brenner and other Hebrew writers, immersed himself in the study of Jewish mysticism and philosophy, and made his literary debut in *Ha-Shiloah*

(1899). He was a delegate to the Fifth Zionist Congress (1901). In a series of articles he vigorously supported the East Africa scheme. After moving to Vilna, he became an editor of *Ha-Zeman*. There he also began to write in Yiddish, which later became his major medium of expression. In 1906 he moved to Warsaw, where he contributed to the Yiddish press.

Zeitlin wrote on literature and on problems of Jewish society and culture. He was greatly concerned with the welfare of his people, and many of his articles were stirring appeals for spiritual and moral regeneration. He also wrote studies on Jewish mysticism and hasidism. His writings reflect a spirit of deep religious devotion. He never found his place in any Jewish political party but fought as an individual for his ideas. During a visit to Palestine in 1925 he became very close to Chief Rabbi Abraham Isaac Kook. In 1942 he was deported from the Warsaw ghetto to the Treblinka extermination camp.

Selections of Zeitlin's writings were published in both Hebrew and Yiddish.

ZEMACH (TZEMAH), SHELOMO. Pioneer of Labor Zionism, educator, and author (b. Plonsk, Russian Poland, 1886; d. Jerusalem, 1974). A Zionist from early youth, Zemach settled in Eretz Israel in 1904 as one of the early immigrants of the Second Aliya. He worked in Jewish agricultural settlements and was one of the founders of Ha-Po'el ha-Tza'ir (1905) and of Ha-Horesh, the first organization of Jewish agricultural laborers. In 1909 he went to France to study at the Sorbonne and at the Nancy agricultural school, where he received a diploma as an agricultural engineer. He spent World War I in Poland as a Hebrew teacher in Warsaw and as an activist in the Zionist movement.

In 1921 he returned to Palestine and became a teacher in the Mikve Yisrael Agricultural School of the Alliance Israélite Universelle, and then for nine years was director of the training department of the Zionist Executive's agricultural experimental station. In 1933 he established the Kadourie Agricultural School on Mount Tabor, serving as its principal for four years.

At the same time he did not neglect his literary work. He published many novels and essays, wrote literary criticism and books on agricultural problems. He served as editor of the literary weekly *Moznayim* and of *Behinot be-Vikoret ha-Sifrut* (1952–57). His selected works (*Ketavim Nivharim*) appeared in 1956. His memoir *Shana Rishona* (First Year) is a classic autobiography of a key member of the Second Aliya.

A. ALPERIN—E. SPICEHANDLER

ZEPHIRAH, BRACHA. Israeli singer (b. Jerusalem, 1911; d. Tel Aviv, 1990). Born to a poor Yemenite family, she was orphaned at the age of three and was raised by volunteer foster families of different ethnic communities in Jerusalem, absorbing their traditional musical repertory. During a brief period of studies in Berlin she met the Russian-born pianist, Nahum Nardi, with whom she embarked on a series of public concerts in Palestine during the 1930s. These were the first public events in which songs of "oriental" Jewish communities—Yemenites, Sephardim, Persians, and Bukharans—were performed in front of a mostly Ashkenazi audience, with improvised piano accompaniment helping to bridge the cultural barrier between traditions.

From 1938 she turned to the group of professional composers who had recently immigrated to the country and commissioned from them precomposed arrangements for her songs. She collaborated especially with Paul Ben-Haim, who also performed with her as pianist in her concerts, and with Oedon Partos, Hanokh Jacoby, Marc Lavry, and Alexander Uriah Boscovitch. For these composers, raised on a purely European heritage, the direct contact with an ethnic singer with professional concert experience served as valuable mediation, and as a source of themes for many of their symphonic and chamber works. In order to expand her repertory Zephirah approached informants from various communities. She included Arabic folk songs in her repertory and also composed songs of her own. A compilation of all the songs is included in her autobiography, *Kolot Rabim* (Many Voices, 1978). In her later years, she was an accomplished painter.

J. HIRSCHBERG

ZERUBAVEL (WITKIN), YA'AKOV. Po'ale Zion pioneer, author, and orator (b. Poltava, Ukraine, Russia, 1886; d. Tel Aviv, 1967). Zerubavel received a traditional Jewish education and learned a trade. He joined a Po'ale Zion group in 1904 and became an ardent disciple and collaborator of Ber Borochov. His literary and oratorical eloquence brought him to prominence in the young movement. After serving a term in a Vilna prison for anti-Tsarist activities, he moved to Galicia and took over the editorship of the Po'ale Zion weekly *Der Yidisher Arbeter*. In 1910 he went to Eretz Israel, where he was cofounder and coeditor (with David Ben-Gurion and Itzhak Ben-Zvi) of *Ha'Ahdut*, the first Po'ale Zion weekly to appear in Hebrew. In 1912 he was sent as the first emissary of the Palestinian Jewish labor movement to other Jewish communities, including those of the United States and Canada.

Zerubavel's literary and political activities, which he resumed on his return to Eretz Israel, were cut short by the outbreak of World War I. Sentenced to prison by the Turkish authorities, he escaped and made his way to the United States, where he spent the next three years writing for and editing Po'ale Zion publications, organizing Po'ale Zion groups, and traveling extensively. After the Revolution of 1917, he returned to Russia and then moved to Poland, where he soon emerged as an outstanding community leader and the most prominent spokesman of Labor Zionism. Following the split in the Po'ale Zion movement, he became a leader in the leftist World Union of Po'ale Zion, of which the Polish Po'ale Zion party he headed was the most important constituent.

Much in demand as a speaker, Zerubavel was constantly on the road, lecturing on political and literary subjects in every major Jewish community of the world. He returned to Palestine in 1935 and was elected to some of the leading bodies of the yishuv, including the Executive Committee of the Histadrut. He served a term on the Executive of the Jewish Agency. Zerubavel was the author of several books, including a biography of Ber Borochov.

C.B. SHERMAN

ZEVIN, SHLOMO YOSEF. Israeli Orthodox rabbi and talmudist (b. Kazimirov, Belorussia, 1885; d. Jerusalem, 1978). He studied at yeshivot in Mir and Bobruisk, and succeeded his father as rabbi of Kazimirov. He was active politically on the eve of the Russian revolution; in 1918, he was a Jewish deputy to the Ukrainian parliament. He and Rabbi Yehezkel Abramsky received permission from the Soviets in 1932 to edit and publish *Yagdil Tora*, a monthly periodical dealing with halakhic and religious matters. In 1934, he settled in Palestine.

He was the founding editor of the Talmudic Encycolpedia (*Encyclopedia Talmudit*), an ambitious multi-volume publication, which is still unfinished. In 1959, he won the Israel Prize for Religious Literature. From 1961, he served as president of Yad Harav Herzog, the World Academy for Torah Research. Besides halakhic works, he collected hasidic tales linked to the weekly synagogue Bible reading.

A member of the Supreme Rabbinical Council, he mediated various rabbinic disputes. G. SHUSTER-BOUSKILA

ZHITLOWSKY, CHAIM. Philosopher, Russian revolutionary, Yiddishist, and exponent of *Galut nationalism (b. Ushachi, Vitebsk Province, Russia, 1865; d. Calgary, Alb., 1943). Although brought up in an Orthodox home, Zhitlowsky was in his twenties when he first concerned himself with Jewish problems. As a student, first in Germany and then in Switzerland, where he received a doctorate in philosophy, he became active in the Socialist movement and was one of the seven founders of the Russian Social Revolutionary party, which was to play an important role in the Russian revolutionary movement.

Zhitlowsky's first work on Jewish issues, published in 1887, met with a negative response in Jewish circles. His pamphlet *A Jew to Jews*, published in Russian in 1892, expounded theories of Jewish national rebirth to which he adhered all his life. In that important work, he presented socialism and Jewish nationalism as two mutually complementary ideals that had equal claims on socially conscious Jews, particularly the Jewish intelligentsia. It was the duty of the Jewish socialist to make the Jewish environment the basis of his operations and to lead the Jewish people to social and national liberation. Zhitlowsky's program rested on the premise that the Jews of the world constituted a nation and that the various Jewish communities were national groups whose normal development had been hampered by anti-Semitic pressure from without and by a faulty economic system from within. He advocated a complete recasting of the occupational distribution of the Jews along "productive" lines, based on agricultural pursuits. The Yiddish language was to be the chief medium of modern Jewish culture. In 1902 he added the demand that the Jews be concentrated in a specific territory.

In 1908 Zhitlowsky settled in New York, where he devoted himself almost exclusively to Jewish causes. He became the most effective opponent of assimilationist concepts in the official Jewish labor movement and the chief theorist of the Yiddishist movement. He was the dominant spirit at the 1908 conference in Czernowitz, Bukovina, at which Yiddish was proclaimed a national language of the Jewish people. An influential Jewish lecturer, he attracted a large following. Besides propagating his brand of Jewish nationalism, he was the first to write books on philosophy in Yiddish.

With respect to Zionism, Zhitlowsky had a checkered career. He was an anti-Zionist at times, a Territorialist at others, and a Zionist on occasion. He joined Po'ale Zion in 1910 and again in 1917, only to drop out each time after periods of membership. A democratic Socialist and an anti-Marxian from his early youth, he disappointed his friends and disciples in the 1930s when he declared himself a Communist fellow traveler. He died while on tour for his newly adopted causes, far from his home and forsaken by most of his former followers. C.B. SHERMAN

ZIFF, WILLIAM BERNARD. Author, publisher, and Zionist activist (b. Chicago, 1898; d. New York, 1953). In 1935 Ziff was president of the Zionist Revisionist Organization of America. Three years later, he wrote *The Rape of Palestine* (1938, 1946), a book in which he charged the British Mandatory government with having deliberately defaulted on the obligations it had assumed toward Palestine. He called for free Jewish immigration to Palestine and conferment of Palestinian citizenship on all stateless Jews.

Ziff was a delegate to the 22nd Zionist Congress (1946). He became prominently associated with the American League for a Free Palestine, urging the Zionist Congress to proclaim a "Hebrew Republic" in Palestine.

Mausoleum of Baron and Baroness Edmond de Rothschild, near Zikhron Ya'akov. [Israel Government Press Office]

ZIKHRON YA'AKOV. Town on the southern spur of Mount Carmel, about 19 mi. (30 km.) south of Haifa. It was founded in 1882 as one of the earliest moshavot by Hovevei Zion from Romania. Baron Edmond de Rothschild took a special interest in the settlement, introducing vineyards as the principal farming branch and constructing there one of his two large wine cellars in the country. Although the original strain of vines had to be uprooted and replaced by another, wine production remained prominent in the village economy. In 1903, the Teachers' Association (*Histadrut ha-Morim*) was founded in Zikhron Ya'akov at a convention addressed by Menahem Ussishkin. Aaron Aaronsohn and his sister Sarah, who activated the *Nili Intelligence group on behalf of the Allies in World War I, lived there and their home was later turned into a museum. In the late 1930s, Zikhron Ya'akov started to become a summer resort, with Bet Daniel of the Bentwich-Friedlaender family as one of the first recreation homes. In the 1950s, new immigrants were absorbed, but growth was slow and in 1987 Zikhron Ya'akov numbered 5,600 inhabitants. In 1954, the remains of Baron de Rothschild were transferred to a mausoleum in a beautiful surrounding park (Ramat ha-Nadiv). The town is named after the baron's father James de Rothschild.

E. ORNI

ZIMBABWE AND ZAMBIA (RHODESIA, SOUTH AND NORTH), ZIONISM IN. The Jewish community of what was then called Rhodesia was founded in the last years of the 19th century by immigrants who had come mainly from England and eastern Europe. The first Rhodesian Zionist Society was founded in Bulawayo in 1898. The total Jewish population of the city at the time was less than 200. In 1899 Morris Landau, president of the society, visited London, whereupon the society was formally constituted a branch of the British Hovevei Zion movement. By 1901, 170 of Bulawayo's 200 Jews were members. Over the years Zionist societies were established also in Salisbury and most of the other centers in Southern Rhodesia (now Zimbabwe) and Northern Rhodesia (now Zambia).

In 1902 the Bulawayo Hovevei Zion Society was affiliated with the South African Zionist Federation, whose headquarters were in Johannesburg (*see* SOUTH AFRICA, ZIONISM IN). Subsequently all the Zionist Societies in Rhodesia were affiliated directly with the South African Zionist Federation.

In 1943 the first Rhodesian Zionist Conference was held. The delegates agreed to establish a Rhodesian Zionist Council to conduct and coordinate Zionist activities in Southern and Northern Rhodesia. The new council became a constituent body of the South African Zionist Federation, with a status similar to that of the provincial Zionist councils in South Africa.

At the 10th Rhodesian Zionist Conference, held in May, 1964, the Rhodesian Zionist Movement assumed autonomous status by constituting itself an independent Zionist territorial federation, under the name Central African Zionist Organization (CAZO), affiliated directly with the World Zionist Organization in Jerusalem. The same year, for the first time in the history of the Rhodesian Zionist Movement, the territory was represented directly by its own delegate at a Zionist Congress, the 26th, held in Jerusalem. Although no longer affiliated with the South African Zionist Federation, the CAZO continued to work closely with it.

The Central African Zionist Organization was not based on individual membership but on the membership of Zionist societies as such, and it also included a number of Jewish congregations. The Executive was composed of representatives from the various Zionist parties and groups. There also was a strong women's Zionist organization, the Women's Zionist Council of Central Africa, with which all women's Zionist societies were directly affiliated. This council was a constituent body of the CAZO, with direct representation on the Executive. A Zionist Youth Council coordinated Zionist youth activities in Rhodesia and Zambia.

In the 1960s the Central African Zionist Organization was responsible for coordinating the day-to-day Zionist activities of the various societies in Rhodesia and Zambia over which it had jurisdiction. The organization engaged in many projects, including the United Israel Appeal, and Jewish National Fund, education, public relations, aliya (immigration), the Women's International Zionist Organization (WIZO), and youth activities. Since April, 1958, it has published its own monthly, the *Central African Zionist Digest*, which is distributed to every Jewish household in Zimbabwe and Zambia. The CAZO also played a vital part in the establishment of Jewish day schools in Salisbury and Bulawayo.

The years 1970–1981 were marked by civil strife in Rhodesia and in common with other members of the white population, many Jews emigrated. It is estimated that about 1,000 immigrated to Israel during that period. In 1981, Rhodesia gained its independence and the new state of Zimbabwe came into being. The new government issued full recognition to the PLO and an office with the privileges of "embassy" was opened in Harare as representative of this organization.

In spite of these developments, the Jewish community, which in 1987 numbered only 1,100, continued to maintain all its communal institutions including the various Zionist societies.

ZIM-ISRAEL SHIPPING COMPANY. *See* TRANSPORTATION IN ISRAEL.

ZION (Tziyon). Originally the name of a Jebusite stronghold in the Jerusalem area, the term "Zion" was applied by the Hebrew prophets to Jerusalem as a whole when referring to the city as a spiritual symbol. Thus the prophets would refer to the people of Jerusalem and of the Land of Judah as Bat Tziyon (Daughter of Zion). As a symbol of the Holy Land, the name Zion became a central concept in the religious life of the Jews in the Diaspora, and in the late 19th century it served as the basis for the terms "Zionism" and "Zionist," coined by Nathan Birnbaum.

ZIONISM. Term coined by Nathan Birnbaum in 1890 for the movement aiming at the return of the Jewish people to the Land of Israel. From 1896 on Zionism referred to the political movement founded by Theodor Herzl, aiming at the establishment of a Jewish National Home in Eretz Israel. Zionism also worked to deepen and intensify Jewish consciousness among Jews the world over. After the establishment of the Jewish State the concept of Zionism was widened to include material and moral support of Israel. *see also* ZIONISM, HISTORY OF; ZIONIST THOUGHT.

ZIONISM, HISTORY OF. Zionism denotes modern Jewish nationalism and the endeavor to restore the Jews to their ancient homeland. It aims at solving the Jewish question by modern means, but its essence is to realize the centuries-old craving to return to Zion. The term "Zionism" was coined by Nathan Birnbaum in his journal *Selbstemanzipation* (1 April 1890) and was adopted by the Zionist movement at its First Congress (1897), but the idea is as old as Jewish history itself; it is an integral part of the Jewish heritage. Wherever they lived throughout the ages, Jews never accepted their existence in the Diaspora as final. The *Galut (exile) was suffered as a penance. The ultimate goal of their aspirations remained immutably the land of Israel. It dominated their minds and hearts, exerting the most comprehensive, potent, and formative influence in their life. It abounded in Jewish liturgy and kept the Messianic idea alive. Emancipation brought in its wake a radical departure from traditional concepts and aspirations. The Great Sanhedrin, convened by Napoleon on 8 February 1807, made the momentous decision that Jews had ceased to be a polity and no longer constituted a national entity; they were an integral part of the nations among whom they lived and entitled to claim the same rights and discharge the same duties as their fellow citizens, from whom they differed only in religion.

However emancipation, at least in central Europe, remained only formal. It gave rise to modern anti-Semitism, which in turn awakened Jewish consciousness.

Moses Hess was the first Jewish thinker in western Europe to take anti-Semitism seriously. The Germans, he proclaimed in his *Rom und Jerusalem* (1862), were anti-Jewish racially. It was therefore futile to expect that reform or emancipation would by some magic render the German Jews socially acceptable. Assimilation was no solution. The Jews were a separate nation, not a religious group. Denial of one's identity was self-deception and could not command respect. The Jews needed a state of their own.

A year earlier (1861) a booklet under the title *Derishat Zion* had been published by Rabbi Zvi *Kalischer of Poznan in German-occupied Poland. Like Rabbi Yehuda *Alkalai, his counterpart in Serbia, Kalischer, by the standards of his time, propounded the revolutionary concept that Israel's redemption could not be brought about by a sudden miracle of divine grace. It depended primarily on the efforts of the Jews themselves. It was their duty to initiate the practical steps in anticipation of the Almighty's blessing. An active resettlement of Eretz Israel fully accorded with the commandments of Judaism. Neither of the rabbis, however, made any impact on their contemporaries, while Moses Hess remained a prophet without much honor. At the same time, the Zionist idea was not confined to Jews alone and was growingly propounded in the west (*See* CHRISTIAN ZIONISM).

It was not until the anti-Jewish pogroms in Russia during 1881 and 1882 that modern Jewish nationalism came into being. The movement was known as Hibbat Zion (Love of Zion) and its adherents, *Hovevei Zion. The experience of the pogroms shattered irreparably the dream of enlightenment and Russification in which some Jewish youth and intelligentsia indulged. Disillusioned and rejected, they sought compensation in a rediscovery of their own national identity. The revival of the Hebrew language and literature was given a new fillip, and the restoration of Jewish national life in Eretz Israel became the central theme in the new thinking. Aspirations for emancipation gave way to self-emancipation.

This was the theme of Leo *Pinsker's pamphlet *Auto-Emancipation* (1882), a classic in Zionist literature. Pinsker was an assimilated Jewish physician in Odessa but the shock of the pogroms made him despair of Russification. Never before had anybody spelled out with such clarity of thought and passionate conviction that the struggle for emancipation led nowhere. He showed that Judeophobia was a psychic aberration that was incurable. One would not combat deep-seated prejudice by reasoning. Everywhere the Jew was a foreigner because he had no country of his own. Even if civil rights were accorded him, his emancipation at best would only be legal, not social. Pinsker saw the only salvation for Jews in a concentration in territory of their own (not necessarily Eretz Israel, though at a later stage he became a Zionist) to forge their national life. Only then would Jews be able to resume their existence among nations as equals.

Hibbat Zion associations sprouted all over Russia. One of the most active and daring was *Bilu. The members, mostly students from Russian universities, were determined to give substance to their new-found ideal. Imbued with the will to build a model society on social justice, they decided to set a personal example, and a number of them made their way to Eretz Israel, founding two settlements. Other Jews from eastern Europe founded other settlements and the modern return to Eretz Israel had been inaugurated (*See* ISRAEL, HISTORY OF).

Although enthusiastic, the pioneers were ill-equipped for their venture. The difficulties were more formidable than they had anticipated. Had it not been for the generous financial support afforded by Baron Edmond de Rothschild of Paris, the infant settlements would have foundered.

In Russia Hibbat Zion also faced its problems. Its conference at Kattowitz in 1884, called by Pinsker to promote and finance Jewish settlement in Eretz Israel, was a modest, though promising, beginning. The movement, however, failed to rally the Jewish masses behind it. They preferred to seek their salvation in the West, primarily in the United States. In addition, wealthy Jews steered clear of it, and, as a result, the necessary funds for settlement in Eretz Israel were not forthcoming. Politically and organizationally, the movement was a failure. Its importance was primarily educational.

The awakening of Jewish nationalism in Germany was slow and confined to academic youth. By 1892 the Jewish societies had confederated into the Verein jüdischer Studenten in Deutschland. The values implanted gave them a sense of dignity and reassurance vis-á-vis an unfriendly environment. One of the young intellectuals, a lawyer by profession, who was to make a particular mark on Zionism in Germany was Max Bodenheimer. He was deeply attached to all that was German, but the growth of anti-Semitism both in Germany and elsewhere distressed him. It transformed his outlook completely. He concluded that it was the homelessness of his people, their minority status among the nations, cut off from the soil, that lay at the root of their misfortune. Bodenheimer reasoned that, if the underlying cause of the problem was Jewish dispersion, the remedy should be sought in the ingathering of a substantial number of Jews in a country of their own. It was in the land of their ancestors that a Jewish nation could revive in a normal social environment, that Jews would acquire a new image and status in the world. He established contact with Nathan Birnbaum in Vienna and with Leo Pinsker in Russia. Of greater practical significance was his acquaintance with David Wolffsohn, who had come to Cologne from Russia. Bodenheimer's idea of the creation of a Jewish state in Eretz Israel fired Wolffsohn's imagination, and in 1893 the two established the Cologne Association for the Promotion of Agriculture and Industry in Eretz Israel, which may be regarded as the beginning of the Zionist movement in Germany.

Theodor Herzl. A campaign to win support was soon launched. However, it was the appearance of Theodor *Herzl's book *The *Jewish State*, in 1896, that gave the most powerful uplift to the morale of the Cologne society. Herzl breathed new life into the east and west European Zionist societies, liberating them from their parochialism and later fusing them into an international movement.

As in the case of Moses Hess, Leo Pinsker, and other individuals, it was anti-Semitism that made Herzl and Max *Nordau, his close collaborator, conscious Jews. Both were steeped in European culture, but the resurgence of modern anti-Semitism wounded their dignity. As the years went by, the feeling grew stronger, but it was not until the Dreyfus trial in 1894–1895 in France that Herzl's hopes of emancipation were irreparably shattered. Contrary to the general belief that hostility to the Jews would disappear, Herzl feared that it would worsen. It was futile to combat anti-

Herzl addressing the 2d Zionist Congress (Basle, 1898). [Zionist Archives]

Semitism, but, he hoped that in the long run anti-Semitism would not harm the Jews and that educationally it might even prove useful. "It forces us," he concluded, "to close ranks, unites us through pressure, and through our unity will make us free." It was this feeling of freedom that made him declare: "We are a people, one people. We recognize ourselves as a nation by our faith." Henceforth he no longer regarded the Jewish question as a social or religious problem but as a national one, to be solved politically by the council of the civilized nations. Sovereignty over a portion of land "large enough to justify the rightful requirements of a nation," to which the Jewish masses would emigrate, would provide the right solution. Pondering the choice between the Argentine and Eretz Israel, Herzl found that the "ever memorable historic home" retained a "force of marvellous potency."

The solution of the problem, however, should not be left to Jews alone. If the Powers, with the concurrence of the sultan, recognized Jewish sovereignty over Eretz Israel, the Jews in return could undertake to regulate Turkish finances; they would form there "a portion of... Europe... an outpost of civilization." The Jewish state would become "something remarkable... a model country for social experiments and a treasure-house for works of art... a destination for the civilized world."

However, Herzl was primarily a man of action. He turned first to Jewish magnates in order to raise the necessary funds but was disappointed. He realized that a national movement had to be shouldered by the people themselves, not by single individuals. It was this reasoning, among others, that prompted him to convene a world Zionist *Congress. It opened on 29 August 1897 in Basle.

In his opening address Herzl declared that the task of the Congress was to lay the foundation of "a refuge for the Jewish nation"; the world had finally recognized that the Jews were a people. The return to their Land should be done openly and in an organized fashion. Herzl formulated the objectives of the newly-founded *World Zionist Organization (WZO) as moderately as possible. In deference to Turkish susceptibilities all references to the idea of Jewish statehood were dropped, and the term *Heimstätte*, which means "homestead" was used. The Congress adopted the *Basle Program as a statement of the basic aims of Zionism.

To obtain international recognition and support for his movement was the second task that Herzl had set for himself. His attempts to achieve a *Charter reached an impasse in his negotiations with both Germany and Turkey. He then shifted his efforts to Britain in the expectation that it would allow him to establish a Jewish colony under its protection somewhere in the neighborhood of Eretz Israel. After a proposal to found a self-governing Jewish colony in the El Arish area or in Sinai fell through, the British Colonial Secretary, Joseph Chamberlain offered instead the Guas Ngishu plateau near Nairobi in East Africa for a Jewish settlement under the British flag. Herzl, pressed by the need to provide a refuge, even temporarily, for the persecuted Russian and Romanian Jews, thought it politically imprudent to reject the offer. At no time did he lose sight of Eretz Israel. At the Sixth Zionist Congress (23–28 August 1903) he assured the delegates that he would in no way deviate from the Basle Program. The fears of some delegates that Herzl might abandon Eretz Israel were unfounded. His main purpose was not necessarily to obtain the East Africa concession but to elicit recognition from the British government. East Africa was only the diplomatic stepping-stone to the main goal. In any case, the proposal was rejected by the Zionist movement which held fast to the determination to return to Eretz Israel, despite the desperate need to find a home as soon as possible for the persecuted masses of east European Jewry.

When Herzl died in 1904, at the age of 44, he had become a legendary figure. He had turned a mystique, a dream, into a political factor. The movement which he brought into being became the most dynamic force in modern Jewish history. He founded its organ, *Die *Welt*, its financial arm, the *Jewish Colonial Trust, and the Congress, which became the embodiment of Zionist parliamentarism.

Ahad Ha-Am. A different genre of Zionism was expounded by *Ahad Ha-Am who shunned politics but instead laid emphasis on cultural Hebrew renaissance. He was the foremost exponent of anti-assimilationism. With assimilation, he maintained, "there is no room... for compromise." He felt that the only chance for Jewry to survive in the modern world was by means of a liberal nationalism based on the ideals of the Hebrew prophets. Unlike that of Herzl and Pinsker, Ahad Ha-Am's Zionism was a response not to anti-Semitism but to assimilation in the West and to ossified rabbinism in the East. Herzl and Pinsker saw the solution in a voluntary mass exodus of Jews from European countries. Ahad Ha-Am, in contrast, doubted whether Eretz Israel could absorb more than a fraction of the Jewish people. Since the Diaspora was to remain a permanent feature of Jewish life and was to contain the majority of Jewish people, the problem was not the plight of the Jewish people, as Herzl believed, but the plight of Judaism. Hence the need for a national spiritual center in Palestine, which would serve as a cultural power-house to restore the cohesion and sense of purpose of the Jewish people, and to counter assimilation. Ahad Ha-Am was one of the first leaders to draw attention to the problem of relations with the Arabs.

Socialist and Religious Zionism. Antecedents of religious Zionism could be traced to rabbis: Alkalai, Kalischer, Gutmacher, Mohilever, and Eliasberg who emphasized the inter-connection between the people of Israel, the Law of Israel, and the Land of Israel. Both Rabbis Mohilever and Reines became stanch supporters of Herzl. The latter, jointly with Rabbi Ze'ev Jawitz, founded the *Mizrachi Movement (Vilna, 1902). Its program was formulated two years later in the first World Convention. It embraced the Basle Program and called for fulfillment of the Torah and Return to Zion. In 1912 some members seceded and joined the newly founded *Agudat Israel.

Socialist Zionism came into being shortly before the Third Zionist Congress. It was founded by Nachman *Syrkin, Hess's disciple. Later it was headed by Ber *Borochov. Both of them rejected the Bund's ideology on the grounds that anti-Semitism was a permanent phenomenon which would not disappear even after a Socialist revolution. Moreover, they maintained, in the Diaspora the Jews could not lead a truly productive way of life. Hence the solution was: mass emigration and a territorial concentration in Eretz Israel in order to found there a new society based on justice and equality. Borochov synthesized the Marxist ideology with nationalism but in later years his rigid determinism and materialism gave way to a more sentimental approach to Zionism. In 1905/6 Socialist-Zionist societies were founded in Russia, Austria, England, United States, and Eretz Israel, and in 1907 the *Po'ale Zion World Movement was founded.

The premature death of Herzl robbed the movement of a leader of international caliber. He was the soul and fountainhead of the Zionist movement and without him it looked as if Zionism might be approaching the end of the road. However, Zionism was too firmly rooted to wither. The East Africa controversy left deep scars and overshadowed the Seventh Congress (27 July—2 August 1905) but, although the debate was acrimonious, it helped to clarify the direction of the movement. At its final session the Congress declared its undivided loyalty to the Basle Program. Another question of primary importance which confronted the Congress was that of orientation. Herzl had given the movement a distinct political complexion, but when his diplomatic *tour de force* proved abortive, there was a demand to change the order of priorities: practical work should be the forerunner of diplomacy, not its consequence; only concrete achievements could form the basis for negotiations; creation of facts should precede the political struggle. However the two schools of thought were not mutually exclusive. The difference was only one of method; the aim remained very much the same and a compromise formula was worked out which read that "parallel to the political-diplomatic activity, systematic development work should be undertaken in Eretz Israel." Any philanthropic or unplanned settlement was rejected.

The Congress elected David *Wolffsohn, Herzl's close collaborator, as the second president of the WZO. He also acted as head of the WZO's Inner Actions Committee, the Executive. After the initial stormy period, the Wolffsohn era (1905–1911) by comparison was uneventful. Yet it was not an unimportant one for it was during this period that the shattered movement was welded together and settlement in Eretz Israel received a new start.

Wolffsohn was succeeded (as chairman) by Professor Otto *Warburg (1911–1920), a distinguished scientist and a respected figure in Germany. His passion was practical work in Eretz Israel. When the Eleventh Congress (2–9 September 1913) took stock of the position it had no reason to be dissatisfied. The machinery ran smoothly and the ideolog-

Group of young immigrants en route to Eretz Israel during Second Aliya. [Israel State Archives]

ical differences had been largely reconciled. Settlement in Eretz Israel had passed the experimental state and the movement was steadily expanding. It was still a minority group within Jewry; its membership did not exceed 130,000 but this did not reflect the number of sympathizers. The budget of the Executive doubled, from 123,000 marks in 1905 to 244,000 marks (equivalent to £12,000) in 1911.

The main achievement was in settlement, chiefly due to Arthur Ruppin and to the pioneers of the Second *Aliya. Between the beginning of 1904 and the outbreak of World War I 35,000 to 40,000 Jews moved to Eretz Israel. Their ambition was to rebuild their own homeland and form the nucleus of a new Jewish society based on social justice.

Private investment, both in rural and urban enterprises, was also encouraged. In 1912 when Ahad Ha-Am, a confirmed pessimist, revisited Eretz Israel he admitted that a miracle had taken place. What had been a vision thirty years earlier had become a reality. A national spiritual center was in the making.

In contrast to their achievements in Eretz Israel, diplomatically the Zionists remained in the wilderness. There was not even one capital in Europe to which they could confidently look for support. Turkey remained as obdurate as ever. It had seemed that the Young Turk Revolution of 24 July 1908 and the overthrow of Hamidean absolutism had ushered in a new era. However, when the Young Turks staged their second coup in April, 1909, the situation changed radically. Ottomanism gave way to Turkism and the dream of a free association of peoples in a multinational and multidenominational empire vanished for ever. Turkey became a centralized state. The recrudescence of Turkish nationalism blighted the Zionists' prospects. In June, 1909, when Wolffsohn arrived in Constantinople for renewed negotiations, the atmosphere was not conducive to a mutual understanding.

Nonetheless, the Zionists continued to protest their loyalty. In his opening address at the Ninth Congress on 26 December 1909, Wolffsohn declared: "We can find no incompatibility between Ottoman interests and Zionist ambitions". Nordau dismissed the allegation that the Zionists nourished separatist aspirations. The Zionists' declarations, although motivated by political expedience, were sincere: loyalty to Turkey became the cornerstone of their policy. However, it was not until 1912 that their position began to improve.

Berlin began to assess Zionism as a factor worthy of consideration while Turkey, realizing the dangers of decentralization implicit in Arab aspirations, revised its policy and abrogated earlier restrictions on the immigration and settlement of Jews in Eretz Israel. On 29 June 1914 Conrad Freiherr von Wangenheim, the German Ambassador to Constantinople, made an unusual declaration to Richard Lichtheim, the Zionist representative, that, should the Zionists in Palestine be persecuted, he would do his best to protect them. The idea emanated from Berlin and stemmed from the conviction that the Zionists were able to do valuable work for Turkey and also benefit Germany by disseminating its cultural and economic influence in the East.

The policy of protection proved invaluable for the preservation of the yishuv during the war, when the attitude of the Turkish authorities in Eretz Israel suddenly changed. It was Ahmed Jamal Pasha, the Commander of the IVth Ottoman Army, and his subordinates, who were responsible for initiating the policy of oppression and banishment. His system of mass deportations would have brought the whole Jewish settlement to complete ruin had not powerful intercessions by the German and American embassies stopped him.

The outbreak of World War I placed the Zionists in an unprecedented predicament. As individuals they discharged their duties in their respective countries of domicile as loyally as other citizens, but the movement was in a quandary, split between two diametrically opposed schools of thought. Chaim Weizmann and his friends, who were convinced that England would win the war, endeavored to unseat the Berlin-led Zionist Executive and transfer the headquarters to New York. In contrast, Zionists in Germany thought that the *Blitzkrieg* pointed to Germany gaining the upper hand, and did their best to maintain their leadership within the movement. There were, however, two inescapable factors which had to be taken into account: first, the fate of Jews in Russia, and second, the security of the yishuv.

The Zionist General Council, which met in Copenhagen on 3–6 December 1914, took note that Germany was the only Power which had some leverage on Turkey and that protection of the Palestine Jews could be effected expeditiously only from Constantinople. It was largely thanks to Richard Lichtheim's connections with the German and American embassies, as well as with the chief rabbi, that the machinery guarding the welfare of the yishuv ran so smoothly. The fate that befell the Armenians illustrated the case.

Consequently, the Council decided on a policy of neutrality, conditioned by the international character of the movement which aimed to solve a problem of international dimensions. It was therefore imperative to win the support of all the powers concerned, without fastening on to one power exclusively. International support, which the Zionists endeavored to secure, in no way ran counter to the principle of neutrality. In keeping with this principle it was decided that, parallel to the activity in Berlin and Constantinople, a diplomatic effort should be mounted in the Entente and neutral countries. This policy remained valid until the end of the war and was vindicated by subsequent events.

In response to steps taken by the Zionist Executive in Berlin and particularly by Lichtheim, its representative in Constantinople, on 22 November 1915 the German government issued instructions to the Consulate in Jerusalem of far-reaching importance. The key phrase read: "It seems politically advisable to show a friendly attitude toward Zionism and its aims." On 29 January 1917 Otto Warburg and Victor Jacobson tried to persuade Dr. Alfred Zimmermann, the German Foreign Minister, that with the American Jewish Congress approaching, it would be beneficial for both Turkey and Germany to issue a public declaration of sympathy with Zionist aspirations in Palestine. Zimmermann was responsive to the idea, particularly as the political climate in Constantinople had changed for the better, but Külmann, the newly-appointed Ambassador, strongly objected. The entry of the United States into the war on the side of the Allies on 6 April 1917 rendered the move impractical.

When the Zionist Executive met in Copenhagen on 29–31 July 1917, it had no reason to be dissatisfied. Despite conditions of war, the cohesion of the movement had not been disrupted and the American and Russian local organizations adhered to the policy laid down in December, 1914.

In the United States the Zionist movement had gone from strength to strength. The Provisional Executive Committee for General Zionist Affairs (created on 30 August, 1914), with Louis D. Brandeis as chairman and Stephen Wise as vice-chairman, rendered a singular service to the well-being of the yishuv. Brandeis' leadership turned the movement from a parochial organization into a force to be reckoned with in Jewish communal life. From an organization with fewer than 5,000 enrolled members in 1914, it reached the figure of almost 150,000. The modest budget of $15,000 in 1914 had increased to $2,500,000 in 1917. One of its greatest assets was the fact that President Wilson had come to believe in the Zionist program as the solution to the Jewish question and had promised his best efforts to implement it.

In Russia too, following the March 1917 Revolution, the rise of Zionism was almost as spectacular. The number of enrolled members, which before the war amounted to 25,000, rose in the spring of 1917 to 140,000. This figure did not include the former Russian territories of Poland, Lithuania, and Bessarabia, then under German and Austrian occupation, where Zionist influence was considerable. In his inaugural address to the Zionist Conference in Petrograd on 6 June 1917, Yehiel Tschlenow confirmed that Zionism had become a mass movement and, as such in a free country, a formidable factor. The Provisional Government was favorably disposed. Former Prime Minister Prince Lwow, his Foreign Minister Miliukov, and other ministers were ready to issue a declaration of sympathy and his successor, Alexander Kerensky, was equally friendly.

Assurances given by the Vatican, the Italian government (May, 1917), as well as a declaration by Jules Cambon (4 June 1917) on behalf of the French government to Nahum *Sokolow, were encouraging. On 18 July, Lord Rothschild and Chaim *Weizmann had submitted to Arthur James Balfour, the British Foreign Secretary, a draft proposal for a pro-Zionist declaration, but attempts to secure the Executive's approval for a pro-British orientation were dismissed. Arthur Hantke complained that Weizmann and Sokolow had acted too independently and consulted neither the Executive nor the Committee in The Hague; the Executive was unaware of the extent to which Weizmann and Sokolow were already committed to Britain. To maintain a balance it was unanimously decided that parallel to the political work in Entente countries, a similar effort should be made in Berlin, Vienna, Sofia, and Constantinople in order to solicit the support of the Central Powers. The movement as a whole had to avoid involvement in power politics or subordination to one of the warring camps.

The information campaign that ensued bore fruit. Important sections of the German press came out strongly in favor of Zionism and a *Pro-Palästina Komitee was founded, the brainchild of Victor Jacobson. The committee included outstanding personalities in German society, politics, science, and letters. However, in spite of repeated efforts by Jews and Gentiles, the much-desired declaration was not forthcoming. Richard Kühlmann, who in the meantime had become Foreign Minister, adopted a negative stance. He equated Zionism with the creation of an independent Jewish state which would be carved out of the Ottoman domain and feared that such a move would undermine the trust between Germany and Turkey. By comparison, the task of Weizmann and Sokolow was easier, since their aspirations fully accorded with British interests. Britain needed Zionism as a useful card to justify the dismemberment of the Ottoman Empire and legitimize its own presence in Palestine. There was undoubtedly a strong undercurrent of sympathy in Britain towards Zionism, which was reflected in the press but, as the official records show, sentiment did not determine state policy.

The Balfour Declaration. One of the primary objectives in issuing the *Balfour Declaration was to swing Jewish opinion towards Britain. This was achieved beyond all expectations. Messages from Jewish communities in various parts of the world poured into London expressing gratitude and appreciation. In Russia the Declaration was greeted with extraordinary enthusiasm, while in the United States it was praised as consonant with the principles of democracy and justice for small nationalities. Even the Jewish communities in Germany and Austria were greatly moved. The *Jüdische Rundschau*, the official Zionist organ, hailed it as an event of "historic importance" and as the first official acknowldegement of Zionism by a Great Power.

The Central Powers could not remain silent. On 17 November 1917 Count Czernin, the Austro-Hungarian Foreign Minister, received Hantke and pledged the support of his government for the realization of Zionist aspirations in Turkey. A month later Talaat Pasha, the Grand Vizier, received Julius Becker, correspondent of the *Vossische Zeitung*, and while dismissing the Balfour Declaration as *"une blague"*, promised to lift all former restrictions on Jewish settlement in Palestine. On 5 January 1918 von dem Bussche-Hadenhausen, Under-Secretary of State of the Foreign Ministry, made a declaration complementary to that of Talaat. The latter maintained the momentum and invited a delegation of Jewish organizations (Vereinigung Jüdischer Organisationen Deutschlands) to Constantinople to negotiate on Immigration, land purchase in Palestine, and autonomy.

On 28 June 1918 Talaat received Victor Jacobson, the head of the delegation and explained the reason for his invitation: *"Les Juifs sont une force, je ne veux pas qu'ils soient contre l'Empire."* He was genuinely interested in satisfying Jewish opinion but the negotiations stumbled on the word "national", which the delegation wished to append to the crucial phrase "Jewish Center in Palestine" in the draft declaration. The only positive result was the expression of sympathy for the Jewish enterprise in Palestine and the abrogation of all former restrictive decrees.

Contrary to the gloomy prognostications in some quarters, Jewry emerged in the aftermath of the Balfour Declaration more united than before. Rifts among those nationally minded were almost completely healed. Non-Zionists also came to terms with the Declaration, although not necessarily with the national concept. Even the Orthodox, the Agudat Israel, formerly bitter opponents of the Zionists, also changed their attitude and declared their readiness to cooperate with them. The Zionists had won a tremendous victory. Weizmann and Sokolow rocketed to fame; the former took command of the Zionist movement, the headquarters of which were subsequently transferred from Berlin to London. The greatest gain was the recognition of the collective Jewish right to Palestine. Moreover, Jews were recognized as a nation. The Balfour Declaration specifically referred to the "Jewish people" and, following its incorporation into the Mandate and approval by the United States, the "Jewish people" became an entity recognized by international law.

I. FRIEDMAN

Aftermath of the Balfour Declaration: 1917–1921. The Balfour Declaration led to a great increase in the strength of the Zionist movement in Russia, Poland, the United States, and elsewhere. The standing of the movement was further enhanced by the appointment in the spring of 1918 of the *Zionist Commission, headed by Weizmann, whose members proceeded to Palestine in order to advise and assist the British military administration there. The international legitimacy of the Zionist Organization was recognized by the major powers in 1919, when Zionist spokesmen, again headed by Weizmann, appeared at the Paris Peace Conference to present their claims (*see* MANDATE FOR PALESTINE).

In spite of these major achievements, however, rumbles of dissatisfaction could be heard from within the movement. These came to a head at the *London Zionist Conference of July, 1920, the first international assembly of the movement since 1913. Weizmann's preeminent role in the movement was formalized at the conference by his election to the presidency of the World Zionist Organization. Although he was elected unopposed, the London Conference inaugurated a conflict within the organization between forces loyal to Weizmann and those who looked for leadership to Justice Louis D. Brandeis, the leading figure in the US branch of the movement. The quarrel reflected fundamentally different conceptions of Zionism. For Brandeis and his associates the political stage in Zionism had ended: thenceforth, they believed, the organization should focus on constructive efforts in Palestine, abandoning any political pretensions. Weizmann and his supporters rejected the notion that the Zionist movement should abdicate any political role. At its final session the London Conference proclaimed the establishment of a £25,000,000 Palestine Foundation Fund (*see* KEREN HA-YESOD). It was hoped that this would provide the essential financial underpinning for the Zionists' activities in Palestine, but the target figure proved to be wildly optimistic.

When Weizmann arrived in the United States in April, 1921 (accompanied by Albert Einstein, Menahem Ussishkin, and others), the quarrel with Brandeis reached its climax. The ostensible issue was the organization of the Keren ha-Yesod, but personality conflicts and the larger conceptual schism exacerbated the argument. In early June, 1921, a special convention of the *Zionist Organization of America (ZOA) in Cleveland upheld Weizmann's program by a vote of 153 to 71. Brandeis did not appear at the convention. After this defeat he resigned as Honorary President of the WZO and he and his supporters withdrew from all official positions in the ZOA. Leadership of the latter passed to a group of Weizmann's supporters, headed by Louis Lipsky. The Brandeis group established a rival fund to the Keren ha-Yesod entitled "Palestine Development Associates", but neither Brandeis nor his supporters ever regained the leadership of American Zionism.

The Brandeis-Weizmann split weakened the Zionist movement particularly in the US, and impaired its fundraising capability. Weizmann's victory in this conflict, however, strengthened his leadership, and enhanced the central authority of the London-based Zionist Executive. Meanwhile, the appointment of Sir Herbert Samuel as first British High Commissioner in Palestine, and the establishment in July, 1920, of a civil administration in the country, marked a decisive stage in the implementation of the Balfour Declaration program.

Zionism in the 1920s. By 1921 Zionism could plausibly claim to be a major political force in world Jewry. This was in spite of the weakness of the movement in the US and the ban on Zionist activity in Russia from the early 1920s onwards. During the inter-war period Poland emerged as the most important center of mass Zionist activity, and the Polish Zionists, headed by leaders such as Yitzhak Grünbaum, advanced to the forefront of the Polish Jewish community and played a significant role in general Polish political life. A major focus of Zionist activity in these years, particularly in Poland, was the establishment of a network of schools in which Hebrew was the language of instruction (*see* TARBUT). Zionist youth movements, of all shades of ideology, played an important role, especially in eastern Europe, and established agricultural training centers (*hakhsharot*). Support for Zionism among Jewish communities in central and western Europe was much less strong. In Germany the movement could muster 20,000 members in the 1920s—an intellectually impressive but politically insignificant minority of the community. In Hungary and France Zionism attracted only small numbers of recruits. In Britain powerful members of the Anglo-Jewish establishment remained hostile to Jewish nationalism. Among Jewish communities in the Moslem world only a handful of enthusiasts rallied to the movement in this period. Nevertheless, at the Twelfth Zionist Congress, held at Carlsbad in 1921, delegates represented a record number of 855,590 shekel-holders.

The party-political constellation within Zionism underwent some important changes in the 1920s. The success of the Bolshevik revolution in Russia led to a split in 1920 within the ranks of the socialist-Zionist Po'ale Zion: the more left-wing faction withdrew altogether from the Zionist Organization. Some of its members subsequently became communists, while others rejoined the Zionist movement. Zionism remained weak among Reform Jews in the west and among Orthodox Jews everywhere. In Poland, Agudat Israel mounted a powerful challenge to the religious-Zionist Mizrachi party for support among Orthodox Jews: in the general election in Poland in 1922, six Agudists were elected to the Sejm (parliament) as against eight Mizrachi representatives. On the right wing of the Zionist movement, Vladimir *Jabotinsky established the *Revisionist party in 1925. Meanwhile women Zionists in many countries formed their own organizations: Hadassah, the American women's Zionist organization, established in 1914, and the Women's International Zionist Organization (WIZO) in other countries. The first conference of WIZO was held in London in 1920.

The period between 1920 and 1929 was one of slow and uneven progress in Zionist activity in Palestine. Severe shortage of funds impaired the ability of the movement to organize mass Jewish immigration on the scale envisaged in the heady aftermath of the Balfour Declaration. Arab anti-Jewish riots in April, 1920, and May, 1921, led the British authorities to adopt a cautious approach to the Jewish National Home. The Third Aliya (1919–23) and the Fourth Aliya (1924–8) brought considerable numbers of middle-class Jews to Palestine. This furthered urban development, most notably the expansion of Tel Aviv, which grew in population from 10,000 to 50,000. By mid-1926 100,000 Jewish immigrants had entered Palestine since the Balfour Declaration. Jewish land ownership grew from 160,000 acres in 1920 to 290,000 in 1929. The formal opening of the Hebrew University of Jerusalem on Mount Scopus in April, 1925, marked the fulfillment of a long-cherished Zionist cultural goal.

A severe economic crisis in Palestine in 1926–7 strained the resources of the Zionist Organization. The British government rejected an application for help in raising a loan of £2,000,000. In these circumstances it became urgently necessary to expand the restricted circles from which most financial support for the Zionist enterprise was drawn. Accordingly, Weizmann initiated negotiations with non-Zionist sympathizers with the Jewish National Home, particularly in the US. His persistent efforts attained fruition in the summer of 1929 with the inauguration of the *Jewish Agency for Palestine at a great convocation in Zurich attended by a galaxy of Jewish leaders, both Zionist and non-Zionist. Although before long the leadership of the expanded Agency became practically synonymous with the Zionist Executive, the establishment of this body represented a major step forward in drawing wealthy American Jews (hitherto mainly hostile or lukewarm towards Zionism) into financial and political support for the Jewish National Home.

The outbreak of severe anti-Zionist disturbances among Arabs in Palestine in August, 1929, led to a prolonged crisis in relations between the Zionists and the British government. In 1930, following the publication of the Passfield White Paper, Weizmann resigned as President of the Zionist Organization and the Jewish Agency in protest against British policy. Although the British government subsequently issued a reinterpretation of policy more favorable to Zionism (*see* MACDONALD LETTER), Weizmann's position within the movement was for the first time seriously weakened. He was viewed as the architect of the Anglo-Zionist alliance: when cracks in the structure of Anglo-Zionist relations began to appear he was inevitably held accountable. At the 17th Zionist Congress at Basle in 1931 Weizmann was fiercely attacked, particularly by the Revisionists. He refused to rescind his resignation and Nahum Sokolow was elected President of the Zionist Organization in his place.

Zionism in the 1930s. In spite of Weizmann's withdrawal from the leadership he continued to exercise authority from behind the scenes, and in fact the movement adhered closely to his policies of cooperation with the British and reconciliation with the Arabs. Weizmann did not go so far as the binationalist supporters of the Berit Shalom, such as Judah Leib Magnes, who expressed readiness to surrender the ultimate objective of a Jewish state in Palestine, but he talked of a settlement on the basis of Arab-Jewish "parity" under the mandatory government. This evoked severe denunciations from the Revisionists, culminating in 1935 in their secession from the Zionist Organization and the establishment of the New Zionist Organization led by Jabotinsky.

The rise of Nazism in Germany and the intensification of anti-Semitism in eastern Europe, most notably Poland, produced a substantial increase in Jewish immigration to Palestine. In the course of the Fifth Aliya (1929–39) more than a quarter of a million Jews entered Palestine. By 1939 the Jewish population of the country numbered 475,000, and the Jewish proportion of the total population had grown to thirty-one percent. The large influx of Jews from Germany (53,000 between 1933 and 1939) brought with it skills, know-how, and capital which transformed the Palestinian Jewish economy. But the quickened pace of development aroused Arab fears and resentment which culminated in the outbreak of a general strike and of a full-scale Arab revolt in 1936. In response, the British government appointed a Royal Commission under Lord Peel (*see* PEEL COMMISSION) which recommended in 1937 the partition of Palestine into independent Jewish and Arab states (with a small residual British mandatory area).

The partition proposal confronted the Zionist movement with a deeply divisive and emotionally charged issue. Weizmann (who had resumed the Presidency of the Organization in 1935) led those who favored acceptance of the principle of partition. He was opposed (from outside the Organization) by Jabotinsky, as well as by such figures as Menahem Ussishkin, Berl Katznelson, and Stephen S. Wise. At tje 20th Zionist Congress at Zurich in July, 1937, Weizmann's policy was, in its essentials, approved by a vote of 299 to 160. It subsequently turned out that the debate had been academic, since the British government, confronted by fierce Arab opposition to the establishment of a Jewish state in any part of Palestine, withdrew its earlier approval of such a scheme.

During the 1930s the influence of the Labor Zionists, and particularly of their Palestinian wing, greatly increased. figures such as David *Ben-Gurion, Moshe *Shertok (Sharett), and Haim *Arlosoroff assumed the leadership of the Palestine Zionist Executive and played an increasing role in the world movement. The assassination of Arlosoroff in 1933, allegedly by Revisionist Zionists, was one of several events that poisoned relations between left and right within the Zionist movement. During the late 1930s these were further strained by the official Zionist policy of *havlaga* (self-restraint) in the face of Arab attacks; the policy was challenged from the right by small groups who advocated (and in some cases practiced) retaliatory terrorism. Throughout this period, however, the *General Zionists (a "non-political" grouping, mainly comprised of liberal, centrist followers of Weizmann and Ussishkin), in alliance with the *Labor Zionists, dominated the Zionist Organization.

The White Paper of 1939, marking a decisive British shift away from the Balfour Declaration policy of support for Zionism, aroused bitter Zionist opposition, but the Zionists were powerless to alter British policy. The 21st Zionist Congress at Geneva in August, 1939, was a sorrowful event. In the course of the proceedings news arrived of the conclusion of the Nazi-Soviet pact, and it became apparent that war was imminent. The business of the Congress was hurriedly concluded, and Weizmann closed the proceedings with an emotional statement: "I have no prayer but this: that we will all meet again alive."

Zionism during World War II. The destruction of the Jewish communities of Nazi-occupied Europe during World War II shattered what had been the heart of the Zionist movement. In some areas Zionists joined Bundists, Communists, and Revisionists in resistance against the Nazis. The whole of Jewry was united in its support of the war against Germany. David Ben-Gurion expressed the outlook of the yishuv with his famous dictum: "We shall fight the war as if there were no White Paper, and fight the White Paper as if there were no war." Inside Europe, the Zionist youth movements played an active role in Jewish resistance to the Nazis and their collaborators.

During the war the main center of Zionist diplomatic activity shifted from Britain to the United States. This move reflected three new facts: first, as a result of the mass slaughter of European Jewry, the US was now the home of the largest concentration of Jews in the world. Secondly, Zionism, hitherto supported only by a minority of American Jews, grew during the war into a dominant political force within American Jewry. Thirdly, the shift reflected the change in relative power within the Grand Alliance as between Britain and the US. New York rather than London was now increasingly seen as the capital of Zionism.

The balance of political leadership in the Zionist movement also changed during the war. Weizmann's policy of reliance on Britain was held to have been discredited and his influence declined. The Palestinian Labor Zionist leaders, Ben-Gurion and Shertok, emerged as the driving force in the movement. The growing importance of American Zionism, however, gave special significance to Americans such as Rabbis Stephen Wise and Abba Hillel *Silver. Within the leadership, the activist and increasingly militant policies of Ben-Gurion in Palestine and Silver in the USA won ground at the expense of the more moderate views of Shertok (who was closely identified with Weizmann) and Wise.

These trends found expression in the *Biltmore Program, adopted by a conference of American Zionists in May, 1942. In this statement all American Zionist organizations went on record as demanding the establishment of a Jewish Commonwealth in Palestine. Although Weizmann had advocated an almost identical objective in an article published prior to the conference, the Biltmore Program was seen as an indication of the decline of his moderating influence within the movement.

The war greatly increased the self-confidence, institutional strength, and military potential of the yishuv. Boom conditions favored the expansion and modernization of the Jewish industrial economy in Palestine. The participation of thousands of Palestinian Jews in the British army provided the yishuv with a vital element of professionally trained soldiers. This had a direct effect in the formation of the elite unit of the Hagana, the Palmah, during the war. Two dissident Jewish underground military forces also became prominent during the war. The Irgun Tzeva'i Le'umi, headed after 1943 by Menahem *Begin, declared "war" on the mandatory government in 1944. Lohamei Herut Israel (Lehi) was a smaller breakaway group from the Irgun. Members of Lehi engaged in contacts with German and Italian agents during the war with a view to collaboration against the British in the Middle East. Lehi was also responsible for the assassination of the British Minister in the Middle East, Lord Moyne, in November, 1944. The actions of these groups were denounced by the mainstream Zionist leadership and enjoyed only minority support among the yishuv.

Zionism after World War II. The revelation at the end of the war of the full effects of Nazi genocide united the great majority of Jews in western countries in support of the Zionist movement. Although the Soviet Union slowly changed its diplomatic posture towards friendship for Zionism, the movement continued to be illegal within Russia. Eastern European countries occupied by the Red Army towards the end of the war also restricted Zionist activity except for the organization of emigration. Jewish communities in Arab countries, faced with growing anti-Zionist and anti-Jewish feeling, hesitated to identify with the official Zionist movement, while holding deeply Zionist views.

The adherence of the British government to a policy of restrictive immigration to Palestine and the British refusal

David Ben-Gurion speaking at a session of the World Zionist Conference held in London, August, 1945. Seated to his left is Rabbi Stephen S. Wise. [Zionist Archives]

to countenance the establishment of a Jewish state led to a crisis in Anglo-Zionist relations. The 22nd Zionist Congress, held at Basle in December, 1946, was the first to convene since before the war. The Revisionist Zionists, whose New Zionist Organization had floundered since the death of Jabotinsky in 1940, rejoined the Zionist Organization and participated in the Congress. The major subject of debate was the British government's invitation to the Zionists to participate in an Arab-Jewish conference on Palestine to be held in London. Weizmann urged participation in the conference and denounced terrorism, but the conference declared that "in existing circumstances the Zionist movement is unable to participate in the London conference." Weizmann resigned as President of the Zionist Organization. He was not replaced and in deference to him the office remained vacant, but his leadership of the movement was effectively at an end.

The failure of the British government to devise a solution to the Arab-Jewish conflict in Palestine led it soon afterwards to turn the entire issue over to the United Nations. During the final stages of the British Mandate in Palestine the Jewish Agency transformed itself into a "state in the making." The "non-Zionist" elements within the Agency had by now shrunk to virtual ciphers, and for all practical purposes the Jewish Agency and the Zionist Organization were synonymous. The various institutions of the Zionist Organization and the representative organs of the yishuv increasingly took on the aspect of government bodies. The Jewish Agency's political department became an embryo Foreign Ministry of the Jewish state. The Hagana emerged as its army, and Zionist representatives at the United Nations were in the forefront of the diplomatic struggle for the establishment of Israel. B. WASSERSTEIN

Since the establishment of the State of Israel. The establishment of the State of Israel in May, 1948, marked the attainment of Zionism's primary political objective. Although the view was advanced, most notably by David Ben-Gurion, that the Zionist movement be regarded as scaffolding which could now be dismantled, this was not the consensus within the movement itself. Most Zionists held to the view that while the establishment of the State of Israel had fulfilled the essential prerequisite for attaining the Zionist idea, the ultimate realization of that idea called for the continued activity and growth of the Zionist movement. The very survival of the State was still threatened by an implacably hostile Arab environment; there was yet to be an "ingathering of the exiles"—meaning at least a substantial part of the Jewish people; the mammoth tasks of absorbing Jewish immigration and developing the economic and social infrastructure of the new State required the help of a strong Zionist movement capable of mobilizing the resources of Diaspora Jewries, especially that of the United States; the Jewish society and culture of Israel had yet to be developed into an exemplary expression of the great values of Judaism and the spiritual center of all Jewry; and, concurrently with all these tasks, within the Diaspora itself the erosive effects of assimilation had to be stemmed, not least through the efforts of Zionists.

Zionist Tasks assumed by the State of Israel. The independent State of Israel quite naturally assumed many of the tasks formerly performed by the World Zionist Organization. (*See* ISRAEL AND THE DIASPORA). Foremost of these was political diplomacy. These tasks were now appropriated by the new State's Foreign Ministry while its newly-created embassies abroad took over most of the political activity previously conducted by territorial Zionist organizations in various countries. Thus, in the State period political policymaking and the conduct of diplomacy ceased to fall within the provenance of the Zionist movement. At the same time the scale of Zionist fundraising was gradually dwarfed by the rapid expansion of Israel's economy in the decades following the emergence of the State. Moreover, the political World Unions functioning within the WZO were overshadowed by their counterparts functioning within Israel's parliamentary system. To be sure, this situation, rooted in the double value accredited to the votes of Zionists within the yishuv, preceded the creation of the State. It had gained momentum from the time of Labor Zionism's ascent to hegemony within the yishuv in the early 1930s. However, in the post-State period as the Diaspora sections of the various Zionist political parties began to atrophy, the domination of the Israeli political structure became complete; the Israeli segments of the Zionist political World Unions constituted 38 percent of the delegates to Zionist Congresses by the 1980s and they also provided the personnel for most of the departmental heads of the WZO-Jewish Agency. Indeed those offices often served as patronage awards for Israeli politicians.

Although in the period of transition from yishuv to statehood, Israel's provisional government had been formed mainly from the ranks of the WZO-Jewish Agency, all governments thereafter were duly elected by the citizens of Israel as a whole and the jurisdiction of Israel's sovereign political structure now extended to its entire population including many who had never been identified with Zionist aims: not only Arabs but also sections of the Jewish Old Yishuv.

In order to distinguish politically and legally between the government of Israel and the Zionist movement, the members of Israel's provisional government (with one exception) resigned their seats on the World Zionist Executive. The office of President of the WZO had been vacant since Chaim Weizmann had not been reelected in 1946. In 1956 Nahum Goldmann was elected president and served until 1968. Since then the office has remained vacant. The key position of chairman of the Executive of the WZO-Jewish Agency in Jerusalem was occupied by Berl Locker from 1948 to 1956. At the 24th Congress in 1956 Nahum Goldmann was elected chairman as well as president, appointing Zalman Shazar as acting chairman in Jerusalem. (Concurrent occupiers of the position of chairman of the executive in New York from 1948 through the 1970s included Abba Hillel Silver, Nahum Goldmann, Rose Halperin, Emanuel Neumann, and Charlotte Jacobsohn). Moshe Sharett was chairman from 1961 until 1965. Arye (Louis) Pincus was acting chairman (1965 to 1968) and chairman from 1968 to 1973; Pinhas Sapir was chairman from June 1974 until August 1975; Josef Almogi from 1976 to 1978; Arye Dulzin (who had twice been acting chairman, in 1973–1974 and again in 1975–1976) was chairman from 1978 to 1987. In 1987 Simcha Dinitz was elected chairman.

The precise formulation of the World Zionist Organization's status in Israeli law and politics was a subject of considerable controversy and debate before finally being settled by the Law on the Status of the World Zionist Organization-Jewish Agency passed by the Knesset in 1952. (*See* ISRAEL AND THE DIASPORA). That law recognized it as "the authorized agency that will continue to operate in the State of Israel for the development and settlement of the country", but did not concede to it the exclusive status of "representative of the Jewish people," as some of the Zionist Organization's leaders wanted. This status was confirmed in the covenant (Amana) signed in July, 1954, between the WZO and the government of Israel.

Functional and Structural Changes in the World Zionist Organization. The 23rd World Zionist Congress, the first since the establishment of the State of Israel, met in Jerusalem in August, 1951, and formulated a new program replacing the original Basle program of 1897. Known as the "*Jerusalem Program," it stated that: "the task of Zionism is the consolidation of the State of Israel, the ingathering of exiles in Eretz Israel, and the fostering of the unity of the Jewish people."

Sporadic efforts followed aimed at reorganizing Zionist structures in the Diaspora in order both to consolidate and to expand the Zionist movement, thereby advancing its aspiration to take the lead in the life of the Jewish people. A major focus of these efforts was the encouragement of greater unity between disparate Zionist parties and organizations which had in the past formed and sustained territorial Zionist federations in some countries but failed to do so in others. In this connection Zionism in the United States constituted the main problem owing to the lack of a unified territorial federation. An example of a Zionist movement which consistently had maintained a unified framework was that of South Africa.

In 1960 a new constitution was adopted which put the WZO on a federative basis and replaced individual membership by shekel-holders with collective representation by Zionist territorial federations as the basis for representation at Zionist Congresses. Whereas until 1960 the number of seats due to each country was computed on the basis of shekel figures, henceforth proportions were stipulated in the constitution (Israel 38 percent, United States 29 percent, and the remaining 33 percent of delegates from other countries to be determined according to the size of the Jewish population and the scale of the Zionist movement there). (*See* WORLD ZIONIST ORGANIZATION).

These efforts at change culminated at the 27th Zionist Congress which met in 1968, about a year after the Six-Day War of June, 1967. The traumatic threat to Israel followed by the euphoria of Israel's victory aroused a tremendous upsurge of Jewish support throughout the Diaspora and constituted a turning point in the consolidation of a broadly Zionist consensus in Jewish life. The 1968 Congress not only reformulated the Jerusalem Program of 1951 but also attempted to make mandatory the establishment in each country of a single Zionist territorial organization subscribing to that program. This resolution became the basis for the formation of the *American Zionist Federation in 1970.

Another far-reaching initiative advanced by the 1968 Congress related to efforts to associate non-Zionist national and international organizations with the World Zionist Organization without requiring them to affiliate with any local Zionist frameworks. Earlier, in late 1964, a Commission on Reorganization was appointed to recommend constitutional reforms to bring the WZO into "accord with contemporary Jewish life and present-day Zionist responsibilities" and to create an effective partnership of all pro-Israel forces.

Presidium and part of the audience at the 25th Zionist Congress (Jerusalem, 1960). [Israel Information Services]

In this vein Aryeh L. Pincus, chairman of the WZO-Jewish Agency (1968–1973), entered into negotiations with Max M. Fisher, chairman of the United Israel Appeal and the Council of Jewish Federations and Welfare Funds in the United States, with a view to a reconstitution of the Jewish Agency. Agreement was duly reached in August, 1970, and the founding assembly of the reconstituted Jewish Agency met in Jerusalem in June, 1971. The WZO retained a fifty percent representation in the Jewish Agency's governing bodies while the chairman of the Executive of the World Zionist Organization, as elected by the Zionist Congress, served automatically also as chairman of the Jewish Agency. The functions of the Jewish Agency and the WZO were separated, the former to be concerned primarily with work in Israel and the latter with work in the Diaspora, chiefly in the fields of youth, education, and culture.

Concurrently with these developments, the WZO's constituent Zionist political parties, known as Zionist World Unions, continued to decline. Soon after the establishment of Israel a marked tendency was evident favoring detachment from dogmatic alignments with Israeli political parties. The question whether, once the sovereign state of Israel existed, it was proper or useful for Diaspora Zionists to be organized in party-political frameworks at all became a major bone of contention within the Zionist movement in various countries. Organizations like Hadassah in the United States and the Confederation of General Zionists throughout the Diaspora formally detached themselves from such party-political connections and restricted themselves in principle to general support for Israel or to particular projects there.

Meanwhile, in fulfillment of its endeavors to broaden its ranks, the WZO incorporated a growing number of Jewish international bodies on the basis of their collective endorsement of the Jerusalem Program (i.e., the individual members of these organizations were not obliged to take up membership of the WZO.) By 1988 there were five such organizations: the World Union for Progressive Judaism (Reform), the World Council of Synagogues (Conservative), the World Union of Synagogues and Congregations (Orthodox), the World Maccabi Union, and the World Sephardi Federation. Their delegates to Congresses, however, were not granted a vote on elections for office, nor did they participate in regional or national elections to Zionist Congresses.

In any case the generations of Diaspora Jews who had grown up after the establishment of the State of Israel, insofar as they were attracted to the cause of Israel, tended to avoid involvement in the Zionist political parties and preferred other agencies whether of a philanthropic or—in the case of the United States—of a political-lobbying nature. Consequently, the Zionist political unions continued to decline both in terms of ideological content and bases of social support.

Zionist Ideological Issues. Much as major functions of the WZO were assumed by the new State, so too Israeli politics subsumed the major ideological issues, notably those concerning the social character of the society, the relationship between state and religion, and aspects of settlement policy. Above all, the intractable problems of Zionist attitudes and policies towards the Arabs of Eretz Israel and the surrounding Arab states—formerly a perennial ideological and policy dilemma for the WZO—now were vested in the Zionist political structures functioning within Israel itself. At most, Zionists situated in the Diaspora could engage vicariously in the partisan controversies generated by these issues.

The Six-Day War of 1967 was a critical turning point in this regard. It generated two acutely conflicting Zionist visions and political programs concerning the balance between striving for peace with the Arab world on the one hand, and maintaining control over the parts of Eretz Israel which fell under Israeli occupation during the Six-Day War, on the other. This issue, above all others, passionately engaged post-State of Israel Zionist political thought and action, giving rise also to a number of extra-parliamentary organizations such as Gush Emunim (The Block of the Faithful), Shalom Akhshav (Peace Now), and Netivot Shalom (Paths to Peace). These groups, no less than the conventional Zionist political parties, all claimed to be the authentic voice of the Zionist tradition and vision. The vitality of Zionist ideology may be said to have become vested in the ongoing struggle over these issues within the policy and society of Israel. In this respect Zionists in the Diaspora, while increasingly engaged in support or opposition to the rival forces in Israel, played no more than a supportive role.

The WZO itself, although reflecting, by dint of its constitution and electoral system, changes in the Knesset elections, could not adopt policy positions on the aforementioned central ideological issue. The change in Israel's political regime inaugurated in 1977, when Menahem Begin became Prime Minister at the head of a coalition which, for the first time, excluded the Israel Labor Party, was duly reflected in the WZO-Jewish Agency by the election of Arye L. Dulzin of the General Zionist Party as chairman of the Executive (1978–1988).

Ideological Reformulations within the World Zionist Organization. The residual ideological issues which did inwardly engage the WZO revolved around reformulations of the movement's purposes in general and the question of personal aliya in particular. The Jerusalem Program of 1951 provided only the vaguest of formulations calling only in general terms for the "ingathering of the exiles." This reflected the lack of consensus favoring reference to personal aliya as a Zionist imperative. In 1968, however, on the crest of the great wave of Jewish identification stimulated by the Six-Day War, a revised Jerusalem Program gained acceptance by the Zionist Congress. Although it too represented a compromise between American and Israeli understanding of Zionism, it referred more specifically to "aliya from all lands" (*for full text see* JERUSALEM PROGRAM). After the passing of this program more specific formulations were passed incrementally by successive Zionist Congresses interspersed with the work of ideological commissions. They laid down "the principles of Zionism" and the "obligations of the individual Zionist." Thus the 28th Congress, held in January, 1972, listed obligations said to "stem from the tasks and functions embraced by the Jerusalem Program" which included: to implement aliya to Israel; to be an active member of the Territorial Organization; to study Hebrew, to give one's children a Jewish education and bring them up towards aliya and Zionist self-fulfillment; to contribute and to be active on behalf of the Zionist funds and to participate actively in the consolidation of Israel's economy; to play an active role in the life of one's community and its institutions, and to endeavor to insure their democratic nature; to strengthen Zionist influence within the community, and to intensify Jewish education; to work for the defense of Jewish rights in the Diaspora. This formulation was endorsed by the 29th Congress, held in February-March, 1978. However, gauged by the actual record of the Zionist leadership in America and some other Diaspora countries, these formulations remained declarative and failed to become either binding or normative. Underlying their indeterminate nature was a deep-seated unwillingness, particularly in the United States of America, to consider their Diaspora situation as one of "galut" (exile) or to regard aliya as a personal imperative. Indeed, when a resolution was passed, at the 28th Congress in 1972, calling for obligatory aliya of Zionist leaders after two terms in office, Hadassah led the opposition to this measure and it was later declared unconstitutional.

This ambiguity over the personal imperative of aliya was compounded by the fact that much the same differences of interpretation over the significance of the term "centrality of Israel" existed among Zionists as among other Jews who, although non-members of Zionist organizations, were also deeply concerned for Israel. This dissension deprived the Zionist Organization's leadership of its former ideological elan. Indeed, it became increasingly difficult to distinguish meaningfully between Zionists and so-called non-Zionists, especially in the United States.

This blurring of a distinction which had been meaningful in the pre-State period became increasingly evident in the relationship between the two partners who reconstituted the Jewish Agency in 1971—the members of the WZO on the one hand, and the leading figures of the major fundraising instrumentalities, especially in the United States, on the other. Something of a turning point was reached in February, 1981, at a special conference held at Caesarea (initiating what became known as the "Caesarea Process") to evaluate the relationship between these partners. There it became apparent that the Jerusalem Program of Zionism—itself a compromise formulation previously hammered out between Israeli and Diaspora Zionist functionaries and leaders—was virtually endorsed by the so-called "non-Zionists" or "fundraisers." Indeed the next Assembly of the Jewish Agency (1983) formally accepted the Jerusalem Program. The epithet "non-Zionist" was thereby nullified to all intents and purposes.

The "Caesarea Process" facilitated more intimate interaction between the two partners in the Jewish Agency and led to increasing involvement of the fund-raiser section in tasks formerly regarded as the exclusive responsibility of the Zionists, such as Jewish education in the Diaspora and even the encouragement of aliya from the western countries. On the other hand, it also led to greater assertiveness by the fundraising activists in the governance of the Jewish Agency, most notably in regard to insistence upon "advise and consent" before the appointment of departmental heads in the Agency. On a number of occasions in the course of the 1980s the fundraisers exercised vetoes on candidates presented by the Israeli sections of the political Zionist World Unions, much to the chagrin of the latter. At the same time, the blurring of ideological distinctions between the two segments of the Jewish Agency raised, with increasing insistence, the question whether the time had not come to fuse the two completely into a unified Jewish Agency framework with a remodeled constitution curtailing or eliminating the domination exercised by the Israeli political parties.

During the first half of the 1980s renewed efforts were made, at the initiative of the WZO chairman, Arye Dulzin, to reexamine the ideological and organizational bases of the Zionist movement. Referred to as the "Herzliya Process", these endeavors took the form of consultations, initially held in Herzliya during 1983, of an Israeli group comprising representative persons from the various Zionist World Unions and organizations, as well as some invited Israeli academics. These were followed by a series of similarly constituted consultations in various regions of the Diaspora. A number of evocative ideological formulations issued from the "Herzliya Process." One was the statement that the Zionist movement's perception of its purposes had changed in the post-State era "from national liberation to national existence." Another was the reformulation of the obligations of a Zionist as "the *mitzvot* of a Zionist." These stated that "aliya is the preeminent duty of a Zionist... each Zionist must accept the obligation to initiate and persevere in that process until he and his family finally come on aliya." In this vein the Zionist General Council in February 1986 resolved that:

> Within the array of Jewish-Zionist obligations there are gradations, like stairs which one climbs from the lowest step to the top; from Zionist-Jewish identification through organizational affiliation, study of the Hebrew language, Jewish education, activity in everything concerning the Jewish community, assistance to Jews in distress and aid to the State of Israel, culminating in aliya and Zionist fulfillment which entails a way of life dedicated to the needs of Israeli society and the State. Through these deeds the Zionist Movement, whose primary task is national liberation, will henceforth also be a movement for national continuity.

Another notable development arising from these deliberations was the formation in 1986 of a *Magshimei Aliya* (Zionist fulfillment through immigration) movement uniting those groups whose members undertook a firm commitment to personal aliya (e.g., the various youth movements and newer organizations of young adults committed to aliya such as Telem and Tehila). This grouping sought the status of an autonomous organization within the WZO. However, as of the 30th Congress held in December, 1987, *Magshimei Aliya* had not attained this objective. Nor was there any evidence that the ideological formulations of the Herzliya Process had more than a declarative impact upon the leadership pattern of the WZO in the various countries of the Diaspora. On the other hand, the effects of changes in the number and relative strength of the WZO's constituent groups and of the Zionist Executive's insistence upon obligatory elections to Congress in all countries was very much in evidence at the 1987 Congress. It resulted in much enlarged representation of newer constituent organizations such as Arzenu (the Zionist organization of the World Union for Progressive Judaism). This changed the balance of forces sufficiently to insure the reinstatement of a Labor party chairman of the executive of the WZO-Jewish Agency in the person of Simcha Dinitz.

Current Dilemmas of the Zionist Movement. In the 1980s, the Zionist Movement of the State of Israel era continued to function in some significant areas of activity but its general condition was giving cause for concern. A number of cumulative vitiating influences took their toll. The low record of aliya up to 1989, fluctuating only between ten and twenty thousand a year during the 1980s (less than half of them from Western countries), raised questions about the attractiveness of Israel as a home for most of Diaspora Jewry. A renewed purpose came with the mass Russian immigration from 1989 onward but the questions remained referring to aliya from the rest of the world. It was also tempered by the consideration that during the 1980s, when opportunities were more open elsewhere, over 90% of those leaving Soviet Russia had gone elsewhere, mostly to the United States. In other countries of Jewish emigration, such as South Africa, only a minority of the Jews leaving went to Israel.

This slap in the face for upholders of the original Zionist vision was compounded by another negative demographic phenomenon—the steady outflow of Israelis, also mainly to North America, referred to pejoratively in Zionist terms as **yerida* (descent). By the mid-1980s the cumulative number of these emigrants from Israel, including many born and educated there, was variously estimated at between 250,000 and 300,000. The demoralizing effect of these factors upon upholders of the Zionist vision was, however, somewhat counterbalanced by authoritative demographic projections which indicated that, notwithstanding *yerida* and intra-Diaspora population movements, all of Diaspora Jewry was undergoing considerable demographic decline. This was mainly owing to low birth rates, but intermarriage was also a cause. Israel's Jewish population, by contrast, still enjoyed positive demographic growth, sufficient to indicate that the percentage of world Jewry domiciled in Israel was steadily rising. Whereas it was only 22.8 percent in 1975, it was likely to reach 34 percent at the turn of the century.

Another unanticipated factor which contradicted fundamental assumptions of the Zionist ideology was the emergence of "anti-Zionism" as a transmutation of anti-Semitism. It had always been a fundament of Zionist analysis that the normalizing of Jewish national existence, which nothing other than a Jewish state could effect, was the only solution for the problem of anti-Semitism. A corollary of this proposition was the expectation that the very existence of a Jewish state would enhance the self-esteem and security of Jews remaining in the Diaspora. Indeed, respect for Jews would replace contempt and the Jewish state would provide not only a refuge for Jews in distress, but in certain circumstances, even reach out to protect them in the Diaspora.

As events after 1948 showed, this vision was realized only in part. Far from disappearing, anti-Semitism proved itself to be highly resilient in assuming the new disguise of "anti-Zionism", insidiously promoted by Arab and Soviet sources. In some cases it assumed terrorist proportions that threatened the physical safety of Jews in Diaspora communities. In 1975 a notorious resolution was passed at the *United Nations branding Zionism "as a form of racism." The fact that thenceforth the WZO found it necessary to devote much attention to the defense of Zionism against this calumny, presented a sharp contrast to the persuasive moral standing which had won worldwide public sympathy for Zionism in the period leading up to the establishment of Israel. Although the UN resolution was rescinded in 1991, the Worldwide fight against anti-Zionism continued.

Against this background, but on another level of discourse, there was a growth of dissension among Jews themselves concerning certain policies and practices of the State of Israel relating to parts of the Land of Israel occupied as a result of the war of June, 1967. These were exacerbated by the Lebanon War, initiated by Israel, in 1982–1984 and by the outbreak in December, 1987, in the Administered Areas of a form of sustained resistance to Israel known as the *intifada*. Although dissent from some of Israel's policies was sharpest among Jews outside the ranks of the Zionist Organization, Zionists too were affected. Among the latter, however, dissension took the form of intensified identification with or, conversely, criticism of, the various conflicting policies functioning within the Israeli polity.

Yet another perennial dilemma of the WZO which has debilitating effects is the blurring of distinctions between members of Zionist organizations and Jews who, although concerned for Israel and committed to supporting it, are not members of any Zionist organization. Attendant upon this dilemma are ambivalence and indecision over the questions whether or not the partnership structure of the Jewish Agency ought to be reconstituted as a unified whole, and whether or not the WZO ought to transform itself into a smaller but more incisively defined ideological movement centered upon the personal imperative of aliya.

Paradoxically, this enervating dilemma of the Zionist movement results from the phenomenal success of Zionism in permeating the broad consensus of Jewry throughout the world; an achievement far beyond the most optimistic expectations of Zionism's founding fathers who had to conduct an arduous minority struggle against ideological opponents, both secularized and religious, occupying the commanding heights of Jewish communal institutions in most Diaspora lands. In the wake of the Holocaust; after the creation of the State of Israel in 1948; and under the impact of the Six-Day War of 1967, the basic postulates of Zionism became progressively more normative as a consensual ideology shared by Jews throughout the world, transcending the variety of religious and secular modes in which modern Jewish identity is expressed.

By the early 1990s the World Zionist Organization still claimed to be the largest international Jewish organization in the world with a total affiliated membership in the Diaspora estimated at one and a half million. Much of this membership, however, was indirect; that is to say through membership of other organizations that had affiliated with the World Zionist Organization. Also in an indirect sense one may add to this the overwhelming majority of Israel's four million Jewish population, who express their participation in the Zionist movement automatically—if mostly unknowingly—via Israel's Knesset elections. Moreover, endorsement of the fundaments of Zionist ideology may be said to exceed these numbers by far; these fundaments include affirmation of the national attributes of Jewish identity, commitment to support of Israel, and recognition of Israel's centrality in determining the collective survival and character of Jews as a distinctive entity in the world.

G. SHIMONI

ZIONIST COMMISSION (Va'ad ha-Tzirim). Commission set up early in 1918 by warrant from the British Foreign Office for the purpose of (1) forming a liaison between the British military administration and the yishuv; (2) coordinating relief work in Palestine and aiding the repatriation of exiles, evacuees, and refugees; (3) assisting in restoring and developing settlements and in organizing the Jewish population in general; (4) assisting Jewish organizations and institutions in Palestine in the resumption of their activities, which had been disrupted by World War I; (5) helping establish friendly relations with the Arabs and other non-Jewish communities; (6) gathering information and reporting on possibilities of further development of Jewish settlements and of the country in general; and (7) investigating the feasibility of plans for establishing a Hebrew University.

The Commission was to include representatives of the

Members of the Zionist Commission arriving in Jerusalem in 1918. Second from the right is Chaim Weizmann. [Zionist Archives]

Jewish communities of the principal Allied countries. At first, the United States, not being at war with Turkey, did not consider it proper to appoint representatives, but in 1919 American Zionists joined the Commission. Because of war conditions, Russian representatives were at first unable to leave for Palestine.

The original members of the Commission arrived in Palestine in April, 1918. They were Chaim Weizmann (chairman), Joseph Cowen, David Eder, Leon Simon, and Israel Sieff (secretary), all from Britain, and Sylvain Lévi, a French anti-Zionist who had been appointed by the French government. Maj. William Ormsby-Gore (later Lord Harlech) was attached to the Commission as liaison officer; he was assisted by James de Rothschild. Later in the year Angelo Levi-Bianchini and Giacomo Artom, who had been appointed by the Italian government, arrived in Palestine to join the Commission.

In its capacity as a liaison body between the Jewish population and the British authorities in Palestine, the Commission took over the political functions of the Palestine Office in Jaffa, which had represented the World Zionist Organization (WZO) in Palestine. The Palestine Office continued its separate existence for another year and a half, but its finances were controlled by the Commission.

The first practical project of the Commission was the establishment of a Relief Department and, with funds supplied by the American Jewish Joint Distribution Committee, it assisted institutions and individuals, especially in Jerusalem, where the population had suffered greatly from starvation and epidemics during the war years. The Commission also endeavored to improve sanitary conditions. After the British occupied northern Palestine (September, 1918), the Commission extended its relief services to that area also.

At the suggestion of General Gilbert Clayton, Chief Political Officer of the Egyptian Expeditionary Force, Weizmann met Emir (later King) Feisal in a desert encampment at Gueira between Akaba and Ma'an (4 June 1918). It was on this occasion that the emir expressed to Weizmann his sympathy with Zionist reconstruction work in Palestine.

In July, 1918, Weizmann presided over the ceremony in which the foundation stones were laid on Mount Scopus for the Hebrew University of Jerusalem. In September he returned to England. David Eder, who headed the Commission's relief activities and who was to remain in Palestine longer than any of the other original members, became acting chairman. Vladimir Jabotinsky, who had arrived in Palestine with the Jewish Legion, joined in the work of the Commission for several months.

In view of the prospects held out by the Balfour Declaration (November, 1917), the Zionists had hoped to be able to inaugurate more ambitious projects once the British occupied all of Palestine. However, the British military authorities, who were generally unsympathetic towards Zionism, declared that as long as the country was under military occupation, it was the duty of the authorities, in accordance with international law, to preserve the status quo. It proved impossible for Jews to purchase land in Palestine. There could be practically no Jewish immigration, since only the repatriation of exiles was permitted by the authorities. Noevertheless, even during the period of military administration the Zionist leaders in Palestine were able to do much to strengthen the communal and economic life of the yishuv. Preparations progressed for the organization of the representative institutions of the yishuv, and the Zionist school system was organized.

In the fall of 1919 the Zionist Commission and the Jaffa Palestine Office were merged, and all departments except the Immigration Department were moved to Jerusalem. However, it was not until the civil administration took power in Palestine after 30 June 1920 that the Zionists could begin new settlement projects. As the sole representative body of the WZO in Palestine, the Commission was active in planning, reconstruction, and immigrant absorption, including participation in land purchases, afforestation and construction projects, support of settlements and new immigrants, and aid to the Hebrew school system.

Eder was succeeded as chairman of the Commission in turn by Eliyahu Ze'ev Lewin-Epstein, Harry Friedenwald, and Robert Szold. Then Eder briefly took charge again. From October, 1919 the Commission was headed by Menahem Ussishkin. The 12th Zionist Congress (1921) replaced the Zionist Commission with the Palestine Zionist Executive, which henceforth was responsible for the administration of Zionist work in Palestine.

T. PRESCHEL—B. WASSERSTEIN

ZIONIST CONGRESSES. *See* CONGRESS, ZIONIST.

ZIONIST EXECUTIVE The Zionist Executive is the executive organ of the World Zionist Organization (WZO). It occupies a place and exercises functions analogous to those of a state government or a company board of directors. According to the Constitution of the WZO, it is "charged with the implementation of the decisions of Congress and General Council and is responsible to those bodies. It shall have the power to acquire rights and to undertake obligations on behalf of the WZO and to represent it externally." The Zionist Executive is charged with the transaction of current business, the normal affairs of the WZO. Until 1921 it was called the Inner (or Small) Actions Committee, in contradistinction to the Greater Actions Committee—today's *Zionist General Council. In the first years of the WZO there was no clear-cut distinction between the jurisdiction of these two bodies: the latter, composed of the representatives of the movement from the various countries, was considered to be the leading organ of the WZO while its actual direction was in the hands of five members of the Greater Actions Committee who, like Herzl, lived in Vienna and constituted the Inner Actions Committee. From the Eighth Zionist Congress (1907), the Inner Actions Committee was elected by the Zionist Congress separately and thus its status was enhanced.

From 1921 the members of the Executive residing in Palestine formed its Palestine branch with its seat in Jerusalem while all the others formed the London branch. Gradually the greater part of the Executive's functions was assigned to its Jerusalem branch while the London branch remained in charge of political activities in general and relations with the mandatory power in particular. After the establishment of the State, the entire Executive moved to Jerusalem with the exception of the members in New York and one representative in London.

According to an express provision of the present Constitution the seat and head office of the Zionist Executive is in Jerusalem, but "divisions of the Executive may be established abroad." Thus the American Section of the Executive has its seat in New York. It has 11 members (1986) including its chairperson. The American Section deals almost exclusively with matters pertaining to Zionist affairs in the USA.

Apart from the sessions of the Executive in Jerusalem, held as a rule every two weeks, "plenary sessions" of the full Executive, including the American members, are held in Jerusalem several times a year. There is no clear-cut delimitation of jurisdiction between the two bodies, but generally speaking plenary sessions deal with policy guidelines and major issues.

A resolution of the 29th Zionist Congress (1978) recommended that, apart from Israel and the USA, Europe, Latin America, and a region composed of South Africa, Australia, and New Zealand, should be represented on the Executive, but this has not yet been effected.

The number of members of the Executive is fixed by the Congress which elects it. It has steadily increased in the course of time, as the following table indicates:

The reason for the proliferation has been not only the growth of the movement but also its increasing diversity. Since the early fifties, when Herut ha-Tzohar joined the Executive, it has been based on a wall-to-wall coalition, with every Zionist party (Zionist World Union) represented. The admission of International Jewish bodies like Maccabi or the Reform Movement has also contributed to the swelling of the Executive because each of them is represented. The proposal made after the 30th Congress to limit constitutionally the number of its members, perhaps to a maximum of 30, was not accepted.

Since 1921 the Zionist Executive has been headed by a chairman, who is elected by Congress separately, while the other members of the Executive are elected en bloc, as a list. The co-chairman of the Executive exercises the functions of the president of the WZO, if this post is vacant—as has been the case since 1968.

The Executive works through Departments and it is its prerogative to set them up—or to abolish them—and to appoint Executive members as heads of departments (others are without portfolio). The Departments of the Executive include those of Organization, Information, Education and Culture, and Torah Education and Culture. The WZO sections of the Jewish Agency Department for Aliya and Absorption deals with immigrants from free countries, while the Agency Aliya Department is in charge of "emergency aliya" (e.g., from Soviet Russia). The WZO section of the Settlement Department deals with settlements in the administered areas, while the Agency Settlement Department is in charge of those in Israel within the pre-1967 borders, a division due to budgetary reasons and to legal requirements and restrictions existing in some countries.

From 1947 to 1971, until the reconstitution of the Jewish Agency, the Zionist Executive was identical with the Executive of the Jewish Agency.

Since 1939, apart from full members, members with limited rights such as deputy members or associate members, have also been included in the Executive.

The Executive elected by the 31st Zionist Congress (1987) consisted, apart from 17 representatives of Zionist World Unions and one of WIZO—all with full voting rights—of five representatives of International Jewish Bodies, members of the WZO like the Maccabi World Union and the Sephardi World Federation whose voting rights are limited. That Congress also decided to set up an Outer Executive consisting of up to 51 members, including all the members of the Inner Executive. The Congress and the Zionist General Council in June 1988 elected 15 members of the Outer Executive bringing their total—together with those of the Inner Executive—to 38. The Presidium of the Zionist General Council was charged with electing additional members and also with defining the jurisdiction of the Outer Executive and its relations with the Inner Executive and other governing bodies of the WZO.

A. ZWERGBAUM

ZIONIST GENERAL COUNCIL (ZGC). The supreme body of the *World Zionist Organization (WZO) in periods between Zionist *Congresses. According to the Constitution of 1960 it may consider and decide upon all matters relating to the WZO—save those within the exclusive jurisdiction of the Zionist Congress (which are not numerous). In particular it inspects and supervises the activities of the *Zionist Executive, which is responsible to the Council: either the Council or its Permanent Budget and Finance Committee considers and decides upon the draft budgets proposed by the Zionist Executive and deals in the inter-Congress period with all budgetary and financial matters of the WZO. Since the 1960 Constitution came into force, every Congress has made use of the possibility to empower the ZGC to amend the Constitution and in fact most of the numerous amendments enacted since 1960 were discussed and passed by the Council rather than by the Congress.

In Herzl's time the ZGC was called Greater Actions Committee; it was composed of 25 members, leading Zionists representing the Zionist territorial organizations of the various countries, and considered the supreme inter-Congress organ of the Movement. The Eighth Zionist Congress (1907) resolved that it should have a membership of no less than 20 and no more than 60 members but the 10th Zionist Congress (1911) reduced it again to the previous 25.

Before the outbreak of World War II the ZGC elected the "Inner Zionist General Council" consisting of 31 members residing in Palestine. The ZGC delegated to it all its authority and powers "if in the event of war there would be no possibility of the ZGC meeting and fulfilling its functions". Thus, indeed, during World War II the Inner Zionist Council exercised all functions of the ZGC safeguarding the continuity and legality of the Movement in crucial times.

The importance, influence, and size of the ZGC increased notably after World War II when Congresses have been held once in four or even five years instead of every second year as had been the case formerly, and for most intents and purposes the ZGC has itself become a miniature Congress.

The ZGC is elected by Congress and reflects its composition because each Congress faction proposes one council member for every five Congress delegates. A remainder of at least three entitles the grouping to an additional Council member. The "key" for the representation of the international Jewish bodies and WIZO is different and is laid down in agreements between them and the WZO: in general, one Council member for three Congress delegates.

In 1986 the ZGC numbered 144 members of whom 20 had limited voting rights, namely the representatives of the international Jewish bodies, and, since 1973, the chairmen of Zionist Federations of countries represented at Congress by at least three delegates.

The sessions of the ZGC are also attended by some 100 members in an advisory capacity without voting rights. These include members of the Executive, representatives of the National Funds, and "Honorary Fellows" (formerly called "virilists")—veteran Zionist leaders. Ordinary sessions of the Council take place at least once every year, usually shortly before or after the sessions of the Jewish Agency Assembly.

Together with the members of the Council, Congress elects a number of deputy members equal to twice the number of its members, to replace members who do not want or are unable to attend a session of the Council, or who wish to renounce their function altogether. Since 1968 the Presidium has also been entitled to replace a member or deputy member "for important reasons" at the request of the grouping concerned, by an "outsider" who was not elected by Congress and this power has been used rather frequently.

The representatives of WIZO and of the Zionist Council for Israel enjoy full voting rights.

The ZGC is headed by a Presidium numbering (1986) 26 members whose composition reflects that of the Council. Its Chairman is also Chairman of the ZGC itself. The functions of the Presidium are not limited to conducting the meetings of the Council and preparing, together with the Zionist Executive, the agenda of the sessions, but it has other tasks including the appointment of committees and office-holders, the enactment of Regulations in the framework of the laws of the WZO or by special authorization of the Congress or Council. The Presidium usually meets once every four to six weeks.

The prestigious Committee for the Amendment of the Constitution, in existence since 1972, has the status of a permanent Committee of the ZGC.

A. ZWERGBAUM

ZIONIST GREATER ACTIONS COMMITTEE. *See* ZIONIST GENERAL COUNCIL.

ZIONIST HISTORIOGRAPHY. Zionist historiography emanated from Zionist ideology and historiosophy, as part of the educational needs and spontaneous development of the Zionist movement. Only in recent years has it become the object of academic research. At the same time, the conception of Zionist history has become an integral part of the internal and external current political debate. From its inception, Zionist ideology was based upon the evaluation of Jewish history in general and of modern Jewish history in particular. On the other hand Zionist ideology provided the "working historian" with the definition of the subject of his study as well as concepts of interpretation. The historical approach to the Zionist movement related in detail to anti-Semitism, to attitudes towards assimilation, to agricultural settlement, etc. The definitions of Zionism as a movement for the "liquidation of the Diaspora"; or for "the creation of a center in the Land of Israel" together with national continuity in the Diaspora; as a movement for the establishment of a state; for the economic regeneration of the Jewish people; for cultural renaissance; or for the perpetuation of

Jewish tradition—all determined the historian's terms of reference to the subject. They are accepted critically by the academic historian.

The spontaneous growth of Zionist historiography is expressed in descriptive memoirs and annals which grew out of the marking of anniversaries, and in meeting the need to present the movement to Jews and to non-Jews, as well as to educate the rising generations. Turning points in the history of the movement, such as Herzl's appearance on the scene, or the fate of the movement after his death, the Balfour Declaration or the establishment of the State of Israel, generated the need to examine the past and to review the movement's development.

Research Sources. The incessant confrontation with the British authorities during the Mandate, as well as with the League of Nations and the United Nations, provided a vast amount of historical material on the relevant issues. Political discussion on the factors that led up to the Balfour Declaration or the nature of the mandatory rule, or the role of the Jews in the development of the country, provide raw material for the historian.

One of the most important incentives to contemporary research is the publication of archival material and new sources. The Zionist sources are partly internal Jewish and Zionist, and partly relate to those movements with which the Jews came into contact. The publication of sources for the study of the period of Hibbat Zion (the new edition of Druyanow edited by Shulamit Laskov); editions of Herzl's writings, diaries, and letters; the publication of Chaim Weizmann's letters in 23 volumes; the publication of the letters and diaries of David Ben-Gurion and Moshe Sharett; the publications of the Israel State Archives—have all contributed greatly to the development of historical research.

At the same time, the archives of Jewish organizations that functioned in Palestine (Alliance Israélite Universelle, the Jewish Colonization Association, and PICA) have been opened to researchers and, together with the Central Zionist Archives and other archives in Israel and in the Diaspora, have provided access to primary source materials. The official archives of Great Britain, the United States, West Germany, and France have enabled research into the variegated background of the Zionist movement.

The transfer of the arena of Zionist activity following World War II also provided new areas for research: the role of the movement in the Middle East, relations with the Arabs in Palestine and with their own national movement, the relations between the Jewish State in the Land of Israel and the Jews in the democratic countries of the west, and the nature of the Zionist movement in the Jewish communities in Asia and Africa.

Progress in the study of the history of the Jewish people at universities in Israel, the USA, and Europe, has transformed the study of Zionism from the concern of journalists, writers, and politicians into an academic subject. Periodicals and publishing houses are now committed to this area of research.

The Role of Zionism. One of the principal concerns of Zionist historiographic research is the relationship between the Zionist movement, Jewish historical continuity, and the background of modern Jewish history. The question facing historians is whether modern nationalism and the modern state in the Land of Israel are the continuation of the historical Jewish yearning throughout the generations, or whether it has introduced a response to the new nature of the "Jewish Question". This "Jewish Question" relates to the granting of citizenship to the Jews, to their economic situation, and to their involvement in the social mobility of the host countries. The Jews are faced with the problem of the collective existence of the Jewish people, and the possibility of persistence of Judaism (according to its various definitions) in the situation prevalent in the modern free world. If the ideological question is to what extent Zionism provides a possible solution to the Jewish problem, then the historical question is the relationship between Zionism and the ideological and sociological processes to which 19th century Jewry was subjected. To what extent did the Emancipation, the Haskala, the religious reform, modernization, secularization, urbanization, migration, lead towards the Zionist solution or to other solutions? In this regard, the ideological basis of the Zionist movement and the formation of social groups which accepted the idea, must be taken into account. Zionist historiography has often been required to relate to Zionism as the sole solution to these processes. A more critical approach considers Zionism as one of the options of Jewish life, in constant contention with other options. The question is whether Zionism is the exclusive expression of the modern concept of *Kelal Israel* (the total Jewish people), which was introduced in the 19th century, or just one of its expressions.

The relationship between Zionism and the development of modern anti-Semitism and political activism on the part of the Jews is also a central issue in the examination of Zionism. To what extent was anti-Semitism the catalyst for the Zionist processes within the Jewish community? Jewish political activism assumed differing forms, and the question to be examined is the relationship between Zionism and this activism.

Another central question is the role of the Land of Israel within Zionism; does it emphasize the relationship with the Jewish religion, or rather the past history of the Jews, or is its essence the ability to establish within its boundaries a free and creative Jewish society? This ties in with the role of the 19th century movement for settlement in Palestine and with the birth of the national movement. In the 19th century the yishuv (the Jewish community in Palestine) grew, even though it was being forged as a Torah-centered community. The relationship between the growth of the Jewish community and nationalist ideologies is a subject under consideration, especially in recent years with the expansion of research into the life of the yishuv. Academic and critical historians are opposed to relating the early stages of Zionist history as a collection of scattered and sporadic ideas concerning the return of Jews to the Land of Israel and the renaissance of the Jewish people. They endeavor to consider these ideas as related to the entire context of the social and ideological development of Jewish society.

This issue is connected with both the Jewish as well as the non-Jewish "harbingers" of Zionism. The ideas of non-Jews regarding the return of the Jews to their land stemmed from a variety of motivations. These motivations were philo-Semitic as well as anti-Semitic, missionary and strategic-political. But the question is whether these were sporadic phenomena, or whether they have a common logic. In other words, to what extent do they reflect the European and American attitude to the Jewish problem, and to what extent did they prepare the ground for Zionism to be accepted by the international community? On the other hand, it may be asked to what extent did they make an impact on the Jewish community itself?

The subject of the Jewish "harbingers" also presents a

problem. Historiography devotes much attention to the question whether Orthodox and non-Orthodox Jews who proposed ideas relating to the return of the Jews to the Land of Israel in the 19th century were harbingers of ideological or social ideas which would later mature within Zionism, or whether they were incidental phenomena or still connected to the Orthodox context. Among the latter were Joseph Salvador, Rabbis Alkalai and Kalischer, Moses Hess, and others.

The public and ideological background to Zionist history has so far featured in general works on Zionist history whose level of conception and expression is uneven. The variety of research published as monographs during the past years has still not reached the stage of a comprehensive presentation. The main general work is Nahum Sokolow's *History of Zionism*, aimed specifically at an English-speaking audience. It is interspersed with topics dealing with English philo-Zionism, the political background of the Zionist movement, as well as literary personalities and movements among the Jews.

In the mid-1930s, Adolf Böhm's *Die Zionistische Bewegung* appeared, still considered to be the best general descriptive work on the Zionist movement; the author was a learned Viennese Jewish businessman active in the Zionist movement. His book provides a description of the Zionist movement's internal development, and deals particularly with the mutual relationship between Jewish nationalism and Zionism in the Diaspora, and the development of the yishuv, in the period up to 1925.

For some time the lectures by Yitzhak Grünbaum served as general historical material in Hebrew for the period up to 1918; this was a descriptive history based on documentation and the memoirs of one of the personalities who lived during that period.

Ben Halpern's *The Idea of the Jewish State* (1961) described the Zionist movement according to its ideological components and according tthe manner in which it was accepted by the Jewish and international communities. Halpern's work differs from the others in that his approach is only partly historical; it is based on a set of analytical terms according to which he examines how revolutionary movements are accepted by society and how they become part of the general social consensus.

After the Six-Day War, Walter Laqueur wrote his *History of Zionism* in which he stressed its ideological-political trends and detailed the confrontation between Israel and the Arab world. In the 1970s and 1980s David Vital produced three volumes on the history of Zionism prior to World War I, from the viewpoint of Herzlian and political Zionism.

Zionism's Beginnings. Historians provide differing approaches as to the actual beginnings of the Zionist movement. There are those who consider the ephemeral associations of the 1860s as constituting a sort of debut of Zionism, while others consider the point of origin to be the 1881 pogroms in Russia, or the advent of the Herzlian period (1897).

The 1860s saw the sprouting of ideas of Jewish prenationalism with Orthodox overtones, or as a reaction to religious Reform; these were linked to proposals concerning the settlement of the Land of Israel prevalent at the time. The center of this movement was Germany, and the leading personalities were Rabbis Kalischer and Alkalai. While historians consider this as the period of the "harbingers", others deem it a phenomenon irrelevant to Zionism as it developed, or even a failure.

Pinpointing the beginning of the history of Zionism to 1881/82 raises historiographic problems, as became clear when the centenary of these events was marked in 1981. Researchers have yet to determine whether the movement was influenced to a major extent by the anti-Semitism and pogroms rampant at the time, or whether it was in line with the structural trends of the period, such as migration, the rise of nationalist awareness among the intellectuals, and the political activism of the various social strata, including the intellectuals ("the revolt in the Diaspora" as Benzion Dinur termed it). The question is whether this activism was the mode of expression only of the Hibbat Zion movement, or of other public movements as well. Further, was this movement a Jewish phenomenon unique to Russian Jewry, or had it begun to flourish among other social groups in the Diaspora, for instance, in the Hapsburg monarchy, etc.

Another dilemma is posed by the relationships between the nationalist movement, the migration movement, and the immigration movement to Eretz Israel. Ths immigrants were only partially connected organizationally, socially, and ideologically to the nationalist movement. Part of the wave of immigration to Eretz Israel known as the "First Aliya" came from Romania, and this was a sort of interim phenomenon between the migration movement as a reaction to persecution and the traditional pre-nationalist or "enlightenment" phenomena. In recent years, progress has been made in the research into Romanian Jewry in general, as well as the study of the movement for settlement in Eretz Israel from Romania.

Latterly, research has focused on the Bilu movement. They have become a symbol of the historical tradition of the period and critical research has pointed up their adventure as well as their failure.

This period raises the question of the relationship between the Zionist movement in the Diaspora and the settlement movement in Eretz Israel. The decisive influence on the settlement movement in Eretz Israel was that of Baron Edmond de Rothschild, a non-Zionist in the conventional sense. In recent years research on the yishuv has intensified, leading to a growth of research into the Zionist movement, as well as into Baron Rothschild's enterprises in the land.

Students of the period posed the question why the movement that flourished in Russia during those years failed. What began as a revolutionary movement, whose aim was to bring the Diaspora to an end through mass immigration to Eretz Israel and the reconstitution of the national homeland, wound up as a tiny movement supporting a number of agricultural villages in Eretz Israel. The answers, partly theoretical and conceptual and partly empirical, are based upon an evaluation of the Russian-Jewish community and the attitude of the notables, the Zionist intellectuals, and the middle class groups toward the ideals of Hibbat Zion. The movement for settlement in Eretz Israel arose in the 1880s in Russia, as a spontaneous movement of associations in various towns: intellectuals did not become the leaders of the movement. In 1884 a central organization was established in Kattowitz, but it lacked a forceful leadership which could implement the movement's ideals. The rifts within the movement between the Odessa Committee and the associations and between the followers of the Enlightenment movement and the ultra-Orthodox, are significant issues for research. Reaction to the movement in other countries is another subject for study.

The movement also faced external obstacles: the objections of the Ottoman government, the lack of public funds, the limited amount of private Jewish capital reaching Eretz Israel and the lack of experience in agricultural settlement, were all prohibiting factors.

The historiography of the 1880s is diverse and includes not only the publication of documents, but also summary works at different levels. Some of these raise basic questions (Citron, Dinaburg) and others present a massive amount of material (Yavnieli, Klausner).

The 90s: The Herzlian Period. Zionist history of the 1890s began with the legalization of the Odessa Committee by the Russian government in February, 1890, and the increased immigration to Eretz Israel in 1890/91. It reached its climax with the advent of Theodor Herzl.

The main conundrum of this period is: was the Herzlian movement a continuation of the earlier Hibbat Zion period in Russia, based on its trials and errors, or was it the outcome of a protest against failure and of the movement's deviation from its original purpose of providing the solution to the "Jewish Problem"? Was the Herzlian movement a direct outcome of the movement that originated in Russia, or was it a movement that arose in western and central Europe as a result of problems such as anti-Semitism, migration, and unemployment of Jews, which exacerbated the material distress of the Jews and stimulated the search for a solution?

The 1890s saw an upsurge of immigration to Eretz Israel. Current research is examining whether the failure of this wave was due to the policy of the Ottoman authorities or the activities of the Hovevei Zion themselves.

During the nineties the idea of the settlement of Eretz Israel and the concept of Jewish nationalism spread throughout the Jewish communities in the Diaspora. The question arises whether the diminution of the Zionist idea, and the abandonment of the concept of ending the Diaspora, helped to spread the idea of agricultural settlement in Eretz Israel among non-nationalist groups which had related to settlement there in a positive manner provided it was not connected to a nationalist idea.

However, during these years there was a spontaneous upsurge of nationalism among groups within the Jewish communities of Europe, especially students. A new class of intellectuals arose against the atmosphere of anti-Semitism, nationalism, and the quest for the essence of Judaism. This provided the basis for Herzl's activities.

On the other hand, these were the years of the growth of the Jewish proletariat and Yiddish culture. The idea of Jewish socialism permeated the Jewish community as an internationalist idea, and later also in a nationalistic form. The Jewish workers' organization, the Bund, was founded in 1897. The relationship between the two movements—the Zionist and the Jewish socialist is a major subject of research.

Zionist historiography has consistently attempted to evaluate the character and teachings of Ahad Ha-Am. The question whether Ahad Ha-Am's ideology was an expression of the failure of the movement and the depletion of its aims, or an expression of the realistic definition of those aims, remains a matter of contention. Were his theories a sign of being resigned to the continued existence of the Diaspora, or recognition of its value? Did they mean the relinquishing of the idea of gathering the entire Jewish people in the Land of Israel, or the recognition of its importance as a center for the continued existence of the Diaspora?

Study of the period of Ahad Ha-Am and the Benei Moshe movement he headed raises the question of the relationship between Zionism and the character of Judaism. In the 1880s the Orthodox Jews considered their approach as providing the content of Jewish nationalism. Ahad Ha-Am proposed an alternative for Jewish cultural continuity not necessarily based on religious belief.

Modern research has concentrated on the question of the intellectual and practical relationship between Orthodox and secular nationalism. The current reality of the relationship between religion, state, and politics in Israel has served to stimulate research, which has uncovered abundant source material, examined them critically, and exposed the intellectual history of Jewish nationalism.

The personality of Theodor Herzl and his historic role is, naturally, a principal subject of Zionist historiography. Although his diaries are among the first historical documents to have been published in Zionist history, the scholarly publication of his writings in their original German is still in progress. However, it cannot be said that the published and archival historical sources have been studied in depth. A number of biographies have been written (the most comprehensive is by Alex Bein), but research in this area has raised the issue of personality and the hero in history in general, and Herzl's specific role in shaping the Zionist movement. Some researchers have examined the effect of the ambience of turn-of-century Vienna on Herzl's attitudes (Schorske); others have stressed the impact of the atmosphere of European colonialism. The role of the Dreyfus affair in Herzl's personal life was dealt with by his biographers. The question arises: was the process leading from the denial of his Judaism to his becoming a Zionist idiosyncratic, or did it reflect a wider social process? Very few from Herzl's milieu, the Viennese and Parisian Jews of his age and class, were attracted by Zionism.

However, more significant than Herzl's personal actions was his role in forging the character of the Zionist movement, whether in its ideological aspect or the organizational and political aspects. What did Herzl add to the understanding of anti-Semitism by those who preceded him (such as Pinsker, with whom he was not acquainted), or to the definition of Jewish nationalist yearnings? The main challenge was to transform the Jewish nation into a political entity, defining its aims, establishing the movement and its institutions, and laying down the methods of action.

A cardinal issue in the research into the period of Herzl is his foreign policy. Was it a failure, which led to a dead end, or did it lay the basis for the movement's development in later years? A recent tendency has been to examine Herzl's policies from the viewpoint of those countries and statesmen with whom he came into contact: Germany, England, Italy, the Vatican, Russia, and Turkey.

Herzl's appearance on the scene had an impact on the Jewish world in general, and he was largely the catalyst for the internal development of Jewish society in general. The declaration of the Jewish nation as a political entity constituted a greater challenge to assimilation than cultural nationalism (such as that of Ahad Ha-Am) or settlement movements like Hovevei Zion. Although Herzl tended not to turn to *Gegenwartsarbeit* (despite his call to the Zionists to "conquer the communities"), he set criteria for the differentiation of the Jewish community in general. Zionist policies were presented, in contrast to apologetics pronounced against anti-Semitism by many Jewish organizations.

Placing Jewish nationalism on a political footing

provoked a dilemma both among religious Jews and young Zionist intellectuals. The religious Jews had to decide whether Jewish political nationalism, aimed at solving Jewish distress by concentrated immigration to Eretz Israel, was preferable from their point of view to the establishment of a few settlements there while also diverting migration to other countries. Political activism advocated revolt against the traditional concept of political passivism. The Jewish intellectuals criticized the internal regime within the Zionist movement and questioned the connection between that and its spiritual content. Members of the Democratic Faction (1901) opposed the autocratic methods of Herzl and his colleagues and claimed that only the leadership of the intellectuals and a sound democratic base could consolidate the movement. Here they differed not only with Herzl but also with the Orthodox, who were represented by the Mizrachi. In recent years important monographs have been written on these issues, as well as biographies dealing with the period (Weizmann, Rabbi Reines).

The Uganda Proposal and Post-Herzlian Period. There have been considerable advances in the study of the British government's proposal for Jewish settlement in East Africa (the Uganda Proposal, 1903). The British side has been examined extensively, and two volumes have been published relating to the controversy within the Zionist movement (M. Heymann). These documents throw light on the complex and fluctuating political attitudes at the time of the dispute, and present a more vivid picture than had been gained from the theoretical debate. The political controversy in Israel after 1967 on the totality of the Land of Israel and its indivisibility has given tangible significance to the question of the attitude to the land itself, and its absolute or relative place in the scale of Zionist values. Debates over the task of the Zionist movement during the European Holocaust raised the question of priorities in the scale of values between the Jewish people and the Land of Israel. The East African controversy also raised the question of allegiance to the organization and loyalty to its leader as against loyalty to an ideal.

In Herzl's time the Zionist Socialist movement was formed. Its multiplicity of approaches: included the implementation of Zionism in the socialist manner, or the harnessing of the Zionist movement to the proletariat, and the construction of a national Jewish economy in Palestine as a response to the needs of the Jewish proletariat. This was a revolutionary challenge to Jewish Socialists (the Bund). It made an important contribution through immigration of pioneers to Palestine; during the period following World War I and had an evergrowing impact on the Zionist movement. This issue has been dealt with in a considerable historical literature that came out of the Zionist movement itself. Recent academic historiography devoted more attention to the sources, expanded the background of the discussion and adopted a critical attitude toward the depiction of this historiography, which set out to provide a basis and justification for the ideology.

The controversy over the East African proposal not only led to a split in the movement and the withdrawal of the Territorialists, but threatened to divide the movement into the very elements which constituted it. At the time of the controversy, the Zionists loyal to Eretz Israel claimed that the dispute was not only political, but rather a basic contradiction between those who considered Zionism as a movement of rescue and subsistence, which emanated from the need to combat anti-Semitism, and those who saw Zionism as a historical movement. The Herzlian Zionists claimed that the opponents of the East African proposal wished to return to the confines of Hibbat Zion.

The historiography of the post-Herzlian period (1904 up to the outbreak of World War I, 1914) endeavors to explain how a common basis was maintained, despite the existence of the different ingredients which joined the Herzlian movement. The decisive question is whether the change in the character of the movement was a divergence from Herzl's political aims or an organic development. This development induced the movement to carry out practical activities in Palestine-Eretz Israel as well as nationalist activities in the Diaspora. The organizational ties between the Zionist movement and national activities in the Diaspora, as well as settlement in Eretz Israel were bones of contention throughout this period. Adolf Böhm, whose description of the period is the most comprehensive, considered the movement's engagement in "work of the present" (*Gegenwartsarbeit*) and settlement activities to be the consequence of its organic development. The evaluation of the personality of David Wolffsohn, who followed Herzl as president of the World Zionist Organization (1905–1911), is relevant to this issue. The internal history of the Zionist organization is permeated with struggles of the "opposition" against Wolffsohn, who considered it essential to continue Herzl's policy. The balance of power between Wolffsohn and the practical Zionists, especially the Russian Zionists, is yet to be assessed.

In 1911, at the Tenth Zionist Congress, Wolffsohn was replaced by Prof. Otto Warburg, who headed an executive representing the main factions of the movement. The executive moved from Cologne to Berlin.

The broadening of the activities of the Zionist Executive has led the research of Zionist history into new areas. Jewish settlement in Eretz Israel has become a topic of research from the time that Arthur Ruppin opened the Palestine Office in Jaffa (1908), and through it the Zionist General Council (Actions Committee) began a systematic centrally-directed Zionist policy in the area of agricultural settlement.

In recent years research has focused on the external politics of the Zionist movement, the so-called "exercises in futile diplomacy." These were attempts to remove the Ottoman limitations on immigration and land purchases and, in the long run, to acquire some sort of autonomous status for the yishuv. Attempted negotiations with the Ottoman authorities by Victor Jacobson and Richard Lichtheim are well documented from the Zionist viewpoint, but no documentation exists of the Ottoman side. Attempts to negotiate with the governments of Germany and England are documented from all parties, and have been described in recent research papers. Documentation of attempts to make contact with Arab elements in Constantinople, as well as in Eretz Israel, is mainly Zionist.

The reorientation that took place in the Zionist movement after Herzl—*Gegenwartsarbeit*, political and cultural nationalist work in the Diaspora—is also reflected in Zionist historiography, beginning with the Helsingfors Conference of Russian Zionists in December, 1906. National Zionist organizations were established in Russia and in the Hapsburg Empire to carry out nationalist activities in the Diaspora, the consequence of which was political representation in elections and also the development of local Jewish nationalism. The aim of these activities could have been the preparation of the Diaspora for a Zionist solution or education towards Jewish nationalism in the Diaspora.

More recent research examines the Jewish communities in general and the function of Zionism within them. Probing Zionism's attitude towards the Jewish community, such studies divide Zionist history (ideological, organizational, and social) according to the various countries. They deal with the influence of the Jewish and non-Jewish environment on the nature of Zionism in each particular country, taking into account local political activity and the ideological and organizational struggle within the Jewish community.

In recent years there has been a major development in Zionist research as regards the study of certain countries: Russia, Germany, Poland, England, South Africa, and the USA. Works on these subjects resulting from academic disciplines are far superior to previous publications in this area, written under the inspiration of *landsmanshaften* and comprising an arbitrary collection of facts and memories. This history of Zionism by country breaks down to a certain extent the general uniform history of Zionism, raising the question whether there was a common denominator to Zionism in the various countries, and what diverse ideological and social factors were active in them.

Related to this aspect is the question of the relationship between eastern European and western European Jewry. To what extent did the acceptance of Zionism and its ideological content differ according to the dividing line between eastern and western European Jewry? The latter underwent a process of emancipation and secular education, and were members of a well-established economic class, while the former lacked civil rights, were more religiously traditional and stemmed from a more popular milieu. Galicia in the Hapsburg empire constituted a bridge between the two: the Jews there held rights, while clinging to their Jewish tradition.

World War I and the Balfour Declaration. With the outbreak of World War I, the Zionist movement was faced with problems for which it was not prepared. The dispersion of the movement throughout many lands necessitated neutrality, despite the fact the the Executive was based in Berlin. Maintaining the security of the yishuv required connections with both the Turks and their German allies. The German conquest of parts of Poland made it possible to carry out public activities formerly forbidden under the Tsar, but presented problems relating to an independent Jewish nationalist policy and the advancement of Jewish culture. The first Russian revolution in March, 1917, brought about a flourishing of unfettered Zionist activities. The growth of nationalism throughout Europe stimulated Jewish nationalism as well. This area has not yet been studied, apart from particular issues, such as the formation of the Jewish legion within the British army.

One of the most researched topics in Zionist historiography is the Balfour Declaration. This act raised the Zionist movement from an ideological and social movement of the Jewish people to a political movement which became an integral part of the alignment of forces in the Middle East. The circumstances of the presentation of the Declaration and its political significance constituted a subject of debate and criticism within the Zionist movement during the mandatory period. These debates led to the publication of the first book on the subject (N. Gelber, 1939). Prior even to the opening of the British official archives. Leonard Stein wrote his classic work, presenting both the Zionist and British sides against the background of World War I, as well as the attitude of the Jews of England, the USA and Russia. The opening of the British official archives lent an impetus to this research, resulting in the publication of a number of new works (M. Verete, I. Friedman, Sanders). However, it cannot be said that research in this area has been exhausted. Only recently a number of books containing documents of importance from the Zionist viewpoint have been published, such as the diaries of S. Tolkowsky and Weizmann's letters relating to the period.

The Balfour Declaration is bound up with a number of other subjects related to processes leading towards it and emerging from it. The historians have examined the political status and the prospects of the Zionist movement against the background of the international relations existing in the pre-World War I period, and especially the Great Powers' alignment around the Ottoman Empire. The relevance of Zionist terminology to the actual situation of power politics existing at the time is in the process of being examined.

The point of departure of this examination is the re-evaluation of the fate of the Ottoman Empire after the entry of Turkey into the war. The definition of Britain's aims as regards the Ottoman lands and its attitude to the demands of its allies (France, Russia, and Italy) are presented as background to the introduction of the Zionist factor. A further aspect for consideration, in addition to the policy of the Great Powers in the Middle East, was the political role of Russian and American Jewry. Here, the question of the British-Zionist connection arises: did the initiative come from the British side, or from the Zionists, and what was the contribution of such Zionist personalities as Weizmann and Sokolow? The research deals with the various versions of the Declaration up to the formulation of the final version, as well as the substantive political value of the Declaration. The negotiations over the Declaration caused a split in the Jewish community between Zionists and anti-Zionists and this, too, is an aspect of the research.

The Period of Weizmann's Leadership. At the end of World War I a new international configuration emerged and the organization of the Jewish people throughout the world underwent a change. The Zionist leadership was replaced, and Chaim Weizmann became the central figure. The focus of history moved to the political scene, firstly regarding Britain and then to the League of Nations in general. The appearance of Zionism on the international stage, the award of the Mandate to Britain, its ratification by the League of Nations, have not yet been examined in full. This research will include the various versions of the proposals submitted by the Zionists to the peace conference, as well as the contacts and concerns of the personalities who laid down the policy.

The center of the Zionist movement moved from Russia to Poland and the USA. The attitude of the Bolshevik authorities to Zionism has been relatively well researched, including the changes in the nationalist policies of the Soviet regime, their attitude to the Jewish community in Russia and the activities of the Soviet Jewish faction in the Communist Party, as well as their attitude to the Hebrew language and literature, to the Zionist movement and to the pioneering movement.

The increased political and economic involvement of the American Zionists, especially the relationships between Chaim Weizmann and Louis Brandeis, has aroused the interest of researchers. Different approaches to Zionism, differing methods of political action, in particular economic and financial policies, led to the fateful split. The main question is whether American lifestyle and culture produced a different type of Zionism from that which evolved in Europe and in Palestine. The struggle for power between the leading personalities, which ended in victory for Weizmann is under examination, as is the accompanying issue of the involvement of non-Zionists in the building of Palestine through the expanded Jewish Agency.

The activities of the Zionist leadership in the twenties were divided between building up Palestine and finding solutions to the situation of the Jews in general. In the mid-twenties the problem of migration from eastern Europe became more crucial as a result of the organizational changes introduced into the region's political structure and economy after World War I, with the creation of nation states (Poland, Lithuania, Latvia, etc.). At the same time, restrictions were introduced on migration to the USA, thus changing a basic condition in existence since the founding of the Zionist movement. The Soviet authorities proposed a solution to the economic problems of the Jews by settlement in the Crimea or Birobidjan, an idea derived from Zionism. These dilemmas raised the problem of Zionist finances and the economic methods of building Palestine. The relationship between public and private capital, the nature of the Zionist funds (especially the Keren ha-Yesod), methods of agricultural settlement, the attitude to urban settlement and urban economy, are currently undergoing examination by means of methods adopted from the discipline of economic history. The immigration policy of the World Zionist Organization as regards the mandatory government has not yet been researched.

Zionist policies differed in the 1920s from what they had been at the end of the war. The focus shifted from the arena of world politics and a comprehensive solution to the Jewish problem. The local political regime in Palestine, as formed by the British mandatory authorities, the problems facing the economy in Palestine, and agricultural settlement in the country, are major points of research. There has been progress in the research of the British mandatory regime in recent years, but the relationship between that regime and Zionist policy has not yet been adequately studied.

The outstanding leader of the Zionist movement in the twenties was Weizmann. Representation at the Zionist Congresses was through national federations and the three political parties: Mizrachi, Po'ale Zion, and the Federations of Ha-Po'el ha-Tza'ir-Tze'irei Zion. The internal political and ideological history of the movement's Executive and its institutions during this period has not yet been researched.

During the twenties, the yishuv, especially the Labor movement, had an ever-increasing influence on the Zionist movement. The Labor movement also influenced its sister movements in the Diaspora, and the He-Halutz movement, as well as the youth movements founded and developed during those years. Study of all these subjects has been advanced in recent years.

The years between 1921 and 1929 are a period of tranquillity as regards "high politics" in connection with Palestine, after the British mandatory government had stabilized and calm prevailed in the country. However, the contradiction between the consolidated mandatory framework and the desire for Zionist fulfillment led to ideological and political ferment. This was expressed in the rise of the Revisionist movement on the one hand and of the Berit Shalom group on the other. Both these movements have been widely researched. The politico-ideological debate in Israel since 1967 has revived the interest in these political traditions. Historical study has been confined to certain specific issues raised by the formation of these movements, such as Weizmann's policies during the years 1922 to 1925, or an evaluation of relationships with the Arabs. From a wider horizon, it might consider the political character of Jewish nationalism and the relationship with Zionist politics of the various social groupings (youth and intellectuals, capitalists or immigrants from different countries—central Europe, Russia and Poland).

The year 1929 returns the focus to the fundamental issue of policies regarding Palestine, with the outbreak of the 1929 riots and attempts at revision of the mandatory policy by the British; the various British Commissions (Shaw, Hope-Simpson) and the International (Wailing/Western Wall) Commission. These events have been subjected to a general survey, but detailed research of all the parties involved (the British, Jews, and Arabs), and the relationships between policies and public opinion, is in its infancy.

The Nazi era. The events of 1929 led to the replacement by a coalition (1931) of Weizmann as leader of the Zionist movement. The history of this issue has been partly examined from the viewpoint of the various political parties, but not from the perspective of the Zionist Organization as a whole.

With the rise of the Nazis to power in 1933, the Zionist movement faced matters of principle as well as practical problems. Dilemmas included the possibility of the continued existence of the Diaspora versus the possibility of Palestine providing an alternative to the Diaspora, and the role of Zionism in guaranteeing the Diaspora's continued existence. On a wider scope, the relationship of Zionism to anti-Semitism and to liberalism is a subject for research.

A concrete issue relating to this period, already widely researched, is the "transfer" agreement between the Jewish Agency and the government of Germany. Meanwhile, research is in progress on the subject of migration of German Jews and their absorption in Palestine.

The mid-thirties saw the failure of the Jewish policy in the Diaspora formulated on the basis of the rights of minorities guaranteed by the Versailles treaty. In 1935 the World Jewish Congress was established with the purpose of defending the rights of Jews. The relationship between the Zionist movement and the struggle for these rights has not yet been examined. On the other hand, much research has focused on efforts made in the twenties to involve non-Zionists in the building of Palestine, within the framework of the expanded Jewish Agency.

The yishuv in the thirties flourished by virtue of increased immigration under the direction of the Jewish Agency (up from 175,000 to 450,000). There was a special combination of ideological and political groupings and social organizations. forming a complex fabric which combined European ideological influences (socialism, communism), the pattern of Jewish society in Europe, and the nature of the structure of the community in Palestine. The organization of the community, "Keneset Israel", the National Council (Va'ad Le'umi), the social strata, and the political parties have not been fully investigated. This study is carried out through both the historical and sociological methods.

The Arab Revolt. The year 1936 and the outbreak of the Arab revolt brings the historiography into the area of the political and constitutional history of Palestine and the reasons for the failure of the mandatory regime. From the Zionist viewpoint this was the failure of Zionist fulfillment.

From the British viewpoint it was their failure to stand by their commitments to both sides and/or the creation of a Palestine entity common to both the Jews and Arabs, while bringing about the establishment of the Jewish national home. The British Public Records Office, on the one hand, and the Central Zionist Archives, on the other, constitute the main sources for this complicated issue.

Zionist-British relationships are being examined on the basis of "high-level" policy laid down in London and of local policy in Palestine. The various factors active in the British government in Palestine—the government offices, the army, public opinion, and local personalities—are being scrutinized along with the ideology and pressure of the Zionist leadership.

The outbreak of the 1936 riots raised the issue of Jewish-Arab relationships which had already been a matter of concern to the Zionist leadership. Instead of a Jewish-Arab arrangement on the basis of Zionist fulfillment, there arose the question of the extent of violence required to attain fulfillment. There was also the question of the manner of the use of violence (defense or attack; the attitude to the local population) in pursuance of the debate over the policy of "restraint" (*havlaga*).

This was the period of the consolidation of the Hagana (founded in 1920) and the Irgun Tzeva'i Le'umi (founded in 1931); these organizations have been described in detail through monumental historical undertakings (the History of the Hagana [Slutzky] and the History of the Irgun [D. Niv]), which also cover large sections of the history of the yishuv.

No less than the Balfour Declaration, the proposals of the Royal Commission led by Lord Peel in 1937 for the partition of Palestine into Jewish and Arab states served as a turning point in the political history of Palestine and, to an extent, in the ideological history of Zionism. From the Zionist viewpoint, this marked the beginning of the end of the fulfillment of Zionism, by the British Mandate and not by virtue of the creation of a Jewish State. It was the end of the attempts to come to an agreement with the Arabs prior to the establishment of a Jewish State.

In recent years a number of studies have been written on British policy, the partition proposal, and the factors that led up to it. Research is also under way on British policy in the Middle East in general, the feasibility of the implementation of partition, and the reasons for the British withdrawal from the partition plan. From the viewpoint of Zionist history, the question is whether this was the last opportunity to save a large proportion of European Jewry in cooperation with the British. The ongoing debate in Israel since 1967 has also raised questions relating to Zionist ideology and the Peel Commission proposals. In this regard, there are discussions of the relationship between ideological loyalties and the exploitation of political situations. Implicit in this issue is the question of the attitude of loyalty to the Jewish people as compared with absolute loyalty to the entire Land of Israel.

The period of World War II transfers the Zionist policy to the international arena. The question arose: did the war impose restrictions on the conflict with Britain and the struggle against the White Paper, or did it open up broader prospects? The participation of Jews in the war within the ranks of the British forces, and the attempts to establish a world "Jewish army", have been researched. The dilemma was the option of an independent Jewish military force (the Hagana and the Palmah) or joining the British army; the status of the Jews and their separate identity were an issue of negotiation between the Jewish Agency and the British authorities and the consideration of the defense of the yishuv against a German invasion, or an Arab uprising, as against the assumption of political roles by the Jewish military forces, and their involvement in the war in general.

Towards a Jewish Political Entity. A further subject of research is the formulation of the political platform of the Zionist movement during the course of World War II. The passage from commitment to the framework of the British Mandate and the Jewish National Home, to the idea of a Jewish State, pointed the research in a variety of directions: the development of Zionist ideology, presentation of alternatives to the British White Paper policy, evaluation of the situation on the international scene and the Middle East during the war as well as in the post-war period, and especially the search for a solution to the Jewish situation. It was on this issue that the contrast between the two leading personalities, Weizmann and Ben-Gurion, became most acute, and this period inspires biographical research regarding both men.

An examination of Zionist policy raises the basic question: to what extent was Zionism able to provide a response to the Jewish question, and to what extent would the solution to the Jewish question be identified with the creation of a Jewish political entity in Palestine?

During the war years American Jewry began to play an increasingly important role in the Zionist political struggle. Research in progress deals with this subject at a number of levels: the changes within the American Zionist movement, the enhancement of the status of Zionism within the general Jewish community, and the political action taken vis-à-vis the American administration, the Senate and the Congress, as well as public opinion.

A central topic of Zionist historiography of this period is the underground organizations in Palestine—the Hagana, the Irgun, and the Lohamei Herut Israel. Historical examination of these organizations cannot be symmetrical: the Hagana was a large organization consisting of a wide variety of political and ideological shades and opinions, functioning under the aegis of the Jewish Agency and political parties active in Palestine; it was only on rare occasions that Hagana leaders made political statements, but the other underground organizations were both ideological and political entities.

A lack of documentary evidence has been largely overcome by recorded oral testimony and memoirs. The role of each of these organizations in forcing the British to leave Palestine, and the defense of the yishuv against Arab attacks, are the main features of the studies, which also relate to the military operations, the political orientation, and relations with the yishuv. The social composition and organizational aspects, as well as the Hagana chain of command have not been examined in depth.

Holocaust Historiography. In recent years a number of research works have been published on the attitude of the Zionist movement to the Holocaust of European Jewry during World War II. This subject is of crucial significance from the viewpoint of Zionist historiography. The Holocaust could be seen as the justification of Zionism or as the destruction of the basis of its very reason. Practical research deals with the possibilities for establishing contacts with the Jews in the countries under Nazi conquest, the possibilities of rescue from these lands, and the alternative potential for providing support and assistance in self-defense. It was expected that Zionist values such as struggle and revolt would be reflected in the behavior of the Jews under Nazi domination.

The theoretical aspects of the Holocaust prove even more profound, and relate to the very essence of Zionism. Questions arise such as whether Zionism was created for the benefit of the Jewish people, or had the Jewish people become a means for its "Utopian" ideal. Should loyalty to the Land of Israel take precedence over loyalty to the Jewish people when they are not analogous? Was the continuity of the yishuv a goal in itself, or did its special attributes derive from the function of its Jewish or Zionist mission? Did the yishuv do all in its power to rescue Jews, or did the challenge of building the country divert its attention from the fate of the Diaspora? Did the concept of selective immigration and the desire to build a national center undermine the possibility of mass immigration of Jews? Did the Zionist movement give up the defense of the rights of Jews in the Diaspora and assistance to liberal regimes? Such dilemmas, in existence since the beginnings of Zionism, became more acute as Jewish distress climaxed during World War II. However, it was clear that no alternative to Palestine did exist for the rescue of Diaspora Jewry, and on the other hand even had the yishuv endangered itself to do so, it had no way to save the Diaspora.

Bound up with the attitude of the Zionist movement to the Holocaust are the actions of the Allied Powers regarding the situation of the Jews during the war. A number of research papers have appeared on this subject.

The Establishment of Israel. An issue around which various aspects of Zionist history converge is the withdrawal of the British forces from Palestine and the establishment of the State of Israel in part of Palestine, in the midst of a war against the armies of the surrounding Arab countries. In this field diplomatic and political history combine with ideological and social history, the military aspect is being increasingly stressed.

The main issue from the viewpoint of Zionist historiography is the quality of Zionist initiative and leadership. With hindsight, the establishment of the State of Israel in the major part of western Palestine was an outstanding political achievement. Historians must determine whether this achievement was a result of Zionist policy or a matter of coincidence and circumstances in which Zionist initiative played only a minor role. Relevant here are the personalities of the Zionist leadership, especially of Weizmann and Ben-Gurion, but also of Nahum Goldmann, Moshe Sneh, Abba Hillel Silver, and Moshe Sharett.

Zionist historiography has had to confront difficult problems in translating ideological orientations, that were a combination of Zionist traditions and the circumstances of World War II, into political formulae. The formulation of the political demands of the Zionist movement caused a serious and profound internal controversy as the choice was made between the formula of a Jewish State or the continuation of the British Mandate, a binational state or an international mandate. The war time constraints combined to stipulate the definition of the status and role of Zionism with regard to the catastrophic Jewish situation. Similarly, the balance of power facing the Zionist movement had to be evaluated. The undermining of the basis of power regarding relations with the British authorities after the issue of the 1929 White Paper made it essential to find new bases for political support.

The first works describing Zionist policy and the establishment of the State of Israel were written at the time of the creation of the State, or soon after (The Esco Foundation for Palestine, J.C. Hurewitz, *The Struggle for Palestine*); other works, combining partial documentation and memoirs, have been written by British authors.

Since 1968 the British Public Record Office files have been available to the public (under the 30 years act), and thus up to 1978 all the documentation relating to the period of the establishment of the State of Israel had been declassified. These documents, together with those of the American National Archives and German documents, have radically changed the historic picture.

Zionist-British relations and Palestine policy have been examined in a large number of monographs, generally based on British and Zionist sources. The expanding sphere of Zionist policy during the period of World War II continued after the war. Zionist policy shifted more and more to the American arena but ties were forged with European states such as France and Italy. The ties with these countries were essential for the implementation of "illegal" immigration. In addition, the Zionist movement began to seek contacts with the USSR. After 1945, Zionist attempts to harness British support for Zionist goals changed to a policy of applying pressure on Britain and finally severing ties with it.

A central issue in this connection relates to the research regarding the decision of the British to leave Palestine and to hand over the Mandate to the United Nations. The question being examined is the date of the decision and whether the decision was sincere or perhaps only a means towards returning to rule the country; was the British decision to leave Palestine motivated by apprehension over the straining of British-American relations, the pressure of British and international public opinion, the general policy towards the Middle East, the constraint of the "illegal" immigration of Jews, or the acts of resistance being carried out by the Jews of Palestine?

The British decision to depart from Palestine could be seen as being opposed to the aspirations of official Zionist policy, or at least as the unexpected outcome of that policy. The Zionist movement now faced a new international array of forces and this has brought the research to examine the attitude to Zionism and the problem of the Jews in the general arena of international relations.

Despite the large number of memoirs, specific research works, and documents published, this research has not yet conclusively analyzed the American policy as regards this issue. The involvement of the President, the State Department, the Congress and American public opinion have been the subject of the publication of a large number of research works.

The UN resolution for the creation of two states in Palestine—Jewish and Arab—on 29 November 1947 led to war between the Palestinian Arabs who refused to accept the UN decision, and the yishuv. After the British left on 14 May 1948, the Arab states joined the fray. The Arab-Israel conflict, especially since 1967, has given rise to a large number of research studies. These cover the historical ties of Islam to Judaism and to Palestine in all their aspects: religious, political, economic, social, ideological, and psychological. The purpose of this research, not as yet exhaustive, is to reconstruct the history of the mutual relationships between Jews and Arabs in the political and economic areas and their mutual images. It is clear that the accusation that the Zionist movement ignored the realistic situation of the country or its inhabitants is baseless although the issue of the attitude to the Arabs was discussed constantly even if solutions were impracticable.

Zionism in Africa and Asia. In recent years, research into the Zionist movement in the countries of Africa and Asia has expanded. The main question being investigated, as regards the history of Zionism in these countries, is whether this was an indigent and authentic growth of Zionism, or an artificial graft of European Zionism (or of the type of Zionism prevalent in the pre-State or post-State of Israel periods). Was the path to Zionism in these communities a result of the transformation they underwent through influences imported from European countries, economic developments and Arab nationalism, or was it the result of the success of Zionism in the Land of Israel? The content of Zionism in these countries, as well as the social issues and the status of the Jewish community, are different from those in Europe, and are unique in themselves, a uniqueness expressed through strong ties to religious tradition.

Although the countries of the Jewish Diaspora in Africa and Asia are of a variegated character and the aspect they share is generally the Moslem religion, the Jewish communities in the Moslem countries were late in undergoing the process of secularization and enlightenment which swept European Jewry. The status of the Jews in traditional Moslem society was different from that of the European Jews. Arab nationalism was also late in developing. The expansion of the European regime and the granting of European citizenship (in the French colonies and protectorates) to Jews introduced European influence. Contact between the Jews in Africa and Asia with world Jewry occurred to a great extent, through the Alliance Israélite Universelle, whose activities were opposed to Zionism up to the establishment of the State of Israel. Zionism was mostly conceived by the Jews of these communities as a continuation of the traditional yearning for the Land of Israel.

In the examination of the history of Zionism in these lands the question arises whether the World Zionist Movement appreciated to its fullest extent the Zionism in these countries or encouraged immigration from them before 1948. A chapter in itself is the formation in Asia and Africa of branches of the Zionist political parties active in Europe and the significance of the contribution in these countries of the European ideological segmentation (the Labor Party, Mizrachi, the Revisionists, He-Halutz, and the youth movements).

Approach to Historiography. The history of Zionism has been researched mainly by critical historians using the classic methods of basing their conclusions on the criticism of sources assembled by them and presenting their research in a narrative way. It was only to a limited extent that critical concepts, beyond those used by their contemporaries, were introduced.

The influence of the social sciences is evident through the introduction of analytical concepts and the expansion of the fields of research. "Modernization", secularization, and political recruitment have begun to appear as concepts of history. The Jewish community in general, and Israeli society, have become accepted subjects of research. Political history, too, has digressed from issues of traditional diplomacy and now deals with the institutional and structural aspects of diplomatic decisions. Despite the intensification of research in recent years, no internal political history of the Zionist movement has yet been written, nor have its economic institutions been fully examined, apart from the Jewish Colonial Trust and the Anglo-Palestine Company. Furthermore, studies are still lacking of the intellectual history, the Hebrew language, education and culture, and the youth movements.

The new analytical approach affected some of the most basic topics of Zionist history, namely the history of land settlement; following the Zionist ideology and orientation this history was set very high on the agenda of the historical tradition. It was recorded in the annals and memoirs of the settlers themselves, of their families, and in publications sponsored by the various settlements.

The sector of the settlement enterprise which was directed by the Zionist Organization is much better documented and described (Bein) than the other sectors. The enterprise of Baron Rothschild as well as of ICA, PICA, private settlements and the urban settlement were less researched.

The opening of the archives of ICA, PICA and other private companies as well as the use of analytical models taken over from geography and sociology contributed towards a considerable progress in this field in recent years. The private sector and the companies not affiliated directly with the Zionist Organization have been described. Likewise the general framework of the settlement, physical and social data of the land and its inhabitants, Turkish and British government policies, the general land market have been studied as abackground to Jewish settlement.

It may be assumed that the future trend of research will depict Zionism against a wider background of Jewish history in general and Middle Eastern politics. Zionism would not appear as an isolated phenomenon but as a part of the social history of the Jews and the intellectual trends of the time. In addition to meticulous research of documents and a fuller narrative of facts, analytical concepts will be used to comprehend this unique and variegated phenomenon.

See also bibliography, pp. 1514–1521.

I. KOLATT

ZIONISTISCHE VEREINIGUNG FUR DEUTSCHLAND (Zionist Organization of Germany). *See* GERMANY, ZIONISM IN.

ZIONIST MOVEMENT, FINANCES. Financial considerations played a major part in the decision to retain the *World Zionist Organization (WZO) intact upon the declaration of the State of Israel in 1948, with the *Jewish Agency (JA) as its operating body in Israel. The newly-formed Israel government would hardly have agreed so readily to the division of functions—which assigned to the JA the responsibility for the vital areas of immigration, absorption, and agricultural settlement—had it not been for the fact that the JA, in undertaking to finance these activities, was relieving the state budget of a major burden at a time of great financial stringency.

The dramatic events leading to the declaration of the State were reflected in the level of giving to campaigns throughout the Diaspora, resulting in a significant increase in funds made available to the JA through the *Keren ha-Yesod. For the first time, the *United Jewish Appeal (UJA) in the US set a goal of $100 million for its 1946 campaign and came close to attaining it; as late as 1942 its income had amounted to less than a quarter of that sum. The 1948 campaign yielded $125 million for UJA in America, and that year also saw a reversal in the ratio by which the UJA's proceeds were divided among its two constituents, the United Palestine Appeal (UPA) and the American Joint Distribution Committee (JDC). Whereas the lion's share had previously gone to the JDC, it was henceforth the UPA which received the bulk of UJA funds. The UPA in turn distributed its income in equal parts to the *Jewish National Fund (JNF) and the Keren ha-Yesod, the financial arm of the JA. The JA's net income from worldwide campaigns in eight months of 1948 amounted to $122,000,000, which represented a substantial part of the total foreign currency income available to Israel from all sources. As Great Britain had ejected the newly independent state from the sterling bloc, the availability of foreign currency became a critical factor in Israel's economy.

There was thus reason to assume that the JA would find the means with which to finance the tasks assigned to it when the division of functions was formally agreed upon at the August, 1948, session of the Zionist General Council. However, it soon became apparent that this was not the case. In the corresponding period of 1949, Keren ha-Yesod income dropped to $84,000,000, even though the number of immigrants increased more than threefold. In the five years from October, 1950 to September, 1955, Keren ha-Yesod's income from worldwide appeals was $266 million (an annual average of $50-$54 million). Generally, four-fifths of this was derived from the UJA in the US; one-fifth from Keren ha-Yesod campaigns in other parts of the world. This amount constituted 60.8% of the JA's total income during that period. Another 24.1% came from the JA's share of German reparations payments, and the rest from loans and grants from the Israeli government (mainly for agricultural settlement) and from contributions to Youth Aliya.

At the root of the decline in Keren ha-Yesod income was a drop in the receipts of Federation campaigns in the US, from $200 million in 1948 to $105 million in 1954. Simultaneously, the UJA's share of these campaigns, which were the main source of its funds, was also declining. It was true that separate campaigns on behalf of Israel were raising an additional $18 million annually, and that these figures did not include the results of the *State of Israel Bond Drive. Taking these into account, overall interest in Israel had scarcely diminished. However, this was scant consolation for the JA, which found itself unable to meet its commitments.

An attempt to increase the share of the JA in the receipts of the UJA was the Israel Emergency Fund, inaugurated in 1956 in connection with the North African immigration of that year. The UJA conducted a special drive whose proceeds were earmarked entirely for the JA. Earlier, the UJA had undertaken a major bank borrowing ("Consolidation Loan"). Though destined in the first instance for the JA, the loan ultimately enabled the Israel government to consolidate its burdensome short-term foreign debt.

Evolution of the Fund-Raising Structure. The worldwide fund-raising structure, as it had evolved over nearly three decades since the establishment of the Keren ha-Yesod in 1919, remained largely in place in the early period of statehood. Over the years it had grown into a rather complex institution.

Following the Balfour Declaration and the victory of the Allied powers in World War I, the WZO decided to create a world-wide fund-raising body called the Keren ha-Yesod (Foundation Fund).

The first American campaign, launched in 1921, brought in about $2 million and remained at the same level for the next several years. This must be judged a rather modest result, considering the dimensions of the need and the fact that the Fund was intended to appeal not only to Zionists but to wealthy non-Zionists as well. However, it faced intense competition from the JDC. By the mid-1920s, it was clear that the JDC intended to turn itself into a permanent feature on the US Jewish scene as an overseas relief agency with its own fund-raising apparatus, and that a *modus vivendi* with the Keren ha-Yesod had to be reached. Simultaneously, to reduce competition among the organizations active in the yishuv, the UPA was founded comprising five of the main groups raising money in the US on behalf of Palestine, chief among them the Keren ha-Yesod.

Most of the potential "big givers" of the time were non-Zionists, and were identified with the JDC. Chaim Weizmann, as president of the WZO, was determined to draw these prominent and wealthy non-Zionists into the upbuilding of the Jewish National Home without involving them in its politics by creating the enlarged Jewish Agency ("enlarged" from its purely Zionist composition). This was accomplished in August, 1929, clearing the way for cooperation with the JDC. That cooperation was first expressed in an Emergency Campaign for the victims of the 1929 Arab rioting in Palestine, and in 1930, in an Allied Jewish Campaign—a forerunner of the UJA—for the needs of both the JA and the JDC.

Also during the 1920s the Federation movement, characterized by the trend to united fund-raising, made constant headway among US Jewish communities. After first encompassing only local charities, the Federations later insisted that the overseas agencies, too, join their local campaigns. As a further decisive step toward the consolidation of fund raising, an agreement to create a "United Jewish Appeal for Refugees and Overseas Needs" was signed under the impact of the *Kristallnacht* pogrom in Nazi Germany in November, 1938. Its two partners were the JDC and the UPA, which had been reconstituted in 1936 as a partnership between the JNF and the Keren ha-Yesod. The National Refugee Service, the main reception agency for European immigrants to the US, was co-opted into the UJA as a beneficiary, but not as a partner.

The American tendency to integrate major fund-raising efforts in a single campaign conducted by the local community did not extend to most of the Keren ha-Yesod campaigns in other parts of the world. With the exception of France and Canada (which followed American patterns of community organization), the Keren Ha-Yesod raised funds exclusively for Israel, usually with the active participation of emissaries from the head office in Jerusalem. Annual campaigns were conducted in 47 countries on all five continents, with the total number of contributors in 1986/1987 set at 227,000, of whom 153,000 lived in English-speaking countries, 43,000 in Europe, and 31,000 in Latin America. Country by country, the largest amount of money was obtained in Canada, followed by Great Britain, South Africa, Australia, and France.

Waning Zionist Influence. In the US, the JNF was dropped from the arrangement in 1952, so that the funds received by the UPA (now UIA̎ United Israel Appeal) from the UJA campaigns were henceforth destined exclusively to the JA. Subsequently, the Keren ha-Yesod itself ceased being an intermediary as it no longer served any real function in the US. The withdrawal of the two major Zionist funds from the US campaign structure had significance beyond eliminating redundancies and bureaucratic deadwood. It was part of the same process that had given rise, in 1929, to the enlarged JA, and that had also been at work in the so-called Silver-Neumann controversy of 1948–49, which resulted in the removal of the two foremost leaders of the Zionist Organization of America from the influential positions they had held in the UJA. The Mapai establishment, which dominated both the Israel government and the JA Executive, was unwilling to leave the flow of UJA funds in the control of elements close to the rival General Zionist party.

While it had been clear for some time that the bulk of UJA funds originated with contributors who were not affiliated with the Zionist movement, the Silver-Neumann episode furnished formal acknowledgement of the waning of Zionist influence on American fund-raising for Israel. Once the articulate and purposeful Zionist leadership had been neutralized in the UPA, the organization lost its *raison d'être*, which was essentially to represent Zionist interests in the UJA nexus.

The UPA's formal structure was retained, and the funds continued to flow through it on the way from the UJA to the JA. In practice, the UJA dealt directly with the JA in everything that concerned the campaign; while the JA transacted most of its business in the US through its American Section.

The next stage in the "de-Zionization" of American fund raising came in 1960, when a new body called the Jewish Agency for Israel, Inc. was set up to control UJA funds destined for Israel. The immediate reason for the reorganization was a ruling by the Internal Revenue Service that tax deductible philanthropic funds sent abroad must be controlled by an American organization, recognized by the Internal Revenue Service. The "Inc." appointed the Jerusalem Jewish Agency as its agent in Israel and allocated its funds to designated areas of JA operations. These did not include such "ideological" departments as Education in the Diaspora, Youth and he-Halutz, and Organization, which henceforth were financed by Keren ha-Yesod income from outside the United States.

The 1971 Reconstitution. From here it was but a short step to the complete separation between WZO and JA, as provided for in the reconstitution of the JA in 1971. In that thoroughgoing revision of the governing structure, the parity principle that had been part of the 1929 agreement was revived in modified form: the WZO relinquished its exclusive control of the JA and reverted to being a 50% partner in it. The 50% share that in 1929 had been allotted to the non-Zionists was now assigned to the leading fund-raising organizations functioning in the Diaspora on behalf of Israel, the Keren ha-Yesod (20%). and the UIA in the US

ZIONIST MOVEMENT FINANCES
FLOW OF FUNDS

Community Federations in US

Local Needs
United Jewish Appeal
JDC
HIAS
US Gov't for East European Refugees
United Israel Appeal
Keren ha-Yesod
Jewish Agency
World Zionist Organization

(30%). The latter had been consolidated (in 1966) with the Jewish Agency for Israel, Inc. into a single corporate body named the United Israel Appeal, which assumed the Inc.'s role as the "principal" of the Jerusalem Agency in the expenditure of UJA funds.

The parity between the "fund-raisers" and the WZO was reflected in the composition of the new governing bodies of the reconstituted Agency, the Assembly and the Board of Governors. Though the Executive continued to direct daily activities as before, it was no longer identical with the Zionist Executive, as it had been ever since the 1929 enlarged Agency ceased functioning with the outbreak of World War II. The membership of the Board of Governors was originally fixed at 38 and then raised to 40, with the aim of having the members of the Zionist Executive constitute the Zionist half of the Board of Governors. It was later increased to 72 (36 from the WZO, 21 from the UIA, and 15 from the Keren ha-Yesod).

In the reconstitution agreement, the WZO was assigned responsibility for the "fulfillment of Zionist programs and ideals," and the JA for immigration and absorption; welfare and health services related to absorption of immigrants; support of education and youth activities, particularly Youth Aliya; absorption in agricultural settlements; and immigrant housing. The new structure for the Agency was given official status in a revision by the Knesset of the Jewish Agency/WZO Status Law first enacted in 1952.

A main concern in the negotiations leading to the reconstitution was the financing of the WZO after the separation of functions. The final agreement provided that the WZO budget be fixed at 10 percent of the JA's total income, with the details of its expenditures to be left entirely to the WZO itself. These funds would come primarily from Keren ha-Yesod campaigns outside the US.

The 1971 reconstitution agreement revalidated the principle, first implemented in 1929, that the JA was the instrument of the Jewish people as a whole, and not only of the Zionist movement. At the same time, the agreement also ushered in the final stage of the UIA's disengagement from the WZO. Where once the Zionist movement had been in complete control of the UIA, it was now represented only by the minority of the UIA Board appointed by the American Zionist groups—19 members out of 63. The majority of the Board came from the UJA and the Federations, so that the UIA, in effect, had become the instrument of the communities. As such, it also appoints, with the active participation of the Federations, its 30% of the governing institutions of the Jewish Agency.

The Flow of Funds. It is a moot question whether the reconstitution had an effect on the flow of funds to the JA, but in 1971/72 (fiscal year ending 31 March), the year the agreement was signed, UIA cash receipts from the UJA came to $186,000,000. This was the largest amount ever, with the exception of 1968 when the Six-Day War emergency drove UIA receipts to an unprecedented $214,000,000. In the 1980s, the UIA consistently provided more than three fourths of the JA's annual operating budgets, which by then stood well above the $400,000,000 mark. Thus in 1985/86, the JA spent some $418,000,000 for its regular budget, of which $308 m. came from the UIA, including $29 m. for *Project Renewal.

TABLE 1
JEWISH AGENCY EXPENDITURES, 1985/86

	in $1,000	%
Immigration and Absorption	71,783	17.15
Rural Settlement	65,437	15.64
Youth Aliya	60,978	14.59
Jewish Education	7,181	1.72
Higher Education	82,132	19.64
Social Programs	14,075	3.38
Vocational Training	15,906	3.80
Housing	13,104	3.14
Other Functions	12,522	2.99
Interest Payments	24,474	5.87
Debt Retirement	37,797	9.05
Administration	12,304	2.93
	417,693	100.00

TABLE 2
JEWISH AGENCY REVENUES, 1985/86

	in $1,000	%
United Israel Appeal (US)	308,246 *	70.25
Keren ha-Yesod	63,354 **	14.47
Israel Education Fund (worldwide)	7,621	1.73
Israel Government Grant	40,474	9.22
Earmarked for Youth Aliya	7,694	1.84
From Rent & Sale of Housing	7,400	1.75
Miscellaneous	3,525	0.84
Total	438,313	100.00
Allocation to WZO	– 27,675	
Net income of Jewish Agency	410,639 ***	

*Does not include $14,238 in interest payments on UIA debts in the US. Includes $24,574 US Government grant for resettlement of Russian immigrants and $15,431 from sale of Israel Education Fund and other assets in Israel.
**Of which $35,679 was allocated to Jewish Agency and $27,675 to WZO.
***Does not include $12,475 carried over from 1984/5 budget.
Source for both Tables: The Jewish Agency for Israel, Finance Department. *Proposed Budget for the Year 1987/88.*

E. STOCK

ZIONIST ORGANIZATION. *See* WORLD ZIONIST ORGANIZATION.

ZIONIST ORGANIZATION OF AMERICA (ZOA). The Federation of American Zionists (popularly known as the American Zionist Federation), which later became the ZOA, was organized at an interstate conference held in New York on July 4, 1898. The lead in organizing the conference was taken by the Federation of Zionists of New York City and vicinity, composed of 36 Zionist groups with an aggregate membership of 5,000. The constituent groups included Hovevei Zion societies and many other clubs, societies, and congregations, as well as new groups that came into being in response to Herzl's *The Jewish State* and the convening of the First Zionist Congress (1897). The conference adopted a constitution for a "National Federation of American Zionists" and elected Professor Richard Gottheil president and Rabbi Stephen S. Wise honorary secretary. Both Gottheil and Wise were to attend the Second Zionist Congress (1898) and, coming under the personal influence of Herzl, remained firmly devoted to his leadership throughout his life.

It is significant that the conference rejected a proposal to apply religious tests to Zionist officials, on the ground that "Zionists have no right to pry into the beliefs and religious views of one another, provided that all were moved by a love of Zion and inspired by the hope of a resettlement within its borders of homeless Jews the world over." In taking this position, the federation characterized itself from the beginning as "general Zionist"—open to all who embraced basic Zionist principles regardless of social and religious ideologies that might otherwise divide them.

Early Years. At this first national gathering American Zionists faced the issue of "political" versus "practical" Zionism. The assembly proclaimed its "belief in the wisdom and urgency of political Zionism" but also "urged upon the International [Zionist] Congress the necessity of supporting the colonies already established in the Holy Land, and if possible, founding new colonies." The ambivalent attitude of the federation on this important issue persisted for years while the federation was still on the periphery of the Zionist movement and hesitated to adopt a strong, definitive position on controversial questions. Although the small inner group of men forming the administration remained thoroughly loyal to Herzl's political Zionism, the same could not be said of followers, who either entertained other views or were uncertain or indifferent.

The early years of the federation were marked by repeated struggles by the Gottheil administration to assert and maintain the central authority of the federation against divisive and separatist influences. There were rival groupings to challenge the federation, striving to achieve recognition and independent status. Prominent among the leaders of the discontented were Rabbi Philip Klein, Dr. Joseph I. Bluestone, and Rev. Dr. Michael Singer, who were persons of consequence devoted to the Zionist idea.

Among the reasons for the occasional rebellions and separatist tendencies were social and cultural differences between persons of Western European origin, generally referred to as "Germans," and Eastern European Jews, generally termed "Russians." The former, representing an earlier migration, constituted a kind of aristocracy and were often referred to as "uptown" Jews. The latter were more recent immigrants, who had arrived in huge numbers in the 1880s and 1890s; they were generally poor and Yiddish-speaking and were referred to as "downtown" Jews. Throughout his administration Gottheil eagerly sought the participation and leadership of other Western, Americanized Jews, whose collaboration he regarded as indispensable to the success of the movement, while "downtown" Jews were at times inclined to question the quality of his Zionism and his leadership. The last organization to resist the centralized authority of the federation was the Chicago-based Knights of Zion, which maintained a separate existence until 1913, when it was finally integrated in the federation.

To strengthen its program of Zionist education and propaganda, the federation established an English monthly magazine, the *Maccabean,* which made its appearance in 1901, with Louis Lipsky as managing editor. This was the beginning of Lipsky's long and prominent career in the organization. It was eight years later, in 1909, that the Yiddish organ of the movement, *Dos Yidishe Folk,* was founded with Senior Abel as editor.

When Wise gave up the position of honorary secretary after one year, he was succeeded by Isidore D. Morrison, who served until 1902. At the Boston Convention held that year, Jacob de Haas, then a resident of London, was elected secretary *in absentia*. Thus, for the first time the organization acquired a full-time administrative head. De Haas entered upon his task with great energy and organizational capacity, and in the ensuing three years the organization was greatly expanded throughout the United States. In 1905 De Haas resigned and moved to Boston.

In these years the federation devoted its efforts increasingly to all the varied forms of Zionist endeavor. Zionist propaganda was carried on continually, and a number of Zionist institutes were established. The first such institute was founded in Philadelphia in 1903; other followed in Pittsburgh, Cleveland, Baltimore, and other cities. Attention was also given to the promotion of the Hebrew language. Shekel campaigns were instituted. Shares of the Jewish Colonial Trust were sold, and activity on behalf of the Jewish National Fund began. The influence of the movement grew.

The Kishinev pogrom of 1903 was a traumatic experience for American Jews. For the first time Eastern and Western Jews joined hands in great demonstrations of grief and protest as well as in philanthropic endeavors to aid the pogrom victims. The convention of the federation, which took place in Pittsburgh that year, highlighted the Zionist reaction. Judah L. Magnes, a young rabbi of great promise, stirred the delegates by his plea to aid and promote the self-defense movement among the Jews of Russia, and thousands of dollars were contributed through the federation.

Gottheil continued to serve as president until the Cleveland Convention of 1904, when he retired for reasons of health. He was succeeded by Dr. Harry Friedenwald of Baltimore, a prominent medical scientist, who also was a Western Jew of German antecedents but was in closer contact with the Russian Jews than his predecessor. Friedenwald retained the office of president until 1912, when Louis Lipsky became chairman of the Executive Committee.

The year 1904 was a difficult one for the movement, marked by the death of Herzl and by the bitter differences that had been aroused by the East Africa scheme. There were a loss of membership in the federation and considerable discouragement, but these were temporary weaknesses.

During Friedenwald's administration the circle that guided and influenced the federation included men and women who favored cultural Zionism as against the political Zionism of the Gottheil administration. In this circle were Dr. Solomon Schechter, head of the Jewish Theological Seminary, Professor Israel Friedlaender, Judah L. Magnes, Henrietta Szold, and Eliyahu Ze'ev Lewin-Epstein. It was part of their Zionist outlook to be vitally concerned not only with the future of Palestine but also with the problems of Jewish life in the Diaspora, specifically in the United States. Schechter exerted a notable Zionist influence on the students of the seminary. He and Friedlaender made the seminary an institution for the graduation not only of rabbis but of Zionists, who carried the message of Zionism to all parts of the country.

During this period the federation could boast also of various affiliates reflecting the Zionist interest. Much attention was given to the problems of youth, including the activities of children's groups variously known as Herzl circles, junior societies, and boys' brigades. *Young Judea initially was formed by the federation in 1909 as its junior department and developed through the earnest efforts of David Schneeberg, a schoolteacher. On the college level, the Zeta Beta Tau fraternity, founded originally in 1898, was the precursor of the Collegiate Zionist League and the Intercollegiate Zionist Association of later years. That association led to the *Avukah, *Masada, and Intercollegiate Zionist Federation of America (IZFA) of more recent times.

The offspring of the federation included also the Order Sons of Zion (*see* B'NAI ZION), a fraternal insurance organization founded in 1907. The Women's Zionist Organization, *Hadassah, was formed by Henrietta Szold in 1912. In addition, special groups for the purchase of land in Eretz Israel were initiated by Simon Goldman of St. Louis toward the close of the first decade of the 20th century and grew in the following decade (*see* AHUZA). All these affiliates added much to the strength and influence of the federation.

After De Haas left for Boston in 1905, Magnes became honorary secretary. Magnes served in that capacity until 1908, when he resigned because of his preoccupation with the projected New York Kehilla. He was succeeded for two years by Rabbi Joseph Jasin, who was followed in 1910 by Henrietta Szold. After an arduous year Miss Szold retired from the position, and the administration was taken over by a collegium consisting of Louis Lipsky as chairman, Bernard A. Rosenblatt as honorary secretary, and Senior Abel.

The year 1908 was politically significant because of the Young Turk Revolution. For the moment it seemed to some Zionists that the revolution presaged a more promising development for Palestine. At the convention held that year, Magnes was so carried away by enthusiasm that he called upon the Zionists to accept the Turkish Revolution as the longed-for basis for the fulfillment of Zionist aims. American Zionists were so far removed from the political realities of the day that the convention apparently endorsed this optimistic assessment, which proved illusory.

Throughout these years important contributions to American Zionism were made by distinguished visitors from Europe and Palestine, among them Nahum Sokolow, Ben-Zion Mossinsohn, and Shemarya Levin. Of all those who came, Levin, a member of the World Zionist Executive, made the greatest and most enduring impact. His repeated visits and his travels throughout the country, the speeches he delivered to innumerable audiences, and his remarkable personality made him the apostle of World Zionism in the eyes of American Jews.

This period also witnessed the escalation of the controversy between American Zionism and the assimilationist viewpoint represented chiefly by the Reform movement. Although the intellectual and moral center of Reform Judaism, the Hebrew Union College in Cincinnati, was outspoken in its anti-Zionist position, some distinguished Reform rabbis gave the fullest support to Zionism and the Zionist movement. A principal pioneer among them was the venerable Bernhard Felsenthal of Chicago, who tirelessly advocated Zionism. Others were Rabbi Gustav Gottheil, Rabbi Max Heller and his son, James G. Heller, Stephen S. Wise, and Judah L. Magnes. But the official negative position of the Reform movement was stated by the Central Conference of American Rabbis (*see* REFORM JUDAISM AND ZIONISM).

There were other groups and sections of American Jewry with which the Zionists carried on lively controversies, in particular, the Jewish Socialists, who condemned Zionism as regressive and reactionary. But the struggle with the Reform assimilationists was the bitterest, perhaps because of the charge of "dual loyalty" that was flung at Zionist adherents.

The year 1914 found the Federation of American

Zionists still small in numbers and financially poor but immeasurably stronger than it had been at the beginning of the century. It had overcome internal crises. It had successfully asserted itself as the paramount Zionist body in the United States, and it had carried on an increasingly successful campaign against anti-Zionist forces. It was also finding its way in the international Zionist movement. Above all, it was making headway among the younger elements of American Jewry.

World War I and the Interwar Years. The outbreak of World War I in 1914 placed new and unexpected burdens upon American Zionism, which suddenly became an important center of World Zionism. Cut off from Allied countries, the Berlin headquarters of the World Zionist Organization (WZO) was able to maintain contact with the neutral United States, and it became necessary to establish a seat of Zionist authority in New York. Shemarya Levin, then visiting the United States and unable to return to his home in Berlin because of the war, joined Louis Lipsky in issuing a call for an extraordinary conference of all American Zionists, which was held on 30 August 1914, in New York. At this conference the Provisional Executive Committee for General Zionist Affairs was formed with Louis D. Brandeis (who had been won to Zionism by De Haas) as its chairman. American Zionism entered a new phase.

In accepting the chairmanship of the Provisional Committee, Brandeis assumed the responsibilities of American Zionist leadership, which in fact involved a trusteeship for the world movement and the Zionist institutions in Palestine. He plunged into the work with vigor, drawing into the circle of Zionist action a number of able associates, among them Felix Frankfurter, Julian W. Mack, Bernard Flexner, Robert Szold, Louis Kirstein, and Mrs. Mary Fels. Under his leadership the financial resources of the organization were greatly expanded and substantial aid was furnished to institutions in Eretz Israel.

The Provisional Committee set up an Emergency Fund to aid the yishuv and Jewish war victims in Europe. It also organized a Transfer Department, which helped persons in the then-neutral United States to send financial aid to Jewish organizations or individuals in Eretz Israel, Egypt, Russia, and Austria-Hungary, and in Constantinople, Damascus, Aleppo, Baghdad, and Beirut. The transfers were effected through the Jewish Colonial Trust in London and a special committee in Vienna. By early 1917 the US Department of State had accorded recognition to the Transfer Department, which was then also serving non-Jews. The Provisional Committee, too, provided the initiative—and helped raise the funds—for a project sponsored by the American Jewish Relief Committee, namely, the dispatch to Jaffa of the United States collier *S.S. Vulcan*, with 900 tons of food. Aboard the ship, loaned by the US Navy Department, were Eliyahu Ze'ev Lewin-Epstein and Louis H. Levin, who supervised the food distribution to Jews, Christians, and Moslems alike.

The organization attracted individual men of prestige as well as greater mass support. It gained steadily in political influence and was enabled to play a decisive role in the events that led to the issuance of the Balfour Declaration in 1917 and in the award of the Mandate for Palestine to Great Britain. This was, in fact, a revolution that lifted American Zionism from its modest position and transformed it into a powerful and dynamic force in American Jewish life. The challenges and opportunities of the war and the high standing of the new, impressive leadership that had appeared made the Zionist appeal almost irresistible.

One of the instruments forged by the movement was the American Jewish Congress. The congress was designed to provide the Jewish community with a representative, democratic body of Zionists and non-Zionists, possessing unchallenged authority to speak and act for all in the postwar settlement. The convocation of the congress (15 December 1918) at first was opposed by the American Jewish Committee and others, but in the end all groups joined in. For the first time American Jews spoke with a united voice, demanding Jewish minority rights in Eastern Europe and a pro-Zionist disposition of Palestine. A representative delegation, headed by Louis Marshall and Julian W. Mack, was elected to present Jewish demands at the Paris Peace Conference.

Among the significant contributions of Brandeis was his open and courageous handling of the issue of "dual loyalty." It was a great service he rendered the cause, when, as an outstanding American, high in the councils of the nation, he defended multiple loyalties insofar as they were not contradictory. By his repeated appearances, his speeches, and his prestige, he greatly reduced the force of the Jewish anti-Zionist opposition.

After Brandeis had been elevated to the Supreme Court in 1916, he continued in the leadership of the Provisional Committee but not as its active chairman. He exerted his influence on President Wilson in connection with the Balfour Declaration. He was succeeded as chairman by Stephen S. Wise. The Provisional Committee continued to function as such until 1918, representing not only the federation but other Zionist parties, such as the Mizrachi and Po'ale Zion groups.

The end of the war brought great changes. At the convention of the federation held in Pittsburgh in 1918, the Provisional Executive Committee was merged with the federation and its branches into what became the Zionist Organization of America (ZOA). This was a fundamental reorganization in which group affiliation of societies was replaced by individual membership, and the geographical district replaced the society as the basic Zionist unit. This convention adopted what became known as the "Pittsburgh Program", essentially a set of principles for the development of Palestine on the basis of social justice. Justice Brandeis was elected honorary president; Judge Julian W. Mack, president; Dr. Stephen S. Wise and Dr. Harry Friedenwald, vice-presidents; Jacob de Haas, exeutive secretary; Louis Lipsky, secretary for organization; Henrietta Szold, secretary for education; and E.Z. Lewin-Epstein, treasurer. The Brandeis administration, substantially unchanged, continued in office until 1921. Meanwhile, the Mizrachi and Po'ale Zion groups became independent entities affiliated with their respective international bodies.

In 1919 Brandeis visited Europe as well as Palestine, where he familiarized himself with the land and its problems. He returned impressed with the need for fighting malaria and improving general health conditions in Palestine. The ZOA Convention, held that year in Chicago, showed unmistakable signs of strained relations between the administration and large sections of the constituency. This situation was caused in part by the retreat of Justice Brandeis behind a veil imposed by his position on the Supreme Court. Another contributing factor was the power exercised by De Haas, who often behaved as the secret emissary of the "silent leader" and by his manner antagonized many rank-and-file Zionists. Undoubtedly there was also tension between the group of Western Jews, strongly entrenched in the leadership, and the Eastern Jews, many of whom were by this time in stable circumstances and felt able to participate more fully in the leadership.

The immediate issue at the Chicago Convention was an organizational question, a proposal for direct representation of the districts and regions in the National Executive Committee. It ended in a verbal duel between the youthful Emanuel Neumann and Stephen S. Wise, who was then at the height of his powers. Neumann's advocacy of a greater measure of democracy won out. As it developed, this was merely a skirmish that presaged an open contest that took place in the next two years.

In 1920 an international Zionist conference, the first to be held since World War I, took place in London. The ZOA was strongly represented by some 40 delegates, headed by Brandeis. By this time Brandeis had formed definite views on how to proceed with the building of the Jewish National Home. He emphasized sound economics and health enterprises in Palestine. He wanted the ZOA to concentrate on gathering private investment capital for specific projects in Paestine and had many reservations concerning the form and purposes of the Keren ha-Yesod which the European leadership wanted to establish as the central, all-inclusive fund to be subscribed by the Jews of the world. Brandeis also wished to entrust the leadership of the movement, insofar as work in Palestine was concerned, to a group of important and wealthy British Jews. At the same time, he declined to accept the leadership of the WZO because of his position on the Supreme Court. His views brought him into conflict with Chaim Weizmann, who was elected president of the WZO. The conference also voted to establish the Keren ha-Yesod as the central fund of the WZO. The American delegates left London dispirited, many of them critical of Brandeis and inclined to support the Weizmann position.

The final clash came in the spring of 1921, when Weizmann went to the United States as head of the WZO delegation, which included Professor Albert Einstein and Menahem Ussishkin. His coming was a signal to his followers in and out of the ZOA administration. Through their efforts and the support of the Yiddish press, the Weizmann delegation was accorded a royal welcome of unprecedented fervor. There followed months of fruitless negotiations between Weizmann and Judge Mack, who was supported by the majority of the ZOA Executive Committee. A minority headed by Lipsky gave full support to Weizmann. The negotiations involved not only technical questions regarding the Keren ha-Yesod but many far-reaching problems, including the issue of "Diaspora nationalism," which was raised by the Brandeis-Mack group. When the negotiations failed to achieve an accommodation between the opposing views, the issue had to be resolved at the ZOA Convention held in Cleveland in June, 1921, which turned out to be one of the most crucial gatherings in the history of American Zionism.

At the very beginning the pro-Weizmann forces were apparently in the majority and succeeded in electing their candidate, Judge Henry J. Dannenbaum of Texas, as permanent chairman of the convention. In the elaborate debate that followed, the Brandeis-Mack position was presented by its most impressive advocates, including Felix Frankfurter, Stephen S. Wise, and Judge Mack himself. They were answered by the spokesmen of the opposition, including Louis Lipsky, Abraham Goldberg, Emanuel Neumann, and Morris Rothenberg. At the conclusion of the debate the convention withheld its confidence from the incumbent administration, whereupon Mack read a statement on behalf of Brandeis and his associates in the administration, declaring their withdrawal from all offices but vowing to remain loyal members of the organization. Lipsky, who had been a member of the administration, had previously resigned to lead the opposition, and it was to him and his principal colleagues that the convention then entrusted the leadership. It elected an administration that included, in addition to Lipsky, Abraham Goldberg, Hermann Conheim, Emanuel Neumann, Bernard A. Rosenblatt, Morris Rothenberg, Peter Schweitzer, and Louis Topkis. The Brandeis group directed its attention to the promotion of business enterprises and, ultimately, the Palestine Economic Corporation.

ZOA delegation with Pres. Warren G. Harding. [Zionist Archives]

From then until 1930 Lipsky was the dominant figure in the ZOA. The Keren ha-Yesod was established with Samuel Untermyer as president and Emanuel Neumann as national director; it met with both a warm welcome and sharp opposition. In the years that followed, several members of the Brandeis group, notably Judge Mack, Stephen S. Wise, and Abba Hillel Silver, resumed active roles in the ZOA and worked for the Keren ha-Yesod.

After the Cleveland Convention of 1921, Hadassah, which had largely supported the Brandeis-Mack administration, asserted its independence of the ZOA. Nevertheless, it continued for a number of years to act as the ZOA's sister organization. Politically, the ZOA scored a remarkable success when the Congress of the United States adopted a joint resolution, approved by President Warren G. Harding on 22 September 1922, endorsing the Balfour Declaration and the idea of the Jewish National Home. The piloting of this resolution through Congress, in the face of anti-Zionist opposition, was largely the work of Elihu D. Stone of Boston, backed and supported by Lipsky and Goldberg.

Raising funds for the work in Palestine through the Keren ha-Yesod, the Jewish National Fund, and other channels remained a principal concern of the ZOA in the inter-war years. There was some rivalry between the Zionist funds and the relief campaigns conducted largely by non-Zionists, but there was no actual conflict between them. In 1925, however, the prominent inclusion in the program of the relief campaign of a provision for settling Russian Jews on the land in the Crimea and the Ukraine provoked disagreement. The provision was regarded with growing suspicion by the Zionist leaders, and the controversy that then developed between the American Zionist movement and the Jewish philanthropic leadership threatened the delicate negotiations that Weizmann was conducting to bring non-Zionist leaders into the expanded Jewish Agency. The American Zionists, for their part, met the situation by adopting Neumann's proposal for uniting all Zionist funds in one appeal, under the title *United Palestine Appeal (UPA). Stephen S. Wise accepted the chairmanship of the UPA, with Neumann as chairman of its Executive Committee. Not only all Zionist funds but also all Zionist parties were represented in this effort; leadership was vested in the ZOA.

The tension between Zionists and non-Zionists continued for a time but was finally overcome by the efforts of both camps, so that by 1929 the public launching of the enlarged Jewish Agency took place in Zurich. The sanguinary Arab riots in Palestine which followed and the sudden death of Louis Marshall, who headed the non-Zionist contingent in the Jewish Agency, coupled with the economic crisis that began that year, had a depressing effect on Zionist activity. A hastily organized ZOA delegation proceeded to Washington to draw the attention of Secretary of State Henry L. Stimson and President Herbert Hoover to the dangerous situation in Palestine, and a large public meeting of protest and mourning was held in New York. An emergency fund was raised to help the victims of the riots.

By 1930 there was a general disposition to reunite all forces in the ZOA, and in the convention held in Cleveland that year foundations were laid for the full return of the Brandeis group. The prevailing mood was rendered gloomier by the publication of the Passfield White Paper, which aroused bitter Jewish opposition. Upon Lipsky's withdrawal from the presidency, the convention elected an administration of 18, with a predominance of the Brandeis group; Robert Szold was subsequently nominated as chairman. Until World War II the office of president was alternated between representatives of the two factions of the ZOA, whose dividing lines had become blurred. The leaders were Morris Rothenberg, Stephen S. Wise, and Solomon Goldman. Brandeis himself remained in the background as the elder stateman whose counsel was in great demand.

When, in the early 1930s, Hitler came to power in Germany, the shadow thrown by the Nazi menace affected all Jews. The ZOA joined with other sections of the Jewish community in expressions of revulsion and protest, and it lent its support to various anti-Nazi moves, including an economic boycott. But all efforts on behalf of European Jewry failed.

World War II and the Postwar Period. Upon the outbreak of World War II in 1939, the World Zionist Executive authorized the leaders of the ZOA to form in America a committee similar to the Provisional Executive Committee that had functioned in World War I. The situation, however, differed from what it had been 25 years earlier because the various Zionist parties in the United States, including Hadassah, had by now fully developed their own identities. There was thus launched the *Emergency Committee for Zionist Affairs, which included representatives of the various parties and groups. Nevertheless, from the committee's inception the principal leadership rested with persons drawn from the ZOA.

During the war an organized effort was undertaken to achieve United States governmental and popular support for the establishment of a Jewish Commonwealth in Palestine. In 1940, largely on the initiative of Emanuel Neumann, a basic political and public relations program began to take shape. These initial efforts culminated in the reorganization in 1943 of the Emergency Committee under the name American Zionist Emergency Council, as a body composed of representatives of the major Zionist groups in the United States, under the leadership of Abba Hillel Silver, who in its early period was cochairman with Stephen S. Wise and later was chairman.

Another development was the mobilization of non-Jewish friends of Zionism through the *American Palestine Committee and the Christian Council on Palestine. Merging later into the American Christian Palestine Committee, these bodies of political leaders, clergymen, educators, and other outstanding citizens proved staunch allies of the Zionist cause.

The *Biltmore Program, which was adopted at an extraordinary conference of American Zionists convened in 1942 largely on the initiative of the ZOA leadership, was a signal contribution to the creation of the Jewish State. In this declaration the goal of Zionism was for the first time clearly defined as the establishment of a Jewish Commonwealth. The Biltmore Program, later adopted by the World Zionist Executive, became also the official position of the entire American Jewish community when it was approved by the *American Jewish Conference, which assembled in 1943 to plan united action on postwar Jewish problems. The action of the conference was assured after a forecful speech by Silver.

At the same time, the ZOA continued its efforts to mobilize maximum political support for the Zionist program. Both the Democratic and the Republican platforms of 1944 included strong pro-Zionist planks. In the fall of that year President Franklin D. Roosevelt sent a strongly worded message to the convention of the ZOA, pledging his support for a Zionist solution of the Palestine problem. In December, 1945, both houses of Congress adopted a concurrent resolution favoring "the upbuilding of Palestine as the Jewish National Home."

These and subsequent political efforts had wide repercussions among American Jews and contributed to a phenomenal growth in the membership of the ZOA during the administrations of Abba Hillel Silver (1945–47) and his successor, Emanuel Neumann (1947–49). All other Zionist organizations shared in the upward trend.

In 1945 President Harry S Truman, moved by humanitarian considerations, sent Earl Harrison to Europe to study the condition of the survivors of the Nazi horror. As a result the President recommended the immediate admission of 100,000 Jews to Palestine. The ZOA leaders, headed by Silver, were prime movers in the chain of events that followed. They strongly criticized the Anglo-American Committee of Inquiry, which had been formed at the suggestion of the British government, denouncing it as a delaying tactic. They likewise opposed, with all the force at their command, the Morrison-Grady Plan, which proposed a tiny Jewish enclave in Palestine. At the 22nd Zionist Congress (1946) they led the militant faction that opposed further efforts toward an accommodation with Great Britain based upon concessions. The uncompromising stand of the Zionist Congress in reaffirming the Biltmore Program was ultimately responsible for Foreign Secretary Ernest Bevin's decision to refer the Palestine issue to the United Nations. This he was moved to do after a long series of fruitless discussions with Zionist representatives in January, 1947.

The active participation of the ZOA in World Zionist affairs continued in 1947 and 1948, when two of its leaders served in the American Section of the Jewish Agency, Silver as chairman and Neumann as a member. Under Silver's guidance there was close coordination between the American Zionist Emergency Council and the Jewish Agency, and all efforts were directed toward ensuring a favorable outcome in the United Nations. While representatives of the Jewish Agency established and maintained contact with the delegates of most of the member nations of the United Nations, the Emergency Council maintained its contact with the United States government and sought to assure its continued support. Eventually, on 29 November 1947, the United Nations adopted a partition proposal sanctioning a Jewish State in part of western Palestine. The following spring Silver officially advised the United Nations of the establishment of the State of Israel (14 May 1948).

Soon thereafter, a controversy developed over the administrative direction of the United Jewish Appeal (UJA). When Silver and Neumann were outvoted in the Jewish Agency in their efforts to preserve Diaspora Zionist influence in the UJA, they resigned as members of the American Section.

There followed a period of public debate between the leadership of the ZOA and leaders of the Jewish Agency and the government of Israel, headed by David Ben-Gurion. At issue were the rights and obligations of American Zionists in the new era. These questions continued to claim the attention of American Zionists and Israelis for a number of years. In 1950, at a conference in Jerusalem

The 1948 convention of the Zionist Organization of America. [Zionist Archives]

President Truman, after addressing the convention of the Zionist Organization of America, in September, 1957, at the Waldorf Astoria Hotel in New York, receives a standing ovation. [Alexander Archer]

attended by many American Jews, a decision was reached to launch the public sale of State of Israel bonds. The ZOA delegation, headed by its president, Benjamin G. Browdy, committed the ZOA to $100,000,000 in bond sales. When the bond campaign was duly launched in the United States, ZOA districts and members played a prominent role in communities throughout the country. At the international mobilzation conference held in Jerusalem in 1958, it was reported that the ZOA had oversubscribed its pledge.

In general, the creation of the State of Israel, its growth, and the successive crises that it had to meet and overcome stimulated Zionist interest and activities in the United States and had a marked effect on the ZOA. This was so despite the opinion expressed by Prime Minister Ben-Gurion to the effect that the continued existence of the Zionist movement in the Diaspora was of doubtful value and that all persons who considered themselves Zionists should settle in Israel. American Zionists gradually adjusted themselves to the new situation. As early as 1948 the representatives of the ZOA, at a meeting of the Zionist Actions Committee in Jerusalem, supported two important measures: (1) a decision to turn to over the government of Israel the Political Department of the Jewish Agency, as well as other departments logically within the purview of the government; and (2) the principle of Hafrada, the formal and legal separation between the Zionist Executive (Jewish Agency) and the government of Israel. The separation of functions and personnel was important in regulating relations between the government and the Zionist movement in the post-State era.

Membership and Program. The membership of the ZOA in the mid-1980s was about 120,000. Its national office was in New York. It continues to stand in the vanguard of the Jewish community with unequivocal support for Israel and involvement in all Jewish communal activity. Emigration of Ethiopian Jewry and their resettlement in Israel, and freedom for and resettlement in Israel of Soviet Jewry are deep concerns of ZOA. ZOA activities on behalf of Soviet Jewry began in the 1930s when ZOA President Morris Rothenberg petitioned the President of the United States to intercede with the Soviets to grant religious freedom for Russian Jewry.

Public affairs issues remain a major thrust of ZOA endeavors to support Israel's position and public image. The campaign to rescind the 1975 UN resolution against Zionism was actively inaugurated by ZOA. The ZOA helped sponsor Resolution 997, which supports any and all means consistent with the US Constitution to close PLO offices throughout the country. On 13 July 1987, ZOA's Metropolitan Region helped introduce a resolution that was passed unanimously by the City Council of New York, which voted to endorse pending legislation in both Houses of Congress.

Masada is ZOA's youth movement. Political rallies, educational and cultural activities, help foster an understanding of and commitment to Zionism. Every year approximately 200 members attend Masada's annual convention where they discuss aliya and Zionist activism. Masada continues in the forefront of Zionist youth organizations by taking over 700 girls and boys to Israel as part of their annual summer program. Garin Masada consists of approximately 40 members who are seriously considering making Israel their home. In 1982–87, 150 Garin members left for Israel.

ZOA is increasingly involved in developing Young Zionist Leadership. The highly successful annual Young Leadership Missions take young men and women to Israel. Upon their return, these young people continue their Zionist education at ZOA seminars designed to bring them into leadership positions in the organization.

The Ivan J. Novick Institute for Israel/Diaspora Relations, another arm of the ZOA, was established in 1984. This Institute was created in order to strengthen the bonds between Israel and the American Jewish community, to bring to Israelis a better understanding of the American Jewish community, and to solidify the centrality of Israel in Jewish life throughout the Diaspora.

In 1984, the Jacob Goodman Institute for Middle East Research and Information was established under the aegis of the ZOA. The Institute works to foster understanding of Zionism in the Jewish and Christian communities. It also combats anti-Zionism by sponsoring analytical and educational forums and publications. In 1984, the Institute inaugurated Christian/Zionist Dialogue thereby projecting the issue of Zionism into the Christian/Jewish agenda. Under its sponsorship, seminars on Propaganda Analysis have been presented on college campuses across the country. The Jacob Goodman Library serves as a resource center and a repository for books and archival materials particularly pertinent to ZOA.

ZOA House, in Tel Aviv. [Zionist Archives]

The ZOA House in Tel Aviv, established in 1953, serves the cultural and educational needs of the American/Israeli community. Kfar Silver, ZOA's educational complex in Ashkelon, established in 1955 is the only American chartered high school in Israel. On the same campus the ZOA established in 1966 the Milly Goodman Academic High School for American children. The school now includes an aviation high school, a technical high school, sports center, and computer programing center. The campus of Kefar Silver and its facilities are also used for annual ZOA Young Zionist summer camps for American high school students.

The ZOA is affiliated with the World Union of General Zionists. It issued regularly the following publications: the **American Zionist*, the official monthly organ for the entire ZOA membership; *ZOA in Review*, a monthly intended for regional and district leadership; *ZINS (Zionist Information Service)*, a weekly news bulletin published simultaneously in English, Yiddish, and Spanish; *Masada Bulletin*, a periodical for ZOA youth; and *ZOA House News*, published bimonthly by the ZOA House in Tel Aviv.

The following served as president of the ZOA (and its predecessor, the Federation of American Zionists): Richard Gottheil (1897–1904); Harry Friedenwald (1904–18); Julian W. Mack (1918–21); Louis Lipsky (1921–30); Robert Szold (1930–32); Morris Rothenberg (1932–36); Stephen S. Wise (1936–38); Solomon Goldman (1938–40); Edmund I. Kaufmann (1940–41); Louis E. Levinthal (1941–43); Israel Goldstein (1943–45); Abba Hillel Silver (1945-47); Emanuel Neumann (1947–49); Daniel Frisch (1949–50); Benjamin G. Browdy (1950–52); Irving Miller (1952–54); Mortimer May (1954-56); Emanuel Neumann (1956–58); Abraham A. Redelheim (1958–60); Max Bressler (1960–62); Max Nussbaum (1962–65); Jacques Torczyner (1965–70); Herman Weisman (1970–74); Joseph P. Sternstein (1974-78); Ivan J. Novick (1978–83); Alleck A. Resnick (1983–86); and Milton S. Shapiro (1986-).

See also UNITED STATES OF AMERICA: RELATIONS WITH ZIONISM AND ISRAEL; UNITED STATES OF AMERICA, ZIONISM IN.

S. CAPLAN—G. HIRSCHLER

ZIONIST SUPREME COURT. The Zionist Supreme Court (ZSC) is the name given in 1979 to the highest judicial body of the World Zionist Organization (WZO), previously called Congress Tribunal. It dates back to the *Organisationsstatut* enacted by the Fifth Zionist Congress in 1901, which provided for a *Kongressgericht* (Congress Court). According to the new constitution of the World Zionist Organization adopted in 1960, the Congress Tribunal combined the functions of the two courts which had existed under the constitution of 1921, the Congress Court and the Court of Honor.

In 1986 the ZSC consisted of a maximum of 30 members, including the president and 6 deputy presidents, all of whom were elected for the duration of the inter-Congress period by the Zionist Congress.

Under article 49 of the constitution, the ZSC was authorized (1) to interpret the constitution; (2) to examine the legality of decisions of central Zionist bodies; (3) to hear and arbitrate certain disputes between Zionist bodies or between a central Zionist body and an individual (except for disputes involving money matters); (4) to deal with objections to decisions to postpone a Zionist Congress or a session of the Zionist General Council; (5) to confirm, annul, or alter the results of Congress elections; (6) to decide complaints lodged by the attorney of the WZO that a certain act constituted an infringement of the constitution or was detrimental to the interests or prestige of the WZO; and (7) to deal with appeals from judgments of judicial bodies of territorial Zionist organizations. Additional jurisdiction was conferred on the ZSC by other enactments as well as resolutions of the governing bodies of the WZO, such as dealing with appeals from the decisions of the Committee for the determination of the number of Congress delegates, of the Central Election Board, etc.

The number of judges forming a bench of the ZSC, apart from exceptional cases, consists of three judges, their chairman being the president of the Court or one of his deputies. The judgments of any bench are final and not subject to further appeal. The cases are conducted under the special Rules of Procedure of the ZSC, which also provides for sanctions to be imposed on Zionist bodies and individuals, ranging from a warning to suspension or cancellation of membership.

The ZSC is busiest before the opening of a Zionist Congress because most cases brought before it pertain to election matters. Though not formally bound by its previous judgments and decisions, it usually decides cases in conformity with the precedents handed down in the course of eight decades. Owing to its impartiality, the high standards of its proceedings, and the eminence of the personalities who have served as presidents of the court (Dr. Max Bodenheimer, Sammy Gronemann, Dr. Aron Barth, Judge Shneur Zalman Cheshin, and Chief Justices Shimon Agranat and Moshe Landau), the ZSC is held in high esteem.

According to an Amendment to the Constitution, adopted in 1976, the members of the Court are elected for two Congress periods (i.e., eight years). Of the 30 members of the Court in 1986, 18 were residents of Israel, seven were from the USA, three from European countries, one from Canada, one from Latin America.

In 1986 the Zionist General Council enacted a far-reaching reform of the process of appointing the members of the ZSC. It provided that while the president himself would also in the future be elected by Congress, the judges whose maximum number was fixed at 30, including no more than three deputy presidents, would be appointed by a special Nominations Committee, consisting of nine members, four of them to be elected by Congress or, in case of replacements by the ZGC, two by the attorney of the WZO and two by the president of the ZSC, who would chair the Nominations Committee. Two members of the Nominations Committee were to be residents of a Diaspora country. The purpose of this reform, following the example of the system of the nomination of judges in the State of Israel, was to bring about, as far as possible, a depoliticization of the appointments of members of the ZSC. While in the exercise of their function they proved to be impartial, Congress, in choosing the candidates, was often influenced by political considerations, which the composition of the new Nominations Committee was intended to relegate to the background.

A. ZWERGBAUM

ZIONIST TERRITORIAL ORGANIZATIONS. Zionist organizations comprising the Zionists living in a particular country. Zionist territorial organizations (ZTOs) have been in existence since the early days of modern Zionism, but their names, patterns, and functions have changed in the course of time. In the beginning, Zionist activities in each country were supervised by territorial committees (*Landescomités*), at lower levels, they were conducted by regional units (*Distrikte*, or Zionist districts) and local societies (*Vereine*) comprising the Shekel payers, that is, individual members of the *World Zionist Organization (WZO). Later, "territorial" organizations became known as Zionist territorial federations (*Landesverbände*); they included all the individual WZO members in the countries concerned.

With the emergence of ideological trends and groupings within the Zionist movement, this simple pattern grew more complex. Those who had adopted a specific Zionist ideology did not belong to the territorial federations but to *separate unions (*Sonderverbände*) such as the Mizrachi (founded in 1902) and the Po'ale Zion (founded in 1907). However, even in later years, after the emergence of additional separate unions, the members of the ZTOs, known as General Zionists, formed the great majority of the movement. Thus, at the 12th Zionist Congress (1921), the General Zionists had 376 delegates, while the delegates affiliated with separate unions numbered 136. The separate unions grew apace, however, and by the 21st Congress (1939), held shortly before World War II, the proportions had been reversed, with the territorial federations represented by 172 delegates and the separate unions by 386. In many cases the General Zionists were divided into two wings, originally designated as A and B. Since the 24th Congress (1956), these two wings have been known as the *World Union of General Zionists and the *World Confederation of General (later United) Zionists, respectively. For all practical purposes, the two are parties in their own right like any others.

As the territorial federations lost their all-inclusive character, the need was increasingly felt for a new comprehensive Zionist framework to embrace all Zionists in a given country, members of separate unions no less than General Zionists or unaffiliated Zionist sympathizers. Therefore, the 19th Congress (1935) called for the establishment of united Zionist federations (*Zionistische Einheitsorganisationen*) that would be based on individual membership. However, the 24th Congress (1956) was willing to settle for the establishment of Zionist federations composed not of individuals but of constituent groups and parties in countries where a more sophisticated organizational structure was not yet in existence.

The 1960 constitution of the WZO considerably changed the status of the Zionist territorial organizations, as they were now called. It differentiated between three types of ZTO: (1) Zionist unions, based on the membership of individual Zionists in a given country; (2) Zionist federations, composed of Zionist groups, political or nonparty; and (3) mixed Zionist federations, based on both individual members and constituent member groups. An Amendment to the Constitution passed in 1973 abolished the second and third type of ZTOS so that only the first remained in force and became universal, but was now called Zionist Federation. Thus, personal membership of individual Zionists in the ZTO became obligatory, being either indirect, for members of Zionist parties and groups, or direct for people who were not affiliated with any Zionist framework but the Zionist Federation itself.

However, there exists also collective membership, not for Zionist bodies or individuals but for national Jewish bodies or territorial branches of international Jewish bodies, such as a territorial organization branch of Maccabi. Although the legal requirement of personal membership of all

Zionists in the Zionist Federation is clear, this principle, while observed in most countries, has not yet been put into practice everywhere. Unless otherwise provided by the Zionist General Council, there should be one ZTO in each country. At the end of the 1980s most countries of the free world where Jews reside in appreciable numbers have a ZTO. There were, however, exceptions. In Great Britain both the Zionist Federation and the Mizrachi had been recognized as ZTOs, each in its own right. On the other hand, no ZTO in the proper sense of the term exists in Israel where a Zionist Council was established in 1969 as the first comprehensive and permanent Zionist structure in the history of the Jewish State. It is a consultative body consisting of representatives of various bodies and groups, party and non-party, including immigrants' associations. Its main objectives are to assist the social and cultural integration of newcomers, to promote contacts with Diaspora Jewry, and to foster a sense of unity with Jews the world over. In the eighties the activities of the Zionist Council for Israel were intensified and their scope extended; e.g., Zionist information work was conducted in schools and development towns, and twinning projects between the latter and Zionist Federations and Jewish communities abroad were launched. These activities were largely due to the initiative of the first Chairman of the Council, Arieh Zimuki. The Council itself has had 10 representatives at the Zionist Congress and three at the Zionist General Council, with voting rights but without the right to join any of the Congress groupings.

The American Zionist Federation is different from all others in several regards: first, obviously, it is by far the largest; second, it was set up and recognized comparatively late—in 1972; third, though admitting individual direct members, its membership is overwhelmingly composed of persons affiliated with constituent bodies of the Federation like Hadassah, Zionist Organization of America (ZOA), etc.; and finally, it is the only Zionist Federation on whose territory a branch of the Zionist Executive is operating (the "American Section of the Executive" in coordination with the AZF).

Under the amendments to the WZO constitution adopted by the 27th Congress, Zionist youth movements and organizations should form an integral part of the ZTOs concerned. Women's organizations, too, should be closely affiliated with them. Under the Constitution of the WZO each Zionist Federation is obligated to admit as members any individual or body that subscribes to the *Jerusalem Program" and to the Statutes of the Federation concerned, unless there are weighty reasons against the admission. A territorial branch or an individual member of a Zionist World Union is to be admitted under any circumstances. Conversely, they are in duty bound to join the Zionist Federation and must not secede from it. A person or body whose admission is refused may appeal to the Territorial Zionist Tribunal and appeal that decision to the Supreme Zionist Court.

The principal functions of the ZTOs are as follows: to encourage and organize immigration to Israel; to foster investments, tourism, and youth work in Israel; to promote hakhshara (agricultural training) and other pioneering activities; to raise money for the national funds and other recognized financial drives for Israel; to disseminate the Hebrew language and advance Hebrew and Jewish education and culture; to engage in Jewish activities and defend Jewish rights in the Diaspora; to represent the Zionist movement in the country concerned; and to disseminate information on Israel and the Zionist movement.

As a rule, a ZTO has the following governing bodies: the Convention (Conference, or General Assembly), which is a counterpart of the Zionist Congress on the territorial level; an Executive Committee for conducting current business; frequently also a Council or other body with supervisory and advisory powers; and a judicial body to settle disciplinary matters and to arbitrate disputes arising from Zionist membership and activities.

To be recognized as a member of the WZO, a ZTO must comply with various requirements laid down in the WZO constitution, one of which is to "act according to the basic principles of justice, equality, and democracy, prevent the membership of bodies or individuals who adhere to or advance discrimination based on origin, nationality, or race, and conduct its affairs having regard to the protection of the requirements of all members."

PRINCIPAL ZIONIST TERRITORIAL ORGANIZATIONS IN 1986

As explained above, Israel cannot be listed here because the Zionist Council for Israel rather than a full-fledged ZTO is functioning there. The position in the United States before the establishment of the American Zionist Federation was similar. Until 1970 most functions performed in other countries by a ZTO were exercised in the United States by Zionist parties and nonpolitical bodies, the most important of which were—in order of the size of their representation at the 30th Zionist Congress—Hadassah, the ZOA, Labor Zionists, Mizrachi-ha-Po'el Mizrachi, United Zionists-Revisionists, Artzenu, and Mapam. The distinctive features of the American Zionist Federation have been enumerated above.

Canada The total membership of the Canadian Zionist Federation in 1985 amounted to just under 50,000 of whom only some 600 were direct members while the overwhelming majority belonged to the Federation through the intermediary of one of its 12 affiliates, the largest of which were Hadassah-WIZO, the (General) Zionist Organization of Canada, and Mizrachi. This Federation is particularly active in the fields of information and public relations.

South Africa The South African Zionist Federation numbered over 35,000 members in 1985, more than a third of the total Jewish population of that country—an exceptionally large proportion. This high membership rate is also due to a special arrangement under which every contributor to the Keren ha-Yesod—United Israel Appeal—is regarded and counted as an organized Zionist. This Federation may serve as a model of an old established (1898) closely-knit and particularly efficient ZTO which dominates the Zionist life of the country.

Australia The membership of the Zionist Federation of Australia—about 30,000—is much higher than the average rate of 10 to 15% of the Jewish population applying in most countries. The various Zionist associations and societies are grouped in Zionist State Councils, a pattern of organization that closely follows the structure of the Commonwealth of Australia. Long before similar affiliations were possible on a global level in the WZO, congregations and other Jewish bodies like educational institutions could be affiliated with the Federation as "Associated Members".

Great Britain The position in Great Britain differs from other countries because two Zionist Federations have existed there for many decades and are recognized as members of the WZO: the general Zionist Federation and the Mizrachi Federation, having between them about 70,000 members of whom some 15% belong to the latter. The general Federation has set up and maintained 10 Jewish Day Schools. Since the seventies, efforts have been made to do away with the anomaly of the existence of two federations and to replace them by a United Zionist Federation. However, various resolutions of the governing bodies of the WZO to this effect, and agreements between the two federations themselves, have not been implemented. On the contrary, after the 30th Zionist Congress, the Likud seceded from the general Federation and formed an association with the Mizrachi Federation.

Central and Eastern Europe Most of the ZTOs in Central and Eastern Europe, once the mainstay of the World Zionist movement, such as those of Poland, Romania, Czechoslovakia, and Yugoslavia, were, after a short-lived restoration following World War II, dissolved by the Communist regimes. Those of Western Germany and Austria are but shadows of their predecessors but do valuable work in the fields of culture and public relations.

Nederlandsche Zionistenbond The Zionist Federation of Holland has always been a closely-knit ZTO based on direct personal membership, even at times when most Zionist federations were loose roof organizations. Therefore, its role in the Zionist life of Holland has always been more important than that of the Zionist parties, whose adherents are only a minority among the membership of the Federation.

Switzerland The prestige and image of the Swiss Zionist Federation in the WZO has always been higher than its small membership would warrant, not only because of its cultural activities and role in fundraising, but also owing to the geographic position of Switzerland and to its tradition. The Swiss and the Swedish Zionist Federations are the only two ZTO's on the Continent of Europe whose existence and work continued without interruption during World War II.

France The number of organized Zionists in France is some 23,000 (1985), little more than 5% of the total Jewish population. The Federation has suffered from periodic splits and secessions of Zionist bodies and groups. Among the numerous Zionist organizations affiliated with the Federation, the largest and probably most active is the French territorial branch of WIZO. While until the sixties immigrants from eastern Europe played the most important part in the Zionist Federation, the great influx of Jews from North Africa to France has left its mark on the membership and leadership of the Federation. The Yiddish-speaking element, which was once predominant, is disappearing and the business of the Federation is now conducted exclusively in French and Hebrew.

Italy In contradistinction to France, the Federazione Sionistica Italiana was established, and is composed almost exclusively, of native-born Italian Jews. The greater part of its 4,800 members—some 18% of the total Jewish population of Italy—are organized in the two largest local branches in Rome and Milan.

Belgium The Zionist Federation of Belgium, operating from two centers, Brussels and Antwerp, has a relatively stronger membership than the French one but the center of gravity of Zionist life still resides more in the Zionist parties than in the Federation.

Latin America The relative strength and the role of the ZTOs in Latin America has increased during the last two decades. Most are characterized by their comparatively recent origin, the eastern European background of most of their members, and consequently, a pattern of organization resembling more closely former Zionist federations in that part of the world than those in English-speaking countries. However, as in France, the Yiddish-speaking founding fathers are being increasingly replaced by the new generation, largely university educated, whose language is Spanish. In Chile, the leading part played by the federation in Jewish life is reminiscent of South Africa, while the membership of the OSA, the Zionist Federation of Argentina, which was only 17,000 in 1982, has grown considerably through the affiliation of Jewish clubs and other non-political elements. Numerically weaker but relatively stronger is the Zionist Organization of Uruguay, with a membership of 14,000 in a total Jewish population of 50,000. Characteristic of the Zionist Federation of Brazil is the existence of two almost independent centers, one in Rio de Janeiro and the other in São Paulo. The Zionist Federation of Mexico is a comprehensive roof organization of a great variety of Zionist bodies, including strong youth groups. Jewish demographic changes—the emigration of Jews from some Latin American countries and their immigration to others—is reflected in the condition and activities of some ZTOs: thus the federations of Bolivia and Ecuador, which were flourishing after World War II, are practically non-existent while the Zionist Federation of Venezuela has become strong and active.

See also separate articles on Zionism in the countries mentioned.

A. ZWERGBAUM

ZIONIST THOUGHT. Zionism is the most fundamental, far-reaching conduit through which the Jewish people came to grips with the modern age, and it has been said, thereby reentered history. Any attempt to define an "ism" is, understandably, suspect, and few movements can vie with Zionism in the richness of its intellectual variety. Still, the major ideologues in the Zionist pantheon, their differences notwithstanding, did concur on the need to champion the revitalization of world Jewry with its return to the Land of Israel, birthplace of that people's identity, to be followed by its sovereign independence and cultural development. Linking the traditionalist aspiration for a return to Zion with 19th century liberal-humanist impulses of national liberation, these thinkers were united in the conviction that only the autonomous exercise of power in the biblically covenanted Eretz Israel would serve as the instrument of collective survival. The Jewish masses, once freed from the ills of exile, would undergo an inner transformation. Reconstitution of a Jewish commonwealth in the Promised Land, moreover, would end not only the 2,000 year-old insecurity of the Jewish people dispersed throughout the globe, but also the malaise which its anomalous existence imposed upon Gentile hosts. Ultimately, the new state was to serve as a model society for the rest of the world.

The earlier forerunners of modern Zionism fused deeply felt religious values with 19th century European nationalism. As early as 1834, the Serbian rabbi and kabbalist Judah *Alkalai insisted, in *Shema Yisrael*, that the creation of Jewish settlements in the Holy Land and military conquest under the first Messiah would bring the final, miraculous Redeemer. *Darkhei No'am* (1839) and *Minhat Yehuda* (1843) appealed for the Jewish nation's mass return to Eretz Israel, a Jewish Assembly to organize mass settlement there, the revival of Hebrew, payments to the Turkish sultan, and a Jewish army. The Polish talmudist Tzevi Hirsch *Kalischer, in such works as *Derishat Zion* (1862) and *Rishon le-Zion*

(1866), particularly extolled agricultural labor on the ancestral soil: it would invigorate the Jewish yishuv; permit greater Torah study and observance of the relevant commandments of the Bible; and, above all, spur the ultimate Redemption.

Their visions evoked only a limited response. Pietists and those in the Holy Land dependent on charity from abroad ("*haluka*") denounced such schemes as heretical. A few Orthodox leaders, including Rabbis Nathan Friedland, Joseph Natonek, Elias Guttmacher, and Azriel Hildesheimer, did adhere to this revolutionary point of view. The traditionally-inclined masses of Eastern Europe, however, feared any movement which smacked of modernity, while *maskilim* (proponents of Enlightenment) and the assimilated Jews of the West optimistically awaited full equality and acceptance as individuals by an enlightened society.

The stress of Alkalai, Kalischer, and a few kindred souls on a religious-nationalist perspective would later make it considerably easier for the founders of the movement to draw upon the masses of East European Jewry and their attachment to the traditional heritage, linking Zionism to messianic prophecy and the historic destiny of the Jewish people. Self-redemption, the rabbis' sharpest break from standard Jewish attitudes —traditional and Reform alike—, was vital to future Zionist thought. Still, these proto-Zionists accepted Emancipation as an instrument for solving the problems of Jewish status, viewing that process as a means to further Orthodox self-preservation. They therefore gave rise to no movement of historical consequence. The same holds true for the major secular pre-Zionist, Moses *Hess.

Hess's *Rome and Jerusalem* (1862), a pioneering work in its analysis of anti-Semitism, the drawbacks of assimilation, and the consequent need for Jewish statehood, anticipates almost every nuance of 20th century Zionist thought. Equally remarkable is the fact that its author, deservedly ranked among the giants of German Socialism, had hitherto espoused Christian eschatology and then Socialism in *The Sacred History of Mankind by a Young Disciple of Spinoza* (1837) and *The European Triarchy* (1841) as essential for the progress of mankind. Hess's faith in the classless society and the perfectability of mankind was shattered by the failed revolutions of 1848 and Hess's subsequent studies in anthropology and anatomy, which convinced the humanitarian Socialist that history produced creative, free "folk types." In his view, Mazzini's liberal nationalism, contrasting with Prussian chauvinism and Russian tyranny, could also liberate Jewry from Papal control and Christian German anti-Semitism. Thus Hess declared: "With the liberation of the Eternal City on the banks of the Tiber, begins the liberation of the Eternal City on the slopes of Moriah."

Jewish life, Hess immediately asserts in *Rome and Jerusalem*, possesses a national character, which is destined to be resurrected with the rest of civilized nations. Assimilation is impossible, particularly in racist Germany. Since the Jewish people alone continues to put forth the demand that a unifying morality should become a daily ideal, its example of an ethical Socialist commonwealth can guide all to the messianic era. The restored Jewish state, founded upon the triumph of productive labor, will become the "moral stay" of the East while sanctifying Western society anew.

Placing Jewry's mission within the broader perspective of world events, Hess gave this cause, ultimately, a wider audience. His eclectic union of Jewish (even Hasidic) tradition with modern secular parlance opened the future possibility, as well, of the broader appeal of Zionism among his own people. Yet his paean to the victory of humanitarianism, his great faith in France, his assumption that monetary compensation or other means would sway the Ottoman Empire to relinquish Palestine—all reflected a progressive idealism without a realistic foundation. East European Jewry, in whom Hess placed his greatest hopes for Jewish nationalism, was oblivious to *Rome and Jerusalem*; the same can be said for contemporary prophets of Socialism and liberalism. The next generation of Jewish intellectuals, confronted by the Russian pogroms of 1881, abandoned Hess's optimistic faith. Rejecting the ideological consensus based on Emancipation and Enlightenment, they made possible the birth of Zionism.

The pogroms which swept across Russia beginning in April, 1881, converted several *maskilim* to Zionism, but none more dramatically than Leo *Pinsker. *Auto-Emancipation!, a Warning to his Kinfolk by a Russian Jew* (1882) expressed the 61-year-old Odessa doctor's prognosis that hopes placed in Emancipation and the amenability of the state had now been proven bankrupt. The savage pogroms, carried out with official sanction while the native intelligentsia kept its silence, proved that Jewish national rehabilitation was the only answer.

This first book in the Zionist canon, only 36 pages in length, called unequivocally for a mass exodus from Europe at once and under Jewish initiative. The "problem of the Jews," their actual physical distress and psychological malaise, demanded a radical alternative to current Jewish life in the Diaspora. Anti-Semitism bore little relationship to education or progress in conventional terms. Rather, "Judeophobia" resulted from the fact that mankind uniquely viewed the homeless Jew as "one of the dead walking among the living." A congress of Jewish notables, Pinsker asserted, had to determine which country was accessible and adapted to satisfy the physical needs of several million Jewish refugees. A stock company would purchase a large piece of land, perhaps Eretz Israel, with a national subscription to follow. The inhospitable nations of Europe could be expected to aid in the departure of the Jews.

This clarion call won few converts in the West, its intended audience, but the Hovevei Zion of Eastern Europe received it enthusiastically. Soon won over to Eretz Israel, which he termed "the precious heritage of our ancestors," the ailing Pinsker tried unsuccessfully to provide leadership to the fledgling movement. At his death in 1891, only twenty-odd settlements had been found4d in Eretz Israel, the movement lacked unity, and the Turkish government decreed a prohibition on further immigration. However, a new Moses, such as the pessimistic physician doubted would arise to guide his people, was also arriving —independently, at Pinsker's conclusions. This Westerner, remarkably ignorant of *Auto-Emancipation!*, would provide the Zionist cause with two ingredients essential for its ultimate success: charisma and international respectability.

Theodor *Herzl elevated Zionism from its comatose state (where it would have been reduced to a narrow philanthropic, emotional cause) into a challenging international issue. The Viennese journalist's contribution in terms of concrete action is readily acknowledged today. Herzl's achievement is equally significant in the realm of thought, most prominently reflected in *The *Jewish State* (1896).

Anti-Semitic excesses in Hungary, Austria, Germany, and France had led this assimilated Jew, as evidence by his play *The New Ghetto* (1894), to rule out both assimilation and conversion as a solution to "the Jewish question." *The Jewish*

State went much further in calling for the restoration of the Jewish State to resolve Jewry's physical distress. In his unequivocally stated view, a company stock venture could consider Argentina or Eretz Israel (the latter, "our ever-memorable historic home," the logical first choice) as the location for a model state. Clearly formulated on principles of social justice—a portrait more fully developed in Herzl's utopian novel **Altneuland* (1902),—this neutral, "aristocratic republic" would favor the equality of all its citizenry and enjoy the finest fruits of Western civilization.

Herzl's ideological postulates were clear: the Jews are a people, one people; this people needs a state for its own sake and to relieve humankind of the Jewish problem; the establishment of the Jewish commonwealth required international sanction and aid; the creation of Jewish sovereignty depends, at the same time, on the skill of the Jewish people itself ("if you wish it, it is no myth"); and the Jewish state must be an exemplary cooperative society. Ever the optimistic West European liberal, Herzl strikingly argued that Jew-hatred could be understood and then rationally dealt with to the satisfaction of Gentile host nations, even as he simultaneously espoused the radical counter-emphasis on dynamically bestirring the masses' innermost desire and will.

This profound thesis impressed a few Western ideologues like playwright Max Nordau and philosopher Nathan Birnbaum (whose German fortnightly *Self-Emancipation* coined the term "Zionism"), but it was the Jewish majority in Eastern Europe which rallied to Herzl's standard. Herzl's proud, outward bearing inspired a harassed people desperately in need of a leader. His fusion of thought and deed made "Zionism" a commonplace in the capitals of Europe and, most important, in the heart of a stricken nation.

All this hardly sat well with *Ahad Ha-Am, the pen name of Asher Ginsberg, who viewed Herzl's "political Zionism" as an artificial creation by Western Jews having little appreciation of things Jewish. What, after all, was specifically Jewish about the commonwealth described in *The Jewish State* (more appropriately translated as "The State of the Jews") and in *Altneuland*? Rather than focus on the problem of the Jews, which he considered dependent on anti-Semitism and an individual concern, Ahad Ha-Am emphasized "the problem of Judaism." The latter, by contrast, arose because a national culture of millennia faced the danger of losing its essential being upon leaving the ghetto walls. This necessitated a return to Jewry's historic roots—Eretz Israel. To live there unhampered, according to its own principles of divinely-inspired justice, Judaism needed not an independent state *à la* Herzl. It required a good-sized settlement of Jews, Ahad Ha-Am concluded, freely creating a unique life style which would radiate the unique values of Judaism throughout the Diaspora.

The mentor of "spiritual" or "cultural" Zionism consistently maintained an elitist stance. *Lo Zeh ha-Derekh*, the essay which catapulted him to prominence in 1889, criticized Hibbat Zion for hurried, mass settlement efforts which bore little relation to reality. A cautious, systematic approach might overcome the facts of limited cultivable land, inevitable Arab opposition, and Turkish intransigence. Finely styled writings such as "Slavery in Freedom" and "Priest and Prophet" saw Western Jews as not free morally or intellectually, oblivious to the truth that only in Eretz Israel can the necessary fusion of the Hebrew spirit and body take place. "Moses" had to serve as the ideal symbol of humility and morality, elevating nationalism to an ethical ideal which hewed to absolute truth and justice. *Al Parashat Derakhim*, Ahad Ha'Am's anthologized essays (1895-1913), doubted the efficacy of Herzlian diplomacy and its ability to protect the Jewish people against cultural sterility and assimilation.

Aside from the ambiguities and inconsistencies contained in his *oeuvre*, Ahad Ha'Am's skepticism, limited program, and deep pessimism hardly met the anxious reality then pressing on the Jews of Europe. However, disciples such as Chaim *Weizmann, Solomon *Schechter, Judah L. *Magnes, Martin *Buber, and Mordecai *Kaplan contributed much to later Zionist and Jewish ideology. Diaspora communities would increasingly assert their ideological stance vis-a-vis the emerging Jewish state in terms mostly from Ahad Ha-Am's lexicon. And every streak in Zionist thought had to take account of the challenges posed by his uncompromising stand against the apotheosis of statism and the promise of quick redemption.

Ahad Ha-Am's concern for the survival of Jewry's collective culture did not go far enough for a younger group of Jewish intellectuals, given their insistence that Zionism called for the metamorphosis of the individual. In this view, **Galut*, with its petrified religious Orthodoxy, had greatly deformed the character of each Jew. Only a new pattern of national life, rooted in the soil of Eretz Israel, freed from the shackles of tradition and wedded to productive labor, would bring about the necessary regeneration of those who settled there. Diaspora Jewry was doomed to atrophy, such voices insisted, even a spiritual center in Eretz Israel reflecting Ahad Ha-Am's normative secular Judaism could not save it.

This school of "*shelilat ha-gola*" (Negation of the Diaspora) received its most trenchant expression in the writings of Micha Joseph *Berdyczewsky (Bin-Gorion), Joseph Hayim *Brenner, and Jacob *Klatzkin (*see* ISRAEL AND THE DIASPORA). Berdyczewsky's nine volumes of disparate essays championed physical strength, the free exercise of the will, and a delight in nature, as practiced by the earliest Hebrews, revolutionaries, and zealots; short stories and novels (and a two-volume *Me-Otzar ha-Aggada*. 1913) lovingly present the vital, mystical wisdom of the common folk in rebellion against static Orthodox practice. The far more pessimistic Brenner, whose novels mercilessly depict the omnipresent sham of Jewish ghetto life in exile, expressed qualified hope in the Second Aliya's worker settlements, the defenders of Tel Hai, the selfless platoons of the Gedud ha-Avoda (Labor Brigade). Convinced that nationalism had replaced spiritual values as the criterion for Jewish identity, Klatzkin (*Tehumim*, 1914) saw no alternative for eath Jew but the choice between life in Eretz Israel as "a nation like all the nations" and eventual disappearance by intermarriage.

These rebel thinkers, as they progressively moved to a sense of two separate entities—religious or assimilated Jew in exile and secular proletarian Hebrew in Eretz Israel—spoke for an increasingly large and influenctial segment within Zionist ranks. David *Ben-Gurion and other future leaders of the Second Aliya envisaged a homeland that would be antithetical to the alleged bankrupt values of past Jewish tradition; Yehezkel *Kaufman's *Gola ve-Nekhar* (1929–1930) developed a nationalist definition similar in several respects to that of Klatzkin. In an extreme form, a faction that dubbed itself "*Canaanites" divorced itself from Judaism, and denied all relation whatever between the yishuv and Diaspora Jewry. However, the great majority of Israeli opinion has rejected this Zionism of catastrophe, a judgment borne out by events of the last two decades.

The spiritual mentor of the Second Aliya's youthful *halutzim* (pioneers) was Aaron David *Gordon, who, in word and deed, embodied these pioneers' idealistic aspirations for regeneration by labor in Eretz Israel. A mystic whose tombstone is fittingly inscribed "*Oved ha-Adam veha-Teva*" (The servant of man and nature). Gordon insisted that physical labor will enable man to rediscover the unity and purpose of the cosmos. Returning to work on the soil of ancient Israel, the Jew would again give full expression to his inner nature and simultaneously, experience that undefined but continous internality of his people. In Eretz Israel, where people and land are organically bound through the generations, a genuine renewal of the individual and the Jewish nation will occur. By creating itself according to the moral law—the essence of Judaism—the yishuv would also set the example of the ideal humanity. Ethical responsibility for all human beings would ultimately ensue.

In such essays as "Human Nation (Man-Nation)" and "Nationalism and Socialism,." this middle-aged intellectual argued that the nation is the "primal force", created by nature as the bridge between the cosmos and an organically united community of individuals. The collective entity known as Israel is the active agent of God's word, with each Jew and the Jewish nation as a whole dedicated to redemption of self and of all life. While, therefore, the Jew—who creates more with the soil of Eretz Israel—has natural rights to the Promised Land, he must treat the Arab indigenous population with humanity and ethical principles on the highest plane.

Gordon's philosophical construct is surely utopian when advocating "the power of truth" to meet the rising Arab nationalist movement, or opposing aggressive class activism to establish a self-reliant Jewish labor community in Eretz Israel. At the same time, the pioneering element in the Zionist movement took heart from his personal example, while he reminded fellow halutzim of the importance of those traditional values which had sustained Jewish life in exile, and that a purely secular nationalism would destroy "our national essence down to its very roots." Finally, his absolute faith helped provide an ethical spark for the secular majority of the yishuv, a spark which Zionism must continue to maintain if it is to survive and grow in a meaningful way.

Where Gordon insisted on an individualist "religion of labor" in Eretz Israel, Nachman *Syrkin believed that a synthesis of European socialism and Jewish nationalism was mandatory to resolve the so-called "Jewish question." The first theoretician of *Socialist Zionism, Syrkin advocated both the organized exodus of the Jewish masses to their own territory and the participation of the majority of Jews, who could not be evacuated soon from a troubled Europe, in the Russian revolutionary cause. His early treatises, *Reflections on the Philosophy of History* (1896) and *Sensation and Idea* (1903), stressed the role of faith and ideas in history, along with the conscious intervention of the individual to bring progress. These general views reinforced Syrkin's particular stance on Jewish matters, first articulated in *Die Judenfrage und der sozialistische Judenstaat* (1898).

The eternal tension between Jew and Gentile, begins *Die Judenfrage*, derives from the Jewish people's loss of national independence. Currently, all classes, contending for power, unite in attacking their common scapegoat: the Jew. Only a classless society in Eretz Israel, with land organized in industrial and agricultural communes of about 10,000-strong each, could save the impoverished masses from economic pressure and anti-Semitism. The Jews there, representing freedom of conscience and the prophetic ideal of universal morality, will "redeem the world" which had crucified Jesus. This update of Hess's ethical Socialism, echoing the French Zionist Bernard Lazare, was soon expanded to advocate participation in the Russian revolutionary movement (*Manifesto to the Jewish Youth*, 1901).

Syrkin's dualistic, seemingly contradictory, conception, which he preached for some thirty years, put him outside the mainstream. Zionists, revolutionaries, and Simon Dubnow's Diaspora nationalists alike opposed his "two-field" concept; the Jews of America, where Syrkin lived during World War I, were reluctant for some time to embrace his class-conscious nationalism. Yet the majority of the Palestinian labor parties adhered to his program of Socialist constructivism after his death, as witnessed by the kibbutz movement and the other voluntary collective institutions established in Eretz Israel. His disciple, Berl *Katznelson, became the dominant theoretician of Mapai; in David Ben-Gurion, Syrkin's expressed hopes for progressive man within the biblical spirit, Israel to be an "*Or la-Goyim*" (a light to the nations), found its epitomization.

Ber *Borochov, operating from the determinist base of Marxist ideology, disparaged this humanitarian Socialism. His pamphlet *The National Question and the Class Struggle* (1905) championed the workers as the only ones aiming at the practical liberation of the nation as a whole and at assuming a "healthy class structure and a sound class struggle." A year later, "Our Platform" insisted that only with a "strategic base" could the Jewish masses expand their narrow labor front and organize against economic exploiters. Their concentration in Eretz Israel to accomplish this end Borochov termed a "stychic process," an inevitable development which would also help attain national-political (but not territorial) autonomy in the Diaspora.

The dialectic materialism of Borochov's original formulation offered no room for the vital aspect of individual will, as Syrkin had argued, or for Zionism's mystical elements. Nor did the Jewish and Arab proletariat in Palestine hew to his "stychic" process. Still, Borochovism provided confidence for thousands of Jewish youth, particularly in Russia, seeking a theory of Zionism based on the premises of Marxist writ. His rigid intellectual synthesis, which also eschewed cooperation with clerical and bourgeois elements, attracted ardent souls otherwise open to Communist and especially Bundist appeals.

In time, Borochov's contact with American Jews during World War I, as well as his observation of the common fate of world Jewry in exile, led to a greater personal appreciation of the role of ideological motivation in solving the Jewish problem. Articles in *Der Yidisher Kemfer* and elsewhere now applauded cooperative settlement in Eretz Israel, a land no longer to be merely a strategic base for the proletariat's class struggle, but a home for all Jews.

"Eretz Israel in Our Program and Tactics," Borochov's last address to the Third All-Russian Po'ale Zion convention a few months before his death in December, 1917, pressed for Eretz Israel as a Jewish home. His direct heirs—the Mapam party, the Kibbutz Artzi, and Kibbutz ha-Me'uhad movements—understood that a people's will had to bring a state into being and then sustain it. At the same time, shorn of its profound, however illogical, mystical element, Zionism is, as the forever agnostic Borochov came to realize, unthinkable.

A small minority especially took this latter view, disagreeing with the predominating school of Zionist thought that the Jewish people could be restructured by resort to contemporary Western liberalism, nationalism, or Socialism, and thus end the unique Jewish problem. Such thoroughly secular responses to modernity, argued these religious Zionists, denied the very essence of Judaism. Their own emphasis on a biblically-rooted sense of "chosenness," the Divine covenant with one historical community realized in the Torah and Eretz Israel, led them to the conclusion that the establishment of a Jewish state forthwith, in the land promised the Patriarchs, was an acting out of the Lord's will. Return to Zion en masse, as Alkalai and Kalischer had posited decades earlier, in conjunction with traditional religious doctrine would hasten the coming of the Messiah.

In such volumes as *Or Hadash al-Tziyon* (1902) and *Sheni ha-Me'orot* (1913), Yitzhak Ya'akov *Reines openly challenged the reigning Orthodox opposition to Zionism, seeing the new movement as God's method for bringing about His people's national restoration and of returning Judiasm to its former spiritual glory. The acknowledged leader of the Mizrachi religious wing within the World Zionist Organization, as well as head of the first modern yeshiva in Eastern Europe, this talmudist averred that Jewry's historic destiny can only be fulfilled in that Promised Land where Torah principles can be nurtured and developed. The Jewish people will then demonstrate that nationalism, instead of being a chauvinistic lust for physical power, is a sacred concept enhanced by religious standards and ethical goals.

Avraham Yitzhak Ha-Kohen *Kook brought to Jewish thought, and to the understanding of Jewish nationalism in particular, a unique mystical dimension. Already as a young rabbi in Latvia, Kook wrote the essay "The Mission of Israel and its Nationhood" (1900), which accepted Zionism as a Divine phenomenon for restoring Jews to the full sense of being rooted in God's world: acceptance of His Torah follows. Only on the holy soil of Eretz Israel, the first Ashkenazi chief rabbi of Palestine later asserted, could the Children of Israel be illuminated by the radiance of the Holy Spirit. There they could synthesize the sacred and profane ("the not-yet holy"), thereby leading mankind, as Yehuda Halevi had postulated long ago, in the task of cosmic return to holiness. *Orot* (1941), *Orot Teshuva* (1924), *Orot ha-Kodesh* (1937), Kook's rapturous poetry, letters, and commentary on the prayer-book—all rooted in kabbalist thought—envisioned renewal of that "sacred connection" between Jewry ("itself Mosaic tradition from Sinai") and Eretz Israel as essential for attaining the messianic age of universal harmony.

Reines and Kook, in their respective fashions, left an indelible legacy on Zinist development. Mizrachi, Ha-Kibbutz ha-Dati, B'nai Akiva, Gush Emunim, modern Orthodox education in Israel and in the United States, are but some manifestations of their impact. By rendering the traditional aspiration for "*reishit tzemihat ge'ulatenu*" (the beginning of the growth of our Redemption) compatible with secular elements, they also facilitated cooperation with the nonobservant majority in Eretz Israel and elsewhere. Kook's poetic mysticism, which saw the selfless dedication of the atheistic chalutzim as also reviving the Divine spark in the national soul of the Jewish people, gave the Zionist effort a firmer sense of worth and fulfillment. And, by giving the nationalist aspects of the Jewish religion vastly greater emphasis than had been assigned to them by Jewish thinkers heretofore, he, more than any other individual, vitalized Jewish tradition and gave it universal import in the modern world.

First to press for the World Zionist Organization's open declaration of its final objective was Vladimir *Jabotinsky, leader of those Revisionist Zionists who demanded "a Jewish State within its historic boundaries." Immediate Jewish control and with it unlimited mass immigration, so as to secure a Jewish majority on both sides of the Jordan River, were deemed essential. The energies of both the Jewish labor and bourgeois classes are necessary for the creation of a Jewish majority, Jabotinsky emphasized. Considering themselves the legitimate heirs of Herzl, in opposition to the "practical" Zionist establishment, Jabotinsky and his followers called for bold diplomatic negotiation to solve Jewry's plight in rational fashion. An army, he argued (much as he had crusaded in Allied circles for the Jewish Legion to help liberate Palestine from Turkish rule during World War I), would help bring order and pride to currently formless Diaspora Jews, as well as reap military and diplomatic objectives. The masses of Eastern Europe, Jabotinsky announced at the first New Zionist Organization rebel congress in 1935, had to be evacuated from "the onrush of lava" threatening them; international sponsorship, he told the Peel Commission two years later, should accomplish this in light of the Jewish people's unique history of persecution. *The Jewish War Front* (1940), published in the year of Jabotinsky's death, called for transferring to Eretz Israel the first million Jews within the first year after the German defeat.

In numerous essays, the Revisionists' charismatic leader applauded Mazzini's notion that the fatherland represented the highest ideal in the world, next to the unfettered individual. Races which maintained their originality in a dynamic manner are to be welcomed, since authentic cultures emphasize the primacy of the specific—but not superior—national experience. The Jews were to be praised for rejecting alien influences, but, in what Jabotinsky termed "this wolfish battle of all against all," defenseless Jewry had to understand that survival demanded activist strength rather than biblically-taught tolerance and compassion. Discipline ably welds the mass into a collective whole; still, freedom of choice and expression must prevail, democracy coming closest to the messianic vision (in the words of his *Autobiography*) of "a glorious anarchic kingdom."

This stormy petrel might be faulted on various grounds: his tendency to glorify power, reflected well in his novel *Samson the Nazirite* (1926), even as he derided the "commufascist" doctrine of totalitarianism; an opponent's disdain for the Socialist halutzim; his excessive liberal confidence in enlightened diplomacy and (until the mid-1930s) in the identity of Zionist and imperial British interests as expressions of European civilization.

On the fundamental issue, however, the future of Jewry's heartland in Eastern Europe, history has proven Jabotinsky correct. While downplaying the Nazi threat, he, almost alone among the Zionist leaders, sensed that what he termed the "zone of Jewish distress" in Eastern and Central Europe was headed for some form of disaster unless there would be a timely transfer of masses of Jews from those countries to Eretz Israel. And given adamant Arab opposition (respectfully analyzed in his 1923 essay "The Iron

Wall"), Jabotinsky clearly saw the only solution to be a Jewish majority quickly, with a formidable army in an independent Jewish state. Betar, the Irgun Tzeva'i Leumi, and Herut—the last led since 1949 by close disciple Menachem Begin—all owed their *raison d'être* to his philosophical construct. As it turned out in ways beyond the ken of even Jabotinsky, Adolf Hitler's fanatical determination and the Allies' indifferent response to Jewry's unparalleled tragedy in World War II proved one of history's bitterest ironies: the Jews of Europe, many of whom fervently dreamed the dream of Zion, did not live to see its realization.

The creation of the State of Israel in 1948, merely three years after World War II, put an official stamp on the Zionist revolution. For the first time in almost 2,000 years, the Jewish people could lay claim, like other ethnic entities, to a national identity in its own country. Zionist ideology played a crucial part in this outcome, giving the Jewish masses of Europe and the settlers of the yishuv, to quote Yaakov Talmon, "the dignity of a hard-pressed nation on the march." Then, too, the institutions and communal villages of Eretz Israel vindicated not only the practical Zionists and the halutzim, but also thinkers like Hess and Borochov, Gordon and Kook. In addition, the Holocaust had provided the ultimate, tragic confirmation of Zionist theory, which had consistently argued that stateless Jewry remained the universal outsider, and that sovereign power, consequently, was the *sine qua non* for physical survival. Zionism thus captured the broadest spectrum of Jewish loyalties, appearing as a synthesis between traditional themes of national redemption and the challenging prospects of modernity.

Four decades later it can be said that Zionism is a half-way revolution. The Jewish state's diverse achievements in this brief time, especially the resettlement of some 1,700,000 immigrants from over 100 countries, and the widespread commitment of world Jewry to Israel, are impressive realities. At the same time, other realities intrude. "Normalization" has neither guaranteed its citizens security nor weakened worldwide anti-Semitism; Diaspora communities remain where they are while young Israelis increasingly leave their homeland; the tensions of Jew vs. Arab and religion vs. secularism have hardly disappeared.

The emphasis of the Pinsker-Herzl-Nordau-Jabotinsky school on "the problem of the Jews" correctly understood the first priority: the rescue of a downtrodden Jewry from the external danger of anti-Semitism. The underlying optimism regarding this problem's solution then led neo-messianists like Syrkin to urge an inner transformation of the Jewish masses along more productive lines. But the internationally sanctioned commonwealth, once established, necessitated the preservation of Jewry's particular identity. Those ideologists who focused on "the problem of Judaism" provide the essential reminder that even a secularized Jewish state could never be "like all the nations." Events have certainly overtaken some aspects of classical Zionist thought, and the prospects for meaningful Jewish continuity give more than a little cause for concern. Yet the experience of the Jews has never conformed to reasonable expectation. Is the reborn State of Israel, then, somehow to be consigned outside the mysterious process to which Jewish destiny has been subject for centuries? The issue is not closed. New theoreticians of Zionism and of the Jewish experience, called to grapple with both "chosenness" and the modern temper, will contribute to its resolution.

M.N. PENKOWER

ZIONIST WORLD UNIONS. The Zionist World Unions (ZWU) are the successors to the *Separate Unions which had legally ceased to exist as a consequence of the promulgation in 1960 of the present Constitution of the WZO. They were recognized as members of the WZO and defined in the amended Article 3 of the Constitution as follows: "Zionist organizations which represent a special ideological point of view within the WZO, have branches in at least 5 countries, and are represented by Congress groupings;" the last clause meaning that they had at least 12 delegates at the previous Congress. The main difference between ZWU and the former Separate Unions is that every member of a territorial branch of a ZWU is to be a member of the Zionist Federation of the country concerned, while this had not been the case in regard to the Separate Unions, and in some countries, they had no connection at all with the Zionist Territorial Organization. On the other hand a Federation must not refuse the admission to its ranks of a territorial branch of a ZWU and conversely such branch is to be affiliated with the Territorial Zionist Federation. Since 1973, the following ZWU's have been in existence and recognized as members of the WZO:

Union of General Zionists
Herut ha-Tzohar
Zionist Labor Movement
Confederation of United Zionists
Mizrachi Ha-Po'el ha-Mizrachi
Mapam
Artzenu

WIZO, though not participating in Congress elections, is also recognized as a ZWU.

The constitutional status of the ZWU's is not as clearly defined and circumscribed as that of the other members of the WZO, the Zionist Federations and the international Jewish bodies, but their actual position is as virtual power centers, strongly influencing the stand taken in votes cast by members of the Executive and the Zionist General Council, the majority of whom have been designated by the ZWU's. On the other hand, the trend for depoliticization of the WZO, expressed in particular by the admission of international Jewish bodies as members of the WZO, has somewhat weakened their position.

A. ZWERGBAUM

ZIONISTS-REVISIONISTS. *See* REVISIONISTS.

ZION MULE CORPS. Jewish auxiliary unit of the British Army formed in 1915. After the outbreak of World War I in 1914, the Turkish authorities expelled from Palestine many thousands of Jews who were not Ottoman subjects. They then went to Egypt. The British administration of Egypt quartered the great majority of them in Alexandria. Vladimir *Jabotinsky, who was in Egypt at the time, communicated to Joseph *Trumpeldor, who had come to Alexandria from Palestine, his idea of organizing a Jewish Legion to fight alongside the British forces against the Turks in Palestine. Trumpeldor enthusiastically agreed with this proposal, and the two men organized a Legion Committee which, in March, 1915, began to recruit volunteers among the Palestinian exiles.

Many Jews were eager to join such a military unit. When the project was submitted to Gen. John Maxwell, commander of the British forces in Egypt, however, he said that army regulations forbade him to enlist foreign nationals as fighting troops. Moreover, he could not promise that the volunteers would be sent to Palestine, for he knew that the British were not then planning an offensive in Palestine. Maxwell suggested that the volunteers form an auxiliary unit in the army to carry provisions and ammunition to the frontline troops in some other sector of the Turkish front. Jabotinsky, the other members of the recruiting committee, and the volunteers all were greatly disappointed and inclined to reject any offer by which the Jewish volunteers would serve as a transport corps only and be employed on a non-Palestinian front. Subsequently the committee was dissolved.

Trumpeldor, on the other hand, wanted to accept the British offer. He argued that there was nothing demeaning in being employed on transport duty; carrying ammunition to the frontline, he said, required no less courage than firing a rifle. In order to get the Turks to leave Palestine, they would have to be defeated, and it made no difference whether one fought them in Palestine or elsewhere.

Trumpeldor helped Col. John Henry *Patterson, who had come to Alexandria from Cairo, to induce the Palestinian exiles to volunteer for the proposed Mule Corps. Most of the volunteers were Palestinian Jews, but there were also some Egyptian Jews. The volunteers were trained and equipped in Egypt; they adopted the Magen David (Shield of David) as their badge. Commands at the training camp were given mostly in Hebrew but occasionally also in English.

On 17 April 1915, the Zion Mule Corps embarked for the battlefront at Gallipoli. The officer in command was Colonel Patterson, who was assisted by British and Jewish officers, including Trumpeldor. The corps performed vitally needed services in carrying food and ammunition to the troops in the frontlines. On occasion its men also participated in the fighting.

In the summer of 1915 Patterson and Trumpeldor returned to Egypt to recruit additional volunteers. They did this with the help of Jewish community leaders. Patterson was in command of the corps until November, 1915, when he was taken ill and was succeeded by Trumpeldor.

With the withdrawal of the Allied forces from Gallipoli at the end of 1915, the Zion Mule Corps was declared disbanded and brought back to Egypt. Despite the pleas of Trumpeldor and his men to be permitted to remain together and prepare for the battle in Palestine, the corps was officially dissolved in the spring of 1916. During the corps' existence 650 men served in it, 562 of them on the Gallipoli front. They suffered 8 dead and 55 wounded.

About 150 of the men of the Zion Mule Corps were accepted in the British Army and were sent to London, where about half of them formed a platoon in the 20th London Regiment. This platoon later formed a nucleus of instructors for the *Jewish Legion, which was formed in 1917.

T. PRESCHEL

ZIPPER, GERSHON. Galician Zionist leader (b. Monastyriska, Galicia, Austria, 1868; d. Lvov, Poland, 1920). Zipper was active in the pre-Herzlian Zionist group Zion in Lvov and played a leading role in spreading Jewish national and Hibbat Zion ideas in Galicia. In 1892 he helped found *Przyszlosc* (The Future), the first national-Jewish periodical in the Polish language. In 1896, soon after the appearance of Herzl's *Jewish State*, he wrote to Herzl, pledging him the support of Galician Jewry.

Subsequently, Zipper became one of the influential figures in the Galician Zionist movement. In 1912, after visiting Eretz Israel, he devoted himself to raising funds for a building for the Hebrew High School in Jerusalem and collected 100,000 francs. In World War I he led the Zionist Organization of Eastern Galicia and founded *Chwila*, the first Zionist daily in the Polish language.

ZISSU, ABRAHAM LEIB, Romanian Zionist leader, writer, journalist, and thinker (b. Piatra Neamtz, Moldavia, 1888; d. Tel Aviv, 1956). He came from a family of Habad hasidim. Although obliged to support his family from an early age, he commenced public activity in his home town in 1908, as cofounder of the Hebrew monthly *Ha-Mekitz* together with writer and historian Menahem Mendel Braunstein (Mibashan), and also contributed to periodicals in Yiddish.

From 1910 Zissu campaigned against anti-Semitism in Romanian student circles. After World War I, he joined the struggle to obtain civil rights for the Jews of Romania and at the same time vigorously combated assimilationist trends among the Jews.

In 1919 he created the first Jewish daily in Romanian, *Mantuirea* (Redemption), which appeared for about two years.

From 1928 to 1941 he engaged principally in political and literary writing. The war brought him to underground Zionist activity, and he spent two months in a political prison camp as a result of his struggle against the Jewish Center (the Romanian *Judenrat*). In early 1944 he became the chairman of the Zionist Executive and the Palestine Office, representing the Jewish Agency in Romania. He worked unstintingly to save Jews and to organize the "illegal" immigration during the critical period 1944–1945. On the eve of the liberation from the Nazis (23 August 1944) he participated in the organization of self-defense by the pioneer Zionist underground.

After the liberation Zissu served as chairman of the Zionist Organization, Jewish Agency representative, chairman of the Romanian delegation to the World Jewish Congress, and organizer of the *Beriha* via Romania. He republished *Mantuirea* and revived the activity of the Jewish Party, fighting for the restoration of the rights of the Jews in Romania.

In 1946 he resigned from all his public offices. In 1950 he was arrested, together with the heads of the Zionist movement, charged with undermining the security of the country, and sentenced to life imprisonment. He was released four years later, and immigrated to Israel in 1956, where he died a few months later. In addition to scores of articles, Zissu's writings include plays and belles-lettres such as: *The Heretic of the Neamtz Monastery, Confession of a Chandelier*, and *Samson and the new Dagon*.

He was widely considered as the spiritual leader of the Zionists in Romania. He had a decisive influence in the consolidation of Zionist ideology among most of the Romanian Zionist leaders between the two world wars despite the fact that he belonged to no faction in the Zionist movement.

E. OFIR

ZITRON, SHEMUEL LEIB. Hebrew author (b. Minsk, Russia, 1860; d. Vilna, Poland, 1930). Zitron lived alternately in Russia and Poland, spending the final decades of his life in Vilna. He attended the yeshiva of Volozhin; later, he pursued secular studies and studied also at the rabbinical seminary in Breslau. It was in Breslau, in 1877, that he began his rich literary career, writing in both Hebrew and Yiddish.

Zitron was active in *Kibbutz Nidhei Yisrael*, a Hovevei Zion society in Minsk, and in the general Hovevei Zion and Zionist movement, especially as a publicist. In 1884 he published a Hebrew translation of Leo Pinsker's *Autoemancipation*. Zitron was on the editorial board of *Ha-Zeman* (1909–14) and from 1911 until his death he wrote a column in *Ha-Olam* on the history of the Hebrew press.

His Hebrew books include a history of the Hibbat Zion movement (1919), written at the request of the Odessa Committee; a book about the key figures in the Zionist movement (1921); a work on Herzl (1921); one on the creators of modern Hebrew literature (1922); and a biographical dictionary of Zionism (*Leksikon Tziyoni*, 1923). These works are valuable because of their wealth of material and the author's personal knowledge of the men and events he describes. Zitron was one of the Hebrew translators of the abridged edition of Heinrich Graetz's *History of the Jews*. He also wrote a number of short stories.

ZLATOPOLSKY, HILLEL. Zionist leader in Russia, and patron of Hebrew cultural institutions (b. Kremenchug, Ukraine, Russia, 1868; d. Paris, 1932). Zlatopolsky grew up in a hasidic environment. After his marriage he moved to Kiev, where he operated a sugar refinery. A prominent Hovev Zion, he became an early adherent of political Zionism and was in charge of the finances of the Russian Zionist Organization. At the Seventh Zionist Congress (1905) he was elected a member of the Greater Actions Committee. He was also an active leader in cultural affairs. He helped found various Hebrew educational and cultural institutions in Kiev and was an ardent supporter of Hebrew periodicals and literary ventures throughout Russia, from *Ha-Shiloah* to *Ha-Am*. Until the Bolsheviks came to power in November, 1917, his home was a center of Hebrew literary and educational activity.

After the revolution Zlatopolsky left Russia and lived mainly in Paris. With Isaac Naiditsch, he helped formulate the philosophy of the *Keren ha-Yesod. He contributed to the Hebrew press articles and feuilletons, some of which were published in book form. His remains were reinterred in Palestine in 1933. G. KRESSEL

ZLOCISTI, THEODOR. Physician and early Zionist (b. Borchestowa, near Danzig, Germany, 1874; d. Haifa, 1943). Zlocisti studied and practiced medicine in Berlin. In 1921 he settled in Palestine, first residing in Tel Aviv where he was a member of the municipal council, and later moving to Haifa.

In 1895 Zlocisti, with Heinrich Loewe, Shemarya Levin, and Leo Motzkin, founded the Jewish Students' Association in Berlin. He joined Herzl soon after the latter's appearance on the Jewish scene and was a delegate to the First (1897) and subsequent Zionist Congresses. During World War I he served as head of the German Red Cross mission in Constantinople and, through his connections with the German Army Staff, tried to persuade the Turkish authorities to abstain from persecuting the Jewish population of Palestine.

Zlocisti made the life and work of Moses Hess his subject of major interest. He wrote a biography of Hess and published his writings. In addition, he wrote poems (published in two volumes) and translated Yiddish poetry into German.

ZOA. *See* ZIONIST ORGANIZATION OF AMERICA.

ZOLLSCHAN, IGNATZ. Anthropologist and Zionist thinker (b. Erlach, Austria, 1877; d. London, 1948). Zollschan studied medicine in Vienna. He settled in Carlsbad and soon was in the midst of a scholarly fight against racial anti-Semitism. After the publication of his book *Das Rassenproblem* (The Race Problem, 1910), he reported to the 10th Zionist Congress in 1911 on the proceedings of the Universal Race Congress in London, which he had attended. In 1933 he sent a memorandum to the 18th Zionist Congress on a plan of action against "scientific" anti-Semitism.

In his work *Revision des jüdischen Nationalismus* (Revision of Jewish Nationalism, 1919), Zollschan rejected Jewish national minority rights in the Diaspora and, consequently, opposed Jewish national political activities. He was one of the founders of the Binyan ha-Aretz group, which demanded exclusive concentration by Zionists on the upbuilding of Palestine. The main concerns of the Jewish people, he wrote, should be the defense of their honor, the struggle against assimilation, and the rebuilding of Palestine. J. FRAENKEL

ZOLOTKOFF, LEON. Newspaper editor, lawyer, and Zionist (b. Vilna, Russia, 1865; d. Long Island, N.Y., 1938). Zolotkoff studied in Vilna and attended the Sorbonne in Paris. He lived for some time in London, where he was active in the Jewish labor movement. Zolotkoff settled in the United States in 1888, received a law degree in Chicago, and practiced law for some time.

Zolotkoff edited the *Courier*, a Yiddish weekly that later became a daily, and *Keren Or* (Ray of Light), a short-lived Hebrew monthly. He was one of the organizers of the Chicago Zionist Organization in 1897, and the same year he helped found the Knights of Zion order in Chicago, of which he became Grand Master. At the First Annual Conference of American Zionists (New York, 1898), Zolotkoff represented eight Zionist groups in Chicago and delivered an important speech. At the 2nd Zionist Congress (1898), to which he was a delegate, he was elected to the Organization Committee. Zolotkoff was a delegate also to several subsequent Congresses. He helped found, and was first editor of, a number of Yiddish and Anglo-Jewish periodicals.

ZONDEK. Family of physicians and researchers.

Bernhard Zondek (b. Wronke, Germany, 1891; d. New York, 1966) received a doctorate in medicine from the University of Berlin in 1919 and served on the staff of the gynecological clinic at Berlin's Charité Hospital until 1929. Zondek was a lecturer (1923–26) and associate professor (1926–33) of gynecology and obstetrics at the University of Berlin, and from 1929 to 1933 he headed the department of gynecology and obstetrics at Berlin-Spandau Hospital. With Dr. Paul Aschheim he developed the Aschheim-

Zondek test to determine pregnancy in the first month.

Forced to flee from Germany when Hitler came to power, Zondek was a member of the Institute of Biochemistry at the University of Stockholm from 1933 until 1934, when he moved to Palestine. Joining the faculty of the Hebrew University of Jerusalem, he served as professor of gynecology and obstetrics at the Hadassah-University Hospital.

A member of the Israel Academy of Sciences and Humanities and of many international professional societies, Zondek was the author of numerous works in his field. He received the Israel Prize (1958).

Hermann Zondek, his brother (b. Wronke, Germany, 1887; d. Jerusalem, 1979), studied at the universities of Göttingen and Freiburg, receiving a doctorate in medicine from the University of Berlin in 1912. He was a lecturer (from 1919) and associate professor (from 1921) at the Friedrich Wilhelm University in Berlin. From 1914–1926 he was head of the internal medicine department at Charité University Hospital in Berlin. In 1926 he became director of the Municipal Hospital Am Urban in Berlin. Forced to flee from Germany when Hitler came to power, he served briefly (1933) on the staff of the Victoria Memorial Jewish Hospital in Manchester, England, and the following year moved to Palestine.

From 1934 to 1959 Zondek was director of the department of internal medicine at the Bikur Holim Hospital in Jerusalem. He was a visiting professor at the Hebrew University of Jerusalem, honorary president of the Advisory Council of the Israel Medical Association, president of the Jerusalem Academy of Medicine, and a member of the Israel Academy of Sciences and Humanities. A member also of several foreign professional societies, he wrote a major work, *Diseases of the Endocrine Glands* (1923; subsequently reedited and expanded in various languages), and numerous papers on diseases of the heart, kidneys, and endocrine system. His memoirs were published in 1982 *Auf festern fusse* (Memoirs of a Jewish Physician).

ZUCKERMAN, BARUCH. Labor Zionist leader (b. Kurenets, Russia, 1887; d. Jerusalem, 1970). While still a yeshiva student, Zuckerman entertained Zionist sympathies, and he was deeply impressed by Herzl's appearance in Vilna in 1903. On his arrival in the United States that year, he immediately became involved in Labor Zionist activities and was one of the founders of the American Po'ale Zion party. In 1905 he went over to the Socialist-Territorialists, remaining with them until his return to Po'ale Zion in 1910.

Zuckerman was soon recognized as the chief exponent of the Labor Zionist movement in the United States, holding high office in it for more than half a century. He edited and contributed to its publications, was the author of most of its pronouncements and the main formulator of its policies. He played a leading role in the foundation of the People's Relief Committee, serving as its executive director from 1915 to 1924. He also had a decisive part in the founding of Farband, the Labor Zionist fraternal order, the Histadrut Campaign, the Jewish Legion of World War I, the American Jewish Congress, and several bodies organized by Po'ale Zion. His wife, Nina, was one of the seven founders of the Pioneer Women.

A member of the Actions Committee of the World Zionist Organization, Zuckerman also served on the Executive of the Jewish Agency and was in charge of its Latin American and Organization Departments from 1948 to 1956. In 1956 he moved to Israel and continued his activities there. His books include a history of the People's Relief Committee and several volumes of memoirs. He also wrote a number of pamphlets.

C.B. SHERMAN

Yizhak Zuckerman.
[Kibbutz Lohamei ha-Geta'ot]

ZUCKERMAN (CUKIERMAN), YIZHAK. A leader of the Warsaw Ghetto uprising (b. Warsaw, 1915; d. Kibbutz Lohamei ha-Geta'ot, 1981). He was one of the four commanders of the Jewish Fighting Organization which offered organized armed resistance to the Nazis from July, 1942. He went on many missions outside the ghetto smuggling assistance into the otherwise closed ghetto via the sewers. He also helped organize a Jewish underground called the Jewish National Council outside of the ghettos to help Jews hiding among the general population.

He took part in the Warsaw Ghetto uprising and the subsequent battles against the Nazis in April, 1943 and survived.

He arrived in Palestine in 1946. With his wife Tzivya *Lubetkin-Zuckerman he was among the founding members of Kibbutz Lohamei ha-Geta'ot.

ZUNSER, ELIAKUM. Yiddish folk poet and singer (b. Vilna, Russia, 1845; d. New York, 1913). Zunser received a traditional education. With the advent of the Hovevei Zion movement he became one of its early adherents. In his poems, some of which he recited at weddings and other festive gatherings, he urged the Jews to settle in Eretz Israel and return to the soil rather than emigrate to the United States. Some of his songs, such as "The Plough," which he translated into Hebrew, were immensely popular. Another song, "Shivat Tziyon" (Return to Zion), was dedicated to the Bilu pioneers. Zunser gave recitals before Hovevei Zion societies in many cities in Russia. In 1889 he went to the United States, where he continued to write nationalist and Zionist poetry.

I. KLAUSNER

TABLE OF ISRAEL LOCALITIES

This table comprises all localities within Israel's pre-1967 borders as well as Jewish settlements beyond them. It is based on the 31 December 1988 list issued by the Israel Bureau of Statistics.

EXPLANATION AND LEGEND

Name: & next to the name of the settlement indicates that it is in the Administered Areas.
@ next to the name, that it is in the Golan Heights.
* next to the name, that it is the subject of an entry in the Encyclopedia.

Affiliation: This shows the countrywide association to which the settlement belongs.

Legend: HI — Hitahdut ha-Ikarim
IH — Ha-Ihud ha-Hakla'i
KA — Kibbutz Artzi ha-Shomer ha-Tza'ir
KD — Kibbutz Dati of Ha-Po'el ha-Mizrachi
MH — Ha-Merkaz ha-Hakla'i
OL — Ha-Oved ha-Le'umi
OTz — Ha-Oved ha-Tzivoni
PAI — Po'alei Agudae Israel
PM — Ha-Po'el ha-Mizrachi moshav movement
Takam — United Kibbutz Movement
TM — Tenu'at ha-Moshavim

Location: N—North; S—South; E—East; W—West; C—Central

Founding Year:
A locality's founding year appears in brackets where the date is that of the rebuilding of an existing settlement after an interval of abandonment.

Municipality, Local Council, Regional Council:
M indicates Municipality; LC, Local Council. Regional Councils are listed by name. These are usually transliterated but some purely geographical names are given in the English form.

Population:
The sign . . indicates that the population figures were not available. The sign — indicates that the place has no permanent inhabitants.

Settlement Form and Observations:
The settlement form indicates besides Israel's unique forms (Kibbutz, Moshav Shitufi, Kehilati = community settlement), towns of over 10,000 inhabitants, and cities with a population exceeding 50,000. Arab localities with less than 10,000 inhabitants are designated "villages," although some have been reclassed recently as "urban localities."
Where the inhabitants are not Jewish, this is indicated, together with the percentages. Where no reference is made to composition, the population is entirely Jewish.
In the Observations column, mention is also made of unusual characteristics of a settlement, or its inhabitants or the circumstances of its foundation. Regular settlements included in the Galilee development project since 1975 are mentioned separately from those which began their existence as *mitzpim.

Name	*Affiliation*	*Region*	*Founding Year*	*Municipality, Local, Regional Council*	*Population 31 Dec. 1988*	*Observations*	*Settlement Form*
Abirim		W. Upper Galilee	1980	Ma'ale Yosef	. .	Founded as Mitzpe	Kehilati
*Abu Ghosh		C. Judean Hills		LC	3,300		Moslem-Arab village
Abu Sinan		W. Upper Galilee		LC	7,130		Arab Village (50% Moslem, 20% Christian, 30% Druze)
Adamit	KA	W. Upper Galilee	1958	Mateh Asher	. .		Kibbutz
Adanim	TM	S. Sharon	1950	S. Sharon	163		Moshav
Aderet	TM	S. Judean Foothills	1961	Mateh Yehuda	353	Adullam project	Moshav
Adi	HI	W. Lower Galilee	1980	Jezreel Valley	322	Founded as Mitzpe	Kehilati

Adirim	TM	Jezreel Valley	1956	Ha-Gilboa	231	Ta'anakh project	Moshav
&Adora	Herut	S. Judean Hills	1984	Hebron Hills	. .		Kehilati
Afek	Takam	Haifa Bay area	1939	Mateh Asher	521	founded as a Tower-and-Stockade settlement	Kibbutz
@Afik	Takam	S. Golan	1967	Golan	267		Kibbutz
*Afikim	Takam	Kinarot Valley	1932	Jordan Valley	1,360		Kibbutz
*Afula		Jezreel Valley	1925	M.	24,500		Town
Agur	TM	S. Judean Foothills	1950	Mateh Yehuda	306		Moshav
Ahi'ezer	PM	C. Coastal Plain	1950	Lod (Lydda) Plain	740		Moshav
Ahihud	TM	W. Upper Galilee	1950	Mateh Asher	445		Moshav
Ahisamakh	TM	S. Sharon	1950	Modi'im	670		Moshav
Ahituv	TM	C. Sharon	1951	Hefer Valley	496		Moshav
Ahuzam	PM	S. Coastal Plain	1950	Lachish	435		Moshav
Ahva	PM	S. Coastal Plain	1976	Be'er Toviya	127		Village
*Akko (Acre)		Akko (Acre)		M.	37,200 (28,750 Jews, 8,450 Arabs [85% Moslems, 15% Christians])		Town
&Alei Zahav	Herut	N. Samaria	1982	Samaria	. .		Kehilati
&Alfei Menashe		N. Samaria	1983	LC	1,910		Urban Locality
*Alma	PM	E. Upper Galilee	1949	Merom ha-Galil	608		Moshav
Almagor	TM	Korazim Region	1961	Jordan Valley	236		Moshav
& Almog	Takam	Dead Sea Region	1977	Pesagot	. .		Kibbutz
&Almon	Amana	N. Judean Hills	1982	Mateh Binyamin	. .		Kehilati
Alon ha-Galil	TM	W. Lower Galilee	1980	Jezreel Valley	. .	Founded as Mitzpe	Moshav
*Alon Shevut		S. Judean Hills	1970	Etzion Bloc	1,450		Rural Locality
Alonei Aba	OTz	W. Lower Galilee	1948	Jezreel Valley	209		Moshav shitufi
@Alonei ha-Bashan	PM	N. Golan	1981	Golan	. .		Moshav shitufi
Alonei Yitzhak		N. Sharon	1949	Menashe	298		Youth village
Alonim	Takam	Jezreel Valley	1938	Jezreel Valley	571	Founded as Tower-and-Stockade	Kibbutz
Aluma		S. Coastal Plain	1965	Shafir	473		Rural center
Alumim	KD	NW Negev	1966	Azata	389		Kibbutz
Alumot	Takam	Kinarot Valley	1941	Jordan Valley	266		Kibbutz
Amasa	Takam	NE Negev	1983	Tamar	. .		Kibbutz
Amatzya	Herut	S. Judean Foothills	1955	Lachish	131	Lachish project	Moshav shitufi
Amiad	Takam	E. Upper Galilee	1946	Upper Galilee	400		Kibbutz
Amikam	Herut	Irron Hills	1950	Alona	176		Moshav
Aminadav	TM	C. Judean Hills	1950	Mateh Yehuda	379		Moshav
Ami'oz	TM	NW Negev	1957	Eshkol	239		Moshav
*Amir	KA	Huleh Valley	1939	Upper Galilee	529	Founded as Tower-and-Stockade	Kibbutz
*Amirim	TM	E. Upper Galilee	1950	Merom ha-Galil	308	Vegetarians and Naturalists	Moshav

Amka	TM	Akko (Acre) Plain	1949	Mateh Asher	466		Moshav
Amnun	OTz	Korazim Region	1983	Jordan Valley	..	Founded as Mitzpe	Moshav
Amuka	—	E. Upper Galilee	1980	Merom ha-Galil	..	Founded as Mitzpe	Kehilati
@Ani'am	TM	C. Golan	1978	Golan	..		Moshav
Ara		Irron Valley			2,090		Moslem-Arab village
Araba		E. Lower Galilee			11,500		Moslem-Arab town
*Arad		NE Negev	1961	LC	13,700		Urban locality
Aramshe		NW Upper Galilee		Mateh Asher	558	Settled Bedouin	Moslem-Arab village
Arara		Irron Valley		LC	7,020		Moslem-Arab village
*Arbel	TM	E. Lower Galilee	1949	Lower Galilee	280		Moshav
& Argaman	Herut	Lower Jordan Valley	1968	Arevot ha-Yarden	..		Moshav
&Ari'el		W. Samaria	1978	LC	6,160		Urban locality
Aro'er		Negev Hills		Masos	2,760	Settled Bedouin	Moslem-Arab urban locality
Arugot	TM	S. Coastal Plain	1949	Be'er Toviya	382		Moshav
Aseret		S. Coastal Plain	1954	Gederot	697		Rural center
Ashalim	Takam	SW Negev	1976	Ramat ha-Negev	109		Moshav shitufi
*Ashdod		S. Coastal Plain	1955	M.	74,700		City
*Ashdot Ya'akov/(Ihud)	Takam	Kinarot Valley	1933	Jordan Valley	570		Kibbutz
*Ashdot Ya'akov/ (Me'uhad)	Takam	Kinarot Valley	1933	Jordan Valley	498		Kibbutz
Asherat	TM	Akko (Acre) Plain	1983	Mateh Asher	..	1977/83 Galilee project	Kehilati
Ashhar	TM	W. Upper Galilee	1986	Misgav	..	Founded as Mitzpe	Kehilati
*Ashkelon		S. Coastal Plain	1948	M.	56,800		City
Aspar	PAI	C. Judea	1983	Etzion Bloc	..		Kehilati
&Ateret	Amana	N. Judean Hills	1981	Mateh Binyamin	..		Kehilati
Atlit (Athlit)		Carmel Coast	1904	LC	2,650		Urban locality
Avdon	TM	W. Upper Galilee	1952	Ma'aleh Yosef	399		Moshav
Avi'el	Herut	Menashe Hills	1949	Alona	269		Moshav
Avi'ezer	PM	C. Judean Foothills	1958	Mateh Yehuda	207	Settlers from Cochin (India)	Moshav
Avigedor	TM	S. Coastal Plain	1950	Be'er Toviya	388	Founded by demobilized soldiers	Moshav
*Avihayil	TM	C. Sharon	1932	Hefer Valley	770		Moshav
Avital	TM	Jezreel Valley	1953	Jezreel Valley	412	Ta'anakh project	Moshav
Avivim	TM	E. Upper Galilee	1960	Mateh Asher	338		Moshav
@Avnei Etan	PM	S. Golan	1978	Golan	..		Moshav
Avtalyon	IH	W. Lower Galilee	1987	Misgav	..		Moshav shitufi
Ayanot		C. Coastal Plain	1930	Gan Raveh	290		Farm School
*Ayelet ha-Shahar	Takam	Huleh Valley	1918	Upper Galilee	951		Kibbutz

Azarya	TM	C. Judean Foothills	1949	Gezer	476		Moshav
*Azor		C. Coastal Plain	1948	LC	6,940		Urban locality
Azri'el	PM	S. Sharon	1951	Lev ha-Sharon	388		Moshav
Azrikam	TM	S. Coastal Plain	1950	Be'er Toviya	499		Moshav
Bahan	Takam	Central Sharon	1953	Hefer Valley	323		Kibbutz
Balfouriya	TM	Jezreel Valley	1922	Jezreel Valley	233		Moshav
Baqa al-Gharbiya		NE Sharon		LC	13,600		Moslem-Arab town
Barak	TM	Jezreel Valley	1956	Ha-Gilboa	265	Ta'anakh project	Moshav
*Bar'am	KA	E. Upper Galilee	1949	Ha-Galil ha-Elyon	436		Kibbutz
Bareket	PM	N. Judean Foothills	1952	Modi'im	522		Moshav
Bar Giyora	Herut	C. Judean Hills	1950	Mateh Yehuda	285	Youth hostel, field school	Moshav
Barka'i	KA	Menashe Hills	1949	Menashe	492		Kibbutz
Barta'a		Menashe Hills			1,480	The village is on the pre-1967 border; the figure is of Israeli citizens	Moslem-Arab village
Bar Yohai		E. Upper Galilee	1979	Merom ha-Galil	85		Industrial center of moshavim
Basmat Tabun		SW Lower Galilee		LC	2,050	Settled by Bedouin	Moslem-Arab urban locality
Batir		C. Judean Hills			. .	Only a small part of the village is within the pre-1967 border	Moslem-Arab village
*Bat Shelomo	HI	Mt. Carmel	1889	Carmel Coast	232		Moshav
*Bat Yam		C. Coastal Plain	1926	M.	133,100		City
Batzera	IH	S. Sharon	1946	Sharon Coast	401		Moshav
&Bedolah	PM	Gaza Strip	1986	Gaza Coast	. .		Moshav
Be'eri	Takam	NW Negev	1946	Eshkol	751	Among the 11 founded in one night	Kibbutz
Be'er Ora		Eilat Hills	1950	Eilot Region		No permanent inhabitants	Gadna youth camp
Be'erot Yitzhak	KD	C. Coastal Plain	1948	Modi'im	409	Transferred from NW Negev	Kibbutz
Be'erotayim	TM	C. Sharon	1949	Hefer Valley	334		Moshav
*Beersheba		N. Negev	(1948)	M.	113,200		City
*Be'er Toviya	TM	S. Coastal Plain	(1930)	Be'er Toviya	651		Moshav
*Be'er Ya'akov		C. Coastal Plain	1907	LC	5,420		Urban locality
Beit Jann		E. Upper Galilee			6,630		Druze village
&Beka'ot	IH	E. Samaria	1972	Arevot ha-Yarden	. .		Moshav
Beko'a	TM	C. Judean Foothills	1951	Mateh Yehuda	424		Moshav
Ben Ami	TM	Akko (Acre) Plain	1952	Mateh Asher	316		Moshav
Benaya	TM	S. Coastal Plain	1949	Brenner	347		Moshav
Benei Atarot	TM	C. Coastal Plain	1948	Modi'im	352	Transferred from Atarot in N. Judea	Moshav

&Benei Atzmon	IH	Gaza Strip	1979	Gaza Coast	342		Moshav
Benei Ayish		C. Coastal Plain	1958	LC	910		Rural locality
*Benei Berak		C. Coastal Plain	1924	M.	109,400		City
Benei Darom	PM	S. Coastal Plain	1949	Yavne Region	280	Transferred from Kefar Darom in Gaza Strip	Moshav shitufi
Benei Deror	TM	S. Sharon	1946	Sharon Coast	281		Moshav shitufi
Benei Re'em	PAI	S. Coastal Plain	1949	Nahal Sorek	505		Moshav
Benei Tziyon	TM	S. Sharon	1947	Sharon Coast	377		Moshav
@Benei Yehuda		S. Golan	1972	Golan	512		Kehilati
*Ben Shemen	TM	N. Judean Foothills	(1949)	Modi'im	281		Moshav
*Ben Shemen		N. Judean Foothills	1921	Modi'im	991		Youth village
Ben Zakai	PM	S. Coastal Plain	1950	Yavne Region	474		Moshav
&Berakha		C. Samaria	1983	Samaria	. .		Rural center
Berekhya	TM	S. Coastal Plain	1950	Ashkelon Coast	531		Moshav
*Beror Hayil	Takam	S. Coastal Plain	1948	Sha'ar ha-Negev	664		Kibbutz
Berosh	TM	W. Negev	1953	Benei Shimon	262		Moshav
&Bet Aba	Herut	W. Samaria	1981	Samaria	351		Kehilati
*Bet Alfa	KA	Harod Valley	1922	Ha-Gilboa	832		Kibbutz
Betar Ilit		S. Judean Hills	1985	Etzion Bloc	. .		Urban locality
Bet Arif	TM	N. Judean Foothills	1951	Modi'im	432		Moshav
&Bet Arye	Herut	N. Judean Hills	1981	Mateh Binyamin	677		Kehilati
Bet Berl		S. Sharon	1947	S. Sharon	329		Study center
Bet Dagan		C. Coastal Plain	1948	LC	2,170		Urban locality
&Bet El (Bethel)	Amana	N. Judean Hills	1977	Mateh Binyamin	1,080		Kehilati
&Bet El B		N. Judean Hills	1978	Mateh Binyamin	620		Yeshiva
Bet Elazari	TM	C. Coastal Plain	1948	Brenner	413		Moshav
Bet Ezra	TM	S. Coastal Plain	1950	Be'er Toviya	454		Moshav
Bet Gamli'el	PM	S. Coastal Plain	1949	Yavne Region	387		Moshav
*Bet Guvrin	Takam	S. Judean Foothills	1949	Yoav	229		Kibbutz
*Bet ha-Arava		Lower Jordan Valley	1980	Megilot	. .		Transitional
Bet ha-Emek	Takam	Akko (Acre) Plain	1949	Mateh Asher	510		Kibbutz
Bet ha-Gadi	PM	NW Negev	1949	Azata	435		Moshav
Bet ha-Levi	TM	C. Sharon	1945	Hefer Valley	252		Moshav
Bet ha-Shita	Takam	Harod Valley	1935	Ha-Gilboa	1,220		Kibbutz
Bet Hanan	TM	C. Coastal Plain	1930	Gan Raveh	442		Moshav
Bet Hananya	TM	N. Sharon	1950	Carmel Coast	251		Moshav
Bet Hashmonai		C. Judean Foothills	1972	Gezer	79		Rural center
Bet Herut	TM	C Sharon	1933	Hefer Valley	374		Moshav
Bet Hillel	TM	Huleh Valley	1940	Mevo'ot ha-Hermon	310		Moshav
Bet Hilkiya	PAI	S. Coastal Plain	1953	Nahal Sorek	280		Moshav
&Bet Horon	Amana	N. Judean Hills	1977	Mateh Binyamin	325		Kehilati
Bet Kama	KA	N. Negev	1949	Benei Shimon	375		Kibbutz

Bet Keshet	Takam	E. Lower Galilee	1944	Lower Galilee	329	First settlement of Palmah	Kibbutz
Bet Lehem ha-Gelilit	TM	W. Lower Galilee	1948	Jezreel Valley	312		Moshav
Bet Me'ir	PM	C. Judean Hills	1950	Mateh Yehuda	365		Moshav
Bet Nehemya	OTz	C. Judean Foothills	1950	Modi'im	402		Moshav
Bet Nekofa	TM	C. Judean Hills	1949	Mateh Yehuda	279		Moshav
Bet Nir	KA	S. Coastal Plain	1955	Yo'av	339		Kibbutz
Bet Oved	TM	C. Coastal Plain	1933	Gan Raveh	279		Moshav
Bet Oren	Takam	Mt. Carmel	1939	Carmel Coast	143	Founded as Tower-and-Stockade	Kibbutz
Bet Raban		S. Coastal Plain	1946	Yavne Region	597		Educational institution
Bet Rimon	KD	E. Lower Galilee	1977	Lower Galilee	127	1977/83 Galilee project	Kibbutz
*Bet She'an (Beth Shean)		Bet She'an Valley	(1948)	LC	13,100		Town
*Bet She'arim	TM	Jezreel Valley	1936	Jezreel Valley	383		Moshav
*Bet Shemesh		C. Judean Foothills	1950	LC	14,200		Town
Bet Shikma	TM	S. Coastal Plain	1950	Ashkelon Coast	447	Moshav	
Bet Tzevi		Carmel Coast	1953	Carmel Coast	400		Educational institution
Bet Uzi'el	PM	C. Coastal Plain	1956	Gezer	265		Moshav
Bet Yanai	IH	C. Sharon	1933	Hefer Valley	307		Moshav
Bet Yehoshu'a	OTz	S. Sharon	1938	Sharon Coast	365	Founded as Tower-and-Stockade	Moshav
Bet Yitzhak-Sha'ar Hefer	IH	C. Sharon	1940	Hefer Valley	1,340		Moshav
Bet Yosef	TM	Bet She'an Valley	1937	Bet She'an Valley	320	Founded as Tower-and-Stockade	Moshav
Bet Za'id		Jezreel Valley	1943	Jezreel Valley	162		Rural locality
Bet Zayit	TM	C. Judean Hills	1949	Mateh Yehuda	800		Moshav
Bet Zera	KA	Kinarot Valley	1926	Jordan Valley	698		Kibbutz
Betzet	TM	Akko (Acre) Plain	1949	Mateh Asher	303		Moshav
Bikura		Bet She'an Valley	1985	Bet She'an Valley			Transitory
Bina		E. Upper Galilee		LC	4,360		Moslem-Arab village
*Binyamina		N. Sharon	1922	LC	3,210		Urban locality
Bir al-Maksur		W. Lower Galilee			4,040	Settled Bedouin	Moslem-Arab village
*Biriya		E. Upper Galilee	1945	Merom ha-Galil	445		Rural locality
Bitan Aharon	IH	C. Sharon	1936	Hefer Valley	353		Moshav
Bit-ha	TM	NW Negev	1950	Merhavim	616		Moshav
Bitzaron	TM	S. Coastal Plain	1935	Be'er Toviya	514		Moshav
Biyada		Akko (Acre) Plain		Mateh Asher	219		Moslem-Arab village
Bu'eina		E. Lower Galilee			4,200		Moslem-Arab village

@Buq'ata		N. Golan		LC	3,530		Druze village
Burgeta	TM	C. Sharon	1949	Hefer Valley	441		Moshav
Bustan ha-Galil	IH	Akko (Acre) Plain	1948	Mateh Asher	551		Moshav
*Caesarea (Kesarya)		N. Sharon	1977		810		Rural locality
Daburiya		E. Lower Galilee		LC	4,970		Moslem-Arab urban locality
*Dafna	Takam	Huleh Valley	1939	Upper Galilee	640	Founded as Tower-and-Stockade	Kibbutz
Daliya	KA	Menashe Hills	1939	Megiddo	849	Founded as Tower-and-Stockade	Kibbutz
Daliyat al-Karmil		Mount Carmel		LC	9,780	97% Druze, 3% Moslem	Druze village
Dalton	PM	E. Upper Galilee	1950	Merom ha-Galil	592		Moshav
*Dan	KA	Huleh Valley	1939	Upper Galilee	554	Founded as Tower-and-Stockade	Kibbutz
*Deganya A	Takam	Kinarot Valley	1909	Jordan Valley	590		Kibbutz
*Deganya B	Takam	Kinarot Valley	1920	Jordan Valley	657		Kibbutz
Dehi		E. Lower Galilee			330		Moslem-Arab Village
Deir al-Assad		W. Lower Galilee		LC	5,140		Moslem-Arab Village
Deir Hana		E. Lower Galilee		LC	5,080		Moslem-Arab Village
Dekel	TM	NW Negev	1982	Eshkol	216	Transferred from Yamit area	Moshav
Devira	KA	N. Negev	1951	Benei Shimon	410		Kibbutz
Devora	TM	Jezreel Valley	1956	Ha-Gilboa	244	Ta'anakh project	Moshav
*Dimona		Negev hills	1955	M.	25,000		Town
Dishon	OTz	E. Upper Galilee	1953	Mevo'ot Hermon	341		Moshav
&Dolev	Amana	N. Judean Hills	1983	Mateh Binyamin	. .		Kehilati
*Dor	TM	Carmel Coast	1949	Carmel Coast	206		Moshav
*Dorot	Takam	NW Negev	1941	Sha'ar ha-Negev	567		Kibbutz
Dovev	TM	E. Upper Galilee	1963	Merom ha-Galil	347		Moshav
Dovrat	Takam	Jezreel Valley	1946	Jezreel Valley	313		Kibbutz
Efal		C. Coastal Plain	1950	Efal (Ono)	999		Aged People's Home
Efal		C. Coastal Plain	1950	Efal (Ono)	. .		Seminary
*&Efrata		S. Judean Hills	1980	LC	1,760		Town
Eilabun		E. Lower Galilee			2,780		Arab urban locality (75% Christian, 25% Moslem)
*Eilat (Elath)		Eilat Hills	1951	M.	24,700		Town
Ein al-Asad		W. Upper Galilee		Merom ha-Galil	511		Druze village
Ein a-Sahla		Irron Hills			757		Moslem-Arab village

Ein Mahil		W. Upper Galilee		LC	6,180		Moslem-Arab urban locality
Ein Naquba		C. Judean Hills		Mateh Yehuda	681		Moslem-Arab village
Ein Qinya		N. Golan		LC	1,340		Druze village
Ein Rafa		C. Judean Hills		Mateh Yehuda	319		Moslem-Arab village
&Elazar	PM	S. Judean Hills	1975	Etzion Bloc	..		Moshav shitufi
&Elei Sinai	Amana	Gaza Strip	1982	Gaza Coast	..	Transferred from Yamit Region	Kehilati
&Eli	Amana	N. Judean Hills	1984	Mateh Binyamin	..		Kehilati
@Eli-Al	TM	S. Golan	1968	Golan	212		Moshav
Elifaz	KA	Eilat Hills	1982	Elot Region	..		Kibbutz
Elifelet	TM	E. Upper Galilee	1949	Upper Galilee	333		Moshav
Elishama	TM	S. Sharon	1951	S. Sharon	411		Moshav
&Elkana		W. Samaria	1977	LC	1,690		Urban locality
Elkosh	TM	W. Upper Galilee	1949	Ma'ale Yosef	243		Moshav
Elon	KA	W. Upper Galilee	1938	Mateh Asher	744	Founded as Tower-and-Stockade	Kibbutz
&Elon Moreh	Amana	C. Samaria	1979	Samaria	773		Kehilati
Elot	Takam	S. Arava Valley	1962	Elot Region	370		Kibbutz
El-Rom	Takam	N. Golan	1971	Golan	232		Kibbutz
Elyakhin		C. Sharon	1950	LC	1,590		Rural locality
Elyakim		Menashe Hills	1949	Megiddo	397		Rural locality
Elyashiv	HI	C. Sharon	1933	Hefer Valley	426		Moshav
Emunim	TM	S. Coastal Plain	1950	Be'er Toviya	459		Moshav
Enat	Takam	S. Sharon	(1925)	S. Sharon	453	See Givat ha-Shelosha	Kibbutz
&Enav	Amana	W. Samaria	1981	Samaria	..		Kehilati
En Ayala	TM	Carmel Coast	1949	Carmel Coast	327		Moshav
En Dor	KA	E. Lower Galilee	1948	Jezreel Valley	598		Kibbutz
*En Gedi	Takam	Dead Sea Shore	1953	Tamar	625		Kibbutz
*En Gev	Takam	Kinarot Valley	1937	Jordan Valley	589		Kibbutz
En ha-Besor	TM	NW Negev	1982	Eshkol	399		Moshav
En ha-Emek		Menashe Hills	1944	Megiddo	411		Rural locality
*En Harod-Ihud	Takam	Harod Valley	1921	Ha-Gilboa	725		Kibbutz
*En Harod-Me'uhad	Takam	Harod Valley	1921	Ha-Gilboa	854		Kibbutz
En Hatzeva		N. Arava Valley	1970	Tamar	..		Transitional
En ha-Horesh	KA	C. Sharon	1931	Hefer Valley	823		Kibbutz
En ha-Mifratz	KA	Haifa Bay area	1938	Mateh Asher	750	Founded as Tower-and-Stockade	Kibbutz
En ha-Natziv	KD	Bet She'an Valley	1946	Bet She'an Valley	595		Kibbutz
En ha-Shelosha	OTz	NW Negev	1950	Eshkol	358		Kibbutz
*En ha-Shofet	KA	Menashe Hills	1937	Megiddo	837		Kibbutz
*En Hod		Mt. Carmel	1954	Carmel Coast	255		Artists' village
En Iron	TM	N. Sharon	1934	Menashe	246		Moshav
En Karmel	Takam	Carmel Coast	1947	Carmel Coast	446		Kibbutz

En Kerem Farm School		C. Judean Hills	1952	Mateh Yehuda	178		Farm School
En Sarid		S. Sharon	1950	Lev ha-Sharon	458		Rural locality
*En Shemer	KA	N. Sharon	(1927)	Menashe	643		Kibbutz
En Tamar	IH	N. Arava Valley	1982	Tamar	. .		Moshav
*En Tzurim	KD	S. Coastal Plain	1949	Shafir	547	Transferred from Etzion Bloc	Kibbutz
En Vered	TM	S. Sharon	1930	Lev ha-Sharon	573	Hityashvut ha-Elef scheme	Moshav
En Ya'akov	TM	W. Upper Galilee	1950	Ma'ale Yosef	335		Moshav
*En Yahav	TM	C. Arava Valley	1951	C. Arava Valley	500		Moshav
@En Zivan	Takam	N. Golan	1968	Golan	221		Kibbutz
Erez	Takam	S. Coastal Plain	1949	Sha'ar ha-Negev	441		Kibbutz
Eshbol	TM	W. Negev	1955	Merhavim	289		Moshav
Eshel ha-Nasi		W. Negev	1952	Merhavim	378		Farm school
Eshta'ol	TM	C. Judean Foothills	1949	Mateh Yehuda	418	Also JNF forest tree nursery	Moshav
Etan	PM	S. Coastal Plain	1955	Shafir	370	Lachish project	Moshav
Etanim		C. Judean Hills	1952	Mateh Yehuda	264		Hospital
&Etz Efrayim		W. Samaria	1985	Samaria	. .		Rural locality
Even Menahem	TM	W. Upper Galilee	1960	Ma'ale Yosef	285		Moshav
Even Sapir	TM	C. Judean Hills	1950	Mateh Yehuda	450		Moshav
Even Shemu'el	TM	S. Coastal Plain	1956	Shafir	521	Lachish project	Rural center
Even Yehuda		S. Sharon	1932	LC	6,060		Urban locality
Even Yitzhak (Gal'ed)	Takam	Menashe Hills	1945	Megiddo	348		Kibbutz
Evron	KA	Akko (Acre) Plain	1945	Mateh Asher	667		Kibbutz
Eyal	Takam	SE Sharon	1949	S. Sharon	353		Kibbutz
Ezer		S. Coastal Plain	1966	Be'er Toviya	92		Rural center
Ezuz		N. Negev Hills	1984	Ramat ha-Negev	. .		Transitory
Fasuta		W. Upper Galilee		LC	2,250		Arab Christian (Greek-Catholic) village
Fureidis		Carmel Coast		LC	6,410		Moslem-Arab urban locality
Ga'ash	KA	S. Sharon	1951	Sharon Coast	549		Kibbutz
Ga'aton	KA	W. Upper Galilee	1948	Mateh Asher	461		Kibbutz
Gadot	Takam	Huleh Valley	1949	Upper Galilee	483	See Mishmar ha-Yarden	Kibbutz
&Gadid	PM	Gaza Strip	1982	Gaza Coast	248		Moshav
Gadish	TM	Jezreel Valley	1956	Ha-Gilboa	263	Ta'anakh project	Moshav
Gal'on	KA	S. Coastal Plain	1946	Yo'av	442	Among the 11 founded in one night	Kibbutz
Gamzu	PAI	C. Judean Foothills	1950	Modi'im	423		Moshav
Ganei Am	OTz	S. Sharon	1934	S. Sharon	205		Moshav
Ganei Hadar		C. Coastal Plain	1958	Gezer	22		Rural locality
&Ganei Tal	PM	Gaza Strip	1979	Gaza Coast	325		Moshav
Ganei Tikva		C. Coastal Plain	1953	LC	8,030		Urban locality
Ganei Yehuda	IH	S. Sharon	1951	S. Sharon	719		Moshav
Ganei Yohanan	TM	C. Coastal Plain	1950	Gezer	283		Moshav
Gan ha-Darom	IH	S. Coastal Plain	1953	Gederot	310		Moshav

Gan ha-Shomeron	IH	N. Sharon	1934	Menashe	397		Moshav
Gan Hayim	TM	S. Sharon	1935	S. Sharon	301		Moshav
&Ganim	OL	N. Samaria	1983	Samaria	. .		Kehilati
Gan Ner	Merkaz Hakla'i	Harod Valley	1987	Ha-Gilboa	. .		Kehilati
&Gan Or	PM	Gaza Strip	1983	Gaza Coast	. .		Moshav
Ganot	IH	C. Coastal Plain	1953	Lod Valley	378		Moshav
Gan Shelomo (Kevutzat Schiller)	Takam	C. Coastal Plain	1927	Brenner	393		Kibbutz
*Gan Shemu'el	KA	N. Sharon	1913	Menashe	1,110		Kibbutz
Gan Sorek	TM	C. Coastal Plain	1950	Gan Raveh	133		Moshav
Gan Yavne		S. Coastal Plain	1931	LC	3,180		Urban locality
Gan Yoshiya	TM	C. Sharon	1949	Hefer Valley	302		Moshav
Gat	KA	S. Coastal Plain	1941	Yo'av	541		Kibbutz
Gat Rimon		S. Sharon	1926	S. Sharon	147		Rural locality
Gazit	KA	E. Lower Galilee	1948	Jezreel Valley	622		Kibbutz
Ge'a	TM	S. Coastal Plain	1949	Ashkelon Coast	455		Moshav
Ge'alya	TM	S. Coastal Plain	1948	Gan Raveh	425		Moshav
*Gedera		S. Coastal Plain	1884	LC	7,190		Urban locality
Gefen	PM	C. Judean Foothills	1955	Mateh Yehuda	289		Moshav
Gelil Yam	Takam	S. Sharon	1943	Sharon Coast	328		Kibbutz
Gerofit	Takam	S. Arava Valley	1963	Elot Region	242		Kibbutz
*Gesher	Takam	Bet She'an Valley	1939	Bet She'an Valley	555	Founded as Tower-and-Stockade	Kibbutz
*Gesher ha-Ziv	Takam	Akko (Acre) Plain	1949	Mateh Asher	470		Kibbutz
@Geshur	KA	S. Golan	1971	Golan	. .		Kibbutz
Ge'ulei Teman (Moshav)	PM	C. Sharon	1947	Hefer Valley	233	First moshav of Yemenite Jews	Moshav
Ge'ulei Teman (Shikun)		C. Sharon	1947	Hefer Valley	84		Rural locality
Ge'ulim	TM	C. Sharon	1945	Hefer Valley	472		Moshav
*Geva	Takam	Harod Valley	1921	Ha-Gilboa	572		Kibbutz
&Geva Binyamin	Amana	N. Judea	1984	Mateh Binyamin	. .		Kehilati
Geva Karmel	TM	Carmel Coast	1949	Carmel Coast	419		Moshav
Gevar'am	Takam	S. Coastal Plain	1942	Ashkelon Coast	260		Kibbutz
*Gevat	Takam	Jezreel Valley	1926	Jezreel Valley	780		Kibbutz
Gevim	Takam	S. Coastal Plain	1947	Sha'ar ha-Negev	383		Kibbutz
*Gevulot	KA	NW. Negev	1943	Eshkol	292		Kibbutz
*Gezer	Takam	C. Judean Foothills	1945	Gezer	271		Kibbutz
@Ghajar		Mt. Hermon Region		LC	1,180		Arab (Nuzairi) village
Gibeton		C. Coastal Plain	1933	Brenner	189		Moshav
Gidona		Harod Valley	1949	Ha-Gilboa	114		Rural locality
Gilat	TM	W. Negev	1949	Merhavim	582		Moshav
&Gilgal	Takam	Lower Jordan Valley	1970	Arevot ha-Yarden	. .		Kibbutz

Gilon	Herut	W. Lower Galilee	1980	Misgav	. .	Founded as Mitzpe	Kehilati
Ginaton	TM	C. Coastal Plain	1949	Modi'im	381		Moshav
*Ginegar	Takam	Jezreel Valley	1922	Jezreel Valley	509		Kibbutz
*Ginosar	Takam	Kinarot Valley	1937	Jordan Valley	717	Founded as Tower-and-Stockade	Kibbutz
Ginot Hadar		S. Sharon	1964	Lev ha-Sharon	80		Rural locality
Gita	TM	W. Upper Galilee	1980	Ma'ale Yosef	. .	Founded as Mitzpe	Kehilati
&Gitit	Herut	E. Samaria	1973	Arevot ha-Yarden	. .		Moshav
*Givat Ada		N. Sharon	1903	LC	1,270		Rural locality
*Gitvatayim		C. Coastal Plain	1922	M	45,600		Town
*Givat Brenner	Takam	C. Coastal Plain	1928	Brenner	1,450		Kibbutz
*Givat ha-Shelosha	Takam	C. Coastal Plain	1925	S. Sharon	448		Kibbutz
Givat Ela	MH	W. Lower Galilee	1988	Jezreel Valley	. .		Kehilati
*Givat Hayim (Ihud)	Takam	Central Sharon	1932	Hefer Valley	887		Kibbutz
*Givat Hayim (Me'uhad)	Takam	Central Sharon	1932	Hefer Valley	1,090		Kibbutz
Givat Hen	TM	S. Sharon	1933	S. Sharon	293		Moshav
Givati	TM	S. Coastal Plain	1950	Be'er Toviya	424		Moshav
Givat Ko'ah	TM	C. Coastal Plain	1950	Modi'im	373		Moshav
Givat Nili	Herut	N. Sharon	1953	Alona	253		Moshav
Givat Oz	KA	Jezreel Valley	1949	Megiddo	501		Kibbutz
Givat Shapira	IH	C. Sharon	1958	Hefer Valley	103		Moshav
Givat Shemesh		C. Judean Hills	1954	Mateh Yehuda	111		Educational institution
Givat Shemu'el		C. Coastal Plain	1942	LC	9,960		Urban locality
Givat Ye'arim	TM	C. Judean Hills	1950	Mateh Yehuda	455		Moshav
Givat Yeshayahu	OTz	C. Judean Foothills	1958	Mateh Yehuda	228	Adullam project	Moshav
@Givat Yo'av	TM	S. Golan	1968	Golan	357		Moshav
&Givat Ze'ev		C. Judean Hills	1983	LC	3,760		Urban locality
Givolim	PM	NW Negev	1952	Azata	247		Moshav
&Givon ha-Hadasha	Amana	N. Judean Hills	1980	Mateh Binyamin	411		Kehilati
Gizo		C. Judean Foothills	1968	Mateh Yehuda	73		Rural locality
Gonen	Takam	Huleh Valley	1951	Upper Galilee	437		Kibbutz
Goren	TM	W. Upper Galilee	1950	Ma'ale Yosef	391		Moshav
Gorenot ha-Galil		W. Upper Galilee	1980	Ma'ale Yosef	. .		Industrial center of moshavim
Ha-Bonim	Takam	Carmel Coast	1949	Carmel Coast	206		Moshav shitufi
Hadar Am	IH	C. Sharon	1933	Hefer Valley	304		Moshav
*Hadera		N. Sharon	1890	M	41,600		Town
Hadid	PM	N. Judean Foothills	1950	Modi'im	459		Moshav
*Hafetz Hayim	PAI	S. Coastal Plain	1944	Nahal Sorek	461		Kibbutz
Haggai	Amana	S. Judean Hills	1984	Hebron Hills	. .		Kehilati

Hagor	TM	S. Sharon	1949	S. Sharon	387		Moshav
Ha-Gosherim	Takam	Huleh Valley	1948	Upper Galilee	505		Kibbutz
Ha-Hoterim	Takam	Carmel Coast	1948	Carmel Coast	605		Kibbutz
*Haifa		Mt. Carmel		M	222,600	90% Jews 6% Arab Christians, 3% Moslems, the rest Bahai and others	City
Hajajra		C. Lower Galilee		Jezreel Valley	571		Moslem-Arab village
&Halamish	Amana	N. Judean Hills	1977	Mateh Binyamin	634		Kehilati
Halutz	TM	W. Upper Galilee	1985	Misgav	..	Founded as Mitzpe	Kehilati
Hamadya	Takam	Bet She'an Valley	1942	Bet She'an Valley	478		Kibbutz
Hamam		Kinarot Valley			730		Arab village
Ha-Ma'pil	KA	C. Coast	1945	Hefer Valley	609		Kibbutz
&Hamra	IH	E. Samaria	1971	Arevot ha-Yarden	...		Moshav
Hani'el	TM	Central Sharon	1950	Hefer Valley	326		Moshav
Hanita	Takam	W. Upper Galilee	1938	Mateh Asher	666	Founded as Tower-and-Stockade	Kibbutz
Ha-Ogen	KA	C. Sharon	1945	Hefer Valley	645		Kibbutz
Ha-On	Takam	Kinarot Valley	1949	Jordan Valley	222		Kibbutz
&Har Adar		N. Judean Hills	1986	Mateh	626		Kehilati
Hararit	HI	W. Lower Galilee	1980	Misgav	..	Founded as Mitzpe	Kehilati
Harashim		W. Upper Galilee	1980	Ma'ale Yosef	..	Founded as Mitzpe	Kehilati
Harduf	Takam	W. Lower Galilee	1980	Jezreel Valley	..	Founded as Mitzpe	Kibbutz
Harel	KA	C. Judean Foothills	1948	Mateh Yehuda	100		Kibbutz
&Har Gilo		S. Judean Hills	1972	Etzion Bloc	298		Rural locality and Field School
Harish		Irron Hills	1982	Menashe	..		Transitory
Harutzim		S. Sharon	1951	Sharon Coast	607		Rural locality
&Hashmona'im		N. Judean Foothills	1985	Mateh Binyamin	..		Rural locality
Ha-Solelim	OTz	W. Lower Galilee	1949	Jezreel Valley	248		Kibbutz
@Haspin		S. Golan	1973	Golan	548	Yeshiva	Kehilati
Hatzav	TM	S. Coastal Plain	1949	Be'er Toviya	642		Moshav
Hatzerim	Takam	W. Negev	1946	Benei Shimon	696	Among the eleven founded in one night	Kibbutz
Hatzeva	TM	C. Arava Valley	1965	C. Arava Valley	482		Moshav
Hatzor Ashdod	KA	S. Coastal Plain	1937	Be'er Toviya	611		Kibbutz
Hatzor ha-Gelilit		Huleh Valley	1953	LC	6,850		Urban locality
Havat Shalem		C. Judean Foothills	1949	Gezer			Transitory
Havatzelet ha-Sharon	IH	C. Sharon	1950	Hefer Valley	366		Moshav
Ha-Yogev	TM	Jezreel Valley	1949	Jezreel Valley	528		Moshav

Hazon	PM	E. Lower Galilee	1969	Merom ha-Galil	465		Moshav
*Ha-Zore'a	KA	Jezreel Valley	1936	Megiddo	1,030		Kibbutz
Ha-Zore'im	PM	E. Lower Galilee	1939	Lower Galilee	416		Moshav
Heletz	TM	S. Coastal Plain	1950	Ashkelon Coast	385		Moshav
Hemed	PM	C. Coastal Plain	1950	Lod Valley	380		Moshav
Hemdat		Lower Jordan Valley	1980	Arevot ha-Yarden	. .		Transitory
Heftzi-Bah	Takam	Harod Valley	1922	Ha-Gilboa	518		Kibbutz
Herev le-Et	IH	C. Sharon	1947	Hefer Valley	425		Moshav
&Hermesh	Herut	N. Samaria	1982	Samaria	. .		Kehilati
Herut	TM	S. Sharon	1930	Lev ha-Sharon	441		Moshav
*Herzliya		S. Sharon	1924	M	71,600		City
Hever		Jezreel Valley	1958		—	Ta'anakh project	Transitory
Hibat Zion	HI	C. Sharon	1933	Hefer Valley	340		Moshav
Hila		W. Upper Galilee	1980	Ma'ale Yosef	. .	Founded as Mitzpe	Kehilati
Hilef		Haifa Region			564		Moslem-Arab village
&Hinanit	TM	N. Samaria	1981	Samaria	. .		Kehilati
Hinaton	Takam	W. Lower Galilee	1984	Jezreel Valley	. .	Founded as Mitzpe	Kibbutz
*Hod ha-Sharon		S. Sharon	1924	LC	24,500		Urban locality
Hodiya	TM	S. Coastal Plain	1949	Ashkelon Coast	396		Moshav
Hofit		C. Sharon	1955	Hefer Valley	916		Rural locality
Hogla	TM	C. Sharon	1933	Hefer Valley	233		Moshav
Holit	Takam	NW Negev	1980	Eshkol	. .	Transferred from Yamit area	Kibbutz
*Holon		C. Coastal Plain	1933	M	146,100		City
&Homesh	OL	N. Samaria	1980	Samaria	. .		Kehilati
Horeshim	KA	S. Sharon	1955	S. Sharon	249		Kibbutz
Hosen	Herut	W. Upper Galilee	1949	Ma'ale Yosef	326		Moshav
Hosha'ya	PM	W. Lower Galilee	1981	Jezreel Valley	. .	Founded as Mitzpe	Kehilati
Hukok	Takam	E. Lower Galilee	1945	Jordan Valley	332		Kibbutz
*Hulda	Takam	C. Judean Foothills	(1930)	Gezer	407		Kibbutz
Hulata	Takam	Huleh Valley	1937	Upper Galilee	557		Kibbutz
Hurfeish		W. Upper Galilee		LC	3,360		Druze village
Ibillin		W. Lower Galilee		LC	6,870		Moslem-Arab village
Ibtin		Haifa region		Zevulun	1,060		Moslem-Arab village
Idan	TM	C. Arava Valley	1980	C. Arava	. .		Moshav
Iksal		E. Lower Galilee		LC	6,480		Moslem-Arab village
*Ilaniya	IH	E. Lower Galilee	1902	Lower Galilee	286		Moshav
Ir Ovot	IH	C. Arava	1979	C. Arava	. .		Moshav shitufi
Isfiya		Mt. Carmel		LC	7,240	80% Druze, 16% Christians, 4% Moslems	Druze village

&Itamar	Amana	Central Samaria	1984	Samaria	. .		Kehilati
&Imanuel		W. Samaria	1983	LC	2,280	Strictly Orthodox settlers	Urban locality
Jaljuliya		S. Sharon		LC	3,940		Arab urban locality
Jat		N. Sharon		LC	5,600		Moslem-Arab village
Jat (Galilee)		W. Upper Galilee		C. Galilee	1,090		Druze village
*Jerusalem		C. Judean Hills		M	493,500	(including 353,900 Jews, 139,600 non-Jews)	City
Jisr a-Zarqa		N. Sharon		LC	6,190	Settled Bedouin	Moslem-Arab village
Jish (Gush Halav)		E. Upper Galilee		LC	1,970	70% Maronite Christians, 30% Moslems	Arab village
Judeida		Akko (Acre) Plain		LC	4,840	90% Moslems, 10% Christians	Arab village
Julis		W. Upper Galilee		LC	3,580		Druze village
Ka'abiya-Tabash		W. Lower Galilee		Jezreel Valley	1,410	Bedouin tribe	Moslem-Arab village
*Kabri	Takam	W. Lower Galilee	1949	Mateh Asher	783		Kibbutz
Kabul		W. Lower Galilee		LC	5,730		Moslem-Arab village
Kadarim	Takam	E. Upper Galilee	1980		. .	Founded as Mitzpe	Kibbutz
&Kadim	OL	N. Samaria	1983	Samaria	. .		Kehilati
Kadima		C. Sharon	1933	LC	3,590		Urban locality
*Kaduri		E. Lower Galilee	1931	Lower Galilee	232		Farm school
Kafr Bara		S. Sharon		LC	1,150		Moslem-Arab village
Kafr Kama		E. Lower Galilee		LC	1,950		Circassian (Moslem) village
Kafr Kana		W. Lower Galilee		LC	10,000	85% Moslems, 15% Christians	Arab village
Kafr Manda		W. Lower Galilee		LC	8,180		Moslem-Arab village
Kafr Misr		E. Lower Galilee			1,260		Moslem-Arab village
Kafr Qara		Menashe Hills		LC	8,610		Moslem-Arab village
Kafr Qasim		S. Sharon		LC	9,250		Moslem-Arab village
Kafr Sumei		E. Upper Galilee		C. Galilee	1,490	82% Druze, 18% Christians	Druze village
Kafr Yasif		Akko (Acre) Plain		LC	5,860	52% Christians, 45% Moslems, 3% Druze	Arab village
Kahal	TM	E. Upper Galilee	1980		. .	1977/83 Galilee Project	Moshav
Kalanit	PM	E. Lower Galilee	1981	Merom ha-Galil	. .	1977/83 Galilee Project	Moshav
&Kalya	Takam	Dead Sea Region	1968	Megilot			Kibbutz
Kamon	HI	W. Lower Galilee	1980	Misgav	. .	Founded as Mitzpe	Kehilati
Kanot		S. Coastal Plain	1951	Be'er Toviya	255		School
Karei Deshe		Kinarot Valley	1954	Jordan Valley	—		Farm
Karkom		Kinarot Valley	1985	Jordan Valley	. .		Kehilati

Karmei Yosef		Central Judean Foothills	1984	Gezer	474		Rural locality
&Karmei Tzur	PM	S. Judean Hills	1984	Etzion Bloc	..		Kehilati
&Karmel	Amana	Judean Desert	1981	Mt. Hebron	..		Moshav shitufi
*Karmiel		W. Lower Galilee	1964	M	20,100		Town
Karmiya	KA	S. Coastal Plain	1950	Ashkelon Coast	316		Kibbutz
&Karnei Shomeron		W. Samaria	1978	Samaria	2,930		Urban locality
&Katif	PM	Gaza Strip	1978	Gaza Coast	..		Moshav shitufi
@Katzerin		S. Golan	1977	LC	2,980		Urban locality
Katzir	HI	Irron Hills	1982	Menashe	..		Kehilati
Kaukab al-Hija		W. Lower Galilee		LC	1,880		Moslem-Arab village
&Kedar	Herut	S. Judean Hills	1982	Etzion Bloc	..		Kehilati
Kedma		S. Coastal Plain	1946	Yo'av	70	Among 11 founded in one night	Rural locality
&Kedumim	Amana	W. Samaria	1977	Samaria	1,490		Kehilati
&Kefar Adumim	Amana	Judean Desert	1979	Mateh Binyamin	522		Kehilati
Kefar Ahim	TM	S. Coastal Plain	1949	Be'er Toviya	278		Moshav
Kefar Aviv	IH	S. Coastal Plain	1951	Gederot	372		Moshav
Kefar Avoda		S. Sharon	1942	Lev ha-Sharon	418		Educational institution for criminal youth
Kefar Aza	Takam	S. Coastal Plain	1951	Sha'ar ha-Negev	618		Kibbutz
Kefar Azar	TM	C. Coastal Plain	1932	Efal (Ono)	430		Moshav
*Kefar Barukh	TM	Jezreel Valley	1926	Jezreel Valley	270		Moshav
Kefar Bialik	IH	Haifa Bay area	1934	Zevulun	574		Moshav
Kefar Bilu	TM	C. Coastal Plain	1932	Gezer	509		Moshav
Kefar Bin Nun	IH	C. Judean Foothills	1952	Gezer	294		Moshav
*Kefar Blum	Takam	Huleh Valley	1943	Upper Galilee	681		Kibbutz
Kefar Dani'el	Takam	C. Judean Foothills	1949	Modi'im	188		Moshav shitufi
*Kefar Darom		Gaza Strip	(1970)	Gaza Coast	..		Transitory
&Kefar Etzion	KD	S. Judean Hills	(1967)	Etzion Bloc	466	See Etzion Bloc	Kibbutz
Kefar Galim		Carmel Coast	1952		385		Marine school
Kefar Gidon		Jezreel Valley	1923		142		Rural locality
*Kefar Giladi	Takam	Huleh Valley	1916	Upper Galilee	708		Kibbutz
Kefar Glickson	OTz	N. Sharon	1939	Menashe	395		Kibbutz
*Kefar ha-Horesh	Takam	W. Lower Galilee	1933	Jezreel Valley	487		Kibbutz
*Kefar ha-Makabi	TM	Haifa Bay Area	1936	Zevulun	351		Kibbutz
Kefar ha-Nagid	TM	S. Coastal Plain	1949	Gan Raveh	406		Moshav
*Kefar ha-Nasi	Takam	Huleh Valley	1948	Upper Galilee	614		Kibbutz
Kefar ha-No'ar ha-Dati	PM	Haifa Bay Area	1937	Zevulun	531		Educational institution
Kefar ha-Rif	IH	S. Coastal Plain	1956	Yo'av	244	Lachish project	Moshav
*Kefar ha-Ro'e	PM	C. Sharon	1934	Hefer Valley	961		Moshav and Yeshiva
*Kefar Habad		C. Coastal Plain	1949	Lod (Lydda) Valley	2,980		Urban locality and educational institutions

@Kefar Haruv	Takam	S. Golan	1974	Golan	232		Kibbutz
*Kefar Hasidim A		Haifa Bay Area	1924	Zevulun	399		Moshav
Kefar Hasidim B		Haifa Bay Area	1950	Zevulun	200		Rural locality
Kefar Hayim	TM	C. Sharon	1933	Hefer Valley	418		Moshav
Kefar Hess	TM	S. Sharon	1933		523		Moshav
*Kefar Hitim	TM	E. Lower Galilee	1936	Lower Galilee	252		Moshav shitufi
Kefar Kisch	TM	E. Lower Galilee	1946	Lower Galilee	309		Moshav
Kefar Maimon	PM	W. Negev	1959	Azata	348		Moshav
*Kefar Malal	TM	S. Sharon	1922	S. Sharon	300		Moshav
Kefar Masaryk	KA	Haifa Bay Area	1938	Mateh Asher	669		Kibbutz
*Kefar Menahem	KA	S. Coastal Plain	1937	Yo'av	575	Founded as Tower-and-Stockade	Kibbutz
Kefar Monash	TM	C. Sharon	1946	Hefer Valley	383		Moshav
Kefar Mordekhai	IH	S. Coastal Plain	1950	Gederot	281		Moshav
Kefar Netter		S. Sharon	1939	Sharon Coast	405		Moshav
Kefar Pines	PM	N. Sharon	1933	Menashe	729		Moshav
Kefar Rosenwald (Zarit)	TM	W. Upper Galilee	1967	Ma'ale Yosef	247		Moshav
Kefar Rosh ha-Nikra	Takam	Akko (Acre) Plain	1949	Mateh Asher	590		Kibbutz
Kefar Ruppin	Takam	Bet She'an Valley	1938	Bet She'an Valley	461		Kibbutz
Kefar Rut	TM	N. Judean Foothills	1977	Modi'im	226		Moshav
*Kefar Sava		S. Sharon	1903	M	54,800		City
Kefar Shamai	PM	E. Upper Galilee	1949	Merom ha-Galil	315	Moshav	
*Kefar Shemaryahu		S. Sharon	1937	LC	1,670		Urban locality
Kefar Shemu'el	OTz	C. Judean Foothills	1950	Gezer	323		Moshav
Kefar Silver		S. Coastal Plain	1957	Ashkelon Coast	327		Educational institution
Kefar Syrkin		S. Sharon	1936		685		Rural locality
Kefar Szold	Takam	Huleh Valley	1942	Upper Galilee	528		Kibbutz
&Kefar Tapuah	PM	W. Samaria	1978	Samaria	..		Kehilati
*Kefar Tavor		E. Lower Galilee	1901	LC	904		Rural locality
Kefar Truman	TM	C. Coastal Plain	1949	Modi'im	300		Moshav
*Kefar Uriya	TM	C. Judean Foothills	(1944)	Mateh Yehuda	285		Moshav
Kefar Veradim		W. Upper Galilee	1984		1,010		Rural locality
*Kefar Vitkin	TM	C. Sharon	1933	Hefer Valley	718		Moshav
Kefar Warburg	TM	S. Coastal Plain	1939	Be'er Toviya	602		Moshav
Kefar Yavetz	PM	S. Sharon	1932	Lev ha-Sharon	273		Moshav
*Kefar Yehezkel	TM	Harod Valley	1921	Ha-Gilbo'a	522		Moshav
*Kefar Yehoshu'a	TM	Jezreel Valley	1927	Jezreel Valley	560		Moshav
*Kefar Yona		S. Sharon	1932	LC	4,060		Urban locality
Kefar Zetim	TM	E. Lower Galilee	1950	Lower Galilee	307		Moshav
@Kela		N. Golan	1984	Golan	..		Transitory

Kelahim	IH	W. Negev	1954	Merhavim	292		Moshav
Kelil	IH	W. Upper Galilee	1979	Mateh Asher	. .	Founded as Mitzpe	Kehilati
Keramim	KA	N. Negev	1980	Benei Shimon	. .		Kibbutz
Kerem Ben Zimra	PM	E. Upper Galilee	1949	Merom ha-Galil	293		Moshav
Kerem Maharal	TM	Mt. Carmel	1949	Carmel Coast	319		Moshav
Kerem Shalom	KA	NW Negev	1956	Eshkol	137		Kibbutz
Kerem Yavne	KD	S. Coastal Plain	1963	Yavne Region	290		Yeshiva
Kesalon	IH	C. Judean Hills	1952	Mateh Yehuda	232		Moshav
@Keshet	PM	C. Golan	1974	Golan	326	Naturalists Vegetarians	Moshav shitufi
Ketura	Takam	S. Arava Valley	1970	Elot Region	199		Kibbutz
Kevutzat *Yavne	KD	S. Coastal Plain	1941	Yavne Region	726		Kibbutz
@Kidmat Tzevi	HI	C. Golan	1985	Golan	. .		Moshav
Kidron	TM	S. Coastal Plain	1949	Brenner	696		Moshav
*Kineret (Moshava)		Kinarot Valley	1909	LC	285		Rural locality
*Kineret (Kevutza)	Takam	Kinarot Valley	1908	Jordan Valley	747		Kibbutz
*Kiryat Anavim	Takam	C. Judean Hills	1920	Mateh Yehuda	403		Kibbutz
&Kiryat Arba		S. Judean Hills	1972	LC	3,750	see Hebron	Urban locality
*Kiryat Ata		Haifa Bay area	1925	M	35,500		Town
*Kiryat Bialik		Haifa Bay area	1934	M	32,600		Town
Kiryat Ekron		C. Coastal Plain	1948	LC	4,430		Urban locality
*Kiryat Gat		S. Coastal Plain	1954	M	27,400		Town
*Kiryat Malakhi		S. Coastal Plain	1951	LC	14,200		Town
*Kiryat Motzkin		Haifa Bay area	1934	M	30,000		Town
&Kiryat Netafim	PM	W. Samaria	1983	Samaria	. .		Kehilati
Kiryat Ono		C. Coastal Plain	1939	LC	22,200		Town
Kiryat Shelomo		S. Sharon	1945	Sharon Coast	. .		Transitory
*Kiryat Shemona		Huleh Valley	1950	M	15,400		Town
*Kiryat Tivon		Haifa Bay area	1937	LC	11,600		Town
Kiryat Yam		Haifa Bay area	1941	M	31,800		Town
Kiryat Ye'arim		C. Judean Hills	1952	Mateh Yehuda	260		Educational institution
Kiryat Ye'arim (Telze-Stone)		C. Judean Hills	1975	Mateh Yehuda	1,230		Rural locality Yeshiva
Kishor	KA	W. Upper Galilee	1976	Misgav	. .	included in 1977/1978 Galilee project exclusively industrial	Kibbutz
Kisra		E. Upper Galilee			2,460		Druze village
Kisufim	Takam	NW Negev	1951	Eshkol	408		Kibbutz
&Kokhav ha-Shahar	Amana	N. Judean Hills	1977	Mateh Binyamin	351		Kehilati
Kokhav Micha'el	TM	S. Coastal Plain	1950	Hof Ashkelon	455		Moshav
Kokhav Ya'akov	Amana	N. Judean Hills	1985	Mateh Binyamin	. .		Kehilati
Kokhav Ya'ir		S. Sharon	1981	LC	2,570		Urban locality
*Korazim	HI	E. Upper Galilee (Korazim Region)	1983	Upper Galilee	. .	Founded as Mitzpe	Moshav

Komemiyut		S. Coastal Plain	1950	Shafir	364		Moshav
Koranit	IH	W. Lower Galilee	1982	Misgav	236	1977/83 Galilee project	Moshav shitufi
Kuseifa		NE Negev		Masos	3,860	Settled Bedouin	Moslem-Arab urban locality
Lachish (Lakhish)	TM	S. Judean Foothills	1955	Lachish	306	Lachish project	Moshav
Lahav	KA	N. Negev	1952	Benei Shimon	450		Kibbutz
Lahavot ha-Bashan	KA	Huleh Valley	1945	Upper Galilee	452		Kibbutz
Lahavot Haviva	KA	N. Sharon	1949	Menashe	290		Kibbutz
Lakiye		Beersheba	1988	Benei Shimon	..	Settled Bedouin	Arab village
Lapidot	TM	W. Upper Galilee	1978	Ma'ale Yosef	..	1977/83 Galilee project	Moshav
*Lavi	KD	E. Lower Galilee	1949	Lower Galilee	742		Kibbutz
Lavon	Takam	W. Lower Galilee	1980	Misgav	..	Founded as Mitzpe 1977/83 Galilee project	Kibbutz
Lehavim		N. Negev	1985	Benei Shimon	1,640		Rural locality
Li-On		S. Judean Foothills	1960	Mateh Yehuda	188	Adullam project	Rural center
Liman	TM	Akko (Acre) Plain	1949	Mateh Asher	323		Moshav
Livnim	TM	W. Lower Galilee	1982	Merom ha-Galil	..	1977/83 Galilee project	Moshav
Lod (*Lydda)		C. Coastal Plain	(1948)	M	41,300	thereof 8,400 non-Jews	Town
*Lohamei ha-Geta'ot	Takam	Akko (Acre) Plain	1949	Mateh Asher	497		Kibbutz
Lotan	Takam	S. Arava Valley	1983	Elot Region	..		Kibbutz
Lotem	Takam	W. Lower Galilee	1978	Misgav	..	1977/83 Galilee project	Kibbutz
Luzit	TM	S. Judean Foothills	1955	Mateh Yehuda	271	Adullam project	Moshav
Lydda see Lod							
Ma'agan	Takam	Kinarot Valley	1949	Jordan Valley	336		Kibbutz
Ma'agan Mikha'el	Takam	Carmel Coast	1949	Carmel Coast	1,130		Kibbutz
&Ma'ale Adumim		Judean Desert	1975	LC	11,800	see Jerusalem	Town
&Ma'ale Amos	Herut	Judean Desert	1981	Etzion Bloc	..		Kehilati
&Ma'ale Efrayim		E. Samaria	1970	LC	1,320		Urban locality
@Ma'ale Gamla	TM	S. Golan	1976		231		Moshav
Ma'ale Gilbo'a	KD	Mount Gilboa	1962	Bet She'an Valley	294		Kibbutz
*Ma'ale ha-Hamisha	Takam	C. Judean Hills	1938	Mateh Yehuda	465	Founded as Tower-and-Stockade	Kubbutz
&Ma'ale Levona		S. Samaria	1983	Mateh Binyamin	..		Kehilati
&Ma'ale Mikhmas	Amana	N. Judean Hills	1981	Mateh Binyamin	214		Kehilati
&Ma'ale Shomeron	Herut	W. Samaria	1980	Samaria	..		Kehilati
*Ma'alot-Tarshiha		W. Upper Galilee	1957	LC	8,770	thereof 3,000 non-Jews	Urban locality
Ma'anit	KA	N. Sharon	1942	Menashe	536		Kibbutz
Ma'as		C. Coastal Plain	1935	S. Sharon	558		Moshav

Mabarot	KA	C. Sharon	1933	Hefer Valley	758		Kibbutz
Mabu'im		W. Negev	1958	Merhavim	219		Rural center
Magal	Takam	N. Sharon	1953	Menashe	456		Kibbutz
Ma'galim		NW Negev	1958	Azata	106		Rural center
Magen	KA	NW Negev	1949	Eshkol	390		Kibbutz
Magen Sha'ul	TM	Mt. Gilbo'a	1976	Ha-Gilboa	261		Moshav
Maghar		E. Lower Galilee		LC	12,400	(ca. 45% Druze, 30% Christians, 25% Moslems)	Arab town
Magshimim	IH	C. Coastal Plain	1979	S. Sharon	350		Moshav
Mahanayim	Takam	Huleh Valley	1939	Upper Galilee	443		Kibbutz
Mahane Baldad		N. Arava Valley	1983	C. Arava Valley			Transitory
Mahane Givat Hananya		E. Lower Galilee	1976	Merom ha-Galil			Transitory
Mahane Yativ		Beersheba Region	1979				Transitory
Mahane Yavor		Acre (Akko) Region	1974	Mateh Asher			Transitory
Mahaseya	PM	C. Judean Foothills	1950	Mateh Yehuda	245		Moshav
Majd al-Kurum		W. Upper Galilee		LC	7,250		Moslem-Arab Urban locality
@Majd a-Shams		N. Golan		LC	6,310		Druze Urban locality
&Makabim		N. Judean Foothills	1986	Gezer	498		Rural locality
Makr		Akko (Acre) Plain		LC	5,920	(ca. 90% Moslems 10% Christians)	Arab Urban locality
Malkiya	Takam	E. Upper Galilee	1949	Upper Galilee	411		Kibbutz
&Malkishu'a	KD	Mt. Gilboa	1976	Bet She'an Valley	..		Kibbutz
Manof	IH	W. Lower Galilee	1980	Misgav	..	1977/83 Galilee project	Moshav
Manot	TM	W. Upper Galilee	1980	Ma'ale Yosef	..	Founded as Mitzpe	Moshav
Manshiyat Zibde		W. Lower Galilee		Jezreel Valley	378	Settled Bedouin	Moslem-Arab village
@Ma'of	IH	N. Golan	1983	Mevo'ot ha-Hermon	..		Moshav
&Ma'on	Amana	Judean Desert	1981	Mt. Hebron	..		Moshav shitufi
Ma'or	TM	N. Sharon	1953	Menashe	349		Moshav
*Ma'oz Hayim	Takam	Bet She'an Valley	1937	Bet She'an Valley	590	Founded as Tower-and-Stockade	Kibbutz
Margaliyot	TM	E. Upper Galilee	1951	Mevo'ot ha-Hermon	288		Moshav
Masad	TM	E. Lower Galilee	1983	Lower Galilee	..	Founded as Mitzpe	Kehilati
*Masada	Takam	Kinarot Valley	1937	Jordan Valley	412		Kibbutz
@Mas'ada		N. Golan		LC	2,280		Druze village
Mash'abei Sadeh	Takam	SW Negev	1949	Ramat ha-Negev	474		Kibbutz
Mashen	TM	S. Coastal Plain	1950	Ashkelon Coast	583		Moshav
Mashhad		E. Lower Galilee		LC	4,160		Moslem-Arab village
Maslul	TM	W. Negev	1950	Merhavim	285		Moshav
&Masu'a	OTz	Lower Jordan Valley	1937	Arevot ha-Yarden	210		Moshav

*Masu'ot Yitzhak	PM	S. Coastal Plain	1949	Shafir	498	Transferred from Etzion Bloc	Moshav shitufi
Mata	TM	Central Judean Hills	1950	Mateh Yehuda	277		Moshav
Matat		W. Upper Galilee	1979	Ma'ale Yosef	. .	Founded as Mitzpe	Kehilati
&Matityahu	PAI	N. Judean Foothills	1981	Mateh Binyamin	215		Moshav shitufi
Matzliah	TM	C. Judean Foothills	1950	Gezer	528	Karaite center	Moshav
Matzuva		W. Upper Galilee	1940	Mateh Asher	620		Kibbutz
Mavki'im	OTz	S. Coastal Plain	1949	Ashkelon Coast	132		Moshav shitufi
Mayan Barukh	Takam	Huleh Valley	1947	Upper Galilee	355		Kibbutz
Mayan Tzevi	Takam	Mt. Carmel	1938	Carmel Coast	585		Kibbutz
Mazkeret Batya		S. Coastal Plain	1883	LC	2,470		Urban locality
Mazor	TM	C. Coastal Plain	1949	Modi'im	396		Moshav
Mazra'a		Akko Plain		Mateh Asher	2,240		Moslem-Arab village
Mefalesim	Takam	S. Coastal Plain	1949	Sha'ar ha-Negev	458		Kibbutz
Megadim	TM	Carmel Coast	1949	Carmel Coast	431		Moshav
*Megiddo	KA	Jezreel Valley	1949	Megiddo	387		Kibbutz
&Mehola	PM	Bet She'an Valley	1968	Arevot ha-Yarden	325		Moshav
Mei Ami	OTz	Irron Hills	1963	Menashe	181		Moshav shitufi
Me'ir Shefeya		Mt. Carmel	(1923)	Carmel Coast	398		Farming School Educational institution
&Mekhora	IH	E. Samaria	1973	Arevot ha-Yarden	118		Moshav
Mele'a	TM	Jezreel Valley	1956	Ha-Gilboa	282	Ta'anakh project	Moshav
Melilot	PM	S. Coastal Plain	1953	Azata	293		Moshav
Menahemya		Kinarot	1902	LC	1,080		Rural locality
*Menara	Takam	E. Upper Galilee	1943	Upper Galilee	291		Kibbutz
Menuha	TM	S. Coastal Plain	1953	Lachish	365	Lachish project	Moshav
Me'ona	TM	W. Upper Galilee	1949	Ma'ale Yosef	376		Moshav
Merav	KD	Bet She'an Valley	1987	Bet She'an Valley	. .		Kibbutz
*Merhavya (Moshav)	TM	Jezreel Valley	1922	Jezreel Valley	279		Moshav
*Merhavya (Kibbutz)	KA	Jezreel Valley	1911	Jezreel Valley	630		Kibbutz
Merkaz Shapira		S. Coastal Plain	1948	Shafir	971		Rural center Yeshiva
@Merom Golan	Takam	N. Golan	1967	Golan	410		Kibbutz
*Meron	PM	E. Upper Galilee	1949	Merom ha-Galil	525		Moshav
Meshar	IH	S. Coastal Plain	1950	Gederot	288		Moshav
Mesilat Zion	TM	C. Judean Foothills	1950	Mateh Yehuda	307		Moshav
Mesilot	KA	Bet She'an Valley	1938	Bet She'an Valley	688	Founded as Tower-and-Stockade	Kibbutz
Metar		N. Negev	1984	LC	1,900		Rural locality
Metav	TM	Jezreel Valley	1954	Ha-Gilboa	340	Ta'anakh project	Moshav

*Metula		E. Upper Galilee	1896	LC	731		Rural locality
&Metzadot Yehuda	Amana	S. Judean Hills	1983	Hebron Hills	. .		Moshav shitufi
Metzar	Takam	S. Golan	1981	Golan	. .		Kibbutz
Metzer	KA	N. Sharon	1953	Menashe	433		Kibbutz
Mevaseret Zion		C. Judean Hills	1951	LC	11,400	Fusion of Ma'oz Zion and Mevaseret Yerushalayim	Town
Mevo Betar	Herut	C. Judean Hills	1950	Mateh Yehuda	199		Moshav
&Mevo Dotan	Amana	N. Samaria	1978	Samaria	. .		Kehilati
@Mevo Hama	Takam	S. Golan	1968	Golan	325		Kibbutz
&Mevo Horon	PAI	N. Judean Hills	1970	Mateh Binyamin	352		Moshav shitufi
Mevo Modi'im	PAI	N. Judean Foothills	1964	Modi'im	180	see Modi'im	Moshav shitufi
Midrakh Oz	TM	Jezreel Valley	1952	Megiddo	448		Moshav
Midreshet Ben-Gurion		Negev Hills	1965	Ramat ha-Negev	672		Farm School Study Center
Midreshet Ruppin		C. Sharon	1948	Hefer Valley	174		Study center
Migdal		Kinarot Valley	1910	LC	1,020		Rural locality
*Migdal ha-Emek		W. Lower Galilee	1952	M	15,000		Town
&Migdalim	Amana	C. Samaria	1983	Samaria	. .		Kehilati
&Migdal Oz	KD	S. Judean Hills	1977	Etzion Bloc	. .		Kibbutz
*Mi'ilya		W. Upper Galilee		LC	2,030		Christian (Greek-Catholic) Arab urban locality
Mikhmanim	HI	W. Lower Galilee	1980	Misgav	. .	Founded as Mitzpe	Kehilati
*Mikhmoret	TM	C. Sharon	1945	Hefer Valley	1,190		Moshav and sea-faring school
*Mikve Yisra'el		C. Coastal Plain	1870		908		Farm school
*Misgav Am	Takam	E. Upper Galilee	1945	Upper Galilee	291		Kibbutz
Misgav Dov	Herut	S. Coastal Plain	1950	Gederot	321		Moshav
Mishmar Ayalon	TM	C. Judean Foothills	1949	Gezer	333		Moshav
Mishmar David	Takam	C. Judean Foothills	1948	Gezer	204		Kibbutz
*Mishmar ha-Emek	KA	Jezreel Valley	1926	Megiddo	813		Kibbutz
Mishmar ha-Negev	Takam	N. Negev	1946	Benei Shimon	671	Among 11 founded in one night	Kibbutz
Mishmar ha-Sharon	Takam	C. Sharon	1933	Hefer Valley	522		Kibbutz
Mishmar ha-Shiva		C. Coastal Plain	1949	Lod (Lydda) Valley	534		Moshav
*Mishmar ha-Yarden	Herut	Huleh Valley	(1949)	Mevo'ot ha-Hermon	329		Moshav
Mishmarot	Takam	N. Sharon	1933	Menashe	325		Kibbutz
Mishmeret	Takam	S. Sharon	1946	Lev ha-Sharon	282		Moshav
Misr		Irron Hills		Menashe	970		Moslem-Arab village
*Mitzpe		E. Lower Galilee	1908	Lower Galilee	107		Rural locality
Mitzpe Aviv	IH	W. Lower Galilee	1981		. .	Founded as Mitzpe	Kehilati

Mitzpe Netofa	Amana	E. Lower Galilee	1979	Lower Galilee	. .	1977/83 Galilee project	Kehilati
*Mitzpe Ramon		Negev Hills	1954	LC	2,610		Urban locality
&Mitzpe Shalem	Takam	Judean Desert	1971	Megilot	. .		Kibbutz
&Mitzpe Yeriho	Amana	Judean Desert	1978	Mateh Binyamin	388		Kehilati
Mivtahim	TM	NW Negev	1950	Eshkol	429		Moshav
Mizra	KA	Jezreel Valley	1923	Jezreel Valley	844		Kibbutz
Moledet (Benei Berit)	TM	E. Lower Galilee	1937	Ha-Gilboa	529	Founded as Tower-and-Stockade	Moshav shitufi
&Morag		Gaza Strip	1972	Gaza Coast			Transitional
Moran	Takam	W. Lower Galilee	1977	Misgav	. .		Kibbutz
Moreshet	IH	W. Lower Galilee	1981	Misgav	. .	1977/83 Galilee project	Moshav
*Motza Ilit		C. Judean Hills	1933	Mateh Yehuda	708		Rural locality
*Motza Tahtit		C. Judean Hills	1894	Mateh Yehuda	47		Rural locality
Mu'awiya		Irron Hills			1,600		Moslem-Arab village
Muqeibila		Irron Hills			1,520		Moslem-Arab village
Musheirifa		Irron Hills			1,750		Moslem-Arab village
Musmus		Irron Hills			2,110		Moslem-Arab village
Na'ala		N. Judean		Mateh Binyamin	. .		Transitory
*Na'an	Takam	C. Coastal Plain	1930	Gezer	1,200		Kibbutz
Nahala	TM	S. Coastal Plain	1953	Yo'av	352		Moshav
*Nahalal	TM	Jezreel Valley	1921	Jezreel Valley	1,030		Moshav
Nahal Amitai		NW Negev	1986	Eshkol			Nahal outpost
&Nahal Avnat		Lower Jordan Valley	1983	Megilot			Nahal outpost
Nahal Be'er Milka		Negev Hills	1983	Ramat ha-Negev			Nahal outpost
&Nahal Bitronit		Lower Jordan Valley	1983				Nahal outpost
&Nahal Doran		S. Judean Hills	1982	Hebron Hills			Nahal outpost
&Nahal Elisha		Lower Jordan Valley		Arevot ha-Yarden			Nahal outpost
&Nahal En Hogla		Lower Jordan Valley	1983				Nahal outpost
Nahal Eshbol		W. Lower Galilee	1979	Misgav			Nahal outpost
&Nahal Eshkolot		S. Judean Hills	1982	Hebron Hills			Nahal outpost
&Nahal Geva'ot		S. Judean Hills	1983	Etzion Bloc			Nahal outpost
&Nahal Ginat		Jezreel Valley	1983	Samaria			Nahal outpost
&Nahali'el	PAI	N. Judean Hills	1984	Mateh Binyamin			Kehilati
&Nahal Irit		N. Samaria	1982	Samaria			Nahal outpost
&Nahal Maskiyot		Lower Jordan Valley	1985	Arevot ha-Yarden			Nahal outpost
&Nahal Negohot		S. Judean Hills	1982	Hebron Hills			Nahal outpost
&Nahal Nimrod		Mt. Hermon	1982	Golan			Nahal outpost
*Nahal Oz	Takam	NW Negev	1951	Sha'ar ha-Negev	495	First settlement founded by Nahal	Kibbutz

&Nahal Rotem		Lower Jordan Valley	1983	Arevot ha-Yarden			Nahal outpost
Nahal Shitim		S. Negev Hills	1984	Eilot Region			Nahal outpost
&Nahal Tzoref		S. Judean Hills	1983	Hebron Hills			Nahal outpost
Nahal Ya'alon		Elat Hills	1984	Elot Region			Nahal outpost
Naham	PM	Judean Foothills	1950	Mateh Yehuda	405		Moshav
*Nahariya		Akko (Acre) Plain	1934	M	29,800		Town
Nahf		W. Lower Galilee		LC	5,660		Moslem-Arab village
Nahsholim	Takam	Carmel Coast	1948	Carmel Coast	453		Kibbutz
Nahshon	KA	C. Judean Foothills	1950	Mateh Yehuda	392		Kibbutz
Nahshonim	KA	S. Sharon	1949	S. Sharon	262		Kibbutz
@ Natur	KA	S. Golan	1980	Golan	. .		Kibbutz
Na'ura		E. Lower Galilee		Ha-Gilboa	1,040		Moslem-Arab village
*Nazareth		W. Lower Galilee		M.	50,600	(73% Moslems, 27% Christians)	Arab city
*Natzerat Ilit Upper Nazareth		W. Lower Galilee	1957	M.	24,900	21,900 Jews, 3,300 Arabs	Town
*Negba	KA	S. Coastal Plain	1939	Yo'av	683	Founded as Tower-and-Stockade	Kibbutz
Nehalim	PM	C. Coastal	1948	Modi'im	1,450	Transferred from Huleh Valley	Moshav
Nehora		S. Coastal Plain	1956	Lachish	413	Lachish Project	Rural center
Nehusha	PM	S. Judean Foothills	(1982)	Mateh Yehuda	198		Moshav
Nein		E. Lower Galilee			887		Moslem Arab village
@Ne'ot Golan	OTz	S. Golan	1967	Golan	. .		Moshav
Ne'ot ha-Kikar	IH	N. Arava Valley	1961	Tamar	255		Moshav
*Ne'ot Mordekhai	Takam	Huleh Valley	1946	Upper Galilee	690		Kibbutz
Nes Amim		Akko (Acre) Plain		Mateh Asher	140		Christian-European settlement
Nes Harim	TM	C. Judean Hills	1950	Mateh Yehuda	405		Moshav
Nesher		Haifa Bay Area	1925	LC	10,600		Town
*Nes Tziyona		C. Coastal Plain	1883	LC	18,600		Town
Neta'im	TM	C. Coastal Plain	1932	Gan Raveh	221		Moshav
*Netanya		C. Sharon	1929	M.	117,800		City
Netef		C. Judean Hills	1982	Mateh Yehuda	. .		Rural locality
Netiv ha-Asara	TM	S. Coastal Plain	1982	Ashkelon Coast	420	Transferred from Yamit area	Moshav
&Netiv ha-Gedud	TM	Lower Jordan Valley	1976	Arevot ha-Yarden	. .		Moshav
Netiv ha-Lamed-He	Takam	S. Judean Foothills	1949	Mateh Yehuda	405		Kibbutz
Netiv ha-Shayara	TM	Akko (Acre) Plain	1950	Mateh Asher	330		Moshav
Netivot		W. Negev	1956	LC	9,730		Town
Netu'a	TM	W. Upper Galilee	1966	Ma'aleh Yosef	275		Moshav
&Netzarim	KD	Gaza Strip	1972	Gaza Coast	. .		Kibbutz
&Netzer Hazani	PM	Gaza Strip	1973	Gaza Coast	328		Moshav

&Netzer Sereni	Takam	C. Coastal Plain	1948	Gezer	570	see also Givat Brenner	Kibbutz
Ne'urim		Central Sharon	1953	Hefer Valley	702	see Ben Shemen	Ed. institution Youth village
*Nevatim	TM	NE Negev	1946	Benei Shimon	537	Among the 11 founded in one night	Moshav
@Neveh Ativ	IH	Mt. Hermon	1972	Golan	..	operates Hermon ski reserve, cable cars	Moshav
Neveh Avot		N. Sharon	1948		794		Aged people's village
&Neveh Dani'el		S. Judean Hills	1982	Etzion Bloc	..		Kehilati
&Neveh Dekalim		Gaza Strip	1980		840		Rural locality
Neveh Efrayim		C. Coastal Plain	1953	LC	2,690		Urban locality
Neveh Etan	Takam	Bet She'an Valley	1938	Bet She'an Valley	318	Founded as Tower-and-Stockade	Kibbutz
Neveh Ilan	Takam	C. Judean Hills	1946	Mateh Yehuda	331	Twice re-founded	Moshav shitufi
Neveh Mikha'el	HI	S. Judean Foothills	1958	Mateh Yehuda	311	Adullam project	Moshav
Neveh Mivtah	TM	S. Coastal Plain	1950	Be'er Toviya	314		Moshav
Neveh Shalom		C. Judean Foothills	1983		..		Rural locality (Jewish-Arab cooperation)
Neveh Ur	Takam	Bet She'an Valley	1949	Bet She'an Valley	339		Kibbutz
Neveh Yam	Takam	Carmel Coast	1939	Carmel Coast	184		Kibbutz
Neveh Yamin	TM	S. Sharon	1949	S. Sharon	651		Moshav
Neveh Yarak	TM	S. Sharon	1951	S. Sharon	481		Moshav
Neveh Zohar		Dead Sea shore	1972	Tamar	..		Rural locality
&Nili	Amana	N. Judean Hills	1981	Mateh Binyamin	292		Kehilati
Nir Akiva	TM	W. Negev	1953	Merhavim	225		Moshav
Nir Am	TM	S. Coastal Plain	1954	Be'er Toviya	411	Lachish project	Moshav
&Niran	Takam	Lower Jordan Valley	1977	Arevot ha-Yarden	..		Kibbutz
Nir Banim	TM	S. Coastal	1954	Be'er Toviya	275	Lachish project	Moshav
Nir David (Tel Amal)	KA	Bet She'an Valley	1936	Bet She'an Valley	729	Founded as Tower-and-Stockade	Kibbutz
Nir Eliyahu	Takam	S. Sharon	1950	S. Sharon	350		Kibbutz
Nir Etzion	PM	Mt. Carmel	1950	Carmel Coast	757	see Etzion Bloc	Moshav shitufi
Nir Galim	PM	S. Coastal Plain	1949	Yavne Region	498		Moshav shitufi
Nir Hen	TM	S. Coastal Plain	1955	Lachish	254	Lachish project	Moshav
*Nirim	KA	NW Negev	(1949)	Eshkol	451	Among 11 founded in one night (1946)	Kibbutz
Nirit	TM	S. Sharon	1982	S. Sharon	..		Kehilati
Nir Moshe	TM	W. Negev	1953	Merhavim	183		Moshav
Nir Oz	KA	NW Negev	1955	Eshkol	441		Kibbutz
Nir Tzevi	IH	C. Coastal Plain	1954	Lod (Lydda) Valley	715		Moshav
Nir Yafeh	TM	Jezreel Valley	1956	Ha-Gilboa	300	Ta'anakh project	Moshav
Nir Yisra'el	OTz	S. Coastal Plain	1949	Ashkelon Coast	376		Moshav

Nir Yitzhak	KA	NW Negev	1949	Eshkol	532		Kibbutz
&Nisanit	Amana	N. Judean Hills	1982	Mateh Binyamin	. .		Kehilati
Nitzana		SW Negev	1983	Ramat ha-Negev			Research site
Nitzana B		SW Negev	1988	Ramat ha-Negev			Transitory
Nitzanei Oz	TM	S. Sharon	1951	Lev ha-Sharon	350		Moshav
Nitzanei Sinai	TN	SW Negev	1986	Ramat ha-Negev	. .		Moshav
*Nitzanim	OTz	S. Coastal Plain	1943	Ashkelon Coast	384		Kibbutz
Nitzanim-Youth Village		S. Coastal Plain	1949	Ashkelon Coast	304		Educational institution
No'am	PM	S. Coastal Plain	1955	Shafir	426	Lachish project	Moshav
Nogah	TM	S. Coastal Plain	1955	Lachish	364	Lachish project	Moshav
Nofekh		C. Coastal Plain	1949	Modi'im	132		Rural locality
&Nofim		W. Samaria	1987	Samaria	. .		Transitory
&Nokedim	Amana	S. Judean Hills	1982	Etzion Bloc	. .		Kehilati
&No'omi	TM	Lower Jordan Valley	1982	Arevot ha-Yarden	. .		Moshav
Nordiya	Herut	S. Sharon	1948	Lev ha-Sharon	363		Moshav shitufi
@Nov	PM	S. Golan	1973	Golan	345		Moshav
Nurit		Mt. Gilboa	1950	Ha-Gilboa			Afforestation center
@Odem	OTz	N. Golan	1976	Golan	. .		Moshav shitufi
*Ofakim		W. Negev	1955	LC	13,400		Town
Ofer	TM	Carmel Coast	1950	Carmel Coast	248		Moshav
&Ofra	Amana	N. Judean Hills	1975	Mateh Binyamin	817		Kehilati
Ohad	TM	NW Negev	1969	Eshkol	205		Moshav
Oholo		Kinarot Valley	1951	Jordan Valley	39		Cultural center
Olesh	TM	Central Sharon	1949	Hefer Valley	479		Moshav
Omen		Jezreel Valley	1958	Ha-Gilboa	. .	Ta'anach settlement project	Transitory
*Omer		N. Negev	1949	LC	5,680		Urban locality
Ometz	TM	Central Sharon	1949	Hefer Valley	223		Moshav
Ora	TM	C. Judean Hills	1950	Mateh Yehuda	349		Moshav
Or Akiva		N. Sharon	1951	LC	7,830	see also Caesarea	Urban locality
Oranim		Haifa Bay Area	1951	Zevulun	125		Teachers' Seminary
Oranit		W. Samaria	1985	Samaria	1,600		Rural locality
Or ha-Ner	Takam	S. Coastal Plain	1957	Sha'ar ha-Negev	370		Kibbutz
Orot	TM	S. Coastal Plain	1952	Be'er Toviya	225		Moshav
@Ortal	Takam	N. Golan	1978	Golan	. .		Kibbutz
Or Yehuda		C. Coastal Plain	1950	LC	20,000		Town
&Otni'el	Amana	S. Judean Hills	1983	Mt. Hebron	. .		Kehilati
Otzem	TM	S. Coastal Plain	1955	Lachish	493	Lachish project	Moshav
Pa'amei Tashaz	TM	W. Negev	1953	Merhavim	301		Moshav
Palmahim	Takam	C. Coastal Plain	1949	Gan Raveh	448		Kibbutz
Paran	TM	C. Arava Valley	1982	C. Arava	296		Moshav
*Pardes Hana-Karkur		N. Sharon	1913	LC	16,200		Town

Pardesiya		S. Sharon	1942	LC	1,010		Rural locality
Parod	Takam	E. Upper Galilee	1949	Merom ha-Galil	315		Kibbutz
Patish	TM	W. Negev	1950	Merhavim	618		Moshav
Pedaya	TM	Lod (Lydda) Region	1951	Gezer	454		Moshav
&Pedu'el	PM	W. Samaria	1984	Samaria	. .		Kehilati
Peduyim	TM	W. Negev	1950	Merhavim	336		Moshav
*Peki'in (Buqei'a)		W. Upper Galilee		Ma'ale Yosef	3,400	70% Druze, 30% Arab Christians	Druze and Arab village
Peki'in Hadasha	TM	W. Upper Galilee	1955	Ma'ale Yosef	218		Moshav
Pelekh	KA	W. Upper Galilee	1980	Misgav	. .	Founded as Mitzpe	Kibbutz
&Penei Haver	Amana	S. Judean Hills	1982	Hebron Hills	. .		Kehilati
Perazon	TM	Jezreel Valley	1953	Ha-Gilboa	330	Ta'anakh project	Moshav
Perigan	OTz	NW Negev	1981	Eshkol	. .	Transferred from Yamit Region	Moshav
&Pesagot		N. Judean Hills	1981	Mateh Binyamin	444		Rural center
*Petah Tikva		C. Coastal Plain	1878	M.	133,600		City
Petahya	OTz	C. Coastal Plain	1951	Gezer	421		Moshav
Petza'el	TM	Lower Jordan Valley	1975	Arevot ha-Yarden	274		Moshav
Pi-Ner	IH	Haifa Region	1987		. .		Kehilati
Porat	PM	S. Sharon	1950	Sharon Coast	472		Moshav
Poriya-Kefar Avoda		E. Lower Galilee	1949	Jordan Valley	143		Rural locality
Poriya-Neveh Oved		E. Lower Galilee	1949	Jordan Valley	663		Rural locality
Qalansuwa		S. Sharon		LC	9,450		Moslem-Arab village
*Ra'anana		S. Sharon	1921	M.	49,400		Town
&Rafiah Yam		TM	1984	Gaza Coast	. .		Kehilati
Rahat		NW Negev		LC	17,900	(settled Bedouin)	Moslem-Arab urban locality
Rakefet	TM	W. Lower Galilee	1981	Misgav	. .	1977/83 Galilee project	Moshav
Rama		E. Upper Galilee		LC	5,750		Arab village
Ramat David	Takam	Jezreel Valley	1926	Jezreel Valley	342		Kibbutz
Ramat Efal		C. Coastal Plain	1969	Efal (Ono)	2,690		Urban locality
*Ramat Gan		C. Coastal Plain	1921	M.	115,700		City
*Ramat ha-Kovesh	Takam	S. Sharon	1932	S. Sharon	646		Kibbutz
*Ramat ha-Sharon		S. Sharon	1923	LC	36,000		Town
Ramat ha-Shofet	KA	Menashe Hills	1941	Megiddo	737		Kibbutz
@Ramat Magshimim	PM	S. Golan	1968	Golan	398		Moshav shitufi
Ramat Pinkas		C. Coastal Plain	1952	Efal (Ono)	571		Rural locality
*Ramat Rahel	Takam	C. Judean Hills	1926	Mateh Yehuda	307		Kibbutz
Ramat Razi'el	Herut	C. Judean Hills	1948	Mateh Yehuda	324		Moshav
Ramat Tzevi	TM	E. Lower Galilee	1942	Ha-Gilboa	338		Moshav
Ramat Yishai		Jezreel Valley	1925	LC	2,080		Urban locality
Ramat Yohanan	Takam	Haifa Bay Area	1932	Zevulun	626		Kibbutz

*Ramleh (Ramla)		C. Judean Foothills		M.	44,500	thereof 37,000 Jews, 7,500 Arabs (c.a. 70% Moslems 30% Christians)	Town
Ram-On	TM	Jezreel Valley	1960	Ha-Gilboa	345	Ta'anakh project	Moshav
@Ramot	TM	S. Golan	1970	Golan	391		Moshav
*Ramot ha-Shavim		S. Sharon	1933	LC	729		Rural locality
Ramot Me'ir	TM	C. Coastal Plain	1949	Gezer	242		Moshav
Ramot Menashe	KA	Menashe Hills	1948	Megiddo	638		Kibbutz
Ramot Naftali	TM	E. Upper Galilee	1945	Mevo'ot ha-Hermon	356		Moshav
Ranen	TM	W. Negev	1950	Merhavim	340		Moshav
Ras Ali		Akko (Acre) Plain			296		Moslem-Arab village
Ravid	Takam	E. Lower Galilee	1981		. .	1977/83 Galilee project	Kibbutz
Regavim	Takam	Menashe Hills	1948	Menashe	348		Kibbutz
Regba	Takam	Akko (Acre) Plain	1946	Mateh Asher	586		Moshav shitufi
&Rehan	OTz	N. Samaria	1977	Samaria	. .		Moshav shitufi
Rehaniya		E. Upper Galilee		Merom ha-Galil	708		Circassian village
Rehov	PM	Bet She'an Valley	1951	Bet She'an Valley	256		Moshav
*Rehovot		C. Coastal Plain	1980	M.	72,500		City
Re'im	Takam	NW Negev	1949	Eshkol	303		Kibbutz
Reina		W. Lower Galilee			7,980		Arab village
Rekhasim		Haifa Bay Area	1957	LC	4,100		Urban locality
Reshafim	KA	Bet She'an Valley	1948	Bet She'an Valley	507		Kibbutz
Retamim	Takam	SW Negev	1983	Ramat ha-Negev	. .		Kibbutz
*Revadim	KA	S. Coastal Plain	1948	Yo'av	372	Transferred from Etzion Bloc	Kibbutz
Revaha	PM	S. Coastal Plain	1953	Shafir	468		Moshav
Revaya	PM	Bet She'an Valley	1952	Bet She'an Valley	220		Moshav
*Revivim	Takam	SW Negev	1943	Ramat ha-Negev	627		Kibbutz
&Rimonim	IM	N. Judean Hills	1977	Mateh Binyamin	. .		Kehilati
Rinatya	TM	C. Judean Foothills	1949	Modi'im	335		Moshav
*Rishon le-Zion		C. Coastal Plain	1882	M.	125,900		City
Rishpon	TM	S. Sharon	1936	Sharon Coast	512		Moshav
&Ro'i	IH	E. Samaria	1976	Arevot ha-Yarden	. .		Moshav
*Rosh ha-Ayin		C. Coastal Plain	1950	LC	11,700		Town
*Rosh Pina		E. Upper Galilee	1882	LC	1,590		Rural locality
&Rosh Tzurim	KD	S. Judean Hills	1969	Etzion Bloc	261		Kibbutz
*Ruhama	KA	S. Coastal Plain	(1944)	Sha'ar ha-Negev	613 414		Kibbutz
Rumana		E. Lower Galilee				Moslem-Arab village	
Rumet Hibb		Lower Galilee		Jezreel Valley	726	Settled Bedouin	Moslem-Arab village
*Sa'ad	KD	NW Negev	1947	Azata	701		Kibbutz

Sa'ar	KA	Akko (Acre) Plain	1948	Mateh Asher	321		Kibbutz
*Safed (Tzefat)		E. Upper Galilee		M.	16,400		Town
Sagib		Beersheba Region		Masos	. .		Bedouin village
Sajur		W. Lower Galilee		Merom ha-Galil	2,160		Moslem-Arab village
Sakhnin		W. Lower Galilee		LC	15,300		Arab town
Salem		Irron Hills			559		Moslem-Arab village
Salema		W. Lower Galilee		Misgav	775		Moslem-Arab village
&Salit	Herut	W. Samaria	1977	Samaria	296		Moshav
Samar	KA	S. Arava	1976	Elot Region	. .		Kibbutz
&Sa-Nur	Amana	N. Samaria	1983	Samaria	. .		Kehilati
Sapir		C. Arava Valley	1979	C. Arava	299		Rural Center
Sarid	KA	Jezreel Valley	1926	Jezreel Valley	726		Kibbutz
*Sasa	KA	E. Upper Galilee	1949	Upper Galilee	458		Kibbutz
*Savyon		C. Coastal Plain	1954	LC	2,470		Urban locality
*Sedeh Boker	Takam	Negev Hills	1952	Ramat ha-Negev	353		Kibbutz
Sedeh David	OTz	S. Coastal Plain	1955	Lachish	392	Lachish project	Moshav
Sedeh Eli'ezer	OTz	Huleh Valley	1952	Mevo'ot ha-Hermon	310		Moshav
Sedeh Eliyahu	KD	Bet She'an Valley	1939	Bet She'an Valley	618		Kibbutz
Sedeh Ilan	PM	E. Lower Galilee	1949	Lower Galilee	324		Moshav
Sedeh Moshe	TM	S. Coastal Plain	1956	Lachish	218	Lachish project	Moshav
Sedeh Nahum	Takam	Bet She'an Valley	1937	Bet She'an Valley	338		Kibbutz
Sedeh Nehemya	Takam	Huleh Valley	1940	Upper Galilee	394		Kibbutz
Sedeh Nitzan	TM	NW Negev	1973	Eshkol	262		Moshav
Sedeh Tzevi	IH	W. Negev	1953	Merhavim	270		Moshav
Sedeh Uziyahu	OTz	S. Coastal Plain	1950	Be'er Toviya	625		Moshav
Sedeh Warburg	IH	S. Sharon	1938	S. Sharon	435		Moshav
*Sedeh Ya'akov	PM	Jezreel Valley	1927	Jezreel Valley	677		Moshav
Sedeh Yitzhak	TM	N. Sharon	1952	Menashe	448		Moshav
Sedeh Yo'av	KA	S. Coastal Plain	1956	Yo'av	282		Kibbutz
Sedei Avraham	TM	NW Negev	1981	Eshkol	. .		Moshav
Sedei Hemed	TM	S. Sharon	1952	S. Sharon	285		Moshav
Sedei Terumot	PM	Bet She'an Valley	1951	Bet She'an Valley	453		Moshav
*Sederot		NE Negev	1951	LC	9,480		Urban locality
*Sedom		Dead Sea Shore		Tamar			Industrial site
Sedot Mikha	TM	S. Judean Foothills	1955	Mateh Yehuda	327	Adullam project	Moshav
*Sedot Yam	Takam	N. Sharon	1940	Carmel Coast	662		Kibbutz
Segev	MH	W. Lower Galilee	1953	Misgav	. .	Re-founded in 1977/83 Galilee project	Kehilati
Segula	TM	S. Coastal Plain	1953	Yo'av	285		Moshav
@Senir	KA	Huleh Valley	1967	Upper Galilee	260		Kibbutz
Sha'ab		W. Lower Galilee		LC	3,500		Moslem-Arab village

Shaikh Danun		W. Upper Galilee		Mateh Asher	1,300		Arab village
@Sha'al	Herut	N. Golan	1976	Golan	..		Moshav
*Sha'alvim	PAI	C. Judean Foothills	1951	Gezer	961		Kibbutz
Sha'ar ha-Amakim	KA	Haifa Bay Area	1935	Zevulun	665		Kibbutz
Sha'ar Efrayim	TM	S. Sharon	1953	Lev ha-Sharon	353		Moshav
*Sha'ar ha-Golan	KA	Kinarot Valley	1937	Jordan Valley	668	Founded as Tower-and-Stockade	Kibbutz
Sha'ar Menashe		N. Sharon	1949	Menashe	1,080		Aged People's village
&Sha'arei Tikva		W. Samaria	1983	Samaria	725		Rural locality
Shadmot Devora	TM	E. Lower Galilee	1939	Lower Galilee	358		Moshav
&Shadmot Mehola	PM	Lower Jordan Valley	1979	Arevot ha-Yarden	..		Moshav
Shahar	TM	S. Coastal Plain	1955	Lachish	383	Lachish project	Moshav
Shaharut		S. Arava Valley	1985	Elot Region			Transitory
Shafir	PM	S. Coastal Plain	1949	Shafir	274		Moshav
&Shalev		Gaza Strip	1987	Gaza Coast	..		Transitory
Shalva	PM	S. Coastal Plain	1952	Shafir	454		Moshav
Shamir	KA	Huleh Valley	1944	Upper Galilee	528		Kibbutz
&Shaked	Herut	N. Samaria	1981	Samaria	291		Kehilati
Shamerat	KA	Akko (Acre) Plain	1948	Mateh Asher	467		Kibbutz
Sandala		Jezreel Valley		Ha-Gilboa	849		Moslem-Arab village
Sharona	TM	E. Lower Galilee	1938	Lower Galilee	375		Moshav
Sharsheret	PM	NW Negev	1951	Azata	342		Moshav
&Shavei Shomeron	Amana	Central Samaria	1977	Samaria	402		Kehilati
*Shavei Zion	IH	Akko (Acre) Plain	1938	LC	678		Moshav shitufi
She'ar Yashuv	OTz	Huleh Valley	1940	Mevo'ot ha-Hermon	263		Moshav
Shedema	IH	S. Coastal Plain	1954	Gederot	187		Moshav
*Shefaram (Shafa Amr)		W. Lower Galilee		M.	19,900	45% Moslems, 35% Christians, 20% Druze	Arab and Druze town
Shefayim	Takam	S. Sharon	1935	Sharon Coast	713		Kibbutz
Shefer	TM	E. Upper Galilee	1950	Merom ha-Galil	232		Moshav
Shekef	Herut	S. Coastal Plain	1982	Lachish	..		Moshav
Shekhanya	IH	W. Lower Galilee	1980	Misgav	135	1977/83 Galilee project	Moshav
*Shelomi		Akko (Acre) Plain	1950	LC	2,210		Urban locality
Sheluhot	KD	Bet She'an Valley	1948	Bet She'an Valley	556		Kibbutz
Shetula	TM	W. Upper Galilee	1969	Ma'ale Yosef	204		Moshav
Shetulim	TM	S. Coastal Plain	1950	Be'er Toviya	529		Moshav
Shezor	TM	W. Upper Galilee	1953	Merom ha-Galil	270		Moshav
Shibli		S. Lower Galilee		LC	2,030	Settled Bedouin	Moslem-Arab urban locality
Shibolim	PM	NW Negev	1952	Azata	320		Moshav
Shilat	OTz	C. Judean Foothills	1977	Modi'im	224		Moshav
&Shiloh	Amana	N. Judean Hills	1979	Mateh Binyamin	608		Kehilati

Shizafon	Takam	S. Arava Valley	1982	Elot Region	. .		Kibbutz
Sho'eva	IH	C. Judean Hills	1950	Mateh Yehuda	349		Moshav, pre-urban Settlements
Shokeda	PM	NW Neğev	1957	Azata	197		Moshav
Shomera	TM	W. Upper Galilee	1949	Ma'ale Yosef	259		Moshav
Shomriya	KA	S. Judean Hills	1984	Benei Shimon	. .		Kibbutz
Shorashim	TM	W. Lower Galilee	1985	Misgav	. .	Included in 1977/83 Galilee project	Moshav shitufi
Shoresh	OTz	C. Judean Hills	1948	Mateh Yehuda	173		Moshav shitufi
Shoshanat ha-Amakim (Amidar)		C. Sharon	1956	Hefer Valley	94		Rural locality
Shoshanat ha-Amakin (Rassco)		C. Sharon	1951	Hefer Valley	673		Rural locality
Shoval	KA	N. Negev	1946	Benei Shimon	574	Among 11 founded in one night	Kibbutz
Shuva	PM	NW Negev	1950	Azata	395		Moshav
Sifsufa	TM	E. Upper Galilee	1949	Merom ha-Galil	426		Moshav
Sitriya	TM	C. Coastal Plain	1949	Gezer	381		Moshav
Sufa	Takam	NW Negev	1981	Eshkol	. .	Transferred from Yamit area	Kibbutz
Sulam		Jezreel Valley			1,560		Moslem-Arab village
&Susya	Amana	Judean Desert	1983	Hebron Hills	. .		Kehilati
Tal-El	TM	W. Upper Galilee	1980	Misgav	. .	Founded as Mitzpe	Kehilati
Talmei Bilu	HI	W. Negev	1953	Merhavim	295		Moshav
Talmei Elazar	IH	N. Sharon	1952	Menashe	259		Moshav
Talmei Eliyahu	TM	NW Negev	1970	Eshkol	246		Moshav
Talmei Yafe	OTz	S. Coastal Plain	1950	Ashkelon Coast	140		Moshav shitufi
Talmei Yehi'el	TM	S. Coastal Plain	1949	Be'er Toviya	376		Moshav
Talmei Yosef	IH	NW Negev	1982	Eshkol	. .	Transferred from Yamit region	Moshav
Tal Shahar	TM	C. Judean Foothills	1948	Mateh Yehuda	374		Moshav
Tamra		W. Lower Galilee		LC	15,400		Arab town
Tamra (Jezreel)		E. Lower Galilee		Ha-Gilboa	937		Arab village
Ta'oz	PM	C. Judean Foothills	1950	Mateh Yehuda	426		Moshav
Tarum	PM	C. Judean Foothills	1950	Mateh Yehuda	358		Moshav
Tayibe		S. Sharon		M	20,000		Moslem-Arab town
Tayibe (Jezreel)		E. Lower Galilee		Jezreel Valley	860		Moslem-Arab village
Te-ashur	TM	W. Negev	1953	Benei Shimon	187		Moshav
&Tefahot	Amana	S. Judean Hills	1983	Hebron Hills	. .	Founded as Mitzpe	Kehilati
&Teko'a	Amana	Judean Desert	1977	Etzion Bloc	372		Kehilati
Tekuma	PM	NW Negev	(1949)	Azata	357	Among 11 founded in one night	Moshav
*Tel Adashim	TM	Jezreel Valley	(1923)	Jezreel Valley	400		Moshav

Telalim	Takam	Negev Hills	1980	Ramat ha-Negev	97		Kibbutz
Telamim	TM	S. Coastal Plain	1950	Lachish	491		Moshav
*Tel-Aviv		C. Coastal Plain	1909	M.	317,800	thereof 11,100 non-Jews	City
&Telem	Herut	S. Judean Hills	1982	Hebron Hills	..		Moshav shitufi
Tel Katzir	Takam	Kinarot Valley	1949	Jordan Valley	412		Kibbutz
*Tel Mond		S. Sharon	1929	LC	3,330		Urban locality
Tel Sheva		N. Negev		LC	4,760	Settled Bedouin	Arab urban locality
Tel Te'omim	PM	Bet She'an Valley	1987	Bet She'an Valley	..		Kehilati
Tel Yitzhak	OTz	S. Sharon	1938	Sharon Coast	644		Kibbutz
*Tel Yosef	Takam	Harod Valley	1921	Ha-Gilboa	495		Kibbutz
&Tene	Amana	S. Judean Hills	1983	Hebron Hills	..		Kehilati
Tenuvot	TM	S. Sharon	1952	Lev ha-Sharon	466		Moshav
*Tiberias		Kinarot Valley		M.	31,200		Town
Tidhar	TM	W. Negev	1953	Benei Shimon	186		Moshav
Tifrah	PAI	W. Negev	1949	Merhavim	891		Moshav
Timrat	MH	S. Lower Galilee	1983	Jezreel Valley	862	1977/83 Galilee project	Rural locality
Timurim	OTz	S. Coastal Plain	1954	Be'er Toviya	357		Moshav shitufi
Tira		S. Sharon		LC	13,000		Moslem-Arab municipality
Tirat Karmel		Mt. Carmel	1949	LC	14,700	see also Haifa	Town
*Tirat Tzevi	KD	Bet She'an Valley	1937	Bet She'an Valley	698		Kibbutz
Tirat Yehuda	PM	C. Coastal Plain	1949	Modi'im	453		Moshav
Tirosh	PM	C. Judean Foothills	1955	Meteh Yehuda	304	Adullam project	Moshav
&Tomer	TM	Lower Jordan Valley	1978	Arevot ha-Yarden	..		Moshav
Tuba-Zanghariya		Huleh Valley			2,830		Moslem-Arab urban locality
Turan		E. Lower Galilee		LC	6,730	ca. 85% Moslems 15% Christians	Arab village
Tushiya		NW Negev	1958	Azata	418		Rural center
Tuval	Takam	W. Upper Galilee	1980	Misgav	121	1977/83 Galilee project	Kibbutz
Tzafririm	TM	S. Judean Foothills	1958	Mateh Yehuda	187	Adullam project	Moshav
Tzafriya	PM	C. Coastal Plain	1949	Lod Valley	604		Moshav
Tze'elim	Takam	NW Negev	1947	Eshkol	456		Kibbutz
Tzefat, see Safed							
Tzelafon	TM	C. Judean Foothills	1950	Mateh Yehuda	456		Moshav
Tzerufa	TM	Carmel Coast	1949	Carmel Coast	402		Moshav
Tzeviya	Takam	W. Lower Galilee	1979	Misgav	..	Founded as Mitzpe	Kibbutz
*Tzipori	TM	W. Lower Galilee	1949	Jezreel Valley	329		Moshav
Tzivon		E. Upper Galilee	1980	Upper Galilee		Founded as Mitzpe	Transitory
Tzofar	TM	C. Arava Valley	1970	Central Arava	..		Moshav

Tzofit	TM	S. Sharon	1933	S. Sharon	355		Moshav
Tzofiya		S. Coastal Plain	1955	Yavne Region			Transitory
Tzohar		NW Negev	1973	Eshkol	293		Rural center
Tzora	Takam	C. Judean Foothills	1948	Mateh Yehuda	925		Kibbutz
Tzorit	Herut	W. Lower Galilee	1981	Misgav	. .	Founded as Mitzpe	Kehilati
Tzova	Takam	C. Judean Hills	1948	Mateh Yehuda	433		Kibbutz
Tzur Hadasa		C. Judean Hills	1960	Mateh Yehuda	197		Rural center
Tzuri'el	TM	W. Upper Galilee	1950	Ma'ale Yosef	247		Moshav
Tzur Moshe	TM	S. Sharon	1937	Lev ha-Sharon	510		Moshav
Tzur Natan	Herut	S. Sharon	1970	S. Sharon	. .		Moshav shitufi
Udim	IH	S. Sharon	1948	Sharon Coast	384		Moshav
*Um al-Fahm		Irron Hills		M.	23,800		Moslem-Arab town
Um al-Ghanam		Irron Hills			863		Moslem-Arab village
Um al-Qutuf		Irron Hills		Menashe	422		Moslem-Arab village
Urim	Takam	NW Negev	1946	Eshkol	620	Among 11 founded in one night	Kibbutz
*Usha		Haifa Bay Area	1937	Zevulun	393		Kibbutz
Uzza	PM	S. Coastal Plain	1950	Safir	591		Moshav
Uzeir		S. Lower Galilee			1,360		Moslem-Arab village
Vardon		S. Coastal Plain	1968	Yo'av	58		Rural center
&Vered Yeriho	IH	Judean Desert	1980	Megilot	. .		Moshav
Ya'ad	TM	W. Lower Galilee	1975	Misgav	249	included in 1977/83 Galilee project	Moshav shitufi
Ya'af		S. Sharon	1968	Lev ha-Sharon	29		Rural center
Ya'ara	TM	W. Upper Galilee	1950	Ma'ale Yosef	329		Moshav
Yad Binyamin		C. Coastal Plain	1949	Nahal Sorek	446		Rural center
Yad ha-Shemona		C. Judean Hills	1978	Mateh Yehuda	76	Gentile-Finnish friends of Israel	Moshav shitufi
Yad Hana	KA	C. Sharon	1950	Hefer Valley	137		Kibbutz
*Yad Mordekhai	KA	S. Coastal Plain	1943	Ashkelon Coast	727		Kibbutz
Yad Netan	OTz	S. Coastal Plain	1953	Lachish	255	Lachish project	Moshav
Yad Rambam	PM	C. Coastal Plain	1955	Gezer	545		Moshav
Ya'el		Jezreel Valley	1960	Ha-Gilboa		Ta'anakh project	Transitory
Yafi'a		S. Lower Galilee		LC	9,330	ca. 80% Moslem, 20% Christian	Arab urban locality
&Yafit	TM	Lower Jordan Valley	1980	Arevot ha-Yarden	. .		Moshav
Yagel	TM	C. Coastal Plain	1950	Lod (Lydda) Valley	391		Moshav
*Yagur	Takam	Haifa Bay area	1922	Zevulun	1,330		Kibbutz
Yahel	Takam	S. Arava Valley	1950	Elot Region	. .	First settlement Reform Jews	Kibbutz
Yakhini	TM	NW Negev	1950	Sha'ar ha-Negev	466		Moshav

&Yakir	Amana	W. Samaria	1981	Samaria	285		Kehilati
Yakum	KA	S. Sharon	1947	Sharon Coast	469		Kibbutz
Yanuh		W. Upper Galilee		Central Galilee	2,240		Druze village
Yanuv	TM	S. Sharon	1950	Lev ha-Sharon	356		Moshav
Yardena	TM	Bet She'an Valley	1952	Bet She'an Valley	326		Moshav
Yarhiv	TM	S. Sharon	1949	S. Sharon	437		Moshav
Yarkona	TM	S. Sharon	1932	S. Sharon	153		Moshav
Yashresh	TM	C. Coastal Plain	1950	Gezer	346		Moshav
Yasur	KA	Haifa Bay area	1949	Mateh Asher	368		Kibbutz
Yated	TM	NW Negev	1983	Eshkol	. .		Moshav
Yatzitz	TM	C. Coastal Plain	1950	Gezer	384		Moshav
*Yavne		S. Coastal Plain	1949	M.	20,800		Town
*Yavne'el		E. Lower Galilee		LC	1,630		Rural locality
Yedida		C. Judean Hills	1964	Mateh Yehuda	124		Educational institution
Yedidya	TM	C. Sharon	1935	Hefer Valley	384		Moshav
Yehi'am	KA	W. Upper Galilee	1946	Mateh Asher	508		Kibbutz
*Yehud		C. Coastal Plain	1948	LC	15,000		Town
*Yeroham		Negev Hills	1958	LC	5,890		Urban locality
Yesha	TM	NW Negev	1957	Eshkol	228		Moshav
Yesodot	PAI	C. Judean Foothills	1948	Nahal Sorek	303		Moshav shitufi
*Yesud ha-Ma'ale		Huleh Valley	1883	LC	759		Rural locality
Yevul	IH	NW Negev	1981	Eshkol	. .		Moshav
Yif'at	Takam	Jezreel Valley	(1926)	Jezreel Valley	850		Kibbutz
Yiftah	Takam	E. Upper Galilee	1948	Upper Galilee	524		Kibbutz
Yinon	TM	S. Coastal Plain	1952	Be'er Toviya	545		Moshav
Yirka		W. Upper Galilee		LC	7,710		Druze urban locality
Yiron	Takam	E. Upper Galilee	1949	Upper Galilee	365		Kibbutz
Yishi	PM	C. Judean Foothills	1950	Mateh Yehuda	452		Moshav
&Yitav	Takam	Lower Jordan Valley	1970	Arevot ha-Yarden	. .		Kibbutz
&Yitzhar	Amana	C. Samaria	1983	Samaria	. .		Kehilati
Yizre'am		S. Coastal Plain	1953	Azata			Transitory
*Yizre'el	Takam	Jezreel Valley	1948	Ha-Gilboa	511		Kibbutz
Yodefat	Takam	W. Lower Galilee	1960	Misgav	217		Moshav shitufi
Yokne'am	IH	Jezreel Valley	1935	Ha-Gilboa	715		Moshav
Yokne'am Ilit		Jezreel Valley	1950	LC	5,700		Urban locality
@Yonatan	PM	C. Golan	1976		. .		Moshav shitufi
Yoshivya	PM	NW Negev	1950	Azata	257		Moshav
*Yotveta	Takam	S. Arava Valley	1951	Elot Region	532		Kibbutz
Yuval	TM	Huleh Valley	1952	Mevo'ot ha-Hermon	314		Moshav
Yuvalim	HI	W. Lower Galilee	1982	Misgav	584		Kehilati
Zalafa		Irron Hills			2,190		Moslem-Arab urban locality
Zamar		C. Sharon	1988	LC		Uniting the 4 villages Bir-a-Gilla, Ibthan, Marja, Yama	Arab urban locality

Zano'ah	PAI	C. Judean Hills	1950	Mateh Yehuda	322		Moshav
Zarazir		S. Lower Galilee		Jezreel Valley	3,550		Moslem-Arab village
Zavdi'el	PAI	S. Coastal Plain	1950	Shafir	373		Moshav
Zekharya	TM	C. Judean Foothills	1950	Mateh Yehuda	423		Moshav
Zerahya	PM	S. Coastal Plain	1950	Shafir	432		Moshav
Zeru'a	PM	NW Negev	1953	Azata	271		Moshav
Zetan	TM	C. Coastal Plain	1950	Lod (Lydda) Valley	561		Moshav
*Zikhron Ya'akov		Mount Carmel	1882	LC	5,860		Askhelon
Zikim	KA	S. Coastal Plain	1949	Askhelon Coast	369		Kibbutz
Zimrat	PM	NW Negev	1957	Azata	362		Moshav
Zohar	IH	S. Coastal Plain	1956	Lachish	386	Lachish project	Moshav

BIBLIOGRAPHY OF ZIONISM

GENERAL WORKS

Ahad Ha'Am (pseud of Asher Ginzberg); *Selected Essays*, tr. by Sir Leon Simon, Jewish Publication Society of America, Philadelphia, 1948.

———:*Essays, Letters, Memoirs*, tr. and ed. by Sir Leon Simon, East and West Library, New York, 1948.

———:*Nationalism and the Jewish Ethic: Basic Writings*, Herzl Press, New York, 1962.

Almog, Shmuel: *Zionism and History*, St. Martin's Press, New York, 1987.

American Jewish Historical Society and Theodor Herzl Foundation: *Conference on the early History of Zionism in America*, ed. by Isidore S. Meyer, New York, 1958.

Avineri, Shlomo: *The Making of Modern Zionism, The Intellectual Origins of the Jewish State*, Basic Books, 1981.

Berman, Morton: *The Bridge to Life: The Saga of the Keren Hayesod*, Keren Ha-Yesod, Tel Aviv, 1970.

Borochov, Ber: *Nationalism and the Class Struggle: A Marxian Approach to the Jewish Problem*, Poale Zion-Zeire Zion of America, New York, 1937.

Brandeis, Louis D.: *Brandeis on Zionism: A Collection of Addresses and Statements*, Zionist Organization of America, Washington, 1942.

Buber, Martin: *On Zion* tr. by Stanley Godman, East and West Library, London, 1973.

Cohen, Israel: *The Zionist Movement*, ed. and rev., with supplementary chapter on Zionism in the United States by Bernard G. Richards, Zionist Organization of America, New York, 1946.

———: *A Short History of Zionism*, Frederick Muller, Ltd., London, 1951.

Cohen, Mitchell.: *Zion and State*, Blackwell, New York, 1987.

Cohen, Naomi W.: *American Jews and the Zionist Idea*, Ktav, New York, 1975.

———: *The Year After the Riots*, Wayne State University Press, Detroit, 1988. Cohen, Stuart A.: *English Zionists and British Jews*, Princeton University Press, 1982.

Davis, Moshe (ed.): The Yom Kippur War: Israel and the Jewish People, Arno Press, New York, 1974. ———: *World Jewry and the State of Israel*, Herzl Press, New York, 1977.

———: *Zionism in Transition*, Herzl Press, New York, 1980.

Dinur, Ben Zion: *Israel and the Diaspora*, Jewish Publication Society, Philadelphia, 1969. Feinstein, Marnin: *American Zionism, 1884–1904*, Herzl Press, New York, 1965.

Fisch, Harold: *The Zionist Revolution: A New Perspective*, St. Martin's Press, New York, 1978.

Frankel, Jonathan: *Prophecy and Politics; Socialism, Nationalism, and the Russian Jews*, Cambridge University Press, Cambridge, 1981.

Friedman, Isaiah: *The Question of Palestine: 1914–1918, British-Jewish-Arab Relations*, Routledge & Kegan Paul, London, 1973.

———: *Germany, Turkey, and Zionism, 1897–1918*, Oxford University Press, Oxford, 1977.

Gilner, Elias: *War and Hope: A History of the Jewish Legion*, Herzl Press, New York, 1969.

Goldman, Guido G.: *Zionism under Soviet Rule, 1917–1928*, Herzl Press, New York, 1960.

Gordon, Aharon D.: *Selected Essays*, League for Labor Palestine, New York, 1938.

Grose, Peter: *Israel in the Mind of America*, Schocken Books, 1983.

Haber, Julius: *The Odyssey of an American Zionist: Fifty Years of Zionist History*, Twayne Publishers, Inc., New York, 1956.

Halkin, Abraham S., Ed.: *The American Jew: A Zionist Analysis*, Theodor Herzl Foundation, New York, 1956.

Halperin, Samuel: *The Political World of American Zionism*, Wayne State University Press, Detroit, 1961.

Halpern, Ben: *A Clash of Heroes, Brandeis, Weizmann and American Zionism*, Oxford University Press, New York, 1987.

———: *The Idea of the Jewish State*, Harvard University Press, Cambridge, Mass., 1961.

Heller, Joseph: *The Zionist Idea*, Schocken Books, Inc., New York, 1949.

Hertzberg, Arthur, (ed.): *The Zionist Idea: A Historical Analysis and Reader*, Doubleday & Company, Inc., and Herzl Press, Garden City, N.Y., 1959.

Herzl, Theodor: *The Jewish State*, Herzl Press, 1970. ———: *Complete Diaries*, ed. by Raphael Patai, 5 vols., Herzl Press, New York, 1960.

———: *Old-New Land (Altneuland)*, tr. by Lotte Levensohn, 2d ed. with rec. footnotes, Bloch Publishing Company, Inc., New York, 1960.
Herzl Year Book, ed. by Raphael Patai, vols. 1–7, Herzl Press, New York, 1958–71
Hess, Moses: *Rome and Jerusalem: A study in Jewish Nationalism*, tr. by Meyer Waxman, 2d ed., Bloch Publishing Company, Inc., New York, 1943.
Jabotinsky, Vladimir: *The War and the Jew*, The Dial Press, Inc., New York, 1942.
———: *The Story of the Jewish Legion*, tr. by Samuel Katz, Bernard Ackerman, New York, 1945.
Jewish Agency for Palestine: *Documents Relating to the Palestine Problem*, London, 1945.
———: *Book of Documents Submitted to the General Assembly of the United Nations Relating to the Establishment of the National Home for the Jewish People*, New York, 1947.
Kallen, Horace M.: *Zionism and World Politics: A Study in History and Social Psychology*, Doubleday Page & Company, New York, 1921.
Kaplan, Mordecai M.: *A New Zionism*, 2d enl.ed., Herzl Press, New York, 1959.
Karp, Abraham J.: *To Give Life: The UJA in the Shaping of the American Jewish Community*, Schocken Books, New York, 1981.
Kobler, Franz: *The Vision Was There: A History of the British Movement for the Restoration of the Jews to Palestine*, Lincoln-Prager, London, 1956.
Kurland, Samuel: *Biluim: Pioneers of Zionist Colonization*, Scopus Publishing Company, Inc., New York, 1943.
Laqueur, Walter: *A History of Zionism*, Schocken Books, New York, 1976.
Learsi, Rufus (pseud. of Israel Goldberg): *Fulfillment: the Epic Story of Zionism*, The World Publishing Company, Cleveland, 1951.
Litvinoff, Barnet: *To the House of Their Fathers: A History of Zionism*, Frederick A. Praeger, Inc., New York, 1965.
Locker, Berl: *Covenant Everlasting*, Sharon Books, New York, 1947.
Mendelsohn, Ezra: *Zionism in Poland: The Formative Years 1915–1926*, Yale University Press, New Haven, 1981.
Nordau, Max: *Max Nordau to His People: A Summons and a Challenge*, Scopus Publishing Company, Inc., New York, 1962.
Parzen, Herbert: *A Short History of Zionism*, Herzl Press, New York, 1962.
Penkower, Monty Noam: *The Emergence of Zionist Thought*, Associated Faculty Press, New York, 1987.
Pinsker, Leo: *Road to Freedom*, Scopus Publishing Company, Inc., New York, 1944.
———: *Auto-Emancipation*, Zionist Organization of America, New York, 1956.
Polish, David: *Renew Our Days: The Zionist Issue in Reform Judaism*, World Zionist Organization, Jerusalem, 1976.
Pragai, Michael J.: *Faith and Fulfilment, Christians and the Return to the Promised Land*, Valentine Mitchell, London, 1985.
Reinharz, Jehuda: *Deutschtum and Judentum; Jewish Liberalism and Zionism in Germany 1893–1914*, Waltham, Mass., 1972.
Rose, Norman: *The Gentile Zionists*, Cass, London, 1973.
Rubenstein, Amnon: *The Zionist Dream Revisited*, Schocken Books, 1984.
Sacher, Harry: *Zionist Portraits, and Other Essays*, Anthony Blond, Ltd., London, 1959.
Samuel, Maurice: *Harvest in the Desert*, Alfred A. Knopf, Inc., New York, 1944.
Sanders, Ronald: *The High Walls of Jerusalem: A History of the Balfour Declaration*, Holt, Reinhart and Winston, New York, 1983.
Schama, Simon: *Two Rothschilds and the Land of Israel*, Collins, London, 1978.
Schroeter, Leonard: *The Last Exodus*, Weidenfeld and Nicolson, London, 1981.
Shapiro, Yonatan: *Leadership of the American Zionist Organization, 1897–1930*, University of Illinois, Urbana, 1971.
Shimoni, Gideon.: *Jews and Zionism: The South African Experience 1910–1967*, Oxford University Press, Cape Town, 1980.
Silver, Abba H.: *Vision and Victory: A Collection of Addresses, 1942–1948*, Zionist Organization of America, New York, 1949.
Simon, Sir Leon: *Studies in Jewish Nationalism*, Longmans, Green & Co., Inc., New York, 1920.
Sokolow, Nahum: *History of Zionism, 1600–1918*, 2 vols., (Longmans, Green & Co., Inc., New York, 1919). Reprint, Ktav Publishing House, N.Y., 1969.
Stein, Leonard J.: *The Balfour Declaration*, Simon and Schuster, New York, 1961.
Stock, Ernest: *Partners and Pursestrings: A History of the United Israel Appeal*, University Press of America, Washington, 1987.
———: *Chosen Instrument. The Jewish Agency in the First Decade of the State of Israel*, Herzl Press, New York, 1988.
Sykes, Christopher: *Two Studies in Virtue*, Alfred A. Knopf, Inc., New York, 1953.
Syrkin, Nachman: *Essays on Socialist Zionism*, Young Po'ale Zion Alliance of America, New York, 1935.
Tuchman, Barbara (Wertheim): *Bible and Sword: England and Palestine from the Bronze Age to Balfour*, New York University Press, New York, 1956.
Urovsky, Melvin, I.: *American Zionism from Herzl to the Holocaust*, Doubleday, New York, 1975.
———: *We are One: American Jewry and Israel*, Anchor Press, New York, 1978.
Vital, David: *The Origins of Zionism*, Oxford University Press, New York, 1975.
———: *Zionism: The Formative Years*, Oxford University Press, New York, 1982.
———: *Zionism: The Crucial Phase*, Clarendon Press, Oxford, 1987.

AUTOBIOGRAPHIES AND BIOGRAPHIES

AHAD HA-AM

Simon, Sir Leon: *Ahad Ha-Am, Asher Ginzberg. A Biography* Jewish Publication Society of America, Philadelphia 1960.

BALFOUR, ARTHUR JAMES

Dugdale, Blanche E.C.B.: *Arthur James Balfour, First Earl of Balfour*, 2 vols., G.P. Hutchinson, London, 1936.

BEGIN, MENACHEM

Haber Eitan: *Menachem Begin: The Legend and the Man*, Delacorte Press, New York, 1978.
Hirschler, Gertrude and Eckman, Lester Samuel: *Menahem Begin*, Bastei Lübbe, New York, 1979.
Malka, Victor: *Menahem Begin*, Paris 1977.
Perlmutter, Amos: *The Life and Times of Menachem Begin*, Doubleday, New York, 1987.
Silver, Eric: *Begin: A Biography*, Weidenfeld and Nicolson, London, 1984.

BEN-GURION, DAVID
Bar-Zohar, Michel: *Ben-Gurion: The Armed Prophet*, tr. by Len Ortzen, Prentice-Hall, Inc., Englewood Cliffs, N.J., 1968.
Ben-Gurion, David: *Israel: A Personal History*, Funk and Wagnalls Inc., New York, 1971.
Litvinoff, Barnet: *Ben-Gurion of Israel*, Frederick A. Praeger Inc., N.Y. 1954.
Samuels, Gertrude: *B-G, Fighter of Goliaths: The Story of David Ben-Gurion*, Thomas Y. Crowell company, New York, 1961.
Teveth Shabtai: *Ben-Gurion: The Burning Ground 1886–1948*, Houghton, Mifflin, Boston, 1987.
BEN-YEHUDA, ELIEZER
St. John, Robert: *Tongue of the Prophets: The Life Story of Eliezer Ben-Yehuda*, Doubleday & Company, Inc., Garden City N.Y., 1952.
BRANDEIS, LOUIS D.
De Haas, Jacob: *Louis D. Brandeis: A Biographical Sketch, with Special Reference to His Contribution to Jewish and Zionist History*, Bloch Publishing Company Inc., New York, 1937.
Gal, Alon: *Brandeis of Boston*, Harvard University Press, Cambridge, Mass., 1980.
BODENHEIMER, MAX I.
Bodenheimer, Max I.: *The Memoirs of M.I. Bodenheimer* tr. by Israel Cohen, Thomas Yoseloff Inc., New York, 1963.
BRODETSKY, SELIG
Brodetsky, Selig: *Memoirs*, Weidenfeld and Nicolson, London, 1960.
DAYAN, MOSHE
Lau-Lavie, Naphtali: *Moshe Dayan: A Biography*, Prayer Book Press, Hartford Conn., 1969.
ESHKOL, LEVI
Prittie, Terence C.F.: *Eshkol: The Man and the Nation*, Pitman Publishing Corporation, New York, 1969.
FRIEDENWALD, HARRY
Levin, Alexandra L.: *Vision: A Biography of Harry Friedenwald*, Jewish Publication Society of America, Philadelphia. 1964.
GOLDMANN, NAHUM
Goldmann, Nahum: *The Autobiography of Nahum Goldman, 60 Years of Jewish Life*, tr. by Helen Sebba, Holl, Rinehart and Winston Inc., New York, 1969.
GORDON, A.D.
Rose, Herbert H.: *The Life and Thought of A.D. Gordon: Pioneer, Philosopher and Prophet of Modern Israel*, Bloch Publishing Company Inc., New York, 1964.
HERZL, THEODOR
Bein, Alex: *Theodore Herzl: A Biography* tr. by Maurice Samuel, Jewish Publication Society of America, Philadelphia, 1956.
Elon, Amos: *Herzl*, Holt, Reinhart and Winston, New York, 1978.
Pawel, Ernst: *The Labyrinth of Exile: A Life of Theodor Herzl*, Farrar, Straus and Giroux, New York, 1989.
HESS, MOSES
Avineri, Shlomo: *Moses Hess: Prophet of Communism and Zionism*, New York University Press, New York, 1985.
Schulman, Mary: *Moses Hess: Prophet of Zionism*, Thomas Yoseloff, Inc., N.Y. 1963.
JABOTINSKY, VLADIMIR
Schechtman, Joseph B.: *The Vladimir Jabotinsky Story* 2 vols., Thomas Yoseloff, Inc., New York, 1956–61.
Shavit, Yaakov, *Jabotinsky and the Revisionist Movement 1925–1948*, Frank Cass, London, 1988.
KATZNELSON, BERL
Shapiro, Anita: *Berl: The Biography of a Socialist Zionist, Berl Katznelson 1887–1944*, Cambridge University Press, Cambridge, 1984.
LEVIN, SHEMARYA
Levin, Shemarya: *Forward from Exile* tr. and ed. by Maurice Samuel, Jewish Publication Society of America, Philadelphia 1967.
MAGNES, JUDAH L.
Bentwich, Norman: *For Zion's Sake: A Biography of Judah L. Magnes, First Chancellor and First President of the Hebrew University of Jerusalem*, Jewish Publication Society of America, Philadephia, 1954.
Goren, Arthur A.: *Dissenter in Zion*, Harvard University Press, Cambridge, Mass. 1982.
MEIR, GOLDA
Meir, Golda: *My Life*, Weidenfeld and Nicolson, London, 1975.
Syrkin, Marie: *Golda Meir: Israel's Leader*, new rev. ed., G.P. Putnam's Sons, New York, 1969.
NORDAU, MAX
Ben-Horin, Meir: *Max Nordau*, Conference of Jewish Social Studies, New York, 1956.
Nordau, Anna (Dons) and Maxa Nordau: *Max Nordau: A Biography* tr. from the French, Nordau Committee, New York, 1943.
PERES, SHIMON
Golan, Matti: *Shimon Peres, A Biography*, Weidenfeld and Nicolson, London, 1982.
Peres, Shimon: *From These Men*, Weidenfeld and Nicolson, London, 1979.
RABIN, YITZCHAK Rabin, Yitzhak: *The Rabin Memoirs*, Weidenfeld and Nicolson, London, 1979.
Slater, Robert: *Rabin of Israel*, Robson Books, London, 1977.
SMOLENSKIN, PERETZ
Freundlich, Charles H.: *Peretz Smolenskin: His Life and Thoughts*, Bloch Publishing Company, Inc., New York, 1966.
SOKOLOW, NACHUM
Kling, Simha: *Nachum Sokolow: Servant of His People* Herzl Press, New York, 1960.
STRICKER, ROBERT
Fraenkel, Joseph Ed.: *Robert Stricker*, Ararat Publishing Society, London, 1950.
SZOLD HENRIETTA
Fineman, Irving: *Woman of Valor: The Life of Henrietta Szold 1860–1945* Simon and Schuster, New York, 1961.
TRUMPELDOR, JOSEPH
Lipovetzky, Pesah: *Joseph Trumpeldor: Life and Works*. World Zionist Organization, Youth and HeHalutz Department, Jerusalem, 1953.
USSISHKIN, MENAHEM
Klausner, Joseph G.: *Menahem Ussishkin: His Life and Work*, Scopus Publishing Company, Inc., New York, 1942.
WEIZMANN, CHAIM
Reinharz, Jehuda: *Chaim Weizmann Vol. I, The Making of a Zionist Leader* Oxford University Press, New York, 1985.
Rose, Norman.: *Chaim Weizmann: a biography*, Viking, New York, 1986.
Weisgal, Meyer W. general editor: *The Letters and Papers of Chaim Weizmann*, 23 volumes, 1968–1980, Vols. I-VII, Oxford University Press, London, Vols VIII-XXIII, Rutgers University, New Jersey.
Weizmann, Chaim: *Trial and Error: The Autobiography of*

Chaim Weizmann, Harper Brothers, New York, 1949.
Weizmann, Chaim: *A Biography by Several Hands* ed. by Meyer W. Weisgal and Joel Carmichael with a preface by David Ben-Gurion, Atheneum Publishers, New York, 1963.
WISE, STEPHEN
Urofsky, Melvin I.: *A Voice That Spoke for Justice: The Life and Times of Stephen S. Wise*, State University of N.Y. Press, 1982.
Wise, Stephen S.: *The Personal Letters of Stephen Wise*, Beacon Press, Boston, 1956.
WOLFFSOHN, DAVID
Cohn, Emil B.: *David Wolffsohn*, Zionist Organization of America, New York, 1944.
ZANGWILL, ISRAEL
Leftwich, Joseph: *Israel Zangwill* Thomas Yoseloff, Inc., New York, 1957.
Wohlgelernter, Maurice: *Israel Zangwill: A study*, Columbia University Press, New York, 1964.

ISRAEL

Archeology, Geography, and Guidebooks

Aharoni, Yohanan: *The Land of the Bible*, trans. from the Hebrew, Westminster Press, Philadelphia, 1979.
Albright, William F.: *The Archaeology of Palestine*, rev. ed., Penguin Books, Inc., Baltimore, 1960.
Avigad, Nahman: *Discovering Jerusalem*, Israel Exploration Society and Shikmona Publishing Co. Inc., Jerusalem, 1980.
Avi-Yonah, Michael (ed.): *A History of the Holy Land*, Weidenfeld and Nicolson, 1969.
Glueck, Nelson: *Rivers in the Desert: A History of the Negev*, Norton Co., New York, 1969.
Orni, Efraim and Efrat, Elisha: *Geography of Israel*, Israel Universities Press, Jerusalem, 1971.
Pearlman, Moshe: *Digging Up the Bible*, Weidenfeld and Nicolson, London, 1980.
Vilnay, Zev: *The Guide to Israel*, 12th ed. rev., Ahiever, Jerusalem, 1969.
———: *The New Israel Atlas*, McGraw-Hill Book Company, New York, 1969.
Yadin, Yigael: *Bar-Kochba* Weidenfeld and Nicolson, London, 1971.
———: *The Message of the Scrolls*, Simon and Schuster, New York, 1957.
———: *Masada: Herod's Fortress and the Zealots' Last Stand*, Random House, Inc., New York, 1966.

History

GENERAL

Bauer, Yehuda: *From Diplomacy to Resistance: A History of Jewish Palestine 1939–1945*, Atheneum, New York, 1973.
Begin, Menahem: *The Revolt: Story of the Irgun*, tr. by Samuel Katz, Henry Schuman, Inc., Publishers, New York, 1951.
Ben-Gurion, David, (ed.): *The Jews in Their Land*, tr. by Doubleday & Company, Inc., Garden City, N.Y., 1966.
Bethell, Nicolas: *The Palestine Triangle*, Andre Deutsch, London, 1979.
Berkman, Ted: *Sabra*, Harper & Row, Publishers, Incorporated, New York, 1969.
Bermant, Chaim I.: *Israel*, Walker & Co., New York, 1967.
Crossman, Richard H.S.: *Palestine Mission: A Personal Record*, Harper & Brothers, New York, 1947.
Crum, Bartley C.: *Behind the Silken Curtain: A Personal Account of Anglo-American Diplomacy in Palestine and the Middle East*, Simon and Schuster, New York, 1947.
Eban, Abba S.: *My People: The Story of the Jews*, Behrman House and Random House, Inc., New York, 1969.
Elston, D.R.: *Israel: The Making of a Nation*, published for the Anglo-Israel Association by the Oxford University Press, New York, 1963.
Esco Foundation for Palestine, Inc.: *Palestine: A Study of Jewish, Arab, and British Policies*, 2 vols., Yale University Press, New Haven, Conn., 1947.
Eytan, Walter: *The First Ten Years: A Diplomatic History of Israel*, Simon and Schuster, New York, 1958.
García-Granados, Jorge: *The Birth of Israel: The Drama as I Saw It*, Alfred A. Knopf, Inc., New York, 1948.
Gervasi, Frank H.: *The Case for Israel*, The Viking Press, Inc., New York, 1967.
Givet, Jacques: *The Anti-Zionist Complex*, SBS Publishing Inc., Englewood, N.J., 1982.
Heschel, Abraham Joshua: *Israel: An Echo of Eternity*, Farrar, Straus & Giroux, Inc., New York, 1969.
Horowitz, David: *State in the Making*, tr. by Julian Meltzer, Alfred A. Knopf, Inc., New York, 1953.
Hurewitz, Jacob C.: *The Struggle for Palestine*, W.W. Norton & Company, Inc., New York, 1968.
Hyamson, Albert Montefiore: *Palestine under the Mandate 1920–1948*, Greenwood Press, Westport, Conn., 1976.
Joseph, Bernard (Dov): *British Rule in Palestine*, Public Affairs Press, Washington, 1948.
———: *The Faithful City: The Siege of Jerusalem, 1948*, Simon and Schuster, New York, 1960.
Katz, Samuel: *Battleground: Fact and Fantasy in Palestine*, Bantam Books, New York and London, 1978.
Kedourie, Elie, and Haim, Sylvia: *Palestine and Israel in the 19th and 20th Centuries*, Frank Cass, London, 1982.
Kedourie, Elie, and Haim, Sylvia, Eds: *Zionism and Arabism in Palestine and Israel*, Frank Cass, London, 1982.
Kisch, Frederick, H.: *Palestine Diary*, Victor Gollancz, Ltd., London, 1938.
Koestler, Arthur: *Promise and Fulfillment: Palestine, 1917–1949*, The Macmillan Company, New York, 1949.
Kollek, Theodore, and Moshe Pearlman: *Jerusalem: A History of 40 Centuries*, Random House, Inc., New York, 1968.
Lall, Arthur S.: *The UN and the Middle East Crisis, 1967*, Columbia University Press, New York, 1968.
Lucas, Noah: *The Modern History of Israel*, Weidenfeld and Nicolson, London 1974.
McDonald, James G.: *My Mission in Israel, 1948–1951*, Simon and Schuster, New York, 1951.
Mandel, Neville J.: *The Arabs and Zionism before World War I*, Berkeley, University of California Press, 1976.
Maoz, Moshe (ed): *Studies on Palestine during the Ottoman Period*, Magnes Press, Jerusalem, 1975.
Meeker, Oden: *Israel: Ancient Land, Young Nation*, Charles Scribner's Sons, New York, 1968.
Meinertzhagen, Richard: *Middle East Diary, 1917–1956*, Thomas Yoseloff, Inc., New York, 1960.
Morris, Yaakov: *Masters of the Desert: 6000 Years in the Negev*, G.P. Putnam's Sons, New York, 1961.
Owen, Edward Roger J. ed.: *Studies in the Economic and Social History of Palestine in the Nineteenth and Twentieth Centuries*, The Macmillan Press, London, 1982.
Parkes, James W.: *A History of Palestine from 135 A.D. to Modern Times*, Oxford University Press, New York, 1949.
Prittie, Terence C.F.: *Israel: The Miracle in the Desert*, rev.ed.,

Penguin Books, Inc., Baltimore, 1968.
Robinson, Donald B., Ed.: *Under Fire: Israel's 20-year Struggle for Survival*, W.W. Norton & Company, Inc., New York, 1968.
Roth, Stephen J. (ed.): *The Impact of the Six-Day War*, The Macmillan Press, London, 1988.
Sachar, Howard M.: *A History of Israel From the Rise of Zionism to Our Times*, Alfred A. Knopf, New York, 1976. *Volume II, From the Aftermath of the Yom Kippur War*, Oxford University Press, New York, 1987.
Sacher, Harry: *Israel: The Establishment of a State*, British Book Centre, New York, 1952.
Samuel, Maurice: *Light on Israel*, Alfred A. Knopf, Inc., New York, 1968.
Samuel, Rinna: *Israel: Promised Land to Modern State*, Golden Press, New York, 1969.
Schechtman, Joseph B.: *The United States and the Jewish State Movement: The Crucial Decade, 1939–1949*, Herzl Press, New York, 1966.
Sharef, Zeev: *Three Days*, tr. by Julian Meltzer, W.H. Allen & Co., Ltd. London, 1962.
Stein, Kenneth W.: *The Land Question in Palestine, 1917–1939*, University of North Carolina Press, Chapel Hill, 1984.
Stock, Ernest: *Israel on the Road to Sinai, 1949–1956, with a Sequel on the Six-day War, 1967*, Cornell University Press, Ithaca, N.Y., 1967.
———: *From Conflict to Understanding: Relations between Jews and Arabs in Israel since 1948*, American Jewish Committee, New York, 1968.
Sykes, Christopher: *Crossroads to Israel*, Indiana University Press, Bloomington, Ind., 1973.
Talmon, Jacob: *Israel Among the Nations*, Weidenfeld and Nicolson, London, 1982.
Wasserstein, Bernard: *The British in Palestine*, Royal Historical Society, London, 1978
Williams, L.F. Rushbrook: *The State of Israel*, The Macmillan Company, New York, 1957.
Yaari, Abraham: *The Goodly Heritage: Memoirs Describing the Life of the Jewish community of Eretz Yisrael from the Seventeenth to the Twentieth Centuries*, Zionist Organization, Youth and HeHalutz Department, Jerusalem, 1958
Zweig, Ron: *Britain and Palestine during the Second World War*, Boydell and Brewer, London, 1986.

GOVERNMENT, POLITICS, AND INTERNATIONAL RELATIONS

Arian, Alan: *Ideological Change in Israel*, The Press of Case Western Reserve University, Cleveland, 1968.
Badi, Joseph: *The Government of the State of Israel*, Twayne Publishers, Inc., New York, 1963.
Becker, Avi: *The United Nations and Israel from Recognition to Reprehension*, Bar-Ilan University, 1985.
Bernstein, Marver H.: *The Politics of Israel*, Princeton University Press, Princeton, N.J., 1957.
Caspi, Dan et al: *The Roots of Begin's Success*, New York, 1984.
Elizur, Yuval and Salpeter, Eliahu: *Who Rules Israel?*, Harper and Row, New York, 1973.
Fein, Leonard J.: *Politics in Israel*, Little, Brown and Company, Boston, 1968.
———: *Israel: Politics and People*, Little, Brown and Company, Boston, 1968.
Fink, Reuben, Ed.: *America and Palestine: The Attitude of Official America and of the American People toward the Rebuilding of Palestine as a Free and Democratic Jewish Commonwealth*, 2d rev. ed., Herald Square Press, New York, 1945.
Frankel, William: *Israel Observed: An Anatomy of the State*, Thames and Hudson, London, 1980 and New York, 1981.
Freedman, Robert O. ed.: *Israel in the Begin Era*, Praeger, New York, 1982.
Freudenheim, Yehoshu'a: *Government in Israel*, Oceana Publications Inc., Dobbs Ferry, N.Y., 1967.
Gavron, Daniel: *Israel After Begin*, Houghton, Mifflin, Boston, 1984.
Haber, Eitan, Ze'ev Schiff and Ehud Ya'ari: *The Year of the Dove*, New York, 1979.
Hebrew University of Jerusalem: *Israel and the United Nations*, Manhattan Publishing Co., New York, 1956.
Horowitz, Dan and Lissak, Moshe: *Origins of the Israel Polity*, University of Chicago Press, Chicago, 1978.
Isaac, Rael Jean: *Israel Divided*, Johns Hopkins University Press, Baltimore, 1976.
Kenen, I.L.: *Israel's Defense Line: Her Friends and Foes in Washington*, Prometheus Books, Buffalo, N.Y., 1981.
Kraines, Oscar: *Government and Politics in Israel*, Houghton Mifflin Company, Boston, 1961.
Kreinin, Mordechai E.: *Israel and Africa: A Study in Technical Cooperation*, Frederick A. Praeger, Inc., New York, 1964.
Landau, Jacob M.: *The Arabs in Israel: A Political Study*, Oxford University Press, New York, 1969.
Laqueur, Walter: *Confrontation: The Middle East and World Politics*, Bantam Books, New York, 1974.
Laufer, Leopold: *Israel and the Developing Countries*, The Twentieth Century Fund, New York, 1967.
Lorch, Netanel: *The Knesset*, Israel Museum, Jerusalem, 1988.
Louvish, Misha: *The Challenge of Israel*, Israel Universities Press, Jerusalem, 1968.
Manuel, Frank E.: *Realities of American-Palestine Relations*, Public Affairs Press, Washington, 1949.
Meyer, Lawrence: *Israel Now*, Delacorte Press, New York, 1982.
Nachmias, David and David Rosenbloom: *Bureaucratic Culture: Citizen and Administration in Israel*, New York, 1978.
O'Brien, Conor Cruise: *The Siege*, Simon and Shuster, New York, 1986.
Oz, Amos: *In the Land of Israel*, Chatto and Windus, London, 1983.
Raphael, Gideon: *Destination Peace: Three Decades of Israeli Foreign Policy*, Weidenfeld and Nicolson, London, 1981.
Ross, Rebecca: *From Moscow to Jerusalem*, New York, 1976.
Rubinstein Amnon: *The Zionist Dream Revisited*, New York, 1974.
Safran, Nadav: *The United States and Israel*, Harvard University Press, Cambridge, Mass., 1963.
Seger, Samuel: *Parliamentary System of Israel*, Syracuse University Press, Syracuse, New York, 1985.
Seligman, Lester G.: *Leadership in a New Nation: Political Development in Israel*, Atherton Press, Inc., New York, 1964.
Shamgar, Meir (Ed.): *Military Government in the Territories Administered by Israel 1967–1980: The Legal Aspects, vol.1*, Hebrew University, Jerusalem, 1982.
Zohar, David: *Political Parties in Israel: The Evaluation of Israeli Democracy*, Praeger, New York, 1974.

ARAB-ISRAELI CONFLICT

Avneri, Arieh L.: *The Claim of Dispossession: Jewish Land-settlement and the Arabs 1878–1948*, Transaction Books,

New Brunswick, N.J., and London, 1984.
Bell, J. Bowyer: *Israel and the Arabs since 1946*, Prentice-Hall, New York, 1950.
Berger, Earl: *The Covenant and the Sword: Arab-Israel Relations, 1948–56*, University of Toronto Press, Toronto, 1965.
Bulloch, John: *Final Conflict*, Century Publishing, London, 1983.
Caplan, Neil: *Palestine Jewry and the Arab Question 1917–1925*, Frank Cass, London, 1978.
Cohen, Aharon: *Israel and the Arab World*, W.H. Allen, London, 1970.
Cohen, Michael J.: *The Origin and Evolution of the Arab-Zionist Conflict*, University of California Press, 1987.
Elazar, Daniel J. (Ed.): *Judea, Samaria and Gaza: Views of the Present and Future*, American Enterprise Institute, Washington and London, 1982.
Flapan, Simha: *Zionism and the Palestinians*, Croom Helm, London, 1979.
Friedlander, Melvin A.: *Sadat and Begin*, Westview Press, Boulder, Colo. 1983.
Gilbert, Martin: *The Arab-Israel Conflict: Its History in Maps*, Weidenfeld and Nicolson, London, 1976.
Gorny, Yosef.: *Zionism and the Arabs 1882–1948*, Oxford University Press, N.Y., 1987.
Katz, Shmuel: *The Hollow Peace*, Dvir and the Jerusalem Post, Jerusalem, 1981.
Khouri, Fred: *The Arab-Israel Dilemma*, Syracuse University Press, New York, 1968.
Laffin, John: *The PLO Connections*, Corgi Books, London, 1983.
Landau, Julian L. (Ed.): *The Media: Freedom or Responsibility (The War in Lebanon, 1982: A Case Study)*, B.A.L. Mass Communications Ltd., Jerusalem, 1984.
Laqueur, Walter (ed.): *The Israel-Arab Reader* Bantam Books, New York, 1969.
———: *The Road to Jerusalem: The Origins of the Arab-Israel Conflict, 1967*, The Macmillan Company, New York, 1968.
Morris, Benny: *The Birth of the Palestinian Refugee Problem, 1947–1949*, Cambridge University Press, Cambridge, 1987.
Nisan, Mordechai: *Israel and the Territories*, Turtledove Publications, Ramat Gan, 1978.
Peters, Joan: *From Time Immemorial: The Origins of the Arab-Jewish Conflict Over Palestine*, Harper and Row, New York, 1984.
Porath, Yehoshua: *The Emergence of the Palestinian —Arab National Movement 1918–1929*, Frank Cass, London, 1974.
———: *The Palestine Arab National Movement*, Frank Cass, London, 1977. Rabinovich, Itamar: *The War for Lebanon*, Cornell University Press, Ithaca, New York, 1984.
Rabinovich, Itamar and Reinharz, Jehuda (eds.): *Israel in the Middle East*, Oxford University Press, New York, 1984.
Randal, J.: *Going All The Way*, Viking Press, New York, 1983.
Sachar, Howard, M.: *Egypt and Israel*, R. Marek, New York, 1981.
Safran, Nadav: From War to War: The Arab-Israeli Confrontation, 1948–1967, Pegasus, New York, 1969.
Safran, Nadav: *Israel: The Embattled Ally*, Belknap Press of Harvard University, Cambridge, Mass. 1978.
Stone, Julius: *Israel and Palestine: Assault on the Law of Nations*, Johns Hopkins University Press, Baltimore and London, 1981.
Teveth, Shabtai: *Ben-Gurion and the Palestine Arabs: From Peace to War*, Oxford University Press, Oxford, 1985.
Timerman, Jacobo: *The Longest War*, Pan Books, London, 1982.
Weizman, Ezer: *The Battle for Peace*, Bantam Books, New York, 1981.

MILITARY

Allon, Yigal: *The Making of the Israeli Army*, Bantam Books, New York, 1970.
Ben-Porat, Yeshayahu, Eitan Haber and Ze'ev Schiff: *Entebbe Rescue*, Dell Publishing Co., New York, 1977.
Churchill, Randolph S., and Winston S. Churchill: *The Six Day War*, Houghton & Brothers, New York, 1947.
Dayan, David: *Strike First! A Battle History of Israel's Six-day War*, tr. by Dov Ben-Abba, Pitman Publishing Corporation, New York, 1968.
Dayan, Moshe: *Breakthrough*, Weidenfeld and Nicolson, London, 1981.
———: *Diary of the Sinai Campaign*, Weidenfeld & Nicolson, London, 1966.
Henriques, Robert D. Q.: *Hundred Hours to Suez: An Account of Israel's Campaign in the Sinai Peninsula*. The Viking Press, Inc., New York, 1957.
Herzog, Chaim: *The Arab-Israel Wars: War and Peace in the Middle East from the War of Independence through Lebanon*, Random House, 1983.
———: *The War of Atonement*, Weidenfeld and Nicolson, London, 1975.
Jansen, Michael: *The Battle of Beirut*, Zed Press, London, 1982.
Kimche, David, and Dan Bawley: *The Sandstorm: The Arab-Israeli War of June 1967; Prelude and Aftermath*, Stein and Day Incorporated, New York, 1968.
Lorch, Netanel: *Israel's War of Independence, 1947–1949*, 2d rev.ed., Hartmore House, Hartford, Conn., 1968.
———: *One Long War: Arab Versus Jew Since 1920*, Keter Publishing House, Jerusalem, 1976. Mardor, Munya: *Haganah*, New American Library, Inc., New York, 1966.
Marshall, Samuel L.A.: *Swift Sword: The Historical Record of Israel's Victory, June, 1967*, American Heritage Publishing Co., Inc., New York, 1967.
O'Ballance, Edgar: *The Sinai Campaign of 1956*, Frederick A. Praeger, Inc., New York, 1960.
Pearlman, Moshe: *The Army of Israel*, Philosophical Library, Inc., New York, 1950.
Schiff, Ze'ev: *A History of the Israeli Army, 1870–1974*, Straight Arrow Books, San Francisco, 1974.
Schiff, Ze'ev and Yaari, Ehud: *Israel's Lebanon War*, Simon and Schuster, New York, 1984.

SOCIETY, IMMIGRATION, AND SETTLEMENT

Bacci, Roberto: *The Population of Israel*, Hebrew University, Jerusalem, 1977
Barer, Shlomo: *The Magic Carpet*, Secker and Warburg, London, 1952.
Bein, Alex: *The Return to the Soil: A History of Jewish Settlement in Israel*, tr. by Israel Schen, Zionist Organization, Jerusalem, 1952.
Ben-Rafael, Eliezer: *The Emergence of Ethnicity, Cultural Groups, and Social Conflict in Israel*, Greenwood Press, Westport, Conn., 1982.
Ben-Yosef, Avraham C.: *The Purest Democracy in the World*, Herzl Press, New York, 1963.
Bettelheim, Bruno: *The Children of the Dream*, The Macmillan Company, New, 1969.

Bondy, Ruth: *The Israelis: Profile of a People*, tr. by Israel Taslitt, Sabra Books, New York, 1969.
Cohen, Mitchell: *Zion and State: Nation, Class, and the Shaping of Modern Israel*, Blackwell, Oxford, 1987.
Darin, Haim: *The Other Society*, Harcourt, Brace & World, Inc., New York, 1963.
Diamond, James S.: *Homeland or Holy Land? The "Canaanite" Critique of Israel*, Indiana University Press, 1986.
Eisenstadt, Samuel N.: *The Absorption of Immigrants*, The Free Press of Glencoe, Ill., Chicago, 1955.
———: *Israeli Society*, Basic Books, Inc., Publishers, New York, 1967.
———: *The Transformation of Israel Society*, West View Press, Boulder, 1985.

Elon, Amos: *The Israelis*, Holt, Rinehart, and Winston, New York, 1971.
Frankenstein, Carl, Ed.: *Between Past and Future*, Henrietta Szold Foundation for Child and Youth Welfare, Jerusalem, 1953.
Habas, Braha: *The Gate Breakers*, tr. by David Segal, Herzl Press, New York, 1953.
Herman, Simon: *Israelis and Jews*, Jewish Publication Society, Philadelphia, 1971.
Hillel, Shlomo: *Operation Babylon*, Doubleday, New York, 1987.
Isaacs, Harold R.: *American Jews in Israel*, The John Day Company, Inc., New York, 1967.
Kallen, Horace: *Utopian at Bay*, Theodor Herzl Foundation, New York, 1958.
Kanovsky, Eliyahu: *The Economy of the Israeli Kibbutz*, distributed for the Center for Middle Eastern Studies of the Harvard University Press, Cambridge, Mass., 1966.
Lapide, Pinchas E.: *A Century of U.S. Aliya*, Association of Americans and Canadians in Israel, Jerusalem, 1961.
Matras, Judah: *Social Change in Israel*, Aldine Publishing Company, Chicago, 1965.
Morris, Yaakov: *On the Soil of Israel: Americans and Canadians in Agriculture*, Association of Americans and Canadians in Israel, Tel Aviv, 1965.
Neubauer, Peter B., Ed.: *Children in Collectives: Child-rearing Aims and Practices in the Kibbutz*, Charles C Thomas, Publisher, Springfield, Ill., 1965.
Patai, Raphael: *Israel between East and West*, 2d ed., rev. and enl., Greenwood Publishing Corp., Westport, Conn., 1970.
Pincus, Chasya: *Come from the Four Winds: The Story of Youth Aliya*, Herzl Press, New York, 1970.
Rabin, Albert I.: *Growing Up in the Kibbutz: Comparison of the Personality of Children Brought Up in the Kibbutz and of Family-reared Children*, Springer Publishing Co., Inc., New York, 1965.
Rapaport, Louis: *Redemption Song: The Story of Operation Moses*, Harcourt Brace Jovanovich, San Diego, 1985.
Sacher, Howard M.: *Aliyah: The Peoples of Israel*, The World Publishing Company, Cleveland, 1961.
———: *From the Ends of the Earth: The Peoples of Israel*, The World Publishing Company, Cleveland, 1964.
Samuel, Edwin: *The Structure of Society in Israel*, Random House, Inc., New York, 1969.
Shavit, Yaakov: *The New Hebrew Nation*, Cass, London, 1987.
Sicron, Moshe: *Immigration to Israel, 1948–1953*, Falk Project for Economic Research in Israel, Jerusalem, 1957.
Smouha Sammy: *Israel, Pluralism and Conflict, Routledge and Kegan Paul, London, 1978.*
Spiro, Melford E.: Kibbutz, Schocken, New York, 1967.
———: *Children of the Kibbutz*, Harvard University Press, Cambridge, Mass., 1958.
Stern, Boris: *The Kibbutz that Was*, Public Affairs Press, Washington, 1965.
Viteles, Harry: *A History of the Co-operative Movement in Israel*, 6 vols., Vallentine, Mitchell & Co. Ltd., London, 1966–70.
Weingarten, Murray: *Life in a Kibbutz*, Zionist Organization, Youth and HeHalutz Department, Jerusalem, 1959.
Weingrod, Alex: *Israel: Group Relations in a New Society*, published for the Institute of Race Relations by Frederick A. Praeger, Inc., New York, 1965.
———: *Reluctant Pioneers: Village Development in Israel*, Cornell University Press, Ithaca, N.Y., 1966.
Weintraub, Dov, and others: *Moshava, Kibbutz, and Moshav: Patterns of Jewish Rural Settlement and Development in Palestine*, Cornell University Press, Ithaca, N.Y., 1969.
Willner, Dorothy: *Nation-building and Community in Israel*, Princeton University Press, Princeton, N.J., 1969.

ECONOMY

Aktzin, Benjamin, and Dror, Yehezkel: *Israel: High-pressure Planning*, Syracuse University Press, Syracuse, N.Y., 1966.
Barkai, Haim: *The Public, Histadrut, and Private Sectors in the Israeli Economy*, Falk Project for Economic Research in Israel, Jerusalem, 1964.
———: *Growth Patterns of the Kibbutz Economy*, North and Holland Publishing Co., Amsterdam, 1977.
Ben-Porath, Yoram (ed.): *The Israel Economy: Maturing through Crisis*, Harvard University Press, Boston, Mass., 1980.
Ginor, Fanny: *Socio-Economic Disparities in Israel*, University of Tel Aviv, Tel Aviv, 1979.
Halevi, Nadav and Klinov-Malul, Ruth: *The Economic Development of Israel*, Frederick Praeger, New York, 1968.
Halperin, Haim: *Agrindus: Integration of Agriculture and Industries*, Frederick A. Praeger, Inc., New York, 1963.
Horowitz, David: *The Economics of Israel*, Pergamon Press, New York, 1967.
Israel Ministry of Commerce and Industry: *Programme for Israel's Industrial Development: Second Outlook, 1965–1970*, tr. by Hannah Schmorak, Government Printer, Jerusalem, 1964.
Patinkin, Don: *The Israel Economy*, Falk Project for Economic Research in Israel, Jerusalem, 1960.
Preuss, Walter: *The Labour Movement in Israel: Past and Present*, tr. by Willy Stadekker, 3d ed., Rubin Mass Publishing House, Jerusalem, 1965.
Rubner, Alex: *The Economy of Israel*, Frederick A. Praeger, Inc., New York, 1960.

EDUCATION, CULTURE, AND RELIGION

Abramov, S. Zalman: *Perpetual Dilemma, Jewish Religion in the Jewish State*, Fairleigh Dickinson University Press, New York —London, 1976.
Badi, Joseph: *Religion in Israel Today*, Bookman Associates, Inc., New York, 1959.
Ben-Dor, Gabriel: *The Druzes in Israel*, Magnes Press, Jerusalem, 1979.
Bentwich, Joseph S.: *Education in Israel*, Jewish Publication Society of America, Philadelphia, 1965.
Braham, Randolph I.: *Israel: A Modern Education System*, U.S. Department of Health, Education, and Welfare, Washington, 1966.

Colbi, Saul: *A History of the Christian Presence in the Holy Land*, University Press of America, Lanham, Md., 1988.
Dana, Nissim (ed.): *The Druze: A Religious Community in Transition*, Turtledove Publications, Jerusalem, 1980.
Gamzu, Haim: *Painting and Sculpture in Israel: Half a Century of the Plastic Arts in Eretz Israel*, tr. by I.M. Lask, Devir Publishers, Tel Aviv, 1958.
Globerson, Aryeh: *Higher Education and Employment in Israel*, Saxon House, Farnborough, England, 1978, New York, 1979.
Goldman, Eliezer: *Religious Issues in Israel's Political Life*, Zionist Organization, Youth and HeHalutz Department, Jerusalem, 1964.
Halkin, Simon: *Modern Hebrew Literature: Trends and Values*, Schocken Books, Inc., New York, 1950.
Jiryis, Sabri: *The Arabs in Israel*, Monthly Review Press, New York, 1976.
Laffin, John: *The Israeli Mind*, Cassell, London, 1979.
Lilker, Shalom: *Kibbutz Judaism*, Herzl Press, New York, 1982.
Litvin, Baruch (ed.): *Jewish Identity*, Feldheim, New York, 1965.
Mari, Sami Khalil: *Arab Education in Israel*, University Press, Syracuse, New York, 1978.
Tammuz, Benjamin, and Wykes-Joyce, Max, (eds.): *Art in Israel*, W.H. Allen and Co., Ltd., London, 1966.
Wallenrod, Reuben: *The Literature of Modern Israel*, Abelard-Schuman, Limited, New York, 1957.
Weiner, Herbert: *The Wild Goats of Ein Gedi*, Doubleday & Company, Inc., Garden City, N.Y., 1961.

DIASPORA—ISRAEL

Baer, Jizchak Fritz: *Galut*, Schocken Books, New York, 1947.
Cohen, Steven M.: *The Attitude of American Jews to Israel and Israelis*, American Jewish Committee, New York, 1983.
Eisen, Arnold: *Galut*, Indiana University Press, Bloomington, 1986.
Herman, Simon: *Jewish Identity*, Herzl Press, New York, 1977.
Liebman, Charles S.: *Pressure without Sanctions: The Influence of World Jewry on Israeli Policy*, Fairleigh Dickinson University Press, Rutherford, 1977.

REFERENCE BOOKS

Bank of Israel: *Annual Report, 1955–1968, 14 vols., Jerusalem, 1956–69.*
Encyclopedia Judaica, 16 vols., Keter Publishing House, Jerusalem 1971. *Encyclopedia Judaica Decennial Book 1973–1982*, Keter Publishing House, 1982, and subsequent yearbooks.
Israel's Foreign Relations Selected Documents 1947–1980, 6 vols., Ministry for Foreign Affairs, Jerusalem 1976–1985.
Israel, Central Bureau of Statistics: *Statistical Abstract, 1949ff.*, Central Bureau of Statistics, Jerusalem.
Political Dictionary of the State of Israel, ed. Susan H. Rolef, MacMillan, New York, 1987.

PERIODICALS

Commentary
Jerusalem Quarterly
Jewish Frontier
Jewish Journal of Sociology
Jewish Spectator
Journal of Palestine Studies
Middle East Review
Midstream
New Outlook
Studies in Zionism, including annual selected and annotated bibliography on the History of Zionism and the State of Israel, Institute for Zionist Research, Tel Aviv University.
Zionist Literature bi-monthly, Zionist Archives, Jerusalem.

S. LANDRESS—E. HOTER—G. WIGODER